Standard Catalog of®

RIFLES & SHOTGUNS

THE COLLECTOR'S PRICE AND REFERENCE GUIDE

JERRY LEE

Published by

Gun Digest® Books, an imprint of F+W Media, Inc.
Krause Publications • 700 East State Street • Iola, WI 54990-0001
715-445-2214 • 888-457-2873
www.krausebooks.com

To order books or other products call toll-free 1-800-258-0929
or visit us online at www.gundigeststore.com

ISBN-13: 978-1-4402-3012-7
ISBN-10: 1-4402-3012-9

Cover Design by Al West
Designed by Kara Grundman, Paul Birling
and Tom Nelsen
Edited by Jerry Lee and Jennifer Pearsall

Printed in the United States of America

CONTENTS

INTRODUCTION

A GUIDE TO PRICING

Prices shown in the *Standard Catalog of Rifles and Shotguns* are designed as a *guide*, not as a quote, and the prices given reflect *retail* values. This is very important to remember. You will seldom realize full retail value if you trade in a gun or sell it to a dealer. In this situation, your gun will be valued at its wholesale price, which is generally substantially below retail value to allow for the seller's profit margin.

It should also be remembered that prices for firearms can vary with the time of the year, the geographical location and the general economy. As might be expected, guns used for hunting are more likely to sell in late summer or early fall as hunting season approaches. However, big-game rifles chambered for powerful magnum cartridges will likely have more appeal in western states than in the east. Semiautomatic rifles or shotguns will not sell well in states where their use for hunting is outlawed, such as Pennsylvania.

It is not practical to list prices in this book with regard to time of year or location so what is given is a reasonable price based on sales at gun shows, auction houses, and information obtained from knowledgeable collectors and dealers. In certain cases there will be no price indicated under a particular condition but rather the notation "N/A" or the symbol "—." This indicates that there is no known price available for that gun in that condition or the sales for that particular model are so few that a reliable price cannot be given. This will usually be encountered only with very rare guns, with newly introduced firearms, or more likely with antique firearms in those conditions most likely to be encountered. Most antique firearms prices are listed in the good, fair and poor categories.

Standard Catalog of Rifles and Shotguns can be used both as an identification guide and as a source of starting prices for a planned firearms transaction. If you start by valuing a given firearm according to the values shown in this book, you will not be too far off the mark.

In the final analysis, a firearm is worth only what someone is willing to pay for it. New trends arise quickly, and there are many excellent bargains to be found in today's market. With patience and good judgment—and with this book under your arm—you, too, can find them.

ABOUT THE EDITOR

Jerry Lee has been editor of several leading magazines in the firearms field including *Guns*, *Petersen's Handguns*, *Rifle Shooter*, and *Wing & Shot*. For many years he also was editor of the *Guns & Ammo* and *Shooting Times* specialty and annual publications. These include such titles as *Book of the 1911*, *Book of the AR-15*, *Combat Arms*, *Surplus Firearms*, *Book of the Model 70*, *Firearms for Law Enforcement*, *Gun Guide*, and many others. He was also responsible for editing the content of custom magazines and catalogs for Smith & Wesson, Remington, Ruger, Mossberg, CZ, Hornady, Nikon, and other manufacturers. Jerry is an NRA Life Member and has written several articles for that organization's website. His passion in firearms mainly centers around Colt handguns, rimfire rifles and 20-gauge shotguns. Jerry and Susan, his wife of more than 40 years, live in West Virginia.

AUCTION HOUSES

Among the many resources used by the editors to determine trends in firearms values are the prices realized at recent auctions. These include the following auction houses, which are considered to be among the very best in the field of modern and antique firearms.

Amoskeag Auctions, 250 Commercial Street, Suite 3011, Manchester, NH 03101; **www.amoskeag-auction.com**
Bonhams & Butterfields, 220 San Bruno Avenue, San Francisco, CA 94103; **www.bonhams.com**
Heritage Auctions, 3500 Maple Avenue, 17th Floor, Dallas, Texas 75219; **www.ha.com**
James D. Julia, Inc., 203 Skowhegan Rd., Fairfield, ME 04937; **www.juliaauctions.com**
Little John's Auctions, 1740 W. La Veta Ave., Orange, CA 92868; **www.littlejohnsauctionservice.com**
Rock Island Auction Co., 7819 42nd Street West, Rock Island, IL 61201; **www.rockislandauction.com**

GRADING SYSTEM

In most cases, the condition of a firearm determines its value. As with all collectible items, a grading system is necessary to give buyers and sellers a measurement that most closely reflects a general consensus on condition. While all grading systems are subjective, the system presented in this publication attempts to describe a firearm in universal terms. It is strongly recommend that the reader be closely acquainted with this grading system before attempting to determine the correct value of a particular firearm.

NIB (NEW IN BOX)

This category can sometimes be misleading. It means that the firearm is in its original factory carton with all of the appropriate papers. It also means the firearm is new, that it has not been fired, and has no wear. This classification brings a substantial premium for both the collector and shooter. It should be noted that NIB values are not the same as MSRP (manufacturer's suggested retail price), but rather are "street prices" that can be considerably lower than the MSRP. A NIB value should closely represent the selling price for a new, unfired gun in the box.

EXCELLENT

Collector quality firearms in this condition are highly desirable. The firearm must be in at least 98 percent condition with respect to blue wear, stock or grip finish, and bore. The firearm must also be in 100 percent original factory condition without refinishing, repair, alterations, or additions of any kind. Sights must be factory original, as well. This grading classification includes both modern and antique (manufactured prior to 1898) firearms.

VERY GOOD

Firearms in this category are also sought after both by the collector and shooter. Modern firearms must be in working order and retain approximately 92 percent original metal and wood finish. It must be 100 percent factory original, but may have some small repairs, alterations, or non-factory additions. No refinishing is permitted in this category. Antique firearms must have 80 percent original finish with no repairs.

GOOD

Modern firearms in this category may not be considered to be as collectible as the previous grades, but antique firearms are considered desirable. Modern firearms must retain at least 80 percent metal and wood finish, but may display evidence of old refinishing. Small repairs, alterations, or non-factory additions are sometimes encountered in this class. Factory replacement parts are permitted. The overall working condition of the firearm must be good, as well as safe. The bore may exhibit wear or some corrosion, especially in antique arms. Antique firearms may be included in this category if the metal and wood finish is at least 50 percent of the factory original.

FAIR

Firearms in this category should be in satisfactory working order and safe to shoot. The overall metal and wood finish on the modern firearm must be at least 30 percent and antique firearms must have at least some original finish or old re-finish remaining. Repairs, alterations, non-factory additions, and recent refinishing would all place a firearm in this classification. However, the modern firearm must be in working condition, while the antique firearm may not function. In either case the firearm must be considered safe to fire if in a working state.

POOR

Neither collectors nor shooters are likely to exhibit much interest in firearms in this condition. Modern firearms are likely to retain little metal or wood finish. Pitting and rust will be seen in firearms in this category. Modern firearms may not be in working order and may not be safe to shoot. Repairs and refinishing would be necessary to restore the firearm to safe working order. Antique firearms in this category will have no finish and will not function. In the case of modern firearms their principal value lies in spare parts. On the other hand, antique firearms in this condition can be used as "wall hangers," or might be an example of an extremely rare variation or have some kind of historical significance.

Example prices are shown for the conditions described above in this format:

NIB	*Exc.*	*V.G.*	*Good*	*Fair*	*Poor*
2250	1800	1500	1250	1000	700

PRICING

Prices given in this book are designed as a guide, not as a quote, and the prices given reflect retail values. This is very important to remember. You will seldom realize full retail value if you trade in a gun or sell it to a dealer. In this situation, your gun will be valued at its wholesale price, which is generally substantially below retail value to allow for the seller's profit margin.

It should also be remembered that prices for firearms can vary with the time of the year, geographical location, and the general economy. As might be expected, guns used for hunting are more likely to sell in late summer or early fall as hunting season approaches. Likewise, big-game rifles chambered for powerful magnum cartridges will likely have more appeal in western states than in the

Deep South, while semi-automatic rifles or shotguns will not sell well in states where their use for hunting is prohibited, such as is the case in Pennsylvania.

It is not practical to list prices in this book with regard to time of year or location. What is given here is a reasonable price based on sales at gun shows, auction houses, and information obtained from knowledgeable collectors and dealers. In certain cases there will be no price indicated under a particular condition, but rather the notation "N/A" or the symbol "—." This indicates that there is no known price available for that gun in that condition or the sales for that particular model are so few that a reliable price cannot be ascertained. This will usually be encountered only with very rare guns, with newly introduced firearms, or more likely with antique firearms in those conditions most likely to be encountered. Most antique firearms will be seen in the Good, Fair and Poor categories.

Standard Catalog of Firearms can be used as an identification guide and as a source of starting prices for a planned firearms transaction. If you begin by valuing a given firearm according to the values shown in this book, you will not be too far off the mark.

In the final analysis, a firearm is worth only what someone is willing to pay for it. New trends arise quickly, and there are many excellent bargains to be found in today's market. With patience and good judgment—and with this book under your arm—you, too, can find them.

ADDITIONAL CONSIDERATIONS

Firearms have been admired and coveted, not only for their usefulness, but also for their grace and beauty. Since the beginning of the 19th century, gun makers have adorned their firearms with engraving, fine woods or special order features that set their products apart from the rest. There is no feasible way to give the collector every possible variation of the firearms presented in this book. However, in a general way, certain special factors will significantly influence the price of a firearm.

Perhaps the most recognizable special feature collectors agree that affects the price of a rifle or shotgun is engraving. The artistry, beauty and intricate nature of engraving draw all collectors toward it. But firearms engraving is a field unto itself requiring years of experience to determine proper chronological methods and the ability to identify the engraver in question.

Factory engraving generally brings more of a premium than after-market engraving. To be able to determine factory work is a difficult task, and can be full of pitfalls. In some cases, factories like Colt and Winchester may have records to verify original factory engraving work, whereas other manufacturers such as Parker, Remington or Savage may not. Whenever a firearm purchase is to be made with respect to an engraved gun, it is in the collector's best interest to secure an expert opinion and or a factory letter prior to the purchase. Engraved firearms are expensive. A mistake could cost the buyer or seller thousands of dollars; proceed with caution.

The 19th and 20th centuries were times when guns were purchased by or given to historically important individuals. Firearms have also been an important part of significant historical events such as the Battle of the Little Bighorn or the Battle of Bull Run. Many of these firearms are in museums where the public can enjoy, see and appreciate them. Others are in private collections that seldom, if ever, are offered for sale. If the collector should ever encounter one of these historically important firearms, it cannot be stressed strongly enough to secure an expert determination as to authenticity. Museum curators are perhaps the best source of information for these types of firearms. As with engraved guns, historical firearms are usually expensive, and without documentation their value is questionable.

Special features and variations are also a desirable part of firearms collecting. As with engraving, special order guns can bring a considerable premium. The Colt factory has excellent records regarding its firearms and will provide the collector with a letter of authenticity. Winchester records are not as comprehensive but rifles made prior to 1908 may have documentation. Other firearm manufacturers either do not have records or do not provide the collector with documentation. This leaves the collector in a difficult position. Special order sights, stocks, barrel lengths, calibers, gauges and chokes must be judged on their own merits. As with other factors, an expert should be consulted prior to purchase. Experienced collectors, researchers, and museums will generally provide the kind of information a collector needs before purchasing a special order or unique firearm.

Perhaps the best advice is for the collector to take his time. Do not be in a hurry, and do not allow yourself to be rushed into making a decision. Learn as much as possible about the firearms you are interested in collecting or shooting. Try to keep current with prices through this publication and the auction houses listed nearby. Go to gun shows, not just to buy or sell, but to observe and learn. It is also helpful to join a gun club or collector's association. These groups have experienced members who are glad to help the beginner or veteran.

Firearms collecting is a rewarding hobby. Firearms are part of our nation's history and represent an opportunity to learn more about their role in the American experience. If done skillfully, firearms collecting can be a profitable hobby as well.

A

A & R SALES SOUTH
El Monte, California

NOTE: A&R Sales South also made frames for custom 1911 builds.

Mark IV Sporter

A semi-automatic copy of the M-14 military rifle. Manufactured in .308 cal. (7.65mm NATO) only.

NIB	Exc.	V.G.	Good	Fair	Poor
950	650	500	375	195	100

ABBEY, F.J. & CO.
Chicago, Illinois

The Abbey Brothers produced a variety of percussion rifles and shotguns which are all of individual design. The prices listed represent what a plain F.J. Abbey & Company firearm might realize.

Rifle

NIB	Exc.	V.G.	Good	Fair	Poor
—	—	1750	800	450	200

Shotgun

NIB	Exc.	V.G.	Good	Fair	Poor
—	—	2500	1750	575	150

ABBEY, GEORGE T.
Utica, New York, and Chicago, Illinois

George T. Abbey originally worked in Utica, New York, from 1845 to 1852. He moved to Chicago in 1852 and was in business until 1874. He manufactured a wide variety of percussion and cartridge firearms. The values listed represent those of his most common products.

Single-Barrel Shotgun

NIB	Exc.	V.G.	Good	Fair	Poor
—	—	1750	850	550	200

Side-by-Side Double-Barrel Shotgun

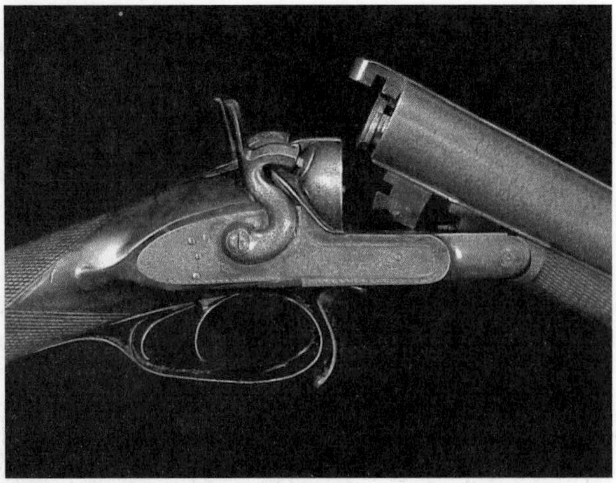

NIB	Exc.	V.G.	Good	Fair	Poor
—	—	2550	1200	675	250

Over-and-Under Double-Barrel Shotgun

NIB	Exc.	V.G.	Good	Fair	Poor
—	—	2750	1300	975	250

ABESSER & MERKEL
Suhl, Germany

Crown Grade

This model is a single-barrel Trap gun with Greener cross bolt-action with two underbolt locks. Offered in 12 gauge with barrel lengths from 28" to 34". Ventilated rib standard. Skip line checkering. Pistol or straight grip stock. Gun weight is between 7 and 7.5 lbs. Engraved receiver with game scenes.

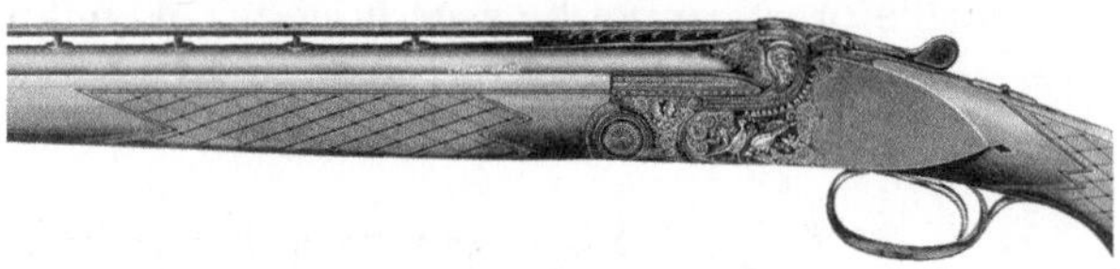

Courtesy Dan Sheil

NIB	Exc.	V.G.	Good	Fair	Poor
—	6000	4925	3825	1000	—

Diamond Grade

This model is a side-by-side gun offered in 12, 16, 20, and 28 gauge as well as .410 bore. Auto ejectors. Double triggers. Full coverage engraving with artistic stock carving behind the frame. Skip line checkering. Many extras offered on this grade will affect price. Barrel lengths from 25" to 32". Weights are from 6.5 lbs. to 7 lbs. Prices are for standard gun with no extras.

Courtesy Dan Sheil

NIB	Exc.	V.G.	Good	Fair	Poor
—	12000	9200	8050	3000	700

NOTE: Add 50 percent for 20 gauge guns and 100 percent for 28 gauge or .410 bore guns.

Empire Grade

This shotgun is a side-by-side with an Anson-Deeley action. The receiver is fully engraved with game birds and fine scroll. The stock is carved behind the action. Checkering is a fine skip line-style. Auto ejectors. Pistol or straight grip stock. With or without Monte Carlo and cheekpiece. Prices listed are for pre-war guns with fluid steel barrels.

Courtesy Dan Sheil

NIB	Exc.	V.G.	Good	Fair	Poor
—	13500	11150	9200	2500	700

NOTE: Add 50 percent for 20 gauge guns and 100 percent for 28 gauge or .410 bore guns.

Excelsior Grade

This side-by-side gun is fitted with engraved side plates. Anson-Deeley action with double triggers. Fine line checkering. Figured walnut stock. All gauges offered from 12 to .410. Barrel lengths from 25" to 32". Many extra cost options available.

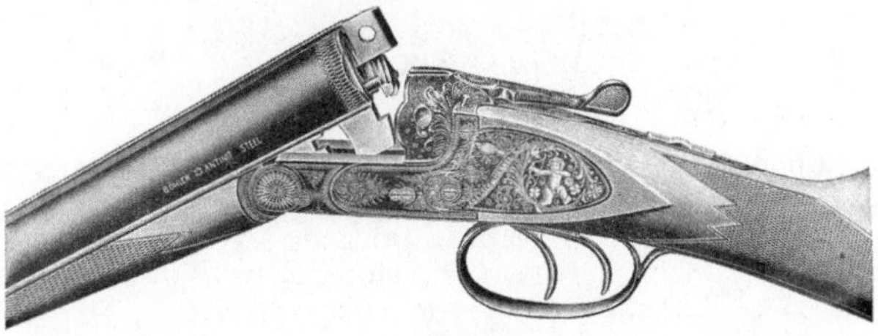

Courtesy Dan Sheil

NIB	Exc.	V.G.	Good	Fair	Poor
—	9000	7500	6500	3100	700

NOTE: Add 50 percent for 20 gauge guns and 100 percent for 28 gauge or .410 bore guns.

Diana Grade

This is an over-and-under combination gun with Greener cross bolt-action. Safety is located on the side of the pistol grip. Iron sights. Set trigger for rifle barrel. A wide variety of centerfire calibers offered with barrel lengths from 26" to 30".

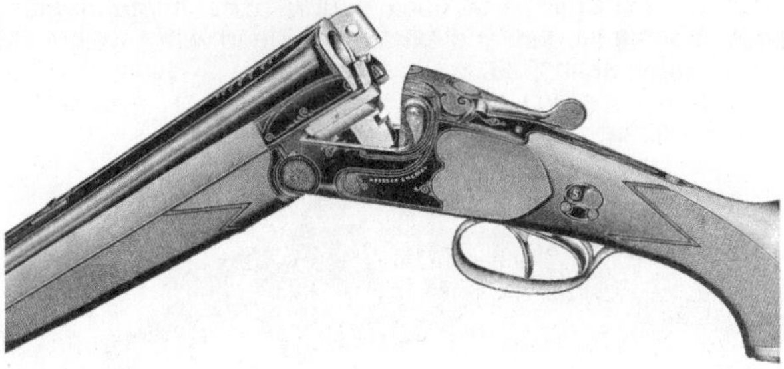

Courtesy Dan Sheil

NIB	Exc.	V.G.	Good	Fair	Poor
—	9500	8250	6250	3200	700

Vandalia Grade

This is an over-and-under gun chambered for 4.75" 12 gauge shells. Barrel lengths from 28" to 32". Walnut stock with pistol or straight grip with skip line checkering. Double triggers with extractors. Premium for factory multi-barrel combinations.

Courtesy Dan Sheil

NIB	Exc.	V.G.	Good	Fair	Poor
—	7250	6000	4500	3300	700

Nimrod

This is a drilling with a Greener cross bolt-action and double under bolt. Safety is located on side of grip. Top two barrels may be 12, 16, or 20 gauge. The bottom barrel is offered in a variety of centerfire calibers. Iron sights. Pistol or straight grip stock. Receiver engraved with game scenes. Add 50 percent for 20 gauge.

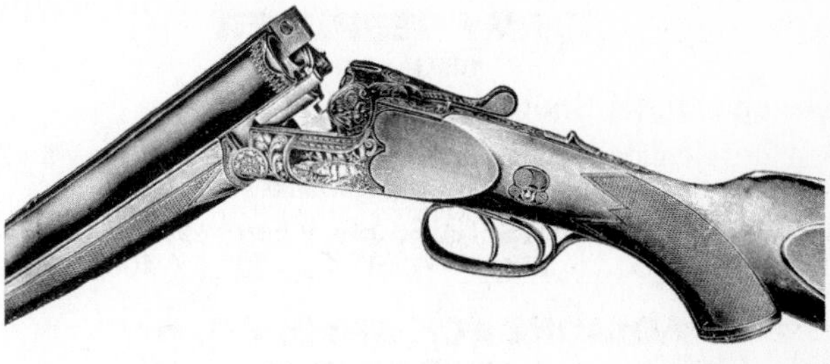

Courtesy Dan Sheil

NIB	Exc.	V.G.	Good	Fair	Poor
—	13000	9950	6000	4995	700

Magazine Rifle

A bolt-action rifle offered in a wide variety of calibers. Barrel lengths from 24" to 30". Calibers from 6.5mm to .404 Rimless. This model may have a Zeiss scope or other special order features that will affect price. Add $2000 for Magnum actions.

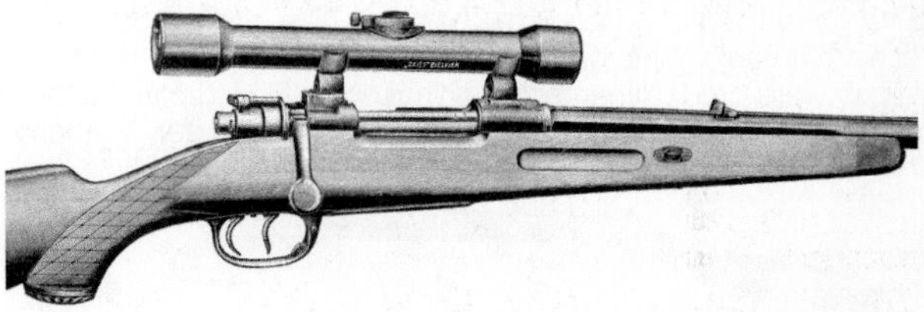

Courtesy Dan Sheil

NIB	Exc.	V.G.	Good	Fair	Poor
—	4900	3950	3350	1100	700

ACME ARMS

New York, New York

A trade name found on .22 and .32 caliber revolvers and 12 gauge shotguns marketed by the Cornwall Hardware Company.

Shotgun

A 12 gauge double-barrel shotgun with external hammers.

NIB	Exc.	V.G.	Good	Fair	Poor
—	400	275	175	125	75

ACTION ARMS LTD.

Philadelphia, Pennsylvania

Timber Wolf Carbine

Introduced in 1989, this slide-action carbine features an 18.5" barrel with adjustable rear sight and blade front sight. Chambered for the .357 Magnum or .38 Special cartridges, it is offered in either blue or hard chrome finish. Weight is approximately 5.5 lbs. Built in Israel by Israel Military Industries.

NIB	Exc.	V.G.	Good	Fair	Poor
850	595	395	300	200	125

Action Arms/IMI Uzi Carbine Models A and B

16-inch-barreled semi-auto version of the Uzi submachine gun chambered in 9mm Parabellum. Add 10 percent for nylon Uzi case and accessories. Built by IMI (Israeli Military Industries).

NIB	Exc.	V.G.	Good	Fair	Poor
1700	1450	1150	850	600	250

ADAMY GEBRUDER

Suhl, Germany

Over-and-Under Shotgun

A 12 or 16 gauge double-barrel over-and-under shotgun with 26" to 30" barrels, double triggers and a walnut stock.

NIB	Exc.	V.G.	Good	Fair	Poor
—	2100	1700	1250	750	400

ADIRONDACK ARMS CO. or A.S. BABBITT CO.

Plattsburgh, New York

Orvil M. Robinson Patent Rifle

The Robinson tube-fed repeating rifle was made in New York between 1870 and 1874. The early models, 1870-1872, are marked "A.S. Babbitt" ; the later models, 1872-1874, "Adirondack Arms Co." The Company was sold to Winchester in 1874, but they never produced the Robinson after that date. The rifle has been found in two styles: The first with small fingers on the hammer to cock and operate the mechanism; the second with buttons on the receiver to retract the bolt and cock the hammer. The rifle was made in .44 cal. with an octagonal barrel usually found in 26" or 28" length. The frames were predominantly brass; but some iron frames have been noted, and they will bring a premium of approximately 25 percent. The barrel and magazine tube have a blued finish.

Courtesy Buffalo Bill Historical Center, Cody, Wyoming

NIB	Exc.	V.G.	Good	Fair	Poor

Orvil M. Robinson Patent Rifle First Model

NIB	Exc.	V.G.	Good	Fair	Poor
—	6500	5200	2700	1300	500

Orvil M. Robinson Patent Rifle Second Model

NIB	Exc.	V.G.	Good	Fair	Poor
—	6500	5200	2700	1300	500

AGUIRRE Y ARANZABAL (AyA)

Eibar, Spain

SIDE-BY-SIDE

Matador Side-by-Side

A 12, 16, 20, 28 or .410 bore boxlock double-barrel shotgun with 26", 28" or 30" barrels, single-selective trigger and automatic ejectors. Blued with a walnut stock. Manufactured from 1955 to 1963.

NIB	Exc.	V.G.	Good	Fair	Poor
—	550	415	350	300	200

NOTE: 28 gauge and .410 add 100 percent.

Matador II Side-by-Side

As above, in 12 or 20 gauge with a ventilated rib.

NIB	Exc.	V.G.	Good	Fair	Poor
—	575	425	375	300	200

Matador III Side-by-Side

As above, with 3" chambers.

NIB	Exc.	V.G.	Good	Fair	Poor
—	600	450	395	325	200

Bolero Side-by-Side

As above, with a non-selective single trigger and extractors. Manufactured until 1984.

NIB	Exc.	V.G.	Good	Fair	Poor
—	500	375	325	295	200

Iberia Side-by-Side

A 12 or 20 gauge Magnum boxlock double-barrel shotgun with 26", 28" or 30" barrels, double triggers and extractors. Blued with a walnut stock.

NIB	Exc.	V.G.	Good	Fair	Poor
—	600	450	395	325	200

Iberia II Side-by-Side

Similar to the above, in 12 or 16 gauge with 28" barrels and 2-3/4" chambers.

NIB	Exc.	V.G.	Good	Fair	Poor
—	625	500	425	325	250

Model 106 Side-by-Side

A 12, 16, or 20 gauge boxlock double-barrel shotgun with 28" barrels, double triggers and extractors. Blued with a walnut stock. Manufactured until 1985.

NIB	Exc.	V.G.	Good	Fair	Poor
—	600	500	400	300	250

Model 107-LI Side-by-Side

As above, with the receiver lightly engraved and an English-style stock. In 12 or 16 gauge only.

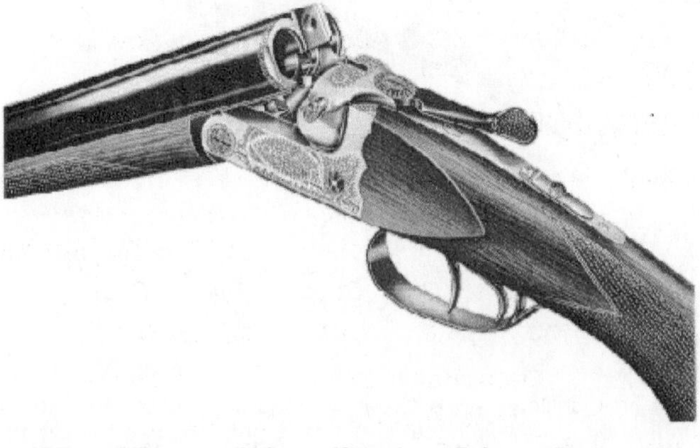

NIB	Exc.	V.G.	Good	Fair	Poor
—	675	575	495	325	275

Model 116 Side-by-Side

A 12, 16 or 20 gauge sidelock double-barrel shotgun with 27" to 30" barrels, double triggers and ejectors. Engraved, blued with a walnut stock. Manufactured until 1985.

NIB	Exc.	V.G.	Good	Fair	Poor
—	1095	975	800	500	350

Model 117 Side-by-Side

As above, with 3" chambers.

NIB	Exc.	V.G.	Good	Fair	Poor
—	1150	1000	850	600	400

Model 117 "Quail Unlimited" Side-by-Side

As above in 12 gauge only with 26" barrels and the receiver engraved "Quail Unlimited of North America." Forty-two were manufactured.

NIB	Exc.	V.G.	Good	Fair	Poor
—	1500	1200	875	650	425

Model 210 Side-by-Side

An exposed hammer, 12 or 16 gauge, boxlock shotgun with 26" to 28" barrels and double triggers. Blued with a walnut stock. Manufactured until 1985.

NIB	Exc.	V.G.	Good	Fair	Poor
—	800	675	550	400	325

Model 711 Boxlock Side-by-Side

A 12 gauge boxlock double-barrel shotgun with 28" or 30" barrels having ventilated ribs, single-selective trigger and automatic ejectors. Manufactured until 1984.

NIB	Exc.	V.G.	Good	Fair	Poor
—	900	800	700	500	350

Model 711 Sidelock Side-by-Side

As above, with sidelocks. Manufactured in 1985 only.

NIB	Exc.	V.G.	Good	Fair	Poor
—	1200	1000	750	500	400

Senior Side-by-Side

A custom order 12 gauge double-barrel sidelock shotgun, gold inlaid and engraved. Made strictly to individual customer's specifications.

NIB	Exc.	V.G.	Good	Fair	Poor
17000	13750	9750	7000	4500	2250

OVER-AND-UNDERS

Model 79 "A" Over-and-Under

A 12 gauge boxlock over-and-under double-barrel shotgun with 26", 28" or 30" barrels, single-selective trigger and automatic ejectors. Blued with a walnut stock. Manufactured until 1985.

NIB	Exc.	V.G.	Good	Fair	Poor
—	1250	1050	925	750	500

Model 79 "B" Over-and-Under

As above, with a moderate amount of engraving.

NIB	Exc.	V.G.	Good	Fair	Poor
—	1350	1150	950	800	575

Model 79 "C" Over-and-Under

As above, with extensive engraving.

NIB	Exc.	V.G.	Good	Fair	Poor
—	2000	1800	1500	1150	675

Model 77 Over-and-Under

As above, patterned after the Merkel shotgun.

NIB	Exc.	V.G.	Good	Fair	Poor
—	3000	2700	2000	1500	1000

Coral "A" Over-and-Under

A 12 or 16 gauge over-and-under boxlock double-barrel shotgun with 26" or 28" barrels having ventilated ribs, double triggers and automatic ejectors. Fitted with a Kersten cross bolt. Manufactured until 1985.

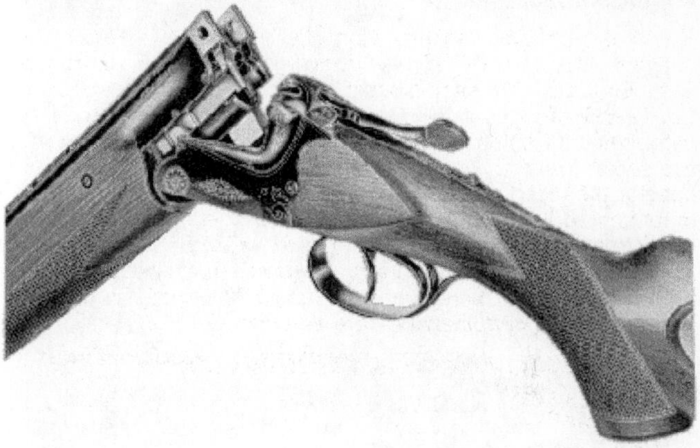

NIB	Exc.	V.G.	Good	Fair	Poor
—	1250	900	700	500	300

Coral "B" Over-and-Under

As above, with an engraved French case hardened receiver.

NIB	Exc.	V.G.	Good	Fair	Poor
—	1400	1100	750	600	350

RECENTLY IMPORTED SHOTGUNS

SIDELOCK/SIDE-BY-SIDE

AyA sidelock shotguns use the Holland and Holland system. They feature double triggers, articulated front trigger, cocking indicators, bushed firing pins, replaceable firing pins, replaceable hinge pins, and chopper lump barrels. Frame and sidelocks are case-colored. These shotguns weigh between 5 and 7 pounds depending on gauge and barrel length. Barrel lengths are offered in 26", 27", 28", and 29" depending on gauge. All stocks are figured walnut with hand checkering and oil finish. These guns are available with several extra cost options that may affect price. Also influencing price of new guns is the fluctuating dollar in relation to Spanish currency.

Model No. 1

This model is offered in 12 gauge and 20 gauge with special English scroll engraving. Fitted with automatic ejectors and straight grip stock with exhibition quality wood.

NIB	Exc.	V.G.	Good	Fair	Poor
—	10500	8000	4750	2300	700

Model No. 1 Round Body

As above, but with a round body action.

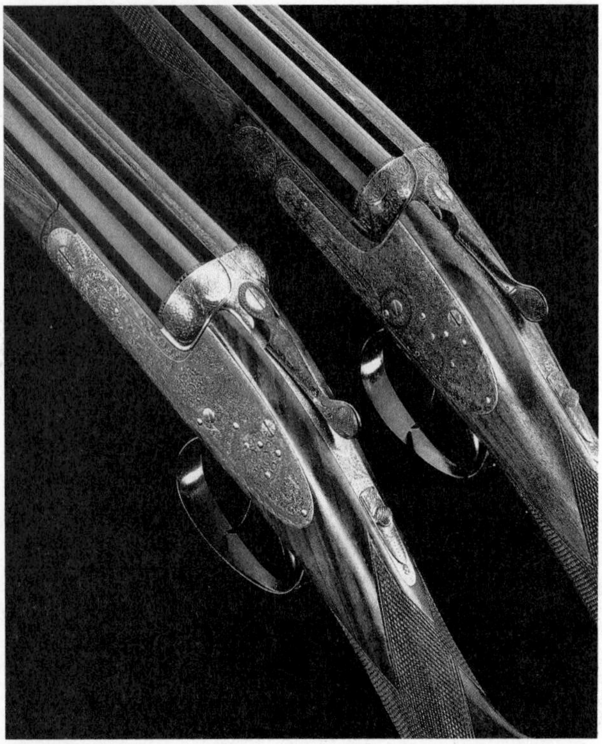

NIB	Exc.	V.G.	Good	Fair	Poor
—	11500	9000	5250	—	—

Model No. 1 Deluxe

A deluxe version of the No. 1 with finer wood and engraving.

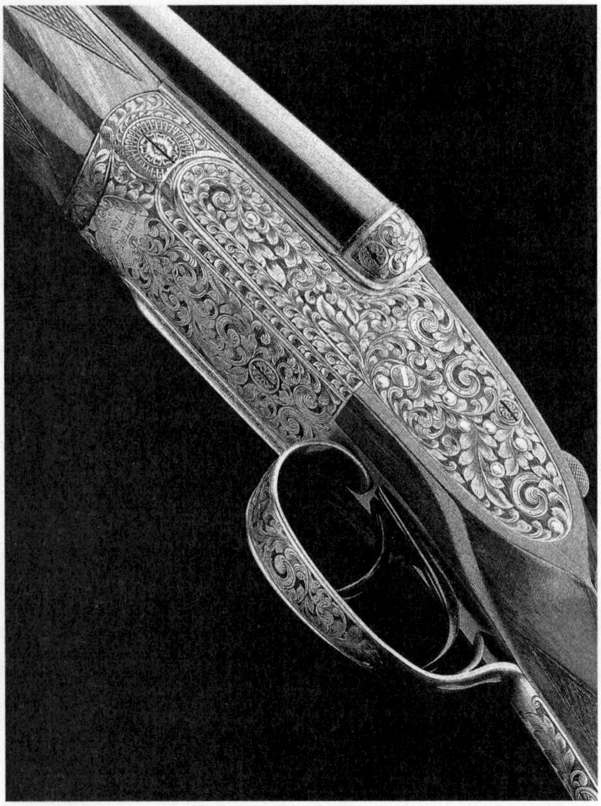

NIB	Exc.	V.G.	Good	Fair	Poor
—	11500	9000	5250	2400	700

NOTE: For round body deluxe add $350.

Model No. 2

This model is offered in 12, 16, 20, and 28 gauge, and .410 bore. It has automatic ejectors and straight-grip, select walnut stock.

NIB	Exc.	V.G.	Good	Fair	Poor
—	5000	4000	2500	1850	700

Model No. 2 Round Body

As above, but with round body action.

NIB	Exc.	V.G.	Good	Fair	Poor
—	5200	4250	2750	1950	700

Model No. 53

Chambered for 12, 16, and 20 gauge. Features three locking lugs and side clips, automatic ejectors and straight grip stock.

NIB	Exc.	V.G.	Good	Fair	Poor
—	3500	4000	2750	1000	700

Model No. 56

This model is available in 12 gauge only and features three locking lugs, side clips, special wide action body, and raised matted rib. Select walnut, straight-grip stock.

NIB	Exc.	V.G.	Good	Fair	Poor
—	8700	6750	5400	2000	1000

Model XXV—Sidelock

Offered in 12 gauge and 20 gauge only this model is fitted with a Churchill-type rib. Automatic ejectors and select straight grip walnut stock are standard.

NIB	Exc.	V.G.	Good	Fair	Poor
—	5250	4250	3200	1750	1000

BOXLOCK SIDE-BY-SIDE

These AyA guns utilize an Anson & Deeley system with double locking lugs with detachable cross pin and separate trigger plate that gives access to the firing mechanism. Frame is case-colored. The barrels are chopper lump, firing pins are bushed, automatic safety and automatic ejectors are standard. Barrel lengths are offered in 26", 27", and 28" depending on gauge. Weights are between 5 and 7 pounds depending on gauge.

Model XXV—Boxlock

This model is available in 12 and 20 gauge only. The select walnut stock is hand checkered with straight grip stock.

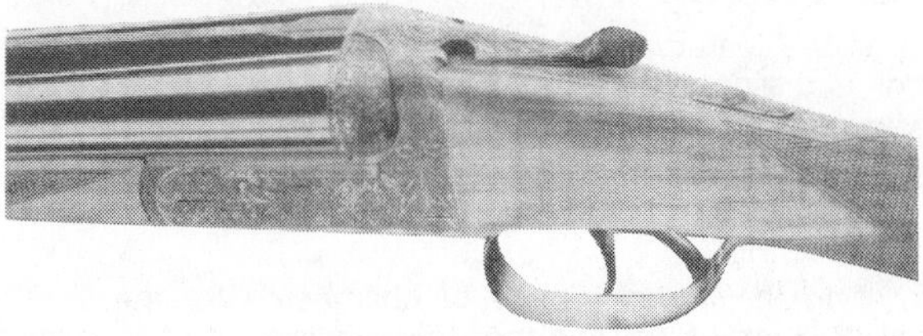

NIB	Exc.	V.G.	Good	Fair	Poor
—	3500	2250	800	600	350

Model No. 4

This model is available in 12, 16, 20, and 28 gauge as well as .410 bore. It is fitted with select hand checkered walnut stock with straight grip. Light scroll engraving on this model. Add 75 percent for 28 and .410.

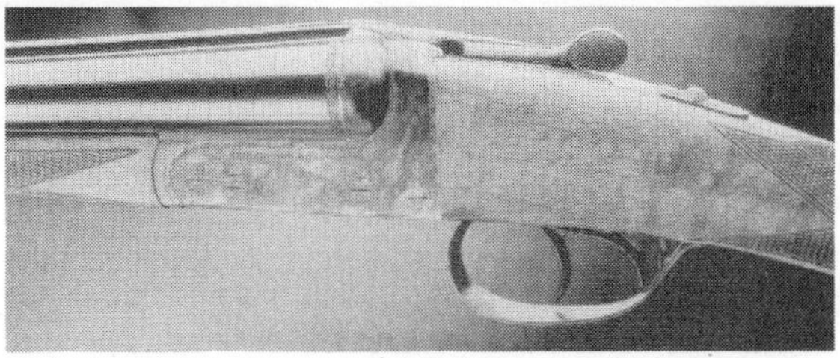

NIB	Exc.	V.G.	Good	Fair	Poor
—	3000	2650	1250	—	—

Model No. 4 Deluxe

Same as above, but with select walnut stock and slightly more engraving coverage. Add 75 percent for 28 and .410.

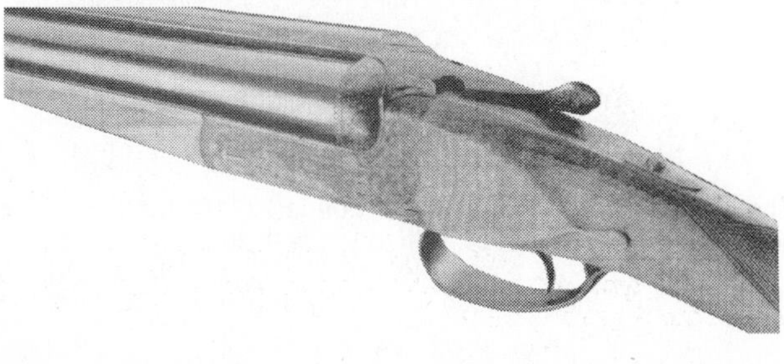

NIB	Exc.	V.G.	Good	Fair	Poor
—	5000	3995	1500	1000	550

OVER-AND-UNDER

These AyA shotguns are similar in design and appearance to the Gebruder Merkel over-and-under sidelocks with three-part forend, Kersten cross bolt, and double under locking lugs.

Model No. 37 Super

This model is available in 12 gauge only with ventilated rib, automatic ejectors, internally gold-plated sidelocks. Offered with three different types of engraving patterns: ducks, scroll, or deep cut engraving. Very few of this model were imported into the U.S.

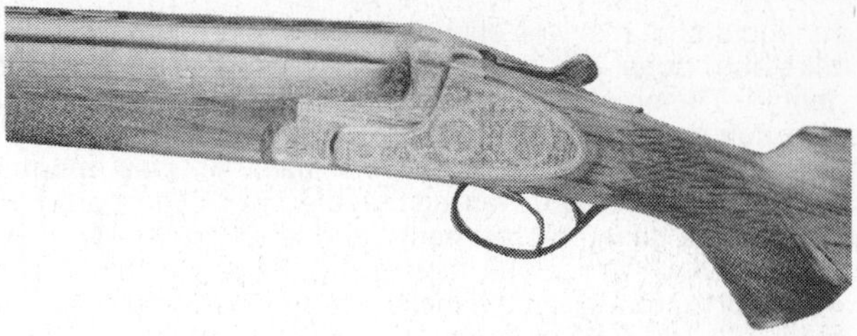

NIB	Exc.	V.G.	Good	Fair	Poor
—	12000	9500	5000	3500	2000

Model Augusta

This is the top-of-the-line AyA model offered in 12 gauge only. It features presentation wood and deep cut scroll engraving. Very few of this model were imported into the U.S.

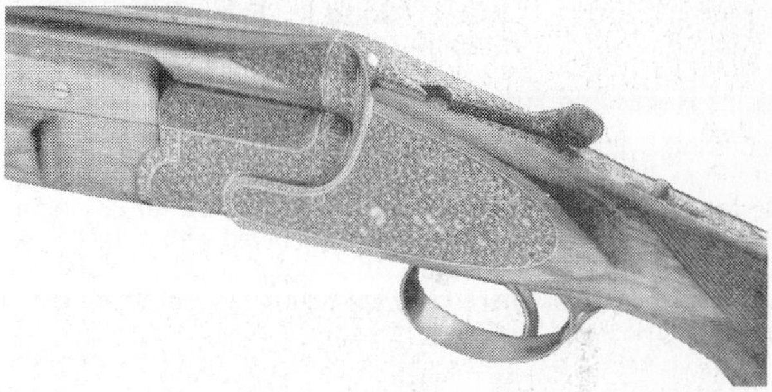

NIB	Exc.	V.G.	Good	Fair	Poor
—	15000	8000	4500	3500	1500

NOTE: For extra cost options add approximately: Pistol grip–$90; Rubber recoil pad–$190; Left-hand gun–$775; Length of pull longer than 15"–$125; Select wood–$235; Deluxe wood–$550; Single non-selective trigger–$400; Single-selective trigger–$600; Chrome-lined barrels–$140; Churchill rib–$375; Raised rib–$180; Extra set of barrels–$1500.

ALLEN, ETHAN

Grafton, Massachusetts

The company was founded by Ethan Allen in the early 1800s. It became a prolific gun-making firm that evolved from Ethan Allen to Allen & Thurber, as well as the Allen & Wheelock Company. It was located in Norwich, Connecticut, and Worchester, Massachusetts, as well as Grafton. It eventually became the Forehand & Wadsworth Company in 1871 after the death of Ethan Allen. There were many and varied firearms produced under all of the headings described above. If one desires to collect Ethan Allen firearms, it would be advisable to educate oneself, as there are a number of fine publications available on the subject. The basic models and their values are listed.

Second Model Pocket Rifle

A rounded-frame, round-grip version of the First Model.

NIB	Exc.	V.G.	Good	Fair	Poor
—	—	—	1550	650	200

Combination Gun

Either an Over/Under or side-by-side rifle chambered for 12 gauge and .38 caliber percussion. The barrels were from 28" to 34" in length. It had two hammers and double triggers with a ramrod mounted either beneath or on the right side of the barrels. The finish was browned with a walnut stock. Examples with a patchbox have been noted. Production was very limited, with the Over/Under versions worth approximately 20 percent more than the side-by-side values given. They were manufactured between the 1840s and the 1860s.

NIB	Exc.	V.G.	Good	Fair	Poor
—	—	6000	4350	1750	600

Drop Breech Rifle

This single-shot rifle was chambered for the .22 through the .44 rimfire cartridges. It had a part-octagon barrel from 23" to 28" in length. The breech was activated by the combination trigger guard action lever. Opening the breech automatically ejected the empty cartridge. The external hammer was manually cocked, and it featured an adjustable sight. The barrel was blued with a case-colored frame and a walnut stock. It was marked "Allen & Wheelock/ Allen's Pat. Sept. 18, 1860." There were approximately 2,000 manufactured between 1860 and 1871.

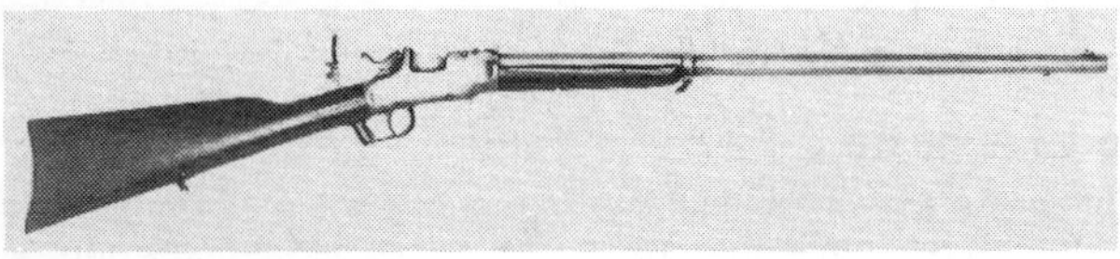

Courtesy Milwaukee Public Museum, Milwaukee, Wisconsin

NIB	Exc.	V.G.	Good	Fair	Poor
—	—	1550	600	200	100

Lipfire Revolving Rifle

A 6-shot, cylinder-type rifle chambered for the .44 caliber lipfire cartridge. It had an unfluted cylinder with slots at its rear to allow for the cartridge lips. The round barrels were 26" to 28" in length with an octagon breech. The finish was blued with a case-colored frame and a walnut buttstock. This model was not marked with the maker's name. There were approximately 100 manufactured between 1861 and 1863.

Courtesy Buffalo Bill Historical Center, Cody, Wyoming

NIB	Exc.	V.G.	Good	Fair	Poor
—	—	18500	7000	2000	775

Double-Barrel Shotgun

A side-by-side gun chambered for 10 or 12 gauge. The barrel length was 28". It was loaded by means of a trapdoor-type breech that had a lever handle. The finish was blued with checkered walnut stock. There were a few hundred manufactured between 1865 and 1871.

NIB	Exc.	V.G.	Good	Fair	Poor
—	—	1800	800	250	125

ALPHA ARMS CO.

Flower Mound, Texas

Alpha Arms Co. produced high-grade bolt-action rifles on a semi-custom basis. It manufactured a number of standard models but offered many options at additional cost. Some of these options were custom sights and finishes and an octagonal barrel. These extra features would add to the value of the models listed. This company operated from 1983 until 1987.

Alpha Jaguar Grade I

Built on a Mauser-type action with barrel lengths from 20" to 24". It was chambered for most calibers between .222 Rem. and .338 Win. Mag. The stock was made from a synthetic laminated material that the company called Alphawood. This model was introduced in 1987 and only produced that year.

NIB	Exc.	V.G.	Good	Fair	Poor
1700	1100	750	500	300	200

Jaguar Grade II

Similar to the Grade I with a Douglas Premium barrel.

NIB	Exc.	V.G.	Good	Fair	Poor
1825	1275	800	500	400	250

Jaguar Grade III

Has the Douglas barrel plus a hand-honed trigger and action and a three-position safety like the Winchester Model 70.

NIB	Exc.	V.G.	Good	Fair	Poor
1950	1500	1050	700	400	200

Jaguar Grade IV

Has all the features of the Grade III with a specially lightened action and sling-swivel studs.

NIB	Exc.	V.G.	Good	Fair	Poor
2000	1750	1200	900	500	250

Alpha Big-Five

Similar to the Jaguar Grade IV chambered for the .300 Win. Mag., .375 H&H Mag. and the .458 Win. Mag. It had a reinforced through-bolt stock to accommodate the recoil of the larger caliber cartridges for which it was chambered. It also had a decelerator recoil pad. This model was manufactured in 1987 only. Add 20 percent for .458.

NIB	Exc.	V.G.	Good	Fair	Poor
2200	1850	1500	950	600	300

Alpha Grand Slam

Features the same high quality as the Jaguar models and is available in a left-hand model. It has a fluted bolt, laminated stock, and a matte blue finish. Deduct 10 percent for left-hand version.

NIB	Exc.	V.G.	Good	Fair	Poor
1700	1500	1250	700	450	250

Alpha Custom

Similar to the Grand Slam with a select grade stock.

NIB	Exc.	V.G.	Good	Fair	Poor
1700	1500	1250	750	500	250

Alpha Alaskan

Similar to the Grand Slam but chambered for the .308 Win., .350 Rem. Mag., .358 Win. and the .458 Win. Mag. It features all stainless steel construction. Add 20 percent for .458.

NIB	Exc.	V.G.	Good	Fair	Poor
2000	1750	1450	850	500	250

AMAC

American Military Arms Corporation
formerly Iver Johnson
Jacksonville, Arkansas

The Iver Johnson Arms Co. was founded in 1871 in Fitchsburg, Massachusetts. It was one of the oldest and most successful of the old-line arms companies on which our modern era has taken its toll. In 1984 the company moved to Jacksonville,

Arkansas; in 1987 it was purchased by the American Military Arms Corporation. This company has released some of the older designs as well as some new models. In 1993 the company went out of business. The original Iver Johnson line is listed under its own heading.

U.S. Carbine .22

This is a semi-automatic, military-style carbine that is patterned after the M1 of WWII fame. It is chambered for the .22 LR cartridge, has an 18.5" barrel and features military-style peep sights and a 15-shot detachable magazine.

NIB	Exc.	V.G.	Good	Fair	Poor
325	250	175	100	75	50

Wagonmaster Lever Action Rifle

This model is chambered for the .22 rimfire cartridge, has an 18.5" barrel and is styled after the Win. 94. The stock has a straight grip; and the forend, a barrel band. There are adjustable sights and a tube magazine that holds 15 LR cartridges.

NIB	Exc.	V.G.	Good	Fair	Poor
295	225	150	100	75	50

Wagonmaster .22 Magnum

This model is the same as the Wagonmaster except that it is chambered for the .22 rimfire magnum.

NIB	Exc.	V.G.	Good	Fair	Poor
325	250	175	125	95	50

Targetmaster Pump-Action Rifle

This model is a slide- or pump-action that is chambered for the .22 rimfire cartridges. It has an 18.5" barrel with adjustable sights and a straight grip stock. It holds 12 LR cartridges.

NIB	Exc.	V.G.	Good	Fair	Poor
325	175	145	115	75	50

Li'L Champ Bolt-Action Rifle

This model is a scaled-down single-shot that is chambered for the .22 rimfire cartridges. It has a 16.25" barrel, adjustable sights, a molded stock, and nickel-plated bolt. This model is 33" overall and is designed to be the ideal first rifle for a young shooter.

NIB	Exc.	V.G.	Good	Fair	Poor
175	125	75	45	35	20

M .30 Cal. Carbine

A military-style carbine styled after the M1 of WWII fame. It is chambered for the .30 Carbine cartridge and has an 18" barrel with military-style sights and hardwood stock. There are detachable 5-, 15-, and 30-round magazines available.

NIB	Exc.	V.G.	Good	Fair	Poor
425	300	225	175	125	90

Paratrooper .30 Carbine

This model is similar to the M1 model with a folding stock.

NIB	Exc.	V.G.	Good	Fair	Poor
495	395	325	250	160	100

Long Range Rifle System/AMAC Model 5100

This is a specialized long-range, bolt-action rifle chambered for the .50 Cal. Browning Machine gun cartridge. It has a 33" barrel and a special muzzlebrake system. A custom order version in the .338 or .416 caliber is also available.

NIB	Exc.	V.G.	Good	Fair	Poor
4100	3550	2900	2000	900	450

AMERICAN ARMS, INC.

North Kansas City, Missouri

SHOTGUNS SIDE-BY-SIDE

York/Gentry

These two designations cover the same model. Prior to 1988 this model was called the York. In 1988 the receiver was casecolored and the designation was changed to the Gentry. This model was chambered for 12, 20, 28 gauge and .410. It had chrome-lined barrels from 26" to 30" in length, double triggers, 3" chambers, and automatic ejectors. The boxlock action featured scroll engraving, and the walnut stock was hand checkered. It was introduced in 1986.

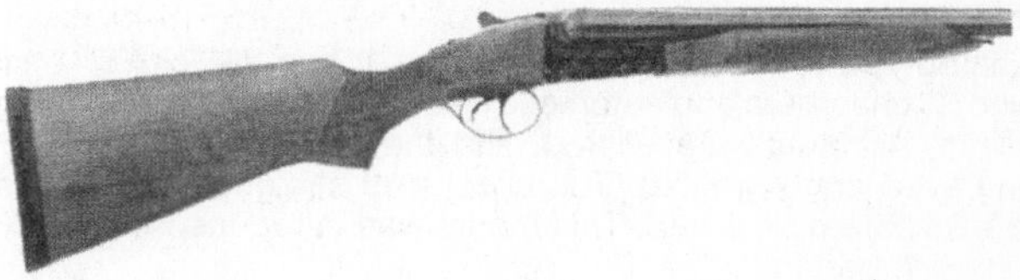

NIB	Exc.	V.G.	Good	Fair	Poor
750	625	450	300	200	150

10 Gauge Magnum Shotgun

A 10 gauge with 3.5" chambers and 32" barrels. It featured a scroll-engraved, chromed boxlock action and double triggers. It was imported from Spain in 1986 only.

NIB	Exc.	V.G.	Good	Fair	Poor
850	750	550	350	250	150

12 Gauge Magnum Shotgun

As above but chambered for 12 gauge 3-1/2" magnum shell.

NIB	Exc.	V.G.	Good	Fair	Poor
800	700	500	300	200	150

Brittany

Chambered for 12 and 20 gauge with 25" or 27" barrels with screw-in choke tubes. It had a solid matted rib and a case-colored, engraved boxlock action. Automatic ejectors and a single-selective trigger were standard on this model, as was a hand checkered, walnut, straight grip stock with semi-beavertail forend. This model was introduced in 1989.

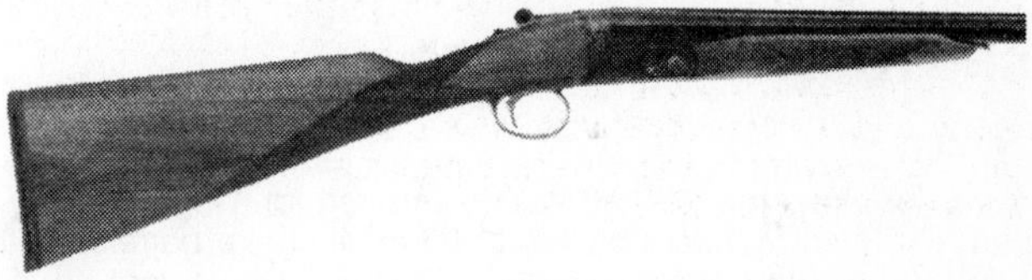

NIB	Exc.	V.G.	Good	Fair	Poor
850	750	600	450	375	200

Turkey Special

A utilitarian model designed to be an effective turkey hunting tool. It is chambered for the Magnum 10 and 12 gauges and has 26" barrels. The finish is parkerized, and the stock is also finished in a non-glare matte. Sling-swivel studs and a recoil pad are standard. This model was introduced in 1987.

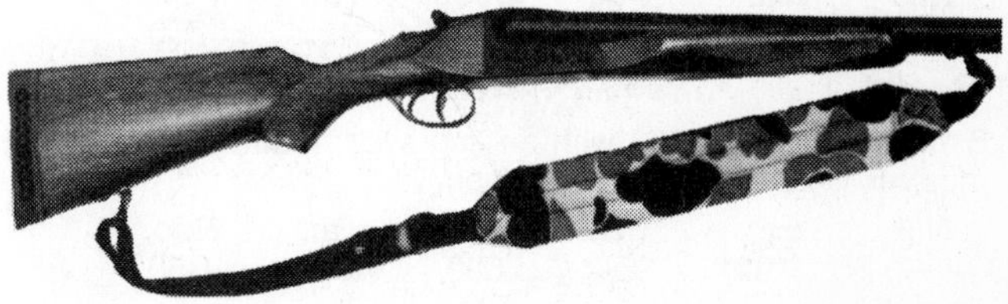

NIB	Exc.	V.G.	Good	Fair	Poor
800	700	450	350	250	150

Waterfowl Special

Similar to the Turkey Special but chambered for the 10 gauge only. It is furnished with a camouflaged sling. Introduced in 1987.

NIB	Exc.	V.G.	Good	Fair	Poor
950	850	550	350	250	150

Specialty Model

Similar to the Turkey Special and offered in 12 gauge 3-1/2" magnum.

NIB	Exc.	V.G.	Good	Fair	Poor
875	750	500	300	200	150

Derby

Chambered for the 12 and 20 gauge. It has 26" or 28" barrels with 3" chambers and automatic ejectors. Either double or single-selective triggers are offered, and the sidelock action is scroll engraved and chromed. The checkered straight grip stock and forearm are oil-finished. This model was introduced in 1986. No longer imported.

NIB	Exc.	V.G.	Good	Fair	Poor
825	700	600	500	350	200

Grulla #2

Top-of-the-line model chambered for 12, 20 and 28 gauge and .410. The barrels are 26" or 28" with a concave rib. The hand-fitted full sidelock action is extensively engraved and case-colored. There are various chokes, double triggers, and automatic ejectors. The select walnut, straight grip stock and splinter forend is hand checkered and has a hand-rubbed oil finish. This model was introduced in 1989. No longer imported.

NIB	Exc.	V.G.	Good	Fair	Poor
2500	1750	1250	900	500	250

SHOTGUNS OVER/UNDER

F.S. 200

A trap or skeet model that was chambered for 12 gauge only. It had 26" Skeet & Skeet barrels or 32" Full choke barrels on the trap model. The barrels were separated and had a vent rib. The boxlock action had a Greener crossbolt and was either black or matte chrome-plated. It featured a single-selective trigger, automatic ejectors, and a checkered walnut pistol grip stock. The F.S. 200 was imported in 1986 and 1987 only.

NIB	Exc.	V.G.	Good	Fair	Poor
—	675	575	465	350	150

F.S. 300

Similar to the F. S. 200 with lightly engraved side plates and a 30" barrel offered in the trap grade. It was imported in 1986 only.

NIB	Exc.	V.G.	Good	Fair	Poor
—	800	675	565	450	250

F.S. 400

Similar to the F.S. 300 with an engraved, matte chrome-plated receiver. It was imported in 1986 only.

NIB	Exc.	V.G.	Good	Fair	Poor
—	1100	950	800	650	350

F.S. 500

Similar to the F.S. 400 with the same general specifications. It was not imported after 1985.

NIB	Exc.	V.G.	Good	Fair	Poor
—	1150	1000	850	700	350

Waterfowl Special

Chambered for the 12 gauge Magnum with 3.5" chambers. It has 28" barrels with screw-in choke tubes. There are automatic ejectors and a single-selective trigger. The finish is parkerized with a matte finished stock, sling swivels, and camouflaged sling and a recoil pad. It was introduced in 1987.

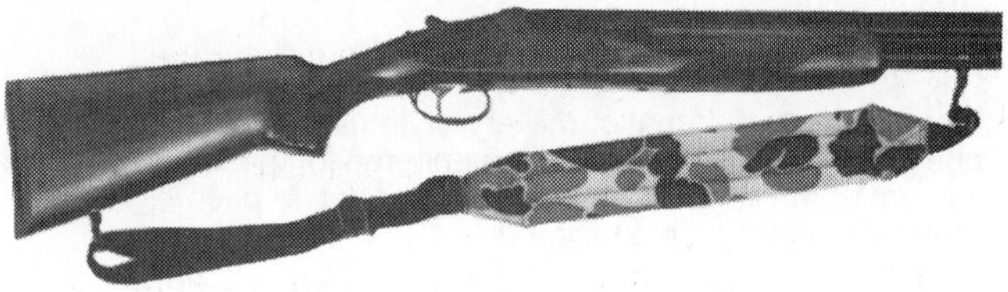

NIB	Exc.	V.G.	Good	Fair	Poor
875	700	500	350	300	150

Waterfowl 10 Gauge

The same as the Waterfowl Special but is chambered for the 10 gauge Magnum with double triggers.

NIB	Exc.	V.G.	Good	Fair	Poor
975	850	600	400	300	200

Turkey Special

Similar to the Waterfowl Special 10 gauge with a 26" barrel with screw-in choke tubes.

NIB	Exc.	V.G.	Good	Fair	Poor
975	850	600	350	300	200

Lince

Chambered for the 12 and 20 gauge and has 26" or 28" barrels with 3" chambers and various chokes. The boxlock action has a Greener crossbolt and was either blued or polished and chrome-plated. The barrels were blued with a ventilated rib. It has a single-selective trigger and automatic ejectors. The Lince was imported in 1986 only.

NIB	Exc.	V.G.	Good	Fair	Poor
—	500	425	350	300	200

Silver Model

Similar to the Lince with a plain, unengraved, brushed-chrome-finished receiver. It was imported in 1986 and 1987.

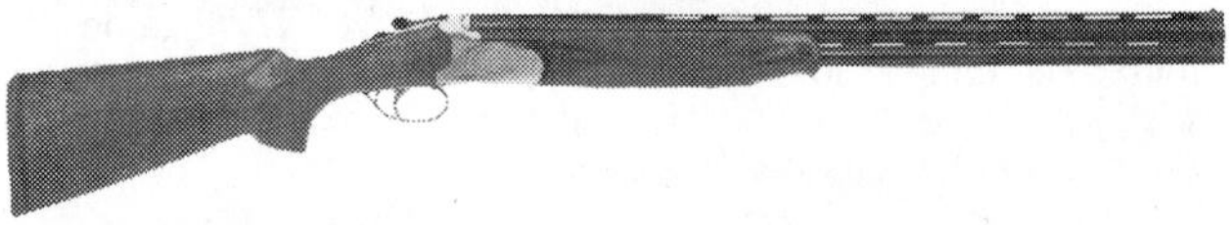

NIB	Exc.	V.G.	Good	Fair	Poor
—	500	425	350	300	200

Silver I

Similar to the Silver but is available in 28 gauge and .410, as well as 12 and 20 gauge. It also has a single-selective trigger, fixed chokes, extractors, and a recoil pad. It was introduced in 1987.

NIB	Exc.	V.G.	Good	Fair	Poor
650	550	325	275	200	175

NOTE: Add $25 for 28 gauge and .410 bore guns.

Silver II

Similar to the Silver I with screw-in choke tubes, automatic ejectors, and select walnut. It was introduced in 1987.

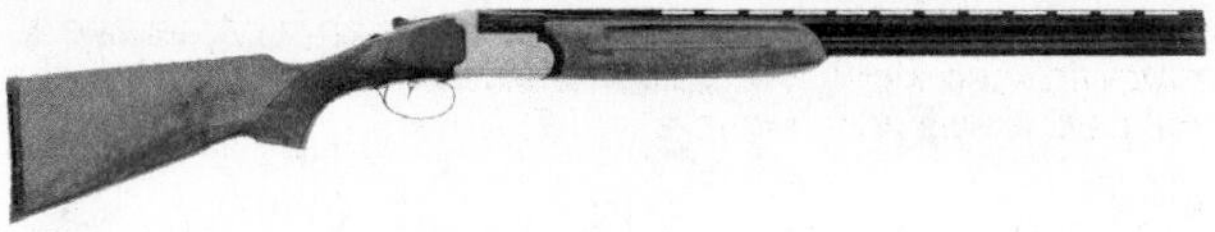

NIB	Exc.	V.G.	Good	Fair	Poor
750	650	450	350	300	150

NOTE: Add $25 for 28 gauge and .410 bore guns.

Silver II Lite

Introduced in 1994 this model is designed as an upland game gun. Offered in 12, 20, and 28 gauge with 26" barrels. Chambered for both 2-3/4" and 3" shells. Frame is made from a lightweight steel alloy. No longer imported.

NIB	Exc.	V.G.	Good	Fair	Poor
875	775	550	400	300	150

Silver Competition/Sporting

Offered in 12 gauge with a choice of 28" or 30" barrels which are made from chrome moly. Barrels have elongated forcing cones, chromed bores and are ported to help reduce recoil. Comes with interchangeable choke tubes. The single-selective trigger is mechanical. Weighs about 7-1/2 pounds. In 1996 a 20 gauge model was added with 28" barrel and 3" chambers.

NIB	Exc.	V.G.	Good	Fair	Poor
950	800	600	400	300	150

Silver Hunter

Introduced in 1999 this model is offered in 12 and 20 gauges with 26" and 28" barrels. Single-selective trigger with extractors. Choke tubes standard. Weight is about 7 lbs.

NIB	Exc.	V.G.	Good	Fair	Poor
625	500	400	300	200	100

Bristol (Sterling)

Chambered for 12 and 20 gauge. It has various barrel lengths with a vent rib and screw-in choke tubes. The chambers are 3", and the chrome-finished action is a boxlock with Greener crossbolt and game scene engraved side plates. There are automatic ejectors and a single-selective trigger. It was introduced in 1986, and in 1989 the designation was changed to the Sterling. No longer imported.

NIB	Exc.	V.G.	Good	Fair	Poor
825	750	675	500	400	200

Sir

Chambered for the 12 and 20 gauge with 3" chambers, various barrel lengths and chokings and a ventilated rib. The chrome-finished sidelock action has a Greener crossbolt and is engraved with a game scene. There are automatic ejectors and a single-selective trigger. This model was imported in 1986. No longer imported.

NIB	Exc.	V.G.	Good	Fair	Poor
—	875	750	625	500	250

Royal

Chambered for the 12 and 20 gauge. It is manufactured in various barrel lengths and chokes with a vent rib and 3" chambers. The chrome-finished sidelock action has a Greener crossbolt and is profusely scroll-engraved. It has automatic ejectors and a single-selective trigger. The select pistol grip walnut stock is hand checkered and oil-finished. This model was imported in 1986 and 1987. No longer imported.

NIB	Exc.	V.G.	Good	Fair	Poor
—	1500	1275	1000	800	400

Excelsior

Similar to the Royal with extensive deep relief engraving and gold inlays. This model was imported in 1986 and 1987. No longer imported.

NIB	Exc.	V.G.	Good	Fair	Poor
—	1750	1500	1200	875	450

SINGLE-BARREL SHOTGUNS

AASB

The standard single-barrel, break-open, hammerless shotgun. It is chambered for 12 and 20 gauge and .410. It has a 26" barrel with various chokes and 3" chambers. It has a pistol grip stock and a matte finish. It was introduced in 1988. No longer imported.

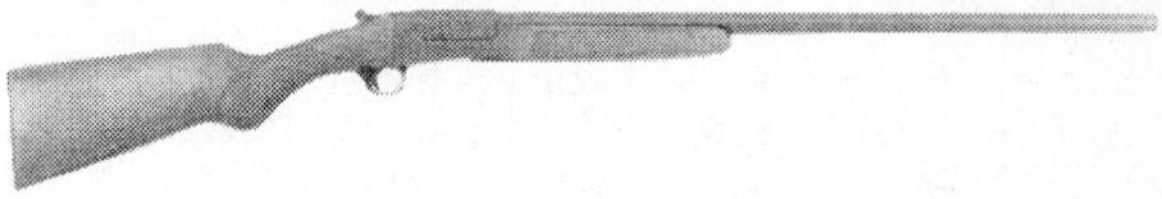

NIB	Exc.	V.G.	Good	Fair	Poor
100	85	75	60	45	25

Campers Special

Similar to the standard model with a 21" barrel and a folding stock. It was introduced in 1988. No longer imported.

NIB	Exc.	V.G.	Good	Fair	Poor
110	95	85	70	50	35

Single-Barrel Shotguns Youth Model

Chambered for the 20 gauge and .410 and has a 12.5" stock with a recoil pad. It was introduced in 1989. No longer imported.

NIB	Exc.	V.G.	Good	Fair	Poor
115	100	80	65	50	35

Slugger

This version has a 24" barrel with rifle sights. It is chambered for the 12 and 20 gauge and has a recoil pad. No longer imported.

NIB	Exc.	V.G.	Good	Fair	Poor
115	100	80	65	50	35

10 Gauge Model

Chambered for the 10 gauge 3.5" Magnum. It has a 32" full choke barrel and a recoil pad. This model was introduced in 1988. No longer imported.

NIB	Exc.	V.G.	Good	Fair	Poor
175	145	100	85	60	45

Combo Model

Similar in appearance to the other single-barrel models but is offered in an interchangeable-barreled rifle/shotgun combination—the 28" barreled .22 Hornet and the 12 gauge, or the 26" barreled .22 LR and 20 gauge. This model was furnished with a fitted hard case to hold the interchangeable barrels. It was introduced in 1989. No longer imported.

NIB	Exc.	V.G.	Good	Fair	Poor
250	200	175	145	110	75

SEMI-AUTO SHOTGUNS

Phantom Field

Chambered for 12 gauge and fitted with choice of 24", 26", or 28" barrels. Fitted with 3" chamber. Gas operated action. Choke tubes standard. Five-round magazine. Checkered walnut stock. Weight is about 7 lbs. Introduced in 1999.

NIB	Exc.	V.G.	Good	Fair	Poor
400	350	300	225	125	75

Phantom Synthetic

Same as model above but furnished with checkered synthetic stock. Weight is about 6.75 lbs. Introduced in 1999.

NIB	Exc.	V.G.	Good	Fair	Poor
400	350	300	225	125	75

Phantom HP

This model features a 19" threaded barrel for external choke tubes. Five-round magazine. Weight is about 6.75 lbs. Introduced in 1999.

NIB	Exc.	V.G.	Good	Fair	Poor
400	375	325	300	150	95

RIFLES

Model ZCY.308

Essentially the same rifle as the ZCY.223 — only it is chambered for the .308 cartridge. This model was imported in 1988 only.

NIB	Exc.	V.G.	Good	Fair	Poor
—	500	425	350	300	200

AKY39

The semi-automatic version of the Soviet AK-47 as it is manufactured by Yugoslavia. It is offered with folding tritium night sights and a wooden fixed stock. It was imported in 1988.

NIB	Exc.	V.G.	Good	Fair	Poor
—	600	475	390	300	200

AKF39

The same rifle as the AKY39 with a metal folding stock.

NIB	Exc.	V.G.	Good	Fair	Poor
—	625	550	475	300	200

AKC47

Basically the same rifle as the AKY39 without the tritium night sights.

NIB	Exc.	V.G.	Good	Fair	Poor
—	575	450	375	300	200

AKF47

The same rifle as the AKC47 with a metal folding stock.

NIB	Exc.	V.G.	Good	Fair	Poor
—	625	550	475	300	200

EXP-64 Survival Rifle

A .22 caliber, semi-automatic takedown rifle. It is self-storing in a floating, oversized plastic stock. The rifle has a 21" barrel with open sights and a crossbolt safety. There is a 10-shot detachable magazine. Importation by American Arms began in 1989.

NIB	Exc.	V.G.	Good	Fair	Poor
165	150	125	95	75	50

SM-64 TD Sporter

A .22 LR semi-automatic with a takedown 21" barrel. It has adjustable sights and a checkered hardwood stock and forend. Importation began in 1989.

NIB	Exc.	V.G.	Good	Fair	Poor
195	155	110	85	65	45

1860 Henry

Replica of lever action Henry rifle. Brass frame. Steel half-octagon barrel with tube magazine. Chambered for .44-40 or .45 Long Colt. Offered in 24" or 18.5" barrels. Weight with 24" barrel is about 9.25 lbs. Built by Uberti.

NIB	Exc.	V.G.	Good	Fair	Poor
950	800	650	400	300	200

1866 Winchester

Replica of Winchester 1866. Offered in .44-40 or .45 Long Colt. Barrel lengths in 24" or 19". Brass frame. Weight is about 8.25 lbs. for 24" barrel model. Built by Uberti.

NIB	Exc.	V.G.	Good	Fair	Poor
825	700	495	300	200	100

1873 Winchester

Replica of Winchester Model 1873. Offered with choice of 24" or 30" barrels. Chambered for .44-40 or .45 Long Colt. Case hardened steel frame. Weight is about 8.25 lbs. for 24" model. Built by Uberti.

NIB	Exc.	V.G.	Good	Fair	Poor
850	725	550	325	225	125

NOTE: Add $80 for 30" barrel.

1885 Single-Shot High Wall

Chambered for .45-70 cartridge this Winchester replica is fitted with a 28" round barrel. Weight is about 8.75 lbs. Built by Uberti.

NIB	Exc.	V.G.	Good	Fair	Poor
850	695	550	350	200	100

Sharps Cavalry Carbine

This Sharps replica is fitted with a 22" round barrel and chambered for the .45-70 cartridge. Adjustable rear sight. Weight is about 8 lbs.

NIB	Exc.	V.G.	Good	Fair	Poor
700	600	425	350	200	100

Sharps Frontier Carbine

Similar to the Cavalry carbine but with a 22" octagonal barrel and double set triggers. Weight is about 7.75 lbs.

NIB	Exc.	V.G.	Good	Fair	Poor
775	625	475	375	225	125

Sharps Sporting Rifle

This model features a 28" octagonal barrel chambered for either the .45-70 or .45-120 cartridge. Double set triggers. Adjustable rear sight. Checkered walnut stock. Weight is about 9 lbs.

NIB	Exc.	V.G.	Good	Fair	Poor
775	625	475	375	225	125

AMERICAN ARMS CO.

Boston, Massachusetts

The history of American Arms is rather sketchy, but it appears the company was formed in 1853 as the G. H. Fox Co. and then became the American Tool & Machine Co. in 1865. In 1870 they formed a new corporation called American Arms Company with George Fox as the principle stockholder. This corporation was dissolved in 1873; a second American Arms Co. was incorporated in 1877 and a third in 1890. It is unclear if these corporations had essentially the same owners, but George H. Fox appears as a principal owner in two of the three. One could assume that financial problems forced them to bankrupt one corporation and reorganize under another. American Arms manufactured firearms in Boston, Massachusetts, from 1866 until 1893. In 1893 they moved to Bluffton, Alabama and manufactured guns until 1901.

Fox Model "Swing Out" Hammer Double

Manufactured from 1870 to 1884, designed by George H. Fox, not to be confused with A.H. Fox. This model is unusual in that the barrel swings to the right for loading and the barrel release is located on the tang. It comes in 10 and 12 gauge, 26", 28", 30" and 32", with twist, Damascus or laminated barrels. Early production models have conventional soldered together barrels. Later variations after 1878 feature a unique design in that the barrels are dovetailed together. These guns could be ordered with several options and choices of finish; this would add premium value to a particular gun.

NIB	Exc.	V.G.	Good	Fair	Poor
—	—	2000	950	400	150

Semi-Hammerless Double

Manufactured from 1892 to 1901. This model features a cocking lever that cocks an internal firing pin. It comes in 12 gauge with 30" twist barrels.

NIB	Exc.	V.G.	Good	Fair	Poor
—	—	1500	750	350	150

Whitmore Model Hammerless Double

Manufactured from 1890 to 1901. It comes in 10, 12, and 16 gauge with 28", 30" or 32" twist, laminated or Damascus barrels. It is marked Whitmore's patent.

Courtesy Nick Niles, Paul Goodwin photo

NIB	Exc.	V.G.	Good	Fair	Poor
—	—	1500	775	375	150

Semi-Hammerless Single-Barrel

Manufactured from 1882 to 1901. It comes in 10, 12, and 16 gauge with 28", 30" or 32" twist or Damascus barrel.

NIB	Exc.	V.G.	Good	Fair	Poor
—	—	1500	750	300	100

AMERICAN GUN CO., NEW YORK

Norwich, Connecticut
Maker—Crescent Firearms Co.

Side-by-Side Shotgun

A typical trade gun made around the turn of the century by the Crescent Firearms Co. to be distributed by H. & D. Folsom. These are sometimes known as "Hardware Store Guns," as that is where many were sold. This particular gun was chambered for 12, 16, and 20 gauges and was produced with or without external hammers. The length of the barrels varied, as did the chokes. Some were produced with Damascus barrels; some, with fluid steel. The latter are worth approximately 25 percent more.NOTE: For a full listing of most of the variations of the Crescent Arms Co., and shotguns marked with American Gun Co. see "Crescent F.A. Co."

AMERICAN INDUSTRIES

Cleveland, Ohio
aka CALICO LIGHT WEAPONS SYSTEMS
Sparks, Nevada

Calico M-100

A semi-automatic carbine that has a 16.1" barrel with a flash suppressor. It is chambered for the .22 LR and features a folding stock, full shrouding hand guards, a 100-round capacity, helical feed, and detachable magazine. It features an ambidextrous safety, pistol grip storage compartment, and a black finished alloy frame and adjustable sights. This model was introduced in 1986.

NIB	Exc.	V.G.	Good	Fair	Poor
500	400	350	250	200	100

Calico M-100P/M-110

Similar to the M-100 .22 rimfire with a 6" barrel with muzzlebrake and no shoulder stock.

NIB	Exc.	V.G.	Good	Fair	Poor
500	400	350	250	200	75

Calico M-100S Sporter/M-105

Similar to the Model 100 handguns with a futuristically styled walnut buttstock and forearm.

NIB	Exc.	V.G.	Good	Fair	Poor
500	400	350	250	200	75

Calico M-101 Solid Stock Carbine

Introduced in 1994 this rifle features a 100-round magazine and a composite buttstock that is removable.

NIB	Exc.	V.G.	Good	Fair	Poor
550	450	400	300	200	75

Calico M-900

A black polymer-stocked rifle that is similar to the M-100S, chambered for the 9mm Parabellum. It has a delayed blowback action and features a stainless steel bolt and alloy receiver. The cocking handle is non-reciprocating, and the rear sight is fixed with an adjustable front. There is a 50-round magazine standard and a 100-round capacity model optional. This model was introduced in 1989.

NIB	Exc.	V.G.	Good	Fair	Poor
750	575	425	350	275	100

Calico M-951

The M-951 is a tactical carbine with a sliding buttstock. The barrel is 16" in length. It weighs about 7 pounds.

NIB	Exc.	V.G.	Good	Fair	Poor
750	575	425	350	275	100

Calico M-951S

Same as above but furnished with more conventional buttstock. Referred to as a light tactical carbine. Weighs about 7-1/4 pounds.

NIB	Exc.	V.G.	Good	Fair	Poor
750	575	425	350	275	100

AMERICAN INTERNATIONAL

Salt Lake City, Utah
aka American Research & Development

American 180 Carbine (SAM-180)

This firearm, imported from Austria, is a semi-automatic, 16.5" barreled carbine chambered for the .22 LR. The sights are adjustable, and the stock is made of high-impact plastic. The unique drum magazine holds 177 rounds and is affixed to the top of the receiver. There is a select-fire version available for law enforcement agencies only and an optional laser lock sight system. Later manufactured by Feather Industries in Boulder, Colorado. It is now known as the SAM-180.

NIB	Exc.	V.G.	Good	Fair	Poor
1400	1200	650	400	200	100

AMERICAN TACTICAL IMPORTS

Rochester, New York

American Tactical Imports GSG-522

Semiauto tactical rifle chambered in .22 LR. Features include 16.25-inch barrel; black finish overall; polymer forend and buttstock; backup iron sights; receiver-mounted Picaatinny rail; 10-round magazine. Several other rifle and carbine versions available. Price: $475.

AMERICAN WESTERN ARMS INC. (AWA)

Delray Beach, Florida

AWA Lightning Rifle LE

A copy of the Colt Lightning slide-action rifle chambered for the .32-20, .38 Special, .38-40, .44-40, or the .45 Colt cartridge. Choice of round barrel lengths in 20" or 24". Engraved AWA logo and stage scene on the receiver. Limited edition to 500 guns.

NIB	Exc.	V.G.	Good	Fair	Poor
1200	950	775	500	300	175

AWA Lightning Rifle

This slide action rifle is chambered for those cartridges above with a 24" barrel length with the choice of round or octagon barrel. Blued finish.

NIB	Exc.	V.G.	Good	Fair	Poor
800	675	500	400	300	175

NOTE: Add $40 for octagon barrel.

AWA Lightning Carbine

As above but with 20" barrel in round or octagon.

NIB	Exc.	V.G.	Good	Fair	Poor
800	675	500	400	300	175

NOTE: Add $40 for octagon barrel.

AMT

formerly Arcadia Machine and Tool
Irwindale, California
See also—Galena Industries Inc.

AMT, one of several companies that succeeded Auto Mag Corp., the original manufacturer of Auto Mag pistols, operated from approx. 1984 to 1998. The prices in this section are for these earlier AMT-built guns. In 1998, Galena Ind. of Sturgis, SD purchased the rights to produce most of the AMT-developed firearms and manufactured several models from 1999 to 2001. In 2005, the rights to several AMT models were acquired by Crusader Gun Co. of Houston, parent company of High Standard Mfg. Co. Also see listing for Auto Mag.

Lightning Rifle

Patterned after the Ruger 10/22 and said to have been discontinued for that reason, this rifle has a 22" barrel and a 25-round, detachable magazine with a folding stock. Introduced in 1986.

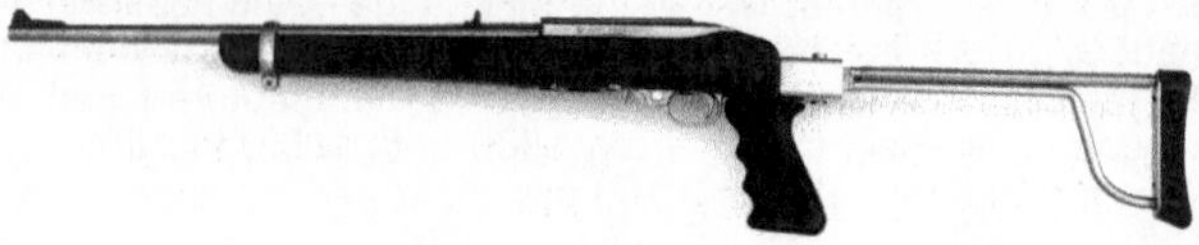

Courtesy J.B. Wood

NIB	Exc.	V.G.	Good	Fair	Poor
375	250	175	125	75	50

Small Game Hunter

As above, with a full stock and 10-round magazine. Introduced in 1986.

NIB	Exc.	V.G.	Good	Fair	Poor
350	225	175	150	125	100

Small Game Hunter II

This semi-automatic rifle is chambered for the .22 LR cartridge. Stock is a checkered black matte nylon and is fitted with a removable recoil pad for ammo, cleaning rod, and knife. Rotary magazine holds 10 rounds. Stainless steel action and barrel. Barrel is a heavyweight target type, 22" long. Weight is 6 lbs.

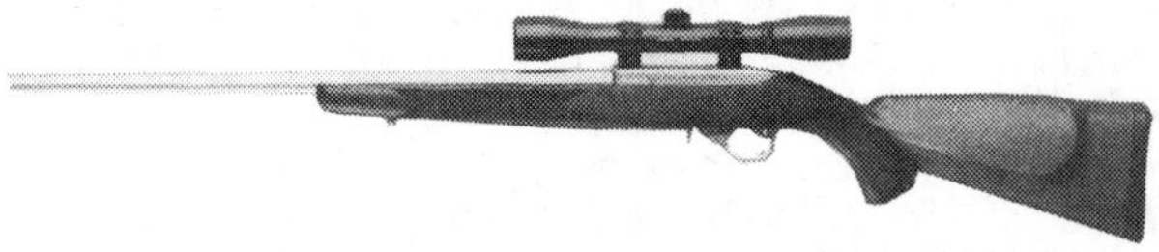

NIB	Exc.	V.G.	Good	Fair	Poor
350	225	175	150	125	100

Hunter Rifle

This semi-automatic rifle is chambered for the .22 Rimfire Magnum cartridge. Stock is checkered black matte nylon. Other features are similar to the Small Game Hunter II including weight.

NIB	Exc.	V.G.	Good	Fair	Poor
375	250	200	150	125	100

Magnum Hunter

Similar to above but chambered for the .22 Magnum cartridge and fitted with a 22" accurized barrel. Barrel and action are stainless steel. It comes standard with a 5-round magazine and composite stock but a laminated stock was available at an extra cost as is a 10-round magazine.

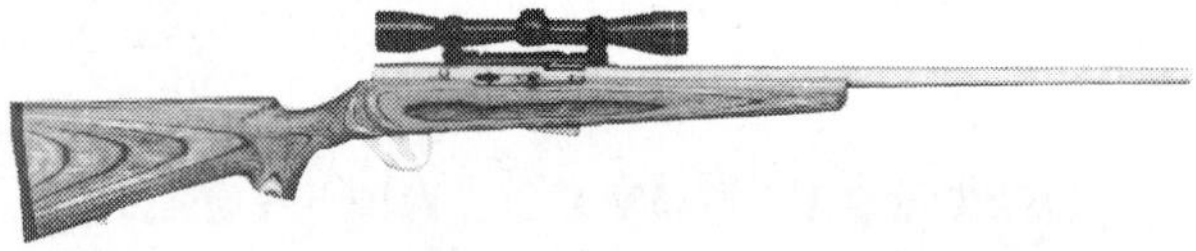

NIB	Exc.	V.G.	Good	Fair	Poor
525	400	350	250	200	150

Target Model

A semi-automatic rifle chambered for .22 LR cartridge and fitted with a 20" target barrel. Weight is about 7.5 lbs. Choice of Fajen or Hogue stock. For Hogue stock deduct $50.00.

NIB	Exc.	V.G.	Good	Fair	Poor
600	500	450	300	200	—

Single-Shot Standard Rifle

Custom-built rifle with choice of barrel length, composite stock, adjustable trigger, post '64 Winchester action, all in stainless and chrome moly steel. Chambered for all standard calibers. First offered in 1996.

NIB	Exc.	V.G.	Good	Fair	Poor
875	675	500	350	200	175

Single-Shot Deluxe Rifle

Custom-built rifle on a Mauser-type action with choice of match grade barrel lengths and custom Kevlar stock. Built from stainless and chrome moly steel. Chambered for all standard calibers. First offered in 1996.

NIB	Exc.	V.G.	Good	Fair	Poor
1800	1400	950	650	400	225

Bolt-Action Repeating Rifle—Standard

Similar in construction and features to the Standard Single-Shot rifle.

NIB	Exc.	V.G.	Good	Fair	Poor
840	675	500	350	200	175

Bolt-Action Repeating Rifle—Deluxe

Similar in construction and features to the Deluxe Single-Shot rifle.

NIB	Exc.	V.G.	Good	Fair	Poor
1800	1400	950	650	400	225

ANSCHUTZ
Ulm, Germany

Orginally founded in 1856 by Julius and Lusie Anschutz, the company was called J.G. Anschutz, and manufactured a wide variety of firearms. In 1950, in Ulm, the new company was founded: J.G. Anschutz GmbH. Values for new guns fluctuate according to currency variations.

Mark 10 Target Rifle

A single-shot, bolt-action rifle that is chambered for the .22 LR cartridge. It has a 26" heavy barrel with adjustable target-type sights. The finish was blued, and the walnut target stock had an adjustable palm rest. It was manufactured between 1963 and 1981.

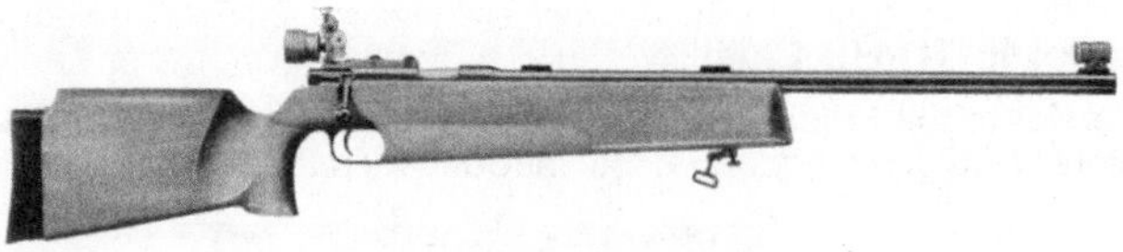

NIB	Exc.	V.G.	Good	Fair	Poor
500	425	350	210	150	100

Model 1403D

A single-shot target rifle chambered for the .22 LR cartridge. It has a 26" barrel and is furnished without sights. It has a fully adjustable trigger and a blued finish with a walnut target-type stock.

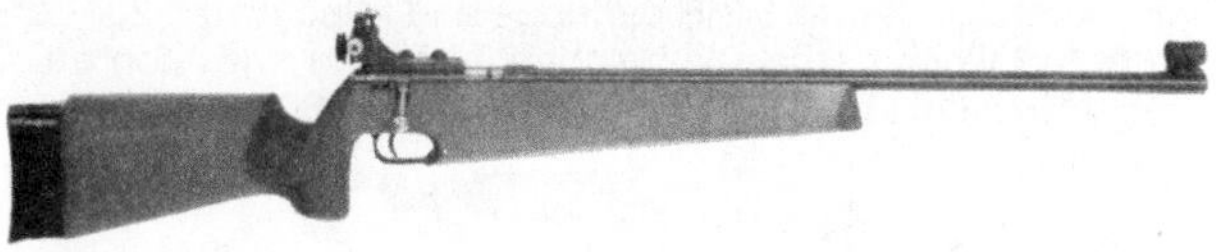

NIB	Exc.	V.G.	Good	Fair	Poor
850	775	675	500	375	250

Model 1407

Similar to the Mark 10 but is furnished without sights. It was known as the "I.S.U." model. It was discontinued in 1981.

NIB	Exc.	V.G.	Good	Fair	Poor
525	450	375	235	175	100

Model 1408

A heavier-barreled version of the Model 1407.

NIB	Exc.	V.G.	Good	Fair	Poor
525	450	375	240	180	105

Model 1411

Designed specifically to be fired from the prone position.

NIB	Exc.	V.G.	Good	Fair	Poor
750	650	450	210	150	100

Model 1413 Match

A high-grade, competition version with a heavy target barrel that is furnished without sights; optional sights extra. The walnut stock has an adjustable cheekpiece.

NIB	Exc.	V.G.	Good	Fair	Poor
775	675	550	400	275	150

Model 1416D HB Classic

This model is chambered for the .22 LR cartridge. Magazine capacity is 5 rounds. Fitted with a match grade trigger and target grade barrel. Checkered walnut stock. Built on the 64 action.

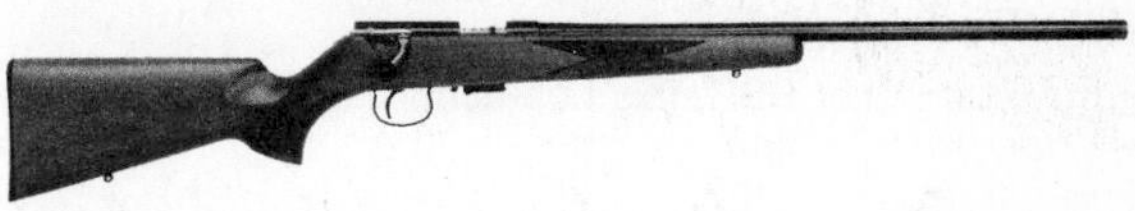

NIB	Exc.	V.G.	Good	Fair	Poor
900	725	595	400	225	125

Model 1416D KL Classic

This sporting rifle is chambered for the .22 LR cartridge and is fitted with an American-style stock of European walnut or hardwood. Built on Anschutz Match 64 action. Left-handed model also offered.

NIB	Exc.	V.G.	Good	Fair	Poor
900	725	595	300	200	100

Model 1416D Custom

Chambered for the .22 LR cartridge, this model features a European-style stock with Monte Carlo cheekpiece, and schnabel fore-end.

NIB	Exc.	V.G.	Good	Fair	Poor
875	650	550	300	200	100

Model 1418D KL Mannlicher

A hunting rifle with a full-length, Mannlicher-type stock made with hand-checkered walnut. Chambered for .22 LR with 5-round magazine. Open iron sights. Weight is about 5.5 lbs.

NIB	Exc.	V.G.	Good	Fair	Poor
1200	950	700	450	200	150

Model 1418/19

A lower-priced sporter model that was formerly imported by Savage Arms.

NIB	*Exc.*	*V.G.*	*Good*	*Fair*	*Poor*
700	650	425	200	125	85

Model 1433D

This is a centerfire version of the Model 54 target rifle chambered for the .22 Hornet. It is a special-order item and features a set trigger and a 4-round, detachable magazine. The finish was blued with a full length Mannlicher stock. It was discontinued in 1986.

NIB	*Exc.*	*V.G.*	*Good*	*Fair*	*Poor*
1500	950	700	400	200	100

Model 1449D Youth

This bolt-action rifle is chambered for the .22 LR cartridge and fitted with a 16" barrel with adjustable rear sight. Stock is European hardwood with 12.25" length of pull. Magazine capacity is 5 rounds. This model is no longer imported.

NIB	*Exc.*	*V.G.*	*Good*	*Fair*	*Poor*
450	300	250	100	75	60

Model Woodchucker

Sold by distributor RSR, this bolt-action .22 caliber is similar to the Model 1449D Youth.

NIB	*Exc.*	*V.G.*	*Good*	*Fair*	*Poor*
450	300	250	100	75	60

Model 1451E Target

This is a single-shot .22 caliber target rifle fitted with a 22" barrel. Can be fitted with either micrometer iron sights or telescope sights. Checkered pistol grip, adjustable buttplate. Weight is about 6.25 lbs.

NIB	*Exc.*	*V.G.*	*Good*	*Fair*	*Poor*
625	500	400	200	125	75

Model 1451R Sporter Target

This is a bolt-action target rifle chambered for the .22 LR cartridge and fitted with a target-style stock and 22" heavy barrel. Furnished with no open sights. Two-stage target trigger is standard. Weight is approximately 6.5 lbs.

NIB	*Exc.*	*V.G.*	*Good*	*Fair*	*Poor*
650	525	425	225	175	100

Model 1451D Custom

Similar to the above model but fitted with a checkered walnut sporting stock with Monte Carlo comb and cheekpiece. Barrel length is 22.75" with open sights. Weight is about 5 lbs.

NIB	*Exc.*	*V.G.*	*Good*	*Fair*	*Poor*
675	550	450	250	150	100

Model 1451D Classic

Similar to the Model 1451 Custom with the exception of a straight walnut stock. Weight is about 5 lbs.

NIB	*Exc.*	*V.G.*	*Good*	*Fair*	*Poor*
700	600	500	300	150	100

Model 1516D KL Classic

Same as above but chambered for .22 Magnum cartridge.

NIB	*Exc.*	*V.G.*	*Good*	*Fair*	*Poor*
775	600	500	300	200	100

Model 1516D KL Custom

Same as above but chambered for .22 Magnum cartridge.

NIB	*Exc.*	*V.G.*	*Good*	*Fair*	*Poor*
850	650	550	450	250	100

Model 1517D Classic

Based on the 64 action this bolt-action rifle is chambered for the .17 HMR cartridge. Fitted with a 23" barrel. Checkered walnut stock. Magazine capacity is 4 rounds for the .17 HMR. Weight is about 5.5 lbs. Introduced in 2003.

NIB	*Exc.*	*V.G.*	*Good*	*Fair*	*Poor*
850	700	575	395	200	125

Model 1517D HB Classic

Similar to the Model 1516D but fitted with a heavy barrel without sights. Weight is about 6.2 lbs. Introduced in 2003.

NIB	*Exc.*	*V.G.*	*Good*	*Fair*	*Poor*
875	725	600	425	200	125

Model 1517D Monte Carlo

Chambered for the .17 HMR cartridge and fitted with a 23" barrel. Checkered walnut stock with schnabel forend and Monte Carlo comb. Weight is about 5.5 lbs. Introduced in 2003.

NIB	*Exc.*	*V.G.*	*Good*	*Fair*	*Poor*
895	745	625	450	200	125

Model 1517MPR Multi Purpose Rifle

Introduced in 2003 this model features a 25.5" heavy barrel without sights, a two-stage trigger, a hardwood stock with beavertail forend. Chambered for the .17 HMR cartridge. Weight is about 9 lbs. **NOTE:** This model is available with a number of extra cost options.

NIB	*Exc.*	*V.G.*	*Good*	*Fair*	*Poor*
925	775	650	475	250	150

Model 1518D Mannlicher

Same as above but chambered for the .22 Magnum.

NIB	Exc.	V.G.	Good	Fair	Poor
1200	950	700	350	225	125

Model 184

A high-grade, bolt-action sporting rifle chambered for the .22 LR cartridge. It has a 21.5" barrel with a folding-leaf sight. The finish is blued with a checkered walnut, Monte Carlo stock with a schnabel forend. It was manufactured between 1963 and 1981.

NIB	Exc.	V.G.	Good	Fair	Poor
575	425	315	225	150	100

Model 54 Sporter

A high-grade, bolt-action sporting rifle chambered for the .22 LR cartridge. It has a 24" tapered round barrel and a 5-shot detachable magazine. It features a folding leaf-type rear sight. The finish is blued with a checkered walnut, Monte Carlo stock. It was manufactured between 1963 and 1981.

NIB	Exc.	V.G.	Good	Fair	Poor
750	675	600	350	250	125

Model 54M

This version is chambered for the .22 rimfire Magnum cartridge.

NIB	Exc.	V.G.	Good	Fair	Poor
800	700	625	375	275	125

Model 141

A bolt-action sporter chambered for the .22 LR cartridge. It has a 23" round barrel with a blued finish and walnut Monte Carlo stock. It was manufactured between 1963 and 1981.

NIB	Exc.	V.G.	Good	Fair	Poor
800	650	450	200	150	100

Model 141M

Chambered for the .22 rimfire Magnum cartridge.

NIB	Exc.	V.G.	Good	Fair	Poor
825	675	475	225	175	100

Model 164

This bolt-action rifle is fitted with a 23" round barrel chambered for the .22 LR cartridge. It has a Monte Carlo stock with open sights. Magazine holds 5 rounds.

NIB	Exc.	V.G.	Good	Fair	Poor
700	625	475	325	175	100

Model 164M

Same as model above but chambered for the .22 Win. Magnum cartridge.

NIB	Exc.	V.G.	Good	Fair	Poor
725	650	500	225	175	100

Model 153

A bolt-action sporting rifle chambered for the .222 Remington cartridge. It has a 24" barrel with folding-leaf rear sight. The finish is blued with a checkered French walnut stock featuring a rosewood forend tip and pistol grip cap. It was manufactured between 1963 and 1981.

NIB	Exc.	V.G.	Good	Fair	Poor
900	750	575	300	225	150

Model 153-S

This version was offered with double-set triggers.

NIB	Exc.	V.G.	Good	Fair	Poor
950	775	615	350	275	150

Model 64

A single-shot, bolt-action rifle that is chambered for the .22 LR cartridge. It has a 26" round barrel and is furnished without sights. The finish is blued, and the walnut target-type stock featured a beaver-tail forearm and adjustable buttplate. It was manufactured between 1963 and 1981.

NIB	Exc.	V.G.	Good	Fair	Poor
600	450	350	200	150	100

Model 64MS

This version was designed for silhouette shooting and has a 21.25" barrel, blued finish, and a target-type walnut stock with a stippled pistol grip.

NIB	Exc.	V.G.	Good	Fair	Poor
950	850	625	400	300	200

Model 64 MPR

This is a multi-purpose target repeater. Chambered for the .22 LR cartridge and fitted with a 25.5" heavy barrel. Offered with optional sights and choice of stainless steel barrel with beavertail or beavertail with swivel rail. Weight is about 9 lbs.

NIB	Exc.	V.G.	Good	Fair	Poor
975	800	695	400	300	200

Model 54.18MS

A high-grade silhouette rifle chambered for the .22 LR cartridge. It has a 22" barrel and a match-grade action with fully adjustable trigger. It is furnished without sights. The finish is blued with a target-type walnut stock.

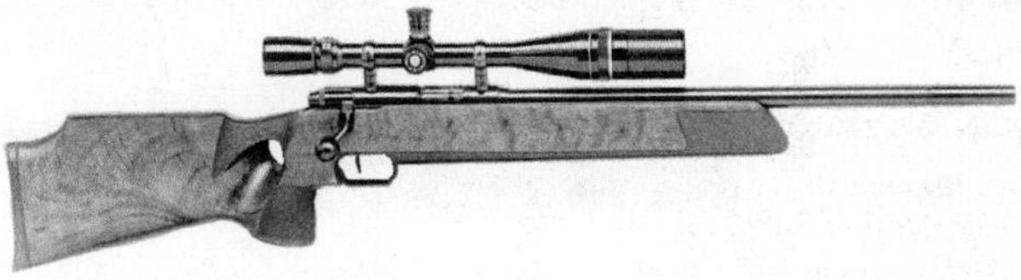

NIB	Exc.	V.G.	Good	Fair	Poor
2150	1500	995	500	300	200

Model 54.MS REP

A repeating rifle with a five-shot, detachable magazine and a thumbhole stock with vented forearm.

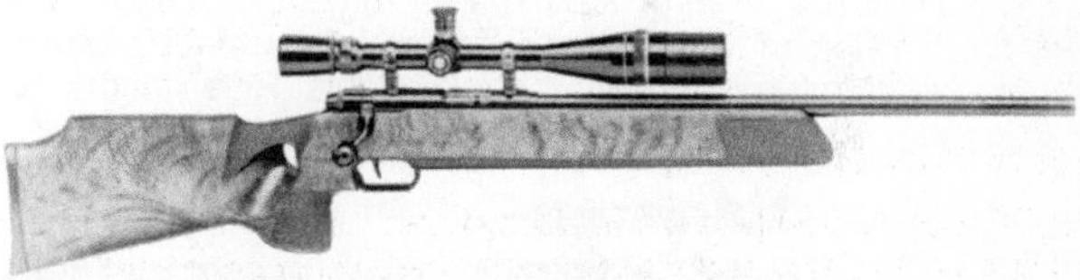

NIB	Exc.	V.G.	Good	Fair	Poor
2100	1600	1050	500	300	200

Model 2000 MK

This single-shot rifle was chambered for the .22 LR cartridge. It has a 26" round barrel with target-type sights. The finish was blued and has a checkered walnut stock. It was not imported after 1988.

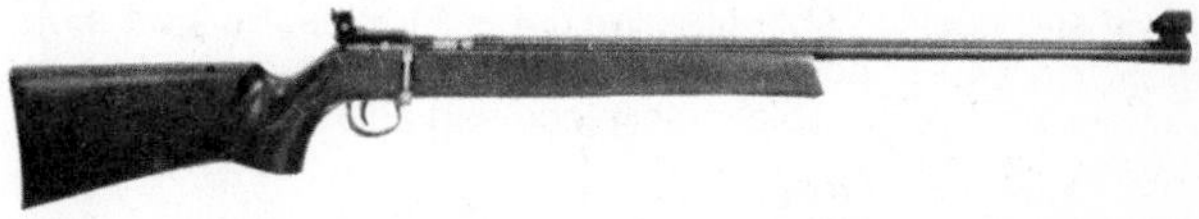

NIB	Exc.	V.G.	Good	Fair	Poor
650	600	450	200	150	100

Model 2007 Supermatch

Introduced in 1993 this target rifle is chambered for the .22 LR cartridge. It has a 19-3/4" barrel fitted to a Match 54 action. Trigger is a two-stage. The stock is standard ISU configuration with adjustable cheekpiece. Weighs about 10.8 pounds. Offered in left-hand model.

NIB	Exc.	V.G.	Good	Fair	Poor
2350	1850	1350	750	350	200

Model 2013 Supermatch

Similar to the above model but fitted with an International stock with palm rest and buttstock hook. Weighs about 12.5 lbs.

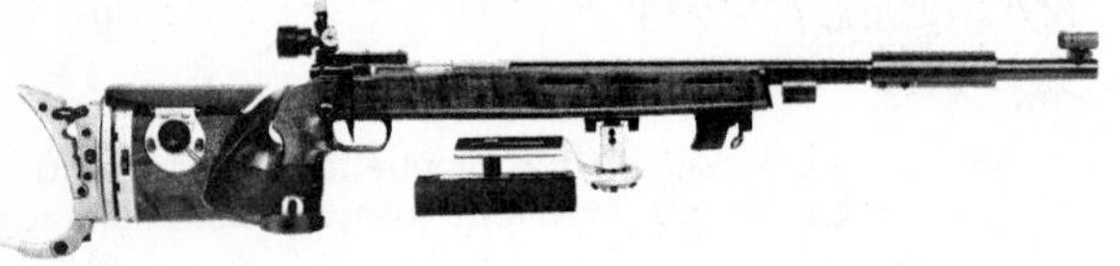

NIB	Exc.	V.G.	Good	Fair	Poor
3200	2600	1850	1250	600	300

Model 1903D

Designed for the advanced junior shooter this target rifle has a 25-1/2" barrel on a Match 64 action with a single stage trigger. The walnut stock is fully adjustable. Weighs about 9.5 pounds and is offered in a left-hand model.

NIB	Exc.	V.G.	Good	Fair	Poor
950	800	700	400	300	200

Model 1803D

A high-grade target rifle chambered for the .22 LR cartridge. It has a 25.5" heavy barrel with adjustable target sights. It features an adjustable trigger. The finish is blued with a light-colored wood stock with dark stippling on the pistol grip and forearm. The stock features an adjustable cheekpiece and buttplate. It was introduced in 1987.

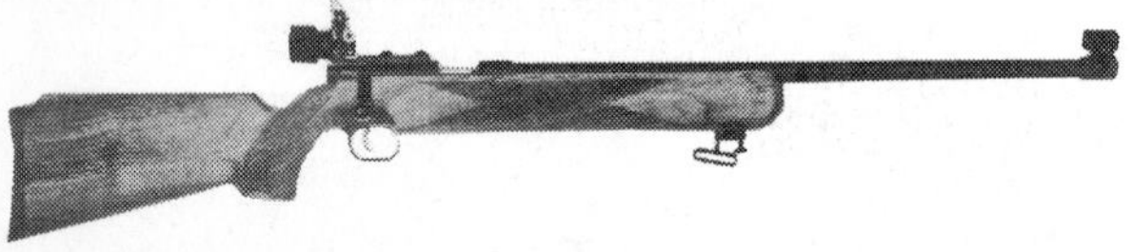

NIB	Exc.	V.G.	Good	Fair	Poor
1200	1000	775	600	450	200

Model 1808D RT Super

A single-shot, running-boar type rifle that is chambered for the .22 LR cartridge. It has a 32.5" barrel furnished without sights. The finish is blued with a heavy target-type walnut stock with thumbhole. It is furnished with barrel weights. Rifle weighs about 9.4 pounds. Also available in a left-hand version.

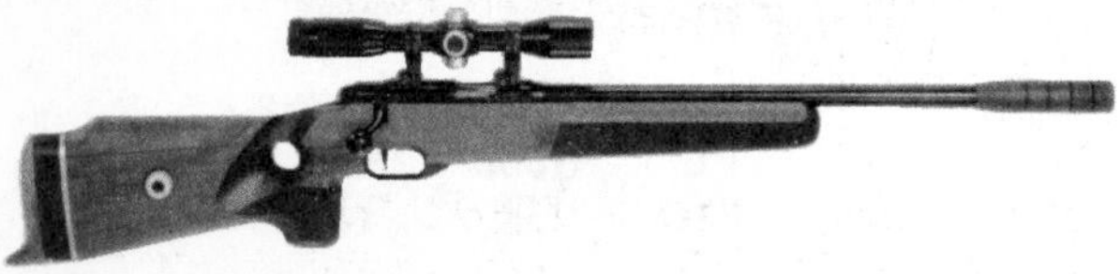

NIB	Exc.	V.G.	Good	Fair	Poor
1500	1300	1150	750	450	250

Model 1907ISU Standard Match

Chambered for the .22 LR cartridge this rifle is designed for both prone and position shooting. Weight is 11.2 lbs. Built on a Match 54 action and fitted with a 26" barrel this rifle has a two-stage trigger with a removable cheekpiece and adjustable buttstock.

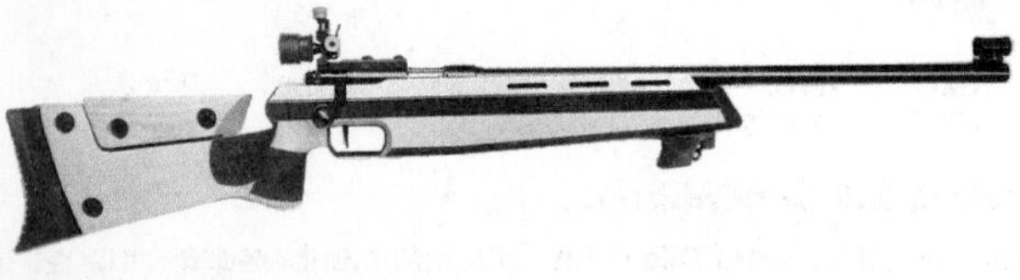

NIB	Exc.	V.G.	Good	Fair	Poor
1600	1350	1000	450	300	200

Model 1910 Super Match II

A high-grade, single-shot target rifle chambered for the .22 LR cartridge. It has a 27.25" barrel and is furnished with diopter-type target sights. The finish is blued with a walnut thumbhole stock with adjustable cheekpiece and buttplate. Hand rest and palm rest are not included.

NIB	Exc.	V.G.	Good	Fair	Poor
2300	1850	1400	900	500	250

Model 1911 Prone Match

This version has a stock designed specifically for firing from the prone position.

NIB	Exc.	V.G.	Good	Fair	Poor
1850	1550	1050	650	400	250

Model 1913 Super Match

A virtually hand-built, match target rifle. It is chambered for the .22 LR cartridge and features a single-shot action. It has adjustable, diopter-type sights on a 27.25" heavy barrel. This is a custom-made gun that features every target option conceivable. The finish is blued with a fully adjustable walnut stock.

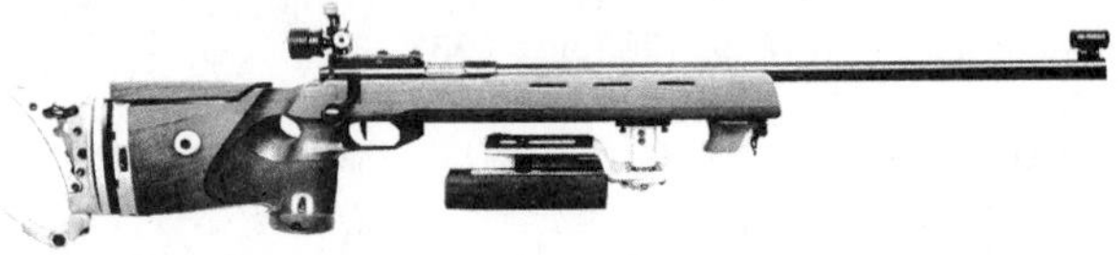

NIB	Exc.	V.G.	Good	Fair	Poor
2700	2100	1600	1000	500	250

Model 1827B Biathlon

A repeating, bolt-action target rifle chambered for the .22 LR cartridge. It is specially designed for the biathlon competition. Production is quite limited and on a custom basis.

NIB	Exc.	V.G.	Good	Fair	Poor
1850	1500	1150	800	400	250

Model 1827BT Biathlon

Similar to the above model but features a straight pull Fortner bolt system. Available in left-hand model.

NIB	Exc.	V.G.	Good	Fair	Poor
2900	2350	1750	1000	500	250

Achiever

Introduced in 1993 this target rifle is chambered for the .22 LR cartridge. Designed for the beginning shooter it is furnished with a 5-shot clip but can be converted to a single-shot with an adaptor. Barrel length is 19-1/2". Action is Mark 2000 with two-stage trigger. Stock pull is adjustable from 12" to 13". Weighs about 5 lbs.

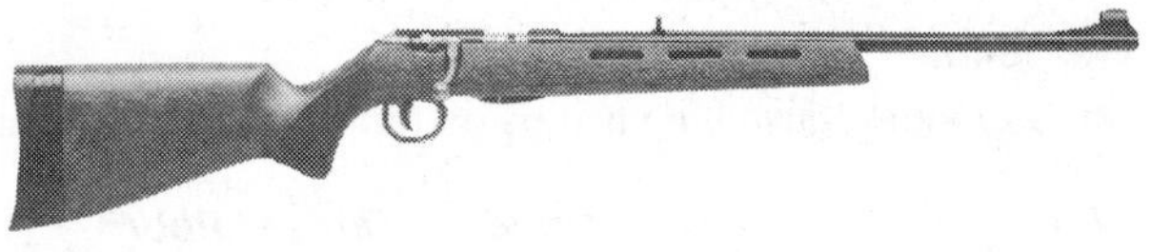

NIB	Exc.	V.G.	Good	Fair	Poor
525	400	295	150	125	100

Achiever Super Target

Designed for the advanced junior shooter this model has a 22" barrel. Weighs about 6.5 lbs.

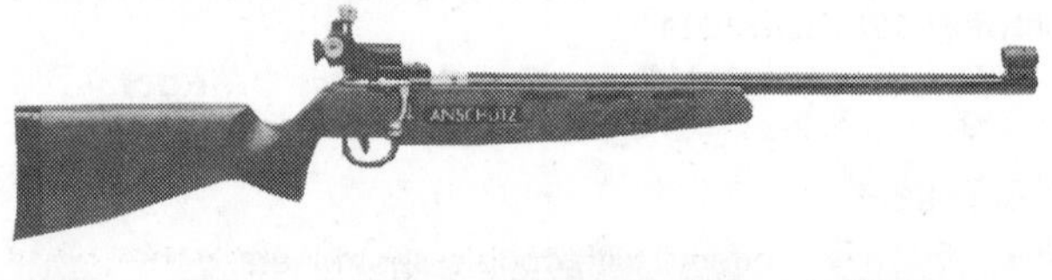

NIB	Exc.	V.G.	Good	Fair	Poor
575	450	325	175	125	100

Bavarian 1700

A classic-style sporting rifle chambered for the .22 LR, .22 rimfire Magnum, .22 Hornet, and the .222 Remington cartridges. It features a 24" barrel with adjustable sights. It has a detachable magazine and a blued finish with a checkered walnut, European-style Monte Carlo stock with cheekpiece. It was introduced in 1988. Values shown are for centerfire.

NIB	*Exc.*	*V.G.*	*Good*	*Fair*	*Poor*
1300	950	600	400	300	200

Classic 1700

Similar in appearance to the Bavarian but furnished with an American-style stock with fluted comb. Furnished in same calibers as Bavarian but weighs 6.75 lbs.

NIB	*Exc.*	*V.G.*	*Good*	*Fair*	*Poor*
1300	950	600	400	300	200

NOTE: For fancy wood stocks "Meister Grade" add $175.

Custom 1700

Similar to the Bavarian and Classic in caliber offerings but offered with a fancy European walnut stock with roll-over cheekpiece with Monte Carlo. The pistol grip has a palm swell and is fitted with a white lined rosewood grip cap with a white diamond insert. Forend is schabel type and stock is checkered in ship line pattern.

NIB	*Exc.*	*V.G.*	*Good*	*Fair*	*Poor*
1650	1275	750	400	300	200

NOTE: For fancy wood stocks "Meister Grade" add $175.

Model 1700 Mannlicher

Similar to the 1700 Classic but fitted with a full-length stock.

NIB	*Exc.*	*V.G.*	*Good*	*Fair*	*Poor*
1550	1200	850	550	350	200

NOTE: For fancy wood stocks "Meister Grade" add $175.

Model 1700 FWT

This model has same specifications as the 1700 Custom but is fitted with a McMillan laminated fiberglass stock. Weighs about 6.25 lbs.

NIB	*Exc.*	*V.G.*	*Good*	*Fair*	*Poor*
1225	900	700	500	300	200

Model 1700 FWT Deluxe

Same as above but fitted with a laminated wood grain stock.

NIB	*Exc.*	*V.G.*	*Good*	*Fair*	*Poor*
1125	900	800	550	300	200

Model 1710 D Classic

Bolt-action .22 caliber rifle with 23.6" barrel with no sights. Walnut stock is checkering. Magazine capacity is 5 rounds. Weight is about 7.3 lbs.

NIB	*Exc.*	*V.G.*	*Good*	*Fair*	*Poor*
1300	1050	800	—	—	—

Model 1710 D HB Classic

Same as above but with heavy barrel. Weight is about 8 lbs.

NIB	*Exc.*	*V.G.*	*Good*	*Fair*	*Poor*
1350	1050	750	475	300	150

Model 1710 D KL Monte Carlo

Same as the Classic but with Monte Carlo stock and folding leaf rear sight with hooded front sight. Weight is about 7.5 lbs.

NIB	*Exc.*	*V.G.*	*Good*	*Fair*	*Poor*
1300	1000	775	425	325	175

Model 1710 D HB Classic 150 Years Anniversary Version

Similar to Model 1710 D HB Classic but with heavy stainless barrel and stock laser-engraved with 150th anniversary and 1901 "Germania" logos. Introduced in 2007. Only 150 units were produced.

NIB	*Exc.*	*V.G.*	*Good*	*Fair*	*Poor*
2100	1700	1200	700	400	200

Model 1712 Silhouette Sporter

Chambered in .22 LR. Features include two-stage trigger, deluxe walnut stock with schnabel, 21.6" blued sightless barrel, 5-shot magazine.

NIB	*Exc.*	*V.G.*	*Good*	*Fair*	*Poor*
1150	925	675	425	200	100

Model 1702 D HB Classic

Chambered in .17 Mach 2. Features include finely-tuned double-stage trigger, walnut stock, 23" blued heavy sightless barrel, 5-shot magazine.

NIB	*Exc.*	*V.G.*	*Good*	*Fair*	*Poor*
1300	1150	700	450	250	125

Model 1502 D HB Classic

Similar to Model 1702 D HB but with single-stage trigger, fewer refinements. Add 10 percent for beavertail forend.

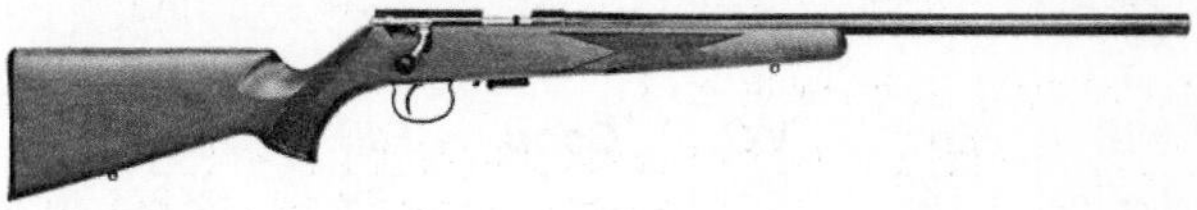

NIB	Exc.	V.G.	Good	Fair	Poor
600	400	300	200	100	50

Anschutz Model 1907 Club

Single-shot economy target rifle chambered in .22 LR. Features include target trigger, short lock time, 26" blued barrel, micrometer rear peep and hood front sights, ambidextrous removable cheekpiece and walnut buttstock with rubber buttplate and stock spacers. Weighs 9.7 lbs. Introduced 2006. MSRP: $1100.

NIB	Exc.	V.G.	Good	Fair	Poor

Model 1717 D Classic

This bolt-action model is chambered for the .17 HMR cartridge. Fitted with a 23.6" barrel with no sights. Checkered walnut stock. Weight is about 7.3 lbs.

NIB	Exc.	V.G.	Good	Fair	Poor
1375	1000	675	475	300	150

Model 1717 D HB Classic

Same as above but with heavy barrel. Weight is about 8 lbs.

NIB	Exc.	V.G.	Good	Fair	Poor
1475	1200	700	495	325	175

Model 1730 D Classic

This bolt-action rifle is chambered for the .22 Hornet cartridge and fitted with a 23.6" barrel. Magazine capacity is 5 rounds. Checkered walnut stock. No sights. Weight is about 7.3 lbs.

NIB	Exc.	V.G.	Good	Fair	Poor
1625	1325	750	525	350	225

Model 1730 D HB Classic

Same as above but fitted with a heavy barrel. Weight is about 8 lbs.

NIB	Exc.	V.G.	Good	Fair	Poor
1550	1250	700	495	325	175

Model 1730 D KL Monte Carlo

This model has a Monte Carlo stock and folding leaf rear sight with hooded front sight. Weight is about 7.5 lbs.

NIB	Exc.	V.G.	Good	Fair	Poor
1625	1325	750	525	350	225

Model 1733D KL Mannlicher

Introduced in 1993 this model features a Mannlicher stock built on a Match 54 action. The stock has a rosewood schnabel tip and checkering is done in a skip-line pattern. Chambered for .22 Hornet. Weighs about 6.25 lbs.

NIB	Exc.	V.G.	Good	Fair	Poor
1450	1150	675	475	300	175

Model 1740 D Classic

This bolt-action model is chambered for the .222 Remington cartridge. Checkered walnut stock with no sights. Magazine capacity is 3 rounds. Weight is about 7.3 lbs.

NIB	Exc.	V.G.	Good	Fair	Poor
1625	1325	750	525	350	225

Model 1740 D HB Classic

Same as above but fitted with a heavy barrel. Weight is about 7.3 lbs.

NIB	Exc.	V.G.	Good	Fair	Poor
1550	1250	700	495	325	175

Model 1740 D KL Monte Carlo

This model is fitted with a Monte Carlo stock and folding leaf rear sight and hooded front sight. Weight is about 7.3 lbs.

NIB	Exc.	V.G.	Good	Fair	Poor
1625	1325	750	525	350	225

Model 520/61

A blowback-operated, semi-automatic rifle that is chambered for the .22 LR cartridge. It has a 24" barrel and a 10-round, detachable magazine. The finish is blued with a checkered walnut stock. This rifle was discontinued in 1983.

NIB	Exc.	V.G.	Good	Fair	Poor
675	550	300	200	100	85

Model 525 Sporter

This semi-automatic rifle is chambered for the .22 LR cartridge. It has a 24" barrel with adjustable sights and a 10-round, detachable magazine. The finish is blued with a checkered Monte Carlo-type stock. It was introduced in 1984. A carbine version with a 20" barrel was originally offered but was discontinued in 1986.

NIB	Exc.	V.G.	Good	Fair	Poor
725	600	450	250	175	100

Exemplar Hornet

Chambered for the .22 Hornet cartridge. It was introduced in 1988.

NIB	Exc.	V.G.	Good	Fair	Poor
1050	850	575	300	200	100

AR-7 INDUSTRIES

Meriden, Connecticut

AR-7 Explorer

Semi-automatic .22 caliber takedown rifle fitted with a 16" barrel and 8-round magazine. Adjustable rear peep sight. Weight is 2.5 lbs.

NIB	Exc.	V.G.	Good	Fair	Poor
200	150	90	65	50	25

AR-7C Explorer

Same as above but with camo stock.

NIB	Exc.	V.G.	Good	Fair	Poor
225	175	100	65	50	25

AR-7 Sporter

Similar to the standard AR-7, but with a metal skeleton stock and aluminum ventilated shrouded barrel. Weight is about 3.8 lbs.

NIB	Exc.	V.G.	Good	Fair	Poor
250	150	120	75	65	35

AR-7 Target

This model features a tubular stock with cantilever 3x9x40mm scope. Fitted with 16" bull barrel. Weight is about 5.7 lbs.

NIB	Exc.	V.G.	Good	Fair	Poor
300	200	150	75	65	35

AR-7 Bolt-Action

This model is similar in all respects to the standard semi-automatic AR-7, but with a bolt action.

NIB	Exc.	V.G.	Good	Fair	Poor
225	120	90	65	50	25

ARMALITE, INC.

Costa Mesa, California
Geneseo, Illinois (current production)

In 1995 Eagle Arms purchased the Armalite trademark and certain other assets. The new companies are organized under the Armalite name. The original company, formed in the mid 1950s, developed the AR-10, which in turn led to the development of the M-16 series of service rifles still in use today. All current models are produced at the Geneseo, Illinois, facility.

AR-17 Shotgun

A gas-operated semi-automatic 12 gauge shotgun, with a 24" barrel and interchangeable choke tubes. The receiver and the barrel are made of an aluminum alloy, with an anodized black or gold finish. The stock and forearm are of plastic. Approximately 2,000 were manufactured during 1964 and 1965. Add 10 percent for gold finish.

NIB	Exc.	V.G.	Good	Fair	Poor
750	625	400	300	225	100

AR-7 Explorer Rifle

A .22 LR semi-auto carbine with a 16" barrel. The receiver and barrel are partially made of an alloy. The most noteworthy feature of this model is that it can be disassembled and the component parts stored in the plastic stock. Manufactured between 1959 and 1973. Reintroduced in 1999.

NIB	Exc.	V.G.	Good	Fair	Poor
225	155	100	75	50	35

AR-7 Custom

As above with a walnut cheekpiece stock, manufactured between 1964 and 1970.

NIB	Exc.	V.G.	Good	Fair	Poor
250	180	125	80	50	35

AR-180

A gas-operated semi-automatic rifle chambered for the .223 or 5.56mm cartridge. The AR-180 is the civilian version of the AR18, which is fully automatic. It is a simple and efficient rifle that was tested by various governments and found to have potential. This rifle was also manufactured by Howa Machinery Ltd. and Sterling Armament Co. of England. The most common version is manufactured by Sterling. Those built by Armalite and Howa bring a small premium.

AR-180 Howa

NIB	Exc.	V.G.	Good	Fair	Poor
1500	1250	900	700	450	200

AR-180 Sterling

NIB	Exc.	V.G.	Good	Fair	Poor
1150	900	700	500	350	175

AR-180B

Similar to the original AR-180. Chambered for the .223 cartridge and fitted with a 19.8" barrel with integral muzzlebrake. Lower receiver is polymer while the upper receiver is sheet steel. Trigger group is standard M15. Accepts standard M15 magazines. Weight is about 6 lbs.

NIB	Exc.	V.G.	Good	Fair	Poor
750	625	500	400	300	125

AR-10A4 Rifle

Introduced in 1995 this model features a 20" stainless steel heavy barrel chambered for the .308 Win. or .243 Win. cartridge. Has a flattop receiver, optional two-stage trigger, detachable carry handle, scope mount. Equipped with two 10-round magazines. Weight is about 9.6 lbs.

NIB	Exc.	V.G.	Good	Fair	Poor
1500	1250	900	700	500	200

NOTE: For stainless steel barrel add $100.

AR-10A4 Carbine

Similar to above model but chambered for .308 Win. cartridge and fitted with a 16" barrel. Flattop receiver. Sold with two 10-round magazines. Weight is approximately 9 lbs.

NIB	Exc.	V.G.	Good	Fair	Poor
1500	1250	900	700	500	200

NOTE: For stainless steel barrel add $100.

AR-10A2 Rifle

This model has a 20" heavy barrel chambered for the .308 cartridge but without the removable carry handle. Weight is about 9.8 lbs.

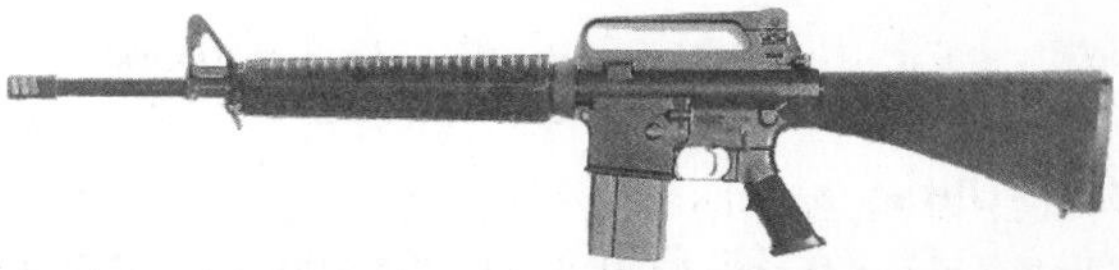

NIB	Exc.	V.G.	Good	Fair	Poor
1500	1250	900	700	500	200

NOTE: For stainless steel barrel add $100.

AR-10A2 Carbine

Similar to model above but fitted with a 16" barrel. Weight is approximately 9 lbs.

NIB	Exc.	V.G.	Good	Fair	Poor
1500	1250	900	700	500	200

NOTE: For stainless steel barrel add $100.

AR-10B

Chambered for the .308 cartridge and fitted with a 20" barrel. The trigger is a single-stage or optional 2-stage match type. This model has several of the early M16 features such as a tapered handguard, pistol grips, and short buttstock in original brown color. Fitted with early charging handle. Limited production. Weight is about 9.5 lbs. Introduced in 1999.

NIB	Exc.	V.G.	Good	Fair	Poor
1600	1250	900	700	500	200

AR-10(T) Rifle

This model features a 24" heavy barrel with a two-stage trigger. The front sight and carry handle are removable. The handguard is fiberglass. Weight is approximately 10.4 lbs.

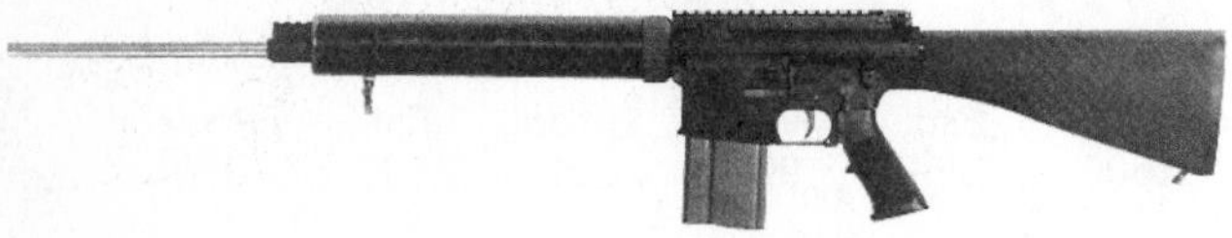

NIB	Exc.	V.G.	Good	Fair	Poor
1850	1400	875	600	450	225

AR-10(T) Carbine

Similar to the AR-10T but fitted with a 16.25" target weight barrel. Weight is approximately 8.5 lbs.

NIB	Exc.	V.G.	Good	Fair	Poor
1850	1400	875	600	450	225

AR-10(T) Ultra

Chambered for the .300 Remington Ultra Short Action Magnum cartridge. Barrel length is 24". Two stage National Match trigger. Offered in choice of green or black stock. Sold with a 5 round magazine.

NIB	Exc.	V.G.	Good	Fair	Poor
1850	1400	875	600	450	225

AR-10 SOF

Introduced in 2003 this model features an M4-style fixed stock. Flattop receiver. Chambered for the .308 cartridge. Offered in both A2 and A4 configurations.

NIB	Exc.	V.G.	Good	Fair	Poor
1850	1400	875	600	450	225

Armalite AR-10 .338 Federal Semi-Auto Rifle

Similar to AR-10 but chambered in .338 Federal. Suggested retail price: Approximately $1500.

NIB	Exc.	V.G.	Good	Fair	Poor
1500	1250	900	700	500	200

M15 SOF

This model is chambered for the .223 cartridge and is fitted with a flattop receiver and M4-style fixed stock. Introduced in 2003. Offered in both A2 and A4 configurations.

NIB	Exc.	V.G.	Good	Fair	Poor
1150	925	675	475	300	150

M15A2 HBAR

This model was introduced in 1995 and features a 20" heavy barrel chambered for .223 cartridge. A2-style forward assist, recoil check brake. Formerly sold with a 10-round magazine. Weight is approximately 8.2 lbs.

NIB	Exc.	V.G.	Good	Fair	Poor
1100	850	600	500	375	125

M15A2 National Match

Chambered for the .223 cartridge this variation features a 20" stainless steel match barrel with two-stage trigger, A2 style forward assist and hard coated anodized receiver. Equipped with a 10-round magazine. Weight is about 9 lbs.

NIB	Exc.	V.G.	Good	Fair	Poor
1475	1200	850	600	375	200

M15A2-M4A1C Carbine

Similar to the M15A2 heavy barrel but with a 16" heavy barrel. Flattop receiver with detachable carry handle. Introduced in 1995.

NIB	Exc.	V.G.	Good	Fair	Poor
1100	900	700	500	300	125

NOTE: Add $100 for Match trigger.

M15A2-M4C Carbine

Similar to the M4A1C Carbine but with the flattop receiver and detachable carry handle.

NIB	Exc.	V.G.	Good	Fair	Poor
1000	850	600	500	300	125

M15A4(T) Eagle Eye

Chambered for the .223 cartridge and fitted with a 24" stainless steel heavy weight barrel this rifle has a National Match two-stage trigger, Picatinny rail, NM fiberglass handguard tube. Sold with a 7-round magazine and 4-section cleaning rod with brass tip, sling, owner's manual, and lifetime warranty.

NIB	Exc.	V.G.	Good	Fair	Poor
1500	1100	800	600	350	150

M15A4 Special Purpose Rifle (SPR)

This model is fitted with a 20" heavy barrel with detachable front sight, detachable carry handle with NM sights, Picatinny rail. Weight is about 7.8 lbs.

NIB	Exc.	V.G.	Good	Fair	Poor
1200	900	750	600	375	175

M15A4 Action Master

This variation features a 20" stainless steel heavy barrel with two-stage trigger, Picatinny rail, and fiberglass handguard tube. Weight is approximately 9 lbs.

NIB	Exc.	V.G.	Good	Fair	Poor
1450	1000	850	600	375	175

M15A4 Eagle Spirit

This version is similar to the Action Master above but fitted with a 16" stainless steel barrel. Weight is about 7.6 lbs.

NIB	Exc.	V.G.	Good	Fair	Poor
1450	1000	850	600	375	175

Armalite M15 A4 Carbine 6.8 & 7.62x39

Shorty, carbine version of AR-15 chambered in 6.8 Remington and 7.62x39. 16" chrome-lined barrel with flash suppressor, front and rear picatinny rails for mounting optics, two-stage tactical trigger. Ten-round magazine. Anodized aluminum/ phosphate finish. Overall length 36.6". Weight: 7 lbs. Suggested retail price: $1107.

AR-30M

Chambered for the .338 Lapua, .300 Winchester Mag., or the .308 Winchester cartridges. Barrel length is 26" with muzzlebrake. Adjustable butt stock. Weight is about 12 lbs. This model is a reduced version of the AR-50.

NIB	Exc.	V.G.	Good	Fair	Poor
1600	1400	1250	1000	500	195

NOTE: Add $150 for .338 Lapua.

AR-50

Introduced in 2000 this rifle is chambered for the .50 BMG cartridge. Fitted with a 31" tapered barrel threaded for recoil check (muzzlebrake). Trigger is single-stage. Stock is a 3-section type with extruded forend. Pachmayr buttplate. Picatinny rail. Buttplate is adjustable. Finish is magnesium phosphated steel and hard anodized aluminum. Bipod. Weight is about 33 lbs.

NIB	Exc.	V.G.	Good	Fair	Poor
3400	2650	2000	1500	750	300

PRE-BAN MODELS

Golden Eagle

Fitted with a 20" stainless extra-heavy barrel with NM two-stage trigger and NM sights. Sold with a 30-round magazine. Weight is about 9.4 lbs.

NIB	Exc.	V.G.	Good	Fair	Poor
1500	1200	950	800	400	200

HBAR

This pre-ban rifle has a 20" heavy barrel, a 30-round magazine, and sling. Weight is approximately 8 lbs.

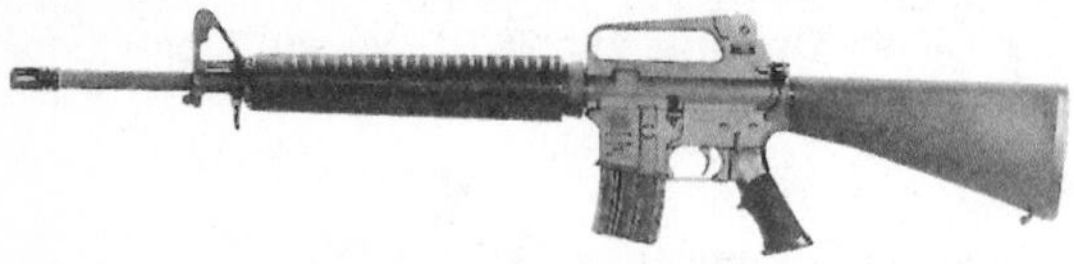

NIB	Exc.	V.G.	Good	Fair	Poor
1300	1000	850	700	350	175

M4C Carbine

This pre-ban variation is fitted with a 16" heavy barrel, collapsible stock, and fixed flash suppressor. Weight is about 6.2 lbs.

NIB	Exc.	V.G.	Good	Fair	Poor
1300	1000	850	700	350	175

ARMES DE CHASSE

Chadds Ford, Pennsylvania

Importer of firearms manufactured by Franchi, P. Beretta, and other arms manufactured in Germany.

Model EJ

An O/U Anson & Deeley action 12 gauge shotgun with double triggers as well as automatic ejectors. Blued barrels, silver finished receiver and checkered walnut stock. Manufactured in Germany and introduced in 1989.

NIB	Exc.	V.G.	Good	Fair	Poor
1500	1250	900	650	500	250

Model EU

As above with a ventilated rib barrel and a nonselective single trigger. Introduced in 1989.

NIB	Exc.	V.G.	Good	Fair	Poor
1600	1300	850	650	500	250

Highlander

A side-by-side double-barrel 20 gauge shotgun with a boxlock action. Available in various barrel lengths and choke combinations, with double triggers and manual extractors. Blued with a checkered walnut stock. Manufactured in Italy and introduced in 1989.

NIB	Exc.	V.G.	Good	Fair	Poor
1350	800	650	350	250	125

Chesapeake

As above but chambered for the 3.5" 12 gauge shell. The bores are chrome-lined and suitable for steel shot. Fitted with automatic ejectors and double triggers. Manufactured in Italy, it was introduced in 1989.

NIB	Exc.	V.G.	Good	Fair	Poor
1450	995	700	475	400	200

Balmoral

English-style straight grip 12, 16, or 20 gauge boxlock shotgun, fitted with false side plates. Receiver and side plates case hardened, the barrels blued. Fitted with a single trigger and automatic ejectors. Manufactured in Italy and introduced in 1989.

NIB	Exc.	V.G.	Good	Fair	Poor
1200	925	725	500	400	200

Model 70E

A 12, 16, or 20 gauge side-by-side shotgun fitted with 27" or 28" barrels. The action based upon the Anson & Deeley design with a Greener crossbolt. The receiver is case hardened, barrels are blued and the walnut stock checkered. Manufactured in Germany and introduced in 1989.

NIB	Exc.	V.G.	Good	Fair	Poor
1225	925	725	500	400	200

Model 74E

As above with game scene engraving and more fully figured walnut stock. Introduced in 1989.

NIB	Exc.	V.G.	Good	Fair	Poor
1475	1050	900	650	500	250

Model 76E

As above with engraved false side plates and fully figured walnut stock. Introduced in 1989.

NIB	Exc.	V.G.	Good	Fair	Poor
2000	1500	1100	750	600	300

ARMSCO FIREARMS CORP.

Ankara, Turkey
U.S.A.—Des Plaines, Illinois

Built by Huglu Hunting Firearms Corporation in Turkey, which was established in 1927. Armsco is the U.S. representive. First year of business in the U.S. was 2002.

SINGLE-SHOT

Model 301A

This single-shot model is offered in 12, 16, 20, 28 gauge as well as .410 bore. Barrel lengths from 22" to 32" depending on gauge. Checkered walnut stock. Weight varies from 5 lbs. to 5.5 lbs. depending on gauge.

NIB	Exc.	V.G.	Good	Fair	Poor
200	150	75	50	35	25

SIDE-BY-SIDE

Model 202B

Boxlock gun offered in 12, 16, 20, and 28 gauge as well as .410 bore with barrel lengths from 22" to 32" depending on gauge. Double triggers. Hand engraved about 50 percent coverage. Fixed chokes or choke tubes. Checkered walnut stock with cheekpiece. Weight is about 6.4 lbs. to 7.3 lbs. depending on gauge.

NIB	Exc.	V.G.	Good	Fair	Poor
550	425	325	200	125	50

Model 202A

Same as above but offered with standard buttstock.

NIB	Exc.	V.G.	Good	Fair	Poor
775	625	450	300	175	75

Model 201A

Offered in gauges from 12 to .410 with sideplates with 50 percent hand engraving. Choice of single or double triggers.

NIB	Exc.	V.G.	Good	Fair	Poor
695	525	450	300	175	75

Model 200A

Boxlock in gauges 12 to .410 with single trigger. Hand engraved 50 percent coverage.

NIB	Exc.	V.G.	Good	Fair	Poor
750	575	450	300	175	75

Model 205A

Offered in gauges 12 to .410 with barrel lengths 22" to 32" depending on gauge. Boxlock frame with 60 percent hand engraving coverage. Single trigger. Checkered walnut stock. Weights are 6.1 lbs. to 6.8 lbs. depending on gauge.

NIB	Exc.	V.G.	Good	Fair	Poor
990	750	600	425	200	100

Model 210AE

Offered in 12, 16, and 20 gauge with single trigger and automatic ejectors. Boxlock frame is 60 percent hand engraved. Optional fixed or choke tubes.

NIB	Exc.	V.G.	Good	Fair	Poor
1250	950	700	450	300	200

Model 210BE

Same as above but with double triggers.

NIB	Exc.	V.G.	Good	Fair	Poor
1150	850	675	450	300	200

OVER-AND-UNDER

Model 104A

Chambered for the 12 through .410 bores with double triggers and barrel lengths from 22" to 32" depending on gauge. Ventilated rib. Checkered walnut stock. Fixed or choke tubes. Weight is from 6.6 lbs. to 7.3 lbs. depending on gauge. Receiver is 15 percent hand engraved.

NIB	Exc.	V.G.	Good	Fair	Poor
425	300	250	200	125	75

Model 103D

Same as model above but with single trigger and schnabel forearm.

NIB	Exc.	V.G.	Good	Fair	Poor
595	475	375	325	175	75

Model 103DE

Same as above but with automatic ejectors.

NIB	Exc.	V.G.	Good	Fair	Poor
750	575	525	425	200	75

Model 103C

Similar to the Model 103D but with blued receiver with gold inlaid birds with 40 percent engraving coverage.

NIB	Exc.	V.G.	Good	Fair	Poor
720	550	525	425	200	75

Model 103CE

Same as above but with automatic ejectors.

NIB	Exc.	V.G.	Good	Fair	Poor
870	650	575	475	225	100

Model 103F

Similar to the Model 103D but with 80 to 100 percent hand engraved side plates.

NIB	Exc.	V.G.	Good	Fair	Poor
850	625	550	450	225	100

Model 103FE

Same as above but with automatic ejectors.

NIB	Exc.	V.G.	Good	Fair	Poor
970	750	600	475	250	125

Model 101SE

Offered in 12 gauge only with 28", 30", or 32" barrels with ventilated rib. Single trigger and automatic ejectors. Hand engraved receiver. Checkered walnut stock. Weight is from 6.6 lbs. to 7.3 lbs. depending on barrel length.

NIB	Exc.	V.G.	Good	Fair	Poor
1325	975	750	450	275	125

Model 101BE

Same as above but with adjustable comb.

NIB	Exc.	V.G.	Good	Fair	Poor
1325	975	750	450	275	125

SEMI-AUTO

Model 401A

This semi-automatic shotgun uses a short-recoil inertia-operated system. Chambered for the 12 gauge shell up to 3". Barrel lengths from 22" to 32". Ventilated rib. Plastic or walnut stock. Fixed or choke tubes. Fully engraved receiver. Weight is from 6.9 lbs. to 7.2 lbs. depending on barrel length. Magazine capacity is 6 rounds.

NIB	Exc.	V.G.	Good	Fair	Poor
425	350	275	225	125	75

Model 401B

Same as model above but with 4-round magazine capacity.

NIB	Exc.	V.G.	Good	Fair	Poor
425	350	275	225	125	75

Model 501GA

This is a gas-operated shotgun chambered for the 3" 12 gauge shell. Barrel lengths are from 22" to 32". Black receiver with 15 percent hand engraving coverage. Magazine capacity is 7 rounds. Walnut or plastic stock. Weight is from 6.8 lbs. to 7.3 lbs. depending on barrel length.

NIB	Exc.	V.G.	Good	Fair	Poor
425	350	275	225	125	75

Model 501GB

Same as above but with 4-round magazine.

NIB	Exc.	V.G.	Good	Fair	Poor
425	350	275	225	125	75

Model 601GB

Same as the Model 501GB but with a full engraving coverage silver receiver.

NIB	Exc.	V.G.	Good	Fair	Poor
450	375	300	250	125	75

Model 601GA

Same as Model 501GA with 7-round magazine capacity.

NIB	Exc.	V.G.	Good	Fair	Poor
450	375	300	250	125	75

Model 701GA

This model is chambered for the 20 gauge 3" shell and fitted with barrel lengths from 22" to 32". Ventilated rib. Walnut stock. Fixed or choke tubes. Magazine capacity is 7 rounds. Weight is 6 lbs. to 6.4 lbs. depending on barrel length.

NIB	Exc.	V.G.	Good	Fair	Poor
450	375	300	225	125	75

Model 701GB

Same as above but with 4-round magazine.

NIB	Exc.	V.G.	Good	Fair	Poor
450	375	300	225	125	75

PUMP ACTION

Model 801A

This is a slide-action 12 gauge shotgun with plastic stock. Barrel length is from 22" to 32". Fixed or choke tubes. Magazine capacity is 7 rounds. Weight is about 7 lbs.

NIB	Exc.	V.G.	Good	Fair	Poor
300	275	250	175	100	50

Model 801B

Same as above but with 4-round magazine.

NIB	Exc.	V.G.	Good	Fair	Poor
300	275	250	175	100	50

ARMSCORP OF AMERICA

Baltimore, Maryland

M14R

A civilian version of the U.S. M14 rifle manufactured from new and surplus parts. Introduced in 1986.

NIB	Exc.	V.G.	Good	Fair	Poor
1350	900	500	300	200	100

M14 National Match

As above but built to A.M.T.U. MIL specifications. Introduced in 1987.

NIB	Exc.	V.G.	Good	Fair	Poor
1650	1250	800	500	400	200

FAL

A civilian version of the FN FAL rifle assembled from new and Argentine surplus parts. Introduced in 1987.

NIB	Exc.	V.G.	Good	Fair	Poor
1600	1250	800	400	300	150

M36 Israeli Sniper Rifle

A specialized weapon built upon the Armscorp M14 receiver in the Bullpup style. Barrel length 22" and of free floating design for accuracy, chambered for the .308 cartridge. There is an integral flash suppressor and a bipod. It is furnished with a 20-shot detachable magazine. This civilian version was first offered for sale in 1989.

NIB	Exc.	V.G.	Good	Fair	Poor
3200	2650	2000	1500	850	400

ARMS CORPORATION OF THE PHILIPPINES

Armscor Precision
Marikina City, Philippines

Armscor Precision is an importer of a variety of firearms made in the Philippines.

SHOTGUNS

Model 30D

A slide-action 12 gauge shotgun fitted with either 28" or 30" barrels with various chokes. The magazine holds 6 cartridges. Weight is about 7.6 lbs.

NIB	Exc.	V.G.	Good	Fair	Poor
200	175	150	125	100	75

Model 30DG

As above with a 20" barrel, fitted with rifle sights and a 7-shot magazine. Weight is about 7.2 lbs.

NIB	Exc.	V.G.	Good	Fair	Poor
175	150	125	100	80	70

Model 30R

As above with shotgun bead sights, 20" or 18.5" barrel. Weight is between 7 and 7.2 lbs. depending on barrel length.

NIB	Exc.	V.G.	Good	Fair	Poor
175	150	125	100	80	70

Model 30RP

As above with an auxiliary black composition pistol grip and an 18.5" barrel.

NIB	Exc.	V.G.	Good	Fair	Poor
175	150	125	100	80	70

Model 30 SAS1

Slide-action 12 gauge with 20" barrel with heat shield. Chambered for the 3" shell. Open cylinder choke. Parkerized finish finish. Weight is about 8 lbs.

NIB	Exc.	V.G.	Good	Fair	Poor
200	150	100	75	50	25

RIFLES

Model M14P

A .22 caliber bolt-action rifle fitted with a 23" barrel, open sights, and a 5-shot detachable magazine. Mahogany stock.

NIB	Exc.	V.G.	Good	Fair	Poor
150	90	75	50	35	25

Model M14D

As above with an adjustable rear sight and checkered stock. Manufactured in 1987 only.

NIB	Exc.	V.G.	Good	Fair	Poor
165	100	85	60	40	25

Model 14Y

This bolt-action rifle is chambered for .22 LR cartridge. It is fitted with an 18" barrel and 10-round magazine. Weight is approximately 5.2 lbs.

NIB	Exc.	V.G.	Good	Fair	Poor
150	125	100	75	50	25

Model 12Y

This bolt-action rifle is a single-shot and chambered for the .22 LR. It is fitted with an 18" barrel. Weight is about 5 lbs.

NIB	Exc.	V.G.	Good	Fair	Poor
125	100	75	50	35	25

Model 1400

This is a bolt-action rifle chambered for the .22 LR cartridge. Fitted with a 22.5" barrel and a 10-round magazine. Weight is about 6.5 lbs.

NIB	Exc.	V.G.	Good	Fair	Poor
225	200	150	125	100	75

Model M1500

A .22 Magnum bolt-action rifle fitted with a 22.5" barrel, open sights, 5-shot magazine and checkered mahogany stock. Weight is approximately 6.5 lbs.

NIB	Exc.	V.G.	Good	Fair	Poor
250	200	150	125	100	75

Model M1600

A .22 caliber copy of the U.S. M16 rifle with an 18" barrel and detachable 15-round magazine. Weight is about 6.2 lbs.

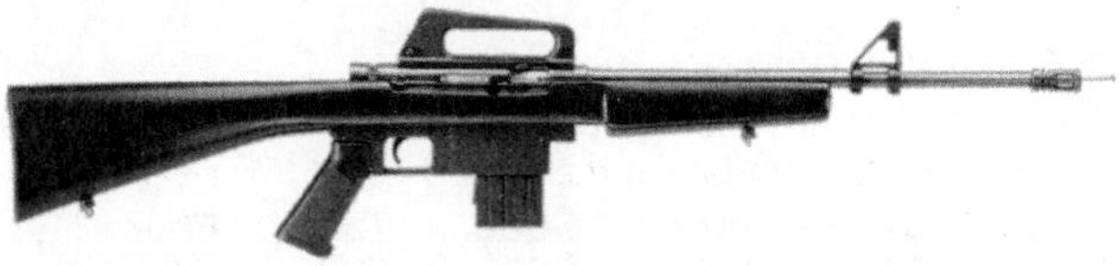

NIB	Exc.	V.G.	Good	Fair	Poor
300	200	125	100	75	50

Model M1600R

As above with a stainless steel collapsible stock and shrouded barrel. No longer in production.

NIB	Exc.	V.G.	Good	Fair	Poor
325	225	150	125	100	75

Model M1600C

As above with a 20" barrel and fiberglass stock. No longer in production.

NIB	Exc.	V.G.	Good	Fair	Poor
300	200	125	100	75	50

Model M1600W

As above with a mahogany stock. No longer in production.

NIB	Exc.	V.G.	Good	Fair	Poor
300	200	125	100	75	50

Model M1800

A .22 Hornet bolt-action rifle fitted with a 22.5" barrel, 5-shot magazine and a mahogany Monte Carlo-style stock. Weight is approximately 6.6 lbs.

NIB	Exc.	V.G.	Good	Fair	Poor
250	200	150	75	50	35

Model 20C

Chambered for .22 LR with a 15-round magazine and fitted with an 18.25" barrel. Weight is about 6.2 lbs.

NIB	Exc.	V.G.	Good	Fair	Poor
175	150	90	70	50	40

Model M20P

A .22 caliber 15-shot semi-automatic rifle fitted with a 20.75" barrel, open sights and plain mahogany stock. Weight is about 6.3 lbs.

NIB	Exc.	V.G.	Good	Fair	Poor
175	150	90	70	50	40

Model M2000

As above with adjustable sights and a checkered stock. Weight is approximately 6.4 lbs.

NIB	Exc.	V.G.	Good	Fair	Poor
175	150	90	70	50	40

Model AK22S

A .22 caliber semi-automatic rifle resembling the Russian AKA47. Barrel length of 18.5", 15-round magazine and mahogany stock. Weight is about 7.5 lbs.

NIB	Exc.	V.G.	Good	Fair	Poor
275	225	195	125	75	50

ARNOLD ARMS

Arlington, Washington

This company offered a wide range of rifles and calibers including its own proprietary cartridges, from the 6mm Arnold to the .458 Arnold. Rifles were built on a choice of actions including the Apollo, Remington, Sako, and Winchester. These action choices affect the base price of the rifle. Went out of business in 2002. Values vary with geography.NOTE: The prices listed are for a base rifle with Remington actions and matte blue finish unless otherwise noted.

Varminter I

This model features a heavy match grade barrel with straight taper. Lengths are from 24" to 26". Calibers are from .222 Rem. to .257 Arnold magnum. Choice of McMillian Varmint stock in various finishes and Pacific Research Varmint stock in flat black. Rifles weigh from 9 to 11 lbs. depending on caliber and configuration.

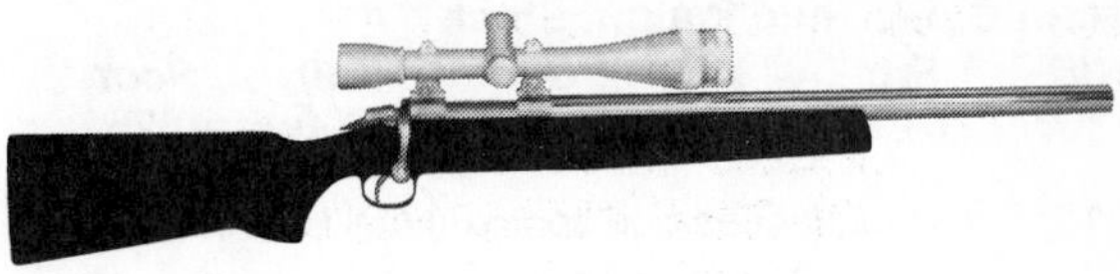

NIB	Exc.	V.G.	Good	Fair	Poor
2600	2000	1450	1050	700	200

NOTE: For Apollo action add approximately $1100.

Varminter II

This variation features a 24" to 26" medium weight match barrel with choice of McMillan or Pacific Research sporter stocks. Choice of triggers. Weight is 7.5 to 9 lbs. depending on configuration. Calibers from .223 Rem. to .257 Arnold Magnum.

NIB	Exc.	V.G.	Good	Fair	Poor
2600	2000	1450	1050	700	200

NOTE: For Apollo action add approximately $1100.

Alaskan Rifle

This is a bolt-action rifle chambered for calibers from .223 to .338 Win. Mag. Barrel lengths are from 22" to 26" depending on caliber. Stocks are synthetic in black woodland or arctic camo. Sights are optional. Rifle is drilled and tapped for scope mounts. Trigger is fully adjustable. Choice of chrome moly steel or stainless steel. Introduced in 1996.

NIB	Exc.	V.G.	Good	Fair	Poor
2600	2000	1450	1050	700	200

NOTE: Add $1100 for Apollo action.

Alaskan Trophy Rifle

Similar to the Alaskan Rifle except chambered for .300 Magnums to .458 Win. Mag. Barrel lengths are 24" to 26" depending on caliber. Choice of walnut, synthetic, or fibergrain stock. Fitted with iron sights. Choice of stainless or chrome moly steel. Introduced in 1996.

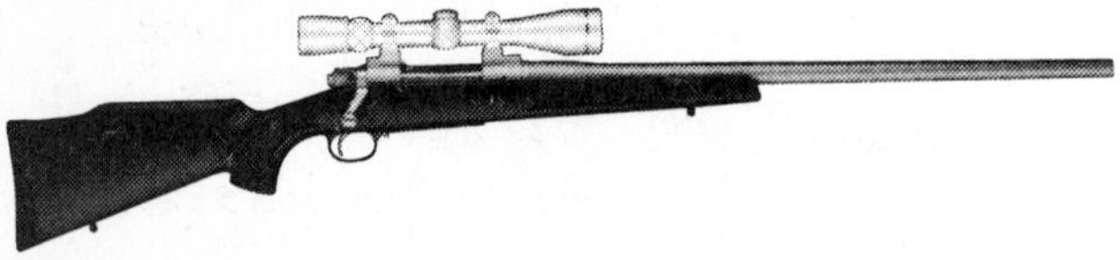

NIB	Exc.	V.G.	Good	Fair	Poor
3100	2500	1450	1050	700	200

NOTE: Add $1100 for Apollo action.

Alaskan Guide Rifle

This model is offered in choice of calibers from .257 to .338 Magnum. Barrel lengths are 22" to 26" depending on caliber. Buyer has a choice of "A" English walnut stock or deluxe synthetic stock. No open sights.

Alaskan Guide Rifle Synthetic Stock

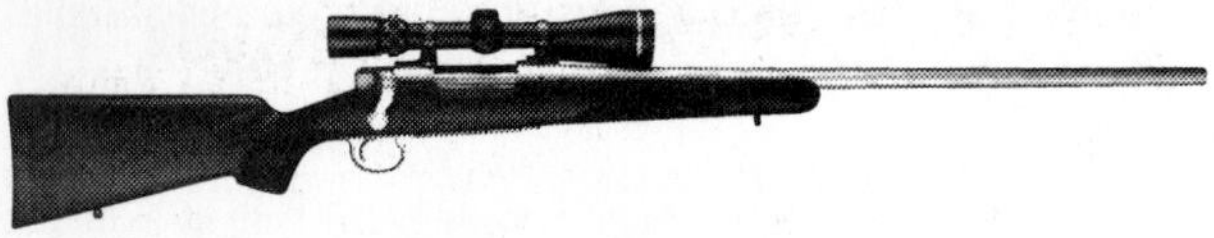

NIB	Exc.	V.G.	Good	Fair	Poor
3700	2900	2200	1400	650	300

Alaskan Guide Rifle Walnut Stock

NIB	Exc.	V.G.	Good	Fair	Poor
4300	3400	2500	1475	700	325

NOTE: For Apollo action add approximately $1100.

Grand Alaskan Rifle

This version is fitted with AAA fancy select or exhibition wood. Built in calibers from 300 Mag. to .458 Win. Mag.

Grand Alaskan Rifle "AAA" English Walnut

NIB	Exc.	V.G.	Good	Fair	Poor
6000	5000	3750	2500	1500	450

Grand Alaskan Rifle "Exhibition" Grade Walnut

NIB	Exc.	V.G.	Good	Fair	Poor
7400	6000	5000	3900	1650	325

NOTE: For Apollo action add $1100.

Safari Rifle

Introduced in 1996 this model features calibers from .223 to .458 Win. Mag. Barrel lengths are from 22" to 26" depending on caliber. The Apollo is a controlled or push feed type with one-piece, cone-head bolt. Fully adjustable trigger with chrome moly or stainless steel construction. Sights are optional but the rifle is drilled and tapped for scope mounts. Choice of A fancy English or AA fancy English walnut.

Safari Rifle "A" Fancy English Walnut

NIB	Exc.	V.G.	Good	Fair	Poor
4300	3500	2700	1650	800	300

Safari Rifle "AA" Fancy English Walnut

NIB	Exc.	V.G.	Good	Fair	Poor
4400	3500	2700	1650	800	300

NOTE: For Apollo action add $1100.

African Trophy Rifle

Similar to the Safari Rifle except stocked in AAA fancy walnut with wraparound checkering.

NIB	Exc.	V.G.	Good	Fair	Poor
6300	5000	3250	2500	1750	300

NOTE: For Apollo action add $1100.

Grand African Rifle

Similar to the Safari rifle with the addition of Exhibition Grade wood. Calibers are from .338 to .458.

NIB	Exc.	V.G.	Good	Fair	Poor
7600	6100	5000	3900	1650	325

NOTE: For Apollo action add $1100.

Serengeti Synthetic Rifle

Similar to the Safari rifle with a fibergrain stock in classic or Monte Carlo style. Checkering or stipple finish. Calibers are .243 to .300 Magnum. Introduced in 1996.

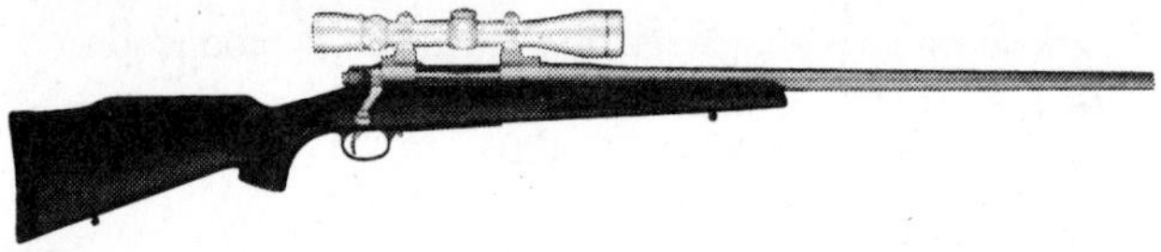

NIB	Exc.	V.G.	Good	Fair	Poor
2600	2100	1600	1150	700	225

NOTE: For Apollo action add $1100.

African Synthetic Rifle

Similar to the Safari rifle with fibergrain stock, checkering or stipple finish. Calibers are .338 Mag. to .458 Mag.

NIB	Exc.	V.G.	Good	Fair	Poor
3300	2600	1800	1400	750	250

NOTE: For Apollo action add $1100.

Neutralizer Rifle Mark I

Built on a Remington 700 or Winchester action this bolt-action rifle is chambered in a choice of calibers from .223 to .300 Win. Mag. Barrel lengths are from 24" to 26" depending on caliber with Magnum barrels up to 28". A fiberglass tactical stock with adjustable cheekpiece and buttplate is standard in various finishes. Winchester action is $400 less.

NIB	Exc.	V.G.	Good	Fair	Poor
2900	2300	1700	1300	700	275

Neutralizer Rifle Mark II

Same as above but with Apollo action.

NIB	Exc.	V.G.	Good	Fair	Poor
4000	3200	2250	1700	900	325

Benchrest Rifles

Custom built. Unable to price individual rifles.

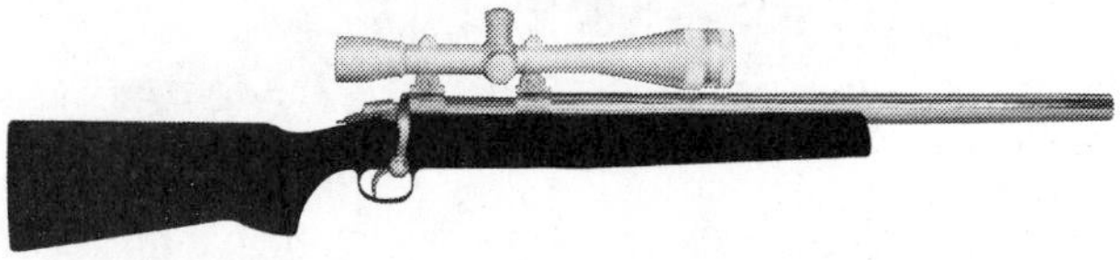

Prone Rifles

Custom built. Unable to price individual rifles.

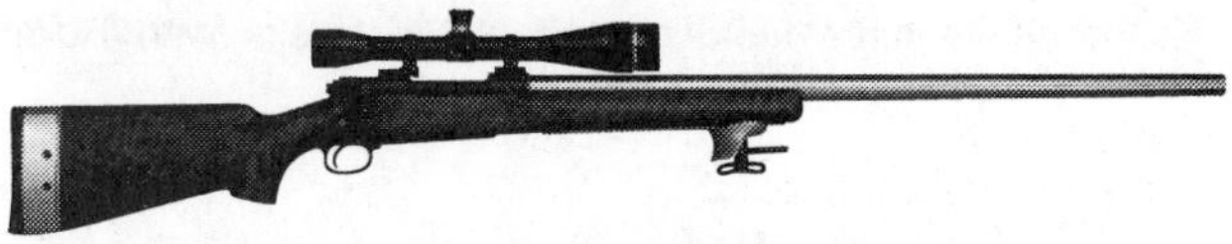

X-Course Rifles

Custom built. Unable to price individual rifles.

1,000 Yard Match Rifles

Custom built. Unable to price individual rifles.

Fully Accurized Production Rifles

These rifles are offered in standard blue or stainless steel with walnut or synthetic stock. Chambered from .223 to .338 Win. mag. and built on Remington, Ruger, or Winchester actions.

NIB	Exc.	V.G.	Good	Fair	Poor
1250	1100	750	600	400	200

ARRIETA S.L.

Elgoibar, Spain

This company produces a wide variety of double-barrel shotguns in a price range from $450 to above $14,000. It is recommended that highly engraved examples, as well as small bore arms, be individually appraised.

490 Eder

A double-barrel boxlock shotgun with double triggers and extractors. Discontinued in 1986.

NIB	Exc.	V.G.	Good	Fair	Poor
—	550	425	325	250	100

500 Titan

A Holland & Holland-style sidelock double-barrel shotgun with French case hardened and engraved locks. Double triggers on extractors. No longer imported after 1986.

NIB	Exc.	V.G.	Good	Fair	Poor
—	675	500	400	300	150

501 Palomara

As above, but more finely finished. Discontinued in 1986.

NIB	Exc.	V.G.	Good	Fair	Poor
—	800	600	500	400	200

505 Alaska

As above, but more intricately engraved. Discontinued in 1986.

NIB	Exc.	V.G.	Good	Fair	Poor
—	900	750	600	500	250

510 Montana

A Holland & Holland-style sidelock double-barrel shotgun with the internal parts gold-plated.

NIB	Exc.	V.G.	Good	Fair	Poor
3200	2750	1250	850	500	250

550 Field

As above, without the internal parts gold-plated.

NIB	Exc.	V.G.	Good	Fair	Poor
3200	2750	1250	850	500	250

557 Standard

As above, but more finely finished.

NIB	Exc.	V.G.	Good	Fair	Poor
3750	3000	1750	1250	800	400

558 Patria

As above, but more finely finished.

NIB	Exc.	V.G.	Good	Fair	Poor
3650	3150	1750	1250	800	400

560 Cumbre

As above, but featuring intricate engraving.

NIB	Exc.	V.G.	Good	Fair	Poor
3800	3200	1800	1200	800	400

570 Lieja

NIB	Exc.	V.G.	Good	Fair	Poor
4400	3500	2000	1500	750	500

575 Sport

NIB	Exc.	V.G.	Good	Fair	Poor
4750	3750	2250	1700	1200	750

578 Victoria

This model is engraved in the English manner with floral bouquets.

NIB	Exc.	V.G.	Good	Fair	Poor
4500	3750	2000	1250	750	350

585 Liria

As above, but more finely finished.

NIB	Exc.	V.G.	Good	Fair	Poor
4800	4000	2250	1500	900	400

588 Cima

NIB	Exc.	V.G.	Good	Fair	Poor
4800	4000	2250	1500	900	400

590 Regina

NIB	Exc.	V.G.	Good	Fair	Poor
4250	3500	2700	1750	1000	500

595 Principe

As above, but engraved with relief-cut hunting scenes.

NIB	Exc.	V.G.	Good	Fair	Poor
7500	6000	4000	3000	2000	1000

600 Imperial

This double-barrel shotgun has a self-opening action.

NIB	Exc.	V.G.	Good	Fair	Poor
6000	5250	3250	2000	1000	500

601 Imperial Tiro

As above, but nickel-plated. Fitted with a self-opening action.

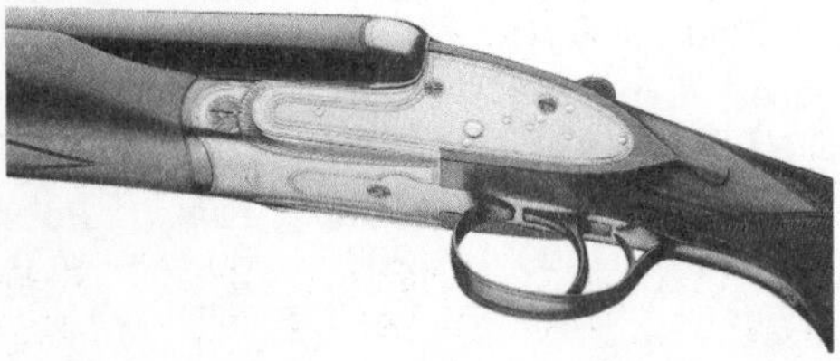

NIB	Exc.	V.G.	Good	Fair	Poor
6750	6000	4000	3000	2000	1000

801

A detachable sidelock, self-opening action, double-barrel shotgun engraved in the manner of Churchill.

NIB	Exc.	V.G.	Good	Fair	Poor
8550	7000	6500	4000	3000	1500

802

As above, with Holland & Holland-style engraving.

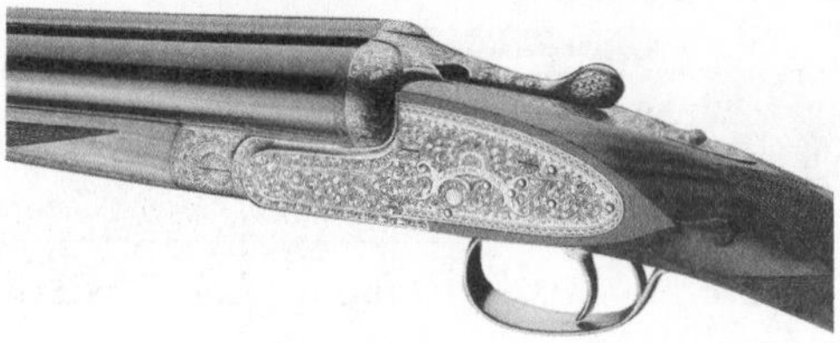

NIB	Exc.	V.G.	Good	Fair	Poor
8550	7000	6500	4000	3000	1500

803

As above, with Purdey-style engraving.

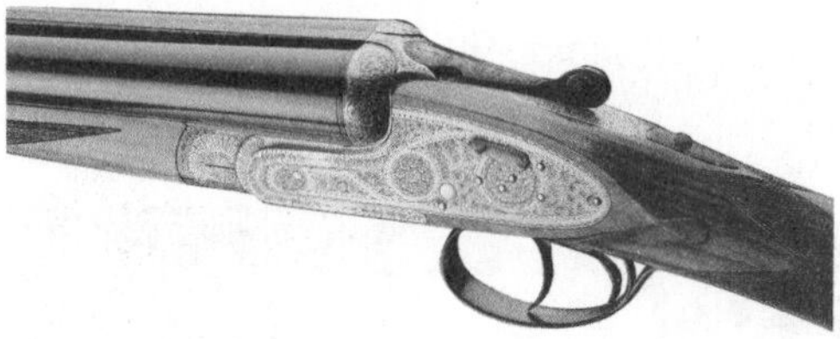

NIB	Exc.	V.G.	Good	Fair	Poor
7050	5000	4000	3000	2000	1000

871

This model features hand detachable sidelocks with Holland ejectors. Scroll engraving.

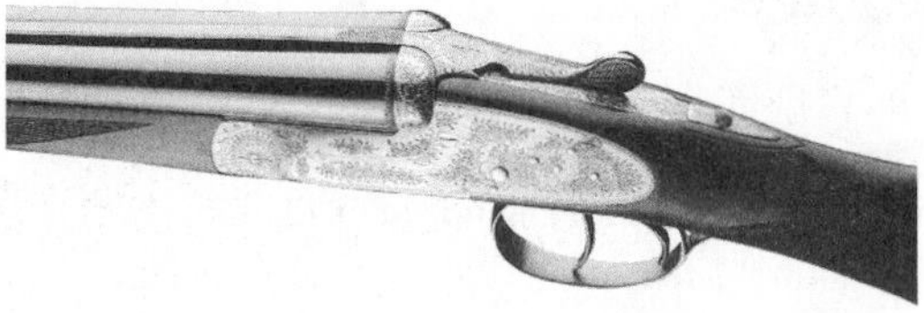

NIB	Exc.	V.G.	Good	Fair	Poor
5300	4400	2500	1500	1000	750

872

This model has same features as the Model 871 with the addition of more engraving coverage using a tighter scroll.

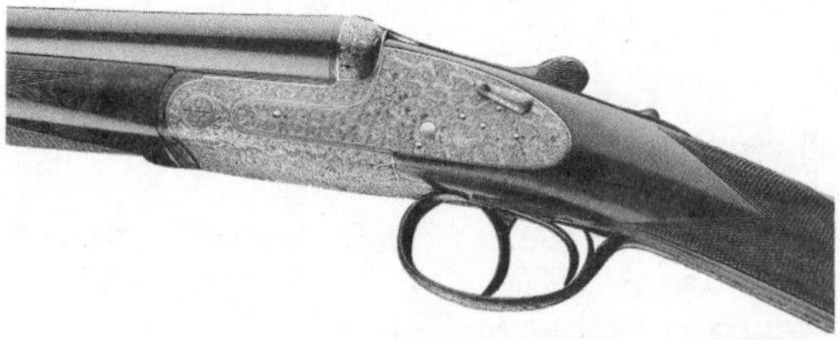

NIB	Exc.	V.G.	Good	Fair	Poor
9800	8250	7000	4000	3000	1000

873

This model features hand detachable sidelocks and game scene engraving.

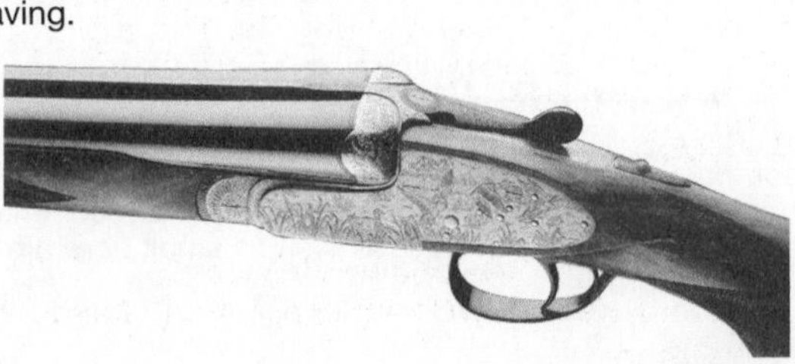

NIB	Exc.	V.G.	Good	Fair	Poor
6850	5800	4500	3000	1500	750

874

Same features as above model but with the addition of a blued frame with gold line outlines.

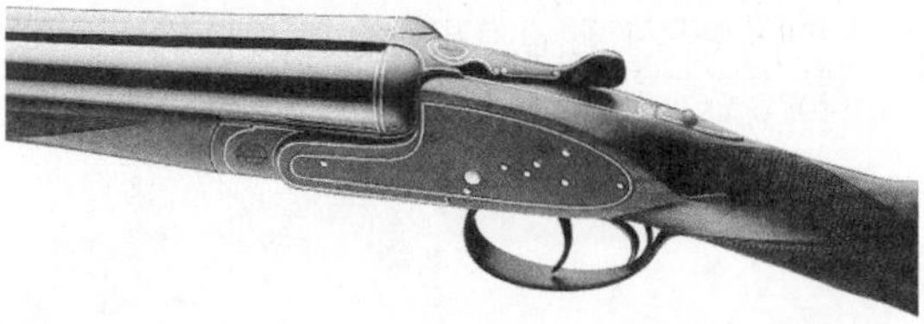

NIB	Exc.	V.G.	Good	Fair	Poor
9000	7750	5500	4500	3000	1000

875

A custom manufactured sidelock, double-barrel shotgun built solely to the customer's specifications.

NIB	Exc.	V.G.	Good	Fair	Poor
15000	11500	8500	6000	3000	1000

R-1 Double Rifle

NIB	Exc.	V.G.	Good	Fair	Poor
15000	12500	10500	6000	3000	1000

R-2 Double Rifle

NIB	Exc.	V.G.	Good	Fair	Poor
18000	16000	14000	11000	5000	2000

NOTE: Add 5 percent for gauges smaller than 16 gauge. Add 10 percent for matched pairs. There are a number of extra cost options that will affect the value of individual guns.

ARSENAL, INC.

Las Vegas, Nevada

SA M-7

Semi-automatic rifles manufactured in U.S. similar to the AK-47 in appearance. Chambered for the 7.62x39 cartridge and fitted with a 16" barrel. Black polymer stock.

NIB	Exc.	V.G.	Good	Fair	Poor
1000	800	550	325	200	125

SA M-7 Classic

As above but with blonde wood stock.

NIB	Exc.	V.G.	Good	Fair	Poor
1050	850	600	325	200	125

SA M-7S

Similar to the SA M-7 but with scope rail added.

NIB	Exc.	V.G.	Good	Fair	Poor
1025	875	575	325	200	125

SA RPK-7

Chambered for the 7.62x39 cartridge this rifle is similar to the RPK. Fitted with a 23" barrel with bipod. Solid blonde wood stock with trap in stock for cleaning kit.

NIB	Exc.	V.G.	Good	Fair	Poor
975	800	595	325	200	125

A-SQUARE

Bedford, Kentucky/Chamberlain, South Dakota

Hannibal Grade

Using the P-17 Enfield action, with a 22" to 26" barrel, this rifle is chambered for 32 calibers from 7mm Rem. Mag. up to and including the .500 A-Square Mag. and .577 Tyrannosaur. Blued with a checkered walnut pistol-grip stock. Introduced in 1986. Weights range from 9 lbs. to 13.25 lbs. depending on caliber. Add 5 percent for Kentucky-built rifles.

NIB	Exc.	V.G.	Good	Fair	Poor
3200	2700	1800	1000	600	350

Caesar Grade

Utilizing a Remington Model 700 action and chambered for the same cartridges as the above, with the exception that A-Square proprietary cartridges are not available. Also made in the left-hand version. Introduced in 1986. Weights are in the 8.5 to 11 lbs. range.

NIB	Exc.	V.G.	Good	Fair	Poor
3200	2700	1800	1000	600	350

Hamilcar Grade

A smaller and lighter version of the Hannibal Grade. It was introduced in 1994. It is designed to be chambered for .30-06 cartridges. Weights are around 8 to 8.5 lbs. Introduced in 1994.

NIB	Exc.	V.G.	Good	Fair	Poor
3200	2700	1800	1000	600	350

Genghis Khan Model

This model is designed for varmint shooting and is fitted with a heavyweight barrel. Offered in .22-250, .243 Win., 6mm Rem., .25-06, .257 Wby., and .264 Win. Barrel length is to customer's specifications, as is length of pull. No iron sights are fitted to this model. Weight is approximately 11 lbs.

NIB	Exc.	V.G.	Good	Fair	Poor
3200	2700	1800	1000	600	350

AUBREY, A.J.

Meriden, Connecticut

Double-Barrel Shotguns

Good quality doubles made for Sears. Value depends on condition, grade, and model. Price range between $100 and $1,500.

AUSTRALIAN AUTOMATIC ARMS LTD.

Tasmania, Australia

SAR

A 5.56mm semi-automatic rifle with a 16.25" or 20" barrel, 5-shot or 20-shot magazine, black plastic stock and forend. Imported from 1986 to 1989.

NIB	Exc.	V.G.	Good	Fair	Poor
1200	950	650	350	250	125

SP

A sporting rifle version of the SAR, fitted with a wood stock and 5-shot magazine. Introduced in 1989.

NIB	Exc.	V.G.	Good	Fair	Poor
975	850	575	300	250	125

AUTO ORDNANCE CORP.

Auto Ordnance makes reproductions of the 1911 Government Model pistol, the Thompson submachine gun (semiauto only) and the M-1 Carbine. Variations of the 1911 are marketed under both the Auto Ordnance and Thompson brand names. In 1999 the company was bought by Kahr Arms and moved from West Hurley, NY to Worcester, MA.

Thompson 1927 A1 Standard (New York Production)

A semi-automatic version of the Thompson submachine gun, chambered for the .45 ACP cartridge with a 16-1/2" barrel that is 18" with compensator. Blued with walnut stock. Weight is 13 lbs.

NIB	Exc.	V.G.	Good	Fair	Poor
1250	850	650	400	300	150

1927 A1 Deluxe/Model T1

As above, with a finned barrel, adjustable sights, pistol grip forearm, and a 50-round drum magazine costing an additional $250. The violin-shaped carrying case adds approximately $150 to the values listed.

NIB	Exc.	V.G.	Good	Fair	Poor
1350	950	695	400	300	150

1927 A1C/Model T5

As above, with an aluminum alloy receiver. Introduced in 1984.

NIB	Exc.	V.G.	Good	Fair	Poor
1175	825	625	400	300	150

1927 A1 Commando/Model T1-C

Introduced in 1998 this version features a 16.5" finned barrel with compensator. The finish is parkerized with black wood finish. Furnished with 30-round magazine and black nylon sling. Weight is about 13 lbs.

NIB	Exc.	V.G.	Good	Fair	Poor
1250	850	650	400	300	150

1927 A3

A .22 caliber variation of the Model 1927 A1 with a 16" barrel and aluminum alloy receiver. No longer in production. Add $500 for drum magazine.

NIB	Exc.	V.G.	Good	Fair	Poor
1350	900	675	550	425	150

T1SB

Short-barreled (10.5" finned and compensated) variant of semi-auto M1. Accepts drum magazines. Requires Form 3. Introduced 2005.

NIB	Exc.	V.G.	Good	Fair	Poor
1500	1150	695	400	300	150

M1SB

Short-barreled (10.5" finned and compensated) variant of semi-auto M1. Does not accept drum magazines. Requires Form 3.

NIB	Exc.	V.G.	Good	Fair	Poor
1500	1150	695	400	300	150

M1 Carbine

Newly-manufactured replica of military M1 carbine chambered in .30 Carbine. Introduced 2005. Birch stock, parkerized finish. (Add 5 percent for walnut stock.)

NIB	Exc.	V.G.	Good	Fair	Poor
950	800	650	500	300	125

AUTO POINTER

Yamamoto Co.
Tokyo, Japan

Auto Pointer Shotgun

A 12 or 20 gauge semi-automatic shotgun with 26", 28" or 30" barrels and an aluminum alloy frame. Blued with a checkered walnut stock. Originally imported by Sloan's but no longer available. Clone of Browning A-5.

NIB	Exc.	V.G.	Good	Fair	Poor
—	475	350	250	175	100

AXTELL RIFLE CO.

(Riflesmith Inc.)
Sheridan, Montana

#1 Long Range Creedmore

This single-shot rifle is chambered for the .40-50BN, .40-70SS, .40-70BN, .40-90, .45-70, .45-90, .45-100. Weight is about 10 lbs. Numerous options will affect price.

NIB	Exc.	V.G.	Good	Fair	Poor
4700	3750	3000	2200	1400	300

New Model Sharps 1877

Chambered for the .45-90, .45-100, and the .45-70 cartridges and fitted with a choice of 30" to 34" half round-half octagon barrel with double-set triggers.

NIB	Exc.	V.G.	Good	Fair	Poor
5200	4000	3250	2500	1500	250

#2 Long Range

The Long Range #2 rifle is chambered for all the same calibers as the #1 Long Range Creedmore. Weight is about 10 lbs.

NIB	Exc.	V.G.	Good	Fair	Poor
3900	3000	1900	900	550	300

Lower Sporting Rifle

Chambered for same calibers as above. Weight is between 9 and 12 lbs. depending on barrel options.

NIB	Exc.	V.G.	Good	Fair	Poor
2600	2000	1375	700	400	200

Business Rifle

Same calibers as above. Weight is about 8.5 lbs.

NIB	Exc.	V.G.	Good	Fair	Poor
2400	1800	1275	700	400	200

Overbaugh Schuetzen

Chambered for the .40-50BN and the .40-50 straight. Weight is 11 to 14 lbs. depending on barrel options.

NIB	Exc.	V.G.	Good	Fair	Poor
4400	3500	3000	2200	1400	300

B

BAER CUSTOM, LES
Hillsdale, Illinois

AR .223 Ultimate Super Varmint

Fitted with a choice of 18", 20", or 24" heavy barrels with 1-in-12 twist. Flat top rail. Choice of single or two-stage trigger. Aluminum free-floating handguard. Bear Coat finish. Introduced in 2000.

NIB	*Exc.*	*V.G.*	*Good*	*Fair*	*Poor*
1975	1600	1300	900	600	300

AR .223 Ultimate Super Match

Introduced in 2002 this model features a wide number of custom features with barrel lengths from 18" to 24". Special match carrier with integral rail system.

NIB	*Exc.*	*V.G.*	*Good*	*Fair*	*Poor*
2125	1700	1400	1000	750	500

AR .223 M4-A2 Flattop

This model features a flat-top rail and match bolt and carrier. The 16" barrel has a integral compensator. Single stage trigger. Knights Armament Systems rail adapter. Bear Coat finish. Introduced in 2000.

NIB	*Exc.*	*V.G.*	*Good*	*Fair*	*Poor*
2175	1725	1425	1025	675	400

AR .223 IPSC Action Model

Similar to the model above but with 18" Super Match heavy barrel with integral compensator. Introduced in 2000.

NIB	*Exc.*	*V.G.*	*Good*	*Fair*	*Poor*
2300	1875	1550	1100	700	450

AR .223 Ultimate NRA Match

This model features numerous custom features and is fitted with a 30" barrel, special front and rear sights.

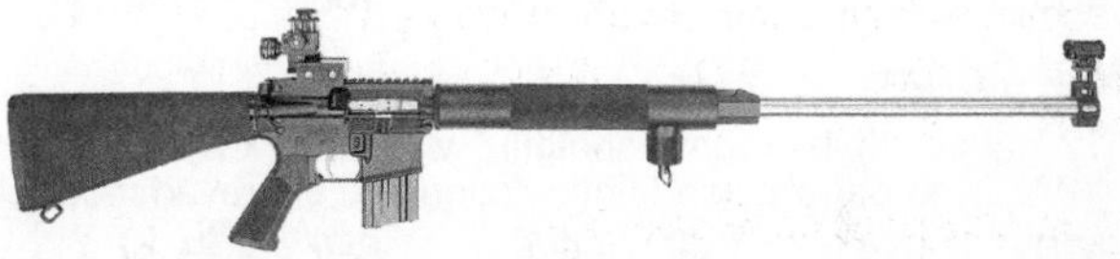

NIB	*Exc.*	*V.G.*	*Good*	*Fair*	*Poor*
2500	2000	1350	900	600	375

NOTE: Add $750 for special sight package.

Thunder Ranch Rifle

This .223 model is fitted with a bench rest 16" barrel. Upper receiver has a carry handle and a top rail. Free floating handguard, jewel two-stage trigger, floading front sight, and many other custom features. Thunder Ranch logo stamped on lower receiver. Weight is about 7.5 lbs. Introduced in 2004.

NIB	*Exc.*	*V.G.*	*Good*	*Fair*	*Poor*
2500	2000	1350	900	600	375

Les Baer Monolith .308 Swat

Military type match sniper rifle chambered in .308 Winchester. Solid full-length Picatinny rail for scope mounting. DuPont-S coating on barrel, two-stage trigger group with choice of 18, 20 (standard) or 24-inch barrel. Two magazines and soft case included. Introduced in 2011.

NIB	*Exc.*	*V.G.*	*Good*	*Fair*	*Poor*
3500	3000	2600	2000	1000	500

BAIKAL

Importer—European American Armory

A custom-made O/U shotgun with detachable sidelocks. Produced in limited quantities and most often to the purchaser's specifications.

Baikal IJ-27E1C

A 12 or 20 gauge Magnum O/U shotgun with 26" Skeet-Skeet or 28" Modified-Full ventilated rib barrels, single-selective trigger and extractors. Blued with a walnut stock.

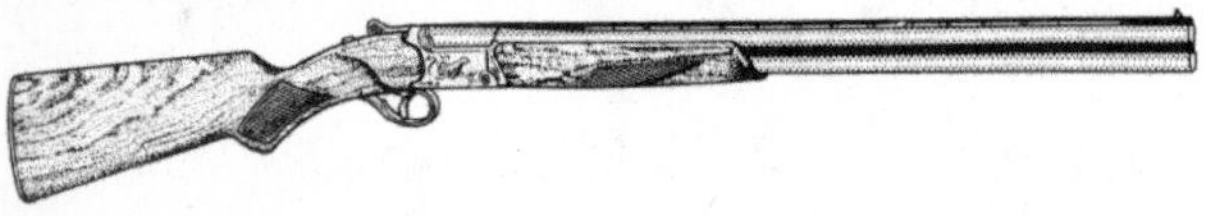

NIB	*Exc.*	*V.G.*	*Good*	*Fair*	*Poor*
375	275	200	150	100	75

Baikal TOZ - 34

A 12 or 28 gauge double-barrel shotgun with 26" or 28" barrels, double triggers, cocking indicators and extractors. Blued with a checkered walnut stock. This model was also available with a silver-plated receiver.

NIB	*Exc.*	*V.G.*	*Good*	*Fair*	*Poor*
400	300	250	200	100	75

Model MC-8-0

A 12 gauge double-barrel shotgun with 26" Skeet-Skeet or 28 Full-Modified barrels, hand fitted action and engraved receiver.

NIB	*Exc.*	*V.G.*	*Good*	*Fair*	*Poor*
2000	1250	950	700	500	250

Model MC-5-105

The Model TOZ-34 with an engraved receiver.

NIB	*Exc.*	*V.G.*	*Good*	*Fair*	*Poor*
1200	850	700	500	300	150

Model MC-7

As above, with a relief engraved receiver.

NIB	*Exc.*	*V.G.*	*Good*	*Fair*	*Poor*
2250	1750	1200	800	550	250

IZH18/MP18

This is a single-barrel shotgun chambered for 12, 20, or .410 bore. Choice of 26.5" or 29.5" barrels. Hardwood stock. Ejectors. Introduced in 1999.

NIB	*Exc.*	*V.G.*	*Good*	*Fair*	*Poor*
95	75	50	35	25	10

IZK18MAX

Similar to the above model but with polished nickel receiver, vent rib, walnut stock, screw-in chokes, and ejectors. Offered in 12 and 20 gauge as well as .410 bore.

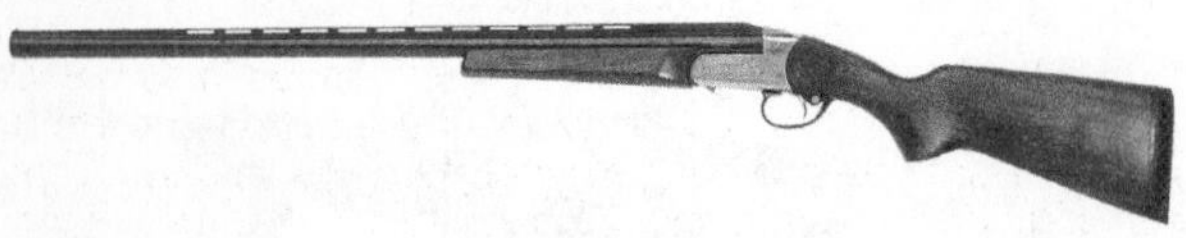

NIB	*Exc.*	*V.G.*	*Good*	*Fair*	*Poor*
170	125	100	75	50	25

IZH43

This side-by-side gun is available in 12, 16, 20, 28, and .410 bore. In barrel lengths for 20" to 28" depending on gauge. Internal hammers. Single-selective trigger, ejectors. Walnut stock.

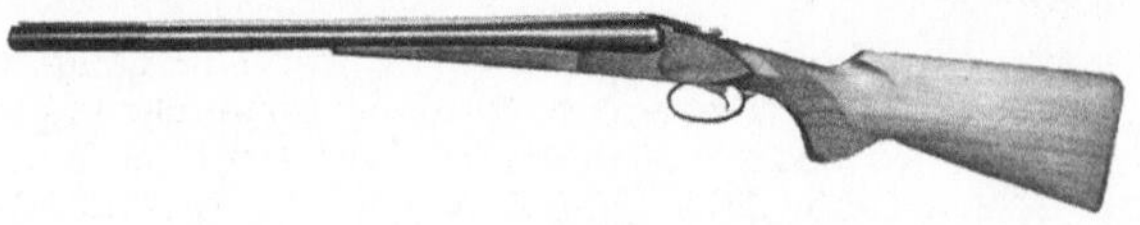

NIB	*Exc.*	*V.G.*	*Good*	*Fair*	*Poor*
350	275	200	150	100	75

NOTE: Add $80 for 28 gauge and .410 bore guns.

IZH43K

Introduced in 1999 this is a 12 or 20 gauge 3" side-by-side external hammer gun with choice of barrel lengths of 18.5", 20", 24", 26", and 28". Single-selective trigger or double trigger. Engraved side plates. Walnut stock with pistol grip. Weight is about 7.3 lbs.

NIB	*Exc.*	*V.G.*	*Good*	*Fair*	*Poor*
375	300	250	175	125	100

NOTE: Deduct $40 for double triggers.

MP213 Coach Gun

Similar to the above model but with internal hammers. Single or double triggers. Weight is about 7 lbs. Barrel inserts for .45-70 were offered.

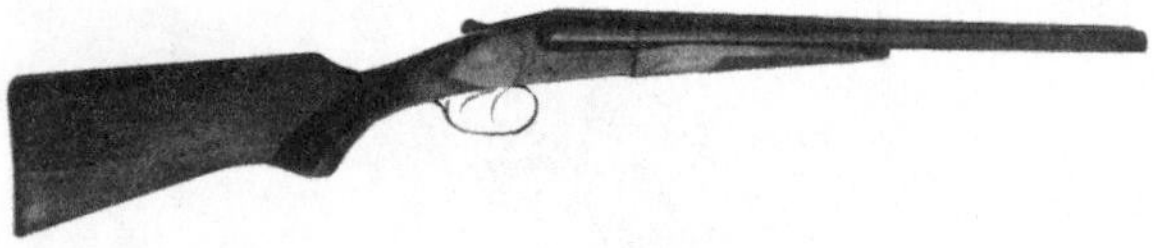

NIB	*Exc.*	*V.G.*	*Good*	*Fair*	*Poor*
650	500	400	350	100	75

NOTE: Add 25 percent for .45-70 inserts.

IZH27

This is an over/under gun chambered for 12, 20, 28, and .410 bore. Choice of 26.5" or 28.5" barrels. Walnut stock. Single trigger with ejectors. Fixed chokes.

NIB	*Exc.*	*V.G.*	*Good*	*Fair*	*Poor*
350	275	200	150	100	75

NOTE: Add $35 for screw-in chokes. Add $85 for 28 gauge and .410 bore guns.

MP233

This over/under gun is chambered for the 12 gauge 3" shell with a choice of 26", 28", or 30" barrels. Walnut checkered stock. Single or double triggers. Screw-in chokes. Removable trigger assembly. Weight is about 7.3 lbs. Introduced in 1999.

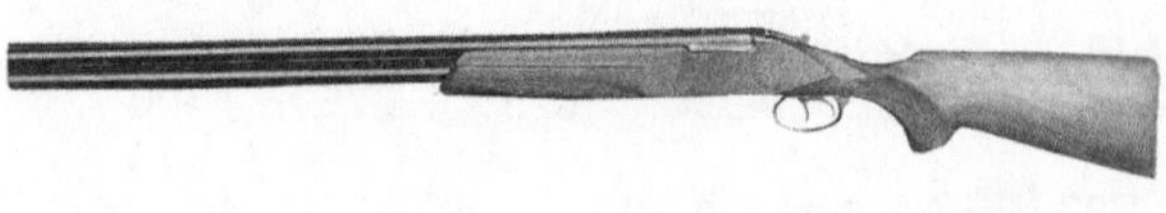

NIB	*Exc.*	*V.G.*	*Good*	*Fair*	*Poor*
700	550400	295	200	175	100

IZH94/MP94

This is an over/under combination gun with a 12 gauge upper barrel and centerfire rifle barrel on the under barrel. Barrel length is 24" or 26". This model is offered as an over/under rifle in calibers .222, .223, 6.5x55, .308, .30-06, or 7.62x39. A .410/.22LR or .410/.22 WMR model is available. Walnut stock single or double trigger. Weight is about 8 - 10 lbs. Open sights.

NIB	Exc.	V.G.	Good	Fair	Poor
525	475	425	350	300	175

NOTE: Deduct 40 percent for .410 .

IZH81

This is a pump-action shotgun chambered for 12 gauge 3" shells. Barrel lengths are a choice of 20", 26", or 28". Five-round detachable magazine. Walnut stock.

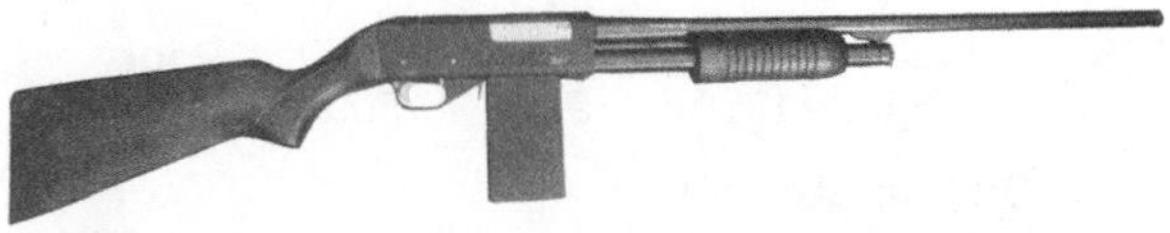

NIB	Exc.	V.G.	Good	Fair	Poor
300	225	165	125	97	50

NOTE: Add $60 for vent rib.

MP131K

This is a pump-action shotgun with a choice of two different feeding sources: a tubular magazine or a detachable 3-round or 5-round box magazine.

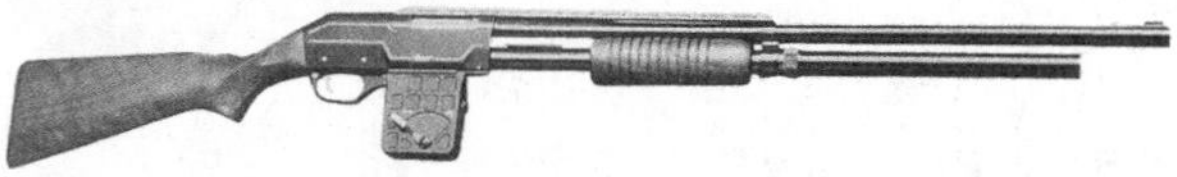

NIB	Exc.	V.G.	Good	Fair	Poor
300	225	165	125	97	50

MP133

This is a slide action shotgun chambered for the 12 gauge 3.5" shell. Available with barrel lengths of 20", 24", 26", or 28". Vent rib or all barrel lengths except 20". Walnut stock. Choke tubes for all barrel lengths except 20" (Cylinder choke). Introduced in 2001.

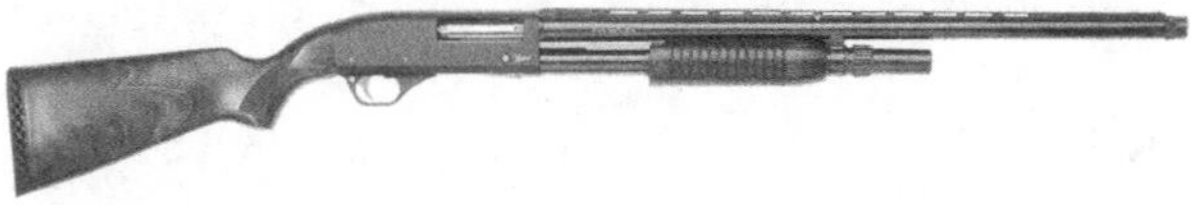

NIB	Exc.	V.G.	Good	Fair	Poor
300	225	165	125	95	50

MP153

This is a semi-automatic shotgun chambered for 12 gauge 3" shell. Choice of 26" or 28" barrels. Choice of walnut or black synthetic stock. Weight is about 7.8 lbs. Screw-in chokes. Introduced in 1999.

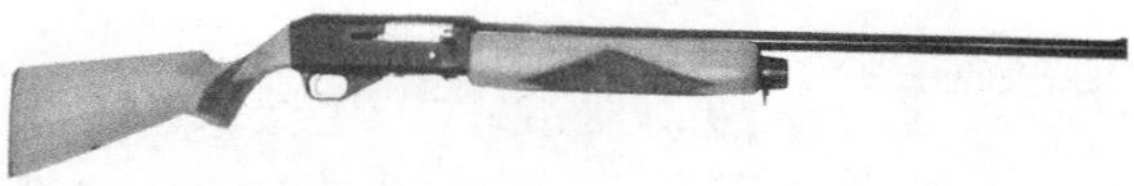

NIB	Exc.	V.G.	Good	Fair	Poor
325	250	190	150	100	65

MP310

Originally imported as the Model IZH2, this O/U is now marketed as the MP310. Offered in 12 gauge, 20 gauge or .410 bore with 26 or 28-inch barrels. Hammer forged barrels, machined steel receiver and monoblock, checkered walnut two-piece stock. Hard chrome-lined barrels, ventilated rib, ejectors, auto safety and single selective trigger.

NIB	Exc.	V.G.	Good	Fair	Poor
475	425	350	300	250	200

MP220

This side-by-side field gun has single selective trigger, ejectors, machined steel boxlock receiver, checkered walnut stock with recoil pad, splinter fore-end, automatic tang safety and screw-in chokes. In 12, 16, 20, 28 gauge and .410 bore. Weight is 8 to 10 lbs.

NIB	Exc.	V.G.	Good	Fair	Poor
300	250	200	175	150	100

BAILONS GUNMAKERS, LTD.

Birmingham, England

Most of the products of this company are produced strictly on custom order.

Hunting Rifle

A bolt-action sporting rifle produced in a variety of calibers with a 24" barrel, open sights, double-set triggers and a 3- or 4-shot magazine. Blued with a well-figured walnut stock. The values listed are for a standard grade rifle.

NIB	Exc.	V.G.	Good	Fair	Poor
3500	2950	2450	1900	675	325

BAKER, M.A.

Fayetteville, North Carolina

In business from 1857 through 1862, Baker produced sporting arms prior to the Civil War. During the Civil War Baker altered muskets and "common rifles." In addition, it is thought that Baker made rifles for the State of North Carolina with lockplates stamped M.A. BAKER/FAYETTEVILLE/N.C. These rifles resembled the U.S. Model 1841 Rifle and had these characteristics: Overall length 51-1/2"; Barrel length 35-1/8"; Caliber .50.

NIB	Exc.	V.G.	Good	Fair	Poor
—	—	26000	13500	3200	1500

BAKER GUN & FORGING CO.

Batavia, New York

The Baker Gun & Forging Company was founded in early 1890, by Elias Baker, brother of William Baker. Made from drop forged parts, Baker single and double barrel shotguns quickly gained a reputation for strength and reliability among shooters of the period. Offered in a wide variety of grades, from plain utilitarian to heavily embellished models, Baker shotguns have in recent years become highly collectable. The company was sold on December 24, 1919, to H. & D. Folsom Arms Company of Norwich, Connecticut. The Folsom Company had for almost 20 years been the Baker Company's sole New York City agent and had marketed at least one Baker model that was only made for them. From 1919 to approximately 1923, Folsom continued to assemble and make Baker shotguns. Late model Bakers were made by the Crescent Firearms Company and have serial numbers with an "F" suffix.

The Baker Gun & Forging Company was the first American arms manufacturer to:
1.Make a single barrel trap shotgun.
2.Make a single barrel trap shotgun with a ventilated rib.
3.Make arms with an intercepting firing pin block safety.
4.Make a double barrel shotgun with hammers directly behind the firing pins.
5.Use a long swinging sear that once adjusted gave consistent trigger pull throughout the working life of an arm.

Those Baker shotguns manufactured between 1913 and 1923 that were engraved by Rudolph J. Kornbrath command substantial price premiums over the values listed.

Baker Trap Gun

A 12 gauge single barrel boxlock shotgun with either a 30" or 32" barrel. Blued, case hardened with a walnut stock.

NIB	Exc.	V.G.	Good	Fair	Poor
—	1800	1450	1050	500	250

Elite Grade

Standard scrollwork and simple game scenes engraved on receiver.

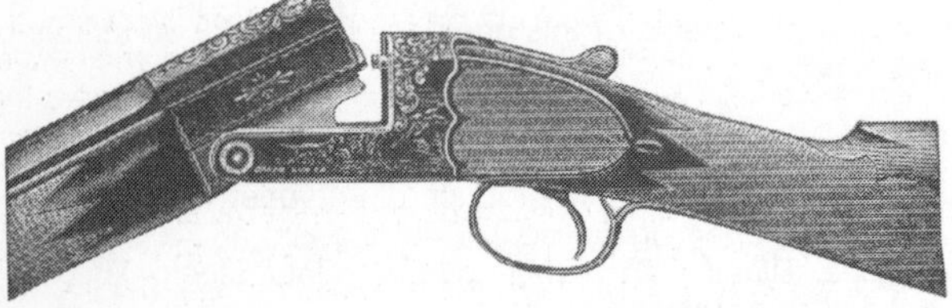

NIB	Exc.	V.G.	Good	Fair	Poor
—	2300	1700	1200	600	250

Superba

Heavily engraved on receiver and sides of barrel breech.

NIB	Exc.	V.G.	Good	Fair	Poor
—	4500	3300	1800	850	500

Expert Grade Double Shotgun

The highest grade shotgun manufactured by the Baker Gun & Forging Company. General specifications as above. The stock of imported English or French walnut. The engraving of full coverage type and partially chiselled. Automatic ejectors and single trigger if requested. Built on special order only.

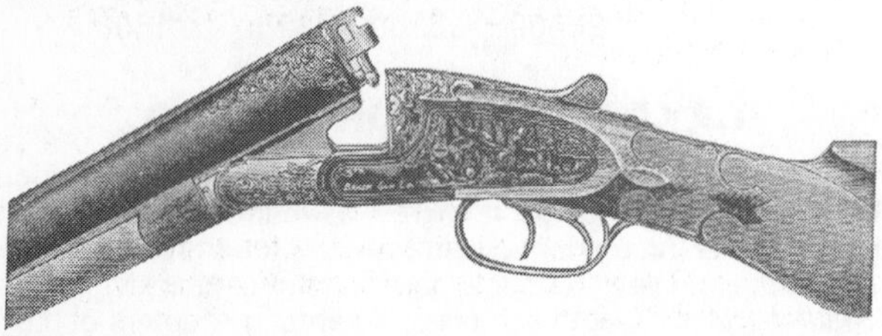

NIB	Exc.	V.G.	Good	Fair	Poor
—	5700	4400	2400	1800	750

Deluxe Grade Double Shotgun

The designation given those Expert Grade shotguns produced by H. & D. Folsom from 1919 to 1923. Characteristics and values identical to those listed for the Baker Expert Grade Double Shotgun.

Black Beauty Double Shotgun

Made solely for H. & D. Folsom Arms Company. A 12 or 16 gauge double barrel shotgun with sidelocks and 26", 28", 30", or 32" barrels in 12 gauge and 26", 28", or 30" barrels in 16 gauge. The barrels are blued, the receiver is case hardened, the sideplates are finished with black oxide and the stock is walnut. Automatic ejectors and single trigger are extra cost options.

NIB	Exc.	V.G.	Good	Fair	Poor
—	1150	1000	850	700	250

Grade S Double Shotgun

As above, with simple engraving.

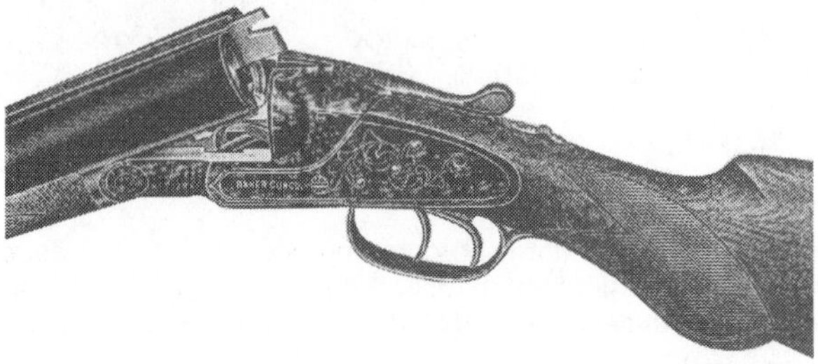

NIB	Exc.	V.G.	Good	Fair	Poor
—	1550	1250	950	500	250

Grade R Double Shotgun

As above, with case hardened sideplates and engraved with simple scrollwork and game scenes.

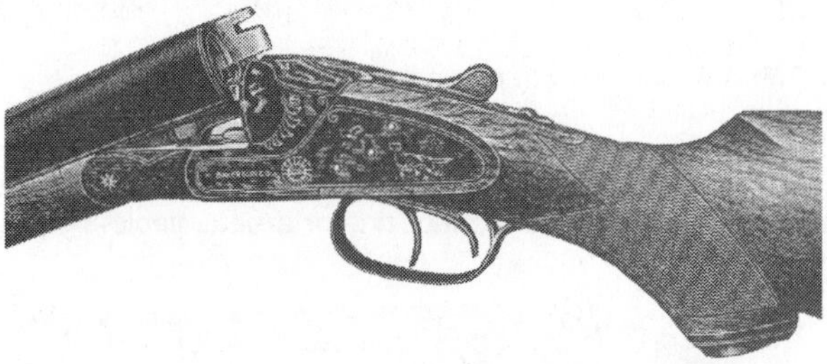

NIB	Exc.	V.G.	Good	Fair	Poor
—	1950	1500	1100	600	300

Paragon Grade Shotgun

As above, with finely cut scrollwork and detailed game scenes engraved on the sideplates. The stock of finely figured walnut.

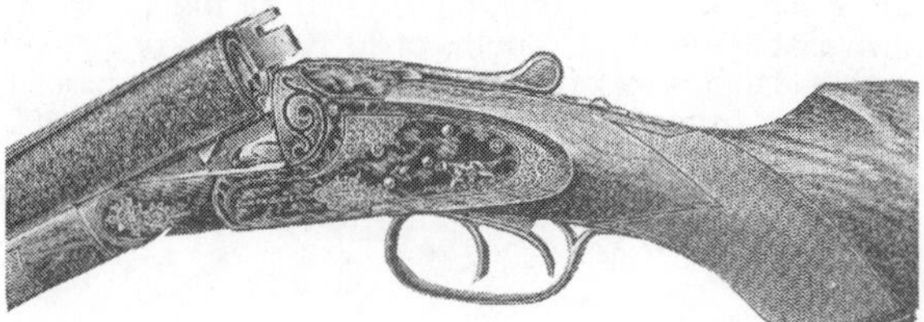

NIB	Exc.	V.G.	Good	Fair	Poor
—	2800	2200	1700	1000	500

Paragon Grade—Model NN

As above, but more finely engraved. Built on special order only. Automatic ejectors.

NIB	Exc.	V.G.	Good	Fair	Poor
—	3950	2900	1950	1400	500

Batavia Special

A 12 or 16 gauge double barrel shotgun with sidelocks and 28", 30", or 32" barrels in 12 gauge and 28" or 30" barrels in 16 gauge. Blued, case hardened with a walnut stock and double triggers.

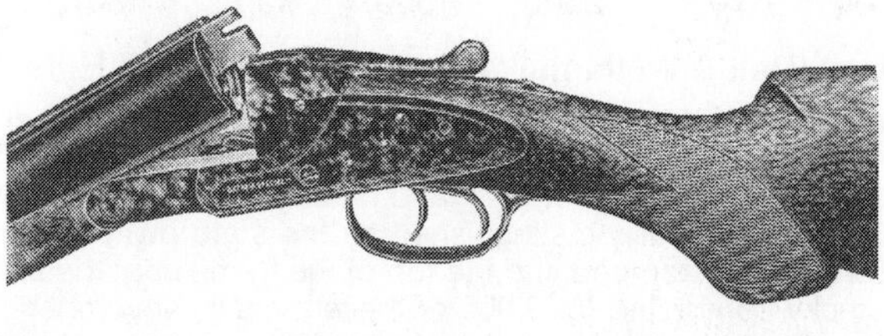

NIB	Exc.	V.G.	Good	Fair	Poor
—	850	550	450	225	175

Batavia Brush Gun

A 12 or 16 gauge double barrel shotgun with sidelocks and 26" barrels. Blued, case hardened with walnut stock. Sling rings and swivels optional.

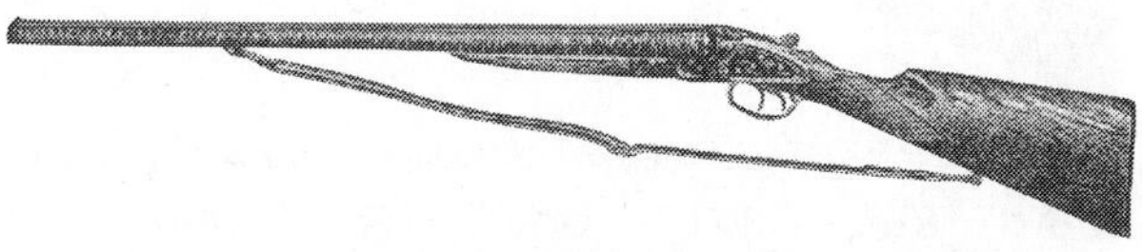

NIB	Exc.	V.G.	Good	Fair	Poor
—	750	600	550	225	175

Batavia Leader

A 12 or 16 gauge double barrel shotgun with sidelocks and 26", 28", 30", or 32" barrels in 12 gauge and 26", 28", or 30" barrels in 16 gauge. Blued, case hardened with a walnut stock and double triggers.

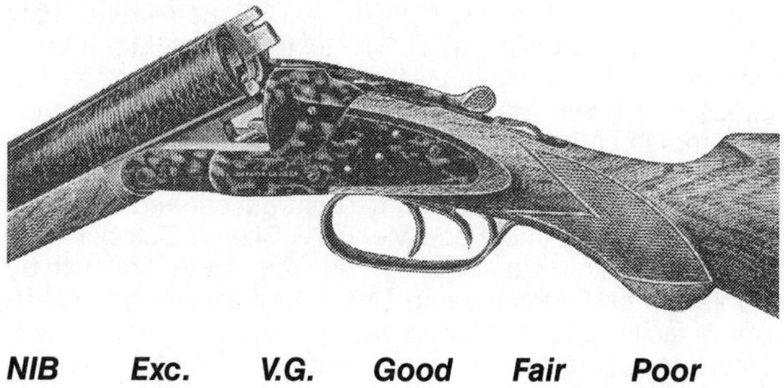

NIB	Exc.	V.G.	Good	Fair	Poor
—	800	575	495	325	275

Batavia Damascus

As above with Damascus barrels.

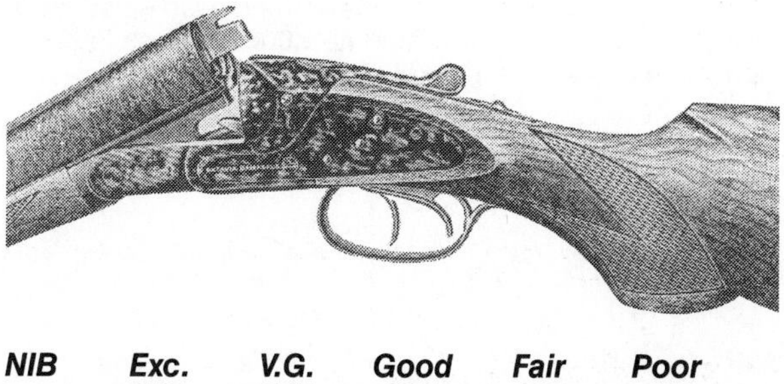

NIB	Exc.	V.G.	Good	Fair	Poor
—	450	375	325	225	175

Baker Hammer Gun

A 10, 12, or 16 gauge double barrel shotgun with sidehammers and 30" and 32" barrels in 10 gauge, 26" to 32" barrels in 12 gauge and 26" to 30" barrels in 16 gauge. Browned, case hardened with walnut stock and double triggers.

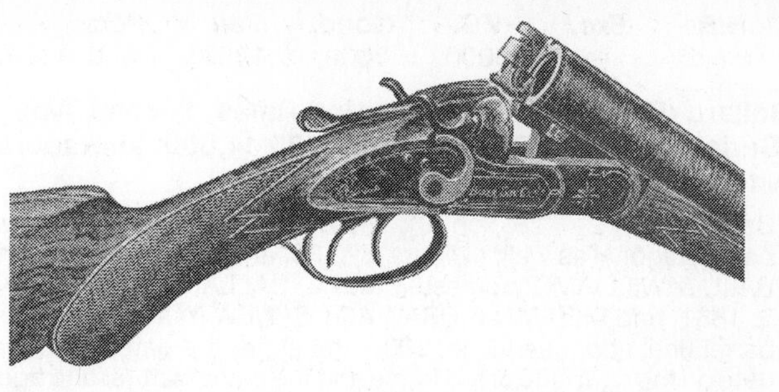

NIB	Exc.	V.G.	Good	Fair	Poor
—	450	350	275	195	100

Batavia Automatic Rifle

A .22 caliber semi-automatic rifle with a 24" round barrel and a detachable 7-shot magazine. Blued with a walnut stock.

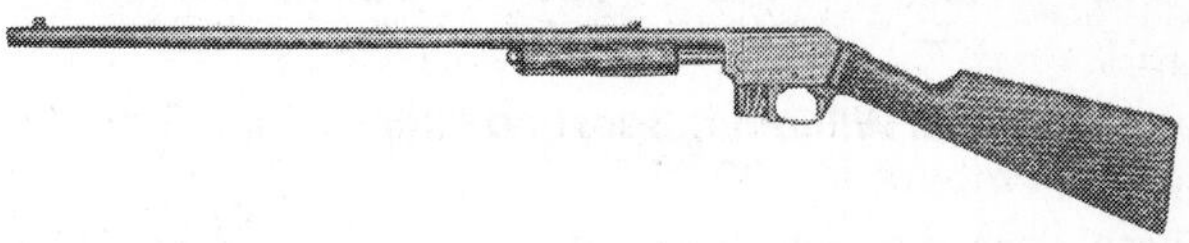

NIB	Exc.	V.G.	Good	Fair	Poor
—	625	550	300	160	70

BALLARD PATENT ARMS

(until 1873; after 1875, see MARLIN)

On Nov. 5, 1861, C.H. Ballard of Worcester, Massachusetts, received a patent for a breechloading mechanism that would remain in production for nearly thirty years. Ballard patented a breechblock that tilted down at its front to expose the breech by activating the lever/triggerguard. During the twelve years that followed, Ballard rifles, carbines, and shotguns were produced by five interrelated companies. Four of these were successive: Ball & Williams, R. Ball & Co. (both of Worcester, Massachusetts), Merrimack Arms & Manufacturing Co. and Brown Manufacturing Company (both of Newburyport, Massachusetts). These four companies produced Ballard arms in a successive serial range (1 through approximately 22,000), all marked upon the top of the frame and the top of the barrel where it joins the frame. In 1863, another company, Dwight, Chapin & Company of Bridgeport, Connecticut, also produced Ballard rifles and carbines in a larger frame size, but in a different serial range (1 through about 1,900), usually marked on the left side of the frame below the agents' mark. The large frame carbines and rifles were produced to fulfill a U.S. War Department contract initially for 10,000 of each, subsequently reduced to 1,000 of each, issued to Merwin & Bray, the sole agents for the Ballard patent arms between 1862 and 1866. Most of the production during this period concentrated on military contracts, either for the U.S. War Department or the state of Kentucky, although the state of New York also purchased 500 for its state militia.

Ballard (Ball & Williams) Sporting Rifles, First Type (Serial numbers 1-100)

Barrel length 24"; caliber .38 rimfire. Markings: BALL & WILLIAMS/ Worcester, Mass., and BALLARD'S PATENT/Nov. 5, 1861 on octagonal barrel. The distinctive feature of the earliest production of the Ballard rifles is the presence of an internal extractor conforming to the patent specifications. After approximately 100 rifles, this feature was dropped in favor of a manual extractor located under the barrel.

Courtesy Milwaukee Public Museum, Milwaukee, Wisconsin

NIB	Exc.	V.G.	Good	Fair	Poor
—	—	5000	3000	1250	500

Ballard (Ball & Williams) Sporting Rifles, Second Type (Serial numbers 200-1600, and 1600-14,000, interspersed with martial production)

Barrel length 24", 28", or 30", usually octagonal, but part round/part octagonal as well; calibers .32, .38, and .44 rimfire. Markings: BALL & WILLIAMS/Worcester, Mass., BALLARD'S PATENT/Nov. 5, 1861, and MERWIN & BRAY, AGT'S/ NEW YORK, on facets of barrel until about serial no. 9000, thereafter the patent name and date on the right side of the frame and the manufacturer and agents on the left side of the frame. On early production (200 to 1500), the extractor knob is smaller and crescent shaped. Early production (prior to about serial no. 10,000) have solid breechblocks; after that number breechblocks are made in two halves. A few of these arms were made with bronze frames to facilitate engraving and plating. These should command a higher premium.

NIB	Exc.	V.G.	Good	Fair	Poor
—	—	2000	1650	730	280

Ballard (Ball & Williams) Sporting Rifles, Third Type (Serial numbers 14,000-15,000)

These arms are essentially the same as the second type in characteristics but have Merwin & Bray's alternate percussion mechanism built into the breechblock. The hammer is accordingly marked on the left side "PATENTED JAN. 5, 1864."

NIB	Exc.	V.G.	Good	Fair	Poor
—	—	1400	1100	550	225

Ballard (Ball & Williams) Military Carbines (Serial numbers 1500-7500, and 8500-10,500)

Overall length 37-1/4"; barrel (bore) length 22"; caliber .44 rimfire. Markings: same as Ballard/Ball & Williams sporting rifles, second type. Additional marks on U.S. War Department purchases include inspector's initials "MM" or "GH" on left side of frame, and "MM" on barrel, breechblock, buttplate, and on left side of buttstock in script within an oval cartouche. Three thousand of the earlier production (serial numbers 1700 through about 5000) of these carbines were sold to the state of Kentucky under an August 1862 contract, extended in April 1863. In November 1863, Kentucky contracted for an additional 1,000 carbines. In the interim, the state of New York purchased 500 for distribution to its militia. The U.S. War Department ordered 5,000 under a contract signed in January of 1864, but Ball & Williams delivered only 1,500 (serial numbers noted in range of 9800 through 10,600) while concentrating production on their more lucrative Kentucky contract. Another 600 of the federal contract were partially inspected (serial numbers about 6500 to 7100-MM in cartouche in stock only) but were rejected because the barrels had been rifled prior to proofing; these were sold to Kentucky in September 1864 on an open market purchase. The carbines marked with federal inspection marks usually bring a premium.

Courtesy Milwaukee Public Museum, Milwaukee, Wisconsin

NIB	Exc.	V.G.	Good	Fair	Poor
—	—	5775	4150	1750	675

Ballard (Ball & Williams) "Kentucky" Half-Stock Rifles

Overall length 45-3/8"; barrel (bore) length 30"; caliber .44 rimfire. These half-stock rifles bear the standard Ball & Williams markings upon their barrels and in addition have the state ownership mark ("KENTUCKY") on the barrel forward of the rear sights. A total of 1,000 (serial numbers about 7100 through 8550) were contracted for by Kentucky in November 1863 and delivered between January and April 1864.

Courtesy Milwaukee Public Museum, Milwaukee, Wisconsin

NIB	Exc.	V.G.	Good	Fair	Poor
—	—	2300	1900	800	350

Ballard (Ball & Williams) "Kentucky" Full-Stock Rifles

Overall length 45-1/4"; barrel (bore) length 30"; caliber .46 rimfire. Marked on the frame with standard Ball & Williams manufacturer (left), agent (left), and patent (right) markings, these rifles are additionally distinguished by the state ownership mark "KENTUCKY" stamped into the top of the frame near the breech. Kentucky contracted for 3,000 of these arms in November 1863, initially in .56 caliber. However, by mutual consent of the state and the contractors, in February 1864 the caliber of the arms was changed to .46. All deliveries were made in this caliber, beginning in July 1864 and continuing until March 1865 (serial numbers 10,400 to 14,500).

Courtesy Milwaukee Public Museum, Milwaukee, Wisconsin

NIB	Exc.	V.G.	Good	Fair	Poor
—	—	2100	1750	620	295

Ballard (Dwight, Chapin & Co.) Carbines

Overall length 37-3/4"; barrel (bore) length 22"; caliber .56 rimfire. Markings: On left side of round-topped frame "BALLARD'S PATENT/NOV. 5 1861" ; on right side of frame "DWIGHT, CHAPIN & CO./BRIDGEPORT CONN." (through serial no. about 125, deleted after that number) over "MERWIN & BRAY/AGT'S N.Y." over serial no. Inspection letters "D" frequently appear on carbines with the Dwight, Chapin, & Co. markings, indicative of preliminary inspection by E. M. Dustin, of the U.S. Ordnance Department.Often mistaken as early Ballard production from a fictitious Fall River, Massachusetts factory, these carbines and their complementing rifles were in fact not placed into production until 1863, as evident by the split, two-piece breechblocks. Both carbines and rifles originated from a contract entered into between the U.S. War Department and Merwin & Bray in October 1862 for 10,000 of each arm, subsequently reduced to 1,000 of each by the Commission on Ordnance and Ordnance Stores. Because Ball & Williams facilities were tied up with Kentucky contracts, Merwin & Bray turned to the small parts maker of Dwight, Chapin & Co. in Bridgeport, Connecticut. Although they tooled for production, they fell short of scheduled delivery dates, and although about 100 carbines had been inspected, no deliveries were accepted (due to caliber problems) by the U.S. government, effectively bankrupting Dwight, Chapin & Co. The completed carbines and unfinished parts were sent to Worcester and assembled by Ball & Williams, and Merwin & Bray sold all 1,000 carbines in Kentucky in April 1864 on an open market purchase.

Courtesy Milwaukee Public Museum, Milwaukee, Wisconsin

NIB	Exc.	V.G.	Good	Fair	Poor
—	—	2450	2000	825	350

Ballard (Dwight, Chapin & Co.) Full-Stock Rifles

Overall length 53"; barrel (bore) length 30"; caliber .56 rimfire. Markings: same as Dwight, Chapin & Co. carbines, but none found with "DWIGHT, CHAPIN & CO./BRIDGEPORT, CONN." stamping above agents marks. The history of these rifles is the same as the .56 caliber carbines, with serial numbers interspersed in the production of the carbines (1 through 1850). Evidently only about 650 of the rifles were completed of the 1,000 set up. Of these, 35 were sold to a U.S. agent in Florida in February 1864 and 600 to Kentucky in April 1864 with the 1,000 carbines.

NIB	Exc.	V.G.	Good	Fair	Poor
—	—	2450	2000	825	350

Ballard (R. Ball & Co.) Sporting Rifles

Overall length varies according to barrel length; barrel (bore) length usually 24", 28", and 30"; calibers .32, .38, .44, and .46 rimfire. Markings: The frame markings of R. Ball & Co. rifles are similar to Ball & Williams production, only eliminating the Ball & Williams marking on the left side. Cartridge size, e.g. "No. 44," usually also stamped upon the top of the barrel or frame. Merwin & Bray's patented alternate ignition device usually present with left side of hammer usually marked "PATENTED JAN. 5, 1864." Serial numbers (which follow in sequence with Ball & Williams production. i.e. after no. about 15,800) appear on top of barrel and top of frame. After William Williams withdrew from the Ball & Williams partnership in mid-1865, the business continued under the name of R. Ball & Co., with Richard Ball's son-in-law, E.J. Halstead, in charge after the former's paralytic stroke in the fall of 1865.

Courtesy Rock Island Auction Company

NIB	Exc.	V.G.	Good	Fair	Poor
—	—	2650	2200	975	400

Ballard (R. Ball & Co.) Carbines

Overall length 37-1/4"; barrel (bore) length 22" caliber .44 rimfire. Markings: same as R. Ball & Co. sporting rifles; "No. 44" on top of frame near breech. Although firm evidence is elusive, approximately 1,000 of these carbines were manufactured in anticipation of a Canadian contract, which never came to fruition. Serial numbers are interspersed with sporting rifles, in the 16,400 through 17,700 range. All are equipped with the Merwin & Bray dual ignition block.

NIB	Exc.	V.G.	Good	Fair	Poor
—	—	1825	1500	580	225

Ballard (Merrimack Arms & Manufacturing Co.) Sporting Rifles

Overall length varies with barrel length; usual barrel lengths 24", 28", 30"; calibers .22, .32, .44, .46, .50 rimfire. Markings: Left side of frame marked with both manufacturing and patent marks, "MERRIMACK ARMS & MFG. CO./NEWBURYPORT, MASS." over "BALLARD'S PATENT/ NOV. 5, 1861." Caliber usually marked on top of barrel or frame, e.g. "No. 38" together with serial no. Left side of hammer marked "PATENTED JAN. 5, 1864" if breech fitted with Merwin & Bray's alternate ignition device. In the spring of 1866, Edward Bray of Brooklyn, New York, and former partner of Joseph Merwin purchased the Ballard machinery from R. Ball & Co. and set up a new plant in Newburyport, Massachusetts primarily for the production of sporting rifles. The glut of surplus arms on the market following the American Civil War, however, forced him into bankruptcy in early 1869, after producing only about 2,000 Ballard rifles, carbines and a limited number of 20 gauge shotguns. Serial numbers continue in the sequence of the Ball & Williams/R. Ball & Co. production (serial numbers about 18,000 through 20,300). Prices of these rifles will vary considerably depending on the degree of finish or engraving.

NIB	Exc.	V.G.	Good	Fair	Poor
—	—	2200	1900	775	350

Ballard (Merrimack Arms & Manufacturing Co.) Carbines

Overall length 37-1/4"; barrel (bore) length 22"; caliber .44 rimfire. Markings: same as Merrimack Arms & Mfg. Co. sporting rifles. In March 1866, the state of New York purchased 100 Ballard carbines (serial numbers about 18,500 to 18,600) for use by its prison guards. In January 1870, an additional 70 (serial numbers 19,400 to 19,500) were purchased from New York City arms merchants Merwin, Hulbert & Co. to arm guards at Sing Sing Prison. Between these two purchases Merrimack Arms & Mfg. Co. had shortened its new "tangless" frames by 1/8", the prime distinction between the two purchases. Despite the rarity of both types of carbines, they do not command high prices.

NIB	Exc.	V.G.	Good	Fair	Poor
—	—	1750	1400	550	300

Ballard (Brown Mfg. Co.) Sporting Rifles

Dimensions: same as Merrimack Arms & Mfg. Co. sporting rifles. Markings: left side of frame marked with manufacturer, "BROWN MFG. CO. NEWBURYPORT, MASS." over patent, "BALLARD'S PATENT/ NOV. 5, 1861." Serial no. on top of barrel and frame. Upon the failure of Merrimack Arms & Manufacturing Company in early 1869, the plant was purchased by John Hamilton Brown, who continued producing Ballard patent rifles until 1873 in a serial range consecutive with that of its three predecessors (Ball & Williams, R. Ball & Co., and Merrimack Arms & Mfg. Co.). Approximately 2,000 Ballard arms were produced during the period of Brown's manufacture of the Ballard (serial numbers about 20,325 through 22,100). Brown made Ballards tend to exhibit finer finishing than earlier produced rifles, accounting for their average higher value. Special features, such as breakdown facility and side extractors (on .22 cal. rifles) will also positively affect the prices.

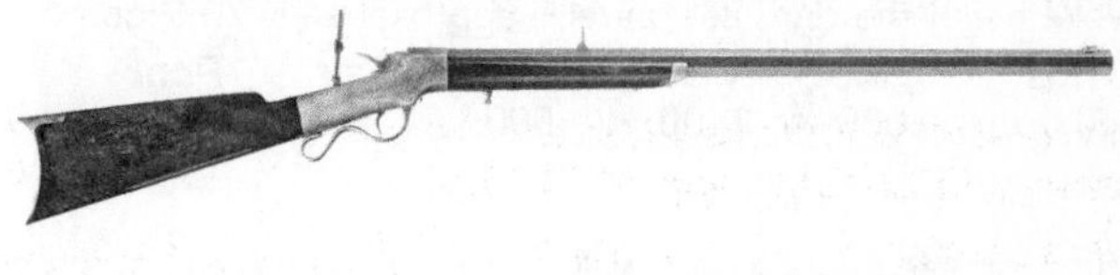

Courtesy Rock Island Auction Company

NIB	Exc.	V.G.	Good	Fair	Poor
—	—	2200	1825	675	350

Ballard (Brown Mfg. Co.) Full-Stock Military Rifles

Overall length 52-1/2" barrel (bore) length 30"; caliber .46 rimfire. Markings: The same as Brown Mfg. Co. sporting rifles, with the addition of the caliber marking, "No. 46," on the top of the barrel forward of the rear sight. The cause for the production of the Ballard/Brown military rifle has yet to be determined, but it has been speculated that they were possibly manufactured in anticipation of a sale to France during the Franco-Prussian War. In any event, the sale was not culminated, and many, if not most, of the estimated 1,000 produced were "sporterized" by shortening the forestock and sold by commercial dealers in the United States. Serial numbers concentrate in the 20,500 through 21,600 range, with sporting rifles interspersed in the sequence. Rifles that have not been sporterized command a premium.

NIB	Exc.	V.G.	Good	Fair	Poor
—	—	2350	1950	800	350

BALLARD RIFLE AND CARTRIDGE CO.

Onsted, Michigan

All models feature American black walnut stocks, case hardening, and rust blued barrels. There are a number of special order features that are available with these rifles.

No. 1-1/2 Hunter's Rifle

This model features a 30" round barrel, single trigger, S lever, plain forend, and rifle buttstock. Blade front sight and Rocky Mountain rear sight are standard. Calibers from .32-40 to .50-70. Weight is about 10.5 lbs.

NIB	Exc.	V.G.	Good	Fair	Poor
3000	2350	1950	1200	700	300

No. 1-3/4 Far West Rifle

Offered with 30" round barrel in standard or heavy weight. Single or double-set triggers, S lever, ring-style lever, blade front sight, and Rocky Mountain rear sight. Offered in calibers from .32-40 to .50-90. Weight with standard 30" barrel is approximately 10.5 lbs., with heavyweight barrel 11.75 lbs.

NIB	Exc.	V.G.	Good	Fair	Poor
2900	2400	1900	1200	700	300

No. 2 Sporting Model

Stocked in plain walnut with crescent butt and offered in 24", 26", 28", or 30" octagon barrel with blade front and Rocky Mountain rear sights. A straight-grip action with S lever, in calibers .38-40, .44-40, and .45 Colt. Discontinued.

NIB	Exc.	V.G.	Good	Fair	Poor
2050	1650	1300	1225	700	300

No. 3 Gallery Rifle

Chambered for the .22 caliber rimfire cartridge this model features a choice of 24", 26", or 30" lightweight octagon barrel with rifle-style buttstock with steel crescent buttplate, S lever, blade and Rocky Mountain sights. Weight with standard 26" barrel is about 7.5 lbs.

NIB	Exc.	V.G.	Good	Fair	Poor
3000	2650	2300	1200	700	300

No. 3F Fine Gallery Rifle

Same as above model but with fancy checkered walnut stock, pistol grip, single or double-set triggers, full-loop lever, light Schuetzen buttstock, Globe front sight and gallery tang sight. Weight with standard 26" barrel is approximately 7.75 lbs.

NIB	Exc.	V.G.	Good	Fair	Poor
3500	3000	2400	1500	750	300

No. 4 Perfection Model

This model features a plain walnut stock with rifle or shotgun butt. Offered in 28", 30" or 32" octagon barrel with blade front sight and Rocky Mountain rear sight. Straight-grip action with single or double-set triggers with S lever or ring lever in calibers from .32-40 to .50-90.

NIB	Exc.	V.G.	Good	Fair	Poor
3400	2900	2300	1200	700	300

No. 4-1/2 Mid Range Model

This model features checkered fancy walnut stock, standard or heavy weight half octagon barrel 30" or 32" with single or double-set triggers, pistol grip, hard rubber or steel shotgun butt, horn forend cap, full-loop lever, and globe front sight. Offered in calibers from .32-40 to .40-70. Weight with standard barrel 10.75 lbs. and with heavy barrel 11.5 lbs.

NIB	Exc.	V.G.	Good	Fair	Poor
3200	2650	2100	1100	600	250

No. 5 Pacific Model

This model features a 30" or 32" octagon barrel in either standard or heavy weight, stocks in rifle or shotgun configuration, double-set triggers, ring lever, blade front sight, and Rocky Mountain rear sight. Calibers from .38-55 to .50-90. Weight with standard 30" barrel is 10.75 lbs., with heavyweight barrel 12 lbs.

NIB	Exc.	V.G.	Good	Fair	Poor
3350	2600	2250	1200	700	300

No. 5-1/2 Montana Model

This model has a fancy walnut stock, double-set triggers, and ring lever. Shotgun steel butt. Barrels are either 28", 30" or 32", extra heavy octagon, in calibers .45-70, .45-110, and .50-90. Under barrel wiping rod. Weight is approximately 14.5 lbs.

NIB	Exc.	V.G.	Good	Fair	Poor
3300	2600	2000	110	600	225

No. 6 Off-Hand Rifle Model (Schuetzen)

This rifle features a fancy walnut checkered stock with hand rubbed finish, heavy Schuetzen buttplate, and horn insert on forend. Choice of 30", 32", or 34" half-octagon barrel with Globe front sight. Straight-grip action with double-set triggers, Schuetzen ball, spur lever and deluxe rust blueing. Offered in .22 LR, .32-40, .38-55, .40-65, and .40-70 calibers.

NIB	Exc.	V.G.	Good	Fair	Poor
3300	2700	2100	1100	600	250

No. 7 Long Range Model

This model features a fancy walnut checkered stock with 32" or 34" standard or heavy weight half octagon barrel. Pistol-grip stock with rubber or steel shotgun butt, single or double-set triggers, full-loop lever, horn forend cap, and globe front sight. Calibers from .32-40 to .45-110. Weight with standard 32" barrel 11.75 lbs., with heavyweight barrel 12.25 lbs.

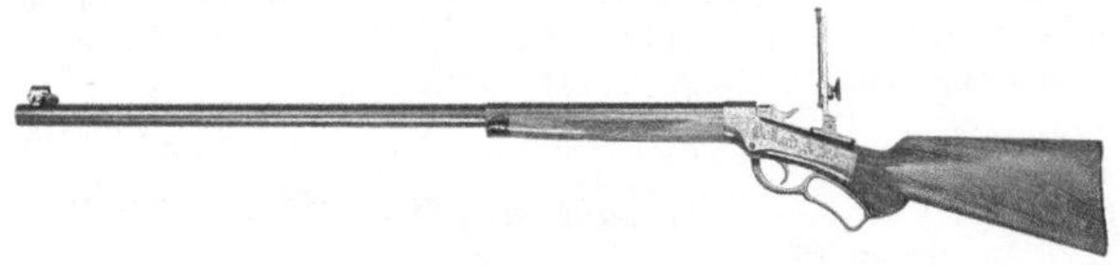

NIB	Exc.	V.G.	Good	Fair	Poor
3100	2550	2200	1100	600	250

No. 8 Union Hill Model

This model features a 30" or 32" half-octagon standard or heavy barrel, single or double-set triggers, pistol-grip stock with cheekpiece, full-loop lever, hook Schuetzen buttplate and fancy walnut checkered stock. Offered in calibers from .22 LR to .40-70. Weight with standard barrel in .32 caliber 10.5 lbs, with heavyweight barrel in .40 caliber 11.5 lbs. This model is not furnished with sights.

NIB	Exc.	V.G.	Good	Fair	Poor
3600	2000	1700	900	450	200

Model 1885 High Wall

This single-shot rifle is chambered for a wide variety of calibers from .18 Bee to .577 Express. Barrel lengths to 34". American walnut stock. Many options to choose from that will affect price. Introduced in 2000.

NIB	Exc.	V.G.	Good	Fair	Poor
3050	2500	2000	1175	650	275

BARRETT F.A. MFG. CO.

Murfreesboro, Tennessee

Barrett MRAD

Chambered in the .338 Lapua Magnum with user-changeable barrel system. Match-grade trigger. Thumb-operated safety can be configured to right or left. Folding stock has adjustable cheekpiece and length of pull. Finished in Barrett's Multi-Role Brown. Introduced in 2011.

NIB	Exc.	V.G.	Good	Fair	Poor
5500	4675	3950	2500	1000	500

Model 82 Rifle

A .50 caliber Browning semi-automatic rifle with a 37" barrel and 11-shot magazine. The barrel fitted with a muzzlebrake, and the receiver with a telescope. Approximate weight 35 lbs. Parkerized. Manufactured from 1985 to 1987.

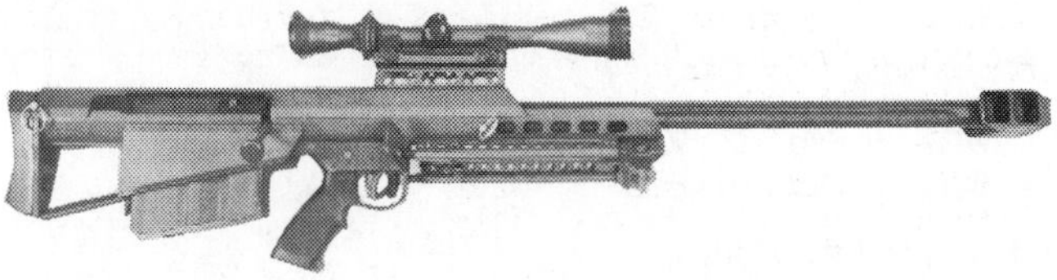

NIB	*Exc.*	*V.G.*	*Good*	*Fair*	*Poor*
8200	6500	4750	2250	1500	400

Model 82A1

As above, with a 29" barrel without sights, and a 10-round magazine. A 10X telescope and iron sights are optional. Comes with hard carrying case. Weight is 28.5 lbs.

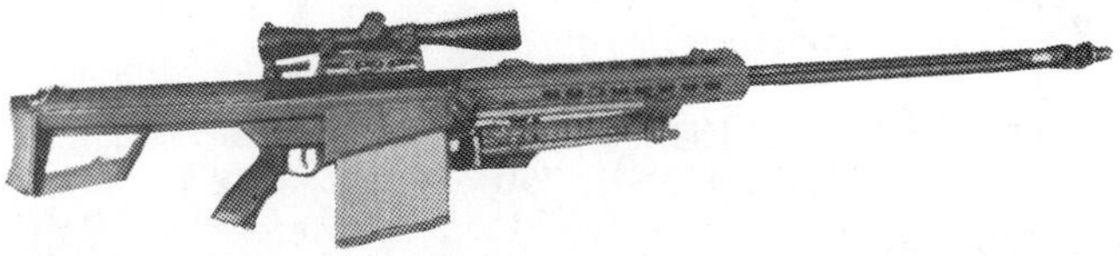

NIB	*Exc.*	*V.G.*	*Good*	*Fair*	*Poor*
9650	7050	4000	2750	1600	400

Model 95M

Introduced in 1995 this .50 caliber BMG bolt-action model features a 29" barrel and 5-round magazine. Scope optional. Weight is 22 lbs.

NIB	*Exc.*	*V.G.*	*Good*	*Fair*	*Poor*
7360	5800	4000	2000	1400	300

Model 99

This model is a single-shot bolt-action rifle chambered for the .50 BMG cartridge. Standard barrel length is 32". Optional barrel lengths of 29" or 25". Rifle weight is about 25 lbs. with 32" barrel.

NIB	*Exc.*	*V.G.*	*Good*	*Fair*	*Poor*
5130	4250	2000	1450	800	200

NOTE: Add $200 for fluted barrel.

Model 99-1

Similar to the Model 99 but fitted with a 29" barrel. Weight is about 21 lbs.

NIB	*Exc.*	*V.G.*	*Good*	*Fair*	*Poor*
4300	3450	1700	1200	600	175

Model 107

Chambered for the .50 caliber cartridge this model is a semi-automatic rifle fitted with a 29" barrel with muzzlebrake. Bipod is detachable and adjustable. M1913 accessory rail. Supplied with two 10-round magazines. Weight is about 32 lbs.

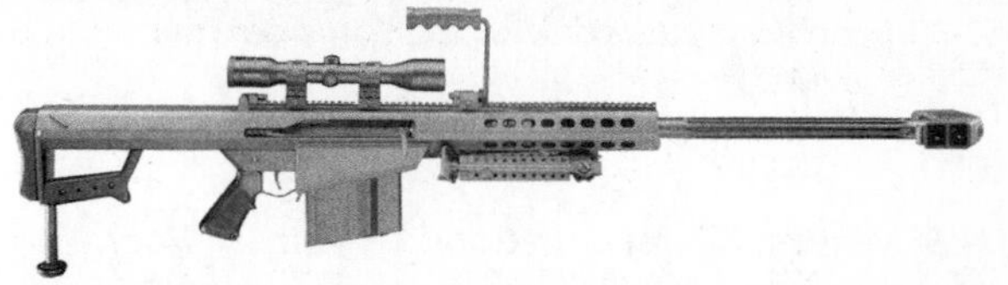

NIB	*Exc.*	*V.G.*	*Good*	*Fair*	*Poor*
9650	7050	4000	2750	1600	400

Model 468

Built on a semi-automatic AR-15 style lower receiver, this rifle features a 16" barrel with muzzlebrake chambered for the 6.8 SPC cartridge. Folding front sight and integrated Rail system. Folding rear sight. Weight is about 7.3 lbs.

NIB	*Exc.*	*V.G.*	*Good*	*Fair*	*Poor*
2800	2100	1450	975	650	225

BAUER F. A. CORP.

Fraser, Michigan

The Rabbit

A .22 caliber by .410 bore combination rifle/shotgun, with a tubular metal stock. Manufactured between 1982 and 1984. Similar to Garcia Bronco.

NIB	*Exc.*	*V.G.*	*Good*	*Fair*	*Poor*
—	325	300	225	125	75

BENELLI

Italy

SHOTGUNS

Model SL-121 V

This is a semi-automatic 12 gauge with 3" chambers and various barrel lengths and chokes. It has a black anodized alloy receiver and was discontinued in 1985.

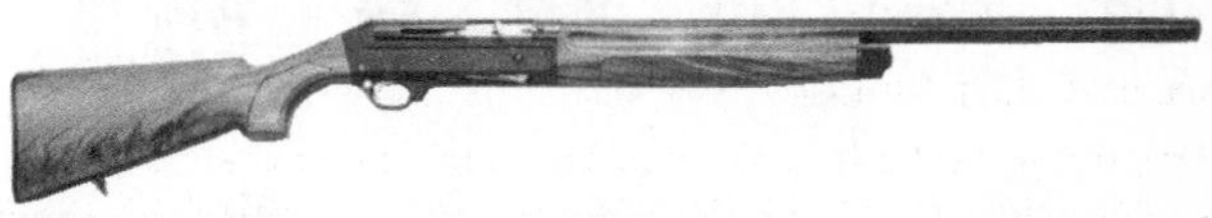

NIB	*Exc.*	*V.G.*	*Good*	*Fair*	*Poor*
500	450	400	350	300	150

Model SL 121 Slug

This model is similar to the SL-121 V with a 21" cylinder-bore barrel and rifle sights. It, too, was discontinued in 1985.

NIB	*Exc.*	*V.G.*	*Good*	*Fair*	*Poor*
500	450	400	350	300	150

Model SL-123 V

This model has the improved, fast, third-generation action. Otherwise it resembles the earlier SL-121.

NIB	Exc.	V.G.	Good	Fair	Poor
550	475	425	350	300	150

Model SL 201

This is a 20 gauge with a 26", Improved Cylinder barrel. It is similar in appearance to the SL-123.

NIB	Exc.	V.G.	Good	Fair	Poor
500	475	425	350	300	150

M3 Super 90

This is an improved version of the Benelli pump action and semi-automatic inertia recoil system. The shotgun can be converted from pump to semi-automatic by turning a spring-loaded ring located at the end of the forearm. It has a rotating bolt system and is chambered for 12 gauge, with a 3" chamber. This model has a 19.75" barrel with cylinder bore and rifle sights with a 7-round tubular magazine. It has a matte black finish and a black fiberglass pistol-grip stock and forearm. This model was introduced in 1986.

NIB	Exc.	V.G.	Good	Fair	Poor
1185	900	700	600	450	300

NOTE: Add $50 for open rifle sights.

M3 Super 90 Folding Stock

Same as above but furnished with a folding tubular steel stock.

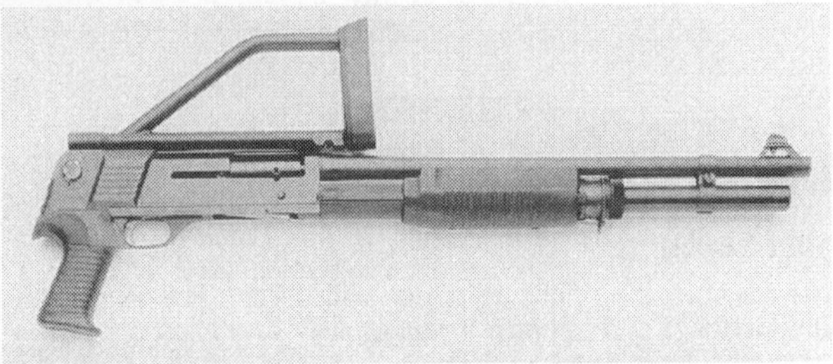

NIB	Exc.	V.G.	Good	Fair	Poor
2000	1500	1150	850	600	300

M4

Adopted by the U.S. Marine Corps this 12 gauge shotgun features a choice of three modular buttstock and two barrel configurations. Top-mounted Picatinny rail. Barrel length is 18.5". Magazine capacity is 6 rounds. Ghost ring sights. Weight is about 8.4 lbs. Matte black finish. Introduced in 2003. The civilian version does not have a collapsible buttstock.

M4 with non-collapsible stock with cheekpiece

M4 with standard stock

NIB	Exc.	V.G.	Good	Fair	Poor
1550	1150	875	725	500	200

M1014 Limited Edition

Introduced in 2003 this version of the M4 is fitted with a skelton buttstock and a special U.S. flag engraving on the receiver. Fitted with an 18.5" barrel and Picatinny rail with ghost ring sights. Limited to 2,500 shotguns.

NIB	Exc.	V.G.	Good	Fair	Poor
1600	1200	900	750	550	250

M1 Practical

This model was designed for IPSC events and features an oversized safety, speed loader, larger bolt handle, muzzlebrake, and adjustable ghost ring sight and optics rail. Offered with 26" barrel with extended magazine tube. Weighs about 7.6 lbs.

NIB	Exc.	V.G.	Good	Fair	Poor
1150	900	750	500	275	125

M1 Super 90 Tactical

This is a semi-automatic 12 gauge shotgun with an inertia recoil system. It features an 18.5" plain barrel with three screw-in choke tubes. Available in either standard polymer stock or pistol-grip stock. Ghost ring sights are standard. Gun weighs 6.5 lbs. First introduced in 1993.

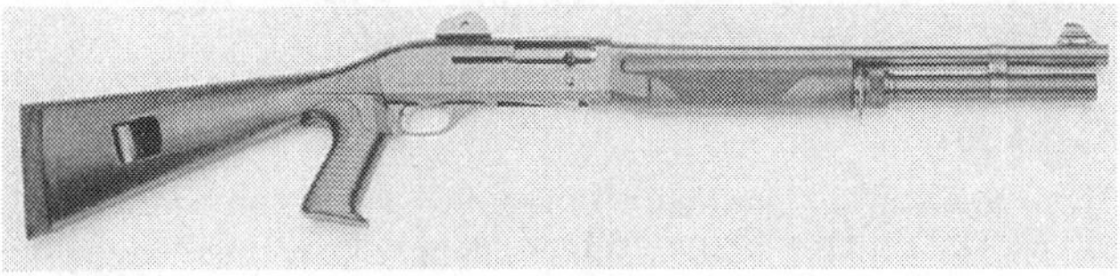

NIB	Exc.	V.G.	Good	Fair	Poor
900	700	600	500	450	250

M1 Super 90 Slug Gun

Equipped with a standard black polymer stock with 19.75" plain barrel. Fitted with a 7-shot magazine. Ghost ring sights are an option. Weighs 6.7 lbs. Camo model introduced in 2000.

NIB	Exc.	V.G.	Good	Fair	Poor
1000	750	550	450	350	250

NOTE: Add $100 for Camo model.

M1 Super 90 Entry Gun

This model is fitted with a black polymer pistol-grip stock with 14" plain barrel. Magazine holds 5 shells. Plain or ghost ring sights available. CAUTION: NFA Weapon, Restricted sale, Class III Transfer required.

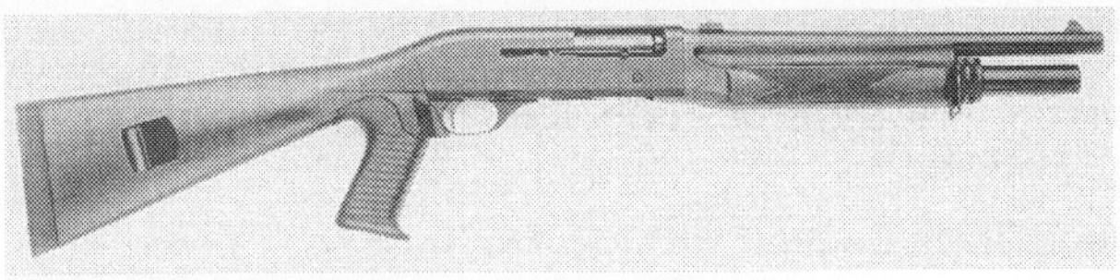

M1 Super 90 Defense Gun

Comes standard with polymer pistol-grip stock, 19.75" barrel, plain sights, or ghost ring sights. Offered in 12 gauge only. Weighs 7.1 lbs.

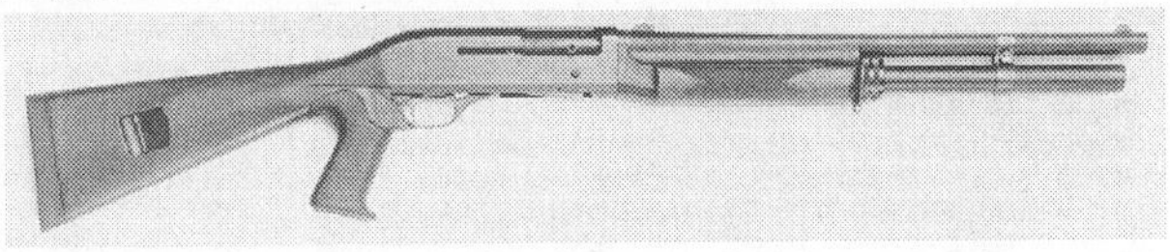

NIB	Exc.	V.G.	Good	Fair	Poor
900	700	600	500	450	250

M1 Super 90 Field

This model is similar to other Super 90 series guns with a 21", 24", 26", or 28" vent rib barrel with screw-in choke tubes. In 1998 this model was available with 24" rifled bore with matte rib. Add $80 for this barrel. Left-hand model added in 2000. In 2001 this model was offered in 20 gauge as well.

NIB	Exc.	V.G.	Good	Fair	Poor
900	650	600	550	450	200

M1 Super 90 Camo Field

Same as above but with camouflage receiver, barrel, buttstock and forearm. Offered in 24", 26", and 28" vent rib barrels. Introduced in 1997. In 1998 this model was also offered with a 21" vent rib barrel. Left-hand model added in 2000. In 2001 this model was offered in 20 gauge as well.

M1 20 gauge

M1 Field Steady Grip

Introduced in 2003 this model features a vertical pistol grip, drilled and tapped receiver and extra Full choke tube. Barrel length is 24". Weight is about 7.3 lbs.

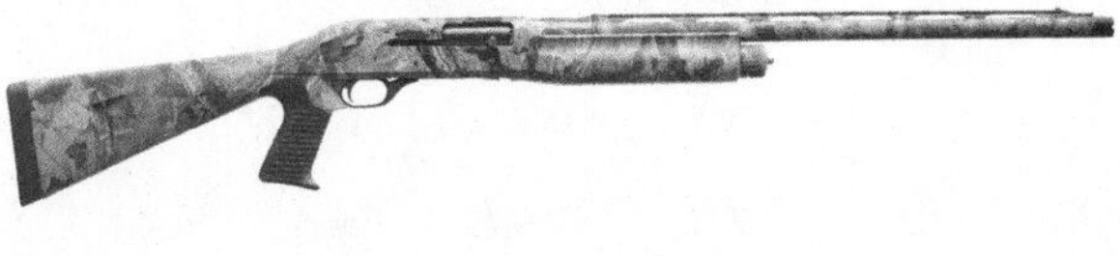

NIB	Exc.	V.G.	Good	Fair	Poor
1175	900	600	325	175	100

M1 Super 90 Sporting Special

Introduced in 1993 this 12 gauge shotgun is similar to the Super 90 with the addition of non-reflective surfaces, 18.5" plain barrel with 3 choke tubes (IC, Mod, Full). The gun is fitted with ghost ring sights.

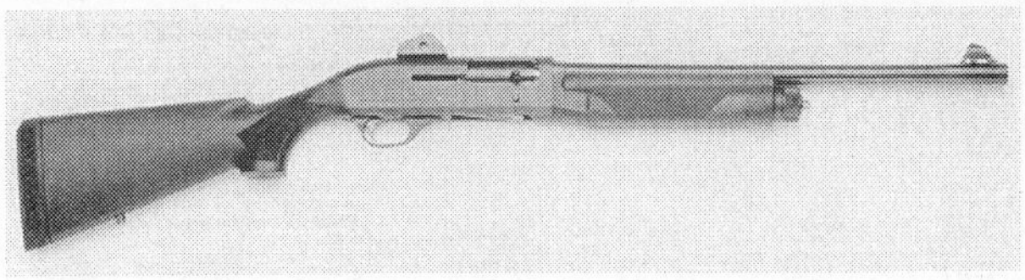

NIB	Exc.	V.G.	Good	Fair	Poor
725	600	500	400	350	200

M2 Practical with ComforTech

Introduced in 2005 this model is chambered for the 12 gauge 3" shell and fitted with a 25" plain barrel with compensator and ghost-ring rear sight. Receiver is fitted with a Picatinny rail. Magazine capacity is 8 rounds. Weight is about 7.6 lbs.

NIB	Exc.	V.G.	Good	Fair	Poor
1335	1000	750	595	400	275

M2 Tactical

This 12 gauge 3" gun is fitted with a 18.5" barrel with choke tubes and choice of rifle or ghost-ring sights. Pistol grip or extended pistol grip. Black synthetic stock. Magazine capacity is 5 rounds. Weight is about 7 lbs.

NIB	Exc.	V.G.	Good	Fair	Poor
1100	850	600	525	300	200

NOTE: Add $70 for ComforTech version and $65 for Ghost-ring sights.

M2 Field with ComforTech

In 12 gauge, this model is offered with a 21", 24", 26" or 28" barrel with a black matte synthetic finish or Max-4, Timber or APG camo. The 20 gauge has a 24" or 26" barrel in black, Timber or APG. Average 12 gauge weight is 7 lbs.; average 20 gauge weight is 5.8 lbs. Add $75 for camo.

NIB	Exc.	V.G.	Good	Fair	Poor
1000	750	500	525	300	200

M2 Field without ComforTech

Same features as above without ComforTech features. Available only in satin walnut with 26" or 28" barrel.

NIB	Exc.	V.G.	Good	Fair	Poor
1075	825	550	525	300	200

Montefeltro Super 90

Introduced in 1987, this model is similar to the Super 90 Field with a checkered walnut stock and forearm with gloss finish. Offered with 21", 24", 26", or 28" vent rib barrel. Available in 12 gauge only with 3" chambers. This shotgun offered in left-hand model also.

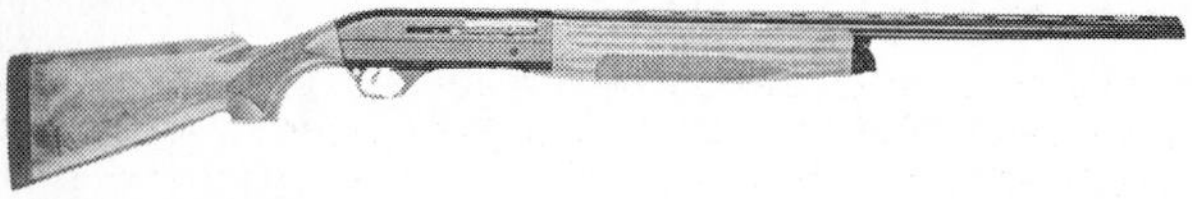

NIB	Exc.	V.G.	Good	Fair	Poor
900	700	600	500	450	350

Montefeltro 20 Gauge

Introduced in 1993, this model features a walnut checkered stock with 26" vent rib barrel. In 1995 a 24" vent rib barrel was offered as well. Gun weighs 5.75 lbs.

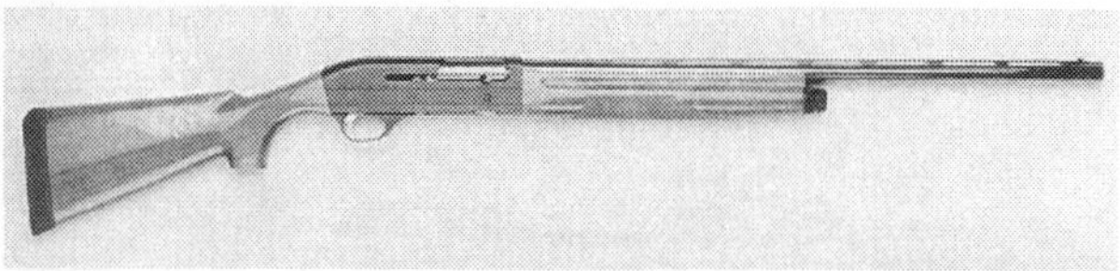

NIB	Exc.	V.G.	Good	Fair	Poor
900	700	600	500	450	350

NOTE: Add $75 for short stock model.

Montefeltro 20 Gauge Camo

Same as above with Realtree Camo finish and offered with 26" vent rib barrel. Introduced in 1998.

NIB	Exc.	V.G.	Good	Fair	Poor
950	750	700	600	500	400

Montefeltro 20 Gauge Limited

Introduced in 1995 this version features a finely etched nickel plate receiver with scroll and game scenes highlighted in gold. The stock is a select grade walnut and is fitted with a 26" vent rib barrel.

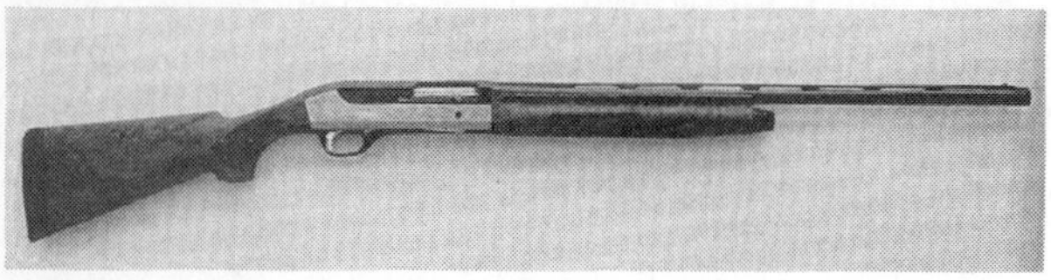

NIB	Exc.	V.G.	Good	Fair	Poor
1750	1250	800	500	400	350

Montefeltro (2005)

This is an updated version of the Montefeltro series of guns with a slight change in the receiver, a different trigger, upgraded wood, and the name "Montefeltro" in gold on the receiver. Offered in 12 or 20 gauge with 3" chambers. Checkered select walnut stock with pistol grip. Choice of 24", 26", or 28" vent rib barrel with choke tubes and red bar front sight. Weight for 12 gauge is about 6.9 lbs. and the 20 gauge is about 5.6 lbs.

NIB	Exc.	V.G.	Good	Fair	Poor
1300	1000	950	700	500	350

SUPER BLACK EAGLE II

This series of guns was introduced in 2005. Major features are a new butt pad, grip, and cryogenically treated barrels for which specially designed longer choke tubes are required. Benelli offers this series with or without "ComforTech" features. This system reduces recoil up to 48 percent and muzzle climb by 15 percent.

Super Black Eagle II with ComforTech

Offered in 12 gauge with 3.5" chambers. Barrel lengths are 24", 26", or 28" with choke tubes and red bar front sight. Available in synthetic or various camo finishes. Magazine capacity is 3 rounds. Weight is about 7.2 lbs. with 26" barrel.

NIB	Exc.	V.G.	Good	Fair	Poor
1465	1100	700	600	365	250

Super Black Eagle II without ComforTech

This model, without ComforTech, has the same options as the one above with the addition of a walnut stock.

NIB	Exc.	V.G.	Good	Fair	Poor
1355	1000	650	575	325	225

NOTE: Add $60 for walnut stock. Add $110 for camo models.

Super Black Eagle II Rifled Slug with ComforTech

This is a 12 gauge 3" chamber gun with 24" rifled barrel with adjustable sights. Available with synthetic stock or Timber HD camo stock. Weight is about 7.4 lbs.

NIB	Exc.	V.G.	Good	Fair	Poor
1535	1150	650	575	325	225

NOTE: Add $120 for Camo version.

Super Black Eagle II Turkey Gun

This 12 gauge 3" chamber shotgun (3.5" chambers on non-ComforTech guns) is fitted with 24" smooth bore barrels with choke tubes. Red bar front sight. Weight is about 7.1 lbs. Available with Timber HD camo stock with or without ComforTech.

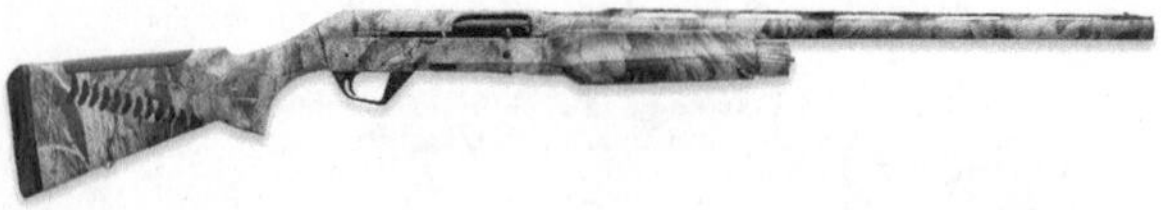

NIB	Exc.	V.G.	Good	Fair	Poor
1455	1050	700	600	365	250

NOTE: Add $130 for ComforTech version.

Super Black Eagle II Steady Grip

This 12 gauge 3.5" chamber gun is fitted with a 24" barrel with red bar front sight. Choke tubes. Stock is camo with steady grip pistol grip. Weight is about 7.3 lbs. This model comes without ComforTech.

NIB	Exc.	V.G.	Good	Fair	Poor
1200	950	650	500	300	200

Super Black Eagle

This model is similar to the Montefeltro Super 90 Hunter with a polymer or walnut stock and forearm. It is offered with a 24", 26", or 28" vent rib barrel with 5 screw-in choke tubes. Chambered for 12 gauge from 2-3/4" to 3-1/2". It was introduced in 1989. The 24" barrel was introduced in 1993.

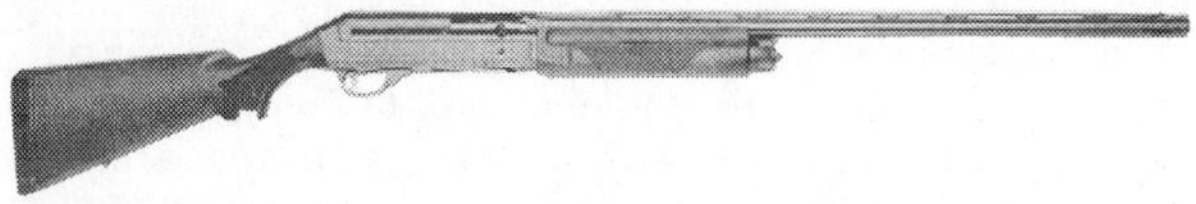

NIB	Exc.	V.G.	Good	Fair	Poor
1200	950	650	500	300	200

Super Black Eagle Left-Hand

Introduced in 1999 this model is the same as the Black Eagle but in a left-hand version. A Camo version is available.

NIB	Exc.	V.G.	Good	Fair	Poor
1200	950	650	500	300	200

Super Black Eagle Custom Slug Gun

This 12 gauge model has a 24" rifled barrel with 3" chamber. It comes standard with matte metal finish. Gun weighs 7.6 lbs.

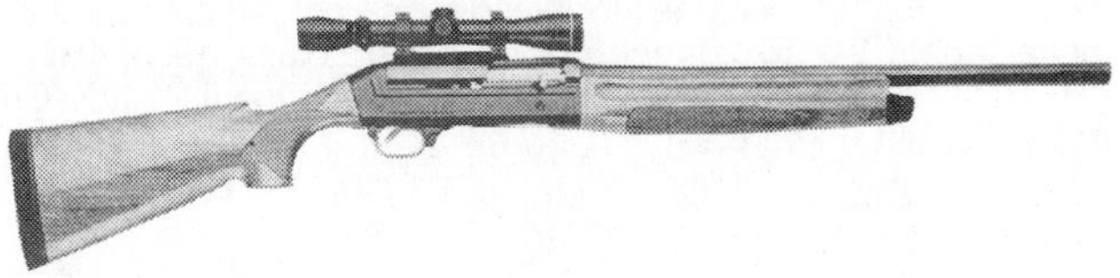

NIB	Exc.	V.G.	Good	Fair	Poor
1100	800	750	600	500	350

Super Black Eagle Camo Gun

Introduced in 1997 this model features 24", 26", or 28' vent rib barrels chambered for 12 gauge shells. Has a Realtree Xtra Brown Camo finish. Stock is camo polymer as is forearm.

NIB	Exc.	V.G.	Good	Fair	Poor
1300	1000	750	600	500	400

Super Black Eagle Steady Grip

Similar to the model above but equipped with a vertical pistol grip. Drilled and tapped receiver. Extra Full choke tube. Barrel length is 24". Weight is about 7.3 lbs. Introduced in 2003.

NIB	Exc.	V.G.	Good	Fair	Poor
1465	1100	650	575	325	225

Super Black Eagle Limited Edition

Introduced in 1997 this shotgun features a 26" vent rib barrel, matte metal finish, and satin select grade wood stock. The nickel plated receiver is finely etched with scroll and game scenes. Limited to 1,000 guns.

NIB	Exc.	V.G.	Good	Fair	Poor
2000	1500	1050	750	525	375

Black Eagle Competition Gun

Offered in 12 gauge only this model is fitted with an etched receiver, mid rib bead, competition stock, and 5 screw-in choke tubes. Available in either 26" or 28" vent rib barrel. The upper receiver is steel while the lower receiver is lightweight alloy. Weighs 7.3 lbs.

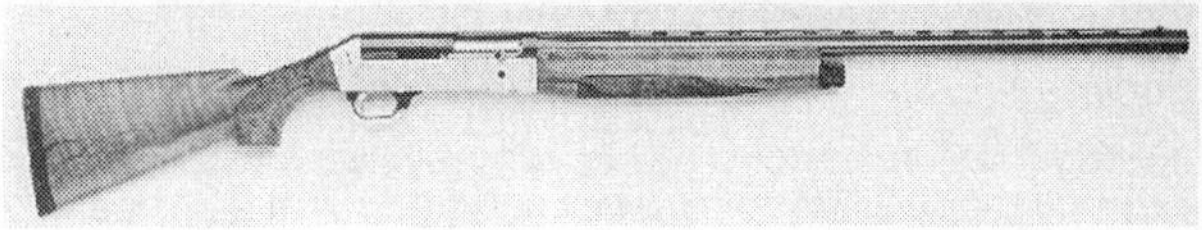

NIB	Exc.	V.G.	Good	Fair	Poor
1300	800	750	700	400	275

Black Eagle

Similar to the Black Eagle Competition Model but with standard grade wood and matte black finish on the receiver. Introduced in 1997.

NIB	Exc.	V.G.	Good	Fair	Poor
900	600	475	325	225	150

BLACK EAGLE EXECUTIVE SERIES

Offered in 12 gauge only this is a special order only shotgun. It is offered with a choice of 21", 24", 26", 28" vent rib barrels. Each grade or level of gun is engraved with increasing levels of coverage. The stock is fancy walnut.

Grade I

NIB	Exc.	V.G.	Good	Fair	Poor
5000	4000	2500	1200	700	300

Grade II

NIB	Exc.	V.G.	Good	Fair	Poor
5700	4500	3000	1500	950	400

Grade III

NIB	Exc.	V.G.	Good	Fair	Poor
6600	5000	3250	1700	1050	550

Legacy

This model features a coin finished alloy receiver and is chambered for the 12 gauge 2-3/4" or 3" shell. It is fitted with a choice of 26" or 28" vent rib barrel with mid and front sights. Weight is about 7.5 lbs. Buttstock and forearm are select walnut.

NIB	Exc.	V.G.	Good	Fair	Poor
1300	800	750	700	400	275

Legacy—20 Gauge

Offered for the first time in 1999 this model is chambered for 20 gauge shells and is fitted with either 24" or 26" vent rib barrels. Weight is about 6 lbs.

NIB	Exc.	V.G.	Good	Fair	Poor
1300	800	750	700	400	275

Legacy Limited Edition

Offered in both 12 and 20 gauge this model features select walnut stock and etched game scenes with gold filled accents. The 12 gauge features waterfowl scenes while the 20 gauge has upland game scenes. The 12 gauge is fitted with a 28" barrel while the 20 gauge has a 26" barrel. This model was introduced in 2000 and is limited to 250 guns in each gauge.

NIB	Exc.	V.G.	Good	Fair	Poor
1600	1200	900	550	375	295

Legacy (2005)

This is a updated version of the Legacy model with changes in the engraving pattern, upgraded wood, improved trigger, and a slightly different receiver style. Offered in 12 and 20 gauge with 3" chambers and choice of 26" or 28" vent rib barrel with choke tubes. Red bar front sight. Checkered select walnut stock with pistol grip. Magazine capacity is 4 rounds. Weight for 12 gauge is about 7.4 lbs. and the 20 gauge is about 5.8 lbs.

NIB	Exc.	V.G.	Good	Fair	Poor
1435	1050	900	575	325	225

NOTE: Add $30 for 20 gauge.

Cordoba

This model, introduced in 2005, is chambered for the 12 gauge 3" shell and fitted with cryogencially treated ported barrels in 28" or 30" lengths with extended choke tubes. Vent rib is 10mm width. Synthetic stock with adjustable length butt pads. Red bar front sight. Weight is about 7.25 lbs.

NIB	Exc.	V.G.	Good	Fair	Poor
1800	1530	1200	850	375	295

Benelli Legacy

Gas-operated semi shotgun chambered for 12, 20 (2-3/4- and 3-inch) and 28 gauge. Features include Inertia Driven system; sculptured lower receiver with classic game scene etchings; highly polished blued upper receiver, giving the Legacy eye-catching originality; AA-Grade walnut stock; gel recoil pad; ported 24- or 26-inch barrel, Crio\xa8 chokes. Weight 7.4 to 7.5 lbs. Legacy Sport (12 gauge only) has more elaborate engraving, optional 30-inch barrel. Prices shown are for 12 or 20 gauge standard model.

NIB	Exc.	V.G.	Good	Fair	Poor
1500	1325	1100	850	500	350

NOTE: Add 10 percent for 28 gauge, 33 percent for Legacy Sport.

Benelli Vinci

Gas-operated semiauto shotgun chambered for 2-3/4- and 3-inch 12-gauge. Features include modular disassembly; interchangeable choke tubes; 24- to 28-inch ribbed barrel; black, MAX-4HD or APG HD finish; synthetic contoured stocks; optional Steady-Grip model. Weight 6.7 to 6.9 lbs.

NIB	Exc.	V.G.	Good	Fair	Poor
1200	1000	850	600	400	300

Benelli Super Vinci

Unlike the Vinci, the Super Vinci fires 12-gauge 2-3/4, 3 and 3-1/2 inch magnum ammunition interchangeably. Barrel lengths: 26 or 28 inches. Features Crio Chokes, red bar front sight, metal bead mid sight. Receiver drilled and tapped for scope mounting. Weight is approx. 7 lbs. Available in black synthetic, Realtree MAX-4 or Realtree APG camo finish. New in 2011.

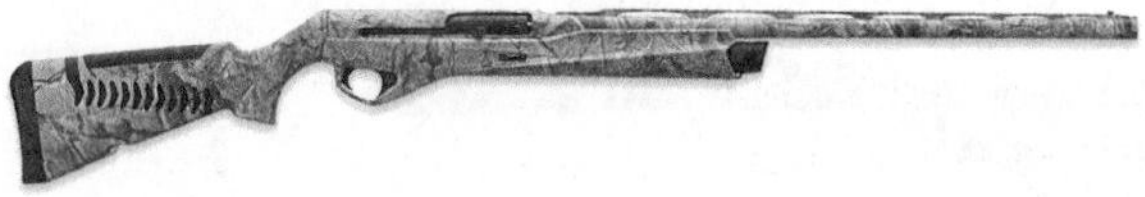

NIB	Exc.	V.G.	Good	Fair	Poor
1400	1150	900	650	450	350

NOTE: Add $100 for camo finish.

Nova

Introduced in 1999 this model features polymer molded frame with steel cage chambered for 3-1/2" shells. Choice of 24", 26", or 28" vent rib barrels. A 18.5" slug barrel is also offered. Two- or four-shot magazine extensions are offered as well. Weight with 28" barrel is 8 lbs. Choice of camo or black synthetic pistol-grip stock. In 2001 this model was offered in 20 gauge as well.

Nova Camo Model

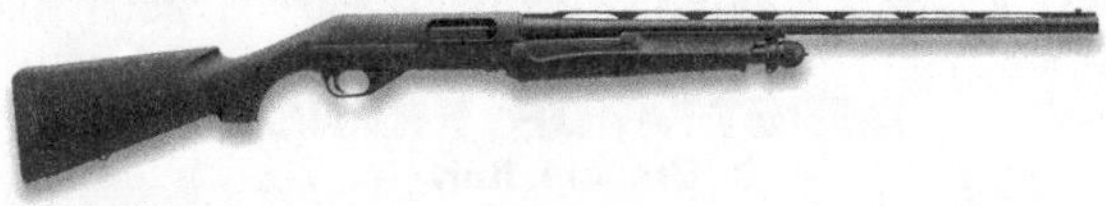

Nova Pump with vent rib barrel

NIB	Exc.	V.G.	Good	Fair	Poor
350	275	225	175	150	75

Nova Slug

This 12 gauge shotgun has a 18.5" cylinder bored barrel with open rifle or ghost-ring sights. Black synthetic stock. Chambered for 2.75" or 3" shells. Magazine capacity is 4 rounds. Weight is about 7.2 lbs. Introduced in 2000.

NIB	Exc.	V.G.	Good	Fair	Poor
350	275	225	200	150	95

NOTE: Add $40 for ghost ring sights.

Nova Rifled Slug

Introduced in 2000 this 12 gauge model features a 24" rifled barrel with open rifle sights. Black synthetic stock or Timber HD camo stock. Chambered for 2.75" or 3" shells. Magazine capacity is 4 rounds. Weight is about 8 lbs.

NIB	Exc.	V.G.	Good	Fair	Poor
525	425	350	250	175	125

NOTE: Add $75 for Camo version.

Nova Field Slug Combo

This 12 gauge 3" gun is equipped with a 26" and 24" barrel. The 26" barrel is fitted with a vent rib and choke tube while the 24" barrel is rifled and fitted with a cantilever scope mount. Black synthetic stock.

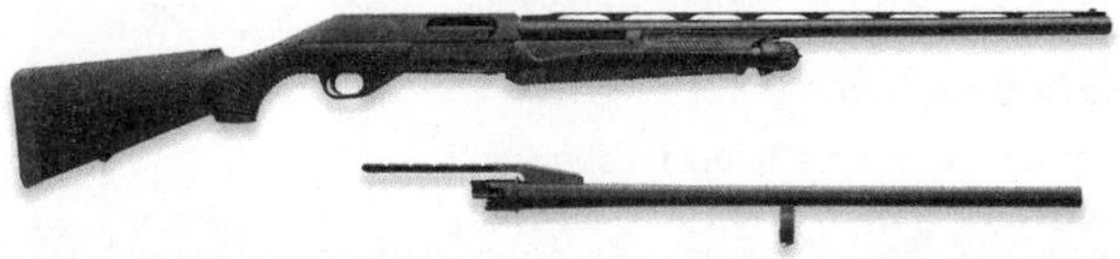

NIB	Exc.	V.G.	Good	Fair	Poor
545	425	325	250	175	125

Nova H2O Pump

Introduced in 2003 this model features a largely polymer exterior with corrosion-resistant finish. Barrel, magazine tube, magazine cap, trigger group and other internal parts are nickel plated. Chambered for 12 gauge. Fitted with an 18.5" barrel. Black synthetic stock. Magazine capacity is 4 rounds. Open rifle sights. Weight is about 7.2 lbs.

NIB	Exc.	V.G.	Good	Fair	Poor
465	375	295	225	150	95

Supernova

Introduced in 2006, the Supernova incorporates Benelli's ComforTech stock system into the Nova pump shotgun. Available in 24", 26" and 28" barrel lengths in matte black synthetic, 24" and 26" barrel lengths in Advantage Timber camo, and 26" and 28" barrel lengths in Max-4 camo. Weight is about 8 lbs. with 28" barrel. All versions are chambered for 3.5" shells. Three choke tubes. Add 15 percent for camo versions.

NIB	Exc.	V.G.	Good	Fair	Poor
475	375	250	175	150	75

Supernova SteadyGrip

As above but with extended pistol grip in 24" barrel only. Matte black synthetic or Advantage Timber stock. Add 15 percent for camo model.

NIB	Exc.	V.G.	Good	Fair	Poor
455	375	250	175	150	75

Supernova Tactical

Matte black synthetic stock with 18" barrel. Available with ComforTech or pistol grip stock. Fixed cylinder bore. Open rifle sights. Ghost ring sights optional.

NIB	Exc.	V.G.	Good	Fair	Poor
400	325	225	150	125	75

Sport Model

This model was introduced in 1997 and is the first shotgun with removable, interchangeable carbon fiber vent ribs. This model is offered in 12 gauge only with choice of 26" or 28" barrels or 20-ga. with 28" barrel. Buttpad is adjustable. Weight is 7 lbs. for 26" models and 7.3 lbs. for 28" models.

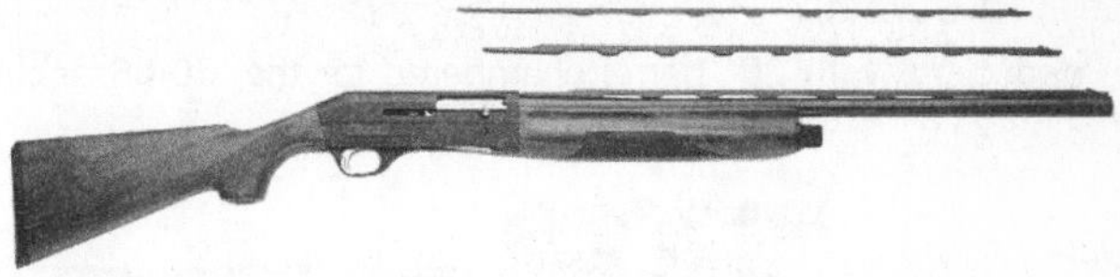

NIB	Exc.	V.G.	Good	Fair	Poor
1300	1000	650	400	250	100

SuperSport with ComforTech

Introduced in 2005 this model is offered in 12 gauge with 3" chamber or 20-ga. with 28" barrel. Choice of 28" or 30" carbon fiber barrel with choke tubes and red bar front sight. Weight is about 7.25 lbs.

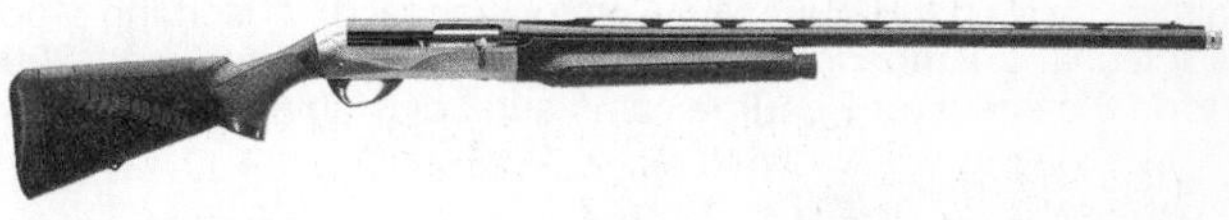

NIB	Exc.	V.G.	Good	Fair	Poor
1670	1250	800	575	395	200

Sport II Model

Introduced in 2003 this model features cryogenically treated barrels and extra-long choke tubes. Chambered for the 12 gauge shell in either 2.75" or 3" with 28" or 30" barrel or 20-ga. with 28" barrel. Vent rib and choke tubes. Magazine capacity is 4 rounds. Red bar front sight. Weight is approximately 7.9 lbs.

NIB	Exc.	V.G.	Good	Fair	Poor
1470	1100	700	475	325	150

Ultra Light

Inertia-driven 12 gauge semi-auto features an alloy receiver, carbon fiber rib and small proportions to bring weight down to about 6 lbs. Walnut stock with Weathercoat finish. Chambered for 3" shells. Offered in 24" or 26" barrel only with 5 Crio chokes. Introduced 2006.

NIB	Exc.	V.G.	Good	Fair	Poor
1435	1050	900	575	325	225

RIFLES

Model R1 Rifle

Introduced in 2003 this rifle is chambered for the .30-06 or .300 Win. Mag cartridge. Barrels are cryogenically treated. Action is gas operated. Interchangeable barrel offered in 20" and 22" in .30-06 and 20" and 24" in .300 Win. Mag. Walnut stock. Detachable magazine has a 4-round capacity. Weight is about 7 to 7.2 lbs. depending on caliber and barrel length. In 2005 the .270 WSM and .300 WSM calibers were added to the R 1 rifle.

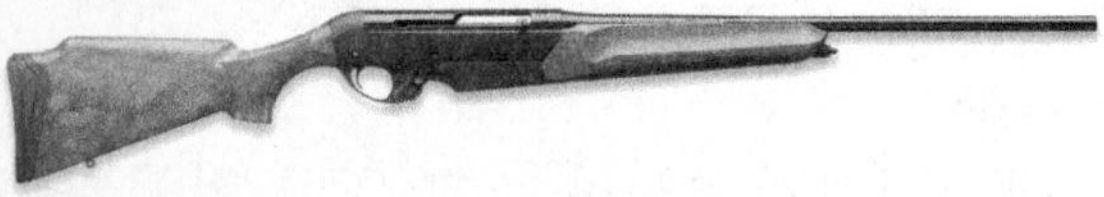

NIB	Exc.	V.G.	Good	Fair	Poor
1080	850	675	500	350	225

Model R1 Carbine

As above but with 20" barrel chambered for the .30-06 or .300 Win. Mag calibers. Weight is about 7 lbs.

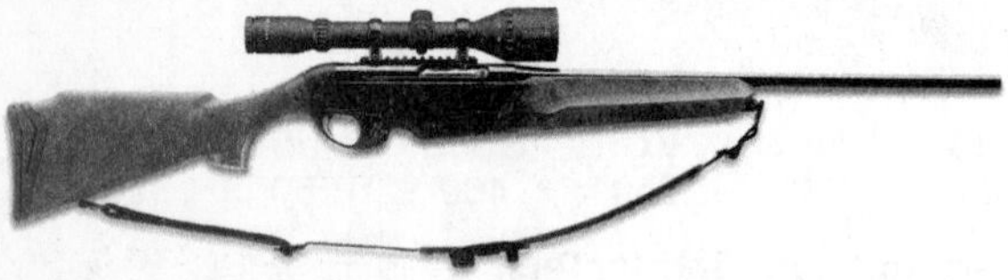

NIB	Exc.	V.G.	Good	Fair	Poor
1080	850	675	500	350	225

R1 ComforTech Rifle

Similar to Model R1 but with ComforTech recoil-absorbing stock. Additional chamberings .270 and .300 WSM. Introduced 2006. Add 10 percent for RealTree camo and adjustable comb.

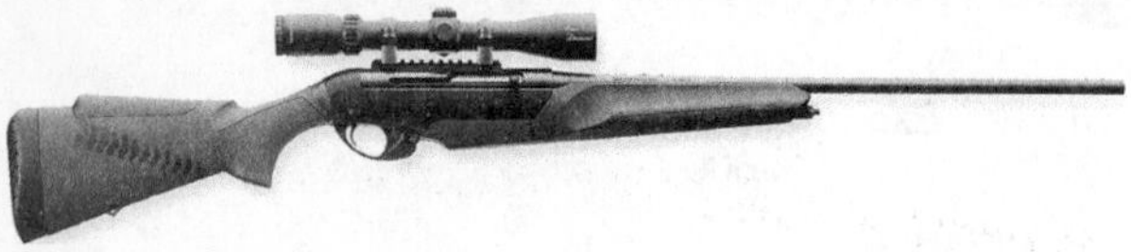

NIB	Exc.	V.G.	Good	Fair	Poor
1350	1100	700	475	325	150

Benelli MR1 Rifle

Gas-operated semiauto rifle chambered in 5.56 NATO. Features include 16-inch 1:9 hard chrome-lined barrel, synthetic stock with pistol grip, rotating bolt, military-style aperture sights with picatinny rail. Comes equipped with 5-round detachable magazine but accepts M16 magazines.

NIB	Exc.	V.G.	Good	Fair	Poor
1135	965	800	550	350	250

BERETTA, DR. FRANCO

Brescia, Italy

Black Diamond Field Grade

The above model is produced in four embellished grades.

NIB	Exc.	V.G.	Good	Fair	Poor
2075	1650	1100	875	450	200

Black Diamond Field Grade Grade One

NIB	Exc.	V.G.	Good	Fair	Poor
2250	1850	1300	850	400	200

Black Diamond Field Grade Grade Two

NIB	Exc.	V.G.	Good	Fair	Poor
2800	2100	1650	1175	500	300

Black Diamond Field Grade Grade Three

NIB	Exc.	V.G.	Good	Fair	Poor
3600	2900	2350	1975	600	300

Black Diamond Field Grade Grade Four

NIB	Exc.	V.G.	Good	Fair	Poor
4350	3600	2850	1750	700	350

Gamma Standard

A 12, 16, or 20 gauge boxlock O/U shotgun with 26" or 28" barrels, single trigger and automatic ejectors. Blued, French case hardened with a walnut stock. Imported from 1984 to 1988.

NIB	Exc.	V.G.	Good	Fair	Poor
900	775	600	425	250	100

Gamma Deluxe

As above, but more finely finished.

NIB	Exc.	V.G.	Good	Fair	Poor
1200	975	800	600	350	125

Gamma Target

As above, in a trap or skeet version. Imported from 1986 to 1988.

NIB	Exc.	V.G.	Good	Fair	Poor
1200	975	800	600	350	125

America Standard

A .410 bore boxlock O/U shotgun with 26" or 28" barrels. Blued, French case hardened with a walnut stock. Imported from 1984 to 1988.

NIB	Exc.	V.G.	Good	Fair	Poor
650	475	325	275	200	100

America Deluxe

As above, but more finely finished.

NIB	Exc.	V.G.	Good	Fair	Poor
695	525	375	300	225	100

Europa

As above, with a 26" barrel and engraved action. Imported from 1984 to 1988.

NIB	Exc.	V.G.	Good	Fair	Poor
800	725	575	425	275	100

Europa Deluxe

As above, but more finely finished.

NIB	Exc.	V.G.	Good	Fair	Poor
850	775	625	475	300	1005

Francia Standard

A .410 bore boxlock double-barrel shotgun with varying barrel lengths, double triggers and manual extractors. Blued with a walnut stock. Imported from 1986 to 1988.

NIB	Exc.	V.G.	Good	Fair	Poor
600	500	375	250	125	100

Alpha Three

A 12, 16, or 20 gauge boxlock double-barrel shotgun with 26" or 28" barrels, single triggers and automatic ejectors. Blued, French case hardened with a walnut stock. Imported from 1984 to 1988.

NIB	Exc.	V.G.	Good	Fair	Poor
750	650	500	325	150	100

Beta Three

A single-barrel, break-open, field-grade gun chambered for all gauges and offered with a ventilated rib barrel from 24" to 32" in length. The receiver chrome-plated, and the stock of walnut. Imported from 1985 to 1988.

NIB	Exc.	V.G.	Good	Fair	Poor
325	225	200	175	125	40

BERETTA, PIETRO

Brescia, Italy

RIFLES

Beretta 1873 Renegade Short Lever-Action Rifle

Lever-action rifle chambered in .45 Colt, .357 Magnum. Patterned after 1873 Winchester. Features include 20" round barrel, blued finish, checkered walnut buttstock and forend, adjustable rear sight and fixed blade front. Ten-round tubular magazine.

NIB	Exc.	V.G.	Good	Fair	Poor
1400	1050	875	595	375	225

Beretta Gold Rush Slide-Action Rifle and Carbine

External replica of old Colt Lightning Magazine Rifle chambered in .357 Magnum and .45 Colt. Features include a 20" round or 24-1/2" octagonal barrel, case-hardened receiver, walnut buttstock and forend, crescent buttplate, 13-round (rifle) or 10-round (carbine) magazine. Available as Standard Carbine, Standard Rifle, or Deluxe Rifle.

Beretta Gold Rush Slide-Action Rifle and Carbine Standard Rifle or Carbine

NIB	Exc.	V.G.	Good	Fair	Poor
1400	1050	875	595	375	225

Cx4 Storm

Introduced in 2003, this semi-automatic carbine has a 16.6" barrel. Chambered for the 9mm, .40 S&W, or .45 ACP cartridge. Synthetic stock with rubber recoil pad has adjustable stock spacers. Ghost ring rear sight with adjustable post front sight. Forward accessory rail. Magazine capacity is 10 rounds for 9mm or .40 S&W and 8 rounds for the .45 ACP model. Weight is about 5.75 lbs.

NIB	Exc.	V.G.	Good	Fair	Poor
650	785	495	350	195	100

AR-70

A .223 caliber, semi-automatic rifle with a 17.7" barrel, adjustable diopter sights, and an 8- or 30-shot magazine. Black epoxy finish with a synthetic stock. Weight is approximately 8.3 lbs. No longer imported into the U.S.

NIB	Exc.	V.G.	Good	Fair	Poor
2100	1900	1500	1000	750	400

BM-59 Standard Grade

A gas operated semi-automatic rifle with detachable box magazine. Chambered for .308 cartridge. Walnut stock. Barrel length is 19.3" with muzzlebrake. Magazine capacity is 5,10, or 20 rounds. Weight is about 9.5 lbs.

NIB	Exc.	V.G.	Good	Fair	Poor
3000	2700	2100	1500	400	200

MODEL 500 CUSTOM

This model was offered in four other grades:

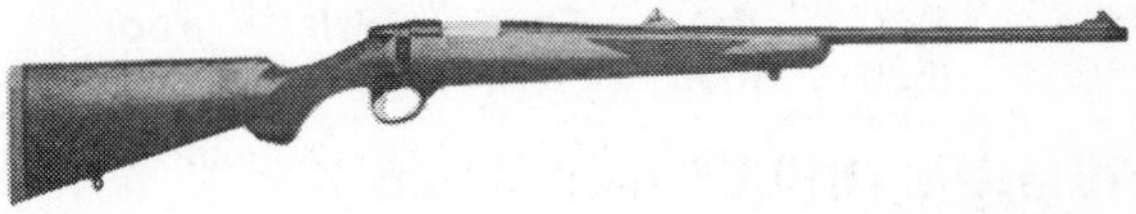

NIB	Exc.	V.G.	Good	Fair	Poor
—	600	525	400	325	275

Model 500S

NIB	Exc.	V.G.	Good	Fair	Poor
—	625	550	425	350	300

Model 500DL

NIB	Exc.	V.G.	Good	Fair	Poor
—	1400	1250	1000	775	650

Model 500DEELL

NIB	Exc.	V.G.	Good	Fair	Poor
—	1600	1450	1200	975	800

Model 500DEELLS

NIB	Exc.	V.G.	Good	Fair	Poor
—	1625	1475	1225	1000	825

Model 501

A .243 or .308 caliber bolt-action rifle with a 23" barrel, furnished without sights and a 6-shot magazine. Blued with a checkered walnut stock. It was discontinued in 1986. It was offered in the same variations as the Model 500 series-501S, 501DL, 501DLS, 501EELL, and 501EELLS. The values for this series are the same as for the 500 series rifles.

Model 502

A .270, 7mm Remington Magnum, and .30-06 caliber bolt-action rifle with a 24" barrel (without sights) and a 5-shot magazine. Blued with a checkered walnut stock. Discontinued in 1986. It is also available in the same variations as the Model 500 and the Model 501 but is valued at approximately 10 percent higher in each variation.

Mato Standard

Same as above but fitted with a matte gray Kevlar and graphite composite stock. Weight is approximately 7.9 lbs.

NIB	*Exc.*	*V.G.*	*Good*	*Fair*	*Poor*
1550	1200	800	600	300	175

Mato Deluxe

This bolt-action rifle was introduced into the Beretta product line in 1997. It is based on the Mauser 98 action and is fitted with a drop-out box magazine. The stock is XXX Claro walnut with a hand-rubbed oil finish and black forend tip. Chambered for .270 Win., .280, .30-06, 7mm Magnum, .300 Magnum, .338 Magnum, and .375 H&H. Weight is about 8 lbs.

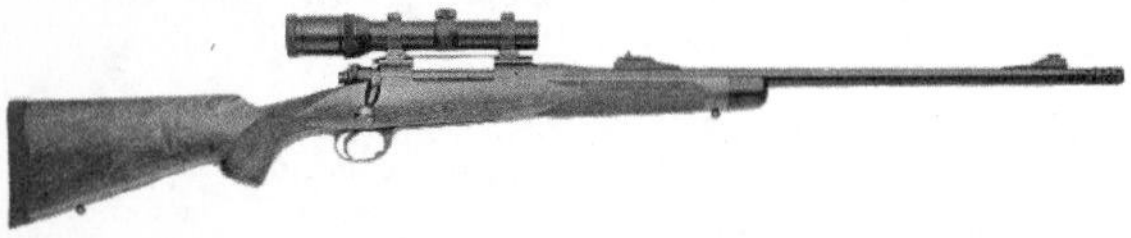

NIB	*Exc.*	*V.G.*	*Good*	*Fair*	*Poor*
2000	1500	1000	750	350	200

PREMIUM RIFLES

Model S689 Sable

A 9.3x74R or the .30-06 caliber O/U rifle with a boxlock action, 23" ribbed barrels and express-type sights. Blued, case hardened or nickel-plated with checkered walnut stock. Double triggers and automatic ejectors. Offered in three grades.

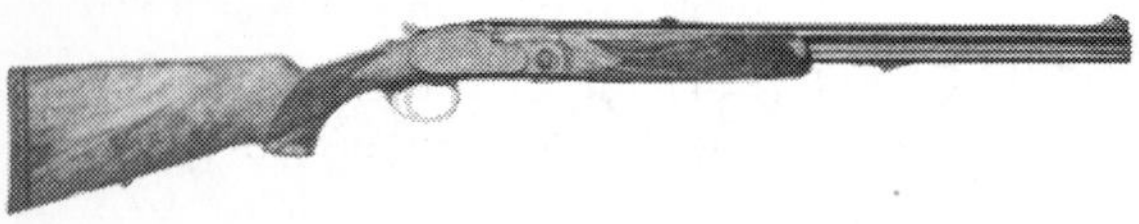

Silver Sable

NIB	*Exc.*	*V.G.*	*Good*	*Fair*	*Poor*
3850	3000	2500	1750	1200	300

Gold Sable

NIB	*Exc.*	*V.G.*	*Good*	*Fair*	*Poor*
6500	5500	4500	3000	1500	350

Diamond Sable

NIB	*Exc.*	*V.G.*	*Good*	*Fair*	*Poor*
12750	10000	7500	5500	2000	1000

NOTE: Extra 20 gauge barrel with forearm add $1,200. Scope with claw mounts add $2,000.

SSO Express

A .375 Holland & Holland and .458 Winchester Magnum caliber O/U, double barrel rifle with 23" barrels, folding express sights, double triggers, and automatic ejectors. Furnished with a fitted case. This firearm is available on a custom order basis and should be individually appraised.

NIB	*Exc.*	*V.G.*	*Good*	*Fair*	*Poor*
18000	13000	9500	6000	3500	2500

SSO5 Express

A more finely finished version of the above.

NIB	*Exc.*	*V.G.*	*Good*	*Fair*	*Poor*
20000	15000	11000	8000	5000	3000

SSO6

This is a premium grade sidelock over-and-under express rifle. Equipped with double triggers. It is offered in 9.3x74R, .375 H&H Magnum, and .458 Win. Magnum. It is fitted with a 24" barrel with express sights. Claw mounts for Zeiss scopes are available from the factory. The receiver is case-colored with light scroll engraving. Special select walnut is used in the stock and forearm with fine line checkering. Stock comes with cheekpiece and rubber recoil pad. Furnished with leather case. Rifle weighs about 11 lbs.

NIB	*Exc.*	*V.G.*	*Good*	*Fair*	*Poor*
55000	45000	34000	24000	15000	10000

SSO6 EELL

Offered in the same calibers as above but furnished with hand engraved game scenes with gold inlays. Walnut stock is special select briar with fine diamond line checkering.

NIB	*Exc.*	*V.G.*	*Good*	*Fair*	*Poor*
65000	50000	40000	30000	18000	10000

Model 455

This is a premium grade side-by-side express rifle with slide locks. Available in these calibers: .375 H&H Magnum, .458 Win. Magnum, .470 Nitro Express, .500 Nitro Express, and .416 Rigby. The receiver is case-colored without engraving and the walnut stock is highly figured with fine line checkering. Comes supplied with express sights. Claw mounts and Zeiss scope offered at customer's request only on .375, .458, and .416. Weighs about 11 lbs.

NIB	*Exc.*	*V.G.*	*Good*	*Fair*	*Poor*
53000	40000	30000	15000	6750	2000

Model 455 EELL

Same as above model but furnished with case-colored game scene engraving with gold inlays. Walnut briar stock with fine diamond line checkering. Supplied with leather case and accessories.

NIB	Exc.	V.G.	Good	Fair	Poor
72500	50000	3500	16500	7500	2500

SHOTGUNS

Beretta shotguns are marked with a symbol or 0 stamping to indicate the type of fixed choke in the barrel or barrels. Usually this stamping is on the side of the barrel in the rear near the receiver on semi-automatics and near the ejectors on double barrel shotguns. Beretta shotguns with screw-in Mobilchoke tubes will have notches cut in them to indicate the amount of choke placed in the tube. The BL series of O/U shotguns were manufactured between 1968 and 1973. They are chambered for 12 or 20 gauge and were offered with 26", 28", or 30" vent ribbed barrels with various choke combinations. They feature boxlock actions and were offered with either single or double triggers, and manual extractors or automatic ejectors. The finishes are blued with checkered walnut stocks. The configurations differ basically in the quality of materials and workmanship and the degree of ornamentation.

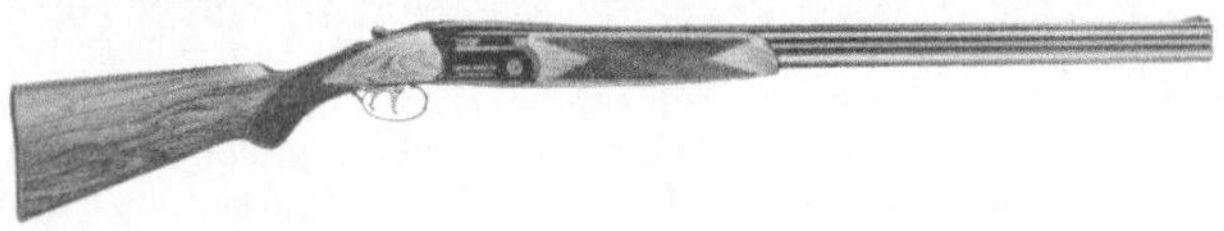

BL-1

NIB	Exc.	V.G.	Good	Fair	Poor
—	500	450	350	225	150

BL-2

NIB	Exc.	V.G.	Good	Fair	Poor
—	425	375	300	250	200

BL-2/S (Speed Trigger)

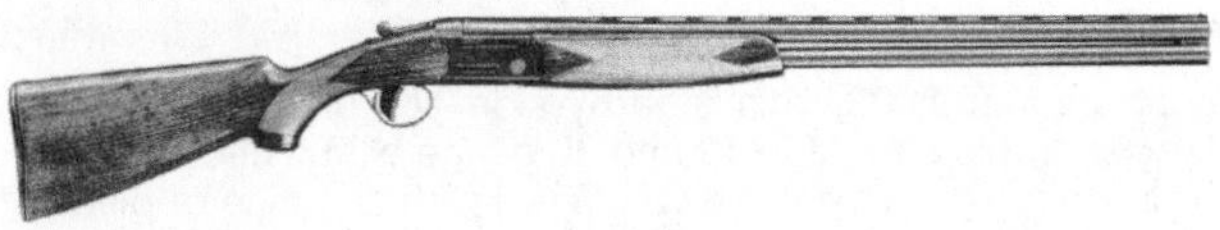

NIB	Exc.	V.G.	Good	Fair	Poor
—	450	400	325	275	225

BL-2 Stakeout

18" barrel.

NIB	Exc.	V.G.	Good	Fair	Poor
—	400	350	275	225	175

BL-3

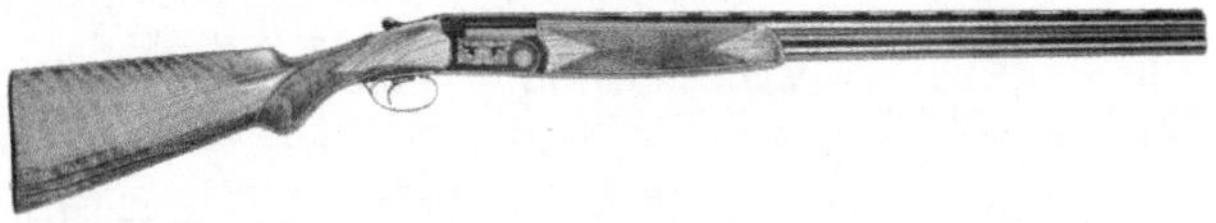

NIB	Exc.	V.G.	Good	Fair	Poor
—	600	550	475	425	350

BL-3 Competition

NIB	Exc.	V.G.	Good	Fair	Poor
—	650	600	525	475	400

BL-4

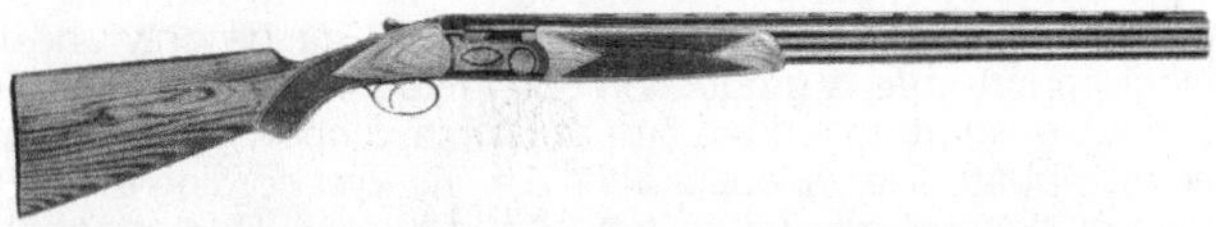

NIB	Exc.	V.G.	Good	Fair	Poor
—	800	750	650	525	425

BL-4 Competition

NIB	Exc.	V.G.	Good	Fair	Poor
—	850	800	700	575	450

BL-5

NIB	Exc.	V.G.	Good	Fair	Poor
—	900	850	725	575	450

BL-5 Competition

NIB	Exc.	V.G.	Good	Fair	Poor
—	950	900	775	600	475

BL-6

Sidelock.

NIB	Exc.	V.G.	Good	Fair	Poor
—	1250	1150	1000	850	675

BL-6 Competition

NIB	Exc.	V.G.	Good	Fair	Poor
—	1300	1200	1050	900	725

Model S55 B

A 12 or 20 gauge O/U shotgun with 26", 28", or 30" ventilated rib barrels, various choke combinations and boxlock action with a single-selective trigger and extractors. Blued with a checkered walnut stock.

NIB	Exc.	V.G.	Good	Fair	Poor
—	550	500	400	325	275

Model S56 E

As above, but more finely finished.

NIB	Exc.	V.G.	Good	Fair	Poor
—	600	550	450	375	325

Model S58 Competition

As above, with either 26" or 30" barrels, wide vent ribs and competition-type stocks.

NIB	Exc.	V.G.	Good	Fair	Poor
—	700	650	550	475	400

Silver Snipe

A 12 or 20 gauge O/U shotgun with 26", 28", or 30" barrels, boxlock action with a double trigger and extractors. Blued with a checkered walnut stock. Manufactured from 1955 through 1967. A single-selective trigger version with ventilated rib and automatic ejectors would be worth approximately 50 percent additional.

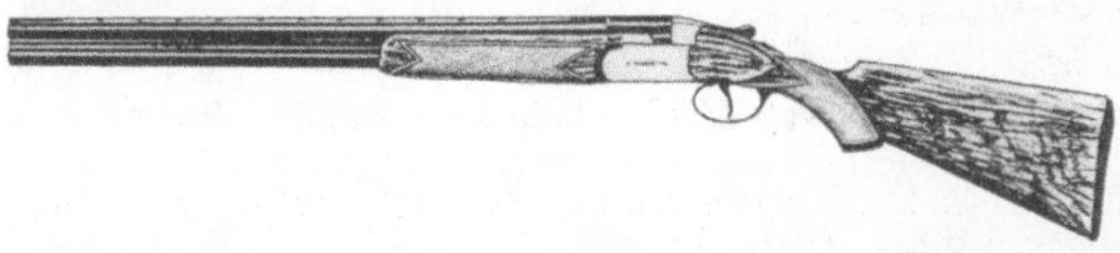

NIB	Exc.	V.G.	Good	Fair	Poor
—	475	375	325	275	200

Golden Snipe

As above with a ventilated rib and automatic ejectors. If it has a single-selective trigger, add 10 percent.

NIB	Exc.	V.G.	Good	Fair	Poor
—	675	600	500	350	200

Model 57 E

As above, but more finely finished. Manufactured between 1955 and 1967.

NIB	Exc.	V.G.	Good	Fair	Poor
—	825	775	600	475	250

ASEL Model

A 12 or 20 gauge O/U shotgun with 26", 28", or 30" ventilated rib barrel with various choke combinations. Single-selective trigger and automatic ejectors. Blued with a checkered pistol-grip stock. Manufactured between 1947 and 1964. Prices listed are for 20 gauge guns.

NIB	Exc.	V.G.	Good	Fair	Poor
—	4250	2500	1200	750	400

NOTE: For 12 gauge guns deduct $1000 from Exc. condition price. For EELL grade add 30 percent.

Model 409 PB

A 12, 16, 20, and 28 gauge boxlock, double-barrel shotgun with 27", 28", or 30" barrels with double triggers and extractors and various choke combinations. Blued with a checkered walnut stock. Manufactured between 1934 and 1964. Add 50 percent for 20 gauge, 100 percent for 28 gauge.

NIB	Exc.	V.G.	Good	Fair	Poor
—	775	700	625	500	250

Model 410

As above, with a 32" Full-choke barrel. Blued with a checkered walnut stock. Introduced in 1934 in 10 gauge only.

NIB	Exc.	V.G.	Good	Fair	Poor
—	1000	925	750	600	300

Model 410 E

More finely finished version of 409PB.

NIB	Exc.	V.G.	Good	Fair	Poor
—	900	825	650	500	275

Model 411 E

The Model 410 with false sideplates and more heavily engraved. Manufactured between 1934 and 1964.

NIB	Exc.	V.G.	Good	Fair	Poor
—	1800	1400	950	800	425

Model 424

A 12 and 20 gauge boxlock shotgun with 26" or 28" barrels, double triggers, various choke combinations, and extractors. Blued with a checkered walnut stock. In 20 gauge it is designated the Model 426 and would be worth an additional 25 percent.

NIB	Exc.	V.G.	Good	Fair	Poor
—	950	875	675	500	225

Model 426 E

As above, with silver inlays and heavier engraving, single-selective trigger and automatic ejectors. Not imported after 1983.

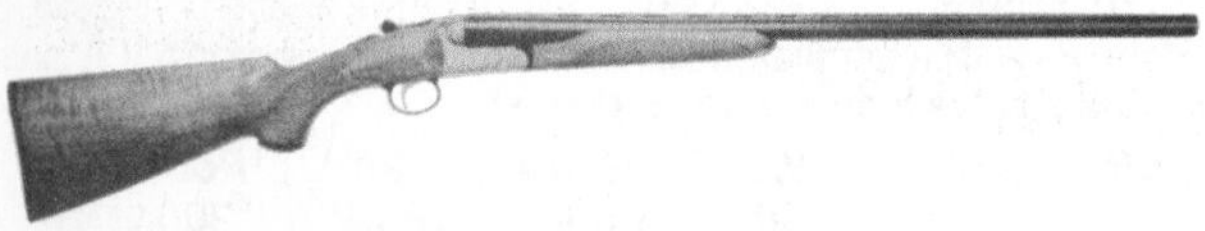

NIB	Exc.	V.G.	Good	Fair	Poor
—	1150	1075	875	700	350

Model 625

A 12 or 20 gauge boxlock, double-barrel shotgun with 26", 28", or 30" barrels, various choke combinations, double triggers and extractors. Moderately engraved and blued with a checkered walnut grip. Imported between 1984 and 1986. Add 50 percent for 20 gauge.

NIB	Exc.	V.G.	Good	Fair	Poor
—	800	750	600	500	250

Silver Hawk

A 10 or 12 gauge boxlock, double-barrel shotgun with 30" barrels, double triggers and extractors. Blued with a silver-finished receiver and a checkered walnut stock. The 10 gauge version would be worth an additional 20 percent. Discontinued in 1967.

NIB	Exc.	V.G.	Good	Fair	Poor
—	500	450	375	250	150

Model 470 Silver Hawk

Introduced in 1997 to commemorate Beretta's 470 years in the gunmaking business, this shotgun is offered in either 12 or 20 gauge configurations. The receiver is silver chrome with engraving. The top lever is checkered with a gold inlaid hawk's head. The gun is fitted with a straight grip stock with splinter forearm of select walnut with oil finish. Choice of 26" or 28" barrels with auto ejection or manual extraction. Weight of 12 gauge about 6.5 lbs. The 20 gauge weighs approximately 6 lbs.

NIB	Exc.	V.G.	Good	Fair	Poor
3600	2800	1500	—	—	—

Model 470 Silver Hawk EL

Introduced in 2002 this model features color case hardened frame with side plates with gold filled game scene engraving. Offered in 12 or 20 gauge with choice of 26" or 28" barrels. Weight is 5.9 lbs. for 20 gauge and 6.5 lbs. for 12 gauge.

NIB	Exc.	V.G.	Good	Fair	Poor
5975	4700	—	—	—	—

471 Silver Hawk

Introduced in 2003, this side-by-side shotgun has a boxlock receiver and is offered in 12 and 20 gauge with a choice of 26" or 28" barrels. This model is also offered with a choice of pistol grip with beavertail fore-end or straight grip stock with splinter fore-end. A straight grip stock with case color receiver is also available at a premium. Select walnut stock with oil finish. Single-selective trigger. Weight is about 6.5 lbs. in 12 gauge and 5.9 lbs. in 20 gauge.

NIB	Exc.	V.G.	Good	Fair	Poor
2875	2250	1300	800	450	300

NOTE: Add $350 for straight grip stock with case color receiver.

BERETTA "SO" SERIES & OTHER PREMIUM SHOTGUNS

These over-and-under shotguns were fitted with side locks, automatic ejectors, single or double triggers. Barrel ranges in length from 26" to 30" with a wide variety of choke combinations. These guns were introduced in 1948 in 12 gauge only and no longer imported as a production gun in 1986. Many of these SO guns were sold through the firm of Garcia, a sporting goods firm and distributor. The various grades are priced according to quality of wood, finish engraving coverage, and the like. Do not confuse these earlier Beretta shotguns with the present line of premium grade Berettas now being imported into the U.S.

Model SO-1

NIB	Exc.	V.G.	Good	Fair	Poor
—	2500	2100	1500	800	400

Model SO-2

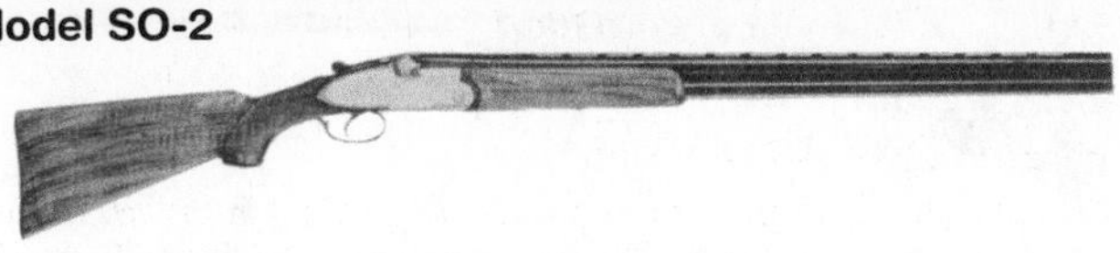

NIB	Exc.	V.G.	Good	Fair	Poor
—	3500	3100	2500	900	500

Model SO-3

NIB	Exc.	V.G.	Good	Fair	Poor
—	5000	4400	3500	1500	1000

Model SO-4 (Garcia SO3EL)

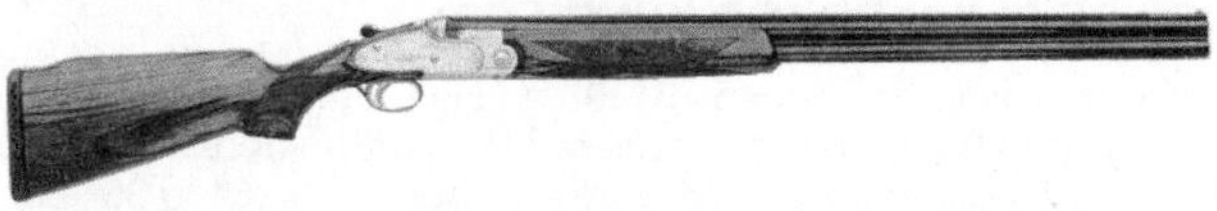

NIB	Exc.	V.G.	Good	Fair	Poor
—	7900	6900	3500	2000	1500

NOTE: For fully engraved Garcia Model SO3-EL add 80 percent.

Model SO-5 (Garcia SO-3 EELL)

NIB	Exc.	V.G.	Good	Fair	Poor
—	—	7900	5900	3500	2500

Model SO-6 (450 or 451 EL) Side-by-Side

This model is fitted with Holland & Holland-style sidelocks and third fastener.

NIB	Exc.	V.G.	Good	Fair	Poor
—	7500	6500	5500	3500	2500

Model SO-7 (451 EELL) Side-by-Side

NIB	Exc.	V.G.	Good	Fair	Poor
—	8900	7900	5900	4000	3000

SO-5 Trap

A premium grade Beretta over-and-under shotgun built for competition trap shooting. Available in 12 gauge with 30" vent rib barrels standard. Barrels in 28" and 32" may be special ordered. Receiver is silver with light scroll engraving. The stock is select highly figured walnut with pistol grip and offered in International or Monte Carlo dimensions. Special trap rubber recoil pad is furnished. Weighs 8 lbs. 2 oz. Furnished with leather case and tools.

NIB	Exc.	V.G.	Good	Fair	Poor
20500	16000	12000	6500	3000	600

SO-5 Trap 2 BBL Set

NIB	Exc.	V.G.	Good	Fair	Poor
23500	18500	13000	6500	3000	600

SO-5 Sporting Clays

Offered in 12 gauge only with choice of 28", 30", or 32" barrels; 26" on special order. Sporting clay dimension walnut stock with pistol grip and rubber recoil pad. Weighs 7 lbs. 8 oz.

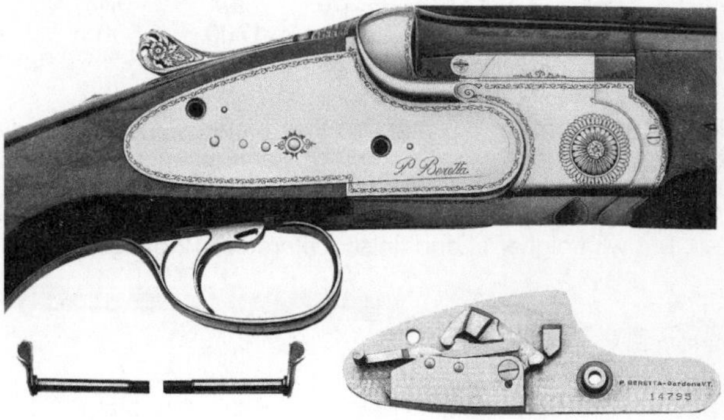

SO-5 sidelocks

NIB	Exc.	V.G.	Good	Fair	Poor
20500	10000	7500	5000	2750	500

SO-5 Skeet

Same general specifications as SO-5 Trap but furnished to skeet dimensions. Offered in 12 gauge only with 26" or 28" vent rib barrels choked skeet. Weighs 7 lbs. 8 oz.

NIB	Exc.	V.G.	Good	Fair	Poor
20500	16000	7500	5000	2750	500

SO-6 EL

This is a premium grade Beretta that is available in several different configurations similar to the SO-5. Available in 12 gauge only. It features a true side lock action, single-selective or nonselective trigger, fixed or screw-in choke tubes. The receiver is offered either in silver finish or case hardened without engraving. The walnut is highly select walnut with fine line checkering. A choice of pistol grip or straight grip is offered. Supplied with a leather fitted hard case. Weighs about 7 lbs. 4 oz. depending on barrel length.

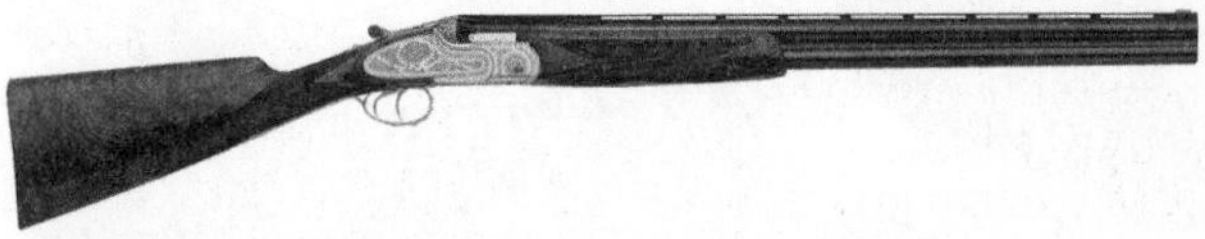

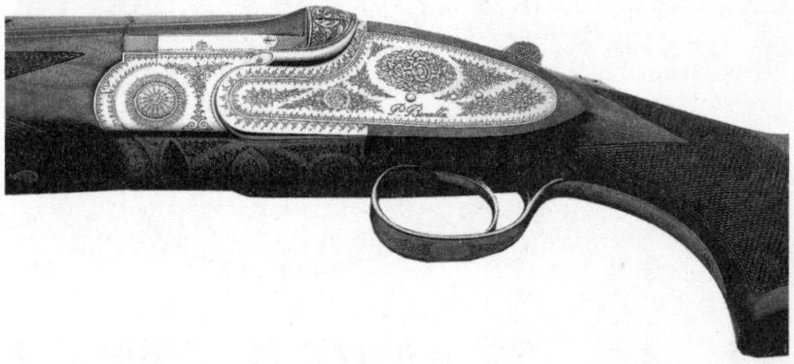

SO-6 receiver

SO-6 Trap

NIB	Exc.	V.G.	Good	Fair	Poor
26500	13000	8500	5000	1700	500

SO-6 Skeet

NIB	Exc.	V.G.	Good	Fair	Poor
26500	13000	8500	5000	1700	500

SO-6 Sporting Clays

NIB	Exc.	V.G.	Good	Fair	Poor
26500	13000	8500	5000	1700	500

SO-6 EELL

A higher grade in the SO-6 series that features a silver receiver with custom engraving with scroll or game scenes. Gold inlays are available on request. Choice of barrel lengths from 26" to 30". Choice of pistol grip or straight grip. All of the same features of the SO-6, but with higher fit and finish. Offered in 12 gauge only.

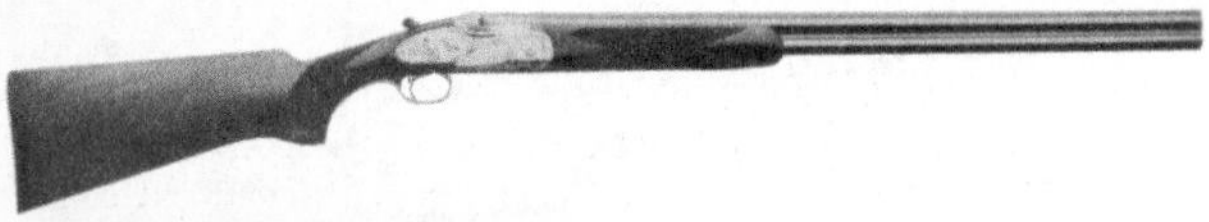

NIB	Exc.	V.G.	Good	Fair	Poor
43750	33500	27000	20000	12000	600

SO-6 EESS

Same specifications as the SO-6 EELL grade but with ruby, sapphire, or emerald side plates with diamond brilliants.

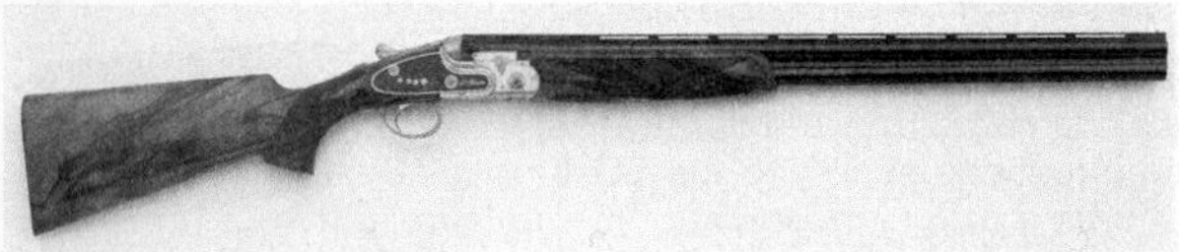

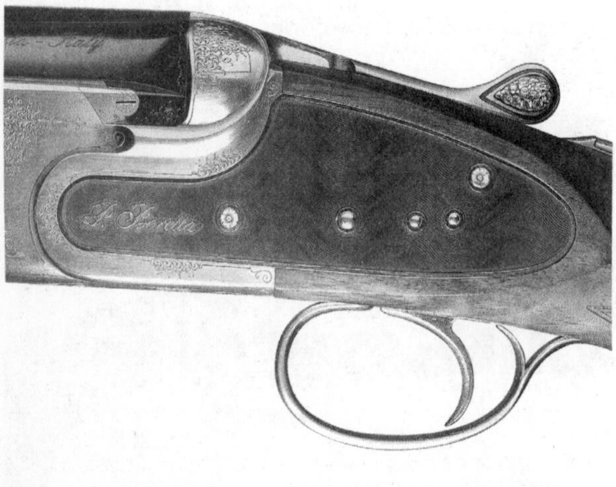

NIB	Exc.	V.G.	Good	Fair	Poor
88850	75000	50000	2250	1750	600

SO-7

One of Beretta's best-grade, sidelock, double-barrel shotgun. It is elaborately engraved and has the highest grade walnut in the stock. No longer in production.

NIB	Exc.	V.G.	Good	Fair	Poor
—	10500	8850	7250	5500	4500

SO-9

This model O/U is Beretta's highest grade. Offered in 12, 20, and 28 gauge, and .410 bore. The true side lock (removable) receiver is highly engraved with scroll or game scenes by Italy's finest craftsmen. Barrel lengths are offered from 26" to 30" with solid hand filed rib. The walnut stock is the finest available with either pistol grip or straight grip. Stock dimensions to customers request. A custom fitted leather case with accessories is supplied with gun. A custom order gun. An independent appraisal is strongly suggested prior to a sale.Suggester Retail Price: From $44,500 to $98,000.

JUBILEE FIELD GRADE (GIUBILEO)

This model was introduced in 1998 and is Beretta's finest boxlock over/under shotgun. The model is fitted with sideplates without screws. Offered in 12, 20, 28, and .410 bore with 26" to 30" barrel depending on gauge. Each gun is richly engraved with fine scroll and signed by master engravers. Highly figured walnut with pistol or straight grip. Weights range from about 7 lbs. in 12 gauge to 5.5 lbs. in .410 bore.

Single Gun

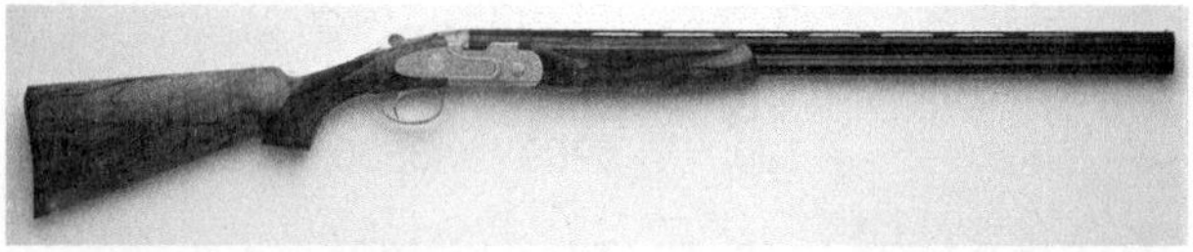

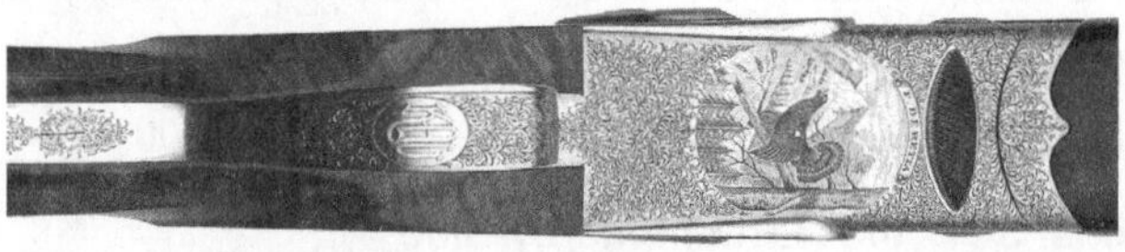

NIB	Exc.	V.G.	Good	Fair	Poor
14750	12000	8250	4500	2200	600

Matched Pair

NIB	Exc.	V.G.	Good	Fair	Poor
32650	—	—	—	—	—

Jubilee Sporting Grade

Similar to the above model in terms of finish but offered in 12 gauge only with choice of 30" or 32" barrels. Pistol grip standard.

NIB	Exc.	V.G.	Good	Fair	Poor
14750	12000	8250	4500	2200	600

NOTE: For 2 barrel combination with 20 gauge barrel and extended chokes add $1,500.

JUBILEE II (GIUBLIO)

This is a side-by-side model offered in 12 or 20 gauge only with straight grip stocks. Choice of 26" or 28" barrels. Full coverage scroll engraving and highly figured walnut. Double triggers are by special order only. The 12 gauge weighs about 6.5 lbs. while the 20 gauge weighs about 6 lbs.

Single Gun

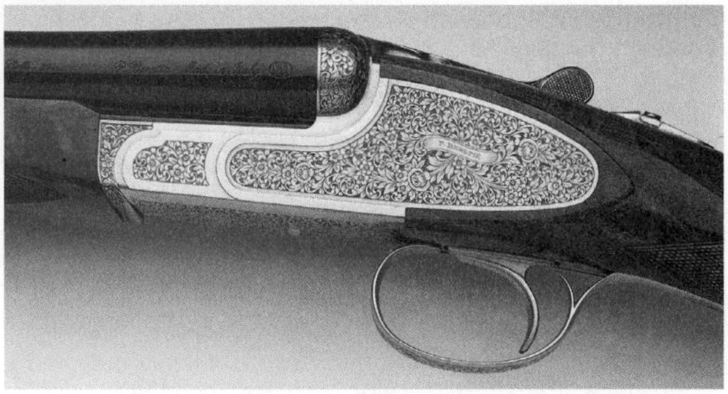

NIB	*Exc.*	*V.G.*	*Good*	*Fair*	*Poor*
14750	12000	8250	4500	2200	600

Matched Pair

NIB	*Exc.*	*V.G.*	*Good*	*Fair*	*Poor*
32650	2600	17000	9200	4000	900

ASE Deluxe Sporting

This boxlock over/under gun is offered in 12 gauge only with choice of 28" or 30" barrels. Classic European scroll engraving. Offered in both field and competition configuration. Weights are about 7.5 lbs. for the 12 gauge.

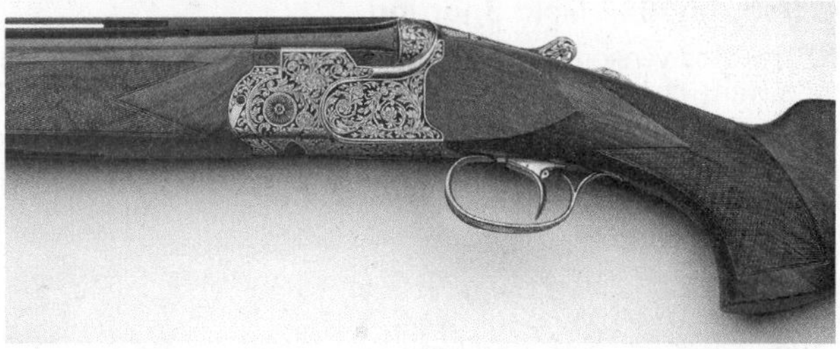

NIB	*Exc.*	*V.G.*	*Good*	*Fair*	*Poor*
25000	18500	12000	900	700	400

MODEL 687 EELL GALLERY SPECIAL

A special version of this model. These are especially engraved guns with upgraded wood that are only made for the Beretta Galleries. Offered in 12, 20, 28, and .410 bore.

Single Gun

NIB	*Exc.*	*V.G.*	*Good*	*Fair*	*Poor*
8500	7300	5900	4500	3300	500

Combo—20/28 Gauge

NIB	*Exc.*	*V.G.*	*Good*	*Fair*	*Poor*
9500	8600	6700	5800	4000	600

Matched Pair

NIB	*Exc.*	*V.G.*	*Good*	*Fair*	*Poor*
17100	15500	11500	8000	4750	700

Imperiale Montecarlo

This is a side-by-side gun chambered for the 12, 20, or 28 gauge shell. True sidelock action. Choice of 26", 27", or 28" barrels with fixed chokes. Other lengths by special request. Weight is about 7.3 lbs. for 12 gauge, 6.5 lbs. for 20 gauge, and 6.2 lbs. for 28 gauge. Master engraved and signed.

Diana

This side-by-side gun is chambered for the 12 or 20 gauge with choice of barrel lengths. Action is true sidelock with exposed hammers. Weight for 12 gauge is about 7.2 lbs. and for the 20 gauge about 6.4 lbs. Master engraved and signed.

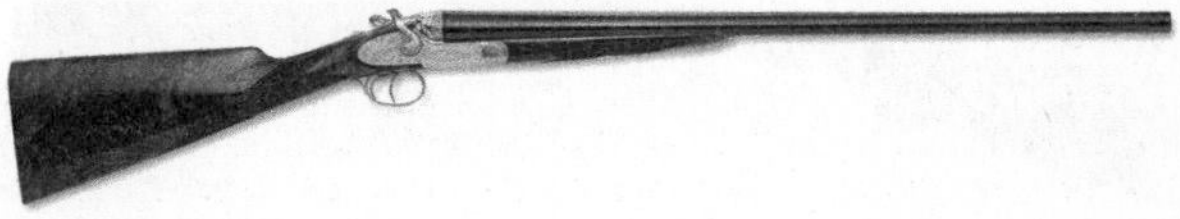

Model 451 Series

A custom order sidelock shotgun. The lowest priced version would be worth approximately $8,000 in excellent condition; and the top-of-the-line model, approximately $25,000. Prospective purchasers are advised to secure a qualified appraisal prior to acquisition.

NIB	*Exc.*	*V.G.*	*Good*	*Fair*	*Poor*
Too Scarce to Value.					

Model 450 Series

This model is the same as the 451 series with the exception of being a Holland & Holland sidelock design. Prospective purchasers are advised to secure a qualified appraisal prior to acquisition.

NIB	*Exc.*	*V.G.*	*Good*	*Fair*	*Poor*
Too Scarce to Value.					

Model 452

This is a premium grade side-by-side shotgun fitted with slide locks (removable). Offered in 12 gauge only with 26", 28", or 30" solid rib barrels. The receiver is a highly polished silver finish without engraving. Triggers may be double, single-selective, or single non-selective. The stock and forearm are special select walnut with fine line checkering with a choice of pistol or straight grip. Comes with leather hard case. Weighs about 6 lbs. 13 oz.

NIB	*Exc.*	*V.G.*	*Good*	*Fair*	*Poor*
24000	19000	14500	8500	4500	2500

Model 452 EELL

Same as above but furnished with fine scroll or game scene engraving. The highest grade of walnut is furnished for the stock and forearm. Leather case with accessories furnished.

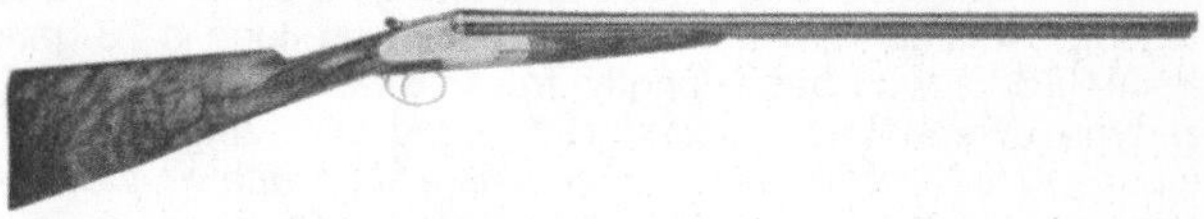

NIB	*Exc.*	*V.G.*	*Good*	*Fair*	*Poor*
31000	27500	19500	11000	7000	600

BERETTA ONYX SERIES

This series designation was first used in 2003 to simplify the product line. Instead of using numeric model references the company now refers to these guns and others by series name.

Onyx

This over-and-under gun is offered in 12, 20, and for 2003, 28 gauge. With a choice of 26" or 28" barrels. It features a boxlock action with select checkered walnut stock, single-selective trigger, schnabel forend and auto safety. Black rubber recoil pad. Blued barrels and action. Weight is about 6.8 lbs. for 12 gauge.

NIB	*Exc.*	*V.G.*	*Good*	*Fair*	*Poor*
1675	1350	950	650	475	200

Onyx Waterfowler 3.5

As above but in 12 gauge with 3.5" chamber and matte black finish.

NIB	Exc.	V.G.	Good	Fair	Poor
1750	1400	1050	700	500	250

White Onyx

Introduced in 2003 this model features a receiver machined in a jeweled pattern with satin nickel alloy. Offered in 12, 20, and 28 gauge with choice of 26" or 28" barrels. Select checkered walnut stock with schnabel forend. Weight is about 6.8 lbs. for 12 gauge.

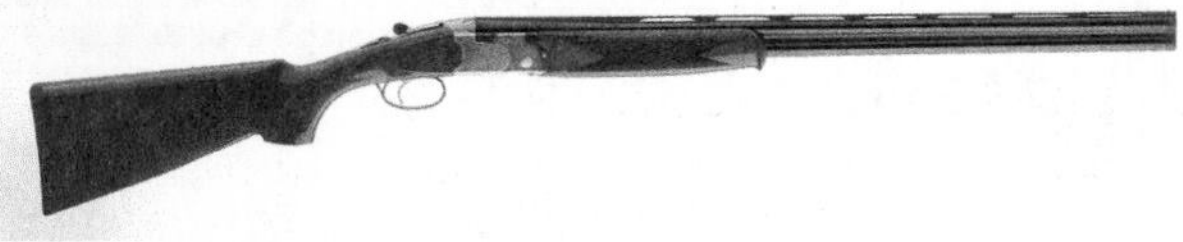

NIB	Exc.	V.G.	Good	Fair	Poor
1775	1425	1250	700	500	250

BERETTA ONYX PRO SERIES

This series designation was first used in 2003 to simplify the product line. Instead of using numeric model references the company now refers to these guns and others by series name.

Onyx Pro

Introduced in 2003 this over-and-under shotgun is offered in 12, 20 and 28 gauge with a choice of 26" or 28" vent rib barrels with choke tubes. Single-selective trigger. Checkered X-Tra wood stock. Gel-Tek recoil pad. Supplied with plastic carry case. Weight is about 6.8 lbs.

NIB	Exc.	V.G.	Good	Fair	Poor
1900	1475	1150	600	400	200

Onyx Pro 3.5

As above in 12 gauge with 3.5" chamber. Weight is approximately 6.9 lbs. Introduced in 2003.

NIB	Exc.	V.G.	Good	Fair	Poor
1970	1550	1250	650	450	225

BERETTA 682 SERIES

Model 682/682 Gold

This is a high-grade, quality-built O/U shotgun. Offered in 12 and 20 gauge, it is also available in some configurations in 28 gauge and .410 bore with barrel lengths from 26" to 34" depending on the type of shooting required. It is fitted with single-selective trigger and automatic ejectors. Barrels are fitted with ventilated rib and various fixed or screw-in choke combinations are available. The stock is a high-grade walnut with fine checkering in stock dimensions to fit the function of the gun. The frame is silver with light scroll borders on most models. This model covers a wide variety of applications and these are listed by grade and/or function: **NOTE:** The Beretta Competition series shotguns have been renamed as of 1994. These shotguns are also referred to as the 682 Gold Competition Series guns, such as Model 682 Gold Trap or Model 682 Gold X Trap Combo and so forth.

682 Super Skeet

This model is offered in 12 gauge only with 28" vent rib barrels choked skeet and skeet. Single-selective trigger and auto ejectors are standard. This Super Skeet features ported barrels and adjustable length of pull and drop. A fitted hard case is standard. Gun weighs 7 lbs. 8 oz.

NIB	Exc.	V.G.	Good	Fair	Poor
2900	1850	1500	1250	750	450

682 Skeet

This is the standard 12 gauge skeet model that features a choice of 26" or 28" vent rib barrels choked skeet and skeet. Walnut stock is of International dimensions with special skeet rubber recoil pad. Gun is supplied with hard case. Weighs 7 lbs. 8 oz.

NIB	Exc.	V.G.	Good	Fair	Poor
2600	1850	1500	1250	750	450

682 4 BBL Set

This skeet gun is fitted with 4 barrels in 12, 20, 28 gauge, and .410 bore. Each barrel is 28", choked skeet and skeet, and fitted with a vent rib.

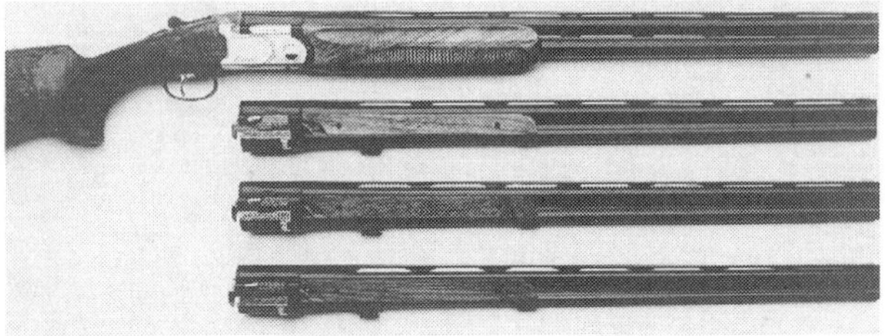

NIB	Exc.	V.G.	Good	Fair	Poor
5500	4000	3500	3000	2000	650

682 Super Sporting/682 Gold Sporting Ported

Built for sporting clays this 12 gauge or 20 gauge model features ported barrel and adjustable length of pull and drop. Fitted with 28" or 30" vent barrel with screw-in chokes; fixed chokes on special order. Checkered walnut stock with pistol grip and recoil pad. Supplied with case. Introduced in 1993. Weight of 12 gauge is 7 lbs. 8 oz. and 20 gauge weighs 6 lbs. 3 oz.

NIB	Exc.	V.G.	Good	Fair	Poor
2400	2000	1600	1100	700	350

682 Sporting/682 Gold Sporting

The standard version of the 12 gauge or 20 gauge Super Sporting model with a choice of 28" or 30" vent rib barrel with screw-in chokes. Checkered walnut stock with recoil pad. Introduced in 1993.

NIB	Exc.	V.G.	Good	Fair	Poor
2900	1950	1500	1250	950	350

682 Sporting Combo

Similar to the 682 Sporting with the addition of two 12 gauge 28" and 30" barrel fitted with screw-in chokes. Supplied with hard case.

NIB	Exc.	V.G.	Good	Fair	Poor
3500	2700	2250	1750	1250	650

682 Super Trap

This 12 gauge trap model (a 20 gauge set of barrels is available on special order) features ported 30" or 32" ventilated rib barrels with either fixed or screw-in chokes. Automatic ejectors are standard as is a single non-selective trigger. The checkered walnut stock can be adjusted for length of pull and drop of comb and is offered in either Monte Carlo or International dimensions. Weight is approximately 8 lbs. 6 oz.

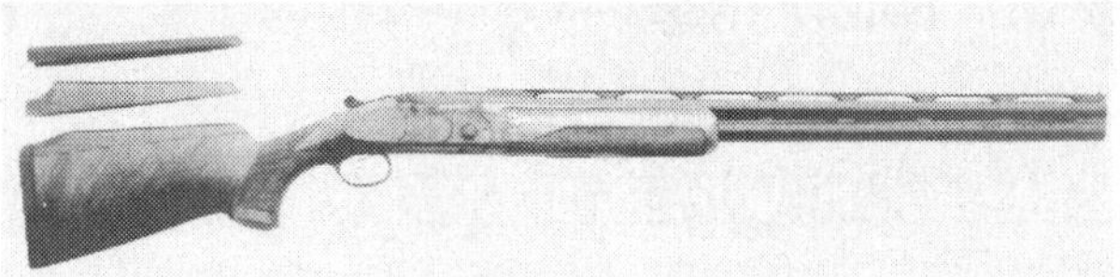

NIB	Exc.	V.G.	Good	Fair	Poor
2900	2150	1700	1250	950	500

682 Top Single Super Trap

Same as the Super Trap but available in a single barrel configuration of either 32" or 34".

NIB	Exc.	V.G.	Good	Fair	Poor
2600	2150	1700	1350	950	500

682 Top Combo Super Trap

This configuration features a single barrel and an O/U barrel, both interchangeable. The combinations are: 30", 32", and 30", 34".

NIB	Exc.	V.G.	Good	Fair	Poor
3300	2975	2350	1750	1250	650

682 Trap

This model is the standard variation Beretta Trap gun. This 12 gauge comes standard with 30" vent rib barrels. However, 28" and 32" barrel can be special ordered. Fixed or screw-in chokes are available. The three-position sliding trigger allows for adjustable length of pull. A checkered walnut stock with recoil pad is standard. Stock is available in either Monte Carlo or International dimensions. Customer has choice of either silver or black receiver. Comes cased.

NIB	Exc.	V.G.	Good	Fair	Poor
2900	1950	1700	1250	900	450

682 Top Single Trap

This 12 gauge single barrel trap gun is available in 32" or 34" vent rib barrel.

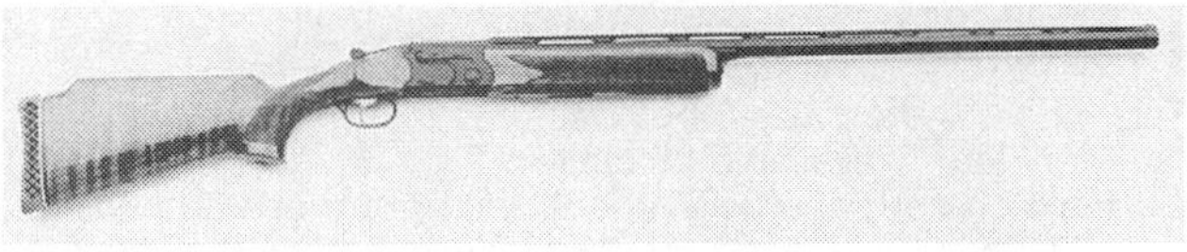

NIB	Exc.	V.G.	Good	Fair	Poor
2400	1950	1750	1250	900	450

682 Mono Combo Trap

A special configuration that features a single barrel with vent rib set to place single barrel in bottom position of what would normally be an O/U setup. A second barrel that is an O/U is also provided as part of the set. Single barrel is 34" and the O/U set is 32" in length.

NIB	Exc.	V.G.	Good	Fair	Poor
2900	2650	2050	1550	950	500

682 Top Combo

This trap combination features a standard placement single barrel with an interchangeable O/U barrel. Barrel available in 30", 32"; 30", 34"; and 32", 34". Barrels are fitted with ventilated rib.

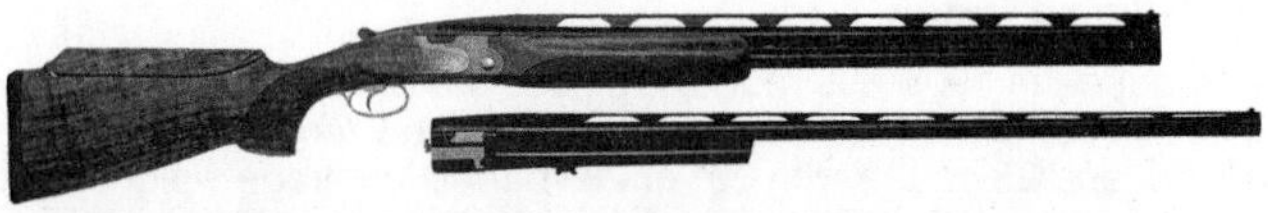

NIB	Exc.	V.G.	Good	Fair	Poor
3000	2750	2050	1350	950	500

682 Gold Trap with Adjustable Stock

Introduced in 1998 this over-and-under features a choice of 30" or 32" barrels with Monte Carlo stock and adjustable drop, cast, and comb. Trigger is adjustable for length of pull. Selected walnut stock with oil finish. Black rubber recoil pad standard. Weight is approximately 8.8 lbs.

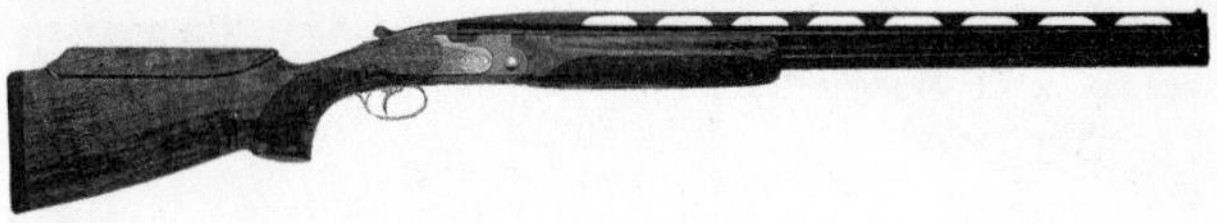

NIB	Exc.	V.G.	Good	Fair	Poor
3950	2900	1950	—	—	—

NOTE: Add $800 for Top Combo set.

682 Gold Skeet with Adjustable Stock

Introduced in 1999 this 12 gauge model features skeet stock with adjustable comb. Stock drop and cast may also be adjusted. Greystone receiver. Comes with case. Offered in choice of 28" or 30" barrels. Single-selective trigger adjustable for length of pull. Black rubber recoil pad standard. Weight is about 7.5 lbs.

NIB	Exc.	V.G.	Good	Fair	Poor
3700	2900	2050	—	—	—

682 Gold "Live Bird"

Introduced in 1995 this model has a gray receiver with select walnut stock. Single-selective is adjustable for length of pull. Offered in 12 gauge only with 30" barrels. Average weight is 8.8 lbs.

NIB	Exc.	V.G.	Good	Fair	Poor
2550	1950	1595	1150	850	400

S682 Gold E Trap

Chambered for 12 gauge 3" chambers with choice of 30" or 32" barrels with overbore and choke tubes. Highly select walnut stock with black rubber pad. Single-selective trigger with adjustable length of pull. Beavertail forend. Adjustable Monte Carlo stock. Front white bead with mid bead sight. Carry case standard. Weight is about 8.8 lbs. Introduced in 2001.

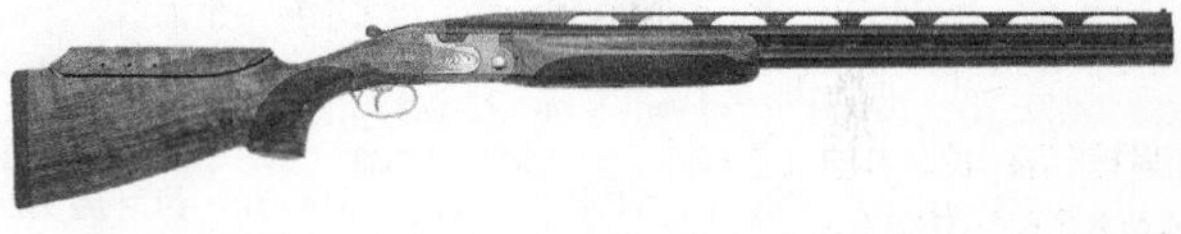

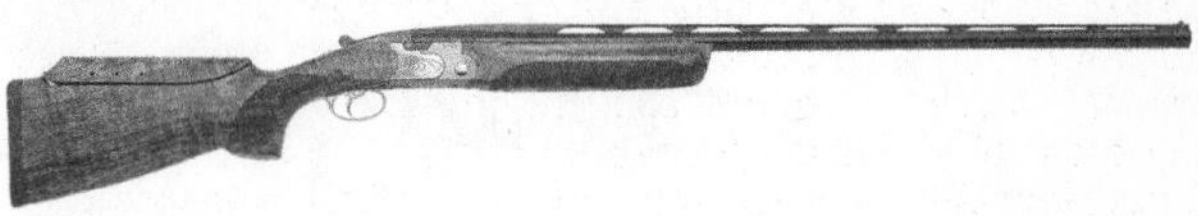

NIB	Exc.	V.G.	Good	Fair	Poor
4600	3700	2750	1800	900	450

S682 Gold E Trap Combo

Offers the same features as the Trap model but with interchangeable over-and-under barrels and top single barrel with under rib. Introduced in 2001.

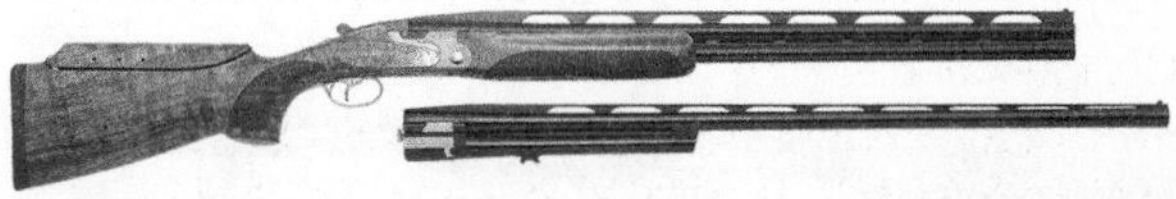

NIB	Exc.	V.G.	Good	Fair	Poor
5600	4400	3100	1700	800	350

S682 Gold E Skeet

This 12 gauge skeet gun features a special skeet-style stock with beavertail forend. Adjustable stock. Barrel lengths are 28" or 30". Single-selective trigger. Weight is about 7.5 lbs. Introduced in 2001.

NIB	Exc.	V.G.	Good	Fair	Poor
4600	3600	2750	1500	625	350

S682 Gold E Sporting

This 12 gauge model has a choice of 28", 30", or 32" barrels with extended choke tubes and tapered top rib with white front sight and mid bead. Sporting clay-style stock of select walnut. Weight is about 7.6 lbs. Introduced in 2001.

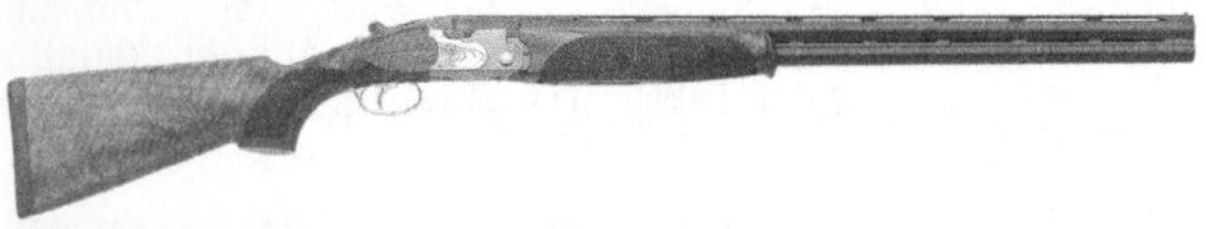

NIB	Exc.	V.G.	Good	Fair	Poor
4150	3200	2350	1200	475	300

Model 685

A lower priced O/U chambered for 12 or 20 gauge with 3" chambers, a satin-chromed boxlock action with a single trigger and extractors. Not imported after 1986.

NIB	Exc.	V.G.	Good	Fair	Poor
—	750	675	550	375	200

BERETTA 686 SERIES

Model 686/686 Silver Perdiz Sporting

This Beretta O/U shotgun is available in a number of different configurations. This basic model features ventilated rib barrels from 24" to 30"; 30" is a special order. Screw-in chokes or fixed chokes are available. All configurations are offered in 12 gauge and 20 gauge with 28 gauge and .410 bore available in special order only. The gun is fitted with checkered American walnut stock with black rubber recoil pad and special grip cap. Some models have silver receiver with scroll engraving and others have black receivers with gold-filled contours. This 686 series was renamed in 1994.

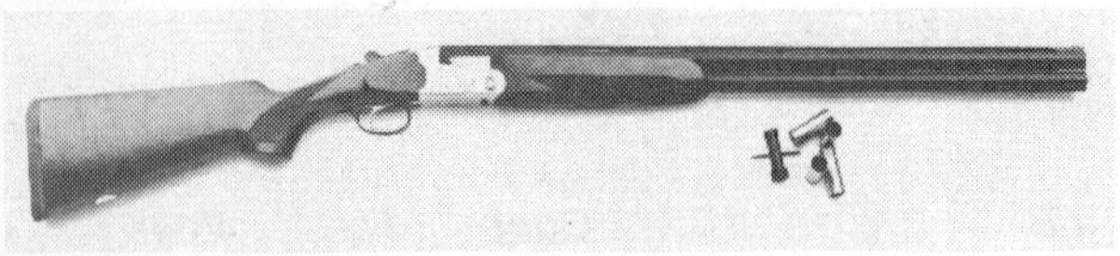

Model 686 Essential/Silver Essential

Introduced in 1994 this 686 model is designed to be an entry level 686. It offers all of the mechanical features of the 686 series without any of the frills. Offered in 12 gauge only with 26" or 28" barrels with open-side rib. Plain walnut stock with checkering and plain blue receiver. Weighs about 6.7 lbs. Renamed the Silver Essential in 1997.

NIB	Exc.	V.G.	Good	Fair	Poor
900	750	600	450	350	200

686 Ultra Light Onyx

This model features a black anodized light alloy receiver accented with an engraved gold-filled "P. Beretta" signature. Available in 12 gauge only with 26" or 28" vent rib barrels. Chokes are either fixed or screw-in type. Weighs 5 lbs. 1 oz.

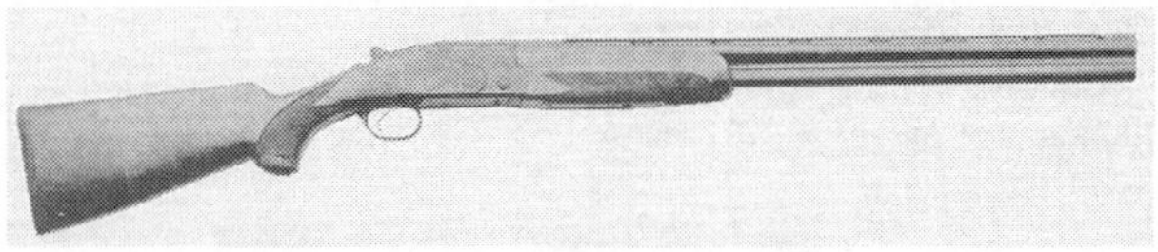

NIB	Exc.	V.G.	Good	Fair	Poor
1050	850	750	600	500	400

686 Onyx

Similar in appearance to the Ultra Light Onyx, but available in either 12 gauge or 20 gauge with vent rib barrel lengths from 26" to 28". Chambers are either 3" or 3.5". Checkered walnut stock offered in pistol grip or straight grip. Choice of choke types. Weight of 12 gauge 6 lbs.13 oz.; 20 gauge 6 lbs. 3 oz. A 12 gauge version with 3-1/2" chambers and 28" barrel is offered (new in 1999) with matte wood finish, matte black receiver, beavertail forend with fingerwells, and silver finish trigger.

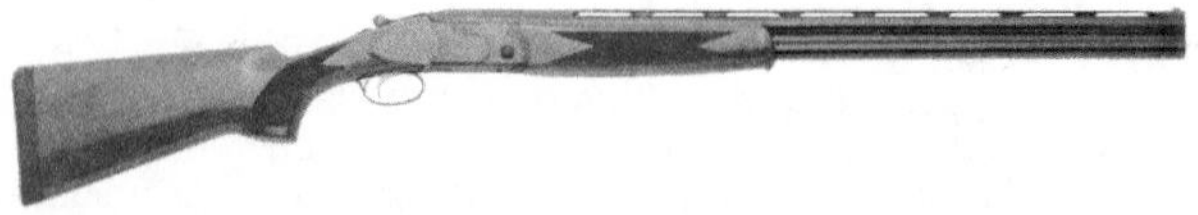

NIB	Exc.	V.G.	Good	Fair	Poor
1800	1350	950	650	500	400

686 Onyx 2 BBL Set

Same as above but supplied with a 20 gauge 28" vent rib barrel and a 28 gauge 26" vent rib barrel.

NIB	Exc.	V.G.	Good	Fair	Poor
2100	1650	1500	800	650	500

686 Silver Receiver

This model is the basic 686. It features a plain semi-matte silver receiver and is available in either 12 or 20 gauge; 28 gauge available on special order. Vent rib barrels are offered in lengths from 24" to 30" with fixed chokes or choke tubes.

NIB	Exc.	V.G.	Good	Fair	Poor
1200	895	775	650	500	400

686 L/686 Silver Perdiz

Same as above but furnished with a scroll engraved silver receiver. Offered in 28 gauge with 26" or 28" vent rib barrels. Gun weighs 5 lbs. 5 oz.

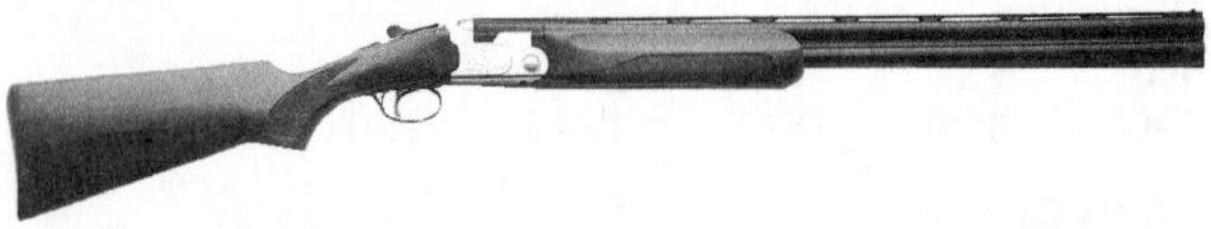

NIB	Exc.	V.G.	Good	Fair	Poor
1200	950	750	650	500	400

686 Silver Pigeon

Introduced in 1996 this model replaces the Silver Perdiz. It has an electroless nickel finish on a scroll engraved receiver. Offered in 12, 20, and 28 gauge with 26" or 28" barrels. Average weight is 6.8 lbs. A new variation, introduced in 1999, features a 20 gauge gun with 28" barrels, straight grip stock, and matte nickel receiver.

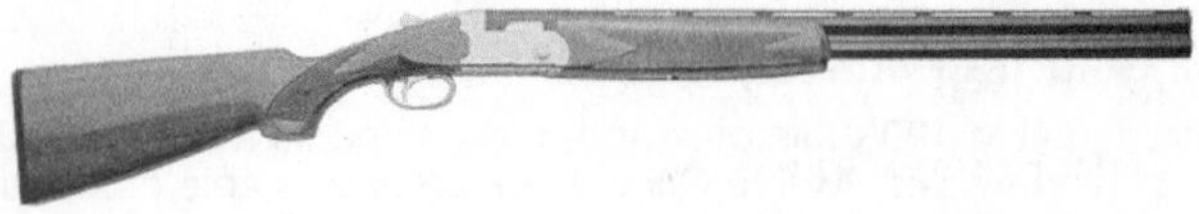

NIB	Exc.	V.G.	Good	Fair	Poor
1800	1450	950	600	400	200

686 Silver Pigeon Sporting

NIB	Exc.	V.G.	Good	Fair	Poor
1500	1050	750	600	400	200

686 Silver Pigeon Trap (30")

NIB	Exc.	V.G.	Good	Fair	Poor
1800	1400	900	700	500	300

686 Silver Pigeon Trap Top Mono (32" or 34")

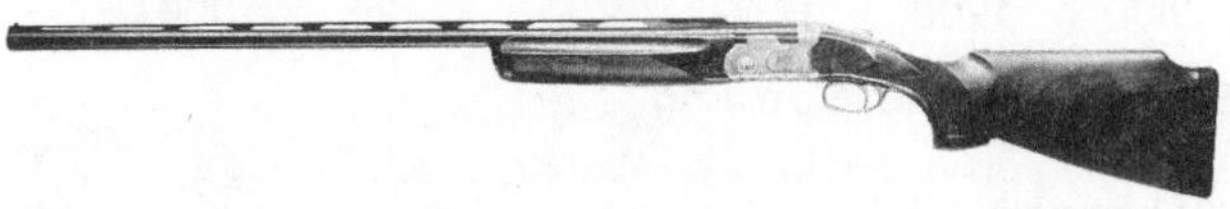

NIB	Exc.	V.G.	Good	Fair	Poor
1800	1400	900	700	500	300

686 Silver Pigeon S

Essentially the same as the Silver Pigeon models but packaged with a carrying case that includes five choke tubes, accessory recoil pad, and sling swivels. A .410-bore offering on a proportionally smaller receiver was added in 2006.

NIB	Exc.	V.G.	Good	Fair	Poor
2000	1600	1275	825	575	350

NOTE: Add $700 for two barrel 20/28 gauge set.

686E Sporting

Offered in 12 or 20 gauge with choice of 28" or 30" barrels. Five Beretta screw-in chokes. Modern ellipsis receiver engraving. Special carrying case. Introduced with new styling in 2001.

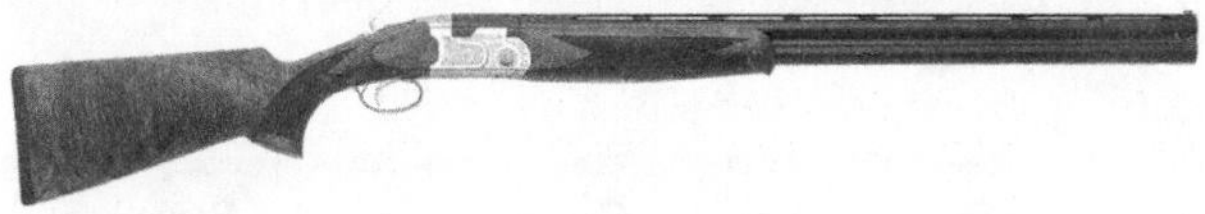

NIB	Exc.	V.G.	Good	Fair	Poor
2100	1700	1350	825	575	350

686 EL/Gold Perdiz

This model is available in 12 gauge or 20 gauge with 26" or 28" vent rib barrels. The receiver is silver with scroll engraving and fitted with side plates. A fitted hard case comes with the gun.

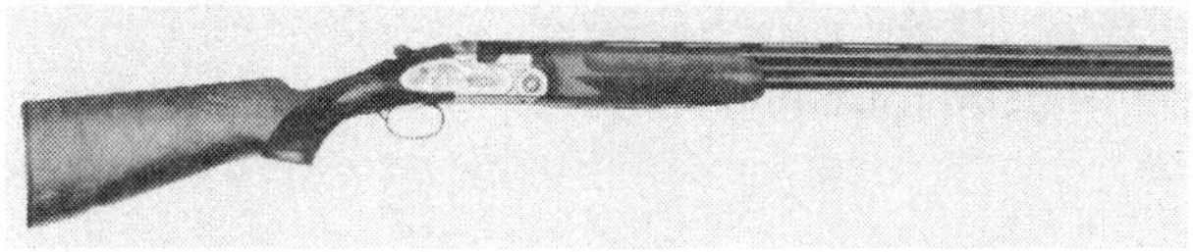

NIB	Exc.	V.G.	Good	Fair	Poor
1900	1350	1100	800	700	350

686 Hunter Sport

A sporting clay 12 gauge or 20 gauge shotgun that features a silver receiver with scroll engraving. Wide 12.5mm target rib. Radiused recoil pad. Offered in 26" or 28" vent rib barrels with screw-in chokes. Offered for the first time in 1993.

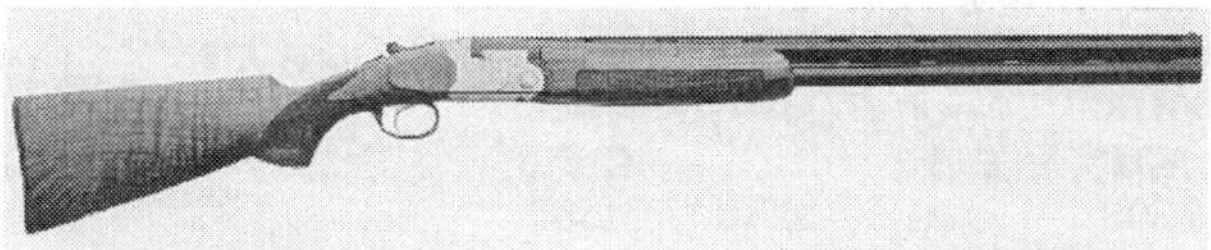

NIB	Exc.	V.G.	Good	Fair	Poor
1200	950	750	600	500	250

686 Onyx Hunter Sport

Same as above but offered in 12 gauge only with matte black finish on receiver and barrels. Weighs 6 lbs.13 oz. Introduced in 1993.

NIB	Exc.	V.G.	Good	Fair	Poor
1100	850	650	600	500	250

WING SERIES

This series designation was first used in 2003 to simplify the product line. Instead of using numeric model references the company now refers to these guns and others by series name.

686 Whitewing

Introduced in the fall of 1998, this over-and-under shotgun is chambered for the 12 gauge shell and fitted with 26" or 28" barrels with Beretta's choke system. The receiver is polished nickel with engraved game scenes, and gold-plated trigger. Walnut pistol-grip stock with gloss finish.

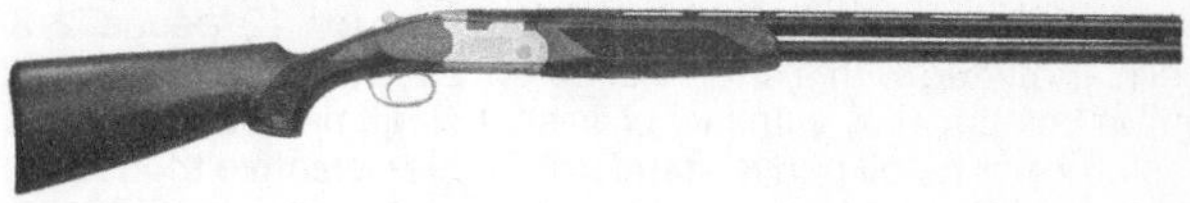

NIB	Exc.	V.G.	Good	Fair	Poor
1350	1025	800	550	375	250

686 Blackwing

This model, introduced in 2002, is similar to the Whitewing model with the exception of a blued receiver and schnabel forend.

NIB	Exc.	V.G.	Good	Fair	Poor
1450	1100	900	600	425	300

686 Sporting Combo

Same specifications as the Hunter Sport with the addition of an interchangeable 30" 12 gauge barrel.

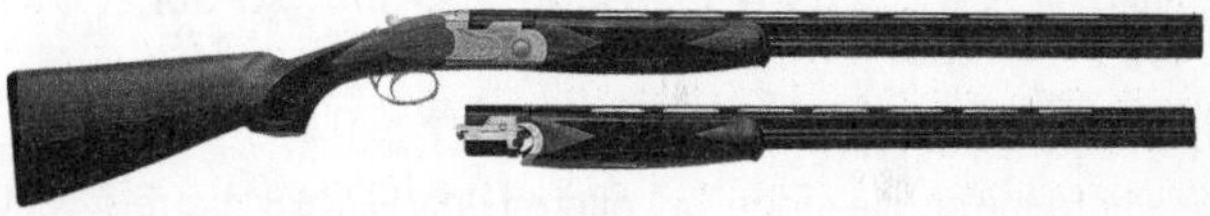

NIB	Exc.	V.G.	Good	Fair	Poor
1900	1600	1250	1000	700	325

686 Collection Trap

Introduced in 1996 this model features a special multi-colored stock and forend. Offered in 12 gauge only with 30" barrels. Factory recoil pad standard. Average weight is 7.7 lbs.

NIB	Exc.	V.G.	Good	Fair	Poor
1500	1000	750	500	400	300

686 Collection Sport

Similar to above but offered with 28" barrels.

NIB	Exc.	V.G.	Good	Fair	Poor
1500	975	750	500	400	300

686 Quail Unlimited 2002 Covey Limited Edition

Offered in 20 or 28 gauge with 26" or 28" vent rib barrels. Choke tubes. Engraved receiver with gold quail inlays. Weight is about 6.8 lbs.

NIB	Exc.	V.G.	Good	Fair	Poor
1950	1550	1250	1000	700	325

686 Ringneck Pheasants Forever

Introduced in 2003 this model is chambered for 12 or 20 gauge and fitted with 26" or 28" vent rib barrels. Checkered walnut stock with pistol grip. Single-selective trigger. Gel-Tek recoil pad. Schnabel forend. Weight is about 6.8 lbs. on 12 gauge.

NIB	*Exc.*	*V.G.*	*Good*	*Fair*	*Poor*
2025	1550	1100	750	450	275

ULTRALIGHT SERIES

This series designation was first used in 2003 to simplify the product line. Instead of using numeric model references the company now refers to these guns and others by series name.

Ultralight

This over-and-under model is chambered for 12 gauge 2-3/4" shells and fitted with a choice of 26" or 28" barrels. The receiver is light aluminum alloy with nickel finish with game scene engraving. Black rubber recoil pad is standard. Single-selective trigger, pistol grip, and schnabel forearm. Weight is approximately 5.75 lbs.

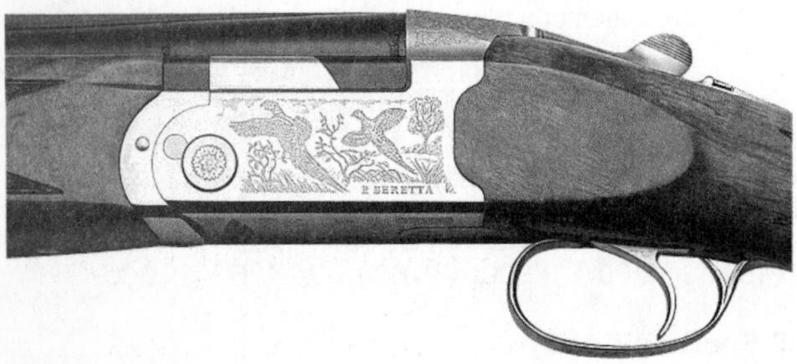

Ultralight Receiver close-up

NIB	*Exc.*	*V.G.*	*Good*	*Fair*	*Poor*
1900	1500	900	600	375	175

Ultralight Deluxe

Similar to the above model but offered only with 28" barrels. Nickel receiver is gold game scene engraved. First offered in 1998.

NIB	*Exc.*	*V.G.*	*Good*	*Fair*	*Poor*
2400	2000	1600	1100	700	350

BERETTA 687/PIGEON SERIES

This series designation was first used in 2003 to simplify the product line. Instead of using numeric model references the company now refers to these guns and others by series name.

Model 687/687 Silver Pigeon Sporting

This model is similar to the Model 686 but in a slightly more ornate version. This series was renamed in 1994.

687 L/Silver Pigeon

This model is offered in 12 gauge or 20 gauge with 26" or 28" vent rib barrels. The boxlock receiver is scroll engraved with game scenes. Auto ejectors and double or single triggers are offered.

NIB	*Exc.*	*V.G.*	*Good*	*Fair*	*Poor*
1800	1100	950	800	650	300

687 Silver Pigeon II

Introduced in 1999, this model features a deep relief game scene engraving on a silver receiver. Select walnut stock with oil finish. Available in 12 gauge only with choice of 26" or 28" vent rib barrels. Single-selective trigger. Weight is about 6.8 lbs.

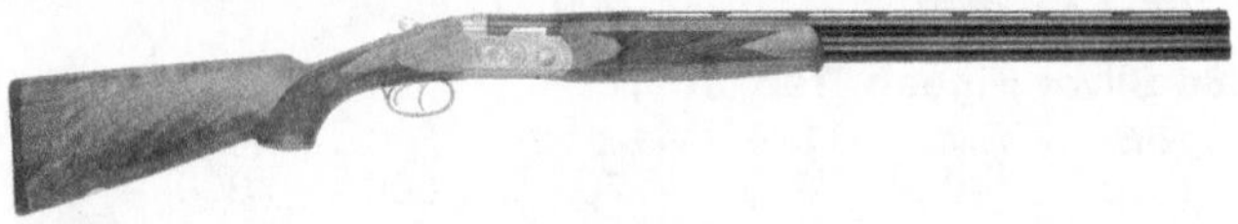

NIB	*Exc.*	*V.G.*	*Good*	*Fair*	*Poor*
2500	1900	1250	700	425	300

687 Silver Pigeon Sporting

A sporting clays version available in 12 or 20 gauge with 28" or 30" barrels.

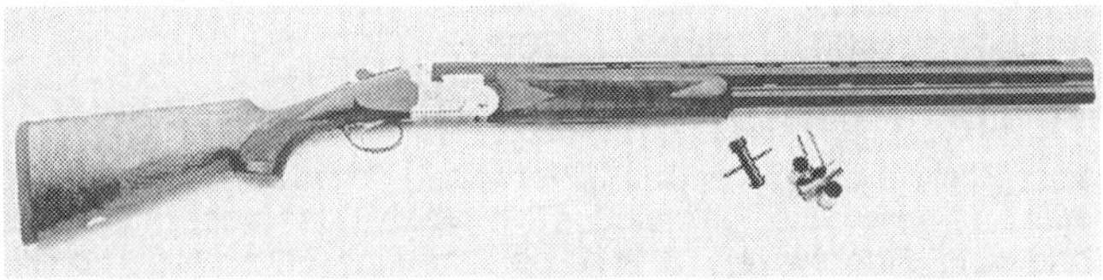

NIB	*Exc.*	*V.G.*	*Good*	*Fair*	*Poor*
1900	1400	1000	700	425	300

687 Silver Pigeon II Sporting

Introduced in 1999, this model features a deep relief engraving with oil finished select walnut stock with schnabel forend. Single-selective trigger. Offered in 12 gauge only with choice of 28" or 30" barrels. Black rubber recoil pad. Weight is about 7.7 lbs.

NIB	*Exc.*	*V.G.*	*Good*	*Fair*	*Poor*
2500	1900	1250	800	475	325

Silver Pigeon S

New in 2007, the Silver Pigeon S Series features scroll and floral engraving on a satin nickel-alloy finished receiver. It is available in 12, 20 and 28 gauge with 26" or 28" barrels, and .410 bore with 28" barrels. All come with five chokes. Weight is about 6.8 lbs.

NIB	*Exc.*	*V.G.*	*Good*	*Fair*	*Poor*
1800	1475	900	600	375	275

Silver Pigeon S Combo

Combo model comes with 26" 20 gauge barrels and 28" 28 gauge barrels.

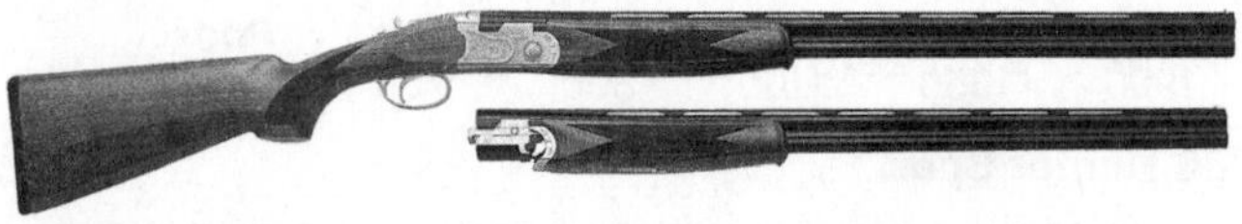

NIB	*Exc.*	*V.G.*	*Good*	*Fair*	*Poor*
2200	1875	100	900	600	300

687 Sporting Combo

Offered in 12 gauge only with two sets of 12 gauge interchangeable vent rib barrels in 28" and 30".

NIB	*Exc.*	*V.G.*	*Good*	*Fair*	*Poor*
2500	2100	1850	1500	750	400

687 Silver Pigeon IV

Introduced in 2003 for the U.S. market this shotgun features a black finish receiver with full scroll engraving with gold-filled game birds. Select oil-finished walnut stock with Gel-Tek recoil pad. Offered in 12, 20, or 28 gauge with 26" or 28" barrels. Single-selective trigger with fluted beavertail forend. Weight is about 6.8 lbs. in 12 gauge.

NIB	Exc.	V.G.	Good	Fair	Poor
2665	1950	1850	1500	750	400

687 Silver Pigeon V

This is the top-of-the-line model in the Silver Pigeon Series. Available in 12, 20 and 28 gauges with 26" and 28" barrels and .410-bore (added in 2006). Pistol-grip stock of richly figured walnut with oil finish. Color case-hardened receiver with gold-filled game bird inlays. English stocked versions of the 20 and 28 gauges and .410 bore were added in 2006.

NIB	Exc.	V.G.	Good	Fair	Poor
3595	2400	1700	1250	750	375

687 EL/687 GOLD PIGEON

This model is offered with scroll engraved gold inlaid game animals. Fitted with side plates. The stock is highly figured walnut with fine line checkering. Available in 12, 20, 28 gauge or .410 bore in 26" or 28" vent rib barrels with screw-in chokes. Comes with fitted hard case. Weights for 12 gauge: 6 lbs. 13 oz.; 20 gauge: 6 lbs. 3 oz.; 28/.410: 5 lbs. 5 oz. Series was renamed in 1994.

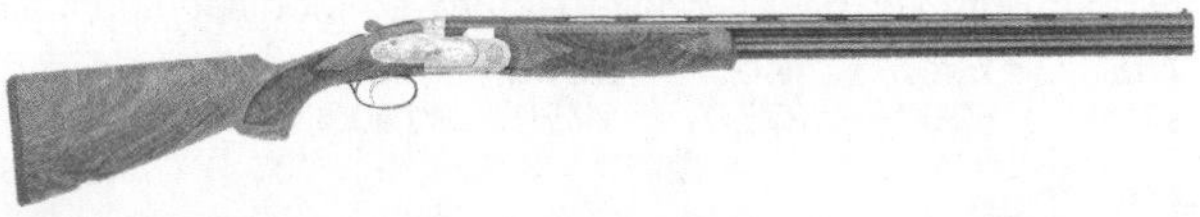

687 EL 12 and 20 gauge

NIB	Exc.	V.G.	Good	Fair	Poor
3400	2450	1800	1200	750	350

687 EL 28/.410

NIB	Exc.	V.G.	Good	Fair	Poor
3450	2500	1850	1250	800	400

687 EL Gold Pigeon Sporting

A sporting clays model chambered for 12 gauge and fitted with 28" or 30" vent rib barrels. Offered new in 1993. Comes with fitted hard case.

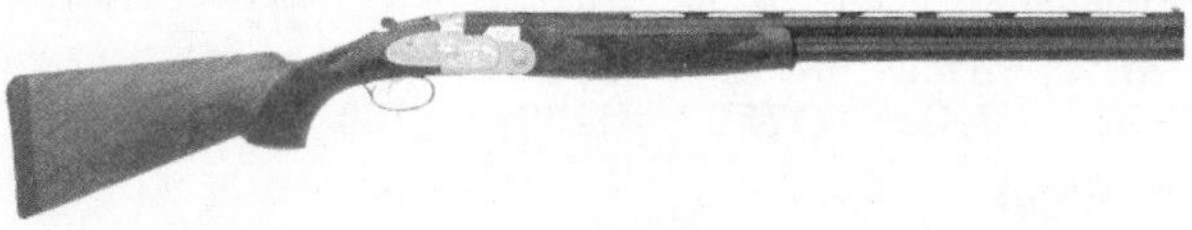

NIB	Exc.	V.G.	Good	Fair	Poor
3400	2450	1750	1250	900	450

687 EELL/DIAMOND PIGEON

Same as above, including gauge and barrel offerings, but furnished with more fully figured walnut and finer checkering. Fitted with side plates that are scroll engraved with fine cut game scenes. This grade is also available in a straight grip English stock version in 20 gauge as well as a combo set of 20 gauge and 28 gauge interchangeable 26" barrels. All 687 EELL Models are fitted with hard case. Series was renamed in 1994.

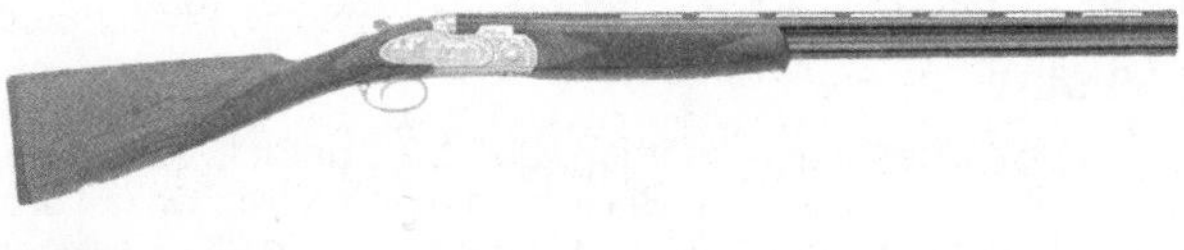

687 EELL 12 and 20 gauge

NIB	Exc.	V.G.	Good	Fair	Poor
5900	3250	2250	1500	1000	400

687 EELL 28 gauge and .410 bore

NIB	Exc.	V.G.	Good	Fair	Poor
6000	3500	2500	1750	1250	450

687 EELL Combo

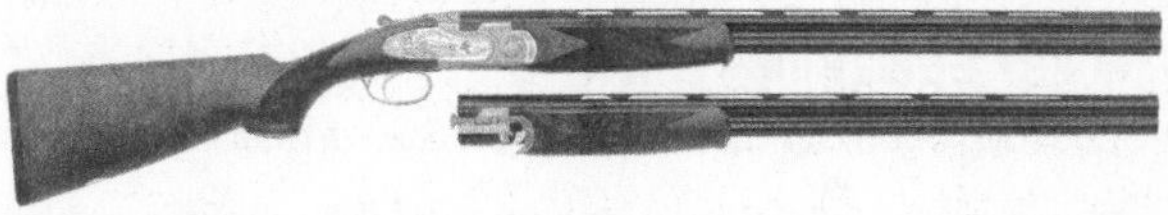

NIB	Exc.	V.G.	Good	Fair	Poor
6900	5250	4000	2250	1300	500

687 EELL DIAMOND PIGEON SKEET

Same as above with the addition of a skeet configuration. A 12 gauge version is offered with 28" vent rib barrels choked skeet and skeet. Weighs about 7 lbs. 8 oz. A 4 barrel set is also offered with interchangeable 12, 20, 28 gauge, and .410 bore barrels choked Skeet and Skeet.

687 EELL 12 gauge

NIB	Exc.	V.G.	Good	Fair	Poor
4800	3700	2500	1750	1450	475

687 EELL 4 BBL Set

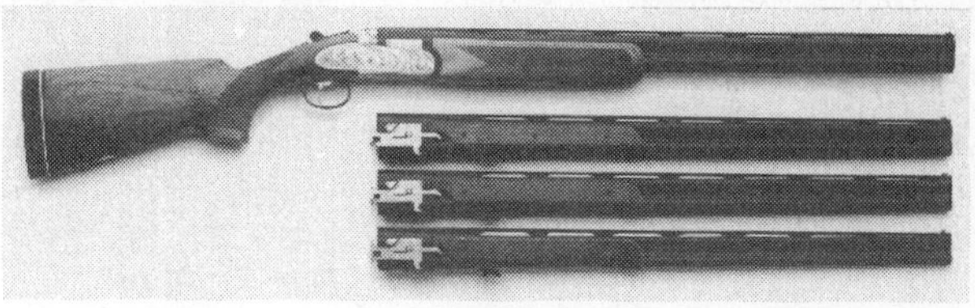

NIB	Exc.	V.G.	Good	Fair	Poor
6400	5000	4500	3750	2500	1500

687 EELL Diamond Pigeon Skeet with Adjustable Stock

Same as the Skeet version above but with adjustable comb, drop and cast. Introduced in 1999.

NIB	Exc.	V.G.	Good	Fair	Poor
6250	4500	3750	2500	1500	500

687 EELL Diamond Pigeon Sporting

A sporting clays version of the 687 EELL in 12 gauge only with 28" vent rib barrels fitted with screw-in chokes.

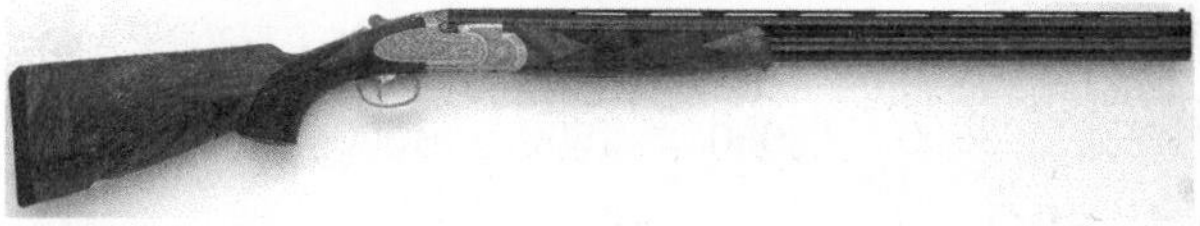

NIB	Exc.	V.G.	Good	Fair	Poor
2000	4750	3500	2500	1750	1200

687 EELL Trap

This model is fitted with either International or Monte Carlo trap stock dimensions. Offered in 12 gauge with 30" vent rib barrels fixed or screw-in choke tubes. Weighs about 8 lbs. 6 oz.

NIB	Exc.	V.G.	Good	Fair	Poor
4000	3000	2500	2000	1500	1000

687 EELL Top Combo

A single barrel trap gun with choice of one single barrel set and one Over/Under steel rod barrel in either 30" and 32" or 32" and 34".

NIB	Exc.	V.G.	Good	Fair	Poor
4700	3500	3000	2250	2000	1000

Model 687 EELL King Ranch

Introduced in 2005. Too scarce to value. Seek a qualified appraisal.

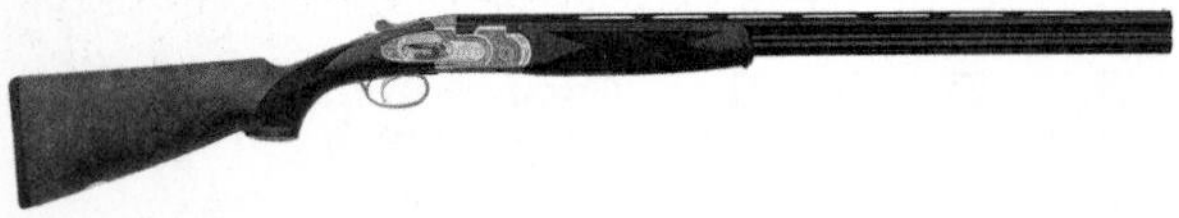

Model 626 Field Grade

A 12 or 20 gauge boxlock double barrel shotgun with a 26" or 28" barrel, various choke combinations, single trigger and automatic ejectors. Engraved, blued with a checkered walnut stock. Imported between 1984 and 1988.

NIB	Exc.	V.G.	Good	Fair	Poor
—	1000	825	700	575	475

626 Onyx

This model is a boxlock side-by-side shotgun offered in 12 gauge and 20 gauge. With choice of 26" or 28" solid rib barrels with screw-in chokes. Double triggers are standard but single trigger is available on request. Receiver is anti-glare black matte finish. Stock is walnut with hand checkering and pistol grip. The 12 gauge weighs 6 lbs. 13 oz. and the 20 gauge weighs 6 lbs. 13 oz.

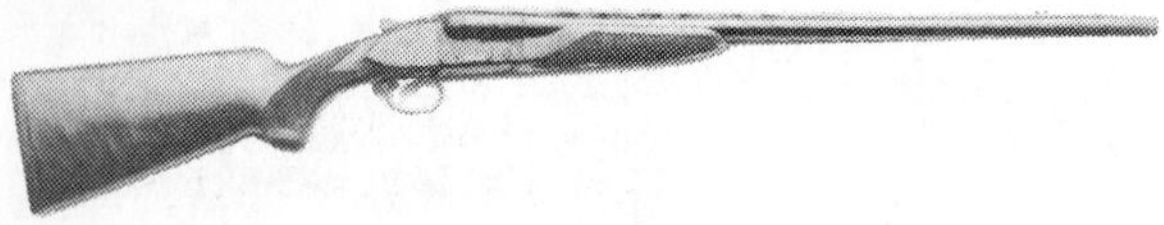

NIB	Exc.	V.G.	Good	Fair	Poor
1350	950	850	750	500	400

627 EL

This model is offered in 12 gauge only with choice of 26" or 28" solid rib barrels. The walnut is highly figured and fine cut checkered. The receiver is silver with side plates engraved with scroll. Comes with hard case.

NIB	Exc.	V.G.	Good	Fair	Poor
2600	2000	1750	1500	1250	650

627 EELL

Same as above but fitted with scroll engraved side plates with game scenes. Walnut is highly figured with fine line checkering. A straight-grip stock is also offered in this model. Comes with hard case.

NIB	Exc.	V.G.	Good	Fair	Poor
3850	3500	3000	2500	1500	1000

Model FS-1

A single-barrel boxlock shotgun in all gauges and a 26" or 28", full choke barrel. Blued with a checkered walnut stock. This model was also known as the "Companion."

NIB	Exc.	V.G.	Good	Fair	Poor
—	300	225	175	125	90

TR-1 Trap

A 12 gauge, single-barrel boxlock trap gun, 32" ventilated rib, full choke barrel. Blued with a checkered, Monte Carlo stock. Manufactured between 1968 and 1971.

NIB	Exc.	V.G.	Good	Fair	Poor
—	375	250	200	150	100

TR-2 Trap

As above, with a high, competition-type vent rib. It was manufactured between 1969 and 1973.

NIB	Exc.	V.G.	Good	Fair	Poor
—	400	275	225	175	125

Mark II Trap

A 12 gauge, boxlock single-barrel trap shotgun with a 32" or 34", full-choke barrel, competition-type rib and automatic ejector. Blued with a checkered, Monte Carlo type, walnut stock. Manufactured between 1972 and 1976.

NIB	Exc.	V.G.	Good	Fair	Poor
—	800	625	525	450	275

Model ASE 90/Gold Series

This is a competition trap model Over/Under shotgun. It features a trigger lock assembly that is removable in the field so a spare can be used in the event of failure. The single non-selective trigger has a three way adjustment. The ventilated rib is wide and the side ribs are also ventilated. Walnut stock and forearms are interchangeable. Special trap recoil pad is standard. Receiver is silver with gold inlays or blued on special order. The ASE 90 weighs about 8 lbs. 6 oz.

ASE 90 Pigeon

Equipped with 28" barrels choked Improved Modified and Full.

NIB	Exc.	V.G.	Good	Fair	Poor
6750	5250	3750	2750	1200	500

ASE 90 Trap

Comes standard with 30" vent rib barrels.

NIB	Exc.	V.G.	Good	Fair	Poor
5950	5250	3750	2750	1200	500

ASE 90 Gold X Trap Combo

Introduced in 1993 this set features a single barrel and interchangeable Over/Under barrels in 30", 32" and 30", 34" combinations.

NIB	Exc.	V.G.	Good	Fair	Poor
6950	2500	1750	1200	700	350

ASE 90 Skeet

This model is a skeet version of the ASE 90 series. Features the same basic specifications as the trap model but configured for competition skeet. Offered in 12 gauge only with 28" Skeet and Skeet chokes. Weighs about 7 lbs. 11 oz.

NIB	Exc.	V.G.	Good	Fair	Poor
5950	2500	1750	1200	700	350

ASE 90 Sporting Clay

Configured for sporting clay competition. Offered in 12 gauge only with 28" or 30" vent rib barrels.

NIB	Exc.	V.G.	Good	Fair	Poor
6950	5200	4000	3000	1500	1000

Model SL-2

A 12 gauge slide action shotgun, 26", 28", or 30", ventilated rib barrels with various chokes. Blued with a checkered walnut stock. Manufactured between 1968 and 1971.

NIB	Exc.	V.G.	Good	Fair	Poor
—	350	300	250	200	150

PIGEON SERIES

As above, in three grades.

Silver Pigeon

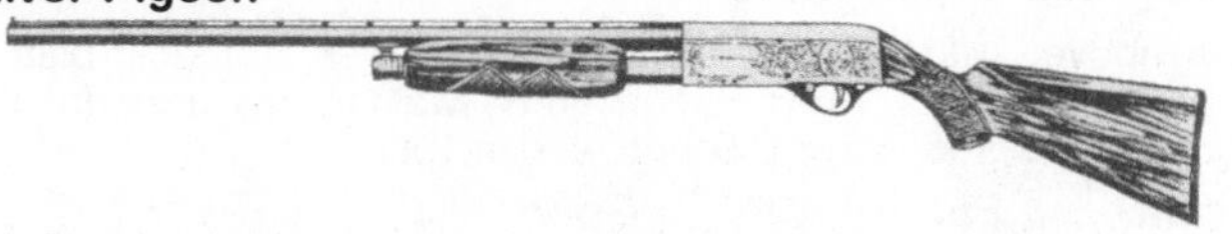

NIB	Exc.	V.G.	Good	Fair	Poor
—	300	250	200	150	110

Gold Pigeon

NIB	Exc.	V.G.	Good	Fair	Poor
—	450	400	300	250	200

Ruby Pigeon

NIB	Exc.	V.G.	Good	Fair	Poor
—	600	550	450	375	275

DT 10 TRIDENT SERIES

These shotguns feature removable trigger mechanism, overbored barrels, and special choke tubes.

Trap

This is a 12 gauge over/under gun with a number of options. The barrel is 30" or 32" and the highly select walnut stock is fitted with a Monte Carlo comb. Stock is also adjustable. Rib type is 3/8" with progressive step. Full black rubber recoil pad. Weight is about 8.8 lbs. A top single model is also offered with 34" barrel. Introduced in 2000.

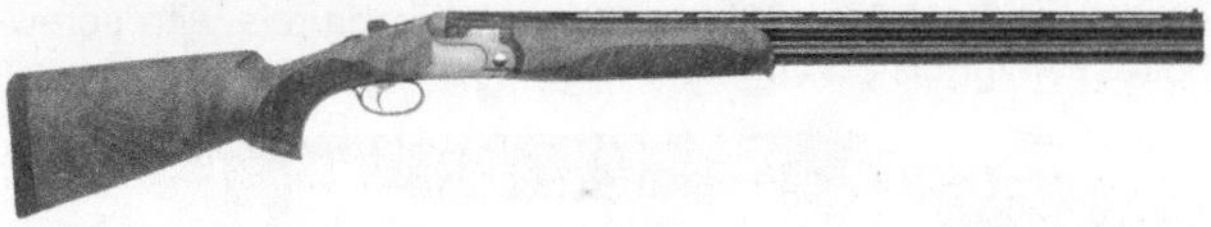

NIB	Exc.	V.G.	Good	Fair	Poor
9450	7000	5000	2750	1600	500

Trap Combo Top

Same as above with both over/under barrels and single barrel combo.

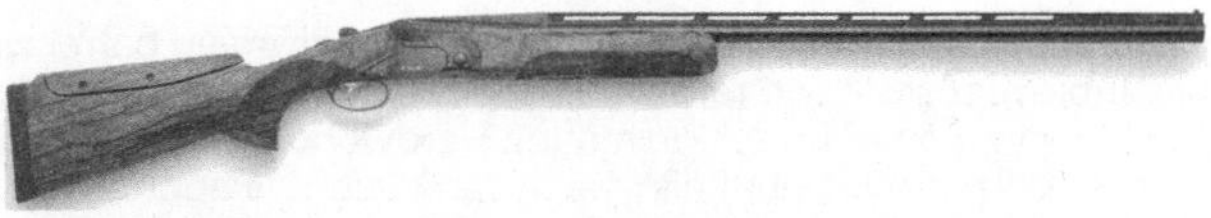

NIB	Exc.	V.G.	Good	Fair	Poor
12995	10500	7500	4700	3000	500

Trap Bottom Single

Introduced in 2001 this model features a choice of 30"/34" barrel combo or 32"/34" barrel combo. Select walnut stock. Fitted with an adjustable point-of-impact rib. Weight is about 8.8 lbs.

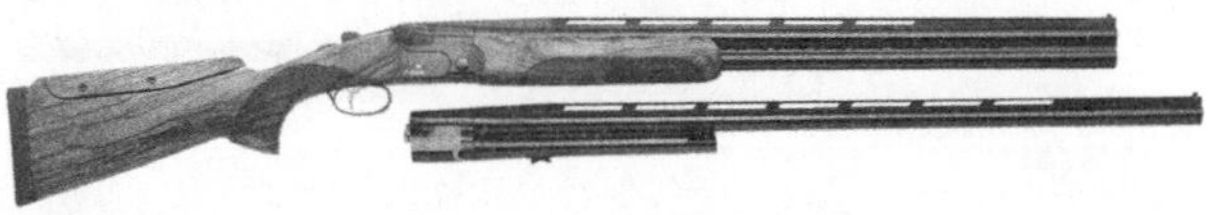

NIB	Exc.	V.G.	Good	Fair	Poor
13250	10500	7500	4700	3000	500

Skeet

This 12 gauge skeet model is fitted with either 28" or 30" barrel. Walnut stock is adjustable. Weight is about 8 lbs. Introduced in 2000.

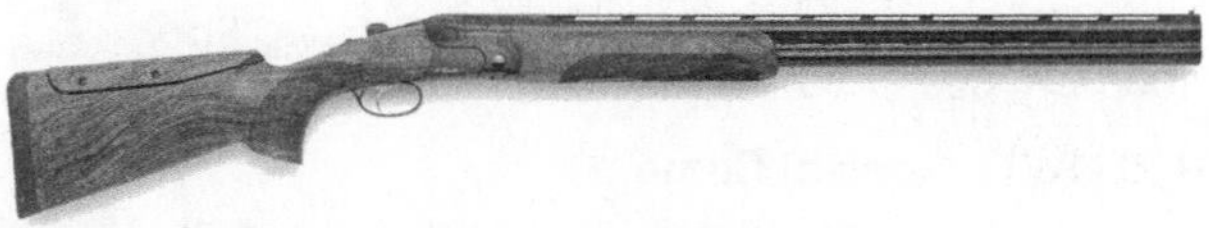

NIB	Exc.	V.G.	Good	Fair	Poor
10450	8000	5000	2850	1875	400

Trident Sporting

This 12 gauge over/under gun is fitted with a choice of 28", 30", or 32" barrels. Highly figured walnut stock with schnabel for-end. Weight is about 8 lbs. Introduced in 2000.

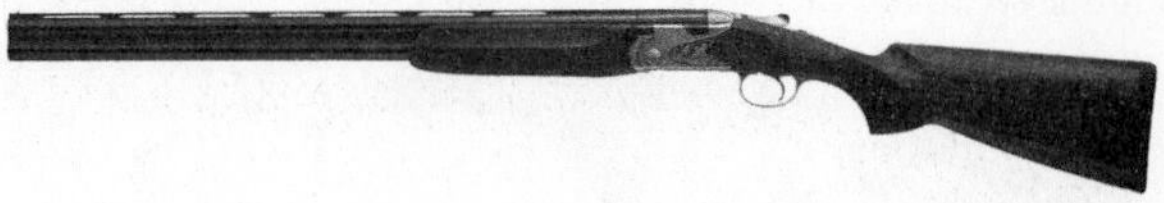

NIB	Exc.	V.G.	Good	Fair	Poor
10500	8000	5000	2850	1875	400

SV10 Perennia

New in 2008, the Perennia over/under is a 3" 12 gauge featuring an oil-finished, select walnut stock and a laser-engraved, nickel high-phosphorous-based finish on the receiver. The barrels are 26" or 28" and feature the Optimachoke HP system introduced in 2008. User-selectable automatic or mechanical shell extraction. Beretta\qs Kick-Off recoil reduction system is available on the 28" Perennia. Includes five choke tubes and plastic carrying case. Add $400 for Kick-Off version.

NIB	Exc.	V.G.	Good	Fair	Poor
3250	2000	1450	800	600	300

SEMI-AUTOMATIC SHOTGUNS

AL SERIES

A 12 or 20 gauge semi-automatic shotgun with 26", 28", or 30" barrels and various choke combinations. Blued with a checkered walnut stock. Manufactured between 1969 and 1976.

AL-1

NIB	Exc.	V.G.	Good	Fair	Poor
—	400	375	300	225	150

AL-2

NIB	Exc.	V.G.	Good	Fair	Poor
—	350	300	250	175	125

AL-2 Competition

NIB	Exc.	V.G.	Good	Fair	Poor
—	400	350	300	225	175

AL-2 Magnum

NIB	Exc.	V.G.	Good	Fair	Poor
—	425	375	325	250	200

AL-3

NIB	Exc.	V.G.	Good	Fair	Poor
—	400	350	300	225	175

AL-3 Deluxe Trap

NIB	Exc.	V.G.	Good	Fair	Poor
—	775	700	600	500	425

Model 301

Improved version of the AL Series manufactured between 1977 and 1982. It is also available as a slug gun with a 22" barrel with rifle sights.

NIB	Exc.	V.G.	Good	Fair	Poor
—	400	350	300	225	175

Model 1200 Field Grade

A 12 gauge semi-automatic shotgun, 28" ventilated rib barrel, screw-in choke tubes and a 4-round, tubular magazine. Matte blued with either a checkered walnut or black synthetic stock. Introduced in 1984.

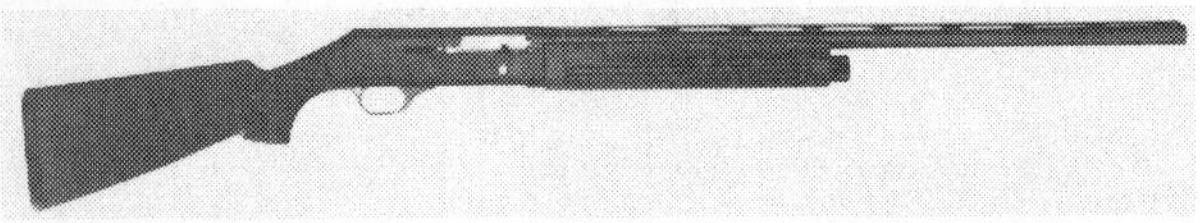

NIB	Exc.	V.G.	Good	Fair	Poor
585	525	425	325	250	200

Model 1200 Magnum

3" chamber.

NIB	Exc.	V.G.	Good	Fair	Poor
585	525	425	325	250	200

Model 1200 Riot

20" cyl. bore barrel.

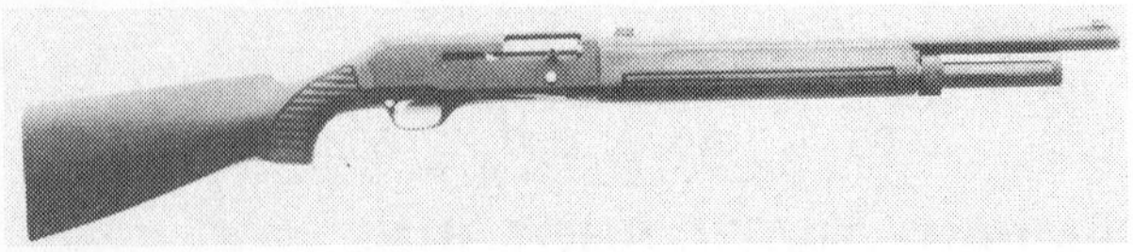

NIB	Exc.	V.G.	Good	Fair	Poor
585	525	425	325	250	200

Model 1201

This 12 gauge semi-automatic shotgun has a short recoil system and features a synthetic stock with matte black finish and lightweight alloy receiver. Available in two basic configurations: the Field Grade with choice of 24", 26", and 28" vent rib barrel with screw-in chokes and Riot Models with 18" plain Cylinder choked barrel with either full stock or pistol-grip-only stock (introduced in 1993). Field Grade weighs about 6 lbs. 12 oz. and the Riot Model about 6 lbs. 5 oz.

Model 1201 Field Grade

NIB	Exc.	V.G.	Good	Fair	Poor
450	400	350	300	200	150

Riot Model

NIB	Exc.	V.G.	Good	Fair	Poor
650	500	400	350	250	175

NOTE: For Riot Models with pistol grip add $40. For Riot Models with Tritium sights add $75. For Ghost Ring sights add $100.

Model 302

A 12 or 20 gauge semi-automatic shotgun using 2.75" or 3" shells interchangeably, various barrel lengths and screw-in choke tubes. Blued with a checkered walnut stock. Manufactured between 1982 and 1987.

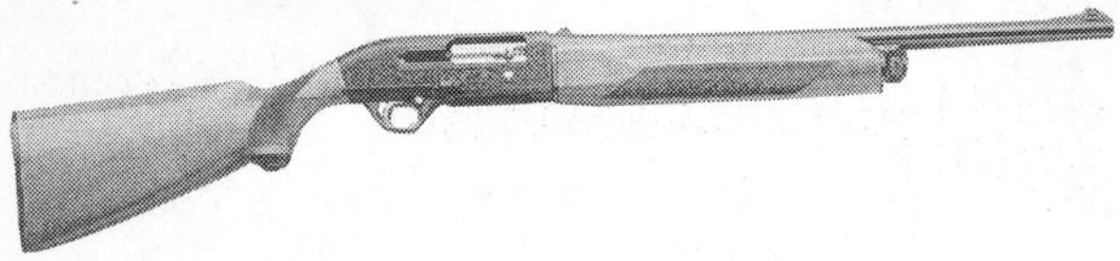

NIB	Exc.	V.G.	Good	Fair	Poor
—	400	350	275	200	150

Model 302 Super Lusso

As above, with a heavily engraved receiver and gold-plated, contrasting parts. Presentation grade walnut was used for the hand checkered stock. Discontinued in 1986.

NIB	Exc.	V.G.	Good	Fair	Poor
—	2150	2000	1600	1050	850

Model Vittoria/Pintail

This semi-automatic 12 gauge shotgun was introduced to the Beretta product line in 1993. It has a short recoil operation and is offered with a 24" or 26" vent rib barrel with screw-in chokes. A 24" rifled choke tube version for slugs is also available. A nonreflective matte finish is put on all wood and metal surfaces. Equipped with sling swivels and walnut stock. Weighs about 7 lbs. Renamed in 1994.

NIB	Exc.	V.G.	Good	Fair	Poor
975	650	500	400	350	250

ES100 Pintail Synthetic

Introduced in 1999, this model is essentially the same as the Pintail model above with the addition of a black synthetic stock. Offered with a choice of 24", 26", or 28" vent rib barrels with screw-in chokes. Weight is about 7 lbs.

NIB	Exc.	V.G.	Good	Fair	Poor
800	650	400	300	200	100

ES100 Pintail Rifled Slug

Introduced in 1997 this model features a 24" fully rifled barrel with adjustable rear sight and removable blade front sight. The receiver is drilled and tapped for scope mount. Hardwood stock with matte finish. Anodized aluminum alloy receiver. Weight is approximately 7 lbs. Fitted with 3" chambers.

NIB	Exc.	V.G.	Good	Fair	Poor
1000	800	600	350	250	100

ES100 Rifled Slug

This variation is the same as the Pintail Rifled Slug model above with the addition of a black synthetic stock. Introduced in 1999.

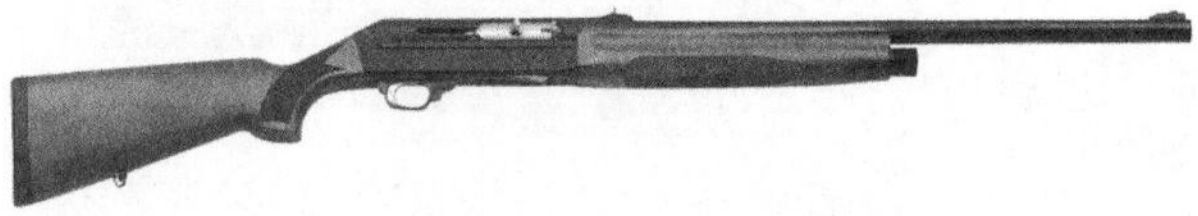

NIB	Exc.	V.G.	Good	Fair	Poor
900	725	475	375	200	150

ES100 Rifled Slug Combo

Same as above but with the addition of a 28" smooth bored barrel.

NIB	Exc.	V.G.	Good	Fair	Poor
1000	800	475	375	200	150

ES100 NWTF Special Camo

This 12 gauge model is fitted with a 24" barrel with 3" chambers. Stock is Mossy Oak camo. Metal is black matte finish. Weight is about 7.3 lbs. Introduced in 1999.

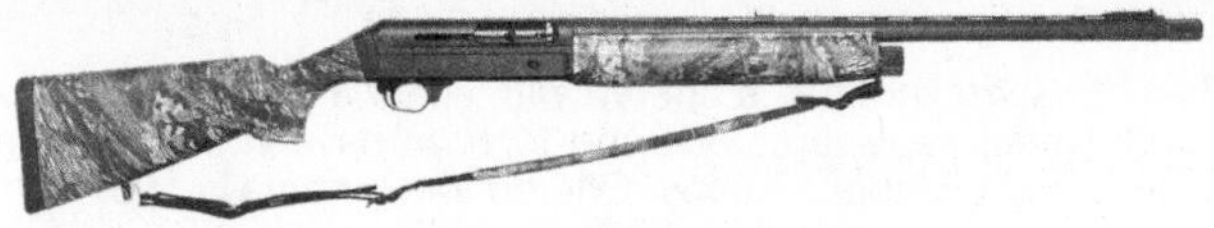

NIB	Exc.	V.G.	Good	Fair	Poor
975	750	550	375	210	150

A-303 SERIES

A 12 or 20 gauge semi-automatic shotgun, 26", 28", 30", or 32" ventilated rib barrels with screw-in choke tubes. Blued with a checkered walnut stock. Introduced in 1987. The various models offered differ slightly in configuration and/or quality of materials.

Model A-303

NIB	Exc.	V.G.	Good	Fair	Poor
650	600	475	375	300	250

Model A-303 Upland

24" barrel.

NIB	Exc.	V.G.	Good	Fair	Poor
680	650	525	425	350	300

Model A-303 Sporting Clay

NIB	Exc.	V.G.	Good	Fair	Poor
735	700	575	475	400	350

Model A-303 Competition (Trap or Skeet)

NIB	Exc.	V.G.	Good	Fair	Poor
675	650	530	425	350	300

Model A-303 Slug Gun

22" barrel with sights.

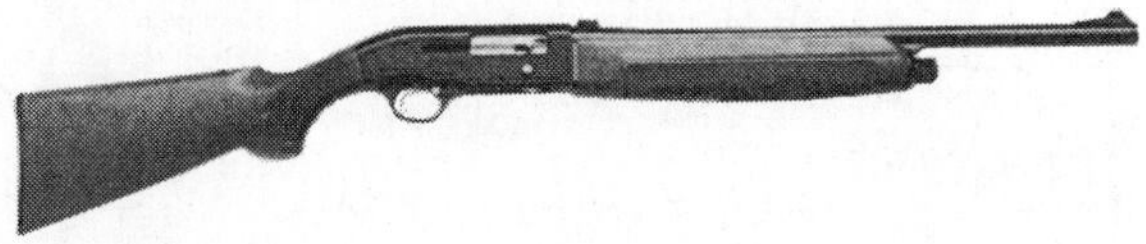

NIB	Exc.	V.G.	Good	Fair	Poor
680	650	525	425	350	300

Model A-303 Youth Gun

This version of the Model 303 is available in 20 gauge with a shorter length of pull, 13.5", than standard. It is fitted with a rubber recoil pad, screw-in choke tubes, and checkered walnut stock.

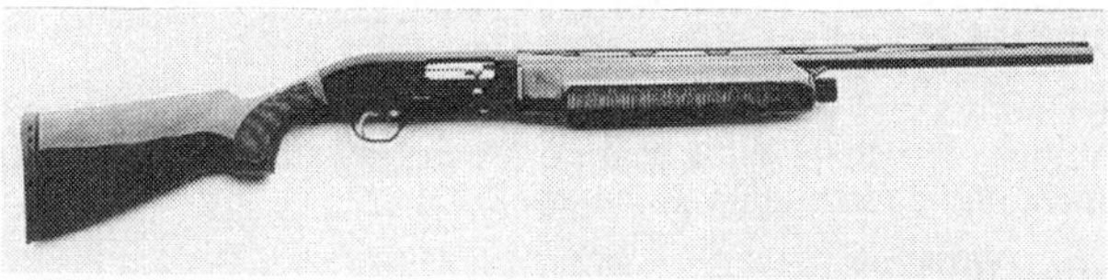

NIB	Exc.	V.G.	Good	Fair	Poor
500	450	400	300	250	200

Model A-303 Ducks Unlimited

A commemorative version of the Model 303. It is chambered for 12 or 20 gauge. There were 5,500 manufactured in 12 gauge in 1986 and 1987. There were 3,500 manufactured in 20 gauge in 1987 and 1988. These are commemorative firearms and are collectible when NIB with all furnished materials.

Model A-303 Ducks Unlimited 12 Gauge

NIB	Exc.	V.G.	Good	Fair	Poor
575	500	425	325	275	225

Model A-303 Ducks Unlimited 20 Gauge

NIB	Exc.	V.G.	Good	Fair	Poor
675	600	525	425	375	325

MODEL AL390/MALLARD SERIES

This series of 12 gauge semi-automatic shotguns features a self-compensating, gas-operating recoil system. All loads from target to 3" Magnums can be used in the same gun. The Field Model features an anodized light alloy receiver with scroll engraving and matte black receiver top. Magazine capacity is 3 rounds. Checkered walnut stock with recoil pad. Available in vent rib barrel lengths from 24" to 30" with 32" on special request. A 22" or 24" slug plain barrel is also available. Chokes are fixed or screw-in at customer's option. Shotgun weighs about 7 lbs. Beginning in 1996 Beretta offered the Silver Mallard shotguns chambered for the 20 gauge shell and available with 24", 26, or 28" barrels. Average weight for these 20 gauge guns is 6.4 lbs.

Field Grade

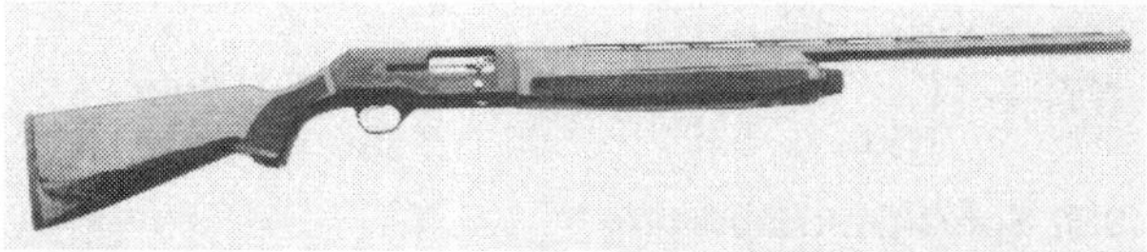

NIB	Exc.	V.G.	Good	Fair	Poor
800	600	450	350	300	200

Slug Gun

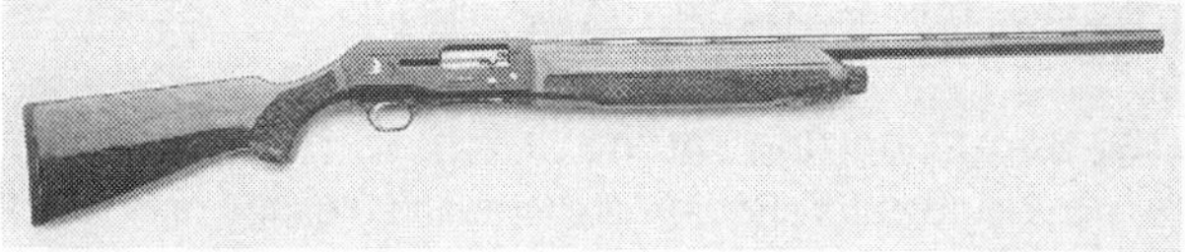

NIB	Exc.	V.G.	Good	Fair	Poor
800	600	450	350	300	200

Synthetic Stock

NIB	Exc.	V.G.	Good	Fair	Poor
800	600	450	350	300	200

Camouflage

NIB	Exc.	V.G.	Good	Fair	Poor
800	600	450	350	300	200

Deluxe Grade/Gold Mallard

Gold-filled game animals and select walnut stock.

NIB	Exc.	V.G.	Good	Fair	Poor
700	650	500	350	300	200

AL390 Trap

NIB	Exc.	V.G.	Good	Fair	Poor
675	600	500	400	300	200

AL390 Super Trap

Features ported barrels in 30" or 32", adjustable length of pull, adjustable comb.

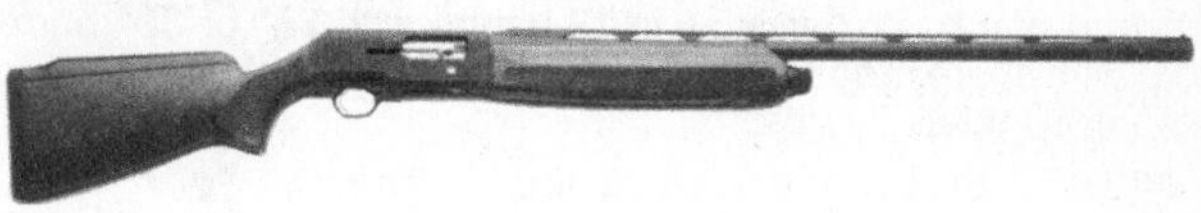

NIB	Exc.	V.G.	Good	Fair	Poor
1000	800	600	500	300	200

AL390 Skeet

NIB	Exc.	V.G.	Good	Fair	Poor
625	550	450	350	250	200

AL390 Super Skeet

Features ported barrel, adjustable cast and length of pull, and adjustable drop. 12 gauge only.

NIB	Exc.	V.G.	Good	Fair	Poor
1000	800	600	500	300	200

AL390 Sporting

NIB	Exc.	V.G.	Good	Fair	Poor
700	550	450	350	250	200

AL390 Sporting 20 gauge

Same as above but in 20 gauge. Introduced in 1997. Weight about 6.8 lbs.

NIB	Exc.	V.G.	Good	Fair	Poor
800	600	450	350	250	200

AL390 Sporting Ported

NIB	Exc.	V.G.	Good	Fair	Poor
725	650	550	400	300	200

AL390 Sport Gold Sporting

Introduced in 1997 this model is similar to above models but with silver sided receiver with gold engraving. Select walnut stock. 12 gauge only with choice of 28" or 30" vent rib barrels. Weight about 7.6 lbs.

NIB	Exc.	V.G.	Good	Fair	Poor
1100	900	700	450	300	175

AL390 Sport Sporting Youth

This semi-automatic shotgun is offered in 20 gauge only with 26" vent rib barrel. Length of pull is 13.5" with adjustable drop and cast on the buttstock. Introduced in 1997. Weight is approximately 6.7 lbs.

NIB	Exc.	V.G.	Good	Fair	Poor
825	675	500	350	200	175

AL390 NWTF Special Youth

Introduced in 1999, this model features a shortened walnut stock with 24" 20 gauge vent rib barrel. Black matte finish. Weight is about 6.4 lbs.

NIB	Exc.	V.G.	Good	Fair	Poor
900	700	525	375	225	175

AL390 Sport Sporting Youth Collection

Same as above but with multi-colored stock and forearm. Introduced in 1997.

NIB	Exc.	V.G.	Good	Fair	Poor
900	750	525	375	225	175

AL390 Sport Diamond Sporting

Introduced in 1998 this model features a silver sided receiver with gold engraving. Select walnut stock with oil finish and adjustable for drop and cast. Available in 12 gauge with 28" or 30" barrels. Sold with spare trigger group and orange front sight beads. Weight is approximately 7.6 lbs.

NIB	Exc.	V.G.	Good	Fair	Poor
3850	3000	1950	1300	600	300

AL390 Camo

This 12 gauge shotgun is offered with either a 24" or 28" vent rib barrel. Barrel, receiver, stock and forearm have woodland camo finish. Weight is about 7.5 lbs. Offered for first time in 1997.

NIB	Exc.	V.G.	Good	Fair	Poor
995	775	595	450	300	150

Waterfowl/Turkey Model

Matte finish.

NIB	Exc.	V.G.	Good	Fair	Poor
550	500	450	350	300	250

NWTF Special Camo

NIB	Exc.	V.G.	Good	Fair	Poor
1100	875	625	500	325	150

NWTF Special Synthetic

NIB	Exc.	V.G.	Good	Fair	Poor
925	750	595	450	300	150

Super Trap

Ported barrels, adjustable comb and length of pull.

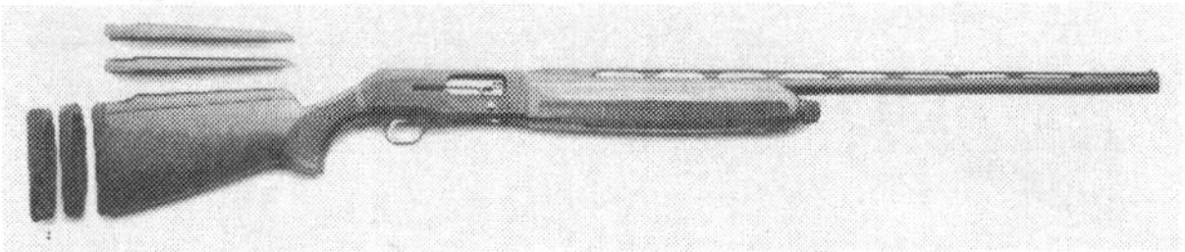

NIB	Exc.	V.G.	Good	Fair	Poor
975	800	650	500	325	175

Super Skeet

Ported barrels, adjustable comb and length of pull.

NIB	Exc.	V.G.	Good	Fair	Poor
950	800	650	500	325	175

3901 SERIES

This series was introduced in 2005 and is built around the A390 shotgun. The 3901 guns feature a gas operating system, choke tubes, and a removable trigger group.

Model 3901

Introduced in 2003, this semi-automatic shotgun is offered in 12 gauge with choice of 26" or 28" barrel. Charcoal gray synthetic stock. Black rubber recoil pad. Non-reflective black finish. Weight is about 7.5 lbs.

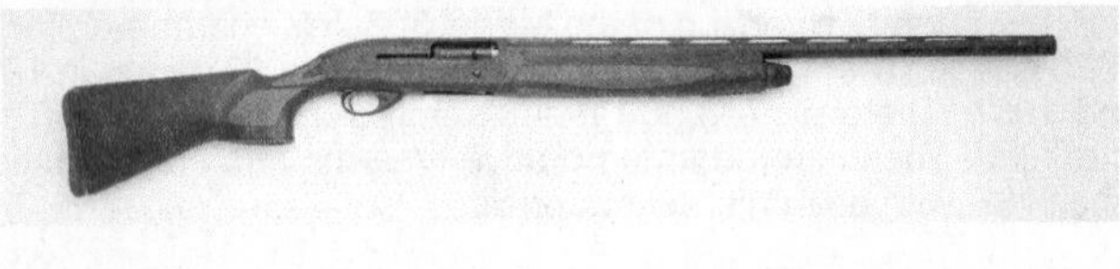

NIB	Exc.	V.G.	Good	Fair	Poor
730	575	450	300	225	175

Model 3901 RL

As above, but in 20 gauge with reduced-length buttstock. Introduced in 2003.

NIB	Exc.	V.G.	Good	Fair	Poor
730	575	450	300	225	175

Model 3901 Camo

This 12 gauge model is offered in Mossy Oak, Shadowgrass camo stock. Choice of 24" or 26" barrel. Introduced in 2003.

NIB	Exc.	V.G.	Good	Fair	Poor
840	650	475	350	250	175

Model 3901 Citizen

Offered in 12 or 20 gauge with choice of 26" or 28" vent rib barrels with choke tubes. Black synthetic stock. Rubber recoil pad. Weight is about 7.6 lbs. for 12 gauge and 7 lbs. for 20 gauge.

NIB	Exc.	V.G.	Good	Fair	Poor
750	600	450	300	225	175

Model 3901 Statesman

As above but with checkered walnut stock.

NIB	Exc.	V.G.	Good	Fair	Poor
850	675	475	325	250	175

Model 3901 Ambassador

This model has all the features of the Statesman but is fitted with a select checkered X-tra wood stock with Gel-Tek recoil pad. Weight for 12 gauge is about 7.2 lbs. and 6.6 lbs. for 20 gauge.

NIB	Exc.	V.G.	Good	Fair	Poor
950	750	525	450	350	200

Model 3901 Target RL

Gas-operated semi-auto chambered in 3" 12-gauge. Specifically designed for smaller-stature shooters with adjustable length of pull from 12 to 13 inches. Stock is adjustable for cast on or cast off. Adjustable comb and Sporting style flat rib. Available in 12 gauge only with 26" or 28" barrel.

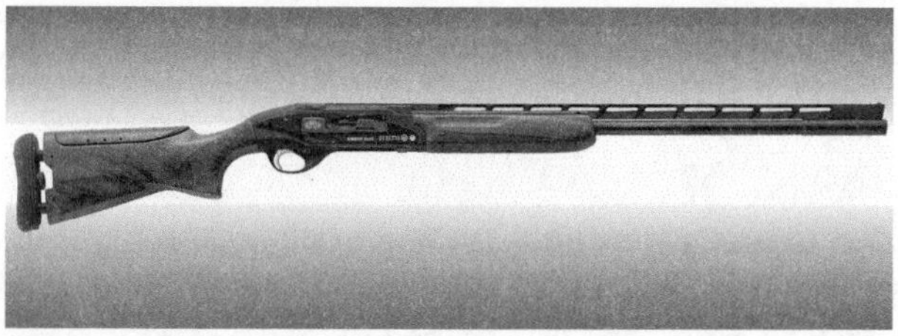

NIB	Exc.	V.G.	Good	Fair	Poor
895	700	550	400	295	175

AL 391 URIKA SERIES

Urika

Introduced in 2000 this semi-automatic shotgun is offered in both 12 and 20 gauge. Choice of barrels from 24" to 30" depending on gauge. Stock is walnut with checkered grip and forend. Rubber recoil pad. Gold trigger. Choke tubes. Weight for 12 gauge is about 7.3 lbs. while the 20 gauge is about 6 lbs.

NIB	Exc.	V.G.	Good	Fair	Poor
850	750	600	450	300	175

Urika Synthetic

Same as above but fitted with a black synthetic stock with gripping inserts. Offered in 12 gauge only. Introduced in 2000.

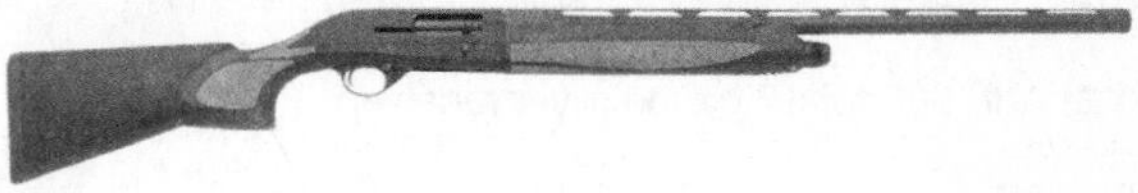

NIB	Exc.	V.G.	Good	Fair	Poor
950	750	625	525	325	200

Urika Camo

This 12 gauge model is offered with either Realtree Hardwoods camo or Advantage Wetlands camo. In 24" or 26" barrels. Weight is about 7.3 lbs. First introduced in 2000.

NIB	Exc.	V.G.	Good	Fair	Poor
1050	800	650	550	300	175

Urika Gold

This model features a 26" or 28" barrels with choke tubes. The black receiver model is offered in both 12 and 20 gauge with a weight of about 7.3 lbs. The silver receiver model (lightweight) is available in 12 gauge only and weighs about 6.6 lbs. Both configurations are fitted with highly figured walnut stock. Gold trigger. Introduced in 2000.

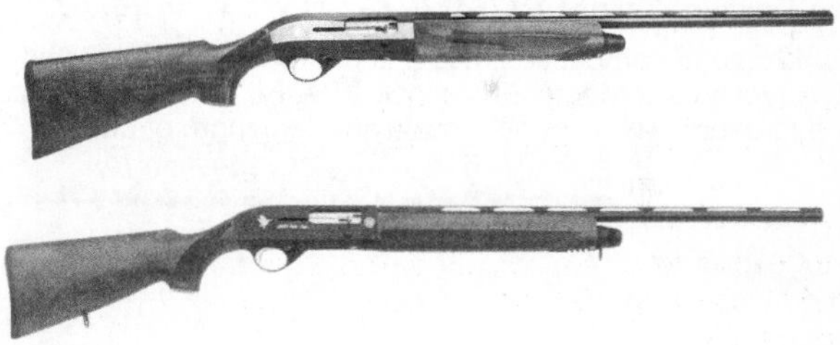

AL391 Gold receiver

NIB	Exc.	V.G.	Good	Fair	Poor
1450	1100	750	675	325	200

Urika Youth

This 20 gauge model features a walnut stock with a shorter length of pull than standard and a 24" barrel. Weight is about 6 lbs. Introduced in 2000.

NIB	Exc.	V.G.	Good	Fair	Poor
1200	950	600	450	275	195

Urika Sporting

This model is offered in both 12 and 20 gauge. Fitted 28" or 30" barrels. Select walnut checkered stock. Gold trigger. Chambered for 3" shells. Weight of 12 gauge is about 7.3 lbs. and the 20 gauge is about 6 lbs. Introduced in 2000.

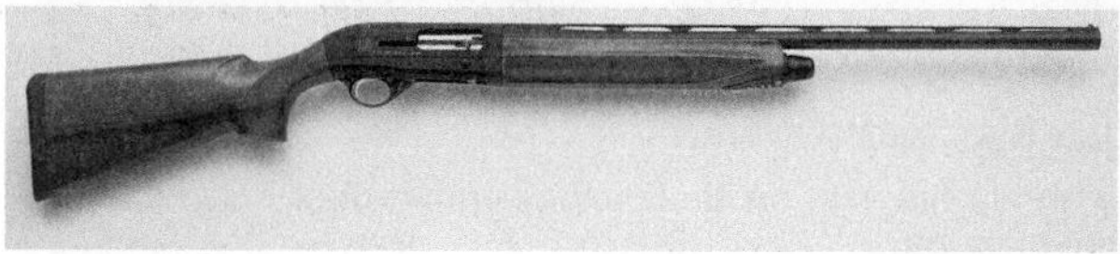

NIB	Exc.	V.G.	Good	Fair	Poor
1100	750	600	500	350	175

Urika Gold Sporting

This model is offered in 12 gauge with a choice of black or silver receiver. The 20 gauge models are offered with black receiver only. Fitted with 28" or 30" barrels. Highly select checkered walnut stock. Chambered for 3" shells. Introduced in 2000.

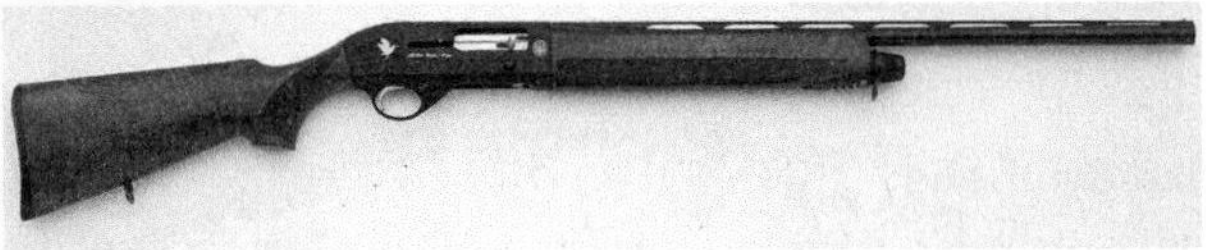

NIB	Exc.	V.G.	Good	Fair	Poor
1295	950	700	600	450	175

NOTE: Add $30 for 12 gauge silver receiver.

Urika Trap

This 12 gauge model is fitted with a choice of 30" or 32" barrels. Select checkered walnut stock with Monte Carlo comb. Chambered for 3" shells. Weight is about 7.2 lbs. Introduced in 2000.

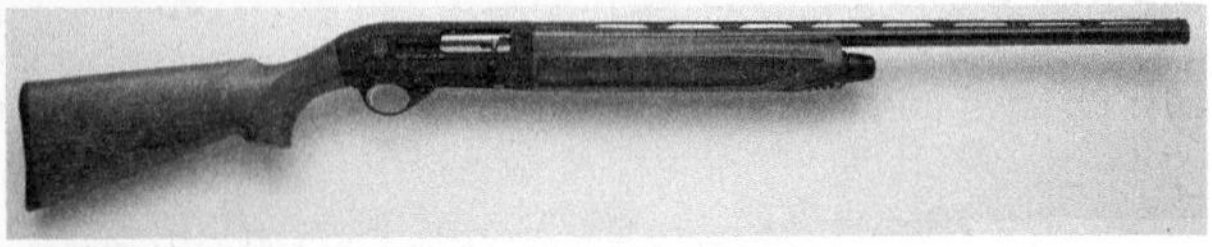

NIB	Exc.	V.G.	Good	Fair	Poor
1000	750	600	500	350	175

Urika Gold Trap

This model is similar to the standard Urika Trap but with highly selected checkered walnut stock and black receiver.

NIB	Exc.	V.G.	Good	Fair	Poor
1295	950	700	600	450	175

Urika Parallel Target RL/SL

This 12 gauge competition model is fitted with 28" or 30" barrels and select walnut Monte Carlo stock. The "RL" has standard stock configurations while the "SL" has a shorter length of pull.

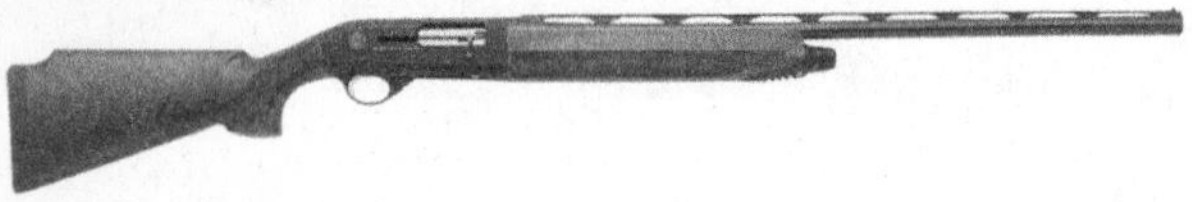

NIB	Exc.	V.G.	Good	Fair	Poor
1100	750	600	500	350	200

URIKA OPTIMA MODELS

First offered in 2003 this shotguns are similar to the standard Urika model but feature Beretta's Optima-Bore overbored barrels with flush Optima-Choke Plus tubes.

Urika Optima

Offered in 12 gauge with 26" or 28" vent rib barrel. Checkered select walnut stock. Gold trigger. Chamber is 3". Weight is about 7.3 lbs.

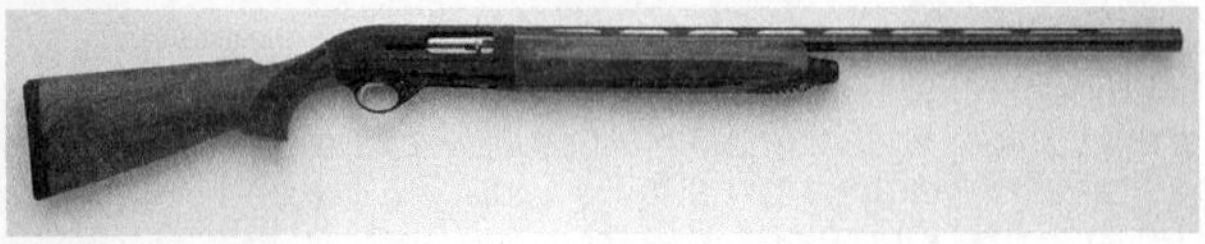

NIB	Exc.	V.G.	Good	Fair	Poor
1500	1175	825	650	450	300

Urika Synthetic Optima

As above but with synthetic stock with rubber inserts. Weight is about 7.4 lbs.

NIB	Exc.	V.G.	Good	Fair	Poor
1300	1105	750	575	400	325

Urika Optima Camo

As above but with camo stock.

NIB	Exc.	V.G.	Good	Fair	Poor
1350	1195	950	625	450	250

URIKA 2 SERIES

Introduced in 2007, the Urika 2 is an enhanced version of the original AL391 Urika. Improvements include the addition of a spinning, self-cleaning action for faster cycling and longer functioning periods between cleanings.

AL391 Urika 2 X-Tra Grain

This series features Beretta\qs wood-enhancement treatment to highlight the color contrast of the wood. Offered in 3" 12 and 20 gauge with 26" and 28" barrels. A 20 gauge youth model with shorter stock and 24" barrel is also offered.

NIB	Exc.	V.G.	Good	Fair	Poor
1000	900	725	575	400	250

AL391 Urika 2 Gold

Select oil-finished wood stock and forend with gold-filled game bird inlays on the receiver. The 12 gauge has a 28" barrel and the 20 gauge has a 26" barrel.

NIB	Exc.	V.G.	Good	Fair	Poor
1350	1075	725	500	375	250

AL391 Urika 2 Kick-Off

These waterfowl models feature Beretta\qs Kick-Off recoil reduction system. Matte black synthetic, Max-4 or Realtree AP finish with 26" or 28" barrel. Deduct 30 percent for models without Kick-Off. Add 10 percent for camo finish.

NIB	Exc.	V.G.	Good	Fair	Poor
1200	950	700	475	350	225

AL391 Urika 2 Sporting X-Tra Grain

Sporting clays models in 12 and 20 gauge with 28" or 30" barrel.

NIB	Exc.	V.G.	Good	Fair	Poor
1200	950	700	475	350	225

AL391 Urika 2 Gold Sporting

Enhanced wood with gold inlays and floral motif engraving on receiver in 12 gauge with 28" or 30" barrel.

NIB	Exc.	V.G.	Good	Fair	Poor
1300	1025	775	525	375	275

AL391 Urika 2 Parallel Target X-Tra Grain

Target model in 12 gauge with 28", 30" or 32" barrel.

NIB	*Exc.*	*V.G.*	*Good*	*Fair*	*Poor*
1250	975	750	525	375	295

AL391 Urika 2 Gold Parallel Target

Enhanced wood with gold inlays and floral motif engraving on receiver in 12 gauge with 30" or 32" barrel.

NIB	*Exc.*	*V.G.*	*Good*	*Fair*	*Poor*
1400	1075	750	525	395	265

AL391 Covey

Introduced in 2003 this model is offered in 20 gauge with a 26" or 28" vent rib barrel. Select walnut stock. Gold-filled game scenes. Weight is about 5.9 lbs. Limited to 1,000 guns.

NIB	*Exc.*	*V.G.*	*Good*	*Fair*	*Poor*
1350	1075	725	500	375	250

AL391 Ringneck

As above but with gold-filled pheasants. In 12 gauge only. Weight is about 7.3 lbs. Limited to 1,000 guns. Introduced in 2003.

NIB	*Exc.*	*V.G.*	*Good*	*Fair*	*Poor*
1360	1075	800	550	400	300

AL391 Teknys

This model features a nickel receiver with polished sides and anti-glare top. Offered in 12 or 20 gauge with 26" or 28" vent rib barrel. X-wood stock with Gel-Tek recoil. Weight is about 7.2 lbs. for 12 gauge and 5.9 lbs. for the 20 gauge. Introduced in 2003.

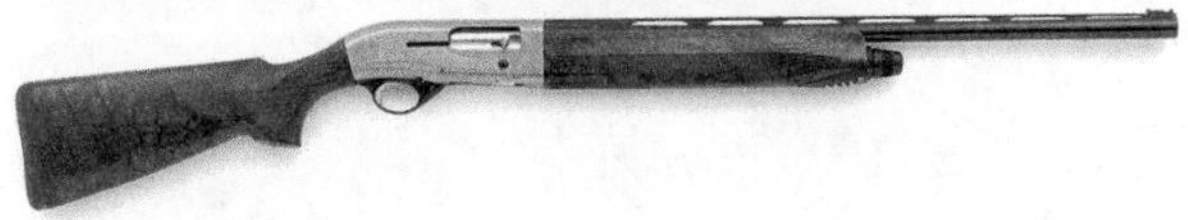

NIB	*Exc.*	*V.G.*	*Good*	*Fair*	*Poor*
1150	900	750	500	350	250

AL391 Teknys Gold

As above, but with engraved hunting scene on the receiver, gold plated trigger, jeweled breech bolt and carrier. Select walnut checkered stock with oil finish. Introduced in 2003.

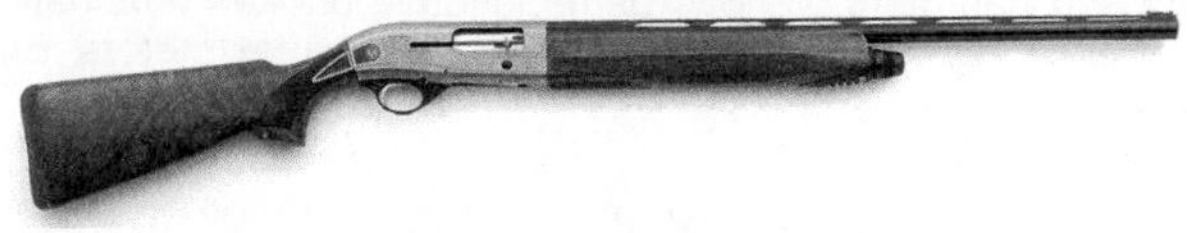

NIB	*Exc.*	*V.G.*	*Good*	*Fair*	*Poor*
1465	1100	850	575	425	325

A391 Teknys Gold Target

Similar to AL391 Teknys Gold but with adjustable comb, 8.5 oz. recoil reducer and additional stepped rib for trap shooting. 30" barrel.

NIB	*Exc.*	*V.G.*	*Good*	*Fair*	*Poor*
1665	1300	975	600	450	350

AL391 Teknys King Ranch

Introduced in 2005.

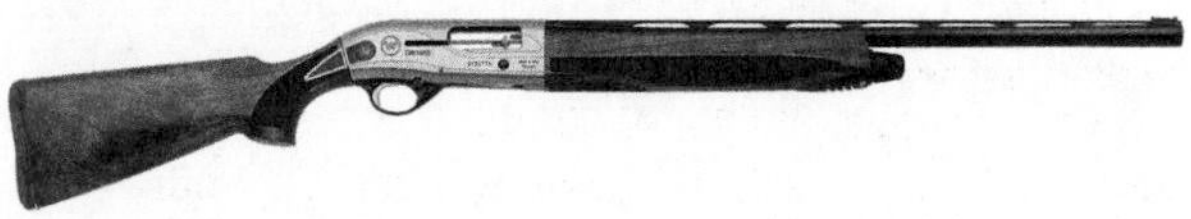

NIB	*Exc.*	*V.G.*	*Good*	*Fair*	*Poor*
1650	1300	1000	725	625	375

AL391 XTREMA SERIES

Xtrema 3.5

Introduced in 2002 this model features an overbuilt Urika to handle 12 gauge 3.5" super magnum loads. Offered with a choice of 24", 26", or 28" vent rib barrels with black synthetic stock or choice of various camo stocks. Weight is about 7.8 lbs.

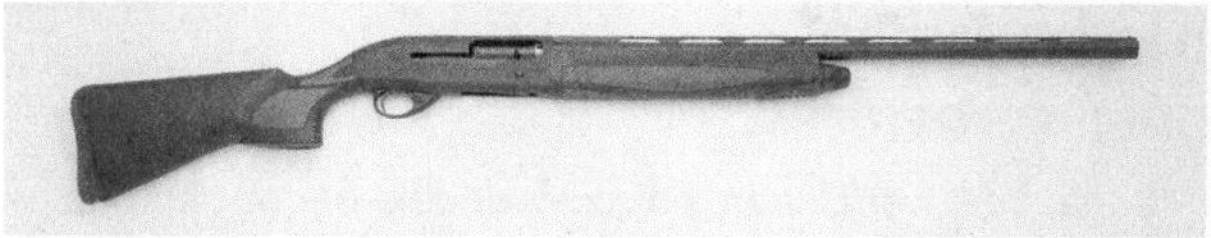

NIB	*Exc.*	*V.G.*	*Good*	*Fair*	*Poor*
1150	900	750	500	350	250

NOTE: Add $100 for camo finish.

AL391 Xtrema2

An upgraded version of the Xtrema with additional recoil-reducing features was introduced in 2005. Available with 24", 26" or 28" barrels with black, Max-4 HD or Hardwoods HD synthetic stock. Optima-Bore five choke system. Optional Kick Off recoil reduction feature available. Add 10 percent for camo finish. Add 30 percent for Kick Off option.

NIB	*Exc.*	*V.G.*	*Good*	*Fair*	*Poor*
1300	950	800	650	400	300

AL391 Xtrema2 Slug Gun

24" rifled barrel version of Xtrema2. Introduced in 2006. Black synthetic only. Add 10 percent for Kick Off option.

NIB	*Exc.*	*V.G.*	*Good*	*Fair*	*Poor*
1200	925	800	650	400	300

UGB25 XCEL

Introduced in 2005 this is a semi-automatic break-open competition Trap gun chambered for the 12 gauge 2.75" shell. The gun is fed from the side with bottom ejection. Choice of 30" or 32" barrel with high trap-style interchangeable rib. Choke tubes. The checkered walnut has an adjustable comb and length of pull. Weight is about 7.7 to 9 lbs. depending on barrel length and rib.

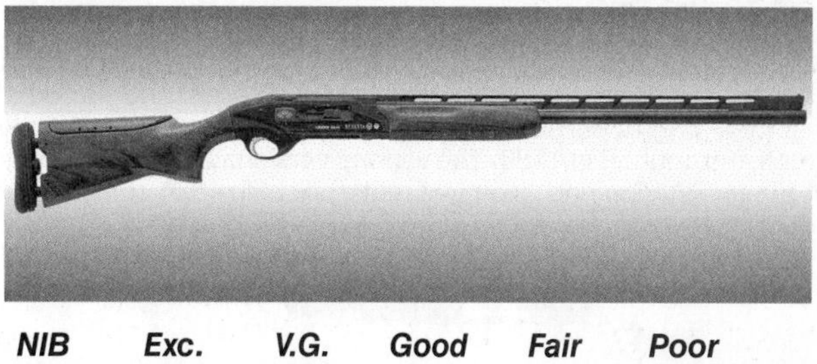

NIB	*Exc.*	*V.G.*	*Good*	*Fair*	*Poor*
3595	2800	2150	1675	850	450

Beretta A400 Xplor Unico Semiauto Shotgun

Self-regulation gas-operated shotgun chambered to shoot all 12-ga, loads from 2-3/4 to 3.5 inches. Features include Kick-Off3 hydraulic damper; 26- or 28-inch "Steelium" barrel with interchangeable choke tubes; anodized aluminum receiver; sculpted, checkered walnut buttstock and forend. Price: $1625.

Beretta TX4 Semiauto Shotgun241

Gas-operated semiauto shotgun chambered for 3-inch 12-ga. shells. Features include 18-inch barrel with interchangeable choke tubes; adjustable ghost ring rear sight with military-style front sight; adjustable length of pull; integral picatinny rail on receiver; 5+1 capacity; soft rubber grip inlays in buttstock and forend. Price: $1450.

BERNARDELLI, VINCENZO

Brescia, Italy

Established in the 1721, this company originally manufactured military arms and only entered the commercial sporting arms market in 1928.

SHOTGUNS

MODEL 115 SERIES

A 12 gauge Over/Under, boxlock, double-barrel shotgun with various barrel lengths and choke combinations, single triggers and automatic ejectors.

Model 115

NIB	Exc.	V.G.	Good	Fair	Poor
1525	1250	900	700	550	300

Model 115S

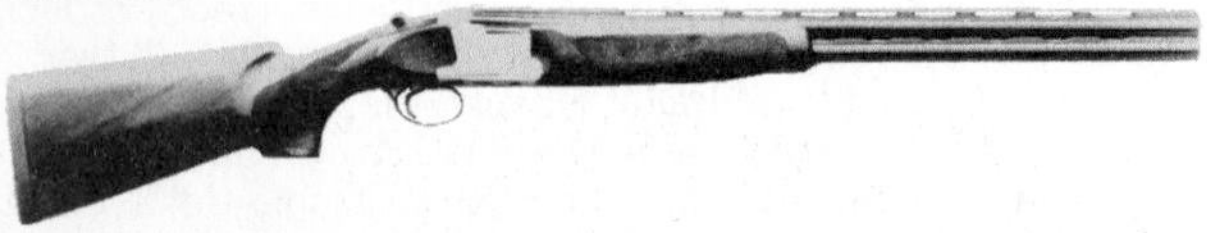

NIB	Exc.	V.G.	Good	Fair	Poor
2000	1750	1200	800	600	300

Model 115L

NIB	Exc.	V.G.	Good	Fair	Poor
2500	2000	1500	900	650	300

Model 115E

NIB	Exc.	V.G.	Good	Fair	Poor
5200	4800	4200	3500	2500	1850

Model 115 Trap

NIB	Exc.	V.G.	Good	Fair	Poor
2200	1950	1400	950	750	600

Model 115S Trap

NIB	Exc.	V.G.	Good	Fair	Poor
2700	2450	1900	1450	1150	900

Model 115E Trap

NIB	Exc.	V.G.	Good	Fair	Poor
5250	4800	4200	3500	2500	1850

MODEL 190 SERIES

A 12 gauge, Over/Under shotgun with various barrel lengths and choke combinations, a single-selective trigger and automatic ejectors. Engraved and silver-finished with a checkered walnut stock. Introduced in 1986. The various versions differ in the degree of ornamentation and quality of materials utilized in construction.

Model 190

NIB	Exc.	V.G.	Good	Fair	Poor
1050	950	750	600	475	400

Model 190MC

NIB	Exc.	V.G.	Good	Fair	Poor
1150	1050	850	700	575	500

Model 190 Special

NIB	Exc.	V.G.	Good	Fair	Poor
1350	1150	950	800	675	600

Model 190 Combo Gun

A .243, .308 or .30-06 caliber and 12, 16, or 20 gauge combination Over/Under rifle shotgun with a boxlock action, double triggers and automatic ejectors. Blued with a checkered walnut stock. Introduced in 1989.

NIB	Exc.	V.G.	Good	Fair	Poor
1625	1425	925	775	650	575

ORIONE SERIES

A 12 gauge boxlock Over/Under shotgun with various barrel lengths and choke combinations. Finishes and triggers were optional, as were extractors or automatic ejectors.

Orione

NIB	Exc.	V.G.	Good	Fair	Poor
1150	900	700	500	400	200

Orione S

NIB	Exc.	V.G.	Good	Fair	Poor
1150	900	700	500	400	200

Orione L

NIB	Exc.	V.G.	Good	Fair	Poor
1250	1000	800	600	500	250

Orione E

NIB	Exc.	V.G.	Good	Fair	Poor
1350	1150	850	600	500	250

S. Uberto I Gamecock

A 12, 16, 20, or 28 gauge boxlock side-by-side shotgun with either 25.75" or 27.5" barrels, various chokes, double triggers and extractors. Automatic ejectors were available and would be worth a 20 percent premium. Blued with a checkered stock.

NIB	Exc.	V.G.	Good	Fair	Poor
—	950	700	500	350	250

Brescia

A 12, 16, or 20 gauge sidelock double-barrel shotgun with exposed hammers, various barrel lengths, choke combinations, a sidelock action, double triggers, and manual extractors. Blued with an English-style, checkered walnut stock.

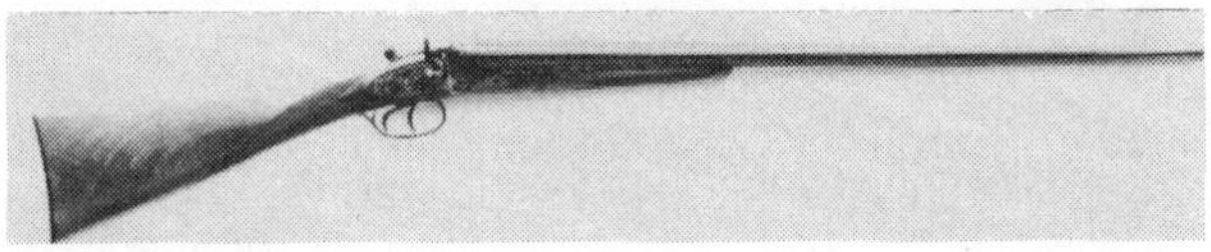

NIB	Exc.	V.G.	Good	Fair	Poor
1850	900	700	450	350	225

Italia

This is a higher grade version of the Brescia.

NIB	Exc.	V.G.	Good	Fair	Poor
2250	1250	750	600	400	250

Italia Extra

This is the highest grade hammer gun that Bernardelli produces.

NIB	Exc.	V.G.	Good	Fair	Poor
5900	2750	1500	1000	750	300

UBERTO SERIES

A 12, 16, 20 or 28 gauge Anson & Deeley boxlock double barrel shotgun with various barrel lengths and choke combinations. The increased value of the various models depends on the degree of engraving, options, and quality of materials and workmanship utilized in their construction.

S. Uberto 1

NIB	Exc.	V.G.	Good	Fair	Poor
1000	800	650	475	350	250

S. Uberto 1E

NIB	Exc.	V.G.	Good	Fair	Poor
1100	900	700	500	350	250

S. Uberto 2

NIB	Exc.	V.G.	Good	Fair	Poor
1500	1100	800	500	350	250

S. Uberto 2E

NIB	Exc.	V.G.	Good	Fair	Poor
1750	1350	950	600	400	250

S. Uberto F.S.

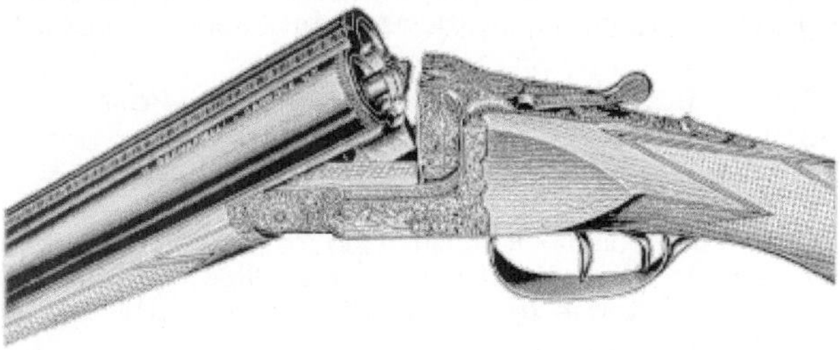

NIB	Exc.	V.G.	Good	Fair	Poor
2000	1500	1100	800	400	250

S. Uberto F.S.E.

NIB	Exc.	V.G.	Good	Fair	Poor
2250	1750	1200	800	400	250

ROMA SERIES

Similar to the S. Uberto Series with false sideplates. The values of the respective variations result from the degree of ornamentation and quality of materials and workmanship utilized in the construction.

Roma 3

NIB	Exc.	V.G.	Good	Fair	Poor
1550	1200	800	600	300	200

Roma 3E

NIB	Exc.	V.G.	Good	Fair	Poor
1750	1300	900	650	300	200

Roma 4

NIB	Exc.	V.G.	Good	Fair	Poor
1950	1400	1100	750	400	250

Roma 4E

NIB	Exc.	V.G.	Good	Fair	Poor
2000	1500	1200	750	400	250

Roma 6

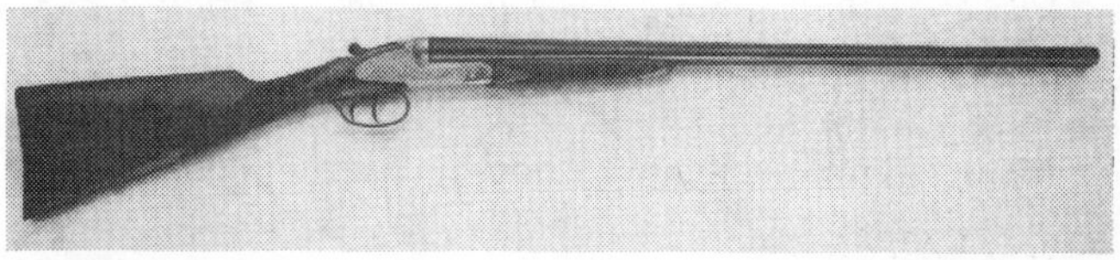

NIB	Exc.	V.G.	Good	Fair	Poor
2100	1750	1400	850	500	250

Roma 6E

NIB	Exc.	V.G.	Good	Fair	Poor
2200	1800	1400	850	500	250

Roma 7

NIB	Exc.	V.G.	Good	Fair	Poor
2900	2500	1800	1200	700	350

Roma 8

NIB	Exc.	V.G.	Good	Fair	Poor
3500	3000	2250	1550	850	400

Roma 9

NIB	Exc.	V.G.	Good	Fair	Poor
4000	3500	2750	1700	950	450

Elio

A 12 gauge boxlock double-barrel shotgun with various barrel lengths and choke combinations, lightweight frame, double triggers and extractors. Scroll-engraved, silver-finished receiver, blued barrels and a select, checkered walnut stock.

NIB	Exc.	V.G.	Good	Fair	Poor
1000	800	600	500	350	250

Elio E

As above, with automatic ejectors.

NIB	Exc.	V.G.	Good	Fair	Poor
1100	900	700	550	350	250

Hemingway

As above, with coin finished receiver, engraved with hunting scenes, 23.5" barrels, double triggers or single trigger and a select, checkered walnut stock. Available in 12, 20 and 28 gauge.

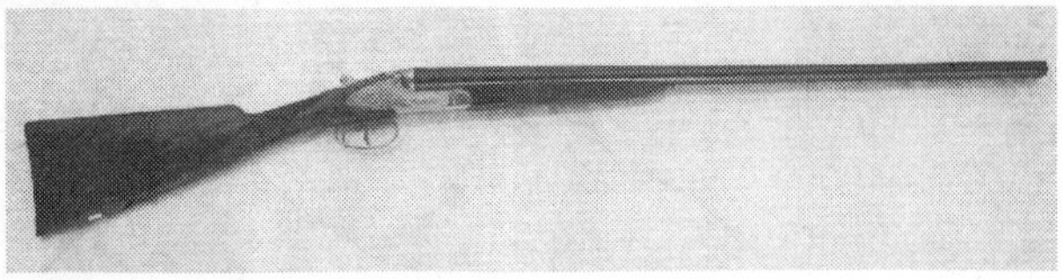

NIB	Exc.	V.G.	Good	Fair	Poor
1750	1350	900	700	400	250

Hemingway Deluxe

Same as above but fitted with full side plates.

NIB	Exc.	V.G.	Good	Fair	Poor
2250	1750	1200	800	400	250

Las Palomas Pigeon Model

A live Pigeon gun in 12 gauge with single trigger.

NIB	Exc.	V.G.	Good	Fair	Poor
3800	3250	2500	2000	1500	750

HOLLAND V.B. SERIES

A 12 or 20 gauge sidelock shotgun with various barrel lengths, detachable Holland & Holland-type locks, single triggers, and automatic ejectors. The models listed vary in the amount of engraving and the quality of their wood. Prospective purchasers are advised to secure a qualified appraisal prior to acquisition.

Holland V.B. Liscio

NIB	Exc.	V.G.	Good	Fair	Poor
8000	5500	4000	3000	2000	1000

Holland V.B. Inciso

NIB	Exc.	V.G.	Good	Fair	Poor
10250	7500	5250	4000	2500	1250

Holland V.B. Lusso

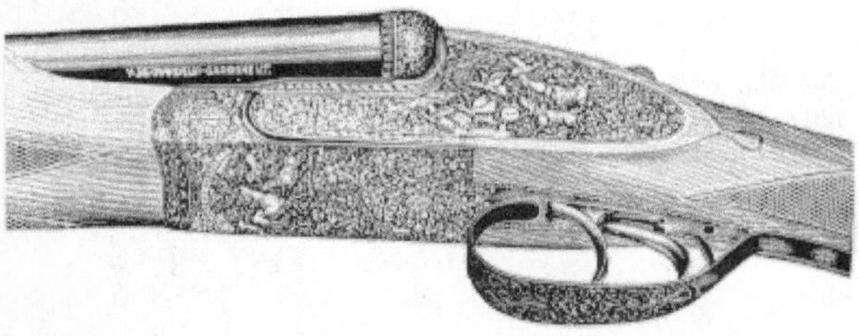

NIB	Exc.	V.G.	Good	Fair	Poor
11000	8000	6000	4500	2500	1250

Holland V.B. Extra

NIB	Exc.	V.G.	Good	Fair	Poor
13000	10000	7500	5500	3000	1500

Holland V.B. Gold

NIB	Exc.	V.G.	Good	Fair	Poor
45000	30000	22500	15000	7500	3000

Luck

An over-and-under shotgun with single-selective trigger or double triggers, automatic ejectors with choice of fixed chokes or choke tubes. Available in 12 gauge. Blued or coin finish receiver.

NIB	Exc.	V.G.	Good	Fair	Poor
1400	1100	850	600	400	200

Giardino/Garden Gun (9mm Rimfire)

This is a semi-automatic shotgun chambered for the 9mm shot cartridge. Fitted with a 4-round magazine. Weight is 5 lbs. MSRP is now (2009) $850!

NIB	Exc.	V.G.	Good	Fair	Poor
800	500	350	250	200	100

RIFLES

Carbina VB Target

A semi-automatic carbine chambered for the .22 LR cartridge. Barrel is 20.8" and magazine capacity is 10 rounds.

NIB	Exc.	V.G.	Good	Fair	Poor
650	550	400	300	200	100

Comb 2000

A rifle shotgun combination in 12 or 16 gauge with a variety of centerfire calibers to choose from. Barrels are 23.5" long. Set trigger, special rib for scope mount and cheekpiece stock with pistol grip. Weight is 6-3/4 lbs.

NIB	Exc.	V.G.	Good	Fair	Poor
2900	2100	1200	800	400	250

Express 2000

An over-and-under double rifle chambered for a variety of European calibers. Fitted with automatic ejectors, double-set triggers or single trigger, muzzle adjustment device. Barrel length is 23.5".

NIB	Exc.	V.G.	Good	Fair	Poor
3350	2550	1700	1200	600	300

Express VB

A side-by-side double rifle chambered for a variety of European calibers up to .375 H&H. Double or single trigger, auto ejectors, and finely engraved receiver with beavertail forearm. Cheekpiece stock with pistol grip.

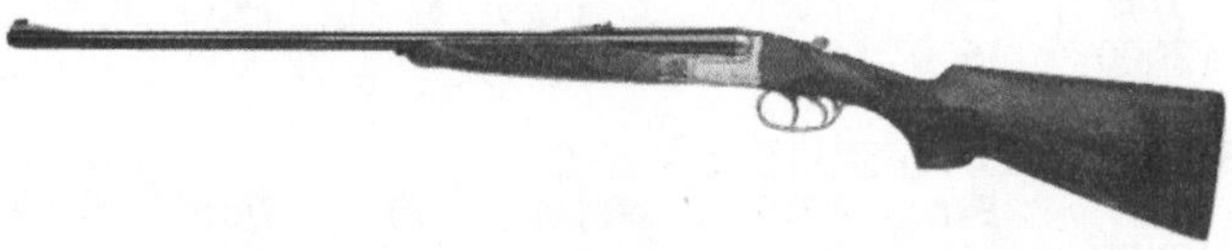

NIB	Exc.	V.G.	Good	Fair	Poor
5900	4900	3750	2000	1000	750

Express VB Deluxe

Same as above but with side plates and select walnut stock finely checkered.

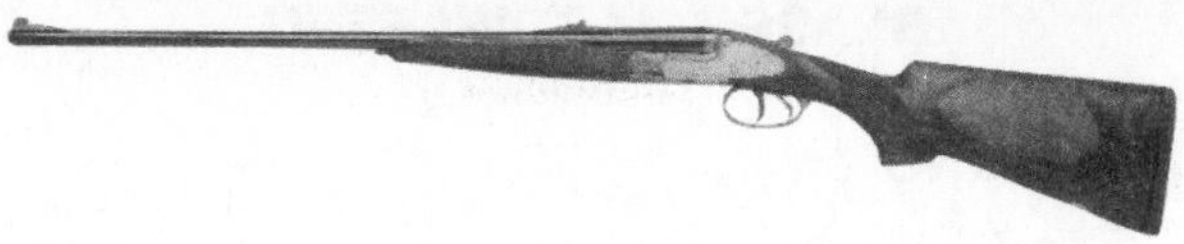

NIB	Exc.	V.G.	Good	Fair	Poor
6300	5200	4000	2000	1000	750

Minerva

A side-by-side double rifle with exposed hammers chambered for the 9.3x74R cartridge. Fitted with fancy walnut stock, double triggers, hand-cut rib, and other high-quality features.

NIB	Exc.	V.G.	Good	Fair	Poor
6700	5900	4550	2500	1200	750

BERTUZZI

Brescia, Italy

SHOTGUNS OVER/UNDER

Zeus

A 12, 16, 20, or 28 gauge sidelock shotgun with automatic ejectors, single-selective trigger, and deluxe checkered walnut stock. Custom order in various barrel lengths and chokes. Engraved. Rarely seen on the used gun market.

NIB
18000-39000

Zeus Extra Lusso

As above, but with best wood and engraving. Cased.

NIB
35000-79000

Zeus Boss System

This gun is chamberd for the 12, 16, 20, or 28 gauge and is fitted with the Boss locking system with ejectors. One-of-a-kind gun with best quality wood and engraving.

NIB
65000-134000

Gull Wing

This is Burtuzzi's best gun with a unique sidelock design mounted on a center plate with a release located on top of the safety to allow sidelock access. These shotguns usually take about three years to build. Consult the distributor about options and availability.

NIB
125000+

Ariete Extra Lusso

This is a best quality hammer gun in all gauges from 12 to 28. Limited quantities.

NIB
65000+

SHOTGUNS SIDE-BY-SIDE

Orione

A 12, 16, 20 or 28 gauge boxlock shotgun with Anson & Deeley through bolt, in various barrel lengths and chokes, single-selective trigger and automatic ejectors. Hand checkered, walnut stock with a semi-beavertail forearm. Engraving.

NIB
25500-39950

Venere

This is a best quality sidelock gun with either a traditional or round frame. Special order to customer specifications. Engraved guns bring a premium.

NIB
29000-69000

Ariete

Best quality hammer gun with or without self cocking hammers and ejectors. Offered in 12 bore through .410. Many options.

NIB
25000-55000

Gull Wing

This is a one-of-a-kind custom built gun with quick release sidelocks. Delivery time about three years. Contact distributor for more information.

NIB
85000+

BIG HORN ARMORY

Cody, Wyoming

Big Horn Armory Model 89 Rifle and Carbine

Lever action rifle or carbine chambered for .500 S&W Magnum. Features include 22-or 18-inch barrel; walnut or maple stocks with pistol grip; aperture rear and blade front sights; recoil pad; sling swivels; enlarged lever loop; magazine capacity 5 (rifle) or 7 (carbine) rounds. Price: $1889.

BIGHORN ARMS CO.

Watertown, South Dakota

Shotgun

A single-shot 12 gauge shotgun with a 26" barrel. Blued with a plastic stock.

NIB	Exc.	V.G.	Good	Fair	Poor
—	195	115	65	50	30

BIGHORN RIFLE CO.

Orem, Utah

Bighorn Rifle

Custom order in any caliber, double-barrel, bolt-action rifle with optional barrel lengths and finishes. Double trigger and walnut stock.

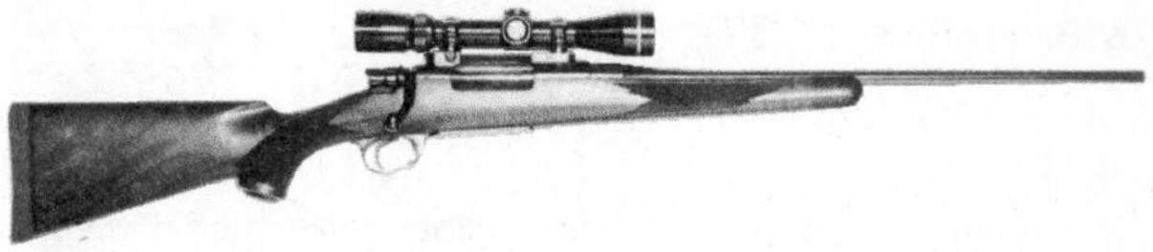

NIB	Exc.	V.G.	Good	Fair	Poor
2500	1750	1500	1000	750	400

BILHARZ, HALL & CO.

CONFEDERATE CARBINES

Bilharz, Hall & Co. Breechloading ("Rising Breech") Carbine

Overall length 40"; barrel length 21"; caliber 54. Markings: either "P" or "P/CS" on upper left side of barrel and top of rising breech. The peculiar feature of this carbine is the manner in which the breechblock exposes the chamber. A box-like chamber at the rear of the barrel rises vertically to expose the chamber for a paper cartridge by activating the lever/triggerguard mechanism. Only 100 of this type were delivered to the Confederacy in September 1862. Two types of front sight blades are known, but neither affects the value.

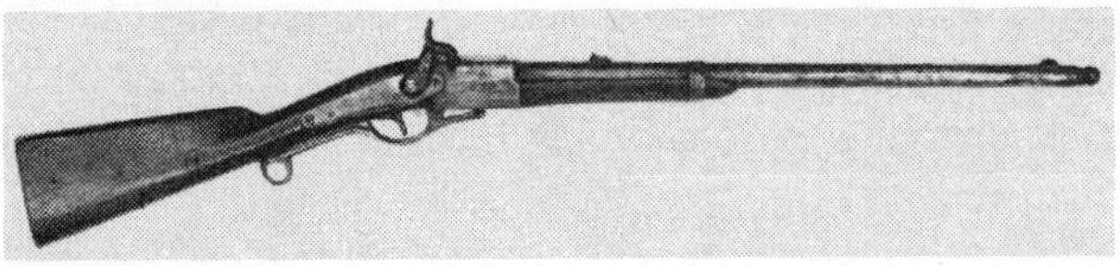

Courtesy Milwaukee Public Museum, Milwaukee, Wisconsin

NIB	Exc.	V.G.	Good	Fair	Poor
—	—	50000	22500	5000	2100

Bilharz, Hall & Co. Muzzleloading Carbine

Overall length 37-1/2"; barrel length 22"; caliber .58. Markings: "P/CS" on upper left of barrel near breech; "CSA" on top near breech. Modeled after the Springfield U.S. M1855 rifle carbine, the Bilharz, Hall & Co. muzzleloading carbine has often been mistakenly identified as a product of D.C. Hodgkins & Sons of Macon, Georgia. Serial numbers (found internally) belie that identification. Instead these arms are part of deliveries made to Richmond from the middle of 1863 until March 1864. Serial numbers, noted in excess of 700, suggest that about 1,000 were produced. Two basic types, the earlier (through serial number 300) were made with brass nosecaps; the later type (about serial number 310 through at least 710) have pewter nosecaps on the short forestock; neither type affects value.

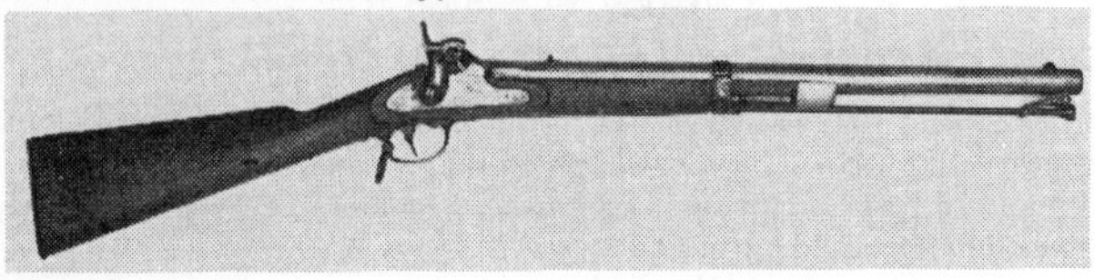

NIB	Exc.	V.G.	Good	Fair	Poor
—	—	25000	10000	3000	1650

BINGHAM LTD.

Norcross, Georgia

PPS 50

A .22 rimfire caliber semi-automatic rifle patterned after the Soviet PPSH submachine gun with 16" barrel and a 50-round drum magazine. Blued, walnut or beech stock with a vented handguard. Manufactured between 1976 and 1985.

NIB	Exc.	V.G.	Good	Fair	Poor
—	575	400	275	225	100

AK-22

A .22 rimfire caliber semi-automatic rifle patterned after the Soviet AK-47 with either a 15- or 29-shot magazine. Walnut or beech stock. Manufactured between 1976 and 1985.

NIB	Exc.	V.G.	Good	Fair	Poor
—	365	225	150	100	75

Bantam

A .22 rimfire or .22 rimfire magnum caliber bolt-action rifle with an 18.5" barrel. Manufactured between 1976 and 1985.

NIB	Exc.	V.G.	Good	Fair	Poor
—	200	85	70	50	35

BLAKE, J. H.

New York, New York

Blake Bolt-Action Rifle

A .30-40 Krag caliber bolt-action rifle with a 30" barrel, and a 7-shot magazine. The stock is secured by three barrel bands. Blued with a walnut stock. Manufactured between 1892 and 1910.

Courtesy Milwaukee Public Museum, Milwaukee, Wisconsin

NIB	Exc.	V.G.	Good	Fair	Poor
—	—	3500	1700	675	200

BLASER JAGDWAFFEN

Germany

SHOTGUNS

Blaser F3

This 12 gauge over/under shotgun with 3" chambers features Grade 4 walnut and is available with 28"-, 30"- or 32" barrels. Includes five choke tubes. Weight is about 8.2 lbs. Introduced 2006.

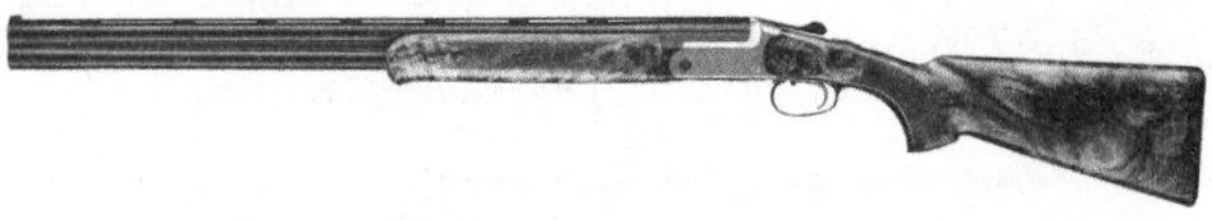

NIB	Exc.	V.G.	Good	Fair	Poor
—	5500	4300	3000	2200	1550

RIFLES

Model K77

A single-shot rifle chambered in a variety of calibers with a 24" barrel and silver-plated as well as engraved receiver. Walnut stock. Introduced in 1988.

NIB	Exc.	V.G.	Good	Fair	Poor
3900	3050	2200	1500	900	450

NOTE: Extra barrels add $750 per barrel.

Model R-84

A bolt-action sporting rifle chambered in a variety of calibers with either a 23" or 24" barrel. Interchangeable barrels are available for this model. Walnut stock. Imported beginning in 1988.

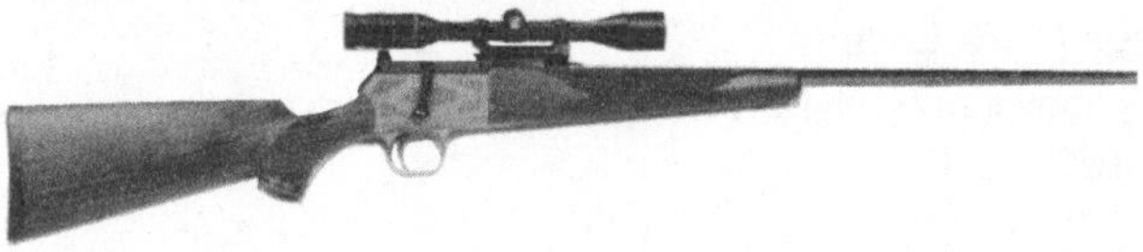

NIB	Exc.	V.G.	Good	Fair	Poor
3700	2850	2000	1800	1100	450

Model R-93 LX

This is a straight-pull-back bolt-action rifle with interchangeable barrels in calibers from .22-250 to .416 Rem. Mag. Barrel length for standard calibers is 22" and for Magnum calibers 26". Magazine capacity is 3 rounds. Receiver is drilled and tapped for Blaser scope mounts. Weight is approximately 7 lbs. Two-piece walnut stock. Introduced by SIGARMS into the U.S. in 1998.

NIB	Exc.	V.G.	Good	Fair	Poor
3000	2400	1700	1200	600	300

NOTE: Add $200 for left-hand rifles, add $800 for .416 Remington Magnum.

Model R-93 Prestige

An updated and upgraded standard model with all the features of the R-93 LX. Light scroll engraving on receiver.

NIB	Exc.	V.G.	Good	Fair	Poor
3275	2750	1800	1300	700	350

Model R-93 Classic

Similar to the model above in choice of calibers and barrel lengths but with the addition of highly figured walnut stock and game scene engraved receiver.

NIB	Exc.	V.G.	Good	Fair	Poor
4500	3300	2400	1750	800	400

NOTE: Add $200 for left-hand rifles, add $800 for .416 Remington Magnum.

Model R-93 Luxus

This is an updated and upgraded model of the R-93 Classic. It features a high grade Turkish walnut stock with ebony forend. Side plates are engraved with game scenes.

NIB	Exc.	V.G.	Good	Fair	Poor
8200	8500	6000	4700	1900	500

Model R-93 Synthetic

Also available in the same wide range of interchangeable barrels and calibers. This model features a one-piece black synthetic stock.

NIB	Exc.	V.G.	Good	Fair	Poor
6300	5200	3950	2900	1500	400

NOTE: Add $200 for left-hand rifles, add $800 for .416 Remington Magnum.

Model R-93 Attache

This model features a custom made stock of highly figured walnut with cheekpiece, leather covered buttplate, silver pistol-grip cap, ebony forend tip, and custom checkering. Sold with a leather carrying case.

NIB	Exc.	V.G.	Good	Fair	Poor
5100	4000	3000	2000	900	400

NOTE: Add $200 for left-hand rifles.

Model R-93 Safari Synthetic

This model is chambered for the .416 Remington Magnum cartridge and fitted with a 24" heavy barrel with open sights. Weight is 9.5 lbs. Black synthetic stock. Other Blaser barrels will interchange on this model.

NIB	Exc.	V.G.	Good	Fair	Poor
2100	1700	1250	875	500	275

Model R-93 Safari LX

Same as the R-93 Safari Synthetic with the exception of a two-piece walnut stock.

NIB	Exc.	V.G.	Good	Fair	Poor
2500	2000	1550	1000	750	350

Model R-93 Safari Classic

This model features an engraved receiver and fancy walnut stock.

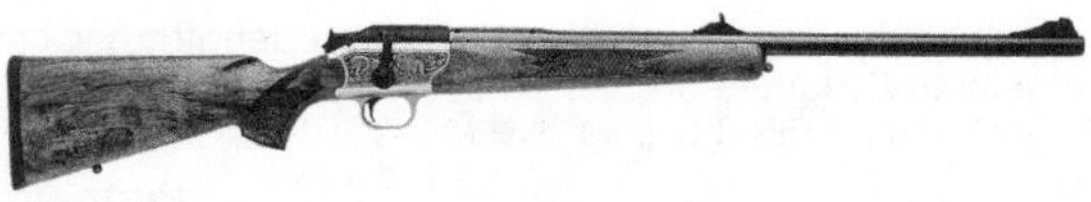

NIB	Exc.	V.G.	Good	Fair	Poor
2500	2000	1550	1000	750	350

Model R-93 Safari Attache

This is a top-of-the-line version of the R-93 series. It features engraved receiver, fancy walnut stock and other custom options found on the R-93 Attache model.

NIB	Exc.	V.G.	Good	Fair	Poor
6000	5000	3950	2900	1500	400

Model R-93 Long Range Sporter

Introduced in 1998, this bolt-action rifle is chambered for the .308 Win. cartridge. The barrel length is 24" without muzzlebrake. Removable box magazine holds 10 rounds. The stock is aluminum and fully adjustable. Weight is approximately 10.4 lbs. No longer in production.

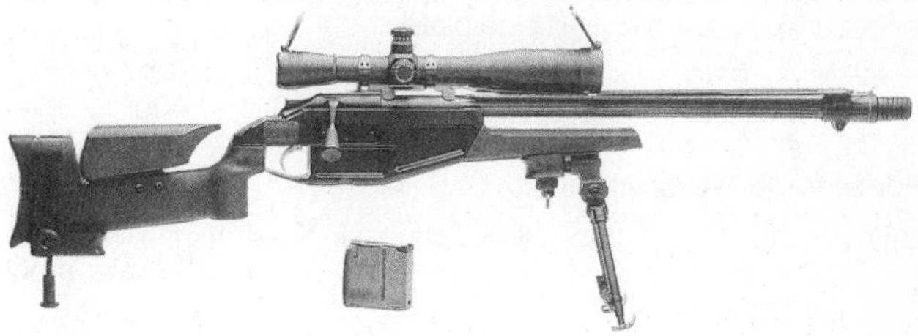

NIB	Exc.	V.G.	Good	Fair	Poor
2200	1775	1250	875	500	275

Model R-93 (LRS2)

This model, introduced in 2000, is a second generation version of the Long Range Sporter model above. It is chambered for the .300 Win. Mag and the .308 both of which are interchangeable. It is also chambered for the .338 Lapua cartridge which does not interchange with the other calibers. The cheekpiece is improved and a new front rail has been added to this model. Barrel length is 24" without muzzlebrake. Weight is about 10.4 lbs.

NIB	Exc.	V.G.	Good	Fair	Poor
3475	2700	1900	1275	800	375

NOTE: For .338 Lapua add $350.

Model R-93 Grand Luxe

Offered in the same wide range of calibers as other Blaser models with the addition of a high grade walnut stock, fully hand engraved receiver, and matching scroll sideplates. Introduced in 1999.

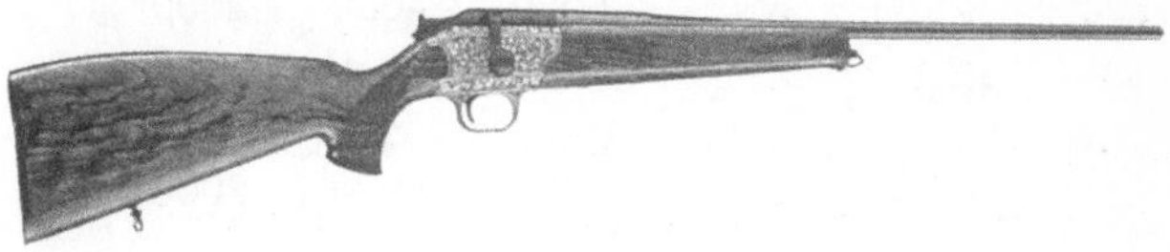

NIB	Exc.	V.G.	Good	Fair	Poor
4675	3700	2800	1300	700	395

NOTE: Add $200 for left-hand rifles.

Model K-95 Standard

This is a single-shot model with break-open action.The receiver is aluminum with engraving on the side plates. Barrel length is 23.6" for standard calibers and 25.6" for magnum calibers. Oil finish Turkish walnut stock. Interchangeable barrels in calibers from .243 to .300 Wby. Magnum. Weight is about 5.5 lbs. Introduced in 2001.

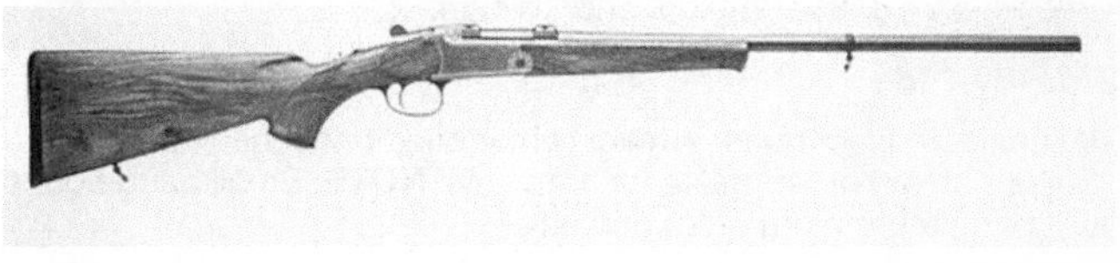

NIB	Exc.	V.G.	Good	Fair	Poor
2500	1950	1500	1150	700	325

Model K-95 Luxus

Same as above but with fancy Turkish walnut stock and hand engraving on receiver and side plates.

NIB	Exc.	V.G.	Good	Fair	Poor
4300	3750	2500	1900	900	400

Model K-95 Stutzen

Introduced in 2003 this break-action single-shot rifle is offered in 23 calibers. Fancy walnut Mannlicher-style, two-piece stock. Interchangeable barrels.

NIB	Exc.	V.G.	Good	Fair	Poor
5400	4650	3200	2250	1000	450

Ultimate Bolt-Action

As above, with a silver-plated and engraved receiver as well as a set trigger.

NIB	Exc.	V.G.	Good	Fair	Poor
7000	5700	1050	825	700	475

SPECIAL ORDER ULTIMATE

The above model is available in a variety of finishes and degrees of decoration.

Ultimate Deluxe

NIB	Exc.	V.G.	Good	Fair	Poor
3250	2600	2050	1750	1400	900

Ultimate Super Deluxe

NIB	Exc.	V.G.	Good	Fair	Poor
4250	3750	3250	2500	2000	1000

Ultimate Exclusive

NIB	Exc.	V.G.	Good	Fair	Poor
5700	5000	4500	3500	2600	1300

Ultimate Super Exclusive

NIB	Exc.	V.G.	Good	Fair	Poor
8900	7900	6800	5000	4000	2000

Ultimate Royal

NIB	Exc.	V.G.	Good	Fair	Poor
11500	9500	7500	6000	4000	2000

NOTE: Extra interchangeable caliber barrels for the above rifles are available at $700 to $1,200 per barrel depending on the grade.

BOSIS, LUCIANO

Brescia, Italy

Bosis is a maker of high-grade sidelock over-and-under and side-by-side guns in gauges 12, 20, 28, and .410. These guns are made on a custom-order basis.

Over-and-Under

Values for used guns in excellent condition begin at $30,000. Secure an expert appraisal prior to sale.

Side-by-Side

Values for used guns in excellent condition begin at $20,000. Secure an expert appraisal prior to sale. **NOTE:** Small gauge guns will bring a premium of 20 percent.

BOSWELL, CHARLES

London, England

One of England's more established makers of best-quality rifles and shotguns. In 1988 the company was purchased by an American consortium and the Cape Horn Outfitters of Charlotte, North Carolina, was appointed their sole agent.

Double Rifle, Boxlock

A .300 Holland & Holland, .375 Holland & Holland or .458 Winchester Magnum double-barrel boxlock rifle with double triggers and a walnut stock. Other features were made to the customer's specifications. A .600 Nitro Express version was also available.

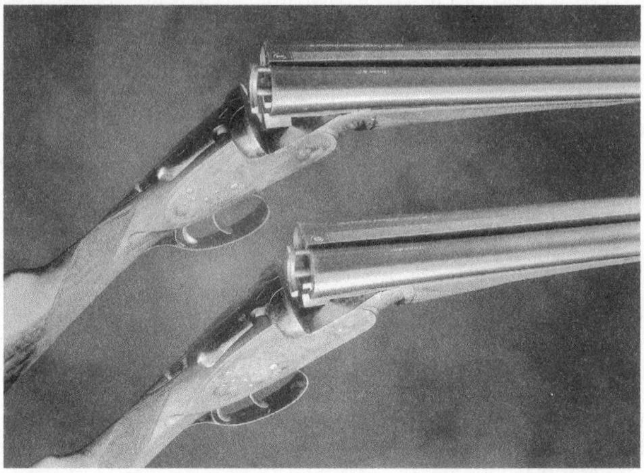

NIB	Exc.	V.G.	Good	Fair	Poor
—	47000	39500	29500	19950	600

NOTE: .600 Nitro Express add 25 percent.

Double Rifle, Sidelock

As above, with Holland & Holland-style sidelocks.

NIB	Exc.	V.G.	Good	Fair	Poor
—	63000	47500	35000	22000	600

NOTE: .600 Nitro Express add 25 percent.

BRAND

Maker—E. Robinson
New York

Brand Breech Loading Carbine

A .50 rimfire caliber carbine with a 22" barrel secured by one barrel band. The frame is marked "Brand's Patent July 29,1862/E. Robinson Manfr/New York." This carbine was produced in limited numbers, primarily for trial purposes.

NIB	Exc.	V.G.	Good	Fair	Poor
—	—	6800	2950	1250	550

BREDA, ERNESTO

Milan, Italy

Andromeda Special

A 12 gauge boxlock shotgun with various barrel lengths and chokes, single-selective triggers and automatic ejectors. Engraved, satin-finished with checkered walnut stock.

NIB	Exc.	V.G.	Good	Fair	Poor
—	1150	775	595	425	300

Vega Special

A 12 gauge boxlock Over/Under shotgun with 26" or 28" barrels, various choke combinations, single-selective trigger and automatic ejectors. Engraved and blued with a checkered walnut stock.

NIB	Exc.	V.G.	Good	Fair	Poor
—	850	700	600	375	275

Vega Special Trap

As above with a competition-styled stock and 30" or 32" barrels with full chokes.

NIB	Exc.	V.G.	Good	Fair	Poor
—	1350	1050	850	500	350

Sirio Standard

Similar to the Vega with extensive engraving and a higher degree of finishing. There is a 28" barreled skeet version available in this model.

NIB	Exc.	V.G.	Good	Fair	Poor
—	2750	2000	1950	1350	650

Standard Semi-Automatic

A 12 gauge semi-automatic shotgun with 25" or 27" ventilated rib barrels, screw-in choke tubes, an engraved receiver, and checkered walnut stock.

NIB	Exc.	V.G.	Good	Fair	Poor
—	375	275	225	175	125

Standard Semi-Automatic Grade I

As above, with more engraving and finer wood.

NIB	Exc.	V.G.	Good	Fair	Poor
—	650	475	325	225	175

Standard Semi-Automatic Grade II

A more elaborately engraved version of the Grade I.

NIB	Exc.	V.G.	Good	Fair	Poor
—	850	600	450	375	250

Standard Semi-Automatic Grade III

The most deluxe version in this line with select walnut and extensive engraving.

NIB	Exc.	V.G.	Good	Fair	Poor
—	1050	800	650	575	250

Magnum Model

Same as the standard but in 12 gauge Magnum.

NIB	Exc.	V.G.	Good	Fair	Poor
—	435	325	250	175	75

Gold Series Antares Standard

A 12 gauge semi-automatic shotgun with a 25" or 27" ventilated rib barrel and screw-in choke tubes. Blued with a checkered walnut stock.

NIB	Exc.	V.G.	Good	Fair	Poor
—	650	425	350	275	225

Gold Series Argus

As above, with alloy frame.

NIB	Exc.	V.G.	Good	Fair	Poor
—	650	475	375	300	250

Gold Series Aries

As above, except in 12 gauge Magnum.

NIB	Exc.	V.G.	Good	Fair	Poor
—	700	495	400	325	275

M1 Garand

Virtual duplicate of the US M1 Garand chambered in .30-06. Made in the mid-1950s by Breda under contract for Denmark. Values shown are for correct, non-import marked specimens. Deduct up to 50 percent for built-up parts guns or non-matching guns.

NIB	Exc.	V.G.	Good	Fair	Poor
—	2200	1595	800	400	250

BRETTON

Ste. Etienne, France

Baby Standard

A 12 or 20 gauge Over/Under shotgun with various barrel lengths and choke combinations and double triggers. Blued, checkered walnut stock.

NIB	Exc.	V.G.	Good	Fair	Poor
1350	975	725	550	400	325

Deluxe Grade

A 12, 16, and 20 gauge Over/Under shotgun. Engraved, coin-finished receiver with walnut stock.

NIB	Exc.	V.G.	Good	Fair	Poor
2150	1875	1400	800	500	325

BRNO ARMS

Uhersky Brod, Czech Republic

NOTE: Some but not all of the BRNO models listed in this section are currently imported into the U.S.

ZG-47

A bolt-action rifle based on the Mauser system. Chambered for .270, 7x57, 7x64, .30-06, 8x57, 8x60, 8x64S, 9.3x62, and on special order 10.75x68. Barrel length is 23.6". Adjustable trigger. Hinged floorplate. Weight is about 7.7 lbs.

Standard

NIB	Exc.	V.G.	Good	Fair	Poor
—	1000	900	800	650	400

Deluxe

NIB	Exc.	V.G.	Good	Fair	Poor
—	1100	950	850	600	450

ZH-SERIES

A double barrel Over/Under boxlock series of shotguns with interchangeable barrels in shotgun and rifle configurations, of various lengths, double triggers and automatic ejectors. The models listed represent the different gauges and/or calibers offered.

ZH-300

NIB	Exc.	V.G.	Good	Fair	Poor
800	675	575	400	325	250

ZH-301

12ga/12ga.

NIB	Exc.	V.G.	Good	Fair	Poor
—	600	500	400	350	200

ZH-302

12ga/12ga Skeet.

NIB	Exc.	V.G.	Good	Fair	Poor
—	600	550	450	400	250

ZH-303 12

12ga/12ga Trap.

NIB	Exc.	V.G.	Good	Fair	Poor
—	600	550	450	400	250

ZH-304

12ga/7x57R.

NIB	Exc.	V.G.	Good	Fair	Poor
—	1000	800	500	400	250

ZH-305

12ga/6x52R.

NIB	Exc.	V.G.	Good	Fair	Poor
—	900	700	500	400	225

ZH-306

12ga/6x50R Mag.

NIB	Exc.	V.G.	Good	Fair	Poor
—	850	650	450	350	200

ZH-308

12ga/7x65R.

NIB	Exc.	V.G.	Good	Fair	Poor
—	850	700	500	400	225

ZH-309

12ga/8x57 JRS.

NIB	Exc.	V.G.	Good	Fair	Poor
—	850	700	500	400	225

ZH-321

16ga/16ga.

NIB	Exc.	V.G.	Good	Fair	Poor
—	750	625	450	400	225

ZH-324

16ga/7x57R.

NIB	Exc.	V.G.	Good	Fair	Poor
—	875	700	500	400	225

ZH-328

16ga/7x65R.

NIB	Exc.	V.G.	Good	Fair	Poor
—	850	700	500	400	225

NOTE: For ZH models with set triggers and cheekpiece add $75. For interchangeable barrels add between $300 and $400 depending on gauge and caliber.

Model 300 Combo

The model ZH-300 with 8 interchangeable barrels in a fitted case. Introduced in 1986.

NIB	Exc.	V.G.	Good	Fair	Poor
8500	6000	4500	2750	2000	1500

Model 500

The model ZH-300 with acid-etched decoration, automatic ejectors and in 12 gauge.

NIB	Exc.	V.G.	Good	Fair	Poor
1100	800	600	425	350	275

ZP-49

A 12 gauge sidelock double-barrel shotgun with double triggers and automatic ejectors. Blued with a walnut stock. Imported in 1986 only.

NIB	Exc.	V.G.	Good	Fair	Poor
—	1050	800	650	450	325

ZP-149

As above, without engraving.

NIB	Exc.	V.G.	Good	Fair	Poor
850	600	500	400	300	200

ZP-349

As above, with the buttstock having a cheekpiece and a beavertail forearm.

NIB	Exc.	V.G.	Good	Fair	Poor
—	800	650	500	350	250

ZBK-100

A single barrel shotgun in 12 or 20 gauge with 27" barrel and walnut stock. Weight is approximately 5.5 lbs.

NIB	Exc.	V.G.	Good	Fair	Poor
250	200	150	125	100	75

RIFLES

ZKW-465 (Hornet Sporter)

A .22 Hornet caliber bolt-action rifle with a 23" barrel, express sights and double-set triggers. Blued with a walnut stock.

NIB	Exc.	V.G.	Good	Fair	Poor
—	1500	1100	950	800	550

Model 21H

A 6.5x57mm, 7x57mm or 8x57mm caliber bolt-action sporting rifle with a 23-5/8" barrel, express sights and double set triggers. Blued with a walnut stock.

NIB	Exc.	V.G.	Good	Fair	Poor
—	1250	1050	900	750	600

Model 22F

As above, with a Mannlicher-style stock. Barrel length is 20-1/2".

NIB	Exc.	V.G.	Good	Fair	Poor
—	1295	1100	900	650	500

Model I

A .22 caliber bolt-action rifle with a 22.75" barrel having folding leaf rear sights. Blued with a walnut stock.

NIB	Exc.	V.G.	Good	Fair	Poor
—	550	400	300	250	200

Model II

As above, with a more finely figured walnut stock.

NIB	Exc.	V.G.	Good	Fair	Poor
—	595	450	350	300	225

ZKM 611

This is a semi-automatic rifle chambered for the .17 HMR or .22 WRM cartridge. It is fitted with a 20" barrel and has a magazine capacity of 6 rounds. Weight is approximately 6.2 lbs.

NIB	Exc.	V.G.	Good	Fair	Poor
700	625	525	300	175	125

ZKM 451

This is a semi-automatic rifle chambered for the .22 LR cartridge and fitted with a 22" barrel. Magazine capacity is 7 rounds. Weight is about 5.25 lbs.

NIB	Exc.	V.G.	Good	Fair	Poor
450	300	250	125	100	75

ZKM 451 LUX

Same as above but with select walnut stock.

NIB	Exc.	V.G.	Good	Fair	Poor
500	350	250	150	125	100

ZBK 680

A .22 Hornet or .222 caliber bolt-action rifle with a 23.5" barrel, double set triggers and 5-shot magazine. Blued with a walnut stock.

NIB	Exc.	V.G.	Good	Fair	Poor
925	750	550	400	325	225

SUPER EXPRESS RIFLE

An Over/Under sidelock double-barrel rifle, with 23.5" barrels, double triggers and automatic ejectors. Engraved, blued with a walnut stock. Available in 6 grades:

NIB	Exc.	V.G.	Good	Fair	Poor

Standard Model

NIB	Exc.	V.G.	Good	Fair	Poor
5500	4150	3000	2500	1750	1250

Grade I

NIB	Exc.	V.G.	Good	Fair	Poor
7500	5900	4750	4500	3600	3250

Grade II

NIB	Exc.	V.G.	Good	Fair	Poor
6500	5150	4000	3500	2750	2250

Grade III

NIB	Exc.	V.G.	Good	Fair	Poor
6250	4900	3950	3250	2750	2250

Grade IV

NIB	Exc.	V.G.	Good	Fair	Poor
6000	4700	3500	3000	2500	2250

Grade V

NIB	Exc.	V.G.	Good	Fair	Poor
5750	3950	3250	2750	2250	1750

Grade VI

NIB	Exc.	V.G.	Good	Fair	Poor
4900	4250	3100	2600	1950	1500

ZH-344/348/349

An over-and-under rifle chambered for 7x57R, 7x65R, or 8x57JRS.

NIB	Exc.	V.G.	Good	Fair	Poor
1500	975	700	550	400	275

Model 98 Standard

This bolt-action rifle is chambered for a variety of calibers from the 7x64 to the 9.3x62. It is fitted with a 23" barrel and figured walnut stock with buttplate and open sights. Weight is approximately 7.25 lbs.

NIB	Exc.	V.G.	Good	Fair	Poor
900	750	400	300	200	150

NOTE: For set trigger add $100.

Model 98 Full Stock

Same as above but with full one-piece stock and set trigger.

NIB	Exc.	V.G.	Good	Fair	Poor
1100	700	500	400	350	200

ZK 99

This is a tip-up centerfire rifle chambered for a wide variety of calibers from 6.5x57R to .30-06. Barrel length is 23" and weight is about 5.75 lbs.

NIB	Exc.	V.G.	Good	Fair	Poor
995	750	550	395	200	150

ZBK 110

This is a single-shot tip-open rifle chambered for the .22 Hornet, .222 Rem., the 5.6x50R Mag., and the 5.6x52R. Barrel length is 23.5". Open sights. Walnut stock without checkering. Weight is about 6 lbs.

NIB	Exc.	V.G.	Good	Fair	Poor
450	350	250	200	150	75

ZBK 110 LUX

Same as above but with select walnut stock with checkering. Open sights.

NIB	Exc.	V.G.	Good	Fair	Poor
440	350	250	200	150	75

ZBK 110 Super Lux

Same as above but with fancy walnut stock with checkering. Open sights.

NIB	Exc.	V.G.	Good	Fair	Poor
650	525	400	300	150	75

BROLIN ARMS

La Verne, California

PUMP-ACTION SHOTGUNS

LAWMAN SERIES - Model HL18SB

This is a pump-action 12 gauge shotgun with an 18.5" barrel, black synthetic stock and bead sights. Weight is about 7 lbs. Introduced in 1997.

NIB	Exc.	V.G.	Good	Fair	Poor
295	250	195	150	95	50

Model HL18SR

Same as above but fitted with rifle sights.

NIB	Exc.	V.G.	Good	Fair	Poor
325	275	225	175	125	65

Model HL18SBN

Same as above but with nickel finish and bead sights.

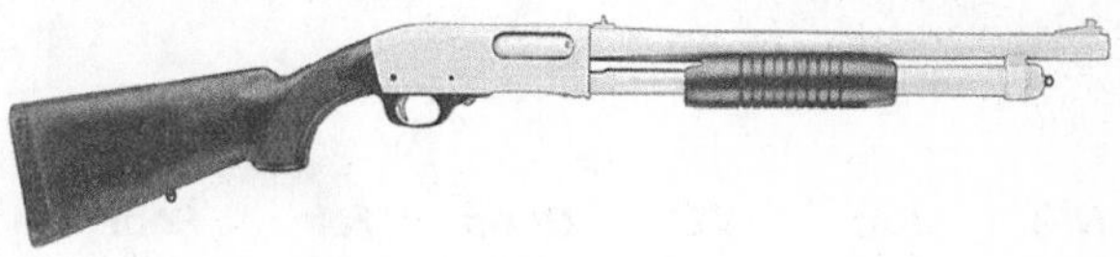

NIB	Exc.	V.G.	Good	Fair	Poor
270	200	150	100	75	50

Model HL18WB

This version has a wood stock and bead sights.

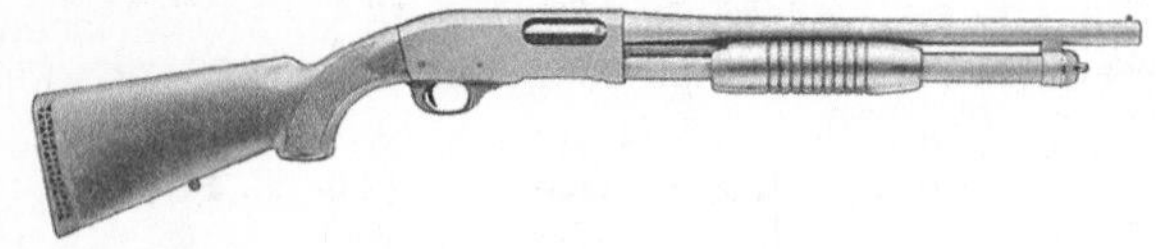

NIB	Exc.	V.G.	Good	Fair	Poor
295	250	195	150	95	50

Model HL18WR

Same as above but fitted with rifle sights.

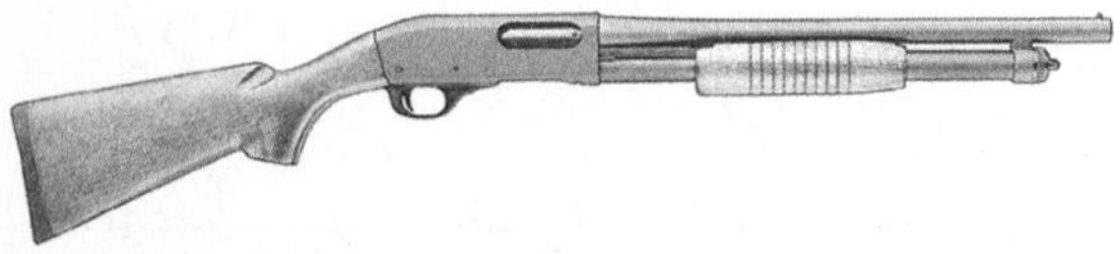

NIB	Exc.	V.G.	Good	Fair	Poor
270	200	150	100	75	50

FIELD SERIES—PUMP ACTION FIELD GUN

Model HF24SB

This is a 12 gauge pump action shotgun with a 24" barrel, matte finish, and black synthetic stock with bead sights. Weight is about 7.3 lbs. Introduced in 1997.

NIB	Exc.	V.G.	Good	Fair	Poor
270	200	150	100	75	50

Model HF28SB

Same as above but fitted with a 28" barrel. Weight is 7.4 lbs.

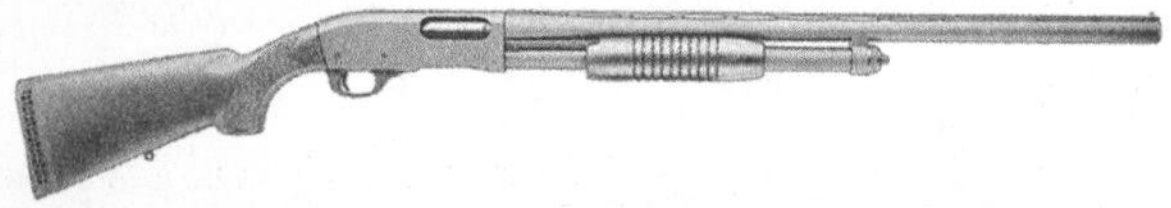

NIB	Exc.	V.G.	Good	Fair	Poor
270	200	150	100	75	50

Model HF24WB

This model features a 24" barrel with wood stock.

NIB	Exc.	V.G.	Good	Fair	Poor
270	200	150	100	75	50

Model HF28WB

Same as above but with 24" barrel.

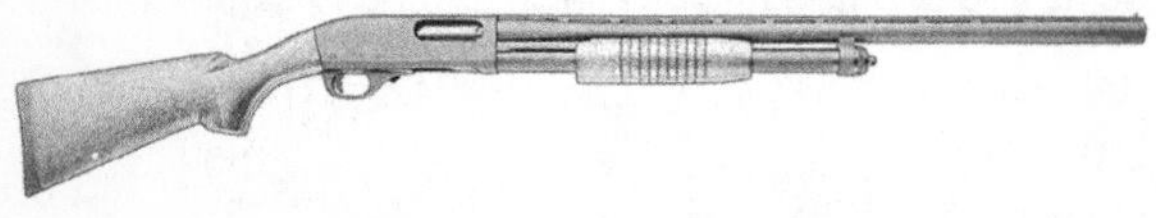

NIB	Exc.	V.G.	Good	Fair	Poor
270	200	150	100	75	50

Slug Special

This slide-action shotgun is chambered for 3" 12 gauge shells and is available with choice of 18.5" or 22" barrels with rifle or ghost ring sights. Available with fixed improved cylinder choke, 4" extended rifled choke, or fully rifled barrel. Choice of wood or synthetic stocks.

NIB	Exc.	V.G.	Good	Fair	Poor
270	200	150	100	75	50

Turkey Special

This 12 gauge 3" model is fitted with a 22" extra full choke vent rib barrel with a choice of wood or synthetic stock.

NIB	Exc.	V.G.	Good	Fair	Poor
270	200	150	100	75	50

FIELD COMBO—TWO BARREL COMBO SET

Model HC28SB

This set consists of an 18.5" barrel and 28" barrel with synthetic stock pistol grip, and bead sights.

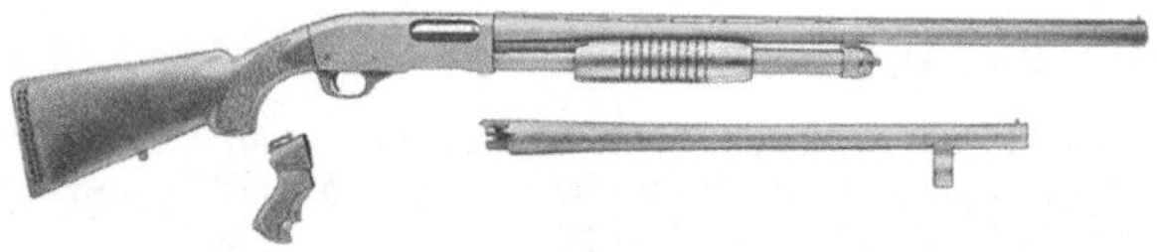

NIB	Exc.	V.G.	Good	Fair	Poor
300	250	200	125	75	50

Model HC28SR

Same as above but with rifle and bead sights.

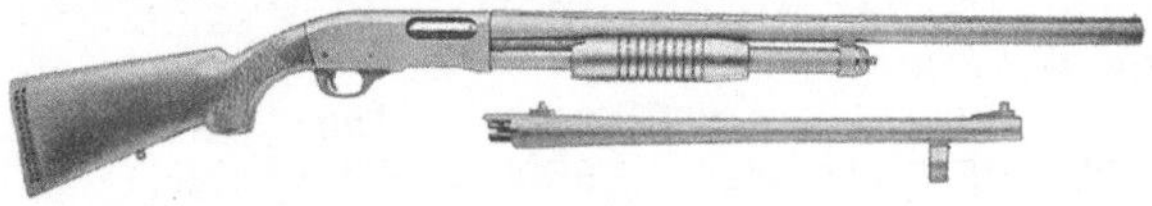

NIB	Exc.	V.G.	Good	Fair	Poor
320	250	200	125	75	50

Model HC28WB

This model features a wood stock, pistol grip, and bead sights.

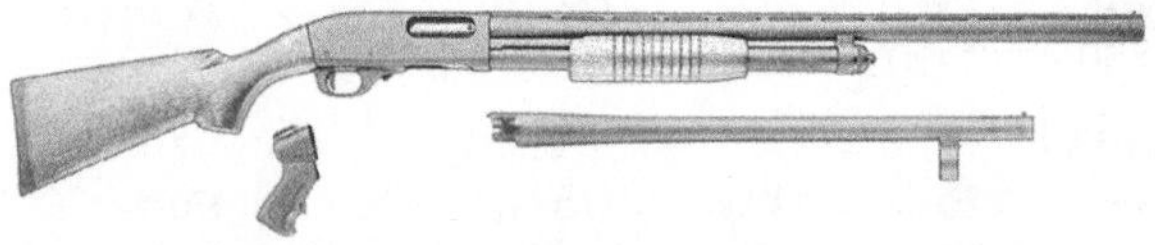

NIB	Exc.	V.G.	Good	Fair	Poor
300	250	200	125	75	50

Model HC28WR

Same as above but with wood stock with rifle and bead sights.

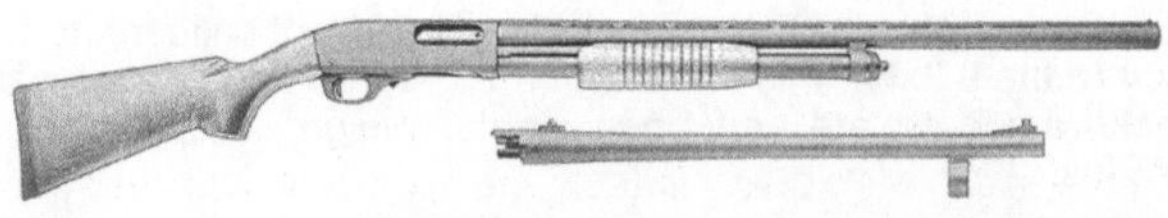

NIB	Exc.	V.G.	Good	Fair	Poor
320	250	200	125	75	50

SEMI-AUTOMATIC SHOTGUNS

BL-12 Security

This 12 gauge shotgun has a 3" chamber and 5 round magazine. It is fitted with a 18.5" vent rib barrel. Synthetic stock is standard.

NIB	*Exc.*	*V.G.*	*Good*	*Fair*	*Poor*
350	325	295	200	150	75

BL-12 Field

Similar to the above model but with a 28" vent rib barrel and choice of wood or synthetic stock.

NIB	*Exc.*	*V.G.*	*Good*	*Fair*	*Poor*
350	325	295	200	150	75

SAS-12 Security

This 12 gauge shotgun is chambered for 2.75" 12 gauge shells and fitted with 24" vent rib barrel or rifle sight barrel. Detachable box magazine; 3 round standard, 5 round optional. Synthetic stock.

NIB	*Exc.*	*V.G.*	*Good*	*Fair*	*Poor*
350	325	295	200	150	75

RIFLES

Mitchell PPS-50

This is a semi-automatic rifle chambered for the .22 LR cartridge. It has a detachable 10-round magazine. It is a copy of the Russian PPSh machine gun used in WWII.

NIB	*Exc.*	*V.G.*	*Good*	*Fair*	*Poor*
400	325	275	225	175	100

MAUSER RIFLES

Lightning Model

This model features a sliding bolt that locks directly into the barrel. Chambered for 7.62x39mm cartridge as well as the .308 Win. Blue finish with choice of colored synthetic stocks. Open sights are standard.

NIB	*Exc.*	*V.G.*	*Good*	*Fair*	*Poor*
550	450	350	325	200	100

Lightning Hunter Model

This model features a detachable magazine, recoil pad, blued finish, checkered wood stock, and choice of open sights or no sights with scope mounts included. Calibers from .243 to .300 Win. Mag.

NIB	*Exc.*	*V.G.*	*Good*	*Fair*	*Poor*
650	500	350	325	200	100

NOTE: Add $50 for open sights, $50 for stainless steel.

Lightning Hunter All Weather Model

Same as above but with black synthetic stock.

NIB	*Exc.*	*V.G.*	*Good*	*Fair*	*Poor*
700	550	350	325	200	100

Lightning Varmint Model

The features of this model are the same as the Lightning Hunter Model with the addition of a heavy fluted barrel with special varmint wood or synthetic stock. Chambered for .22-250 and .243 cartridges.

NIB	*Exc.*	*V.G.*	*Good*	*Fair*	*Poor*
900	700	550	450	300	125

Lightning Sniper

This model features a heavy fluted barrel with detachable magazine and a choice of special wood or synthetic stock with built-in bi-pod rail. Offered in .308 or 300 Win. Mag. calibers.

NIB	*Exc.*	*V.G.*	*Good*	*Fair*	*Poor*
1000	800	600	450	300	125

Lightning Professional

This model has a heavy fluted barrel, no sights, and recoil compensator. A tuned trigger system is standard. All weather adjustable stock with pistol grip. Available in .308 or .300 Win. Mag. calibers.

NIB	*Exc.*	*V.G.*	*Good*	*Fair*	*Poor*
900	700	550	395	300	125

Model 2000 Classic

The 2000 Classic features an interchangeable caliber system for cartridges in the same action length. Detachable magazine. High-grade walnut stock with cut checkering and rosewood forend. Single set trigger is standard. Offered in .270, .308, .30-06, 7mm Rem. Mag., and .300 Win. Mag.

NIB	*Exc.*	*V.G.*	*Good*	*Fair*	*Poor*
1500	1250	800	495	300	125

Model 2000 Varmint

This model features a heavy fluted barrel with special varmint wood stock with accessory rail. Offered in .22-250, and .243 calibers. Standard without sights.

NIB	*Exc.*	*V.G.*	*Good*	*Fair*	*Poor*
2200	1700	1200	800	400	200

Model 2000 Sniper

This model features an interchangeable caliber system, heavy fluted barrel, no sights, single set trigger, all-weather stock with built-in bi-pod rail. Offered in .308 and .300 Win. Mag. calibers.

NIB	*Exc.*	*V.G.*	*Good*	*Fair*	*Poor*
2200	1750	1250	800	400	200

Model 20/22

This is a high-quality .22 bolt-action rifle chambered for the .22 LR or .22 Magnum cartridge. Available in both a standard and deluxe configuration. Add $100 for deluxe version.

NIB	*Exc.*	*V.G.*	*Good*	*Fair*	*Poor*
750	575	475	395	300	125

Model 1898 Commemorative

This model celebrates the 100 year anniversary of the '98 Mauser. Chambered for the 8mm Mauser cartridge. This is a limited edition rifle.

NIB	*Exc.*	*V.G.*	*Good*	*Fair*	*Poor*
2300	1750	1400	1000	675	300

Model 98

This is the original Mauser action built to Safari calibers. Chambered for .375 H&H or .416 Rigby.

NIB	*Exc.*	*V.G.*	*Good*	*Fair*	*Poor*
10000	8000	6250	5000	1500	400

BROWN, E.A. MANUFACTURING CO.

Alexandria, Minnesota

Brown Model 97D Single-Shot Rifle

This is a single-shot falling block rifle chambered for calibers from .17 Ackley to .45-70 Gov't. Barrel lengths up to 26". Sporter-style stock with pistol grip, cheekpiece, and schnabel forend. Blue/black finish. Weight is about 6 lbs. No sights.

NIB	*Exc.*	*V.G.*	*Good*	*Fair*	*Poor*
1200	1000	750	600	400	200

BROWN PRODUCTS, INC., ED

Perry, Missouri

NOTE: There are a number of extra options available on Ed Brown handguns and rifles that may affect values. In August of 2010, Ed Brown announced that he would no longer be accepting orders for new rifles and, for an indefinite period of time, would be focusing on his core business of handguns. Rifle parts and limited services remain available.

Savanna

Fitted with a long action and chambered for calibers from .257 Ackley to .338 Win. Mag. Barrel is a lightweight 24" for standard calibers and a 24" medium weight for magnum calibers. Talley scope mounts included. Fiberglass stock, recoil pad, steel trigger guard and floorplate are standard.

NIB	*Exc.*	*V.G.*	*Good*	*Fair*	*Poor*
3800	3000	1995	1500	900	400

Damara

Similar to Savanna but in a lightweight configuration with natural-finish stainless barrel.

NIB	*Exc.*	*V.G.*	*Good*	*Fair*	*Poor*
3200	2650	2000	1300	650	400

Varmint

This is a custom-made rifle with a short single-shot action, 26" medium weight barrel or 24" heavyweight barrel. H-S Precision stock. Available in calibers from .222 to 6.5/.284.

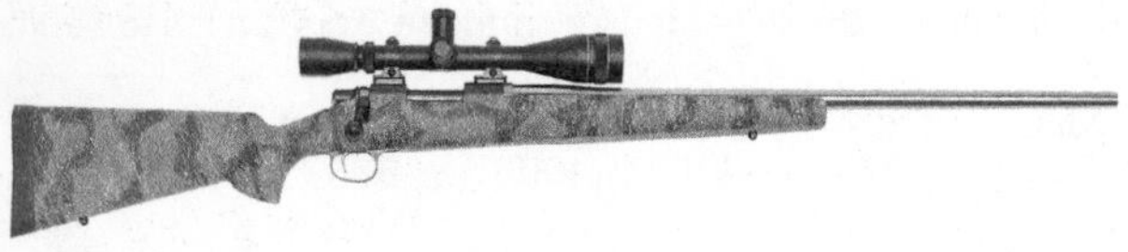

NIB	*Exc.*	*V.G.*	*Good*	*Fair*	*Poor*
3500	2800	2000	1300	750	400

Bushveld

This model is based on a Dakota controlled feed action. Fitted with a 24" medium or heavyweight barrel. Calibers from .330 Dakota to .458 Win. Mag. Detachable box magazine. Monte Carlo fiberglass stock, recoil pad, steel trigger and floorplate are standard as is Talley scope mounts. Weight is approx. 8.5 lbs.

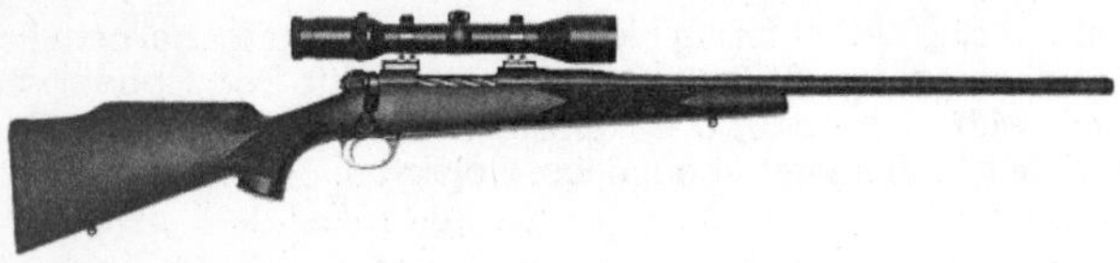

NIB	*Exc.*	*V.G.*	*Good*	*Fair*	*Poor*
4400	3250	2000	1500	900	400

Express

Centerfire bolt-action rifle chambered for a wide variety of large Africa-class calibers. Dropped box magazine, fully controlled feed, fluted bolt, McMillan stock, iron sights.

NIB	*Exc.*	*V.G.*	*Good*	*Fair*	*Poor*
3600	2900	2350	1600	800	400

Marine Sniper

Duplicate of Vietnam-era McMillan sniper rifle, controlled feed, fluted bolt, hinged floorplate, woodland camo stock, blackened stainless steel barrel and receiver. Offered in .308 and .300 Win. Mag. calibers. Weight is about 9.25 lbs.

NIB	*Exc.*	*V.G.*	*Good*	*Fair*	*Poor*
3700	2950	2350	1600	900	400

Light Tactical

This is a short-action rifle with light weight floorplate and trigger guard. Fitted with a 21-inch medium-weight barrel. Black fiberglass stock with aluminum bedding block. Available in calibers from .22-250 to .308.

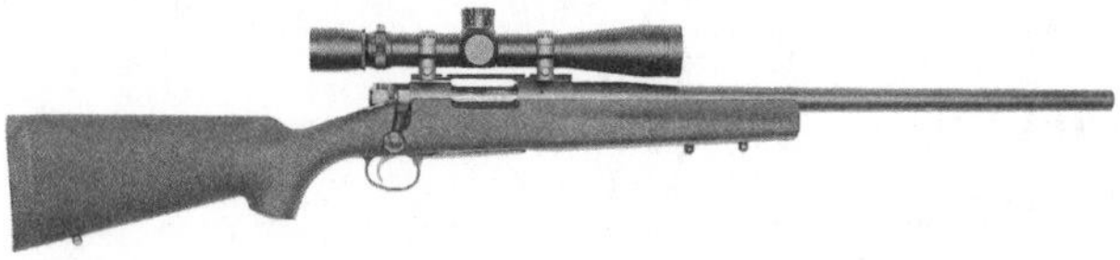

NIB	*Exc.*	*V.G.*	*Good*	*Fair*	*Poor*
4100	2950	2000	1500	900	400

Tactical

This is similar to the above model but built on a long action with heavy weight 26-inch blued barrel. McMillan A-3 black tactical stock. Available in .308 and .300 Win. Mag.

NIB	*Exc.*	*V.G.*	*Good*	*Fair*	*Poor*
3900	3350	2500	1600	950	400

Ozark

This rifle is built on a short action with a blind magazine. A 21-inch lightweight barrel is fitted for standard calibers and a medium weight 21-inch barrel for magnum calibers. Chambered for calibers from .22-250 to .308. Talley scope mounts are included as is a fiberglass stock, recoil pad, steel trigger guard and floorplate.

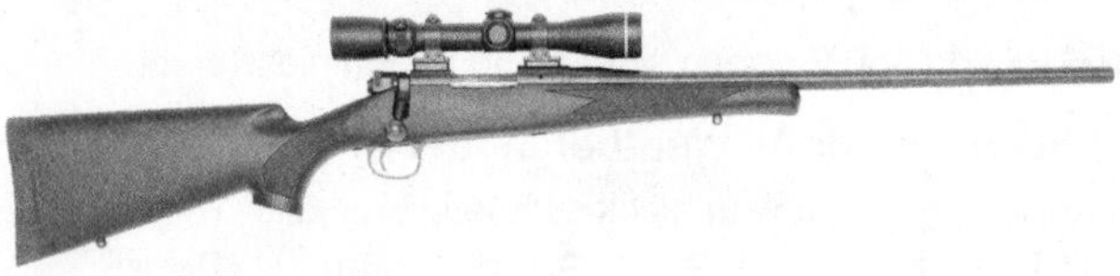

NIB	*Exc.*	*V.G.*	*Good*	*Fair*	*Poor*
3800	3000	1995	1500	900	400

Denali

This is a lighter-weight version of the Ozark with a 22-inch super light-weight barrel. Chambered for calibers .25-06 to .300 WSM. Weight is about 6.75 lbs.

NIB	*Exc.*	*V.G.*	*Good*	*Fair*	*Poor*
3800	3000	1995	1500	900	400

Peacekeeper

This is a single-shot long-action rifle chambered for .30-378 Wby., .338-378 Wby., or the .338 Lapua caliber. Fitted with a heavy 26-inch barrel with muzzlebrake. Fiberglass tactical stock with recoil pad. Leupold Mark 4 scope mounts standard. Weight is approx. 13 lbs.

NIB	Exc.	V.G.	Good	Fair	Poor
4500	3250	2100	1300	800	400

BROWNING ARMS CO.

Morgan, Utah

BUCK MARK SERIES

Buck Mark Standard Stainless URX

.22 LR semi-auto. 5.5" stainless bull barrel; 34 oz. Ambidextrous rubberized grip and adjustable sights. (Also available in alloy steel.) Introduced 2006.

NIB	Exc.	V.G.	Good	Fair	Poor
400	325	275	200	125	100

SHOTGUNS

SUPERPOSED SHOTGUNS

This series of Over/Under, double-barrel shotguns is chambered for 12, 20, and 28 gauges, as well as the .410 bore and is offered with vent rib barrels from 26.5" to 32" in length. It features various choke combinations. This shotgun is built on a boxlock action and features either double or single-selective triggers and automatic ejectors. There were a number of versions offered that differ in the amount of ornamentation and the quality of the materials and workmanship utilized in manufacture. Values for small-bore models are generally higher. This series was introduced in 1930 and is manufactured by Fabrique Nationale in Belgium. For factory restored guns or very fine non-factory restorations Superposed guns will bring close to factory original prices.For extra factory installed barrels add $1000 to $2500 depending on the grade of the gun.

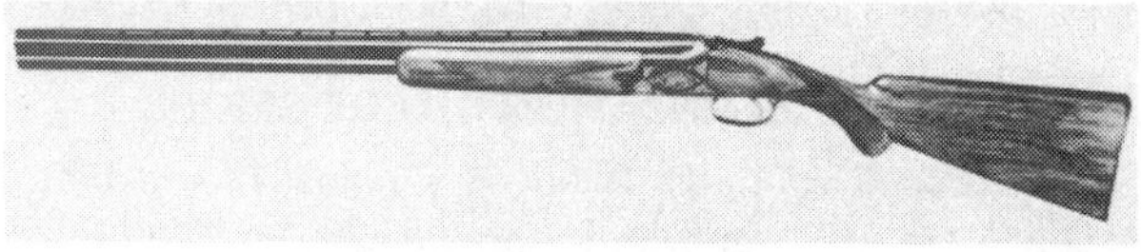

PRE-WAR SUPERPOSED, 1930-1940

Browning Superposed shotgun prices are divided into three different categories. The first category is for pre-war guns built from 1930 to 1940. These pre-war Superposed guns were manufactured in 12 gauge only from serial number 1 to around 17,000. These shotguns were offered in four different grades: Grade I, Pigeon, Diana, and Midas.

Grade I

Rock Island Auction Company, August, 2004

NIB	Exc.	V.G.	Good	Fair	Poor
—	2500	1950	1200	450	300

Pigeon

NIB	Exc.	V.G.	Good	Fair	Poor
—	4900	3800	2800	1500	800

Diana

NIB	Exc.	V.G.	Good	Fair	Poor
—	7000	6000	4700	2000	900

Midas

NIB	Exc.	V.G.	Good	Fair	Poor
—	11500	8900	5000	2500	1000

NOTE: For twin-single triggers add 15 percent. For vent rib add 10 percent. For recoil pads or shorter than standard stocks deduct 25 percent.

SUPERPOSED FROM 1947-1959

The second category of Superposed was produced and sold from 1947 to 1959. These were built in 12 and 20 gauge as well as the 28 gauge and .410 bore which were introduced in 1959. These shotguns were graded using a Roman numeral system instead of names. They are: Grade I, Grade II, Grade III, Grade IV, Grade V, and Grade VI. The values listed are for 12 gauge. Add the premium or deductions as listed. The number of 28 gauge and .410 bore guns sold in late 1959 number less than 100. **NOTE:** The number of Grade VIs sold in North America is unknown, but it was most likely very small. This is a very rare grade. Proceed with caution.

Grade I

NIB	Exc.	V.G.	Good	Fair	Poor
3700	2500	1400	900	300	250

Grade II

NIB	Exc.	V.G.	Good	Fair	Poor
5000	4000	2500	1200	600	375

Grade III

NIB	Exc.	V.G.	Good	Fair	Poor
6250	5500	3900	2200	750	450

Grade IV

NIB	Exc.	V.G.	Good	Fair	Poor
9500	8500	4500	2400	1200	550

Grade V

NIB	Exc.	V.G.	Good	Fair	Poor
8500	7000	4000	2400	1200	650

Grade VI

NIB	Exc.	V.G.	Good	Fair	Poor
15000	13000	7900	4000	2200	850

NOTE: 20 gauge add 60 percent. 28 gauge add 100 percent (1959 only). 410 add 100 percent (1959 only). Trap deduct 40 percent. Standard weight 12 gauge Grade I deduct 10 percent.

SUPERPOSED FROM 1960-1976

Browning Superposed shotguns built from 1960 to 1976 revert back to the older grade names. They are Grade I, Pigeon, Pointer, Diana, and Midas. These shotguns were available in 12, 20, and 28 gauge as well as .410 bore. This last production period is a little more complicated due to manufacturing changes that some collectors consider important such as round knobs, long tangs.Prices listed reflect Superposed field guns produced from 1960 to 1965 in round pistol grip knob with long trigger guard tang in 12 gauge. For all other variations during this period one should consider:For salt wood damage deduct a minimum of 60 percent. For round knob short tang (circa 1966-1969) deduct 50 percent. For flat knob short tang (circa 1969-1971) deduct 50 percent. For flat knob long tang (circa 1971-1976) deduct 25 percent. For New Style Skeet and Lightning Trap (recoil pad, flat knob, full beavertail forearm) with long trigger guard tang (1971-1976) deduct 35 percent; with short trigger guard tang deduct 40 percent; if Broadway rib deduct an additional 10 percent. For skeet chokes on field guns deduct 5 percent. For recoil pads on 2-3/4" chambered field guns deduct 20 percent. For Master engraver signed guns (Funken, Watrin, Vrancken) add 10 percent. For Standard weight Grade I guns deduct 10 percent. For shorter than standard stock length deduct 25 percent. For barrel lengths of 32" add 10 percent. For 20 gauge add 50 percent. For 28 gauge add 100 percent. For .410 bore add 60 percent.

Grade I

NIB	Exc.	V.G.	Good	Fair	Poor
4000	3250	1500	700	500	250

Pigeon Grade

NIB	Exc.	V.G.	Good	Fair	Poor
6500	5500	3800	2000	1000	600

Pointer Grade—Rare

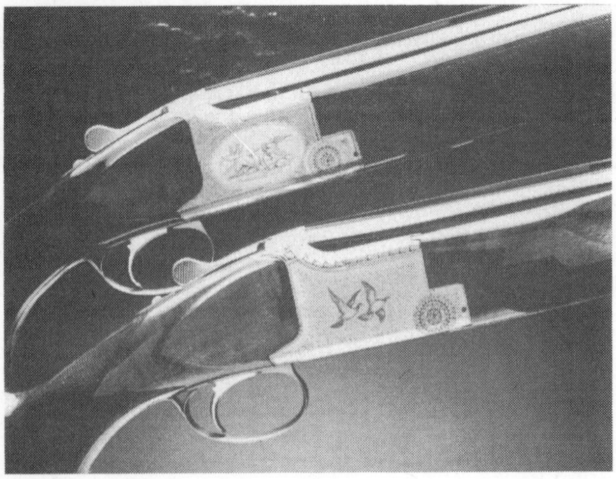

NIB	Exc.	V.G.	Good	Fair	Poor
9500	8050	5600	3000	2000	1000

Diana Grade

NIB	Exc.	V.G.	Good	Fair	Poor
9500	8250	5700	3000	2000	1000

Midas Grade

Comment: FN also built Exhibition Grades that were sold in this country under the Browning name. Collectors consider a true Exhibition Grade as one not having a "C" prefix in the serial number. These particular guns are considered quite desirable and should be appraised on an individual basis. Superposed in this catageory can range in price from $10,000 to $20,000 depending on gauge, engraving coverage, and options.The second type of Exhibition Grade is know as the "C" type that was first sold in the United States from about 1973 to 1977 and is so called because of the "C" prefix in the serial number. There were about 225 of these guns sold in the United States. They came in quite a few grades and some were specially ordered. Although the lower grades are not considered by some to be true exhibitions (pre-C series) the highest "C" series grades are a match to the best of the older exhibitions. In 2000, an all option Superlight 2 barrel set with sideplates engraved by Vranken sold for $22,000. Generally, depending on the gun, prices will range between $6,000 and $25,000. These "C" grade guns should also be appraised individually.

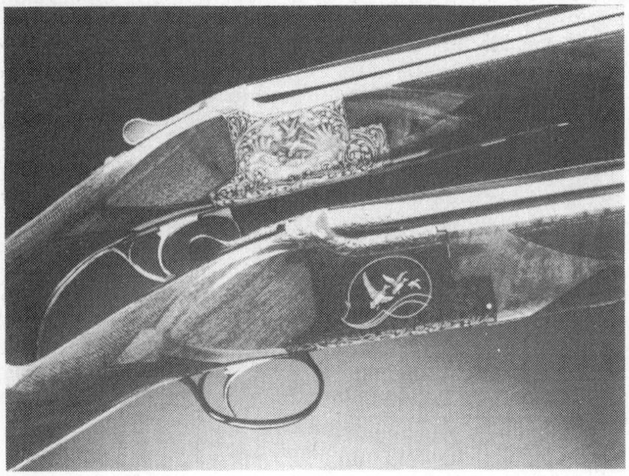

NIB	Exc.	V.G.	Good	Fair	Poor
13000	12000	9000	7000	5000	4000

SUPERPOSED SUPERLIGHT

This model was first introduced in 1967 in 12 gauge and in 1969 in 20 gauge. Special order 28 gauge as well as .410 bore are also seen. It was offered in 26.5" barrel lengths with 27.5" barrls in 12 gauge and 28" barrels in smaller bores available on special order. It features a rounded frame and straight grip stock with tapered solid or vent rib barrels. Regular production on the Superlight ended in 1976 for the grades listed. Production did continue for the Superlight in the P series begun in 1977.

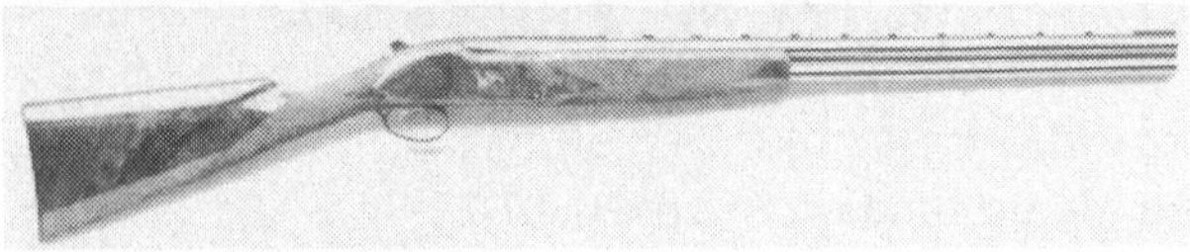

Grade I

NIB	Exc.	V.G.	Good	Fair	Poor
4500	3750	1800	700	500	250

Pigeon Grade

NIB	Exc.	V.G.	Good	Fair	Poor
7000	5900	4000	2500	1000	800

Pointer Grade—Rare

NIB	Exc.	V.G.	Good	Fair	Poor
10000	9000	6000	3500	2000	1000

Diana Grade

NIB	Exc.	V.G.	Good	Fair	Poor
11000	8500	6500	3500	2000	1000

Midas Grade

NIB	Exc.	V.G.	Good	Fair	Poor
13500	12000	9000	7000	5000	4000

NOTE: For 20 gauge guns add a 50 percent premium. For 28 gauge guns add a 100 percent premium. For .410 bore guns add 30 percent premium for high grades guns and 30 percent for Grade I.

SUPERPOSED PRESENTATION GRADE SERIES

The superposed shotguns listed were manufactured between 1977 and 1984 by FN in Belgium. The models listed differ in the amount of ornamentation and the quality of materials and workmanship utilized in construction. This series was also available in a superlight configuration. **NOTE:** Due to the tremendous variation of P-Series guns, prices here reflect the Superlight configuration. An all option superlight with a checkered butt, oil finish, and three piece forend will bring 25-30 percent more. For all other variations one should consider:For trap guns deduct 35 percent. For new style skeet deduct 30 percent. For skeet choked field guns deduct 5 percent. For recoil pads on field guns deduct 30 percent. For flat knob long tang hunting guns with no options deduct 35 percent. For flat knob long tang hunting guns with all options add 25 percent. For guns signed by J. Baerten add 5 percent. For P-4V guns with no gold deduct 20 percent. For hand filed vent rib add 5 percent.For Presentation Grade guns with extra sets of barrels add approximately $1,500 to $2,500 depending on gauge and combination. For P1, P2, and P3 grades add the premium listed:

For 20 gauge guns—55 percent.
For .28 gauge guns—100 percent.
For .410 bore—30 percent.For the P4 grade add the premium listed:
For 20 gauge guns—55 percent.
For 28 gauge guns—100 percent.
For .410 bore—40 percent.

Presentation 1 (without gold inlays)

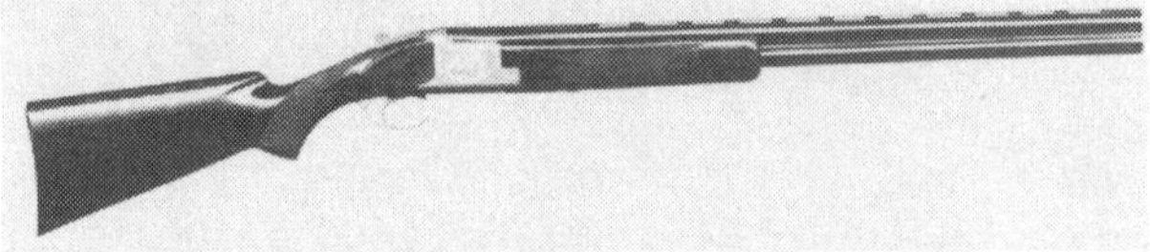

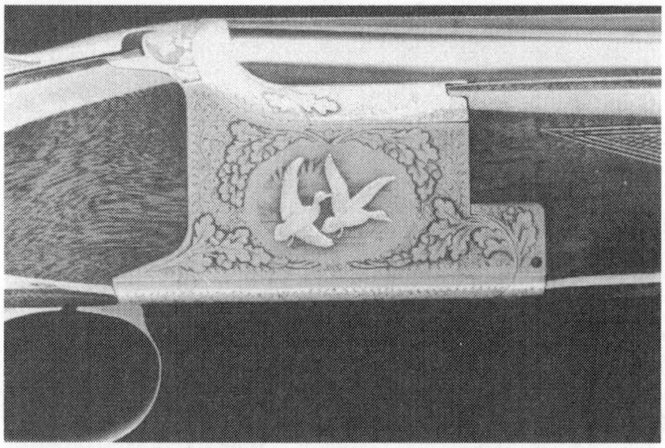

NIB	Exc.	V.G.	Good	Fair	Poor
4500	3700	1900	1000	600	500

Presentation 1 Gold-inlaid

NIB	Exc.	V.G.	Good	Fair	Poor
6250	5000	3250	1400	700	500

Presentation 2 (without gold inlays)

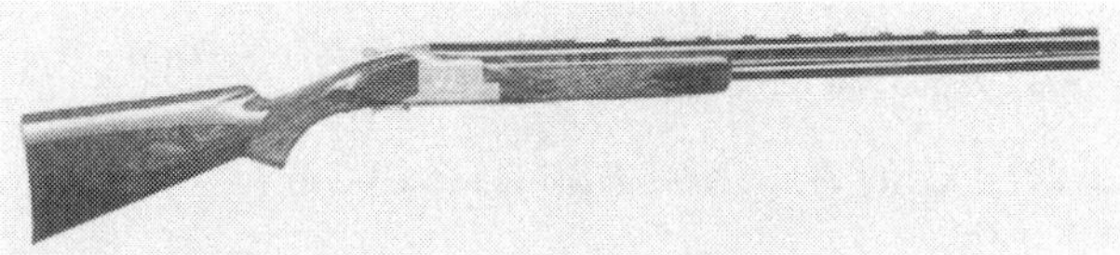

NIB	Exc.	V.G.	Good	Fair	Poor
6250	5250	3700	1800	1000	600

Presentation 2 Gold-inlaid

NIB	Exc.	V.G.	Good	Fair	Poor
8500	7500	4950	2500	1500	1000

NOTE: For early hand-engraved P3 models (approximately 25 produced) add 40 percent. These early guns are rare, proceed with caution.

Presentation 3 Gold-inlaid

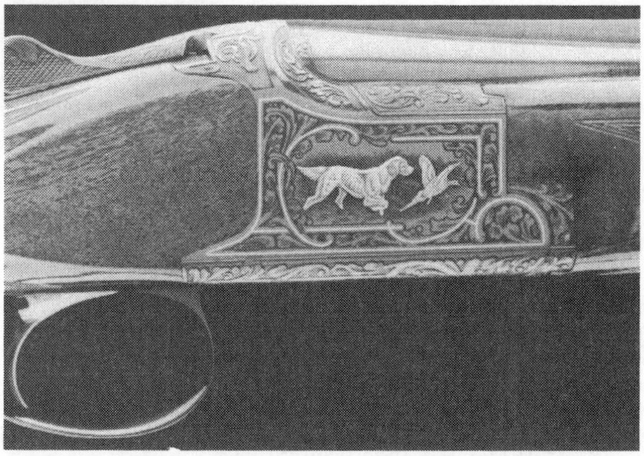

NIB	Exc.	V.G.	Good	Fair	Poor
10500	8500	5500	4000	2000	1300

Presentation 4 Gold-inlaid

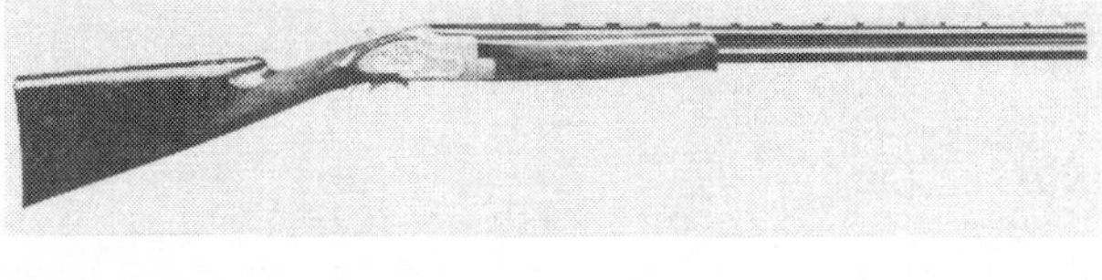

NIB	Exc.	V.G.	Good	Fair	Poor
14000	12500	9800	6750	5000	3500

NOTE: For P4 Grade guns with no gold deduct approximately 20 percent.

SUPERPOSED WATERFOWL LIMITED EDITION SERIES

This model was issued in three different versions: Mallard, Pintail, and Black Duck. Each edition was limited to 500 guns, all in 12 gauge.

1981 Mallard Issue

NIB	Exc.	V.G.	Good	Fair	Poor
8200	7000	4900	3300	1900	1100

1982 Pintail Issue

NIB	Exc.	V.G.	Good	Fair	Poor
8200	7000	4900	3300	1900	1100

1983 Black Duck Issue

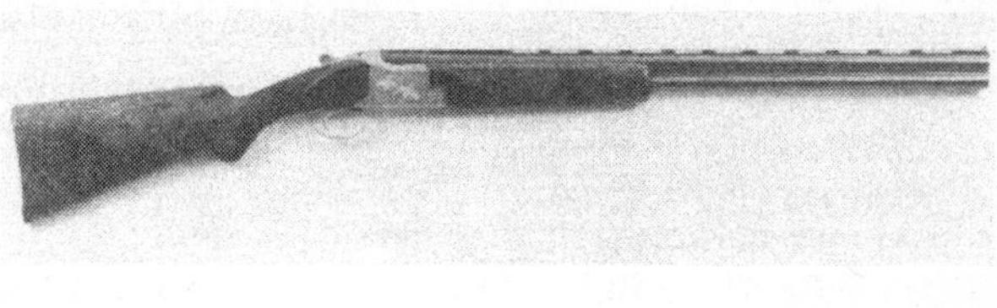

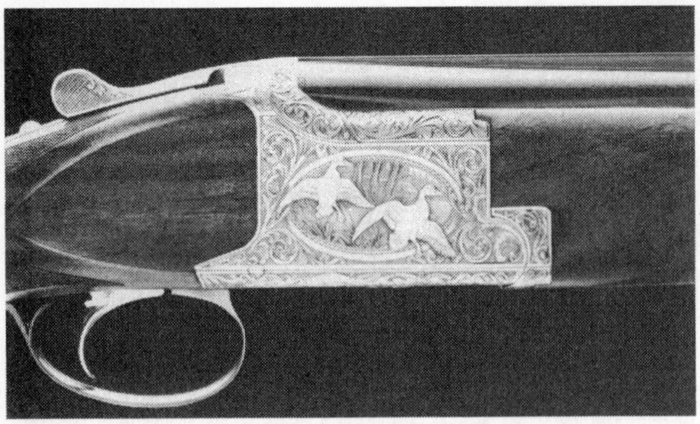

NIB	Exc.	V.G.	Good	Fair	Poor
8200	7000	4900	3300	1900	1100

Bicentennial Model

Produced in 1976 to commemorate the 200 year anniversary of America. A total of 53 guns were built in this special edition. All of these Superposed were 12 gauge with 28" barrels and each was numbered for one of the fifty states plus the District of Columbia. Two additional guns were built for the Smithsonian Institution and the Liege Firearms Museum. All were fitted with side plates with gold inlays. To reflect true value guns must be in unfired condition in their original case with all the papers.

NIB	Exc.	V.G.	Good	Fair	Poor
12000	9000	5950	2750	1500	1000

NOTE: Price often depends on the state.

FN/Browning Superposed

A number of FN Browning Superposed B-25 shotguns were imported into this country by Browning in various grades. These Superposed were intended originally for FN's European market. There are a large number of variations and grades. It is strongly suggested that an expert appraisal be sought prior to the sale. As a general rule these prices for NIB guns are: A grade-$1,200-1,600; B grade $1,600-2,500; C grade $2,500-3,500; D grade $3,500-5,000. These guns are marked with both the Browning and FN barrel address.

Classic

Produced in 1986 this model was offered in 20 gauge with 26" barrels. About 2,500 guns were produced. Silver gray receiver with engraving.

NIB	Exc.	V.G.	Good	Fair	Poor
4000	3200	2650	2000	800	300

Gold Classic

This shotgun was similar to the above model but more finely finished and engraved with gold inlays. About 350 of these guns were built in 1986.

NIB	Exc.	V.G.	Good	Fair	Poor
10500	7500	4995	2450	1750	400

CUSTOM SHOP B25 & B125 SUPERPOSED

These special order Superposed are currently available with a delivery time of 6 to 8 months. A number of options are offered that affect price. B125 guns are assembled in Belgium with components made in other countries to hold down costs. The B25 is made entirely in Belgium and is the more expensive version of the Superposed. Prices listed are retail only. **NOTE:** Retail prices for current production guns change often. Contact Browning for the present prices.

B-125

TrapRetail Price—$8,125

12 Gauge Sporting

A StyleRetail Price—$4,475
B StyleRetail Price—$4,800
C StyleRetail Price—$5,275

12 & 20 Gauge Hunting and Superlight

A StyleRetail price—$4,475
B StyleRetail price—$4,800
C StyleRetail price—$5,275

B-25

Grade IRetail price—$19,500
Pigeon GradeRetail price—$21,000
Pointer GradeRetail price—$23,000
Diana GradeRetail price—$24,000
Midas GradeRetail price—$30,000

Custom Shop BSL

This is a side-by-side shotgun is equiped with Browning sidelock barrel, Holland & Holland-type locks with double trigger and auto ejectors. The gun is assembled and finished by Labeau-Courally. It is offered in both 12 and 20 gauge. Engraved grayed receiver or case colored receiver. Introduced into the Browning product line in 2001.

Case Colored Receiver (BSL Grade LC1)

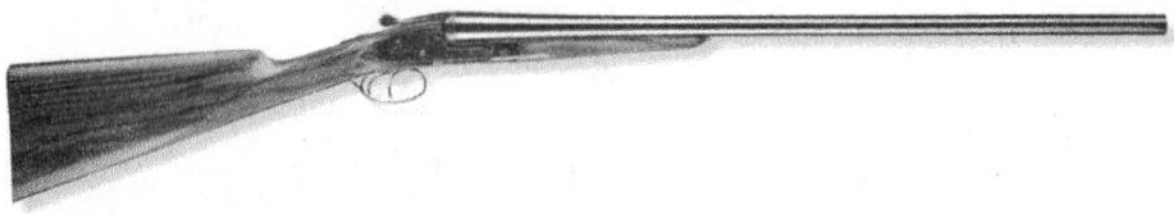

NIB	Exc.	V.G.	Good	Fair	Poor
13000	11000	9000	—	—	—

Engraved Gray Receiver (BSL Grade LC2)

NIB	Exc.	V.G.	Good	Fair	Poor
18000	15000	12500	—	—	—

Liege

This is an Over/Under shotgun chambered for 12 gauge. It was offered with 26.5", 28", or 30" vent rib barrels with various choke combinations. It features a boxlock action with a nonselective single trigger and automatic ejectors. The finish is blued with a checkered walnut stock. There were approximately 10,000 manufactured between 1973 and 1975. U.S. versions were marked Browning Arms Company on the barrel.

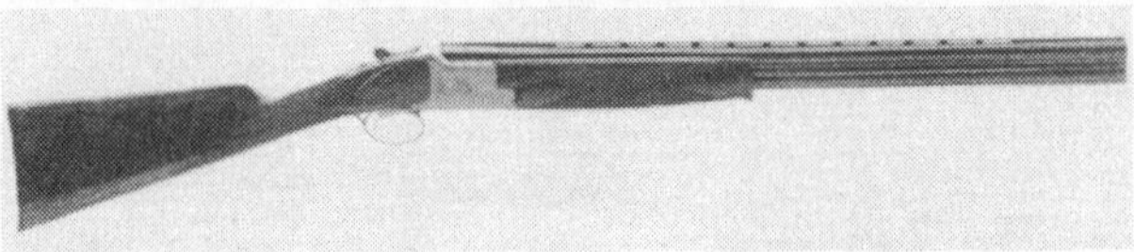

NIB	Exc.	V.G.	Good	Fair	Poor
1500	850	650	450	300	200

B27

This improved version of the Liege was imported into the U.S., some without the Browning Arms Company markings and only the FN barrel address. Others may have both barrel addresses. It was offered in a number of variations that differed in the amount of ornamentation and quality of materials and workmanship utilized. It features the same action as the Liege Over/Under gun.

Standard

NIB	*Exc.*	*V.G.*	*Good*	*Fair*	*Poor*
1200	950	650	350	250	200

Deluxe

NIB	*Exc.*	*V.G.*	*Good*	*Fair*	*Poor*
1600	1200	850	500	350	250

Deluxe Trap

NIB	*Exc.*	*V.G.*	*Good*	*Fair*	*Poor*
1600	1200	850	450	300	250

Deluxe Skeet

NIB	*Exc.*	*V.G.*	*Good*	*Fair*	*Poor*
1600	1200	850	450	300	250

Grand Deluxe

NIB	*Exc.*	*V.G.*	*Good*	*Fair*	*Poor*
2000	1500	1000	650	500	400

City of Liege Commemorative

250 manufactured.

NIB	*Exc.*	*V.G.*	*Good*	*Fair*	*Poor*
2500	1650	1000	600	450	300

ST-100

This is an Over/Under trap gun that features separated barrels with an adjustable point of impact. It is chambered for 12 gauge and has a 30" or 32" barrel with full choke and a floating ventilated rib. It features a single trigger and automatic ejectors. The finish is blued with a checkered walnut stock. It was manufactured by FN between 1979 and 1981.

NIB	*Exc.*	*V.G.*	*Good*	*Fair*	*Poor*
3750	2700	1800	1000	700	400

CITORI SERIES

This is an Over/Under, double-barrel shotgun chambered for all gauges and offered with vent rib barrels of 26" through 30" in length. It has a boxlock action with a single-selective trigger and automatic ejectors. The various grades differ in the amount of ornamentation and the quality of materials and workmanship utilized in construction. This series is manufactured in Japan by B.C. Miroku and was introduced in 1973. **NOTE:** For all Citori models, add a 15-20 percent premium for 28 gauge and .410.

NIB	*Exc.*	*V.G.*	*Good*	*Fair*	*Poor*
2750	1700	1400	1000	700	400

Grade I

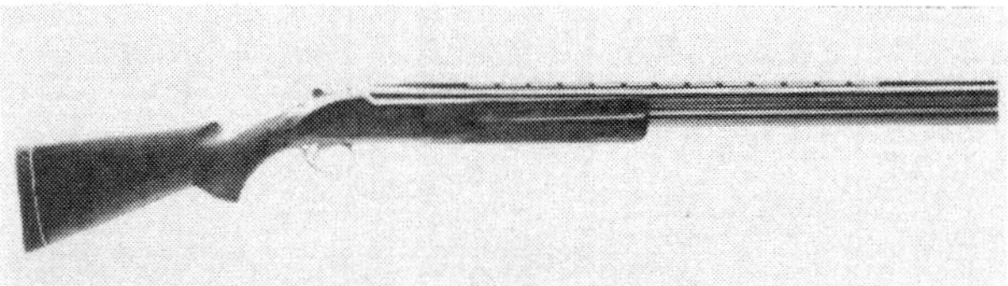

NIB	*Exc.*	*V.G.*	*Good*	*Fair*	*Poor*
1200	900	725	550	425	300

NOTE: Add premium of 30 percent for 16 gauge guns.

Upland Special—Grade I

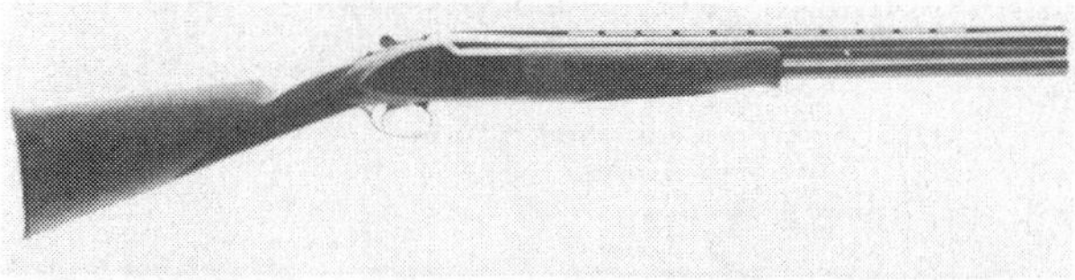

NIB	*Exc.*	*V.G.*	*Good*	*Fair*	*Poor*
1350	950	700	600	400	300

Grade II—1978 to 1983

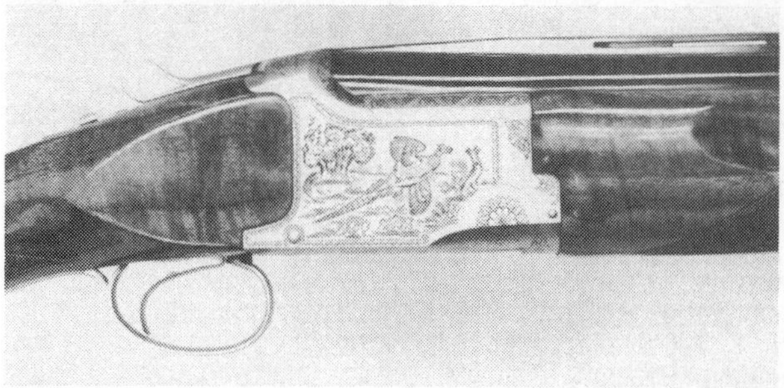

NIB	*Exc.*	*V.G.*	*Good*	*Fair*	*Poor*
—	1500	1300	1000	650	400

Grade II—Choke Tubes

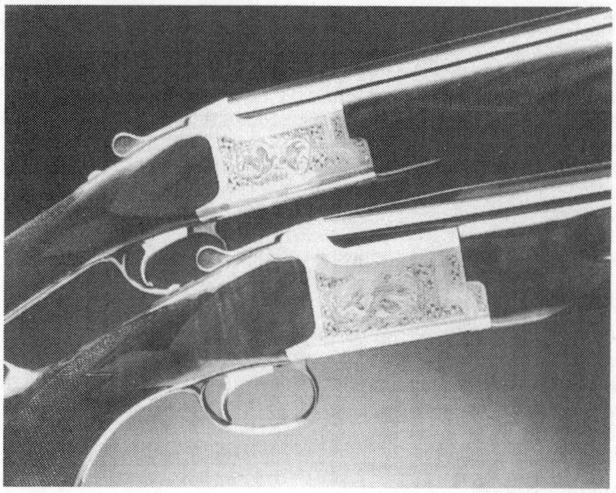

NIB	*Exc.*	*V.G.*	*Good*	*Fair*	*Poor*
1600	1400	1000	775	650	400

Grade V—1978 to 1984

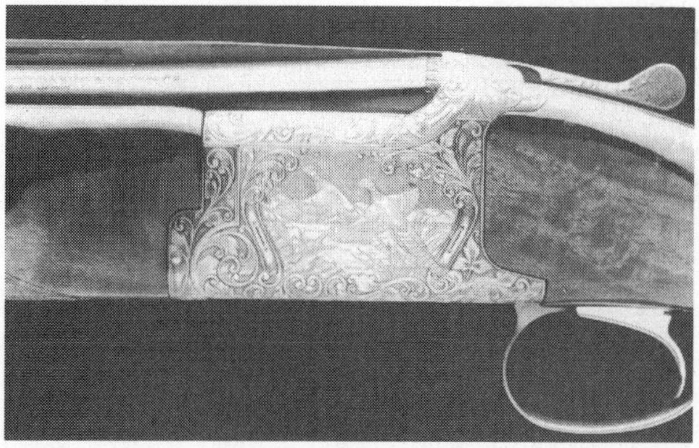

NIB	*Exc.*	*V.G.*	*Good*	*Fair*	*Poor*
2900	2300	1600	950	750	400

Grade V with sideplates—1981 to 1984

NIB	*Exc.*	*V.G.*	*Good*	*Fair*	*Poor*
2950	2500	2100	1500	800	400

NOTE: Add 10 percent for small gauges.

Grade VI—Choke Tubes

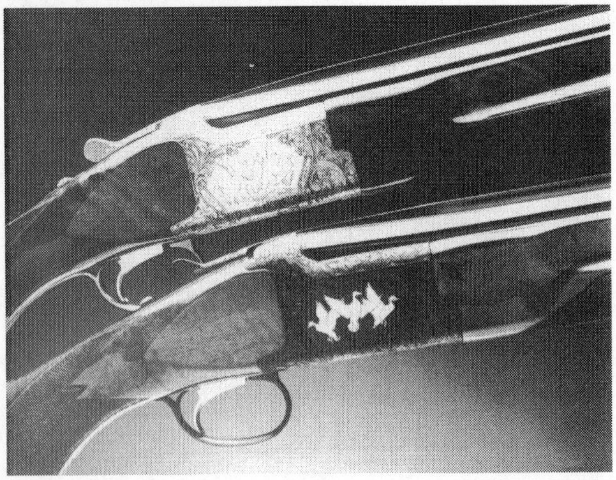

NIB	*Exc.*	*V.G.*	*Good*	*Fair*	*Poor*
1950	1650	1200	1000	750	500

Citori Hunter

This model features a full pistol-grip stock with beavertail forearm with high-gloss walnut. Chambered for 12 with 2.75", 3", or 3.5" chambers and choice of 26", 28" or 30" barrels in 12 gauge. The 20 gauge models have a choice of 26" or 28" barrels. Twelve gauge guns weigh from 7 lbs. 13 ozs. to 8 lbs. 9 ozs. depending on barrel length. Twenty gauge guns weigh about 6.75 lbs.

NIB	*Exc.*	*V.G.*	*Good*	*Fair*	*Poor*
1500	1100	850	650	550	450

NOTE: Add $75 for 3.5" models.

Citori Sporting Hunter

This model has the same features as the Hunting model with the exception of the stock configuration. The Sporting Hunter has a Sporting model buttstock and a Superposed style forearm. Fitted with a contoured sporting recoil pad. Introduced in 1998.

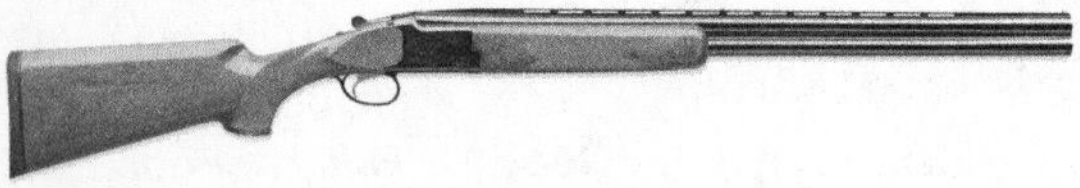

NIB	*Exc.*	*V.G.*	*Good*	*Fair*	*Poor*
1550	1400	1050	750	550	450

NOTE: Add $75 for 3.5" models.

Citori Satin Hunter

This model is chambered for 12 gauge shells, has a hunting-style stock, choice of 26" or 28" barrels, and a special satin wood finish with matte black receiver and barrels. Offered in Grade I only. Weight is about 8 lbs. Introduced in 1999.

NIB	*Exc.*	*V.G.*	*Good*	*Fair*	*Poor*
1250	1000	825	700	500	375

NOTE: Add $100 for 3.5" chamber.

Citori Satin Hunter Micro Midas

A budget-priced Citori with the same features and handling qualities that have made other Citoris so popular. Available in 12 or 20 gauge with 24 or 26-inch barrels. Satin-finished walnut stock with 13-inch length of pull. Vector-Pro lengthened forcing cones. Weight: 6 lbs. 3 oz. to 6 lbs. 10 oz. New in 2011.

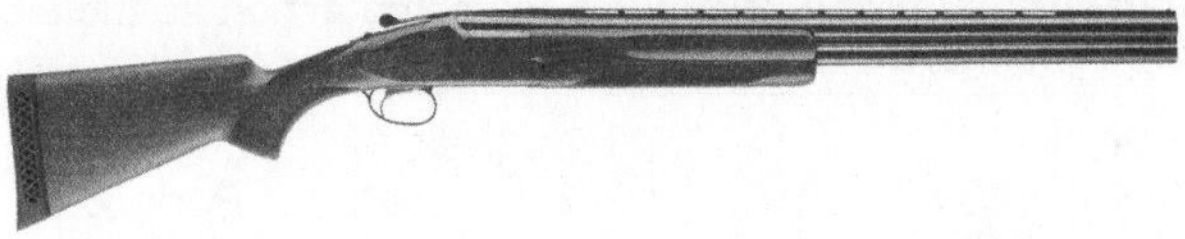

NIB	*Exc.*	*V.G.*	*Good*	*Fair*	*Poor*
1300	1050	900	800	500	300

CITORI LIGHTNING

This is a lightweight version that features a slimmer profile and has a checkered, round-knob, pistol-grip stock. It is offered in all gauges and in the same barrel lengths as the standard Citori. It features screw-in choke tubes known as Invectors. It was introduced in 1988. Offered in 12, 20 and 28 gauge and .410 bore. Weights are 6.5 lbs. to 8 lbs. depending on gauge and barrel length. The models differ in the amount of ornamentation and quality of materials and workmanship utilized.

Grade I

NIB	*Exc.*	*V.G.*	*Good*	*Fair*	*Poor*
1650	1200	900	600	450	375

Grade III

NIB	*Exc.*	*V.G.*	*Good*	*Fair*	*Poor*
2450	1900	1400	975	600	450

Grade IV

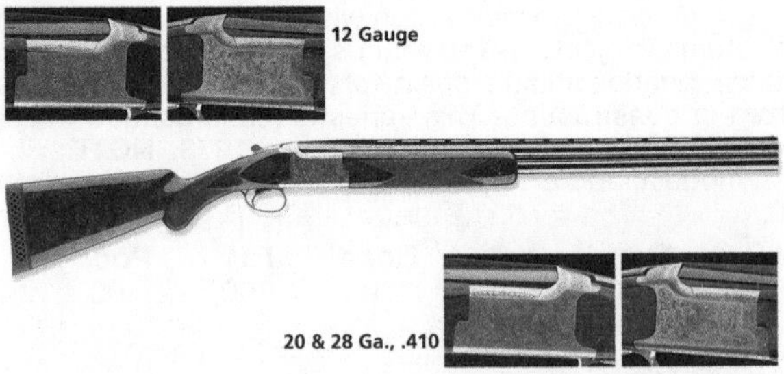

NIB	*Exc.*	*V.G.*	*Good*	*Fair*	*Poor*
2610	1950	1450	1025	650	500

Grade VI

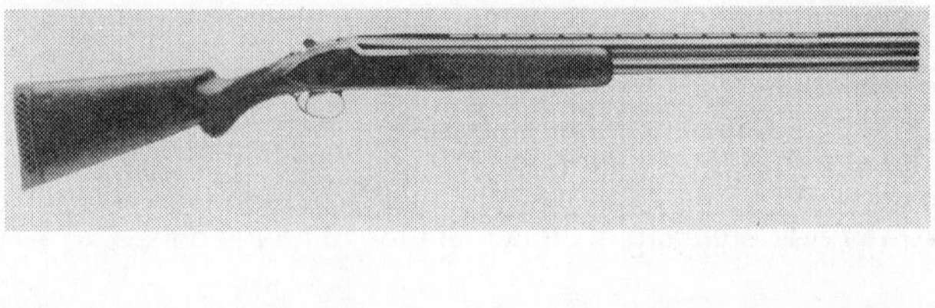

NIB	Exc.	V.G.	Good	Fair	Poor
3800	3000	2250	1500	700	550

Grade VII

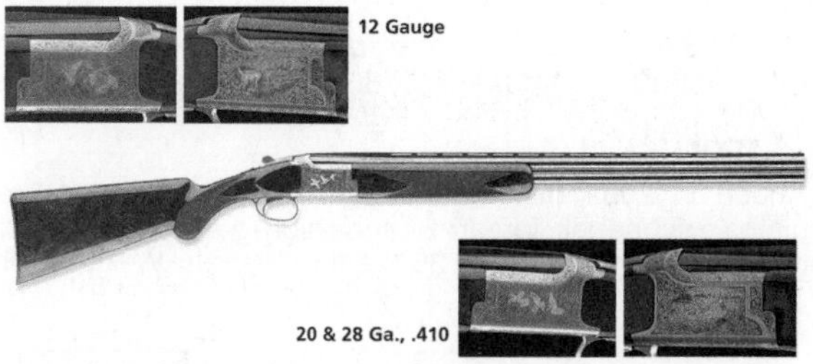

NIB	Exc.	V.G.	Good	Fair	Poor
4145	3100	2500	1750	775	575

NOTE: Add $300 for 28 and .410 models.

Feather

Introduced in 1999 this model features a lightweight alloy receiver. Offered in 12 gauge Grade I only with choice of 26" or 28" barrels. Weight with 28" barrels is about 7 lbs. 11 ozs. In 2000 this model was offered in 20 gauge as well with 26" or 28" barrels with 3" chambers. Weight of 20 gauge is about 6.5 lbs.

NIB	Exc.	V.G.	Good	Fair	Poor
1870	1400	975	595	400	300

Feather Combo

This model features a 20 gauge and 28 gauge barrel, both 27" long. The 20 gauge with 3" chambers the 28 gauge with 2.75" chambers. Pistol grip stock. Weight is about 6.25 lbs. Supplied with Browning luggage case. Introduced in 2000.

NIB	Exc.	V.G.	Good	Fair	Poor
3035	2250	1700	1250	700	550

Citori Feather XS

This model is offered in 12, 20, 28, and .410 bore. It has a lightweight alloy receiver. Fittted with a walnut stock with pistol grip, black recoil pad and schnabel forearm. Triple trigger system and Hi-Viz Comp sight system standard. Weight is about 7 lbs. for 12 gauge; 6.5 lbs. for 20 gauge; 6 lbs. for 28 gauge; and 6 lbs. for .410 bore. Introduced in 2000.

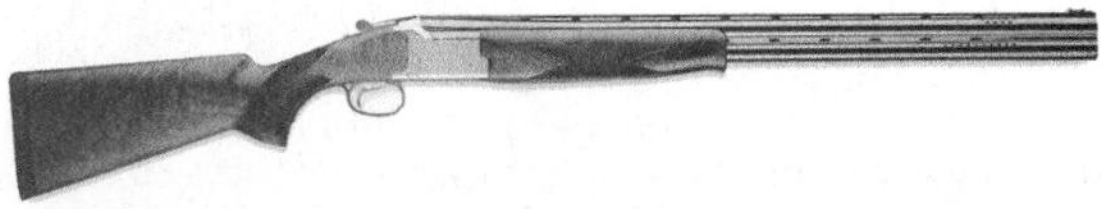

NIB	Exc.	V.G.	Good	Fair	Poor
2000	1500	1200	900	600	400

Citori Superlight Feather

Chambered for the 12 or 20 gauge with straight grip stock and schnabel forearm. This model has an alloy receiver. Checkered walnut stock. Offered with 26" barrels. Weight is about 6 lbs. Introduced in 2002.

NIB	Exc.	V.G.	Good	Fair	Poor
1940	1450	1100	800	550	350

Citori Super Lightning Grade I

Introduced in 2005 this12 or 20 gauge model features a blued receiver with gold line border. Checkered satin finished select walnut stock with pistol grip and Schnabel forearm. Barrels are 26" or 28" with choke tubes. Recoil pad on 12 gauge. Weight is about 8 lbs. for the 12 gauge and 6.75 lbs. for the 20 gauge.

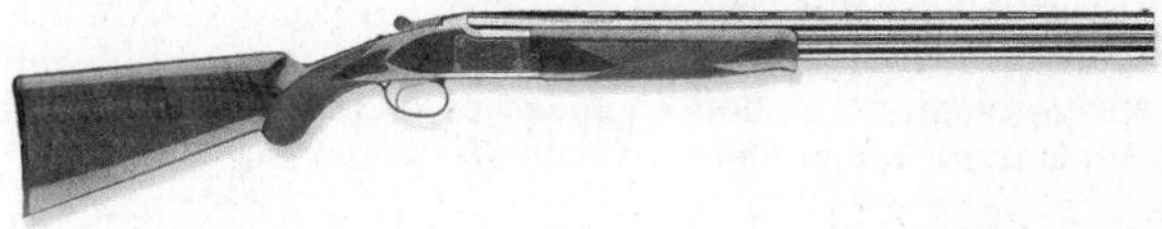

NIB	Exc.	V.G.	Good	Fair	Poor
1865	1400	1050	750	500	300

Citori Classic Lightning Grade I

Offered in 12 or 20 gauge with choice of 26" or 28" vent rib barrels with choke tubes. Receiver is scroll engraved on a silver nitride finish. Checkered select walnut stock with oil finish. Forearm is Lightning style. Recoil pad on 12 gauge. Weight is about 8 lbs. for 12 gauge and about 6.75 lbs. for the 20 gauge. Introduced in 2005.

NIB	Exc.	V.G.	Good	Fair	Poor
1890	1425	1075	775	525	325

Citori Classic Lightning Feather Grade I

This model, introduced in 2005, features a high relief engraved alloy receiver. Chambered for the 12 or 20 gauge and fitted with 26" or 28" vent rib barrels with choke tubes. Checkered select stock with Schnable forearm. Recoil pad on 12 gauge. Weight is about 7 lbs. for 12 gauge and about 6.25 lbs. for 20 gauge.

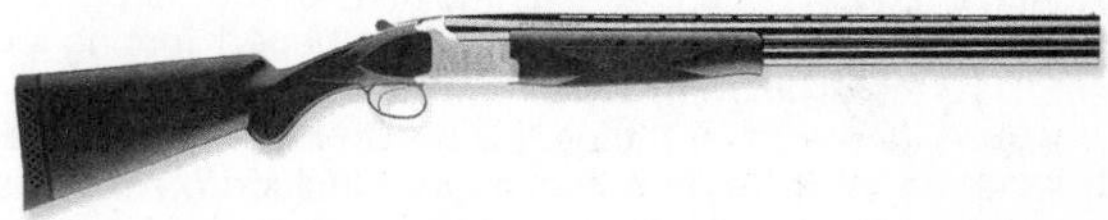

NIB	Exc.	V.G.	Good	Fair	Poor
1950	1450	1100	775	525	325

Citori 525 Sporting

Introduced in 2002 this model is chambered for the 12 or 20 gauge and fitted with a choice of 28" or 30" vent rib ported barrels. The stock is redesigned with a Euro checkering pattern and more pronounced palm swell. Weight is about 8 lbs. for the 12 gauge and 7 lbs. for the 20. In 2003 this model was offered in both 28 gauge and .410 bore.

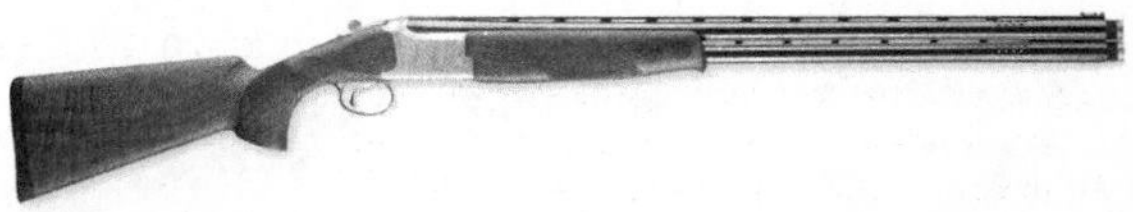

NIB	Exc.	V.G.	Good	Fair	Poor
2320	1750	1250	800	550	350

NOTE: Add $275 for adjustable comb.

Citori 525 Field

As above but with a choice of 26" or 28" barrels. Barrels are unported. Ventilated recoil pad. Introduced in 2002. In 2003 this model was offered in both 28 gauge and .410 bore.

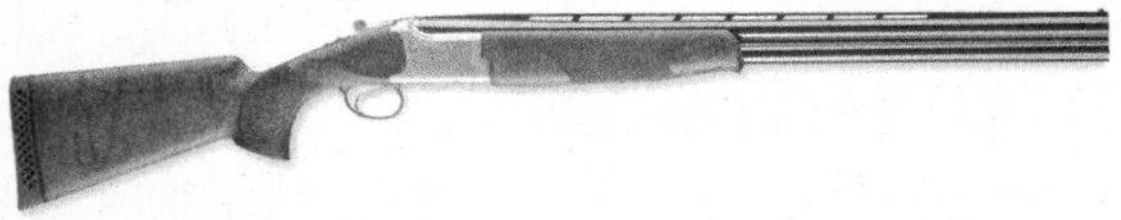

NIB	Exc.	V.G.	Good	Fair	Poor
1980	1475	950	700	500	325

Citori 525 Golden Clays Sporting

This model has the same features as the 525 Sporting but with an oil-finished high stock and engraved receiver with gold inlays. In 2003 this model was offered in both 28 gauge and .410 bore.

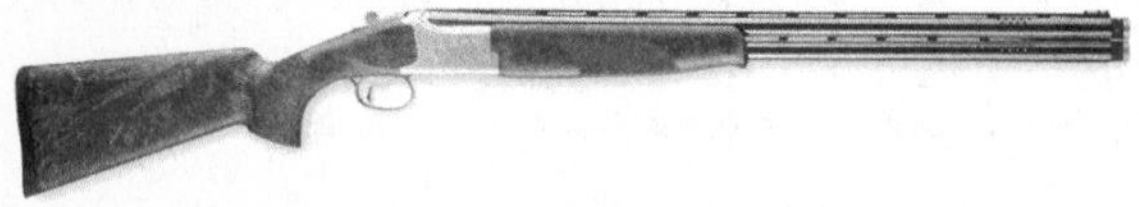

NIB	Exc.	V.G.	Good	Fair	Poor
4450	3250	2600	1950	1200	550

Citori 525 Feather

This lightweight Citori features an alloy receiver with a steel breech face and high-relief engraving. The stock and Schnabel forend are Grade II/III oil finished walnut. Available in 12, 20 and 28 gauges and .410 bore with 26" or 28" barrels. All but 28 gauge have 3" chambers. Weight is about 6.9 lbs. in 12 gauge and 5.5 to 5.7 lbs. in others. Three choke tubes.

NIB	Exc.	V.G.	Good	Fair	Poor
2300	1750	1250	800	550	350

Citori 625 Sporting

Introduced in 2008, this 2.75" 12 gauge has 28", 30" or 32" ported barrels with Browning\qs Vector Pro lengthened forcing cones system. The stock and Schnabel forend are Grade III/IV walnut. The steel receiver has a silver nitride finish with high-relief engraving and gold embellishment. Five choke tubes included. Weight is 7.9 to 8.2 lbs. Add 5 percent for adjustable comb stock.

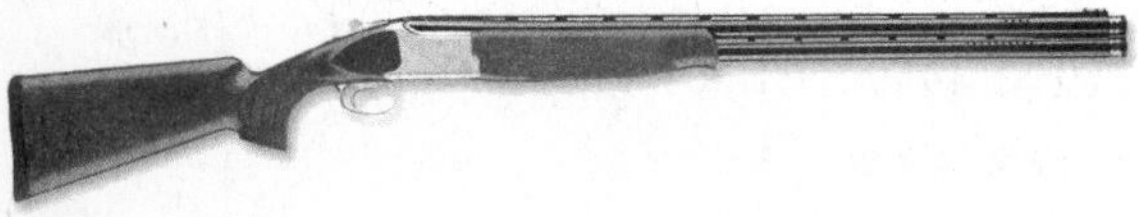

NIB	Exc.	V.G.	Good	Fair	Poor
3500	2700	1975	1200	850	550

Citori 625 Sporting Left Hand

As above but configured for left-hand shooters.

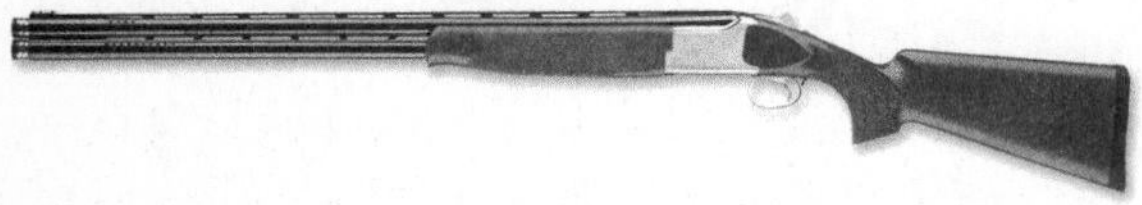

NIB	Exc.	V.G.	Good	Fair	Poor
3500	2700	1975	1200	850	550

Citori 625 Field

26" or 28" barrels and a gloss oil finish Grade II/III walnut stock and schnabel forend. Steel receiver with silver nitride finish and high-relief engraving. Three choke tubes. Chambered for 12, 20, 28 gauge and .410. Weight: 7 lbs., 14 oz. to 6 lbs., 12 oz.

NIB	Exc.	V.G.	Good	Fair	Poor
2400	1900	1400	975	600	450

Citori Esprit

Introduced in 2002 this model features removable decorative sideplates, schnabel forearm, and high-grade walnut stock. Offered in 12 gauge only with 28" vent rib barrels. Weight is about 8.25 lbs.

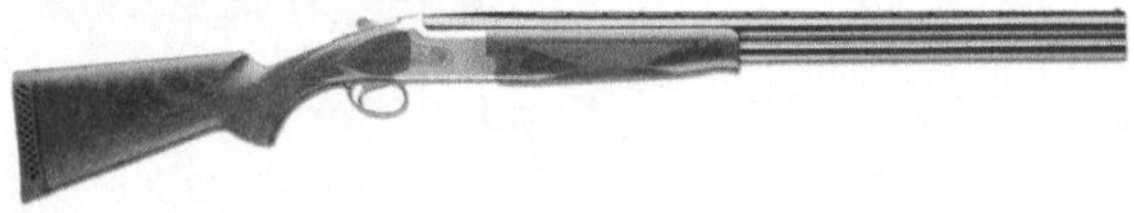

NIB	Exc.	V.G.	Good	Fair	Poor
2450	1975	1400	975	600	450

Citori Sporting Clays

Specifically designed for sporting clays shooting. Offered in 12 gauge only, each model is back-bored, ported and fitted with Invector-Plus choke tubes. Barrels are chrome-plated. Receiver is blued with gold inscription. Pigeon Grade has gold detailing and high grade gloss walnut stock. Signature Grade features a red and black print on the stock with gold decals. Trigger is adjustable to three length of pull positions. Comes with three interchangeable trigger shoes. Each model is fitted with rubber recoil pad.

NIB	Exc.	V.G.	Good	Fair	Poor
2450	1975	1400	975	600	450

Citori Lightning Sporting Model

This model features a rounded pistol grip and Lightning forearm with choice of high or low vent rib. Chambered for 3" shells. Offered in 28" or 30" barrels. Weighs about 8.5 lbs. Introduced in 1989.

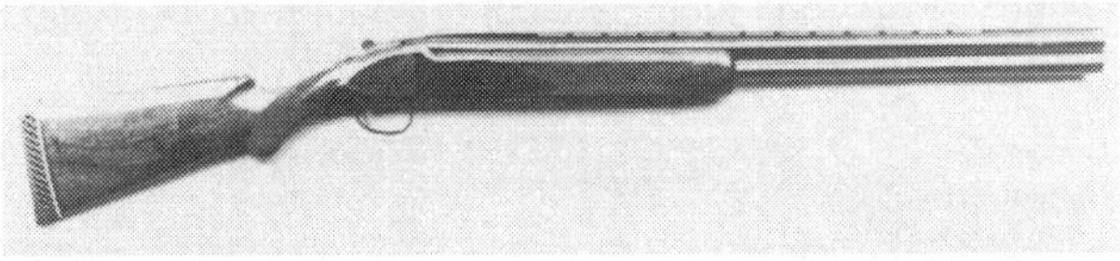

NIB	Exc.	V.G.	Good	Fair	Poor
1400	1000	800	600	450	300

Citori Lightning Sporting Model Pigeon Grade

NIB	Exc.	V.G.	Good	Fair	Poor
1450	1100	900	650	450	300

Citori Lightning Sporting Model Golden Clays

First introduced in 1994.

NIB	Exc.	V.G.	Good	Fair	Poor
2800	2250	1650	900	450	300

Citori Privilege

This high-grade model features game scene engraved sideplates, unique checkering pattern, oil finish high-grade walnut stock with pistol grip. Offered in 12 gauge only with choice of 26" or 28" barrels. Weight is about 8 lbs. Introduced in 2000. In 2001 a 20 gauge version with 26" or 28" barrels was introduced.

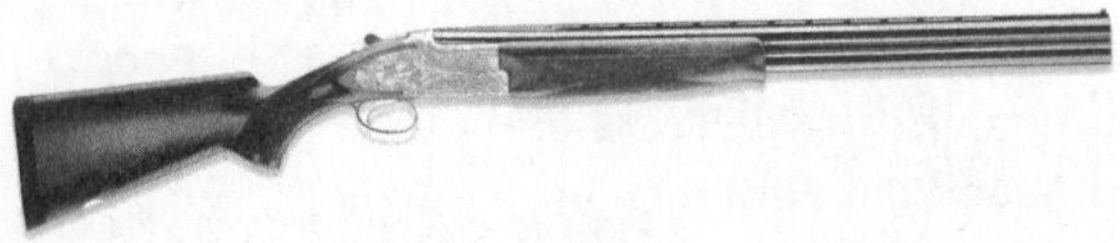

NIB	Exc.	V.G.	Good	Fair	Poor
5475	4250	3500	2800	1300	550

Citori XS Sporting Clays

Introduced in 1999, this model features silver nitride receiver with gold accents and European-style stock with schnabel forend. Available in 12 or 20. Choice of 28", 30" or 32" barrels. Weight varies from 8 lbs. in 12 gauge to 7 lbs. for the 20 gauge.

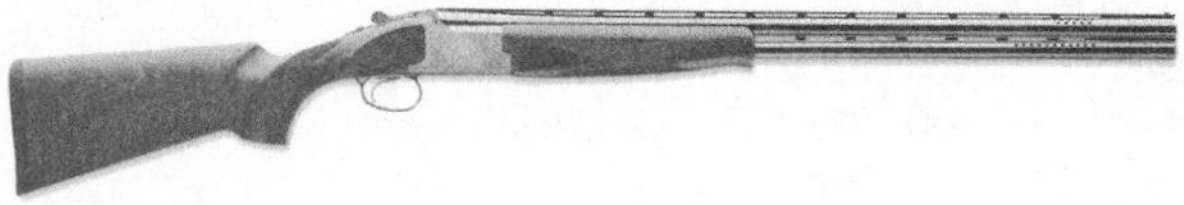

NIB	Exc.	V.G.	Good	Fair	Poor
2600	2050	1450	1000	625	475

Citori Ultra XS Skeet

This model is offered in 12 gauge only with choice of 28" or 30" ported barrels chambered for 2.75" shells. Semi-beavertail forearm. Triple trigger system standard. Adjustable comb optional. Walnut stock with pistol grip and black recoil pad. Weight is about 7.75 lbs. Introduced in 2000. In 2001 a 20 gauge version was introduced with a choice of 28" or 30" barrels.

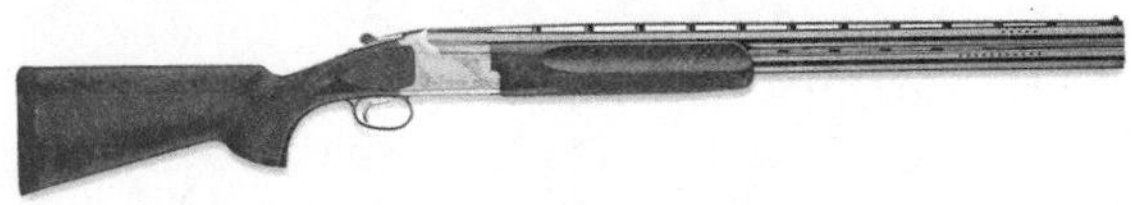

NIB	Exc.	V.G.	Good	Fair	Poor
2535	1900	1375	950	600	450

NOTE: Add $275 for adjustable comb.

Citori XS Special

This is a 12 gauge 2.75" chamber gun with choice of 30" or 32" vent rib barrels with porting and extended choke tubes. Checkered walnut stock with adjustable comb and pistol grip. Semi-beavertail forearm. Silver engraved receiver. Weight is about 8.7 lbs.

NIB	Exc.	V.G.	Good	Fair	Poor
2825	2100	1550	1100	675	475

CITORI PLUS

This model features an adjustable point of impact from 3" to 12" above point of aim. Receiver on Grade I is blued with scroll engraving. Walnut stock is adjustable and forearm is a modified beavertail style. Available in 30" or 32" barrels that are backbored and ported. Non-ported barrels are optional. Weighs about 9 lbs. 6 oz. Introduced in 1989.

Citori Plus Grade I

NIB	Exc.	V.G.	Good	Fair	Poor
1300	1075	750	500	400	300

Citori Plus Pigeon Grade

NIB	Exc.	V.G.	Good	Fair	Poor
1850	1500	950	700	500	300

Citori Plus Signature Grade

NIB	Exc.	V.G.	Good	Fair	Poor
1750	1450	950	700	500	300

Citori Plus Golden Clays

NIB	Exc.	V.G.	Good	Fair	Poor
2850	2295	1500	900	450	300

Trap Combination Set

This version is offered in Grade I only and features a 34" single barrel and a 32" set of Over/Under barrels. It is furnished in a fitted case and has been discontinued.

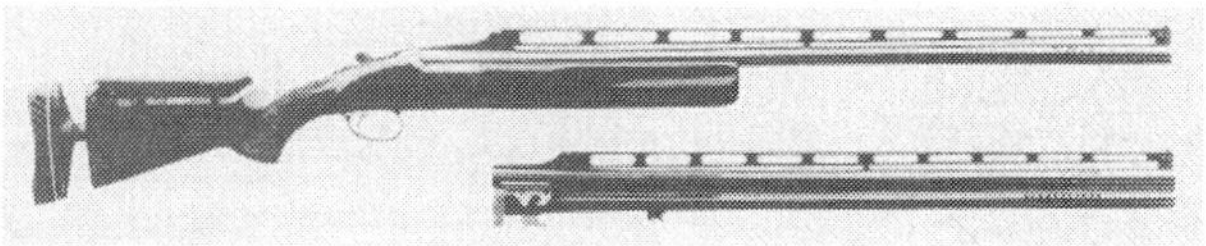

NIB	Exc.	V.G.	Good	Fair	Poor
—	1950	1350	950	800	700

GTI MODEL

This model features a 13mm wide rib, ventilated side ribs, pistol-grip stock, semi-beavertail forearm. Offered in 28" or 30" barrel. Weighs about 8 lbs. This model not offered in Pigeon Grade. Introduced in 1989.

Grade I

NIB	Exc.	V.G.	Good	Fair	Poor
1200	975	750	600	450	300

Signature Grade

NIB	Exc.	V.G.	Good	Fair	Poor
1200	975	750	600	450	300

Golden Clays

NIB	Exc.	V.G.	Good	Fair	Poor
2575	1975	1250	900	450	300

ULTRA SPORTER—SPORTING CLAYS

This model was introduced in 1995 and replaces the GTI model. It features a 10mm to 13mm tapered rib and is offered with either a blued or gray receiver with walnut stock with pistol grip and semi-beavertail forearm. Fitted with adjustable comb. Adjustable length of pull. Offered in 12 gauge only with 28" or 30" barrels. Average weight is 8 lbs.

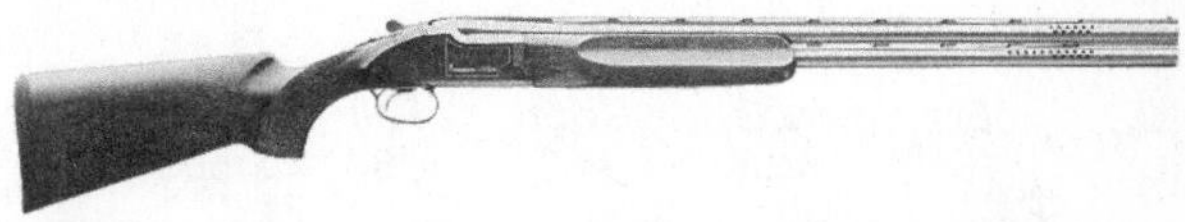

NIB	Exc.	V.G.	Good	Fair	Poor
1550	1200	800	550	400	300

Ultra Sporter Sporting Clays—Golden Clays

NIB	Exc.	V.G.	Good	Fair	Poor
2900	2300	1600	1100	750	400

NOTE: For Ultra Sporters with adjustable comb add $200 to NIB price.

Citori Superlight

This is a lighter-weight version of the Citori chambered for all gauges and offered with the same features as the Lightning Series. The grades differ in the amount of ornamentation and quality of materials and workmanship utilized. This series was introduced in 1983.

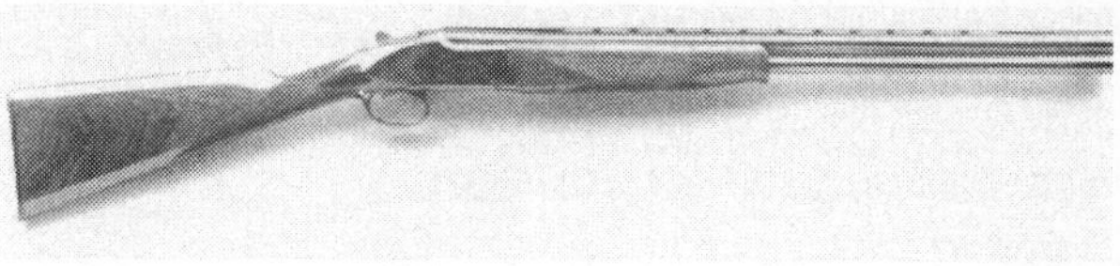

Citori Superlight Feather

Introduced in 1999 this model features a straight grip stock with schnabel forend. Lightweight alloy receiver. Offered in 12 gauge Grade I only with choice of 26" or 28" barrels. Weight with 28" barrels is about 6 lbs. 6 ozs.

NIB	Exc.	V.G.	Good	Fair	Poor
1700	1250	895	600	475	350

Micro Lightning

Offered in 20 gauge only and has reduced dimensions for smaller shooters. Available with 24" vent rib barrels. Weighs 6 lbs. 3 oz. Introduced in 1991.

NIB	Exc.	V.G.	Good	Fair	Poor
1100	895	700	600	400	300

GRAN LIGHTNING

This is essentially a Grade I Lightning with a high grade select walnut stock with satin finish. Receiver and barrels are blued. Offered in 12 gauge and 20 gauge with choice of 26" or 28" vent rib barrels. Choke tubes standard. Weighs about 8 lbs. in 12 gauge and 6 lbs. 11 oz. in 20 gauge. Introduced in 1990. In 2004 the 28 gauge and .410 bore were added.

NIB	*Exc.*	*V.G.*	*Good*	*Fair*	*Poor*
2550	1900	1300	975	650	350

Grade I

NIB	*Exc.*	*V.G.*	*Good*	*Fair*	*Poor*
1300	975	750	500	425	350

Grade III

NIB	*Exc.*	*V.G.*	*Good*	*Fair*	*Poor*
1625	1375	1050	750	550	450

Grade V

Discontinued 1984.

NIB	*Exc.*	*V.G.*	*Good*	*Fair*	*Poor*
—	1800	1350	950	750	500

Grade VI

NIB	*Exc.*	*V.G.*	*Good*	*Fair*	*Poor*
2000	1750	1300	1000	800	500

Citori White Lightning

Introduced in 1998 this model features a silver nitride scroll engraved receiver. Offered in 3" 12 and 3" 20 gauge with choice of 26" or 28" barrels. In 2004 this model is also available in 28 gauge as well as .410 bore. Weight is approximately 8 lbs. for 12 gauge models and 6.8 lbs. for 20 gauge models. Invector-Plus chokes standard. Lightning-style stock.

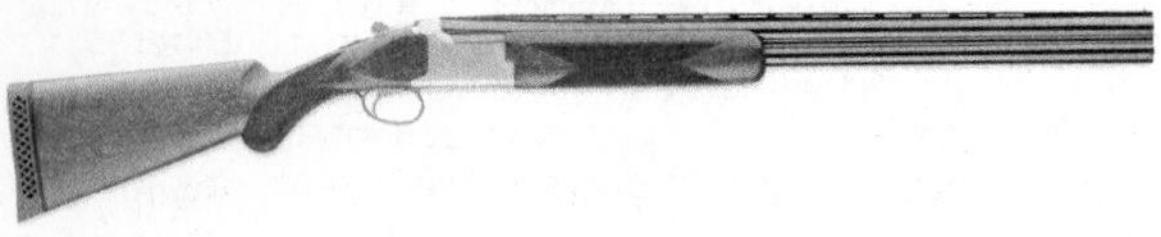

NIB	*Exc.*	*V.G.*	*Good*	*Fair*	*Poor*
1500	1200	950	700	600	375

NOTE: Add $75 for 28 and .410 models.

Citori White Upland Special

Introduced in 2000 this model features a shortened straight-grip stock, schnabel forearm, and 24" barrel. Fitted with 2.75" chambered for 12 gauge and 20 gauge only. Weight is about 6.75 lbs.

NIB	*Exc.*	*V.G.*	*Good*	*Fair*	*Poor*
1650	1200	975	725	625	395

CITORI SKEET

This series of guns was chambered for all gauges and was designed for competition skeet shooting. It is similar to the standard Citori with a high-post target rib and 26" or 28" barrels. The versions differ in the amount of engraving and the quality of materials and workmanship utilized.

Grade I

NIB	*Exc.*	*V.G.*	*Good*	*Fair*	*Poor*
1000	925	750	550	425	350

Grade II

Discontinued 1983.

NIB	*Exc.*	*V.G.*	*Good*	*Fair*	*Poor*
—	1000	900	750	450	300

Grade III

NIB	*Exc.*	*V.G.*	*Good*	*Fair*	*Poor*
1500	1200	900	750	450	300

Grade V

NIB	*Exc.*	*V.G.*	*Good*	*Fair*	*Poor*
1600	1200	900	750	450	300

Grade VI

NIB	*Exc.*	*V.G.*	*Good*	*Fair*	*Poor*
2000	1750	1200	900	450	300

Golden Clays

First introduced in 1994.

NIB	*Exc.*	*V.G.*	*Good*	*Fair*	*Poor*
2400	2000	1500	900	450	300

CITORI SKEET - 3 GAUGE SET

Consists of 20 gauge, 28 gauge, and .410 bore interchangeable 28" vent rib barrels. Introduced in 1987.

Grade I

NIB	*Exc.*	*V.G.*	*Good*	*Fair*	*Poor*
2200	1950	1700	1250	900	700

Grade III

NIB	*Exc.*	*V.G.*	*Good*	*Fair*	*Poor*
2600	2250	1900	1400	1100	800

Set Grade VI

NIB	*Exc.*	*V.G.*	*Good*	*Fair*	*Poor*
3000	2500	2000	1500	1200	900

CITORI SKEET - 4 GAUGE SET

This set has a 12 gauge, 20 gauge, 28 gauge, and .410 bore interchangeable vent rib barrels in either 26" or 28" lengths. Introduced in 1981.

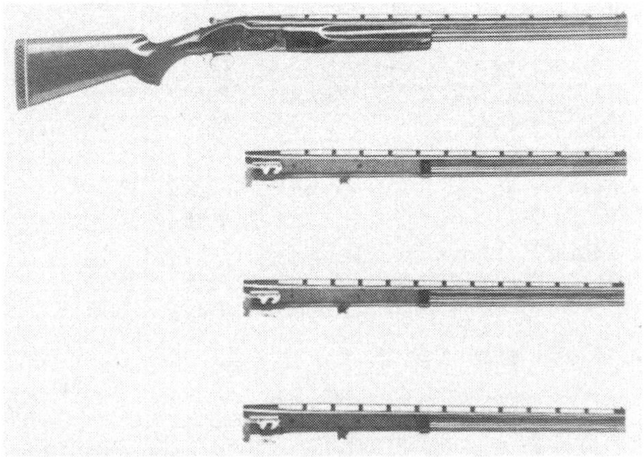

Grade I

NIB	*Exc.*	*V.G.*	*Good*	*Fair*	*Poor*
3400	2750	2250	1700	1250	900

Grade III

NIB	*Exc.*	*V.G.*	*Good*	*Fair*	*Poor*
3500	2900	2500	1900	1350	900

Grade VI

NIB	Exc.	V.G.	Good	Fair	Poor
3900	3300	2900	2250	1400	950

CITORI TRAP

This version is similar to the standard Citori, offered in 12 gauge only with 30" or 32" barrels. It features a high rib and a Monte Carlo-type stock with recoil pad. The versions differ as to the amount of ornamentation and the quality of materials and workmanship utilized.

Grade I

NIB	Exc.	V.G.	Good	Fair	Poor
1200	975	750	550	425	350

Plus Trap

Adjustable rib and stock. Introduced in 1989.

NIB	Exc.	V.G.	Good	Fair	Poor
1700	1450	1000	750	600	500

Grade II

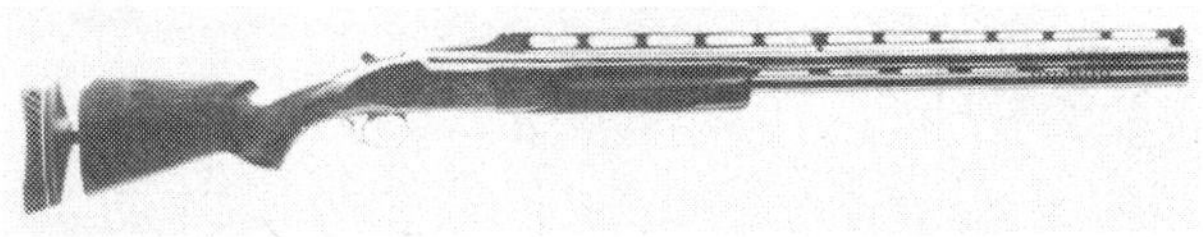

Discontinued 1983.

NIB	Exc.	V.G.	Good	Fair	Poor
—	1200	1000	675	450	350

Grade III

NIB	Exc.	V.G.	Good	Fair	Poor
1600	1450	1000	750	600	500

Grade V

NIB	Exc.	V.G.	Good	Fair	Poor
—	1500	1350	900	650	450

Grade VI

NIB	Exc.	V.G.	Good	Fair	Poor
2200	1900	1550	1250	1000	800

CITORI XT TRAP

Introduced in 1999, this Trap model is fitted with contoured beavertail with Monte Carlo stock with or without adjustable comb. The grayed receiver is highlighted in gold with light scroll work. Choice of 32" or 30" barrels. Weight is approximately 8 lbs. 11 ozs.

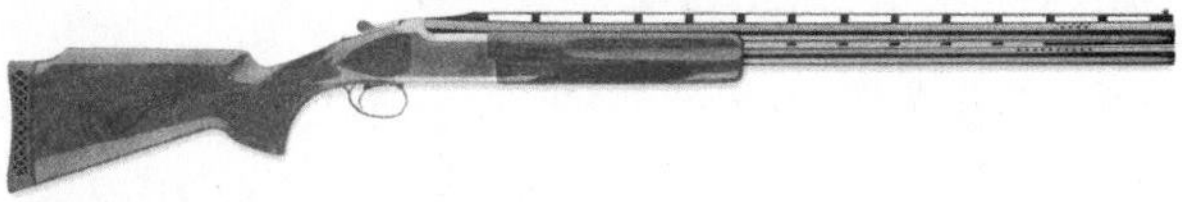

NIB	Exc.	V.G.	Good	Fair	Poor
2500	1700	1200	900	650	395

NOTE: Add $275 for adjustable comb.

Golden Clays

First introduced in 1994.

NIB	Exc.	V.G.	Good	Fair	Poor
2950	2250	1500	900	450	300

Signature Grade

NIB	Exc.	V.G.	Good	Fair	Poor
2150	1750	900	600	450	300

Gold

Introduced in 2005 this model features a gold game scene engraving pattern on a silver receiver. Choice of 30" or 32" vent rib ported barrels with choke tubes. Checkered select walnut stock with adjustable comb and semi-beavertail forearm. Stock also has adjustable length of pull and recoil reduction system. Weight is about 9 lbs.

NIB	Exc.	V.G.	Good	Fair	Poor
4520	3300	2900	2250	1400	650

Model 325 Sporting Clays

Introduced in 1993 this model has a European design that features a scroll-engraved, grayed receiver schnabel forearm, 10mm wide vent rib, three interchangeable and adjustable trigger shoes, and back-bore barrels that are ported and fitted with choke tubes. Available in 12 gauge and 20 gauge. The 12 gauge is offered with 28", 30", or 32" barrels while the 20 gauge is offered with 28" or 30" barrel fitted with conventional chokes. The 12 gauge weighs about 7 lbs. 14 oz., while the 20 gauge weighs about 6 lbs. 12 oz.

NIB	Exc.	V.G.	Good	Fair	Poor
1550	1200	900	700	450	300

SPECIAL SPORTING

Similar to the Sporting model but fitted with a 2-3/4" chamber and choice of 28", 30", or 32" barrels. Barrels are ported. Barrels are also fitted with a high post rib. Stock has a full pistol grip and optional adjustable comb. Depending on barrel length weighs about 8.3 lbs.

NIB	Exc.	V.G.	Good	Fair	Poor

Grade I

NIB	Exc.	V.G.	Good	Fair	Poor
1350	975	750	600	450	300

Signature Grade

NIB	Exc.	V.G.	Good	Fair	Poor
1350	1000	750	600	450	300

Pigeon Grade

NIB	Exc.	V.G.	Good	Fair	Poor
1500	1300	850	600	450	300

Golden Clays

NIB	Exc.	V.G.	Good	Fair	Poor
2600	1975	1250	900	450	300

Model 425 Sporting Clays

This Citori over-and-under gun is offered in both 12 and 20 gauge with a choice of 28" and 30" barrel with 32" barrels available on the 12 gauge as well. The 425 is adjustable for length of pull and has an adjustable comb. Barrels are fitted with a 10mm wide rib. Invector chokes are standard. Average weight is 7 lbs. 14 oz. Introduced in 1995.

NIB	Exc.	V.G.	Good	Fair	Poor
1650	1200	850	600	450	300

Model 425 Golden Clays

Same as above but with high-grade wood and engraved receiver.

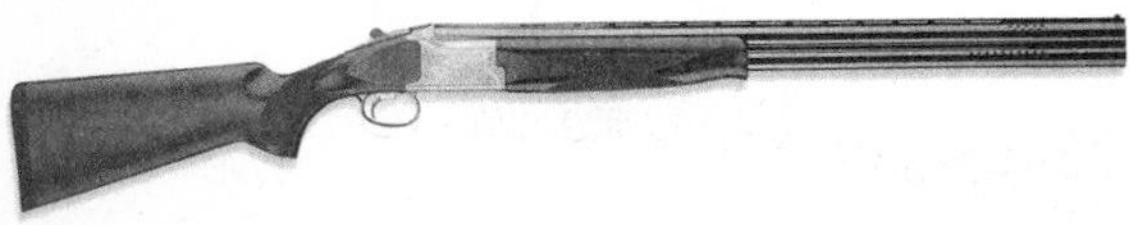

NIB	Exc.	V.G.	Good	Fair	Poor
3000	2450	1650	1100	600	300

NOTE: For Model 425 with adjustable comb add $200 to NIB price.

Light Sporting 802ES (Extended Swing)

Introduced in 1996 this model features a 28" vent rib barrel with 2" stainless steel extension tubes for an extended swing of 30". An additional 4" extension is also included. Thus the barrel can be 28", 30" or 32" according to needs. Chambered for 12 gauge with adjustable length of pull. Walnut stock with pistol grip and schnabel forearm. Weight is about 7.5 lbs.

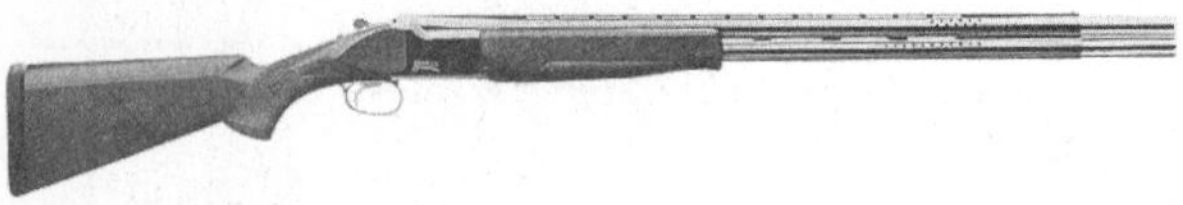

NIB	Exc.	V.G.	Good	Fair	Poor
—	1500	900	700	500	250

Citori Plus Combo

This model features a single-barrel trap and an interchangeable Over/Under set of barrels. Other features are similar to Citori Plus Grade 1. Barrel combinations are 32" Over/Under with 34" single barrel or 30" Over/Under barrel with 32" or 34" single barrel. Introduced in 1989.

NIB	Exc.	V.G.	Good	Fair	Poor
2500	2100	1750	1100	700	450

Citori Ultra XS Prestige

New in 2008, this 12 gauge sporting clays model features an adjustable comb and Grade III/IV walnut stock with right hand palm swell. Ported barrels are 28", 30" or 32". Gold accented, high relief Ultra XS Special engraving on the steel/silver nitride finish receiver. Weight is about 8 lbs.

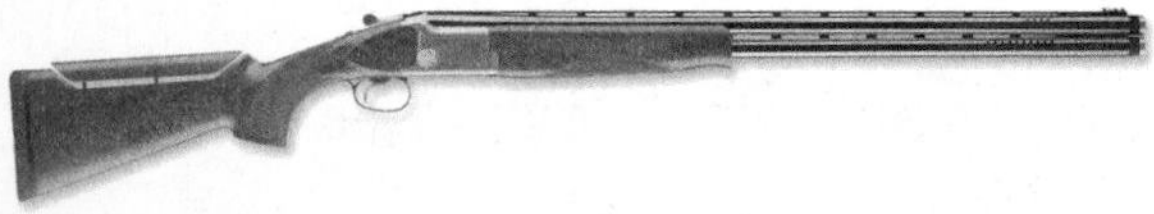

NIB	Exc.	V.G.	Good	Fair	Poor
4500	3300	2900	2250	1400	600

BT-99 SERIES

BT-99

This is a break-open, single-barrel trap gun chambered for 12 gauge only. It is offered with a 32" or 34", vent rib barrel with screw-in choke tubes. It features a boxlock action with automatic ejectors. The finish is blued with a checkered walnut stock and beavertail forearm. It was introduced in 1968 by B.C. Miroku.

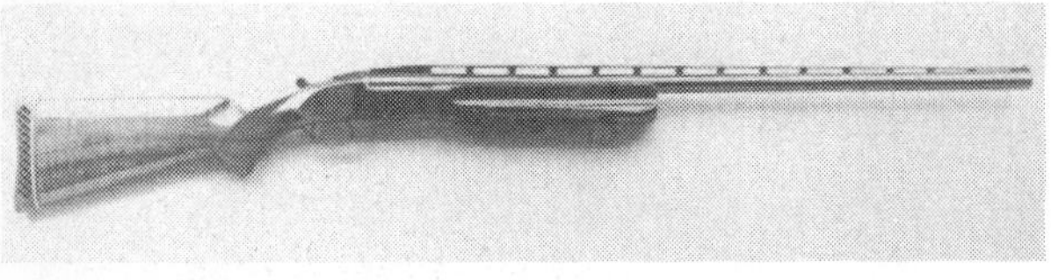

NIB	Exc.	V.G.	Good	Fair	Poor
1500	1100	800	500	400	350

Stainless

First introduced in 1993.

NIB	Exc.	V.G.	Good	Fair	Poor
1675	1250	900	700	550	350

Signature Grade I

First introduced in 1993.

NIB	Exc.	V.G.	Good	Fair	Poor
1300	1050	700	600	500	300

Pigeon Grade

First introduced in 1993.

NIB	Exc.	V.G.	Good	Fair	Poor
1600	1250	800	650	500	300

Golden Clays

First introduced in 1994. In 2003 this model was offered with an adjustable comb. Weight is about 9 lbs. Available with either a 32" or 34" barrel.

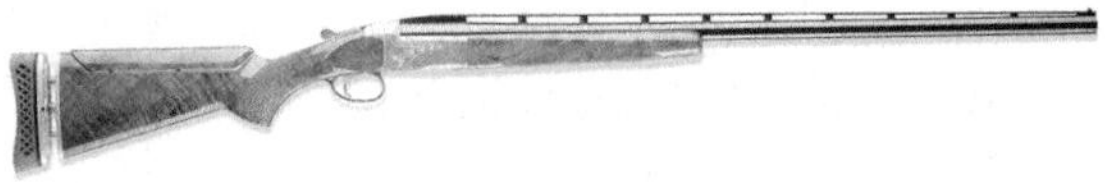

NIB	Exc.	V.G.	Good	Fair	Poor
3700	2500	1750	1100	500	300

BT-99 PLUS

This version features an adjustable vent rib and a recoil reduction system. It has an adjustable stock and recoil pad, as well as a back-bored barrel. It was introduced in 1989.

NIB	Exc.	V.G.	Good	Fair	Poor
1350	1200	900	700	500	300

Pigeon Grade

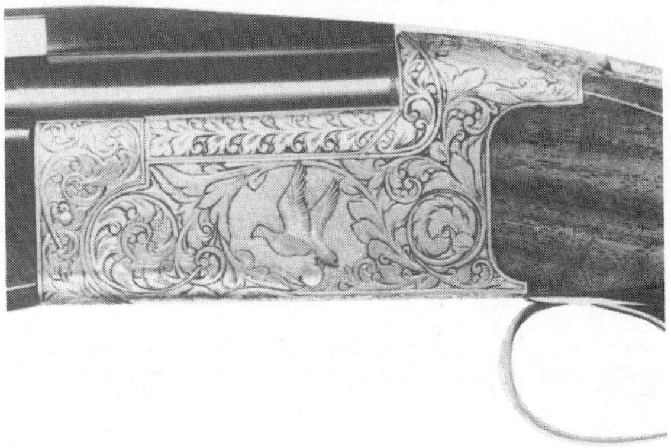

NIB	Exc.	V.G.	Good	Fair	Poor
1700	1300	900	800	550	350

Signature Grade

NIB	Exc.	V.G.	Good	Fair	Poor
1600	1200	850	700	500	300

Stainless—Grade I

Same as standard version but offered in stainless steel. First introduced in 1993. Available in 32" and 34" barrels. Weighs about 8 lbs. 11 oz.

NIB	Exc.	V.G.	Good	Fair	Poor
1700	1350	900	700	500	350

Golden Clays

First introduced in 1994.

NIB	Exc.	V.G.	Good	Fair	Poor
2700	2250	1750	900	450	300

Plus Micro

Slightly reduced dimensions and offered in barrel lengths from 28" to 34". Weighs about 8 lbs. 6 oz. Introduced in 1991.

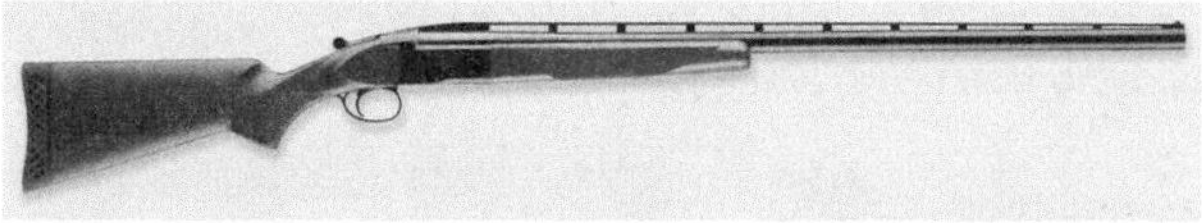

NIB	Exc.	V.G.	Good	Fair	Poor
1350	1100	900	700	500	300

Grade III

New in 2008, this BT-99 features a gloss finish Monte Carlo Grade III/IV walnut stock and gold accented high relief engraving on the receiver. Add 10 percent for adjustable comb stock.

NIB	Exc.	V.G.	Good	Fair	Poor
2400	1950	1250	750	550	350

MODEL BT-100

First introduced in 1995 this single-barrel trap features an adjustable trigger pull and length of pull. The stock is either a Monte Carlo version or an adjustable comb version. Barrel is either 32" or 34". Choice of blue or stainless finish. Weight is about 8.9 lbs.

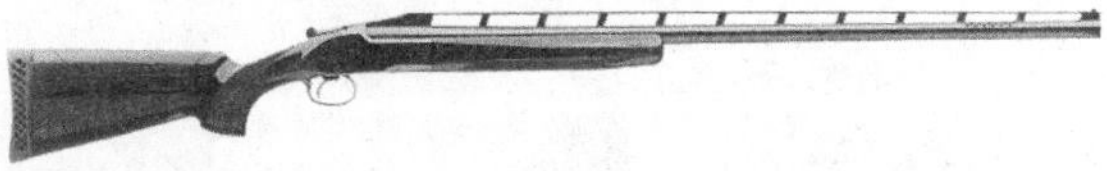

NIB	Exc.	V.G.	Good	Fair	Poor
2500	1900	1200	700	500	300

Satin

Introduced in 1999, this model features a matte black receiver and barrels without ejector selector. Available in 32" or 34" barrels. Available in Grade I only.

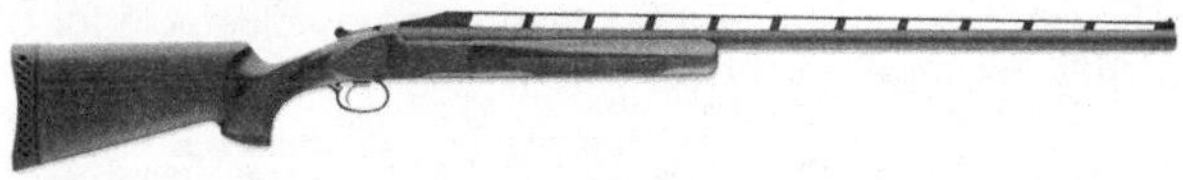

NIB	Exc.	V.G.	Good	Fair	Poor
1950	1300	1050	600	400	200

Thumbhole

This model is the same as the standard BT-100, but with the additional feature of a thumbhole stock. Offered in both blue and stainless.

NIB	Exc.	V.G.	Good	Fair	Poor
2575	2000	1350	1000	600	400

Recoilless Trap

First introduced in 1993 this model features an advanced design that eliminates recoil up to 72 percent. The receiver is a special bolt-action single-shot. Receiver is black anodized. It is fitted with an adjustable ventilated rib so the point of impact can be moved. Adjustable length of pull. The Standard Model is a 12 gauge with 30" barrel while the Micro Model is fitted with 27" barrels. Choke tubes are supplied. Standard Model weighs 9 lbs. 1 oz., while the Micro Model weighs 8 lbs. 10 oz.

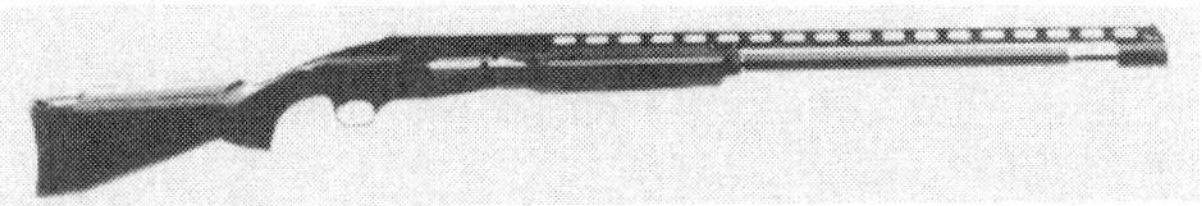

NIB	Exc.	V.G.	Good	Fair	Poor
1700	1400	900	700	500	350

BSS

This is a side-by-side, double-barrel shotgun chambered for 12 or 20 gauge. It was offered with a 26", 28", or 30" barrel with various choke combinations. It features a boxlock action and automatic ejectors. Early guns had a nonselective single trigger; late production, a selective trigger. The finish is blued with a checkered walnut stock and beavertail forearm. It was manufactured between 1978 and 1987 by B.C. Miroku.

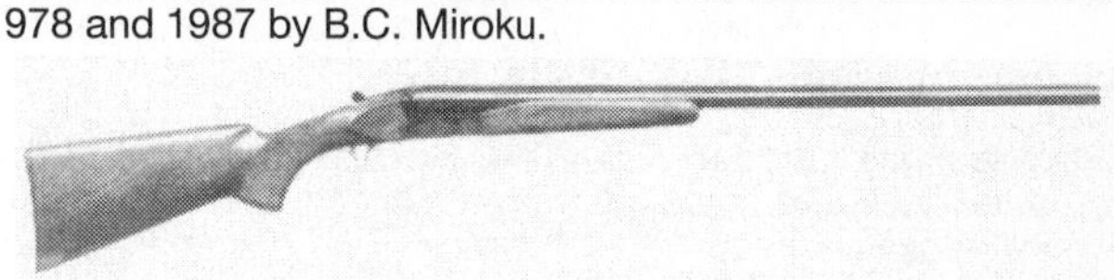

NIB	Exc.	V.G.	Good	Fair	Poor
—	2500	1650	975	650	400

NOTE: Single-selective trigger add 20 percent. 20 gauge add 20 percent.

BSS Grade II

This version features game scene engraving and a satin, coin finished receiver. It was discontinued in 1984.

NIB	Exc.	V.G.	Good	Fair	Poor
—	2750	1950	1350	850	500

BSS Sporter

This version features an English-style, straight-grip stock and a splinter forearm. The stock was oil-finished. It was offered with a 26" or 28" barrel.

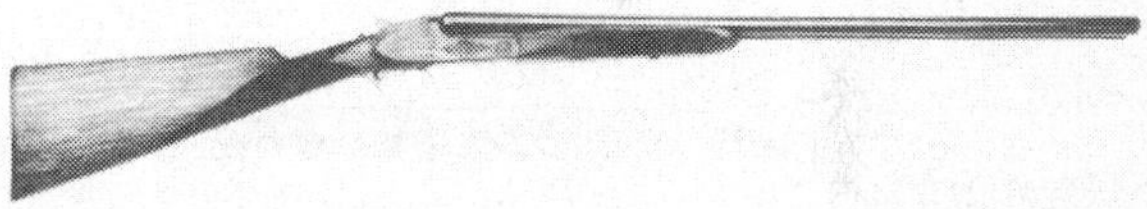

NIB	Exc.	V.G.	Good	Fair	Poor
—	2400	1550	975	650	400

NOTE: For 20 gauge add 20 percent.

BSS Sidelock

This version features an engraved sidelock action and was offered in 12 or 20 gauge. It was offered with a 26" or 28" barrel and has a straight-grip stock and splintered forearm. It was manufactured in Korea between 1983 and 1987. **NOTE:** The last few dozen 12 gauge sidelocks produced were an uncatalogued version of earlier guns. These guns had very finely engraved game scenes with English scroll. Add a 30 percent premium for this variation.

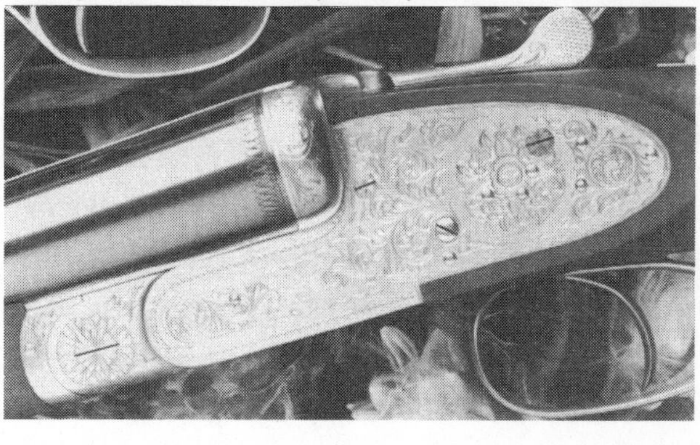

NIB	Exc.	V.G.	Good	Fair	Poor
4000	3500	2200	1750	800	500

NOTE: Add 30 percent to above prices for 20 gauge guns.

CYNERGY SERIES

This series was introduced in 2004. Browning calls it the third generation over-and-under gun. The Cynergy has a number of new design features such as a monolock hinge system for a lower profile, an inflex recoil pad, a new mechanical trigger system, an adjustable comb, back-bored barrels, and impact ejectors.

Field

This 12 gauge 3" model features a checkered walnut stock and forearm. Silver nitrate receiver with engraving. Choice of 26" or 28" vent rib barrels with choke tubes. Weight is about 7.75 lbs. A synthetic stock with adjustable comb is also offered.

NIB	Exc.	V.G.	Good	Fair	Poor
2050	1800	1400	1000	575	325

NOTE: Deduct $40 for synthetic stock.

Classic Field

This more traditionally styled 12 gauge was added to the Cynergy line in 2006. It features a steel receiver with silver nitride finish and game bird scenes on each side. Satin finish walnut stock and Schnabel style forend. Three choke tubes. Available in barrel lengths of 26" and 28" with an average weight of 7.75 lbs.

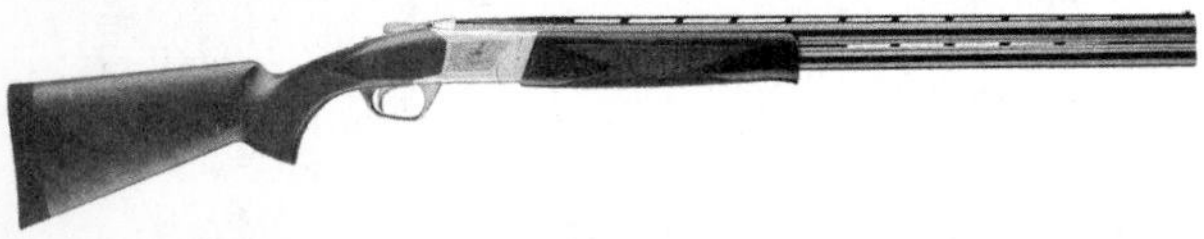

NIB	Exc.	V.G.	Good	Fair	Poor
2150	1850	1400	1000	575	325

Field Small Gauge

Introduced in 2005 this model is chambered for the 20 or 28 gauge or .410 bore. Choice of 26" or 28" vent rib barrels. Weight is about 6.25 lbs.

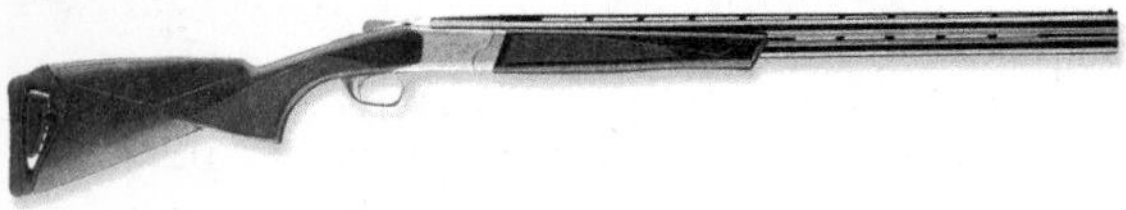

NIB	Exc.	V.G.	Good	Fair	Poor
2100	1850	1450	1050	575	325

Cynergy Sporting

As above but with higher grade walnut stock and choice of 28", 30", or 32" vent rib barrels with choke tubes. Ported barrels. Hi-Viz front sight. Weight is about 8 lbs. A synthetic stock with adjustable comb is also offered.

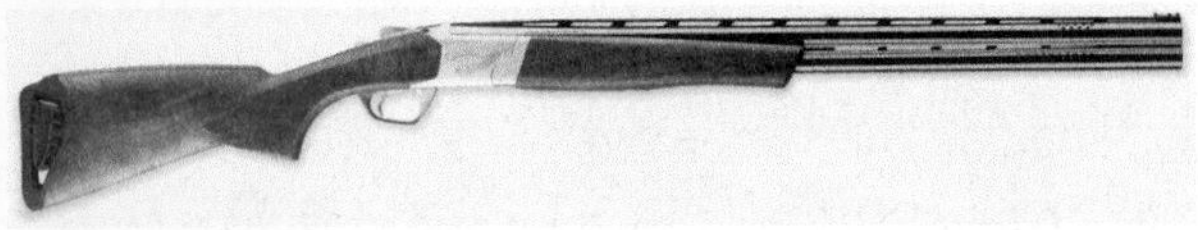

NIB	Exc.	V.G.	Good	Fair	Poor
2500	1900	1200	900	500	300

NOTE: For synthetic stock deduct $40.

Classic Sporting

New for 2006, this traditionally styled version of the Cynergy Sporting is available in 12 gauge with 28", 30" or 32" ported barrels. Oil finish walnut stock with Schnabel forend and Browning logo on steel receiver with silver nitride finish. Three Invector-Plus Midas Grade choke tubes. Average weight 7.75 lbs.

NIB	Exc.	V.G.	Good	Fair	Poor
2750	2200	1800	900	500	300

Classic Field Grade III

Similar to Classic Cynergy Field but with full coverage high-relief engraving on receiver and top lever, gloss finish Grade III/IV walnut.

NIB	Exc.	V.G.	Good	Fair	Poor
3400	2600	2000	1650	950	550

Classic Field Grade IV

Similar to Cynergy Classic Field Grade III but with more extensive, gold-highlighted engraving.

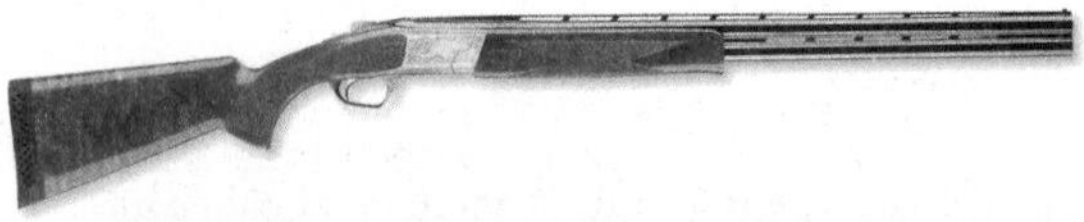

20 GA.

12 GA.

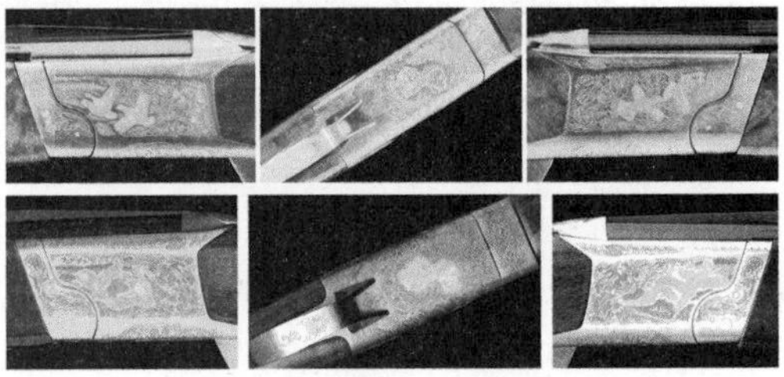

NIB	Exc.	V.G.	Good	Fair	Poor
5100	4200	3450	2300	1400	600

Sporting, Adjustable Comb

Similar to Cynergy Sporting but with a comb adjustable for cast and drop. Average weight 8.2 lbs. Introduced 2006.

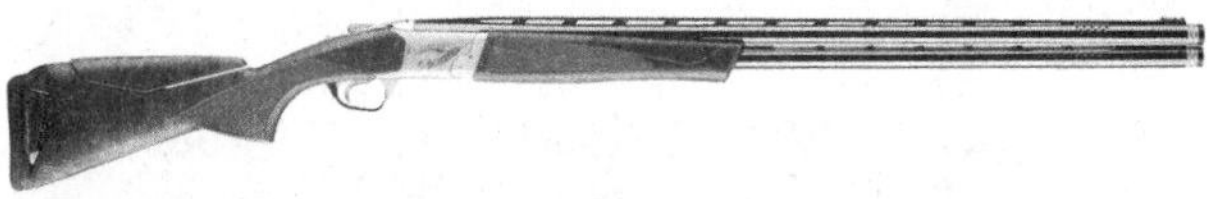

NIB	Exc.	V.G.	Good	Fair	Poor
2900	2000	1475	1050	750	450

Sporting Small Gauge

As above but in 20" or 28" gauge. Choice of 28", 30", or 32" ported barrels in 20 gauge and 28" or 30" ported barrels in 28 gauge. Weight is about 6.25 to 6.5 lbs. depending on barrel length. Introduced in 2005.

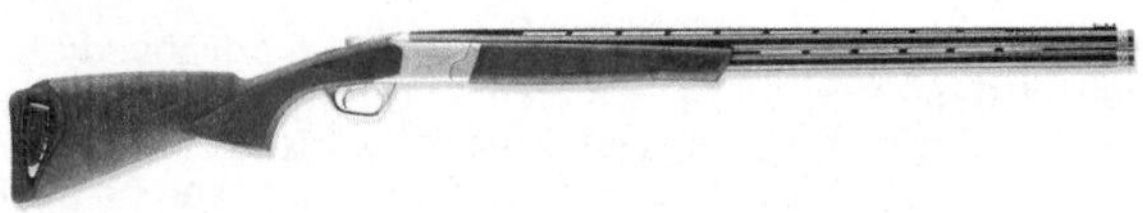

NIB	Exc.	V.G.	Good	Fair	Poor
2300	1750	1200	850	625	400

Feather

This lightweight Cynergy 12 gauge was introduced in 2006, followed by 20 and 28 gauge and .410 bore versions in 2008. Satin finish walnut stock. Weight is about 6.5 lbs. in 12 gauge and about 5 lbs. in others.

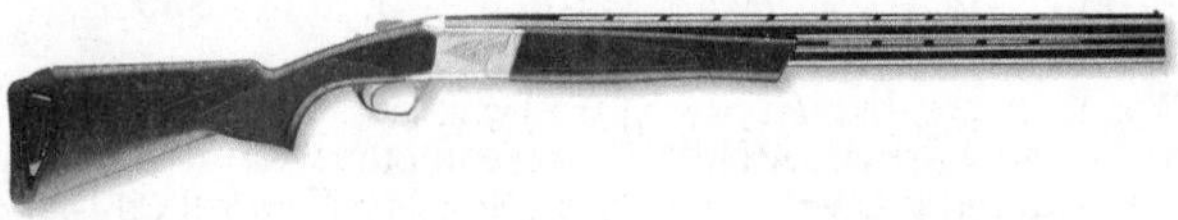

NIB	Exc.	V.G.	Good	Fair	Poor
2400	1800	1300	950	675	450

Feather Composite

As above but with synthetic stock and forend in 12 gauge only.

NIB	Exc.	V.G.	Good	Fair	Poor
2300	1700	1200	950	675	450

Euro Sporting

Sporting clays and skeet version comes in 2.75" 12 and 20 gauge with 28", 30" or 32" barrels. Stock is oil finish Grade III/IV walnut. Three choke tubes. Weight is about 8 lbs. in 12 gauge and 6.5 lbs. in 20 gauge.

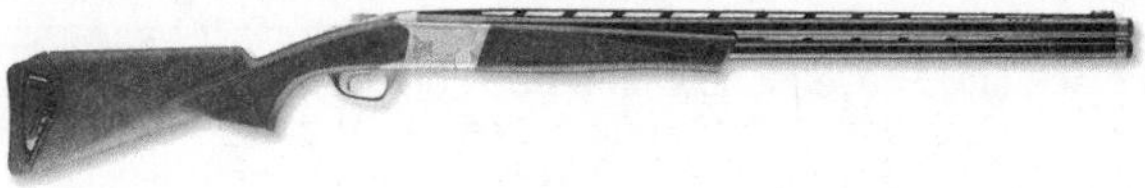

NIB	Exc.	V.G.	Good	Fair	Poor
3500	2800	2200	1650	950	550

Euro Field

Similar to Cynergy Euro Sporting but has Invenctor Plus tubes in 12 and 20 gauge, standard Invector tubes on 28 gauge and .410.

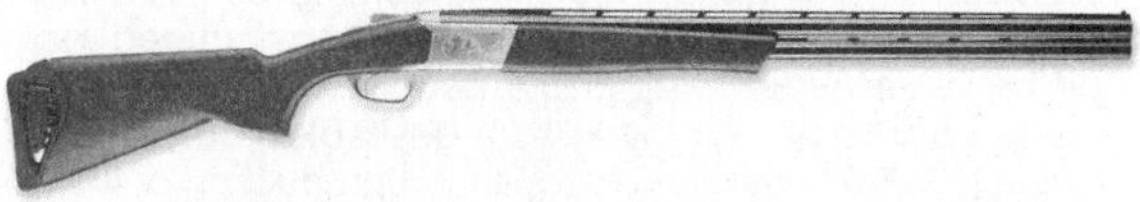

NIB	Exc.	V.G.	Good	Fair	Poor
2500	1900	1200	700	500	300

Euro Sporting Composite with Adjustable Comb

Similar to Euro Sporting Composite but with adjustable comb.

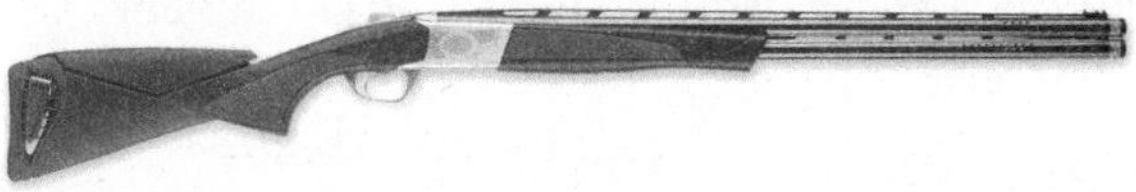

NIB	Exc.	V.G.	Good	Fair	Poor
3400	2600	2000	1650	950	550

Classic Trap Unsingle Combo

Trap shotgun in 12 gauge comes with a double barrel set in 32/34", 32/32", 30/34" or 30/32". Gloss finish Monte Carlo Grade III/IV walnut stock with right hand palm swell and adjustable comb. Weight is about 8.9 lbs. Four choke tubes. Aluminum fitted carrying case.

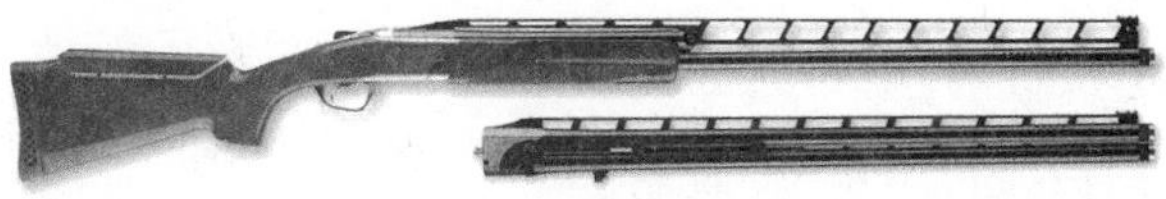

NIB	Exc.	V.G.	Good	Fair	Poor
4800	3800	2900	2250	1400	600

AUTO-5 SHOTGUN

Early Production Auto-5

This series of recoil-operated, semi-automatic shotguns was designed by John M. Browning and was offered in 12 or 16 gauge. The barrel lengths were 26", 28", 30", or 32" with various chokes and ribs. It has a unique, square-back action that has become instantly recognizable. The finish is blued with a checkered, walnut, round-knob stock. The various versions differ in the amount of ornamentation, type of rib, and quality of materials and workmanship utilized in construction. This series was manufactured in Belgium by FN between 1903 and 1939. The first example appeared in the United States in 1923. Pre-WWI 16 gauge guns, introduced in 1936, had 2-9/16" chambers; early models should be inspected by a qualified gunsmith before firing. **NOTE:** For 16 gauge not converted to 2-3/4" chamber deduct 30 percent. Grade III or Grade IV prices are not nearly as affected by chamber length because of their rarity. Original pre-war barrels were serial numbered to the gun. For extra barrels serial numbered to the gun add $100 for plain barrels, $200 for matte rib barrels, $275 for vent rib barrels. For extra barrels on Grade IV guns add an additional 30 percent to these barrel prices. Prices given are for guns with original barrels serial numbered to the gun. Remember the safety is located in front of the trigger guard. Deduct 10 to 25 percent for "suicide safety" in trigger guard.

Grade I—Plain Barrel

NIB	Exc.	V.G.	Good	Fair	Poor
—	500	400	300	250	150

Grade I—Matte Rib

NIB	Exc.	V.G.	Good	Fair	Poor
—	750	600	400	300	175

Grade I—Vent Rib

NIB	Exc.	V.G.	Good	Fair	Poor
—	825	650	475	375	200

Grade II—Plain Barrel

NIB	Exc.	V.G.	Good	Fair	Poor
—	950	800	700	250	150

Grade II—Matte Rib

NIB	Exc.	V.G.	Good	Fair	Poor
—	1150	850	750	350	175

Grade II—Vent Rib

NIB	Exc.	V.G.	Good	Fair	Poor
—	1400	1000	800	400	200

Grade III—Plain Barrel

NIB	Exc.	V.G.	Good	Fair	Poor
—	1900	1500	850	500	250

Grade III—Matte Rib

NIB	Exc.	V.G.	Good	Fair	Poor
—	3000	2500	1350	600	250

Grade III—Vent Rib

NIB	Exc.	V.G.	Good	Fair	Poor
—	3500	3000	1350	600	300

Grade IV—Plain Barrel

NIB	Exc.	V.G.	Good	Fair	Poor
—	4000	3250	2250	850	350

Grade IV—Matte Rib

NIB	Exc.	V.G.	Good	Fair	Poor
—	4850	4150	3000	1000	400

Grade IV—Vent Rib

NIB	Exc.	V.G.	Good	Fair	Poor
—	5500	4750	3500	1500	500

American Browning Auto-5

This recoil-operated, semi-automatic shotgun was another variation of the early-production Auto-5. It was chambered for 12, 16, or 20 gauge and was manufactured by the Remington Company for Browning. It is quite similar to Remington's Model 11 shotgun but features the Browning logo and a different type of engraving. There were approximately 45,000 manufactured between 1940 and 1942.

NIB	Exc.	V.G.	Good	Fair	Poor
—	675	575	450	375	200

NOTE: Vent rib add 20 percent. 20 gauge add 10 percent.

MID-PRODUCTION AUTO-5—FN MANUFACTURE STANDARD WEIGHT

This version of the recoil-operated, semi-automatic Auto-5 shotgun was manufactured by FN in Belgium between 1952 and 1976. It was offered in 12 or 16 gauge with 26" through 32" barrels with various chokes. The finish is blued with a checkered walnut stock and a black buttplate that was marked "Browning Automatic" with "FN" in center oval. Guns made prior to 1967 will be found with round knob pistol grips. The flatbottom variation was introduced in 1967.

Plain Barrel

NIB	Exc.	V.G.	Good	Fair	Poor
750	600	475	400	250	175

Matte Rib

NIB	Exc.	V.G.	Good	Fair	Poor
825	725	500	400	275	200

Vent Rib

NIB	Exc.	V.G.	Good	Fair	Poor
950	800	600	450	300	250

NOTE: Add 25 percent for guns with round-knob pistol grip and 35 percent for straight-grip stock. Add 20 percent for 20 gauge guns. Add 40 percent for 16 and 20 gauge guns NIB.

Auto-5 Lightweight

This version was chambered for 12 or 20 gauge and featured a lighter-weight, scroll-engraved receiver. It was manufactured between 1952 and 1976 by FN. The 20 gauge was not introduced until 1958.

NIB	Exc.	V.G.	Good	Fair	Poor
895	750	600	450	275	200

NOTE: Vent rib add 20 percent. For 20 gauge add 20 percent.

Auto-5 Magnum

This version featured 3" chambers and was offered with 26" through 32", full-choke barrels. It was manufactured between 1958 and 1976 by FN. The 12 gauge was introduced in 1958 and the 20 gauge brought out in 1967.

NIB	Exc.	V.G.	Good	Fair	Poor
—	950	750	550	375	200

NOTE: Vent rib add 20 percent. Add 10 to 15 percent for 20 ga.

Auto-5 Skeet

This version is similar to the Lightweight Model, chambered for 12 or 20 gauge with a 26" or 28", vent rib, skeet-choked barrel.

NIB	Exc.	V.G.	Good	Fair	Poor
—	795	575	525	425	250

Auto-5 Trap Model

This version is similar to the standard-weight model except chambered for 12 gauge only, with a 30", vent rib, full-choke barrel. It was manufactured by FN until 1971.

NIB	Exc.	V.G.	Good	Fair	Poor
—	675	550	475	300	225

Sweet Sixteen

This version is similar to the standard-weight and is chambered for 16 gauge only. It has a gold-plated trigger and was manufactured by FN between 1936 and 1976. **NOTE:** Not all A-5 16-gauges are Sweet Sixteens. Look for the gold-plated trigger, "Sweet Sixteen" script, and the lack of a suicide safety.

NIB	Exc.	V.G.	Good	Fair	Poor
1500	950	700	400	300	200

NOTE: Matte rib add 25 percent. Vent rib add 50 percent.

Two Millionth Commemorative

This version commemorated the two millionth Auto-5 shotgun produced by FN. It was engraved with a special high-polish blue finish and high-grade, checkered walnut in the stock. It was furnished in a black fitted case along with a book on the Browning Company. There were 2,500 manufactured between 1971 and 1974. As with all commemoratives, it must be NIB to realize its top potential.

NIB	Exc.	V.G.	Good	Fair	Poor
3000	1850	950	625	475	300

LATE PRODUCTION AUTO-5—B.C. MIROKU MANUFACTURE

In 1976 production of the Auto-5 shotgun was begun by B.C. Miroku in Japan. This move was accomplished after approximately 2,750,000 Auto-5 shotguns were manufactured by FN in Belgium between 1903 and 1976. The Japanese-manufactured guns, in the opinion of many knowledgeable people, show no less quality or functionality but are simply not as desirable from a collector's standpoint. In 1999 Browning discontinued production of the Auto-5 shotgun. **NOTE:** Since the discontinuance of the Auto-5, values for Japanese examples have risen, approaching those of Belgian guns.

Light 12

This version is chambered for 12 gauge 2-3/4" chamber only and is offered with a lightweight receiver. The barrel has a vent rib and choke tubes. It was introduced in 1975.

NIB	Exc.	V.G.	Good	Fair	Poor
750	650	500	400	350	250

Light 20

This version is similar to the Light 12 except chambered for 20 gauge only.

NIB	Exc.	V.G.	Good	Fair	Poor
800	650	550	425	350	250

Magnum

This version features 3" chambers and is offered with 26", 28", 30", or 32" barrels. It was introduced in 1976 by Miroku and discontinued in 1996.

NIB	Exc.	V.G.	Good	Fair	Poor
900	775	575	450	325	250

Buck Special

This version has a 24" barrel cylinder-bored with adjustable sights. It was introduced by Miroku in 1976.

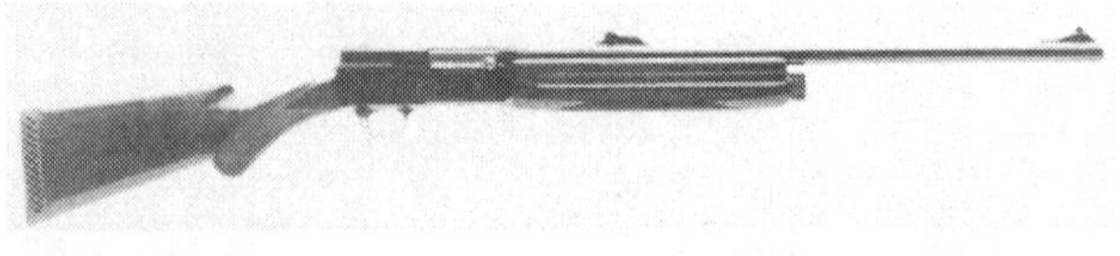

NIB	Exc.	V.G.	Good	Fair	Poor
725	625	500	425	300	200

LATE PRODUCTION AUTO-5—B.C. MIROKU MANUFACTUREE

Skeet

This is a competition model that features 26" or 28", skeet-bored barrels with a vent rib. It was manufactured between 1976 and 1983 by Miroku.

NIB	Exc.	V.G.	Good	Fair	Poor
825	550	450	350	—	200

LATE PRODUCTION AUTO-5—B.C. MIROKU MANUFACTURE

Sweet Sixteen

This version is similar to the Belgian-produced Sweet Sixteen, but is offered standard with a vent rib and screw-in Invector choke tubes. It was introduced in 1988 by Miroku and discontinued in 1992.

NIB	Exc.	V.G.	Good	Fair	Poor
1350	1100	750	550	375	225

DU 50th Anniversary

This was a high-grade version of the Auto-5 produced to commemorate the 50th anniversary of Ducks Unlimited. It is highly engraved and features high-gloss bluing and a fancy checkered walnut stock. There were approximately 5,500 manufactured by Miroku in 1987. They were auctioned by the Ducks Unlimited chapters to raise money for the organization, and because of this fact, it is difficult to furnish an accurate value. This is a commemorative firearm and, as such, must be NIB with all furnished materials to command premium collector value. We furnish what we feel is a general value.

NIB	Exc.	V.G.	Good	Fair	Poor
3000	2000	800	600	450	300

DU Sweet Sixteen

This was a special version of the Miroku-manufactured Sweet Sixteen that was auctioned by the Ducks Unlimited chapters in 1988. There were 5,500 produced. All specifications and cautions that were furnished for the 50th Anniversary gun also apply here.

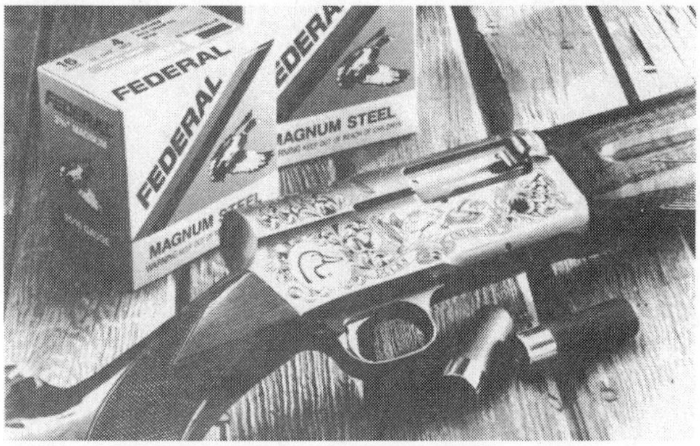

NIB	Exc.	V.G.	Good	Fair	Poor
2500	1500	850	600	400	300

AUTO-5 CLASSIC

This is a special limited edition series of A-5 shotguns built in 12 gauge only. The Classic is photo-etched with game scenes on a silver gray receiver. 5,000 of these guns were manufactured in 1984. The Gold Classic is similar in appearance but features gold inlays and is limited to 500 guns.

Classic

NIB	Exc.	V.G.	Good	Fair	Poor
2000	1675	1200	750	525	300

Gold Classic

Produced by FN.

NIB	Exc.	V.G.	Good	Fair	Poor
8500	7000	5000	3000	1400	650

Auto-5 Light Buck Special

This model is a lightweight version of the Buck Special. Chambered for the 2-3/4" shell and fitted with a 24" vent rib barrel. Conventional choked for slug or buckshot. Barrel has adjustable rear sight and ramp front sight. Weighs 8 lbs.

NIB	Exc.	V.G.	Good	Fair	Poor
850	650	550	450	375	225

AUTO-5 STALKER

New for 1992 this model is available in either a lightweight version or a Magnum version. The Light Stalker is available in 12 gauge with either 26" or 28" barrel with choke tubes. The Magnum Stalker is offered in 12 gauge (3" chamber) with 28" or 30" barrel and choke tubes. The Light Stalker weighs 8 lbs. 4 oz. and the Magnum Stalker weighs 8 lbs. 11 oz.

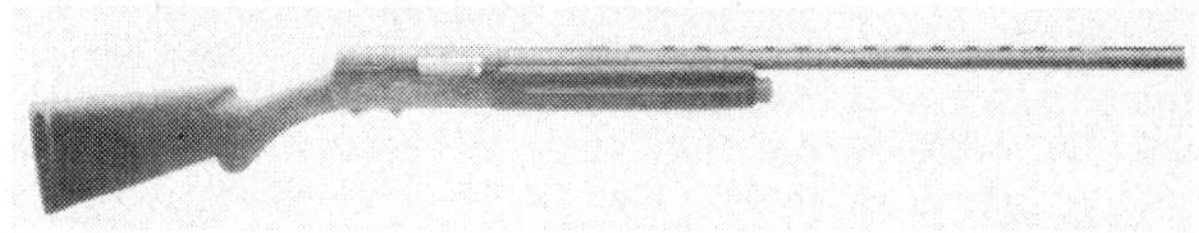

Light Stalker

NIB	Exc.	V.G.	Good	Fair	Poor
775	600	550	400	300	225

Magnum Stalker

NIB	Exc.	V.G.	Good	Fair	Poor
800	650	600	375	275	250

Auto-5 Final Tribute Limited Edition

Introduced in 1999, this commemorative A-5 is limited to 1,000 shotguns. It represents the final production of this model. Chambered for the 12 gauge shell and fitted with a 28" vent rib barrel this shotgun has a special engraved receiver.

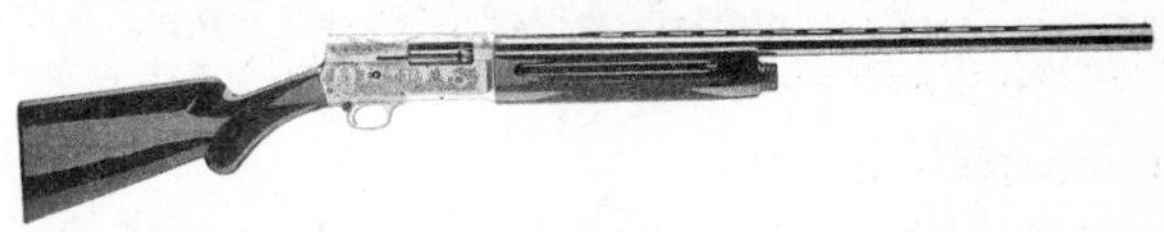

NIB	Exc.	V.G.	Good	Fair	Poor
5000	3750	2500	2000	1300	500

Double Automatic Shotgun

This is a short recoil-operated, semi-automatic shotgun chambered for 12 gauge only. It was offered with a 26", 28", or 30" barrel that was either plain or vent ribbed. It has various chokes. The receiver is steel, and the finish is blued or silver with a checkered walnut stock. The tubular magazine holds only two shots—hence its name. It was manufactured between 1954 and 1972.

NIB	Exc.	V.G.	Good	Fair	Poor
—	625	500	350	275	225

NOTE: Vent rib add 25 percent.

Twelvette Double Auto

This version is similar to the Double Automatic except that it has an aircraft aluminum alloy frame color-anodized in either blue, silver, green, brown, or black. Red-, gold-, or royal blue-colored receivers were the rarest colors and would command approximately a 50 to 75 percent premium. It was offered with either a plain or vent rib barrel. There were approximately 65,000 produced between 1954 and 1972.

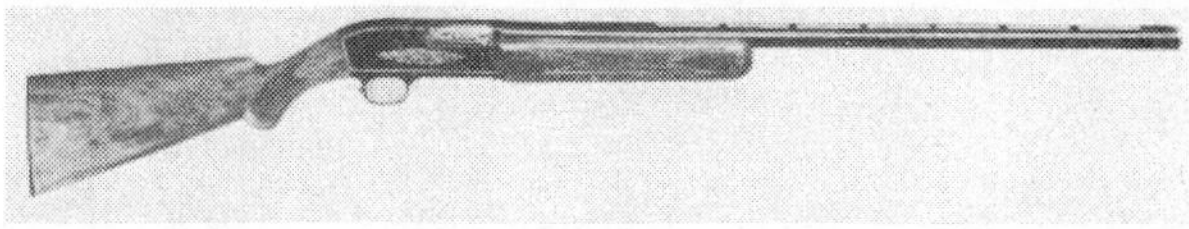

NIB	Exc.	V.G.	Good	Fair	Poor
—	775	595	350	275	225

NOTE: Vent rib add 25 percent.

Twentyweight Double Auto

This version is similar in all respects to the Twelvette except that it is three-quarters of a pound lighter and was offered with a 26.5" barrel. It was manufactured between 1952 and 1971.

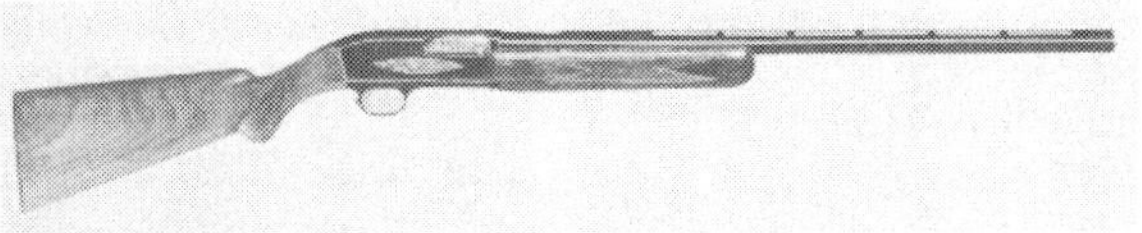

NIB	Exc.	V.G.	Good	Fair	Poor
—	750	595	375	300	250

NOTE: Vent rib add 25 percent.

2000 SERIES

B-2000

This is a gas-operated, semi-automatic shotgun chambered for 12 or 20 gauge and offered with a 26", 28", or 30", vent rib barrel with various chokes. The finish is blued with a checkered walnut stock. This shotgun was assembled in Portugal from parts that were manufactured by FN in Belgium. There were approximately 115,000 imported between 1974 and 1981.

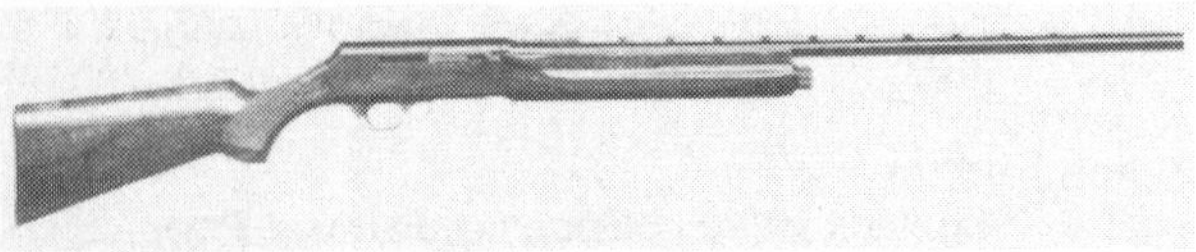

NIB	Exc.	V.G.	Good	Fair	Poor
625	550	475	300	225	175

Magnum

This version features a barrel with 3" chambers and was offered standard with a recoil pad.

NIB	Exc.	V.G.	Good	Fair	Poor
775	575	500	300	225	175

Buck Special

This version has a 24", cylinder-bored barrel with rifle sights.

NIB	Exc.	V.G.	Good	Fair	Poor
625	475	425	275	225	175

Trap

This version has a 30", full-choke barrel with a floating rib and a Monte Carlo-type trap stock.

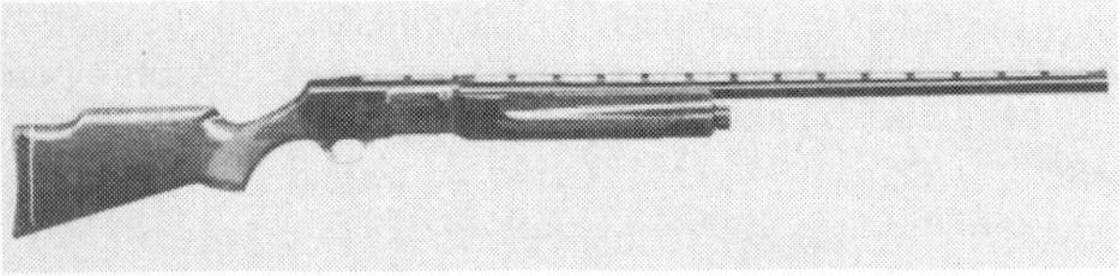

NIB	Exc.	V.G.	Good	Fair	Poor
600	475	425	275	225	175

Skeet

This version features a 26", skeet-bored barrel with a floating vent rib and a skeet-type stock.

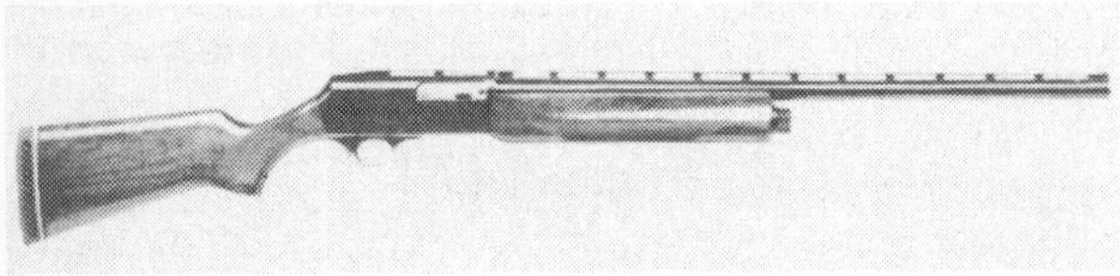

NIB	Exc.	V.G.	Good	Fair	Poor
—	595	450	375	275	200

NOTE: Add 20 percent for 20 gauge guns.

B-80

This is a gas-operated, semi-automatic shotgun chambered for 12 or 20 gauge. It features 3" magnum potential by simply exchanging the barrel. It features various-length barrels and was offered with screw-in Invector chokes as of 1985. The receiver is either steel or lightweight aluminum alloy. The finish is blued with a checkered walnut stock. This gun was assembled in Portugal from parts manufactured by Beretta in Italy. It was manufactured between 1981 and 1988.

NIB	Exc.	V.G.	Good	Fair	Poor
—	550	450	375	325	225

NOTE: Add 20 percent for 20 gauge guns.

B-80 Buck Special

This version features a 24", cylinder-bored barrel with rifle sights. It was discontinued in 1984.

NIB	Exc.	V.G.	Good	Fair	Poor
—	495	400	350	300	200

B-80 DU Commemorative

This version was produced to be auctioned by American Ducks Unlimited chapters. In order to realize the collector potential, it must be NIB with all supplied materials. Values supplied are general.

NIB	Exc.	V.G.	Good	Fair	Poor
950	650	550	425	325	275

GOLD SERIES

Gold 10

Introduced for the first time in 1993 this is a gas-operated 5-shot semi-automatic shotgun chambered for the 10 gauge shell. Offered with 26", 28", or 30" vent rib barrel. The standard model has a walnut stock, blued receiver and barrel while the Stalker Model is fitted with a graphite composite stock with nonglare finish on receiver and barrel. Both models are fitted with choke tubes. Weighs about 10 lbs. 10 oz.

NIB	Exc.	V.G.	Good	Fair	Poor
950	700	550	450	300	150

Gold Evolve

Introduced in 2004 this model is an updated version of the original Gold gun. It features newly designed receiver, magazine cap, ventilated rib design, checkering pattern and Hi-Viz sights. Offered in 12 gauge 3" with choice of 26", 28", or 30" barrel with choke tubes. Weight is about 7 lbs. for the 28" model.

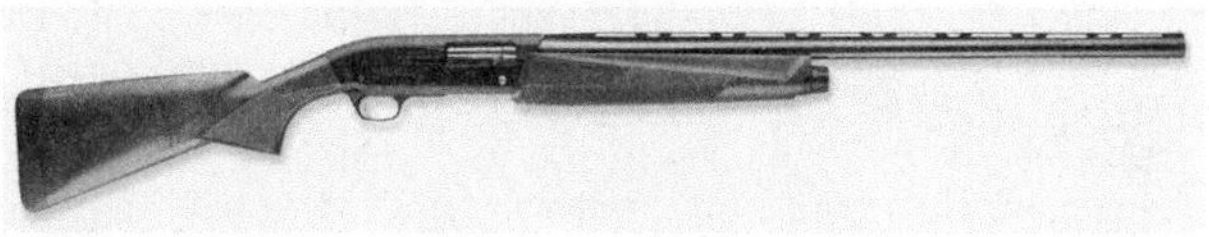

NIB	Exc.	V.G.	Good	Fair	Poor
1195	875	700	525	400	225

Gold Light 10 Gauge Camo

This 10 gauge model is offered with 26" or 28" barrels with Mossy Oak or Shadow Grass camo. Lightweight alloy receiver reduces weight to 9 lb. 10 oz. Introduced in 2001.

NIB	Exc.	V.G.	Good	Fair	Poor
1275	975	775	595	450	250

Gold 10 Gauge Combo

This 10 gauge model has a choice of two vent rib barrels in lengths of 24" and 26", or 24" and 28". Walnut stock with black ventilated recoil pad. Weight with 28" barrels is about 10 lbs. 10 ozs.

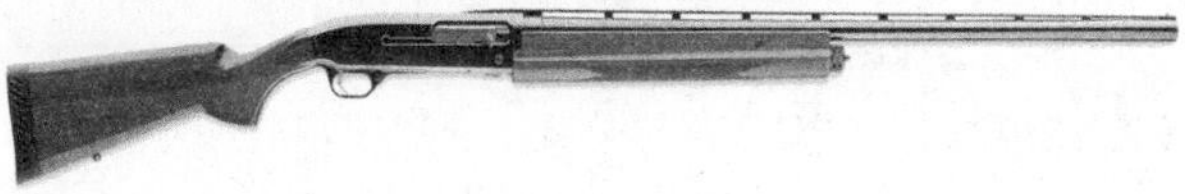

NIB	Exc.	V.G.	Good	Fair	Poor
1150	800	675	500	375	250

Gold Stalker

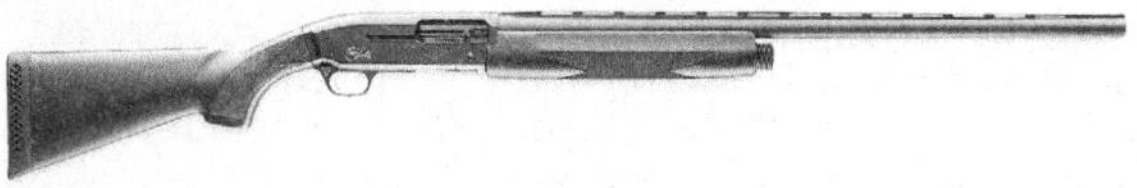

NIB	Exc.	V.G.	Good	Fair	Poor
1025	725	550	450	300	150

Gold Classic Stalker

Introduced in 1999 this model features a classic Browning squared receiver and fully adjustable stock. This model is chambered for 12 gauge shells with choice 26" or 28" vent rib barrels. Gun has 3" chambers. Black synthetic stock. Weight is about 7 lbs. 3 ozs.

NIB	Exc.	V.G.	Good	Fair	Poor
850	675	550	400	275	125

Gold 3-1/2" 12 Gauge

Introduced in 1997 this model features a 3-1/2" chamber. It can operate 2-3/4", or 3" shells as well. Choice of barrel lengths from 26" to 30". Invector-Plus chokes. Magazine capacity is four 2.75" shells or three 3" shells or three 3.5" shells. The weight is approximately 7 lbs. 10 oz.

NIB	Exc.	V.G.	Good	Fair	Poor
1000	795	595	450	200	150

Gold 12 Gauge Hunter

Introduced in 1994 this semi-automatic shotgun is built on the same gas operating system as the Gold 10. Offered with 26", 28", or 30" barrel it has a magazine capacity of four 3" shells. Walnut stock has full checkered pistol grip with black rubber recoil pad. Invector-Plus choke tubes supplied. Weighs about 7.5 lbs. Also available (1998) in Stalker version with non-glare matte metal parts and stocks.

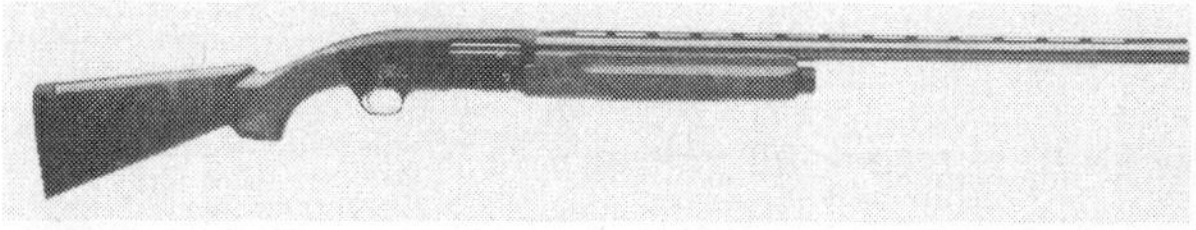

NIB	Exc.	V.G.	Good	Fair	Poor
750	525	400	300	200	150

Gold Classic Hunter

Introduced in 1999, this model features a squared receiver, fully adjustable stock, selected walnut stock, and deep blued barrels. Choice of 26", 28", or 30" vent rib barrel. Offered with 3" chamber 12 gauge only.

NIB	Exc.	V.G.	Good	Fair	Poor
850	600	500	400	275	225

Gold Classic 20 Gauge

Offered with choice of 26" or 28" vent rib barrels with select walnut stock. Adjustable comb. Squared receiver. Weight is about 6 lbs. 12 ozs. Introduced in 1999.

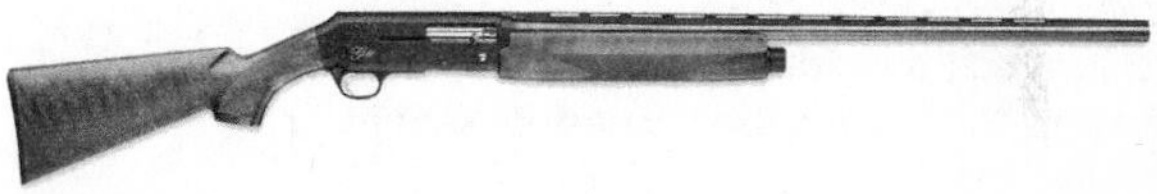

NIB	Exc.	V.G.	Good	Fair	Poor
795	600	500	400	275	225

Gold Classic High Grade

Introduced in 1999, this model features a traditional square receiver with engraved silver gray finish. Offered in 12 gauge only with 3" chambers and 28" vent rib barrel. Select walnut stock. Weight is about 7 lbs. 6 ozs.

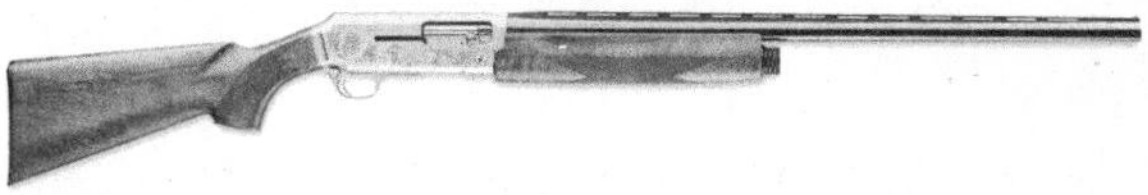

NIB	Exc.	V.G.	Good	Fair	Poor
1500	1200	775	500	225	165

Gold Deer Hunter

Introduced in 1997, this model features a choice of a fully rifled barrel or a smooth bore barrel with Invector choke system. Both versions come with a cantilever scope mount. Stock and forearm are of select walnut. Receiver has non-glare black finish. Barrel is satin finish. Barrel length is 22" on both barrels. Weight is about 7 lbs. 12 oz. Price listed are for smoothbore barrel.

NIB	Exc.	V.G.	Good	Fair	Poor
875	650	500	400	200	150

NOTE: For fully rifled version add $40.

Gold Deer Hunter—20 gauge

Same as above but chambered for 20 gauge 3" shell. Furnished with fully rifled 22" barrel. Cantilever scope mount. Introduced in 2001.

NIB	Exc.	V.G.	Good	Fair	Poor
1025	900	625	495	300	200

Gold Deer Stalker

This model, introduced in 1999, is the same as the model above but fitted with a black synthetic stock.

NIB	Exc.	V.G.	Good	Fair	Poor
950	700	600	500	300	150

Gold Deer—Mossy Oak

Introduced in 1999 with camo finish.

NIB	Exc.	V.G.	Good	Fair	Poor
825	675	575	450	200	125

Gold Waterfowl—Mossy Oak Shadow Grass 12 Gauge 3.5" Chamber, Shadow Grass

NIB	Exc.	V.G.	Good	Fair	Poor
1275	900	725	550	375	150

Gold 12 Gauge 3" Chamber

NIB	Exc.	V.G.	Good	Fair	Poor
1100	775	650	575	375	150

Gold 12 Gauge 3.5" Chamber Ultimate Turkey Gun

NIB	Exc.	V.G.	Good	Fair	Poor
1280	1000	900	725	375	200

Gold Hunter

Chambered for 12 and 20 gauge and offered in 26" or 28" barrel lengths. Weighs about 6.8 lbs.

NIB	Exc.	V.G.	Good	Fair	Poor
750	625	400	300	200	150

Gold Sporting Clays

Introduced in 1996, this model features a ported barrel in 28" or 30" lengths. Recoil pad is standard. Weight is about 7.5 lbs.

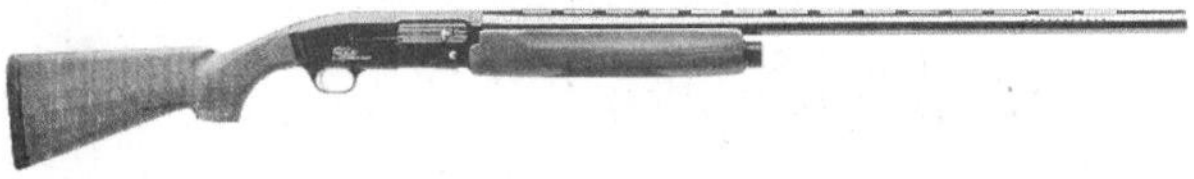

NIB	Exc.	V.G.	Good	Fair	Poor
800	675	475	375	200	150

Gold Ladies/Youth Sporting Clays

Offered in 12 gauge only with 2.75" chambers this model features a 28" vent rib barrel. Overall dimensions have been adjusted to fit women. Black solid recoil pad. Weight is about 7 lbs. 6 ozs. Introduced in 1999.

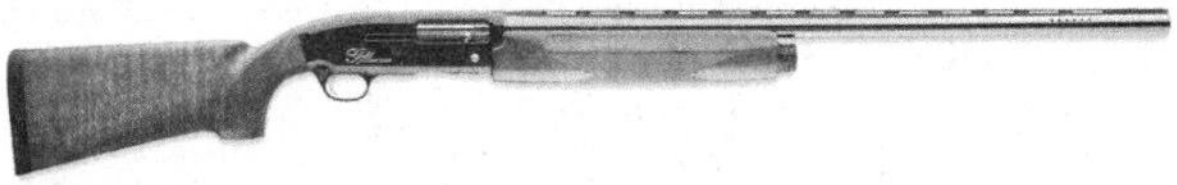

NIB	Exc.	V.G.	Good	Fair	Poor
1200	895	625	450	300	125

Gold "Golden Clays" Ladies Sporting Clays

Introduced in 2005 this 12 gauge 2.75" chambered gun is fitted with a 28" vent rib ported barrel with 4 choke tubes. Silver receiver is engraved with gold enhancements. Weight is about 7.75 lbs.

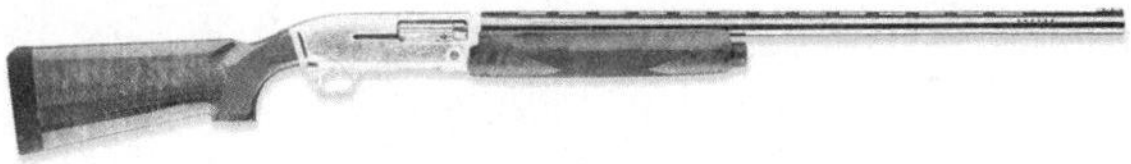

NIB	Exc.	V.G.	Good	Fair	Poor
1900	1375	1050	800	575	300

Gold "Golden Clays" Sporting Clays

As above but with standard stock dimensions and choice of 28" or 30" barrels. Introduced in 2005.

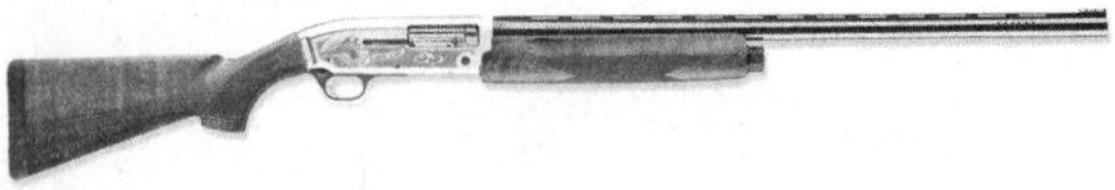

NIB	Exc.	V.G.	Good	Fair	Poor
1800	1300	1050	800	575	300

Gold Micro

Introduced in 2001 this model features a 20 gauge gun with 26" barrel, smaller pistol grip, shorter length of pull, and back-bored barrel with choke tubes. Weight is about 6 lb. 10 oz.

NIB	Exc.	V.G.	Good	Fair	Poor
925	650	575	475	300	125

Gold Upland

Offered in 12 or 20 gauge. The 12 gauge offered with 24" barrel and the 20 gauge with 26" barrel. Straight grip stock with 3" chamber. Weight is 7 lbs. for 12 gauge and 6.75 lbs. for 20 gauge. Introduced in 2001.

NIB	Exc.	V.G.	Good	Fair	Poor
950	700	600	475	300	125

Gold Fusion

This model features a new style vent rib, adjustable comb pro-comp sight, and five choke tubes. Offered in 12 gauge with 3" chambers with 26" or 28" barrels. Introduced in 2001. In 2002 this model was offered in 20 gauge as well as 12 with choice of 26" or 28" vent rib barrel. Weight for 12 gauge is about 7 lbs. anbd for 20 gauge about 6.5 lbs.

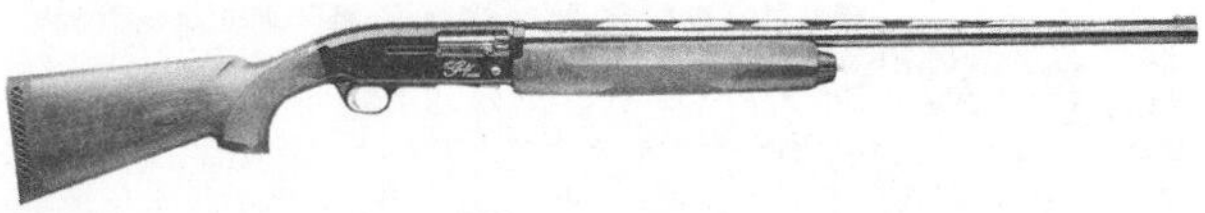

NIB	Exc.	V.G.	Good	Fair	Poor
900	725	650	495	300	125

Gold Fusion High Grade

Similar to the Gold Fusion with the addition of a high grade Turkish walnut stock, silver nitride receiver with game scene in gold. Five choke tubes and a hard case are standard. Introduced in 2005.

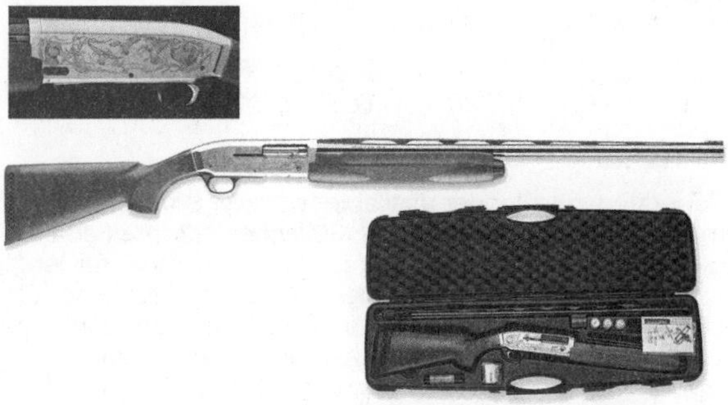

NIB	Exc.	V.G.	Good	Fair	Poor
1600	1250	900	625	450	300

Golden Clays

Introduced in 1999, this model features chambered for the 12 gauge shell with 2.74" chambers. Choice of 28" or 30" vent rib ported barrels. Engraved silver gray receiver. Select walnut stock. Weight is about 7 lbs. 3 ozs.

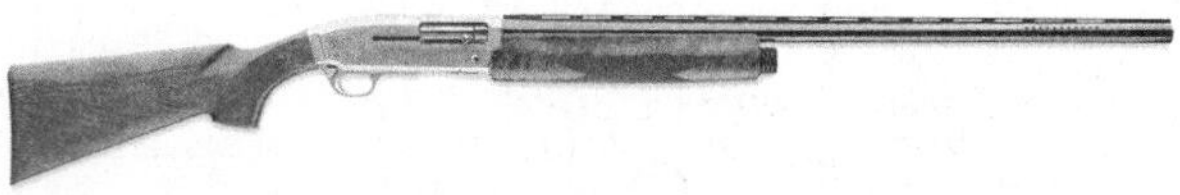

NIB	Exc.	V.G.	Good	Fair	Poor
1250	1000	825	675	425	300

500 SERIES

A-500G/A-500R

This is a self-adjusting, gas-operated, semi-automatic shotgun chambered for 12 gauge only. It is offered with 26", 28", or 30" barrels with a vent rib and screw-in Invector choke tubes. It has 3" chambers and can fire any load interchangeably. The finish is blued with a checkered walnut stock and recoil pad. It features light engraving. It was introduced in 1987. At this time (2008) the recoil version (A-500R) has a slightly better reputation for functioning than the gas-operated A-500G, but values are roughly similar.

NIB	Exc.	V.G.	Good	Fair	Poor
575	490	425	350	275	225

A-500G Sporting Clays

This gas-operated version is designed for sporting clays and features a choice of 28" or 30" vent rib barrel with semi-gloss finish with gold lettering "Sporting Clays." Ventilated recoil pad standard. Weighs about 8 lbs.

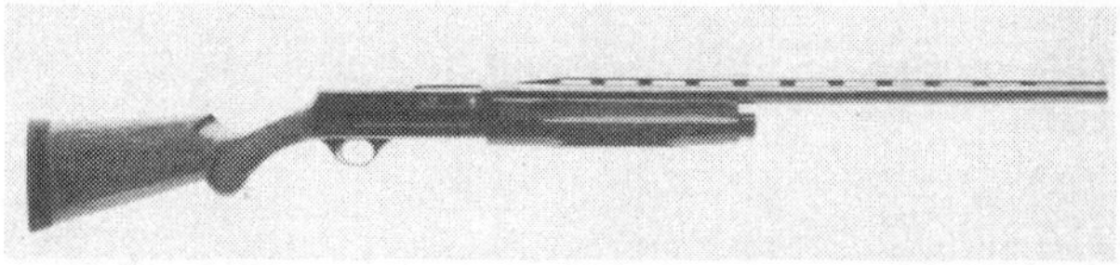

NIB	Exc.	V.G.	Good	Fair	Poor
550	425	350	300	200	150

A-500R Hunting Model

Similar in appearance to the A-500G with the exception that this model operates on a short recoil design. The buttstock features a full pistol grip. Available with 26", 28", or 30" vent rib barrels. Choke tubes standard. Weighs about 7 lbs. 13 oz.

NIB	Exc.	V.G.	Good	Fair	Poor
475	385	300	250	200	150

A-500R Buck Special

Same as Hunting Model with the addition of adjustable rear sight and contoured front ramp sight with gold bead. Choke tubes standard, as is 24" barrel. Weighs 7 lbs. 11 oz.

NIB	Exc.	V.G.	Good	Fair	Poor
500	425	350	300	225	150

SILVER SERIES

This value-priced series of gas-operated autoloaders was introduced in 2006. All models feature a semi-humpback design and aluminum alloy receiver. Weights vary from 7.25 to 7.5 lbs. depending on barrel length and stock material. Three choke tubes provided with all models.

Silver Hunter

This version features a satin finish walnut stock and forend. It is available with a 3" chamber in 26", 28" and 30" barrel lengths or with a 3.5" chamber in 26" or 28" barrel length. Add 15 percent for 3.5" chamber. A 20 gauge version with 26" or 28" barrel became available in 2008.

NIB	Exc.	V.G.	Good	Fair	Poor
850	700	575	400	295	200

Silver Stalker

Similar to Silver Hunter but with matte black composite stock and forend. Sling swivel studs. 3.5" chamber only.

NIB	Exc.	V.G.	Good	Fair	Poor
825	675	550	375	275	175

Silver Micro

This is a 20 gauge with a 26" barrel and shorter stock dimensions for smaller shooters.

NIB	Exc.	V.G.	Good	Fair	Poor
825	695	550	375	275	175

Silver Sporting Micro

This 2.75" 12 gauge includes adjustment spacers for changing stock length. Barrel is 28". Three choke tubes included. Weight is about 7 lbs.

NIB	Exc.	V.G.	Good	Fair	Poor
1150	900	725	600	375	250

Silver NWTF

New in 2008, this 3" 12 gauge turkey gun is fully camouflaged with Mossy Oak\qs New Break-Up pattern. The 24" barrel is outfitted with fiber-optic rifle sights. Weight is about 7 lbs. Add 10 percent for 3.5" chamber.

NIB	Exc.	V.G.	Good	Fair	Poor
1100	900	725	600	375	250

Silver Rifled Deer

New in 2008, this 3" 12 gauge slug gun features a rifled barrel with cantilever scope mount. Finishes include satin walnut, black composite and Mossy Oak New Break-Up camo. Add 10 percent for camo finish.

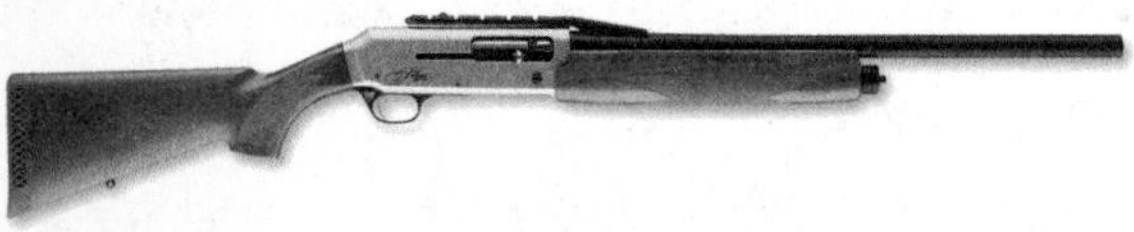

NIB	Exc.	V.G.	Good	Fair	Poor
1100	900	725	600	375	250

Silver–Mossy Oak

Similar to Silver Stalker but in choice of Mossy Oak New Break-Up with 26" barrel or Mossy Oak New Shadow Grass with 26" or 28" barrel.

NIB	Exc.	V.G.	Good	Fair	Poor
925	650	575	475	300	125

Gold Superlite Hunter

Introduced in 2006, this gun uses an aluminum alloy receiver and alloy magazine tube to reduce weight to about 7 lbs. in 12 gauge. Gloss finish walnut stock. Available with 3" or 3.5" chamber and 26" or 28" barrel. Magazine cut-off feature on 3.5" model. A 6.5 lb. 20 gauge with 3" chamber and 26" or 28" barrel is also offered. Three choke tubes. Add 15 percent for 3.5" chamber.

NIB	Exc.	V.G.	Good	Fair	Poor
900	650	575	475	300	125

Gold Superlite FLD Hunter

Similar to Gold Superlite Hunter but with semi-humpback style receiver and satin finish walnut stock and 3" chamber only. Magazine cut-off on 12 gauge models. Adjustable shim system and three choke tubes.

NIB	Exc.	V.G.	Good	Fair	Poor
925	650	575	475	300	125

Gold Superlite Micro

Similar to Gold Superlite Hunter but with compact dimensions for smaller shooters. Only in 20 gauge with 26" barrel. Weighs about 6.25 pounds. Three choke tubes.

NIB	Exc.	V.G.	Good	Fair	Poor
925	650	575	475	300	125

MAXUS SERIES

Introduced in 2009 as a replacement for the Gold line.

Maxus

Autoloading shotgun chambered for 3" or 3-1/2" shells. Aluminum receiver, lightweight profile 26" or 28" barrel with vent rib, composite stock, Vector Pro lengthened forcing cone, DuraTouch Armor Coating overall. Handles shorter shells interchangeably. Weight: 6-7/8 lbs.

Maxus Stalker

Matte black finish overall. Add $150 for 3-1/2".

NIB	Exc.	V.G.	Good	Fair	Poor
1200	975	800	625	475	300

Maxus Mossy Oak Duck Blind

Mossy Oak Duck Blind finish overall. Add $150 for 3-1/2".

NIB	Exc.	V.G.	Good	Fair	Poor
1300	975	800	625	475	300

Maxus Hunter

Gas-operated auto-loader available with 3 or 3-1/2-inch magnum chambers. Barrel lengths: 26, 28, 30 inches (22 for rifled version). Lengthened forcing cone. Stock is shim-adjustable for length of pull, cast and drop. Glossy-finished walnut stock with 22-line checkering. Also offered in Mossy Oak Break-Up Infinity camo, and as Rifled Deer version with Mossy Oak Break-up Infinity camo. Weight: approx. 7 pounds. Introduced in 2011.

NIB	Exc.	V.G.	Good	Fair	Poor
1200	1000	850	650	400	300

Maxus Sporting Carbon

Gas-operated 12-gauge auto-loader with 3-inch chamber. Aluminum alloy receiver has satin nickel finish, laser engraving. Barrel length: 28 or 30 inches. Gloss-finished high-grade walnut stock. Also available with carbon fiber stock and as Rifled Deer Stalker version with cantilevered scope base and 22-inch barrel. New 2011.

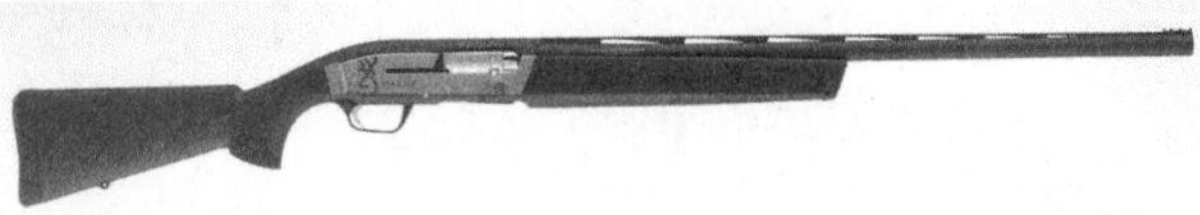

NIB	Exc.	V.G.	Good	Fair	Poor
1390	1200	950	700	450	350

NOTE: Deduct 15 percent for Deer Stalker/Carbon

BPS SERIES

This is a slide-action shotgun chambered for 10, 12, or 20 gauge. It is offered with various length vent rib barrels with screw-in Invector chokes. It features 3" magnum chambers and a bottom-ejection system that effectively makes it ambidextrous. It has double slide bars and a 5-shot tubular magazine. It is constructed of all steel. It was introduced by B.C. Miroku in 1977.

Field Grade

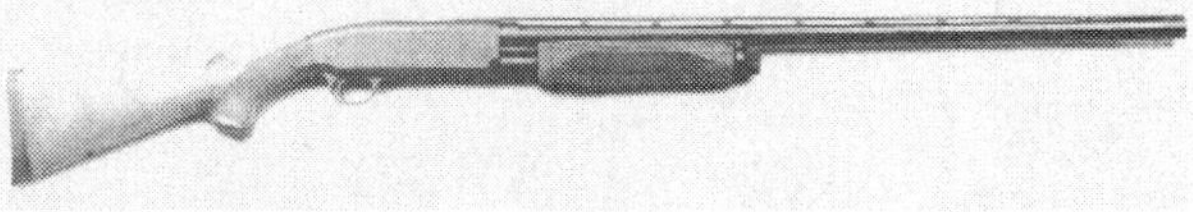

NIB	*Exc.*	*V.G.*	*Good*	*Fair*	*Poor*
350	300	275	200	200	150

Field Grade 28 Gauge

Introduced in 1994. Weight approximately 7 lbs.

NIB	*Exc.*	*V.G.*	*Good*	*Fair*	*Poor*
425	325	295	225	210	150

Magnum Model

10 or 12 gauge, 3.5" chambers.

NIB	*Exc.*	*V.G.*	*Good*	*Fair*	*Poor*
510	400	350	300	250	150

Waterfowl Camo (1999)

Waterfowl Camo (1999) BPS 12 Gauge

NIB	*Exc.*	*V.G.*	*Good*	*Fair*	*Poor*
525	425	350	300	250	150

Waterfowl Mossy Oak Break-Up

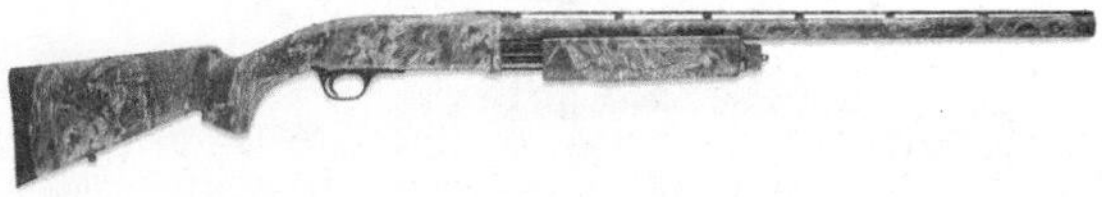

Waterfowl Mossy Oak Break-Up BPS 12 Gauge

NIB	*Exc.*	*V.G.*	*Good*	*Fair*	*Poor*
575	475	375	325	250	150

Mossy Oak New Break-up

Similar to BPS Hunter but with Mossy Oak New Break-up camo finish overall; 3" and 3-1/2" 12-gauge only.

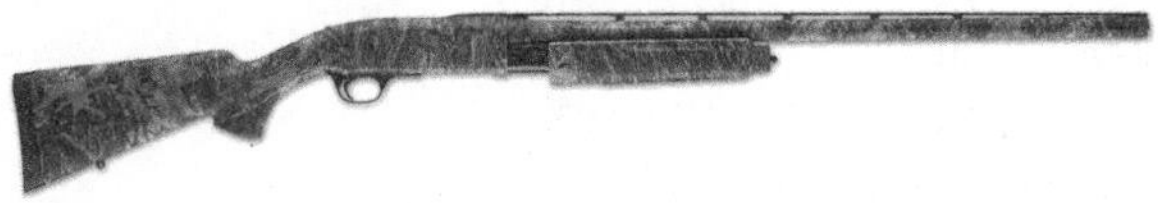

NIB	*Exc.*	*V.G.*	*Good*	*Fair*	*Poor*
750	625	400	300	200	150

Mossy Oak Duck Blind

Similar to above but with Mossy Oak Duck Blind finish overall.

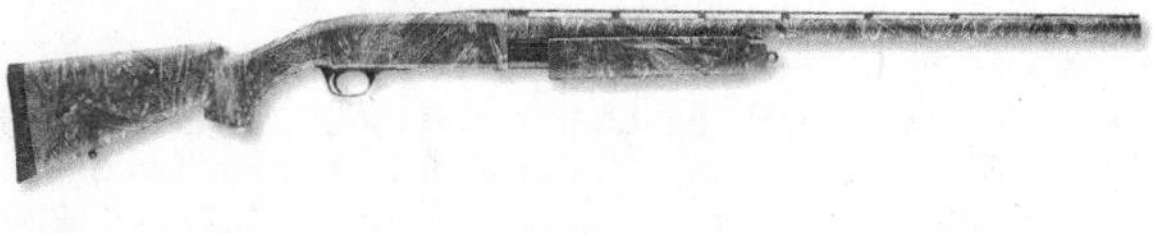

NIB	*Exc.*	*V.G.*	*Good*	*Fair*	*Poor*
750	625	400	300	200	150

Rifled Deer Mossy Oak New Break-up

Similar to BPS Rifled Deer Hunter but with Mossy Oak New Break-up camo finish overall.

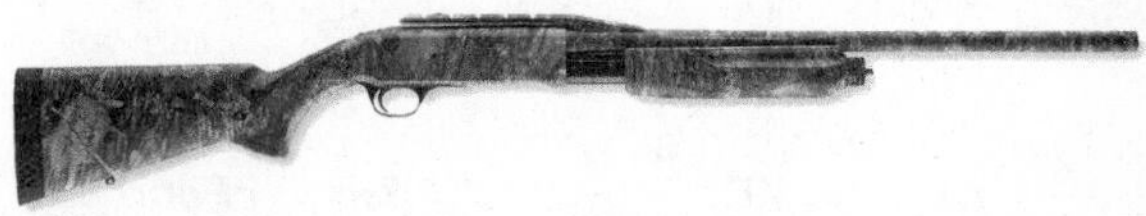

NIB	*Exc.*	*V.G.*	*Good*	*Fair*	*Poor*
750	625	400	300	200	150

10 Gauge Mossy Oak Shadow Grass Camo (1999)

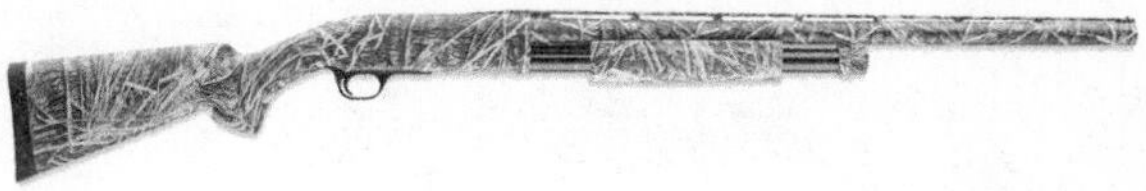

NIB	*Exc.*	*V.G.*	*Good*	*Fair*	*Poor*
575	475	375	325	175	125

BPS NWTF SERIES

This model is finished in a Mossy Oak Breakup pattern and bears the NWTF logo on the buttstock. Fitted with a 24" barrel, Hi-Viz front sight, Extra Full extended turkey choke. Introduced in 2001. Offered in the configurations listed.

BPS 10 Gauge

NIB	*Exc.*	*V.G.*	*Good*	*Fair*	*Poor*
625	475	400	325	200	125

BPS 12 Gauge 3.5" Chamber

NIB	*Exc.*	*V.G.*	*Good*	*Fair*	*Poor*
625	475	400	325	200	125

BPS 12 Gauge 3" Chamber

NIB	*Exc.*	*V.G.*	*Good*	*Fair*	*Poor*
550	450	375	325	200	125

Stalker

Matte finish, black stock.

NIB	*Exc.*	*V.G.*	*Good*	*Fair*	*Poor*
435	390	325	275	200	150

Stalker—Combo

A combination of a 28" vent rib barrel and a choice of 22" fully rifles barrel or 20.5" Invector barrel with Extra Full turkey choke. Introduced in 2000.

NIB	*Exc.*	*V.G.*	*Good*	*Fair*	*Poor*
650	525	475	325	200	125

10 Gauge Turkey

Fitted with a 24" vent rib barrel and black synthetic stock with black solid recoil pad, this model was introduced in 1999. Weight is about 9 lbs. 2 ozs.

NIB	*Exc.*	*V.G.*	*Good*	*Fair*	*Poor*
525	425	375	325	200	125

Game Gun

These models are designed for turkey and deer with 20.5" barrels with Invector chokes or rifled barrels. Deer model has 5" rifled choke tube while the turkey model has Extra Full choke tube. The Cantilever model has a fully rifled barrel. Weight is approximately 7.7 lbs. Introduced in 1998. Add $30 for deer model and $60 for Cantilever model.

NIB	Exc.	V.G.	Good	Fair	Poor
450	350	300	250	200	125

Micro 20 Gauge

This model features a 22" vent rib barrel with shorter pistol grip stock and lighter weight. Weight is about 6.75 lbs. Introduced in 2001.

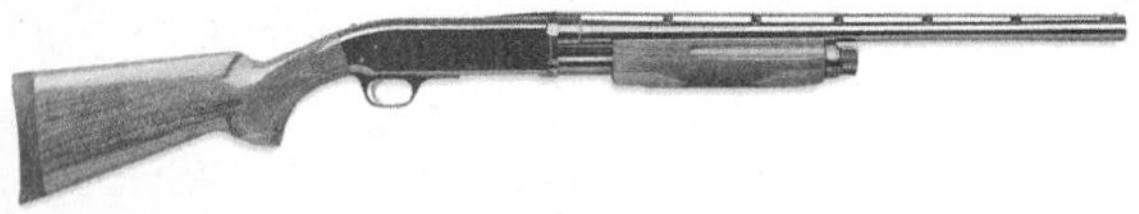

NIB	Exc.	V.G.	Good	Fair	Poor
450	350	300	250	200	125

Upland Special

This model is chambered for the 20 gauge shell and fitted with a 22" vent rib barrel. The walnut stock is a straight grip. Weight is about 6.5 lbs. This model comes in 12 or 20 gauge with a 22" barrel and straight grip stock. A 16 gauge version with a 24" or 26" barrel was introduced in 2008. A very beautiful little pump.

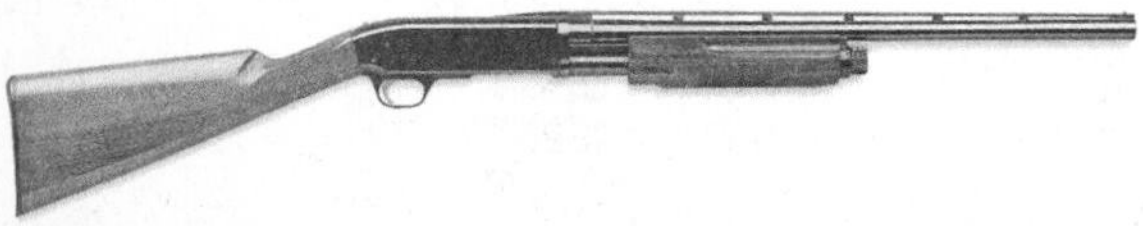

NIB	Exc.	V.G.	Good	Fair	Poor
550	375	300	275	200	125

Small Gauge

Introduced in 2000 this model is chambered for the 28 gauge and the .410 bore. The 28 gauge is offered with a choice of 26" or 28" vent rib barrel with Invector chokes. The .410 is available with 26" vent rib barrel with Invector chokes. Both the 28 gauge and .410 bore weigh about 6.75 lbs.

NIB	Exc.	V.G.	Good	Fair	Poor
525	450	325	275	200	125

Pigeon Grade

Furnished in 12 gauge only with high grade walnut stock and gold trimmed receiver.

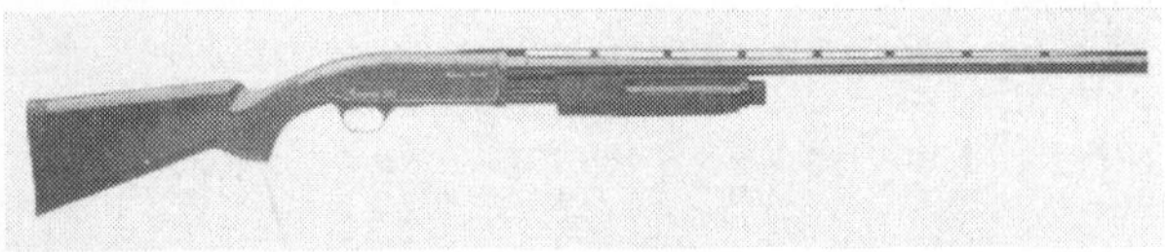

NIB	Exc.	V.G.	Good	Fair	Poor
500	400	300	225	175	125

Game Gun

Offered in 12 gauge only this model is available in either a Turkey Special or a Deer Special. Both have 20.5" plain barrel and drilled and tapped receivers. The stock is walnut. The turkey gun is fitted with an Extra Full choke. The deer gun has a special rifled choke tube for slugs. Both weigh about 7 lbs. 7 oz.

NIB	Exc.	V.G.	Good	Fair	Poor
300	250	175	125	100	50

Trap Model

NIB	Exc.	V.G.	Good	Fair	Poor
—	375	325	275	200	150

BPS Micro Trap

Similar to BPS TrapModel but with compact dimensions (13-3/4" length of pull, 48-1/4" overall length). 12 gauge only.

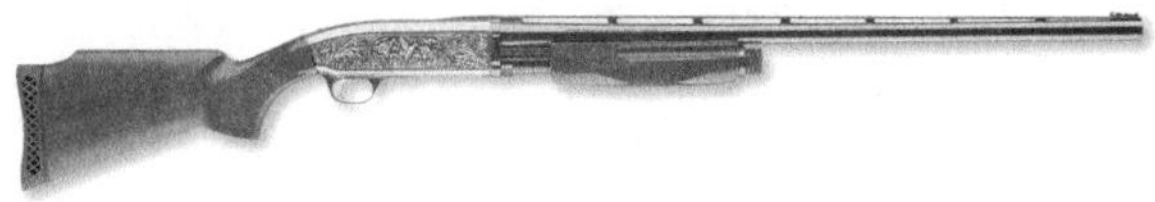

NIB	Exc.	V.G.	Good	Fair	Poor
700	—	—	—	—	—

CAUTION: Do not interchange Invector choke tubes with Invector-Plus choke tubes. May cause personal injury.

Youth Model

Short stock, 22" barrel.

NIB	Exc.	V.G.	Good	Fair	Poor
435	390	325	275	200	150

Waterfowl Deluxe

This version is chambered for 12 gauge with a 3" chamber and features an etched receiver with a gold-plated trigger. Otherwise, it is similar to the standard BPS.

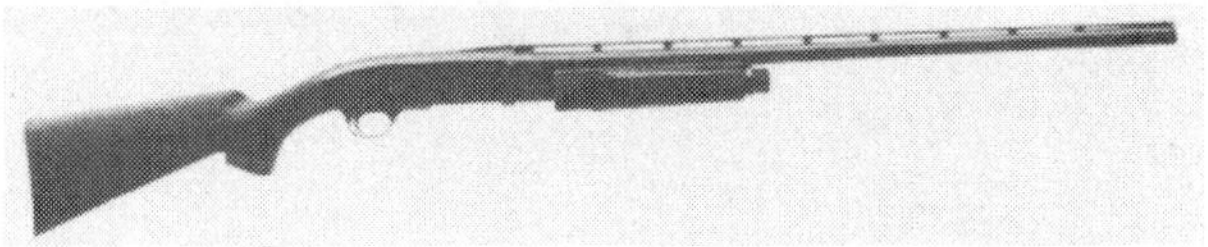

NIB	Exc.	V.G.	Good	Fair	Poor
—	600	525	425	325	250

BPS Ducks Unlimited Versions

These were limited-edition guns produced to be auctioned by Ducks Unlimited. They were furnished with a case and must be NIB with furnished materials to realize their collector potential.

NIB	Exc.	V.G.	Good	Fair	Poor
650	525	425	325	250	175

MODEL 12

Grade I

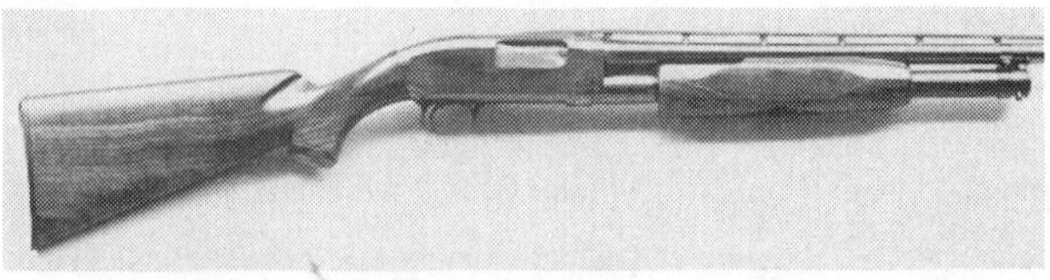

This is a slide-action shotgun chambered for 20 and 28 gauge with a 26", modified choke, vent rib barrel. It is a reproduction of the Winchester Model 12 shotgun. It has a 5-round, tubular magazine with a floating, high-post rib. It has a takedown feature and is blued with a walnut stock. Introduced in 1991, total production was limited to 7,000 guns.

NIB	Exc.	V.G.	Good	Fair	Poor
825	625	425	300	250	200

Grade V

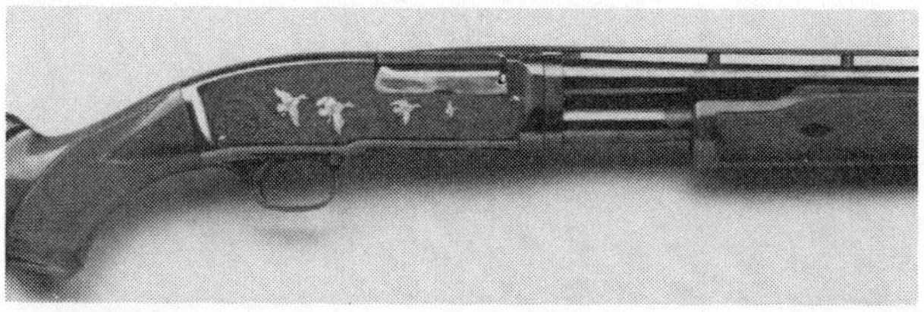

This is an extensively engraved version of the Grade I Model 12. It features a select walnut stock with deluxe checkering and a high-gloss finish. There are gold inlays. It was introduced in 1991, and production was limited to 5,000 guns. Discontinued 1992.

NIB	Exc.	V.G.	Good	Fair	Poor
1200	950	700	450	300	200

NOTE: For 28 gauge add 30 percent.

LIMITED EDITION MODEL 42

A new version of the .410 bore pump shotgun that was last produced by Winchester in 1963. Available in two grades both fitted with 26" vent rib barrels. The Grade I features a plain blued receiver with walnut stock. The Grade V features a blued receiver with scroll engraving and gold inlays. Both models are choked Full and weigh 6 lbs. 4 oz.

Grade I

NIB	Exc.	V.G.	Good	Fair	Poor
900	600	500	400	300	200

Grade V

NIB	Exc.	V.G.	Good	Fair	Poor
1150	900	700	500	350	200

A-Bolt Shotgun

Introduced in 1995 this bolt-action shotgun was offered in 12 gauge with 3" chamber. Rifled barrel version is 22" long while the Invector barrel version is 23" long with a 5" rifle tube installed. Has a 2-shot detachable magazine. Average weight is about 7 lbs. **NOTE:** This is considered the Rolls-Royce of bolt shotguns and is becoming quite desirable. Manufacture ceased in 1998.

A-Bolt Shotgun Hunter Version

NIB	Exc.	V.G.	Good	Fair	Poor
1000	850	750	500	300	100

A-Bolt Shotgun Stalker Version

NIB	Exc.	V.G.	Good	Fair	Poor
900	750	650	400	200	100

NOTE: For Invector rifled choke tube model deduct $50.

RIFLES

HIGH-POWER BOLT-ACTION RIFLE

This was a high-grade, bolt-action sporting rifle manufactured by FN in Belgium (from 1959 to 1975) or Sako of Finland (from 1961 to 1975). It was built on either a Mauser or a Sako action and chambered for a number of popular calibers from the .222 Remington up to the .458 Winchester Magnum. There were three basic grades that differed in the amount of ornamentation and the quality of materials and workmanship utilized. Certain calibers are considered to be rare and will bring a premium from collectors of this firearm. We recommend securing a qualified appraisal on these rifles if a transaction is contemplated. We furnish general values only. **NOTE:** From 1959 through 1966 FN Mauser actions with long extractors were featured. These Mauser actions will bring a premium depending on caliber. From 1967 on, FN Supreme actions with short extractors were used. Only .30-06 and .270 calibers continued with long extractor Mauser actions. CAUTION: For buyer and seller alike some rare calibers may be worth as much as 100 percent or more over prices listed for rare calibers such as .284 Win., .257 Roberts, 300 H&H, and .308 Norma Magnum. The High-Power bolt-action rifles seemed to be particularly hard hit by salt wood. That is why short extractors rifles bring less than long extractor guns. No factory replacement stocks are known to still be available. Deduct 20-25 percent for short extractor rifles. Proceed with caution.

Safari Grade

Standard model, standard calibers.

NIB	Exc.	V.G.	Good	Fair	Poor
—	1350	1100	850	400	300

Medallion Grade

Scroll engraved, standard calibers.

NIB	Exc.	V.G.	Good	Fair	Poor
—	2500	1900	1400	750	400

Olympian Grade

Extensive game scene engraving, standard calibers.

NIB	Exc.	V.G.	Good	Fair	Poor
—	6300	5250	4250	2500	1500

Model BBR

This is a bolt-action sporting rifle chambered for various popular calibers. It has a 24" barrel with an adjustable trigger and fluted bolt. It features a detachable magazine under the floorplate and was furnished without sights. The finish is blued with a checkered, walnut, Monte Carlo stock. It was manufactured between 1978 and 1984 by Miroku.

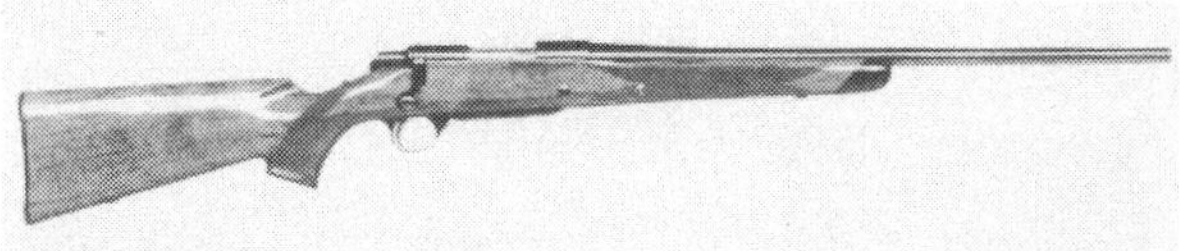

NIB	Exc.	V.G.	Good	Fair	Poor
—	575	400	350	275	200

BOSS™ SYSTEM

Introduced by Browning in 1994 this new accuracy system allows the shooter to fine-tune his Browning rifle to the particular load he is using. Consists of a tube on the end of the rifle muzzle that allows the shooter to select the best setting for the ammunition type. The system also reduces recoil. BOSS stands for Ballistic Optimizing Shooting System. This option will add approximately

$80 to the value of the particular Browning rifle on which it is fitted.

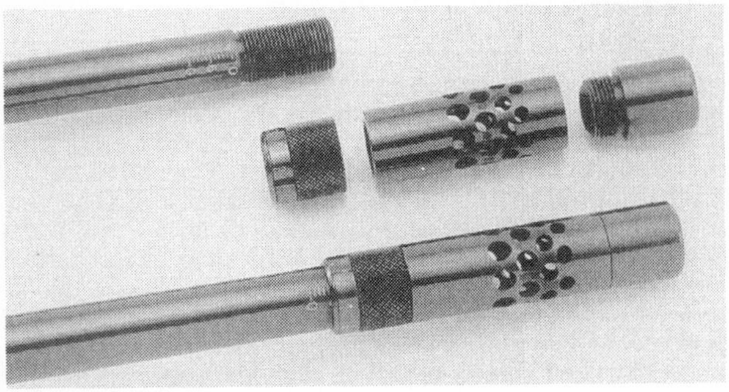

X-BOLT SERIES

Introduced in 2008, the X-Bolt series of rifles features an adjustable three-position Feather Trigger system, a newly-designed bolt release, an improved scope mounting system, tang safety, and a generally slimmer, sleeker profile.

Composite Stalker

Features include steel receiver with matte blue finish, free-floating crowned barrel, matte black composite stock with palm swell, Inflex recoil pad. Various barrel lengths depending on chambering, which include both medium and long cartridges ranging from .243 Winchester to .338 Winchester Magnum. Introduced in 2008.

NIB	Exc.	V.G.	Good	Fair	Poor
850	700	600	500	350	200

Stainless Stalker

Similar to above but with stainless steel receiver and barrel. Various barrel lengths depending on chambering, which include both medium and long cartridges ranging from .243 Winchester to .375 H&H Magnum. Introduced in 2008.

NIB	Exc.	V.G.	Good	Fair	Poor
850	700	600	500	350	200

Hunter

Similar to above but with sculpted, satin-finished walnut stock with cut checkering and low-luster blued barrel and receiver. Various barrel lengths depending on chambering, which include both medium and long cartridges ranging from .243 Winchester to .338 Winchester Magnum. LH model available.

NIB	Exc.	V.G.	Good	Fair	Poor
850	700	600	500	350	200

Medallion

Similar to above but with high-gloss finish and engraved, blued barrel and receiver. Various barrel lengths depending on chambering, which include both medium and long cartridges ranging from .243 Winchester to .375 H&H Magnum. Introduced in 2008. Available in left-hand version.

NIB	Exc.	V.G.	Good	Fair	Poor
1000	850	700	600	500	350

Micro Hunter

Similar to Browning X-Bolt Hunter but with compact dimensions (13-5/16" length of pull, 41-1/4" overall length). LH available.

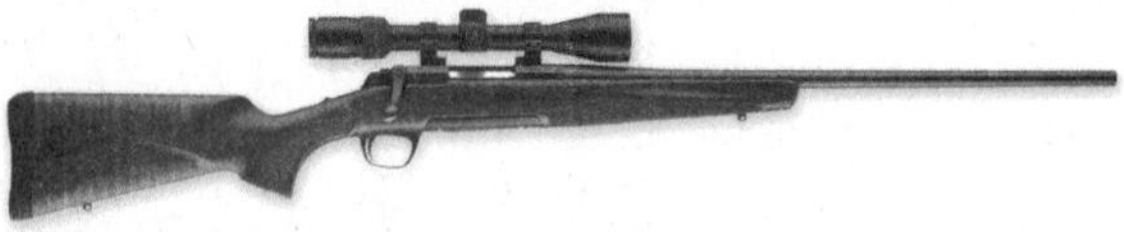

NIB	Exc.	V.G.	Good	Fair	Poor
800	700	600	500	350	200

Varmint Stalker

Similar to X-Bolt Stalker but with medium-heavy free-floated barrel, target crown, composite stock. .223, .22-250, .243 Winchester and .308 Winchester only.

NIB	Exc.	V.G.	Good	Fair	Poor
1000	850	700	600	500	350

RMEF White Gold

Similar to X-Bolt Medallion but with gold-engraved matte stainless finish and Rocky Mountain Elk Foundation grip cap. Chambered in .325 WSM only.

NIB	Exc.	V.G.	Good	Fair	Poor
1300	1000	850	650	550	375

X-Bolt RMEF Special Hunter

Similar to above but with matte blued finish without gold highlights.

NIB	Exc.	V.G.	Good	Fair	Poor
900	700	600	500	350	200

A-BOLT SERIES

NOTE: In 2004 new calibers were offered for the A-Bolt series depending on model. They are the .25 WSSM and the .223 Rem. SSA.All A-Bolt II Descriptions: "II" designation dropped from A-Bolt name in 2006.

A-Bolt Hunter

This is the current bolt-action rifle manufactured by B.C. Miroku. It is chambered for various popular calibers and offered with a 22", 24", or 26" barrel. It has either a short or long action, an adjustable trigger, and a detachable box magazine that is mounted under the floorplate. It is furnished without sights and is blued with a checkered walnut stock. It was introduced in 1985.

NIB	Exc.	V.G.	Good	Fair	Poor
575	400	350	300	250	200

A-Bolt II Hunter

Introduced in 1994 this new model features a newly designed anti-bind bolt and improved trigger system. In 2001 the .300 Winchester Short Magnum cartridge was offered for this model. In 2003 a left-hand model was introduced.

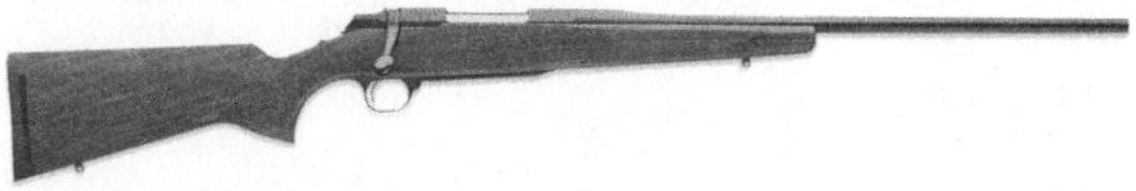

NIB	Exc.	V.G.	Good	Fair	Poor
795	575	400	300	250	200

A-Bolt II Hunter WSSM

Similar to the A-Bolt Hunter but chambered for the .223 WSM and .243 WSM cartridges. The stock design is also different from the A-Bolt Hunter with the addition of a longer pistol grip and thicker forearm. Weight is about 6.25 lbs. Introduced in 2003.

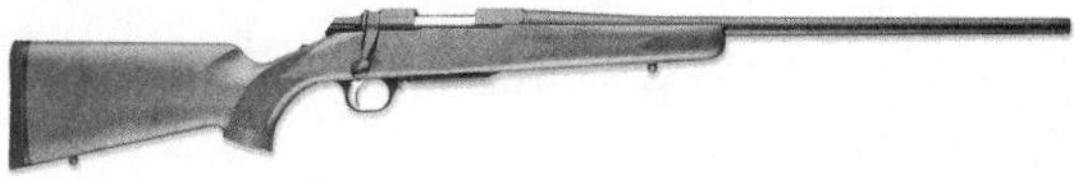

NIB	Exc.	V.G.	Good	Fair	Poor
795	575	400	300	250	200

A-Bolt II Micro Hunter

Introduced in 1999, this model features a shorter length of pull and a shorter barrel length than the Hunter model. Offered in .22 Hornet, .22-250, 7mm-08, .308, .243, and .260 calibers. Weight is about 6 lbs. In 2003 the .270 WSM, 7mm WSM, and .300 WSM calibers were added for this model as well as a left-hand version.

NIB	Exc.	V.G.	Good	Fair	Poor
650	525	350	250	200	150

NOTE: Add $30 for left-hand model and $30 for WSM calibers.

A-Bolt II Classic Hunter

This model features a Monte Carlo stock, low luster bluing, select walnut, and double bordered checkering. Offered in .30-06, .270, 7mm Rem. Mag., and .300 Win. Mag. No sights. Weight is about 7 lbs. Introduced in 1999.

NIB	Exc.	V.G.	Good	Fair	Poor
675	500	395	250	200	150

A-Bolt Stainless Hunter

This model features a black composite stock, stainless steel receiver and barrel, no sights. Chamberings range from .243 Winchester to .300 WSM. Weight is about 6-1/2 lbs. Introduced in 2008.

NIB	Exc.	V.G.	Good	Fair	Poor
800	650	450	300	250	200

A-Bolt Classic Hunter WSSM

As above but chambered for the .223 WSSM and .243 WSSM cartridges. Weight is about 6.25 lbs. Introduced in 2003.

NIB	Exc.	V.G.	Good	Fair	Poor
800	650	450	300	250	200

A-Bolt Mountain Ti

This model features a lightweight stainless steel 23" barrel, titanium receiver, and lightweight fiberglass stock. Chambered for the .270 WSM, 7mm WSM, and the .300 WSM cartridges. Weight is about 5.5 lbs. Calibers: .243, 7mm-08, .308, .325 WSM. Introduced in 2004.

NIB	Exc.	V.G.	Good	Fair	Poor
1695	1300	1050	800	575	350

A-Bolt Composite Stalker

Supplied with composite stock and matte finish bluing. Offered in .338 Win. Mag., .300 Win. Mag., 7mm Rem. Mag., .25-06, .270, .280, .30-06. Introduced in 1988. In 2001 the .300 Winchester Short Magnum cartridge was offered for this model. Calibers: .223 WSSM, .243 WSSM, .25 WSSM, .223, .243, .7mm-08, .270 WSM, 7mm WSM, .300 WSM, .325 WSM, .25-06, .270, .280, .30-06, 7mm RM, .300 WM, .338 WM. Add 10 percent for BOSS or left-hand version.

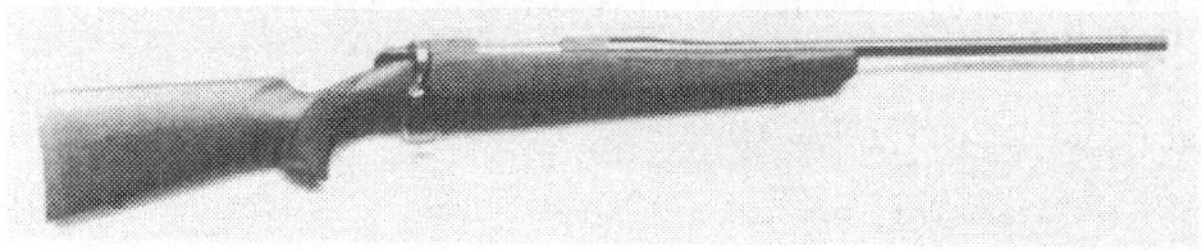

NIB	Exc.	V.G.	Good	Fair	Poor
550	350	300	250	200	150

A-Bolt II Composite Stalker

Same as above but with 1994 improvements.

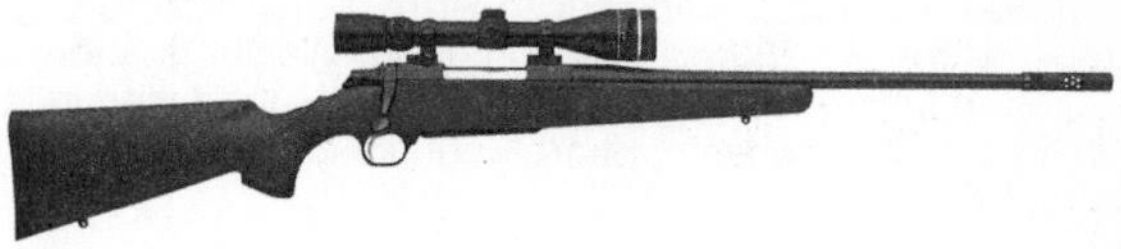

NIB	Exc.	V.G.	Good	Fair	Poor
670	525	400	300	250	200

NOTE: Add $80 for BOSS system.

A-Bolt Composite Stalker WSSM

As above but chambered for the .223 WSSM or the .243 WSSM cartridge. Weight is about 6 lbs. Introduced in 2003.

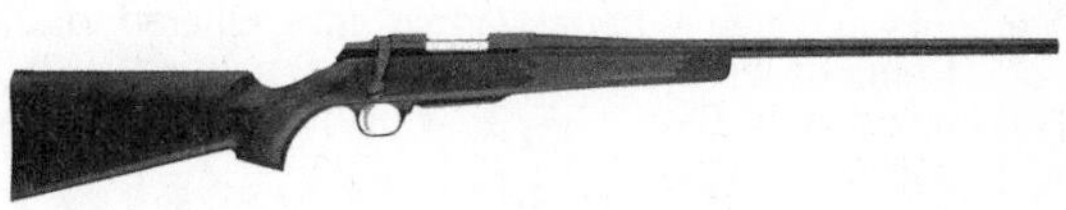

NIB	Exc.	V.G.	Good	Fair	Poor
700	550	400	300	250	200

A-Bolt Stainless Stalker

Bolt-action rifle. Calibers: .223 WSSM, .243 WSSM, .25 WSSM, .223, .243, .7mm-08, .270 WSM, 7mm WSM, .300 WSM, .325

WSM, .25-06, .270, .280, .30-06, 7mm RM, .300 WM, .338 WM, .375 H&H. Barrel: 22-inch, 23-inch, 24-inch, 26-inch stainless steel, sightless (except for .375 H&H). Magazine: Detachable box. Stock: Black composite. Add 10 percent for BOSS system and left-hand version.

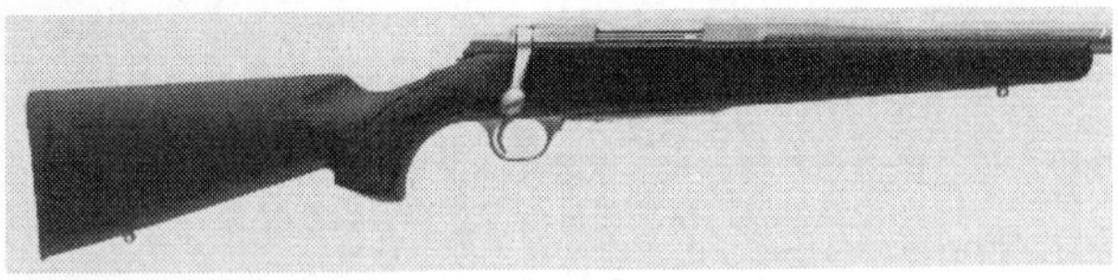

NIB	Exc.	V.G.	Good	Fair	Poor
600	450	400	350	300	250

NOTE: For .300 and .338 calibers add $30.

A-Bolt II Composite Stainless Stalker

Same as above but with 1994 improvements.

NIB	Exc.	V.G.	Good	Fair	Poor
850	650	550	400	300	250

NOTE: For Magnum calibers add $30. For BOSS system add $110.

A-Bolt Stainless Stalker, WSSM

As above but chambered for the .223 WSSM and .243 WSSM calibers. Stock design is slightly different from standard A-Bolt Stalker. Weight is about 6 lbs. Introduced in 2003.

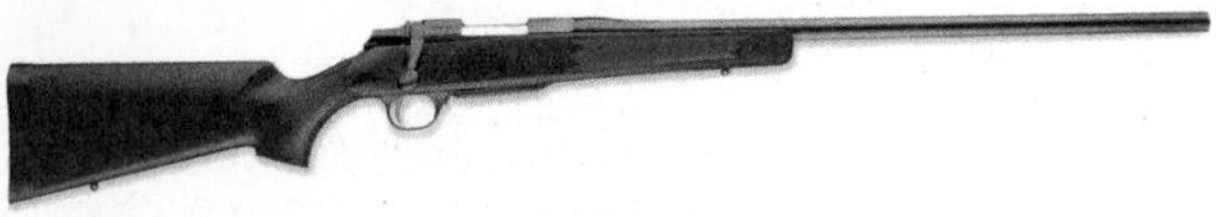

NIB	Exc.	V.G.	Good	Fair	Poor
880	675	550	400	300	250

A-Bolt Carbon Fiber Stainless Stalker

This model features a Christensen Arms patent carbon barrel. Chambered for .22-250 or .300 Win. Mag. Weight is about 6.25 lbs. for short action and 7 lbs. for long action. Introduced in 2000. In 2001 the .300 Winchester Short Magnum cartridge was offered for this model.

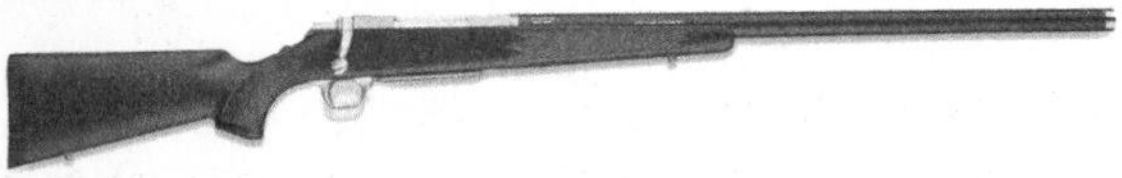

NIB	Exc.	V.G.	Good	Fair	Poor
1400	1200	1000	900	700	350

A-Bolt II Heavy Barrel Varmint

Introduced in 1994 this model features all of the A-Bolt II improvements in a heavy barrel varmint rifle. Offered in .22-250 and .223 Rem. calibers with 22" barrel. Equipped with black laminated wood stock.

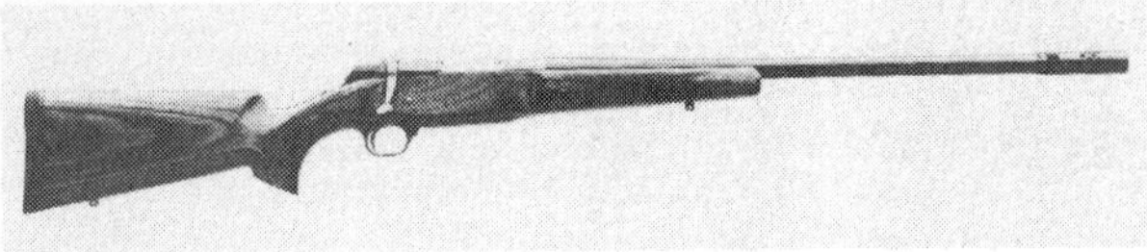

NIB	Exc.	V.G.	Good	Fair	Poor
685	600	525	425	325	250

A-Bolt Varmint Stalker

Introduced in 2002 this model features a new armor coated synthetic stock. Matte blue metal finish. Chambered for the .223 Rem. and .22-250 Rem. cartridges. Fitted with a 24" barrel on the .223 and a 26" barrel on the .22-250. Weight is about 8 lbs.

NIB	Exc.	V.G.	Good	Fair	Poor
790	650	525	425	325	250

A-Bolt Varmint Stalker WSSM

As above but chambered for the .223 WSSM and .243 WSSM cartridges. Weight is about 7.75 lbs. Introduced in 2003.

NIB	Exc.	V.G.	Good	Fair	Poor
815	650	525	425	325	250

A-Bolt Eclipse M-1000

Thumbhole stock. Calibers: .270, .30-06, 7mm RM, .22-250, .308, .270 WSM, .7mm WSM, .300 WSM. Add 10 percent for BOSS. The rifle is fitted with a 26" barrel with BOSS system. The stock is a laminated hardwood with gray/black finish. The forearm is a benchrest style. Weight is approximately 9 lbs. 13 oz.

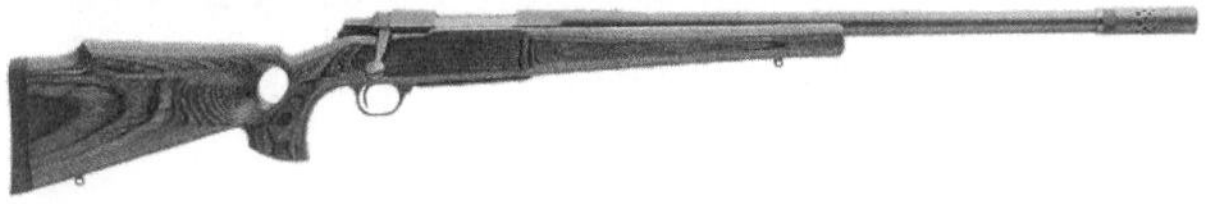

NIB	Exc.	V.G.	Good	Fair	Poor
1135	700	625	450	350	250

A-Bolt Eclipse M-1000 WSM & Stainless

Introduced in 2004 this model is offered in all of the WSM calibers. The M-1000 is blued with a heavy barrel, while the stainless is fitted with a heavy bull barrel. Barrel length is 26". Weight is 9.85 lbs. No sights.

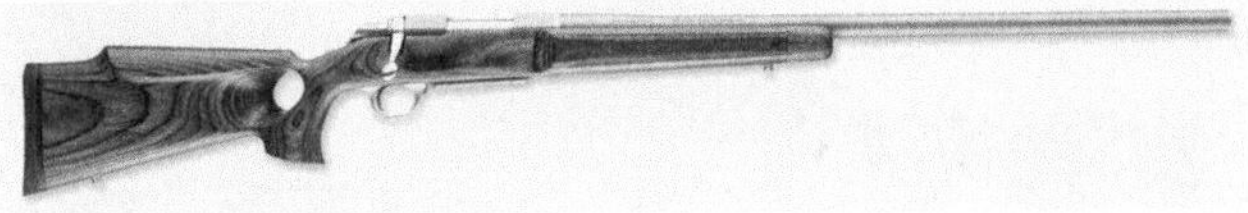

NIB	Exc.	V.G.	Good	Fair	Poor
1050	825	675	500	350	200

NOTE: Add $200 for the stainless model.

A-Bolt Eclipse Varmint

Introduced in 1996 this model features a thumbhole stock made from gray/black laminated hardwood. Offered in two version: a short-action, heavy-barrel version, and a long and short action with standard-weight barrel. Eclipse Varmint weighs about 9 lbs. and the standard-barrel version weighs about 7.5 lbs. depending on caliber.

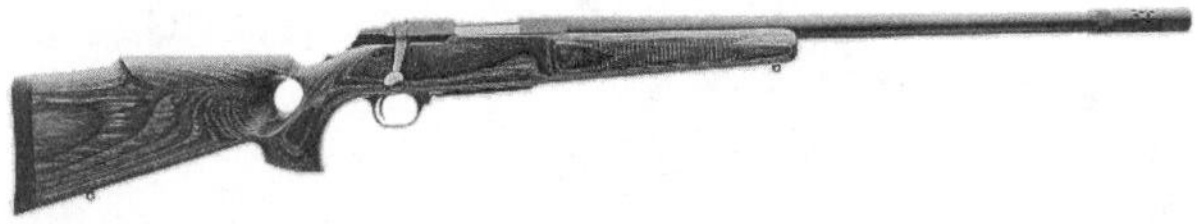

NIB	Exc.	V.G.	Good	Fair	Poor
950	800	600	500	400	250

Euro-Bolt

First introduced in 1993 this A-Bolt variation features a rounded bolt shroud, Mannlicher-style bolt handle, continental-style stock with cheekpiece, schnabel-style forearm. The finish is a low-luster blue. Offered in .270, .30-06, and 7mm Rem. Mag. calibers. Weighs about 7 lbs.

NIB	Exc.	V.G.	Good	Fair	Poor
650	500	450	350	250	150

A-Bolt II Euro Bolt

Same as above but with 1994 improvements.

NIB	Exc.	V.G.	Good	Fair	Poor
850	500	450	350	250	150

NRA A-Bolt Wildlife Conservation Collection

Commemorates NRA's Environment Conservation and Hunting Outreach Program. Caliber: .243 Win. Barrel: 22-inch blued sightless. Stock is satin-finish walnut with NRA Heritage logo lasered on buttstock. MSRP: $797.

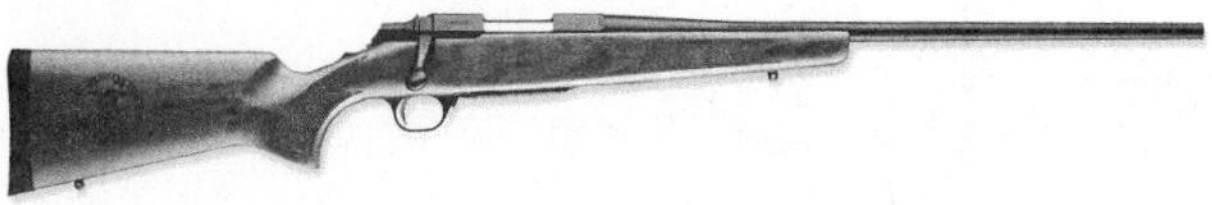

A-Bolt Medallion Model

Calibers: .223 WSSM, .243 WSSM, .25 WSSM, .223, .243, .7mm-08, .270 WSM, 7mm WSM, .300 WSM, .325 WSM, .25-06, .270, .280, .30-06, 7mm RM, .300 WM, .338 WM. Add 10 percent for BOSS or left-hand version.

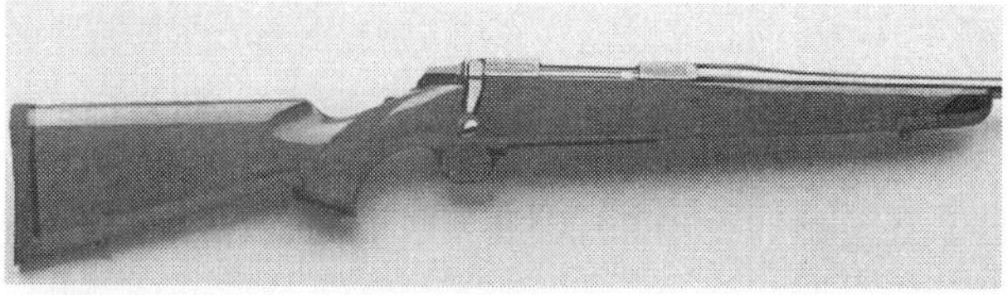

NIB	Exc.	V.G.	Good	Fair	Poor
800	600	500	400	300	250

NOTE: Add $35 for .300 and .338 calibers.

A-Bolt II Medallion

Same as above but with 1994 improvements. In 2003 this model was offered in a left-hand version.

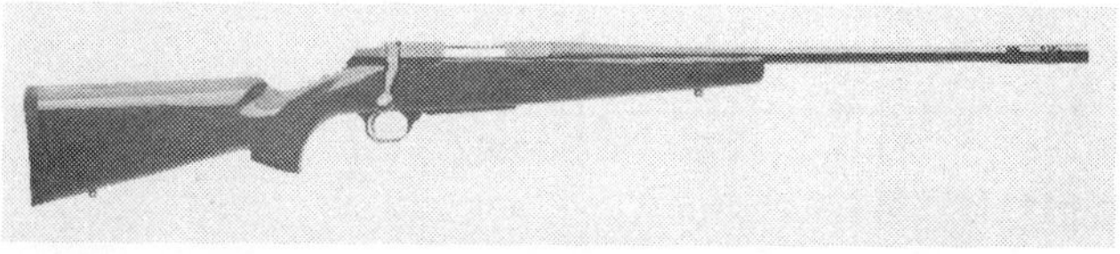

NIB	Exc.	V.G.	Good	Fair	Poor
765	600	450	350	300	250

A-Bolt II Medallion WSSM

As above but chambered for the .223 WSSM or the .243 WSSM cartridge. Weight is about 6.25 lbs. Introduced in 2003.

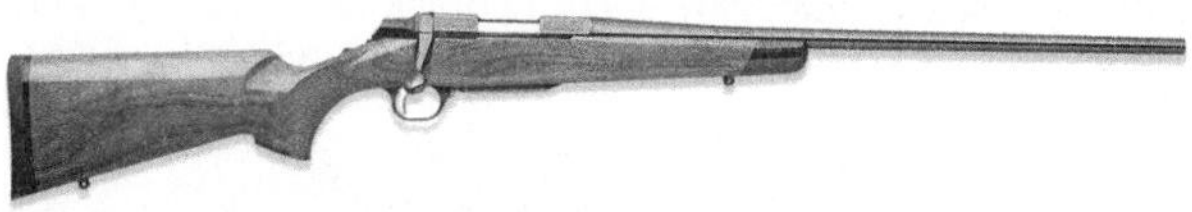

NIB	Exc.	V.G.	Good	Fair	Poor
795	650	525	450	400	325

A-Bolt Gold Medallion

This version has a fancy grade walnut stock with a cheekpiece. It is lightly engraved and has gold-inlaid letters. It was introduced in 1988.

NIB	Exc.	V.G.	Good	Fair	Poor
690	625	550	450	400	325

A-Bolt II Gold Medallion

Same as above but with 1994 improvements.

NIB	Exc.	V.G.	Good	Fair	Poor
690	625	550	450	400	325

A-Bolt II White Gold Medallion

This model features a gold engraved stainless receiver and barrel, select walnut stock with brass spacers and rosewood caps. European-style cheekpiece. No sights. Introduced in 1999. Offered in .30-06, .270, 7mm Rem. Mag., and .300 Win. Mag. Weight is about 7 lbs. 8 ozs.

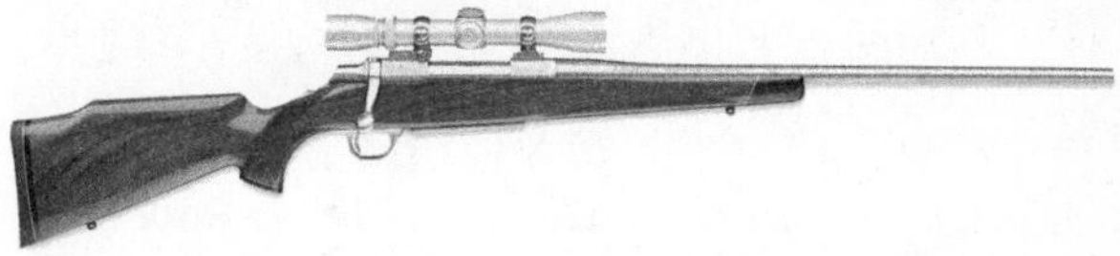

NIB	Exc.	V.G.	Good	Fair	Poor
1100	800	650	500	425	350

A-Bolt White Gold Medallion, RMEF

Introduced in 2003 this model is a special edition for the Rocky Mountain Elk Foundation. Chambered for the 7mm Rem. Mag. and fitted with a 26" barrel. Both action and barrel are stainless steel. Special RMEF logo on the grip cap. Weight is about 7.75 lbs. Add 5 percent for WSM calibers.

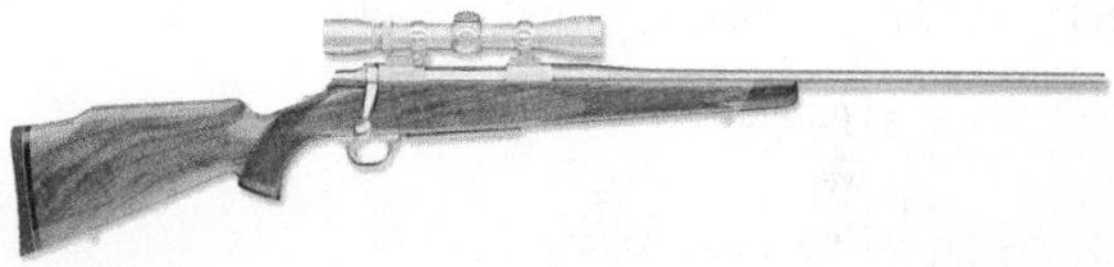

NIB	Exc.	V.G.	Good	Fair	Poor
1200	950	750	600	450	325

A-Bolt Custom Trophy

Introduced in 1998 this model features gold highlights on the barrel and receiver, select walnut stock, with shadowline cheekpiece and skeleton pistol grip. The barrel is octagonal. Chambered for .270 and .30-06 with 24" barrel and 7mm Rem. Mag. and .300 Win. Mag. with 26" barrel. Weight varies from 7 lbs. 11 oz. to 7 lbs. 3 oz. depending on caliber.

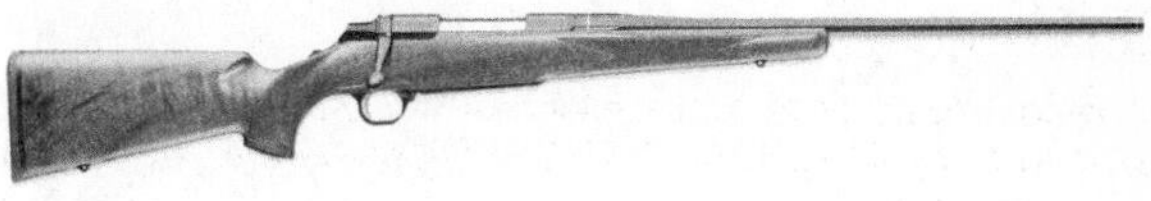

NIB	Exc.	V.G.	Good	Fair	Poor
1300	1000	800	650	425	300

A-Bolt Big Horn Sheep Issue

This is a high-grade version of the A-Bolt chambered for the .270 cartridge. It features a deluxe skipline checkered walnut stock with a heavily engraved receiver and floorplate. It has two gold sheep inlays. There were 600 manufactured in 1986 and 1987.

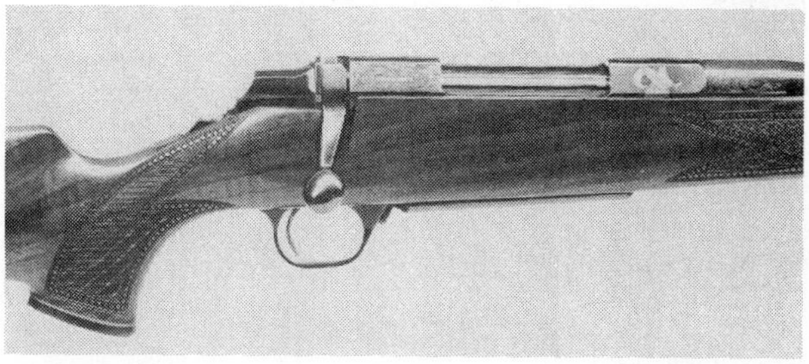

NIB	Exc.	V.G.	Good	Fair	Poor
1050	800	600	450	400	325

Micro-Medallion Model

This is a smaller version of the A-Bolt Hunter chambered for popular cartridges that fit a short action. It has a 20" barrel without sights and a 3-round magazine. It was introduced in 1988.

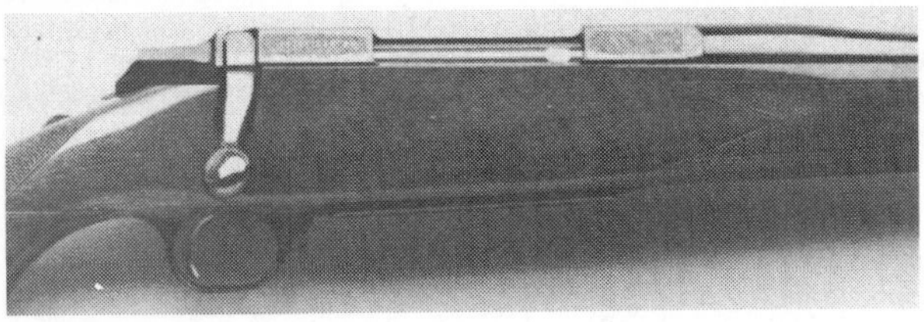

NIB	Exc.	V.G.	Good	Fair	Poor
525	475	400	350	300	250

A-Bolt II Micro-Medallion

Same as above but with 1994 improvements.

NIB	Exc.	V.G.	Good	Fair	Poor
525	475	400	350	300	250

A-Bolt Pronghorn Issue

This is a deluxe version of the A-Bolt chambered for the .243 cartridge. It is heavily engraved and gold inlaid and features a presentation-grade walnut stock with skipline checkering and pearl-inlaid borders. There were 500 manufactured in 1987.

NIB	Exc.	V.G.	Good	Fair	Poor
1300	1000	750	500	400	325

A-Bolt Special Hunter RMEF

Similar to A-Bolt Hunter but honors Rocky Mountain Elk Foundation. Chambered in .325 WSM. Satin finish. Introduced 2007.

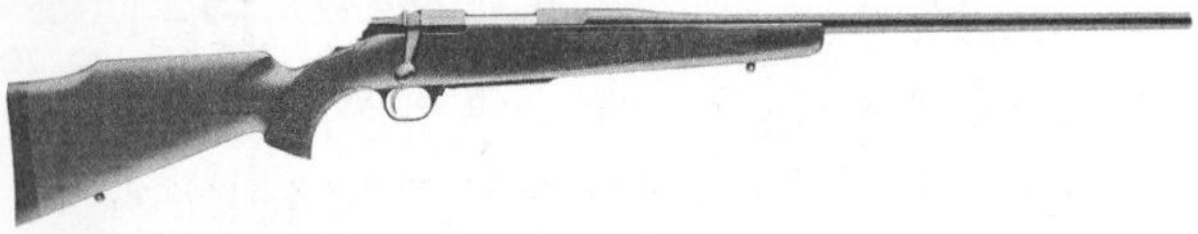

NIB	Exc.	V.G.	Good	Fair	Poor
800	600	500	400	300	250

A-Bolt White Gold RMEF

Similar to A-Bolt Special Hunter RMEF but with stainless barrel and receiver and glossy finish. Introduced 2007.

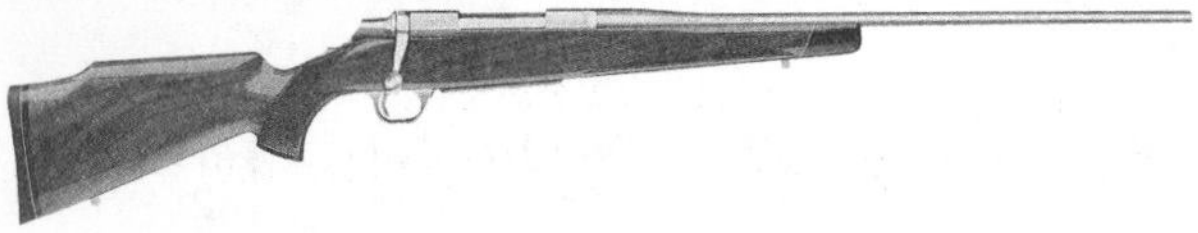

NIB	Exc.	V.G.	Good	Fair	Poor
1100	775	600	475	325	200

A-Bolt Target

Similar to A-Bolt but with 28" heavy bull blued barrel, blued receiver, satin finish gray laminated stock with adjustable comb and semi-beavertail forend. Chambered in .223, .308 Winchester and .300 WSM.

NIB	Exc.	V.G.	Good	Fair	Poor
1275	1000	800	650	425	300

A-Bolt Target Stainless

Similar to above but with stainless receiver and barrel.

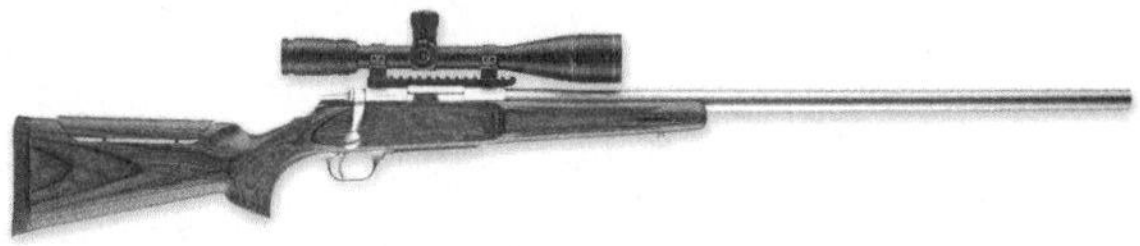

NIB	Exc.	V.G.	Good	Fair	Poor
1500	1275	1000	800	650	425

Acera Straight Pull Rifle

Introduced in 1999, this model features a straight action bolt system. It is chambered for the .30-06 with a 22" barrel and the .300 Win. Mag. with 24" barrel. Open sights are optional as is the BOSS system. Detachable box magazine. Checkered walnut stock. Prices listed are for .30-06 with no sights and no BOSS.

NIB	Exc.	V.G.	Good	Fair	Poor
1100	775	600	475	325	200

NOTE: Add $100 for .300 Win. Mag with no sights and no BOSS.

Grade I A-Bolt .22

This is a bolt-action sporting rifle chambered for the .22 LR or .22 Magnum cartridges. It features a 60-degree bolt and a 22" barrel available either with or without open sights. It has a 5-round, detachable magazine and an adjustable trigger. The finish is blued with a checkered walnut stock. It was introduced in 1986.

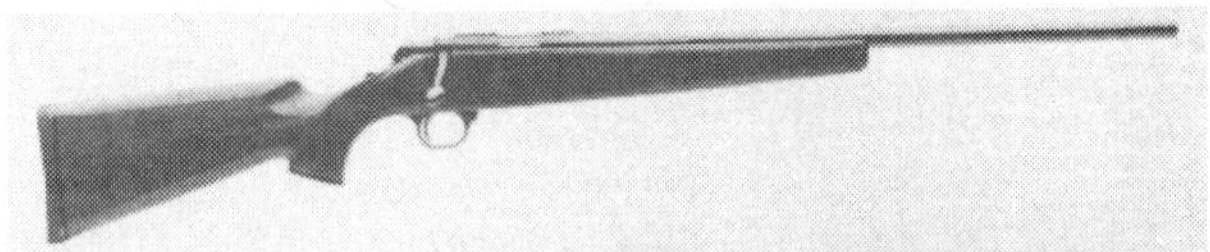

NIB	Exc.	V.G.	Good	Fair	Poor
340	275	210	150	125	100

NOTE: .22 Magnum add 15 percent.

Gold Medallion A-Bolt .22

This deluxe, high-grade version features a select stock with rosewood pistol-grip cap and forend tip. It is lightly engraved and has gold-filled letters. It was introduced in 1988.

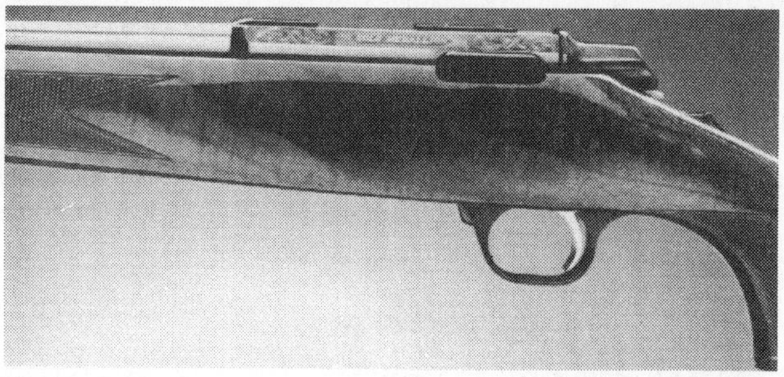

NIB	Exc.	V.G.	Good	Fair	Poor
450	400	350	300	225	175

T-Bolt Model T-1

This is a unique, straight-pull, bolt-action sporting rifle chambered for .22 caliber cartridges. It has a 22" barrel with open sights and a 5-round magazine. The finish is blued with a plain walnut stock. It was manufactured between 1965 and 1974 by FN. Many T-Bolt rifles were affected by salt wood. Proceed with caution. Reintroduced 2006 with rotary magazine.

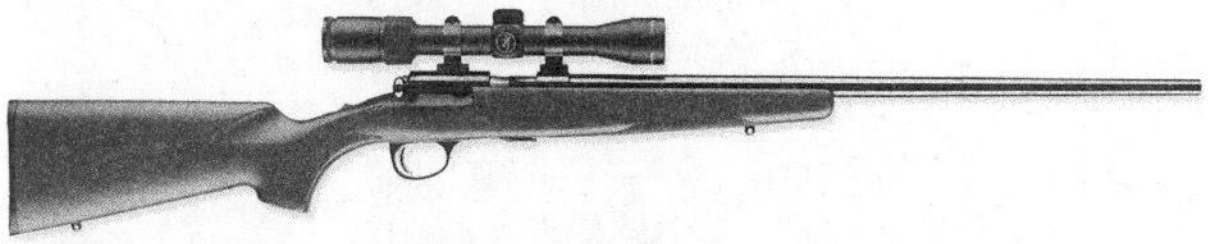

NIB	Exc.	V.G.	Good	Fair	Poor
—	550	395	350	150	100

T-Bolt Model T-2

This version is similar to the T-1 with a select, checkered walnut stock and a 24" barrel.

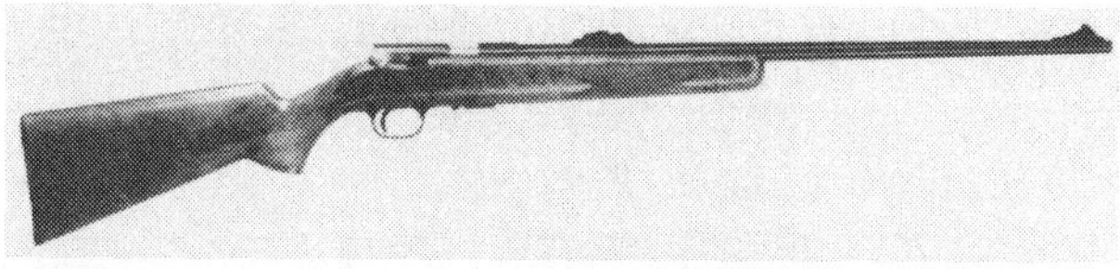

NIB	Exc.	V.G.	Good	Fair	Poor
—	600	450	375	250	200

T-Bolt (2006)

Reintroduction of classic and collectible T-bolt straight-pull .22 rifle. Introduced in 2006. Chambered for .17 HMR, .22 WMR or .22 LR.

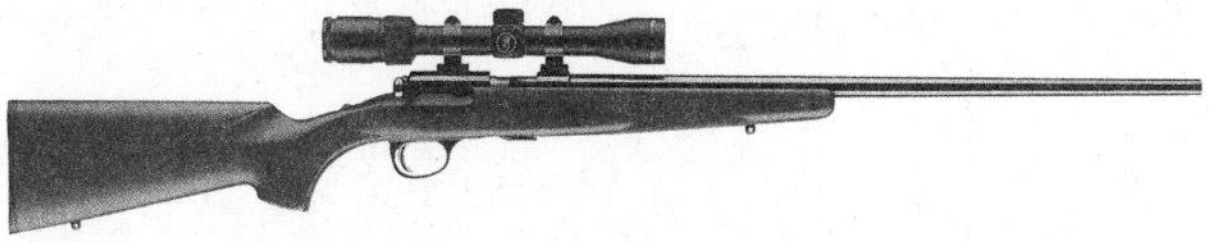

NIB	Exc.	V.G.	Good	Fair	Poor
600	475	450	375	250	200

T-Bolt Target/Varmint

Similar to reintroduced T-Bolt but with floating heavy target barrel and other accurizing refinements. Introduced 2007.

NIB	Exc.	V.G.	Good	Fair	Poor
650	525	500	425	300	250

T-Bolt Target/Varmint Stainless

Similar to above but with stainless steel receiver and barrel. Introduced 2008.

NIB	Exc.	V.G.	Good	Fair	Poor
850	725	650	525	350	325

T-Bolt Composite Hunter

Sporter version of the new T-Bolt with black composite Monte Carlo stock and glossy blue barrel and receiver. Chambered in .17 HMR, .22 WMR or .22 LR. Scope not included. Introduced 2008.

NIB	Exc.	V.G.	Good	Fair	Poor
675	525	500	425	300	250

T-Bolt Composite Target/Varmint

Sporter version of the new T-Bolt Target/Varmint with black composite Monte Carlo stock and glossy blue barrel and receiver. Chambered in .17 HMR, .22 WMR or .22 LR. Scope not included. Introduced 2008.

NIB	Exc.	V.G.	Good	Fair	Poor
700	550	525	450	325	275

T-Bolt Composite Target/Varmint Left Hand

Similar to T-Bolt Composite Target/Varmint but in left-hand version.

NIB	Exc.	V.G.	Good	Fair	Poor
725	550	525	450	325	275

T-Bolt Sporter

Sporter version of the new T-Bolt with satin walnut stock and bright blue barrel and receiver. Scope not included. Introduced 2008.

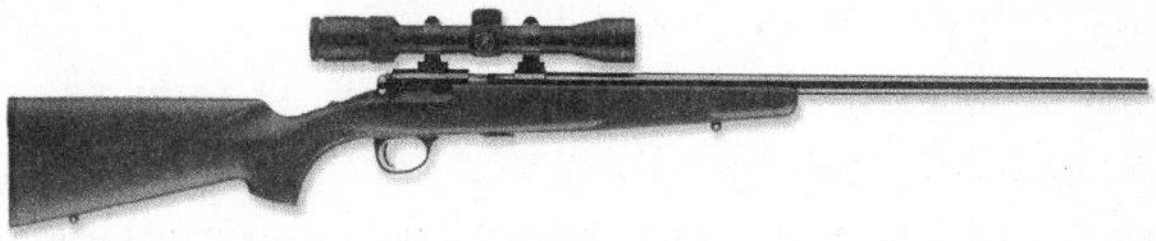

NIB	Exc.	V.G.	Good	Fair	Poor
700	550	525	450	325	275

T-Bolt Sporter Left Hand

Similar to Browning T-Bolt Sporter but in left-hand version.

NIB	Exc.	V.G.	Good	Fair	Poor
700	550	525	450	325	275

T-Bolt Composite Sporter Left Hand

Similar to Browning T-Bolt Sporter Left Hand but with composite stock.

NIB	Exc.	V.G.	Good	Fair	Poor
700	550	525	450	325	275

Model 52 Limited Edition

This model is based on the design of the original Winchester Model 52 .22 caliber bolt-action rifle. Fitted with a 24" barrel and walnut stock with oil finish. Metal pistol-grip cap and rosewood forend tip. Drilled and tapped for scope. Five-round detachable magazine. Blued finish. Weight is about 7 lbs. From 1991 to 1992 5,000 Model 52s were built.

NIB	Exc.	V.G.	Good	Fair	Poor
850	750	650	550	—	350

BPR-22

This is a short-stroke, slide action rifle chambered for the .22 LR and Magnum cartridges. It has a 20.25" barrel with open sights and an 11-round, tubular magazine. The finish is blued with a checkered walnut stock. It was manufactured between 1977 and 1982.

NIB	Exc.	V.G.	Good	Fair	Poor
—	500	350	215	125	95

NOTE: Add $100 for models chambered for .22 Magnum.

BPR-22 Grade II

This version is engraved and has a select walnut stock.

NIB	Exc.	V.G.	Good	Fair	Poor
—	600	400	275	225	150

NOTE: Add 20 percent for models chambered for .22 Magnum.

Trombone Model

This is a slide-action rifle chambered for the .22 LR cartridge. It has a 24" barrel with open sights and a takedown design. It has a tubular magazine and a hammerless action. There were approximately 150,000 manufactured by FN between 1922 and 1974. Approximately 3,200 were imported by Browning in the 1960s. They are marked with either the FN barrel address or the Browning Arms address. The Browning-marked guns are worth approximately 20 percent additional. The values given are for FN-marked guns.

NIB	Exc.	V.G.	Good	Fair	Poor
1000	750	600	450	375	275

.22 CALIBER SEMI-AUTO

This is a blowback-operated, semi-automatic rifle chambered for the .22 Long Rifle or Short cartridge. It features a take-down barrel design with a 19.25" barrel and an 11-round, tubular magazine inside the buttstock. It is loaded through a hole in the middle of the buttstock. The finish is blued with a checkered walnut stock and beavertail forearm. This lightweight, compact firearm was manufactured by FN between 1956 and 1974 for U.S. marked guns. There are a number of versions that differ in the amount of ornamentation and the quality of materials and workmanship.

Grade I

NIB	Exc.	V.G.	Good	Fair	Poor
750	525	400	325	220	125

NOTE: For Grade I short add 20 percent. Early Wheel Sight manufactured 1956-1960 add 10 percent.

Grade II—French Grayed Receiver

NIB	Exc.	V.G.	Good	Fair	Poor
1600	1200	900	700	300	200

NOTE: For Grade II short add 300 percent.

Grade III

French grayed receiver.

NIB	Exc.	V.G.	Good	Fair	Poor
3250	2700	1900	1200	700	400

NOTE: For premium engravers add 40 percent to Grade III. For Grade III short add 800 percent. For unsigned Grade III, 1956-1960 deduct 20 percent.

.22 SEMI-AUTO/MODEL SA-22 (MIROKU MFG.)

This model is similar to the Belgian FN except that it was produced as of 1976 by B.C. Miroku in Japan. Collector interest is not as high as in the FN version.

Grade I

NIB	Exc.	V.G.	Good	Fair	Poor
700	575	400	275	125	100

Grade II

Discontinued 1984.

NIB	Exc.	V.G.	Good	Fair	Poor
900	700	525	375	225	150

Grade III

Discontinued 1983.

NIB	Exc.	V.G.	Good	Fair	Poor
1000	775	600	500	300	200

Grade VI

Gold plated animals.

NIB	Exc.	V.G.	Good	Fair	Poor
1100	850	700	525	325	275

BAR-22

This is a blowback-operated, semi-automatic rifle chambered for the .22 LR cartridge. It has a 20.25" barrel with open sights and a 15-round, tubular magazine. It features a polished, lightweight alloy receiver. It was finished in blue with a checkered walnut stock. It is manufactured between 1977 and 1985 by Miroku.

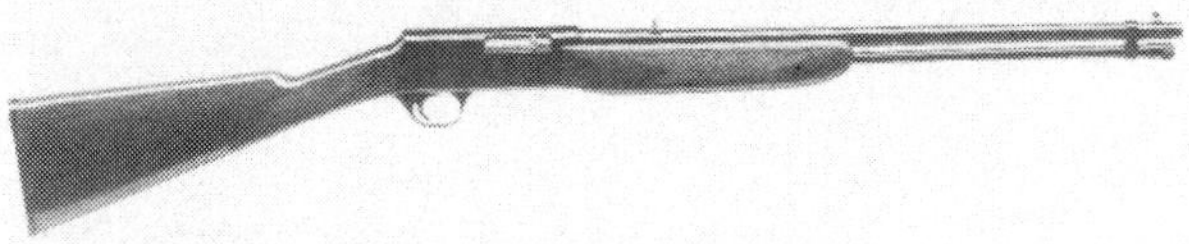

NIB	Exc.	V.G.	Good	Fair	Poor
—	600	525	290	160	125

Grade II

This is a deluxe version with an engraved, silver-finished receiver. It has a select walnut stock. It was discontinued in 1985.

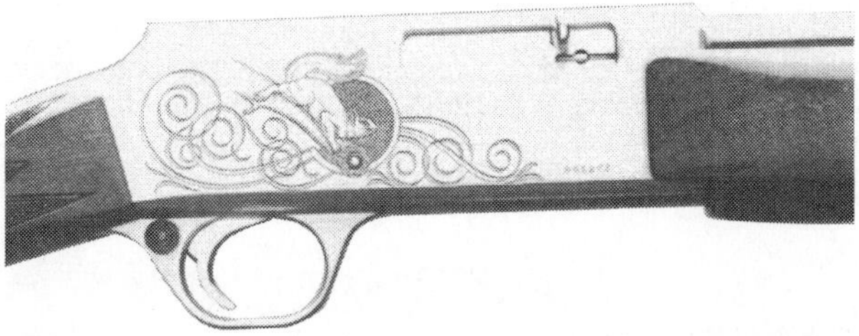

NIB	Exc.	V.G.	Good	Fair	Poor
—	695	575	375	175	150

BUCK MARK RIFLE

This model uses the same design as the Buck Mark pistol. It is fitted with an 18" barrel (heavy on the target model) and thumbhole pistol grip. Magazine capacity is 10 rounds. Integral rail scope mount. Introduced in 2001. Weight is about 4.25 lbs. for Sporter and 5.5 lbs. for the Target model.

Target Model

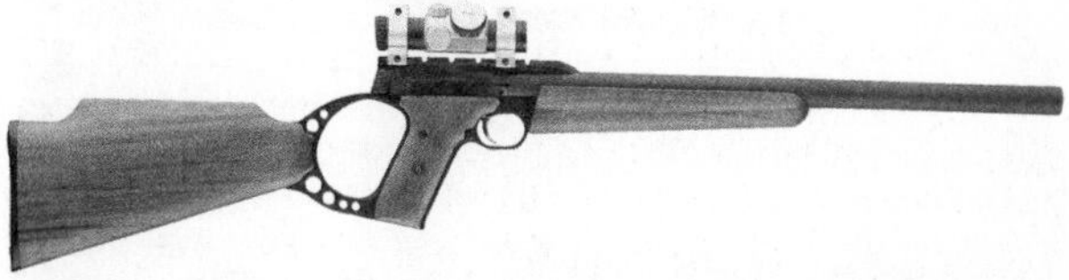

NIB	Exc.	V.G.	Good	Fair	Poor
595	460	325	250	195	125

Sporter Model

NIB	Exc.	V.G.	Good	Fair	Poor
590	450	325	250	195	125

Patent 1900 High Power

This is a semi-automatic sporting rifle chambered for the .35 Remington cartridge. It is similar in configuration to the Remington Model 8 rifle. It has a 22" barrel with open sights and a 5-round, integral magazine. The finish is blued with a plain walnut stock. There were approximately 5,000 manufactured between 1910 and 1931. A deluxe model with a ribbed barrel and checkered walnut stock was also available and would be worth approximately 15 percent additional. Very rare in the USA.

NIB	Exc.	V.G.	Good	Fair	Poor
—	1500	1000	700	475	300

BAR HIGH POWER RIFLE

This is a gas-operated, semi-automatic sporting rifle chambered for various popular calibers from the .243 up to the .338 Magnum cartridges. It was offered with either a 22" or 24" barrel with folding leaf sight until 1980. The finish is blued with a checkered walnut stock. The various grades offered differed in the amount of ornamentation and the quality of materials and workmanship utilized. Earlier models were manufactured in Belgium by FN; these guns would be worth approximately 15 percent additional over guns assembled in Portugal from parts manufactured by FN. The early .338 Magnum model is rarely encountered and would be worth approximately 25 percent additional. The Grade I values furnished are for Portuguese-assembled guns from 1977 until the introduction of the BAR Mark II in 1993. This model was introduced in 1967 and discontinued in 1977.

Grade I

NIB	Exc.	V.G.	Good	Fair	Poor
1000	725	650	475	225	100

Grade I Magnum

NIB	Exc.	V.G.	Good	Fair	Poor
1150	750	675	400	250	125

Grade II Deluxe

1967-1974.

NIB	Exc.	V.G.	Good	Fair	Poor
1200	900	825	475	300	175

Grade II Deluxe Magnum

1968-1974.

NIB	Exc.	V.G.	Good	Fair	Poor
1275	950	850	500	325	200

Grade III

Discontinued 1984. **NOTE:** The Grade III was offered in two variations. The first was hand-engraved and produced in Belgium. The second was photo-etched and built in Belgium and assembled in Portugal. This second variation will not be as valuable as the first.

NIB	Exc.	V.G.	Good	Fair	Poor
1450	1200	900	600	375	250

Grade III Magnum

Discontinued 1984.

NIB	Exc.	V.G.	Good	Fair	Poor
1500	1300	950	650	400	275

NOTE: Prices indicated above are for 1970 through 1974 production. For guns assembled in Portugal deduct 30 percent. .338 Win. Mag caliber is rare in Grade III; add 75 percent premium.

Grade IV

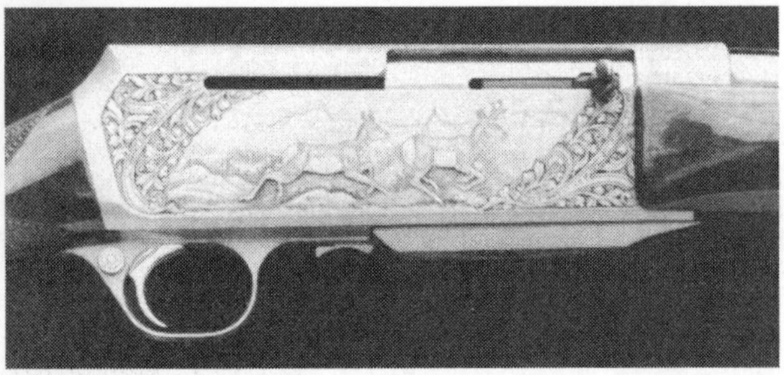

Gamescene engraved. This grade was hand-engraved from 1970 through 1976 then was etched thereafter. Grade IV rifles were discontinued in 1984.

NIB	Exc.	V.G.	Good	Fair	Poor
1900	1500	1050	800	650	400

NOTE: Pre-1977 rifles add 40 percent. Premium engraving add 10 percent.

Grade IV Magnum

NIB	Exc.	V.G.	Good	Fair	Poor
2000	1600	1075	850	650	425

Grade V

Gold Inlaid. 1971-1974.

NIB	Exc.	V.G.	Good	Fair	Poor
5500	4800	3500	2800	1200	600

Grade V Magnum

1971-1974.

NIB	Exc.	V.G.	Good	Fair	Poor
5600	4900	3600	2900	1250	600

NOTE: For special order variations on Grade V rifles add up to 100 percent.

North American Deer Rifle Issue

This is a deluxe version of the BAR chambered for .30-06 only. It features a photo etched, silver-finished receiver and a deluxe, checkered walnut stock. There were 600 produced and furnished with a walnut case and accessories. This model was discontinued in 1983. As with all commemoratives, it must be NIB to command premium values.

NIB	Exc.	V.G.	Good	Fair	Poor
4000	3600	2400	1800	450	250

BAR Mark II Safari Rifle

This is an improved version of the BAR first introduced by Browning in 1967. Announced in 1993 this Mark II design uses a new gas system with a newly designed buffering system to improve reliability. This model also has a new bolt release lever, a new easily removable trigger assembly. Available with or without sights. Walnut stock with full pistol grip and recoil pad on magnum gun are standard. The receiver is blued with scroll engraving. Rifles with magnum calibers have a 24" barrel while standard calibers are fitted with a 22" barrel. Available in .243, .308, .270, .30-06, 7mm Rem. Mag., .300 Win. Mag., .338 Win. Mag. Standard calibers weigh about 7 lbs. 9 oz. and magnum calibers weigh about 8 lbs. 6 oz.

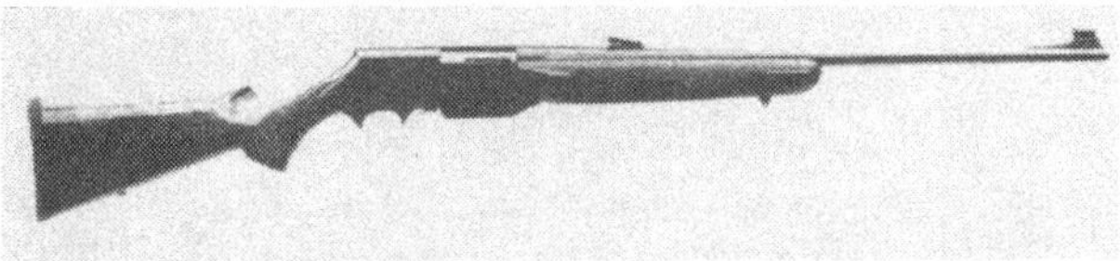

NIB	Exc.	V.G.	Good	Fair	Poor
825	750	600	450	250	150

NOTE: Add 30 percent for .270 Wby. Mag., which was made for one year only.

BAR Mark II Lightweight

This version of the Mark II was introduced in 1997 and features a lightweight alloy receiver and shortened 20" barrel. It is offered in .30-06, .270 Win., .308 Win., and .243 Win. calibers. It is not offered with the BOSS system. Weight is approximately 7 lbs. 2 oz.

NIB	Exc.	V.G.	Good	Fair	Poor
900	725	550	425	175	125

BAR Composite Stalker

Introduced in 2001 this model features a composite buttstock and forend with removable magazine. It is offered in short action (.243 and .308) with sights, and in standard action (.270 and .30-06) with no sights. In magnum calibers (7mm, .330 Win., and .338) it is offered with no sights and with the BOSS system as well.

NIB	Exc.	V.G.	Good	Fair	Poor
900	725	550	425	175	125

NOTE: For magnum calibers add $75, and for BOSS add $140.

BAR High Grade Models

These models will feature high grade walnut stock with highly polished blued barrel. Receivers will be grayed with game animals: mule deer and whitetail on the standard calibers (.270 and .30-06) and elk and moose on magnum calibers (7mm magnum and .300 Win. Mag).

NIB	Exc.	V.G.	Good	Fair	Poor
1825	1450	1100	800	550	400

BAR Short Trac

Introduced in 2004 this model features the ability to chamber magnum cartridges. Offered in .270 WSM, 7mm WSM, .325 WSM and .300 WSM as well as .243 and .308. Fitted with a 23" barrel in magnum calibers and 22" barrel in non-magnum. Receiver is alloy steel. Redesigned stock adjustable length of pull. Weight is about 7.25 lbs. for magnum calibers and 6 75 lbs. for others. Add 10 percent for camo finish.

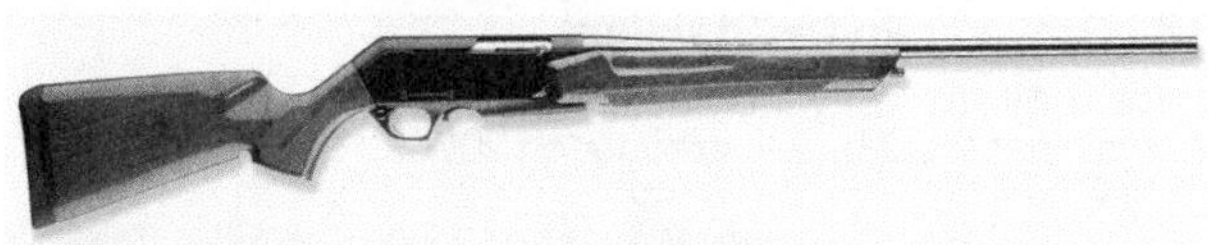

NIB	Exc.	V.G.	Good	Fair	Poor
950	650	450	350	250	200

BAR Long Trac

Similar to the above model but made for long action calibers such as .270, .30-06, 7mm Rem. Mag, and .300 Win. Mag. Barrel length is 22" for the .270 and .30-06 and 24" for the other two calibers. Weight is about 7 lbs. for .270 and .30-06 and 7.5 lbs. for 7mm and .300. Introduced in 2004. Add 10 percent for camo finish.

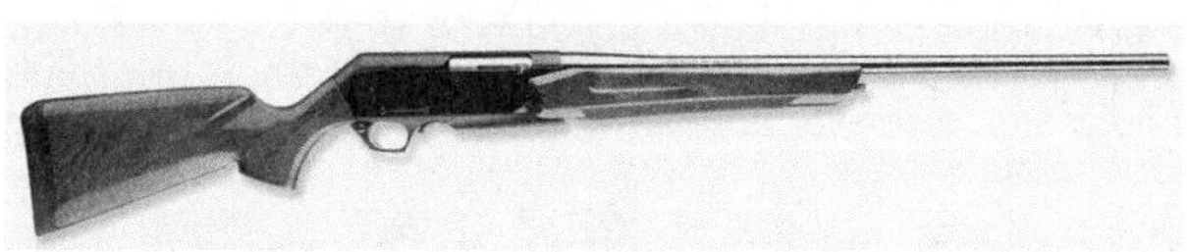

NIB	Exc.	V.G.	Good	Fair	Poor
950	650	450	350	250	200

NOTE: Add $75 for magnum calibers.

BAR ShortTrac Stalker

Similar to BAR ShortTrac but with matte blue barrel and composite stock. Introduced 2006.

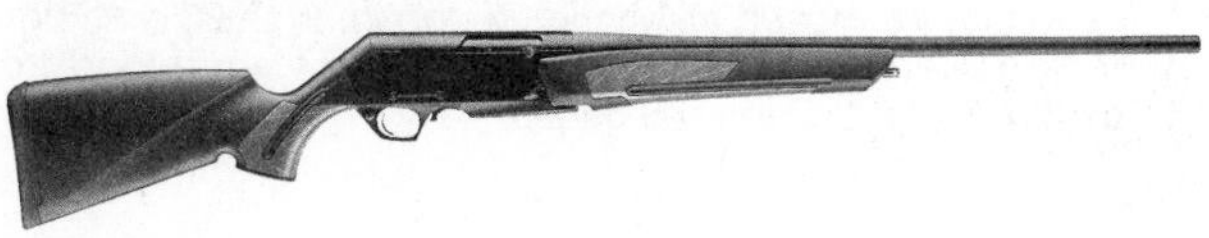

NIB	Exc.	V.G.	Good	Fair	Poor
850	670	550	450	350	250

BAR LongTrac Stalker

Long-action version of the BAR ShortTrac Stalker.

NIB	Exc.	V.G.	Good	Fair	Poor
850	670	550	450	350	250

BAR ShortTrac Left-Hand

Similar to BAR ShortTrac but in left hand. Introduced 2007.

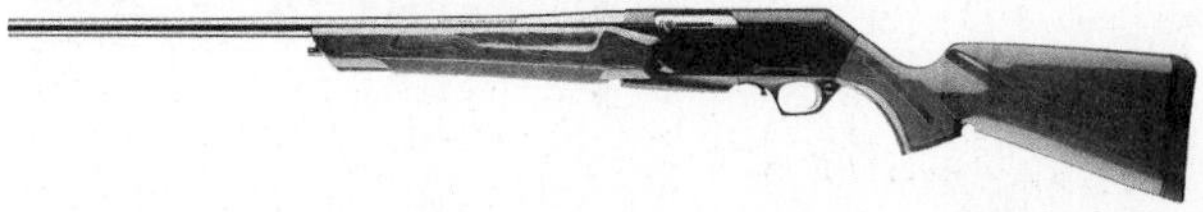

NIB	Exc.	V.G.	Good	Fair	Poor
950	650	450	350	250	200

BAR ShortTrac Mossy Oak New Break-up

Similar to BAR ShortTrac but with Mossy Oak Break-up finish overall.

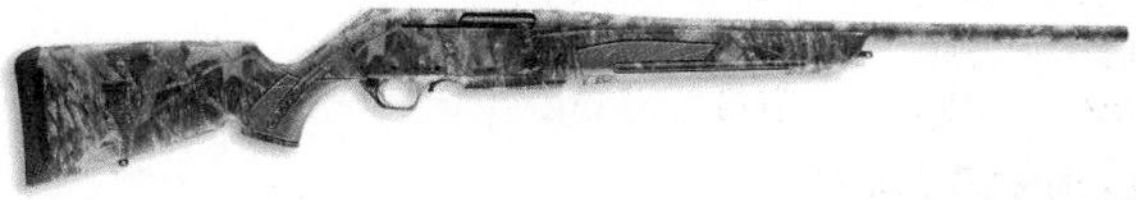

NIB	Exc.	V.G.	Good	Fair	Poor
1275	1000	750	600	475	350

BAR ShortTrac Digital Green

Similar to above but with Digital Green camo finish overall.

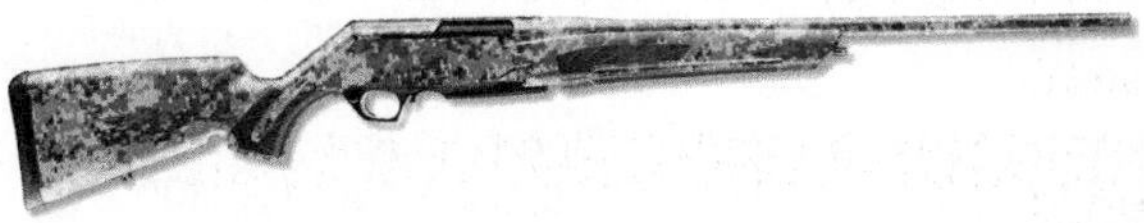

NIB	Exc.	V.G.	Good	Fair	Poor
1275	1000	750	600	475	350

BAR LongTrac Left-Hand

Similar to BAR Long-Trac but in left hand. Introduced 2007.

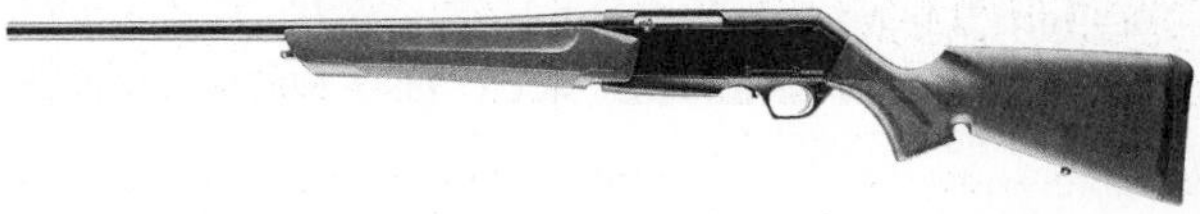

NIB	Exc.	V.G.	Good	Fair	Poor
950	1000	750	600	475	350

BAR LongTrac Mossy Oak New Break-up

Similar to BAR LongTrac but with Mossy Oak Break-up finish overall.

NIB	Exc.	V.G.	Good	Fair	Poor
1275	1000	750	600	475	350

Model BPR

The initials "BPR" stand for Browning Pump Rifle. It was introduced in 1997 and is similar in appearance to the BAR. Offered in both long action and short action calibers with barrel lengths from 22" to 24". Short action calibers are: .243 Win., and .308 Win. Long Action calibers are: .270 Win., .30-06, 7mm Rem. Mag., and .300 Win. Mag. Weight is about 7 lbs. 3 oz. Discontinued 2003.

NIB	Exc.	V.G.	Good	Fair	Poor
800	675	525	400	300	200

BL-22 Grade I

This is a lever-action rifle chambered for the .22 rimfire cartridge. It has an 18" barrel with a tubular magazine and a folding leaf rear sight. It is a Western-style firearm that features an exposed hammer. The finish is blued with a walnut stock. It was introduced in 1970 by Miroku.

NIB	Exc.	V.G.	Good	Fair	Poor
450	350	200	150	125	100

BL-22 Grade II

This version is similar with a scroll-engraved receiver and a checkered, select walnut stock.

NIB	Exc.	V.G.	Good	Fair	Poor
475	350	225	175	150	125

BL-22 Field Series Grade I

Introduced in 2005 this rifle features a satin nickel receiver. Walnut stock with no checkering. Blued trigger. Magazine capacity is 16 rounds. Weight is about 5 lbs.

NIB	Exc.	V.G.	Good	Fair	Poor
495	375	350	200	150	100

BL-17 Field Series Grade I

As above but chambered for the .17 Mach 2 cartridge. Weight is about 5.2 lbs.

NIB	Exc.	V.G.	Good	Fair	Poor
515	400	350	200	150	100

BL-22 Field Series Grade II

As above but with checkered stock, gold trigger, and scroll engraving on the receiver.

NIB	Exc.	V.G.	Good	Fair	Poor
555	425	350	200	150	125

BL-17 Field Series Grade II

As above but chambered for the .17 Mach 2 cartridge.

NIB	Exc.	V.G.	Good	Fair	Poor
545	425	350	200	150	125

BL-22 Grade II Octagon

Introduced in 2005 this model has a 24" octagon barrel chambered for the .22 Long and Long Rifle cartridges. Receiver is silver nitride with scroll engraving and gold trigger. Magazine capacity is 16 rounds. Gold bead front sight. Weight is about 5.25 lbs.

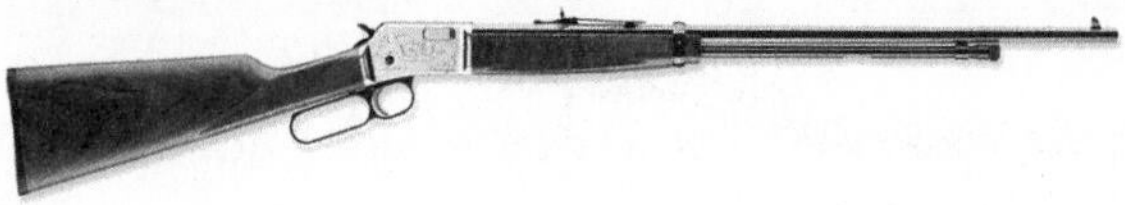

NIB	Exc.	V.G.	Good	Fair	Poor
725	550	375	275	200	150

BL-17 Grade II Octagon

As above but chambered for the .17 Mach 2 cartridge. Magazine capacity is 16 rounds. Weight is about 5.35 lbs. Introduced in 2005.

NIB	Exc.	V.G.	Good	Fair	Poor
750	575	375	275	200	150

BL-22 Classic

This model was introduced in 1999 and has the same features as the BL-22 Grade I.

NIB	Exc.	V.G.	Good	Fair	Poor
425	375	275	200	175	125

BL-22 NRA Grade 1

Similar to BL-22 Grade 1 but with NRA logo lasered on buttstock.

NIB	Exc.	V.G.	Good	Fair	Poor

BL-22 Gray Laminate Stainless

Similar to BL-22 but with gray laminated stock, nickeled receiver and stainless steel barrel. Introduced 2006.

NIB	Exc.	V.G.	Good	Fair	Poor
725	550	375	275	200	150

Browning BL-22 Micro Midas

Chambered for the .22 LR. Designed for younger shooters with 12-inch length of pull. Lever action with short 33-degree throw. Full-length tubular magazine, American walnut stock, gloss finish, straight grip. Receiver is steel with blued finish and grooved for scope mounts. New 2011.

NIB	Exc.	V.G.	Good	Fair	Poor
400	350	300	250	200	150

Model 81 BLR

This is a contemporarily designed, lever-action sporting rifle chambered for various popular calibers from .22-250 up to .358 Winchester. It has a 20" barrel with adjustable sights. It features a 4-round, detachable magazine and a rotary locking bolt. The finish is blued with a checkered walnut stock and recoil pad. It was introduced in 1971 and manufactured that year in Belgium. In 1972 manufacture moved to Miroku in Japan. In 2003 a straight-grip stock was introduced and WSM calibers were added from .270 to .300. Weight is about 6.5 lbs.

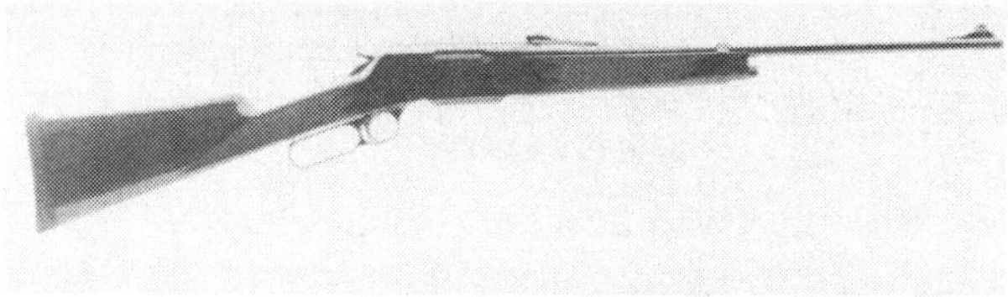

NIB	Exc.	V.G.	Good	Fair	Poor
895	675	500	300	200	150

NOTE: Belgian-manufactured version add 20 percent.

BLR Lightweight Takedown

Similar to BLR Lightweight but with takedown feature. Introduced 2007.

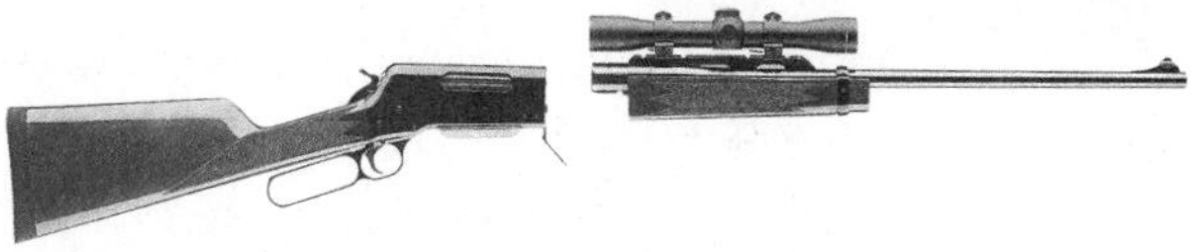

NIB	Exc.	V.G.	Good	Fair	Poor
775	650	575	375	200	150

BLR Lightweight 81 Stainless Takedown

Similar to above but with stainless steel barrel and receiver. Introduced 2008.

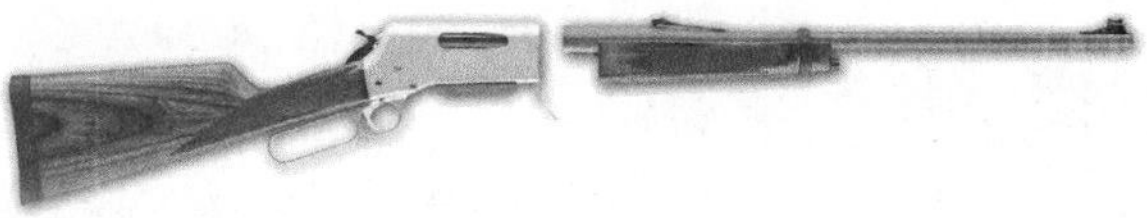

NIB	Exc.	V.G.	Good	Fair	Poor
975	850	695	475	350	225

Model B-78

Introduced in 1973 this single-shot, lever-action falling block was offered in several calibers from .22-250 to .45-70. Barrel lengths from 24" to 26" in either round or octagonal shape with no sights except .45-70. Checkered walnut stock. First built in 1973 and discontinued in 1983.

NIB	Exc.	V.G.	Good	Fair	Poor
1100	750	550	300	200	100

NOTE: Add 15 percent for .45-70 caliber.

Model 53

Offered in 1990 this model is a reproduction of the Winchester Model 53 and like the original is chambered for the .32-20 cartridge. This is a limited edition offering confined to 5,000 rifles. It features hand-cut checkering, high-grade walnut stock with full pistol grip and semi-beavertail forend. Pistol grip is fitted with a metal grip cap. Barrel length is 22" and the finish is blue.

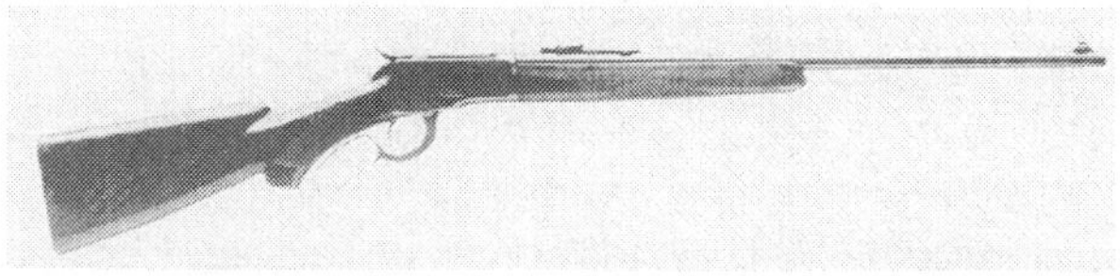

NIB	Exc.	V.G.	Good	Fair	Poor
725	625	550	450	325	200

Model 65 Grade I

This was a limited-edition, lever-action rifle chambered for the .218 Bee cartridge. It has a tapered, round, 24" barrel with open sights. It was patterned after the Winchester Model 65 rifle. It has a 7-round, tubular magazine. The finish is blued with a plain walnut stock and metal buttplate. There were 3,500 manufactured in 1989.

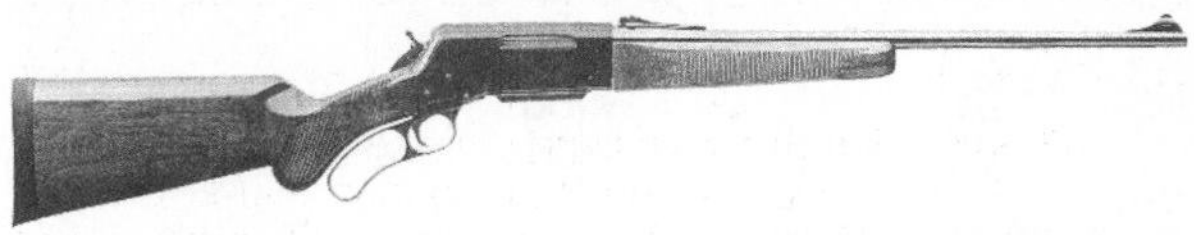

NIB	Exc.	V.G.	Good	Fair	Poor
850	675	500	300	—	150

Model 65 High Grade

This is a deluxe version that features a silver-finished, scroll engraved receiver with gold animal inlays and a gold-plated trigger. It features a select, checkered walnut stock. There were 1,500 manufactured in 1989.

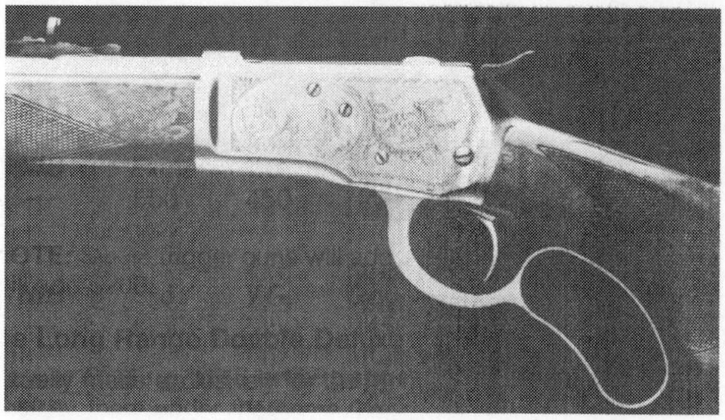

NIB	Exc.	V.G.	Good	Fair	Poor
1650	1200	825	500	400	300

Model 71 Grade I

This was a reproduction of the Winchester Model 71, chambered for the .348 cartridge. It has either a 20" or 24" barrel with open sights and a 4-round, tubular magazine. The finish is blued with a plain walnut stock. There were 4,000 20" carbines and 3,000 24" rifles manufactured in 1986 and 1987.

NIB	Exc.	V.G.	Good	Fair	Poor
—	950	750	595	400	250

Model 71 High Grade

This version was similar to the Grade I except that it had a scroll engraved, grayed receiver with a gold-plated trigger and gold inlays. There were 3,000 rifles and 3,000 carbines manufactured in 1986 and 1987.

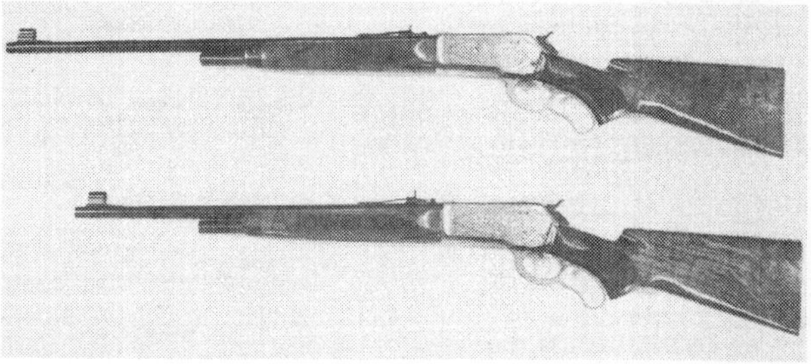

NIB	Exc.	V.G.	Good	Fair	Poor
—	1400	950	750	500	325

Jonathan Browning Mountain Rifle

Same as above but without fancy wood, case, or engraving. Also chambered for .45 or .54 caliber.

NIB	Exc.	V.G.	Good	Fair	Poor
800	500	400	300	—	175

Model 1878 (Original)

Based on John M. Browning's first patent this single-shot rifle was the only firearm manufactured by the Browning brothers. Offered in several calibers, only a few hundred probably exist with the Ogden, Utah, barrel address. This design was later sold to Winchester and sold under that company's name as the Model 1885 High Wall.

NIB	*Exc.*	*V.G.*	*Good*	*Fair*	*Poor*
—	1500	12500	8500	3500	1000

Model 1885 High Wall

This is a single-shot rifle with falling block action and octagonal free-floating barrel similar to the Model 78. Introduced in 1985. The stock is a high grade walnut with straight grip and recoil pad. Furnished with 28" barrel it is offered in these calibers: .223, .22-250, .270, .30-06, 7mm Rem. Mag., .45-70 Gov't. Weighs about 8 lbs. 12 oz.

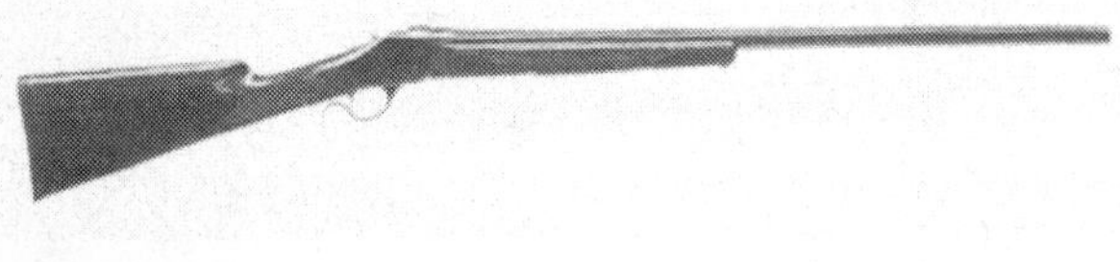

NIB	*Exc.*	*V.G.*	*Good*	*Fair*	*Poor*
1275	950	650	500	200	100

Model 1885 Low Wall

Introduced in 1995 this rifle is similar to the above but in a more accurate version of the original Low Wall. The thin octagon barrel is 24" in length. Trigger pull is adjustable. The walnut stock is fitted with a pistol grip and schnabel forearm. Offered in .22 Hornet, .223 Rem. and the .243 Win. calibers. Weight is about 6.4 lbs.

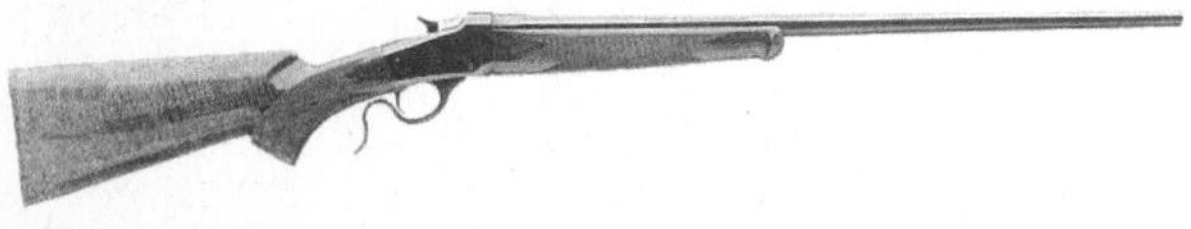

NIB	*Exc.*	*V.G.*	*Good*	*Fair*	*Poor*
1150	850	550	400	300	150

Model 1885 Low Wall Traditional Hunter

Introduced in 1998 this model is similar to the Low Wall but with a half-octagon half-round 24" barrel chambered for the .357 Magnum, .44 Magnum, and .45 Colt cartridges. Case colored receiver and crescent butt with tang sight are also features. Weight is approximately 6.5 lbs.

NIB	*Exc.*	*V.G.*	*Good*	*Fair*	*Poor*
1150	850	550	400	300	150

Model 1885 BPCR (Black Powder Cartridge Rifle)

This model was introduced in 1996 for BPCR metallic silhouette shoots. Chambered for the .45-70 or .40-60 caliber the receiver is case colored and the 28" round barrel is fitted with vernier sight with level. The walnut stock has a checkered pistol grip and is fitted with a tang sight. Weight is approximately 11 lbs.

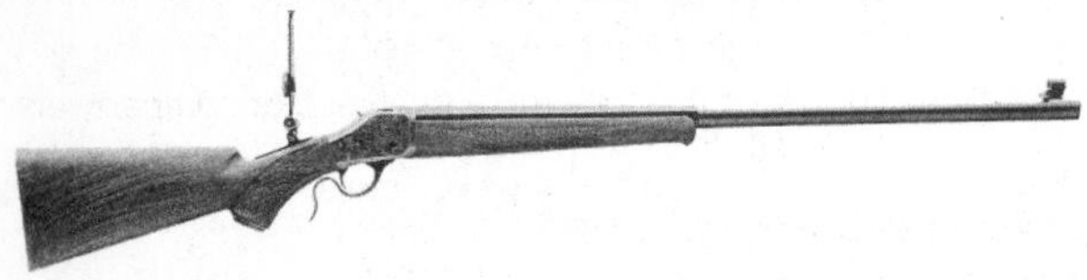

NIB	*Exc.*	*V.G.*	*Good*	*Fair*	*Poor*
1600	1300	800	400	300	150

Model 1885 BPCR Creedmore Type

Introduced in 1998 this model is chambered for the 45/90 cartridge and features a 34" heavy half-round barrel with long range tang sight and wind gauge front sight. Weight is approximately 11 lbs. 13 oz.

NIB	*Exc.*	*V.G.*	*Good*	*Fair*	*Poor*
1500	1250	875	750	525	300

Model 1885 High Wall Traditional Hunter

This variation of the Model 1885 series was introduced in 1997. It is fitted with an oil finish walnut stock with crescent buttplate. The barrel is octagonal and 28" in length. The rear sight is buckhorn and the rifle is fitted with a tang-mounted peep sight. The front sight is gold bead classic style. The rifle is chambered for the .30-30, .38-55, and .45-70 cartridges. Weight is approximately 9 lbs. In 1998 the .454 Casull caliber was added to this rifle.

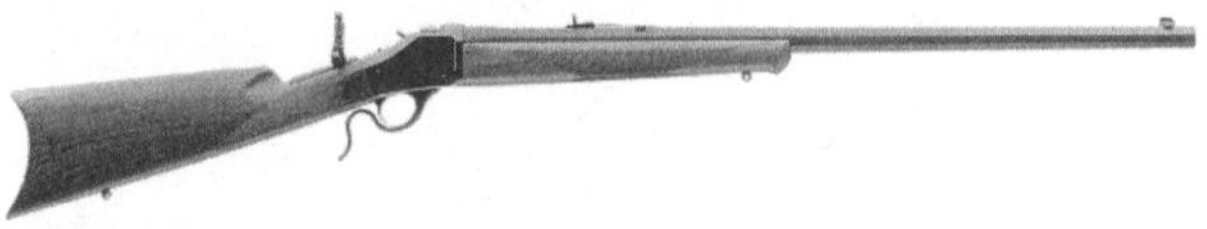

NIB	*Exc.*	*V.G.*	*Good*	*Fair*	*Poor*
1200	950	700	575	400	275

Model 1886 Grade I

This was a lever action sporting rifle patterned after the Model 1886 Winchester rifle. It was chambered for the .45-70 cartridge and has a 26", octagonal barrel with a full-length, tubular magazine. The finish is blued with a walnut stock and crescent buttplate. There were 7,000 manufactured in 1986.

NIB	*Exc.*	*V.G.*	*Good*	*Fair*	*Poor*
1350	950	725	600	450	300

Model 1886 Grade I Carbine

NIB	*Exc.*	*V.G.*	*Good*	*Fair*	*Poor*
950	650	550	400	325	250

Model 1886 High Grade

This deluxe version of the Model 1886 features game scene engraving with gold accents and a checkered, select walnut stock. "1 of 3,000" is engraved on the top of the barrel. There were 3,000 manufactured in 1986.

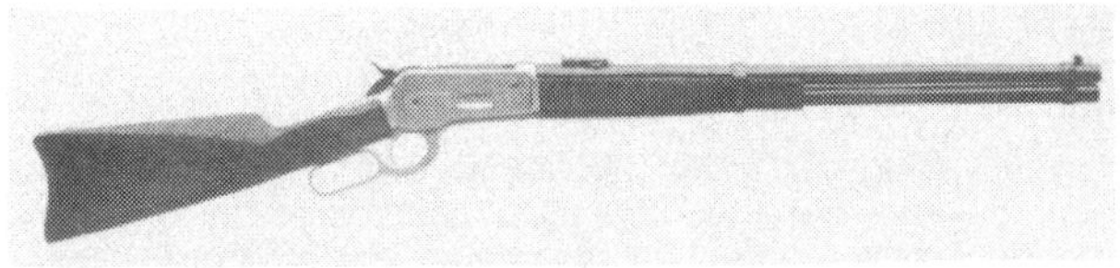

NIB	*Exc.*	*V.G.*	*Good*	*Fair*	*Poor*
1600	1150	900	700	550	425

Model 1886 High Grade Carbine

NIB	*Exc.*	*V.G.*	*Good*	*Fair*	*Poor*
1200	950	750	600	450	300

Model 1886 Montana Centennial

This version is similar to the High Grade with a different engraving pattern designed to commemorate the centennial of the State of Montana. There were 2,000 manufactured in 1986. As with all commemoratives, it must be NIB with all supplied materials to command collector interest.

NIB	*Exc.*	*V.G.*	*Good*	*Fair*	*Poor*
1300	950	750	600	450	375

B-92 Carbine

This is a lever action sporting rifle patterned after the Winchester Model 92. It was chambered for the .357 Mag. and the .44 Mag.

cartridges. It has a 20" barrel with an 11-round, tubular magazine. The finish is blued with a walnut stock. It was discontinued in 1986.

NIB	Exc.	V.G.	Good	Fair	Poor
—	700	625	400	250	120

NOTE: Add 10 percent for Centennial Model. For .357 Magnum add 30 percent.

Model 1895 Grade I

This is a lever action sporting rifle chambered in .30-40 Krag and the .30-06 cartridge. It was patterned after the Model 1895 Winchester rifle. It has a 24" barrel and a 4-round, integral box magazine. It has a buckhorn rear sight and a blade front. The finish is blued with a walnut stock. There were 6,000 manufactured in .30-06 and 2,000 chambered for the .30-40 Krag. It was manufactured in 1984.

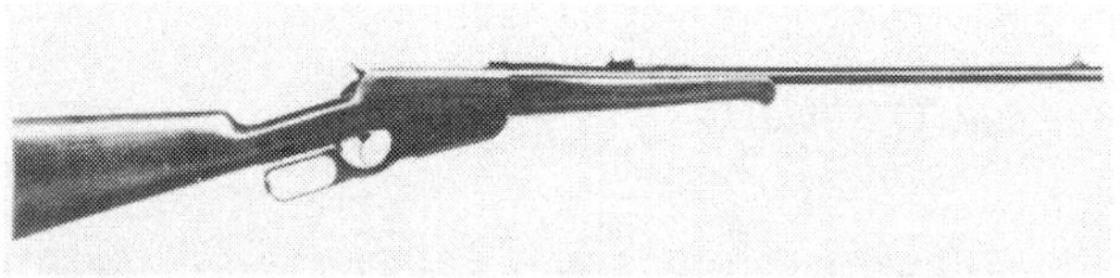

NIB	Exc.	V.G.	Good	Fair	Poor
—	950	675	475	375	275

Model 1895 High Grade

This is the deluxe engraved version of the Model 1895. It has gold-inlaid game scenes and a gold-plated trigger and features a checkered select walnut stock. There were 2,000 produced in 1984—1,000 in each caliber.

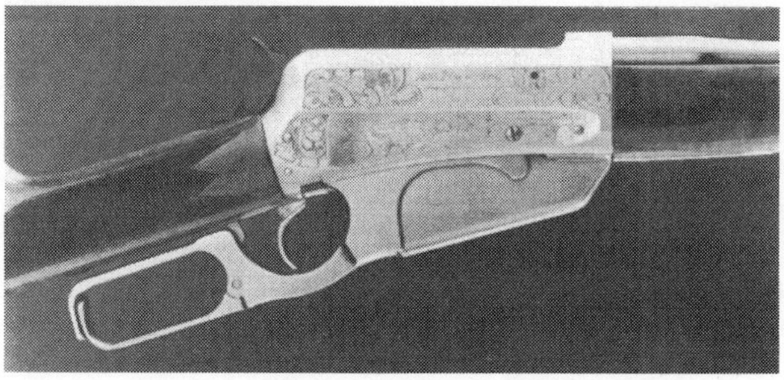

NIB	Exc.	V.G.	Good	Fair	Poor
—	1500	1250	900	700	400

Express Rifle

This is an Over/Under, superposed rifle chambered for the .270 Winchester or the .30-06 cartridges. It has 24" barrels with folding express sights and automatic ejectors. It features a single trigger. The receiver is engraved and is finished in blue with a deluxe checkered walnut stock. Introduced in 1980 and discontinued in 1986.

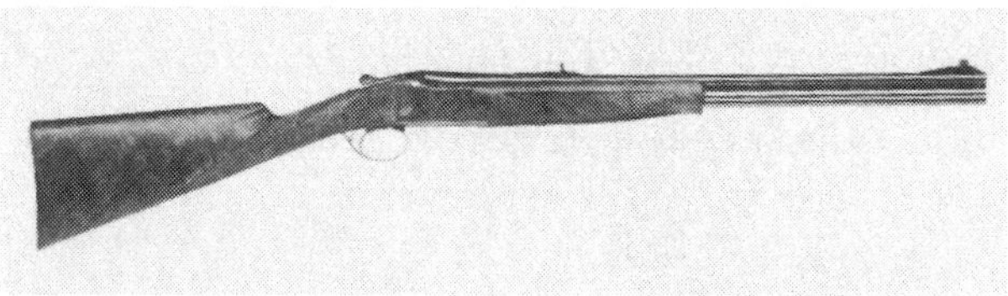

NIB	Exc.	V.G.	Good	Fair	Poor
—	6500	3950	2000	1100	800

Custom Shop Express Rifles

Produced in two different models; the Herstall and the CCS 375. Both are custom-built with choice of engraving patterns.

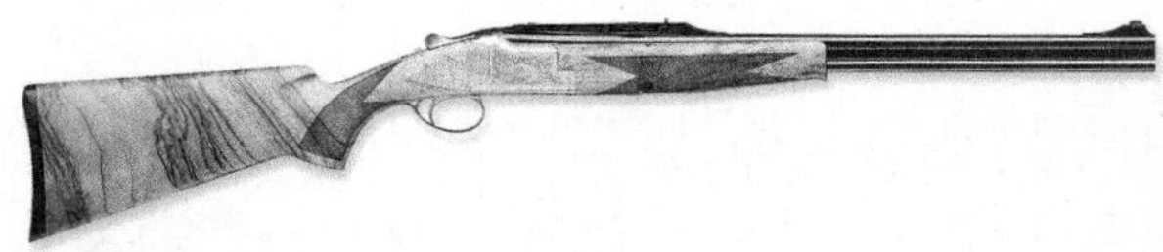

NIB	Exc.	V.G.	Good	Fair	Poor
N/A	23000	17500	12000	5500	700

Continental Set

This consists of an Express Rifle chambered for the .30-06 cartridge and furnished with an extra set of 20 gauge, Over/Under barrels. The shotgun barrels are 26.5" in length. There is a single trigger, automatic ejectors, and a heavily engraved receiver. The select walnut stock is hand checkered and oil-finished. It was furnished with a fitted case. There were 500 manufactured between 1978 and 1986.

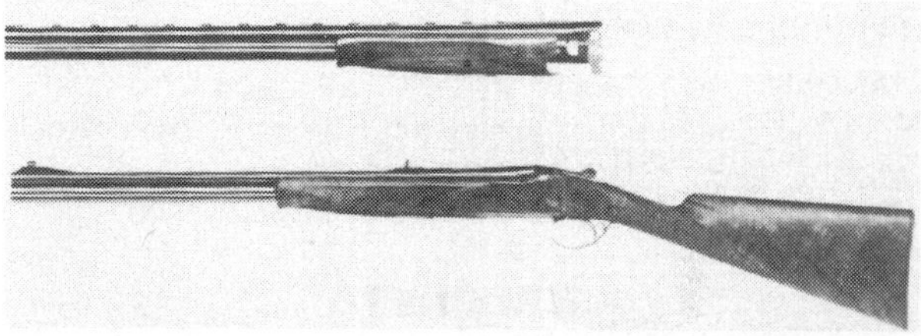

NIB	Exc.	V.G.	Good	Fair	Poor
12000	9250	5500	3250	1300	1000

BROWN MANUFACTURING CO.

Newburyport, Massachusetts

SEE—Ballard Patent Arms

Brown Mfg. Co./Merrill Patent Breechloading Rifles

Overall length 54-3/4"; barrel (bore) length 35"; caliber .577. Markings: On breechblock-bolt mechanism, "BROWN MFG. CO. NEWBURYPORT, MASS./PATANTED OCT. 17, 1871." The patent issued to George Merrill in 1871, permitted the Brown Manufacturing Co. to alter probably up to 1,000 English P1853 rifle-muskets to a single-shot breechloading system. The large bolt handle projecting upward at the end of the breech readily distinguishes these arms.

Courtesy Milwaukee Public Museum, Milwaukee, Wisconsin

NIB	Exc.	V.G.	Good	Fair	Poor
—	—	2500	1250	800	300

BROWN PRECISION, INC.

Los Molinos, California

Although known as a manufacturer of stocks, this company also produced custom-order rifles.

High Country Standard

A .243 to .30-06 bolt-action rifle with a 22" barrel and Kevlar stock.

NIB	Exc.	V.G.	Good	Fair	Poor
985	775	600	500	400	200

NOTE: Gray camo stock, stainless barrel and Leupold 2.5 x 10 scope add $650.

Open Country Varmint Rifle

Similar to the above, with a heavy barrel. Introduced in 1989.

NIB	Exc.	V.G.	Good	Fair	Poor
1100	800	650	550	400	200

Law Enforcement Model

A .308 caliber Remington Varmint action rifle with a 20" barrel, Zeiss telescope and Kevlar stock.

NIB	Exc.	V.G.	Good	Fair	Poor
1050	800	650	550	400	200

Pro-Hunter

A .375 Holland & Holland or .458 Winchester Magnum bolt-action rifle. Blued, electroless nickel-plated or Teflon coated.

NIB	Exc.	V.G.	Good	Fair	Poor
1800	1400	950	700	500	250

Brown Precision Rifle

A .270 or .30-06 bolt-action rifle with a 22" featherweight barrel and Kevlar stock.

NIB	Exc.	V.G.	Good	Fair	Poor
600	475	350	250	150	100

Blaser Rifle

Built on the Camex-Blaser action with a Brown Precision stock.

NIB	Exc.	V.G.	Good	Fair	Poor
1600	1300	850	550	400	200

BRUCHET

Ste. Etienne, France

Model A

A 12 or .410 bore side-by-side shotgun with double triggers, and automatic ejectors. The barrel lengths and chokes are to customer specifications. Produced on a limited basis (50 per year) since 1982. Base price is listed.

NIB	Exc.	V.G.	Good	Fair	Poor
3600	2750	1900	1450	1000	500

Model B

As above, with a finer finish and a spring-assisted action opener. Imported since 1982.

NIB	Exc.	V.G.	Good	Fair	Poor
6950	5250	4000	3000	2250	1250

BSA GUNS LTD.

Birmingham, England

Established in 1861, this firm has produced a wide variety of firearms over the years. The more common of these arms that are currently available in the United States are listed.

SINGLE-SHOT

No. 12 Cadet Martini

A .310 caliber single-shot Martini action rifle with a 29" barrel, adjustable sights and straight-gripped walnut stock. Approximately 80,000 were manufactured from 1911 to 1913. Many of those imported into the United States were altered to .22 caliber.

NIB	Exc.	V.G.	Good	Fair	Poor
—	750	500	300	150	100

Centurian Match Rifle

As above, in .22 caliber with a 24" barrel, adjustable sights and a pistol-grip walnut stock.

NIB	Exc.	V.G.	Good	Fair	Poor
—	600	450	300	200	100

Model 13 Sporter

As above, in .22 Hornet with hunting sights.

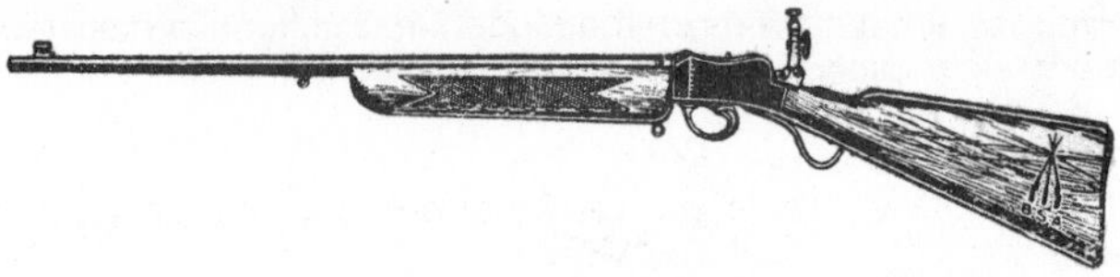

NIB	Exc.	V.G.	Good	Fair	Poor
—	650	425	300	225	100

Martini International Match

As above, with a heavy match barrel, ISU-style sights and a match stock. Manufactured from 1950 to 1953.

NIB	Exc.	V.G.	Good	Fair	Poor
—	750	575	325	250	125

Martini International Light

As above, with a 26" barrel of lighter weight.

NIB	Exc.	V.G.	Good	Fair	Poor
—	750	575	325	250	125

Martini International ISU

As above, meeting ISU specifications with a 28" barrel. Manufactured from 1968 to 1976.

NIB	Exc.	V.G.	Good	Fair	Poor
—	850	675	400	325	200

BOLT-ACTIONS

Royal

A bolt-action sporting rifle manufactured in a variety of calibers and a 24" barrel, with a checkered French walnut stock.

NIB	Exc.	V.G.	Good	Fair	Poor
—	550	500	250	200	100

Majestic Deluxe

A .22 Hornet, .222, .243, 7x57mm, .308 or .30-06 bolt-action sporting rifle with a 22" barrel, having a folding rear sight and a checkered walnut stock with a schnabel forend tip. Imported from 1959 to 1965.

NIB	Exc.	V.G.	Good	Fair	Poor
—	550	350	250	200	100

Majestic Deluxe Featherweight

As above, in .270 or .458 Magnum with a thinner barrel. Add 25 percent for .458. Add 75 percent for .458.

NIB	Exc.	V.G.	Good	Fair	Poor
—	550	350	250	200	100

Monarch Deluxe

As above, drilled and tapped for telescopic sight and also available in a heavy barreled varmint version in .222 or .243 caliber. Imported from 1966 to 1974.

NIB	Exc.	V.G.	Good	Fair	Poor
—	550	375	275	225	100

HERTERS U9

The firm of Herters, Inc. of Waseca, Minnesota, imported BSA rifle actions beginning in 1965 that were used for custom-made rifles. Commencing in 1986, BSA began production of a new line of bolt-action sporting rifles on the Model CF-2 action. The standard production models are listed.

Sporter/Classic

A hunting rifle available in a variety of calibers with a checkered walnut stock. Introduced in 1986.

NIB	Exc.	V.G.	Good	Fair	Poor
—	450	325	275	200	100

Varminter

As above, with a matte-finished heavy barrel in .222, .22-250 or .243 caliber. Introduced in 1986.

NIB	Exc.	V.G.	Good	Fair	Poor
—	350	275	225	175	100

Stutzen Rifle

As above, with a 20.5" barrel and a Mannlicher-style stock.

NIB	Exc.	V.G.	Good	Fair	Poor
—	475	350	275	225	100

Regal Custom

As above, with an engraved receiver, checkered walnut stock and an ebony forend. Imported only in 1986.

NIB	Exc.	V.G.	Good	Fair	Poor
—	925	750	600	500	250

CFT Target Rifle

A .308 caliber single-shot version of the above with a 26.5" barrel and adjustable sights. Imported only in 1987.

NIB	Exc.	V.G.	Good	Fair	Poor
—	750	600	550	400	200

SHOTGUNS

Royal

This side-by-side is chambered for either 12 or 20 gauge 3" shells. Choice of 26" or 28" barrels with multi chokes. Checkered select walnut stock with straight grip. Splinter forearm. Case colored receiver with side plates. Single selective trigger. Recoil pad standard. Weight is about 7.25 lbs. for 12 gauge and about 6.75 lbs. for the 20 gauge.

NIB	Exc.	V.G.	Good	Fair	Poor
1500	1150	900	675	—	—

Classic

This side-by-side gun is offered in 12, 16, 20, 28 gauge as well as .410 bore. Choice of 26" or 28" barrels except for 28 and .410 where 26" barrels are the only length offered. Checkered walnut stock with pistol grip. Case colored box lock receiver with scroll engraving. Semi-beavertail forearm. Recoil pad standard. Choke tubes standard. Weight is about 7.25 lbs. for 12 gauge, 6.75 lbs. for 16 gauge, 6.6 lbs. for 20 gauge, 6.25 lbs. for 28 gauge. .410 bore weighs about 6.5 lbs.

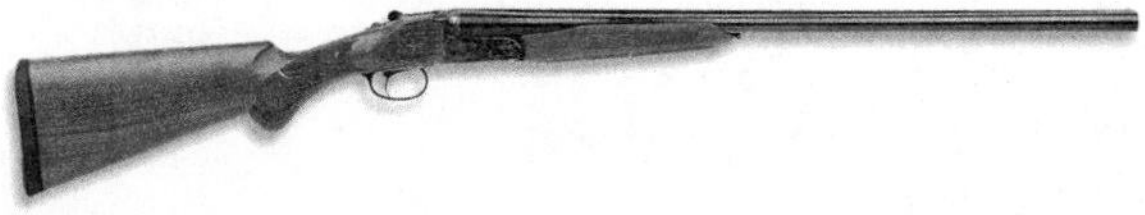

NIB	Exc.	V.G.	Good	Fair	Poor
1300	975	800	600	400	200

Falcon

This is an over and under gun in either 12 or 20 gauge 3" chambers. Choice of 26" or 28" barrels with ventilated rib and choke tubes. Checkered walnut stock with pistol grip. Case colored scroll engraved receiver. Single selective trigger. Automatic ejectors. Recoil pad is standard. Weight is about 7.25 lbs. for the 12 gauge and 7 lbs. for the 20 gauge.

NIB	Exc.	V.G.	Good	Fair	Poor
1200	900	875	500	300	150

Falcon Sporting

Similar to the Falcon but offered only in 12 gauge with 2.75" chambers. Choice of 2" or 30" ventilated rib barrels with 5 chokes tubes. Barrels are ported. Checkered walnut stock with Schnabel forearm. Weight is about 7.7 lbs.

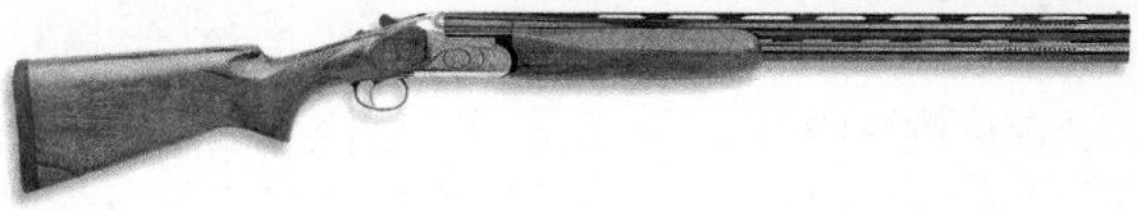

NIB	Exc.	V.G.	Good	Fair	Poor
1250	950	775	475	275	125

Silver Eagle

This over and under gun is chambered for either the 12 or 20 gauge 3" shell. Fitted with 26" or 28" vent rib barrels with choke tubes. Checkered walnut stock with pistol grip. Single selective trigger. Blued box lock receiver. Recoil is standard. Weight for 12 gauge is about 7.2 lbs. and 6.75 lbs. for the 20 gauge.

NIB	Exc.	V.G.	Good	Fair	Poor
490	375	300	250	200	125

Silver Eagle II

Similar to the Silver Eagle above with the addition of automatic ejectors.

NIB	Exc.	V.G.	Good	Fair	Poor
590	425	275	225	175	100

200 Series

This is a series of semi-automatic shotgun chambered for 12, 16, 20, 28 gauge as well as the .410 bore. The 12, 16, and 20 gauge guns are offered with choice of 26" or 28" vent rib barrels with choke tubes. The 28 and .410 are available in 26" barrels only. All gauges are offered with a choice of walnut or synthetic stocks. The 20 gauge gun is offered in a youth model with shortened stock. All gauges have 3" chambers except for the 28 gauge with 2.75" chambers. Weights range from 7.4 lbs. to 6.5 lbs.

NIB	Exc.	V.G.	Good	Fair	Poor
390	290	225	200	100	75

NOTE: Add $70 for walnut stock.

300 SM Series

This semi-automatic series is offered in 12 gauge only with 3.5" chambers. Choice of 24", 26", or 28" vent rib barrels with choke tubes. Synthetic stock. Weights are about 7.3 lbs.

NIB	Exc.	V.G.	Good	Fair	Poor
420	315	250	225	175	100

BULLARD REPEATING ARMS CO.
Springfield, Massachusetts

Designed by James H. Bullard, the rifles listed were manufactured in competition with those produced by the Whitney Arms Company and the Winchester Repeating Arms Company. Approximately 12,000 were made between 1886 and 1890.

Small Frame

A .32-40 and .38-45 caliber lever action rifle with a 26" octagonal barrel and either a half or full length magazine tube. Blued or case hardened with a walnut stock. The receiver is stamped "Bullard Repeating Arms Company/Springfield, Mass., U.S.A. Pat. Aug. 16, 1881." The caliber is marked on top of the frame.

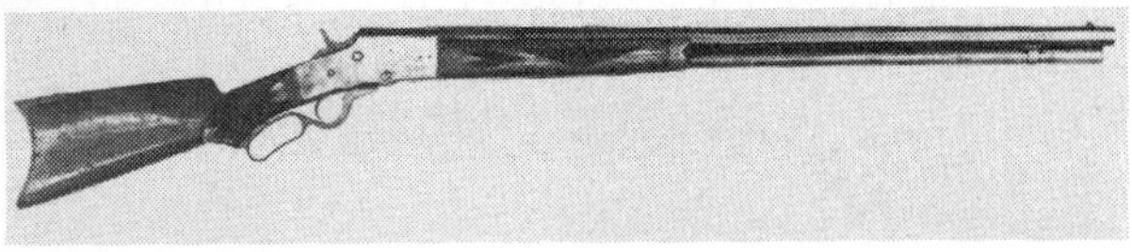

Courtesy Milwaukee Public Museum, Milwaukee, Wisconsin

NIB	*Exc.*	*V.G.*	*Good*	*Fair*	*Poor*
—	—	4000	2050	675	300

Large Frame

A .40-75 through .45-85 caliber lever action rifle with 28" octagonal barrel. Other features and markings as above. Can be custom ordered in .50-95 and .50-115.

NIB	*Exc.*	*V.G.*	*Good*	*Fair*	*Poor*
—	—	5150	2500	875	400

Carbine

A .45-70 caliber lever action rifle with a 22" round barrel and a sliding dust cover on the receiver. Marking and finish as above.

NIB	*Exc.*	*V.G.*	*Good*	*Fair*	*Poor*
—	—	7950	3800	1500	500

Musket

A .45-70 caliber lever action rifle with a 30" round barrel with a full-length stock secured by two barrel bands. There is a rod under the barrel, military sights, and the same sliding cover on the receiver as found on the Carbine. There have been examples noted without the manufacturer's markings.

NIB	*Exc.*	*V.G.*	*Good*	*Fair*	*Poor*
—	—	7500	3500	1500	500

BURGESS GUN CO.
Buffalo, New York

SEE—Colt and Whitney

One of the most prolific 19th century designers was Andrew Burgess who established his own company in 1892. The Burgess Gun Company manufactured slide action shotguns and rifles operated by a unique pistol grip prior to their being purchased by the Winchester Repeating Arms Company in 1899. Arms based on Burgess' patents were manufactured by a variety of American gun makers. Serial numbers for all Burgess shotguns begin at 1000.

12 Gauge Slide Action Shotgun

A 12 gauge slide-action shotgun with a 28" or 30" barrel. Blued with a walnut stock. This model was available with 6 grades of engraving. The values listed are for the standard, plain model.

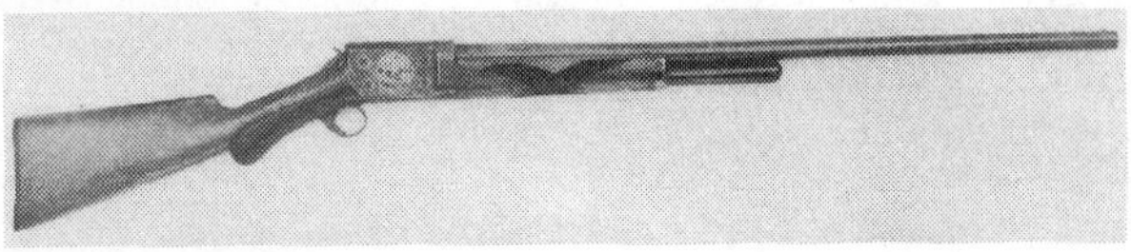

Burgess engraving grades (1-4)

NIB	*Exc.*	*V.G.*	*Good*	*Fair*	*Poor*
—	—	1700	700	250	125

Folding Shotgun

As above, with a 19.5" barrel that is hinged so that it may be folded back against the buttstock.

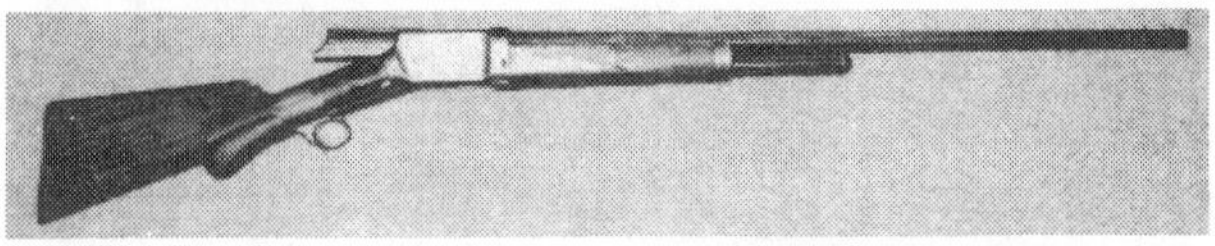

NIB	*Exc.*	*V.G.*	*Good*	*Fair*	*Poor*
—	—	4550	1750	650	300

Slide Action Rifle

An extremely rare rifle based upon the shotgun design described above. Manufactured in at least three calibers with varying barrel lengths. Blued with a walnut stock.

NIB	*Exc.*	*V.G.*	*Good*	*Fair*	*Poor*
—	—	3950	1500	500	250

BUSHMASTER FIREARMS INC.
Windham, Maine

Bushmaster XM15-E2S Target Model

Furnished with a 20" heavy barrel and A-2 stock. Weight is 8.35 lbs.

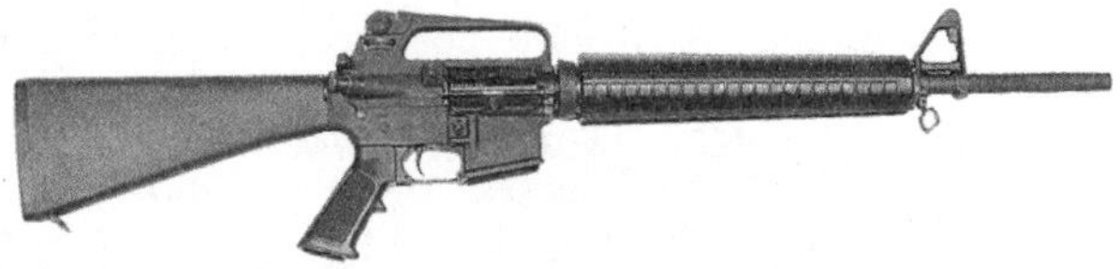

NIB	*Exc.*	*V.G.*	*Good*	*Fair*	*Poor*
800	675	550	400	300	200

NOTE: Add $10 for 24" barrel and $20 for 26" barrel. Add $75 for A3 carry handle.

Bushmaster XM15-E2S V-Match Competition Rifle

This model is a specially designed competition rifle with 20", 24", or 26" barrel lengths. Fitted with a black anodized aluminum handguard. Weight is about 8.1 lbs.

NIB	*Exc.*	*V.G.*	*Good*	*Fair*	*Poor*
950	800	700	450	350	250

NOTE: Add $75 for A3 carry handle.

Bushmaster XM15-E2S V-Match Carbine

As above but with 16" barrel. Weight is about 6.9 lbs.

NIB	*Exc.*	*V.G.*	*Good*	*Fair*	*Poor*
900	700	575	450	350	250

NOTE: Add $75 for A3 carry handle.

Bushmaster XM15-E2S Shorty Carbine

This "post-ban" model of the M16 is a gas-operated semi-automatic rifle chambered for the .223 Remington cartridge. It is fitted with a heavy 16" barrel and a 30-round magazine. Overall length is 35" and empty weight is 6.72 lbs.

NIB	Exc.	V.G.	Good	Fair	Poor
—	675	550	450	300	200

NOTE: Add $50 for fluted barrel. Add $75 for A3-type carry handle.

Bushmaster XM15-E2S Dissipator

Similar to the above model with a 16" barrel but fitted with a longer plastic handguard to give a longer sight radius. Weight is 7.2 lbs.

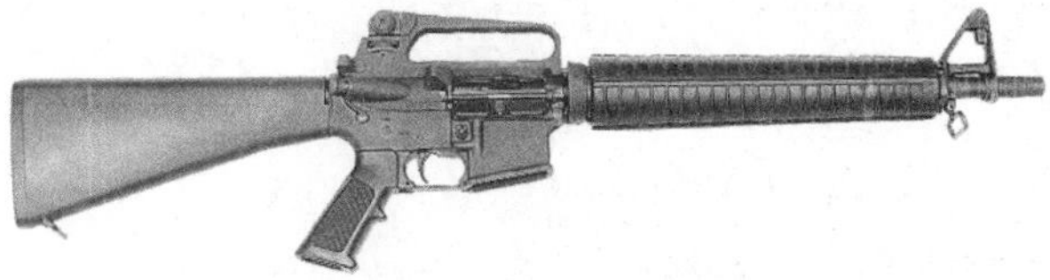

NIB	Exc.	V.G.	Good	Fair	Poor
950	775	600	450	300	200

NOTE: Add $75 for A3 carry handle.

Bushmaster M4 Post-Ban Carbine

Introduced in 2001 this rifle features a 14.5" barrel with permanently attached Mini Y Comp muzzlebrake (total length 16") and pinned, fixed-length Tele-style stock. Chambered for .223 caliber. M16A2 rear sight. Supplied with 10-round magazine. Weight is about 6.6 lbs.

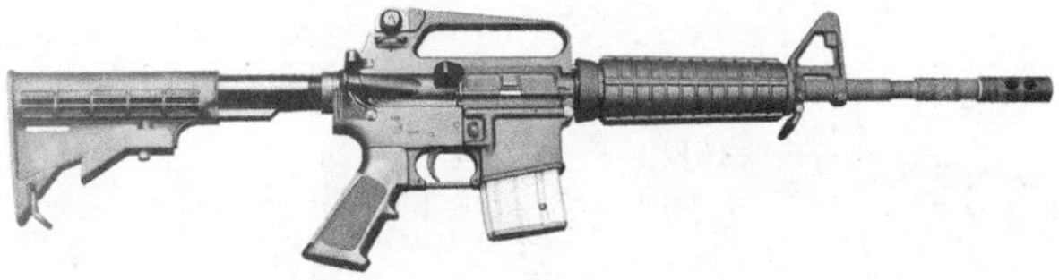

NIB	Exc.	V.G.	Good	Fair	Poor
1050	900	750	450	300	200

Bushmaster M4A3 Post-Ban Carbine

Same as above but with removable carry handle. Introduced in 2001.199

NIB	Exc.	V.G.	Good	Fair	Poor
1125	975	825	500	400	300

Bushmaster DCM Competition Rifle

This model features a 20" extra heavy barrel with free floating forend. Competition sights and trigger. Supplied with buttstock weight and hard carrying case. 10-round magazine.

NIB	Exc.	V.G.	Good	Fair	Poor
1350	1075	800	600	500	350

Bushmaster 11.5" Barrel Carbine

AR-style carbine chambered in 5.56/.223. Features include an 11.5" chrome-lined barrel with permanently attached BATF-approved 5.5" flash suppressor, fixed or removable carry handle, optional optics rail, 30-round magazine. Overall length 31.625". Weight: 6.46 or 6.81 lbs.

NIB	Exc.	V.G.	Good	Fair	Poor
900	775	600	450	300	200

Bushmaster Heavy-Barreled Carbine

AR-style semi-auto carbine chambered in 5.56/.223. Features include a chrome-lined, heavy profile 16" vanadium steel barrel, fixed or removable carry handle, six-position telestock. Overall length 32.5". Weight: 6.93 lbs. to 7.28 lbs.

NIB	Exc.	V.G.	Good	Fair	Poor
1000	850	700	550	300	200

Bushmaster Modular Carbine

AR-style carbine chambered in 5.56/.223. Features include 16" chrome-lined chrome-moly vanadium steel barrel, skeleton stock or six-position telestock, clamp-on front sight and detachable flip-up dual aperture rear, 30-round magazine. Overall length 36.25". Weight: 7.3 lbs.

NIB	Exc.	V.G.	Good	Fair	Poor
1450	1200	1000	750	400	250

Bushmaster M17S Bullpup

This model is a gas-operated semi-automatic rifle in the bull-pup design. Chambered for the .223 cartridge and fitted with a 21.5" barrel. Weight is 8.2 lbs.

NIB	Exc.	V.G.	Good	Fair	Poor
1000	875	675	400	300	200

Bushmaster Gas Piston Rifle

Semi-auto AR-style rifle chambered in .223. Features include a 16" barrel, telescoping stock, carry handle, 30-round magazine, and piston assembly rather than direct gas impingement. Overall length 32.5". Weight: 7.46 lbs.

NIB	Exc.	V.G.	Good	Fair	Poor
1750	1375	1050	800	650	300

Bushmaster 6.8 SPC Carbine

AR-style semi-auto rifle chambered in 6.8 SPC. Features include 16" M4 profile barrel with Izzy muzzle brake, 26-round magazine, six-position telestock. Available in A2 (fixed carry handle) or A3 (removable carry handle) configuration. Overall length 32.75". Weight: 6.57 lbs. Also chambered in 7.62x39mm.

NIB	Exc.	V.G.	Good	Fair	Poor
1750	1375	1050	800	650	300

Carbon 15 9mm Carbine

Semi-auto carbine chambered in 9mm Parabellum. Carbon fiber frame, 16-inch steel barrel, six-position telescoping stock, 30-rd. detachable magazine. Introduced 2006.

NIB	Exc.	V.G.	Good	Fair	Poor
1000	850	700	550	475	300

Carbon 15 Top Loading Rifle

Semi-auto rifle chambered in .223. Carbon fiber frame, 16-inch steel barrel, retractable stock, Picatinny rail, 10-rd. fixed magazine. Based on AR-15. Introduced 2006.

NIB	Exc.	V.G.	Good	Fair	Poor
1000	850	700	550	475	300

Predator

Semi-auto rifle chambered in .223. 20-inch DCM-type barrel, fixed composite buttstock, 2-stage competition trigger, Picatinny rail, 1/2" scope risers. Based on AR-15. Introduced 2006.

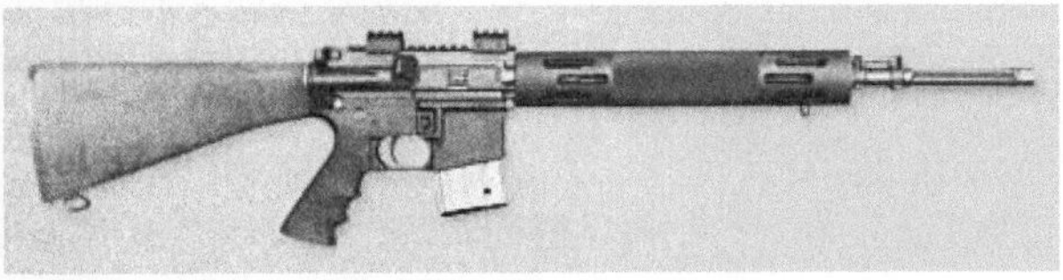

NIB	Exc.	V.G.	Good	Fair	Poor
1100	900	750	600	525	325

Carbon 15 .22 Rimfire Rifle

Similar to Shorty carbine but chambered in .22 LR. Blowback; 10-rd. magazine. MSRP: $790.

NIB	Exc.	V.G.	Good	Fair	Poor
625	495	350	275	200	150

Bushmaster .308 Hunter

Designed for the hunter, chambered in .308 Winchester with a 20-inch heavy-fluted barrel with chrome lined bore and chamber. Features include 5-round magazine, mid-length gas system, two .75-inch mini risers for optics mounting, Hogue rubberized pistol grip, standard A2 stock. Vista Hunter has A2 grip. Approx. weight 8.5 pounds.

NIB	Exc.	V.G.	Good	Fair	Poor
1400	1100	925	775	500	300

NOTE: Add $100 for Vista Hunter if NIB .

Bushmaster ORC Series

The Optics Ready Carbine series is for shooters who wish to add various optical holograph, red dot or scope sights. Chambered in .223/5.56 with magazine capacity of 30 rounds or .308 with 20-round magazine. The gas piston system taps gas from the barrel much like AK and FAL designs. Provides a cleaner operation with less recoil. Detented plug in the gas block allows for easy cleaning. Barrel length is 16 inches, weight is 6.6 pounds (.223) to 7.75 pounds (.308).

NIB	Exc.	V.G.	Good	Fair	Poor
1125	965	825	700	500	300

NOTE: Add $60 for .308 chambering.

Bushmaster .450 Carbine

Chambered for the .450 Bushmaster cartridge, providing big-bore power in the AR platform. Developed with Hornady Mfg. the cartridge propels a 250-grain bullet at 2200 fps, ideal for most North American big game. Barrel length of 16 or 20 inches, A3 flattop receiver with Picatinny rail, weight is approx. 8.5 pounds.

NIB	Exc.	V.G.	Good	Fair	Poor
1200	1025	900	750	550	350

Bushmaster BA50 .50 BMG Rifle and Carbine

A bolt-action, 10-round repeater intended for long-range target shooting. 30-inch barrel, muzzle brake. Carbine has 20-inch barrel.

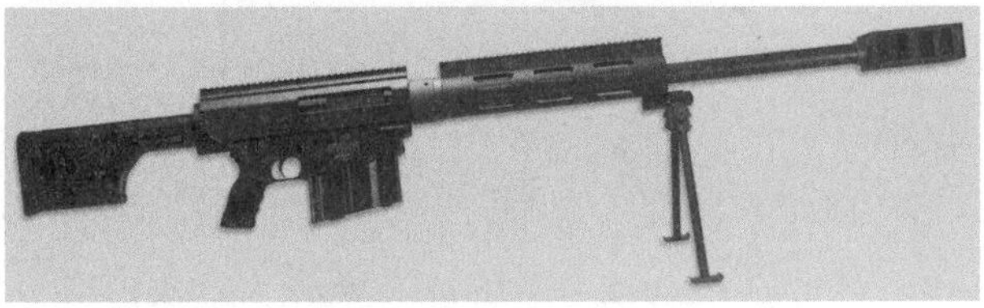

NIB	Exc.	V.G.	Good	Fair	Poor
5000	4200	3700	3000	—	—

C

CABANAS, INDUSTRIAS S.A.

Aguilas, Mexico

This company manufactures a variety of bolt-action single-shot rifles that utilize .22 caliber blanks to propel a .177 caliber pellet. Scarce, but not especially valuable.

Mini-82 Youth

NIB	Exc.	V.G.	Good	Fair	Poor
75	65	50	40	30	20

R-83 Larger Youth

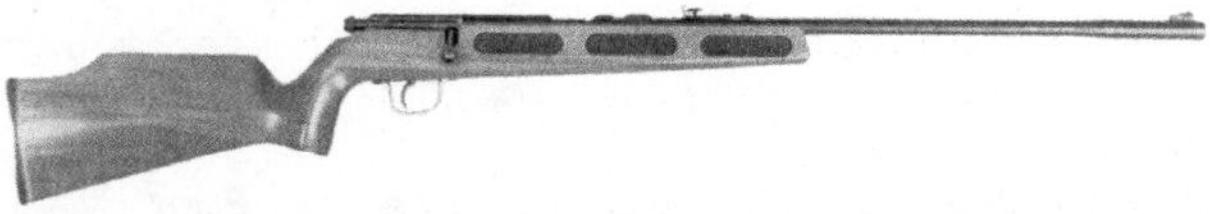

NIB	Exc.	V.G.	Good	Fair	Poor
85	75	60	50	40	30

Safari A

NIB	Exc.	V.G.	Good	Fair	Poor
100	90	75	50	40	30

Varmint

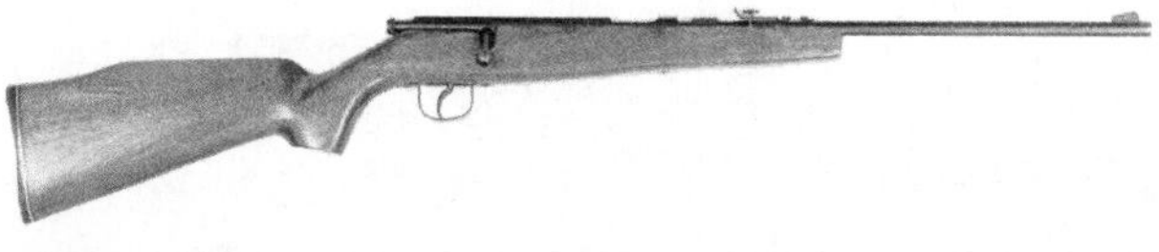

NIB	Exc.	V.G.	Good	Fair	Poor
125	110	90	75	—	35

Espronceda IV

NIB	Exc.	V.G.	Good	Fair	Poor
125	110	90	75	50	35

Leyre

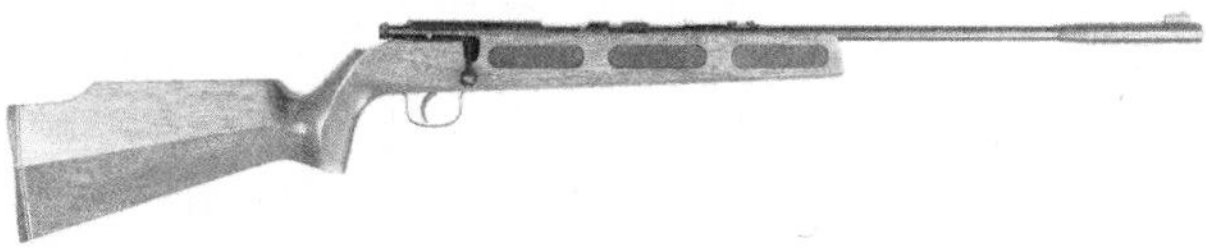

NIB	Exc.	V.G.	Good	Fair	Poor
140	125	100	85	65	50

Master

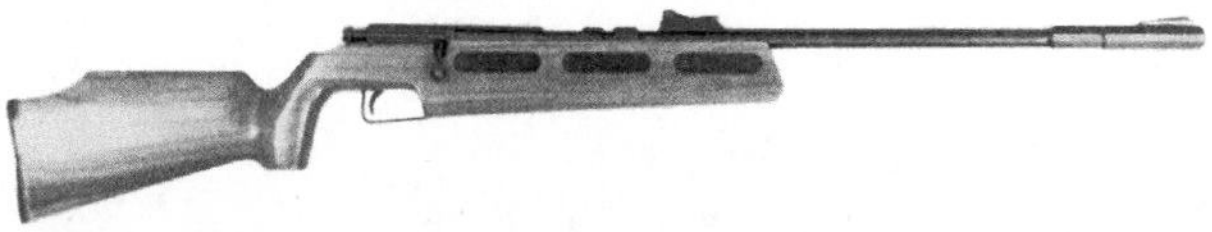

NIB	Exc.	V.G.	Good	Fair	Poor
150	130	110	100	75	60

CASARTELLI, CARLO

Brescia, Italy

Sidelock Shotgun

Custom order sidelock shotgun that is available in any gauge, barrel length, choke, automatic ejectors and single-selective trigger and choice of engraving style.

NIB	Exc.	V.G.	Good	Fair	Poor
16000	14500	10500	8250	6000	4000

Kenya Double Rifle

Custom order, full sidelock rifle that is available in all standard and magnum calibers.

NIB	Exc.	V.G.	Good	Fair	Poor
33000	29000	24000	18900	13000	9000

Africa Model

A bolt-action rifle built on a square-bridge magnum Mauser action. It is chambered for the heavy magnum calibers and can be taken down for transport. The other features are on a custom order basis.

NIB	Exc.	V.G.	Good	Fair	Poor
9750	8800	7500	5750	4750	3750

Safari Model

Built on a standard Mauser bolt-action and is chambered for the non-magnum calibers.

NIB	Exc.	V.G.	Good	Fair	Poor
8000	7200	5800	4500	3250	2500

CENTURY INTERNATIONAL ARMS CO.

St. Albans, Vermont

Century International Arms is a leading importer of military firearms primarily of foreign manufacture. These low-cost firearms are excellent shooters and many have been restocked to make satisfactory hunting rifles. The listing offers a representative sample of imports from Century. The company is always providing new surplus firearms that may not appear in this edition.

Centurion Shotgun

This is a new over/under shotgun in 12, 20, and 28 gauge as well as .410 bore with 2-3/4" chambers. The walnut stock is checkered. The receiver is blue. Offered in 28" vent-rib barrels in full and modified chokes. Weight is about 7.35 lbs. for the 12 gauge and 5.3 lbs. for the .410 bore.

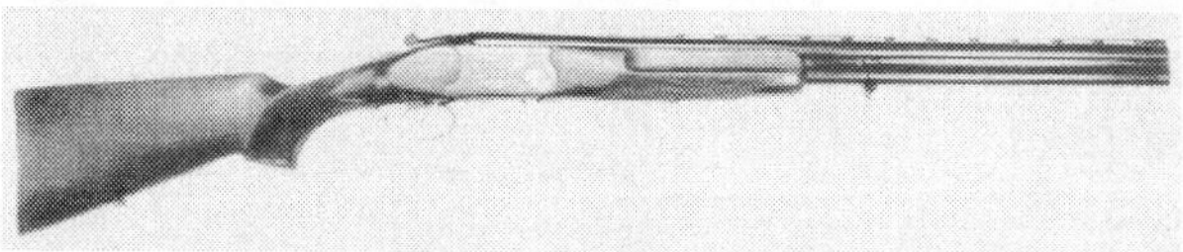

NIB	Exc.	V.G.	Good	Fair	Poor
—	375	325	225	175	125

Centurion 98 Sporter

This is a refinished and rebuilt on a surplus German Mauser 98 action with new commercial 22" barrel. No sights. A synthetic stock with recoil pad is standard. Chambered for .270 or .30-06. Weighs about 7 lbs. 13 oz.

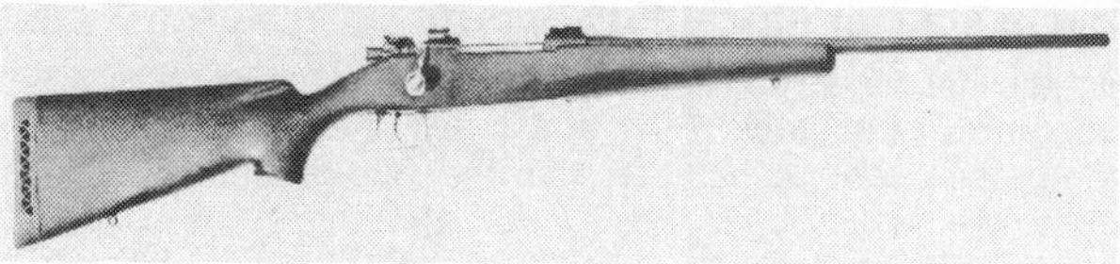

NIB	Exc.	V.G.	Good	Fair	Poor
—	300	250	175	150	100

Century Centurion 14

This bolt-action rifle uses an Enfield Pattern 14 action drilled and tapped for scope mount. Barrel is 24" and chambered for 7mm Rem. Mag. Walnut stock is checkered with pistol grip and Monte Carlo comb. No sights.

NIB	Exc.	V.G.	Good	Fair	Poor
350	300	250	175	150	100

Enfield Sporter No. I Mark III

This refinished rifle has a cut down Sporter-style stock. Action and sights are original. Caliber is .303.

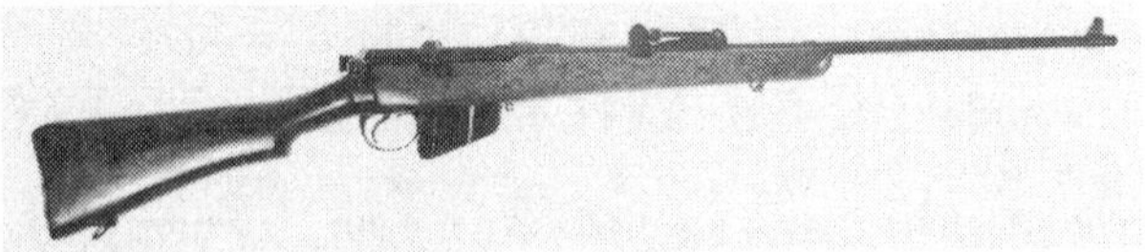

NIB	Exc.	V.G.	Good	Fair	Poor
—	250	200	150	100	50

Enfield Sporter No. 4 Mark I

With new walnut stock.

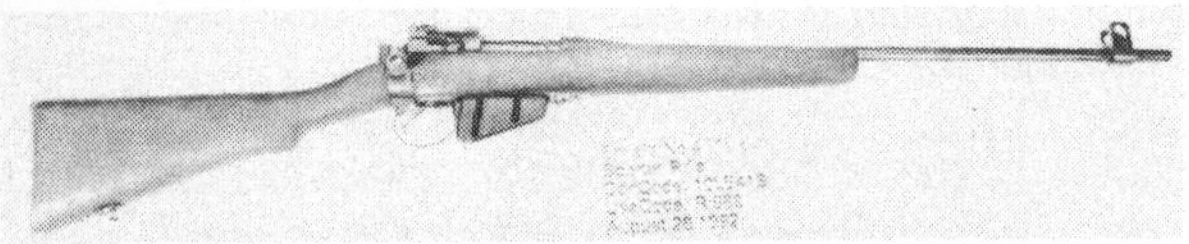

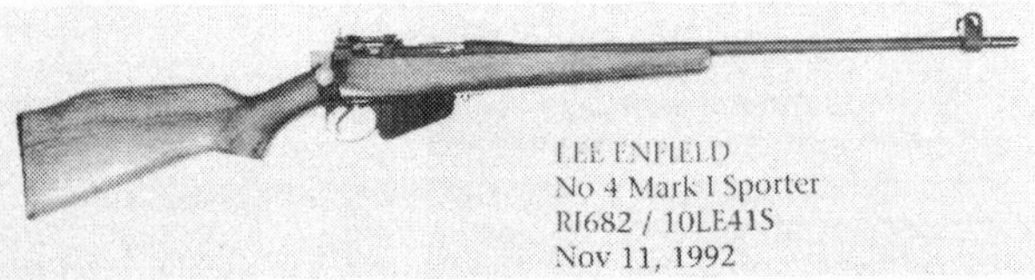

NIB	Exc.	V.G.	Good	Fair	Poor
—	260	210	150	100	50

TOZ-17

An original Russian rifle chambered for the .22 LR. Has a 21" barrel and 5-round magazine. Checkered stock and iron sights. Weighs about 5.4 lbs.

NIB	Exc.	V.G.	Good	Fair	Poor
—	175	135	110	50	40

TOZ-17-1

Same as above with hooded front sight and tangent rear sight. Receiver is grooved for scope mount.

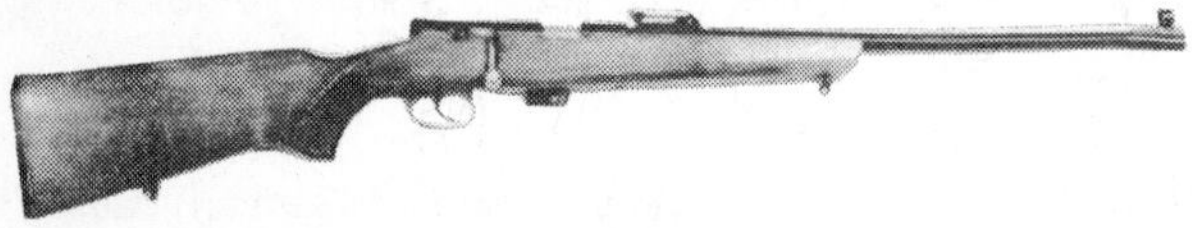

NIB	Exc.	V.G.	Good	Fair	Poor
—	185	145	120	60	50

Mexican Mauser Model 1910 Sporter

This rifle has been converted from a military rifle to a sporter by cutting down the stock. The metal is refinished and the barrel has been rebored and rechambered for the .30-06 cartridge. The box magazine holds 5 rounds. Barrel is 23" and rifle weighs about 8 lbs.

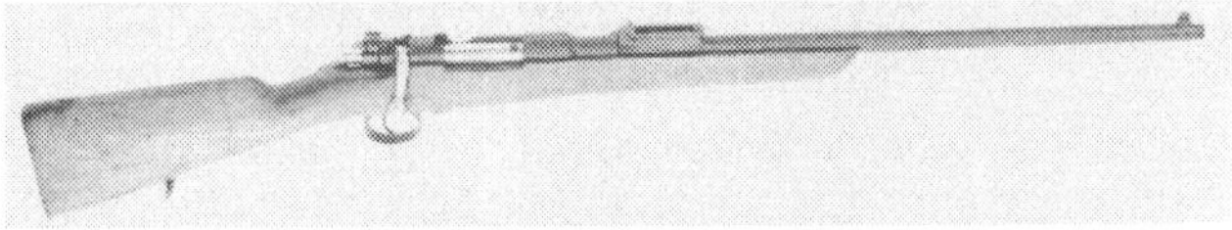

NIB	Exc.	V.G.	Good	Fair	Poor
—	185	145	120	60	50

FAL Sporter

This is a refinished FAL receiver and barrel installed in a synthetic thumbhole stock. The flash suppressor and bayonet lug have been removed. Barrel is 20.75" and weight is approximately 10 lbs.

NIB	Exc.	V.G.	Good	Fair	Poor
1300	1000	775	500	350	150

M-14 Rifle

Imported from China by Century International this rifle features a 22" barrel chambered for the .308 Win. cartridge. Stock is walnut with rubber pad. Parkerized finish. Weight is approximately 8.25 lbs.

NIB	Exc.	V.G.	Good	Fair	Poor
750	650	550	300	150	100

Tiger Dragunov Rifle

This is a shortened version of the Russian SVD sniper rifle. Fitted with a 20.8" barrel and chambered for the 7.62x54R cartridge the rifle is sold with a 5-round magazine and a 4x range finding scope. Imported from Russia. Weight is about 8.5 lbs.

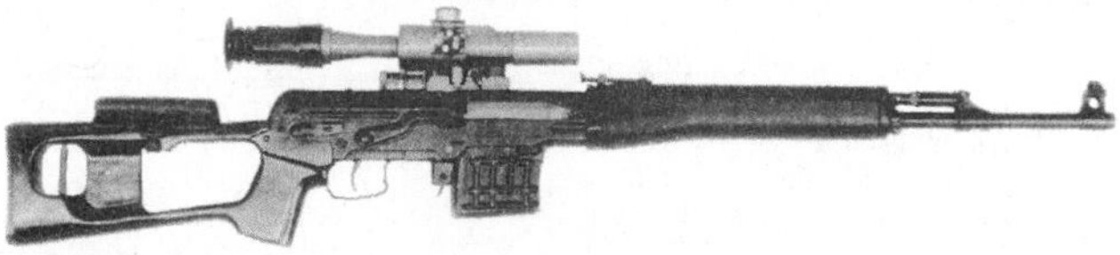

NIB	Exc.	V.G.	Good	Fair	Poor
1350	1100	800	500	350	150

CETME

Madrid, Spain

Cetme Autoloading Rifle

A .308 caliber semi-automatic rifle with a fluted chamber, a 17.74" barrel, an aperture rear sight and a 20-round detachable magazine. Black with a military-style wood stock. It is identical in appearance to the H&K 91 assault rifle.

NIB	Exc.	V.G.	Good	Fair	Poor
2500	2000	1500	900	550	300

CHAMPLIN FIREARMS

Enid, Oklahoma

Champlin Firearms Company manufactures custom order rifles built to the customer's specifications. Prospective purchasers are advised to secure a qualified appraisal prior to purchase.

Bolt-Action Rifle

These arms featured round or octagonal barrels, set triggers, a variety of sights and well figured walnut stocks.

NIB	Exc.	V.G.	Good	Fair	Poor
5500	—	3500	2900	2200	1500

CHAPMAN CHARLES
Chattanooga, Tennessee

Chapman produced a limited number of percussion carbines and rifles during the Civil War. Carbines had an overall length of 39-1/2" and .54 caliber barrels 24" in length. Their furniture was of brass. Chapman rifles resembled the U.S. Model 1841 Rifle, but did not have patchboxes. Overall length 48-1/2", barrel length 33", caliber .58. Chapman rifles and carbines are marked "C. CHAPMAN" on the lockplates.Prospective purchasers are strongly advised to secure an expert appraisal prior to acquisition.

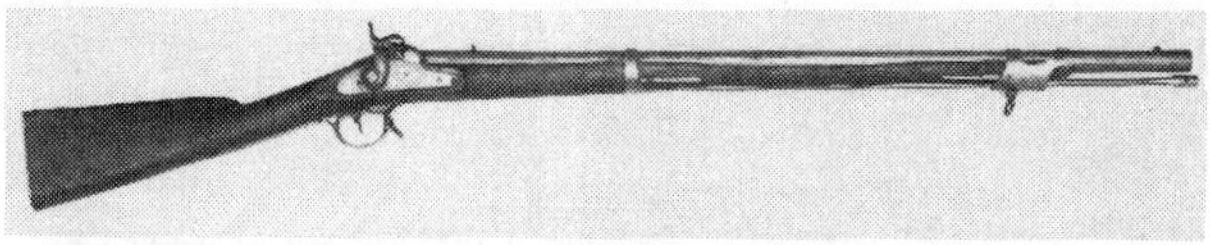

Courtesy Milwaukee Public Museum, Milwaukee, Wisconsin

NIB	Exc.	V.G.	Good	Fair	Poor
—	—	38000	17500	3000	1000

CHAPUIS ARMES
France

RG Progress

A 12, 16, or 20 gauge boxlock shotgun. Most options are available on order.

NIB	Exc.	V.G.	Good	Fair	Poor
2500	2250	2000	1800	1250	900

RG Express Model 89

A 7 x 65R, 8 x 57 JRS, 9.3 x 74R, and .375 Holland & Holland caliber sidelock, double-barreled rifle. The other features are at the customer's order.

NIB	Exc.	V.G.	Good	Fair	Poor
6500	5750	4800	4000	3000	1500

Utility Grade Express Model

A side-by-side boxlock-action double rifle with case colored or coin finish receiver. Offered in a variety of calibers: 9.3x74R, 8x57JRS, 7x65R, 8x75RS, and .30-06. Checkered walnut stock with pistol grip.

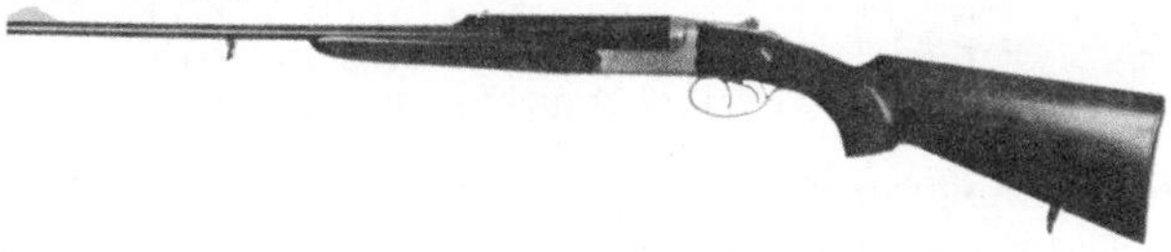

NIB	Exc.	V.G.	Good	Fair	Poor
6000	4800	4000	3000	1500	750

St. Bonnet Model

This model is a side-by-side shotgun with sideplates on a boxlock-action. Scroll engraved case colored receiver. Straight grip stock and double triggers. Offered in 12, 16, or 20 gauge.

NIB	Exc.	V.G.	Good	Fair	Poor
4000	3250	2000	1250	800	500

AFRICAN PH MODEL GRADE I

A boxlock-action double rifle offered in a wide variety of calibers. Caliber determines retail price. Hand engraved case colored receiver. Pistol grip stock with European-style cheekpiece.

.470 Nitro & .416 Rigby

NIB	Exc.	V.G.	Good	Fair	Poor
12500	9500	8500	6000	3750	700

375 H&H

NIB	Exc.	V.G.	Good	Fair	Poor
9500	7500	6250	4000	2500	600

.300 Win. Mag.

NIB	Exc.	V.G.	Good	Fair	Poor
8500	6500	5250	3000	1750	500

.30-06, 9.3x74 R

NIB	Exc.	V.G.	Good	Fair	Poor
8000	6000	5000	3000	1750	500

Grade II

Same as above but with master engraving with game scenes. Add 20 percent to 25 percent to above NIB prices.

CHARTER 2000, INC.
Shelton, Connecticut

Field King Rifle

Available with blue or stainless steel finish and chambered for .25-06, .270, .30-06, or .308 with 22" barrel. Magazine capacity is 4 rounds. Checkered fiberglass stock with cheekpiece. Weight is about 8 lbs.

NIB	Exc.	V.G.	Good	Fair	Poor
300	225	175	125	—	50

Field King Carbine

Same as above but with 18" barrel with compensator (20" total) and chambered for .308.

NIB	Exc.	V.G.	Good	Fair	Poor
350	250	200	150	—	50

CHARTER ARMS CORP.
Ansonia, Connecticut/Shelton, Connecticut

AR-7 Explorer Rifle

A .22 caliber semi-automatic rifle with a 16" barrel, 8-shot magazine and hollow plastic stock which can house the barrel when detached.

NIB	Exc.	V.G.	Good	Fair	Poor
175	125	80	60	40	25

CHEYTAC
Arco, Idaho

M-200

This bolt action rifle is chambered for the .408 CheyTac cartridge. Detachable barrel length is 30" with muzzlebrake. Magazine capacity is 7 rounds. Integral bipod. No sights, but receiver has attachable Picatinny rail. Weight is about 27 lbs.

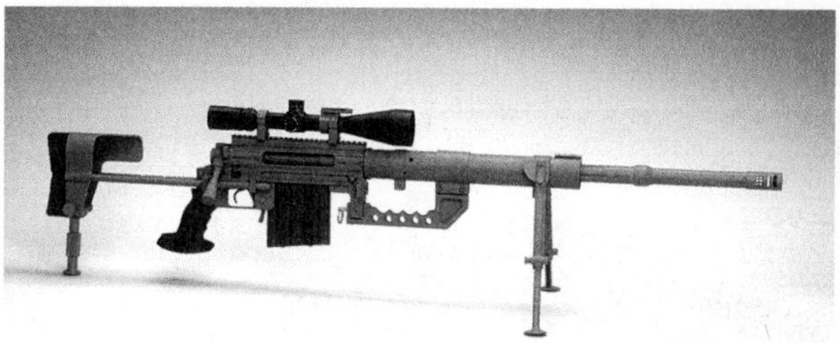

NIB	Exc.	V.G.	Good	Fair	Poor
10995	8250	6900	5400	3000	700

M-310

This is a single shot bolt action rifle chambered for the .408 CheyTac cartridge. Fitted with a 25" barrel with muzzlebrake. McMillian A-5 stock with adjustable cheekpiece. Match grade trigger. Picatinny rail. Weight is about 16.5 lbs.

NIB	Exc.	V.G.	Good	Fair	Poor
4395	3250	2750	1875	1300	500

CHIPMUNK RIFLES/ROGUE RIFLE CO.

Lewiston, Idaho

Chipmunk Single-Shot Standard Rifle

A .22 or the .22 rimfire Magnum caliber bolt-action rifle with 16.25" barrel, and open sights. Weight is approximately 3.5 lbs.

NIB	Exc.	V.G.	Good	Fair	Poor
185	150	125	100	80	60

Deluxe Chipmunk

As above, with a hand-checkered walnut stock.

NIB	Exc.	V.G.	Good	Fair	Poor
230	180	135	100	80	60

Chipmunk .17 HMR

Similar to the Standard Model but chambered for the .17 HMR cartridge. Introduced in 2002.

NIB	Exc.	V.G.	Good	Fair	Poor
200	160	125	100	75	45

Chipmunk TM

Introduced in 2002 this model features a micrometer rear sight. Stock has accessory rail installed and is adjustable for length of pull. Barrel is an 18" heavy type. Weight is about 5 lbs.

NIB	Exc.	V.G.	Good	Fair	Poor
325	250	150	125	100	75

CHRISTENSEN ARMS

Fayette, Utah

NOTE: There are a number of custom options offered by this company for its rifles. Many of these options may affect price. Prices listed are for standard models with standard features.

Carbon One

This is a bolt-action rifle with Remington 700 action chambered for .17 through .243 caliber. It is fitted with a custom trigger, Match grade stainless steel barrel and black synthetic stock. Weight is about 6 lbs.

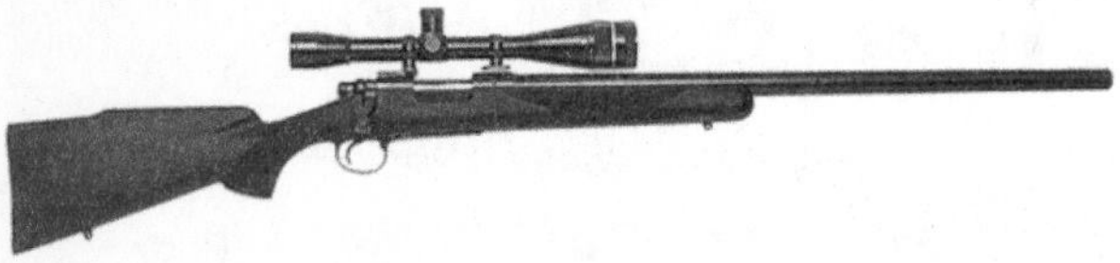

NIB	Exc.	V.G.	Good	Fair	Poor
3900	2750	1900	1200	700	500

Carbon Lite

This model is similar to above but weighs about 5 lbs.

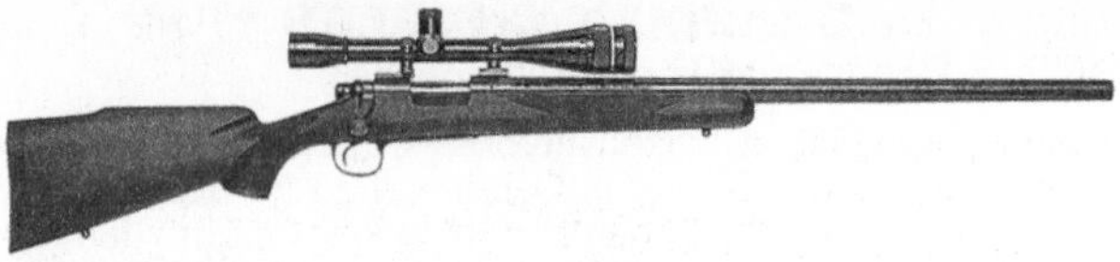

NIB	Exc.	V.G.	Good	Fair	Poor
3900	2750	1900	1200	700	500

Carbon King

This model utilizes a Remington 700 BDL long action and is chambered for .25 caliber through .30-06. Stainless steel barrel, custom trigger, and black synthetic stock are standard. Weight is approximately 6.5 lbs.

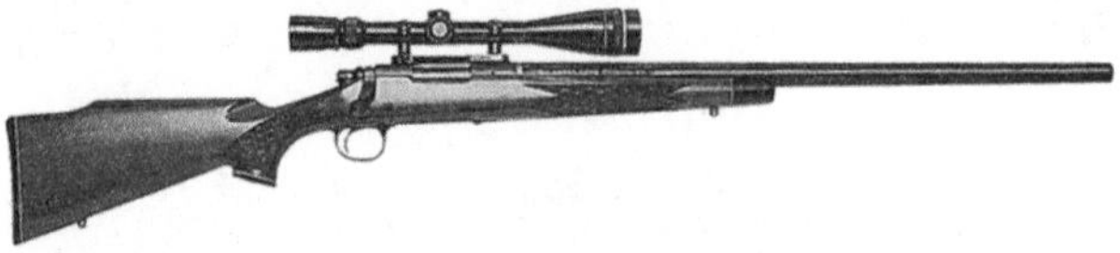

NIB	Exc.	V.G.	Good	Fair	Poor
3900	2750	1900	1200	700	500

Carbon Cannon

Similar to above model and chambered for belted magnum calibers. Weight is about 7 lbs.

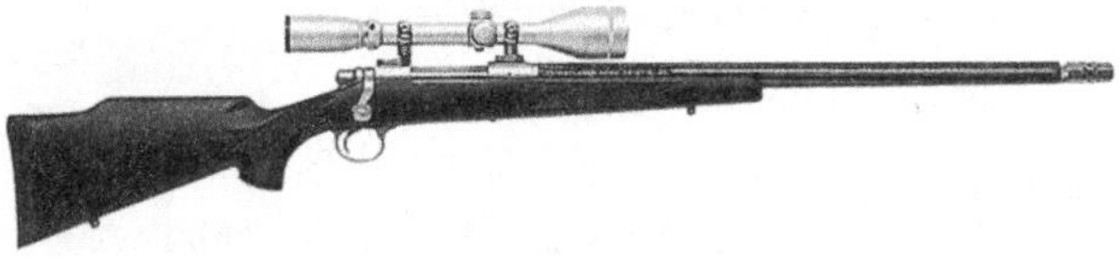

NIB	Exc.	V.G.	Good	Fair	Poor
3900	2750	1900	1200	700	500

Carbon Challenge I

This rifle is built on a Ruger 10/22 action. It is fitted with a Volquartsen trigger, stainless steel bull barrel and black synthetic stock. Weight is appr. 3.5 lbs. Add 20 percent for .17 caliber.

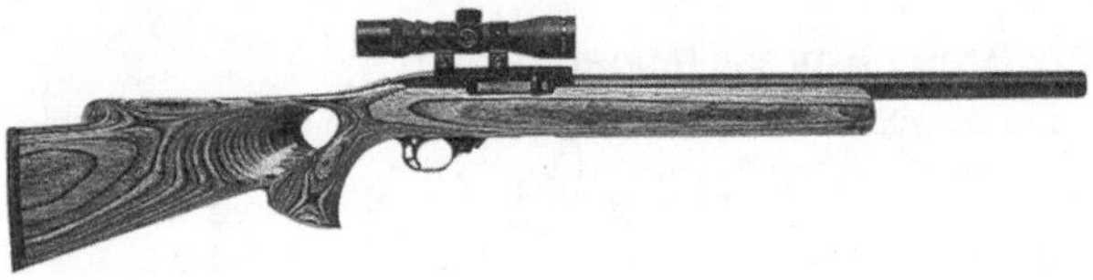

NIB	Exc.	V.G.	Good	Fair	Poor
1800	1300	875	600	400	175

Carbon Challenge II

Similar to above model but fitted with an AMT action and trigger. Weight is about 4.5 lbs. Discontinued.

NIB	Exc.	V.G.	Good	Fair	Poor
1295	995	700	550	325	125

Carbon Tactical

This bolt-action model uses a Remington 700 BDL action and is available in most any caliber. It is fitted with a custom trigger, Match grade stainless steel barrel and black synthetic stock. Weight is about 7 lbs.

NIB	Exc.	V.G.	Good	Fair	Poor
3900	2750	1900	1200	700	500

Carbon Conquest

Chambered for the .50 caliber BMG cartridge this rifle is built on a McMillan stainless steel bolt-action with magazine capacity of 5 rounds. Barrel length is 32" with muzzlebrake. Composite stock. Weight is about 20 lbs.

NIB	Exc.	V.G.	Good	Fair	Poor
6250	4000	3250	1700	875	400

NOTE: For single-shot model deduct $1,000.

Carbon One Hunter

Semi-custom bolt action rifle built around choice of receivers; steel barrel encased in carbon alloy shroud; synthetic stock. All popular calibers. Weight: 6.5-7 lbs.

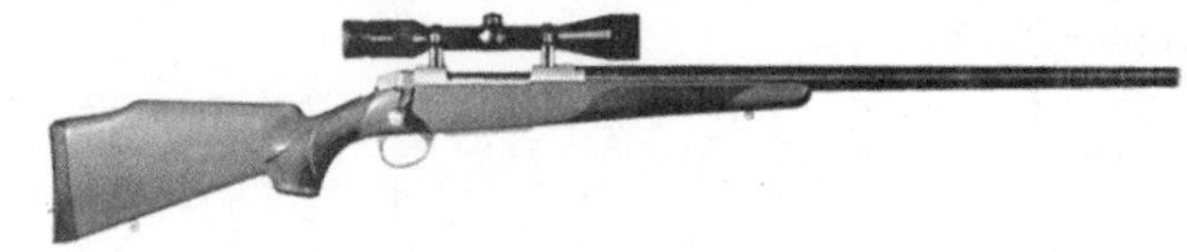

NIB	Exc.	V.G.	Good	Fair	Poor
1500	1300	875	550	375	125

Carbon Ranger Repeater

Semi-custom bolt-action rifle chambered in .50 BMG. Five-shot magazine; steel Pac-Nor barrel encased in carbon alloy. Muzzle brake. Weight: 20 lbs.

NIB	Exc.	V.G.	Good	Fair	Poor
5250	4600	3500	2350	1400	400

Carbon Ranger Single Shot

Similar to repeater but single shot.

NIB	Exc.	V.G.	Good	Fair	Poor
4700	4000	300	2000	1100	375

CHURCHILL

Various European Manufacturers and Importers

SIDE-BY-SIDES

Windsor I

A 10, 12, 16, 20, 28, and .410 bore Anson & Deeley double-barrel boxlock shotgun with barrel lengths from 23" through 32", various choke combinations, double triggers and extractors. Scroll-engraved, silver-finished, with checkered walnut pistol grip and forend.

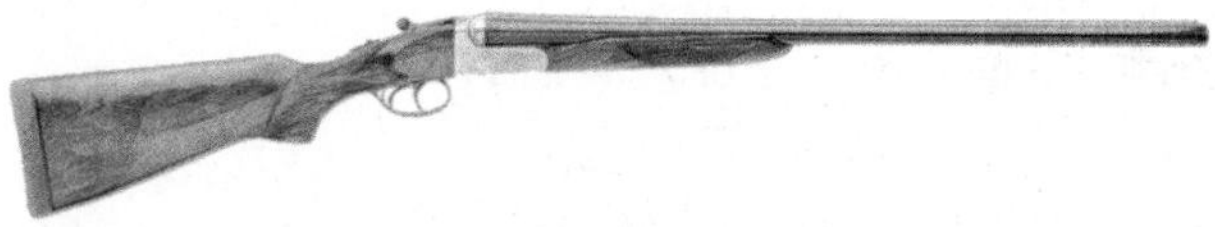

NIB	Exc.	V.G.	Good	Fair	Poor
800	600	500	400	300	200

Windsor II

As above, in 10, 12, and 20 gauge only with automatic ejectors. Not imported after 1987.

NIB	Exc.	V.G.	Good	Fair	Poor
800	600	550	450	350	250

Windsor VI

As above with sidelocks. Chambered for 12 and 20 gauge only with automatic ejectors. Not imported after 1987.

NIB	Exc.	V.G.	Good	Fair	Poor
1100	800	750	650	500	350

Royal

A 12, 20, 28 and .410 bore boxlock double-barrel shotgun with various barrel lengths and chokes, double triggers and extractors. Case hardened with checkered walnut stock. Introduced in 1988.

NIB	Exc.	V.G.	Good	Fair	Poor
650	500	425	350	275	125

OVER/UNDERS

Monarch

A 12, 20, 28, or .410 bore Over/Under shotgun with a boxlock-action, 25", 26", or 28" ventilated-rib barrels, either double- or a single-selective trigger, extractors, and a checkered walnut stock.

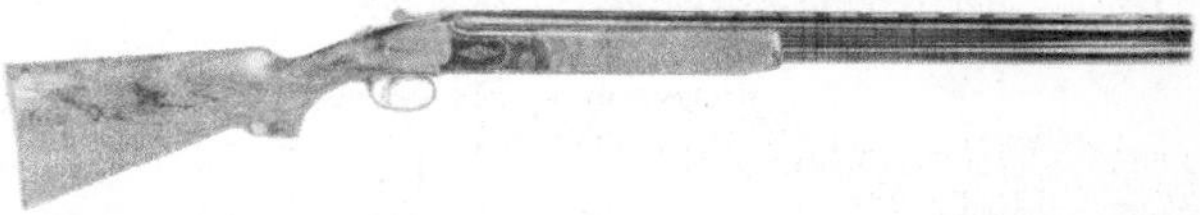

NIB	Exc.	V.G.	Good	Fair	Poor
600	475	425	375	300	150

Windsor III

A 12 and 20 and .410 bore boxlock double-barrel shotgun with 27" or 30" ventilated-rib barrels, extractors, a single-selective trigger, scroll-engraved, silver finished and a checkered walnut stock.

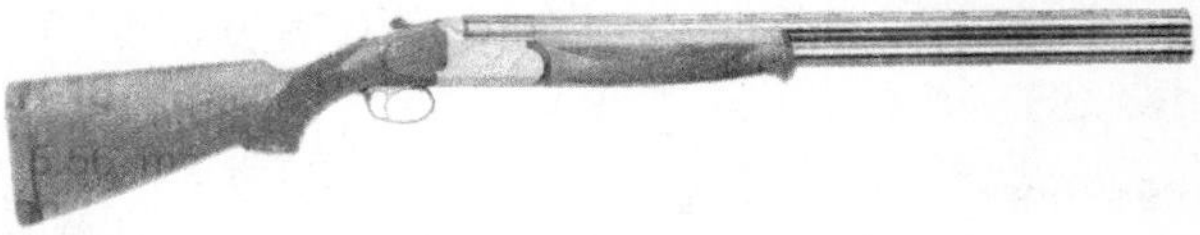

NIB	Exc.	V.G.	Good	Fair	Poor
700	575	525	475	400	200

Windsor IV

As above, with screw-in choke tubes standard. Introduced in 1989.

NIB	Exc.	V.G.	Good	Fair	Poor
975	775	650	500	425	200

Regent

As above, in 12 and 20 gauge with 27" ventilated-rib barrels, screw-in choke tubes, scroll-engraved false sideplates, automatic ejectors, a single-selective trigger, and a checkered walnut stock. Not imported after 1986.

NIB	Exc.	V.G.	Good	Fair	Poor
950	750	650	550	450	250

Regent II

As above with finer overall finishing.

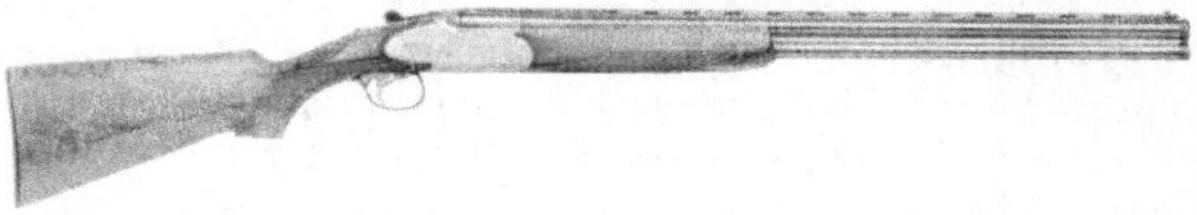

NIB	Exc.	V.G.	Good	Fair	Poor
1250	1000	850	750	500	250

Regent Shotgun/Rifle Combination

A .222, .223, .243, .270, .308, or .30-06 caliber/12 gauge Over/Under rifle/shotgun with a 25" ventilated rib, automatic ejectors and single-selective trigger. Silver finished, scroll engraved with a checkered walnut stock.

NIB	Exc.	V.G.	Good	Fair	Poor
1050	825	725	600	450	250

Windsor Grade Semi-Automatic

A 12 gauge semi-automatic shotgun with 26", 28", or 30" ventilated-rib barrels and screw-in choke tubes. An etched and anodized alloy receiver with a checkered walnut stock.

NIB	Exc.	V.G.	Good	Fair	Poor
500	375	325	275	225	175

Regent Grade Semi-Automatic

Chambered for 12 gauge with choice of 26", 28", or 30" barrels. Standard chokes or choke tubes. Walnut stock with pistol grip. Introduced in 1984 and discontinued in 1986. Weight is about 7-1/2 lbs.

NIB	Exc.	V.G.	Good	Fair	Poor
500	375	325	275	225	175

Windsor Grade Slide-Action

A 12 gauge slide-action shotgun with a 26" through 30" ventilated-rib barrel, various chokes, double slide rails, and an anodized alloy receiver. Checkered walnut stock. Discontinued in 1986.

NIB	Exc.	V.G.	Good	Fair	Poor
—	500	375	300	250	175

RIFLES

Highlander

A .25-06 through .300 Winchester Magnum caliber bolt-action rifle with a 22" barrel, with or without sights, a 3-shot magazine, and a checkered walnut stock.

NIB	Exc.	V.G.	Good	Fair	Poor
575	425	375	300	250	200

Regent

As above, with a Monte Carlo-style comb and cheekpiece. Discontinued in 1988.

NIB	Exc.	V.G.	Good	Fair	Poor
—	650	500	425	350	275

CHURCHILL, E. J. LTD.

London, England

One of One Thousand Rifle

A .270 to .458 Magnum caliber bolt-action rifle with 24" barrel and a select French walnut stock with a trap pistol-grip cap and recoil pad. Only 100 produced for the 20th anniversary of Interarms in 1973.

NIB	Exc.	V.G.	Good	Fair	Poor
—	1750	1050	850	700	550

Premier Over-and-Under

This is a sidelock ejector gun available in 12, 20 or 28 gauge. Single- or double-trigger with choice of finish. Barrel lengths built to order. Deluxe Turkish walnut with choice of grip. Fine scroll engraving. Weight for 12 gauge gun about 7 lbs., for 20 gauge guns about 6.75 lbs. Many extra cost options available.

NIB	Exc.	V.G.	Good	Fair	Poor
47000	36500	26000	20000	10000	800

NOTE: Add $3,000 for 28 gauge guns.

Premier Side-by-Side

Similar to the over-and-under gun but with side-by-side barrels. Also offered in 16 gauge as well as 12, 20, and 28 gauge. Weights are about 6.5 lbs. for 12 gauge; 6 lbs. for 16 gauge; and 5.8 lbs. for 20 gauge. Many extra options are available.

NIB	Exc.	V.G.	Good	Fair	Poor
38000	30000	20000	16500	7000	600

NOTE: Add $3,000 for 28 gauge guns.

Premier Double Rifle

Similar in construction to the side-by-side shot this rifle is chambered for the .300 H&H, .375 H&H, or .500 Nitro Express. Weight is 9.5 lbs. for the .300, 9.75 lbs. for the 375, and 12.5 lbs. for the .500. Many extra-cost options.

NIB	Exc.	V.G.	Good	Fair	Poor
55000	45000	35000	20000	13000	800

NOTE: Add $3,000 for .500 N.E. guns.

Baronet Magazine Rifle

This rifle uses the standard Mauser 98 action with fully adjustable trigger, 3 position safety, and box release floor plate. Barrel length is custom to order. Border engraving. Chambered for the .30-06 or .375 H&H. Weight for .30-06 is about 8.5 lbs., for the .375 about 9 lbs. Many extra-cost options offered. Seek an expert opinion prior to a sale.

NIB	Exc.	V.G.	Good	Fair	Poor
13000	9750	7000	45000	2750	575

CIMARRON F. A. CO.

Fredericksburg, Texas

In business since 1984 this company imports quality single-action revolvers and rifles from Uberti, Armi San Marco, and Pedersoli. **NOTE:** Cimarron also sells Uberti-manufactured blackpowder Colt reproductions, from the Patterson to the Model 1862 Pocket. For prices and specifications on these models see the Uberti section.

RIFLES

Model 1865 Spencer

Chambered for the .56-50 centerfire cartridge.

NIB	Exc.	V.G.	Good	Fair	Poor
1350	975	775	650	375	250

Henry Civil War Model

Offered in .44 WCF or .45 Long Colt with 24-1/4" barrel.

NIB	Exc.	V.G.	Good	Fair	Poor
1200	925	750	625	350	200

NOTE: For charcoal blue or white finish add $80.

Henry Civilian Model

Same as above but without military markings.

NIB	Exc.	V.G.	Good	Fair	Poor
1200	925	750	625	350	200

Model 1866 Yellowboy Carbine

Reproduction of the Winchester model 1866. Fitted with a 19" barrel and chambered for .38 Special, .44 WCF, or .45 Long Colt.

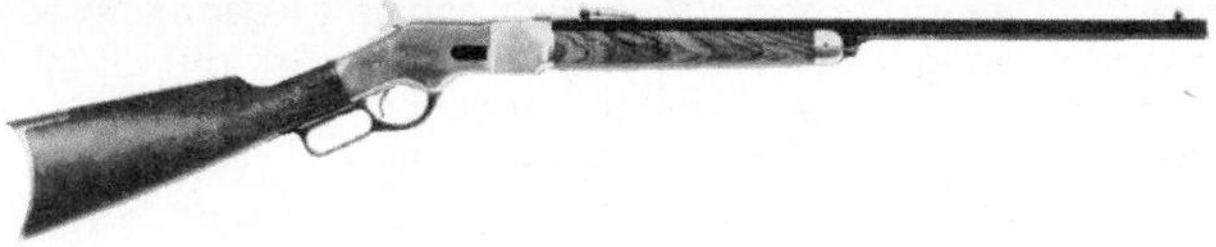

NIB	Exc.	V.G.	Good	Fair	Poor
985	750	600	525	300	150

NOTE: For charcoal blue add $40.

Model 1866 Yellowboy Rifle

Same as above but fitted with a 24-1/4" barrel.

NIB	Exc.	V.G.	Good	Fair	Poor
985	750	600	525	300	150

NOTE: For charcoal blue add $40.

Model 1866 Yellowboy Trapper

As above but with a 16" barrel.

NIB	Exc.	V.G.	Good	Fair	Poor
950	725	600	525	300	150

Model 1873 Winchester Rifle

This lever-action rifle is offered in .357 Magnum, .44 WCF, or .45 Long Colt. Fitted with a 24-1/4" barrel.

NIB	Exc.	V.G.	Good	Fair	Poor
1150	925	750	675	400	200

NOTE: For charcoal blue add $40. For pistol grip option add $140.

Model 1873 Long Range Rifle

Similar to the Model 1873 but fitted with a 30" barrel. For pistol grip option add $140.

NIB	Exc.	V.G.	Good	Fair	Poor
1175	950	775	675	400	200

NOTE: For 1 of 1000 engraving option add $1,250.

Model 1873 Carbine

Same as the standard Model 1873 but fitted with a 19" barrel.

NIB	Exc.	V.G.	Good	Fair	Poor
1150	925	750	675	400	200

NOTE: For charcoal blue add $40.

Model 1873 Short Rifle

This model is fitted with a 20" barrel. Production ceased in 1998.

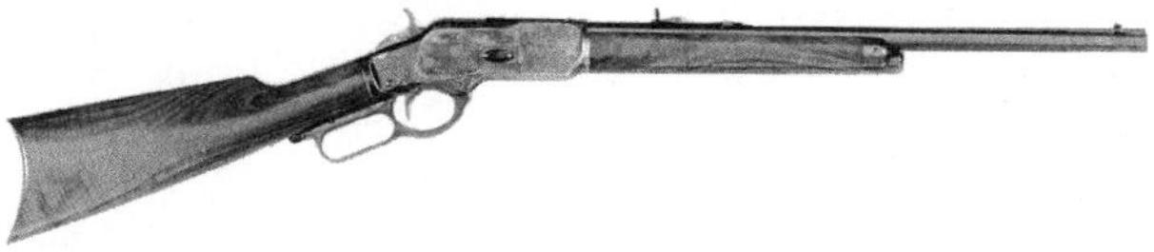

NIB	Exc.	V.G.	Good	Fair	Poor
1150	925	750	675	400	200

NOTE: For charcoal blue add $40.

Model 1873 Trapper

As above but with 16" barrel.

NIB	Exc.	V.G.	Good	Fair	Poor
1150	925	750	675	400	200

Model 1873 Deluxe Sporting Rifle

This model is fitted with a 24" barrel, checkered walnut stock with pistol grip.

NIB	Exc.	V.G.	Good	Fair	Poor
1220	925	850	725	400	200

Model 1873 Evil Roy Rifle

This model is chambered for the .357 or .45 Colt cartridge and fitted with a 20" barrel.

NIB	Exc.	V.G.	Good	Fair	Poor
1150	925	750	675	400	200

Model 1873 Larry Crow Signature Series Rifle

Chambered for the .357 or .45 Colt cartridge and fitted with a 20" barrel.

NIB	Exc.	V.G.	Good	Fair	Poor
1045	825	750	675	400	200

Model 1892 Solid Frame Rifle

Offered with either 20" or 24" octagon barrels and chambered for the .357, .44WCF, or .45 Colt cartridges.

NIB	Exc.	V.G.	Good	Fair	Poor
850	675	575	450	300	150

Model 1892 Takedown Rifle

As above but with takedown feature.

NIB	Exc.	V.G.	Good	Fair	Poor
975	775	675	525	375	200

Billy Dixon Model 1874 Sharps (Pedersoli)

A reproduction of the Model 1874 Sharps rifle chambered for the .45-70 cartridge. Fitted with a 32" tapered octagon barrel. Stock is hand checkered with oil finish walnut. Double set triggers standard. First introduced to the Cimarron product line in 1997.

NIB	Exc.	V.G.	Good	Fair	Poor
1650	1225	1100	700	500	250

Remington Rolling Block

This Remington reproduction was introduced to Cimarron in 1997 and represents the Rolling Block Sporting rifle with 30" tapered octagon barrel and chambered for .45-70 cartridge. Hand-checkered, satin-finished walnut stock.

NIB	Exc.	V.G.	Good	Fair	Poor
1300	1000	900	550	300	175

Adobe Walls Rolling Block

This model is chambered for the .45-70 cartridge and is fitted with a 30" octagon barrel. Hand-checkered walnut stock with hand finishing. Case colored receiver and German silver nose cap. Weight is about 10.13 lbs. Introduced in 2004.

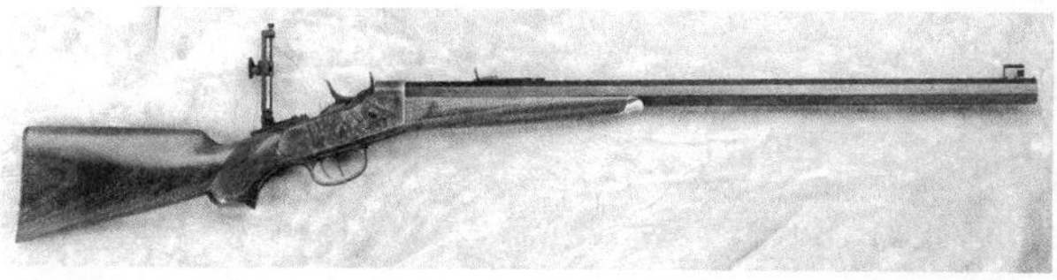

NIB	Exc.	V.G.	Good	Fair	Poor
1425	1050	950	600	350	225

Model 1885 High Wall

Reproduction of the Winchester Model 1885 chambered for .45-70, .45-90, .45-120, .40-65, .348 Win., .30-40 Krag, or .38-55 cartridges. Fitted with a 30" barrel. Walnut stock and case colored receiver.

NIB	Exc.	V.G.	Good	Fair	Poor
995	800	650	500	300	125

Model 1885 Deluxe High Wall

As above but with checkered walnut stock with pistol grip.

NIB	Exc.	V.G.	Good	Fair	Poor
1175	875	700	550	300	125

Model 1885 Low Wall

Introduced in 2004 this model is chambered for the .22 Long Rifle, .22 Hornet, .30-30, .32-20, .38-40, .357 Mag, .44-40, and .44 Mag cartridges. Hand checkered walnut stock with pistol grip. Octagon barrel is 30" long. Single or double-set trigger.

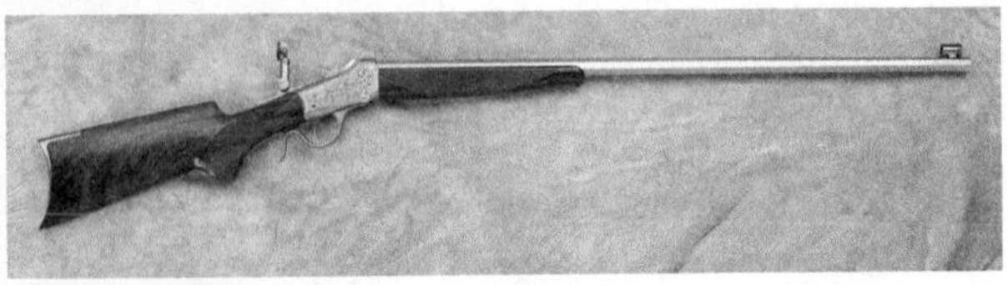

NIB	Exc.	V.G.	Good	Fair	Poor
1175	850	700	550	300	125

Texas Ranger Carbine

This model is a copy of the Sharps Model 1859 Military Carbine. Round barrel is 22" long. Receiver is case colored. Stock is American black walnut. Chambered for the .45-70 cartridge. Marked "T*S" on the barrel. Introduced in 2004.

NIB	Exc.	V.G.	Good	Fair	Poor
1200	900	725	600	350	150

Sharps Silhouette

Offered in .45-70 or .40-65 calibers with 32" octagon barrel. Introduced in 1998.

NIB	Exc.	V.G.	Good	Fair	Poor
1095	850	700	600	350	150

Quigley Sharps Sporting Rifle

This rifle is chambered for the .45-70 or .45-120 caliber and fitted with a heavy 34" octagon barrel. Introduced in 1998.

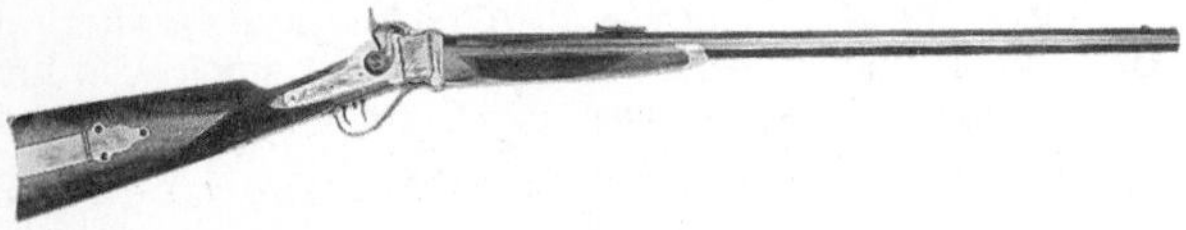

NIB	Exc.	V.G.	Good	Fair	Poor
1725	1350	1175	700	450	275

Billy Dixon Model 1874 Sharps (Armi-Sport)

Fitted with a 32" barrel and chambered for the .45-70, .45-90, or the .50-70. Introduced in 1995.

NIB	Exc.	V.G.	Good	Fair	Poor
1350	1025	875	500	300	150

Sharp's No. 1 Sporting Rifle

Plain walnut stock with pistol grip. Fitted with a 32" barrel. Chambered for the .45-70 cartridge.

NIB	Exc.	V.G.	Good	Fair	Poor
1350	1050	900	500	300	150

Pride of the Plains Model

Based on the Sharps Model 1874 Sporting Rifle, this model, chambered for the .45-70 cartridge, features a 32" octagon barrel, hand-checkered walnut stock with pistol grip, coin nickel receiver, Creedmore tang sight, and target front sight with inserts. Introduced in 2004.

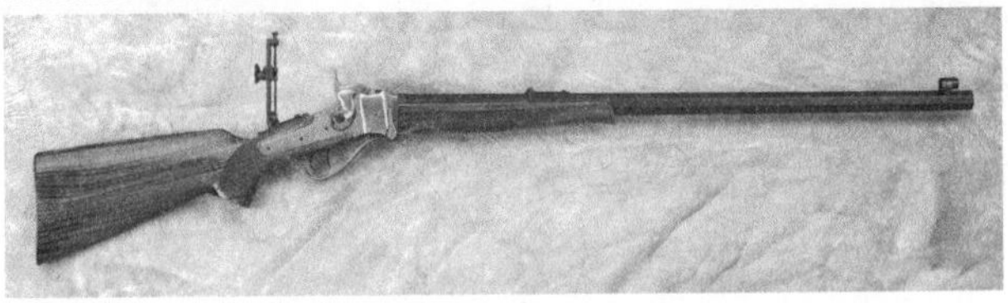

NIB	Exc.	V.G.	Good	Fair	Poor
1620	1200	925	500	300	150

Professional Hunter Model

This model is the basic Sharps Model 1874 chambered for the .45-70 cartridge. Fitted with a 32" barrel, case colored receiver, walnut stock with shotgun butt and double-set triggers. Introduced in 2004.

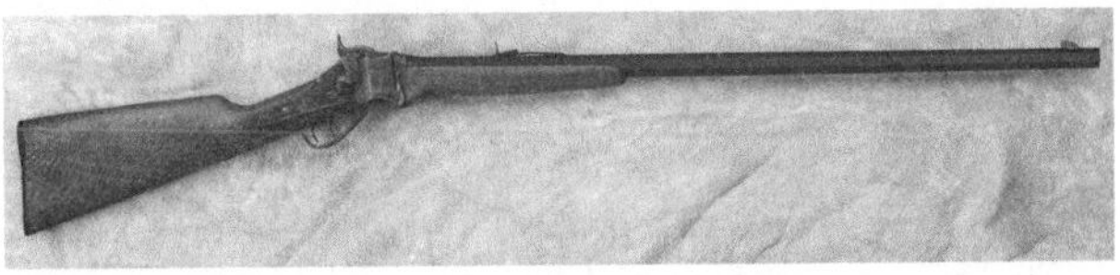

NIB	Exc.	V.G.	Good	Fair	Poor
1160	850	725	500	300	150

Big Fifty Model

Chambered for the .50-90 cartridge and fitted with a 34" half-octagon barrel. Fancy walnut stock with hand checkering and pistol grip. Case colored receiver, German silver nose cap, and Hartford-style Soule Creedmore sights with spirit level and globe front sight. Weight is about 11 lbs. Introduced in 2004.

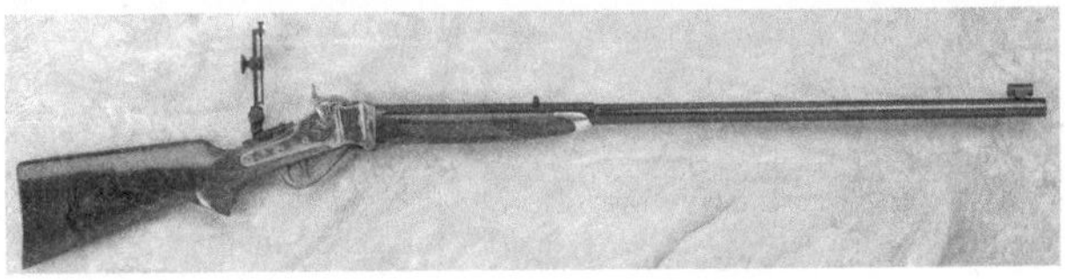

NIB	Exc.	V.G.	Good	Fair	Poor
1890	1400	1150	700	450	275

Springfield Trapdoor Carbine

Based on the famous Springfield design. Chambered for the .45-70.

NIB	Exc.	V.G.	Good	Fair	Poor
995	800	625	425	250	125

Springfield Trapdoor Officer's Model

This is the Officer's version of the Springfield Trapdoor model. Chambered for .45-70.

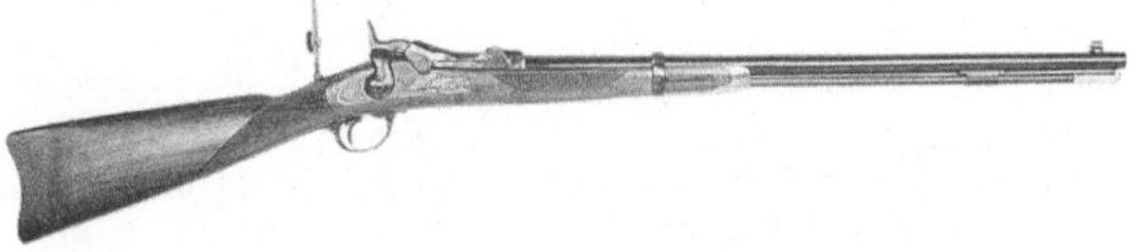

NIB	Exc.	V.G.	Good	Fair	Poor
1150	900	775	500	275	150

CLAPP, HOFFMAN & CO. CLAPP, GATES & CO. RIFLES

Alamance, North Carolina

Maker of Confederate Civil War rifles, 1862 - 1864. Overall length: Types I, II, & III 51-1/4" to 52", Type IV varies between 46-1/2" and 51"; barrel length: Types I, II, & III 35-1/4" to 36", Type IV varies between 31-1/4" and 35-7/8"; caliber: Types I, II, & III .50, Type IV .577; markings: none. Despite the absence of makers marks, the Clapp, Gates & Co. products are readily distinguished by their part-round, part-octagonal (octagonal section on Types I to III, about 4" long, 4-3/4" to 5-1/2" on Type IV rifles) barrels having only a slightly raised bolster projecting from the upper right quarter. This small bolster accommodates the boxlock that distinguished the first 100 rifles produced. This gave way to a standard percussion lock on subsequent production, which required that the hammer bend sharply to the left to strike the cone. Type I and Type II rifles were adapted to a "footprint" saber bayonet lug on the right side of the barrel; Types III and IV also had a saber bayonet lug on the right side of the barrel but of the standard pattern. Types III and IV are distinguished by their caliber, the former being .50, the latter .577. Prices reflect Type II through IV production; Type I (while extant) has never been offered for sale and would presumably bring a significantly higher premium.

NIB	*Exc.*	*V.G.*	*Good*	*Fair*	*Poor*
—	—	39500	19500	3900	1200

CLASSIC DOUBLES

Tochigi City, Japan

Importer of Japanese shotguns formerly imported by Winchester as the Model 101 and Model 23. These models were discontinued by Winchester in 1987 and imported by Classic Doubles until 1990.

Model 201 Classic

A 12 or 20 gauge boxlock side-by-side double-barrel shotgun with 26" ventilated-rib barrels, screw-in choke tubes single-selective trigger and automatic ejectors. Blued with checkered walnut stock and beavertail forearm.

NIB	*Exc.*	*V.G.*	*Good*	*Fair*	*Poor*
2400	1950	1700	1500	1250	900

Model 201 Small Bore Set

As above, with a smaller receiver and two sets of barrels chambered for 28 gauge and .410. The barrels are 28" in length.

NIB	*Exc.*	*V.G.*	*Good*	*Fair*	*Poor*
4100	3500	2950	2250	1750	1250

Model 101 Classic Field Grade I

A 12 or 20 gauge Over/Under shotgun with 25.5" or 28" ventilated-rib barrels, screw-in choke tubes, automatic ejectors and a single-selective trigger. Engraved, blued with checkered walnut stock.

NIB	*Exc.*	*V.G.*	*Good*	*Fair*	*Poor*
2000	1750	1500	1250	1000	700

Classic Field Grade II

As above, in 28 gauge and .410, highly engraved with a coin-finished receiver and a deluxe walnut stock with a round knob pistol grip and fleur-de-lis checkering.

NIB	*Exc.*	*V.G.*	*Good*	*Fair*	*Poor*
2500	2000	1750	1500	1250	900

Classic Sporter

As above, in 12 gauge only with 28" or 30" barrels, ventilated rib and screw-in choke tubes. The frame is coin-finished with light engraving and a matted upper surface to reduce glare. The stock is select walnut. This model was designed for sporting clays.

NIB	*Exc.*	*V.G.*	*Good*	*Fair*	*Poor*
2250	1800	1500	1250	1000	700

Waterfowl Model

As above with 30" barrels, 3" chambers, vent-rib, and screw-in choke tubes. The overall finish is a subdued matte with light engraving.

NIB	*Exc.*	*V.G.*	*Good*	*Fair*	*Poor*
1650	1350	1000	850	650	500

Classic Trap Over-and-Under

Designed for competition trap shooting with 30" or 32" barrels, a ventilated center and top rib, automatic ejectors, screw-in choke tubes, and a single trigger. Blued with light engraving and a walnut stock in straight or Monte Carlo style.

NIB	*Exc.*	*V.G.*	*Good*	*Fair*	*Poor*
2250	1750	1500	1250	1000	700

Classic Trap Single

As above, with a single 32" or 34" barrel.

NIB	*Exc.*	*V.G.*	*Good*	*Fair*	*Poor*
2250	1800	1500	1250	1000	700

Classic Trap Combo

As above, with a single barrel and a set of over-and-under barrels.

NIB	*Exc.*	*V.G.*	*Good*	*Fair*	*Poor*
3000	2500	2000	1750	1250	1000

Classic Skeet

As above, with 27.5" barrels.

NIB	*Exc.*	*V.G.*	*Good*	*Fair*	*Poor*
2250	1750	1500	1250	1000	700

Classic Skeet 4 Gauge Set

As above, furnished with four sets of barrels chambered for 12, 20, 28 gauge, and .410.

NIB	*Exc.*	*V.G.*	*Good*	*Fair*	*Poor*
4150	3750	3000	2500	1850	1500

CLERKE PRODUCTS

Santa Monica, California

Hi-Wall

A copy of the Winchester Model 1885 High Wall rifle with the action activated by a lever, and the receiver is case colored. This rifle is chambered for almost all of the modern calibers and features a 26" barrel and a walnut stock with a pistol grip and a schnabel forend. It was manufactured between 1972 and 1974.

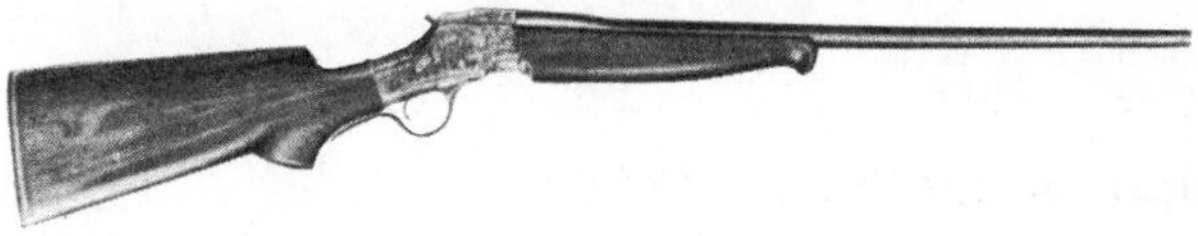

NIB	*Exc.*	*V.G.*	*Good*	*Fair*	*Poor*
975	850	650	425	300	200

Deluxe Hi-Wall

As above, with a half-round/half-octagonal barrel, select walnut stock, and a recoil pad. It was manufactured between 1972 and 1974.

NIB	*Exc.*	*V.G.*	*Good*	*Fair*	*Poor*
1100	975	750	525	400	250

COBRAY INDUSTRIES

S.W.D., Inc.
Atlanta, Georgia

TM-11 Carbine

Similar to the MII and M12 pistols in 9mm caliber, with a 16.25" shrouded barrel and a telescoping metal shoulder stock.

NIB	*Exc.*	*V.G.*	*Good*	*Fair*	*Poor*
—	450	350	225	150	100

TM-12 Carbine

As above but chambered for the .380 ACP cartridge.

NIB	Exc.	V.G.	Good	Fair	Poor
—	450	350	225	150	100

Terminator Shotgun

A single-shot 12 or 20 gauge shotgun that fires from an open bolt position. The cocked bolt is released to slam home on the shell when the trigger is pulled. The 18" barrel is cylinder bored. There is a telescoping wire stock and the finish is Parkerized. We have seen many of these advertised at sky-high prices, but junk is junk.

NIB	Exc.	V.G.	Good	Fair	Poor
—	175	125	80	60	40

CODY, MICHAEL & SONS

Nashville, Tennessee

Received a contract with the State of Tennessee for "Mississippi" rifles with brass patchboxes in late 1861. Barrel length 36"; caliber .54. Cody often used reworked Model 1817 Rifle barrels and sporting pattern single screw lockplates. Rifles are unmarked except for large engraved serial number on top of breech plug tang.

NIB	Exc.	V.G.	Good	Fair	Poor
—	—	29500	13000	2150	775

COLT'S PATENT FIRE ARMS MANUFACTURING COMPANY

Hartford, Connecticut

COLT REVOLVING LONG GUNS 1837-1847

First Model Ring Lever Rifle

This was actually the first firearm manufactured by Colt; the first revolver appeared a short time later. There were 200 of the First Models made in 1837 and 1838. The octagonal barrel of the First Model is 32" long and browned, while the rest of the finish is blued. The stock is varnished walnut with a cheekpiece inlaid with Colt's trademark. The ring lever located in front of the frame is pulled to rotate the 8-shot cylinder and cock the hammer. The rifle is chambered for .34, .36, .38, .40, and .44 caliber percussion. The cylinder is roll-engraved, and the barrel is stamped "Colt's Patent/Patent Arms Mfg. Co., Paterson, N. Jersey." This model has a top strap over the cylinder. They were made both with and without an attached loading lever. The latter is worth approximately 10 percent more.

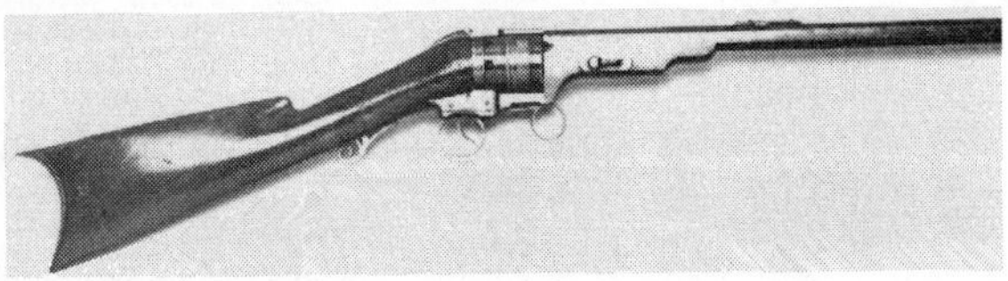

Courtesy Bonhams & Butterfields, San Francisco, California

NIB	Exc.	V.G.	Good	Fair	Poor
—	—	—	90000	40000	9750

Second Model Ring Lever Rifle

This model is quite similar in appearance to the First Model. Its function is identical. The major difference is the absence of the top strap over the cylinder. It had no trademark stamped on the cheekpiece. The Second Model is offered with a 28" and a 32" octagonal barrel and is chambered for .44 caliber percussion, holding 8 shots. There were approximately 500 produced from 1838-1841. The presence of an attached cheekpiece would add approximately 10 percent to the value.

Courtesy Bonhams & Butterfields, San Francisco, California

NIB	Exc.	V.G.	Good	Fair	Poor
—	—	—	80000	19500	8000

Model 1839 Shotgun

This model is quite similar in appearance to the 1839 Carbine. It is chambered for 16 gauge and holds six shots. It has a Damascus pattern barrel, and the most notable difference is a 3.5" (instead of a 2.5") long cylinder. There were only 225 of these made from 1839-1841. The markings are the same as on the Carbine.

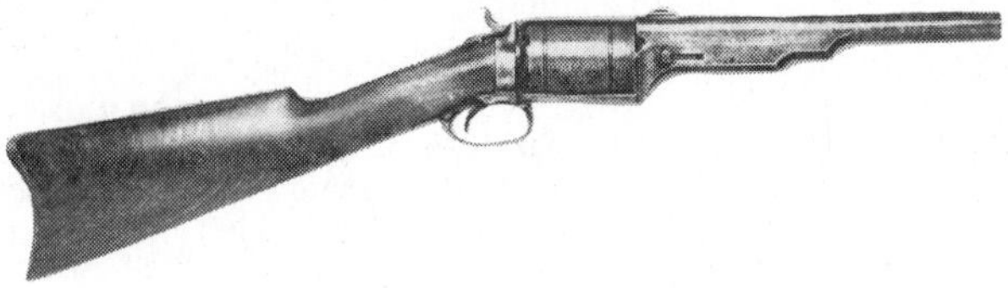

Courtesy Bonhams & Butterfields, San Francisco, California

NIB	Exc.	V.G.	Good	Fair	Poor
—	—	37500	29500	11000	6000

Model 1839 Carbine

This model has no ring but features an exposed hammer for cocking and rotating the 6-shot cylinder. It is chambered for .525 smoothbore and comes standard with a 24" round barrel. Other barrel lengths have been noted. The finish is blued, with a browned barrel and a varnished walnut stock. The cylinder is roll-engraved, and the barrel is stamped "Patent Arms Mfg. Co. Paterson, N.J.-Colt's Pt." There were 950 manufactured from 1838-1841. Later variations of this model are found with the attached loading lever standard, and earlier models without one would bring approximately 25 percent additional. There were 360 purchased by the military and stamped "WAT" on the stock. These would be worth twice what a standard model would bring.

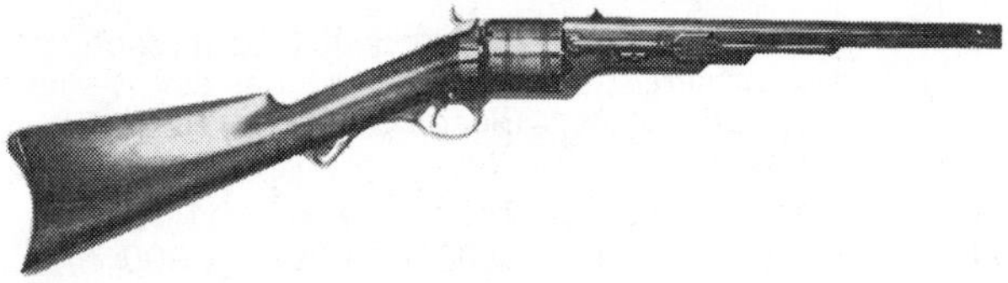

Courtesy Bonhams & Butterfields, San Francisco, California

NIB	Exc.	V.G.	Good	Fair	Poor
—	—	6300	45000	13500	7900

Model 1839/1850 Carbine

In 1848 Colt acquired a number of Model 1839 Carbines (approximately 40) from the state of Rhode Island. In an effort to make them marketable they were refinished and the majority fitted with plain cylinders (brightly polished) having integral ratchets around the arbor hole. Barrel length 24"; caliber .525; barrel browned; cylinder polished; frame blued; furniture case hardened; walnut stock varnished.

NIB	Exc.	V.G.	Good	Fair	Poor
—	—	70000	55000	18500	6500

Model 1854 Russian Contract Musket

In 1854 Colt purchased a large number of U.S. Model 1822 flintlock muskets that the company altered to percussion cap ignition and rifled. The reworked muskets are dated 1854 on the barrel tang and at the rear of the lockplate. In most instances the original manufactory marks, such as Springfield or Harpers Ferry at the rear of the lockplate, have been removed, while the U.S. and eagle between the hammer and bolster remain. The percussion nipple bolster is marked COLT'S PATENT. Some examples have been noted with the date 1858. Barrel length 42"; caliber .69; lock and furniture burnished bright; walnut stock oil finished.

NIB	Exc.	V.G.	Good	Fair	Poor
—	15000	10000	5000	1500	750

COLT SIDE HAMMER LONG GUNS

MODEL 1855 SPORTING RIFLE, 1ST MODEL

This is a 6-shot revolving rifle chambered for .36 caliber percussion. It comes with a 21", 24", 27", or 30" round barrel that is part octagonal where it joins the frame. The stock is walnut with either an oil or a varnish finish. The frame, hammer, and loading lever are case colored; the rest of the metal, blued. The hammer is on the right side of the frame. The 1st Model has no forend, and an oiling device is attached to the barrel underlug. The trigger guard has two spur-like projections in front and in back of the bow. The roll-engraved cylinder scene depicts a hunter shooting at five deer and is found only on this model. The standard stampings are " Colt's Pt./1856" and "Address S. Colt Hartford, Ct. U.S.A."

Early Model

Low serial numbers with a hand-engraved barrel marking "Address S. Colt Hartford, U.S.A."

NIB	Exc.	V.G.	Good	Fair	Poor
—	—	16500	15000	5500	1500

Production Model

NIB	Exc.	V.G.	Good	Fair	Poor
—	—	15000	12000	3000	1000

Carbine

Identical to the 1st Model Rifle but offered with a 15" and 18" barrel.

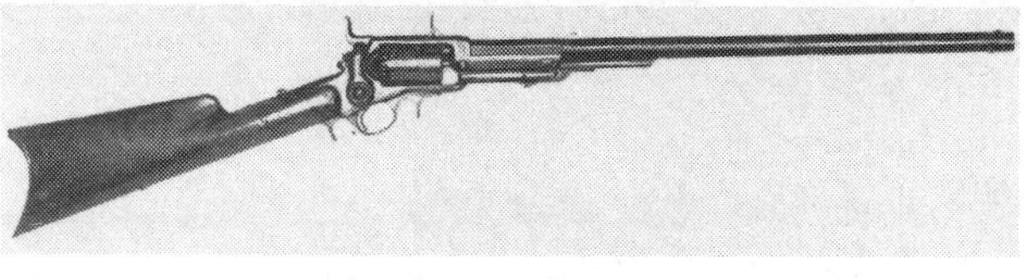

Courtesy Milwaukee Public Museum, Milwaukee, Wisconsin

NIB	Exc.	V.G.	Good	Fair	Poor
—	—	12500	9500	3000	1000

Model 1855 Half Stock Sporting Rifle

Although this rifle is quite similar in appearance and finish to the 1st Model, there are some notable differences. It features a walnut forend that protrudes halfway down the barrel. There are two types of trigger guards—a short projectionless one or a long model with a graceful scroll. There is a 6-shot model chambered for .36 or .44 caliber or a 5-shot model chambered for .56 caliber. The cylinder is fully fluted. The markings are "Colt's Pt/1856" and "Address Col. Colt/Hartford Ct. U.S.A." There were approximately 1,500 manufactured between 1857 and 1864.

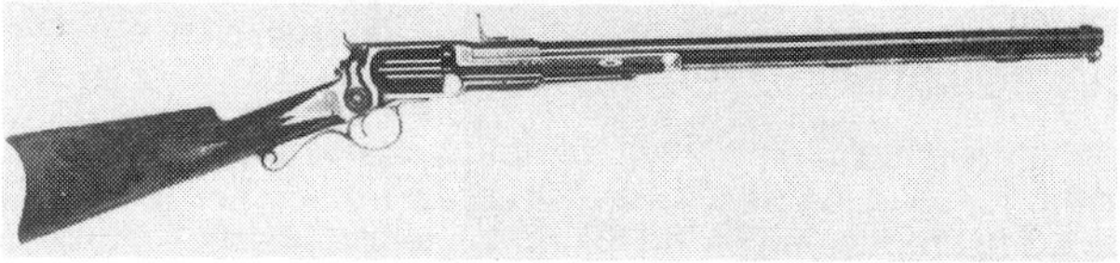

Courtesy Milwaukee Public Museum, Milwaukee, Wisconsin

NIB	Exc.	V.G.	Good	Fair	Poor
—	—	12500	9500	3500	1000

Model 1855 Full Stock Military Rifle

This model holds 6 shots in its .44 caliber chambering and 5 shots when chambered for .56 caliber. It is another side hammer revolving rifle that resembles the Half Stock model. The barrels are round and part-octagonal where they join the frame. They come in lengths of 21", 24", 27", 31", and 37". The hammer and loading lever are case colored; the rest of the metal parts, blued. The walnut buttstock and full length forend are oil finished, and this model has sling swivels. The cylinder is fully fluted. Military models have provisions for affixing a bayonet and military-style sights and bear the "U.S." martial mark on examples that were actually issued to the military. The standard stampings found on this model are "Colt's Pt/1856" and "Address Col. Colt Hartford, Ct. U.S.A." There were an estimated 9,300 manufactured between 1856 and 1864.

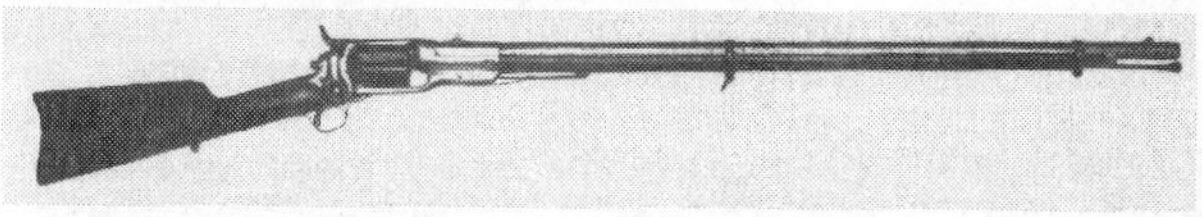

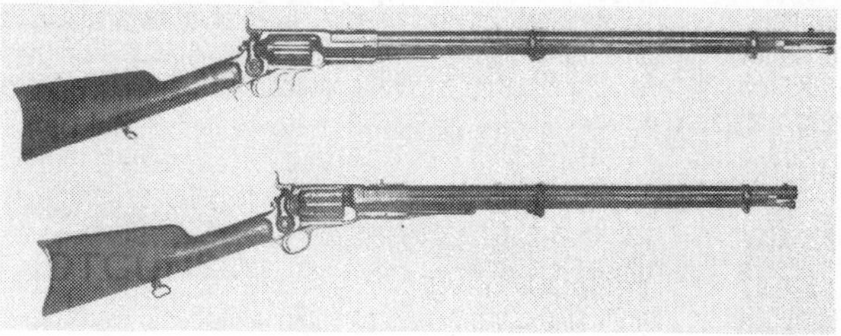

Courtesy Milwaukee Public Museum, Milwaukee, Wisconsin

Model 1855 Full Stock Military Rifle Martially Marked Models

NIB	Exc.	V.G.	Good	Fair	Poor
—	—	42500	25000	9500	2000

Model 1855 Full Stock Military Rifle Without Martial Markings

NIB	Exc.	V.G.	Good	Fair	Poor
—	—	13500	9750	3500	1000

Model 1855 Full Stock Sporting Rifle

This model is similar in appearance to the Military model, with these notable exceptions. There is no provision for attaching a bayonet, there are no sling swivels, and it has sporting-style sights. The buttplate is crescent shaped. This model has been noted chambered for .56 caliber in a 5-shot version and chambered for .36, .40, .44, and .50 caliber in the 6-shot variation. They are quite scarce in .40 and .50 caliber and will bring a 10 percent premium. The standard markings are "Colt's Pt/1856" and "Address Col. Colt/Hartford Ct. U.S.A." Production on this model was quite limited (several hundred at most) between the years 1856 and 1864.

NIB	Exc.	V.G.	Good	Fair	Poor
—	—	20000	13500	4000	1000

Model 1855 Revolving Carbine

This model is similar in appearance to the 1855 Military Rifle. The barrel lengths of 15", 18", and 21" plus the absence of a forend make the standard Carbine Model readily identifiable. The markings are the same. Approximately 4,400 were manufactured between 1856 and 1864.

NIB	Exc.	V.G.	Good	Fair	Poor
—	—	13500	9500	4000	1000

Model 1855 Artillery Carbine

Identical to the standard carbine but chambered for .56 caliber only, it has a 24" barrel, full-length walnut forend, and a bayonet lug.

NIB	Exc.	V.G.	Good	Fair	Poor
—	—	23500	17000	5500	1500

Model 1855 British Carbine

This is a British-proofed version with barrel lengths of up to 30". It has a brass trigger guard and buttplate and is chambered for .56 caliber only. This variation is usually found in the 10000-12000 serial number range.

NIB	Exc.	V.G.	Good	Fair	Poor
—	—	18500	13000	3750	1000

MODEL 1855 REVOLVING SHOTGUN

This model very much resembles the Half Stock Sporting Rifle but was made with a 27", 30", 33", and 36" smoothbore barrel.

It has a 5-shot cylinder chambered for .60 or .75 caliber (20 or 10 gauge). This model has a case-colored hammer and loading lever; the rest of the metal is blued, with an occasional browned barrel noted. The buttstock and forend are of walnut, either oil or varnish-finished. This model has no rear sight and a small trigger guard with the caliber stamped on it. Some have been noted with the large scroll trigger guard; these would add 10 percent to the value. The rarest shotgun variation would be a full stocked version in either gauge, and qualified appraisal would be highly recommended. This model is serial numbered in its own range, #1-#1100. They were manufactured from 1860-1863.

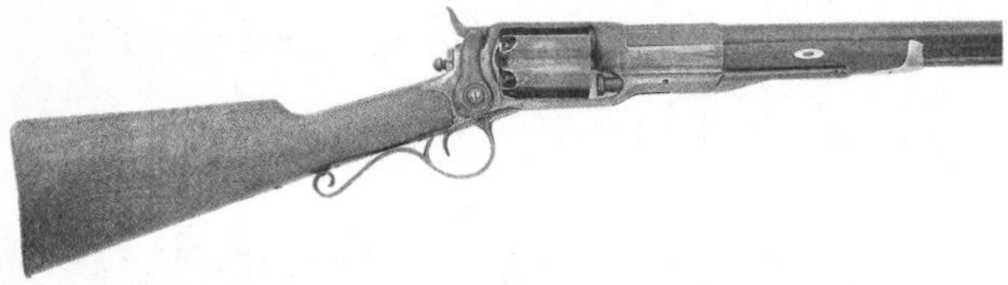

Courtesy Amoskeag Auction Company

.60 Caliber (20 gauge)

NIB	Exc.	V.G.	Good	Fair	Poor
—	—	22500	10000	3500	1000

.75 Caliber (10 gauge)

NIB	Exc.	V.G.	Good	Fair	Poor
—	—	22500	10000	3500	1000

Model 1861 Single-Shot Rifled Musket

With the advent of the Civil War, the army of the Union seriously needed military arms. Colt was given a contract to supply 112,500 1861-pattern percussion single-shot muskets. Between 1861 and 1865, 75,000 were delivered. They have 40" rifled barrels chambered for .58 caliber. The musket is equipped with military sights, sling swivels, and a bayonet lug. The metal finish is bright steel, and the stock is oil-finished walnut. Military inspector's marks are found on all major parts. "VP" over an eagle is stamped on the breech along with a date. The Colt address and a date are stamped on the lockplate. A large number of these rifles were altered to the Snyder breech loading system for the Bey of Egypt.

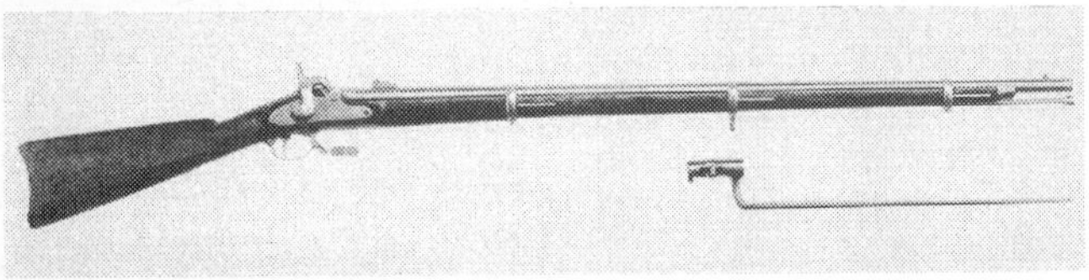

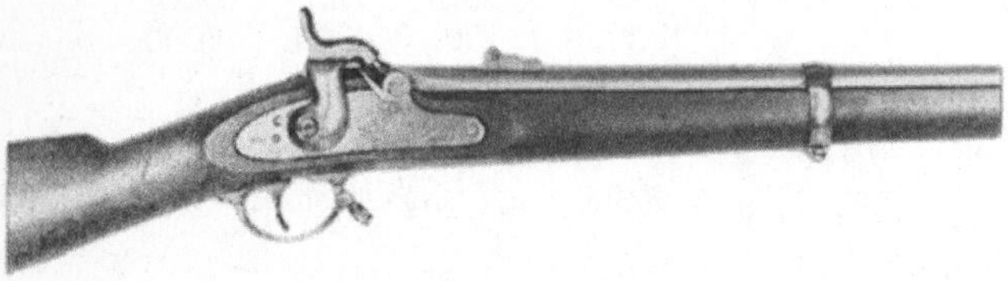

Courtesy Milwaukee Public Museum, Milwaukee, Wisconsin

Model 1861 Single-Shot Rifled Musket Production Model

NIB	Exc.	V.G.	Good	Fair	Poor
—	—	5500	2000	750	450

COLT ANTIQUE LONG ARMS

BERDAN SINGLE-SHOT RIFLE

This is a scarce rifle on today's market. There were approximately 30,200 manufactured, but nearly 30,000 of them were sent to Russia. This rifle was produced from 1866-1870. It is a trapdoor-type action chambered for .42 centerfire. The standard model has a 32.5" barrel; the carbine, 18.25". The finish is blued, with a walnut stock. This rifle was designed and the patent held by Hiram Berdan, Commander of the Civil War "Sharpshooters" Regiment. This was actually Colt's first cartridge arm. The 30,000 rifles and 25 half-stocked carbines that were sent to Russia were in Russian Cyrillic letters. The few examples made for American sales have Colt's name and Hartford address on the barrel.

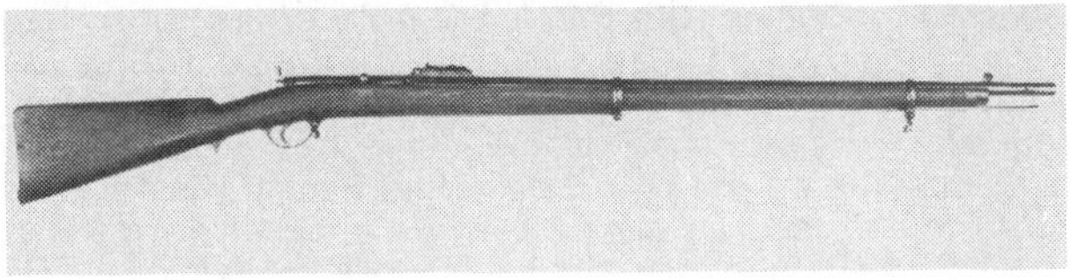

Courtesy Milwaukee Public Museum, Milwaukee, Wisconsin

Rifle Russian Order

30,000 manufactured.

NIB	Exc.	V.G.	Good	Fair	Poor
—	15000	10000	5000	1500	750

Carbine Russian Order

25 manufactured.

NIB	Exc.	V.G.	Good	Fair	Poor
—	18000	12500	6500	1800	750

Rifle U.S. Sales

100 manufactured.

NIB	Exc.	V.G.	Good	Fair	Poor
—	15000	10000	5000	1500	750

Carbine U.S. Sales

25 manufactured.

NIB	Exc.	V.G.	Good	Fair	Poor
—	18000	12500	6500	1800	750

Colt-Franklin Military Rifle

This is a rifle that was not a successful venture for Colt. The patents were held by William B. Franklin, a vice-president of the company. This was a bolt-action rifle with a primitive, gravity-fed box magazine. It is chambered for the .45-70 government cartridge, has a 32.5" barrel, and is blued, with a walnut stock. The rifle has the Colt Hartford barrel address and is stamped with an eagle's head and U.S. inspectors marks. There were only 50 of these rifles produced, and it is believed that they were prototypes intended for government sales. This was not to be, and production ceased after approximately 50 were manufactured in 1887 and 1888.

NIB	Exc.	V.G.	Good	Fair	Poor
—	—	9500	5000	2000	1100

COLT-BURGESS LEVER-ACTION RIFLE

This represented Colt's only attempt to compete with Winchester for the lever-action rifle market. It is said that when Winchester started to produce revolving handguns for prospective marketing, Colt dropped the Burgess from its line. This rifle is chambered for .44-40. It has a 25.5" barrel and a 15-shot tubular magazine. The Carbine version has a 20.5" barrel and 12-shot magazine. The finish is blued, with a case-colored hammer and lever. The stock is walnut with an oil finish. The Colt Hartford address is on the barrel, and "Burgess Patents" is stamped on the bottom of the lever. There were 3,775 rifles manufactured—1,219 with round barrels and 2,556 with octagonal barrels. There were also 2,593 Carbines. The Burgess was produced from 1883-1885.

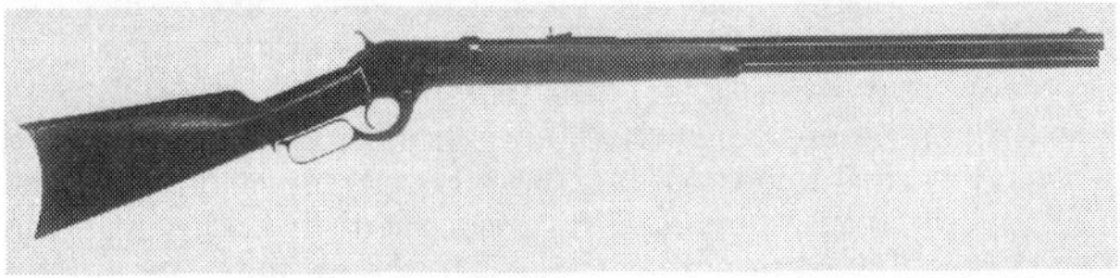

Courtesy Buffalo Bill Historical Center, Cody, Wyoming

Rifle Octagonal Barrel.

NIB	Exc.	V.G.	Good	Fair	Poor
—	—	5500	3500	1500	550

Rifle Round Barrel.

NIB	Exc.	V.G.	Good	Fair	Poor
—	—	5200	3500	1500	550

Rifle Carbine

NIB	Exc.	V.G.	Good	Fair	Poor
—	—	6000	5000	2000	950

Baby Carbine

Lighter frame and barrel (RARE).

NIB	Exc.	V.G.	Good	Fair	Poor
—	—	10000	6000	2500	1150

LIGHTNING SLIDE-ACTION, MEDIUM-FRAME

This was the first slide-action rifle Colt produced. It is chambered for .32-20, .38-40, and .44-40 and was intended to be a companion piece to the SAAs in the same calibers. The rifle has a 26" barrel with 15-shot tube magazine; the carbine, a 20" barrel with 12-shot magazine. The finish is blued, with case-colored hammer; the walnut stock is oil-finished; and the forend, usually checkered. The Colt name and Hartford address are stamped on the barrel along with the patent dates. There were approximately 89,777 manufactured between 1884 and 1902.

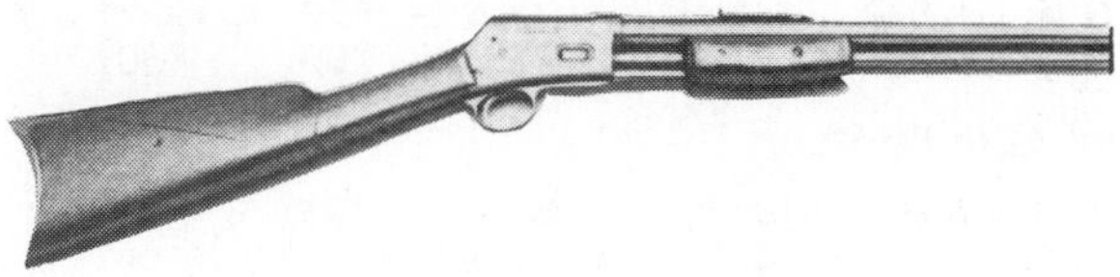

Courtesy Bonhams & Butterfields, San Francisco, California

Rifle

NIB	Exc.	V.G.	Good	Fair	Poor
—	—	2750	1250	750	400

Carbine

NIB	Exc.	V.G.	Good	Fair	Poor
—	—	3500	1750	800	500

Military Rifle or Carbine

.44-40 caliber, short magazine tube, bayonet lug, and sling swivels.

NIB	Exc.	V.G.	Good	Fair	Poor
—	—	5000	2000	1000	600

Baby Carbine

Courtesy Richard M. Kumor Sr.

1 lb., lighter version of standard carbine.

NIB	Exc.	V.G.	Good	Fair	Poor
—	—	8750	5500	1250	750

San Francisco Police Rifle

.44-40 caliber, #SFP 1-SFP401 on bottom tang.

NIB	Exc.	V.G.	Good	Fair	Poor
—	—	9000	6000	1800	1000

Lightning Slide-Action Small-Frame

This is a well-made rifle and the first of its type that Colt manufactured. It is chambered for the .22 Short and Long. The standard barrel length is 24"; the finish, blued with a case-colored hammer. The stock is walnut; some were checkered; some, not. The barrel is stamped with the Colt name and Hartford address and the patent dates. There were 89,912 manufactured between 1887 and 1904.

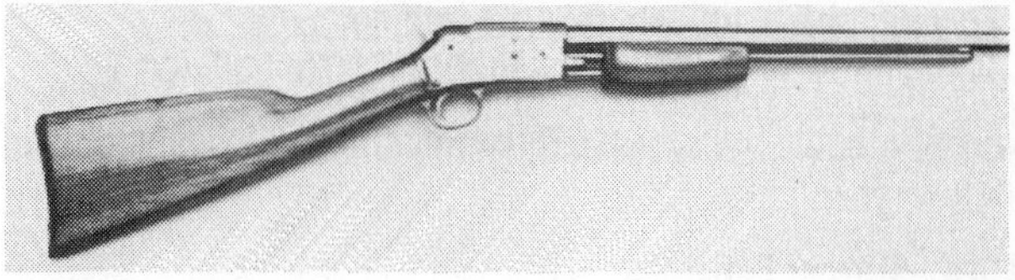

Courtesy Bonhams & Butterfields, San Francisco, California

NIB	Exc.	V.G.	Good	Fair	Poor
—	3250	1100	700	500	300

LIGHTNING SLIDE-ACTION, LARGE-FRAME (EXPRESS)

This rifle is similar in appearance to the medium-frame Lightning, though larger in size. It is chambered in larger rifle calibers of the era, from .38-56 up to .50-95 Express. The larger calibers are more desirable from a collector's standpoint. The rifle has a 28" barrel; the carbine, a 22" barrel. The finish is blued, with a case-colored hammer. The stock is oiled walnut; the forend, checkered. The Colt name and Hartford address are stamped on the barrel along with the patent dates. This rifle is quite large and has come to be known as the "Express model." Colt manufactured 6,496 between 1887 and 1894.

Rifle

28" octagonal barrel.

NIB	Exc.	V.G.	Good	Fair	Poor
—	—	7500	3750	750	500

Rifle

28" round barrel.

NIB	Exc.	V.G.	Good	Fair	Poor
—	—	7500	3750	750	500

Carbine

22" barrel.

NIB	Exc.	V.G.	Good	Fair	Poor
—	—	9000	5500	2500	750

Baby Carbine

22" barrel 1 lb. lighter.

NIB	Exc.	V.G.	Good	Fair	Poor
—	—	12500	6500	2500	950

Model 1878 Double-Barrel Shotgun

This model is chambered in 10 or 12 gauge and has 28", 30", or 32" barrels. It is a sidelock double-trigger hammer gun with case-colored locks and breech. The barrels are browned Damacus-patterned. The checkered walnut stock is varnished or oil-finished. The Colt's Hartford address is stamped on the barrel rib; and Colt's name, on the lock. This has been regarded as one of the finest shotguns made in America, although Colt had difficulty competing with the less expensive European imports of the day. They ceased production after only 22,690 were manufactured between 1878 and 1889.

NIB	Exc.	V.G.	Good	Fair	Poor
—	—	4500	2250	750	300

NOTE: Fully engraved model add 300 percent.

Model 1883 Double-Barrel Shotgun

This model is a hammerless boxlock, chambered for 8, 10 or 12 gauge. The barrels are 28", 30", or 32"; and it features double triggers. The frame and furniture are case-colored; the barrels, browned with Damascus pattern. The checkered walnut stock is varnished or oil-finished. Colt's Hartford address is stamped on the barrel rib. "Colt" is stamped on each side of the frame.

Again, as in the Model 1878, this is rated as one of the finest of all American-made shotguns. There were many special orders, and they require individual appraisal. Colt manufactured 7,366 of these guns between 1883 and 1895.

NIB	Exc.	V.G.	Good	Fair	Poor
—	3000	2000	1400	775	400

NOTE: Fully engraved model add 300 percent. For 8 gauge add 200 percent.

Double-Barrel Rifle

This is one of the rarest of all Colt firearms and is a prize for the Colt collector. There were only 35 of these guns manufactured. They were said to be the special interest of Caldwell Hart Colt, Samuel Colt's son, who was an avid arms collector. It is said that most of the 35 guns produced wound up in his collection or those of his friends. This gun is chambered for .45-70 or one of the larger variations thereof. It is an exposed hammer sidelock with double triggers. The locks, breech, and furniture are case-colored; the barrels, browned or blued. The barrels are 28" in length, and the checkered stock was oil-finished or varnished walnut. The barrel rib is stamped with the Colt name and Hartford address. The locks are also stamped "Colt." One must exercise extreme caution in dealing with this model as there have been Model 1878 shotguns converted into double rifles. Colt manufactured the 35 guns over the period 1879-1885.

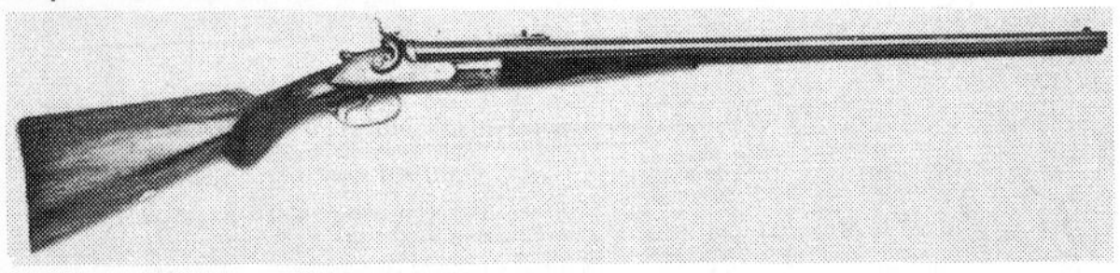

Courtesy Bonhams & Butterfields, San Francisco, California

NIB	Exc.	V.G.	Good	Fair	Poor
—	95000	75000	35500	—	—

COLT MODERN LONG ARMS

Colteer I-22

This is a single-shot bolt-action rifle chambered for .22 LR or .22 Magnum. It has a plain uncheckered walnut stock, 20" barrel, and adjustable sights. There were approximately 50,000 manufactured between 1957 and 1966.

NIB	Exc.	V.G.	Good	Fair	Poor
—	300	175	125	90	25

Stagecoach

This is a semi-automatic, saddle ring carbine. It is chambered for .22 LR and has a 16.5" barrel and a 13-shot tubular magazine. The stock is fancy walnut, and the receiver has the stagecoach holdup scene roll-engraved on it. There were approximately 25,000 manufactured between 1965 and 1975.

NIB	Exc.	V.G.	Good	Fair	Poor
—	450	350	200	150	100

Colteer

This is a less-expensive version of the Stagecoach. It features a 19.5" barrel, has a 15-shot tubular magazine, and is stocked in a plainer grade walnut. There is no roll engraving. Approximately 25,000 were manufactured between 1965 and 1975. Add 50 percent for .22 rimfire magnum.

NIB	Exc.	V.G.	Good	Fair	Poor
—	400	300	175	100	90

Coltsman Bolt-Action Rifle

The Coltsman was manufactured for Colt by Kodiak Arms. It utilizes either a Mauser or Sako action. The rifle is offered in .243, .308, .30-06, and .300 Winchester Magnum. It has a barrel length of 22", 24" in the Magnum chambering. The stock is checkered American walnut. There were approximately 10,000 manufactured between 1958 and 1966. There is a deluxe version that features a higher-grade, skipline-checkered walnut stock and rosewood forend tip; this is called "The Coltsman Custom."

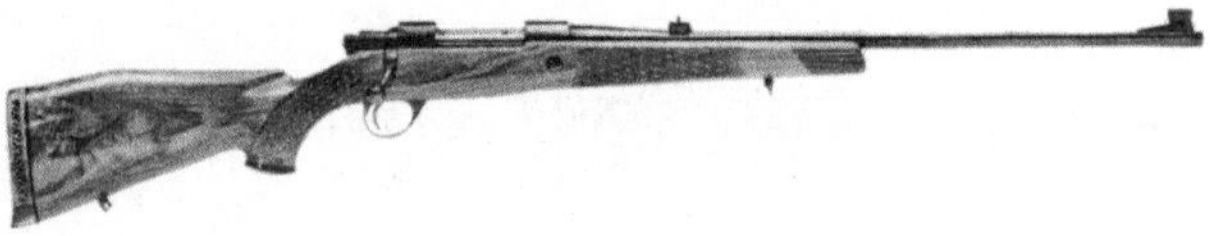

NIB	Exc.	V.G.	Good	Fair	Poor
—	650	550	450	350	250

NOTE: Coltsman Custom add 50 percent.

Coltsman Pump Shotgun

This model was manufactured by Jefferson Arms, utilizing an aluminum alloy frame made by Franchi. It is chambered for 12, 16, and 20 gauge and has a 26" or 28" plain barrel. There were approximately 2,000 manufactured between 1961 and 1965.

NIB	Exc.	V.G.	Good	Fair	Poor
—	350	300	275	200	150

Semi-Auto Shotgun

This shotgun was manufactured for Colt by the firm of Luigi Franchi in Italy. It features an aluminum alloy receiver and is chambered for 12 or 20 gauge. The barrel length is 26", 28", 30", or 32"—either vent-rib or plain. A deluxe version, "The Custom Auto," features a fancy walnut stock and a hand engraved receiver. There were approximately 5,300 manufactured between 1962 and 1966.

NIB	Exc.	V.G.	Good	Fair	Poor
—	375	325	300	225	175

NOTE: Custom Auto add 25 percent.

Double-Barrel Shotgun

During 1961 and 1962, Colt had approximately 50 side-by-side shotguns made for them by a French gun manufacturer. They have the Colt name on the breech area of the barrels and are in the 467000-469000 serial range. There is little information available on this gun, and Colt never went past the test-market stage.

NIB	Exc.	V.G.	Good	Fair	Poor
—	1200	950	650	500	400

Colt Light Rifle

Introduced in 1999, this bolt-action rifle is offered in both long and short action calibers from .243 to .300 Win. Mag. Fitted with a 24" barrel and adjustable trigger. Stock is black synthetic. Action and barrel are matte black. Long action calibers. Weight about 6 lbs., with short action rifle about 5.4 lbs. Adjustable trigger. No sights.

NIB	Exc.	V.G.	Good	Fair	Poor
—	700	600	500	400	200

Colt Sauer Bolt-Action Rifle

This is a high quality and unique rifle manufactured for Colt by the firm of J.P. Sauer & Son of Germany. The rifle features a non-rotating bolt that makes the Colt Sauer action smoother functioning than most. It has a 24" barrel, skipline-checkered walnut stock with rosewood forend tip, pistol grip cap, and recoil pad. There are five basic configurations: the Standard Action, chambered for .25-06, .270 Winchester, and .30-06; the Short Action, chambered for .22-250, .243 Winchester, and .308 Winchester; the Magnum Action, chambered for .7mm Remington Magnum, .300 Winchester Magnum, and .300 Weatherby Magnum; also the "Grand Alaskan" and the "Grand African," heavier versions chambered for .375 Holland & Holland Magnum and .458 Winchester Magnum, respectively. These rifles were all discontinued by Colt in 1985.

Colt Sauer Short Action

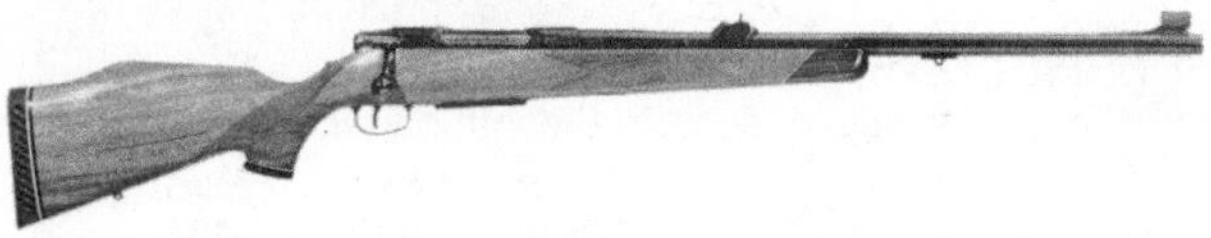

NIB	Exc.	V.G.	Good	Fair	Poor
—	1995	1850	1500	800	500

NOTE: Prices here are for short actions. Standard Action add $50. Magnum Action add 20 percent. "Grand Alaskan" add 50 percent. "Grand African" add 75 percent.

Colt Sauer Drilling

This is a rather unique firearm and one with which many American enthusiasts are not familiar—a 3-barreled gun. It features a side-by-side shotgun in 12 gauge over a .30-06 or .243 rifle barrel. The name was based on the German word for three, as this is where the concept was developed. They are quite popular in Europe where the game preserve style of hunting is prevalent but have little use in America where our hunting seasons don't often overlap. This drilling has 25" barrels and pop-up sights for the rifle barrel and is nicely engraved. It was discontinued by Colt in 1985.

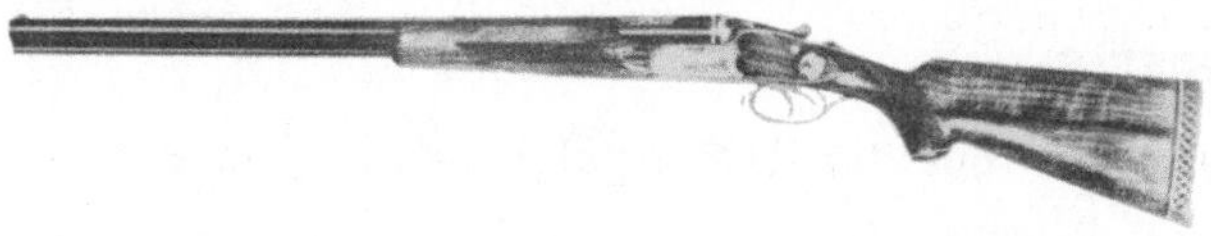

NIB	Exc.	V.G.	Good	Fair	Poor
—	4500	2950	2000	1500	1100

Colt-Sharps Rifle

Introduced in 1970 as the last word in sporting rifles, the Colt-Sharps is a falling-block action that was advertised as a modern Sharps-Borchardt. This undertaking was first-class all the way. The finish is high polish blue with a deluxe-grade hand-checkered walnut stock and forend. This rifle is chambered for .17 Remington, .22-250, .243, .25-06, 7mm Remington Magnum, .30-06, and .375 Holland & Holland Magnum; and it was offered cased with accessories. This model was manufactured between 1970 and 1977. Add 25 percent for .375.

NIB	Exc.	V.G.	Good	Fair	Poor
6000	4900	3200	1550	800	500

COLT AR-15 & SPORTER RIFLES

PRICING NOTICE: It is estimated that the value of pre-ban AR-15s declined 10-15 percent since the 1994-2004 Assault Weapons ban has lapsed but the market has once again spiked due to demand. The pricing status of the AR-15 is still volatile.

AR-15 Sporter (Model #6000)

A semi-automatic rifle firing from a closed bolt was introduced into the Colt product line in 1964. Similar in appearance and function to the military version, the M-16. Chambered for the .223 cartridge. It is fitted with a standard 20" barrel with no forward assist, no case deflector, but with a bayonet lug. Weighs about 7.5 lbs. Dropped from production in 1985.

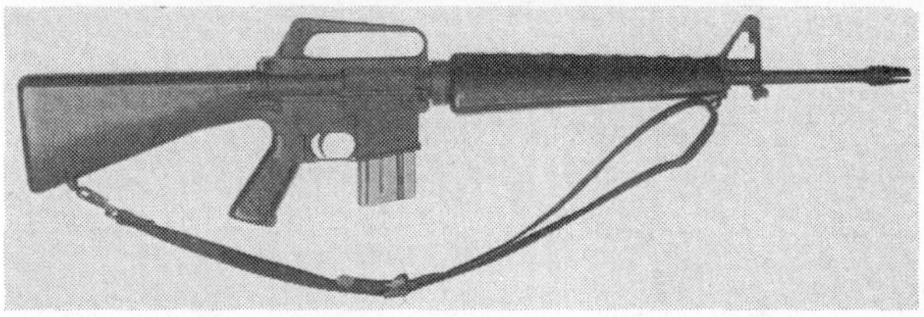

NIB	Exc.	V.G.	Good	Fair	Poor
2150	1800	1600	1500	600	400

AR-15 Sporter w/Collapsible Stock (Model #6001)

Same as above but fitted with a 16" barrel and folding stock. Weighs approximately 5.8 lbs. Introduced in 1978 and discontinued in 1985.

NIB	Exc.	V.G.	Good	Fair	Poor
2750	2450	2100	1800	600	400

AR-15 Carbine (Model #6420)

Introduced in 1985 this model has a 16" standard weight barrel. All other features are the same as the previous discontinued AR-15 models. This version was dropped from the Colt product line in 1987.

NIB	Exc.	V.G.	Good	Fair	Poor
2200	1900	1700	1600	600	400

AR-15 9mm Carbine (Model #6450)

Same as above, chambered for 9mm cartridge. Weighs 6.3 lbs.

NIB	Exc.	V.G.	Good	Fair	Poor
2250	1950	1750	1650	700	400

AR-15A2 Sporter II (Model #6500)

Introduced in 1984 this was an updated version with a heavier barrel and forward assist. The AR sight was still utilized. Weighs approximately 7.8 lbs.

NIB	Exc.	V.G.	Good	Fair	Poor
1850	1500	1300	1050	550	400

AR-15A2 Government Model Carbine (Model #6520)

Added to the Colt line in 1988 this 16" standard barrel carbine featured for the first time a case deflector and the improved A2 rear sight. This model is fitted with a 4-position telescoping buttstock. Weighs about 5.8 lbs.

NIB	Exc.	V.G.	Good	Fair	Poor
2300	2000	1750	1650	700	400

AR-15A2 Government Model (Model #6550)

This model was introduced in 1988 is the rifle equivalent to the Carbine. It features a 20" A2 barrel, forward assist, case deflector, but still retains the bayonet lug. Weighs about 7.5 lbs. Discontinued in 1990. USMC model.

NIB	Exc.	V.G.	Good	Fair	Poor
2300	2000	1750	1650	700	400

AR-15A2 H-Bar (Model #6600)

Introduced in 1986 this version features a special 20" heavy barrel. All other features are the same as the A2 series of AR15s. Discontinued in 1991. Weighs about 8 lbs.

NIB	Exc.	V.G.	Good	Fair	Poor
1950	1750	1500	950	700	500

AR-15A2 Delta H-Bar (Model #6600DH)

Same as above but fitted with a 3x9 scope and detachable cheekpiece. Dropped from the Colt line in 1990. Weighs about 10 lbs.

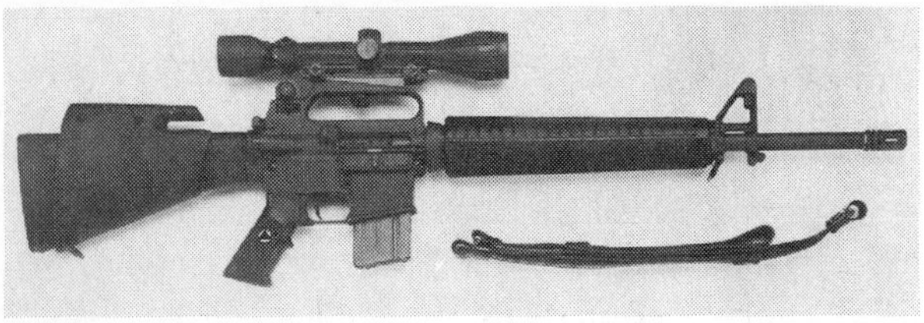

NIB	Exc.	V.G.	Good	Fair	Poor
2350	2100	1800	1650	850	600

Sporter Lightweight Rifle

This lightweight model has a 16" barrel and is finished in a matte black. It is available in either a .223 Rem. caliber (Model #6530) that weighs 6.7 lbs., a (Model #6430) 9mm caliber weighing 7.1 lbs., or a (Model #6830) 7.65x39mm that weighs 7.3 lbs. The .223 is furnished with two five-round box magazines as is the 9mm and 7.65x39mm. A cleaning kit and sling are also supplied with each new rifle. The buttstock and pistol grip are made of durable nylon and the handguard is reinforced fiberglass and aluminum lined. The rear sight is adjustable for windage and elevation. These newer models are referred to simply as Sporters and are not fitted with a bayonet lug and receiver block has different size pins.

NIB	Exc.	V.G.	Good	Fair	Poor
1500	1300	1000	600	400	300

NOTE: The Model 6830 will bring about $25 less than the above prices.

Sporter Target Model Rifle (Model #6551)

This 1991 model is a full size version of the Lightweight Rifle. The Target Rifle weighs 7.5 lbs. and has a 20" barrel. Offered in .223 Rem. caliber only with target sights adjustable to 800 meters. New rifles are furnished with two 5-round box magazines, sling, and cleaning kit.

NIB	Exc.	V.G.	Good	Fair	Poor
1400	1200	1000	650	400	300

NOTE: For post-9/94 guns deduct 30 percent.

Sporter Match H-Bar (Model #6601)

This 1991 variation of the AR-15 is similar to the Target Model but has a 20" heavy barrel chambered for the .223 caliber. This model weighs 8 lbs. and has target type sights adjustable out to 800 meters. Supplied with two 5-round box magazines, sling, and cleaning kit.

NIB	Exc.	V.G.	Good	Fair	Poor
1400	1200	1000	650	400	300

AR-15 (XM16E1)

This rifle was made upon request for foreign contracts. Very rare. Proceed with caution. This variation will command a premium price over the standard AR-15 rifle. Secure an appraisal before a purchasee.

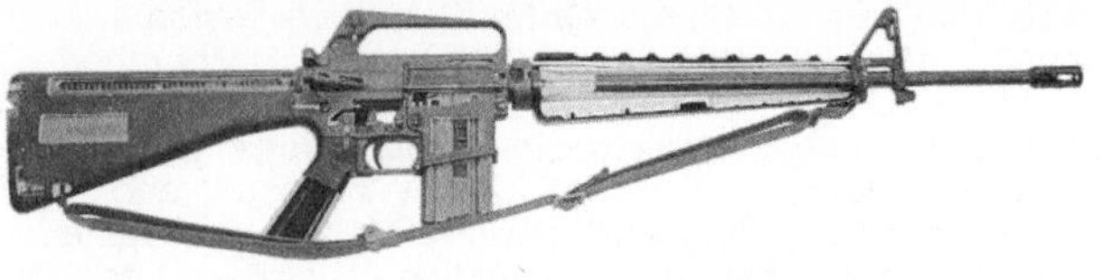

Courtesy Richard M. Kumor, Sr.

Sporter Match Delta H-Bar (Model #6601 DH)

Same as above but supplied with a 3x9 scope. Weighs about 10 lbs. Discontinued in 1992.

NIB	Exc.	V.G.	Good	Fair	Poor
2100	1800	1600	1300	600	400

Colt Match Target M4

Similar to above but with carbine-length barrel.

NIB	Exc.	V.G.	Good	Fair	Poor
2200	1900	1600	1300	600	400

Sporter Competition H-Bar (Model #6700)

Introduced in 1992, the Competition H-Bar is available in .223 caliber with a 20" heavy barrel counterbored for accuracy. The carry handle is detachable with target sights. With the carry handle removed the upper receiver is dovetailed and grooved for Weaver-style scope rings. This model weighs approximately 8.5 lbs. New rifles are furnished with two 5-round box magazines, sling, and cleaning kit.

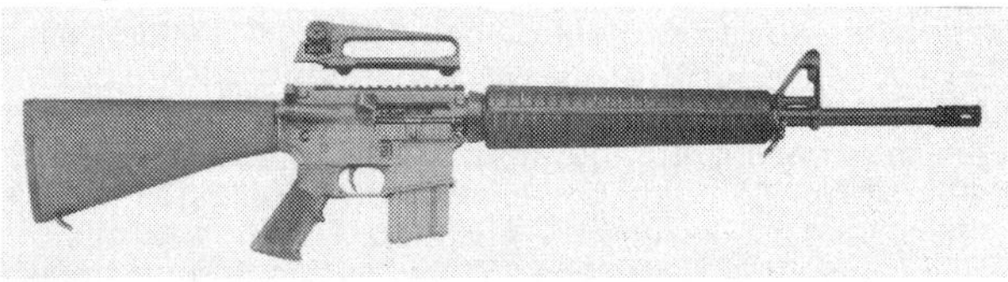

NIB	Exc.	V.G.	Good	Fair	Poor
1800	1500	1300	1000	500	350

NOTE: For post-9/94 guns deduct 35 percent.

Sporter Competition H-Bar Select w/scope (Model #6700CH)

This variation is identical to the Sporter Competition with the addition of a factory mounted scope. The rifle has also been selected for accuracy and comes complete with a 3-9X rubber armored variable scope, scope mount, carry handle with iron sights, and nylon carrying case.

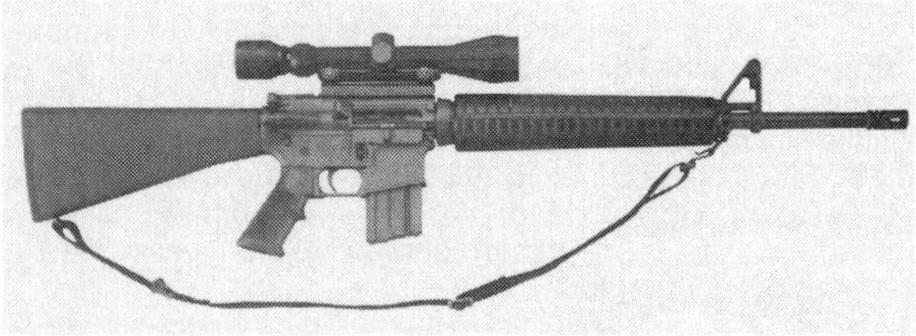

NIB	Exc.	V.G.	Good	Fair	Poor
2000	1800	1400	1000	600	400

AR-15 Carbine Flat-top Heavyweight/Match Target Competition (Model #6731)

This variation in the Sporter series features a heavyweight 16" barrel with flat-top receiver chambered for the .223 cartridge. It is equipped with a fixed buttstock. Weight is about 7.1 lbs.

NIB	Exc.	V.G.	Good	Fair	Poor
1200	1000	800	600	400	300

AR-15 Tactical Carbine (Model #6721)

This version is similar to the above model with the exception of the buttstock which is telescoping and adjusts to 4 positions. Chambered for the .223 cartridge with a weight of about 7 lbs. A majority of these guns were for law enforcement only. Only 134 rifles are pre-ban.

NIB	*Exc.*	*V.G.*	*Good*	*Fair*	*Poor*
1400	1200	1000	800	600	400

NOTE: 100 percent premium if serial number is below BD000135.

Sporter H-Bar Elite/Accurized Rifle (Model #6724)

This variation was introduced in 1996 and features a free floating 24" stainless steel match barrel with an 11 degree target crown and special Teflon coated trigger group. The handguard is all-aluminum with twin swivel studs. Weight is approximately 9.26 lbs.

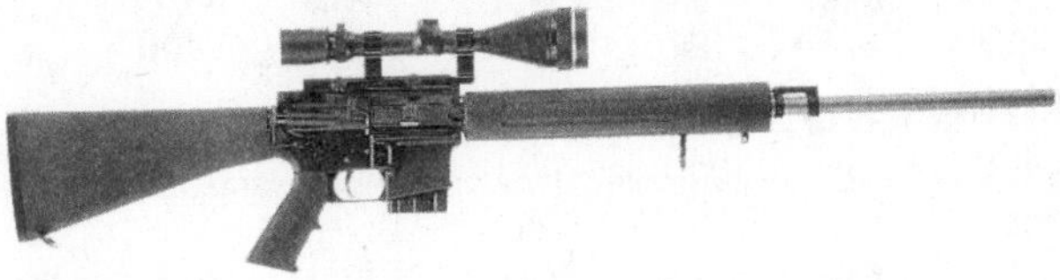

NIB	*Exc.*	*V.G.*	*Good*	*Fair*	*Poor*
1500	1250	900	550	400	300

Colt SP901

New hunting type modular rifle chambered in .308 Winchester with interchangeable upper receiver in .223 Remington. Fully floating 16-inch chrome lined barrel. One-piece monolithic receiver ready for optical sights. Adjustable front and rear sights. Ambidextrous magazine release, bolt catch and safety. Scheduled to be introduced in late 2011. Price: TBA

Colt SP6920

Sporter version of the classic Colt M4 carbine. Chambered for .223 Remington with chrome-lined bore with 6 grooves, 1-7-inch right hand twist. Four-position collapsible stock. Flattop receiver with removable carry handle. Matte black finish. Introduced in 2011.

NIB	*Exc.*	*V.G.*	*Good*	*Fair*	*Poor*
975	850	725	600	400	200

Colt SP6940

Same gun as SP6920 but with one-piece upper receiver, fully floated barrel which allows easier mounting of optical, laser or light accessories. No carry handle. Matte black finish. Introduced in 2011.

NIB	*Exc.*	*V.G.*	*Good*	*Fair*	*Poor*
1275	1075	900	700	500	300

COLT BLACKPOWDER ARMS

Brooklyn, New York

These blackpowder revolvers and rifles were made under license from Colt. Imported from Italy. No longer in business.

Colt 1861 Musket

This Civil War musket is chambered in the .58 caliber. Lockplate, hammer, buttplate, and three barrel bands, and 40" barrel are finished bright. The stock is a one-piece oil-finish affair. Bayonet and accessories are extra.

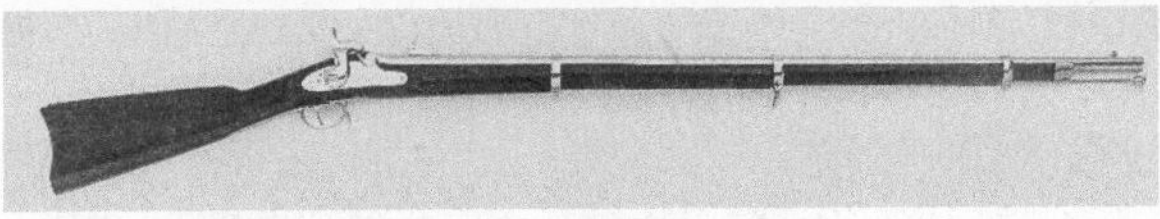

NIB	*Exc.*	*V.G.*	*Good*	*Fair*	*Poor*
800	650	500	325	275	150

Colt 1861 Musket—Artillery Model

Same as above but fitted with a 31-1/2" barrel.

NIB	*Exc.*	*V.G.*	*Good*	*Fair*	*Poor*
800	650	500	325	275	150

Colt 1861 Musket Presentation 1 of 1000

Limited to 1,000 guns these are special finished with a high polish and Colt's signature in gold on the trigger guard. Sold with special custom wooden case.

NIB	*Exc.*	*V.G.*	*Good*	*Fair*	*Poor*
1650	1300	750	600	450	300

Colt 1861 Musket Presentation 1 of 1000—Artillery Model

Same as above but 31-1/2" barrel.

NIB	*Exc.*	*V.G.*	*Good*	*Fair*	*Poor*
1650	1300	750	600	450	300

Colt Gamemaster .50

Introduced in 1997 this rifle issimilar to the above in general outline and is in .50 caliber. It is fitted with a 31.5" barrel and weighs about 13 lbs.

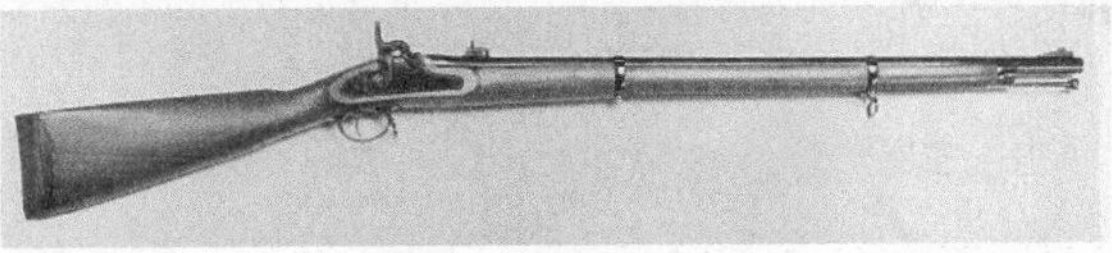

NIB	*Exc.*	*V.G.*	*Good*	*Fair*	*Poor*
800	650	475	300	225	125

COMMANDO ARMS

Knoxville, Tennessee

Formerly known as Volunteer Enterprises. The name change took place in 1978.

Mark III Carbine

A .45 ACP caliber semi-automatic rifle with a 16.5" barrel, a peep rear sight and a vertical foregrip. Manufactured between 1969 and 1976.

NIB	*Exc.*	*V.G.*	*Good*	*Fair*	*Poor*
675	550	375	300	225	150

Mark 9 Carbine

As above, in 9mm caliber.

NIB	*Exc.*	*V.G.*	*Good*	*Fair*	*Poor*
675	550	375	300	225	150

Mark .45

The new designation for the Mark III after the company changed its name.

NIB	*Exc.*	*V.G.*	*Good*	*Fair*	*Poor*
675	550	375	300	225	150

CONNECTICUT SHOTGUN MANUFACTURING COMPANY

New Britain, Connecticut

RBL Side-By-Side Shotgun

Round-action SXS shotguns made in the USA. Chambered in 12, 16, 20 and 28 gauge with scaled frames. Barrel lengths 26", 28", 30" and 32" with five TruLock choke tubes. Deluxe fancy-grade walnut buttstock and forend, Quick Change recoil pad in two lengths. Various dimensions and options available depending on gauge. Values shown are for 12 gauge.

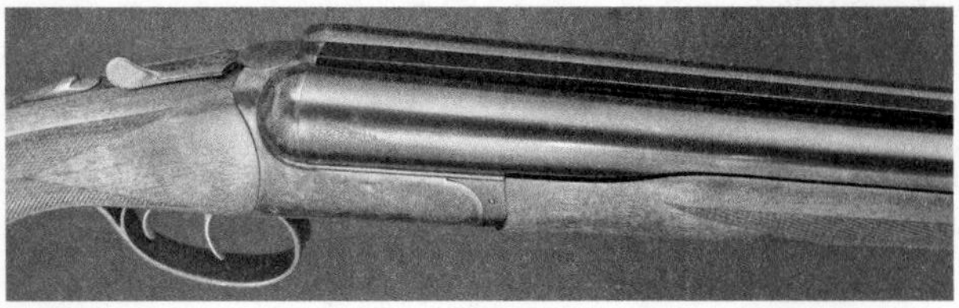

NIB	Exc.	V.G.	Good	Fair	Poor
4000	2950	2000	1275	800	400

NOTE: For 16 gauge add 10 percent, for 20 or 28 gauge add 20 percent.

A-10 American

Sidelock design in 12, 20 or 28 gauge with XX grade walnut stock and light scroll engraving. Offered in standard barrel lengths from 26 to 32 inches. Options include higher-grade wood and engraving. Prices shown are for standard mode. Introduced in 2010

NIB	Exc.	V.G.	Good	Fair	Poor
7500	6000	4500	3500	—	—

Model 21

This is a faithful rendition of the famous Winchester side-by-side shotgun that was in production from 1931 to 1959 and on custom-order from 1960 to 1993. Made in all gauges and standard barrel lengths with many options. Each gun is custom made to order. Introduced in 2002. Prices are for standard 12, 16 and 20-gauge models.

NIB	Exc.	V.G.	Good	Fair	Poor
15000	12000	9500	7000	3500	—

NOTE: Add $3000 for 28 or .410, plus $10,000 if made on optional small frame.

Model 21 Grand American

As above with high-grade, gold-inlayed engraving, AAA-grade walnut stock with elaborate checkering and carving patterns. Comes with two sets of barrels.

NIB	Exc.	V.G.	Good	Fair	Poor
25000	20000	17500	15000	8000	—

NOTE: Add $3000 for 28 or .410, plus $10,000 if made on optional small frame.

CONNECTICUT VALLEY ARMS CO.

Norcross, Georgia

RIFLES

Express Rifle

A .50 caliber double-barrel percussion rifle with 28" barrels. Blued with a walnut stock.

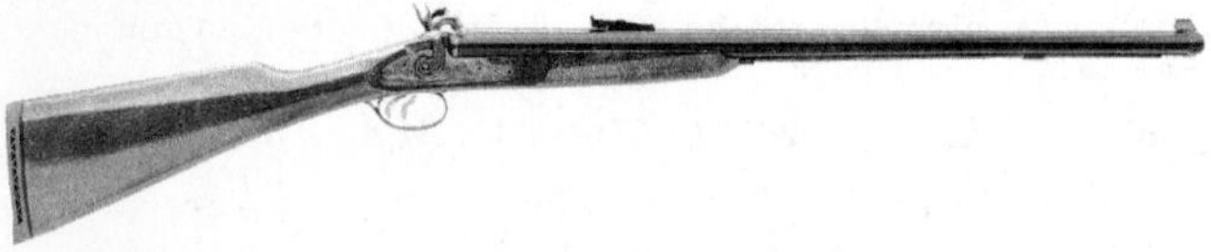

NIB	Exc.	V.G.	Good	Fair	Poor
625	475	425	375	325	200

NOTE: Deluxe version add 25 percent.

Over-and-Under Rifle

A .50 caliber double-barrel over-and-under rifle with 26" barrels. Blued with a walnut stock.

NIB	Exc.	V.G.	Good	Fair	Poor
600	475	425	375	325	200

Hawken Rifle

A .50 caliber with a 28" octagonal barrel, double set triggers and a walnut stock.

NIB	Exc.	V.G.	Good	Fair	Poor
450	325	275	225	150	100

Presentation Grade Hawken

As above, with an engraved lock, patchbox, and finely figured stock.

NIB	Exc.	V.G.	Good	Fair	Poor
550	425	375	325	275	200

Pennsylvania Long Rifle

A .50 caliber flintlock rifle with a 40" octagonal barrel, double set triggers and a walnut stock.

NIB	Exc.	V.G.	Good	Fair	Poor
475	400	350	300	250	175

Kentucky Rifle

A .45 caliber percussion rifle with a 33.5" octagonal barrel and walnut stock.

NIB	Exc.	V.G.	Good	Fair	Poor
275	225	175	150	100	75

Mountain Rifle

A .50 or .54 caliber percussion half-stock rifle.

NIB	Exc.	V.G.	Good	Fair	Poor
300	225	175	125	100	75

Blazer Rifle

A .50 caliber percussion rifle with a 28" octagonal barrel and walnut stock.

NIB	Exc.	V.G.	Good	Fair	Poor
150	125	100	85	65	45

Apollo Shadow SS

Introduced in 1993 this rifle features an in-line stainless steel bolt spring-action, a 24" blued round barrel with octagonal one piece receiver, drilled and tapped. Stock is black hardwood-textured with Dura Grip with pistol grip and recoil pad. Offered in either .50 or .54 caliber. Weighs about 9 lbs.

NIB	Exc.	V.G.	Good	Fair	Poor
175	150	125	100	75	50

Apollo Classic

Similar to the above Apollo Model but with dark brown stained laminated hardwood stock with pistol grip, raised comb, and recoil pad. Weighs about 8-1/2 lbs.

NIB	Exc.	V.G.	Good	Fair	Poor
215	175	150	125	100	75

Apollo Carbelite

Offered in .50 caliber with percussion bolt and 27" blued round taper barrel with octagonal receiver, drilled and tapped. Fitted with Carbelite composite stock with Monte Carlo and cheekpiece with pistol grip. Weighs approximately 7-1/2 lbs.

NIB	Exc.	V.G.	Good	Fair	Poor
280	225	175	150	100	75

Apollo Starfire

Chambered for the .50 caliber bullet this rifle is an in-line type with 24" stainless steel barrel with synthetic stock with checkered pistol grip, raised comb, and cheekpiece. Weight is about 6.5 lbs.

NIB	Exc.	V.G.	Good	Fair	Poor
225	175	150	125	100	75

Apollo Eclipse Rifle

Offered in either .50 or .54 caliber with 24" round barrel with blued steel receiver. Synthetic stock with checkered pistol, raised comb, and cheekpiece. Approximate weight is 6.5 lbs.

NIB	Exc.	V.G.	Good	Fair	Poor
175	150	125	100	85	65

Apollo Dominator

Fitted with a synthetic thumbhole stock and a 24" round barrel this rifle is chambered for the .50 caliber bullet. Introduced in 1996. Weight is approximately 8.5 lbs.

NIB	Exc.	V.G.	Good	Fair	Poor
300	225	175	150	100	75

Apollo Brown Bear

This .50 caliber rifle is fitted with a hardwood stock with pistol grip with raised comb and cheekpiece. The barrel is round and 24". Introduced in 1996. Weight is about 6.5 lbs.

NIB	Exc.	V.G.	Good	Fair	Poor
200	175	150	125	100	75

Frontier Carbine

Fitted with a 24" blued barrel this rifle is offered in .50 caliber percussion or flintlock. Case hardened lock with hardwood stock. Weighs about 6-3/4 lbs.

NIB	Exc.	V.G.	Good	Fair	Poor
150	125	100	85	75	50

Plainsman Rifle

This .50 caliber percussion rifle has a 26" octagonal barrel with case hardened lock and hardwood stock. Weight is about 6-1/2 lbs.

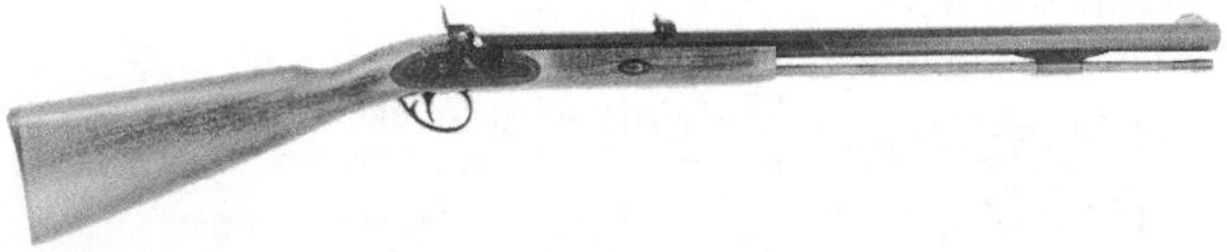

NIB	Exc.	V.G.	Good	Fair	Poor
130	115	100	85	75	50

Panther Carbine

This percussion rifle is available in either .50 or .54 caliber. It is fitted with a 24" blued octagonal barrel with Hawken-style case hardened lock. Stock is textured black Dura Grip over hardwood with Monte Carlo comb, cheekpiece, and pistol grip. Weight approximately 7-1/2 lbs.

NIB	Exc.	V.G.	Good	Fair	Poor
150	125	100	85	75	50

Bushwacker Rifle

This .50 caliber percussion rifle is fitted with a 26" octagonal barrel with case hardened engraved lock and brown stained hardwood stock with rounded nose. Weight is about 7-1/2 lbs.

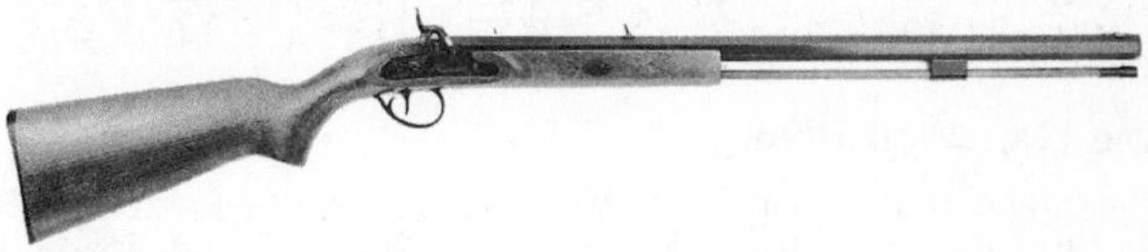

NIB	Exc.	V.G.	Good	Fair	Poor
135	115	100	85	75	50

Trophy Carbine

This carbine is fitted with a 24" half-round half-octagon barrel with Hawken-style lock. The stock is walnut with Monte Carlo comb, cheekpiece, and pistol grip. Offered in .50 or .54 caliber percussion and weighs about 6-3/4 lbs.

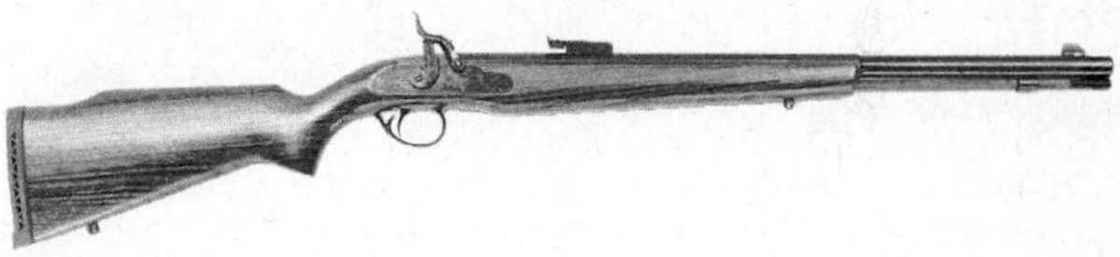

NIB	Exc.	V.G.	Good	Fair	Poor
215	175	150	125	100	75

Varmint Rifle

This is a lightweight percussion rifle in .32 caliber with 24" octagon barrel and case-colored lock. The stock is hardwood. Weighs about 6-3/4 lbs.

NIB	Exc.	V.G.	Good	Fair	Poor
175	150	125	100	85	75

Woodsman Rifle LS

Introduced in 1994 this rifle features a 26" blued octagon barrel with dark brown stained laminated hardwood stock. Offered in .50 or .54 caliber percussion. Weighs about 6-1/2 lbs.

NIB	Exc.	V.G.	Good	Fair	Poor
135	115	100	85	75	50

Frontier Hunter Carbine

Offered in either .50 or .54 caliber this percussion rifle is fitted with a 24" blued octagon barrel and case hardened 45\xfb offset hammer. The stock is dark stained laminated hardwood. Weighs about 7-1/2 lbs.

NIB	Exc.	V.G.	Good	Fair	Poor
170	150	125	100	75	50

Grey Wolf Rifle

Offered in either .50 or .54 caliber percussion this rifle is fitted with a 26" matte blue octagon barrel with a case hardened engraved lock. The stock is matte gray composite with raised comb, checkered pistol grip, and buttplate. Weighs about 6-1/2 lbs.

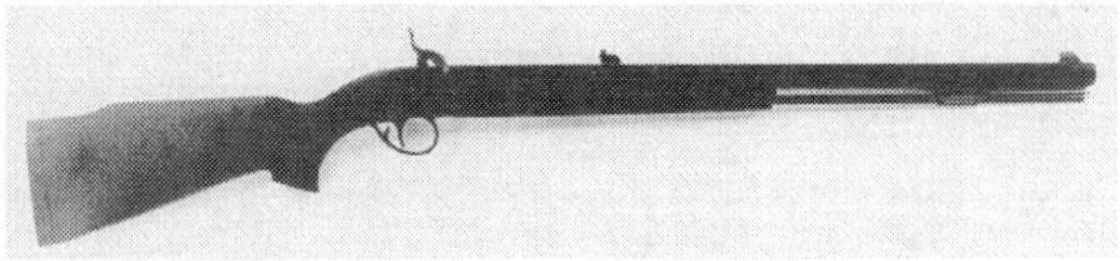

NIB	Exc.	V.G.	Good	Fair	Poor
160	125	100	85	75	50

Lone Grey Wolf Rifle

Introduced in 1994 this .50 caliber percussion rifle features a 26" matte blued octagon barrel. The trigger guard is oversized. The composite stock is black and has a raised comb, checkered pistol grip, and recoil pad. Weighs about 6-1/2 lbs.

NIB	Exc.	V.G.	Good	Fair	Poor
185	150	125	100	75	50

Timber Wolf Rifle

Introduced in 1994 this model is similar to the above model but is furnished with Realtree composite stock with raised comb, checkered pistol grip, and buttplate. Weighs about 6-1/2 lbs.

NIB	Exc.	V.G.	Good	Fair	Poor
185	165	140	100	75	50

Tracker Carbine LS

Introduced in 1994 this carbine is fitted with a 21" blued, half-round, half-octagon barrel with a Hawken-style lock. The stock is laminated dark brown with matte finish, and straight grip. Chambered for .50 caliber percussion. Weighs about 6-1/2 lbs.

NIB	Exc.	V.G.	Good	Fair	Poor
185	165	140	100	75	50

Stag Horn

Introduced in 1996 this in-line rifle is chambered for the .50 or .54 caliber bullet. The round barrel is 24" with blued finish. The stock is synthetic with checkered pistol grip, raised comb, and cheekpiece. Weight is about 6.5 lbs.

NIB	Exc.	V.G.	Good	Fair	Poor
175	150	125	100	85	65

Electra

A .50-caliber inline muzzleloader that uses electronic-arc ignition rather than caps or primers. Powered by common 9v battery. Finishes include stainless/camo, stainless/black composite, and blued/black composite. Introduced in 2007. Price given is for stainless/camo version.

NIB	Exc.	V.G.	Good	Fair	Poor
600	500	400	300	200	100

SHOTGUNS

Brittany 11 Shotgun

A .410 bore double-barrel percussion shotgun with 24" barrels, double triggers and a walnut stock.

NIB	Exc.	V.G.	Good	Fair	Poor
425	350	250	150	125	75

Trapper Shotgun

A 12 gauge percussion single barrel shotgun with a 28" barrel threaded for choke tubes, and a walnut stock.

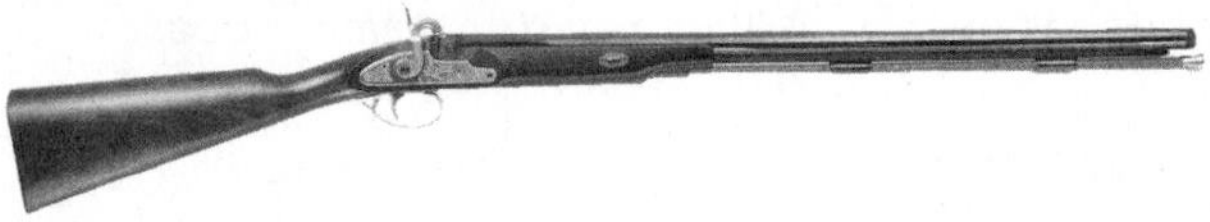

NIB	Exc.	V.G.	Good	Fair	Poor
275	250	225	175	150	100

Classic Turkey Double-Barrel Shotgun

This is a 12 gauge percussion breech-loading shotgun with 28" barrel. The checkered stock is European walnut with straight grip. Weighs about 9 lbs.

NIB	Exc.	V.G.	Good	Fair	Poor
495	375	275	200	175	100

Trapper Shotgun

This is a single barrel 12 gauge shotgun with a 28" barrel. The stock is a straight grip hardwood with checkering. Supplied with three interchangeable chokes. Weighs about 6 lbs.

NIB	Exc.	V.G.	Good	Fair	Poor
295	250	200	150	100	75

CONTENTO/VENTUR

A 12 gauge Over/Under shotgun with 32" barrels, screw-in choke tubes, a high ventilated rib, automatic ejectors, and a standard single-selective trigger. Checkered, with Monte Carlo walnut stock.

SIDE-BY-SIDE

Model 51

A 12, 16, 20, 28, and .410 bore boxlock double-barrel shotgun with 26", 28", 30", and 32" barrels, various chokes, extractors and double triggers. Checkered walnut stock. Introduced in 1980 and discontinued in 1985.

NIB	Exc.	V.G.	Good	Fair	Poor
—	500	350	300	225	150

Model 52

As above in 10 gauge.

NIB	Exc.	V.G.	Good	Fair	Poor
—	500	350	300	225	150

Model 53

As above, with scalloped receiver, automatic ejectors and available with a single-selective trigger. Discontinued in 1985.

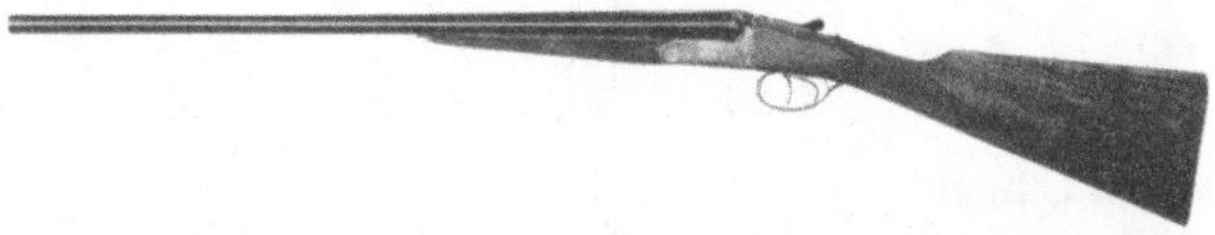

NIB	Exc.	V.G.	Good	Fair	Poor
—	550	400	350	250	200

NOTE: Single-selective trigger add 25 percent.

Model 62

A 12, 20, or 28 gauge Holland & Holland sidelock shotgun with various barrel lengths and chokes, automatic ejectors, cocking indicators, a floral engraved receiver, a checkered, walnut stock. Discontinued in 1982.

NIB	Exc.	V.G.	Good	Fair	Poor
—	1150	800	750	600	450

Model 64

As above, but more finely finished. No longer in production.

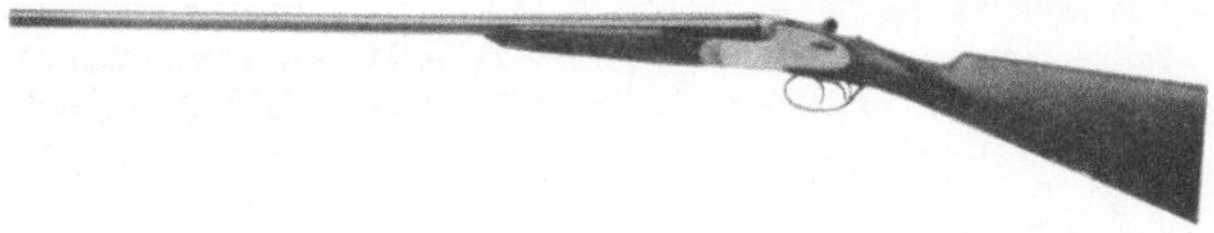

NIB	Exc.	V.G.	Good	Fair	Poor
—	1250	900	850	700	550

OVER/UNDER

NIB	Exc.	V.G.	Good	Fair	Poor
—	1250	900	750	600	500

Mark 2

As above, with an extra single barrel and fitted in a leather case.

NIB	Exc.	V.G.	Good	Fair	Poor
—	1500	1200	1050	900	800

Mark 3

As above, but engraved with a finely figured walnut stock.

NIB	Exc.	V.G.	Good	Fair	Poor
—	1850	1500	1250	1100	950

Mark 3 Combo

As above, with an extra single barrel and fitted in a leather case.

NIB	Exc.	V.G.	Good	Fair	Poor
—	3200	2600	2250	1750	1300

CONTINENTAL ARMS CO.

Norwich, Connecticut

Double Rifle

A .270, .303, .30-40, .30-06, .348, 375 H&H, .400 Jeffreys, .465, .475, .500, and .600 Nitro Express caliber Anson & Deeley boxlock double-barreled rifle with 24" or 26" barrels, and double triggers. Checkered walnut stock.

NIB	Exc.	V.G.	Good	Fair	Poor
—	6500	4500	3750	3000	2250

COOK & BROTHER RIFLES AND CARBINES

New Orleans

In early 1861, Ferdinand W.C. Cook and his brother, Francis L. Cook, both English emigres, joined to form Cook & Brother in New Orleans to manufacture rifles and carbines following the English P1853 series for the newly seceded state of Louisiana and its neighbors. Between June 1861 and the federal occupation of New Orleans in April 1862, this firm produced about 200 cavalry and artillery carbines and about 1000 rifles. Having successfully moved the armory's machinery before federal occupation, the firm continued manufacture of rifles in Selma, Alabama, during 1862, probably completing another 1,000 rifles with the New Orleans lock markings from the parts brought with them. Re-established in Athens, Georgia, in early 1863, the firm continued to build both carbines and rifles, manufacturing more than 5,500 above the New Orleans production through 1864. The firm's products were clearly among the best small arms made within the Confederacy.

Cook & Brother Rifles (New Orleans & Selma production)

Overall length 48-3/4"; barrel length 33"; caliber .58. Markings: representation of a Confederate flag ("Stars & Bars") and "COOK & BROTHER/N.O./1861 (or) 1862" on lock; same usually on barrel, together with serial number and "PROVED" near breech. Rifles in the early production have long range rear sights and unusual two piece block and blade front sights as well as an integral bayonet lug with guide on right side of barrel. Later production utilizes a brass clamping ring for the bayonet, a block open rear sight and a simple block and blade front sight. Earlier production will claim a premium if in good condition.

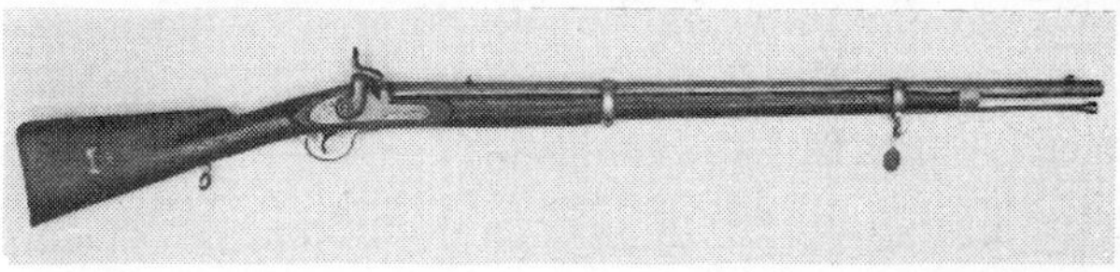

Courtesy Milwaukee Public Museum, Milwaukee, Wisconsin

NIB	Exc.	V.G.	Good	Fair	Poor
—	—	35000	15500	3000	1650

Cook & Brother Carbines (New Orleans production)

Overall length 40" (artillery), 37" (cavalry); barrel length 24" (artillery), 21" to 21-1/2" (cavalry); caliber .58. Markings: As on Cook & Brother rifles (New Orleans production) artillery and cavalry carbines were produced in New Orleans in a separate serial range from the rifles. Total production is thought not to have exceeded 225, divided evenly between 1861 and 1862 dates. In addition to the overall and barrel lengths, the main difference between the artillery and cavalry carbines is the manner in which they were carried. The former bears standard sling rings on the upper band and the trigger guard strap, the latter has a bar with a ring on the left side of the stock. Both are exceedingly rare.

NIB	Exc.	V.G.	Good	Fair	Poor
—	—	20000	8500	5000	1500

Cook & Brother Rifles (Athens production)

Overall length 49"; barrel length 33"; caliber .58. Markings: representation of a Confederate flag ("Stars & Bars") and "COOK & BROTHER/ATHENS GA./date (1863 or 1864), and serial number on lock; "PROVED" on barrel near breech; serial number on various metal parts. After re-establishing their plant at Athens, Georgia, in the spring of 1863, Cook & Brother continued to manufacture rifles in a consecutive serial range after their New Orleans/Selma production (beginning about serial number 2000) and continued to make arms well into 1864 (through at least serial number 7650) until Sherman's army threatened the plant and necessitated the employment of its workforce in a military capacity as the 23rd Battalion Georgia State Guard.

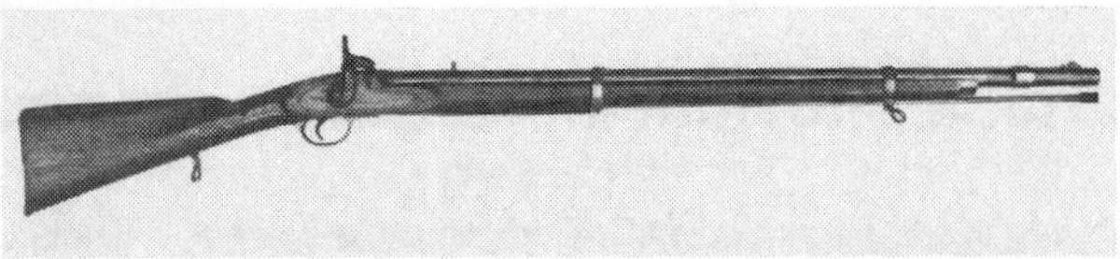

Courtesy Milwaukee Public Museum, Milwaukee, Wisconsin

NIB	Exc.	V.G.	Good	Fair	Poor
—	—	21000	9300	3000	900

Cook & Brother Carbines (Athens production)

Overall length 40" (artillery) or 37" (cavalry); barrel lengths 24" (artillery) or 21" to 21-1/2" (cavalry); caliber .58. Markings: same as on Athens production rifles. Artillery and cavalry carbines were manufactured in the same serial range as the Athens production rifles (about 2000 through 7650). As in New Orleans production, the artillery and cavalry carbines are distinguished from one another by their respective lengths. Unlike New Orleans/Selma production, however, some of the cavalry carbines are mounted with sling swivels of the artillery style, while others bear the sling ring on the left side and additionally have a swivel ring to secure the ramrod.

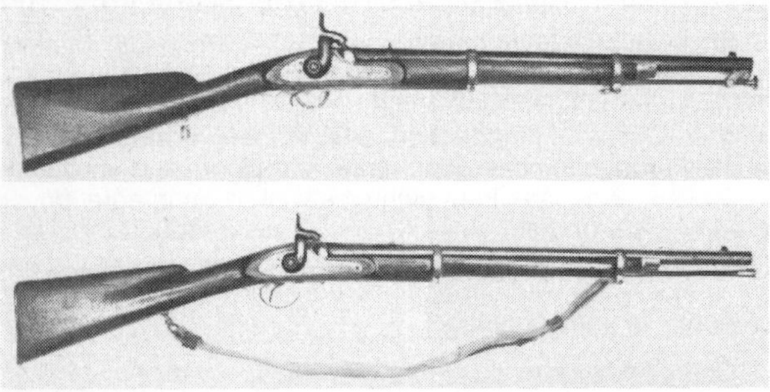

Courtesy Milwaukee Public Museum, Milwaukee, Wisconsin

NIB	Exc.	V.G.	Good	Fair	Poor
—	—	27500	9800	3900	1250

COOPER ARMS

Stevensville, Montana

MODEL 36 MARKSMAN

This is a premium bolt-action rifle chambered for the .22 LR cartridge and in centerfire calibers of .17 CCM and .22 Hornet. The 23" Shilen barrel is mated to a solid bar stock receiver. High grade walnut is used in stocks that are fine-lined checkered.

Standard

NIB	Exc.	V.G.	Good	Fair	Poor
1600	900	700	500	300	2000

Classic

NIB	Exc.	V.G.	Good	Fair	Poor
1800	1200	800	600	400	200

Custom Classic

NIB	Exc.	V.G.	Good	Fair	Poor
2000	1650	1150	850	600	300

Western Classic

Octagon barrel and case color metal.

NIB	Exc.	V.G.	Good	Fair	Poor
2400	1900	1350	900	700	300

BR-50 w/Jewell Trigger

NIB	Exc.	V.G.	Good	Fair	Poor
1800	1450	1100	800	600	300

IR-50-50 w/Jewell Trigger

NIB	Exc.	V.G.	Good	Fair	Poor
1800	1450	1100	800	600	300

Featherweight w/Jewell Trigger

NIB	Exc.	V.G.	Good	Fair	Poor
1800	1450	1100	800	600	300

MODEL 38/40

This bolt-action rifle is chambered for the .17 AK Hornet, .22 K Hornet, or the .22 Hornet.

Classic

NIB	Exc.	V.G.	Good	Fair	Poor
1800	1500	1100	800	600	300

Custom Classic

NIB	Exc.	V.G.	Good	Fair	Poor
2000	1750	1250	850	600	300

Western Classic

NIB	Exc.	V.G.	Good	Fair	Poor
2200	1800	1250	850	600	300

MODEL 21

This bolt-action rifle is chambered for these cartridges: .221 Fireball, .222, .223, 6x45, 6x47, .17 Mach IV, and the .17 Rem. A 24" stainless steel Shilen match grade barrel is fitted. AAA claro walnut is used. Oval forearm, ambidextrous palm swell, 22 lpi checkering, oil finish, and Pachmayr buttpad are all standard features. Weighs approximately 8 lbs.

Varmint Extreme

NIB	Exc.	V.G.	Good	Fair	Poor
1600	1250	900	700	500	250

Classic

NIB	Exc.	V.G.	Good	Fair	Poor
1600	1250	900	700	500	250

Custom Classic

NIB	Exc.	V.G.	Good	Fair	Poor
1900	1700	1300	850	600	300

Western Classic

NIB	Exc.	V.G.	Good	Fair	Poor
2200	1800	1250	850	600	300

Benchrest w/Jewell Trigger

NIB	Exc.	V.G.	Good	Fair	Poor
2100	1800	1250	850	600	300

MODEL 22

This is a bolt-action single rifle chambered for a variety of calibers: 6mm PPC, .22-250, .220 Swift, .243, .25-06, .308, .22 BR, 7.62x39, 6.5x55. A Pachmayr decelerator pad is standard. Weight is approximately 8.5 lbs.

Pro Varmint Extreme

NIB	Exc.	V.G.	Good	Fair	Poor
1750	1500	1200	800	600	300

Benchrest w/Jewell Trigger

NIB	Exc.	V.G.	Good	Fair	Poor
2100	1800	1300	900	650	300

Repeater

Same as above but with magazine and chambered for .22-25, .308, 7mm-08, and .243.

NIB	Exc.	V.G.	Good	Fair	Poor

Repeater Classic

NIB	Exc.	V.G.	Good	Fair	Poor
2400	2000	1750	1250	800	325

Repeater Custom Classic

NIB	Exc.	V.G.	Good	Fair	Poor
2650	2200	1850	1400	900	400

Repeater Western Classic

NIB	Exc.	V.G.	Good	Fair	Poor
2200	1800	1250	850	600	300

Model 52 Classic

Long-action repeater offered virtually any centerfire caliber from .22-250 to .340 Weatherby. Model 52 Classic has oil-finished AA Claro walnut stock, hand checkering, matte finish. Also offered with synthetic stock as Excalibur. Custom Classic has more extensive checkering, ebony fore-end cap. Western Classic available in any caliber, has octagon barrel, case-hardened action, engraving. Introduced in 2007.

NIB	Exc.	V.G.	Good	Fair	Poor
1500	1300	1000	800	500	300

NOTE: Add $150 for Excalibur, $1200 for Custom Classic, $2000 for Western Classic.

Model 54

Similar to above except with short action and in these calibers: .22-250, .243 Win., .250 Sav., .260 Rem., 7mm-08 Rem., .308 Win. Optional models same as Model 52 plus three varmint variants.

NIB	Exc.	V.G.	Good	Fair	Poor
1500	1300	1000	800	500	300

NOTE: Add $150 for Excalibur, $400 for Varmint Extreme, $1200 for Custom Classic, $2000 for Western Classic.

Model 57

Bolt-action repeater chambered for the following rimfire calibers: .17 Mach II, .17 HMR, .22 LR, or .22 Win. Mag. Offered in several versions including standard model with checkered walnut stock, matte finish, steel grip cap.

NIB	Exc.	V.G.	Good	Fair	Poor
1400	1200	950	750	500	300

NOTE: Add $500 for Custom Classic, $1200 for Western Classic

COSMI, A. & F.

Torrette, Italy

SEMI-AUTOMATIC

A 12 and 20 gauge top-break semi-automatic shotgun with various barrel lengths and chokes, an 8-shot magazine, and a ventilated rib. This is basically a custom-built, made-to-order gun. There is a standard and a deluxe model, with differences in the degree of embellishment.

Standard Model

NIB	Exc.	V.G.	Good	Fair	Poor
14000	8500	4750	3250	2200	1500

Deluxe Model

NIB	Exc.	V.G.	Good	Fair	Poor
15500	9500	6000	4250	3250	1750

CPA RIFLES

Dingman's Ferry, Pennsylvania

This company builds rifles based on the Stevens Model 44-1/2. Several different configurations are offered, which are listed. Note there there are a number of special order options and custom features available at extra charge that will affect value.

Schuetzen Rifle

This model is usually built to order as to stock style, caliber, and barrel size, shape and length. Many calibers are available from .22 Short to .40-65 Winchester. Sights are extra.

NIB	Exc.	V.G.	Good	Fair	Poor
2900	2250	1600	975	600	300

Silhouette Rifle

This model as produced is approved for BPCR competition by the NRA. This model has either a sporting-style stock with low comb or the Model 52 style with more drop. Calibers are from .38-55 to .45-110 with other calibers available. Standard barrel is #4 part octagon 30" in length. Sights are extra.

NIB	Exc.	V.G.	Good	Fair	Poor
2550	1900	1350	700	550	250

Sporting Rifle

This model uses a sporting-style stock with standard forearm with Schnabel tip. Rifles are offered in rimmed calibers including .222, .225, .22 Hornet and others. Standard barrels are round or part octagon with weights from #1 to #5 and up to 28" in length. Sights are extra.

NIB	Exc.	V.G.	Good	Fair	Poor
2475	1900	1350	700	550	250

Varmint Rifle

As above but with a semi-beavertail forearm.

NIB	Exc.	V.G.	Good	Fair	Poor
2475	1900	1350	700	550	250

CRESCENT F. A. CO.

Norwich, Connecticut

The company made good quality inexpensive single and double-barrel shotguns at its Norwich works, beginning about 1892. It was bought by H&D Folsom of New York City, large importers and distributors of firearms and sporting goods, so they could add an American-made sidelock hammer, side-by-side to their extensive range of imported guns. The Crescent guns were offered in 12, 16, 20, and 28 gauges and later, 44XL shot caliber with Damascus twist laminated or Armory steel barrels depending on the shooter's wants. In 1898 VL&D said these were the best American hammer guns in the market for the money.Huge quantities of these "Hardware Guns" were produced in a profusion of private brands as well as in Folsom's house brand "American Gun Co. of NY." In 1922 the Crescent brand replaced the "American Gun Co. of NY" and can be found on many thousands of doubles. In 1905 Crescent's first hammerless sidelock was introduced as the American Gun Co. "Knickerbocker" Model No. 6. This very popular model became the Crescent "Peerless" No. 6 in 1922. In 1928 it became the Crescent "Empire" No. 60 and in 1931 the Crescent-Davis "New Empire" No. 88, "New Empire" No. 9, and "Empire" No. 9.Crescent was bought by J. Stevens Arms Co., Division of Savage Arms Corp. about 1930. It was merged with Davis-Warner Arms Corp. successors to N.R. Davis & Sons Co. and became Crescent-Davis Arms Corp. In 1932 the operation was moved to the Stevens plant at Springfield, Mass. where some sidelock doubles were assembled, Crescent-Davis brand guns remained in Steven's full line catalog until 1941 but from 1937 to 1941 the doubles sold in the C-D brand were on either Stevens or Davis boxlock frames.

DOUBLES

Triumph—Hammerless Boxlock

NIB	Exc.	V.G.	Good	Fair	Poor
—	800	650	425	300	200

Model 2655—Laminated Barrels Hammer Sidelock

NIB	Exc.	V.G.	Good	Fair	Poor
—	575	450	325	200	150

Model 2665—Damascus Barrels Hammer Sidelock

NIB	Exc.	V.G.	Good	Fair	Poor
—	575	450	325	200	150

Crescent American Hammer Gun No. 0—Hammer Sidelock

NIB	Exc.	V.G.	Good	Fair	Poor
—	400	325	250	200	100

American Machine Made 2641—Hammer Sidelock

NIB	Exc.	V.G.	Good	Fair	Poor
—	450	350	300	250	200

American Machine Made 2650—Hammer Sidelock

NIB	Exc.	V.G.	Good	Fair	Poor
—	575	450	325	200	150

American Machine Made 2660—Damascus Barrels Hammer Sidelock

NIB	Exc.	V.G.	Good	Fair	Poor
—	700	550	400	275	175

American Gun Co. NY No. 1 Armory—Hammerless Sidelock

NIB	Exc.	V.G.	Good	Fair	Poor
—	450	325	250	200	100

American Gun Co. NY No. 2—Hammerless Sidelock

NIB	Exc.	V.G.	Good	Fair	Poor
—	575	450	300	250	200

American Gun Co. No. 3—Damascus Barrels Hammer Sidelock

NIB	Exc.	V.G.	Good	Fair	Poor
—	700	550	425	300	250

American Gun Co. No. 4—Hammer Sidelock

NIB	Exc.	V.G.	Good	Fair	Poor
—	800	650	525	400	300

American Gun Co. No. 5—Damascus Barrels Hammer Sidelock

NIB	Exc.	V.G.	Good	Fair	Poor
—	925	800	650	450	350

Folsom Arms Co. No. 0 Armory—Hammer Sidelock

NIB	Exc.	V.G.	Good	Fair	Poor
—	450	325	250	200	100

Folsom Arms Co. No. 2—Hammer Sidelock

NIB	Exc.	V.G.	Good	Fair	Poor
—	575	450	300	200	150

Folsom Arms Co. No. 3—Damascus Barrel

NIB	Exc.	V.G.	Good	Fair	Poor
—	700	550	425	300	200

Knickerbocker No. 6 Armory—Hammerless Sidelock

Courtesy Nick Niles, Paul Goodwin photo

NIB	Exc.	V.G.	Good	Fair	Poor
—	450	325	250	200	100

Knickerbocker No. 7—Hammerless Sidelock

NIB	Exc.	V.G.	Good	Fair	Poor
—	450	325	250	200	100

Knickerbocker No. 8—Damascus Barrels Hammerless Sidelock

NIB	Exc.	V.G.	Good	Fair	Poor
—	575	450	300	250	200

New Knickerbocker Armory—Hammerless Sidelock

NIB	Exc.	V.G.	Good	Fair	Poor
—	450	325	250	200	100

New Knickerbocker WT—Hammerless Sidelock

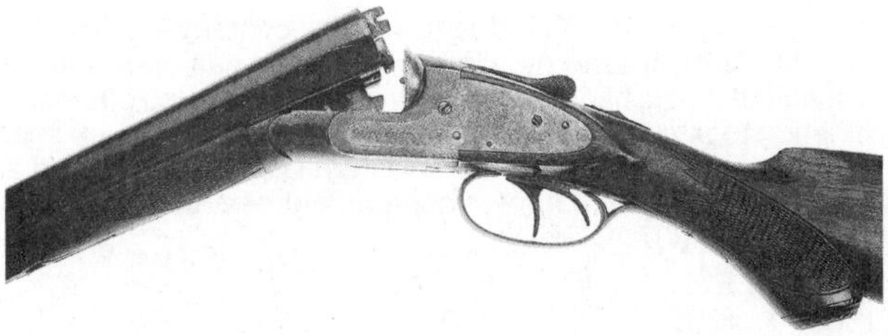

Courtesy Nick Niles, Paul Goodwin photo

NIB	Exc.	V.G.	Good	Fair	Poor
—	500	375	250	200	150

New Knickerbocker Damascus Barrels—Hammerless Sidelock

NIB	Exc.	V.G.	Good	Fair	Poor
—	575	450	300	250	200

American Gun Co. Small Bore No. 28—Straight Stock Hammer Sidelock

NIB	Exc.	V.G.	Good	Fair	Poor
—	925	775	650	400	300

American Gun Co. Small Bore No. 44—Straight Stock Hammer Sidelock

NIB	Exc.	V.G.	Good	Fair	Poor
—	1025	825	700	475	350

American Gun Co. No. 0—Armory Straight Stock—Hammer Sidelock

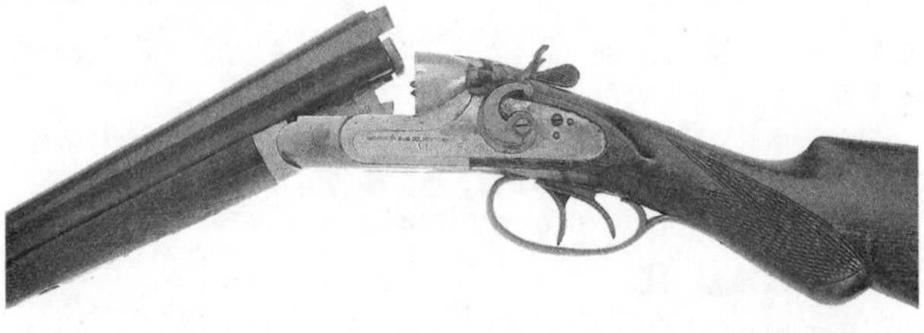

Courtesy Nick Niles, Paul Goodwin photo

NIB	Exc.	V.G.	Good	Fair	Poor
—	400	300	250	200	100

American Gun Co. No. 28—Nitro Straight Stock—Hammer Sidelock

NIB	Exc.	V.G.	Good	Fair	Poor
—	925	775	650	400	300

American Gun Co. No. 44—Nitro Straight Stock—Hammer Sidelock

NIB	Exc.	V.G.	Good	Fair	Poor
—	1025	825	700	475	350

American Gun Co. Midget Field No. 28—Hammer Sidelock

NIB	Exc.	V.G.	Good	Fair	Poor
—	925	775	650	400	300

American Gun Co. Midget Field No. 44—Hammer Sidelock

Courtesy Nick Niles, Paul Goodwin photo

NIB	Exc.	V.G.	Good	Fair	Poor
—	1025	825	700	500	350

Crescent 1922 Model No. 66—Quail—Hammerless Sidelock

NIB	Exc.	V.G.	Good	Fair	Poor
—	700	550	400	275	175

Crescent Firearms Co. No. 0—Hammer Sidelock

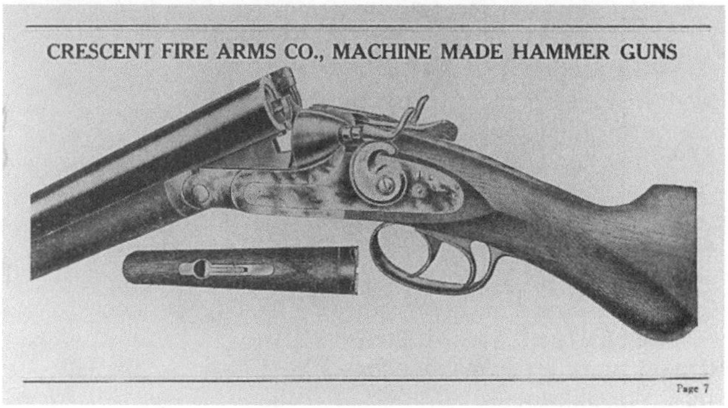

NIB	Exc.	V.G.	Good	Fair	Poor
—	450	350	250	200	150

Crescent Firearms Co. No. 0—Nickel—Hammer Sidelock

NIB	Exc.	V.G.	Good	Fair	Poor
—	600	450	350	250	200

Crescent Firearms Co. No. 6—Peerless—Hammerless Sidelock

NIB	Exc.	V.G.	Good	Fair	Poor
—	450	350	250	200	150

Crescent Firearms Co. No. 6E—Peerless Engraved—Hammerless Sidelock

NIB	Exc.	V.G.	Good	Fair	Poor
—	700	550	400	275	175

Crescent Firearms Co. No. 66—Quail—Hammerless Sidelock

NIB	Exc.	V.G.	Good	Fair	Poor
—	750	550	425	300	200

Crescent Firearms Co. No. 60—Empire—Hammerless Sidelock

Courtesy Nick Niles, Paul Goodwin photo

NIB	Exc.	V.G.	Good	Fair	Poor
—	500	400	350	300	200

Crescent Firearms Co. No. 6—Peerless—Hammerless Sidelock

Courtesy Nick Niles, Paul Goodwin photo

NIB	Exc.	V.G.	Good	Fair	Poor
—	450	350	300	200	150

Crescent Firearms Co. No. 44—Improved—Hammer Sidelock

NIB	Exc.	V.G.	Good	Fair	Poor
—	800	600	500	400	300

Crescent Empire No. 60—Hammerless Sidelock

NIB	Exc.	V.G.	Good	Fair	Poor
—	400	300	250	200	100

New Crescent Empire Red Butt—Hammerless Sidelock

NIB	Exc.	V.G.	Good	Fair	Poor
—	450	350	250	200	150

Crescent New Empire No. 88—Hammerless Sidelock

NIB	Exc.	V.G.	Good	Fair	Poor
—	450	350	250	200	150

Crescent New Empire No. 9—Hammerless Sidelock

Courtesy Nick Niles, Paul Goodwin photo

NIB	Exc.	V.G.	Good	Fair	Poor
—	400	300	250	200	100

Crescent Certified Empire No. 60—Hammerless Sidelock

NIB	Exc.	V.G.	Good	Fair	Poor
—	450	300	250	200	150

Crescent Certified Empire No. 9—Hammerless Sidelock

NIB	Exc.	V.G.	Good	Fair	Poor
—	500	375	300	250	200

Crescent Certified Empire No. 88—Hammerless Sidelock

Courtesy Nick Niles, Paul Goodwin photo

NIB	Exc.	V.G.	Good	Fair	Poor
—	575	450	400	350	300

Crescent Davis No. 600—Hammerless Boxlock

Courtesy Nick Niles, Paul Goodwin photo

NIB	Exc.	V.G.	Good	Fair	Poor
—	450	350	300	250	200

Crescent Davis No. 900—Hammerless Boxlock

NIB	Exc.	V.G.	Good	Fair	Poor
—	575	450	400	350	300

Single-Shot

Made in 12, 16, 20, and 28 gauge and .410. Barrel lengths were 26", 28", 30", and 32", with various chokes. It had an exposed hammer, fluid steel barrel, and walnut pistol grip stock.

NIB	Exc.	V.G.	Good	Fair	Poor
—	200	125	100	75	50

Brand Names Used by Crescent Arms

American Bar Lock Wonder made for Sears, Roebuck & Co.
American Boy made for Townley Metal & Hardware Co.
American Gun Co. (H & D Folsom house brand)
American Gun Company of New York
American Nitro
Armory Gun Co.Baker Gun Co. (if no foreign proof marks)
T. Barker New York-if a sidelock hammerless double without proofs.
Bellmore Gun Co.Berkshire No. 3000 made for Shapleigh Hardware Co. of St. Louis, MO
Black Beauty-hammerless doubles
Bluefield Clipper
Bluegrass Arms Co. made for Belknap Hardware Co. of Louisville, KY
Blue Whistler
Bridge Black PrinceBridge Gun Co.
Bridge Gun Works
Bridgeport Arms Co. (if no foreign proof marks)
Bright Arms Co.
Canadian Belle
Carolina Arms Co. made for Smith Wadsworth Hardware Co. of Charlotte, NC
Caroline Arms
Central Arm Co. made for Shapleigh Hardware Co. of St. Louis, MO
Chatham Arms Co.
Cherokee Arms Co. made for C. M. McClung Co. of Knoxville, TN
Chesapeake Gun Co.
Chicago Long Range Wonder 1908-1918 made for Sears, Roebuck & Co. of Chicago, IL
Colonial
Columbian New York Arms Co.
Compeer made for Van Camp Hardware & Iron Co. of Indianapolis, IN
Connecticut Arms Co.
Cumberland Arms Co.
Crescent Fire Arms Co.
Creve Cour (if no foreign proof marks) made for Isaac Walker Hardware Co. of Peoria, IL
CrusoDaniel Boone Gun Co. made for Belknap Hardware Co. of Louisville, KY
Delphian Arms Co. (some models without foreign proof marks) made for Supplee-Biddle Hardware Co. of Philadelphia, PA
Delphian Manufacturing Co. (some models)
Diamond Arms Co. (some models) made for Shapleigh Hardware Co. of St. Louis, MO
Dunlap Special made for Dunlap Hardware Co. of Macon, GAE.C. Mac made for E.C. Meacham Arms Co. of St. Louis, MO
Elgin Arms Co. made for Strauss & Schram and Fred Biffar & Co. both of Chicago, IL
Elmira Arms Co.
Empire Arms Co. made for Sears, Roebuck & Co. of Chicago, IL
Empire State Arms Co.
Enders Oakleaf made for Shapleigh Hardware Co. of St. Louis, MO
Enders Special Service made for Shapleigh Hardware Co.
Enders Royal Service made for Shapleigh Hardware Co.
Essex made for Belknap Hardware Co. of Louisville, KY
Excel made for Montgomery Ward & Co. of Chicago, IL
Farwell Arms Co. made for Farwell, Ozmun & Kirk of St. Paul, MN
Faultless made for John M. Smythe Co. of Chicago, IL
Faultless Goose Gun made for John M. Smyth Co. of Chicago, IL
The Field after 1894
Folsom Arms Co. (also used by H & D Folsom on Belgian imports)
F.F. Forbes (H & D Folsom house brand)
Fort Pitt Arms Co.
Fremont Arms Co. (also used on Belgian imports)
Gold Medal Wonder
Greenfield (some models) made for Hibbard, Spencer, Bartlett & Co. of Chicago, ILH.B.C. (some models) made for Hudson's Bay Co. of Canada
H.S.B. & Co. (some models) made for Hibbard, Spencer,Bartlett & Co. of Chicago, IL
Hanover Arms Co. (if no foreign proof marks)
S.H. Harrington (if no foreign proof marks)
Hartford Arms Co. made for both Simmons Hardware and Shapleigh Hardware Co. of St. Louis, MO
Harvard (H & D Folsom house brand)
Hermitage (some models) made for Grey-Dusley Hardware Co. of Nashville, TN
Hip Spe Bar (some models) made for Hibbard, Spencer, Bartlett & Co. of Chicago, IL
Hibbard (some models) made for Hibbard, Spencer, Bartlett & Co. of Chicago, IL
Howard Arms Co. made for Fred Biffar & Co. of Chicago, IL
Hudson (some models) made for Hibbard, Spencer, Bartlett & Co. of Chicago, IL
Hunter made for Belknap Hardware Co. Louisville, KY
Interstate Arms Co. made for Townley Metal & Hardware Co. of Kansas City, MO
Jackson Arms Co. made for C.M. McClung & Co. of Knoxville, TN
Joseph Arms Co. Norwich, Conn.
K K and Keen Kufter (some models) made for Shapleigh Hardware Co. of St. Louis, MO
Kingsland Special and Kingsland 10 Star made for Geller, Ward & Hasner of St. Louis, MO
Kirk Gun Co. made for Farwell, Ozmun & Kirk of St. Paul, MN
Knickerbocker (up to 1915, H & D Folsom house brand)
Knockabout (before 1925) made for Montgomery Ward & Co. of Chicago, IL
Knoxall (only hammerless doubles)
Laclede Gun Co.
Lakeside made for Montgomery Ward & Co. of Chicago, IL

Leader Gun Co. made for Charles Williams Stores of New York, NY
Lee's Special and Lee's Munner Special made for Lee Hardware Co. of Salina, KS
Long Range Marvel, Long Range Winner, and Long Range Wonder made between 1893 to 1909 for Sears, Roebuck & Co. of Chicago, IL
F.A. LoomisMarshwoodMassachusetts Arms Co. made before 1920 for Blish, Mizet and Silliman Hardware Co. of Atchison, KS
Mears (if no foreign proof marks)
Metropolitan made for Siegal-Cooper Co. of New York, NY
Minnesota Arms Co. made for Farwell, Ozmun, Kirk & Co. of St. Paul, MN
Mississippi Arms Co. St. Louis (some models) made for Shepleigh Hardware Co. of St. Louis, MO
Mississippi Valley Arms Co. (some models) made for Shapleigh Hardware Co. of St. Louis, MO
Mohawk made for Glish, Mizet and Lilliman Hardware Co. of Atchinson, KS
Monitor
R. Murdock, National Firearms Co. (some models)
National Arms Co. hammer doubles (without foreign proof marks) and hammerless doubles made for May Hardware Co. of Washington, D.C. and Moskowitz and Herbach Co. of Philadelphia, PA
New Britain Arms Co.'s Monarch
New Elgin Arms Co.
New EmpireNew England (some models after 1914) made for Sears, Roebuck & Co.
New England Arms Co. (some models)
Newport Model CN made for Hibbard, Spencer, Bartlett and Co. of Chicago
Newport Model WN (some models) made for Hibbard, Spencer, Bartlett and Co. of Chicago
New Rival made for Van Camp Hardware and Iron Co. of Indianapolis, IN
New York Arms Co. made for Garnet Carter Co. of Chattanooga, TN
New York Machine Made (some models)
New York Match Gun (some models)
New York Nitro Hammerless
Nitro Bird made for Conover Hardware Co. of Kansas City, MO
Nitro Hunter made for Belknap Hardware Co. of Louisville, KY
Nitro King 1908 to 1917 made for Sears, Roebuck & Co. of Chicago, IL
Norwich Arms Co.
Not-Noc Manufacturing Co. made for Belknap Hardware Co. of Louisville, KY and Canton Hardware Co. of Canton, OH
Osprey made for Lou J. Eppinger, Detroit, MI
Oxford made for Belknap Hardware Co. of Louisville, KY
Peerless (H & D Folsom house brand)
Perfection made for H. G. Lipscomb & Co. of Nashville, TN
Piedmont made for Piedmont Hardware Co. of Danville, PA
Piedmont Arms Co.
Pioneer Arms (if no foreign proof marks) made for Kruse and Baklmann Hardware Co. of Cincinnati, OH
Quail (H & D Folsom house brand)
Queen City made for Elmira Arms Co. of Elmira, NY
Red Chieftan (model 60) made for Supplee Biddle Hardware Co. of Philadelphia, PARev-O-Noc (some models) made for Hibbard, Spencer, Bartlett & Co. of Chicago, IL
Rich-Con made for Richardson & Conover Hardware Co.Charles Richter (some models) made for New York Sporting Goods Co. of New York, NY
Rickard Arms Co. made for J. A. Rickard Co. of Schenectady, NYRival (some models) made for Van Camp Hardware and Iron Co. of Indianapolis, IN
Rocket SpecialRoyal Service made for Shapleigh Hardware Co. of St. Louis, MO
Rummel Arms Co. made for A. J. Rummel Arms Co. of Toledo, OH
Ruso (if no foreign proof marks)St. Louis Arms Co. (sidelock hammerless doubles) made for Shapleigh Hardware Co. of St. Louis, MO
Seminole (hammerless) unknown
Shue's Special made for Ira M. Shue of Hanover, PA
Smithsonian (some models)
John M. Smythe & Co. made for John M. Smythe Hardware Co. of Chicago, IL
Southern Arms Co. (some models)
Special Service made for Shapleigh Hardware Co. of St. Louis, MO
Spencer Gun Co. made for Hibbard, Spencer, Bartlett & Co. of Chicago, IL
Sportsman (some models) made for W. Bingham & Co. of Cleveland, OH
Springfield Arms Co. used until 1930. (H & D Folsom house brand). This brand was also used by Stevens and James Warner guns.Square Deal made for Stratton, Warren Hardware Co. of Memphis, TN
Star Leader (some models)
State Arms Co. made for J.H. Lau & Co. of New York, NY
Sterling Arms Co.
Sullivan Arms Co. made for Sullivan Hardware Co. of Anderson, SC
Superior (some models) made for Paxton & Gallagher Co. of Omaha, NE
Syco (some models) made for Wyeth Hardware Co. of St. Joseph, MO
Ten Star & Ten Star Heavy Duty (if no foreign proof marks) made for Geller, Ward & Hasner Co. of St. Louis, MO
Tiger (if no foreign proof marks) made for J.H. Hall & Co. of Nashville, TN
Townley's Pal and Townley's American Boy made for Townley Metal & Hardware Co. of Kansas City, MO
Trap's Best made for Watkins, Cottrell Co. of Richmond, VA
Triumph (some models) made for Sears, Roebuck & Co. of Chicago, IL
Tryon Special (some models) made for Edward K. Tryon Co. of Philadelphia, PA
U.S. Arms Co. (if no foreign proof marks) made for Supplee-Biddle Hardware Co. of Philadelphia, PA
U.S. FieldUtica Firearms Co. (some models) made for Simmons Hardware Co. of St. Louis, MO
Victor & Victor Special made for Hibbard, Spencer, Bartlett & Co. of Chicago, IL
Virginia Arms Co. made for Virginia-Carolina Co. of Richmond, VA
Volunteer (some models) made for Belknap Hardware Co. of Louisville, KY
Vulcan Arms Co. made for Edward K. Tryon Co. of Philadelphia, PA
Warren Arms Co. (if no foreign proof marks)
Washington Arms Co. (some models)
Wauregan (some models)
Wautauga (some models) made for Wallace Hardware Co. Morristown, TN
Wildwood made for Sears, Roebuck & Co. of Chicago, IL
Wilkinson Arms Co. (if no foreign proof marks) made for Richmond Hardware Co. of Richmond, VA
Wilshire Arms Co. made for Stauffer, Eshleman & Co. of New Orleans, LA
Winfield Arms Co. (H & D Folsom house brand)
Winoca Arms Co. made for Jacobi Hardware Co. of Philadelphia, PA
Witte Hardware Co. (some models) made for Witte Hardware Co. of St. Louis, MO

Wolverine Arms Co. made for Fletcher Hardware Co. of Wilmington, NC
Worthington Arms Co. made for George Worthington Co. of Cleveland, OH

CROSSFIRE
LaGrange, Georgia

This combination rifle/shotgun is manufactured by Saco Defense, Inc. for Crossfire. It is the first production firearm to combine the shotgun and rifle into a pump action, multi-shot weapon.

MK-1

This model is designed to fire both a .223 Rem. cartridge and a 12 gauge 3" shotgun shell from two different barrels. It is a dual action long gun operated with a pump action. Overall length of the gun is 38". The shotgun has a 4-round detachable magazine while the rifle has an AR-15 type 5-round magazine. Shotgun barrel is furnished with choke tubes. Offered in black oxide finish or camo finish. Weight is approximately 8.6 lbs. Introduced in 1999.

NIB	*Exc.*	*V.G.*	*Good*	*Fair*	*Poor*
2200	1700	1350	775	500	250

NOTE: Add $100 for camo finish.

CUSTOM GUN GUILD
Doraville, Georgia

Wood Model IV

A falling block single-shot rifle produced in a number of popular calibers with barrel lengths from 22" to 28". The stock of select checkered walnut. This is a lightweight rifle, at approximately 5.5 lbs. It was manufactured for one year only, 1984, and is not often encountered on today's market.

NIB	*Exc.*	*V.G.*	*Good*	*Fair*	*Poor*
—	3750	2750	2500	1750	1000

CZ
Strakonice, Czech Republic

This firm is a separate company from the one located in Uhershy Brod. Prior to the collapse of the Soviet Union both companies were owned and operated by the state.

RIFLES

CZ Model 3

This bolt-action rifle, introduced in 2004, is produced in the U.S.A. Offered in both right- and left-hand configurations. Chambered for the Winchester Short Magnums: .270, 7mm, and .300. Walnut stock with choice of stainless steel or blue finish. Fitted with a 24" barrel. No sights. Magazine is 3 rounds. Weight is about 7.5 lbs.

NIB	*Exc.*	*V.G.*	*Good*	*Fair*	*Poor*
970	675	575	400	200	100

NOTE: Add $30 for stainless steel.

CZ 452-2E LUX

This bolt-action rifle is chambered for the .22 LR or .22 Win. Mag. cartridge. It is fitted with a 24.8" barrel with hooded front and adjustable rear sight. Trigger is adjustable for pull. The pistol grip stock is a European-style Turkish walnut. Supplied with a 5-round magazine. Blued finish. Weight is approximately 6.6 lbs.

NIB	*Exc.*	*V.G.*	*Good*	*Fair*	*Poor*
490	350	225	150	125	100

NOTE: Add $40 for .22 WMR.

CZ ZKM-452D

As above, with a walnut, Monte Carlo-style stock.

NIB	*Exc.*	*V.G.*	*Good*	*Fair*	*Poor*
—	425	300	225	150	100

CZ 452-2E ZKM Style

Similar to the above model but chambered for .22 LR only and fitted with a black synthetic stock and matte nickel finish. Fitted with a 22.5" barrel. Weight is about 6 lbs.

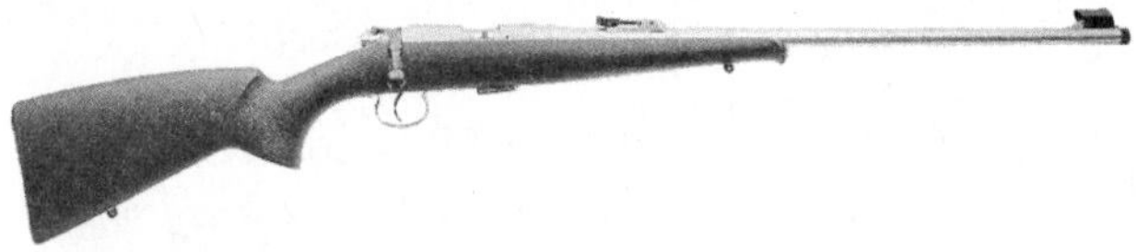

NIB	*Exc.*	*V.G.*	*Good*	*Fair*	*Poor*
475	325	225	175	125	100

CZ 452 Training Rifle

Chambered for the .22 LR cartridge and fitted with a 24.8" barrel. Detachable magazine has a 5-round capacity. Beechwood stock. Adjustable sights. Weight is about 5.4 lbs.

NIB	*Exc.*	*V.G.*	*Good*	*Fair*	*Poor*
375	275	175	150	125	100

CZ 452 American Classic

This model is chambered for the .22 LR and .22 Win. Mag. cartridge and features an American-style Circassian walnut stock with 18 lpi checkering. Fitted with a 21" barrel with recessed target crown. Supplied with a 5-round magazine. Blued finish. Weight is about 6.5 lbs. Introduced in 1999. In 2005 the .17 Mach 2 caliber was offered.

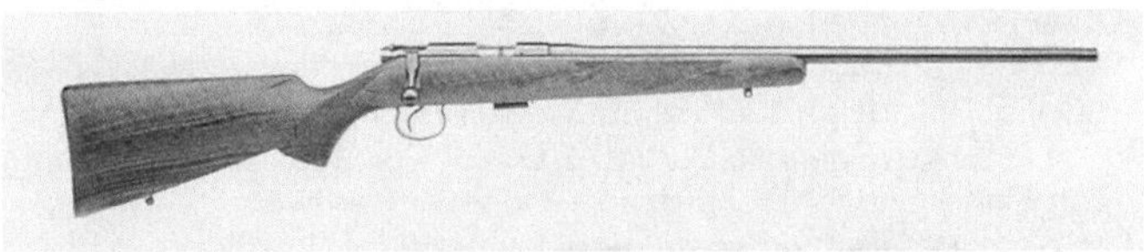

NIB	*Exc.*	*V.G.*	*Good*	*Fair*	*Poor*
465	350	250	150	12	100

NOTE: Add $40 for .22 WMR. or .17 HMR.

CZ 452 Varmint

This bolt-action rifle is chambered for the .22 LR cartridge and is fitted with a 20" barrel. American-style Turkish walnut stock. Blued finish. Weight is about 7.5 lbs. In 2005 the .17 Mach 2 was offered.

NIB	*Exc.*	*V.G.*	*Good*	*Fair*	*Poor*
420	300	250	200	150	125

NOTE: Add $20 for .17 Mach 2 caliber.

CZ 452 Scout

This model is designed for the younger shooter and features a shortened buttstock, 16.2" barrel, and reduced weight receiver. Chambered for the .22 LR cartridge. Open adjustable sights. Weight is 3.9 lbs. Introduced in 2000.

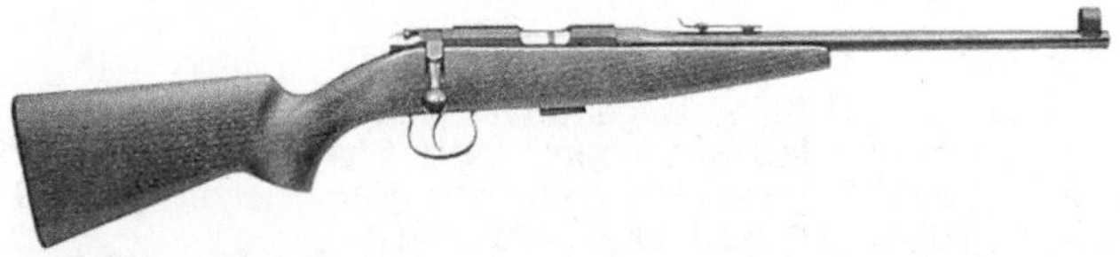

NIB	*Exc.*	*V.G.*	*Good*	*Fair*	*Poor*
275	200	150	125	100	75

CZ 452 Style

Chambered for the .22 LR cartridge and fitted with a 22.5" barrel, this model features a synthetic stock with matte nickel finish. Magazine capacity is 5 or 10 rounds. Weight is about 5.3 lbs.

NIB	*Exc.*	*V.G.*	*Good*	*Fair*	*Poor*
400	300	250	225	125	75

CZ 452 Silhouette

Designed for small silhouette competition shooting, this .22 caliber rifle has a synthetic stock and blued finish. Barrel length is 22.5". Weight is about 5.3 lbs.

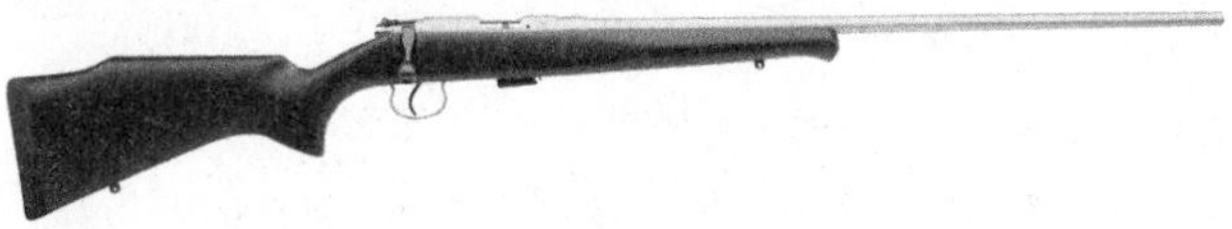

NIB	*Exc.*	*V.G.*	*Good*	*Fair*	*Poor*
400	300	250	225	125	75

CZ 452 FS

This model, introduced in 2004, is chambered for the .22 Long Rifle or .22 WMR cartridge and fitted with a full-length Turkish walnut stock. Barrel length is 20.5". Adjustable sights. Weight is about 6.5 lbs.

NIB	*Exc.*	*V.G.*	*Good*	*Fair*	*Poor*
475	350	265	200	150	100

CZ 513 Basic

This model is a simplified version of the CZ 452. It features a plain beechwood stock with no checkering. Iron sights. Chambered for the .22 Long Rifle cartridge. Barrel length is 21". Weight is about 5.4 lbs. Introduced in 2004.

NIB	*Exc.*	*V.G.*	*Good*	*Fair*	*Poor*
275	200	170	125	100	75

CZ 511

This is a semi-automatic rifle chambered for the .22 LR cartridge. Fitted with a 22" barrel. Two-position rear sight. Supplied with an 8-round magazine. Cross bolt safety. Turkish walnut stock. Blued finish. Weight is approximately 5.4 lbs.

NIB	*Exc.*	*V.G.*	*Good*	*Fair*	*Poor*
400	335	250	175	125	75

CZ Model 527

This bolt-action model is chambered for the .22 Hornet, .222 Rem., and the .223 Rem. The rear sight is adjustable and the checkered stock is walnut. Barrel length is 23.6" and magazine capacity is 5 rounds. Weight is approximately 6.2 lbs.

NIB	*Exc.*	*V.G.*	*Good*	*Fair*	*Poor*
600	500	400	300	225	125

CZ 527 American Classic

Introduced in 1999, this model features a 20.5" barrel with American-style Turkish walnut stock. Weight is approximately 7.6 lbs. Blued finish. In 2005 this model was chambered for the .204 Ruger cartridge with 22" barrel.

NIB	*Exc.*	*V.G.*	*Good*	*Fair*	*Poor*
600	500	400	300	200	100

NOTE: Add $170 for English walnut stock, $200 for fancy American walnut, $30 for maple, and $30 for laminate stock.

CZ 527 Lux

This is a bolt-action center fire rifle chambered for the .22 Hornet, .222 Rem., or the .223 Rem. cartridge. Fitted with a 23.6" barrel with a hooded front sight and fixed rear sight. The trigger is an adjustable single-set type. The Turkish walnut stock is in the Bavarian style. Blued finish. Supplied with a 5-round magazine. Weight is approximately 6.6 lbs.

NIB	Exc.	V.G.	Good	Fair	Poor
600	475	350	250	150	100

CZ 527 Premium (Lux)

Introduced in 2000 this model features hand fitted actions, fancy walnut stock, 18 lpi checkering, and satin finish. Offered in .22 Hornet and .223 Rem. Barrel length is 22". Magazine capacity is 5 rounds. Weight is about 6.2 lbs.

NIB	Exc.	V.G.	Good	Fair	Poor
650	525	400	300	175	125

CZ 527 FS

Similar to the above model but fitted with a 20.5" barrel with Mannlicher-style stock. Blued finish. Weight is about 6 lbs.

NIB	Exc.	V.G.	Good	Fair	Poor
690	525	400	300	175	125

CZ 527 Varmint

Chambered for the .17 Remington or .204 Ruger cartridge and fitted with a 24" heavy barrel. Checkered Turkish walnut stock. No sights. Detachable magazine. Weight is about 7.2 lbs.

NIB	Exc.	V.G.	Good	Fair	Poor
600	475	350	175	125	100

CZ 527 Varmint Laminate

Chambered for the .223 Rem. cartridge and fitted with a 24" heavy barrel. Gray laminate stock. Magazine capacity is 5 rounds. Weight is about 8 lbs. Introduced in 2002.

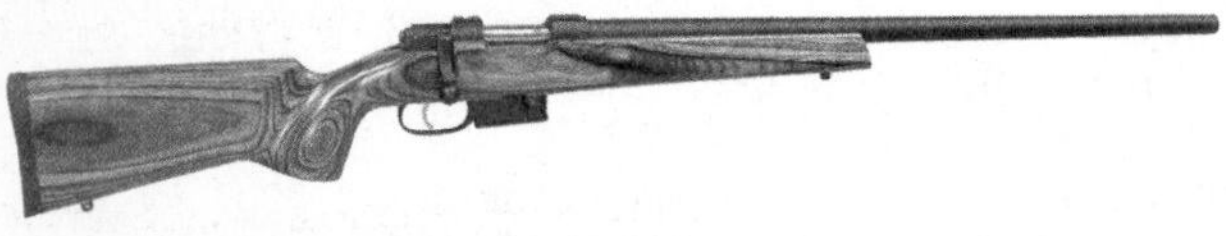

NIB	Exc.	V.G.	Good	Fair	Poor
695	525	400	300	200	100

CZ 527 Varmint

As above but with an H-S Kevlar stock. Weight is about 7.5 lbs. Introduced in 2002. In 2004 this model was also offered with a Turkish walnut stock.

NIB	Exc.	V.G.	Good	Fair	Poor
800	625	400	300	200	100

CZ 527 Carbine

This model, introduced in 2000, is chambered for the 7.62x39 cartridge and fitted with a 18.5" barrel. Detachable magazine capacity is 5 rounds. Open sights. Weight is about 6 lbs.

NIB	Exc.	V.G.	Good	Fair	Poor
600	475	350	225	175	100

CZ 527 Prestige

An upgraded CZ 527 American with jeweled bolt and semi-fancy Turkish walnut with hand rubbed finish. Chambered for the .22 Hornet or .223 Remington cartridges. Barrel length is 21.9". Weight is about 6.2 lbs. Introduced in 2001.

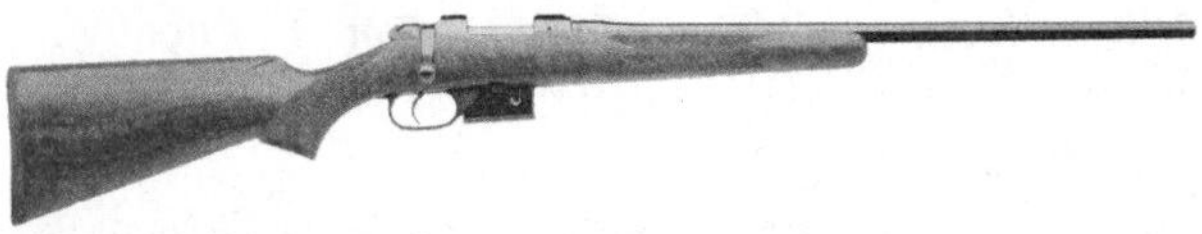

NIB	Exc.	V.G.	Good	Fair	Poor
880	675	600	475	275	150

CZ Model 537

This bolt-action rifle is chambered for the .270, .308, and .30-06 cartridges. The rear sight is adjustable and the stock is checkered walnut. Barrel length is 23.6". Magazine capacity is 5 rounds. Weight is approximately 7.9 lbs. Discontinued.

NIB	Exc.	V.G.	Good	Fair	Poor
600	475	375	250	200	100

CZ 550 American Classic

Similar to the Model CZ 550 this rifle is chambered for the .243, .308, .270,and .30-06 cartridges. It is fitted with a 20.5" barrel and American-style Turkish walnut stock. No sights. Supplied with 5-round internal magazine. Blued finish. Weight is about 7.6 lbs. Introduced in 1999.

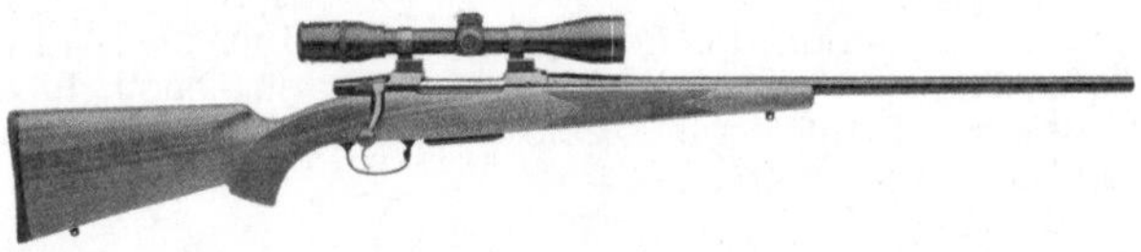

NIB	Exc.	V.G.	Good	Fair	Poor
620	500	400	300	200	100

CZ Model 550

Chambered for the .243, .270, .308, and .30-06 cartridges, this bolt-action rifle features a 24" barrel and high comb walnut stock. No open sights. Weight is about 7.25 lbs.

NIB	Exc.	V.G.	Good	Fair	Poor
700	525	400	300	200	100

CZ Model 550 Battue Lux

Chambered for the .30-06 cartridge. Ramp rear sight. Barrel length is 20.25". Weight is approximately 7.25 lbs. Checkered walnut stock.

NIB	Exc.	V.G.	Good	Fair	Poor
700	525	400	300	200	100

CZ Model 550 FS Battue

Same as above but with full-length stock.

NIB	Exc.	V.G.	Good	Fair	Poor
750	600	500	375	200	100

CZ Model 550 Minnesota

This model is chambered for the .270 Win. and .30-06 calibers. Barrel length is 23.5". Weight is approximately 7.25 lbs. No sights. Supplied with recoil pad.

NIB	Exc.	V.G.	Good	Fair	Poor
650	550	450	325	225	125

CZ Model 550 Minnesota DM

Same as above but with detachable magazine. Calibers are .270 Win. and .308.

NIB	Exc.	V.G.	Good	Fair	Poor
725	575	475	350	225	125

CZ 550 Prestige

This model is similar to the CZ 550 American with the added features of jeweled bolt, semi-fancy walnut and hand rubbed finish. Chambered for the .270 or .30-06 cartridges with 23.6" barrel. Weight is approximately 7.3 lbs. Introduced in 2001.

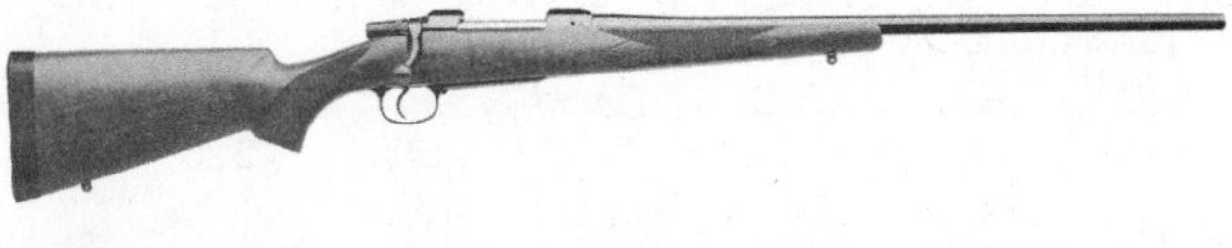

NIB	Exc.	V.G.	Good	Fair	Poor
700	625	550	425	300	175

CZ 550 Lux

This rifle is chambered for the 7x57, 6.5x55 SE, and the 9.3x62 cartridges. Barrel length is 23.6". Fixed magazine capacity is 5 rounds. Bavarian-style stock with Turkish walnut. Open sights. Weight is about 7.3 lbs.

NIB	Exc.	V.G.	Good	Fair	Poor
575	450	375	200	150	75

CZ 550 Varmint

This model is chambered for the .308 Win. cartridge and is fitted with a 25.6" heavy barrel. No sights. Checkered walnut varmint-style stock. Ventilated recoil pad. Single set trigger. Detachable magazine holds 4 rounds. Weight is about 9.3 lbs. In 2004 an HS Precision Kevlar stock was also offered on this model.

NIB	Exc.	V.G.	Good	Fair	Poor
650	500	400	300	200	100

NOTE: Add $200 for Kevlar stock.

CZ 550 Varmint Laminate

As above but with a gray laminate stock and offered in .22-250. Introduced in 2002.

NIB	Exc.	V.G.	Good	Fair	Poor
750	600	450	350	200	125

CZ 550 Safari Magnum

Chambered for the .300 Win. Mag., .375 H&H, .458 Win. Mag., and the .416 Rigby cartridges, this bolt-action rifle is fitted with a 25" barrel and 5-round internal magazine. Sights are one standing and two folding express rear with a hooded front sight. Blued finish. Bavarian-style Turkish walnut stock. Weight is about 9.2 lbs.

NIB	Exc.	V.G.	Good	Fair	Poor
925	750	500	400	300	200

CZ 550 American Safari Magnum

Introduced in 2004 this model is similar to the Safari Magnum above but with an American pattern stock. Offered with American walnut, brown laminate, or camo laminate stock. This model is also offered with fancy American walnut stock.

NIB	Exc.	V.G.	Good	Fair	Poor
925	750	500	400	300	200

NOTE: For laminate stock add $200, for fancy wood stock add $600.

CZ 550 Ultimate Hunting Rifle

Similar to CZ550 Safari Magnum but chambered for .300 WM only and with custom select wood. 23.6-inch barrel. Accuracy guaranteed at one MOA to 1000 yards. Introduced 2006.

NIB	Exc.	V.G.	Good	Fair	Poor
3600	3000	2450	1500	675	300

CZ 550 Premium

Introduced in 2000 this model features a hand fitted action with fancy walnut stock and 18 lpi checkering. Chambered for .30-06 and .270 Win. cartridges. Barrel length is 23.6". Weight is about 7.3 lbs.

NIB	Exc.	V.G.	Good	Fair	Poor
925	750	500	400	300	200

CZ 550 Medium Magnum

This model is designed around a mid-sized magnum action. Fitted with a 23.6" barrel and has a fixed magazine capacity of 5 rounds. Chambered for the .300 Win. Mag or the 7mm Rem. Mag. Single set trigger and adjustable rear sight. Weight is about 7.3 lbs. Introduced in 2001.

NIB	Exc.	V.G.	Good	Fair	Poor
700	575	425	300	200	100

CZ 550 Safari Classic Custom

Chambered for the .404 Jeffery, .450 Rigby, or the .505 Gibbs. Fancy grade checkered walnut stock. Single set trigger. Express sights.

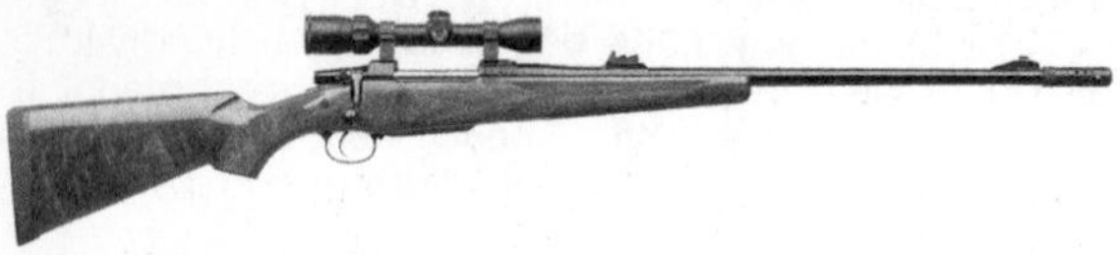

NIB	Exc.	V.G.	Good	Fair	Poor
2400	2000	1400	750	400	300

NOTE: Add $100 for .505 Gibbs.

CZ-581

A 12 gauge O/U double-barrel boxlock shotgun with 28" ventilated rib barrels, single trigger, and automatic ejectors. Blued with a walnut stock.

NIB	Exc.	V.G.	Good	Fair	Poor
875	700	600	450	400	200

CZ-584

A combination 12 gauge/7x57Rmm, .222 or .308 caliber Over/Under combination rifle/shotgun with 24.5" ventilated rib barrels, single triggers and automatic ejectors. Blued with a walnut stock.

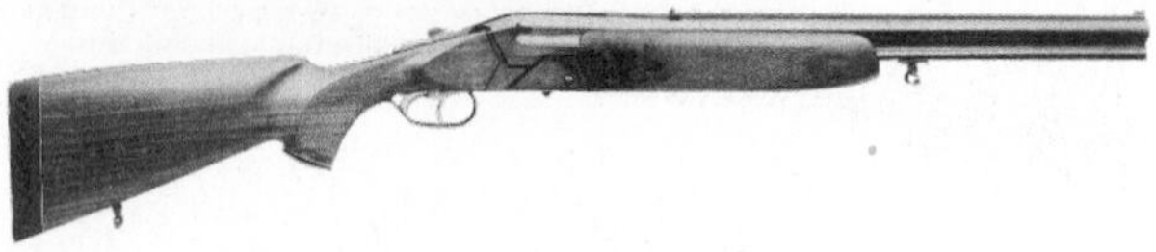

NIB	Exc.	V.G.	Good	Fair	Poor
1000	775	600	500	400	200

CZ ZKK 600

Offered in 7x57mm, 7x64mm, .270, or .30-06. Features a Mauser-type bolt-action with controlled feed, non-rotating extractor, and dovetailed receiver in three action lengths.

NIB	Exc.	V.G.	Good	Fair	Poor
750	625	500	425	325	175

NOTE: Add $100 to prices for pop-up receiver sight that was discontinued in 1977.

CZ ZKK 601

As above, in .243 or .308 caliber.

NIB	Exc.	V.G.	Good	Fair	Poor
700	600	500	425	325	175

CZ ZKK 602

As above, in .300 Holland & Holland, .375 Holland & Holland or .458 Winchester Magnum.

NIB	Exc.	V.G.	Good	Fair	Poor
800	700	600	500	400	200

CZ 700 Sniper M1

Introduced in 2001 this rifle is chambered for the .308 Winchester cartridge and fitted with a 25.6" heavy barrel. Receiver has permanently attached Weaver rail. Laminated stock has adjustable cheekpiece and buttplate with adjustable trigger. Magazine capacity is 10 rounds. Weigh is approximately 12 lbs.

NIB	Exc.	V.G.	Good	Fair	Poor
2350	1800	1300	700	400	200

CZ 750 Sniper

Bolt-action rifle; .308 Win. 10-shot detachable magazine, 26-inch blued barrel, two scope mount systems, polymer stock, weighs 12 lbs. Introduced 2006.

NIB	Exc.	V.G.	Good	Fair	Poor
2000	1750	1550	1050	600	325

CZ 455

Updated version of the popular CZ 452. Action forged from steel billets. Walnut stock, cut checkering, oil finish. No sights furnished, 20-1/2 inch barrel. Trigger adjustable for weight and pull. Detachable magazine. Available with CZ Switch Barrel Set in .22 LR and .17 HMR. Single barrel guns chambered for the .22LR, .22 WMR or .17 HMR.

NIB	Exc.	V.G.	Good	Fair	Poor
350	300	250	220	170	100

CZ 512

Rimfire, semi-automatic rifle. Dual guide rods for smooth operation. Hammer forged barrel, adjustable sights. Receiver is machined for 11mm dovetail mounts. Field stripping via a coin, modular design for simple takedown. Aluminum upper receiver with polymer lower. Beechwood stock. Chambered for the .22LR and .22 WMR.

NIB	Exc.	V.G.	Good	Fair	Poor
400	350	295	220	185	125

CZ 550 Urban Sniper

Compact profile in a modern sniper rifle. Free floating 16" barrel with target crown. Surefire muzzle brake with suppressor compatibility. Bell & Carlson fiberglass stock, aluminum bedding block, oversized bolt handle and single stage trigger. Available with a 5 or 10 round magazine. Chambered for the .308 Winchester with other calibers on request.

NIB	Exc.	V.G.	Good	Fair	Poor
2000	1725	1400	950	500	300

SHOTGUNS

CZ 712

This is a gas-operated semi-automatic 12 gauge 3" chamber shotgun built on a lightweight alloy receiver. Offered with a choice of 26" or 28" vent rib barrels. Magazine is 4 rounds. Checkered walnut stock with blued finish. Weight is about 7 lbs. Introduced in 2004.

NIB	Exc.	V.G.	Good	Fair	Poor
425	325	275	200	150	100

CZ 720

This model is similar to the above but chambered for the 20 gauge 3" shell. Offered with a choice of 26" or 28" vent rib barrels. Walnut stock. Weight is about 6 lbs. Introduced in 2004.

NIB	Exc.	V.G.	Good	Fair	Poor
425	325	275	200	150	100

Redhead

This over and under is available in 12, 20, or 28 gauge with choke tubes, and .410 bore with fixed chokes. Barrel lengths are 26" or 28". Single-selective trigger with extractors on 28 and .410 models. Checkered walnut stock with pistol grip. Receiver finish is silver. Weight from 8 lbs. to 6 lbs. depending on gauge.

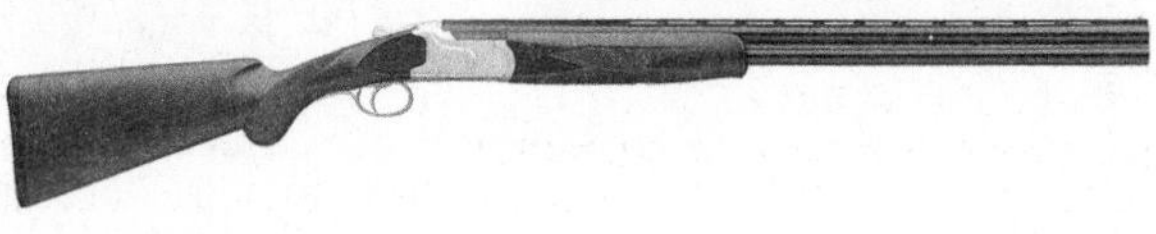

NIB	Exc.	V.G.	Good	Fair	Poor
795	625	500	350	200	150

Canvasback

This over and under gun is offered in 12 or 20 gauge fitted with 26" or 28" barrels with choke tubes. Single-selective trigger with extractors. Black receiver finish. Weight is about 7.5 lbs.

NIB	Exc.	V.G.	Good	Fair	Poor
695	550	450	350	200	150

Woodcock

Available in 12, 20, 28 and .410 bore with 26" or 28" barrel with chokes tubes except for fixed chokes on the .410. Single-selective trigger with ejectors except for the 12 and 20 gauge. Receiver is case colored with sideplate. Checkered walnut stock with pistol grip.

NIB	Exc.	V.G.	Good	Fair	Poor
1055	825	625	450	300	225

NOTE: Add $75 for 28 and .410 models.

Woodcock Custom Grade

Similar to the Woodcock model, but stocked with Grade IV walnut and offered only in 20 gauge with 28" barrels.

NIB	Exc.	V.G.	Good	Fair	Poor
1500	1250	975	600	400	200

Mallard

This 12 or 20 gauge over and under gun is fitted with double triggers and extractors. Barrel length is 28". Checkered walnut stock with pistol grip. Coin finish receiver.

NIB	Exc.	V.G.	Good	Fair	Poor
695	550	450	350	200	150

Durango

This side-by-side gun is offered in 12 or 20 gauge with 20" barrels with choke tubes. Extractors. Case colored receiver. Single trigger. Checkered walnut with pistol grip.

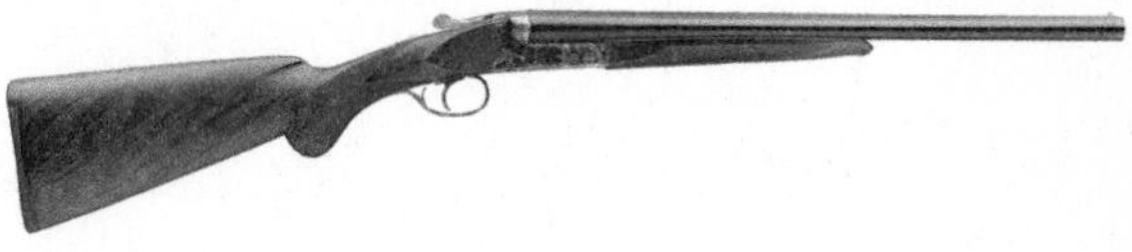

NIB	Exc.	V.G.	Good	Fair	Poor
795	625	550	400	300	200

Amarillo

As above but with double triggers.

NIB	Exc.	V.G.	Good	Fair	Poor
700	550	425	350	250	150

Ringneck

This side-by-side gun is chambered for the 12, 16, 20, 28, or .410 bore with 26" or 28" barrels with choke tubes. Case colored receiver with side plates. Single-selective trigger with extractors. Checkered walnut stock with pistol grip. Add $100 for 16 gauge.

NIB	*Exc.*	*V.G.*	*Good*	*Fair*	*Poor*
870	675	575	400	300	200

NOTE: Add $175 for 28 and .410 models.

Ringneck Custom Grade

Select Grade IV walnut is used in the manufacture of this 20 gauge with 28" barrels.

NIB	*Exc.*	*V.G.*	*Good*	*Fair*	*Poor*
1200	1000	700	450	300	200

Bobwhite

As above but with straight grip stock and double triggers.

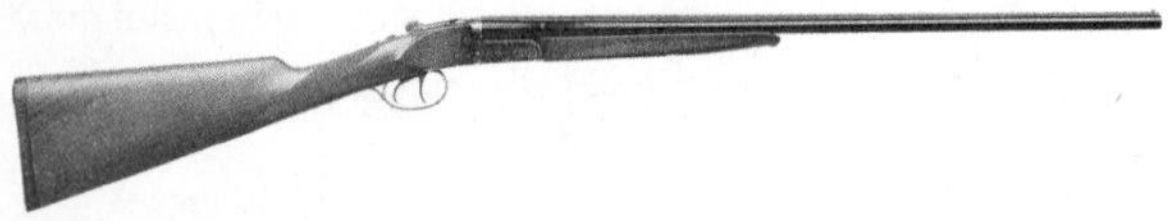

NIB	*Exc.*	*V.G.*	*Good*	*Fair*	*Poor*
795	625	550	400	300	200

Partridge

New in 2008, this side-by-side is available in 12, 20 and 28 gauge and .410 bore with 3" chambers (2.75" in 28 gauge), each with a frame scaled to its bore size. White chrome-plated receiver with scroll engraving. Boxlock action and double triggers. Straight grip stock and splinter forend. Barrels are 28" in 12 and 20 gauge and 26" in 28 and .410. Includes five choke tubes (.410 is choked IC/MOD). Add 20 percent for 28 gauge and .410 bore.

NIB	*Exc.*	*V.G.*	*Good*	*Fair*	*Poor*
795	625	550	400	300	200

Grouse

New in 2008, the Grouse is a single trigger side-by-side in 12, 20 and 28 gauge and .410 bore with 3" chambers (2.75" in 28 gauge). White chrome-plated receiver with scroll engraving. Prince of Wales grip and semi-beavertail Schnabel forend. Barrels are 28" in 12 and 20 gauge and 26" in 28 and .410. Includes five choke tubes (.410 is choked IC/MOD). Add 20 percent for 28 gauge and .410 bore.

NIB	*Exc.*	*V.G.*	*Good*	*Fair*	*Poor*
995	800	700	550	450	300

CZ Sporting

This dedicated sporting clays over/under is a 12 gauge with an adjustable comb stock and forend of #3 Circassian walnut. It features chrome-lined barrels back-bored to .736 and automatic ejectors. Barrels are 30" or 32". Five choke tubes included. Weight is about 9 lbs.

NIB	*Exc.*	*V.G.*	*Good*	*Fair*	*Poor*
2400	1800	1300	700	400	200

Hammer Coach

12-gauge cowboy gun with double triggers, color case hardened receiver, external hammers and Turkish walnut pistol grip stock and forend. Fixed IC and modified chokes. Introduced 2006.

NIB	*Exc.*	*V.G.*	*Good*	*Fair*	*Poor*
795	625	550	400	300	200

D

DAEWOO
Pusan, Korea

DR200

Introduced in 1996 this post-ban semi-automatic rifle is chambered for the .223 Rem. cartridge. It features a black matte finish with a synthetic thumbhole stock. Barrel length is 18.3". Uses AR-15 magazines, not included with the rifle. Weight is about 9 lbs.

NIB	*Exc.*	*V.G.*	*Good*	*Fair*	*Poor*
975	875	500	400	300	150

K-2/AR-100 (Max I)

A 5.56mm caliber pre-ban semi-automatic rifle with an 18" barrel, gas-operated rotary bolt-action, magazines interchangeable with those from the M-16. Black. Introduced in 1985, but is no longer imported.

NIB	*Exc.*	*V.G.*	*Good*	*Fair*	*Poor*
1450	1200	950	700	500	400

K1A1 (Max II)

This rifle is quite similar to the K-2/AR-100 but with a folding composite stock.

NIB	*Exc.*	*V.G.*	*Good*	*Fair*	*Poor*
1450	1200	950	700	500	400

DAISY
Rogers, Arkansas

VL Presentation Model

As above, with a walnut stock. Approximately 4,000 were made in 1968 and 1969.

NIB	*Exc.*	*V.G.*	*Good*	*Fair*	*Poor*
275	150	125	100	75	50

VL Cased Presentation Model

As above, with a gold plaque inlaid in the stock and with a fitted case containing 300 VL cartridges.

NIB	*Exc.*	*V.G.*	*Good*	*Fair*	*Poor*
325	200	175	125	100	75

Model 2201/2211

A bolt-action single-shot rifle chambered for .22 LR cartridge. Fitted with a 19" barrel with octagon shroud. Ramp blade front sight with adjustable notch rear sight. Synthetic stock on Model 2211 and walnut stock on Model 2201. Trigger is adjustable. Weight is about 6.5 lbs.

NIB	*Exc.*	*V.G.*	*Good*	*Fair*	*Poor*
200	150	100	60	50	25

Model 2202/2212

Similar to the above model in appearance but fitted with a 10-round rotary magazine. The synthetic stock is Model 2212 and the walnut stock is Model 2202. Weight is about 6.5 lbs.

NIB	*Exc.*	*V.G.*	*Good*	*Fair*	*Poor*
200	150	100	60	50	25

Model 2203/2213

This is a semi-automatic rifle chambered for .22 long rifle cartridge. Has a 7-round magazine and a 19" barrel. The synthetic stock is Model 2213 and the walnut stock is Model 2203. Weight is approximately 6.5 lbs.

NIB	*Exc.*	*V.G.*	*Good*	*Fair*	*Poor*
225	175	125	75	75	50

DAKIN GUN CO.
San Francisco, California

Model 100

A 12 and 20 gauge boxlock double-barrel shotgun with 26" or 28" barrels, various chokes, extractors and double triggers. Engraved, blued, with a checkered walnut stock. Manufactured in the 1960s.

NIB	*Exc.*	*V.G.*	*Good*	*Fair*	*Poor*
—	475	325	275	200	100

Model 147

As above, with ventilated rib barrels.

NIB	*Exc.*	*V.G.*	*Good*	*Fair*	*Poor*
—	450	375	250	200	100

Model 160

As above with a single-selective trigger.

NIB	*Exc.*	*V.G.*	*Good*	*Fair*	*Poor*
—	700	600	450	250	150

Model 215

As above, but more finely finished.

NIB	*Exc.*	*V.G.*	*Good*	*Fair*	*Poor*
—	1800	1600	1100	500	250

Model 170

A 12, 16, and 20 gauge Over/Under shotgun with 26" or 28" ventilated rib barrels, various chokes, and double triggers. Blued and lightly engraved. Discontinued in the 1960s.

NIB	*Exc.*	*V.G.*	*Good*	*Fair*	*Poor*
—	500	425	350	275	150

DAKOTA ARMS, INC.
Sturgis, South Dakota

This company was formed by Don Allen. He was a fine craftsmen in the field of custom rifles. The company offers four basic models with a number of options to fit the customers' needs or wants. The workmanship and materials are of the highest quality. In business since 1987, the company was purchased by Remington Arms Co. in 2009. **NOTE:** All prices are base prices. Dakota offers a number of extra cost options that can greatly affect the value of its rifles and shotguns.

RIFLES

Dakota 76 Classic

A .257 Roberts, .270 Winchester, .280 Remington, .3006, 7mm Remington Magnum, .338, .300 Winchester Magnum, and the

.458 Winchester Magnum bolt-action rifle with a 23" barrel, and Mauser-type extractor. Checkered walnut stock. Manufactured in 1987.

NIB	Exc.	V.G.	Good	Fair	Poor
5000	4250	3000	1650	800	400

Dakota 76 Varmint

Introduced in 1996 this rifle is chambered for a variety of cartridges from the .22 Hornet to the 6mm PPC. This is a single-shot bolt-action design available in right- or left-hand versions. Barrel length is 24". The Varmint-style stock is semi-fancy walnut with oil finish and no checkering. Many extra cost options are offered for this model. This model is no longer in production as of 1998.

NIB	Exc.	V.G.	Good	Fair	Poor
5000	42500	3000	1650	800	400

Varmint Grade

Offered in a wide variety of calibers from the .222 Rem. to the .22-250 Rem. Furnished with X grade English walnut. This model was discontinued in 1998.

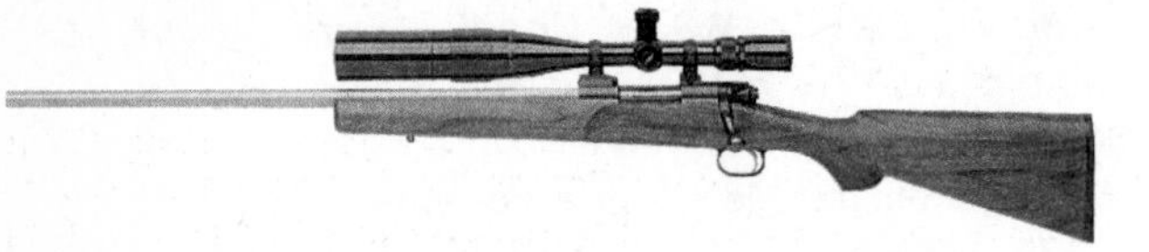

NIB	Exc.	V.G.	Good	Fair	Poor
2500	1850	1500	1100	600	300

Varmint Hunter

This model is built on a Model 97 action. Standard features are fiberglass stock, round-action single-shot, adjustable trigger, and black recoil pad. Barrel length is 24". Offered in calibers from .220 Swift to .308 Winchester. Weight is about 8 lbs. Introduced in 1999.

NIB	Exc.	V.G.	Good	Fair	Poor
2195	1750	1000	750	600	300

Safari Grade

Chambered in .375 Holland & Holland, .458 Winchester Magnum, and other short Magnum calibers. Features an ebony forend tip, one-piece magazine assembly and open sights. Weighs approximately 8-1/2 lbs.

NIB	Exc.	V.G.	Good	Fair	Poor
6495	5250	2000	1350	700	350

Alpine Grade

As above, but lighter in weight and chambered for .22-250, .243, 6mm, 250-3000, 7mm/08, .308, and .358. Introduced in 1989.

NIB	Exc.	V.G.	Good	Fair	Poor
5400	3950	3000	2000	700	350

African Grade

As above in .416 Rigby, .416 Dakota, .404 Jeffery, and .450 Dakota with walnut especially selected for strength, with crossbolts through the stock. Weighs between 9 and 10 lbs.

NIB	Exc.	V.G.	Good	Fair	Poor
7995	5750	4500	2200	1075	400

Model 10 Single-Shot

Built on a single-shot falling action this rifle features a 23" barrel and choice of XX grade wood with oil finish. Fine line checkering, steel gripcap, and 1/2" recoil pad are also standard. Weighs about 5.5 lbs.

NIB	Exc.	V.G.	Good	Fair	Poor
5200	4000	2750	1550	900	400

Model 10 Single-Shot Magnum

Same as above but in calibers .338 Win. Mag to .416 Dakota. Weight about 6.5 lbs.

NIB	Exc.	V.G.	Good	Fair	Poor
5895	4600	3200	1900	1000	450

Dakota .22 Long Rifle Sporter

Fitted with a 22" barrel and X grade oil finish walnut with fine line checkering and steel gripcap. A 1/2" black recoil pad is standard. Weighs about 6-1/2 lbs. This model ceased production in 1998.

NIB	Exc.	V.G.	Good	Fair	Poor
1750	1300	800	650	500	275

Dakota .22 Long Rifle Sporter (New Model)

This is a reintroduction (2003) of the Dakota .22 rifle.

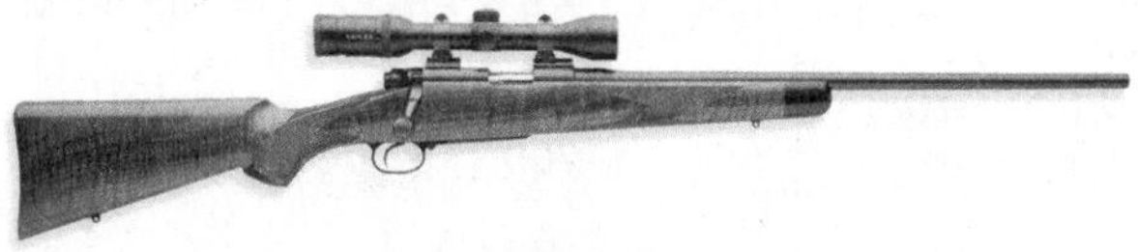

NIB	Exc.	V.G.	Good	Fair	Poor
3000	2500	2000	1350	700	350

Model 97 Long Range Hunter

Introduced in 1997 this bolt-action rifle is offered in 13 calibers: .250-6, .257 Roberts, .270 Win., .280 Rem., 7mm Rem. Mag., 7mm Dakota Mag., .30-06, .300 Win. Mag., .300 Dakota Mag., .338 Win. Mag., .330 Dakota Mag., .375 H&H, .375 Dakota Mag. Barrel lengths depend on caliber but are either 24" or 26". The trigger is fully adjustable. Many other special features. Stock is black synthetic with one-piece bedding. Black recoil pad is standard. Weight is approximately 7.7 lbs.

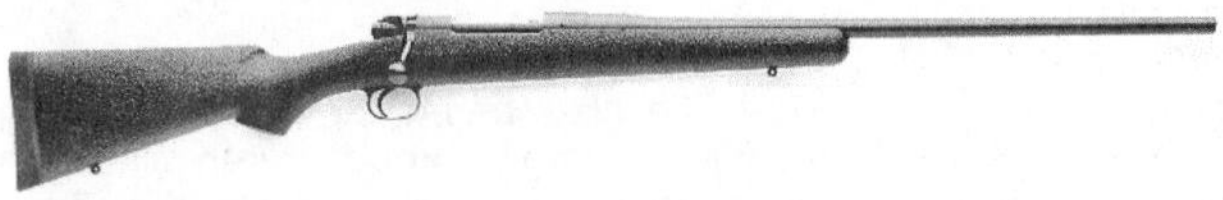

NIB	Exc.	V.G.	Good	Fair	Poor
2800	2400	2200	1500	800	375

Model 97 Lightweight Hunter

Introduced in 1998 this rifle features barrel lengths from 22" to 24" in both short- and long-actions. A special lightweight composite stock is used. Calibers offered range from .22-250 to .330 Dakota Magnum. Weights are between 6.15 to 6.5 lbs. depending on caliber and barrel length.

NIB	Exc.	V.G.	Good	Fair	Poor
2000	1500	1100	800	500	375

NOTE: Add 50 to 70 percent for Deluxe with AAA grade wood.

Model T-76 Longbow Tactical Rifle

This long range tactical bolt-action rifle is available in 3 calibers: .338 Lapua, .300 Dakota Mag., and .330 Dakota Mag. The fiberglass stock is an A-2 McMillan in black or olive green. Adjustable length of pull with bipod spike in forearm. The 28" stainless steel is .950 diameter at the muzzle with muzzlebrake. The rifle is sold with a number of accessories such as a case with bipod, tool kit and tool box. Weight is about 13.7 lbs.

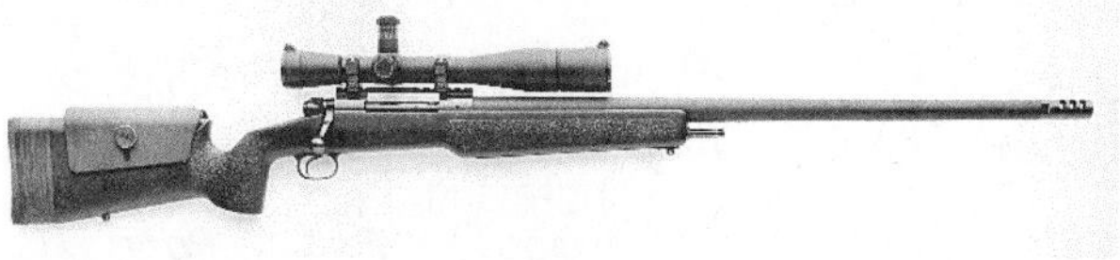

NIB	Exc.	V.G.	Good	Fair	Poor
4600	4250	3000	1650	800	400

MODEL 76 TRAVELER

This model was introduced in 1999 and is built on a modified Model 76 design and stocked in wood. Disassembly is threadless. It is offered in standard length action, short magnum-action, and long-actions in both left and right hand. Offered in three grades.

Traveler Classic

NIB	Exc.	V.G.	Good	Fair	Poor
4495	3200	2575	1700	600	350

Traveler Safari

NIB	Exc.	V.G.	Good	Fair	Poor
5495	3900	2575	1700	600	350

Traveler African

NIB	Exc.	V.G.	Good	Fair	Poor
5995	4500	3100	2200	900	450

Classic Predator

This bolt action rifle is chambered for the .17 VarTarg, .17 Rem., .17 Tactical, .20 VarTarg, .20 Tactical, .20 PPC, .204 Ruger, .221 Rem. Fireball, .222 Rem., .222 Rem. Mag., .223 Rem., .22 BR, 6 PPC, and the 6 BR. Fitted with a 22" stainless steel barrel, Checkered special select Claro walnut stock with cheekpiece.

NIB	Exc.	V.G.	Good	Fair	Poor
4495	3500	2650	1700	800	375

Serious Predator

As above but with AAA Claro walnut stock.

NIB	Exc.	V.G.	Good	Fair	Poor
5000	4250	3000	1650	800	400

All-Weather Predator

As above but with varmint style composite stock.

NIB	Exc.	V.G.	Good	Fair	Poor
3395	2795	2100	1500	00	300

Double Rifle

Available in most common calibers. Fitted with exhibition walnut with pistol grip. Barrel is 25". Round-action with selective ejectors, recoil, pad and hard case. Prices listed are for guns without engraving.

NIB	Exc.	V.G.	Good	Fair	Poor
42000	35000	28500	17000	3500	800

Little Sharps Rifle

Introduced in 2003 this is a smaller version (20 percent) of the full size Sharps rifle. Standard rifle has a 26" octagon barrel, straight grips stock with XX walnut, steel buttplate and blade front sight. Offered in calibers from .17 HMR to .30-40 Krag. Weight is around 8 lbs.

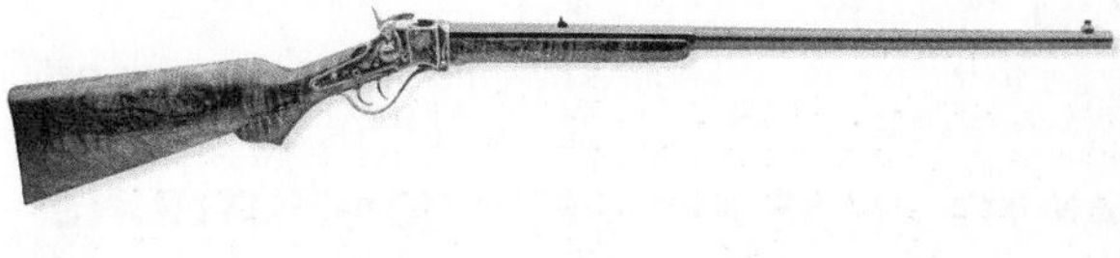

NIB	Exc.	V.G.	Good	Fair	Poor
5500	3950	2750	2000	1500	400

Limited Edition .30-06 Model 76

Ultra-decked-out version of Model 76; commemorates 100th anniversary of .30-06 cartridge; production limited to 101 units. Introduced 2006.

NIB	Exc.	V.G.	Good	Fair	Poor
8000	5500	4000	2650	1700	500

Limited Edition .30-06 Model 10

Ultra-decked-out version of Model 10; commemorates 100th anniversary of .30-06 cartridge; production limited to 101 units. Introduced 2006.

NIB	Exc.	V.G.	Good	Fair	Poor
8000	5500	4000	2650	1700	500

SHOTGUNS

Classic Grade

This grade features a case colored round-action with straight grip and fancy walnut oil finish stock. Forearm is splinter type. Double trigger standard with choice of chokes. This model is no longer in production.

NIB	Exc.	V.G.	Good	Fair	Poor
7950	5200	4400	3000	2000	600

Premier Grade

This grade features a case colored round-action with 50 percent engraving coverage. Exhibition grade English walnut stock with straight grip and splinter forearm. Oil rubbed finish. Double triggers are standard with choice of chokes.

NIB	Exc.	V.G.	Good	Fair	Poor
13950	9500	7000	4750	2900	500

NOTE: Add 10 percent for 28 gauge and .410 bore.

Dakota American Legend

Introduced in 1996, this side-by-side shotgun is offered in 12, 20 and 28 gauge, and .410 bore with 27" barrels, concave rib, splinter forearm, double triggers, straight grips stock, and full scroll engraving on the frame. Many additional extra cost options are offered that can greatly affect the price. The base price is listed.

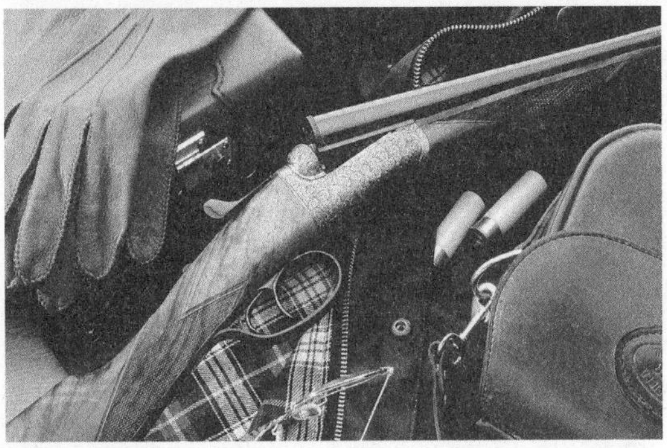

NIB	Exc.	V.G.	Good	Fair	Poor
18000	14000	11500	7900	5000	600

Dakota Shotgun

Similar to the American Legend but offered in two grades of finish. These new grades were first offered in 1997.

DAKOTA ARMS INC.—FERLIB SHOTGUNS

In 2000 Dakota Arms Inc. became the exclusive importer of Ferlib shotgun in the U.S. The models listed are imported and sold by Dakota Arms Inc.

Model 7

NIB	Exc.	V.G.	Good	Fair	Poor
10950	8000	6500	5000	4000	700

Model 7 Prince Model

NIB	Exc.	V.G.	Good	Fair	Poor
11950	9000	7500	6000	4500	700

Model 7 Prince Model Side Lever

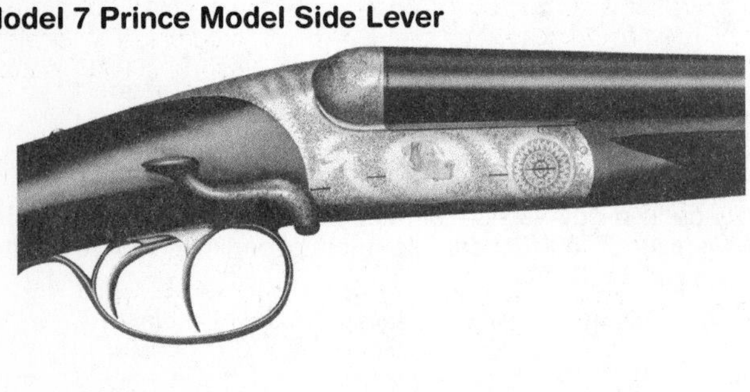

NIB	Exc.	V.G.	Good	Fair	Poor
14500	10500	8500	7000	5500	700

Model 7 Rex

NIB	Exc.	V.G.	Good	Fair	Poor
14950	11000	8500	7000	5500	700

Model 7 Premier

NIB	Exc.	V.G.	Good	Fair	Poor
16950	12500	10000	7200	5500	600

Model 7 Sideplate Model

NIB	Exc.	V.G.	Good	Fair	Poor
14400	10500	8500	7000	5500	700

Model 7 Sideplate Model with Gold

NIB	Exc.	V.G.	Good	Fair	Poor
15100	11250	10000	7200	5500	600

Model 7 Sideplate with Scroll

NIB	Exc.	V.G.	Good	Fair	Poor
14000	10500	8500	7000	5500	700

Model 7 Hammer Gun

NIB	Exc.	V.G.	Good	Fair	Poor
19000	14000	12000	10000	5000	700

Model 7 H.H. Model—no engraving

NIB	Exc.	V.G.	Good	Fair	Poor
20000	15000	13000	11000	570	675

Model 7 Esposizione

NIB	Exc.	V.G.	Good	Fair	Poor
25500	18000	13000	10000	7000	700

Model 7 L'Inglesina

NIB	Exc.	V.G.	Good	Fair	Poor
25500	18000	13000	10000	7000	700

Model 7 Model E "Fantasy"

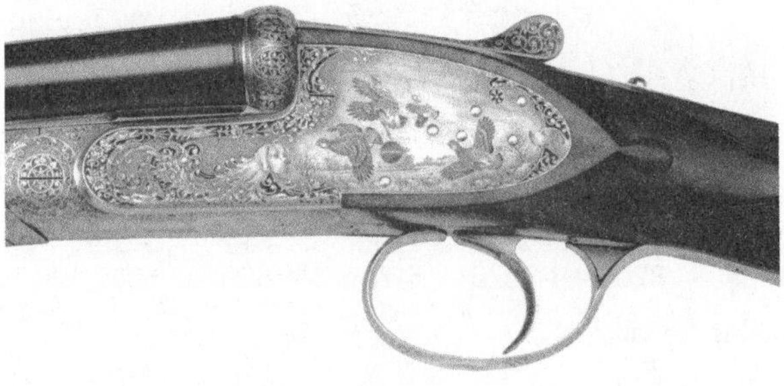

NIB	Exc.	V.G.	Good	Fair	Poor
39500	27500	22000	15500	11000	700

Model 7 Boss—no engraving

NIB	Exc.	V.G.	Good	Fair	Poor
29500	20000	15000	10000	7000	750

DAKOTA ARMS INC.—SIACE SHOTGUNS

Imported from Italy in 2004 and called the Dakota SuperLight. These shotguns are side-by-sides with boxlock actions.

Field

Available in 12, 20, 24, and 28 gauge as a well as 16, 32 and .410. Case colored receiver with select Turkish walnut. Checkereing is 24 lpi. Double triggers. Border engraving. Weight is about 5.5 lbs. for the 20 gauge.

NIB	Exc.	V.G.	Good	Fair	Poor
4500	3500	2400	1775	1100	500

NOTE: Add $600 for 16, 32, and .410 bores.

Field Grade II

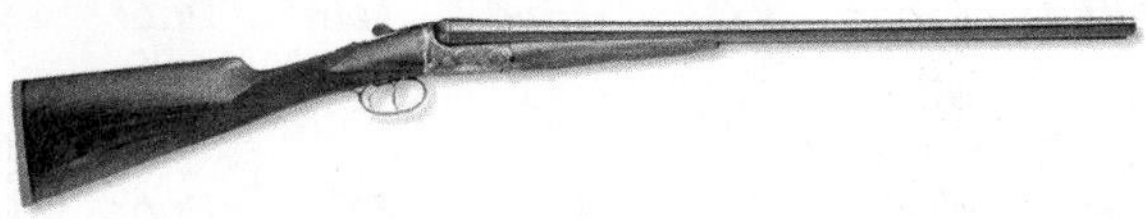

As above but with 65 percent coverage of English scroll.

NIB	Exc.	V.G.	Good	Fair	Poor
5500	4250	3200	1600	800	400

NOTE: Add $700 for 16, 32, and .410 bores.

Field Grade III

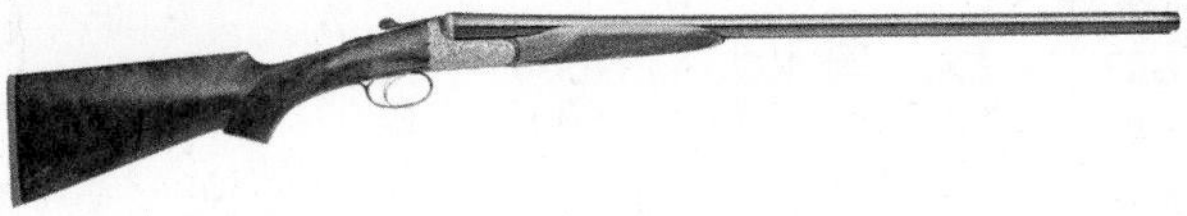

As above but with deeply cut vine and leaf scroll with deluxe Turkish walnut and 65 percent coverage of English scroll.

NIB	Exc.	V.G.	Good	Fair	Poor
6500	5000	4000	3000	1650	400

NOTE: Add $800 for 16, 32, and .410 bores.

DALY, CHARLES

An importer of German, Japanese, and Italian shotguns and combination guns.

CHARLES DALY, EARLY PRUSSIAN GUNS

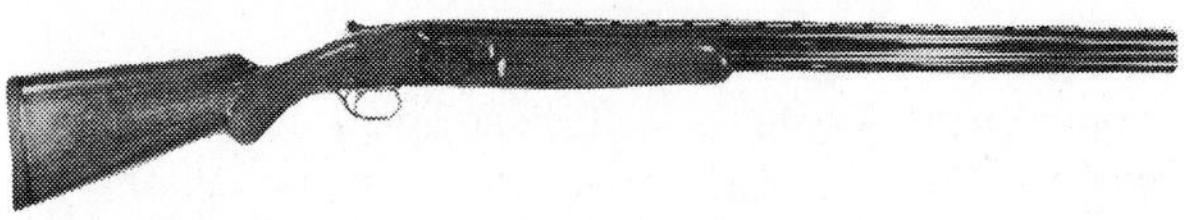

Commanidor Over-and-Under Model 100

A boxlock over-and-under Anson & Deeley action shotgun chambered all gauges, choice of barrel length and chokes, double triggers (standard) or single-selective trigger. Blued with a checkered walnut stock. Manufactured in Belgium in the late 1930s.

NIB	Exc.	V.G.	Good	Fair	Poor
—	1000	750	475	275	200

Commanidor Over-and-Under Model 200

As above, with a better-grade walnut stock.

NIB	Exc.	V.G.	Good	Fair	Poor
—	1100	850	550	300	200

Superior Side-by-Side

As above, with an Anson & Deeley boxlock action and double triggers. Blued with a walnut stock. Not manufactured after 1933.

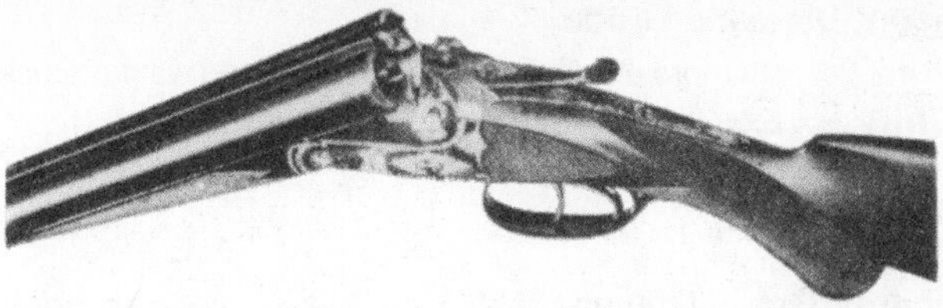

NIB	Exc.	V.G.	Good	Fair	Poor
—	1400	950	650	450	250

Empire Side-by-Side

As above, but engraved with a better grade of walnut.

NIB	Exc.	V.G.	Good	Fair	Poor
—	2750	2000	1750	1250	600

Diamond Grade Side-by-Side

A deluxe version of the above.

NIB	Exc.	V.G.	Good	Fair	Poor
—	5750	4500	3750	3000	1200

Regent Diamond Grade Side-by-Side

A custom order version of the above.

NIB	Exc.	V.G.	Good	Fair	Poor
—	11500	8500	7000	5500	2500

Empire Over-and-Under

A 12, 16, and 20 gauge Anson & Deeley boxlock shotgun with choice of barrel length and choke, double triggers and automatic ejectors. Engraved with fine quality scrollwork and walnut stock. Discontinued in 1933.

NIB	Exc.	V.G.	Good	Fair	Poor
—	3500	2750	2000	1150	500

Diamond Grade Over-and-Under

As above, but more finely finished.

NIB	Exc.	V.G.	Good	Fair	Poor
—	5500	3750	3250	2500	1250

SEXTUPLE SINGLE-BARREL TRAP

Empire Grade

A 12 gauge boxlock single-barrel shotgun with 30"-34" Full choke barrels, ventilated rib and automatic ejectors. The strong action features six locking lugs. Engraved with a walnut stock. Manufactured after 1933.

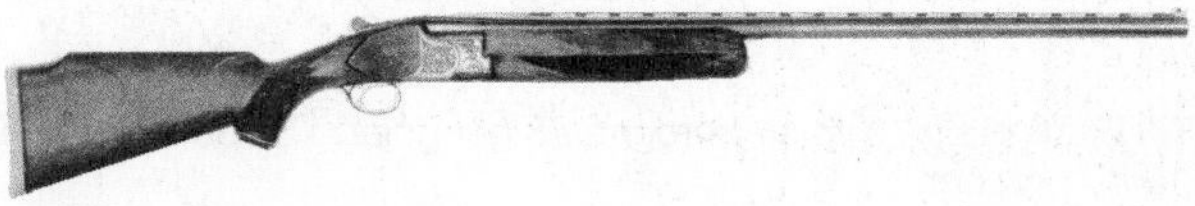

NIB	Exc.	V.G.	Good	Fair	Poor
—	2950	2450	1850	1500	750

Regent Diamond Grade

As above, with more engraving and a better grade walnut stock.

NIB	Exc.	V.G.	Good	Fair	Poor
—	7500	6300	5500	4500	2000

DRILLINGS

Superior Grade Drilling

A 12, 16, and 20 gauge Over/Under rifle/shotgun with a rifle barrel in .25-20, .25-35, or .30-30. Engraved with a walnut stock. Not manufactured after 1933.

NIB	Exc.	V.G.	Good	Fair	Poor
—	3700	2450	1800	1450	800

Diamond Grade Drilling

As above, with more engraving and a better grade of walnut in the stock.

NIB	Exc.	V.G.	Good	Fair	Poor
—	5250	4500	3750	3000	1500

Regent Diamond Grade Drilling

As above, with elaborate engraving and the highest quality walnut stock.

NIB	Exc.	V.G.	Good	Fair	Poor
—	12500	9500	7200	5800	3000

CHARLES DALY, B.C. MIROKU GUNS

Empire Grade Side-by-Side

A 12, 16, and 20 gauge Anson and Deeley boxlock shotgun with 26", 28", and 30" barrels, various chokes, extractors, and a single trigger. Blued with a checkered walnut stock. Manufactured between 1968 and 1971.

NIB	Exc.	V.G.	Good	Fair	Poor
—	750	550	375	200	100

NOTE: Add 10 percent for ventilated rib barrels and/or 20 gauge.

Superior Grade Single Barrel Trap

A 12 gauge boxlock shotgun with 32" or 34" ventilated rib barrels, Full choke, and automatic ejector. Blued with Monte Carlo walnut stock. Manufactured between 1968 and 1976.

NIB	Exc.	V.G.	Good	Fair	Poor
—	675	525	450	350	200

OVER-AND-UNDERS

A 12, 20, and 28 gauge and .410 bore boxlock shotgun with 26", 28", and 30" barrels with ventilated ribs. Various choke combinations were offered with single-selective triggers and automatic ejectors. Blued with checkered walnut stocks. The differences between the grades are the degree and quality of the engraving and the grade of walnut used for the stock. The smaller-bore guns bring a premium as listed. Manufactured between 1963 and 1976 by B.C. Miroku.

Venture Grade

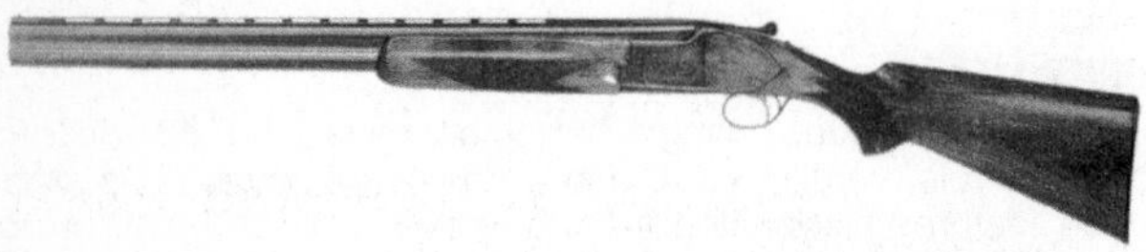

NIB	Exc.	V.G.	Good	Fair	Poor
—	750	675	500	375	200

NOTE: 20 gauge add 10 percent. 28 gauge add 20 percent. .410 add 30 percent.

Venture Grade Skeet or Trap

Offered with either 26" Skeet & Skeet or 30" Full choke.

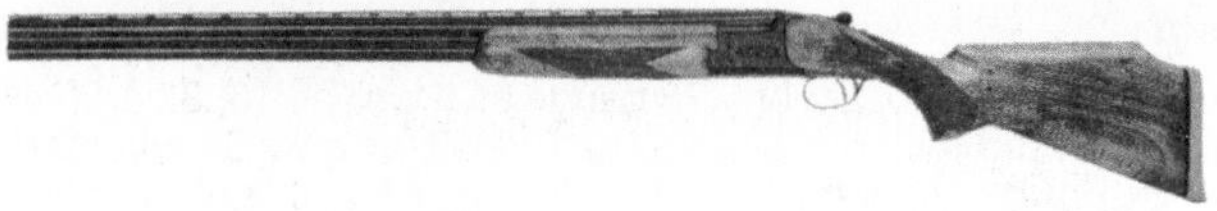

NIB	Exc.	V.G.	Good	Fair	Poor
—	600	550	475	375	200

NOTE: 20 gauge add 10 percent. 28 gauge add 20 percent. .410 add 30 percent.

Field Grade

Chambered for 12 and 20 gauge only.

NIB	Exc.	V.G.	Good	Fair	Poor
—	650	575	500	425	200

Superior Grade

NIB	Exc.	V.G.	Good	Fair	Poor
—	750	675	600	525	200

Superior Grade Trap

NIB	Exc.	V.G.	Good	Fair	Poor
—	800	600	525	425	200

Diamond Grade

NIB	Exc.	V.G.	Good	Fair	Poor
—	1800	1400	975	650	300

Diamond Grade Trap or Skeet

With either 26" Skeet & Skeet or 30" Full choke barrels and Monte Carlo stocks.

NIB	Exc.	V.G.	Good	Fair	Poor
—	1500	1100	800	650	350

NOTE: Wide rib add 5 percent.

CHARLES DALY, ITALIAN MANUFACTURE

Manufactured by the firm of Breda in Milan, Italy. The semi-automatic "Novamatic" was produced in 1968. All other models began Italian production in 1976. Imported by KBI, Inc. until 2010.

Novamatic Lightweight

A 12 gauge semi-automatic shotgun with a 26" or 28" ventilated-rib barrel and screw-in choke tubes. The receiver is alloy, with checkered walnut stock. Imported under the Daly name in 1968 only.

NIB	Exc.	V.G.	Good	Fair	Poor
—	400	325	275	175	125

Novamatic Trap

As above, with a Monte Carlo stock and a 30" full choke barrel.

NIB	Exc.	V.G.	Good	Fair	Poor
—	415	340	290	200	150

Charles Daly Automatic

A 12 gauge Magnum semi-automatic shotgun with 26" or 28" ventilated rib barrels, screw-in choke tubes and a 5-shot magazine. There is a slug gun available with rifle sights. Checkered walnut grip in two versions—a pistol grip and an English-style straight grip.

NIB	Exc.	V.G.	Good	Fair	Poor
—	475	395	300	225	150

NOTE: The choke-tube model would be worth a 10 percent premium.

Field Grade

Introduced in 1999, this model has several variations all in 12 gauge. The standard gun has a choice of 24", 26", 28", or 30" barrels with screw-in chokes and synthetic stocks. A slug gun is offered with 22" barrel in blue or nickel finish. A full coverage camo model is offered in the same configurations as the field grade.

NIB	Exc.	V.G.	Good	Fair	Poor
425	365	255	200	150	100

NOTE: Add $30 for nickel slug gun, add $100 for camo gun.

Superior Grade Hunter

Offered in 12 gauge with choice of 26", 28", or 30" vent-rib barrels. Walnut stock with hand checkering. Gold trigger and gold highlights. Introduced in 1999.

NIB	Exc.	V.G.	Good	Fair	Poor
550	425	365	245	160	100

Superior Grade Sporting

Same as above but with a 28" or 30" ported barrel and select walnut stock.

NIB	Exc.	V.G.	Good	Fair	Poor
570	450	365	245	160	100

Superior Grade Trap (Semi-Automatic Shotguns)

This 12 gauge model is offered with a choice of 30" or 32" vent-rib barrel. Walnut stock with hand checkering. Introduced in 1999.

NIB	Exc.	V.G.	Good	Fair	Poor
625	475	390	270	185	100

Field Hunter VR-MC

This series of 3" semi-automatic 12 gauges is finished in one of four Realtree/Advantage camo patterns or matte black. Barrels are 24", 26" or 28". Advantage Timber model is available in 20 gauge and black matte is available in 20 and 28 gauge. Add 15 percent for camo.

NIB	Exc.	V.G.	Good	Fair	Poor
425	365	255	200	150	100

Field Hunter VR-MC Youth

As above but with a 1.6-inch shorter stock and 22" barrel. In 20 gauge only.

NIB	Exc.	V.G.	Good	Fair	Poor
400	345	230	165	125	100

Superior II

New in 2007, the Superior II line of semi-autos features oil-finished Turkish walnut stocks and three chokes.

NIB	Exc.	V.G.	Good	Fair	Poor
600	525	395	275	200	100

Superior II Hunter

Available in 12 and 20 gauge with 26" or 28" barrel and 28 gauge with 26" barrel.

NIB	Exc.	V.G.	Good	Fair	Poor
600	525	395	275	200	100

Superior II Sport

In 12 gauge only with 28" or 30" ported barrel and wide rib.

NIB	Exc.	V.G.	Good	Fair	Poor
600	525	395	275	200	100

Superior II Trap

In 12 gauge, 30" ported barrel only with Monte Carlo comb and wide rib.

NIB	Exc.	V.G.	Good	Fair	Poor
650	550	425	275	200	100

Field Hunter Maxi-Mag VR-MC Semi-Auto

This 3.5" 12 gauge comes in one of three Realtree/Advantage camos and matte black with 24", 26" or 28" ported barrel. Add 15 percent for camo.

NIB	Exc.	V.G.	Good	Fair	Poor
425	365	255	200	150	100

TURKISH SHOTGUNS

Model 105

This 3" 12 gauge over-and-under features an engraved nickel-plated steel receiver, double triggers and extractors. Chokes are fixed Modified and Full with 28" barrels or Modified and Improved Cylinder with 26" barrels.

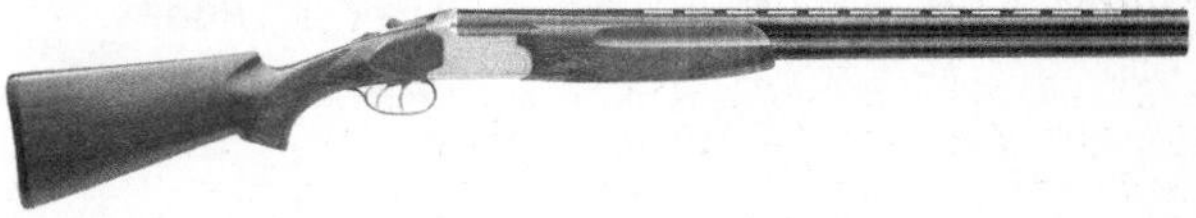

NIB	Exc.	V.G.	Good	Fair	Poor
600	450	395	300	175	100

Model 106/206

Similar to Model 105 but in 12, 20 and 28 gauge and .410 bore. The Model 106 has a blued receiver with raised gold ducks and a rounded pistol grip. All but the .410 include three screw-in chokes. Barrels are 26" or 28" in 12 and 20 gauge and 26" in 28 gauge and .410. Frames are scaled to gauge.

NIB	Exc.	V.G.	Good	Fair	Poor
650	495	395	300	175	100

NOTE: Add $50 for 28 and .410. Add $50 for model 206 with SST, ejectors.

Model 306

This 3" side-by-side is offered in 12 and 20 gauge with 26" or 28" barrels. Turkish walnut stock, gold-plated single selective trigger and extractors. Three choke tubes.

NIB	Exc.	V.G.	Good	Fair	Poor
400	350	295	175	115	75

PUMP SHOTGUNS

Field Grade

This 12 gauge pump gun is offered with 24", 26", 28", or 30" barrels. With fixed chokes. A slug gun is offered with 18.5" barrels with blue or nickel finish. A camo version is also offered. First introduced in 1999. This model is also offered in 20 gauge in both full size and youth.

NIB	Exc.	V.G.	Good	Fair	Poor
300	225	165	125	100	65

NOTE: Add $10 for nickel gun, add $80 for full camo gun.

Field Tactical

This pump gun is chambered for the 12 gauge shell and fitted with an 18.5" barrel with fixed blade front sight . An 18.5" slug barrel with adjustable sights is also offered. Black synthetic stock. Blued or nickel finish.

NIB	Exc.	V.G.	Good	Fair	Poor
350	275	190	150	125	75

NOTE: Add $30 for nickel finish.

Field Hunter MM (Maxi-Mag)

This is a 12 gauge pump gun chambered for the 3.5" Magnum shell. Offered with choice of 24", 26", or 28" vent-rib ported barrels. Black synthetic stock with camo stock also available. Weight is about 6.75 lbs.

NIB	Exc.	V.G.	Good	Fair	Poor
275	225	150	125	100	65

NOTE: Add $50 for camo finish.

Field Hunter Maxi-Mag VR-MC Pump

Newer versions of the Maxi-Mag are recognized by an updated forend and availability in Timber or Hardwoods camo or matte black. All are 3.5" 12 gauges with a 24", 26" or 28" ported barrel. Add 15 percent for camo.

NIB	Exc.	V.G.	Good	Fair	Poor
350	300	255	200	150	100

OVER-AND-UNDER GUNS

Charles Daly Field Grade Over-and-Under

A 12, 20, 28, and .410 gauge over-and-under shotgun with 26" or 28" chrome-lined ventilated rib barrels with a crossbolt boxlock-action, single-selective trigger, and extractors. Blued with a stamped checkered walnut stock. Introduced in 1989. Weight for 12 gauge guns about 7 lbs. Weight for 28 and .410 guns about 6.75 lbs.

NIB	Exc.	V.G.	Good	Fair	Poor
900	775	575	400	250	200

NOTE: Add $150 for ejectors.

Charles Daly Field Ultra Light

Introduced in 1999, this model is offered in either 12 or 20 gauge with 26" barrel choked Improved Cylinder/Modified. The receiver is aluminum alloy. Walnut stock with pistol grip and slim forend. Weight is approximately 5.5 lbs.

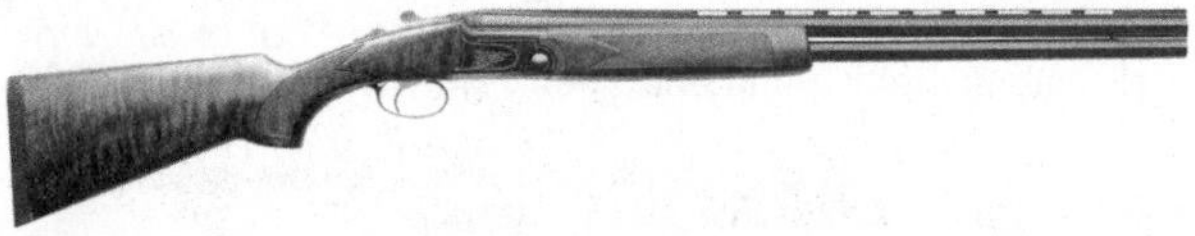

NIB	Exc.	V.G.	Good	Fair	Poor
950	850	650	450	—	—

Charles Daly Empire Over-and-Under

As above with automatic ejectors, screw-in choke tubes, and a silver-finished receiver. The walnut stock is hand-checkered. Introduced in 1989.

NIB	Exc.	V.G.	Good	Fair	Poor
1150	1000	750	500	400	200

Empire II EDL Hunter

Offered in 12, 20, 28, and .410 bores this gun features 26" or 28" vent rib barrels (26" only on 28 or .410), choke tubes on the 12 and 20 gauge guns and fixed chokes on the 28 and .410 guns. Receiver has game scene engraving with nine gold enlays. Weight is 6.25 to 7.25 lbs. depending on gauge.

NIB	Exc.	V.G.	Good	Fair	Poor
2000	1500	1100	700	375	200

Empire Sporting

This model is offered in 12 gauge with a choice of 28" or 30" barrels. Fitted with a Monte Carlo stock and automatic ejectors.

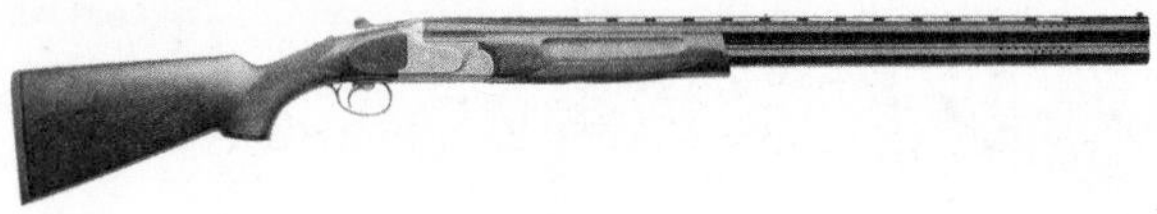

NIB	Exc.	V.G.	Good	Fair	Poor
1850	1425	1000	600	375	200

Empire Grade Combination

This is an over-and-under with a 12 gauge top barrel and a rifle lower barrel. Rifle calibers are .22 Hornet, .223 Rem., .22-250, .243, .270, .308 and .30-06. Barrel length is 23.5". Weight is about 7.25 lbs.

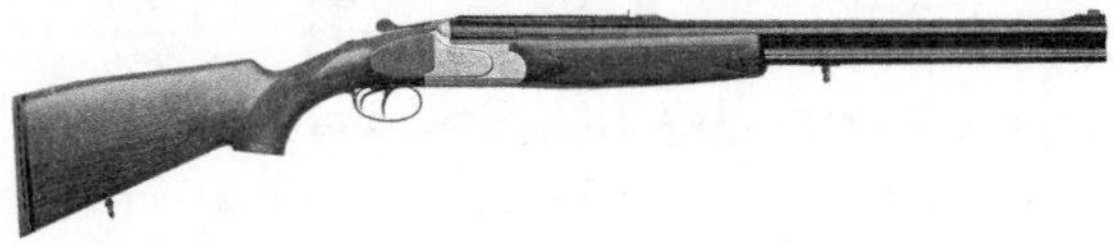

NIB	Exc.	V.G.	Good	Fair	Poor
2190	1600	1150	800	375	200

Empire Trap

This 12 gauge model features a Monte Carlo stock with 30" barrels.

NIB	Exc.	V.G.	Good	Fair	Poor
2250	1650	1200	750	325	150

Empire Trap Mono

This is a single barrel trap gun with choice of 30" or 32" barrels. Automatic ejectors and Monte Carlo fully adjustable stock.

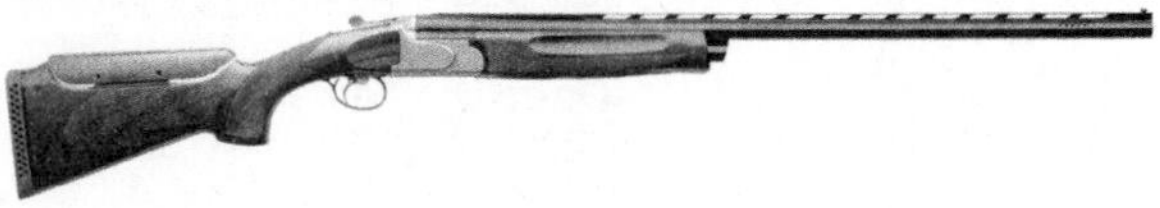

NIB	Exc.	V.G.	Good	Fair	Poor
2450	1800	1250	900	375	175

NOTE: Deduct $600 for non-adjustable stock.

Empire Grade Trap Combo

This model features a 30" over/under barrel with an additional 32" single barrel. Buttstock has fully adjustable comb. Introduced in 1999.

NIB	Exc.	V.G.	Good	Fair	Poor
4000	3000	2000	1450	675	375

NOTE: Deduct $600 for non-adjustable stock.

Diamond Grade Over-and-Under

As above in 12 and 20 gauge Magnum with various barrel lengths and screw-in choke tubes, single trigger, automatic ejectors, and select walnut stock. Extra fancy walnut stock and hand engraved frame.

NIB	Exc.	V.G.	Good	Fair	Poor
5750	4250	2500	1250	900	450

Diamond Grade Sporting

This 12 gauge model features a choice of 28" or 30" barrels with automatic ejectors and Monte Carlo stock.

NIB	Exc.	V.G.	Good	Fair	Poor
5900	4500	2750	1250	900	450

Diamond Grade Trap or Skeet

As above, with 26" or 30" barrels. Available in 1989.

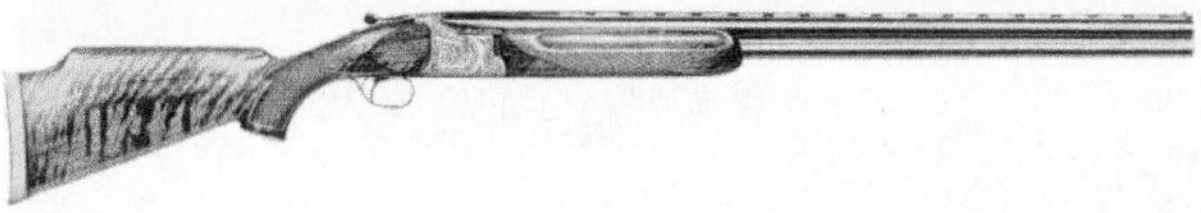

NIB	Exc.	V.G.	Good	Fair	Poor
5900	4500	2750	1250	900	400

Diamond Grade Mono

This model has a fully adjustable stock. Barrel choice is 30". Automatic ejectors are standard.

NIB	Exc.	V.G.	Good	Fair	Poor
6500	5250	3750	1750	900	400

Diamond Grade Trap Combo

This model has a fully adjustable stock. Choice of 30" over/under barrels and 32" single barrel.

NIB	Exc.	V.G.	Good	Fair	Poor
7500	5700	4250	2650	1000	450

Presentation Grade Over-and-Under

As above, with a Purdy-type boxlock action and engraved false sideplates. The stock is of deluxe French walnut. Discontinued in 1986.

NIB	Exc.	V.G.	Good	Fair	Poor
—	5500	3750	1650	900	450

Superior II Over-and-Under

A 12, 20, 28, and .410 gauge over-and-under shotgun with 26" or 28" ventilated rib barrels, various chokes, single trigger, and automatic ejectors. Engraved, blued with a walnut stock. Weight for 12 and 20 gauge guns about 7 lbs. For 28 and .410 guns weight is about 6.75 lbs.

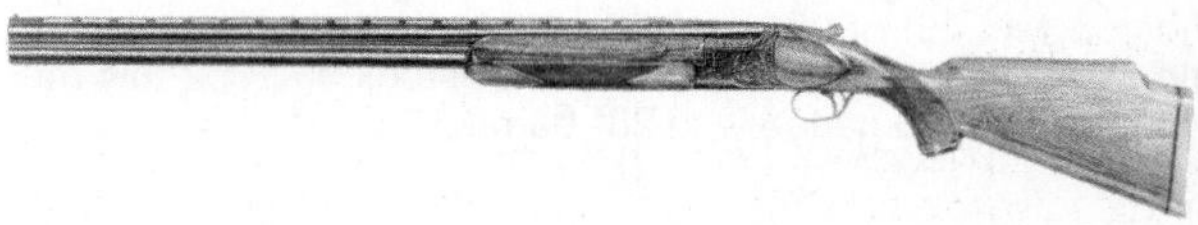

NIB	Exc.	V.G.	Good	Fair	Poor
625	550	350	300	200	150

Superior II Grade Sporting

This 12 gauge model is fitted with a choice of 28" or 30" barrels. Monte Carlo stock and automatic ejectors.

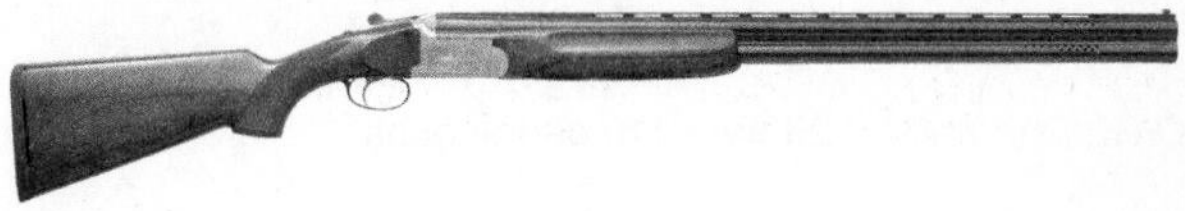

NIB	Exc.	V.G.	Good	Fair	Poor
650	575	375	325	225	165

Superior Grade Trap (Over-And-Under Guns)

This 12 gauge gun is fitted with 30" barrels, Monte Carlo stock and automatic ejectors.

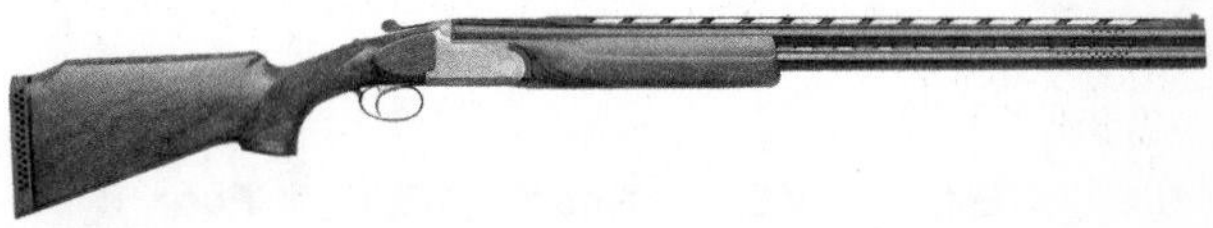

NIB	Exc.	V.G.	Good	Fair	Poor
1700	1250	900	625	425	200

Superior Grade Combination

This is an over-and-under with a 12 gauge top barrel and a rifle lower barrel. Rifle calibers are .22 Hornet, .223 Rem., and .30-06. Barrel length is 23.5". Weight is about 7.25 lbs.

NIB	Exc.	V.G.	Good	Fair	Poor
1480	1100	800	550	350	175

SIDE-BY-SIDE GUNS

Field Hunter

A side-by-side boxlock gun chambered for 10, 12, 20, 28 and .410. Barrel length from 26" to 32" depending on gauge. Extractors are standard. Add $100 for ejectors. Weight from 8.75 lbs. to 6.75 lbs. depending on gauge. Nickel receiver with game scene engraving.

NIB	Exc.	V.G.	Good	Fair	Poor
1190	850	600	400	250	100

NOTE: Add $40 for 28 and .410 guns, add $100 for automatic ejectors.

Superior Hunter

A 12, 20, and 28 gauge as well as .410 bore boxlock double-barrel shotgun with 26" or 28" barrels, various chokes, a boxlock action and single trigger. Blued with a walnut stock. In 2002 this model was offered in 10 gauge with 28" barrels.

NIB	Exc.	V.G.	Good	Fair	Poor
1660	1200	850	600	350	150

NOTE: Add $50 for 28 and .410 gauge guns.

Empire Side-by-Side

Offered in 12 and 20 gauge with 26" or 28" barrels. Chokes are fixed. Weight is about 7 lbs. Silver receiver with game scene engraving, straight stock, splinter forearm, automatic ejectors.

NIB	Exc.	V.G.	Good	Fair	Poor
2120	1500	1100	700	400	200

Diamond Side-by-Side

Offered in 12, 20, 28, and .410 with 26" or 28" barrels and fixed chokes. Fancy walnut straight grip stock, hand detachable sidelocks, 100 percent hand engraving coverage. Hand fit and finished. Weight for 12 and 20 gauge guns is about 6.75 lbs., while the 28 and .410 guns weigh about 5.75 lbs. This model is generally made on special order only.

NIB	Exc.	V.G.	Good	Fair	Poor
6700	5000	3500	1500	750	350

NOTE: Add $450 for 28 and .410 bores.

Country Squire Side-by-Side Folding

This model features a folding stock with 25.5" barrels, gold double triggers and walnut stock. Chokes are Full and Full.

NIB	Exc.	V.G.	Good	Fair	Poor
475	375	275	200	145	100

Country Squire Over-and-Under Folding

Same as the model above but with over-and-under vent-rib barrels 25.5" in length.

NIB	Exc.	V.G.	Good	Fair	Poor
550	450	325	250	175	125

RIFLES

Field Grade Mauser 98

This bolt-action rifle is offered in a wide variety of calibers from .243 Win. to .458 Win. Mag. Barrel length is 23" for all calibers. Stock is black synthetic. Open sights. Add $175 for .375 H&H and .458 Win. Mag.

NIB	Exc.	V.G.	Good	Fair	Poor
460	350	300	225	150	100

NOTE: Add $50 for stainless steel.

Field Grade Mini-Mauser 98

This version is chambered for short cartridges such as the .22 Hornet, .223, .22-250, and 7.62x39mm. Barrel length is 19.25". Magazine capacity is 5 rounds.

NIB	Exc.	V.G.	Good	Fair	Poor
600	475	350	250	175	125

Superior Grade Mauser 98

This model is similar to the Field Grade Mauser with the addition of a hand-checkered walnut stock.

NIB	Exc.	V.G.	Good	Fair	Poor
600	425	325	225	165	100

Superior Grade Mini-Mauser 98

Same as the Field Grade Mini-Mauser with the addition of a hand-checkered walnut stock.

NIB	Exc.	V.G.	Good	Fair	Poor
600	450	325	250	150	100

Field Grade Rimfires

Chambered for .22 LR cartridge and fitted with a 22" barrel in the bolt-action version, 20" barrel in semi-auto version or 17.5" barrel in bolt-action. Youth model, or 16.25" barrel in bolt-action single-shot True Youth model.

NIB	Exc.	V.G.	Good	Fair	Poor
120	100	75	50	25	10

NOTE: Add $25 for True Youth model.

Superior Grade Rimfire

Chambered for .22 LR or .22 Mag, or .22 Hornet in bolt-action or .22 LR semi-auto. Walnut stock with checkering. Open sights.

NIB	Exc.	V.G.	Good	Fair	Poor
175	125	100	75	50	25

NOTE: Add $20 for .22 Mag. model and $170 for .22 Hornet model.

Superior II Grade Rimfire

This version was introduced in 2005 and is chambered for the .22 Long Rifle, .22 WMR, or the .17 HMR cartidges. Fitted with a 22" barrel with open sights on the .22 LR and drilled and tapped for scope mounts on the .22 WMR and .17 HMR models. Oiled walnut stocks with checkering.

NIB	Exc.	V.G.	Good	Fair	Poor
260	200	175	150	125	100

NOTE: Add $40 for .22 Mag. model and $75 for .17 HMR.

Empire Grade Rimfire

Empire Grade has select walnut stock with 24 lpi hand-cut checkering. Grip and forearm caps highly polished and blued metal finish. Same configurations as Superior Grade rifles.

NIB	Exc.	V.G.	Good	Fair	Poor
335	275	225	175	125	100

NOTE: Add $20 For .22 Mag. model and $100 for .22 Hornet model.

Superior Grade Express Rifle

Chambered for the .30-06 cartridge and fitted with 23.5" barrel. Open sights with dovetail receiver for scope mounting. Silver receiver with game scene engraving. Checkered walnut stock with sling swivels. Weight is about 7.75 lbs.

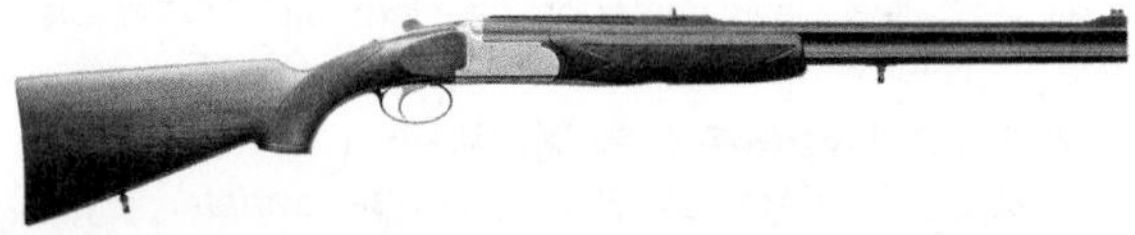

NIB	Exc.	V.G.	Good	Fair	Poor
3250	2700	1800	1475	1000	500

Empire Express Rifle

Chambered for the .30-06, .375H&H, or .416 Rigby cartridge with open sights and dovetail receiver for scope mounting. Barrel length is 23.5". Checkered walnut stock with Bavarian-style cheekpiece. Silver game scene engraved receiver. Weight is about 8 lbs.

NIB	Exc.	V.G.	Good	Fair	Poor
3600	3000	2300	1775	1250	600

NOTE: Add $700 for .375 H&H and .416 Rigby models.

DAN ARMS OF AMERICA

Allentown, Pennsylvania

These are Italian-made shotguns manufactured by Silmer and imported by Dan Arms of America. Production ceased in 1988.

SIDE-BY-SIDES

Field Grade

A boxlock shotgun chambered for all gauges with 26" or 28" barrels, various choke combinations, double triggers and extractors. Blued with a walnut stock.

NIB	Exc.	V.G.	Good	Fair	Poor
—	325	265	225	150	125

Deluxe Field Grade

As above, with a single trigger and automatic ejectors.

NIB	Exc.	V.G.	Good	Fair	Poor
—	465	400	325	250	200

OVER/UNDERS

Lux Grade I

A 12 and 20 gauge Over/Under shotgun with a 26", 28" or 30" ventilated rib barrels, double triggers and extractors. Blued finish with a walnut stock.

NIB	Exc.	V.G.	Good	Fair	Poor
—	325	265	200	150	100

Lux Grade II

As above, in 12 gauge only with a single trigger.

NIB	Exc.	V.G.	Good	Fair	Poor
—	350	300	250	200	150

Lux Grade III

As above, in 20 gauge only with automatic ejectors.

NIB	Exc.	V.G.	Good	Fair	Poor
—	400	325	275	225	175

Lux Grade IV

As above in 12 gauge only with screw-in choke tubes.

NIB	Exc.	V.G.	Good	Fair	Poor
—	450	375	325	275	200

Silver Snipe

A 12 or 20 gauge shotgun manufactured to custom order with engraved false sideplates and a select walnut stock.

NIB	Exc.	V.G.	Good	Fair	Poor
—	1250	1000	800	600	350

DARNE, S. A.

St. Etienne, France

Darne Side-by-Side Shotguns

A 12, 16, 20, or 28 gauge sliding breech double-barrel shotgun manufactured in a variety of barrel lengths and with numerous optional features. Manufactured from 1881 to 1979.NOTE: Darnes have been undergoing a surge in popularity in the last few years because of their unique design. Depending on the circumstances, and the amount of factory engraving and ornamentation present, individual examples may bring considerably in excess of the values listed below. Deduct 25 percent for 2.5-inch chambers.

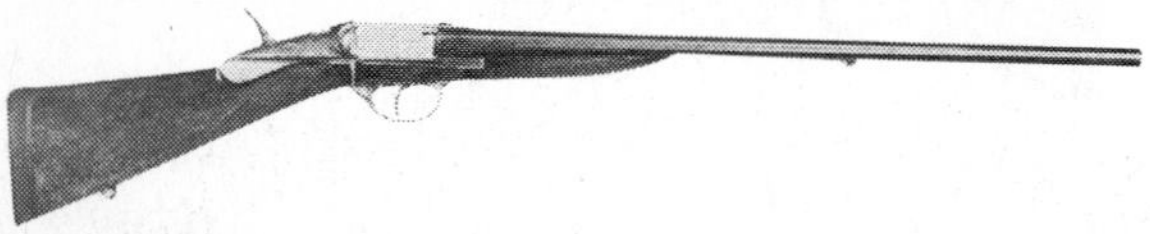

Model R11

NIB	Exc.	V.G.	Good	Fair	Poor
—	3500	2600	1950	800	550

Model R13

NIB	Exc.	V.G.	Good	Fair	Poor
—	3800	9600	2250	1100	750

Model R15

NIB	Exc.	V.G.	Good	Fair	Poor
—	4000	3000	2450	1500	750

Model V19

NIB	Exc.	V.G.	Good	Fair	Poor
—	4500	3600	2950	2050	1250

Model V22

NIB	Exc.	V.G.	Good	Fair	Poor
—	5000	4100	3500	2500	1700

Model V Hors Series No. I

NIB	Exc.	V.G.	Good	Fair	Poor
—	7500	5500	4050	3250	1500

DAVENPORT FIREARMS CO.

Providence, Rhode Island
Norwich, Connecticut

DOUBLE-BARREL SHOTGUNS

William Hastings Davenport's company also made and marked double-barrel, visible hammer guns in Providence, R.I. on Orange St., 1880-1882 and in Norwich, Conn. ca. 1890-1909. All are monbloc designs of which there were four models. The 1st model made at Providence, ca. 1881, had hammers rising out of the boxlock frame. The 2nd model, made in Norwich, Conn. about 1898, is a typical boxlock. The 3rd model made in Norwich, Conn., ca. 1909, has small sidelocks set in larger boxlock frames. Its barrels have unnotched extensions and notched underlugs. The 4th model, also from Norwich, possibly made after the 1901 takeover by Hopkins & Allen, also has sidelocks set in boxlock frames but the barrels have half moon lugs and notched barrel extensions. Few Davenport doubles are seen although single barrel guns are often found.

1st Model

NIB	Exc.	V.G.	Good	Fair	Poor
—	1200	875	500	400	300

2nd Model

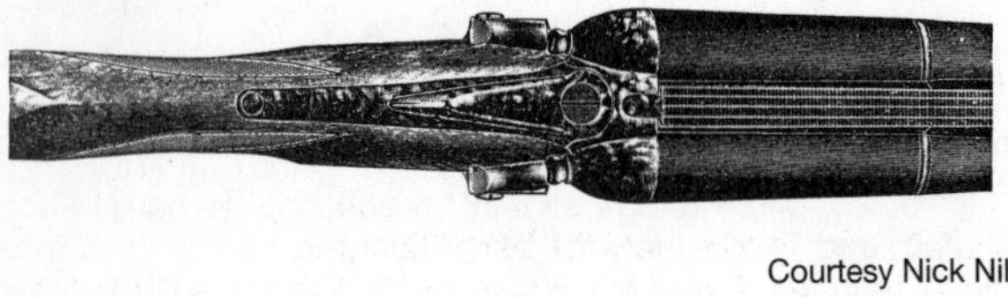

Courtesy Nick Niles

NIB	Exc.	V.G.	Good	Fair	Poor
—	700	450	300	200	150

3rd Model

NIB	Exc.	V.G.	Good	Fair	Poor
—	1200	875	500	400	300

4th Model

NIB	Exc.	V.G.	Good	Fair	Poor
—	900	450	300	250	200

Single Barrel Shotgun

A 10, 12, 16, or 20 gauge side-hammer single-barrel shotgun with 26" to 36" barrels and extractors. Blued, case hardened with a walnut stock. Manufactured from approximately 1880 to 1915.

NIB	Exc.	V.G.	Good	Fair	Poor
—	—	450	300	150	75

8 Gauge Goose Gun

As above, in 8 gauge.

NIB	Exc.	V.G.	Good	Fair	Poor
—	—	550	250	175	100

Falling Block Single-Shot Rifle

A .22, .25, or .32 rimfire single-shot rifle with a 24" round barrel and exposed hammer. Blued with a walnut stock. The barrel marked "The W.H. Davenport Fire Arms Co. Norwich, Conn. U.S.A. Patented Dec. 15, 1891." Manufactured between 1891 and 1910.

NIB	Exc.	V.G.	Good	Fair	Poor
—	—	675	425	325	200

Arms bearing this name were manufactured in Spain by Fabrica De Armas.

Model 63B

A 12, 16, 20, 28, or .410 bore double-barrel boxlock shotgun with 25" to 30" barrels. Engraved, nickel-plated with a walnut stock. Made from 1963 to 1976.

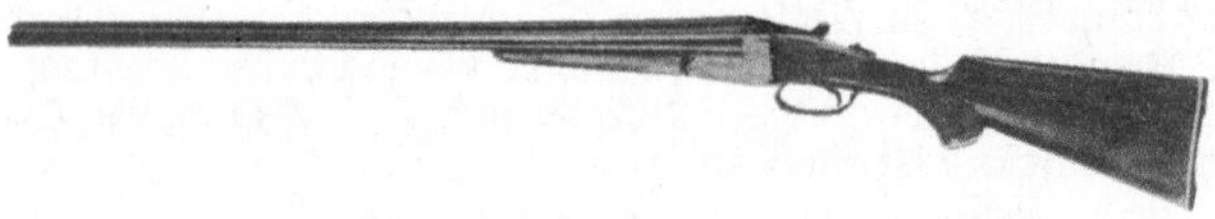

NIB	Exc.	V.G.	Good	Fair	Poor
—	350	225	200	150	100

Model 69 SL

A 12 or 20 gauge sidelock double-barrel shotgun with 26" or 28" barrels and finished as above.

NIB	Exc.	V.G.	Good	Fair	Poor
—	425	350	300	225	125

Stagecoach Model 73

A 12 or 20 gauge Magnum sidelock double-barrel shotgun with 20" barrels and exposed hammers.

NIB	Exc.	V.G.	Good	Fair	Poor
—	300	250	175	150	100

DAVIS, N.R. & CO. DAVIS, N.R. & SONS

Manufacturer of percussion, and later, cartridge shotguns from 1853 to 1919. The cartridge shotguns embodied Nathan R. Davis' patented improvements of 1879, 1884, and 1886. Though only made in plain, serviceable grades, Davis shotguns were extremely well made and lived up to the company's motto "As Good as the Best."

Grade A and B Hammerless Shotguns

Made in 12 or 16 gauge with 28", 30", or 32" barrels.

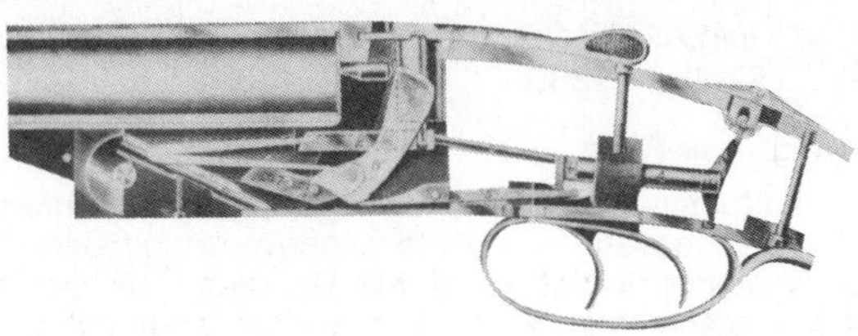

NIB	Exc.	V.G.	Good	Fair	Poor
—	900	675	400	200	100

Grade C Hammerless Shotgun

Made in 10 gauge with 30" or 32" barrels.

NIB	Exc.	V.G.	Good	Fair	Poor
—	900	675	400	200	100

Grade D and DS Hammer Shotguns

Made in 12 or 16 gauge with 28", 30", or 32" barrels.

NIB	Exc.	V.G.	Good	Fair	Poor
—	875	675	425	200	100

Grade E and F Single-Barrel Shotguns

Made in 12 or 16 gauge with 30" or 32" barrels.

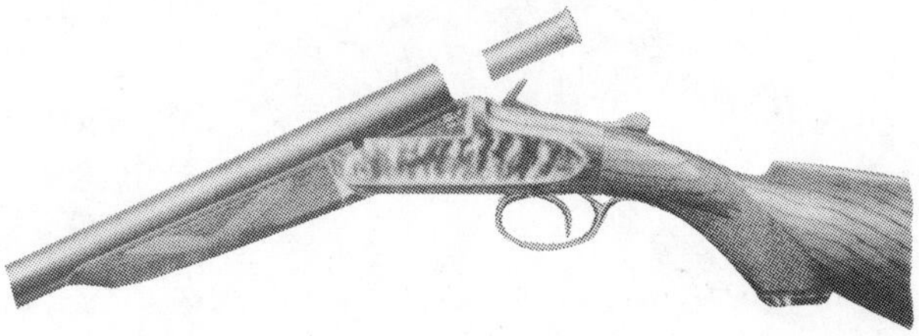

NIB	Exc.	V.G.	Good	Fair	Poor
—	350	250	125	75	50

N.R. DAVIS BRANDS

1st Button Opener—Hammer Boxlock

NIB	Exc.	V.G.	Good	Fair	Poor
—	475	325	250	150	100

1st Sidelever—Hammer Boxlock

NIB	Exc.	V.G.	Good	Fair	Poor
—	475	325	250	150	100

2nd Sidelever—Hammer Boxlock

Courtesy Nick Niles, Paul Goodwin photo

NIB	Exc.	V.G.	Good	Fair	Poor
—	475	325	250	150	100

1st Toplever—Hammer Boxlock

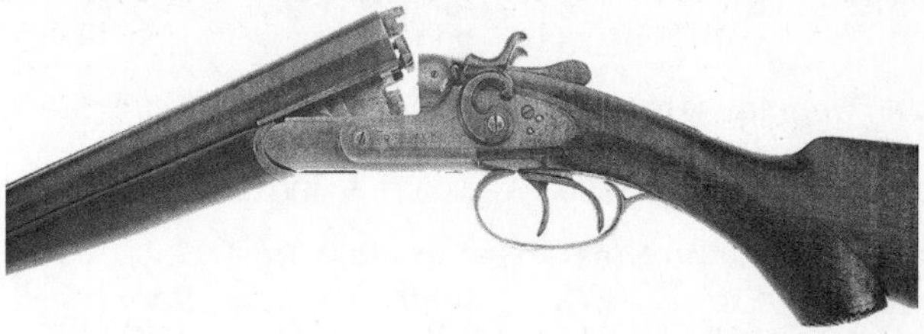

Courtesy Nick Niles, Paul Goodwin photo

NIB	Exc.	V.G.	Good	Fair	Poor
—	475	325	250	150	100

2nd Toplever—Hammer Boxlock

NIB	Exc.	V.G.	Good	Fair	Poor
—	475	325	250	150	100

3rd Toplever—Hammer Boxlock

NIB	Exc.	V.G.	Good	Fair	Poor
—	475	325	250	150	100

1879 1st Model—Hammer Boxlock

NIB	Exc.	V.G.	Good	Fair	Poor
—	475	325	250	150	100

1879 2nd Model—Damascus Barrels—Hammer Boxlock

NIB	Exc.	V.G.	Good	Fair	Poor
—	475	325	250	150	100

1885 "Hammerless" —Hammerless Boxlock

NIB	Exc.	V.G.	Good	Fair	Poor
—	475	325	250	150	100

1886 Rival—Hammerless Boxlock

NIB	Exc.	V.G.	Good	Fair	Poor
—	350	275	200	150	100

1886 Rival Improved—Hammerless Boxlock

NIB	Exc.	V.G.	Good	Fair	Poor
—	350	275	200	150	100

1897 "G" —Hammer Sidelock

NIB	Exc.	V.G.	Good	Fair	Poor
—	350	275	200	150	100

N.R. DAVIS & SONS BRAND

Hammerless 1900—Hammerless Boxlock

NIB	Exc.	V.G.	Good	Fair	Poor
—	350	275	200	150	100

Hammerless A—Damascus Barrels—Hammerless Boxlock

NIB	Exc.	V.G.	Good	Fair	Poor
—	350	275	200	150	100

Hammerless B—Hammerless Boxlock

NIB	Exc.	V.G.	Good	Fair	Poor
—	350	275	200	150	100

Hammerless C—Engraved Damascus Barrel—Hammerless Boxlock

NIB	Exc.	V.G.	Good	Fair	Poor
—	400	325	250	150	100

Hammerless D—Engraved—Hammerless Boxlock

NIB	Exc.	V.G.	Good	Fair	Poor
—	475	375	300	250	200

New Model—Hammerless Boxlock

NIB	Exc.	V.G.	Good	Fair	Poor
—	350	275	200	150	100

"D.S." Straight Stock—Engraved—Hammerless Boxlock

NIB	Exc.	V.G.	Good	Fair	Poor
—	350	275	200	150	100

Davis Special—Hammerless Boxlock

NIB	Exc.	V.G.	Good	Fair	Poor
—	925	650	500	400	250

Davis "B" Manga Steel—Hammerless Boxlock

NIB	Exc.	V.G.	Good	Fair	Poor
—	925	650	500	400	250

DAVIS-WARNER BRANDS

See – Davis-Warner.

CRESCENT-DAVIS BRANDS

Model No. 600—Hammerless Boxlock

NIB	Exc.	V.G.	Good	Fair	Poor
—	700	550	300	200	100

Model No. 900—Hammerless Boxlock

NIB	Exc.	V.G.	Good	Fair	Poor
—	700	550	300	200	100

DAVIS-WARNER ARMS CORPORATION

Norwich, Connecticut

Established in 1917, when N.R. Davis & Sons purchased the Warner Arms Company. Manufactured shotguns, as well as revolvers and semi-automatic pistols. Ceased operations in 1930. The Crescent Arms Company purchased the proprietary rights to the name and briefly assembled shotguns under the name (probably from parts acquired in the purchase) until Crescent was in turn purchased by J.C. Stevens.Initially, the Davis-Warner shotguns were identical to those made by Davis (page 360), but they subsequently made a Davis Grade B.S. Hammerless, Davis-Warner Expert and Davis Grade D.S. The pistols made by the company included .32 caliber revolvers and two Browning Patent semi-automatics made in Belgium for the company.

Davis Grade B.S. Hammerless Shotgun

Made in 12, 16, or 20 gauge with 28", 30", or 32" barrels.

Courtesy William Hammond

NIB	Exc.	V.G.	Good	Fair	Poor
—	875	650	400	200	100

Davis-Warner Expert Hammerless

Made in 12, 16, or 20 gauge with 26", 28", 30", or 32" barrels.

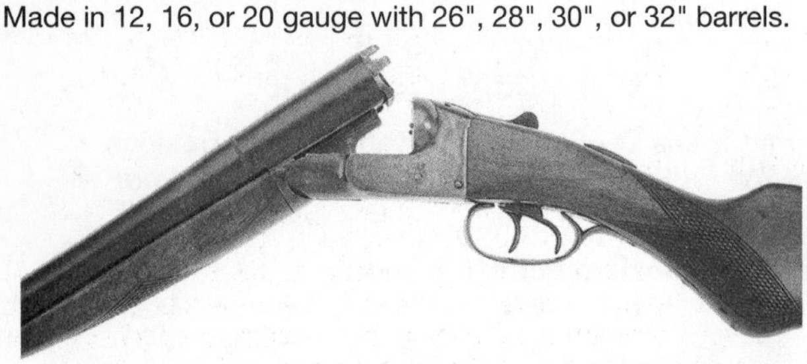

Courtesy Nick Niles, Paul Goodwin photo

NIB	Exc.	V.G.	Good	Fair	Poor
—	875	650	400	200	100

"BS" —Hammerless Boxlock

NIB	Exc.	V.G.	Good	Fair	Poor
—	350	275	200	150	100

"Maximin" —Hammerless Boxlock

Courtesy Nick Niles, Paul Goodwin photo

NIB	Exc.	V.G.	Good	Fair	Poor
—	475	325	250	200	150

"DS" —Hammerless Boxlock

NIB	Exc.	V.G.	Good	Fair	Poor
—	350	275	200	150	100

Deluxe—Hammerless Boxlock

NIB	Exc.	V.G.	Good	Fair	Poor
—	350	275	200	150	100

Premier—Hammerless Boxlock

NIB	Exc.	V.G.	Good	Fair	Poor
—	350	275	200	150	100

Peerless Ejector—Hammerless Boxlock

Courtesy Nick Niles, Paul Goodwin photo

NIB	Exc.	V.G.	Good	Fair	Poor
—	475	325	250	200	150

Hypower—Hammerless Boxlock

NIB	Exc.	V.G.	Good	Fair	Poor
—	475	325	250	200	150

Ajax (Model 800)

Courtesy Nick Niles, Paul Goodwin photo

NIB	Exc.	V.G.	Good	Fair	Poor
—	475	325	250	150	100

Ajax—Hammerless Boxlock

Courtesy Nick Niles, Paul Goodwin photo

NIB	Exc.	V.G.	Good	Fair	Poor
—	350	275	200	150	100

Certified (Savage)

Courtesy Nick Niles, Paul Goodwin photo

NIB	Exc.	V.G.	Good	Fair	Poor
—	475	325	250	150	100

Deluxe Special (Model 805)

Automatic ejectors.

NIB	Exc.	V.G.	Good	Fair	Poor
—	575	450	300	200	150

Premier Special (Model 802)

NIB	Exc.	V.G.	Good	Fair	Poor
—	575	450	300	200	150

Premier (Model 801)

NIB	Exc.	V.G.	Good	Fair	Poor
—	475	325	250	150	100

DEMRO

Manchester, Connecticut

XF-7 Wasp Carbine

A 9mm or .45 caliber semi-automatic carbine with a 16.5" barrel and folding stock. Fires from open bolt.

NIB	Exc.	V.G.	Good	Fair	Poor
—	750	600	450	300	150

T.A.C. Model 1

As above, with a fixed stock.

NIB	Exc.	V.G.	Good	Fair	Poor
—	750	600	450	300	150

DERINGER RIFLES AND PISTOLS, HENRY

Philadelphia, Pennsylvania

Henry Deringer Sr. and his son, Henry Jr., were well established in Philadelphia by the close of the War of 1812, having made both sporting and military rifles at that place since the turn of the century. Henry Jr. continued in the gun trade until the outbreak of the American Civil War, primarily producing flintlock and percussion military rifles, at least 2,500 "Northwest guns" and 1,200 rifles for the Indian trade, a few percussion martial pistols, but most importantly the percussion pocket pistols that became so popular that they took on his misspelled name as a generic term, the "derringers."

Deringer U.S. M1814 Military Rifle

Overall length 48-1/2"; barrel length 32-3/4"; caliber .54. Markings: on lockplate, "US/H. DERINGER/PHILADA," on top flat of barrel, "H. DERINGER/PHILADA" and standard U.S. proofmarks. The U.S. M1814 rifle is distinguished by its part octagonal barrel, whose bands were secured by wedge-shaped spring bands, and the distinctive finger ridges on the triggerguard strap. Henry Deringer Sr. received a contract for 2,000 of these rifles in 1814, but delivered only 50 that year, devoting his resources instead to a more lucrative Pennsylvania state contract for rifles.

NIB	Exc.	V.G.	Good	Fair	Poor
—	—	9000	2950	1500	850

Deringer U.S. M1817 Military Rifle (Types I & II)

Overall length 51-1/4"; barrel length 36"; caliber .54. Markings: on lockplate, "US/H. DERINGER/PHILADA" forward of cock, date on tail; standard U.S. proofmarks on barrel. The U.S. M1817 "common" rifle followed much of the same design elements as its predecessor, the U.S. M1814 rifle; however, the barrel is fully round with its bands secured by full band springs, and on the earlier production, the finger ridges on the triggerguard strap were eliminated in favor of a plain strap formed into a handgrip. On the 6,000 rifles manufactured under his 1840 contract, Deringer eliminated the "pistol grip" in favor of a plain strap, distinguishing Type 11 production from Type 1. As one of the four major contractors for the U.S. M1817 rifle, Deringer produced a total of 111,000 rifles for the U.S. War Department. Many of the rifles from first two contracts (2,000 in 1821, 3,000 in 1823) were distributed to Southern states under the 1808 Militia Act. Accordingly, Deringer M1817 rifles altered to percussion by traditional Southern methods may generate a premium.

Deringer U.S. M1817 Military Rifle (Types I & II) (in flintlock)

NIB	Exc.	V.G.	Good	Fair	Poor
—	—	8000	3500	1750	800

Deringer U.S. M1817 Military Rifle (Types I & II) (altered to percussion)

NIB	Exc.	V.G.	Good	Fair	Poor
—	—	4000	1250	600	400

Deringer Original Percussion Martial Rifles (Types I & II)

Overall length 51-1/4"; barrel length 36"; caliber .54. Markings: Type I-on lockplate forward of hammer "DERINGER/PHILA" ; also known to exist with standard U.S. M1817 lock markings and barrel marks; Type II-on lockplate forward of hammer "US/ DERINGER/PHILADELA" or "DERINGER/PHILADELA" and same on top of barrel.Although the Type I rifle of this series appears at first glance to be a late contract rifle altered to percussion by means of the cone-in barrel method, in fact it is an original percussion rifle made by Deringer from modified spare parts that remained after the completion of his 1840 contract. The Type 11 rifle also evidences having been made from modified parts; however, its cone is set in an elongated bolster brazed to the right side of the barrel. Speculation concerning these rifles is rampant; however, the available evidence indicates that Deringer produced about 600 of these most likely produced at the beginning of the American Civil War.

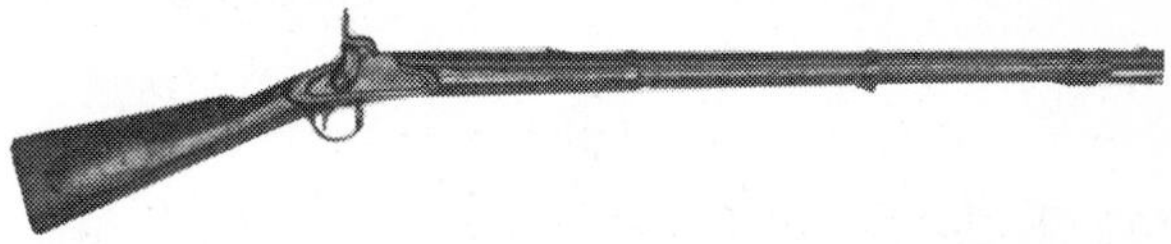

Courtesy Milwaukee Public Museum, Milwaukee, Wisconsin

NIB	Exc.	V.G.	Good	Fair	Poor
—	—	4750	1550	800	450

Deringer Original Percussion Rifle-Muskets

Overall length 57-3/4"; barrel length 42"; caliber .69. Markings: on lock forward of hammer, "US/DERINGER/PHILADELA." Just as the original percussion rifle appears to be an altered arm, the rare Deringer rifle muskets at first appear to have been flintlocks. However, these arms are original percussion, having been made from spare or rejected parts from the U.S. M1816 muskets. The brazed bolsters are identical in style to that of the Type 11 original percussion rifles made by Deringer. Barrels are rifled with seven grooves, and the barrels accordingly bear a rear sight. Deringer probably assembled a hundred of these rifles in 1861 to arm some company of Pennsylvania's early war regiments.

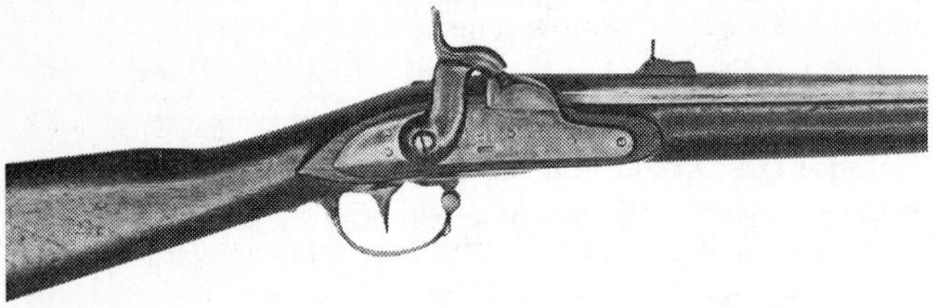

Courtesy Milwaukee Public Museum, Milwaukee, Wisconsin

NIB	Exc.	V.G.	Good	Fair	Poor
—	—	4000	1300	725	450

DESENZANI, LABORATORIES ARMI

Brescia, Italy

OVER-AND-UNDER

These custom made guns are all unique. Used guns in excellent condition will bring $35,000. Values increase depending on the smaller gauges and amount amd coverage of engraving.

SIDE-BY-SIDE

These custom made guns are all unique. Used guns in excellent condition will bring $25,000. Values increase depending on the smaller gauges and amount amd coverage of engraving.

DESERT EAGLE, ISRAELI MILITARY INDUSTRIES

Mountain Eagle Rifle

A limited edition rifle (1,000) with a Sako action and composite stock. Chambered for the .270, .280, .30-06, .300 Win., .338 Win, 7mm Mag. Introduced in 1994. Additional calibers are .300 Weatherby, .375 H&H, .416 Rem., and 7mm STW. Barrel length is 24". Average weight is about 7.74 lbs.

NIB	Exc.	V.G.	Good	Fair	Poor
2295	1700	1150	800	400	175

NOTE: For muzzlebrake add $150. For .375 H&H and .416 Rem. add $300. For left-hand actions add $100.

Mountain Eagle Varmint Edition

Chambered for the .222 Rem. and the .223 Rem. cartridges and fitted with a 26" stainless Krieger barrel. Kevlar-graphite stock. Weight is approximately 9 lbs. 13 oz.

NIB	Exc.	V.G.	Good	Fair	Poor
2295	1750	1150	800	400	175

MAGNUM LITE RIMFIRE RIFLES

These rifles are built with Ruger 10/22 actions and graphite barrels. There are several variations depending on stock configuration.

Hogue and Fajen Scope-Hi Stock

NIB	Exc.	V.G.	Good	Fair	Poor
650	495	400	300	200	125

Fajen Thumbhole Sporter

NIB	Exc.	V.G.	Good	Fair	Poor
700	550	450	300	200	125

Fajen Thumbhole Silhouette

NIB	Exc.	V.G.	Good	Fair	Poor
800	650	500	300	200	125

Turner Barracuda

NIB	Exc.	V.G.	Good	Fair	Poor
800	650	500	300	200	125

NOTE: For Clark Custom Upgrades add $130 to price of each Magnum Lite rifle.

MAGNUM LITE CENTERFIRE RIFLES

These rifles are built on Sako actions and are fitted with graphite barrels. Introduced in 1999. Offered in two configurations, both with synthetic stock.

Heavy Barrel

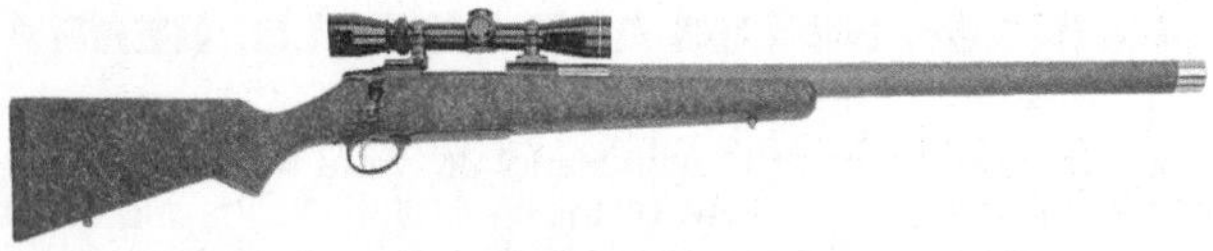

Fitted with a 26", 1.2" diameter barrel with a 1-in-14 twist. Chambered for .223 cartridge. Weight is approximately 7.8 lbs.

NIB	Exc.	V.G.	Good	Fair	Poor
2295	1700	1150	800	400	295

Sport Taper Barrel

Fitted with a 24" tapered barrel and chambered for the .280 Rem., 7mm Mag, .30-06, .300 Win. Mag. Weight is about 6.4 lbs.

NIB	Exc.	V.G.	Good	Fair	Poor
2295	1700	1150	800	400	295

Tactical Rifle

Introduced in 2000 this rifle features a 26" match grade barrel chambered for the .223, .22-250, .308, or .300 Win. Mag. cartridges. The barrel is made from carbon fiber. The action is a Remington Model 700. H-S Precision tactical stock with adjustable comb. Adjustable trigger. Weight is approximately 8.3 lbs.

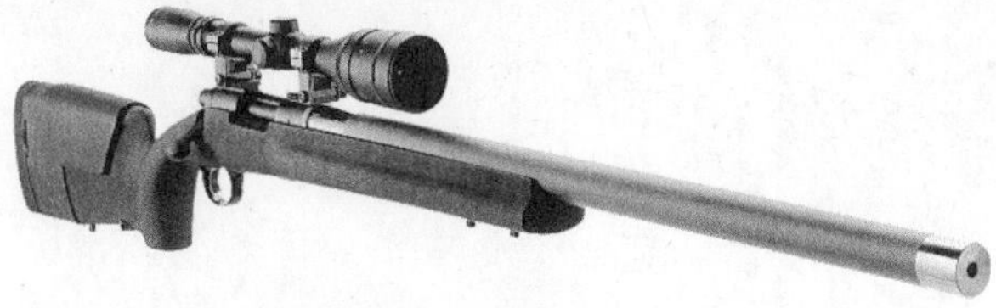

NIB	Exc.	V.G.	Good	Fair	Poor
2400	1800	1250	850	400	295

DESTROYER CARBINE

Spain

Destroyer Carbine

A 9mm Bayard/Large caliber bolt-action rifle with a 20" barrel and 7-shot magazine. Full length stock with two barrel bands.

NIB	Exc.	V.G.	Good	Fair	Poor
—	500	395	200	100	35

DIAMOND

Turkey

Gold Series Auto

Chambered for the 12 gauge shell with 3" chamber. Barrel length is 28". Turkish walnut stock or synthetic stock. Black receiver with gold-filled engraving. Also available with 24" slug barrel with sights.

NIB	Exc.	V.G.	Good	Fair	Poor
350	300	200	150	100	75

NOTE: Add $50 for walnut stock.

Gold Series Pump

Offered with the same features as the semi-auto Gold gun but with a slide-action.

NIB	Exc.	V.G.	Good	Fair	Poor
300	250	175	125	100	75

Note: Add $25 for walnut stock.

Silver Series Mariner Semi-Auto

This is a 12 gauge stainless steel and anodized alloy semi-auto gun with 3" chambers and fitted with 22" vent-rib barrel and synthetic stock.

NIB	Exc.	V.G.	Good	Fair	Poor
425	350	275	200	150	100

Silver Series Mariner Pump

A 12 gauge pump gun with 20" slug barrel and symthetic stock. Stainless steel and alloy.

NIB	Exc.	V.G.	Good	Fair	Poor
350	275	200	150	100	75

Diamond Elite Semi-Auto

This 12 gauge 3" chamber shotgun is offered with 22" to 28" barrels with 3 choke tubes. Engraved receiver.

NIB	Exc.	V.G.	Good	Fair	Poor
325	275	200	150	100	75

Diamond Elite Pump

As above but in a slide-action configuration.

NIB	Exc.	V.G.	Good	Fair	Poor
250	200	200	150	100	75

Diamond Panther Semi-Auto

A 12 gauge gun with 3" chambers with 20" or 28" vent-rib barrel. Furnished with three choke tubes. Synthetic stock.

NIB	Exc.	V.G.	Good	Fair	Poor
325	275	200	150	100	75

Diamond Elite Pump

As above but with slide-action. Also offered with 18.5" slug barrel.

NIB	Exc.	V.G.	Good	Fair	Poor
300	250	175	125	100	75

DOUBLESTAR, CORP.

Winchester, Kentucky

Star EM-4

Chambered for the .223 cartridge and fitted with a 16" barrel. Rifle is supplied with A-2 or flat top upper and Colt M-4 handguard.

NIB	Exc.	V.G.	Good	Fair	Poor
915	750	600	500	275	125

Star-15

This model has a 20" barrel, A-2 buttstock, and A-2 handguard. Supplied with A-2 or flat top upper.

NIB	Exc.	V.G.	Good	Fair	Poor
775	625	575	450	225	100

Star Lightweight Tactical Rifle

Fitted with a 15" fluted barrel with permanently attached muzzlebrake. Fitted with a shot tactical buttstock. Supplied with an A-2 or flat top upper.

NIB	Exc.	V.G.	Good	Fair	Poor
880	700	575	450	225	100

Star Carbine

This model has a 16" match grade barrel. Supplied with either an A-2 buttstock or non-collapsing CAR buttstock. Upper receiver is A-2 style or flat top.

NIB	Exc.	V.G.	Good	Fair	Poor
775	625	575	450	225	100

Star DS-4 Carbine

This model features a 16" M-4 barrel with 6 position buttstock, oval handguard, and A2 flash hider. Weight is about 6.75 lbs. Choice of A2 or flattop upper receiver.

NIB	Exc.	V.G.	Good	Fair	Poor
875	700	575	450	225	100

Star Super Match Rifle

Choice of match grade barrel lengths of 16", 20", 22", or 24". Rifle supplied with flat top upper or tactical Hi-Rise upper.

NIB	Exc.	V.G.	Good	Fair	Poor
875	700	575	450	225	100

Star Critterslayer

This model is fitted with a 24" fluted super match barrel with a flat top upper and free floating handguard. Match 2 stage trigger. Fitted with a Harris LMS swivel bipod and Ergo grip with palm swell.

NIB	Exc.	V.G.	Good	Fair	Poor
1300	1000	750	600	395	175

DSC Expedition Rifle

Offered with a 16" or 20" lightweight barrel with integral muzzle-brake. Stock, sights, and receiver are A2 configuration.

NIB	Exc.	V.G.	Good	Fair	Poor
825	650	575	450	225	100

DSC Star-15 CMP Service Rifle

Fitted with a 20" chrome lined heavy match barrel. National Match front and rear sights. CMP free float handguard. National Match trigger. A2 upper receiver.

NIB	Exc.	V.G.	Good	Fair	Poor
1000	750	650	575	450	225

DSC Star CMP Improved Service Rifle

Similar to the above model but with 20" Wilson Arms premium grade heavy match barrel. McCormick single- or two-stage Match trigger and Tippie Competition rear sight.

NIB	Exc.	V.G.	Good	Fair	Poor
1299	975	825	650	575	300

DSC Star 15 Lightweight Tactical

This model is fitted with a 16" fluted heavy barrel with tactical "shorty" A-2 buttstock.

NIB	Exc.	V.G.	Good	Fair	Poor
880	700	575	450	225	100

DSC Star Dissipator

This model features a 16" barrel with full length handguard. Available with A2 or flattop upper receiver.

NIB	Exc.	V.G.	Good	Fair	Poor
875	700	575	450	225	100

DSC Star 15 9mm Carbine

Chambered for the 9mm cartridge and fitted with a 16" heavy barrel. A2 or flattop upper receiver. Available with A2 or CAR buttstock.

NIB	Exc.	V.G.	Good	Fair	Poor
995	750	650	575	450	225

DOUG TURNBULL RESTORATION, INC.

Bloomfield, New York

This company began operation in 1983 as a one-man shop. Today the company numbers 14 people and does finish work for most major firearms manufacturers. The company also installs Miller single triggers. The models listed are a series of special run firearms produced by Turnbull.

Colt/Winchester Cased Set

A cased set with a Colt Model 1873 engraved revolver and a Winchester Model 1894. Colt is chambered for the .45 Colt cartridge and fitted with a 7.5" barrel. Engraving is "B" coverage. Model 1894 is chambered for the .45 Colt cartridge and is in the saddle ring configuration. Engraving pattern is #9 with deer. Checkered walnut stock. Limited to five sets total. Serial numbers 160DT to 164DT.

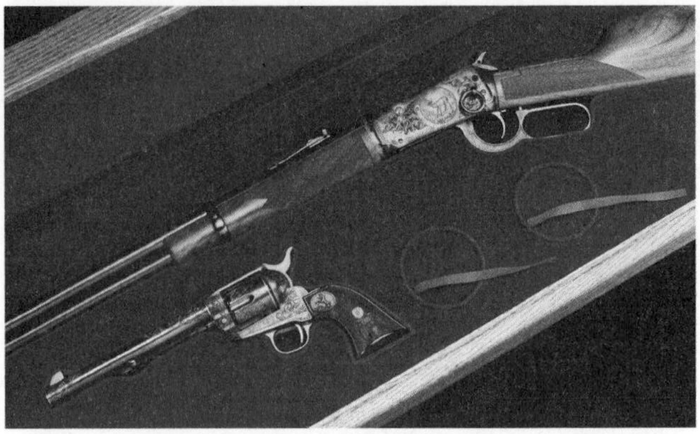

NIB	Exc.	V.G.	Good	Fair	Poor
5750	4300	3750	2500	1500	600

Theodore Roosevelt Winchester Model 1876

This custom rifle is limited to 25 pieces and will be serial numbered from TR01 to TR-25. Each rifle is engraved and checkered in the style of the original and chambered for the .45-70 cartridge. It is fitted with a 28" half round barrel. Gold inlaid stock oval. A portion of the proceeds of each rifle goes to benefit the Doug Turnbull Conservation Laboratory at the National Firearms Museum.

NIB	Exc.	V.G.	Good	Fair	Poor
29000	—	—	—	—	—

DPMS

St. Cloud, Minnesota

Panther Bull A-15

This A-15 type rifle is chambered for the .223 cartridge and fitted with a 20" stainless steel bull barrel. A2-style buttstock. No sights. Barrel has 1:9 twist. Flat top receiver. Handguard is aluminum free float tube. Upper and lower receivers are hard coated black. Weight is about 9.5 lbs. Each rifle comes standard with two 7-round magazines, sling, and cleaning kit.

NIB	Exc.	V.G.	Good	Fair	Poor
900	700	550	400	275	125

Panther Bull 24

Similar to the model above but fitted with a 24" bull barrel. Flat top receiver. Weight is about 10 lbs.

NIB	Exc.	V.G.	Good	Fair	Poor
950	750	600	400	275	125

Panther Deluxe Bull 24 Special

This model is fitted with a 24" stainless steel fluted bull barrel. Adjustable A2 style buttstock. Flat top receiver. Adjustable sniper pistol grip. Weight is about 10 lbs.

NIB	Exc.	V.G.	Good	Fair	Poor
1150	900	750	400	275	125

Panther Extreme Super Bull 24

This model is fitted with a 24" stainless steel extra heavy bull barrel (1.150" dia.). Skeletonized stock. Flat top receiver. Weight is about 11.75 lbs.

NIB	Exc.	V.G.	Good	Fair	Poor
1200	800	650	400	275	125

Panther Bulldog

Fitted with a 20" stainless steel fluted bull barrel with black synthetic A2-style buttstock. Flat top receiver. Adjustable trigger. Weight is about 10 lbs.

NIB	Exc.	V.G.	Good	Fair	Poor
1200	975	800	400	275	125

Panther Bull Sweet 16

This model is fitted with a 16" stainless steel bull barrel with flat top receiver. Weight is about 7.75 lbs.

NIB	Exc.	V.G.	Good	Fair	Poor
1100	900	550	400	275	125

Panther Bull SST 16

Similar to the model above but with stainless steel lower receiver. Weight is about 9 lbs.

NIB	Exc.	V.G.	Good	Fair	Poor
1300	975	650	400	275	125

Panther Bull Classic

This model is fitted with a 20" 4150 steel bull barrel. Square front post sight, adjustable A2 rear sight. Weight is about 9.75 lbs.

NIB	Exc.	V.G.	Good	Fair	Poor
1200	800	650	400	275	125

Panther Arctic

This model is similar to the model above but with 20" fluted bull barrel and flat top receiver. Black A2-style buttstock with white coat finish on receiver and handguard. Black Teflon finish on barrel. Weight is about 8.25 lbs.

NIB	Exc.	V.G.	Good	Fair	Poor
1075	850	700	400	275	125

Panther Classic

Fitted with a 20" 4150 steel heavy barrel with square front post sight and A2 rear sight. A2 round handguard. Weight is about 9.5 lbs.

NIB	Exc.	V.G.	Good	Fair	Poor
800	600	500	400	275	125

Panther DCM

This model is similar to the model above but with 20" stainless steel heavy barrel and NM rear sight. DCM free-float handguard. Adjustable trigger. Weight is about 9.5 lbs.

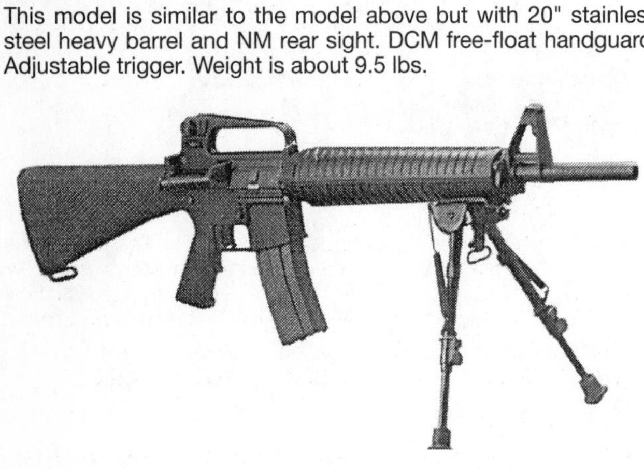

NIB	Exc.	V.G.	Good	Fair	Poor
950	750	600	400	275	125

Panther Classic 16 Post Ban

This model is fitted with a 1" 4150 steel heavy barrel. A2-style sights. Round handguard. Weight is about 7.25 lbs.

NIB	Exc.	V.G.	Good	Fair	Poor
775	600	500	400	275	125

Panther Free Float 16 Post Ban

Similar to the model above with 16" barrel but fitted with a vented free-floated barrel and vented free-float tube handguard. Weight is approximately 7.25 lbs.

NIB	Exc.	V.G.	Good	Fair	Poor
825	650	550	400	275	125

Panther Southpaw Post Ban

This model is fitted with a 20" 4150 steel heavy barrel with A2-style sights. Upper receiver has been modified for left-hand ejection. Weight is about 9.5 lbs.

NIB	Exc.	V.G.	Good	Fair	Poor
875	700	600	400	275	125

Panther Race Gun

Similar to Panther Bull but with 24-inch fluted bull barrel. Sights: JP Micro adjustable rear, JP front sight adjustable for height. Includes Lyman globe and Shaver inserts.

NIB	Exc.	V.G.	Good	Fair	Poor
1875	1500	800	500	275	125

Panther Tuber

Similar to Panther Bull 24 but with 16-inch barrel with cylindrical aluminum shroud.

NIB	Exc.	V.G.	Good	Fair	Poor
700	600	500	400	275	125

Single Shot Rifle

AR-15-style single-shot rifle with manually-operated bolt, no magazine.

NIB	Exc.	V.G.	Good	Fair	Poor
775	500	400	275	125	100

Panther Pardus

Similar to Panther Post-ban but with 16-inch bull barrel, telescoping buttstock and tan Teflon finish. Introduced 2006.

NIB	Exc.	V.G.	Good	Fair	Poor
1200	850	700	400	275	200

Panther 20th Anniversary Rifle

Similar to Panther Post-ban but with 20-inch bull barrel and engraved, chrome-plated lower receiver. Introduced 2006.

NIB	Exc.	V.G.	Good	Fair	Poor
2500	2000	1550	800	500	300

Panther 6.8 Rifle

Similar to Panther DCM but with 20-inch chrome-moly barrel and chambered for 6.8x43 Remington SPC. Introduced 2006.

NIB	Exc.	V.G.	Good	Fair	Poor
1000	850	700	400	275	125

Panther Mark 12

Similar to Panther but with flash hider and other refinements. Introduced 2007.

NIB	Exc.	V.G.	Good	Fair	Poor
1300	850	700	400	275	125

Panther SDM-R

Similar to Panther but with stainless steel barrel and Harris bipod. Introduced 2007.

NIB	Exc.	V.G.	Good	Fair	Poor
1200	850	700	400	275	125

LRT-SASS

Semi-automatic rifle based on AR-15 design. Chambered in .308 Win. With 18-inch stainless steel barrel with flash hider, collapsible Vitor Clubfoot carbine stock and 19-rd. detachable magazine. Introduced 2006.

NIB	Exc.	V.G.	Good	Fair	Poor
1900	1600	1475	1000	600	350

LR-260

Similar to LRT-SASS but with 24-inch stainless steel barrel and chambered in .260 Remington. Also available with 20-inch chrome-moly barrel as LR-260H. Introduced 2006.

NIB	Exc.	V.G.	Good	Fair	Poor
1775	1400	1100	800	500	300

LR-243

Similar to LR-260 but with 20-inch chrome-moly barrel and chambered in .243 Win. Introduced 2006.

NIB	Exc.	V.G.	Good	Fair	Poor
1775	1400	1100	800	500	300

LR-204

Similar to LRT-260 but chambered in .204 Ruger. Introduced 2006.

NIB	Exc.	V.G.	Good	Fair	Poor
1775	1400	1100	800	500	300

5.56 Panther Oracle

Semi-auto AR-style rifle chambered in 5.56 NATO. Features include 16-inch 4140 chrome-moly 1:9 barrel; phosphated steel bolt; oval Glacier Guard hand guard; flattop upper with Picatinny rail; aluminum lower; two 30-round magazines; Pardus 6-position telescoping stock. Also available on larger platform in .308 Winchester/7.62 NATO.

NIB	Exc.	V.G.	Good	Fair	Poor
700	575	500	400	300	200

Panther 3G1

Semi-auto AR-style rifle chambered in 5.56 NATO. Features include 18-inch 416 stainless 1:9 barrel; phosphated steel bolt; VTAC modular hand guard; flattop upper with Picatinny rail; aluminum lower; two 30-round magazines; Magpul CTR adjustable stock.

NIB	Exc.	V.G.	Good	Fair	Poor
1000	850	700	600	400	300

Prairie Panther

Semi-auto AR-style rifle chambered in 5.56 NATO. Features include 20-inch 416 stainless fluted heavy 1:8 barrel; phosphated steel bolt; free-floated carbon fiber hand guard; flattop upper with Picatinny rail; aluminum lower; two 30-round magazines; skeletonized Zytel stock; finished in King\qs Desert Shadow camo overall.

NIB	Exc.	V.G.	Good	Fair	Poor
1400	1100	850	700	450	300

Panther RAPTR

Semi-auto AR-style rifle chambered in 5.56 NATO. Features include 16-inch 4140 chrome-moly 1:9 barrel; phosphated steel bolt; ERGO Z-Rail 4-rail hand guard; front vertical grip; standard A2 sights; aluminum lower; four 30-round magazines. Price: $1649.

NIB	Exc.	V.G.	Good	Fair	Poor
1350	1025	800	625	350	250

Panther REPR

Semi-auto AR-style rifle chambered in .308 Win./7.62 NATO. Features include 18-inch 416 stainless steel 1:10 barrel; phosphated steel bolt; 4-rail free-floated hand guard; no sights; aluminum lower; two 19-round magazines; Coyote Brown camo finish overall.

NIB	Exc.	V.G.	Good	Fair	Poor
2100	1850	1400	1000	650	350

Panther 308 Mk12

Semi-auto AR-style rifle chambered in .308 Win./7.62 NATO. Features include 16-inch 4140 chrome-moly heavy 1:10 barrel; phosphated steel bolt; 4-rail free-floated hand guard; flip-up front and rear sights; aluminum lower; two 19-round magazines; matte black finish overall; Magpul CTR adjustable stock.

NIB	Exc.	V.G.	Good	Fair	Poor
1400	1100	850	700	450	300

Panther A-15 Pump Rifle

This model has a 20" 4150 steel heavy barrel with A2-style sights. Fitted with an A2 compensator and modified to slide-action. Weight is about 8.5 lbs.

NIB	Exc.	V.G.	Good	Fair	Poor
1400	1050	700	600	500	300

DSA, INC.

Barrington, Illinois

DSA, Inc. began selling its rifles to the public in 1996. Based on actual blueprints of the famous FN/FAL rifle, DSA rifles are made in the US. All SA58 rifles are fitted with fully adjustable gas system, Type I, II, or III forged receiver, hand-lapped barrel, muzzlebrake, elevation adjustable post front sight, windage adjustable rear peep sight with 5 settings from 200 to 600 meters, detachable metric magazine, adjustable sling and hard case.

SA58 24" Bull

Fitted with a 24" stainless steel barrel with .308 match chamber. Overall length is 44.5". Weight is approximately 11.5 lbs.

NIB	Exc.	V.G.	Good	Fair	Poor
2100	1800	1150	800	500	300

SA58 21" Bull

Same as the above but fitted with a 21" stainless steel barrel. Weight is about 11.1 lbs.

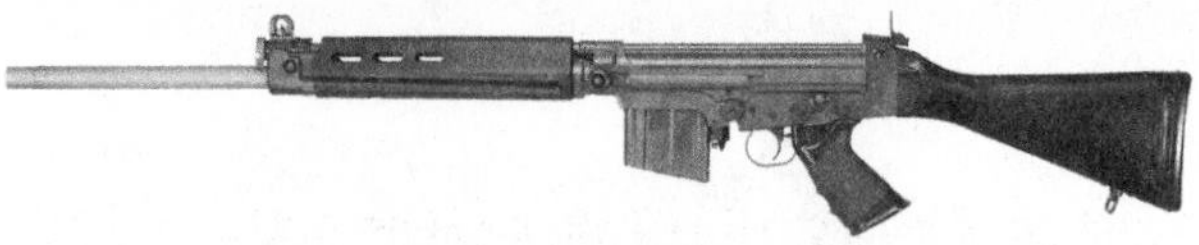

NIB	Exc.	V.G.	Good	Fair	Poor
2100	1800	1150	800	500	300

NOTE: Add $250 for stainless steel.

SA58 Medium Contour

This model is offered with a 21" barrel in either stainless steel or blued steel. Weight is about 10.5 lbs.

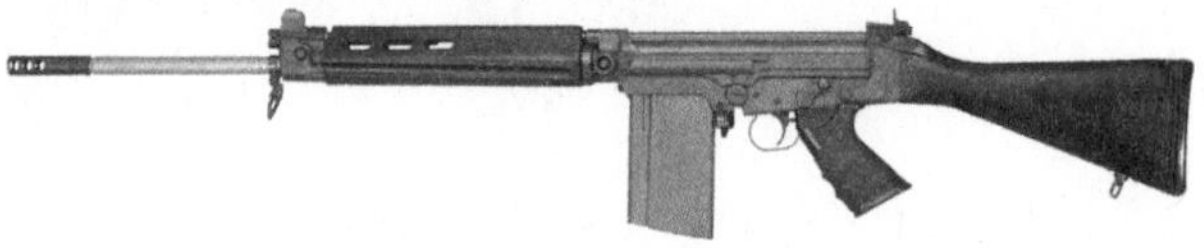

Medium contour stainless steel

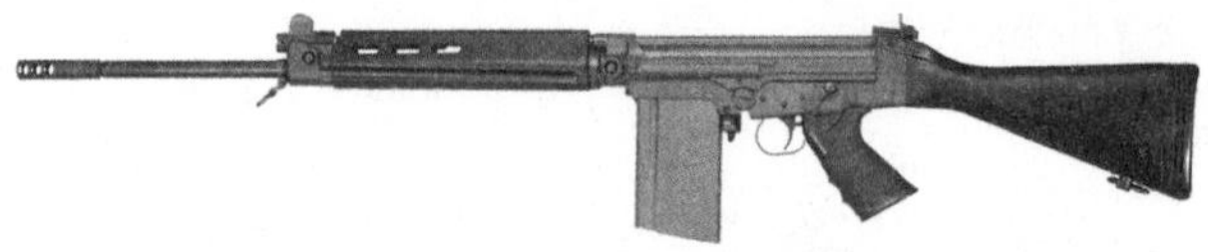

Medium contour blued

NIB	Exc.	V.G.	Good	Fair	Poor
2100	1800	1150	800	500	300

SA58 Carbine

This model is fitted with a 16.25" barrel. Barrel is cut for factory light bipod. Blued finish. A stainless steel version is also available. Overall length is 37.5". Weight is about 8.35 lbs.

NIB	Exc.	V.G.	Good	Fair	Poor
2100	1800	1150	800	500	300

NOTE: Add $250 for stainless steel.

SA58 Standard

This model has a 21" barrel cut for factory light bipod. Weight is about 8.75 lbs. Blued finish.

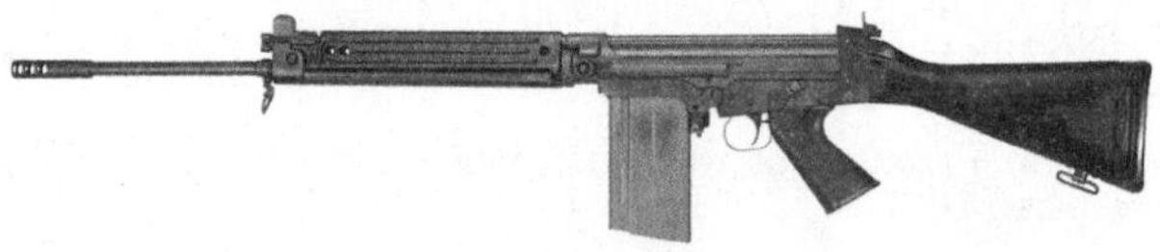

NIB	Exc.	V.G.	Good	Fair	Poor
2100	1800	1150	800	500	300

SA58 Tactical

Fitted with a 16.25" fluted barrel, black synthetic stock, Type I receiver, adjustable sights, and detachable magazine. Blued finish. Weight is about 8.25 lbs.

NIB	Exc.	V.G.	Good	Fair	Poor
2100	1800	1150	800	500	300

SA58 Congo

This .308 model features a 18" bipod-cut barrel with short Belgian-style flash hider. Type I receiver with carry handle. Synthetic buttstock and pistol grip. Aluminum lower. Detachable magazine. Adjustable sights. Weight is about 8.6 lbs.

NIB	Exc.	V.G.	Good	Fair	Poor
2250	1900	1250	800	500	300

SA58 Para Congo

This model is fitted with a Type II receiver with carry handle and a 18" bipod-cut barrel with short Belgian-style flash hider. Steel lower. Folding steel Para stock. Adjustable sights. Weight is about 9.85 lbs.

NIB	Exc.	V.G.	Good	Fair	Poor
2250	1900	1250	800	500	300

SA58 Predator

Offered in .308, .260 Rem., or .243. This rifle has a Type I receiver, a 16" medium carbine barrel with target crown or 19" medium barrel with target crown. Green furniture. Aluminum lower. Picatinny rail. Weight is about 9 lbs. with 16" barrel.

NIB	Exc.	V.G.	Good	Fair	Poor
1950	1650	1250	800	475	200

SA58 Graywolf

This .308 model is fitted with a 21" match grade barrel with target crown. Type I receiver. Aluminum lower. Extended safety. Picatinny rail. Target pistol grip with standard or X-series buttstock. Versa-pod bipod. Weight is about 13 lbs.

NIB	Exc.	V.G.	Good	Fair	Poor
2100	1600	1250	800	500	300

SA58 T48 Replica

Chambered for the .308 cartridge and fitted with a 21" barrel with replica Browning flash hider. Supplied with 10- or 20-round fixed magazine with stripper clip top cover. Wooden stock. Weight is about 9.7 lbs.

NIB	Exc.	V.G.	Good	Fair	Poor
1950	1650	1250	800	475	200

SR58 Medium Contour Stainless Steel

Similar to SA50 Standard but with flash hider and stainless steel lower, top cover and loading handle. Introduced 2006.

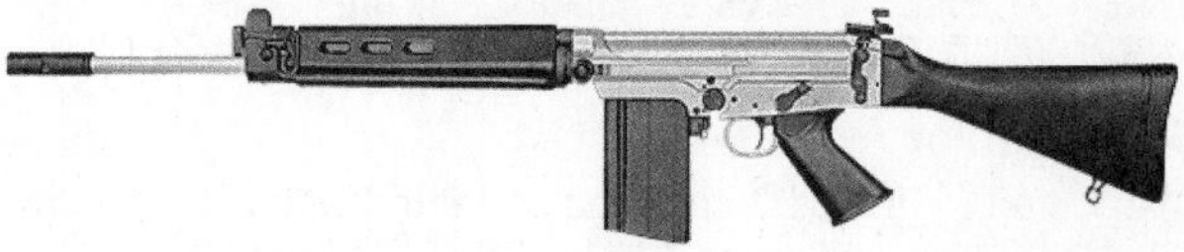

NIB	Exc.	V.G.	Good	Fair	Poor
1700	1400	900	700	600	300

DS-MP1 .308 Custom Bolt Action

Based on Remington 700 short action. 22-inch stainless steel recessed Badger match barrel, black Duracote finish, black McMillan synthetic stock and Picatinny rail. Introduced in 2006.

NIB	Exc.	V.G.	Good	Fair	Poor
2100	1800	1150	800	500	300

DS-AR

S1 Rifle

Introduced in 2004 this 5.56 caliber rifle features a 20" or 24" bull barrel with Picatinny gas black sight base. Flattop receiver. Free floating aluminum handguard. A2 stock. Ten-round magazine. Discontinued.

NIB	Exc.	V.G.	Good	Fair	Poor
1150	850	600	425	225	150

CVI Carbine

Similar to the model above but with a 16" barrel with forged front sight base and integral muzzlebrake. D-4 handguard. Fixed CAR buttstock. Ten-round magazine. Discontinued.

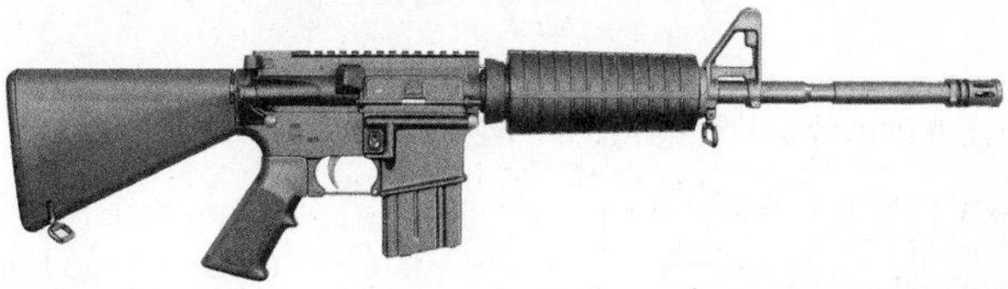

NIB	Exc.	V.G.	Good	Fair	Poor
1150	850	600	425	225	150

LE4 Carbine

As above but with pre-ban features. For law enforcement only. Discontinued.

NIB	Exc.	V.G.	Good	Fair	Poor
1150	850	600	425	225	150

DS-AR S Series Rifle

Introduced in 2005 this rifle is chambered for the .223 cartridge and fitted with a choice of 16", 20", or 24" stainless steel match grade bull barrel. A2 stock with free floating handguard. Flattop receiver, National Match 2 stage trigger. Magazine capacity is 10, 20, or 30 rounds.

NIB	Exc.	V.G.	Good	Fair	Poor
1350	1050	800	525	225	150

DS-AR Carbine

Chambered for the .223 cartridge and fitted with a 16" D4 barrel with flash hider. Choice of fixed or collapsible stock. Choice of forged flattop or A2 upper receiver. Magazine capacity is 10, 20, or 30 rounds. Introduced in 2005.

NIB	Exc.	V.G.	Good	Fair	Poor
1350	1050	800	525	225	150

DS-AR Rifle

As above but with 20" heavy barrel with flash hider and fixed stock. Introduced in 2005.

NIB	Exc.	V.G.	Good	Fair	Poor
1350	1050	800	525	225	150

DS-AR DCM Rifle

Chambered for the .223 cartridge with Wylde chamber. Fitted with a 20" match grade Badger barrel. DCM free float handguard system. National Match two-stage trigger. National Match rear sight. A2 upper receiver. Introduced in 2005.

NIB	Exc.	V.G.	Good	Fair	Poor
1595	1250	950	625	425	225

DS-AR CQB MRP

Introduced in 2005 this model features a 16" chrome lined barrel with A2 flash hider. Collapsible stock with MRP quad rail. Monolithic rail platform upper. Flattop or A2 upper receiver. Supplied with 30-round magazine.

NIB	Exc.	V.G.	Good	Fair	Poor
2595	1850	1400	1025	600	300

DSA Z4 Gas Trap Carbine (GTC)

This model, introduced in 2005, is fitted with a 16" chrome lined barrel with M4 profile fluted with Vortec flash hider. Collapsible 6-position stock with free float tactical rail. Gas trap system. Flattop upper receiver. Magazine capacity is 10, 20, or 30 rounds.

NIB	Exc.	V.G.	Good	Fair	Poor
1675	1250	950	625	425	225

BOLT ACTION RIFLES

DS-MP1

This is a bolt action rifle chambered for the .308 cartridge. It is built on a custom Remington 700 action and fitted with a 21" Badger barrel with target crown. Black McMillan A5 stock. Matte black finish. Introduced in 2004.

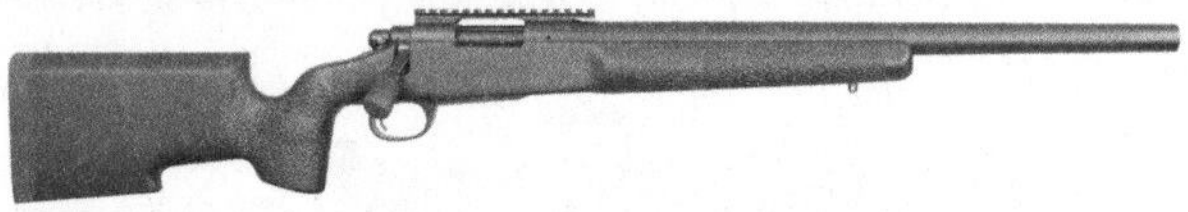

NIB	Exc.	V.G.	Good	Fair	Poor
2800	2100	1675	1050	650	425

DUBIEL ARMS CO.

Sherman, Texas

Established in 1975 by Joseph Dubiel and Dr. John Tyson. They are engaged in the manufacture of high-quality, custom built, bolt-action rifles. The rifles are constructed from patented Dubiel actions that feature a 5-lug bolt locking mechanism and a 36-degree bolt rotation. They are chambered for all calibers from .22-250 through .458 Winchester Magnum. Barrel lengths, weights, and stock styles are made to the customer's order. Douglas Premium barrels and Canjar triggers are used, and there are six basic stock designs available. The rifles are guaranteed to group in 1.5" at 100 yards with factory ammunition. The values listed are basic retail prices.

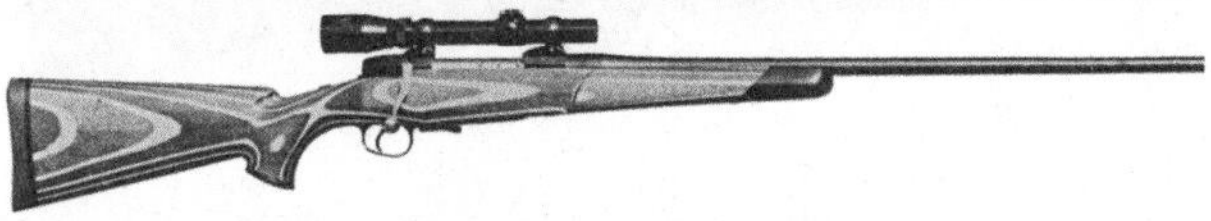

NIB	Exc.	V.G.	Good	Fair	Poor
2750	2000	1500	950	700	—

DUMOULIN

Herstal, Belgium

The guns produced by Ernest Dumoulin are essentially handmade to the customer's order. They are of the highest quality, both in materials and workmanship. There are many options available that have a tremendous impact on value fluctuations. The models and values listed here are base prices.

SHOTGUNS

Europa Model

A side-by-side double-barrel chambered for 12, 20, and 28 gauge and .410 bore. It is available in any length barrel and choke combination, with an Anson & Deeley boxlock action and automatic ejectors. One has the option of double- or single-selective triggers and a choice of six different moderate engraving patterns. The select walnut stock is oil-finished. This model was introduced in 1989. Basic values are listed.

NIB	Exc.	V.G.	Good	Fair	Poor
3500	2750	1950	1250	800	400

Leige Model

A side-by-side double chambered for 12, 16, 20, and 28 gauge. It is similar to the Europa, with a greater degree of finish and more engraving. The walnut is of a higher grade. This model was introduced in 1986.

NIB	Exc.	V.G.	Good	Fair	Poor
5750	4200	2750	1500	950	425

Continental Model

A side-by-side chambered for 12, 20, and 28 gauge and .410. Barrel lengths and chokes are on a custom-order basis. This is a true sidelock action with automatic ejectors and choice of triggers. There are six different engraving patterns, and the stock is made of high grade, hand-checkered, oil-finished walnut. This model was introduced in 1989.

NIB	Exc.	V.G.	Good	Fair	Poor
7500	6000	4500	3000	1500	400

Etendart Model

A side-by-side chambered for 12, 20, and 28 gauge. This best grade side-by-side is built on a purely made-to-order basis. It is profusely engraved and uses exhibition grade walnut in its stock. There are 12 different engraving patterns from which to choose, and the cost is according to embellishments chosen. Values given here are for the basic model.

NIB	Exc.	V.G.	Good	Fair	Poor
14500	11000	8500	4000	3000	700

Superposed Express International

An Over/Under chambered for 20 gauge and is furnished with a set of rifle barrels in the customer's choice of seven calibers. The walnut is of a deluxe grade, and engraving is available at extra cost. This is a made-to-order gun, and the value here is for the most basic model. This gun was discontinued in 1985.

NIB	Exc.	V.G.	Good	Fair	Poor
—	2500	2000	1250	750	400

Boss Royal Model

The best grade Over/Under, chambered for 12, 20, and 28 gauge. It is a full sidelock gun that is made to the customer's specification using the finest materials and workmanship available. This model was introduced in 1987.

NIB	Exc.	V.G.	Good	Fair	Poor
18500	15000	12000	8000	4500	700

Eagle Model Combination Gun

This model has a rifle barrel or the shotgun barrel that is chambered for 12 or 20 gauge. The rifle calibers available are .22 Hornet, .222 Remington, .222 Remington Magnum, 6mm, .243, .25-06, .30-06, 6.5 x 57R, 7 x 57R, 8 x 57JRS, and 9.3 x 74R. The action is a boxlock with automatic ejectors, and the other specifications are on a custom-order basis. This model was introduced in 1989.

NIB	Exc.	V.G.	Good	Fair	Poor
2750	2250	1500	950	750	400

DOUBLE RIFLES

Europa I

A made-to-order, Over/Under, double-barreled rifle available in the same calibers as the Eagle Combination gun. It has an Anson & Deeley boxlock and all other options to the customer's specifications.

NIB	Exc.	V.G.	Good	Fair	Poor
6000	4700	3500	4000	1250	500

Continental I Model

A more deluxe Over/Under rifle with a true sidelock-action. The calibers are the same as the Europa. The specifications are to the customer's order with 12 engraving patterns to choose from at extra cost. This model was introduced in 1989.

NIB	Exc.	V.G.	Good	Fair	Poor
9000	7150	5500	4000	2000	600

Pionier Express Rifle

A side-by-side double rifle chambered for the .22 Hornet through the .600 Nitro Express. It has the Anson & Deeley boxlock-action and is quite deluxe throughout. The specifications are to the customer's order, and there are basically 12 models available (P-1 through P-XII). The differences among these models are in the degree of ornamentation and quality of the walnut used for the stock. Values range from approximately $10,000 to $15,000 for the basic models.

Aristocrat Model

A low-profile single-shot chambered for all calibers up to .375 Holland & Holland. This is a deluxe, made-to-order rifle with exhibition-grade walnut and 12 engraving patterns available.

NIB	Exc.	V.G.	Good	Fair	Poor
—	9500	7500	5800	3000	700

BOLT-ACTION RIFLES

Centurion Model

A custom-order rifle built on a Mauser or Sako action and chambered for all calibers from .270 to .458 Winchester Magnum. The barrel lengths available were 21.5", 24", and 25.5"; and there were many engraving options from which to choose. The stock is of deluxe French walnut, with rosewood forend tip and pistol gripcap. This rifle was discontinued in 1986.

NIB	Exc.	V.G.	Good	Fair	Poor
11	800	650	500	400	300

Centurion Classic

Similar to the Mauser-actioned Centurion chambered for the non-Magnum calibers only. The walnut used for the stock is a better grade.

NIB	Exc.	V.G.	Good	Fair	Poor
1275	950	750	600	500	400

Diane

A more deluxe version of the Centurion Classic.

NIB	Exc.	V.G.	Good	Fair	Poor
1800	1550	1250	900	650	500

Amazone

A 20" barreled, full-length stocked, upgraded version of the Diane.

NIB	Exc.	V.G.	Good	Fair	Poor
2100	1750	1400	950	700	500

Bavaria Deluxe

Similar to the Centurion, with the same barrel lengths and calibers available. The engraving styles available are more deluxe. This model was discontinued in 1985.

NIB	Exc.	V.G.	Good	Fair	Poor
2350	1800	1400	950	700	500

Safari Model

Similar to the Bavaria Deluxe, but it is chambered for the heavy Magnum calibers only.

NIB	Exc.	V.G.	Good	Fair	Poor
3275	2700	1900	1450	900	500

Safari Sportsman

Built on a Magnum Mauser action and is chambered for the .375 Holland & Holland, .404 Jeffreys, .416 Rigby, and the .505 Gibbs. This is a true big game rifle that was made available in 1986.

NIB	Exc.	V.G.	Good	Fair	Poor
4500	3650	2400	1550	1100	—

African Pro

A more deluxe version of the Safari Sportsman, with a folding leaf rear sight, hooded front sight, and an ebony or buffalo horn forend tip.

NIB	Exc.	V.G.	Good	Fair	Poor
5200	3950	2700	1700	1300	750

E

EAGLE ARMS
Division of Armalite
Geneseo, Illinois

PRE-BAN MODELS

Golden Eagle

This model is identical in design to the AR-15. Fitted with a 20" stainless steel extra-heavy barrel with National Match sights and two-stage trigger. Weight is about 9.4 lbs.

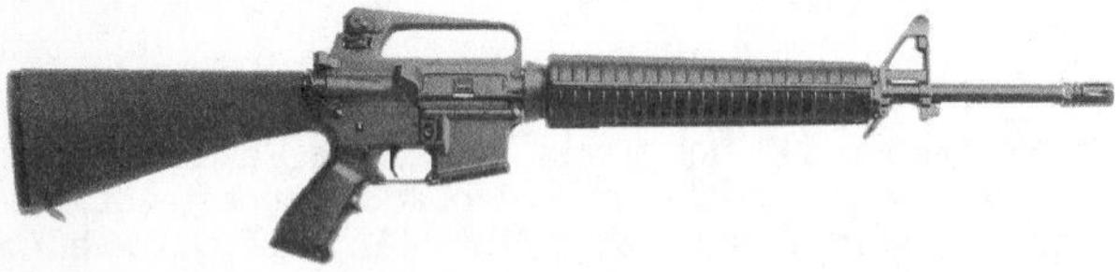

NIB	Exc.	V.G.	Good	Fair	Poor
1050	950	750	575	400	225

HBAR

Similar to the above model but with a heavy 20" barrel. Weight is approximately 8 lbs.

NIB	Exc.	V.G.	Good	Fair	Poor
1250	950	750	575	400	225

SPR

This is similar to the above model with the exception of a detachable carry handle. Weight is about 7.6 lbs.

NIB	Exc.	V.G.	Good	Fair	Poor
1250	950	750	575	400	225

M4C Carbine

This model features a 16" barrel with a 4.33" flash suppressor. Retractable stock. Weight is approximately 6.2 lbs.

NIB	Exc.	V.G.	Good	Fair	Poor
1250	950	750	575	400	225

M4A1C Carbine

Similar to the above model but with detachable carry handle. Weight is about 6 lbs.

NIB	Exc.	V.G.	Good	Fair	Poor
1250	950	750	575	400	225

POST-BAN MODEL

Golden Eagle

This model features a 20" stainless steel extra-heavy barrel with two-stage trigger. Weight is about 9.2 lbs.

NIB	Exc.	V.G.	Good	Fair	Poor
1050	850	750	575	400	225

ENDERS, CARL
Suhl, Germany

Side-by-Side Shotgun

Percussion damascus double-barrel side-by-side in 12 gauge. Ornate checkering with cheekpiece and engraved metal work. This firm made high-quality firearms, mostly side-by-side guns. The gun pictured was made circa 1850-1860. The firm was in business from about 1835 to approximately 1890.

Courtesy Jim Cate

NIB	Exc.	V.G.	Good	Fair	Poor
—	—	1250	550	300	150

ERA
Brazil

Era Double Barrel Shotgun

An inexpensive shotgun chambered for 12 and 20 gauge, as well as .410. It was offered with 26", 28", or 30" barrels with various choke combinations. It has double triggers and extractors, with a checkered hardwood pistol-grip stock. This gun is also available as a Quail model with a 20" barrel and as a Riot model with an 18" barrel. These two models are not offered in .410 bore.

NIB	Exc.	V.G.	Good	Fair	Poor
—	200	150	125	100	75

Era Over-and-Under Shotgun

Chambered for 12 or 20 gauge, with 28" ventilated rib barrels that were choked full and modified. It is a boxlock with double triggers, extractors, and a hardwood stock. It was also offered in a trap model and a skeet model chambered for 12 gauge only and appropriately choked. These latter two models would be worth a 10 percent premium over the values listed.

NIB	Exc.	V.G.	Good	Fair	Poor
—	325	275	250	200	150

ERMA WERKE WAFFENFABRIK
Erfurt, Germany
Post-war
Dachau, Germany

Known primarily as a manufacturer of submachine guns, but they are also in the handgun and rifle business. In 1933 they answered the German army's need for an inexpensive practice weapon by producing a .22 rimfire conversion unit for the Luger pistol. This was marketed commercially and was available for many years. The success of this unit led the company to produce other inexpensive target and plinking pistols. After the war they were reorganized in the western sector and resumed submachine gun production. In 1964 they returned to the sporting firearms business with the introduction of their .22 rimfire Luger-lookalike pistol. Since then, they have produced many like-quality firearms. They were imported by Excam of Hialeah, Florida. This association is now terminated, and they are currently imported by Beeman Precision in Santa Rosa, California, and Mandell Shooting Supplies in Scottsdale, Arizona.

RIFLES

EM1.22

A semi-automatic .22 rimfire version of the M1 Carbine. It has an 18" barrel and a 15-round magazine. It was manufactured between 1966 and 1976.

NIB	Exc.	V.G.	Good	Fair	Poor
—	350	225	150	125	100

EG-72, EG-722

A 15-shot slide-action carbine chambered for .22 rimfire, with a 18.5" barrel and open sights. The finish is blued, and it was manufactured between 1970 and 1985.

NIB	Exc.	V.G.	Good	Fair	Poor
—	250	165	100	75	50

EG-712, EG-73

A lever copy of the Winchester 94 Carbine chambered for the .22 rimfire or the .22 rimfire Magnum (EG-73). It has an 18.5" barrel and holds 15 shots in a tubular magazine. It was manufactured between 1973 and 1985.

NIB	Exc.	V.G.	Good	Fair	Poor
—	250	175	150	125	100

SR-100

This is long-range precision bolt-action rifle chambered for .308 Win., .300 Win. Mag., or .338 Lapua calibers. Barrel length on the .308 Win. caliber is 25.25", other calibers are 29.25". All barrels are fitted with a muzzlebrake. Trigger is adjustable. Stock is laminated with thumbhole and adjustable recoil pad and cheekpiece. Weight is approximately 15 lbs.

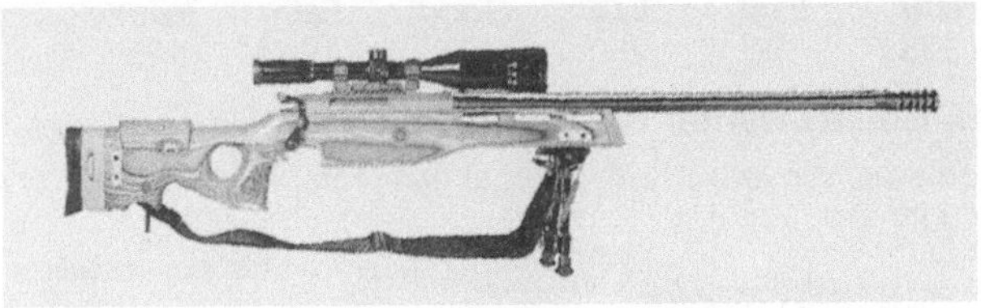

NIB	Exc.	V.G.	Good	Fair	Poor
8800	7000	5000	2750	1300	600

ESCORT

Turkey

SEMI-AUTOMATIC SHOTGUNS

Model AS

This 12 gauge 3" model is fitted with a 28" vent rib barrel with choke tubes. Walnut stock. Black finish. Magazine capacity is 4 rounds. Weight is about 7 lbs.

NIB	Exc.	V.G.	Good	Fair	Poor
450	365	245	200	150	100

NOTE: Add $45 for TriViz model.

Model PS

This 12 gauge 3" model is similar to the above but with a black polymer stock and black finish. Also offered in Shadow Grass camo or Mossy Oak Break-Up camo. Choice of Spark or TriViz front sights. Barrel length is 28" except for TriViz variation with 24" barrel. Weight is about 7 lbs. Add 10 percent for camo.

NIB	Exc.	V.G.	Good	Fair	Poor
450	365	245	200	150	100

Model PS AimGuard

This 12 gauge 3" model is fitted with a 20" fixed choke barrel in Cylinder bore. Black polymer stock with black finish. Magazine capacity is 5 rounds. Weight is about 6.4 lbs.

NIB	Exc.	V.G.	Good	Fair	Poor
400	295	200	125	100	75

Combo Model

This 12 gauge 3" model is offered with two sets of barrels: one 28" with Full choke tube and the other 24" with Turkey choke tube. Polymer stock with Mossy Oak Break-Up. Receiver is fitted with a dovetail mount. Weight is about 7 lbs.

NIB	Exc.	V.G.	Good	Fair	Poor
575	425	365	295	200	100

PUMP ACTION SHOTGUNS

Field Hunter

This 12 gauge 3" model is fitted with a 28" vent rib barrel with choke tubes. Offered with a black polymer stock of Mossy Oak Break-Up or Shadow Grass camo pattern. A 24" barrel with TriViz is also offered. Magazine capacity is 4 rounds. Weight is about 7 lbs.

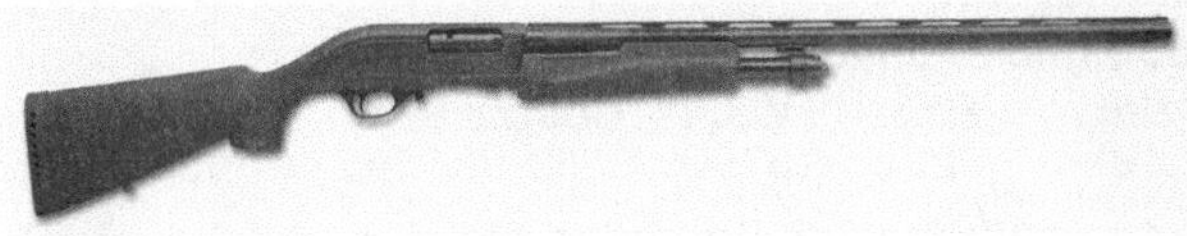

NIB	Exc.	V.G.	Good	Fair	Poor
325	225	165	135	100	75

NOTE: For camo finish add $50. For TriViz sights add $100.

AimGuard

This 12 gauge 3" model is fitted with a 20" barrel with fixed Cylinder bore choke. Black polymer stock. Magazine capacity is 5 rounds. Weight is about 6.4 lbs. Add 10 percent for 18" barrel and nickel finish.

NIB	Exc.	V.G.	Good	Fair	Poor
325	225	165	135	100	75

Escort Semi-Auto Slug Gun

This slug gun is available in 12 or 20 gauge. Rifled barrel is 22 inches long with 1:26-inch twist. Self-regulating gas piston. It has Hi-Viz sights and is equipped with a cantilevered scope base. Black synthetic stock. Overall length, 42 inches. Weight: 6.3 lbs. (20 ga.), 7 lbs. (12 ga.).

NIB	Exc.	V.G.	Good	Fair	Poor
530	475	375	300	250	200

Escort Pump Slug Gun

Same specifications as semi-auto except slide action. Weight: 6 lbs. (20 ga.), 6.7 lbs. (12 ga.).

NIB	Exc.	V.G.	Good	Fair	Poor
430	385	290	250	200	150

EUROARMS OF AMERICA

Winchester, Virginia

An importer of blackpowder muzzle-loading firearms, primarily replicas of early American weapons.

RIFLES

The rifles listed are modern replicas of early American and British firearms. They are of good quality and are quite serviceable. There is little collector interest, and they are listed along with their values.

Cook & Brother Carbine

NIB	Exc.	V.G.	Good	Fair	Poor
595	500	375	250	195	100

1863 J.P. Murray

NIB	Exc.	V.G.	Good	Fair	Poor
595	500	375	250	195	100

1853 Enfield Rifled Musket

NIB	Exc.	V.G.	Good	Fair	Poor
610	525	375	250	195	100

1858 Enfield Rifled Musket

NIB	Exc.	V.G.	Good	Fair	Poor
610	525	375	250	195	100

1861 Enfield Musketoon

NIB	Exc.	V.G.	Good	Fair	Poor
500	375	250	195	100	65

1803 Harper's Ferry

NIB	Exc.	V.G.	Good	Fair	Poor
595	500	375	250	195	100

1841 Mississippi Rifle

NIB	Exc.	V.G.	Good	Fair	Poor
595	500	375	250	195	100

Pennsylvania Rifle

NIB	Exc.	V.G.	Good	Fair	Poor
400	350	275	225	150	100

Hawken Rifle

NIB	Exc.	V.G.	Good	Fair	Poor
400	350	275	225	150	100

Cape Gun

NIB	Exc.	V.G.	Good	Fair	Poor
450	395	325	275	200	150

Buffalo Carbine

NIB	Exc.	V.G.	Good	Fair	Poor
450	395	325	275	200	150

1862 Remington Rifle

NIB	Exc.	V.G.	Good	Fair	Poor
450	395	325	275	200	150

Zouave Rifle

NIB	Exc.	V.G.	Good	Fair	Poor
450	395	325	275	200	150

Duck Gun

A single-barreled percussion fowling piece chambered for 8, 10, or 12 gauge. It has a 33" smooth-bore barrel and a case-colored hammer and lock. The stock is walnut with brass mountings. This model was introduced in 1989. Add 20 percent for 8 gauge.

NIB	Exc.	V.G.	Good	Fair	Poor
450	395	325	275	200	150

Standard Side-by-Side

A side-by-side, chambered for 12 gauge percussion. It has 28" barrels with engraved locks and a walnut stock.

NIB	Exc.	V.G.	Good	Fair	Poor
475	400	350	295	200	125

EUROPEAN AMERICAN ARMORY CORP.

EAA Bounty Hunter Shotgun—External Hammers

This is a side-by-side shotgun with external hammers chambered for 10, 12, 16, 20, 28, and .410 bores. It is offered in barrel lengths of 20", 24", and 26".

NIB	Exc.	V.G.	Good	Fair	Poor
375	300	250	175	150	125

EAA Bounty Hunter Shotgun—Traditional

Same as above but with internal hammers. Offered in 12 or 20 gauge.

NIB	Exc.	V.G.	Good	Fair	Poor
300	250	200	150	100	75

EAA PM2 Shotgun

This is a pump-action 12 gauge shotgun with 6-round box magazine. Barrel length is 20" and finish is either blue or chrome. Stock is black composite. Weight is 6.8 lbs. This model was discontinued in 1993.

NIB	Exc.	V.G.	Good	Fair	Poor
450	350	300	250	200	150

NOTE: Add $100 for optional night sights.

EAA HW 60 RIFLE

This German-made target rifle is chambered for the .22 LR. It features an adjustable trigger and other target and match grade components. The barrel length is 26.8", the stock is stippled walnut, and the finish is blue. Weighs approximately 10.8 lbs.

Target Grade

NIB	Exc.	V.G.	Good	Fair	Poor
700	595	500	400	300	200

Match Grade

NIB	Exc.	V.G.	Good	Fair	Poor
795	675	550	450	350	250

EAA SABATTI

These firearms are made by the Sabatti firm in Gardone, Italy. It is a old line company, having been in the firearms business since 1674. The company also produces and supplies component parts to many of Italy's premier gun makers. These shotguns and rifles are manufactured for the cost-conscious buyer.

Falcon

This is a field grade Over/Under shotgun with checkered walnut stock with pistol grip, boxlock action, double triggers, and extractors. Offered in 12 or 20 gauge with 3" chambers. Also available in 28 gauge and .410 bore with 26" or 28" barrels. Barrel lengths are available in 26", 28", or 30". Chokes are fixed.

NIB	Exc.	V.G.	Good	Fair	Poor
575	425	400	350	300	250

Falcon 28/.410

NIB	Exc.	V.G.	Good	Fair	Poor
625	480	425	375	325	275

EAA Sporting Clay Basic

This model features a single-selective trigger, extractors, checkered walnut stock with pistol grip, extra wide rib, and blued receiver with scroll engraving. Offered in 12 gauge only with 28" fixed choke barrel.

NIB	Exc.	V.G.	Good	Fair	Poor
350	275	250	200	150	100

EAA Sporting Clay Pro

This model is similar to the basic sporting clay model with the addition of a select walnut stock, screw-in choke tubes, automatic ejectors, recoil pad. Comes with hard shell case.

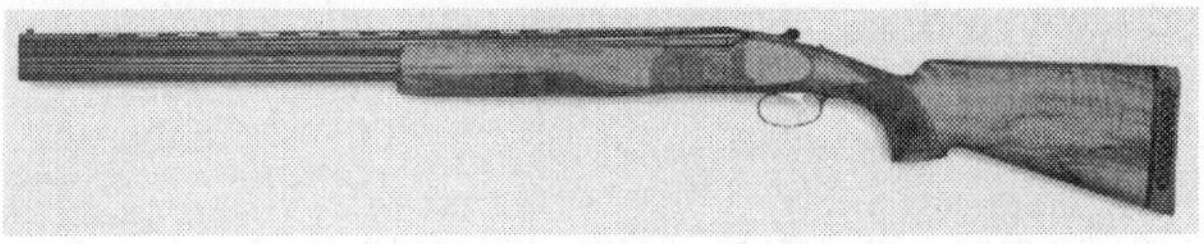

NIB	Exc.	V.G.	Good	Fair	Poor
950	720	650	550	450	300

EAA Sporting Clay Pro Gold

Same as above but with gold inlay receiver.

NIB	Exc.	V.G.	Good	Fair	Poor
1000	750	650	550	450	300

EAA Saba

This model is a side-by-side shotgun that features an engraved silver boxlock receiver, double or single triggers, selective ejectors, solid raised matted rib, and select European walnut checkered stock. Offered in 12, 20, and 28 gauge as well as .410 bore. Barrel length are 26" or 28" with fixed chokes.

NIB	Exc.	V.G.	Good	Fair	Poor
775	600	500	400	300	250

EAA/BAIKAL SHOTGUNS

SEE—Baikal

EAA/Saiga Shotgun

A semi-automatic shotgun based on the AK-47 design. Chambered for the 12, 20 and .410 bore. Barrel length are 20", 24", 26", or 28". Blued finish with optional camo finish. Detachable 5-round box magazine. Introduced in 1999.

NIB	Exc.	V.G.	Good	Fair	Poor
600	525	450	350	200	125

NOTE: Deduct $175 for .410 variation.

EAA/Saiga Rifle

Same as above but chambered for 7.62x39 or .308 cartridge. Fitted with a 20" barrel. Choice of wood or synthetic stock. Introduced in 1999.

NIB	Exc.	V.G.	Good	Fair	Poor
550	450	300	200	125	75

NOTE: Add $100 for .308 caliber.

EAA Rover 870

This is a high-quality bolt-action rifle. The walnut stock is checkered with rubber recoil pad. Adjustable rear sight and receiver is drilled and tapped for scope mount. Barrel length is 22". Chambered for these cartridges: .22-250, .243, .25-06, .270, .308, .30-06, 7mm Rem. Mag., .300 and .338 Win. Mag.

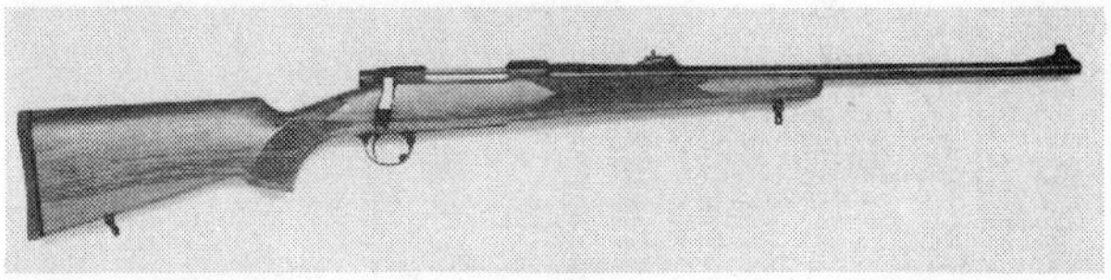

NIB	Exc.	V.G.	Good	Fair	Poor
585	445	375	300	200	125

EAA SP 1822

This Sabatti rifle is chambered for the .22 LR. It is a semi-automatic carbine with a two-piece adjustable stock.

NIB	Exc.	V.G.	Good	Fair	Poor
225	175	125	100	85	60

EAA SP 1822H

This a heavy barrel version of the above model without sights. The receiver is fitted with scope mount base.

NIB	Exc.	V.G.	Good	Fair	Poor
225	175	125	100	85	60

EAA SP 1822TH

This variation also has a heavy barrel without sights but with base mounts. A one-piece Bell and Carlson thumb hole stock is the feature of this model.

NIB	Exc.	V.G.	Good	Fair	Poor
350	260	225	175	125	90

EVANS REPEATING RIFLE CO.

Mechanic Falls, Maine

Incorporated in 1873, this firm produced repeating rifles based upon patents issued to Warren R. Evans (1868-1871) and later George F. Evans (1877, 1878 and 1879). The most distinctive feature of these arms is that they used a butt magazine operating on the principle of an Archimedean screw. Distributed by Merwin, Hulbert & Company, as well as Schuyler, Hartley & Graham, Evans rifles met with some success. One of their earliest advocates was William F. Cody (Buffalo Bill). The company ceased operations in 1879, after approximately 15,000 arms had been made.

LEVER-ACTION RIFLE

This rifle is totally unique for a number of reasons. It holds the most rounds of any repeating rifle that did not have a detachable magazine, with capacities up to 38 rounds on some models. This rifle was chambered for its own cartridge—the .44 Evans of which there were two versions: a 1" cartridge in the "Old Model" and the "Transition Model" and a 1.5" cartridge in the "New Model." The finish on these rifles is blued, with nickel-plated levers and buttplates noted on some examples. The stocks are walnut. There were approximately 12,250 of all models manufactured between 1873 and 1879.

OLD MODEL

This variation is chambered for the 1" .44 Evans cartridge and has a butt stock that covers only the top half of the revolving 34-shot magazine located in the butt of the rifle. The buttplate appears as if it is reversed, and the markings on the "Old Model" are "Evans Repeating Rifle/Pat. Dec. 8, 1868 & Sept. 16, 1871." There are three versions of the Old Model listed. They were manufactured between 1874 and 1876 and serial numbered 1-500.

Military Musket

This version has a 30" barrel, with two barrel bands and provisions for a bayonet. There were only 50 estimated manufactured.

NIB	Exc.	V.G.	Good	Fair	Poor
—	—	3750	1700	500	200

Sporting Rifle

Approximately 300 of this model produced with a 26", 28", or 30" octagonal barrel.

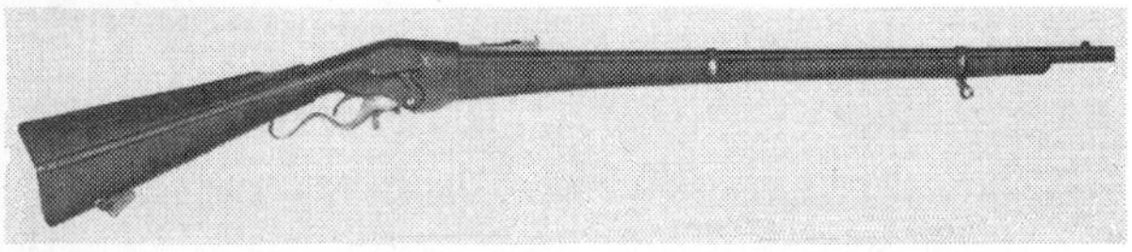

Courtesy Milwaukee Public Museum, Milwaukee, Wisconsin

NIB	Exc.	V.G.	Good	Fair	Poor
—	—	1950	900	500	200

Carbine

This variation has a 22" barrel, with one barrel band and a sling swivel. There were 150 produced.

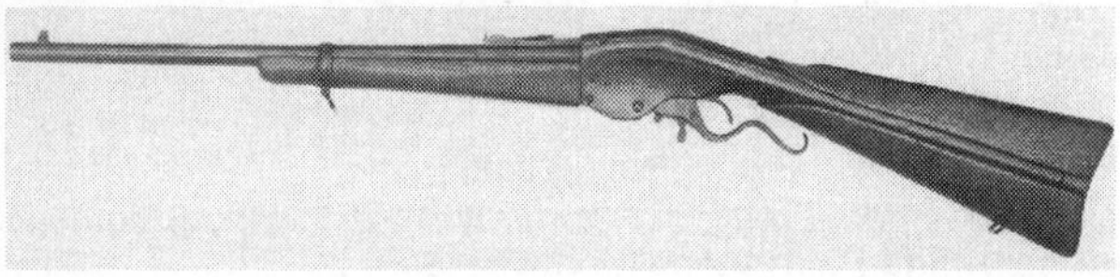

Courtesy Milwaukee Public Museum, Milwaukee, Wisconsin

NIB	Exc.	V.G.	Good	Fair	Poor
—	—	3500	1450	500	200

TRANSITIONAL MODEL

Has a buttstock that covers both the top and bottom of the rotary magazine, with an exposed portion in the middle of the butt. The buttplate does not have the backward appearance, and the barrel is marked "Evans Repeating Rifle Mechanic Falls Me./Pat Dec. 8, 1868 & Sept. 16, 1871." This version was manufactured in 1876 and 1877 and was serial numbered between 500-2185, for a total of approximately 1,650 manufactured.

Military Musket

Has a 30" barrel and two barrel bands. 150 were produced.

NIB	Exc.	V.G.	Good	Fair	Poor
—	—	3000	1750	650	200

Carbine

Four hundred-fifty of these were produced, with a 22" barrel and one barrel band.

NIB	Exc.	V.G.	Good	Fair	Poor
—	—	2950	1700	600	200

Sporting Rifle

Has a 26", 28", or 30" barrel. There were 1,050 produced.

NIB	Exc.	V.G.	Good	Fair	Poor
—	—	2250	1000	300	150

"Montreal Carbine"

A special issue marked "Montreal," sold by R.H. Kilby, Evans' Canadian sales agent. There were between 50 and 100 produced.

NIB	Exc.	V.G.	Good	Fair	Poor
—	—	3250	1150	450	250

NEW MODEL

Approximately 10,000 of the New Model were produced, chambered for the 1.5" .44 Evans cartridge with a magazine capacity reduced to 28. The frame was redesigned and rounded at the top, and the forend fit flush to the receiver. The lever and hammer are streamlined, and there is a dust cover over the loading gate. The markings are the same as on the Transitional Model with "U.S.A." added to the last line. This version was not serial numbered, and any numbers found are assembly numbers only.

Military Musket

3,000 produced, with a 30" barrel and two barrel bands.

NIB	Exc.	V.G.	Good	Fair	Poor
—	—	3950	1750	450	275

Carbine

4,000 produced with a 22" barrel, one barrel band, and a sling swivel.

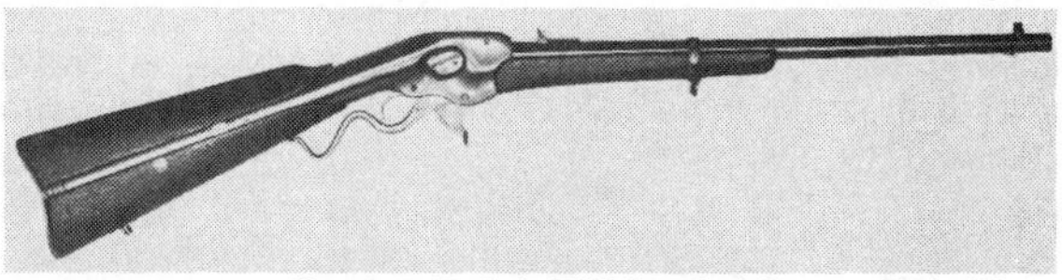

Courtesy Buffalo Bill Historical Center, Cody, Wyoming

NIB	Exc.	V.G.	Good	Fair	Poor
—	—	2150	950	500	250

Sporting Rifle

3,000 produced with 26", 28", or 30" octagonal barrels.

NIB	Exc.	V.G.	Good	Fair	Poor
—	—	2500	2000	800	300

EXCEL INDUSTRIES

Chino, California

Accelerator Rifle

As above but with an 18" fluted stainless steel barrel and black polymer pistol-grip stock. Fully adjustable removable sights on a Weaver rail. Weight is about 8 lbs. Introduced in 2004.

NIB	Exc.	V.G.	Good	Fair	Poor
465	350	275	195	150	100

EXEL ARMS OF AMERICA

Laurona & Ugartechia

—Lanber

This firm was engaged in the import of Spanish shotguns. They ceased importing them in 1967, and the specific models will be found listed under the manufacturers' names.

F

FABARM

Brescia, Italy

In 1998 H&K took over the importation of the Fabarm shotgun line in the U.S.

SEMI-AUTOMATIC SHOTGUNS

Ellegi Standard

A gas-operated, semi-automatic shotgun chambered for 12gauge. It has a 28" vent-rib barrel with choice of choke. The re-ceiver is blue anodized alloy with a photo-etched game scene,and the stock and forearm are checkered walnut. This model wasintroduced in 1989.

NIB	Exc.	V.G.	Good	Fair	Poor
700	625	525	450	350	250

The Ellegi Model is available in six other configurations. The differences are in the barrel length and choke, type of choke tubes, and finish. Basically the guns are quite similar to the standard model. These variations are listed.

Ellegi Standard Ellegi Multichoke

NIB	Exc.	V.G.	Good	Fair	Poor
700	625	525	450	350	250

Ellegi Standard Ellegi Innerchoke

NIB	Exc.	V.G.	Good	Fair	Poor
725	650	550	475	375	275

Ellegi Standard Ellegi Magnum

NIB	Exc.	V.G.	Good	Fair	Poor
725	650	550	475	375	275

Ellegi Standard Ellegi Super Goose

NIB	Exc.	V.G.	Good	Fair	Poor
800	725	625	550	450	350

Ellegi Standard Ellegi Slug

NIB	Exc.	V.G.	Good	Fair	Poor
775	700	600	525	425	325

Ellegi Standard Ellegi Police

NIB	Exc.	V.G.	Good	Fair	Poor
575	500	450	400	300	225

SLIDE-ACTION SHOTGUNS

Model S.D.A.S.S.

Chambered for 12 gauge with a 3" chamber. It is offered with a20" or 24.5" barrel threaded for external choke tubes. This modelhas an 8-shot tube magazine, twin action bars, an alloy receiver,and a matte black finish. It is a defensive-type shotgun and hasbeen imported since 1989.

NIB	Exc.	V.G.	Good	Fair	Poor
350	275	200	150	100	75

The Special Police and the Martial Model are variations of the basic slide-action and differ in barrel length and choke. The Police Model has a shrouded barrel.

Model S.D.A.S.S. Special Police

NIB	Exc.	V.G.	Good	Fair	Poor
525	475	425	350	275	200

Model S.D.A.S.S. Martial Model

NIB	Exc.	V.G.	Good	Fair	Poor
475	425	375	300	225	175

SINGLE-SHOT SHOTGUNS

Omega Standard

Has an alloy receiver and is chambered for 12 and 20 gauge, as well as .410. It has 26" or 28" barrels with various chokes. The finish is black with a beech stock. It was introduced in 1989.

NIB	Exc.	V.G.	Good	Fair	Poor
150	125	100	75	50	40

Omega Goose Gun

Chambered for 12 gauge only, with a 35.5" full-choke barrel.

NIB	Exc.	V.G.	Good	Fair	Poor
195	140	125	100	75	50

SIDE-BY-SIDE SHOTGUNS

Beta Model

This double-barrel is chambered for 12 gauge only, with choice of barrel length and choke. It has a boxlock action with false side plates. It has a single trigger and automatic ejectors, and the finish is blued with a checkered, select walnut stock. This model was introduced in 1989.

NIB	Exc.	V.G.	Good	Fair	Poor
925	850	750	600	450	300

Beta Europe

A deluxe version that features single-selective triggers and a game scene engraved, coin-finished receiver. The stock is the straight English style with a splinter forend. This model was introduced in 1989.

NIB	Exc.	V.G.	Good	Fair	Poor
1750	1500	1250	1000	750	500

OVER/UNDER SHOTGUNS

Field Model

Chambered for 12 gauge and has 29" vent-rib barrels with various chokes. The receiver is coin-finished, and the stock is checkered walnut. This Model was discontinued in 1985.

NIB	Exc.	V.G.	Good	Fair	Poor
900	700	600	500	400	300

Gamma Field

Chambered for 12 or 20 gauge and is offered with 26", 28", or 29" vent-rib barrels and various choke combinations. Screw-in choke tubes are available and would be worth a 10 percent premium. This model has a boxlock, coin-finished receiver that is moderately engraved and a checkered walnut stock.

NIB	Exc.	V.G.	Good	Fair	Poor
925	850	775	650	500	350

Gamma Paradox Gun

Chambered for 12 gauge only, and the top barrel is rifled for accurate placement of slugs. The barrels are 25" long with vent-rib, and the bottom barrel has three screw-in choke tubes. This model has a single-selective trigger and automatic ejectors. The finish is similar to the Field Model. It was introduced in 1989.

NIB	Exc.	V.G.	Good	Fair	Poor
1000	900	825	750	600	450

Gamma Trap or Skeet

Competition-grade guns with either a 27.5" barrel with five screw-in choke tubes on the skeet model or a 29" barrel with screw-in trap chokes. Both models feature single-selective triggers and automatic ejectors; and the trap model has a Monte Carlo stock. They have moderately engraved, coin-finished boxlock actions and were introduced in 1989.

NIB	Exc.	V.G.	Good	Fair	Poor
1000	900	825	750	600	450

Gamma Sporting Competition Model

Designed for Sporting Clays and is chambered for 12 gauge only. The 29" barrel has a wide rib and is furnished with five screw-in choke tubes. It has a single-selective trigger, automatic ejectors, and a checkered walnut stock with a competition recoil pad. It is finished like the skeet and trap models and was introduced in 1989.

NIB	Exc.	V.G.	Good	Fair	Poor
1000	900	825	750	600	450

CURRENTLY IMPORTED SHOTGUNS (H&K-POST 1997) SEMI-AUTOMATIC & PUMP SHOTGUNS

Camo Lion

Introduced in 1999, this 12 gauge model features a ported barrel system in 24", 26", or 28" lengths. Wetlands camo finish. Five chokes tubes and hard plastic case included. Weight is about 7 lbs.

NIB	Exc.	V.G.	Good	Fair	Poor
800	650	450	300	175	100

Red Lion

This is a 12 gauge semi-auto with 3" chambers, three-shot magazine, matte finish, walnut stock, rubber vented recoil pad with leather cover, and set of five choke tubes. Available with 24", 26", or 28" vent-rib barrel. Weight is about 7 lbs.

NIB	Exc.	V.G.	Good	Fair	Poor
800	650	450	300	175	100

Red Lion Ducks Unlimited 2001

This model is offered only through the Ducks Unlimited banquet program only. This is a 12 gauge 28" barrel with select walnut stock. Oil finish. Unique serial numbers from 0001DU2001 to 3600DU2001. Receiver is engraved with waterfowl scene and DU logo. Comes with lockable case. Limited to 3,600 shotguns.

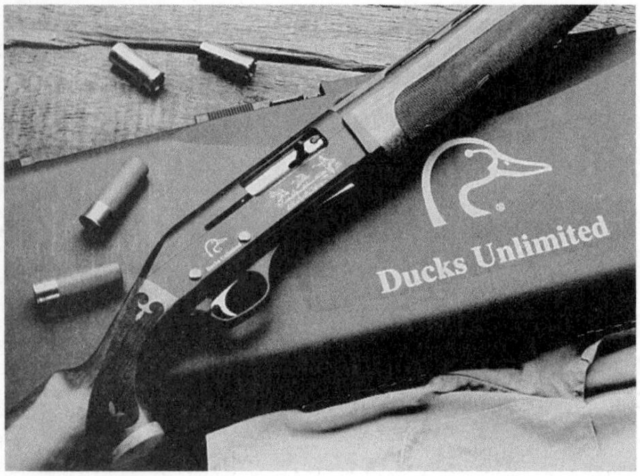

NIB	Exc.	V.G.	Good	Fair	Poor
975	775	625	500	325	200

Gold Lion

Has many of the features of the Red Lion model with the addition of a high-grade oil-finished walnut stock with Olive wood pistol grip cap. Trigger is gold plated.

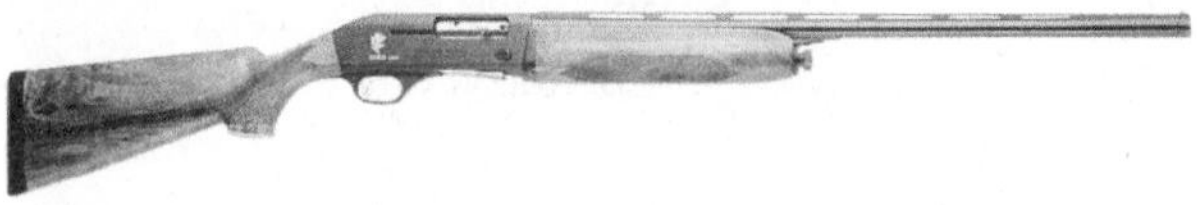

NIB	Exc.	V.G.	Good	Fair	Poor
800	650	450	300	175	100

Gold Lion Mark III

This semi-automatic model is an improved version of the Gold Lion with the addition of an enhanced walnut stock, lightweight receiver with scroll and engraving and gold enlays. Fitted with a 28" TriBore barrel and chambered for the 3" 12 gauge shell. Supplied with five choke tubes. Weight is about 7.2 lbs.

NIB	Exc.	V.G.	Good	Fair	Poor
975	775	625	500	325	200

Sporting Clays Lion

This model, introduced in 1999, features a ported barrel and special "TriBore" system. Offered in 12 gauge with 28" barrel. Walnut stock with rubber recoil pad, gold-plated trigger, matte blue finish, red front sight bar, 10mm channeled rib, two extra front sights (green and white), and a set of five choke tubes. Weight is about 7.2 lbs.

NIB	Exc.	V.G.	Good	Fair	Poor
975	775	625	500	325	200

Rex Lion

Introduced in 2002 this model features a 12 gauge gun with 3" chambers with 26" or 28" vent-rib barrel. Choke tubes. High-grade walnut stock with Olive wood grip cap. Silver and black frame with scroll engraving with gold inlay. Weight is about 7 lbs. A limited edition.

NIB	Exc.	V.G.	Good	Fair	Poor
1050	800	650	450	300	175

Sporting Clays Extra

Introduced in 2000 this model features a 28" or 30" vent-rib barrel with carbon fiber finish on both barrel and receiver. This model also supplied with eight competition choke tubes. Stock is adjustable. Supplied with fitted luggage case. Weight is about 7.3 lbs.

NIB	Exc.	V.G.	Good	Fair	Poor
850	675	450	300	175	100

Tactical Semi-Auto

This is a 12 gauge semi-automatic shotgun fitted with a 20" barrel threaded for chokes. Receiver-mounted Picatinny rail. Flip-up front sight. Optional magazine extension has 7-round capacity. Also optional pistol grip. Weight is about 6.6 lbs. Introduced in 2001.

NIB	Exc.	V.G.	Good	Fair	Poor
650	550	400	265	150	100

Home Security HD

This semi-automatic shotgun is chambered for the 12 gauge 3" shell. Fitted with a 20" plain barrel with cylinder screw-in choke. Matte black finish. Black polymer stock. Magazine capacity is 5 rounds. Weight is about 7.5 lbs.

NIB	Exc.	V.G.	Good	Fair	Poor
600	475	300	225	150	100

H368

This 12 gauge 3" model features a 28" tri-bore vent rib barrel, matte black synthetic stock or Realtree camo stock. Lightweight alloy matte black receiver. Magazine capacity is 2 rounds. Weight is about 7.2 lbs. Introduced in 2003. Also available in a left-hand model.

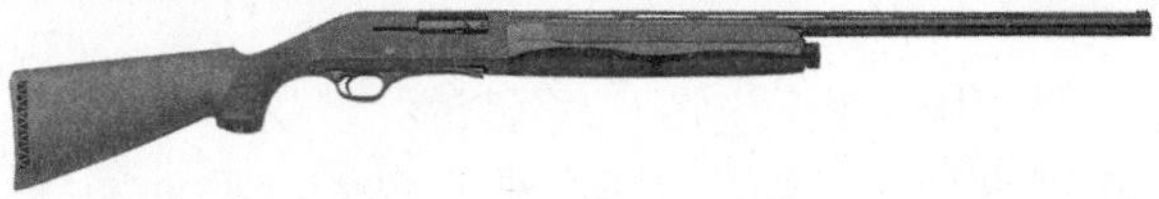

H368 Composite model

H368 Camo model

NIB	Exc.	V.G.	Good	Fair	Poor
650	550	400	265	150	100

NOTE: Add $60 for camo stock and $90 for left-hand model.

SLIDE ACTION

FP6 Field Pump

Introduced in 2001 this model features a black alloy receiver with screw-in chokes. Chambered for 12 gauge with 28" barrel. Black synthetic stock. Optional 24" rifles barrel. Weight is about 7 lbs.

NIB	Exc.	V.G.	Good	Fair	Poor
375	350	275	225	175	100

FP6 Field Pump Camo

Same as above but with Mossy Oak Break-up camo pattern.

NIB	Exc.	V.G.	Good	Fair	Poor
375	350	275	225	175	100

FP6

This model is a 12 gauge slide-action shotgun with 3" chamber, 20" barrel with heat shield, black polymer stock, threaded barrel for exterior chokes. Weight is about 6.6 lbs. This model is also available with a carbon fiber finish.

NIB	Exc.	V.G.	Good	Fair	Poor
500	400	300	200	125	100

FP6 with Rail

Introduced in 1999, this model is similar to the standard FP6 with the addition of a Picatinny rail mounted on the top of the receiver. Also fitted with a flip-up front sight. In 2003 this model was offered with a 20" tri-bore barrel with barrel threaded choke, new style front sight, and ghost ring rear sight.

NIB	Exc.	V.G.	Good	Fair	Poor
510	410	300	200	125	100

NOTE: This model is also available with 14" barrel. This requires a BATF tax and all NFA rules apply to purchase and sale of this restricted shotgun. An accessory wire stock and pistol grip are available for an additional $150.

OVER/UNDER GUNS

Max Lion

This over/under gun is chambered for the 12 or 20 gauge, 3" shell and fitted with single-selective trigger, auto ejectors, high grade walnut stock, leather covered recoil pad, set of five choke tubes and a fitted luggage-style case. Choice of 26", 28", or 30" barrels on 12 gauge guns and 26" or 28" on 20 gauge guns. Weight is about 7.5 lbs. for 12 gauge and 7 lbs. for 20 gauge.

NIB	Exc.	V.G.	Good	Fair	Poor
1200	900	700	550	300	175

NOTE: In 1999 the Max Lion was offered with the TriBore barrel system. For models with this system add $70 to above NIB prices.

Max Lion Light

Introduced in 2000 this model features 24" barrels in both 12 and 20 gauge. Receiver has gold game bird inlay. Single trigger, automatic ejectors and select walnut stock. Weight is about 7 lbs.

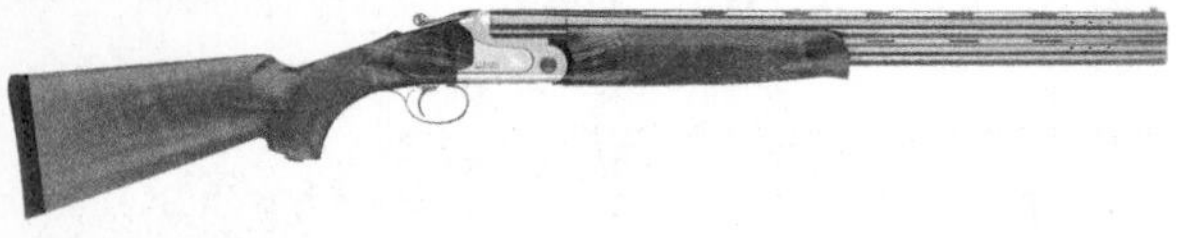

NIB	Exc.	V.G.	Good	Fair	Poor
1200	900	700	550	300	175

Max Lion Paradox

Introduced in 2002 this model features a 12 gauge 3" gun with 24" barrels. The bottom barrel is rifled. Case hardened receiver with checkered walnut stock. Weight is about 7.6 lbs.

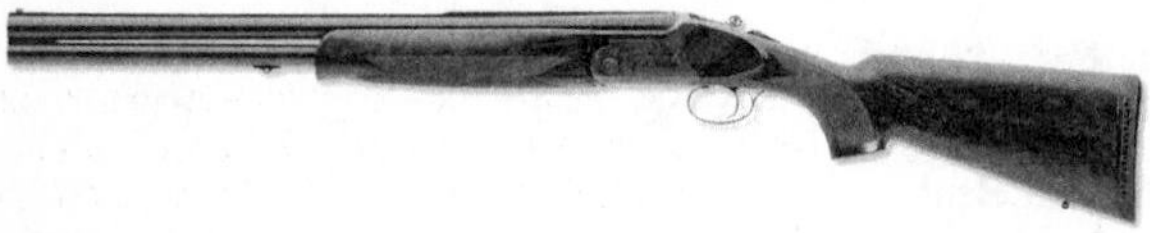

NIB	Exc.	V.G.	Good	Fair	Poor
1425	1175	900	700	550	300

Sporting Clays Competition Lion

This model is available in 12 or 20 gauge with 28" 10mm channeled rib barrels. Single-selective trigger and automatic ejectors. Recoil reducer installed in buttstock. Ported barrels. Set of 5 choke tubes standard. Leather covered recoil pad. High grade walnut stock. Introduced in 1999.

NIB	Exc.	V.G.	Good	Fair	Poor
925	825	600	500	300	150

Sporting Clays Max Lion

Chambered for the 12 gauge 3" shell and fitted with a 32" tri-bore vent rib barrel. Select walnut stock with hand checkering, adjustable trigger, and leather covered recoil pad. Engraved gold inlay receiver is case colored. Supplied with eight choke tubes. Weight is approximately 7.9 lbs. Introduced in 2003.

NIB	Exc.	V.G.	Good	Fair	Poor
925	825	600	500	300	150

Sporting Clays Competition Extra

This 12 gauge model features a a choice of 28" or 30" barrels. Walnut stock is adjustable. Finish is carbon fiber. Gun is supplied with set of eight choke tubes. Introduced in 2000. Weight is about 7.8 lbs.

NIB	Exc.	V.G.	Good	Fair	Poor
1000	775	625	500	400	150

Black Lion Competition

Similar to the Max Lion in choice of gauges and barrel lengths and features but with less figured walnut stock and black receiver finish.

NIB	Exc.	V.G.	Good	Fair	Poor
1050	795	650	525	425	175

Monotrap

This is a single barrel trap gun with 30" vent-rib barrel. Forearm has built-in recoil reduction system. Single-selective trigger and automatic ejectors. Adjustable comb. This shotgun is a 12 gauge built on a 20 gauge receiver. Weight is about 6 lbs. Introduced in 2000.

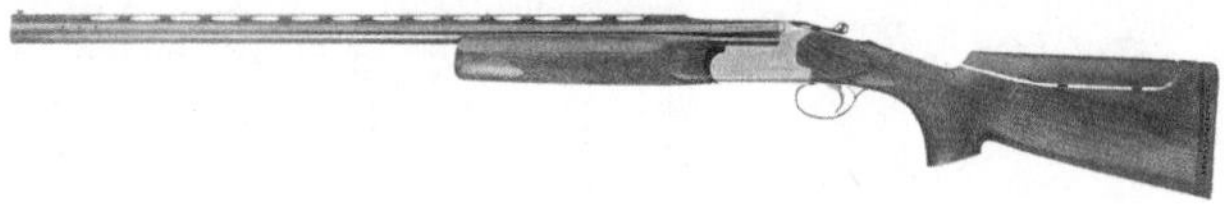

NIB	Exc.	V.G.	Good	Fair	Poor
1800	1350	1100	750	600	500

Silver Lion

This model is available in both 12 and 20 gauge and with 26", 28" barrel and 30" barrels in 12 gauge. The silver finish receiver is etched and stock is high quality walnut with leather covered pad. Scalable forearm is standard and is single-selective trigger and auto ejectors. Five chokes tubes are included. Weight is about 7.5 lbs. for 12 gauge guns and 7 lbs. for 20 gauge.

Silver Lion 12 gauge

Silver Lion 20 gauge

NIB	Exc.	V.G.	Good	Fair	Poor
925	825	600	500	300	150

Silver Lion Youth

This 20 gauge over-and-under features a shortened buttstock and 24" ported barrels. Single-selective trigger and automatic ejectors standard. Walnut stock. Rubber recoil pad. Silver steel receiver. Weight is approximately 6 lbs. Introduced in 1999.

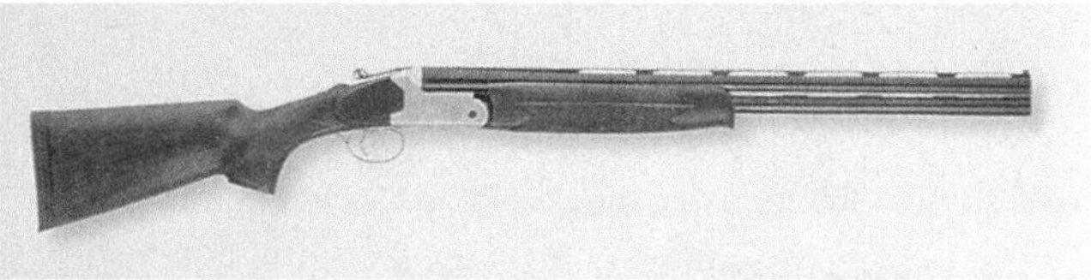

NIB	Exc.	V.G.	Good	Fair	Poor
800	775	675	500	325	150

Super Light Lion Youth

Similar to the Silver Lion Youth model but chambered for 12 gauge shells. Aluminum receiver and 24" ported barrels. Introduced in 1999. Weight is about 6.5 lbs.

NIB	Exc.	V.G.	Good	Fair	Poor
800	775	675	500	325	150

Ultra Mag Lion

This model is a 12 gauge gun with 3.5" chambers, black receiver, single-selective trigger, auto ejectors, blackened walnut stock, leather covered recoil pad, and set of five choke tubes. Barrel length is 28". Weight is 7.9 lbs.

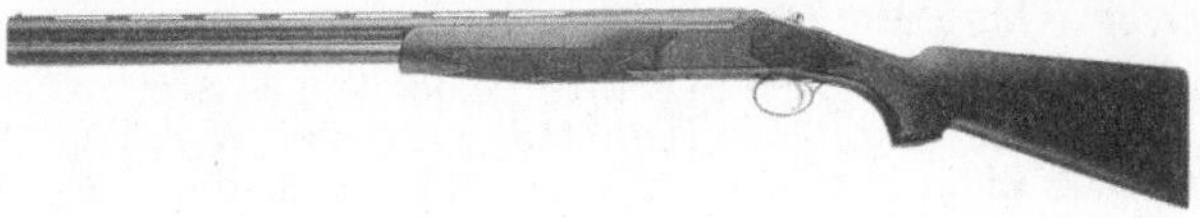

NIB	Exc.	V.G.	Good	Fair	Poor
800	775	675	500	325	150

Super Light Lion

This model features a lightweight alloy receiver with 12 gauge 24" barrels, single-selective trigger, non-auto ejectors, walnut stock, five choke tubes, and leather covered recoil pad. Weight is about 6.5 lbs.

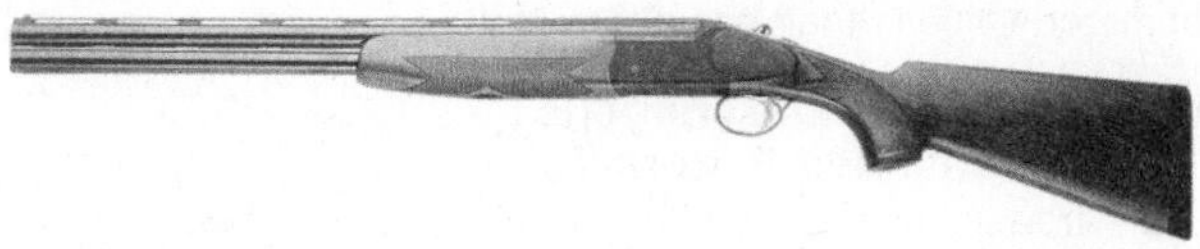

NIB	Exc.	V.G.	Good	Fair	Poor
800	775	675	500	325	150

NOTE: For TriBore system add $125.

Camo Turkey Mag.

Introduced in 1999, this model features an unported TriBore 20" barrel. Receiver has Picatinny rail on top. Full extra brown camo finish. Chambered for 12 gauge with 3.5" chambers. Weight is about 7.5 lbs.

NIB	Exc.	V.G.	Good	Fair	Poor
925	825	600	500	300	150

Ultra Camo Mag. Lion

This 12 gauge 3.5" model is fitted with 28" barrels. Wetlands camo pattern finish. Non-automatic ejectors. Weight is about 8 lbs. Introduced in 1999. Standard with steel screw-in chokes and regular screw-in chokes.

NIB	Exc.	V.G.	Good	Fair	Poor
925	825	600	500	300	150

SIDE-BY-SIDE GUNS

NIB	Exc.	V.G.	Good	Fair	Poor

Classic Lion Grade I

Offered in 12 gauge with 3" chambers, single-selective trigger, auto-ejectors, walnut stock, buttplate, and fitted with 26" barrels. Weight is about 7 lbs.

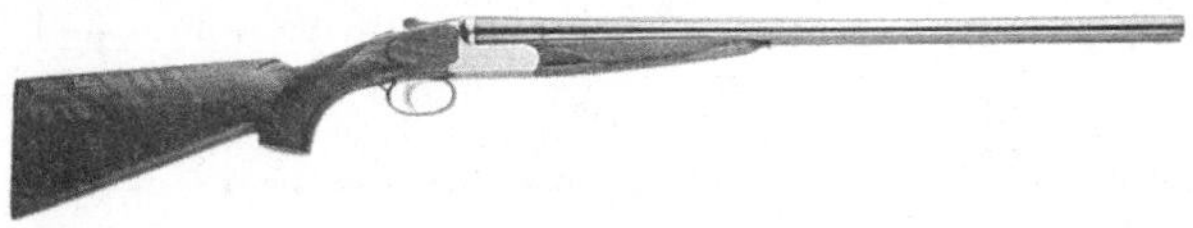

NIB	Exc.	V.G.	Good	Fair	Poor
1200	925	825	600	500	300

Classic Lion Grade II

Similar to the Grade I but with the addition of oil finished stock and removable sideplates with game scene engraving. Weight is 7.2 lbs.

NIB	Exc.	V.G.	Good	Fair	Poor
1200	925	825	600	500	300

Classic Lion Elite

Introduced in 2002, this 12 gauge model features 26" or 28" barrels with case colored receiver and straight grip stock. Fixed chokes. Weight is about 7 lbs.

NIB	Exc.	V.G.	Good	Fair	Poor
1300	1025	850	650	525	315

FABBRI, ARMI

Gardone V.T., Italy

Fabbri Armi currently manufactures one of the best shotguns in the world. They are available as a custom made-to-order item, and they are not often seen in the used gun market. The values for guns of this nature and quality are impossible to accurately establish in a book of this nature as there are so many options and conditions that make the prices fluctuate greatly. We give an estimated figure as a base starting point. See Karl Lippard's book Fabbri Shotguns, Colorado Springs, Colorado, VM Publications, 1998, for more value details

Side-by-Side Shotgun

Chambered for 12 or 20 gauge with all other features on a custom-order basis. This model is no longer in production.

NIB	Exc.	V.G.	Good	Fair	Poor
39500	27000	18500	15000	10000	8000

NOTE: Deduct $10,000 for Type One Model.

Over-and-Under Shotgun

Chambered for 12 or 20 gauge with all other features on a custom-order basis. Prices listed are for Boehler barrels.

NIB	Exc.	V.G.	Good	Fair	Poor
41500	26000	18500	15000	10000	8000

NOTE: Add 50 percent for vacuum arc remelted steel barrels. Deduct 50 percent for Phoenix barrels.

FABRIQUE NATIONALE

Herstal, Belgium

In 1889 Fabrique Nationale (or FN) was founded by a group of Belgian investors for the purpose of manufacturing Mauser rifles for the Belgian army. This was to be accomplished under license from Mauser, with the technical assistance of Ludwig Loewe of Berlin. A few years later, in the late 1890s, John Browning arrived in Europe seeking a manufacturer for his semi-automatic shotgun. He had severed his ties with Winchester after a disagreement. This led to a long association that worked out extremely well for both parties. Later Browning became associated with Colt, and the world market was divided—with the Eastern Hemisphere going to FN and the Western Hemisphere to Colt.In this section, we list arms that bear the FN banner. The FN-manufactured firearms produced under the Browning banner are listed in the Browning section of this book.

RIFLES

Model 1889

NIB	Exc.	V.G.	Good	Fair	Poor
—	350	250	200	125	100

Model 1949 or SAFN 49

NIB	Exc.	V.G.	Good	Fair	Poor
—	600	500	300	225	150

Model 30-11 Sniper Rifle

NIB	Exc.	V.G.	Good	Fair	Poor
—	5000	4500	3500	2750	2000

FN-FAL

50.00—21" Rifle Model

NIB	Exc.	V.G.	Good	Fair	Poor
3000	2750	2250	2000	1850	1000

50.63—18" Paratrooper Model

NIB	Exc.	V.G.	Good	Fair	Poor
3800	3350	2950	2750	2450	1100

50.64—21" Paratrooper Model

NIB	Exc.	V.G.	Good	Fair	Poor
3300	3000	2700	2200	1900	1000

50.41—Synthetic Butt H-Bar

NIB	Exc.	V.G.	Good	Fair	Poor
2800	2400	2000	1800	1200	1000

50.42—Wood Butt H-Bar

NIB	Exc.	V.G.	Good	Fair	Poor
2800	2400	2000	1800	1200	1000

FN FAL "G" SERIES (TYPE I RECEIVER)

Standard

NIB	Exc.	V.G.	Good	Fair	Poor
6500	5000	4000	3000	2000	1000

Lightweight

NIB	Exc.	V.G.	Good	Fair	Poor
6500	5000	4000	3000	2000	1000

FN CAL

NIB	Exc.	V.G.	Good	Fair	Poor
7000	6500	5000	3000	1500	1000

FNC

Standard

Fixed stock, 16" or 18" barrel.

NIB	Exc.	V.G.	Good	Fair	Poor
3000	2800	2500	2000	1500	1000

FNC Paratrooper Model

Folding stock, 16" or 18" barrel.

NIB	Exc.	V.G.	Good	Fair	Poor
3000	2800	2500	2000	1500	1000

NOTE: The above prices are for Belgian-made guns only.

Musketeer Sporting Rifles

A bolt-action rifle built on the Mauser-action chambered for various popular cartridges. It has a 24" barrel and is blued, with a checkered walnut stock. It was manufactured between 1947 and 1963.

NIB	Exc.	V.G.	Good	Fair	Poor
—	450	350	300	250	200

Deluxe Sporter

A higher-grade version of the Musketeer with the same general specifications. It was also manufactured between 1947 and 1963.

NIB	Exc.	V.G.	Good	Fair	Poor
—	550	450	400	275	200

FN Supreme

Chambered for the popular standard calibers and has a 24" barrel with an aperture sight and a checkered walnut stock. It was manufactured between 1957 and 1975.

NIB	Exc.	V.G.	Good	Fair	Poor
—	800	650	500	400	400

Supreme Magnum Model

Similar to the standard Supreme except that it is chambered for .264 Win. Mag., 7mm Rem. Mag., and .300 Win. Mag. It is furnished with a recoil pad and was manufactured between the same years as the standard model.

NIB	Exc.	V.G.	Good	Fair	Poor
—	800	650	500	400	400

FAMARS, A. & S.

Brescia, Italy

The Famars shotgun is one of the world's finest and is available on a custom-order basis. This makes it quite difficult to accurately establish values in a book of this nature. We list them and give an estimated value in their basic form only.

Engraving Pattern Descriptions (Older Discontinued Patterns)

S2—Traditional fully engraved fine English scroll with coverage highlighting selected areas of the receiver and forend metal. Wood grade is AA.

S3—Traditional hand-engraved scroll with some open areas around the scroll coverage on the receiver and forend metal. Wood grade is AAA.

S4—Traditional full coverage, intricate and high in detail. Patterns may be English, German, or game scene. Wood grade is AAAA.

S5—Grade S4 patterns with animals inlaid in 24k gold. Wood grade is AAAA.

S4E—Extremely high detail scenes and elaborate ornamental work where the subject matter is selected by the customer. Wood grade is AAAAA.

S5E—Similar to the S4E level but with raised or flush gold inlay work. Wood grade is AAAAA.

SXO—The best work by the world's best engravers. Museum quality. Wood grade is AAAAAA.

ZEUS

An engraved side-by-side boxlock in 12, 20, 28, and .410 bore.

In the white

NIB	Exc.	V.G.	Good	Fair	Poor
19000	12000	9000	6500	4750	750

D2 pattern

NIB	Exc.	V.G.	Good	Fair	Poor
20000	12000	9000	6500	4750	750

S3 pattern

NIB	Exc.	V.G.	Good	Fair	Poor
22000	20000	12000	9000	6500	900

NOTE: Add 10 percent for smaller gauges.

TRIBUTE

An engraved side-by-side droplock offered in 12 or 20 gauge.

In the white

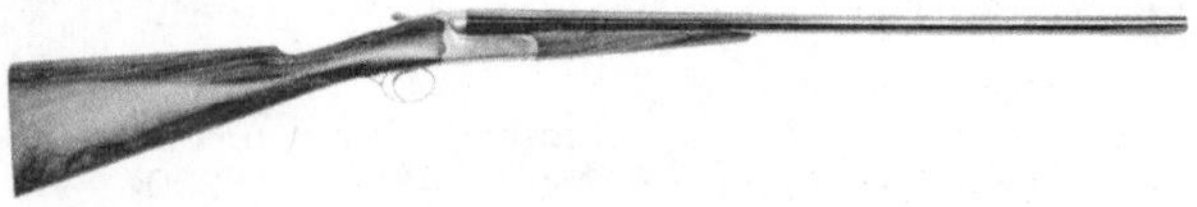

NIB	Exc.	V.G.	Good	Fair	Poor
21400	20800	12000	9000	6500	900

D2 pattern

NIB	Exc.	V.G.	Good	Fair	Poor
22600	20500	12000	9000	6500	900

S3 pattern

NIB	Exc.	V.G.	Good	Fair	Poor
24300	22000	12000	9000	6500	900

VENUS

A side-by-side sidelock shotgun with choice of engraving patterns and coverage. Offered in 12, 20, 28, or .410 bore.

In the white

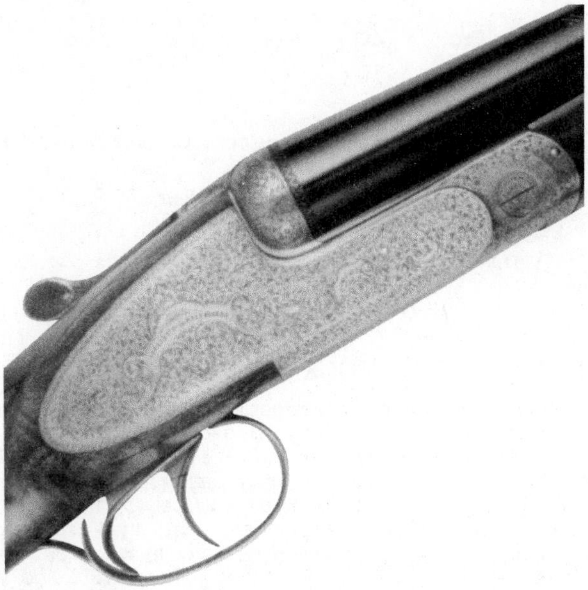

NIB	Exc.	V.G.	Good	Fair	Poor
32700	30500	20000	12000	9000	900

D2 pattern

NIB	Exc.	V.G.	Good	Fair	Poor
33900	31500	—	—	—	—

D3 pattern

NIB	Exc.	V.G.	Good	Fair	Poor
37000	10500	—	—	—	—

D4 pattern

NIB	Exc.	V.G.	Good	Fair	Poor
42800	39000	—	—	—	—

D5 pattern

NIB	Exc.	V.G.	Good	Fair	Poor
48200	42000	—	—	—	—

D4E pattern

NIB	Exc.	V.G.	Good	Fair	Poor
53500	47500	—	—	—	—

D5E pattern

NIB	Exc.	V.G.	Good	Fair	Poor
58500	51500	—	—	—	—

DXO pattern

NIB	Exc.	V.G.	Good	Fair	Poor
85000	55000	—	—	—	—

VENERI

A side-by-side sidelock shotgun.

NIB	Exc.	V.G.	Good	Fair	Poor
32000	30000	—	—	—	—

D2 pattern

NIB	Exc.	V.G.	Good	Fair	Poor
32700	30500	—	—	—	—

JOREMA ROYAL

An over-and-under shotgun with sidelocks. Offered in 12, 20, 28, and .410 bore

In the white

NIB	Exc.	V.G.	Good	Fair	Poor
32700	26000	—	—	—	—

S2 pattern

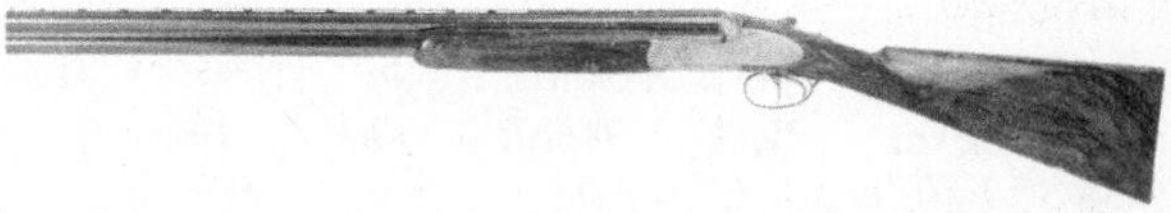

NIB	Exc.	V.G.	Good	Fair	Poor
33900	20000	—	—	—	—

S3 pattern

NIB	Exc.	V.G.	Good	Fair	Poor
37300	29500	—	—	—	—

S4 pattern

NIB	Exc.	V.G.	Good	Fair	Poor
42900	33500	—	—	—	—

S5 pattern

NIB	Exc.	V.G.	Good	Fair	Poor
48200	29500	—	—	—	—

S4E pattern

NIB	Exc.	V.G.	Good	Fair	Poor
53500	42500	—	—	—	—

S5E pattern

NIB	Exc.	V.G.	Good	Fair	Poor
53500	42500	—	—	—	—

SXO pattern

NIB	Exc.	V.G.	Good	Fair	Poor
85000	66500	—	—	—	—

NOTE: Add 15 percent for smaller gauges.

EXCALIBER BL

An over-and-under shotgun with removable trigger group. Offered in 12, 20, 28, and .410 bore with single trigger.

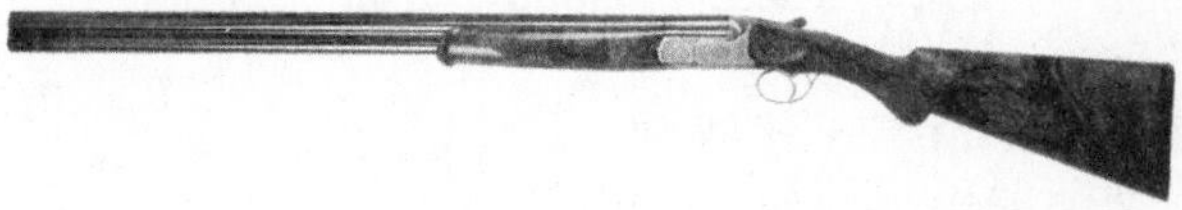

NIB	Exc.	V.G.	Good	Fair	Poor
11800	6500	—	—	—	—

Extra

Finer engraving than standard.

NIB	Exc.	V.G.	Good	Fair	Poor
15455	8900	—	—	—	—

Prestige

Finer engraving than BL Extra.

NIB	Exc.	V.G.	Good	Fair	Poor
17820	10750	—	—	—	—

BLX

Over-and-under shotgun with sideplates.

NIB	Exc.	V.G.	Good	Fair	Poor
11150	9000	—	—	—	—

BLX Extra

Same as above but with finer engraving.

NIB	Exc.	V.G.	Good	Fair	Poor
16759	14000	—	—	—	—

BLX Prestige

Finer engraving than the BLX Extra.

NIB	Exc.	V.G.	Good	Fair	Poor
16900	13750	—	—	—	—

SL

Over-and-under shotgun with sidelocks.

NIB	Exc.	V.G.	Good	Fair	Poor
26125	14800	—	—	—	—

SL Extra

Same as above with finer engraving.

NIB	Exc.	V.G.	Good	Fair	Poor
30000	16000	—	—	—	—

SL Prestige

Finer engraving than the SL Extra.

NIB	Exc.	V.G.	Good	Fair	Poor
33000	18000	—	—	—	—

Express

An over-and-under double rifle in calibers from 7x65R to .375 H&H.

NIB	Exc.	V.G.	Good	Fair	Poor
20196	11500	—	—	—	—

Express Extra

Same as above but with finer engraving.

NIB	Exc.	V.G.	Good	Fair	Poor
27060	12000	—	—	—	—

Express Prestige

Finer engraving than the Express Extra.

NIB	Exc.	V.G.	Good	Fair	Poor
32065	15250	—	—	—	—

African Express

A side-by-side boxlock double rifle. Calibers from .22 Long Rifle to .600 NE.

NIB	Exc.	V.G.	Good	Fair	Poor
34000	17500	—	—	—	—

Venus Express Professional

A side-by-side double rifle with sidelocks.

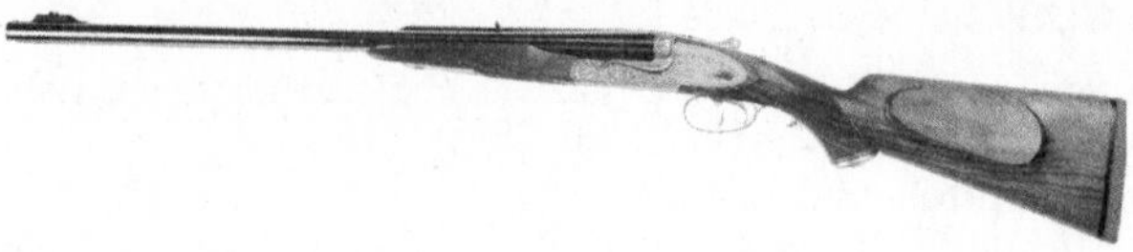

NIB	Exc.	V.G.	Good	Fair	Poor
45000	34500	—	—	—	—

Venus Express Extra

A side-by-side double rifle with sidelocks. Calibers from .375 H&H to .500 NE.

NIB	Exc.	V.G.	Good	Fair	Poor
95750	50000	—	—	—	—

FARROW ARMS CO.

Holyoke, Massachusetts
Mason, Tennessee

FARROW FALLING BLOCK RIFLE

Designed by W.M. Farrow, a target shooter who had worked on the Ballard rifles for the Marlin company. The Farrow rifles are chambered for various calibers and have barrel lengths from 28"-36" of octagonal configuration. They feature tang sights and are either all blued or have a nickel-plated receiver. The stocks are walnut. There were two grades offered that varied according to the grade of wood used. These rifles are quite scarce on today's market, and the number manufactured between 1885 and 1900 is unknown.

No. 1 Model

Fancy walnut with checkering and a Schutzen buttplate.

NIB	Exc.	V.G.	Good	Fair	Poor
—	—	13500	4500	1950	750

No. 2 Model

Plainer wood and no checkering.

NIB	Exc.	V.G.	Good	Fair	Poor
—	—	11000	3300	1600	500

FAYETTEVILLE ARMORY PISTOLS AND RIFLES

Fayetteville, North Carolina

In 1861, the U.S. Arsenal at Fayetteville, North Carolina, was seized by the officials of that state and later turned over to the government of the Confederate States of America. While still controlled by the state of North Carolina, a number of inferior flintlock arms were altered at the arsenal from flint to percussion, including a number of U.S. M1836 pistols and U.S. M1819 Hall rifles (the latter also shortened and remodeled into cavalry carbines). In accordance with an agreement between the governors of Virginia and North Carolina, the rifle machinery seized at the former U.S. Armory at Harpers Ferry, Virginia, was also sent to Fayetteville, where in 1862 the Confederacy began the construction of rifles modeled after the U.S. M1855 rifle. Production continued until 1865 when the advance of Sherman's armies necessitated the evacuation of the armory.

Fayetteville Armory Rifles (Types I through IV)

Overall length 49-1/8"; barrel length 33"; caliber .58. Markings: on barrel, an eagle over "C.S.A./FAYETTEVILLE" forward of the hammer and the date on the rounded tail. "CSA" also found on buttplates; date on top of barrel; proofmarks (eagle head, "V" and "P") on left quarter of barrel near breech.From 1862 to early 1865, the Fayetteville Armory produced four variants of the old U.S. M1855 rifle on the machinery that had been lent to North Carolina by Virginia after its capture in April 1861. The earliest 1862 production (Type I) utilized unmilled lockplates captured at Harpers Ferry and are distinguished by having a "hump" (where the Maynard primer would have been milled) that extends to the arc of the hammer. Type II production utilized the newly made locks received from Richmond during the balance of 1862; they had a relatively low "hump" whose upper surface matched the contour of the stock. By the end of 1862, Fayetteville was producing its own lock, the plate of which resembled the U.S. M1861 rifle musket, but with a distinctive "S" shaped hammer. This lock distinguishes both type III and type IV production. All rifles made through 1863 continued to bear a saber bayonet lug on the right side of the barrel. In 1864, however, this was eliminated in favor of a triangular socket bayonet. The absence of the saber bayonet lug and remodeled front sight distinguishes type IV production. Because the barrel machinery went to Richmond, production at Fayetteville was continually hindered, seldom reaching more than 300 per month in the three years that the Fayetteville rifle was manufactured. (Note: The rarity of Type I production will usually generate a premium for that variant.)

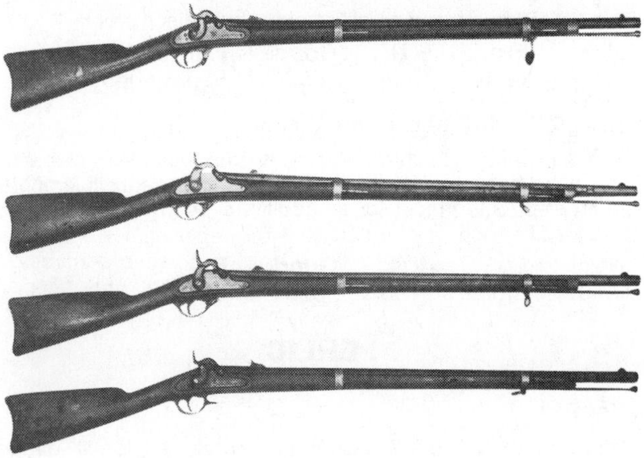

Courtesy Milwaukee Public Museum, Milwaukee, Wisconsin

NIB	***Exc.***	***V.G.***	***Good***	***Fair***	***Poor***
—	—	27500	10500	4000	800

FEATHER INDUSTRIES, INC.

Trinidad, Colorado

AT-22

A blowback-operated semi-automatic chambered for the .22 LR cartridge. It has a removable, shrouded 17" barrel and a folding metal stock. There are adjustable sights, and the finish is black. There is a detachable 20-round magazine. This model was introduced in 1986.

NIB	***Exc.***	***V.G.***	***Good***	***Fair***	***Poor***
450	200	175	150	110	75

AT-9

Similar to the AT-22 except that it is chambered for the 9mm Parabellum cartridge and has a 16" barrel and 32-round magazine. It was introduced in 1988.

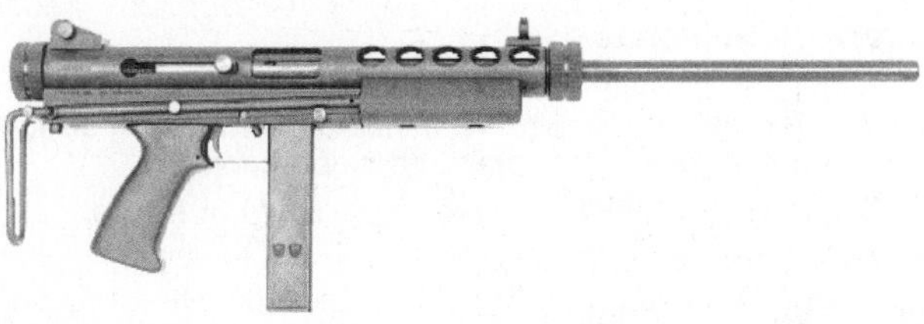

NIB	***Exc.***	***V.G.***	***Good***	***Fair***	***Poor***
800	675	300	250	175	125

KG-9

A 9mm, semi-automatic assault rifle that was introduced in 1989.

NIB	***Exc.***	***V.G.***	***Good***	***Fair***	***Poor***
725	500	425	375	300	250

KG-22

Similar in appearance to the KG-9 except that it is chambered for .22 LR and has a 20-round detachable magazine. It was introduced in 1989.

NIB	***Exc.***	***V.G.***	***Good***	***Fair***	***Poor***
400	275	225	175	125	100

SAR-180

The current incarnation of the old American 180, which was manufactured in Austria a number of years ago. It is chambered for .22 LR and has a 17.5" barrel. It is a blowback-operated semi-automatic that has a 165-round drum magazine that sits on top of the action on the flat side. The rear sight is adjustable, and the finish is blued with a walnut stock, pistol grip, and forend. This model was revived by Feather Industries in 1989.

NIB	***Exc.***	***V.G.***	***Good***	***Fair***	***Poor***
750	675	600	475	300	200

FEDERAL ENGINEERING CORP.

Chicago, Illinois

XC-220

A blowback-operated, semi-automatic rifle chambered for the .22 LR cartridge. It has a 16.5" barrel and a steel receiver that is blued. The stock is black synthetic. This model was introduced in 1984.

NIB	***Exc.***	***V.G.***	***Good***	***Fair***	***Poor***
650	450	375	225	175	125

XC-450

Similar in appearance to the XC-220 except that it is chambered for the .45 ACP cartridge. It has a 30-round detachable magazine.

NIB	***Exc.***	***V.G.***	***Good***	***Fair***	***Poor***
750	525	450	400	300	250

XC-900

A 9mm Parabellum version of the same basic firearm. It has a 32-round magazine and was introduced in 1984.

NIB	***Exc.***	***V.G.***	***Good***	***Fair***	***Poor***
750	525	450	400	300	250

FEDERAL ORDNANCE, INC.

South El Monte, California

An importer as well as a manufacturer that basically fabricates new and custom firearms out of existing older military parts. The firearms they import are military surplus weapons. The firearms covered here are of Federal Ordnance manufacture.

M-14 Semi-Automatic

A semi-automatic version of the M-14 service rifle. It is constructed of a newly manufactured receiver that has no selector and select surplus G.I. parts. The rifle is refinished to original specifications and furnished with a 20-round magazine and either a wood or fiberglass stock. This model was introduced in 1986. Although this model is a battle rifle and falls into the category affected by the wild price fluctuations we have been experiencing, prices for this gun have stayed fairly stable due to a fairly constant supply. This model has been manufactured since 1986.

NIB	Exc.	V.G.	Good	Fair	Poor
—	750	600	550	450	375

Model 713 Mauser Carbine

A 16"-barreled version of the Mauser with a fixed walnut stock. It has a standard magazine and is chambered for 7.63mm or 9mm Parabellum. It is refinished and was introduced in 1987.

NIB	Exc.	V.G.	Good	Fair	Poor
—	1250	1000	900	700	575

Model 713 Deluxe

Chambered for 7.63mm and has a 16" barrel with a detachable shoulder stock made of deluxe walnut. It has been modified to accept detachable magazines and is furnished with two 20-shot units. It has a 1000-meter adjustable sight and is furnished in a fitted leather case. There were only 1,500 manufactured in 1986.

NIB	Exc.	V.G.	Good	Fair	Poor
2000	1750	1500	1250	1000	800

FEG (FEGYVER ES GAZKESZULEKGYAR)

Budapest, Hungary

Rudolf Frommer was a first-class engineer who became associated with Fegyvergyar in 1896. In 1900 he became the manager and held that position until his retirement in 1935. He died one year later in 1936. His designs were successful and prolific. They were used militarily and sold on the commercial market as well.

RIFLES

SA-2000-M

Introduced in 1999, this model is a semi-automatic rifle chambered for the 7.62x39mm cartridge or the .223 cartridge. Fitted with a detachable 10-round magazine, synthetic stock and muzzlebrake.

NIB	Exc.	V.G.	Good	Fair	Poor
575	450	350	250	150	95

AMD-65 AK47

Hungarian AK-47 clone chambered in 7.62xc39. Fixed or folding-stock versions are available.

NIB	Exc.	V.G.	Good	Fair	Poor
650	495	375	275	175	125

FEINWERKBAU

Oberndorf, Germany

Known predominately for the production of high quality, extremely accurate air rifles and pistols. They also produce some of the most accurate target .22 caliber firearms in the world today. These firearms are listed:

Model 2000 Universal

A single-shot, bolt-action target rifle chambered for the .22 rimfire cartridge. It has a 26.5" barrel with adjustable aperture sights and a fully adjustable trigger. There were four different stock configurations offered with stippled pistol grips and forearms. An electronic trigger was available as a $450 option. This model was discontinued in 1988.

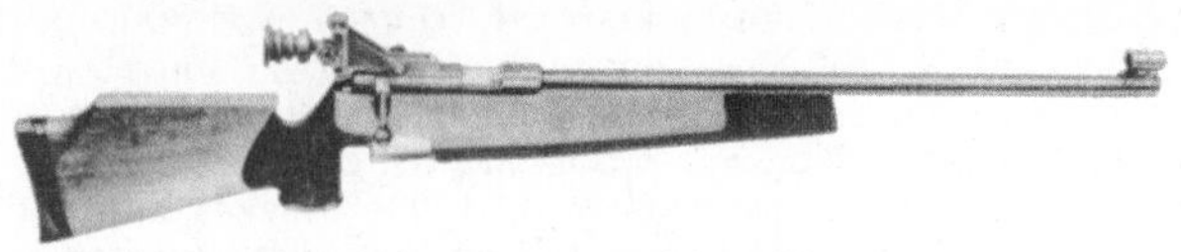

NIB	Exc.	V.G.	Good	Fair	Poor
—	1800	1250	950	650	550

Mini 2000

Has a 22" barrel, and the electronic trigger was available at the additional cost.

NIB	Exc.	V.G.	Good	Fair	Poor
—	1550	1050	850	550	450

Match Rifle

Has a 26.75" barrel and an adjustable cheekpiece stock.

NIB	Exc.	V.G.	Good	Fair	Poor
—	1650	1095	850	550	450

Model 2600 Ultra Match Free Rifle

Similar to the Model 2000, with a laminated thumbhole stock and a heavy 26" barrel, fully adjustable sights, and trigger. It is offered with an electronic trigger for an additional $400. This model was introduced in 1986.

NIB	Exc.	V.G.	Good	Fair	Poor
1950	1400	1150	850	650	550

FERLIB

Gardone V.T., Italy

Model F.VI

A high-grade, side-by-side shotgun chambered for all gauges and is essentially custom-ordered. It is available in various barrel lengths and chokes and has an Anson and Deeley boxlock-action, double triggers, and automatic ejectors. The action is case-colored, and the stock is hand-checkered select walnut. Single-selective triggers are available for an additional $375.

NIB	Exc.	V.G.	Good	Fair	Poor
4750	3600	—	—	—	—

NOTE: 28 gauge and .410 add 10 percent.

Model F.VII

Has a scroll-engraved, coin-finished frame but otherwise is similar to the Model F.VI. Single trigger option and small gauge premium are the same.

NIB	Exc.	V.G.	Good	Fair	Poor
12000	8500	—	—	—	—

Model F.VII/SC

A more deluxe version with gold inlays and a game scene-engraved receiver. Options and premium are the same.

NIB	Exc.	V.G.	Good	Fair	Poor
13000	9500	—	—	—	—

Model F.VII Sideplate

Features false sideplates that are completely covered with game scene engraving. This model is standard with a single-selective trigger, but the small gauge premium is applicable.

NIB	Exc.	V.G.	Good	Fair	Poor
15000	10500	—	—	—	—

Model F.VII/SC Sideplate

The false sideplate model with gold inlays accenting the full coverage engraving.

NIB	Exc.	V.G.	Good	Fair	Poor
16000	11500	—	—	—	—

NOTE: 28 gauge and .410 add 10 percent.

Hammer Gun

Features a boxlock action with external hammers. Its other features are custom ordered to the purchaser's specifications.

NIB	Exc.	V.G.	Good	Fair	Poor
20000	14500	—	—	—	—

F.I.E.

Hialeah, Florida

Firearms Import and Export was engaged in the business of importing the Franchi shotgun (which is listed under its own heading) and the Arminius revolver (which is made in Germany). They were also distributors for the Titan semi-automatic pistols, which are manufactured in the U.S.A. They were also importing a series of 9mm pistols from Italy that are produced by Tanfoglio and known as the TZ series. F.I.E. was no longer in business as of 1990.

Model 122

A bolt-action rifle chambered for .22 rimfire, with a 21" barrel and adjustable sights. It has a 10-shot magazine and a walnut Monte Carlo stock. It was introduced in 1986.

NIB	Exc.	V.G.	Good	Fair	Poor
200	100	75	50	35	25

Single-Shot

Brazilian made and chambered for 12 or 20 gauge and .410. It is a single-barreled break open, with 25" through 30" barrel and various chokes. It is blued with a wood stock and was introduced in 1985.

NIB	Exc.	V.G.	Good	Fair	Poor
150	100	60	45	35	25

S.O.B.

Similar to the single-shot, with an 18.5" barrel and a pistol grip instead of a standard stock. This model was discontinued in 1984.

NIB	Exc.	V.G.	Good	Fair	Poor
165	110	60	45	35	25

Sturdy Over-and-Under

Chambered for 12 and 20 gauge and has 3" chambers and 28" vent-rib barrels with various chokes. This is an over-and-under with double triggers and extractors. The frame is engraved and silver finished. It was manufactured in Italy by Maroccini and imported between 1985 and 1988.

NIB	Exc.	V.G.	Good	Fair	Poor
400	300	225	175	150	100

Brute

A side-by-side chambered for 12 and 20 gauge and .410. It has 19" barrels, double triggers, and extractors. It has a wood stock and was dropped from the line in 1984.

NIB	Exc.	V.G.	Good	Fair	Poor
300	200	125	100	75	50

SPAS-12

A unique shotgun in that it can function as a pump or an automatic with the touch of a button. It is a paramilitary-type shotgun chambered for 12 gauge, with a 21.5" barrel and a 9-shot tube magazine. It has an alloy receiver and a folding stock. The finish is all black. This model is manufactured by Franchi in Italy.

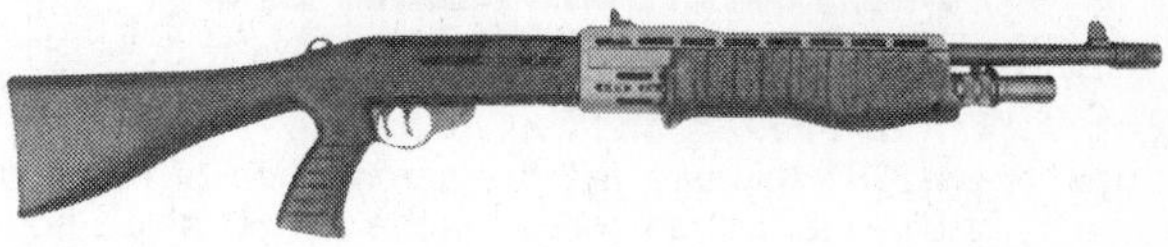

NIB	Exc.	V.G.	Good	Fair	Poor
1500	1100	900	700	400	300

Law-12

A paramilitary-type, 12-gauge, semi-automatic shotgun that is gas-operated and has a 9-shot tube magazine. The barrel is 21.5" in length and choked cylinder bore. It has a military special black finish and a black synthetic stock.

NIB	Exc.	V.G.	Good	Fair	Poor
850	650	400	300	200	100

SAS-12

A paramilitary-type, slide-action shotgun chambered for 12 gauge. It has a 21.5" barrel, choked cylinder bore. The finish is similar to the LAW-12, and it is manufactured by Franchi in Italy.

NIB	Exc.	V.G.	Good	Fair	Poor
850	650	500	400	300	200

FINNISH LION

Valmet, Sweden

ISU Target Rifle

A single-shot, bolt-action rifle chambered for the .22 rimfire cartridge. It has a 27" heavy barrel and a target stock with accessories. It features target adjustable sights and was manufactured between 1966 and 1977.

NIB	Exc.	V.G.	Good	Fair	Poor
—	475	325	275	200	125

Champion Free Rifle

Has a 29" heavy barrel and double-set triggers. Otherwise it is similar to the ISU model. It was manufactured between 1965 and 1972.

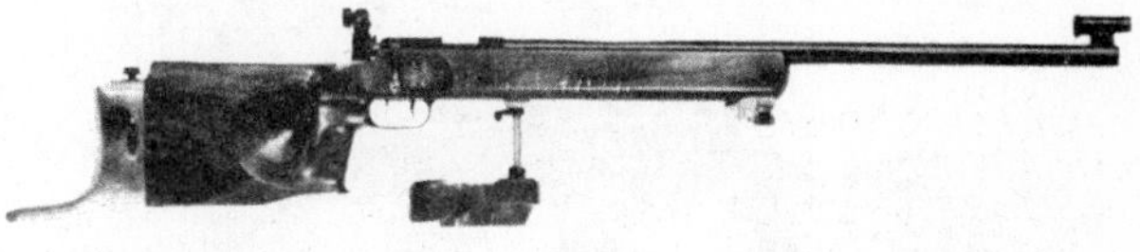

NIB	Exc.	V.G.	Good	Fair	Poor
—	900	750	600	375	275

Match Rifle

Similar to the Champion rifle, with a thumbhole stock and an adjustable buttplate. It was manufactured between 1937 and 1972.

NIB	Exc.	V.G.	Good	Fair	Poor
—	900	750	600	375	275

FLETCHER BIDWELL, LLC

Viroqua, Wisconsin

Spencer 1860 Military Carbine

Introduced in 2001 this is a faithful reproduction of the original Spencer Carbine. It is chambered for the .56-50 black powder cartridge but in centerfire. Fitted with a blued 22" round barrel. Magazine capacity is 7 rounds in butt tube. Bone charcoal case hardened receiver. Walnut stock. Blade front sight with ladder rear sight adjustable to 800 yards. Weight is about 9 lbs. Built in U.S.

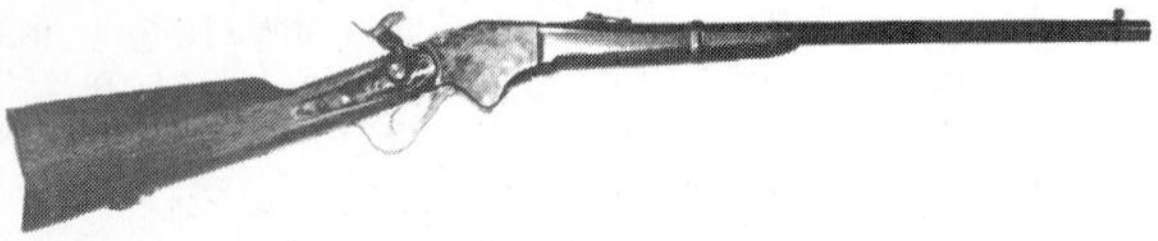

NIB	Exc.	V.G.	Good	Fair	Poor
2750	1950	1500	900	625	400

FLORENCE ARMORY

Florence, Guilford Counry, North Carolina

Founded in 1862 as a repair facility to alter sporting arms for military use. Majority of work done by H.C. Lamb & Company. In 1862, Captain Z. Coffin ordered stocks, barrels and locks to assemble newly made rifles. Furniture of these arms varied, either being supplied by Glaze & Company or being the remainders from Searcy & Moore's production. Number made estimated to be in excess of 300 rifles in both .50 and .54 calibers. These arms (particularly the barrels) exhibit characteristics of North Carolina contract pieces.

NIB	Exc.	V.G.	Good	Fair	Poor
—	—	29500	12500	4000	1450

FNH USA, INC.

McLean, Virginia

This company is a subsidary of FN Herstal in Belgium. It is essentially the sales and marketing arm for FN in the U.S. market.

FN RIFLES

These rifles are produced at FN manufacturing in the U.S.

FNAR

Semi-auto chambered in .308 Winchester. Cold hammer-forged 16-inch standard or 20-inch heavy barrel. Magazine capacity: 5 or 10 rounds. Weight: 8.5 to 10 lbs. Receiver-mounted optical rail with additional rails on fore-end. Matte black synthetic stock with fully adjustable comb and length of pull via interchangeable inserts. Match-grade model available.

NIB	Exc.	V.G.	Good	Fair	Poor
1600	1350	1050	800	450	300

FN A1 SPR

Chambered for the .308 7.62x51mm cartridge. Bolt-action. Fitted with a 24" heavy barrel with no sights. Choice of hinged floorplate or detachable box magazine. Stock is McMillan A3 tactical. Weight is about 10.75 lbs.

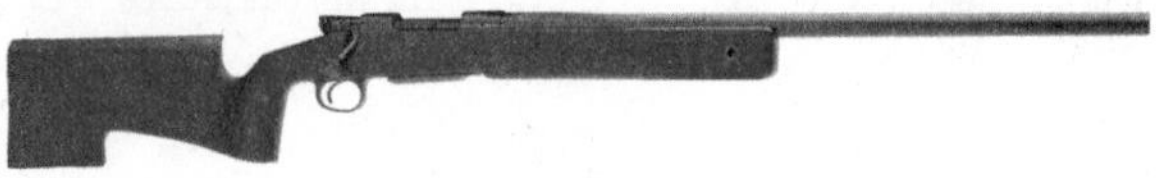

NIB	Exc.	V.G.	Good	Fair	Poor
1600	1350	1175	900	725	375

FN A1a SPR

Similar to the above model but fitted with a 20" heavy fluted barrel. McMillan A3 tactical stock. Weight is about 9.75 lbs.

NIB	Exc.	V.G.	Good	Fair	Poor
1600	1350	1175	900	725	375

FN A2 SPR

Fitted with a 24" heavy barrel with McMillan A4 tactical stock and Badger Ordinance scope base. Weight is about 10.75 lbs.

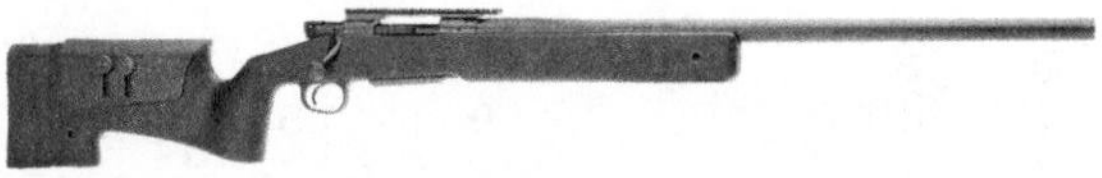

NIB	Exc.	V.G.	Good	Fair	Poor
2190	1750	1550	1275	900	400

FN A3 SPR

This model has a 24" heavy barrel with McMillan A4 adjustable stock, Badger Ordinance scope base and Badger Ordinance or FN scope rings. Supplied with FNH Parker-Hale type or Harris bipod. Weight is about 10.75 lbs.

NIB	Exc.	V.G.	Good	Fair	Poor
2450	1950	1650	1375	950	450

FN A4 SPR

Fitted with a 24" heavy barrel with McMillan A4 adjustable tactical stock. Scope base and rings standard. Choice of several tactical scopes. Bipod. Sling. Drag bag. Kill flash. Tool kit. Cleaning kit. Hard case. Weight is about 10.75 lbs.

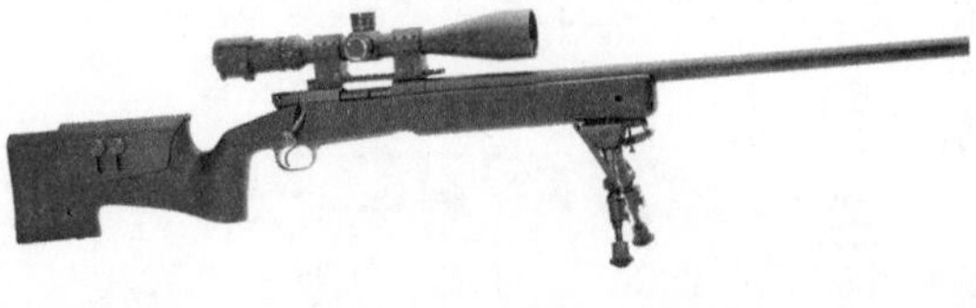

NIB	Exc.	V.G.	Good	Fair	Poor
5725	4350	3000	2350	1200	700

NOTE: Price listed does not include scope.

FN A5 SPR

This model has a 20" heavy fluted barrel threaded for a suppressor. Special McMillan tactical stock. The rest of the features are the same as the FN A4 model.

NIB	Exc.	V.G.	Good	Fair	Poor
7600	5750	4000	2400	1600	700

NOTE: Price listed do not include scope.

FN A5a SPR

This model has a 20" heavy fluted barrel threaded for a suppressor. Special SPR McMillan adjustable tactical stock. Weight is about 9.75 lbs.

NIB	Exc.	V.G.	Good	Fair	Poor
2460	1975	1650	1375	950	450

FN PBR (Patrol Bolt Rifle)

Introduced in 2004 this rifle is chambered for the .308 cartridge. Offered with four different barrel lengths: 18", 20", 22", or 24". Fitted with a two-piece MIL spec M1913 rail. Black Hogue stock. Magazine capacity is 4 rounds. Weight is about 9 lbs.

NIB	Exc.	V.G.	Good	Fair	Poor
2300	1895	1475	1050	700	400

PGM PRECISION RIFLES

These rifles are made by PGM Precision, a subsidary of FN, in Poisy Cedex, France.

Ultima Ratio Intervention

This bolt-action rifle is chambered for the .308 7.62x51mm cartridge and fitted with a 23.6" ribbed barrel with integral muzzle-brake. Folding bipod. Stock, trigger group, and action are fixed to a rigid metal girder. Stock is adjustable. No sights. Magazine capacity is 5 or 10 rounds. Weight is about 13.25 lbs. depending on configuration.

NIB	Exc.	V.G.	Good	Fair	Poor
9000	7995	6000	3250	1795	700

Ultima Ratio Commando I

Similar to the above model but with 18.5" fluted barrel with muzzlebrake. Weight is about 12 lbs.

NIB	Exc.	V.G.	Good	Fair	Poor
9100	8050	6100	3250	1795	700

Ultima Ratio Commando II

Similar to the Commando I but with folding stock.

NIB	Exc.	V.G.	Good	Fair	Poor
8320	—	—	—	—	—

FN-Mini-Hecate

Chambered for the .308 cartridge this bolt-action rifle features a free-loading interchangeable 18.5", 19.7", 21.7", or 23.6" match-grade barrel. Collapsible buttstock. Magazine capacity is 10 rounds. Weight is about 14 lbs. Introduced in 2001.

NIB	Exc.	V.G.	Good	Fair	Poor
9100	8050	6100	3250	1795	700

.338 Lapua

Similar to the Mini-Hecate but chambered for the .33 Lapua cartridge and fitted with a 27.2" barrel with integral muzzlebrake. Collapsible buttstock. Weight is about 15 lbs. Magazine capacity is 10 rounds.

NIB	Exc.	V.G.	Good	Fair	Poor
10500	9000	7750	6000	3750	1475

Hecate II

Chambered for the .50 BMG cartridge. Fitted with a 27.6" heavy barrel with integral muzzlebrake. Bipod. Adjustable stock. Magazine capacity is 7 rounds. Weight is about 36 lbs. Pricing not available.

OM .50 Nemesis

Chambered for the .50 caliber Browning cartridge (12.7x99mm) this bolt-action rifle features an adjustable buttstock, bipod, and other characteristics that make it a long range material rifle. Weight is approximately 28 lbs. Pricing not available.

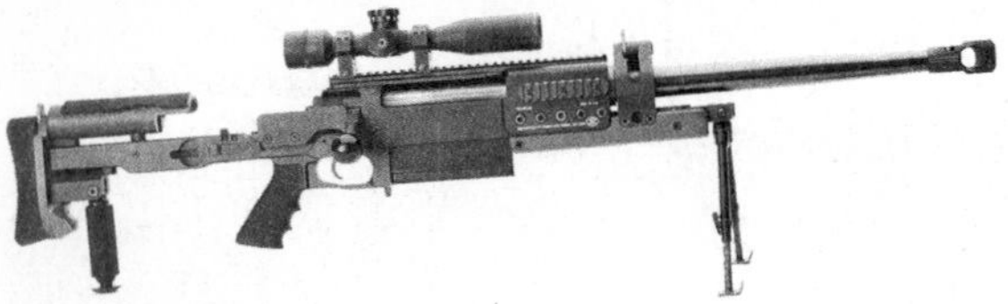

SHOTGUNS

FN Police Shotgun

This is a slide-action 12 gauge shotgun chambered for the 3" 12 gauge shell. Barrel length is 18". Magazine capacity is 7 rounds. Black synthetic stock. Corrosion-resistant finish. Weight is about 6.5 lbs.

NIB	Exc.	V.G.	Good	Fair	Poor
350	275	200	150	125	100

FN Tactical Police

Similar to the standard model but with ported barrel and collapsible stock with pistol grip. Weight is about 6.5 lbs.

NIB	Exc.	V.G.	Good	Fair	Poor
550	475	400	300	200	100

FN Self-Loading Police

This shotgun is a gas-operated semi-automatic shotgun fitted with a picatinny rail and short stock. Chambered for the 12 gauge shell. Magazine capacity is 6 rounds. Weight is about 7.75 lbs.

NIB	Exc.	V.G.	Good	Fair	Poor
700	600	500	400	300	200

FOGARTY

American Repeating Rifle Co.
Boston, Massachusetts

FOGARTY REPEATING RIFLE AND CARBINE

A limited number of repeating rifles and carbines based upon Valentine Fogarty's patents were produced between 1866 and 1867. The calibers of these arms varies and the normal barrel lengths are 20" and 28". Blued, casehardened with walnut stocks. The American Repeating Rifle Company was purchased by the Winchester Repeating Arms Company in 1869.

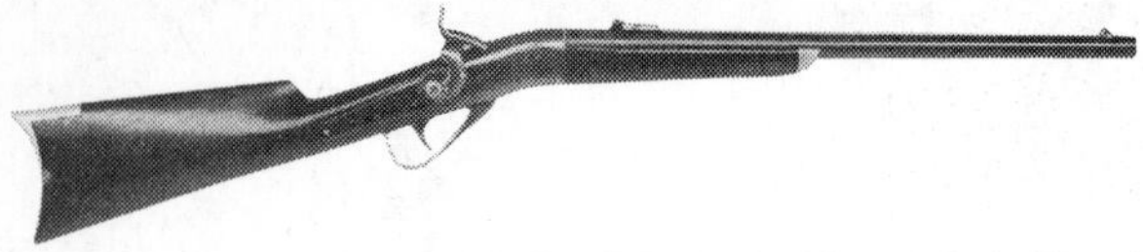

Courtesy Buffalo Bill Historical Center, Cody, Wyoming

NIB	Exc.	V.G.	Good	Fair	Poor
—	—	9500	4050	1250	450

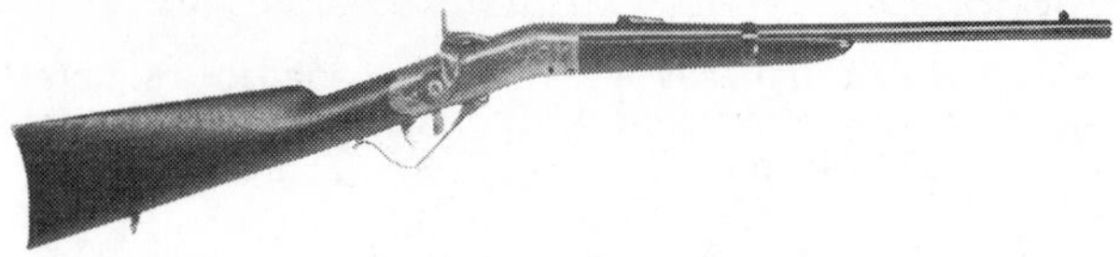

Courtesy Buffalo Bill Historical Center, Cody, Wyoming

NIB	Exc.	V.G.	Good	Fair	Poor
—	—	9500	4050	1250	450

FOLSOM, H&D ARMS CO.

Large distributor of double and single barrel shotguns produced by Crescent Firearms Co., Norwich, Connecticut. Folsom owned and later sold to Savage Arms Co. the Crescent Firearms Co., Davis Warner Co., and Baker Gun Co. around 1930. For more information see also Crescent Firearms Co.

FOREHAND & WADSWORTH

Worcester, Massachusetts

Established in 1871 and operated under the above name until 1890 when it became the Forehand Arms Company. Hopkins & Allen purchased the company in 1902.

Forehand Arms Co. 1898-1902 Double-Barrel Shotguns

Good quality hammer and hammerless doubles but few produced until taken over by Hopkins and Allen Firearms Co. Values from $100 to $1,000 depending on grade and condition.

FOX, A. H.

Philadelphia, Pennsylvania

Ansley H. Fox established the Fox Gun Company in Baltimore, Maryland, in 1896. Subsequently, he made arms under the name Philadelphia Gun Company. As of 1905, he operated under the name A.H. Fox. In 1930, this company was purchased by the Savage Arms Company who continued manufacturing all grades of Fox shotguns. As of 1942, the Savage Company only made the plainer grades. **NOTE:** Fox Model B double shotguns see Savage Arms Co.

Sterlingworth

A 12, 16, or 20 gauge boxlock double-barrel shotgun with 26", 28", or 30" barrels, double triggers and extractors. Automatic ejectors were also available and would add approximately 30 percent to the values listed. Blued, casehardened with a walnut stock. Manufactured from 1911 to 1946.

Courtesy Nick Niles, Paul Goodwin photo

NIB	Exc.	V.G.	Good	Fair	Poor
—	2000	1600	1000	500	275

NOTE: 20 gauge add 50 percent. Add 25 percent for 16 gauge.

Sterlingworth Deluxe

As above, with an ivory bead, recoil pad and optional 32" barrel.

NIB	Exc.	V.G.	Good	Fair	Poor
—	2500	1900	1250	700	400

NOTE: 20 gauge add 50 percent. Add 25 percent for 16 gauge.

SP Grade

A 12, 16, or 20 gauge boxlock double-barrel shotgun with varying length barrels, double triggers and extractors.

NIB	Exc.	V.G.	Good	Fair	Poor
—	1600	1325	1050	450	225

NOTE: 20 gauge add 35 percent. Automatic ejectors add 15 percent. Add 25 percent for 16 gauge.

HE Grade

Similar to the early A Grade and offered in 12 and 20 gauge. Chambers were 2-1/4" standard with 3" chambers available on request. This model is marked on the barrel "Not Warranted." this referred to pattern density, not barrel quality. Only sixty 20 gauge HE Grades appear in factory records. Manufactured from 1923 to 1942.

NIB	Exc.	V.G.	Good	Fair	Poor
—	3250	2800	2225	1000	650

NOTE: Single-selective trigger add 20 percent. Add 30 percent premium for 20 gauge.

HIGH GRADE GUNS A-FE

The Fox Company as well as the Savage Arms Company produced a variety of shotguns decorated in varying grades. They were available in 12, 16, and 20 gauge. As the value for these arms depends on the particular features of these arms, prospective purchasers are advised to secure a qualified appraisal prior to acquisition. **NOTE:** A 25 percent premium should be added to the grades below for small gauge guns and guns with single selective trigger.

A Grade

Built from 1905 to 1942.

NIB	Exc.	V.G.	Good	Fair	Poor
—	2100	1700	1225	600	400

AE Grade (Automatic Ejectors)

Built from 1905 to 1946.

NIB	Exc.	V.G.	Good	Fair	Poor
—	2400	2000	1600	900	700

B Grade

Built from 1905 to 1918.

NIB	Exc.	V.G.	Good	Fair	Poor
—	3100	2700	1950	1100	500

BE Grade

Built from 1905 to 1918.

NIB	Exc.	V.G.	Good	Fair	Poor
—	3500	3050	2500	1500	900

C Grade

Built from 1905 to 1913.

NIB	Exc.	V.G.	Good	Fair	Poor
—	3300	2700	2150	1100	550

CE Grade

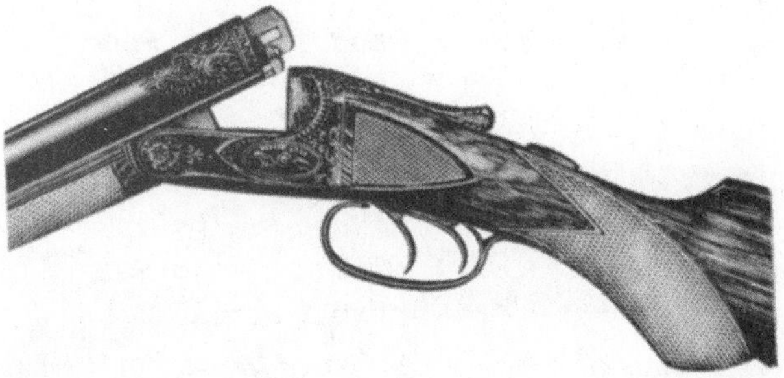

Built from 1905 to 1946.

NIB	Exc.	V.G.	Good	Fair	Poor
—	3800	3350	2550	1700	950

XE Grade

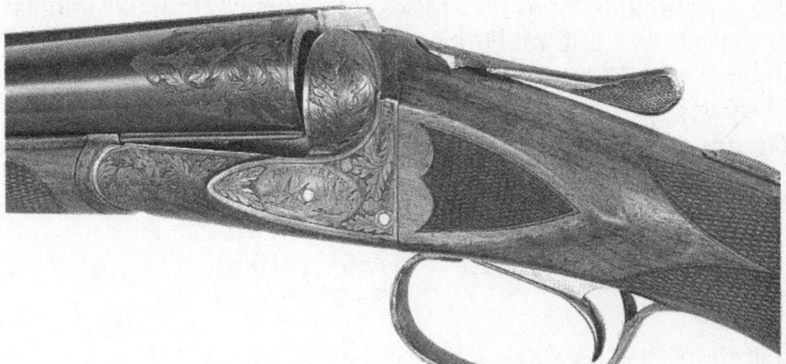

Courtesy William Hammond

Built from 1914 to 1945.

NIB	Exc.	V.G.	Good	Fair	Poor
—	6500	5900	4150	2250	1100

D Grade

Built from 1906 to 1913.

NIB	Exc.	V.G.	Good	Fair	Poor
—	9300	8000	5150	2750	1000

DE Grade

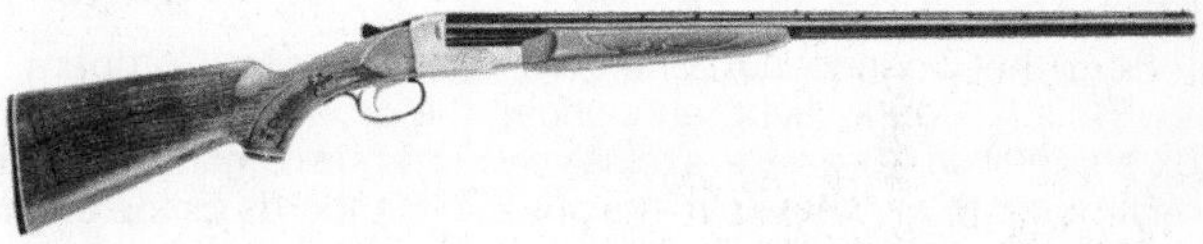

Built from 1906 to 1945.

NIB	Exc.	V.G.	Good	Fair	Poor
—	9800	8500	5700	3300	1500

F Grade

Built from 1906 to 1913.

NIB	Exc.	V.G.	Good	Fair	Poor
—	25000	16800	9000	5700	3000

FE Grade

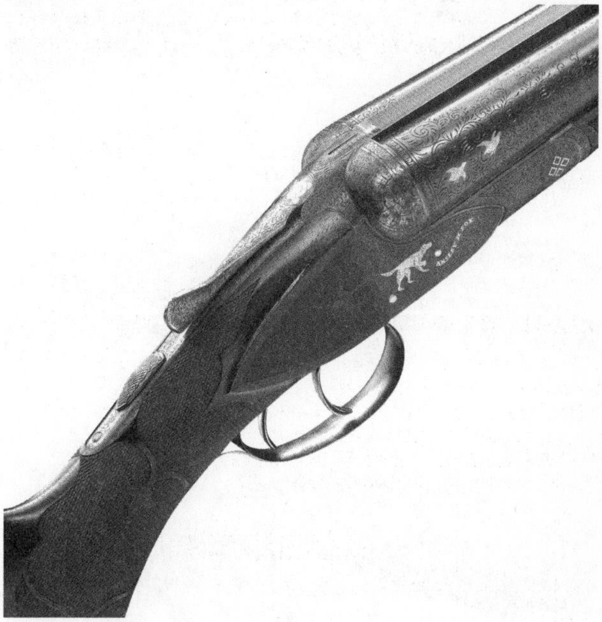

Built from 1906 to 1940.

NIB	Exc.	V.G.	Good	Fair	Poor
—	28000	21000	11500	7700	5000

SINGLE BARREL TRAP GUNS

A 12 gauge single barrel boxlock shotgun with 30" or 32" ventilated rib barrels and automatic ejector. There were approximately 571 single-barrel trap guns manufactured. Produced in four grades as listed:

J Grade

Built from 1919 to 1936.

NIB	*Exc.*	*V.G.*	*Good*	*Fair*	*Poor*
—	3100	2400	1750	1050	600

K Grade

Built from 1919 to 1931. Approximately 75 built.

NIB	*Exc.*	*V.G.*	*Good*	*Fair*	*Poor*
—	4350	3300	2450	1650	950

L Grade

Built from 1919 to 1931. Approximately 25 built.

NIB	*Exc.*	*V.G.*	*Good*	*Fair*	*Poor*
—	5750	3900	3150	2150	1200

M Grade

Built from 1919 to 1932. A total of 9 guns built.

NIB	*Exc.*	*V.G.*	*Good*	*Fair*	*Poor*
—	15000	10000	6500	4700	2500

RECENTLY MANUFACTURED A.H. FOX SHOTGUNS

In 1993 the Connecticut Shotgun Manufacturing Company of New Britain, Connecticut, announced the production of the A.H. Fox shotgun in 20 gauge exclusively. The gun is hand-built and constructed to the same dimensions and standards as the original Fox. The gun is offered in five grades with many standard features and several optional ones as well. Each shotgun is built to order. Because these guns are newly built and have no pricing history, only manufacturer's retail price for the base gun will be given. Extra sets of barrels, single triggers, and other extra costs options will greatly affect price.

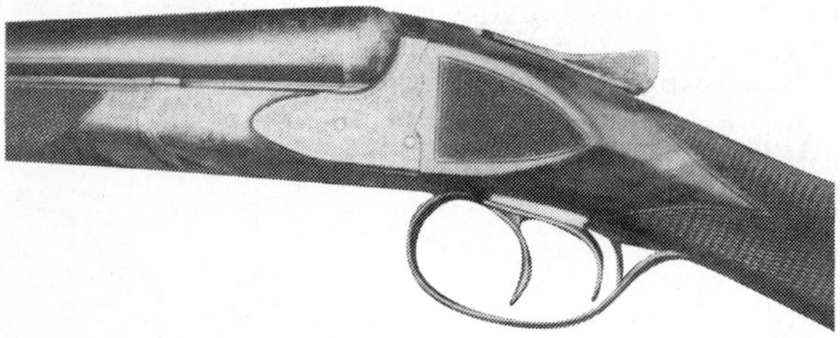

CE Grade

Retail price: $15,500

XE Grade

Retail price: $17,000

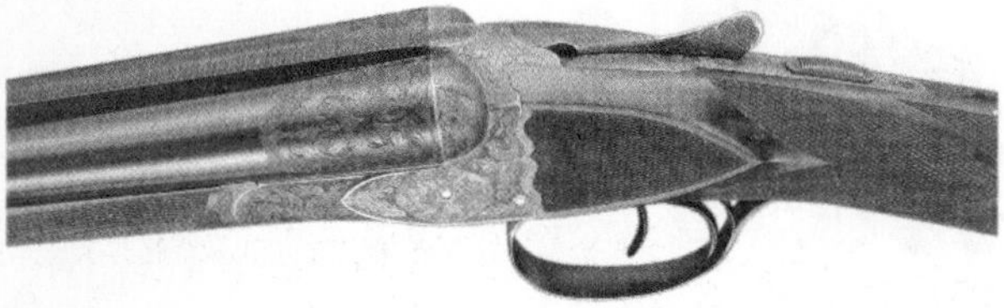

DE Grade

Retail price: $20,500

FE Grade

Retail price: $25,500

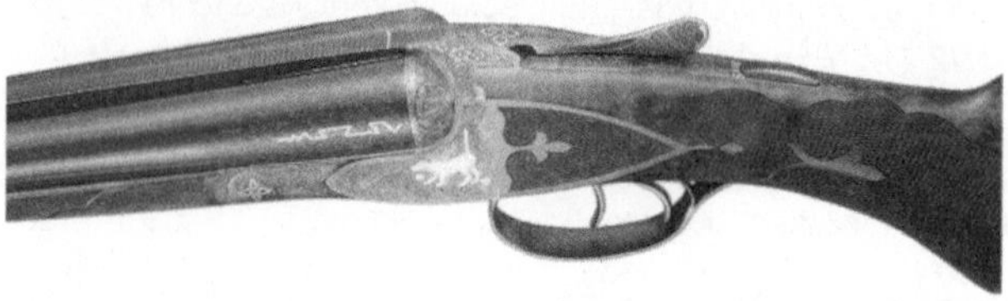

Exhibition Grade

This is the company's highest grade and features any optional detail the customer desires including custom engraving and exhibition quality wood. Retail price: On request from CSMC.

FRANCHI, L.

Brescia, Italy

SIDE-BY-SIDE-SHOTGUNS

Astore

A 12 gauge boxlock shotgun manufactured in a variety of barrel lengths with double triggers and automatic ejectors. Blued with a straight walnut stock. Manufactured from 1937 to 1960.

NIB	*Exc.*	*V.G.*	*Good*	*Fair*	*Poor*
2900	1600	750	500	350	200

Astore II

As above, but more finely finished.

NIB	*Exc.*	*V.G.*	*Good*	*Fair*	*Poor*
3150	1850	900	700	450	250

Astore 5

As above, but more finely finished.

NIB	*Exc.*	*V.G.*	*Good*	*Fair*	*Poor*
3350	2150	1250	950	600	300

Airone

Similar to the Astore. Manufactured during the 1940s.

NIB	*Exc.*	*V.G.*	*Good*	*Fair*	*Poor*
2900	1600	750	500	350	200

SIDELOCK DOUBLE-BARREL SHOTGUNS

A 12, 16, or 20 gauge sidelock double-barrel shotgun manufactured in a variety of barrel lengths with a single-selective trigger and automatic ejectors. Produced in the following grades they differ as to engraving coverage and quality of wood:

Condor

NIB	*Exc.*	*V.G.*	*Good*	*Fair*	*Poor*
7500	6500	4500	3500	2500	1250

Imperial

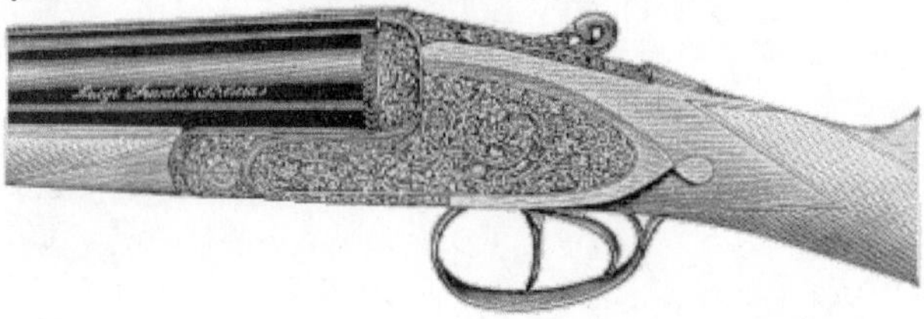

NIB	*Exc.*	*V.G.*	*Good*	*Fair*	*Poor*
10000	8500	6000	4500	3250	1500

Imperiales

NIB	Exc.	V.G.	Good	Fair	Poor
10500	9000	6500	5000	3500	1500

No. 5 Imperial Monte Carlo

NIB	Exc.	V.G.	Good	Fair	Poor
15000	12500	9000	7500	5000	2000

No. 11 Imperial Monte Carlo

NIB	Exc.	V.G.	Good	Fair	Poor
16000	13500	10000	8000	5500	2000

Imperial Monte Carlo Extra

NIB	Exc.	V.G.	Good	Fair	Poor
20000	17500	12500	9500	7500	3500

Highlander

Introduced in 2003 this model features either a 12, 20, or 28 gauge gun fitted with 26" barrels and fixed chokes. Select walnut straight grip stock with splinter forend. Coin finished steel receiver. Single trigger. Weight is 6.4 lbs. for 12 gauge; 5.8 lbs. for 20 gauge, and 5.7 lbs. for 28 gauge.

NIB	Exc.	V.G.	Good	Fair	Poor
1800	1600	1200	850	475	300

NOTE: Add $150 for 28 gauge.

OVER/UNDER SHOTGUNS

Priti Deluxe Model

A 12 or 20 gauge Over/Under boxlock double-barrel shotgun with 26" or 28" ventilated rib barrels, single trigger and automatic ejectors. Introduced in 1988.

NIB	Exc.	V.G.	Good	Fair	Poor
400	350	300	250	200	150

Falconet

A 12, 16, 20, and 28 gauge as well as .410 bore boxlock double-barrel shotgun with single-selective trigger and automatic ejectors. The receiver was anodized in tan, ebony, or silver finishes. Manufactured from 1968 to 1975.

NIB	Exc.	V.G.	Good	Fair	Poor
650	550	425	350	250	200

NOTE: Silver receiver add 10 percent. 28 gauge and .410 add 25 percent.

Falconet Skeet

As above, with a 26" skeet barrel with a wide rib and the receiver casehardened. Manufactured from 1970 to 1974.

NIB	Exc.	V.G.	Good	Fair	Poor
950	850	700	550	450	250

Falconet International Skeet

As above, but more finely finished.

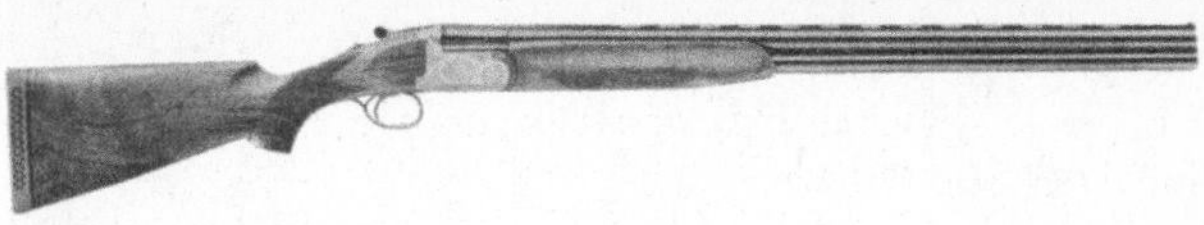

NIB	Exc.	V.G.	Good	Fair	Poor
1050	950	750	600	475	250

Falconet Trap

As above, with a 30" modified and full choke barrel, and trap stock. Manufactured from 1970 to 1974.

NIB	Exc.	V.G.	Good	Fair	Poor
1000	900	700	550	450	250

Falconet International Trap

As above, but more finely finished.

NIB	Exc.	V.G.	Good	Fair	Poor
1050	950	750	600	475	250

Peregrine Model 451

A 12 gauge boxlock double-barrel shotgun with 26" or 28" ventilated rib barrels, alloy receiver, single-selective trigger and automatic ejectors. Manufactured in 1975.

NIB	Exc.	V.G.	Good	Fair	Poor
800	675	495	375	275	200

Peregrine Model 400

As above, with a steel frame.

NIB	Exc.	V.G.	Good	Fair	Poor
850	775	600	400	300	200

Aristocrat

Similar to the above, with 26", 28", or 30" ventilated rib barrels. Manufactured from 1960 to 1969.

NIB	Exc.	V.G.	Good	Fair	Poor
850	725	600	400	300	200

Aristocrat Magnum

As above, with 3" chambers and 32" full choke barrels.

NIB	Exc.	V.G.	Good	Fair	Poor
895	775	675	450	300	200

Aristocrat Silver King

As above, with a French case hardened receiver, and available in four grades of decoration.

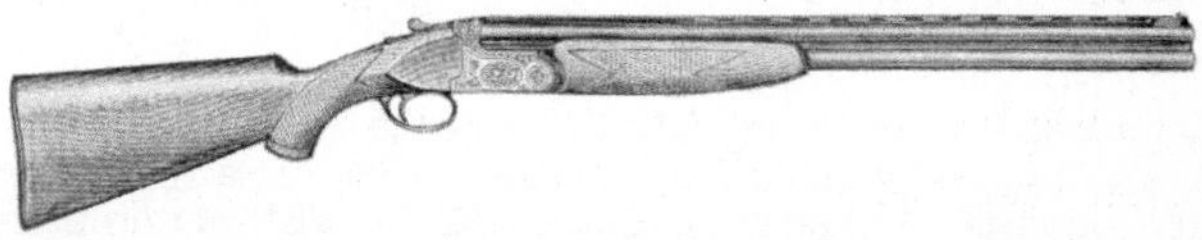

NIB	Exc.	V.G.	Good	Fair	Poor
950	875	775	475	350	200

Aristocrat Deluxe

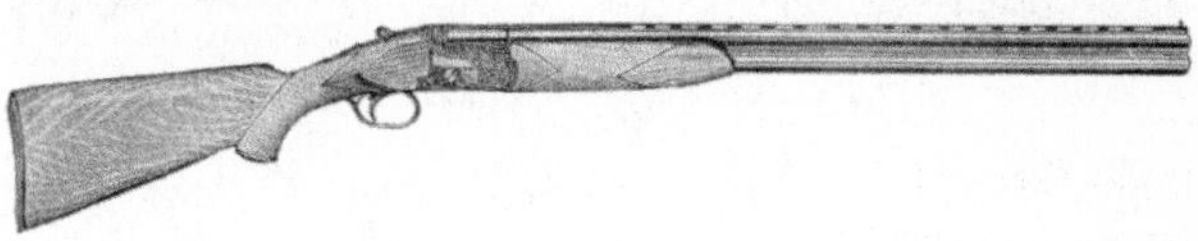

NIB	Exc.	V.G.	Good	Fair	Poor
1250	1000	875	575	400	200

Aristocrat Supreme

NIB	Exc.	V.G.	Good	Fair	Poor
1650	1400	950	700	575	250

Aristocrat Imperial

NIB	Exc.	V.G.	Good	Fair	Poor
2950	2450	1950	1250	950	450

Aristocrat Monte Carlo

NIB	Exc.	V.G.	Good	Fair	Poor
3750	3200	2950	2000	1500	750

Model 2003 Trap

A 12 gauge boxlock double-barrel shotgun with 30" or 32" ventilated rib barrels, single-selective trigger and automatic ejectors. Manufactured in 1976.

NIB	Exc.	V.G.	Good	Fair	Poor
1450	1300	900	650	500	250

Model 2004 Trap

A single-barreled version of the Model 2003.

NIB	Exc.	V.G.	Good	Fair	Poor
1450	1300	900	650	500	250

Model 2005 Combination Trap

The Model 2003 with both a single and set of Over/Under barrels.

NIB	Exc.	V.G.	Good	Fair	Poor
2800	2400	1950	1200	950	450

Model 3000 "Undergun"

As above, with a single barrel fitted with a high ventilated rib so that it fires from the lower barrel position.

NIB	Exc.	V.G.	Good	Fair	Poor
3050	2850	2200	1500	1200	600

Alcione Classic

Introduced in 2004 this 12 gauge 3" model features 26" or 28" ventilated rib barrels. Side rib is ventilated. Walnut stock with schnabel forend. Optional 20 gauge barrels. Weight is about 7.5 lbs.

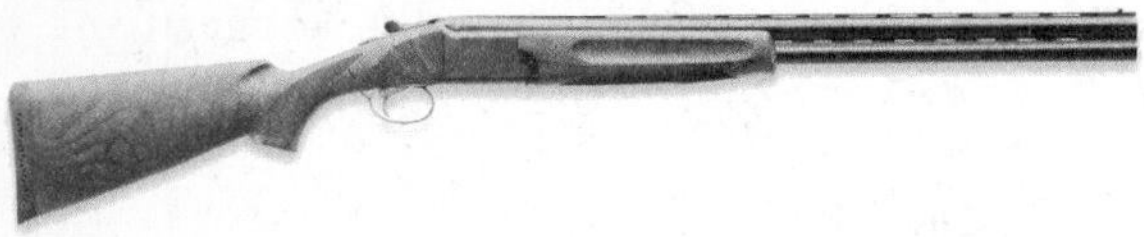

NIB	Exc.	V.G.	Good	Fair	Poor
1300	975	800	600	500	250

Alcione T (Titanium)

Introduced in 2002 this model is similar to the Alcione Field but has an aluminum alloy frame with titanium inserts. Available in 12 and 20 gauge with 3" chambers. Choice of 26" or 28" vent rib barrels with choke tubes. Weight is about 6.8 lbs. for 12 and 20 gauge.

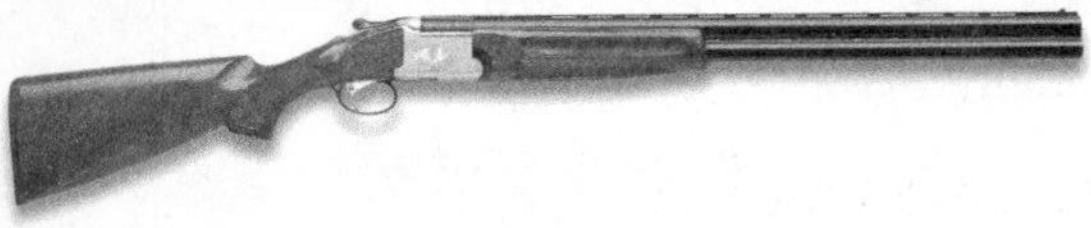

NIB	Exc.	V.G.	Good	Fair	Poor
1400	1150	950	700	600	300

Alcione T Two Barrel Set

As above but with a two-barrel set: One 12 gauge 28" and the other is a 20 gauge 26". Introduced in 2004.

NIB	Exc.	V.G.	Good	Fair	Poor
1600	1275	1100	800	650	350

Alcione Field Model

A 12 gauge boxlock double-barrel shotgun with 26" or 28" ventilated rib barrels, single-selective trigger and automatic ejectors. Engraved silver receiver. Weight is about 7.5 lbs.

NIB	Exc.	V.G.	Good	Fair	Poor
1200	995	800	525	300	150

Alcione Sporting

This over/under gun is designed for sporting clays competition. Fitted with mechanical triggers and ported barrels. Offered in 12 gauge only with 30" barrels. Select walnut stock. Removable sideplates. Weight about 7.5 lbs.

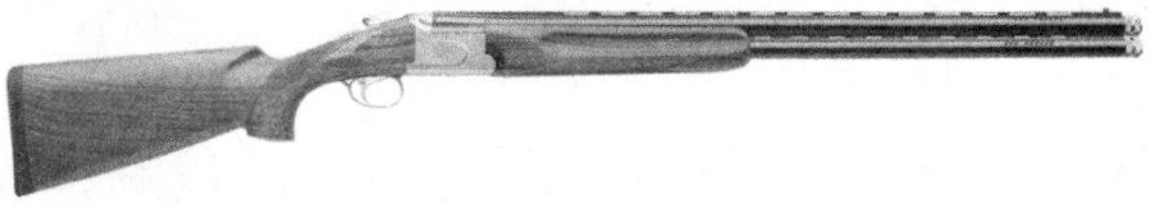

NIB	Exc.	V.G.	Good	Fair	Poor
1550	1250	995	775	400	00

Alcione LF

This 12 or 20 gauge model features barrels of 26" and 28" in 12 gauge and 26" in 20 gauge. Both gauges are chambered for 3" shells. Walnut stock. Receiver is aluminum alloy with etched games scenes with gold fill. Weight is about 6.8 lbs.

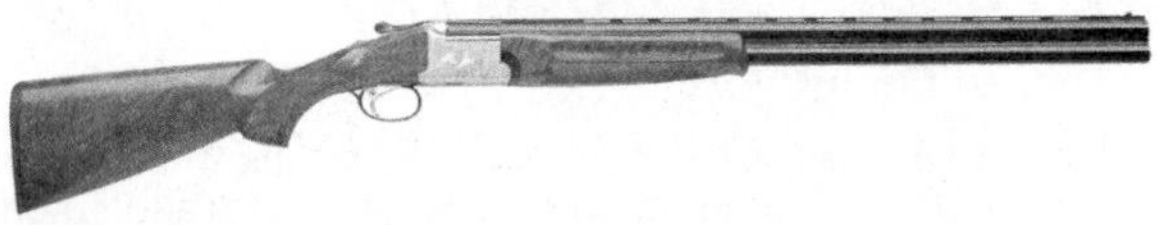

NIB	Exc.	V.G.	Good	Fair	Poor
1300	1050	700	450	300	200

Alcione SL Sport

As above, but more finely finished and with a French casehardened receiver.

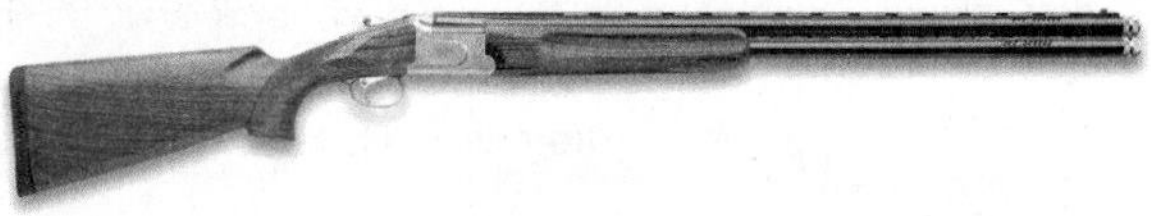

NIB	Exc.	V.G.	Good	Fair	Poor
1375	1125	775	525	375	275

Alcione SP

Chambered for the 12 gauge shell and fitted with 28" vent rib barrels with choke tubes. Full slide lock-style side plates with engraving and gold pheasants and mallards. Weight is about 7.5 lbs. Introduced in 2003.

NIB	Exc.	V.G.	Good	Fair	Poor
1700	1450	975	700	575	345

ALCIONE SIDEPLATES

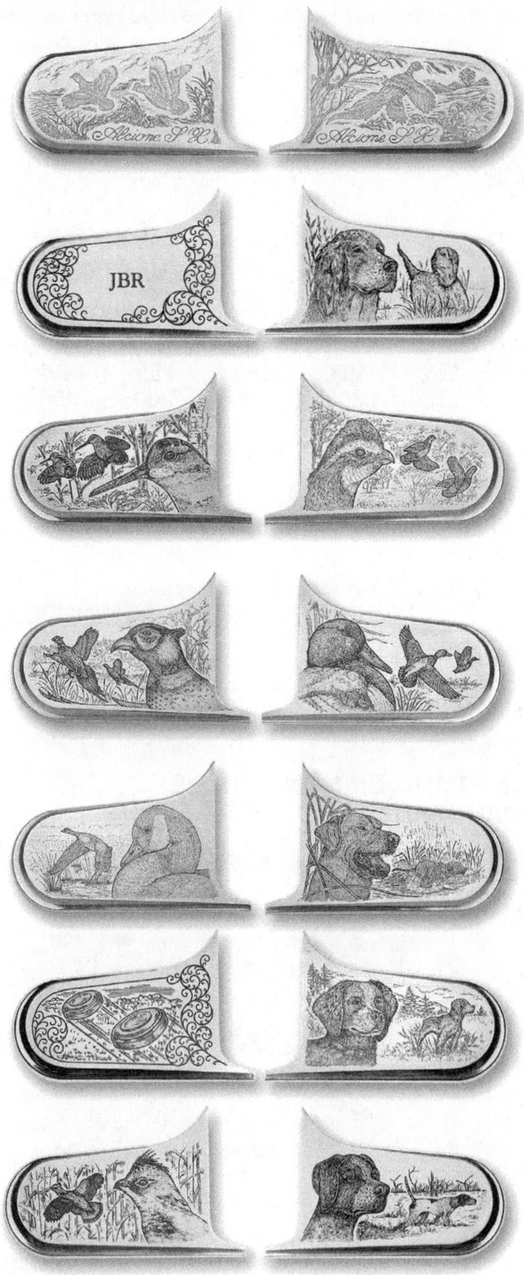

Alcione Classic SX

This 12 gauge 3" model is similar to the Alcione Field SX above but with blued receiver. Available with choice of 26" or 28" vent rib barrels. An extra 12 gauge 30" ported barrel and 20 gauge barrels are also optional. Weight is about 7.5 lbs. Introduced in 2004.

NIB	*Exc.*	*V.G.*	*Good*	*Fair*	*Poor*
1400	1150	950	700	600	300

Alcione Field SX

This model is fitted with a high grade walnut stock, fine checkering, and engraved receivers with gold filled etched side plates. Offered with 28" or 26" barrels. Weight is about 7.3 lbs.

NIB	*Exc.*	*V.G.*	*Good*	*Fair*	*Poor*
1600	1250	995	775	400	00

Veloce

Introduced in 2001 this model is chambered for the 20 or 28 gauge only with 26" or 28" barrels for 20 gauge guns and 26" barrels for 28 gauge guns. Aluminum alloy receiver. Engraved side plates with gold filled game scenes. Mechanical trigger. Select walnut stock. Weight of 20 gauge guns is about 5.8 lbs. and 28 gauge guns about 5.5 lbs.

NIB	*Exc.*	*V.G.*	*Good*	*Fair*	*Poor*
1375	1125	775	525	375	275

Veloce English Stock

Introduced in 2002 this model is similar ot the Veloce but with a straight-grip stock. Offered in 20 and 28 gauge with 26" vent-rib barrels. Choke tubes. Weight is about 5.7 lbs. in 20 gauge and 5.5 lbs. in 28 gauge.

NIB	*Exc.*	*V.G.*	*Good*	*Fair*	*Poor*
1400	1150	950	700	600	300

Veloce Grade II

This 20 or 28 gauge model features an extra-select-grade walnut stock with gold-filled birds and scroll engraving. The 20 gauge is offered with either a 26" or 28" vent-rib barrel, while the 28 gauge is fitted with a 26" vent-rib barrel. The 20 gauge gun weighs about 5.75 lbs., while the 28 gauge gun weighs about 5.5 lbs.

NIB	*Exc.*	*V.G.*	*Good*	*Fair*	*Poor*
1600	1275	1100	800	650	350

Veloce Squire Set

This model features a two-barrel set in 20 and 28 gauge. Each barrel set is fitted with 26" vent-rib barrels. Select walnut stock, gold-embelished game scenes, jeweled monoblocs, and filigreed top lever. Weight is about 5.5 lbs. Introduced in 2003.

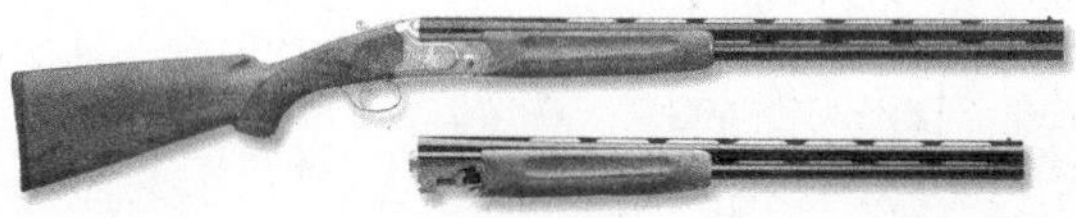

NIB	*Exc.*	*V.G.*	*Good*	*Fair*	*Poor*
2100	1775	1600	1200	800	400

FRANCHI RENAISSANCE

The Renaissance Series was introduced in 2006. These over-and-unders feature ultra-light alloy receivers, oil-finished walnut stocks, Prince of Wales pistol grips, cut checkering and Twin

Shock Absorber recoil pads with gel insert. The 3" 12 and 20 gauges have 26" or 28" barrels; the 28 gauge has a 26" barrel. Weights average 6.2 lbs. in 12 gauge, 5.8 lbs. in 20 gauge and 5.5 lbs. in 28 gauge. Add 5 percent to values shown for 28 gauge.

Field

Walnut stock with engraved receiver.

NIB	Exc.	V.G.	Good	Fair	Poor
1600	1250	995	775	400	00

Classic

A-Grade walnut with gold inlaid receiver.

NIB	Exc.	V.G.	Good	Fair	Poor
1650	1300	1050	825	450	250

Elite

AA-Grade Walnut with gold inlaid receiver.

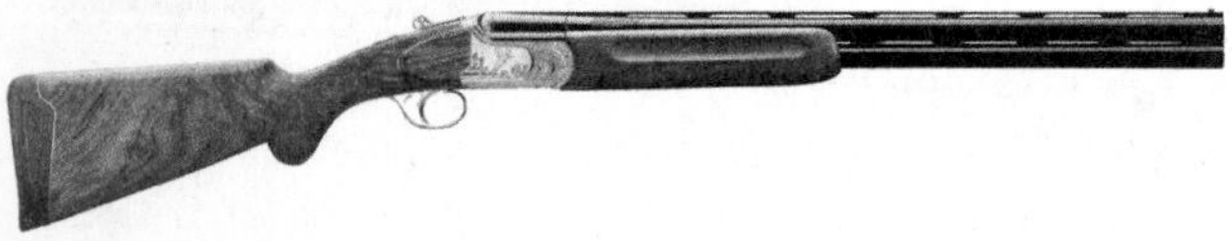

NIB	Exc.	V.G.	Good	Fair	Poor
1900	1550	1295	1050	650	275

Sporting

This 3" 12 gauge model was introduced in 2007. It features a 30" barrel, A-Grade walnut stock, engraved receiver with gold inlay and adjustable comb. Weight is about 7.9 lbs.

NIB	Exc.	V.G.	Good	Fair	Poor
1975	1625	1350	1300	825	325

SEMI-AUTOMATIC SHOTGUNS

AL48

A 12 or 20 gauge semi-auto shotgun with 24" to 30" ventilated-rib barrels (those made after 1989, threaded for choke tubes) and an alloy receiver. Walnut stock. Manufactured since 1950. Values shown are for current production.

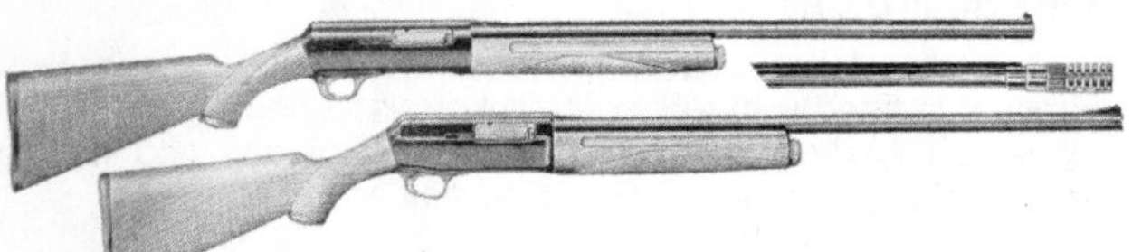

NIB	Exc.	V.G.	Good	Fair	Poor
725	550	300	250	150	100

NOTE: Magnum Model add 10 percent. Add $75 for 28 gauge model.

AL 48 Short Stock (Modern)

Same as above but in 20 gauge with shorter length of pull. First imported in 2000.

NIB	Exc.	V.G.	Good	Fair	Poor
700	525	275	250	150	100

AL 48 Deluxe English Stock (Modern)

Similar to the standard AL 48 but with straight grip stock. Offered in 20 and 28 gauge with 26" vent-rib barrel with choke tubes. Weight is about 5.5 lbs. Introduced in 2002.

NIB	Exc.	V.G.	Good	Fair	Poor
800	625	375	275	175	100

Hunter Model AL48 (1950-1970)

As above with an etched receiver and more finely figured wood.

NIB	Exc.	V.G.	Good	Fair	Poor
550	350	300	250	200	150

NOTE: Magnum Model add 10 percent.

Eldorado AL48 (1954-1975)

As above, but more finely finished. Manufactured from 1954 to 1975.

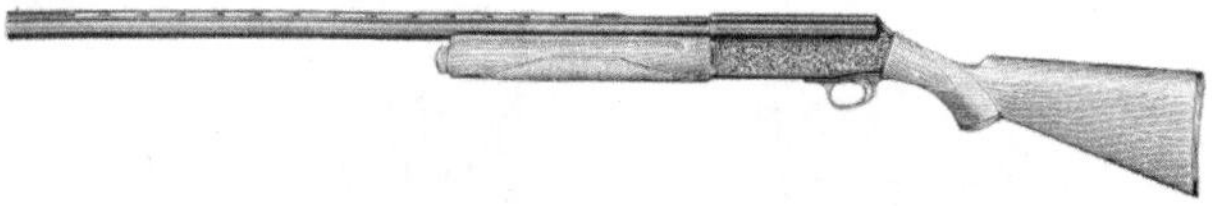

NIB	Exc.	V.G.	Good	Fair	Poor
600	425	325	250	200	150

CROWN GRADE, DIAMOND GRADE, IMPERIAL GRADE

As above, with hand-done engraving and finely figured walnut stocks.

Crown Grade

NIB	Exc.	V.G.	Good	Fair	Poor
1800	1450	1200	800	475	250

Diamond Grade

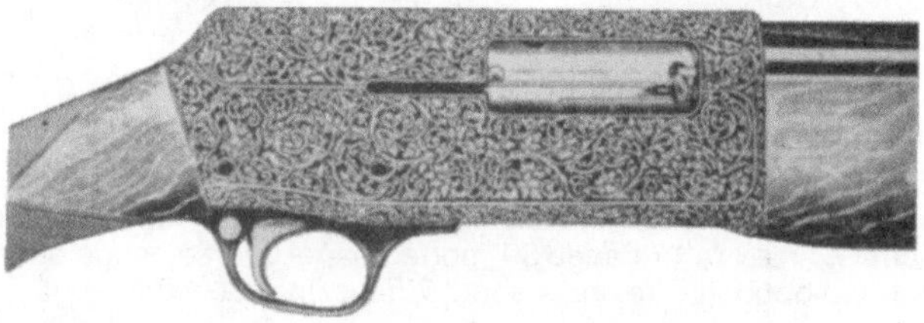

NIB	Exc.	V.G.	Good	Fair	Poor
2300	1850	1375	900	575	300

Imperial Grade

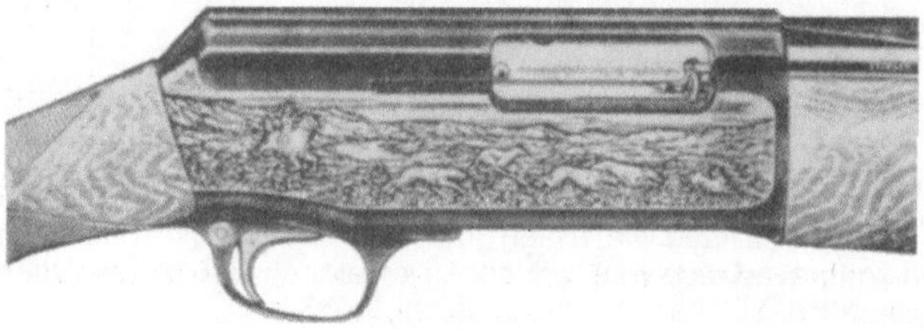

NIB	Exc.	V.G.	Good	Fair	Poor
2800	2450	1850	1250	950	450

Model 500

A 12 gauge semi-automatic shotgun with a 28" ventilated-rib barrel and walnut stock. Introduced in 1976.

NIB	Exc.	V.G.	Good	Fair	Poor
500	425	375	295	150	100

NOTE: Deluxe version add 10 percent.

Model 520 "Eldorado Gold"

An engraved and gold-inlaid version of the above.

NIB	Exc.	V.G.	Good	Fair	Poor
1250	1050	850	550	300	150

Model 530 Trap

The Model 500 with a 30" or 32" ventilated-rib barrel and trap stock.

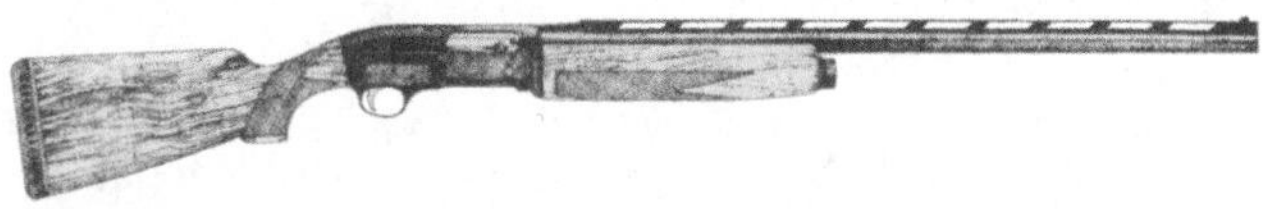

NIB	Exc.	V.G.	Good	Fair	Poor
675	600	500	400	300	150

Prestige Model

A 12 gauge semi-automatic shotgun manufactured in a variety of barrel lengths. After 1989 the barrels threaded for choke tubes. Alloy receiver and walnut stock.

NIB	Exc.	V.G.	Good	Fair	Poor
675	550	475	350	250	150

Elite Model

As above, with an etched receiver and more finely figured stock.

NIB	Exc.	V.G.	Good	Fair	Poor
700	600	525	350	250	150

SPAS12

A 12 gauge slide-action/semi-automatic shotgun with a 21.5" barrel and 9-shot magazine. Anodized, black finish with a composition folding or fixed stock.

NIB	Exc.	V.G.	Good	Fair	Poor
1450	1000	800	600	475	300

Black Magic Game Model

A 12 gauge Magnum semi-automatic shotgun with 24" to 28" ventilated rib barrels threaded for choke tubes, gold anodized alloy receiver, blackened barrel and walnut stock. Also available in trap or skeet configuration.

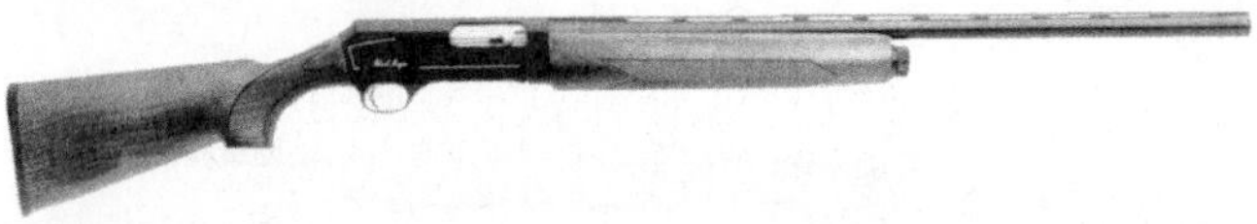

NIB	Exc.	V.G.	Good	Fair	Poor
750	600	525	300	250	100

NOTE: Skeet Model add 10 percent. Trap Model add 15 percent.

Black Magic Hunter

A 12 or 20 gauge Magnum double-barrel shotgun with 28" ventilated-rib barrels threaded for choke tubes, single-selective triggers and automatic ejectors. Blued with a walnut stock. Introduced in 1989.

NIB	Exc.	V.G.	Good	Fair	Poor
700	550	475	300	250	100

Black Magic Lightweight Hunter

As above, with 26" barrels and 2.75" chambers.

NIB	Exc.	V.G.	Good	Fair	Poor
975	850	650	400	300	150

Variomax 912

Introduced in 2001 this model is chambered for the 12 gauge 3.5" shell. It is offered with a choice of 24", 26", 28", or 30" barrels with vent-rib. Black synthetic stock. Weight is about 7.6 lbs. Choke tubes. In 2002 a walnut stock was added as an option.

NIB	Exc.	V.G.	Good	Fair	Poor
700	550	475	300	250	100

NOTE: Add $50 for walnut stock.

Variomax 912 Camo

Same as above but with Advantage Timber camo finish.

NIB	Exc.	V.G.	Good	Fair	Poor
750	600	525	300	250	10

Variomax 912 SteadyGrip

Introduced in 2005 this model features a extended pistol grip and Advantage H-D camo stock with 24" vent rib barrel and choke tubes. Weight is about 8 lbs.

NIB	Exc.	V.G.	Good	Fair	Poor
775	625	550	325	265	10

Variopress 612 Sporting

This is a 12 gauge semi-automatic gas-operated shotgun with 30" ported barrel. Extended choke tubes. Select walnut stock with stock drop kit. Magazine capacity is 5 rounds. Weight is about 7 lbs. First imported in 2000.

NIB	Exc.	V.G.	Good	Fair	Poor
700	550	475	300	250	100

Variopress 612 Field

This 12 gauge model is offered with barrel lengths from 24" to 28". Stock configurations are walnut, synthetic, or camo. Magazine capacity is 5 rounds. Weight is about 7 lbs. depending on barrel length.

NIB	*Exc.*	*V.G.*	*Good*	*Fair*	*Poor*
700	550	475	300	250	100

Variopress 612 Defense

This 12 gauge gun is fitted with an 18.5" barrel and black synthetic stock. Matte black finish. Choke is cylinder. Weight is about 6.5 lbs. Magazine capacity is 5 rounds. First imported in 2000.

NIB	*Exc.*	*V.G.*	*Good*	*Fair*	*Poor*
600	500	425	350	250	150

Variopress 620 Field

This model is offered in 20 gauge with a choice of walnut or camo stock. Barrel lengths from 24" to 28". Magazine capacity is 5 rounds. Weight is about 6 lbs.

NIB	*Exc.*	*V.G.*	*Good*	*Fair*	*Poor*
700	550	475	300	250	100

NOTE: Add $50 for camo stock.

Variopress 620 Short Stock

Same as above but with 12.5" length of pull and walnut stock. First imported in 2000.

NIB	*Exc.*	*V.G.*	*Good*	*Fair*	*Poor*
700	550	475	300	250	100

MODEL 712

This is semi-automatic shotgun chambered for the 12 gauge 3" shell. Available with choice of 24", 26", or 28" vent rib barrels with choke tubes. Also offered in several different finishes: Weathercoat (synthetic wood), Max-4 camo and Timber HD. Choice of synthetic wood, black synthetic, or camo stock. Weight is about 6.8 lbs. to 7 lbs., depending on stock and barrel length. Introduced in 2004.

WeatherCoat

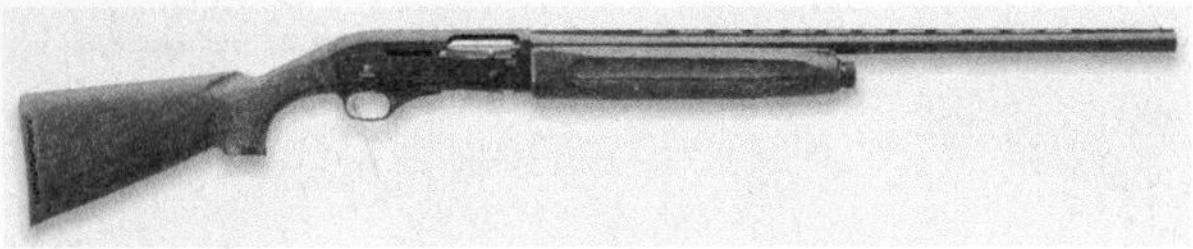

NIB	*Exc.*	*V.G.*	*Good*	*Fair*	*Poor*
700	600	500	375	200	100

Camo

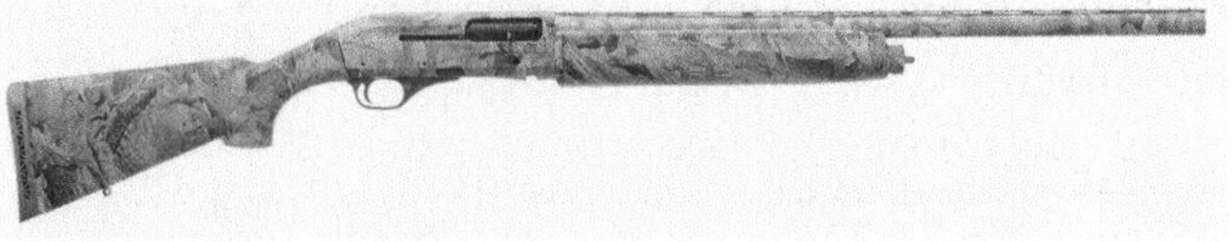

NIB	*Exc.*	*V.G.*	*Good*	*Fair*	*Poor*
725	625	525	400	225	125

Synthetic

NIB	*Exc.*	*V.G.*	*Good*	*Fair*	*Poor*
775	650	550	425	250	150

MODEL 720

Similar to the Model 712 but chambered for the 20 gauge 3" shell. Offered with 24", 26", or 28" vent rib barrels. Choice of Max-4, Timber HD finish or walnut stock with 12.5" lop. Introduced in 2004.

Camo

NIB	*Exc.*	*V.G.*	*Good*	*Fair*	*Poor*
750	650	550	425	250	150

Walnut Short Stock

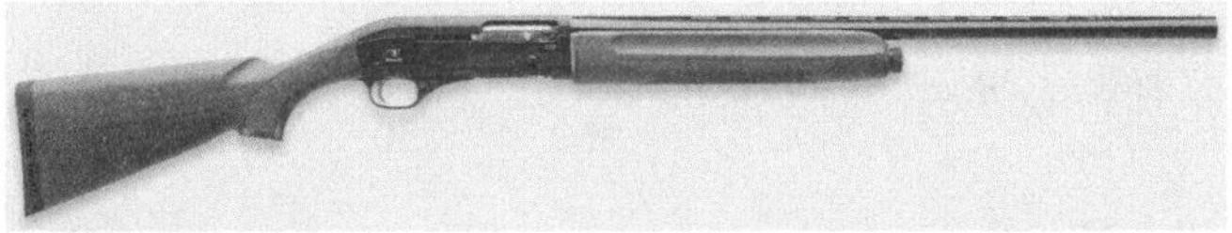

NIB	*Exc.*	*V.G.*	*Good*	*Fair*	*Poor*
725	625	525	400	225	125

WeatherCoat

Introduced in 2005 with 28" vent rib barrel. Weight is about 6.2 lbs.

NIB	*Exc.*	*V.G.*	*Good*	*Fair*	*Poor*
775	650	550	425	250	150

I-12

Introduced in 2005 this 12 gauge model is offered with 3" chambers and choice of 24", 26", or 28" vent rib barrels. Available with synthetic, walnut, Max-4, or Timber H-D stock. Choke tubes. Weight is about 7.5 lbs. depending on barrel length.

NIB	*Exc.*	*V.G.*	*Good*	*Fair*	*Poor*
1200	900	600	500	350	200

White Gold

Similar to Inertia I-12 but with highly figured walnut stock and white gold game bird scene on a satin nickel receiver. Introduced in 2006. Available only with 28" barrel. Weight is about 7.7 lbs.

NIB	Exc.	V.G.	Good	Fair	Poor
1400	1050	750	600	425	250

RIFLES

Centennial Semi-Automatic

A .22 caliber semi-automatic rifle with a 21" barrel, adjustable sights, Alloy receiver and walnut stock. Manufactured in 1968 only.

NIB	Exc.	V.G.	Good	Fair	Poor
550	375	325	250	175	125

NOTE: Deluxe Engraved Model add 20 percent.

FRANCOTTE, A.

Liege, Belgium

Jubilee

A 12, 16, 20, and 28 gauge Anson & Deeley boxlock double-barrel shotgun with various barrel lengths and chokes, automatic ejectors, double triggers and walnut stock.

NIB	Exc.	V.G.	Good	Fair	Poor
—	1650	1350	1100	850	450

Jubilee No. 14

Courtesy William Hammond

NIB	Exc.	V.G.	Good	Fair	Poor
—	2450	2050	1700	1300	650

Jubilee No. 18

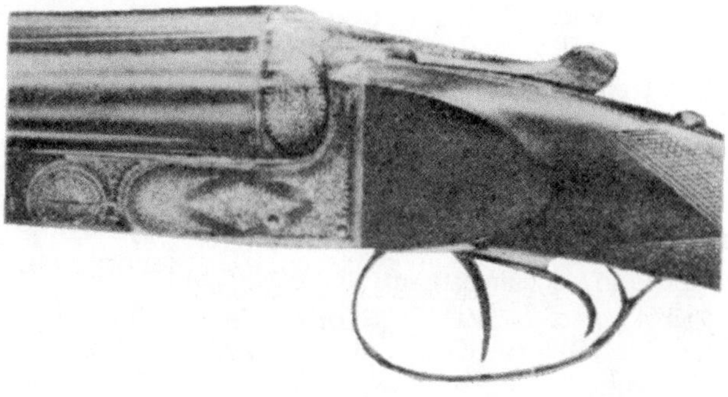

NIB	Exc.	V.G.	Good	Fair	Poor
—	2950	2450	2200	1500	750

Jubilee No. 20

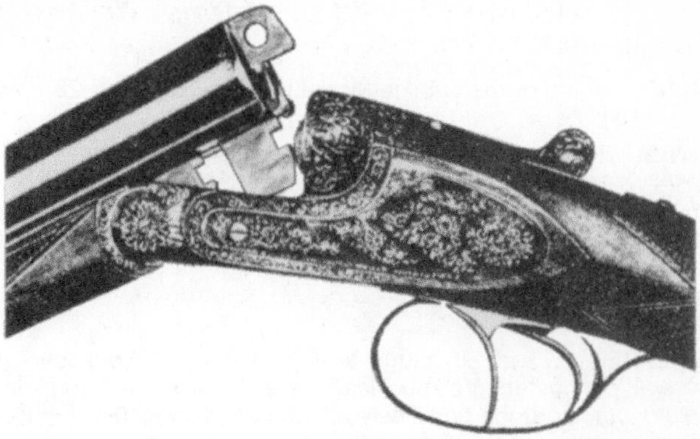

NIB	Exc.	V.G.	Good	Fair	Poor
—	3450	2700	2250	1750	900

Jubilee No. 25

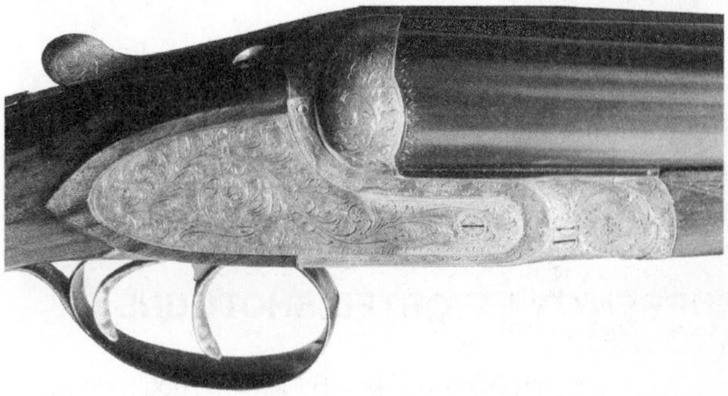

NIB	Exc.	V.G.	Good	Fair	Poor
—	3950	3250	2750	2000	1000

Jubilee No. 30

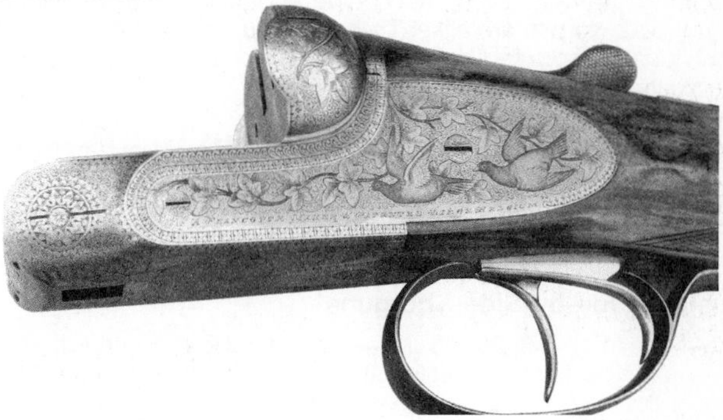

Courtesy William Hammond

NIB	Exc.	V.G.	Good	Fair	Poor
—	5000	4200	3500	3000	1500

Jubilee Eagle Grade No. 45

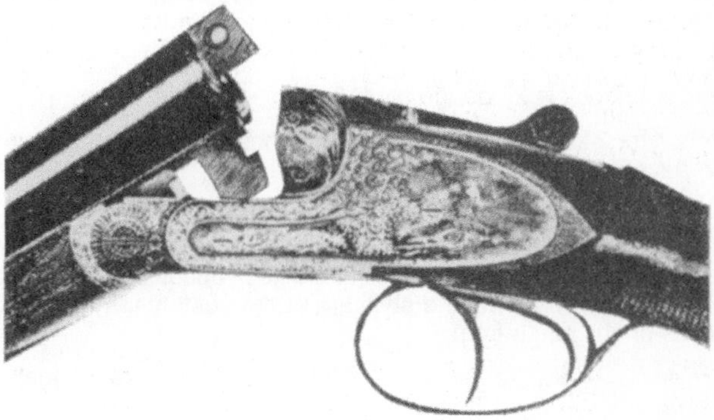

NIB	Exc.	V.G.	Good	Fair	Poor
—	3950	3200	2500	2000	1000

Knockabout

A plain version of the Jubilee Model in 12, 16, 20, and 28 gauge and .410 bore.

NIB	Exc.	V.G.	Good	Fair	Poor
—	1450	1300	850	650	500

NOTE: 20 gauge add 20 percent; 28 gauge add 30 percent; .410 add 40 percent.

Sidelock Side-by-Side

A 12, 16, 20, and 28 gauge and .410 bore sidelock shotgun ordered per customer's specifications. Extensive scroll engraving, deluxe walnut stock and finely checkered. The .410 will bring a premium of from $1,200-$1,500.

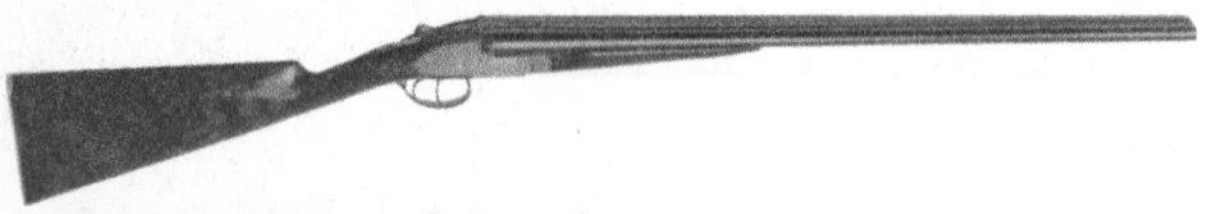

NIB	Exc.	V.G.	Good	Fair	Poor
13000	11500	8000	6500	5000	3500

Deluxe Sidelock Side-by-Side

As above, with gold-inlaid hunting scenes.

NIB	Exc.	V.G.	Good	Fair	Poor
16500	13500	10000	8000	5750	4800

CURRENTLY IMPORTED SHOTGUNS AND RIFLES

Francotte currently imports side-by-side boxlock or sidelock shotguns, double rifles, and single-shot rifles as well as bolt-action rifles into the United States through Armes De Chasse. These shotguns and rifles are all custom built to the customer's specifications. Gauge (including 24 and 32 gauge), caliber, barrel length, engraving, wood type and style are all individually produced. No two are alike. These shotguns and rifles should be individually appraised before the sale. Prices listed are subject to fluctuations in international currency.

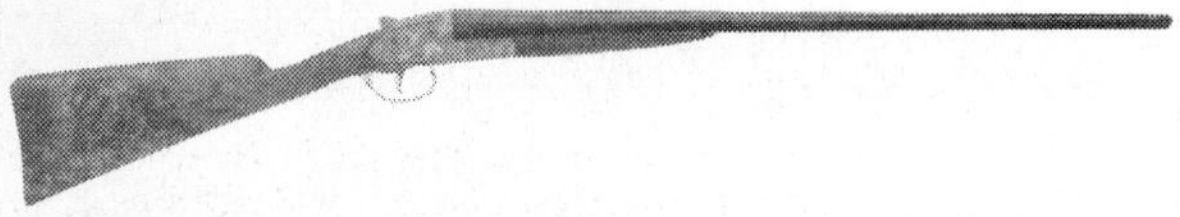

Custom Side-by-Side Shotguns

Available in 12, 16, 20, 28 gauge and .410 bore in either boxlock or sidelock actions. Barrel length, engraving, wood type and style are at the customer's discretion. Retail prices range from:

Basic Boxlock with 27.5" barrels and walnut stock with double triggers in 12, 16, and 20 gauge without engraving—$18,000

Basic Boxlock in 28 gauge or .410 bore without engraving—$14,000

Basic Boxlock with 26.5" or 28" barrels and deluxe walnut stock with scroll engraving, and double triggers in 12, 16, and 20 gauge—$23,000

Basic Boxlock in 28 gauge or .410 bore—$28,000

Prices for 24 and 32 gauge are extra. These prices do not include engraving.

Custom Double Rifles

These custom built double rifles are offered in calibers from 9.3x74R to .470 Nitro Express in boxlock or sidelock actions. Barrel length, engraving, wood type and style are at the customer's discretion. Retail prices range from:

Prices for 24 and 32 gauge are extra. These prices do not include engraving.

Boxlock in 9.3x74R, 8x57JRS and other European calibers-$14,000

Boxlock in.375 H&H and.470 NE—$19,000Sidelock in 9.3x74R, etc.—$23,700.

Sidelock in large calibers—$32,000

Custom Single-Shot Mountain Rifles

These single-shot rifles are offered in rimmed cartridges but rimless cartridge rifles can be built on special request. Barrel length, engraving, wood type and style are at the customer's discretion. Retail prices range from:

Boxlock in rimmed calibers—Prices start at $13,000.

Sidelock in 7x65R and 7mm Rem. Mag.—Prices start at $24,000

Custom Bolt-Action Rifles

These bolt-action rifles utilize a Mauser 98 type action with adjustable trigger. They are offered in calibers from .17 Bee to .505 Gibbs. Barrel lengths are 21" to 24.5", engraving wood type and style are at the customers' discretion. Retail prices range from:

Standard bolt-action calibers: .270, .30-06, 7x64, 8x60S and 9.3x62—Prices start at $7,650

Short-action calibers: .222, .223—Prices start at $9,100

Magnum-action calibers: 7mm Rem. Mag., .300 Win. Mag., .338 Win. Mag., .375 H&H, and .458 Win. Mag.—Prices start at $8,400

African calibers: .416 Rigby, .460 Wby., .505 Gibbs—Prices start at $12,250.

NOTE: Please note that the prices listed are for the basic models. They do not reflect the extensive list of options available on these custom firearms.

FRANKLIN, C. W.

Liege, Belgium

Manufacturer of utilitarian shotguns with either exposed or enclosed hammers. Circa 1900.

Single-Barrel

NIB	Exc.	V.G.	Good	Fair	Poor
—	150	75	50	35	20

Damascus Barrel Double

NIB	Exc.	V.G.	Good	Fair	Poor
—	250	150	125	100	65

Steel Barrel Double

NIB	Exc.	V.G.	Good	Fair	Poor
—	300	175	150	125	90

FRANKONIA JAGD

Favorit, Germany

NOTE: Seldom seen in USA. Values extremely variable, based on local market, chambering, and other factors.

Favorit Standard

Chambered for various European calibers, this bolt-action rifle has a 24" barrel and set triggers. Blued, with a checkered walnut stock.

NIB	Exc.	V.G.	Good	Fair	Poor
—	450	295	260	175	125

Favorit Deluxe

As above, with a more finely figured stock.

NIB	Exc.	V.G.	Good	Fair	Poor
—	475	325	275	200	150

Safari Model

As above, in Magnum calibers.

NIB	Exc.	V.G.	Good	Fair	Poor
—	1400	950	675	275	200

Heeren Rifle

A best quality single-shot rifle with a 26" octagonal barrel, double-set triggers, and adjustable sights. Engraved with hand checkered, high-grade walnut. Blued. Produced in a variety of calibers.

NIB	Exc.	V.G.	Good	Fair	Poor
—	5000	3050	2500	1700	1250

FRASER, DANIEL & SON

Edinburgh, Scotland

This renowned rifle maker was an apprentice of Alexander Henry. Fraser had retail stores at these addresses:

FRIGON

Clay Center, Kansas

An importer of guns manufactured by Marocchi of Italy.

FT I

A 12 gauge boxlock single-barrel shotgun with a 32" or 34" ventilated rib barrel, full choke, automatic ejector and interchanged stock. Blued. Introduced in 1986.

NIB	Exc.	V.G.	Good	Fair	Poor
950	750	650	550	450	300

FTC

As above, with two sets of barrels (a single ventilated rib trap barrel and a set of Over/Under ventilated rib barrels). In a fitted case. Introduced in 1986.

NIB	Exc.	V.G.	Good	Fair	Poor
1750	1400	1150	800	650	500

FS-4

A four gauge set (12, 20, and 28 gauge and .410 bore). Introduced in 1986.

NIB	Exc.	V.G.	Good	Fair	Poor
2500	2100	1750	1500	1100	750

FRUHWIRTH

Austria

M1872 Fruhwirth System Rifle

An 11mm bolt-action rifle with a 25" barrel and 6-shot magazine. Blued with a full-length walnut stock.

NIB	Exc.	V.G.	Good	Fair	Poor
—	650	425	300	195	100

FUNK, CHRISTOPH

Suhl, Germany

Christoph Funk began his gun business before 1900. The vast majority of long guns were best quality. Some collectors believe that J.P. Sauer built receivers for Funk but this is not known for certain. Funk produced shotguns, shotgun-rifle combinations, and double rifles. Some were exported to England and the U.S. Most of the U.S. imports are in the more common North American calibers such as .300 Savage, 30-30, 32-20 Winchester, and 12 or 16 gauge. Most are found with only a right-hand extension arm which locks into the receiver, but some higher grades have both extension arms. The quality of these guns is extremely high. Guns were probably not made after 1940. Quality of engraving and caliber determines value. American calibers will command a higher price. Prices listed are for American calibers.

Courtesy Jim Cate

NIB	Exc.	V.G.	Good	Fair	Poor
—	2950	2250	1450	600	400

Prewar Drilling in 16 or 12 gauge

NIB	Exc.	V.G.	Good	Fair	Poor
—	—	—			

FURR ARMS

Prescott, Arizona
J. & G. Sale, Inc.

In addition to producing reproductions of various cannon, this company also manufactured one-tenth to three-quarter scale reproductions of Gatling guns. Furr products are highly desirable in some circles, with the Gatling .22 reproductions typically commanding prices in excess of $18,000 in mint, unfired condition.

FYRBERG, ANDREW

Worcester and Hopkinton, Massachusetts

Double-Barrel Shotguns

Fyrberg did work for Iver Johnson and C.S. Shattuck Co. of Hatfield, Mass. He began producing a hammerless double about 1902, a well designed boxlock with coil mainsprings. An estimated 2,000 were produced at Hopkinton and Worcester, Mass. Some have been made at Meriden, Conn. Sears cataloged the Fyrberg guns in 1902 to about 1908.

NIB	Exc.	V.G.	Good	Fair	Poor
—	525	425	300	200	150

G

GALEF (ZABALA)

Zabala Hermanos & Antonio Zoli
Spain

Zabala Double

A 10, 12, 16, and 20 caliber boxlock shotgun with a 22" to 30" barrel and various chokes. Hardwood stock. Add 50 percent for 10 gauge.

NIB	*Exc.*	*V.G.*	*Good*	*Fair*	*Poor*
—	450	300	175	100	75

Companion

A folding 12 to .410 bore single-shot underlever shotgun with a 28" or 30" barrel.

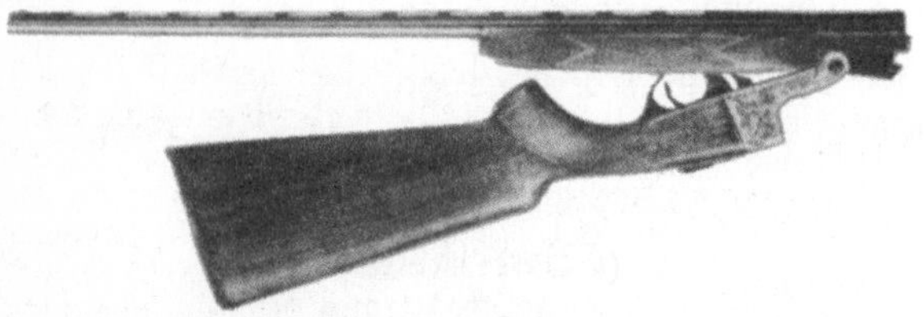

NIB	*Exc.*	*V.G.*	*Good*	*Fair*	*Poor*
—	200	145	105	50	25

Monte Carlo Trap

A 12 gauge underlever single-shot shotgun with a 32" ventilated rib barrel.

NIB	*Exc.*	*V.G.*	*Good*	*Fair*	*Poor*
—	325	275	150	100	75

Silver Snipe, Golden Snipe, and Silver Hawk

SEE—Antonio Zoli

GALIL

Israel Military Industries
Israel

Model AR

NIB	*Exc.*	*V.G.*	*Good*	*Fair*	*Poor*
2800	2400	2000	1500	900	700

Model ARM

NIB	*Exc.*	*V.G.*	*Good*	*Fair*	*Poor*
3000	2700	2000	1500	900	700

Sniper Rifle

NIB	*Exc.*	*V.G.*	*Good*	*Fair*	*Poor*
8500	7500	6000	4000	3000	2000

Hadar II

NIB	*Exc.*	*V.G.*	*Good*	*Fair*	*Poor*
1300	1100	800	650	500	400

GALLAGER

Richardson & Overman
Philadelphia, Pennsylvania

Gallager Carbine

A .50 caliber single-shot percussion carbine with a 22.25" barrel, saddle ring and walnut stock. Blued and case hardened. Approximately 23,000 were made during the Civil War.

Percussion Model

As above, in .56-62 rimfire caliber. Approximately 5,000 of this model were made.

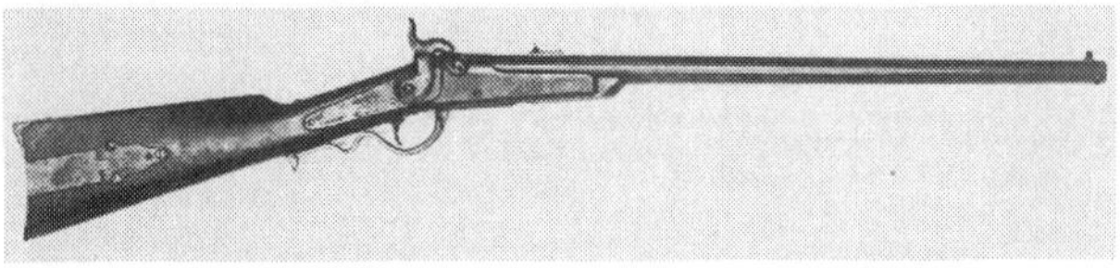

Courtesy Milwaukee Public Museum, Milwaukee, Wisconsin

NIB	*Exc.*	*V.G.*	*Good*	*Fair*	*Poor*
—	—	3900	2450	1500	500

Spencer Cartridge Model

NIB	*Exc.*	*V.G.*	*Good*	*Fair*	*Poor*
—	—	3425	1950	1350	400

GAMBA, RENATO

Gardone V. T., Italy

SIDE-BY-SIDE SHOTGUNS

Hunter Super

A 12 gauge Anson & Deeley boxlock double-barrel shotgun with a variety of barrel lengths and chokes, double triggers and extractors. Engraved and silver-plated.

NIB	*Exc.*	*V.G.*	*Good*	*Fair*	*Poor*
1250	900	700	550	450	250

Principessa

A 12, 20 or 28 gauge boxlock shotgun. Engraved, checkered stock.

NIB	*Exc.*	*V.G.*	*Good*	*Fair*	*Poor*
1850	1250	900	700	500	250

Oxford 90

A 12 or 20 gauge sidelock shotgun with various barrel lengths and chokes, the Purdey locking system, double triggers, and automatic ejectors. Walnut stock.

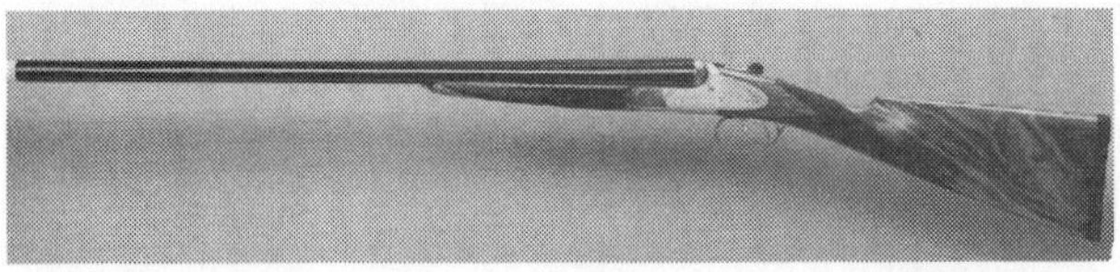

NIB	*Exc.*	*V.G.*	*Good*	*Fair*	*Poor*
4250	3250	1700	900	600	300

Oxford Extra

Same as above but with fine engraving.

NIB	*Exc.*	*V.G.*	*Good*	*Fair*	*Poor*
5200	4000	2250	1500	900	450

Gamba 624 Prince

Fitted with a Wesley Richards-type frame, select walnut stock, and fine hand engraving. Offered in 12 gauge with 28" barrels.

NIB	Exc.	V.G.	Good	Fair	Poor
4800	3900	2500	1500	850	400

Gamba 624 Extra

Same as above but with deep floral engraving.

NIB	Exc.	V.G.	Good	Fair	Poor
8000	5000	4500	2500	1250	600

London

A 12 or 20 gauge Holland & Holland sidelock shotgun with various barrel lengths and chokes, double- or single-selective trigger, automatic ejectors. Walnut stock.

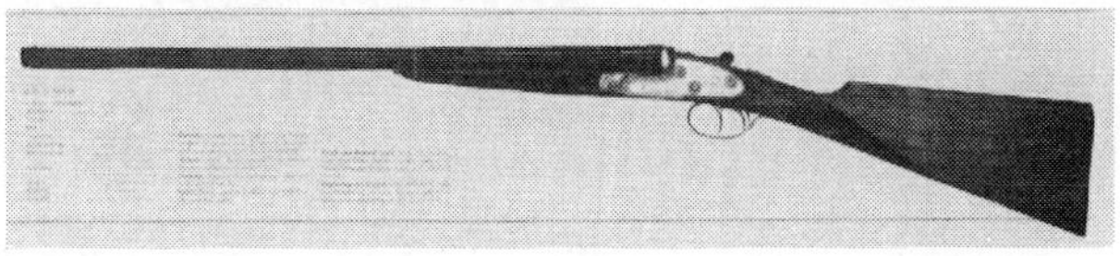

NIB	Exc.	V.G.	Good	Fair	Poor
7000	5500	4500	2500	1250	700

London Royal

As above with engraved hunting scenes.

NIB	Exc.	V.G.	Good	Fair	Poor
8000	6500	5000	3750	2000	950

Ambassador Gold and Black

A 12 and 20 gauge Holland & Holland sidelock shotgun with various barrel lengths and choke combinations, single-selective trigger, automatic ejectors, and a single gold line engraved on the barrels and the frame. Walnut stocks.

NIB	Exc.	V.G.	Good	Fair	Poor
25000	19000	13500	9500	5000	2500

Ambassador Executive

Gamba's best quality shotgun produced in 12 or 20 gauge to the customer's specifications.

NIB	Exc.	V.G.	Good	Fair	Poor
28000	20000	15000	10000	5000	2500

OVER-AND-UNDER SHOTGUNS

Country Model

A 12 and 20 gauge Over/Under shotgun with 28" or 30" barrels with ventilated rib, double triggers, extractors, and walnut stock.

NIB	Exc.	V.G.	Good	Fair	Poor
650	550	400	300	275	200

Grifone Model

A 12 and 20 gauge Over/Under shotgun with 26", 28", or 30" ventilated-rib barrels, a single-selective trigger, and automatic ejectors. The boxlock action is silver-plated, with walnut stock. Available with screw-in chokes, and this would add 10 percent to the values.

NIB	Exc.	V.G.	Good	Fair	Poor
800	650	550	350	250	200

Europa 2000

A 12 gauge Over/Under shotgun in various barrel lengths and choke combinations, single-selective trigger, and automatic ejectors. Engraved, silver-plated, boxlock action with false sideplates and walnut stock.

NIB	Exc.	V.G.	Good	Fair	Poor
1250	900	700	550	350	250

Grinta Trap and Skeet

A 12 gauge Over/Under shotgun with 26" Skeet or 30" Full choke barrels, a single-selective trigger, automatic ejectors, and some engraving. Walnut stock.

NIB	Exc.	V.G.	Good	Fair	Poor
1350	900	700	550	350	250

Victory Trap and Skeet

As above, but more finely finished.

NIB	Exc.	V.G.	Good	Fair	Poor
1650	1150	850	600	400	250

Edinburg Match

As above, with slightly different engraving patterns.

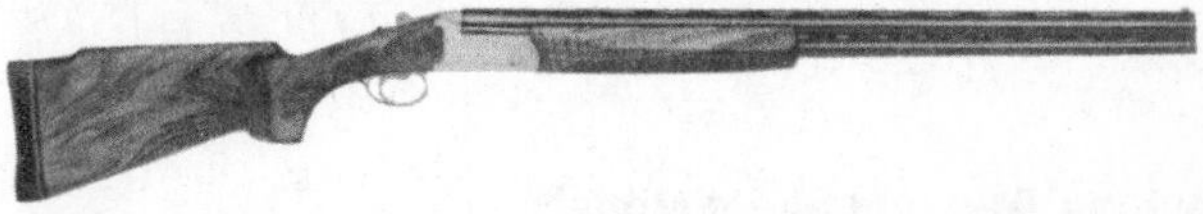

NIB	Exc.	V.G.	Good	Fair	Poor
1250	1000	800	600	400	250

Boyern 88 Combination Gun

A 12 gauge combination Over/Under rifle/shotgun with double triggers, and extractors. Engraved game scenes and coin-finished with walnut stock.

NIB	Exc.	V.G.	Good	Fair	Poor
1250	900	700	500	400	250

DAYTONA SERIES

This is a competition shotgun, first introduced into the US in 1986 as the Type I. The Type I was available in different configurations with the base model selling for about $4,000 until 1991. In 1994 Gamba introduced the Daytona in a wide variety of configurations and grades under a new designation called the Type II. The primary difference was in the location of the stock bolt. Only about 80 Daytona Type II shotguns are allocated to the US per year. They are a high quality shotgun with an excellent reputation. Prices are listed for 12 gauge guns. 20 gauge guns are available on special request.

Daytona Trap

Offered in 12 gauge with 30" or 32" barrels. Select walnut stock with hand checkering. Removable trigger group, improved Boss lock-up, and boxlock receiver.

NIB	Exc.	V.G.	Good	Fair	Poor
5900	4750	3000	2250	1200	600

Daytona Sporting

Available in 12 gauge with 30" barrel with screw-in chokes and single-selective trigger.

NIB	Exc.	V.G.	Good	Fair	Poor
4000	3250	2500	1900	1200	700

Daytona Skeet

Offered in 12 gauge with 29" barrels and single-selective trigger.

NIB	Exc.	V.G.	Good	Fair	Poor
4000	3250	2500	1900	1200	700

Daytona America Trap

Offered in 12 gauge with 30" or 32" barrels, high adjustable rib, adjustable stock, and single trigger.

NIB	Exc.	V.G.	Good	Fair	Poor
4000	3250	2500	1900	1200	700

Daytona Game

Offered in 12 gauge with 28" barrels and single trigger.

NIB	Exc.	V.G.	Good	Fair	Poor
3900	3500	3000	2250	1200	700

NOTE: Add $300 for black frame with gold inlaid names and logo.

DAYTONA GRADE 6 ENGRAVING

Fine English scroll hand engraving edged with gold line work.

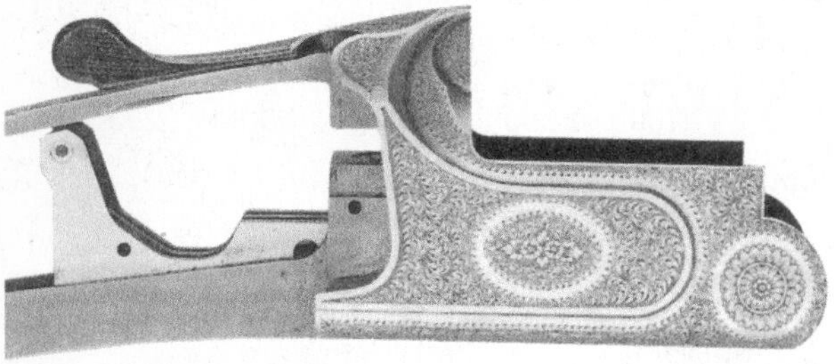

Daytona Trap and Skeet Models

NIB	Exc.	V.G.	Good	Fair	Poor
13000	5000	4000	3000	1500	700

Daytona Sporting Model

NIB	Exc.	V.G.	Good	Fair	Poor
13500	5000	4000	3000	1500	700

DAYTONA GRADE 5 ENGRAVING

Deep relief floral engraving with gold inlaid griffons.

Daytona Trap and Skeet Models

NIB	Exc.	V.G.	Good	Fair	Poor
14000	9000	6500	5000	2500	1200

Daytona Sporting Model

NIB	Exc.	V.G.	Good	Fair	Poor
14500	9000	6500	5000	2500	1200

DAYTONA GRADE 4 ENGRAVING

A flying eagle in a landscape and very fine English scroll by master engravers.

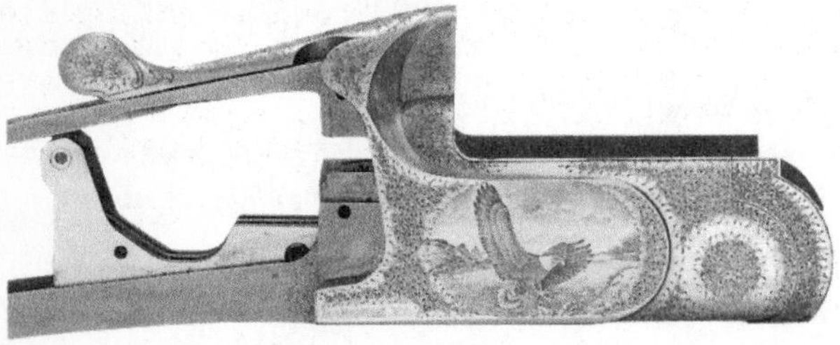

Daytona Trap and Skeet Models

NIB	Exc.	V.G.	Good	Fair	Poor
16250	10000	7500	5500	3000	1500

Daytona Sporting Model

NIB	Exc.	V.G.	Good	Fair	Poor
16750	10000	7500	5500	3000	1500

DAYTONA SL GRADE 3 ENGRAVING

Fitted with sideplates with engraved game scenes and fine English scroll by master engravers.

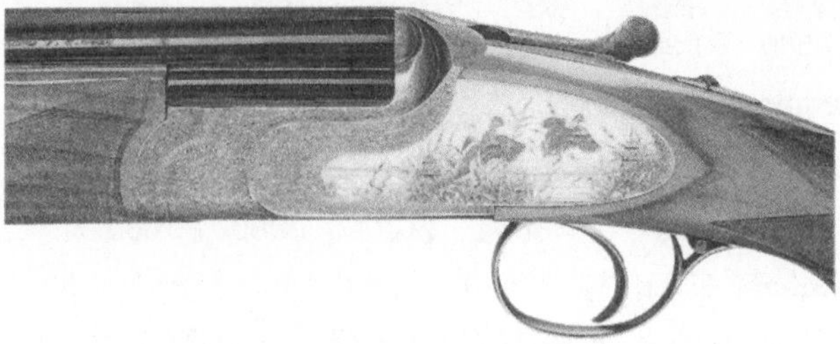

Daytona Trap and Skeet Models

NIB	Exc.	V.G.	Good	Fair	Poor
18750	15000	11000	7500	3500	1750

Daytona Sporting Model

NIB	Exc.	V.G.	Good	Fair	Poor
19250	11000	9000	6500	3500	1750

Daytona Game

NIB	Exc.	V.G.	Good	Fair	Poor
18750	11000	9000	6500	3500	1750

Daytona SLHH Grade 2 Engraving

Fitted with sideplates and Boss lock-up system, automatic ejectors, figured walnut stock, and fine game scene engraving signed by a master. Offered in 12 gauge with 28" barrels.

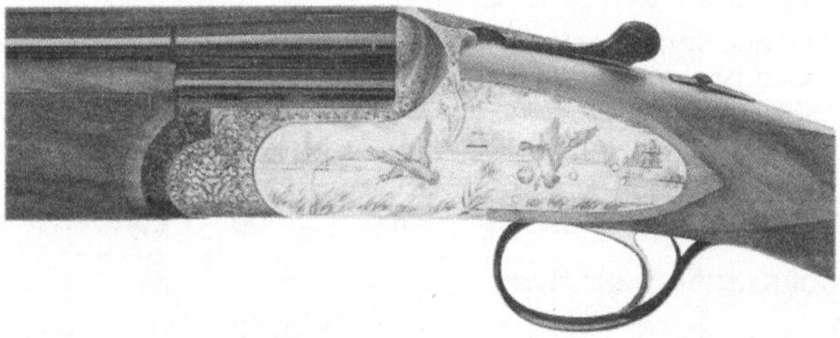

NIB	Exc.	V.G.	Good	Fair	Poor
36250	16000	12500	9500	6000	3000

Daytona SLHH Grade 1 Gold Engraving

Same as above but with gold inlaid game scenes and floral-style engraving signed by master engraver. Offered in 12 gauge with 28" barrels.

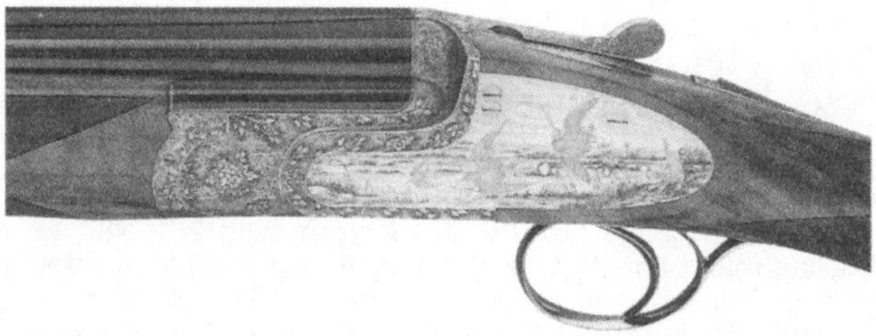

NIB	Exc.	V.G.	Good	Fair	Poor
43500	17000	13000	9500	5500	2500

Daytona SLHH "One of Thousand"

Same as above but game scene is executed at customers direction and is a totally custom ordered gun. Available in all configurations.

NIB	Exc.	V.G.	Good	Fair	Poor
125000	70000	35000	15500	7500	600

Concorde Game Shotguns

This over-and-under model is offered as a slightly less expensive alternative to the Daytona Series guns. The base gun is available with a blued or chromed action. Extra barrel are interchangeable in both 12 and 20 gauges with 28" barrels and single triggers.

NIB	Exc.	V.G.	Good	Fair	Poor
6000	4250	3000	1500	750	450

Concorde Trap

Available in 12 gauge with 30" or 32" barrels with single trigger.

NIB	Exc.	V.G.	Good	Fair	Poor
—	2000	1500	1000	600	450

Concorde Skeet

Available in 12 gauge with 29" barrels and single trigger.

NIB	Exc.	V.G.	Good	Fair	Poor
6000	4250	3000	1500	750	450

Concorde Sporting

Offered in 12 gauge with 30" barrels, screw-in chokes, and single-selective trigger.

NIB	Exc.	V.G.	Good	Fair	Poor
6100	2900	2000	1500	900	500

Concorde Game Grade 7 Engraving

Game scene engraving with fine English scroll.

NIB	Exc.	V.G.	Good	Fair	Poor
8700	4000	3250	2250	1200	600

Concorde Game Grade 8 Engraving

English scroll engraving.

NIB	Exc.	V.G.	Good	Fair	Poor
6250	3000	2500	1750	1000	500

Concorde 2nd Generation

Similar to the Concorde series but with fixed trigger group. Black or chrome frame. Automatic ejectors. Select walnut stock. Choice of 12 or 20 gauge with 28" or 30" barrels and single trigger. Introduced in 2002.

NIB	Exc.	V.G.	Good	Fair	Poor
6100	4850	3200	1950	750	300

Le Mans

This model is chambered for the 12 gauge shell and fitted with a choice of 28" or 30" barrels. Automatic ejectors. Single-selective trigger. Five choke tubes. Introduced in 2002.

NIB	Exc.	V.G.	Good	Fair	Poor
1750	1200	850	625	475	200

Hunter II

This 12 gauge model has an alloy frame with reinforced barrel with automatic ejectors. Five choke tubes. Single-selective trigger. Barrel lengths of 26" to 27.5". Introduced in 2002.

NIB	Exc.	V.G.	Good	Fair	Poor
1600	1100	750	525	375	150

RIFLES

Safari Express

A 7x65R, 9.3x74R, or .375 H&H caliber boxlock double-barrel rifle with 25" barrels, open sights, double triggers, automatic ejectors, and a coin-finished scroll engraved receiver. Walnut stock.

NIB	Exc.	V.G.	Good	Fair	Poor
8500	6500	4500	1750	750	350

Mustang

A 5.6x50, 6.5x57R, 7x65R, .222 Rem., .270 Win., or .30-06 caliber sidelock single barrel rifle with double-set triggers, engraved sidelock action and walnut stock.

NIB	Exc.	V.G.	Good	Fair	Poor
8500	6500	4500	1750	750	350

RGZ 1000

7x64, .270 Win., 7mm Rem. Mag., and .300 Win. Mag. caliber Mauser 98 bolt-action with a 20.5" barrel. Walnut pistol grip stock with a cheekpiece.

NIB	Exc.	V.G.	Good	Fair	Poor
1100	900	750	550	400	200

RGX 1000 Express

As above, with double-set triggers and a 23.75" barrel.

NIB	Exc.	V.G.	Good	Fair	Poor
1250	950	750	550	400	200

GARAND

(U.S. M1 Rifle)
U.S. Rifle, CAL. M1 (Garand)

SCOPE VARIANTS (SNIPER RIFLES)

NOTE: Sniper rifles must have sales or varification papers.

NIB	Exc.	V.G.	Good	Fair	Poor
—	3000	2500	1000	600	500

M1C

NIB	Exc.	V.G.	Good	Fair	Poor
—	10000	8000	5000	—	—

MC 1952 (USMC Issue) M1D

NIB	Exc.	V.G.	Good	Fair	Poor
—	3800	3000	2000	—	—

NATIONAL MATCH

Type I

NIB	Exc.	V.G.	Good	Fair	Poor
—	4500	2500	1800	—	—

Type II

NIB	Exc.	V.G.	Good	Fair	Poor
—	3200	2200	1500	—	—

NOTE: For history, technical data, descriptions, and prices see the Standard Catalog of Military Firearms under United States, Rifles.Pricing Note: Prices listed are for rifles in original, unaltered condition. Rifles also must include sale papers if necessary. For rifles that have been refinished or restored deduct about 50 percent.

Rebuilt Rifle, any manufacture

NIB	Exc.	V.G.	Good	Fair	Poor
—	900	550	425	—	—

DCM Rifles

NIB	Exc.	V.G.	Good	Fair	Poor
—	850	575	450	—	—

Navy Trophy Rifles U.S.N. Crane Depot Rebuild

NIB	Exc.	V.G.	Good	Fair	Poor
—	1800	1000	900	—	—

AMF Rebuild

NIB	Exc.	V.G.	Good	Fair	Poor
—	1000	900	750	—	—

H&R Rebuild

NIB	Exc.	V.G.	Good	Fair	Poor
—	900	800	700	—	—

NOTE: These rifles MUST be original and validated by experts.

Springfield Armory Production Gas trap sn: ca 81-52,000

NIB	Exc.	V.G.	Good	Fair	Poor
—	40000	35000	25000	—	—

Gas tap/modified to gas port

NIB	Exc.	V.G.	Good	Fair	Poor
—	5000	3500	2500	—	—

Pre-Dec. 7, 1941 gas port production pn sn: ca 410,000

NIB	Exc.	V.G.	Good	Fair	Poor
—	4000	2200	1300	=900	400

WWII Production sn: ca 410,000-3,880,000

NIB	Exc.	V.G.	Good	Fair	Poor
—	1400	1100	900	750	500

Post-WWII Production sn: ca 4,200,000-6,099,361

NIB	Exc.	V.G.	Good	Fair	Poor
—	1100	850	650	500	450

Winchester Educational Contract sn: 100,000-100,500

NIB	Exc.	V.G.	Good	Fair	Poor
—	10000	6000	4500	2000	700

Winchester sn: 100,501-165,000

NIB	Exc.	V.G.	Good	Fair	Poor
—	6500	4500	3000	1100	550

Winchester sn: 1,200,00-1,380,000

NIB	Exc.	V.G.	Good	Fair	Poor
—	5500	4500	2500	750	400

Winchester sn: 2,305,850-2,536,493

NIB	Exc.	V.G.	Good	Fair	Poor
—	3500	2800	1500	500	300

Winchester sn: 1,601,150-1,640,000 "win-13"

NIB	Exc.	V.G.	Good	Fair	Poor
—	3500	2200	1800	1500	850

Harrington & Richardson Production

NIB	Exc.	V.G.	Good	Fair	Poor
—	1800	1200	900	600	300

International Harvester Production

NIB	Exc.	V.G.	Good	Fair	Poor
—	2200	1500	800	500	250

International Harvester/with Springfield Receiver (postage stamp)

NIB	Exc.	V.G.	Good	Fair	Poor
—	2800	1500	1000	—	—

International Harvester/with Springfield Receiver (arrow head)

NIB	Exc.	V.G.	Good	Fair	Poor
—	2800	1500	1000	—	—

International Harvester/with Springfield Receiver (Gap letter)

NIB	Exc.	V.G.	Good	Fair	Poor
—	2800	1500	1000	—	—

International Harvester/with Harrington & Richardson Receiver

NIB	Exc.	V.G.	Good	Fair	Poor
—	1900	1200	900	—	—

British Garands (Lend Lease)

NIB	Exc.	V.G.	Good	Fair	Poor
—	1300	1200	875	500	275

M1 Garand Cutaway

NIB	Exc.	V.G.	Good	Fair	Poor
—	3000	2500	1000	600	500

NOTE: For examples with documentation add 300 percent.

GARBI
Eibar, Spain

Model 51-B

A 12 gauge boxlock shotgun, also available in 16 and 20 gauge, with double triggers, automatic ejectors, case hardened or coin-finished receiver and walnut stock.

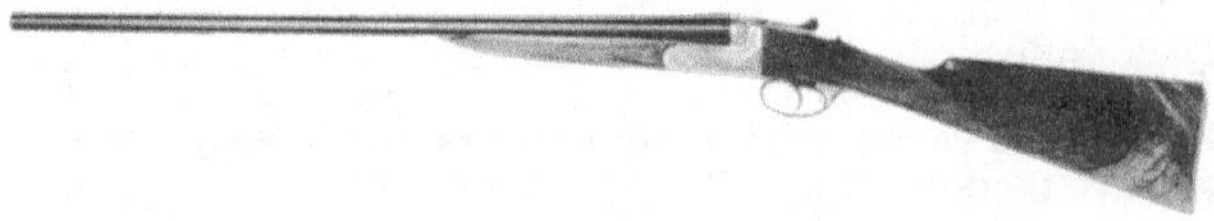

NIB	Exc.	V.G.	Good	Fair	Poor
1750	1200	850	600	—	—

Model 62-B

A 12 gauge sidelock shotgun, also chambered for 16 and 20 gauge with double triggers, extractors and cocking indicators. Engraved, case hardened or coin-finished receiver and walnut stock.

NIB	Exc.	V.G.	Good	Fair	Poor
1500	1050	850	650	325	175

Model 71

A 12, 16, or 20 gauge Holland & Holland sidelock shotgun with various barrel lengths and choke combinations, automatic ejectors and a single-selective trigger. Engraved with fine English-style scrollwork and walnut stock. Discontinued in 1988.

NIB	Exc.	V.G.	Good	Fair	Poor
2500	2000	1800	1500	700	225

Model 100

A 12, 16, or 20 gauge Holland & Holland sidelock shotgun with chopper-lump barrels, automatic ejectors, and a single trigger. Engraved in the Purdey style, with walnut stock.

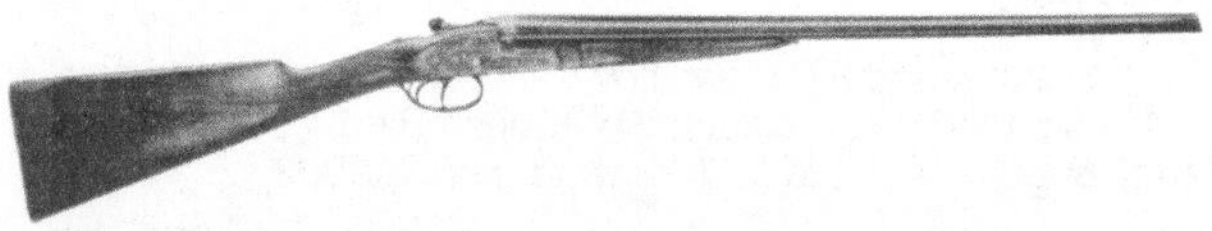

NIB	Exc.	V.G.	Good	Fair	Poor
3500	3000	2500	2000	900	250

Model 101

As above, with floral engraving. Discontinued in 1988 in this form, then furnished with hand-engraved Continental scroll with round body action.

NIB	Exc.	V.G.	Good	Fair	Poor
6100	5250	3250	2500	1000	350

Model 102

As above, with Holland & Holland style, engraving and also in 28 gauge. Discontinued in 1988.

NIB	Exc.	V.G.	Good	Fair	Poor
4500	3750	3200	1600	600	250

Model 103A

This model has Purdey-style engraving with high grade wood and checkering.

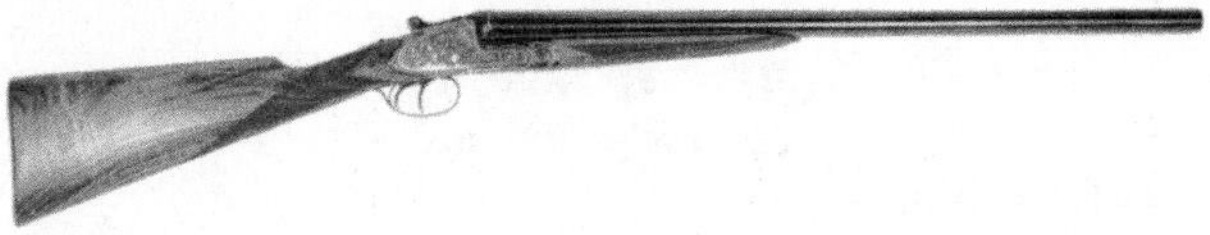

NIB	Exc.	V.G.	Good	Fair	Poor
14100	10000	7500	5500	2750	1000

Model 103A Royal

Same as above but with special high quality engraving, very fancy wood, hand matted rib.

NIB	Exc.	V.G.	Good	Fair	Poor
16000	12500	8500	6500	3750	1200

Model 103B

In 12, 16, 20, or 28 gauge, Holland & Holland sidelock shotgun with various barrel lengths and choke combinations, chopper-lump barrels, Holland & Holland easy-opening mechanism, automatic ejectors, single-selective trigger, and Purdey-type scroll engraving.

NIB	Exc.	V.G.	Good	Fair	Poor
21600	16750	10500	7750	6000	1500

Model 103B Royal

Same as above but with high quality engraving, very fancy wood, hand matted rib.

NIB	Exc.	V.G.	Good	Fair	Poor
22500	18000	13000	8500	4200	1600

Model 120

As above, with engraved hunting scenes. Discontinued in 1988.

NIB	Exc.	V.G.	Good	Fair	Poor
21600	16750	10500	7750	6000	1500

Model 200

As above, Magnum proofed, double locking screws and 100 percent floral scroll engraving.

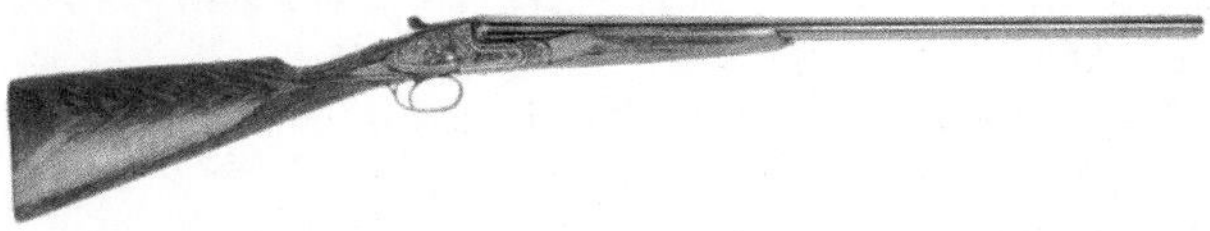

NIB	Exc.	V.G.	Good	Fair	Poor
17100	13500	9500	6500	300	1250

Model Special

A special order gun. Too rare to price.

Express Rifle

This is a best-quality sidelock side-by-side double rifle. Stock has pistol grip and cheekpiece. Choice of English scroll or floral engraving. Calibers are 7x65R, 9.3x74R, or .375 H&H.

NIB	Exc.	V.G.	Good	Fair	Poor
21000	15000	12000	7750	6000	1500

GARCIA

(formerly Firearms International of Wash., D.C.)

Garcia Bronco

A single-shot .410 shotgun or .22 LR or .22 Magnum rifle with swing out action, modeled somewhat after the old Hamilton No. 7. Barrel length is 18.5". Stock is a one-piece metal skeletonized affair. Weight is approximately 3.5 lbs. Introduced in 1968 and discontinued in 1978. Built in U.S.A.

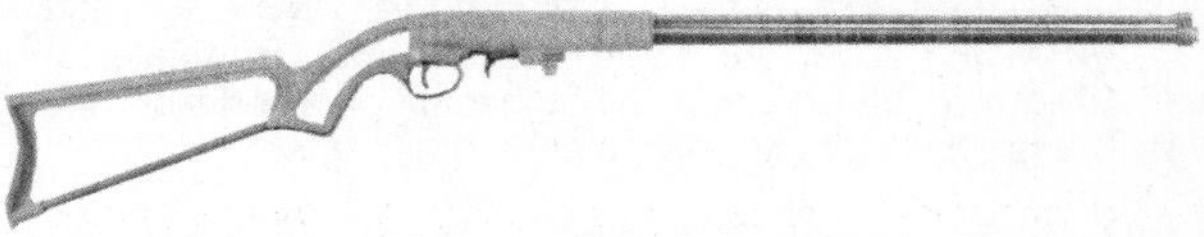

NIB	Exc.	V.G.	Good	Fair	Poor
350	250	225	125	90	50

Garcia Bronco .22/.410

This is an over-and-under shotgun/rifle combination. The over barrel is .22 Long Rifle and the under barrel is chambered for .410 bore. Barrel length is 18.5". One-piece metal skeletonized stock. Introduced in 1976 and discontinued in 1978. Weight is about 4 lbs.

NIB	Exc.	V.G.	Good	Fair	Poor
500	375	295	200	115	75

Garcia Musketeer

This model is a bolt-action rifle chambered for the .243, .264, .270, .30-06, .307 Win. Mag., .308 Norma, 7mm Rem. Mag., and .300 Win. Mag. Fitted with a checkered walnut stock, open sights, pistol grip, hinged floorplate, and adjustable trigger. Introduced in 1970 and discontinued in 1972.

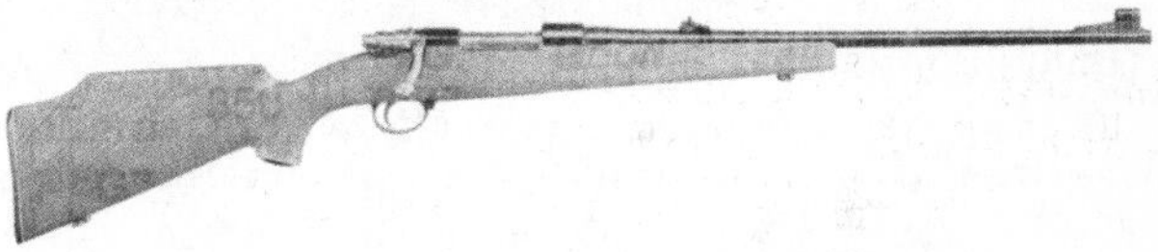

NIB	Exc.	V.G.	Good	Fair	Poor
600	500	350	250	200	150

GEHA

Germany

An altered Mauser 98 rifle rebarreled for use with 12 gauge shotgun shells. Barrel length 26.5", military stock shortened to half length and the butt inlaid with a brass medallion marked "Geha." Manufactured from approximately 1919 to 1929.

NIB	Exc.	V.G.	Good	Fair	Poor
—	375	225	150	100	75

GENEZ, A. G.

New York, New York

Located at 9 Chambers Street, Genez made a wide variety of firearms during his working life (ca. 1850 to 1875). The most commonly encountered of his arms today are single-shot percussion pistols and percussion double-barrel shotguns. More rarely seen are single-shot percussion target rifles. A number of the arms he made were decorated by Louis D. Nimschke. Genez products signed by Nimschke command considerable premiums over the values for the standard firearms listed.

Double-Barrel Shotgun

Most often encountered in 12 gauge with varying barrel lengths; blued steel furniture, and walnut stock.

NIB	Exc.	V.G.	Good	Fair	Poor
—	—	2800	1950	500	250

GEORGIA ARMORY

Milledgeville, George

Established in 1862, this concern produced a rifle based upon the U.S. Model 1855 Harper's Ferry Rifle. Nearly identical in all respects to the Harpers Ferry, the Georgia Armory rifle had a lockplate patterned after the U.S. Model 1841 Rifle. Lock marked "G.A. ARMORY" over the date (1862 or 1863). Buttplate tangs marked with serial numbers. The highest known serial number is 309. These rifles were fitted with saber bayonets.

NIB	Exc.	V.G.	Good	Fair	Poor
—	—	65000	22000	10500	3000

GEVARM

St. Etienne, France

Model A-6

This .22 caliber semi-automatic rifle fires from an open bolt. It is fitted with a one-piece stock. Furnished with a 8-round magazine. The E-1 20 magazine will not fit the A-6 without hand fitting. Add 15 percent for higher-end A7 model. These rifles are increasingly popular on the secondary market because of their open-bolt design.

NIB	Exc.	V.G.	Good	Fair	Poor
—	800	695	475	275	165

E-1 Autoloading Rifle

A .22 caliber semi-automatic rifle with a 19" barrel, 8-shot magazine, blued with walnut grips. Two-piece stock. A 20-round magazine is an option.

NIB	Exc.	V.G.	Good	Fair	Poor
—	550	450	295	200	150

GIB

Eibar, Spain

10 Gauge Shotgun

A 10 gauge Magnum boxlock double-barrel shotgun with 32" matte-ribbed barrels. Case hardened, blued with walnut grips.

NIB	Exc.	V.G.	Good	Fair	Poor
—	700	495	275	150	100

GIBBS

New York, New York

Gibbs Carbine

A .52 caliber single-shot percussion carbine with a sliding 22" round barrel. Blued, case hardened with a walnut stock. The lock marked with an American eagle and "Wm. F. Brooks/Manf New York/1863." The breech marked "L.H. Gibbs/Patd/Jany 8, 1856." There were only 1,050 produced.

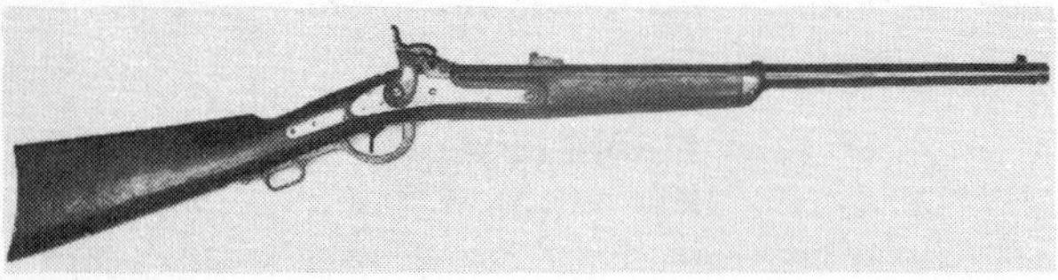

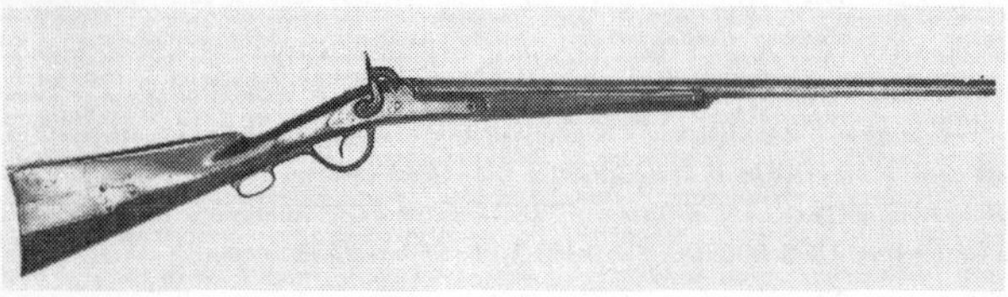

Courtesy Milwaukee Public Museum, Milwaukee, Wisconsin

NIB	Exc.	V.G.	Good	Fair	Poor
—	—	5950	2200	900	350

GIBBS, J. & G. / LATER GIBBS, GEORGE

Bristol, England

Established in 1835, this concern continues in business to this day.

J. & G. Gibbs	4 Redcliffe Street	1835-1842
George Gibbs	142 Thomas Street	
	Clare Street	
	39 Corn Street	

While initially known for exceptionally accurate single-shot rifles, the firm subsequently established a reputation for first quality bolt-action magazine rifles in a variety of large bore calibers. Bolt rifles by Gibbs, Rigby and others havebecome extremely desirable, especially in the African chamberings.

GIBBS GUNS, INC.

Greenback, Tennessee

Mark 45 Carbine

A .45 ACP caliber semi-automatic rifle with a 16.5" barrel, a 5-, 15-, 30-, or 90-shot magazine. Blued, with a walnut buttstock and forend. A nickel-plated model was available as an option and would bring approximately $25 additional. Discontinued in 1988.

NIB	Exc.	V.G.	Good	Fair	Poor
650	475	275	200	125	100

GIBBS RIFLE COMPANY

Martinsburg, West Virginia

SEE—Parker-Hale

This company imports Parker Hale black powder replicas and WW II surplus military firearms such as the Mauser Model 1888, Model 71/84, and the Israeli K98. The company also produced historical remakes and specialty rifles.

Enfield No. 5 Jungle Carbine

This is a remake of the original British rifle. Chambered for the .303 cartridge and fitted with a 20" barrel with flash hider. Magazine capacity is 10 rounds. Weight about 7.75 lbs. New stock.

NIB	Exc.	V.G.	Good	Fair	Poor
350	295	200	150	100	50

Enfield No. 7 Jungle Carbine

This model is chambered for the .308 Winchester cartridge. Fitted with a 20" barrel with flash hider. Magazine capacity is 12 rounds. Adjustable rear sight. Original wood. Weight is about 8 lbs.

NIB	Exc.	V.G.	Good	Fair	Poor
350	295	200	150	100	50

Quest Extreme Carbine

An updated design of the No. 5 Jungle Carbine. Chambered for .303 cartridge with 20" barrel. Nickel finish and new hardwood stock. Brass butt trap. Weight is about 7.75 lbs.

NIB	Exc.	V.G.	Good	Fair	Poor
350	295	200	150	100	50

Quest II Extreme Carbine

Updated version of the No. 7 Jungle Carbine with nickel finish, see through scope mount and hardwood stock. Chambered for the .308 cartridge. Magazine capacity is 12 rounds. Barrel length is 20" and weight is about 8 lbs.

NIB	Exc.	V.G.	Good	Fair	Poor
350	295	200	150	100	50

Quest III Extreme Carbine

Similar to Quest II but with synthetic stock.

NIB	Exc.	V.G.	Good	Fair	Poor
350	295	200	150	100	50

Summit 45-70 Carbine

This bolt-action is built on the Enfield No. 4 action and rebarreled to .45-70 caliber. Fitted to a 21" barrel. MIL SPEC peep sight and checkered walnut stock. Weight is about 8.5 lbs.

NIB	Exc.	V.G.	Good	Fair	Poor
400	325	225	175	125	75

Mauser M71/84

Chambered for the 11mm Mauser cartridge and fitted with a 31.5" barrel. This model has been arsenal reconditioned but is otherwise original.Weight is about 10 lbs.

NIB	Exc.	V.G.	Good	Fair	Poor
300	250	175	150	100	50

Mauser M88 Commission Rifle

Fitted with a 30" barrel and chambered for the 8mm cartridge. This model has been arsenal reconditioned but is otherwise original. Weight is about 10 lbs.

NIB	Exc.	V.G.	Good	Fair	Poor
200	175	120	100	65	50

GOLDEN EAGLE

Nikko Limited
Tochigi, Japan

SHOTGUNS

Golden Eagle Model 5000 Grade I

A 12 or 20 gauge Over/Under shotgun with of 26", 28", and 30" barrels with ventilated ribs and various choke combinations, a single-selective trigger and automatic ejectors. Blued, with a walnut stock that has an eagle's head inlaid into the pistol grip cap. Manufactured between 1976 and the early 1980s.

NIB	Exc.	V.G.	Good	Fair	Poor
1500	900	750	600	475	250

Grade I Skeet

As above, with a 26" or 28" barrel having a wide competition rib.

NIB	Exc.	V.G.	Good	Fair	Poor
1300	900	750	600	475	250

Grade I Trap

Similar to the skeet model, with a 30" or 32" barrel.

NIB	Exc.	V.G.	Good	Fair	Poor
1300	900	750	600	475	250

Model 5000 Grade II

As above, but more finely finished with an eagle's head inlaid in the receiver in gold.

NIB	Exc.	V.G.	Good	Fair	Poor
1500	1000	800	600	475	250

Grandee Grade III

As above, but more elaborately engraved.

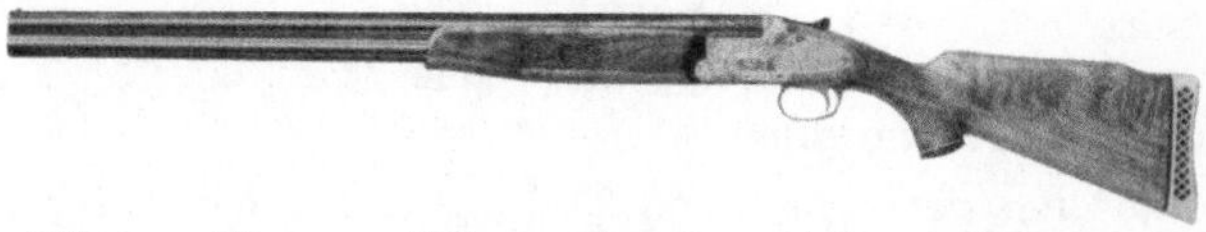

NIB	Exc.	V.G.	Good	Fair	Poor
2500	2000	1750	1400	850	500

RIFLES

Model 7000 Grade I

A Mauser bolt-action rifle chambered for all popular American calibers with a 24" or 26" barrel, walnut stock and a rosewood pistol-grip cap and forend tip.

NIB	Exc.	V.G.	Good	Fair	Poor
700	600	500	375	300	200

Model 7000 African

As above in .375 H&H and .458 Win. Mag. caliber with open sights.

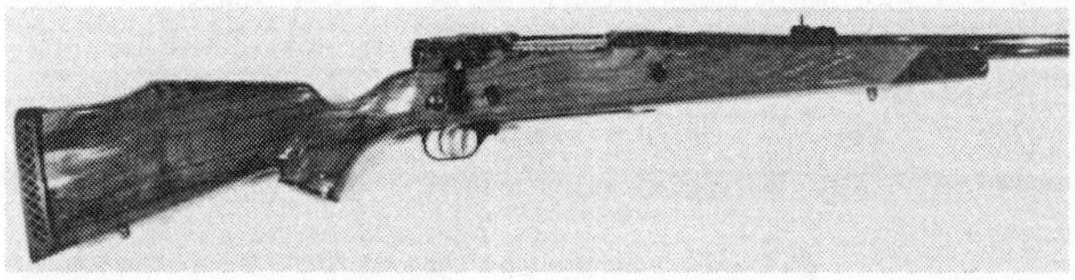

NIB	Exc.	V.G.	Good	Fair	Poor
800	650	550	400	325	250

Model 7000 Grade II

As above, but engraved.

NIB	Exc.	V.G.	Good	Fair	Poor
900	750	625	450	350	275

GONCZ CO.

Hollywood, California

GC Carbine

A 7.63mm Mauser, 9mm Parabellum, .38 Super, and .45 ACP caliber semi-automatic rifle with a 16.1" barrel. Black with a walnut stock. Later production models were stainless steel.

NIB	Exc.	V.G.	Good	Fair	Poor
650	500	395	275	200	125

GC Stainless

As above, in stainless steel. Introduced in 1987.

NIB	Exc.	V.G.	Good	Fair	Poor
800	550	425	325	250	175

GC Collector's Edition

A limited edition with hand-polished finish.

NIB	Exc.	V.G.	Good	Fair	Poor
875	600	500	425	350	225

Halogen Carbine

The GC Carbine with a powerful light source mounted under the barrel. Chambered for 9mm and .45 ACP only.

NIB	Exc.	V.G.	Good	Fair	Poor
750	500	395	275	200	125

Laser Carbine

As above, with a laser sighting system effective to 400 yards.

NIB	Exc.	V.G.	Good	Fair	Poor
1500	1250	1000	750	650	500

GRANGER, G.
St. Etienne, France

Side-by-Side Shotgun

A custom-order 12, 16, and 20 gauge boxlock double-barrel shotgun. Manufactured since 1902. ecause the gun is imported the value of the dollar frequently determines price movement.

NIB	Exc.	V.G.	Good	Fair	Poor
—	16500	13000	8500	4250	1500

GRAS
France

Model 1874

An 11mm caliber bolt-action rifle with a 32" barrel with a walnut stock, a barrel band and a metal tip. The bayonet is a spike blade with a wood handle and a brass butt cap.

NIB	Exc.	V.G.	Good	Fair	Poor
—	500	375	225	150	75

GREENE
Milbury, Massachusetts

Greene Breechloading Rifle

A .53 caliber single-shot bolt-action percussion rifle with a 35" barrel, under hammer and full length walnut stock secured by three barrel bands. Marked "Greene's Patent/Nov. 17, 1857." Approximately 4,000 were made by the A.H. Waters Armory between 1859 and 1862.

NIB	Exc.	V.G.	Good	Fair	Poor
—	—	3250	1050	400	200

GREENER, W. W. LTD.
Birmingham, England

Perhaps the best known manufacturer of double-barrel shotguns in England during the 19th Century. Greener was also a prolific author. His name will forever be associated with the "Greener Crossbolt." Greener hammer-model shotguns were quite popular in the United States during the last half of the 19th century. The company is still in business in Birmingham and makes a limited number of custom guns. Current prices on the used gun market range for basic boxlock, non-ejector models in the $1,500 to $2,000 range. Top of the line models from the first half of the 20th centuy can bring $100,000 or more. Because of the wide range of models and grades, a professional appraisal would be necessary before any transaction.

GREIFELT & CO.
Suhl, Germany

OVER/UNDER SHOTGUNS

Grade No. 1

NOTE: 28 gauge and .410 add 25 percent.

NIB	Exc.	V.G.	Good	Fair	Poor
—	3750	3250	2950	1750	1000

Grade No. 3

Similar to the No. 1, with less engraving. Manufactured prior to WWII.

NIB	Exc.	V.G.	Good	Fair	Poor
—	3250	2700	1850	1250	750

NOTE: 28 gauge and .410 add 25 percent.

Model 143E

The post-war version of the No. 1. Not made in 28 gauge or .410 bore.

NIB	Exc.	V.G.	Good	Fair	Poor
—	2750	2300	1650	1200	750

Combination Gun

A combination Over/Under rifle/shotgun manufactured in all bores and a variety of rifle calibers with 24" or 26" barrels. Made prior to 1939.

NIB	Exc.	V.G.	Good	Fair	Poor
—	5800	4750	3950	2500	1250

NOTE: Deduct 40 percent if rifle caliber is obsolete. 28 gauge and .410 add 25 percent. Automatic ejectors add 10 percent.

SIDE-BY-SIDE SHOTGUNS

Model 22

A 12 or 20 gauge boxlock double-barrel shotgun with 28" or 30" barrels, sideplates, double triggers and extractors. Blued, case hardened with a walnut stock. Manufactured after 1945.

NIB	Exc.	V.G.	Good	Fair	Poor
—	2500	1950	1500	500	200

Model 22E

As above, with automatic ejectors.

NIB	Exc.	V.G.	Good	Fair	Poor
—	2750	2300	1650	550	225

Model 103

A 12 and 16 gauge boxlock shotgun with a 28" or a 30" barrel, double triggers and extractors. Walnut stock with a pistol or straight English-style grip. Post-war model.

NIB	Exc.	V.G.	Good	Fair	Poor
—	2250	1800	1350	400	175

Model 103E

As above, with automatic ejectors.

NIB	Exc.	V.G.	Good	Fair	Poor
—	2500	1950	1500	500	200

Drilling

A 12, 16, or 20 gauge double-barrel shotgun fitted with a rifle barrel, chambered for a variety of cartridges. Barrel length 26", boxlock-action, double triggers, extractors and folding rear sight. Manufactured prior to 1939.

NIB	Exc.	V.G.	Good	Fair	Poor
—	3750	3200	2950	900	300

NOTE: Deduct 40 percent if rifle caliber is obsolete. 20 gauge add 10 percent.

GRENDEL, INC.
Rockledge, Florida

SRT-20F Compact Rifle

A .308 caliber bolt-action rifle with 20" finned match grade barrel, 9-shot magazine, a folding synthetic stock, integral bipod and no sights.

Courtesy Jim Supica, Old Town Station

NIB	Exc.	V.G.	Good	Fair	Poor
575	500	425	325	250	100

SRT-24

As above, with a 24" barrel. Discontinued in 1988.

NIB	Exc.	V.G.	Good	Fair	Poor
600	525	450	350	275	100

R-31 Carbine

This semi-automatic carbine was introduced in 1991 and is chambered for the .22 WMR cartridge. Fitted with a 16" barrel with muzzlebrake and a telescoping tubular stock. Magazine capacity is 30 rounds. Weight is about 4 lbs. Discontinued in 1994.

NIB	Exc.	V.G.	Good	Fair	Poor
300	250	200	150	125	100

GRIFFIN & HOWE
New York, New York

Established in 1923, this firm manufactured on custom order a variety of bolt-action sporting rifles. These rifles have an excellent reputation and are quite desirable.

GRULLA
Eibar, Spain

Model 216RL

This side-by-side shotgun is offered in 12, 16, 20, and 28 gauge, as welll as .410 bore. Barrel length is 28". Articulated double triggers. Action body is H&H side locks. Select walnut with straight grip and splinter forend. Fixed chokes. Choice of different styles of engraving. Weight range from 7.1 lbs. for 12 gauge to 6 lbs. for .410 bore.

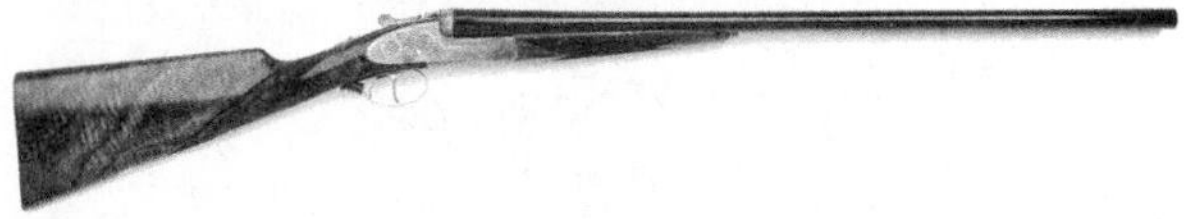

NIB	Exc.	V.G.	Good	Fair	Poor
9000	5750	3500	2000	1350	500

NOTE: Add $300 for 28 gauge and .410 bore.

Royal

As above but fitted with a 7-pin H&H-style lock.

NIB	Exc.	V.G.	Good	Fair	Poor
9500	6250	3800	2500	1750	750

GUERINI, CAESAR
Italy

This line of Italian over-and-under guns was introduced into the U.S.A. in 2004.

Flyway

This over-and-under 12 gauge 3" gun is offered with either 28" or 30" vent-rib barrels with choke tubes. Checkered walnut stock with pistol grip. Trap-style forearm with finger grooves. Single-selective trigger and ejectors. Weight is about 8 lbs. depending on barrel length.

NIB	Exc.	V.G.	Good	Fair	Poor
2795	2300	1750	1300	900	500

Woodlander

This model is offered in 12, 20 and 28 gauge with choice of 26" or 28" vent-rib barrels and choke tubes. Frame is case hardened with gold ruffed grouse on bottom of receiver. The checkered Circassian walnut stock with straight grip is oil finished. Single-selective trigger and ejectors. Weight is about 6.25 lbs. for the 20 gauge and 6.15 lbs. for the 28 gauge.

NIB	Exc.	V.G.	Good	Fair	Poor
2795	2300	1750	1300	900	500

Magnus Light

This model is offered in 12, 20, or 28 gauge with choice of 26" or 28" vent-rib barrels with choke tubes. Alloy frame with Tinaloy finish with side plates. Scroll engraved with gold game birds. Checkered walnut stock with Prince of Wales-style pistol grip. Weight of 12 gauge is about 6 lbs.; 20 gauge is 5.4 lbs. and the 28 gauge is about 5.25 lbs.

NIB	Exc.	V.G.	Good	Fair	Poor
3500	2995	2000	1500	1000	500

Magnus

Similar to the Magnus Light but with case hardened steel receiver. Weight is about 6.75 lbs. for the 12 gauge, 6.5 lbs. for the 20 gauge, and 6.25 lbs. for the 28 gauge.

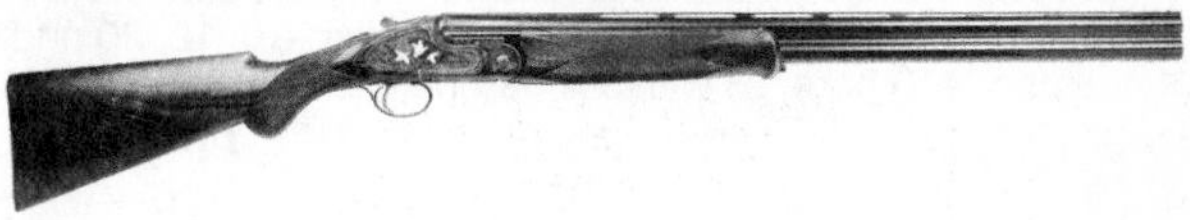

NIB	Exc.	V.G.	Good	Fair	Poor
3500	2995	2000	1500	1000	500

Tempio

This over-and-under gun is offered in 12, 20, and 28 gauge with choice of 26" or 28" barrels with choke tubes. Checkered Circassian walnut stock with Prince of Wales-style pistol grip. Alloy receiver is a gray finish of Tinaloy. Engraved with scroll and gold game birds. Single-selective trigger with ejectors. Weight is about 6.8 lbs. for 12 gauge, 6.4 lbs. for 20 gauge, and 6.25 lbs. for the 28 gauge.

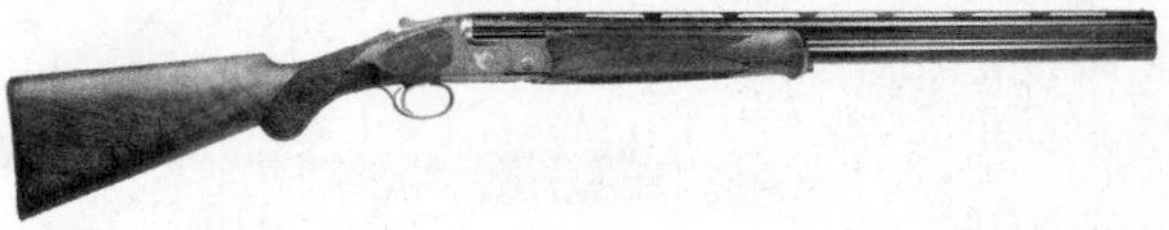

NIB	Exc.	V.G.	Good	Fair	Poor
2450	2000	1500	1050	600	250

Forum/Forum Sporting

This model is offered in 12, 20 and 28 gauge, with choice of 26" or 28" barrels on the Forum and 30", 32", or 34" on the Forum Sporting. Gun has silver receiver with scroll and game scene engraving with side plates.

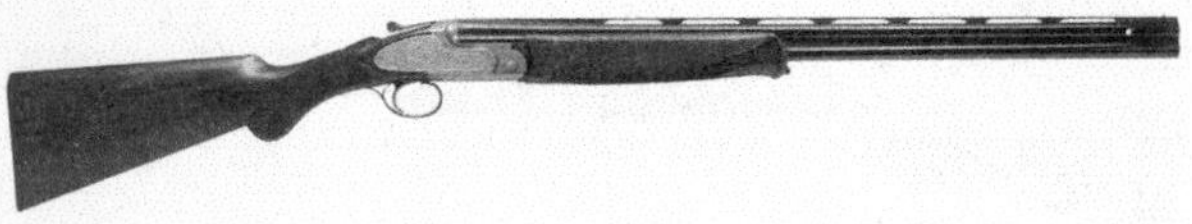

NIB	*Exc.*	*V.G.*	*Good*	*Fair*	*Poor*
7250	6000	4750	3250	1600	700

NOTE: Add $300 for Forum Sporting.

Summit Sporting/Summit Limited

Offered in 12, 20, or 28 gauge with choice of 30" or 32" vent-rib barrels with extended choke tubes. Alloy receiver with engraving. Single-selective trigger is adjustable for length of pull. Ejectors. Checkered walnut stock with pistol grip. Weight of 12 gauge is about 8 lbs., the 20 gauge about 7.5 lbs., and the 28 gauge about 7.45 lbs.

NIB	*Exc.*	*V.G.*	*Good*	*Fair*	*Poor*
2950	2300	1650	1200	750	300

NOTE: For Summit Limited add $300.

Magnus Sporting

This model is similar to the Summit but with upgraded wood and sidelock-style receiver with scroll engraving and gold game birds.

NIB	*Exc.*	*V.G.*	*Good*	*Fair*	*Poor*
3500	2900	2300	1650	1000	500

Essex

New in 2006, this over-and-under with oil-finished stock and coin finished receiver with scroll engraving is available in 12, 20 and 28 gauges and .410 bore, all with 3" chambers.

NIB	*Exc.*	*V.G.*	*Good*	*Fair*	*Poor*
4250	3500	2300	1650	1000	500

GUSTAF, CARL

Eskilstuna, Sweden

Bolt-Action Rifle

A 6.5x55, 7x64, .270, 7mm Magnum, .308, .30-06, and 9.3x62 caliber bolt-action rifle with a 24" barrel. Blued with a walnut stock in either the classic style or with a Monte Carlo cheekpiece. Manufactured between 1970 and 1977.

NIB	*Exc.*	*V.G.*	*Good*	*Fair*	*Poor*
—	700	600	450	325	150

Bolt-Action Rifle Grade II

As above, with better walnut and a rosewood pistol grip cap and forend tip.

NIB	*Exc.*	*V.G.*	*Good*	*Fair*	*Poor*
—	850	650	475	375	175

Bolt-Action Rifle Grade III

As above, with a high-gloss finish and a finely figured walnut stock.

NIB	*Exc.*	*V.G.*	*Good*	*Fair*	*Poor*
—	950	700	550	475	275

Deluxe Bolt-Action

As above, with an engraved floorplate and trigger guard, a Damascened bolt, and a high-grade French walnut stock. Manufactured between 1970 and 1977.

NIB	*Exc.*	*V.G.*	*Good*	*Fair*	*Poor*
—	1250	900	650	450	300

Varmint Model

A .222, .22-250, .243, and 6.5x55 caliber bolt-action rifle with 27" barrel and a large bolt knob made of Bakelite. Furnished without open sights and has a heavy target-type stock. Manufactured in 1970 only.

NIB	*Exc.*	*V.G.*	*Good*	*Fair*	*Poor*
—	700	600	450	325	150

Grand Prix Target

A .22 caliber single-shot, bolt-action rifle with a 27" barrel and adjustable weights. Furnished without sights and with an adjustable butt target stock. Only manufactured in 1970.

NIB	*Exc.*	*V.G.*	*Good*	*Fair*	*Poor*
—	700	600	450	325	150

Model 2000

A 6.5x55, .243, .270, .308, and .30-06 caliber bolt-action rifle with a 60 percent bolt lift and a cold swagged barrel and action. Furnished with open sights. Blued, walnut stock with a Monte Carlo cheekpiece. Manufactured until 1985.

NIB	*Exc.*	*V.G.*	*Good*	*Fair*	*Poor*
—	675	575	400	300	150

GWYN & CAMPBELL

Hamilton, Ohio

Union Carbine

A .52 caliber single-shot breech loading percussion carbine with a round/octagonal 20" barrel marked "Gwyn & Campbell/ Patent/1862/ Hamilton,O." Blued, case hardened with a walnut stock. Approximately 8,500 were made between 1862 and 1865.

Courtesy Milwaukee Public Museum, Milwaukee, Wisconsin

NIB	*Exc.*	*V.G.*	*Good*	*Fair*	*Poor*
—	—	4000	1975	500	300

H

HALL, ALEXANDER

New York, New York

Revolving Rifle

A .58 caliber percussion revolving rifle with a 15-shot open centered cylinder. The frame was made of brass, the barrel and cylinder of iron and the stock of walnut. Manufactured during the 1850s in limited quantities. This is a very rare firearm.

NIB	*Exc.*	*V.G.*	*Good*	*Fair*	*Poor*
—	—	27500	12500	3750	1300

HALL-NORTH

Middletown, Connecticut

MODEL 1840 CARBINE

This carbine was manufactured by Simeon North and was chambered for .52 caliber percussion. It is a single-shot, breech-loading, smoothbore with a 21" round barrel. It has a full-length stock held on by two barrel bands. There is a ramrod mounted under the barrel, and the mountings are of iron. The lock is case hardened, and the barrel is brown. The stock is walnut. The markings are "US/S. North/Midltn/Conn." There are two distinct variations, both produced under military contract.

Type 1 Carbine

This model has a squared, right-angled breech lever mounted on the trigger plate. There were 500 of these manufactured in 1840.

NIB	*Exc.*	*V.G.*	*Good*	*Fair*	*Poor*
—	—	9000	4000	1750	1000

Type 2 Carbine

This variation features a curved, breech-operating lever that is known as a fishtail. There were approximately 6,000 of these manufactured from 1840 to 1843. Some have an 8" bar and ring.

NIB	*Exc.*	*V.G.*	*Good*	*Fair*	*Poor*
—	—	7500	2500	1100	550

HAMBUSH, JOSEPH

Ferlach, Austria

Boxlock Side-by-Side Shotgun

A custom-order boxlock double-barrel shotgun chambered for all gauges, single-selective or double trigger and automatic ejectors. It features workmanship of a high order, and all specification could vary with the customer's wishes. Engraved with hunting scenes. This is a rare gun and is not often encountered on today's market.

NIB	*Exc.*	*V.G.*	*Good*	*Fair*	*Poor*
—	1950	1100	950	575	375

NOTE: Pricing is only estimated as not enough are traded to provide accurate values.

Sidelock Side-by-Side Shotgun

Similar to the above, but features a full sidelock-action.

NIB	*Exc.*	*V.G.*	*Good*	*Fair*	*Poor*
—	3800	2500	1750	1600	1350

HAMILTON RIFLE COMPANY

Plymouth, Michigan

Manufacturer of inexpensive .22 caliber rifles established by Clarence J. Hamilton and his son Coello. The company was established in 1898 in Plymouth, Michigan. The company ceased production in 1945. Over 1 million rifles were produced between 1900 and 1911.NOTE: Despite the fact that there were many Hamilton rifles sold, most of these little guns were used hard and many did not survive. Hamilton rifles in excellent condition are hardly ever encountered. No prices are quoted for rifles in this condition as few exist. Further information about these rifles is gratefully accepted by the editor.

Model 7

The first rifle produced by the company, it was made entirely of castings and stampings. It was nickel plated. Chambered for the .22 Short cartridge with an 8" brass-lined barrel that pivots for loading. The stock was a metal skeleton. Production ceased in 1901 with a total of 44,000 rifles produced.

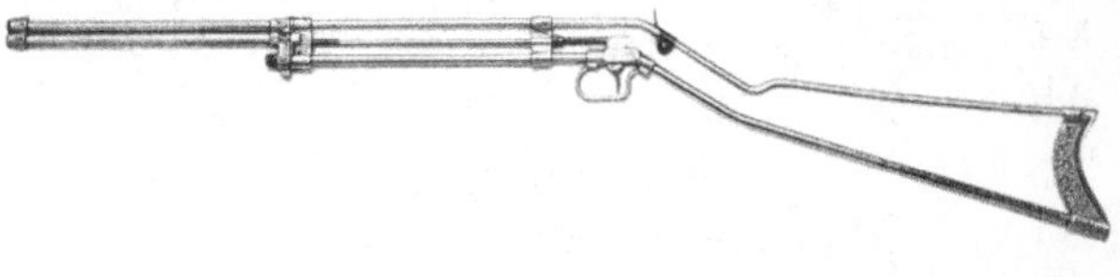

Courtesy William F. Krause

Hamilton Model 7

NIB	*Exc.*	*V.G.*	*Good*	*Fair*	*Poor*
—	750	500	450	300	195

Model 11

Similar to the Model 7 but fitted with a board-like walnut stock. There are markings stamped into the buttstock: HAMILTON RIFLES CO., PLYMOUTH, MICH., PAT. PENDING NO.11. The Model 11 was produced from 1900 to 1902 and approximately 22,000 were sold.

NIB	*Exc.*	*V.G.*	*Good*	*Fair*	*Poor*
—	700	475	300	200	150

Model 23

This was the first bolt-action rifle made by the company. The receiver is a steel tube with a loading port in the top where the barrel joins the receiver. The bolt handle is located at the extreme rear of the bolt. The cocking knob must be operated manually. Walnut stock either rounded or flat. Chamber for the .22 Short and .22 Long cartridges. 15" brass lined barrel. Blued finish. Weighs about 3 lbs. Produced from 1905 to 1909. About 25,000 guns were sold.

NIB	Exc.	V.G.	Good	Fair	Poor
—	700	475	300	200	150

Model 27

Single-shot tip-up .22 caliber rifle with stamped steel receiver. Barrel length 16" brass lined or 14-7/8"; overall length 30". First produced in 1906.

NIB	Exc.	V.G.	Good	Fair	Poor
—	475	300	200	150	100

Model 027

As above with a walnut stock. First produced in 1908.

NIB	Exc.	V.G.	Good	Fair	Poor
—	495	300	200	150	100

Model 31

Introduced in 1910 this single-shot rifle is chambered for the .22 Short and Long cartridge. Fitted with a 15-3/4" barrel with brass liner. It is a tip-up design. Blued finish. Weighs about 2.25 lbs.

NIB	Exc.	V.G.	Good	Fair	Poor
—	725	575	400	250	200

Model 35 or Boys' Military Rifle

Single-shot .22 caliber rifle with a full-length oval walnut straight-grip stock and 15-3/4" brass lined barrel. Produced from 1915 to 1918. Sold with a stamped steel bayonet. Few bayonets survive.

NIB	Exc.	V.G.	Good	Fair	Poor
—	950	700	450	250	125

NOTE: Add $150 for bayonet to above prices.

Model 39

This was the only repeating rifle built by the company. It is a hammerless slide-action design with a tubular magazine. Magazine capacity is 15 rounds of .22 Short. Barrel length is 16" with brass liner. Walnut stock with blade front sight. Produced from 1922 to 1930. Weighs about 4 lbs.

NIB	Exc.	V.G.	Good	Fair	Poor
—	575	300	200	150	100

Model 43

This is a bolt-action design with the loading port on the top of the barrel. There is no external cocking knob but the bolt is pulled to the rear when in the locked position. Chambered for the .22 Short and .22 Long cartridges. 15.75" brass lined barrel. Fitted with an oval walnut stock with blade front sight and open non-adjustable rear sight. Weighs about 3 lbs. Built from 1924 to 1932.

NIB	Exc.	V.G.	Good	Fair	Poor
—	575	300	200	150	100

Model 47

This is a bolt-action single-shot rifle with the loading port located on top of the barrel. It was chambered for the .22 Short and Long cartridges. The cocking knob is located at the rear of the bolt handle. Early Model 47 were built with 16" brass lined barrels. Later examples were fitted with 18.25" steel lined barrels. Early guns had an oval buttstock while later guns had a pistol grip stock. Very late guns had an all-steel barrel. Produced from 1927 to 1932.

NIB	Exc.	V.G.	Good	Fair	Poor
—	575	475	300	200	150

Model 51

This was a conventional type bolt-action rifle with the cocking knob located at the rear of the bolt. Two styles of buttstocks were used: a flat style or later an oval shape. This was the first Hamilton rifle chambered for the .22 LR cartridge. Barrel was 20" steel. Finish was blue. Weight was approximately 3.5 lbs. Produced from 1935 to 1941.

NIB	Exc.	V.G.	Good	Fair	Poor
—	550	400	250	200	150

Model 55

This bolt-action rifle was chambered for the .22 Short, Long, and LR cartridges. Fitted with a 20" steel barrel with bead front sight and open adjustable rear sight. Walnut stock. This is the rarest Hamilton rifle. Only one example is known. Produced from late 1941 to early 1942.

NIB	Exc.	V.G.	Good	Fair	Poor
—	1000	—	—	—	—

HAMMERLI, SA

Lenzburg, Switzerland

Model 45 Smallbore Rifle

A .22 caliber bolt-action single-shot, with a 27.5" heavy barrel, an aperture rear and globe target front sight and a match rifle-type thumbhole stock. Manufactured between 1945 and 1957.

NIB	Exc.	V.G.	Good	Fair	Poor
—	825	700	595	450	250

Model 54 Smallbore Rifle

As above, with an adjustable buttplate. Manufactured between 1954 and 1957.

NIB	Exc.	V.G.	Good	Fair	Poor
—	850	725	625	475	275

Model 503 Smallbore Free Rifle

Similar to the Model 54, with a free rifle-style stock.

NIB	Exc.	V.G.	Good	Fair	Poor
—	800	675	575	450	225

Model 506 Smallbore Match Rifle

The later version of the Smallbore target series. Manufactured between 1963 and 1966.

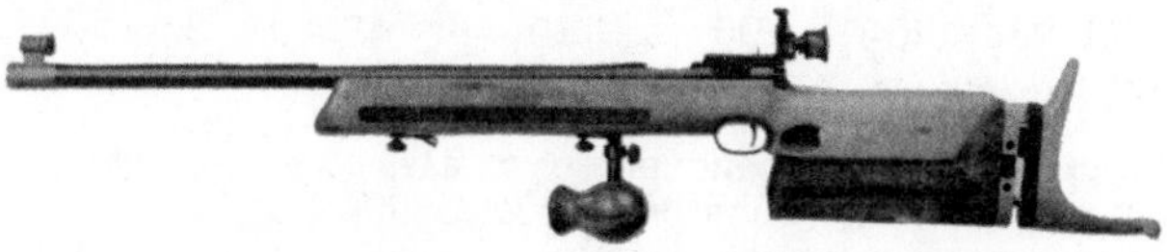

NIB	Exc.	V.G.	Good	Fair	Poor
—	850	725	625	475	275

Olympic 300 Meter

A 7x57, .30-06, or .300 H&H Magnum caliber bolt-action, single-shot, rifle with a 20.5" heavy barrel, an aperture rear, globe target front sight, double-set triggers and a free rifle-type, adjustable thumbhole stock with a wide beavertail forearm and schuetzen-style buttplate. Manufactured between 1945 and 1959.

NIB	Exc.	V.G.	Good	Fair	Poor
—	1050	900	725	550	325

Sporting Rifle

A bolt-action, single-shot rifle chambered for many popular calibers (American and European), double-set triggers and a classic-style stock.

NIB	Exc.	V.G.	Good	Fair	Poor
—	800	675	575	450	225

HANUS, BILL

Newport, Oregon

Bill Hanus Classic

Built in Spain by Ignacio Ugartechea these side-by-side shotguns are offered in 16, 20, 28 gauge, as well as .410 bore. They are fitted with 27" barrel with concave ribs and are choked IC/M. Stock is straight grip with splinter forearm. Double triggers are standard as are automatic ejectors.

NIB	Exc.	V.G.	Good	Fair	Poor
2000	1700	1350	900	625	350

HARRINGTON & RICHARDSON, INC.

Madison, North Carolina

Established in 1877 by G.H. Harrington and W.A. Richardson. The arms originally produced by this company were marketed under the trade name Aetna. In November 2000 the Marlin Firearms Company purchased the assets of Harrington & Richardson. In 2008 it was announced that H&R/NEF/Marlin had been acquired by Remington Arms, and that H&R's Gardner, Mass., plant would be closed and absorbed into Remington's existing production facilities.

SHOTGUNS

HAMMERLESS DOUBLE

A 10 or 12 gauge Anson & Deeley hammerless boxlock double-barrel shotgun with 28", 30", or 32" Damascus barrels in various choke combinations, double triggers and extractors. Engraved, case hardened and walnut stock. Four grades were available. They differ in the amount of engraving and the quality of materials and workmanship utilized. Approximately 3,500 were manufactured between 1882 and 1885.

D Grade

NIB	Exc.	V.G.	Good	Fair	Poor
—	650	550	425	300	175

C Grade

NIB	Exc.	V.G.	Good	Fair	Poor
—	750	650	500	400	275

B Grade

NIB	Exc.	V.G.	Good	Fair	Poor
—	900	750	600	500	350

A Grade

NIB	Exc.	V.G.	Good	Fair	Poor
—	2000	1750	1500	1000	550

Harrich No. 1

A 12 gauge boxlock single barrel shotgun with a 32" or 34", ventilated rib, full-choke barrel and automatic ejector. Engraved, blued with a checkered, walnut stock. Imported between 1971 and 1975.

NIB	Exc.	V.G.	Good	Fair	Poor
—	1750	1500	1150	850	650

Single-Barrel Shotguns

Harrington & Richardson manufactured a series of single-barrel, break-open shotguns between 1908 and 1942. They were chambered for various gauges and had various barrel lengths and chokes. The finishes were blued with walnut stocks. There is little collector interest in these guns and, if in sound condition, are desirable as shooters only. They are the Models 3, 5, 6, 7, 8, and 9, as well as a hinged-frame, folding design.

NIB	Exc.	V.G.	Good	Fair	Poor
—	125	100	85	65	40

Turkey Mag

A single-shot break-open side release gun chambered for the 12 gauge 3-1/2" shell with screw-in Full choke. The hardwood stock has a Mossy Oak finish. Barrel length is 24" with a bead front sight. Weight is about 6 lbs.

NIB	Exc.	V.G.	Good	Fair	Poor
175	150	125	100	75	50

Youth Turkey Gun

Similar in appearance to the Turkey Mag. but on a smaller scale. Chambered for the 20 gauge 3" shell with 22" barrel. Weighs about 5.5 lbs.

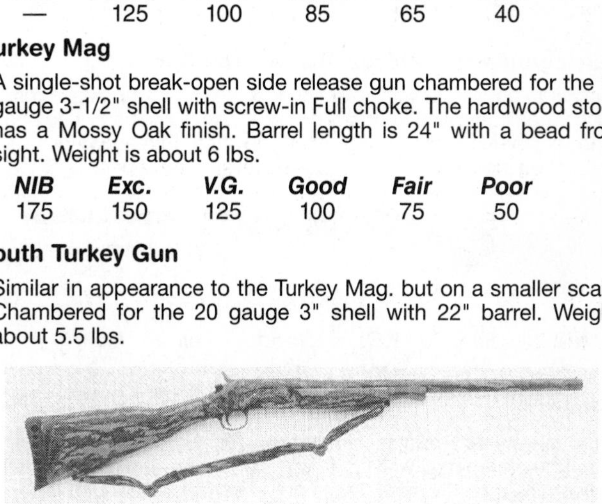

NIB	Exc.	V.G.	Good	Fair	Poor
165	140	115	90	60	40

Topper (New Production)

This is a break-open side release single-shot available in 12 and 20 gauge as well as .410 bore. The 12 gauge is offered with a 28" barrel while the others are fitted with 26" barrels. Blued finish with hardwood stock in black finish with semi-pistol grip. Weight is approximately 6 lbs.

NIB	Exc.	V.G.	Good	Fair	Poor
150	100	80	60	45	30

Topper Deluxe

NIB	Exc.	V.G.	Good	Fair	Poor
170	125	90	70	50	40

Topper Jr. in 20 Gauge and .410 Bore Only

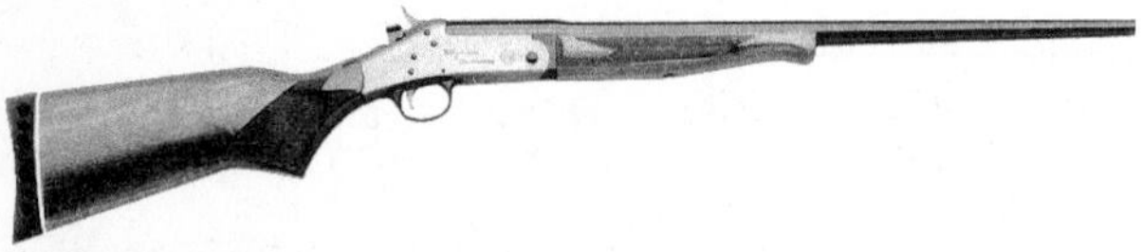

NIB	Exc.	V.G.	Good	Fair	Poor
150	100	80	60	45	30

Topper Jr. Classic

Similar to the Topper Jr. Features a black walnut stock with butt checkering. White line spacer and black recoil pad. Weighs about 7.5 lbs.

NIB	Exc.	V.G.	Good	Fair	Poor
150	100	80	60	45	30

Topper Deluxe Slug

This 12 gauge single-shot has a 24" fully rifled barrel with built-in compensator.

NIB	Exc.	V.G.	Good	Fair	Poor
150	115	90	70	50	40

Topper Deluxe Classic

Introduced in 2004, this 12 gauge 3" single shot gun is fitted with a 28" vent rib barrel with screw-in modified choke. American black walnut stock with pistol grip and ventilated recoil pad. Barrel has black finish while the receiver has a nickel finish. Weight is about 5.5 lbs. In 2005 this model was offered in 20 gauge.

NIB	Exc.	V.G.	Good	Fair	Poor
245	200	150	100	75	50

Harrington & Richardson Topper Trap Gun

Similar to above but with select checkered walnut stock and forend with fluted comb and full pistol grip; 30" barrel with two white beads and screw-in chokes (Improved Modified Extended included); deluxe Pachmayr trap recoil pad. Suggested retail price $360.

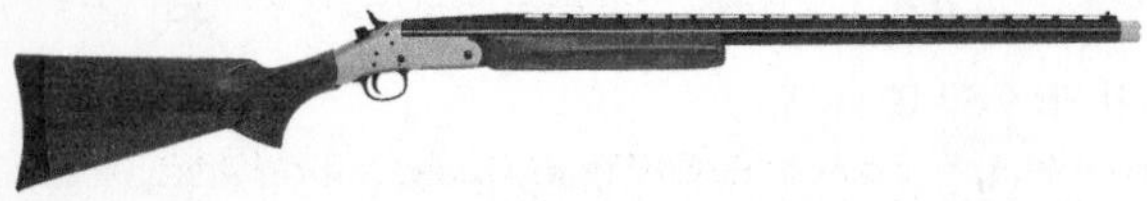

NIB	Exc.	V.G.	Good	Fair	Poor
350	275	200	165	145	75

Tamer

This single-shot gun is chambered for the .410 shell with 3" chamber. It is fitted with a 19-1/2" barrel and had a matte nickel finish. The stock is matte black polymer. Weighs about 6 lbs.

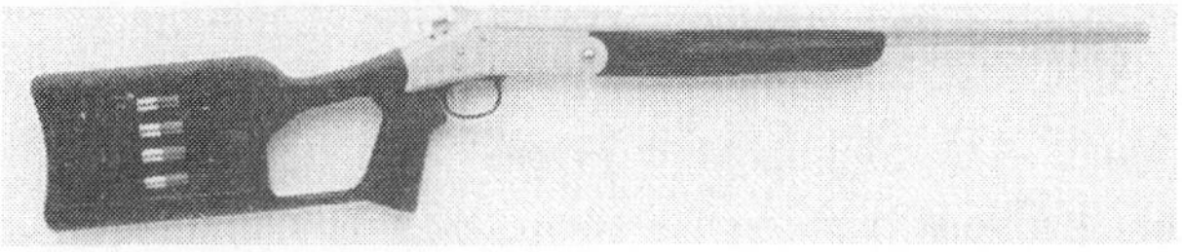

NIB	Exc.	V.G.	Good	Fair	Poor
160	125	90	60	45	30

Ultra Slug Hunter

Introduced in 1995 this model uses a heavy 10 gauge action fitted with a 24" 12 gauge barrel. Weight is about 8 lbs.

NIB	Exc.	V.G.	Good	Fair	Poor
150	115	90	70	50	40

ULTRA SLUG HUNTER DELUXE

20 Gauge

Introduced in 1997 this model is chambered for 20 gauge shells and features a hand checkered camo laminated wood stock. Fitted with a fully rifled heavy slug barrel 24" long.

NIB	Exc.	V.G.	Good	Fair	Poor
315	250	200	150	100	75

12 Gauge

Same as above but in 12 gauge with 3" chamber.

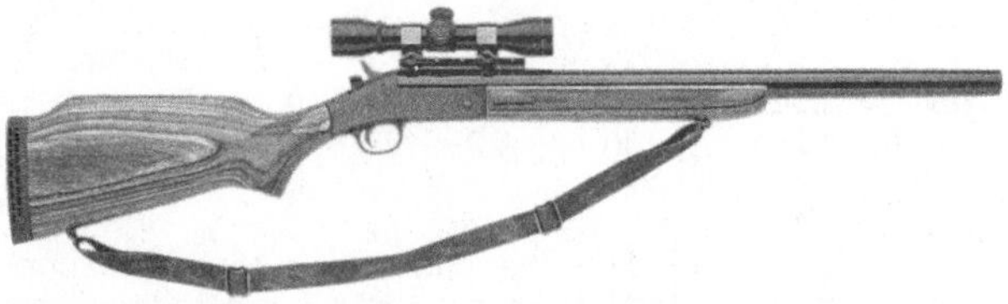

NIB	Exc.	V.G.	Good	Fair	Poor
315	250	200	150	100	75

Ultra Slug Youth Model

As above but chambered for 20 gauge shell. Weight is approximately 7 lbs.

NIB	Exc.	V.G.	Good	Fair	Poor
260	200	150	100	60	45

Ultra Slug Hunter Bull Barrel

Same as above but chambered for 20 gauge.

NIB	Exc.	V.G.	Good	Fair	Poor
150	100	80	60	45	30

Ultra Slug Hunter Thumbhole Stock

Similar to above but with laminated thumbhole stock and blued or stainless steel finish. Weight: 8.5 lbs. Add 10 percent for stainless.

NIB	Exc.	V.G.	Good	Fair	Poor
350	275	—	—	—	—

Ultra Slug Youth Bull Barrel

Same as above but with 22" barrel.

NIB	Exc.	V.G.	Good	Fair	Poor
150	100	80	60	45	30

Harrington & Richardson Ultra Lite Slug Hunter

Single-shot break-open shotgun. 12- or 20-gauge with 3" chamber; fully rifled 24" barrel; hardwood stock with walnut finish, full pistol grip, recoil pad and sling swivels. No iron sights; scope base included. Overall length 40" , weight 5.25 lbs. 20-ga. Youth Model has 20" rifled barrel. Deluxe Model has checkered laminated stock and forend.

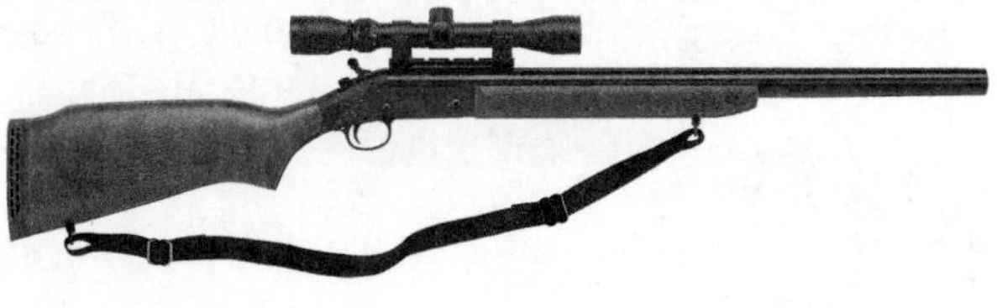

NIB	Exc.	V.G.	Good	Fair	Poor
275	225	150	100	75	50

Camo Laminate Turkey NWTF Edition

Introduced in 1999 this single barrel model features a 12 gauge 3.5" 22" barrel choked Turkey full. Polished receiver has laser engraved NWTF logo. Stock is hand checkered and is hardwood laminate with a green, brown, and black pattern. Ventilated recoil pad and sling swivels and camo sling are standard.

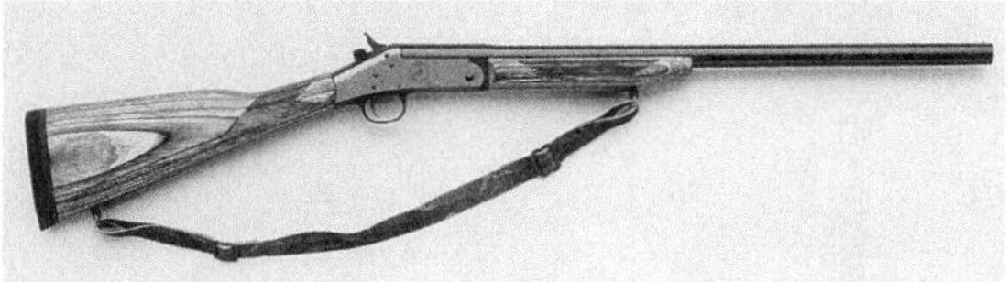

NIB	Exc.	V.G.	Good	Fair	Poor
250	200	150	100	75	50

Camo Laminate Turkey Youth NWTF Edition

Similar to the Camo Turkey above but chambered for 20 gauge with 3" chambers. Stock is laminated hardwood but with special shorter dimensions.

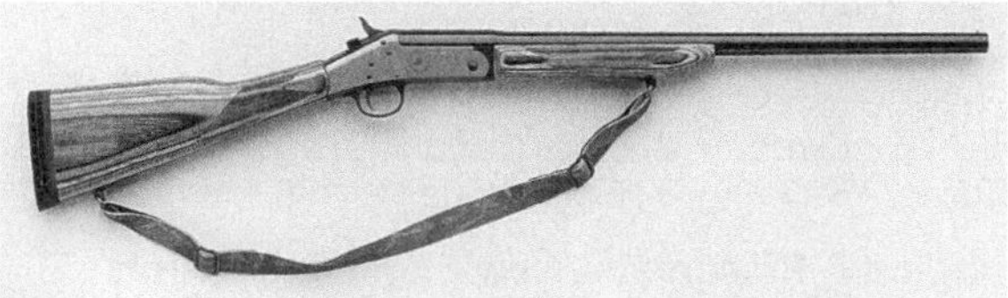

NIB	Exc.	V.G.	Good	Fair	Poor
250	200	150	100	75	50

Topper (Old Production)

A single-shot, break-open shotgun chambered for various gauges with various barrel lengths, chokes. Blued, with a hardwood stock. Introduced in 1946.

NIB	Exc.	V.G.	Good	Fair	Poor
—	145	95	75	60	40

Model 088

An external hammer single-shot, break-open shotgun chambered for all gauges with various barrel lengths, chokes and an automatic ejector. Blued, with a case colored frame and hardwood stock.

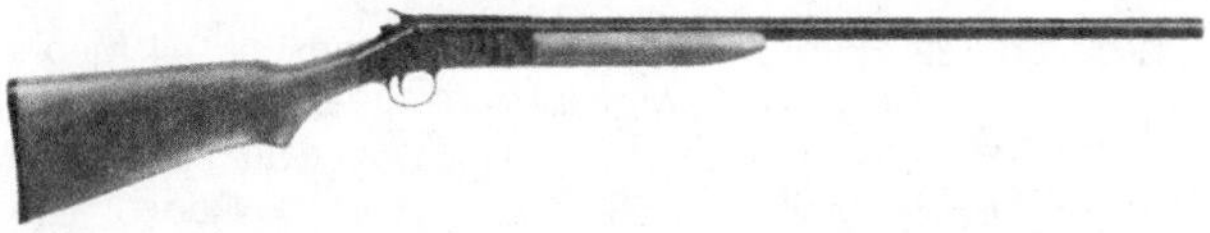

NIB	Exc.	V.G.	Good	Fair	Poor
—	80	65	50	40	30

Model 099

As above, but matte, electroless, nickel-plated.

NIB	Exc.	V.G.	Good	Fair	Poor
—	110	95	75	60	40

Model 162

A 12 or 20 gauge boxlock single-shotgun with a 24" barrel with rifle sights.

NIB	Exc.	V.G.	Good	Fair	Poor
—	125	100	80	65	45

Model 176

A 10-gauge, 3.5" Magnum caliber boxlock single barrel shotgun with a heavyweight 36" barrel and a Full choke. Manufactured between 1977 and 1985.

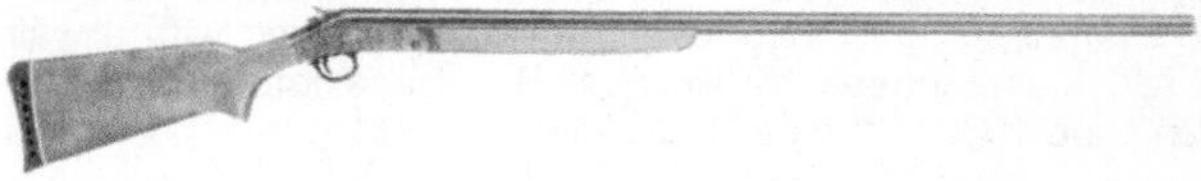

NIB	Exc.	V.G.	Good	Fair	Poor
—	225	175	115	75	45

Model 400

A 12, 16, or 20 gauge slide-action shotgun with a 28" Full choke barrel. Blued, with a hardwood stock. Manufactured between 1955 and 1967.

NIB	Exc.	V.G.	Good	Fair	Poor
—	150	125	100	75	50

Model 401

As above, with a variable choke device. Manufactured between 1956 and 1963.

NIB	Exc.	V.G.	Good	Fair	Poor
—	175	150	125	90	65

Model 402

As above, in a .410 bore. Manufactured between 1959 and 1967.

NIB	Exc.	V.G.	Good	Fair	Poor
—	175	150	125	90	65

Model 440

A 12, 16, or 20 gauge slide-action shotgun with a 26", 28", or 30" barrel in various chokes. Blued, with a hardwood stock. Manufactured between 1968 and 1973.

NIB	Exc.	V.G.	Good	Fair	Poor
—	150	125	100	75	50

Model 442

As above with a ventilated-rib barrel and a checkered stock. Manufactured between 1969 and 1973.

NIB	Exc.	V.G.	Good	Fair	Poor
—	175	150	125	90	65

Model 403

A .410 bore semi-automatic shotgun with a 26", Full choke barrel. Blued, with a hardwood stock. Manufactured in 1964.

NIB	Exc.	V.G.	Good	Fair	Poor
—	300	250	175	100	75

Model 404

A 12, 20, or .410 bore boxlock double-barrel shotgun with 26" or 28" barrels, double triggers and extractors. Blued with a walnut stock. Manufactured by Rossi in Brazil and imported between 1969 and 1972.

NIB	Exc.	V.G.	Good	Fair	Poor
—	175	150	125	90	65

Pardner Pump Field Gun Full-Dip Camo

Pump-action shotgun with steel receiver, double action bars, cross-bolt safety, easy take-down. 28" barrel with 3" chamber and ventilated rib, screw-in Modified choke tube. Synthetic stock with ventilated recoil pad and grooved fore-end with Realtree APG-HDTM full camo dip finish. Overall length 48-1/8" , weight 7-1/2 lbs. Also available in several variations with hardwood stock or black synthetic stock. Suggested retail for full camo version $278.

Excell

Introduced in 2005 this semi-auto shotgunis chambered for the 12 gauge 3" shell and fitted with a 28" vent rib barrel with choke tubes. Checkered black synthetic stock. Magazine capacity is 5 rounds. Weight is about 7 lbs.

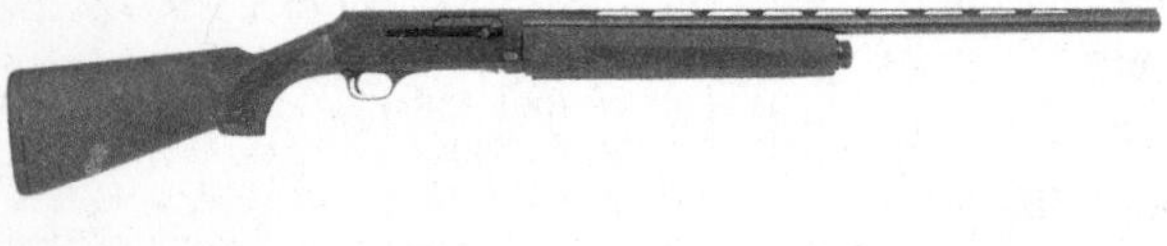

NIB	Exc.	V.G.	Good	Fair	Poor
400	365	295	200	150	100

Excell Waterfowl

As above but with Real Tree Advantage Wetlands camo finish. Introduced in 2005.

NIB	Exc.	V.G.	Good	Fair	Poor
425	375	325	225	175	125

Excell Turkey

This model is fitted with a 22" barrel with choke tubes and fiber optic front sight. Real Tree Advantage Hardwoods camo finish. Weight is 7 lbs. Introduced in 2005.

NIB	Exc.	V.G.	Good	Fair	Poor
425	375	325	225	175	125

Excell Combo

This model has a black synthetic stock and two barrels: 28" vent rib with choke tubes, and 24" rifled barrel. Weight is about 7 lbs. depending on barrel length. Introduced in 2005.

NIB	Exc.	V.G.	Good	Fair	Poor
450	395	350	250	195	145

Pinnacle

This is an over-and-under gun chambered for the 12 or 20 gauge with 3" chambers. Barrel length for the 12 gauge is 28" and for the 20 gauge 26"; both with vent ribs. Choke tubes. Checkered walnut stock with recoil pad and pistol grip. Weight is about 6.75 lbs. for the 12 gauge and 6.25 lbs. for the 20 gauge. Introduced in 2005.

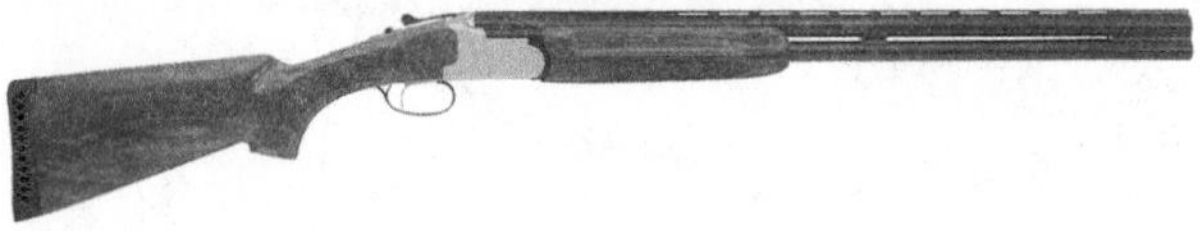

NIB	Exc.	V.G.	Good	Fair	Poor
700	600	500	325	175	125

Model 1212

A 12 gauge over-and-under boxlock shotgun with 28" ventilated rib barrels. Blued with a walnut stock. Also available with 30" barrels having 3" chambers. Manufactured by Lanber Arms of Spain and imported after 1976.

NIB	Exc.	V.G.	Good	Fair	Poor
—	450	375	325	200	125

Long Tom Classic

Introduced in 1996 this limited edition single-barrel shotgun features a case hardened frame with 32" Full choked barrel. Stock is hand-checkered black walnut with crescent buttplate. Chambered for 12 gauge. Weight is about 7.5 lbs.

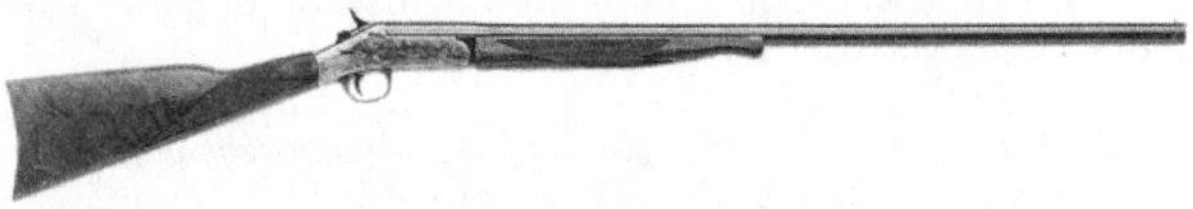

NIB	Exc.	V.G.	Good	Fair	Poor
425	395	325	250	175	125

Harrington & Richardson/New England Firearms Handi-Rifle/Slug Gun Combos

Single-shot break-open rifle/shotgun combos (one rifle barrel, one shotgun barrel per combo) chambered in .44 Magnum/12-ga. rifled slug and .357 Magnum/20-ga. rifled slug. Rifle barrels are not interchangeable; shotgun barrels are interchangeable. Stock is black matte high-density polymer with sling swivel studs, molded checkering and recoil pad. Rifle barrel 22" for both calibers; shotgun barrels 28" (12 ga.) and 24" (20 ga.) fully rifled. No iron sights; scope rail included. Overall length 38" (both rifle chamberings); 42" (12-ga.) and 40" (20 ga.). Weight 7 - 8 lbs.

NIB	Exc.	V.G.	Good	Fair	Poor
—	300	250	175	100	75

RIFLES

Model 058

A 20-gauge, .22 Hornet, .30-30, .357 Magnum, or .44 Magnum caliber rifle/shotgun outfit with interchangeable barrels. Blued with a hardwood stock.

NIB	Exc.	V.G.	Good	Fair	Poor
—	200	150	100	75	50

Model 258

As above, but with a matte, electroless nickel-plate finish.

NIB	Exc.	V.G.	Good	Fair	Poor
—	225	175	125	100	75

Reising Model 60

A .45 ACP caliber semi-automatic rifle with an 18.25" barrel and a 12- or 20-round detachable magazine. Blued, with a walnut stock. It operates on a retarded blowback system and was developed to be used as a police weapon. Manufactured between 1944 and 1946.

Courtesy Richard M. Kumor, Sr.

NIB	Exc.	V.G.	Good	Fair	Poor
—	2000	1600	1000	450	250

Model 65 Military (Model 58C)

A .22 LR caliber semi-automatic rifle with a 23" barrel and Redfield peep sights. Blued, with a walnut stock. Manufactured between 1944 and 1956.

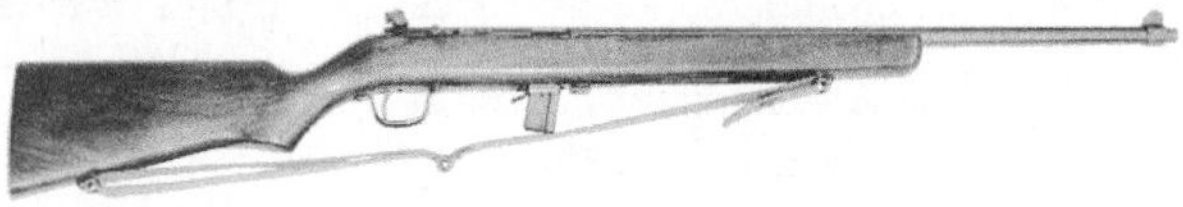

Courtesy Richard M. Kumor, Sr.

NIB	Exc.	V.G.	Good	Fair	Poor
—	500	300	200	125	90

NOTE: Add 100 percent if USMC marked.

Model 150

A .22 LR caliber semi-automatic rifle with a 20" barrel and a 5-shot magazine. Blued, with a walnut stock. Manufactured between 1949 and 1953.

NIB	Exc.	V.G.	Good	Fair	Poor
—	100	80	60	45	30

Model 155 (Shikari)

This is a single-shot, break-open rifle chambered for the .44 Magnum or the .45-70 cartridge. It has a 20" barrel with fixed sights. The finish is blued, with a full-length walnut stock. It was introduced in 1972.

NIB	Exc.	V.G.	Good	Fair	Poor
—	375	300	225	150	100

Model 157

As above in .22 Magnum, .22 Hornet, and .30-30 caliber.

NIB	Exc.	V.G.	Good	Fair	Poor
—	350	275	200	125	75

Model 158

A .357 or .44 Magnum single-shot side lever rifle with a 22" barrel. Blued, case hardened with a walnut stock. Available with an interchangeable 26" 20 gauge barrel. Manufactured prior to 1986.

NIB	Exc.	V.G.	Good	Fair	Poor
—	350	275	200	125	75

Model 300 Ultra

A .22-250 up to the .300 Winchester Magnum caliber, bolt-action rifle with a 22" or 24" barrel and without sights. High polished blue, and checkered walnut stock. Manufactured between 1965 and 1978.

NIB	Exc.	V.G.	Good	Fair	Poor
—	450	400	350	275	175

Model 301 Carbine

As above with an 18" barrel and a full-length, Mannlicher-style stock.

NIB	Exc.	V.G.	Good	Fair	Poor
—	450	400	350	275	175

Model 317 Ultra Wildcat

A .17 Rem., .17-223, .222 Rem., and the .223 Rem. caliber short Sako bolt-action rifle with a 20" barrel furnished without sights. Blued, with a checkered walnut stock. Manufactured between 1968 and 1976.

NIB	Exc.	V.G.	Good	Fair	Poor
—	550	400	350	275	175

Handi-Rifle

Break-action single-shot rifle that\qs been around in one form another since God invented dirt. Side lever release, automatic ejection, hardwood stock, transfer bar passive safety. Available in nearly every conceivable rimfire and centerfire chambering (except the biggest centerfires) and now made under the auspices of Marlin, this rifle is as good a bargain today as it ever was. Some newer models feature factory scopes, bull barrels, thumbhole stocks and other niceties, but they\qre still Handi-Rifles. Value is generally under $300 even in New or Excellent condition, sometimes remarkably under. NOTE: The latest iteration of the Handi-Rifle (2008) is available in a wide variety of chamberings, from .223 to .500 S&W Magnum.

Synthetic Handi-Rifle

Basic Handi-Rifle design but with synthetic buttstock and forend (either grooved or beavertail). Available with iron sights or picatinny rail for mounting optics.

NIB	Exc.	V.G.	Good	Fair	Poor
275	200	175	150	100	50

Stainless Handi-Rifle

Similar to above but with stainless barrel. Chambered in .223, .270 or .30-06.

NIB	Exc.	V.G.	Good	Fair	Poor
295	225	200	175	115	75

Synthetic Handi-Rifle/Slug Gun Combo

Similar to above but with extra slug barrel. Available in .44 Mag/12 ga. and .357 Magnum/20 ga. Introduced in 2008.

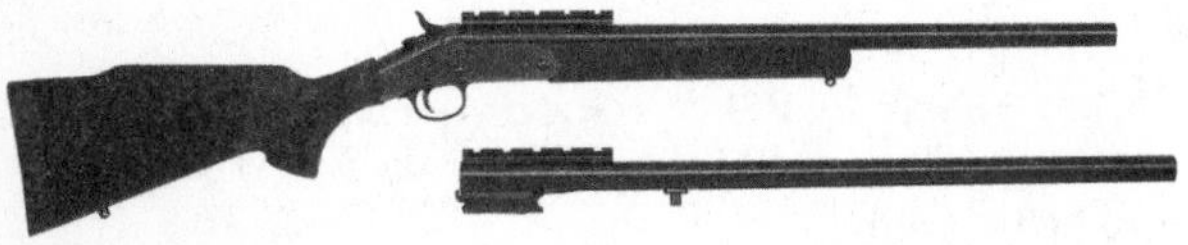

NIB	Exc.	V.G.	Good	Fair	Poor
—	325	300	225	175	100

Superlite Handi-Rifle Compact

Similar to Synthetic Handi-Rifle but weighs only 5.5 lbs. Chambered in .223 and .243. Also available with optional scope.

NIB	Exc.	V.G.	Good	Fair	Poor
295	225	200	175	115	75

Ultra Varmint Rifle

This single-shot rifle is chambered for the .223 Rem. or the .22-250 cartridge. It is fitted with a 22" heavy barrel. The stock is hand checkered curly maple (older models) or laminated (newer models) with Monte Carlo cheekpiece. Comes with picatinny rail for mounting optics. Weighs about 7.5 lbs.

NIB	Exc.	V.G.	Good	Fair	Poor
350	295	175	125	75	50

Ultra Varmint Thumbhole

Similar to above but with laminated thumbhole stock.

NIB	Exc.	V.G.	Good	Fair	Poor
375	325	200	150	100	75

Stainless Steel Ultra Varmint Thumbhole

Similar to above but with stainless teel barrel and matte nickel receiver.

NIB	Exc.	V.G.	Good	Fair	Poor
375	325	200	150	100	75

Ultra Varmint Fluted

Introduced in 2005 this model is chambered for the .204 Ruger, .22-250, or the .223 Rem. cartridge. Fitted with a 24" fluted barrel with no sights. Stock is black synthetic with vertical adjustable adjustment knob, recoil pad, and adjustable bipod mount. Weight is about 7 lbs.

NIB	Exc.	V.G.	Good	Fair	Poor
350	295	175	125	75	50

Model 317P

As above, but more finely finished. Manufactured between 1968 and 1976.

NIB	Exc.	V.G.	Good	Fair	Poor
—	500	475	425	375	250

Ultra Rifle—Hunting

Single-shot rifle chambered for .25-06, .308 Win., and .357 Rem. Max. The .25-06 has a 26" barrel, the other two are fitted with 22" barrels. A Cinnamon laminated stock is standard. Weight is about 7 lbs. In 2001 the .450 Marlin cartridge was added.

NIB	Exc.	V.G.	Good	Fair	Poor
275	200	175	150	100	50

Harrington & Richardson/New England Firearms Stainless Ultra Hunter with Thumbhole Stock

Single-shot break-open rifle chambered in .45-70 Government. 24" stainless steel barrel and receiver with scope mount rail; hammer extension; cinnamon laminate thumbhole stock. Overall length 40" ; weight 8 lbs.

NIB	Exc.	V.G.	Good	Fair	Poor
375	325	200	150	100	75

Ultra Rifle—Varmint

Same as above but chambered for .223 Rem. with 22" barrel. Laminated stock with checkered pistol grip.

NIB	Exc.	V.G.	Good	Fair	Poor
375	325	200	150	100	75

Ultra .22 Magnum Rifle

Same as above but chambered for the .22 Winchester Magnum. Introduced in 2001.

NIB	Exc.	V.G.	Good	Fair	Poor
295	225	200	175	115	75

Ultra Rifle—Comp

Introduced in 1997 this single-shot rifle features an integral muzzlebrake on the end of the barrel. Available in .270 Win. and .30-06 calibers with 24" barrels. Camo laminated stock.

NIB	Exc.	V.G.	Good	Fair	Poor
295	225	200	175	115	75

Ultra Rifle Rocky Mountain Elk Foundation Commemorative

A limited edition single rifle chambered for the .35 Whelen cartridge. Selected laminated stock with Monte Carlo. Barrel length is 26".

NIB	Exc.	V.G.	Good	Fair	Poor
—	450	400	350	275	175

Sportster .17 HMR

A .17 HMR version of the Handi-Rifle with black polymer Monte Carlo stock and picatinny rail for moutning optics. Overall length 38-1/4 inches.

NIB	Exc.	V.G.	Good	Fair	Poor
—	250	200	150	100	50

Sportster

A .22 LR or .22 WMR version of the Handi-Rifle with black polymer stock, flued forend and iron sights. Overall length 36-1/4".

NIB	Exc.	V.G.	Good	Fair	Poor
—	175	150	100	75	50

Sportster Compact

Similar to above but in .22 LR only and two inch shorter length of pull.

NIB	Exc.	V.G.	Good	Fair	Poor
—	150	125	100	75	50

Buffalo Classic

This rifle was first produced in 1995. It is chambered for the .45-70 and .38-55 cartridges. Barrel length is 32" with no sights but dovetail front and drilled and tapped rear. Hand checkered walnut stock with case colored crescent steel buttplate. Weight is approximately 8 lbs. Since its introduction in 1995 there have been about 2,000 guns produced. The factory anticipates about 1,000 of these rifles being built each year.

NIB	Exc.	V.G.	Good	Fair	Poor
375	315	225	175	125	50

Wesson & Harrington Brand 125th Anniversary Rifle

Introduced in 1996 this rifle commemorates the 125th anniversary of the partnership. This special rifle is chambered for the .45-70 Government cartridge. The receiver is hand engraved. The barrel length is 32". The stock is American black walnut with crescent steel butt.

NIB	Exc.	V.G.	Good	Fair	Poor
395	325	250	200	150	75

Ultra Rifle Whitetails Unlimited 1997 Commemorative Edition

Introduced in 1997 and chambered for the .45-70 Govt. cartridge this model features a hand checkered black walnut stock. Special laser engraving on the action and pewter finished medallion inletted into stock. Barrel length is 22".

NIB	Exc.	V.G.	Good	Fair	Poor
325	275	225	175	125	75

CR Carbine

Single-shot rifle based on the Handi-Rifle design. Two-piece checkered walnut stock with schnabel forend. Marble\qs front and rear sights, Crescent steel buttplate. Chambered in .45 Colt. Introduced in 2007.

NIB	Exc.	V.G.	Good	Fair	Poor
375	315	225	150	100	50

Model 333

The Model 300 in 7mm Mag. caliber. Manufactured in 1974.

NIB	Exc.	V.G.	Good	Fair	Poor
—	250	200	175	125	100

Model 340

A .243 to .308 Winchester caliber bolt-action rifle with a 22" barrel and a 5-shot magazine. Blued, with a checkered walnut stock.

NIB	Exc.	V.G.	Good	Fair	Poor
—	400	350	300	225	150

Model 360 Ultra Automatic

A .243 Win. and the .308 Win. caliber semi-automatic rifle with a 22" barrel, adjustable sights and a 3-shot detachable magazine. Blued, with a checkered walnut stock. Manufactured between 1965 and 1978.

NIB	Exc.	V.G.	Good	Fair	Poor
—	425	375	275	195	100

Model 451 Medalist

A .22 LR caliber bolt-action rifle with a 26" barrel, open sights and a 5-shot detachable magazine. Blued, with a walnut stock. Manufactured between 1948 and 1961.

NIB	Exc.	V.G.	Good	Fair	Poor
—	175	150	125	100	75

Model 700

A .22 rimfire Magnum caliber, semi-automatic rifle with a 22" barrel, adjustable sights and a 5-round, detachable magazine. Blued, with a checkered walnut stock. Manufactured between 1977 and 1985.

NIB	Exc.	V.G.	Good	Fair	Poor
—	225	200	150	125	85

Model 700 DL

As above, with a checkered walnut stock and with a 4X scope. Manufactured until 1985.

NIB	Exc.	V.G.	Good	Fair	Poor
—	300	250	200	150	100

Model 750

A .22 LR bolt-action single-shot rifle with a 22" barrel with sights and a short stock. Blued, and the stock is hardwood.

NIB	Exc.	V.G.	Good	Fair	Poor
—	100	80	60	45	25

Model 865

A .22 LR caliber bolt-action rifle with a 22" barrel, open sights and a 5-shot magazine. Blued, with a hardwood stock.

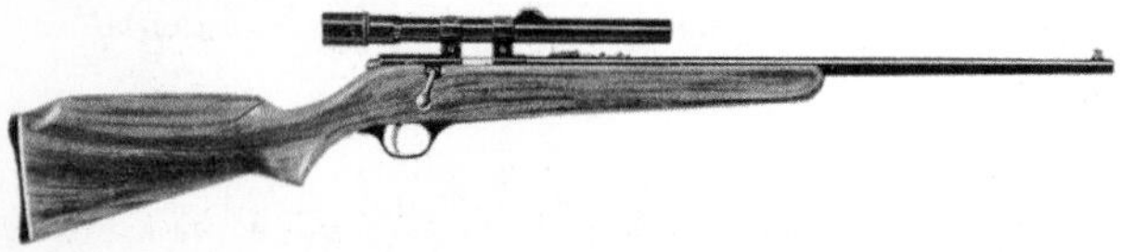

NIB	Exc.	V.G.	Good	Fair	Poor
—	100	80	60	45	25

Model 5200

A .22 LR caliber bolt-action, single-shot rifle with a 28" heavy barrel without sights, and an adjustable trigger. Blued, with a target-type walnut stock.

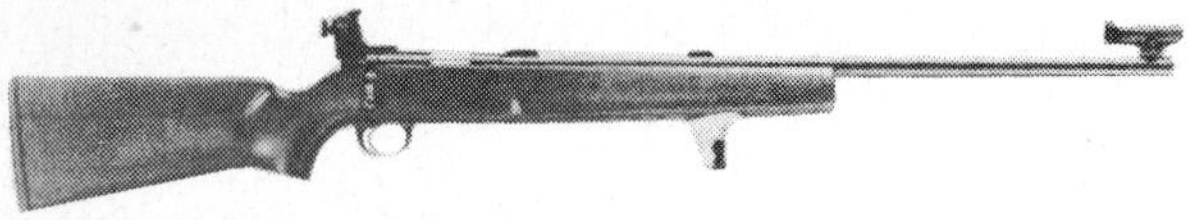

NIB	Exc.	V.G.	Good	Fair	Poor
—	400	350	300	225	125

Model 5200 Sporter

A .22 LR caliber bolt-action rifle with a 24" barrel, adjustable sights and a 5-shot magazine. Blued with a walnut stock. Not manufactured after 1983.

NIB	Exc.	V.G.	Good	Fair	Poor
—	400	350	300	225	125

100th Anniversary Officer's Model

A commemorative replica of the Officer's Model 1873 Trapdoor Springfield Rifle, with a 26" barrel. Engraved, and an anniversary plaque mounted on the stock. Blued, with a case colored receiver and a pewter forend tip. There were 10,000 manufactured in 1971. As with all commemoratives, this model is most desirable when NIB with all supplied material.

NIB	Exc.	V.G.	Good	Fair	Poor
850	695	500	375	250	175

CUSTER MEMORIAL ISSUE

A limited production issue commemorating George Armstrong Custer's Battle of the Little Bighorn. Heavily engraved and gold inlaid with a high-grade checkered walnut stock. Furnished in a mahogany display case that included two books dealing with the subject. There were two versions produced—an Officer's Model, of which 25 were issued commemorating the 25 officers that fell with Custer, and another version commemorating the 243 enlisted men who lost their lives at the Little Bighorn. As with all commemoratives, to be collectible they must be NIB with all furnished material.

Officer's Model

25 manufactured.

NIB	Exc.	V.G.	Good	Fair	Poor
3000	2000	1600	1200	500	200

Enlisted Men's Model

243 manufactured.

NIB	Exc.	V.G.	Good	Fair	Poor
1500	1000	600	400	250	150

Model 171

A reproduction of the Model 1873 Trapdoor Springfield Carbine with a 22" barrel. Blued, with a case colored receiver and a walnut stock.

NIB	Exc.	V.G.	Good	Fair	Poor
—	500	450	300	200	125

Model 171-DL

As above, but more finely finished.

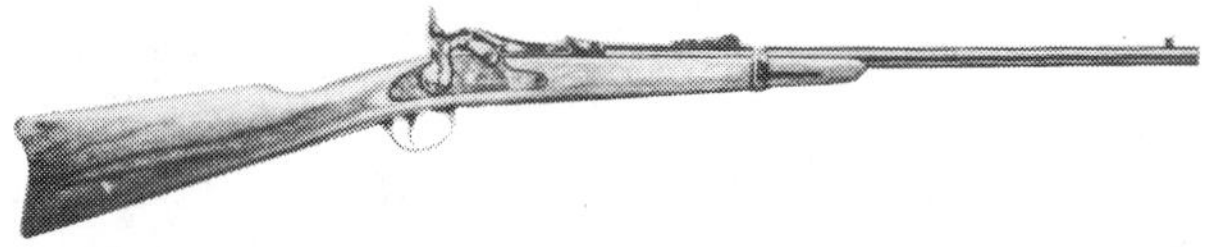

NIB	Exc.	V.G.	Good	Fair	Poor
—	550	500	325	250	175

Model 174

A plain copy of the Springfield Model 1873 Carbine in .45-70 caliber with a 22" barrel. Manufactured in 1972.

NIB	Exc.	V.G.	Good	Fair	Poor
—	525	400	325	250	175

Model 178

A copy of the Springfield Model 1873 rifle with a 32" barrel. Manufactured from 1973 to 1984.

NIB	Exc.	V.G.	Good	Fair	Poor
—	525	400	325	250	175

HARRIS GUNWORKS

Phoenix, Arizona

NOTE: There are a wide range of extra costs options for all Harris Gunworks models that in many cases will dramatically affect price.

National Match Rifle

Introduced in 1989 this model features a bolt-action rifle chambered for the 7mm-08 or .308 with 5-round magazine. It is fitted with a 24" stainless steel match grade barrel with Canjar trigger. The stock is fiberglass with adjustable buttplate. Weight is about 11 lbs.

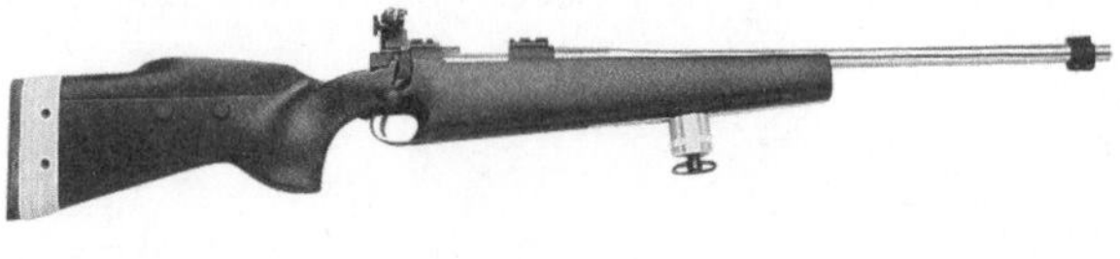

NIB	Exc.	V.G.	Good	Fair	Poor
3500	2750	1750	950	600	300

Model 86 Sniper Rifle

Chambered for .308, .30-06, .300 Win. Mag. with 24" heavy match grade barrel. The stock is a special design McHale fiberglass with textured grip and forearm. Fitted with a recoil pad. Supplied with a bipod. Weight is about 11.25 lbs.

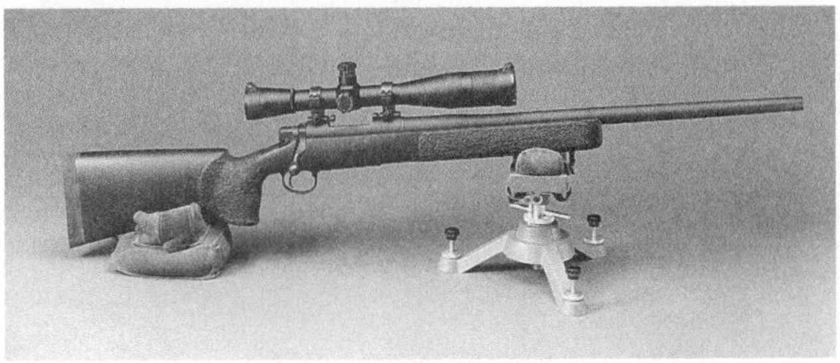

NIB	*Exc.*	*V.G.*	*Good*	*Fair*	*Poor*
2700	2100	1600	1000	600	350

NOTE: Add $100 for take-down model.

Model 87 Series

These are single-shot rifles chambered for .50 BMG. Fitted with a 29" barrel with muzzlebrake. Fiberglass stock. Introduced in 1987. Weight is approximately 21.5 lbs.

NIB	*Exc.*	*V.G.*	*Good*	*Fair*	*Poor*
6000	4750	3000	2000	1000	500

NOTE: For Model 87R 5-shot repeater add $600. For Model 87 5-shot repeater add $400. For Model 92 Bullpup add $300.

Model 88

These bolt-action .50 BMG rifles are offered in two different configurations. One is fitted with a 20" carbon graphite barrel with add-on recoil arrestor with black teflon finish. The second variation is fitted with a 16.5" stainless steel barrel with integral recoil arrestor. Both rifles weigh about 14 lbs. Titanium action is available for further weight reduction.

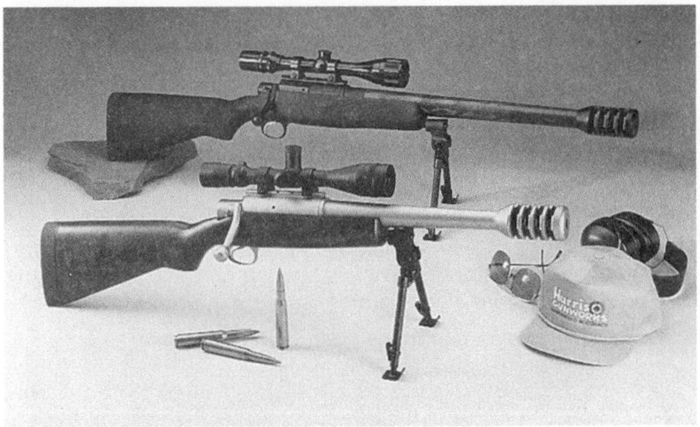

NIB	*Exc.*	*V.G.*	*Good*	*Fair*	*Poor*
6000	4750	3000	2000	1000	500

Model 89 Sniper Rifle

This bolt-action rifle is chambered for .308 cartridge. Fitted with a 28" barrel. Supplied with a bipod. Stock is fiberglass with adjustable length of pull and fitted with a recoil pad. Weight is about 15.25 lbs.

NIB	*Exc.*	*V.G.*	*Good*	*Fair*	*Poor*
2700	2100	1600	1000	600	350

Model 93

Bolt-action .50 BMG rifle with folding hinge stock assembly. Furnished with a 10-round or 20-round magazine. Barrel length is 29". Weight is approximately 21 lbs.

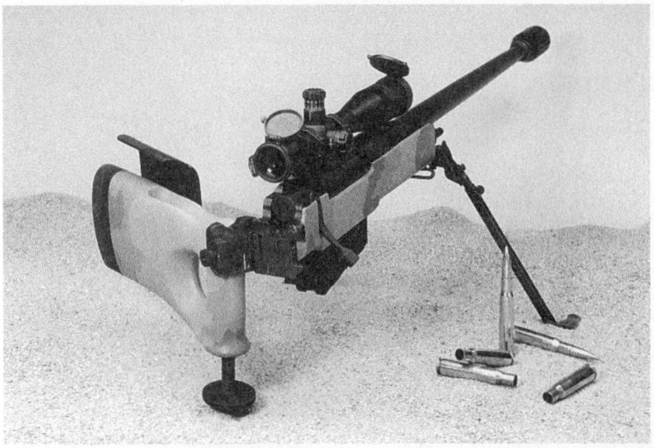

Model 93 folding model

NIB	*Exc.*	*V.G.*	*Good*	*Fair*	*Poor*
6000	4750	3000	2000	1000	500

Model 95

This is a lightweight variation of the .50 BMG models featuring Titanium and graphite. Supplied with bipod. Barrel length is 29". Weight is approximately 18 lbs.

NIB	*Exc.*	*V.G.*	*Good*	*Fair*	*Poor*
6000	4750	3000	2000	1000	500

Model 96

This is a gas-operated semi-automatic .50 BMG sniper rifle. Barrel length is 29". Detachable 5-round magazine. Weight is approximately 25 lbs.

NIB	*Exc.*	*V.G.*	*Good*	*Fair*	*Poor*
7500	6500	4000	2500	1500	750

Long Range Rifle

Chambered for a variety of cartridges such as the .300 Win. Mag., 7mm Rem. Mag., .300 Phoenix, .338 Lapua. This is a single-shot rifle fitted with a 26" match grade stainless steel barrel. Fiberglass stock with adjustable buttplate and cheekpiece. Weight is about 14 lbs.

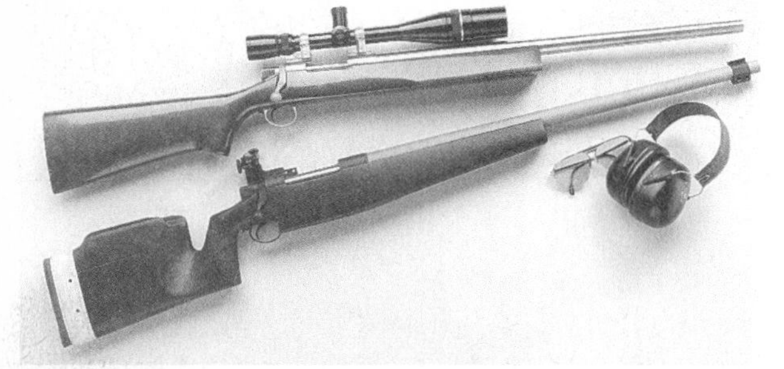

NIB	Exc.	V.G.	Good	Fair	Poor
3900	2850	1500	1000	700	350

Target/Benchrest Rifle

Offered in .243, .308, 6mm BR, 6mm PPC, and 6mm Rem. This model is custom built for the customer. Available in both left- and right-hand. Weight is about 11 lbs.

NIB	Exc.	V.G.	Good	Fair	Poor
3500	2750	1750	950	600	300

Antietam Sharps Rifle

This is a replica of the Sharps Model 1874 sidehammer introduced in 1994. Chambered for the .40-65 or the .45-70. Choice of 30" or 32" octagon or round barrel. Stock is fancy walnut with either straight, pistol grip, or Creedmoor with schnabel forearm. Many optional sights offered. Weight is about 11.25 lbs.

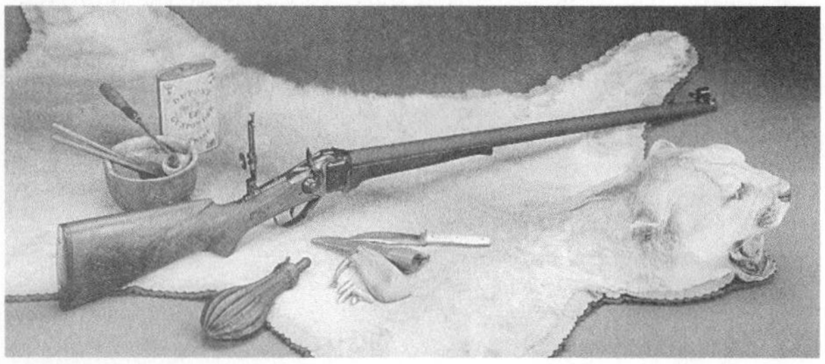

NIB	Exc.	V.G.	Good	Fair	Poor
2600	1950	1200	800	450	200

Signature Classic Sporter

This is a left- or right-handed bolt-action model introduced in 1987 with a choice of calibers from .22-250 to .375 H&H. Barrel lengths are 22", 24", or 26" depending on caliber. Choice of fiberglass stocks in green, beige, brown, or black. A wood stock is optional. Weight is about 7 lbs. for short action calibers.

NIB	Exc.	V.G.	Good	Fair	Poor
3150	2550	1500	1150	500	250

Signature Classic Stainless Sporter

Same as above but with barrel and action made from stainless steel. A .416 Rem. Mag is available in this variation also. This model is also available with interchangeable barrels.

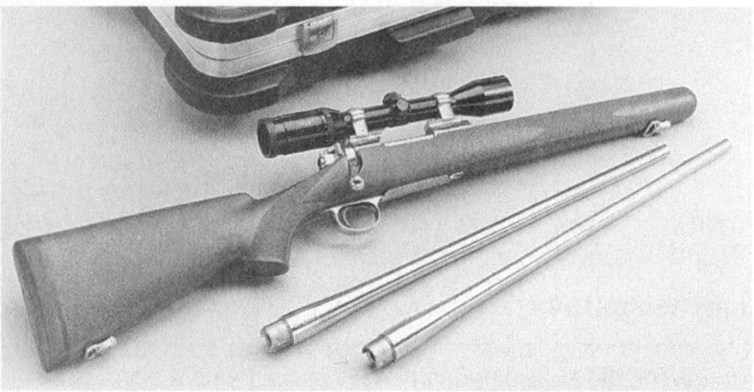

NIB	Exc.	V.G.	Good	Fair	Poor
3200	2650	1600	1250	600	300

NOTE: Add $600 for interchangeable barrels.

Signature Super Varminter

Similar to the Classic Sporter except fitted with a heavy contoured barrel, adjustable trigger, and special hand-bedded fiberglass stock. Chambered for .223, .22-250, .220 Swift, .243, 6mm Rem., .25-06, 7mm-08, 7mm BR, .308, .350 Rem. Introduced in 1989.

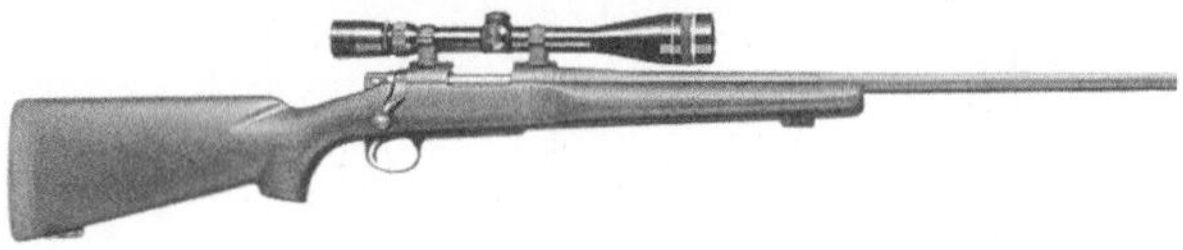

NIB	Exc.	V.G.	Good	Fair	Poor
2900	2250	1600	1050	700	350

Signature Alaskan

Similar to the Classic Sporter except fitted with a match grade barrel with single leaf rear sight. Nickel finish. Walnut Monte Carlo stock with cheekpiece and palm swell grip. Chambered for .270 to .375 H&H. Introduced in 1989.

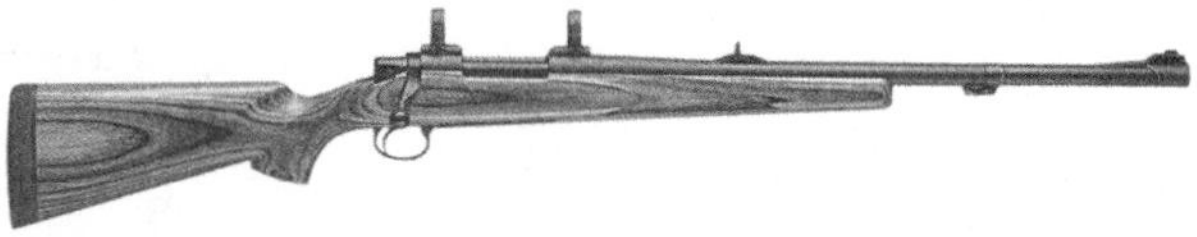

NIB	Exc.	V.G.	Good	Fair	Poor
3950	3200	2200	1500	700	350

Signature Titanium Mountain Rifle

Similar to the Classic Sporter except action is made of titanium alloy and barrel of chrome-moly steel. Stock is graphite reinforced fiberglass. Chambered for .270 to .300 Win. Mag. Weight is about 5.5 lbs. Introduced in 1989.

NIB	Exc.	V.G.	Good	Fair	Poor
3500	2750	1750	950	600	300

NOTE: Add $400 for graphite steel barrel.

Sportsman 97

This bolt-action rifle is chambered for a variety of calibers from .270 Win. to .338 Win. The stock is fancy grade walnut, Bastogne, or English. A Talon action is fitted.

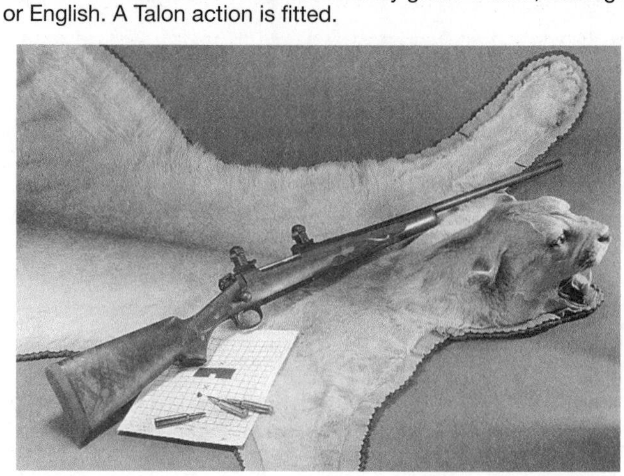

NIB	Exc.	V.G.	Good	Fair	Poor
2900	2250	1600	1050	700	350

Talon Safari Rifle

This bolt-action rifle is chambered for 16 different calibers from .300 Win. Mag. to .460 Weatherby Mag. The finish is a matte black with fiberglass Safari stock. Weight is between 9 and 10 lbs. depending on caliber.

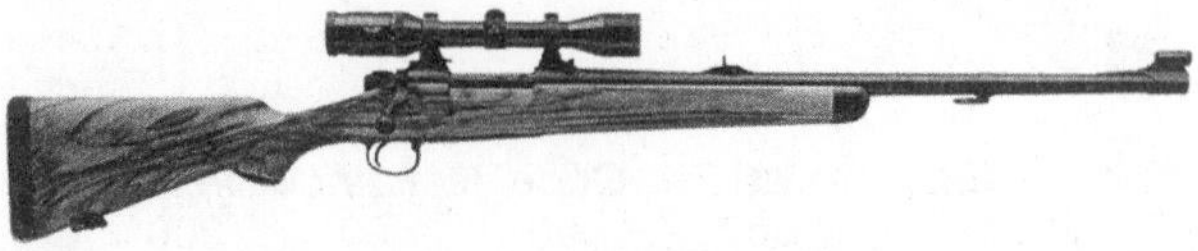

NIB	Exc.	V.G.	Good	Fair	Poor
4200	3350	2200	1600	1200	600

Talon Sporter Rifle

This bolt-action rifle, introduced in 1991, uses a pre-64 Model 70 type action with cone breech. Barrel and action are stainless steel. Chambered for a wide variety of calibers from .22-250 to .416 Rem. Mag. Choice of walnut or fiberglass stock. Most barrel lengths are 24". Weight is about 7.5 lbs. depending on caliber.

NIB	Exc.	V.G.	Good	Fair	Poor
3150	2550	1500	1150	500	250

DOUBLE RIFLE/SHOTGUN

This side-by-side gun is offered in .470 NE or .500 NE as well as 12 and 20 gauge guns. Engraved receiver, AAA fancy walnut stocks and 3-leaf express sights are standard. Offered in boxlock and side lock models.

Boxlock

NIB	Exc.	V.G.	Good	Fair	Poor
15000	12500	9000	5000	2750	1500

SideLock

NIB	Exc.	V.G.	Good	Fair	Poor
21000	16500	12000	7500	3100	1750

HATFIELD RIFLE COMPANY

St. Joseph, Missouri

Squirrel Rifle

A flintlock or percussion rifle in .32 to .50 caliber with a 39" barrel, double set triggers, adjustable sights, brass mounts and maple stocks. Available in a wide variety of forms, which affect the values. The values listed are for plain, standard models.

NIB	Exc.	V.G.	Good	Fair	Poor
550	400	350	300	225	150

SHOTGUNS

Uplander Grade I

A 20 gauge boxlock double-barrel shotgun with a 26" improved cylinder and modified barrel with a matte raised rib, single-selective trigger and automatic ejectors. Case hardened, blued with a deluxe-grade, hand-checkered walnut stock. Introduced in 1987.

NIB	Exc.	V.G.	Good	Fair	Poor
1250	1050	750	600	475	200

Uplander Pigeon Grade II

As above, with scroll engraving with a fitted leather case.

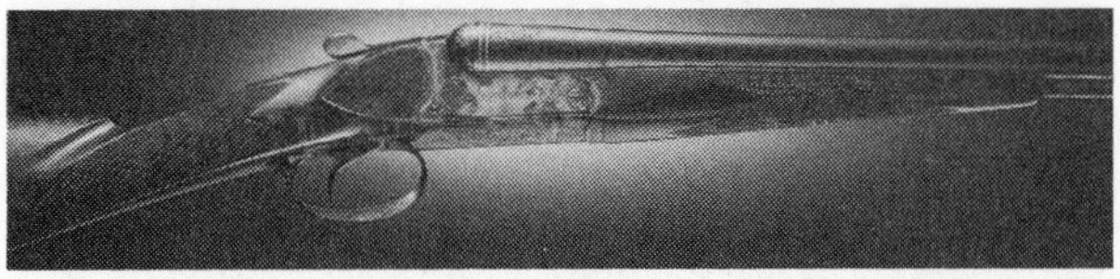

NIB	Exc.	V.G.	Good	Fair	Poor
2250	1750	1275	900	650	500

Uplander Super Pigeon Grade III

As above, with deep-relief cut engraving and a leather case.

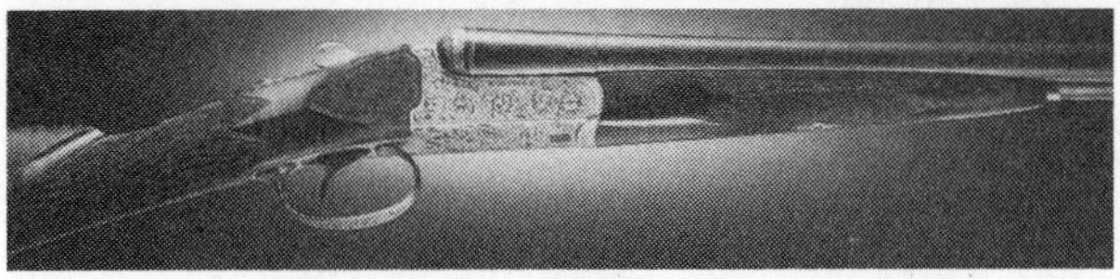

NIB	Exc.	V.G.	Good	Fair	Poor
2500	2200	1700	1400	1000	700

Uplander Woodcock Grade V

As above, with seven 24 kt. gold inlays and best quality engraving. Furnished with a leather case.

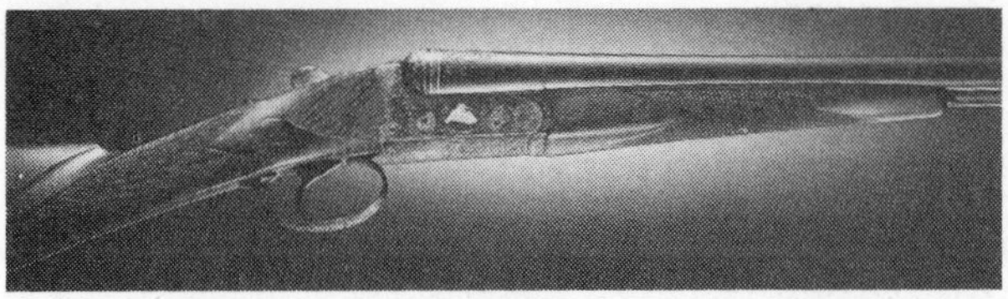

NIB	Exc.	V.G.	Good	Fair	Poor
5600	5000	4250	3500	2750	2000

HAWKEN

St. Louis, Missouri

During the early part of the 19th century, Jacob and Samuel Hawken manufactured a variety of flintlock, percussion and cartridge rifles, shotguns and pistols. They are best known, however, for half stock Plains Rifles. Though of a plain nature, these arms were recognized for their accuracy and dependability. Early Hawken rifles will be worth a substantial premium over later examples. Some examples in very good condition may be worth as much as $50,000. Proceed with caution.

HEAVY EXPRESS INC.

Colorado Springs, Colorado

This company built custom-built rifles using its proprietary nonbelted cartridges from .260 Heavy Express Magnum to the .416 Heavy Express Magnum. The company's rifles were built on Ruger Model 77 Mark II and Winchester Model 70 Classic actions. Barrels are 4140 chrome-moly blue and 416R stainless steel. Stocks include factory walnut, laminated, or composite designs. The prices listed are for the basic guns. Options are not included and will affect price.

Heavy Express Premier—Ruger M77 Mk II

This rifle is chambered for the .260 HE Mag, .284 HE Mag., or .300 HE Mag. Choice of walnut, laminated, or composite stocks.

NIB	Exc.	V.G.	Good	Fair	Poor
1500	1150	800	600	350	175

NOTE: Add $200 for stainless steel.

Heavy Express Monarch—Winchester M70 Classic

Same as above but built on a Winchester M70 Classic action. Choice of stocks.

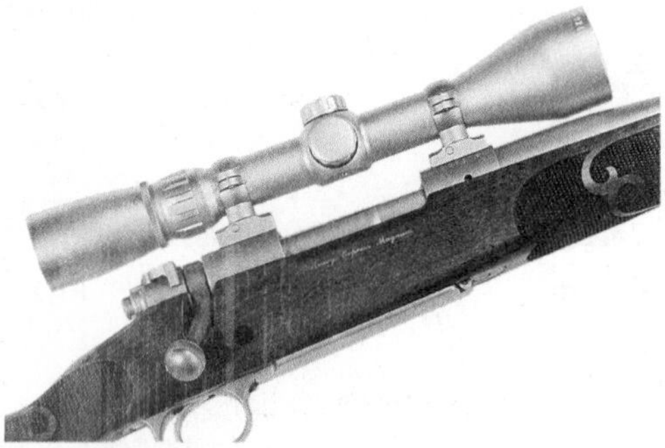

Close-up of Model 70 Classic stainless steel action

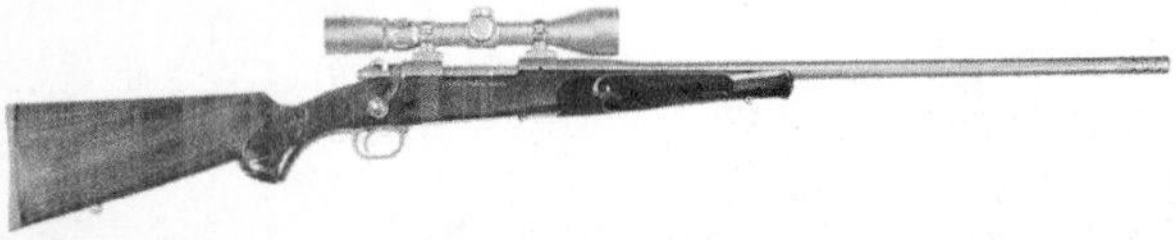

NIB	Exc.	V.G.	Good	Fair	Poor
1775	1400	1000	750	500	250

NOTE: Add $200 for stainless steel.

Heavy Express Monarch—Ruger 77 MK II

This rifle is built on a Ruger M77 action and is chambered for the .338, .350, .375, .416, and .460 HE Magnum cartridges. Choice of stocks.

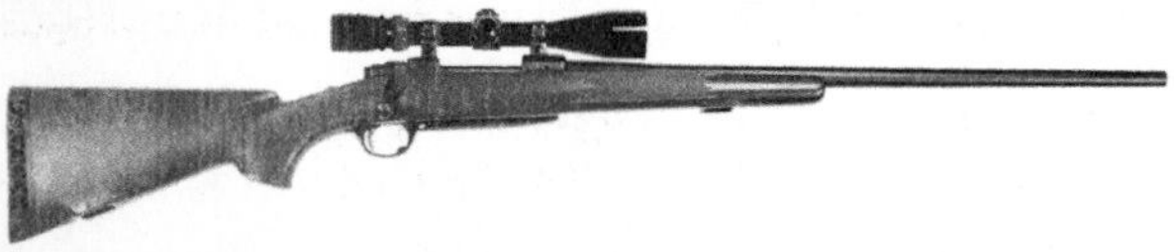

NIB	Exc.	V.G.	Good	Fair	Poor
1775	1400	1000	750	500	250

NOTE: Add $200 for stainless steel.

Heavy Express Single-Shot—Ruger #1

This rifle is chambered in .300, .338, .350, and .416 HE Magnum cartridges. Choice of stocks.

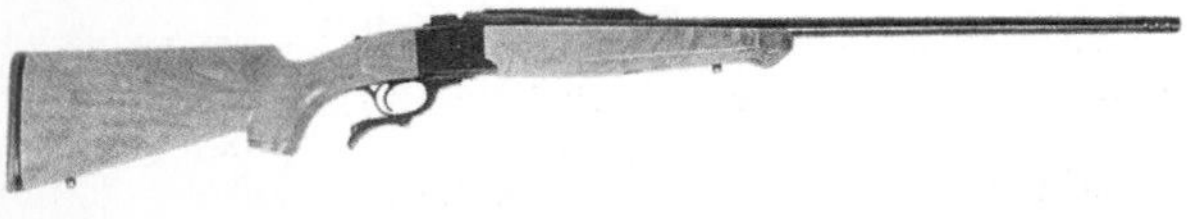

NIB	Exc.	V.G.	Good	Fair	Poor
1775	1400	1000	750	500	250

NOTE: Add $200 for stainless steel.

Heavy Express Premier—Winchester M70 Classic

This rifle is built on a Ruger M77 Mk II action in .260 HE Mag., .284 HE Mag., or .300 HE Mag. Choice of stocks.

NIB	Exc.	V.G.	Good	Fair	Poor
1500	1150	800	500	400	200

NOTE: Add $200 for stainless steel.

HECKLER & KOCH

Oberndorf/Neckar, Germany

At the end of WWII, the French dismantled the Mauser factory as part of their reparations; and the buildings remained idle until 1949, when firearms production was again allowed in Germany. Heckler & Koch was formed as a machine tool enterprise and occupied the vacant Mauser plant. In the early 1950s Edmund Heckler and Theodor Koch began to produce the G3 automatic rifle based on the Spanish CETME design and progressed to machine guns and sub-machine guns and eventually to the production of commercial civilian rifles and pistols. In 1990 the company got into financial difficulties because of a failed contract bid. In December 1990 the French state consortium GIAT announced the purchase of Heckler and Koch, but a little more than a year later the contract was canceled. Later in 1991 the company was purchased by Royal Ordnance of Britain. In 2002 the company was sold to a combined group of European investors and long-time company managers.

Model 91 A2

This rifle is recoil-operated, with a delayed-roller lock bolt. It is chambered for the .308 Winchester cartridge and has a 17.7" barrel with military style aperture sights. It is furnished with a 20-round detachable magazine and is finished in matte black with a black plastic stock. Some areas of the country have made its ownership illegal.

NIB	Exc.	V.G.	Good	Fair	Poor
4000	3000	2000	1500	1150	800

Model 91 A3

This model is simply the Model 91 with a retractable metal stock.

NIB	Exc.	V.G.	Good	Fair	Poor
4200	3250	2250	1700	1350	900

Model 93 A2

This model is similar to the Model 91 except that it is chambered for the .223 cartridge and has a 16.4" barrel. The magazine holds 25 rounds, and the specification are the same as for the Model 91.

NIB	Exc.	V.G.	Good	Fair	Poor
4000	3000	2000	1500	1150	800

Model 93 A3

This is the Model 93 with the retractable metal stock.

NIB	Exc.	V.G.	Good	Fair	Poor
4200	3250	2250	1700	1350	900

Model 94 A2

This is a carbine version chambered for the 9mm Parabellum cartridge, with a 16.5" barrel. It is a smaller-scaled weapon that has a 15-shot magazine.

NIB	Exc.	V.G.	Good	Fair	Poor
4000	3750	3500	3100	2500	1250

Model 94 A3

This model is a variation of the Model 94 with the addition of a retractable metal stock.

NIB	Exc.	V.G.	Good	Fair	Poor
4200	3950	3750	3300	2700	1000

Model 270

This model is chambered for the .22 LR cartridge. It is a sporting-styled rifle with a 16.5" barrel. It is furnished with either a 5- or a 20-round magazine and is blued, with a checkered walnut stock. This rifle was discontinued in 1985.

NIB	Exc.	V.G.	Good	Fair	Poor
800	675	500	350	250	150

Model 300

This model is similar to the Model 270 except that it is chambered for the .22 rimfire Magnum cartridge. It was not imported after 1988.

NIB	Exc.	V.G.	Good	Fair	Poor
800	675	500	350	250	150

Model 630

This model is chambered for the .223 and features the same roller-delayed semi-automatic action as found on the paramilitary-type weapons. This is a sporting-style rifle that has a polished blue finish and a checkered walnut stock. The barrel is 17.7" long, and the magazines offered hold either 4 or 10 rounds. Importation was discontinued in 1986.

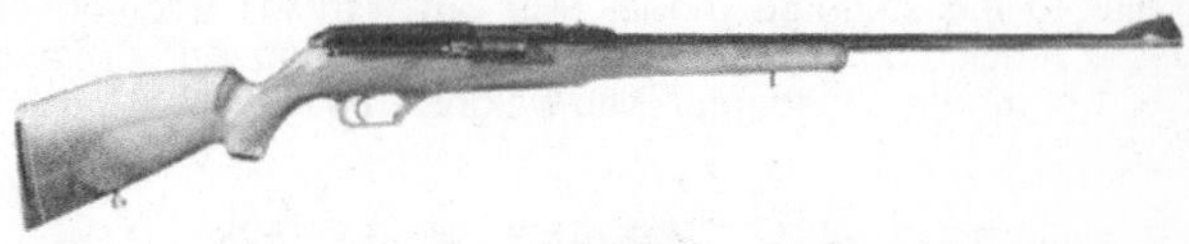

NIB	Exc.	V.G.	Good	Fair	Poor
1795	1350	900	650	450	300

Model 770

This model is similar to the Model 630 except that it is chambered for the .308 Winchester cartridge and has 19.7" barrel. It was not imported after 1986.

NIB	Exc.	V.G.	Good	Fair	Poor
1795	1350	900	650	450	300

Model 940

This model is essentially the same as the Model 770 except that it is chambered for the .30-06 cartridge. It has a 21" barrel and was not imported after 1986.

NIB	Exc.	V.G.	Good	Fair	Poor
2000	1600	1000	600	400	300

Model SL6

This is Heckler & Koch's current sporting rifle chambered for the .223 cartridge. It has a 17.7" barrel and features the same basic action as the military versions. It has a matte black finish and a walnut stock with a vented walnut hand guard. The magazine holds 4 rounds.

NIB	Exc.	V.G.	Good	Fair	Poor
1600	1300	950	650	350	300

Model SL7

This model is similar to the SL6 except that it is chambered for the .308 Winchester cartridge and has a 3-round magazine.

NIB	Exc.	V.G.	Good	Fair	Poor
1600	1300	950	650	350	300

Model SR9

This model was introduced into the U.S. market after the federal government prohibited the importation of H&K's other semi-automatic rifles. The SR9 is similar to the HK91 but has been certified by the BATF as a sporting rifle. This model features a special thumb hole stock made of Kevlar reinforced fiberglass. The action is a delayed-roller locked bolt semi-automatic design chambered for the .308 Winchester cartridge. The barrel is 19.7" in length and features adjustable rear sight with hooded front sight. The rifle weighs 10.9 lbs.

NIB	Exc.	V.G.	Good	Fair	Poor
2900	2400	2000	1400	700	500

Model SR9 (T) Target

Similar to the standard model SR9 but with the addition of a special MSG90 adjustable buttstock, PSG-1 trigger group, and a PSG-1 contoured hand grip. Rifle weighs 10.6 lbs.

NIB	Exc.	V.G.	Good	Fair	Poor
3000	2500	2200	1650	950	600

Model SR9 (TC) Target Competition

Similar to the Model SR9 (T) but with the addition of the PSG-1 adjustable buttstock. Rifle weighs 10.9 lbs.

NIB	Exc.	V.G.	Good	Fair	Poor
3300	3000	2300	1950	1100	700

BASR Model

This is a bolt-action rifle chambered for various popular calibers. It has a stainless steel barrel and was essentially custom built to the customer's specifications. The stock is of Kevlar. This model is quite rare because only 100 were manufactured in 1968.

NIB	Exc.	V.G.	Good	Fair	Poor
—	4000	3600	2750	1300	800

PSG-1

This rifle is a high precision sniping rifle that features the delayed-roller semi-automatic action. It is chambered for the .308 Winchester cartridge and has a 5-shot magazine. Barrel length is 25.6". It is furnished with a complete array of accessories including a 6x42-power illuminated Hensoldt scope. Rifle weighs 17.8 lbs.

NIB	Exc.	V.G.	Good	Fair	Poor
14500	12500	9000	7500	6000	4000

Model SL8-1

This is a new generation .223 rifle modeled after the military Model G36 and introduced in 2000. It is built of carbon fiber polymer and is gas operated. Thumbhole stock with cheekpiece. Barrel length is 20.8". Magazine capacity is 10 rounds. Adjustable sights. Weight is approximately 8.6 lbs.

NIB	Exc.	V.G.	Good	Fair	Poor
1800	1625	1050	700	500	325

SLB 2000

Introduced in 2001 this gas-operated semi-automatic rifle is chamberd for the .30-06 cartridge. The receiver is built of lightweight alloy. The barrel is 16.7" in length and will accept interchangeable barrels at some future date. Oil finished walnut stock. Open sights with both barrel and receiver drilled and tapped for scope mounts. Magazine capacity is 2, 5, or 10 rounds. Weight is about 7.25 lbs.

NIB	Exc.	V.G.	Good	Fair	Poor
1800	1300	1050	775	400	225

Model MR556A1

Direct descendant of the HK416, Semi-automatic, gas-piston operating system. Free floating rail hand-guard system with four Picatinny rails for mounting of optical or lighting accessories. Two-stage trigger. Retractable butt-stock can be locked in any position to suit individual requirements. Chambered for the 5.56x45mm NATO round. Magazine capacities: 10, 20 or 30 rounds. New for 2011.

NIB	Exc.	V.G.	Good	Fair	Poor
2900	2475	2100	1300	650	300

Model USC

Introduced in 2000 this semi-automatic blowback carbine is derived from H&K's UMP submachine gun. Chambered for the .45 ACP cartridge and fitted with a 16" barrel. Skeletonized stock. Accessory rail on top of receiver. Adjustable sights. Magazine capacity is 10 rounds. Weight is approximately 6 lbs.

NIB	Exc.	V.G.	Good	Fair	Poor
1700	1275	1000	750	400	200

HENRY, ALEXANDER

Edinburgh, Scotland

Noted for both the rifling system he developed and the falling block single-shot rifles he made, Alexander Henry conducted business at these locations:, 12 South Street, Andrew Street1853-1858

8 South Street, Andrew Street1858-1862
12 South Street, Andrew Street1862-1871
12 and 14 South Street, Andrew Street1871-1875
12 South Street, Andrew Street1875-1895
18 Frederick Street1895-1911
22 Frederick Street1911-

Single-Shot Rifle

A high-grade single-shot that features a true falling-block action that is activated by a side lever on the action. It was available in the popular European cartridges of the era, and the barrel length varies from 22" to 28" in length. This rifle exhibits fine quality materials and workmanship. The select-grade walnut stock and schnabel forend are hand checkered. The finish of the rifle is scroll-engraved and blued. This company manufactured firearms from 1869 until 1895.

NIB	Exc.	V.G.	Good	Fair	Poor
—	—	3800	1500	700	400

Double Rifle

A side-by-side, double-barreled Express Rifle chambered for the .500/450 Black Powder Express cartridge. It has Damascus barrels and double triggers. This gun is hammerless and features ornate scroll engraving as well as a high-grade hand checkered walnut stock and forend. It was furnished with a fitted leather case and accessories. This rifle was manufactured in the 1890s.

NIB	Exc.	V.G.	Good	Fair	Poor
—	—	9000	5000	1750	800

HENRY REPEATING ARMS COMPANY

Brooklyn, New York

Henry Lever-Action

Chambered for the .22 LR, Long, and Short cartridges It is fitted with a 18.25" barrel and weighs 5.5 lbs. Magazine capacity is 15 for the .22 LR cartridge. Rear sight is adjustable and the front sight is hooded.

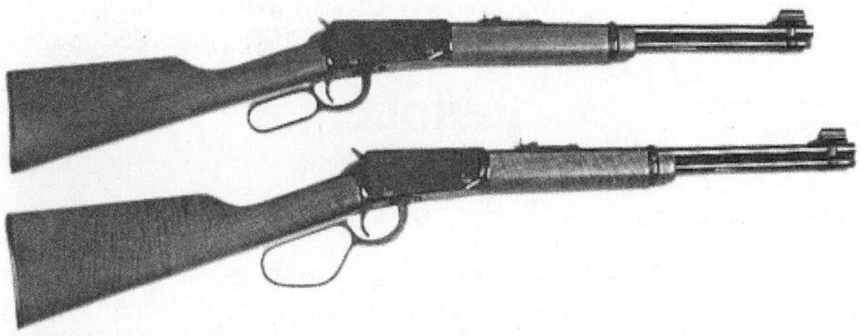

NIB	Exc.	V.G.	Good	Fair	Poor
280	200	155	125	75	50

Henry Carbine

Similar to the above model but with an overall length of 34". It features a large loop lever.

NIB	Exc.	V.G.	Good	Fair	Poor
280	200	155	125	75	50

Henry Youth Model

Similar to the carbine model above but with an overall length of 33".

NIB	Exc.	V.G.	Good	Fair	Poor
280	200	155	125	75	50

Henry Lever-Action .22 Magnum

Fitted with a 19.5" barrel with a tubular magazine capacity of 11 rounds. Checkered deluxe walnut stock. Weight is about 5.5 lbs.

NIB	Exc.	V.G.	Good	Fair	Poor
350	300	250	195	125	75

Henry Lever-Action Frontier Model

Similar to Henry Lever Action but with 20-inch octagon barrel. Chambered in .22 WMR and .17HMR. Introduced 2006.

NIB	Exc.	V.G.	Good	Fair	Poor
375	300	250	175	115	85

Henry Golden Boy

This lever-action rifle is chambered for the .22 LR, Short, or Long cartridges as well as the .22 WRM cartridge in a separate model. Fitted with a brass receiver and 20" octagon barrel. Walnut stock. Weight is about 6.75 lbs.

NIB	Exc.	V.G.	Good	Fair	Poor
550	400	295	200	125	85

NOTE: Add $70 for .22 WRM model or .17 HMR. Add $20 for large loop lever. Add $600 for hand-engraved model.

Henry Golden Boy Deluxe

Chambered for the .22 Long Rifle cartridge and fitted with a 20" octagon barrel. Fancy walnut stock. Deeply engraved receiver.

NIB	Exc.	V.G.	Good	Fair	Poor
1250	995	650	400	200	125

Henry Deluxe Engraved Golden Boy Magnum

Similar to Golden Boy Deluxe but chambered in .22 WMR. Features deluxe deep-cut German-style engraving on receiver. Introduced 2006.

NIB	Exc.	V.G.	Good	Fair	Poor
1275	1000	675	425	225	150

Henry Varmint Express

This lever-action rifle is chambered for the .17 HMR cartridge and fitted with a 20" round barrel. Checkered American walnut stock. Scope mount included. Magazine capacity is 11 rounds. Weight is about 5.75 lbs.

NIB	Exc.	V.G.	Good	Fair	Poor
45	350	225	175	100	75

Henry Big Boy

This lever-action model is chambered for the .44 Magnum or .45 Colt cartridge. Octagonal barrel is 20". Magazine capacity is 10 rounds. American walnut stock with straight grip. Weight is about 8.7 lbs. .357 Magnum added 2006.

NIB	Exc.	V.G.	Good	Fair	Poor
725	595	400	300	200	150

Henry Big Boy Deluxe Engraved .44 Magnum

Similar to Henry Big Boy but with deluxe deep-cut German-style engraving on receiver. Introduced 2006.

NIB	Exc.	V.G.	Good	Fair	Poor
1350	1100	850	550	275	175

Big Boy .44 Magnum "Wildlife Edition"

Similar to Big Boy .44 Magnum but with forend and buttstock laser-engraved with whitetail deer scenes. Introduced in 2007.

NIB	Exc.	V.G.	Good	Fair	Poor
875	750	625	500	250	125

Big Boy .45 Colt "Cowboy Edition"

Similar to Big Boy .45 Colt but with forend and buttstock laser-engraved with Old West scenes. Introduced in 2007.

NIB	Exc.	V.G.	Good	Fair	Poor
1350	1100	850	550	275	175

Henry 30-30

Caliber: .30-30 Winchester. Features a 20-inch barrel, straight-grip American walnut stock with rubber butt-pad, XS Ghost Ring sights, blue finish, weight of 7 lbs. Also available with brass receiver, octagon barrel and adjustable Marble's buck-horn rear sight, bead front.

NIB	Exc.	V.G.	Good	Fair	Poor
650	575	500	400	300	200

NOTE: Add 30 percent for brass receiver/octagon barrel.

HENRY MARE'S LEG

Caliber: .45 Colt or .22 S/L/LR. Has large-loop lever based on rifle seen in classic Steve McQueen western TV series "Wanted: Dead or Alive." Barrel length is 12.9 inches, overall length 25 inches. Weight: 5.8 lbs. (.45 Colt), 4.5 lbs. (.22). Lanyard ring, blue finish, straight-grip walnut stock. Sights are Marble's adjustable semi-buckhorn rear and brass bead front (.45 Colt): adjustable rear and hooded front (.22).

Mare's Leg .45 Colt

NIB	Exc.	V.G.	Good	Fair	Poor
800	675	500	400	300	200

Mare's Leg .22

NIB	Exc.	V.G.	Good	Fair	Poor
315	275	220	175	110	85

Henry Pump-Action Rifle

Introduced in 1999 this .22 caliber is fitted with a 18.25" barrel and chambered for the .22 LR cartridge. Walnut stock and adjustable rear sight. Weight is approximately 5.5 lbs. Add

NIB	Exc.	V.G.	Good	Fair	Poor
350	250	185	135	100	75

Henry U.S. Survival Rifle

This model is an improved version of the AR-7 .22 caliber survival rifle issued to the Air Force. It is a breakdown design and features a waterproof stock, a steel-lined barrel and adjustable sights. Furnished with two 8-round magazines. Overall length when broken down is 16.5".

NIB	Exc.	V.G.	Good	Fair	Poor
250	175	115	85	65	40

Henry Pump-Action .22 Octagon Rifle

Similar to Henry Pump-Action Rifle but with 20-inch octagon barrel. Introduced 2006. Add 10 percent for .22 WMR.

NIB	Exc.	V.G.	Good	Fair	Poor
495	350	225	150	125	75

Henry Mini Bolt

This single-shot bolt-action .22 caliber rifle is designed for young shooters. Barrel length is 16.25". Overall length is 30.25" Stainless steel barrel and receiver. Colored stocks available. Adjustable sights. Weight is about 3.25 lbs.

NIB	Exc.	V.G.	Good	Fair	Poor
210	165	100	75	50	25

Henry Acu-Bolt

Chambered for the .22 LR, .22 WMR, or the .17 HMR cartridges and fitted with a 20" barrel. Fiberglass stock. Scope mounts. Weight is about 4.25 lbs. Add 10 percent for factory scope.

NIB	Exc.	V.G.	Good	Fair	Poor
315	275	200	150	100	75

HEROLD

Franz Jaeger
Suhl, Germany

Bolt-Action Rifle

A .22 Hornet bolt-action sporting rifle with a 24" ribbed barrel, adjustable sights, double set triggers and walnut stock. Imported by Charles Daly and Stoeger Arms prior to WWII.

NIB	Exc.	V.G.	Good	Fair	Poor
—	1500	850	600	400	250

HERTER'S

Waseca, Minnesota

An importer and retailer of European-made firearms. Active until approximately 1980.

J-9 or U-9 Hunter

Mauser-action sporting rifles manufactured in England (J-9) and Yugoslavia (U-9), with 24" barrels and Monte Carlo-style walnut stocks.

NIB	Exc.	V.G.	Good	Fair	Poor
—	475	200	155	100	75

J-9 or U-9 Presentation or Supreme

As above, with checkering and sling swivels.

NIB	Exc.	V.G.	Good	Fair	Poor
—	550	325	200	150	100

HESSE ARMS

Inver Grove Heights, Minnesota

FAL-H RIFLES

All FAL-H rifles include these features: military spec internalparts, new or as new barrel, military finish, post ban legal muzzlebrake, one magazine, new metric pattern Type 3 receiver, adjustable gas system, refinished or new pistol grip, hard case,carry handle, sling, and manual. All rifles chambered for .308Winchester cartridge. Additional calibers in .22-250 and .243 arealso available. Weights are from 8.5 to 14 lbs. depending on model.

NOTE: Value on Hesse Arms products can fluctuate widely .

FALO Tactical Rifle

This model features a free floating handguard assembly.

NIB	Exc.	V.G.	Good	Fair	Poor
1150	900	700	400	200	100

FALO Heavy Barrel

This model features a heavy barrel and is based on the Israeli FALO rifle.

NIB	Exc.	V.G.	Good	Fair	Poor
950	750	600	400	200	100

FAL-H High Grade

This model is available in any configuration and features a new walnut stock, pistol grip, and handguard. Trigger is gold plated.

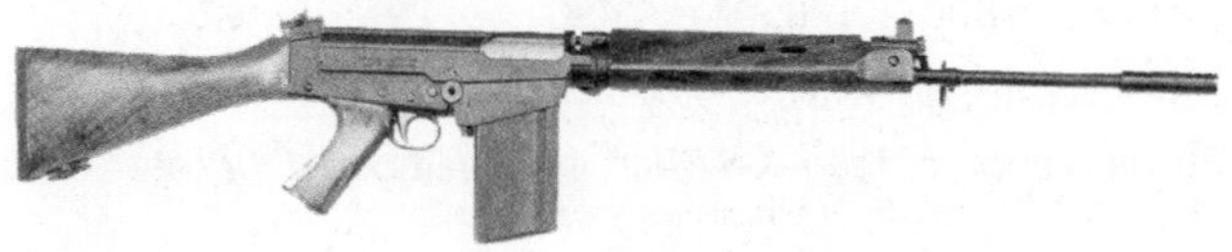

NIB	Exc.	V.G.	Good	Fair	Poor
1350	1050	850	500	300	150

FAL-H Standard Grade

This is standard model that is similar in appearance to the original FAL.

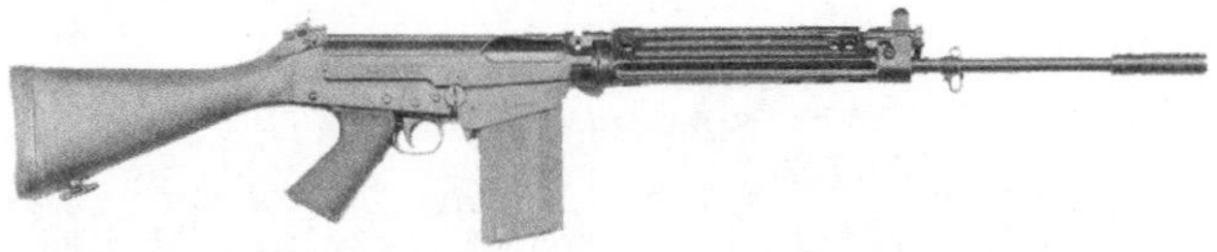

NIB	Exc.	V.G.	Good	Fair	Poor
950	750	600	400	200	100

FAL-H Congo Rifle

This model features a 16" barrel.

NIB	Exc.	V.G.	Good	Fair	Poor
1000	800	650	400	200	100

FALO Congo Rifle

Similar to the model above but fitted with a 16" heavy barrel.

NIB	Exc.	V.G.	Good	Fair	Poor
1000	800	650	400	200	100

HAR-15 RIFLES

All of the HAR-15 rifles have these features: military spec internal parts, heavy match grade barrels, post ban legal muzzle-brake, A2 upper receiver, A2 round handguards with heat shields, A2 stock, A2 lower receiver. Each rifle comes with hard case, manual, and sling. Rifles are chambered for .223 Remington but can be chambered in other calibers as well. These are: .17 Rem. add $145, 9mm NATO add $85, 6mm PPC add $145, 6mmx45 add $95, .300 Fireball add $195, 7.62x39 add $45.

Omega Match

Fitted with a 1" diameter stainless steel barrel, adjustable match trigger, E2 stock, flat top receiver, free floating handguard.

NIB	Exc.	V.G.	Good	Fair	Poor
1000	800	650	400	200	100

HAR-15A2 Standard Rifle

This model has all of the standard features offered for HAR-15 rifles.

NIB	Exc.	V.G.	Good	Fair	Poor
725	575	475	325	150	75

HAR-15A2 National Match

This model is fitted with special bolt carrier, adjustable match trigger. Designed as Match grade rifle.

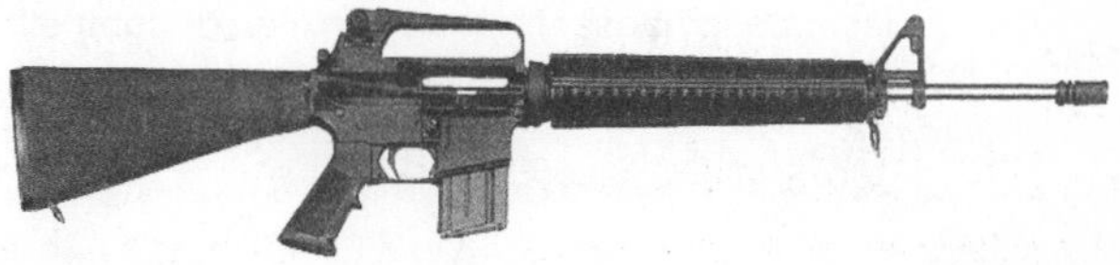

NIB	Exc.	V.G.	Good	Fair	Poor
1000	800	650	400	200	100

HAR-15A2 Bull Gun

This model is fitted with a 1" stainless steel barrel with special front sight base.

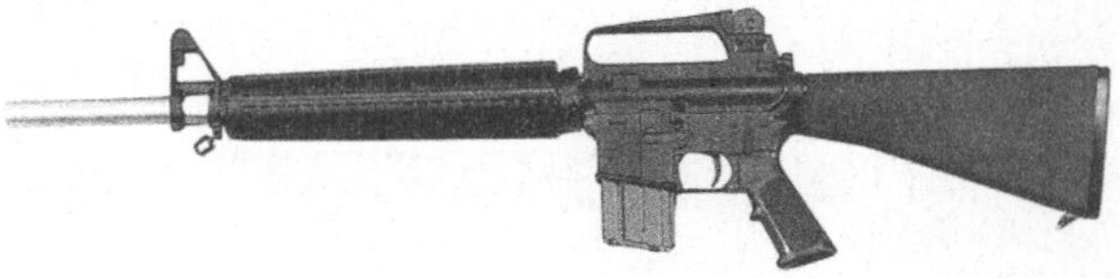

NIB	Exc.	V.G.	Good	Fair	Poor
775	600	475	225	150	75

HAR-15A2 Dispatcher

Fitted with a 16" barrel with full length handguard.

NIB	Exc.	V.G.	Good	Fair	Poor
725	575	450	225	150	75

HAR-15A2 Carbine

Fitted with a 16" heavy barrel and a non-collapsing stock with short handguard.

NIB	Exc.	V.G.	Good	Fair	Poor
725	575	475	225	150	75

H-22 RIFLES

All H-22 rifles include these features: new internal parts interchangeable with Ruger 10/22 rifle, heavy stainless steel barrel with match chamber, stainless steel receiver, laminated stock, hard case, magazine, and manual. All rifle are chambered for .22 LR. For an additional $250 charge any H-22 rifle can be converted to .22 Magnum. Weight of these rifles is approximately 7 lbs.

H-22 Tigershark

Special forearm and skeleton stock with heavy fluted barrel. Special trigger pack with over travel screw and glass bedded stock.

NIB	Exc.	V.G.	Good	Fair	Poor
800	650	525	375	195	125

H-22 Competition Rifle

This model features a gloss finished laminated competition thumbhole stock.

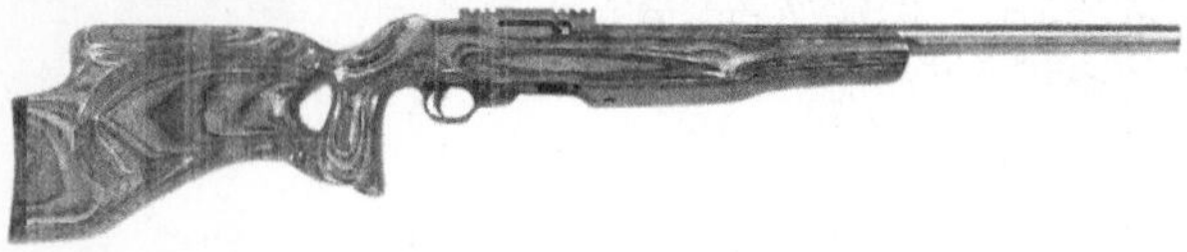

NIB	Exc.	V.G.	Good	Fair	Poor
550	450	350	225	150	75

H-22 Wildcat

This model has a screwed-in heavy barrel and a special laminated stock.

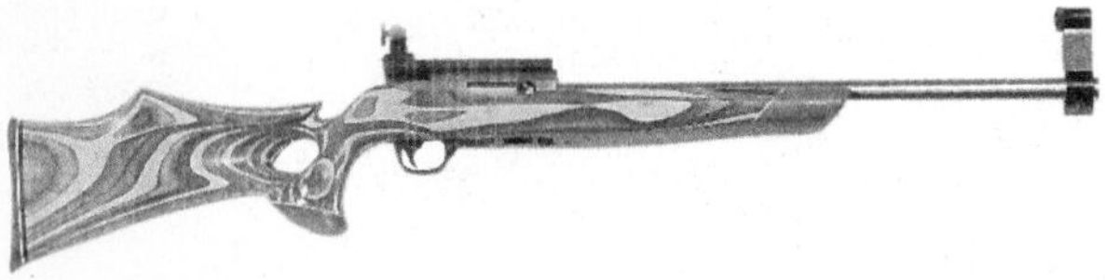

NIB	Exc.	V.G.	Good	Fair	Poor
550	450	350	225	150	75

H-22 Standard Rifle

Has all the standard features of the H-22 rifle including a buttstock with cheekpiece.

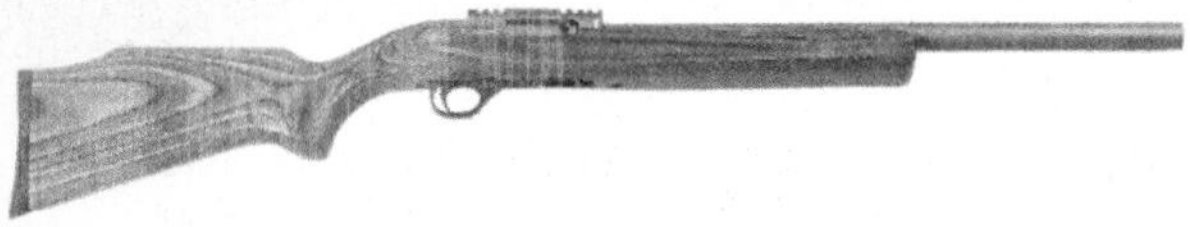

NIB	Exc.	V.G.	Good	Fair	Poor
475	375	300	200	125	50

M14-H Standard Rifle

This is a semi-automatic version of the M14 rifle chambered for the .308 cartridge. It is fitted with a new receiver, walnut stock or synthetic stock. Each rifle is sold with a sling, annual, and 10-round magazine and an extra original M145 stock.

NIB	Exc.	V.G.	Good	Fair	Poor
1000	800	650	400	200	100

M14-H Brush Rifle

This model has the same features as the standard rifle but with an 18" barrel.

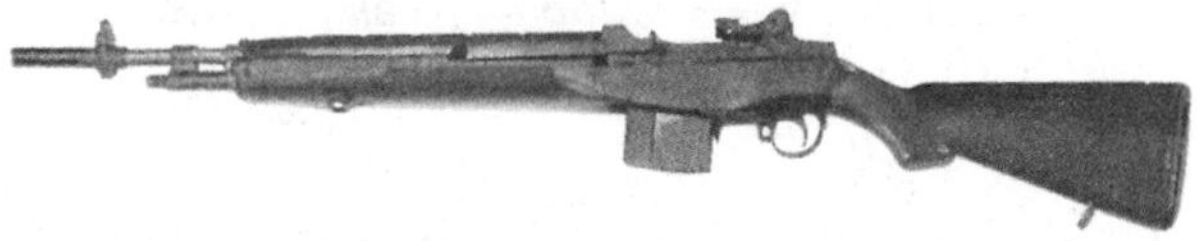

NIB	Exc.	V.G.	Good	Fair	Poor
1050	800	650	450	225	125

Hesse Model 47 Rifle

This is a copy of the AK-47 and it is chambered for the 7.63x39 cartridge. It is also available in .223 caliber.

NIB	Exc.	V.G.	Good	Fair	Poor
600	475	375	275	150	75

HEYM, F. W.

Suhl, Germany

Established in 1865 in Suhl, Germany, this company was reestablished after WWII in Munnerstadt. The company remained there until 1996 when it moved back to a suburb of Suhl. Post-war arms were originally imported by Paul Jaeger of Grand Junction, Tennessee.

SINGLE-SHOT RIFLES

Model HR-30

Built on the Ruger No. 1 falling-block-action and chambered for most calibers with a 24" round barrel or a 26" barrel in the magnum calibers. There is a quarter rib with express sights, and the single-set trigger is made by Canjar. The rifle is engraved with a game scene motif, and the stock is deluxe, hand checkered French walnut with a classic European-style cheekpiece. French case hardened and blued.

NIB	Exc.	V.G.	Good	Fair	Poor
—	5000	3900	3250	1750	1250

Model HR-38

As above, with an octagonal barrel.

NIB	Exc.	V.G.	Good	Fair	Poor
—	5200	4250	3500	2000	1500

DOUBLE RIFLES

Model 22 Safety

An over-and-under combination rifle/shotgun chambered for 16 or 20 gauge over .22 Hornet, .22 WMR, .222 Remington, .222 Remington Magnum, .223, 5.6x50Rmm, 6.5x57Rmm, and

7x57Rmm with 24" barrels. Boxlock action with a single trigger, automatic ejectors, and automatic decocking mechanism. French case hardening, blued with a walnut stock.

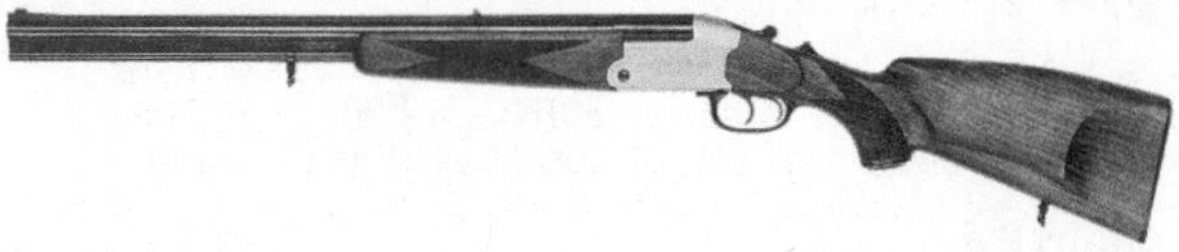

NIB	Exc.	V.G.	Good	Fair	Poor
—	3500	3000	2750	1200	900

Model 77B/55B Over-and-Under Rifle

An over-and-under rifle manufactured in a variety of calibers with 25" barrels having open sights: and a boxlock-action with Kersten double cross bolts. The action is heavily engraved with a game scene motif and is silver plated. This model has double triggers, cocking indicators, automatic ejectors, and select walnut stock. The barrels machined to accept a Zeiss scope with claw mounts.

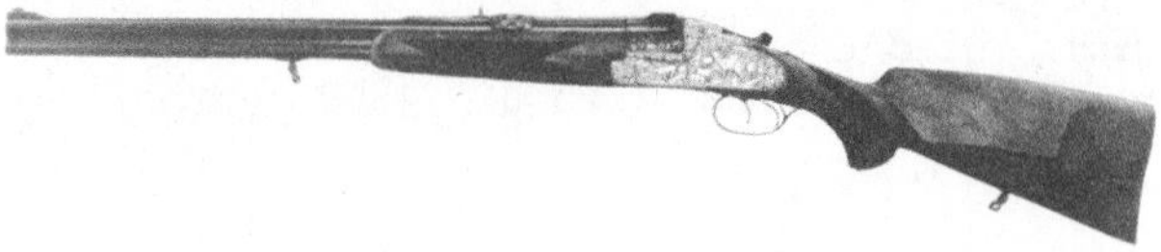

NIB	Exc.	V.G.	Good	Fair	Poor
—	6000	5500	4000	3250	2500

Model 55BSS

As above with sidelocks.

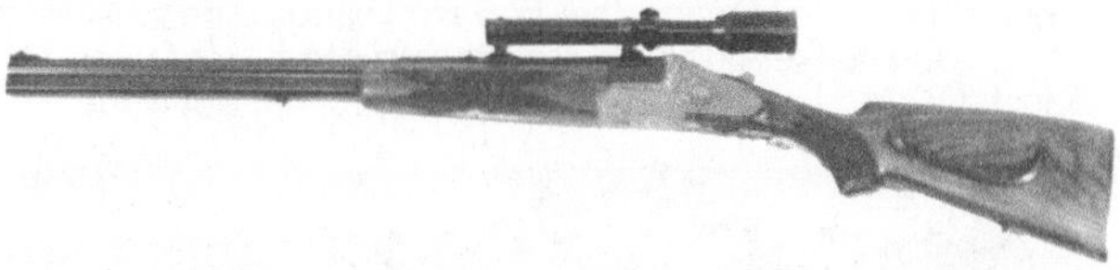

NIB	Exc.	V.G.	Good	Fair	Poor
—	10500	9500	8500	5000	3500

Model 55BF/77BF

Similar to the Model 55B, except one barrel is rifled and the other smooth in 12, 16, or 20 gauge.

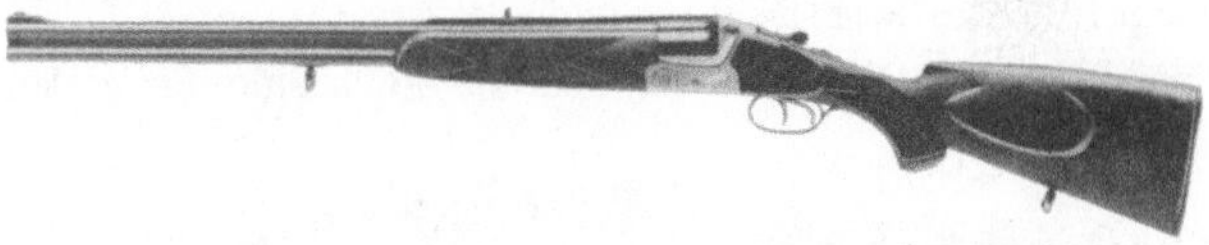

NIB	Exc.	V.G.	Good	Fair	Poor
—	6000	5500	5000	3250	2500

Model 55BFSS

As above, with sidelocks.

NIB	Exc.	V.G.	Good	Fair	Poor
—	10500	9500	8500	5000	3500

Model 88 B

A large bore double-barrel boxlock rifle with 24" barrels, automatic ejectors, double triggers, and select walnut stock.

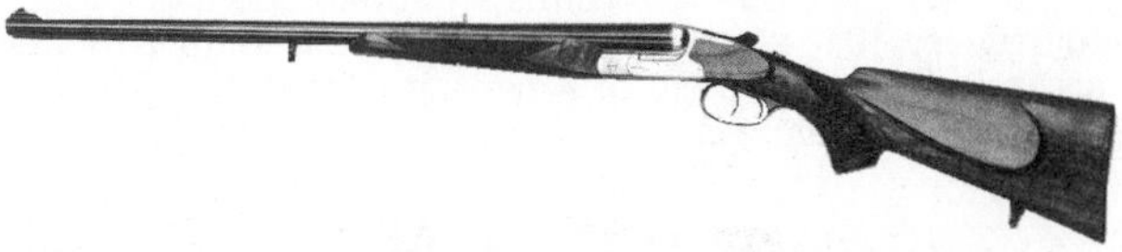

NIB	Exc.	V.G.	Good	Fair	Poor
—	10500	9750	8750	5500	4000

Model 88 BSS

As above with sidelocks.

NIB	Exc.	V.G.	Good	Fair	Poor
—	15000	13500	10500	6500	5250

Model 88 Safari

As above, but chambered for .375 Holland & Holland, .458 Winchester Magnum, .470, or .500 Nitro Express calibers with 25" barrels.

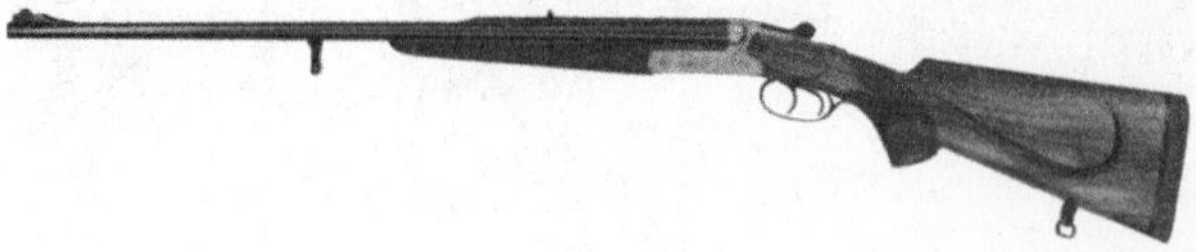

NIB	Exc.	V.G.	Good	Fair	Poor
—	14500	13000	10000	7000	4750

DRILLINGS

Model 33

A boxlock drilling manufactured in a variety of American and European calibers and gauges with 25" barrels, double triggers and extractors. Case hardened, blued with a walnut stock.

NIB	Exc.	V.G.	Good	Fair	Poor
—	7000	6000	5250	3750	2000

Model 33 Deluxe

Same as above but with game scene engraving.

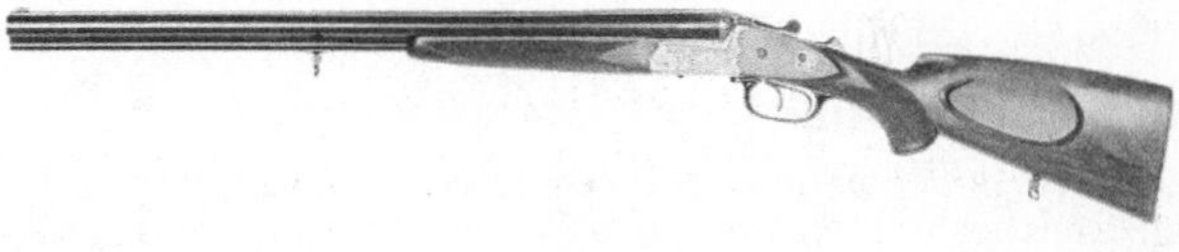

NIB	Exc.	V.G.	Good	Fair	Poor
—	8500	7000	5750	4500	2500

Model 37

Similar to the Model 33 Standard but with full sidelocks.

NIB	Exc.	V.G.	Good	Fair	Poor
—	17500	13000	9500	6000	2500

Model 37 Deluxe

Similar to the above Model 37 but with hand engraved scroll work and fancy walnut stock.

NIB	Exc.	V.G.	Good	Fair	Poor
—	20000	16500	12000	6000	3000

BOLT-ACTION RIFLES

Model SR-20

A Mauser-action sporting rifle manufactured in a variety of calibers with 21", 24", or 26" barrels, open sights, adjustable trigger or set trigger. Blued with a walnut stock.

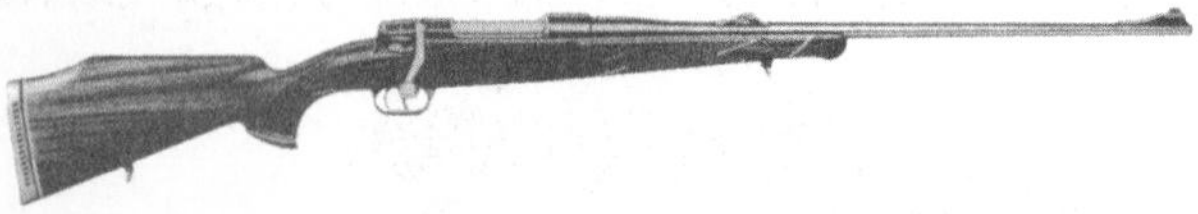

NIB	Exc.	V.G.	Good	Fair	Poor
2450	2250	1650	750	600	450

Model SR-20 Alpine

As above with a 20" barrel and Mannlicher stock. Introduced in 1989.

NIB	Exc.	V.G.	Good	Fair	Poor
3650	3250	2750	1250	850	600

SR-20 Classic Safari

As above, but chambered for .404 Jeffries, .425 Express, and the .458 Winchester Magnum with a 24" barrel having express sights. Introduced in 1989.

NIB	Exc.	V.G.	Good	Fair	Poor
4500	4000	3750	2000	1250	750

SR-20 Classic Sportsman

This model features a round barrel without sights. Chambered for many calibers from .243 to .375 H&H. Introduced in 1988. Add $100 for Magnum calibers.

NIB	Exc.	V.G.	Good	Fair	Poor
2650	2250	1900	900	500	300

SR-20 Trophy

Similar to the above Classic Sportsman model but with German bead ramp sight and open quarter rib rear sight. Select walnut stock with oil finish. Octagonal barrel and rosewood grip cap.

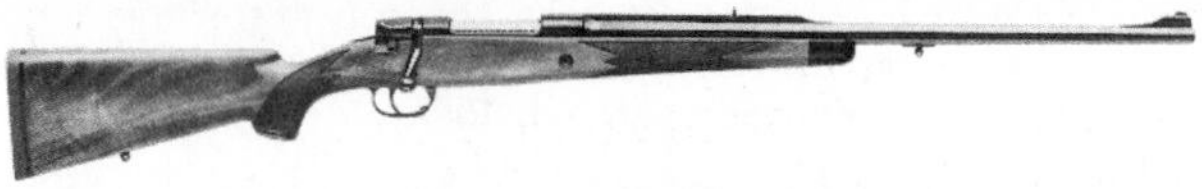

NIB	Exc.	V.G.	Good	Fair	Poor
3500	3000	2250	1800	900	300

Magnum Express

This bolt-action rifle is chambered for .338 Lapua, .375 H&H, .416 Rigby, .500 Nitro Express, .500 A-Square, and a few were built in .600 Nitro Express. Fitted with a 24" barrel. Adjustable front sight, three leaf rear express sight. Select hand checkered European walnut stock, and many other special features. Introduced in 1989.

NIB	Exc.	V.G.	Good	Fair	Poor
6800	5500	4000	2500	1750	500

NOTE: Add $4,000 for 600 N.E.

HI-POINT FIREARMS

MKS Supply
Dayton, Ohio

.40 S&W Carbine

.40 S&W semi-auto carbine. Features include all-weather, black, polymer stock, 10 shot magazine, 17.5-inch barrel, sling swivels, grip mounted clip release, quick on & off thumb safety, rear peep sight, 32.5-inch OAL and a scope mount. Add $85 for red dot sight.

NIB	Exc.	V.G.	Good	Fair	Poor
275	200	150	100	75	50

Model 995 Carbine

Similar to .40 S&W Carbine but chambered for 9mm Parabellum.

NIB	Exc.	V.G.	Good	Fair	Poor
285	210	160	110	75	50

HIGGINS, J. C.

Chicago, Illinois

The Sears, Roebuck & Company of Chicago used the trade name J.C. Higgins on the firearms and other sporting goods it sold between 1946 and 1962. Arms bearing this tradename were manufactured by a variety of American gunmakers. See High Standard, Mossberg, etc.

HIGH STANDARD

New Haven, Connecticut 1932-1945
Hamden, Connecticut 1946-1977
East Hartford, Connecticut 1977-1984

NOTE: See High Standard Manufacturing Co., Houston, TX at the end of this semi-auto pistol section.

SHOTGUNS

SEMI-AUTOMATIC SHOTGUNS

Supermatic Field

NOTE: Slight premium for 20 gauge.

NIB	Exc.	V.G.	Good	Fair	Poor
—	300	250	195	100	75

Supermatic Special

Like the Supermatic Field except with 27" barrel with six-position click-stop adjustable choke. Supermatic Special models were superceded by models in the Supermatic Deluxe group beginning in 1966. The 12 gauge guns have 2-3/4" chambers.

NIB	Exc.	V.G.	Good	Fair	Poor
—	300	250	195	100	75

Supermatic Deluxe

Gas-operated semi-automatic shotgun. Blued finish, Checkered pistol grip walnut stock and forearm. Four-round magazine capacity. The adjustable choke had 6 click-stop positions. Recoil pad beginning 1966. The 12 gauge guns have 2-3/4" chambers while the 20 gauge guns have 3" chambers.

NIB	Exc.	V.G.	Good	Fair	Poor
—	325	275	210	125	95

NOTE: Add $20 premium for vent rib versions.

Supermatic Duck

Gas-operated semi-automatic shotgun chambered for 3" magnum and suitable for all 2-3/4" shells. Blued finish. Checkered pistol-grip walnut stock and forearm. Magazine capacity: five 2-3/4" shells, four 3" shells. Recoil pad.

NIB	Exc.	V.G.	Good	Fair	Poor
—	325	275	210	125	95

NOTE: Add $20 premium for vent rib versions.

Supermatic Deer Gun

Like Supermatic Deluxe with rifle sight. Recoil pad. Receiver tapped for peep sight on catalog number 8246. The 12 gauge guns have 2-3/4" chambers.

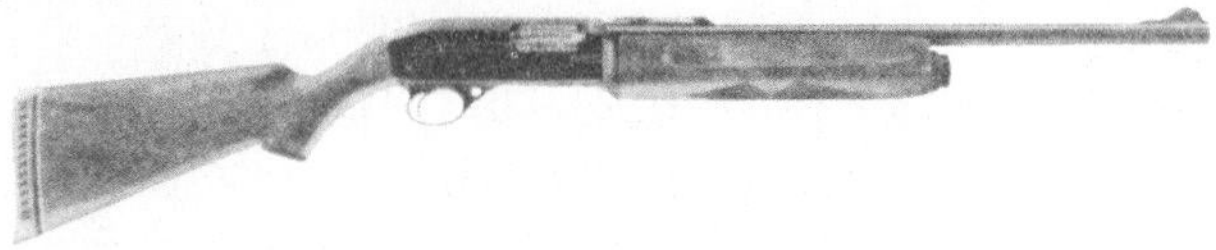

NIB	Exc.	V.G.	Good	Fair	Poor
—	300	250	195	100	75

Supermatic Skeet

Same features as Supermatic Deluxe except select American walnut stock and forearm and no recoil pad. The 12 gauge guns have 2-3/4" chambers while the 20 gauge guns have 3" chambers.

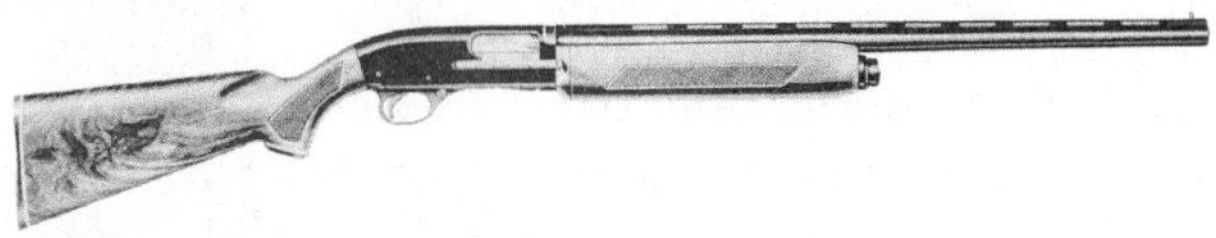

NIB	Exc.	V.G.	Good	Fair	Poor
—	325	275	210	125	95

Supermatic Trap

Same features as Supermatic Deluxe except select American walnut stock and forearm. Recoil pad. Catalog number 8266 is the Executive Trap model with Fajen Monte Carlo stock. The 12 gauge guns have 2-3/4" chambers.

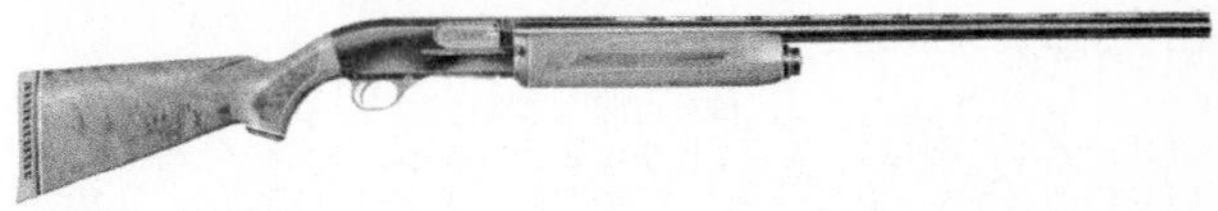

NIB	Exc.	V.G.	Good	Fair	Poor
—	325	275	210	125	95

PUMP SHOTGUNS

Model 200

An economy 12 gauge pump shotgun sold as part of a promotional package beginning in 1971. The package included the Model 200, a zippered gun case, a plastic trigger lock, and G-96 gun lubricant. Prices are for gun alone. Add $30 for gun with complete promotional package.

NIB	Exc.	V.G.	Good	Fair	Poor
—	175	130	105	90	65

Flite King Field

Slide-action shotgun. Blued finish, plain pistol grip walnut stock and forearm. Catalog number 8450, magazine capacity: five 2-1/2" shells, four 3" shells. The 12 gauge guns have 2-3/4" chambers while the 20 gauge guns have 3" chambers.

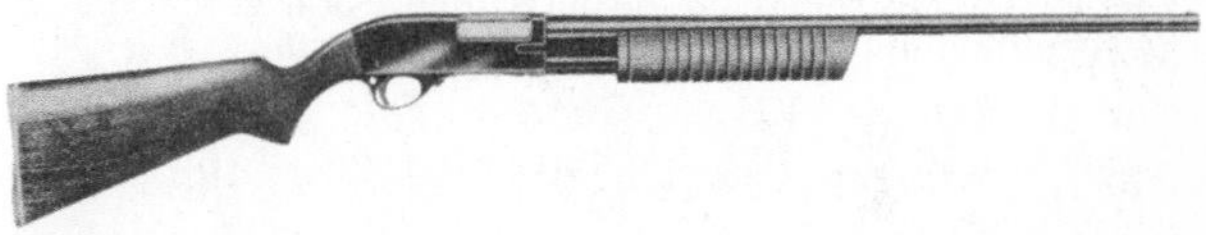

NIB	Exc.	V.G.	Good	Fair	Poor
—	250	195	150	100	65

NOTE: Add 50 percent for .410 bore.

Flite King Brush

Like the Flite King Field except has adjustable rifle sights. Receiver is tapped for the Williams sight and provision exist for sling swivels. Deluxe models have Williams receiver sight, a leather sling with swivels, and a recoil pad. The 12 gauge guns have 2-3/4" chambers.

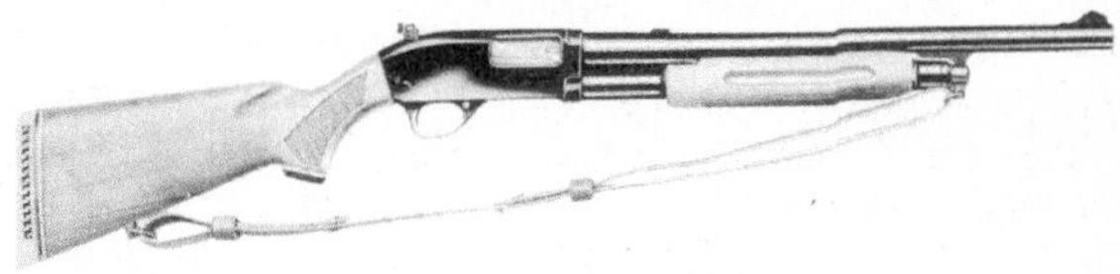

Flite King Brush Deluxe

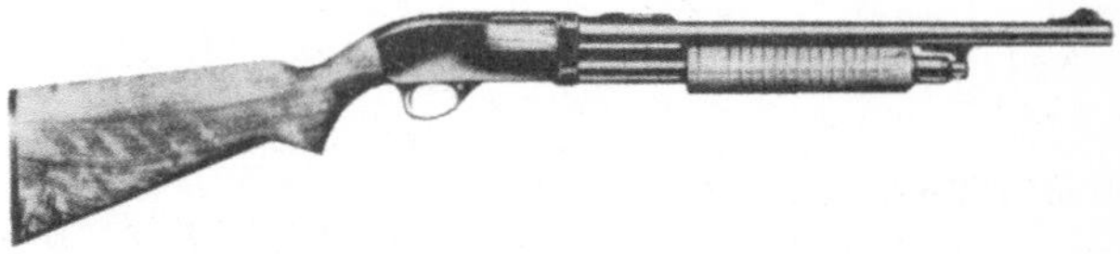

NIB	Exc.	V.G.	Good	Fair	Poor
—	265	205	160	100	75

NOTE: Add $10 premium for deluxe model.

Flite King Special

Like the Flite King Field except for a 27" barrel with 6-click-stop adjustable choke. The 12 gauge guns have 2-3/4" chambers while the 20 gauge guns have 3" chambers.

NIB	Exc.	V.G.	Good	Fair	Poor
—	250	195	150	100	65

Flite King Deluxe

Slide-action shotgun. Blued finish, checkered pistol grip walnut stock and forearm. Five-round magazine capacity. Available with and without a vent rib. 8411 and 6411 were the boys "Converta Pump" sold with two stocks: one youth size and one full size. The adjustable choke had six click-stop positions. Recoil pad beginning 1966 except .410 models.The 12 gauge guns have 2-3/4" chambers, the 16 gauge has 2-3/4" chambers, the 20 gauge guns have 3" chambers, the 28 gauge has 2-3/4" chambers, and the .410 bore has 3" chambers.

NIB	Exc.	V.G.	Good	Fair	Poor
—	265	205	160	100	75

NOTE: Add $20 for vent rib.

Flite King Citation

Like the Flite King Trophy without the vent rib. Catalog number 8130 has a compensator integral with the 6 position click stop adjustable choke. The 12 gauge guns have 2-3/4" chambers while the 16 gauge guns have 2-3/4" chambers as well.

NIB	Exc.	V.G.	Good	Fair	Poor
—	250	195	150	100	65

Flite King Trophy

Slide-action shotgun. Blued finish, checkered pistol grip walnut stock and forearm. Five-round magazine capacity. Ventilated rib. Catalog number 8140 has a compensator integral with the adjustable choke. The 12 gauge guns have 2-3/4" chambers while the 20 gauge guns have 3" chambers.

NIB	Exc.	V.G.	Good	Fair	Poor
—	250	195	150	100	65

Flite King Skeet

Same features as Flite King Deluxe except select American walnut stock and forearm and no recoil pad. The 12 gauge guns have 2-3/4" chambers, the 20 gauge guns have 3" chambers, the 28 gauge has 2-3/4" chambers, and the .410 bore has 3" chambers.

NIB	Exc.	V.G.	Good	Fair	Poor
—	290	200	150	100	75

Flite King Trap

Same features as Flite King Deluxe except select American walnut stock and forearm. Recoil pad. 8166 is the Executive Trap model with Fajen Monte Carlo stock. Catalog number 6165 is a model with provisions for interchangeable barrels. The 12 gauge guns have 2-3/4" chambers.

NIB	Exc.	V.G.	Good	Fair	Poor
—	275	185	150	100	75

NOTE: Add $25 for Fajen Monte Carlo stock.

BOLT-ACTION

Model 514

The Sears version of this shotgun was recalled for safety considerations in the late 1990s. The catalog numbers listed are from a parts book which does not provide production dates.

NIB	Exc.	V.G.	Good	Fair	Poor
—	135	85	60	45	25

POLICE SHOTGUNS

Semi-Automatic

A gas-operated semi-automatic 12 gauge shotgun. Plain oiled pistol grip walnut stock and forearm. Magazine capacity is four. Recoil pad.

NIB	Exc.	V.G.	Good	Fair	Poor
—	265	205	160	100	75

Model 10-A

A gas-operated semi-automatic 12 gauge shotgun in bullpup configuration with pistol grip. Integral carrying handle and integral flashlight on top of gun. Magazine capacity is four.

NIB	Exc.	V.G.	Good	Fair	Poor
—	900	725	575	325	225

Model 10-B

A gas-operated semi-automatic 12 gauge shotgun in bullpup configuration with pistol grip. Fitted with a integral folding carrying handle and mounting provisions for a flashlight. Magazine capacity is four. Carrying case catalog number 50284 and attachable flashlight catalog number 50285 sold optionally.

NIB	Exc.	V.G.	Good	Fair	Poor
—	900	725	575	325	225

NOTE: Values are for gun with flashlight.

Pump

A slide-action 12 gauge shotgun. Plain pistol-grip oiled walnut stock and forearm—changed from walnut to stained and lacquered birch in the mid 1970s. 8111/8113 magazine capacity six. 8104/8129 magazine capacity five. A 1963 flyer mentions the #8105 Flite King Brush 20" and the #8107 Flite King Deluxe 20" as riot guns. The data on the #8105 and #8107 is listed under Flite King Brush.

NIB	Exc.	V.G.	Good	Fair	Poor
—	230	160	125	100	75

IMPORTED SHOTGUNS

Supermatic Shadow Automatic

A gas-operated semi-automatic shotgun in 12 and 20 gauge, interchangeable barrels. Checkered walnut stock and forearm. Special "airflow" rib. Imported from Nikko in Japan.

NIB	Exc.	V.G.	Good	Fair	Poor
—	395	280	200	130	100

Supermatic Shadow Indy Over-and-Under

A boxlock over-and-under 12 gauge shotgun with selective auto ejectors and single trigger. Receiver is fully engraved. Skipline checkered walnut stock with pistol grip. Ventilated forearm. Recoil pad. Special "airflow" rib. Imported from Nikko in Japan.

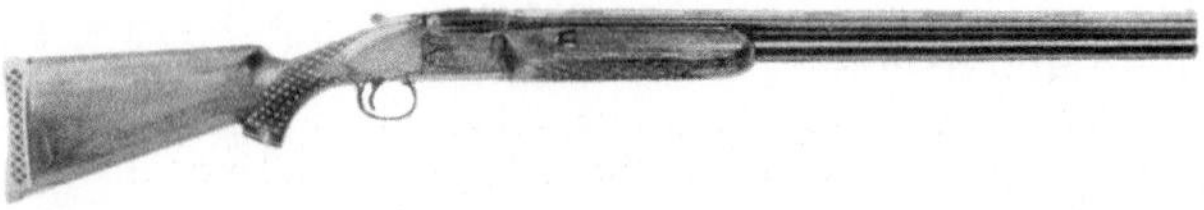

NIB	Exc.	V.G.	Good	Fair	Poor
—	860	730	625	475	350

Supermatic Shadow Seven Over-and-Under

Like the Shadow Indy but with a standard size vent rib, conventional forearm, no recoil pad, standard checkering, and less engraving. Imported from Nikko in Japan.

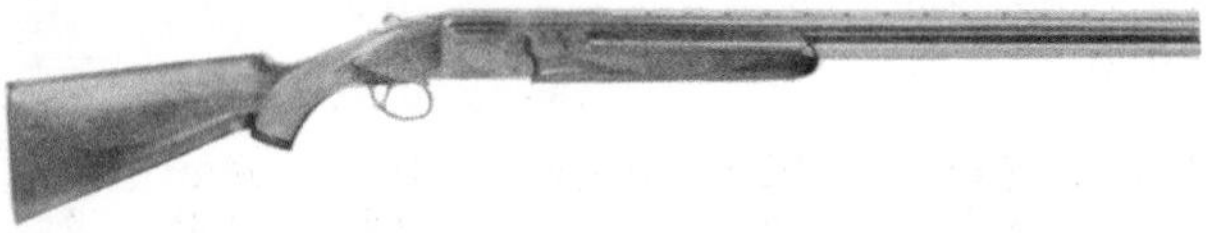

NIB	Exc.	V.G.	Good	Fair	Poor
—	695	585	480	350	300

RIFLES

RIMFIRE PUMP

Sport King/Flite King

A .22 caliber slide-action rifle capable of using S / L / LR ammunition interchangeably. 24" barrel, open sights, and a tubular magazine. Magazine capacity 21 S, 17 L or 15 LR.

NIB	Exc.	V.G.	Good	Fair	Poor
—	175	110	80	65	45

Sport King Field

A .22 caliber semi-auto rifle capable of using S / L / LR ammunition interchangeably. 22.25" barrel, open sights, and a tubular magazine. Magazine capacity 21 S, 17 L, or 15 LR. Walnut stock.

NIB	Exc.	V.G.	Good	Fair	Poor
—	165	95	70	60	40

Sport King Special

Like the Sport King Field except Monte Carlo walnut stock with pistol grip.

NIB	Exc.	V.G.	Good	Fair	Poor
—	185	130	100	60	40

Sport King Deluxe/Sport King

The Sport King Special with a new name. Catalog number 6005 is also the same gun but called just Sport King. A promotional package was offered that included the Sport King rifle, a zippered gun case, a plastic trigger lock, and G-96 gun lubricant. This package was catalog number 8007.

NIB	Exc.	V.G.	Good	Fair	Poor
—	215	145	110	80	50

NOTE: Add a 10 percent premium for complete 8007 package in original box.

Sport King Carbine

A .22 carbine semi-automatic rifle capable of using S / L / LR ammunition interchangeably. 18.25" barrel, open sights, and a tubular magazine. Magazine capacity 17 S, 14 L, or 12 LR. Straight grip walnut stock with barrel band and sling.

NIB	Exc.	V.G.	Good	Fair	Poor
—	195	145	110	80	50

Hi-Power Field Grade

A .270 or .30-06 caliber bolt-action rifle with a 22" barrel, open sights and a 4-shot magazine. Blued with a walnut stock.

NIB	Exc.	V.G.	Good	Fair	Poor
—	350	265	225	150	100

Hi-Power Deluxe

Like the Field Grade except has a Monte Carlo-style stock.

NIB	Exc.	V.G.	Good	Fair	Poor
—	400	330	275	175	130

HOLDEN, C. B.

Worcester, Massachusetts

Open Frame Rifle

A .44 rimfire single-shot rifle with a 28" barrel, open sights, silver plated bronze frame and walnut stock. The barrel marked "C.B. Holden Worcester-Mass." Produced in limited quantities during the mid-1860s.

NIB	Exc.	V.G.	Good	Fair	Poor
—	—	2600	1850	675	300

HOLECK, EMANUEL

Czechoslovakia

Holeck Rifle

Chambered for the .276 cartridge this semi-automatic rifle was submitted for testing for U.S. military trials in the 1920s. Barrel length is 21.5" with upper portion slotted for operating handle. Rotating dial at barrel band. Rarely encountered.

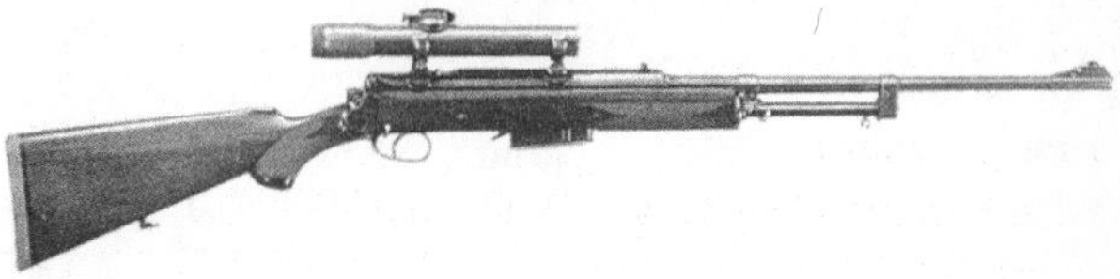

NIB	Exc.	V.G.	Good	Fair	Poor
—	4250	—	—	—	—

NOTE: Thanks to Jim Supica for the research found in his Old Town Station Dispatch, in which one of these rifles was offered for sale.

HOLLAND & HOLLAND, LTD.

London, England

Established in 1835, Holland & Holland has manufactured a wide variety of shotguns and rifles during its existence. The greater part of these arms are made to custom order.

DOUBLE RIFLES

No. 2 Grade Double Rifle

A sidelock double-barrel rifle produced in a variety of calibers with 24" barrels, double triggers, automatic ejectors and express sights. Obsolete cartridges could be worth less.

NIB	Exc.	V.G.	Good	Fair	Poor
—	19500	15500	10200	7700	4000

Royal Side-by-Side Rifle

Price depends on caliber.

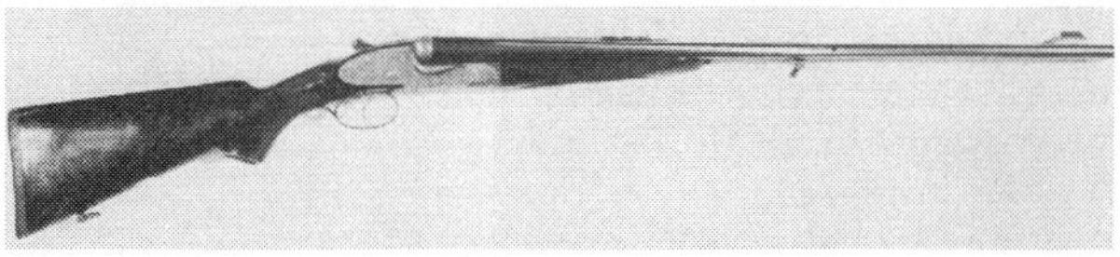

H&H .700 Bore Side-by-Side Rifle

A .700 Holland & Holland double-barrel rifle with a weight of approximately 18 lbs. Currently manufactured. Because of the uniqueness of the piece, buyers should seek qualified appraisal.

BOLT-ACTION RIFLES

Best Quality Rifle

Price depends on caliber and extra cost options. Retail prices for magazine rifles begin around $30,000, depending on the value of the dollar. Due to the uniqueness of each rifle an independent appraisal is a must prior to a sale.

HOLLOWAY ARMS CO.

Ft. Worth, Texas

HAC Model 7

A 7.62x54mm semi-automatic rifle with a 20" barrel, adjustable sights, integral telescope mount and 20-shot magazine. Black anodized finish with folding stock. No longer in production.

NIB	Exc.	V.G.	Good	Fair	Poor
2500	2000	1750	1200	600	500

HAC Model 7C

As above, with a 16" barrel.

NIB	Exc.	V.G.	Good	Fair	Poor
2750	2500	2000	1400	700	500

HAC Model 7S

As above, with a heavy barrel.

NIB	Exc.	V.G.	Good	Fair	Poor
2850	2650	2100	1500	700	500

HOPKINS & ALLEN

Norwich, Connecticut

SEE—Bacon Arms Co. & Merwin Hulbert & Co.

Falling Block Rifle

A .22 to .38-55 caliber single-shot rifle with a 24", 26", or 28" octagonal barrel. Blued with a walnut stock. Manufactured between 1888 and 1892.

NIB	Exc.	V.G.	Good	Fair	Poor
—	—	1250	650	325	175

Schuetzen Rifle

A .22 or .25-20 caliber single-shot rifle with a 26" octagonal barrel, double-set trigger and a Schuetzen-type buttplate. Blued with a walnut stock.

NIB	Exc.	V.G.	Good	Fair	Poor
—	—	2750	1025	550	200

Double-Barrel Shotguns

Hopkins & Allen also made good quality single and double-barrel shotguns in large numbers. Many were sold under private brand names such as Seminole and King Nitro. Both hammer and hammerless versions were offered. Values vary from $100 to $1,000 depending on model and condition.

HORSLEY, THOMAS

York, England

SEE—British Double Guns

HOWA MACHINE COMPANY

Japan

This company manufactured bolt-action rifles for Smith & Wesson until 1985 and then for Mossberg in 1986 and 1987. From 1988 to 2000 Howa firearms were imported by Interarms of Alexandria, Virginia. These rifles are now imported by Legacy Sports of Alexandria, Virginia.

Model 1500 Hunter

A .22-250, .223, .243, .270, 7mm Remington Magnum .308, .30-06, .300 Win. Mag., and .338 Winchester Magnum caliber bolt-action sporting rifle with a 22" or 24" barrel and 3- or 5-shot magazine. Blued or stainless steel with a checkered walnut stock. In 2002 this rifle was offered with black polymer stock. Weight is approximately 7.6 lbs.

NIB	Exc.	V.G.	Good	Fair	Poor
700	575	450	325	225	175

NOTE: Add $70 for stainless steel.

Model 1500 JRS Classic

Offered in blue or stainless steel with laminated stock, these rifles are chambered for the .223 through .338 Win. Mag calibers. Barrel length is 22" or 24", depending on caliber. Weight is about 8 lbs.

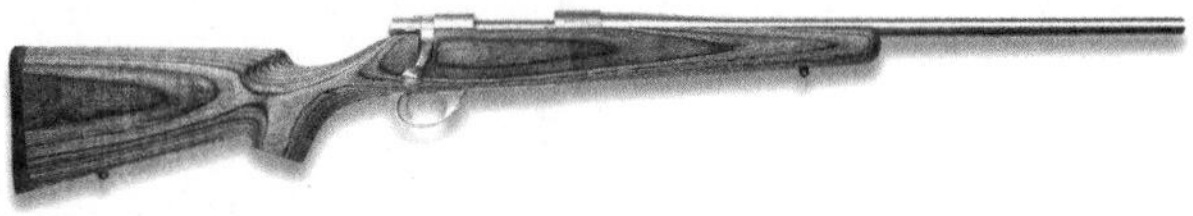

NIB	Exc.	V.G.	Good	Fair	Poor
750	6254	500	375	250	195

NOTE: Add $70 for stainless steel.

Model 1500 Mountain

Introduced in 2004 this bolt-action model is chambered for the .243, .308, or 7mm-08 cartridges. Fitted with a 20" contoured barrel with no sights. Blued finish with black hardwood stock. Stainless steel offered in .308 only. Magazine capacity is 5 rounds. Weight is about 6.4 lbs.

NIB	Exc.	V.G.	Good	Fair	Poor
700	575	450	325	225	175

NOTE: Add $115 for stainless steel.

Model 1500 Trophy

As above, but with more finely figured walnut stocks and checkering. Introduced in 1988. No longer imported.

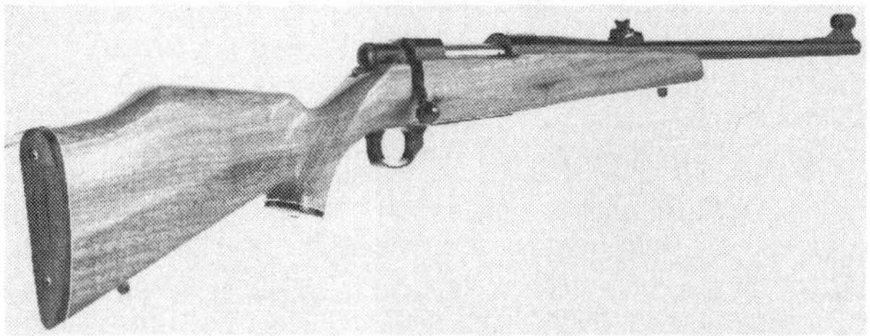

NIB	Exc.	V.G.	Good	Fair	Poor
750	625	500	375	250	195

Model 1500 Varmint

As above, in .22-250 or .223 caliber with a 24" heavy barrel. Choice of walnut or synthetic stock, in blue or stainless. Weight is about 9.3 lbs. Introduced in 1988.

NIB	Exc.	V.G.	Good	Fair	Poor
750	625	500	375	250	195

NOTE: Add $70 for stainless steel and $20 for walnut stock.

Model 1500 Varmint Supreme

This model features a stainless steel barrel chambered for the .223, .22-250, .308, and .243 with no sights. Choice of black synthetic, or laminated stock with Monte Carlo comb.

NIB	Exc.	V.G.	Good	Fair	Poor
750	625	500	375	250	195

NOTE: Add $110 for thumbhole stock.

Model 1500 Lightning Rifle

Introduced in 1993, this model has a black composite checkered stock with schnabel forend. The buttstock is Monte Carlo. Choice of blue or stainless steel. Offered in .223, .22-250, .243, .270, .308, .30-06, 7mm Rem. Mag., .300 and .338 Win. Mag. Weighs about 7.5 lbs.

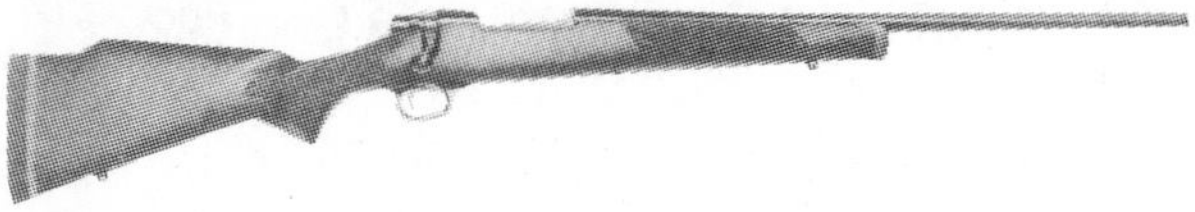

NIB	Exc.	V.G.	Good	Fair	Poor
700	575	450	325	225	175

NOTE: Add $70 for stainless steel.

Model 1500 Youth

This model is chambered for the .243, .308, or 7mm-08 cartridge. Barrel length is 20". Black hardwood stock with 1" shorter length of pull than standard. Weight is about 6.3 lbs. Introduced in 2004.

NIB	Exc.	V.G.	Good	Fair	Poor
650	525	400	275	175	125

NOTE: Add $115 for stainless steel .308 version.

Model 1500 Thumbhole Sporter

As above but with thumbhole stock. Weight is about 8.25 lbs.

NIB	Exc.	V.G.	Good	Fair	Poor
800	625	500	400	275	150

NOTE: Add $70 for stainless steel.

Model 1500 Custom

Chambered for the .300 WSM or .300 Win. Magnum cartridge this rifle is fitted with a 22" or 24" barrel, depending on caliber. Polymer or laminated stock. Weight is around 8 lbs. Blued or stainless steel.

NIB	Exc.	V.G.	Good	Fair	Poor
950	800	700	495	325	175

NOTE: Add $70 for stainless steel.

Realtree Camo Rifle

Introduced in 1993, this bolt-action model features a composite stock and a 22" barrel. Both the metal and stock finish are a brown leaf pattern. The receiver is a mono-block system. The floorplate is hinged and the magazine holds 5 rounds. The receiver is drilled and tapped for scope mounts. Fitted with a sling swivel and recoil pad. Offered in .30-06 and .270 calibers. Weighs 8 lbs.

NIB	Exc.	V.G.	Good	Fair	Poor
650	525	400	275	175	125

Texas Safari Rifle

Chambered for the .270 Win. or .300 Win. Magnum cartridge, this rifle is modified by gunsmith Bill Wiseman. Blue Teflon finish and 22" or 24" barrel depending on caliber. Laminated stock. Weight is about 7.8 lbs.

NIB	Exc.	V.G.	Good	Fair	Poor
1200	800	650	525	400	150

Model 1500 PCS (Police Counter Sniper)

This bolt-action is offered in .308 Winchester and fitted with a 24" heavy barrel. Magazine capacity is 5 rounds. Available in blue or stainless steel and walnut or synthetic stock. Weight is approximately 9.3 lbs.

NIB	Exc.	V.G.	Good	Fair	Poor
1200	800	650	525	400	150

H-S PRECISION, INC.

Rapid City, South Dakota

SPR Sporter Rifle

This bolt-action rifle is offered in both long and short actions with any standard SAAMI caliber. Match grade stainless steel barrel lengths are 22", 24", or 26" with optional muzzlebrake available. Synthetic stock is offered in various colors. Weight is between 7.5 and 7.75 lbs. depending on barrel length. Magazine capacity is 4 rounds for standard calibers and 3 rounds for magnum calibers.

NIB	Exc.	V.G.	Good	Fair	Poor
2375	1800	1400	900	500	250

SPL Lightweight Sporter

Introduced in 2005 this model features a 22", 24", or 26" fluted barrel with choice of short or long action calibers. Detachable magazine. No sights. Pro-series synthetic stock. Weight is under 7 lbs.

NIB	Exc.	V.G.	Good	Fair	Poor
2400	1825	1425	925	525	275

PHR Professional Hunter Rifle

This bolt-action rifle is chambered for magnum calibers only and is fitted with 24" or 26" stainless steel match grade fluted barrel (except .416 Rigby). Built in recoil reduced in synthetic stock with choice of colors. Matte black finish. Weight is between 7.75 lbs. and 8.25 depending on barrel length and caliber. Offered in any standard SAAMI caliber. Magazine capacity is 3 rounds.

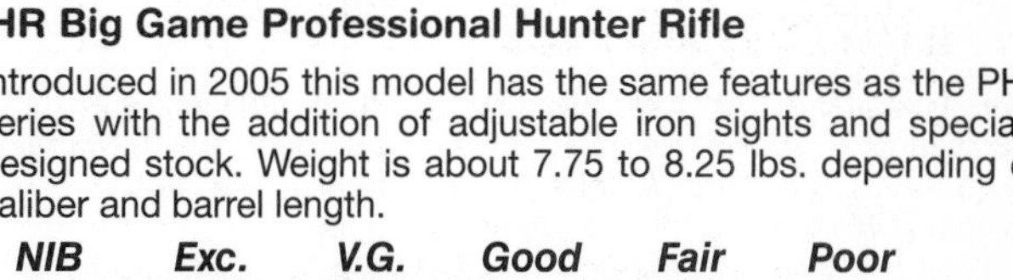

NIB	Exc.	V.G.	Good	Fair	Poor
2600	2050	1650	1050	575	300

BHR Big Game Professional Hunter Rifle

Introduced in 2005 this model has the same features as the PHR series with the addition of adjustable iron sights and specially designed stock. Weight is about 7.75 to 8.25 lbs. depending on caliber and barrel length.

NIB	Exc.	V.G.	Good	Fair	Poor
2750	2250	1850	1175	625	350

PHL Professional Hunter Lightweight Rifle

This model features a weight of 5.75 lbs. Fitted with a Pro-Series stock and choice of 20" or 22" contoured fluted stock. Matte black teflon finish. Detachable magazine. Chambered for short action calibers. Introduced in 2005.

NIB	Exc.	V.G.	Good	Fair	Poor
2750	2250	1850	1175	625	350

VAR Varmint Rifle

Offered in long or short action with .17 Rem., 6mm PPC, and .223 Rem. in single-shot. Fitted with match grade stainless steel fluted barrel in 24" or 26" lengths. Also available is a lightweight 20" barrel. Synthetic stock in choice of colors with 20" barrel guns offered with thumbhole stocks. Black matte finish. Weight is between 8 and 8.25 lbs. for standard rifles and 7.5 and 7.75 lbs. for 20" barrel guns. Available in any standard SAAMI caliber.

NIB	***Exc.***	***V.G.***	***Good***	***Fair***	***Poor***
2600	2050	1650	1050	575	300

Varmint Take-Down Rifle

This take-down bolt-action rifle is offered in a stainless steel long or short action with 24" stainless steel match grade fluted barrel. Matte black finish. Weight is between 8.5 and 9 lbs.

NIB	***Exc.***	***V.G.***	***Good***	***Fair***	***Poor***
3700	2900	2050	1450	600	400

NOTE: Add $1,000 for extra barrel with same head size caliber and $1,200 for extra barrel with different head size caliber.

Professional Hunter Take-Down Rifle

This take-down rifle is offered in magnum and super magnum calibers with 24" fluted stainless steel barrel. Built in recoil reducer. Matte black finish. Weight is between 8.25 and 8.75 lbs.

NIB	***Exc.***	***V.G.***	***Good***	***Fair***	***Poor***
3900	3100	2250	1650	750	450

HTR Heavy Tactical Rifle

This bolt-action model features a stainless steel long or short action with fluted stainless steel 24" heavy barrel. Stock is synthetic with adjustable cheekpiece and length of pull. Any standard SAAMI caliber is available. Weight is about 10.75 to 11.25 lbs. Matte black finish.

NIB	***Exc.***	***V.G.***	***Good***	***Fair***	***Poor***
2750	2250	1850	1175	625	350

Short Tactical

Chambered for the .308 cartridge and fitted with a 20" fluted barrel with matte teflon finish. Pro-Series tactical stock.

NIB	***Exc.***	***V.G.***	***Good***	***Fair***	***Poor***
2750	2250	1850	1175	625	350

RDR Rapid Deployment Rifle

This is similar to the model above but with 20" stainless steel fluted barrel and smaller stock. Thumbhole stock on request. Magazine is 4 rounds. Matte black finish. Offered in any short action SAAMI calibers. Weight is between 7.5 and 7.75 lbs.

NIB	***Exc.***	***V.G.***	***Good***	***Fair***	***Poor***
2750	2250	1850	1175	625	350

TTD Tactical Take-Down System

This take-down rifle is chambered for any standard SAAMI caliber and fitted with a 24" fluted heavy stainless steel barrel. Magazine capacity is 4 rounds for standard calibers and 3 rounds for magnum calibers. Synthetic stock that is adjustable for length of pull and cheekpiece. Matte black finish. Weight is between 11.25 and 11.75 lbs.

NIB	***Exc.***	***V.G.***	***Good***	***Fair***	***Poor***
3900	3100	2250	1650	750	450

HUGLU

Turkey

SIDE-BY-SIDES

Bobwhite

Offered in 12, 20, 28 gauge as well as .410 bore with 26" or 28" barrel with choke tubes. The .410 bore has fixed chokes. Double triggers with no auto ejectors. Manual safety. Box lock receiver with silver finish. Walnut stock with round knob pistol grip and splinter schnabel forend.

NIB	***Exc.***	***V.G.***	***Good***	***Fair***	***Poor***
700	550	400	275	175	125

NOTE: Add $200 for 28 gauge or .410 models.

Ringneck

Similar to the Bobwhite but with single trigger and case colored frame with side plates. Choice of round knob pistol grip or straight grip. Forend is beavertail schnabel.

NIB	***Exc.***	***V.G.***	***Good***	***Fair***	***Poor***
1000	750	600	495	300	150

NOTE: Add $200 for 28 gauge or .410 models.

OVER-AND-UNDER

Woodcock

This gun is available in 12, 20, or 28 gauge as well as .410 bore. Choice of 26" or 28" vent rib barrels with choke tubes, except for fixed chokes on the .410. Single trigger. No auto ejectors. Manual safety. Receiver finish is case colored. Checkered walnut stock with round knob pistol grip and schnabel forend.

NIB	***Exc.***	***V.G.***	***Good***	***Fair***	***Poor***
1050	825	600	495	300	150

NOTE: Add $150 for 28 gauge or .410 models.

Woodcock Deluxe

As above but in 12 gauge with auto ejectors and side plates.

NIB	***Exc.***	***V.G.***	***Good***	***Fair***	***Poor***
1200	900	750	550	350	185

Redhead

Available in 12, 20, 28, and .410. Choice of 26" or 28" vent rib barrels with choke tubes, except for .410 with fixed chokes. The 20 gauge is also offered with 24" barrels. Single trigger, no auto ejectors, and manual safety. Boxlock receiver with silver finish. Checkered walnut stock with round knob pistol grip and schnabel forearm.

NIB	***Exc.***	***V.G.***	***Good***	***Fair***	***Poor***
800	625	500	400	275	150

NOTE: Add $150 for 28 gauge or .410 models.

Redhead Deluxe

As above but in 12 and 20 gauge only with 26" or 28" barrels. Auto ejectors.

NIB	Exc.	V.G.	Good	Fair	Poor
900	750	675	395	200	100

Mallard

This 12 or 20 gauge gun is fitted with 28" vent rib barrels with choke tubes. Double triggers and no auto ejectors. Silver receiver. Checkered walnut stock with round knob pistol grip and schnabel forend.

NIB	Exc.	V.G.	Good	Fair	Poor
550	425	300	200	150	75

Canvasback

This gun is available in 12, 20, 28, and .410 bore. Choice of 26" or 28" vent rib barrels with choke tubes, except for the .410 with fixed chokes. Single trigger with no auto ejectors and manual safety. Black boxlock receiver. Checkered walnut stock with round knob pistol grip and schnabel forend.

NIB	Exc.	V.G.	Good	Fair	Poor
800	625	500	400	275	150

NOTE: Add $150 for 28 gauge or .410 models.

Canvasback Deluxe

As above but in 12 and 20 gauge only with auto ejectors.

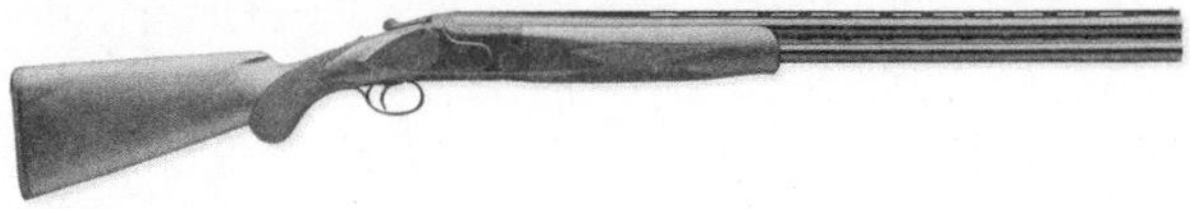

NIB	Exc.	V.G.	Good	Fair	Poor
900	750	675	395	200	100

COWBOY & SINGLE-SHOT

Cottontail

This is a single-barrel shotgun in 12 or 20 gauge as well as .410 bore with choice of 24" or 28" barrels. Modified choke. No auto ejectors. Silver receiver with blued barrel. Checkered walnut stock with pistol grip.

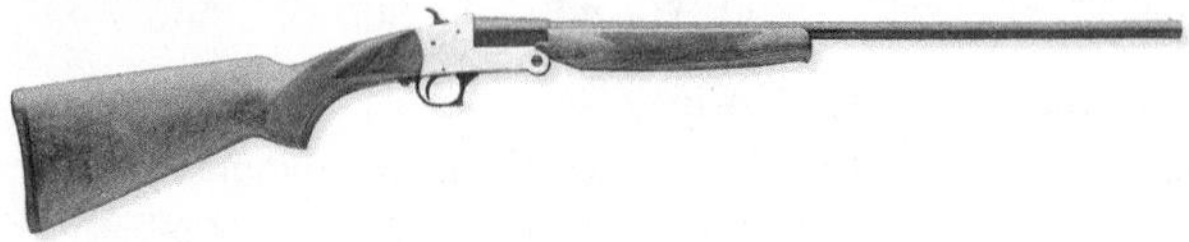

NIB	Exc.	V.G.	Good	Fair	Poor
200	150	100	75	50	25

Durango

This side-by-side shotgun is chambered for the 12 or 20 gauge with single trigger and choke tubes. Barrel lengths are 20". No auto ejectors. The boxlock receiver is case colored. Checkered walnut grips with round knob pistol grip and schnabel forend.

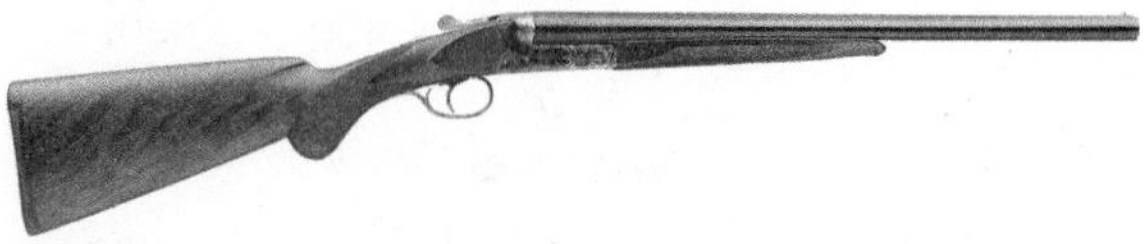

NIB	Exc.	V.G.	Good	Fair	Poor
850	650	500	400	275	150

Amarillo

Similar to the Durango but with a flat-side receiver.

NIB	Exc.	V.G.	Good	Fair	Poor
700	525	400	300	195	125

SEMI-AUTOMATICS

Sharptail

This 12 gauge 3" gun is fitted with a choice of 26" or 28" vent rib barrels with choke tubes. Black receiver. Checkered walnut stock with pistol grip. Weight is about 7.3 lbs.

NIB	Exc.	V.G.	Good	Fair	Poor
550	425	300	200	150	95

Canadian

As above but with an alloy frame and matte black finish. Weight is about 7 lbs.

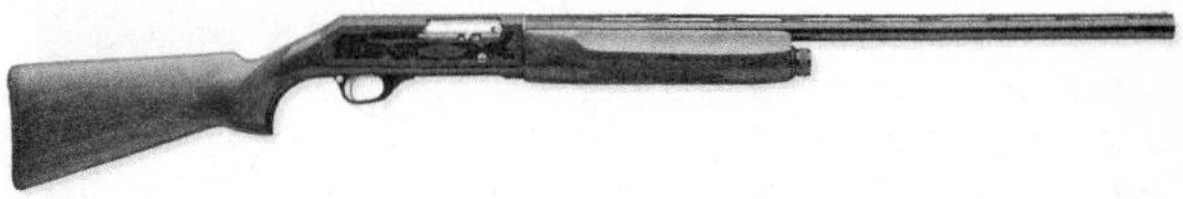

NIB	Exc.	V.G.	Good	Fair	Poor
650	525	400	275	165	115

Teal

This model is a 20 gauge with 3" chambers and a choice of 26" or 28" vent rib barrels with choke tubes. Black alloy receiver. Checkered walnut stock with pistol grip.

NIB	Exc.	V.G.	Good	Fair	Poor
550	425	300	200	150	95

COMPETITION GUNS

Vandalia Trap

This 12 gauge trap gun is offered with either a single barrel/double barrel combo; single barrel only, or double barrel only. Five choke tubes. Engraved silver receiver. Checkered walnut stock with pistol grip and adjustable comb.

NIB	Exc.	V.G.	Good	Fair	Poor
1900	1400	995	650	395	200

NOTE: For Combo model add $300.

English Sporter

This is a sporting clays model chambered for the 12 gauge shell and fitted with a 30" barrel with ten choke tubes. Black receiver. Adjustable comb with checkered walnut stock with pistol grip.

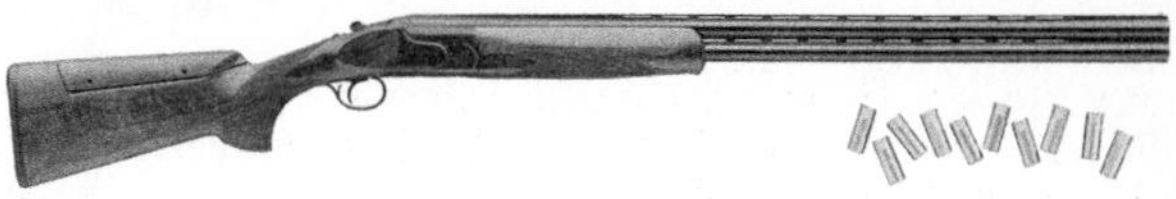

NIB	Exc.	V.G.	Good	Fair	Poor
1900	1400	995	650	395	200

CUSTOM GRADES

Custom Grade II

This is a custom-built side-by-side gun in the customer's choice of gauge. Engraved case colored receiver with side plates. Choice of barrel lengths. Select walnut stock with hand checkering and round knob pistol grip.

NIB	Exc.	V.G.	Good	Fair	Poor
2200	1600	1200	950	500	300

Custom Grade IV

This custom-built side-by-side features a silver scroll engraved receiver with side plates. Straight grip stock. Choice of bore and barrel lengths.

NIB	Exc.	V.G.	Good	Fair	Poor
2800	1900	1400	650	600	350

Custom Grade IV with Upgrade

This is an over-and-under gun with extra fancy walnut stock and elaborately engraved silver receiver. Choice of gauge and barrel lengths.

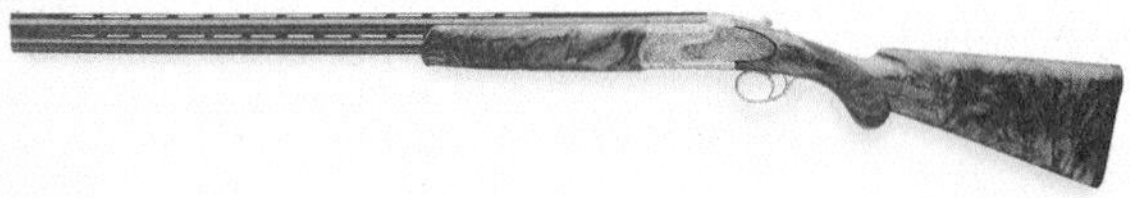

NIB	Exc.	V.G.	Good	Fair	Poor
3150	2200	1600	750	650	350

Custom Grade VI

This is the highest grade offered with the finest walnut stock and engraving.

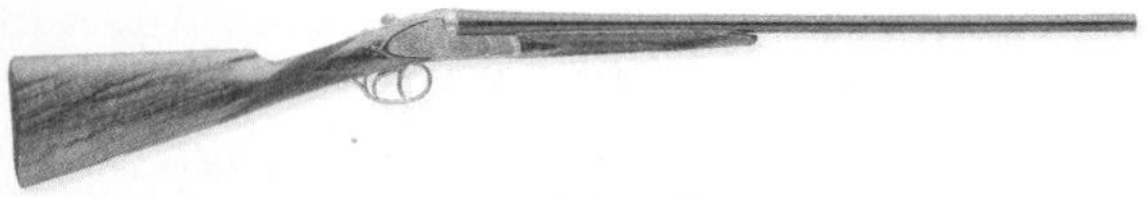

NIB	Exc.	V.G.	Good	Fair	Poor
3500	26500	1900	950	775	475

HUNGARY

SA-85M

This is pre-ban semi-automatic copy of the AKM rifle. Chambered for the 7.62x39mm cartridge. Fixed or folding stock.

NIB	Exc.	V.G.	Good	Fair	Poor
1800	1600	1200	850	600	500

HUSQVARNA

Husqvarna, Sweden

DOUBLE SHOTGUNS

A number of pre-war Husqvarna side-by-side shotguns have been imported over the years. While sturdy, excellent shotguns, their collector value is rather limited. Those following values apply only to modern, fluid-steel (nitro proofed) guns.

NIB	Exc.	V.G.	Good	Fair	Poor
—	500	425	350	300	250

BOLT-ACTION RIFLES

Hi-Power

A bolt-action sporting rifle manufactured in a variety of calibers with a 24" barrel, open sights and beechwood stock. Manufactured between 1946 and 1951.

NIB	Exc.	V.G.	Good	Fair	Poor
—	500	375	275	200	150

Model 1100 Deluxe

As above, with a walnut stock. Manufactured between 1952 and 1956.

NIB	Exc.	V.G.	Good	Fair	Poor
—	550	400	325	250	200

Model 1000 Super Grade

As above, with a Monte Carlo-style stock. Manufactured between 1952 and 1956.

NIB	Exc.	V.G.	Good	Fair	Poor
—	575	475	350	250	200

Model 3100 Crown Grade

A bolt-action sporting rifle manufactured in a variety of calibers with a 24" barrel, walnut stock with a black composition forend tip and pistol grip cap. Manufactured between 1954 and 1972.

NIB	Exc.	V.G.	Good	Fair	Poor
—	575	475	350	300	200

Model 4100 Lightweight

As above, with a schnabel forend tip. Manufactured between 1954 and 1972.

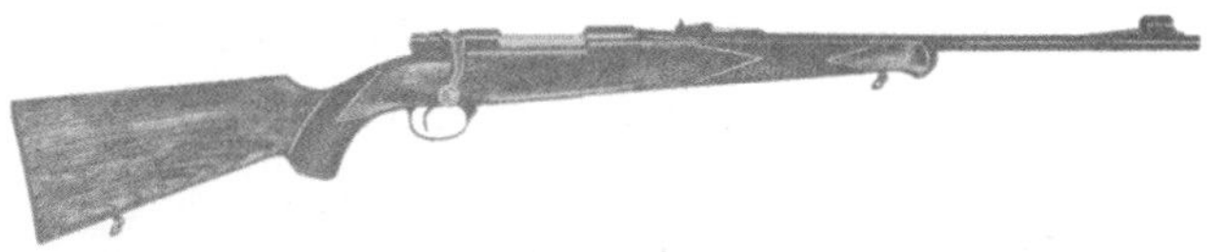

NIB	Exc.	V.G.	Good	Fair	Poor
—	575	475	350	300	200

Model 456

As above, with a full length Mannlicher-style stock. Manufactured between 1959 and 1970.

NIB	Exc.	V.G.	Good	Fair	Poor
—	600	500	375	325	200

Model 6000

The Model 4100 with express folding sights and a finely figured walnut stock. Manufactured between 1968 and 1970.

NIB	Exc.	V.G.	Good	Fair	Poor
—	600	500	400	300	200

Model 9000 Crown Grade

A bolt-action sporting rifle manufactured in a variety of calibers with a 23.5" barrel, open sights, adjustable trigger and walnut stock. Manufactured in 1971 and 1972.

NIB	Exc.	V.G.	Good	Fair	Poor
—	500	425	350	300	250

Model 8000 Imperial Grade

As above, with an engraved magazine floor plate, machine jeweled bolt and finely figured walnut stock. Manufactured in 1971 and 1972.

NIB	Exc.	V.G.	Good	Fair	Poor
—	675	550	475	400	300

HYPER

Jenks, Oklahoma

Single-Shot Rifle

A custom made falling block-action single-shot rifle manufactured in a variety of calibers, barrel lengths, barrel types, and stock styles. Manufactured until 1984.

NIB	Exc.	V.G.	Good	Fair	Poor
—	2750	2000	1750	1450	800

I

IAB
Industria Armi Bresciane
Brescia, Italy

S-300

A 12 gauge boxlock single-barrel trap gun with 30" or 32" barrels having a wide ventilated rib and walnut trap-style stock.

NIB	Exc.	V.G.	Good	Fair	Poor
—	1600	1325	1050	850	450

C-300 Combo

A 12 gauge over-and-under boxlock double-barrel shotgun with 30" or 32" barrels, single-selective trigger, automatic ejectors, trap-style walnut stock, accompanied by two extra single barrels.

NIB	Exc.	V.G.	Good	Fair	Poor
—	2850	2300	1875	1500	800

C-300 Super Combo

As above, but more finely finished.

NIB	Exc.	V.G.	Good	Fair	Poor
—	3600	2800	2275	1750	900

IAI-AMERICAN LEGENDS
Houston, Texas

M-888 M1 Carbine

A re-creation of the U.S. M1 Carbine in .30 caliber. Barrel length is 18". Weight is about 5.5 lbs. Uses surplus magazines of 15 to 30 rounds. Comes with 10-round magazine. Options of wooden or metal handguard and walnut or birchwood stock.

NIB	Exc.	V.G.	Good	Fair	Poor
675	575	400	325	200	100

M-333 M1 Garand

Remanufactured to GI specifications. Fitted with 24" barrel and GI wood stock. Eight-round capacity. Parkerized finish. Weight is about 9.5 lbs.

NIB	Exc.	V.G.	Good	Fair	Poor
900	800	625	495	350	150

IAR
San Juan Capistrano, California

An importer of Italian made reproduction pistol and rifles. For a complete listing see ***Uberti***.

IGA
Veranopolis, Brazil

Single-Barrel Shotgun

A 12 or 20 gauge or .410 bore single barrel shotgun with an exposed hammer, 28" barrel and hardwood stock.

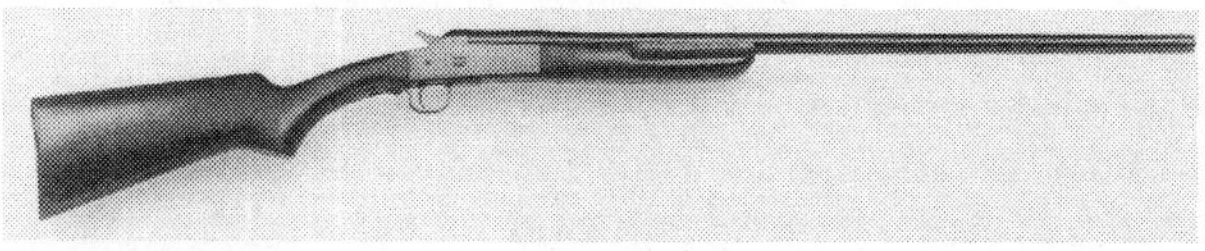

NIB	Exc.	V.G.	Good	Fair	Poor
150	90	75	50	40	30

Single-Barrel Shotgun Youth Model

Offered in 20 gauge and .410 bore this model features a 22" barrel and shorter than standard buttstock. Weighs 5 lbs.

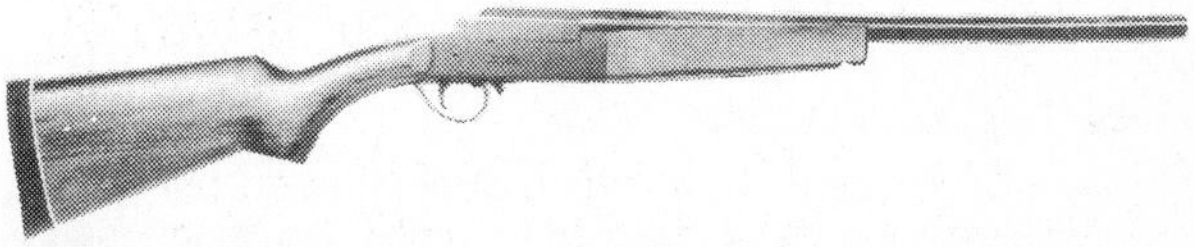

NIB	Exc.	V.G.	Good	Fair	Poor
150	100	80	60	50	35

Coach Gun

A 12 and 20 gauge as well as .410 bore boxlock double-barrel shotgun with 20" barrels, double triggers and extractors. Blued with a hardwood stock.

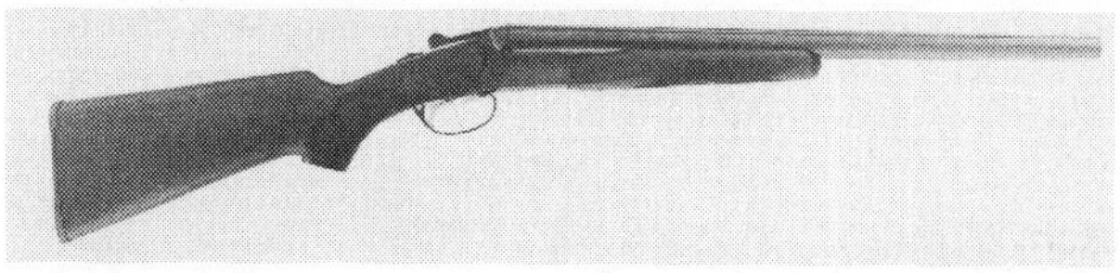

NIB	Exc.	V.G.	Good	Fair	Poor
425	325	250	150	100	75

NOTE: Add $50 for nickel finish. Add $60 for engraved butt stock.

Standard Side-by-Side Uplander Model

Offered in 12, 20, 28 gauge, and .410 bore with 26" and 28" barrels. Checkered hardwood stock with pistol grip or straight grip in 20 gauge only. Weighs 6.75 lbs.

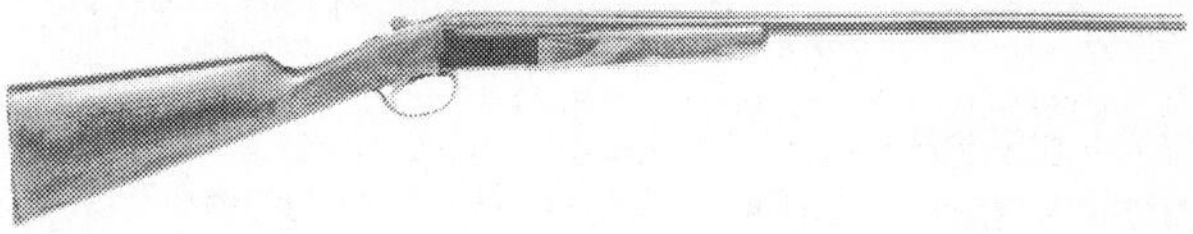

NIB	Exc.	V.G.	Good	Fair	Poor
425	325	250	150	100	75

NOTE: Add $40 for choke tubes.

Uplander Youth Model

Same as above but offered in .410 bore with 24" barrel or 20 gauge with 24" barrels. Shorter length of pull. Recoil pad standard.

NIB	Exc.	V.G.	Good	Fair	Poor
450	325	250	150	100	75

Uplander Supreme

Introduced in 2000 this model features a high grade walnut stock with checkering, single-selective trigger, choke tubes, and automatic ejectors. Offered in 12 and 20 gauge with 26" or 28" barrels. Chambered for 3" shells. Soft rubber recoil pad standard.

NIB	Exc.	V.G.	Good	Fair	Poor
600	450	375	300	200	100

Standard Over-and-Under Condor I

This model is offered in 12 or 20 gauge with 26" or 28" barrels. Fitted with extractors and single trigger. Choke tubes are standard. Checkered hardwood stock with pistol grip and recoil pad. Weighs 8 lbs.

NIB	Exc.	V.G.	Good	Fair	Poor
425	300	225	200	150	100

Condor II

Same as above but with double triggers and plastic buttplate.

NIB	Exc.	V.G.	Good	Fair	Poor
400	250	200	150	100	75

Condor Supreme Deluxe

This model is similar to the standard Condor model but has a high grade walnut stock, hand checkering, recoil pad, single-selective trigger, and automatic ejectors. Offered in 12 and 20 gauge with 26" or 28" vent rib barrels. Chambered for 3" shells. Choke tubes standard. First offered in 2000.

NIB	Exc.	V.G.	Good	Fair	Poor
550	400	325	200	150	100

Deluxe Over-and-Under ERA 2000

Offered in 12 gauge only with 26" or 28" barrels. Fitted with single trigger and extractors. Choke tubes are standard. Barrels are chrome lined and stock is hand checkered.

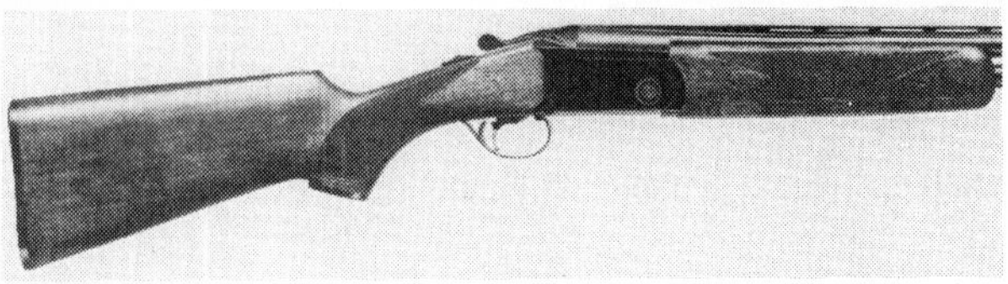

NIB	Exc.	V.G.	Good	Fair	Poor
450	325	250	150	100	75

INTERARMS
Alexandria, Virginia

An importer of arms made by Howa Machine, Star and Walther. This firm is no longer in business.

Mark X Viscount

Bolt-action sporting rifle made in a variety of calibers with a 24" barrel, open sights, adjustable trigger and magazine holding either 3 or 5 cartridges. Manufactured in Yugoslavia. Blued with a walnut stock.

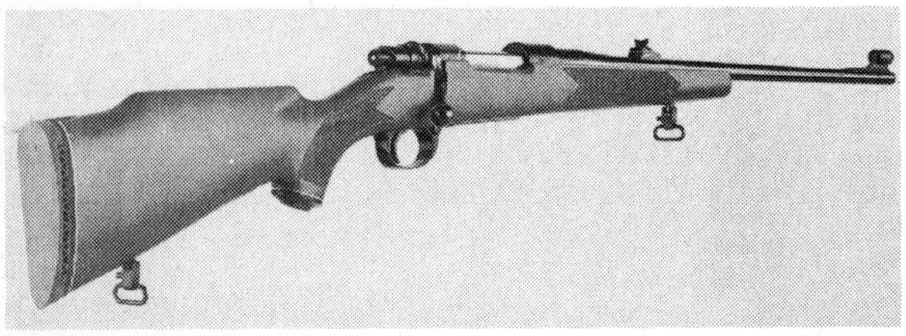

NIB	Exc.	V.G.	Good	Fair	Poor
450	300	250	200	175	125

Mark X Lightweight

As above, with a 20" barrel and composite stock. Introduced in 1988.

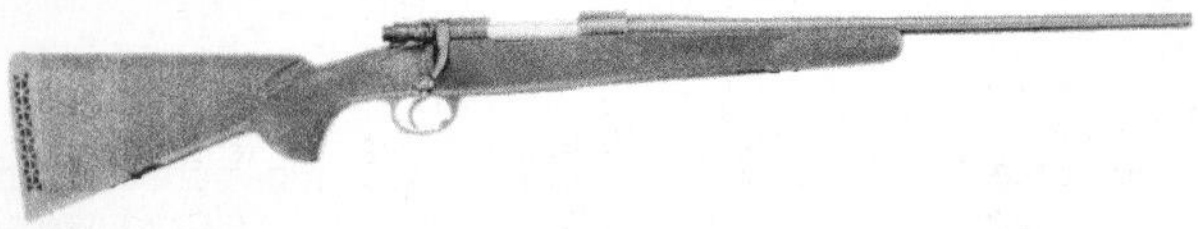

NIB	Exc.	V.G.	Good	Fair	Poor
450	300	250	200	175	125

Mini Mark X

As above, with a short action in .223 caliber only with a 20" barrel, open sights, adjustable trigger and 5-shot magazine. Introduced in 1987.

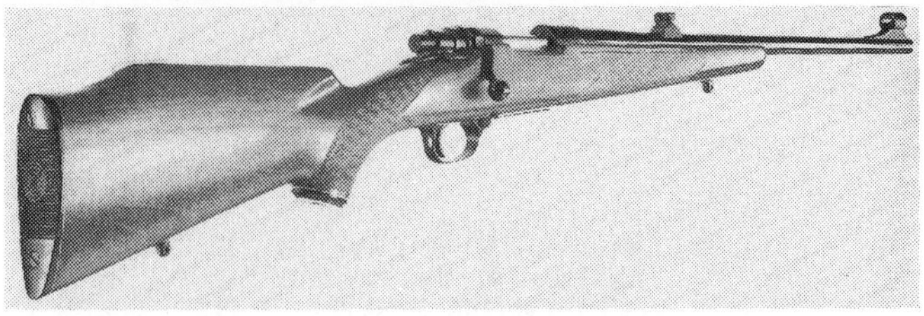

NIB	Exc.	V.G.	Good	Fair	Poor
450	300	250	200	175	125

Mark X American Field

As above, with a finely figured walnut stock, ebony forend tip, pistol grip cap, sling swivels and recoil pad. Introduced in 1984.

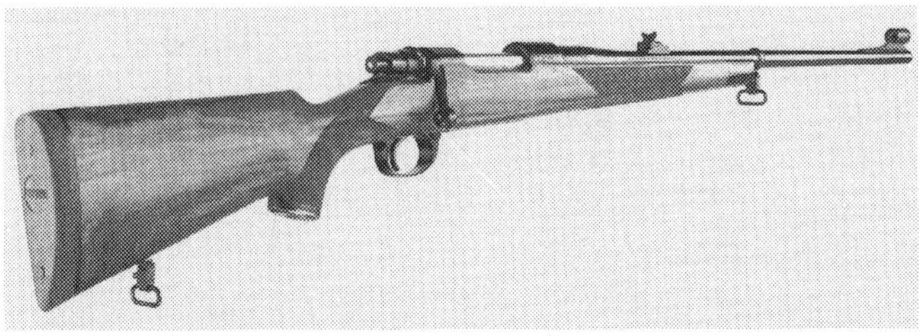

NIB	Exc.	V.G.	Good	Fair	Poor
525	400	350	300	250	175

Whitworth Express Rifle

A .375 Holland & Holland or .458 Winchester Magnum bolt-action sporting rifle with a 24" barrel, express sights and 3-shot magazine. Blued with a walnut stock. Introduced in 1974.

NIB	Exc.	V.G.	Good	Fair	Poor
950	750	550	350	250	200

Whitworth Mannlicher Carbine

A .243, .270, 7x57mm, .308, and the .30-06 caliber bolt-action rifle with a 20" barrel, open sights, sling swivels and a full length stock. Manufactured between 1984 and 1987.

NIB	Exc.	V.G.	Good	Fair	Poor
—	725	550	375	250	200

Cavalier

A bolt-action sporting rifle made in a variety of calibers with a modern styled stock having a rollover cheekpiece. Discontinued.

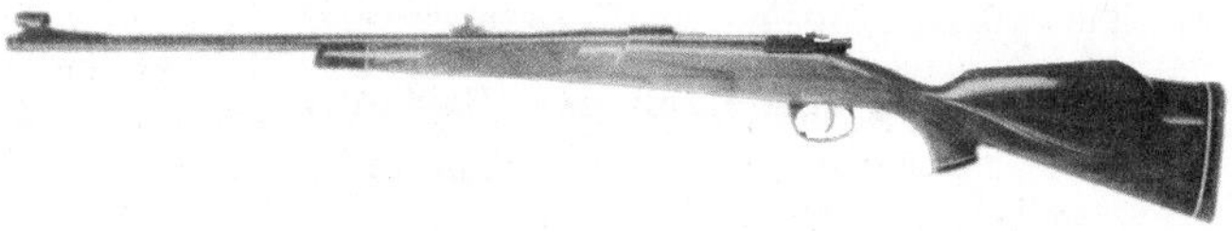

NIB	Exc.	V.G.	Good	Fair	Poor
—	500	400	350	200	150

Mannlicher Carbine

As above, with a 20" barrel and full length stock. Discontinued.

NIB	Exc.	V.G.	Good	Fair	Poor
—	600	500	425	275	195

Continental Carbine

As above, with double set triggers. Discontinued.

NIB	Exc.	V.G.	Good	Fair	Poor
—	625	525	450	300	225

Alaskan Model

Similar to the Mark X, in .375 Holland & Holland or .458 Winchester Magnum with a 24" barrel. Discontinued in 1985.

NIB	Exc.	V.G.	Good	Fair	Poor
—	950	750	550	350	200

INTRATEC USA, INC.

Miami, Florida

TEC-9C

Similar to TEC-9 pistol, but with a 16" barrel and a folding stock. Manufactured in 1987.

NIB	Exc.	V.G.	Good	Fair	Poor
—	450	350	295	200	100

ITHACA GUN CO.

Ithaca, New York

This material was supplied by Walter C. Snyder and is copyrighted in his name. Used with the author's permission. The Ithaca Gun Company was founded by William Henry Baker, John VanNatta, and Dwight McIntyre. Gun production started during the latter half of 1883 at an industrial site located on Fall Creek, Ithaca, New York. Leroy Smith joined the company by 1885 and George Livermore joined the firm in 1887. By 1894 the company was under the exclusive control of Leroy Smith and George Livermore. Many of the company's assets were purchased by the Ithaca Acquisition Corporation in 1987 and moved to King Ferry, New York, where it operated until May, 1996. Now dba Ithaca Gun Company of Upper Sandusky, Ohio.

HAMMER MODELS

ITHACA BAKER MODEL

The first model produced by the company was designed by W.H. Baker and was manufactured from 1883 through 1887. It was offered in six grades; Quality A ($35) through Quality F ($200) in either 10 or 12 gauge. All Ithaca-produced Baker models had exposed hammers. Grades above Quality B are seldom encountered and an expert appraisal is recommended.

Quality A

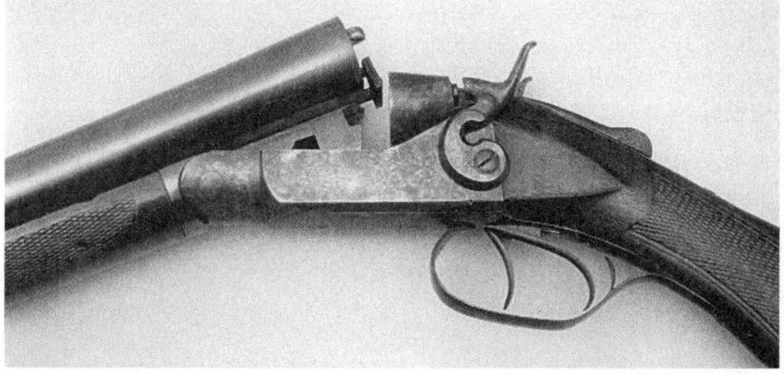

Courtesy Walter C. Snyder

NIB	Exc.	V.G.	Good	Fair	Poor
—	900	500	300	200	100

Quality B

NIB	Exc.	V.G.	Good	Fair	Poor
—	1850	1350	750	300	100

NEW ITHACA GUN

The New Ithaca Gun was introduced in 1888 and discontinued during 1915. Like its predecessor, it was introduced in the same seven grades, Quality A through Quality F. Later, the Quality F was discontinued. By 1900, a "condensed steel" barreled model, named Quality X, was introduced. The New Ithaca Gun was produced in gauges 10, 12, and 16, and very rarely, 20. Lower grade models carried the logo, "New Ithaca Gun," usually within a banner, on each side of the frame. Like its predecessor, grades above Quality B are seldom encountered, and an expert appraisal is recommended. Sixteen gauge guns command a 30 percent price premium. The extremely rare 20 gauge model requires an expert appraisal.

Quality A

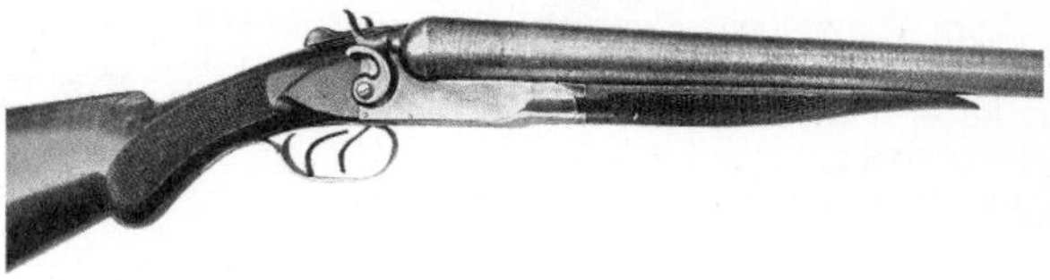

Courtesy Walter C. Snyder

NIB	Exc.	V.G.	Good	Fair	Poor
—	1100	775	295	175	100

Quality AA

NIB	Exc.	V.G.	Good	Fair	Poor
—	1100	775	295	175	100

Quality B

NIB	Exc.	V.G.	Good	Fair	Poor
—	1300	875	450	225	100

Quality X

NIB	Exc.	V.G.	Good	Fair	Poor
—	1300	875	450	225	100

THE "NEW DOUBLE BOLTED HAMMER GUN"

During 1915, the Ithaca Gun Company replaced the New Ithaca Gun with a model it referred to as "our new model two bolt hammer gun." The new hammer gun had coil springs powering the external hammers. The "two bolt" lock up was accomplished by a bottom bolt and by the top lever engagement with the rear nub of the rib extension. Lower grade models were marked on both sides of the frame with a setter dog and the logo, "Ithaca Gun Co." The 1915 catalog is the last year hammer guns were advertised but the old records indicate a few were sold as late as 1919.Grades offered were X, A, AA, B, C, D, and E. The 1915 catalogue advertised a price of $29 for an A Quality model and $150 for the elaborately engraved Quality E. All grades were available in 10, 12, and 16 gauges. Like the New Ithaca Gun, grades above Quality B are seldom encountered, and an expert appraisal is recommended. Sixteen gauge guns command a 30 percent price premium. The extremely rare 20 gauge model requires an expert appraisal.

Quality A

NIB	Exc.	V.G.	Good	Fair	Poor
—	1300	875	350	225	100

Quality AA

NIB	Exc.	V.G.	Good	Fair	Poor
—	1600	1075	450	250	100

Quality B

NIB	Exc.	V.G.	Good	Fair	Poor
—	1600	1075	450	250	100

Quality X

NIB	Exc.	V.G.	Good	Fair	Poor
—	1600	1075	450	250	100

HAMMERLESS MODELS

The first hammerless Ithaca gun was introduced in 1888. All Ithaca double guns were discontinued in 1948.The gauge and grade can usually be found on the left front corner of the water table of the frame, the serial number is usually found on the right side of the same water table, on the barrel flats, and on the forend iron.

CRASS MODEL

The Crass Model, named after Ithaca's Frederick Crass who designed it, was introduced in 1888. It was offered in Quality 1 through Quality 7. The Quality 1P, a model with no engraving, was introduced in 1898. The Crass Model underwent three major frame redesigns before it was discontinued during 1901. The gun was available in 10, 12, and 16 gauge. Automatic ejectors were introduced in 1893 and were available in any quality gun at extra cost. **NOTE:** Sixteen gauge guns will command a 20 percent price premium. Guns above Quality 4 are seldom encountered, and an expert appraisal is necessary. For automatic ejectors add $250. The serial number range for the Crass Model is approximately 7000 to 50000.

Quality 1

NIB	*Exc.*	*V.G.*	*Good*	*Fair*	*Poor*
—	900	575	400	225	100

Quality 1-1/2

NIB	*Exc.*	*V.G.*	*Good*	*Fair*	*Poor*
—	900	575	400	225	100

Quality 1P

NIB	*Exc.*	*V.G.*	*Good*	*Fair*	*Poor*
—	900	575	400	225	100

Quality 2

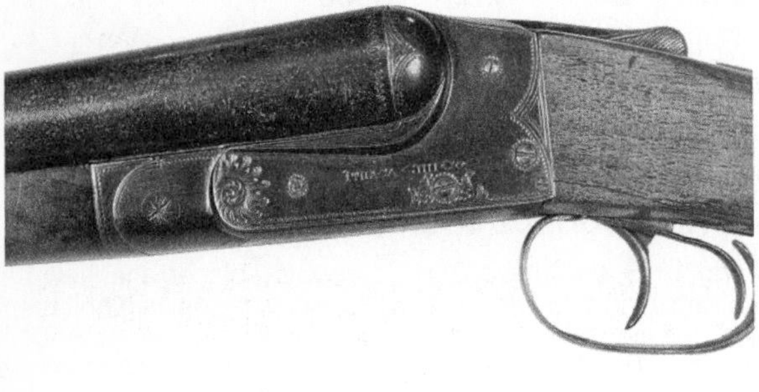

Courtesy Walter C. Snyder

NIB	*Exc.*	*V.G.*	*Good*	*Fair*	*Poor*
—	1300	875	600	250	100

Quality 3

NIB	*Exc.*	*V.G.*	*Good*	*Fair*	*Poor*
—	1800	1300	775	325	100

Quality 4

NIB	*Exc.*	*V.G.*	*Good*	*Fair*	*Poor*
—	2250	1850	1075	325	100

LEWIS MODEL

Chester Lewis, an Ithaca Gun employee, was credited with the design of the gun that now bears his name. The gun was bolted through the rib extension in addition to the traditional under bolt. The model was available from 1901 through 1906, and was offered in Qualities 1 through 7. It was made in 10, 12, and 16 gauge, and after 1906, 20 gauge. Automatic ejectors were offered at added cost.Qualities offered: 1, 1 Special, 1-1/2, 2, 3, 4, 5, 6, 7. The 1 Special had Nitro Steel barrels. **NOTE:** Automatic ejectors add about $250 to grades below Quality 4. The serial number range for the Lewis Model is approximately 55000 to 123600.

Quality 1

NIB	*Exc.*	*V.G.*	*Good*	*Fair*	*Poor*
—	900	575	325	175	100

Quality 1 Special

NIB	*Exc.*	*V.G.*	*Good*	*Fair*	*Poor*
—	900	575	325	175	100

Quality 1-1/2

NIB	*Exc.*	*V.G.*	*Good*	*Fair*	*Poor*
—	950	600	350	200	100

Quality 2

NIB	*Exc.*	*V.G.*	*Good*	*Fair*	*Poor*
—	1150	725	500	225	100

Quality 3

NIB	*Exc.*	*V.G.*	*Good*	*Fair*	*Poor*
—	1850	1500	850	425	100

Quality 4

NIB	*Exc.*	*V.G.*	*Good*	*Fair*	*Poor*
—	2700	2350	1900	475	100

Quality 5

NIB	*Exc.*	*V.G.*	*Good*	*Fair*	*Poor*
—	3700	3150	2100	725	300

Quality 6

NIB	*Exc.*	*V.G.*	*Good*	*Fair*	*Poor*
—	6300	4750	3200	775	300

Quality 7

NIB	*Exc.*	*V.G.*	*Good*	*Fair*	*Poor*
—	6300	4750	3200	775	300

MINIER MODEL

The Minier Model, named after Ithaca's David Minier, was introduced in 1906 and was available through 1908. It was offered in Qualities Field through 7 and any grade could be ordered with ejectors. The Minier Model was the first Ithaca gun to use coil springs to power the internal hammers. This model was triple bolted, e.g., two fastenings at the rib extension and the under bolt. Gauges 10, 12, 16, and 20 were offered. Grades offered: Field, 1, 1 Special, 1-1/2, 2, 3, 4, 5, 6, 7. **NOTE:** Automatic ejectors add $250 to guns below Quality 4. The serial number range for the Minier Model is approximately 130000 to 151000.

Field Grade

NIB	*Exc.*	*V.G.*	*Good*	*Fair*	*Poor*
—	1150	725	500	225	100

Quality 1

NIB	*Exc.*	*V.G.*	*Good*	*Fair*	*Poor*
—	1150	725	500	225	100

Quality 1 Special

NIB	*Exc.*	*V.G.*	*Good*	*Fair*	*Poor*
—	1150	725	500	225	100

Quality 1-1/2

NIB	*Exc.*	*V.G.*	*Good*	*Fair*	*Poor*
—	1150	725	500	225	100

Quality 2

NIB	Exc.	V.G.	Good	Fair	Poor
—	1350	700	475	225	100

Quality 3

NIB	Exc.	V.G.	Good	Fair	Poor
—	2250	1200	575	450	100

Quality 4

NIB	Exc.	V.G.	Good	Fair	Poor
—	2700	1325	875	450	100

Quality 5

NIB	Exc.	V.G.	Good	Fair	Poor
—	3700	3150	2100	725	300

Quality 6

NIB	Exc.	V.G.	Good	Fair	Poor
—	5250	4100	1550	725	300

Quality 7

NIB	Exc.	V.G.	Good	Fair	Poor
—	6800	4300	1700	800	300

FLUES MODEL

The Flues Model Ithaca gun was built on a three-piece lock mechanism invented and patented by Emil Flues. Introduced in 1908, it remained in production through 1926 when it was replaced by the Ithaca New Double. It was offered in gauges 10, 12, 16, 20, and 28, and enjoyed the longest production life of any Ithaca double gun. Several grades were offered beginning with the Field grade and ending with the Sousa Special. The Flues Model had the same bolting system as used on the Minier Model. Any grade could have been ordered with automatic ejectors at extra cost. A single-selective trigger made by the Infallible Trigger company was offered after 1914 and was the first single trigger offered from the company. Qualities offered were: Field, 1, 1 Special, 1-1/2, 2, 3, 4, 5, 6, 7, and Sousa. **NOTE:** Add $200 for factory-ordered single trigger, add $200 for automatic ejectors on grades lower than Grade 4. Small gauges command a price premium. A 20 gauge gun may command up to a 50 percent price premium; a 28 gauge field grade perhaps as much as 200 percent. The serial number range for the Flues is approximately 175000 to 399000. Expert appraisals are recommended on higher-grade, small-gauge models as they are seldom encountered.

Field Grade

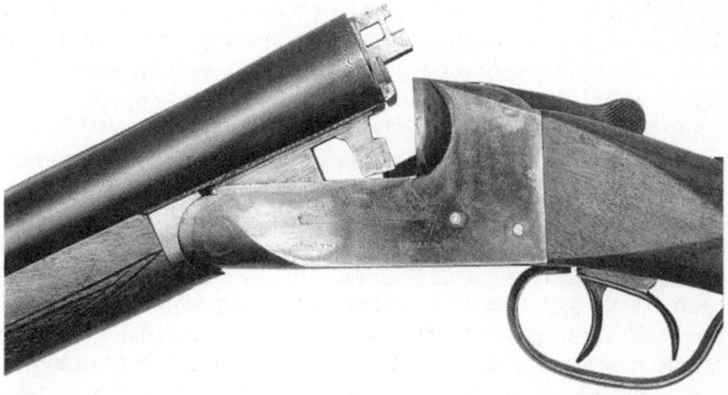

NIB	Exc.	V.G.	Good	Fair	Poor
—	1100	700	375	250	100

Grade 1

NIB	Exc.	V.G.	Good	Fair	Poor
—	1100	700	375	250	100

Grade 1 Special

NIB	Exc.	V.G.	Good	Fair	Poor
—	1100	700	375	250	100

Grade 1-1/2

NIB	Exc.	V.G.	Good	Fair	Poor
—	1250	850	500	350	100

Grade 2

NIB	Exc.	V.G.	Good	Fair	Poor
—	1350	900	575	400	100

Grade 3

NIB	Exc.	V.G.	Good	Fair	Poor
—	2300	1600	800	500	100

Grade 4

NIB	Exc.	V.G.	Good	Fair	Poor
—	2300	1600	800	500	100

Grade 5

NIB	Exc.	V.G.	Good	Fair	Poor
—	2800	2200	1650	600	200

Grade 6

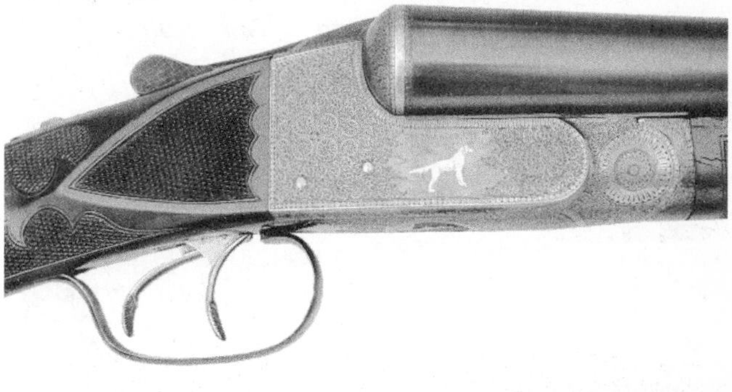

Courtesy Walter C. Snyder

NIB	Exc.	V.G.	Good	Fair	Poor
—	11000	6000	2750	1100	300

Grade 7

NIB	Exc.	V.G.	Good	Fair	Poor
—	11500	7000	3000	1250	300

Sousa

NIB	Exc.	V.G.	Good	Fair	Poor
—	17000	12000	7500	3750	N/A

THE NEW ITHACA DOUBLE

The New Ithaca Double, commonly referred to as the NID, was manufactured from 1926 to 1948. It has the distinction of being the last double gun manufactured by the factory. The NID was bolted by a single rotary top bolt and was considered of all Ithaca double guns manufactured up to that time. External cocking indicators were standard on all NID models until about 1934, when they were eliminated from the design. Selective and non-selective single triggers and automatic ejectors were optional at additional costs. A special variation of the NID was introduced in 1932 to accommodate 10 gauge 3-1/2" magnum ammunition and was named, appropriately, the Magnum 10. All NID were available in grades Field, 1, 2, 3, 4, 5, 7, and Sousa (renamed the $1,000 grade after 1936). Gauges Magnum 10, standard 10, 12, 16, 20, 28, and .410 bore were offered. **NOTE:** Like most collectible double guns, the smaller gauges command a price premium over the 12 gauge model. A 16 gauge field grade may command a 25 percent price premium, a 20 gauge field grade may command up to a 50 percent price premium, and the 28 gauge, and .410 caliber field-grade models perhaps as much as 250-300 percent. It is recommended that an expert opinion be sought for the valuation of high-grade, small-gauge models. Of late, the Magnum 10 gauge model also commands a price premium. Few of these guns trade, and the advice of an expert appraiser is suggested. Non-selective single trigger add $150. Single-selective trigger add $250. Ventilated rib add $300. Automatic ejectors for grade below Grade 4 add $300. Beavertail forearm add $200. Monte Carlo buttstock add $300.

Field Grade

NIB	*Exc.*	*V.G.*	*Good*	*Fair*	*Poor*
—	1100	700	375	250	100

Grade 1

NIB	*Exc.*	*V.G.*	*Good*	*Fair*	*Poor*
—	1350	850	475	250	100

Grade 2

Courtesy Walter C. Snyder

NIB	*Exc.*	*V.G.*	*Good*	*Fair*	*Poor*
—	1650	900	725	350	100

Grade 3

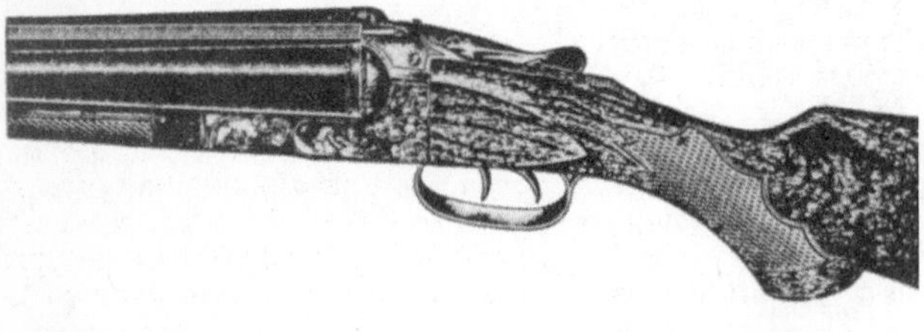

NIB	*Exc.*	*V.G.*	*Good*	*Fair*	*Poor*
—	2600	1600	1075	425	100

Grade 4

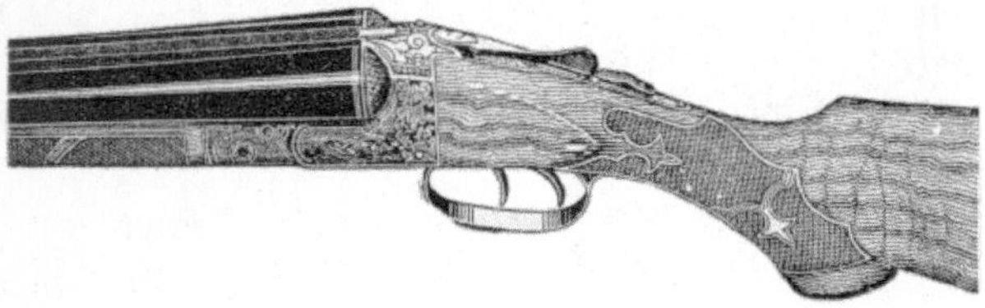

NIB	*Exc.*	*V.G.*	*Good*	*Fair*	*Poor*
—	3250	2700	1600	475	100

Grade 5

NIB	*Exc.*	*V.G.*	*Good*	*Fair*	*Poor*
—	4300	3400	2200	775	200

Grade 7

NIB	*Exc.*	*V.G.*	*Good*	*Fair*	*Poor*
—	12000	7500	4250	1100	300

Sousa Grade

NIB	*Exc.*	*V.G.*	*Good*	*Fair*	*Poor*
—	28000	15000	8000	4000	800

THE NEW ITHACA DOUBLE (MODERN-1999)

SPECIAL FIELD GRADE

This side-by-side double is offered in 16, 20, 28, and .410 bore with a choice of matted rib barrel lengths of 26", 28", or 30". Ivory bead front sight. The action is case colored with light line border engraving. The stock is feather crotch black walnut with 22 lpi checkering. Choice of pistol or straight grip. Double trigger is standard. Weight in 20 gauge is about 5 lbs. 14 oz. 28 gauge is about 5 lbs. 8 oz., and .410 bore weighs about 5 lbs. 5 oz.

NIB	*Exc.*	*V.G.*	*Good*	*Fair*	*Poor*
6200	4750	4000	1700	800	300

Grade 4E

This model is also available in 16, 20, 28, and .410 with 26", 28", and 30" barrels. This model has gold plated triggers jeweled barrel flats and hand tuned locks. Black walnut stock has 28 lpi checkering with a fleur-de-lis pattern. Pistol or straight grip stock. Action is hand engraved with three game scenes and bank note scroll. Case colored frame.

NIB	Exc.	V.G.	Good	Fair	Poor
8000	6000	3000	1750	775	300

Grade 7E

This model has all of the gauges and barrel lengths of the above guns. Action is hand engraved with gold two tone inlays. Exhibition grade black walnut stock with elaborate patterns. Custom built dimensions.

NIB	Exc.	V.G.	Good	Fair	Poor
11000	8750	7500	4250	1100	300

Sousa Grade

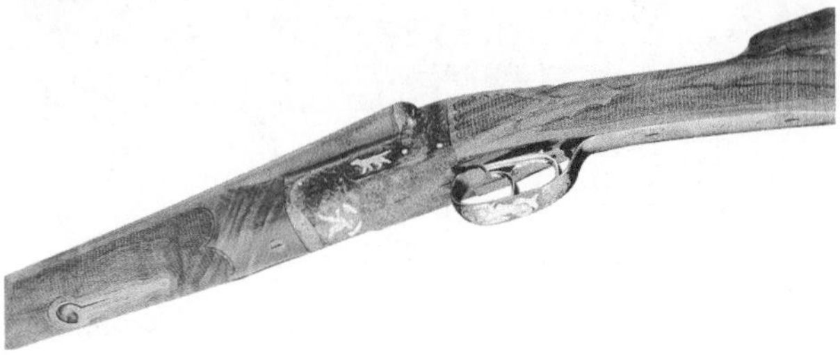

The famous Sousa mermaid in raised gold inlay

This model, available in the same gauges and barrel lengths as the above guns is stocked with presentation grade black walnut, hand carved with 32 lpi checkering. The action is hand engraved with bank note scroll and gold inlays. The entire gun is hand fitted and polished. Extremely limited availability. Special order only.

NIB	Exc.	V.G.	Good	Fair	Poor
18000	12500	—	—	—	—

LEFEVER ARMS COMPANY, INC.

During 1921, Ithaca Gun, under the name "Lefever Arms Company, Inc." introduced a line of lower-cost, box-lock guns. See the Lefever Arms Company section of this book for prices concerning those guns.

WESTERN ARMS CORPORATION

During 1929 the Ithaca Gun Company created the Western Arms Corporation, which introduced a new, low-cost double gun. That new double gun was named The Long Range Double and it was produced in 12, 16, and 20 gauges, and .410 caliber. Twenty gauge guns often command a 20 percent premium, a .410 caliber can command up to a 250 percent premium. This model was last made at the start of World War II.

The Long Range Double

The Long Range Double had walnut stocks that were not checkered.

NIB	Exc.	V.G.	Good	Fair	Poor
—	550	450	200	150	N/A

NOTE: Single trigger guns will add $100 and automatic ejectors will add $200.

The Long Range Double Deluxe

Usually made exclusively for the Montgomery Ward Company and sold by them under the name, Western Field Deluxe. This model had a line checkering pattern at the grip and on the splinter forend. Many of the Ithaca produced Western Field Deluxe guns had automatic ejectors and that fact was stamped into the right barrel.

NIB	Exc.	V.G.	Good	Fair	Poor
—	575	475	300	150	N/A

NOTE: Single triggers add $100. Automatic ejectors add $200.

ITHACA SINGLE-BARREL TRAP GUNS

The Ithaca Gun Company introduced a single-barrel trap gun in 1914. This gun was based upon the Emil Flues three piece lock design used for the double gun and has become known as the Flues Model Single-Barrel Trap. The Flues Model was discontinued during 1922 and was replaced that year by a model designed by Ithaca's Frank Knickerbocker, commonly referred to as the "Knick." The Knick Model was discontinued in 1988, shortly after the Ithaca Acquisition Corp. purchased the assets of the Ithaca Gun Company. For many years, The Ithaca Single-Barrel Trap Gun was the gun of choice for many champion shooters.

FLUES MODEL SINGLE-BARREL TRAP GUN (1914 TO 1922)

The Flues Model trap gun was introduced in 1914 and offered in Grades 4, 5, 6, and 7. A lower cost Victory grade was introduced in 1919 and the highest cost variety, the Sousa Special was introduced in 1918. All Flues model trap guns were made within the same serial number sequence as the double guns but do have the letter "T" for Trap following the serial number. All Flues Models with the exception of the Victory Grade were produced with an automatic ejector. A rubber anti-recoil pad was an option. Guns having a pre-1916 engraving pattern will command the highest prices.

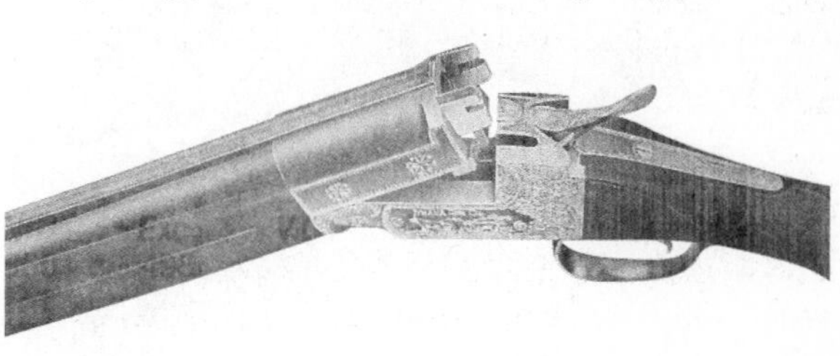

Courtesy Walter C. Snyder

Victory Grade

NIB	Exc.	V.G.	Good	Fair	Poor
—	1300	900	700	300	N/A

Grade 4E

NIB	Exc.	V.G.	Good	Fair	Poor
—	2350	1900	1300	400	N/A

Grade 5E

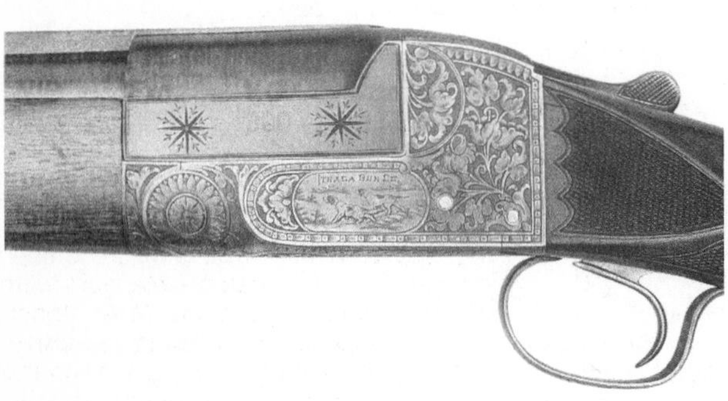

NIB	Exc.	V.G.	Good	Fair	Poor
—	4200	3100	2550	600	N/A

Grade 6E

NIB	Exc.	V.G.	Good	Fair	Poor
—	6300	5250	3200	900	N/A

Grade 7E

NIB	Exc.	V.G.	Good	Fair	Poor
—	8350	6200	4100	1050	N/A

Sousa Grade

NIB	Exc.	V.G.	Good	Fair	Poor
—	16500	11000	9000	2500	N/A

KNICK MODEL SINGLE-BARREL TRAP

The Knick Model trap gun was introduced during 1922 and was based on a design credited to Frank Knickerbocker. The design was simple and very serviceable, had been in continues production until 1988 when it was discontinued. The model was available in Victory, 4, 5, 7, and Sousa Special Grades. The Sousa was replaced by the $1,000 Grade in about 1936, which was replaced by the $2,000 Grade by 1952, the $2,500 Grade by 1960, the $3,000 Grade by 1965, the $5,000 Grade by 1974, and finally, the Dollar Grade in the early 1980s as the cost of production increased. All Knick models were produced with an automatic ejector and a rubber anti-recoil pad.

Victory Grade

Courtesy William Hammond

NIB	Exc.	V.G.	Good	Fair	Poor
2500	1350	900	700	300	N/A

Grade 4E

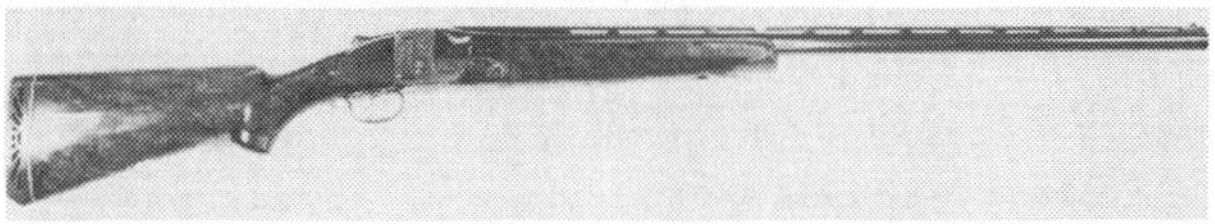

Courtesy C. Hadley Smith

NIB	Exc.	V.G.	Good	Fair	Poor
3300	2450	1950	1100	500	N/A

Grade 5E

NIB	Exc.	V.G.	Good	Fair	Poor
5500	4400	3300	2750	875	N/A

Grade 7E

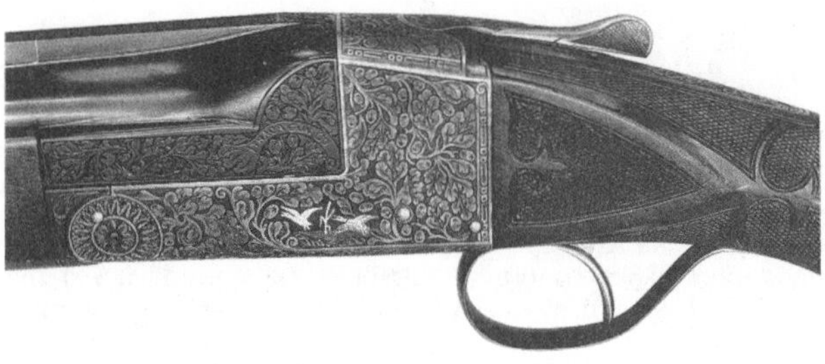

NIB	Exc.	V.G.	Good	Fair	Poor
8800	5500	4450	3300	1100	N/A

Sousa Grade

NIB	Exc.	V.G.	Good	Fair	Poor
19000	11000	6600	4400	N/A	N/A

$1,000 to $2,500 Grades

NIB	Exc.	V.G.	Good	Fair	Poor
16500	13500	8800	6500	2200	N/A

$3,000 through the Dollar Grade

NIB	Exc.	V.G.	Good	Fair	Poor
13500	11000	6500	5500	2200	N/A

Century Grade Trap (SKB)

A 12 gauge boxlock single barrel shotgun with a 32" or 34" ventilated rib barrel and automatic ejector. Blued with a walnut stock. Manufactured by SKB during the 1970s.

NIB	Exc.	V.G.	Good	Fair	Poor
—	900	700	550	350	300

Century II (SKB)

An improved version of the above model.

NIB	Exc.	V.G.	Good	Fair	Poor
—	950	700	600	450	350

Model 66 Supersingle —1963-1978

A 12, 20 or .410 bore lever action single-shot shotgun with a 24" barrel. Blued with a walnut stock. The 20 gauge and .410 bore command a 50 percent premium.

Courtesy C. Hadley Smith

NIB	Exc.	V.G.	Good	Fair	Poor
300	180	150	125	100	50

Model 66 Youth Grade

A special gun offered for the youth market in 20 gauge and .410 bore.

NIB	Exc.	V.G.	Good	Fair	Poor
300	180	150	125	100	50

Model 66 Buck Buster (RS Barrel)

As above, in 20 gauge with a Deerslayer 22" barrel fitted with rifle sights.

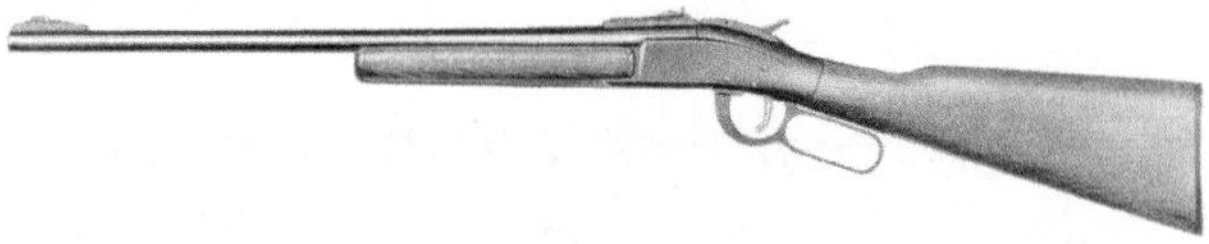

NIB	Exc.	V.G.	Good	Fair	Poor
325	250	200	150	125	75

Model 66 Vent Rib

NIB	Exc.	V.G.	Good	Fair	Poor
325	250	200	150	125	75

ITHACA AUTO & BURGLAR GUN NFA, CURIO OR RELIC

The Ithaca Auto & Burglar Gun is a double-barreled 20 gauge smooth bore pistol manufactured by Ithaca Gun Company, Ithaca, New York, from 1922 to 1934. Total production was approximately 4,500. They were made by modifying Ithaca\qs standard field grade double-barrel shotgun by shortening the barrels and fitting the receiver with a pistol grip. Standard factory guns had blued 10" barrels, case hardened receivers with the legend Auto & Burglar Gun/ Ithaca Gun Co./Ithaca, New York, and the figure of a pointing dog stamped on each side. The barrel length on 21 guns inspected varied to 10.25" (typically in increments divisible by .125"), apparently from inexact factory quality control. Ithaca set a $37.50 retail price when the gun was in production, but some dealers sold it for $40 or more. Production was halted when the government ruled the Ithaca Auto & Burglar Gun to be a "firearm" in the "any other weapon" category under the National Firearms Act (NFA) of 1934.There are two variations, termed Model A and Model B. Model A utilizes the so-called Flues frame (named after Emil Flues, who designed it in 1908), and its distinctive grip has a curving butt and a large spur. Model A is designed for 2.5" shells, and is not considered safe to fire using modern ammunition. Approximately 2,500 Model A Auto & Burglar Guns were manufactured from 1922 to 1925, when the Flues model was discontinued.Model B utilizes the so-called N.I.D. frame (short for New Ithaca Double), introduced in 1926 and discontinued in 1948. The N.I.D. is designed for modern ammunition and 2.75" shells, has cocking indicators, and a different pistol grip that is perpendicular to the barrel and which lacks the distinctive spur. Some Model Bs have been observed with rosettes or "stars" engraved in each side of the receiver; their significance is unknown at this time, but they probably are decorations. Approximately 2,000 Model B Auto & Burglar Guns were manufactured from 1926 to 1934.

Model A Serial numbered from 343336 to 398365

NIB	Exc.	V.G.	Good	Fair	Poor
—	2500	2000	1750	900	500

Model B Serial numbered from 425000 to 464699

NIB	Exc.	V.G.	Good	Fair	Poor
—	2750	2200	2000	950	550

NOTE: Nonstandard or special order guns command premiums of 100 percent or more. Original holsters (marked Auto and Burglar Gun/made by/ITHACA GUN CO./ithaca, n.y.) are extremely rare and worth $300 to $500 or more.

ITHACA MODEL 37 REPEATER

The Ithaca Model 37 Repeater was introduced in 1937 in 12 gauge, 1938 in 16 gauge, and in 1939 in 20 gauge. It underwent very few design changes throughout its long life which ended 1987 when the Ithaca Acquisition Corp. acquired the assets of the Ithaca Gun Company during 1987 and renamed the gun the Model 87. The name has recently been changed again to the M37 after the assets of the Ithaca Acquisition Corp. were purchased in May of 1996 by the Ithaca Gun Company, LLC. All Model 37 guns were chambered only for 2-3/4" ammunition until 1983, when the Magnum with 3" chamber was introduced to some configurations. Most Model 37 guns had blued metal and walnut stocks with the exception of the Model 37 Field Grade series which had matte finished metal and Birch stocks. Sixteen gauge guns were discontinued in 1973. Ithaca Gun closed in April, 2005, but reopened in 2006 as Ithaca Guns USA of Upper Sandusky, Ohio. **NOTE:** Twenty gauge guns made before 1968 will generally command a price premium.

Model 37/Standard Grade—1937-1983

Guns made before 1968 will enjoy a 15 percent price premium; those made before World War II, a 30 percent price premium.

Courtesy C. Hadley Smith

NIB	Exc.	V.G.	Good	Fair	Poor
—	350	200	175	125	75

Model 37S/Skeet Grade—1937-1953

Guns made before World War II will enjoy a 50 percent price premium.

NIB	Exc.	V.G.	Good	Fair	Poor
—	600	400	350	250	100

Model 37T/Trap—1937-1953

Guns made before World War II will enjoy a 50 percent price premium.

NIB	Exc.	V.G.	Good	Fair	Poor
—	600	400	350	250	100

Model 37T/Target—1954-1961

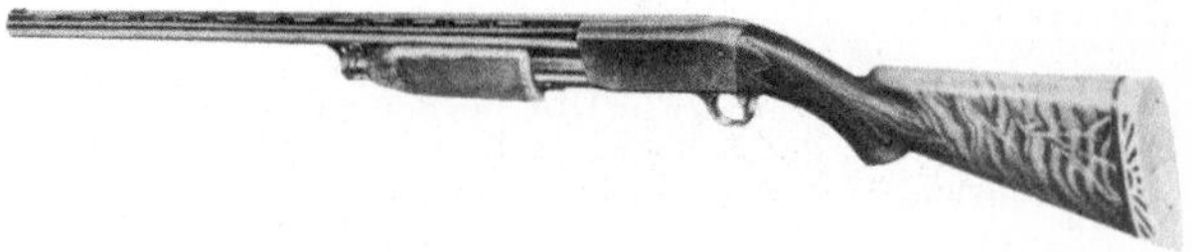

NIB	Exc.	V.G.	Good	Fair	Poor
—	600	400	350	250	100

Model 37R/Solid Rib—1940-1967

Guns made before World War II will enjoy a 50 percent price premium.

Courtesy Walter C. Snyder

NIB	Exc.	V.G.	Good	Fair	Poor
—	400	275	225	200	75

Model 37 Military Marked (WWII)

This is one of the scarcest military shotguns. It was built in three different configurations; 30" barrel, 20" barrel, and 20" barrel with handguard and bayonet lug (Trench Gun). A scarce shotgun, proceed with caution.

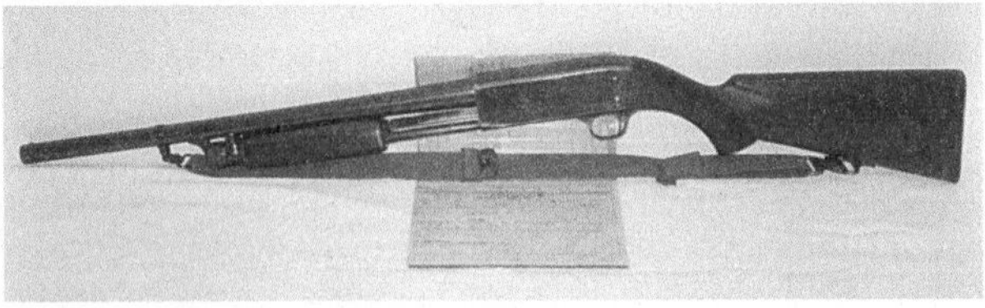

NIB	Exc.	V.G.	Good	Fair	Poor
—	2000	1800	1500	—	—

NOTE: Add $200 for government release papers and 150 percent for Trench Gun configuration.

Model 37RD/Deluxe Solid Rib—1954-1962

Courtesy C. Hadley Smith

NIB	Exc.	V.G.	Good	Fair	Poor
—	500	375	300	200	100

Model 37 Deerslayer—1959-1987

All Deerslayer models made before 1968 will enjoy a 10 percent to 20 percent price premium.

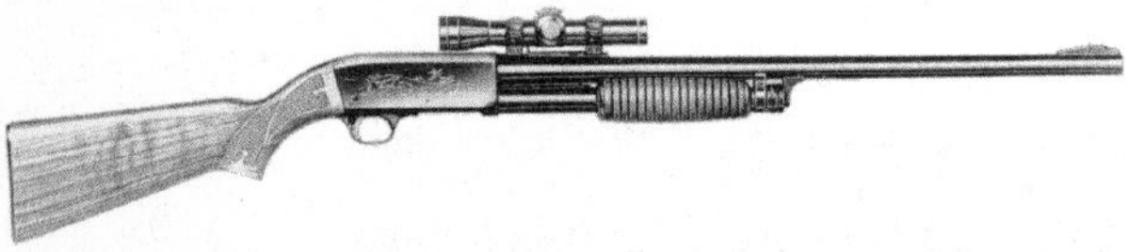

Courtesy C. Hadley Smith

NIB	Exc.	V.G.	Good	Fair	Poor
—	300	250	200	125	75

Model 37 Deluxe Deerslayer—1959-1971

NIB	Exc.	V.G.	Good	Fair	Poor
—	300	250	225	125	75

Model 37 Super Deluxe Deerslayer—1959-1987

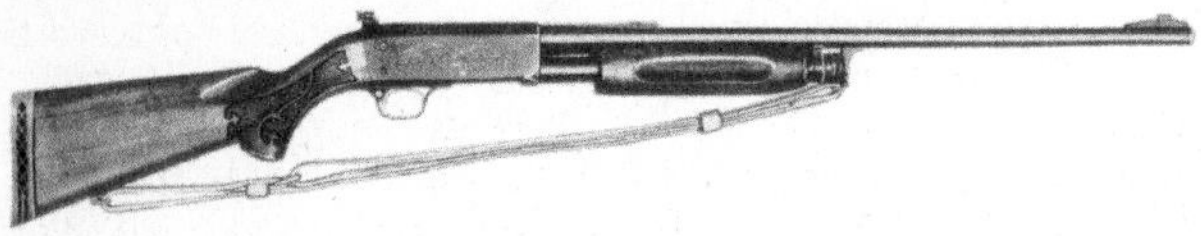

Courtesy C. Hadley Smith

NIB	Exc.	V.G.	Good	Fair	Poor
—	450	325	275	200	100

Model 37 Supreme Grade—1967-1987

NIB	Exc.	V.G.	Good	Fair	Poor
—	700	450	350	200	100

Model 37 Field Grade Standard—1983-1985

NIB	Exc.	V.G.	Good	Fair	Poor
—	350	200	150	125	75

Model 37 Field Grade Vent—1983-1986

NIB	Exc.	V.G.	Good	Fair	Poor
—	350	250	200	125	75

Model 37 Basic Featherlight—1979-1983

Manufactured in 12 gauge only.

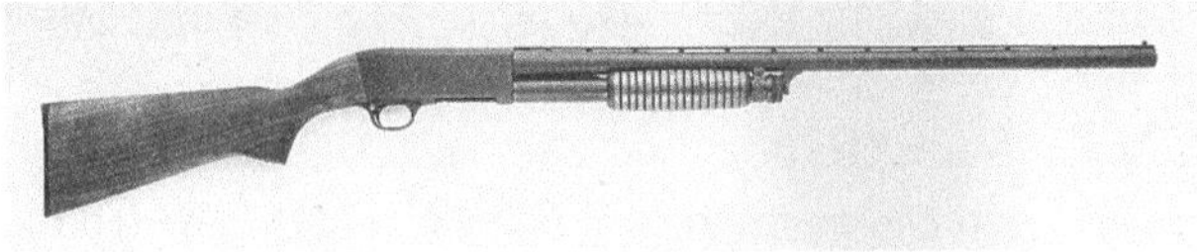

Courtesy Walter C. Snyder

NIB	Exc.	V.G.	Good	Fair	Poor
—	300	250	200	125	75

Model 37V/Vent Rib—1961-1983

Guns made before 1968 will enjoy a 10 percent to 20 percent price premium.

NIB	Exc.	V.G.	Good	Fair	Poor
—	350	300	175	150	75

Model 37RV/Deluxe Vent Rib—1961-1966

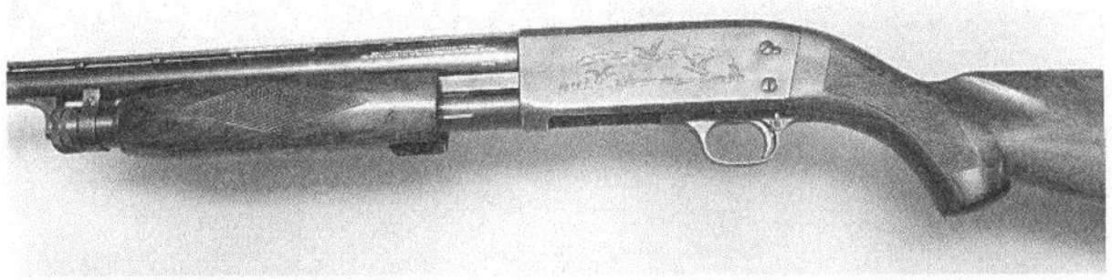

NIB	Exc.	V.G.	Good	Fair	Poor
—	750	500	300	200	75

Model 37D/Deluxe—1955-1977

Guns made before 1968 will enjoy a 10 percent to 20 percent price premium.

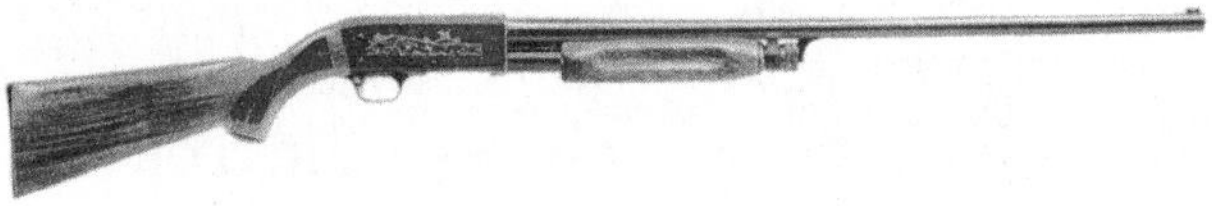

Courtesy C. Hadley Smith

NIB	Exc.	V.G.	Good	Fair	Poor
—	400	250	175	125	75

Model 37DV/Deluxe Vent Rib—1961-1987

Guns made before 1968 will enjoy a 10 percent to 20 percent price premium.

NIB	Exc.	V.G.	Good	Fair	Poor
—	450	300	200	150	100

Model 37 Magnum 3" Chamber—1978-1987

NIB	Exc.	V.G.	Good	Fair	Poor
—	400	300	225	125	75

Model 37 Field Grade Magnum—1984-1987

NIB	Exc.	V.G.	Good	Fair	Poor
—	300	225	175	125	75

Model 37 UltraLight—1978 to 1987

The UltraLight had an aluminum alloy frame and trigger plate. The barrels are marked Ultra Featherlight and the serial number is prefaced with the mark, "ULT." Both the 12 and 20 gauges were offered.

NIB	Exc.	V.G.	Good	Fair	Poor
—	475	400	300	150	100

Model 37 English UltraLight—1982-1987

This gun is the same as the Model 37 UltraLight, but has an English-style straight grip stock.

NIB	Exc.	V.G.	Good	Fair	Poor
—	500	450	350	150	100

Model 37 Camo

Introduced in 1985, this model is available with either a green or brown camouflage finish and was offered only in 12 gauge.

NIB	Exc.	V.G.	Good	Fair	Poor
—	350	300	200	150	100

Model 37 Bicentennial

A special model produced during 1976 to commemorate the 200 year anniversary of the United States. The gun came with a full-length trunk-style hard case and a pewter belt buckle number to the gun. The serial number was prefaced with "U.S.A."

NIB	Exc.	V.G.	Good	Fair	Poor
650	500	300	200	125	75

NOTE: Subtract 35 percent if the original case and belt buckle are missing.

Model 37 Ducks Unlimited Commemorative, Auction Grade

Special edition made during 1977. Serial number sequence was 40-DU0001 to 40-DU1125.

NIB	Exc.	V.G.	Good	Fair	Poor
650	400	300	150	100	75

Model 37 Ducks Unlimited Commemorative, Trade Grade

Special edition made during 1977. Lower grade version of the Auction Grade. Serial number preceded with the mark, DU37040.

NIB	Exc.	V.G.	Good	Fair	Poor
450	400	350	200	N/A	N/A

Model 37 2500 Series Centennial

A commemorative Model 37 12 gauge shotgun with silver-plated receiver and press checkered stocks. Manufactured in 1984.

NIB	Exc.	V.G.	Good	Fair	Poor
800	500	300	150	100	75

Model 37 Presentation Series Centennial

A commemorative Mode 37 12 gauge with a gold-plated receiver and high grade hand checkered stocks. It was manufactured during 1980, but is still available as of August 1997.

NIB	Exc.	V.G.	Good	Fair	Poor
1500	800	500	150	100	—

HI-GRADE ITHACA MODEL 37 GUNS

The Ithaca Gun company offered custom engraving services either from its in-house engraver, one of which was retained until about 1972, or through an outside contract engraver who was usually William Mains. Many customers requested some degree of custom work and guns with various patterns turn up from time to time. There were four standard engraving patterns offered to customers, Grade 1, Grade 2, Grade 3, and the very elaborate $1,000 Grade pattern. Increasing production costs forced the $1,000 Grade to become the $2,000 Grade, the $2,500, and finally the $3,000 Grade over the years. **NOTE:** All factory engraved Model 37 guns are rare and require an expert appraiser to determine an accurate value.

$1,000 Grade

The Model 37 with an engraved receiver, gold inlays, and a well-figured walnut stock. Manufactured between 1940 and 1942.

NIB	Exc.	V.G.	Good	Fair	Poor
10000	5000	3000	2000	N/A	N/A

$2,000 Grade

Manufactured from 1946 to 1957.

NIB	Exc.	V.G.	Good	Fair	Poor
10000	5000	3000	2000	N/A	N/A

$3,000 Grade

NIB	Exc.	V.G.	Good	Fair	Poor
8000	4000	2500	1500	N/A	N/A

MODEL 37 LAW ENFORCEMENT WEAPONS

The Ithaca Gun Company entered the law enforcement market in 1962 when it introduced the Model 37 Military and Police (M&P) and the Model 37DS Police special (DSPS). The M&P Model was styled after the riot guns made for various military contracts. The DSPS was styled after the Ithaca Deerslayer. Both models were offered with 8-shot capacity after 1968. A chrome finish was an available option after 1976. Both models usually had ring turned slide handles. Only those models available to the general public, i.e. barrel lengths of 18" or longer, are listed. Add 25 percent if marked with police department.

Model 37 Military and Police (M&P)—1962-1986

NIB	Exc.	V.G.	Good	Fair	Poor
550	450	250	200	125	75

NOTE: Add 20 percent for an 8-shot model in NIB or EXC. condition, and add an additional 15 percent for chrome plated models in similar condition.

Model 37 DS Police Special—1962-1986

NIB	Exc.	V.G.	Good	Fair	Poor
575	450	250	200	125	75

NOTE: Add 20 percent for an 8-shot model in NIB or EXC. condition, and add an additional 15 percent for chrome plated models in similar condition.

ITHACA MODEL 87 REPEATER

During 1987 many of the assets of the bankrupt Ithaca Gun Company were purchased by the Ithaca Acquisition Corporation. Manufacture of the Model 37 was resumed that summer after the gun was renamed the Model 87. Many of the Models offered by the old company were continued. All Model 87 field guns were produced with ventilated ribs. All Deerslayer models continued the rifle sights used on the Model 37 guns.

Model 87 Basic—1989-1994

Early models had birch stocks, later production had walnut stocks. All had ring turned slide handles.

NIB	Exc.	V.G.	Good	Fair	Poor
350	300	250	175	125	75

Model 87 Magnum

The Model 87 was manufactured in the styles listed as of 1989:

NIB	Exc.	V.G.	Good	Fair	Poor
400	350	300	225	150	100

Model 87 Field Grade—1987-1990

Stocks were walnut with pressed checkering.

NIB	Exc.	V.G.	Good	Fair	Poor
325	250	200	175	125	75

Model 87 Camo—1987-1994

NIB	Exc.	V.G.	Good	Fair	Poor
300	250	200	175	125	75

Model 87 Turkey Gun—1987-1996

Courtesy C. Hadley Smith

NIB	Exc.	V.G.	Good	Fair	Poor
325	250	200	175	125	75

Model 87 Deluxe—1987-1996

The buttstocks and slide handle were walnut with a machine cut checkered pattern.

Courtesy C. Hadley Smith

NIB	Exc.	V.G.	Good	Fair	Poor
375	300	250	200	125	75

Model 87 Ultralite—1987-1990

All IAC manufactured Ultralite guns carry the old Model 37 serial number.

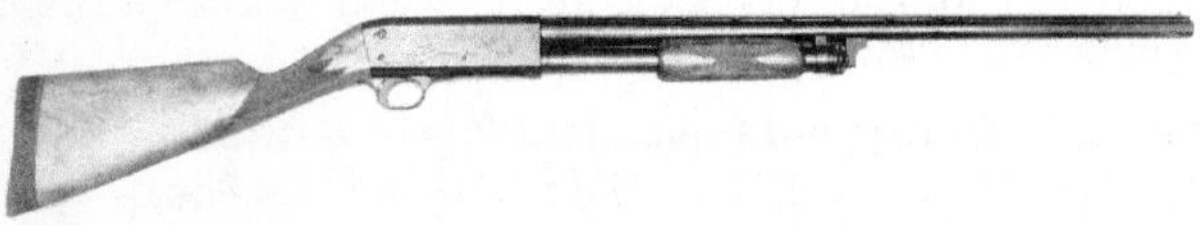

Courtesy C. Hadley Smith

NIB	Exc.	V.G.	Good	Fair	Poor
500	350	250	175	125	75

Model 87 English—1993-1996

Hand-checkered walnut stocks. The slide handle was styled after the pre-war Model 37 slide handle.

NIB	Exc.	V.G.	Good	Fair	Poor
400	350	250	175	125	75

Model 87 Ultralite Deluxe

NIB	Exc.	V.G.	Good	Fair	Poor
400	350	300	250	125	75

Model 87 Supreme Grade—1987-1996

High grade walnut stocks with hand checkering. Metal had extra fine polish and finish.

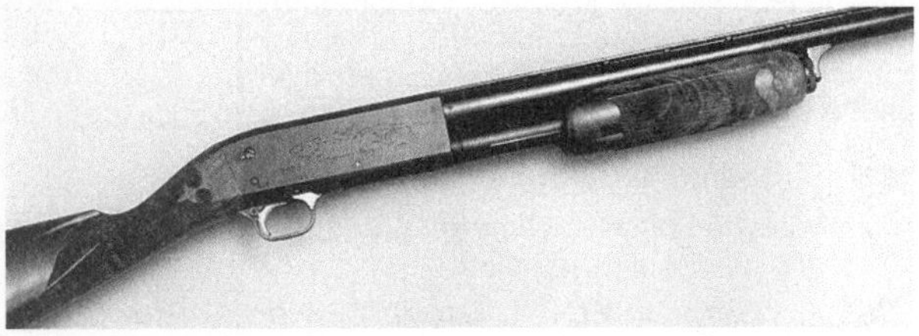

Courtesy C. Hadley Smith

NIB	Exc.	V.G.	Good	Fair	Poor
1000	700	500	300	250	100

Model 87 Deerslayer Basic—1989-1996

Walnut, oil finish butt and slide handle stocks. Slide handle was classic ring turned style.

NIB	Exc.	V.G.	Good	Fair	Poor
300	275	250	200	125	75

Model 87 Deerslayer—1989-1996

It was sometimes advertised as the Model 87 Deerslayer Field. Buttstock and slide handle were walnut and usually had a pressed checkered pattern. The slide handle was the beavertail style.

Courtesy C. Hadley Smith

NIB	Exc.	V.G.	Good	Fair	Poor
350	300	250	200	125	75

Model 87 Deluxe Deerslayer—1989-1996

Butt stock and slide handle were walnut with a machine-cut checkering pattern. The slide handle was beavertail.

NIB	Exc.	V.G.	Good	Fair	Poor
400	350	250	200	125	75

Model 87 Deerslayer II—1988-1996

This model had a fixed rifle barrel and a Monte Carlo buttstock. A small number of guns were specially made with a fast twist barrel to handle Brenneke ammunition and are marked "BRENNEKE" on the receiver.

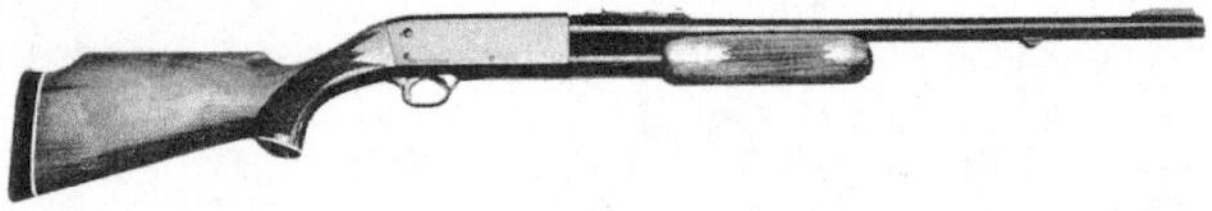

Courtesy C. Hadley Smith

NIB	Exc.	V.G.	Good	Fair	Poor
550	450	350	200	125	75

NOTE: Brenneke-marked guns will command a 30 percent price premium.

Model 87 Home Protection and Law Enforcement Models

The Ithaca Acquisition Corporation continued production of many of the law enforcement firearms produced by the Ithaca Gun Company. Only those models available to the general public are listed.

Model 87 Military & Police—1987-1996

Generally produced with a non-checkered walnut buttstock and a ring turned slide handle, both of which were oil finished. Add 20 percent for an 8-shot model in NIB or excellent condition.

NIB	Exc.	V.G.	Good	Fair	Poor
450	395	275	200	125	75

NOTE: Add an additional 15 percent for chrome plated models in similar condition.

Model 87 DS Police Special—1987-1996

Produced with either a pressed checkered or a non-checkered walnut buttstock, and a ring-turned slide handle, both lacquer finished. The metal was usually finished with a commercial polished blue but a chrome-plated finish was also available.

NIB	Exc.	V.G.	Good	Fair	Poor
450	395	275	200	125	75

NOTE: Add 20 percent for an 8-shot model in NIB or excellent condition, and add an additional 15 percent for a chrome plated models in similar condition.

NEW MODEL 37

During 1996, the assets of the bankrupt Ithaca Acquisition Corporation were purchased by a new company named the Ithaca Gun Company, LLC. One of the first public actions of the new firm was to rename the Model 87 the Model 37, before resuming production later that year, the serial number of the new Model 37 is prefaced with the letter "M." A used market for the new Model 37 has not been established at this time. Suggested retail prices for each model currently produced are listed.In 2001 a Legacy Edition upgrade featuring a laser carved handwritten message in the stock was available for an additional $125.

MODEL 37 DEERSLAYER II

This model is offered in both 12 and 20 gauge. Fitted with either 20" or 25" barrels with rifled bores. These barrel are fixed to the receiver. Magazine capacity is 5 rounds. Walnut stock. Weight is approximately 7 lbs. In 2001 a 16 gauge version with fixed rifled barrel was offered.

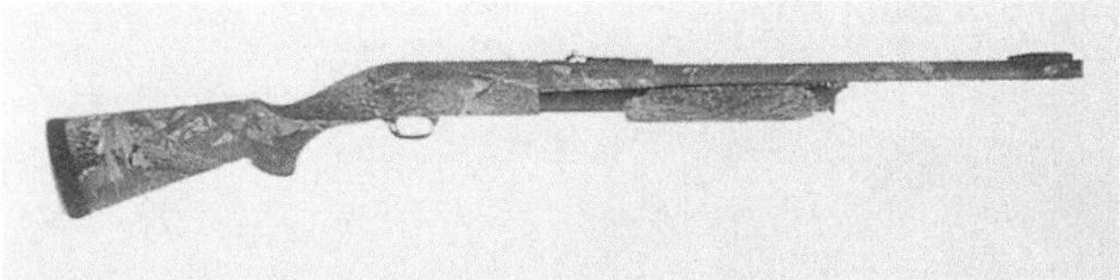

NIB	*Exc.*	*V.G.*	*Good*	*Fair*	*Poor*
640	500	375	275	200	100

Smooth Bore Deluxe

Offered in 12, 16, or 20 gauge with interchangeable barrels in 20" or 25" with smoothbore for deer. Walnut stock. Magazine capacity is 5 rounds. Weight is approximately 6.75 lbs.

NIB	*Exc.*	*V.G.*	*Good*	*Fair*	*Poor*
675	400	350	275	200	100

Rifled Deluxe

Same as above but in 12 and 20 gauge only with rifled barrels.

NIB	*Exc.*	*V.G.*	*Good*	*Fair*	*Poor*
675	400	350	275	200	100

Ithaca Gun Company Deerslayer III Slug Shotgun

Updated, slug-only version of the classic Model 37 pump-action shotgun. 12 or 20 gauge. Fully rifled, heavy fluted 26" barrel with 1:28 twist. Bottom ejection. Fancy black walnut stock and forend, blued barrel and receiver.

Same as above but in 12 and 20 gauge only with rifled barrels.

NIB	*Exc.*	*V.G.*	*Good*	*Fair*	*Poor*
1350	1000	750	500	300	150

Ithaca Gun Company Model 37 28 Gauge

28-ga. pump action shotgun. Scaled down receiver with traditional Model 37 bottom ejection and easy takedown. 26" or 28" barrel, black walnut stock and forend. Available in Fancy "A," Fancy "AA," and Fancy "AAA" grades with increasingly elaborate receiver engraving and decoration. Special order only. Values shown are for "Fancy A" grade

NIB	*Exc.*	*V.G.*	*Good*	*Fair*	*Poor*
1000	750	575	400	300	200

Model 37 Deluxe Field

This model is offered in 12, 16, and 20 gauge with interchangeable vent rib barrels of 26", 28", or 30" (12 gauge only). Walnut stock. Magazine capacity is 5 rounds. Weight is about 7 lbs.

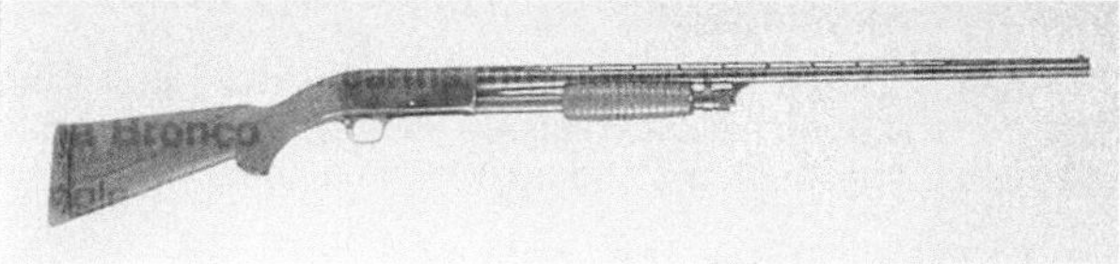

NIB	*Exc.*	*V.G.*	*Good*	*Fair*	*Poor*
625	475	375	250	150	100

Model 37 Deluxe Field English Style

This model is offered in 20 gauge only with 24", 26", or 28" vent rib barrels. Walnut stock. Weight is about 7 lbs. Magazine capacity is 5 rounds.

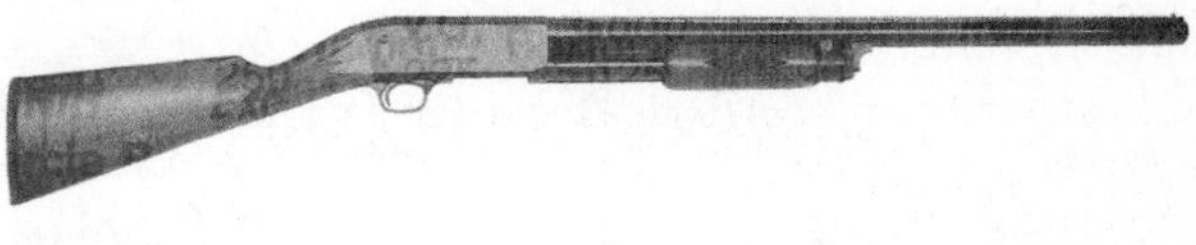

NIB	*Exc.*	*V.G.*	*Good*	*Fair*	*Poor*
650	475	375	250	150	100

Model 37 Ultra Featherlight Grouse Special

Based on the Classic Model 37 with bottom ejection this model features an aluminum receiver and 24" vent rib barrel with choke tubes. Straight grip stock of American black walnut.

NIB	*Exc.*	*V.G.*	*Good*	*Fair*	*Poor*
650	525	395	275	150	100

Model 37 Ultra Featherlight Youth

Similar to the above model but with a 22" barrel and 12.75" length of pull buttstock with ventilated recoil pad.

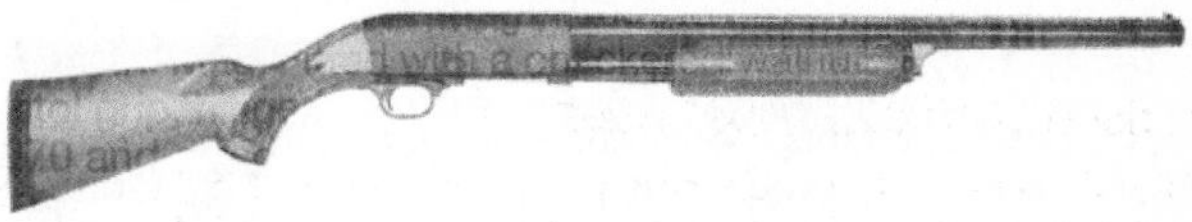

NIB	*Exc.*	*V.G.*	*Good*	*Fair*	*Poor*
600	475	375	250	150	100

Model 37 Sporting Clays

This model features a choice of 24", 26", or 28" wide vent rib barrels with Briley choke tubes. Receiver has an antiqued finish with scroll engraving and high grade American black walnut.

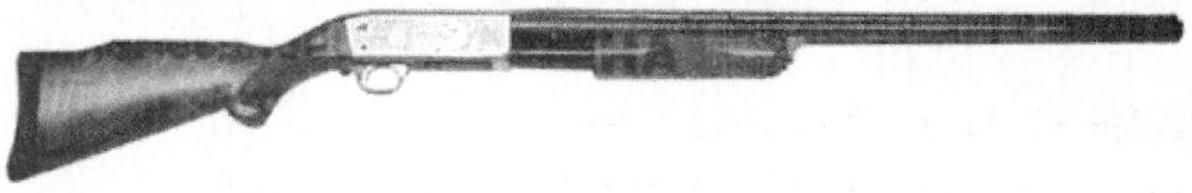

NIB	*Exc.*	*V.G.*	*Good*	*Fair*	*Poor*
1350	1000	750	575	300	150

Model 37 Trap

This model has similar features as the sporting clays but with 30" wide vent rib barrel.

NIB	*Exc.*	*V.G.*	*Good*	*Fair*	*Poor*
1350	1000	750	500	300	150

Model 37 Women's Endowment Shotgun

Offered in 16 or 20 gauge with straight grip stock and a length of pull designed for the woman's height of 5\q5". American walnut stock with cut checkering.

NIB	*Exc.*	*V.G.*	*Good*	*Fair*	*Poor*
635	500	375	250	150	100

Model 37 Turkeyslayer

This model is offered in 12 gauge with 22" Full choke barrel. Choice of 22" ported barrel. Also, a 20 gauge youth model is offered with 22" barrel. Camo stock is standard. Weight is about 7 lbs.

NIB	Exc.	V.G.	Good	Fair	Poor
600	475	375	250	150	10

NOTE: Add $15 for ported barrel option.

Model 37 Waterfowler

Available in 12 gauge only with 28" steel shot barrel. Camo pattern stock. Weight is about 7 lbs. Magazine capacity is 5 rounds.

NIB	Exc.	V.G.	Good	Fair	Poor
595	475	375	250	150	10

Model 37 New Classic

Available in 12, 20, or 16 gauge with hand checkered walnut stock with choice of pistol grip or straight grip and high polish bolt and other component parts. Sunburst recoil pad. Interchangeable vent rib barrels in either 26" or 28". Weight is about 7 lbs.

NIB	Exc.	V.G.	Good	Fair	Poor
810	625	475	375	250	150

Model 37 Turkeyslayer

The first version of this model was made from 1996 to 2004 with a 22-inch barrel and camo stock. It was offered in 12 or 20 gauge. A later model, introduced in 2010, is in 12 gauge only with a 24-inch fixed barrel and synthetic stock with a matte black or camo finish. Also available with laminated thumb-hole stock. Other features include a Briley extended and ported extra-full turkey choke, lengthened forcing cone, Pachmayr Decelerator recoil pad, Tru-Glo fiber optic front sight. Weight: 7.6 pounds with standard stock, 8.2 pounds with thumb-hole.

NIB	Exc.	V.G.	Good	Fair	Poor
575	500	450	400	300	200

Model 37 Home Defense

In 12 or 20 gauge with 18.5 or 20-inch barrel, rifle sights, matte blue finish. Black synthetic or wood stock, 20-inch fixed barrel, rifle sights. Magazine holds 8 rounds (12 ga. only) or 5 rounds (12 or 20 ga.).

NIB	Exc.	V.G.	Good	Fair	Poor
425	385	340	295	250	200

Model 37 Hogslayer

In 12-gauge with 20-inch rifled barrel with rifle sights, matte blued finish. Tubular magazine holds 8 rounds. Matte blued barrel and action. Synthetic stock.

NIB	Exc.	V.G.	Good	Fair	Poor
450	400	355	300	250	200

MODEL 51 SERIES

A 12 or 20 gauge semi-automatic shotgun with 26", 28", or 30" ventilated rib barrels. Blued with a walnut stock. Manufactured from 1970 to 1985 as listed.

Model 51A Standard

Plain barrel.

Courtesy C. Hadley Smith

NIB	Exc.	V.G.	Good	Fair	Poor
—	400	325	250	150	75

NOTE: Vent rib add $100.

Model 51A Magnum

3" chamber.

NIB	Exc.	V.G.	Good	Fair	Poor
—	425	350	275	175	75

NOTE: Vent rib add $100.

Model 51A Waterfowler

Matte finished.

NIB	Exc.	V.G.	Good	Fair	Poor
—	425	350	275	175	75

Model 51A Deerslayer

Courtesy C. Hadley Smith

NIB	Exc.	V.G.	Good	Fair	Poor
—	325	275	225	150	75

Model 51A Turkey Gun

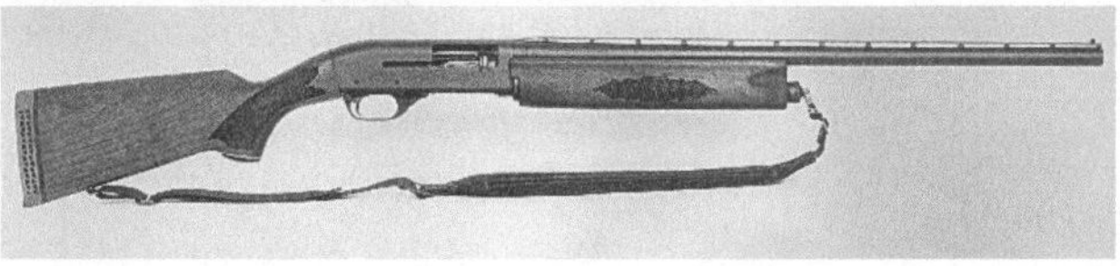

Courtesy C. Hadley Smith

NIB	Exc.	V.G.	Good	Fair	Poor
—	425	350	275	175	75

Model 51 Supreme Trap

NIB	Exc.	V.G.	Good	Fair	Poor
—	425	375	325	250	75

Model 51 Supreme Skeet

NIB	Exc.	V.G.	Good	Fair	Poor
—	450	400	350	275	200

Model 51 Ducks Unlimited Commemorative

NIB	Exc.	V.G.	Good	Fair	Poor
600	500	375	325	275	200

Model 51 Presentation

Engraved receiver.

NIB	Exc.	V.G.	Good	Fair	Poor
1500	1250	1000	750	500	300

NOTE: The market for Ithaca Mag-10s has declined somewhat with the success of the 3.5-inch 12-ga. load. This is apparently because most owners consider their Mag-10s as hunting weapons, not collectors' pieces. Nevertheless, NIB or Excellent+ examples still command fairly high prices, if the right buyer can be found.

MAG-10 SERIES

A 10 gauge Magnum semi-automatic shotgun manufactured in a variety of barrel lengths, styles and finishes. Manufactured from 1975 to 1986 as listed.

Standard Grade

NIB	Exc.	V.G.	Good	Fair	Poor
—	750	600	650	300	250

Standard Vent Rib Grade

NIB	Exc.	V.G.	Good	Fair	Poor
—	850	675	700	550	250

Deluxe Vent Rib Grade

NIB	Exc.	V.G.	Good	Fair	Poor
—	1000	750	775	600	250

Supreme Grade

NIB	Exc.	V.G.	Good	Fair	Poor
—	1100	850	850	700	250

Roadblocker—Military and Police Model

NIB	Exc.	V.G.	Good	Fair	Poor
—	750	600	650	300	250

Presentation Grade

Engraved, gold-inlaid, 200 made.

NIB	Exc.	V.G.	Good	Fair	Poor
1875	1500	1100	900	750	300

National Wild Turkey Federation

Shotguns manufactured by Perazzi and Japanese firms that were marketed by Ithaca are listed under the respective manufacturer's name.

1985 manufacture.

NIB	Exc.	V.G.	Good	Fair	Poor
850	700	600	550	450	350

RIFLES

Model X5-C

A .22 caliber semi-automatic rifle with a 7-shot magazine. A 10-shot magazine was available as an extra cost option. Blued with a walnut stock. Manufactured between 1958 and 1964.

NIB	Exc.	V.G.	Good	Fair	Poor
400	200	150	100	75	50

Model X5T Lightning

A .22 caliber tubular feed auto-loading rifle produced between 1959 and 1963. Some models were stocked with curly maple stocks. These guns will command a 25 percent price premium.

NIB	Exc.	V.G.	Good	Fair	Poor
450	175	150	100	75	50

Model X-15 Lightning

Similar to the above, but manufactured between 1964 and 1966.

NIB	Exc.	V.G.	Good	Fair	Poor
450	175	150	100	75	50

Model 49 Saddlegun—1961-1979

A .22 caliber lever action single-shot rifle with an 18.5" barrel, fixed sights, alloy receiver and hardwood stock. It was offered chambered for the .22 Magnum in 1962. Deduct 20 percent for .22 LR.

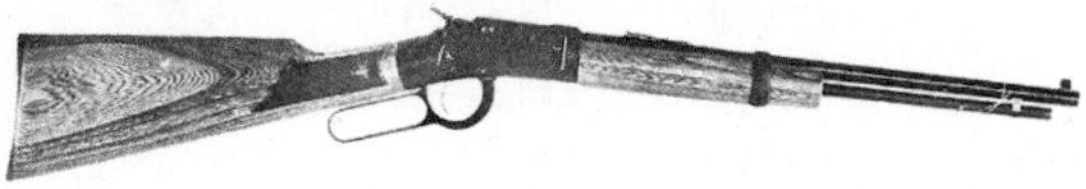

Courtesy C. Hadley Smith

NIB	Exc.	V.G.	Good	Fair	Poor
350	220	175	100	50	25

Model 49 Saddlegun Deluxe Grade

Fitted with gold plated trigger, hammer, and equipped with sling and sling swivels.

NIB	Exc.	V.G.	Good	Fair	Poor
400	250	200	125	50	25

Model 49 Saddlegun Presentation Grade

High grade wood and engraved frame.

NIB	Exc.	V.G.	Good	Fair	Poor
425	300	250	200	50	25

Model 49R—1968-1971

A lever action .22 caliber tubular feed repeater. Magazine capacity is 15 LR cartridges.

NIB	Exc.	V.G.	Good	Fair	Poor
350	250	200	150	50	25

Model 72 Saddlegun—1973-1979

A .22 or .22 Magnum caliber lever action rifle with an 18.5" barrel, tubular magazine, open sights and walnut stock. Made by Erma in Germany.

NIB	Exc.	V.G.	Good	Fair	Poor
300	250	225	200	100	25

LSA-55 OR 65 SERIES

A bolt-action sporting rifle manufactured in a variety of calibers and barrel lengths by Tikka of Finland. Imported between 1969 and 1977 in the models listed.

LSA-55 Standard

NIB	Exc.	V.G.	Good	Fair	Poor
—	500	350	300	250	175

LSA-55 Deluxe

NIB	Exc.	V.G.	Good	Fair	Poor
—	600	375	325	275	200

LSA-55 Varmint Heavy Barrel

NIB	Exc.	V.G.	Good	Fair	Poor
—	600	400	350	300	225

LSA-65 Long Action

NIB	Exc.	V.G.	Good	Fair	Poor
—	500	350	300	250	175

LSA-65 Deluxe

NIB	Exc.	V.G.	Good	Fair	Poor
—	600	375	325	275	200

LSA-55 Turkey Gun

A 12 gauge by .222 Remington caliber over-and-under combination rifle/shotgun with 24.5" barrels, single trigger, exposed hammer and walnut stock. Manufactured in Finland by Tikka between 1970 and 1981.

NIB	Exc.	V.G.	Good	Fair	Poor
—	900	700	450	350	275

IVER JOHNSON ARMS, INC.

Middlesex, New Jersey

SEE—AMAC

Established in 1883 in Fitchburg, Massachusetts, this company has produced a wide variety of firearms during its existence.

Model X

Bolt action .22 caliber single-shot rifle fitted with 22" barrel with open sights, pistol grip. Manufactured between 1927 and 1932.

NIB	Exc.	V.G.	Good	Fair	Poor
—	175	110	90	70	40

Model XA

As above but with Lyman receiver sight, swivels, leather strap, and ivory bead. Manufactured between 1927 and 1932.

NIB	Exc.	V.G.	Good	Fair	Poor
—	325	225	175	130	80

Model 2X

Fitted with a 24" heavy barrel and adjustable sights. Manufactured between 1932 and 1955.

NIB	Exc.	V.G.	Good	Fair	Poor
—	400	300	250	150	100

Li'L Champ

Chambered for the .22 LR cartridge this is a bolt-action single-shot rifle that weighs about 3 lbs.

NIB	Exc.	V.G.	Good	Fair	Poor
—	125	85	70	50	30

Long Range Rifle

This is a single-shot bolt-action rifle chambered for the .50 caliber Browning cartridge. Fitted with a 29" fluted barrel and adjustable trigger. Bipod. Comes supplied with a 20 power Leupold scope. Limited production. Weight is about 36 lbs. Manufactured between 1988 and 1993.

NIB	Exc.	V.G.	Good	Fair	Poor
—	4600	4000	3000	2500	1000

JJ 9mm Carbine

This is a copy of the U.S. military M1. Blued finish and hardwood stock. Magazine is 20 rounds. Chambered for the 9mm cartridge. Built between 1985 and 1986.

NIB	Exc.	V.G.	Good	Fair	Poor
—	500	400	250	175	100

NOTE: Add 10 percent for folding stock. Deduct 5 percent for plastic stock.

Delta-786 Carbine

Similar to the M1 carbine but in 9mm only. Matte finish. Manufactured in 1989.

NIB	Exc.	V.G.	Good	Fair	Poor
—	500	400	250	175	1000

Carbine .30 Caliber

Similar to the M1 carbine and chambered for the .30 carbine cartridge. Offered in various stock configurations. Built from 1985 to 1986 and again in 1988 to 1993.

NIB	Exc.	V.G.	Good	Fair	Poor
—	600	485	315	250	150

NOTE: For paratrooper model add $50, for Johnson 5.7mm caliber deduct $75, no premium for stainless steel.

U.S. Carbine .22 Caliber

Same as above but chambered for the .22 LR or .22 Magnum cartridge. Built in 1985 and 1986 and again in 1988. Fitted with 15-round magazine.

NIB	Exc.	V.G.	Good	Fair	Poor
—	350	295	225	150	75

Slide Action Targetmaster

Chambered for the .22 LR or .22 Magnum cartridge this rifle has a 15-round tubular magazine. Manufactured between 1985 and 1988 and again in 1990.

NIB	Exc.	V.G.	Good	Fair	Poor
—	250	170	125	100	50

Wagonmaster Model EW .22 HBL Lever Action

Chambered for the .22 LR or .22 Magnum cartridge and fitted with a hardwood stock. Blued finish. Grooved scope mounts. Built in 1985 and 1986 and again between 1988 and 1990.

NIB	Exc.	V.G.	Good	Fair	Poor
—	250	175	130	100	50

Model IJ .22 HB Semi-Automatic (Trail Blazer)

Chambered for .22 LR only with 10-round magazine. Manufactured in 1985 only.

NIB	Exc.	V.G.	Good	Fair	Poor
—	225	130	100	60	40

SHOTGUNS

Champion

A single barrel shotgun manufactured in a variety of gauges as well as .44 or .45 caliber with 26" to 32" barrels, external hammers, and automatic ejectors. Blued with a walnut stock. Manufactured between 1909 and 1956.

NIB	Exc.	V.G.	Good	Fair	Poor
—	250	200	150	75	25

Matted Rib Grade

As above, in 12, 16, or 20 gauge with a matte rib barrel. Manufactured between 1909 and 1948.

NIB	Exc.	V.G.	Good	Fair	Poor
—	275	225	175	95	50

Trap Grade

As above, in 12 gauge with a 32" ventilated rib barrel. Manufactured between 1909 and 1942.

NIB	Exc.	V.G.	Good	Fair	Poor
—	525	350	275	175	100

Hercules Grade

A boxlock double-barrel shotgun manufactured in a variety of gauges with 26" to 32" barrels, double triggers and extractors. Blued with a walnut stock.

NIB	Exc.	V.G.	Good	Fair	Poor
—	1350	1050	775	550	350

NOTE: Add premium for these features:
Single trigger—50 percentEjectors—50 percent
28 gauge—200 percent.410 bore—150 percent
20 gauge—75 percent16 gauge—20 percent
Engraving—200 percentVent rib—25 percent

Skeeter Model

As above, but more finely finished. Discontinued in 1946.

NIB	Exc.	V.G.	Good	Fair	Poor
—	2250	1600	1050	750	300

NOTE: Add premium for these features:
Single trigger—50 percentEjectors—50 percent
28 gauge—200 percent.410 bore—150 percent
20 gauge—75 percent16 gauge—20 percent
Engraving—200 percentVent rib—25 percent

Super Trap

A 12 gauge boxlock double barrel shotgun with a 32" full choked barrels, and extractors. Discontinued in 1942.

NIB	Exc.	V.G.	Good	Fair	Poor
—	2650	2000	1350	850	350

NOTE: Add 50 percent for Miller single selective trigger and 35 percent for non-selective single trigger.

Silver Shadow

A 12 gauge boxlock over-and-under shotgun with a 26" or 28" ventilated rib barrels, double triggers and extractors. Blued with a walnut stock. Manufactured in Italy and imported by Iver Johnson.

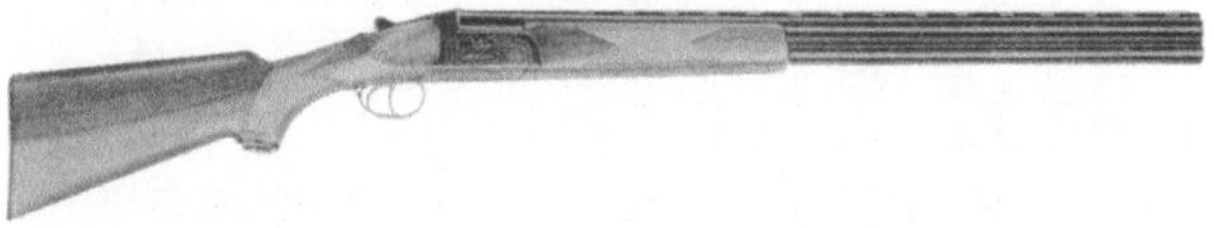

NIB	Exc.	V.G.	Good	Fair	Poor
—	550	400	350	300	200

NOTE: Also available with a single trigger, which would increase the values listed by approximately 25 percent.

J

JACQUITH, ELIJAH

Brattleboro, Vermont

Revolving Under Hammer Rifle

An extremely rare .40 caliber percussion revolving rifle with a 34" round-octagonal barrel and 8-shot cylinder. It is believed that approximately 25 of these rifles were made in 1838 and 1839. The barrel marked "E. Jaquith Brattleboro. Vt." Prospective purchasers should secure a qualified appraisal prior to acquisition.

NIB	Exc.	V.G.	Good	Fair	Poor
—	—	18000	7250	2200	2200

JEFFERY, W. J. & CO. LTD.

London, England

This company produced high quality shotguns and rifles. Their products have been used by wealthy sportsmen for many years. They produced guns under their own banner and also as contractors for other distributors. They made the guns sold by the Army & Navy Department Store in London. Guns of this type were basically custom-ordered and as such are extremely hard to evaluate on a general basis. We supply estimated values for standard models.

Single-Shot

Built on the Farquharson Falling Block action and was chambered for many calibers up to the .600 Nitro Express. This was also a custom-order gun, and the barrel length was optional. There are usually folding express sights, and the finish is usually blued with a select, hand-checkered walnut stock. These were high quality firearms, and the values would be determined, for the most part, by the options and embellishments on the particular specimen. Individual appraisal is definitely advised. The caliber in which a rifle is chambered will also have an effect on the value. Obsolete calibers bring less, and the larger express calibers bring more.

NIB	Exc.	V.G.	Good	Fair	Poor
—	9000	6750	3750	21700	900

Boxlock Double Rifle

A boxlock chambered for many different calibers. It can be found with either a top or underlever action and has folding express sights. The stock and forearm are select, hand-checkered walnut, and the finish is usually blue. This was a custom-order proposition, and values can be affected by many variables such as caliber, options, and embellishment. Damascus barreled hammerguns are worth approximately 50 percent less.

NIB	Exc.	V.G.	Good	Fair	Poor
—	22000	15250	10950	3850	2500

Sidelock Double Rifle

Has detachable sidelocks and otherwise is comparable to the boxlock version.

NIB	Exc.	V.G.	Good	Fair	Poor
—	35000	22500	12250	7000	4000

JENKS CARBINE

Manufacturer—N. P. Ames

Springfield, Massachusetts

Jenks "Mule Ear Carbine"

A .54 caliber percussion side hammer carbine with a 24.5" round barrel and full length stock secured by two barrel bands. The lock case hardened, the barrel browned and the furniture of brass. The lock marked "N.P.Ames/Springfield/ Mass." The barrel stamped "Wm.Jenks/USN" followed by the inspector's initials. The buttstock carries an inspector's cartouche. Approximately 4,250 were made between 1841 and 1846. Some were marked "USR" for the "U.S. Revenue Cutter Service," and these would bring approximately an 80 percent premium over the values listed. However, prospective purchasers should secure a qualified appraisal prior to acquisition.

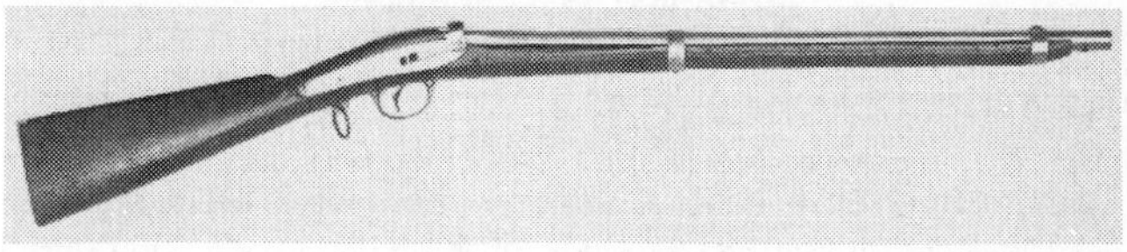

Courtesy Milwaukee Public Museum, Milwaukee, Wisconsin

NIB	Exc.	V.G.	Good	Fair	Poor
—	—	4500	3750	1500	600

Jenks Navy Rifle

As above, with a 30" round barrel and full-length stock secured by three barrel bands. Approximately 1,000 were made for the U.S. Navy in 1841.

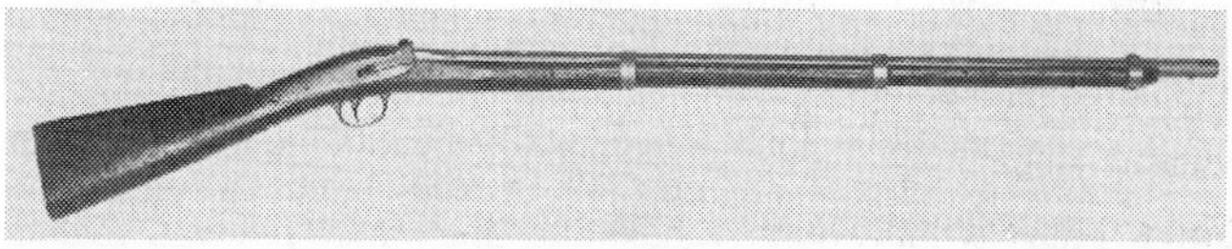

Courtesy Milwaukee Public Museum, Milwaukee, Wisconsin

NIB	Exc.	V.G.	Good	Fair	Poor
—	—	5000	4250	1750	750

JENKS-HERKIMER

New York

Manufacturer—E. Remington & Son

Jenks Carbine

Identical to the Jenks Carbine listed in the previous entry except that the barrel length is 24.25" and the lock is fitted with a Maynard tape primer. The lock marked "Remington's/Herkimer/ N.Y." The barrel is marked "W. Jenks/USN/RC/P/Cast Steel." Approximately 1,000 of these carbines manufactured circa 1846.

NIB	Exc.	V.G.	Good	Fair	Poor
—	—	5000	4250	1750	750

JENKS-MERRILL

Baltimore, Maryland

An alteration of the Jenks Carbine listed previously to a breech loading system developed by J.H. Merrill. The conventional sidelock marked "J. H. Merrill Balto./Pat. July 1858." The breech retains the mark "Wm.Jenks/USN." Approximately 300 were altered between 1858 and 1860.

NIB	Exc.	V.G.	Good	Fair	Poor
—	—	9750	8500	3500	950

JOSLYN

Milbury, Massachusetts

Manufacturer—A.H. Waters

Model 1855 Carbine

A .54 caliber breech loading single-shot percussion carbine witha 22.5" barrel secured to the forend by one barrel band. Blued,case hardened with brass mounts. The lock marked "A.H.Waters& Co./Milbury, Mass.," and the patent dates stamped on thebreech lever. Approximately 1,000 manufactured in 1855 and1856.

NIB	Exc.	V.G.	Good	Fair	Poor
—	—	2750	2000	950	300

Model 1855 Rifle

Similar to the above, in .58 caliber with a 38" barrel secured bythree barrel bands. Several hundred were made in 1856.

NIB	Exc.	V.G.	Good	Fair	Poor
—	—	4500	3250	1100	400

JOSLYN

Springfield, Massachusetts
Manufacturer—Springfield Armory

Joslyn Breechloading Rifle

The first mass-produced, true breechloading cartridge firearm manufactured in a national armory. The actions were supplied by the Joslyn Firearms Company, and the rifles were chambered for the .56-50 rimfire cartridge. This rifle has a 35.5" round barrel and a full-length stock that is held on by three barrel bands. The lock is marked "U.S./Springfield" with "1864" at the back. The barrel is marked "B. F. Joslyn's Patent/ Oct. 8th, 1861 / June 24th, 1862." There were approximately 3,000 of these manufactured circa 1865. They were probably issued to Union forces, but it is unknown if they saw action before the end of the Civil War.

NIB	Exc.	V.G.	Good	Fair	Poor
—	—	5500	3495	1950	500

.50-70 Alteration

Approximately 1,600 Joslyn rifles were rechambered to fire the .50-70 centerfire cartridge. The conversion consisted of rechambering and drilling a new firing pin hole after the rimfire pin was sealed. There was no specific serial number range in which these conversions were done. Most of these weapons were eventually converted to smoothbores and sold in Africa. The original military specimens are extremely scarce.

NIB	Exc.	V.G.	Good	Fair	Poor
—	—	6000	4200	2500	750

JOSLYN FIREARMS COMPANY

Stonington, Connecticut

Model 1862 Carbine

A .52 rimfire breechloading single-shot carbine with a 22" round barrel secured by one barrel band. Blued, case hardened with brass mounts. The lock marked "Joslyn Firearms Co./Stonington/ Conn.," and the patent date marked on the barrel. The trigger plate is 8" long, and the upper tang measures 4.5". Approximately 4,000 manufactured in 1862.

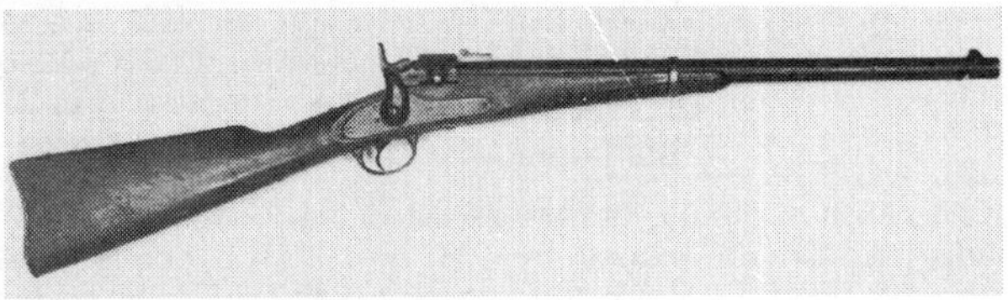

Courtesy Milwaukee Public Museum, Milwaukee, Wisconsin

NIB	Exc.	V.G.	Good	Fair	Poor
—	—	4500	3700	1500	400

Model 1864 Carbine

As above, with case hardened iron mounts, a 7" trigger plate and 2" upper tang. Approximately 12,000 were made in 1864 and 1865.

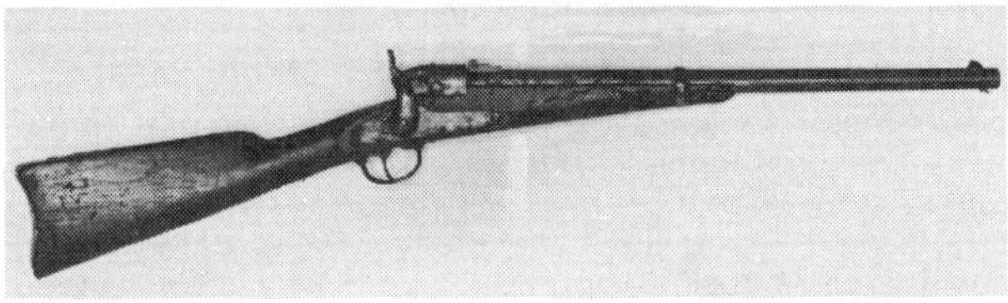

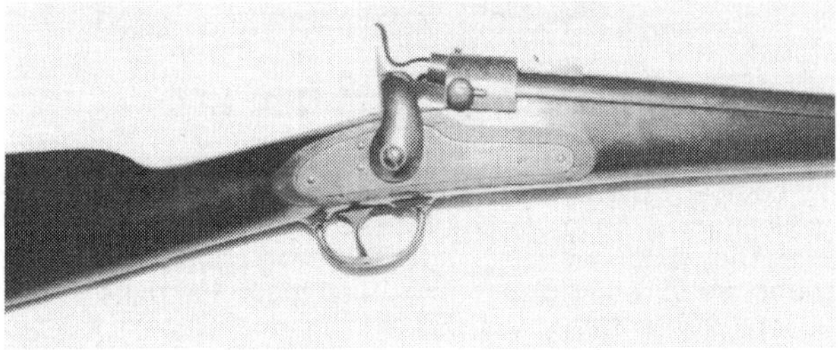

Courtesy Milwaukee Public Museum, Milwaukee, Wisconsin

NIB	Exc.	V.G.	Good	Fair	Poor
—	—	4200	3300	1100	400

JUSTICE, P. S.

Philadelphia, Pennsylvania

Percussion Rifle

A .58 caliber percussion rifle with a 35" round barrel secured by two barrel bands, browned barrel, polished lock and brass furniture. The lock marked "P.S. Justice/Philada." Approximately 2,500 were manufactured in 1861.

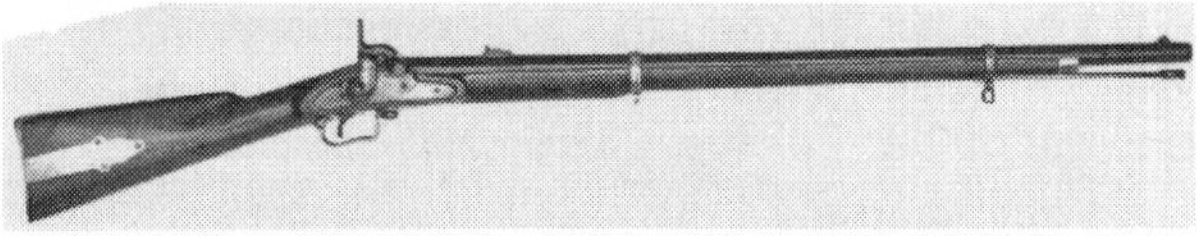

Courtesy Milwaukee Public Museum, Milwaukee, Wisconsin

NIB	Exc.	V.G.	Good	Fair	Poor
—	—	2300	1900	875	450

K

KASSNAR IMPORTS, INC.

Harrisburg, Pennsylvania

Standard Over-and-Under

A 12, 20, 28 or .410 bore boxlock double-barrel shotgun with 26" or 28" barrels, ventilated ribs, single trigger and extractors. Blued with a walnut stock.

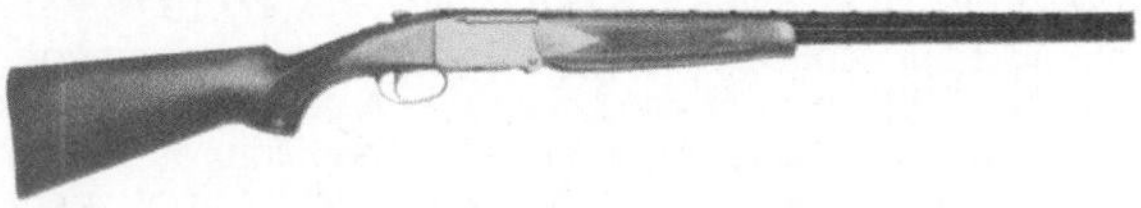

NIB	Exc.	V.G.	Good	Fair	Poor
350	275	225	200	150	100

Deluxe Over-and-Under

As above, with a more finely figured stock.

NIB	Exc.	V.G.	Good	Fair	Poor
400	325	250	225	175	100

Standard Side-by-Side

A 20, 28 or .410 bore boxlock folding double-barrel shotgun with 26" barrels, double triggers and extractors. Blued with a walnut stock.

NIB	Exc.	V.G.	Good	Fair	Poor
250	200	175	150	100	75

Deluxe Side-by-Side

As above, in .410 bore only and with more finely figured wood.

NIB	Exc.	V.G.	Good	Fair	Poor
300	250	200	175	125	75

KEBERST INTERNATIONAL

Kendall International
Paris, Kentucky

Keberst Model 1A

A .338 Lapua Magnum, .338-416 Rigby, and the .338-06 caliber bolt-action rifle with a 24" barrel having an integral muzzle-brake, and fitted with a 3-9 power Leupold telescope. Matte blued with a camouflaged composition stock. Manufactured in 1987 and 1988.

NIB	Exc.	V.G.	Good	Fair	Poor
—	3750	3000	2500	1800	900

KEL-TEC CNC INDUSTRIES

Cocoa, Florida

SUB-2000 Rifle

Introduced in 1996 this is a semi-automatic rifle chambered for the 9mm or .40 S&W cartridge. The barrel length is 16.1". The rifle can be folded closed with an overall length of 16". Weight is approximately 4.6 lbs. Different grip assembly can be fitted to this rifle allowing for the use of different magazines.

NIB	Exc.	V.G.	Good	Fair	Poor
375	295	175	125	75	50

SU-16

This semi-automatic gas operated rifle is chambered for the .223 cartridge. It is fitted with an 18" barrel. This rifle has several unique features: the forend folds down to form a bipod, the stock can store spare magazines and the rifle folds into two parts for carry. Weight is about 5 lbs. SU-16A, 18.5-inch barrel; SU-16B, 16-inch lightweight barrel; SU-16C, 16-inch barrel, folding stock; SU-16CA, 16-inch standard barrel and standard stock.

NIB	Exc.	V.G.	Good	Fair	Poor
625	525	400	295	200	125

PLR-16

A 5.56 mm NATO gas-operated, semi-automatic AR-15-style long-range pistol. Windage-adjustable rear sight. Picatinny rail. Muzzle threaded for muzzle-brake. 9.2" barrel, 51 oz. 10-round or M-16 magazine. Blued finish, polymer construction. Introduced 2006.

NIB	Exc.	V.G.	Good	Fair	Poor
650	550	425	325	200	100

RFB Rifle

Bullpup semi-auto rifle with 32", 24" or 18" barrel, black laminated stock, third swivel for bipod. Forward ejection; takes FAL-type magazines. Chambered in .308 Winchester. Announced in 2007. Price shown is for sporter. As of early 2009 this rifle had not entered production.

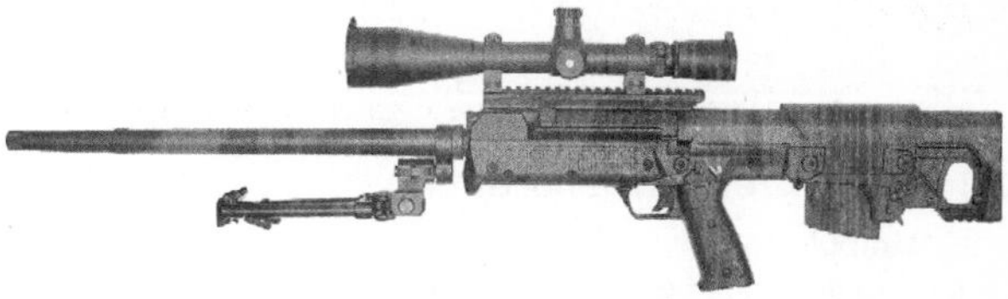

NIB	Exc.	V.G.	Good	Fair	Poor
1850	1600	—	—	—	—

KEMPER, SHRIVER & COMPANY

Nashville, Tennessee

Delivered rifles made from sporting arm parts to the Ordnance Department at Nashville from December 1861 to March 1862. In all 150 arms were assembled. Overall length 48-1/2"; octagonal barrels shortened 33" and bored to .48 caliber; some fitted with saber bayonet lugs; stocks of military with brass furniture.

NIB	Exc.	V.G.	Good	Fair	Poor
—	—	4750	2000	1500	700

KESSLER ARMS CORPORATION

Silver Creek, New York

Bolt-Action Shotgun

A 12, 16, or 20 gauge shotgun with 26" or 28" barrels. Blued with a walnut stock. Manufactured between 1951 and 1953.

NIB	Exc.	V.G.	Good	Fair	Poor
—	125	75	50	30	20

Levermatic Shotgun

A 12, 16, or 20 gauge lever-action shotgun with a 26" or 28" barrel. Blued with a walnut stock. Manufactured between 1951 and 1953. A nice low-end collectible.

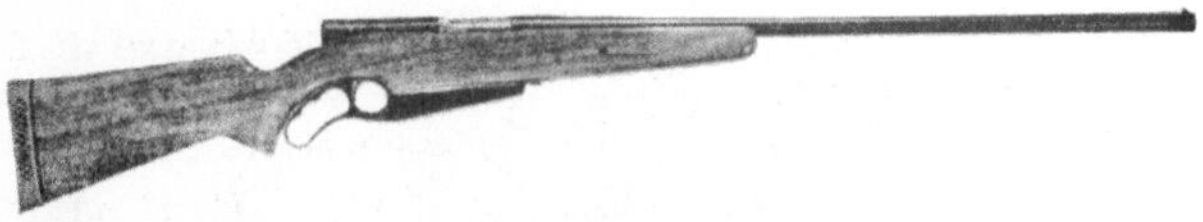

NIB	Exc.	V.G.	Good	Fair	Poor
—	300	275	200	150	75

KETTNER, EDWARD

Suhl, Germany

Drilling

This is a high-quality three-barreled firearm chambered for 12x12 gauge or 16x16 gauge over various metric rifle cartridges. The barrels are 25" in length and feature ejectors, selective triggers, and pop-up rifle sights that appear when the rifle barrel is selected. This gun is deep-relief engraved in the German style and has a high-grade checkered walnut stock. It was manufactured between 1922 and 1939.

NIB	Exc.	V.G.	Good	Fair	Poor
—	—	3200	1700	900	500

K.F.C. (KAWAGUCHIYA FIREARMS CO.)

Japan

E-1 Trap or Skeet Over-and-Under

A 12 gauge boxlock double-barrel shotgun with 26" or 30" barrels, competition rib, single-selective trigger, and automatic ejectors. Engraved, blued with a walnut stock. Manufactured until 1986.

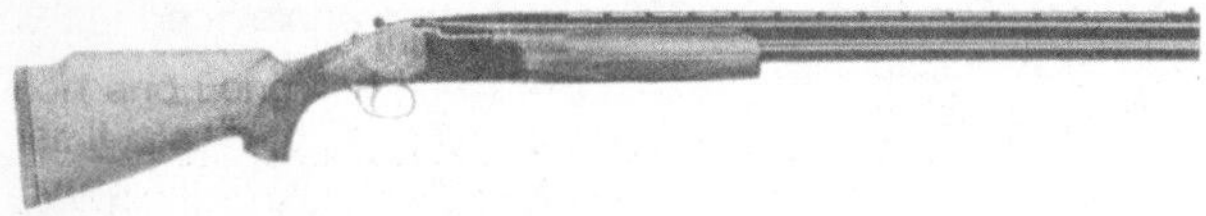

NIB	Exc.	V.G.	Good	Fair	Poor
—	950	800	700	500	300

E-2 Trap or Skeet Over-and-Under

As above, but more finely finished.

NIB	Exc.	V.G.	Good	Fair	Poor
—	1400	1250	1000	750	350

Field Grade Over-and-Under

As above, with a narrow rib and 26" or 28" barrels. Discontinued in 1986.

NIB	Exc.	V.G.	Good	Fair	Poor
—	650	575	500	400	275

Model 250

A 12 gauge semi-automatic shotgun with 26", 28", or 30" barrels fitted for choke tubes. Matte blued with a walnut stock. Manufactured from 1980 to 1986.

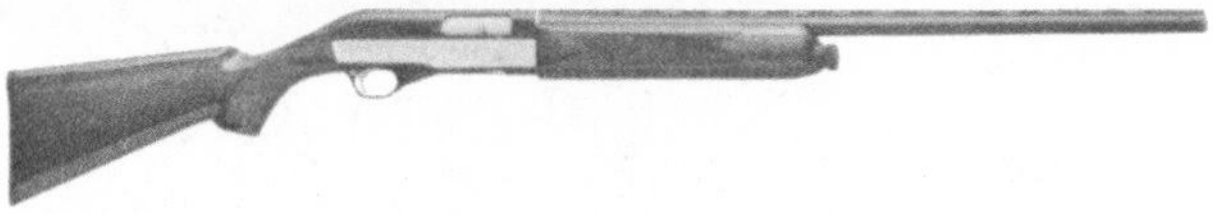

NIB	Exc.	V.G.	Good	Fair	Poor
—	350	300	275	200	100

KIMBER MFG., INC.

Yonkers, New York

Kimber of Oregon was established in April 1979 by Greg and Jack Warne. The company produced high quality rimfire and centerfire rifles until going out of business in early 1991. Kimber produced approximately 60,000 rifles during its operation. In April 1993, Greg Warne opened Kimber of America in Clackamas, Oregon. This new company presently manufactures the same high-quality rifles built on an improved Model 82 Sporter action and stock, but in rimfire only. In 1995 the company expanded its product line to include centerfire rifles as well as a 1911 .45 ACP semi-automatic pistol line. In 1997 manufacturing operations were consolidated in the New York pistol factory and the two factories in Oregon were closed.

DISCONTINUED MODELS

Model 82 Classic

A .22, .22 Magnum, or .22 Hornet bolt-action rifle with a 22" barrel furnished without sights and 4- or 5-shot magazine. Blued with a walnut stock. Discontinued in 1988.

NIB	Exc.	V.G.	Good	Fair	Poor
—	700	600	550	450	350

NOTE: For Model 82 Series rifles in .22 Magnum caliber add 10 percent. For rifles chambered for .22 Hornet add 15 percent.

Cascade Model

As above, with a Monte Carlo-style stock.

NIB	Exc.	V.G.	Good	Fair	Poor
—	750	650	600	500	400

Custom Classic Model

As above, in .218 Bee or .25-20.

NIB	Exc.	V.G.	Good	Fair	Poor
—	800	725	650	400	300

Mini Classic

The Model 82 with an 18" barrel. Manufactured in 1988.

NIB	Exc.	V.G.	Good	Fair	Poor
—	600	550	475	400	300

Deluxe Grade

Similar to the Custom Classic. Introduced in 1989.

NIB	Exc.	V.G.	Good	Fair	Poor
1000	850	650	550	450	350

Model 82A Government

A .22 caliber bolt-action rifle with a 25" heavy barrel fitted with telescope mounts. Matte blued with a walnut stock. Introduced in 1987.

NIB	Exc.	V.G.	Good	Fair	Poor
675	550	450	375	300	200

Continental

Similar to the Custom Classic with a 20" barrel, open sights, and full length Mannlicher-style stock. Introduced in 1987.

NIB	Exc.	V.G.	Good	Fair	Poor
850	750	650	500	400	300

Super Continental

As above, but more finely finished. Discontinued in 1988.

NIB	Exc.	V.G.	Good	Fair	Poor
1200	1100	1000	750	600	300

Super America

The Model 82 but more finely finished. Discontinued in 1988.

NIB	Exc.	V.G.	Good	Fair	Poor
1500	1200	950	850	650	500

Super Grade

As above, introduced in 1989.

NIB	Exc.	V.G.	Good	Fair	Poor
1200	1000	900	750	600	475

Centennial

A commemorative rifle moderately engraved including a special match barrel, skeleton buttplate, hand-selected walnut stock, and light engraving. Issued to commemorate the 100th anniversary of the .22 LR cartridge. One hundred were manufactured in 1987.

NIB	Exc.	V.G.	Good	Fair	Poor
2500	2250	2000	1750	1500	1150

Brownell

In 1986, 500 commemorative rifles were produced in honor of Leonard Brownell, featuring a high-grade, Mannlicher-style, full-length walnut stock.

NIB	Exc.	V.G.	Good	Fair	Poor
1500	1250	1000	800	600	500

MODEL 84 SERIES—DISCONTINUED MODELS

A bolt-action rifle manufactured in a variety of smallbore calibers with a 22" or 24" barrel and 5-shot magazine. Blued with a walnut stock. Variations are listed.

NIB	Exc.	V.G.	Good	Fair	Poor
1500	1250	1000	800	600	500

Classic Model

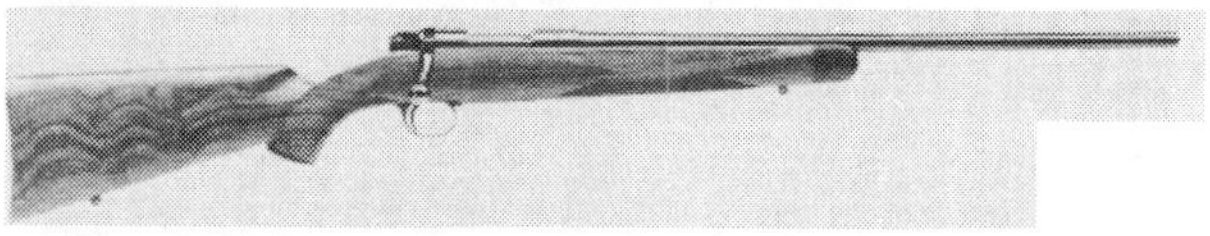

NIB	Exc.	V.G.	Good	Fair	Poor
700	650	600	400	250	200

Custom Classic Model

NIB	Exc.	V.G.	Good	Fair	Poor
900	800	700	500	350	200

Deluxe Grade Sporter

NIB	Exc.	V.G.	Good	Fair	Poor
1200	1000	850	750	500	250

Continental

NIB	Exc.	V.G.	Good	Fair	Poor
975	900	800	700	500	250

Super Continental

NIB	Exc.	V.G.	Good	Fair	Poor
1300	1100	850	700	575	250

Super America

NIB	Exc.	V.G.	Good	Fair	Poor
1500	1000	925	825	600	300

Super Grade

NIB	Exc.	V.G.	Good	Fair	Poor
1250	1100	1000	850	650	300

Ultra Varmint

As above, with a 24" stainless steel barrel and laminated birch wood stock. Introduced in 1989.

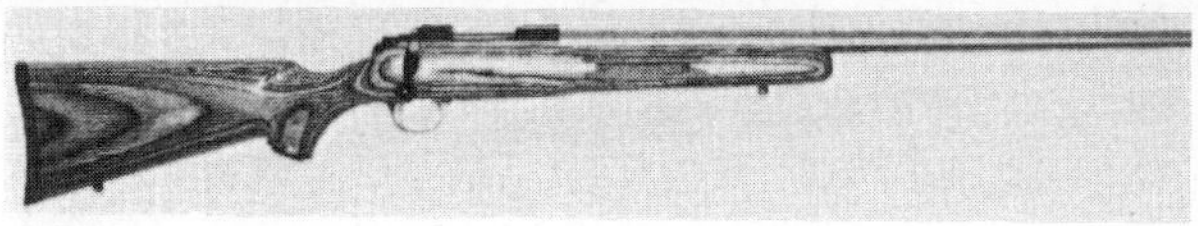

NIB	Exc.	V.G.	Good	Fair	Poor
1150	1000	900	750	550	250

Super Varmint

As above with a walnut stock. Introduced in 1989.

NIB	Exc.	V.G.	Good	Fair	Poor
1250	1100	1000	850	650	300

MODEL 89 SERIES/BGR (BIG GAME RIFLES)

A bolt-action sporting rifle produced in .270 Winchester to .375 Holland & Holland caliber with a 22" or 24" barrel. Blued with a walnut stock. The variations of this model are listed.

NIB	Exc.	V.G.	Good	Fair	Poor
—	1000	850	675	500	400

Classic Model

NIB	Exc.	V.G.	Good	Fair	Poor
800	650	550	400	300	200

Custom Classic Model

NIB	Exc.	V.G.	Good	Fair	Poor
1000	850	650	450	350	250

Deluxe Grade

NIB	Exc.	V.G.	Good	Fair	Poor
1400	1150	900	650	450	250

Super America

NIB	Exc.	V.G.	Good	Fair	Poor
1800	1250	900	700	500	250

Super Grade

NIB	Exc.	V.G.	Good	Fair	Poor
1800	1250	900	700	500	250

MODEL 82C SERIES

NOTE: In 1998 the Model 82C series rifles went out of production.

Model 82C Classic

Bolt-action rifle chambered for the .22 LR cartridge. Receiver drilled and tapped for sights. Fitted with a 22" barrel. Detachable magazine holds 4 rounds. Stock is plain with standard grade Claro Walnut. Checkering is 18 lines to the inch with 4 point side panel pattern. Red rubber butt pad and polished steel pistol grip cap are standard. Weight is approximately 6-1/2 lbs.

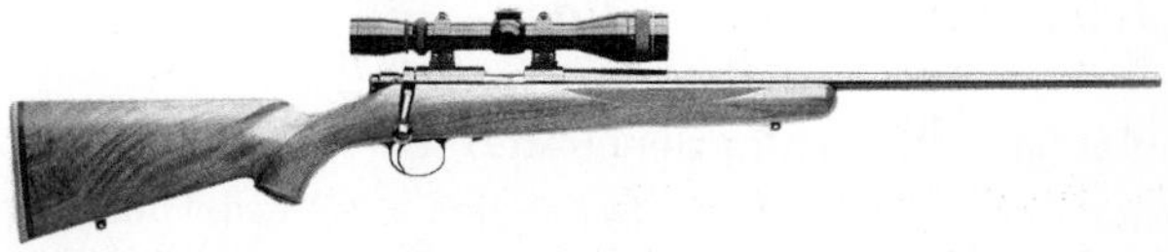

NIB	Exc.	V.G.	Good	Fair	Poor
900	650	500	400	—	—

Model 82C Super America

Same as above but fitted with AAA fancy grade Claro Walnut with ebony tip and beaded cheekpiece. Hand checkering is 22 lpi in a full-coverage pattern. Steel buttplate and steel pistol grip cap are standard.

NIB	Exc.	V.G.	Good	Fair	Poor
2200	1500	1100	750	300	300

Model 82C Custom Match

This bolt-action .22 caliber has a 22" barrel. The stock is AA French walnut with full coverage checkering. Finish is rust blued. Weight is about 6.75 lbs.

NIB	Exc.	V.G.	Good	Fair	Poor
2000	1600	950	700	400	200

Model 82C Custom Shop SuperAmerica (Basic)

Same as above but furnished with a number of special order options that greatly affect the value. Seek an independent appraisal before the sale.

Model 82C Stainless Classic Limited Edition

Introduced in 1996 this limited edition Model 82C is chambered for the .22 long rifle cartridge The stainless steel barrel is 22" long. A 4-shot magazine is included. Production limited to about 600 rifles.

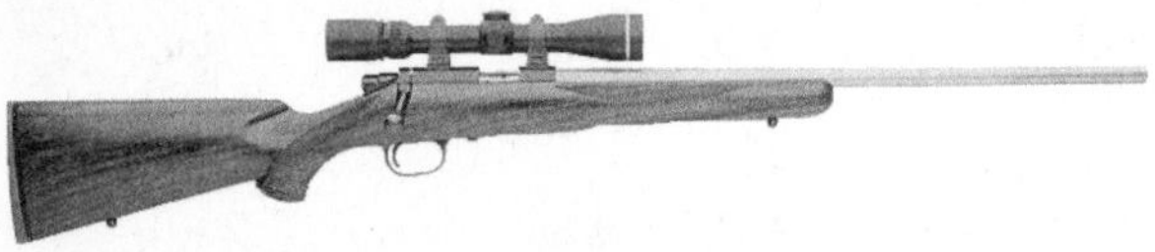

NIB	Exc.	V.G.	Good	Fair	Poor
1900	1750	1100	800	500	300

Model 82C SVT (Short Varmint/Target)

First introduced in 1996 this .22 caliber rifle is a single-shot. It is fitted with an 18" stainless steel fluted barrel. The walnut stock is a target style with no checkering. Weight is about 7.5 lbs.

NIB	Exc.	V.G.	Good	Fair	Poor
1350	1050	700	500	400	175

Model 82C HS (Hunter Silhouette)

Introduced in 1997 this model features a 24" half-fluted barrel. Chambered for .22 Long Rifle cartridge. Stock is American walnut with high comb. Trigger is fully adjustable. Four-round magazine is standard. Weight is about 7 lbs.

MODEL 84C SERIES

NOTE: In 1998 the Model 84C series rifle went out of production.

Model 84C Single-Shot Varmint

Chambered for the .17 Rem. or .223 Rem. cartridge this rifle is fitted with a 25" stainless steel fluted barrel. Claro walnut stock with varmint-style forearm. Weight is approximately 7.5 lbs.

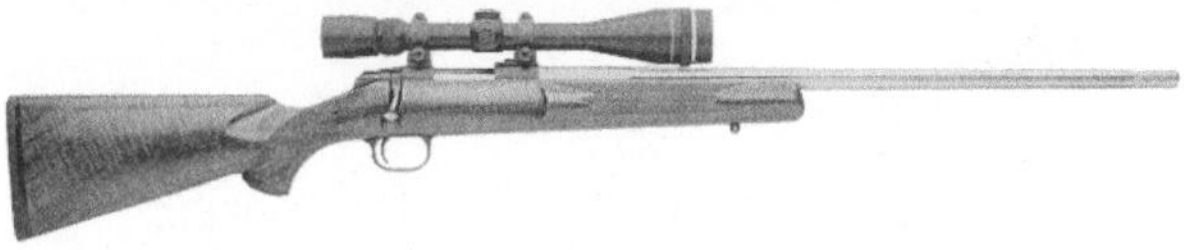

NIB	Exc.	V.G.	Good	Fair	Poor
1500	1175	900	600	400	200

Sporterized Model 98 Swedish Mausers

These are reconditioned and reworked Mausers that are fitted with new match grade stainless steel fluted barrels in 24" or 26" depending on caliber. The stock is new synthetic checkered. Chambered in .257 Roberts, .270 Win., .280 Rem., .30-06, 7mm Rem. Mag, .300 Win. Mag., .338 Win. Mag., and the .220 Swift with a 25" barrel.Suggested retail price is $535 for standard calibers and $560 for Magnums.

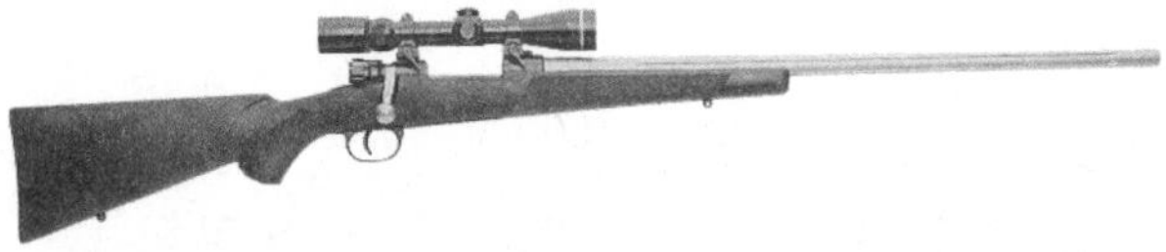

Sporterized Model 96 Swedish Mausers

Similar to the above in terms of reworking and reconditioning. Chambered for these calibers:.22-250 w/stainless steel heavy barrel fluted—Retail $500..243 Win.—$400 to $465 depending on finish. 6.5x55mm-—$340 to $370 depending on finish.7mm-08 Rem.—$415 to $465 depending on finish..308 Win.—$415 to $520 epending on finish and barrel configuration.

RECENT PRODUCTION MODELS

17 SERIES

This series of .17 Mach 2 rifles was introduced in 2005. Features are similar to the 22 Series.

Hunter

Fitted with a 22" light sporter barrel with no sights. Checkered walnut stock with black pad and clear stock finish. Magazine capacity is 5 rounds. Weight is about 6.5 lbs.

NIB	Exc.	V.G.	Good	Fair	Poor
900	700	500	375	250	125

SVT (Short Varmint/Target) (Centerfire)

This model is fitted with a 18.25" stainless steel bull fluted barrel with no sights. Checkered walnut stock with black pad and oil finish. Magazine capacity is 5 rounds. Weight is about 7.9 lbs.

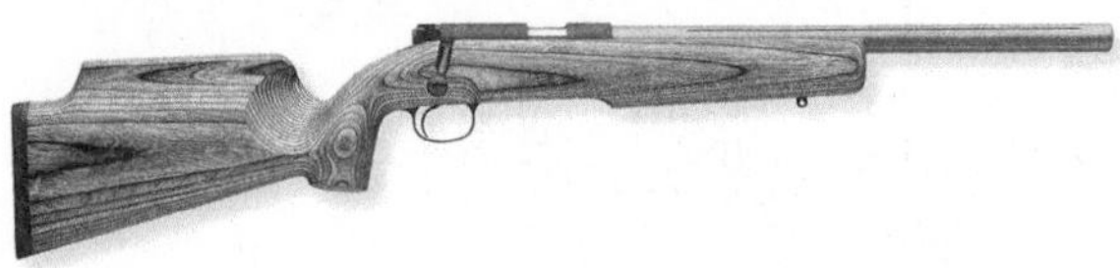

NIB	Exc.	V.G.	Good	Fair	Poor
1200	950	775	575	350	150

Pro Varmint

This model features a 20" stainless steel heavy sporter fluted barrel with no sights. Stock is gray laminate with oil finish and no checkering. Magazine capacity is 5 rounds. Weight is about 6.75 lbs.

NIB	Exc.	V.G.	Good	Fair	Poor
1150	875	675	500	325	150

Classic Varmint

Fitted with a 20" heavy sporter fluted barrel with no sights. Checkered walnut stock with oil finish. Magazine capacity is 5 rounds. Weight is about 6.5 lbs.

NIB	Exc.	V.G.	Good	Fair	Poor
1200	950	775	575	350	150

22 SERIES

In 1999 Kimber introduced a new line of bolt-action .22 caliber rimfire rifles. First deliveries were made early in 2000. This series is built on a totally new design from bolt, to magazine, to barrel. All rifles in this series have a 5-round magazine capacity. This line replaces the Model 82-C series of rifles.

Classic

This .22 caliber rifle is fitted with a 22" barrel with fully adjustble trigger. Stock is A grade Claro walnut with 18 lpi checkering. Fitted with a Model 70 style safety. Blued finish. Weight is about 6.5 lbs.

NIB	Exc.	V.G.	Good	Fair	Poor
1200	950	775	575	350	150

Custom Classic

Fitted with a 22" barrel, ebony forend tip, hand-rubbed oil finish, and 24 lpi checkering, This rifle was introduced in 2003. Weight is about 6.5 lbs.

NIB	Exc.	V.G.	Good	Fair	Poor
1425	1100	850	675	450	150

Super America

This model features a 22" barrel with fully adjustable trigger. Stock is AAA grade Claro walnut with 22 lpi wrap-around checkering and ebony forend tip. Black recoil pad. Weight is about 6.5 lbs.

NIB	Exc.	V.G.	Good	Fair	Poor
1900	1400	1075	775	500	200

SVT (Short Varmint/Target)

Fitted with an 18" fluted stainless steel barrel and gray laminated wood stock with high target comb. This model weighs about 7.5 lbs. In 2004 this model was also offered in the .17 Mach 2 caliber.

NIB	Exc.	V.G.	Good	Fair	Poor
1150	875	675	500	325	150

Classic Varmint

Introduced in 2003, this model features a 20" barrel with hand-rubbed oil finish and 20 lpi checkering. Weight is about 6.5 lbs. In 2004 this model is also available in the .17 Mach 2 caliber.

NIB	Exc.	V.G.	Good	Fair	Poor
1150	875	675	500	325	150

Pro Varmint

This model features a heavy fluted 20" stainless steel barrel and a gray laminated stock. No sights. Magazine capacity is 5 rounds. Weight is about 6.75 lbs. Introduced in 2004. This model is also available in .17 Mach 2 caliber.

NIB	Exc.	V.G.	Good	Fair	Poor
1200	950	775	575	350	150

HS (Hunter Silhouette)

This model is fitted with a 24" medium sporter match grade barrel with match chambered and half fluting. Walnut stock with 18 lpi checkering and Monte Carlo comb. Weight is about 7 lbs.

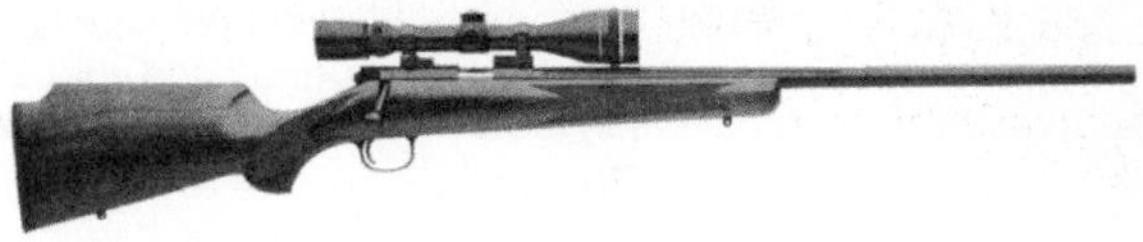

NIB	Exc.	V.G.	Good	Fair	Poor
900	700	500	375	250	125

Hunter

This is a lower-priced version of the Classic.

NIB	Exc.	V.G.	Good	Fair	Poor
800	650	550	400	300	200

Custom Match Limited Edition

Introduced in 2004 this is a limited edition of 300 rifles. This rifle features a checkered French walnut stock of AAA wood and several custom features. Serial numbered from KAN25001-KAN25300.

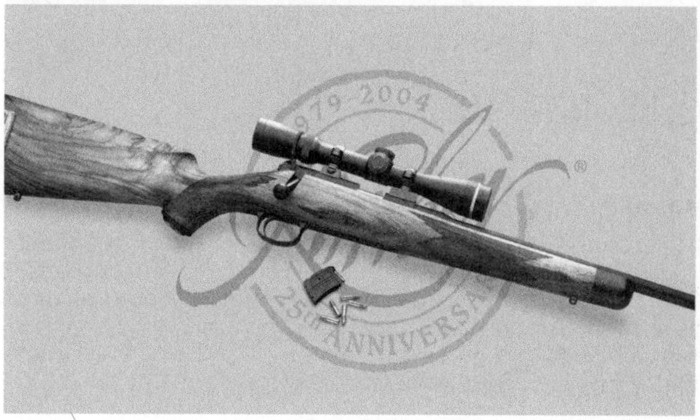

NIB	Exc.	V.G.	Good	Fair	Poor
2850	2300	—	—	—	—

MODEL 84M SERIES

Classic

Introduced in 2001 this centerfire bolt-action rifle is chambered for the .243 Win., .260 Rem., 7mm-08 Rem., and the .308 Win. In 2005 this model was offered chambered for the .22-250 cartridge. Fitted with a 22" light sporter match grade barrel Claro walnut stock with 20 lpi checkering and satin wood finish. Matted blue finish. Fitted with a 1" Pachmayr Decelerator recoil pad. Weight is about 5.75 lbs.

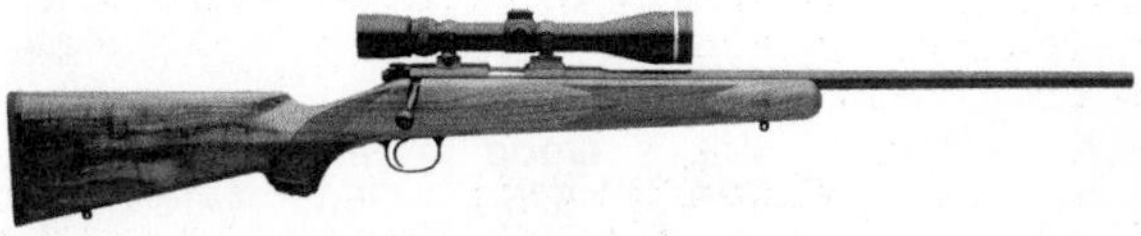

NIB	Exc.	V.G.	Good	Fair	Poor
1100	895	700	475	300	150

Montana

This model is essentially a stainless steel version of the Model 84M Classic with a black synthetic stock. Weight is about 5.25 lbs. Introduced in 2003.

NIB	Exc.	V.G.	Good	Fair	Poor
1200	950	775	575	350	150

SuperAmerica

This model was first offered in 2003 and is available in .243, .260 Rem., 7mm-08 Rem., and .308 Win. Fitted with a 22" barrel. In 2005 this model was offered chambered for the .223 cartridge. Stock is select walnut with 24 lines-to-the-inch checkering and fitted with an ebony forend tip, cheekpiece, and hand-rubbed oil finish. Weight is approximately 5.75 lbs. depending on caliber. Magazine capacity is 5 rounds.

NIB	Exc.	V.G.	Good	Fair	Poor
1800	1350	1000	650	325	175

Pro Varmint

This rifle is chambered for the .22-250 Win. cartridge and fitted with a 24" stainless steel fluted barrel with no sights. In 2005 offered in 204 Ruger and .223 calibers. Gray laminted stock. Magazine capacity is 5 rounds. Weight is 7.25 lbs. Introduced in 2004.

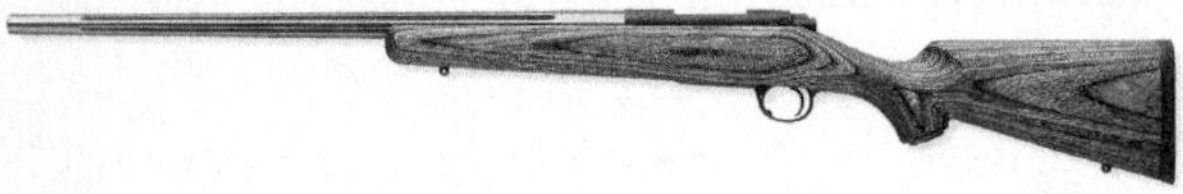

NIB	Exc.	V.G.	Good	Fair	Poor
1075	800	575	400	300	150

Varmint

Similar to the Classic but fitted with a stainless steel 26" match grade barrel. Chambered for the .22-250 Rem. cartridge. In 2005 offered in the .204 Ruger caliber. Fitted with a .5" solid recoil pad. Weight is approximately 7.4 lbs.

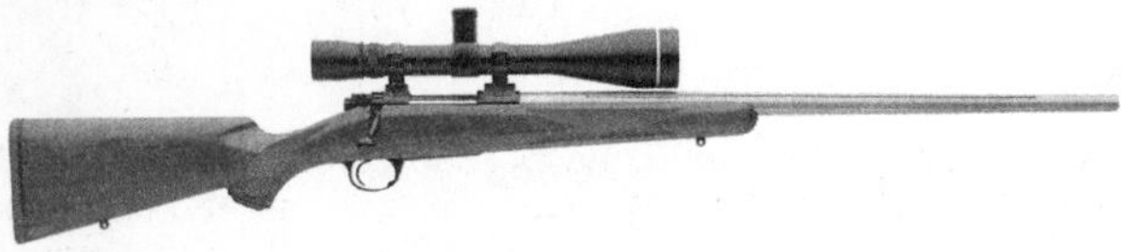

NIB	Exc.	V.G.	Good	Fair	Poor
1000	750	500	375	300	150

SVT

Stocked in gray laminate with Monte Carlo comb. Barrel length is 18.25" in stainless steel and fluted. Chambered for the .223 cartridge. Magazine capacity is 5 rounds. Weight is about 8.3 lbs.

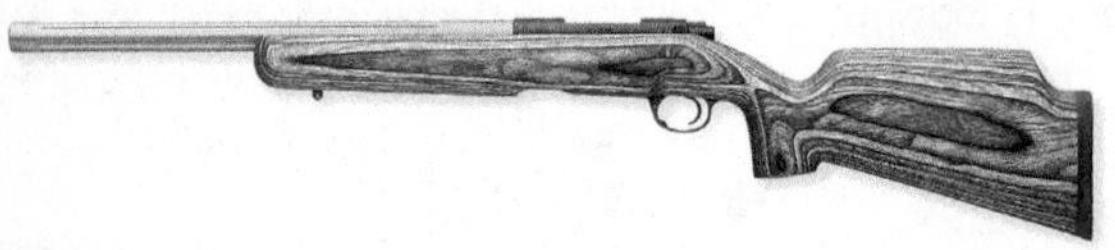

NIB	Exc.	V.G.	Good	Fair	Poor
1200	950	775	575	350	150

LongMaster VT

This bolt-action rifle is chambered for the .22-250 cartridge and is fitted with a 26" fluted stainless steel match grade barrel. Special laminated target stock. Weight is about 10 lbs. No sights. Introduced in 2002.

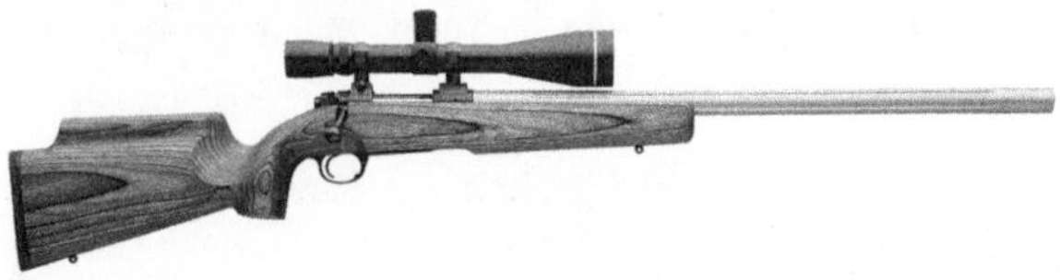

NIB	Exc.	V.G.	Good	Fair	Poor
1200	950	775	575	350	150

LongMaster Classic

Same features as the Model 84M Classic but with 24" fluted stainless steel barrel chambered for the .308 Win. cartridge. In 2005 offered in .223 caliber. Checkered walnut stock. Weight is about 7.25 lbs. Introduced in 2002.

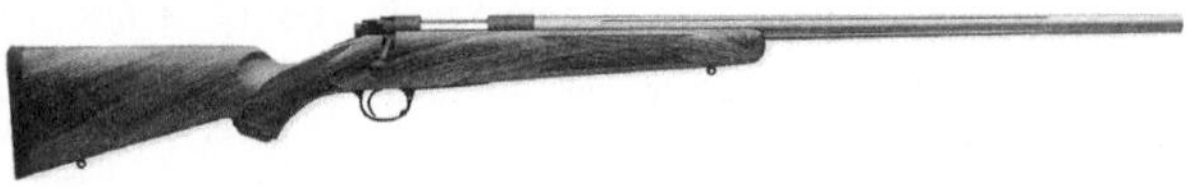

NIB	Exc.	V.G.	Good	Fair	Poor
1200	950	775	575	350	150

LongMaster Pro

This model, introduced in 2003, is a single-shot bolt-action rifle fitted with a 24" fluted heavy barrel chambered for the .308 Win. or .22-250 cartridge. Fitted with a synthetic benchrest stock. Weight is about 7.25 lbs.

NIB	Exc.	V.G.	Good	Fair	Poor
1350	1050	700	500	400	175

Tactical

Based on Model 84 action but with 24" mediumweight fluted match barrel, black laminated stock, third swivel for bipod. Chambered in .308 Winchester. Introduced in 2007.

NIB	Exc.	V.G.	Good	Fair	Poor
1075	800	575	400	300	150

Kimber Model 84L Classic Rifle

Bolt action rifle chambered in .270 Win. and .30-06. Features include 24-inch sightless matte blue sporter barrel; hand-rubbed A-grade walnut stock with 20 lpi panel checkering; pillar and glass bedding; Mauser claw extractor; 3-position M70-style safety; 5-round magazine; adjustable trigger.

NIB	Exc.	V.G.	Good	Fair	Poor
1000	850	720	400	300	200

Kimber 84L Montana

Long action variation of Model 84 action. Chambered in .25-06 Remington, .270 Winchester, .280 Ackley Improved and .30-06 Springfield. Capacity is 4 rounds in blind magazine. Kevlar-reinforced carbon fiber stock. Match-grade barrel, chamber and trigger. Free-floating 24-inch barrel is both pillar and glass bedded. Model 70-type 3-position safety. Weight is under 6 pounds. Introduced in 2011.

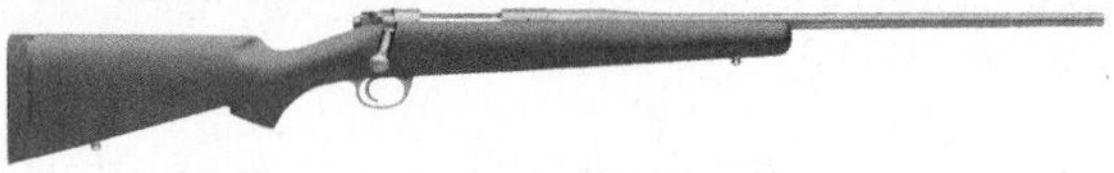

NIB	Exc.	V.G.	Good	Fair	Poor
1150	1000	850	600	300	200

MODEL 8400 SERIES

This series was introduced in 2003 and features the smallest action size compatible with the WSM family of cartridges.

Classic

This model is fitted with a select walnut stock with 20 lpi checkering. Chambered for the WSM calibers: .270, 7mm, .300, and .325. Barrel length is 24" with no sights. Magazine capacity is 3 rounds. Weight is about 6.6 lbs.

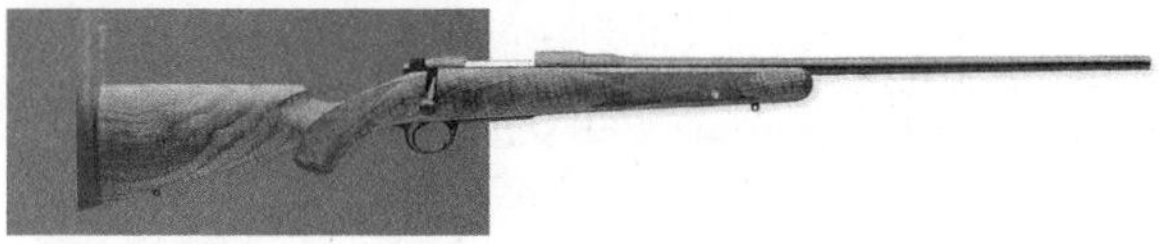

NIB	Exc.	V.G.	Good	Fair	Poor
1000	795	600	475	300	150

NOTE: Add $140 for French walnut.

Montana

This model features a 24" stainless steel barrel with no sights. Stock is black synthetic with no checkering. Same calibers as the Classic. Weight is about 6.25 lbs.

NIB	Exc.	V.G.	Good	Fair	Poor
1350	1050	700	500	400	175

SuperAmerica

This model is fitted with a AAA walnut stock with 24 lpi checkering. Cheekpiece and ebony forend tip are standard. Barrel length is 24" with no sights and chambered for the same calibers as the Classic. Weight is about 6.6 lbs.

NIB	Exc.	V.G.	Good	Fair	Poor
1875	1350	1000	650	325	175

Classic Select Grade

Similar to 8400 Classic but with hand-rubbed, oil-finished select stock of Claro or French walnut. Introduced 2006.

NIB	Exc.	V.G.	Good	Fair	Poor
1100	895	700	475	300	150

Tactical

24" heavyweight match barrel, stippled black McMillan stock, third swivel for bipod. Chambered in .308 Winchester. Introduced in 2007.

NIB	Exc.	V.G.	Good	Fair	Poor
1650	1200	800	550	300	150

Advanced Tactical

Similar to Model 8400 Tactical but with KimPro II Dark Earth finish, fully-adjustable stock and hard case. Introduced in 2007.

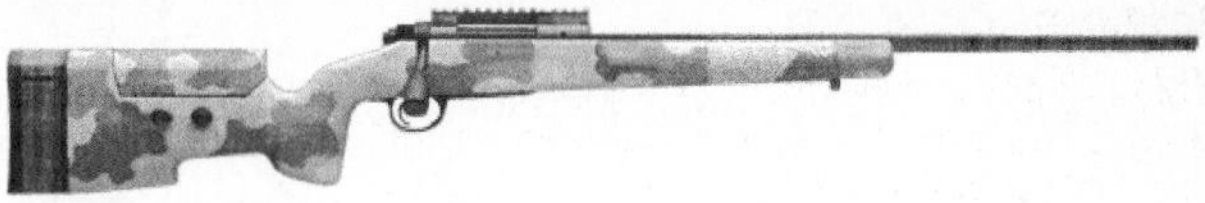

NIB	Exc.	V.G.	Good	Fair	Poor
1800	1350	1000	650	325	175

Patrol Rifle

Bolt action tactical rifle chambered in .308 Win. Features include 20-inch 1:12 fluted sightless matte blue heavy barrel; black epoxy-coated laminated wood stock with 20 lpi panel checkering; pillar and glass bedding; Mauser claw extractor; 3-position M70-style safety; 5-round magazine; adjustable trigger. Price: $1476.

SHOTGUNS

AUGUSTA SHOTGUNS

These shotguns are made in Italy for Kimber. Based on a Boss-type action, each model is fitted with H-Viz sights and Pachmayr Decelerator recoil pads. Back bored. Single-selective trigger and automatic ejectors. Introduced in 2002.

Sporting

Chambered for the 12 gauge shell and fitted with a choice of barrel lengths from 28.5" to 32". Checkered walnut stock with pistol grip and schnabel forearm. Blued finish with silver frame. Weight is about 7.75 lbs.

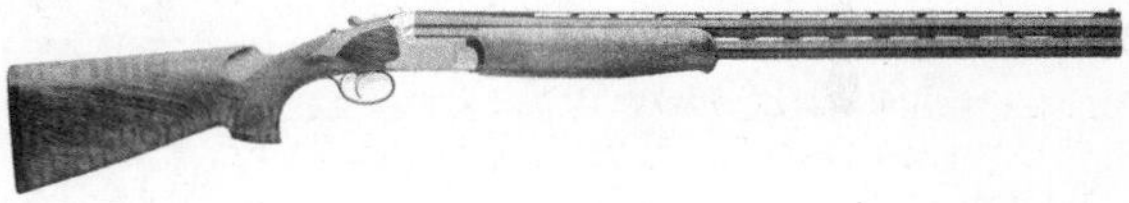

NIB	Exc.	V.G.	Good	Fair	Poor
6250	4500	3000	1750	600	300

Field

Also chambered for the 12 gauge shell and choice of barrel lengths from 26" to 27.5". Checkered with pistol grip and beavertail forearm. Weight is about 7 lbs.

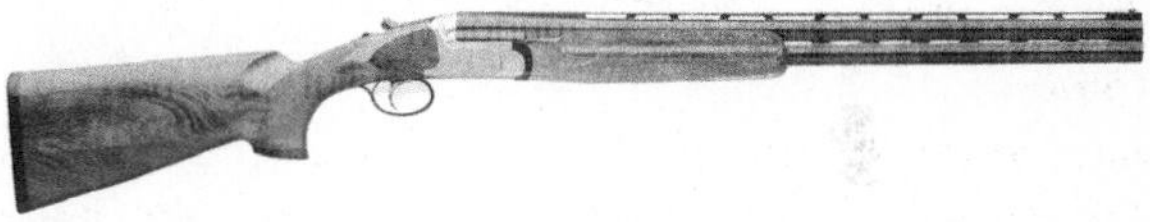

NIB	Exc.	V.G.	Good	Fair	Poor
5650	3900	2650	1500	475	225

Trap

This 12-gauge model is offered in barrel lengths from 30" to 34". Beavertail forearm. Wide ramped ventilated rib. Weight is about 7.75 lbs.

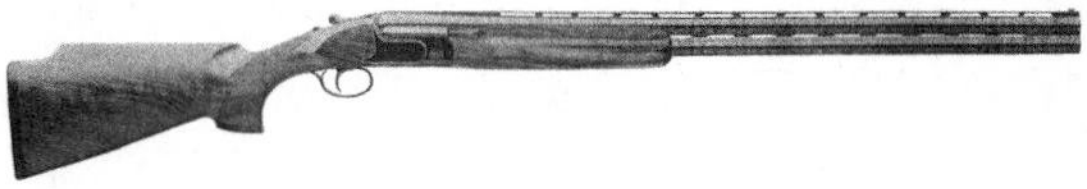

NIB	Exc.	V.G.	Good	Fair	Poor
6250	4500	3000	1750	600	300

Skeet

This 12-gauge gun has a choice of 26" or 27.5" barrels. Barrels are fitted with an 11mm flat rib. Checkered walnut stock with beavertail forearm. Weight is about 7.5 lbs.

NIB	Exc.	V.G.	Good	Fair	Poor
6250	4500	3000	1750	600	300

VALIER SHOTGUNS

These side-by-side guns were introduced into the Kimber line in 2005.

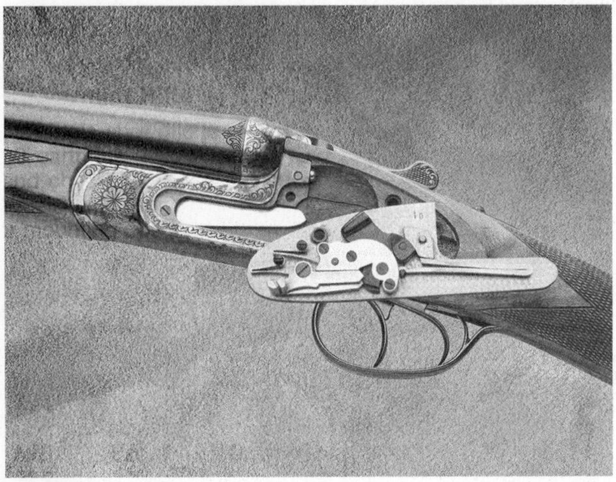

Grade I

A lightweight, properly-scaled side-by-side in 16- and 20-gauge. Double triggers and extractors. Choked IC and Mod. Color case-hardened receiver, straight stock and splinter forend. Hand checkered wood at 24 lpi. Chambered for 2.75" shells in 16 gauge and 3" shells in 20 gauge.

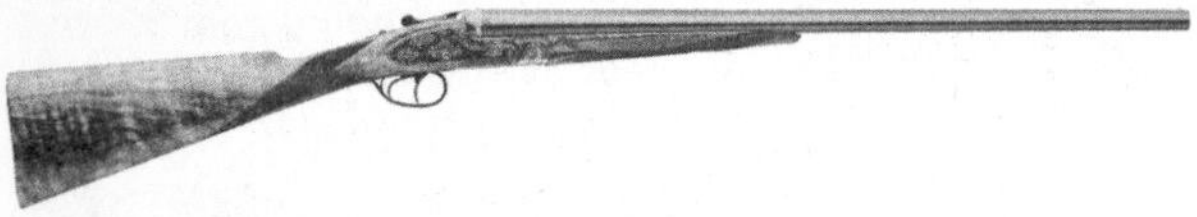

NIB	*Exc.*	*V.G.*	*Good*	*Fair*	*Poor*
3300	2900	2300	1250	600	300

Grade II

Similar to Valier Grade I but with higher grade wood and choice of color case, blued or bone charcoal receiver in 20 gauge; bone charcoal only in 16 gauge. Automatic ejectors.

NIB	*Exc.*	*V.G.*	*Good*	*Fair*	*Poor*
4900	3500	2700	1500	700	300

MARIAS SHOTGUNS

Grade I

This single-trigger sidelock over-and-under features scroll hand engraving and bone charcoal case colors with 24 lpi checkered wood. Grade I is available with 28" barrels and Prince of Wales stock in 12 and 20 gauge. Chambered for 3" shells. Automatic ejectors. Comes with 5 choke tubes.

NIB	*Exc.*	*V.G.*	*Good*	*Fair*	*Poor*
4600	3300	2300	1200	600	300

Grade II

Similar to Marias Grade I but with higher grade wood. Available in 12 gauge with PW stock or 20 gauge with PW or straight stock in 26", 28" or 30" barrels.

NIB	*Exc.*	*V.G.*	*Good*	*Fair*	*Poor*
4900	3500	2700	1500	700	300

KLEINGUENTHER/KDF, INC.

Kleinguenther Distinctive Firearms
Seguin, Texas

Condor

A 12 gauge boxlock over-and-under shotgun with 28" barrels with ventilated ribs, single-selective trigger and automatic ejectors. Blued with a walnut stock. Manufactured in Italy.

NIB	*Exc.*	*V.G.*	*Good*	*Fair*	*Poor*
—	700	600	525	375	275

Brescia

A 12 gauge boxlock double-barrel shotgun with 28" barrels, double triggers and extractors. Blued with a walnut stock. Manufactured in Italy.

NIB	*Exc.*	*V.G.*	*Good*	*Fair*	*Poor*
—	400	325	300	200	125

K-14 Insta Fire Rifle

A bolt-action sporting rifle manufactured in a variety of calibers with 24" or 26" barrels furnished without sights. Blued with a Monte Carlo-style walnut stock.

NIB	*Exc.*	*V.G.*	*Good*	*Fair*	*Poor*
—	1750	1350	1100	500	250

K-15

Similar to the above, with a 60-degree bolt angle and an accurized barrel guaranteed to fire a .5" group at 100 yards. Manufactured with a variety of optional features.

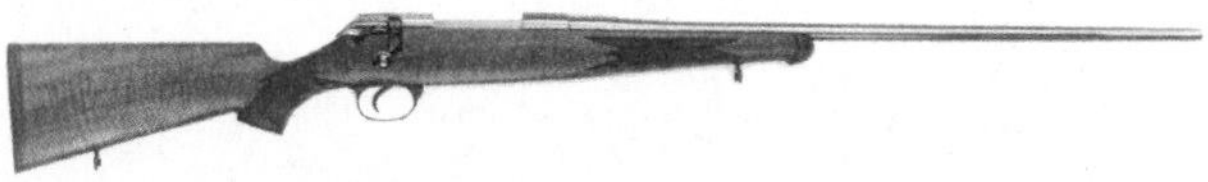

NIB	*Exc.*	*V.G.*	*Good*	*Fair*	*Poor*
—	1750	1350	1100	500	250

K-15 Pro-Hunter

As above, matte blued or electroless nickel-plated with a fiberglass stock.

NIB	*Exc.*	*V.G.*	*Good*	*Fair*	*Poor*
—	1750	1350	1100	500	250

K-15 Swat Rifle

A 7.62x54mm caliber bolt-action rifle with a 24" or 26" barrel furnished without sights, 4-shot magazine and Parkerized finish. Walnut stock.

NIB	*Exc.*	*V.G.*	*Good*	*Fair*	*Poor*
—	1800	1400	1150	700	350

K-15 Dangerous Game

As above, in .411 KDF caliber.

NIB	*Exc.*	*V.G.*	*Good*	*Fair*	*Poor*
—	2500	2000	1300	1000	700

K-16

A bolt-action sporting rifle manufactured in a variety of calibers with a 24" or 26" barrel furnished without sights, single stage adjustable trigger, accurized barrel and Dupont Rynite stock. Produced with a variety of optional features.

NIB	Exc.	V.G.	Good	Fair	Poor
—	1750	1350	1100	500	250

Titan Menor

A .222 or .223 caliber bolt-action rifle with a 24" or 26" barrel furnished without sights and Monte Carlo-style or standard schnabel tipped walnut stock. Blued.

NIB	Exc.	V.G.	Good	Fair	Poor
—	1200	900	550	400	200

Titan II Standard

As above, with a mid-sized action.

NIB	Exc.	V.G.	Good	Fair	Poor
—	1200	900	550	400	200

Titan II Magnum

As above, with a long action. Discontinued in 1988.

NIB	Exc.	V.G.	Good	Fair	Poor
—	1350	1100	675	450	200

Titan .411 KDF Mag.

As above, in .411 KDF with a 26" barrel having an integral muzzlebrake. Blued or electroless nickel-plated with a walnut stock. Discontinued in 1988.

NIB	Exc.	V.G.	Good	Fair	Poor
—	2500	2000	1300	1000	700

K-22

A .22 caliber bolt-action rifle with a 21" free floating barrel furnished without sights, adjustable trigger, and 5-shot magazine. Also known as the Mauser 201.

NIB	Exc.	V.G.	Good	Fair	Poor
—	500	400	300	175	100

K-22 K-22 Deluxe

NIB	Exc.	V.G.	Good	Fair	Poor
—	525	425	325	200	125

K-22 K-22 Deluxe Custom

NIB	Exc.	V.G.	Good	Fair	Poor
—	650	550	450	375	225

K-22 K-22 Deluxe Special Select

NIB	Exc.	V.G.	Good	Fair	Poor
—	1150	850	750	650	325

Model 2005

A .22 caliber semi-automatic rifle with a 19.5" barrel, open sights, and 5-shot magazine. Blued with a walnut stock. Also available in a deluxe model. Imported in 1986.

NIB	Exc.	V.G.	Good	Fair	Poor
250	175	150	100	75	50

Model 2107

A .22 or .22 Magnum caliber bolt-action rifle with a 19.5" barrel, open sights, and 5-shot magazine. Blued with a walnut stock.

NIB	Exc.	V.G.	Good	Fair	Poor
—	375	325	250	150	100

Model 2112

The deluxe version of the Model 2107.

NIB	Exc.	V.G.	Good	Fair	Poor
—	400	325	275	175	125

KNICKERBOCKER

Made by Crescent Fire Arms Co.

Double-Barrel Shotgun

Knickerbocker was a popular Dutch name for a New Yorker and was used as a brand on many hammerless sidelock doubles made by Crescent Firearms Co. Valued from $100 to $700 depending on model and condition.

KNIGHT RIFLES

Centerville, Iowa

This company was started in 1985 by Tony Knight. The company produces in-line blackpowder muzzleloading rifles and a complete line of accessories

Disc Magnum

Available in .50 caliber with a choice of blued or stainless steel 24"" or 26" barrel. Adjustable rear sight. Checkered stock with palm swell and rubber recoil pad. Stock also offered in black or camo. Adjustable trigger. Weight is approximately 8 lbs.

NIB	Exc.	V.G.	Good	Fair	Poor
450	350	300	250	200	150

NOTE: Add $50 for camo finish, $70 for stainless steel.

Bighorn Magnum

Available in .50 caliber with choice of 22" or 26" blued or stainless steel barrel. Adjustable rear sight. Checkered stock with rubber recoil pad. Stock also offered in black or camo. Adjustable trigger. Weight is about 7.7 lbs.

NIB	Exc.	V.G.	Good	Fair	Poor
325	250	200	175	150	100

NOTE: Add $50 for camo finish, $70 for stainless steel.

T-Bolt Magnum

Available in .50 caliber with choice of blue or stainless steel 22" or 26" barrel. Adjustable rear sight. Composite stock with rubber recoil pad. Stock also available in camo. Adjustable trigger. Weight is about 8 lbs.

NIB	Exc.	V.G.	Good	Fair	Poor
400	325	275	225	150	100

NOTE: Add $50 for camo finish, $70 for stainless steel.

LK-93 Wolverine

Available in .50 or .54 caliber with a choice of 22" blued or stainless steel barrel. Adjustable rear sight. Composite skeleton or thumbhole stock. Stock also available in black or camo. Adjustable trigger. Weight is about 6.5 lbs.

NIB	Exc.	V.G.	Good	Fair	Poor
265	200	150	100	75	25

NOTE: Add $50 for camo finish, $70 for stainless steel, $40 for thumbhole stock.

LK-93 Wolverine Youth

Same as model above but with shorter length of pull. Offered in black stock only.

NIB	Exc.	V.G.	Good	Fair	Poor
275	225	175	125	100	75

American Knight

Available in .50 caliber with 22" blued barrel. Adjustable rear sight. Black composite stock. Non-adjustable trigger. Weight is approximately 6.3 lbs.

NIB	Exc.	V.G.	Good	Fair	Poor
200	150	100	75	50	25

MK-85 Hunter

This model is offered in .50 or .54 caliber with blued finish and walnut stock.

NIB	Exc.	V.G.	Good	Fair	Poor
550	450	375	325	250	200

MK-85 Predator

This is a stainless steel version of the Hunter model. Offered with composite stock or various camo finishes.

NIB	Exc.	V.G.	Good	Fair	Poor
650	525	450	300	250	200

NOTE: Add $50 for camo finish.

MK-85 Stalker

This model is offered in .50 or .54 caliber with a variety of stock options. Standard stock is composite. Blued finish.

NIB	Exc.	V.G.	Good	Fair	Poor
565	450	375	325	250	200

NOTE: Add $50 for camo finish.

MK-85 Knight Hawk

This model is offered in .50 or .54 caliber with black composite stock and stainless steel.

NIB	Exc.	V.G.	Good	Fair	Poor
750	600	500	400	300	200

MK-86 Shotgun

Available in 12 gauge with 24" extra full choked barrel. Black composite stock with blued finish.

NIB	Exc.	V.G.	Good	Fair	Poor
600	475	375	250	200	150

NOTE: Add $70 for stainless steel.

Knight Rolling Block Rifle

Rolling-block blackpowder rifle similar in design to the old Remington rolling block design. 209 primer ignition, .50 caliber barrel rifled for sabots. Finishes include blued/composite, stainless/camo, and all-camo. Introduced in 2007. Values shown are for stainless.

NIB	Exc.	V.G.	Good	Fair	Poor
375	300	200	125	100	50

Knight Long Range Hunter

.45-, .50- or .52-caliber bolt-action muzzleloader with 27" fluted stainless barrel. Said to shoot 4" 3-shot groups at 200 yards. Laminated stock. Introduced in 2007.

NIB	Exc.	V.G.	Good	Fair	Poor
525	400	300	200	100	50

KNIGHT'S MANUFACTURING CO.

Vero Beach, Florida

STONER SR-15 RIFLES

SR-15 Match

Chambered for .223 Win. and fitted with a target contour 20" free floating barrel. Two-stage match trigger. Flat top receiver. No sights. Weight is approximately 7.9 lbs.

NIB	Exc.	V.G.	Good	Fair	Poor
1850	1400	1050	750	500	200

SR-15 M-5 Rifle

This .223 is fitted with a 20" standard weight barrel with two-stage target trigger. Handguard employs RAS accessory system. Fitted with flip-up low profile rear sight. Weight is about 7.6 lbs.

NIB	Exc.	V.G.	Good	Fair	Poor
1700	1250	950	700	400	200

SR-15 E3 URX Carbine

Similar to SR-15 M5 but with 16-inch barrel, telescoping buttstock and vertical forend grip. Introduced 2006.

NIB	Exc.	V.G.	Good	Fair	Poor
2100	1700	1250	950	500	200

SR-15 M-4 Carbine

This model also includes the RAS system and has a flip-up rear sight. Two-stage target trigger and 16" lightweight barrel. Weight is about 6.8 lbs.

NIB	Exc.	V.G.	Good	Fair	Poor
1700	1250	950	700	400	200

STONER SR-25 RIFLES

SR-25 Match

This rifle is chambered for the .308 caliber and fitted with a 24" target contour free floating barrel. Special rifling and twist rate. No sights. Weight is about 10.75 lbs.

NIB	Exc.	V.G.	Good	Fair	Poor
3495	2600	1850	950	600	400

SR-25 Lightweight Match

This .308 rifle is fitted with a 20" free floating barrel. No sights. Weight is about 9.5 lbs.

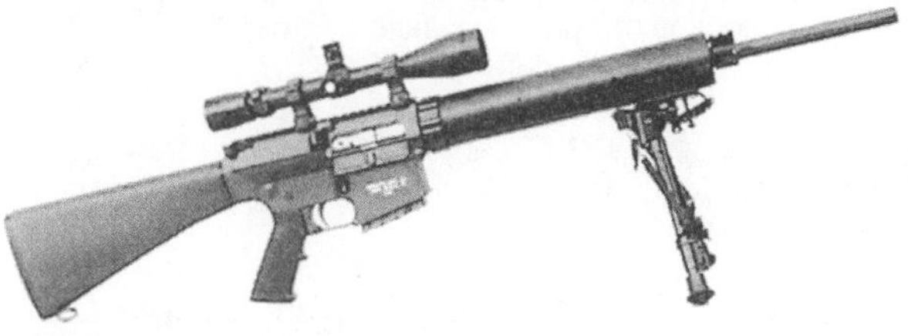

NIB	Exc.	V.G.	Good	Fair	Poor
2995	2250	1500	900	550	350

SR-25 Stoner Carbine

Fitted with a 16" free floating barrel and special short non-slip handguard. Weight is about 7.75 lbs.

NIB	Exc.	V.G.	Good	Fair	Poor
2995	2250	1500	900	—	—

SR-25 Competition Match

This rifle is chambered for either .308 or .260 cartridge and has a 26" match barrel. Fitted with a special forearm which rotates in 15 degree increments. Trigger is adjustable two-stage with extended trigger guard. Special bolt stop and charging handle. Adjustable buttstock. This model may be fitted with several extra costs options that will affect price.

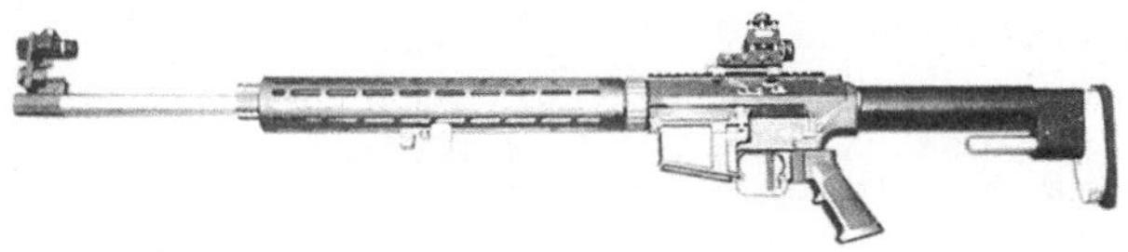

NIB	Exc.	V.G.	Good	Fair	Poor
6000	4750	3000	1750	1000	600

SR-25 Mk11 Mod 0 Match Rifle

Introduced in 2004 this rifle features a heavy 20" free floating target grade barrel.

NIB	Exc.	V.G.	Good	Fair	Poor
5295	3900	2500	1650	100	475

SR-50 Rifle

This is a semi-automatic rifle chambered for the .50 BMG cartridge. Magazine feed. Weight is approximately 31 lbs.

NIB	Exc.	V.G.	Good	Fair	Poor
7000	5500	4000	3000	2000	750

KONGSBERG

Norway

Thumbhole Sporter

Introduced in 1993, this bolt-action rifle is chambered of the .22-250 and .308 Win. cartridges. It is fitted with a 23" heavy barrel. The stock is American walnut with stippled thumbhole grip and wide forend. Cheekpiece is adjustable for height. Weight is about 8.5 lbs. Available in both right- and left-hand configurations.

NIB	Exc.	V.G.	Good	Fair	Poor
1575	1250	900	550	350	200

NOTE: Add 10 percent for left-hand model.

Classic Rifle

This model was also introduced in 1993 and is chambered for a wide variety of calibers from .22-250 to .338 Win. Mag. Fitted with a 23" barrel for standard calibers and a 26" barrel for magnum calibers. European walnut stock with straight comb. Hand checkered. Open sights. Weight is about 7.5 lbs. depending on caliber. Offered in both left- and right-hand configurations.

NIB	Exc.	V.G.	Good	Fair	Poor
995	800	650	375	225	125

NOTE: Add 10 percent for left-hand models and 10 percent for magnum calibers.

KRICO

Stuttgart, West Germany

Sporting Rifle

A .22 Hornet or .222 caliber bolt-action rifle with 22", 24", or 26" barrels, single or double set trigger, adjustable sights and a 4-shot magazine. Blued with a walnut stock. Manufactured between 1956 and 1962.

NIB	Exc.	V.G.	Good	Fair	Poor
—	650	550	475	375	275

Sporting Carbine

As above, with a 20" barrel and full length stock.

NIB	Exc.	V.G.	Good	Fair	Poor
—	675	575	500	400	300

Varmint Special Rifle

The Sporting Rifle with a heavier barrel.

NIB	Exc.	V.G.	Good	Fair	Poor
—	650	550	475	375	275

Model 300

A .22 caliber bolt-action rifle with a 23.5" barrel, 5-shot magazine and grooved receiver. Blued with a walnut stock. Imported prior to 1989.

NIB	Exc.	V.G.	Good	Fair	Poor
—	700	600	550	400	300

Model 302 and 304

Variations of the above. Discontinued in 1986.

NIB	Exc.	V.G.	Good	Fair	Poor
—	700	600	550	400	300

Model 311 Smallbore

A .22 caliber bolt-action rifle with a 22" barrel, double set triggers, adjustable sights and a 5- or 10-shot magazine. Blued with walnut stock. Not imported after 1988.

NIB	Exc.	V.G.	Good	Fair	Poor
—	325	275	225	150	100

Model 320

As above, with a 19.5" barrel and full length stock. Discontinued in 1988.

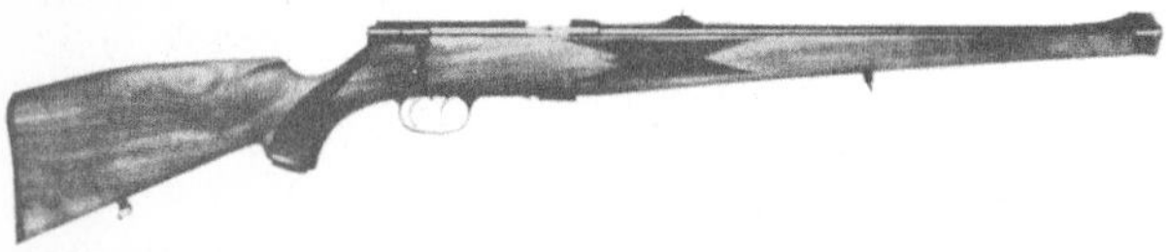

NIB	Exc.	V.G.	Good	Fair	Poor
—	700	600	550	400	300

Model 340

A .22 caliber bolt-action rifle with a 21" heavy barrel furnished without sights, adjustable trigger and 5-shot magazine. Blued with a walnut stock. Not imported after 1988.

NIB	Exc.	V.G.	Good	Fair	Poor
—	750	625	575	425	325

Model 340 Mini-Sniper

As above, but matte finished, barrel fitted with a muzzlebrake and stock with a raised cheekpiece as well as ventilated hand guard.

NIB	Exc.	V.G.	Good	Fair	Poor
—	1000	850	750	500	400

Model 340 Kricotronic

The Model 340 fitted with an electronic trigger. Not imported after 1988.

NIB	Exc.	V.G.	Good	Fair	Poor
—	1450	1000	850	600	500

Model 360S Biathlon Rifle

Introduced in 1991 this model features a .22 Long Rifle straight pull bolt-action with 5-round magazine and fitted with a 21.25" barrel. Walnut stock with high comb and adjustable buttplate. Fully adjustable match peep sight. Fitted with 17 oz. match trigger. Weight is approximately 9.25 lbs.

NIB	Exc.	V.G.	Good	Fair	Poor
1950	1350	850	500	300	150

Model 360S2 Biathlon Rifle

Same as above but fitted with a black epoxy finished walnut stock with pistol grip. Weight is 9 lbs.

NIB	Exc.	V.G.	Good	Fair	Poor
1500	1250	800	400	200	100

Model 400 Match

Chambered for the .22 LR or the .22 Hornet this bolt-action rifle is fitted with a heavy match 23" barrel and a 5-round magazine. The match-style stock is of European walnut. Fitted with a double set of match triggers. Weight is about 8.8 lbs.

NIB	Exc.	V.G.	Good	Fair	Poor
900	775	650	500	300	150

Model 400 Sporter

A .22 Hornet caliber bolt-action rifle with a 23.5" barrel, open sights and 5-shot magazine. Blued with a walnut stock. Not imported after 1988.

NIB	Exc.	V.G.	Good	Fair	Poor
—	750	625	550	425	325

Model 420

As above, with a 19.5" barrel, double set triggers, and a full-length stock. Discontinued in 1988.

NIB	Exc.	V.G.	Good	Fair	Poor
—	900	750	675	500	400

Model 440

Similar to the Model 340. Not imported after 1988.

NIB	Exc.	V.G.	Good	Fair	Poor
—	950	800	700	500	375

Model 500 Kricotronic Match Rifle

Chambered for the .22 LR this bolt-action rifle is fitted with a 23.6" barrel with tapered bore. Walnut stock with match-type adjustable buttplate. Electronic ignition system gives fastest lock time. Weight is approximately 9.4 lbs.

NIB	Exc.	V.G.	Good	Fair	Poor
3900	3000	2400	1650	1000	400

Model 600 Sporter

A .17 Remington to .308 Winchester caliber bolt-action rifle with a 23.5" barrel, open sights and 3-shot magazine. Blued with a walnut stock. Not imported after 1988.

NIB	Exc.	V.G.	Good	Fair	Poor
—	1150	950	875	700	575

Model 600 Sniper Rifle

This bolt-action rifle is chambered for the .222, .223, .22-250, .243, and 308. It is fitted with a 25.6" heavy barrel with flack hider. The stock is walnut with adjustable rubber buttplate. Magazine holds 4 rounds. Weight is about 9.2 lbs.

NIB	Exc.	V.G.	Good	Fair	Poor
2900	2100	1500	1100	600	300

Model 600 Match Rifle

Chambered for the same calibers as the 600 Sniper with the addition of the 5.6x50 Mag. Fitted with a 23.6" barrel. The match stock is vented in forearm for cooling. Wood is walnut with cheekpiece. Weight is approximately 8.8 lbs.

NIB	Exc.	V.G.	Good	Fair	Poor
1500	1100	750	600	300	150

Model 620

As above, with a 20.5" barrel, double set triggers, and full-length stock.

NIB	Exc.	V.G.	Good	Fair	Poor
1500	1100	750	600	300	150

Model 640 Varmint Rifle

Similar to the above, in .22-250, .222 or .223 caliber with a 23.5" heavy barrel. Not imported after 1988.

NIB	Exc.	V.G.	Good	Fair	Poor
—	1250	1025	925	775	625

Model 640 Sniper Rifle

As above, but matte finished. Discontinued in 1988.

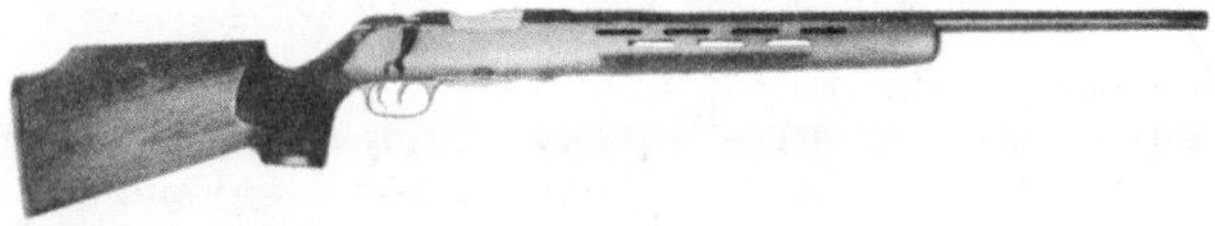

NIB	Exc.	V.G.	Good	Fair	Poor
1500	1100	750	600	300	150

Model 640 Deluxe Sniper Rifle

As above, in .223 or .308 caliber with a 23" barrel, stippled stock, and adjustable trigger. Not imported after 1988.

NIB	Exc.	V.G.	Good	Fair	Poor
—	1700	1250	1000	750	650

Model 700 Sporter

A .270 or .30-06 caliber bolt-action rifle with a 23.5" barrel, open sights, single set trigger, and 3-shot magazine. Blued with a walnut stock. Discontinued in 1988.

NIB	Exc.	V.G.	Good	Fair	Poor
—	1050	850	750	600	500

Model 720

As above, with a 20.5" barrel, double set triggers, and full-length stock. Discontinued in 1988.

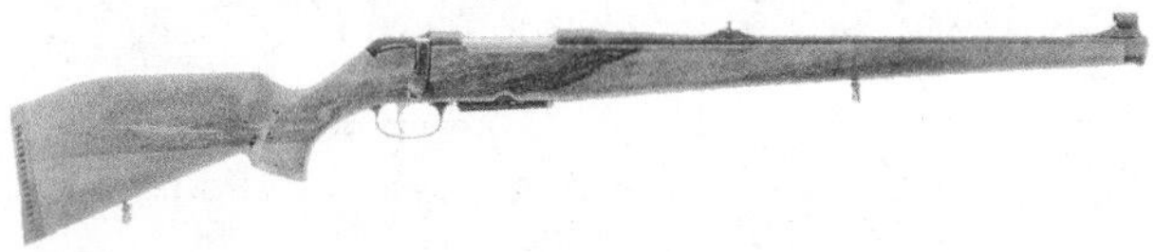

NIB	Exc.	V.G.	Good	Fair	Poor
—	1200	900	750	600	500

Model 720 Limited Edition

As above, in .270 caliber only with gold-plated furniture and gold highlighted engraving. Not imported after 1988.

NIB	Exc.	V.G.	Good	Fair	Poor
—	2500	2000	1750	1400	900

KRIEGHOFF, HEINRICH, GUN CO.

Ulm, Germany

DRILLINGS AND COMBINATION GUNS

Plus Model

A three-barrel combination rifle/shotgun produced in a variety of gauges and calibers with 25" barrels, double triggers, and automatic ejectors. Blued with a walnut stock. Introduced in 1988.

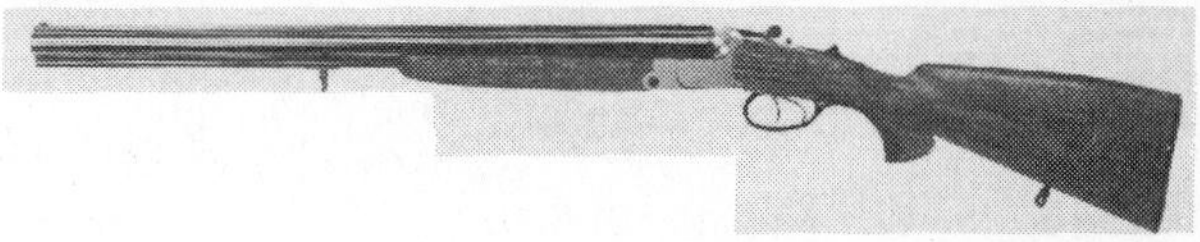

NIB	Exc.	V.G.	Good	Fair	Poor
6600	5250	4100	3500	2000	750

Trumpf Model

A combination rifle/shotgun produced in a variety of calibers and gauges with 25" barrels and double triggers. Blued with a walnut stock.

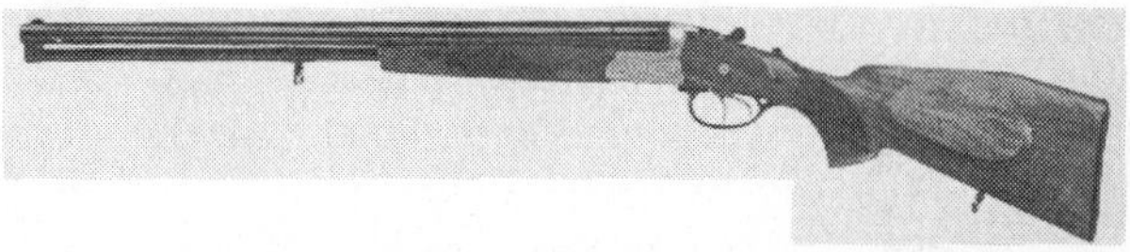

NIB	Exc.	V.G.	Good	Fair	Poor
11000	7700	5100	3500	2000	750

Trumpf Dural

As above, lightweight boxlock with a Duraluminum frame.

NIB	Exc.	V.G.	Good	Fair	Poor
11000	7700	5100	3500	2000	750

NOTE: For single trigger add $1,850. For free-floating barrel add $450.

Neptun Model

A combination over-and-under rifle/shotgun with sidelocks produced in a variety of gauges and calibers. Engraved, blued with a walnut stock.

NIB	Exc.	V.G.	Good	Fair	Poor
15000	12000	10500	5000	2500	1500

Neptun Dural

As above, lightweight boxlock with a Duraluminum frame.

NIB	Exc.	V.G.	Good	Fair	Poor
15000	12000	10500	5000	2500	1500

Neptun Primus Model

The Neptun with relief engraving and detachable sidelocks.

NIB	Exc.	V.G.	Good	Fair	Poor
20000	17000	14000	7500	3500	2000

Neptun Primus Dural

As above, lightweight sidelock with a Duraluminum frame.

NIB	Exc.	V.G.	Good	Fair	Poor
20000	18000	14000	7500	3500	2000

DOUBLE RIFLES

Teck Over-and-Under

A boxlock over-and-under rifle manufactured in a variety of calibers with 25" barrels, double triggers, extractors, and express sights. Blued with a walnut stock.

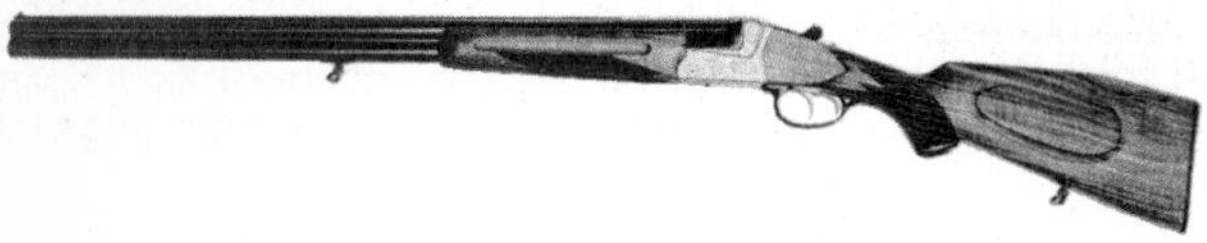

NIB	Exc.	V.G.	Good	Fair	Poor
9000	8250	6600	5000	2250	1500

NOTE: For .458 Win. Mag add $1,500.

Ulm Model

As above, with sidelocks.

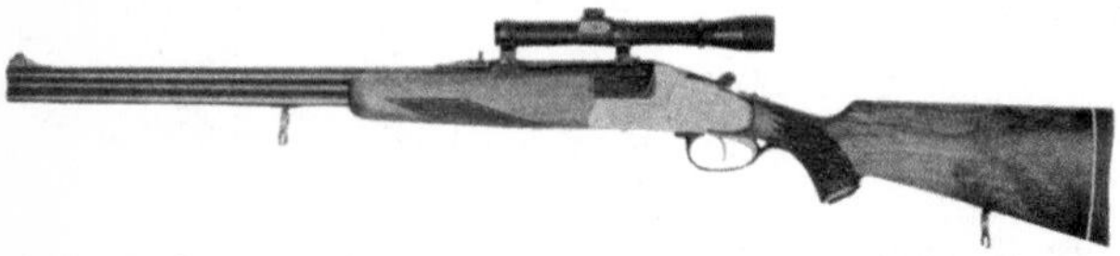

NIB	Exc.	V.G.	Good	Fair	Poor
15000	12000	10500	7500	3000	2000

Ulm Primus

As above, with detachable sidelocks.

NIB	Exc.	V.G.	Good	Fair	Poor
23500	19500	16500	11500	7000	3000

Ultra

This boxlock over-and-under rifle is offered with several different options such as same caliber rifle barrels or different caliber rifle barrels. Built on a 20 gauge frame with game scene engraving. Weights are depending on calibers and combinations of calibers but are between 6.5 lbs. and 8 lbs.

NIB	Exc.	V.G.	Good	Fair	Poor
7500	6100	4400	3000	1500	800

Classic

This is a side-by-side rifle with sideplates. Offered in 7x65R to 9.3x74R calibers with an optional interchangeable 20 gauge shotgun barrel. Single trigger. Choice of standard stock with cheekpiece or classic Bavaria style. Weight is approximately 7.25 to 8 lbs. depending on calibers.

NIB	Exc.	V.G.	Good	Fair	Poor
8800	6900	5000	3500	2000	800

Classic Big Five

Similar to the Classic but chambered for .375 H&H, .375 NE, .458 Win. Mag., .416 Rigby, .470 NE, and .500 NE 3". Double trigger with hinged front trigger. Weighs approximately 9.25 to 10 lbs. depending on caliber. Interchangeable barrel are optional.

NIB	Exc.	V.G.	Good	Fair	Poor
10900	82500	5100	3500	2000	750

NOTE: There are many optional engraving patterns available for these double rifles that may affect price. Consult an expert prior to a sale.

SHOTGUNS

MODEL 32 STANDARD

A 12, 20, 28 or .410 bore boxlock over-and-under shotgun with 26.5" to 32" barrels, single-selective trigger and automatic ejectors. Blued with a walnut stock. Discontinued in 1980.

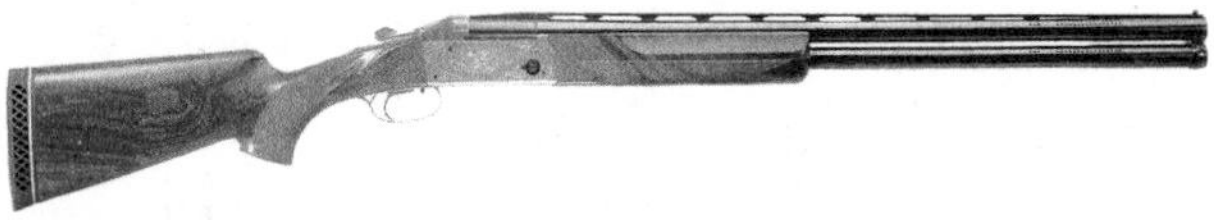

NIB	Exc.	V.G.	Good	Fair	Poor
—	3000	2500	2000	1100	750

NOTE: 28 gauge or .410 two barrel set add 50 percent. Four-barrel Skeet set add 100 percent.

San Remo Grade

NIB	Exc.	V.G.	Good	Fair	Poor
—	5000	3750	1900	1400	1000

Monte Carlo Grade

NIB	Exc.	V.G.	Good	Fair	Poor
—	6250	4850	2750	1650	1250

Crown Grade

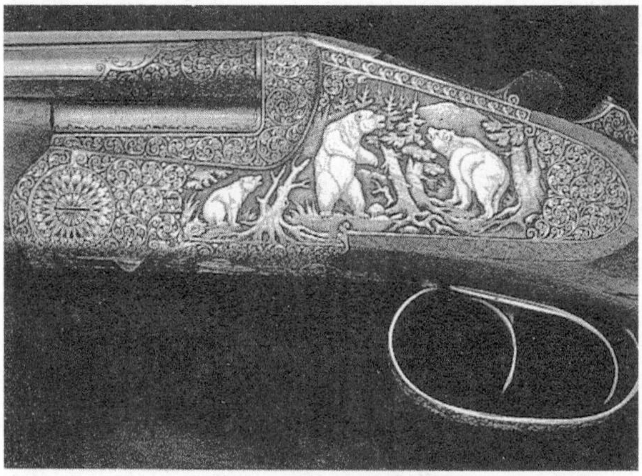

Courtesy Bonhams & Butterfields

NIB	Exc.	V.G.	Good	Fair	Poor
—	8700	6500	4300	2200	1500

Super Crown Grade

NIB	Exc.	V.G.	Good	Fair	Poor
18000	14700	10500	6850	3750	2000

Single Barrel Trap Gun

The Model 32 with a single 32" to 34" barrel.

NIB	Exc.	V.G.	Good	Fair	Poor
—	3950	3250	1700	1075	600

Teck

Similar to the Teck double rifle but offered in 12 and 16 gauge.

NIB	Exc.	V.G.	Good	Fair	Poor
12000	10000	7500	4550	3000	1750

Teck Dural

Same as above but with lightweight aluminum frame.

NIB	Exc.	V.G.	Good	Fair	Poor
12000	10000	7500	4550	3000	1750

Ulm

This sidelock over-and-under is offered in both 12 and 16 gauge.

NIB	Exc.	V.G.	Good	Fair	Poor
20000	16500	13000	8000	4500	3000

Ulm Dural

This is a lightweight version of the above model.

NIB	Exc.	V.G.	Good	Fair	Poor
20000	16500	13000	8000	4500	3000

Ulm Primus

This is a deluxe version of the Ulm series with sidelocks and extensive engraving.

NIB	Exc.	V.G.	Good	Fair	Poor
30000	22250	16500	12000	7000	3500

Ulm Primus Dural

This is a lightweight version of the above model.

NIB	Exc.	V.G.	Good	Fair	Poor
30000	22250	16500	12000	7000	3500

Ultra

This is a lightweight over-and-under gun offered in 12 or 20 gauge.

NIB	Exc.	V.G.	Good	Fair	Poor
—	6250	4850	2750	1650	1250

KS-5 Single Barrel Trap

This model is a boxlock 12 gauge only trap gun with 32" or 34" ventilated tapered rib barrel and case hardened frame with a satin gray finish. The barrel features an adjustable point of impact and is offered with screw-in choke tubes. Weight is approximately 8.6 lbs.

NIB	Exc.	V.G.	Good	Fair	Poor
8000	7500	5900	3650	1250	800

KS-5 Special

Same as above but furnished with adjustable rib and adjustable comb.

NIB	Exc.	V.G.	Good	Fair	Poor
8250	7750	6100	3900	1500	1000

K-80 TRAP

This is a boxlock 12 gauge shotgun built to trap dimensions. This model is offered in many variations. Available in over-and-under trap with choice of 30" or 32" vent tapered step rib barrels. Also a single barrel is offered in 32" or 34" tapered step rib lengths. These single barrels are adjustable for point of impact. A top single barrel is available as well in 34" length. Trap combos are offered also. All barrels are offered with or without choke tubes. The checkered walnut stock is offered in Monte Carlo or straight trap dimensions. Trap guns weigh approximately 8.75 lbs. Prices listed are for Standard Grade.

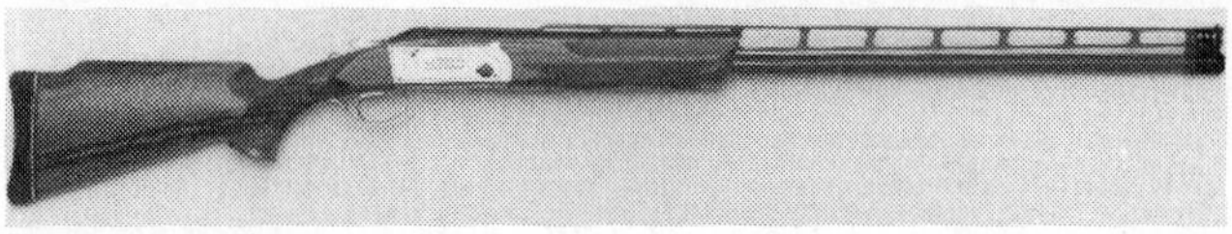

Over-and-Under Trap

NIB	Exc.	V.G.	Good	Fair	Poor
12000	10500	7400	4850	2000	1000

Unsingle Trap

NIB	Exc.	V.G.	Good	Fair	Poor
12500	11000	8250	5400	2250	1250

Top Single Trap

NIB	Exc.	V.G.	Good	Fair	Poor
13250	11200	9500	6400	3300	1500

Trap Combos

NIB	Exc.	V.G.	Good	Fair	Poor
13000	10700	9600	7400	4300	1900

NOTE: Bavaria Grade add 70 percent. Danube Grade add 100 percent. Gold Target Grade add 200 percent.

K-20 Sporting and Field

Compact frame variation of the K-80, chambered in 20 or 28 gauge, or .410 bore. Barrels are 30 or 32 inches with five choke tubes and tapered flat rib. Checkered walnut stock, auto ejectors and single selective trigger. Weight is approx. 7-1/4 lbs. Available with extra sets of barrels in other two gauges.

NIB	Exc.	V.G.	Good	Fair	Poor
9000	8000	7000	4000	2200	1000

K-80 Sporting Clays

The frame is the same as the trap model with the addition of a lightweight alloy model and is available in 12 gauge only. Barrel lengths for standard weight model are 28", 30", or 32" with tapered flat rib. The lightweight model is offered with 28" or 30" flat rib barrels. Select European walnut stock with hand checkering and supplied with a #3 Sporting stock with schnabel forearm. The standard weight model weighs about 8.25 lbs. while the lightweight model weighs 7.75 lbs. Prices listed are for the Standard Grade.

NIB	Exc.	V.G.	Good	Fair	Poor
9500	8000	7000	4000	2200	1000

NOTE: Bavaria Grade add 70 percent. Danube Grade add 100 percent. Gold Target Grade add 200 percent.

K-80 SKEET

This model is offered in a number of variations. The standard weight skeet with 28" or 30" tapered or parallel ribs, lightweight skeet with 28" or 30" tapered or parallel ribs, International skeet with 28" parallel broadway rib, and the 4 barrel skeet set in 12, 20, and 28 gauge as well as .410 bore with 8mm rib. Stock is hand-checkered select European walnut with a choice of several skeet dimensions. Values listed are for Standard Grade.

Standard Weight Skeet

NIB	Exc.	V.G.	Good	Fair	Poor
7500	6250	4950	3300	2200	1000

Lightweight Skeet

NIB	Exc.	V.G.	Good	Fair	Poor
7500	6250	4950	3300	2200	1000

International Skeet

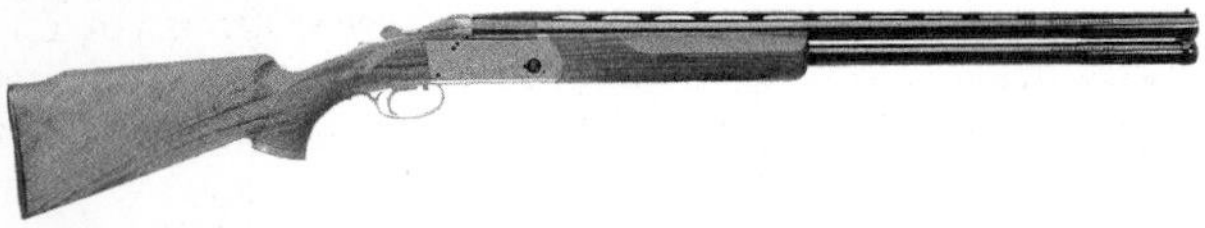

NIB	Exc.	V.G.	Good	Fair	Poor
7500	6250	4950	3300	2200	1000

4 Barrel Set

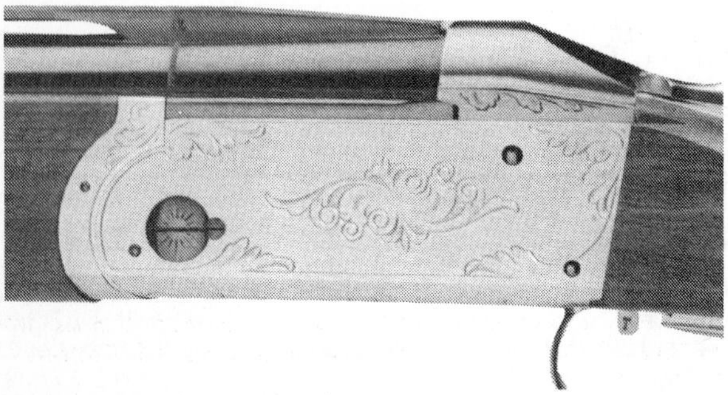

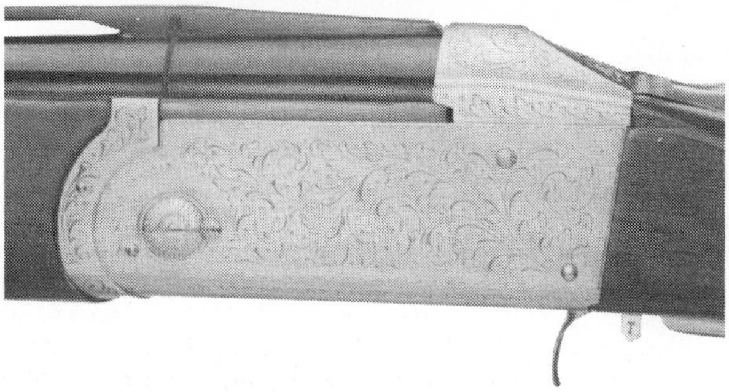

NIB	Exc.	V.G.	Good	Fair	Poor
17000	10000	7600	4400	3300	2200

NOTE: Bavaria Grade add 70 percent. Danube Grade add 100 percent. Gold Target Grade add 200 percent. Optional Engravings available by special order on NIB or Exc. conditions guns: Parcours add $1500. Parcours Special add $2800. Super Scroll add $1100. Gold Super Scroll add $2900. Custom Bavaria $4700 over Bavaria Grade price.

L

LAKELANDER
Gulfport, Mississippi

Model 389 Premium

This bolt action rifle is chambered for .270 Win., .308 Win., and .30-06 calibers. It is fitted with a 22" lightweight barrel. The stock is oil finished walnut with diamond checkering. Rosewood forend cap, black recoil pad, and Monte Carlo buttstock. Weight is approximately 7.6 lbs. Introduced in 1997.

NIB	*Exc.*	*V.G.*	*Good*	*Fair*	*Poor*
1750	1350	950	700	375	200

Model 389 Classic

Similar to the Premium grade rifle above but offered with traditional stock and checkering and less fancy walnut stock. Weight is approximately 7.3 lbs. Introduced in 1997.

NIB	*Exc.*	*V.G.*	*Good*	*Fair*	*Poor*
1725	1325	925	675	350	150

Model 389 Match-Maker

This bolt action is chambered for the .308 cartridge and is fitted with a 21.7" barrel. The stock is target style with adjustable chin support with benchrest-style buttpad. Weight is approximately 8.4 lbs. Introduced in 1997.

NIB	*Exc.*	*V.G.*	*Good*	*Fair*	*Poor*
2250	1850	1350	850	575	250

NOTE: Add $50 for magnum calibers.

LAMB, H. C. & CO.
Jamestown, North Carolina

Muzzle Loading Rifle

Chambered for .58 caliber and utilizes the percussion ignition system. It has a 33" barrel and a full-length oak stock held on by two barrel bands. There is a ramrod mounted under the barrel that is made of iron. All other trim is brass, and there is a bayonet lug at the muzzle. This rifle was made for the Confederacy; and the workmanship was crude, as it was on most CSA weapons. The stock is marked "H.C.Lamb & Co., N.C." There were supposedly 10,000 rifles ordered, but actually there were approximately 250 manufactured between 1861 and 1863. The rarity of the guns of the Confederacy gives them a great deal of collector appeal.

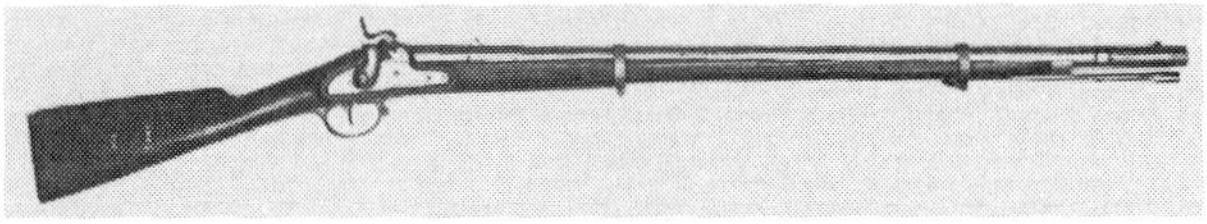

Courtesy Milwaukee Public Museum, Milwaukee, Wisconsin

NIB	*Exc.*	*V.G.*	*Good*	*Fair*	*Poor*
—	—	35000	15000	2750	500

LAMES
Chiavari, Italy

Skeet or Trap Grade

An over-and-under shotgun chambered for 12 gauge with either 26" skeet-and-skeet barrels or 30" or 32" full-choked barrels. It has a competition-style wide vent rib and automatic ejectors. The trigger is single-selective, and the finish is blued. The trap gun has a Monte Carlo stock of checkered walnut. Both models feature recoil pads.

NIB	*Exc.*	*V.G.*	*Good*	*Fair*	*Poor*
—	700	575	4575	375	200

California Trap Grade

This over-and-under is similar to the standard trap model, with separated barrels. All other features are the same.

NIB	*Exc.*	*V.G.*	*Good*	*Fair*	*Poor*
—	775	650	575	475	225

Field Grade

Similar in design to the standard trap model, with 3" chambers and barrel lengths of 26", 28", or 30" and a field dimensioned stock. It features various choke combinations and was also available with the separated barrels of the California Trap for an additional 20 percent in cost.

NIB	*Exc.*	*V.G.*	*Good*	*Fair*	*Poor*
—	475	450	350	250	150

LANBER ARMAS S.A.
Vizcaya, Spain

Model 2072 Slug

Fixed choke double barrel slug gun with 3" chambers and 20" barrel with fiber-optic rifle sights. Weight is about 6 lbs. A hard-to-find gun.

NIB	*Exc.*	*V.G.*	*Good*	*Fair*	*Poor*
900	800	650	475	300	200

Model 844 ST

A 12-gauge over-and-under shotgun with 26" or 28" vent rib barrels. The chokes vary, and the gun features a single-selective trigger, extractors, and an engraved receiver with a blued finish and a walnut stock. This gun was manufactured until 1986.

NIB	*Exc.*	*V.G.*	*Good*	*Fair*	*Poor*
—	425	350	300	250	175

Model 844 MST

Similar to the Model 844 ST except that it is chambered for 3" Magnum and has 30" Full and Modified choked barrels.

NIB	*Exc.*	*V.G.*	*Good*	*Fair*	*Poor*
—	525	450	300	250	175

Model 844 EST

Similar to the others, but it features automatic ejectors.

NIB	*Exc.*	*V.G.*	*Good*	*Fair*	*Poor*
—	575	425	350	300	200

Model 844 EST CHR

Has automatic ejectors and double triggers. All other features are the same as the EST.

NIB	*Exc.*	*V.G.*	*Good*	*Fair*	*Poor*
—	550	400	325	275	175

Model 2004 LCH

An over-and-under chambered for 12 gauge and features 28" vent rib barrels with screw-in choke tubes. It has a single-selective trigger, automatic ejectors, and an engraved boxlock action that is matte finished, with a hand-checkered walnut stock. This model was also discontinued in 1986.

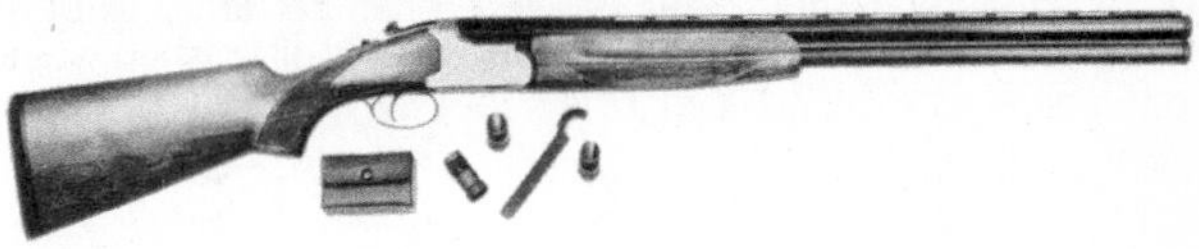

NIB	Exc.	V.G.	Good	Fair	Poor
—	775	650	550	475	375

Model 2008 LCH and Model 2009 LCH

The trap and skeet versions of the series. The basic differences are in the barrel lengths and the stock dimensions.

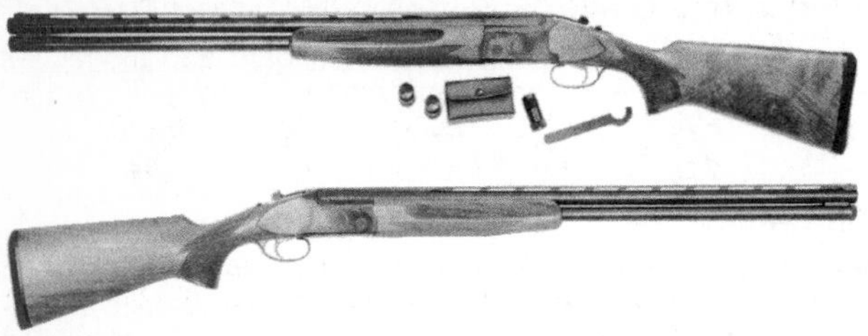

NIB	Exc.	V.G.	Good	Fair	Poor
—	900	750	650	575	475

Model 2067

This 20 gauge over/under with 3" chambers has 28" barrels, auto ejectors and an oil-finished walnut stock. Weight is about 6.6 lbs.

NIB	Exc.	V.G.	Good	Fair	Poor
775	650	550	450	375	200

Model 2077 Hunter Light

This is a 2.75" 12 gauge with 26" barrels and a lightweight alloy receiver. Weight is about 6.2 lbs.

NIB	Exc.	V.G.	Good	Fair	Poor
850	725	575	475	400	200

Model 2087 Hunter

This 12 gauge comes with 3" chambers, auto ejectors, oil-finished walnut stock and 28" or 30" barrel. Weight is about 7 lbs.

NIB	Exc.	V.G.	Good	Fair	Poor
775	650	550	450	375	200

Model 2097 Sporting

Sporting clays model in 12 gauge with 3" chambers and 28" or 30" barrels. Weight is about 7.7 lbs. Add $50 for Sporting LUX model.

NIB	Exc.	V.G.	Good	Fair	Poor
850	725	575	475	400	200

Model 2088 Rival I

Sporting clays model is a 2.75" 12 gauge with 28" barrels and case-hardened receiver. Weight is about 7.6 lbs.

NIB	Exc.	V.G.	Good	Fair	Poor
1600	1300	850	600	400	200

Model 2089 Rival II

This 2.75" 12 gauge sporting clays gun has 30" barrels, one fixed and the other threaded for choke tubes. Blued receiver. Weight is about 7.9 lbs.

NIB	Exc.	V.G.	Good	Fair	Poor
1600	1300	850	600	400	200

Model 2070 Becada

This 3" 12 gauge gun developed for woodcock hunting features one fixed choke barrel and one barrel threaded for chokes. Barrel length is 23". Weight is about 6 lbs.

NIB	Exc.	V.G.	Good	Fair	Poor
850	725	575	475	400	200

Model 2531 Victoria I

This 12 gauge semi-automatic has a 3" chamber and 28" barrel with an internal choke tube system. The stock is oil finished walnut and the receiver is blued. Weight is about 6.8 lbs.

NIB	Exc.	V.G.	Good	Fair	Poor
600	500	400	300	200	100

Model 2532 Victoria II

Similar to above and available with a 26" or 28" barrel.

NIB	Exc.	V.G.	Good	Fair	Poor
625	525	425	325	225	100

Model 2532 Victoria II EXT

Similar to above but with a 24.5" barrel and external choke tube system.

NIB	Exc.	V.G.	Good	Fair	Poor
625	525	425	325	225	100

Model 2534

This lighter version of the 2532 weighs about 6.4 lbs. with a 26" barrel.

NIB	Exc.	V.G.	Good	Fair	Poor
625	525	425	325	225	100

Model 2533 Victoria LUX

Semi-automatic 3" 12 gauge features a brushed silver finish, scrollwork and gold mallard on the receiver. The barrel is 26" or 28" and weight is about 6.8 lbs.

NIB	Exc.	V.G.	Good	Fair	Poor
650	550	450	350	250	100

Model 2533 Victoria LUX EXT

As above but with 24.5" barrel and external choke tube system.

NIB	Exc.	V.G.	Good	Fair	Poor
650	550	450	350	250	100

Model 2535 Victoria Slug

Dedicated slug gun has fiber-optic rifle sights atop a 24", fixed cylinder barrel.

NIB	Exc.	V.G.	Good	Fair	Poor
650	550	450	350	250	100

LANCASTER, CHARLES

London, England

4 Barreled Shotgun

This company also produced a shotgun in the 4 barrel configuration. It is chambered for 12 or 16 gauge and has 28" barrels. The gun is, as one would imagine, quite heavy and poorly balanced; and it was not a great success.

NIB	Exc.	V.G.	Good	Fair	Poor
—	—	6250	4000	2000	1000

Bolt Action Rifle

A high-grade sporting rifle chambered for various different calibers. The barrel is 24" in length; and the finish is blued with a classic-styled, hand-checkered walnut stock. This rifle was discontinued in 1936.

NIB	Exc.	V.G.	Good	Fair	Poor
—	3500	1900	1250	800	600

LAR MFG. CO.

West Jordan, Utah

Grizzly 50 Big Boar

A single-shot breech loading rifle chambered for the .50 caliber BMG cartridge. The barrel is 36" in length and the rifle weighs approximately 30 lbs.

NIB	Exc.	V.G.	Good	Fair	Poor
2350	2000	1550	1100	550	300

NOTE: Add $100 for Parkerized finish. Add $250 for nickel frame, and $350 for full nickel finish.

LASALLE
France

Slide-Action Shotgun

Chambered for 12 or 20 gauge and is offered with a 26", 28", or 30" barrel with improved-cylinder, modified, or full chokes. The receiver is alloy, anodized blue and the vent rib barrel is blued. The stock is checkered walnut.

NIB	Exc.	V.G.	Good	Fair	Poor
—	275	225	200	150	100

Semi-Automatic Shotgun

A gas-operated semi-automatic shotgun chambered for 12 gauge only, with the same barrel length and choke combinations as are available on the slide-action model. The receiver is also alloy, and the stock is checkered walnut.

NIB	Exc.	V.G.	Good	Fair	Poor
—	325	250	200	175	100

LAURONA
Eibar, Spain

The list of models listed was compiled by Thomas E. Barker of Galaxy Imports, Ltd., Inc.

OVER-AND-UNDERS

Model 67

The first over-and-under Laurona chambered for 12 gauge only with double triggers and 28" vent rib barrels with extractors. The boxlock action and barrels are blued, and the stock is checkered walnut in 20 lpi skip line checkering.

NIB	Exc.	V.G.	Good	Fair	Poor
—	200	150	100	75	50

Model 71

Similar to the Model 67 with minor cosmetic changes and improvements to facilitate ease of manufacturing. Receiver is bright chromed with roll engraving depicting dogs on the right side and birds on the left. This model was imported and sold by Sears & Robuck in about 1973 and 1974. The earlier models had traditional solid center ribbed blued barrels, the later models having black chrome finished solid ribbed barrels.

NIB	Exc.	V.G.	Good	Fair	Poor
—	225	175	125	100	75

MODEL 82

Similar to the Model 71 with auto-ejectors. Chambered for 12 gauge only. All barrels separated without center rib with Black Chrome finish and hard chrome bores with long forcing cones in chambers. Firing pins changed to traditional round type. Many internal parts improved for reliability. Checkering changed from skip diamond to standard 20 lpi. In most respects the 82 Models are representative of present-day Laurona over-and-under shotguns and will share most internal parts.

Game

Barrels are 28" with 2-3/4" or 3" chambers, long forcing cones, hard chrome bores, 5mm rib, and chokes ****/**(IC/IM) or ***/*(M/F). Finish on barrels is black chrome with nickel receiver with Louis XVI style engraving. Tulip forend, field-style stock with plastic buttplate. Weighs approximately 7 lbs.

NIB	Exc.	V.G.	Good	Fair	Poor
—	250	200	175	125	100

Super Game

Similar to the Model 82 Game except with more elaborate and very delicate engraving

NIB	Exc.	V.G.	Good	Fair	Poor
—	350	250	150	125	100

Trap Combi

Similar to the Model 82 Game except for 28" or 29" barrels. The rib is 8mm. The Trap stock is fitted with a rubber recoil pad. Weight is about 7.4 lbs.

NIB	Exc.	V.G.	Good	Fair	Poor
—	450	400	350	300	200

Trap Competition

Similar to the Model 82 Trap Combi except for the 13mm aluminum rib with long white sight. Engraving consist of motifs on sides of receiver. Beavertail fluted forend and Monte Carlo Trap stock with black rubber special Trap recoil pad. Weight is approximately 8 lbs.

NIB	Exc.	V.G.	Good	Fair	Poor
—	500	400	300	250	200

Super Trap (U only)

Similar to the Model 82 Trap Competition except for special trap Pachmayr recoil pad with imitation leather face. Engraving very delicate fine scroll. Weight is 7 lbs., 12 oz.

NIB	Exc.	V.G.	Good	Fair	Poor
—	575	475	350	300	250

Super Skeet

Similar to the Model 82 Super Trap except fitted with 28" barrels choked sheet with field-style buttstock with plastic buttplate. Weight is approximately 7 lbs.

NIB	Exc.	V.G.	Good	Fair	Poor
—	500	400	300	250	200

Pigeon Competition

Similar to the Model 82 Trap Competition except fitted with 28" barrels. Recoil pad is special competition-style Pachmayr with imitation leather face. Weight is about 7 lbs., 13 oz.

NIB	Exc.	V.G.	Good	Fair	Poor
—	550	450	350	300	250

Super Pigeon

Similar to the Model 82 Super Trap except fitted with 28" barrels. Weight is approximately 7 lbs., 9 oz.

NIB	Exc.	V.G.	Good	Fair	Poor
—	575	475	350	300	250

NOTE: The Super Models listed have nickel-finish receivers featuring delicate fine scroll engraving with black chrome relief. All barrels have a very durable rust-resistant black chrome finish.

Model 84S Super Game

Similar to the Model 82 Super Game except for the new single-selective trigger which is designated by "S" in the model number. Chambered for the 12 gauge 3" magnum with 28" barrels with 8mm rib. Weight is approximately 7 lbs.

NIB	Exc.	V.G.	Good	Fair	Poor
—	500	400	350	200	100

NOTE: The Super Game models listed were available with an extra set of 20 gauge multi-choke barrels in 26" or 28". Add $400 to Exc. value for these barrels. For models with cast-on stocks for left-hand shooters add $50 to Exc. value.

Model 83MG Super Game

Similar to the Model 82 Super Game except this model was the advent of Laurona's new multi-choke. CAUTION! The Laurona multi-choke is not compatible with any other brand of screw-in chokes because of the black chrome plating on the metric threads. Do not attempt to interchange with other guns. Barrel for this model in 12 gauge are 28" in length and for the 20 gauge 26" or 28". Both are chambered for the 3" shell. Rib is 8mm. Weight is about 7 lbs.

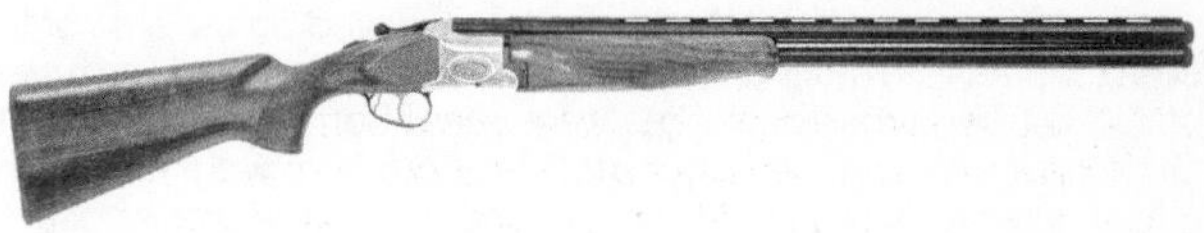

NIB	Exc.	V.G.	Good	Fair	Poor
—	500	400	350	200	100

Model 85MS Super Game

Similar to the Model 83MG Super Game except for the single-selective trigger. Chambered for the 12 or 20 gauge 3" Magnum. Weight is about 7 lbs.

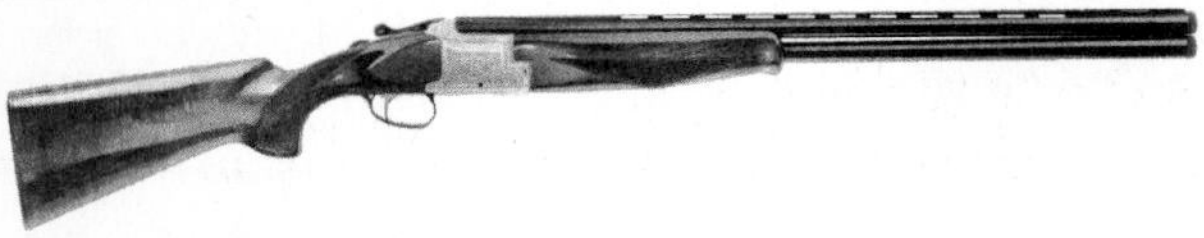

NIB	Exc.	V.G.	Good	Fair	Poor
—	700	650	450	250	200

Model 84S Super Trap

Single-selective trigger with 29" barrels. Chambered for 2-3/4" shells with long forcing cones. The aluminum rib is 13mm wide. Auto ejectors. Receiver is nickel plated with fine scroll engraving with black chrome relief. Beavertail forearm and choice of Monte Carlo or standard Trap stock. Weight is about 7 lbs., 12 oz.

NIB	Exc.	V.G.	Good	Fair	Poor
—	800	750	550	350	250

Model 85MS Super Trap

Similar to the Model 82S Super Trap except multi-choke in bottom barrel with fixed choke on top barrel. Weight is about 7 lbs., 12 oz.

NIB	Exc.	V.G.	Good	Fair	Poor
—	900	825	700	500	300

Model 85MS Super Pigeon

Similar to the Model 85MS Super Trap except with 28" barrels with fixed IM choke on top barrel and multi-choke on bottom barrel. Intended for live bird competition. Weight is about 7 lbs., 4 oz.

NIB	Exc.	V.G.	Good	Fair	Poor
—	950	900	800	600	300

Model 85MS Special Sporting

Similar to the Model 85MS Super Pigeon except for field-style buttstock with plastic buttplate. Intended for upland game. Weight is approximately 7 lbs., 4 oz.

NIB	Exc.	V.G.	Good	Fair	Poor
—	950	900	800	600	300

Model 84S Super Skeet

Similar to the Model 85MS Special Sporting except choked skeet and skeet. Weight is approximately 7 lbs.

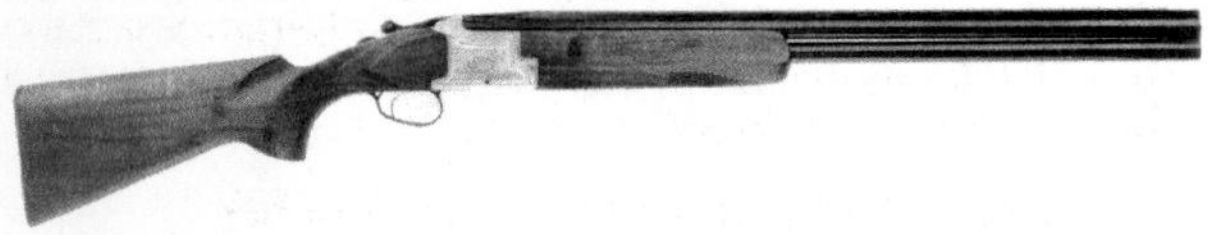

NIB	Exc.	V.G.	Good	Fair	Poor
—	950	900	800	600	300

300 SILHOUETTE

These guns are basically the same as the Super series above with these exceptions: They are readily identified by the white and black chrome stripped receiver with the model engraved on the side of the receiver. Barrels are multi-choked on both bores and have 11mm steel ribs. NOTE: Two types of chokes were used. Some guns came with knurl head-type as in the Super models and others were made with the flush invector style. A later option for ease of changing chokes is the knurl long choke, which is a flush-type with a knurl head added. Both later type chokes, the flush and the knurl long-type, can be used in the early multi-choke models with some extension showing.

Trap

This model has barrels 29" with 2-3/4" chambers and long forcing cones with hard chrome bores and 11mm rib. Beavertail forearm and straight comb trap stock fitted with a ventilated black rubber recoil pad are standard. Weight is approximately 8 lbs.

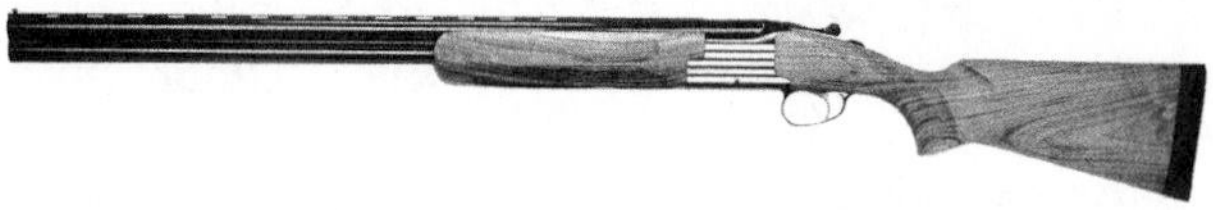

NIB	Exc.	V.G.	Good	Fair	Poor
—	750	500	300	200	100

Sporting Clays

Similar to the Model 300 Trap except with 28" barrels. Some guns came with 3" chambers. The buttstock is field style with plastic buttplate or hard rubber sporting clays pad. Weight is about 8 lbs.

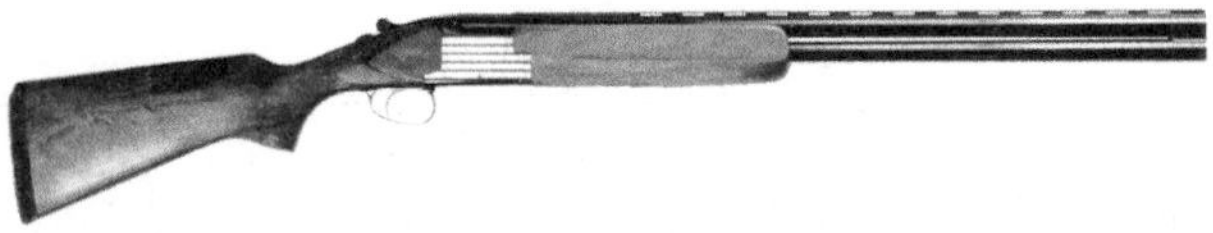

NIB	Exc.	V.G.	Good	Fair	Poor
—	750	500	300	200	100

Ultra Magnum

Similar to the Model 300 Sporting Clays except with 3-1/2" chamber in 12 gauge for waterfowl hunting. Weight is about 7 lbs., 8 oz.

NIB	Exc.	V.G.	Good	Fair	Poor
—	850	600	450	275	150

SIDE-BY-SIDE BOXLOCKS

Models with "X" after the model number were made after 1975 and finished with non-rusting black chrome on barrels and action with hard chrome bores. Guns were made in 12, 16, and 20 bore. Smaller gauges were made on special order. Side-by-side shotguns were discontinued by Laurona after 1978 to concentrate on the over-and-under market.

Model 11

Boxlock action with triple Greener-type round crossbolt. Independent firing pins bushed into the face of the action. Barrels of "Bellota" steel. Made in 12, 16, and 20 gauge.

NIB	Exc.	V.G.	Good	Fair	Poor
—	400	350	300	200	150

Model 13

Similar to the Model 11 except with Purdey-type bolting system. Extractor of double radius.

NIB	Exc.	V.G.	Good	Fair	Poor
—	400	350	300	200	150

Model 13X

Barrels and action finished in black chrome and hard chrome bores.

NIB	Exc.	V.G.	Good	Fair	Poor
—	500	400	300	250	200

Model 13E

Similar to the Model 13 except with automatic ejectors.

NIB	Exc.	V.G.	Good	Fair	Poor
—	500	400	300	250	200

Model 13XE

Similar to the Model 13E except black chrome finish and hard chrome bores.

NIB	Exc.	V.G.	Good	Fair	Poor
—	600	500	400	350	300

Model 15 Economic Pluma

Similar to the Model 13 except first model has hard chrome bores.

NIB	Exc.	V.G.	Good	Fair	Poor
—	450	400	300	250	200

Model 15X

Similar to the Model 15 except black chrome finish and hard chrome bores.

NIB	Exc.	V.G.	Good	Fair	Poor
—	500	400	300	250	200

Model 15E Economic Pluma

Similar to the Model 15 except with automatic ejectors.

NIB	Exc.	V.G.	Good	Fair	Poor
—	550	450	350	300	250

Model 15XE

Similar to the Model 15E except black chrome finish and hard chrome bores.

NIB	Exc.	V.G.	Good	Fair	Poor
—	600	500	400	350	300

Model 52 Pluma

Boxlock action with back of action scalloped and artistically engraved in fine English-style scroll. Churchill rib and double radius extractor. Hard chrome bores. Weight is about 6 lbs.

NIB	Exc.	V.G.	Good	Fair	Poor
—	750	650	500	400	350

Model 52E Pluma

Similar to the Model 52 except with automatic ejectors. Weight is approximately 6 lbs., 2 oz.

NIB	Exc.	V.G.	Good	Fair	Poor
—	850	750	600	500	450

SIDE-BY-SIDE SIDELOCKS

Model 103

Blued sidelock with some light border engraving. Triple Purdey-type bolting system. Extractor of double radius. Barrels of special "Bellota" steel with hard chrome bores. Made in 12, 16, and 20 gauge.

NIB	Exc.	V.G.	Good	Fair	Poor
—	900	800	700	500	400

Model 103E

Similar to the Model 103 except with automatic ejectors.

NIB	Exc.	V.G.	Good	Fair	Poor
—	1000	800	700	600	500

Model 104X

Case-colored sidelocks with Purdey-type bolting system. Extractor with double radius. Fine double safety sidelocks. Gas relief vents. Articulated trigger. Hard chrome bores. Demi-block barrels of special "Bellota" steel. Black chrome barrels. Produced in 12, 16, and 20 gauge with smaller bores available on special order.

NIB	Exc.	V.G.	Good	Fair	Poor
—	1200	1000	800	700	600

Model 104XE

Same as Model 104X but with Holland automatic selective ejectors.

NIB	Exc.	V.G.	Good	Fair	Poor
—	1350	1100	900	800	700

Model 105X Feather

Same as the Model 104X but with concave rib. Weight in 12 gauge is approximately 6 lbs., 2 oz.

NIB	Exc.	V.G.	Good	Fair	Poor
—	1250	1000	800	700	600

Model 105XE Feather

Same as Model 105X but with Holland automatic selective ejectors.

NIB	Exc.	V.G.	Good	Fair	Poor
—	1400	1250	1000	800	750

Model 502 Feather

Fine sidelock with Purdey-type bolting system. Very fine double safety sidelocks, hand detachable. Gas relief vents. Holland automatic selective ejectors. Articulated trigger. Inside hard chromed demi-block barrels of special "Bellota" steel. Outside Black Chrome finish. Fine English-style scroll engraving. Marble gray or Laurona Imperial finish. Churchill or concave type rib. Weight: 12 gauge is approximately 6.25 lbs. Offered in 12, 16, and 20 gauge.

NIB	Exc.	V.G.	Good	Fair	Poor
—	2200	1800	1600	1500	1400

Model 801 Deluxe

Same as the Model 502 Feather but engraving is a true deluxe Renaissance style. Fully handmade with Imperial finish. First grade walnut stock and forearm.

NIB	Exc.	V.G.	Good	Fair	Poor
—	4400	4000	3750	2750	2250

Model 802 Eagle

Same as the Model 801 Deluxe except highly artistic base relief hand engraving of hunting scenes.

NIB	Exc.	V.G.	Good	Fair	Poor
—	5000	4500	4000	3500	3250

LAW ENFORCEMENT ORDNANCE CORP.

Ridgeway, Pennsylvania

Striker 12

A semi-automatic shotgun designed for self-defense. It is chambered for 12 gauge and has an 18.25" cylinder bored barrel. The unique feature about this gun is its 12-round drum magazine. The barrel is shrouded, and the stock folds. A fixed-stock model is also available. This gun was introduced primarily as a law enforcement tool, and the original models had 12" barrels and were legal for law enforcement agencies and Class 3 licensed individuals only. This shotgun is no longer imported into the U.S. This shotgun is now classified as a Class III weapon and subject to restrictions of the B.A.T.F. Be certain that the particular shotgun is transferable before purchase. If there are any questions contact B.A.T.F. before purchase. Striker 12 shotguns in excellent condition may sell for as much as $1500.

LAZZERONI ARMS COMPANY

Tucson, Arizona

Model 2000ST-F

This model, as with all Lazzeroni models, is chambered for the company's own proprietary calibers. The 6.17 (.243) Spitfire, 6.53 (.257) Scramjet, 6.71 (.264) Phantom, 7.21 (.284) Tomahawk, 7.82 (.308) Patriot, and the 8.59 (.338) Galaxy. Fitted with a 27" match grade barrel with fully adjustable trigger, and removable muzzlebrake. Conventional fiberglass stock.

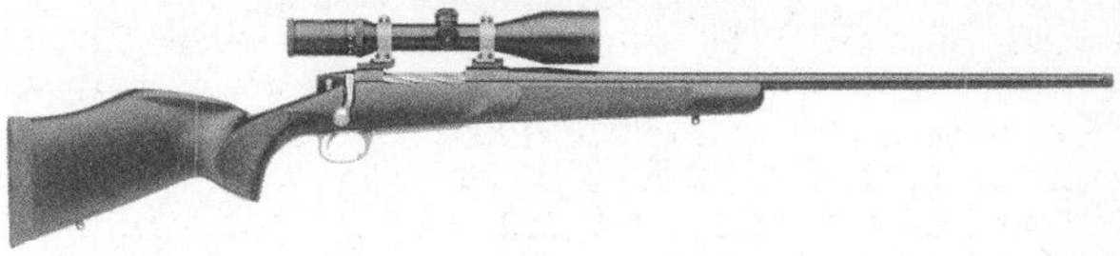

NIB	Exc.	V.G.	Good	Fair	Poor
3700	3000	2200	1500	800	300

Model 2000ST-W

As above but fitted with a conventional black wood laminate stock. No longer offered.

NIB	Exc.	V.G.	Good	Fair	Poor
4800	3900	2700	1750	1000	350

Model 2000ST-FW

As above but fitted with a conventional fiberglass stock and an additional black wood laminate stock. No longer offered.

NIB	Exc.	V.G.	Good	Fair	Poor
5300	4250	3000	2000	1200	500

Model 2000ST-28

This model is a 28" barrel variation of the Model 2000 ST chambered for the 7.82 Warbird cartridge. Introduced in 1999.

NIB	Exc.	V.G.	Good	Fair	Poor
5300	4250	3000	2000	1200	500

Model 2000SLR

This model has a 28" extra-heavy fluted barrel with conventional fiberglass stock. Chambered for the 6.53 Scramjet, 7.21 Firehawk, and the 7.82 Warbird.

NIB	Exc.	V.G.	Good	Fair	Poor
3900	3100	2300	1600	900	400

Model 2000SP-F

This model is fitted with a 23" match grade and Lazzeroni thumbhole fiberglass stock. Chambered for all Lazzeroni calibers.

NIB	Exc.	V.G.	Good	Fair	Poor
3700	3000	2200	1500	800	300

Model 2000SP-W

Same as above but with black wood laminate thumbhole stock. No longer offered.

NIB	Exc.	V.G.	Good	Fair	Poor
4800	3900	2700	1750	1000	350

Model 2000SP-FW

Same as above model but supplied with two stocks: a thumbhole fiberglass stock and a black wood laminate stock. No longer offered.

NIB	Exc.	V.G.	Good	Fair	Poor
5300	4250	3000	2000	1200	500

Model 2000SA

Designed as a lightweight mountain rifle. Chambered for .308, .284, or .338 propriety calibers. Barrel length is 24" and fluted except for .338 caliber. Offered in both right- and left-hand models. Stock has Monte Carlo cheekpiece. Weight is approximately 6.8 lbs.

NIB	Exc.	V.G.	Good	Fair	Poor
4000	3100	2300	1600	900	400

Model 2000DG

Offered in Saturn and Meteor calibers only and fitted with a 24" barrel this rifle weight about 10 lbs. Fibergrain stock finish, removable muzzlebrake, and threaded muzzle protector are standard.

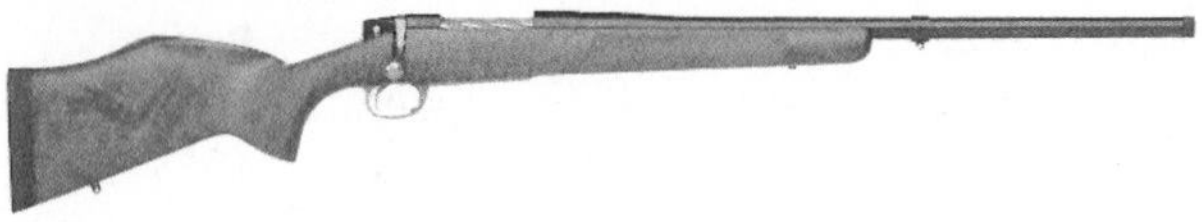

NIB	Exc.	V.G.	Good	Fair	Poor
4400	3500	2700	1850	1050	450

Model 700ST

This rifle is built around a modified Remington 700 action and fitted with a 26" barrel. Chambered for all Lazzeroni long action calibers except Saturn and Meteor. Weight is about 8 lbs. synthetic stock.

NIB	Exc.	V.G.	Good	Fair	Poor
2400	1850	1550	1200	900	200

Swarovski P.H. 3-12x50 Rifle

NIB	Exc.	V.G.	Good	Fair	Poor
1400	1150	925	600	400	150

Savage 16 LZ

Introduced in 2001 this model features a 24" stainless steel barrel, synthetic stock. It is chambered for the 7.82 Patriot and 7.21 Tomahawk cartridges. Weight is approximately 6.8 lbs. Base price is listed.

NIB	Exc.	V.G.	Good	Fair	Poor
900	775	500	375	200	100

Sako TRG-S

This model is fitted with a 26" stainless steel barrel and synthetic stock. It is chambered for the 7.82 Warbird and 7.21 Firebird cartridges. Weight is about 7.9 lbs. Base price is listed.

NIB	Exc.	V.G.	Good	Fair	Poor
1400	1150	925	600	400	150

Model 2005 Global Hunter

Features include a precision CNC-machined 17R stainless steel receiver; stainless steel, match-grade button-barrel; Jewel competition trigger; titanium firing pin; slim line graphite/composite stock; precision-machined aluminum-alloy floorplate/trigger guard assembly; Vais muzzle brake; and Limbsaver\xa8 recoil pad. Base price is listed.

NIB	Exc.	V.G.	Good	Fair	Poor
6900	5900	4700	3250	1500	500

LE FORGERON

Liege, Belgium

Model 6020 Double Rifle

A boxlock-actioned side-by-side rifle that is chambered for the 9.3x74R cartridge. It has 25" barrels with double triggers and automatic ejectors. The finish is blued, and the pistol grip stock is checkered walnut.

NIB	Exc.	V.G.	Good	Fair	Poor
—	6100	4950	4400	3300	1250

Model 6040

Simply the Model 6020 with false sideplates. All other specifications are the same.

NIB	Exc.	V.G.	Good	Fair	Poor
—	6900	5750	4950	3850	1500

Model 6030

A double rifle that has a true sidelock action and is engraved. It has a deluxe French walnut stock.

NIB	Exc.	V.G.	Good	Fair	Poor
—	11000	8800	8000	6100	2000

Boxlock Shotgun

This is a side-by-side, double-barreled shotgun chambered for 20 or 28 gauge. The barrel lengths are optional, as are the choke combinations. This gun has a single-selective trigger and automatic ejectors. It is engraved and blued, with a deluxe French walnut stock.

NIB	Exc.	V.G.	Good	Fair	Poor
—	5500	4400	3600	2500	1000

NOTE: False sideplates add 20 percent.

Sidelock Shotgun

Has similar specifications to the boxlock except that it has a true sidelock action and is generally more deluxe in materials and workmanship.

NIB	Exc.	V.G.	Good	Fair	Poor
—	13000	12000	9350	7250	2500

LE MAT
Paris, France

LeMat Revolving Carbine

Chambered for the centerfire, rimfire cartridges, or percussion. Barrel are half round half octagon and 20" in length. Chambered for a variaty of calibers but in percussion usually .42 caliber with a .62 caliber smoothbore lower barrel.

Courtesy Little John's Auction Service, Inc., Paul Goodwin photo

NIB	Exc.	V.G.	Good	Fair	Poor
—	—	31500	25000	11000	3000

LEBEAU COURALLY
Liege, Belgium

This company has been in business since 1865 and has made more guns for royalty than any other gun company in the world. The prices listed are for guns without engraving. There are other extra-cost options that will affect price. All guns are built to order, and there is virtually no upper end for the values for these infrequently-encountered guns. Values are certainly well in excess of $30,000 for any model in Very Good or better condition.

LEE FIREARMS CO.
Milwaukee, Wisconsin

Lee Single-Shot Carbine

A rare single-shot break-open carbine that pivots to the right side for loading. It is chambered for the .44 rimfire cartridge and has a 21.5" barrel with a hammer mounted in the center of the frame. The carbine has a walnut buttstock but no forearm and is marked "Lee's Firearms Co. Milwaukee, Wisc." There were approximately 450 manufactured between 1863 and 1865. There are few surviving examples, and one should be wary of fakes.

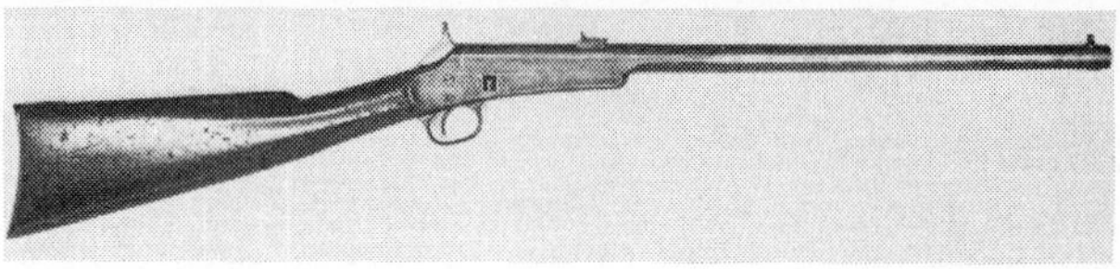

Courtesy Milwaukee Public Museum, Milwaukee, Wisconsin

NIB	Exc.	V.G.	Good	Fair	Poor
—	—	6500	2200	900	400

Lee Sporting Rifle

Similar to the military carbine except that it has a longer octagonal barrel. The barrel length was varied, and there were more of these manufactured. The survival rate appears to have been better than for the carbine model.

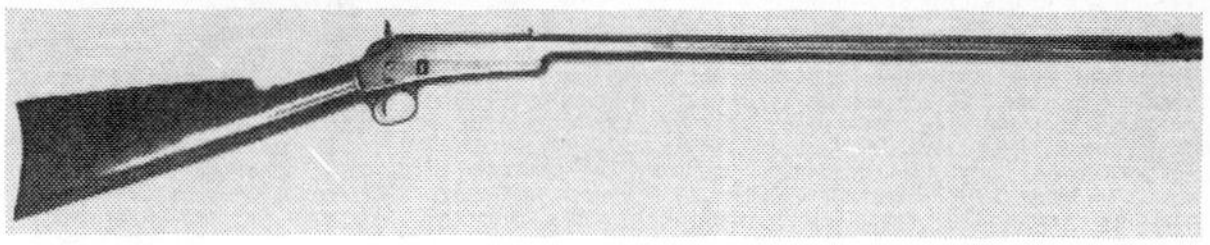

Courtesy Milwaukee Public Museum, Milwaukee, Wisconsin

NIB	Exc.	V.G.	Good	Fair	Poor
—	—	1750	700	300	150

LEFEVER ARMS CO.
Syracuse, New York

Founded by Dan Lefever, who was a pioneer in the field of breech-loading firearms. This company was founded in 1884, with Lefever as the president. He was referred to as "Uncle Dan" within the firearms industry. He was responsible for many improvements in the double-barrel shotgun design. He developed the automatic hammerless system in the late 1880s. He also developed a compensating action that allowed simple adjustments to compensate for action wear. In 1901 he was forced out of the company and organized another company—the D.M. Lefever, Sons & Company—also in Syracuse. Dan Lefever died in 1906, and his new company went out of business. The original company was acquired by Ithaca in 1916. They continued to produce Lefever guns until 1948.

SIDEPLATED SHOTGUN

A double-barrel, side-by-side shotgun chambered for 10, 12, 16, or 20 gauge. It was offered with 26", 28", 30", or 32" barrels with various choke combinations. The barrels are either Damascus or fluid steel. Damascus guns have become collectible and in better condition—very good to excellent—can bring nearly the same price as the fluid-steel guns. It features a fractional sidelock because the hammers were mounted in the frame and the sears and cocking indicators were mounted on the sideplates. After serial number 25,000, the entire locking mechanism was frame mounted and only the cocking indicators remained on the side plates. Double triggers are standard. The finish is blued, with a checkered walnut stock. There are a number of variations that differ in the amount of ornamentation and the quality of materials and workmanship utilized in their construction. Automatic ejectors are represented by the letter "E" after the respective grade designation. This shotgun was manufactured between 1885 and 1919. We strongly recommend that a qualified appraisal be secured if a transaction is contemplated. There was also an Optimus Grade and a Thousand Dollar Grade offered. These are extremely high-grade, heavily ornamented firearms inlaid with precious metals. They are extremely rare, and evaluating them on a general basis is impossible.

H Grade

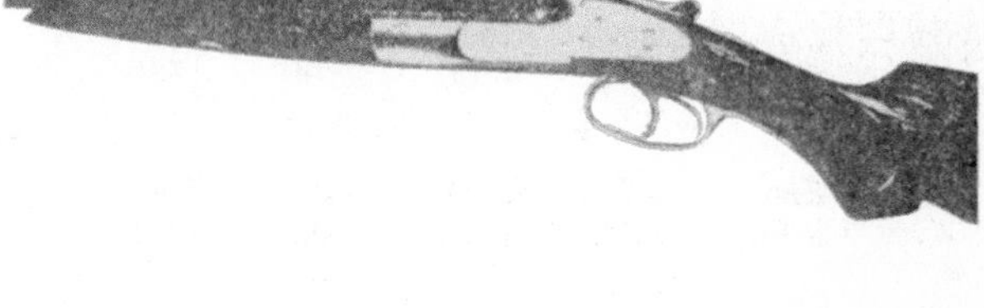

NIB	Exc.	V.G.	Good	Fair	Poor
—	1600	1250	950	550	350

HE Grade

NIB	Exc.	V.G.	Good	Fair	Poor
—	2400	1900	1550	900	650

G Grade

NIB	Exc.	V.G.	Good	Fair	Poor
—	1900	1500	1200	700	425

GE Grade

NIB	Exc.	V.G.	Good	Fair	Poor
—	2800	2150	1800	1000	650

F Grade

NIB	Exc.	V.G.	Good	Fair	Poor
—	2400	1900	1550	900	650

FE Grade

NIB	Exc.	V.G.	Good	Fair	Poor
—	3400	2650	2200	1300	800

E Grade

NIB	Exc.	V.G.	Good	Fair	Poor
—	3700	2950	2400	1400	900

EE Grade

Courtesy Rock Island Auction Company

NIB	Exc.	V.G.	Good	Fair	Poor
—	4800	3850	3100	1850	1150

D Grade

NIB	Exc.	V.G.	Good	Fair	Poor
—	4700	3650	3000	1800	1100

DS Grade

NIB	Exc.	V.G.	Good	Fair	Poor
—	1450	1150	900	500	300

DE Grade

Courtesy Rock Island Auction Company

NIB	Exc.	V.G.	Good	Fair	Poor
—	7250	5750	4600	2800	1750

DSE Grade

NIB	Exc.	V.G.	Good	Fair	Poor
—	1750	1400	1150	700	500

C Grade

NIB	Exc.	V.G.	Good	Fair	Poor
—	6250	4950	4200	2400	1500

CE Grade

NIB	Exc.	V.G.	Good	Fair	Poor
—	8750	6950	5650	3400	2100

B Grade

NIB	Exc.	V.G.	Good	Fair	Poor
—	8250	6550	5300	3200	2000

BE Grade

NIB	Exc.	V.G.	Good	Fair	Poor
—	10250	8150	6600	4000	2500

A Grade

NIB	Exc.	V.G.	Good	Fair	Poor
—	15250	12150	10100	6000	3700

AA Grade

NIB	Exc.	V.G.	Good	Fair	Poor
—	20400	16200	13200	8000	5000

NOTE: For all models listed: 20 gauge add 25 percent. Single-selective trigger add 10 percent.

LEFEVER ARMS COMPANY, INC. (ITHACA)

During 1916, the Ithaca Gun company purchased the gunmaking assets of the Syracuse, New York based, Lefever Arms Company. Between then and World War I, they continued to manufacture the same sideplate gun that had been made in Syracuse until about 1919 when they were discontinued. Prices for those guns are listed above. During 1921, Ithaca Gun Company, under the name the Lefever Arms Company, Inc., introduced a line of lower costs, boxlock guns. Eventually, six different models were produced. Ithaca's Lefever guns were produced in 12, 16, and 20 gauges, and in .410 bore. Twenty gauge guns often command a price premium of 50 percent; a .410 bore gun may command up to a 200 percent premium.

Nitro Special

A side-by-side, double-barrel shotgun chambered for 12, 16, or 20 gauge, as well as .410. The barrels were offered in lengths of 26" to 32" with various choke combinations. It features a boxlock action with double triggers and extractors standard. The finish is blued, with a case-colored receiver and a checkered walnut stock. This model was manufactured between 1921 and 1948 and, incredible as it may seem, its price at introduction was $29. Add 100+ percent for .410.

NIB	Exc.	V.G.	Good	Fair	Poor
—	600	400	250	200	100

NOTE: Single-selective trigger add $100. Automatic ejectors add $200.

Long Range Single-Barrel Trap and Field (Model 2)

Manufactured from 1927 to 1947, the Model 2 was a single-barrel gun with no rib. Like the Nitro Special, it had walnut stocks that were line cut checkered at the grip area of the buttstock and on the forend.

NIB	Exc.	V.G.	Good	Fair	Poor
—	500	300	200	100	100

Single-Barrel Trap Ventilated Rib (Model 3)

Manufactured from 1927 to 1942, the Model 3 was a single-barrel gun with the same ventilated rib that was used on the "Knick" trap gun. The walnut stocks had line cut checkering at the grip area of the buttstock and on the forend.

NIB	Exc.	V.G.	Good	Fair	Poor
—	1200	500	250	100	100

Double-Barrel Ventilated Rib Trap (Model 4)

Manufactured during 1929 but catalogued until 1939, the Model 4 was a double-barrel gun with a ventilated rib barrel. The walnut stocks had line cut checkering at the grip area of the buttstock and on the beavertail forend. Only about 200 units were produced.

NIB	Exc.	V.G.	Good	Fair	Poor
—	2000	1200	1000	700	100

A Grade (Model 5)

Manufactured from 1936 to 1939, the A Grade was a double-barreled gun. The walnut stocks had pointed checkering cut at the grip area of the buttstock and on the splinter forend. A line engraving outlined its nicely sculptured frame.

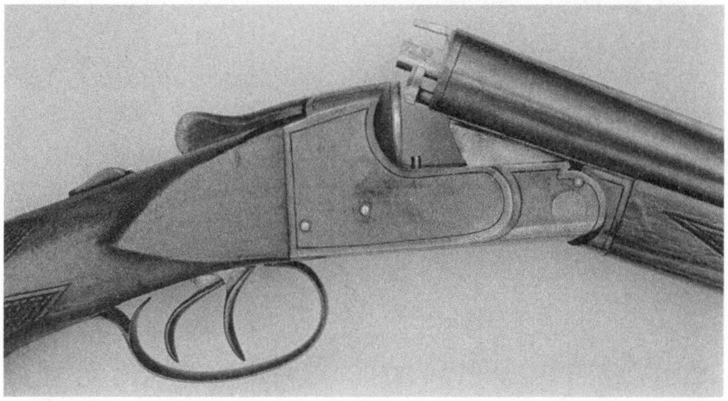

Photo by Walter C. Snyder

NIB	Exc.	V.G.	Good	Fair	Poor
—	900	600	400	300	100

NOTE: Single trigger add $200, automatic ejectors add $200, beavertail forend add $300.

Skeet Special (Model 6)

Manufactured from 1936 to 1939, the A Grade was a double-barreled gun. The walnut stocks had pointed checkering cut at the grip area of the buttstock and on the beavertail forend. A beavertail forend, single trigger, automatic ejectors, a recoil pad, and ivory center and front sight were standard. The frame was sculptured and line engraved like the Model 5.

NIB	Exc.	V.G.	Good	Fair	Poor
—	1500	1200	1000	400	100

LEFEVER, D. M., SONS & COMPANY

Syracuse, New York

"Uncle Dan" Lefever founded the Lefever Arms Company in 1884. In 1901 he was forced out of his company and founded the D.M. Lefever, Sons & Company. He continued to produce high-grade, side-by-side shotguns, but of a totally new boxlock design. There were approximately 1,200 shotguns of all variations produced during this period, making them extremely rare and difficult to evaluate on a general basis. We list the models and average values but strongly suggest securing qualified appraisal if a transaction is contemplated.

LEFEVER DOUBLE-BARREL SHOTGUN

A side-by-side, double-barrel shotgun chambered for 12, 16, or 20 gauge. It was offered with various-length barrels and choke combinations that were made to order. It features double triggers and automatic ejectors. A single-selective trigger was available as an option. The finish is blued, with a checkered walnut stock. The individual grades differ in the amount of ornamentation and the general quality of the materials and workmanship utilized in their construction. This model was discontinued in 1906.There are an "Optimus" and an "Uncle Dan" grade, which are top-of-the-line models, that features extremely high quality in materials and workmanship and a great deal of ornamentation. This firearm is extremely rare and seldom found in today's market. It is impossible to evaluate it on a general basis.

O Excelsior Grade—Extractors

NIB	Exc.	V.G.	Good	Fair	Poor
—	2750	2200	1750	950	700

Excelsior Grade—Auto Ejectors

NIB	Exc.	V.G.	Good	Fair	Poor
—	3250	2700	2100	1250	900

F Grade, No. 9

NIB	Exc.	V.G.	Good	Fair	Poor
—	3250	2950	2350	1500	1100

E Grade, No. 8

NIB	Exc.	V.G.	Good	Fair	Poor
—	4300	3700	3200	2400	1700

D Grade, No. 7

NIB	Exc.	V.G.	Good	Fair	Poor
—	4800	4100	3550	2750	2000

C Grade, No. 6

NIB	Exc.	V.G.	Good	Fair	Poor
—	5400	4750	3850	3000	2500

B Grade, No. 5

NIB	Exc.	V.G.	Good	Fair	Poor
—	6900	6000	4950	3500	3000

AA Grade, No. 4

NIB	Exc.	V.G.	Good	Fair	Poor
—	9500	8200	6750	4200	2750

NOTE: For all models listed: 20 gauge add 50 percent. Single-selective trigger add 25 percent.

LEMAN, H. E.

Lancaster, Pennsylvania

Leman Militia Rifle

A .58 caliber percussion muzzleloader that has a 33" round barrel. The stock is full-length and is held on by two barrel bands. There is a ramrod mounted under the barrel. The trim is brass; and the barrel is browned, with a case-colored lock. The lock is marked "H.E.Leman/Lancaster, Pa." There were approximately 500 manufactured between 1860 and 1864. They are believed to have been used by the Pennsylvania State Militia in the Civil War.

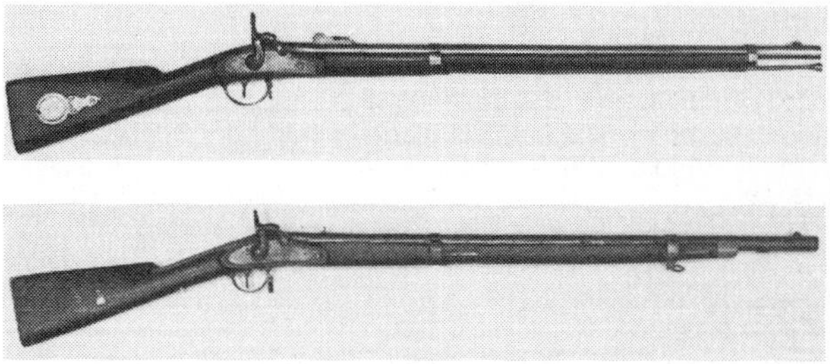

Courtesy Milwaukee Public Museum, Milwaukee, Wisconsin

NIB	Exc.	V.G.	Good	Fair	Poor
—	—	4750	2000	750	300

LIEGEOISE D ARMES

Liege, Belgium

Side-by-Side Boxlock Shotgun

This double-barreled gun is chambered for 12 and 20 gauge. The barrels are 28" or 30" in length, and the choke combinations are varied. It has a single trigger and automatic ejectors. The action is moderately engraved; and the finish is blued, with a checkered walnut stock.

NIB	Exc.	V.G.	Good	Fair	Poor
—	900	700	500	400	200

LINS, A. F.
Philadelphia, Pennsylvania

Rifled Musket

A single-shot, muzzleloading, percussion rifle chambered for .58 caliber. It has a 39" barrel and a full-length walnut stock held on by three barrel bands. There is an iron ramrod mounted under the barrel. The mountings are iron, and there is a bayonet lug combined with the front sight. The lock is marked "A. Fred. Lins/ Philada." This is a rare weapon that was used by Union forces in the Civil War. There were approximately 200 manufactured in 1861 and 1862.

Courtesy Milwaukee Public Museum, Milwaukee, Wisconsin

NIB	Exc.	V.G.	Good	Fair	Poor
—	—	5500	2000	825	300

LITTLE SHARPS RIFLE MFG. CO.
Big Sandy, Montana

Little Sharps Rifle

This hand-built reproduction of the single-shot Sharps rifle is 20 percent smaller than the original. Chambered for a wide variety of calibers from .22 Long Rifle to .375 LSR. A number of extra cost options are available for this rifle. The price listed is for the basic model.

NIB	Exc.	V.G.	Good	Fair	Poor
3250	2750	2000	1500	900	500

LJUTIC INDUSTRIES
Yakima, Washington

Bi-Matic Semi-Automatic

A custom-built, gas-operated, semi-automatic shotgun that is known for its low level of felt recoil. It is chambered for 12 gauge and has 26" to 32" barrels choked for either skeet or trap. The stock specifications are to the customer's order. Add 15 percent for interchangeable chokes.

NIB	Exc.	V.G.	Good	Fair	Poor
2750	2100	1300	800	400	200

Dynatrap Single-Barrel

A single-shot trap gun chambered for 12 gauge. It has a 33" vent rib full-choke barrel and features a push-button opener and a manual extractor. The stock is made to trap specifications. There are many options that affect the value.

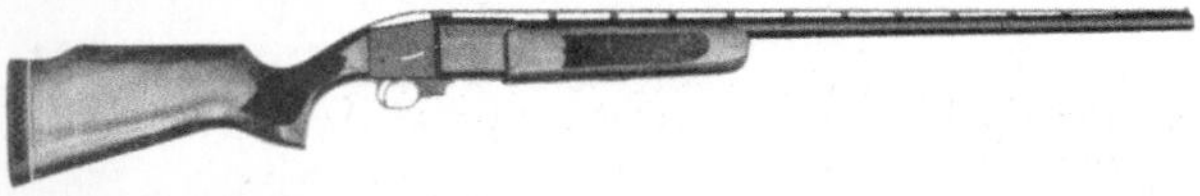

NIB	Exc.	V.G.	Good	Fair	Poor
2500	1500	1000	800	400	200

Model X-73 Single-Barrel

Similar features to the Dynatrap, with a high competition rib. Appraisal is recommended. Add 15 percent for interchangeable chokes.

NIB	Exc.	V.G.	Good	Fair	Poor
2750	2100	1300	800	400	200

Mono Gun Single-Barrel

Chambered for 12 gauge and has a 34" vent rib barrel. It is essentially a custom-order proposition that is available with a standard, as well as a release, trigger. There are many value-affecting options available. Add 15 percent for interchangeable chokes.

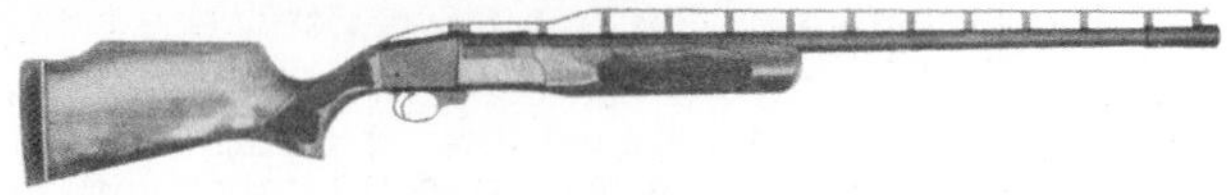

NIB	Exc.	V.G.	Good	Fair	Poor
2750	2100	1300	800	400	200

LTX Model

A deluxe version of the Mono Gun with a 33" medium-height vent rib and a high-grade walnut stock with fine hand checkering. Options raise values drastically. 27502100130080040020

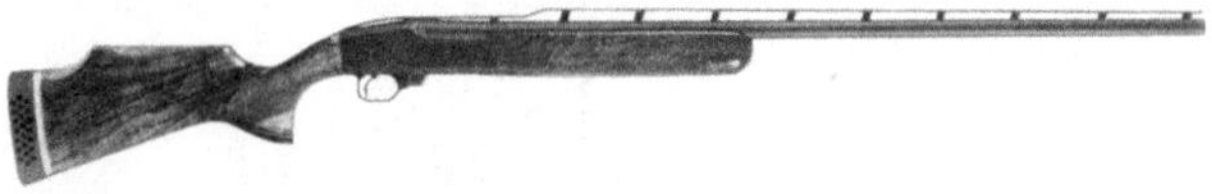

NIB	Exc.	V.G.	Good	Fair	Poor
3000	2250	1600	1300	800	200

Space Gun

A unique single-barrel gun chambered for 12 gauge, with trap choking. It has a stock and forearm that reminds one of a crutch in appearance but which allows the shooter to have in-line control with little felt recoil. The barrel, forearm, and stock are all on one line. There is a recoil pad and a high ventilated rib.

NIB	Exc.	V.G.	Good	Fair	Poor
3750	3000	2250	1500	900	200

Bi-Gun Over-and-Under

An over-and-under double chambered for 12 gauge. It has 30" or 32" vent ribbed barrels that are separated. The choking is to trap specifications, and the stock is deluxe hand-checkered walnut.

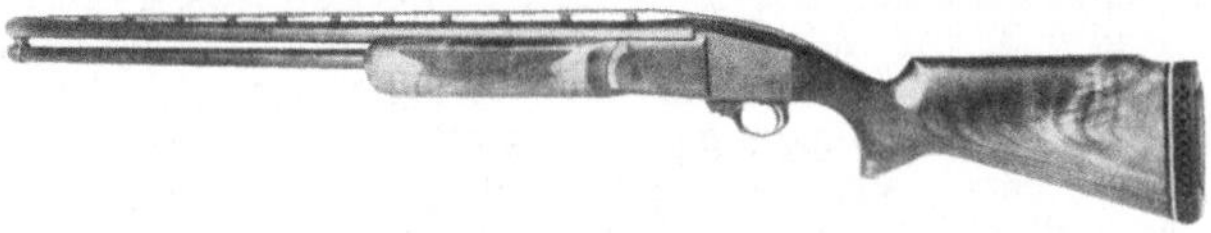

NIB	Exc.	V.G.	Good	Fair	Poor
7250	6000	4000	1000	600	200

Bi-Gun Combo

The over-and-under Bi-Gun supplied with a high ribbed single-barrel in addition to the separated over-and-under barrels.

NIB	Exc.	V.G.	Good	Fair	Poor
10000	7000	4000	2000	1000	200

LM-6 Super Deluxe

This is a custom-built over-and-under gun made to the customer's specifications. Available in 12 gauge with barrel lengths from 28" to 34". All other specifications are custom. .

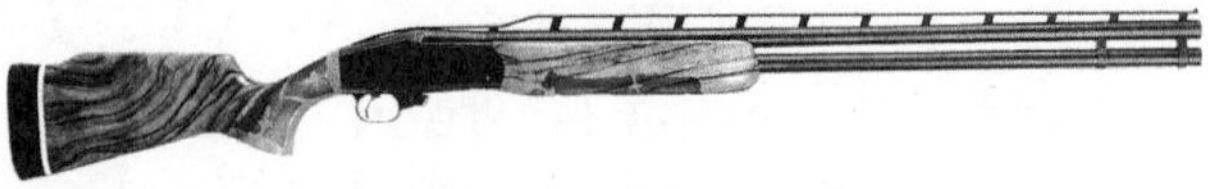

NIB	Exc.	V.G.	Good	Fair	Poor
7750	6800	5750	4000	1600	200

NOTE: Extra single-barrel add $7,000.

LONDON ARMOURY COMPANY
London

This firm was established in 1856, by Robert Adams. In addition to marketing revolvers based upon Adams' designs, the London Armoury Company were major retailers of other arms, particularly Enfield Pattern 53 Percussion Rifles. During the 1870s, the

London Armoury distributed Colt pistols. During its business life, the London Armoury Company was located at these addresses:

Henry Street	1857-1863
36 King William Street	1864-1868
54 King William Street	1868-1883
118 Queen Victoria Street	1884-1886
114 Queen Victoria Street	1887-1905
1 Lawrence Pounty Hill	1905-1910
31 Bury Street, St. James	1910-1939
10 Ryder Street, St. James	1940-1950

Although the firm continued in business after 1950, its operations were restricted to the trade of used arms.

LONE STAR RIFLE COMPANY

Conroe, Texas

This company builds custom blackpowder rifles. They are built on the rolling block design and are offered in two basic configurations. There are a wide number of options that will affect the price of these rifles.

Sporting Rifle

This is a basic configuration that features a straight grip stock with semi-crescent butt. Offered in a wide variety of calibers from .32-40 to .50-90. Barrel lengths, barrel configurations, wood, triggers, sights, engraving, finishes, hammers, and accessories will greatly affect the final price.Basic retail price: $2195.

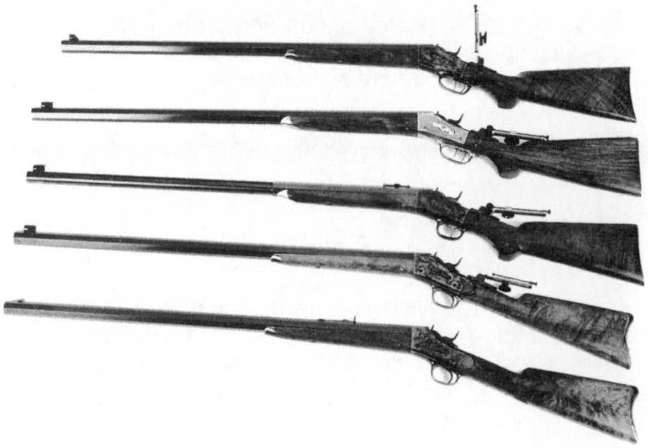

Target Rifle

This is a basic configuration that features a straight grip stock with semi-crescent butt. Offered in a wide variety of calibers from .32-40 to .50-90. Barrel lengths, barrel configurations, wood, triggers, sights, engraving, finishes, hammers, and accessories will greatly affect the final price.Basic retail price: $2195.

LUNA

Zella-Mehlis, Germany

Target Rifle

A .22 or .22 Hornet caliber Martini action single-shot rifle with a 20" barrel, adjustable sights, and walnut stock. Manufactured prior to WWII.

NIB	Exc.	V.G.	Good	Fair	Poor
—	1800	1350	850	500	250

LYMAN

Middletown, Connecticut

Lyman In-Line

Introduced in 1998 this in-line muzzleloader is offered in either .50 or .54 caliber. Fitted with a 22" barrel. Hardwood stock. Add $80 for stainless steel version.

NIB	Exc.	V.G.	Good	Fair	Poor
300	250	200	125	75	50

Deerstalker Rifle

Available in either .50 or .54 caliber percussion or flintlock. Fitted with a 24" barrel and hardwood stock. A stainless steel version is also offered for an additional $80.

NIB	Exc.	V.G.	Good	Fair	Poor
375	250	200	150	100	50

Deerstalker Carbine

Same as above but with 21" barrel. Offered in .50 caliber only.

NIB	Exc.	V.G.	Good	Fair	Poor
375	250	200	150	100	50

Great Plains Rifle

This rifle is offered in .50 or .54 caliber flint or percussion. Barrel length is 32". Hardwood stock.

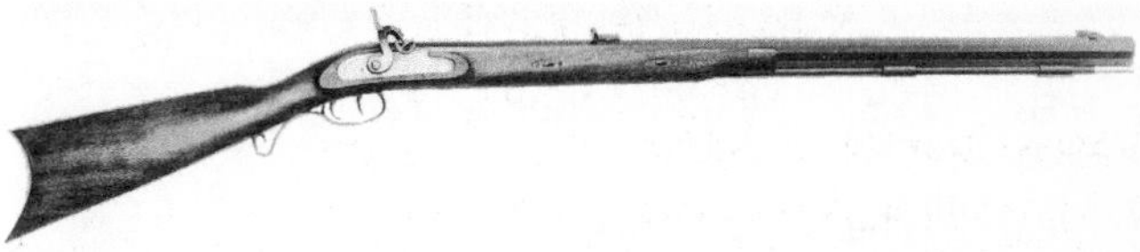

NIB	Exc.	V.G.	Good	Fair	Poor
525	400	300	175	125	100

NOTE: Add $25 for flintlock version and $10 for left-hand rifles. Early models in Excellent condition are showing significant collector potential.

Trade Rifle

This rifle is offered in either .50 or .54 caliber with 28" octagonal barrel and hardwood stock. Polished brass furniture. Add $25 for flintlock rifle.

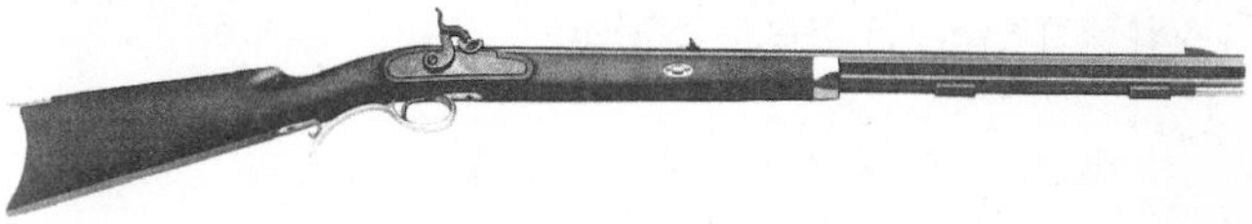

NIB	Exc.	V.G.	Good	Fair	Poor
300	250	200	125	75	50

M

M.O.A. CORP.
Dayton, Ohio

Carbine

As above with an 18" barrel. Discontinued.

NIB	Exc.	V.G.	Good	Fair	Poor
1000	675	525	350	275	150

MADSEN
Copenhagen, Denmark

Model 47

NIB	Exc.	V.G.	Good	Fair	Poor
—	700	525	400	275	125

MAGNUM RESEARCH, INC.
Minneapolis, Minnesota

SEE ALSO—Desert Eagle

MagnumLite Graphite Rifle

Bolt action rifle built on Remington or Sako action with H-S Precision or Hogue stock. Chambered in .22-250, .223, 7mm Rem. Mag., .280, or .30-06.

NIB	Exc.	V.G.	Good	Fair	Poor
2300	1650	1295	600	300	150

MagnumLite MLR-1722 Rifle

Semi-auto rimfire rifle with graphite barrel and black Hogue overmolded stock. 10-shot rotary magazine.

NIB	Exc.	V.G.	Good	Fair	Poor
665	525	400	250	175	100

MagnumLite MLR-1722 .17 Mach-2 Rifle

Similar to above but chambered in .17 Mach-2.

NIB	Exc.	V.G.	Good	Fair	Poor
665	525	400	250	175	100

MagnumLite MLR-1722 .22 WMR Graphite Rifle

Semi-auto rimfire rifle with graphite barrel and skeletonized laminated stock with thumbhole in a variety of laminate colors. Chambered in .22 WMR.

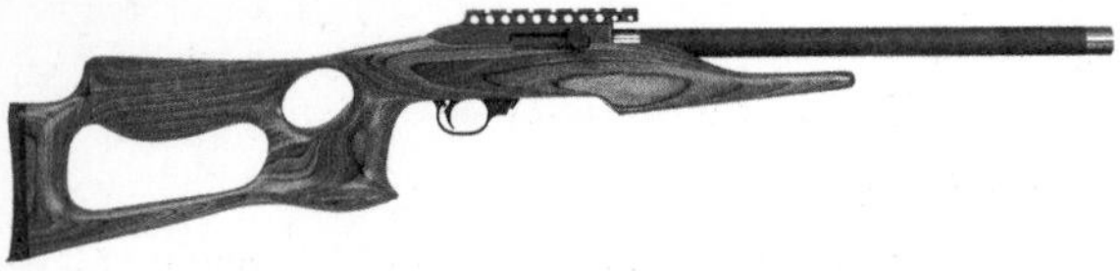

NIB	Exc.	V.G.	Good	Fair	Poor
765	600	450	250	175	100

MagnumLite MLR-1722 .17 HMR Graphite Rifle

Similar to above but with conventional Hogue overmolded stock. Chamberd in 17 HMR.

NIB	Exc.	V.G.	Good	Fair	Poor
765	600	450	250	175	100

MagnumLite MLR-1722 .17 HMR Stainless Steel Rifle

Similar to above but with stainless steel receiver and barrel.

NIB	Exc.	V.G.	Good	Fair	Poor
665	525	400	250	175	100

MALIN, F. E.
London, England

Boxlock and sidelock shotguns made by Malin were imported into the United States for a number of years. As these arms were all essentially built to specific customer's requirements, standard values cannot be provided.

Boxlock Basic Model

Features an Anson & Deeley action and high-grade walnut. All other specification were on a custom-order basis. This gun should definitely be individually appraised as values will fluctuate greatly with options.

NIB	Exc.	V.G.	Good	Fair	Poor
4800	4000	3500	2500	1850	1000

NOTE: Estimated value only.

Sidelock Basic Model

Features a Holland & Holland-type detachable sidelock action, and all other features (as on the boxlock) were on a custom-order basis. This model should also be appraised individually.

NIB	Exc.	V.G.	Good	Fair	Poor
7000	6000	4750	3000	2500	1250

NOTE: Estimated value only.

MANNLICHER SCHOENAUER
Steyr, Austria

NOTE: For military models and their history, technical data, descriptions, and prices see the Standard Catalog of Military Firearms under Austria-Hungary. For currently imported Mannlicher models, see Steyr.

Model 1903 Carbine

A 6.5x54mm caliber bolt-action rifle with a 17.7" barrel. Rotary magazine capacity is 5 rounds. Folding rear leaf sight, double set triggers, and full-length walnut stock. Discontinued prior to WWII.

NIB	Exc.	V.G.	Good	Fair	Poor
—	2200	1650	1300	1000	550

Model 1905 Carbine

As above but chambered for the 9x56mm cartridge. Discontinued prior to WWII.

NIB	Exc.	V.G.	Good	Fair	Poor
—	1850	1500	1000	750	550

Model 1908 Carbine

As above but chambered for the 7x57mm or 8x56mm cartridge. Discontinued prior to WWII.

NIB	Exc.	V.G.	Good	Fair	Poor
—	1950	1600	1000	750	550

Model 1910 Carbine

As above but chambered for the 9.5x57mm cartridge. Discontinued prior to WWII.

NIB	Exc.	V.G.	Good	Fair	Poor
—	1850	1500	1000	750	550

Model 1924 Carbine

As above but chambered for the .30-06 cartridge. Discontinued prior to WWII.

NIB	Exc.	V.G.	Good	Fair	Poor
—	2750	2250	1750	1000	550

High Velocity Rifle

As above, but in 7x64mm Brenneke, .30-06, 8x60Smm Magnum, 9.3x62mm, and the 10.75x68mm caliber with a 23.5" barrel and folding leaf sight. Half-length walnut stock. Discontinued prior to WWII.

NIB	Exc.	V.G.	Good	Fair	Poor
—	2750	2250	1750	1000	550

NOTE: Takedown Model add 75 percent.

Model 1950

A .257 Roberts, .270 Winchester, and .30-06 caliber bolt-action rifle with a 24" barrel and 5-shot rotary magazine. Blued with a half length walnut stock. Manufactured between 1950 and 1952.

NIB	Exc.	V.G.	Good	Fair	Poor
—	1600	1250	800	650	450

Model 1950 Carbine

As above, with a 20" barrel and a full-length stock.

NIB	Exc.	V.G.	Good	Fair	Poor
—	1600	1250	800	650	450

Model 1950 6.5 Carbine

As above, in 6.5x54mm Mannlicher Schoenauer caliber with a 18.5" barrel and full-length stock.

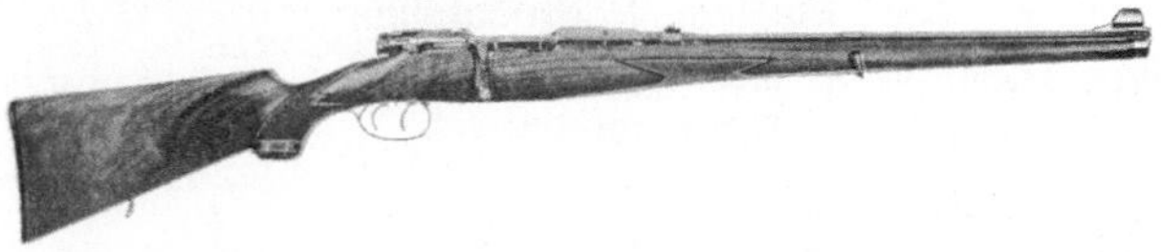

NIB	Exc.	V.G.	Good	Fair	Poor
—	1650	1200	850	650	300

Model 1952

Similar to the above, with a turned back bold handle. Manufactured between 1952 and 1956.

NIB	Exc.	V.G.	Good	Fair	Poor
—	2100	1850	1300	650	300

Model 1952 Carbine

Similar to the Model 1950 carbine, but additionally in 7x57mm caliber. Manufactured between 1952 and 1956.

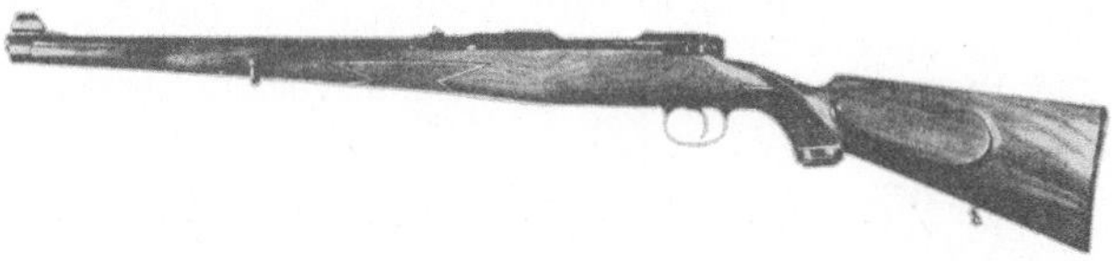

NIB	Exc.	V.G.	Good	Fair	Poor
—	2100	1850	1300	650	300

Model 1952 6.5mm Carbine

As above, in 6.5x54mm Mannlicher Schoenauer caliber with an 18.5" barrel. Manufactured between 1952 and 1956.

NIB	Exc.	V.G.	Good	Fair	Poor
—	1850	1500	850	650	300

Model 1956 Rifle

A .243 or .30-06 caliber bolt-action rifle with a 22" barrel and Monte Carlo-style stock. Manufactured between 1956 and 1960.

NIB	Exc.	V.G.	Good	Fair	Poor
—	2100	1700	950	650	300

Model 1956 Carbine

As above, with a 20" barrel and full-length stock. Manufactured between 1956 and 1960.

NIB	Exc.	V.G.	Good	Fair	Poor
—	2100	1700	950	650	300

Model 1961 MCA Rifle

As above, but modified for easier use with a telescopic sight.

NIB	Exc.	V.G.	Good	Fair	Poor
—	1550	1250	1000	800	650

Model 1961 MCA Carbine

As above, with a 20" barrel and half-length stock.

NIB	Exc.	V.G.	Good	Fair	Poor
—	1550	1250	1100	700	600

Model M72 LM Rifle

Fitted with a 23" fluted barrel, double set or single trigger and full-length stock. Manufactured between 1972 and 1980.

NIB	Exc.	V.G.	Good	Fair	Poor
—	1300	1050	700	550	450

MARATHON PRODUCTS, INC.

Santa Barbara, California

.22 First Shot

A .22 caliber single-shot bolt-action rifle with a 16.5" barrel and overall length of 31". Blued with a walnut stock. Manufactured between 1985 and 1987.

NIB	Exc.	V.G.	Good	Fair	Poor
—	75	55	45	30	25

.22 Super Shot

As above, with a 24" barrel. Manufactured between 1985 and 1987.

NIB	Exc.	V.G.	Good	Fair	Poor
—	75	55	45	30	25

Centerfire Rifle

A bolt-action sporting rifle manufactured in a variety of calibers with a 24" barrel, open sights, adjustable trigger and 5-shot magazine. Blued with a walnut stock. Manufactured in 1985 and 1986.

NIB	Exc.	V.G.	Good	Fair	Poor
—	325	250	200	150	125

MARBLE'S ARMS & MFG. CO.

Gladstone, Michigan

Marble's Game Getter Gun NFA, curio or relic

Marble's suspended sales of the Game Getter in the United States after the Treasury Department ruled it was a "firearm" under the NFA, but continued sales abroad. Its retail price in 1934 was about $24 (12" or 15" barrels) to $26 (18" barrels). The Bureau of Internal Revenue removed the 18" barrel variation from the NFA in a Letter Ruling dated March 1, 1939. Today, the 12" and 15" barrel variations are controlled under the NFA in the "any other weapon" category. If the shoulder stock is removed from a 12", 15", or 18" barreled Game Getter, however, ATF has ruled it to be an NFA "firearm" subject to a $200 transfer tax.

Model 1908

Serial numbered from A to M; then 001 to 10000.

NIB	Exc.	V.G.	Good	Fair	Poor
—	1800	1200	750	550	425

Model 1921

RIGHT SIDE:

Calibers 22 & 44 Calibers 22 & 44
Patent Allowed Patent Allowed

Each of the markings on the right side is enclosed within an elongated circle.

OTHER CHARACTERISTICS:

Separate flat buttplate attached with two screws up to approximately serial number 1200; afterwards, a flattened buttplate was integrally formed from the same round steel used to form the skeleton stock. Early stocks have drop adjustment with a knurled collar 3/8" diameter by 13/16" long; at approximately serial number 2500, the collar was changed to 1/2" by 5/8" long. The hammer spur is curved down up to approximately serial number 2,000, then the curve at hammer is up.The Model 1908 was originally designed for .22 short, long or LR and .44 shot and ball ammunition, but the most satisfactory load was the long-cased .44-40 that held the shot in place with a disk and mouth crimp. The 1915 Marble's catalog stated the Model 1908 was available for use with the 2" .410 shotgun shell; chambering is slightly different from that of the .44-40, but is seldom encountered.Production of the Model 1908 was not resumed because of World War I. To meet the continuing demand for this extremely popular firearm, Marble's produced an entirely new gun in 1921. The grip, folding stock (made from cold-rolled sheet metal and nickel-plated), and other features were redesigned. The serial number range for the Model 1921 is 10001 (shipped in October 1921) to 20076. Most production of the Model 1921 apparently ended around the time of World War II; however, factory records disclose that Marble's was exporting 15" barrel Model 1921s into Canada in 1955, where their registration was not required at that time. Marble's also assembled approximately 200 Model 1921s from parts circa 1960-61, and sold them (without the holster) for $200 each.The Model 1921 was originally designed from the 2" .410 shotgun shell, but Marble's changed the extractor marking on some guns to 2-1/2" or 2 1/2" to indicate factory rechambering for the 2.5" shell, which has been reported to have started in 1924. However, the change to a 2-1/2" chamber may not have been uniform, because both 2" and 2-1/2" marked guns have been observed in low (14000) and high (19000) serial number ranges. The lowest serial number with 2" marking observed so far is 14601. The range from approximately 14500 to 17000 have plastic rather than walnut grips, a single-bladed rear sight rather than multiple-blade, and blued rather than case-hardened hammer. Outside this range, only 19288 has the 2" marking; and number 19692 is marked 2-1/2". No Model 1921 Game Getters are known to have been factory chambered for the 3" .410 shell.The markings on the Model 1921 are:

LEFT SIDE:

Marble'S Game Getter Gun Marble Arms & Mfg.Co.
Gladstone, Mich.U.S.A.

RIGHT SIDE:

UPPER BARREL 22 S.L. LR.&N.R.A
LOWER BARREL .44GG & .410 2"OTHER

CHARACTERISTICS:

Other barrel markings for the Model 1921 in .410 are .410 2-1/2" and .410 2-1/2"; the latter appears in the serial number range from approximately 15000 to 16600, and in the low 19000 range. Plastic grips were used in the serial range from approximately 14600 to 17000.The Model 1921 was originally designed for the 2" .410 shotgun shell, but Marble's changed the extractor marking on some guns to 2-1/2" or 2-1/2" to indicate factory rechambering for the 2.5" shell, apparently on a random or special-order basis (both 2" and 2-1/2" marked guns have been observed in low (14000) and high (19000) serial number ranges). The lowest serial number with 2?" marking observed so far is 14601. The range from approximately 14500 to 17000 have plastic rather than walnut grips, single-bladed rear sight rather than multiple-blades, and blued rather than case hardened hammer. Outside this range, only 19288 has the 2?" marking; number 19692 is marked 2-1/2". No Model 1921 Game Getters are known to have been factory chambered for the 3" .410 shell.

NIB	Exc.	V.G.	Good	Fair	Poor
—	1800	1200	750	550	425

NOTE: Boxed guns (wooden box, Model 1908; cardboard box, Model 1921) with accessories, or 18" barrel variations, nonstandard calibers (.25-20, .32-20, .38-40, etc.) command premiums of 50 to 200 percent or more; an original holster is $75 to $150. Two new-in-box Model 1908 with 15" and 18" barrels sold for $2,700 and $3,600, respectively, in 1994. An original wooden Model 1908 box alone may sell for $500 to $900. All 18" barrel variations are rare.

MARLIN FIREARMS CO.

Madison, North Carolina

NOTE: Marlin, along with its subsidiaries Harrington & Richardson/ NEF, is now owned by Remington Arms.

Ballard Rifles

Established by John Mahlon Marlin in 1863. Marlin manufactured pistols until 1875 when he began production of Ballard rifles. In 1881 he made his first lever-action repeating rifle for which his company became famous.

BALL & WILLIAMS BALLARDS

First Model

This model was the first Ballard produced. It was introduced in 1861 and was offered with a 24" or 28" octagonal barrel. The frame is case colored, and the barrel is blued. The walnut stock is varnished. The major identifying feature of this model is the inside extractor. This was the only Ballard that had this feature before Marlin began to manufacture the rifle in 1875. The barrel is stamped "Ball & Williams/Worchester, Mass." and "Ballards Patent/Nov. 5, 1861." There were approximately 100 manufactured and serial numbered from 1-100.

NIB	Exc.	V.G.	Good	Fair	Poor
—	—	3000	2500	900	400

Military Rifle

There is not enough known about these rifles and probably never will be. They were chambered most frequently for the .44 and .54 rimfire cartridges and feature the outside tangs and extractors. They were offered with a 30" round barrel and full-length forearm. There are three barrel bands and sling swivels. The government ordered only 35 of these for use in the Civil War; and if one was to be definitely authenticated as a genuine martial specimen, it would be quite valuable. Many of these rifles were marked "Kentucky" on top of the receiver because the militia of that state armed its men with the Ballard rifles and carbines. This marking was a sales aid used by the company and does not indicate militia ownership. Thenumber manufactured is not known. Barrel markings are as on the First Model.

NIB	Exc.	V.G.	Good	Fair	Poor
—	—	5000	2850	1250	300

Civil War Military Carbine

This model has a 22" part-round, part-octagonal barrel and is chambered for the .44 rimfire cartridge. It has the outside tang and extractor. The stock and forearm are walnut with a barrel band sling swivel. The buttstock bears an oval cartouche surrounding the inspector's marks, "MM." These letters also appear stamped on major metal parts. There were 1,509 ordered by the government for use in the Civil War. The barrel was marked the same as the rifle.

NIB	Exc.	V.G.	Good	Fair	Poor
—	—	5500	3750	1500	500

Sporting Rifle

This model is chambered for the .32, .38, and .44 rimfire cartridges. The octagonal barrel is 24", 26", or 28" in length and is blued. The frame is case colored. The stock and forearm are varnished walnut, and there is a knob that protrudes in front of the frame to operate the outside manual extractor. There is a crescent buttplate standard. There were approximately 6,500 manufactured, and barrel markings are the same as on the First Model.

NIB	Exc.	V.G.	Good	Fair	Poor
—	—	2000	1550	500	200

Sporting Carbine

This model is similar in appearance to the Sporting Rifle with a 22" part-round, part-octagonal barrel. It is chambered for the .44 and .54 caliber cartridge, and the sling swivel is found on a barrel band in the front. The knob on the bottom activates the outside extractor. There have been some encountered with "Kentucky" stamped on the top, but this does not affect the value. The markings are the same as on the previous models. There are no production figures available, but some estimate approximately 2,000 were manufactured.

NIB	Exc.	V.G.	Good	Fair	Poor
—	—	2200	1750	600	250

Dual Ignition System

This system allows the use of the rimfire cartridge or percussion method by simply turning the striker on the hammer from one position to the other. This model features a percussion nipple mounted on the breechblock, and the hammer is marked "Patented Jan. 5, 1864." The patent was held by Merwin and Bray. This swivel system is usually found on the sporting models and would increase the value of the weapon by 20 percent.

MERRIMACK ARMS CO. AND BROWN MANUFACTURING CO.

The values for the Ballard rifles manufactured by these two firms are the same, and the specifications are similar. The identifying difference is in the markings, "Merrimack Arms & Mfg. Co./ Newburyport Mass." or "Brown Mfg. Co. Newburyport, Mass." Merrimack produced approximately 3,000 of these rifles between 1867 and 1869 serial numbered in the 18000-20000 range. Brown produced approximately 1,800 between 1869 and 1873 in the 20000-22000 serial number range.

Sporting Rifle

This model was produced in .22 (rare), .32, .38, .44, .46, and .52 caliber rimfire or percussion, as most encountered featured the dual ignition system and had the nipple in the breechblock. They have either a round or octagonal barrel in 24", 26", or 28" lengths. The appearance and finish is similar to the Ball & Williams rifles; and the major difference is the inside tang. The extractor was still outside mounted and manually activated. Exact production breakdown is unknown. There is no premium for the dual ignition system on these later guns.

NIB	Exc.	V.G.	Good	Fair	Poor
—	—	1700	1250	450	200

Sporting Carbine

This model is quite similar in appearance to the Sporting Rifle, with a 22" part-round, part-octagonal barrel.

NIB	Exc.	V.G.	Good	Fair	Poor
—	—	1800	1350	550	300

Military Rifle

The Military Rifle is similar to the sporting version except that it has a 30" round barrel and full-length forearm with three barrel bands. It is chambered for the .44 and .52 caliber rimfire or percussion with the dual ignition system.

NIB	Exc.	V.G.	Good	Fair	Poor
—	—	2000	1500	650	300

Shotgun

This model is similar to the Sporting Rifle in appearance but is chambered for 24 gauge, with a 30" round barrel. There is a groove milled in the top of the frame to use as a sight. The butt-plate is shotgun-style instead of the usual crescent shape.

NIB	Exc.	V.G.	Good	Fair	Poor
—	—	1200	800	350	200

MARLIN-BALLARD RIFLES

Commencing in 1875 the Ballard single-shot rifle was made by John Marlin for Schoverling and Daly. In 1881 the business was incorporated and became the Marlin Firearms Co. All the Ballards made from then until 1891, when they were discontinued, were produced under this banner. The only real difference in the rifles manufactured during these periods was in the markings. The earlier rifles are stamped "J.M. Marlin New Haven. Conn. U.S.A./ Ballards Patent. Nov. 5, 1861" ; and the post-1881 models are stamped "Marlin Firearms Co. New Haven Ct. U.S.A./Patented Feb. 9, 1875/Ballards Patent Nov. 5, 1861."

Ballard Hunters Rifle

This model resembles the earlier Brown Manufacturing Company rifles, and it utilizes many leftover parts acquired by Marlin. It is chambered for the .32, .38, and .44 rimfire and centerfire and features John Marlin's unique reversible firing pin that allows the same gun to use both rimfire and centerfire ammunition simply by rotating the firing pin in the breechblock. This model still had the external ejector and bears the J.M. Marlin markings. There were approximately 500 manufactured in the 1 to 500 serial range. They were produced in 1875 and 1876.

NIB	Exc.	V.G.	Good	Fair	Poor
—	—	3700	2750	950	400

Ballard No. 1 Hunters Rifle

This model bears the early J.M. Marlin marking only, as it was manufactured from 1876 until 1880 and was discontinued before the incorporation. It has a 26", 28", and 30" barrel and is chambered for the .44 rimfire or centerfire cartridge. It has the reversible firing pin and also the new internal extractor. Production figures are not available, but the serial number range is between 500 and 4000.

NIB	Exc.	V.G.	Good	Fair	Poor
—	—	4500	3000	1000	400

Ballard No. 1-1/2 Hunters Rifle

This model is similar to the No. 1 except that it is chambered for the .45-70, .40-63, and the .40-65 cartridges and does not have the reversible firing pin. The barrel length is 30" and 32". It was manufactured between 1879 and 1883. This model is found with both early and later markings.

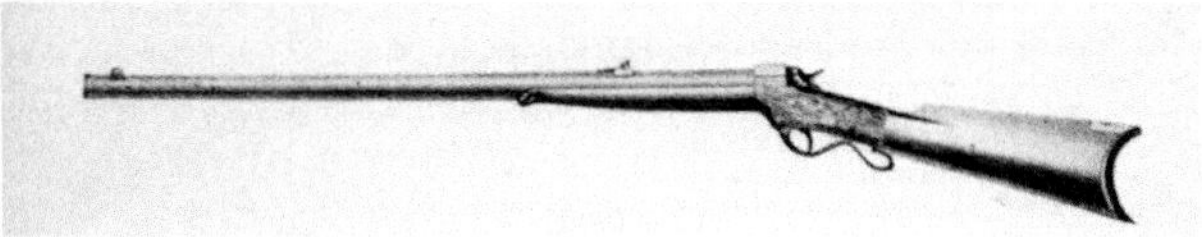

Photo by Lt. Col. William S. Brophy from Marlin Firearms with permission

NIB	Exc.	V.G.	Good	Fair	Poor
—	—	5200	3750	1500	500

Ballard No. 1-3/4 "Far West" Hunters Rifle

This model was made by J. M. Marlin only and is similar to the 1-1/2, the difference being the addition of double-set triggers and a ring on the opening lever. It was manufactured in 1880 and 1881.

NIB	Exc.	V.G.	Good	Fair	Poor
—	—	6300	4750	2000	600

Ballard No. 2 Sporting Rifle

This model is chambered for the .32, .38 rimfire or centerfire cartridges, and the .44 centerfire. It has the reversible firing pin and was offered in 26", 28", and 30" barrel lengths. This model features "Rocky Mountain" sights and was manufactured between 1876 and 1891. It is found with both early and late markings.

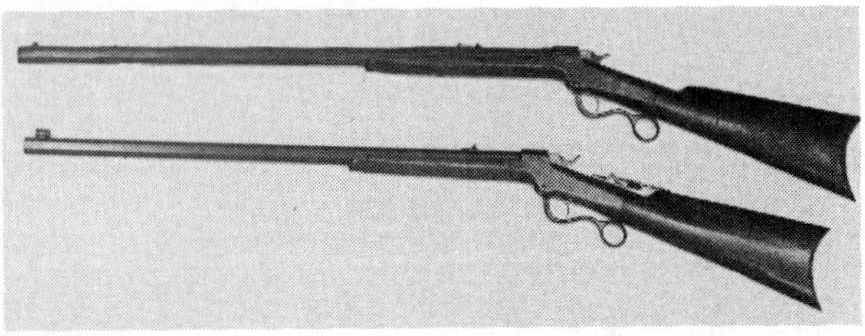

Courtesy Milwaukee Public Museum, Milwaukee, Wisconsin

NIB	Exc.	V.G.	Good	Fair	Poor
—	—	3200	2000	650	200

Ballard No. 3 Gallery Rifle

This model is similar to the No. 2 rifle but is chambered for the .22 rimfire cartridge and has a manually operated external extractor. The sights are the same; and a 24" barrel was offered in addition to the 26", 28", and 30". This rifle was manufactured between 1876 and 1891.

NIB	Exc.	V.G.	Good	Fair	Poor
—	—	3200	2000	650	200

Ballard No. 3F Gallery Rifle

This is a deluxe version of the No. 3. It has a pistol-grip stock, a nickel-plated Schutzen-style buttplate, and an opening lever like a repeating rifle. It features a 26" octagonal barrel and an oil-finished stock. It was manufactured in the late 1880s and is quite scarce in today's market.

No. 3 F Fine Gallery Rifle.

Photo by Lt. Col. William S. Brophy from Marlin Firearms with permission

NIB	Exc.	V.G.	Good	Fair	Poor
—	—	6500	4250	1750	500

Ballard No. 4 Perfection Rifle

This model is chambered for a number of centerfire calibers from .32-40 to .50-70. The barrel lengths are from 26" to 30", and the sights are of the "Rocky Mountain" type. This model was manufactured between 1876 and 1891.

Courtesy Rock Island Auction Company

NIB	Exc.	V.G.	Good	Fair	Poor
—	—	6500	4250	1750	500

Ballard No. 3-1/2 Target Rifle

This model is similar to the No. 4 Perfection Rifle except that it has a checkered stock with a shotgun-style buttplate, a 30" barrel, and a tang peep sight with globe front sight. It was chambered for the .40-65 cartridge and was manufactured from 1880-1882.

NIB	Exc.	V.G.	Good	Fair	Poor
—	—	6500	4250	1750	500

Ballard No. 4-1/2 Mid Range Rifle

This model is also a variation of the No. 4 Perfection model. It has a higher-grade checkered stock with a shotgun buttplate. It has a 30" part-round, part-octagonal barrel and is chambered for the .38-40, .40-65, and the .45-70 cartridges. It features a Vernier tang peep sight and a globe front sight. It was manufactured between 1878 and 1882.

NIB	Exc.	V.G.	Good	Fair	Poor
—	—	6750	4500	2000	500

Ballard No. 4-1/2 A-1 Mid Range Target Rifle

This is a deluxe version of the No. 4-1/2" rifle. It features scroll engraving on the frame with "Ballard A-1" on the left and "Mid-Range" on the right. It is chambered for the .38-50 and the .40-65 cartridge and has a high-grade checkered stock with a horn forend tip. The sights are the highest-grade Vernier tang sight and a spirit lever front sight. The shotgun or rifle-style butt was optional. This model was manufactured between 1878 and 1880.

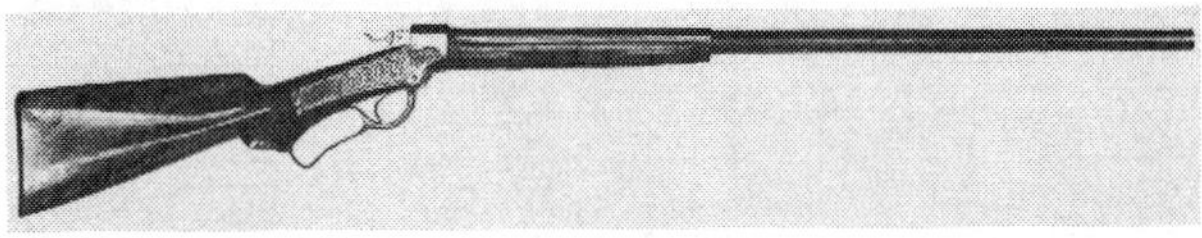

Courtesy Milwaukee Public Museum, Milwaukee, Wisconsin

NIB	Exc.	V.G.	Good	Fair	Poor
—	—	9000	7250	3500	750

Ballard No. 5 Pacific Rifle

This model has a 30" or 32" medium to heavyweight barrel, with a ramrod mounted underneath. It is chambered for many different calibers from .38-50 to .50-70. This model features "Rocky Mountain" sights, a crescent butt, double-set triggers, and a ring-style opening lever. It was manufactured between 1876 and 1891.

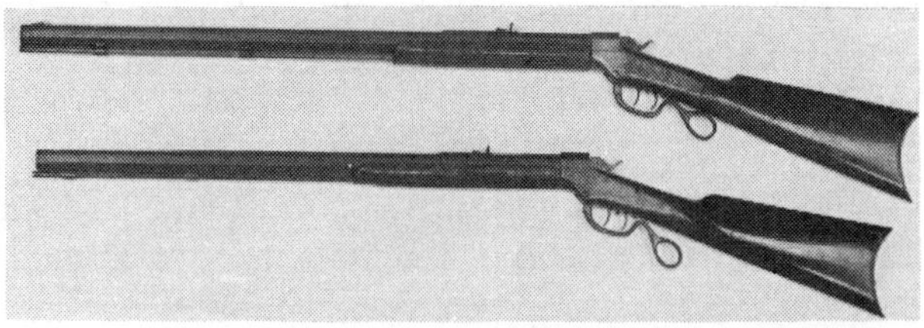

Courtesy Milwaukee Public Museum, Milwaukee, Wisconsin

NIB	Exc.	V.G.	Good	Fair	Poor
—	—	5500	4750	2000	500

Ballard No. 5-1/2 Montana Rifle

This model is similar to the Pacific Rifle, with an extra heavyweight barrel, and is chambered for the .45 Sharps cartridge only. It features a checkered steel shotgun-style buttplate. It was manufactured from 1882-1884 and has the late markings only.

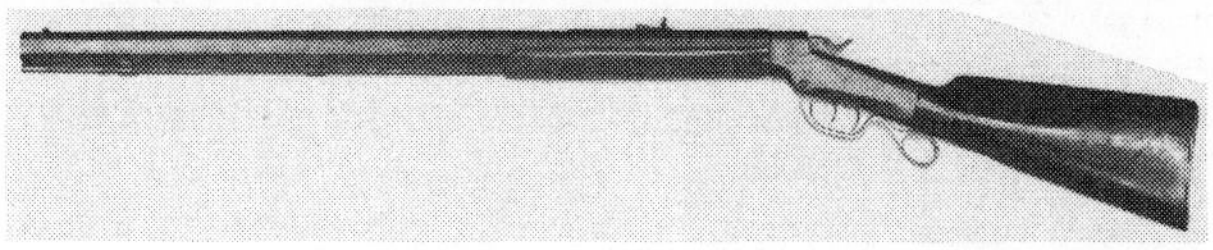

Courtesy Milwaukee Public Museum, Milwaukee, Wisconsin

NIB	Exc.	V.G.	Good	Fair	Poor
—	—	15000	10000	5500	1250

Ballard No. 6 Schuetzen Off Hand Rifle

This model has a 30" or 32" octagonal barrel and is chambered for the .40-65, .44-75, and the .38-50 cartridges. The stock is of select walnut in the high-combed Schuetzen style. The buttplate is nickel-plated, and the receiver is not engraved. The sights are Vernier tang type on the rear and a spirit lever front. The triggers are double set, and the opening lever has a ring and a spur. This model is marked J.M. Marlin only and was manufactured between 1876 and 1880.

NIB	Exc.	V.G.	Good	Fair	Poor
—	—	—	6500	2500	500

Ballard No. 6 Schuetzen Rifle

This model is similar to the Off Hand model but was produced by the later Marlin Firearms Company and was so marked. It is a more deluxe version with checkered stock, horn forend tip, and a fully engraved receiver. This model was chambered for the .32-40 and the .38-55 cartridges and was manufactured between 1881 and 1891.

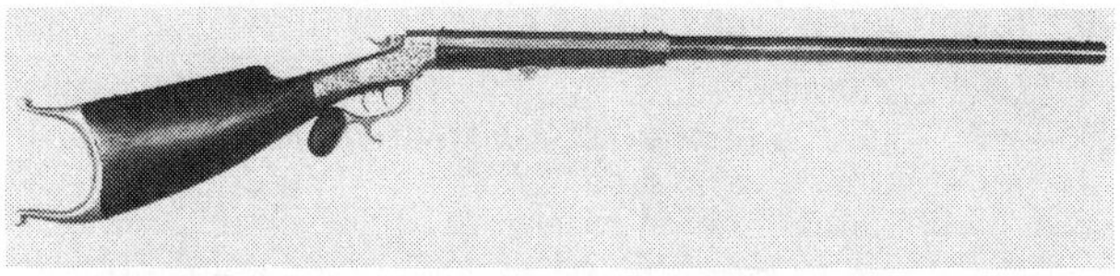

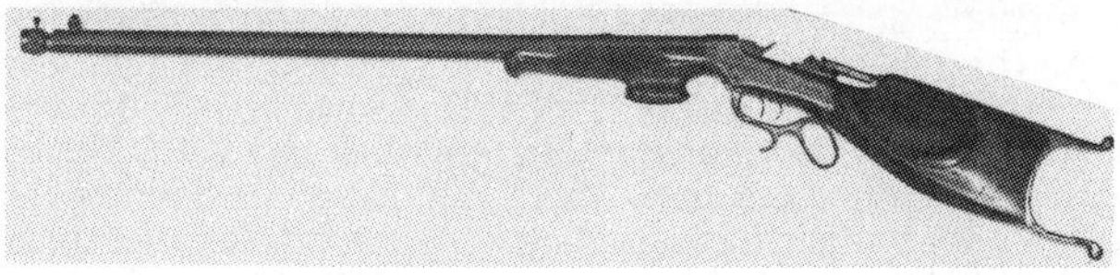

Courtesy Milwaukee Public Museum, Milwaukee, Wisconsin

NIB	Exc.	V.G.	Good	Fair	Poor
—	—	13000	8500	4500	1250

Ballard No. 6-1/2 Off Hand Mid Range Rifle

This model is chambered for the .40-54 Everlasting cartridge only. It has a 28" or 30" part-round, part-octagonal barrel, a Schuetzen-style stock, and a plain non-engraved receiver. It was manufactured between 1880 and 1882.

NIB	Exc.	V.G.	Good	Fair	Poor
—	20000	9500	5500	2500	500

Ballard No. 6-1/2 Rigby Off Hand Mid Range Rifle

This model is chambered for the .38-50 and the .40-65 cartridges. It features the Rigby ribbed-style barrel in 26" and 28" lengths, with Vernier rear and globe front sights and a high grade, checkered walnut, Schuetzen-style stock with horn forend tip, and pistol-grip cap. The buttplate is nickel-plated, and the opening lever is of the ring type with a single trigger and extensively engraved receiver. This model was manufactured from 1880 to 1882.

No. 6½ Off-Hand Rifle.

Photo by Lt. Col. William S. Brophy from Marlin Firearms with permission

NIB	Exc.	V.G.	Good	Fair	Poor
—	—	14500	9000	5500	1250

Ballard No. 6-1/2 Off Hand Rifle

This model is chambered for the .32-40 and .38-55 cartridges and features barrel lengths of 28" and 30". It has a checkered, high-grade walnut, Schuetzen-style stock with nickel-plated buttplate. The forend tip and pistol-grip cap are of horn, and the receiver is engraved. This model has a single trigger, full-ring opening lever, Vernier tang rear sight, and spirit lever front sight. The 6-1/2 Off Hand was made by the Marlin Firearms Company between 1883 and 1891 and is found with the later markings only.

NIB	Exc.	V.G.	Good	Fair	Poor
—	—	14000	9000	5500	1250

Ballard No. 7 "Creedmore A-1" Long Range Rifle

This model is commonly chambered for the .44-100 or the .45-100 cartridges. It has a 34" part-round, part-octagonal barrel and a high grade checkered pistol-grip stock, with a horn forend tip and shotgun-style butt. The sights are a special 1,300-yard Vernier tang rear and a spirit level front. There is another sight base on the heel of the stock for mounting the rear sight for ultra long-range shooting. The opening lever is similar to a repeating rifle, and a single trigger is featured. The receiver is engraved and marked "Ballard A-1" on the left and "Long Range" on the right. This model was manufactured between 1876 and 1886 and is found with both early and late markings.

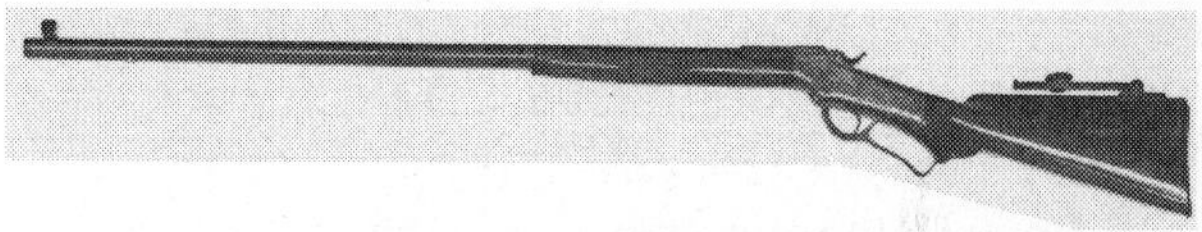

Courtesy Milwaukee Public Museum, Milwaukee, Wisconsin

NIB	Exc.	V.G.	Good	Fair	Poor
—	—	15000	9700	5500	1250

Ballard No. 7 Long Range Rifle

This model is similar to the "Creedmore A-1" but is slightly less deluxe. The engraving is less elaborate, and the lettering on the receiver is absent. This model was manufactured between 1883 and 1890 and is found with the later markings only.

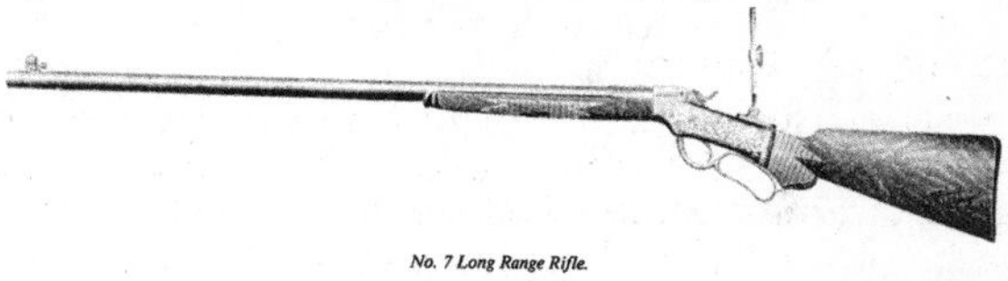

No. 7 Long Range Rifle.

Photo by Lt. Col. William S. Brophy from Marlin Firearms with permission

NIB	Exc.	V.G.	Good	Fair	Poor
—	—	13500	8000	4500	850

Ballard No. 7A-1 Long Range Rifle

This model is a higher grade version of the "Creedmore A-l," with fancier walnut and a checkered straight stock. Better sights and deluxe engraving are also featured. This model was manufactured between 1879 and 1883 and is found with both markings.

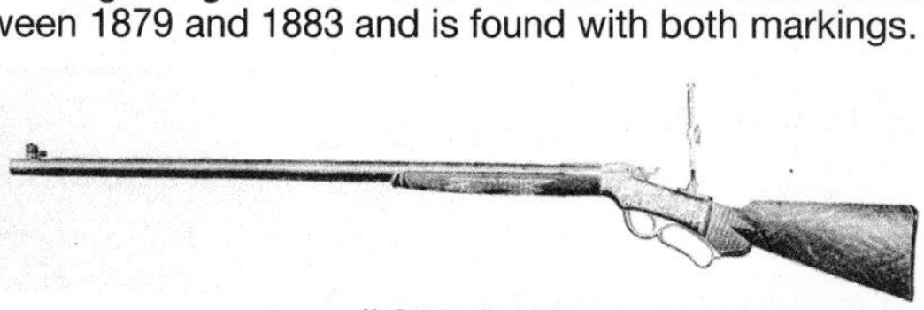

No. 7 A-1 Long Range Rifle.

Photo by Lt. Col. William S. Brophy from Marlin Firearms with permission

NIB	Exc.	V.G.	Good	Fair	Poor
—	—	16000	1000	5500	1250

Ballard No. 7A-1 Extra Grade Long Range Rifle

This is the highest grade version of the No. 7 rifles. It features a 34" "Rigby" -type ribbed, round barrel. This was usually a special-order rifle with most features to customer specifications. The model was manufactured in limited numbers between 1879 and 1883. It is found with both markings.

Photo by Lt. Col. William S. Brophy from Marlin Firearms with permission

NIB	Exc.	V.G.	Good	Fair	Poor
—	—	19500	11500	6500	1500

Ballard No. 8 Union Hill Rifle

This model has a 28" and 30" part-round, part-octagonal barrel and is chambered for the .32-40 and the .38-55 cartridges. It has a checkered pistol-grip stock with nickel-plated buttplate; and the opening lever is fully enclosed ring, as on the repeaters. There is a double-set trigger and a tang peep with globe front sight. The receiver is not engraved. This model was manufactured between 1884 and 1890 and is found only with the late markings. This was one of the most popular rifles in the Ballard line.

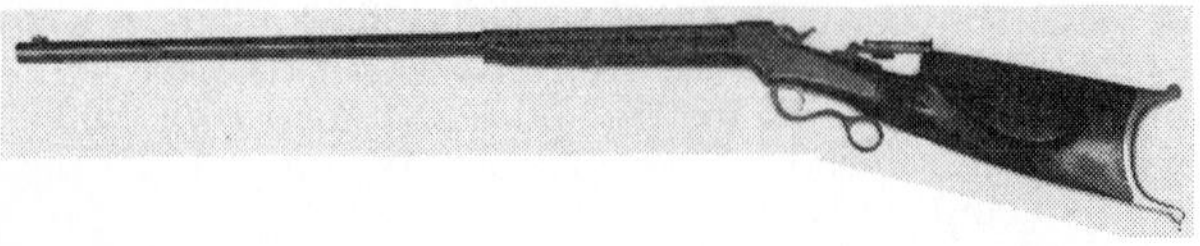

Courtesy Milwaukee Public Museum, Milwaukee, Wisconsin

NIB	Exc.	V.G.	Good	Fair	Poor
—	—	7000	4250	1750	500

Ballard No. 9 Union Hill Rifle

This model is similar to the No. 8 except that it features a single trigger and better sights. It was manufactured between 1884 and 1891 and has the later markings only.

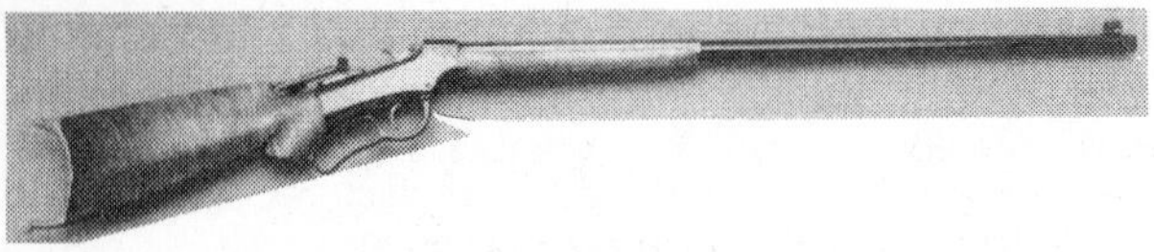

Courtesy Bonhams & Butterfields, San Francisco, California

NIB	Exc.	V.G.	Good	Fair	Poor
—	—	7000	4250	1750	500

Ballard No. 10 Schuetzen Junior Rifle

This model is simply a heavier barreled version of the No. 9. The barrel is 32" long, and the checkered pistol-grip stock is of the off-hand style. The rear sight is a Vernier Mid Range model, and the front sight is a spirit-level type. This was a popular model that was manufactured between 1885 and 1891. It is found with the later markings only.

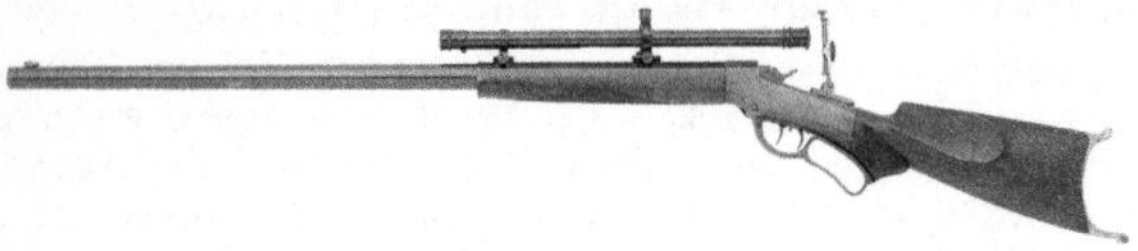

Courtesy Amoskeag Auction Company

NIB	Exc.	V.G.	Good	Fair	Poor
—	—	7000	4750	2000	650

EARLY PRODUCTION MARLIN RIFLES

Model 1881 Lever-Action Rifle

This was the first of the Marlin lever-action rifles and has always been regarded as a high quality rifle. It is capable of handling the large calibers and was well received by the shooting public. The rifle is chambered for the .32-40, .38-55, .40-60, .45-70, and the .45-85. The 24", 28", or 30" octagonal barrel is standard. Round barrels were offered and are scarce today. There is a tubular magazine beneath the barrel, and the rear sight is the buckhorn type with a blade on the front. This model ejects its empty cartridges from the top. The finish is blued, with a case colored hammer, lever, and buttplate. The walnut stock is varnished. There were approximately 20,000 manufactured between 1881 and 1892 but this is not easy to ascertain, as the factory records on Marlin rifles are quite incomplete.

Courtesy Bonhams & Butterfields, San Francisco, California

NIB	Exc.	V.G.	Good	Fair	Poor
—	—	4500	2000	750	300

Model 1881 Lever-Action Rifle Lightweight Model

Thinner frame, lever, and barrel .32-40 and .38-55 caliber only-24" and 28" barrel.

NIB	Exc.	V.G.	Good	Fair	Poor
—	—	4200	1750	600	300

NOTE: Add 200-300 percent premium for 1st Models prior to serial number 600. Add 15 percent premium for .45-70 caliber.

Model 1888 Lever-Action Rifle

This model is chambered for the .32-20, .38-40, and the .44-40 cartridges. This is a shorter action that was designed (chiefly by Lewis Hepburn) to handle the pistol cartridges for which it was chambered. The standard barrel was octagonal, but round barrels were available as special-order items. This is a top ejecting action. It has a buckhorn rear and a blade front sight. The finish is blued with a case colored hammer, lever, and buttplate. The walnut stock is varnished. There were approximately 4,800 manufactured in 1888 and 1889. As with most of these fine old rifles, many special-order options were available that affect today's market value. Individual appraisal would be necessary for these special models, to ascertain both value and authenticity.

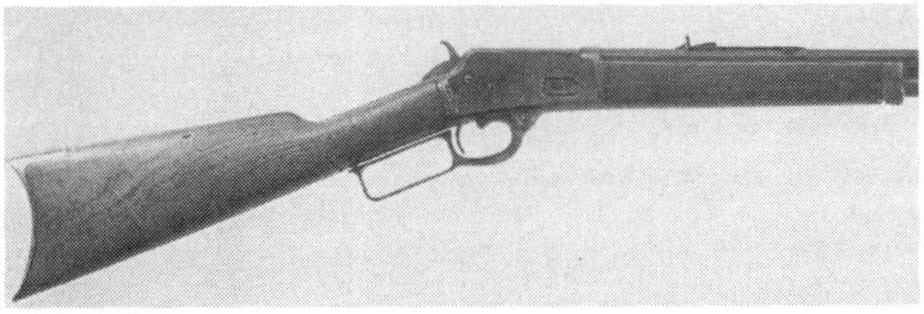

Thinner frame, lever, and barrel .32-40 and .38-55 caliber only-24" and 28" barrel.

NIB	Exc.	V.G.	Good	Fair	Poor
—	—	3500	2500	600	350

NOTE: Add 40 percent premium for half octagon barrel. Add 20 percent premium for round barrel.

MODEL 1889 LEVER-ACTION RIFLE

This was Marlin's first side-eject, solid-top rifle. It is chambered for .25-20, .32-20, .38-40, and the .44-40 cartridges. It features either octagonal or round barrels in lengths from 24" to 32" with buckhorn rear and blade front sights. The finish is blued with a case colored hammer, lever, and buttplate. The plain walnut stock is varnished. The barrel is stamped "Marlin Fire-Arms Co. New Haven Ct. U.S.A./Patented Oct.11 1887 April 2.1889." This model features a lever latch, and many options were offered. Again one must urge individual appraisal on such variations. Values fluctuate greatly due to some seemingly insignificant variation. There were approximately 55,000 manufactured between 1889 and 1899.

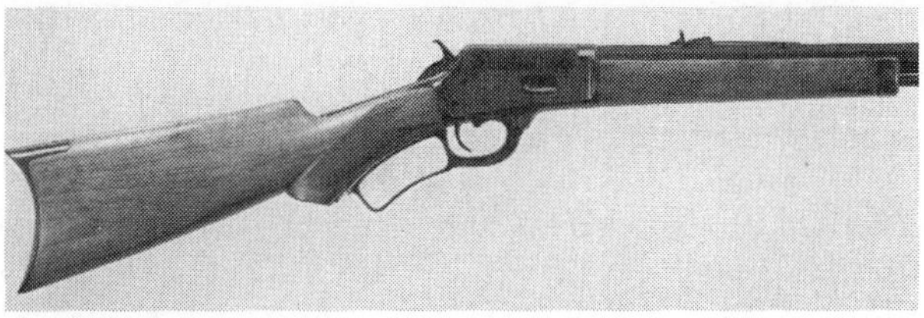

Production Model

24" barrel.

NIB	Exc.	V.G.	Good	Fair	Poor
—	—	1700	1000	450	150

Short Carbine

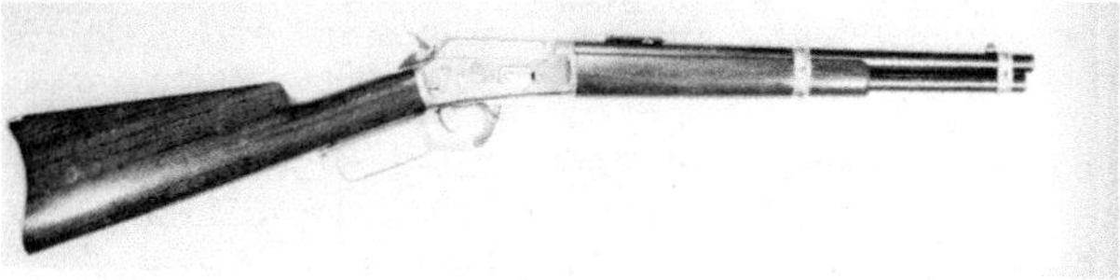

Photo by Lt. Col. William S. Brophy from Marlin Firearms with permission

15" barrel. 327 produced.

NIB	Exc.	V.G.	Good	Fair	Poor
—	—	5000	2250	1000	500

Carbine 20" Barrel and Saddle Ring on Left Side of Receiver

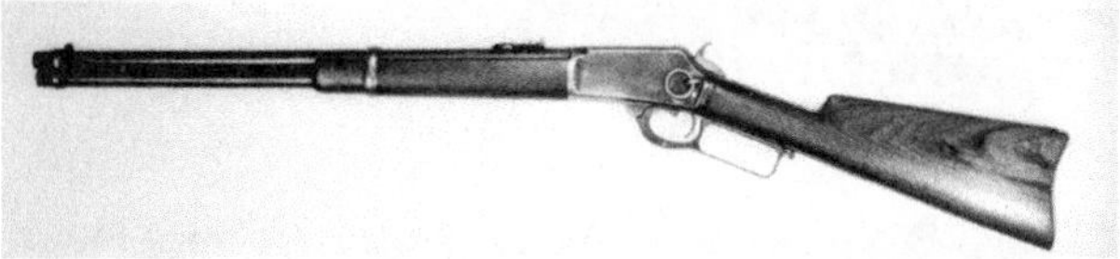

Photo by Lt. Col. William S. Brophy from Marlin Firearms with permission

15" barrel. 327 produced.

NIB	Exc.	V.G.	Good	Fair	Poor
—	—	2250	1250	500	250

Musket

30" barrel with full-length stock, 68 made in .44-40.

NIB	Exc.	V.G.	Good	Fair	Poor
—	—	6500	3000	1250	650

Model 1891 Lever-Action Rifle

This was Marlin's first rifle designed to fire the .22 rimfire and the first repeating rifle to accept the .22 Short, Long, and LR cartridges interchangeably. It was also chambered for the .32 rimfire and centerfire. The 24" octagonal barrel is standard, with a buckhorn rear and blade front sight. The finish is blued with a case colored hammer, lever, and buttplate. The stock is plain walnut. The first variation is marked "Marlin Fire-Arms Co. New Haven, Ct. U.S.A./ Pat'd Nov.19.1878.April 2.1889. Aug.12 1890" on the barrel, with the solid-topped frame marked "Marlin Safety." The second variation was marked the same with "March 1,1892" added. There were approximately 18,650 manufactured between 1891 and 1897.

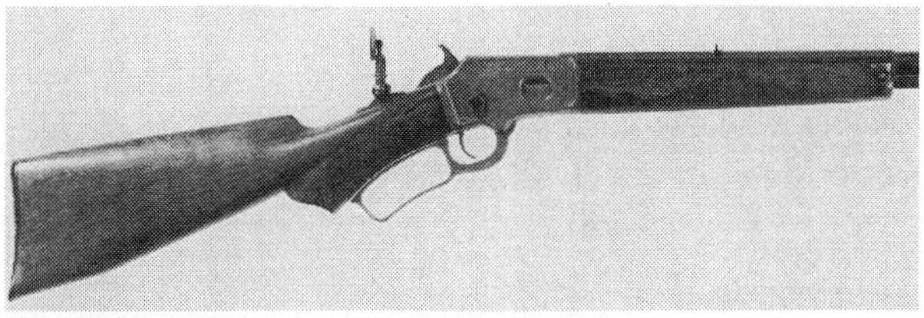

1st Variation

.22 rimfire only, side loading, appr. 5,000 made.

NIB	Exc.	V.G.	Good	Fair	Poor
—	—	2500	1000	550	300

2nd Variation

.22 and .32 rimfire, .32 centerfire, tube loading, Model 1891 on later model tangs (3rd variation).

NIB	Exc.	V.G.	Good	Fair	Poor
—	—	1500	500	300	150

NOTE: Add 20 percent for .22 rifle with "1891" stamped on tang. Deduct 50 percent for .32 caliber.

MODEL 1892 LEVER-ACTION RIFLE

This is basically an improved version of the Model 1891 and is similar to the second variation of the 1891. The only notable exceptions were the tang marking "Model 1892" and "Model 92" on later models. The .22 rimfire was scarce in the Model 1892. There were approximately 45,000 manufactured between 1895 and 1916. There were many options, and these special-order guns must be individually appraised to ascertain value and authenticity.

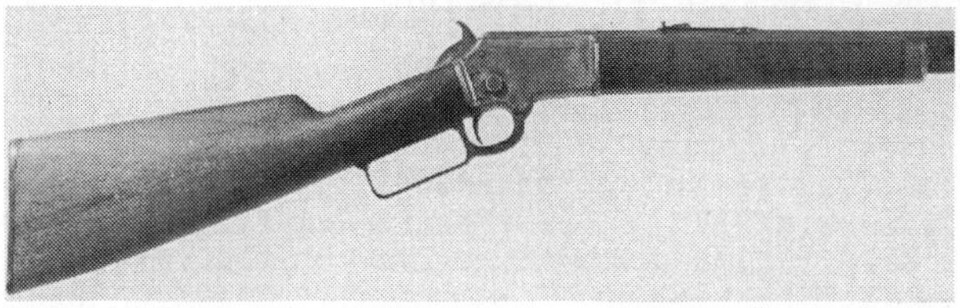

NIB	Exc.	V.G.	Good	Fair	Poor
—	—	1350	400	250	150

NOTE: Antique (pre-1898) add 20 percent.

.32 Rimfire and Centerfire

.22 and .32 rimfire, .32 centerfire, tube loading, Model 1891 on later model tangs (3rd variation).

NIB	Exc.	V.G.	Good	Fair	Poor
—	—	950	350	150	100

MODEL 1893 LEVER-ACTION RIFLE

This model was the first rifle Marlin designed for the then new smokeless powder cartridges. It is chambered for the .25-36, .30-30, .32 Special, .32-40, and the .38-55. It was offered standard with either a round or octagonal barrel, in lengths of 24" to 32". Buckhorn rear and blade front sights were also standard. The receiver, lever, hammer, and buttplate are case colored, and the rest is blued. The stock is varnished walnut.As with all of these early Marlins, many options were offered and, when encountered, will drastically alter the value of the particular rifle. For this reason we supply the values for the basic model and urge securing competent appraisal on non-standard specimens. The barrel on earlier guns is marked "Marlin FireArms Co. New Haven, Ct.U.S.A./ Patented Oct.11. 1887.April 2.1889.Aug.1.1893." In 1919 the markings were changed to "The Marlin Firearms Corporation/ New Haven, Conn.U.S.A.Patented." The rifles manufactured after 1904 are marked "Special Smokeless Steel" on the left side of the barrel. The upper tang is marked "Model 1893" on early guns; and "Model 93," on later specimens. There were approximately 900,000 manufactured between 1893 and 1935. Factory records are incomplete on the Model 1893.

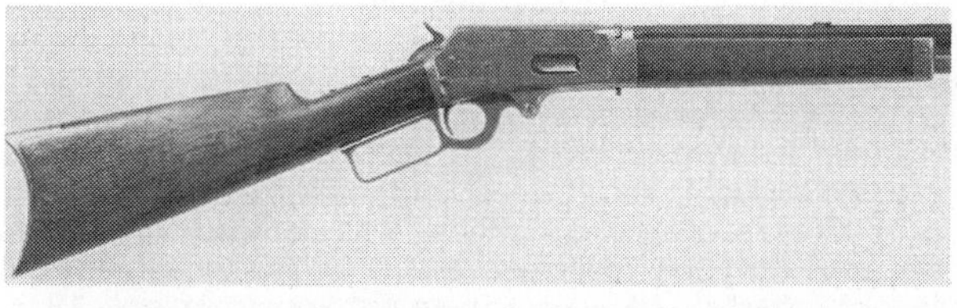

Antique Production (Pre-1898)

Courtesy Bonhams & Butterfields, San Francisco, California

NIB	Exc.	V.G.	Good	Fair	Poor
—	2250	1000	650	450	275

Modern Production 1899-1935

NIB	Exc.	V.G.	Good	Fair	Poor
—	1750	850	550	350	225

NOTE: Add 100 percent premium for musket. Deduct 50 percent for B model with blued receiver.

MODEL 1894 LEVER-ACTION RIFLE

This model is similar to the Model 1893, with a shorter action. It is chambered for the .25-20, .32-20, .38-40, and the .44-40. 24" to 32" round or octagonal barrels with full-length magazine tubes are standard, as are buckhorn rear and blade front sights. The finish is case colored receiver, lever, hammer, and buttplate, with the rest blued. The walnut stock is varnished. The first versions were marked "Marlin Fire-Arms Co., New Haven, Ct.U.S.A./Patented Oct.11, 1887. April 2,1889." The top of the frame is marked "Marlin Safety," and the model designation is not stamped on the tang. These early rifles were chambered for .38-40 and .44-40 only. The later rifles added the patent date "Aug. 1, 1893" ; and "Model 1894" was stamped on the tang. On the latest versions this was shortened to "Model 94." There were approximately 250,000 manufactured between 1894 and 1935. This model was also produced with a great many options. Individual appraisal should be secured when confronted with these features.

Antique Production (Pre-1898)

NIB	Exc.	V.G.	Good	Fair	Poor
—	1850	1150	650	450	275

Modern Production (1899-1935)

NIB	Exc.	V.G.	Good	Fair	Poor
—	1600	850	550	350	225

NOTE: Add 100 percent premium for musket. Add 25 percent premium for saddle ring carbine. Add 30 percent premium for "Baby" carbine.

MODEL 1895 LEVER-ACTION RIFLE

This is a large rifle designed to fire the larger hunting cartridges. It is chambered for the .33 W.C.F., .38-56, .40-65, .40-70, .40-83, .45-70, and the .45-90. It came standard with round or octagonal barrels from 26" to 32" in length. A bull-length magazine tube was also standard, as were buckhorn rear and blade front sights. The finish is case colored receiver, lever, and hammer; the rest is blued with a varnished walnut stock. The barrel markings are the same as the Model 1894, and the top tang is marked "Model 1895." After 1896 "Special Smokeless Steel" was stamped on the barrel. There were also many options available for this model, and they have a big effect on the value. There were approximately 18,000 manufactured between 1895 and 1917.

Antique Production (Pre-1898)

NIB	Exc.	V.G.	Good	Fair	Poor
—	3750	2850	2000	1250	600

Modern Production (1899-1917)

NIB	Exc.	V.G.	Good	Fair	Poor
—	2400	1500	875	650	500

MODEL 1897 LEVER-ACTION RIFLE

This model is an improved version of the Model 1892. It was chambered for the .22 rimfire only and came standard with a 24", 26", or 28" round, octagonal, or part-round, part-octagonal barrel. The standard sights are buckhorn rear and blade front, and all were manufactured as takedown rifles. They have case colored receiver, lever, and hammer. The rest is blued, and the walnut stock is varnished. There were approximately 125,000 manufactured between 1897 and 1917. In 1922 production was begun with the designation changed to Model 39 which is produced to this day. There were also options offered with this rifle that have great effect on the value; take this into consideration and seek qualified appraisal.

Standard Production Rifle

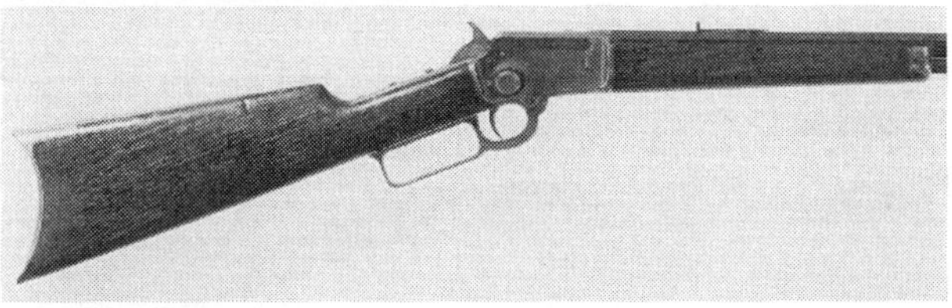

NIB	Exc.	V.G.	Good	Fair	Poor
—	2200	1500	1100	650	200

NOTE: For first year production antique add 40 percent.

Deluxe Rifle

Checkering and fancy pistol-grip stock.

NIB	Exc.	V.G.	Good	Fair	Poor
—	3000	2000	1500	850	300

MODERN PRODUCTION MARLIN RIFLES

Model 18 Slide-Action Rifle

This model is chambered for the .22 rimfire cartridges. It was offered standard with a 20" round or octagonal barrel, open sights, and a straight walnut stock. It has an exposed hammer and blued finish with blued steel buttplate. There is a half-length tubular magazine, and the stock features a quick takedown screw on the top tang which was marked "Model 18." This rifle was manufactured between 1906 and 1909.

Photo by Lt. Col. William S. Brophy from Marlin Firearms with permission

NIB	Exc.	V.G.	Good	Fair	Poor
—	650	495	200	150	80

Model 20 Slide-Action Rifle

The Model 20 was chambered for the .22 rimfire cartridges and was offered standard with a 24" octagonal barrel and open sight, with an exposed hammer. This rifle was only made as a "Takedown" receiver model and is blued, with a straight walnut stock. It was manufactured between 1907 and 1922.

NIB	Exc.	V.G.	Good	Fair	Poor
—	600	450	200	125	75

Model 25 Slide-Action Rifle

This model was chambered for the .22 Short only and was not a commercial success. The 23" round or octagonal barrel is standard, as are open sights. It is called a takedown model, but only the stock is removable—the receiver does not separate. It has an exposed hammer, tubular magazine, and straight walnut stock. The finish is blued. This rifle was manufactured in 1909 and 1910.

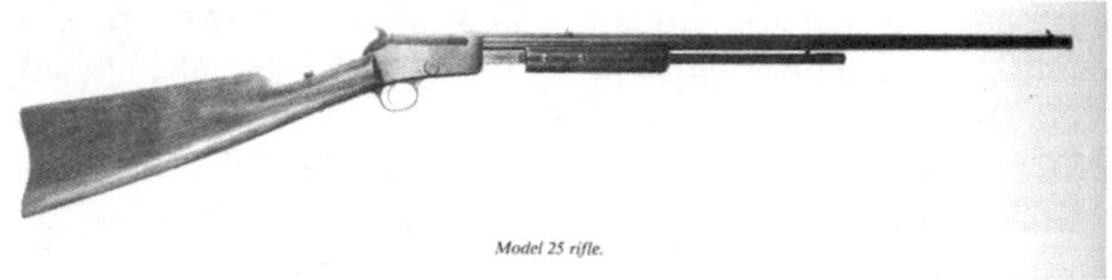

Model 25 rifle.

Photo by Lt. Col. William S. Brophy from Marlin Firearms with permission

NIB	Exc.	V.G.	Good	Fair	Poor
—	850	625	475	300	175

Model 27 Slide-Action Rifle

This is a centerfire rifle chambered for the .25-20 and .32-20 cartridges. Also chambered for the .25 caliber rimfire cartridge. It features a 24" octagonal barrel with two-thirds-length magazine tube that holds 7 shots. It has open sights, a blued finish, and straight walnut stock with crescent buttplate. It was manufactured in from 1910 to 1916.

NIB	Exc.	V.G.	Good	Fair	Poor
—	950	700	475	275	100

NOTE: Deduct 20 percent for rifles chambered for the .25 rimfire.

Model 27S Slide-Action Rifle

The Model 27S is similar to the Model 27 but with a sliding button on the right side of the receiver that permitted the gun to be opened while a cartridge was in the chamber. It was offered with a round (1913) or octagonal 24" barrel. The .25 rimfire cartridge was added in 1913 to those already available. This model was introduced in 1910 and was manufactured until 1932. Deduct 20 percent for rifles chambered for the .25 rimfire.

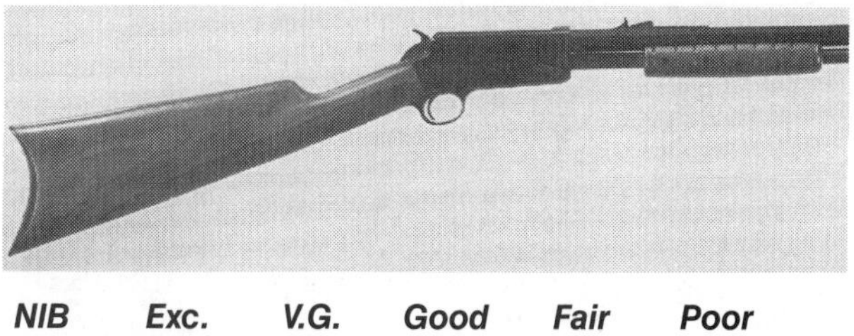

NIB	Exc.	V.G.	Good	Fair	Poor
—	950	700	475	275	100

Model 29 Slide-Action Rifle

This model is identical to the Model 20 with a 23" round barrel and smooth walnut forend instead of a grooved one as found on the Model 20. It was manufactured between 1913 and 1916. Deduct 20 percent for rifles chambered for the .25 rimfire.

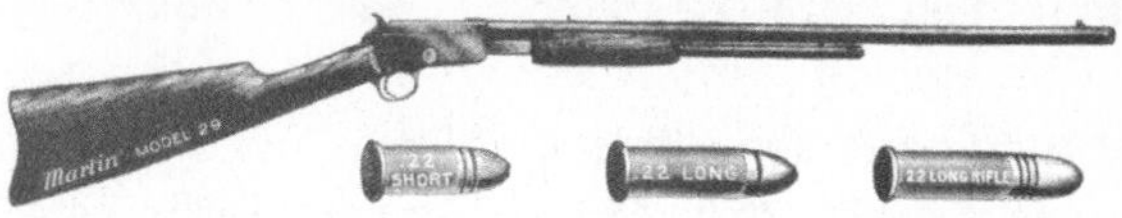

Photo by Lt. Col. William S. Brophy from Marlin Firearms with permission

NIB	Exc.	V.G.	Good	Fair	Poor
—	600	450	300	225	75

Model 32 Slide-Action Rifle

This model was the first of the hammerless slide-action rifles. It is chambered for the .22 rimfire and has a 24" octagonal barrel and half-length magazine tube. The Model 32 is a takedown rifle with adjustable sights and features "Ballard" rifling. It is blued, with a pistol-grip walnut stock. The advent of WWI and the need for Marlin to produce military arms cut short the production of this model. It was manufactured in 1914 and 1915 only.

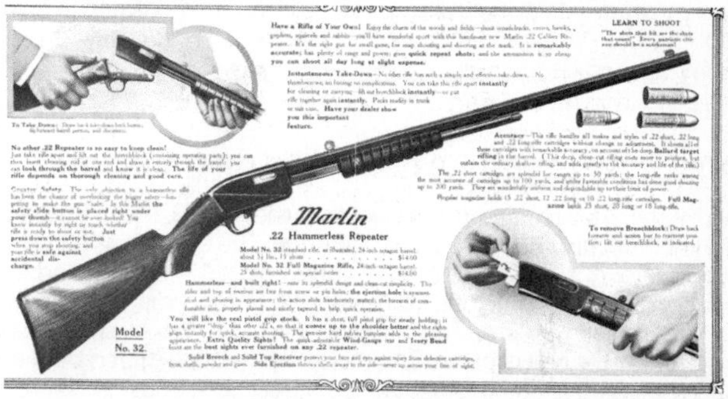

Photo by Lt. Col. William S. Brophy from Marlin Firearms with permission

NIB	Exc.	V.G.	Good	Fair	Poor
—	750	525	300	150	100

Model 37 Slide-Action Rifle

This model is the same as the Model 29 with a 24" round barrel and full-length magazine tube. It was manufactured between 1913 and 1916.

Photo by Lt. Col. William S. Brophy from Marlin Firearms with permission

NIB	Exc.	V.G.	Good	Fair	Poor
—	500	350	200	125	75

Model 38 Slide-Action Rifle

This was the hammerless model introduced after the end of WWI to replace the Model 32. It is similar in appearance but features a Rocky Mountain adjustable rear and an ivory bead front sight instead of the distinctive round Swebilius sight on the Model 32. The Model 38 was manufactured between 1920 and 1930.

NIB	Exc.	V.G.	Good	Fair	Poor
—	500	400	300	175	115

Model 40 Slide-Action Rifle

This model is identical to the Model 27S centerfire rifle except that the barrel is marked "Marlin-Rockwell." The top tang is stamped "Marlin/Mod. 40." This is a rare model, and not many marked in this manner have been noted.

NIB	Exc.	V.G.	Good	Fair	Poor
—	750	575	375	225	150

Model 47 Slide-Action Rifle

This model is similar to the Model 20, with a 23" round barrel and an improved magazine tube. The Model 47 has a case colored receiver and a checkered buttstock. This model was not offered for sale nor was it listed in Marlin's catalog but was offered free of charge to anyone purchasing four shares of Marlin stock for $100. One other fact about this model is that it was the first Marlin to be case colored with the new cyanide method; this created a tiger-striped pattern that is peculiar to the Model 47 Rifle.

NIB	Exc.	V.G.	Good	Fair	Poor
—	750	600	400	250	160

MODEL 1936 LEVER-ACTION RIFLE OR CARBINE

This model is a direct descendant of the Model 1893. It is chambered for the .30-30 and the .32 Special cartridge. The stock is streamlined with a pistol grip added and a 20" round barrel. A barrel band and improved sights are utilized. It has a 7-shot tube magazine and a semi-beavertail forearm. The receiver, lever, and hammer are case colored; and the rest is blued. This model was manufactured between 1936 and 1948. It was designated the Model 36 in 1937.

1st Variation (early 1936)

This variation has a slight "fish-belly" forearm, long tang, case colored receiver, lever, and hammer, with no serial number prefix. These are rare.

NIB	Exc.	V.G.	Good	Fair	Poor
—	1200	850	400	175	125

2nd Variation (late 1936-1947)

This variation has thicker forearm, short tang, and "B" serial number prefix.

NIB	Exc.	V.G.	Good	Fair	Poor
—	1000	650	300	150	100

(1937-1948)

First and Second variations both have case colored receiver and "C" serial number prefix. Second variation tapped for receiver sight.

NIB	Exc.	V.G.	Good	Fair	Poor
—	800	600	400	195	125

(1937-1948) Third Variation—Blued Receiver

NIB	Exc.	V.G.	Good	Fair	Poor
—	600	400	300	175	100

Model 36 Sporting Carbine

This model is similar to the 1936 Carbine, with a 20" barrel. It features a two-thirds-length magazine tube and holds 6 shots instead of 7. The front sight is a ramp sight with hood.

NIB	Exc.	V.G.	Good	Fair	Poor
—	800	600	400	195	125

Model 36A-DL Lever-Action Rifle

This model is similar to the Model 36A, with a deluxe checkered stock. It features sight swivels and is furnished with a leather sling.

NIB	Exc.	V.G.	Good	Fair	Poor
—	800	650	400	225	150

MODEL 336

Information on the Model 336 were provided by Doug Murray, author and publisher of The 336 (1983).NOTE: Beginning in the 1980s, Marlin used the "S" suffix on its model numbers (e.g., 336CS, 1895S, etc.), to designate models with the new crossbolt safety. This suffix has now been dropped in most cases, even though the safety remains.

Model 336 Carbine (R.C. Regular Carbine)

This model was introduced in 1948 and was an improved version of the Model 36. It features a new-type round bolt, chrome-plated with improved extractor and redesigned cartridge carrier that improved feeding. It is chambered for the .30-30 and the .32 Special cartridges and has a 20" tapered round barrel with Ballard-type rifling. The finish is blued, with the receiver top matted to reduce reflections. The pistol-grip stock and semi-beavertail forend are of American walnut. It features Rocky Mountain-style rear and bead front sights, and the hammer is lowered to facilitate scope mounting.

NIB	Exc.	V.G.	Good	Fair	Poor
—	475	325	175	125	100

Model 336C

The same as the Model 336 Carbine. In 1951 the catalog model designation was changed. In 1952 the .35 Remington cartridge was added to the line. In 1963 the .32 Special was discontinued.

NIB	Exc.	V.G.	Good	Fair	Poor
—	475	325	175	125	100

Model 336A

This model is similar to the 336C, with a 24" barrel and steel forend tip instead of a barrel band. The magazine tube is two-thirds-length and holds 6 shots. This model was introduced in 1948 and built until 1962. It was reintroduced in 1973 and discontinued in 1980. In 1950 the .35 Rem. was introduced, and in 1960 the .32 Special was discontinued.

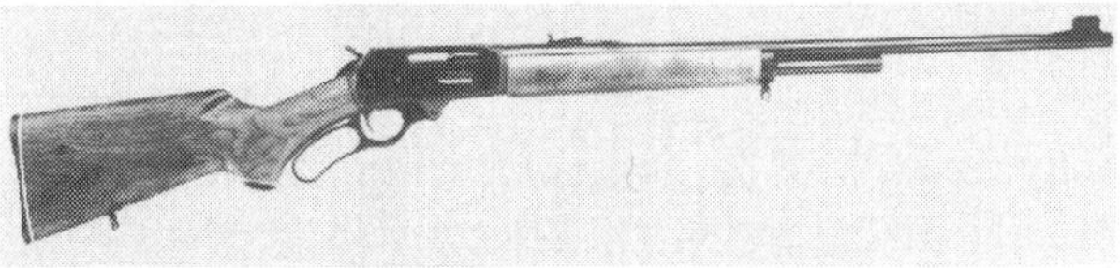

NIB	Exc.	V.G.	Good	Fair	Poor
—	475	325	175	125	100

Model 336ADL

This model differs from the Model 336A by having a deluxe wood checkered stock and forend, quick detachable swivels, better grade finish, and a sling.

NIB	Exc.	V.G.	Good	Fair	Poor
—	650	500	300	150	125

Model 336SC (Sporting Carbine)

This is basically a 336A with forend tip and two-thirds magazine but has a 20" barrel instead of the 24" found on the 336A.

NIB	Exc.	V.G.	Good	Fair	Poor
—	400	300	200	150	100

Model 336SD (Sporting Deluxe Carbine)

This is the 336 SC in a deluxe checkered stock version, with quick detachable swivels and supplied with a sling.NOTE: This is a scarce model as only 4,392 were built.

NIB	Exc.	V.G.	Good	Fair	Poor
—	1000	750	400	200	125

Model 336 MicroGroove Zipper

This model was advertised as a fast-handling, lever-action carbine chambered for the .219 Zipper cartridges flat trajectory, varmint-type round. It has a 20" heavy barrel, which was the feature that doomed it to failure as this was too short to coax the maximum performance and accuracy from the cartridge. The "MicroGroove" rifling that was used did not yield long barrel life; and the model survived from 1955 through 1959, when it was discontinued. It is externally similar to the 336 SC.

NIB	Exc.	V.G.	Good	Fair	Poor
—	1600	950	550	300	150

NOTE: First few thousand Zippers made in standard weight barrels, not heavy weight. These are scarce and found in the "M" prefix code number. Add 100 percent.

Model 336T (Texan)

This is a straight-stock version of the 336C, chambered for the .30-30 cartridge, with an 20" barrel. Also produced in .35 Rem. from 1953 to 1964, and .44 Mag. from 1965 to 1967. It was manufactured from 1953-1983.

NIB	Exc.	V.G.	Good	Fair	Poor
—	650	475	395	250	175

Model 336DT

A deluxe-stock version of the "Texan," with the map of Texas and a longhorn carved on the butt. It was manufactured between 1962 and 1964. Calibers are .30-30 and .35 Rem.

NIB	Exc.	V.G.	Good	Fair	Poor
—	700	550	425	275	175

Model 336 "Marauder"

This is simply a 336T with a 16.25" barrel and a slimmer forend. It is chambered for either the .30-30 or .35 Remington cartridges, has a gold trigger, and is drilled and tapped for both scope mounts and receiver sights. It was manufactured in 1963 and 1964.

NIB	Exc.	V.G.	Good	Fair	Poor
—	750	675	550	300	150

Model 336 .44 Magnum

This is the 336 "Marauder" with a 20" MicroGroove barrel chambered for the .44 Magnum cartridge. It holds 10 shots and was introduced in 1963. Not very successful, reportedly because of feeding difficulties.

NIB	Exc.	V.G.	Good	Fair	Poor
—	600	450	295	150	100

Model 336 "Centennial"

In 1970 a 100th year medallion was embedded into the buttstock of the 336 Carbines, the 336 Texan, and the 444 Rifle.

NIB	Exc.	V.G.	Good	Fair	Poor
—	625	500	375	250	150

1970 100th Year Commemorative Matched Pair

This is a deluxe octagonal barreled .30-30 with an engraved receiver and deluxe wood with an inlaid medallion, accompanied by a matching Model 339 .22 rimfire rifle. They are numbered the same and are furnished in a deluxe luggage case. There were 1,000 sets manufactured in 1970. These are commemoratives, and as such it should be noted that collectors usually will only show interest if they are new and uncocked in the original packaging. All accessories and brochures should be included for them to be worth top dollar. Once a commemorative has been used, it has no more value than as a shooter.

NIB	Exc.	V.G.	Good	Fair	Poor
1800	1400	900	600	400	300

Model 336 "Zane Grey Century"

This model was introduced in 1972, the 100th anniversary of the birth of Zane Grey, the famous Western author. This model has a 22" octagonal barrel chambered for the .30-30. The stock is high grade walnut and features a brass buttplate and pistol-grip cap. A Zane Grey medallion is inlaid into the receiver. There were 10,000 manufactured in 1972. This is a commemorative rifle and must be new in the box to generate the top collector appeal.

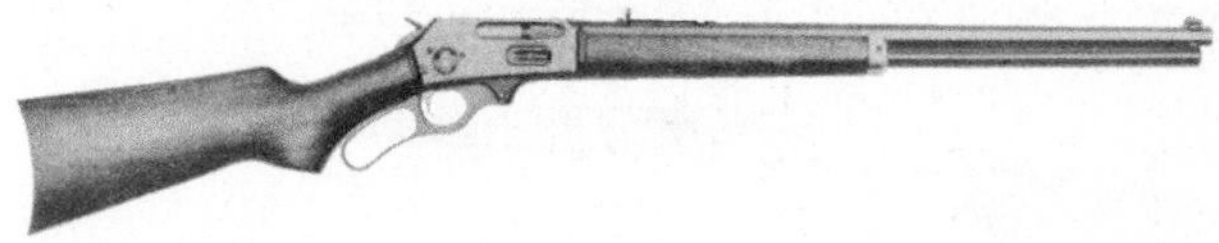

NIB	Exc.	V.G.	Good	Fair	Poor
600	425	275	200	150	100

Model 336 Octagon

This model was introduced to utilize the octagonal barrel making equipment that was on hand from the manufacture of the commemoratives. It is essentially a 336T with a 22" tapered octagonal barrel chambered for .30-30 only. It features a full-length magazine tube, slim forend with steel cap, and a classic-style hard rubber buttplate. The walnut stock is straight, and the lever is square. The finish, including the trigger, is blued. This model was made in 1973 only.

NIB	Exc.	V.G.	Good	Fair	Poor
725	600	500	325	175	150

Model 336ER (Extra Range)

This model was introduced in 1983 and was advertised as being chambered for the .307 Winchester and the .356 Winchester cartridges. The .307 was never produced. The .356 Winchester was supposed to add new capabilities to this classic rifle, but it never caught on with the shooting public and was discontinued in 1986 after only 2,441 Model ERs were manufactured. It has a 20" barrel and 5-shot tube magazine.

NIB	Exc.	V.G.	Good	Fair	Poor
—	825	550	300	250	150

Model 336C

This is the current carbine model of this line. It has a hammer-block safety and is chambered for the .30-30, .35 Remington, and until 1988 the .375 Winchester. The barrel is 20", and the magazine tube holds 6 shots. The pistol-grip stock and semi-beavertail forearm are American walnut. This model has been manufactured since 1984. The 1983 model was known as the 336C and had no hammer-block safety. Weight is approximately 7 lbs.

NIB	Exc.	V.G.	Good	Fair	Poor
475	350	225	200	175	150

Model 336SS

Similar to the Model 336C but in .30-30 only and with stainless steel barrel and receiver.

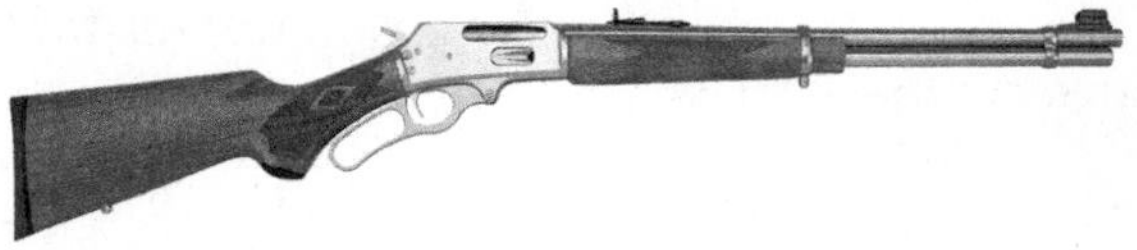

NIB	Exc.	V.G.	Good	Fair	Poor
525	400	250	200	150	100

Model 336LTS

This is the latest version of the old "Marauder" carbine. It was dubbed the LTS or "Lightweight" model instead of the Marauder as it was feared that the latter designation would be inappropriate in today's society. The model features a 16.5" barrel with full-length tube magazine that holds 5 shots. The walnut stock has a straight grip, and there is a barrel band on the forearm. The butt has a rubber rifle pad. This model was introduced in 1988. Discontinued.

NIB	Exc.	V.G.	Good	Fair	Poor
675	450	300	250	200	150

Model 336 Cowboy

This model is similar to the Model 336 CS. It is available in both .30-30 and .38-55 calibers. It is fitted with 24" tapered octagon barrel. Rear sight is Marble buckhorn. Tubular magazine holds 6 rounds. Straight grip walnut stock has a hard rubber buttplate. Weight is about 7.5 lbs. First introduced in 1999.

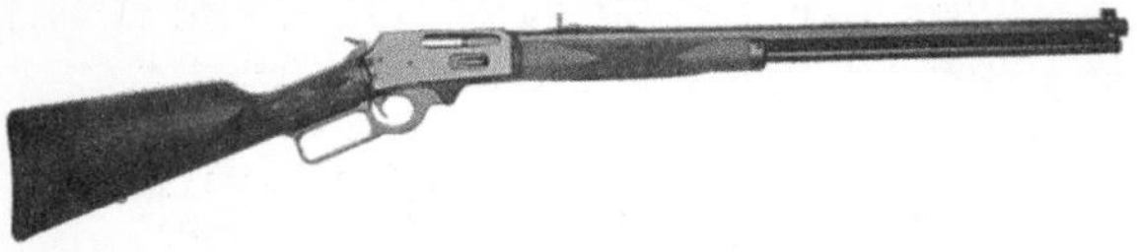

NIB	Exc.	V.G.	Good	Fair	Poor
875	650	525	325	175	150

Model 336M

Introduced in 2000, this model is chambered for the .30-30 cartridge. It features a stainless steel receiver and barrel; all other parts are nickel plated. Barrel length is 20". Magazine capacity is 6 rounds. Checkered walnut stock has a Mar-Shield finish. Rubber buttpad. Weight is about 7 lbs. Marlin's first stainless steel rifle.

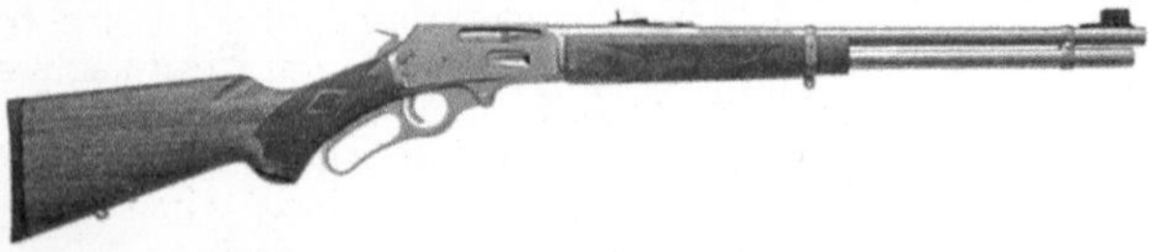

NIB	Exc.	V.G.	Good	Fair	Poor
675	550	425	275	175	125

Model 336CC

Chambered for the .30-30 cartridge and fitted with a 20" barrel this model features a Mossy Oak Break-Up camo finish. Adjustable rear sight. Weight is about 7 lbs. Introduced in 2001.

NIB	Exc.	V.G.	Good	Fair	Poor
500	390	325	250	200	100

Model 336W

Similar to Model 336C but in .30-30 only and with gold-plated trigger and hardwood stock. Also available with factory-mounted 3x9 scope. Add 10 percent for scope package.

NIB	Exc.	V.G.	Good	Fair	Poor
450	395	325	250	200	100

Model 336Y "Spike Horn"

Chambered for the .30-30 cartridge and fitted with a 16.5" barrel, this rifle features a checkered walnut stock with pistol grip. Magazine capacity is 5 rounds. Adjustable rear sight. Weight is about 6.5 lbs. Introduced in 2003.

NIB	Exc.	V.G.	Good	Fair	Poor
575	425	300	200	150	100

Model 336XLR

Lever-action chambered in 30/30 or .35 Remington, with 5-shot tubular magazine, 24-inch stainless steel barrel, along with stainless steel receiver, trigger, trigger guard plate, magazine tube, loading gate, and lever. Full pistol grip, swivel studs, and Ballard-type rifling precision fluted bolt. Features solid top receiver with side-ejection, adjustable folding semi-buckhorn rear sight, ramp front sight, tapped for scope mount. Designed for Hornady LEVERevolution cartridges. Introduced 2006.

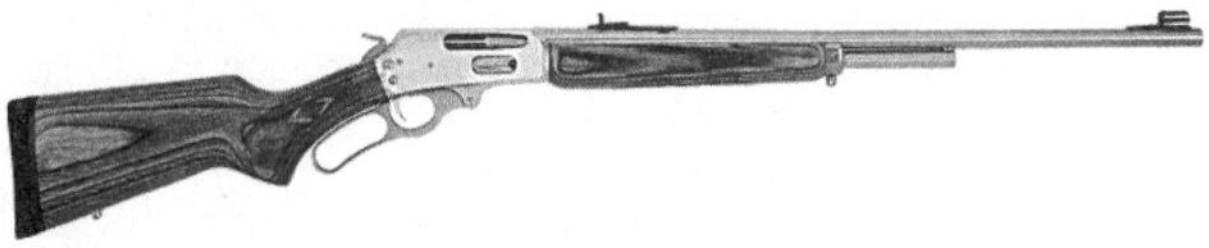

NIB	Exc.	V.G.	Good	Fair	Poor
625	500	375	250	175	100

Marlin 336BL

Lever action rifle chambered for .30-30. Features include 6-shot full length tubular magazine; 18-inch blued barrel with Micro-Groove rifling (12 grooves); big-loop finger lever; side ejection; blued steel receiver; hammer block safety; brown laminated hardwood pistol-grip stock with fluted comb; cut checkering; deluxe recoil pad; blued swivel studs.

NIB	Exc.	V.G.	Good	Fair	Poor
525	400	250	200	150	100

Marlin 336 Deluxe

Lever action rifle chambered in .30-30. Features include 6-shot tubular magazine; side ejection; solid top receiver; highly polished deep blue finish; hammer block safety; #1 grade full fancy American black walnut stock and forend; 20-inch barrel with Micro-Groove rifling (12 grooves); adjustable semi-buckhorn folding rear, ramp front sight with brass bead and Wide-Scan\xaa hood. Solid top receiver tapped for scope mount; offset hammer spur (right or left hand) for scope use. Price: N/A.

Model 30AS

This model is similar to the 336 CS, but the stock is made of walnut-finished hardwood instead of genuine American walnut. It is chambered for .30-30 only.

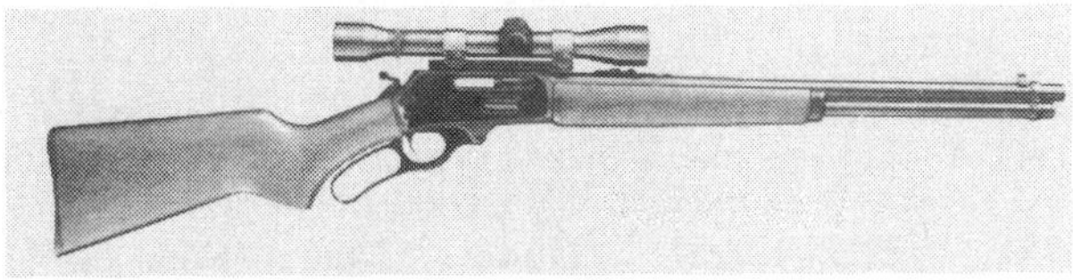

NIB	Exc.	V.G.	Good	Fair	Poor
395	285	200	175	125	100

Model 444 Lever-Action

This model was introduced in 1965. It is chambered for the .444 Marlin. The rifle is essentially a Model 336 action modified to accept the larger cartridge. It has a 24" round barrel that was cut back to 22" in 1971. It holds 5 shots total and, when introduced, featured a straight-gripped Monte Carlo stock and semi-beavertail forend with barrel band. Another band holds the two-thirds-length magazine tube in place. In 1971 the stock was changed to a pistol grip without the Monte Carlo comb.

NIB	Exc.	V.G.	Good	Fair	Poor
—	600	450	300	175	125

Model 444S

This model was introduced in 1972 and is essentially the later 444 with a steel forend tip instead of the barrel bands.

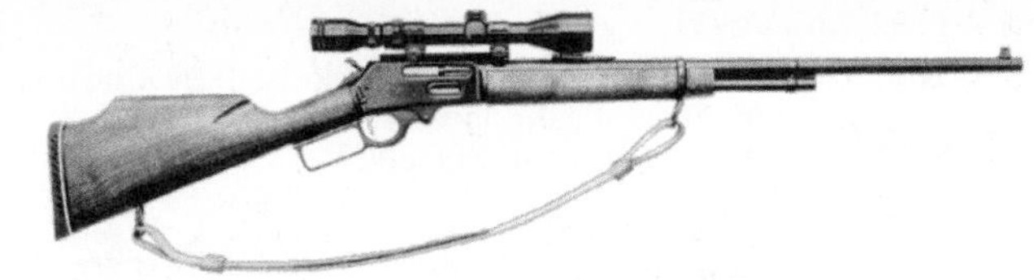

NIB	Exc.	V.G.	Good	Fair	Poor
—	500	350	175	150	125

Model 444SS

In 1984 the company added a crossbolt hammer-block safety to the 444 S and redesignated it the 444 SS. This Model is currently in production as the Model 444, the "S" suffix having been dropped.

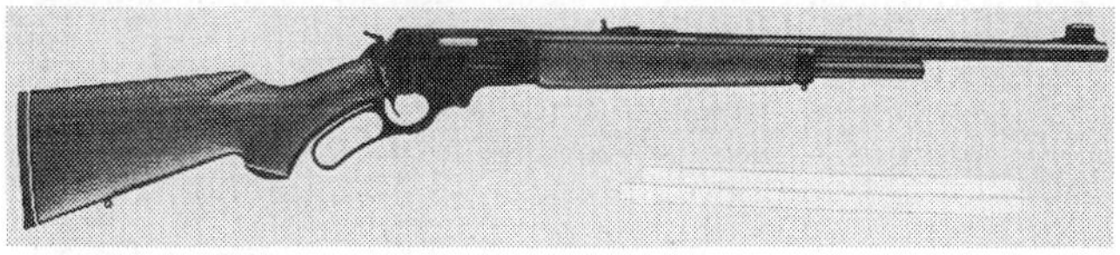

NIB	Exc.	V.G.	Good	Fair	Poor
550	395	300	225	150	125

Model 444P Outfitter

Introduced in 1999 this model is chambered for the .444 Marlin cartridge. It is fitted with a 18.5" ported barrel. Tubular magazine capacity is 5 rounds. Walnut stock with straight grip and ventilated recoil pad standard. Weight is approximately 6.75 lbs.Discontinued 2002.

NIB	Exc.	V.G.	Good	Fair	Poor
725	600	425	335	275	200

Model 444XLR

Similar to Model 1895XLR but chambered in .444 Marlin. Introduced 2006.

NIB	Exc.	V.G.	Good	Fair	Poor
625	500	375	250	175	100

Model 1894 Lever-Action

The production of the Model 336 in .44 Magnum was a frustrating experience as the action was simply too long for a short pistol case. In 1969 Marlin reintroduced the Model 1894 chambered for the .44 Magnum cartridge. The barrel is 20", and the full-length magazine tube holds 10 rounds. It features an adjustable rear and a ramp-type front sight. The finish is blued, with a matted receiver top. The walnut stock has a straight grip; and the forend, a barrel band. From 1969 to 1971 there was a brass saddle ring.

NIB	Exc.	V.G.	Good	Fair	Poor
525	375	300	200	150	100

Model 1894 Octagon Barrel

This is basically the same as the Model 1894, with a 20" octagonal barrel and a steel forend tip instead of the barrel band. There were 2,957 manufactured in 1973 only.

NIB	Exc.	V.G.	Good	Fair	Poor
—	650	525	350	225	100

Model 1894 Sporter

This variation has a 20" round barrel, half-length magazine tube that holds 6 shots, and a hard rubber classic-style buttplate. Only 1,398 were manufactured in 1973.

NIB	Exc.	V.G.	Good	Fair	Poor
625	475	325	250	175	125

Model 1894P

This model was introduced in 2000 and is chambered for the .44 Magnum or .44 Special cartridges. Barrel length is 16.25". Magazine capacity is 8 rounds. Adjustable rear sight. Blued finish with bead blasted receiver top. Drilled and tapped for scope mount. Weight is about 5.75 lbs.

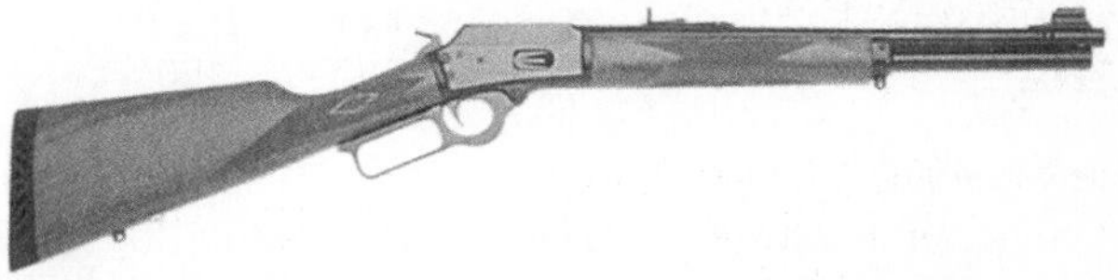

NIB	Exc.	V.G.	Good	Fair	Poor
600	450	375	300	150	100

Model 1894CS Lever-Action

This model is chambered for the .38 Special and .357 Magnum cartridges. It features an 18.5" round barrel, with full-length magazine tube and two barrel bands. It holds 9 shots and has a walnut straight-grip stock. This model was manufactured between 1969 and 1984. In 1984 a hammer-block crossbolt safety was added, and the model number was changed to 1894 CS. All other specifications remained the same. The Model is now known, again, as the Model 1894C.

NIB	Exc.	V.G.	Good	Fair	Poor
—	525	375	275	125	100

Model 1894M Lever-Action Rifle

This model is similar to the other 1894 rifles except that it is chambered for the .22 Magnum cartridge and features an outside loading tube magazine that holds 11 shots. The barrel is 20" long, and there is a steel forend tip instead of a barrel band. This model was manufactured between 1983 and 1988 and was only produced with the crossbolt safety.

NIB	Exc.	V.G.	Good	Fair	Poor
—	550	450	325	275	150

Model 1894S Lever-Action Rifle

This model was introduced in 1984. It is chambered for the .41 Magnum and the .44 Special/.44 Magnum cartridges. In 1988 the .45 Colt chambering was offered. This model has a 20" barrel and a straight-grip stock. The forend has a steel cap. This model is currently produced as the Model 1894 and features the hammer-block safety.

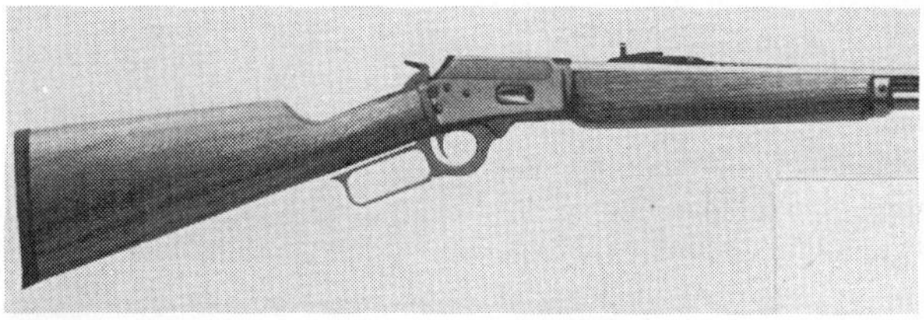

NIB	Exc.	V.G.	Good	Fair	Poor
550	450	375	275	175	125

Model 1894CL (Classic) Lever-Action Rifle

This model was introduced in 1988 and is the same basic rifle chambered for the old .25-20 and .32-20 cartridges. The rifle is also chambered for the .218 Bee cartridge. The barrel is 22", and the half-length magazine tube holds 6 shots. The walnut stock has no white spacers and has a black buttplate. Discontinued in 1993. **NOTE:** Collector interest has been growing in this model since it was discontinued in 1993.

NIB	*Exc.*	*V.G.*	*Good*	*Fair*	*Poor*
750	550	450	300	250	150

Model 1894CL (Classic) New

Reintroduced in 2005 this model is chambered for the .32-20 cartridge and fitted with a 22" barrel with open sights. Tubular magazine capacity is 6 rounds. Checkered straight grip walnut stock. Weight is about 6 lbs. Discontinued.

NIB	*Exc.*	*V.G.*	*Good*	*Fair*	*Poor*
700	600	475	395	300	125

Model 1894 Century Limited

An anniversary edition of the Marlin Model 1894 is limited to 2,500 rifles chambered in .44-40 caliber. Frame engraved and case colored. It is fitted with a 24" octagon barrel with 10-round magazine tube. The stock is semi-fancy walnut with straight grip and cut checkering with brass crescent buttplate.

NIB	*Exc.*	*V.G.*	*Good*	*Fair*	*Poor*
950	700	425	300	200	100

Model 1894 Century Limited Employee Edition

Same as above but limited to 100 rifles. The gun has a finer grade wood and the Marlin Man on the Horse logo is inlaid in gold on the right side of the receiver.

NIB	*Exc.*	*V.G.*	*Good*	*Fair*	*Poor*
1500	825	700	425	300	200

Model 1894 Cowboy

Introduced in 1996 this lever-action rifle features a 24" tapered octagon barrel with a 10-round tubular magazine. It is chambered for the .45 Long Colt, a popular cartridge for "Cowboy Action Shooting." Straight-grip checkered stock with blued steel forearm cap. Weight is approximately 7.5 lbs.

NIB	*Exc.*	*V.G.*	*Good*	*Fair*	*Poor*
750	600	450	300	225	150

Model 1894 Cowboy 32

As above but chambered for the .32 H&R Magnum cartridge. Introduced in 2004.

NIB	*Exc.*	*V.G.*	*Good*	*Fair*	*Poor*
750	600	450	300	225	150

Model 1894 Cowboy II

Introduced in 1997 and is the same as the Model 1894 Cowboy but is chambered for several cartridges. Available in .44-40, .357 Mag., .38 Special, and .44 Mag/.44 Special.

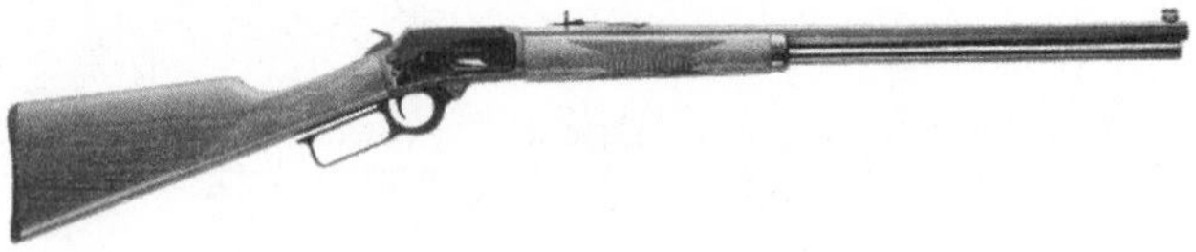

NIB	*Exc.*	*V.G.*	*Good*	*Fair*	*Poor*
650	525	300	225	150	100

Model 1894CP

This model is chambered for the .375 Magnum cartridge and fitted with a 16.25" ported barrel. Tubular magazine holds 8 rounds. Checkered American black walnut stock. Adjustable semi-buckhorn rear sight. Receiver drilled and tapped for scope mount. Weight is about 5.75 lbs. Introduced in 2001.

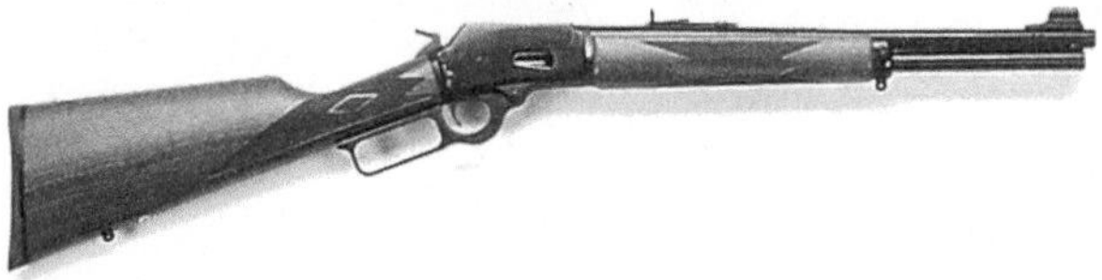

NIB	*Exc.*	*V.G.*	*Good*	*Fair*	*Poor*
626	575	450	300	225	100

Model 1894SS

This lever-action rifle is chambered for the .44 Magnum and .44 Special cartridges. Fitted with a 20" barrel with 10-round magazine. Stainless steel barrel and receiver. Checkered walnut stock with straight grip. Rubber buttpad. Weight is about 6 lbs. Introduced in 2002.

NIB	*Exc.*	*V.G.*	*Good*	*Fair*	*Poor*
650	500	400	300	200	100

Model 1894PG

Introduced in 2003, this lever-action model is chambered for the .44 Rem. Mag cartridge and fitted with a 20" barrel. Checkered walnut stock with pistol grip. Magazine capacity is 10 rounds. Adjustable rear sight. Blued finish. Weight is about 6.5 lbs.

NIB	*Exc.*	*V.G.*	*Good*	*Fair*	*Poor*
575	450	300	225	150	100

Model 1894FG

This lever-action model is chambered for the .41 Rem. Magnum cartridge and fitted with a 20" barrel. Checkered walnut stock with pistol grip. Magazine capacity is 10 rounds. Weight is about 6.5 lbs. Introduced in 2003.

NIB	Exc.	V.G.	Good	Fair	Poor
600	450	300	225	150	100

Model 1894 Cowboy

Fitted with a 20" barrel and chambered for the .38 Special cartridge, this rifle is designed for Cowboy Action Shooting. Special hand-tuned parts. Magazine capacity is 10 rounds. Walnut stock with straight grip. Case colored receiver, bolt, trigger plate, and lever. Weight is about 6 lbs. Introduced in 2002. In 2003 this model was offered chambered for the .45 Colt cartridge.

NIB	Exc.	V.G.	Good	Fair	Poor
825	750	600	500	300	150

Marlin 1894 Deluxe

Lever action rifle chambered in .44 Magnum/.44 Special. Features include 10-shot tubular magazine; squared finger lever; side ejection; richly polished deep blued metal surfaces; solid top receiver; hammer block safety; #1 grade fancy American black walnut straight-grip stock and forend; cut checkering; rubber rifle butt pad; Mar-Shield finish; blued steel fore-end cap: swivel studs; deep-cut Ballard-type rifling (6 grooves). Price: N/A.

Marlin 1894CSS

Lever action rifle chambered in .357 Magnum/.38 Special. Features include 9-shot tubular magazine; stainless steel receiver, barrel, lever, trigger and hammer; squared finger lever; side ejection; solid top receiver; hammer block safety; American black walnut straight-grip stock and forend; cut checkering; rubber rifle butt pad; Mar-Shield finish. Price: N/A.

Marlin 1894 CSBL

Chambered in .357/.38 Special with 7-round capacity. Barrel is 16-1/4 inches, stock gray/black laminated. Other features include Marlin's Big Loop lever, stainless steel barrel, receiver, trigger guard plate and loading gate. Ghost-ring sighting system with mounting rail for optical sights. Introduced in 2011.

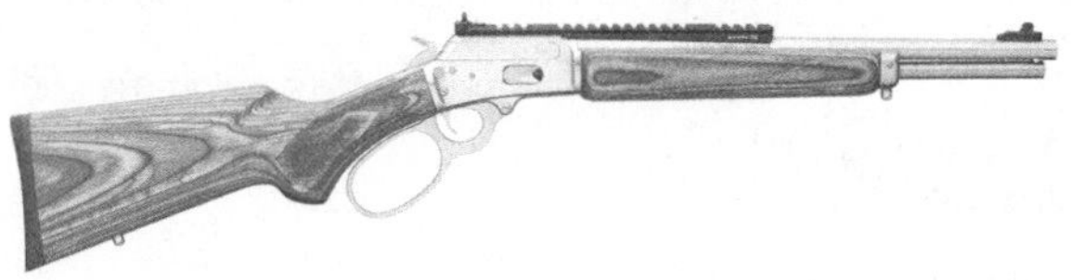

NIB	Exc.	V.G.	Good	Fair	Poor
800	725	600	500	400	300

Model 1895 and 1895SS Lever-Action

The Model 1895 was reintroduced on the Model 336 action that had been modified to handle the .45-70 cartridge. This was done to capitalize on the nostalgia wave that descended on the country in the early 1970s. This model features a 22" round barrel with a two-thirds-length magazine tube that holds 4 shots. The walnut stock had a straight grip until the Model 1895 S was released in 1980, when a pistol-grip stock was used. In 1983 the Model 1895 SS with the crossbolt hammer-block safety was added; it is currently produced in this configuration.

NIB	Exc.	V.G.	Good	Fair	Poor
600	5000	325	200	150	100

NOTE: For early "B" prefix guns below serial number 12000 add 25 percent.

Model 1895M

Similar to the Model 1895 but chambered in .450 Marlin.

NIB	Exc.	V.G.	Good	Fair	Poor
600	5000	325	200	150	100

Model 1895 Century Limited

Chambered for the .45-70 cartridge this model features a 4-shot tubular magazine, 24" half round/half octagon barrel, semi-fancy walnut stock with pistol grip. The receiver is French greyed and engraved with the Marlin Man on one side and two bears on the other. Weight is about 7.5 lbs. Discontinued. 299 produced.

NIB	Exc.	V.G.	Good	Fair	Poor
1200	1050	700	500	300	150

Model 1895 Century Limited Employee Edition

Similar to the above model but limited to 100 rifles. The company logo is inlaid in gold on the right side and the left side has two cow elk and a bull elk.

NIB	Exc.	V.G.	Good	Fair	Poor
1450	1200	800	600	400	200

Model 1895G "Guide Gun"

This model is chambered for the .45-70 Government cartridge. It has a 18.5" ported barrel. Straight grip walnut stock with cut checkering and ventilated recoil pad. Adjustable rear sight. Weight is about 6.75 lbs. Introduced in 1998.

NIB	Exc.	V.G.	Good	Fair	Poor
650	550	450	350	250	150

Model 1895GS Guide Gun

Introduced in 2001, this .45-70 rifle is fitted with a 18.5" ported barrel with 4-round magazine. Stainless steel receiver and barrel. American black walnut stock with cut checkering and ventilated recoil pad. Adjustable rear semi-buckhorn sight. Weight is about 7 lbs. Early models had ported barrel, now discontinued.

NIB	Exc.	V.G.	Good	Fair	Poor
6	75	550	450	350	100

Model 1895 Cowboy

This rifle is chambered for the .45-70 cartridge and fitted with a 26" tapered octagon barrel. Tubular magazine has a 9-round capacity. Adjustable semi-buckhorn rear sight. American black stock with cut checkering. Hard rubber butt. Weight is about 8 lbs. Introduced in 2001.

NIB	Exc.	V.G.	Good	Fair	Poor
650	550	450	350	200	100

Model 1895XLR

Lever-action chambered in .45-70 Government or .450 Marlin with a 4-shot tubular magazine, 24-inch stainless steel barrel, along with stainless steel receiver, trigger, trigger guard plate, magazine tube, loading gate, and lever. Full pistol grip, swivel studs, and

Ballard-type rifling precision fluted bolt. Features solid top receiver with side-ejection, adjustable folding semi-buckhorn rear sight, ramp front sight, tapped for scope mount. Designed for Hornady LEVERevolution cartridges. Introduced 2006.

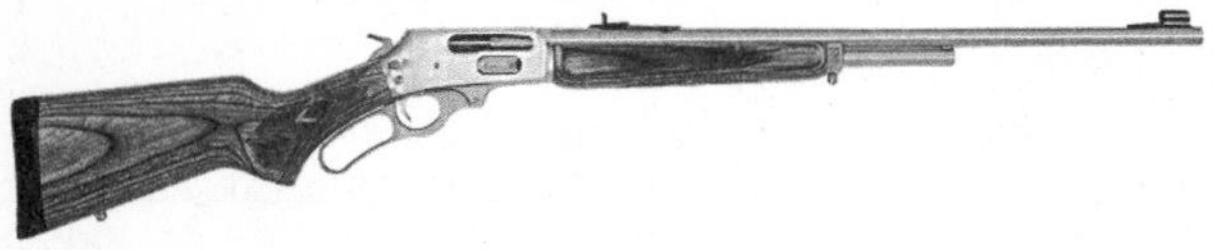

NIB	Exc.	V.G.	Good	Fair	Poor
700	600	525	400	300	150

Model 1895MXLR

Similar to Model 1895XLR but chambered in .450 Marlin. Introduced 2006.

NIB	Exc.	V.G.	Good	Fair	Poor
700	600	525	400	300	150

Marlin Model 1895 SBLR

Similar to Model 1895GS Guide Gun but with stainless steel barrel (18-1/2"), receiver, large loop lever and magazine tube. Black/gray laminated buttstock and forend, XS ghost ring rear sight, hooded ramp front sight, receiver/barrel-mounted top rail for mounting accessory optics. Chambered in .45-70 Government. Overall length 42-1/2". Weight: 7-1/2 lbs.

NIB	Exc.	V.G.	Good	Fair	Poor
875	700	600	525	400	150

Marlin 1895GBL

Lever action rifle chambered in .45-70 Government. Features include 6-shot, full-length tubular magazine; 18-1/2-inch barrel with deep-cut Ballard-type rifling (6 grooves); big-loop finger lever; side ejection; solid-top receiver; deeply blued metal surfaces; hammer block safety; pistol-grip two tone brown laminate stock with cut checkering; ventilated recoil pad; Mar-Shield finish, swivel studs. Price: N/A

Model 308MXLR

Similar to the Model 1895MXLR but chambered in the proprietary .308 Marlin Express cartridge.

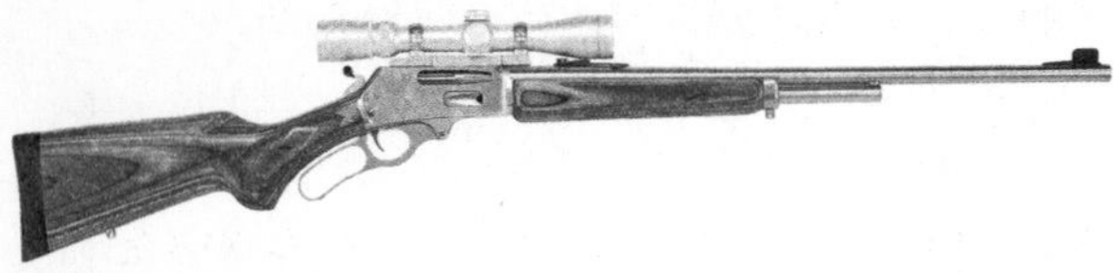

NIB	Exc.	V.G.	Good	Fair	Poor
700	600	525	400	300	150

Model 308MX

Similar to the Model 308MXLR but with blued receiver and barrel.

NIB	Exc.	V.G.	Good	Fair	Poor
550	450	350	250	150	100

Marlin Model 338MXLR

Lever-action rifle chambered for .338 Marlin Express. 24" stainless steel barrel, stainless steel receiver, lever and magazine tube. Black/gray laminated checkered stock and forend. Hooded ramp front sight and adjustable semi-buckhorn rear; drilled and tapped for scope mounts. Receiver-mounted crossbolt safety. Overall length 42-1/2". Weight: 7-1/2 lbs.

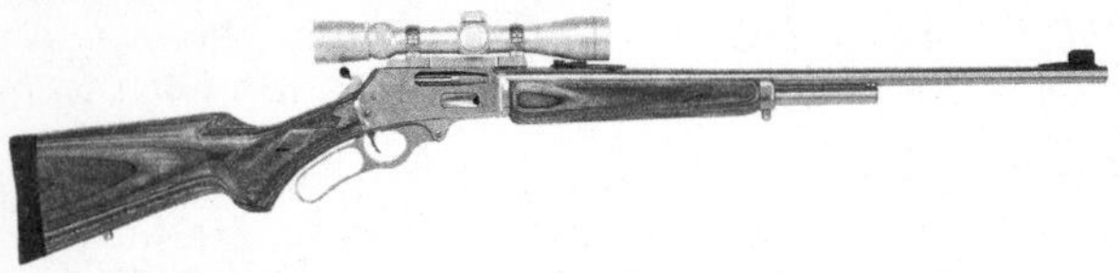

NIB	Exc.	V.G.	Good	Fair	Poor
700	600	525	400	300	150

Model 338MX

Similar to Model 338MXLR but with blued metal and walnut stock and forend.

NIB	Exc.	V.G.	Good	Fair	Poor
550	450	350	250	150	100

Model 1897 Century Limited

Introduced in 1997 this model is chambered for the .22 caliber cartridge and commemorates the 100th anniversary of the Model 1897. It is fitted with a 24" half round/half octagon barrel with adjustable Marble rear sight and Marble front sight with brass bead. Blued receiver is engraved and gold inlayed with semi-fancy walnut stock and hard rubber buttplate. Weight is about 6.5 lbs.

NIB	Exc.	V.G.	Good	Fair	Poor
900	700	575	475	300	200

Model 1897 Century Limited Employee Edition

Similar to the model above but with additional gold engraving on the lever. Limited to 100 rifles.

NIB	Exc.	V.G.	Good	Fair	Poor
1300	1150	900	700	400	250

Model 1897 Cowboy

This .22 caliber lever-action rifle is fitted with a 24" tapered octagon barrel with adjustable Marble buckhorn sight and Marble front sight with brass bead. Full-length tubular magazine holds 26 Shorts, 21 Longs, and 19 LR cartridges. Walnut straight grip stock with hard rubber buttplate. Weight is 7.5 lbs. Introduced in 1999.

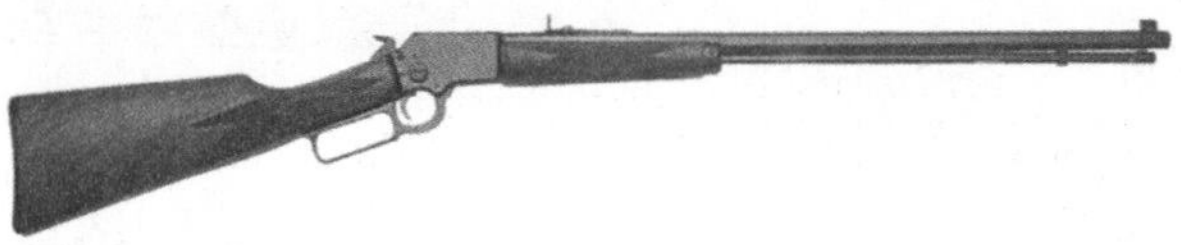

NIB	Exc.	V.G.	Good	Fair	Poor
700	550	450	350	200	100

Model 1897 Annie Oakley

Introduced in 1998 this .22 caliber model features an 18.5" tapered octagon barrel, adjustable Marble rear sight and Marble front sight. The blued receiver is roll engraved with gold signature. Stock is straight grip with blued end cap and hard rubber buttplate. Weight is approximately 5.5 lbs.

NIB	Exc.	V.G.	Good	Fair	Poor
700	600	400	300	200	125

Model 1897 Texan

Chambered for the .22 caliber cartridge and fitted with a 20" octagon barrel, this rifle has a walnut stock with straight grip. Magazine capacity is 14 to 21 cartridges depending on type. Weight is about 6 lbs. Introduced in 2002.

NIB	Exc.	V.G.	Good	Fair	Poor
700	600	400	300	200	125

Marlin Glenfield Lever-Action Rifles

The Glenfield line of rifles was designed to be sold in large outlet chain stores and were simply cheaper versions that were to be sold for less money. The rifles functioned fine, but birch was used instead of walnut and pressed checkering instead of handcut. These rifles were manufactured under the Glenfield name between 1964 and 1983. There are five models of Lever-Action Glenfields: the 36G, 30, 30A, 30 GT, and the 30 AS. They are chambered for the .30-30 cartridge, and the basic differences are slight and, in most cases, merely cosmetic. They are good, serviceable rifles but have little or no collector interest or investment potential.

NIB	Exc.	V.G.	Good	Fair	Poor
295	250	200	150	125	100

Model 30AW

This lever-action rifle is chambered for the .30-30 cartridge. It has a 20" barrel and 6-round magazine tube. The stock is walnut finished birch with pistol-grip cap and hard rubber buttplate. Introduced in 1998.

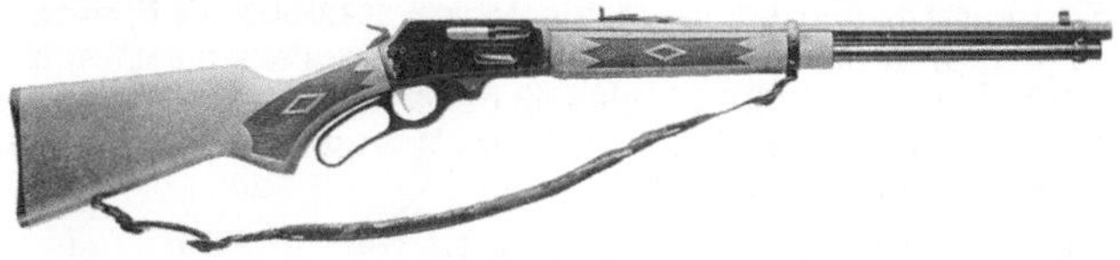

NIB	Exc.	V.G.	Good	Fair	Poor
300	250	200	150	125	100

Model 39 Lever-Action Rifle

This model originally evolved from the Model 1891 invented by L.L. Hepburn. The 1891 rifle became the 1892 and eventually developed into the takedown Model 1897. The latter two were produced until 1915, when they were discontinued in favor of machine gun production for WWI. In 1922, when the company was sold to John Moran and became the Marlin Firearms Corp., the .22 rimfire lever-action was reintroduced as the Model 39. It has been in production in one form or another ever since.

MODEL 39

As it was introduced in 1922, the Model 39 was chambered for the .22 rimfire and had a 24" octagonal barrel and a takedown receiver. It has a full-length magazine tube which holds 25 Shorts, 20 Longs, or 18 LR cartridges. Most Model 39s had a spring-loaded button outer magazine tube release. Very early variations had the Model '97 type knurled latch release. As the Model 39As were being phased in around 1939 many have the more modern removable inner magazine tube. It has a solid top frame and side ejection, a Rocky Mountain rear, and ivory bead front sight. The receiver, lever, and hammer are case colored; the barrel is blued. The pistol-grip stock and steel-capped forearm are varnished walnut. This model was manufactured in this form between 1922 and 1938 with a number of options that could affect value and would warrant individual appraisal. Model 39s with a "star" stamped on the tang were considered high grade guns by the factory inspector and will command a premium in better condition examples. **NOTE:** Model 39s made prior to 1932 that have either no prefix or the prefix S on the serial number should not be used with high-speed ammunition. The prefix HS indicates the improved bolt that is safe for this ammunition.

Standard Rifle

NIB	Exc.	V.G.	Good	Fair	Poor
—	1500	850	475	300	200

Deluxe Rifle

Factory checkering, fancy wood and "star" stamp on tang.

NIB	Exc.	V.G.	Good	Fair	Poor
—	2500	1500	750	400	250

MODEL 39A LEVER-ACTION RIFLE

This is an improved version of the Model 39. It has a heavier, tapered round barrel and semi-beavertail forearm and a redesigned pistol-grip stock. The rubber buttplate was replaced by one of a synthetic fiber; otherwise, specifications were similar to the Model 39. This model was manufactured from 1939 to 1960. Several variations are listed.

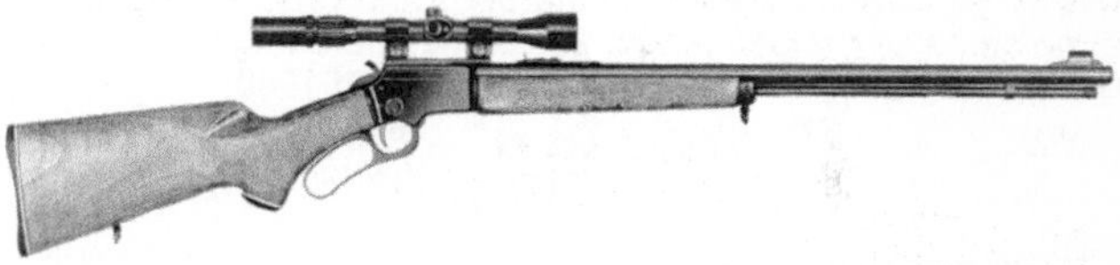

Factory checkering, fancy wood and "star" stamp on tang.

Pre-war Variations

(1939-1941) case colored receiver, no serial number prefix (1939) or "B" prefix (1940-1941).

NIB	Exc.	V.G.	Good	Fair	Poor
—	1200	800	450	250	150

Post-war Variations

(1945-1953) Serial number prefixes up to letter "K." Ballard-type deep rifling.

NIB	Exc.	V.G.	Good	Fair	Poor
—	700	575	425	250	200

NOTE: Add 20 percent premium of C prefix 1st post-war variation with figured wood.

Post-war Variations

(1954-1956) Serial number prefixes L, M, N, with MicroGroove barrel.

NIB	Exc.	V.G.	Good	Fair	Poor
—	600	495	395	225	125

"Golden 39A's" (1954-1963)

Gold trigger, MicroGroove rifling. Serial number prefixes L through W.

NIB	Exc.	V.G.	Good	Fair	Poor
—	550	450	325	195	125

MODEL 39A MOUNTIE

This is basically a carbine version of the Model 39A. It features a 20" tapered round barrel, straight-grip walnut stock, and slimmed-down forearm. It was manufactured between 1953 and 1960.

1st Variation

K prefix and 24" barrel, fat forearm.

NIB	Exc.	V.G.	Good	Fair	Poor
—	600	450	300	200	100

NOTE: Add 20 percent for slim forearm.

Standard

NIB	Exc.	V.G.	Good	Fair	Poor
—	450	325	175	125	100

Model 39A 1960 Presentation Model

Released in 1960, this was Marlin's 90th Anniversary model. It is similar to the 39A but has a chrome-plated barrel and receiver with a high grade, checkered walnut stock and forend. There is a squirrel carved on the right side of the buttstock. There were 500 produced in 1960. This is a commemorative and as such will be desirable to collectors only if NIB with all boxes and papers with which it was originally sold.

NIB	Exc.	V.G.	Good	Fair	Poor
1200	900	500	300	175	125

Model 39M Mountie 1960 Presentation Model

This is the carbine version of the 90th Anniversary model. This is the same as the 39A with a 20" barrel and straight-grip stock. There were 500 of this model manufactured in 1960.

NIB	Exc.	V.G.	Good	Fair	Poor
1200	900	500	300	175	125

Model 39ADL Lever-Action Rifle

This model is the same as the 90th Anniversary issue except that it is blued instead of chrome-plated. There were 3,306 manufactured between 1960 and 1963.

NIB	Exc.	V.G.	Good	Fair	Poor
1000	850	500	300	175	125

Model Golden 39A Lever-Action Rifle

This model is similar to the 39A, with a gold-plated trigger and sling swivels. It was manufactured between 1960 and 1983.

NIB	Exc.	V.G.	Good	Fair	Poor
—	650	550	400	250	125

Model 39 Carbine

This is a slimmer, lighter version of the Model 39A. It features a slimmer forend and thinner barrel. There were 12,140 manufactured between 1963 and 1967.

NIB	Exc.	V.G.	Good	Fair	Poor
—	550	400	250	175	100

Model 39 Century Limited

The introduction of this model marked the 100th Anniversary of the Marlin Company. This model features a 20" octagonal barrel with semi-buckhorn rear and brass blade front sight. The stock is fancy walnut, with a straight grip and a brass forend tip and buttplate. There is a medallion inlaid into the right side of the receiver and a brass plate on the stock. There were 34,197 manufactured in 1970. As a commemorative this model needs to be as it came from the factory to command collector interest.

NIB	Exc.	V.G.	Good	Fair	Poor
950	550	300	150	125	100

Model 39A Article II

This model commemorated the National Rifle Association's 100th Anniversary in 1971. It has a 24" octagonal barrel, high grade walnut pistol-grip stock, and brass forend tip and buttplate. The right side of the receiver has the NRA's Second Amendment "Right to Keep and Bear Arms" medallion inlaid. Manufactured in 1971.

NIB	Exc.	V.G.	Good	Fair	Poor
750	450	300	150	125	100

Model 39M Article II

This model is the same as the Model 39A Article II except that it is a carbine version with a 20" octagonal barrel and a straight grip stock. There were 3,824 manufactured in 1971. As commemoratives NIB condition is essential to collector interest.

NIB	Exc.	V.G.	Good	Fair	Poor
775	475	325	175	150	100

Model 39A Octagon

This model was produced because the company had the machinery and some leftover barrels from the two commemorative models produced in 1970 and 1971. This was a regular production run that was meant to be used and was not a special issue. It has a 24", tapered octagonal barrel and is chambered for the .22 rimfire cartridges. It has a pistol-grip walnut stock, with steel forend tip. There were 2,551 manufactured in 1972 and 1973. This was not a commercially successful model, and it was discontinued for that reason.

NIB	Exc.	V.G.	Good	Fair	Poor
800	600	400	250	200	175

Model 39M Octagon

This is the 20", octagonal barreled carbine version with a straight-grip stock. There were 2,140 manufactured in 1973.

NIB	Exc.	V.G.	Good	Fair	Poor
750	600	400	250	200	175

Model 39D Lever-Action Rifle

This is essentially the Model 39M carbine, 20" barrel version with a pistol-grip stock. It was manufactured in 1971 and reintroduced in 1973. The 1971 version has white line spacers and pistol-grip caps. The 1973 version has neither of these features.

NIB	Exc.	V.G.	Good	Fair	Poor
—	625	475	325	195	125

Golden 39A Lever-Action Rifle

This is the current production model of this extremely popular .22 rifle. It features the hammer-block crossbolt safety and sling swivel studs. It is similar in appearance to its predecessors. Takedown style.

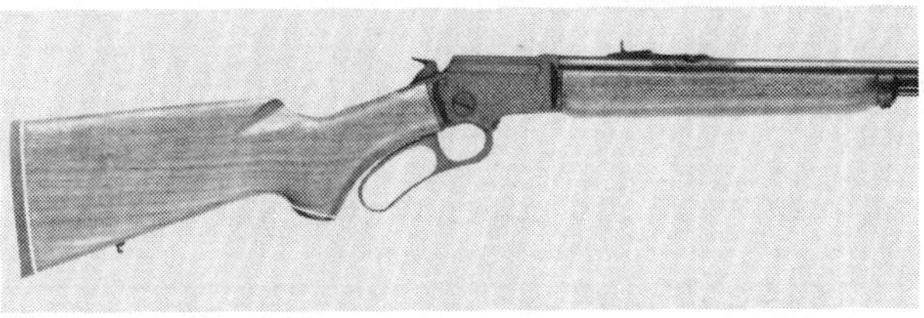

NIB	Exc.	V.G.	Good	Fair	Poor
650	550	425	325	225	200

Model 39TDS Lever-Action Rifle

Similar to the Model 39AS, with a 20" carbine barrel and straight-grip stock. It replaced the Model 39M and was introduced in 1988. Superseded by the current Golden 39A, which is a takedown design.

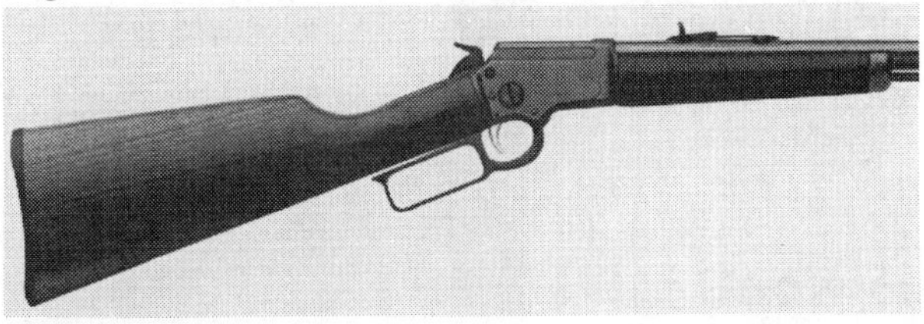

NIB	Exc.	V.G.	Good	Fair	Poor
600	475	300	200	150	100

Model 39AWL

This is a limited edition of 2,000 rifles distributed solely through Wal-Mart. Fitted with a 24.5" octagon barrel, select checkered walnut stock, gold filled engraving, and stamped "Wildlife For Tomorrow."

NIB	Exc.	V.G.	Good	Fair	Poor
750	600	400	300	200	125

Model 56 Levermatic Rifle

This is a streamlined version of the lever-action. It features a short lever throw and a one-piece walnut stock. The 22" barrel is round and is chambered for the .22 rimfire cartridges. There is a 7-shot detachable magazine, open sights, and a gold-plated trigger. The receiver on this model was made of aluminum after 1956. There were 31,523 manufactured between 1955 and 1964.

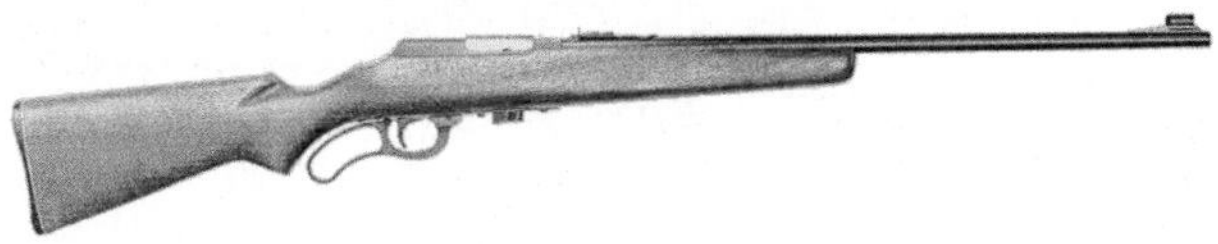

NIB	Exc.	V.G.	Good	Fair	Poor
—	325	225	150	75	50

Model 56 "Clipper King" Levermatic

This is the same as the Model 56 except that it is specially packaged and comes with a 4X .22 scope. The name "Clipper King" is stamped on the barrel, and the buttplate is red hard rubber. There were only 152 of these manufactured in 1959.

NIB	Exc.	V.G.	Good	Fair	Poor
—	350	250	175	100	75

Model 57 Levermatic Rifle

This model is similar to the Model 56, with a tube magazine and Monte Carlo stock. In 1960 Marlin went back to a steel receiver on this model. There were 34,628 manufactured from 1959 to 1965.

NIB	Exc.	V.G.	Good	Fair	Poor
—	325	225	150	75	50

Model 57M Levermatic Rifle

This is the Model 57 chambered for the .22 Magnum cartridge. There were 66,889 manufactured between 1959 and 1969.

NIB	Exc.	V.G.	Good	Fair	Poor
—	450	350	250	175	100

Model 62 Levermatic Rifle

This model is similar in appearance to the Model 57 except that it is chambered for the centerfire .256 Magnum cartridge and has a 4-shot magazine. In 1966 the .30 carbine cartridge was added. This model has a 23" "MicroGroove" barrel with open sights and a walnut one-piece stock. The first 4,000 Model 62s were shipped without serial numbers in violation of federal law. The company recalled the rifles for numbering; and, to this day, the owner of a centerfire Model 62 can return the rifle for numbering. There were 15,714 manufactured between 1963 and 1969. Add 15 percent for .256. **NOTE:** From 1969 to 1972, the first digit of the serial number indicates the year of manufacture. In 1973, the system was changed by having the first two digits subtracted from 100 to find the year of production. For example: 2717793=100-27=1973.

NIB	Exc.	V.G.	Good	Fair	Poor
—	600	475	375	225	100

MARLIN: MISCELLANEOUS RIMFIRE BOLT-ACTION RIFLES

The Marlin Firearms Company produced a great many bolt-action rifles, both single-shot and repeaters, starting in 1930 and continuing today. These rifles were low-priced and designed primarily as utility rifles. They also manufactured many autoloaders of the same type during these years. The Glenfield name will also be found on these models, as many were produced to be marketed by the large chain outlets. These rifles have limited value as collectibles at the present time, but no one can deny that they're durable, accurate, good-natured little rifles.

Single Shot

Model 65	1935-37
Model 65E	1935-37
Model 100	1935-59
Model 100S	1937-38
Model 101	1941-77
Model 101 DL	1941-45
Model 100 SB	1941
Model 101	1959
Model 122	1962-65

Repeater

Model 80	1935-59
Model 80E	1935-39
Model 81	1939
Model 81E	1939
Model 81DL	1939
Model 80B	1940
Model 80BE	1940
Model 81B	1940
Model 81BE	1940
Model 80 CSB	1941
Model 80DL	1941-64
Model 80C	1941-71
Model 980	1966-71
Model 780	1971-88
Model 781	1971-88
Model 782	1971-88
Model 783	1971-88
Model 880	1988-Pres.
Model 881	1988-Pres.
Model 882	1988-Pres.
Model 883	1988-Pres.

AUTOLOADERS

Model 50	1931-34	Model 98	1950-61
Model 50E	1931-34	Model 99	1959-61
Model A-1	1935-46	Model 99C	1962-78
Model A-1 E	1935-46	Model 99G	1960-65
Model A-1C	1940-46	Model DL	1960-65
Model A-1 DL	1940-46	Model 60	1960-Pres.
Model 88-C	1947-56	Model 49	1968-71
Model 88-DL	1953-56	Model 49DL	1971-78
Model 89-C	1950-61	Model 990	1979-87
Model 89-DL	1950-61	Model 995	1979-Pres.

The year of manufacture of Marlin modern production rifles made between 1946 and 1968 can be determined by the letter prefix on the serial number.

The prefixes are as follows:

1946–C	1951–H	1956–N	1961–U	1966–AB
1947–D	1952–J	1957–P	1962–V	1967–AC
1948–E	1953–K	1958–R	1963–W	1968–AD
1949–F	1954–L	1959–S	1964–Y, Z	
1950–G	1955–M	1960–T	1965–AA	

Model 70P "Papoose"

Semi-automatic takedown carbine chambered for the .22 rimfire family of cartridges. It has a 16.25" barrel and a 7-shot detachable magazine. It is supplied with 4X scope and bright red case that will float if dropped overboard. The stock is walnut-finished birch, with a pistol grip and rubber buttplate. It was introduced in 1986.

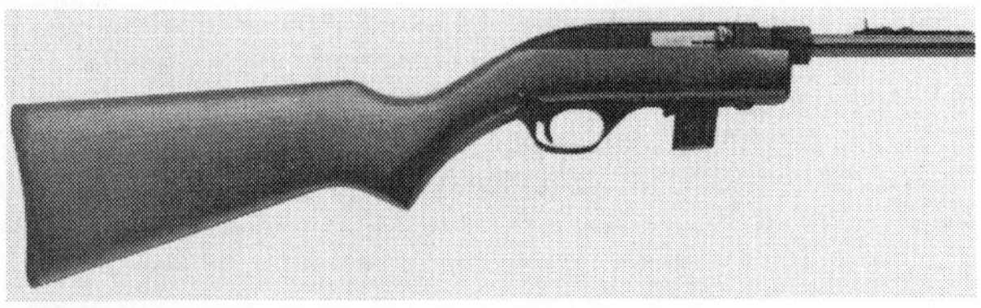

NIB	Exc.	V.G.	Good	Fair	Poor
275	200	150	100	75	50

Model 70PSS

Same as Model 70P above but furnished with a 10-round magazine and finished in stainless steel with synthetic stock. Automatic last shot bolt hold-open.

NIB	Exc.	V.G.	Good	Fair	Poor
245	175	125	100	85	60

Model 70HC

This is the Model 70 .22 rimfire semi-auto that has been produced since 1983 with a high-capacity, 25-round "Banana" magazine.

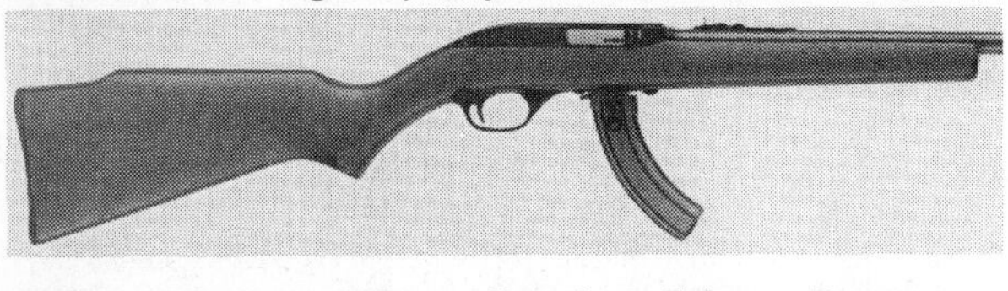

NIB	Exc.	V.G.	Good	Fair	Poor
200	160	140	110	85	75

Model 9 Camp Carbine

This model has a 16.5" barrel and is chambered for the 9mm Parabellum pistol cartridge. It has a 12- or 20-shot detachable magazine, walnut-finished hardwood pistol-grip stock, and a sandblasted matte-blued finish. There are open sights, and the receiver is drilled and tapped for scope mounting. This model was introduced in 1985.

NIB	Exc.	V.G.	Good	Fair	Poor
625	500	395	250	175	125

Model 9N

Similar to the Model 9mm Carbine but furnished with nickel-plated metal parts.

NIB	Exc.	V.G.	Good	Fair	Poor
650	525	425	275	195	125

Model 45 Camp Carbine

This is the same as the 9mm version but is chambered for the .45 ACP cartridge and has a 7-shot detachable magazine. This is a very hot collectible.

NIB	Exc.	V.G.	Good	Fair	Poor
675	600	425	300	225	175

Model 922M

First offered in 1993 this model is a semi-automatic .22 Win. Magnum Rimfire rifle. It features a 7-shot clip, 20.5" MicroGrove barrel. The receiver is sandblasted and drilled and tapped for scope mounting. Monte Carlo black walnut stock with rubber rifle buff pad. Adjustable rear sight and ramp front sight with hood. Rifle weighs 6.5 lbs.

NIB	Exc.	V.G.	Good	Fair	Poor
550	450	375	225	150	125

Model 995

Semi-automatic .22 LR only rifle features a 7-shot clip, 18" MicroGroove barrel. Receiver is grooved for scope mount and receiver has a serrated non-glare top. Adjustable sights. Monte Carlo American black walnut stock with checkered pistol grip and forearm. White buttplate spacer is standard. Rifle weighs 5 lbs. Introduced in 1979.

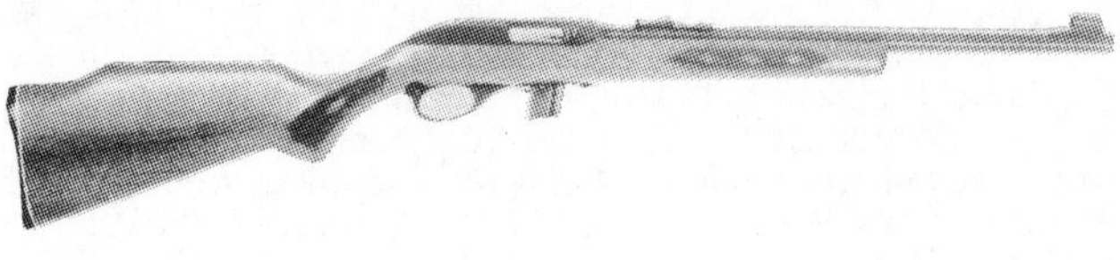

NIB	Exc.	V.G.	Good	Fair	Poor
175	110	80	70	60	40

Model 995SS

Same as above but with stainless steel finish and black fiberglass stock. Introduced in 1995.

NIB	Exc.	V.G.	Good	Fair	Poor
195	125	100	85	60	50

Model 990L

This semi-automatic .22 LR Marlin features a tubular 14-round magazine with 22" MicroGrove barrel. The trigger is gold plated. The receiver is grooved for a scope mount while the stock is a two-tone brown birch Monte Carlo. Rubber rifle buttpad is standard. Rifle weighs 5.75 lbs.

NIB	Exc.	V.G.	Good	Fair	Poor
150	120	100	80	65	50

Model 7000

This model was first offered in 1997 and is a semi-automatic .22 caliber rifle with 18" heavy barrel. Magazine holds 10 rounds. Black synthetic stock with Monte Carlo comb and molded checkering. Receiver grooved for scope mount. No sights included. Weight about 6 lbs.

NIB	Exc.	V.G.	Good	Fair	Poor
200	150	125	100	75	50

Model 7000T

This target rifle is fitted with an 18" barrel with recessed muzzle. No sights. The stock is laminated red, white, and blue with pistol grip. Serrated rubber buttplate is adjustable for length of pull, height, and angle. Weight is about 7.5 lbs. Introduced in 1999.

NIB	Exc.	V.G.	Good	Fair	Poor
425	375	325	275	150	100

Model 795

Similar to the Model 7000 above but with an 18" standard weight barrel. Weight is about 5 lbs. Also available with 4X scope.

NIB	Exc.	V.G.	Good	Fair	Poor
150	115	—	—	—	—

NOTE: Add $5 for scope.

Model 795SS

As above but with stainless steel action and barrel with black fiberglass stock. Weight is about 4.5 lbs. Introduced in 2002.

NIB	Exc.	V.G.	Good	Fair	Poor
200	150	125	100	75	50

Model 60

This semi-automatic 14-shot .22 caliber LR features a 22" MicroGroove barrel with adjustable rear sight. Receiver is grooved for scope mount and stock is birch with Monte Carlo comb. Rifle weighs 5.5 lbs. Introduced in 1960.

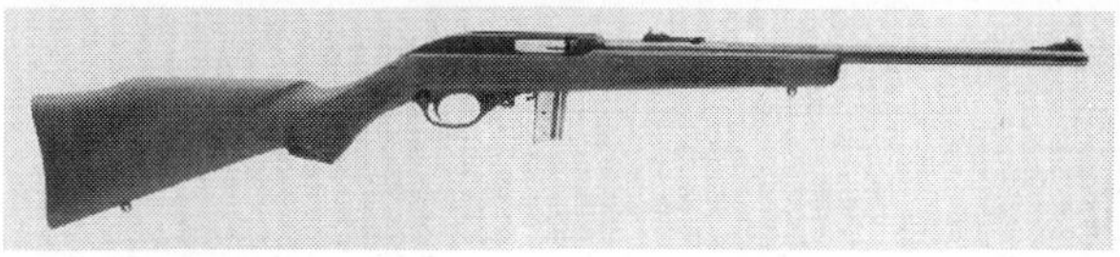

NIB	Exc.	V.G.	Good	Fair	Poor
175	125	90	60	50	40

Model 60SS

Introduced in 1993 this model is similar to the Model 60 except that it features a stainless barrel, bolt, and magazine tube. All other metal parts are nickel plated. The stock is a two-tone black and gray laminated birch Monte Carlo.

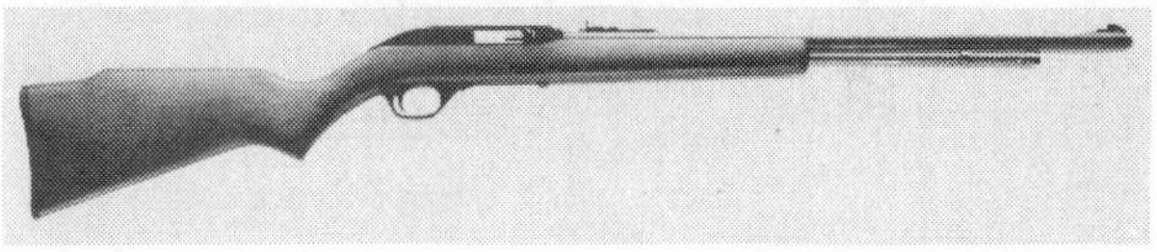

NIB	Exc.	V.G.	Good	Fair	Poor
275	225	150	125	75	50

Model 60SN

Similar to Model 60SS but with black synthetic stock with molded checkering and swivel studs. Blued metal. Introduced in 2007. Available with factory-mounted 3x9 scope. Add 10 percent for scope package.

NIB	Exc.	V.G.	Good	Fair	Poor
200	150	125	100	75	50

Model 60S-CF

Similar to Model 60SN but with carbon fiber-dipped black synthetic stock, giving it a – quote – "racy, high tech look." Woo-hoo!

NIB	Exc.	V.G.	Good	Fair	Poor
250	225	175	125	100	75

Model 60SB

Introduced in 1998 this model features a stainless steel 22" barrel, bolt and magazine tube. The stock is birch with Monte Carlo and hard rubber buttplate.

NIB	Exc.	V.G.	Good	Fair	Poor
175	125	90	60	50	40

Model 60SSK

Similar to the Model 60SB with the addition of a black synthetic Monte Carlo stock with checkering.

NIB	Exc.	V.G.	Good	Fair	Poor
195	195	150	125	100	75

Model 60C

Similar to the Model 60 but with RealTree camo finish. Introduced in 2000.

NIB	Exc.	V.G.	Good	Fair	Poor
195	195	150	125	100	75

Model 60DL

Introduced in 2004 this model features a Monte Carlo hardwood stock with Walnutone walnut pattern finish with full pistol grip. Weight is about 5.5 lbs.

NIB	Exc.	V.G.	Good	Fair	Poor
175	125	90	60	50	40

Marlin 60DLX

Semiauto rifle chambered for .22 LR. Features include 14-shot tubular magazine; side ejection; manual and automatic last-shot bolt hold-opens; receiver top with serrated, non-glare finish; cross-bolt safety; steel charging handle; Monte Carlo American walnut-finished hardwood; full pistol grip; tough Mar-Shield finish; 19-inch barrel with Micro-Groove\xa8 rifling. Limited availability. Price: N/A.

Model 2000

This is a bolt-action single-shot target rifle chambered for the .22 LR. The barrel is a 22" long MicroGroove design with match chamber and recessed muzzle. The rear sight is a fully adjustable target peep sight with a hooded front sight supplied with 10 aperture inserts. The stock is a Marlin blue fiberglass/Kevlar material with adjustable buttplate. There is an aluminum forearm rail with forearm stop and quick detachable swivel. Rifle weighs 8 lbs. Discontinued.

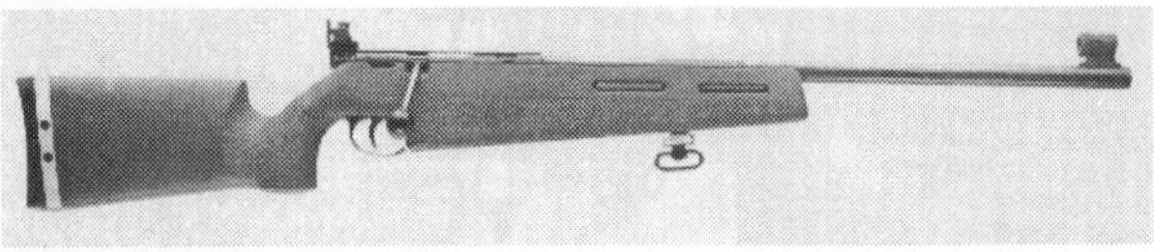

NIB	Exc.	V.G.	Good	Fair	Poor
425	325	250	200	150	125

Model 2000A

This is a 1996 version of the Model 2000 introduced in 1994 that features an adjustable comb and an ambidextrous pistol grip. A Marlin logo is molded into the side of the buttstock. Weighs approximately 8-1/2 lbs. Discontinued.

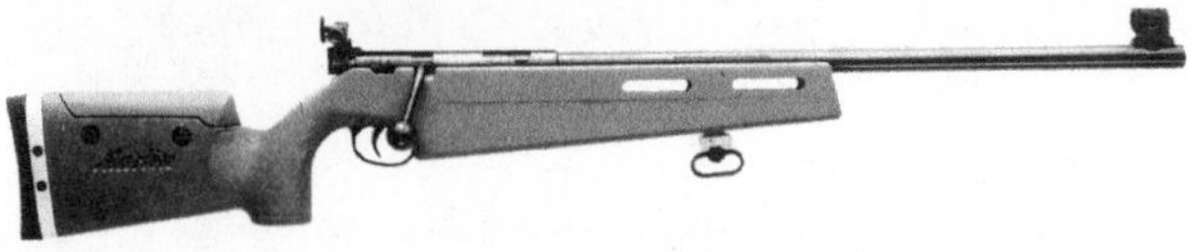

NIB	Exc.	V.G.	Good	Fair	Poor
425	350	250	200	150	125

Model 2000L

Introduced in 1996 this version of the Model 2000 features a black/grey laminated stock. It is fitted with a heavy 22" barrel with a match chamber. Fitted with a two-stage target trigger and a rubber buttplate that is adjustable for length of pull, height and angle. Weight is about 8 lbs. Discontinued.

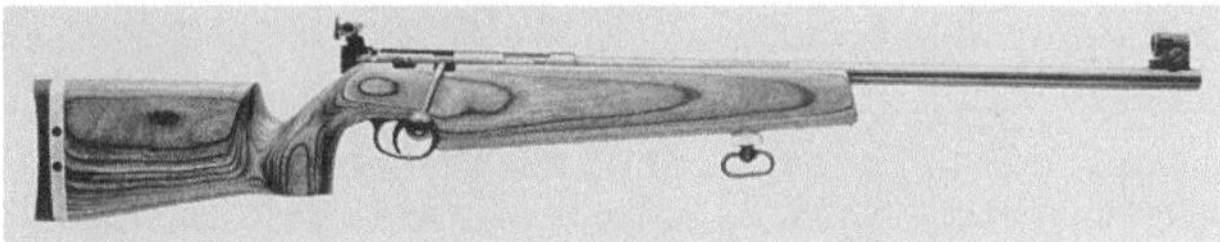

NIB	Exc.	V.G.	Good	Fair	Poor
450	400	300	250	175	125

Model 880

This is a bolt-action clip-fed rifle chambered for the .22 LR caliber. The clip is a 7-shot magazine. The MicroGroove barrel is 22" and has adjustable folding rear sight and ramp front sight with hood. Rifle weighs 5.5 lbs. and was introduced in 1988. Discontinued in 2004.

NIB	Exc.	V.G.	Good	Fair	Poor
160	135	110	90	75	50

Model 880SS

Introduced in 1994 this .22 caliber rifle features a synthetic stock and a stainless steel receiver and barrel. The barrel is 22" long and a 7-shot magazine is standard. Discontinued in 2004.

NIB	Exc.	V.G.	Good	Fair	Poor
250	175	150	125	75	60

Model 880SQ

Similar to the Model 880 but fitted with a 22" heavy barrel and no sights. Introduced in 1996. Weight is approximately 7 lbs. Discontinued in 2004.

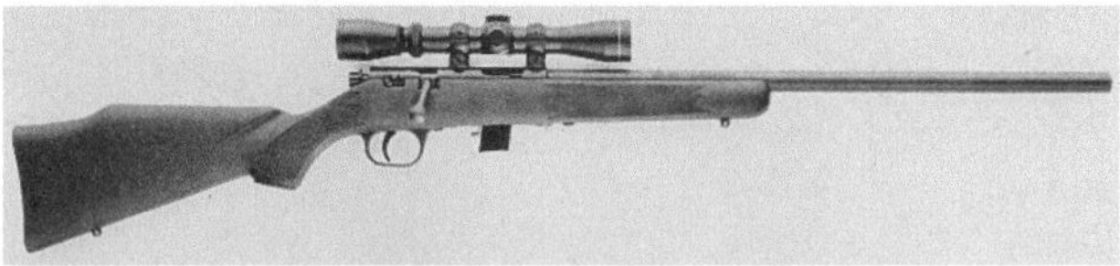

NIB	Exc.	V.G.	Good	Fair	Poor
285	225	200	150	100	75

Model 881

Bolt-action .22 caliber rifle has a tubular magazine that holds 25 Shorts, 19 longs, and 17 LR. A 22" MicroGroove barrel has adjustable folding rear sight and ramp front sight with hood. Stock is black walnut with Monte Carlo and a rubber rifle buttpad with sling swivels. Rifle weighs 6 lbs. First offered in 1988. Discontinued in 2004.

NIB	Exc.	V.G.	Good	Fair	Poor
175	150	125	100	80	60

Model 882SS

This bolt-action magazine rifle is chambered for the .22 Magnum cartridge. It has a stainless steel barrel and action with black synthetic stock. It has Marlin "Fire Sights" installed. Introduced in 1998. Discontinued in 2004.

NIB	Exc.	V.G.	Good	Fair	Poor
225	175	150	100	75	50

Model 25N

A Marlin promotional model. Bolt-action rifle chambered for the .22 LR only. Seven-shot clip magazine with a 22" MicroGroove barrel. Receiver grooved for scope mount. Walnut finished birch stock. Gun weighs 5.5 lbs.

NIB	Exc.	V.G.	Good	Fair	Poor
125	90	80	70	50	40

Model 25NC

Similar to the model above but with Mossy Oak Break-Up camo finish. Introduced in 2000.

NIB	Exc.	V.G.	Good	Fair	Poor
125	100	80	70	50	40

Model 25MN

Same as above but chambered for the .22 Win. Magnum Rimfire cartridge. Gun weighs 6 lbs.

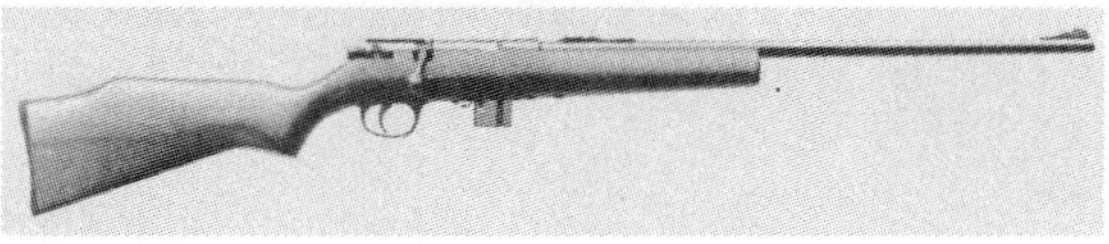

NIB	Exc.	V.G.	Good	Fair	Poor
175	150	125	100	80	60

Model 25MNC

Similar to the above model but with Mossy Oak Break-Up camo finish. Weight is about 6 lbs. Introduced in 2001.

NIB	Exc.	V.G.	Good	Fair	Poor
195	160	125	100	80	60

Model 17V

Introduced in 2002 this bolt-action rifle is chambered for the .17 Hornady Magnum Rimfire cartridge. Fitted with a 22" heavy barrel. Hardwood stock. No sights. Magazine capacity is 7-round detachable magazine. Weight is about 6 lbs.

NIB	Exc.	V.G.	Good	Fair	Poor
225	200	150	115	90	50

Model 17VS

As above but with stainless steel heavy barrel and action and laminated stock. Weight is about 7 lbs. Discontinued.

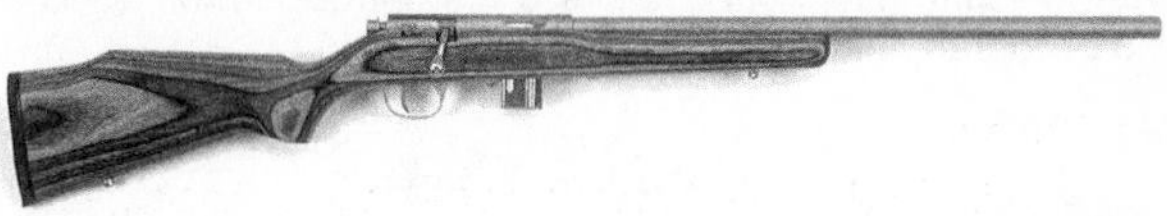

NIB	Exc.	V.G.	Good	Fair	Poor
285	225	200	150	100	75

Model 15YN

A Marlin promotional model referred to as the "Little Buckaroo." A bolt-action .22 caliber single-shot rifle for the beginner. Features a MicroGroove 16.25" barrel adjustable rear sight and receiver grooved for scope mount. Birch stock. Rifle weighs 4.25 lbs.

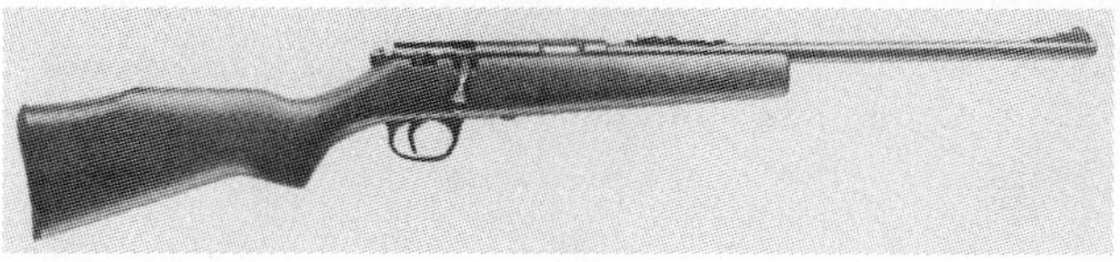

NIB	Exc.	V.G.	Good	Fair	Poor
125	100	75	60	50	40

Model 15N

This bolt-action rifle is chambered for .22 S, L and LR. It is fitted with an adjustable rear sight. It has a full size birch interchangeable with the Model 15YN. Weight is about 4.25 lbs. Introduced in 1998.

NIB	Exc.	V.G.	Good	Fair	Poor
185	145	100	75	60	40

Model 15YS (Youth)

This is single-shot bolt-action rifle with a shorter-than-standard length of pull. Barrel length is 16.25". Hardwood stock. Weight is about 4.25 lbs. Introduced in 2002.

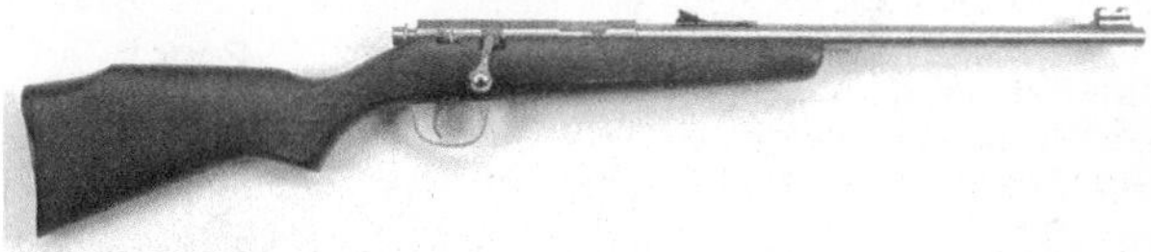

NIB	Exc.	V.G.	Good	Fair	Poor
175	140	110	65	50	35

Model 81TS

This is a bolt-action rifle chambered for the .22 Short, Long, and LR cartridges. It is fitted with a 22" barrel and has a tubular magazine. It comes with a black Monte Carlo synthetic stock and adjustable rear sight. Weight is about 6 lbs. Introduced in 1998. Discontinued in 2004.

NIB	Exc.	V.G.	Good	Fair	Poor
175	140	110	65	50	35

Model 882

Bolt-action rifle chambered for .22 Win. Magnum Rimfire cartridge. A 7-shot clip is standard. A MicroGroove 22" barrel with adjustable rear sight and ramp front sight with hood. Receiver grooved for scope mount. Black walnut stock with Monte Carlo and rubber rifle butt. Rifle weighs 6 lbs. Introduced in 1988 and still in production. Discontinued in 2004.

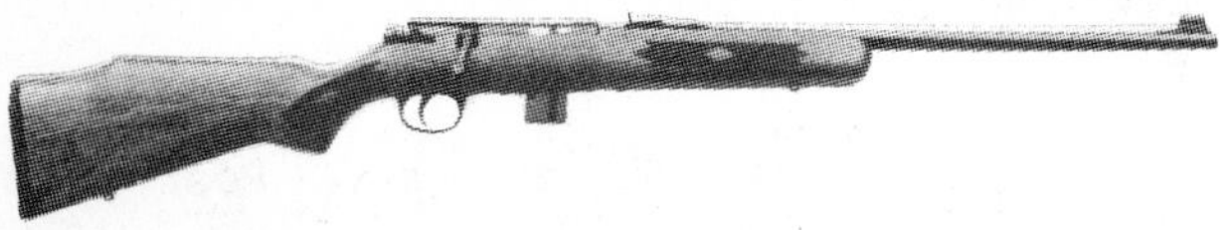

NIB	Exc.	V.G.	Good	Fair	Poor
285	225	200	150	100	75

Model 882L

Same as above but furnished with a two-tone brown hardwood Monte Carlo stock. Rifle weighs 6.25 lbs. Discontinued in 2004.

NIB	Exc.	V.G.	Good	Fair	Poor
275	215	190	145	90	60

Model 882SS

Same as above but furnished in stainless steel. With black fiberglass stock. Introduced in 1995. Discontinued in 2004.

NIB	Exc.	V.G.	Good	Fair	Poor
285	225	200	150	100	75

Model 882SSV

This variation of the Model 882, introduced in 1997, is all in stainless steel and chambered for the .22 WMR cartridge. It is fitted with a nickel plated 7-round magazine and 22" barrel. The stock is black synthetic with molded checkering. Receiver is grooved for scope mount. 1" brushed aluminum scope ring mounts included. Weighs about 7 lbs. Discontinued in 2004.

NIB	Exc.	V.G.	Good	Fair	Poor
285	225	200	150	100	75

Model 83TS

Chambered for the .22 Win. Mag cartridge and fitted with a 22" barrel with 12-round tubular magazine. Adjustable rear sight. Bolt-action with synthetic stock. Weight is about 6 lbs. Introduced in 2001. Discontinued in 2004.

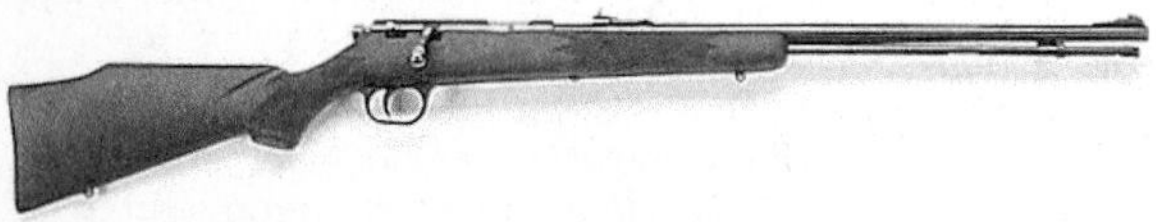

NIB	Exc.	V.G.	Good	Fair	Poor
250	200	165	145	100	75

Model 883

Bolt-action rifle chambered for .22 Win. Magnum cartridge with 12-shot tubular magazine. Furnished with a 22" MicroGroove barrel and adjustable rear sight, ramp front sight with hood. Checkered American black walnut stock with Monte Carlo. Rifle weighs 6 lbs. Introduced in 1988. Discontinued in 2004.

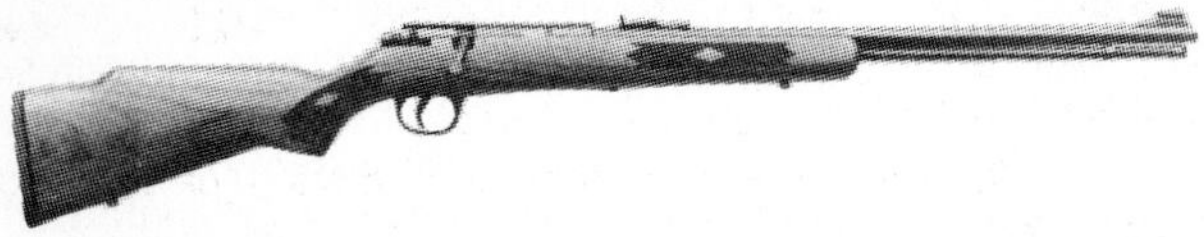

NIB	Exc.	V.G.	Good	Fair	Poor
285	225	200	150	100	75

Model 883N

Same as above but furnished with stainless steel barrel, receiver, front breech bolt, and striker. All other metal parts, except for sights, are nickel plated. Discontinued in 2004.

NIB	Exc.	V.G.	Good	Fair	Poor
285	225	200	150	100	75

Model 883SS

Introduced in 1993 this model is similar to the Model 883 but with all metal parts in stainless steel or nickel and the stock is a two-tone brown birch Monte Carlo that is not checkered. Discontinued in 2004.

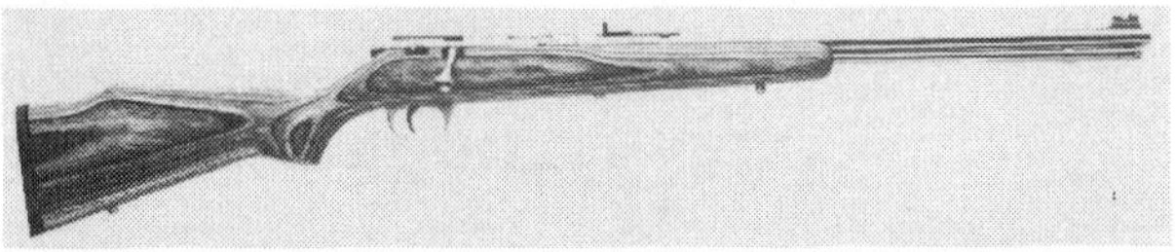

NIB	Exc.	V.G.	Good	Fair	Poor
275	215	190	145	90	60

Model 717M2

Introduced in 2005 this semi-automatic model is chambered for the .17 Mach 2 cartridge. Laminated hardwood stock with Monte Carlo comb. Fitted with an 18" barrel with iron sights. Magazine capacity is 7 rounds. Weight is about 5 lbs.

NIB	Exc.	V.G.	Good	Fair	Poor
300	250	200	175	150	125

MODEL 900 SERIES

This bolt action rimfire series was introduced into the Marlin line in 2004 and features a T-900 fire control system. This is a trigger and safety system that features a wide serrated trigger and improved trigger pull. The safety activitation is also improved. The 900 series also features drilled and tapped receivers on all models.

Model 983T

Chambered for the .22 WMR cartridge and fitted with a 22" barrel. Monte Carlo black fiberglass stock with checkering. Adjustable sights. Tubular 12-round magazine. Weight is about 6 lbs.

NIB	Exc.	V.G.	Good	Fair	Poor
285	225	200	150	100	75

Model 983S

As above but with laminated two-tone stock.

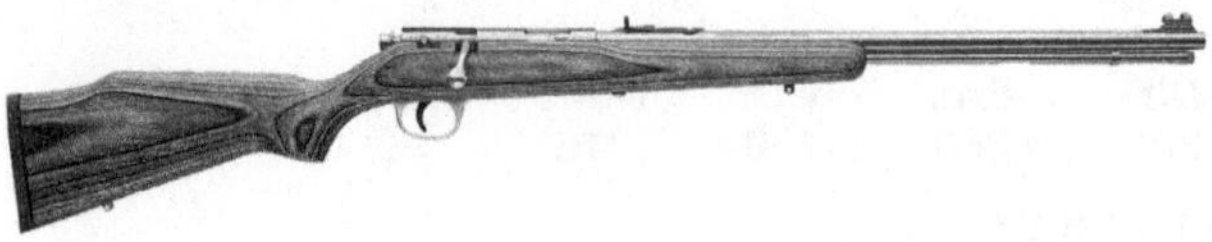

NIB	Exc.	V.G.	Good	Fair	Poor
285	225	200	150	100	75

Model 983

This .22 WMR model features a Monte Carlo stock of American black walnut with full pistol grip and checkering.

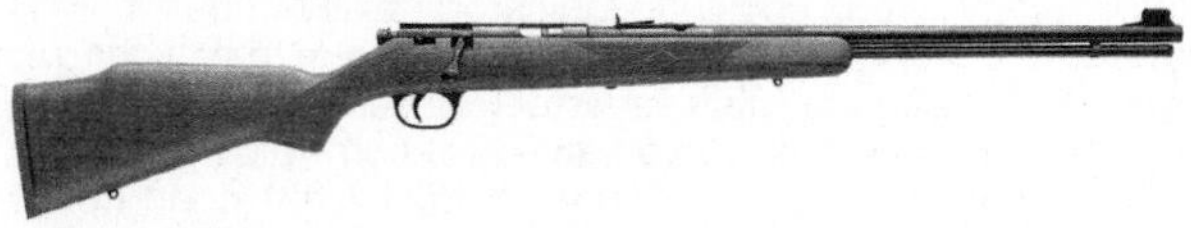

NIB	Exc.	V.G.	Good	Fair	Poor
285	225	200	150	100	75

Model 917

Bolt-action rifle chambered in .17 Hornady Mag. Rimfire; 7-shot clip magazine; fiberglass-filled synthetic stock with full pistol grip; swivel studs and molded-in checkering. Adjustable open rear sight, ramp front. 22-inch barrel. Introduced 2006.

NIB	Exc.	V.G.	Good	Fair	Poor
285	225	200	150	100	75

Model 917V

This model is chambered for the .17 HMR cartridge and fitted with a 22" heavy barrel. Hardwood Monte Carlo stock with full pistol grip. No sights. Detachable magazine with 7-round capacity. Weight is about 6 lbs.

NIB	Exc.	V.G.	Good	Fair	Poor
285	225	200	150	100	75

Model 917VR

Similar to Model 917 but with fiberglass-filled synthetic stock. Introduced 2006.

NIB	Exc.	V.G.	Good	Fair	Poor
285	225	200	150	100	75

Model 917VS

As above but with gray/black laminated hardwood stock. No sights. Magazine is nickel plated. Weight is about 7 lbs. Scope bases included.

NIB	Exc.	V.G.	Good	Fair	Poor
285	225	200	150	100	75

Marlin Model 917VS-CF

Similar to Model 917VS but with carbon fiber-patterned stock.

NIB	Exc.	V.G.	Good	Fair	Poor
285	225	200	150	100	75

Model 917VSF

Chambered for the .17 HMR cartridge and fitted with a 22" heavy stainless steel fluted barrel with no sights. Nickel magazine capacity is 7 rounds. Laminated gray stock with Monte Carlo comb. Weight is about 6.75 lbs. Introduced in 2005.

NIB	Exc.	V.G.	Good	Fair	Poor
300	250	200	175	150	125

Model 917VT

Similar to above but with laminated brown thumbhole stock. Introduced 2008.

NIB	Exc.	V.G.	Good	Fair	Poor
350	300	250	175	145	110

Model 917VST

Similar to above but with laminated gray/black thumbhole stock. Introduced 2008.

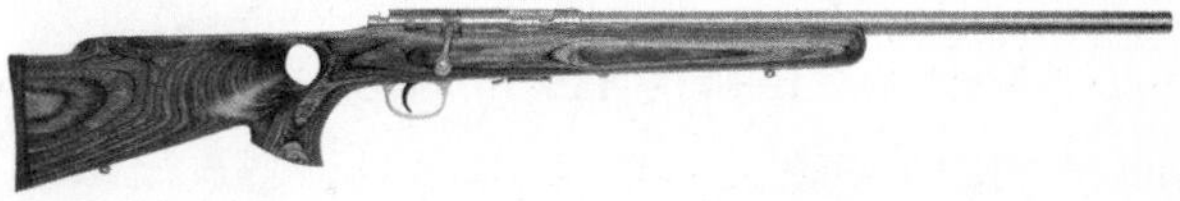

NIB	Exc.	V.G.	Good	Fair	Poor
400	350	295	245	125	100

Model 917M2

This model is chambered for the .17 Mach 2 cartridge and fitted with a 22" heavy barrel. Monte Carlo hardwood stock with full pistol grip. No sights but scope bases included. Magazine capacity is 7 rounds. Weight is about 5.5 lbs.

NIB	Exc.	V.G.	Good	Fair	Poor
300	250	200	175	150	125

Model 917M2S

As above but with Monte Carlo gray/black laminated stock with full pistol grip. Stainless steel barrel and receiver. Nickel plated magazine.

NIB	Exc.	V.G.	Good	Fair	Poor
325	275	225	200	175	125

Model 982S

This model is chambered for the .22 WMR cartridge and fitted with a 22" stainless steel barrel with adjustable sights. Black fiberglass stock with Monte Carlo and full pistol grip. Detachable 7-round nickel magazine. Weight is about 6 lbs.

NIB	Exc.	V.G.	Good	Fair	Poor
285	225	200	150	100	75

Model 982L

As above but for a gray/black laminated stock. Weight is about 6.25 lbs.

NIB	Exc.	V.G.	Good	Fair	Poor
300	250	200	175	150	125

Model 982

Similar to 982S but with American black walnut checkered stock with Monte Carlo and full pistol grip. Adjustable sights. Weight is about 6 lbs.

NIB	Exc.	V.G.	Good	Fair	Poor
285	225	200	150	100	75

Model 982VS

As above but with black fiberglass Monte Carlo stock. Heavy 22" stainless steel barrel. Nickel plated 7-round magazine. No sights. Weight is about 7 lbs.

NIB	Exc.	V.G.	Good	Fair	Poor
325	275	225	200	175	125

Model 982VS-CF

As above but with synthetic stock with dipped carbon-fiber textured finish.

NIB	Exc.	V.G.	Good	Fair	Poor
325	275	225	200	175	125

Model 925M

As above but with hardwood stock and full pistol grip. Fitted with 22" standard weight barrel. Adjustable sights. Weight is about 6 lbs.

NIB	Exc.	V.G.	Good	Fair	Poor
250	200	165	145	100	75

Marlin Model 925RM

Similar to Model 925M but with black fiberglass-filled synthetic stock.

NIB	Exc.	V.G.	Good	Fair	Poor
250	200	165	145	100	75

Model 925MC

As above but with Monte Carlo stock with Mossy Oak Break-up camo stock. Weight is about 6 lbs.

NIB	Exc.	V.G.	Good	Fair	Poor
285	225	200	150	100	75

Model 980V

This model is chambered for the .22 LR cartridge and fitted with a 22" heavy barrel. Black fiberglass stock with Monte Carlo and full pistol grip. No sights. Magazine capacity is 7 rounds. Weight is about 7 lbs.

NIB	Exc.	V.G.	Good	Fair	Poor
285	225	200	150	100	75

Model 980S

As above but with standard weight 22" barrel and 7-round nickel plated magazine and stainless steel barrel and receiver. Adjustable sights. Weight is about 6 lbs.

NIB	Exc.	V.G.	Good	Fair	Poor
285	225	200	150	100	75

Model 980S-CF

As above but with carbon fiber stock. Introduced in 2007.

NIB	Exc.	V.G.	Good	Fair	Poor
285	225	200	150	100	75

Model 981T

This model is chambered to handle interchangeably the .22 Short, Long, or LR cartridges in a tubular magazine. Black Monte Carlo fiberglass stock with full pistol grip. Adjustable sights. Fitted with a standard weight 22" barrel. Weight is about 6 lbs.

NIB	Exc.	V.G.	Good	Fair	Poor
285	225	200	150	100	75

Marlin 981TS

Bolt action rifle chambered in .22 S/L/LR. Features include tubular magazine (holds 25 Short, 19 Long or 17 Long Rifle cartridges; thumb safety; red cocking indicator; black fiberglass-filled synthetic stock with full pistol grip; molded-in checkering and swivel studs; 22-inch stainless steel barrel with Micro-Groove rifling (16 grooves). Adjustable semi-buckhorn folding rear sight, ramp front with high visibility, orange front sight post; cutaway Wide-Scan hood. Receiver grooved for scope mount; drilled and tapped for scope bases. Price: N/A.

Model 925

This model is chambered for the .22 LR cartridge and fitted with a 22" standard weight barrel with adjustable sights. Monte Carlo hardwood stock with full pistol grip. Seven-round magazine. Weight is about 5.5 lbs.

NIB	Exc.	V.G.	Good	Fair	Poor
225	175	150	125	95	75

Model 925R

As above but with factory-mounted 3x9 scope.

NIB	Exc.	V.G.	Good	Fair	Poor
250	200	165	145	100	75

Model 925C

As above but with Monte Carlo hardwood stock with Mossy Oak Break-up camo pattern. Adjustable sights.

NIB	Exc.	V.G.	Good	Fair	Poor
250	200	165	145	100	75

Model 915Y Compact

Single shot .22 rimfire rifle with 16-1/4-inch barrel, hardwood stock with impressed checkering and iron sights.

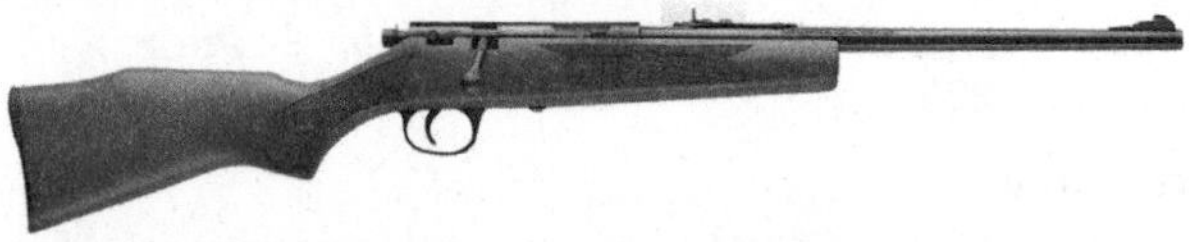

NIB	Exc.	V.G.	Good	Fair	Poor
200	150	125	100	75	50

Model 915YS Compact

Similar to above but with stainless steel receiver and barrel , no checkering and fiber optic sights.

NIB	Exc.	V.G.	Good	Fair	Poor
225	175	150	125	95	75

Model 322 Bolt-Action Rifle

This model is chambered for the .222 cartridge and has a 24" medium-weight barrel with MicroGroove rifling. It has a checkered walnut pistol-grip stock. The magazine holds 4 shots, and the adjustable trigger and sights are Sako products. The Sako receiver is fitted for Sako scope mounting bases. Non-Sako receivers were apparently also used. The MicroGroove rifling in the barrel was not successful for this caliber, and accuracy fell off after as few as 500 shots—so this model was dropped and replaced. The serial numbers were Sako, and there were 5,859 manufactured between 1954 and 1959.

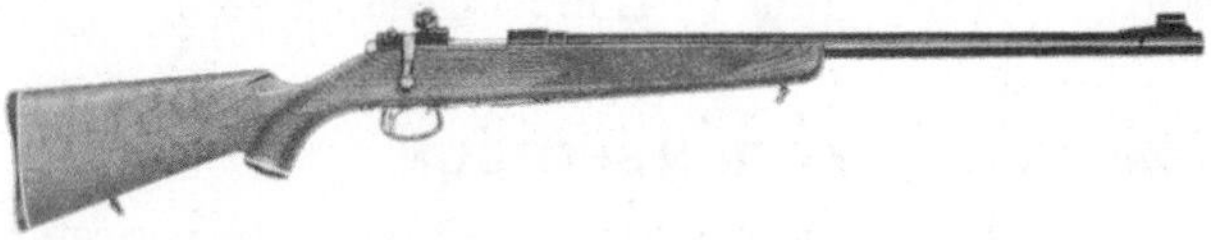

NIB	*Exc.*	*V.G.*	*Good*	*Fair*	*Poor*
—	950	600	500	325	200

Model 422 Bolt-Action Rifle

This model is the successor to the Model 322. It is simply the same rifle fitted with a 24", featherweight, stainless steel barrel and named the "Varmint King." The stock features a Monte Carlo stock with a cheekpiece. There were only 354 manufactured between 1956 and 1958.

NIB	*Exc.*	*V.G.*	*Good*	*Fair*	*Poor*
—	950	600	500	325	200

Model 455 Bolt-Action Rifle

This model is built on the Fabrique Nationale Belgian Mauser action. It is chambered for the .308 and the .30-06 cartridges. It has a stainless steel barrel made by Marlin and has a 5-shot magazine. It has a Bishop checkered walnut stock with detachable sling swivels and a leather sling. The rear sight is a Lyman 48, and the front is a ramp type with a detachable hood. The receiver is drilled and tapped for scope mounts. The trigger is an adjustable Sako unit. There were 1,079 manufactured in .3006 and only 59 in .308 between 1955 and 1959.

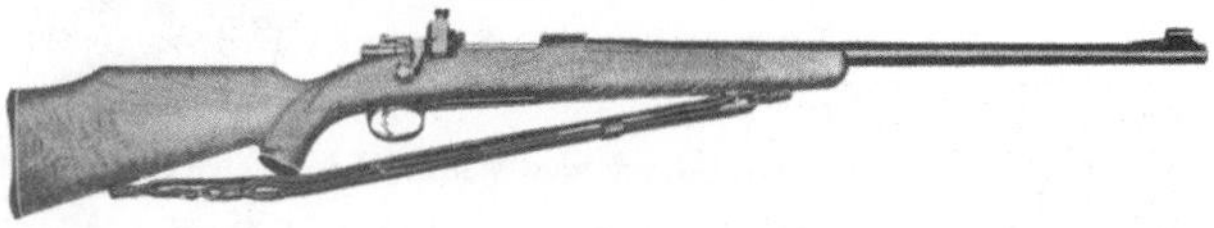

NIB	*Exc.*	*V.G.*	*Good*	*Fair*	*Poor*
—	700	595	425	300	200

Model MR-7

Introduced in 1996, this was an American made bolt-action centerfire rifle of a totally new design. Chambered for the .25-06 (first offered in 1997), .243, .270 Win. .280, .308, or .30-06 cartridges it is fitted with a 22" barrel. It has an American black walnut stock and a 4-shot detachable box magazine. Offered with or without sights. Weight is approximately 7.5 lbs. Discontinued 1999.

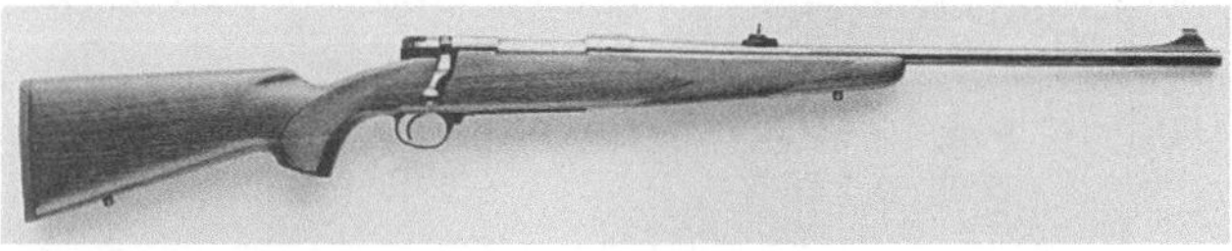

NIB	*Exc.*	*V.G.*	*Good*	*Fair*	*Poor*
450	350	300	250	175	150

Model MR-7B

Similar to the MR-7 but fitted with a 4-round blind magazine and birch stock. Offered in .30-06 or .270 with or without sights. Introduced in 1998. Discontinued.

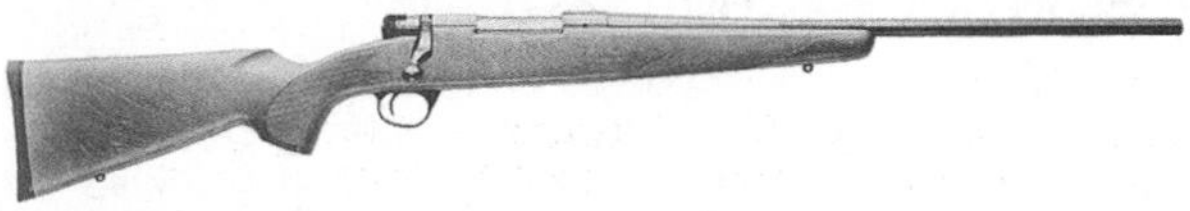

NIB	*Exc.*	*V.G.*	*Good*	*Fair*	*Poor*
375	300	250	175	150	100

Model XL7 Bolt Action Rifle

Introduced in 2008, this is a centerfire bolt-action rifle with adjustable Pro-Fire trigger system. 4+1 capacity . Chambered in .25-06, .270 and .30-06 with a crowned, precision-rifled 22-inch barrel that is joined to the receiver with a pressure nut. Black synthetic stock with raised cheekpiece and Soft-Tech recoil pad. No sights; drilled and tapped for mounts. Add $50 for factory scope package.

NIB	*Exc.*	*V.G.*	*Good*	*Fair*	*Poor*
325	275	225	200	175	125

Model XL7C Bolt Action Rifle

Similar to above but with RealTree APG HD camo finish.

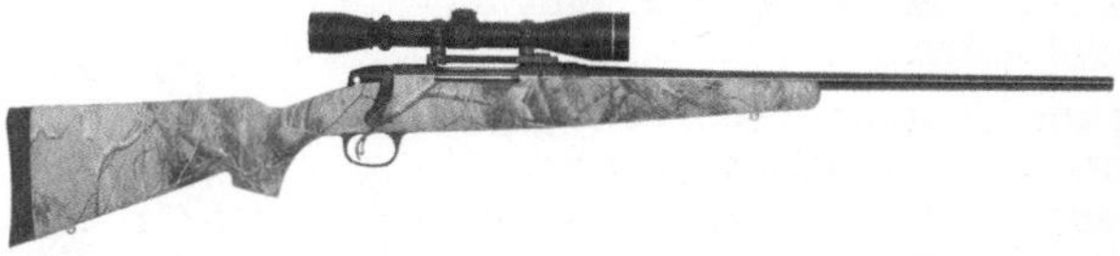

NIB	*Exc.*	*V.G.*	*Good*	*Fair*	*Poor*
350	300	250	175	145	110

Marlin XS7 Short-Action Bolt Action Rifle

Similar to Model XL7 but chambered in 7mm-08, .243 Winchester and .308 Winchester. Add $50 for factory scope package.

NIB	*Exc.*	*V.G.*	*Good*	*Fair*	*Poor*
325	275	225	200	175	125

Marlin Model XS7Y Youth Rifle

Similar to above but with smaller dimensions .

NIB	*Exc.*	*V.G.*	*Good*	*Fair*	*Poor*
325	275	225	200	175	125

Marlin Model XS7C Camo

Similar to above but with Realtree APG HD camo stock.

NIB	*Exc.*	*V.G.*	*Good*	*Fair*	*Poor*
350	300	250	175	145	110

Marlin XS7S

Bolt action rifle; similar to Model XS7 but with stainless steel barrel, receiver and trigger group. Short action. Price: N/A.

Marlin XL7

Entry-level bolt action rifle chambered in .25-06 Rem., .270 Win., .30-06 Spr. Features include 4+1 magazine capacity; pillar bedded 22-inch barrel; Pro-Fire adjustable trigger system; 2-position safety; red cocking indicator; swivel studs; matte blue/ black finish; black synthetic stock with molded in checkering and Soft-Tech recoil pad. No sights. Price: N/A.

MARLIN SHOTGUNS

MODEL 1898 SLIDE-ACTION SHOTGUN

This model was made in 12 gauge, with an exposed hammer. It has a takedown receiver and walnut pistol-grip stock and forend. There is a 5-shot tube magazine, and the barrel lengths are from 26" and 32". They were manufactured between 1898 and 1905.

Shotgun Grade A

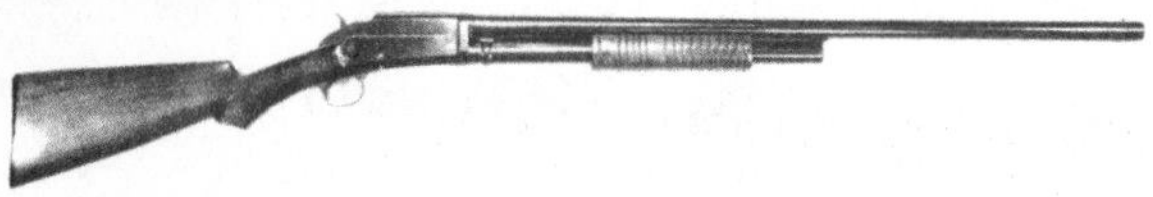

Photo by Lt. Col. William S. Brophy from Marlin Firearms with permission

This variation has a 38", 30", or 32" barrel, is Full choke, and is the plainest grade.

NIB	Exc.	V.G.	Good	Fair	Poor
—	475	425	325	125	75

Shotgun Grade A Brush or Riot

This is the same shotgun with a 26" cylinder-bore barrel.

NIB	Exc.	V.G.	Good	Fair	Poor
—	425	375	250	150	100

Shotgun Grade B

This is the same as the Grade A with a special smokeless steel barrel and a checkered stock.

NIB	Exc.	V.G.	Good	Fair	Poor
—	675	550	350	150	100

Shotgun Grade C

This is a more deluxe version with engraving and fancier wood.

NIB	Exc.	V.G.	Good	Fair	Poor
—	1150	850	550	275	125

Shotgun Grade D

This variation has a Damascus barrel and the greatest amount of engraving.

NIB	Exc.	V.G.	Good	Fair	Poor
—	2100	1400	900	450	250

MODEL 16 SLIDE-ACTION SHOTGUN

This model is exactly the same as the Model 1898 except that it is chambered for 16 gauge only. The four grades are the same also. They were manufactured between 1903 and 1910.

Grade A

NIB	Exc.	V.G.	Good	Fair	Poor
—	500	450	400	250	150

Grade B

NIB	Exc.	V.G.	Good	Fair	Poor
—	650	550	400	200	100

Grade C

NIB	Exc.	V.G.	Good	Fair	Poor
—	1100	850	500	300	150

Grade D

NIB	Exc.	V.G.	Good	Fair	Poor
—	2000	1400	950	425	250

Model 17 Slide-Action Shotgun

This model is an exposed-hammer gun with a solid frame and a straight-grip stock. It is chambered for 12 gauge, with a 30" or 32" barrel. The Model 17 was manufactured between 1906 and 1908.

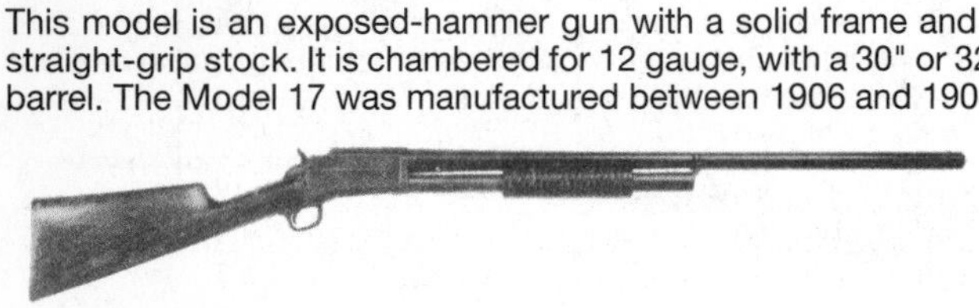

NIB	Exc.	V.G.	Good	Fair	Poor
—	525	450	275	150	75

Model 17 Brush Gun

This variation is similar to the standard Model 17, with a 26" cylinder-bore barrel.

NIB	Exc.	V.G.	Good	Fair	Poor
—	550	475	325	200	100

Model 17 Riot Gun

This variation has a 20" cylinder-bore barrel.

NIB	Exc.	V.G.	Good	Fair	Poor
—	600	525	325	150	125

MODEL 19 SLIDE-ACTION SHOTGUN

This is a takedown gun, chambered for 12 gauge. It is basically an improved and lightened version of the Model 1898. It is available in the same four grades. It was manufactured in 1906 and 1907.

Grade A

NIB	Exc.	V.G.	Good	Fair	Poor
—	500	450	250	150	100

Grade B

NIB	Exc.	V.G.	Good	Fair	Poor
—	600	550	500	350	225

Grade C

NIB	Exc.	V.G.	Good	Fair	Poor
—	750	675	5550	425	300

Grade D

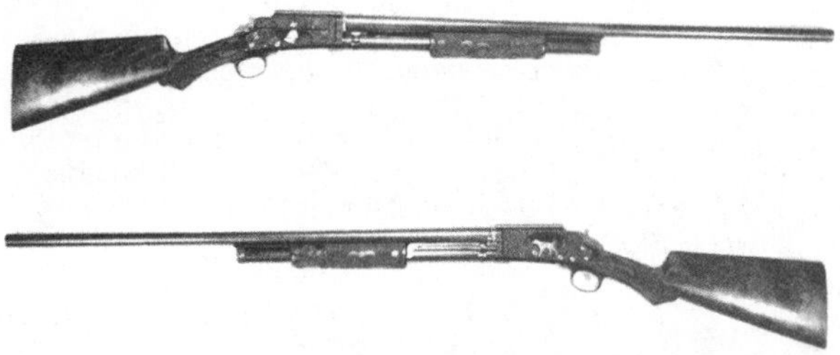

Photo by Lt. Col. William S. Brophy from Marlin Firearms with permission

NIB	Exc.	V.G.	Good	Fair	Poor
—	1850	1500	1050	400	200

MODEL 21 "TRAP" SLIDE-ACTION SHOTGUN

This model is basically the same as the Model 19 with a straight-grip stock. The 1907 catalog listed it as a Trap model. This model was manufactured in 1907 and 1908. The four grades are similar to the previous models.

Grade A

NIB	Exc.	V.G.	Good	Fair	Poor
—	450	450	300	200	100

Grade B

NIB	Exc.	V.G.	Good	Fair	Poor
—	600	550	350	200	100

Grade C

NIB	Exc.	V.G.	Good	Fair	Poor
—	750	675	500	350	200

Grade D

NIB	Exc.	V.G.	Good	Fair	Poor
—	1600	1300	1050	700	550

MODEL 24 SLIDE-ACTION SHOTGUN

This model is actually an improved version of the Model 21. It has a pistol-grip stock and exposed hammer. It features an automatic recoil lock on the slide and a matte rib barrel. Otherwise, it is quite similar to its predecessor. It was manufactured between 1908 and 1917.

Grade A

Photo by Lt. Col. William S. Brophy from Marlin Firearms with permission

NIB	Exc.	V.G.	Good	Fair	Poor
—	475	400	350	150	100

Grade B

NIB	Exc.	V.G.	Good	Fair	Poor
—	600	550	450	350	225

Grade C

NIB	Exc.	V.G.	Good	Fair	Poor
—	750	675	550	425	300

Grade D

NIB	Exc.	V.G.	Good	Fair	Poor
—	1600	1300	900	600	400

Marlin "Trap Gun"

This model is unique in that it has no numerical designation and is simply known as the "Trap Gun." It is a takedown gun with interchangeable barrels from 16" to 32". It has a straight-grip buttstock and is quite similar in appearance to the Model 24. It was manufactured between 1909 and 1912.

NIB	Exc.	V.G.	Good	Fair	Poor
—	1000	700	525	350	200

Model 26 Slide-Action Shotgun

This model is similar to the Model 24 Grade A, with a solid frame. It has 30" or 32" barrels.

NIB	Exc.	V.G.	Good	Fair	Poor
—	525	450	325	125	100

Model 26 Brush Gun

This model has a 26" cylinder-bored barrel.

NIB	Exc.	V.G.	Good	Fair	Poor
—	550	475	325	200	100

Model 26 Riot Gun

This variation has a 20" cylinder-bored barrel.

NIB	Exc.	V.G.	Good	Fair	Poor
—	600	525	325	150	125

MODEL 28 HAMMERLESS SLIDE-ACTION SHOTGUN

This model was the first of the Marlin hammerless shotguns. It is a takedown 12 gauge, with barrels from 26" to 32" in length. The stock has a pistol grip, and it comes in four grades like its predecessors. The Model 28 was manufactured between 1913 and 1922.

Grade A

NIB	Exc.	V.G.	Good	Fair	Poor
—	400	335	200	100	70

Grade B

NIB	Exc.	V.G.	Good	Fair	Poor
—	600	550	350	350	225

Grade C

NIB	Exc.	V.G.	Good	Fair	Poor
—	750	625	550	425	300

Grade D

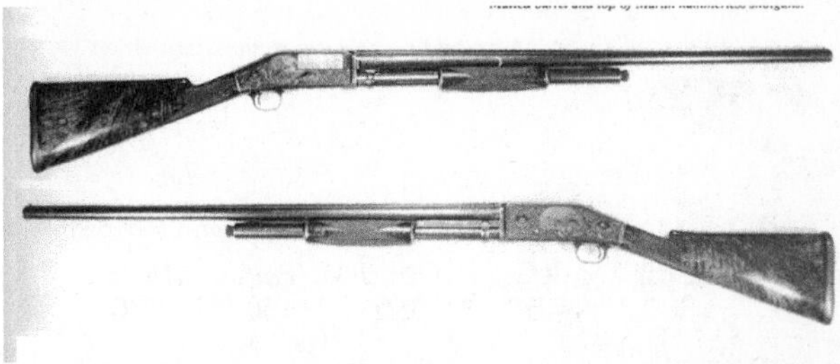

Photo by Lt. Col. William S. Brophy from Marlin Firearms with permission

NIB	Exc.	V.G.	Good	Fair	Poor
—	1700	1200	800	600	300

Model 28TS Trap Gun

This variation is the same as the Model 28 with a 30" Full choke barrel with matte rib and a high-comb straight grip stock. It was manufactured in 1915.

NIB	Exc.	V.G.	Good	Fair	Poor
—	725	600	525	425	300

Model 28T Trap Gun

This variation is the deluxe model, similar to the Model 28TS, with engraving, high-grade walnut, and hand checkering. It was manufactured in 1915.

NIB	Exc.	V.G.	Good	Fair	Poor
—	750	625	550	425	300

MODEL 30 SLIDE-ACTION SHOTGUN

This model is an improved version of the Model 16, 16 gauge shotgun. Its features are similar, with the addition of the improved takedown system and the automatic recoil lock on the slide. This model was manufactured between 1910 and 1914.

Grade A

NIB	Exc.	V.G.	Good	Fair	Poor
—	550	475	350	200	100

Grade B

NIB	Exc.	V.G.	Good	Fair	Poor
—	600	550	450	200	100

Grade C

NIB	Exc.	V.G.	Good	Fair	Poor
—	750	675	550	250	150

Grade D

NIB	Exc.	V.G.	Good	Fair	Poor
—	1400	1200	1000	700	550

Model 30 Field Grade

This model is similar to the Model 30 Grade B, with a 25" modified-choke barrel and a straight-grip stock. It was manufactured in 1913 and 1914.

NIB	Exc.	V.G.	Good	Fair	Poor
—	450	375	250	150	100

MODEL 31 SLIDE-ACTION SHOTGUN

This model is a smaller version of the Model 28 hammerless takedown shotgun, chambered for 16 and 20 gauge. It was produced with barrel lengths of 26" and 28" and was available in the usual four grades, with various different chokes. This model was manufactured between 1915 and 1922.

Grade A

Photo by Lt. Col. William S. Brophy from Marlin Firearms with permission

NIB	Exc.	V.G.	Good	Fair	Poor
—	500	450	350	150	100

Grade B

NIB	Exc.	V.G.	Good	Fair	Poor
—	600	550	450	250	150

Grade C

NIB	Exc.	V.G.	Good	Fair	Poor
—	750	675	550	300	150

Grade D

NIB	Exc.	V.G.	Good	Fair	Poor
—	1400	1200	1000	600	300

Model 42/42A Slide-Action Shotgun

This model was originally listed as the Model 42; but in the second year of production, the designation was changed to 42/A for no more apparent reason than standardization of models. This model is similar to the Model 24 except that the barrel markings are different. It is still an exposed hammer takedown gun chambered for 12 gauge. It was manufactured between 1922 and 1933.

NIB	Exc.	V.G.	Good	Fair	Poor
—	375	325	200	150	100

Model 43A Slide-Action Shotgun

This hammerless model was quite similar to the Model 28, with different markings and less attention to finishing detail. It was manufactured between 1923 and 1930.

NIB	Exc.	V.G.	Good	Fair	Poor
—	400	350	250	150	75

Model 43T Slide-Action Shotgun

This model is the same as the Model 43A takedown hammerless with a 30" or 32" matte rib barrel. The straight-grip stock is of high grade walnut, with a non-gloss oil finish and fitted recoil paid. This model was manufactured between 1922 and 1930.

NIB	Exc.	V.G.	Good	Fair	Poor
—	500	450	350	200	100

Model 43TS Slide-Action Shotgun

This is a custom-order version of the Model 43T, the same in all respects except that the stock could be ordered to any specifications the shooter desired. It was manufactured between 1922 and 1930.

NIB	Exc.	V.G.	Good	Fair	Poor
—	700	625	550	250	150

Model 44A Slide-Action Shotgun

This model is similar to the Model 31 and was advertised as its successor. It is a hammerless takedown chambered for the 20 gauge. It features an improved bolt opening device located in the trigger guard area instead of at the top of the receiver and has a shorter 4-shot magazine tube. The model was manufactured from 1922 until 1933.

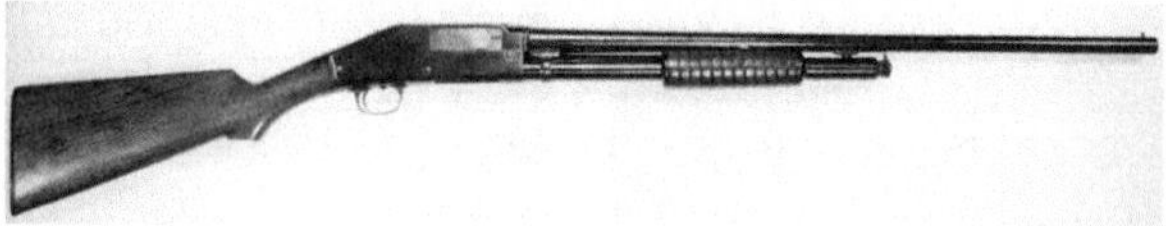

Photo by Lt. Col. William S. Brophy from Marlin Firearms with permission

NIB	Exc.	V.G.	Good	Fair	Poor
—	475	400	275	150	100

Model 44S Slide-Action Shotgun

This model is similar to the Model 44A, with a higher grade walnut stock that featured hand-cut checkering.

NIB	Exc.	V.G.	Good	Fair	Poor
—	500	425	300	200	100

Model 49 Slide-Action Shotgun

This model is a 12-gauge, exposed-hammer takedown that combines features of the Model 42 and the Model 24. It is basically a lower-priced model that was never listed in the Marlin catalog. This model was part of Frank Kenna's money-raising program—anyone who purchased four shares of stock for $25 per share was given one, free of charge. This model was manufactured between 1925 and 1928.

NIB	Exc.	V.G.	Good	Fair	Poor
—	700	625	550	250	150

Model 53 Slide-Action Shotgun

This model is a hammerless, takedown, 12 gauge that was not in production for long. It is theorized that the Model 53 was produced to use up old parts on hand when the Model 43 was introduced. It was manufactured in 1929 and 1980.

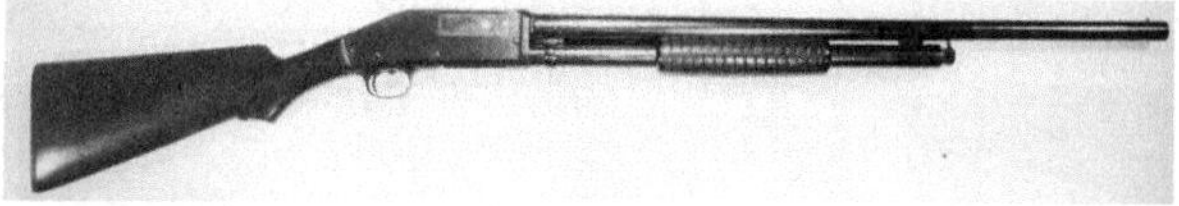

Photo by Lt. Col. William S. Brophy from Marlin Firearms with permission

NIB	Exc.	V.G.	Good	Fair	Poor
—	450	400	275	175	125

Model 60 Single-Barrel Shotgun

This is a break-open, exposed-hammer, top lever-opening 12 gauge with either 30" or 32" full-choke barrel. It has a pistol grip stock. There were approximately 60 manufactured in 1923.

NIB	Exc.	V.G.	Good	Fair	Poor
—	400	350	250	150	75

Model 63 Slide-Action Shotgun

This was the last of the slide-action shotguns produced by Marlin until the Model 120 in 1971. It is a hammerless, takedown 12 gauge and replaced the Model 43A in the Marlin catalog. This model had improvements over the earlier guns, but its introduction during the Depression did little to bolster sales. This model was also offered free of charge to anyone purchasing four shares of Marlin stock at $25 per share. It was manufactured between 1931 and 1933.

NIB	Exc.	V.G.	Good	Fair	Poor
—	500	450	350	200	100

Model 63T Slide-Action Shotgun

This is the trap-grade version of the Model 63. It has a better grade hand-checkered stock, with a fitted recoil pad and oil finish. It was manufactured between 1931 and 1933.

NIB	Exc.	V.G.	Good	Fair	Poor
—	600	525	450	200	125

Model 63TS Slide-Action Shotgun

This variation is the same as the Model 63T except that the stock dimensions were custom-made to the customer's specifications. It was manufactured between 1931 and 1933.

NIB	Exc.	V.G.	Good	Fair	Poor
—	700	625	550	250	150

Model .410 Lever-Action Shotgun (Original)

This was a unique venture for the Marlin Company—a lever-action shotgun based on the Model 1893 action with a longer loading port, modified tube magazine that held 5 shots, and a smoothbore barrel chambered for the .410 shot shell. The finish of this gun is blued, with a walnut pistol grip stock and grooved beavertail forend. It has a hard rubber rifle-type buttplate. The model was available with either a 22" or 26" full-choke barrel. This gun was also part of the stock purchase plan and was given free of charge to anyone purchasing four shares at $25 per share. It was also cataloged for sale and was manufactured between 1929 and 1932.

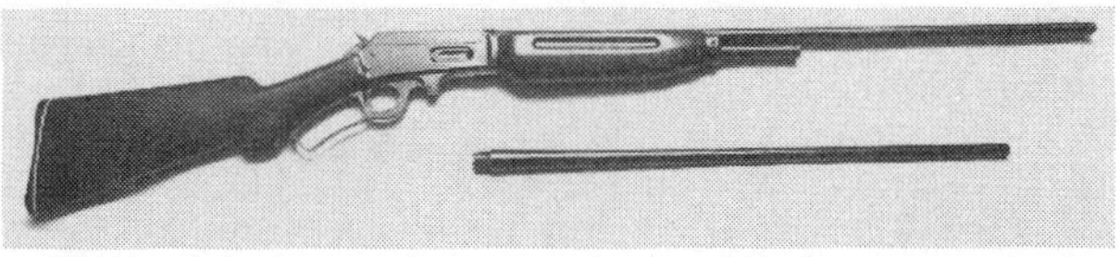

Courtesy Mike Stuckslager

NIB	Exc.	V.G.	Good	Fair	Poor
—	1600	1000	650	500	200

Model .410 Deluxe (Original)

This variation was never cataloged and is essentially the same as the standard version with a hand-checkered stock. The forend does not have the grooves found on the standard model. Be wary of fakes!

NIB	Exc.	V.G.	Good	Fair	Poor
—	2200	1200	800	400	200

Model .410 (New)

A lever-action shotgun chambered for the 2.5-inch .410 shotshell. Checkered walnut stock, fluorescent front sight. Based on the Model 336 action. Discontinued.

NIB	Exc.	V.G.	Good	Fair	Poor
700	625	550	450	300	—

Model 410XLR 410 XLR

New in 2009, this is the latest Marlin .410 shotgun. It's built on the M1895 chassis and is chambered for 2.5-inch .410 sheels. Receiver and barre; are stainless and the stock is laminated wood.

NIB	Exc.	V.G.	Good	Fair	Poor
750	675	575	450	300	—

Model 90 Over-and-Under Shotgun

This gun was produced in response to a request from Sears Roebuck that Marlin should manufacture an over-and-under shotgun for Sears to market in their stores. The guns produced for Sears have the prefix 103 in their serial numbers and were marked "Ranger" before WWII and "J.C. Higgins" after the war. Prior to 1945 they were not marked Marlin; after that date Sears requested that the company stamp their name on the guns. They were also produced as the Marlin Model 90 during the same period and were chambered for 12, 16, and 20 gauge, as well as .410 bore. The 16 and 20 gauge guns were first offered in 1937 with 26" or 28" barrels. In 1939 the .410 bore was first offered with 26" barrel and 3" chambers. The barrels are either 26", 28", or 30", with various chokes. The action is a boxlock with extractors. Guns made prior to 1950 were solid between the barrels; after that date there was a space between the barrels. They can be found with double or single triggers and a checkered walnut stock. A ventilated rib was also offered as an option beginning in 1949. Be aware that this model was also available as a combination gun in .22 LR/.410, .22 Hornet/.410, and .218 Bee/.410. There were approximately 34,000 Model 90s manufactured between 1937 and 1963.

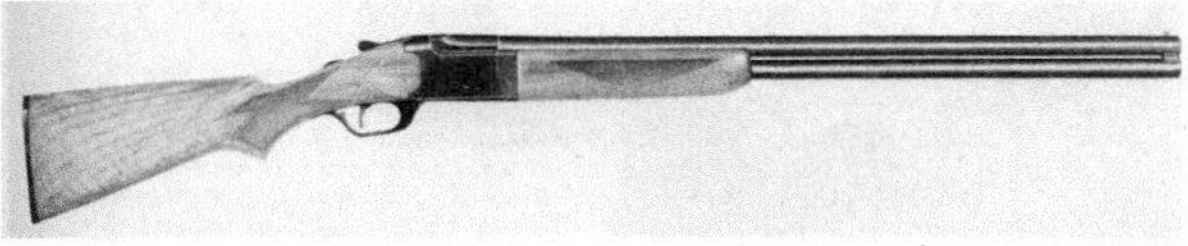

Photo by Lt. Col. William S. Brophy from Marlin Firearms with permission

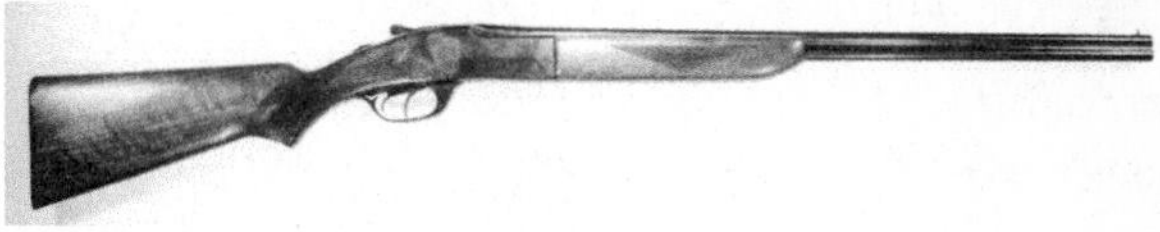

Photo by Lt. Col. William S. Brophy from Marlin Firearms with permission

NIB	Exc.	V.G.	Good	Fair	Poor
—	550	425	350	275	200

NOTE: Single trigger add 33 percent. Add 25 percent for 20 gauge guns and 125 percent for .410 bores. Add a 150 percent premium for combination guns. There are other rare gauge and barrel combinations that may affect value.

Premier Mark I Slide-Action Shotgun

This model was made by Manufrance and called the LaSalle. Marlin was able to purchase them without the barrels at a good enough price for them to barrel and market them under their own name. This model is 12 gauge only, with an alloy receiver and seven interchangeable barrels in 26"-30" lengths and various chokes. The plain stock is French walnut. The biggest problem with this gun is that the light weight (six pounds) produced severe recoil, and it was less than enjoyable to shoot. This model was in production from 1959 through 1963, with approximately 13,700 sold.

NIB	Exc.	V.G.	Good	Fair	Poor
—	325	225	175	150	100

Premier Mark II

This model is similar to the Mark I, with light engraving and a checkered stock.

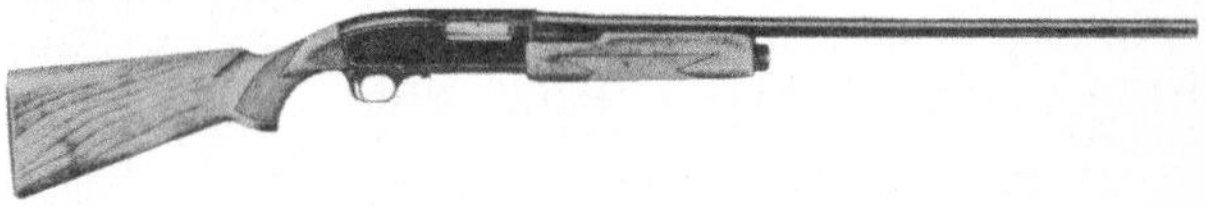

NIB	Exc.	V.G.	Good	Fair	Poor
—	325	225	175	150	100

Premier Mark IV

This model is similar to the Mark II, with more engraving on the receiver.

NIB	Exc.	V.G.	Good	Fair	Poor
—	325	225	175	150	100

NOTE: Add 10 percent for vent rib.

Model 120 Slide-Action Shotgun

This model was styled to resemble the Winchester Model 12 and was advertised as an all steel and walnut shotgun. It was offered with interchangeable barrels from 26" to 40", and various chokes were available. The checkered stock is of walnut, with a fitted recoil pad. The tube magazine holds 5 shots, 4 in 3". There was a Trap Model available (1973-1975), as well as a slug gun (1974-1984). This model was manufactured between 1971 and 1985. A really nice gun, if a bit heavy. Add 10 percent for 36-inch "Long Tom" barrel.

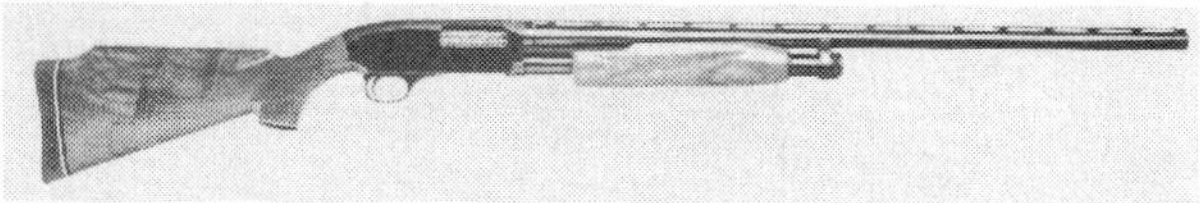

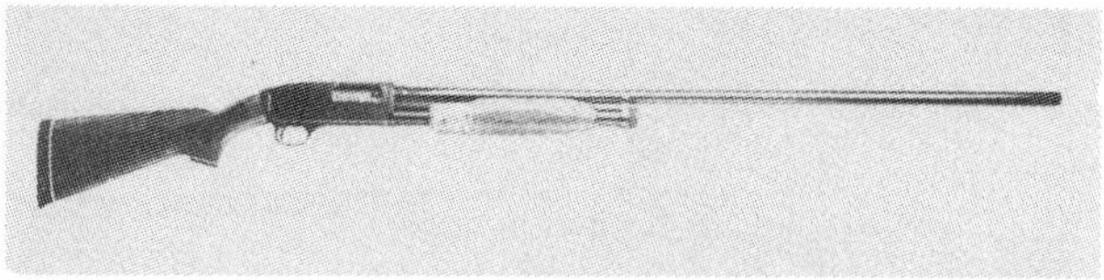

NIB	*Exc.*	*V.G.*	*Good*	*Fair*	*Poor*
—	350	300	250	150	125

Model 778 Slide-Action Shotgun (Glenfield)

This model is similar to the Model 120, with a walnut finished hardwood stock instead of walnut, and the Glenfield name stamped on it. It was manufactured between 1979 and 1984.

NIB	*Exc.*	*V.G.*	*Good*	*Fair*	*Poor*
—	275	225	175	125	100

Model 50DL

This bolt-action 12 gauge shotgun is available with a 28" modified barrel, black synthetic stock. Ventilated recoil pad is standard. Brass bead front sight. Weight is approximately 7.5 lbs.

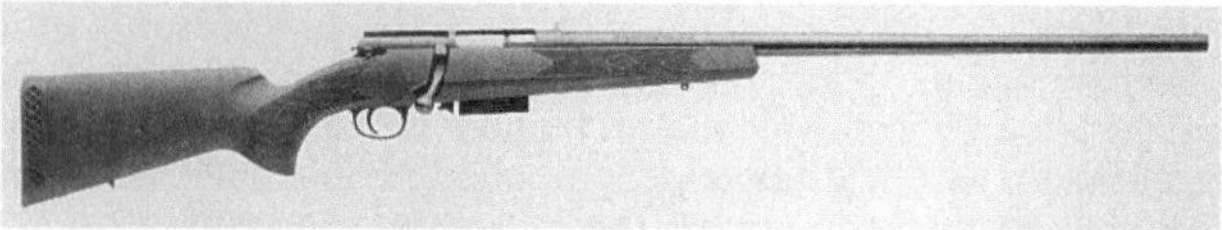

NIB	*Exc.*	*V.G.*	*Good*	*Fair*	*Poor*
300	275	225	150	125	100

Model 55 Bolt-Action Shotgun

This model is chambered for 12, 16, and 20 gauge, with Full or adjustable choke and barrels of 26" or 28". It is a bolt-action with 2-shot box magazine. The pistol grip stock is plain. This model was manufactured between 1950 and 1965.

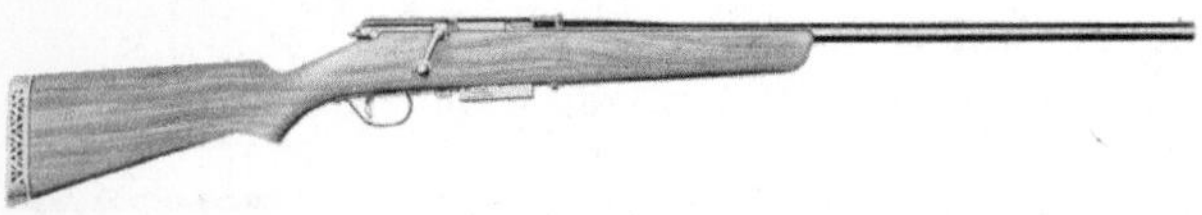

NIB	*Exc.*	*V.G.*	*Good*	*Fair*	*Poor*
—	225	175	100	50	25

Model 55 Swamp Gun

This is simply the Model 55 with a 3" Magnum, 20" barrel and an adjustable choke. It was manufactured between 1963 and 1965.

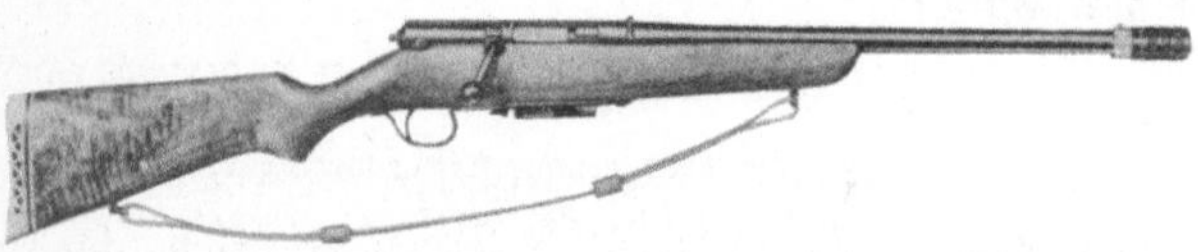

NIB	*Exc.*	*V.G.*	*Good*	*Fair*	*Poor*
—	300	250	175	75	50

Model 55 Goose Gun

This is the Model 55 with a 3" chambered, 36" Full choke 12-ga. barrel and a recoil pad and sling. It was introduced in 1962.

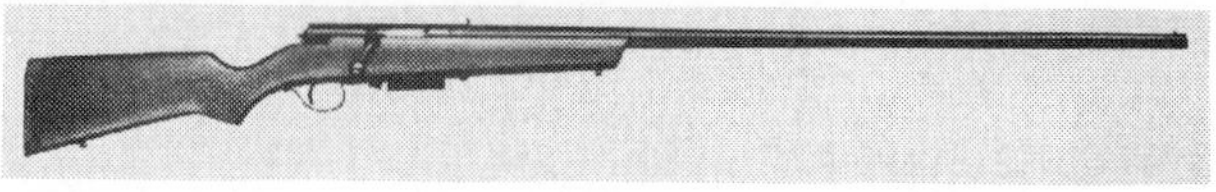

NIB	*Exc.*	*V.G.*	*Good*	*Fair*	*Poor*
375	250	175	150	75	50

Model 55S Slug Gun

This is the Model 55 with a 24" cylinder-bore barrel and rifle sights. It was manufactured between 1974 and 1983.

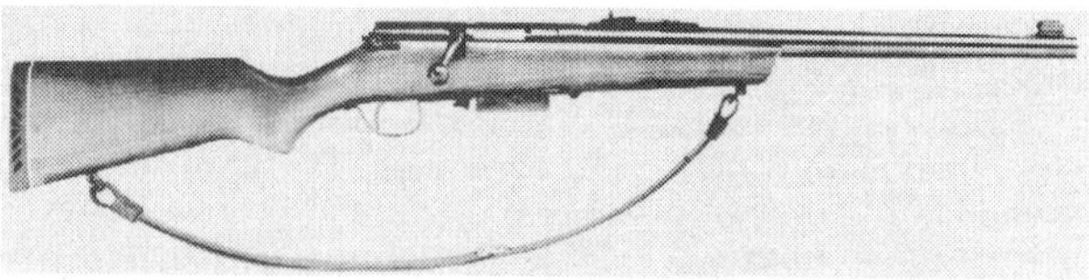

NIB	*Exc.*	*V.G.*	*Good*	*Fair*	*Poor*
—	250	200	150	100	50

Model 5510 Bolt-Action Shotgun Goose Gun

This model is chambered for the 3.5" 10 gauge. It has a 34" Full choke barrel and a recoil pad and sling. It was manufactured between 1976 and 1985.

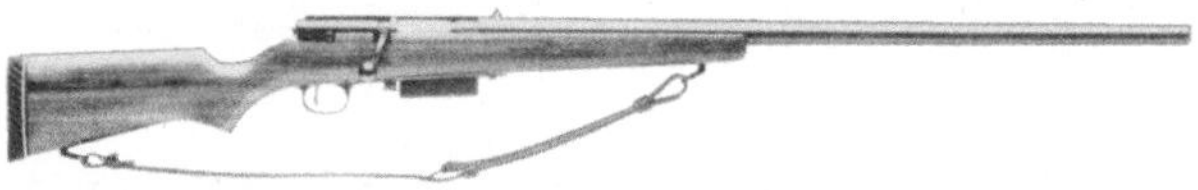

NIB	*Exc.*	*V.G.*	*Good*	*Fair*	*Poor*
—	400	300	250	175	100

Model 55GDL

This bolt-action shotgun is fitted with a 36" full choke barrel and reinforced black synthetic stock. Magazine holds two rounds. Ventilated recoil pad is standard. First introduced in 1997. Weight is about 8 lbs. Discontinued.

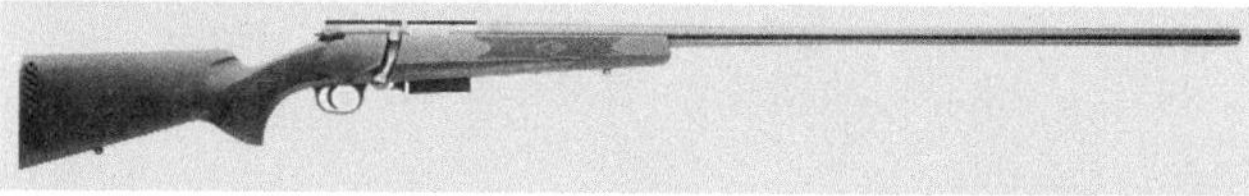

NIB	*Exc.*	*V.G.*	*Good*	*Fair*	*Poor*
350	325	275	200	150	100

Model 512 Slugmaster

Introduced in 1994 this bolt-action shotgun features a rifled 21" barrel. It is equipped with a two-shot detachable magazine and a ventilated recoil pad. A special scope is also provided. Weight is approximately 8 lbs. Discontinued.

NIB	*Exc.*	*V.G.*	*Good*	*Fair*	*Poor*
350	325	275	200	150	100

Model 512DL Slugmaster

Introduced in 1997 this bolt-action model features a black synthetic stock with a fully rifled 21" barrel chambered for the 12 gauge shell. A two-round magazine is standard. Adjustable rear sight with ramp front sight. Receiver drilled and tapped for scope mount. Weight is about 8 lbs. In 1998 this model was furnished with "Fire Sights." Discontinued.

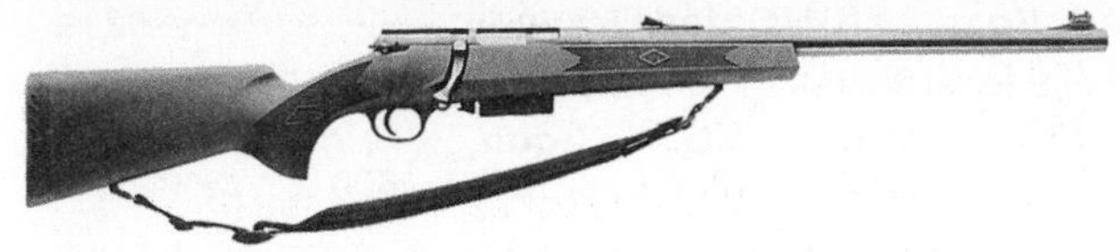

Model 512 DL with Fire Sights

NIB	Exc.	V.G.	Good	Fair	Poor
395	250	200	150	125	100

Model 512P

Introduced in 1999 this model is similar to the Model 512 DL with the addition of a 21" fully rifled and ported barrel. Fire sights are standard. Weight is about 8 lbs. Discontinued.

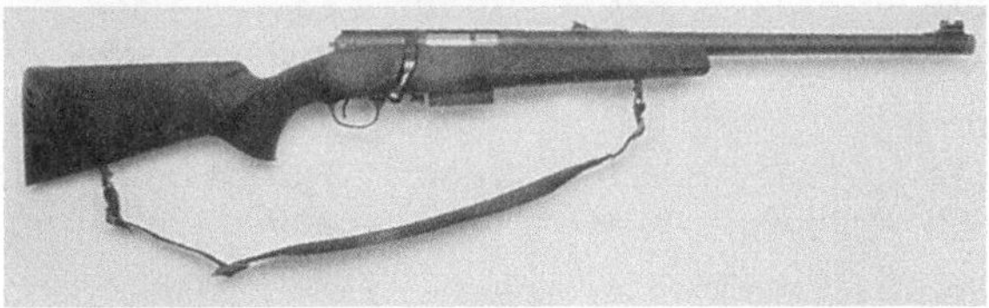

NIB	Exc.	V.G.	Good	Fair	Poor
395	250	200	150	125	100

Model 25MG

This bolt-action .22 Win. Mag shotshell-only gun is fitted with a 22" smoothbore barrel. It has a 7-round magazine. Hardwood stock. Weight is about 6 lbs. First introduced in 1999.

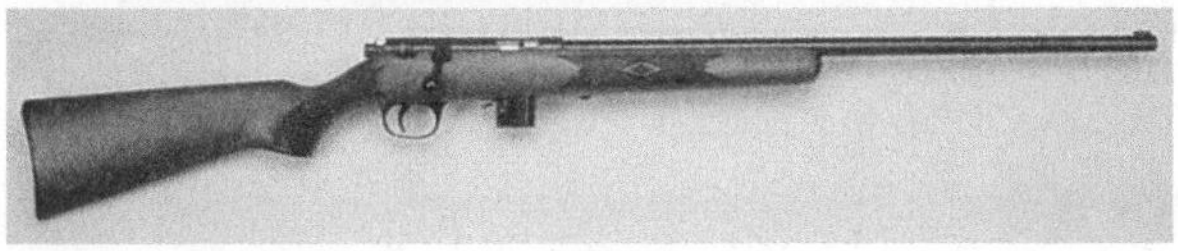

NIB	Exc.	V.G.	Good	Fair	Poor
225	175	145	125	100	75

MODERN LC SMITH SHOTGUNS

NOTE: The modern line of L.C. Smith shotguns is made in Europe and imported into the USA under the Marlin name.

Model LC410-DB

A side-by-side .410 bore, with fleur-de-lis checkered walnut stock, single selective trigger, selective automatic ejectors, three choke tubes (IC, M, F) and 26" chrome-lined barrels with solid rib, and bead front sight. Its case-colored receiver has gold game bird embossed on the side and bottom.

NIB	Exc.	V.G.	Good	Fair	Poor
1600	1175	900	700	500	300

Model LC28-DB

Similar to above but in 28 gauge.

NIB	Exc.	V.G.	Good	Fair	Poor
1750	1275	900	700	500	300

Model LC12-DB

This 12-gauge double barrel features 3" chambers, a single trigger, selective automatic ejectors, three choke tubes (IC, M, F), 28" barrels with a solid rib and a bead front sight. Its walnut stock is checkered, and has a fluted comb, a beavertail forearm and a recoil pad. Case-coloring on receiver and side plates.

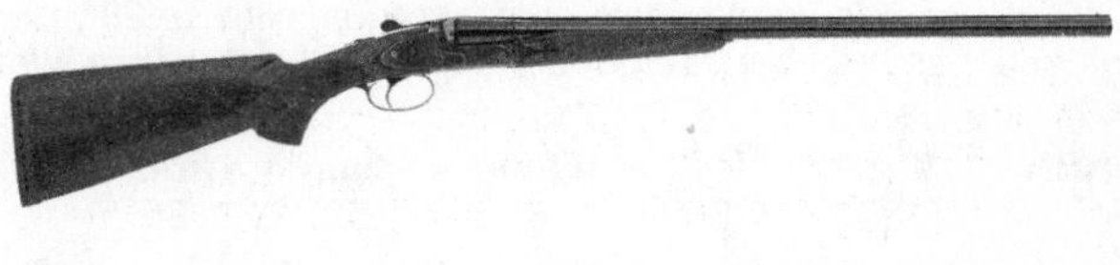

NIB	Exc.	V.G.	Good	Fair	Poor
1100	950	800	575	400	250

Model LC20-DB

Similar to above but in 20 gauge.

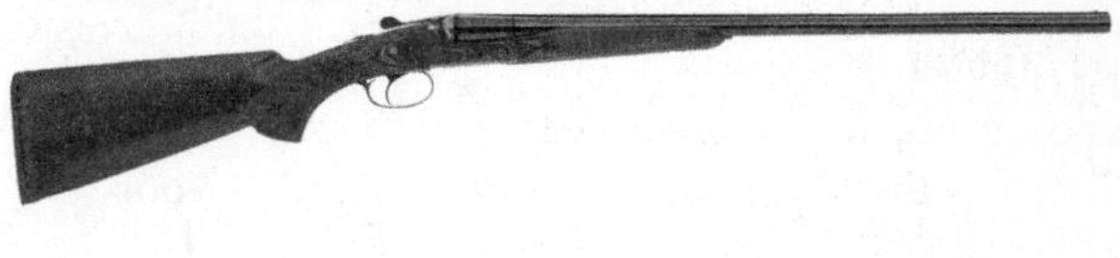

NIB	Exc.	V.G.	Good	Fair	Poor
1100	950	800	575	400	250

Model LC12-OU

This over-and-under features 3" chambers, a single selective trigger, selective automatic ejectors, automatic safety, three choke tubes (IC, M, F), 28" barrels with ventilated rib and bead front sight. It has a checkered walnut stock with a fluted comb and recoil pad and features case-coloring on its receiver and sideplates.

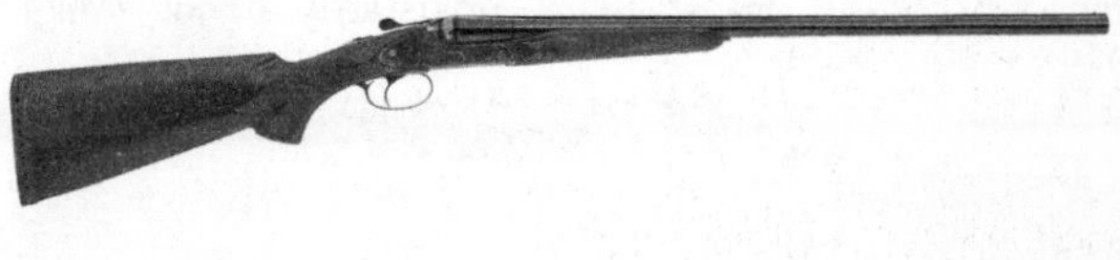

NIB	Exc.	V.G.	Good	Fair	Poor
950	825	600	450	300	200

Model LC20-OU

Similar to above but in 20 gauge.

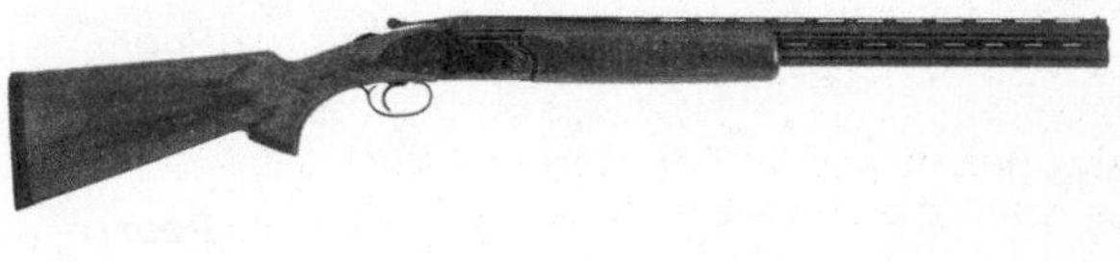

NIB	Exc.	V.G.	Good	Fair	Poor
950	825	600	450	300	200

MODERN MUZZLELOADERS

Model MLS-50/54

These Marlin in-line muzzleloaders were introduced in 1997. They are stainless steel and available in either .50 or .54 caliber. The barrel is 22" long. Adjustable Marble rear sight, ramp front sight with brass bead. Drilled and tapped for scope mount. Black synthetic stock with molded in checkering. Weight is about 7 lbs. Discontinued, and not particularly easy to take down for cleaning.

NIB	Exc.	V.G.	Good	Fair	Poor
300	225	200	150	75	50

MAROCCHI ARMI

Brescia, Italy

Model 2000

A 12 gauge Magnum single-shot shotgun with a 28" barrel, exposed hammer and automatic ejector. Blued with a walnut stock.

NIB	Exc.	V.G.	Good	Fair	Poor
—	100	80	65	50	35

Field Master I

A 12 gauge over-and-under shotgun with 26" or 28" ventilated rib barrels fitted for choke tubes, single trigger and automatic ejectors. Blued, French case hardened with a walnut stock.

NIB	Exc.	V.G.	Good	Fair	Poor
—	500	395	300	200	150

Field Master II

As above, with a single-selective trigger.

NIB	Exc.	V.G.	Good	Fair	Poor
—	525	450	350	225	175

CONQUISTA SERIES

Grade I is the standard grade with a special polished steel finish and machined engraved. The stock and forearm are select walnut and hand checkered 20 lpi.Grade II has roll engraved game scenes. The stock is select figured walnut.Grade III is hand engraved by a master engraver featuring game scenes. Finely figured walnut stock.

SPORTING CLAYS MODEL

Offered in 12 gauge with 28", 30", or 32" ventilated rib barrels. Screw in chokes are standard. Adjustable trigger. Weight is approximately 8 lbs.

Grade I

NIB	Exc.	V.G.	Good	Fair	Poor
1950	1700	1175	850	600	300

Grade II

NIB	Exc.	V.G.	Good	Fair	Poor
2350	1900	1475	950	700	350

Grade III

NIB	Exc.	V.G.	Good	Fair	Poor
3350	2850	1825	1150	800	400

Sporting Light Grade I

Same as above but slightly smaller dimensions. Available in 28" or 30" barrel length. Weight is about 7.5 lbs.

NIB	Exc.	V.G.	Good	Fair	Poor
2050	1700	1175	850	600	300

Sporting Clays Left-Hand Model Grade I

Same as Sporting Clays Model but designed for the left-handed shooter.

NIB	Exc.	V.G.	Good	Fair	Poor
2150	1700	1175	850	600	300

Lady Sport Model Grade I

Offered in 12 gauge only with choice of 28" or 30" vent rib barrels. Slightly smaller dimensions for women. Weight 7.75 lbs.

NIB	Exc.	V.G.	Good	Fair	Poor
2150	1700	1175	850	600	300

Lady Sport Model Spectrum Grade—Colored Frame

NIB	Exc.	V.G.	Good	Fair	Poor
2100	1750	1200	850	600	300

Lady Sport Left-Handed Grade I

Same as above but for left-handed shooters.

NIB	Exc.	V.G.	Good	Fair	Poor
2100	1750	1200	850	600	300

Lady Sport Left-Handed Spectrum Left-Handed

NIB	Exc.	V.G.	Good	Fair	Poor
2175	1800	1225	850	600	300

TRAP MODEL

Built for the competition shooter this model features a choice of 30" or 32" vent rib barrels. Trap dimension stock. Weight approximately 8.25 lbs.

Grade I

NIB	Exc.	V.G.	Good	Fair	Poor
2025	1750	1200	850	600	300

Grade II

NIB	Exc.	V.G.	Good	Fair	Poor
2400	1950	1500	1000	750	350

Grade III

NIB	Exc.	V.G.	Good	Fair	Poor
3400	2700	18900	1500	800	400

SKEET MODEL

This model is designed for the competition shooter. Only a 28" vent rib barrel is offered as standard. Skeet dimension stock. Skeet chokes. Weight is approximately 7.75 lbs.

Grade I

NIB	Exc.	V.G.	Good	Fair	Poor
2025	1750	1200	850	600	300

Grade II

NIB	Exc.	V.G.	Good	Fair	Poor
2425	1950	1525	1000	750	350

Grade III

NIB	Exc.	V.G.	Good	Fair	Poor
3400	2700	1900	1500	800	400

Classic Doubles Model 92

Offered in 12 gauge only with 30" vent rib barrels. Adjustable trigger. Walnut stock with 18 lpi checkering. Weight is approximately 8.12 lbs.

NIB	Exc.	V.G.	Good	Fair	Poor
1650	1350	875	600	500	250

Model 99 Grade I

This over-and-under gun features a silver-grayed receiver, boxlock action with single-selective trigger, pistol-grip stock and schnabel forearm. Sporting models are offered with 28", 30", or 32" barrels. Trap models are offered with 30" or 32" barrels, and skeet models with 28" or 30" barrels. All barrels are supplied with five extended choke tubes.

NIB	Exc.	V.G.	Good	Fair	Poor
3125	2350	1800	750	700	300

Model 99 Grade III

This model has all of the above features in addition to five flush-mounted choke tubes and silver game scene engraved receiver.

NIB	Exc.	V.G.	Good	Fair	Poor
5200	3400	2200	950	800	300

MASQUELIER S. A.

Liege, Belgium

Carpathe

A .243, .270, .7x57mm, 7x65Rmm, or .30-06 caliber single-shot rifle with a 24" barrel, adjustable trigger and adjustable sights.

Blued, with an engraved receiver and walnut stock. Imported until 1986.

NIB	Exc.	V.G.	Good	Fair	Poor
—	3750	2950	1950	1250	750

Express

A .270, .30-06, 8x57JRSmm, or 9.3x74Rmm caliber over-and-under double-barrel rifle with 24" barrels, single-selective trigger and automatic ejectors. Blued, engraved with a walnut stock. Not imported after 1986.

NIB	Exc.	V.G.	Good	Fair	Poor
—	3800	2950	1950	1250	750

Ardennes

As above, but made on custom order only. Discontinued in 1986.

NIB	Exc.	V.G.	Good	Fair	Poor
—	8000	6000	3750	2500	1000

Boxlock Side-by-Side Shotgun

A 12 gauge boxlock double-barrel shotgun manufactured in a variety of barrel lengths with a single-selective trigger and automatic ejectors. Blued with a walnut stock. Imported prior to 1987.

NIB	Exc.	V.G.	Good	Fair	Poor
—	4750	3500	2500	1500	850

Sidelock Side-by-Side Shotgun

Similar to the above, but with detachable sidelocks and finely engraved. Imported prior to 1987.

NIB	Exc.	V.G.	Good	Fair	Poor
—	14500	11750	7000	5000	1750

MASSACHUSETTS ARMS CO.

Chicopee Falls, Massachusetts

Maynard Carbine

This is a single-shot breechloader chambered for .35 or.50 caliber percussion. The barrel is round and 20" in length. The trigger guard is the lever that pivots the barrel in break-open fashion when it is lowered. The finish is blued, with a case colored frame. The buttstock is walnut, and there is no forend. This carbine was designed by the same Maynard who invented the tape primer system. There are two models—a 1st and a 2nd. They were made for both sporting use and as a U.S. Martial carbine. The 2nd Model was used considerably during the Civil War.

1st Model

This model is marked "Maynard Patentee/May 27, 1851/June 17, 1856." It has an iron patchbox and a curved buttplate. It has a Maynard tape primer system and a tang sight. Later production was fitted with a sling swivel. There are approximately 400 of these carbines that are U.S. marked, but the total manufactured in the late 1850s is unknown.

Courtesy Milwaukee Public Museum, Milwaukee, Wisconsin

1st Model U.S. Martially Marked

NIB	Exc.	V.G.	Good	Fair	Poor
—	—	6500	4050	2000	700

1st Model Commercial Model

NIB	Exc.	V.G.	Good	Fair	Poor
—	—	4000	3000	1250	400

2nd Model

This model is chambered for .50 caliber only and does not have the tape primer system or the tang sight. There is no patchbox, and the buttplate is not as curved as on the 1st Model. It is marked "Manufactured By/Mass. Arms Co./Chicopee Falls." There were approximately 20,000 manufactured between 1860 and 1865. This model was used by Union forces during the Civil War.

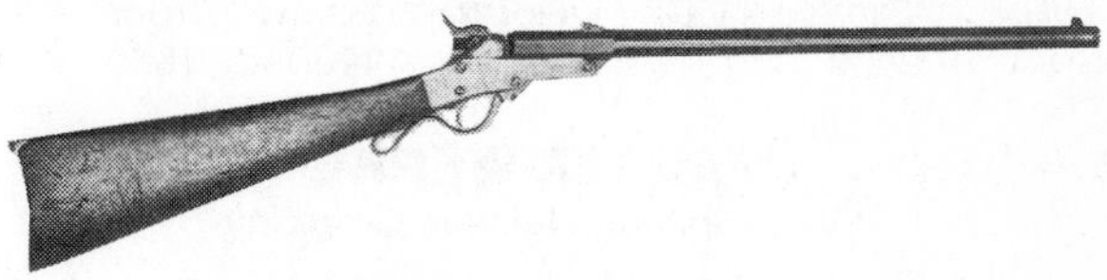

Courtesy Milwaukee Public Museum, Milwaukee, Wisconsin

NIB	Exc.	V.G.	Good	Fair	Poor
—	—	2500	2050	700	500

Maynard Patent Sporting Rifles

Sporting rifles bearing the designations Model 1865, 1873 and 1882 were manufactured in a wide variety of calibers, gauges, stock styles, finishes, and options.

Courtesy Milwaukee Public Museum, Milwaukee, Wisconsin

NIB	Exc.	V.G.	Good	Fair	Poor
—	—	2500	1650	660	200

MATEBA ARMS

Italy

AutoRevolver Carbine

Similar in principle to handgun by the same maker but with 16" or 18" barrel and walnut buttstock, pistol grip and forend.

NIB	Exc.	V.G.	Good	Fair	Poor
1800	1300	1000	700	500	300

MAUNZ MFG., INC.

Maumee, Ohio

Manufacturer (1970s-1980s) of high-end law enforcement and competition rifles based primarily on the M14 military rifle.

Model 77 Service Match Rifle

Semi-auto rifle chambered in .308 Winchester and other chamberings on custom order. 22-inch barrel standard; medium and heavy barrels also available. Charcoal gray parkerized finish. Custom rifles had heavyweight Kevlar or graphite/fiberglass stocks covered in black gelcoat. Red/white/blue stocks were also produced. 300 produced.

NIB	Exc.	V.G.	Good	Fair	Poor
—	2500	2250	2000	1850	1500

Model 87 Maunz Match Rifle

Semi-auto rifle chambered in .308 Winchester and 6.30 Maunz; Limited .338 and .45 Maunz chamberings on custom order. Sold only to Master competitors and American Shooters Union members.

NIB	Exc.	V.G.	Good	Fair	Poor
—	2500	2200	2000	1500	1200

Model 57 M1A

Semi-auto rifle chambered in .30-06, .276 and .308 Winchester, also .45 Maunz (rare). M1 Garand receiver with M14 parts and National Match barrels. Custom-built glass-bedded stock. Approximately 200 made.

NIB	Exc.	V.G.	Good	Fair	Poor
—	1500	1250	1000	800	600

Model 67 Match Grade for Practice

Semi-auto rifle chambered in .308 Winchester, 6.30 Maunz and .45 Maunz. Camp Perry stamped. Not allowed for Service Rifle competition. Combination of M1 Garand and M14 parts. Approximately 250 made.

NIB	Exc.	V.G.	Good	Fair	Poor
—	2000	1800	1500	1200	1500

MAUSER WERKE

Oberndorf-am-Neckar, Germany

Established in 1869 by Peter and Wilhelm Mauser, this companycame under the effective control of Ludwig Loewe and Companyof Berlin in 1887. In 1896 the latter company was reorganized un-der the name *Deutsches Waffen und Munition* or as it is betterknown, DWM.

NOTE: For historical information, technical details, and photosand prices see the *Standard Catalog of Military Firearms*.

EARLY SPORTING RIFLES

A wide variety of commercial Model 98 Sporting Rifles were made, most of which had 23.5" ribbed barrels, open sights, 5-shot magazines, single or double set triggers, and either full or semi-pistol grip stocks.

NOTE: The values listed here are representative.

NIB	Exc.	V.G.	Good	Fair	Poor
—	375	325	300	275	200

Model EN310

A .22 caliber single-shot bolt-action rifle with a 19.75" barrel, open sights, and plain walnut stock. Manufactured before WWII.

NIB	Exc.	V.G.	Good	Fair	Poor
—	250	225	200	150	100

Type A—Short Action

NIB	Exc.	V.G.	Good	Fair	Poor
—	4500	3900	3300	1850	70000

Model EL320

As above, with a 23.5" barrel and checkered walnut stock.

NIB	Exc.	V.G.	Good	Fair	Poor
—	275	250	225	175	125

Type A—Medium Action

NIB	Exc.	V.G.	Good	Fair	Poor
—	3500	2900	2350	1600	700

Model KKW

A .22 caliber single-shot bolt-action rifle with a 26" barrel, ladder rear sight and full-length walnut stock. Manufactured prior to WWII.

NIB	Exc.	V.G.	Good	Fair	Poor
—	400	350	300	225	150

Type A—Long Action

NIB	Exc.	V.G.	Good	Fair	Poor
—	4500	3900	3300	1850	700

Model MS350B

A .22 caliber bolt-action rifle with a 26.75" barrel, adjustable rear sight and 5-shot magazine. Blued with a walnut stock.

NIB	Exc.	V.G.	Good	Fair	Poor
—	475	400	350	275	200

Type B

NIB	Exc.	V.G.	Good	Fair	Poor
—	3500	2900	2300	1400	500

Model ES340B

Similar to the above, but in single-shot form.

NIB	Exc.	V.G.	Good	Fair	Poor
—	375	300	250	175	100

Type K

NIB	Exc.	V.G.	Good	Fair	Poor
—	4500	3900	3300	1850	700

Model MM41OBN

A .22 caliber bolt-action rifle with a 23.5" barrel, adjustable sights, and 5-shot magazine. Blued with a walnut stock.

NIB	Exc.	V.G.	Good	Fair	Poor
—	400	350	300	200	125

Type M

NIB	Exc.	V.G.	Good	Fair	Poor
—	4500	3900	3300	1850	700

Model MS420B

As above, with a 26.75" barrel and target-style stock.

NIB	Exc.	V.G.	Good	Fair	Poor
—	400	350	300	200	125

Type S

NIB	Exc.	V.G.	Good	Fair	Poor
—	4500	3900	3300	1850	700

CARBINE MODELS

Cone Hammer Flat Side Carbine

A 7.63mm caliber carbine with an 11.75" barrel, early adjustable sight, flat frame and detachable buttstock. Prospective purchasers should secure a qualified appraisal prior to acquisition. Too rare to price. **NOTE:** Watch for fakes.

Large Ring Hammer Transitional Carbine

Similar to the above, with milled frame panels. Prospective purchasers should secure a qualified appraisal prior to acquisition.

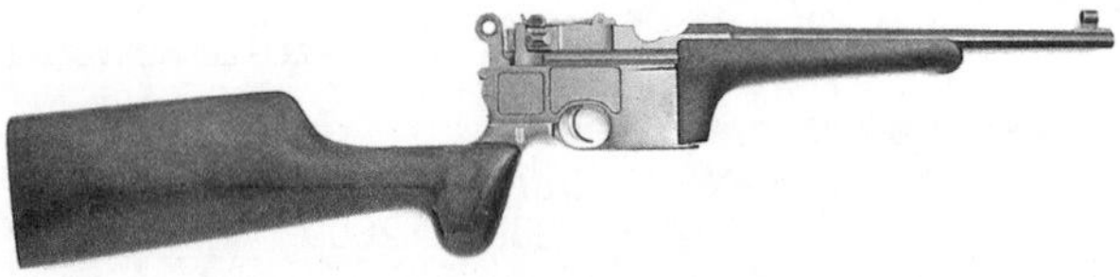

NIB	Exc.	V.G.	Good	Fair	Poor
—	25000	18000	11000	5000	3000

Large Ring Hammer Flatside Carbine

Similar to the above, with a 14.5" barrel. Prospective purchasers should secure a qualified appraisal prior to acquisition.

NIB	Exc.	V.G.	Good	Fair	Poor
—	22000	17000	10000	5000	3000

Small Ring Hammer Carbine

Similar to the above, with the hammer having a smaller diameter hole at its tip. Prospective purchasers should secure a qualified appraisal prior to acquisition. Some late carbines were chambered for the 9mm export.

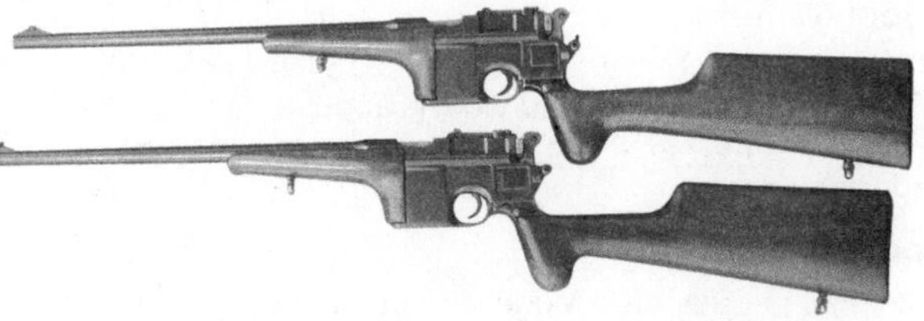

Courtesy Gale Morgan

NIB	Exc.	V.G.	Good	Fair	Poor
—	23000	18000	15000	6000	4000

CHINESE COPIES

Shansei Arsenal Model

Approximately 8,000 Model 96 pistols were manufactured in .45 ACP caliber.Copies of the Model 96 were made by Unceta (Astra) and Zulaica y Cia (Royal) and marketed by the firm of Beistegui Hermanos. These copies are covered in their own sections of this text. **NOTE:** Within the past several years, a large quantity of Model 96 pistols exported to or made in China have been imported into the United States. It has been reported that some newly made copies of the Shansei .45 were recently exported from China. Proceed with caution.

Courtesy Gale Morgan

NIB	Exc.	V.G.	Good	Fair	Poor
—	5000	3500	2250	1500	1300

MAUSER RIFLES & PISTOLS—RECENT PRODUCTION

NOTE: In February 1999 SIGARMS announced the acquisition of the Mauser line of small arms. With the acquisition, SIG assumes the rights to the Mauser name and will integrate the Mauser product line into SIGARMS' line of small arms.

Model 2000

A .270, .308, or the .30-06 caliber bolt-action rifle with a 24" barrel, open sights and a 5-shot magazine. Blued, with a checkered walnut stock. Manufactured between 1969 and 1971 by Heym.

NIB	Exc.	V.G.	Good	Fair	Poor
—	600	450	300	200	150

Model 3000

As above, with a 22" barrel, no sights and Monte Carlo-style stock. Manufactured from 1971 to 1974 by Heym.

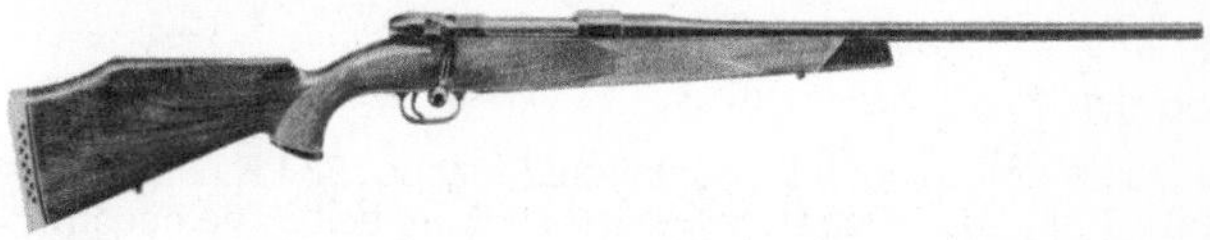

NIB	Exc.	V.G.	Good	Fair	Poor
—	600	450	300	200	150

Model 3000 Magnum

As above, in 7mm Rem. Mag., .300 Win. Mag. and the .375 H&H Mag. caliber with a 26" barrel and a 3-shot integral magazine. Blued, with a checkered walnut stock. Produced by Heym.

NIB	Exc.	V.G.	Good	Fair	Poor
—	675	525	375	250	200

Model 4000

Similar to the Model 3000, but in .222 or .223 caliber with folding open sights. Produced by Heym.

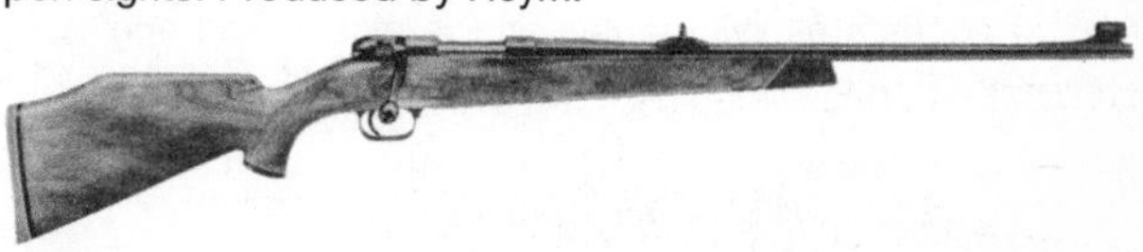

NIB	Exc.	V.G.	Good	Fair	Poor
—	550	400	250	200	150

Model 225

A .243 to. 300 Weatherby Magnum caliber bolt-action rifle with a 24" or 26" barrel, no sights, adjustable trigger or 3- or 5-shot magazine. Blued with a walnut stock.

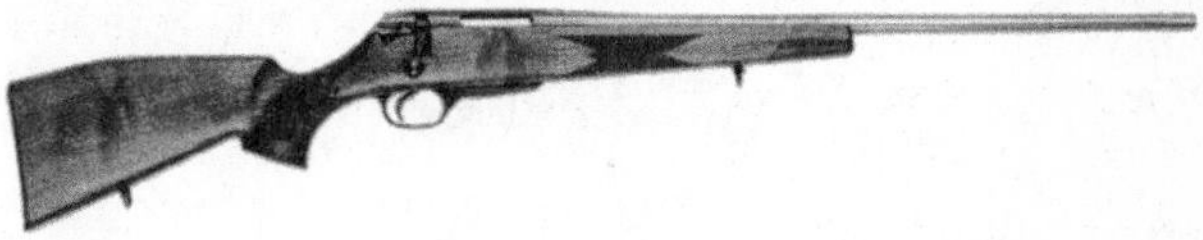

NIB	Exc.	V.G.	Good	Fair	Poor
1400	1250	1000	750	600	500

Model ES340

A .22 caliber single-shot bolt-action rifle with a 25.5" barrel, open sights, and walnut stock. Manufactured before WWII.

NIB	Exc.	V.G.	Good	Fair	Poor
—	300	250	225	175	125

Model DSM34

Similar to the above, with a 25" barrel and full-length walnut stock. Manufactured prior to WWII.

NIB	Exc.	V.G.	Good	Fair	Poor
—	325	275	250	200	150

Model MS420B

Similar to the above, with a 25" barrel and 5-shot magazine. Manufactured before WWII.

NIB	Exc.	V.G.	Good	Fair	Poor
—	375	325	300	275	200

Model ES350

A .22 caliber single-shot bolt-action rifle with a 27.5" barrel and checkered pistol grip walnut stock. Manufactured before WWII.

NIB	Exc.	V.G.	Good	Fair	Poor
—	450	400	375	350	275

Model M410

Similar to the above, with a 23.5" barrel and 5-shot magazine. Manufactured before WWII.

NIB	Exc.	V.G.	Good	Fair	Poor
—	375	325	300	275	200

Model M420

As above, with a 25.5" barrel.

Model 107

This is a bolt-action rifle chambered for the .22 LR. Barrel length is 21.6" and box magazine has a 5-shot capacity. The beechwood checkered Monte Carlo stock is full size with pistol grip, plastic buttplate. The rear sight is adjustable. Metal finish is blue. Weighs about 5 lbs.

NIB	Exc.	V.G.	Good	Fair	Poor
265	225	180	150	125	100

Model 201 Standard

This model features a 21" medium heavy free-floating barrel. The receiver accepts all rail mounts and is also drilled and tapped for scope mount. Magazine capacity is 5-shot. Chambered for. 22 LR or .22 WMR cartridge. The beechwood stock is hand checkered with plastic buttplate. The Monte Carlo stock is fitted with cheekpiece. Weighs about 6.5 lbs.

NIB	Exc.	V.G.	Good	Fair	Poor
400	325	250	200	150	100

Model 66 Standard

This is a centerfire bolt-action rifle fitted with a European Walnut hand-checkered oil finish stock. Stock is half stock design. Rosewood forends and pistol grip caps are standard. Fitted with rubber recoil pad and 1" quick disconnect sling swivels. Barrels are interchangeable on this model. Barrels with standard calibers is 24" and approximate weight is 7.5 lbs. Standard calibers are: .243 Win., .270, .308, .30-06, 5.6x57, 6.5x57, 7.64, and 9.3x62.

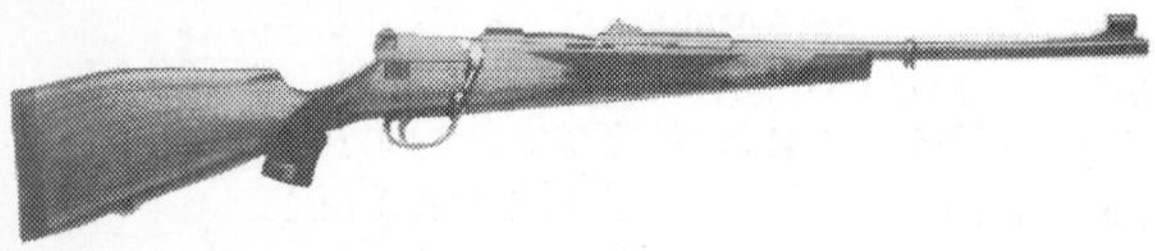

NIB	Exc.	V.G.	Good	Fair	Poor
1400	1150	850	700	550	350

Model 66 Magnum

Same as above but chambered for 7mm Rem. Mag., .300 and .338 Win. Mag., 6.5x68, 8x86S, 9.3x64. Fitted with a 26" barrel and weighs about 7.9 lbs.

NIB	Exc.	V.G.	Good	Fair	Poor
1500	1250	950	800	600	400

Model 66 Safari

Same as above but chambered for .375 H&H and .458 Win. Mag. Fitted with a 26" barrel and weighs about 9.3 lbs.

NIB	Exc.	V.G.	Good	Fair	Poor
2250	1575	1100	850	650	400

Model 66 Stuzen

Same as the Standard Model 66 but fitted with a full stock. Barrel length is 21" and calibers are same as Standard. Weighs about 7.5 lbs.

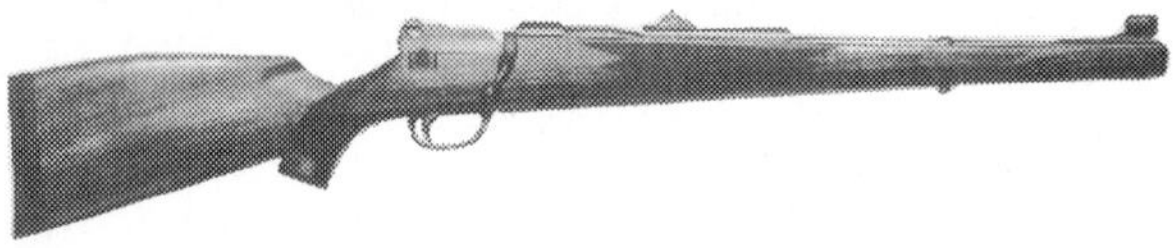

NIB	Exc.	V.G.	Good	Fair	Poor
1500	1250	950	800	600	400

IDF Mauser Rifle Model 66SP

This is a bolt-action rifle chambered for the .308 Win. cartridge. Adjustable trigger for pull and travel. Barrel length is 27". Specially designed stock has broad forend and a thumb hole pistol grip. Cheekpiece is adjustable as is the recoil pad. Supplied with case. This rifle is military issue. Fewer than 100 imported into the U.S. by Springfield Armory.

NIB	Exc.	V.G.	Good	Fair	Poor
2250	1575	1100	850	650	400

Model 77

Fitted with a 24" barrel this bolt-action rifle is chambered for the .243, .270, 6.5x57, 7x64, .308, and .30-06 calibers. Detachable box magazine. Set trigger. Walnut stock with cheekpiece and hand checkering. Weight is about 7.25 lbs.

NIB	Exc.	V.G.	Good	Fair	Poor
1250	950	800	650	450	200

Model 77 Ultra

This model is fitted with a 20" barrel and chambered for the 6.5x57, 7x64, and .30-06 calibers. Weight is about 7.5 lbs.

NIB	Exc.	V.G.	Good	Fair	Poor
1250	950	800	650	450	200

Model 77 Mannlicher

Similar to the Ultra Model but with a full-length Mannlicher stock. Set trigger. Weight is about 7.5 lbs.

NIB	Exc.	V.G.	Good	Fair	Poor
1250	950	800	650	450	200

Model 77 Big Game

Chambered for the .375 H&H Magnum cartridge and fitted with a 26" barrel. Weight is about 8.5 lbs.

NIB	Exc.	V.G.	Good	Fair	Poor
1400	1100	900	750	500	200

Model 86-SR

Introduced in 1993 this bolt-action .308 is sometimes referred to as the Specialty Rifle. Fitted with a laminated wood and special match thumbhole stock or fiberglass stock with adjustable cheekpiece. Stock has rail in forearm and an adjustable recoil pad. Magazine capacity is 9 rounds. Finish is a non-glare blue. The barrel length with muzzlebrake is 28.8". Many special features are found on this rifle from adjustable trigger weight to silent safety. Mauser offers many options on this rifle as well that will affect the price. Weight is approximately 11 lbs.

NIB	Exc.	V.G.	Good	Fair	Poor
3300	2950	2500	1750	1250	750

Model 93 SR

Introduced in 1996 this is a tactical semi-automatic rifle chambered for the .300 Win. Mag. or the .338 Lapua cartridge. Barrel length is 25.5" with an overall length of 48.4". Barrel is fitted with a muzzlebrake. Magazine capacity is 6 rounds for .300 and 5 rounds for .338 caliber. Weight is approximately 13 lbs.

NIB	Exc.	V.G.	Good	Fair	Poor
3300	2950	2500	1750	1250	750

Model 96

This bolt-action rifle is chambered for the .25-06, .270 Win., 7x64, .308, or .30-06 cartridge. It is fitted with a 22" barrel (24" Magnum calibers) and has a 5-round top loading magazine. Receiver is drilled and tapped. Checkered walnut stock. No sights. Approximately weight is 6.25 lbs.

NIB	Exc.	V.G.	Good	Fair	Poor
700	600	500	300	125	100

Model 98 (SIG Arms)

Built in Germany this bolt-action rifle features a select walnut stock with oil finish. Express rear sight and single stage trigger. Chambered for the .416 Rigby, .450 Dakota, .458 Lott, and .500 Jeffery. Weight is approximately 8.8 lbs.

NIB	Exc.	V.G.	Good	Fair	Poor
1000	—	—	—	—	—

NOTE: Add $1,000 for .500 Jeffery.

Model 99 Standard

This model is a bolt-action centerfire sporting rifle. It is offered with two stock designs: a classic with straight oil finish stock or high luster with cheekpiece and schnabel forend and Monte Carlo with rosewood forend tip and pistol grip cap. Chambered for standard calibers: .243, .25-06, .270, .308, .30-06, 5.6x57, 6.5x57, 7x57, 7x64. Barrel length is 24". Weight about 8 lbs.

NIB	Exc.	V.G.	Good	Fair	Poor
900	700	600	500	400	300

Model 99 Magnum

Same as above but chambered for magnum calibers: 7mm Rem. Mag., .257 Wby., .270 Wby., .300 Wby., .300 and .338 Win. Mag., 8x68S, and 9.3x64. Fitted with 26" barrel. Weighs about 8 lbs.

NIB	Exc.	V.G.	Good	Fair	Poor
950	750	650	550	400	300

MAVERICK ARMS, INC.

Subsidiary of O. F. Mossberg & Sons, Inc.
Eagle Pass, Texas

Model 88

A 12 gauge Magnum slide-action shotgun with 28" or 30" barrels, anodized receiver and composition stock. Introduced in 1989.

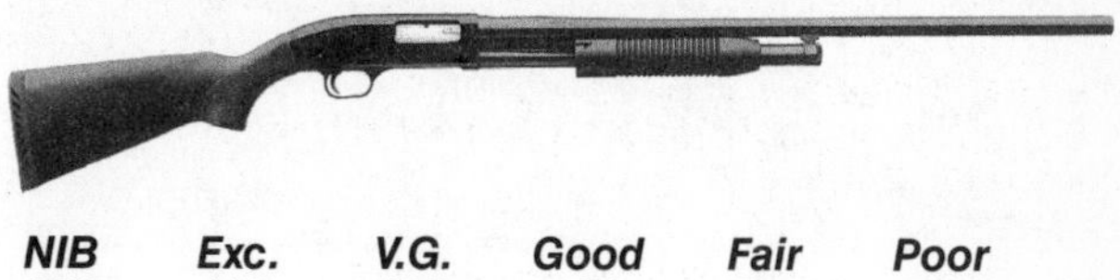

NIB	Exc.	V.G.	Good	Fair	Poor
250	150	125	100	75	50

Model 88 Slug Pump Shotgun

A 12-gauge Magnum pump-action shotgun with an interchangeable Cylinder-bore barrel. Black synthetic stock and forearm, blued metal finish, 6-shot magazine. Add $20 for rifled 24" barrel with adjustable rifle sights.

NIB	Exc.	V.G.	Good	Fair	Poor
295	200	100	75	60	50

Model 88 Six-Shot Security Model

A 12-gauge Magnum pump-action shotgun with a 6-shot magazine and an interchangeable 18-1/2" Cylinder-bore fixed choke barrel. A rugged black synthetic stock and forearm, blued metal finish and brass front sight bead are also included. Add 5 percent for Eight-Shot Security Model with 20" Cylinder-bore fixed choke barrel. Add 10 percent for heat shield.

NIB	Exc.	V.G.	Good	Fair	Poor
295	200	100	75	60	50

M. B. ASSOCIATES-GYROJET

San Ramon, California

Established in 1960 by R. Maynard and Art Biehl, M. B. Associates produced the Gyrojet pistols and carbines from 1962 to 1970. Basically a hand held rocket launcher, shooting a 12mm or 13mm spin stablized rocket cartridge, composed of four-part solid rocket fuel. The nose of the round was forced rearward onto a stationary firing pin, igniting the fuel, expelling the round and recocking for the next shot. These were not very accurate and led to MBA's demise. Ammunition typically sells for $35 per round or more. Dave Rachwal.

Mark I Model A Carbine

13mm, black anodized finish with walnut stock and carrying handle.

NIB	Exc.	V.G.	Good	Fair	Poor
—	2495	2195	1700	1000	600

Mark I Model B Carbine

13mm, antique nickel finish with walnut stock. This was the sporter carbine and had a flared muzzle and sleek lines.

NIB	Exc.	V.G.	Good	Fair	Poor
—	1495	800	900	400	200

McMILLAN & CO. INC., G. (LATER: HARRIS/MCMILLAN GUNWORKS, HARRIS GUNWORKS)

Phoenix, Arizona

Competition Model

A custom order bolt-action rifle in .308, 7mm-08, and the .300 Winchester Magnum caliber with the barrel length, stock type, and dimensions to the customer's specifications. Introduced in 1988.

NIB	Exc.	V.G.	Good	Fair	Poor
1700	1500	1150	800	600	300

Model 86 Sniper's Rifle

A custom order rifle in .308 Winchester or the .300 Winchester Magnum calibers with a synthetic stock and a choice of scope systems. Introduced in 1988.

NIB	Exc.	V.G.	Good	Fair	Poor
3250	2700	1900	1100	600	300

Model 86 System

As above, with the Ultra scope, mounting system, bipod, and fitted case. Introduced in 1988.

NIB	Exc.	V.G.	Good	Fair	Poor
3700	3250	2300	1800	850	550

Model 87 Long Range Snipers Rifle

A large stainless steel, single-shot bolt-action rifle in .50 BMG caliber featuring a 29" barrel with an integral muzzlebrake. Camouflaged synthetic stock. Weight 21 lbs. Accurate to 1,500 meters. Introduced in 1988.

NIB	Exc.	V.G.	Good	Fair	Poor
6000	5200	4000	2750	1000	500

Model 87 System

As above, with a bipod and a 20X Ultra scope, mounting system, and a fitted case. Introduced in 1988.

NIB	Exc.	V.G.	Good	Fair	Poor
6500	5700	4400	3150	1200	600

Signature Model

A bolt-action sporting rifle manufactured in a variety of calibers up to .375 Holland & Holland with a 22" or 24" stainless barrel, composition stock and either 3- or 4-shot magazine. Introduced in 1988.

NIB	Exc.	V.G.	Good	Fair	Poor
2200	1750	1250	800	600	300

Signature Stainless

Same as model above but barrel and action made of stainless steel. Fiberglass stock. Left- or right-hand model. The .416 Rigby is also offered in this configuration. Introduced in 1990.

NIB	Exc.	V.G.	Good	Fair	Poor
2500	2050	1650	1000	750	400

Signature Alaskan

This model, introduced in 1989, is offered in .270 .280 Rem., .30-06, 7mm Rem. Mag., .300 Win. Mag., .300 Wby. Mag., .358 Win. Mag., .340 Wby. Mag., .375 H&H. Match grade barrel from 22" to 26" in length. Single leaf rear sight and barrel band front sight.

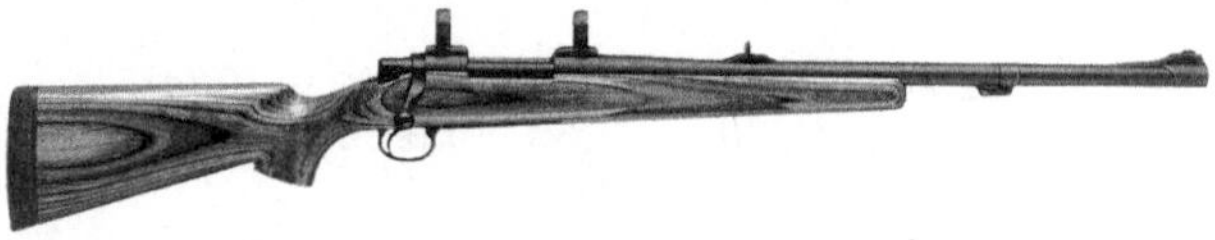

NIB	Exc.	V.G.	Good	Fair	Poor
3000	2700	2000	1500	950	500

Signature Titanium Mountain

Offered in calibers from .270 Win. to 7mm Rem. Mag. Match grade barrel is produced from titanium. Stock is graphite. Weight is about 6.5 lbs.

NIB	Exc.	V.G.	Good	Fair	Poor
3500	3000	2500	1800	950	500

Signature Varminter

Available in calibers such as .223, .22-250, .220 Swift, .243, 6mm Rem., .25-06, 7mm-08, .308. Barrel lengths from 22" to 26". Heavy barrel configuration with hand bedded fiberglass stock. Field bipod is standard. Introduced in 1989.

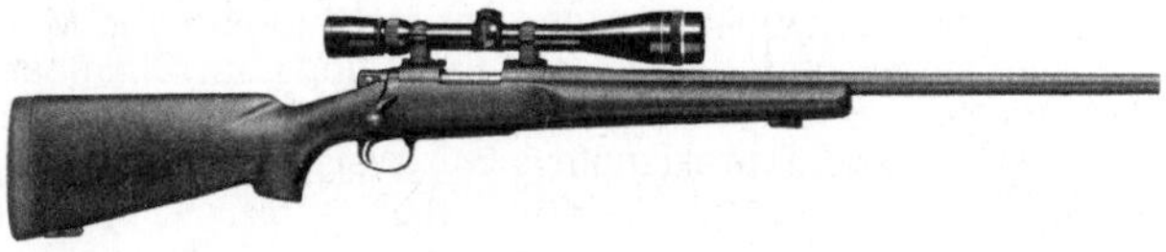

NIB	Exc.	V.G.	Good	Fair	Poor
2500	2000	1500	900	600	400

Talon Safari

Bolt-action rifle offered in various calibers from .300 Win. Mag. to .458 Win. Mag. Stainless steel barrel is 24". Four-round magazine. Fiberglass stock. Introduced in 1989. Weight is approximately 10 lbs.

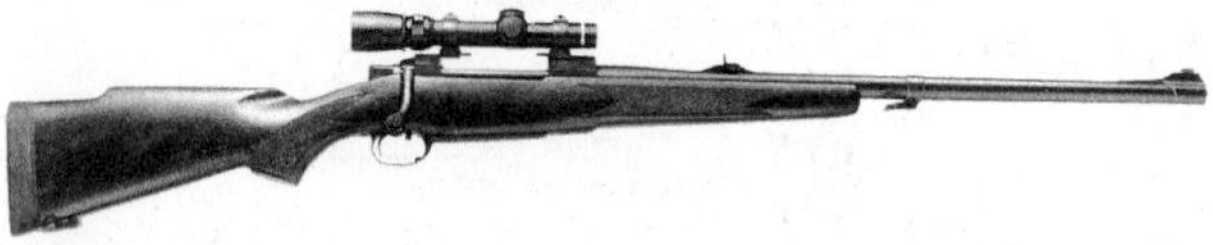

NIB	Exc.	V.G.	Good	Fair	Poor
3750	3250	2200	6500	950	500

Talon Sporter

Offered in calibers from .25-06 to .416 Rem. Mag. 24" barrel with no sights. Built on a pre-1964 Winchester Model 70 action. Choice of walnut or fiberglass stock. Weight is about 7.5 lbs.

NIB	Exc.	V.G.	Good	Fair	Poor
2500	2000	1750	1250	600	250

Model 300 Phoenix Long Range Rifle

Introduced in 1992 and chambered for the .300 Phoenix cartridge. Fitted with a 28" barrel with no sights. Fiberglass stock. Weight is approximately 12.5 lbs.

NIB	Exc.	V.G.	Good	Fair	Poor
3000	2500	2050	1450	600	350

Model 40 Sniper

This bolt-action rifle chambered for the .308 cartridge was introduced in 1990. Fitted with a 24" match grade heavy weight barrel. No sights. Weight is about 9 lbs.

NIB	Exc.	V.G.	Good	Fair	Poor
2500	2000	1500	1150	500	300

Model 92 Bullpup

This is a single-shot rifle chambered for the .50 caliber BMG. Fitted with a 26" barrel and no sights. Fiberglass bullpup stock. First introduced in 1995.

NIB	Exc.	V.G.	Good	Fair	Poor
4500	3750	2800	2200	1000	500

Model 93 SN

This is a bolt-action rifle chambered for the .50 BMG and fitted with a 29" barrel with muzzlebrake. Magazine holds 10 rounds. No sights. Weight is approximately 21.5 lbs. Folding fiberglass stock. Introduced in 1995.

NIB	Exc.	V.G.	Good	Fair	Poor
4750	4250	3500	2450	1450	750

McMillan LRHR

Long Range Hunting Rifle, rifle designed for precision shooting. Custom made, benchrest tolerances in a long or short action. Chambered in .243 Winchester, .308 Winchester, 7mm Remington, .300 Winchester and .338 Lapua Magnum. Action is pillar bedded. Barrel lengths: 24, 26 or 27-inches, depending on caliber. McMillan A-3 fiberglass stock is standard

NIB	Exc.	V.G.	Good	Fair	Poor
4750	4000	3000	2500	—	—

MERCURY
Eibar, Spain

Double-Barreled Shotgun

A 10, 12, or 20 gauge Magnum boxlock double-barrel shotgun with 28" or 32" barrels, double triggers and extractors. Blued with a walnut stock. Add 75 percent for 10 ga.

NIB	Exc.	V.G.	Good	Fair	Poor
—	325	250	225	175	125

NOTE: 10 gauge add 25 percent.

Model 622 VP

A .22 caliber semi-automatic rifle with a 20" barrel, open sights and 7-shot magazine. Blued with a walnut stock. Manufactured by Robar & Son.

NIB	Exc.	V.G.	Good	Fair	Poor
—	325	275	250	200	125

MERIDEN FIREARMS CO.
Meriden, Connecticut

Double-Barrel Shotguns

From 1905-1918 Meriden Fire Arms Co. successor to A.J. Aubrey, made 12, 16, and 20 gauge sidelock double-barrel shotguns. These were better quality hammer and hammerless side-by-sides fitted with twist, laminated, Damascus, and steel barrels in grades A to G. Some of these guns were beautifully engraved by the same artisans who worked for Parker Bros. and other Connecticut gunmakers. Prices in 1910 ranged from $40 to $250 but they represented great value for the money as they were superior to the popular Crescent guns which they closely resembled. Current values depend on model, grade, gauge, and condition. It is difficult to find examples in excellent condition as these were sold by Sears to customers who put them to hard use. In good condition their current values range from $250 for plain Janes to $3,500 or more for the top grades, of which few specimens are known.

Single-Barrel Shotguns and Rifles

Meriden Fire Arms Co. also made many single-barrel shotguns and rifles whose current values are determined by growing collector interest and condition.

MERKEL, GEBRUDER
Suhl, Germany

An Introduction to Merkel Brother's Guns by Dan SheilMerkel Brothers shotgun and rifle makers began production around the turn of the century in Suhl, Germany. Merkel made a number of different models but the company was most well known for its over-and-under shotgun. It also made bolt-action rifles, side-by-side double express rifles, falling block single-shot rifles, side-by-side shotguns, drillings, and just about anything in the way of firearms its customers desired.Perhaps the company's greatest productive era fell between the end of World War I and the 1950s. During the 1930s most of the live pigeon shoots were won with Merkel shotguns. However, there seems to be a difference of opinion about when Merkel built its best quality guns. This is not an easy question to answer. Most shooters and collectors feel that pre-World War II guns are the best examples of Merkel craftsmanship. But, in my opinion, some of the finest Merkels I have seen were produced immediately after World War II. Outstanding examples of Merkel's quality continue to appear up to the construction of the Berlin Wall in 1961.Another area of controversy is the high grade Merkel 300 series shotgun. Many have compared this gun to the Italian and British makers and believe it is a mass produced gun. This is not the case because all Merkel shotguns are handcrafted and as far as I know barrels will not interchange unless they are supplied with the gun from the factory. While the 100 and 200 series guns may be mass produced, the 300 series is not, and that is easy to determine by looking at the serial number together with the date stamped on the barrel. Very few 300 series guns were produced in a given period.In terms of durability, strength, and reliability, there is not an over-and-under shotgun that is built as strong as the Merkel. It has two Kersten style locking lugs on the upper barrel that fit into the face of the receiver while the bottom has two under lugs that give the gun a rugged four position locking system. I don't think I have ever heard of a Merkel being sent back to the gunmaker or a gunsmith to have the frame tightened. It just is not necessary; the guns will not shoot loose.With respect to value, the Merkel over-and-under guns have been sleepers in the gun industry for a number of years. Until recently they have not brought the price that they deserve. I am specifically talking about the 300 series; the 303 Luxus and the 304. Generally speaking all of the special order Merkel over-and-under shotguns have done well. I think the shooting public will begin to recognize the quality and craftsmanship built into every one of these fine guns.One last comment regarding special order Merkels and the company's reputation for building just about anything the customer wanted.

It is impossible to cover all of the variations that the company produced in its long history, but the buyer should be aware that he may encounter some different and uncataloged Merkels along the way.In August 1993 Merkel Brothers declared bankruptcy. The assets of the company were reportedly purchased by Steyr. GSI, Inc. Trussville, Alabama currently imports Merkel guns.NOTE: Merkel is now owned by Heckler & Koch.Editor's Comment: The Merkel gun prices listed are based on either one or two factors: 1) they are no longer in production or 2) the guns were built prior to the Berlin Wall, which generally bring a premium. An additional factor was introduced in 1994 when the factory began to use an alpha numeric serial number system. This new system dates the guns from 1994. The prices listed for new Merkels are influenced by the value of the dollar to the German Deutschemark.

SIDE-BY-SIDE SHOTGUNS

Model 8

This model has a self-cocking Deeley boxlock action side-by-side with cocking indicators. The locking mechanism is a Greener cross-bolt with double-barrel locking lug. Triggers are single-selective or double. The safety is automatic and tang mounted. This model has an extractor. Offered in 12 and 16 gauge with 28" solid rib barrels or 20 gauge with 26.75" barrels. Available with straight or pistol grip oil-finished walnut stock. Receiver is case colored with light scroll engraving. The 12 and 16 gauge guns weigh about 6.8 lbs. while the 20 gauge weighs approximately 6 lbs.

NIB	*Exc.*	*V.G.*	*Good*	*Fair*	*Poor*
1500	1150	900	600	500	400

Model 117/117E

Offered in 12 and 16 gauge with various barrel lengths, this model featured a boxlock action with double triggers and extractors. Ejectors were available under the "E" designation. The boxlock action body was scrupled at the rear with fine line scroll engraving.

NIB	*Exc.*	*V.G.*	*Good*	*Fair*	*Poor*
—	6000	4350	1950	1000	500

Model 118/118E

Also offered in 12 and 16 gauge this model is similar to above model with slightly more engraving and better wood. This model also has some engraving coverage on the breech end of the barrels.

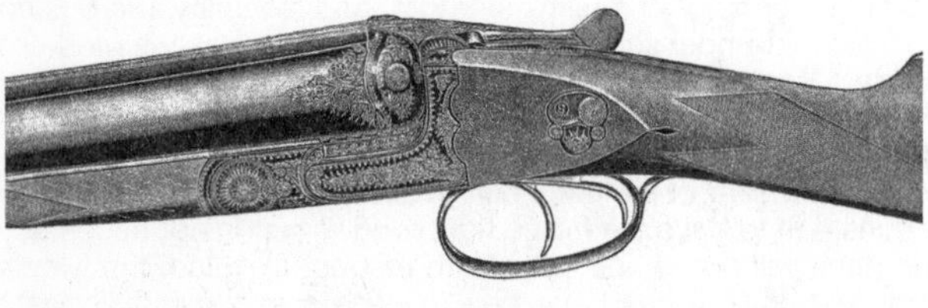

NIB	*Exc.*	*V.G.*	*Good*	*Fair*	*Poor*
—	7100	4900	2800	1200	650

Model 124/125

Similar to the above models but supplied with extractors for the Model 124 and ejectors for the Model 125. Both models have more engraving coverage with game scenes. Finer checkering and fancy wood is seen on this model.

Model 124

NIB	*Exc.*	*V.G.*	*Good*	*Fair*	*Poor*
—	5400	4350	2500	1500	700

Model 125

NIB	*Exc.*	*V.G.*	*Good*	*Fair*	*Poor*
—	6000	4600	3500	2000	1000

Model 130

This was one of Merkel's highest side-by-side shotguns. It featured a sidelock action, extra fancy wood, fine line checkering, and full coverage game scene engraving.

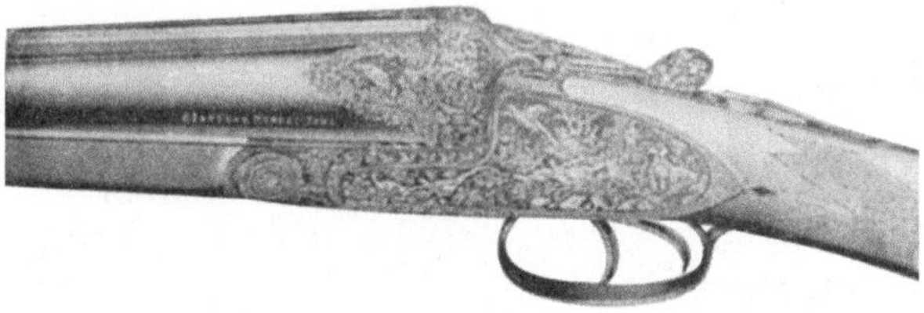

NIB	*Exc.*	*V.G.*	*Good*	*Fair*	*Poor*
—	25500	17500	10000	3200	300

Model 126

Similar to the Model 130 but fitted with removable sidelocks.

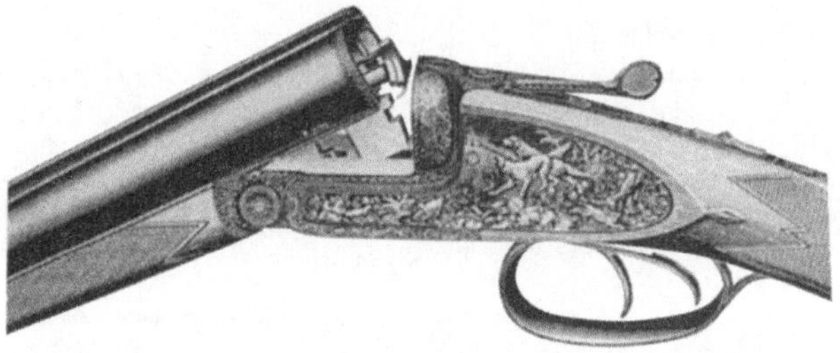

NIB	*Exc.*	*V.G.*	*Good*	*Fair*	*Poor*
—	18500	15500	82700	4500	300

Model 170

This model was offered in 12 gauge only with automatic ejectors. The boxlock action was engraved with fine full coverage scroll.

NIB	*Exc.*	*V.G.*	*Good*	*Fair*	*Poor*
—	6000	4900	3900	2500	300

Model 127

This model was Merkel's finest side-by-side shotgun. The sidelock action featured full coverage fine line scroll engraving of the best quality.

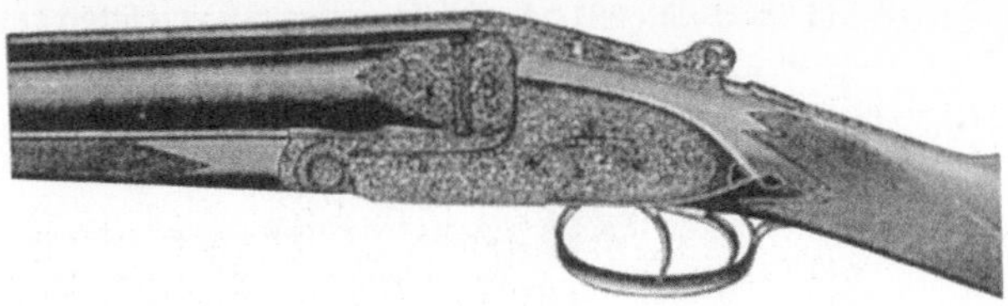

NIB	Exc.	V.G.	Good	Fair	Poor
—	25000	19500	14500	6000	300

Model 47E

Same as above but fitted with ejectors. Offered in 12, 16, or 20 gauge. Supplied with fitted luggage case.

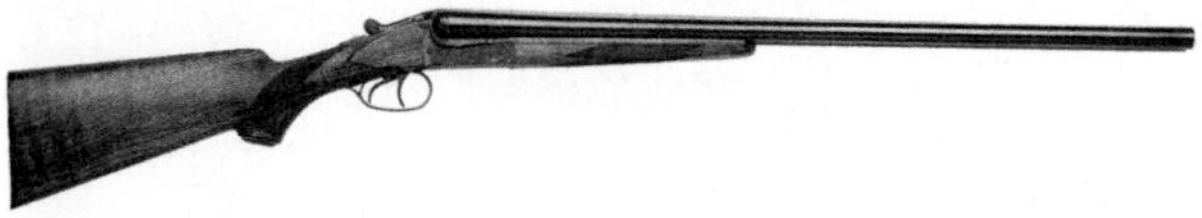

NIB	Exc.	V.G.	Good	Fair	Poor
5000	3700	2300	1200	600	200

Model 147

Same as Model 8 but with silver grayed receiver with fine engraved hunting scenes, engraved border, and screws. This model has been discontinued.

NIB	Exc.	V.G.	Good	Fair	Poor
3700	3250	2300	1100	600	200

Model 147E

Same as above but fitted with ejectors. Offered in 12, 16, 20, or 28 gauge. Supplied with fitted luggage case.

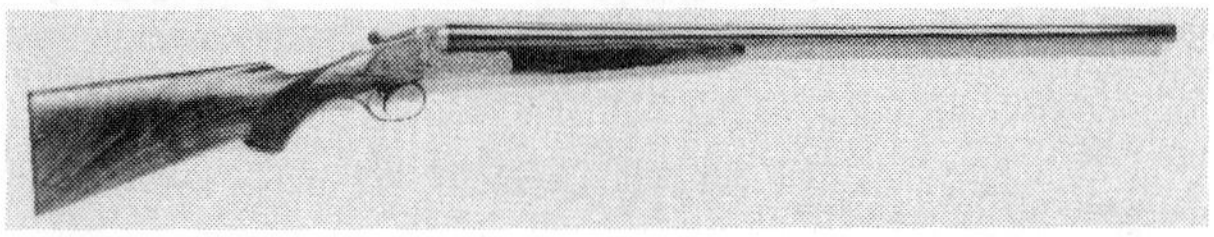

NIB	Exc.	V.G.	Good	Fair	Poor
5750	3850	2700	1500	1000	300

Model 147EL

Similar to the Model 147E but with fancy walnut stock. Supplied with fitted luggage case.

NIB	Exc.	V.G.	Good	Fair	Poor
6000	4950	3400	2200	1000	3000

Model 122

This model features the same specifications as the above models but has false sideplates. This model is fitted with ejectors and the receiver is silver grayed with fine engraved hunting scenes on false sideplates, engraved border, and screws.

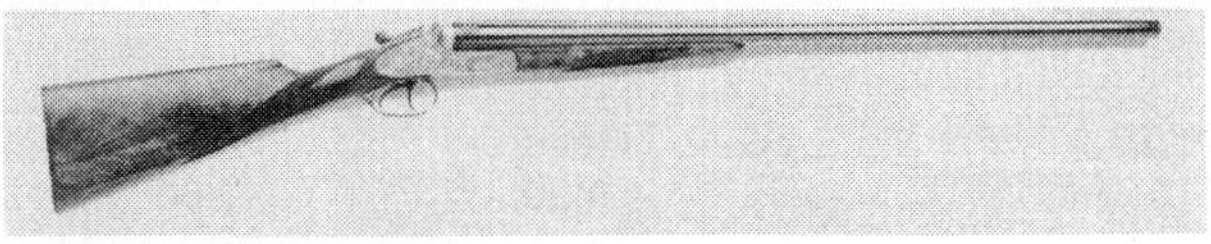

NIB	Exc.	V.G.	Good	Fair	Poor
5750	4500	3000	1900	950	300

Model 47SL

Same as above but with scroll engraving in place of hunting scenes.

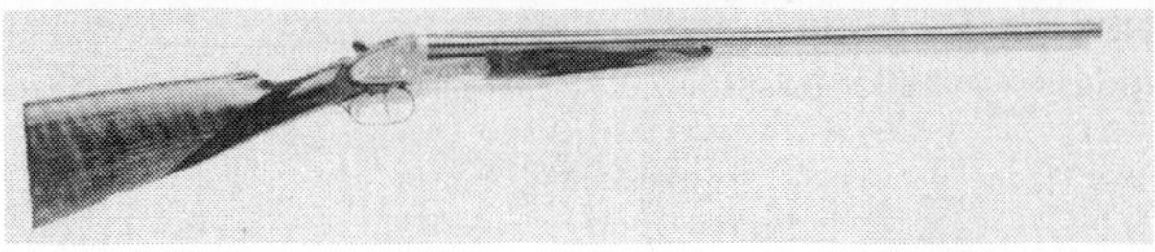

NIB	Exc.	V.G.	Good	Fair	Poor
8200	6100	4400	3000	1750	300

Model 147SL

This model features true Holland and Holland-style sidelocks with cocking indicators. Gauge and barrel lengths are as above. Stock is fancy walnut. However, 20 gauge gun weighs 6.4 lbs., 28 gauge gun weighs about 6.1 lbs.

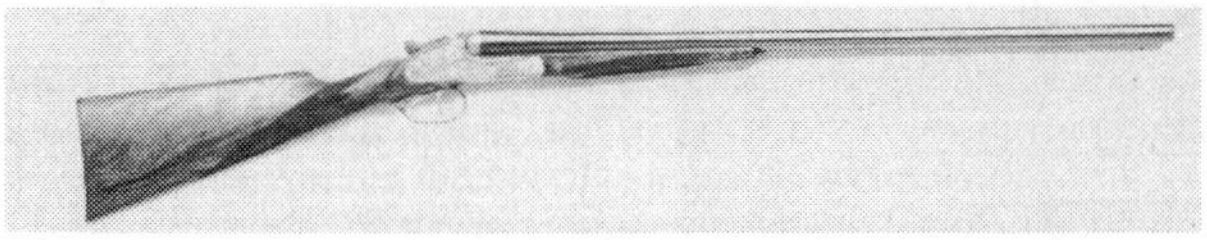

NIB	Exc.	V.G.	Good	Fair	Poor
10000	7000	5500	3850	2250	300

Model 147SSL

Similar to the Model 147SL but fitted with removable side plates. Fancy walnut stock. Supplied with fitted luggage case.

NIB	Exc.	V.G.	Good	Fair	Poor
8800	6500	5200	3000	2500	300

Models 247S/347S

These models are the same as the Model 147S with the exception of the types of engraving.

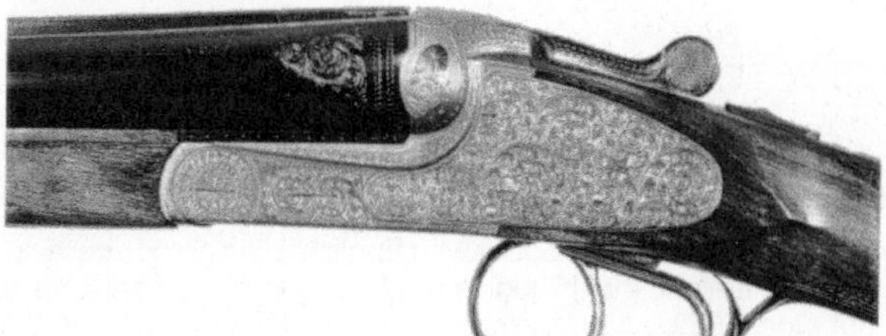

Model 247S

Large scroll engraving.

NIB	Exc.	V.G.	Good	Fair	Poor
7700	5800	4400	2500	2000	300

Model 347S

Medium scroll engraving.

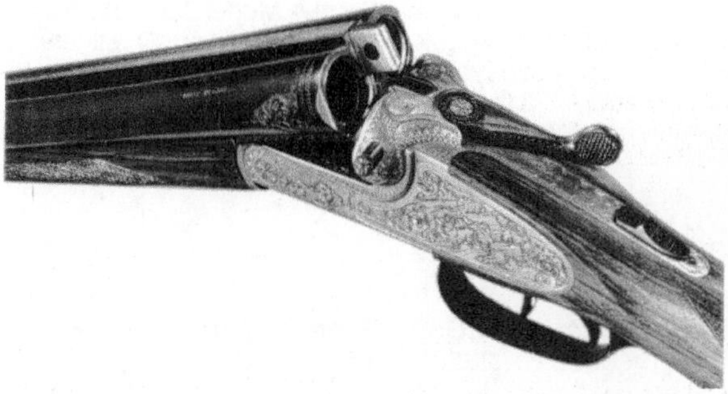

NIB	Exc.	V.G.	Good	Fair	Poor
7100	6100	4950	3850	2250	300

Model 447SL

Small scroll engraving.

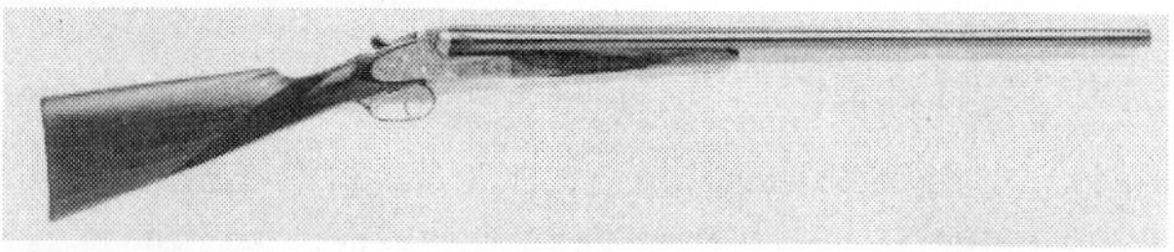

NIB	Exc.	V.G.	Good	Fair	Poor
9900	7300	6000	4400	2700	300

NOTE: For wood upgrade add $1,200. For custom stock dimensions add $ 1,400. For left-hand stocks add $900.

Model 280

This is a boxlock gun chambered for the 28 gauge shell and fitted with 28" barrels choked Improved Cylinder and Modified. Double triggers with ejectors. Straight-grip walnut stock. Scroll engraving with case colored receiver. Weight is about 5.2 lbs.

NIB	Exc.	V.G.	Good	Fair	Poor
4900	3600	2650	1900	950	300

Model 280EL

This model features an Anson & Deely boxlock action with engraved hunting scenes on a silver-grayed action. Double triggers. Fancy walnut with straight grip stock. Offered in 28 gauge with 28" barrels. Fitted luggage case standard. Weight is about 5.2 lbs. First imported in 2000.

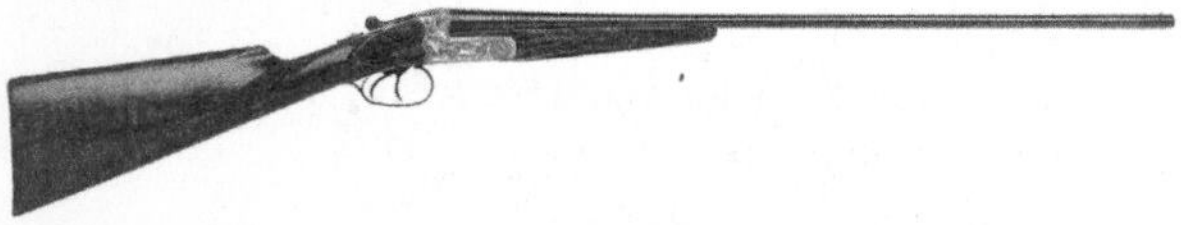

NIB	Exc.	V.G.	Good	Fair	Poor
7500	5500	3850	2500	1500	300

Model 280SL

Similar to the Model 280EL, but with English-style scroll engraving on H&H style sidelocks with choice of pistol-grip or straight-grip fancy walnut stock. Fitted luggage case standard. First imported in 2000.

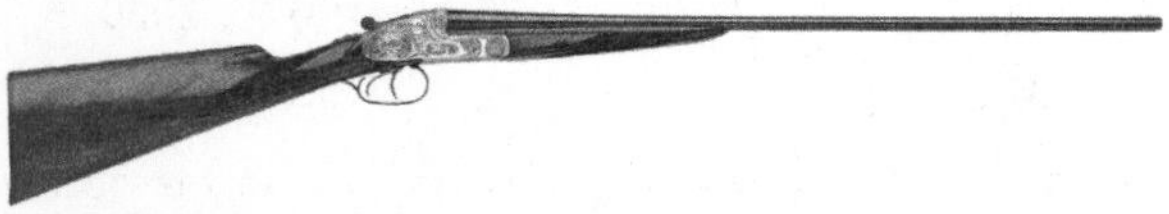

NIB	Exc.	V.G.	Good	Fair	Poor
10100	7700	5500	3600	1700	300

Model 360

This boxlock model is the same as the Model 280 but chambered for the .410 bore. Straight grip walnut stock. Scroll engraving on case colored receiver. Barrel is 28" choke Modified and Full. Weight is about 5.2 lbs.

NIB	Exc.	V.G.	Good	Fair	Poor
4800	3600	2650	1400	800	300

Model 360EL

This model is the same as the Model 280EL but chambered for the .410 shell and fitted with 28" barrels. Fancy walnut and fitted case. Weight is about 5.5 lbs. First imported in 2000.

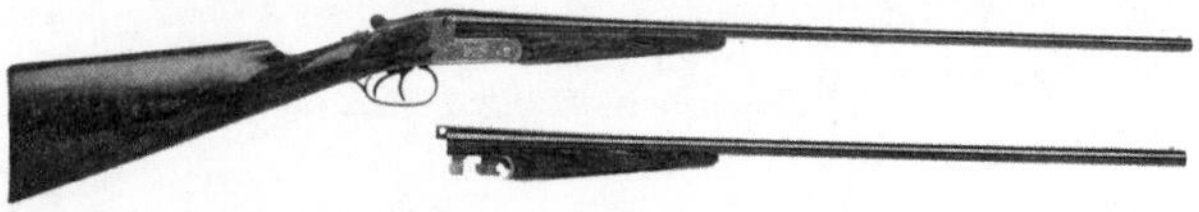

NIB	Exc.	V.G.	Good	Fair	Poor
7500	5700	4100	2750	1300	300

Model 360SL

Same as the Model 360EL but with English-style scroll engraving on H&H style sidelocks and choice of pistol grip or straight grip stock. First imported in 2000.

NIB	Exc.	V.G.	Good	Fair	Poor
10500	8100	5900	3750	1600	300

Model 280/360 Two Barrel Set

This set consists of a 28 gauge 28" barrel and a .410 bore 28" barrel with scroll engraving and oil finish walnut stock. Double triggers and straight grip stock.

NIB	Exc.	V.G.	Good	Fair	Poor
10500	8100	5900	3750	1600	500

Model 280/360EL Two Barrel Set

This set consists of a 28 gauge 28" barrel and a .410 bore 28" barrel with engraved hunting scenes and fancy walnut stock. Double triggers and straight-grip stock. First imported in 2000.

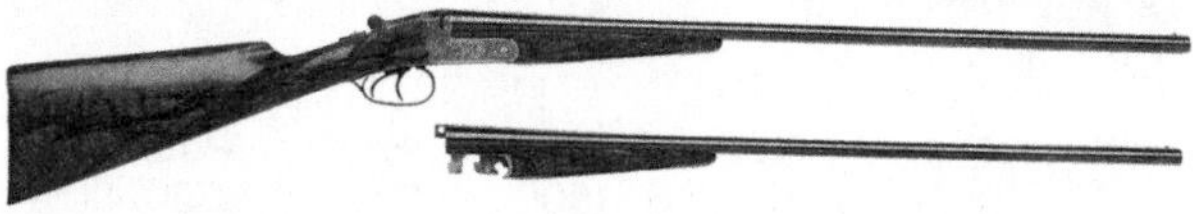

NIB	Exc.	V.G.	Good	Fair	Poor
10500	8100	5900	3750	1600	500

Model 280/360SL Two Barrel Set

Same as above but with English-style scroll engraving and choice of pistol-grip or straight-grip stock. First imported in 2000.

NIB	Exc.	V.G.	Good	Fair	Poor
15500	11500	8000	5500	3500	500

Model 1620

This is a boxlock side-by-side gun chambered for the 16 gauge shell. Fitted with 28" barrels with double triggers. Barrel chokes Improved Cylinder and Modified. Ejectors. Straight-grip walnut stock with oil finish. Case colored receiver finish. Light scroll engraving. Fitted luggage case. Weight is about 6.1 lbs.

NIB	Exc.	V.G.	Good	Fair	Poor
4650	3600	2500	1800	1000	300

NOTE: For two-barrel set add $2,300. Second set is 20 gauge with 28" barrels.

Model 1620E

Similar to Model 1620 but with fine engraved hunting scenes on silver-grayed receiver.

NIB	Exc.	V.G.	Good	Fair	Poor
5000	4000	3000	2000	1000	300

Model 1620EL

As above but with high-grade walnut straight-grip stock and deeply engraved hunting scenes.

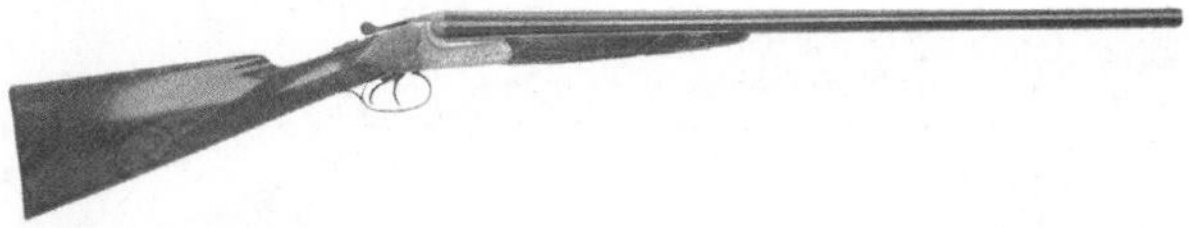

NIB	Exc.	V.G.	Good	Fair	Poor
6000	5000	3850	2200	1100	300

NOTE: For two-barrel set add $2,900. Second set is 20 gauge with 28" barrels.

Model 1620SL

Similar to the 1620 models above but with grayed sidelocks with deeply engraved hunting scenes. High-grade walnut stock with oil finish. Weight is 6.6 lbs.

NIB	Exc.	V.G.	Good	Fair	Poor
11000	8400	6100	3750	1800	500

NOTE: For two-barrel set add $3,800. Second set is 20 gauge with 28" barrels.

Model 1622

Introduced in 2006, this 16-gauge boxlock side-by-side features full sideplates, case hardened receiver with cocking indicators, ejectors, single selective or double triggers and pistol grip or English style stock. Fixed IC and Mod. chokes. Add 50 percent for 2-barrel set (second set is 28" 20 gauge).

NIB	Exc.	V.G.	Good	Fair	Poor
4000	3200	2550	1700	1400	300

Model 1622E

Similar to 1622 but with fine engraved hunting scenes on silver-grayed receiver.

NIB	Exc.	V.G.	Good	Fair	Poor
7500	5700	4100	2750	1300	300

Model 1622EL

Similar to Model 1622E but with luxury grade wood. Add 30 percent for 2-barrel set (second set is 28" 20 gauge).

NIB	Exc.	V.G.	Good	Fair	Poor
8800	6500	5200	3000	2500	300

OVER-AND-UNDER SHOTGUNS

Model 102E

This was Merkel's standard over-and-under boxlock model. Offered in 12 gauge with 28" barrels or 16 gauge with 26" barrels. Both are fitted with double triggers, semi-pistol grip, and ejectors.

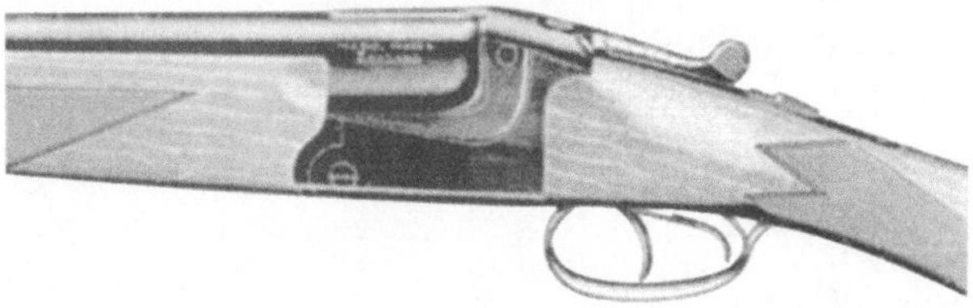

NIB	Exc.	V.G.	Good	Fair	Poor
—	1800	1450	1100	650	400

Model 103E

Similar to the standard but with more English scroll engraving coverage and better wood. This model was offered in 12, 16, and 20 gauge.

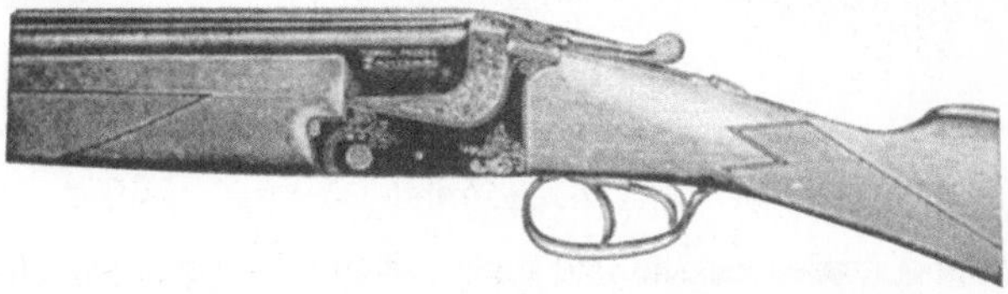

NIB	Exc.	V.G.	Good	Fair	Poor
—	2450	1650	1350	950	600

Model 204E

This model is essentially a Model 203E with finer engraving. This model was discontinued prior to 1939.

NIB	Exc.	V.G.	Good	Fair	Poor
—	6600	4900	3300	2200	1750

Model 301E

This is a boxlock model with scalloped action chambered for the 12, 16, 20, 24, 28, and 32 gauge. The engraving is an English scroll and the trigger guard is horn. Double triggers and pistol grip are standard. This model was produced prior to 1939.

NIB	Exc.	V.G.	Good	Fair	Poor
—	4900	4000	2500	2000	1850

Model 302E

Similar to the Model 301E but fitted with side plates. The full-coverage engraving features game scenes. This model produced prior to WWII.

NIB	Exc.	V.G.	Good	Fair	Poor
—	13250	11000	8250	4400	2000

Model 303 Luxus

This over-and-under Merkel is custom built to the customer's specifications. Each gun is unique and should be appraised by a knowledgeable individual who is familiar with quality European shotguns.

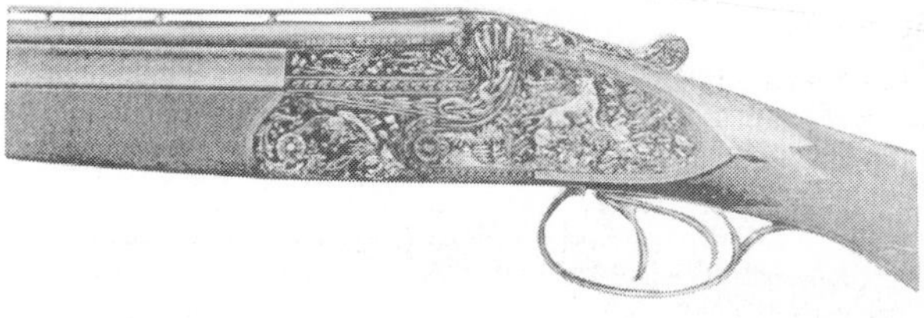

NIB	Exc.	V.G.	Good	Fair	Poor
22000	—	—	—	—	—

Model 304E

This pre-war model was the highest grade in Merkel's over-and-under shotgun line. A sidelock gun with full coverage scroll engraving of the highest quality. Fine line checkering and extra fancy wood make this gun difficult to appraise due to its rarity.

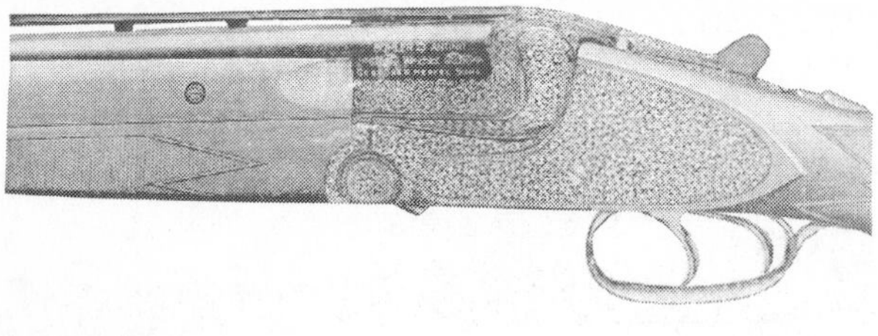

Model 400E

A higher grade over-and-under fitted with Kersten crossbolt, finer engraving, and fancy wood. Merkel offered this grade in 12, 16, 20, 24, 28, and 32 gauge with choice of barrel lengths. This model was produced prior to 1939.

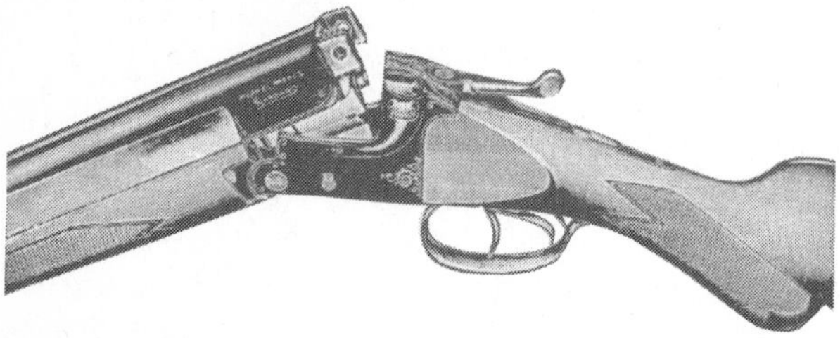

NIB	*Exc.*	*V.G.*	*Good*	*Fair*	*Poor*
—	1950	1450	1000	600	400

Model 401E

Similar to the model above but with full coverage game scene engraving.

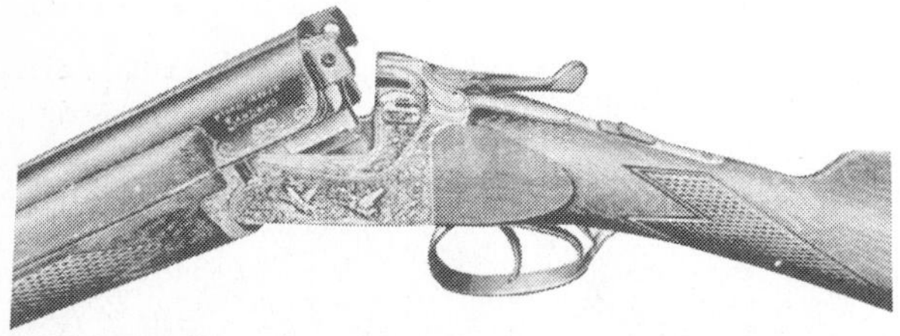

NIB	*Exc.*	*V.G.*	*Good*	*Fair*	*Poor*
—	2750	2000	1350	800	600

Model 200E

The action on this model is a self cocking Blitz where the hammers are attached to the trigger plates. The locking mechanism is a Kersten double cross bolt lock with release. Trigger may be either single-selective or double. The manual safety is mounted on the tang. Fitted with coil spring ejectors. Offered in 12 and 16 gauge with 28" solid rib barrels or 20 gauge with 26.75" barrels. The oil-finished stock is offered with straight or pistol grip. The receiver is case colored with engraved border and screws. The 12 gauge weighs 7 lbs., the 16 gauge 6.8 lbs., and the 20 gauge 6.4 lbs.

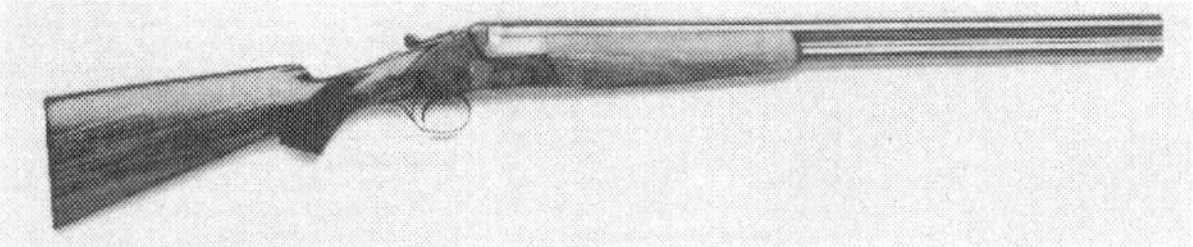

NIB	*Exc.*	*V.G.*	*Good*	*Fair*	*Poor*
2900	2200	1650	1000	800	500

Model 201E

Same as Model 200E but with silver grayed receiver with fine engraved hunting scenes, engraved border, and screws.

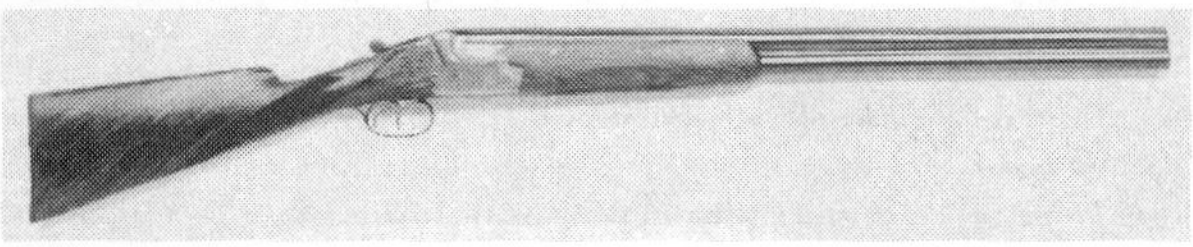

NIB	*Exc.*	*V.G.*	*Good*	*Fair*	*Poor*
3700	3100	2500	1650	1000	750

Model 202E

This model has the same basic specifications as the Model 201E but is fitted with false side plates with cocking indicators.

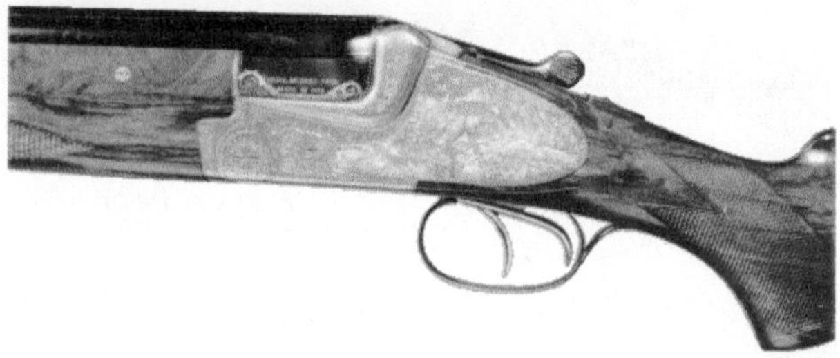

NIB	*Exc.*	*V.G.*	*Good*	*Fair*	*Poor*
8200	5500	3850	2500	1500	1000

Model 200ES

This model features a Blitz action with cocking indicators and Kersten double cross bolt lock with release. The trigger is single-selective with tang-mounted manual safety. Coil spring ejectors are standard. Offered in 12 gauge only with 26.75" or 28" ventilated rib barrel. The walnut stock has skeet dimensions with pistol grip. Receiver is silver grayed with 112 coverage scroll engraving, engraved borders, and screws. Weighs approximately 7.3 lbs.

NIB	*Exc.*	*V.G.*	*Good*	*Fair*	*Poor*
4400	3600	2750	2200	1500	1000

Model 200ET

Same as Model 200ES, but in a trap configuration. The ventilated rib barrel length offered is 30".

NIB	*Exc.*	*V.G.*	*Good*	*Fair*	*Poor*
4700	3850	3000	2250	1750	1000

Model 200SC (Sporting Clays)

Introduced in 1995 this model is offered in 12 gauge only with 3" chambers and 30" barrels with ventilated rib. It is fitted with a single-selective trigger adjustable for length of pull. It has a special walnut oil finished stock with 26 lpi checkering. Pistol grip and Pachmayr Sporting Clays recoil pad is standard. Weight is approximately 7.6 lbs.

NIB	*Exc.*	*V.G.*	*Good*	*Fair*	*Poor*
7200	6000	3300	1500	900	450

NOTE: With Briley choke tubes add $500.

Model 201ES

Same as Model 200SC but with full coverage scroll engraving.

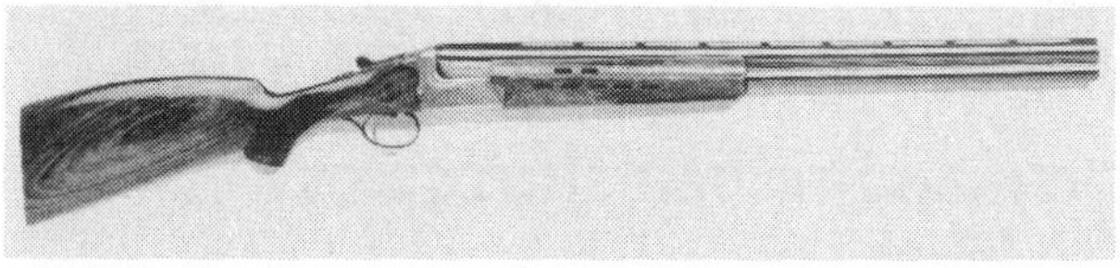

NIB	*Exc.*	*V.G.*	*Good*	*Fair*	*Poor*
4950	4050	3300	2500	2000	1000

Model 201ET

Same as Model 210ES but fitted with a 30" barrel and trap stock dimensions.

NIB	*Exc.*	*V.G.*	*Good*	*Fair*	*Poor*
4950	4100	3300	2750	2000	1000

Model 203E

This model has true Holland & Holland-style sidelocks with cocking indicators. These sideplates are removable with cranked screw. The gauge selection and barrel are the same as those listed above. The silver grayed receiver has English-style large scroll engraving. This model has been discontinued.

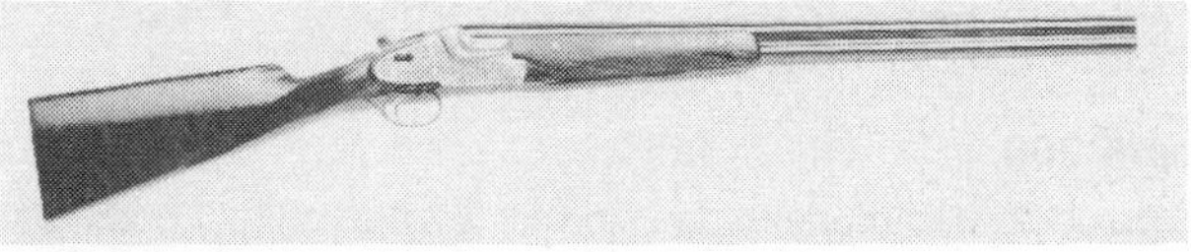

NIB	Exc.	V.G.	Good	Fair	Poor
13500	10400	8250	5000	2500	1000

Model 303E

Same as Model 203E but with detachable sidelock plates with integral retracting hook. The Model 303E also has medium scroll work engraving and Holland & Holland-type ejectors.

NIB	Exc.	V.G.	Good	Fair	Poor
18700	16500	13400	7500	5000	2500

Model 303EL

This model features H&H-style sidelocks that are quick detachable without tools. Receiver is engraved with hunting scenes. Offered in 12, 20 and 28 gauge. Double triggers and fancy walnut stock with pistol or straight grip. Weight for 12 gauge is about 7 lbs, for the 20 gauge about 6.4 lbs, and for the 28 gauge about 6.4 lbs. Fitted luggage case standard.

NIB	Exc.	V.G.	Good	Fair	Poor
26000	18700	13000	7500	5000	2500

Model 2000EL

This model features a Kersten cross bolt lock, scroll engraving on a silver grayed receiver and a modified Anson & Deely boxlock action. This gun is offered in 12, 20, or 28 gauge with ejectors, single-selective or double triggers, fancy wood, and choice of pistol or straight grip stock. Weight is about 7 lbs. for 12 gauge, 6.4 lbs. for 20 gauge, and 6.4 lbs. for 28 gauge.

NIB	Exc.	V.G.	Good	Fair	Poor
7200	5100	3600	2200	1500	750

Model 2000EL Sporter

Similar to the above model but fitted with 30" barrels on the 12 gauge, and 28" barrels on the 20 and 28 gauge.

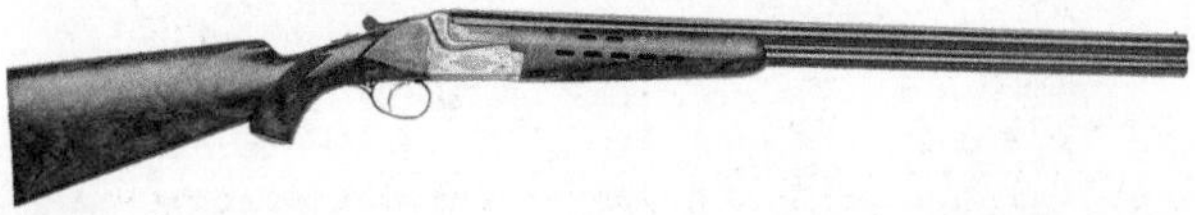

NIB	Exc.	V.G.	Good	Fair	Poor
7200	5200	3600	2200	1500	750

Model 2000CL

Introduced in 2005 this model is chambered for the 12, 20, or 28 gauge with 28" barrels choked improved cylinder and modified. Scroll engraved receiver with case colors. Single selective trigger with auto ejectors. High grade wood with semi-pistol grip and straight grip.

NIB	Exc.	V.G.	Good	Fair	Poor
7700	5800	3750	2200	1500	750

Model 2000CL Sporter

As above but with 30" barrel for the 12 gauge with vent rib and 28" barrels with solid rib for the 20 and 28 gauge guns. Pistol grip stock. Introduced in 2005.

NIB	Exc.	V.G.	Good	Fair	Poor
8100	6100	3750	2200	1500	750

NOTE: Deduct $500 for 20 and 28 gauge models.

Model 2001EL

Similar to the Model 2000 but with finely engraved hunting scenes. This model is offered in 28 gauge as well as 12 and 20 gauge.

NIB	Exc.	V.G.	Good	Fair	Poor
9800	7200	4950	2900	2000	1000

Model 2001EL Sporter

Same as above but with 30" barrels for 12 gauge, 28" barrels for 20 and 28 gauge.

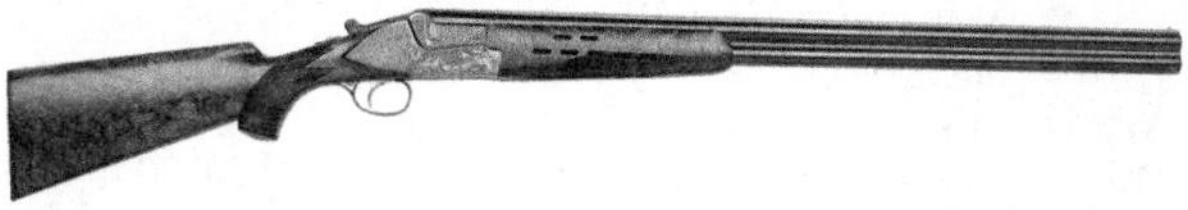

NIB	Exc.	V.G.	Good	Fair	Poor
11000	7300	5300	3600	2000	1000

Model 2002EL

This model features finely engraved hunting scenes with arabesque style. Offered in 12, 20 and 28 gauges.

NIB	Exc.	V.G.	Good	Fair	Poor
11000	8800	6000	4400	2200	1200

Model 2016EL

This is a 16 gauge gun with 28" barrels and single non-selective trigger and ejectors. Fixed chokes. Checkered walnut stock with semi-pistol grip. Scroll engraving on the case colored receiver. Weight is about 6.6 lbs.

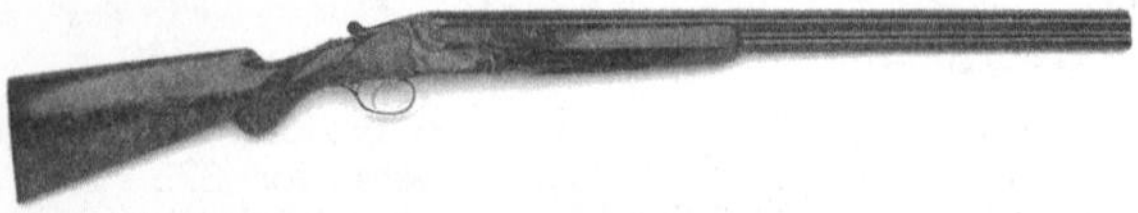

NIB	Exc.	V.G.	Good	Fair	Poor
6495	5000	3600	2200	1500	750

Model 2016EL Two Barrel Set

As above but with extra set of 20 gauge 28" barrels with fixed chokes.

NIB	Exc.	V.G.	Good	Fair	Poor
10600	7900	5500	3600	2000	1000

Model 2116EL

This 16 gauge model is similar to the above but with game scene engraving on the case colored receiver.

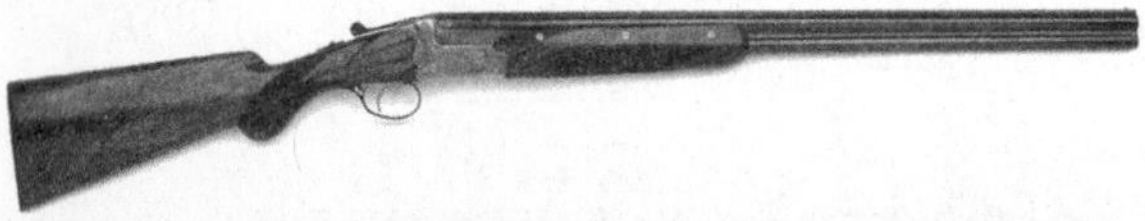

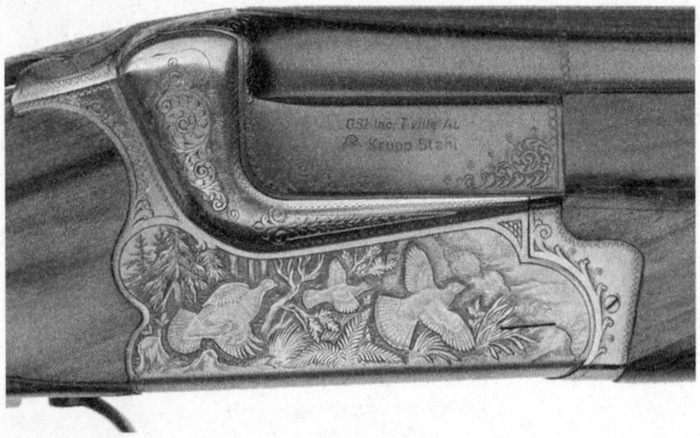

NIB	Exc.	V.G.	Good	Fair	Poor
9100	6800	4400	2900	2000	1000

Model 2116EL Two Barrel Set

As above with extra set of 20 gauge 28" barrels with fixed chokes.

NIB	Exc.	V.G.	Good	Fair	Poor
13000	9300	6950	4400	2900	2000

RIFLE/SHOTGUN COMBINATION GUNS

Model 410E

Merkel's base boxlock model with ejectors. Produced prior to WWII.

NIB	Exc.	V.G.	Good	Fair	Poor
—	2500	1950	1350	750	500

Model 411E

Similar to the above but with the addition of a small coverage of scroll engraving.

NIB	Exc.	V.G.	Good	Fair	Poor
—	2750	2200	1650	1100	600

Model 300

A boxlock hammerless four barrel shotgun/rifle combination. The shotgun barrels were 12, 16, or 20 gauge, while the top rifle barrel was .22 rimfire with the bottom rifle barrel .30-30 or .25-35. Probably any combination of rifle and shotgun could be used as this was a special order gun. Very rare.

Model 311E

This combination gun has additional English scroll engraving.

NIB	Exc.	V.G.	Good	Fair	Poor
—	8600	7200	5500	2250	1250

Model 312E

This model is fitted with sideplates and game scene engraving.

NIB	Exc.	V.G.	Good	Fair	Poor
—	10400	9000	7500	4000	2000

Model 313E

This model has sidelocks with fine, full coverage scroll engraving. An expert appraisal is recommended due to this model's rarity and unique features.

NIB	Exc.	V.G.	Good	Fair	Poor
—	13000	11750	8800	4400	2000

Model 314E

This sidelock model is also rare and unique. An expert appraisal is recommended prior to a sale. Extra barrels will frequently be seen with this model.

SINGLE-SHOT AND BOLT-ACTION RIFLES

Merkel built special single-shot rifles and bolt-action rifles. These guns were produced prior to WWII and are seldom seen in the United States. The buyer should exercise caution and seek expert assistance prior to a sale.

Model 180

This is a top lever single rifle with double under lugs built on a boxlock action. The stock is 3/4 with pistol grip. Commonly referred to as a stalking rifle. Offered in a variety of European calibers. A rare Merkel.

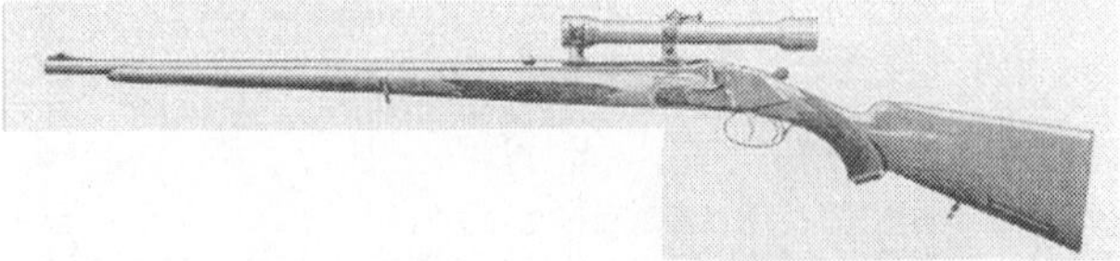

NIB	Exc.	V.G.	Good	Fair	Poor
—	3300	2400	1650	1000	500

Model 183

This top lever model features a Holland & Holland-type sidelock action with the sidelock on the left side and the removable side plate on the right side. Fitted with a straight-grip stock and full-length forearm with sling swivels, fine line checkering, and fancy wood. A rare rifle.

NIB	Exc.	V.G.	Good	Fair	Poor
—	8300	5500	3850	2000	1200

Model 190

This is Merkel's version of a Sporting rifle built on a Mauser action. Offered in a variety of European calibers. These were special order rifles and will be seen in a variety of configurations.

NIB	Exc.	V.G.	Good	Fair	Poor
—	3300	2500	1650	1100	650

DOUBLE RIFLES—COMBINATION GUNS—DRILLINGS

Side-by-Side Double Rifles Model 128E

This side-by-side rifle is a droplock design with scroll and game scene engraving. The wood is Circassian walnut with fine line checkering. Offered in a variety of European calibers.

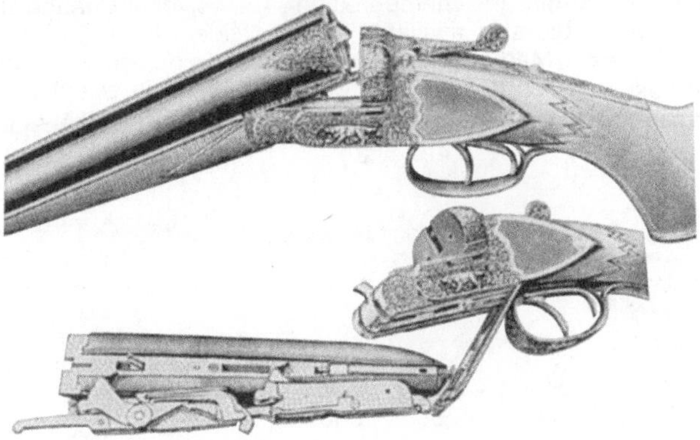

Model 132E

Similar to the Model 128E but with full coverage scroll engraving and fancy wood.

Model 140-1

This model features a Greener cross bolt, scroll engraving with case hardened receiver. Extractors and double triggers with pistol grip stock are standard. Offered in a wide variety of European and American calibers.

NIB	Exc.	V.G.	Good	Fair	Poor
6500	5200	4100	2900	2000	1000

Model 140-1.1

Same as above model but with finely engraved hunting scenes.

NIB	Exc.	V.G.	Good	Fair	Poor
7400	6100	4400	2900	2000	1000

Model 140-2

This double rifle has an Anson & Deely boxlock action. Double triggers. Barrel length is 23.6". Chambered for .375 H&H, .416 Rigby, and the .470 NE. Pistol grip stock with cheekpiece on oil finish walnut. Weight is about 10.7 lbs. depending on caliber.

NIB	Exc.	V.G.	Good	Fair	Poor
11500	8250	6000	3750	2200	1500

Model 140-2.1

This model is similar to the one above but is engraved with African game scenes.

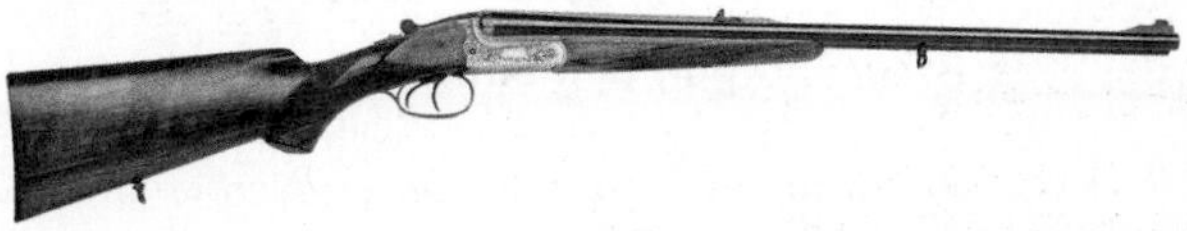

NIB	Exc.	V.G.	Good	Fair	Poor
13400	9300	6600	3750	2200	1500

Model 150-1

This model features an arabesque engraving on a silver greyed receiver. Extractors, double triggers, and pistol grip are standard.

NIB	Exc.	V.G.	Good	Fair	Poor
8250	6600	5100	3000	2000	900

Model 150-1.1

Same as above model but with finely engraved hunting scenes.

NIB	Exc.	V.G.	Good	Fair	Poor
9500	7700	6000	3500	2500	1000

Model 160S Luxus Double Rifle

This double rifle is part of the Luxus series and features on the highest quality sidelock action, wood, and fittings. It is offered in .222 Rem., 5.6x5OR Mag., .243, 6.5x57R, 7x57, 7x65, .3006, .30R Blaser, 8x57IRS, 8x57RS, .308 Win., and 9.3x74R. Weighs approximately 8 lbs. An expert appraisal should be sought prior to a sale due to the unique nature of this model.

NIB	Exc.	V.G.	Good	Fair	Poor
15000	12500	8500	5750	300	1600

Model 160S-2.1

Same as above but with finely engraved hunting scenes. Chambered for the .470 Nitro Express. Weight is about 11 lbs.

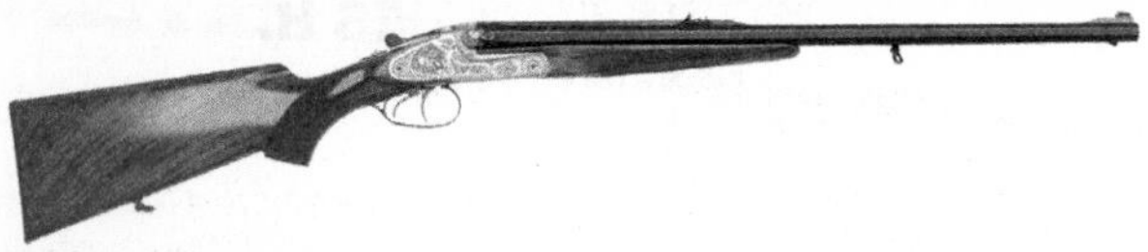

NIB	Exc.	V.G.	Good	Fair	Poor
28500	20750	16500	12000	7500	1500

Model 211E Rifle/Shotgun Combination

This over-and-under model features a gray metal boxlock action with hunting scenes. The top barrel is available in 12, 16, or 20 gauge and the bottom barrel is offered in .22 Hornet, 5.6R Mag., 5.6R, .222 Rem., .243 Win., 6.5x55, 6.5x57R, 7x57R, 7x65R, .30-06, 8x57IRS, 9.3x74R, and .375 H&H Mag. The barrel has a solid rib and the trigger is single-selective. The select walnut stock is hand checkered. Weight is about 7 lbs.

NIB	Exc.	V.G.	Good	Fair	Poor
6600	4950	3850	2250	1500	700

Model 210E Rifle/Shotgun Combination

Same as above model but features a scroll engraved case hardened receiver. This model has been discontinued.

NIB	Exc.	V.G.	Good	Fair	Poor
6900	5500	4400	2750	1200	700

Model 211E Rifle/Shotgun Combination

Similar to the above model but with finely engraved hunting scenes.

NIB	Exc.	V.G.	Good	Fair	Poor
8300	6600	4900	3000	1500	750

Model 213E Rifle/Shotgun Combination

This combination gun features sidelocks with English style large scroll engraving on a silver grayed receiver. Also is fitted with double triggers and pistol grip with cheekpiece.

NIB	Exc.	V.G.	Good	Fair	Poor
13000	10000	8200	5500	1900	900

Model 313E Rifle/Shotgun Combination

Same as above model but with finer scroll engraving and fancy wood.

NIB	Exc.	V.G.	Good	Fair	Poor
19000	15000	8250	6500	2000	1000

Model 220E Over-and-Under Double Rifle

This is a boxlock design with a Kersten double cross bolt, scroll engraved case hardened receiver, Blitz action, double triggers, and pistol-grip stock with cheekpiece.

NIB	Exc.	V.G.	Good	Fair	Poor
10000	6600	4950	3800	1700	825

Model 221E Over-and-Under Double Rifle

Similar to the model above but with game scene engraving on a silver grayed receiver.

NIB	Exc.	V.G.	Good	Fair	Poor
12500	9350	6300	4500	2300	900

Model 223E Over-and-Under Double Rifle

This model is fitted with sidelocks and features English-style arabesque engraving in large scrolls on silver grayed receiver.

NIB	Exc.	V.G.	Good	Fair	Poor
16000	14000	11000	8000	4200	1000

Model 240-1

This is a boxlock double rifle and shotgun chambered for the 7x65R, .30R Blaser, 6.5x57R, 8x57IRS, 9.3x74R, .30-06, and the .308 Win. Shotgun barrels are 20 gauge. Fitted with 23.6" barrels and double triggers. Ejectors. Scroll engraving. Walnut stock with pistol grip and cheekpiece. Weight is about 10 lbs.

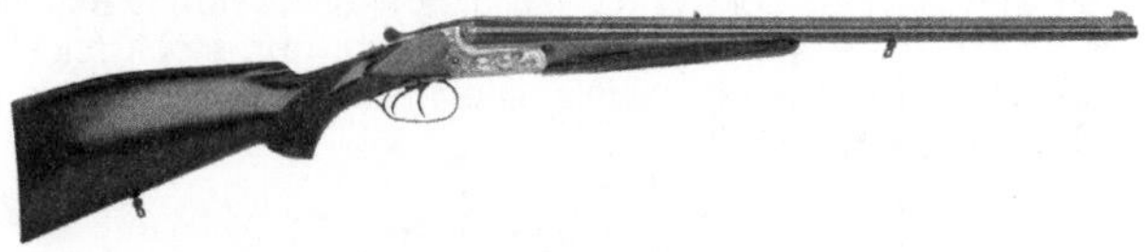

NIB	Exc.	V.G.	Good	Fair	Poor
8000	6300	5000	4000	3000	1300

Model 240-1.1

As above but with hunting scene engraving on grayed receiver.

NIB	Exc.	V.G.	Good	Fair	Poor
9100	7100	6000	5000	4000	1500

Model 323E Over-and-Under Double Rifle

Similar to the above model but with finer engraving.

NIB	Exc.	V.G.	Good	Fair	Poor
25000	19000	13500	9500	3200	1500

Model 95K Drilling

This model is a three-barrel shotgun/rifle combination. The top two barrels are chambered for 12, 16, or 20 gauge and the bottom barrel is available in rifle calibers from .22 Hornet to .375 H&H Mag. The action is a boxlock design with scroll engraving on borders and screws. The stock is select grade walnut with raised comb, pistol grip with cap, cheekpiece, and plastic butt-plate. Weighs about 7.7 lbs. This model has been discontinued.

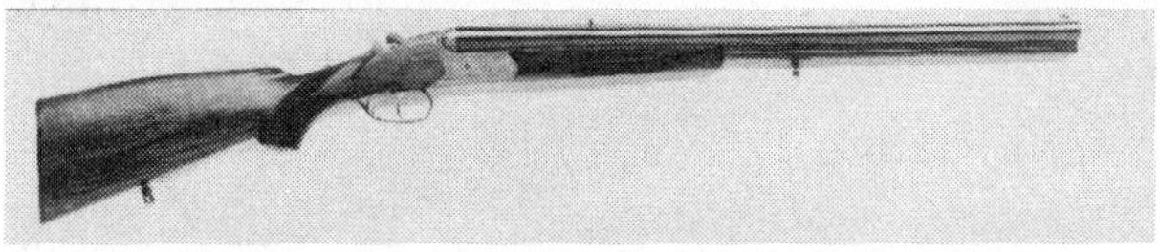

NIB	Exc.	V.G.	Good	Fair	Poor
9400	7400	4700	3000	2000	1000

Model 96K

Similar to the above model but with scroll engraving on a case hardened frame.

NIB	Exc.	V.G.	Good	Fair	Poor
9800	7800	5000	3700	2200	1000

Model 96K—Engraved

Same as above but with finely engraved hunting scenes with arabesque engraving on a silver grayed receiver.

NIB	Exc.	V.G.	Good	Fair	Poor
11000	8500	5500	4000	2700	1100

K-SERIES STALKING RIFLES

Model K-1 Jagd

Introduced in 2003 this single-shot break-open rifle is chambered for the .243, 270, 7x57R, .308 Win., .30-06, 7mm Rem. Mag., .300 Win. Mag., and the 9.3x74R cartridge. Fitted with a 23.6" barrel. Hunting scene engraving. Weight is about 5.4 lbs.

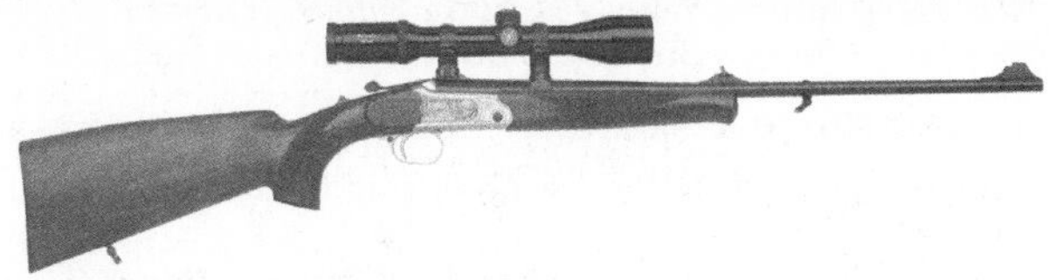

NIB	Exc.	V.G.	Good	Fair	Poor
4200	2750	1900	1600	1100	600

BOLT ACTION RIFLES

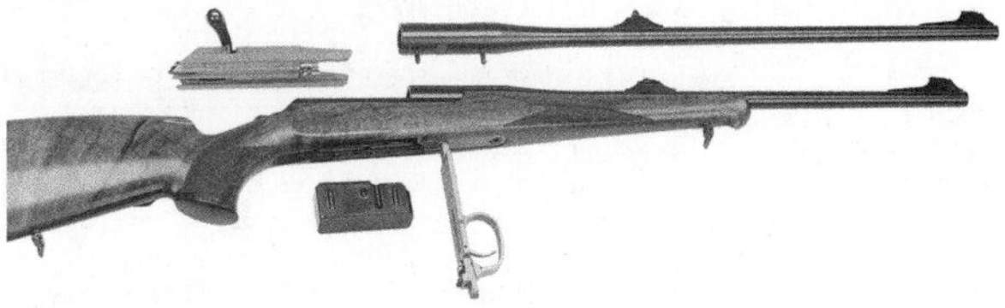

KR-1 Premium

A short stroke bolt action rifle chambered for .243, .308 or .30-06 and 7mm Rem. mag., and .300 Win. mag. calibers. Barrel length for standard calibers is 20" or 22", and for magnum calibers 22" or 24". Checkered walnut stock with hog-back comb. Magazine capacity is 3 rounds. Single set trigger. Interchangeable barrels. Arabesque engraving on bolt housing and trigger plate. Select walnut stock with Bavarian cheekpiece. Weight is about 6.4 lbs. depending on caliber and barrel length. Introduced in 2005.

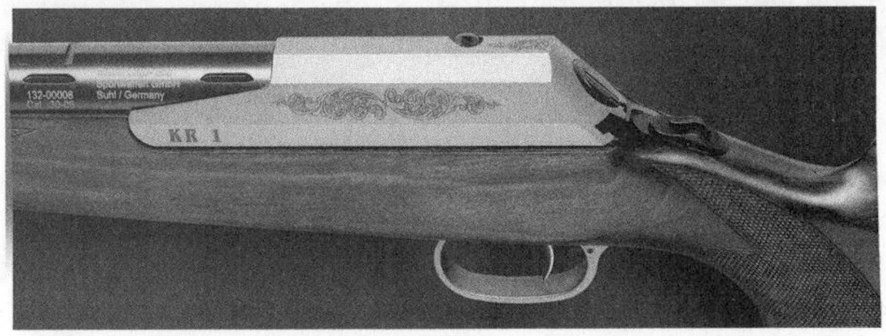

NIB	Exc.	V.G.	Good	Fair	Poor
3550	2900	2200	1650	900	450

NOTE: Add $200 for magnum calibers.

KR-1 Weimar

As above but with rounded bolt housing with hand chiselled engraving with game scenes. Trigger and lock bolt head are gold titanium nitride plated. Select walnut stock with rosewood forearm tip and Bavarian double fold cheekpiece. Introduced in 2005.

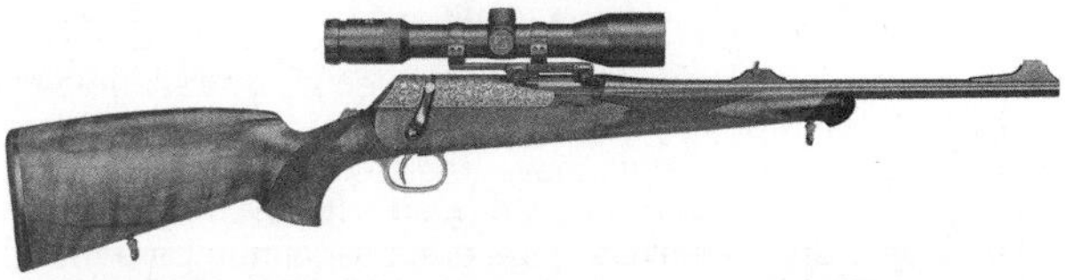

NIB	Exc.	V.G.	Good	Fair	Poor
11000	8800	7100	5500	3000	600

NOTE: Add $200 for magnum calibers.

MERRILL, JAMES H.

Baltimore, Maryland

Merrill Rifle

A single-shot breechloading rifle that is chambered for .54 caliber and utilizes the percussion ignition system. The breech opens for loading by lifting and pulling back on a lever. The barrel is 33" in length, and there is a full-length walnut stock held on by two barrel bands. The mountings and patch box are brass; and the lock is case colored, with a browned barrel. The lock is marked "J.H. Merrill Balto./Pat. July 1858." There are military acceptance marks on the stock. There were approximately 775 of these rifles manufactured and purchased by the government for use during the Civil War. They were made in 1864 and 1865.

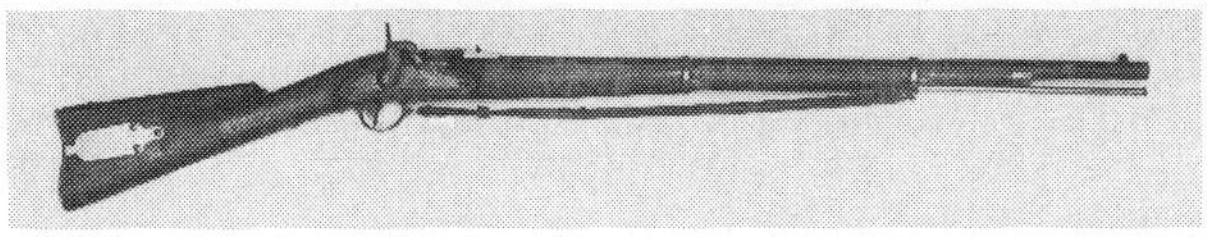

Courtesy Milwaukee Public Museum, Milwaukee, Wisconsin

NIB	Exc.	V.G.	Good	Fair	Poor
—	—	7800	6350	2750	750

Merrill Carbine

Similar in appearance to the rifle except that the barrel length is 22" and the stock is only half-length with one barrel band. There are some variations that are quite subtle in appearance but which have a considerable effect on values. We recommend that an independent appraisal be secured. The values given are for the standard 1st and 2nd Types. There were approximately 15,000 total manufactured, and most were used in the Civil War.

Merrill Carbine 1st Type

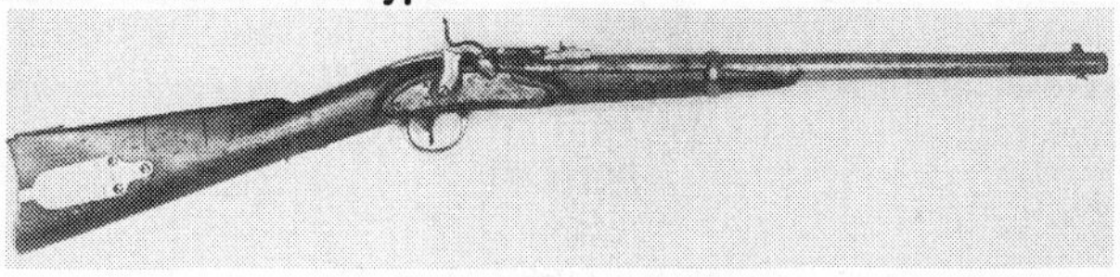

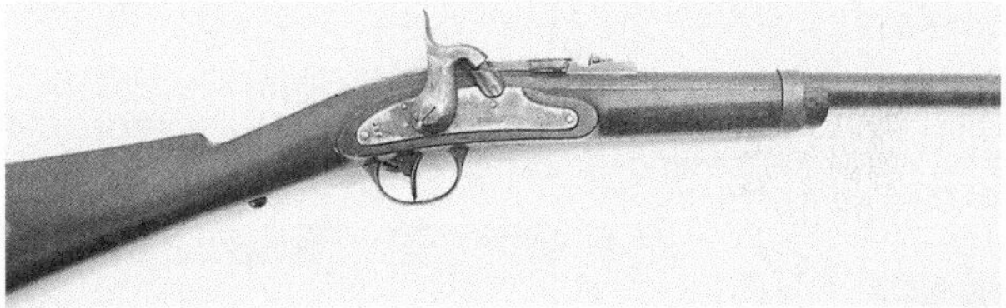

Courtesy Milwaukee Public Museum, Milwaukee, Wisconsin

No eagle stamped on the lock, and the breech lever is flat.

NIB	Exc.	V.G.	Good	Fair	Poor
—	—	3750	2750	1500	500

Merrill Carbine 2nd Type

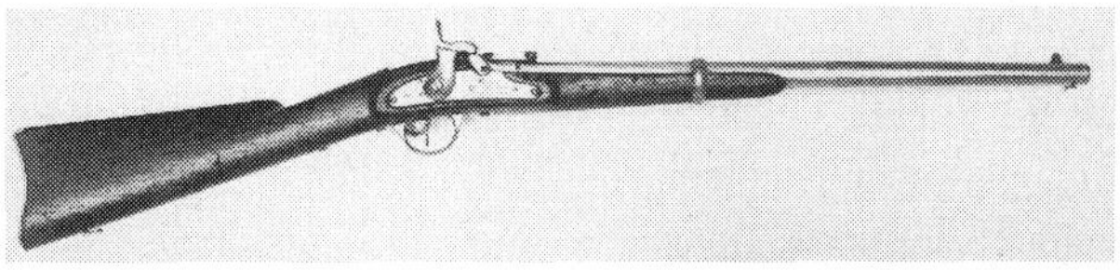

Courtesy Milwaukee Public Museum, Milwaukee, Wisconsin

NIB	Exc.	V.G.	Good	Fair	Poor
—	—	4250	3000	1750	600

MERRILL, LATROBE & THOMAS

S. Remington—Maker
Ilion, New York

Carbine

A .58 caliber breech loading percussion carbine with an overall length of 38" and barrel length of 21". The lock marked "S. Remington/ Ilion, N.Y." and the barrel "Merrill, Latrobe & Thomas/

Baltimore, Md./Patent Applied For." Approximately 170 were made in 1855.

NIB	Exc.	V.G.	Good	Fair	Poor
—	—	45000	35000	12500	700

MERWIN HULBERT & CO.

New York, New York

Merwin Hulbert & Co., New York City. Founder Joseph Merwin had previously been involved in Merwin & Bray. Merwin Hulbert & Co. or its principals were also involved in Phoenix Rifle, Evans Rifle Company, American Cartridge Company, and Hopkins & Allen of Norwich, CT. Most Merwin Hulbert revolvers will be marked with the Hopkins & Allen name, in addition to Merwin Hulbert. They were made for a fairly brief period, with most production apparently taking place during the 1870s & early 1880s.There has been some confusion over a classification system for MH revolvers. The system adopted here is based on the distinctions listed in Art Phelps' book, The Story of Merwin Hulbert & Co. Firearms. We believe this is the first time the Phelps system has been adapted to a list format.

SMALL FRAME MERWIN HULBERT POCKET REVOLVERS

Merwin Hulbert Rifles

The Merwin Hulbert rifles are very similar in design to Hopkins & Allen single-shot breech loaders. Advertised in .22 and .32 rimfire, as well as .32 WCF, .38 WCF, and .44 WCF. May have been offered in .32-40 and .38-55 chamberings. A 20 ga. shotgun barrel was offered separately for these rifles. Features included set trigger, rebounding hammer, pistol grip stock, & takedown. Seldom encountered, the Merwin Hulbert name on these should bring a premium over standard Hopkins & Allen single-shot rifles. A small frame "Merwin Hulbert & Co's. Junior" rifle was also offered, chambered for .22 rimfire.

MIIDA

Japan

Marubeni America Corp.

Model 612

A 12 gauge boxlock over-and-under shotgun with 26" or 28" ventilated rib barrels, single-selective trigger and automatic ejectors. Blued with a walnut stock. Imported between 1972 and 1974.

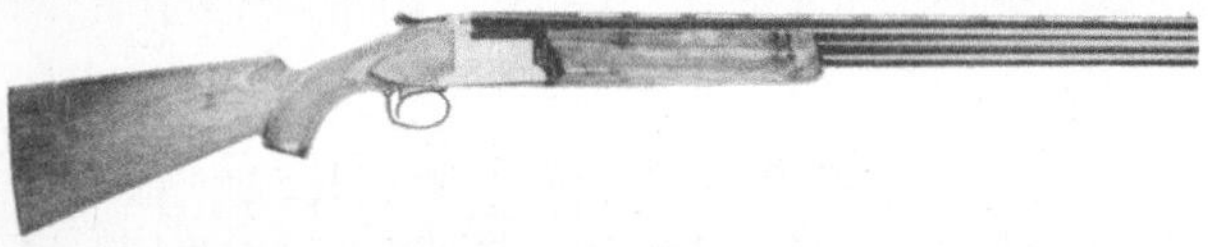

NIB	Exc.	V.G.	Good	Fair	Poor
—	900	750	600	400	250

Model 612 Skeet

As above, with 27" Skeet choked barrels and some engraving. Imported between 1972 and 1974.

NIB	Exc.	V.G.	Good	Fair	Poor
—	900	750	600	400	250

Model 2100 Skeet

Similar to the Model 612 but with more engraving coverage.

NIB	Exc.	V.G.	Good	Fair	Poor
—	950	800	650	450	300

Model 2200 Trap or Skeet

As above, with either 30" trap or 27" skeet bored barrels and more finely engraved. Imported between 1972 and 1974.

NIB	Exc.	V.G.	Good	Fair	Poor
—	1100	850	700	450	300

Model 2300 Trap or Skeet

A more finely finished Model 2200. Imported from 1972 until 1974.

NIB	Exc.	V.G.	Good	Fair	Poor
—	1200	900	750	500	300

Model GRT Trap or GRS Skeet

A 12 gauge boxlock shotgun fitted with false sideplates, 27" skeet or 29" Full choked barrels, single-selective trigger and automatic ejector. Imported between 1972 and 1974.

NIB	Exc.	V.G.	Good	Fair	Poor
—	2250	1850	1250	800	500

MILLER ARMS

Sturgis, South Dakota

NOTE: There are a large number of extra costs options avialable for these rifles.

Standard Rifle

This is single shot falling block rifle. Fitted with a 26" round barrel chambered for centerfire cartridges up to .375 caliber. Stock is checkered XXX walnut with pistol grip. Quarter rib scope base. Weight depends on caliber.

NIB	Exc.	V.G.	Good	Fair	Poor
4500	3500	2000	1300	700	350

Low Boy

This model features a 24" half round/half octagon barrel. All other features as above.

NIB	Exc.	V.G.	Good	Fair	Poor
5000	4000	2250	1300	700	350

Model F

This model is similar to the standard rifle with the addition of a 26" octagon barrel with tang sight and globe front sight. All calibers to .45-110.

NIB	Exc.	V.G.	Good	Fair	Poor
6000	4750	3000	2200	1300	500

MILTECH

Los Altos, California

This company rebuilds and refinishes selected military firearms. All firearms are thoroughly inspected for safety and are considered safe to shoot. All firearms have their original receivers and markings. These rifles are not stamped with the Miltech name but do have a unique Miltech pine crate serial numbered to the gun as standard. The company will verify that it did the rebuild if asked. All guns come with manual, sling, and other selected accessories depending on model.

German Mauser Model 98k

NIB	Exc.	V.G.	Good	Fair	Poor
1495	1150	900	750	550	300

M1 Garand

NIB	Exc.	V.G.	Good	Fair	Poor
1595	1200	850	700	500	300

NOTE: For International Harvester and Winchester add $225.

M1D Garand

NIB	Exc.	V.G.	Good	Fair	Poor
2950	2500	1900	1350	700	400

Gallery of Rifles and Shotguns

The original big gun bad boy, Barrett outdoes itself with the M107A1, a semi-auto .50-cal. with a butt-stock monopod, thermal-guard cheek-piece, reconfigurable rear grip, all which weigh four pounds less than the original.

Your daughter will trade in her dolls in a heartbeat for a chance to join you on the range with her own Thompson/Center Hot Shot in hot pink! Always safe until the hammer's cocked, this .22LR is a great starter youth gun.

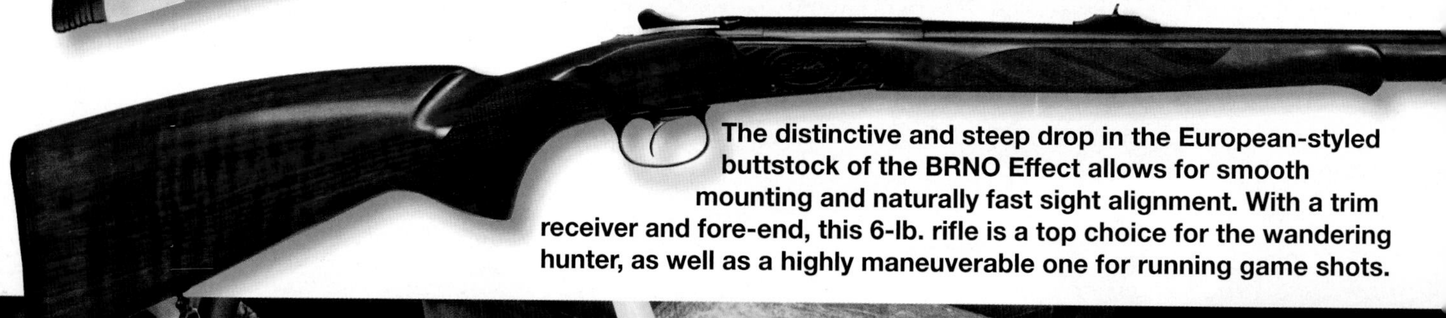

The distinctive and steep drop in the European-styled buttstock of the BRNO Effect allows for smooth mounting and naturally fast sight alignment. With a trim receiver and fore-end, this 6-lb. rifle is a top choice for the wandering hunter, as well as a highly maneuverable one for running game shots.

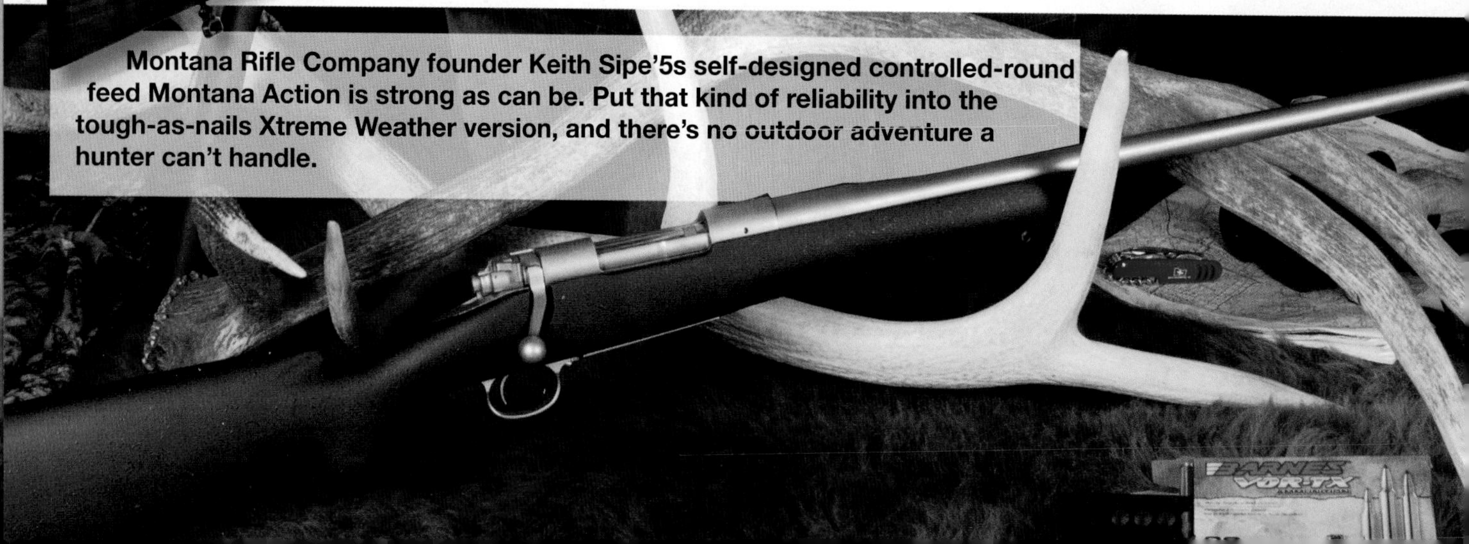

Montana Rifle Company founder Keith Sipe'5s self-designed controlled-round feed Montana Action is strong as can be. Put that kind of reliability into the tough-as-nails Xtreme Weather version, and there's no outdoor adventure a hunter can't handle.

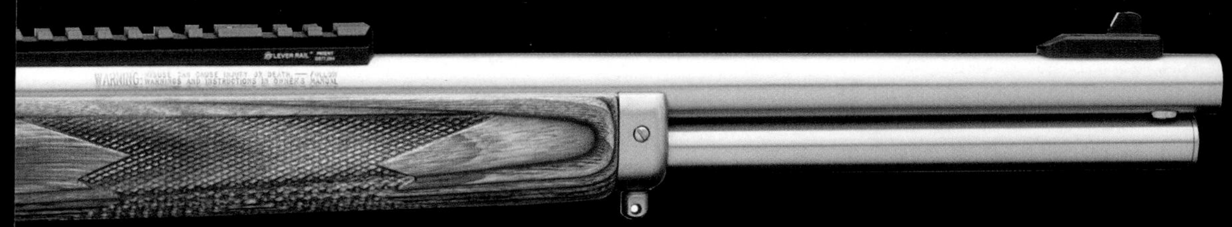

The .45-70 Gov't. cartridge is all the rage these days, and no one does a lever action for this cartridge like Marlin does. Its 1895SBL, with laminate stock, stainless hardware, and gloved hand accessible oversized loop, is an ultimate pack saddle gun for back-country wilderness hunts.

If you have a bevy of Africa's exotic game in your sights, then Dakota's 76 African Traveler is a rifle for the challenge. The two-piece take-down design lets users add on extra barrels within like cartridge families, providing the ability to span plains game to dangerous game with one gun.

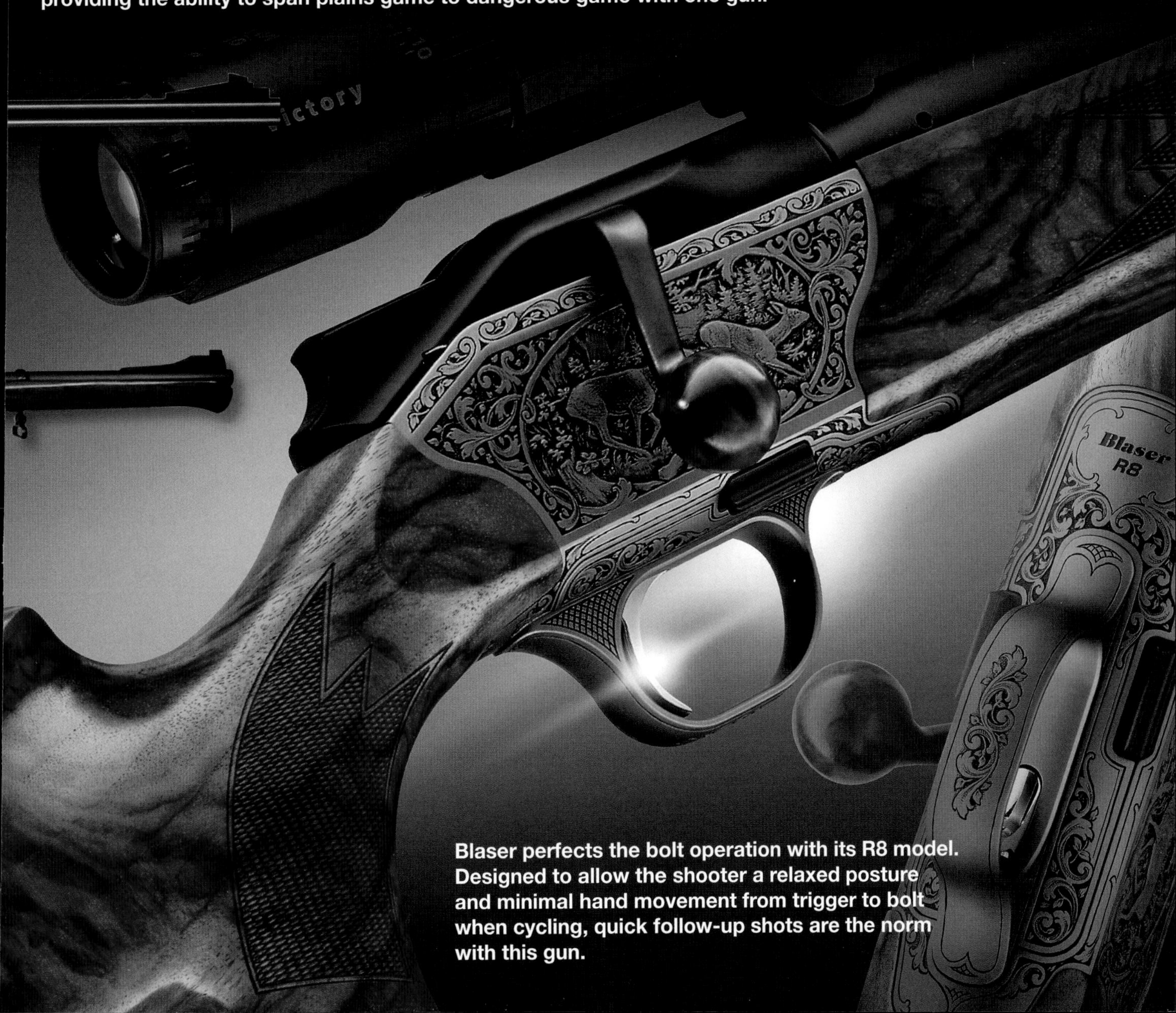

Blaser perfects the bolt operation with its R8 model. Designed to allow the shooter a relaxed posture and minimal hand movement from trigger to bolt when cycling, quick follow-up shots are the norm with this gun.

Sure, you could use this gun for home defense, but if you really want to be prepared, take FNH's SLP tac shotgun to every three-gun competition you can find. FNH declares the wicked-fast SLP has more tactical division wins than any other tac shotgun out there.

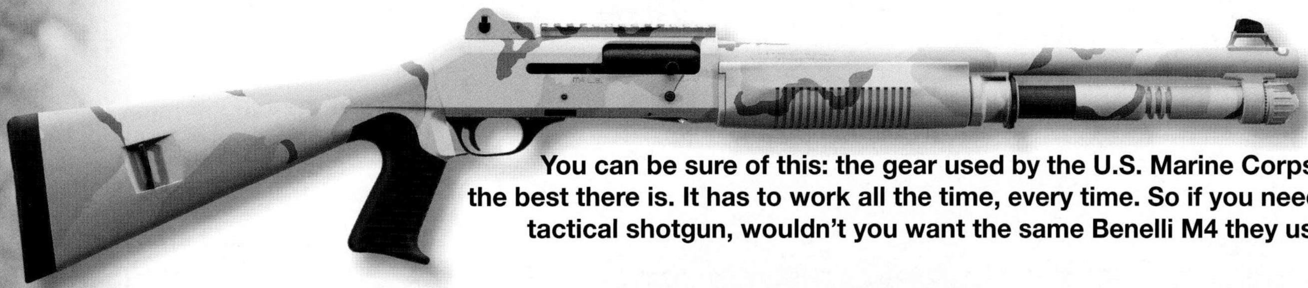

You can be sure of this: the gear used by the U.S. Marine Corps is the best there is. It has to work all the time, every time. So if you need a tactical shotgun, wouldn't you want the same Benelli M4 they use?

The Remington 1100 Competition gives clay games shooters the gun they love in the field tweaked to bust orange discs. With overbored 30-in. barrel, extended Briley target chokes, and an in-stock recoil reducing system, all that's left to say is "PULL!"

Shot-to-shot recovery time in Benelli's Super Sport is 69% faster than with many other semi-autos, thanks to Benelli's unique ComforTech system, gel butt pad and comb top, and muzzle porting that also stifles felt recoil by almost 50%.

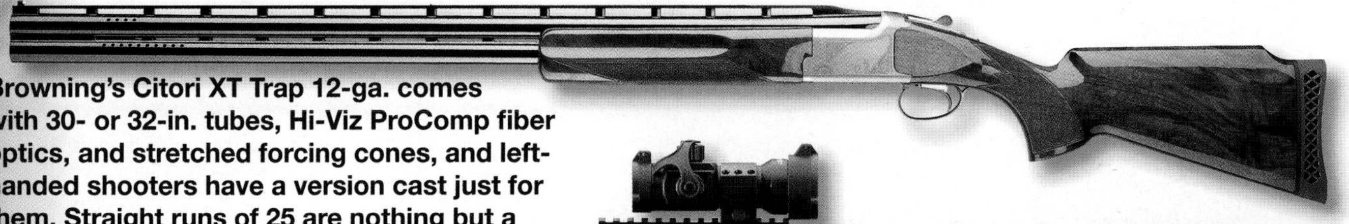

Browning's Citori XT Trap 12-ga. comes with 30- or 32-in. tubes, Hi-Viz ProComp fiber optics, and stretched forcing cones, and left-handed shooters have a version cast just for them. Straight runs of 25 are nothing but a walk in the park.

The Coach gun from Stoeger goes tactical, in the company's Double Defense version. Barrels are ported topside to keep muzzle rise minimal, while accessory rails top and bottom accommodate a variety of add-ons.

Mossberg's reputation for building simple, reliable, and practical shotguns is complete with the 500 JIC—Just In Case—Cruiser. The breakdown, pistol-griped 12-ga. and companion survival kit come housed in a floating carry tube. Hike on!

One of the most durable short-barreled shotguns on the market today, Mossberg's 5901A1 Mariner sees duty in the home, for backup needs in outdoor conditions, for daily law enforcement use, and for fun and games in 3-gun competitions.

The problem with competition semi-auto shotguns is that it's sometimes difficult to tell if a gun is safe. Beretta fixed that with its break-open semi-auto UGB25 Xcel. The ingenious design provides same point of impact from shot to shot, while providing other shooters on the line clear visbility of an open and unloaded gun.

M1 Carbine

NIB	Exc.	V.G.	Good	Fair	Poor
1295	1050	800	575	375	200

NOTE: For Rockola and Winchester add $200-300.

Model 1941 Johnson

NIB	Exc.	V.G.	Good	Fair	Poor
5000	4000	3000	2000	1000	500

Model 1903 Springfield

NIB	Exc.	V.G.	Good	Fair	Poor
1495	1150	900	750	550	300

Model 1903A3 Springfield

NIB	Exc.	V.G.	Good	Fair	Poor
1495	1150	900	750	550	300

Model 1903 Mark I Springfield

NIB	Exc.	V.G.	Good	Fair	Poor
1550	1225	975	800	575	325

Model 1917 U.S. Enfield

NIB	Exc.	V.G.	Good	Fair	Poor
1495	1150	900	750	550	300

MIROKU B. C.

Miroku, Japan

Firearms produced by this manufacturer have been imported and marketed by a variety of companies such as Charles Daly, Browning, Winchester, and SKB.

MITCHELL ARMS, INC.

Santa Ana, California

An importer and distributor of foreign-made firearms, this company is no longer in business. However, some Mitchell models were available under Brolin Arms through 1998. Brolin Arms was no longer in business as of 1999.This company also imported Yugoslavian-manufactured semi-automatic AK-47 rifles in 7.62x39mm, as well as 7.62x54mm.

Galil

A .22 or .22 Magnum caliber copy of the Galil rifle. Introduced in 1987.

NIB	Exc.	V.G.	Good	Fair	Poor
500	400	300	150	125	100

MAS

A .22 or .22 Magnum caliber copy of the French MAS Bullpup Service Rifle. Introduced in 1987.

NIB	Exc.	V.G.	Good	Fair	Poor
400	325	200	150	125	100

AK-22

A .22 or .22 Magnum caliber copy of the AK-47 rifle. Introduced in 1985.

NIB	Exc.	V.G.	Good	Fair	Poor
400	300	250	125	100	75

M-16

A .22 rimfire copy of the Colt AR-15. Introduced in 1987.

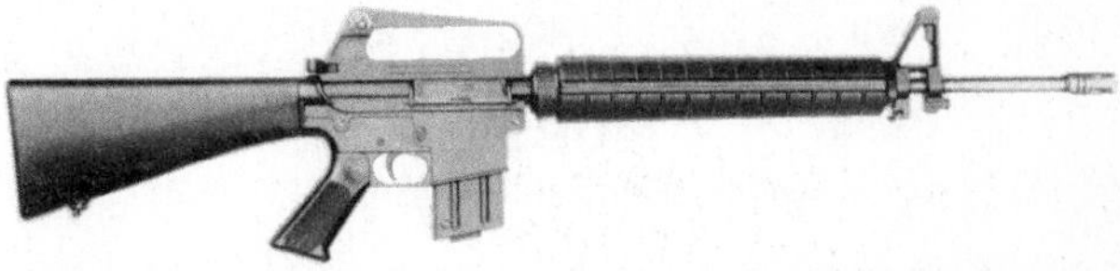

NIB	Exc.	V.G.	Good	Fair	Poor
325	250	150	125	100	75

PPSH-30/50

A .22 or .22 Magnum caliber copy of the PPSH Submachine gun.

NIB	Exc.	V.G.	Good	Fair	Poor
375	325	225	150	75	60

MITCHELL'S MAUSERS

Fountain Valley, California

Black Arrow

This is a .50 caliber bolt-action rifle with 5-round box magazine. Fitted with a recoil compensator. Iron sights. Bipod.

NIB	Exc.	V.G.	Good	Fair	Poor
6500	5000	4000	2700	1600	500

Escalade

This is a slide-action shotgun chambered for the 12 gauge shell. Fitted with a choice of 18.5" barrel, 28" vent rib barrel, or 22" barrel with Turkey choke. Turkish walnut stock. Blued.

NIB	Exc.	V.G.	Good	Fair	Poor
395	300	250	200	150	100

Sabre

This is a semi-automatic 12 gauge shotgun with choice of 22" vent rib barrel or 28" vent rib barrel. Blued.

NIB	Exc.	V.G.	Good	Fair	Poor
495	400	350	300	250	150

Mauser M98 Basic

This bolt-action rifle is fitted with a Mauser 98 action and offered in most standard hunting calibers.

NIB	Exc.	V.G.	Good	Fair	Poor
7900	6000	4500	2275	1500	400

NOTE: For magnum calibers add $2,000.

Mauser M98 Varmint

As above but chambered for .22-250 or .220 Swift.

NIB	*Exc.*	*V.G.*	*Good*	*Fair*	*Poor*
6900	5000	3500	1775	1000	300

Mauser M98 African/Alaskan

Chambered for heavy calibers up to .500 Jeffries.

NIB	*Exc.*	*V.G.*	*Good*	*Fair*	*Poor*
12000	9000	6500	2500	1500	500

MK ARMS, INC.

Irvine, California

Model 760

A 9mm caliber semi-automatic carbine with a 16" shrouded barrel, fixed sights, and 14-, 24- or 36-shot magazine. Parkerized with a folding stock. Introduced in 1983.

NIB	*Exc.*	*V.G.*	*Good*	*Fair*	*Poor*
950	700	575	400	250	125

MORSE

Greenville, South Carolina
State Armory

Morse Carbine

Overall length 40"; barrel length 2"; caliber .50 (other calibers are known to have been made on an experimental basis). The round barrel is blued, the frame is of brass and the stock is of either walnut or beechwood. Approximately 1,000 were manufactured during the Civil War.

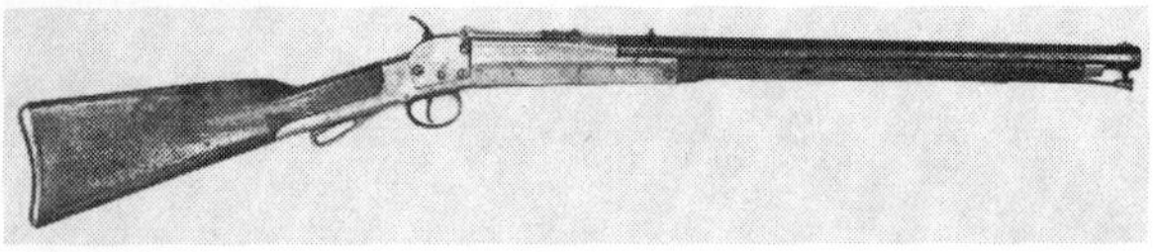

Courtesy Milwaukee Public Museum, Milwaukee, Wisconsin

NIB	*Exc.*	*V.G.*	*Good*	*Fair*	*Poor*
—	—	27000	23000	7500	1500

MOSSBERG, O. F. & SONS, INC.

North Haven, Connecticut

Founded by Oscar F. Mossberg in 1892 at Fitchburg, Massachusetts, this company for a time was located at Chicopee Falls, Massachusetts, and since 1919 has been in North Haven, Connecticut. It is the oldest family-owned firearms manufacturer in America.

RIFLES

Model K Rifle

A .22 caliber slide-action rifle with a 22" barrel, tubular magazine, internal hammer and takedown system. Blued with a walnut stock. Discontinued in 1931.

NIB	*Exc.*	*V.G.*	*Good*	*Fair*	*Poor*
—	175	150	125	75	50

Model M Rifle

As above, with a 24" octagonal barrel. Manufactured from 1928 and 1931.

NIB	*Exc.*	*V.G.*	*Good*	*Fair*	*Poor*
—	175	150	125	75	50

Model L Rifle

Beginning in 1930, the Mossberg company manufactured a variety of utilitarian single-shot and repeating bolt-action rifles. Later they introduced a similar line of semi-automatic rifles. As these arms were intended for extensive use and were low-priced, the values for them may be categorized as listed.

NIB	*Exc.*	*V.G.*	*Good*	*Fair*	*Poor*
—	450	325	250	175	100

Bolt-Action Rifles

NIB	*Exc.*	*V.G.*	*Good*	*Fair*	*Poor*
—	100	80	65	45	20

Semi-Automatic Rifles

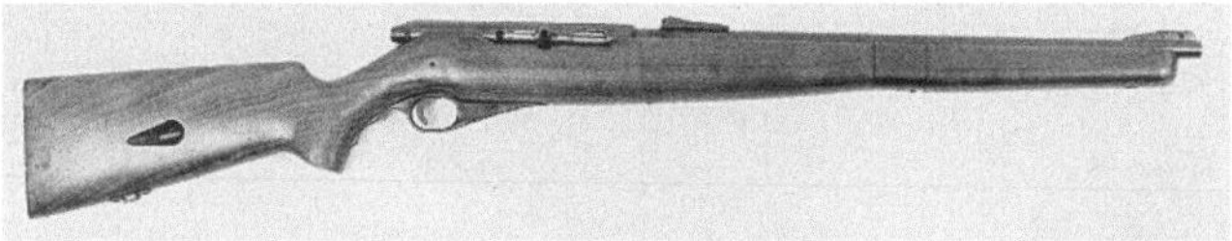

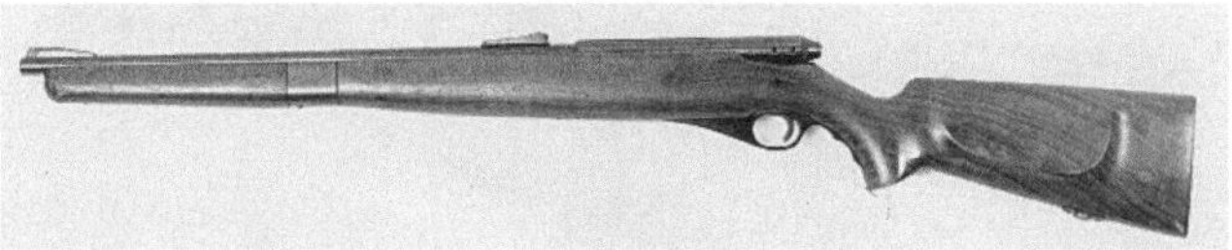

NIB	*Exc.*	*V.G.*	*Good*	*Fair*	*Poor*
—	125	100	80	60	40

Model 400 Palomino

A .22 caliber lever-action rifle with a 22" barrel, open sights and tubular magazine. Also made with an 18.5" barrel. Blued with a walnut stock. Manufactured from 1959 to 1964.

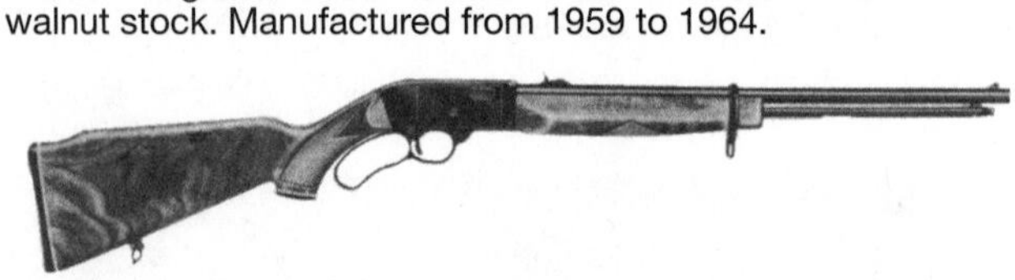

NIB	*Exc.*	*V.G.*	*Good*	*Fair*	*Poor*
—	250	200	150	100	50

Model 702 Plinkster

Introduced in 2004 this 22 caliber semi-automatic rifle is fitted with a 18" barrel with adjustable sights. Detachable 10-round magazine. Blued finish and choice of black synthetic, hardwood, synthetic thumbhole, solid pink, pink camo, or Mossy Oak New Break-up camo finish stock. Weight is about 4 lbs. Also available as scope package (add 10 percent) and with tiger maple or carbon fiber stock and chromed barrel and receiver. By 2008, a variety of color and stock options – including a modern synthetic version of Mossberg's old flip-down forend and thumb-hole stocks – had been added to the line, and these will bring more or less than the values listed, according to local demand.

NIB	*Exc.*	*V.G.*	*Good*	*Fair*	*Poor*
175	145	110	75	50	25

Model 702 International Plinkster

This model features a 21" chrome barrel with iron sights. Black synthetic stock. Weight is about 4.5 lbs.

NIB	*Exc.*	*V.G.*	*Good*	*Fair*	*Poor*
195	160	125	90	65	40

Model 702 Plinkster Autoloading Rifle with Muzzle Brake

Semiauto rifle chambered in .22 LR. Features include a black synthetic stock with Schnabel, 10-round detachable box magazine, 21-inch matte blue barrel with muzzle brake, receiver grooved for scope mount. Price: $271.

Model 817 Varmint

Introduced in 2008, this offering by Mossberg International features a 21-inch free-floating blued or brushed chrome barrel, hardwood or black synthetic stock, factory Weaver mounts, detachable box magazine and .17 HMR chambering.

NIB	*Exc.*	*V.G.*	*Good*	*Fair*	*Poor*
235	200	165	125	75	50

Mossberg Tactical .22

An AR-styled rimfire auto-loading rifle with an 18-inch, free-floating barrel. Matte blue finish. Matte black synthetic stock with fixed or adjustable length of pull. Magazine capacity, 10 or 25 rounds. Quad fore-end for unlimited mounting opportunities of optical or light systems. Peep rear and front post sight are standard.

NIB	*Exc.*	*V.G.*	*Good*	*Fair*	*Poor*
235	200	160	120	100	80

Model 100 ATR (All-Terrain Rifle)

Introduced in 2005, this bolt action rifle is chambered for the .270 or .30-06 calibers. Fitted with a 22" barrel with no sights. Choice of black synthetic, synthetic walnut, or camo stock. Matte blue or all-weather finish. Weight is about 7 lbs. .243, 308. Also available as 3X9 scope package (add 10 percent).

NIB	*Exc.*	*V.G.*	*Good*	*Fair*	*Poor*
360	300	250	200	150	100

Model 100 ATR Night Train

Similar to above but with black synthetic stock, factory-mounted 4x16 scope, bipod and .308 Winchester chambering. Introduced 2008.

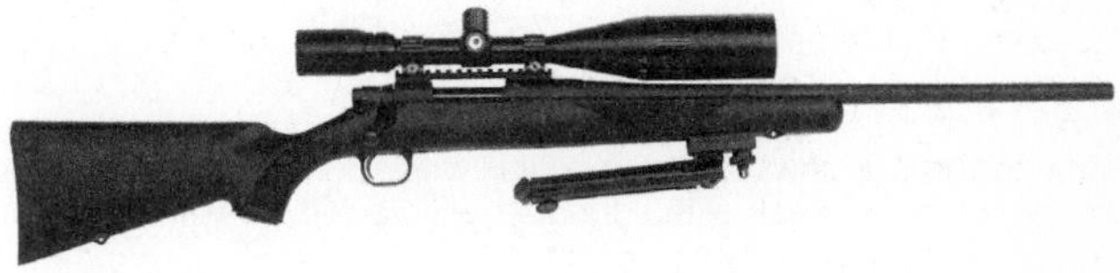

NIB	*Exc.*	*V.G.*	*Good*	*Fair*	*Poor*
375	325	275	225	165	125

Model 100 ATR Super Bantam

Similar to Model 100 ATR but chambered only in .243 and .308. No sights. Synthetic black stock adjustable for length of pull. Introduced in 2007.

NIB	*Exc.*	*V.G.*	*Good*	*Fair*	*Poor*
360	300	250	200	150	100

Model 800

A bolt-action rifle manufactured in a variety of calibers with a 22" barrel and folding leaf rear sight. Blued with a walnut stock. Introduced in 1967.

NIB	*Exc.*	*V.G.*	*Good*	*Fair*	*Poor*
—	225	200	150	100	75

Model 800D

As above, with a comb stock, rosewood forend tip and pistol grip cap. Manufactured from 1970 to 1973.

NIB	*Exc.*	*V.G.*	*Good*	*Fair*	*Poor*
—	300	250	200	150	100

Model 800V

As above, with a 24" heavy barrel not fitted with sights. Introduced in 1968.

NIB	*Exc.*	*V.G.*	*Good*	*Fair*	*Poor*
—	225	200	150	100	75

Model 800M

As above, with a Mannlicher-style stock.

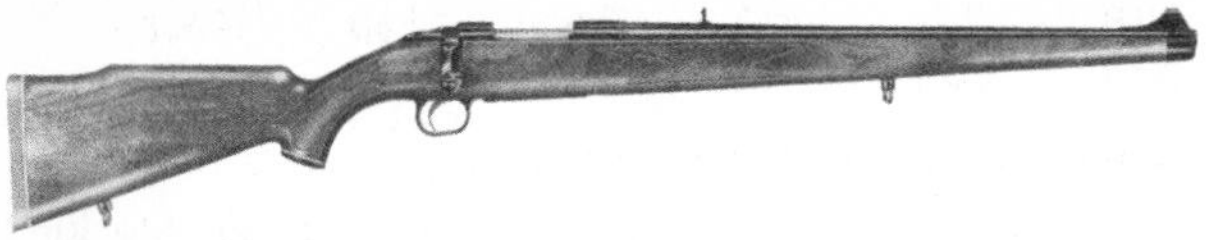

NIB	Exc.	V.G.	Good	Fair	Poor
—	275	250	200	150	100

Model 800SM

As above, with a 4X scope.

NIB	Exc.	V.G.	Good	Fair	Poor
—	300	275	225	150	100

Model 801 Half-Pint Plinkster

Entry-level .22 LR single-shot rifle with removable magazine plug to allow insertion of 10-round magazine. Sixteen-inch barrel, hardwood stock, adjustable open sights. Overall weight 4 lbs. Introduced 2008.

NIB	Exc.	V.G.	Good	Fair	Poor
150	125	100	75	50	25

Model 802 Plinkster Bolt Action

Bolt-action rifle chambered in .22 LR with 18-inch steel barrel and black synthetic stock with schnabel. Also available with 4X scope package (add 10 percent). Introduced 2006.

NIB	Exc.	V.G.	Good	Fair	Poor
150	125	100	75	50	25

Model 817 Plinkster Rifle

Similar to Model 802 Plinkster but chambered in .17 HMR. Introduced in 2007.

NIB	Exc.	V.G.	Good	Fair	Poor
175	150	125	100	75	50

Model 810

A .270 to .338 Winchester Magnum caliber bolt-action rifle with a 22" or 24" barrel fitted with a folding rear sight. Blued with a Monte Carlo-style stock. Introduced in 1970.

NIB	Exc.	V.G.	Good	Fair	Poor
—	275	250	200	150	100

Model 472C

A .30-30 or. 35 Remington Caliber lever-action rifle with a 20" barrel, open sights, and tubular magazine. Blued with a walnut stock. Introduced in 1972.

NIB	Exc.	V.G.	Good	Fair	Poor
—	250	195	150	100	75

Model 472P

As above, with a pistol grip stock and not fitted with a saddle ring.

NIB	Exc.	V.G.	Good	Fair	Poor
—	250	195	150	100	75

Model 472 One in Five Thousand

As above, with an etched receiver, brass buttplate, saddle ring and barrel band. A total of 5,000 were made in 1974.

NIB	Exc.	V.G.	Good	Fair	Poor
—	400	350	300	200	150

Model 479 PCA

Similar to the Model 472C in .30-30 caliber with a 20" barrel. Blued with a walnut stock.

NIB	Exc.	V.G.	Good	Fair	Poor
—	250	195	150	100	75

Model 479 RR

As above, with a gold-plated trigger and barrel band as well as "Roy Rogers" signature. A total of 5,000 were made in 1983.

NIB	Exc.	V.G.	Good	Fair	Poor
—	325	250	200	150	100

Model 464 Lever Action Centerfire Rifle

Side-loading, top-ejecting lever rifle with button-rifled 20-inch barrel, blued finish and hardwood stock. Straight or pistol-grip stock.Tang-mounted thumb safety. Chambered in .30-30.

NIB	Exc.	V.G.	Good	Fair	Poor
—	400	350	300	200	150

Model 464 Lever Action Rimfire Rifle

A rimfire version of the above with 18-inch barrel.

NIB	Exc.	V.G.	Good	Fair	Poor
—	375	–	–	–	–

SSi-One Sporter

Introduced in 2000 this is a single-shot rifle chambered for the .223, .243, 270 Win., .308, and .30-06 cartridges. Fitted with a 24" barrel without sights. Matte blue finish. Checkered walnut stock. Weight is about 8 lbs. Interchangeable barrels including 12 gauge.

NIB	Exc.	V.G.	Good	Fair	Poor
475	375	300	225	175	125

SSi-One Varmint

Similar to the above model but fitted with a 24" bull barrel chambered for the .22-250 cartridge. Walnut stock. Weight is about 10 lbs. Introduced in 2000. Interchangeable barrels.

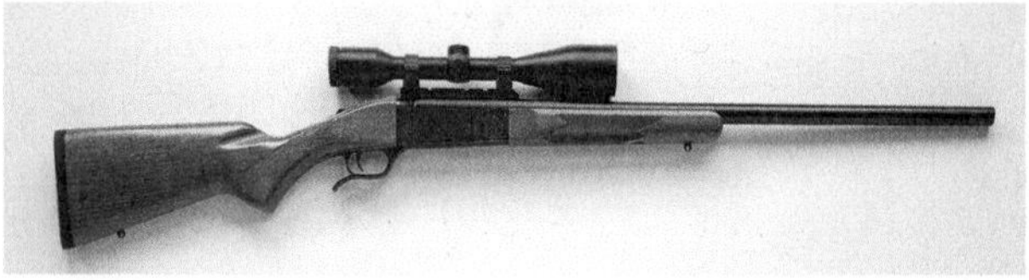

NIB	Exc.	V.G.	Good	Fair	Poor
475	375	300	225	175	125

SSi-One Slug

This model is similar to the other SSi-One guns but is fitted with a 24" fully rifled 12 gauge barrel. Walnut stock. Weight is about 8 lbs. Interchangeable barrels. Introduced in 2000.

NIB	Exc.	V.G.	Good	Fair	Poor
475	375	300	225	175	125

SSi-One Turkey

Same as above but with 24" smoothbore barrel. Will handle 3.5" magnum 12 gauge shells. Weight is about 7.5 lbs. Introduced in 2001.

NIB	Exc.	V.G.	Good	Fair	Poor
475	375	300	225	175	125

MODEL 1500 SERIES

A .223 to .338 Winchester Magnum bolt-action rifle with a 22" or 24" barrel, 5- or 6-shot magazine and various sights. Blued with a hardwood or walnut stock. Manufactured by Howa in Japan and also known as the Smith & Wesson Model 1500. Offered in 1986 and 1987.

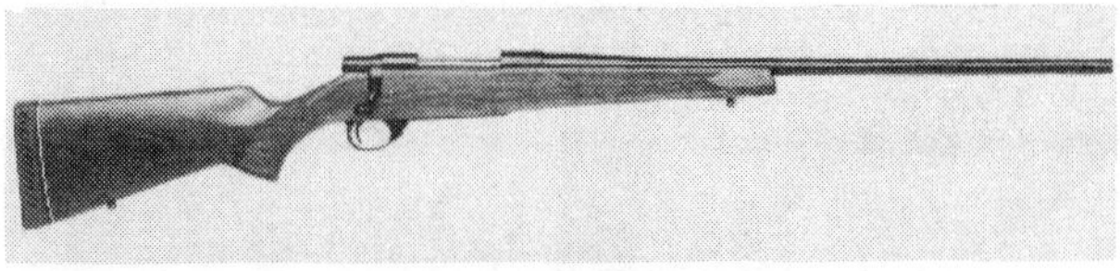

Model 1500 Mountaineer Grade I

NIB	Exc.	V.G.	Good	Fair	Poor
—	350	250	225	150	125

Model 1500 Mountaineer Grade II

NIB	Exc.	V.G.	Good	Fair	Poor
—	325	275	250	175	125

Model 1500 Varmint

24" heavy barrel.

NIB	Exc.	V.G.	Good	Fair	Poor
—	350	300	275	200	150

Model 1550

As above, but in .243, .270 or .30-06 caliber. Offered in 1986 and 1987.

NIB	Exc.	V.G.	Good	Fair	Poor
—	325	275	250	175	125

Model 1700 LS

Similar to the above, and in the same calibers with a 22" barrel not fitted for sights, machine jeweled bolt and knurled bolt handle. Blued with a walnut stock and schnabel forend. Offered in 1986 and 1987.

NIB	Exc.	V.G.	Good	Fair	Poor
—	400	350	275	200	150

Mossberg 4x4 Rifle

Bolt-action centerfire rifle chambered in .25-06, .270, .30-06, 7mm Rem Mag, .300 Win Mag, .338 Win Mag. Barrel length 22" (iron sight) or 24" (sightless). Detachable box magazine, two-position safety. Walnut, laminated or black synthetic stock with lightening cutouts in butt and forend. Scope package also available. Introduced in 2007.

NIB	Exc.	V.G.	Good	Fair	Poor
475	375	300	225	175	125

Mossberg 4X4 Classic Stock Synthetic

Similar to above but with black synthetic stock and Marinecote metal surfaces.

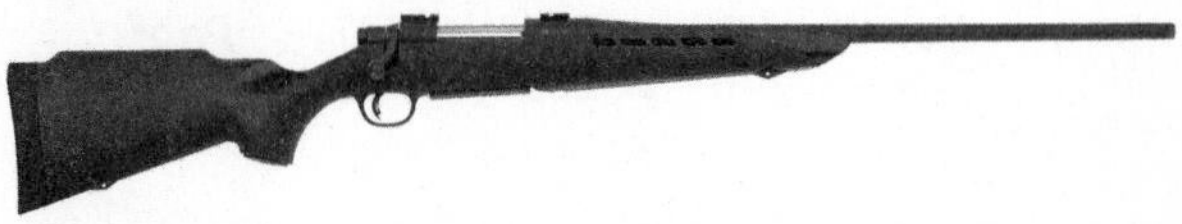

NIB	Exc.	V.G.	Good	Fair	Poor
—	450	350	275	200	125

Mossberg 4X4 Scoped Combo

Similar to above but with matte blue finish and 3x9 scope.

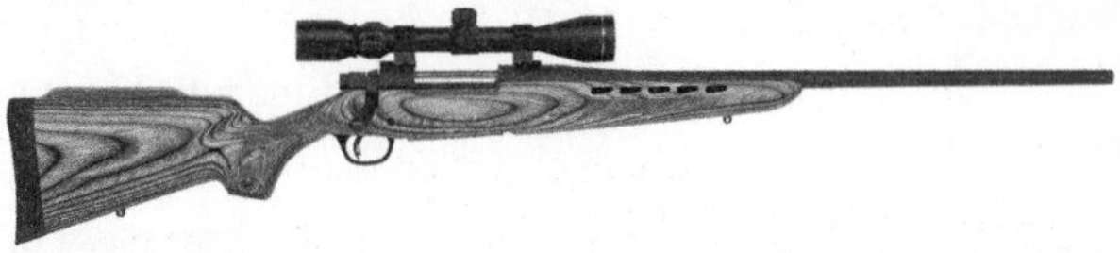

NIB	Exc.	V.G.	Good	Fair	Poor
—	450	350	275	200	125

Mossberg 4X4 Classic Walnut Stock

Similar to above but with checkered walnut stock. Suggested retail price: To be announced.

NIB	Exc.	V.G.	Good	Fair	Poor
—	500	450	350	225	150

SHOTGUNS

Mossberg manufactured a variety of shotguns that were sold at low to moderate prices. The values for these arms are approximately all the same.

Mossberg: Miscellaneous Bolt-Action Shotguns

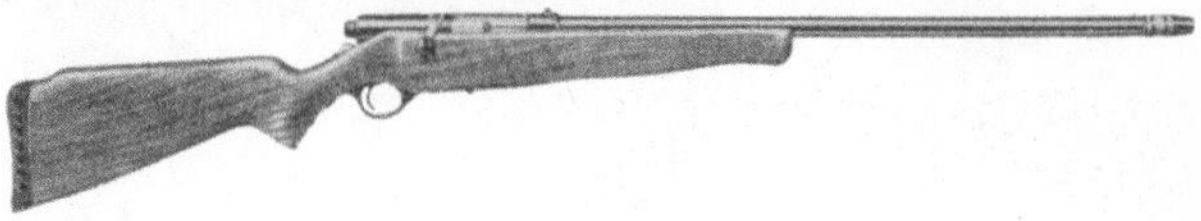

NIB	Exc.	V.G.	Good	Fair	Poor
—	150	125	90	65	35

Model 695

Introduced in 1969 this bolt-action shotgun is chambered for the 12 gauge shell. Barrel length is 22" with either a rifled bore or plain bore. Finish is matte blue. In 1997 this model was offered with a 22" plain ported barrel with rifled bore. Magazine capacity is 3 rounds. Weight is about 7.5 lbs.

NIB	Exc.	V.G.	Good	Fair	Poor
275	225	175	150	125	100

Model 695 Camo

Introduced in 2000 this model is the same as the standard Model 695 with the addition of Woodlands camo finish.

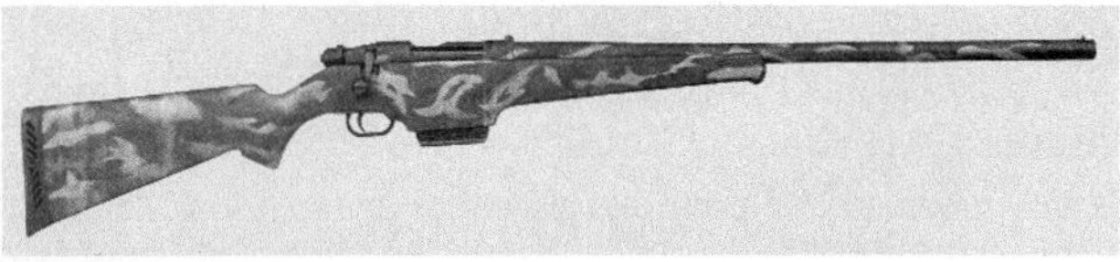

NIB	Exc.	V.G.	Good	Fair	Poor
375	325	275	250	195	150

Model 200K

A 12 gauge slide-action shotgun with a 28" barrel and Mossberg select choke. Blued with a composition slide handle and walnut stock. Manufactured from 1955 to 1959.

NIB	Exc.	V.G.	Good	Fair	Poor
—	150	125	100	75	50

MODEL 500 SERIES

A 12, 20 or .410 bore slide-action shotgun manufactured in a variety of barrel lengths and styles, as listed.

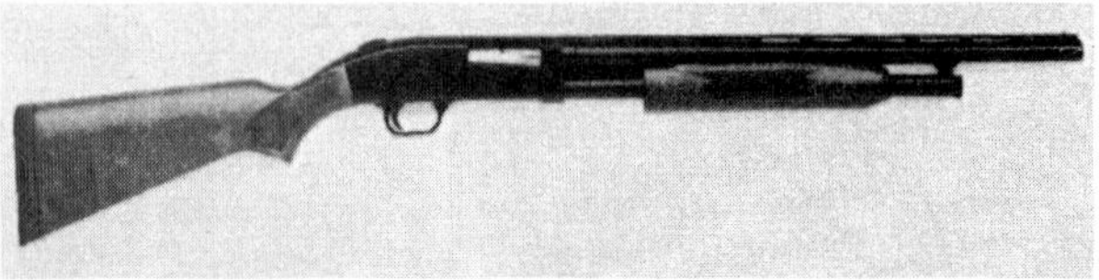

Regal

NIB	Exc.	V.G.	Good	Fair	Poor
—	250	200	150	100	75

Field Grade

NIB	Exc.	V.G.	Good	Fair	Poor
285	250	200	150	100	75

Steel Shot

Chrome bore.

NIB	Exc.	V.G.	Good	Fair	Poor
—	300	250	200	125	100

Slugster

Crown grade, iron sights.

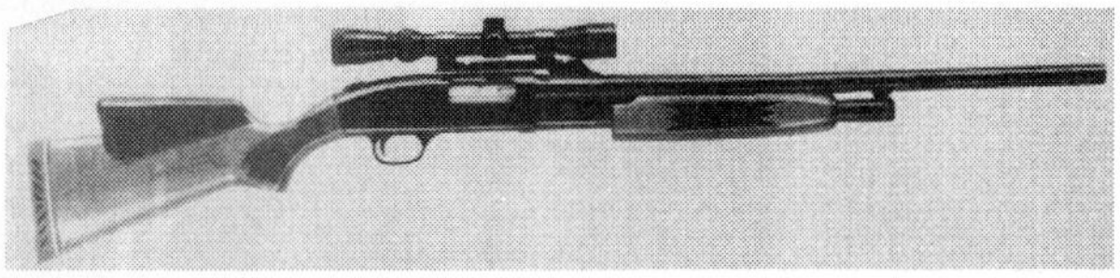

NIB	Exc.	V.G.	Good	Fair	Poor
—	275	250	200	150	100

Camper

18.5" barrel, camo case.

NIB	Exc.	V.G.	Good	Fair	Poor
—	295	275	225	175	100

Hi-Rib Trap

NIB	Exc.	V.G.	Good	Fair	Poor
—	275	250	200	150	100

Super Grade

NIB	Exc.	V.G.	Good	Fair	Poor
—	300	275	225	175	100

Pigeon Grade

NIB	Exc.	V.G.	Good	Fair	Poor
—	375	300	250	200	125

Pigeon Grade Trap

NIB	Exc.	V.G.	Good	Fair	Poor
—	450	375	300	250	175

Persuader

Riot gun, 18.5" barrel in 12 gauge. 20" barrel in 20 gauge (added 2008).

NIB	Exc.	V.G.	Good	Fair	Poor
300	275	225	175	100	75

Mariner

Marinecote finish.

NIB	Exc.	V.G.	Good	Fair	Poor
400	325	225	200	150	125

Cruiser

Pistol grip only.

NIB	Exc.	V.G.	Good	Fair	Poor
375	300	250	200	125	100

Bantam

Introduced in 1996 this model is slightly smaller overall than the full-size guns. Chambered for the 20 gauge shell it is fitted with a 22" shotgun barrel or 24" rifled vent rib barrel. Walnut stock. Weight is about 6.9 lbs.

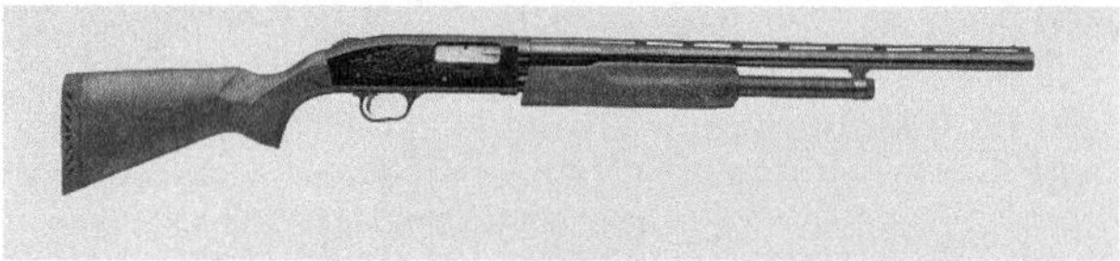

NIB	Exc.	V.G.	Good	Fair	Poor
275	225	200	150	125	100

Super Bantam Field

Introduced in 2005 this model features a 20 gauge 3" chamber with 22" ventilated rib barrel with choke tubes. Blued finish. Synthetic stock with adjustabe length of pull. Weight is about 5.25 lbs.

NIB	Exc.	V.G.	Good	Fair	Poor
315	275	175	125	100	75

Super Bantam Turkey

This 20 gauge 3" model has a 22" vent rib ported barrel with extra full choke. Synthetic camo stock. Adjustable stock for lop. Weight is about 5.25 lbs. Introduced in 2005.

NIB	Exc.	V.G.	Good	Fair	Poor
375	325	250	175	150	100

Super Bantam Slug

This 20 gauge model features a full rifled 24" ported barrel with adjustable sights. Synthetic stock with blue or camo finish. Weight is about 5.25 lbs. Introduced in 2005. In 2008, a version with an integrated scope base was added to this series.

NIB	*Exc.*	*V.G.*	*Good*	*Fair*	*Poor*
375	325	250	175	150	100

Super Bantam Combo

This model introduced in 2005, features a 22" vent rib barrel with choke tubes and a 24" fully rifled ported barrel. Camo finish with adjustable lop synthetic stock. Weight is about 5.25 lbs.

NIB	*Exc.*	*V.G.*	*Good*	*Fair*	*Poor*
400	325	275	200	150	125

Bullpup

A 12 gauge slide-action Bullpup shotgun with an 18.5" or 20" shrouded barrel. Matte black finish with a composition stock. Introduced in 1986. Discontinued. Values shown are for 6-shot version. Add 215 percent for 8-shot.

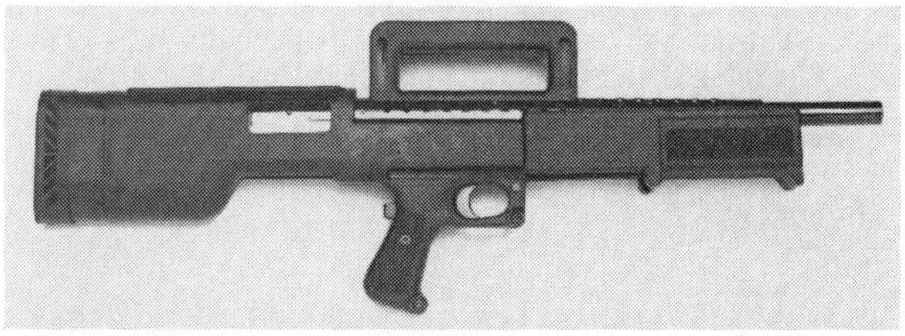

NIB	*Exc.*	*V.G.*	*Good*	*Fair*	*Poor*
600	500	375	250	150	100

Slug Gun Viking Grade

Introduced in 1996 this model is a 12 gauge gun with 24" rifled barrel with iron sights and green synthetic stock. NOTE: In 1997 Mossberg introduced ported barrels on some of its slug models. These ported barrels will be seen on rifled barrels only.

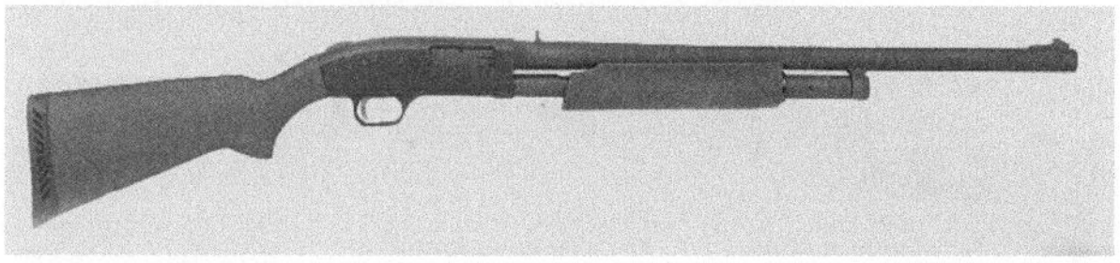

NIB	*Exc.*	*V.G.*	*Good*	*Fair*	*Poor*
300	275	225	175	100	75

Grand Slam Turkey

This 12 or 20 gauge 3" gun was introduced in 2004. Offered with a 20" vent rib barrel with adjustable fiber optic sights and ported Extra Full choke tube. Available in Real Tree Hardwood or Mossy Oak Break-Up camo pattern. Weight is about 7 lbs. for the 12 gauge gun and about 6.75 lbs. for the 20 gauge.

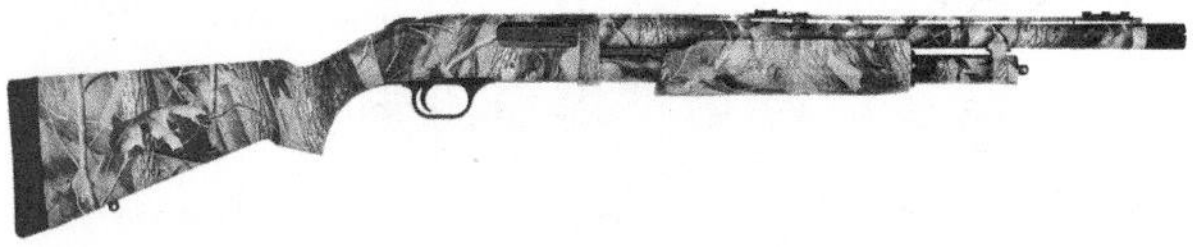

NIB	*Exc.*	*V.G.*	*Good*	*Fair*	*Poor*
375	325	250	175	150	100

Flyway Series

Introduced in 2005 this model is a 12 gauge 3.5" gun with 28" vent rib barrel with fiber optic front sight. Choke tubes. Advantage camo synthetic stock. Weight is about 7.5 lbs.

NIB	*Exc.*	*V.G.*	*Good*	*Fair*	*Poor*
400	325	225	200	150	125

Combo

The 500 series has a total of nine combination sets available to choose from. They are a combination of shotgun barrels and rifled barrels for different hunting applications they are offered in both 12 and 20 gauge sets of the same gauge only.

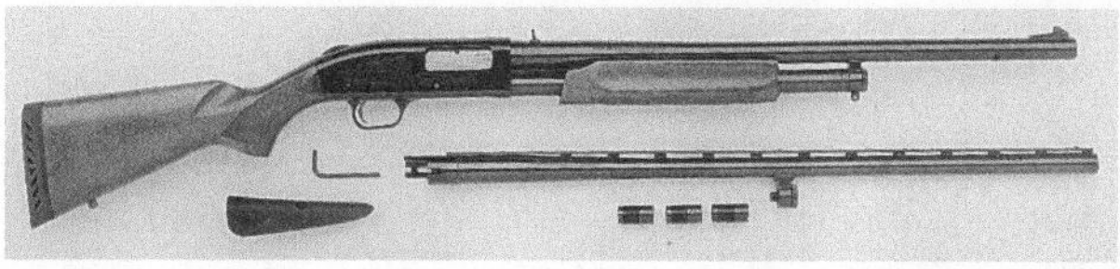

NIB	*Exc.*	*V.G.*	*Good*	*Fair*	*Poor*
400	325	275	225	175	125

USA

Introduced in 1997 this model is similar to the military model. It has a Parkerized finish with heavy-duty sling swivels. Fitted with a plain 20" barrel choked Cylinder. Stock is black synthetic. Magazine capacity is 6 rounds. Weight is about 7.2 lbs.

NIB	*Exc.*	*V.G.*	*Good*	*Fair*	*Poor*
250	200	175	150	125	100

HS (Home Security)

This shotgun is chambered for the .410 shell and fitted with an 18.5" barrel. Five-round magazine capacity. Synthetic stock and blue finish. NOTE: In 1999 Mossberg offered a .50 muzzleloader 24" fully rifled barrel that will fit directly onto any six-shot Model 500.

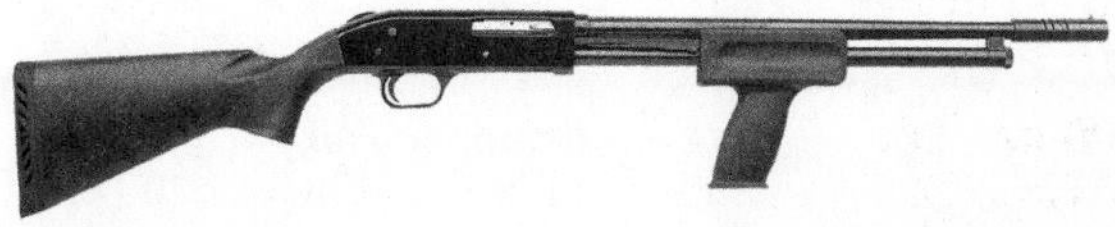

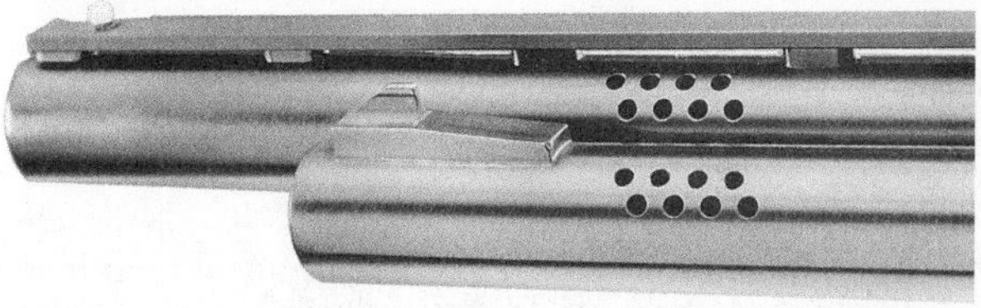

Porting on most 500 series and 835 series vent rib and slug barrels

NIB	*Exc.*	*V.G.*	*Good*	*Fair*	*Poor*
350	325	275	225	200	150

Rolling Thunder

This home defense/tactical model is a 3" 12 gauge featuring a pistol grip, 23" barrel with heat shield and recoil-reducing stabilizer and six-round capacity.

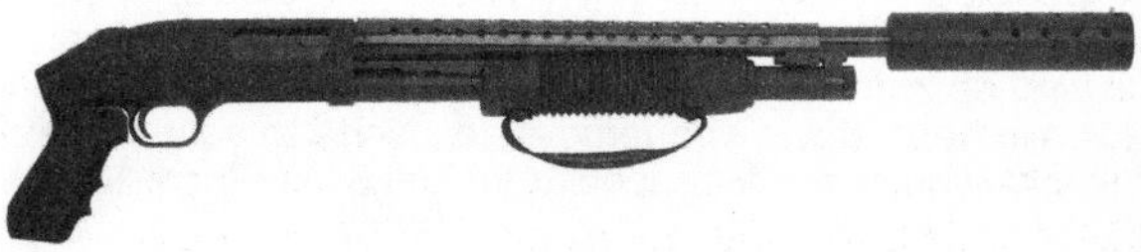

NIB	*Exc.*	*V.G.*	*Good*	*Fair*	*Poor*
400	325	275	225	175	125

Tactical Cruiser "Door Buster"

Similar to above but with serrated muzzle. A TALO exclusive.

NIB	*Exc.*	*V.G.*	*Good*	*Fair*	*Poor*
525	425	325	225	175	125

Tactical

The Model 500 Tactical 8-shot pump has a 20-inch barrel and ghost ring sights. Black synthetic, pistol-grip stock can be adjusted to provide a 10-3/4 to a 14-5/8-inch length of pull. Weight: 6-1/4 lbs. Capacity: 7+1. Matte blue finish.

NIB	Exc.	V.G.	Good	Fair	Poor
480	440	400	370	320	280

SHOTGUNS

MODEL 500 SERIES

JIC (Just In Case)

This survival model is a 3" 12 gauge featuring a pistol grip, 18.5" barrel and a weatherproof pack tube. Three different models available with different finishes and accessory packages. Add 15 percent for nickel finish.

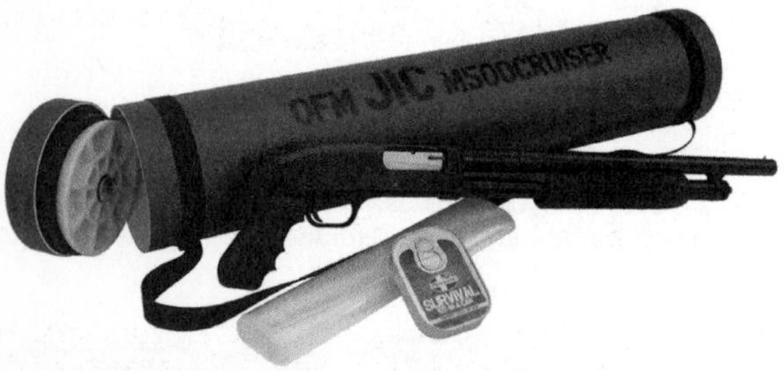

NIB	Exc.	V.G.	Good	Fair	Poor
375	325	250	175	150	100

JIC II

Takedown pump-action shotgun chambered in 3-inch 12 gauge. Similar to other JIC models but features matte black finish overall and comes packaged in black nylon zippered case. Price: $435.

Model 505 Youth

Offered in 20 gauge or .410 bore this model is fitted with a 20" vent rib barrel with choke tubes for the 20 gauge and fixed modified choke for the .410 bore. Wood stock with recoil pad. Blued finish. Weight is about 5.25 lbs.

NIB	Exc.	V.G.	Good	Fair	Poor
315	275	175	125	100	75

Mossberg 510 Mini Shotgun

Compact pump-action shotgun based on Model 500 action, chambered in 3-inch 20 gauge and .410. Features include an 18.5-inch vent rib barrel with interchangeable (20) or fixed (.410) choke, black synthetic stock with removable inserts to adjust LOP from 12 to 14+ inches, 4-shot capacity. Weight 5 lbs. Price: $364.

Model 535 ATS (All Terrain Shotgun) Field

Introduced in 2005 this 12 gauge 3.5" model features a 28" vent rib barrel with choke tubes. Blued finish with checkered wood stock with pistol grip. Weight is about 6.75 lbs.

NIB	Exc.	V.G.	Good	Fair	Poor
375	325	250	175	150	100

Model 535 ATS Turkey

As above but with 22" vent rib barrel with extra full choke and fiber optic front sight. Synthetic stock with matte blue or camo finsh. Weight is about 6.5 lbs. Introduced in 2005.

NIB	Exc.	V.G.	Good	Fair	Poor
375	325	250	175	150	100

NOTE: Add $55 for camo finish.

Model 535 ATS Waterfowl

This model is fitted with 28" vent rib barrel with choke tubes and fiber optic front sight. Synthetic stock with matte blue or camo finish. Weight is about 6.75 lbs. Introduced in 2005.

NIB	Exc.	V.G.	Good	Fair	Poor
375	325	250	175	150	100

NOTE: Add $55 for camo finish.

Model 535 ATS Slugster

Fitted with a fully rifled 24" vent rib barrel with adjustable sights. Choice of matte blue or camo finish and synthetic stock. Weight is about 7 lbs.

NIB	Exc.	V.G.	Good	Fair	Poor
375	325	250	175	150	100

Model 535 ATS Combos

This set is offered in several different configurations: Field/Deer, 28" and 24"; Turkey/Deer, 22" and 24"; and Turkey/Slug/Waterfowl, 22" and 28". Weights are from 6.5 to 7 lbs. depending on barrel length. Introduced in 2005.

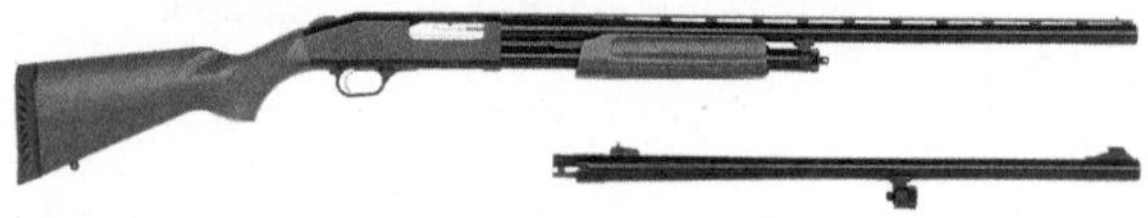

NIB	Exc.	V.G.	Good	Fair	Poor
475	400	350	225	150	175

NOTE: Add $55 for camo finish.

MODEL 590 SERIES

Special Purpose

Fitted with a 20" shrouded barrel, bayonet lug, Parkerized or blued finish. Speed feed stock and ghost ring sights. Introduced in 1987. Weight is about 7.25 lbs.

NIB	*Exc.*	*V.G.*	*Good*	*Fair*	*Poor*
325	275	200	175	125	100

Model 590 Mariner

Marinecote finish.

NIB	*Exc.*	*V.G.*	*Good*	*Fair*	*Poor*
425	350	275	225	150	100

Model 590DA

This 12 gauge model, introduced in 2000, features a 6-round tubular magazine and an 18.5" barrel. Choice of plain bead sight or ghost ring sights. Choke is fixed Modified. Weight is about 7 lbs. A 14" barreled model is also offered but NFA rules apply.

NIB	*Exc.*	*V.G.*	*Good*	*Fair*	*Poor*
500	400	300	200	150	100

NOTE: Add $50 for Ghost Ring sights.

Model 590 Bullpup

The Model 500 with a 20" barrel and 9-shot magazine. Introduced in 1989. Discontinued.

NIB	*Exc.*	*V.G.*	*Good*	*Fair*	*Poor*
600	500	400	250	200	125

Model 590A1 Blackwater

The 590A1 Blackwater pump is a 12 gauge with 3-inch chamber, a 20-inch-long heavy-walled barrel, measures 41 inches overall, and has ghost ring/AR-style sights. Length of pull is 13-7/8 inches. Features a synthetic Speedfeed stock and Parkerized finish. Thumb safety is atop the receiver. Capacity is 8+1 rounds, weight is 7-1/4 lbs. Blackwater logo etched on receiver.

NIB	*Exc.*	*V.G.*	*Good*	*Fair*	*Poor*
585	500	425	350	300	150

Model 590 Tri Rail

The Tri-Rail Model 590 pump gun is chambered for 3-inch 12-gauge loads and features a protective heat shield on its 20-inch barrel. Overall length is 40-7/8-inches. Has synthetic Speedfeed stock, bead front sight. Features a Tri-Rail fore end with removable side rails and an integral bottom rail. Extended magazine gives the gun an 8+1 capacity. Matte blue finish. Length of pull is 13.8-inches. Weight: 7-1/4 lbs.

NIB	*Exc.*	*V.G.*	*Good*	*Fair*	*Poor*
540	490	440	390	300	150

Model 590 A1

The Model 590A1 features an adjustable aluminum stock and ghost ring sights. Heavy-walled barrel is 20-inches long. Length of pull can be adjusted between 10-1/2 and 14-1/4-inches. Weight: 7-1/2 lbs. Capacity: 8+1. Parkerized finish.

NIB	*Exc.*	*V.G.*	*Good*	*Fair*	*Poor*
480	420	325	250	200	125

MODEL 835 SERIES

Ulti-Mag

A 12 gauge Magnum slide-action shotgun with a choice of 24" or 28" ventilated rib barrel fitted for choke tubes, 6-shot magazine and either composition camo or walnut stock. Barrel is ported. Introduced in 1988. In 1998 this model was offered with Shadow Grass camo pattern on both stock and barrel. In 1999 this model was offered with Woodland camo. Weight is 7.3 to 7.7 lbs. In 2000 this model was offered with Realtree Hardwoods camo finish.

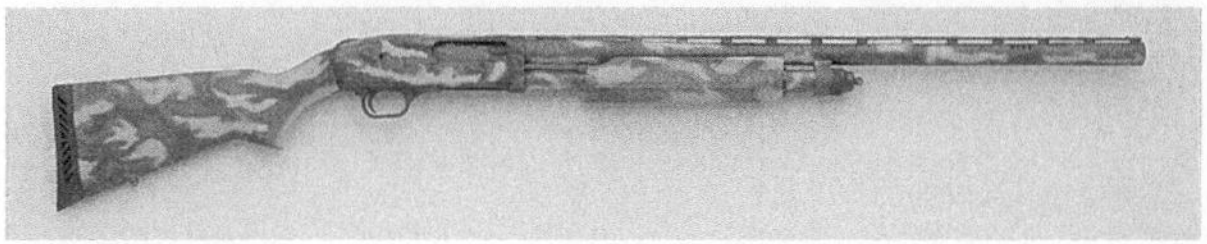

NIB	*Exc.*	*V.G.*	*Good*	*Fair*	*Poor*
425	350	275	225	150	100

Ulti-Mag Viking Grade

Introduced in 1996 this model features a 12 gauge 3.5" magnum chambered with green synthetic stock and Modified choke tube. Furnished with 28" vent rib barrel.

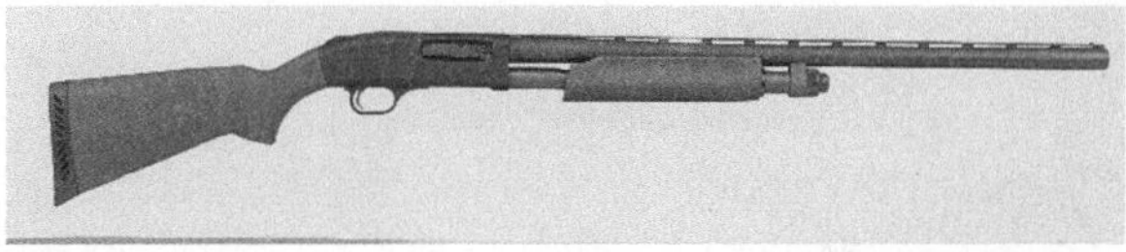

NIB	*Exc.*	*V.G.*	*Good*	*Fair*	*Poor*
300	250	200	175	125	100

Ulti-Mag Crown Grade

The Crown Grade features checkered walnut stock with fluted comb. It is chambered for the 12 gauge with 3.5" chamber. Offered in 24" or 28" vent rib barrels with blued or camo finish. Weight is about 7.3 to 7.7 lbs.

NIB	*Exc.*	*V.G.*	*Good*	*Fair*	*Poor*
375	300	225	200	150	100

Ulti-Mag Crown Grade Combo Model

Same as above but offered with both a 28" vent rib barrel and a 24" rifled barrel with iron sights.

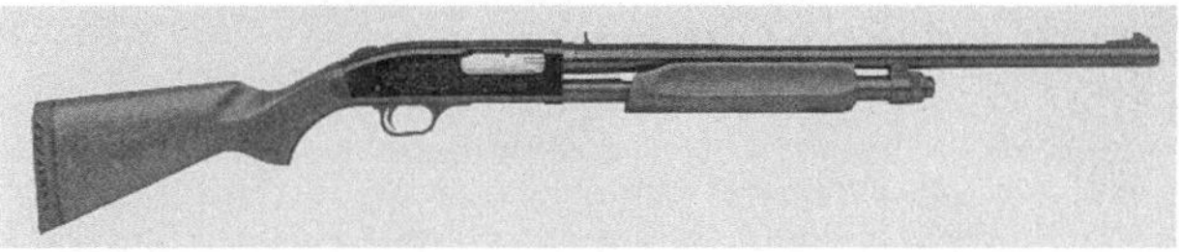

NIB	*Exc.*	*V.G.*	*Good*	*Fair*	*Poor*
425	325	250	225	175	150

Ulti-Mag Grand Slam Turkey

Introduced in 2004 this 12 gauge 3.5" model features a 20" vent rib overbored barrel with Extra Full ported choke tube. Magazine capacity is 6 rounds for 2.75" shells, 5 rounds for 3", and 4 rounds for 3.5" shells. Adjustable fiber optic sights. Available in Real Tree Hardwoods camo or Mossy Oak Break-Up. Weight is about 7.25 lbs.

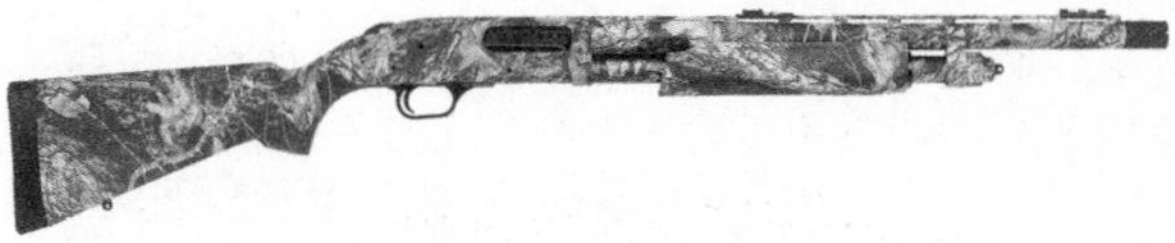

NIB	*Exc.*	*V.G.*	*Good*	*Fair*	*Poor*
400	325	275	225	175	125

Ulti-Mag Thumbhole Turkey

New in 2006, this dedicated pump-action 12 gauge turkey gun features a thumbhole stock and overbored barrel. Chambered for 3.5 inch shells. X-Factor ported choke tube. Barrel is 20 inches and has adjustable fiber-optic front and rear sights. Weight is about 7.75 lbs. Available in Mossy Oak New Break-Up camo or Realtree Hardwoods Green camo.

NIB	Exc.	V.G.	Good	Fair	Poor
475	400	325	250	200	125

Ulti-Mag Tactical Turkey

Same as above but with extended pistol grip stock that is adjustable for length of pull from 10.75" to 14.5".

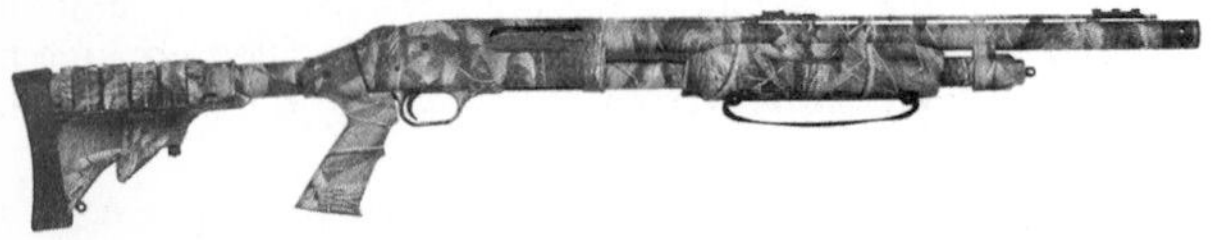

NIB	Exc.	V.G.	Good	Fair	Poor
475	400	325	250	200	125

Wild Turkey Federation

As above, with a Wild Turkey Federation medallion inlaid in the stock. Introduced in 1989.

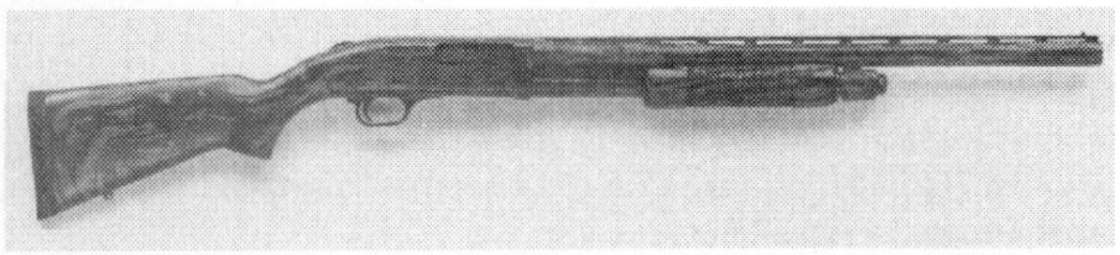

NIB	Exc.	V.G.	Good	Fair	Poor
475	400	325	250	200	125

American Field

This 12 gauge model has a checkered walnut stock, 28" ventilated rib barrel with Modified choke tube. Weight is about 7.7 lbs.

NIB	Exc.	V.G.	Good	Fair	Poor
300	275	225	200	150	100

MODEL 935 MAGNUM SERIES

The 935 Magnum series of guns was introduced in 2004.

Magnum Waterfowl Camo

This 12 gauge 3.5" semi-automatic shotgun is available with either a 26" or 28" vent rib overbored barrel with fiber optic bead and choke tubes. Offered with choice of Mossy Oak Break-Up or Advantage Max-4 camo pattern. Magazine capacity is 5 rounds of 3" and 4 rounds of 3.5". Weight is about 7.75 lbs.

NIB	Exc.	V.G.	Good	Fair	Poor
600	500	400	250	200	125

935 Magnum Slugster

Similar to above but with 24" fully rifled barrel, rifle sights, Realtree AP camo overall.

NIB	Exc.	V.G.	Good	Fair	Poor
600	500	400	250	200	125

935 Magnum Turkey/Deer Comb

Similar to above but with interchangeable 24" Turkey barrel, Mossy Oak New Break-up camo overall.

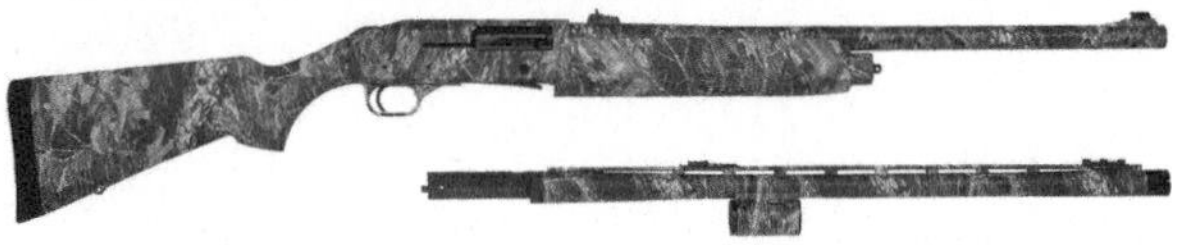

NIB	Exc.	V.G.	Good	Fair	Poor
700	600	500	350	275	150

Magnum Turkey Camo

This 12 gauge 3.5" model features a 24" vent rib overbored barrel with adjustable fiber optic sights. Ultra Full choke tube. Offered in Mossy Oak Break-Up or Hardwoods HD-Green. Weight is about 7.75 lbs.

NIB	Exc.	V.G.	Good	Fair	Poor
600	500	400	250	200	125

Magnum Waterfowl Synthetic

This 12 gauge 3.5" gun features a choice of 26" or 28" vent rib overbored barrel with choke tubes. Fiber optic bead. Matte black finish with black synthetic stock. Weight is about 7.75 lbs.

NIB	Exc.	V.G.	Good	Fair	Poor
550	450	350	250	150	125

Magnum Turkey Synthetic

As above but with 24" vent rib overbored barrel with Ultra Full choke tube. Weight is about 7.75 lbs.

NIB	Exc.	V.G.	Good	Fair	Poor
550	450	350	250	150	125

Magnum Waterfowl/Turkey Combo

Similar to above but with 24" Turkey and 28" Waterfowl barrels, Mossy Oak New Break-up finish overall. Suggested retail price: To be announced.

Grand Slam Turkey

This 12 gauge 3.5" model features a a 22" vent rib overbored barrel with Extra Full ported choke tube. Adjustable fiber optic sights. Offered in Real Tree Hardwoods green or Mossy Oak Break-Up camo pattern. Camo sling included. Weight is about 7.5 lbs.

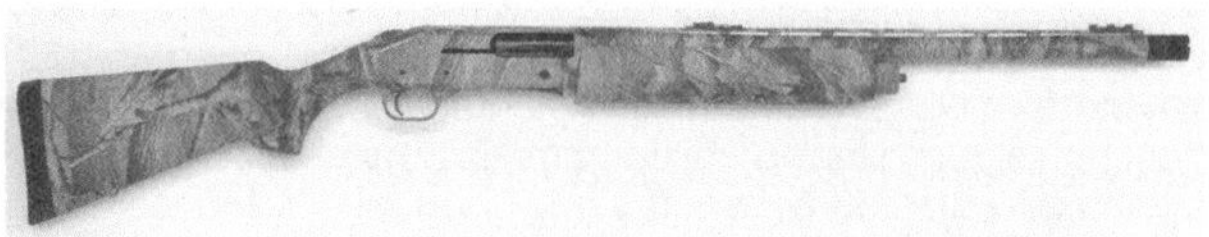

NIB	Exc.	V.G.	Good	Fair	Poor
650	550	450	275	225	150

MODEL 930 SERIES

This is a 12 gauge 3" chamber semi-automatic shotgun series introduced in 2005.

Field

This 12 gauge 3" gun is fitted with either 26" or 28" vent rib barrels with choke tubes. The barrel is ported. Checkered walnut stock with recoil pad. Magazine capacity is 5 rounds. Blued finish. Weight is about 7.75 lbs.

NIB	*Exc.*	*V.G.*	*Good*	*Fair*	*Poor*
525	425	325	225	175	125

Turkey

Fitted with a synthetic stock and 24" vent rib ported barrel. Chokes are extra full extended tubes. Offered with matte blue finish or camo finish. Weight is about 7.5 lbs.

NIB	*Exc.*	*V.G.*	*Good*	*Fair*	*Poor*
500	400	300	200	150	100

NOTE: Add $100 for camo finish.

Waterfowl

This model is fitted with a 28" vent rin ported barrel with choke tubes. Choice of matte blue or camo finish. Weight is about 7.75 lbs.

NIB	*Exc.*	*V.G.*	*Good*	*Fair*	*Poor*
500	400	300	200	150	100

NOTE: Add $100 for camo finish.

Slugster

This model features a 24" vent rib ported barrel with choice of plain or Monte Carlo synthetic stock. Matte blue or camo finish. Weight is about 7.5 lbs.

NIB	*Exc.*	*V.G.*	*Good*	*Fair*	*Poor*
525	425	325	225	175	125

NOTE: Add $100 for camo finish.

Tactical

This 3" 12 gauge has an 18.5" barrel and cylinder bore. Synthetic stock with matte black finish.

NIB	*Exc.*	*V.G.*	*Good*	*Fair*	*Poor*
500	400	300	200	150	100

Mossberg 930 Tactical Autoloader with Heat Shield

Similar to Model 930 Tactical but with ventilated heat shield handguard. Price: $626.

Road Blocker

Similar to above but with muzzle brake.

NIB	*Exc.*	*V.G.*	*Good*	*Fair*	*Poor*
525	425	325	225	175	125

SPX

Billed as a "home security" model, the 3" 12 gauge SPX has a seven-round magazine tube, 18.5" barrel, picatinny rail, ghost ring rear sight and fiber-optic front sight. Deduct 10 percent for white dot sights.

NIB	*Exc.*	*V.G.*	*Good*	*Fair*	*Poor*
600	500	400	275	150	125

Home Security/Field Combo

Combo unit with 18.5" Cylinder bore barrel and 28" ported Field barrel; black synthetic stock and matte black finish. Suggested retail price: To be announced.

Model 3000

A 12 or 20 gauge slide-action shotgun manufactured in a variety of barrel lengths and styles. Blued with a walnut stock. Also known as the Smith & Wesson Model 3000.

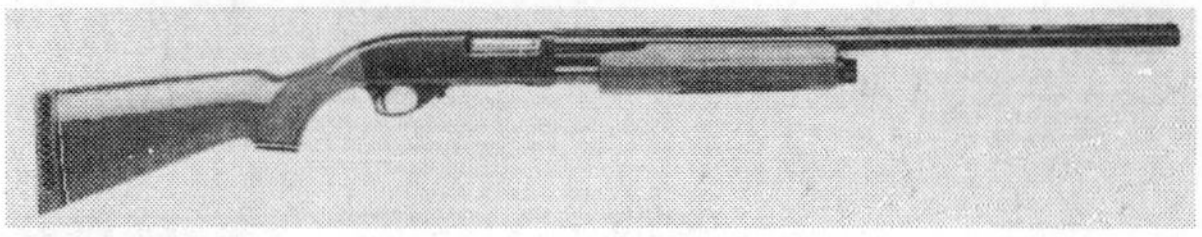

NIB	*Exc.*	*V.G.*	*Good*	*Fair*	*Poor*
—	325	250	175	125	75

Model 3000 Waterfowler

As above, but matte finished, fitted with sling swivels and accompanied by a camouflage sling. Produced in 1986.

NIB	*Exc.*	*V.G.*	*Good*	*Fair*	*Poor*
—	350	275	200	150	100

Model 3000 Law Enforcement

As above, with an 18.5" or 20" cylinder-bore barrel. Manufactured in 1986 and 1987.

NIB	*Exc.*	*V.G.*	*Good*	*Fair*	*Poor*
—	375	275	200	150	100

Model 1000

A 12 or 20 gauge semi-automatic shotgun manufactured in a variety of barrel lengths and styles, the receiver of an aluminum alloy and blued. Also known as the Smith & Wesson Model 1000. Offered in 1986 and 1987.

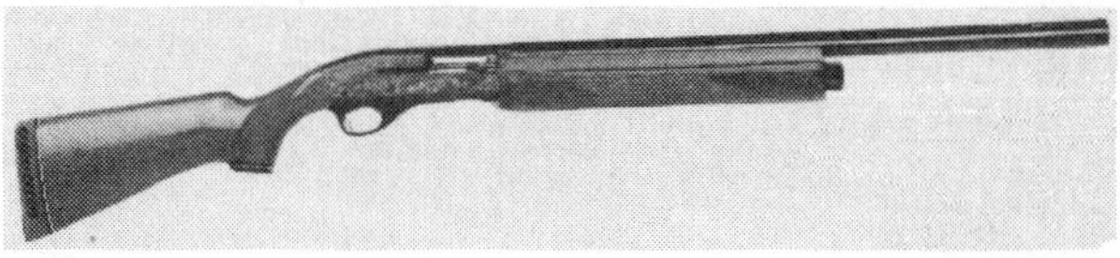

NIB	*Exc.*	*V.G.*	*Good*	*Fair*	*Poor*
—	300	250	200	150	100

Model 1000 Slug

As above, with a 22" barrel fitted with rifle sights. Offered in 1986 and 1987.

NIB	*Exc.*	*V.G.*	*Good*	*Fair*	*Poor*
—	325	250	200	125	100

MODEL 1000 SUPER SERIES

As above, with a steel receiver and a self-regulating gas system that allows the use of either standard or Magnum shells.

NIB	Exc.	V.G.	Good	Fair	Poor
—	375	300	250	150	100

Model 1000 Super Waterfowler

Matte finish.

NIB	Exc.	V.G.	Good	Fair	Poor
—	375	300	250	150	100

Model 1000 Super Slug

Rifle sights.

NIB	Exc.	V.G.	Good	Fair	Poor
—	375	300	250	150	100

Model 1000 Super Trap

30" high rib barrel.

NIB	Exc.	V.G.	Good	Fair	Poor
—	395	325	275	175	125

Model 1000 Super Skeet

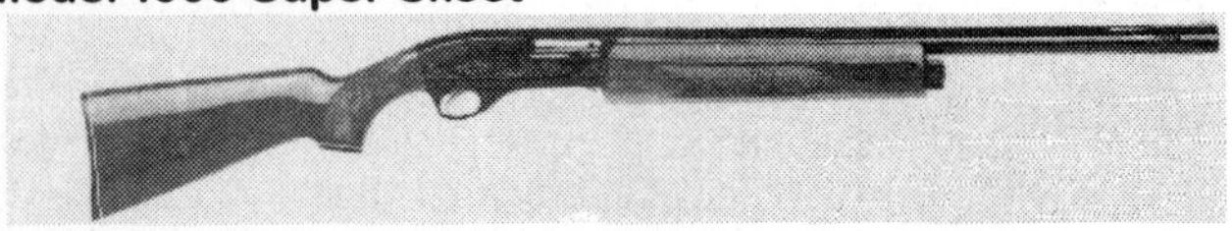

25" barrel.

NIB	Exc.	V.G.	Good	Fair	Poor
—	395	325	275	175	125

Model 5500 MKI I

A 12 gauge semi-automatic shotgun supplied with either a 26" barrel for 2.75" shells or a 28" barrel for 3" shells. Blued with a walnut stock. Introduced in 1989.

NIB	Exc.	V.G.	Good	Fair	Poor
300	235	200	175	150	125

MODEL 9200 SERIES

This model has a variety of configurations. It is a 12 gauge semi-automatic with a choice of walnut stock or camo synthetic stock. Barrel lengths are from 22" to 28". Weights range from 7 to 7.7 lbs.

Viking Grade

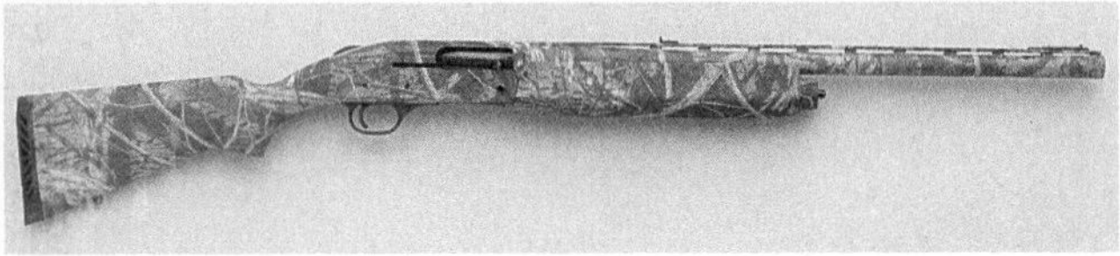

Mossy Oak Shadow Branch Camo

NIB	Exc.	V.G.	Good	Fair	Poor
350	300	275	200	100	75

USST Crown Grade

NIB	Exc.	V.G.	Good	Fair	Poor
400	350	300	200	100	75

Model 9200 Combos

NIB	Exc.	V.G.	Good	Fair	Poor
475	425	350	250	150	100

Model 9200 Special Hunter

28" vent rib barrel with synthetic stock.

NIB	Exc.	V.G.	Good	Fair	Poor
475	425	350	250	150	100

Model 9200 Deer Combo

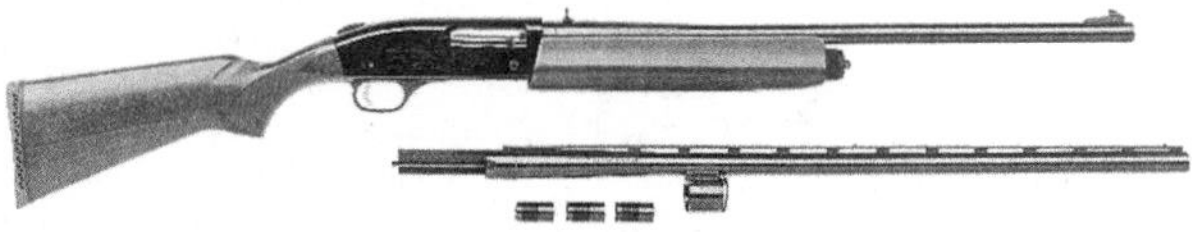

NIB	Exc.	V.G.	Good	Fair	Poor
475	425	350	250	150	100

Model 9200 Turkey Camos

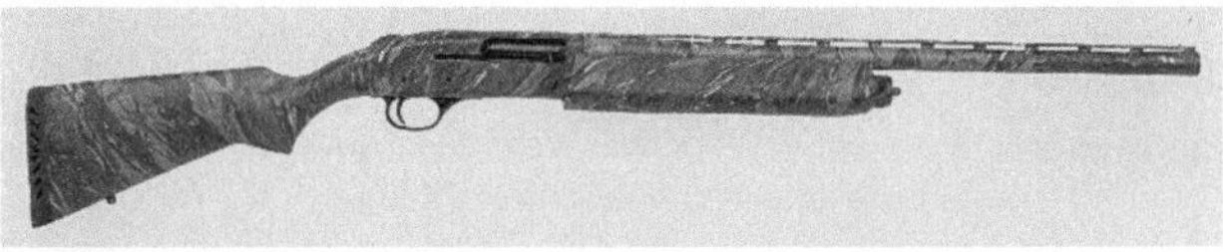

NIB	Exc.	V.G.	Good	Fair	Poor
475	425	350	250	150	100

Model 9200 Crown Grade Bantam

NIB	Exc.	V.G.	Good	Fair	Poor
395	350	300	250	125	75

Model 9200 Jungle Gun

This is a 12 gauge aut loader fitted with a plain 18.5" barrel with bead sight. Barrel choked Cylinder. Chambers are 2-3/4". Magazine capacity is 5 rounds. Parkerized finish. Synthetic stock.

NIB	Exc.	V.G.	Good	Fair	Poor
525	450	325	200	150	125

Model SA-20

This synthetic-stocked, matte black 20 gauge autoloader is chambered for 3-inch shells. It has a 28" or 26" vent-rib barrel and comes with five choke tubes. Weight is about 6 lbs. The Bantam model has a 1-inch shorter length of pull and 24" barrel and weighs about 5.6 lbs. Introduced in 2008.

NIB	Exc.	V.G.	Good	Fair	Poor
400	350	300	200	100	75

SA-20 Tactical

Mossberg's SA-20 Tactical Autoloader is in 20 gauge only. Easy-Load elevator facilitates fast, one-handed reloading. Top-mounted Picatinny-style rail accommodates optical sights, while the magazine tube rail allows mounting lights, lasers and other accessories. Ghost ring rear and fiber optic front sights. Gas-operated action. Capacity: 4+1. Cylinder-bore barrel is 20-inches long. Available with conventional black synthetic or synthetic pistol grip stock. Weight is approx. 6 pounds.

NIB	*Exc.*	*V.G.*	*Good*	*Fair*	*Poor*
480	440	400	370	320	280

RESERVE SERIES

Introduced in 2005 this is an over-and-under gun in 12, 20, 28 gauge as well as .410 bore. Made in Turkey.

Silver Reserve Field

Offered in 12 gauge with 28" vent rib barrels, 20 gauge with 26" or 28" vent rib barrels, 28 gauge with 26" vent rib barrels, .410 with 26" vent rib barrels. All gauge have choke tubes except for the .410 with fixed chokes. Steel silvered receiver with scroll engraving and game senes in gold. Checkered walnut stock with recoil pad. Single trigger. Weight is from 6 lbs. to 7.7 lbs. depending on gauge. Add 20 percent for 28 and .410.

NIB	*Exc.*	*V.G.*	*Good*	*Fair*	*Poor*
500	400	300	200	150	100

Silver Reserve Sporting

As above but in 12 gauge only with 28" vent 10mm rib barrels with choke tubes and ported barrels. Weight is about 7.7 lbs.

NIB	*Exc.*	*V.G.*	*Good*	*Fair*	*Poor*
650	550	425	300	225	125

Silver Reserve Side-by-Side

New in 2008, the side-by-side version of the Silver Reserve comes in 12 gauge with 28" or 26" barrels and 20 and 28 gauge with 26" barrels. The stock and forend is select black walnut with satin finish. The receiver is satin-finished silver with scroll engraving and barrels are blued. Bores are chrome-plated. All models come with five choke tubes. Weight is 6.4 to 6.5 lbs. for 20 and 28 gauges; 7.2 lbs. for 12 gauge.

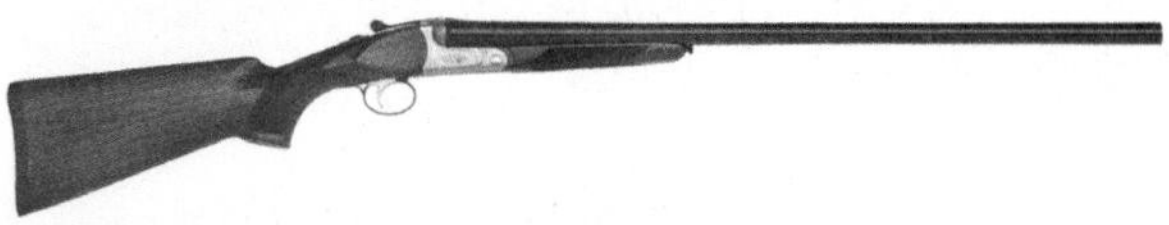

NIB	*Exc.*	*V.G.*	*Good*	*Fair*	*Poor*
750	650	550	400	250	150

Onyx Reserve Sporting SxS

Similar to Silver Reserve Sporting but with blued receiver.

NIB	*Exc.*	*V.G.*	*Good*	*Fair*	*Poor*
675	575	450	300	175	125

Onyx Reserve Side-by-Side

This model is similar to the Silver Reserve but with a blued receiver.

NIB	*Exc.*	*V.G.*	*Good*	*Fair*	*Poor*
800	700	575	400	225	150

MOUNTAIN ARMS

Ozark, Missouri

Wildcat

Similar to Rau Arms Wildcat (q.v.) and Garcia Bronco but with plastic stock inserts. A takedown model was offered as well. Estimated 6,243 produced 1971-1978. The first several thousand bore the Rau Arms label.

NIB	*Exc.*	*V.G.*	*Good*	*Fair*	*Poor*
225	175	125	100	65	35

MOUNTAIN RIFLES, INC.

Palmer, Alaska

Mountaineer

This bolt-action rifle, introduced in 1997, is built on a Remington action with Model 70 style bolt release. A factory muzzlebrake is installed with open sights. A Timney trigger is standard. Stock is fiberglass. Finish is Parkerized. This model is chambered for many different calibers, from .223 Rem. to .416 Rem., including Dakota and Weatherby cartridges. Weight starts at about 6 lbs. and is dependent on caliber. There are several options that will affect price. A left-hand model is offered as an option.

NIB	*Exc.*	*V.G.*	*Good*	*Fair*	*Poor*
2195	1750	1400	1100	750	300

Super Mountaineer

Similar to the Mountaineer model but the bolt is fluted and hollow. Barrel is match grade stainless steel with muzzlebrake. Kevlar/Graphite stock. Wide variety of calibers. Weight starts at about 4.25 lbs. depending on caliber.

NIB	*Exc.*	*V.G.*	*Good*	*Fair*	*Poor*
2895	2350	1900	1500	1000	400

Pro Mountaineer

This model is built on a Winchester Model 70 action. Premium match grade barrel with muzzlebrake. Model 70 trigger. Stainless steel matte finish. Kevlar/Graphite stock. Wide variety of calibers. Weight starts at about 6 lbs.

NIB	*Exc.*	*V.G.*	*Good*	*Fair*	*Poor*
2895	2350	2350	1900	1500	400

Pro Safari

This model is built on an MRI action with controlled feed. Premium match grade barrel. Timney trigger. Matte blue finish. Exhibition grade walnut stock with custom bottom metal. Weight starts at about 7 lbs. depending on caliber. Caliber from .223 to .458 Lott.

NIB	*Exc.*	*V.G.*	*Good*	*Fair*	*Poor*
4495	3500	2300	1750	1200	500

Ultra Mountaineer

Built on an MRI action with premium match grade barrel and muzzlebrake. Timney trigger. Parkerized finish. Kevlar/Graphite stock. Calibers from .223 to .505 Gibbs. Weight begins at 5 lbs. depending on caliber.

NIB	Exc.	V.G.	Good	Fair	Poor
2995	2500	2200	1900	1500	400

NOTE: Add $500 for Rigby-length calibers.

MURFEESBORO ARMORY

Murfeesboro, Tennessee

Established in 1861 by William Ledbetter. Made copies of U.S. Model 1841 Rifle complete with patchbox and double strapped nose cap. Barrel bands pinned to stock. Between 270 and 390 made from October of 1861 through March of 1862. Overall length 48-3/4"; barrel length 33"; .54 caliber. Unmarked except for serial number on various parts including the barrel.

NIB	Exc.	V.G.	Good	Fair	Poor
—	—	27500	16500	6600	2000

MURRAY, J. P.

Columbus, Georgia

Percussion Rifle

A .58 caliber percussion rifle with a 33" barrel, full stock and brass mounts. Also made with a 23.5" to 24" barrel as a carbine. The lock marked "J.P. Murray/Columbus Ga." Several hundred were manufactured between 1862 and 1864.

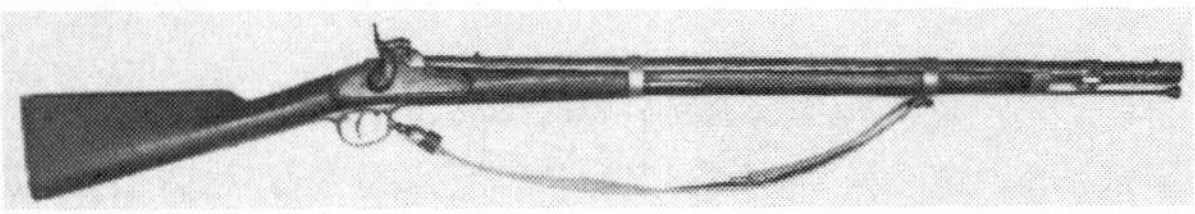

Courtesy Milwaukee Public Museum, Milwaukee, Wisconsin

NIB	Exc.	V.G.	Good	Fair	Poor
—	—	50000	33000	14000	1500

MUSGRAVE

Republic of South Africa

RSA NR I Single-Shot Target Rifle

A .308 caliber single-shot bolt-action rifle with a 26" barrel, match sights, adjustable trigger and target-style stock. Made of walnut. Manufactured between 1971 and 1976.

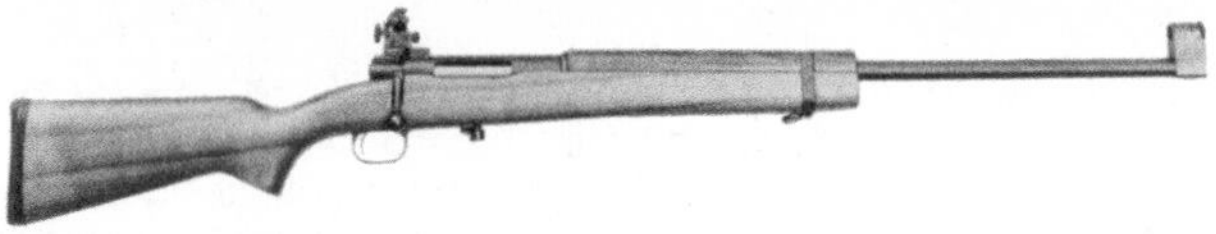

NIB	Exc.	V.G.	Good	Fair	Poor
—	550	425	300	225	125

Valiant NR6

A .243, .270, .308, .30-06, and 7mm Remington Magnum caliber bolt-action sporting rifle with a 24" barrel, open sights and English-style stock. Imported from 1971 to 1976.

NIB	Exc.	V.G.	Good	Fair	Poor
—	450	350	275	175	125

Premier NR5

As above, with a 26" barrel and pistol-grip Monte Carlo-style stock. Discontinued in 1976.

NIB	Exc.	V.G.	Good	Fair	Poor
—	550	450	325	225	150

MUSKETEER RIFLES

Firearms International/Garcia
Washington, D.C.

Sporter

A .243 to .300 Winchester Magnum caliber bolt-action rifle with a 24" barrel without sights, and Monte Carlo-style stock. Imported between 1963 and 1972. Add 20 percent for magnum chamberings.

NIB	Exc.	V.G.	Good	Fair	Poor
—	500	375	275	195	120

Deluxe Sporter

As above, with an adjustable trigger and more finely figured walnut stock.

NIB	Exc.	V.G.	Good	Fair	Poor
—	550	400	300	200	125

Carbine

The Sporter with a 20" barrel.

NIB	Exc.	V.G.	Good	Fair	Poor
—	500	375	275	195	120

N

NAVY ARMS COMPANY

Martinsburg, West Virginia

Not a manufacturer but an importer. Founded in 1957 by Val Forgett to enhance the shooting of blackpowder firearms without destroying the originals. The first replica was the Colt 1851 Navy. Thus, the name of the new company, "Navy Arms." In the early 1980s Navy Arms began importing surplus firearms from European countries. Navy Arms continues to offer both blackpowder replicas and foreign imports. For a short period of time the company imported double-barrel shotguns. This was discontinued in 1990. Most if not all of the guns listed below are also to be found under the manufacturers' names as well as those of other importers.

SHOTGUNS

Model 83

A 12 or 20 gauge Magnum Over/Under shotgun manufactured in a variety of barrel lengths and styles with double triggers and extractors. Blued, engraved, with a walnut stock. Introduced in 1985.

NIB	*Exc.*	*V.G.*	*Good*	*Fair*	*Poor*
500	400	275	200	175	100

Model 93

As above, with automatic ejectors.

NIB	*Exc.*	*V.G.*	*Good*	*Fair*	*Poor*
575	475	300	250	200	100

Model 95

As above, with a single trigger and screw-in choke tubes.

NIB	*Exc.*	*V.G.*	*Good*	*Fair*	*Poor*
600	500	350	250	200	100

Model 96 Sportsman

As above, in 12 gauge only with a gold-plated receiver.

NIB	*Exc.*	*V.G.*	*Good*	*Fair*	*Poor*
600	500	350	250	200	100

Model 100

A 12, 20, 28 or .410 bore Over/Under boxlock shotgun with 26" ventilated rib barrels, single trigger and extractors. Blued, chrome-plated, with a walnut stock. Introduced in 1989. Add 20 percent for .410.

NIB	*Exc.*	*V.G.*	*Good*	*Fair*	*Poor*
450	350	200	150	100	75

Model 100 Side-by-Side

A 12 or 20 gauge Magnum boxlock double-barrel shotgun with 27.5" barrels, double triggers and extractors. Blued with a walnut stock. Imported between 1985 and 1987.

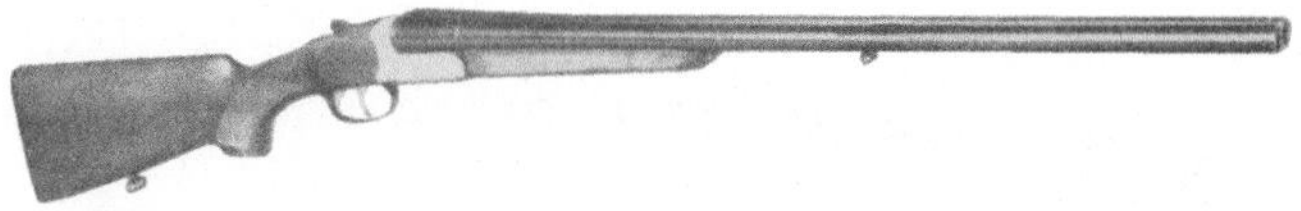

NIB	*Exc.*	*V.G.*	*Good*	*Fair*	*Poor*
—	475	350	250	200	100

Model 150

As above, with automatic ejectors.

NIB	*Exc.*	*V.G.*	*Good*	*Fair*	*Poor*
—	495	375	300	225	125

Model 105

A 12, 20 or .410 bore folding single barrel shotgun with a 26" or 28" barrel, chrome-plated engraved receiver, blued barrel and hardwood stock. Introduced in 1985.

NIB	*Exc.*	*V.G.*	*Good*	*Fair*	*Poor*
125	80	75	65	50	35

Model 105 Deluxe

As above, with vent rib barrel and a checkered walnut stock.

NIB	*Exc.*	*V.G.*	*Good*	*Fair*	*Poor*
150	100	85	75	60	45

REPLICA LONG GUNS

Harpers Ferry Flint Rifle

This model is a copy of the 1803 rifle in the original .54 caliber. It features a rust blued 35" barrel. Weight is 8.5 lbs.

NIB	*Exc.*	*V.G.*	*Good*	*Fair*	*Poor*
600	475	350	300	200	100

Harpers Ferry "Journey of Discovery" Rifle

Similar to the Harpers Ferry Flint Rifle above but with oil finished walnut stock, brass fittings brass patchbox engraved "Lewis and Clark \xd4 Journey of Discovery';1803 to 1806." Introduced in 2003.

NIB	*Exc.*	*V.G.*	*Good*	*Fair*	*Poor*
775	600	475	275	175	100

Brown Bess Musket

This replica is a copy of the second model used between 1760 and 1776. Bright finish on metal and one-piece walnut stock with polished brass locks. Barrel is 42" and weight is 9.5 lbs.

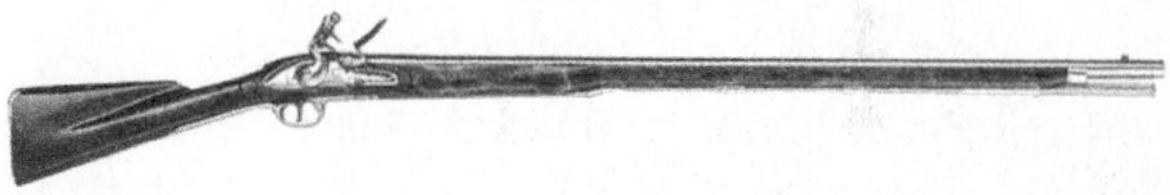

NIB	*Exc.*	*V.G.*	*Good*	*Fair*	*Poor*
800	625	500	300	200	100

Brown Bess Carbine

Same as above but fitted with a 30" barrel. Weighs 7.75 lbs.

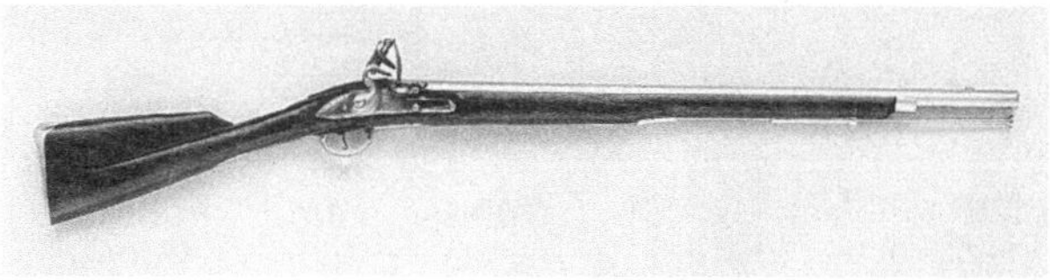

NIB	*Exc.*	*V.G.*	*Good*	*Fair*	*Poor*
800	625	500	300	200	100

1777 Charleville Musket

Copy of French flintlock in .69 caliber. Fittings are steel with brass front sight and brass flashpan. Barrel length is 44.625" and weight is about 8.75 lbs

NIB	*Exc.*	*V.G.*	*Good*	*Fair*	*Poor*
900	700	550	400	300	150

1777 Standard Charleville Musket

Same as above with polished steel barrel and select walnut stock.

NIB	Exc.	V.G.	Good	Fair	Poor
900	700	550	400	300	150

1816 M.T. Wickham Musket

Furnished in .69 caliber with steel ramrod with button head. Brass flashpan and walnut stock are standard.

NIB	Exc.	V.G.	Good	Fair	Poor
600	550	450	350	250	200

1808 Springfield Musket

This model is a U.S. copy of the 1763 Charleville musket with 1808 Springfield markings. Barrel length is 44" and weight is 8.75 lbs.

NIB	Exc.	V.G.	Good	Fair	Poor
950	800	600	400	200	100

Pennsylvania Long Rifle

This model is offered in either percussion or flintlock ignition and is offered in a choice of .32 caliber or .45 caliber. It has an octagonal 40.5" rust blued barrel, polished lock, double set triggers, and brass furniture on a walnut stock. Weighs 7.5 lbs.

Pennsylvania Long Rifle Percussion

NIB	Exc.	V.G.	Good	Fair	Poor
450	375	250	200	150	100

Pennsylvania Long Rifle Flintlock

NIB	Exc.	V.G.	Good	Fair	Poor
475	400	275	225	150	100

Kentucky Rifle

Offered in either percussion or flintlock ignition it has a blue steel barrel, case colored lockplate, and a polished brass patch box inletted into a walnut stock. The barrel length is 35" and the rifle is available in .45 oz. 50 caliber. Weight is 6 lbs. 14 oz.

Kentucky Rifle Percussion

NIB	Exc.	V.G.	Good	Fair	Poor
475	325	200	150	100	75

Kentucky Rifle Flintlock

NIB	Exc.	V.G.	Good	Fair	Poor
495	335	225	150	100	75

Mortimer Flintlock Rifle

Offered in .54 caliber with rust blued barrel, walnut stock with cheekpiece and checkered straight grip. It also has a external safety and sling swivels. Barrel length is 36" and weight is 9 lbs. Optional shotgun barrel. Made by Pedersoli.

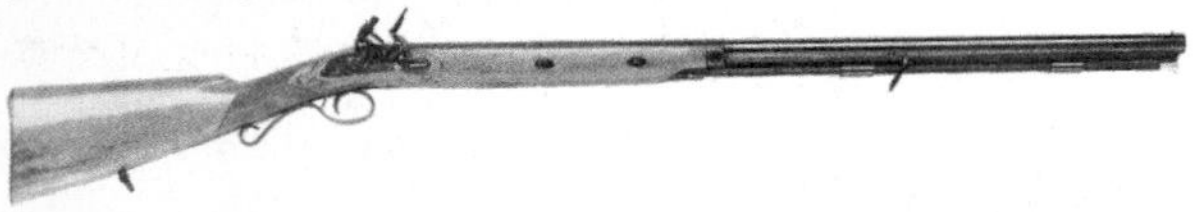

NIB	Exc.	V.G.	Good	Fair	Poor
900	750	600	500	450	150

NOTE: Optional shotgun barrel add $240.

Tryon Creedmoor Rifle

This .45 caliber model features a heavy blued 33" octagonal barrel, hooded front sight, adjustable tang sight, double set triggers, sling swivels, and a walnut stock. Weighs about 9.5 lbs.

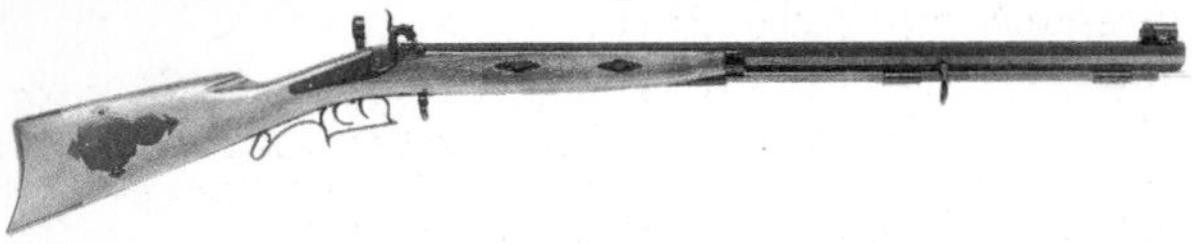

NIB	Exc.	V.G.	Good	Fair	Poor
800	600	525	450	400	150

Standard Tryon Rifle

Same as above but without target sights.

NIB	Exc.	V.G.	Good	Fair	Poor
700	500	350	300	250	200

Deluxe Tryon Rifle

Same as above but with polished and engraved lock and patch box.

NIB	Exc.	V.G.	Good	Fair	Poor
750	525	375	325	250	200

Parker-Hale Whitworth Rifle

This is a replica of a British sniper rifle, .451 caliber, used by the Confederates during the Civil War. Round barrel is 36" and features a globe front sight and ladder rear sight. The walnut stock is hand checkered. Weighs 9 lbs. 10 oz.

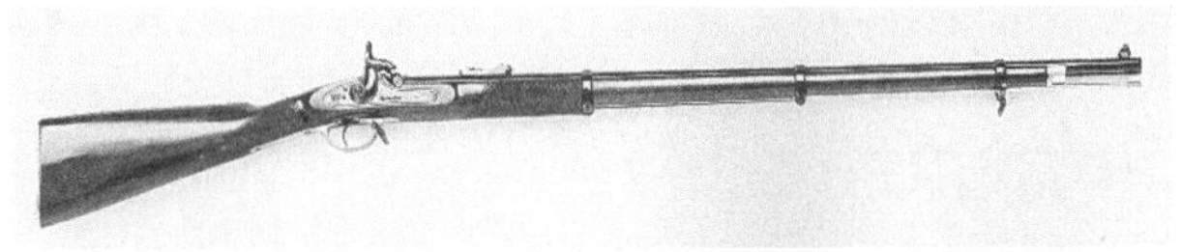

NIB	Exc.	V.G.	Good	Fair	Poor
850	675	600	450	300	150

NOTE: Limited edition telescope add $150.

Parker-Hale Volunteer Rifle

A .451 caliber rifle with hand checkered walnut stock. Fitted with 32" barrel with globe front sight and ladder rear sight. Weighs 9.5 lbs.

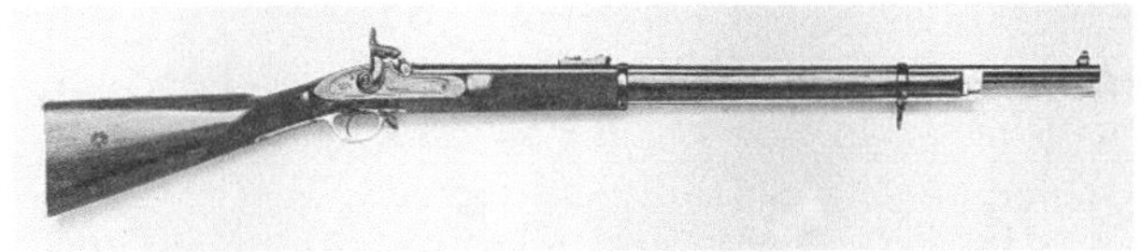

NIB	Exc.	V.G.	Good	Fair	Poor
825	650	550	400	300	150

Parker-Hale 3 Band Volunteer Rifle

Same basic specifications as Whitworth rifle but furnished with Alexander Henry rifling.

NIB	Exc.	V.G.	Good	Fair	Poor
750	650	600	400	250	50

Rigby Target Rifle

The 1880s replica is chambered for the .451 caliber. It is fitted with adjustable front sight and vernier tang sight. The lock, breech plug, trigger guard, buttplate, and escutcheons are case colored. Barrel length is 32" and weight is 7 lbs. 12 oz.

NIB	Exc.	V.G.	Good	Fair	Poor
700	500	450	300	200	100

1861 Springfield Rifle

This .58 caliber replica is fitted with an 1855-style hammer. Barrel length is 40" and weight is 10 lbs. 4 oz.

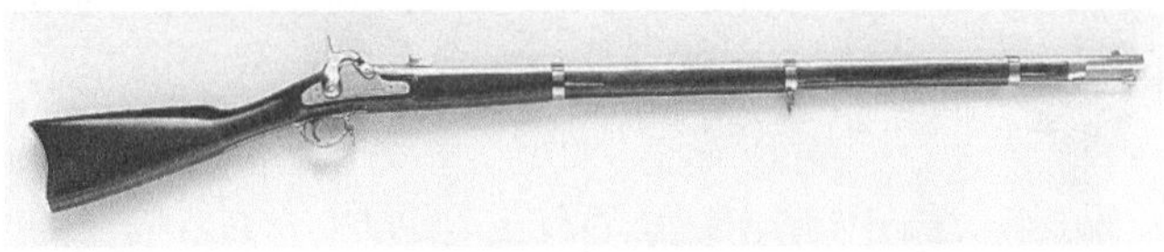

NIB	Exc.	V.G.	Good	Fair	Poor
550	425	350	300	200	100

Model 1873 Springfield Officer's Trapdoor

This model features a single set trigger, case colored breechblock, deluxe walnut stock, adjustable rear peep sight with Beech front sight. Chambered for the .45-70 cartridge and fitted with a 26" round barrel. Weight is about 8 lbs. Introduced in 2003.

NIB	*Exc.*	*V.G.*	*Good*	*Fair*	*Poor*
900	750	495	350	300	200

1862 C.S. Richmond Rifle

This Confederate rifle is .58 caliber and is a faithful reproduction of those produced at the Richmond Armory. Barrel length is 40". Weighs 10 lbs. 4 oz.

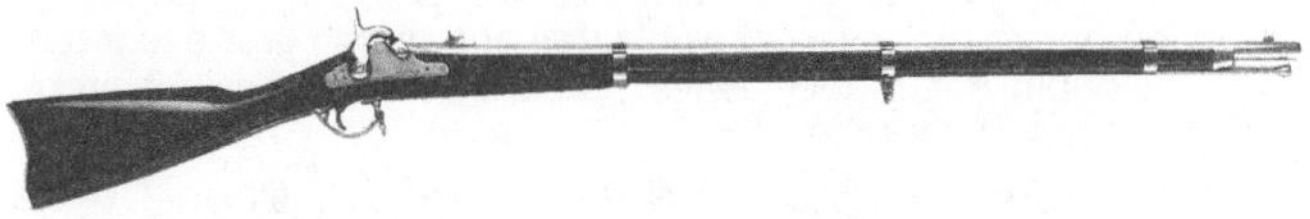

NIB	*Exc.*	*V.G.*	*Good*	*Fair*	*Poor*
550	425	350	300	200	100

J.P. Murray Carbine

This Confederate cavalry .58 caliber carbine has a case colored lock and brass furniture on a walnut stock. Barrel length is 23.5" and weight is 8 lbs. 5 oz.

NIB	*Exc.*	*V.G.*	*Good*	*Fair*	*Poor*
495	325	250	200	150	100

1863 Springfield Rifle

An exact replica of the famous Springfield Musket. Barrel is 40" with 3 barrel bands. All metal parts are finished bright. Weighs 9.5 lbs.

NIB	*Exc.*	*V.G.*	*Good*	*Fair*	*Poor*
550	425	350	300	200	100

1841 Mississippi Rifle

Also known as the "Yager" rifle; offered in either .54 or .58 caliber. Barrel length is 33" and weighs 9.5 lbs.

NIB	*Exc.*	*V.G.*	*Good*	*Fair*	*Poor*
450	325	250	200	150	100

Zouave Rifle

This Civil War replica is a .58 caliber with polished brass hardware and blued 33" barrel. Weighs 9 lbs.

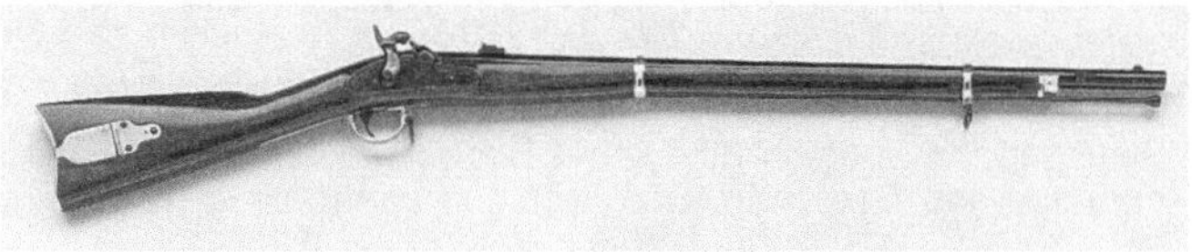

NIB	*Exc.*	*V.G.*	*Good*	*Fair*	*Poor*
450	325	250	200	150	100

Parker-Hale 1861 Musketoon

Made by Gibbs Rifle Company using 130-year-old gauges for reference. This .577 caliber replica features a 24" barrel with folding ladder military sight. The stock is walnut and the lock is case colored. All furniture is polished brass. Weighs 7.5 lbs.

NIB	*Exc.*	*V.G.*	*Good*	*Fair*	*Poor*
400	325	250	200	150	100

Navy Arms Musketoon

Same as above but manufactured in Italy.

NIB	*Exc.*	*V.G.*	*Good*	*Fair*	*Poor*
400	325	250	200	150	100

Parker-Hale 1858 Two Band Musket

This .577 caliber model is based on the 1858 Enfield naval pattern. Fitted with a military sight graduated to 1,100 yards. Case colored lock and walnut stock with brass fittings. Barrel length is 33" and weighs 8.5 lbs.

NIB	*Exc.*	*V.G.*	*Good*	*Fair*	*Poor*
550	425	350	300	200	100

Navy Arms 1858 Two Band Musket

Same as above but built in Italy.

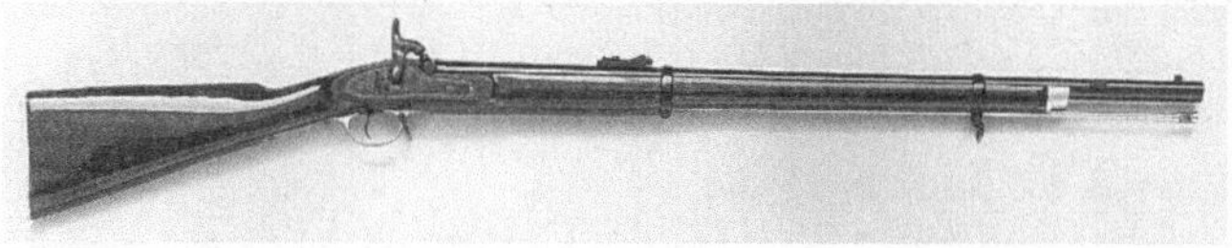

NIB	*Exc.*	*V.G.*	*Good*	*Fair*	*Poor*
450	325	250	200	150	100

Parker-Hale Three Band Musket

This replica is based on the design produced between 1853 and 1863. The rear sight is based on an 1853 model graduated to 900 yards. Is fitted with a case colored lock and walnut stock with brass furniture. Barrel is 39" and weighs 9 lbs.

NIB	*Exc.*	*V.G.*	*Good*	*Fair*	*Poor*
600	475	400	300	200	100

Navy Arms Three Band Musket

Same as above but produced in Italy.

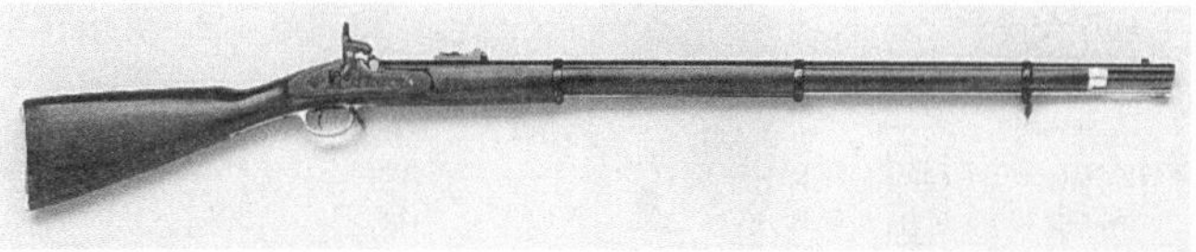

NIB	*Exc.*	*V.G.*	*Good*	*Fair*	*Poor*
475	350	300	250	200	100

Navy Arms Revolving Carbine

Fitted with a 20" barrel and chambered for the .357 Magnum, .44-40, or .45 Colt cartridge. This model has a revolving 6-shot cylinder. Straight-grip stock with brass buttplate and trigger guard. The action is based on the Remington Model 1874 revolver. Introduced in 1968 and discontinued in 1984.

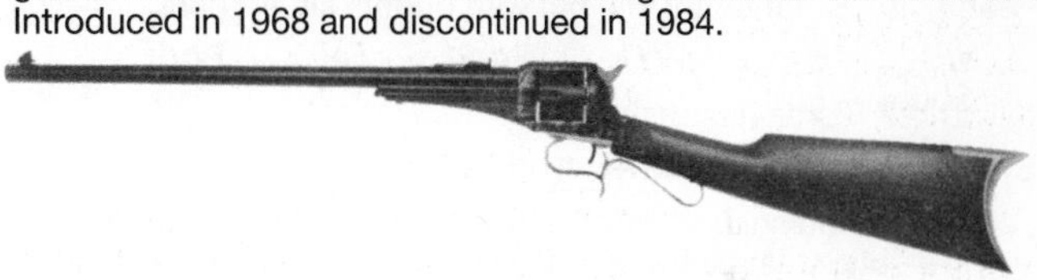

NIB	*Exc.*	*V.G.*	*Good*	*Fair*	*Poor*
600	500	400	300	200	100

1859 Sharps Infantry Rifle

This is a .54 caliber copy of the three band Sharps. Barrel length is 30". Case hardened receiver and patch box. Blued barrel and walnut stock. Weight is about 8.5 lbs.

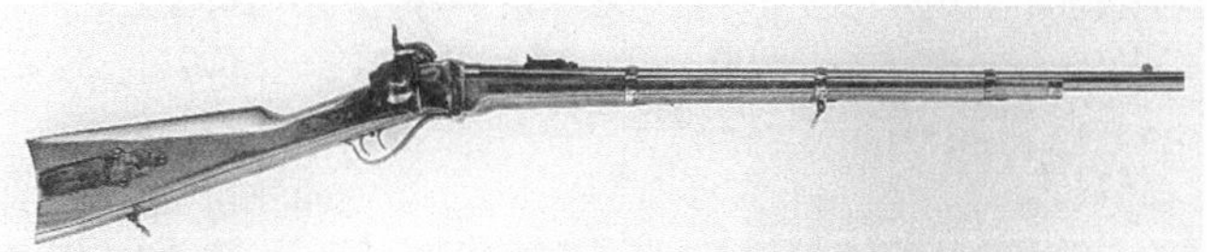

NIB	*Exc.*	*V.G.*	*Good*	*Fair*	*Poor*
1150	800	600	400	300	150

1859 Berdan Sharps Rifle

Similar to the 1859 Sharps above but with double set triggers.

NIB	*Exc.*	*V.G.*	*Good*	*Fair*	*Poor*
1200	850	650	450	325	150

1873 Sharps No. 2 Creedmore

Chambered for the .45-70 cartridge and fitted with a 30" round barrel. Polished nickel receiver. Target-grade rear tang sight and front globe sight with inserts. Checkered walnut stock with pistol grip. Weight is about 10 lbs. Introduced in 2002.

NIB	*Exc.*	*V.G.*	*Good*	*Fair*	*Poor*
1425	1000	750	550	375	200

Sharps #2 Silhouette Rifle

This model is identical to the standard No. 2 above but with a full octagon barrel. Weight is about 10.5 lbs. Introduced in 2003.

NIB	Exc.	V.G.	Good	Fair	Poor
1325	1000	750	550	375	200

Sharps #2 Sporting Rifle

Same as the No. 2 standard rifle but with case colored receiver. Introduced in 2003.

NIB	Exc.	V.G.	Good	Fair	Poor
1425	1000	750	550	375	200

1873 Sharps Quigley

This model is chambered for the .45-70 cartridge and fitted with a heavy 34" octagon barrel. Case hardened receiver with military patchbox. Open sights. Weight is about 13 lbs. Introduced in 2002.

NIB	Exc.	V.G.	Good	Fair	Poor
1490	1100	850	625	395	225

1874 Sharps Infantry Rifle

This model is fitted with a 30" round barrel and chambered for the .45-70 cartridge. Blued barrel with case hardened receiver. Walnut stock with 3 barrel bands. Weight is about 8.5 lbs.

NIB	Exc.	V.G.	Good	Fair	Poor
1150	800	600	400	300	150

1874 Sharps Sniper Rifle

Same as 1874 Infantry rifle but with double set triggers.

NIB	Exc.	V.G.	Good	Fair	Poor
1200	850	650	450	325	150

Sharps Cavalry Carbine

A breech-loading .54 caliber carbine with 22" blued barrel. Military-style sights, walnut stocks, and saddle bar with ring are standard. Weighs 7 lbs. 12 oz.

NIB	Exc.	V.G.	Good	Fair	Poor
1050	800	600	400	300	150

Sharps Cavalry Carbine Cartridge Model

Same as above but chambered for the .45-70 Government cartridge.

NIB	Exc.	V.G.	Good	Fair	Poor
1150	800	600	400	300	150

1874 Sharps Plains Rifle

This model features a case colored receiver, blued barrel, and checkered walnut stock. Offered in .44-70 or .54 caliber percussion. Barrel length is 28.5". Weight is 8 lbs. 10 oz.

NIB	Exc.	V.G.	Good	Fair	Poor
1150	800	600	400	300	150

1874 Sharps Sporting Rifle

Similar to the above model but features a full pistol grip, 32" medium weight octagonal barrel, double set triggers, and case colored frame. Weight is about 10.75 lbs.

NIB	Exc.	V.G.	Good	Fair	Poor
1325	1000	750	550	375	200

1874 Sharps Buffalo Rifle

Chambered for the .45-70 or .45-90 and fitted with a 28" heavy octagon barrel. Buttstock is checkered. Weight is approximately 12 lbs.

NIB	Exc.	V.G.	Good	Fair	Poor
1325	1000	750	550	375	200

1874 Sharps No. 3 Long Range Rifle

Built by Pedersoli this rifle is fitted with a 34" medium weight octagon barrel, globe target front sight and match grade rear tang sight. Double set trigger. Case hardened frame. Walnut stock. Weight is about 11 lbs.

NIB	Exc.	V.G.	Good	Fair	Poor
1800	1325	950	725	400	300

1873 Winchester Rifle

This replica features a case colored receiver, blued octagon 24" barrel, and walnut stocks. Offered in either .44-40 or .45 Long Colt. Weighs about 8 lbs. 4 oz.

NIB	Exc.	V.G.	Good	Fair	Poor
900	725	600	500	400	200

1873 Winchester Carbine

Same specifications as rifle above but fitted with a 19" round barrel, blued receiver, and saddle ring. Weighs 7 lbs. 4 oz.

NIB	Exc.	V.G.	Good	Fair	Poor
900	725	600	500	400	200

1873 Winchester Sporting Rifle

This model features a 24.25" octagonal barrel, case colored receiver, and checkered pistol grip. Offered in .44-40 or. 45 Long Colt. Weighs about 8 lbs. 14 oz.

NIB	Exc.	V.G.	Good	Fair	Poor
950	750	650	525	400	200

1873 Sporting Long Range Rifle

Similar to the Sporting Rifle above but chambered for the .44-40 cartridge and fitted with a 30" octagon barrel. Long-range rear tang sight. Weight is about 7.5 lbs. Introduced in 2002.

NIB	Exc.	V.G.	Good	Fair	Poor
1075	850	750	625	500	250

1873 Border Model

Introduced in 2000 this model features a 20" blued octagon barrel with buckhorn rear sight. Magazine capacity is 10 rounds. Checkered pistol-grip stock is walnut with oil finish. Chambered for the .357 Mag., .44-40, or .45 Colt cartridge.

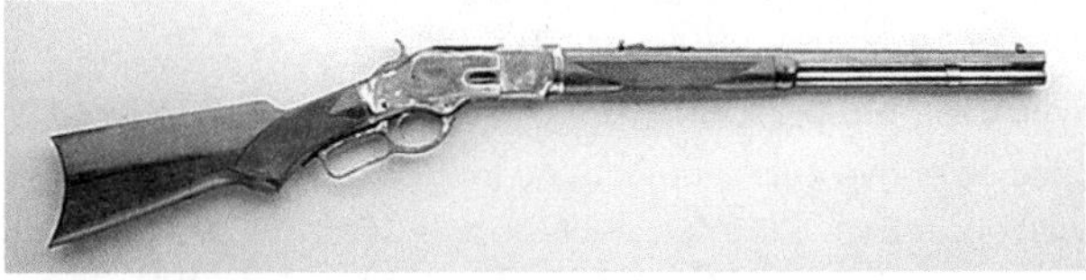

NIB	Exc.	V.G.	Good	Fair	Poor
975	800	700	550	450	225

1866 "Yellowboy" Rifle

This model features a brass receiver, 24" octagon barrel, and walnut stocks. Weighs 8.5 lbs.

NIB	Exc.	V.G.	Good	Fair	Poor
850	675	525	450	300	150

1866 "Yellowboy" Carbine

Same as above but fitted with a 19" round barrel and saddle ring. Weighs 7 lbs. 4 oz.

NIB	*Exc.*	*V.G.*	*Good*	*Fair*	*Poor*
850	675	525	450	300	150

1866 "Yellowboy" Short Rifle

Introduced in 2000 this model features a 20" barrel with buckhorn rear sight. Walnut stock with oil finish. Receiver is yellow brass. Chambered for the .38 Special, .44-40, or .45 Colt cartridge. Magazine capacity is 10 rounds.

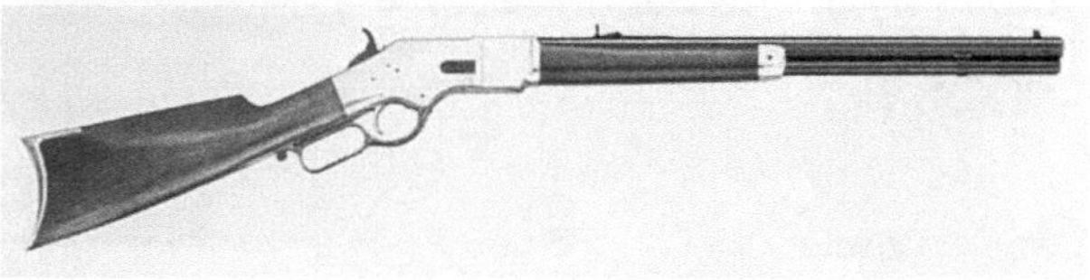

NIB	*Exc.*	*V.G.*	*Good*	*Fair*	*Poor*
850	675	525	450	300	150

Iron Frame Henry

This is a replica of the famous and rare .44-40 Iron Frame Henry that features a case colored frame. Barrel length is 24" and rifle weighs 9 lbs.

NIB	*Exc.*	*V.G.*	*Good*	*Fair*	*Poor*
925	750	650	500	400	200

Blued Iron Frame Henry

Same as above but furnished with a highly polished blued receiver.

NIB	*Exc.*	*V.G.*	*Good*	*Fair*	*Poor*
925	750	650	500	400	200

Military Henry

Based on the brass frame military version of the Henry rifle this model is furnished with sling swivels mounted on the left side. The buttplate is fitted with a trap door. Caliber is .44-40 and barrel length is 24". Weighs 9 lbs. 4 oz.

NIB	*Exc.*	*V.G.*	*Good*	*Fair*	*Poor*
900	725	625	500	400	200

Henry Carbine

This is the brass frame carbine version and features a 22" barrel. Chambered for the .44-40 cartridge. Weighs 8 lbs. 12 oz.

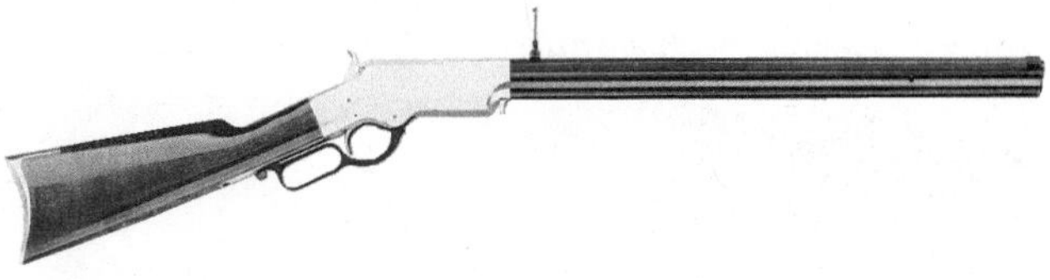

NIB	*Exc.*	*V.G.*	*Good*	*Fair*	*Poor*
875	700	600	500	400	200

Henry Trapper

This replica is not based on an actual Henry. Fitted with a unique 16.5" barrel, this brass frame model weighs 7 lbs. 7 oz. Chambered for the .44-40 cartridge.

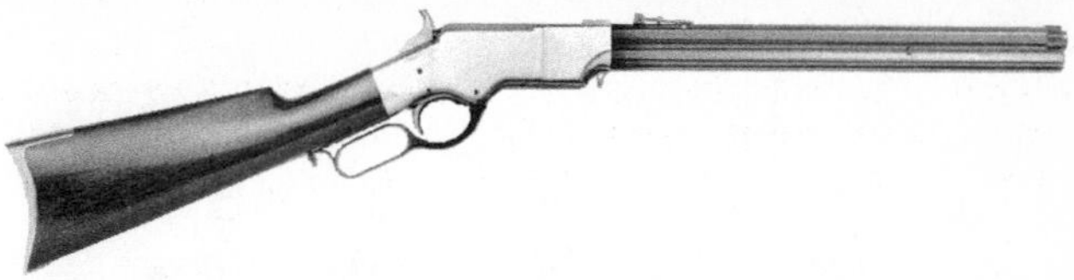

NIB	*Exc.*	*V.G.*	*Good*	*Fair*	*Poor*
875	700	600	500	400	200

1892 Rifle

This lever-action rifle is chambered for the .357 Mag., .44-40, .45 Colt, or .32-20 cartridge. Octagon barrel is 24.25". Walnut stock, crescent butt and blued or case colored receiver. Weight is about 6.25 lbs.

NIB	*Exc.*	*V.G.*	*Good*	*Fair*	*Poor*
525	425	350	300	250	200

1892 Short Rifle

Same as above but with 20" octagon barrel. Weight is about 6.25 lbs.

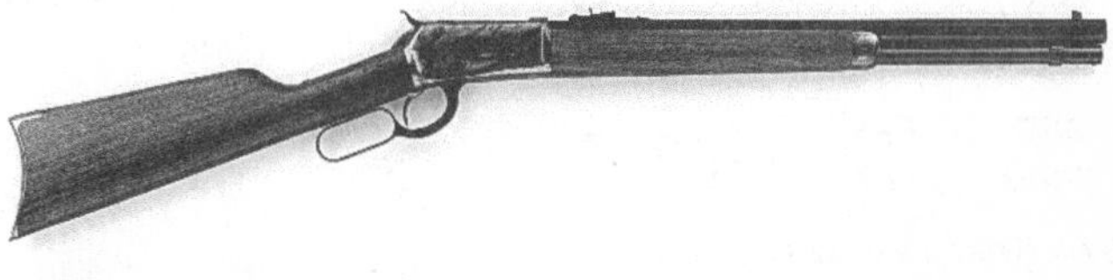

NIB	*Exc.*	*V.G.*	*Good*	*Fair*	*Poor*
525	425	350	300	250	200

1892 Carbine

Similar to the short rifle but fitted with a 20" round barrel and saddle ring on left side of receiver. Weight is about 5.75 lbs.

NIB	*Exc.*	*V.G.*	*Good*	*Fair*	*Poor*
450	350	300	250	200	150

1892 Brass Frame Carbine

Same as above but with polished brass receiver.

NIB	*Exc.*	*V.G.*	*Good*	*Fair*	*Poor*
450	350	300	250	200	150

1892 Brass Frame Rifle

This model is the same as the rifle but with polished brass receiver.

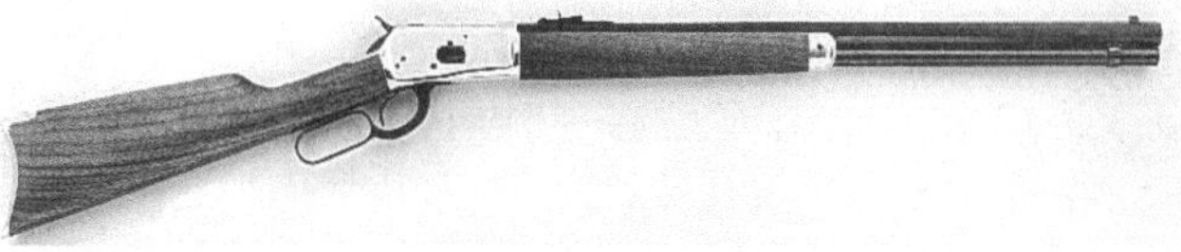

NIB	*Exc.*	*V.G.*	*Good*	*Fair*	*Poor*
525	425	350	300	250	200

No. 2 Creedmoor Target Rifle

This is a reproduction of the Remington No. 2 Creedmoor. It features a case colored receiver, tapered 30" octagonal barrel, hooded front sight, Creedmoor tang sight, and walnut stock with checkered pistol grip. Furnished in .45-70 Government. Weighs 9 lbs.

NIB	*Exc.*	*V.G.*	*Good*	*Fair*	*Poor*
900	725	625	500	400	200

Rolling Block Buffalo Rifle

This rifle is a replica of the Remington Buffalo rifle. It is fitted with a 26" or 30" octagonal or half octagonal barrel, case colored receiver, blade front sight, notch rear sight, brass trigger guard, with walnut stocks. Tang is drilled and tapped for tang sight.

NIB	Exc.	V.G.	Good	Fair	Poor
750	600	475	300	200	100

Rolling Block Buffalo Rifle Half Octagon Barrel Model

NIB	Exc.	V.G.	Good	Fair	Poor
750	600	475	300	200	100

"John Bodine" Rolling Block Rifle

Chambered for the .45-70 cartridge and fitted with a 30" octagon barrel. Double set triggers. Match-grade rear tang sight. Weight is about 12 lbs. Introduced in 2002.

NIB	Exc.	V.G.	Good	Fair	Poor
1550	1150	800	575	350	200

1885 High Wall

Chambered for the .45-70 cartridge this rifle is fitted with a 30" medium heavy octagon barrel. Case colored receiver, target sights and walnut stocks. Also available with 28" round barrel.

NIB	Exc.	V.G.	Good	Fair	Poor
900	725	600	500	400	200

NOTE: Reduce price by $100 for Buckhorn sights and $60 for 28" barrel.

1873 Springfield Infantry Rifle

A copy of the Trapdoor Springfield. Chambered for .45-70 and fitted with a 32.5" barrel. Walnut stock and case hardened breechlock. Weight is approximately 8.25 lbs.

NIB	Exc.	V.G.	Good	Fair	Poor
975	800	600	500	400	200

1873 Springfield Cavalry Carbine

Same as above but with 22" barrel. Weight is about 7 lbs.

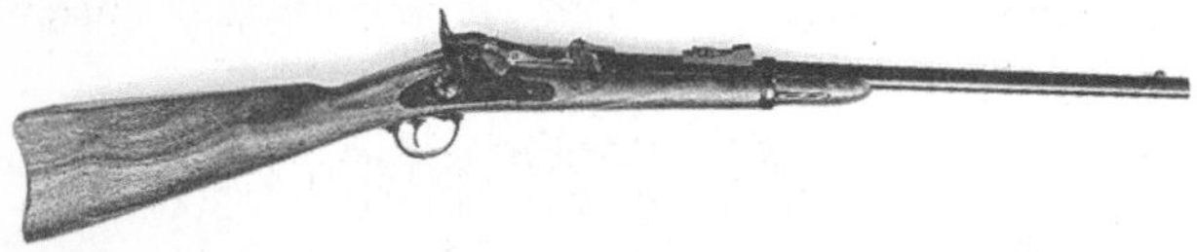

NIB	Exc.	V.G.	Good	Fair	Poor
875	700	600	500	400	200

Ithaca/Navy Hawken Rifle

Offered in either .50 or. 54 caliber percussion. Features a 31.5" rust blued octagon barrel. The percussion lockplate is case colored, while the rest of the hardware is blued with the exception of the nose cap and escutcheons. Weighs about 9 lbs. 13 oz.

NIB	Exc.	V.G.	Good	Fair	Poor
350	300	250	200	150	100

Hawken Rifle

This model features a case colored lock, 28" blued octagon barrel, adjustable sights, double set triggers, and hooked breech. The polished brass furniture and patch box are mounted on a walnut stock. Weighs about 8.5 lbs.

NIB	Exc.	V.G.	Good	Fair	Poor
300	200	175	125	95	60

Hawken Hunter Rifle

Offered in .50, .54, or .58 caliber, this model features blued hardware, adjustable sights, case colored lock, and hooked breech. The walnut stock is hand checkered with a cheekpiece. Rubber recoil pad is standard. Barrel length is 28".

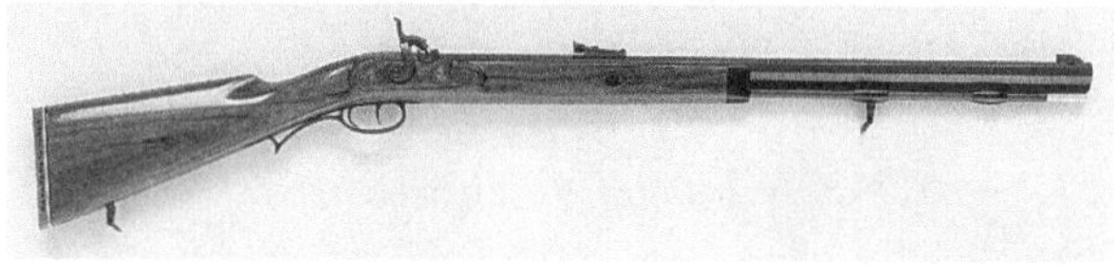

NIB	Exc.	V.G.	Good	Fair	Poor
295	190	150	100	75	60

Hawken Hunter Carbine

Same as above but fitted with a 22.5" barrel. Weighs about 6 lbs. 12 oz.

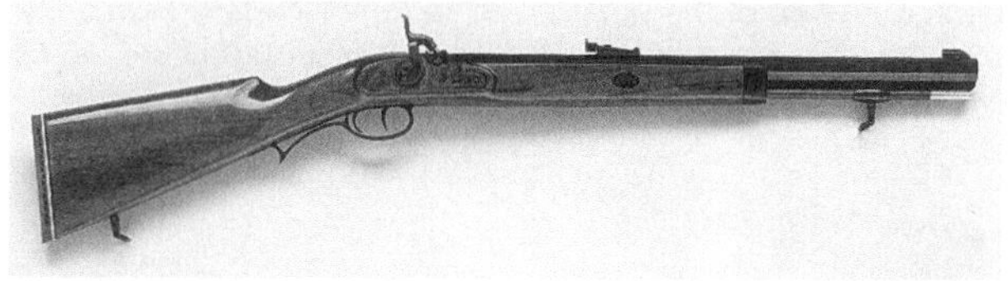

NIB	Exc.	V.G.	Good	Fair	Poor
295	190	150	100	75	60

Kodiak MKIV Double Rifle

Built in Europe by Pedersoli, this model is chambered for the .45-70 cartridge and features a walnut stock with cheekpiece and hand checkering. Barrel length is 24" with adjustable sights. Engraved sideplates are polished bright. Sling swivels standard. Weighs 10.2 lbs.

NIB	Exc.	V.G.	Good	Fair	Poor
4500	3350	2500	1500	600	400

Mortimer Flintlock or Percussion Shotgun

Replica of 12 gauge English Mortimer. This model features a waterproof pan, roller frizzen (flintlock only); external safety. All parts are case colored. Barrel is 36" long. Weighs 7 lbs.

NIB	Exc.	V.G.	Good	Fair	Poor
975	800	600	500	400	200

Fowler Shotgun

This 12 gauge model is a side-by-side with straight gripstock. The gun features a hooked breech and 28" blued barrels. The sideplates are engraved and case colored. Double triggers and checkered walnut stock are standard. Weighs 7.25 lbs.

NIB	Exc.	V.G.	Good	Fair	Poor
550	395	300	250	200	100

Navy Arms Steel Shot Magnum

Same as above but in 10 gauge. Weighs 7 lbs. 9 oz.

NIB	Exc.	V.G.	Good	Fair	Poor
575	400	295	125	100	75

T&T Shotgun

This turkey and trap model has a straight grip stock and 28" barrel choked Full and Full. Locks are case colored and engraved. Walnut stock is checkered. Weighs 7.5 lbs.

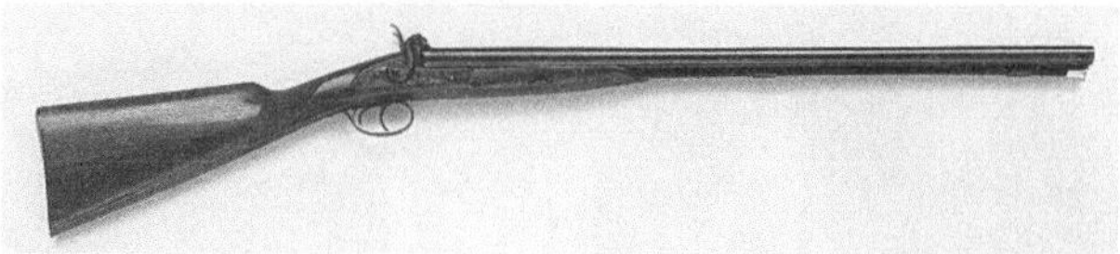

NIB	*Exc.*	*V.G.*	*Good*	*Fair*	*Poor*
550	395	300	250	200	100

Japanese Tanegashima Matchlock

This model is a .50 caliber with 41" barrels. Weighs 8.5 lbs.

NIB	*Exc.*	*V.G.*	*Good*	*Fair*	*Poor*
1150	800	600	400	300	150

MILITARY SURPLUS ARMS

SKS Type 56 w/Scope Rail

This semi-automatic gas operated rifle is chambered for the 7.62x39 cartridge. It has a 10-round clip. This model is fitted with a scope rail on the left side of the receiver. Barrel length is 20.5". Weight is 8 lbs.

NIB	*Exc.*	*V.G.*	*Good*	*Fair*	*Poor*
400	325	250	200	150	100

Standard SKS Type 56

Same as above without the scope rail.

NIB	*Exc.*	*V.G.*	*Good*	*Fair*	*Poor*
400	325	250	200	150	100

Standard SKS Type 56 With Scope and Bipod

As above but fitted with a 2.75 power Type 89 scope and RPK style folding bipod.

NIB	*Exc.*	*V.G.*	*Good*	*Fair*	*Poor*
400	325	250	200	150	100

SKS "Cowboy's Companion" Carbine

Barrel length on this version is 16.5". Weighs 7 lbs. 8 oz.

NIB	*Exc.*	*V.G.*	*Good*	*Fair*	*Poor*
400	325	250	200	150	100

SKS "Cowboy's Companion" Carbine Military Version

This is the military version of the "Cowboy's Companion" fitted with a short cruciform folding bayonet.

NIB	*Exc.*	*V.G.*	*Good*	*Fair*	*Poor*
400	325	250	200	150	100

SKS "Hunter" Carbine

This model has a checkered composite Monte Carlo stock with full length pull. Comes with 5-round magazine.

NIB	*Exc.*	*V.G.*	*Good*	*Fair*	*Poor*
400	325	250	200	150	100

TU-KKW Training Rifle

Based on the 98 Mauser and chambered for the .22 LR cartridge. It is fitted with military sights, bayonet lug, cleaning rod and take down disc. Comes with detachable 5-round box magazine. Barrel length is 26" and weighs 8 lbs.

NIB	*Exc.*	*V.G.*	*Good*	*Fair*	*Poor*
325	275	200	150	100	60

TU-KKW Sniper Trainer

Same as above but fitted with a 2.75 power Type 89 scope and quick detachable mounting system.

NIB	*Exc.*	*V.G.*	*Good*	*Fair*	*Poor*
375	325	275	200	150	100

TU-33/40 Carbine

This model is based on the WWII Mauser G 33/40 mountain carbine. Chambered for the .22 LR or 7.62x39 cartridge. Barrel length is 20.75" and weighs 7.5 lbs.

NIB	*Exc.*	*V.G.*	*Good*	*Fair*	*Poor*
325	275	200	150	100	—

JW-15 Rifle

This model is a bolt-action design based on the BRNO Model 5 action. Chambered for the .22 LR it features adjustable sights, sling swivels, an detachable 5-round magazine. The top of the receiver is dovetailed for easy scope mounting. Barrel is 24" long and rifle weighs 5 lbs. 12 oz.

NIB	*Exc.*	*V.G.*	*Good*	*Fair*	*Poor*
100	80	70	60	50	35

Martini Target Rifle

A .444 or .45-70 caliber single-shot Martini-action rifle with a 26" or 30" octagonal barrel, tang sight, and walnut stock. Offered between 1972 and 1984.

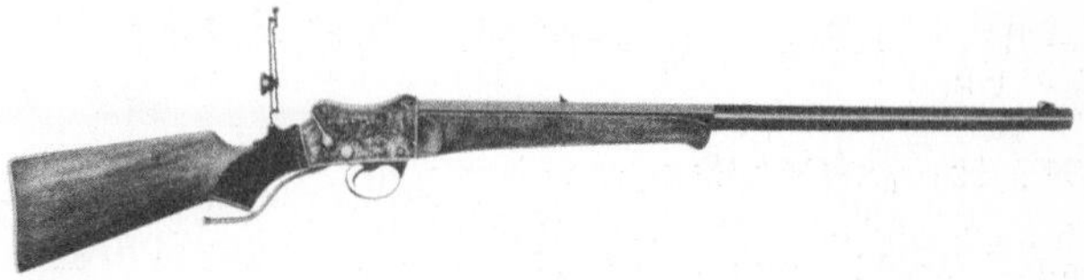

NIB	*Exc.*	*V.G.*	*Good*	*Fair*	*Poor*
—	625	500	400	300	150

RPKS-74

A 5.56mm or 7.62x39mm caliber semi-automatic rifle with a 19" barrel patterned after the Russian AK series rifles.

NIB	*Exc.*	*V.G.*	*Good*	*Fair*	*Poor*
550	450	375	275	200	10

No. 5 Enfield Jungle Carbine

This replica is chambered for .303 British cartridge and fitted with cupped buttplate and flashider. Barrel length is 20.5". Magazine capacity is 10 rounds. Weight is approximately 7 lbs.

NIB	*Exc.*	*V.G.*	*Good*	*Fair*	*Poor*
375	325	275	200	150	100

No. 6 Enfield Jungle Carbine

This reproduction is chambered for .303 British with 20.5" barrel with flashider. Weight is about 7 lbs. Ten-round magazine.

NIB	*Exc.*	*V.G.*	*Good*	*Fair*	*Poor*
375	325	275	200	150	100

Ishapore 2A No. 1 MK III Rifle

This is a refinished rifle with 25" barrel and chambered for .308 Win. cartridge. Magazine capacity is 12 rounds. Weight is about 9.3 lbs.

NIB	Exc.	V.G.	Good	Fair	Poor
350	250	200	150	100	75

2A Tanker Carbine

This is a replica with a short 20" barrel. Chambered for .308 Win. Magazine capacity is 12 rounds. Weight is approximately 8.7 lbs.

NIB	Exc.	V.G.	Good	Fair	Poor
375	325	275	200	150	100

MK III Tanker Carbine

Similar to the above model but chambered for the .303 British cartridge. Magazine capacity is 10 rounds.

NIB	Exc.	V.G.	Good	Fair	Poor
375	325	275	200	150	100

Lithgow No. 1 MK III Rifle

These rifles are in unissued condition. Barrel length is 25". Chambered for .303 British cartridge. Magazine capacity is 10 rounds. Weight is about 9 lbs.

NIB	Exc.	V.G.	Good	Fair	Poor
400	325	250	200	150	100

No. 1 MK III Enfield Rifle

These rifles are standard MK III S.M.L.E. rifles that have been refinished. Barrel length is 25.25". Magazine capacity is 10 rounds of .303 British. Weight is about 9 lbs.

NIB	Exc.	V.G.	Good	Fair	Poor
375	325	275	200	150	100

No. 4 Tanker Carbine

This is a cut-down version of the No. 4 MK I Enfield. Barrel length is 20.5". Chambered for .303 with magazine capacity of 10 rounds. Weight is approximately 8.2 lbs.

NIB	Exc.	V.G.	Good	Fair	Poor
350	250	200	150	100	75

No. 4 MK I Enfield Rifle

This is a reconditioned rifle. Barrel length is 25". Magazine capacity is 10 rounds of .303 British. Weight is about 8.6 lbs.

NIB	Exc.	V.G.	Good	Fair	Poor
350	250	200	150	100	75

Savage No. 4 MK I Rifle

Chambered for .303 British cartridge with 25" barrel. Stocks are unissued. Magazine capacity is 10 rounds. Weight is approximately 8.7 lbs.

NIB	Exc.	V.G.	Good	Fair	Poor
375	325	275	200	150	100

NESIKA BAY PRECISION, INC.

Sturgis, South Dakota

Hunting Rifles

Offered in a number of different calibers with several stock options to choose from. All rifles are fitted with adjustable trigger.

NIB	Exc.	V.G.	Good	Fair	Poor
4000	2900	2300	1500	750	400

Varmint Rifles

Offered in a variety of calibers and barrel lengths and weights. Single shot or repeater.

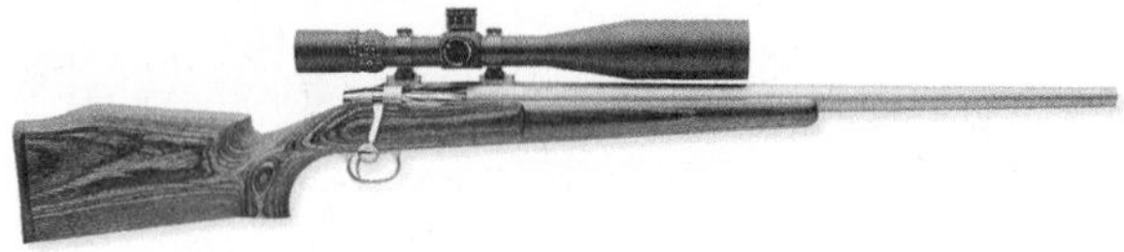

NIB	Exc.	V.G.	Good	Fair	Poor
3500	2900	2300	1500	750	400

Urban Tactical Rifle

Chambered for the .308 cartridge and fitted with a 20" fluted barrel. Detachable box magazine. Weight is about 10 lbs. Add 5-10 percent for Heavy Tactical version.

NIB	Exc.	V.G.	Good	Fair	Poor
5800	4800	3500	2700	800	500

NOTE: For .300 win. Mag add $100.

NEW ENGLAND FIREARMS CO.

Gardner, Massachusetts

New England Firearms Company is owned by Marlin.

Excell

Introduced in 2005 this model is chambered for the 12 gauge 3" shell and fitted with a 28" vent rib barrel with choke tubes. Checkered black synthetic stock. Magazine capacity is 5 rounds. Weight is about 7 lbs.

NIB	Exc.	V.G.	Good	Fair	Poor
450	375	295	225	150	100

Excell Waterfowl

As above but with Real Tree Advantage Wetlands camo finish. Introduced in 2005.

NIB	Exc.	V.G.	Good	Fair	Poor
475	400	325	250	175	125

Excell Turkey

This model is fitted with a 22" barrel with choke tubes and fiber optic front sight. Real Tree Advantage Hardwoods camo finish. Weight is 7 lbs. Introduced in 2005.

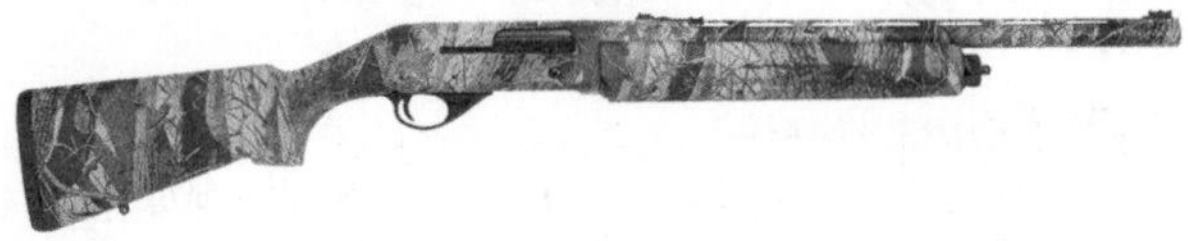

NIB	Exc.	V.G.	Good	Fair	Poor
475	400	325	250	175	125

Excell Combo

This model has a black synthetic stock and two barrels: 28" vent rib with choke tubes, and 24" rifled barrel. Weight is about 7 lbs. depending on barrel length. Introduced in 2005.

NIB	Exc.	V.G.	Good	Fair	Poor
500	425	345	260	185	135

Pardner

A 12, 16, 20 or .410 bore single-shot shotgun with a 24", 26", or 28" barrel. Blued with a walnut stock. Introduced in 1987.

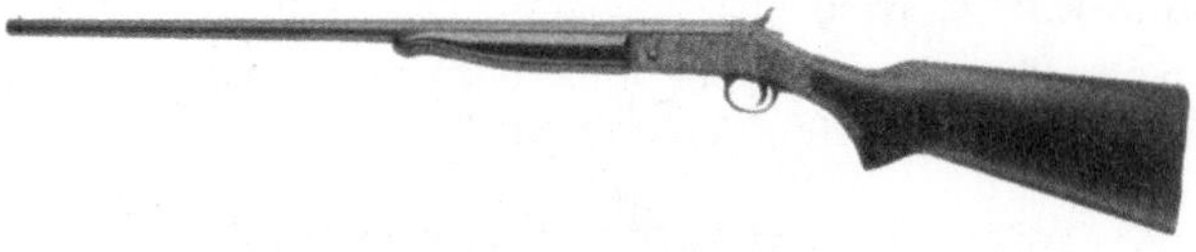

NIB	Exc.	V.G.	Good	Fair	Poor
150	100	80	70	60	40

Pardner Youth

Similar to the above model but offered only in 20 and 28 gauge as well as .410. Fitted with a 26" barrel. Weight is between 5 and 6 lbs.

NIB	Exc.	V.G.	Good	Fair	Poor
150	100	80	70	60	40

Special Purpose

This is a similar model but it is offered only in 10 gauge. It is available in several different configurations: A 10 gauge model with hardwood stock with 28" barrel, a camo model with 28" barrel, a camo model with 32" barrel choked Modified, and a black matte finish model with 24" barrel with screw-in turkey Full choke. Weight is about 9.5 lbs.

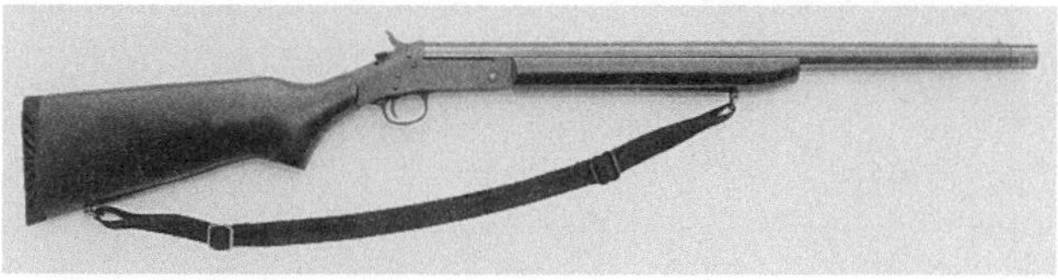

NIB	Exc.	V.G.	Good	Fair	Poor
250	175	125	100	75	50

Pardner Pump Turkey

This model is chambered for the 12 gauge 3" shell and fitted with 22" barrel with turkey choke tube. Magazine capacity is 5 rounds. Weight is about 7.5 lbs. Introduced in 2005.

NIB	Exc.	V.G.	Good	Fair	Poor
275	225	175	125	100	75

Pardner Pump Walnut Shotgun

12- or 20-gauge pump-action shotgun with American walnut furniture, 28- or 26-inch vent rib barrel, 3-inch chamber and screw-in choke tube. Weight 7-1/2 lbs.

NIB	Exc.	V.G.	Good	Fair	Poor
—	275	225	175	125	100

Pardner Pump Synthetic Shotgun

Similar to above but with black synthetic buttstock and forend.

NIB	Exc.	V.G.	Good	Fair	Poor
—	225	175	150	100	75

Pardner Pump Field Shotgun

Similar to above but with Realtree APG HD camo finish.

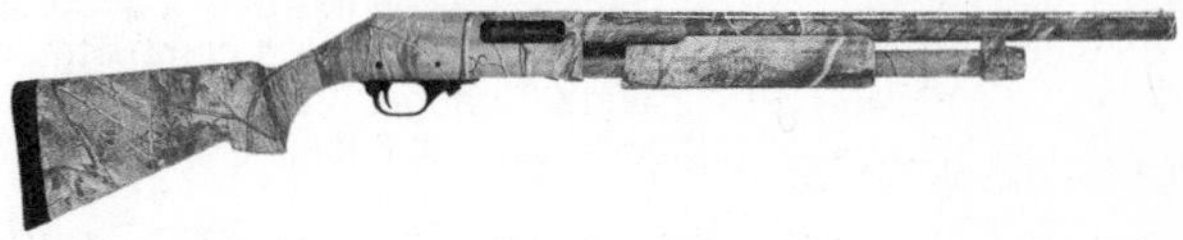

NIB	Exc.	V.G.	Good	Fair	Poor
—	275	225	175	125	100

Pardner Pump Compact Field Shotgun

Similar to above but with 1-1/4-inch shorter length of pull and 21 inch barrel.

NIB	Exc.	V.G.	Good	Fair	Poor
—	225	175	150	100	75

Pardner Pump Compact Walnut Shotgun

Similar to Pardner Pump Walnut model but with 1-1/4 inch shorter length of pull and 21 inch barrel. Weight 6-1/4 lbs.

NIB	Exc.	V.G.	Good	Fair	Poor
—	225	175	150	100	75

Pardner Pump Compact Synthetic Shotgun

Similar to above but with black synthetic buttstock and forend.

NIB	Exc.	V.G.	Good	Fair	Poor
—	225	175	150	100	75

Pardner Pump Combo

Introduced in 2005 this model features two 12 gauge 3" barrels. One 28" with vent rib and choke tubes, and the other 22" rifled slug barrel. Walnut stock. Weight is about 7.5 lbs. depending on barrel length.

NIB	Exc.	V.G.	Good	Fair	Poor
275	225	175	125	100	75

Pardner Pump Protector

Similar to Pardner Pump but with matte black finish throughout and synthetic buttstock and forend. Also available with carbon fiber dipped stock.

NIB	Exc.	V.G.	Good	Fair	Poor
—	225	175	150	100	75

Pardner Pump Turkey

Similar to Pardner Pump but with Realtree APG HD full-camo dip or Realtree Hardwoods camo finish. Fiber optics front and rear sights. Comes with screw-in XF Turkey choke tube.

NIB	Exc.	V.G.	Good	Fair	Poor
—	275	225	175	125	100

Survivor

Based on a single-shot break-action design this rifle or shotgun is fitted with a synthetic stock with integral storage compartments. Offered in .410/.45 Colt, 12 and 20 gauge, .223 Rem., and .357 Mag. Barrel length is 22". Weight is about 6 lbs.

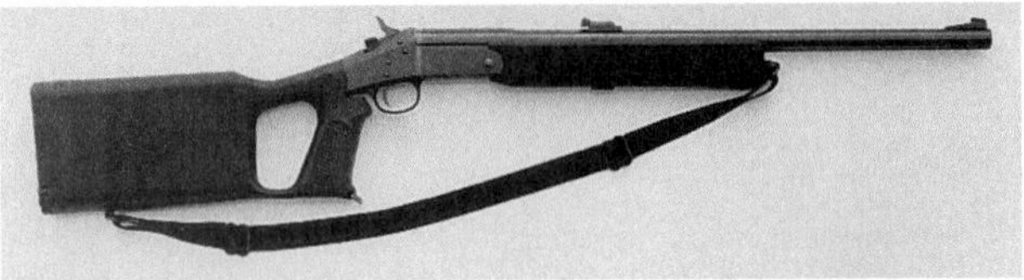

NIB	Exc.	V.G.	Good	Fair	Poor
200	175	150	125	100	75

Handi-Rifle (aka Handi-Gun)

.22 Hornet, .223, .243, .270, .280, .30-30, .44 Magnum, or .45-70 caliber version of the above with a 22" barrel fitted with open sights. Blued, with a walnut stock. Introduced in 1989. In 2003 this model was offered in stainless steel. In 2004 the .22-250, .25-06, and .204 calibers were added. In 2005 the .500 S&W was added.

NIB	Exc.	V.G.	Good	Fair	Poor
275	200	150	125	100	75

Tracker

This single-shot break-open shotgun is offered in both 12 and 20 gauge with rifled barrel or cylinder bore barrel. Both are 24" in length. Equipped with adjustable rifle sights. Weight is about 6 lbs.

NIB	Exc.	V.G.	Good	Fair	Poor
150	125	100	75	60	50

Super Light Rifle

This single-shot rifle is chambered for the .22 Hornet or .223 Rem. It is fitted with a 20" light weight barrel. Choice of scope mount and no sights or adjustable rear sight and ramp front sight. Black polymer stock with semi-beavertail forend. Weight is about 5.5 lbs.

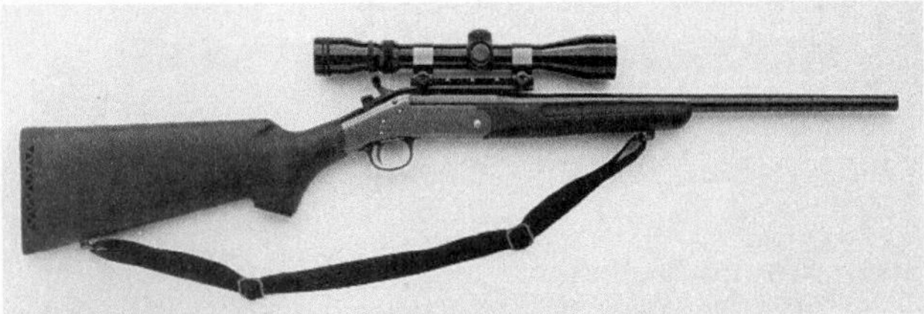

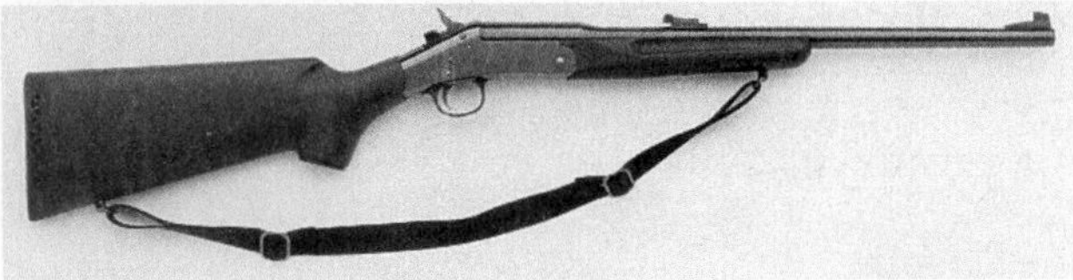

NIB	Exc.	V.G.	Good	Fair	Poor
175	125	100	75	60	50

Huntsman

This is a blackpowder gun with break-open action hardwood pistol-grip stock. Fitted with a 24" barrel. Chambered for .50 or .45 caliber slug. Recoil pad. Weight is about 6.5 lbs. Introduced in 2002.In 2003 this model was offered in stainless steel.

NIB	Exc.	V.G.	Good	Fair	Poor
175	125	100	75	60	50

Handi-Rifle Combo

Combination two-barrel set of .50 blackpowder barrel and .243 Win. barrel. Hardwood stock. No iron sights.

NIB	Exc.	V.G.	Good	Fair	Poor
275	225	175	125	100	—

Sportster

This is a single shot .22 caliber short/LR or .22 WMR rifle with a 20" barrel. No iron sights. Black polymer Monte Carlo stock with matte black metal finish. Scope mount rail. Weight is about 5.5 lbs.

NIB	Exc.	V.G.	Good	Fair	Poor
175	125	100	75	60	50

Sportster Youth

As above but with standard stock. Weight is about 5.25 lbs.

NIB	Exc.	V.G.	Good	Fair	Poor
175	125	100	75	60	50

Sportster .17 HMR

This single-shot model is chambered for the .17 HMR cartridge and fitted with a 22" heavy varmint barrel. No iron sights. Black polymer Monte Carlo stock with matte black metal finish. Weight is about 7 lbs.

NIB	Exc.	V.G.	Good	Fair	Poor
175	125	100	75	60	50

Sportster .17 M2

As above but chambered for the .17 Mach2 cartridge. Introduced in 2005.

NIB	Exc.	V.G.	Good	Fair	Poor
175	125	100	75	60	50

Sportster SL

This is a semi-automatic rifle chambered for the .22 LR cartridge. Fitted with a 19" barrel. Walnut finished hardwood stock with Monte Carlo and pistol grip. Adjustable sights. Ten-round magazine. Weight is about 5.5 lbs. Introduced in 2004.

NIB	Exc.	V.G.	Good	Fair	Poor
150	125	100	75	60	50

Sportster Versa-Pack

This is a two-barrel set with a 22" .410 barrel and the other a 20" .22 caliber barrel. Hardwood stock with straight grip. Iron sights. Weight about 5.5 lbs.

NIB	Exc.	V.G.	Good	Fair	Poor
250	175	125	100	75	50

NEWTON ARMS CO.

Buffalo, New York

Also known as the Buffalo Newton Rifle Company and the Charles Newton Rifle Company. In operation from 1913 to 1932.NOTE: Any of the rifles listed chambered for a Newton caliber will bring a premium over standard calibers of about 25 percent.

Newton-Mauser Rifle

A .256 Newton caliber bolt-action rifle with a 24" barrel and double set triggers. Blued with a walnut stock. Manufactured circa 1914.

NIB	Exc.	V.G.	Good	Fair	Poor
—	—	1300	850	500	300

Standard Rifle First Type

A .22, .256, .280, .30, .33, and .35 Newton as well as .30-06 caliber bolt-action rifle with a 24" barrel, open or aperture sights and double set triggers. Blued with a walnut stock. Manufactured between 1916 and 1918.

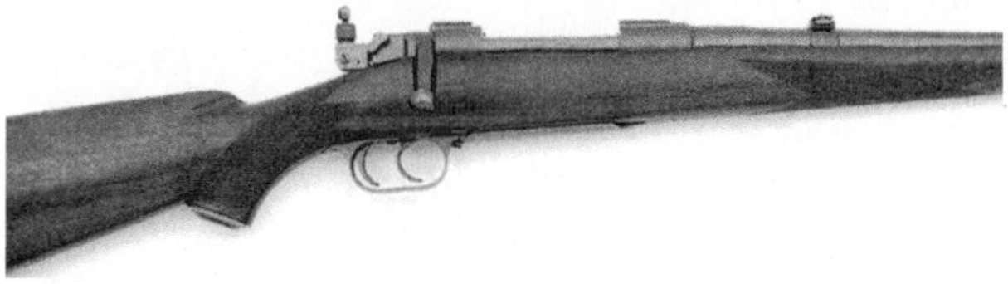

Courtesy Amoskeag Auction Company, Inc.

NIB	Exc.	V.G.	Good	Fair	Poor
—	2500	2150	1500	900	400

Standard Rifle Second Model

A .256, .30, or .35 Newton as well as .30-06 caliber bolt-action rifle as above, but with an Enfield-style bolt handle. Manufactured after 1918.

NIB	Exc.	V.G.	Good	Fair	Poor
—	2500	2150	1500	900	400

Buffalo Newton Rifle

As above, but marked "Buffalo Newton Rifle Company."

NIB	Exc.	V.G.	Good	Fair	Poor
—	2000	1650	1000	600	300

NOBLE

Haydenville, Massachusetts

In business between 1946 and 1971, this company manufactured a variety of plain, utilitarian firearms. In general, these arms are all worth approximately the same, that is, less than $200 in excellent condition. Noble firearms represent an attractive opportunity for the beginning collector as most can be had very inexpensively.

RIFLES

Model 10

A .22 caliber bolt-action single rifle with a 24" barrel. Pistol grip stock with no checkering. Open sights. Produced in the late 1950s.

NIB	Exc.	V.G.	Good	Fair	Poor
—	75	60	50	40	30

Model 20

A .22 caliber bolt-action rifle fitted with a 22" barrel. Open sights. Produced from the late 1950s to the early 1960s.

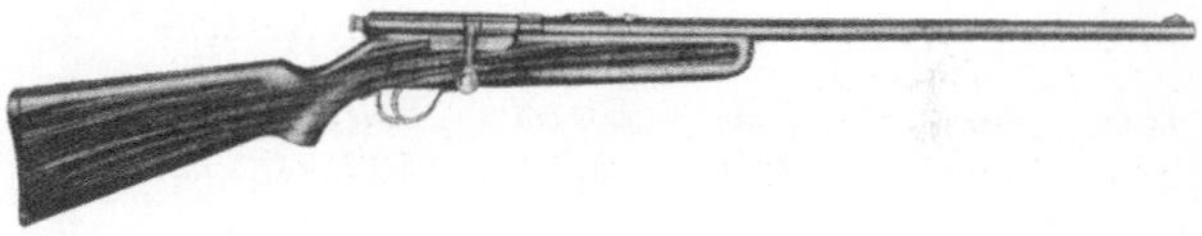

NIB	Exc.	V.G.	Good	Fair	Poor
—	75	60	50	40	30

Model 33

This is a .22 caliber slide-action rifle fitted with a 24" barrel and tubular magazine and Tenite stock. Produced from the late 1940s to the early 1950s.

NIB	Exc.	V.G.	Good	Fair	Poor
—	80	70	60	50	40

Model 33A

Same as above but fitted with a wood stock.

NIB	Exc.	V.G.	Good	Fair	Poor
—	75	60	50	40	30

Model 222

This is a single-shot bolt-action rifle chambered for the .22 caliber cartridge. Plain pistol-grip stock.

NIB	Exc.	V.G.	Good	Fair	Poor
—	85	75	60	50	40

Model 235

A rather dopey but kinda cute .22 caliber slide-action rifle with a 24" barrel and tubular magazine. Plain pistol-grip stock and groved slide handle.

NIB	Exc.	V.G.	Good	Fair	Poor
—	200	125	75	60	50

Model 275

A .22 caliber lever-action rifle with tubular magazine. Fitted with a 24" barrel. The plain stock has a semi-pistol grip.

NIB	Exc.	V.G.	Good	Fair	Poor
—	175	100	80	60	50

SHOTGUNS

Model 40

This is a hammerless slide-action shotgun chambered for the 12 gauge shell. It is fitted with a tubular magazine and 28" barrel with multi choke. Plain pistol stock with grooved slide handle.

NIB	Exc.	V.G.	Good	Fair	Poor
—	125	100	85	70	50

Model 50

Same as above but without the multi choke.

NIB	Exc.	V.G.	Good	Fair	Poor
—	115	90	80	65	50

Model 60

A hammerless slide-action shotgun in 12 or 16 gauge with tubular magazine and fitted with a 28" barrel with adjustable choke. Plain pistol grip stock with grooved slide handle.

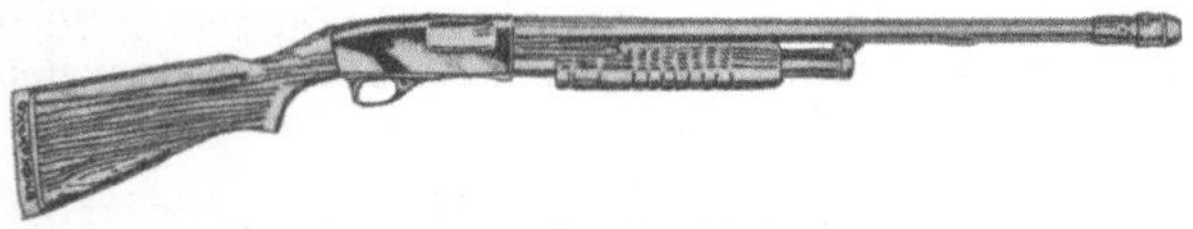

NIB	Exc.	V.G.	Good	Fair	Poor
—	175	150	125	100	75

Model 65

Same as above but without adjustable choke.

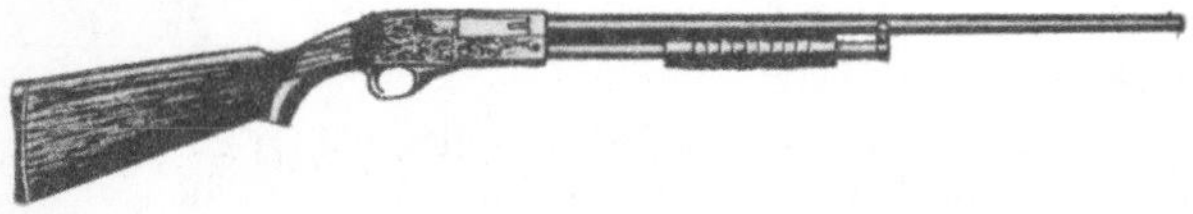

NIB	Exc.	V.G.	Good	Fair	Poor
—	150	125	100	75	60

Model 66CLP

Offered in 12 or 16 gauge this slide-action shotgun is fitted with a 28" plain barrel and a keyed lock fire control system.

NIB	Exc.	V.G.	Good	Fair	Poor
—	160	140	110	85	70

Model 66RCLP

Similar to above but fitted with a 28" vent rib barrel and checkered pistol-grip stock. Adjustable choke is standard.

NIB	Exc.	V.G.	Good	Fair	Poor
—	200	175	150	125	100

Model 66RLP

Same as above but without adjustable choke.

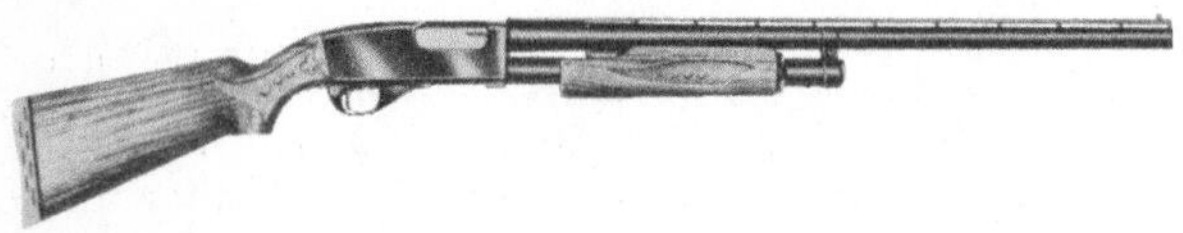

NIB	Exc.	V.G.	Good	Fair	Poor
—	175	150	125	100	75

Model 66XL

Similar to the above models but with plain barrel, and checkering only on the slide handle.

NIB	Exc.	V.G.	Good	Fair	Poor
—	150	125	100	75	60

Model 70CLP

Similar to the Model 66 series but offered in .410 bore with 26" barrel and adjustable choke. Both the buttstock and slide handle are checkered.

NIB	Exc.	V.G.	Good	Fair	Poor
—	175	150	125	100	75

Model 70RCLP

This variation is fitted with a 26" ventilated rib barrel.

NIB	Exc.	V.G.	Good	Fair	Poor
—	200	175	150	125	100

Model 70RLP

This model has a vent rib barrel and no adjustable choke.

NIB	Exc.	V.G.	Good	Fair	Poor
—	175	150	125	100	75

Model 70XL

This version has no adjustable choke but is fitted with a 26" vent rib barrel. Stock is checked.

NIB	Exc.	V.G.	Good	Fair	Poor
—	125	100	80	70	60

Model 602RCLP

This is a hammerless slide-action shotgun chambered for the 20 gauge shell. It is fitted with a 28" vent barrel and adjustable choke. Checkered pistol grip stock with slide handle.

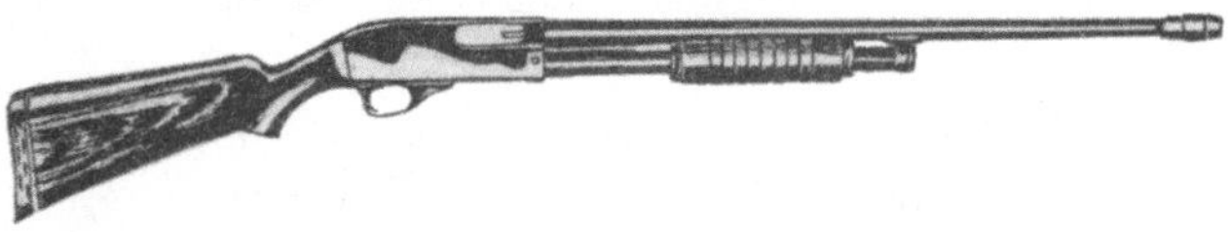

NIB	Exc.	V.G.	Good	Fair	Poor
—	225	200	175	125	100

Model 602CLP

Same as above but with plain barrel.

NIB	Exc.	V.G.	Good	Fair	Poor
—	175	150	125	100	75

Model 602RLP

Same as Model RCLP except without the addition of an adjustable choke device.

NIB	Exc.	V.G.	Good	Fair	Poor
—	200	175	150	125	100

Model 602XL

Same as above but with only the slide handle checkered.

NIB	Exc.	V.G.	Good	Fair	Poor
—	150	125	100	75	60

Model 662

This 20 gauge slide-action shotgun has a plain aluminum barrel with checkered pistol grip and slide handle. The receiver is made from aluminum. Produced in the late 1960s.

NIB	Exc.	V.G.	Good	Fair	Poor
—	200	175	150	125	100

Model 80

This model is a semi-automatic inertia-operated shotgun chambered for the .410 shell. It is fitted with a 26" barrel, plain pistol stock with slotted forearm. Produced in the early to mid 1960s.

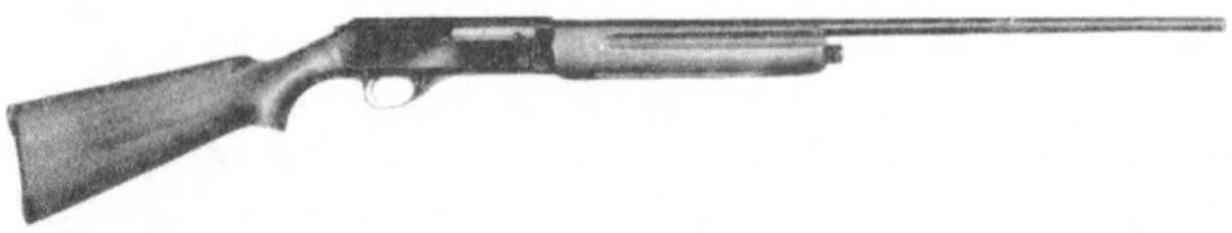

NIB	Exc.	V.G.	Good	Fair	Poor
—	250	200	150	125	100

Model 166L

This is a 12 gauge slide-action shotgun with a key lock system. It is fitted with a 24" barrel bored for rifled slug. Lyman peep rear sight with post front sight. Checkered pistol and slide handle.

NIB	*Exc.*	*V.G.*	*Good*	*Fair*	*Poor*
—	250	200	150	125	100

Model 420

This shotgun is a box lock design side-by-side with double triggers and offered in 12, 16, 20 gauge, as well as .410 bore. Barrel lengths are 28" for all gauges except .410 where it is 26". Lightly engraved frame. Checkered walnut stock and splinter forearm.

NIB	*Exc.*	*V.G.*	*Good*	*Fair*	*Poor*
—	300	250	200	150	100

Model 450E

This model is similar to the Model 420 with the addition of automatic ejectors and not offered in .410 bore. Checkered pistol grip stock with beavertail forearm. Produced in the late 1960s.

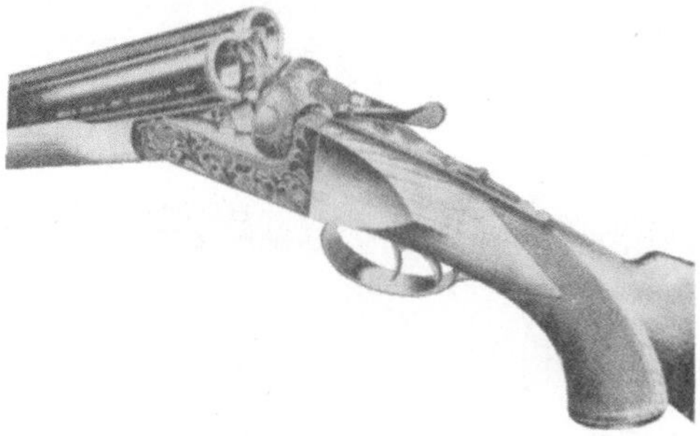

NIB	*Exc.*	*V.G.*	*Good*	*Fair*	*Poor*
—	350	275	225	175	125

NORINCO

Peoples Republic of China
China North Industries Corp.

Norinco is a state-owned conglomerate in China that exported firearms to the United States from 1988 to 1995. Importation of Norinco firearms was banned in conjunction with the 1994 Crime Bill and various trade sanctions against China, with the exception of several shotguns that were marketed between 1999 and 2002.

ATD .22

A .22 caliber semi-automatic rifle with a 19.4" barrel and 11-shot magazine located in the butt. Blued with a hardwood stock. Importation began in 1987.

NIB	*Exc.*	*V.G.*	*Good*	*Fair*	*Poor*
200	150	125	100	75	50

EM-321

A .22 caliber slide-action rifle with a 19.5" barrel and 10-shot tubular magazine. Blued with a hardwood stock. Introduced in 1989.

NIB	*Exc.*	*V.G.*	*Good*	*Fair*	*Poor*
150	100	85	75	65	50

Model HL-12-203 Shotgun

A 12 gauge boxlock Over/Under shotgun with 30" ventilated rib barrels fitted for choke tubes, single trigger and automatic ejectors. Blued with a hardwood stock. Introduced in 1989.

NIB	*Exc.*	*V.G.*	*Good*	*Fair*	*Poor*
400	325	275	225	175	125

Model HL-12-102 Shotgun

A 12 gauge slide-action shotgun with a 28" barrel and 3-shot magazine. Blued with a hardwood stock. Introduced in 1989.

NIB	*Exc.*	*V.G.*	*Good*	*Fair*	*Poor*
275	225	200	175	125	100

Model 97 Hammer Pump

Similar in appearance to the Winchester Model 1897 shotgun. Fitted with a 20" barrel with cylinder choke. Hardwood stock.

NIB	*Exc.*	*V.G.*	*Good*	*Fair*	*Poor*
375	275	200	150	100	75

SKS Rifle

A 7.62x39mm caliber semi-automatic rifle with a 20.5" barrel, folding bayonet and either a 10-shot fixed magazine or 30-shot detachable magazine. Blued with a hardwood stock. Importation began in 1988.

NIB	*Exc.*	*V.G.*	*Good*	*Fair*	*Poor*
—	400	300	225	150	100

Type 84S AK

Similar to the AKS service rifle, in 5.56mm caliber with a 16" barrel and 30-shot magazine.

NIB	*Exc.*	*V.G.*	*Good*	*Fair*	*Poor*
900	800	700	550	350	200

Type 84S-1

As above, with an underfolding metal stock.

NIB	*Exc.*	*V.G.*	*Good*	*Fair*	*Poor*
1050	900	750	575	375	225

Type 84S-3

As above, with a composition stock.

NIB	*Exc.*	*V.G.*	*Good*	*Fair*	*Poor*
1000	850	700	600	400	225

NOSLER CUSTOM

Bend, Oregon

Nosler Custom Model 48 Sporter

Bolt-action centerfire rifle chambered in various calibers, 24" barrel, round top receiver, onyx gray composite stock. Introduced 2007. Price shown includes scope. Limited edition series has high grade walnut stock, double square bridge action with integral scope bases. Only 500 made.

NIB	*Exc.*	*V.G.*	*Good*	*Fair*	*Poor*
2495	2000	1600	900	500	300

NOTE: Add 50 percent for limited edition model.

O

OHIO ORDNANCE INC.

Chardon, Ohio

Model 1918A3 Self-Loading Rifle

This rifle is a semi-automatic version of the famed Browning Automatic Rifle. It is chambered for the .30-06 cartridge and has a 20-round magazine. It was introduced in this configuration in 1996. Subtract 10 percent for bakelite stock.

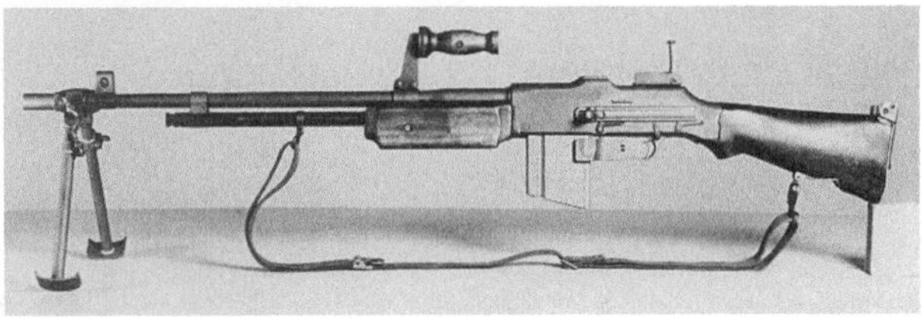

NIB	Exc.	V.G.	Good	Fair	Poor
3800	3300	2500	1850	1500	750

Colt Browning Water Cooled Gun

Introduced in 2001, this is a semi-automatic version of the famous Browning Model 1928 belt-fed machine gun. This model features a .30-06 or 7.65 Argentine caliber belt-fed gun with tripod, wooden ammo box, water hose, water can, and one 250 cloth belt.

NIB	Exc.	V.G.	Good	Fair	Poor
3700	3300	2500	1850	1500	750

NOTE: Add $200 for .308 or 8mm caliber guns.

1919A4

Semi-auto version of the air-cooled, belt-fed .30-caliber 1919 machine gun. Chambered for .308/7.62 NATO.

NIB	Exc.	V.G.	Good	Fair	Poor
3250	2800	2000	1250	1100	500

OLYMPIC ARMS, INC.

Olympia, Washington

RIFLES

SGW Ultra Match (PCR-1)

A match grade copy of the AR-15 with a 20" or 24" barrel and not fitted with a carrying handle. Weight is about 10 lbs.

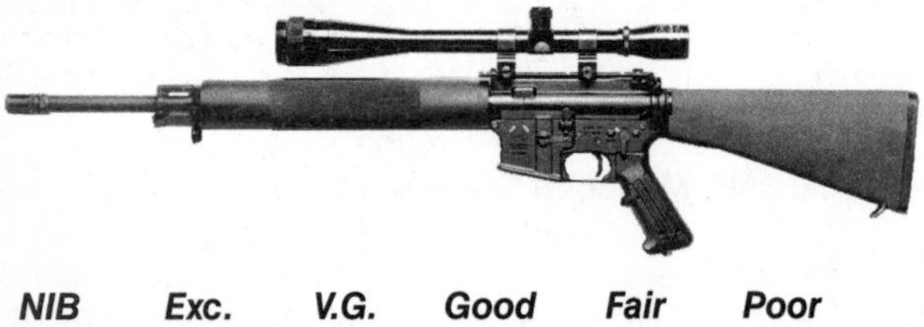

NIB	Exc.	V.G.	Good	Fair	Poor
1250	1000	800	500	400	200

Model PCR-2

Similar to the above model but fitted with a 16" match grade barrel, post front and E2 rear sight. Weight is approximately 8.2 lbs.

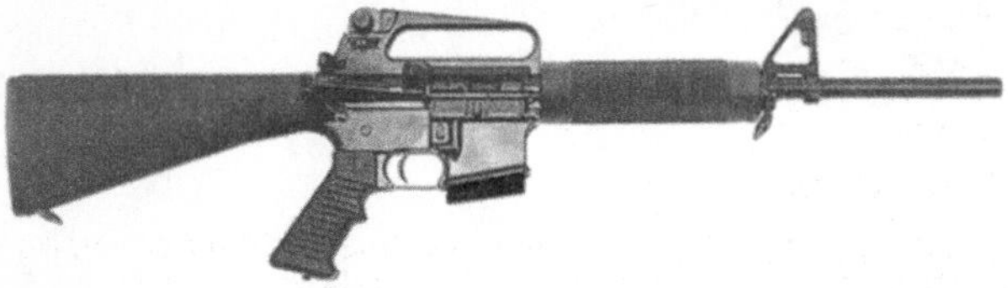

NIB	Exc.	V.G.	Good	Fair	Poor
1300	1050	850	550	450	225

Model PCR-3

Same as above model but with forged T-12 upper receiver.

NIB	Exc.	V.G.	Good	Fair	Poor
1300	1050	850	550	450	225

Model PCR-4

This version is fitted with a 20" steel barrel with post front sight and A-1 style rear sight. Weight is approximately 8.5 lbs.

NIB	Exc.	V.G.	Good	Fair	Poor
900	725	575	450	350	150

Model PCR-5

Similar to the above but fitted with a 16" barrel. Weight is about 7 lbs.

NIB	Exc.	V.G.	Good	Fair	Poor
900	725	575	450	350	150

Model PCR-6

This AR-15 style rifle is chambered for the 7.62x39 Russian caliber. It is fitted with a 16" barrel with a post front sight and a A-1 style rear sight. Weight is about 7 lbs.

NIB	Exc.	V.G.	Good	Fair	Poor
900	725	575	450	350	150

Model PCR-7 "Eliminator"

This model is a shortened version of the PCR-4. It is fitted with a 16" barrel, A2 handguard, A2 stock, and an A2 pistol grip. Weight is about 7.6 lbs.

NIB	Exc.	V.G.	Good	Fair	Poor
900	725	575	450	350	150

Model PCR-Service Match

This .223 caliber rifle has a 20" stainless steel match barrel. It is fitted with a post front sight and a E-2 style rear sight. Weight is about 8.7 lbs.

NIB	Exc.	V.G.	Good	Fair	Poor
1100	800	675	500	300	150

Ultra CSR Tactical Rifle

This is a bolt-action rifle chambered for the .308 Winchester cartridge. Barrel length is 26". Magazine capacity is 5 rounds. Tactical-style stock is black synthetic with aluminum bedding block. Comes complete with scope rings and Harris bipod in a hardcase. Weight is approximately 9.4 lbs.

NIB	Exc.	V.G.	Good	Fair	Poor
1100	800	675	500	300	150

Model CAR-97

Chambered for the .223 cartridge or optional 9mm, .40 S&W, or .45 ACP pistol cartridges. Fitted with a 16" barrel and non-collapsible CAR-style stock. Overall length is 34". Weight is about 7 lbs.

NIB	Exc.	V.G.	Good	Fair	Poor
900	725	575	450	350	150

NOTE: Add $50 for pistol cartridge conversion.

UM-1P

Gas-operated .223 semi-auto target rifle based on AR-15 chassis. Features include 24-inch stainless steel bull barrel, anodized finish, pistol grip with bottom swell, Picatinny rail, Harris bipod, and competition trigger.

NIB	Exc.	V.G.	Good	Fair	Poor
900	725	575	450	350	150

UM-1

Similar to UM-1P but with 20-inch stainless steel bull barrel, standard pistol grip, no bipod.

NIB	Exc.	V.G.	Good	Fair	Poor
900	725	575	450	350	150

SM-1P

Tricked-out AR-15 in .223 with 20-inch stainless steel barrel, free-floating sleeve handguard, carry handle upper or Picatinny rail flattop, pneumatic recoil buffer, Bob Jones interchangeable sight system, competition trigger, and Maxhard receivers.

NIB	Exc.	V.G.	Good	Fair	Poor
1300	1050	850	550	450	225

SM-1

Similar to SM-1P but with standard receivers, trigger and sights. No pneumatic recoil buffer.

NIB	Exc.	V.G.	Good	Fair	Poor
1000	700	575	450	300	150

ML-1

Similar to SM-1 but with 16-inch barrel with flash hider, 6-position collapsible buttstock and free-floating aluminum tube handguard.

NIB	Exc.	V.G.	Good	Fair	Poor
1000	700	575	450	300	150

ML-2

Similar to ML-1 but with flat-top upper receiver with Picatinny rails, standard buttstock and bull barrel.

NIB	Exc.	V.G.	Good	Fair	Poor
1000	700	575	450	300	150

Model K8

Similar to ML-2 but with 20-inch barrel and extended aluminum tube handguard.

NIB	Exc.	V.G.	Good	Fair	Poor
1000	700	575	450	300	150

Model K8-MAG

Similar to K8 but with 24-inch bull barrel and chambered in .223 WSM, .243 WSM or .25 WSM.

NIB	Exc.	V.G.	Good	Fair	Poor
1000	700	575	450	300	150

K3B

Features include 16-inch chrome-moly barrel with flash-hidefully adjustable rear sight, 6-position collapsible buttstock and carbine-length handguard.

NIB	Exc.	V.G.	Good	Fair	Poor
900	725	575	450	350	150

K3B-M4

Similar to K3B but with M4S fiberite handguard with heatshield and 32.25-inch overall length.

NIB	Exc.	V.G.	Good	Fair	Poor
900	725	575	450	350	150

K3B-CAR

Similar to K3B but with 30.5-inch overall length.

NIB	Exc.	V.G.	Good	Fair	Poor
900	725	575	450	350	150

K3B-FAR

Similar to K3B but with Featherweight barrel and weight of 5.84 lbs.

NIB	Exc.	V.G.	Good	Fair	Poor
900	725	575	450	350	150

K4B

Similar to K3B but with 20-inch barrel and rifle-length fiberite handguard.

NIB	Exc.	V.G.	Good	Fair	Poor
900	725	575	450	350	150

K4B-A4

Similar to K4B but with ventilated FIRSH rifle-length handguard.

NIB	Exc.	V.G.	Good	Fair	Poor
950	775	600	475	375	175

LTF

Features include 16-inch chrome-moly barrel, free-floating FIRSH handguard with Picatinny rails, ACE FX skeleton stock, ERGO pistol grip and multiple-aperture flipup sight system.

NIB	Exc.	V.G.	Good	Fair	Poor
1100	800	675	500	350	150

LT-M4

Similar to LTF but with 16-inch stainless steel barrel.

NIB	Exc.	V.G.	Good	Fair	Poor
1100	800	675	500	350	150

K16

Similar to K8 but with 16-inch bull chrome-moly barrel.

NIB	Exc.	V.G.	Good	Fair	Poor
800	625	475	400	300	125

GI-16

Basic AR-15-inspired semi-auto rifle chambered in .223. 16-inch chrome-moly barrel with flash-hider, 6-position collapsible buttstock, carbine-length handguard and rear sight adjustable for windage only.

NIB	Exc.	V.G.	Good	Fair	Poor
900	725	575	450	350	150

Plinker Plus

Similar to GI-16 but with standard buttstock.

NIB	Exc.	V.G.	Good	Fair	Poor
800	625	475	400	250	100

Plinker Plus 20

Similar to Plinker Plus but with 20-inch barrel and rifle-length handguard.

NIB	Exc.	V.G.	Good	Fair	Poor
850	675	525	425	300	125

K7 Eliminator

Similar to K4B but with 16-inch barrel with extended handguard and sight radius of 20-inch-barreled models.

NIB	Exc.	V.G.	Good	Fair	Poor
900	725	575	450	350	150

K30

Similar to GI-16 but chambered in .30 Carbine. Includes mag well insert to accept military-spec magazines.

NIB	Exc.	V.G.	Good	Fair	Poor
900	725	575	450	350	150

K9/K10/K40/K45

Similar to K30 but chambered, respectively, for 9mm Parabellum, 10mm, .40 S&W and .45ACP. Models use converted surplus military magazines.

NIB	Exc.	V.G.	Good	Fair	Poor
900	725	575	450	350	150

K9-GL/K40-GL

Similar to K9 and K40 but accept standard Glock pistol magazines.

NIB	Exc.	V.G.	Good	Fair	Poor
900	725	575	450	350	150

Model OA-93-CAR

Features include OA-93 FT recoil-reducing upper, 16-inch chrome-moly barrel with Phantom flash hider, and side-folding buttstock.

NIB	Exc.	V.G.	Good	Fair	Poor
1000	700	575	450	300	150

Olympic Arms Gamestalker

Sporting AR-style rifle chambered in .223, .243 and .25 WSSM and .300 OSSM. Features include forged aluminum upper and lower; flat top receiver with Picatinny rail; gas block front sight; 22-inch stainless steel fluted barrel; free-floating slotted tube handguard; camo finish overall; ACE FX skeleton stock. Price: $1,359.

OMEGA

Geneseo, Illinois
Springfield Armory

Over-and-Under Shotgun

A 12, 20, 28 or .410 bore boxlock over-and-under shotgun with 26" or 28" ventilated rib barrels, single trigger and extractors. Blued with a walnut stock.

NIB	Exc.	V.G.	Good	Fair	Poor
—	450	300	200	150	125

Side-by-Side Double Barreled Shotgun

A 20, 28 or .410 bore boxlock double-barrel shotgun with 26" barrels, double triggers and extractors. Blued with a hardwood stock.

NIB	Exc.	V.G.	Good	Fair	Poor
—	350	250	150	100	75

Single Barreled Shotgun

A 12, 20 or .410 bore single barrel shotgun manufactured in a variety of barrel lengths and fitted with an extractor. Blued with a hardwood stock.

NIB	Exc.	V.G.	Good	Fair	Poor
—	125	85	65	50	35

OMEGA FIREARMS CO.

Flower Mound, Texas

Bolt-Action Rifle

A .25-06 to .358 Norma Magnum bolt-action rifle with a 22" or 24" barrel, octagonal bolt, adjustable trigger and rotary magazine. Blued with a two-piece walnut or laminated stock. Discontinued circa 1975.

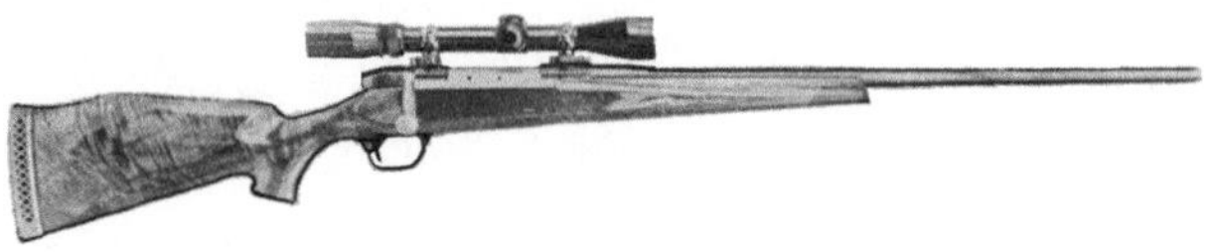

NIB	Exc.	V.G.	Good	Fair	Poor
—	800	650	550	424	200

OPUS SPORTING ARMS, INC.

Long Beach, California

Opus One

A .243, .270, or .30-06 caliber bolt-action rifle with a 24" barrel, well figured walnut stock and an ebony pistol grip cap as well as forend tip. Built on a Model 70 Winchester action. Manufactured in 1987 and 1988.

NIB	Exc.	V.G.	Good	Fair	Poor
—	2250	1600	1150	700	350

Opus Two

As above, in 7mm Remington Magnum and .300 Winchester Magnum.

NIB	Exc.	V.G.	Good	Fair	Poor
—	2500	1750	1250	750	350

Opus Three

As above, in .375 Holland & Holland and .458 Winchester Magnum.

NIB	Exc.	V.G.	Good	Fair	Poor
—	3000	2000	1500	900	500

OVERTON, JOHN

Nashville, Tennessee

Formerly armorer at Harpers Ferry Armory. He delivered 81 rifles copying the U.S. Model 1841 but with a saber bayonet lug on the right side of the barrel. Unmarked externally but are serial numbered internally. Overall length ca. 48-3/4"; barrel length 33"; .54 caliber.

NIB	Exc.	V.G.	Good	Fair	Poor
—	—	18500	14000	5500	2000

P

PAGE-LEWIS ARMS CO.
Chicopee Falls, Massachusetts

Model A Target

A .22 caliber single-shot lever-action rifle with a 20" barrel and open sights. Blued with a walnut stock. Manufactured from 1920 to 1926.

NIB	Exc.	V.G.	Good	Fair	Poor
—	300	225	175	125	100

Model B Sharpshooter

As above, with a 24" barrel and longer forend.

NIB	Exc.	V.G.	Good	Fair	Poor
—	300	225	175	125	100

Model C Olympic

As above, with a 24" barrel and improved sights.

NIB	Exc.	V.G.	Good	Fair	Poor
—	375	275	200	150	100

Challenge Model 49

Single shot .22 LR boy's rifle, manufactured c. 1925-1930. Stamped on top of barrel "Page Lewis Arms Co., Chicopee Falls, Mass USA/22 LR" Model 49. 22" long barrel, fixed front and rear sights.

NIB	Exc.	V.G.	Good	Fair	Poor
—	150	100	75	50	35

PALMER
Windsor, Vermont
E. G. Lamson & Co.

Palmer Bolt-Action Carbine

A .50 caliber single-shot bolt-action carbine with a 20" round barrel, walnut half stock and full sidelock. Blued and case hardened. The receiver marked "Wm. Palmer / Patent / Dec.22, 1863" and the lock "G.Lamson & Co./ Windsor, Vt." Approximately 1,000 were made in 1865.

NIB	Exc.	V.G.	Good	Fair	Poor
—	3000	2250	1500	700	250

PARA USA (PARA-ORDNANCE)
Pineville, North Carolina

Previously known as Para-Ordnance of Scarborough, Ontario, Canada. In 2009 the company relocated to Pineville, North Carolina.

TTR Rifle Series

Para's Tactical Target Rifle is based on the AR platform with 16.5-inch barrel, 30-round magazine. Chambered in .223 Rem./5.56x45 NATO. Flat Top upper receiver, full-length Picatinny rail, short or long-rail forearm, adjustable buttstock. Delayed impingement gas system, front and rear flip-up sights. Accepts all M16 and AR-15 magazines.

NIB	Exc.	V.G.	Good	Fair	Poor
1950	1700	1450	1100	900	400

PARKER BROS.
Meriden, Connecticut

Perhaps the best known of all American shotgun manufacturers. Established by Charles Parker shortly after the Civil War, this company has produced a wide variety of shotguns in a number of different styles over the years. In the early 1930s the company was purchased by Remington Arms Company.

VH

A 12, 16, 20, 28 or .410 bore boxlock double-barrel shotgun manufactured in a variety of barrel lengths with double triggers and extractors. Blued, case hardened receiver with a walnut stock. Only 2,297 guns had single triggers. Only 3,983 guns had straight grip stocks.*Approximately 78,659 were made: 10 gauge—20, 12 gauge—51,901, 16 gauge—14,446, 20 gauge—10,406, 28 gauge—1,417, .410 bore—469.NOTE: Also made with automatic ejectors and known as the Model VHE. The E suffix was used on all models to denote automatic ejectors.

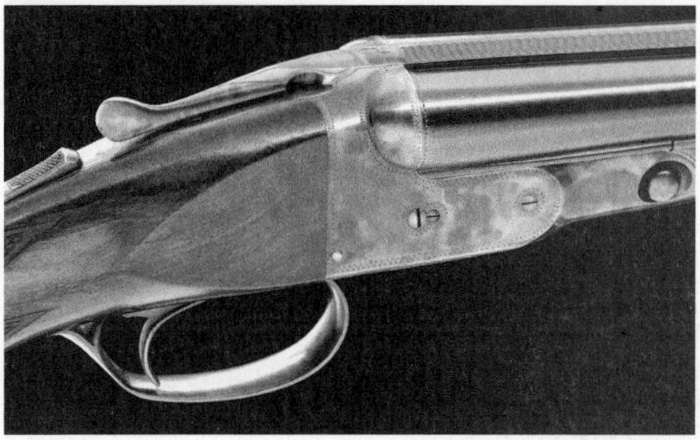

Courtesy Bonhams & Butterfields

NIB	Exc.	V.G.	Good	Fair	Poor
—	4250	3700	2950	2000	1000

NOTE: VHE add 40 percent, 20 gauge add 60 percent, 28 gauge add 500 percent, .410 add 500 percent.

PH

Similar to the above, but with a small amount of scroll engraving. slightly better grade of walnut.*Approximately 1,339 were made: 10 gauge—798, 12 gauge—839, 16 gauge—208, 20 gauge—204, 28 gauge—only 5, .410 bore—only 4.

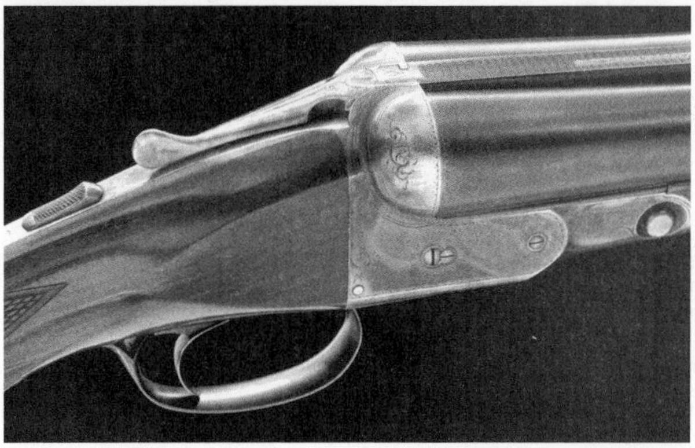

Courtesy Bonhams & Butterfields

NIB	Exc.	V.G.	Good	Fair	Poor
—	4700	4000	3350	2100	1000

NOTE: PHE (ejectors) add 40 percent. For 20 gauge add 60 percent. For the extremely rare 28 and .410 models, prices can command a 1000 percent premium.

GH

Similar to the above, with a modest amount of scroll and game scene engraving and the barrels marked "Parker Special

Steel." Only about 430 G grades were built with straight grip stocks.*Approximately 4,291 were made: 8 gauge—11, 10 gauge—63, 12 gauge—2,501, 16 gauge—607, 20 gauge—990, 28 gauge—91, .410 bore—28.

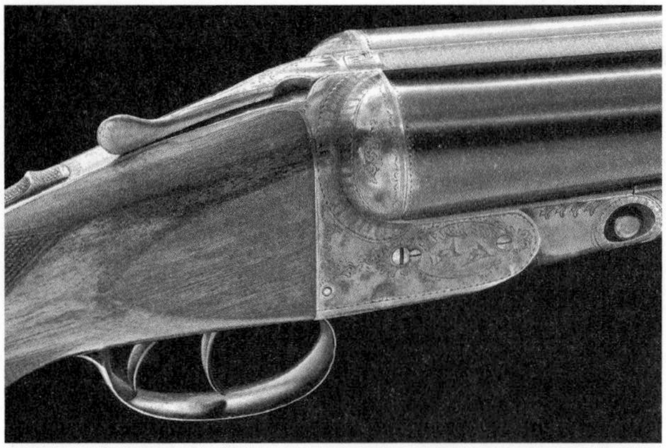

NIB	Exc.	V.G.	Good	Fair	Poor
—	6000	5000	4000	3000	1000

NOTE: GHE add 35 percent, 16 gauge add 15 percent, 20 gauge add 50 percent, 28 gauge add 300 percent, .410 add 500 percent.

DH

As above, but more finely finished. Engraving coverage more profuse. Most modern D grade guns were fitted with Titanic barrels. Only about 280 were built with Parker single triggers, and only about 280 were built with ventilated ribs.*Approximately 9,346 were made: 8 gauge—10, 10 gauge—45, 12 gauge—6,330, 16 gauge—1,178, 20 gauge—1,536, 28 gauge—187, .410 bore—60.

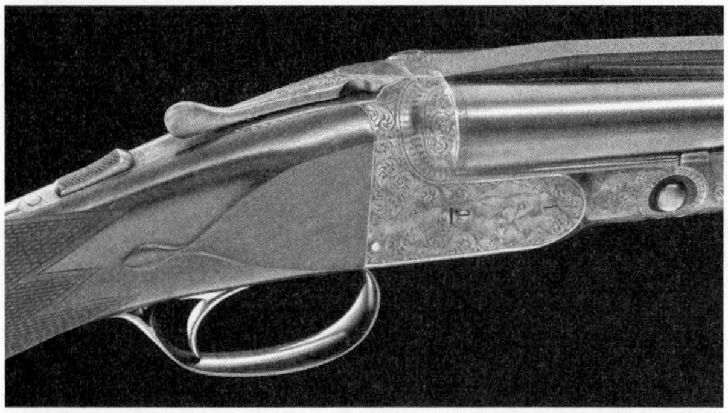

Courtesy Bonhams & Butterfields

NIB	Exc.	V.G.	Good	Fair	Poor
—	7500	6000	5000	3500	1000

NOTE: DHE add 35 percent, 16 gauge add 15 percent, 20 gauge add 50 percent, 28 gauge add 300 percent, .410 add 500 percent.

CH

As above, with more scroll and game scene engraving coverage. Marked with Acme steel barrels. Only about 93 C grades had straight-grip stocks.*Approximately 697 were made: 8 gauge—only 2, 10 gauge— only 9, 12 gauge—410, 16 gauge—105, 20 gauge—149, 28 gauge—only 16, .410 bore—only 6.

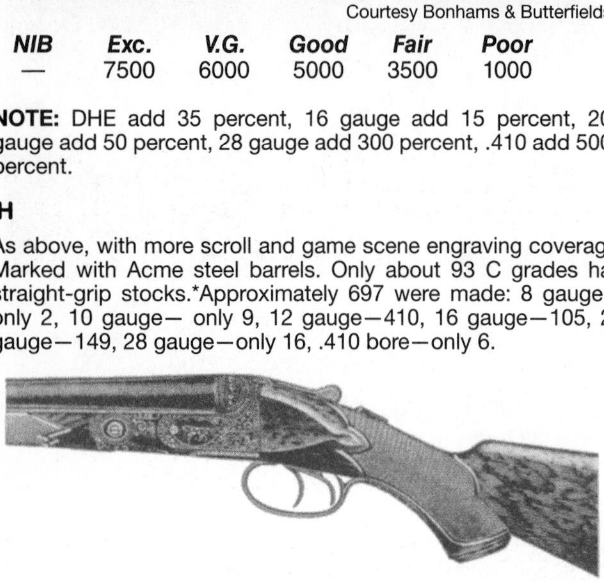

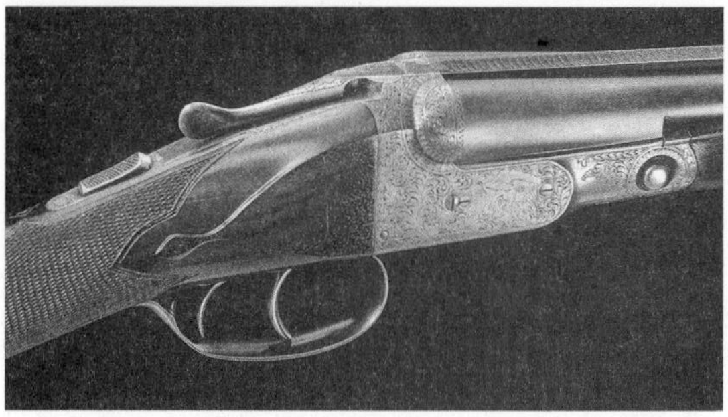

NIB	Exc.	V.G.	Good	Fair	Poor
—	14000	12500	9000	6500	1500

NOTE: CHE add 35 percent, 16 gauge add 10 percent, 20 gauge add 40 percent, 28 gauge add 400 percent, .410 add 700 percent.

BH

As above, but offered in a variety of different styles of engraved decoration. Only about 66 guns had straight-grip stocks, 29 had beavertail forends, 20 were built with vent ribs, and 57 had single triggers.*Approximately 512 were made: 10 gauge—only 2, 12 gauge—317, 16 gauge—71, 20 gauge—109, 28 gauge—13.NOTE: Prospective purchasers are advised to secure a qualified appraisal prior to acquisition.

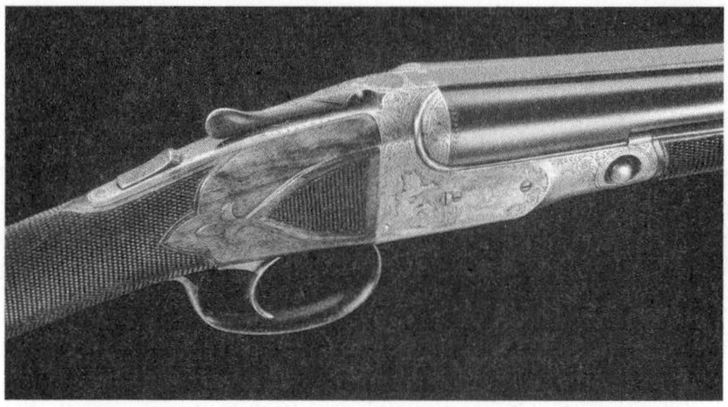

NIB	Exc.	V.G.	Good	Fair	Poor
—	18000	16000	13000	10000	2500

NOTE: BHE add 35 percent, 16 gauge add 15 percent, 20 gauge add 50 percent, 28 gauge add 450 percent.

AH

As above, but highly engraved with finely figured walnut stocks. Most had Acme steel barrels. About 42 A grade guns were built with straight grip stocks.*Approximately 167 were made: 10 gauge—only 1, 12 gauge—92, 16 gauge—23, 20 gauge—44, 28 gauge—only 6, .410 bore— only 1.

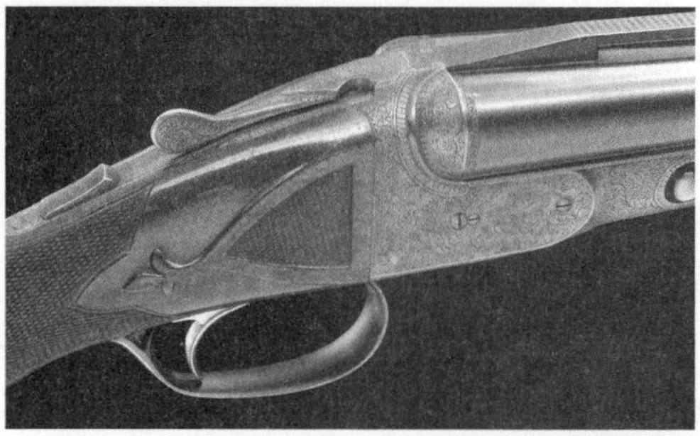

Courtesy Bonhams & Butterfields

NIB	Exc.	V.G.	Good	Fair	Poor
—	30000	27500	20000	15000	2500

NOTE: AHE add 30 percent, 16 gauge add 25 percent, 20 gauge add 75 percent, 28 gauge add 450 percent, .410 add 600 percent.

AAH

As above, with either Whitworth or Peerless barrels and not made in .410 bore. The engraving is more extensive and of the first quality. Only one AA grade has a ventilated rib, ten were built with single trigger and 95 had straight grip stocks.*Approximately 238 were made: 10 gauge—only 2, 12 gauge—185, 16 gauge—19, 20 gauge—27, 28 gauge—only 5.NOTE: Due to the rarity of this grade prospective purchasers are advised to secure a qualified appraisal prior to acquisition.

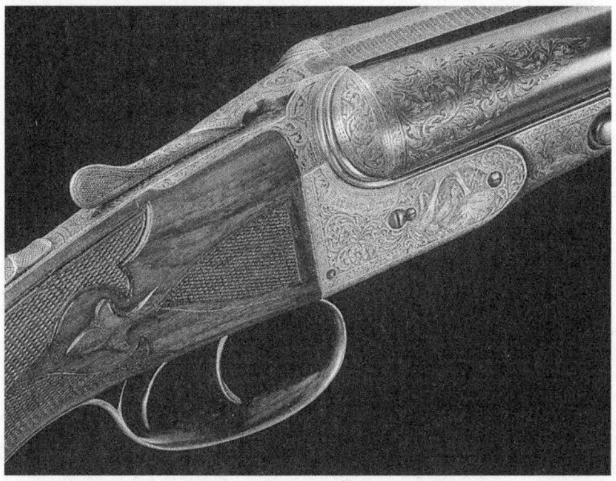

NIB	Exc.	V.G.	Good	Fair	Poor
—	50000	45000	37500	20000	3000

NOTE: AAHE add 30 percent, 16 gauge add 35 percent, 20 gauge add 75 percent, 28 gauge add 250 percent.

A-1 Special

As above, but made strictly on special order and not manufactured in .410 bore. Two A-1 Specials were built with ventilated rib, 7 had single triggers, 3 had beavertail forends, and 24 were built with straight-grip stocks.*Approximately 79 were made: 12 gauge—55, 16 gauge—only 6, 20 gauge—11, and 28 gauge—only 7.

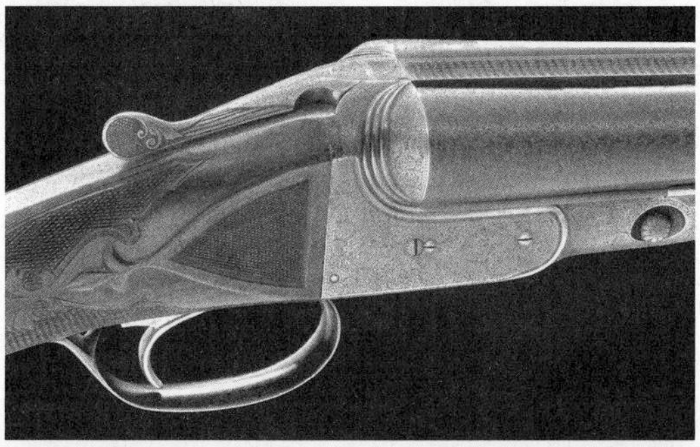

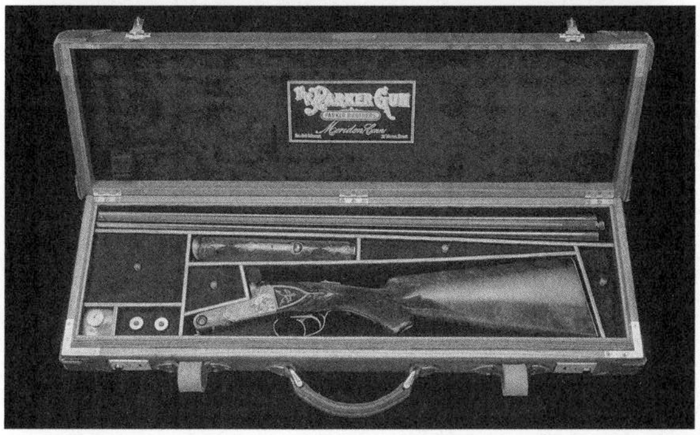

Courtesy Bonhams & Butterfields

NIB	Exc.	V.G.	Good	Fair	Poor
—	90000	80000	65000	35000	5000

NOTE: 16 gauge add 35 percent, 20 gauge add 75 percent, 28 gauge add 400 percent.

SINGLE-BARREL TRAP

A 12 gauge single-shot shotgun with a 30", 32", or 34" barrel, automatic ejector and walnut stock. Produced in a variety of grades as listed. Prospective purchasers are advised to secure a qualified appraisal prior to acquisition.

S.C. Grade

NIB	Exc.	V.G.	Good	Fair	Poor
—	7500	6500	4000	2000	1000

S.B. Grade

NIB	Exc.	V.G.	Good	Fair	Poor
—	9000	7500	5500	2400	1600

S.A. Grade

NIB	Exc.	V.G.	Good	Fair	Poor
—	14000	13000	10000	5000	2000

S.A.A. Grade

NIB	Exc.	V.G.	Good	Fair	Poor
—	25000	20000	15000	10000	5000

S.A-1 Special Grade

NIB	Exc.	V.G.	Good	Fair	Poor
—	30000	25000	18000	12000	5000

Under Lifter Hammer Gun

A side hammer double-barrel shotgun manufactured in a variety of gauges with the barrel release located in front of the triggerguards. Damascus barrels, case hardened locks, blued furniture with walnut stocks. Manufactured during the 1870s and later.

NIB	Exc.	V.G.	Good	Fair	Poor
—	6000	3200	1500	800	600

Trojan

A 12, 16, or 20 gauge boxlock double-barrel shotgun manufactured in a variety of barrel lengths with double triggers and extractors. Only 27 Trojans were built with single triggers. Blued, case hardened receiver with a walnut stock.*Approximately 33,000 were made: 12 gauge—21,977, 16 gauge—6,573, 20 gauge—5450, 28 gauge—None.

NIB	Exc.	V.G.	Good	Fair	Poor
—	3500	3000	2000	1000	600

NOTE: 20 gauge add 40 percent.

PARKER-HALE LTD.

Birmingham, England

Model 1200

A .22-250 to .300 Winchester Magnum bolt-action rifle with a 24" barrel and open sights. Blued, with walnut stock.

NIB	Exc.	V.G.	Good	Fair	Poor
700	550	450	400	350	250

Model 1100 Lightweight

As above, with a 22" barrel and 4-shot magazine. Introduced in 1985.

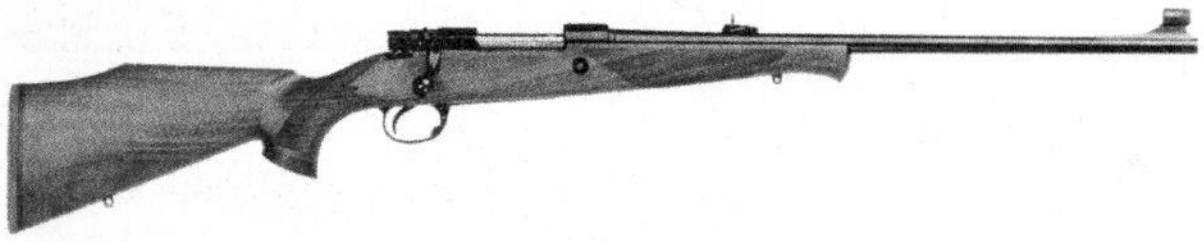

NIB	Exc.	V.G.	Good	Fair	Poor
600	475	400	300	250	200

Model 81 Classic

A .22-250 to 7mm Remington Magnum bolt-action rifle with a 24" barrel and open sights. Blued with a walnut stock. Introduced in 1985.

NIB	Exc.	V.G.	Good	Fair	Poor
875	750	600	500	400	350

Model 81 African

As above, but in .375 Holland & Holland caliber. Introduced in 1986.

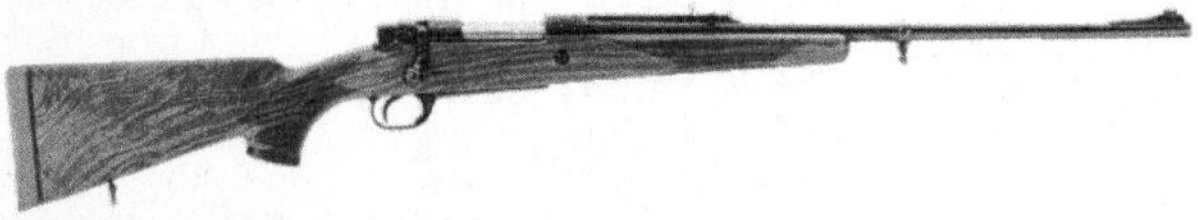

NIB	Exc.	V.G.	Good	Fair	Poor
1750	1200	1100	700	500	350

Model 84 Target

Similar to the Model 81, but in .308 caliber with adjustable rear sights and an adjustable cheekpiece.

NIB	Exc.	V.G.	Good	Fair	Poor
1300	1000	800	600	450	250

Model 85 Sniper

As above, with a telescope and bipod.

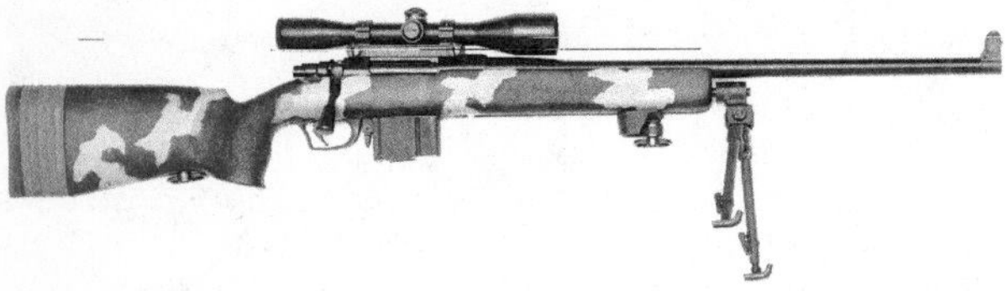

NIB	Exc.	V.G.	Good	Fair	Poor
3250	2500	975	—	—	—

Model 640E Shotgun

A 12, 16, or 20 gauge boxlock double-barrel shotgun manufactured in a variety of barrel lengths with double triggers and extractors. Blued, French case hardened with a walnut stock. Introduced in 1986.

NIB	Exc.	V.G.	Good	Fair	Poor
575	450	400	300	250	200

Model 640A

As above, with a pistol grip, beavertail forend, and single trigger. Introduced in 1986.

NIB	Exc.	V.G.	Good	Fair	Poor
675	550	500	400	300	200

Model 645E

As above, but more finely finished and engraved.

NIB	Exc.	V.G.	Good	Fair	Poor
700	550	500	400	300	200

Model 670E

A sidelock double-barrel shotgun made on special order. Introduced in 1986.

NIB	Exc.	V.G.	Good	Fair	Poor
3000	2500	1850	1200	750	400

PARKER REPRODUCTIONS

Japan

This company had exact reproductions of Parker D, DHE, B and A-1 Special shotguns made in Japan. They are of the finest quality and workmanship. The styles of engraving and features of these shotguns correspond exactly to the original Parker Arms. The following following values are a starting point.

DHEGrade

This side-by-side shotgun is offered in 12 gauge, 20 gauge, and 28 gauge. Barrel lengths are 26" or 28" with sold matte rib. Stocks are select walnut with choice of pistol or straight grip. Choice splinter or beavertail forearms are offered. Single or double triggers are available as well. The receiver is case colored and scroll engraved with game scenes to match the original Parker DHE grade. Weight of 12 gauge is 6.75 lbs., 20 gauge is 6.5 lbs., and 28 gauge weighs 5.3 lbs.

DHEGrade 12 or 20 Gauge

NIB	Exc.	V.G.	Good	Fair	Poor
6500	5000	3950	2200	1200	400

NOTE: For 28 gauge add 10 percent.

16/20 Combination

Introduced in 1993 and limited to 500 sets. Offered with 28" barrels only this set features a 16 gauge barrel on a 20 gauge frame. Weighs 6.25 lbs.

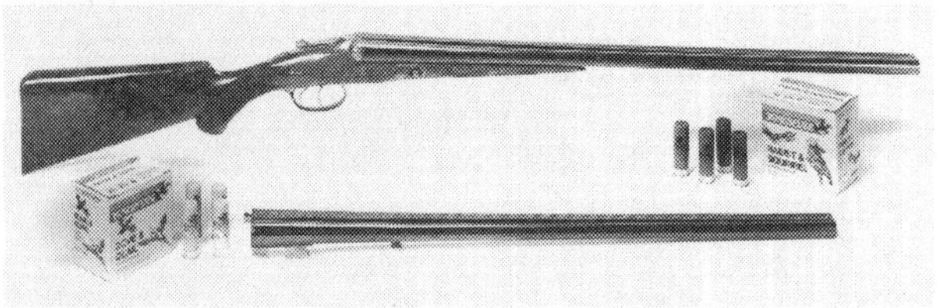

NIB	Exc.	V.G.	Good	Fair	Poor
11000	8900	7500	3500	200050	650

16/20 Combination 28 Gauge

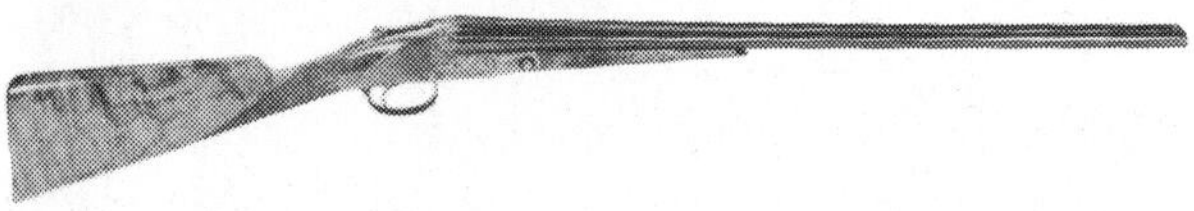

NIB	Exc.	V.G.	Good	Fair	Poor
6000	4250	3000	2000	1400	400

16/20 Combination 28 Gauge/.410 Bore Combination

NIB	Exc.	V.G.	Good	Fair	Poor
11000	8900	7500	3500	200050	650

NOTE: Add $990 for an additional barrel and $170 for beavertail forearm. For the D Grade, three-barrel sets are offered in 16/20/20 combinations for an additional $2300.

DHE Grade Steel-Shot Special

Offered in 12 gauge only with 28" barrels. Fitted with 3" chambers and special chrome lined barrels. Weighs 7 lbs.

NIB	Exc.	V.G.	Good	Fair	Poor
6000	5000	3950	2200	1200	400

BHEGrade Limited Edition

This model features engraving similar to the original Parker BHE Grade. Fancy walnut stocks with fine line checkering was standard. It was offered in 12 gauge, 20 gauge, and 28 gauge. A 28 gauge/.410 bore combination was also offered. Only 100 shotguns in this grade were produced in 1989.

NIB	Exc.	V.G.	Good	Fair	Poor
8500	6500	5000	2250	900	450

BHEGrade Limited Edition 2-Barrel Set

NIB	Exc.	V.G.	Good	Fair	Poor
15000	11500	9500	4000	2000	750

A-1 Special

Introduced in 1988, this grade featured fine scroll engraving and presentation French walnut with custom checkering pattern. The stock was hand carved with fleur-de-lis and features 32 lpi checkering. The grip cap was rosewood and gold or gold initial plate on straight grip guns. Gold wire was used on the breech end on the barrels. Serial numbers were in gold relief as were the word "SAFE" and "L" and "R" on models with selective single trigger. Barrel flats and frame water table were jeweled. This grade was offered in 12, 20, and 28 gauge with a few early guns sold with 28 gauge/.410 bore combinations. Furnished with English-style oak-and-leather case with canvas and leather cover, engraved snap caps, and engraved oil bottle.

A-1 Special 12 or 20 Gauge

NIB	Exc.	V.G.	Good	Fair	Poor
22000	17500	13000	9500	5000	700

A-1 Special 28 Gauge

NIB	Exc.	V.G.	Good	Fair	Poor
19500	14000	9500	7000	3500	600

A-1 Special Custom Engraved

This model is a custom A-1 Special hand-engraved to each individual customer's specifications. Only a limited number of these shotguns were built. Initial price in 1989 was $10,500. The sky's the limit on a gun of this sort.

PEABODY

Providence, Rhode Island
Providence Tool Company

NOTE: For historical information, photos, and data on Peabody military rifles see the Standard Catalog of Military Firearms.

Peabody Rifle and Carbine

A .43 Spanish, .443, .45 Peabody, .45-70, .50 or .50-70 caliber single-shot rifle with a 33" or 20" (carbine) barrel and either a full-length or half stock. The receiver marked "Peabody's Patent July 22, 1862 / Mannf'd by Providence Tool Co. Prov. R.I." Blued, with a walnut stock. Produced in large quantities during the 1860s and 1870s.

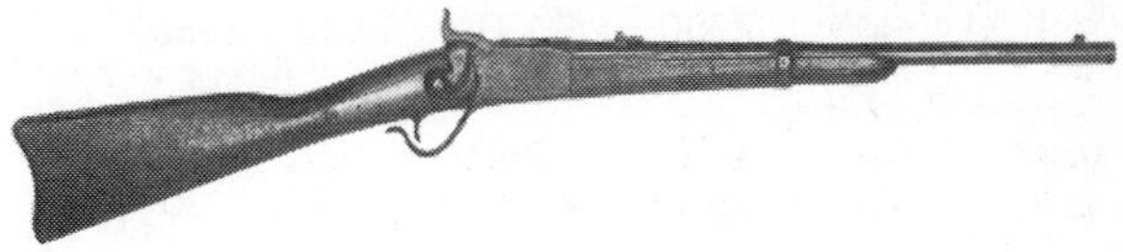

Courtesy Milwaukee Public Museum, Milwaukee, Wisconsin

NIB	Exc.	V.G.	Good	Fair	Poor
—	—	1950	900	300	100

Sporting Rifle

As above, in a sporting configuration with either 26" or 28" barrels. The frame marked, "Peabody's Patent, July 22, 1862 / Manf'd by Providence Tool Co., Prov. R.I." Blued, case hardened with a walnut stock. Manufactured from approximately 1866 to 1875.

NIB	Exc.	V.G.	Good	Fair	Poor
—	—	5500	3000	1100	400

PEABODY-MARTINI SPORTING RIFLES

NOTE: For historical information, photos, and data on Peabody-Martini military rifles see the Standard Catalog of Military Firearms.

Creedmoor

A .40-90 or .44-100 caliber Martini-action single-shot rifle with a 32" round/octagonal barrel, butt-mounted vernier rear sight, combination wind gauge and spirit level front sight. The receiver marked, "Peabody & Martini Patents" and the barrel "Manufactured by the Providence Tool Co. Providence R.I. U.S.A." Blued, case hardened with a walnut stock.

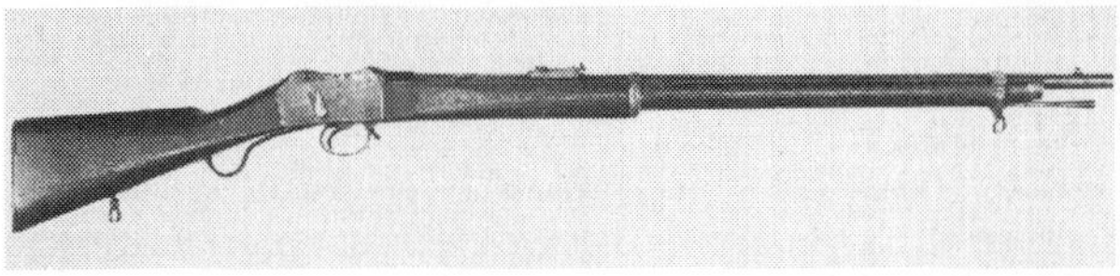

Courtesy Milwaukee Public Museum, Milwaukee, Wisconsin

NIB	Exc.	V.G.	Good	Fair	Poor
—	—	8250	3850	1650	550

Creedmoor Mid-Range

Similar to the above, but in .40-70 or .40-90 caliber with a 28" round/octagonal barrel, vernier tang sight and wind gauge front sight. Blued, case hardened with a walnut stock.

NIB	Exc.	V.G.	Good	Fair	Poor
—	—	6600	3700	1400	400

What Cheer

The Creedmoor without a pistol grip.

NIB	Exc.	V.G.	Good	Fair	Poor
—	—	6600	3600	1350	400

What Cheer Mid-Range

The Mid-Range Creedmoor without a pistol grip.

NIB	Exc.	V.G.	Good	Fair	Poor
—	—	5500	3100	1100	300

Kill Deer

A .45-70 caliber single-shot Martini-action rifle with 28" or 30" round/octagonal barrels, adjustable tang rear sight and globe front sights. Blued, case hardened with a walnut stock.

NIB	Exc.	V.G.	Good	Fair	Poor
—	—	8250	4700	1650	500

PEDERSEN, JOHN D.

Denver, Colorado & Jackson, Wyoming

Pedersen Rifle

NIB	Exc.	V.G.	Good	Fair	Poor
—	15000	7500	5000	2500	500

Pedersen Carbine

NIB	Exc.	V.G.	Good	Fair	Poor
—	17500	8500	6000	3000	—600

PEDERSEN CUSTOM GUNS

North Haven, Connecticut

A division of the O.F. Mossberg Company operated between 1973 and 1975.

Model 4000 Shotgun

The Mossberg Model 500 slide-action shotgun in 12, 20 or .410 bore with 26", 28", or 30" ventilated rib barrels. Blued, engraved with a walnut stock. Manufactured in 1975.

NIB	Exc.	V.G.	Good	Fair	Poor
—	400	350	250	200	100

Model 4000 Trap

Chambered for 12 gauge only with 30" Full choke barrel. Monte Carlo stock with factory recoil pad.

NIB	Exc.	V.G.	Good	Fair	Poor
—	500	400	300	200	100

Model 4500

As above, but with a reduced amount of engraving.

NIB	Exc.	V.G.	Good	Fair	Poor
—	425	325	225	175	100

Model 4500 Trap

Same as the Model 4000 Trap but with less engraving.

NIB	Exc.	V.G.	Good	Fair	Poor
—	400	350	250	200	100

Model 1500

A 12 gauge Magnum over-and-under shotgun with 26", 28", or 30" ventilated rib barrels, single-selective trigger and automatic ejectors. Blued with a walnut stock. Weight is about 7.5 lbs. depending on barrel length. Manufactured between 1973 and 1975.

NIB	Exc.	V.G.	Good	Fair	Poor
—	900	775	550	300	200

Model 1500 Skeet

Similar to the above model but fitted with a skeet-style stock, 27" barrels and skeet chokes.

NIB	Exc.	V.G.	Good	Fair	Poor
—	950	825	600	350	200

Model 1500 Trap

This model is fitted with a Monte Carlo-style stock a choice of 30" or 32" barrels.

NIB	Exc.	V.G.	Good	Fair	Poor
—	950	825	600	350	200

MODEL 1000

As above, but manufactured in two grades of decoration. Manufactured between 1973 and 1975.

Grade I

NIB	Exc.	V.G.	Good	Fair	Poor
—	1750	1250	800	500	200

Grade II

NIB	Exc.	V.G.	Good	Fair	Poor
—	1500	1000	750	400	200

MODEL 1000 MAGNUM

This model is chambered for the 12 gauge 3" shell and fitted with 30" barrels.

Grade I

NIB	Exc.	V.G.	Good	Fair	Poor
—	1600	1200	800	500	200

Grade II

NIB	Exc.	V.G.	Good	Fair	Poor
—	1400	1100	750	400	200

MODEL 1000 SKEET

Offered in 12 gauge only with 26" or 28" barrels. Skeet-style stock and skeet chokes.

Grade I

NIB	Exc.	V.G.	Good	Fair	Poor
—	1750	1250	800	400	200

Grade II

NIB	Exc.	V.G.	Good	Fair	Poor
—	1500	1000	750	400	200

MODEL 1000 TRAP

This model is chambered for 12 gauge and fitted with 30" or 32" barrels. Trap-style Monte Carlo stock.

Grade I

NIB	Exc.	V.G.	Good	Fair	Poor
—	1600	1200	800	500	200

Grade II

NIB	Exc.	V.G.	Good	Fair	Poor
—	1400	1100	750	400	200

MODEL 2000

A 12 or 20 gauge boxlock double-barrel shotgun with 26", 28", or 30" barrels, single-selective trigger and automatic ejectors. Produced in two grades of decoration. Manufactured in 1973 and 1974.

Grade I

NIB	Exc.	V.G.	Good	Fair	Poor
—	2000	1500	1000	600	200

Grade II

NIB	Exc.	V.G.	Good	Fair	Poor
—	1750	1250	800	400	200

Model 2500

A 12 or 20 gauge boxlock double-barrel shotgun with 26" or 28" barrels, double triggers and automatic ejectors. Blued with a walnut stock.

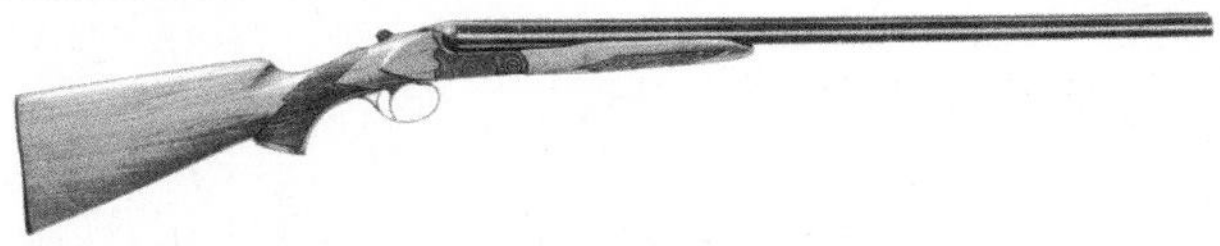

NIB	Exc.	V.G.	Good	Fair	Poor
—	400	300	250	150	200

MODEL 3000

A Mossberg Model 810 bolt-action rifle manufactured in .270 to .338 Winchester Magnum caliber with a 22" or 24" barrel with open sights. Produced in three grades.

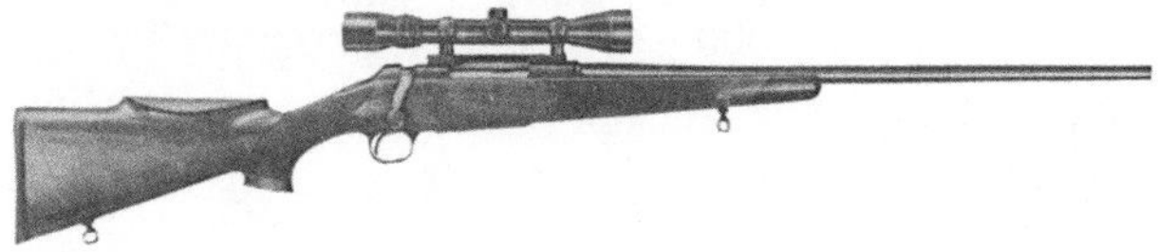

Grade III—Plain

NIB	Exc.	V.G.	Good	Fair	Poor
—	450	400	350	150	200

Grade II

NIB	Exc.	V.G.	Good	Fair	Poor
—	525	425	350	150	200

Grade I

NIB	Exc.	V.G.	Good	Fair	Poor
—	800	650	500	200	200

Model 4700

The Mossberg Model 472 lever-action in .30-30 or .35 Remington caliber with a 24" barrel and 5-shot tubular magazine. Blued with a walnut stock.

NIB	Exc.	V.G.	Good	Fair	Poor
—	450	375	275	175	100

PEDERSOLI, DAVIDE

Brescia, Italy

Davide Pedersoli & C. was founded in 1957 by the late Davide Pedersoli. In the nearly half-century since, Pedersoli has established itself as a manufacturer of extremely high-quality replica and modern firearms. Pedersoli products are frequently marked with the importer's or retailer's name (e.g., Dixie Gun Works or Cabela's) rather than the Pedersoli brand, usually at widely varying discounts. Many muzzleloading rifles and pistols are available in kit form at reduced prices.NOTE: Rapidly-fluctuating currency markets can result in values for newly-imported Pedersoli guns being 10-15 percent higher than the values listed below.

RIFLES

Swivel-Breech Rifle

Muzzleloading over-under rotating percussion rifle in .45, .50, or .54 caliber. Browned barrel, walnut stock. Discontinued.

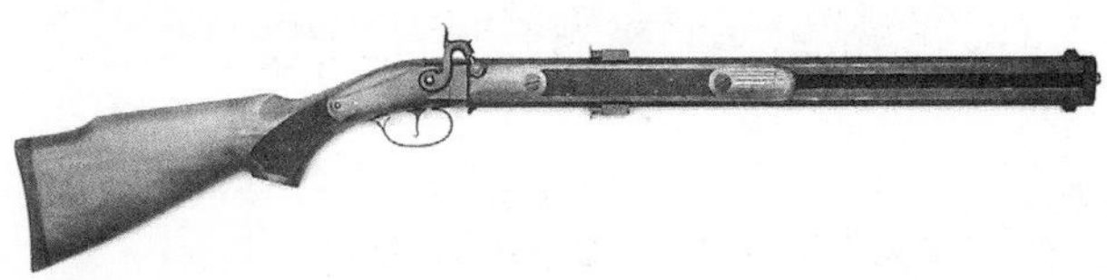

NIB	Exc.	V.G.	Good	Fair	Poor
700	625	500	350	175	100

Bristlen A. Morges Target Rifle

Recreation of 1850-vintage percussion target rifle made by Marc Bristlen of Morges, Switzerland. Schuetzen-style buttplate, double triggers, false muzzle. Shoots .35- or .45-caliber elongated conical. Add 20 percent for deluxe model.

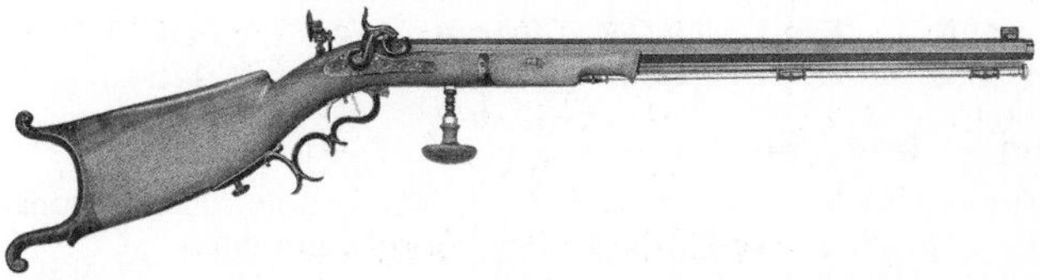

NIB	Exc.	V.G.	Good	Fair	Poor
1350	900	600	500	400	200

Waadtlander Target Rifle

Similar to Bristel A. Morges target rifle but rifled for .45-caliber round ball. Add 20 percent for deluxe version.

NIB	Exc.	V.G.	Good	Fair	Poor
1350	900	600	500	400	200

Swiss Rifle

Similar to Waadtlander Target Rifle but in flintlock with 29.5" barrel.

NIB	Exc.	V.G.	Good	Fair	Poor
1350	900	600	500	400	200

Wurttemberg Mauser

Replica of 1857 Mauser military percussion rifle made from 1857 to 1856. Shoots .54 Minie ball. Designed for 100m target shooting.

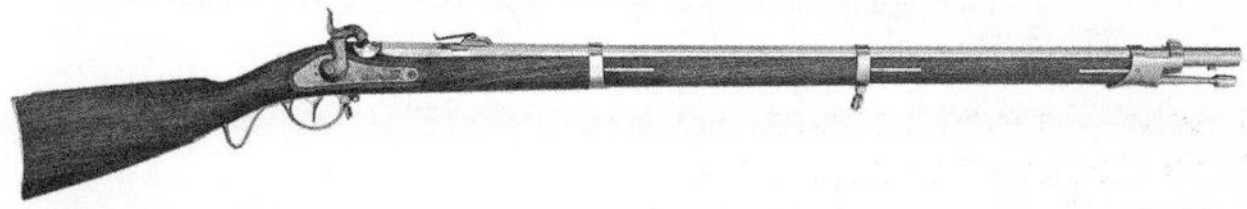

NIB	Exc.	V.G.	Good	Fair	Poor
1000	850	700	575	400	125

Gibbs Rifle

Recreation of the 1865-vintage long-range percussion rifle made by George Gibbs of London. Shoots elongated .40- or .45-caliber conicals.

NIB	Exc.	V.G.	Good	Fair	Poor
1350	900	600	500	400	200

Tryon Rifle

Recreation of noteworthy American percussion plains rifle c. 1850. .45-, .50-, or .54-caliber. Add 10 percent for Creedmore model; 20 percent for deluxe target model.

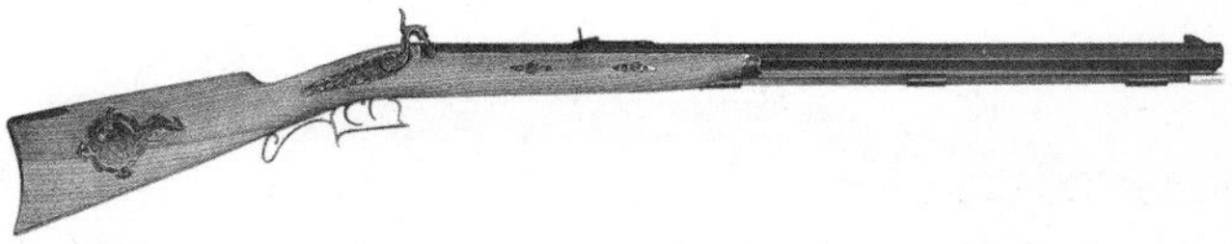

NIB	Exc.	V.G.	Good	Fair	Poor
750	600	450	300	150	75

Mortimer Rifle

Recreation of arms made c. 1850 by H. W Mortimer & Son of London. Percussion and flint versions available. Various configurations including Whitworth, Vetterli, and 12-ga. fowler.

NIB	Exc.	V.G.	Good	Fair	Poor
1050	875	600	500	400	175

Indian Trade Musket

Recreation of 18th-century flintlock smoothbore fusil as typified by colonial and early 19th-century trading companies.

NIB	Exc.	V.G.	Good	Fair	Poor
825	750	650	500	400	175

Frontier Rifle

Recreation of typical American hunting rifle c. 1800 - 1840. .32-, .36-, .45-, .50- and .54-caliber versions available in flintlock and percussion. Various barrel lengths.

NIB	Exc.	V.G.	Good	Fair	Poor
750	600	450	300	150	75

Kentucky Rifle

Recreation of Pennsylvania-style rifle c. 1800. .32-, .45- and .50-caliber percussion or flintlock. Add 35 percent for "Silver Star" model.

NIB	Exc.	V.G.	Good	Fair	Poor
750	600	450	300	150	75

Alamo Rifle

Recreation of long rifle used in Mexican War of the 1840s. Double triggers; .32-, .45- or .50-caliber.

NIB	Exc.	V.G.	Good	Fair	Poor
825	750	650	500	400	175

Cub

Scaled-down Pennsylvania-type rifle in .36, .45 or .50 caliber. Percussion or flint. Add 25 percent for flint.

NIB	Exc.	V.G.	Good	Fair	Poor
550	425	350	250	200	100

Country Hunter

Exceedingly simple half-stock .50-caliber percussion or flintlock rifle.

NIB	Exc.	V.G.	Good	Fair	Poor
500	425	350	250	200	100

Jager Rifle

Massive, decidedly Germanic .54-caliber percussion or flintlock rifle based on Teutonic hunting arms c. 1750-1850.

NIB	Exc.	V.G.	Good	Fair	Poor
950	875	700	550	375	200

Leger 1763 Charleville Musket

Recreation of Revolution-era .69-caliber smoothbore flintlock musket.

NIB	Exc.	V.G.	Good	Fair	Poor
1050	875	600	500	400	175

Revolutionnaire 1777 Musket

Similar to Charleville musket but in detail patterned after muskets used in French Revolution.

NIB	Exc.	V.G.	Good	Fair	Poor
1050	875	600	500	400	175

Corrige An IX

Similar to Revolutionnaire 1777 musket but differing in details of frizzen, etc.

NIB	Exc.	V.G.	Good	Fair	Poor
1050	875	600	500	400	175

An IX Dragoon Musket

Similar to Corrige An IX musket but with 40.5" cavalry-length barrel.

NIB	Exc.	V.G.	Good	Fair	Poor
1050	875	600	500	400	175

Austrian 1798 Flintlock Musket

Similar to 1777 musket but with Austrian modifications in barel bands, bayonet mount, etc.

NIB	Exc.	V.G.	Good	Fair	Poor
1050	875	600	500	400	175

Prussian 1809 Flintlock Musket

Similar to French 1777 musket but in .75 caliber with "Potsdam" markings.

NIB	Exc.	V.G.	Good	Fair	Poor
1050	875	600	500	400	175

Brown Bess Flintlock Musket

Recreation of legendary .75-caliber smoothbore musket as used by British troops before, during and after the American Revolutionary War.

NIB	Exc.	V.G.	Good	Fair	Poor
950	875	700	550	375	200

Springfield 1795 Musket

Recreation of America's first indigenous military arm. .69-caliber smoothbore.

NIB	Exc.	V.G.	Good	Fair	Poor
950	875	700	550	375	200

Harper's Ferry 1816 Musket

Recreation of U.S. martial .69-caliber smoothbore flintlock musket.

NIB	Exc.	V.G.	Good	Fair	Poor
950	875	700	550	375	200

Rocky Mountain Hawken

Faithful recreation of legendary plains rifle. .54 caliber.

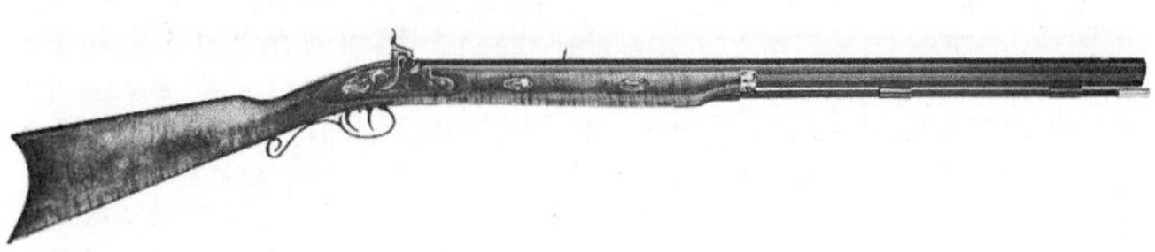

NIB	Exc.	V.G.	Good	Fair	Poor
850	695	550	400	250	125

Springfield 1861 Rifle

Recreation of .58-caliber percussion rifle as used in American Civil War.

NIB	Exc.	V.G.	Good	Fair	Poor
950	875	700	550	375	200

Kodiak Combination Gun

Percussion side-by-side rifle/shotgun combination gun with 12-ga. smoothbore barrel and .50-, .54- and .58-caliber rifled barrel.

NIB	Exc.	V.G.	Good	Fair	Poor
1100	850	600	425	300	200

Kodiak Double Rifle

Side-by-side double percussion rifle in .50, .54, .58 and .72 caliber. Sights regulated to 75 yards.

NIB	Exc.	V.G.	Good	Fair	Poor
1200	950	700	475	325	200

Rolling Block Rifle

Replica of famous Remington rolling block single-shot rifle 1867 – c. 1890. Various centerfire chamberings and configurations including Baby carbine. Prices shown are for standard version in .45-70.

NIB	Exc.	V.G.	Good	Fair	Poor
950	875	700	550	375	200

1859 Sharps Cavalry Carbine

Replica of Sharps percussion carbine with 22" barrel, patchbox and elvator sight; .54 caliber. Also available as Infantry Rifle with 30" barrel.

NIB	Exc.	V.G.	Good	Fair	Poor
895	825	775	675	475	200

1862 Robinson Confederate Sharps

Similar to 1859 Sharps carbine but with different barrel band, receiver details, and rear sight.

NIB	Exc.	V.G.	Good	Fair	Poor
800	675	575	400	300	125

Sharps 1863 Sporting Rifle

Replica of Sharps sporting rifle with 32" barrel, set trigger and sculpted forend; .45 or .54 caliber. .45 version rifled for elongated conicals.

NIB	Exc.	V.G.	Good	Fair	Poor
850	725	625	450	350	150

1874 Sharps

High-quality replica of first Sharps chambered for metallic cartridges. Chamberings include .45-70, .45-90, .45-110, .45-120, .50-70 and .50-90. Several variations available including Sporting Standard Sporting, Cavalry Rifle, Cavalry Carbine, Sporting Deluxe, Sporting Extra Deluxe, Silhouette Standard, Silhouette Deluxe, Boss, Business Rifle, Buffalo, Billy Dixon, Long Range, Quigley, Creedmore #2 and Competition Standard. Prices given are for Standard Sporting model.

NIB	Exc.	V.G.	Good	Fair	Poor
1100	850	600	425	300	200

1873 Trapdoor Springfield

Replica of famous single-shot cartridge rifle chambered in .45-70. Several variations available including Standard Rifle, Standard Carbine, Officer's Model and Long Range Model. Add 30 percent for Deluxe models. Prices given are for Standard Rifle.

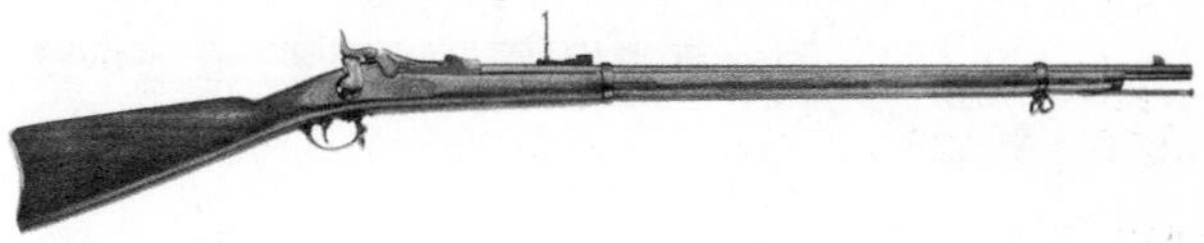

NIB	Exc.	V.G.	Good	Fair	Poor
1100	850	600	425	300	200

Kodiak Mark IV Express Rifle

Side-by-side double rifle chambered for .45-70 cartridge.

NIB	Exc.	V.G.	Good	Fair	Poor
4500	3750	3000	2000	900	300

Pedersoli Lightning Rifle

Updated replica of Model 1883 Colt Lightning Magazine Rifle. Pump action with magazine disconnector. Chambered for .44-40 and .45 Colt.

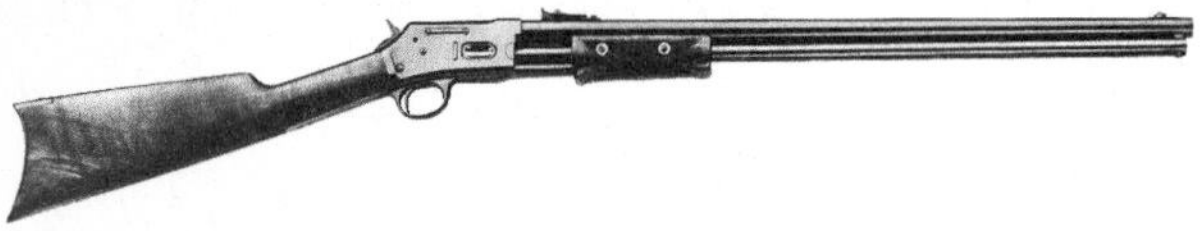

NIB	Exc.	V.G.	Good	Fair	Poor
1100	850	600	425	300	200

SHOTGUNS

Double Percussion Shotgun

Side-by-side muzzleloading shotgun in 20, 12 and 10 gauge. Interchangeable chokes. Camo models available. Prices given are for basic version in 12 ga.

NIB	Exc.	V.G.	Good	Fair	Poor
650	550	475	300	175	125

Coach Shotgun

Side-by-side 12-ga. percussion shotgun with 20" barrels. Discontinued.

NIB	Exc.	V.G.	Good	Fair	Poor
600	525	450	275	150	125

Mortimer Shotgun

Recreation of 12-ga. fowlers made c. 1830 to 1850 by H. W Mortimer & Son of London. Percussion and flint versions available.

NIB	Exc.	V.G.	Good	Fair	Poor
1100	850	600	425	300	200

MODERN MUZZLELOADERS

Denali

In-line 50-caliber muzzleloader with lever-operated break-open action. Walnut/blue or camo/blue finish. Add 15 percent for camo.

NIB	Exc.	V.G.	Good	Fair	Poor
380	350	275	200	100	50

Brutus 94

Inline .50-caliber muzzleloader. Blued/composite, blued/synthetic or stainless/blued/walnut finish. Add 15 percent for camo.

NIB	Exc.	V.G.	Good	Fair	Poor
350	300	200	125	100	75

Brutus Ovation

Inline .50-caliber muzzleloader with interchangeable barrels. Developed in cooperation with Mid-Western Outdoor Specialties and so marked. One-piece stock. Blued/hardwood or blued/camo finish. Add 15 percent for camo.

NIB	Exc.	V.G.	Good	Fair	Poor
350	300	200	125	100	75

Rolling Block Percussion Rifle

.50-caliber muzzleloading version of Remington rolling block rifle. Blued/hardwoods or blued/camo finish.

NIB	Exc.	V.G.	Good	Fair	Poor
350	300	200	125	100	75

PERAZZI

Brescia, Italy

This company was founded in 1957. During the 1970s Ithaca and Winchester imported and sold Perazzi shotguns. Perazzi has now taken over its own importation and distribution in the United States with the creation of Perazzi USA, Inc. Many shooters consider the Perazzi to be the finest currently produced shotgun in the world.Perazzi has an extensive variety of models to choose from. In addition, each model may be available in different grades. These grades are based on the type of finish, engraving, and wood quality. The vast majority of Perazzi shotguns that are sold in this country are Standard Grade guns. According to Perazzi USA, these Standard Grade guns account for approximately 98 percent of North American sales. Therefore, it is unlikely that the shooter or collector will encounter high-grade Perazzi guns. It should be pointed out that in some models no Extra Grade or Extra Gold Grade shotguns have ever been sold in the United States.For the benefit of the reader an approximate description of each grade follows. It is a general description because the Perazzi customer may order practically any combination of finishes or engraving patterns he or she desires. Use this list as a general guide. It is strongly suggested that anyone wanted to know more about Perazzi guns buy a copy of Karl Lippard's book, Perazzi Shotguns. He can be reached at P.O. Box 60719, Colorado Springs, CO, 719-444-0786. PRICING NOTE: Because of the difficulty in pricing grades above the SCO Grade because of their rarity and custom configurations these grades are not priced.ADDITIONAL NOTE: Perazzi shotguns are a highly specialized field with fluctuating values and nearly endless variations. The following information is of the most general nature and is not intended to be comprehensive. An arbitrary value of $700 has been entered for examples in Poor condition; we have never personally seen a Perazzi in less than Good condition, except for fire-damaged examples or other basket cases.

OUT-OF-PRODUCTION SHOTGUNS

NOTE: Very high premiums on early SCO and higher grades.

COMP 1-SB TRAP Standard Grade

This model is a single barrel trap gun in 12 gauge only with 32" or 34" vent rib barrel.

NIB	Exc.	V.G.	Good	Fair	Poor
—	2250	1500	1000	750	500

COMP 1-TRAP Standard Grade

This is an over-and-under version of the above model.

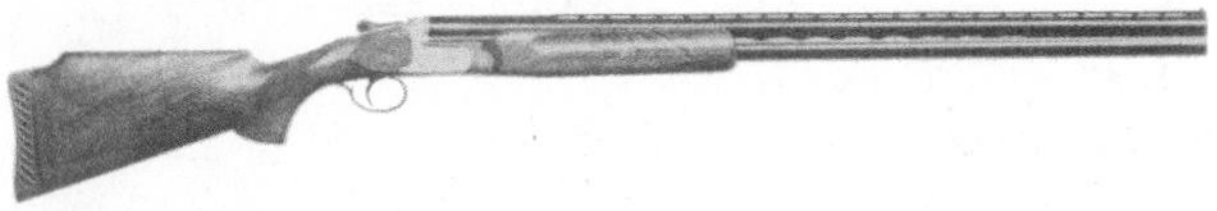

NIB	Exc.	V.G.	Good	Fair	Poor
—	4800	4000	3000	2250	500

Light Game Model Standard Grade

Offered in 12 gauge with a 27.5" vent rib barrel. Trigger group is not detachable. Produced between 1972 and 1974.

NIB	Exc.	V.G.	Good	Fair	Poor
—	6250	4750	3000	1400	500

NOTE: Deduct 25 percent for skeet chokes.

MT-6 Model Standard Grade

This model was offered in 12 gauge with a tapered vent rib. The trigger group was not removable. Discontinued in 1983.

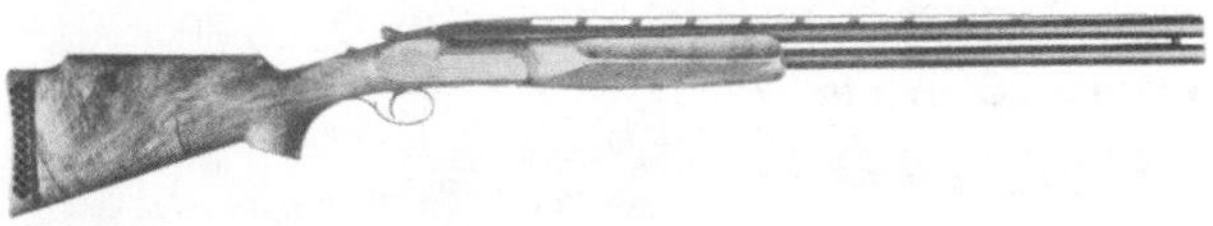

NIB	Exc.	V.G.	Good	Fair	Poor
—	3100	2500	1900	1000	400

NOTE: Deduct 20 percent for 27.375" barrels.

MX3

This model was discontinued in 1988 and was available in 12 gauge only for single barrel Trap, over-and-under trap, combination trap, skeet, and sporting configurations.

Standard Grade

NIB	Exc.	V.G.	Good	Fair	Poor
—	3500	3000	2250	1750	400

SC3 Grade

NIB	Exc.	V.G.	Good	Fair	Poor
—	5000	4000	3000	2200	500

SCO Grade

NIB	Exc.	V.G.	Good	Fair	Poor
—	6500	5500	4000	2500	500

Gold Grade

NIB	Exc.	V.G.	Good	Fair	Poor
10000	8500	5900	2700	—	700

NOTE: Add 50 percent to above prices for Combination Trap Guns.

GRAND AMERICAN SPECIAL

This model was introduced in 1988 and features a high ramped rib similar to the MX3 model. The forend was grooved. Discontinued in 1991. It was offered in single barrel trap, combination trap, and over-and-under trap configurations.

Standard Grade

NIB	Exc.	V.G.	Good	Fair	Poor
—	5250	4250	3500	2000	700

SC3 Grade

NIB	Exc.	V.G.	Good	Fair	Poor
—	6500	5250	4500	3000	700

SCO Grade

NIB	Exc.	V.G.	Good	Fair	Poor
—	8000	6500	5500	3750	700

Gold Grade

NIB	Exc.	V.G.	Good	Fair	Poor
—	10000	7500	6000	4000	700

Grade w/Sideplates

NIB	Exc.	V.G.	Good	Fair	Poor
—	13500	10000	7500	6000	700

Gold Grade w/Sideplates

NIB	Exc.	V.G.	Good	Fair	Poor
—	15000	12000	8500	6500	700

SHO Model

NOTE: This over-and-under sidelock model is available in 12 gauge only in both Type 1 and Type 2 configurations. Type 1 does not have rebounding firing pins and is worth approximately 50 percent less than Type 2 models that are fitted with rebounding firing pins. There are no parts available in this country or at the factory for Type 1 guns. An expert appraisal is recommended for this model due to its unique features.The SHO model features a silver finish with fine scroll engraving with game scenes to customer's specifications. Select walnut stock built to customer's dimensions with fine line checkering. A custom built shotgun. Special order only. The sky's the limit.

DHO Model

This is a side-by-side shotgun offered in 12 gauge only. It has full sidelocks and a silver receiver finish with scroll and game scene engraving of the same quality as the SHO Model. Fancy walnut stock with fine line checkering. An expert appraisal is recommended for this model due to its unique features. Special order only. The sky's the limit.

DHO Extra Gold

Available in any gauge and barrel length combination. Only the finest presentation walnut and checkering. A totally custom built shotgun. Special order only. Special order only. The sky's the limit.

RECENT PRODUCTION SHOTGUNS

MX9

Introduced in 1993 this model features removable inserts on rib to adjust point of impact and a walnut stock with adjustable comb. Offered in 12 gauge with 32" or 34" barrel with screw-in chokes in Trap configuration and single barrels in Trap/Combo models. A competition version is also offered with unique vent rib inserts to correct for point of impact.The trigger group is removable. Available in several different grades of ornamentation.

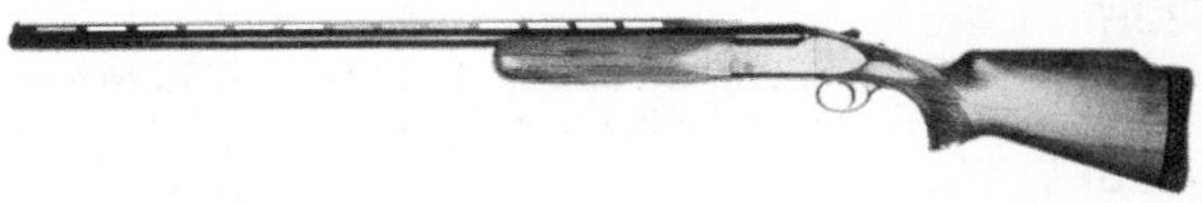

Standard Grade

NIB	Exc.	V.G.	Good	Fair	Poor
—	6500	5000	3500	1800	700

SC3 Grade

NIB	Exc.	V.G.	Good	Fair	Poor
—	11500	6000	5000	3000	700

SCO Grade

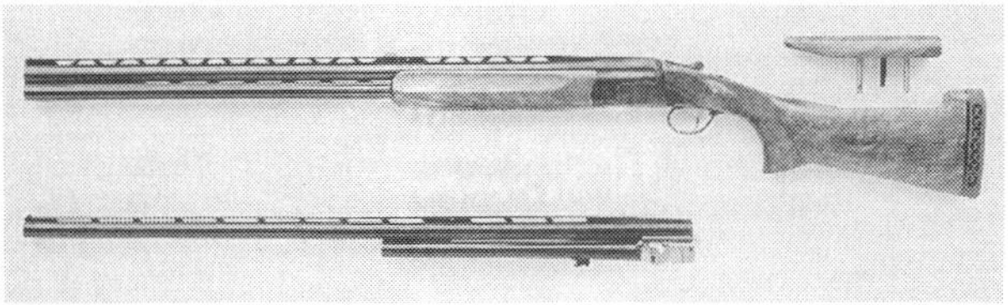

NIB	Exc.	V.G.	Good	Fair	Poor
—	18000	8000	7000	3500	7000

Standard Grade Trap Combo MX 9

NIB	Exc.	V.G.	Good	Fair	Poor
—	9500	6500	5000	3500	900

MX10

This model was introduced in 1993. Its Single Barrel Trap models feature a different method of rib height and pattern adjustment. This model also has an adjustable stock. Available in 12 gauge with 32" or 34" barrels. Trap/Combo models are offered in 12 gauge with 29.5" or 31.5" over-and-under barrels with 32" or 34" single barrel. Chokes are fixed. Competition models are offered in 12 gauge and 20 gauge with choice of 29.5" or 31.5" barrel for 12 gauge and 29.5" barrel for 20 gauge. The ventilated rib height is adjustable as is the comb position on the stock. Trigger is removable.

Standard Grade

NIB	Exc.	V.G.	Good	Fair	Poor
—	8250	7000	6000	4300	700

SC3 Grade

NIB	Exc.	V.G.	Good	Fair	Poor
—	10000	8500	7000	5200	700

SCO Grade

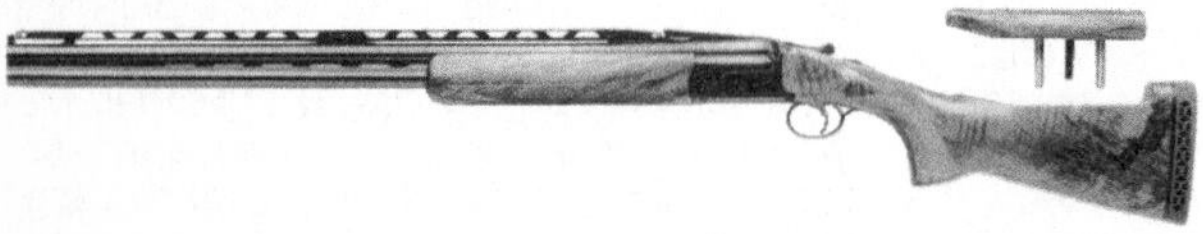

NIB	Exc.	V.G.	Good	Fair	Poor
—	13500	11000	8500	6750	700

Standard Grade Combo Model

NIB	Exc.	V.G.	Good	Fair	Poor
—	15000	13000	10500	5000	700

TM I SPECIAL

This basic single barrel Perazzi Trap model is offered in 12 gauge with 32" or 34" barrel. Trigger is adjustable.

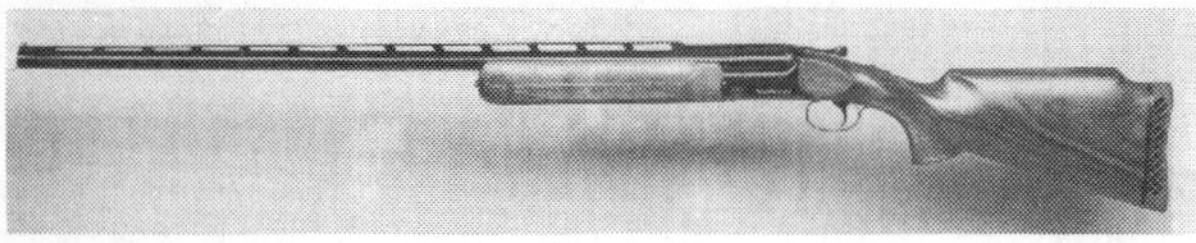

Standard Grade

NIB	Exc.	V.G.	Good	Fair	Poor
—	4000	2000	1250	850	700

TMX SPECIAL

Similar to TM I Special with select walnut.

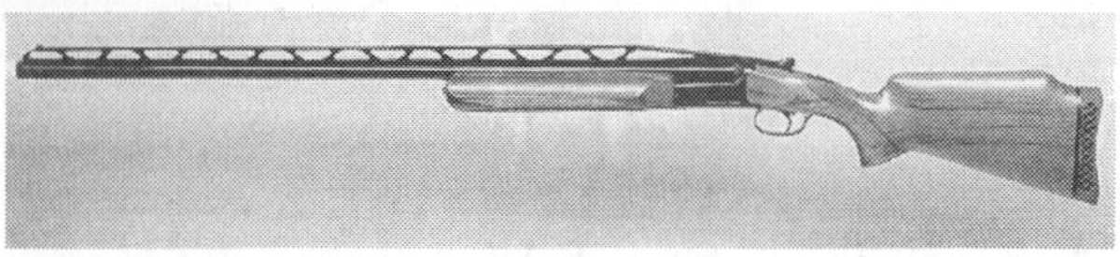

Standard Grade

NIB	Exc.	V.G.	Good	Fair	Poor
—	5000	4200	2700	1900	700

SCO Grade

NIB	Exc.	V.G.	Good	Fair	Poor
—	8000	6000	5000	2100	700

MX8 SPECIAL

This model features a low contour vent rib, adjustable trigger, and grooved forend.NOTE: Some SCO engraving patterns on early models have sold in the $30,000 to $45,000 price range. depending on the engraver. Get an expert appraisal. Beware of counterfeits.

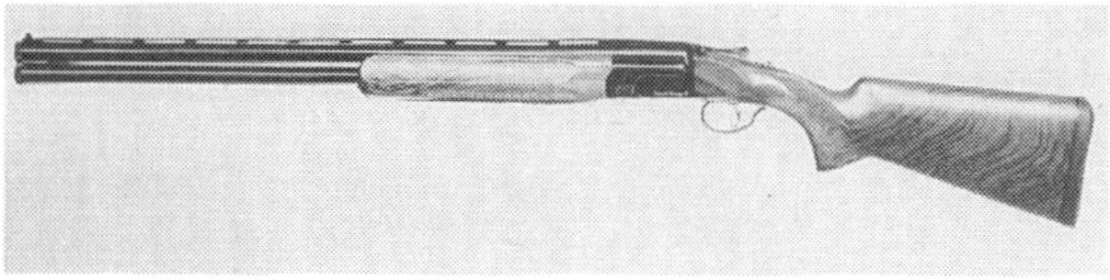

Special Standard Grade

NIB	Exc.	V.G.	Good	Fair	Poor
—	5500	4000	3000	2000	700

Special SC3 Grade

NIB	Exc.	V.G.	Good	Fair	Poor
—	7500	5500	3800	2500	700

Special SCO Grade

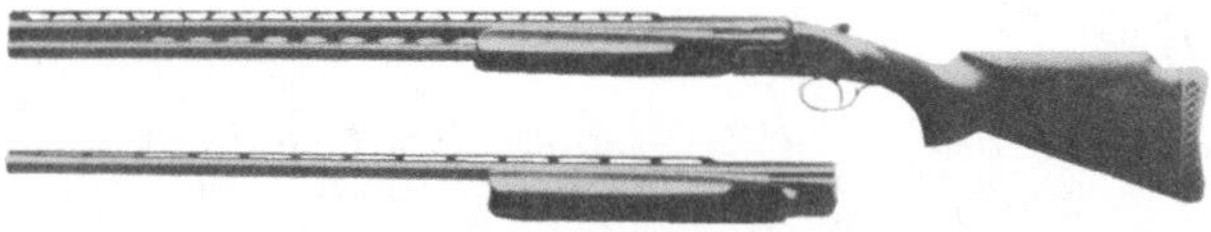

NIB	Exc.	V.G.	Good	Fair	Poor
—	13000	10500	8000	5000	700

Special Standard Grade MX 8 Trap Combo

NIB	Exc.	V.G.	Good	Fair	Poor
—	7500	5000	3500	2000	700

MX8/20

This model was first introduced in 1993. It features a removable trigger group. Available in 20 gauge only with choice of 27.5", 28.375", 29.5" flat ventilated rib barrels. Choice of fixed or screw-in chokes on sporting model. Stock is custom made to customer's dimensions with beavertail forend.

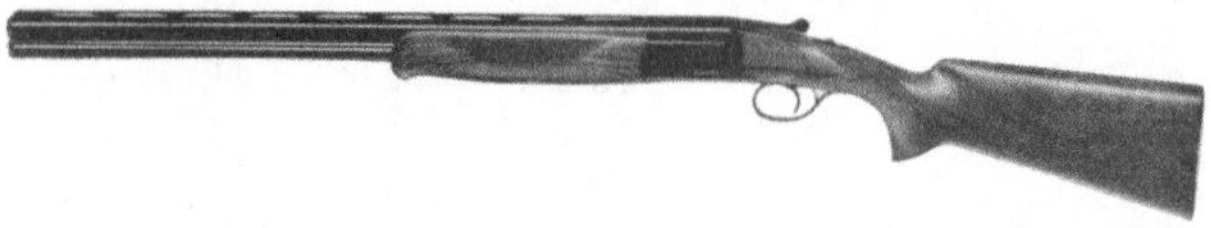

Standard Grade

NIB	Exc.	V.G.	Good	Fair	Poor
—	5500	4000	3000	2000	700

SC3 Grade

NIB	Exc.	V.G.	Good	Fair	Poor
—	7500	5500	4000	2750	700

SCO Grade

NIB	Exc.	V.G.	Good	Fair	Poor
—	10000	7500	5500	3250	700

MX8/20-8/20C

Introduced in 1993 and offered in 20 gauge with 26" or 27.625" vent rib barrels. The trigger group on this model is removable. The stock is a high-grade walnut custom made to customers' specifications. The forend is round. The MX8/20 is supplied with fixed chokes while the MX8/20C has 5 screw-in choke tubes. Add $400 for MX8/20C values.

Standard Grade

NIB	Exc.	V.G.	Good	Fair	Poor
—	6000	4500	3000	1750	700

SC3 Grade

NIB	Exc.	V.G.	Good	Fair	Poor
—	8000	6000	4250	2000	700

SCO Grade

NIB	Exc.	V.G.	Good	Fair	Poor
—	11500	8500	7000	4000	700

MX7 Standard Grade

Introduced in 1993. This an over-and-under trap model that is offered in 12 gauge with 29.5" or 31.5" over-and-under barrels with either 32" or 34" single barrel. This model has a non-renewable trigger group feathering fixed coil spring trigger mechanism. The trigger is selective and works in conjunction with the safety catch. The vent rib is ramped on the Combo Trap model. The walnut is custom made to the customer's dimensions.

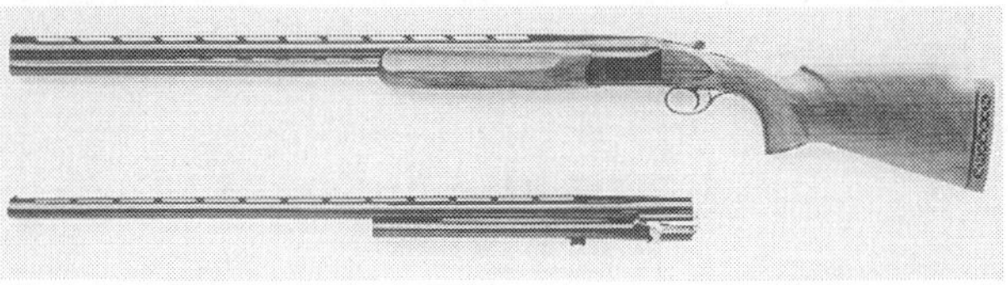

NIB	Exc.	V.G.	Good	Fair	Poor
—	4500	3200	2500	1750	700

MX7C Standard Grade

Introduced in 1993 this model is offered in 12 gauge with a non-renewable trigger group. It has a coil spring mechanism, fully selective in conjunction with the safety. Offered in 27.5", 29.5", or 31.5" flat vent rib barrels. Screw-in chokes are standard. Walnut stock is custom made to customer's dimensions. The forend is beavertail.

NIB	Exc.	V.G.	Good	Fair	Poor
—	5500	4000	3000	2000	700

DB81 SPECIAL

This model, offered in 12 guage only, features a high ramped ventilated rib. Trigger is adjustable with internal selector. Barrel length are 29.5" or 31.5".Add $1,000 for two forends and two triggers for Trap/Combo models.

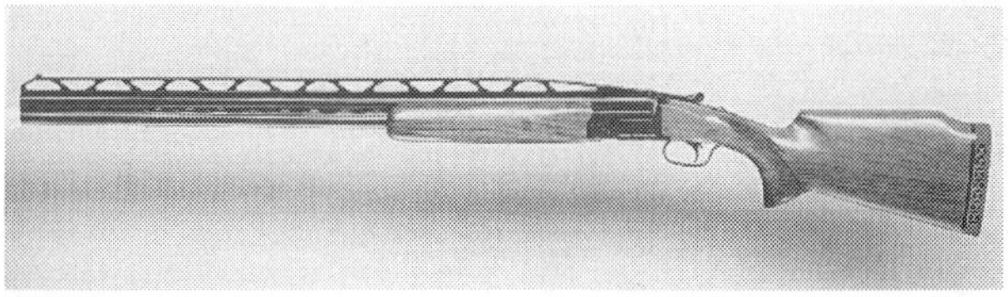

Standard Grade

NIB	Exc.	V.G.	Good	Fair	Poor
—	8700	6500	5200	2500	700

SC3 Grade

NIB	Exc.	V.G.	Good	Fair	Poor
—	11000	8000	7000	3500	700

SCO Grade

NIB	Exc.	V.G.	Good	Fair	Poor
—	17500	12500	10000	6500	700

COMPETITION MODELS

Competition versions are over-and-under shotguns in trap, skeet, pigeon, and sporting models. Stock dimensions are based on the particular model chosen. Trap models feature trap stock dimensions and forearm designed for that purpose. The other models also have their own particular specifications. However, prices are based on a common style referred to by Perazzi as Competition. Thus, all models within this group are priced the same regardless of specific type.

Mirage Special Standard Grade

This model features an adjustable trigger and is available in 12 gauge with choice of 27.5", 28.375", 29.5", or 31.5" ventilated rib barrels.

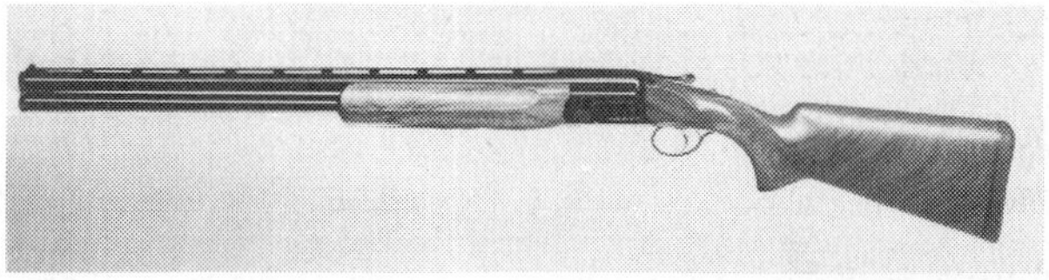

NIB	Exc.	V.G.	Good	Fair	Poor
—	5500	3750	2500	1100	700

Mirage Special Sporting Standard Grade

Similar to the Mirage Special listed above, but with external trigger selection and screw-in chokes. Offered in 12 gauge only with choice of 27.5", 28.375", or 29.5" vent rib barrels.

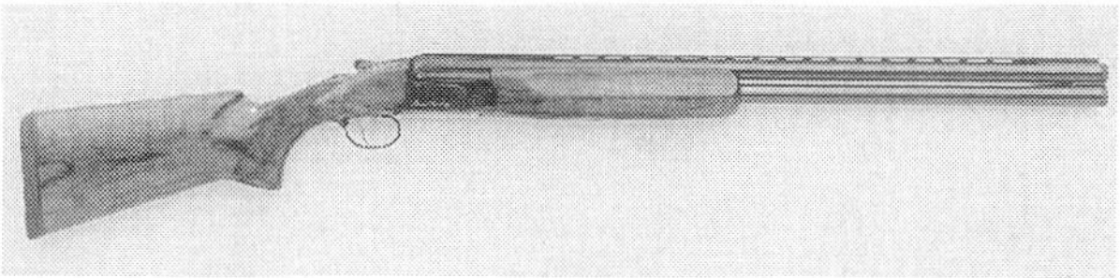

NIB	Exc.	V.G.	Good	Fair	Poor
—	4500	3250	2500	1100	700

Mirage Special Sporting Classic Standard Grade

This model features the same basic specifications as the Mirage Special Sporting with the addition of a scroll border on the receiver and triggerguard. The wood is of slightly higher quality. Offered in 12 gauge only with 27.5", 28.375", or 29.5" vent rib barrels.

NIB	Exc.	V.G.	Good	Fair	Poor
—	4500	3250	2500	1100	700

Mirage MX8 Standard Grade

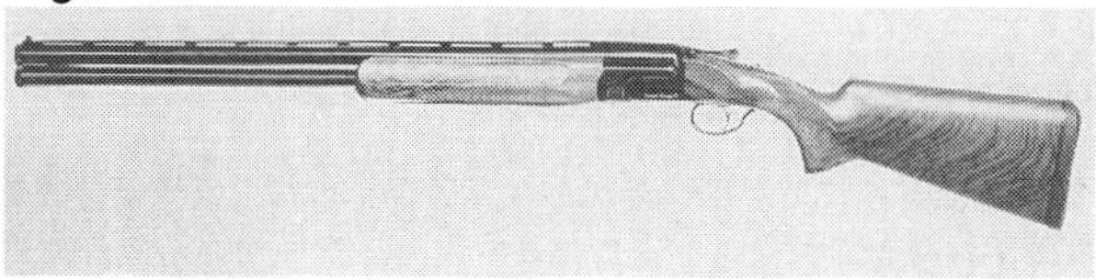

NIB	Exc.	V.G.	Good	Fair	Poor
—	5800	4250	3000	1500	700

SCO Model SCO Grade

This model is similar to the MX8 but offered only in 12 gauge with barrel length from 27.5" to 31.5". The trigger is adjustable instead of removable.

NIB	Exc.	V.G.	Good	Fair	Poor
—	10500	6000	4500	3000	700

MIRAGE SPECIAL 4-GAUGE SET

Similar to the Mirage Special in appearance and specifications but fitted with four barrel sets with 27.62" barrels in 12, 20, 28 gauge, and .410 bore. For 28.37" barrels add $2,000 and for 29.5" barrels add $3,000.

Standard Grade

NIB	Exc.	V.G.	Good	Fair	Poor
—	—	10000	7000	4500	700

SC3 Grade

NIB	Exc.	V.G.	Good	Fair	Poor
—	21000	15000	10000	7500	700

SCO Grade

NIB	Exc.	V.G.	Good	Fair	Poor
—	28000	19000	12500	8500	700

MX12/12C

Offered in 12 gauge only with 26.75" or 27.5" vent rib barrels. The single-selective trigger is nonrefillable. The walnut stock is fitted with a schnabel forend and the receiver has a light-scroll engraved border. The MX12 is supplied with fixed chokes while the MX12C is fitted with 5 screw-in choke tubes. Add $400 to MX12 prices to get MX12C values.

Standard Grade

NIB	Exc.	V.G.	Good	Fair	Poor
—	4500	3250	2000	1200	700

SC3 Grade

NIB	Exc.	V.G.	Good	Fair	Poor
—	6500	4750	3250	2000	700

SCO Grade

NIB	Exc.	V.G.	Good	Fair	Poor
—	10000	7000	5000	3500	700

MX20/20C

This model is offered in 20 gauge. It features a nonremovable trigger group. The frame is smaller than 12 gauge. Offered with 26" or 27.5" vent rib barrels. The MX20 has fixed chokes while the MX20C is supplied with 5 screw-in choke tubes. Add $400 to MX20 prices to get MX20C values.

Standard Grade

NIB	Exc.	V.G.	Good	Fair	Poor
—	5500	4250	3200	2000	1000

SC3 Grade

NIB	Exc.	V.G.	Good	Fair	Poor
—	6500	4750	3000	2500	1000

SCO Grade

NIB	Exc.	V.G.	Good	Fair	Poor
—	19500	17000	13500	9000	3000

MX28 AND MX410

Introduced in 1993 these two models feature a nonremovable trigger group and a special small frame for each. The MX28, .28 gauge, weighs about 5.5 lbs. while the MX410, .410 bore, weighs slightly less. Both are supplied with fixed chokes, flat ribs, custom made stocks, and round forends. Each model is offered with a choice of 26" or 27.5" barrels. Both the MX28 and MX410 are priced the same.

Standard Grade

NIB	Exc.	V.G.	Good	Fair	Poor
—	12000	10750	8000	6000	1000

SCO Grade

NIB	Exc.	V.G.	Good	Fair	Poor
—	18000	16000	13500	9000	2000

PERRY PATENT FIREARMS CO.

Newark, New Jersey

Perry Carbine

A .54 caliber breech-loading percussion carbine with a 20.75" barrel and half-length walnut stock secured by one barrel band. Blued with a case hardened lock. Approximately 200 were made.

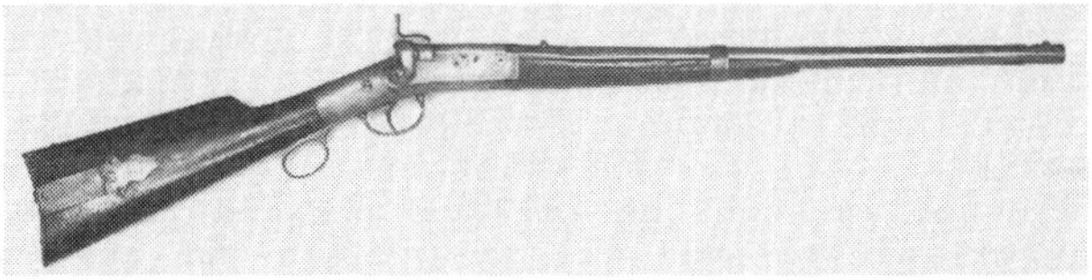

Courtesy Milwaukee Public Museum, Milwaukee, Wisconsin

NIB	Exc.	V.G.	Good	Fair	Poor
—	27500	13000	8250	3600	1000

PERUGINI & VISINI

Brescia, Italy

Arms by this maker were imported by W.L. Moore of Westlake Village, California.

Liberty Model

A side-by-side 12, 20, 28 and .410 gauge shotgun with 28" barrels. Anson & Deeley action with a double Purdy lock. Blued overall with checkered walnut stock.

NIB	Exc.	V.G.	Good	Fair	Poor
7500	6000	4500	2500	1250	750

Classic Model

A 12 or 20 gauge double-barrel shotgun with a Holland & Holland-style sidelock and a double Purdy lock. The barrels are 28" in length. Single trigger and automatic ejectors. The sidelocks and mounts and engraved and blued. Well figured and checkered walnut stock.

NIB	Exc.	V.G.	Good	Fair	Poor
15000	11500	9500	4000	2000	1000

Bolt-Action Rifle

A Mauser-type bolt-action rifle available in a variety of chamberings, with 24" or 26" barrels. Sights not furnished. Well figured checkered walnut stock.

NIB	Exc.	V.G.	Good	Fair	Poor
6500	4250	3000	1500	900	500

Deluxe Bolt-Action Rifle

As above with first quality walnut stocks and a case.

NIB	Exc.	V.G.	Good	Fair	Poor
7500	5000	3500	1500	1000	600

Eagle Single-Shot

An Anson & Deeley single-shot rifle fitted with either 24" or 26" barrels, open sights, automatic ejector and adjustable trigger. Stock of checkered walnut.

NIB	Exc.	V.G.	Good	Fair	Poor
7500	4250	4000	1500	1000	600

Boxlock Express Rifle

An Anson & Deeley action double-barrel rifle chambered for .444 Marlin or 9.3x74R cartridges. The barrel length is 24" and is fitted with express sights. Double triggers and automatic ejectors. Receiver case hardened and the barrels as well as mounts blued. Checkered walnut stock.

NIB	*Exc.*	*V.G.*	*Good*	*Fair*	*Poor*
7000	5500	3750	2000	1500	500

Magnum Over-and-Under

An Anson & Deeley action over-and-under rifle available .375 Holland & Holland and .458 Winchester Magnum. The barrels are 24" in length and fitted with express sights. Double triggers and automatic ejectors. Receiver and barrels blued, the stock of checkered walnut.

NIB	*Exc.*	*V.G.*	*Good*	*Fair*	*Poor*
7000	5500	3750	2000	1500	500

Super Express Rifle

A Holland & Holland-style sidelock double-barrel rifle. Having 24" barrels fitted with express sights. Available in a variety of chamberings. The receiver and sidelocks are either case hardened or finished in the bright and fully engraved. Checkered walnut stock.

NIB	*Exc.*	*V.G.*	*Good*	*Fair*	*Poor*
20000	17500	13000	10000	6500	1000

Victoria Side-by-Side Rifle

Similar to the Boxlock Express Rifle but chambered for .30-06, 7x65R, or 9.3x74R cartridges. Either 24" or 26" barrels were available. Double triggers and automatic ejectors. Blued with minimal engraving. Stock of checkered walnut.

NIB	*Exc.*	*V.G.*	*Good*	*Fair*	*Poor*
6500	5250	4000	3000	1500	750

Selous Side-by-Side Rifle

First quality double-barrel express rifle with 24" or 26" barrels. Fully detachable Holland & Holland-style sidelocks, double triggers and automatic ejectors. Fully engraved with well figured checkered walnut stocks.

NIB	*Exc.*	*V.G.*	*Good*	*Fair*	*Poor*
22500	17500	12500	6000	3000	1500

PGM PRECISION

France

Model PGM

This is a highly sophisticated semi-automatic rifle designed and built on a modular component system. Barrel change is fast and available calibers are .308 Win., .300 Savage, 7mm-08, .243, and .22-250. Match grade barrel length is 23.4". Fully adjustable trigger and buttstock with adjustable bipod. Five-round magazine is standard. Weight is approximately 13 lbs.

NIB	*Exc.*	*V.G.*	*Good*	*Fair*	*Poor*
13500	9000	7000	3500	1750	1000

PIOTTI

Brescia, Italy

This Italian gunmaking firm is located in Gardone Val Trompia in the province of Brescia. Its shotguns are hand crafted and limited to a few each year. Each gun is made to individual specifications. Many consider them one of the best double shotguns made in the world today. Actions are either Anson & Deeley boxlock or Holland & Holland sidelock. Several features are offered on these shotguns at no additional cost: type of stock and forearm, barrel length and chokes, rib, action shape and finish.Other features are considered extra cost options and will affect the value of the gun. There are: single triggers, detachable sidelocks, automatic safety, recoil pads, upgraded wood, engraving, and multi-gauge sets. With the exception of a few grades Piotti guns are available in 10, 12, 16, 20, and 28 gauge, as well as .410 bore. Depending on gauge barrel lengths are from 25" to 32".

Model Piuma (BSEE)

This model is the firm's standard boxlock offering. Available in 12 gauge to .410 bore it features ejectors and a scalloped frame. Fine scroll and rosette engraving is standard.NOTE: Around serial number 9000, or 1989, Piotti began building the Model BSEE to the same standards as the King Model. Therefore, guns below serial number 9000 deduct about 40 percent from prices listed.

NIB	*Exc.*	*V.G.*	*Good*	*Fair*	*Poor*
14250	10500	7500	6000	4000	700

Westlake Model

This was Piotti's second quality model. It features a case colored receiver with gold line work. Offered in 12, 16, and 20 gauge. Discontinued in 1989.

NIB	*Exc.*	*V.G.*	*Good*	*Fair*	*Poor*
13000	10500	8000	6000	3500	700

Over-and-Under Gun

This model features King 2 engraving which has a light border scroll with 10 percent coverage. Custom engraving patterns available at extra charge.

NIB	*Exc.*	*V.G.*	*Good*	*Fair*	*Poor*
44750	33500	25000	17500	10000	1000

Model King No. I

This model features a sidelock with fine line scroll engraving with full coverage. A gold crown is inlaid on the top lever prior to 1989. H&H or Purdey-style engraving. Select walnut with hand checkering is standard. Chambered from 10 gauge to .410 bore.

NIB	*Exc.*	*V.G.*	*Good*	*Fair*	*Poor*
26750	20000	15000	12500	8000	700

Monte Carlo Model

This model was a less expensive version of the King Model. It had H&H or Purdey-style engraving. It was discontinued in 1989 and was upgraded and became part of the King Model. This occured around serial number 9000.

NIB	*Exc.*	*V.G.*	*Good*	*Fair*	*Poor*
14000	10000	7000	6000	3500	700

Model King Extra

This model is similar to the King No. 1 but with the addition of a number of engraving styles from English to game scenes with gold inlays. Because of the wide variety of engraving patterns offered on this model it is advisable to secure a qualified appraisal before purchase.

Model Lunik

This model is fitted with Holland & Holland sidelocks. Engraving is Renaissance-style relief cut scroll engraving. A gold crown is inlaid on the top lever. Offered in gauges from 10 to .410 bore.

NIB	Exc.	V.G.	Good	Fair	Poor
28600	21000	16000	12000	7000	—700

MODEL MONACO

This sidelock model features all of the best that Piotti has to offer and extra attention is paid to hand work and fitting. Only the finest European hardwoods are used. Available in 10 gauge to 410 bore. Offered with three different types of engraving designated No. 1, No. 2, and No. 4.

Monaco No. 1 or No. 2

NIB	Exc.	V.G.	Good	Fair	Poor
35500	26500	20000	16500	12000	700

Monaco No. 3

NIB	Exc.	V.G.	Good	Fair	Poor
38500	28500	22500	18000	13000	700

Monaco No. 4

NIB	Exc.	V.G.	Good	Fair	Poor
46750	35000	27500	20000	17500	700

PLAINFIELD MACHINE CO.

Dunelien, New Jersey

Super Enforcer

A cut-down version of the U.S. M1 Carbine with a 12" barrel and pistol grip. The finish is blued and stocks are walnut.

NIB	Exc.	V.G.	Good	Fair	Poor
—	600	475	375	225	100

M1 Carbine

A commercial reproduction of the U.S. M1 Carbine. The finish is blued. Walnut stock.

NIB	Exc.	V.G.	Good	Fair	Poor
—	400	350	225	150	100

M1 Paratrooper Carbine

As above with a telescoping wire buttstock and walnut forend.

NIB	Exc.	V.G.	Good	Fair	Poor
—	475	375	275	200	125

POLY-TECHNOLOGIES, INC./POLY-TECH

China

SKS

A semi-automatic rifle chambered for the 7.62x39mm cartridge with a 20.5" barrel and 10-shot fixed magazine. Based on the Soviet Siminov carbine. Finish is blued, and the stock and hand guard are made of a Chinese hardwood.

NIB	Exc.	V.G.	Good	Fair	Poor
425	375	200	150	100	50

AKS-762

A semi-automatic version of the Chinese-type 56 Assault rifle chambered for the 7.62x39mm cartridge with a 16.5" barrel. Furnished with a 20-round magazine and a Chinese bayonet. The finish is blued, and the stock is hardwood. Add 15 percent for milled receiver.

NIB	Exc.	V.G.	Good	Fair	Poor
950	800	675	500	350	200

NOTE: For folding stock model add $250.

AK-47/S

Chambered for the 7.62x39 cartridge.

NIB	Exc.	V.G.	Good	Fair	Poor
1350	1150	850	750	600	400

NOTE: For folding stock model add $350. With a Soviet-style bayonet add $15.

M-14/S

A reproduction of the U.S. M14 rifle chambered for the 7.62mm cartridge with a 22" barrel and 20-round magazine. Finish is blued and the stock is of hardwood.

NIB	Exc.	V.G.	Good	Fair	Poor
1000	875	675	500	350	200

PORTER, P. W.

New York, New York

TURRET RIFLE

A 9-shot vertical cylinder .44 caliber rifle with either a 26" or 28" octagonal barrel. The only markings are "Address P.W. Porter/New York." Four variations of this rifle are known and the 22" barreled carbine would command a 25 percent premium. Approximately 1,250 were manufactured during the 1850s.

1st Model with Canister Magazine

Fitted with a 30-shot round canister magazine over the turret, this model was made in Tennessee and is extremely rare. Most often the canisters are not encountered and values reflect this. Approximately 25 were made.

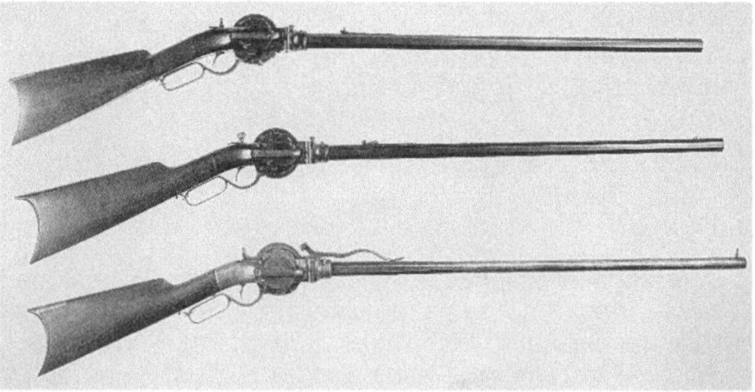

NIB	Exc.	V.G.	Good	Fair	Poor
—	—	37500	30000	13500	2000

2nd Model (New York)

NIB	Exc.	V.G.	Good	Fair	Poor
—	—	15000	12000	5125	1000

3rd Model (New York)

This model has a screw-off cover over the magazine.

NIB	Exc.	V.G.	Good	Fair	Poor
—	—	13000	1050	5200	1000

4th Model (New York)

As above but without an automatic primer magazine and the nipples are exposed.

NIB	Exc.	V.G.	Good	Fair	Poor
—	—	10500	8800	4150	750

PRAIRIE GUN WORKS

Winnipeg, Manitoba, Canada

M-15

This is a lightweight mountain rifle chambered for .22-250, 6mm-284, .25-284, 6.5-284, 7mm-08, .308 Win., and most short calibers. Built on a Remington 700 action with 20" lightweight barrel. Stock is Kevlar and comes in either green, black or gray. Barrel length is usually 20". Weight is approximately 4.75 lbs.

NIB	Exc.	V.G.	Good	Fair	Poor
2600	2200	1750	1200	800	500

M-18

Similar to the above model but chambered for long action calibers and fitted with barrel lengths from 22" to 24". Weight is approximately 5.25 lbs.

NIB	Exc.	V.G.	Good	Fair	Poor
2600	2200	1750	1200	800	500

PRANDELLI & GASPARINI

Brescia, Italy

Boxlock Side-by-Side Shotgun

A good quality double-barrel 12 or 20 gauge shotgun with 26" or 28" barrels. Single-selective trigger, automatic ejectors and an Anson & Deeley action. Blued, stock of select walnut.

NIB	Exc.	V.G.	Good	Fair	Poor
—	2500	1750	1100	700	450

Sidelock Side-by-Side Shotgun

Similar to the above, but with full sidelocks.

NIB	Exc.	V.G.	Good	Fair	Poor
—	3500	2650	1500	900	500

Boxlock Over-and-Under Shotgun

An over-and-under double-barrel 12 or 20 gauge shotgun with 26" or 28" barrels, single triggers and automatic ejectors. Blued, with select walnut stock.

NIB	Exc.	V.G.	Good	Fair	Poor
—	2750	1850	1200	900	350

Sidelock Over-and-Under Shotgun

As above with full sidelocks.

NIB	Exc.	V.G.	Good	Fair	Poor
—	3000	2500	1800	950	450

PRATT, GEORGE

Middletown, Connecticut

Trap Gun

A doubled-barreled, stationary burglar alarm or animal trap gun that is chambered for .38 caliber centerfire. The barrel is 4" in length, and all of the components are made of cast iron with a galvanized finish. Barrels and action are mounted on a round base, which can turn 360 degrees. The patent date "Dec. 18, 1883" is marked on the gun. Many were manufactured between 1880 and the early 1890s.

NIB	Exc.	V.G.	Good	Fair	Poor
—	—	1800	1200	500	150

PREMIER

Italy and Spain

A trade name used by various retailers on shotguns manufactured in Italy and Spain that were imported during the late 1950s and early 1960s.

Regent Side-by-Side Shotgun

A double-barrel shotgun with 26" to 30" barrels available in all standard gauges. Receiver blued, stock of walnut. Normally found with a pistol grip and beavertail forend.

NIB	Exc.	V.G.	Good	Fair	Poor
—	450	250	200	150	100

Regent Magnum

As above but chambered for the 3.5" 10 gauge Magnum cartridge. Barrels 32" in length and choked Full and Full.

NIB	Exc.	V.G.	Good	Fair	Poor
—	500	300	250	200	150

Brush King

Identical to the Regent Model except that it is fitted with 22" Modified and Improved Cylinder barrels and a straight-grip English-style stock.

NIB	Exc.	V.G.	Good	Fair	Poor
—	500	375	250	200	150

Ambassador Model

A more ornate version of the Regent Model.

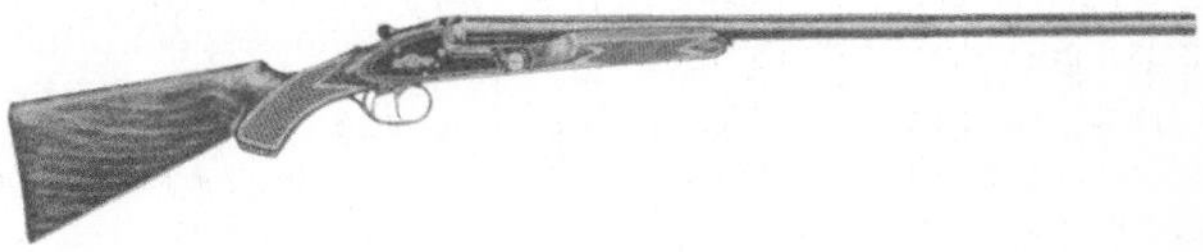

NIB	Exc.	V.G.	Good	Fair	Poor
—	600	450	300	250	175

Presentation Custom Grade

A custom-order shotgun with game scenes as well as gold and silver inlays.

NIB	Exc.	V.G.	Good	Fair	Poor
—	2500	1750	1250	850	400

PRINZ

Germany

Grade 1 Bolt-Action Rifle

A high quality bolt-action rifle chambered for the .243, .30-06, .308, 7mm Remington Magnum or the .300 Winchester Magnum cartridges. Barrel length 24", double-set triggers available. Finish is blued, stock is of oil-finished select walnut. Introduced in 1989.

NIB	Exc.	V.G.	Good	Fair	Poor
1200	950	700	450	325	150

Grade 2 Bolt-Action Rifle

As above with a rosewood forend tip and pistol grip cap.

NIB	Exc.	V.G.	Good	Fair	Poor
1300	1075	750	475	350	175

Tip Up Rifle

A high quality single-shot rifle available in a variety of American cartridges. Barrel length 24" and not furnished with sights. Finish blued, stock of select walnut.

NIB	Exc.	V.G.	Good	Fair	Poor
3000	2250	1700	1135	850	300

Model 85 "Princess"

A combination 12 gauge shotgun and rifle with 24" or 26" barrels, double triggers, and automatic ejectors. Finish blued, stock of select walnut.

NIB	Exc.	V.G.	Good	Fair	Poor
3500	2850	2100	1650	1000	300

PROFESSIONAL ORDNANCE, INC.

Ontario, California

NOTE: This company has been purchased by Bushmaster.

Carbon-15 Rifle—Type 97

Similar to the Carbon-15 Pistol Type 97 but fitted with a 16" barrel, quick detachable buttstock, quick detach compensator, Weaver type mounting base. Overall length is 35". Weight is about 3.9 lbs.

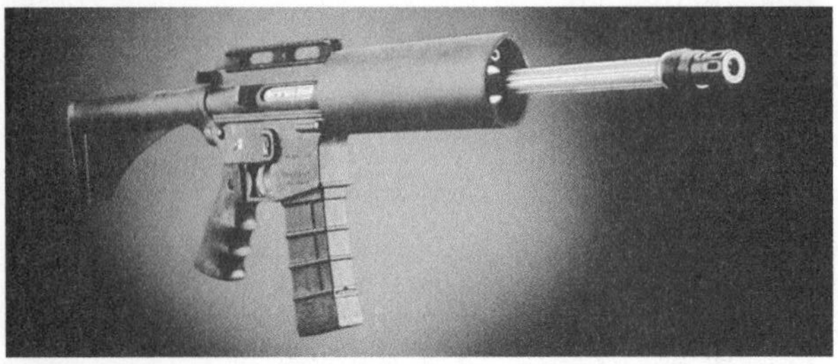

NIB	Exc.	V.G.	Good	Fair	Poor
950	725	600	500	350	150

Carbon-15 Rifle—Type 97S

Introduced in 2000 this rifle incorporated several new features. Its foregrip is double walled and insulated with a sheet of ultra-lightweight amumina silica ceramic fiber. The recoil buffer has been increased in size by 30 percent for less recoil. A new ambidextrous safety has been added, and a new multi carry silent sling with Hogue grip is standard. Weight is approximately 4.3 lbs.

NIB	Exc.	V.G.	Good	Fair	Poor
1285	950	700	550	375	150

Carbon-15 Rifle—Type 21

This model is fitted with a 16" light profile stainless steel barrel. Quick detachable stock, weaver mounting base. Introduced in 1999. Weight is approximately 3.9 lbs.

NIB	Exc.	V.G.	Good	Fair	Poor
1150	900	650	500	325	125

PULASKI ARMORY

Pulaski, Tennessee

Founded in 1861, this firm produced rifles for the State of Tennessee. Overall length 48-1/2" to 49-1/2"; round barrels 32-1/2" to 33-1/4"; caliber .54. Resemble U.S. Model 1841 Rifles except without patchbox. Had single screw sporting locks with diamond-shaped ferrules. Usually marked on barrel "PULASKI T. C.S.A. 61." Production estimated to be about 300.

NIB	Exc.	V.G.	Good	Fair	Poor
—	—	16500	10000	5000	1500

PUMA

Model 92 Rifle

This model is a copy of the Winchester lever-action rifle. It is fitted with a 24" octagon barrel and chambered for the .44 Magnum, .357 Magnum, .454 Casull or .45 Colt cartridge. Offered in a variety of finishes such as stainless steel, blued, blued and brass, and blued and case colored. Fitted with a cresent butt and hardwood stock.

NIB	Exc.	V.G.	Good	Fair	Poor
550	425	350	275	200	100

NOTE: Add $50 for stainless steel

Model 92 Trapper

Introduced in 2004 this model features a 16" barrel with large-loop lever and saddle ring. Available in all of the calibers noted above.

NIB	Exc.	V.G.	Good	Fair	Poor
550	425	350	275	200	100

PPS22

New in 2009, this is a .22 LR version of the Soviet PPSh submachinegun. Comes with one 50-round drum magazine.

NIB	Exc.	V.G.	Good	Fair	Poor
575	475	350	275	200	100

PURDEY, J. & SONS LTD.

London, England

Perhaps the finest manufacturer of shotguns, double-barrel and bolt-action rifles in the world. Virtually all their products are made on special order and it is impossible to establish general values for their products. Prospective purchasers are advised to seek qualified guidance prior to the acquisition of any arms made by this maker. The prices listed are for standard guns with no extras.

Hammerless Ejector Side-by-Side Game Gun

Available in 12, 16, 20, 28, and .410 bore. Engraved sidelocks.

NIB	Exc.	V.G.	Good	Fair	Poor
88000	—	—	—	—	—

NOTE: For 28 and .410 bore guns add an additional $3,000.

Hammerless Ejector Over-and-Under Gun

This gun is offered in 12, 16, 20, 28, and .410 bore with sidelocks.

NIB	Exc.	V.G.	Good	Fair	Poor
100,000	—	—	—	—	—

NOTE: For 28 and .410 bore guns add an additional $3,500.

Double-Barreled Rifle

A side-by-side double rifle with sidelocks. It can be built in any caliber. Prices listed are for new guns in various bore sizes:.300 bore—$77,000.375 bore—$77,500
.470 bore—$80,500.577 bore—$90,000
.600 bore—$92,000

Q

QUACKENBUSH

Herkimer, New York

Quackenbush Safety Cartridge Rifle

A single-shot, takedown boy's rifle chambered for .22 rimfire cartridges in either .22 Short or .22 Long. Barrel length 18". Weight was about 4.5 lbs. All metal parts nickel-plated. The breech swings to the side for loading. Stock of walnut. Manufactured between 1886 and about 1920. Approximately 50,000 were produced. Quackenbush also made nickel-plated nutcrackers. Who'd'a thought?

NIB	Exc.	V.G.	Good	Fair	Poor
—	—	800	650	300	150

Junior Safety Rifle

Same as above but with skeleton stock. Built between 1893 and 1920. About 7,000 guns were manufactured. Weight was about 4 lbs.

NIB	Exc.	V.G.	Good	Fair	Poor
—	—	950	600	200	100

Bicycle Rifle

Chambered for the .22 cartridge, this rifle was fitted with a 12" barrel. Skeleton wire pistol grip.

NIB	Exc.	V.G.	Good	Fair	Poor
—	—	1300	750	350	150

R

RANGER ARMS, INC.

Gainesville, Texas

.22 Rifle

A bolt-action rifle produced in .22 LR with a checkered walnut Monte Carlo stock. Manufactured in the early 1970s.

NIB	Exc.	V.G.	Good	Fair	Poor
—	200	150	100	75	50

Statesman

A bolt-action rifle produced in various centerfire calibers with a 22" barrel, no sights, and a checkered walnut stock. Standard finish blued. Manufactured in the early 1970s.

NIB	Exc.	V.G.	Good	Fair	Poor
—	900	750	600	350	200

Statesman Magnum

As above, but chambered for magnum calibers and with a 24" barrel.

NIB	Exc.	V.G.	Good	Fair	Poor
—	950	800	650	375	200

Senator

As above with a better finish.

NIB	Exc.	V.G.	Good	Fair	Poor
—	1000	850	700	525	250

Senator Magnum

As above chambered for magnum cartridges.

NIB	Exc.	V.G.	Good	Fair	Poor
—	1150	900	750	575	250

Governor

As above with better walnut and finer lined checkering.

NIB	Exc.	V.G.	Good	Fair	Poor
—	1300	1050	800	600	300

Governor Magnum

As above chambered for magnum cartridges.

NIB	Exc.	V.G.	Good	Fair	Poor
—	1540	1200	950	750	300

RAPTOR ARMS CO.

Shelton, Connecticut

Raptor Bolt-Action Rifle

An economy-class bolt rifle introduced in 1997 and chambered for the .270, .30-06, .243, .25-06, and .308 calibers. Fitted with a 22" barrel and black synthetic checkered stock. An upgrade model was available with wooden stock. Adjustable trigger. Weight is about 7.5 lbs. MSRP in 1999 was $249.

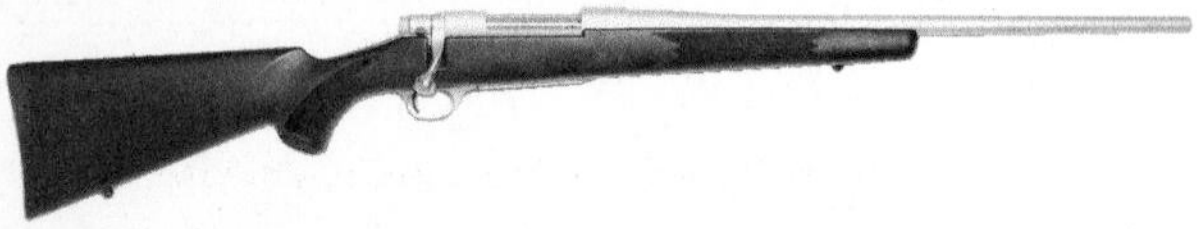

NIB	Exc.	V.G.	Good	Fair	Poor
275	225	175	125	100	75

Peregrine Bolt-Action Rifle

Similar to above but with checkered hardwood stock. Special order.

NIB	Exc.	V.G.	Good	Fair	Poor
275	225	175	125	100	75

RAU ARMS CORP.

El Dorado, Kansas

WILDCAT

Single-shot pivoting-barrel .22 rimfire rifle with skeletonized stock with walnut or mahogany inset. Forend acts as extractor. Similar in overall look to FIE/Garcia Bronco but in .22 only. Mfd. 1969-1970 with c.2500-3000 produced. Later produced by Mountain Arms (q.v.).

Model 500

Blued with walnut stock insert.

NIB	Exc.	V.G.	Good	Fair	Poor
300	200	150	100	75	45

Model 600 Deluxe

Chrome finish with mahogany stock insert.

NIB	Exc.	V.G.	Good	Fair	Poor
325	225	175	125	95	50

RAVELL

Barcelona, Spain

Maxim Double Rifle

A Holland & Holland-styled sidelock double-barrel rifle available in either .375 Holland & Holland or 9.3x74R with 23" barrels having express sights. Double triggers and automatic ejectors. The sidelocks and mounts engraved, stock of well figured walnut normally fitted with a recoil pad.

NIB	Exc.	V.G.	Good	Fair	Poor
4500	3500	2750	1850	1250	850

READ & WATSON

Danville, Virginia

During 1862 and 1863, Read & Watson produced approximately 900 altered Hall rifles for the State of Virginia. These arms were made from Hall rifles issued to the state prior to the Civil War. The original breech loading mechanisms were removed and a brass breech piece or receiver was secured in their place. New buttstocks were fitted and the original Hall furniture was reused. Carbines have an overall length of 42-1/8"; barrel length of 26" and are of .52 caliber. Position and style of serial numbers varies.

NIB	Exc.	V.G.	Good	Fair	Poor
—	—	18500	15500	7100	1000

REEDER, GARY CUSTOM GUNS

Flagstaff, Arizona

This company offers complete guns as listed below. It also offers custom options built on customer guns as well. An extensive number of custom options is available on any of these models. Prices listed below reflect the standard for that particular model. Retail prices only are listed below due to lack of active secondary market for these limited edition guns. Reeder is a custom manufacturer, or restylist, working primarily with Ruger frames. Only a representative sampling of his works is presented here, and the values are estimates ony. Since many of Reeder's guns are made to custom specs, their value is largely a matter of finding the right buyer.

American Hunter

Built on a Winchester Model 94 big bore frame and chambered for the .444 Marlin cartridge. Black Chromix finish. Ghost ring rear sight. Special engraving. Checkering walnut stock.

NIB	Exc.	V.G.	Good	Fair	Poor
1350	1125	900	—	—	—

Alaskan Classic

Built on a Marlin Model 1895 frame and chambered for the .45-70 cartridge. Barrel length is 16.5". Black Chromix finish. Ghost ring rear sight. Special engraving. Checkering walnut stock.

NIB	Exc.	V.G.	Good	Fair	Poor
1500	1295	950	—	—	—

Buffalo Hunter

Built on a Marlin Model 1895 frame and chambered for the .475 GNR cartridge. Barrel length is 18". Full length magazine tube. Black Chromix finish. Peep rear sight. Special engraving. Checkering walnut stock.

NIB	Exc.	V.G.	Good	Fair	Poor
1500	1295	950	—	—	—

Big 5 Classic

This single-shot rifle is built on the customer's Ruger No. 1 rifle. Chambered for the .500 Jeffery cartridge. Fitted with a heavy barrel to customer's length and muzzlebrake. Tuned action. Buttstock weight added. Game scene engraved.

NIB	Exc.	V.G.	Good	Fair	Poor
2200	1725	1150	—	—	—

REMINGTON ARMS COMPANY, INC.

Madison, North Carolina

Founded in 1816 by Eliphalet Remington, this company has the distinction of being the oldest firearms manufacturing firm in the United States. Since 1856 it has been known by four different names: between 1856 and 1888, E. Remington & Sons; 1888-1910, Remington Arms Company; 1910-1925, Remington Arms U.M.C. Company (Union Metallic Cartridge Company); and 1925 to the present, Remington Arms Company.

RIFLES

Model 1841 "Mississippi Rifle"

A .54 caliber percussion rifle with a 33" barrel and full stock secured by two barrel bands. The lock (marked Remington's Herkimer N.Y.) is case hardened, the barrel browned and the furniture of brass. The stock is fitted with a brass patch box on the right side. Approximately 20,000 were made between 1846 and 1855.

Paul Goodwin photo

NIB	Exc.	V.G.	Good	Fair	Poor
—	—	2000	1750	750	400

Model 1861 U.S. Rifle Musket

A .58 caliber percussion rifle with a 40" barrel and full length stock secured by three barrel bands. The lock marked "Remington's Ilion, N.Y." Finished in the white with a walnut stock. Approximately 40,000 were made between 1864 and 1866.

Paul Goodwin photo

NIB	Exc.	V.G.	Good	Fair	Poor
—	—	3000	1250	500	200

Model 1863 Zouave Rifle

A .58 caliber percussion rifle with a 33" barrel and full length stock secured by two barrel bands. The lock case hardened and marked "Remington's Ilion N.Y.," the barrel blued and the furniture of brass. Approximately 12,500 were manufactured between 1862 and 1865.

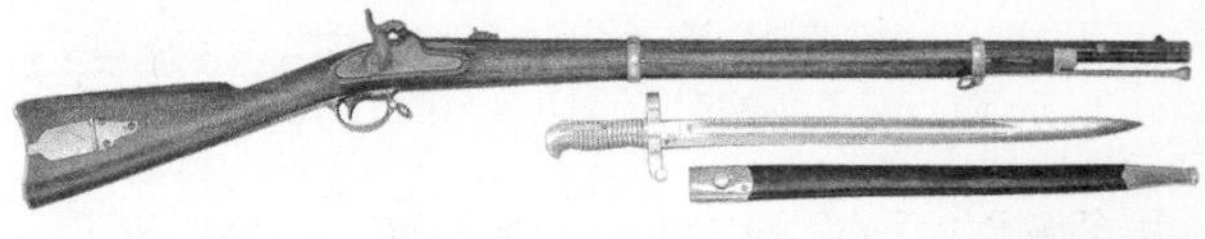

Paul Goodwin photo

NIB	Exc.	V.G.	Good	Fair	Poor
—	—	3000	2250	1500	500

Breech-Loading Carbine

A .46 or .50 rimfire single-shot rolling block carbine with a 20" barrel. Blued, case hardened with a walnut stock. The tang marked "Remington's Ilion, N.Y. Pat. Dec. 23, 1863 May 3 & Nov. 16, 1864." The .50 caliber version is worth approximately 15 percent more than the .46 caliber. Approximately 15,000 .50-caliber variations were made, most of which were sold to France. Approximately 5,000 carbines were made in .46 caliber. Manufactured from 1864 to 1866.

Paul Goodwin photo

NIB	Exc.	V.G.	Good	Fair	Poor
—	—	3750	1500	500	200

Revolving Rifle

A .36 or. 44 caliber revolving rifle with either 24" or 28" octagonal barrels with a 6-shot cylinder. The trigger guard formed with a scrolled finger extension at the rear. Blued, case hardened with a walnut stock. These rifles are also encountered altered to cartridge and would be worth approximately 20 percent less than the percussion values listed below. The barrel marked "Patented Sept. 14, 1858 E. Remington & Sons, Ilion, New York, U.S.A. New Model." The .44 caliber model will bring a premium of about 15 percent and is rare. Approximately 1,000 were manufactured between 1866 and 1879.

Courtesy Buffalo Bill Historical Center, Cody, Wyoming

Courtesy Milwaukee Public Museum, Milwaukee, Wisconsin

NIB	Exc.	V.G.	Good	Fair	Poor
—	—	11500	8000	5500	900

Remington-Beals Rifle

A .32 or .38 caliber sliding barrel single-shot rifle with octagonal barrels of 24", 26", or 28" length. The barrel can be moved forward by lowering the trigger guard/lever. This model is to be found with either frames made of brass or iron, the latter being worth approximately 20 percent more than the values listed below. Walnut stock. The barrel marked "Beals Patent June 28, 1864 Jan. 30, 1866 E. Remington & Sons, Ilion, New York." Approximately 800 were manufactured between 1866 and 1888. A few examples are known to have been factory engraved. Prospective purchasers are advised to secure a qualified appraisal prior to acquisition.

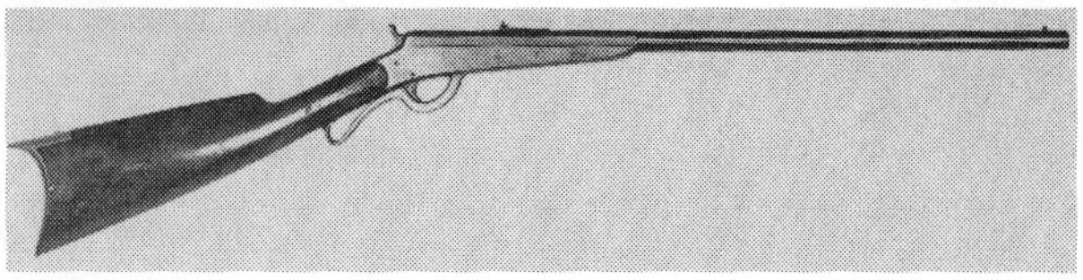

Courtesy Milwaukee Public Museum, Milwaukee, Wisconsin

NIB	Exc.	V.G.	Good	Fair	Poor
—	—	—	950	400	150

U.S. Navy Rolling Block Carbine

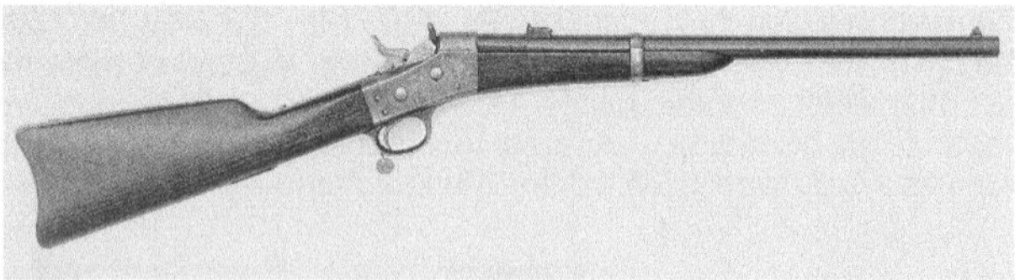

NIB	Exc.	V.G.	Good	Fair	Poor
—	—	—	2750	1000	350

Model 1867 Navy Cadet Rifle

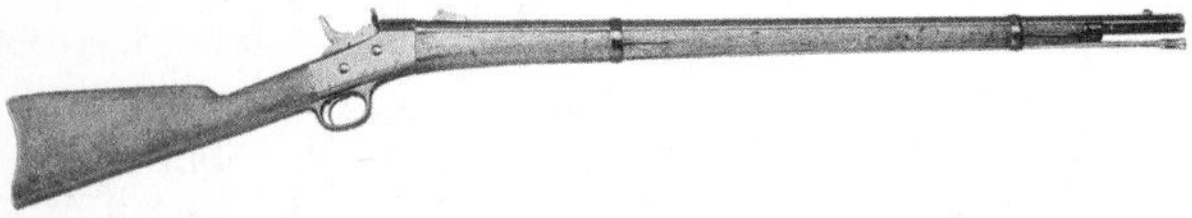

Paul Goodwin photo

NIB	Exc.	V.G.	Good	Fair	Poor
—	—	2750	1400	700	350

Rolling Block Military Rifles

NIB	Exc.	V.G.	Good	Fair	Poor
—	—	900	750	400	100

NO. 1 ROLLING BLOCK SPORTING RIFLE

Standard No. 1 Sporting Rifle

A single-shot rolling block rifle produced in a variety of calibers from .40-50 to .50-70 centerfire as well as .32, .44 and .46 rimfire. Standard barrel lengths were either 28" or 30" and of octagonal form.

Courtesy Milwaukee Public Museum, Milwaukee, Wisconsin

NIB	Exc.	V.G.	Good	Fair	Poor
—	—	—	3750	1500	500

Long-Range Creedmoor Rifle

A .44-90, .44-100, or .44-105 caliber rolling block rifle with a 34" half-octagonal barrel, long-range vernier tang sights and globe front sights. Blued, case hardened with a walnut stock and a checkered pistol grip. This rifle was available with a number of optional features and a qualified appraisal should be secured if those features are in doubt. Produced from 1873 to 1890.

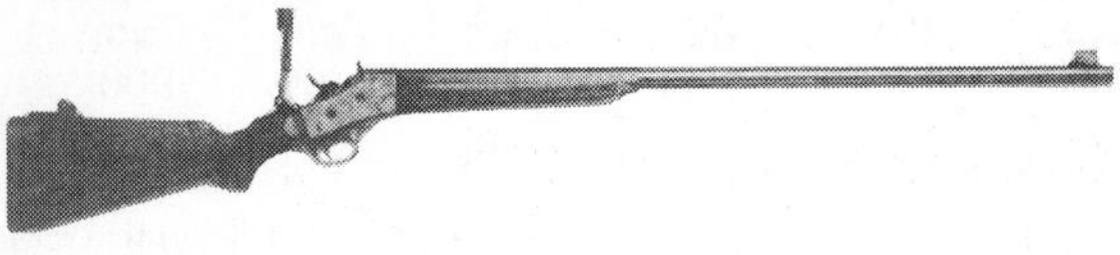

Courtesy Bonhams & Butterfields, San Francisco, California

NIB	Exc.	V.G.	Good	Fair	Poor
—	—	8500	5750	2500	500

Mid-Range Target Rifle

As above, except chambered for .40-70, .44-77, .45-70, or .50-70 caliber with 28" or 30" half-octagonal barrels. Produced from 1875 to 1890.

NIB	Exc.	V.G.	Good	Fair	Poor
—	—	6000	2750	1750	300

Short-Range Rifle

As above, chambered for cartridges between .38 and .44 caliber with 26" or 30" round or octagonal barrels. Open rear sight with beach front sight. The walnut stock is checkered. Produced from 1875 to 1890.

NIB	Exc.	V.G.	Good	Fair	Poor
—	—	5000	2750	1675	250

Black Hills Rifle

As above, in .45-60 caliber with a 28" round barrel fitted with open sights and a plain straight grip stock. Produced from 1877 to 1882.

NIB	Exc.	V.G.	Good	Fair	Poor
—	—	5000	2750	1675	250

Shotgun

As above, in 16 gauge with either a 30" or 32" Damascus or fluid steel barrels. Produced from 1870 to 1892.

NIB	Exc.	V.G.	Good	Fair	Poor
—	2800	1650	1200	750	150

Baby Carbine

As above, with a 20" thin round barrel chambered for the .44-40 cartridge and fitted with a saddle ring on the left side of the frame. Blued, case hardened with a walnut stock and a carbine buttplate. Manufactured from 1892 to 1902.

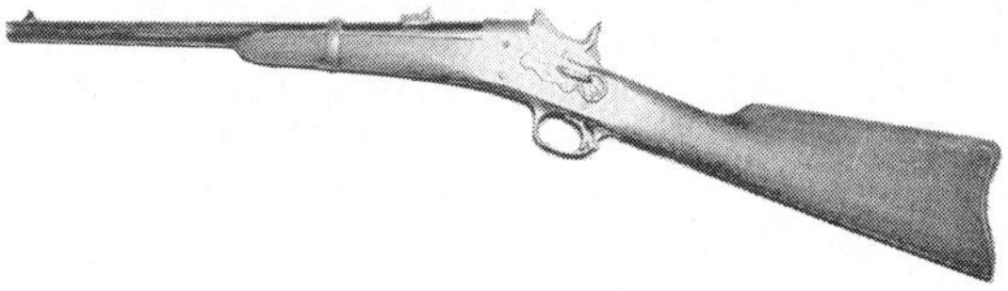

NIB	Exc.	V.G.	Good	Fair	Poor
—	8000	4250	2250	900	200

Model 1-1/2 Sporting Rifle

A lightweight variation of the above using a 1.25" wide, No. 1 rolling block action. Chambered for rimfire cartridges from .22 to the .38 Extra Long, as well as centerfire cartridges from .32-20 to the .44-40. Medium weight octagonal barrels from 24" to 28" in length, with open rear and a blade-type front sight. Blued, case hardened with a walnut stock. There were several thousand manufactured between 1888 and 1897.

Paul Goodwin photo

NIB	Exc.	V.G.	Good	Fair	Poor
—	—	2000	950	400	100

Model 2 Sporting Rifle

As above, using a No. 2 action and chambered for various cartridges from .22 to .38 caliber with 24" or 26" octagonal barrels. Blued, case hardened with a walnut stock. This model was produced with a number of optional features that affect its value. Prospective purchasers are advised to secure a qualified appraisal prior to acquisition. Manufactured from 1873 to 1910.

Paul Goodwin photo

NIB	Exc.	V.G.	Good	Fair	Poor
—	—	1500	600	250	100

No. 4 Rolling Block Rifle

Built on the lightweight No. 4 action, this rifle was available in .22, .25 Stevens, or .32 caliber, with either a 22.5" or 24" octagonal barrel. Blued, case hardened with a walnut stock. A takedown version was also made and these are worth approximately 10 percent more than the values listed. Approximately 50,000 were made between 1890 and 1933.

NIB	Exc.	V.G.	Good	Fair	Poor
—	900	700	400	200	75

Model No. 4 S Military Rifle

At the request of the United States Boy Scouts in 1913, the Remington Company designed a military style rifle having a 28" barrel and full length forend secured by one barrel band. A short upper hand guard was also fitted and a bayonet stud is to be found at the muzzle. In 1915 the designation of this model was changed from "Boy Scout" to "Military Model." Approximately 15,000 were made between 1913 and 1923.

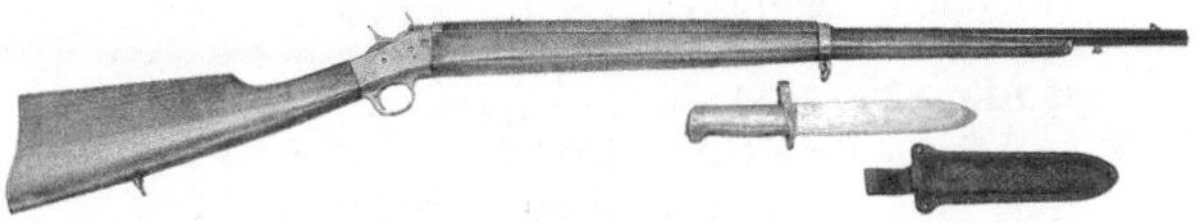

Paul Goodwin photo

NIB	Exc.	V.G.	Good	Fair	Poor
—	—	2250	950	400	275

No. 5 Rolling Block Rifle

Built on the No. 5 action, this rifle was designed for smokeless cartridges and was made in a variety of barrel lengths, calibers and in a carbine version. Blued, case hardened with a walnut stock.

NIB	Exc.	V.G.	Good	Fair	Poor
—	—	2250	800	350	100

No. 5 Sporting or Target Rifle

Chambered for the .30-30, .303 British, 7mm, .30 U.S., .32-40, .32 U.S., and the .38-55 cartridges. This rifle was offered with 28" or 30" round barrels and features a plain, straight-grip stock with a half-length forend. It has open rear sights and was available with double-set triggers that would add approximately 10 percent to the value. It was manufactured between 1898 and 1905.

NIB	Exc.	V.G.	Good	Fair	Poor
—	—	5750	2250	850	300

Model 1897

A 7x57mm and .30 U.S. caliber full stock rolling block rifle. The Model 1902 is of identical form except that it was fitted with an automatic ejector. Manufactured from 1897 to 1902.

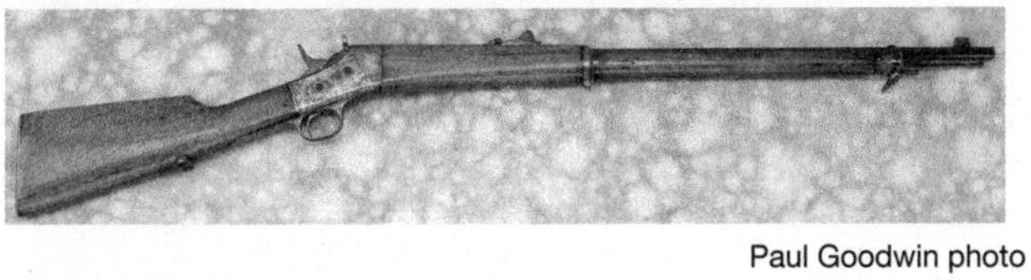

Paul Goodwin photo

NIB	Exc.	V.G.	Good	Fair	Poor
—	2800	1250	550	250	100

Carbine

As above, fitted with a 20" round barrel and a half-length forend secured by one barrel band.

NIB	Exc.	V.G.	Good	Fair	Poor
—	—	1750	750	350	100

No. 6 Rolling Block Rifle

A lightweight, small rifle designed expressly to be used by young boys. It is chambered for the .22 rimfire cartridge, as well as the .32 Short or Long. It was also produced with a smoothbore barrel to be used with shot cartridges. The round barrel is 20" in length. It has a takedown action with a barrel held on by a knurled knob underneath the frame. It is a lightweight rolling block, with a thin operating knob on the breech. The finish is blued overall. Early models featured a case-colored frame, and these versions would be worth approximately 10 percent additional. It has a straight-grip walnut stock with a small forearm. Over 250,000 manufactured between 1902 and 1903.

Paul Goodwin photo

NIB	Exc.	V.G.	Good	Fair	Poor
—	750	475	300	100	75

No. 7 Rolling Block Rifle

Readily identifiable by its accentuated checked pistol grip, this model was available in .22 or .25-10 Stevens caliber with 24", 26", or 28" half octagonal barrels. Fitted with a tang mounted aperture rear sight. Blued, case hardened with a walnut stock. Approximately 1,000 were made between 1903 and 1911.

NIB	Exc.	V.G.	Good	Fair	Poor
—	6500	5000	3000	2000	500

REMINGTON-HEPBURN RIFLES

Remington-Hepburn No. 3 Rifle

A lever activated falling block single-shot rifle designed by Lewis Hepburn available in a variety of calibers from .22 Winchester centerfire to .50-90 Sharps with octagonal or round barrels of 26", 28", or 30" length. Blued, case hardened with a walnut stock. This model was available with a variety of optional features that affect the value considerably. Prospective purchasers are advised to secure a qualified appraisal prior to acquisition. Approximately 10,000 were made between 1883 and 1907.

NIB	Exc.	V.G.	Good	Fair	Poor
—	—	4000	2000	1200	300

Remington-Hepburn No. 3 Match Rifle

As above, but fitted with a high comb buttstock and a nickel-plated Schuetzen buttplate. Manufactured in various calibers from

.25-20 Stevens to .40-65 with 30" half octagonal barrels. This model was made in two versions: "A Quality" with a plain stock, tang mounted rear sight and a Beach front sight, and; "B Quality" with a checkered walnut stock having a cheek rest, checkered forend, vernier rear sight and a combination wind gauge and spirit level front sight. Double set triggers were also available and these would add approximately 10 percent to the values listed below. Approximately 1,000 were made between 1883 and 1907.

Remington-Hepburn No. 3 Match Rifle A Quality

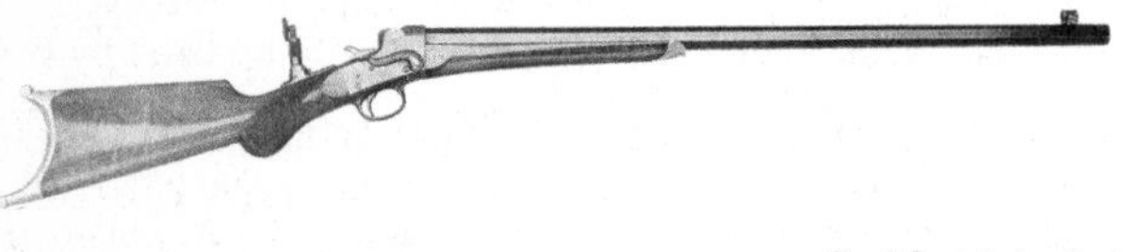

Paul Goodwin photo

NIB	Exc.	V.G.	Good	Fair	Poor
—	—	7500	4750	1800	350

Remington-Hepburn No. 3 Match Rifle B Quality

Paul Goodwin photo

NIB	Exc.	V.G.	Good	Fair	Poor
—	—	8250	5000	1900	500

Remington-Hepburn No. 3 Long-Range Creedmoor Rifle

As above, in .44 caliber with a 32" or 34" half-octagonal barrel, long-range vernier rear sight, combination wind gauge and spirit level front sight, deluxe checkered walnut stock and a rubber shotgun buttplate. Produced with a number of optional features that affect the value. Prospective purchasers are advised to secure a qualified appraisal prior to acquisition. Manufactured from 1880 to 1907.

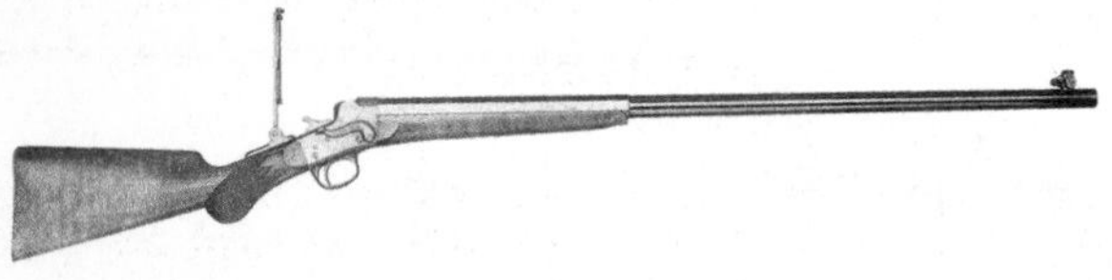

Paul Goodwin photo

NIB	Exc.	V.G.	Good	Fair	Poor
—	—	7500	4750	1800	350

Remington-Hepburn No. 3 Mid-Range Creedmoor Rifle

As above, but chambered for the .40-65 cartridge and fitted with a 28" barrel.

NIB	Exc.	V.G.	Good	Fair	Poor
—	—	5000	2250	950	350

REMINGTON-HEPBURN NO. 3 LONG-RANGE MILITARY RIFLE

This is a rare variation that is chambered for the .44-20 Remington cartridge. It has a round 34" barrel and a full-length forearm held on by two barrel bands. The finish is blued and case-colored, and the stock is walnut. There are two basic versions. The plain grade has an uncheckered, straight-grip stock with military-type sights. There is also a fancy grade that features a high-grade, checkered, pistol-grip stock with a full-length, checkered forend, vernier tang sight, and wind gauge, spirit lever front sight. There were a few manufactured in the 1880s.

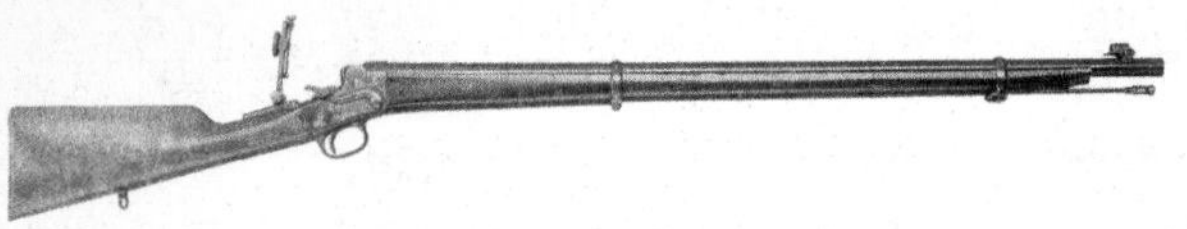

Paul Goodwin photo

Plain Grade

NIB	Exc.	V.G.	Good	Fair	Poor
—	—	4500	2500	1200	400

Fancy Grade

NIB	Exc.	V.G.	Good	Fair	Poor
—	—	7500	3750	1500	600

REMINGTON-HEPBURN NO. 3 SCHUETZEN MATCH RIFLE

As above, with the exception that instead of the side lever, the action is raised or lowered by means of the lever on the trigger guard. Chambered for various popular cartridges and offered with a 30" or 32" part-octagonal, heavy barrel. It features a vernier tang sight with a hooded front sight. It was standard with double-set triggers and a palm rest. The finish is blued and case-colored, with a high-grade checkered walnut stock and forend. It has an ornate, Swiss-type Schuetzen buttplate and is also known as the "Walker-Hepburn Rifle." There were two versions available. One, a standard breechloader with the Remington Walker-marked barrel; and the other, a muzzleloading variation that was fitted with a removable false muzzle. This version was supplied with a brass bullet starter and other accessories. Prospective purchasers are advised to secure a qualified appraisal prior to acquisition.

Breechloading Version

NIB	Exc.	V.G.	Good	Fair	Poor
—	—	27500	12500	3500	900

Muzzleloading Version

NIB	Exc.	V.G.	Good	Fair	Poor
—	—	42500	17500	5000	1500

Remington-Hepburn No. 3 High-Power Rifle

The Model No. 3 was also made available in a variety of smokeless cartridges: .30-30, .30-40, .32 Special, .32-40 and .38-55. Standard barrel lengths were 26", 28", or 30". Produced from 1900 to 1907.

NIB	Exc.	V.G.	Good	Fair	Poor
—	4000	2500	1750	650	250

REMINGTON-KEENE MAGAZINE RIFLE

A bolt-action rifle chambered for the .40, .43, and .45-70 centerfire cartridges with 22", 24.5", 29.25", or 32.5" barrels. It is readily identifiable by the exposed hammer at the end of the bolt. Blued, case hardened hammer and furniture, with a walnut stock. The receiver marked "E. Remington & Sons, Ilion, N.Y." together with the patent dates 1874, 1876, and 1877. The magazine on this rifle was located beneath the barrel and the receiver is fitted with a cut-off so that the rifle could be used as a single-shot. Approximately 5,000 rifles were made between 1880 and 1888 in the variations listed.

Sporting Rifle

24.5" barrel.

Paul Goodwin photo

Remington-Keene Repeating Sporting Rifle Fancy Grade

NIB	Exc.	V.G.	Good	Fair	Poor
—	3450	2000	750	350	150

Navy Rifle

As above, with a 29.25" barrel.

NIB	Exc.	V.G.	Good	Fair	Poor
—	—	—	4500	1750	450

Carbine

As above, with a 22" barrel and a half-length forend secured by one barrel band.

NIB	Exc.	V.G.	Good	Fair	Poor
—	—	5750	3250	1250	350

REMINGTON-LEE RIFLES

Remington-Lee Magazine Rifle

Designed by James Paris Lee, rifles of this type were originally manufactured by the Sharps Rifle Company in 1880. The Remington Company began production of this model in 1881 after the Sharps Company ceased operations. Approximately 100,000 Lee magazine rifles were made between 1880 and 1907. Their variations are listed.

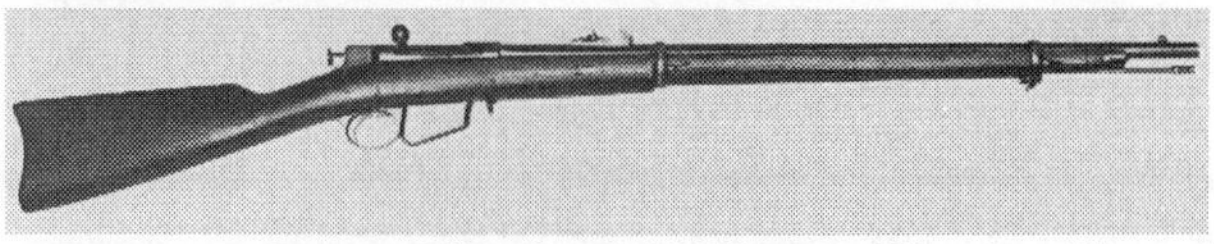

Courtesy Milwaukee Public Museum, Milwaukee, Wisconsin

Remington-Lee Model 1879 Sharps Mfg.

Barrel length 28" with a full-length stock secured by two barrel bands. The barrel marked "Sharps Rifle Co. Bridgeport, Conn." and "Old Reliable" in a rectangular cartouche. Approximately 300 were made prior to 1881.

NIB	Exc.	V.G.	Good	Fair	Poor
—	—	4750	3000	2000	600

Remington-Lee Model 1879 U.S. Navy Model

NIB	Exc.	V.G.	Good	Fair	Poor
—	—	2250	1600	750	250

Remington-Lee Model 1879 Sporting Rifle

Barrel length 28" or 30", .45-70 or .45-90 caliber, checkered pistol-grip stock with a sporting-style forend. Markings on the receiver as above. Approximately 450 made.

NIB	Exc.	V.G.	Good	Fair	Poor
—	—	2500	1750	700	250

Remington-Lee Model 1879 Military Rifle

Identical to the Navy model, except chambered for the .43 Spanish cartridge. A limited number were also produced in .45-70 caliber. The Spanish versions are worth approximately 25 percent less than the values listed below. Approximately 1,000 were made. The majority of these rifles were made for export.

NIB	Exc.	V.G.	Good	Fair	Poor
—	—	1250	750	500	150

Remington-Lee Model 1882 Army Contract

NIB	Exc.	V.G.	Good	Fair	Poor
—	—	2000	1250	750	300

Remington-Lee Model 1885 Navy Contract

NIB	Exc.	V.G.	Good	Fair	Poor
—	—	2400	1750	750	300

Remington-Lee Model 1882 & 1885 Military Rifles

Barrel length 32", full-length stock secured by two barrel bands, chambered for .42 Russian, .43 Spanish, .45 Gardner or .45-70 cartridges. The values for those rifles not in .45-70 caliber would be approximately 25 percent less than those listed. Approximately 10,000 Model 1882 rifles were made and 60,000 Model 1885 rifles. The two models can be differentiated by the fact that the cocking piece on the bolt of the Model 1885 is larger. The majority of these rifles were made for foreign contracts and commercial sales.

NIB	Exc.	V.G.	Good	Fair	Poor
—	—	1795	950	400	150

Remington-Lee Model 1882 & 1885 Sporting Rifle

As above, chambered for .45-70 and .45-90 caliber with 26" or 30" octagonal barrels and walnut sporting stocks. Approximately 200 were made.

NIB	Exc.	V.G.	Good	Fair	Poor
—	—	2400	1750	750	200

Remington-Lee Model 1882 & 1885 Carbine

As above, with a 24" barrel and a half-length forend secured by one barrel band. Prospective purchasers are advised to secure a qualified appraisal prior to acquisition.

NIB	Exc.	V.G.	Good	Fair	Poor
—	—	2400	1750	750	200

REMINGTON-LEE MODEL 1899

Designed for use with smokeless and rimless cartridges, this model is marked on the receiver "Remington Arms Co. Ilion, N.Y. Patented Aug. 26th 1884 Sept. 9th 1884 March 17th 1885 Jan 18th 1887." Produced from 1889 to 1907 in the variations listed.

Military Rifle

NIB	Exc.	V.G.	Good	Fair	Poor
—	—	1250	500	200	100

Military Carbine

NIB	Exc.	V.G.	Good	Fair	Poor
—	—	1750	700	300	100

Remington-Lee Sporting Rifle

As above, with a 24", 26", or 28" round or octagonal barrel and a half-length sporting stock with a checkered pistol grip. Approximately 7,000 were manufactured.

NIB	Exc.	V.G.	Good	Fair	Poor
—	—	1250	500	200	100

Remington Lebel Bolt-Action Rifle

NIB	Exc.	V.G.	Good	Fair	Poor
—	—	750	450	150	100

Remington Mosin-Nagant Bolt-Action Rifle

NIB	Exc.	V.G.	Good	Fair	Poor
—	—	600	300	100	75

U.S. Model 1917 Magazine Rifle

NIB	Exc.	V.G.	Good	Fair	Poor
—	—	1250	600	150	100

REMINGTON-WHITMORE MODEL 1874

A sidelock double-barrel shotgun, combination shotgun/rifle or double-barrel rifle with 28" or 30" fluid steel barrels. Also available with Damascus barrels. The barrels released by pushing forward the top lever. Blued, case hardened with a straight or semi-pistol grip walnut stock. The barrels marked "A. E. Whitmore's Patent Aug. 8, 1871, April 16, 1872." The rib between the barrels is marked "E. Remington & Sons, Ilion, N.Y." Several thousand were manufactured between 1874 and 1882.

Shotgun

NIB	Exc.	V.G.	Good	Fair	Poor
—	—	1750	850	450	100

Combination Gun (Rare)

NIB	Exc.	V.G.	Good	Fair	Poor
—	—	4250	3200	1500	300

Double Rifle

Very rare.

NIB	Exc.	V.G.	Good	Fair	Poor
—	—	9000	4250	1500	500

Model 1882 Shotgun

A sidelock double-barrel 10 or 12 gauge shotgun with 28" or 30" fluid steel or Damascus barrels. Blued, case hardened with a checkered pistol grip stock and hard rubber buttplate. The barrels are marked "E. Remington & Sons, Ilion, N.Y." and the lock is marked "Remington Arms Co." This model has a conventional top lever that moves to the side. Offered with optional engraving, and such models should be individually appraised. Approximately 7,500 were manufactured between 1882 and 1889.

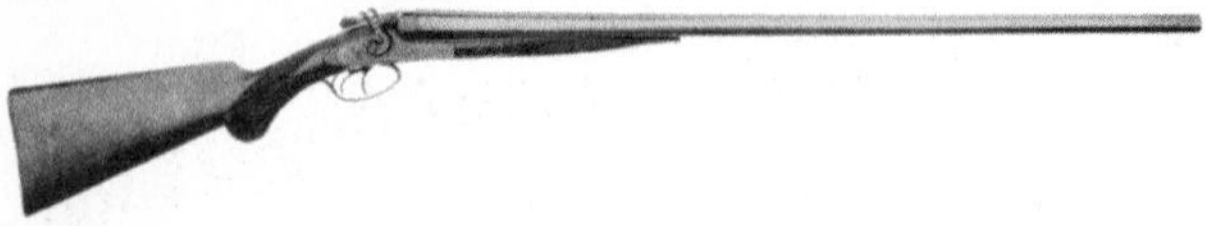

NIB	Exc.	V.G.	Good	Fair	Poor
—	—	1750	750	300	100

Model 1883 through 1889 Shotgun

A sidelock 10, 12, or 16 gauge double-barrel shotgun with fluid steel or Damascus barrels 28" to 32" in length. The models 1883, 1885, 1887, and 1889 are all somewhat alike, varying only in the form of their hammers and internal mechanisms. Blued, case hardened, checkered pistol-grip stock with a grip cap. Available in a variety of styles including highly engraved models that should be individually appraised. Approximately 30,000 were made between 1883 and 1909.

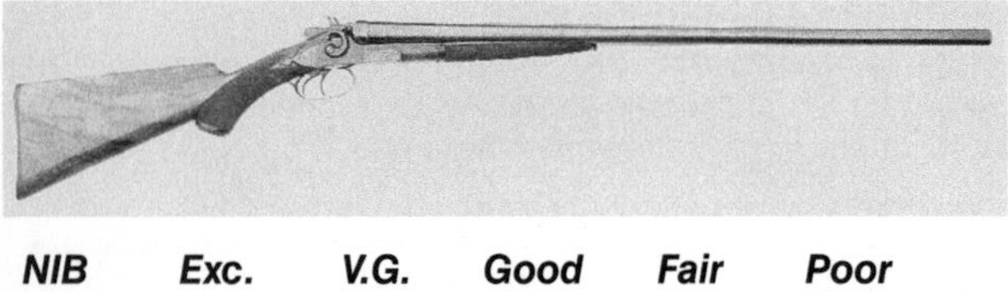

NIB	Exc.	V.G.	Good	Fair	Poor
—	—	1200	2000	800	200

Model 1893 (No. 9)

Single-barrel hammer gun in 10, 12, 16, 20, 24, and 28 gauge. Barrel lengths from 28" to 34". Case colored frame with hard rubber buttplate.

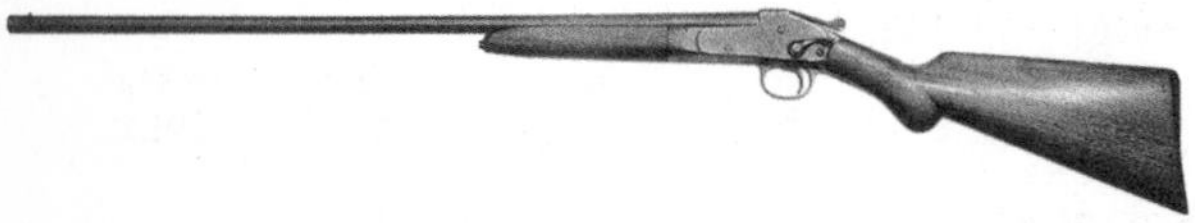

Courtesy William F. Krause

NIB	Exc.	V.G.	Good	Fair	Poor
—	—	—	600	250	100

Hammerless Shotgun Model 1894

A boxlock 10, 12, or 16 gauge double shotgun with fluid steel or Damascus barrels 26" to 32" in length. Blued, case hardened with a pistol-grip stock. Available in a variety of styles and it is advised that highly engraved examples should be individually appraised.

NIB	Exc.	V.G.	Good	Fair	Poor
—	—	1750	750	300	100

NOTE: Fluid steel barrels add 25 percent premium.

Model 1900 Shotgun

As above, in 12 and 16 gauge only. The same cautions apply to highly engraved examples.

NIB	Exc.	V.G.	Good	Fair	Poor
—	—	1500	600	250	100

MODEL 8

A .25, .30, .32, or .35 Remington semi-automatic rifle featuring a 22" barrel with open sights. The barrel is covered by a full- length tube that encloses the recoil spring. Blued with walnut stock. Approximately 60,000 were made between 1906 and 1936 in the styles listed. Add 35 percent for .25 Remington.Some collectors will pay, and demand, prices substantially in excess of those listed below for Grades C, D and E.

Standard Grade

Courtesy Remington Arms

NIB	Exc.	V.G.	Good	Fair	Poor
—	900	700	550	250	125

Model 8A

Checkered stock.

NIB	Exc.	V.G.	Good	Fair	Poor
—	1000	800	600	300	150

Model 8C

NIB	Exc.	V.G.	Good	Fair	Poor
—	2500	1500	900	500	300

Model 8D Peerless

Light engraving.

NIB	Exc.	V.G.	Good	Fair	Poor
—	5000	3500	1750	800	400

Model 8E Expert

NIB	Exc.	V.G.	Good	Fair	Poor
—	7500	4000	2250	1100	450

Model 8F Premier

Heavily engraved.

Paul Goodwin photo

NIB	Exc.	V.G.	Good	Fair	Poor
—	10000	7500	3750	1600	700

MODEL 81 WOODSMASTER

An improved variation of the Model 8, chambered for the same calibers (bu not the .25, apparently) as well as the .300 Savage cartridge. Produced from 1936 to 1950 in the styles listed. Add 300 percent for police model with detachable 15-round magazine.

Standard Grade

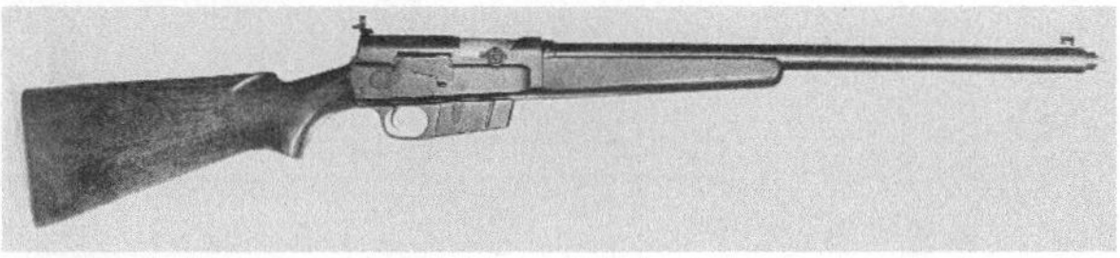

NIB	Exc.	V.G.	Good	Fair	Poor
—	900	750	500	250	125

Model 81A

NIB	Exc.	V.G.	Good	Fair	Poor
—	650	450	300	175	125

Model 81D Peerless

Engraved.

NIB	Exc.	V.G.	Good	Fair	Poor
—	7500	4000	2250	1100	450

Model 81F Premier

Heavily engraved.

NIB	Exc.	V.G.	Good	Fair	Poor
—	10000	7500	3750	1600	700

MODEL 12 OR 12A

A .22 caliber slide-action rifle with a 22" round or octagonal barrel having open sights. Blued with a walnut stock. Manufactured from 1909 to 1936 in the styles listed.

Model 12A

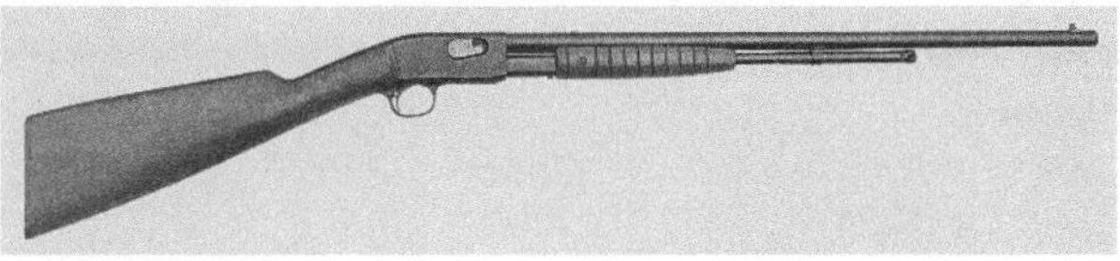

NIB	Exc.	V.G.	Good	Fair	Poor
—	800	600	300	225	150

Model 12B

.22 Short, Gallery Model.

NIB	Exc.	V.G.	Good	Fair	Poor
—	1100	900	700	400	150

Model 12C

24" octagon barrel.

NIB	Exc.	V.G.	Good	Fair	Poor
—	1000	750	500	300	175

Model 12C N.R.A. Target

Limited production.

NIB	Exc.	V.G.	Good	Fair	Poor
—	1300	1100	825	500	300

Model 12CS

.22 Remington Special.

NIB	Exc.	V.G.	Good	Fair	Poor
—	1000	900	700	400	175

Model 12D Peerless

Light engraving.

NIB	Exc.	V.G.	Good	Fair	Poor
—	5000	3750	1800	1000	500

Model 12E Expert

NIB	Exc.	V.G.	Good	Fair	Poor
—	7500	4000	2250	1200	800

Model 12F Premier

Heavily engraved.

Paul Goodwin photo

NIB	Exc.	V.G.	Good	Fair	Poor
—	9000	5250	3150	1500	800

MODEL 121 AND/OR 121A

A .22 caliber slide-action rifle with a 24" round barrel. Blued with a walnut stock. Manufactured from 1936 to 1954 in the styles listed.

Model 121 and/or 121A Standard Grade

NIB	Exc.	V.G.	Good	Fair	Poor
—	600	500	300	175	100

Model 121D Peerless

Engraved.

NIB	Exc.	V.G.	Good	Fair	Poor
—	5000	3750	1800	1000	500

Model 121F Premier

Heavily engraved.

NIB	Exc.	V.G.	Good	Fair	Poor
—	9000	5250	3150	1500	800

Model 121S

.22 WRF.

NIB	Exc.	V.G.	Good	Fair	Poor
—	850	700	400	350	250

Model 121SB—Smoothbore

There are four different variations of this smoothbore rifle. Seek expert advice before a sale.

NIB	Exc.	V.G.	Good	Fair	Poor
—	1000	800	650	400	300

MODEL 14 OR 14A

A .25, .30, .32 or .35 Remington caliber slide-action rifle with a 22" round barrel and open sights. Blued, plain walnut stock. Manufactured from 1912 to 1936. Add 85 percent for .25 Remington.

NIB	Exc.	V.G.	Good	Fair	Poor
—	900	750	500	300	200

Model 14R

As above, with an 18.5" barrel.

NIB	Exc.	V.G.	Good	Fair	Poor
—	1500	800	500	300	200

Model 14-1/2

As above, except chambered for the .38-40 or .44-40 cartridge with a 22.5" barrel. A carbine with an 18.5" barrel known as the Model 14-1/2R, would be worth approximately 10 percent more than the values listed. Manufactured from 1912 to 1922.

NIB	Exc.	V.G.	Good	Fair	Poor
—	2000	1250	700	350	250

Model 16

A .22 caliber (Remington Automatic, not interchangeable with anything else) semi-automatic rifle with a 22" barrel and open sights. Blued with a walnut stock. Later production examples were known as the Model 16A. Manufactured from 1914 to 1928.

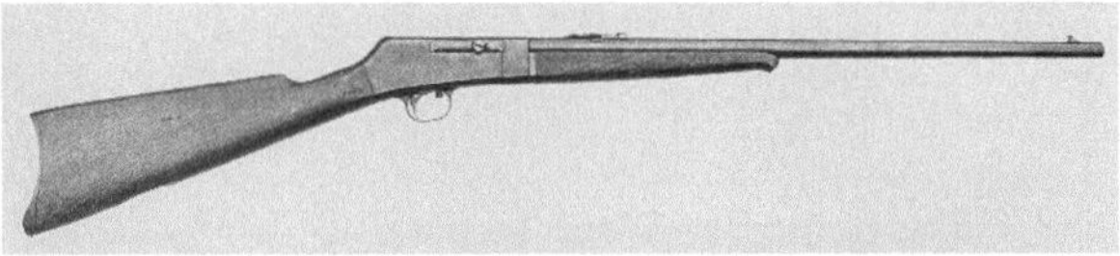

Courtesy Remington Arms

NIB	Exc.	V.G.	Good	Fair	Poor
—	500	375	250	125	75

Model 141

A .30, .32, or .35 Remington caliber slide-action rifle with a 24" barrel having open sights. Blued with a plain walnut stock. Later production versions of this rifle were known as the Model 141A. Manufactured from 1936 to 1950.

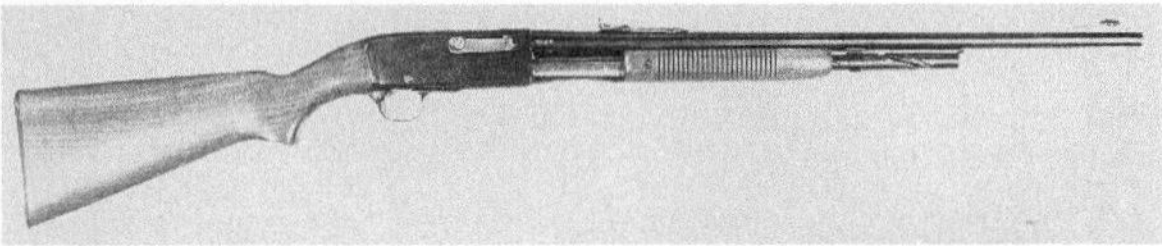

Courtesy Remington Arms

NIB	Exc.	V.G.	Good	Fair	Poor
—	650	500	350	250	175

Model 25

A .25-20 or .32-20 caliber slide-action rifle with a 24" barrel having open sights. Blued with a walnut stock. Later production examples were known as the Model 25A and a carbine version with an 18" barrel as the Model 25R. Manufactured from 1923 to 1936.

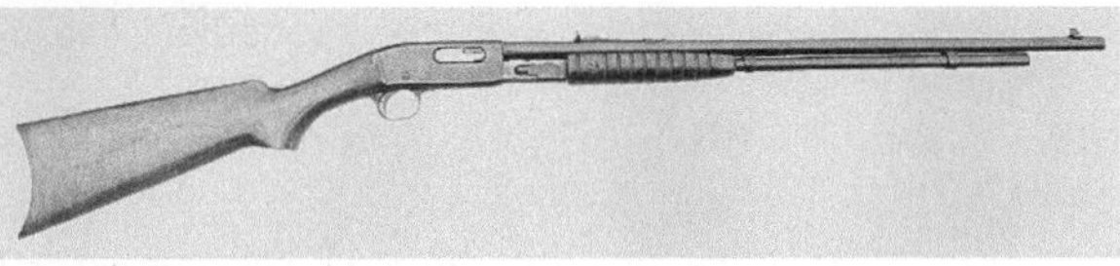

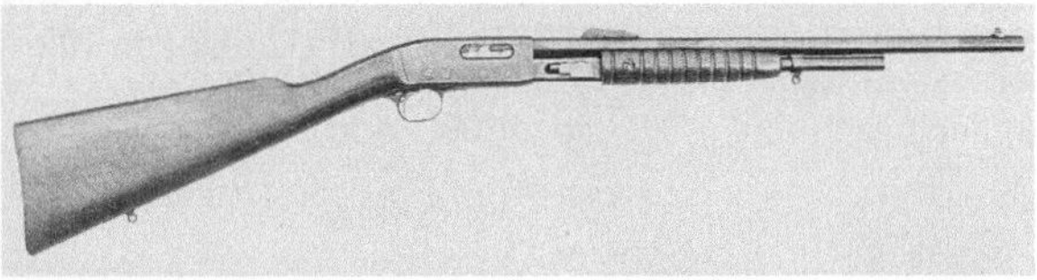

Courtesy Remington Arms

Model 25

NIB	Exc.	V.G.	Good	Fair	Poor
—	1000	750	400	250	200

NOTE: For rifles with 18" barrels add 100 percent.

Model 24

Designed by John M. Browning, this semi-automatic rifle is of .22 caliber with a 19" barrel and open sights. Blued with a walnut pistol grip stock. Later production versions were known as the Model 24A. Produced from 1922 to 1935.

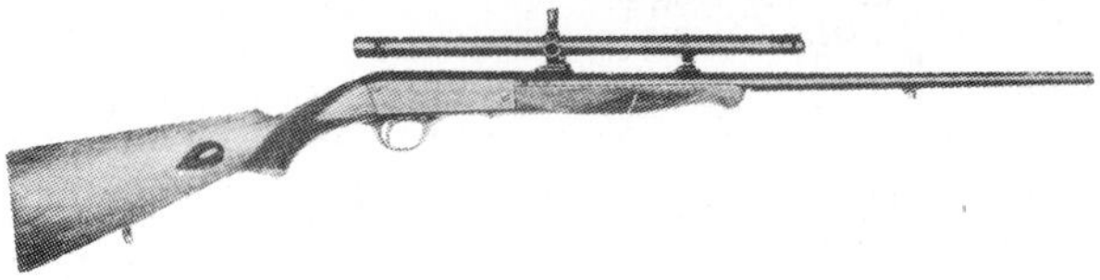

Courtesy Wallis & Wallis, Lewes, Sussex, England

NIB	Exc.	V.G.	Good	Fair	Poor
—	750	500	295	150	100

MODEL 241 SPEEDMASTER

A .22 caliber takedown semi-automatic rifle with a 24" barrel and open sights. Blued with a walnut stock. Later production versions were known as the Model 241A. Approximately 56,000 were made between 1935 and 1949 in the styles listed.

Model 241

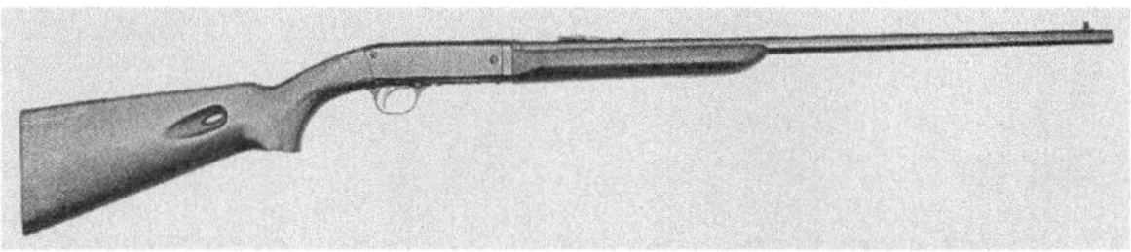

Courtesy Remington Arms

NIB	Exc.	V.G.	Good	Fair	Poor
—	450	350	250	200	150

Model 241D Peerless

Engraved.

NIB	Exc.	V.G.	Good	Fair	Poor
—	5000	3750	1800	1000	500

Model 241E Expert

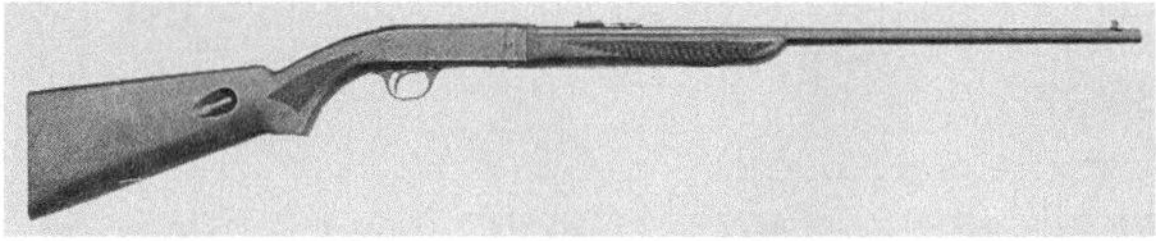

NIB	Exc.	V.G.	Good	Fair	Poor
—	7500	4000	2250	1200	800

Model 241F Premier

Heavily engraved.

NIB	Exc.	V.G.	Good	Fair	Poor
—	9000	5250	3150	1500	800

Model 550A

A .22 Short, Long, or LR caliber semi-automatic rifle with a 24" barrel and open sights. Blued with a walnut pistol-grip stock. Approximately 220,000 were made between 1941 and 1971.

NIB	Exc.	V.G.	Good	Fair	Poor
—	350	275	150	100	75

Model 550P

As above, with an aperture rear sight.

NIB	Exc.	V.G.	Good	Fair	Poor
—	375	300	175	125	100

Model 55-2G

As above, except fitted with a shell deflector and a screw eye for securing it to a shooting gallery counter.

NIB	Exc.	V.G.	Good	Fair	Poor
—	500	375	225	135	75

Model 30A "Express"

A sporting rifle using the U.S. Model 1917 Enfield bolt-action chambered for various Remington cartridges as well as the 7x57mm and .30-06 cartridges. Barrel length 22". Checkered walnut stock. A carbine model fitted with a 20" barrel was known as the Model 30R. Manufactured from 1921 to 1940.

Courtesy Remington Arms

NIB	Exc.	V.G.	Good	Fair	Poor
—	950	700	475	175	100

Model 30S

As above, chambered for the .257 Roberts, 7x57, and the .30-06 cartridges and with 24" barrel with a Lyman receiver sight. Select checkered walnut stock. Manufactured from 1930 to 1940.

NIB	Exc.	V.G.	Good	Fair	Poor
—	1300	975	495	250	150

Model 41A "Targetmaster"

This is a bolt-action rimfire rifle chambered for the .22 caliber Short, Long, LR. It is fitted with a 27" barrel with an open rear sight and bead front sight. The pistol-grip stock is plain. It was produced from 1936 to 1940.

NIB	Exc.	V.G.	Good	Fair	Poor
—	300	200	150	100	50

Model 41AS

Same as above but chambered for the .22 Remington Special or .22 WRF cartridge.

NIB	Exc.	V.G.	Good	Fair	Poor
—	275	175	125	100	75

Model 41P

Same as Model 41A with the addition of a rear peep sight and hooded front sight.

NIB	Exc.	V.G.	Good	Fair	Poor
—	325	225	175	125	50

Model 41SB

Same as Model 41A except for use with .22 shot cartridge. Barrel is smoothbore.

NIB	Exc.	V.G.	Good	Fair	Poor
—	350	275	195	150	75

Miscellaneous Remington Bolt Action Rimfires, 1930-1970

From 1930 to 1970 the Remington Company produced a variety of single-shot and repeating .22 caliber rifles. The values for these are much the same, consequently, they are listed for reference only.

Model 33	Model 510 X
Model 33 NRA	Model 511 A
Model 34	Model 511 P
Model 34 NRA	Model 511 X
Model 341 A	Model 512 A
Model 341 P	Model 512 P
Model 341 SB	Model 512 X
Model 510	Model 514
Model 510 P	Model 514 P
Model 510 SB	Model 514 BC

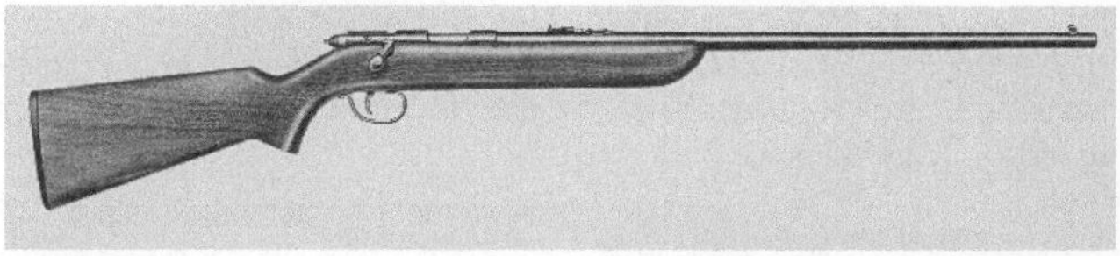

Model 510

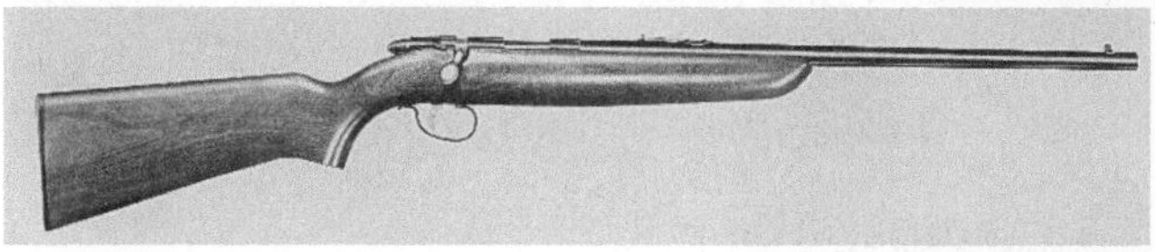

Courtesy Remington Arms

Model 510 Carbine

NIB	Exc.	V.G.	Good	Fair	Poor
—	300	200	125	750	50

Model 37

A .22 caliber bolt-action magazine target rifle with a heavy 28" barrel featuring target-sights and telescope bases. Blued with a walnut target style stock. Manufactured from 1937 to 1940.

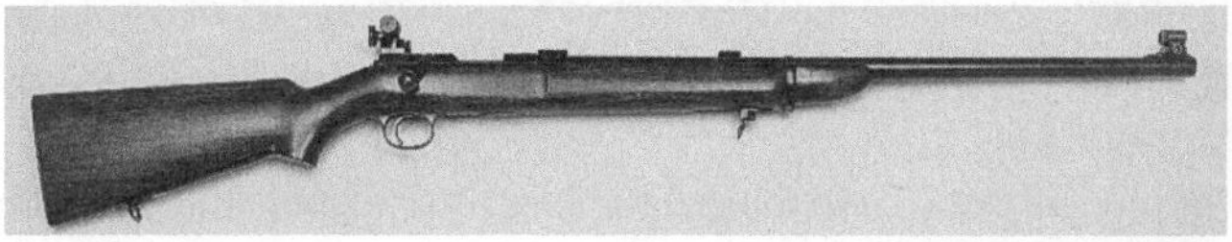

Courtesy Remington Arms

NIB	Exc.	V.G.	Good	Fair	Poor
—	600	500	400	300	250

Model 37-1940

As above, with an improved lock, trigger pull and redesigned stock. Manufactured from 1940 to 1954.

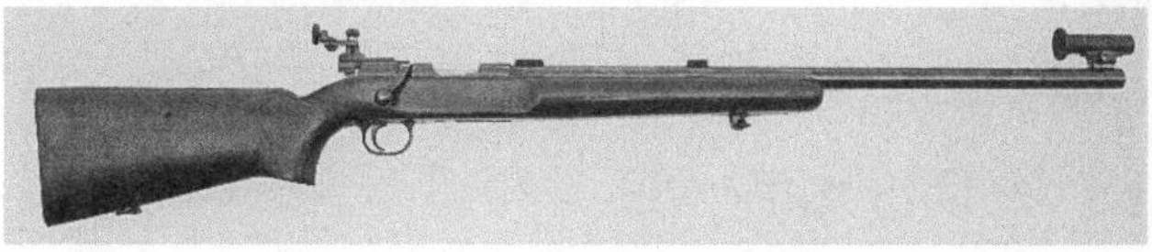

Courtesy Remington Arms

NIB	Exc.	V.G.	Good	Fair	Poor
—	900	750	500	300	200

Model 504

Introduced in 2004 this .22 caliber bolt action rifle is fitted with a 20" barrel with no sights. American walnut stock with checkering and pistol grip. Satin blue metal finish. Six round flush mounted detachable magazine. Receiver is drilled and tapped for scope mounts. Weight is about 6 lbs. Discontinued 2006.

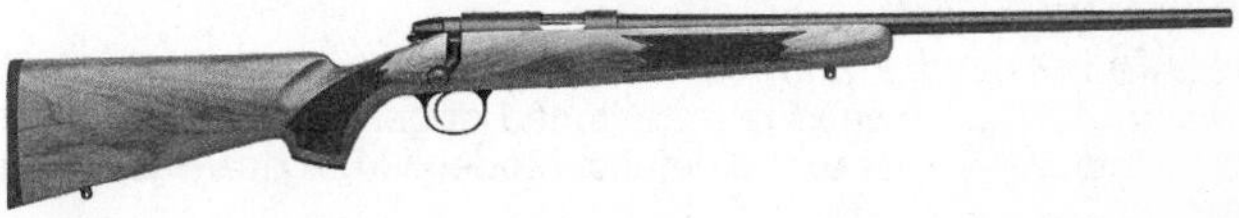

NIB	Exc.	V.G.	Good	Fair	Poor
650	550	400	300	200	100

Model 504 Custom

Introduced in 2005 this model features a fancy walnut stock.

NIB	Exc.	V.G.	Good	Fair	Poor
1000	850	625	400	225	125

Model 504-T LS HB

Introduced in 2005 this model features a 20" heavy barrel with blued finish. Chambered for the .22 Long Rifle or the .17 HMR cartridge. Brown laminate stock with Monte Carlo comb. Weight is about 8.5 lbs.

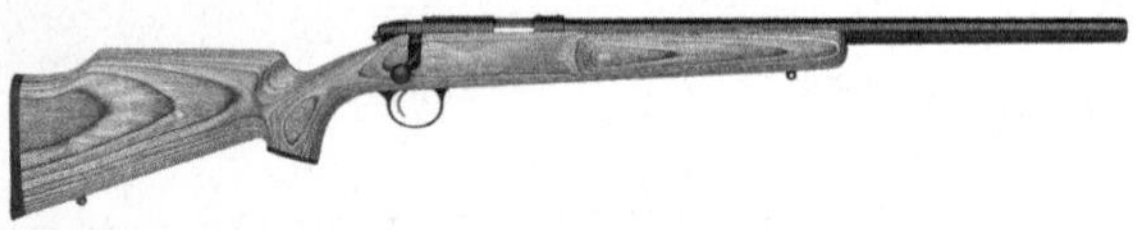

NIB	Exc.	V.G.	Good	Fair	Poor
800	675	475	275	250	150

Model 541 S Custom

A .22 caliber bolt-action magazine rifle with a 24" barrel. Blued with a scroll engraved receiver, and checkered walnut stock having a rosewood pistol grip cap and forend tip. Manufactured from 1972 to 1984.

NIB	Exc.	V.G.	Good	Fair	Poor
—	600	500	375	200	125

Model 541T

As above, drilled and tapped for telescopic sights. Introduced in 1986.

NIB	Exc.	V.G.	Good	Fair	Poor
375	275	200	175	125	75

Model 541T Heavy Barrel

This model is the same as the standard 541-T with the exception of a 24" heavy barrel. First introduced in 1993.

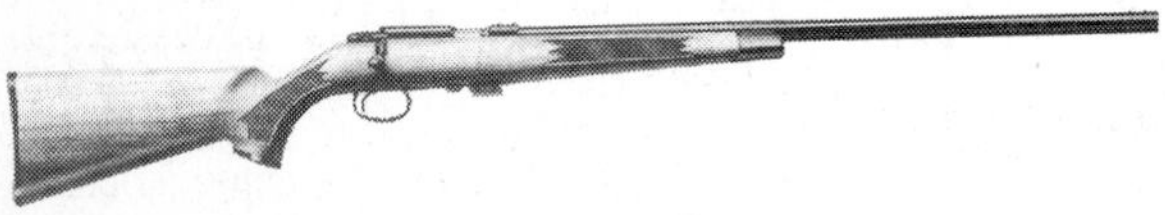

NIB	Exc.	V.G.	Good	Fair	Poor
450	350	300	250	200	125

Model 547

High-quality magazine-fed .17 or .22 rimfire sporter with walnut stock, crowned muzzle, tuned rigger and other goodies. Suspiciously similar to the defunct Model 504. A dealer exclusive for 2007.

NIB	Exc.	V.G.	Good	Fair	Poor
1000	775	600	400	275	200

Model 511 Scoremaster

A .22 caliber bolt-action magazine sporting rifle with a 22" barrel. Blued with a walnut stock. Six- round magazine.

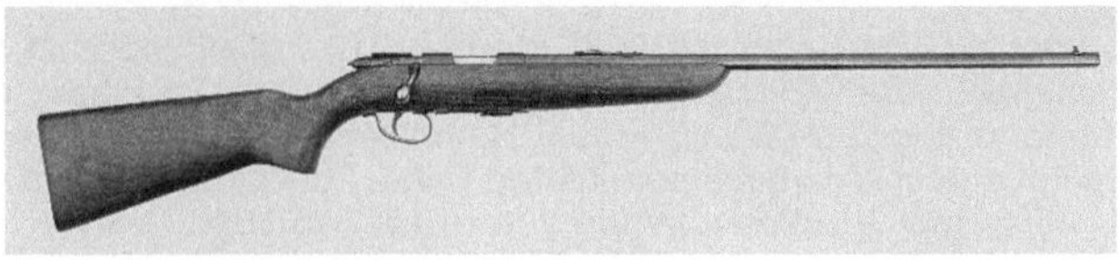

NIB	Exc.	V.G.	Good	Fair	Poor
—	325	250	175	125	75

Model 512

Bolt-action .22 rimfire repeater identical to 511 except with tubular magazine located beneath the barrel. Capacity is 15 LR, 17 Long and 22 Short cartridges. Manufactured from 1940 to 1962. All 500 series models (510, 511, 512, 513 and 521) feature a red cocking indicator at the rear of the bolt.

NIB	Exc.	V.G.	Good	Fair	Poor
—	350	275	200	150	100

Model 513 TR Matchmaster

A .22 caliber bolt-action magazine target rifle with a heavy 27" barrel and Redfield aperture rear sight. Blued with a target-style walnut stock. Manufactured from 1940 to 1969.

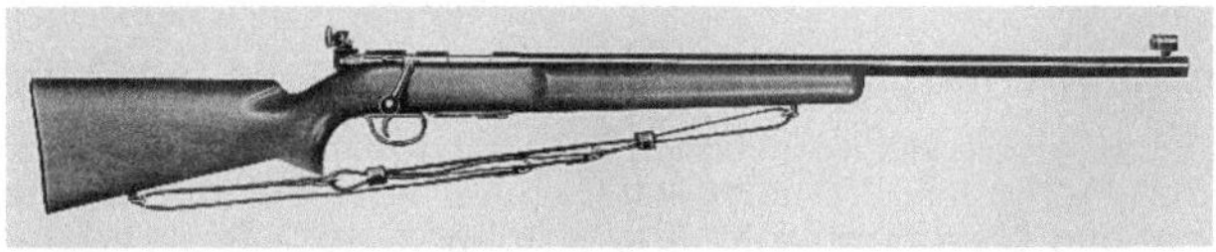

NIB	Exc.	V.G.	Good	Fair	Poor
—	400	300	200	150	100

Model 513 S

As above, with Marble sights and a checkered walnut sporting-style stock. Manufactured from 1941 to 1956.

NIB	Exc.	V.G.	Good	Fair	Poor
—	750	625	475	375	225

Model 521 TL Jr.

A .22 caliber bolt-action magazine target rifle with a heavy 25" barrel and Lyman sights. Blued with a target-style walnut stock. Manufactured from 1947 to 1969.

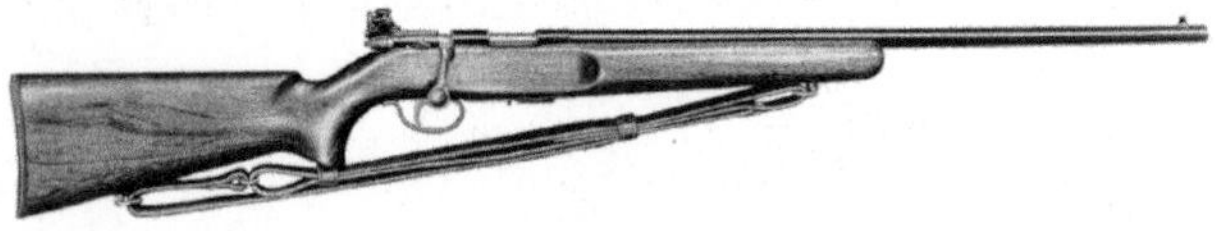

NIB	Exc.	V.G.	Good	Fair	Poor
—	350	250	175	125	75

MODEL 760

A slide-action sporting rifle chambered for various popular centerfire cartridges from the .222 up to the .35 Remington cartridge, with a 22" round barrel and open sights. It features a detachable box magazine. Blued with a checkered, walnut, pistol-grip stock. Manufactured between 1952 and 1982. Examples of this rifle chambered for the .222, .223, .244, and the .257 Roberts are worth a premium of 100 to 200 percent over other calibers. This model was produced in the styles listed.

Standard Model

NIB	Exc.	V.G.	Good	Fair	Poor
—	500	395	275	195	150

Model 760 Carbine

18.5" barrel.

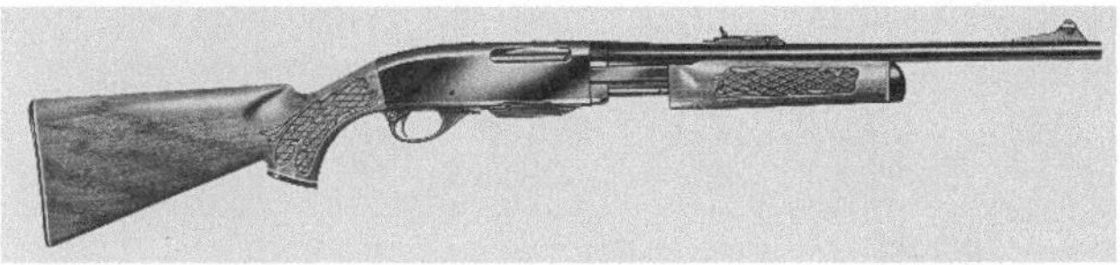

NIB	Exc.	V.G.	Good	Fair	Poor
—	525	395	275	195	150

Model 760D Peerless

Engraved.

NIB	Exc.	V.G.	Good	Fair	Poor
—	5000	3500	2250	1100	450

Model 760F Premier

Game scene engraved.

NIB	Exc.	V.G.	Good	Fair	Poor
—	9000	6000	4500	1700	550

Model 760F Gold Inlaid

NIB	Exc.	V.G.	Good	Fair	Poor
—	10000	7000	5250	2200	750

Model 760 Bicentennial

1976 only.

NIB	Exc.	V.G.	Good	Fair	Poor
—	550	495	295	200	150

Model 760 ADL

NIB	Exc.	V.G.	Good	Fair	Poor
—	525	395	275	195	150

Model 760 BDL

Basketweave checkering.

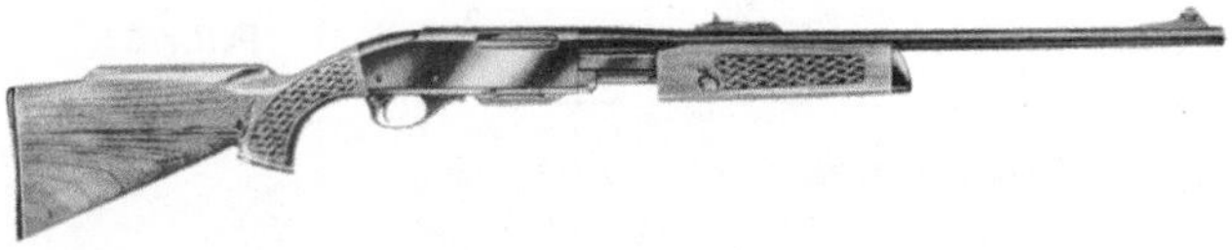

NIB	Exc.	V.G.	Good	Fair	Poor
—	525	395	275	195	150

Model 552A Speedmaster

A .22 caliber semi-automatic rifle with a 23" barrel and open sights. Blued with a pistol grip walnut stock. Manufactured from 1959 to 1988.

NIB	Exc.	V.G.	Good	Fair	Poor
—	295	225	150	75	50

Model 552 BDL

As above, with a more fully figured stock and impressed checkering. Introduced in 1966.

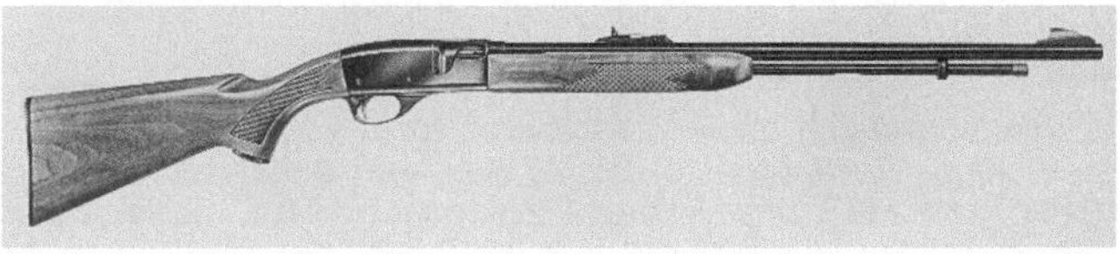

Courtesy Remington Arms

NIB	Exc.	V.G.	Good	Fair	Poor
425	300	225	150	100	75

Model 552 BDL Deluxe Speedmaster NRA Edition

Introduced in 2005 this model features a walnut stock with checkering and high gloss finish. Blued receiver and barrel with NRA logos etched on both sides of the receiver.

NIB	Exc.	V.G.	Good	Fair	Poor
520	400	300	195	125	95

Model 572 Fieldmaster

A .22 caliber slide-action rifle with a 21" barrel and open sights. Blued with a walnut stock. Manufactured from 1955 to 1988.

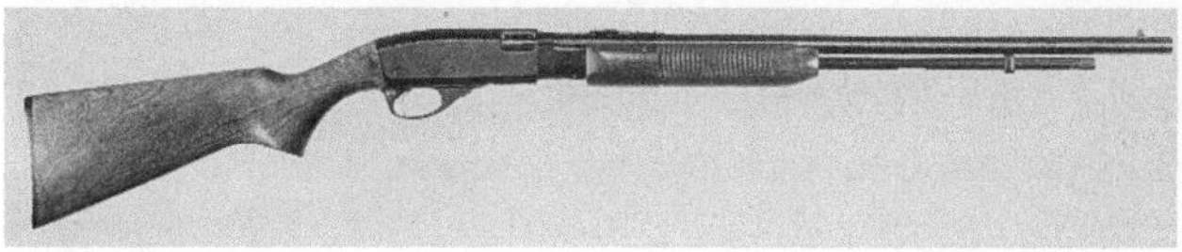

Courtesy Remington Arms

NIB	Exc.	V.G.	Good	Fair	Poor
—	295	225	150	75	50

Model 572 BDL

As above, but with a more fully figured walnut stock with impressed checkering. Introduced in 1966.

NIB	Exc.	V.G.	Good	Fair	Poor
425	300	225	150	110	85

Model 572SB

This is the same as the Model 572 but it has a smoothbore barrel and is chambered for the .22 LR shot cartridge.

NIB	Exc.	V.G.	Good	Fair	Poor
325	275	200	125	75	60

Model 572 BDL Smoothbore

Similar to Model 572 but with unrifled barrel for use with shot cartridges. Introduced as a special production item in 2007.

NIB	Exc.	V.G.	Good	Fair	Poor
425	300	225	150	110	85

Model 580

A .22 caliber single-shot bolt-action rifle with a 24" barrel, open sights and a Monte Carlo-style stock. Blued. Manufactured from 1968 to 1978.

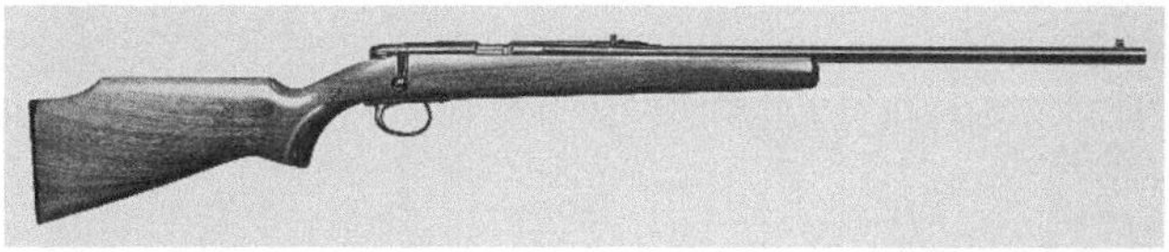

Courtesy Remington Arms

NIB	Exc.	V.G.	Good	Fair	Poor
—	250	200	150	75	50

Model 580 BR

Same as above but with 1" shorter buttstock.

NIB	Exc.	V.G.	Good	Fair	Poor
250	200	150	175	75	50

Model 580 SB

This is the same as the Model 580 except with a smoothbore barrel for .22 LR shot cartridges.

NIB	Exc.	V.G.	Good	Fair	Poor
300	250	175	125	75	50

Model 581

A .22 caliber bolt-action magazine rifle, blued with a 24" barrel and walnut stock. Manufactured from 1967 to 1983.

NIB	Exc.	V.G.	Good	Fair	Poor
300	250	175	125	75	50

Model 581 Left-Hand

Same as above but built for a left-handed shooter.

NIB	Exc.	V.G.	Good	Fair	Poor
295	250	175	125	75	50

Model 581-S

As above, fitted with a 5-round detachable magazine. Introduced in 1986.

NIB	Exc.	V.G.	Good	Fair	Poor
300	250	175	125	75	50

Model 582

As above, fitted with a tubular magazine in place of the detachable box magazine. Manufactured from 1967 to 1983.

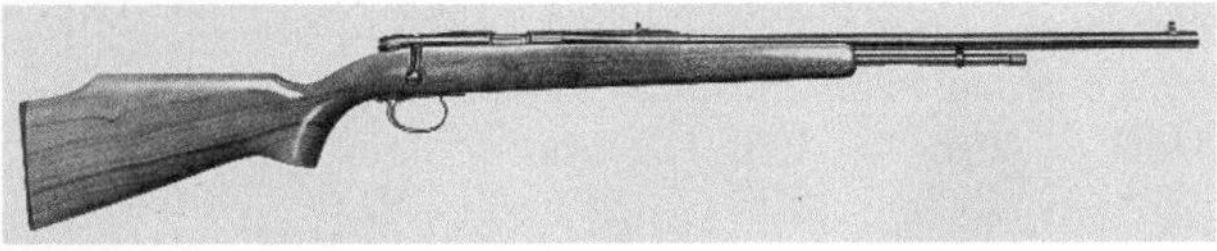

Courtesy Remington Arms

NIB	Exc.	V.G.	Good	Fair	Poor
300	250	175	125	75	50

Model 591

A 5mm rimfire Magnum bolt-action rifle with a 24" barrel and Monte Carlo-style stock. Approximately 20,000 were made between 1970 and 1973.

NIB	Exc.	V.G.	Good	Fair	Poor
450	300	225	175	125	75

Model 592

As above, with a tubular magazine. Approximately 7,000 were made.

NIB	Exc.	V.G.	Good	Fair	Poor
450	300	225	175	125	75

Model 740

A semi-automatic rifle with a 22" barrel and detachable box magazine. Chambered in .244 Rem., .280 Rem., .308 or .30-06. Blued with a plain walnut stock. Also available with an 18.5" barrel that would be worth approximately 10 percent more than the values listed below. 30 percent premium for .244 Remington. Manufactured from 1955 to 1960.

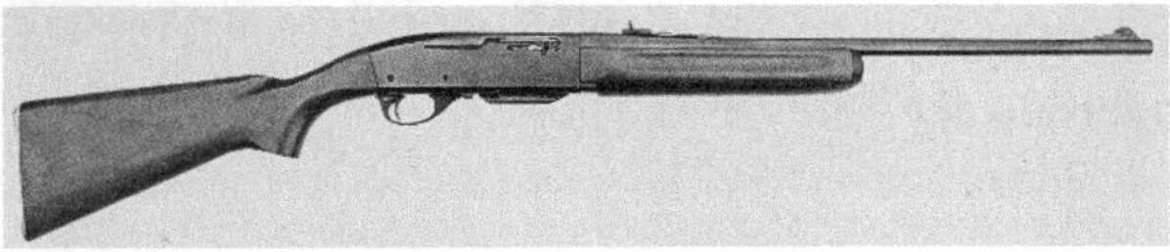

NIB	Exc.	V.G.	Good	Fair	Poor
—	300	225	200	150	100

Model 740 ADL

As above, with a checkered walnut stock with a pistol grip.

NIB	Exc.	V.G.	Good	Fair	Poor
—	350	250	225	150	100

Model 740 BDL

As above, with a more finely figured walnut stock.

NIB	Exc.	V.G.	Good	Fair	Poor
—	400	275	250	150	100

Model 742

A 6mm Remington, .243, .280, .30-06, or .308 caliber semi-automatic rifle with a 22" barrel and 4-shot magazine. Also available with an 18" barrel in calibers .308 and .30-06 that are worth approximately 10 percent more than the values listed below. Blued with a checkered walnut stock. Manufactured from 1960 to 1980.

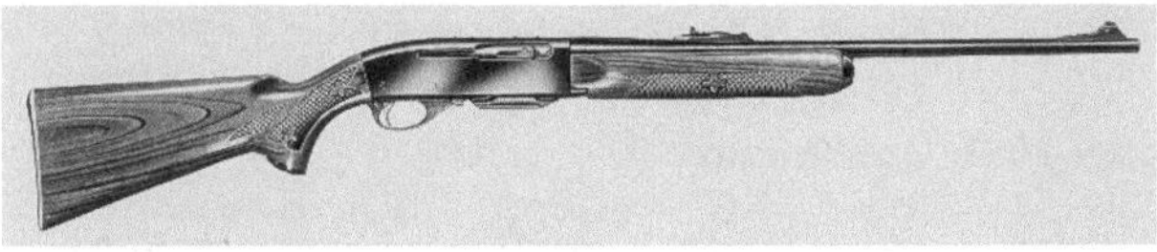

Courtesy Remington Arms

NIB	Exc.	V.G.	Good	Fair	Poor
—	350	275	250	150	100

Model 742 BDL Standard Grade

As above, with a Monte Carlo-style stock and basketweave checkering.

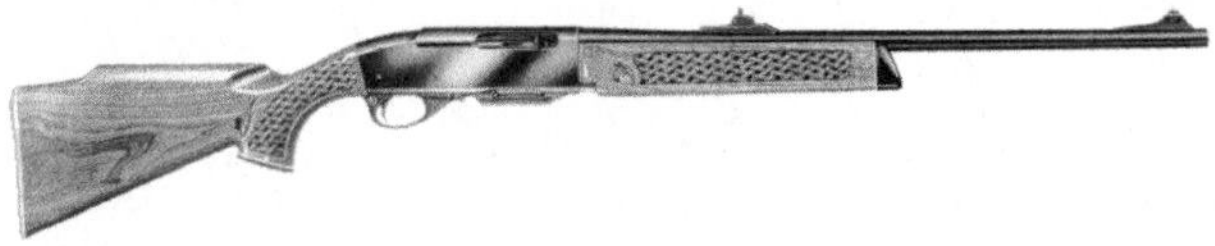

NIB	Exc.	V.G.	Good	Fair	Poor
—	375	275	225	175	125

Model 742D Peerless

Engraved.

NIB	Exc.	V.G.	Good	Fair	Poor
—	5000	3500	2250	1100	450

Model 742F Premier (Game Scene)

NIB	Exc.	V.G.	Good	Fair	Poor
—	9000	6000	4500	1700	550

Model 742F Premier (Gold Inlaid)

NIB	Exc.	V.G.	Good	Fair	Poor
—	10000	7000	5250	2200	750

Model 742 Bicentennial

Mfg. 1976 only.

NIB	Exc.	V.G.	Good	Fair	Poor
—	550	495	295	200	150

Model 76 Sportsman

A .30-06 slide-action rifle with a 22" barrel and 4-shot magazine. Blued with walnut stock. Manufactured from 1985 to 1987.

NIB	Exc.	V.G.	Good	Fair	Poor
—	325	225	175	125	75

Model 7600 Standard Grade

A variation of the above, chambered for a variety of cartridges from 6mm Remington to .35 Whelen with a 22" barrel and a detachable magazine. Also available with an 18.5" barrel. Blued with a checkered walnut stock. In 1996 fine line engraving on the receiver was offered as standard.

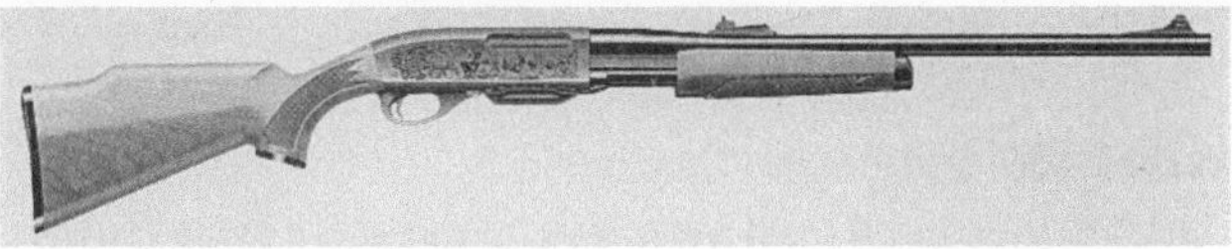

Model 7600 with engraving Courtesy Remington Arms

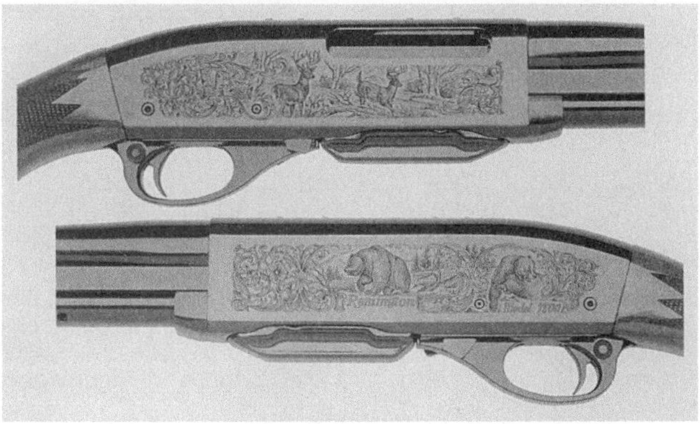

Close-up of engraving on Model 7600 Courtesy Remington Arms

NIB	Exc.	V.G.	Good	Fair	Poor
615	450	325	225	150	100

Model 7600D Peerless

Engraved.

NIB	Exc.	V.G.	Good	Fair	Poor
—	5000	3500	2250	1100	450

Model 7600F Premier

Game scene engraved.

NIB	Exc.	V.G.	Good	Fair	Poor
—	9000	6000	4500	1700	550

Model 7600 Premier

Gold inlaid.

NIB	Exc.	V.G.	Good	Fair	Poor
—	10000	7000	5250	2200	750

Model 7600 Synthetic

Same as the standard grade Model 7600 with black synthetic stock. A .30-06 carbine version is also available. Introduced in 1998.

NIB	Exc.	V.G.	Good	Fair	Poor
510	375	275	200	150	100

Model 7600 Special Purpose

The same configuration as the standard Model 7600 but equipped with a special finish on both the wood and metal that is nonreflective. First offered in 1993.

NIB	Exc.	V.G.	Good	Fair	Poor
600	475	350	225	150	100

Model 7600P Patrol Rifle

Introduced in 2002 this rifle is chambered for the .308 cartridge. It is fitted with a 16.5" barrel. Synthetic stock with matte black finish. Parkerized finish on metal. Wilson Combat rear ghost-ring sights with AO front sight. Weight is about 7 lbs.

NIB	Exc.	V.G.	Good	Fair	Poor
600	475	350	225	150	100

Model 7600 Buckmasters ADF (American Deer Foundation)

Introduced in 1997 and built only for that year this model is chambered for the .30-06 cartridge and is a limited edition item. Fitted with a 22" barrel and special fine line engraved receiver.

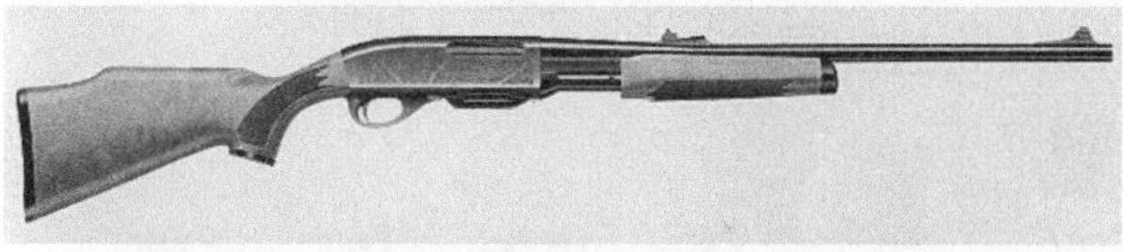

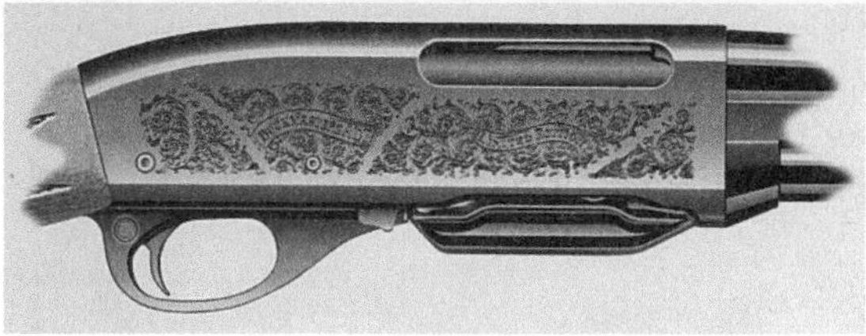

Close-up detail on engraving for Model 7600

NIB	Exc.	V.G.	Good	Fair	Poor
600	475	350	225	150	100

MODEL 7600 CUSTOM GRADE

This Custom Shop model is available in three levels of engraving, gold inlay, wood grade and finish, metal work finish, recoil pad/buttplate, and dimensions. Each gun should be individually appraised prior to a sale.

D Grade

NIB	Exc.	V.G.	Good	Fair	Poor
—	5000	3500	2250	1100	450

F Grade

NIB	Exc.	V.G.	Good	Fair	Poor
—	9000	6000	4500	1700	550

F Grade with Gold Inlay

NIB	Exc.	V.G.	Good	Fair	Poor
—	10000	7000	5250	2200	750

Model Six

A centerfire slide-action rifle with a 22" barrel and a 4-shot detachable magazine. Blued with a walnut stock. Manufactured from 1981 to 1987.

NIB	Exc.	V.G.	Good	Fair	Poor
—	450	350	275	200	125

Model 7615 Tactical Pump Carbine

Pump-action rifle based on Model 7600 action and chambered in .223 Remington with 16-1/2" barrel. Folding synthetic stock. Introduced in 2007.

NIB	Exc.	V.G.	Good	Fair	Poor
600	475	350	225	150	100

Model 7615 Special Purpose Synthetic

Similar to Model 7615 Tactical but with fixed stock and picatinny rail. A dealer exclusive for 2007.

NIB	Exc.	V.G.	Good	Fair	Poor
625	500	375	250	175	125

Model 7615 Camo Hunter

Similar to Model 7615 Tactical but with fixed buttstock and entirely camo-finished except for action parts and trigger guard assembly. Introduced in 2007.

NIB	Exc.	V.G.	Good	Fair	Poor
650	525	400	265	195	150

Model 7615 Ranch Carbine

Similar to Model 7615 Tactical but with fixed buttstock, walnut buttstock and forend, and 18-1/2" barrel. No iron sights but drilled and tapped for scope mounts. Introduced in 2007.

NIB	Exc.	V.G.	Good	Fair	Poor
625	500	375	250	175	125

Model 74 Sportsman

A .30-06 caliber semi-automatic rifle with a 22" barrel and a 4-shot detachable magazine. Blued with a walnut stock. Manufactured from 1985 to 1987.

NIB	Exc.	V.G.	Good	Fair	Poor
—	350	250	175	125	75

Model Four

As above, with a select Monte Carlo-style stock. Manufactured from 1982 to 1987.

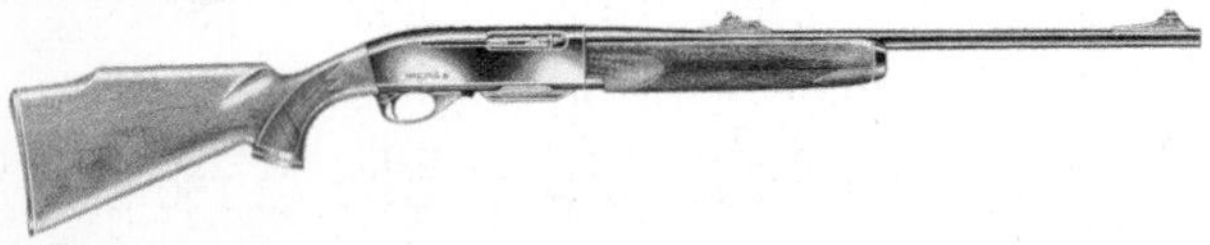

NIB	Exc.	V.G.	Good	Fair	Poor
—	500	400	350	275	175

Model 7400

This is a semi-automatic rifle with a 22" barrel. It is chambered for the .243, .270, .280, .30-06, .308, and the .35 Whelen. Blued with a checkered walnut stock. Average weight is about 7.5 lbs. Introduced in 1982. In 1996 this model was offered with fine line engraving on the receiver as standard.

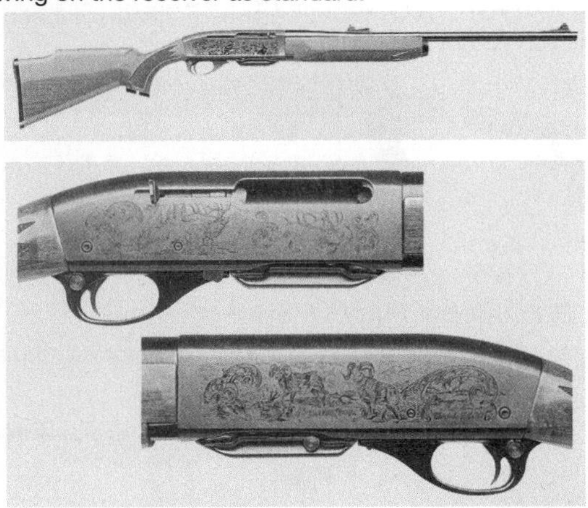

Courtesy Remington Arms

Model 7400 with engraving

NIB	Exc.	V.G.	Good	Fair	Poor
600	475	350	250	200	100

Model 7400 Synthetic

Similar to the Model 7400 with black nonreflective synthetic stock. A .30-06 carbine is also offered. Introduced in 1998.

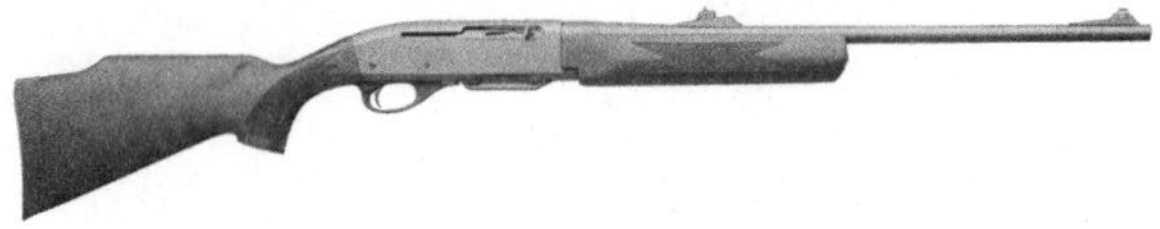

NIB	Exc.	V.G.	Good	Fair	Poor
550	400	300	200	150	100

Model 7400 Weathermaster

Introduced in 2003 this semi-automatic model features a weather-resistant black synthetic stock and matte nickel-plated receiver, barrel, and magazine. Barrel length is 22" with iron sights. Chambered for the .30-06 or .270 Win. cartridges. Weight is about 7.5 lbs.

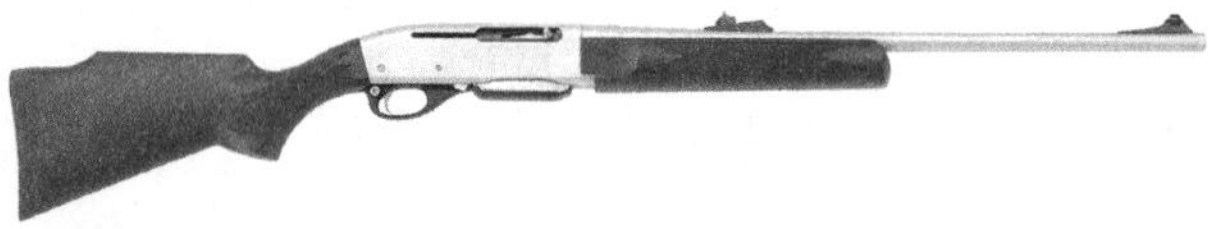

NIB	Exc.	V.G.	Good	Fair	Poor
650	525	400	300	200	100

Model 7400 Carbine

Same as above but with 18.5" barrel and chambered for the .30-06 cartridge.

NIB	Exc.	V.G.	Good	Fair	Poor
550	400	300	200	150	100

Model 7400 Special Purpose

The same configuration as the standard Model 7400 but equipped with a special finish on both the wood and metal that is nonreflective. First offered in 1993.

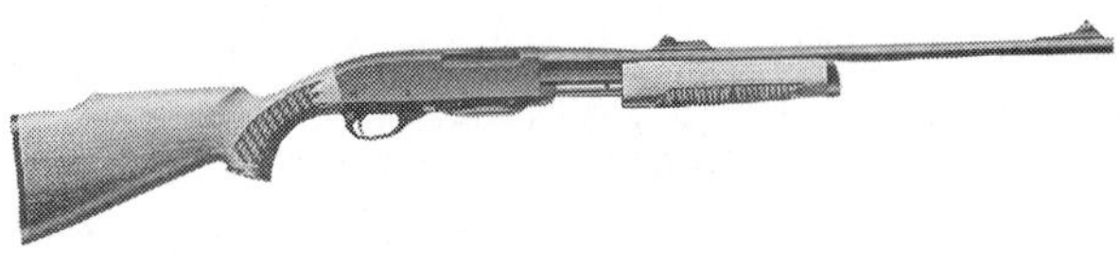

NIB	Exc.	V.G.	Good	Fair	Poor
450	350	300	250	200	100

Model 7400 Buckmasters ADF (American Deer Foundation)

Introduced in 1997, and built only in that year this model is limited. Chambered for the .30-06 cartridge and fitted with a 22" barrel. Special fine line engraving and polished blue finish. American walnut stock with Monte Carlo and cut checkering. Weight is 7.5 lbs.

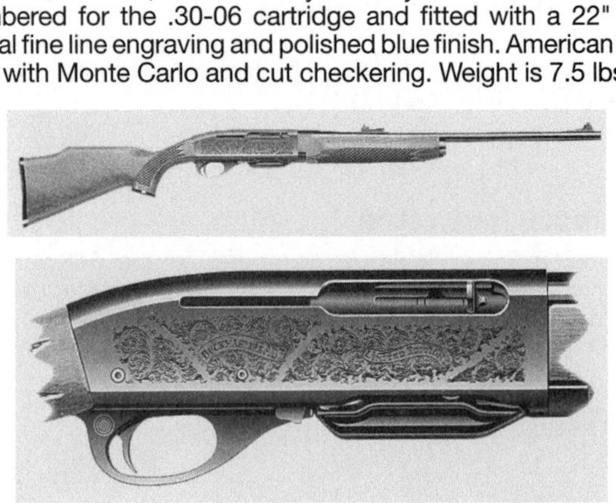

Close-up detail on engraving for Model 7400 Buckmasters ADF

NIB	Exc.	V.G.	Good	Fair	Poor
600	500	400	300	200	100

Model 7400 Custom Grade

This Custom Shop model is available in three levels of engraving, gold inlay, wood grade and finish, metal work finish, recoil pad/buttplate, and dimensions. Each gun should be individually appraised prior to a sale.

Model 7400 Custom Grade F Grade

NIB	Exc.	V.G.	Good	Fair	Poor
—	9000	6000	4500	1700	550

Model 7400 Custom Grade F Grade with Gold Inlay

NIB	Exc.	V.G.	Good	Fair	Poor
—	10000	7000	5250	2200	750

Model 750 Woodsmaster

Wood-stocked version of Model 7400 semi-auto. Rifle version has 22" barrel; carbine has 18.5" barrel. Introduced 2006.

NIB	Exc.	V.G.	Good	Fair	Poor
650	550	400	275	175	100

Model 750 Synthetic

Similar to Model 750 Woodsmaster but with black synthetic stock and forend. Introduced in 2007.

NIB	Exc.	V.G.	Good	Fair	Poor
625	550	400	300	225	125

Model R-15 VTR Predator Rifle

AR-style rifle chambered for .223 Remington or .204 Ruger. Supplied with one 5-shot magazine but accepts AR-style higher-cap magazines. 22-inch fluted barrel; fixed stock. Finish: Advantage MAX-12 HD overall.

NIB	Exc.	V.G.	Good	Fair	Poor
1100	900	695	500	250	125

Model R-15 VTR Predator Carbine

Similar to above but with 18-inch barrel.

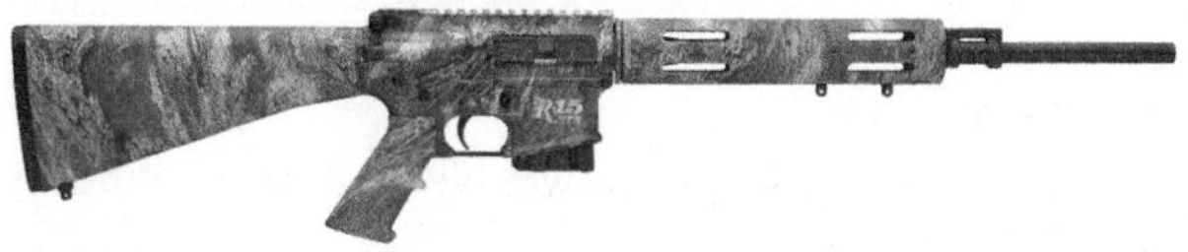

NIB	Exc.	V.G.	Good	Fair	Poor
1100	900	695	500	250	125

Model R-15CS VTR Predator Carbine

Similar to above but with collapsible buttstock.

NIB	Exc.	V.G.	Good	Fair	Poor
1145	950	750	550	275	150

Model R-15 Hunter

Similar to R-15 but in .30 Remington AR or .450 Bushmaster, 22" barrel, Realtree AP HD camo.

NIB	Exc.	V.G.	Good	Fair	Poor
1200	975	750	550	275	150

Model R-15 VTR Byron South Edition

.223, 18" barrel, Advantage MAX-1 HD camo.

NIB	Exc.	V.G.	Good	Fair	Poor
1200	975	750	550	275	150

Model R-15 VTR SS Varmint

As above but with 24" stainless steel barrel.

NIB	Exc.	V.G.	Good	Fair	Poor
1200	975	750	550	275	150

Model R-15 VTR Thumbhole

Similar to R-15 Hunter but with thumbhole stock.

NIB	Exc.	V.G.	Good	Fair	Poor
1300	1075	850	595	295	150

Model R-25 Modular Repeating Rifle

Enhanced AR-style semi-auto rifle chambered in .243, 7mm-08 and .308 Winchester. Features include 20" chrome-moly barrel, single-stage trigger, four-round magazine, aluminum alloy upper and lower Mossy Oak Treestand camo finish overall. Overall length 38-1/4", weight: 7-3/4 lbs.

NIB	Exc.	V.G.	Good	Fair	Poor
1375	1100	850	650	275	150

REMINGTON'S "NYLON SERIES" .22 RIFLES

Model 10 Nylon

Bolt action single shot. Approximately 10,700 (approx. 2000 smoothbore and only 200 of those with 24" barrel) produced from 1962-1964. Mohawk brown nylon stock with white accents, chrome spoon style bolt handle, safety engages upon cocking, .22 short, long, and long rifle. This model is available in both rifled and smoothbore versions (smoothbore barrels are marked "smoothbore" and in barrel lengths of 19-1/2" and 24". Add 100 percent+ for the 24" versions. Add 100 percent+ for NIB.

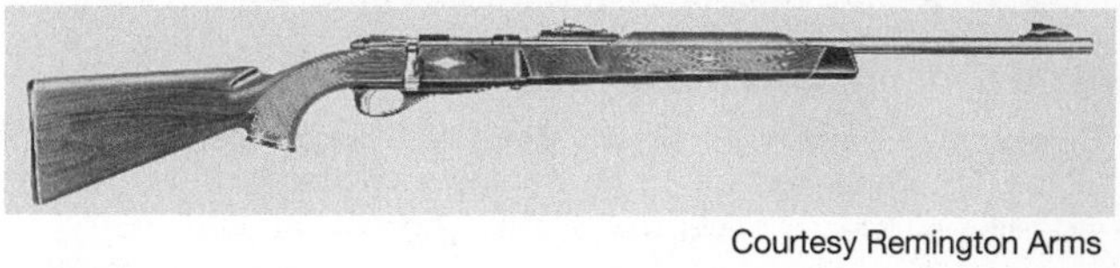

Courtesy Remington Arms

10

NIB	Exc.	V.G.	Good	Fair	Poor
—	700	600	500	300	200

10 (SB)

NIB	Exc.	V.G.	Good	Fair	Poor
—	1000	800	700	500	450

Model 11 Nylon

Bolt action repeater, 6- or 10-round metal box magazine. Approximately 22,500 produced from 1962-1964. Mohawk brown nylon stock with white accents, chrome spoon style bolt handle, manual right side safety. .22 short, long or long rifle. Barrel lengths of 19-1/2" and 24". Add 100 percent for the 24" version.

NIB	Exc.	V.G.	Good	Fair	Poor
—	475	375	300	275	175

Model 12 Nylon

Bolt action repeater, 14 round external tubular magazine under the barrel. Approximately 27,600 produced from 1962-1964. Mohawk brown nylon stock with white accents, chrome spoon style bolt handle, manual right side safety. .22 short, long or long rifle. Barrel lengths of 19-1/2" and 24". Add 100 percent for 24" version.

NIB	Exc.	V.G.	Good	Fair	Poor
—	475	375	300	275	175

MODEL 66 NYLON

Semi-automatic, 19-1/2" barrel, 14 round tubular magazine, fed through the buttplate. In excess of 1,000,000 produced from 1959-1987. Seven different variations of style and color were sold. Non-serialized prior to the 1968 gun control act of 1968. An "A" prefix was added to the serialization in 1977. Add 100 percent+ for NIB.

66 (MB) "Mohawk" Brown

Blued metal parts, dark chocolate brown stock with white accents, .22 LR ONLY. 1959-1987. Approx. 678,000.

66 (SG) "Seneca" Green

Blued metal parts, dark olive green stock (often confused with MB in artificial light) with white accents, .22 LR ONLY, 1959-1962. Approx. 45,000.

66 (AB) "Apache" Black

Bright chrome plated metal parts, black stock with white accents, .22 LR ONLY.1962-1983. Approx. 220,000.

66 (BD) "Black Diamond"

Blued metal parts, black stock with black diamonds in the forend. The remainder of accents are white, .22 LR ONLY, 1978-1987. Approx. 56,000.

66 (GS) "Gallery Special"

Blued metal parts, Dark brown stock with white accents. Barrel marked .22 SHORT. Distinguished by shell deflector over ejection port and a loop on the forend for the counter chain. 1961-1981. Approx. 6500.

66 (AN) "150th Anniversary Rifle"

Blued metal parts, dark brown stock with white accents, .22 LR ONLY. Distinguished by 150th Anniversary stamping on the left side of the receiver cover. 1966 ONLY. Approx. 4000.

66 (BI) "Bicentennial Rifle"

Blued metal parts, dark brown stock with white accents, .22 LR ONLY. Distinguished by the eagle and 1776/1976 stamping on the left side of the receiver cover. 1976 ONLY. Approx. 10,000.

66 (MB)

NIB	Exc.	V.G.	Good	Fair	Poor
—	250	175	150	125	100

66 (SG)

NIB	Exc.	V.G.	Good	Fair	Poor
—	550	450	325	275	175

66 (AB)

NIB	Exc.	V.G.	Good	Fair	Poor
—	500	425	350	250	125

66 (BD)

NIB	Exc.	V.G.	Good	Fair	Poor
—	425	375	300	250	150

66 (GS)

NIB	Exc.	V.G.	Good	Fair	Poor
—	1200	950	700	450	300

66 (AN)

NIB	Exc.	V.G.	Good	Fair	Poor
—	850	650	450	300	250

66 (BI)

NIB	Exc.	V.G.	Good	Fair	Poor
—	750	500	325	275	200

NOTE: One should expect 100 percent+ premium for new in the box examples.

MODEL 76 NYLON

Lever action repeater. The only lever action Remington ever produced. 19-1/2" barrel, 14 round tubular magazine, fed through the buttplate. Produced from 1962-1964 in three different variations. Add 100 percent+ for NIB.

76 (MB) "Trailrider"

Blued metal parts, dark brown stocks with white accents. Approximately 25,300 produced.

76 (AB) "Trailrider"

Bright chrome metal parts, black stock with white accents. Approximately 1600 produced.

76 (not cataloged)

Blued metal parts, black stock with white accents. Production numbers do not exist.

76 (MB)

NIB	Exc.	V.G.	Good	Fair	Poor
—	1700	600	500	375	250

76 (AB)

NIB	Exc.	V.G.	Good	Fair	Poor
—	2000	800	700	500	400

76 (Not cataloged)

NIB	Exc.	V.G.	Good	Fair	Poor
—	1800	675	600	400	300

MODEL 77 NYLON

Known as the 77 (MB): Semi-automatic,19-1/2" barrel, 5 round plastic box magazine. Blued metal parts, dark brown stock with white accents. .22 LR ONLY. 1970-1971. Approx. 15,300 produced. This model was replaced by the Model 10C in 1972. Add 100 percent for NIB.

NIB	Exc.	V.G.	Good	Fair	Poor
—	500	375	300	200	150

Model 10C Nylon

Known as the 10C. An identical copy of the 77 (MB), except that the box magazine capacity was increased to 10 rounds. 1972-1978. Approx. 128,000 produced. Add 50 percent for NIB.

NIB	Exc.	V.G.	Good	Fair	Poor
—	325	275	225	175	100

Model 77 Apache Nylon

Known as the "APACHE 77." Semi-automatic, 19-1/2" barrel, 10 round plastic box magazine. Metal parts coated with a black "teflon-like" finish, bright green stock with swirls of orange brown and black (highly variable), not to be confused with the 66 (SG). This rifle was contracted as an "exclusive" run, marketed by K-Mart. The number manufactured is hazy, but estimates run from 54,000 to over 100,000. Produced from 1987-1989. Add 100 percent for NIB.

NIB	Exc.	V.G.	Good	Fair	Poor
—	350	250	200	140	120

Model 522 Viper

Introduced in 1993 the Model 522 Viper is a new Remington .22 rimfire caliber semi-automatic design. The black stock is made from synthetic resin, while the receiver is made from a synthetic as well. It features a 20" barrel and a 10-shot detachable clip. The rifle weighs 4.6 lbs.

NIB	Exc.	V.G.	Good	Fair	Poor
160	120	100	80	60	40

Model 597

Introduced in 1997 this automatic .22 LR rimfire rifle features a carbon steel barrel with alloy receiver. All metal has a nonreflective matte black finish. Stock is dark gray synthetic. Barrel length is 20" and weight is approximately 5.5 lbs.

NIB	Exc.	V.G.	Good	Fair	Poor
225	150	100	70	50	25

Model 597 Sporter

Introduced in 1998 this version of the Model 597 has a blued finish with a hardwood stock with beavertail-style forearm. Magazine capacity is 10 rounds.

NIB	Exc.	V.G.	Good	Fair	Poor
225	150	100	70	50	25

Model 597 Stainless Sporter

Same as the Model 597SS but fitted with a hardwood stock. Introduced in 2000.

NIB	Exc.	V.G.	Good	Fair	Poor
275	200	150	100	75	25

Model 597 LSS

This version of the Model 597 is similar to the above but with the addition of a laminated stock and stainless steel finish.

NIB	Exc.	V.G.	Good	Fair	Poor
300	225	175	125	100	50

Model 597 SS

This version is also chambered for the .22 LR and has a stainless steel barrel on an alloy receiver. The stock is gray synthetic with beavertail style forearm. Magazine capacity is 10 rounds. Weight is about 5.5 lbs. Introduced in 1998.

NIB	Exc.	V.G.	Good	Fair	Poor
240	175	125	100	75	25

Model 597 HB

Introduced in 2001 this model features a 20" carbon steel heavy barrel chambered for the .22 LR cartridge. Fitted with a brown laminated stock. No sights. Weight is about 6 lbs.

NIB	Exc.	V.G.	Good	Fair	Poor
275	225	165	125	75	25

Model 597 HB Magnum

Same as model above but chambered for the .22 Winchester Magnum cartridge. Introduced in 2001.

NIB	Exc.	V.G.	Good	Fair	Poor
425	325	200	165	125	50

Model 597 Magnum

This model features a 20" carbon steel barrel, alloy receiver, and black synthetic stock. It is chambered for the .22 Win. Magnum cartridge. Weight is approximately 6 lbs.

NIB	Exc.	V.G.	Good	Fair	Poor
350	250	200	150	100	50

Model 597 Magnum LS

Chambered for the .22 Magnum. The receiver and barrel are blued with a gray laminated hardwood stock with beavertail- style forearm. Magazine capacity is 10 rounds. Introduced in 1998. In 2003 this model was also offered chambered for the .17 HMR cartridge.

NIB	Exc.	V.G.	Good	Fair	Poor
375	275	195	145	100	50

Model 597 Custom Target

This model is available on special order from the Custom Shop. It is chambered for the .22 LR cartridge and has a 20" stainless steel heavy target barrel without sights. The stock is a green, laminated-wood target style with pistol grip. Trigger is custom tuned. Weight is approximately 7.5 lbs. Introduced in 1998.

NIB	Exc.	V.G.	Good	Fair	Poor
600	475	400	275	200	150

Model 597 Custom Target Magnum

Similar to the model above but chambered for the .22 Win. Mag. Weight is approximately 8 lbs. Introduced in 1998. This is special order item only.

NIB	Exc.	V.G.	Good	Fair	Poor
750	600	500	375	250	175

Model 597 LSS

Similar to Model 597 but with laminated stock, stainless barrel and 3-9X scope. Dealer exclusive for 2007.

NIB	Exc.	V.G.	Good	Fair	Poor
275	200	150	100	75	25

Model 597 Synthetic Scope Combo

"Package rifle" similar to Model 597 but with 3-9X scope included. Introduced in 2007.

NIB	Exc.	V.G.	Good	Fair	Poor
300	225	175	125	100	50

Model 597 TVP (Target/Varmint/Plinker)

Ultra-funky .22 LR autoloader built on the Model 597 chassis. Features include bolt-guidance system with twin, tool-steel guide rails; laminated, skeletonized wood stock; non-glare matte finish; 10-shot metal detachable magazine; and last-shot hold-open bolt for added safety. Scope rail. Introduced in 2008.

NIB	Exc.	V.G.	Good	Fair	Poor
530	465	395	275	175	125

Model 597 Yellow Jacket

Similar to above but with yellow and black laminated stock.

NIB	Exc.	V.G.	Good	Fair	Poor
500	395	225	150	100	75

Model 597 Blaze Camo

A Model 597 with synthetic stock molded in screamin' blaze orange and black.

NIB	Exc.	V.G.	Good	Fair	Poor
275	225	165	125	75	25

Model 597 Pink Camo

Similar to above but with a pink – yes, pink – and black camo-pattern stock.

NIB	Exc.	V.G.	Good	Fair	Poor
275	225	165	125	75	25

Model 597 FLX

Similar to Model 597 Blaze/Pink camo but with FLX Digital Camo stock.

NIB	Exc.	V.G.	Good	Fair	Poor
275	225	165	125	75	25

Model 597 AAC

Same features as other 597 models except has 16.5-inch barrel that will accept AAC flash hider, muzzle break or suppressor. Staggered-stack magazine holds 10 rounds. Weight is 5.5 pounds.

NIB	Exc.	V.G.	Good	Fair	Poor
195	165	140	115	100	75

Remington 597 VTR - Quad Rail

Semiauto rifle chambered in .22 LR, styled to resemble AR. Features include matte blued finished and black synthetic stock; 16-inch barrel; Pardus A2-style collapsible pistol-grip stock; quad-rail free-floated tube; 10-round magazine.

Remington 597 VTR A-2 Fixed Stock

Similar to Remington 597 VTR - Quad Rail but with fixed A2-style stock and standard handguard with quad rail.

Remington 597 VTR Collapsible Stock

Similar to 597 VTR A-2 Fixed Stock but with Pardus A2-style collapsible pistol-grip stock.

Remington 597 VTR A-TACS Camo

Semiauto rifle chambered in .22 LR, styled to resemble AR. Features include ATACS camo finish overall; 16-inch barrel; Pardus A2-style collapsible pistol-grip stock; round handguard without rails; receiver-mounted optics rail; 10-round magazine.

NIB	Exc.	V.G.	Good	Fair	Poor
400	360	325	275	210	150

NOTE: Add 30 percent for A-TACS Camo model.

Model Five

.22 rimfire bolt-action sporter. Calibers: .22 LR or .22 WMR or .17 HMR; five-shot detachable magazine. Barrel: 22" blued with iron sights; receiver blued for scope mounts. Stock: laminated walnut with QD swivels. Add 10 percent for .22 WMR. Introduced 2006.

NIB	Exc.	V.G.	Good	Fair	Poor
300	250	175	125	75	25

Model 40X Target Rifle

A .22 caliber rimfire single-shot bolt-action rifle with a heavy 28" barrel fitted with Redfield Olympic sights or telescopic sight bases. Blued with a walnut target style stock having a hard rubber butt-plate. Manufactured from 1955 to 1964.

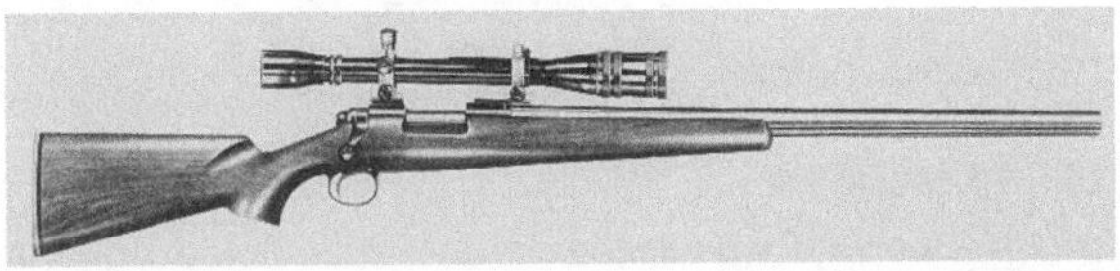

Courtesy Remington Arms

NIB	Exc.	V.G.	Good	Fair	Poor
—	750	550	425	350	300

Model 40X Sporter

As above, with a 24" barrel, 5-shot magazine and a walnut sporting style stock. Fewer than 700 were made between 1969 and 1980.

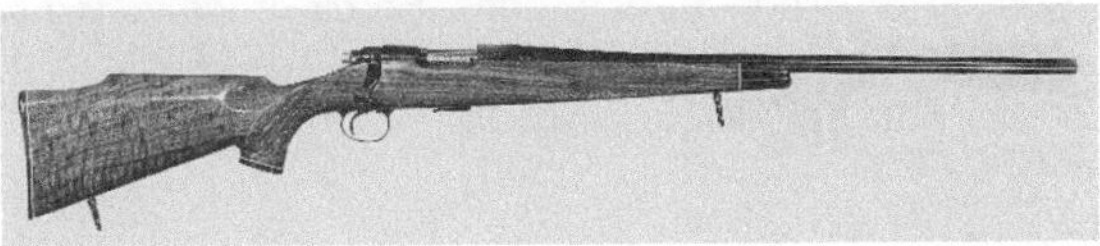

Courtesy Remington Arms

NIB	Exc.	V.G.	Good	Fair	Poor
—	2500	1700	1200	500	275

Model 40X Centerfire

As above, chambered for .222, .222 Magnum, .308, or .30-06 centerfire cartridges. Manufactured from 1961 to 1964.

NIB	Exc.	V.G.	Good	Fair	Poor
—	700	500	400	300	200

Model 40XB Rangemaster Centerfire

This model is built in the Custom Shop and features stainless steel barrel, receiver, and bolt. The receiver is drilled and tapped and fitted with a 27-1/4" heavy target barrel. The trigger is fully adjustable. There is a choice of walnut stock or synthetic stock. Starting in 1998 this model was offered with a special laminated thumbhole stock. Offered in calibers from .222 to .300 Win. Mag. This rifle is built to order. Made since 1964.

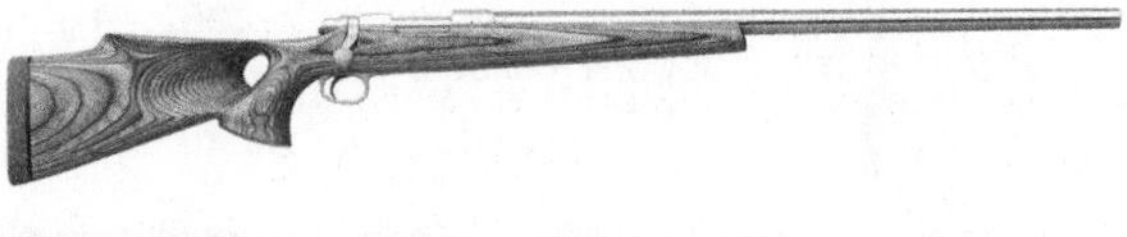

NIB	Exc.	V.G.	Good	Fair	Poor
2100	1800	1325	1000	600	250

Model 40XB BR

This is a bench rest Custom Shop version of the above model. This rifle has a 22" stainless heavy barrel chambered for the .22 BR Remington. Adjustable trigger. Built to order.

NIB	Exc.	V.G.	Good	Fair	Poor
—	1000	850	600	450	200

Model 40XB Tactical Rifle

First offered in 2003 this bolt-action rifle features a Teflon coated stainless steel 27.25" barrel chambered for the .308 Win. cartridge. Fitted with a H.S. Precision tactical stock with vertical pistol grip. Remington 40-X trigger.

NIB	Exc.	V.G.	Good	Fair	Poor
2400	2100	1600	1200	700	350

Remington 40XS Tactical

Bolt action rifle chambered in .308 Winchester or .338 Lapua Magnum. Features include 416 stainless steel Model 40-X 24-inch 1:12 barreled action; black polymer coating; McMillan A3 series stock with adjustable length of pull and adjustable comb; adjustable trigger and all-steel trigger guard; Harris bipod with quick adjust swivel lock Leupold Mark IV 3.5-10x40mm long range M1 scope with Mil Dot reticle; Badger Ordnance all-steel Picatinny scope rail and rings.

NIB	Exc.	V.G.	Good	Fair	Poor
5400	4700	4000	3000	—	—

NOTE: Deduct 50 percent if without Leupold scope, Harris Bipod, Badger Ordnance Picatinny rail.

Model 40XR KS Sporter

This Custom Shop version is also chambered for the .22 LR and is fitted with a 24" barrel. Fully adjustable trigger.

NIB	Exc.	V.G.	Good	Fair	Poor
1300	1000	850	600	450	350

Model XC KS

This is a Custom Shop position rifle with 24" stainless steel heavy barrel chambered for .223 Rem. and .308 Win. cartridges. Kevlar stock with palm rail. Weight is approximately 11 lbs.

NIB	Exc.	V.G.	Good	Fair	Poor
2650	2225	1850	1400	800	400

Model 673 Guide Rifle

Introduced in 2003 this bolt-action rifle features a 22" vent rib barrel chambered for the 6.5 mm Rem. Mag, .308, .300 RUM, or.350 Rem. Mag cartridge. Adjustable rear sight. The stock is dark and light tan laminate with checkering. Magazine capacity is three rounds. Weight is about 7.5 lbs. Discontinued 2006. Slight premium for .300 RUM.

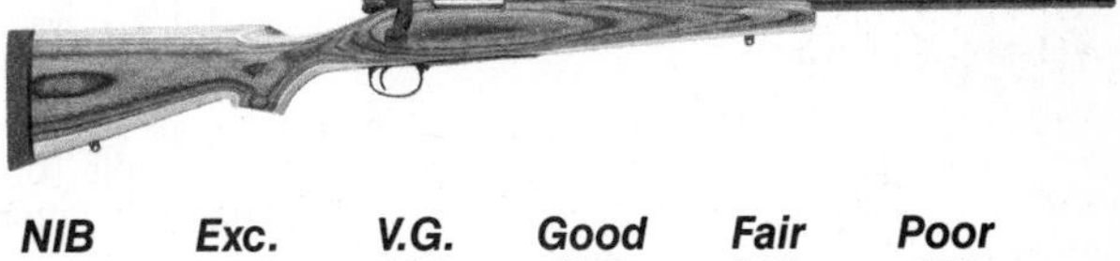

NIB	Exc.	V.G.	Good	Fair	Poor
650	525	400	300	200	150

Model 720A

A .257 Roberts, .270, or .30-06 bolt-action sporting rifle with a 22" barrel and a 5-shot integral magazine. Blued with a checkered walnut stock. Approximately 2,500 were manufactured in 1941.

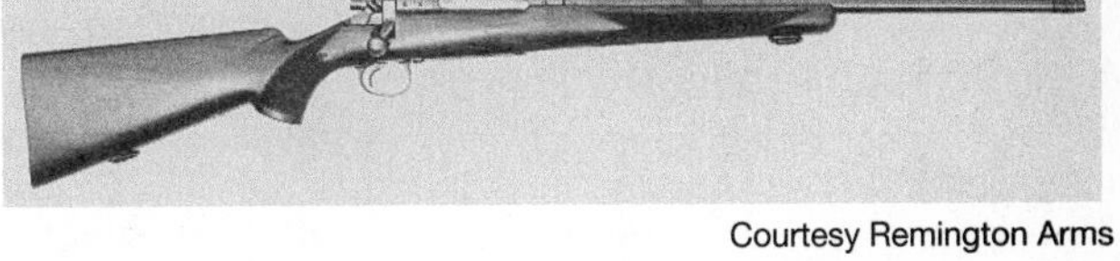

Courtesy Remington Arms

NIB	Exc.	V.G.	Good	Fair	Poor
—	2400	1875	1300	700	400

NOTE: Deduct 40 percent if .30-06 caliber.

MODEL 721

A .264 Magnum, .270, .280 or .30-06 bolt-action rifle with a 24" barrel and a 4-shot magazine. Blued with a plain walnut stock. Manufactured from 1948 to 1962. ADL model has checkered stock. BDL has high grade stock.

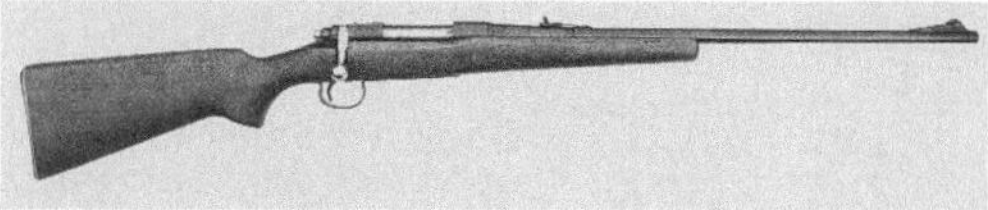

Courtesy Remington Arms

Standard Version

NIB	Exc.	V.G.	Good	Fair	Poor
—	450	350	200	150	100

ADL

NIB	Exc.	V.G.	Good	Fair	Poor
—	475	375	250	200	125

BDL

NIB	Exc.	V.G.	Good	Fair	Poor
—	450	375	300	250	150

Model 721A Magnum

.300 H&H.

NIB	Exc.	V.G.	Good	Fair	Poor
—	550	400	350	275	150

Model 722

A short-action variation of the Model 721 chambered for .222 Rem., .222 Rem. Magnum, .243 Win., .244 Rem., .257 Roberts, .300 Savage, .308 Winchester. The BDL models featured high-grade, select walnut stocks; ADL had checkered stocks. Made from 1948 to 1962.

NIB	Exc.	V.G.	Good	Fair	Poor
—	450	350	200	150	100

NOTE: Add 25 percent for BDL, 10 percent for ADL. Add 25 percent for .222 Rem. Mag., .243, .257 or .308 chamberings.

Model 725 ADL

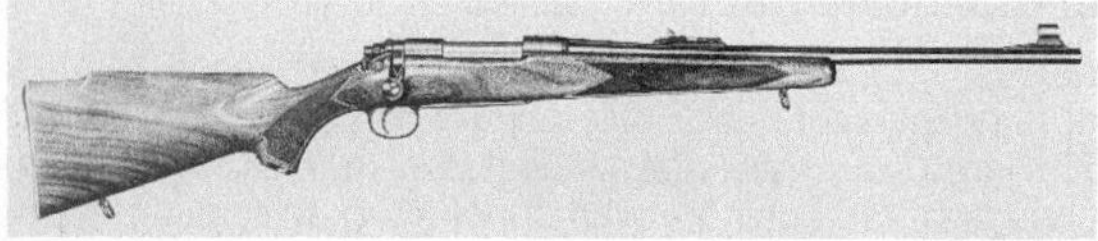

Courtesy Remington Arms

NIB	Exc.	V.G.	Good	Fair	Poor
—	800	525	275	225	150

Model 725 Kodiak

A .375 Holland & Holland Magnum or .458 Winchester Magnum, bolt-action sporting rifle with a 26" barrel, muzzlebrake, open sights and 3-shot magazine. Blued with a checkered walnut stock. Manufactured in 1961. Very limited production.

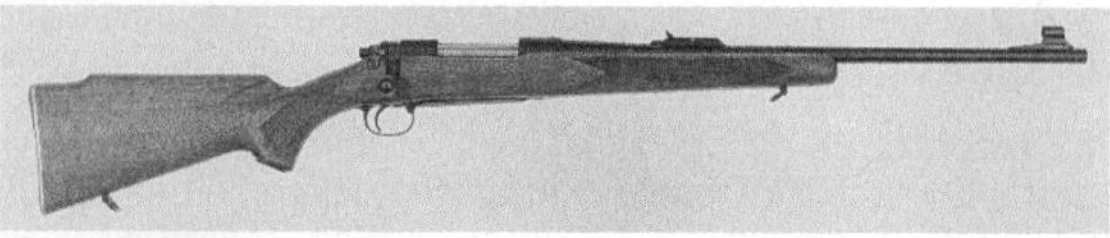

NIB	Exc.	V.G.	Good	Fair	Poor
—	3000	2500	2000	1000	300

Model 78 Sportsman

A centerfire bolt-action sporting rifle with a 22" barrel and 4-shot magazine. Blued with a walnut stock. Introduced in 1985. Calibers: .223, .243, .270, .308, .30-06.

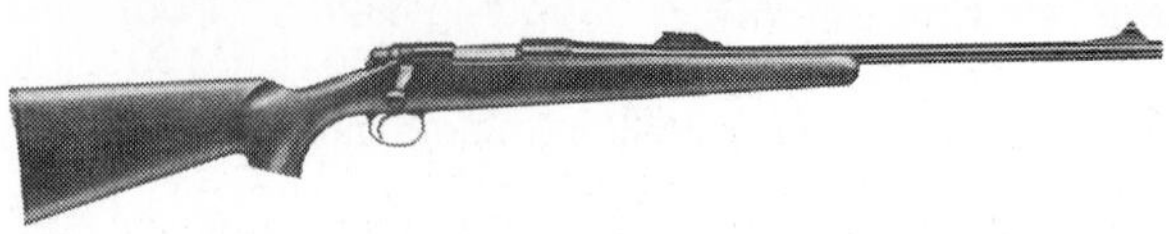

NIB	Exc.	V.G.	Good	Fair	Poor
335	275	225	200	150	100

Model 600

A centerfire bolt-action sporting rifle with an 18.5" ventilated rib barrel and a checkered walnut stock. Manufactured from 1964 to 1967. Calibers: .222 Rem., .223 Rem., 6mm Rem., .243, .308, .35 Rem.

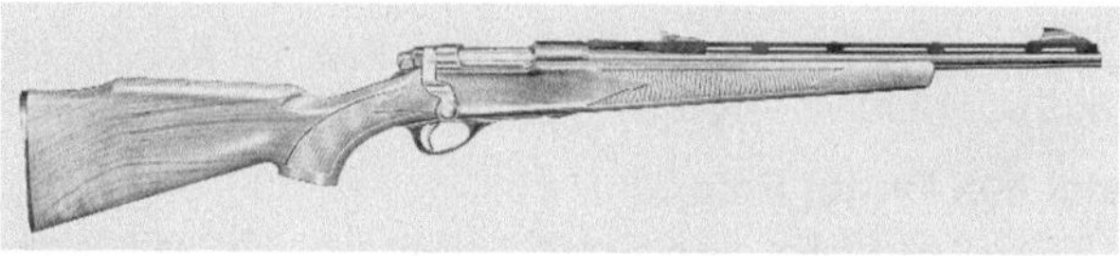

Courtesy Remington Arms

NIB	Exc.	V.G.	Good	Fair	Poor
—	550	450	350	225	150

NOTE: Add 100 percent for .223 Rem.

Model 600 Mohawk

As above, but with a plain barrel and chambered only for the .222 Remington, .243 Winchester or .308 Winchester cartridges. Manufactured from 1971 to 1979.

NIB	Exc.	V.G.	Good	Fair	Poor
—	450	375	225	175	125

Model 600 Magnum

As above, chambered for the 6.5mm Remington Magnum and .350 Remington Magnum cartridges. Stock of laminated walnut and beechwood. Manufactured from 1965 to 1967.

NIB	Exc.	V.G.	Good	Fair	Poor
—	1000	750	600	450	200

Model 660

An improved version of the Model 600. Manufactured from 1968 to 1971.

NIB	Exc.	V.G.	Good	Fair	Poor
—	550	425	350	250	200

Model 660 Magnum

As above, but chambered for either the 6.5mm Remington Magnum or .350 Remington Magnum cartridges and fitted with a laminated stock.

NIB	Exc.	V.G.	Good	Fair	Poor
—	1000	750	600	450	200

MODEL 700 SERIES

Model 700 ADL

A centerfire bolt-action sporting rifle with either a 20", 22" or 24" barrel, open sights and a 4-shot magazine. Blued with a checkered Monte Carlo-style walnut stock. Introduced in 1962. This model was available in most popular calibers from .222 Rem. to .300 Win. Mag.

NIB	Exc.	V.G.	Good	Fair	Poor
425	325	250	200	150	100

Model 700 ADL Synthetic

This model features a black matte metal finish with 22" barrel or 24" on Magnums. The synthetic stock is black with checkering, recoil pad, and sling swivel studs. Receiver is drilled and tapped for scope. Offered in .243, .270, .30-06 and 7mm Rem. Mag. In 1998 this model was available in .223 Rem. and .300 Win. Mag.

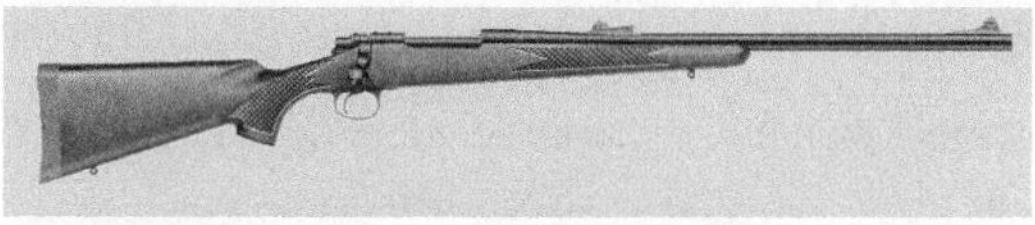

Courtesy Remington Arms

NIB	*Exc.*	*V.G.*	*Good*	*Fair*	*Poor*
350	300	250	200	150	100

Model 700 ADL Synthetic Youth

Introduced in 1998 this model has a shortened synthetic stock with a 13" lop. Offered in .243 and .308 calibers.

NIB	*Exc.*	*V.G.*	*Good*	*Fair*	*Poor*
400	300	250	200	150	100

Model 700 BDL

Same as above, with a hinged floorplate, cut checkering, black forend tip and pistol grip cap. Offered in a wide variety of calibers from the .17 Rem. to the .338 Rem. Ultra Mag. Weights are between 7.25 lbs. to 7.62 lbs. depending on caliber and barrel length.

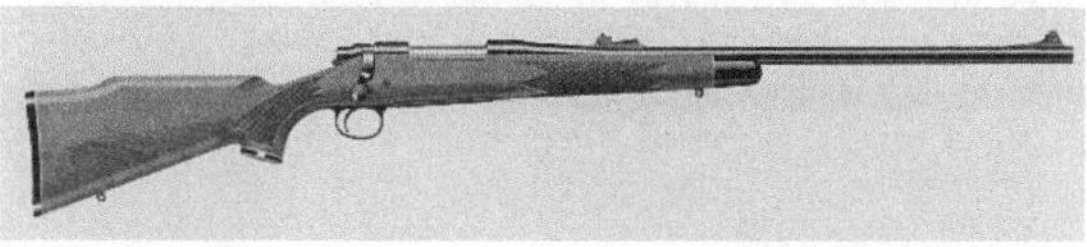

Courtesy Remington Arms

NIB	*Exc.*	*V.G.*	*Good*	*Fair*	*Poor*
715	525	400	275	225	150

Model 700 BDL LH (Left-Hand)

This model is also offered in selected calibers for left-hand shooters. They are: .270 Win., 7mm Rem. Mag., .30-06, and .300 Rem. Ultra Mag.

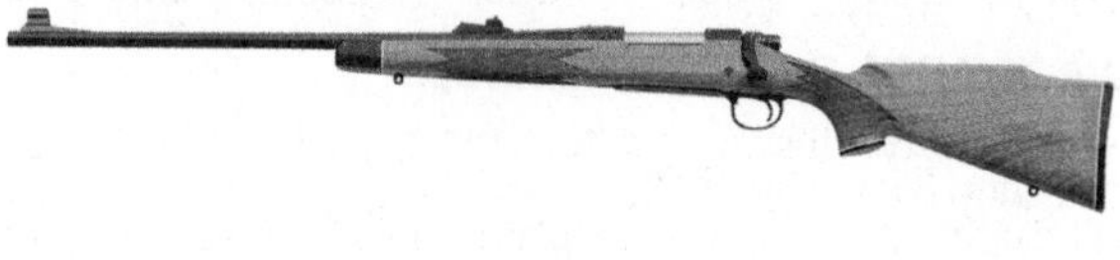

NIB	*Exc.*	*V.G.*	*Good*	*Fair*	*Poor*
800	700	500	325	250	150

Model 700 BDL (DM)

Same as above but introduced in 1995 with detachable magazine.

NIB	*Exc.*	*V.G.*	*Good*	*Fair*	*Poor*
715	525	400	300	225	150

Model 700 BDL LSS

This is a Model 700, introduced in 1996, with a synthetic stock and stainless steel bolt, floor plate, trigger guard, and sling swivels. The action and barrel are stainless steel as well. In 1997 the .260 Rem. cartridge was also available.

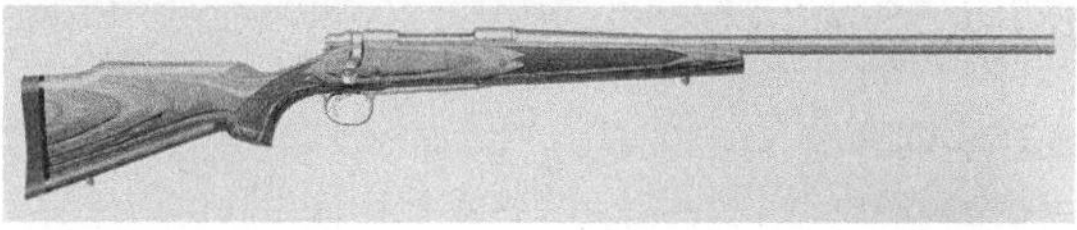

Courtesy Remington Arms

NIB	*Exc.*	*V.G.*	*Good*	*Fair*	*Poor*
600	475	400	350	300	200

Model 700 BDL SS DM—Magnum Rifle

Introduced in 1996 this Model 700 version is fitted with a factory installed muzzlebrake on its Magnum calibers: 7mm Rem. Mag., .300 Win. Mag., .300 Wthby. Mag., and the .338 Win. Mag. and the .338 Rem. Ultra Mag. Weight is approximately 7.5 lbs. In 1997 the 7mm STW cartridge was added to this model.

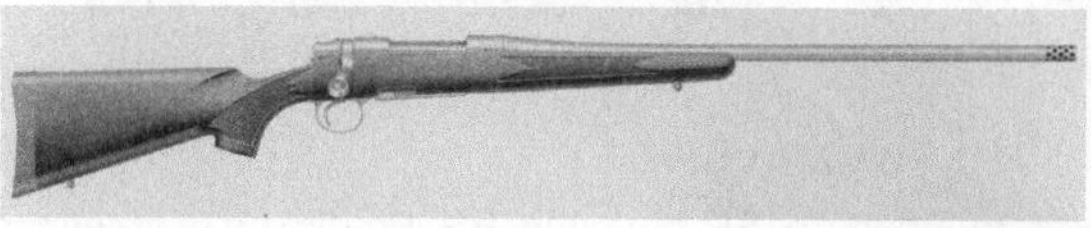

Courtesy Remington Arms

NIB	*Exc.*	*V.G.*	*Good*	*Fair*	*Poor*
675	500	400	300	200	150

Model 700 BDL SS Short Action

Fitted with stainless steel 24" and chambered for the 7mm Rem. Ultra Mag. and the .300 Rem. Ultra Mag. Black synthetic stock. No sights. Weight is about 7.325 lbs. Introduced in 2003.

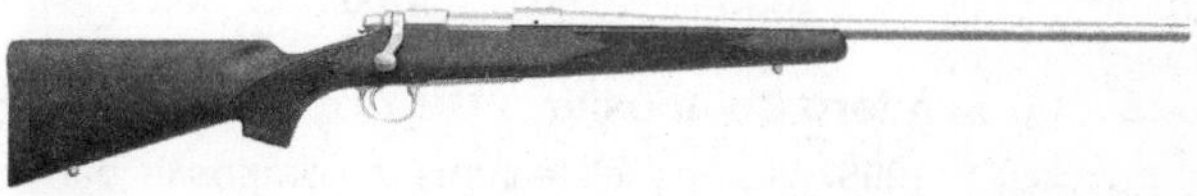

NIB	*Exc.*	*V.G.*	*Good*	*Fair*	*Poor*
775	625	500	395	300	175

Model 700 BDL SS Camo Special Edition (RMEF)

This is a special edition rifle for the Rocky Mountain Elk Foundation. Fitted with a 24" barrel and chambered for the .300 Rem. Ultra Mag cartridge. Camo stock with stainless steel receiver and barrel. Weight is about 7.5 lbs. Introduced in 2001. In 2002 the 7mm Rem. Ultra Mag chambering was added for one year only. In 2003 the .300 Rem. Ultra Mag was offered.

NIB	*Exc.*	*V.G.*	*Good*	*Fair*	*Poor*
835	650	500	395	300	175

Model 700 EtronX

Introduced in 2000 this rifle features a new technology that electronically discharges the round resulting in nearly instant ignition. LED located on top of the grip that shows safe or fire and chamber status. There is also a low battery indicator and malfunction indicators as well. The rifle is fitted with a 26" stainless steel fluted barrel. The stock is fiberglass and graphite reinforced with Kevlar. Chambers are .220 Swift, .22-250 Rem., and .243 Win. cartridges. Average weight is about 8.88 lbs. The gun was a flopperoo but is now considerable an almost-prime collectible. Discontinued 2004.

NIB	*Exc.*	*V.G.*	*Good*	*Fair*	*Poor*
1450	1300	1150	700	500	300

Model 700 Sendero

This Model 700 configuration is chambered for the .25-06, .270, 7mm Rem. Mag., .300 Win. Mag. It is fitted with a synthetic stock and a 26" heavy barrel.

NIB	*Exc.*	*V.G.*	*Good*	*Fair*	*Poor*
600	475	400	300	200	150

Model 700 Sendero SF

Introduced in 1996 this model features a stainless steel fluted barrel. It has a synthetic stock with full length bedding. It weighs about 8.5 lbs. Chambered for same calibers as the standard Sendero above except for the .270. In 1997 the 7mm STW cartridge was made available for this model. In 2003 the 7mm Rem. Ultra Mag. and the .300 Rem. Ultra Mag. were added calibers.

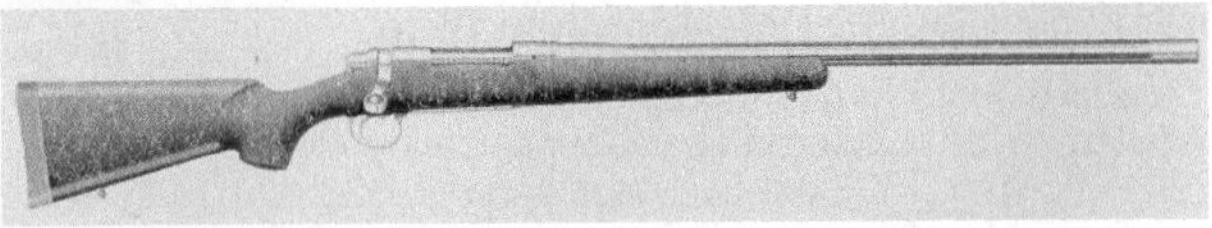

Courtesy Remington Arms

NIB	Exc.	V.G.	Good	Fair	Poor
1015	800	600	450	350	200

Model 700 Sendero SF-II

Similar to Sendero SF but with HS Precision synthetic stock. Chambered in .264 WM, 7mm RM, 7mm RUM, .300 WM, and .300 RUM. Introduced 2006.

NIB	Exc.	V.G.	Good	Fair	Poor
1150	985	835	700	500	300

Model 700 Sendero Composite

Introduced in 1999, this model features a composite barrel of graphite fiber with a stainless steel liner. Stock is synthetic. Calibers available are .25-06, 7mm STW, and .300 Win. Mag. Barrel length is 26". Weight is just under 8 lbs.

NIB	Exc.	V.G.	Good	Fair	Poor
1675	1250	975	700	475	300

Model 700 Mountain Rifle

As above, with a tapered 22" lightweight barrel, blued with checkered walnut stock. Introduced in 1986.

NIB	Exc.	V.G.	Good	Fair	Poor
425	325	250	200	150	100

Model 700KS Mountain Rifle

As above, with a lightweight Kevlar stock. Introduced in 1986.

NIB	Exc.	V.G.	Good	Fair	Poor
750	700	600	500	400	300

Model 700 Mountain Rifle (DM)

Same as standard Mountain Rifle but introduced in 1995 with detachable magazine. In 1998 this model was available in .260 Rem. caliber.

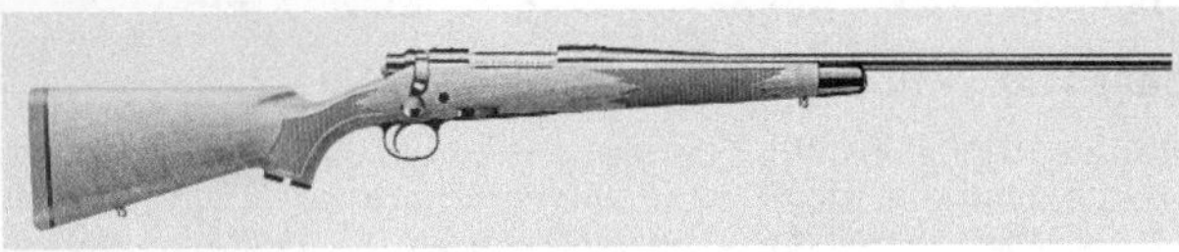

Courtesy Remington Arms

NIB	Exc.	V.G.	Good	Fair	Poor
780	575	425	300	250	175

Model 700 Safari Grade

As the Model 700BDL chambered for 8mm Remington Magnum, .375 Holland & Holland, .416 Remington Magnum or .458 Winchester Magnum cartridges, 24" barrel and 3-shot magazine. Blued with a finely figured walnut checkered stock. The Model KS Safari Grade was fitted with a Kevlar stock and would be worth approximately 20 percent more than the values listed. Introduced in 1962.

NIB	Exc.	V.G.	Good	Fair	Poor
875	750	600	500	400	300

Model 700 RS

As above, chambered for the .270 Winchester, .280 Remington, or .30-06 cartridges, 22" barrel and 4-shot magazine. Blued with a DuPont Rynite stock. Manufactured during 1987 and 1988.

NIB	Exc.	V.G.	Good	Fair	Poor
—	550	425	350	250	150

Model 700 FS

As above, with a Kevlar stock.

NIB	Exc.	V.G.	Good	Fair	Poor
—	550	475	400	300	200

Model 700 BDL European

Available for the first time in 1993, this model features an oil finish stock with Monte Carlo comb and raised cheekpiece. The checkering is fine line. In addition the rifle has a hinged floorplate, sling swivel studs, hooded ramp front sight, and adjustable rear sight. Offered in these calibers: .243, .207, .280, 7mm-08, 7mm Mag. .30-06, and .308.

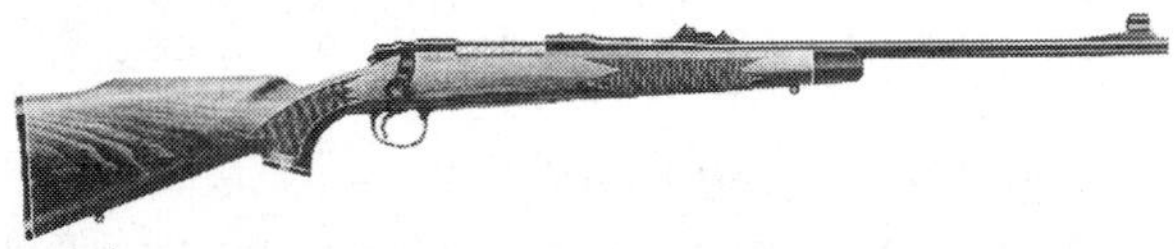

NIB	Exc.	V.G.	Good	Fair	Poor
675	400	350	300	250	200

Model 700 BDL Stainless Synthetic

Offered in 1993 this model features a stainless steel receiver, barrel, and bolt. Synthetic stock has straight comb, raised cheekpiece, and hinged floor plate. Metal is finished in a black matte nonreflective finish. Available in 14 calibers from .223 to .338 Win. Mag. All barrel lengths regardless of caliber are 24".

NIB	Exc.	V.G.	Good	Fair	Poor
550	450	350	300	200	150

Model 700 BDL Stainless Synthetic (DM)

Same as above but introduced in 1995 with detachable magazine.

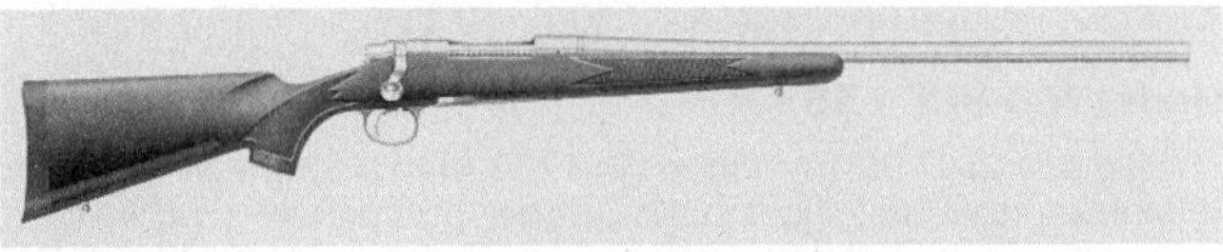

Courtesy Remington Arms

NIB	Exc.	V.G.	Good	Fair	Poor
575	475	350	300	200	150

Model 700 CDL

This model was introduced in 2004 and features a classic-style checkered walnut stock with black forend tip and grip cap. Hinged floor plate. Chambered for the .243, .270, 7mm-08, 7mm Rem. Mag., 7mm Rem. Ultra Mag, .30-06, .300 Win. Mag, and .300 Rem. Ultra Mag. Standard calibers are fitted with a 24" barrel while magnum calibers have a 26" barrel. Weight is about 7.5 lbs. depending on caliber.

NIB	Exc.	V.G.	Good	Fair	Poor
740	550	400	295	200	125

Model 700 CDL SF (2009)

Similar to above but chambered in .257 Roberts.

NIB	Exc.	V.G.	Good	Fair	Poor
740	550	400	295	200	125

Model 700 CDL Boone and Crockett

Similar to Model 700 CDL but with B&C laser-engraved barrel. A dealer exclusive for 2007.

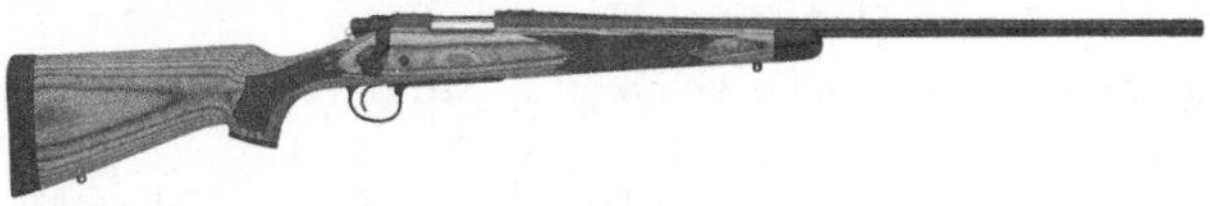

NIB	Exc.	V.G.	Good	Fair	Poor
750	560	400	295	200	125

Model 700 CDL SF Ltd.

Similar to Model 700 CDL but with engraved floorplate and stainless, fluted barrel. Chambered in .30-06 and .17 Remington Fireball. 2006 "Centennial" model commemorates the centennial of the .30-06 cartridge and was introduced in 2006 for one year only. Reintroduced in .260 Remington in 2008. .280 Remington added 2010.

NIB	Exc.	V.G.	Good	Fair	Poor
1100	900	675	450	275	150

Model 700 Mountain Rifle Stainless Synthetic

This model is the same as the Mountain Rifle but with stainless steel receiver, bolt, and barrel. Offered in .25-06 Rem., .270, .280, and .30-06. All calibers are supplied with a 22" barrel. In 1998 this model was available in .260 Rem. caliber.

NIB	Exc.	V.G.	Good	Fair	Poor
830	600	450	300	225	150

Model 700 LSS Mountain Rifle

This model, introduced in 1999, is fitted with a two-tone laminated stock with black forend tip and cheekpiece. Stainless steel barrel and action. Offered in .260 Remington, 7mm-08 Rem., .270 Win., and .30-06. Barrel length is 22". Weight is approximately 6.5 lbs.

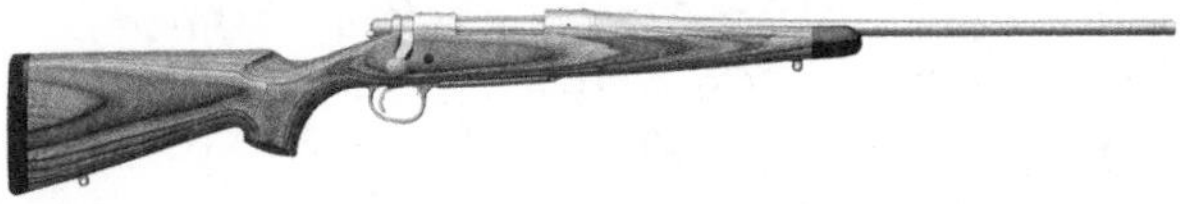

NIB	Exc.	V.G.	Good	Fair	Poor
830	625	450	300	200	100

Model 700 Titanium

Introduced in 2001 this model features a titanium receiver drilled and tapped for scope mounts. Fitted with a 22" stainless steel barrel chambered for both long and short calibers. Synthetic stock. Weight is approximately 5.25 lbs. In 2002 the .308 Win. chambering was added.

NIB	Exc.	V.G.	Good	Fair	Poor
1270	950	700	500	300	175

Model 700 Varmint Special Synthetic

The stock on this model is reinforced with DuPont Kevlar, fiberglass, and graphite. Rifle is offered with a heavy barrel and all metal has a fine matte black finish. The barrel rest on a machined aircraft-grade aluminum bedding stock. The receiver is drilled and tapped for scope mounts. Offered in .22-250, .223, and .308 calibers. In 1993 the .220 Swift was added to the line. This model was later dropped from the product line. In 2000 it was reintroduced in all calibers above but the .220 Swift.

NIB	Exc.	V.G.	Good	Fair	Poor
600	475	400	350	300	200

Model 700 VS SF (Varmint Synthetic Stainless Fluted)

Introduced in 1994 this model features a stainless steel barrel, receiver and action. It is fitted with a 26" heavy varmint barrel that has a spherical concave crown contour. Six flutes reduce barrel weight and help cooling. A synthetic stock made from fiberglass reinforced with graphite is standard. The stock is dark gray. Offered in .223, .220 Swift, .22-250, and .308 calibers. The .243 Win. cartridge was added to this model in 1997. The rifle weighs about 8-3/8 lbs. In 1998 the barrel was fluted and ported.

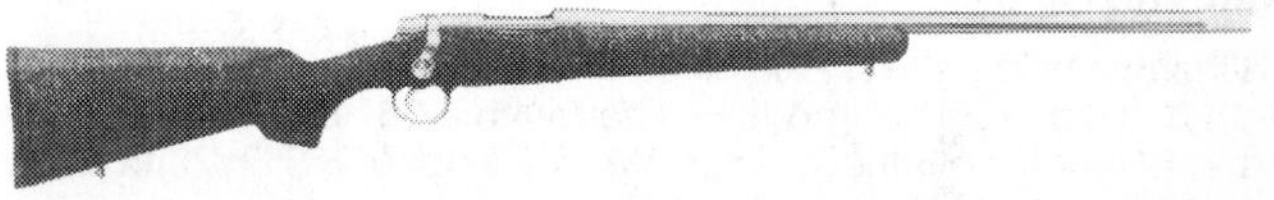

NIB	Exc.	V.G.	Good	Fair	Poor
800	650	500	400	300	150

Model 700 Varmint Special Wood

Same as above but furnished with walnut stock and offered in these calibers: .222, .22-250, .223, 6mm, .243, 7mm-08, and .308.

NIB	Exc.	V.G.	Good	Fair	Poor
825	675	525	400	300	150

Model 700 Varmint Laminated Stock (VLS)

Same as above but furnished with special laminated stock. Introduced in 1995.The 7mm-08 Rem. cartridge was added to this model in 1997. In 1998 a beavertail forend was added to this model, as well as the .260 Rem and the 6mm Rem. calibers.

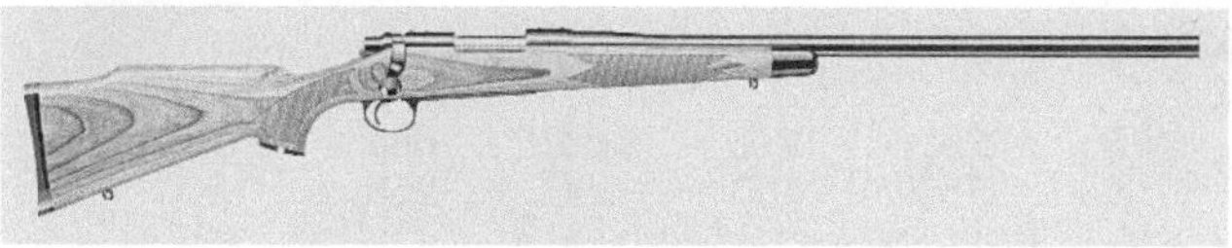

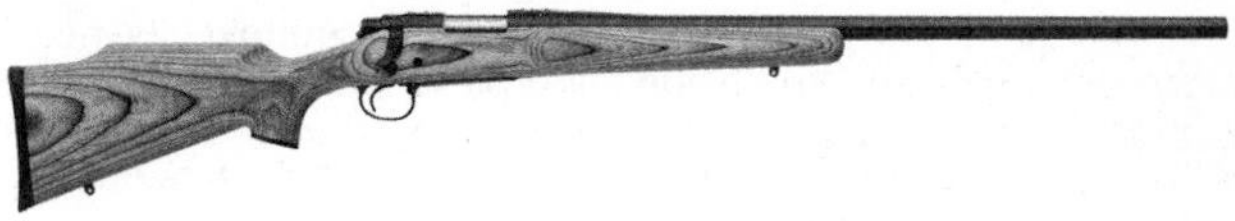

Courtesy Remington Arms

Model 700 VLS with beavertail forearm

NIB	Exc.	V.G.	Good	Fair	Poor
750	575	425	300	250	150

Model 700 VS Composite (Varmint Synthetic Composite)

This model is fitted with a graphite fiber composite barrel and chambered for the .223 Rem., .22-250, or .308 cartridges. Stock is synthetic. Barrel lengths are 26". Weight is 7.9 lbs. Introduced in 1999.

NIB	Exc.	V.G.	Good	Fair	Poor
1675	1250	950	600	425	300

Model 700 LV SF (Light Varmint)

This model, introduced in 2004, features a black synthetic stock with 22" stainless steel fluted barrel. Chambered for the .17 Rem, .221 Rem Fireball, .223, and .22-250. Weight is about 6.75 lbs.

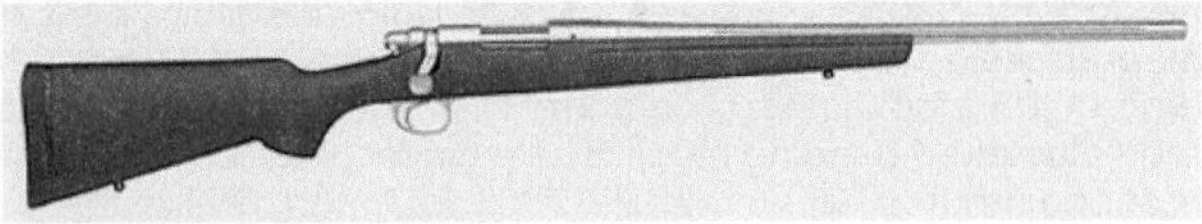

NIB	Exc.	V.G.	Good	Fair	Poor
950	700	475	300	225	125

Model 700 VS SF II

Introduced in 2005 this model features a varmint synthetic stock with stainless steel action and stainless fluted barrel chambered for the .204 Ruger, .220 Swift, 223, and .22-250. Barrel length is 26". Weight is about 8.5 lbs.

NIB	Exc.	V.G.	Good	Fair	Poor
1025	775	600	475	250	125

Model 700 VSF

Chambered for the .17 Remington Fireball, .204 Ruger, .220 Swift, .223 or .22-250 this model is fitted with a 26" blued fluted heavy barrel and tan synthetic stock. Weight is about 8.5 lbs. Introduced in 2005.

NIB	Exc.	V.G.	Good	Fair	Poor
930	700	475	300	225	125

Model 700 LSS LH (Laminated Stock SS Left-Hand)

Introduced in 1998 this model features a stainless steel barreled action with satin finish. Stock is similar to the BDL style with Monte Carlo comb and cheekpiece with hinged floor plate. Barrel is 24" with no sights. Offered in .270, .30-06, 7mm Rem. Mag, and .300 Win. Mag.

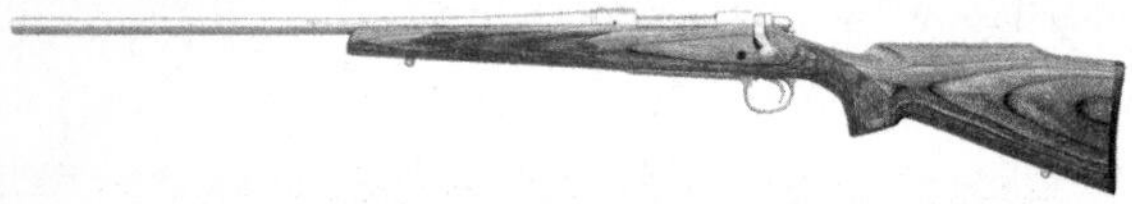

NIB	Exc.	V.G.	Good	Fair	Poor
700	550	400	300	250	150

Model 700 SPS

This model introduced in 2005, features an improved synthetic stock, RS recoil pad and hinged floorplate. Chambered for short, standard, and long action calibers. Supplied with sling swivels studs. Matte blue finish. Weight is about 7.5 lbs. depending on caliber and barrel length.

NIB	Exc.	V.G.	Good	Fair	Poor
575	450	300	200	150	100

Model 700 SPS Model 700 SPS Synthetic Left Hand

Similar to Model 700 SPS but configured for left-handed shooters.

NIB	Exc.	V.G.	Good	Fair	Poor
575	450	300	200	150	100

Model 700 SPS Varmint

Varmint version of Model 700 SPS with 26" heavy-contour barrel and synthetic stock with weight-reducing cuts in the forend. Available in a variety of chamberings from .17 Remington Fireball to .308 Winchester. Introduced in 2007.

NIB	Exc.	V.G.	Good	Fair	Poor
575	450	300	200	150	100

Model 700 SPS Dangerous Game

Similar to 700 SPS but chambered in .375 H&H Magnum. A TALO exclusive.

NIB	Exc.	V.G.	Good	Fair	Poor
675	550	400	275	200	150

Model 700 SPS Stainless

As above but with matte stainless steel barrel and action. No Ultra magnum calibers offered in this configuration. Introduced in 2005.

NIB	Exc.	V.G.	Good	Fair	Poor
610	475	350	225	150	100

Model 700 SPS DM

This model is the same as the Model SPS but with detachable magazine. Matte blue finish. Introduced in 2005.

NIB	Exc.	V.G.	Good	Fair	Poor
575	450	300	200	150	100

Model 700 SPS Youth

Offered in both long and short action calibers this model features barrel lengths of 20" and 22" depending on caliber. Weight is about 7 lbs. Introduced in 2005.

NIB	Exc.	V.G.	Good	Fair	Poor
525	425	275	175	125	100

Model 700 SPS Tactical

Similar to Model 700 Police but with 20" barrel and in .223 and .308. Laser-engraved tactical barrel. A dealer exclusive for 2007.

NIB	Exc.	V.G.	Good	Fair	Poor
800	675	500	375	250	175

Remington Model 700 SPS Tactical AAC

A Special Purpose Synthetic version of the Model 700 with a 20-inch heavy-contour, hammer-forged barrel with threaded muzzle.

Chambered in .308 Winchester. Hogue Overmolded Ghillie Green pillar-bedded stock with semi-beavertail forearm, Super-Cell recoil pad. Remington X-Mark Pro externally adjustable trigger. Black oxide finish. Weight: 7.5 pounds.

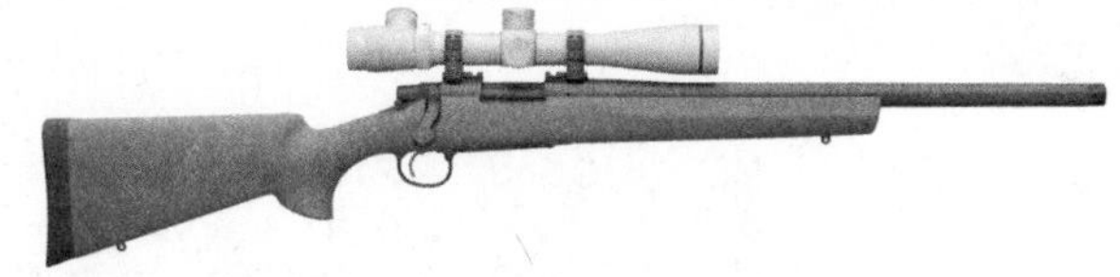

NIB	*Exc.*	*V.G.*	*Good*	*Fair*	*Poor*
650	550	475	400	300	200

Remington 700 VTR A-TACS Camo with Scope

Bolt action rifle chambered in .223 and .308 Win. Features include ATACS camo finish overall; triangular contour 22-inch barrel has an integral muzzle brake; black overmold grips; 1:9 (.223 caliber) or 1:12 (.308) twist; factory-mounted scope.

NIB	*Exc.*	*V.G.*	*Good*	*Fair*	*Poor*
875	750	625	550	380	225

Model 700 XCR

Introduced in 2005 this model features a stainless steel action and barrel with synthetic stock, rubber grip and forearm panels. Hinged floorplate. RS recoil pad. Chambered for the .270 Win., .280 Rem., 7mm Ultra Mag., .30-06, .300 WSM, and the .300 Win. Mag. cartridges. Barrel lengths are 24" and 26" depending on caliber. Weight is around 7.5 lbs. depending on caliber.

NIB	*Exc.*	*V.G.*	*Good*	*Fair*	*Poor*
865	650	500	375	295	125

NOTE: Add $25 for magnum calibers.

Model 700 XCR (Rocky Mountain Elk Foundation)

As above but with camo stock, engraved floorplate and 7mm Rem. Mag. caliber. Introduced in 2005.

NIB	*Exc.*	*V.G.*	*Good*	*Fair*	*Poor*
865	650	500	375	295	125

Remington 700 XCR II

Bolt action rifle chambered in .25-06 Remington, .270 Win, .280 Remington, 7mm Remington Mag., 7mm Remington Ultra Mag., .300 WSM, .300 Win Mag., .300 Remington Ultra Mag, .338 Win. Mag., .338 Remington Ultra Mag, .375 H&H, .375 Remington Ultra Mag., .30-06 Springfield. Features include black TriNyte corrosion control system coating; coated stainless steel barrel and receiver; olive drab green Hogue overmolded synthetic stock; SuperCell recoil pad; X-Mark Pro Trigger System; 24- or 26-inch barrel, depending on chambering.

NIB	*Exc.*	*V.G.*	*Good*	*Fair*	*Poor*
825	735	600	500	350	200

Remington 700 XCR II - BoneCollector Edition

Similar to Remington 700 XCR II but with Realtree AP HD camo stock.

NIB	*Exc.*	*V.G.*	*Good*	*Fair*	*Poor*
900	785	675	550	380	225

Model 700 Classic

This limited edition model was furnished with a straight comb, satin finished walnut stock, sling swivel studs, and hinged magazine floorplate. The series began in 1981 and each year Remington offered the Model 700 Classic in a special chambering, concluding the series in 2005.

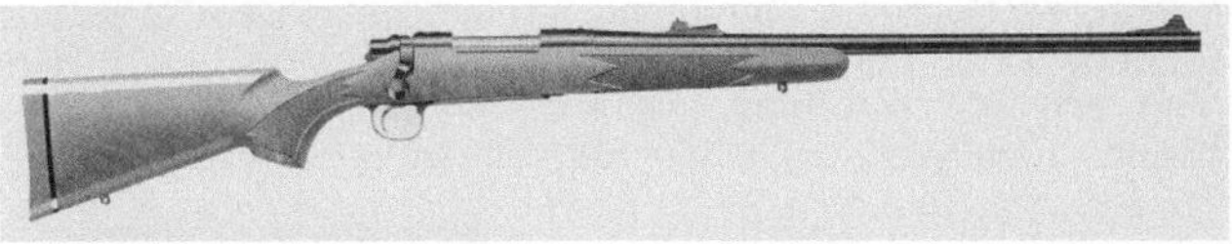

Courtesy Remington Arms

A list of chamberings by year.

1981—7MM Mauser	1994—6.5X55
1982—.257 Roberts	1995—.300 Win. Mag.
1983—.300 H&H Mag.	1996—.375 H&H Mag.
1984—.250-3000	1997—.280 Rem.
1985—.350 Rem. Mag.	1998—8mm Rem. Mag.
1986—.264 Win. Mag.	1999—.17 Remington
1987—.338 Win. Mag.	2000—.223 Remington
1988—.35 Whelen	2001—7mm-08
1989—.300 Wthby. Mag.	2002—.221 Rem.Fireball
1990—.25-06 Rem.	2003—.300 Savage
1991—7mm Wthby. Mag.	2004—8mm Mauser
1992—.220 Swift	2005—.308 Winchester
1993—.222 Rem.	

NIB	*Exc.*	*V.G.*	*Good*	*Fair*	*Poor*
900	700	600	500	350	250

NOTE: Add 25 percent for .250 Savage, .257 Roberts, 6.5x55 or 7x57.

Model 700 Custom

A special order rifle available in either American, English, or California walnut. Stock can be fitted to customer's own dimensions. Engraving is available as is a large selection of calibers. Model 700 Custom rifles should be priced individually and an appraisal should be obtained.

Model 700 Custom "C" Grade

Introduced in 2003 this Custom Shop bolt-action rifle is fitted with fancy walnut with Monte Carlo stock and rosewood forend tip and grip cap. Offered in all standard calibers. Barrel length is 24" for all calibers except Ultra Mags. which are 26".

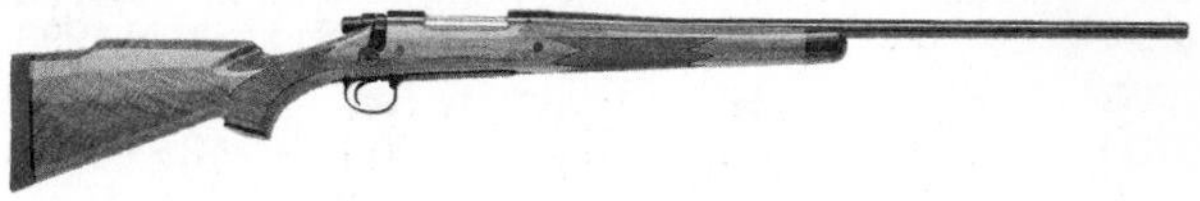

Model 700 AWR (Alaskan Wilderness Rifle)

This model is built in the Custom Shop and features a blind magazine and stainless steel components on a black matte synthetic stock. Fitted with a 24" barrel, all metal parts are finished in a black satin. Offered in .300 Weatherby Magnum, 7mm Rem. Mag., .300 Win. Mag., .338, and .375 calibers. In 1998 the 7mm STW was added as an additional caliber to this model. Weighs about 6-3/4 lbs. Built to order.

Model 700 APR (African Plains Rifle)

This Custom Shop model features a hinged floorplate, a 26" barrel, and blue metal finish. The stock is a laminated Monte Carlo style with cheekpiece and is fitted with black rubber recoil pad. Offered in same calibers as Model 700 AWR. Weighs about 7-3/4 lbs.

Model 700 ABG (African Big Game)

This Custom Shop rifle is fitted with a laminated stock, matte finished receiver and barrel, and 3-round detachable magazine. Chambered for the .375 Rem. Ultra Mag, .375 H&H, .416 Rem. Mag, and .458 Win. Mag. Introduced in 2001. Many extra cost options are offered for Custom Shop firearms.

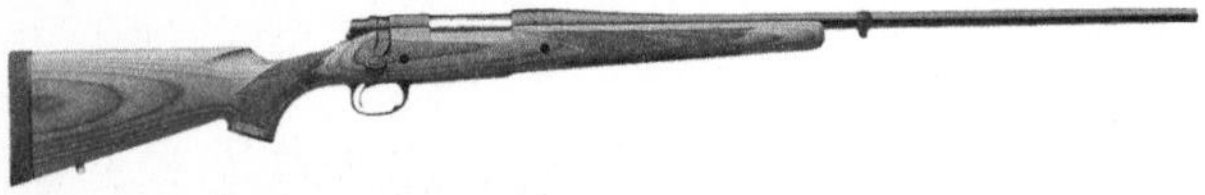

Model 700 Safari KS Stainless

A new addition to the Remington line in 1993, the Safari KS Stainless has a special reinforced Kevlar stock in a nonreflective gray finish. Checkering is 18 lines to the inch. Offered in these calibers: .375 H&H Mag., .416 Rem. Mag., and the .458 Win. Mag.

NIB	*Exc.*	*V.G.*	*Good*	*Fair*	*Poor*
925	800	650	450	300	200

Model 700 Police

Chambered for the .223 cartridge and fitted with a 26" heavy barrel (1-9" twist), black synthetic stock, and Parkerized finish.

NIB	*Exc.*	*V.G.*	*Good*	*Fair*	*Poor*
850	675	500	395	200	125

Model 700 Police DM

Same as above but chambered for .308 Win. (1-12" twist) or .300 Win. Mag (1-10" twist). Detachable magazine standard.

NIB	*Exc.*	*V.G.*	*Good*	*Fair*	*Poor*
850	675	500	395	200	125

NOTE: Add $20 for .300 Win. Mag model.

Model 700 Police Lightweight Tactical

This model is chambered for the .308 Win. cartridge and fitted with a 20" fluted barrel (1-12" twist). Stock is slim composite Kevlar with dual front swivel studs. Parkerized finish. Detachable magazine. Weight is approximately 7.5 lbs. Introduced in 1998.

NIB	*Exc.*	*V.G.*	*Good*	*Fair*	*Poor*
700	550	400	300	200	125

Model 700 XCR Tactical Long Range Rifle

Chambered in .223 Rem., .300 Lapua and .338 WM; 26" crowned stainless varmint contour barrel; olive drab Bell & Carlson synthetic stock. Coated overall with TriNyte Corrosion Control finish. Introduced in 2007.

NIB	*Exc.*	*V.G.*	*Good*	*Fair*	*Poor*
925	800	675	500	300	150

NOTE: Add 50 percent for .338 Lapua.

Model 700 XCR Compact Tactical

Similar to above but with Black TriNyte PVD coating OD green stock; hinged floorplate magazine; dual front swivel studs and rear stud; free-floating 20-inch barrel with LTR-style fluting; 40-X externally adjustable trigger; tactical-style 1 in 9" (223 caliber) or 1 in 12" twist (308 caliber). Chambered in .223 and .308.

NIB	*Exc.*	*V.G.*	*Good*	*Fair*	*Poor*
1400	1150	875	650	475	200

Model 700 Target Tactical Rifle

Bolt-action rifle chambered in .308 Winchester. Features include a 26" triangular counterbored barrel with 1: 11-1/2 rifling, textured green Bell & Carlson varmint/tactical stock with adjustable comb and length of pull, adjustable trigger, satin black oxide finish on exposed metal surfaces, hinged floorplate, SuperCell recoil pad, matte blue on exposed metal surfaces. Overall length 45-3/4". Weight: 11-3/4 lbs. Suggested retail price: To be announced.

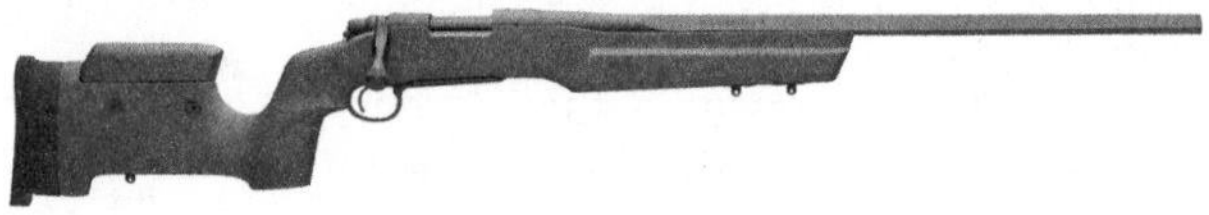

NIB	*Exc.*	*V.G.*	*Good*	*Fair*	*Poor*
1800	1550	1175	850	675	300

Model 700 VTR Varmint-Tactical Rifle

Bolt-action rifle chambered in .17 Remington Fireball, .204 Ruger, .22-250, .223 Remington, .243 Winchester, and .308 Winchester. Features include a 22" triangular counterbored barrel, olive drab overmolded or Digital Tiger TSP Desert Camo stock with vented semi-beavertail forend, tactical-style dual swivel mounts for bipod, matte blue on exposed metal surfaces. Overall length 41-5/8". Weight: 7-1/2 lbs.

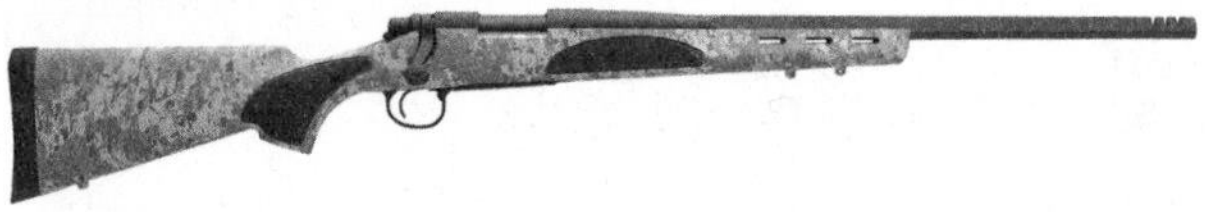

NIB	*Exc.*	*V.G.*	*Good*	*Fair*	*Poor*
750	625	500	375	200	125

Model 700 VTR Varmint-Tactical Rifle Desert Recon

Similar to above but with Digital Desert Camo stock and chambered for .223 and .308 Winchester only.

NIB	*Exc.*	*V.G.*	*Good*	*Fair*	*Poor*
750	625	500	375	200	125

Model 700 XHR Extreme Hunting Rifle

Bolt-action rifle chambered in .243 Winchester, .25-06, .270 Winchester, 7mm-08, 7mm Remington Magnum, .300 Winchester Magnum, 7mm Remington Ultra Mag, .30-06, and .300 Remington Ultra Mag. Features include a 24", 25" or 26" triangular magnum-contour counterbored barrel, adjustable trigger, synthetic stock finished in Realtree AG HD camo, satin black oxide finish on exposed metal surfaces, hinged floorplate, SuperCell recoil pad. Overall length 41-5/8" to 46-1/2". Weight: 7-1/4 lbs. to 7-5/8 lbs.

NIB	*Exc.*	*V.G.*	*Good*	*Fair*	*Poor*
850	675	500	395	200	125

Model 700 SPS Buckmasters Edition

Similar to Model 700 SPS but with engraved floorplate and camo stock. Also available in Youth model chambered in .243 only. Introduced in 2007.

NIB	Exc.	V.G.	Good	Fair	Poor
500	450	400	350	300	150

Model 700 Alaskan Ti

Lightweight (6.25 lbs.) version of Model 700 with titanium receiver, 24" fluted stainless barrel and Bell & Carlson synthetic stock. Chambered in a variety of long, short, and super-short cartridges. Introduced in 2007.

NIB	Exc.	V.G.	Good	Fair	Poor
1600	1350	1050	775	500	200

Model 700 LSS 50th Anniversary of the .280 Remington

Similar to Model 700 LSS but in .280 Remington. A dealer exclusive for 2007.

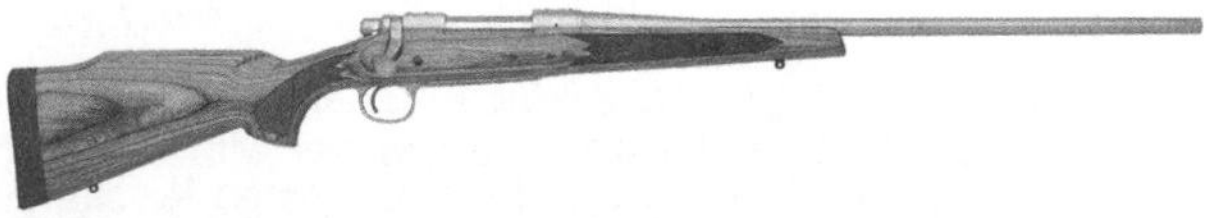

NIB	Exc.	V.G.	Good	Fair	Poor
800	675	500	375	250	175

Model 700 VL SS Thumbhole

Similar to Model 700 VS Composite but with brown laminated thumbhole stock and stainless steel barrel. Introduced in 2007.

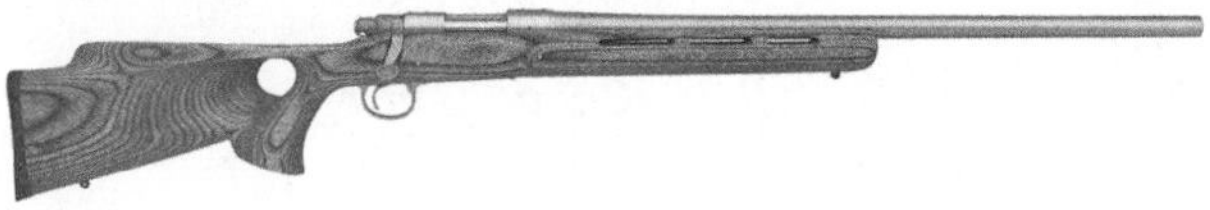

NIB	Exc.	V.G.	Good	Fair	Poor
725	575	400	300	200	125

Model 700 Tactical Weapons System

This set is designed for law enforcement use and features a Model 700 Police chambered for the .308 Win. cartridge, a 24" barrel (1-12" twist), and detachable magazine. Also furnished with a Leupold VARI X III scope with rings and base, and a Harris 1A2 bipod, sling, lens covers, and case.

NIB	Exc.	V.G.	Good	Fair	Poor
2500	2000	1650	1150	800	500

Model 700 ML

This model was introduced in 1996. It is an in-line design and the first built on a modern action. It is chambered for the .50 or .54 caliber bullet. It is fitted with a synthetic stock and rubber recoil pad. The barrel length is 24" and the approximate weight is 7.75 lbs. A camo stock option was added to this model in 1997. Discontinued 2006.

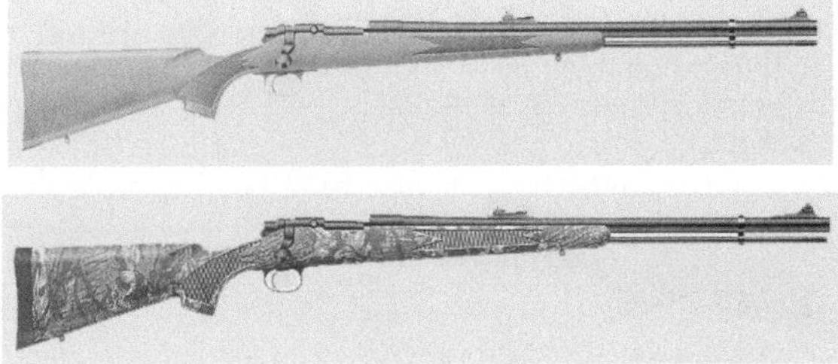

Courtesy Remington Arms

Remington Model 700 ML Camo

NIB	Exc.	V.G.	Good	Fair	Poor
350	250	200	150	100	75

Model 700 ML Custom

Introduced in 1997 this new model is similar to the above model but features a satin metal finish and gray laminated thumbhole stock with roll-over cheekpiece. Discontinued.

NIB	Exc.	V.G.	Good	Fair	Poor
550	425	350	275	200	100

Model 700 MLS

Same as above but with stainless steel barrel and action. Discontinued.

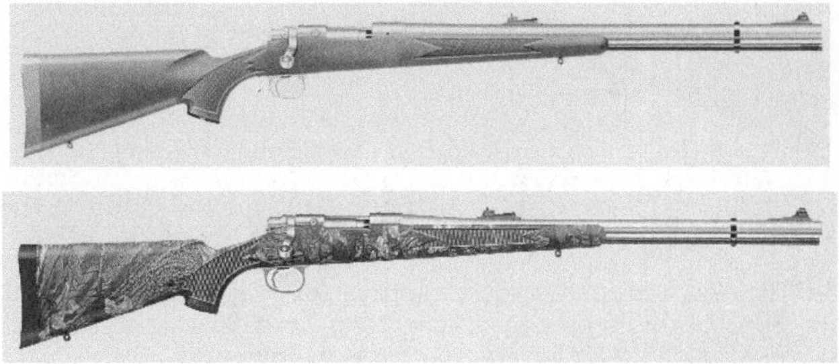

Courtesy Remington Arms

Remington Model 700 MLS Camo

NIB	Exc.	V.G.	Good	Fair	Poor
400	300	250	200	150	100

Model 700 MLS Custom

Similar to the above model but with a satin stainless steel finish and a two-toned gray laminated thumbhole stock with roll-over cheekpiece. Introduced in 1997. Discontinued.

NIB	Exc.	V.G.	Good	Fair	Poor
600	475	375	325	225	125

Model 700 ML Youth

This model is similar to the Model ML with a shortened stock with 13" lop with a rubber recoil pad. Discontinued.

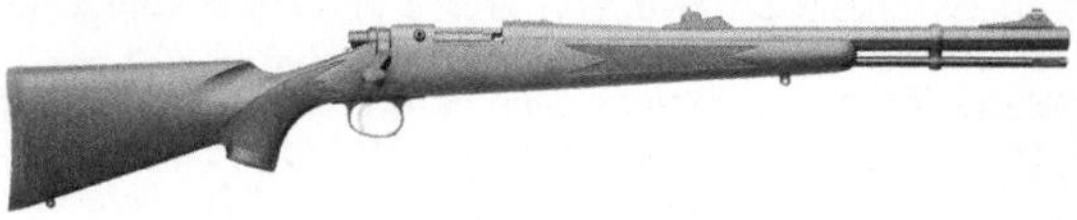

NIB	Exc.	V.G.	Good	Fair	Poor
370	300	250	200	150	100

Model 710

Introduced in 2001 this rifle is chambered for the .270 Win. or .30-06 cartridge. Fitted with a 22" barrel and dark gray synthetic stock. Detachable box magazine. Supplied with pre-mounted Bushnell Sharpshooter 3-9x scope. Barrel finish is ordnance gray steel with a matte finish. Weight is about 7.12 lbs. In 2004 the 7mm Rem. Mag. and .300 Win Mag chamberings were added. In 2005 the receiver was extruded solid steel. Calibers: .243, 7mm RM, .300 WM.

NIB	Exc.	V.G.	Good	Fair	Poor
375	285	225	195	150	100

Model 710 Youth

Similar to Model 710 but with 20" barrel and 39.5" overall length. Chambered in .243 Win. Introduced 2006.

NIB	Exc.	V.G.	Good	Fair	Poor
375	285	225	195	150	100

Model 788

A centerfire bolt-action sporting rifle with either a 22" or 24" barrel and a plain walnut stock. An 18" barrel carbine was also manufactured and is worth approximately 10 percent more than the values listed below. Manufactured from 1967 to 1983.

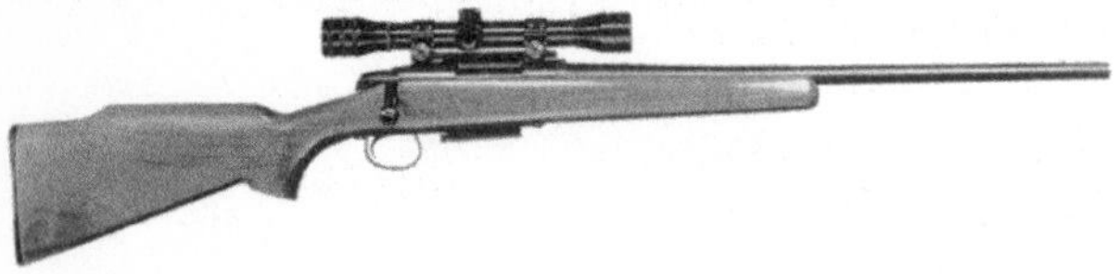

NIB	Exc.	V.G.	Good	Fair	Poor
—	500	425	375	300	250

NOTE: Add a 30 percent premium for .44 Magnum, 25 percent for .30-30, and 20 percent premium for 7mm-08 caliber. Add 40 percent premium for left-hand models in 6mm and .308.

Model Seven

A centerfire bolt-action sporting rifle with an 18.5" barrel and 4- or 5-shot magazine. Blued with a checkered walnut stock. Chambered for .223 Rem., .243 Rem., 7mm-08 Rem., .308 Win., and for 1997 the .260 Rem. cartridge. Introduced into the Remington product line in 1982.

NIB	Exc.	V.G.	Good	Fair	Poor
600	475	325	275	200	100

Model Seven FS

As above with a Kevlar stock. Introduced in 1987.

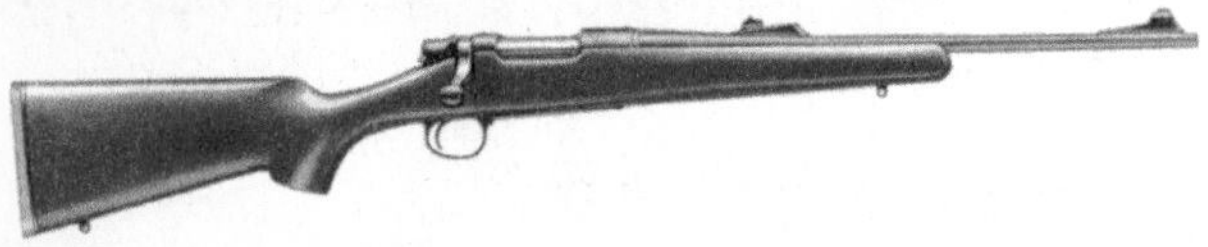

NIB	Exc.	V.G.	Good	Fair	Poor
600	525	450	375	275	150

Model Seven Synthetic

Updated Synthetic short-action series in .223 Remington, .243 Winchester, .260 Remington, 7mm-08 Remington and .308 Winchester. Twenty-inch satin blue carbon steel barrel and matte black stock. Externally adjustable X-Mark Pro trigger is standard. No sights furnished. Weight: 6.5 pounds. Compact version has 18-inch barrel, chambered in .243 or 7mm-08 only.

NIB	Exc.	V.G.	Good	Fair	Poor
585	500	425	365	300	200

Model Seven SS (Stainless Synthetic)

Introduced in 1994 this model features a stainless steel barrel, receiver, and bolt with a matte finish. It is fitted with a 20" barrel, and a hinged floorplate. The synthetic stock is textured black. Available in .243, 7mm-08, and .308. In 1997 the .260 Rem. cartridge was also offered. Weight approximately 6.25 lbs.

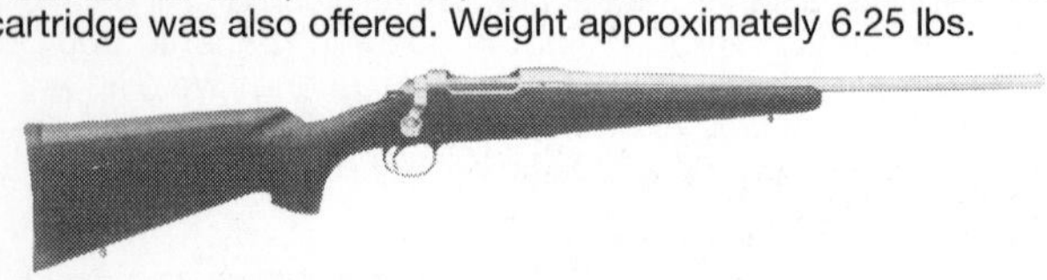

NIB	Exc.	V.G.	Good	Fair	Poor
625	450	350	300	200	150

Model Seven LSS

This model has a stainless steel barrel and action but is fitted with a satin finished laminated stock. Chambered for .22-250, .243, and 7mm-08 Rem. Weight is about 6.5 lbs. Introduced in 2000.

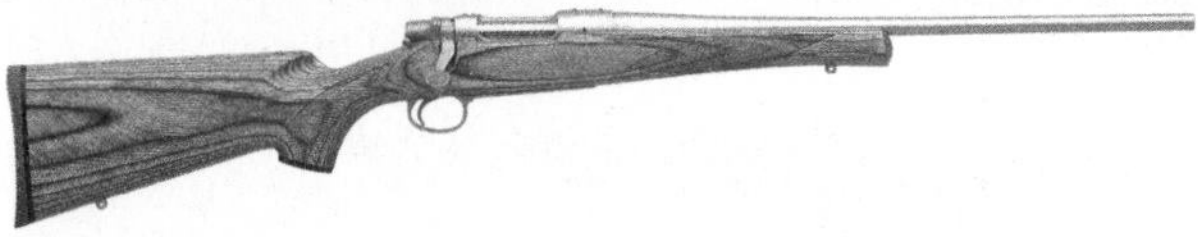

NIB	Exc.	V.G.	Good	Fair	Poor
625	500	375	300	200	100

Model Seven LS

This model offers a laminated stock but with a carbon steel blued barrel. Offered in five calibers: .22-250, .243, .260 Rem., 8mm-08 Rem., and .308 Win. Weight is about 6.5 lbs. Introduced in 2000.

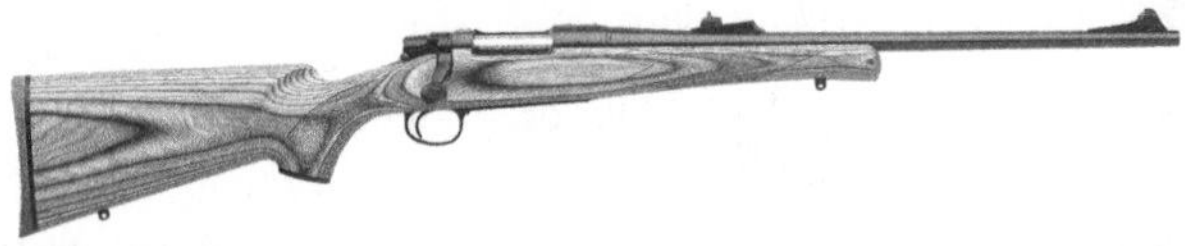

NIB	Exc.	V.G.	Good	Fair	Poor
625	500	375	300	200	100

Model Seven MS

First introduced in 1993 and available through the Remington Custom Shop. This rifle features a 20" barrel with Mannlicher stock made from select grain wood and laminated for strength. Available in most short-action calibers including .222 Rem., .223 Rem., .22-250, .243 Win., 6mm Rem., .250 Savage, .257 Roberts, .260 Rem., 7mm-08, .308 Win., .35 Rem., .350 Rem. Mag.

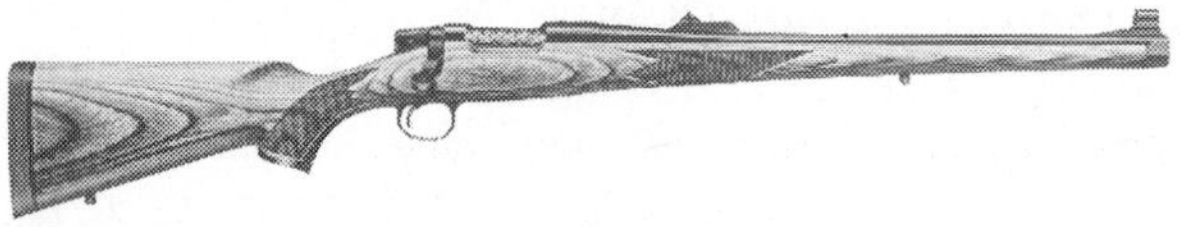

NIB	Exc.	V.G.	Good	Fair	Poor
2000	1800	1500	500	350	250

NOTE: Add 20 percent for .250 Savage, .257 Roberts, .35 Rem.

Model Seven AWR

The Alaskan Wilderness Model has a black synthetic stock, stainless steel action, and a 22-inch barrel with a black matte Teflon finish. Weight: 6-1/8 lbs. Detachable 3-shot magazine. It was available from the Remington Custom Shop from 2002 - 2008 and chambered only in 6.8 Rem. SPC, 7mm Rem. SAUM or .300 Rem. SAUM. It was replaced by the Model Seven AWR II in 2008. This model came with a 20 or 22-inch stainless steel barrel, Bell & Carlson olive green fiberglass stock and hinged floorplate. Chamberings include .260 Rem., .270 WSM, 7mm-08, 7mm Rem. SAUM, .308 Win., .300 WSM, .300 Rem. SAUM and .350 Rem. Mag.

NIB	Exc.	V.G.	Good	Fair	Poor
2000	1800	1500	500	350	250

NOTE: Add 10 percent for AWR II

Model Seven Youth

First offered in 1993 this variation is a youth version of the standard Model 7. The buttstock is 1" shorter than standard. Available in 6mm, .243, and 7mm-08. In 1998 this model was available in .260 Rem. caliber.

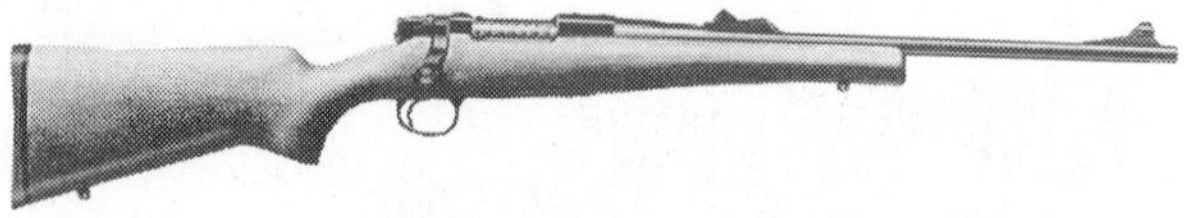

NIB	Exc.	V.G.	Good	Fair	Poor
600	495	350	225	175	100

Model Seven CDL

Similar to Model Seven but with satin walnut.satin blue finish, sightless barrel, and Limbsaver recoil pad. Introduced 2006.

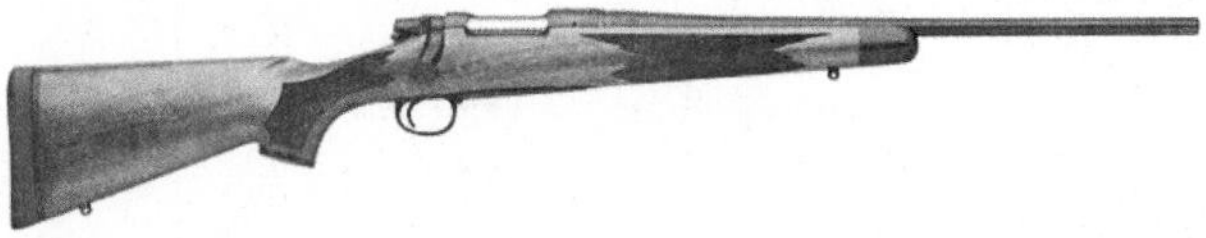

NIB	Exc.	V.G.	Good	Fair	Poor
775	625	550	400	275	150

Model Seven XCR Camo

Similar to Model Seven LSS but with camo stock, fluted barrel and weather-resistant coating. Chambered in .243, 7mm-08, .308, .270 WSM and .300 WSM. Introduced in 2007.

NIB	Exc.	V.G.	Good	Fair	Poor
775	650	500	395	275	175

Model Seven 25th Anniversary Version

Similar to Model Seven but in 7mm-08 only with 25th anniversary medallion inset at the pistol grip cap area, high-sheen blued finish on the receiver, bolt and 22" standard-contour barrel, X-Mark Pro Trigger and SuperCell recoil pad. Introduced 2008.

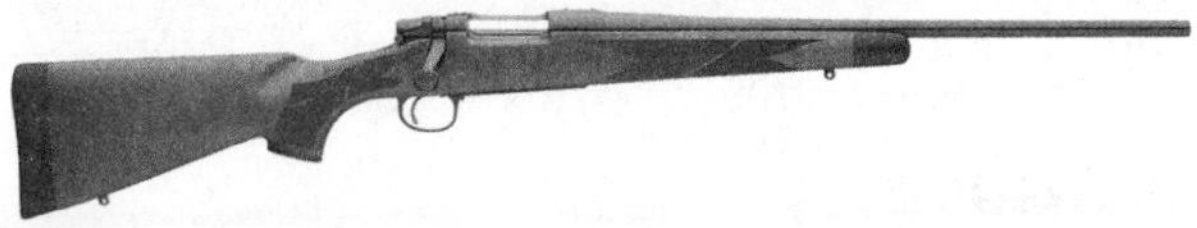

NIB	Exc.	V.G.	Good	Fair	Poor
950	700	550	350	250	150

Model Seven Predator

Similar to Model Seven but with full coverage in Mossy Oak\xa8 Brush\xa8 camo; fluted, magnum contour 22" barrel, synthetic stock as on Model Seven XCR; X-Mark Pro Trigger. Chambered in .17 Remington Fireball, .204, .223, .22-250 and .243.

NIB	Exc.	V.G.	Good	Fair	Poor
800	650	500	395	275	175

Model 770

Package rifle similar to Model 710 but with redesigned bolt assembly and magazine catch. Chambered in .243, .270, 7mm-08, .308, .30-06, and .300 WM. Also available in Youth model chambered in .243 only. Introduced in 2007. In 2008 a version with stainless steel barrel and receiver and full camo finish was introduced.

NIB	Exc.	V.G.	Good	Fair	Poor
400	300	225	175	100	50

Model 770 Youth

Similar to Model 770 but with shorter stock and barrel.

NIB	Exc.	V.G.	Good	Fair	Poor
375	275	200	165	90	50

Model 715 Sportsman

Similar to Model 770. A dealer exclusive for 2007.

NIB	Exc.	V.G.	Good	Fair	Poor
375	275	200	165	90	50

Model 798

Long-action sporting rifle built on reworked 98 Mauser action. Calibers: .243, .308, .30-06, .270, .300 WM, .375 H&H, .458 WM. Barrel: 22" or 24" blued sightless. Stock: Brown laminated with recoil pad. Claw extractor, 2-position safety, hinged floorplate. Add 10 percent for Magnum chamberings; add 30 percent for .375 and .458. Introduced 2006.

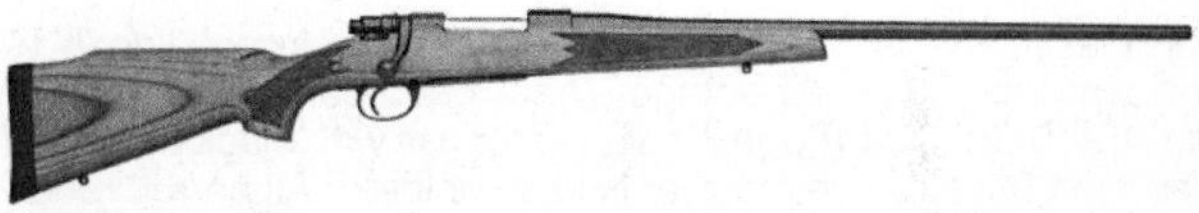

NIB	Exc.	V.G.	Good	Fair	Poor
575	400	300	200	125	100

Model 798 Stainless Laminate

Similar to Model 798 but with laminated stock and stainless barrel. Chambered in .243, .25-06, .270, .30-06, 7mm Mag, .300 WM and .375 H&H Mag. Introduced in 2007. Add 25 percent for .375.

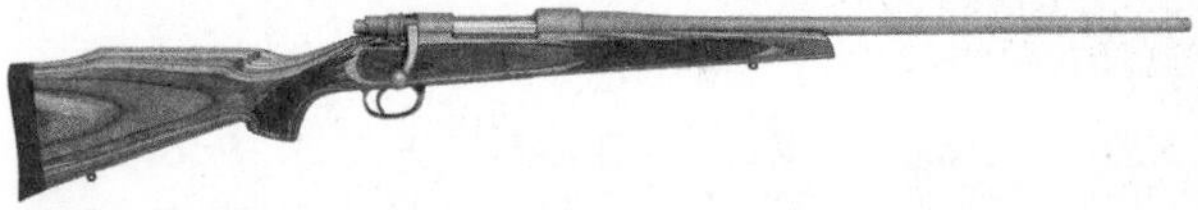

NIB	Exc.	V.G.	Good	Fair	Poor
650	475	350	250	175	125

Model 798 SPS

Similar to Model 798 but with blued barrel and black synthetic stock. Introduced 2008.

NIB	Exc.	V.G.	Good	Fair	Poor
575	400	300	200	125	100

Model 798 Safari

Similar to Model 798 but chambered in .375 H&H or .458 Winchester Magnum. Introduced 2008.

NIB	Exc.	V.G.	Good	Fair	Poor
850	700	575	400	325	250

Model 799

Similar to Model 798 but short-action without recoil pad. Calibers:

.22 Hornet, .222 Remington, .22-250, .223, 762X39. Introduced 2006.

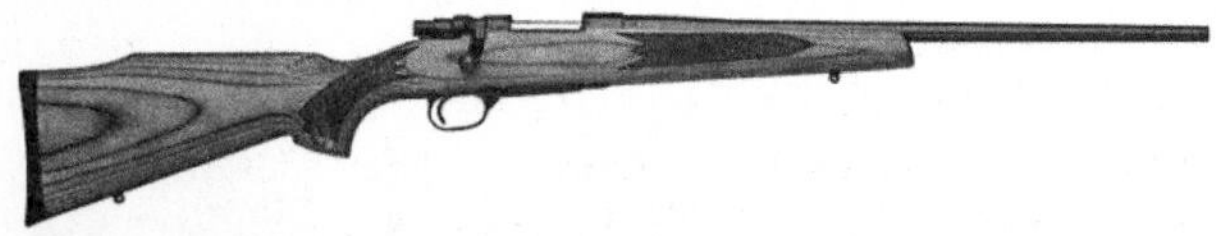

NIB	Exc.	V.G.	Good	Fair	Poor
525	400	300	200	125	100

Model 1816 Commemorative Flint Lock Rifle

Introduced in 1995. It features a 39", .50 caliber octagonal barrel. Stock is hand finished extra fancy curly maple. Built for one year only. Special order only.

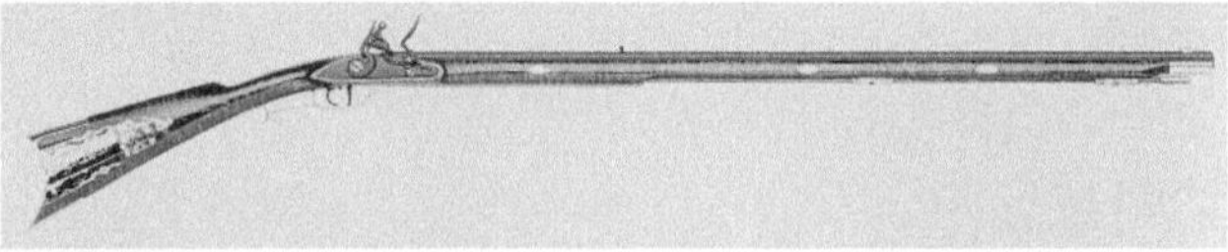

Courtesy Remington Arms

NIB	Exc.	V.G.	Good	Fair	Poor
1825	1200	850	700	500	300

Remington No. 1 Rolling Block Mid-Range

This classic rifle was reintroduced into the Remington line in 1997 and features a 30" half octagon, half-round barrel chambered for the .45-70 Govt. cartridge. Designed for use with black powder and lead cast bullets. The receiver is case colored. All barrel, receiver, and metalwork markings match the original rifle. Rear tang-mounted vernier sight and front globe sight with interchangeable inserts. A single set trigger is standard. Steel buttplate. Weight is approximately 9.75 lbs.

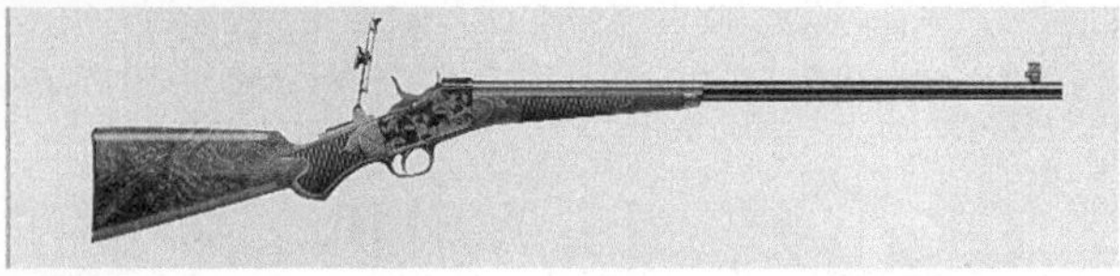

NIB	Exc.	V.G.	Good	Fair	Poor
2200	1900	1500	1200	700	400

Remington Mid-Range Sporter Rolling Block

Introduced in 1998 this model features a 30" round barrel with pistol grip sporter stock. Adjustable rear sight. Chambered for .30-30, .444 Marlin, and .45-70 Govt. A number of extra cost options are available for this model including barrels, sights, fancy wood, etc. Prices listed below are for standard model.

NIB	Exc.	V.G.	Good	Fair	Poor
1800	1600	1350	900	600	350

Model SPR18 Single Shot Rifle

A break-action rifle with silvertone receiver and fluted barrel. Calibers: .223, .243, .270, .30-06, .308. Weight: 6-3/4 lbs. Imported; introduced 2005.

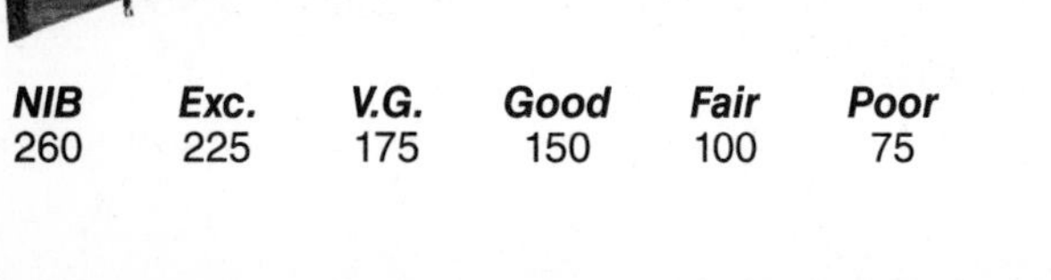

NIB	Exc.	V.G.	Good	Fair	Poor
260	225	175	150	100	75

Model SPR22 Double Rifle

Lever-operated break-action SXS double rifle in .30-06 and .45-70. Double triggers, tang safety. Barrels can be regulated via jackscrew. Imported; introduced 2005.

NIB	Exc.	V.G.	Good	Fair	Poor
1000	850	700	600	450	300

Model SPR94 Combo Gun

Over/under rifle shotgun. Combinations: .410/.22 rimfire, .410/.17HMR, .41o/.22WMR, 12-ga./.223, 12-ga./.30-06, 12-ga./.308. Double triggers, tang safety. Imported; introduced 2005.

NIB	Exc.	V.G.	Good	Fair	Poor
850	700	600	450	300	200

Model 412

Compact single-shot chambered for .22 LR. 19.5" blued barrel, hardwood stock. Introduced 2006.

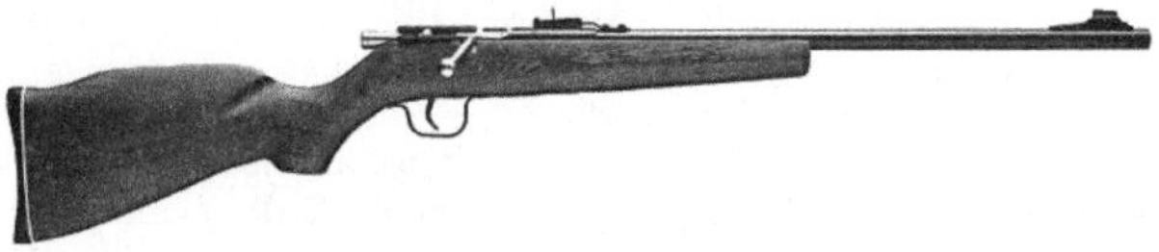

NIB	Exc.	V.G.	Good	Fair	Poor
165	125	100	75	50	25

SHOTGUNS

Model 10A

A 12, 16, or 20 gauge slide-action shotgun with barrels ranging from 26" to 32". Takedown, blued with a plain walnut stock. Manufactured from 1907 to 1929.

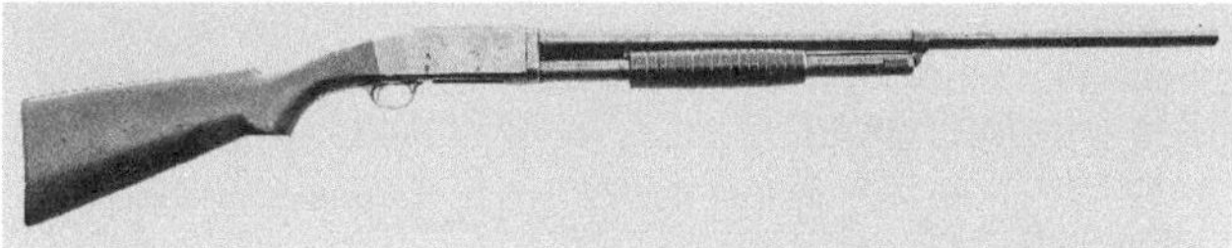

Courtesy Remington Arms

NIB	Exc.	V.G.	Good	Fair	Poor
—	375	300	250	200	100

Model 11

A 12, 16, or 20 gauge semi-automatic shotgun with barrels ranging in length from 26" to 32". Designed by John M. Browning and produced under license from Fabrique Nationale. Blued with a checkered walnut stock. Approximately 300,000 were made from 1911 to 1948. Solid rib or vent rib add 30 percent to listed values.

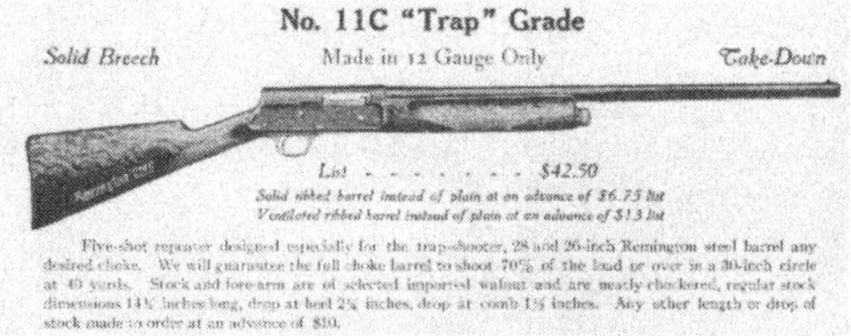

NIB	Exc.	V.G.	Good	Fair	Poor
—	550	400	300	200	100

Model 11B Special

Engraved.

NIB	Exc.	V.G.	Good	Fair	Poor
—	900	750	600	300	200

Model 11D Tournament

NIB	Exc.	V.G.	Good	Fair	Poor
—	1000	895	675	500	300

Model 11E Expert

Engraved.

NIB	Exc.	V.G.	Good	Fair	Poor
—	4500	3250	2700	1500	300

Model 11F Premier

Heavily engraved.

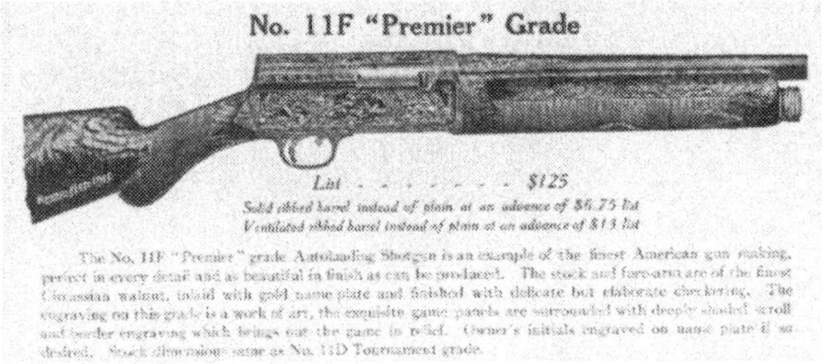

NIB	Exc.	V.G.	Good	Fair	Poor
—	9000	7000	5000	3500	500

Model 11R

20" barrel riot gun.

NIB	Exc.	V.G.	Good	Fair	Poor
—	475	350	250	175	100

Model 17

A 20 gauge slide-action shotgun with barrels ranging in length from 26" to 32". Takedown, blued with a plain walnut stock. Approximately 48,000 were made from 1917 to 1933.

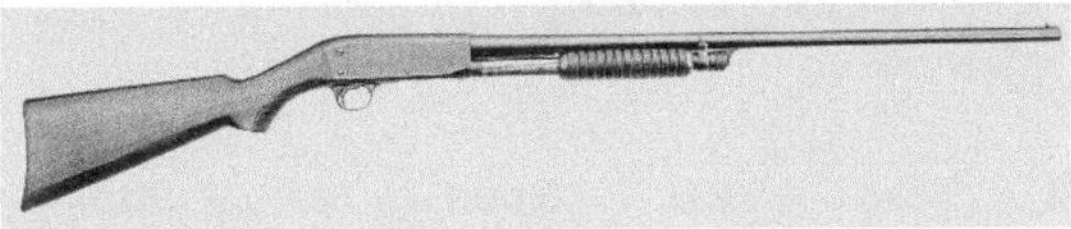

Courtesy Remington Arms

NIB	Exc.	V.G.	Good	Fair	Poor
—	395	300	250	175	100

NOTE: Vent rib add 25 percent.

Model 29

As above, chambered for 12 gauge cartridges. Approximately 24,000 manufactured from 1929 to 1933.

NIB	Exc.	V.G.	Good	Fair	Poor
—	450	350	300	200	175

NOTE: For guns with 32" barrels add 40 percent. Vent rib add 25 percent.

Model 31

A 12, 16, or 20 gauge slide-action shotgun with barrels ranging in length from 26" to 32" and a magazine capacity of either 2 or 4 rounds. Takedown, blued with a walnut stock. Approximately 160,000 were made from 1931 to 1949.

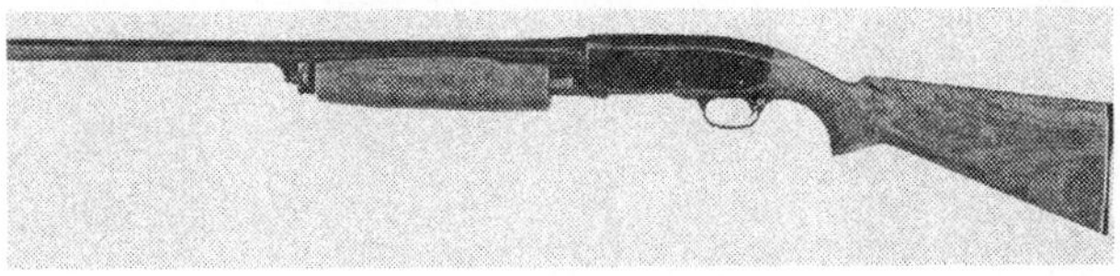

NIB	Exc.	V.G.	Good	Fair	Poor
—	450	325	275	200	125

NOTE: For guns with 32" barrel add 50 percent. For early models with checkered stocks add 40 percent. Solid rib or vent rib add 25 percent. For early banded barrels add 25 percent.

MODEL 870 SERIES

Model 870 Wingmaster

A 12, 16, or 20 gauge slide-action shotgun with 26", 28", or 30" barrels and a 5-shot tubular magazine. Blued with a plain walnut stock. Manufactured from 1950 to 1963.

NIB	Exc.	V.G.	Good	Fair	Poor
—	350	225	200	150	100

NOTE: Vent rib add 10 percent.

Model 870 Field Wingmaster

As above, with a checkered walnut stock and screw-in choke tubes. Introduced in 1964. In 1980 the 16 gauge was dropped as an offering but was later reinstated (see below).

NIB	Exc.	V.G.	Good	Fair	Poor
550	450	300	225	150	100

Model 870 Field Wingmaster 16 Gauge

In 2002 the 16 gauge was reintroduced into the Wingmaster line. Offered with 26" or 28" vent rib barrel with choke tubes. Walnut stock with blued finish. Weight is about 7 lbs. Offered in 16 gauge in other configurations listed.

NIB	Exc.	V.G.	Good	Fair	Poor
600	475	375	250	200	100

Model 870 Wingmaster NRA Edition

This is a 12 gauge 3" gun with a 28" vent rib barrel with choke tubes. Walnut stock with checkering. Blued receiver with NRA logos on both sides. Introduced in 2005.

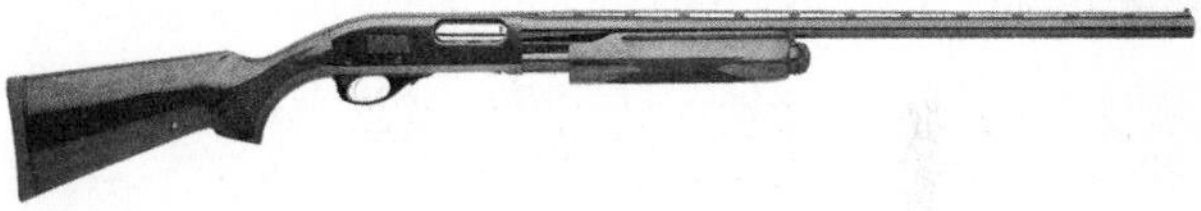

NIB	Exc.	V.G.	Good	Fair	Poor
550	450	300	225	150	100

Model 870 Wingmaster Jr.

Introduced in 2005 this model features a 20 gauge gun with 18.75" vent rib barrel with choke tubes. Checkered walnut stock with recoil pad. Blued finish. Weight is about 6 lbs.

NIB	Exc.	V.G.	Good	Fair	Poor
550	450	300	225	150	100

Model 870 Field Wingmaster Small Bores

Introduced in 1999 this model is now offered in both 28 gauge and .410 bore. Checkered walnut stock. High polish blue finish. Both guns are fitted with 25" barrels. The 28 gauge has Rem chokes while the .410 comes with fixed Modified chokes. Weight is approximately 6 lbs. Price listed is for the .410 bore.

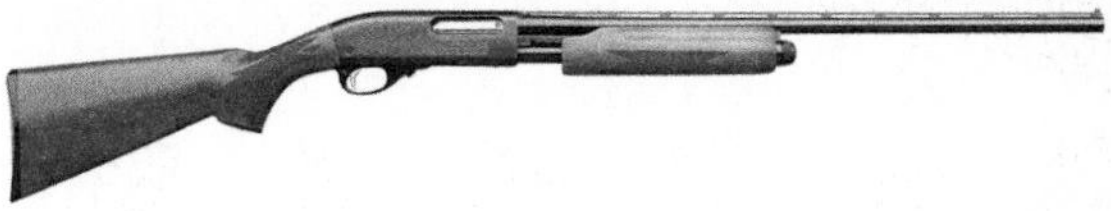

NIB	Exc.	V.G.	Good	Fair	Poor
600	475	395	300	275	200

NOTE: Add $50 for 28 gauge gun.

Model 870 Magnum

As above, chambered for 12 or 20 gauge 3" Magnum shells. Introduced in 1964. Choke tubes introduced in 1987.

NIB	Exc.	V.G.	Good	Fair	Poor
575	425	300	225	150	100

Model 870 Express

As above, for 3", 12 gauge shells with a 28" ventilated rib and one choke tube. Parkerized with a matte finished stock. Introduced in 1987.

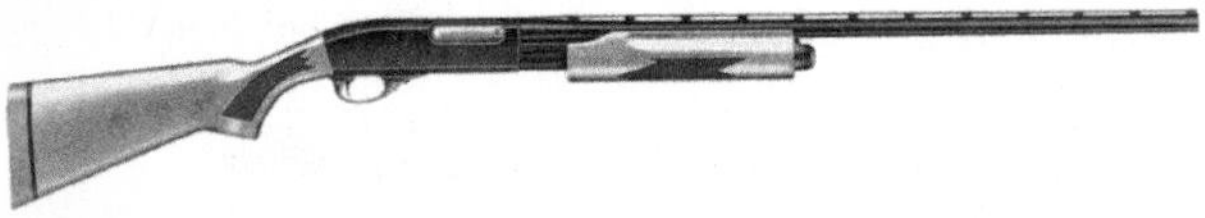

NIB	Exc.	V.G.	Good	Fair	Poor
330	250	200	150	100	75

Model 870 Express Synthetic

NIB	Exc.	V.G.	Good	Fair	Poor
330	250	200	150	100	75

Model 870 Express Synthetic Youth

NIB	Exc.	V.G.	Good	Fair	Poor
300	250	200	150	100	75

Model 870 Express Jr. NWTF Edition

This 20 gauge model is fitted with a 18.75" vent rib barrel with choke tubes. Synthetic stock has a camo finish. Metal is matte black. Weight is about 6 lbs. Introduced in 2005.

NIB	Exc.	V.G.	Good	Fair	Poor
320	250	200	150	100	75

Model 870 Express Super Magnum

Introduced in 1998, this 870 is similar to the 870 Express but is chambered for 3.5" 12 gauge. Offered in walnut stock with blued 28" barrel, matte black synthetic with 26" or 28" barrel or various camo finishes. Also available as a combo with extra 20" rifled deer barrel. Add $100 for camo. Add 20 percent for combo with deer barrel. Introduced in 1998.

NIB	Exc.	V.G.	Good	Fair	Poor
425	330	225	175	125	100

Model 870 Express Super Magnum Fall Flight

Chambered for the 12 gauge with either 2.75", 3", or 3.5" shells. Fitted with 30" vent rib barrel with choke tubes. Skyline Fall Flight camo finish. Weight is about 7.75 lbs. Introduced in 2005.

NIB	Exc.	V.G.	Good	Fair	Poor
475	375	275	225	175	150

Remington 870 Express Synthetic Super Mag Turkey-Waterfowl Camo

Pump action shotgun chambered in 12-ga., 2-3/4 to 3-1/2 inch. Features include full Mossy Oak Bottomland camo coverage; 26-inch barrel with HiViz fiber-optics sights; Wingmaster HD Waterfowl and Turkey Extra Full RemChokes; SuperCell recoil pad; drilled and tapped receiver. Price:

NIB	Exc.	V.G.	Good	Fair	Poor
515	440	375	315	200	150

Remington 870 Super Mag Turkey-Predator Camo with Scope

Pump action shotgun chambered in 12-ga., 2-3/4 to 3-1/2 inch. Features include 20-inch barrel; TruGlo red/green selectable illuminated sight mounted on pre-installed Weaver-style rail; black padded sling; Wingmaster HD\xaa Turkey/Predator RemChoke; full Mossy Oak Obsession camo coverage; ShurShot pistol grip stock with black overmolded grip panels; TruGlo 30mm Red/Green Dot Scope pre-mounted.

NIB	Exc.	V.G.	Good	Fair	Poor
575	500	425	350	200	150

Model 870TA Trap

As above, with a competition ventilated rib and checkered stock. Produced in 12 gauge only. Discontinued in 1986.

NIB	Exc.	V.G.	Good	Fair	Poor
500	400	300	200	150	100

Model 870TB Trap

As above, with a 28" or 30" Full choke, ventilated rib barrel and a trap-style walnut stock. Manufactured from 1950 to 1981.

NIB	Exc.	V.G.	Good	Fair	Poor
—	450	325	275	200	125

Model 870TC Trap

As above, with a finely figured walnut stock and screw-in choke tubes.

NIB	Exc.	V.G.	Good	Fair	Poor
575	475	400	350	250	150

Model 870 Express Deer Gun

This model is fitted with a 20" fully rifled barrel, iron sights, and Monte Carlo stock. Also offered with a 20" IC rifle sighted barrel. Available in 12 gauge only.

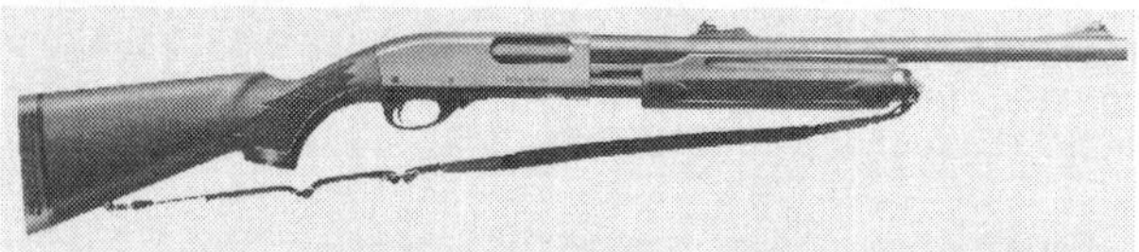

NIB	Exc.	V.G.	Good	Fair	Poor
370	275	200	150	125	100

Model 870 Express Deer/Turkey Combo

This 3" 12 gauge has a 21-inch barrel threaded for Remchokes for turkey hunting and a 23" rifled slug barrel with cantilever scope mount for deer hunting. Receiver and barrel are matte black; synthetic stock is Mossy Oak Break-Up camo.

NIB	Exc.	V.G.	Good	Fair	Poor
625	500	425	350	250	150

Model 870 Express Left-Hand

Left-hand version of the Express model fitted with a 28" vent rib barrel and checkered hardwood stock. Black matte finish.

NIB	Exc.	V.G.	Good	Fair	Poor
360	275	200	150	100	75

Remington 870 Express Synthetic Turkey Camo

Pump action shotgun chambered for 2-3/4 and 3-inch 12-ga. Features include 21-inch vent-rib bead-sighted barrel; standard Express finish on barrel and receiver; Turkey Extra Full RemChoke; synthetic stock with integrated sling swivel attachment.

NIB	Exc.	V.G.	Good	Fair	Poor
445	385	325	275	200	150

MODEL 870 SERIES

Model 870 Express Super Magnum Turkey

This 12 gauge gun will handle 2.75", 3", or 3.5" shells. Fitted with a 23" vent rib barrel, black synthetic stock, and matte black metal finish. Weight is about 7.25 lbs. Introduced in 1999.

NIB	Exc.	V.G.	Good	Fair	Poor
390	290	200	150	100	75

Model 870 Express Synthetic Deer

This model is fitted with a 20" fully rifled barrel with adjustable rifle sights. Black synthetic stock with Monte Carlo comb and matte black finish. Weight is about 7 lbs. Introduced in 1999.

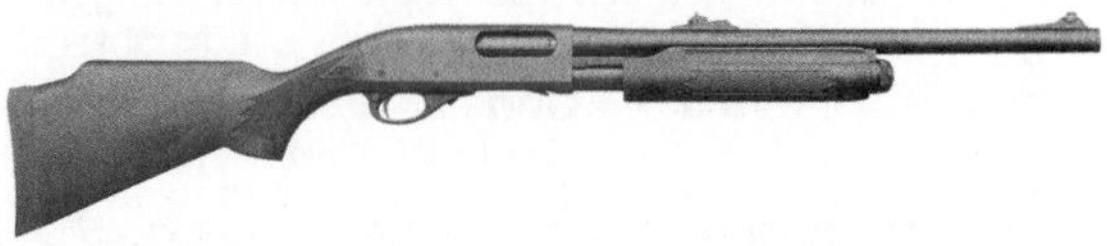

NIB	Exc.	V.G.	Good	Fair	Poor
370	275	200	150	100	75

Model 870 Express Compact Deer

20 gauge; similar to Model 870 Express Synthetic Deer but with smaller dimensions.

NIB	Exc.	V.G.	Good	Fair	Poor
425	300	200	150	100	75

Model 870 Express Compact Pink Camo

20 gauge; similar to Model 870 Express but with pink camo synthetic stock.

NIB	Exc.	V.G.	Good	Fair	Poor
370	275	200	150	100	75

Model 870 Express Compact Synthetic

Similar to above but with matte black synthetic stock.

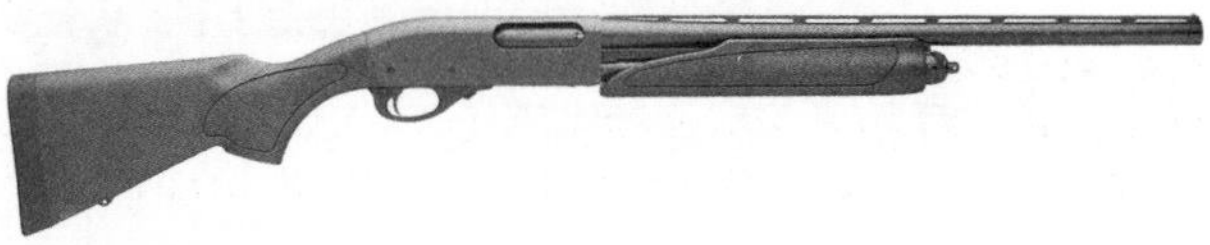

NIB	Exc.	V.G.	Good	Fair	Poor
370	275	200	150	100	75

Model 870 Express Compact Camo

Similar to above but with camo buttstock and forend.

NIB	Exc.	V.G.	Good	Fair	Poor
395	295	215	150	100	75

Model 870 Express Compact Jr.

Similar to above but with shorter barrel and LOP.

NIB	Exc.	V.G.	Good	Fair	Poor
370	275	200	150	100	75

Model 870 Express Combos

Offered in both 12 and 20 gauge with a 26" vent rib modified barrel and a 20" fully rifled deer barrel.

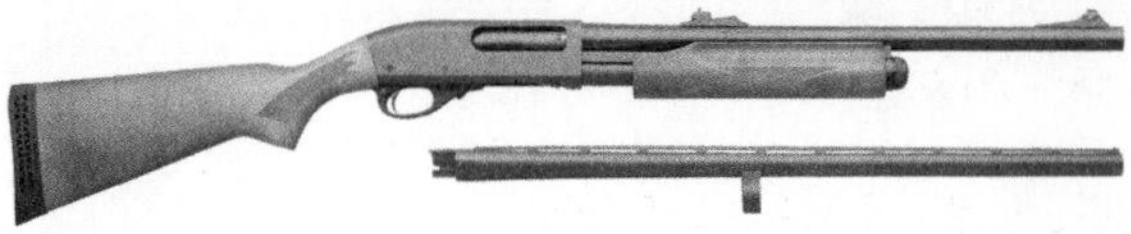

NIB	Exc.	V.G.	Good	Fair	Poor
500	395	250	200	150	100

Model 870 Express Youth Gun

Available in 20 gauge only, this shotgun is built for children. It has a 13" length of pull, a 21" vent rib barrel, and is sold with a Modified Rem. choke tube.

NIB	Exc.	V.G.	Good	Fair	Poor
330	250	200	150	125	100

Model 870 Express Turkey

Furnished in 12 gauge with 21" vent rib barrel with extra-full Remington choke Turkey tube.

NIB	Exc.	V.G.	Good	Fair	Poor
345	250	175	150	125	100

Model 870 Express Camo Turkey

Similar to the Express Turkey but with complete coverage of camo stock. Metal is matte black.

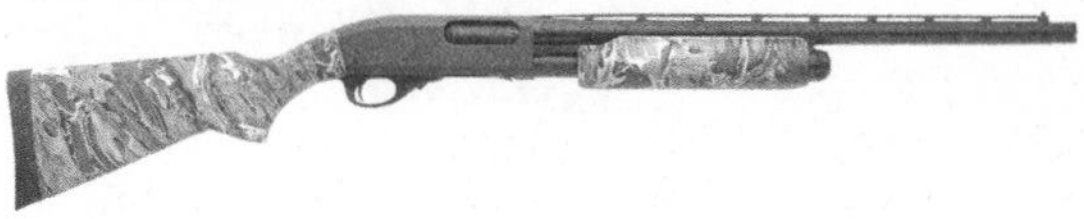

NIB	Exc.	V.G.	Good	Fair	Poor
400	300	225	150	100	75

Model 870 20 Gauge Express Youth Camo Turkey

Similar to the Model 870 Express Camo but in 20 gauge with shortened stock (13" lop).

NIB	Exc.	V.G.	Good	Fair	Poor
400	300	225	150	100	75

Model 870 Express Small Game

Offered in 20 gauge or .410, this model has a nonreflective metal and wood finish. The .410 bore is furnished with a 25" vent rib Full choke barrel, while the 20 gauge is available with a 26" or 28" vent rib barrel with Modified Rem. choke tube.

NIB	Exc.	V.G.	Good	Fair	Poor
225	200	175	150	125	100

Model 870 Express HD (Home Defense)

Introduced in 1995 this model features an 18" 12 gauge barrel with cylinder barrel with front bead sight. Weight approx. 7.25 lb.

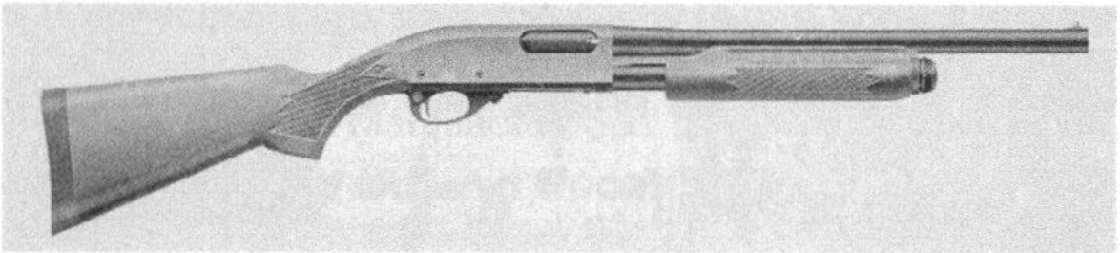

Courtesy Remington Arms

NIB	Exc.	V.G.	Good	Fair	Poor
345	250	175	150	125	100

Model 870 Classic Trap

Introduced in 2000 this model features special fine line engraving with gold inlays. Stock is select walnut with Monte Carlo comb, 30" barrel with a contoured vent rib. Ventilated recoil pad with white-line spacers. Choke tubes. Weight is about 8 lbs.

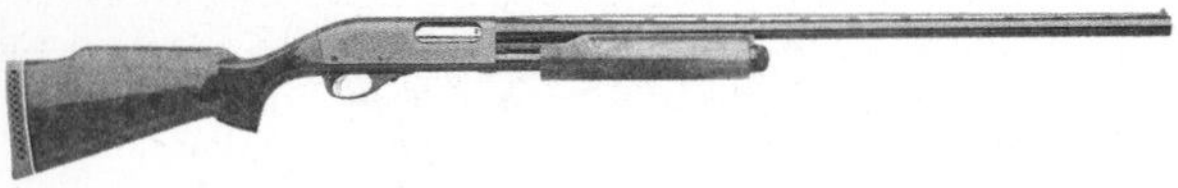

NIB	Exc.	V.G.	Good	Fair	Poor
675	550	450	300	200	—

Model 870 Special Field

This Remington pump-action shotgun is available in either 12 or 20 gauge and features an English-style straight grip stock, 21" vent rib barrel and slim shortened slide handle. In 12 gauge the gun weighs 7 lbs. and in 20 gauge it weighs 6.25 lbs. Comes with a set of Remington choke tubes.

NIB	Exc.	V.G.	Good	Fair	Poor
650	550	375	250	150	100

Model 870 Rifle Deer Gun

This new 20 gauge model was introduced in 1994 and features a fully rifled 20" barrel. It has a new scope rail design that is more rigid. The finish is blue and the Monte Carlo stock is walnut. Is equipped with recoil pad and checkering.

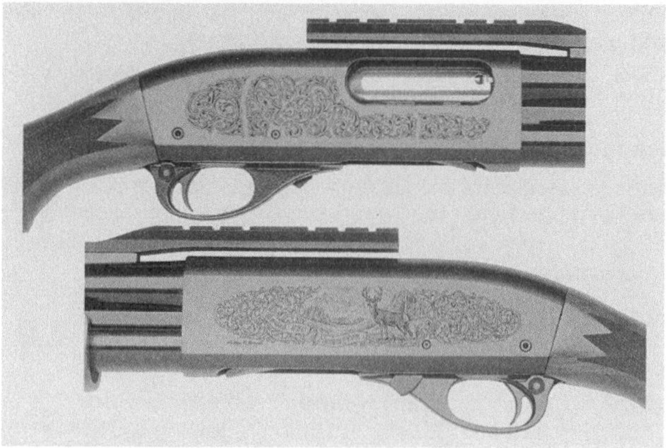

Close-up of engraving detail on Model 870 Deer Gun

NIB	Exc.	V.G.	Good	Fair	Poor
450	400	350	300	200	100

Model 870 Brushmaster Deer Gun

This 12 gauge slide-action shotgun is fitted with a 20" Remington choke plain barrel and Monte Carlo stock. Available for either left-hand or right-hand shooters.

NIB	Exc.	V.G.	Good	Fair	Poor
350	300	250	200	150	100

Model 870 Express Youth Turkey Camo

Similar to the model above but chambered for the 20 gauge shell and finished with Realtree Camo. Weight is about 6 lbs.

NIB	Exc.	V.G.	Good	Fair	Poor
400	300	225	150	125	100

Model 870 Youth Deer Gun

Chambered for the 20 gauge shell and fitted with a 21" full choked barrel. Realtree Camo finish. Magazine capacity is 4 rounds. Weight is about 6 lbs.

NIB	Exc.	V.G.	Good	Fair	Poor
350	300	250	200	150	100

Model 870 Security

Offered in 12 gauge only this personal protection shotgun has an 18.5" Cylinder-choked plain barrel with front bead sight.

NIB	Exc.	V.G.	Good	Fair	Poor
350	300	250	200	150	100

Model 870 SPS-Camo

Offered in 12 gauge only and a choice of 26" or 28" vent rib barrel with Rem. choke tubes. The wood and metal are finished in a brown camo color. Introduced in 2001.

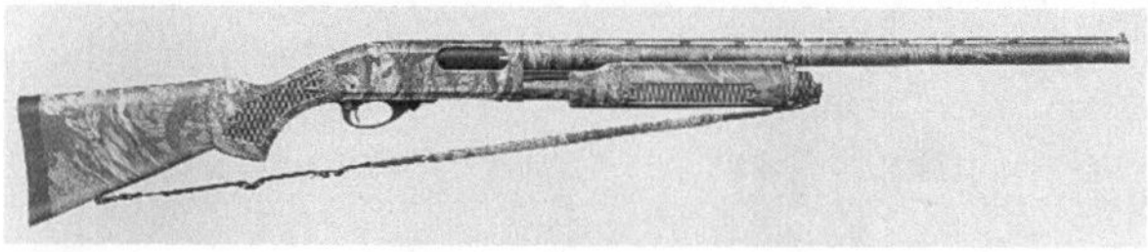

NIB	Exc.	V.G.	Good	Fair	Poor
600	425	325	225	175	125

Model 870 SPS Super Magnum Camo

This model is chambered for 12 gauge shells with chambers that will handle both 3" magnum and 3.5" magnum shells as well as all 2.75" shells. Barrel is 23" with ventilated rib and Rem. chokes. Finish is Mossy Oak camo. Weight is about 7.25 lbs. Introduced in 1999.

NIB	Exc.	V.G.	Good	Fair	Poor
600	425	325	225	175	125

Model 870 SPS-BG Camo

Available for the first time in 1993 this model features a 12 gauge 20" plain barrel with IC and Turkey Super Full Rem. choke tubes. The wood and metal are finished in a brown camo color.

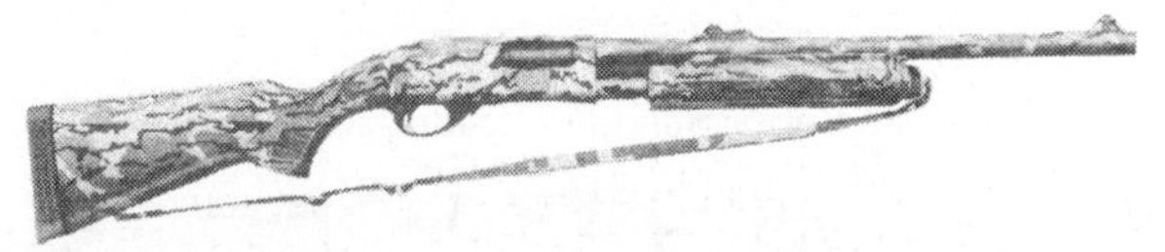

NIB	Exc.	V.G.	Good	Fair	Poor
400	300	225	175	125	100

Model 870 SPS Fully Rifled Deer Gun

This 20 gauge model features an 18.5" fully rifled heavy barrel with no sights. Receiver has a cantilever scope mount. Black synthetic stock. Black matte finish. Weight is about 8 lbs. Magazine capacity is 4 rounds. Introduced in 2004.

NIB	Exc.	V.G.	Good	Fair	Poor
500	375	250	175	125	100

Model 870 SPS Super Slug Deer Gun

This model features a 23" fully rifled modified contour barrel which is equipped with a barrel mounted cantilever scope mount. Stock is black synthetic. Weight is approximately 8 lbs. Introduced in 1999.

NIB	Exc.	V.G.	Good	Fair	Poor
600	425	325	250	175	100

Model 870 SPS-T

This 12 gauge model comes standard with a 21" vent rib barrel, Rem. choke tubes in IC and Turkey Super Full, black synthetic stock, and black matte finish.

NIB	Exc.	V.G.	Good	Fair	Poor
575	475	400	350	250	150

Model 870 SPS-T Camo

Same as above with the exception of a 21" vent rib barrel with IC and Turkey Super Full Rem. choke tubes. Both wood and metal are finished in a green camo color.

NIB	Exc.	V.G.	Good	Fair	Poor
600	425	325	250	175	100

Model 870 SPS-T Youth Turkey Camo

This shotgun is finished in Mossy Oak Break-Up and chambered for the 12 gauge shell. Fitted with a 20" Super Full choke. Weight is about 7.125 lbs. Introduced in 2001.

NIB	Exc.	V.G.	Good	Fair	Poor
565	450	325	250	175	125

Model 870 SPS-T Super Magnum Camo

This 12 gauge model will handle 2.75", 3", and 3.5" shells. Fitted with a 23" barrel with Rem chokes. Finish is Mossy Oak camo. Weight is about 7.25 lbs. Introduced in 1999.

NIB	Exc.	V.G.	Good	Fair	Poor
615	425	325	250	175	125

Model 870 SPS-T Camo NWTF 25th Anniversary

This model, fitted with a 21" barrel has special fiber optic sighting system. NWTF logo on left side of receiver. Introduced in 1998.

NIB	Exc.	V.G.	Good	Fair	Poor
600	450	325	250	175	125

Model 870 SPS-T Super Mag

Similar to Model 870 SP-T Thumbhole but with pistol-grip stock and vent-rib barrel.

NIB	Exc.	V.G.	Good	Fair	Poor
630	450	350	275	200	150

Model 870 SPS-T/20

This 20-gauge turkey gun features a 3" chamber, 23" vent rib barrel, R3 recoil pad and full coverage in Mossy Oak New Break-Up camo. Drilled and tapped for scope mount.

NIB	Exc.	V.G.	Good	Fair	Poor
550	450	325	250	195	150

Model 870 SPS-T Camo

Chambered for the 20 gauge 3" shell and fitted with a 20" barrel with full choke. Stock is Mossy Oak camo. Fiber optic front sight. Weight is about 6 lbs. Introduced in 2003.

NIB	Exc.	V.G.	Good	Fair	Poor
600	450	325	250	175	125

Model 870 SP-T Super Magnum Thumbhole

This 12 gauge 3.5" gun is fitted with a 23" barrel with choke tubes. Mossy Oak Obsession finish. Open sights with fiber-optic front sight. Weight is about 8 lbs. Introduced in 2005.

NIB	Exc.	V.G.	Good	Fair	Poor
650	500	350	250	175	125

Model 870 Dale Earnhardt Limited Edition

This is a 12 gauge with a 28" vent rib barrel with choke tubes. Checkered walnut stock. The receiver is engraved with Earnhardt's likeness and gold signature. High polish blue finish. Weight is about 8 lbs. Introduced in 2005.

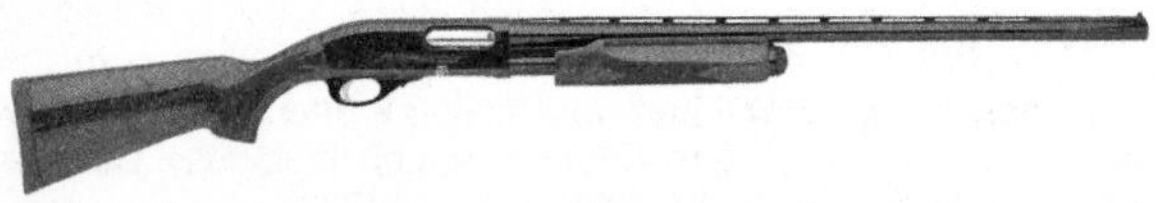

NIB	Exc.	V.G.	Good	Fair	Poor
650	500	350	250	175	125

Model 870 Marine Magnum

This 12 gauge shotgun has a nickel finish on the inside and outside of the receiver and barrel. Synthetic stock is checkered. The 18" barrel is bored cylinder and is fitted with a 7-round magazine. Sling swivel studs are standard.

NIB	Exc.	V.G.	Good	Fair	Poor
560	325	275	225	175	125

Model 870 SPS

Offered in 12 gauge only with synthetic stock and black matte finish. The barrel is either 26" or 28" with ventilated rib and Rem. choke tubes.

NIB	Exc.	V.G.	Good	Fair	Poor
325	275	225	175	125	100

Model 870 SPS-Deer

Available with a 20" rifle with plain barrel, this 12 gauge shotgun has a black synthetic stock and black matte finish. First introduced in 1993.

NIB	Exc.	V.G.	Good	Fair	Poor
550	450	325	250	195	150

Model 870 Police

This model comes in a wide variety (21) of 12 gauge configurations. Fitted with barrel from 14" (Class III), 18", or 20". Most with Parkerized finish, although some variations have blued finish. Wood stock, folding stock, Speedfeed stock, or synthetic stock. Rifle or bead sights, and some configurations with Ghost-ring and tritium night sights. Some variations have 7- or 8-round magazine extensions depending on barrel length.

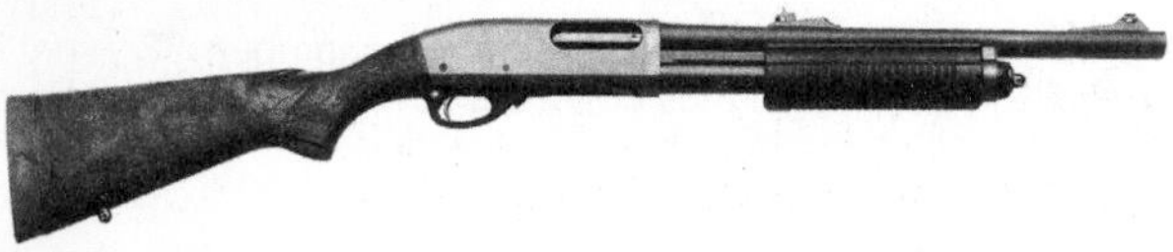

NIB	Exc.	V.G.	Good	Fair	Poor
650	525	400	300	225	125

Model 870 Tac-2 SpecOps Stock

Tactical 3" 12 gauge is available with a Knoxx pistol-grip or folding stock. Barrel is 18" with fixed Cylinder choke. Magazine capacity is 6 shells. Weight is 7 lbs.

NIB	Exc.	V.G.	Good	Fair	Poor
615	425	325	250	175	125

Model 870 Tac-3 Speedfeed IV

Tactical 3" 12 gauge with pistol-grip stock and 20" barrel. Extended 7-round magazine. Weight is 7.5 lbs.

NIB	Exc.	V.G.	Good	Fair	Poor
600	450	325	250	175	125

Model 870 Tac-3 Folder

As above but with Knoxx Spec-Ops folding stock. Weight is 7 lbs.

NIB	Exc.	V.G.	Good	Fair	Poor
600	450	325	250	175	125

Remington 870 Express Tactical A-TACS Camo

Pump action shotgun chambered for 2-3/4- and 3-inch 12-ga. Features include full A-TACS digitized camo; 18-1/2-inch barrel; extended ported Tactical RemChoke; SpeedFeed IV pistol-grip stock with SuperCell recoil pad; fully adjustable XS\xa8 Ghost Ring Sight rail with removable white bead front sight; 7-round capacity with factory-installed 2-shot extension; drilled and tapped receiver; sling swivel stud.

NIB	Exc.	V.G.	Good	Fair	Poor
600	525	450	375	275	185

MODEL 870 SERIES

Model 870 Custom Grade

This Custom Shop model is available in three levels of engraving, gold inlay, wood grade and finish, metal work finish, recoil pad/buttplate, and dimensions.

Grade D Grade

NIB	Exc.	V.G.	Good	Fair	Poor
3000	200	1100	—	—	—

Grade F Grade

NIB	Exc.	V.G.	Good	Fair	Poor
6000	4000	2250	—	—	—

Grade F Grade with Gold Inlay

NIB	Exc.	V.G.	Good	Fair	Poor
10000	7500	5000	—	—	—

Model 870 SP-T Thumbhole

Introduced in 2005, this 3.5" 12 gauge is designed specifically for turkey hunting with full coverage in Mossy Oak Obsession camo and thumbhole stock. The 23" barrel features fiber-optic adjustable rifle sights and is drilled and tapped for scope mounting. Includes R3 recoil pad, sling, swivels and turkey super full choke tube.

NIB	Exc.	V.G.	Good	Fair	Poor
615	425	325	250	175	125

Model 870 Special Purpose Thumbhole

Laminated stock 12 gauge slug gun with 3" chamber and 23" fully rifled cantilever barrel.

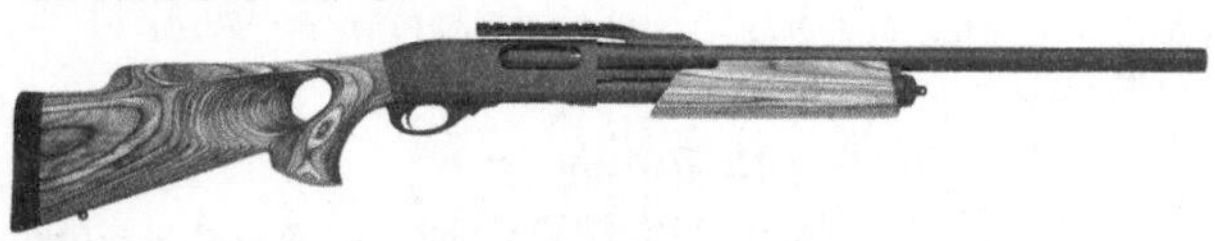

NIB	Exc.	V.G.	Good	Fair	Poor
525	475	350	275	200	150

Model 870 XCS Marine Magnum

New in 2007, this weather-resistant 870 is a 3" 12 gauge with full black TriNyte coverage, 18" fixed Cylinder barrel and 7 round capacity. Weight is 7.5 lbs.

NIB	Exc.	V.G.	Good	Fair	Poor
675	495	400	300	200	125

Model 870 SPS MAX Gobbler

This dedicated turkey gun is a 3.5" 12 gauge featuring a length-adjustable Knoxx SpecOps stock, 23" barrel, fiber-optic rifle sights, Super Full turkey choke tube and full coverage in Realtree APG camo. Drilled and tapped for Weaver style mount. Weight is 8 lbs.

NIB	Exc.	V.G.	Good	Fair	Poor
650	550	425	350	225	150

Model 870 20 Ga. Lightweight Magnum

Fixed-choke, high-gloss 3-inch version of the Model 870 Wingmaster. with impressed checkering. Introduced mid-1980s. Also chambers 2.75-inch shells. Discontinued.

NIB	Exc.	V.G.	Good	Fair	Poor
550	450	325	250	195	150

Model 870 Wingmaster 100th Anniversary

This Commemorative Edition 12 gauge celebrating 100 years of Remington pump shotguns (dating from the introduction of the Model 10 in 1908) was introduced in 2008 and offered only for one year. Gold-inlaid logos on both sides of receiver and "B" Grade American Walnut stock with high-gloss finish. Includes three choke tubes.

NIB	Exc.	V.G.	Good	Fair	Poor
875	600	475	350	200	125

Model 870 with Claro Walnut

This 2008 upgrade to the 870 Wingmaster features a semi-fancy claro walnut stock and forend. It is available in 3-inch 12- and 20-gauge with 28" and 26" barrels, respectively. Three choke tubes included.

NIB	Exc.	V.G.	Good	Fair	Poor
875	600	475	350	200	125

Model 870 Express Magnum ShurShot Cantilever

This 3-inch 12 gauge has a 23", fully rifled barrel with cantilever scope mount. Matte black finish. Weight is about 7.75 lbs.

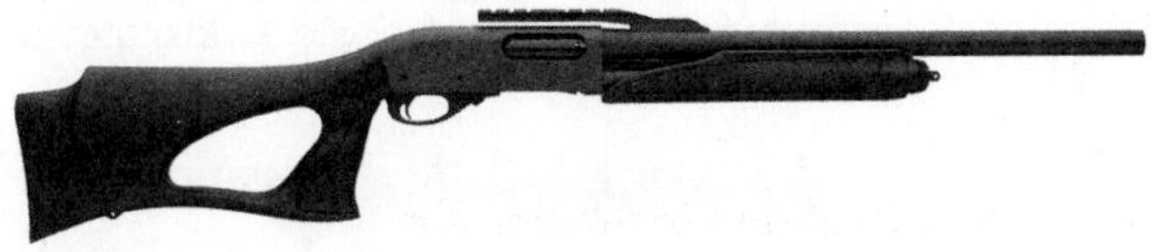

NIB	Exc.	V.G.	Good	Fair	Poor
550	450	325	250	195	150

Model 870 SPS ShurShot Synthetic Super Slug

Pump-action shotgun based on 870 platform. Chambers 12-gauge 2-3/4" and 3" shells interchangeably. Extra-heavy (1" dia.) 25-1/2" fully rifled barrel pinned to receiver. SuperCell recoil pad. Drilled and tapped for scope mounts with Weaver rail included. Matte black metal surfaces, Mossy Oak Treestand ShurShot buttstock and forend. Overall length 47". Weigh: 7-7/8 lbs.

NIB	Exc.	V.G.	Good	Fair	Poor
550	450	325	250	195	150

Model 870 Express Super Magnum Waterfowl

Introduced in 2008, this dedicated waterfowl gun is completely finished in Mossy Oak Duck Blind camo. The 3.5" 12 gauge has a 28" barrel, HiViz single bead sight and weighs about 7.5 lbs. Includes one choke tube.

NIB	Exc.	V.G.	Good	Fair	Poor
350	300	250	200	150	100

Model 870 Express Magnum ShurShot Turkey

This turkey-dedicated model has a matte black finish with a ShurShot pistol grip/thumbhole stock and forend finished in Mossy Oak Obsession camo. The 3-inch 12 gauge has a 21-inch barrel. Includes a Turkey Extra Full choke tube. Weight is about 7.5 lbs.

NIB	Exc.	V.G.	Good	Fair	Poor
500	400	325	250	175	100

Model 870 SPS ShurShot Turkey

New in 2008, this 12 gauge 870 is chambered for shells up to 3.5". It features Remington's ShurShot pistol grip/thumbhole stock and is fully covered in Realtree's APG HD camo. It has a 23-inch non-vent-rib barrel outfitted with fiber-optic rifle-type sights and includes an extended Turkey Rem Choke. Weight is about 7.5 lbs.

NIB	Exc.	V.G.	Good	Fair	Poor
625	495	400	300	200	125

Model 870 Express Tactical

Similar to Model 870 but in 12 gauge only (2-3/4" and 3" interchangeably) with 18-1/2" barrel, Tactical RemChoke extended/ported choke tube, black synthetic buttstock and forend, extended magazine tube, gray powdercoat finish overall. 38-1/2" overall length. Weight: 7-1/2 lbs.

NIB	Exc.	V.G.	Good	Fair	Poor
575	465	325	250	195	150

Model 870 Express Tactical with Ghost Ring Sights

Similar to Model 870 Express Tactical but with top-mounted accessories rail and XS ghost ring rear sight.

NIB	Exc.	V.G.	Good	Fair	Poor
625	495	400	300	200	125

Model 870 Tactical Desert Recon

This tactical version 870 features Digital Tiger desert camo on the synthetic stock and forend and an olive-drab powder-coated barrel and receiver. It is available with an 18" (six-round mag. capacity) or 20" (seven-round mag. capacity) barrel. Speedfeed I (shell holding) or Speedfeed IV (pistol grip) stock. Add 10 percent for Speedfeed IV stock.

NIB	Exc.	V.G.	Good	Fair	Poor
625	495	400	300	200	125

Model 887 Nitro Mag Pump Shotgun

Pump-action shotgun based on the Model 870. Chambers 3-1/2", 3" and 2-3/4" 12-gauge shells interchangeably. Black matte ArmorLokt rustproof coating throughout. SuperCell recoil pad. 28" barrel with solid rib and Hi-Viz front sight with interchangeable light tubes. Black synthetic stock with contoured grip panels.

NIB	Exc.	V.G.	Good	Fair	Poor
445	385	325	275	200	150

Model 887 Nitro Mag Waterfowl

Similar to above but with Advantage Max-4 camo overall.

NIB	Exc.	V.G.	Good	Fair	Poor
450	400	350	300	200	100

Remington 887 Bone Collector Edition

Pump action shotgun chambered in 12-ga., 2-3/4 to 3-1/2 inch. Features include ArmorLokt rustproof coating; synthetic stock and fore-end; 26-inch barrel; full camo finish; integral swivel studs; SuperCell recoil pad; solid rib and HiViz front sight. Bone Collector logo.

NIB	Exc.	V.G.	Good	Fair	Poor
560	475	400	335	250	150

Remington 887 Nitro Mag Camo Combo

Pump action shotgun chambered in 12-ga., 2-3/4 to 3-1/2 inch. Features include 22-inch turkey barrel with HiViz fiber-optic rifle sights and 28-inch waterfowl with a HiViz sight; extended Waterfowl and Super Full Turkey RemChokes are included; SuperCell recoil pad; synthetic stock and fore-end with specially contoured grip panels; full camo coverage.

NIB	Exc.	V.G.	Good	Fair	Poor
625	535	460	385	325	200

Remington 887 Nitro Mag Tactical

Pump action shotgun chambered in 12-ga., 2-3/4 to 3-1/2 inch. Features include 18-1/2-inch barrel with ported, extended tactical RemChoke; 2-shot magazine extension; barrel clamp with integral Picatinny rails; ArmorLokt coating; synthetic stock and fore-end with specially contour grip panels.

NIB	Exc.	V.G.	Good	Fair	Poor
450	400	350	275	200	150

Model 48 Sportsman

A 12, 16, or 20 gauge semi-automatic shotgun with 26", 28", or 32" barrels and a 3-shot tubular magazine. Blued with a checkered walnut stock. Approximately 275,000 were made from 1949 to 1959.

NIB	Exc.	V.G.	Good	Fair	Poor
—	325	300	250	175	100

NOTE: Vent rib add 20 percent.

Model 11-48

As above, with the addition of 28 gauge and .410 bore. Approximately 425,000 were made from 1949 to 1968. 225 percent premium for 28 ga.

NIB	Exc.	V.G.	Good	Fair	Poor
—	300	250	200	150	75

Model 58 Sportsman

A 12, 16, or 20 gauge semi-automatic shotgun with 26", 28", or 30" barrels and a 3-shot tubular magazine. The receiver is scroll engraved and blued. Checkered walnut stock. Approximately 270,000 were made from 1956 to 1963.

NIB	Exc.	V.G.	Good	Fair	Poor
—	300	250	200	150	75

Model 878 Automaster

As above, in 12 gauge only. Approximately 60,000 were made from 1959 to 1962.

NIB	Exc.	V.G.	Good	Fair	Poor
—	350	250	175	125	75

MODEL 1100 SERIES

A 12, 16, 20 or 28 gauge or .410 bore semi-automatic shotgun with barrels ranging in length from 26" to 30". Fitted with choke tubes after 1987. Blued with a checkered walnut stock. Manufactured beginning in 1963.

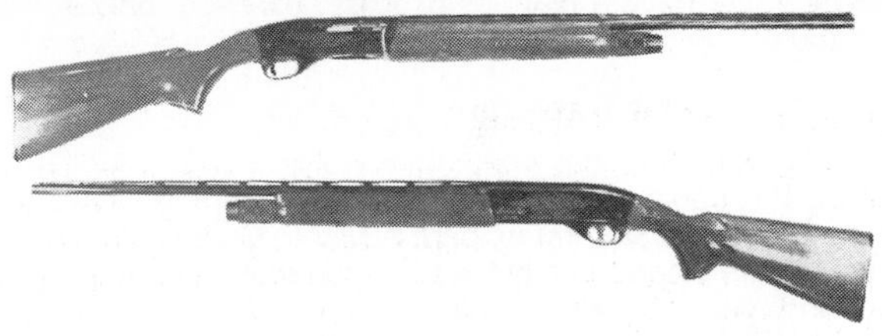

NIB	Exc.	V.G.	Good	Fair	Poor
550	450	350	200	150	100

NOTE: The smaller bore versions are worth approximately 20 percent more than the values listed.

Model 1100 Classic Field

Introduced in 2003 this shotgun is chambered for the 16 gauge shell and fitted with a choice of 26" or 28" vent rib barrel with Remington choke tubes. Checkered walnut stock with pistol grip. High polish blue finish. Magazine capacity is four rounds. Weight is about 7 to 7.25 lbs. depending on barrel length.

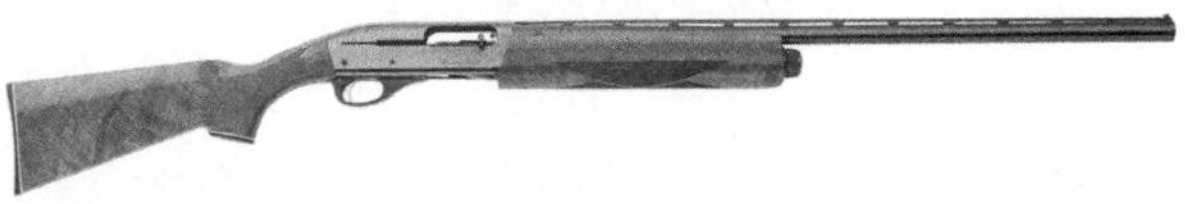

NIB	Exc.	V.G.	Good	Fair	Poor
800	600	450	300	200	100

Model 1100 Small Game

Available in 20, 28 gauge or .410 bore fitted with 25" vent rib barrels. The 28 gauge and .410 have fixed chokes while the 20 gauge has Rem. choke tubes.

NIB	Exc.	V.G.	Good	Fair	Poor
500	450	400	350	250	150

Model 1100 Youth Gun

Offered in 20 gauge only with a 21" vent rib 2-3/4" barrel. The stock has a special 13" length of pull. Gun is supplied with a set of Rem. choke tubes.

NIB	Exc.	V.G.	Good	Fair	Poor
600	400	350	300	200	150

Model 1100 Youth Synthetic

Fitted with a 21" vent rib barrel this 20 gauge gun has a 1" shorter length of pull than standard. Matte black finish. Black synthetic stock. Weight is approximately 6.5 lbs. Introduced in 1999.

NIB	Exc.	V.G.	Good	Fair	Poor
575	400	300	225	150	100

Model 1100 Youth Synthetic Camo

Same as model above but with RealTree camo finish and chambered for 20 gauge 3" magnum shells. Weight is about 6.75 lbs. Introduced in 1999.

NIB	Exc.	V.G.	Good	Fair	Poor
695	475	325	225	175	100

Model 1100 Tournament Skeet

Offered in 20, 28 gauge, and .410 bore. The 28 gauge and .410 come with 25" Skeet choked vent rib barrels while the 20 gauge is supplied with a 26" Skeet choked vent rib barrel.

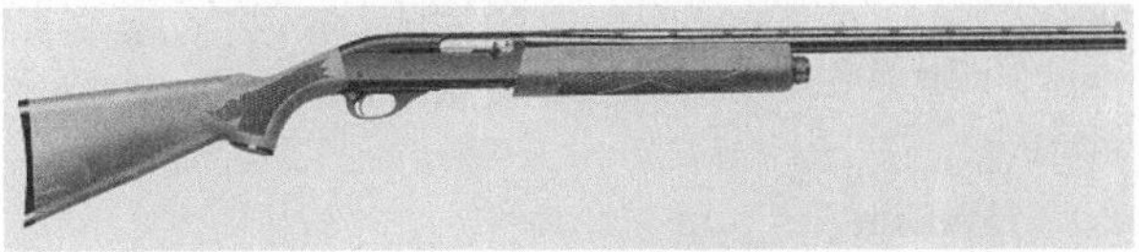

Courtesy Remington Arms

NIB	Exc.	V.G.	Good	Fair	Poor
800	650	500	400	250	150

Model 1100 Tournament Skeet, 12 Gauge

Introduced in 2003 this model is fitted with a 26" light contour vent rib barrel. Stock is semi-fancy walnut. Receiver is rolled-marked "tournament skeet." Supplied with extended choke tubes and gold-plated trigger. Weight is about 7.75 lbs.

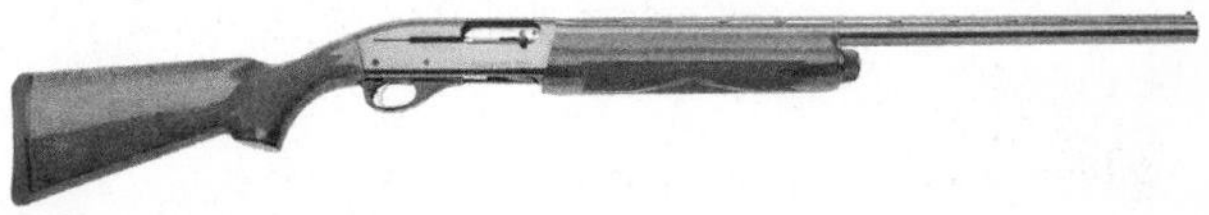

NIB	Exc.	V.G.	Good	Fair	Poor
650	500	400	300	200	100

Model 1100 Classic Trap

This model features a 30" low-profile vent rib barrel. The stock is semi-fancy walnut with Monte Carlo comb and ventilated recoil pad. Receiver has fine line engraving with gold inlays and the trigger is gold. Weight is about 8.25 lbs.

NIB	Exc.	V.G.	Good	Fair	Poor
850	725	600	475	350	200

Model 1100 Sporting 12

Introduced in 2000 this 12 gauge model features a 28" low profile vent rib barrel. Stock is walnut with cut checkering and Sporting Clays-style recoil pad. Gold trigger and fine line engraving on the receiver. Weight is about 8 lbs.

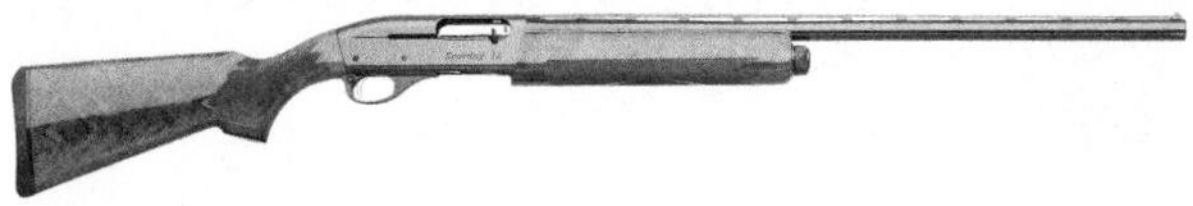

NIB	Exc.	V.G.	Good	Fair	Poor
725	650	475	400	300	150

Model 1100 Sporting 20

This model has a high grade walnut stock with glass finish and recoil pad. It is fitted with a 28" barrel with target sights. Interchangeable chokes. Introduced in 1998.

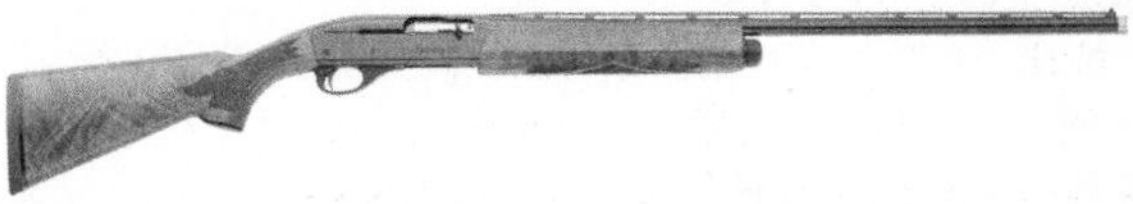

NIB	Exc.	V.G.	Good	Fair	Poor
700	625	425	400	300	150

Model 1100 Sporting 28

Introduced in 1996 this version is chambered for the 28 gauge shell. It is fitted with interchangeable chokes and a 25" vent rib barrel. The stock is walnut with Tournament grade checkering and recoil pad.

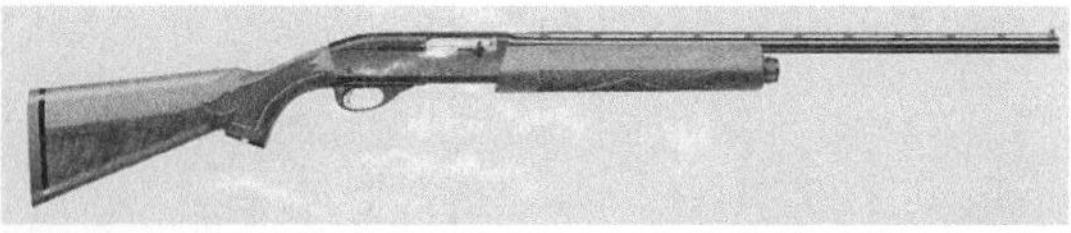

Courtesy Remington Arms

NIB	Exc.	V.G.	Good	Fair	Poor
825	700	575	475	350	200

Model 1100 Competition Master

Introduced in 2003 this model features a 12 gauge gun chambered for the 2.75" shell. Fitted with a 22" vent rib barrel with Remington chokes and fiber optic front sight. Has a gray synthetic stock with matte black finish on receiver and barrel. Magazine extension has eight-round capacity. Receiver mounted ammo carrier for seven extra shells. Weight is about 8 lbs. Designed for practical shooting competition.

NIB	Exc.	V.G.	Good	Fair	Poor
725	600	425	400	300	150

Model 1100 Competition

Introduced in 2005 this model is chambered for the 12 gauge shells with 2.75" chamber. Fitted with a 30" target style barrel with 10mm vent rib. Extended choke tubes. Receiver is nickel plated. Stock is semi-fancy American walnut with checkering and high gloss finish. Adjustable comb offered as option. Weight is about 8 lbs.

NIB	Exc.	V.G.	Good	Fair	Poor
950	775	650	525	350	175

Model 1100 LT-20

This 20 gauge model features a choice of 26" or 28" vent rib barrels with Rem choke tubes. It has a blue finish and walnut Monte Carlo stock. Recoil pad and cut checkering are standard. Weight is 6.75 to 7 lbs. depending on barrel length.

NIB	Exc.	V.G.	Good	Fair	Poor
600	450	400	300	200	150

Model 1100 LT-20 "Limited"

20 gauge lightweight Mode l 1100 Field gun with stock 1-inches shorter than standard, and 23" barrel for youthful, beginner shooters of smaller stature.

Courtesy Thorton D'Arc

NIB	Exc.	V.G.	Good	Fair	Poor
675	525	475	375	275	200

NOTE: In September 1980, Remington announced the Model 1100 Limited Edition "One of Three Thousand." This was a high grade gun with positive cut checkered fancy American walnut wood with a fitted rosewood grip cap and thin brown butt pad. It is 14K gold trimmed and etched with a hunting scenes on the receiver. All metal parts including the receiver, barrel, bolt and magazine cap have a high-luster finish. Available only in 1980. NIB: $3000.

Model 1100 TBMC Trap Gun

12 gauge with 30-inch, vent rib barrel in full or modified trap chokes. This gun featured a figured and checkered stock and fore-end, and had a rubber recoil pad. A Monte Carlo style stock was optional. A left-hand version of this gun was also available Due to a shortage of American walnut, in mid-year Remington began fitting some Model 1100 and Model 870 Field Grade shotguns with lightweight mahogany stocks and forends.

NIB	Exc.	V.G.	Good	Fair	Poor
725	650	475	400	300	150

Model 1100 LT-20 Deer Gun

Same as above but fitted with a 21" barrel with adjustable sights and an improved cylinder choke. Satin finish with American walnut stock. Weight is approximately 6.5 lbs.

NIB	Exc.	V.G.	Good	Fair	Poor
525	450	400	300	200	150

Model 1100 LT-20 Synthetic

Same as above but fitted with a synthetic stock with recoil pad.

NIB	Exc.	V.G.	Good	Fair	Poor
550	375	325	275	200	150

Model 1100 LT-20 Magnum

This 20 gauge Model 1100 is chambered for the 3" 20 gauge shell. It is fitted with a 28" vent rib barrel with interchangeable chokes. Checkered walnut stock. Weight is about 7 lbs.

NIB	Exc.	V.G.	Good	Fair	Poor
575	395	400	300	200	150

Model 1100 LT-20 Synthetic Camo NWTF 25th Anniversary

This model is fitted with a 21" barrel with special fiber optic sighting system. NWTF logo on left side of receiver. Introduced in 1998.

NIB	Exc.	V.G.	Good	Fair	Poor
650	525	450	300	250	125

Model 1100 Synthetic

Introduced in 1995 this model is furnished with a black synthetic stock with black matte metal finish. Available in both 12 and 20 gauge. Weight is about 6.75 to 7 lbs. depending on barrel length. In 2003 this model was offered chambered for the 16 gauge shell.

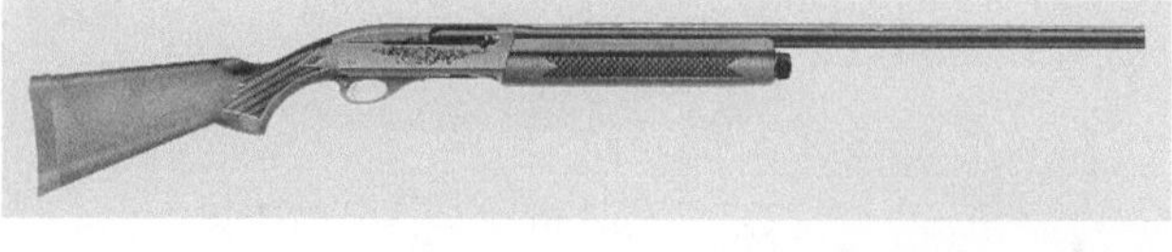

Courtesy Remington Arms

NIB	Exc.	V.G.	Good	Fair	Poor
550	450	350	250	200	100

Model 1100 Synthetic Deer Gun

Same as above but fitted with a 21" fully rifled barrel with cantilever rail for scope mounting. Furnished with 2-3/4" chamber. Stock is black synthetic with checkering and Monte Carlo-style cheekpiece. Recoil pad is standard.

NIB	Exc.	V.G.	Good	Fair	Poor
525	450	400	300	200	150

Model 1100 Competition Synthetic

The 1100 Competition Synthetic is super-tuned for competitive shooters. Overbored 30-inch barrel with lengthened forcing cones. Optimized for 2-3/4-inch target loads and light field loads. Receiver and all internal parts have nickel-Teflon finish. Synthetic stock has SuperCell recoil pad. Twelve-gauge only; weight: 8-1/4 lbs.

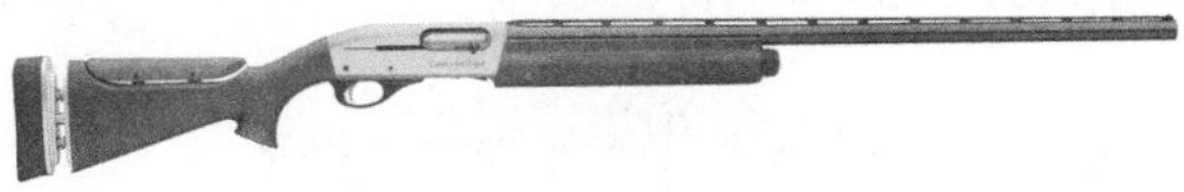

NIB	Exc.	V.G.	Good	Fair	Poor
900	800	675	525	400	250

MODEL 1100 CUSTOM GRADE

This Custom Shop model is available in three levels of engraving, gold inlay, wood grade and finish, metal work finish, recoil pad/buttplate, and dimensions. Each gun should be individually appraised prior to a sale.

D Grade

NIB	Exc.	V.G.	Good	Fair	Poor
3000	200	1100	—	—	—

F Grade

NIB	Exc.	V.G.	Good	Fair	Poor
6000	4000	2250	—	—	—

F Grade with Gold Inlay

NIB	Exc.	V.G.	Good	Fair	Poor
10000	7500	5000	—	—	—

Model 1100 G3

Introduced in 2006, this updated 1100 features a Realwood high gloss semi-fancy stock and forend. Available in 12 and 20 gauges with 26" or 28" barrel and chambered for 3" shells. Includes five Pro Bore chokes for 12 gauge and five Rem chokes for 20 gauge, R3 recoil pad and high-grade travel case. A left-handed version was added to this line in 2008.

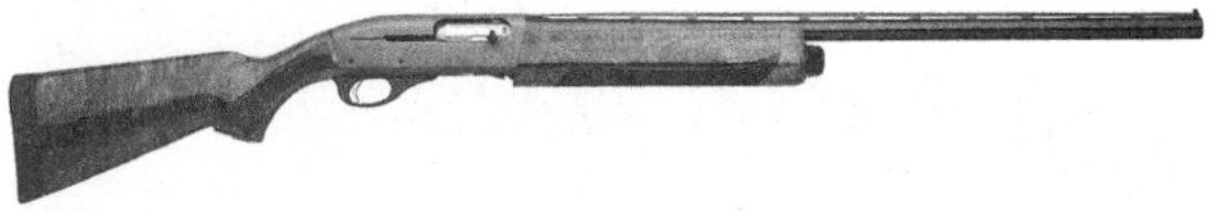

NIB	Exc.	V.G.	Good	Fair	Poor
825	600	450	300	225	150

Model 1100 Tactical Speedfeed IV

All-black 2.75" 12 gauge has an 18" barrel with fixed Improved Cylinder choke and Speedfeed IV stock. Extended 6-round magazine. Weight is 7.5 lbs.

NIB	Exc.	V.G.	Good	Fair	Poor
825	600	450	300	225	150

Model 1100 Tactical Standard Stock

Tactical 2.75" 12 gauge has 22" barrel threaded for Remchokes. Extended 8-round magazine.

NIB	Exc.	V.G.	Good	Fair	Poor
825	600	450	300	225	150

Model 1100 Premier Sporting

Introduced in 2008 as a dedicated sporting clays gun, the Premier Sporting comes in 12, 20 and 28 gauge and .410 bore with 2.75" chamber (3" in .410). Polished nickel receiver with fine-line embellishments and gold accents. Stock and forend are semi-fancy American walnut with high-gloss finish. A full line of Briley choke tubes and Premier Sporting hard case are included. Weights are about 8 lbs. in 12 gauge; 7 lbs. in 20 gauge; and 6.5 lbs. in 28 gauge and .410. Add 5 percent for 28 and .410.

NIB	Exc.	V.G.	Good	Fair	Poor
1150	1000	850	675	475	300

MODEL 11-87 SERIES

Model 11-87 Premier

A 3", 12 gauge semi-automatic shotgun with 26" to 32" ventilated rib barrels having screw-in choke tubes. Blued with a checkered walnut stock. Weight is approximately 7.75 lbs. Introduced in 1987. In 1999 this model was offered in a left-hand version.

Model 11-87 Premier left-hand model

NIB	Exc.	V.G.	Good	Fair	Poor
700	600	450	300	200	150

Model 11-87 Premier 20 Gauge

Introduced in 1999 this model is built on a small frame receiver. It will chamber both 2.75" and 3" shells. Available in both 26" and 28" vent rib barrels with twin beads. Barrels are built for Rem. chokes. Stock is walnut with gloss finish. Weight is about 7 lbs.

NIB	Exc.	V.G.	Good	Fair	Poor
675	575	425	300	225	125

Model 11-87 Dale Earnhardt Tribute

Introduced in 2003 to honor Dale Earnhardt this 12 gauge gun is fitted with a 28" vent rib barrel and walnut stock with checkering. Engraved on the receiver is a likeness of Earnhardt, his signature, and scroll work. Inlayed in gold. Serial numbers start with "DE3." Weight is about 7.75 lbs.

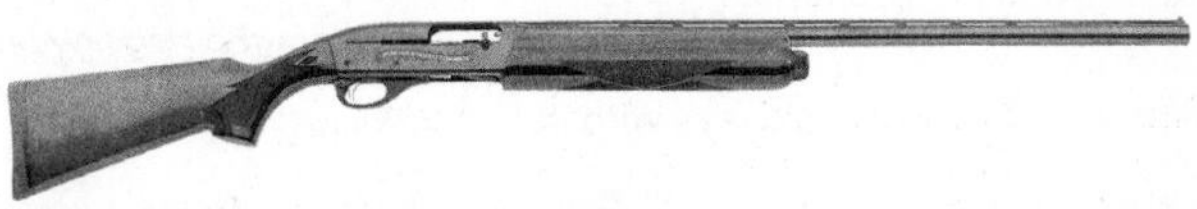

NIB	Exc.	V.G.	Good	Fair	Poor
675	575	425	300	225	125

Model 11-87 Upland Special

This model is offered in 12 or 20 gauge with 23" barrel with twin bead sights. Chambered for 3" shells. Stock is walnut with straight grip. Choke tubes standard. Weight is about 7.25 for 12 gauge and 6.5 lbs. for 20 gauge. Introduced in 2000.

NIB	Exc.	V.G.	Good	Fair	Poor
725	600	450	300	225	125

Model 11-87 Premier Cantilever Scope Mount Deer Gun

This semi-automatic model has a Monte Carlo stock and the option of a barrel-mounted scope (not included). Optional with a fully rifled barrel 21" long with a 1-in-35" twist. Also available in a 21" nonrifled barrel with Rifled and IC Rem. choke tubes. Available in 12 gauge only. Sling swivel studs and camo are standard.

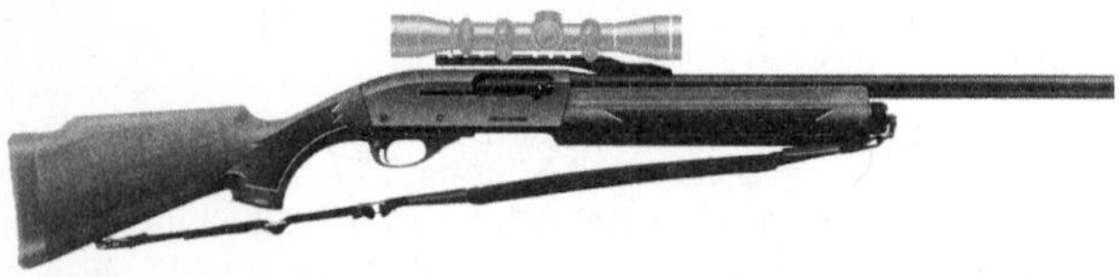

NIB	Exc.	V.G.	Good	Fair	Poor
800	675	400	300	200	150

Model 11-87 Premier Trap

Available in either right- or left-hand models. Is available with either a straight or Monte Carlo comb, 2.75" chamber, 30" vent rib overbored barrel and special Rem. Trap choke tubes. This model is set up to handle 12 gauge target loads only.

NIB	Exc.	V.G.	Good	Fair	Poor
525	475	425	300	200	150

Model 11-87 Premier SC (Sporting Clays)

This model features a special target stock with a 3.16" length of pull longer than standard and 1/4" higher at the heel. The butt pad is radiused at the heel and rounded at the toe. The receiver top, barrel, and rib have a fine matte finish on the blueing. The vent rib is a medium wide 8mm with stainless steel mid bead and a Bradley-style front bead sight. Gun is supplied new with these Rem. choke tubes: Skeet, Improved Skeet, Improved Cylinder, Modified, and Full. Supplied from the factory with a two-barrel custom fitted hard case.

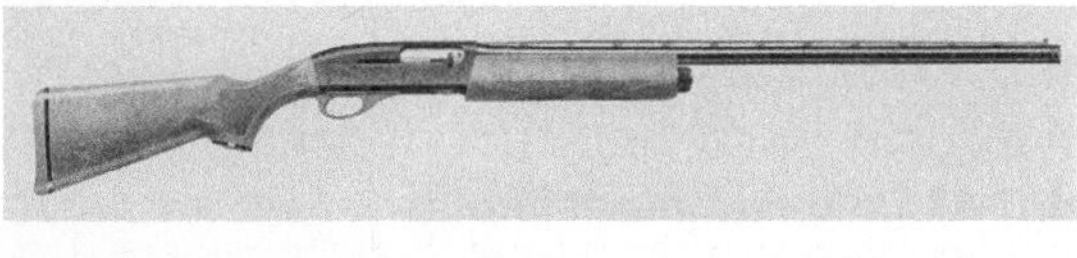

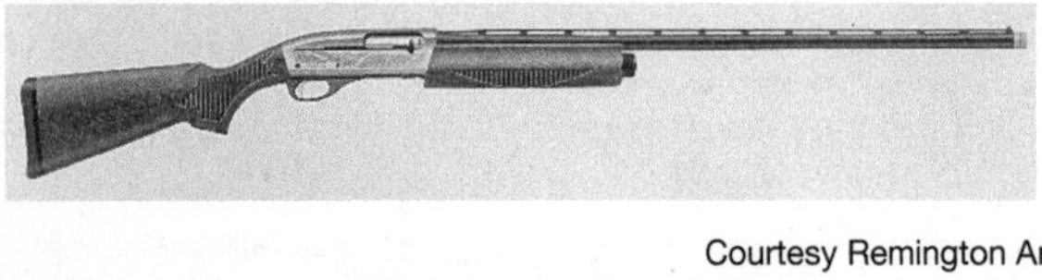

Courtesy Remington Arms

Model 11-87 Sporting Clays with new engraving

NIB	Exc.	V.G.	Good	Fair	Poor
750	600	450	350	200	150

Model 11-87 SC NP (Sporting Clays Nickel-Plated)

Same as above but with nickel-plated receiver.

NIB	Exc.	V.G.	Good	Fair	Poor
800	650	500	400	300	200

Model 11-87 SPS-BG Camo

This 12 gauge model is fitted with a rifle sighted 21" barrel with a brown camo finish on the stock and metal parts. Introduced in 1993.

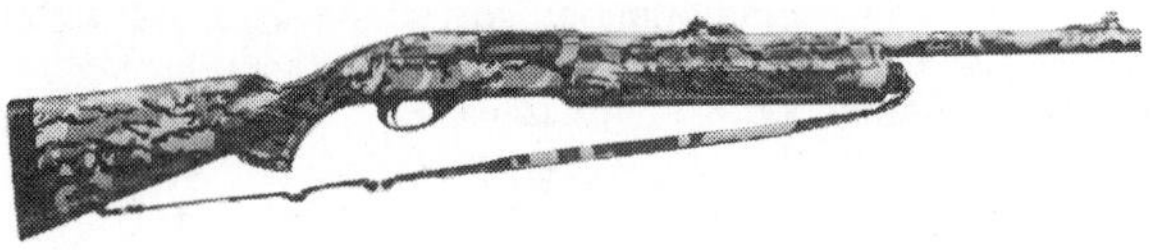

NIB	Exc.	V.G.	Good	Fair	Poor
525	475	425	300	200	150

Model 11-87 SPS-T Camo

Same as above but supplied with a 21" vent rib barrel with IC and Turkey Super Full Rem. choke tubes. Camo finish is green. Introduced in 1993.

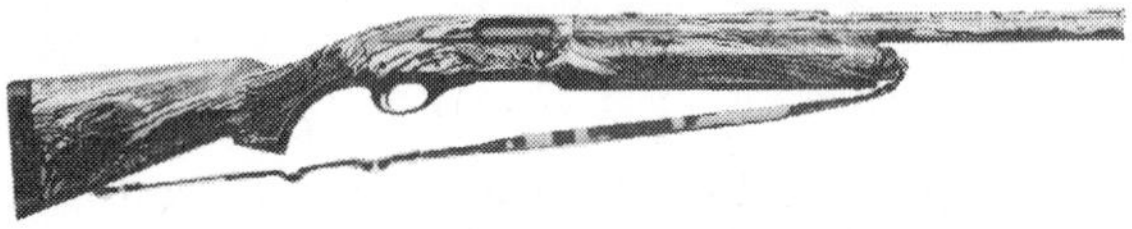

NIB	Exc.	V.G.	Good	Fair	Poor
550	450	350	250	200	150

Model 11-87 SPS

This 12 gauge model is furnished with a 26" or 28" vent rib barrel with IC, Mod., and Full Rem. choke tubes. The stock is a black synthetic material and the metal is finished in a black matte. In 1997 a camo version of this model was introduced.

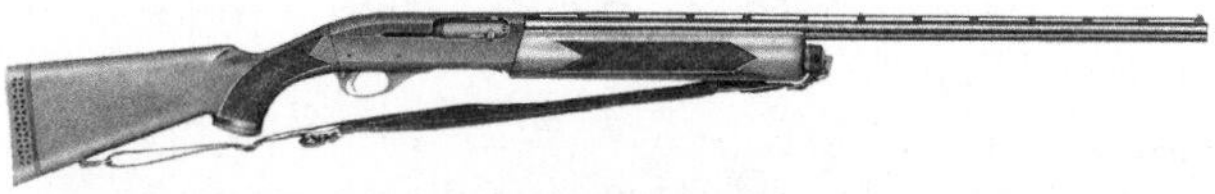

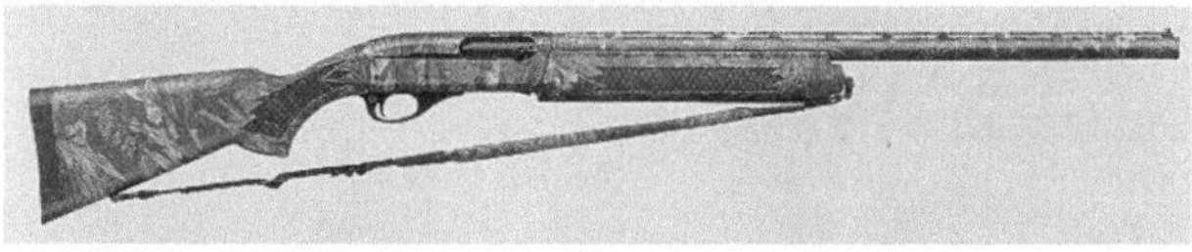

Remington Model 11-87 SPS Camo

NIB	Exc.	V.G.	Good	Fair	Poor
500	400	300	250	200	150

Model 11-87 SPS-Deer

The same as above but fitted with a 21" rifled, sighted barrel. First introduced in 1993.

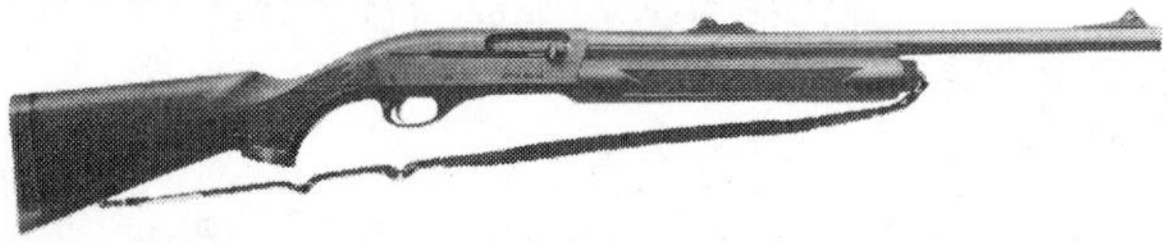

NIB	Exc.	V.G.	Good	Fair	Poor
525	475	425	300	200	150

Model 11-87 Waterfowl

This 12 gauge gun is fitted with a 28" vent rib barrel with choke tubes and Hi-Viz sights. Camo pattern is Mossy Oak Shadow-grass. Weight is about 8.25 lbs. Introduced in 2004.

NIB	Exc.	V.G.	Good	Fair	Poor
925	700	600	500	350	175

Model 11-87 SPS-T

Same as above but fitted with a 21" vent rib barrel with IC and Turkey Super Full Rem. choke tubes. In 1997 a camo version of this model was introduced.

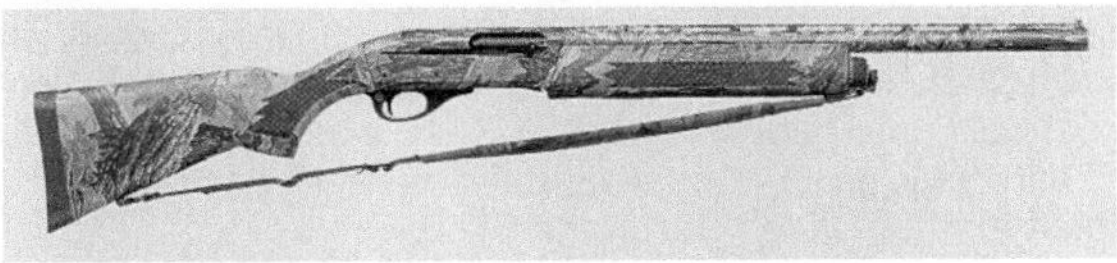

Remington Model 11-87 SPS-T Camo

NIB	Exc.	V.G.	Good	Fair	Poor
525	475	425	300	200	150

Model 11-87 SPS-T Camo NWTF 25th Anniversary

This model has a 21" barrel with special fiber optic sighting system. NWTF logo on left side of receiver. Introduced in 1998.

NIB	Exc.	V.G.	Good	Fair	Poor
700	595	425	300	200	150

Model 11-87 SP Super Magnum

Introduced in 2000 this model is chambered for the 12 gauge 3.5" Magnum shell. Fitted with a 26" or 28" vent rib barrel. Walnut stock with flat finish. Recoil pad. Matte black finish. Weight is about 8.25 lbs.

NIB	Exc.	V.G.	Good	Fair	Poor
675	500	350	300	125	100

Model 11-87 SPS Super Magnum

Same as above but with a black synthetic stock. Introduced in 2000. Weight is about 8.25 lbs.

NIB	Exc.	V.G.	Good	Fair	Poor
675	500	350	300	125	100

Model 11-87 SPS-T Super Magnum (NWTF Edition)

Introduced in 2005 this model features a 12 gauge 3.5" chamber with 23" barrel with choke tubes and iron sights. Mossy Oak Obsession camo stock with Monte Carlo comb. Weight is about 8 lbs.

NIB	Exc.	V.G.	Good	Fair	Poor
950	775	650	525	350	175

Model 11-87 Police

Offered chambered for 12 gauge shells, this model features a synthetic stock, 18" barrel with bead, rifle, or Ghost Ring sights, and 7-shot magazine extension.

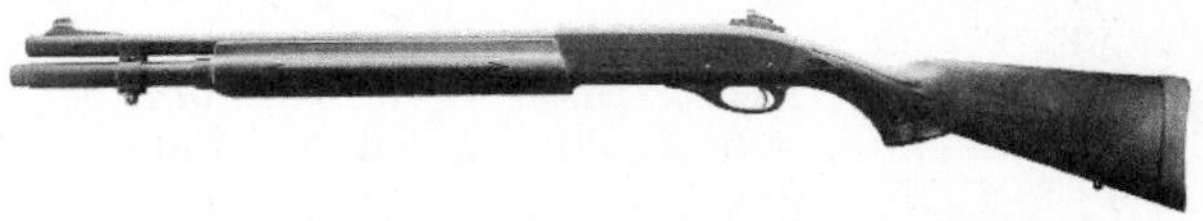

NIB	Exc.	V.G.	Good	Fair	Poor
675	500	350	300	125	100

NOTE: Add $20 for rifle sights and $60 for Ghost Ring sights.

MODEL 11-87 CUSTOM GRADE

This Custom Shop model is available in three levels of engraving, gold inlay, wood grade and finish, metal work finish, recoil pad/buttplate, and dimensions.

D Grade

NIB	Exc.	V.G.	Good	Fair	Poor
3000	200	1100	—	—	—

F Grade

NIB	Exc.	V.G.	Good	Fair	Poor
6000	4000	2250	—	—	—

F Grade with Gold Inlay

NIB	Exc.	V.G.	Good	Fair	Poor
10000	7500	5000	—	—	—

Model 11-87 Sportsman Synthetic

Introduced in 2005, this model features a black synthetic stock with choice of 12 or 20 gauge 3" chambers; 26" or 28" barrels with Mod. choke tube. Weight is about 7.75 to 8.25 lbs. depending on gauge and barrel length.

NIB	Exc.	V.G.	Good	Fair	Poor
675	500	350	300	125	100

Model 11-87 Sportsman Super Magnum

In 2008, Remington added this 3.5-inch version of the 11-87 Sportsman. It has a 28-inch barrel and weighs 8.25 lbs.

NIB	Exc.	V.G.	Good	Fair	Poor
750	625	550	400	300	200

Model 11-87 Sportsman Rifled

This is a 12 gauge 3" gun with 21" rifled barrel with cantilever scope mount. Black synthetic stock with black metal finish. Weight is about 8.5 lbs. Introduced in 2005.

NIB	Exc.	V.G.	Good	Fair	Poor
675	500	350	300	125	100

Model 11-87 Sportsman Youth

This is a 20 gauge 3" gun with 21" vent rib barrel with choke tubes. Black synthetic stock, length of pull is 13". Weight is about 6.5 lbs. Introduced in 2005.

NIB	Exc.	V.G.	Good	Fair	Poor
600	450	400	300	200	150

Model 11-87 Sportsman Compact Synthetic

Similar to Model 1-87 black synthetic but with reduced overall dimensions.

NIB	Exc.	V.G.	Good	Fair	Poor
700	595	500	350	225	150

Model 11-87 Sportsman Youth Camo

Same as above but with full coverage in Mossy Oak Break-Up camo.

NIB	Exc.	V.G.	Good	Fair	Poor
750	625	550	400	300	175

Model 11-87 Sportsman NRA Edition

This 12 gauge, 3" model is fitted with a 28" vent rib barrel with choke tubes. Synthetic stock with Mossy Oak New Break-Up camo. NRA logo on the left side of the matte black receiver. Introduced in 2005.

NIB	Exc.	V.G.	Good	Fair	Poor
675	500	350	300	125	100

Model 11-87 SP Thumbhole

Laminated, thumbhole-stock 12 gauge slug gun with 3" chamber and 21" fully rifled cantilever barrel.

NIB	Exc.	V.G.	Good	Fair	Poor
700	595	500	350	225	150

Model 11-87 SPS-T Super Magnum

Similar to Model 11-87 SP Thumbhole but with pistol-grip stock and vent rib barrel.

NIB	Exc.	V.G.	Good	Fair	Poor
750	625	550	400	300	200

Model 11-87 SP-T Thumbhole

This 12 gauge with 3.5" chamber is made specifically for turkey hunting. Camouflaged in Mossy Oak Obsession with an R3 recoil pad and thumbhole stock. The 23" barrel has fiber-optic adjustable rifle sights and is drilled and tapped for scope mounting. Includes a turkey super full choke tube and sling/swivels. Introduced 2006.

NIB	Exc.	V.G.	Good	Fair	Poor
750	625	550	400	300	200

Model 11-87 Sportsman Camo

New in 2007, the camo version of the Sportsman comes in 12 and 20 gauge with 26" or 28" barrel. Finished in Mossy Oak Break-Up camo.

NIB	Exc.	V.G.	Good	Fair	Poor
750	625	550	400	300	200

Model 11-87 Sportsman Camo Rifled

Camo 12 gauge slug gun with 21" barrel and cantilever scope mount.

NIB	Exc.	V.G.	Good	Fair	Poor
750	625	550	400	300	200

Model 11-87 Sportsman Camo Youth

Youth model in 20 gauge with shorter length of pull was introduced in 2007. Weight is about 6.5 lbs.

NIB	Exc.	V.G.	Good	Fair	Poor
700	595	500	350	225	150

Remington 11-87 Sportsman Field

Semiauto shotgun chambered in 12 and 20 ga., 2-3/4- and 3-inch. Features include 26- (20) or 28-inch (12) barrel; vent rib; RemChokes (one supplied); sati-finished walnut stock and forend with fleur-de-lis pattern; dual sights; nickel-plated bolt and trigger: Suggested retail price: Starting at $845.

Remington 1187 Sportsman Camo

Similar to 1187 Sportsman Field but with synthetic stock and forend in Mossy Oak New Break-Up Camo. Price: $879.

Remington 11-87 Sportsman Super Mag Synthetic

Semiauto shotgun chambered in 12-ga. 3-1/2-inch. Features include black matte synthetic stock and forend; rubber overmolded grip panels on the stock and fore-end; black padded sling; HiViz sights featuring interchangeable light pipe; 28-inch vent-rib barrel; SuperCell recoil pad; RemChoke. Price: $859.

Remington 11-87 Sportsman Super Mag Shurshot Turkey

Similar to 11-87 Sportsman Super Mag Synthetic but with ambidextrous ShurShot pistol-grip stock; full Realtree APG HD coverage; 23-inch barrel with fully adjustable TruGlo rifle sights. Wingmaster HD Turkey Choke included. Price: $972.

Model 11-87 SPS Super Magnum Waterfowl

This 3.5" 12 gauge is finished in Mossy Oak Duck Blind camo. It has a 30" barrel and includes three chokes. Weight is 8.25 lbs.

NIB	Exc.	V.G.	Good	Fair	Poor
950	775	650	525	350	175

Model 11-87 Sportsman Super Mag ShurShot Turkey

New in 2008, this specialized turkey shotgun with ShurShot stock is a 3.5-inch-chamber 12 gauge with a 23-inch non-vent-rib barrel. It comes with fiber-optic rifle-type sights, and a synthetic stock and forend. The gun is fully covered in Realtree APG HD camo. Weight is about 7.6 lbs.

NIB	Exc.	V.G.	Good	Fair	Poor
800	695	550	450	300	175

Model 11-87 Sportsman Super Magnum Waterfowl

As above, but with full coverage in Mossy Oak Duck Blind camo and shell-holding Speedfeed stock and three choke tubes.

NIB	Exc.	V.G.	Good	Fair	Poor
850	725	595	475	325	195

Model 11-87 Sportsman ShurShot Cantilever

This dedicated slug gun in 3-inch 12-gauge features a 23-inch, fully rifled barrel with cantilever scope mount. It is matte black with synthetic stock and forend finished in Realtree Hardwoods HD camo. Weight is about 8 lbs.

NIB	*Exc.*	*V.G.*	*Good*	*Fair*	*Poor*
850	725	595	475	325	195

Model 11-96 Euro Lightweight

Introduced in 1996 this model is based on the Model 11-87 action. Two vent rib barrel lengths are offered: 26" and 28" supplied with three Rem chokes. Fine line engraving on the receiver and checkered Claro walnut stocks are standard. Blued finish. Weight is approximately 7 lbs. Made for one year only.

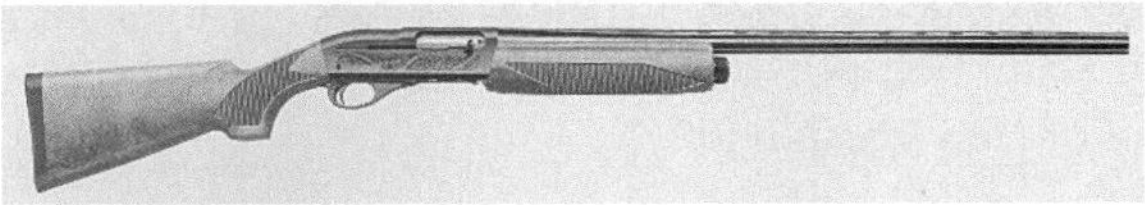

NIB	*Exc.*	*V.G.*	*Good*	*Fair*	*Poor*
1000	875	625	500	325	200

Model SP-10

A 3.5", 10 gauge semi-automatic shotgun with 26" or 30" ventilated rib barrels having screw-in choke tubes. Matte blued with a checkered walnut stock.

NIB	*Exc.*	*V.G.*	*Good*	*Fair*	*Poor*
1500	1275	950	775	600	300

Model SP-10 Magnum Camo

A new model introduced in 1993, this 10 gauge semi-automatic is designed for the turkey or deer hunter. Available with either 26" or 30" vent rib barrel or a 22" deer barrel. An additional barrel option is a 23" vent rib barrel with a camo finish. All barrels are fitted with Remington choke tubes.

NIB	*Exc.*	*V.G.*	*Good*	*Fair*	*Poor*
1550	1325	1000	825	625	325

Model SP-10 Magnum Camo NWTF 25th Anniversary

This model has a special fiber optic sighting system. The "NWTF" logo is on the left side of the receiver. Barrel length is 23". Introduced in 1998.

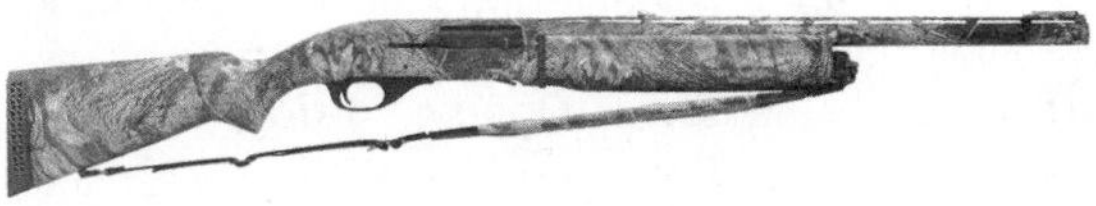

NIB	*Exc.*	*V.G.*	*Good*	*Fair*	*Poor*
1550	1325	1000	825	625	325

Model SP-10 Synthetic

This model features a black synthetic stock with 26" barrel chambered for 10 gauge shells. Matte black metal finish. Choke tubes standard. Introduced in 2000. Weight is about 10 lbs.

NIB	*Exc.*	*V.G.*	*Good*	*Fair*	*Poor*
1300	1150	900	775	575	300

Model SP-10 RC/VT

This 10 gauge gun was introduced in 2005 and is fitted with a 26" vent rib barrel with choke tubes. Mossy Oak Obsession finish. Weight is about 10.75 lbs.

NIB	*Exc.*	*V.G.*	*Good*	*Fair*	*Poor*
1300	1150	900	775	575	300

Model SP-10 Custom Grade

This Custom Shop model is available in three levels of engraving, gold inlay, wood grade and finish, metal work finish, recoil pad/buttplate, and dimensions.

Model SP-10 Magnum Waterfowl

New in 2007, this waterfowl-specific model is a synthetic-stock 3.5" 10 gauge with Mossy Oak Duck Blind camo finish and 26" barrel. Includes three Briley ported choke tubes. Weight is about 10.9 lbs.

NIB	*Exc.*	*V.G.*	*Good*	*Fair*	*Poor*
1550	1325	1000	825	625	325

Model SP-10 Magnum Thumbhole Camo

Special turkey model features a synthetic thumbhole stock and complete Mossy Oak Obsession camo finish. Barrel is 23". Briley ported turkey choke included. Weight is 10.9 lbs.

NIB	*Exc.*	*V.G.*	*Good*	*Fair*	*Poor*
1650	1500	1200	900	675	350

Model 105CTi

New in 2006, this ultralight gas-operated 12 gauge autoloader features advanced recoil reduction and bottom feed and ejection. Available with 26" or 28" barrel. Satin finish walnut stock. Chambered for 3" shells. Includes three Pro Bore chokes. Weighs about 7 lbs.

NIB	*Exc.*	*V.G.*	*Good*	*Fair*	*Poor*
1175	950	800	600	475	275

Versa Max

The Versa Max gas-operated semi-auto, shoots everything from 2-3/4-inch target loads to 3-1/2-inch magnums. Synthetic stock in black and camo finishes is fully adjustable for length-of-pull, drop-of-comb and cast. Twelve-gauge only; 26- and 28-inch barrels; 7.7 lbs. Introduced in 2011.

NIB	Exc.	V.G.	Good	Fair	Poor
1325	1150	1000	850	600	300

MODEL 11-87 SERIES

MODEL 32

A 12 gauge over-and-under shotgun with 26", 28", or 30" separated barrels and a single-selective trigger. Approximately 15,000 were made from 1932 to 1942.

Standard Grade

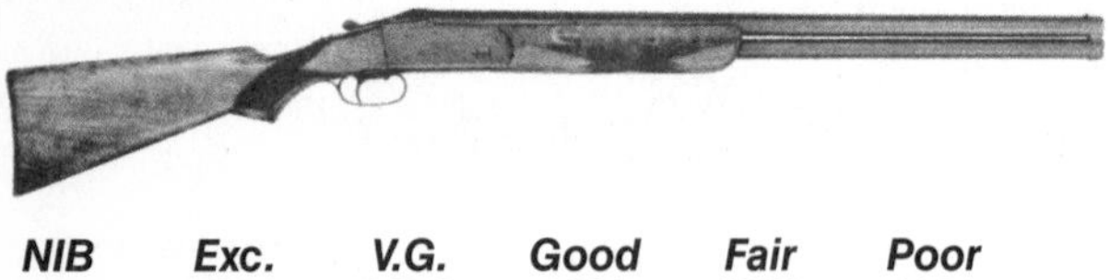

NIB	Exc.	V.G.	Good	Fair	Poor
—	2500	2250	1600	1250	1000

NOTE: Solid or vent rib add 10 percent.

Skeet

NIB	Exc.	V.G.	Good	Fair	Poor
—	2750	2250	1950	1500	1250

TC

NIB	Exc.	V.G.	Good	Fair	Poor
—	2750	2500	2250	1750	1450

TC 32D Grade

NIB	Exc.	V.G.	Good	Fair	Poor
3000	200	1100	—	—	—

TC 32F Grade

NIB	Exc.	V.G.	Good	Fair	Poor
6000	4000	2250	—	—	—

TC 32E Expert

NIB	Exc.	V.G.	Good	Fair	Poor
10000	7500	5000	—	—	—

MODEL 3200

A 12 gauge over-and-under shotgun with 26", 28", or 30" separated ventilated rib barrels, single-selective trigger, and automatic ejector. Blued with a checkered walnut stock. Manufactured from 1972 to 1984.

Field Grade

NIB	Exc.	V.G.	Good	Fair	Poor
—	800	725	600	450	300

Magnum

3" chambers.

NIB	Exc.	V.G.	Good	Fair	Poor
—	1000	850	750	550	300

Skeet

NIB	Exc.	V.G.	Good	Fair	Poor
—	1200	995	800	600	300

4-Gauge Set

NIB	Exc.	V.G.	Good	Fair	Poor
—	5500	4750	3500	2450	1500

Trap

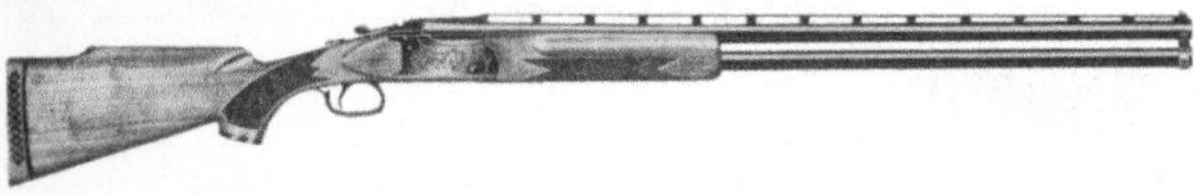

NIB	Exc.	V.G.	Good	Fair	Poor
—	1200	995	800	600	300

Special Trap

Deluxe wood.

NIB	Exc.	V.G.	Good	Fair	Poor
—	1350	1150	750	700	300

Competition Trap

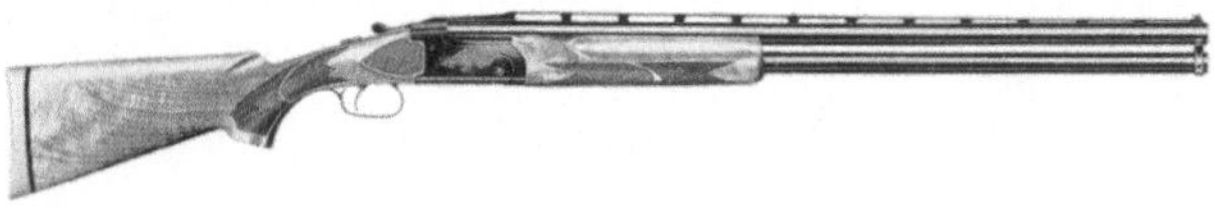

Engraved.

NIB	Exc.	V.G.	Good	Fair	Poor
—	2750	2000	1350	950	300

Premier

Heavily engraved.

NIB	Exc.	V.G.	Good	Fair	Poor
—	5500	4750	3900	—	—

"One of One Thousand"

1,000 produced.

NIB	Exc.	V.G.	Good	Fair	Poor
—	3500	3000	2500	—	—

Model 300 Ideal

This 12 gauge over-and-under shotgun, was introduced in 2000, and is offered with a choice of 26", 28", or 30" barrels. Single-selective trigger and automatic ejectors. Metal finish is blue. Stock is walnut with semi-gloss finish. Solid black recoil pad. Weight is about 7.62 lbs. for 28" barrels. Dropped from production in 2001.

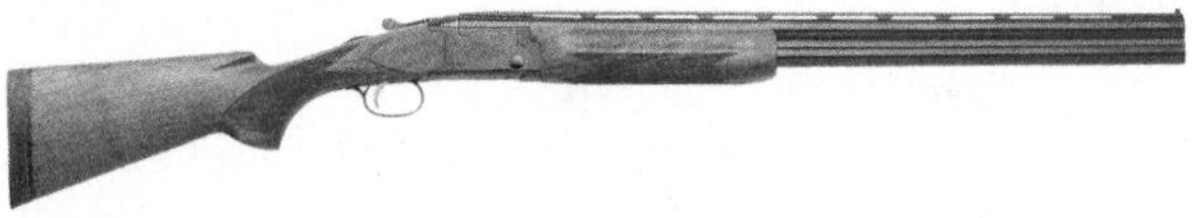

NIB	Exc.	V.G.	Good	Fair	Poor
1650	1400	1150	700	575	300

Model 90-T Single-Barrel Trap

Offered in 12 gauge only, this single-barrel Trap shotgun is fitted with either a 32" or 34" overbored Full choke barrel.

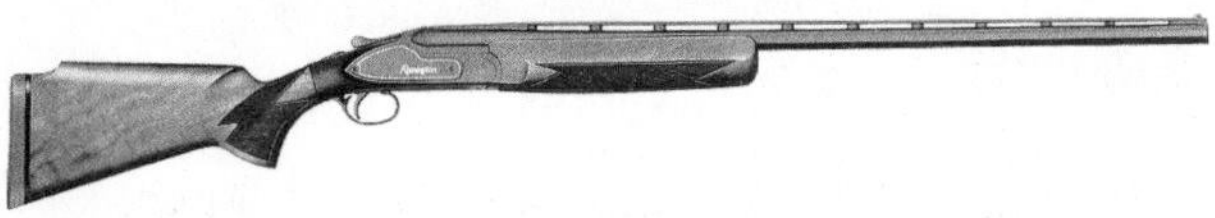

NIB	Exc.	V.G.	Good	Fair	Poor
3600	2500	1450	1100	600	300

Model 90-T Single-Barrel Trap (High Rib)

The same shotgun as described above with the exception of an adjustable high rib for shooters who prefer a more open target picture and higher head position.

NIB	Exc.	V.G.	Good	Fair	Poor
3600	2500	1450	1100	600	300

Model 332

A reintroduction, in 2002, of the famous Remington Model 32 this model features a mechanical set trigger, automatic ejectors with a choice of vent rib barrel lengths in 26", 28", and 30". Checkered walnut stock. Black oxide metal finish. Chambered for the 12 gauge with 3" chambers. Weight is about 7.75 lbs. depending on barrel length.

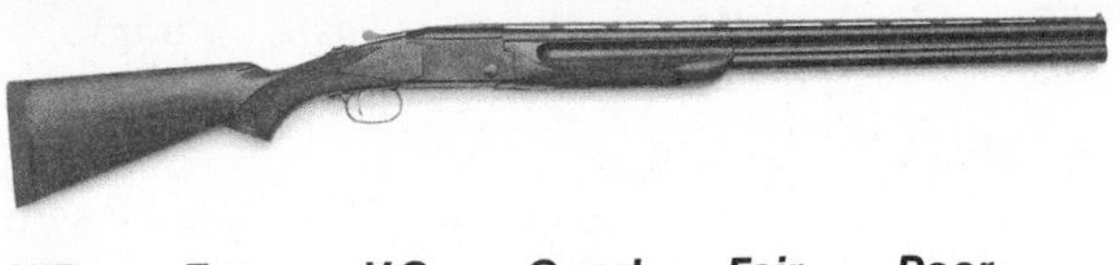

NIB	Exc.	V.G.	Good	Fair	Poor
1250	900	750	600	400	250

Remington Peerless

Introduced in 1993, this new Remington over-and-under shotgun is offered in 12 gauge only. Available in 26", 28", and 30" vent rib barrel lengths and fitted with Remington choke tubes (IC, M, F). The sideplates are removable and the stock is American walnut. Production stopped in 1998.

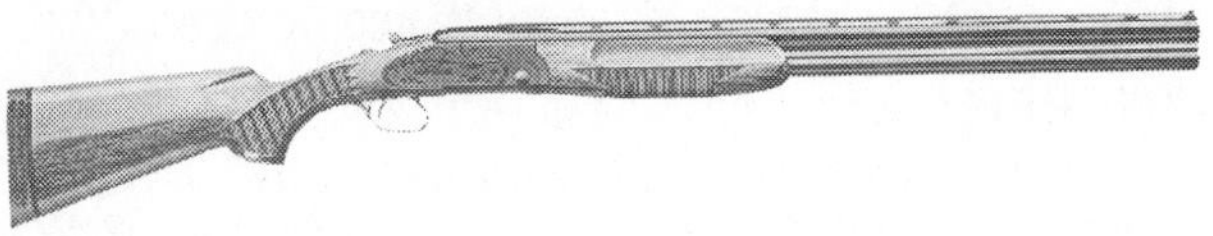

NIB	Exc.	V.G.	Good	Fair	Poor
1250	900	750	600	400	250

Model 396 Sporting

Introduced in 1996 this over-and-under shotgun is designed for sporting clays shooting. It is offered in 12 gauge only with 30" barrels. Chokes are interchangeable Rem. choke system. Fancy American stock with satin finish. Scroll engraving on the receiver and blue finish. Weight is about 8 lbs.

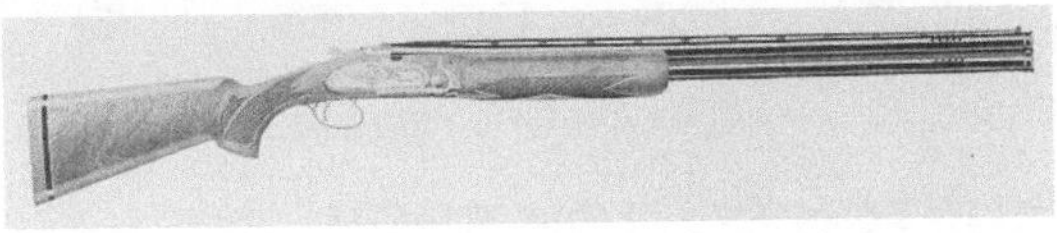

Courtesy Remington Arms

NIB	Exc.	V.G.	Good	Fair	Poor
2150	1700	1150	875	500	300

Model 396 Skeet

Same but with a choice of 28" or 30" barrels.

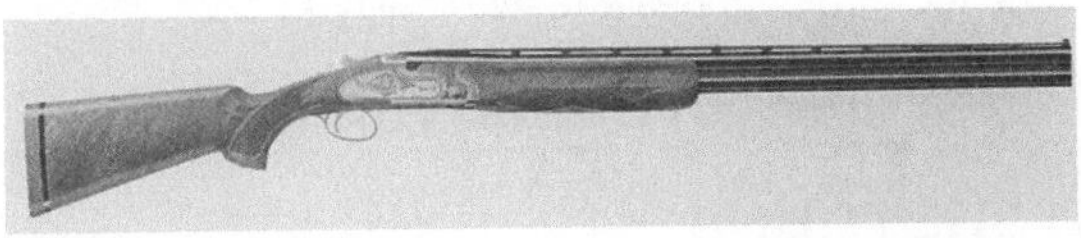

Courtesy Remington Arms

NIB	Exc.	V.G.	Good	Fair	Poor
2150	1700	1150	875	500	300

Model 396 Custom Grade

This Custom Shop model is available in three levels of engraving, gold inlay, wood grade and finish, metal work finish, recoil pad/buttplate, and dimensions. Each gun should be individually appraised prior to a sale.

PREMIER SERIES O/U

Introduced in 2006, the Italian-made over-and-unders in the Premier Series feature premium figured walnut stocks, Schnabel forends, ProBore chokes, 3" chambers (2.75" in 28 gauge) and include a hardside case.

Premier STS Competition

This 12 gauge with 28", 30" or 32" overbored barrels has an engraved, nickel-plated receiver and high-gloss finished stock. Weight is about 7.8 lbs. Add 15 percent for adjustable-stock model.

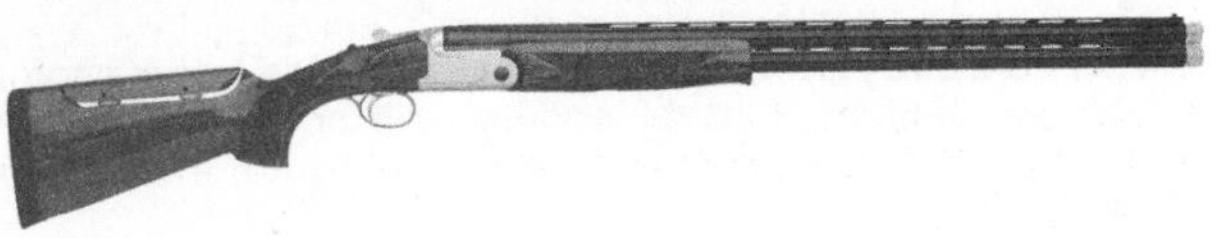

NIB	Exc.	V.G.	Good	Fair	Poor
1500	1300	950	700	550	300

Premier Field Grade

Available in 12, 20 and 28 gauges with satin finish and nickel receiver. Available with 26" or 28" barrels. Includes three flush chokes. Weight is about 6.5 lbs. for 20 and 28 gauges and 7.5 lbs. for 12 gauge.

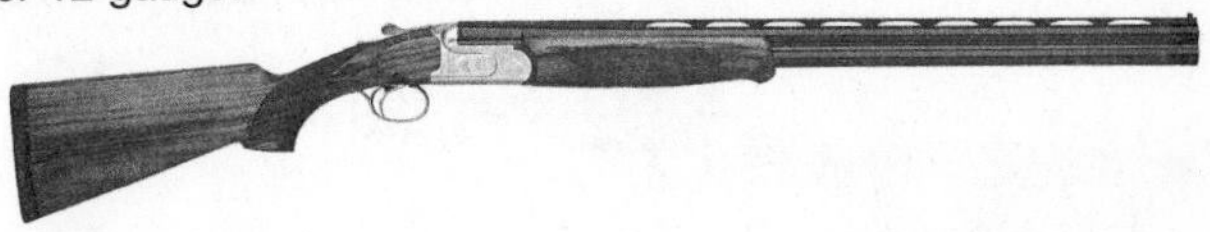

NIB	Exc.	V.G.	Good	Fair	Poor
1400	1200	900	650	500	300

Premier Upland Grade

As above but with oil finish stock and case colored receiver with gold game bird scene.

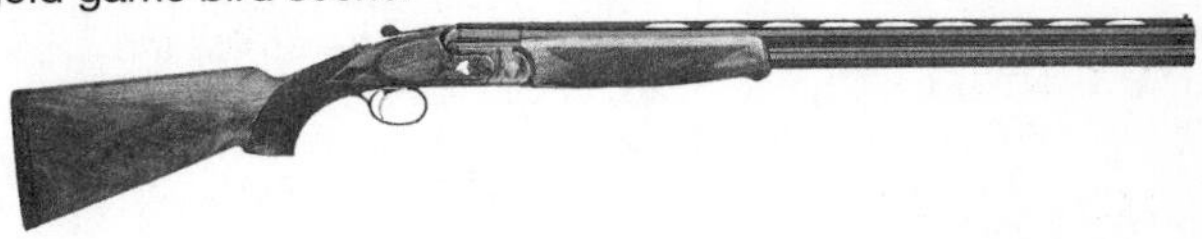

NIB	Exc.	V.G.	Good	Fair	Poor
1450	1250	900	675	525	300

Premier RGS

This special Conservation Gun of the Year in 2007 for the Ruffed Grouse Society is a 20 gauge with 26" barrels, satin oil finished stock and satin black oxide receiver. Includes five choke tubes. Weight is 6.5 lbs.

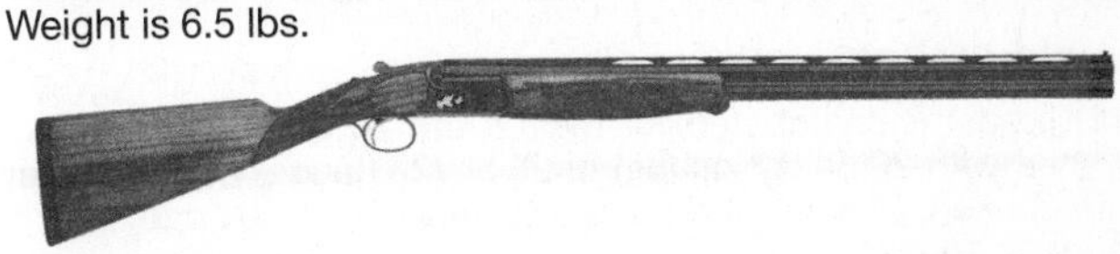

NIB	Exc.	V.G.	Good	Fair	Poor
1650	1400	1150	700	575	300

Remington Parker AAHE Double

Built to order, this side-by-side double is exact in every respect to the original Parker Brothers shotguns made from the 1860s to 1937, and again until 1942 after Remington purchased the company. In 2006, Remington with Connecticut Shotgun Mfg. Co., to build the high-grade AAHE model. It is offered in 28 gauge only with many options including stock dimensions and engraving patterns. Prices start at $49,000.

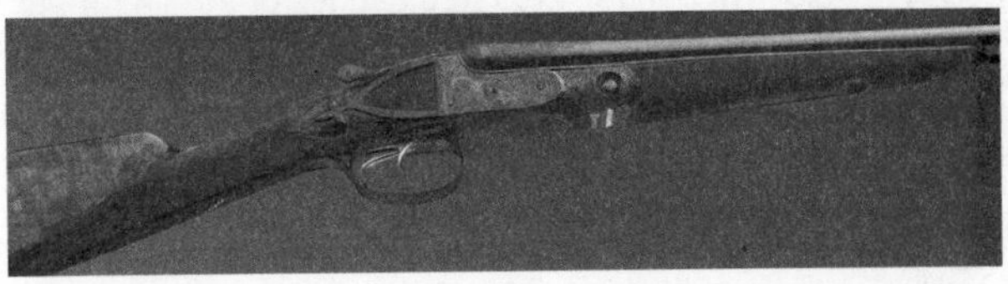

SPARTAN GUNWORKS BY REMINGTON

This line of imported firearms was introduced into the Remington line in 2004. No longer a separate brand.

Model SPR 210

This is a side-by-side gun with single-selective trigger and auto ejectors. The box lock receiver is nickel and is fitted with 26" or 28" barrels with choke tubes in 12 and 20 gauge, and fixed chokes in 28 and .410 bore. This model is also offered with 20" barrel with choke tubes and blued receiver. Checkered walnut stock with recoil pad. Weight is about 6.75 lbs. depending on gauge and barrel length.

NIB	Exc.	V.G.	Good	Fair	Poor
475	400	350	225	175	100

NOTE: Add $30 for 28 and .410 bore models.

Model SPR 220

This is a double trigger model with 20" barrels with choke tubes. Extractors. Nickel or blued receiver. Walnut stock with recoil pad. Weight is about 6.25 lbs.

NIB	Exc.	V.G.	Good	Fair	Poor
425	375	300	200	150	100

Model SPR 310

This model is an over-and-under gun chambered for the 12, 20, 28, and .410 bore. Choice of 26" or 28" vent rib barrels with choke tubes or 26" barrels for the 28 and .410. Single selective trigger and auto ejectors. Checkered walnut stock with recoil pad. Weight is about 7.5 lbs.

NIB	Exc.	V.G.	Good	Fair	Poor
475	400	350	225	175	125

Model SPR 310S

This model is chambered for the 12 and 20 gauge 3" shell and is fitted with 29.5" (12 gauge) or 28.5" (20 gauge) ported barrels with choke tubes. Checked walnut stock with recoil pad. Weight is about 7.5 lbs.

NIB	Exc.	V.G.	Good	Fair	Poor
700	600	475	350	275	200

Model SPR 100/Sporting

This is a single shot gun chambered for the 12, 20 , or .410 bore and fitted with 29.5" (12 gauge), 28.5" (20 gauge), or 26" (.410) barrel. Single trigger with ejectors or extractors. A youth model is also offered with 24" barrel chambered for the .410 bore. Checkered walnut stock with recoil pad. Weight is about 6.25 lbs.

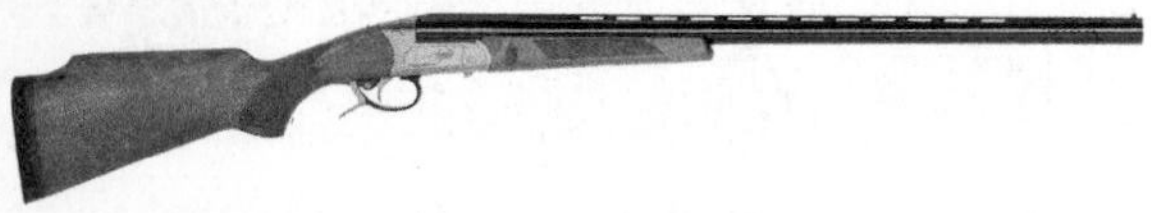

NIB	Exc.	V.G.	Good	Fair	Poor
250	175	125	100	75	50

NOTE: Add $40 for Sporting models.

Model SPR 18

This is a single shot rifle chambered for the .223, .243, .270, or .30-06 calibers. Nickel receiver. Fitted with a 23.5" barrel with iron sights. Checkered walnut stock with recoil pad. Weight is about 6.75 lbs.

NIB	Exc.	V.G.	Good	Fair	Poor
275	200	150	125	95	75

Model SPR 22

This model is a side-by-side double rifle chambered for the .30-06 or .45-70 calibers and fitted with 23.5" barrels. Blued receiver and checkered walnut stock with recoil pad. Weight is about 7.5 lbs.

NIB	Exc.	V.G.	Good	Fair	Poor
1000	825	700	575	400	250

Model SPR 94

This model features and under-and-under rifle/shotgun combination. Chambered for the .410/17HMR, .410/.22WMR, 12/.223, 12/.30-06, or 12/.308. Fitted with a 24" barrel with iron sights. Checkered walnut stock with recoil pad. Blued receiver. Weight is about 8 lbs. depending on combination.

NIB	Exc.	V.G.	Good	Fair	Poor
375	300	225	150	100	75

NOTE: Add 30 percent for centerfire models.

REMINGTON CUSTOM SHOP

The Remington Custom Shop builds a number of specialty rifles and shotguns as well as specific custom guns for its customers. Remington will build a wide number of special features from special wood type, finish, and styling options to engraving. These special order features add considerably to the cost of a gun and will affect its price. The Custom Shop can be reached at 1-800-243-9700 for current prices and availability.

REMINGTON 180TH ANNIVERSARY LIMITED EDITION RIFLES AND SHOTGUNS

Remington manufactured 180 each of these firearms to commemorate the founding of the company in 1816: Model 700, Model 7600, Model 7400, Model 870, and Model 11-87. These firearms featured fine line hand engraving with gold embellishments. The rifles were chambered for the .30-06 cartridge with 22" barrels and the shotguns were chambered for the 12 gauge shell with 26" vent rib barrels with Rem chokes. All guns had blue finishes with high gloss semi-fancy walnut stocks. If sold in a five-gun set each should have matching serial numbers. The suggested retail price for the five-gun set was $6,925 in 1996.

Individual guns carried these suggested retail prices:

Model 700 180th Anniversary Commemorative—$1,372
Model 7400 180th Anniversary Commemorative—$1,372
Model 7600 180th Anniversary Commemorative—$1,332
Model 870 180th Anniversary Commemorative—$1,305
Model 11-87 180th Anniversary Commemorative—$1,465

RENETTE, GASTINNE

Paris, France

Model 105

An Anson & Deeley action 12 or 20 gauge double-barrel shotgun available in a variety of barrel lengths, with double triggers and automatic ejectors. Blued, case hardened with a checkered walnut stock.

NIB	Exc.	V.G.	Good	Fair	Poor
—	4000	3200	2500	1700	300

Model 98

As above, except more finely finished.

NIB	Exc.	V.G.	Good	Fair	Poor
—	5200	4500	3500	2800	300

Model 202

A 12 or 20 gauge sidelock double-barrel shotgun made only on custom order. French case hardened and blued with a checkered walnut stock.

NIB	Exc.	V.G.	Good	Fair	Poor
—	9000	7000	5000	3450	300

Model 353

A custom manufactured double-barrel shotgun with detachable sidelocks. Highly finished.

NIB	Exc.	V.G.	Good	Fair	Poor
—	35000	30000	1700	8000	500

RIFLES

Type G Rifle

A .30-06, 9.3x74R, or .375 Holland & Holland double-barrel rifle with 24" barrels, express sights, double triggers and automatic ejectors. Engraved, blued with a checkered walnut stock.

NIB	Exc.	V.G.	Good	Fair	Poor
—	5500	3700	3000	2000	650

Type R Deluxe

As above, engraved with hunting scenes and with a more finely figured walnut stock.

NIB	Exc.	V.G.	Good	Fair	Poor
—	7000	5000	3400	2900	750

Type PT President

As above, inlaid in gold with extremely well figured walnut stock.

NIB	Exc.	V.G.	Good	Fair	Poor
—	8000	6400	4000	3500	950

Mauser Bolt-Action

A custom-made bolt-action rifle built on a Mauser action. Choice of calibers and stock styles. Base price listed.

NIB	Exc.	V.G.	Good	Fair	Poor
—	11000	9000	6500	3000	750

Deluxe Mauser Bolt-Action

Same as above but with fancy wood and other options.

NIB	Exc.	V.G.	Good	Fair	Poor
—	20000	14000	9000	6500	1250

REUTH, F.

Hartford, Connecticut

Animal Trap Gun

A cast iron .28 to .50 caliber percussion trap gun with either single or double-barrels 3.5" or 5" in length. This firearm fires a barbed arrow and is triggered by a cord attached to an animal trap or bait. The barrels marked "F. Reuth's Patent, May 12, 1857." Several hundred were made between 1858 and 1862.

NIB	Exc.	V.G.	Good	Fair	Poor
—	—	2000	1650	550	150

NOTE: The single-barrel model is more common than the double-barrel and is worth approximately 20 percent less.

RHEINMETALL

Sommerda, Germany

Dreyse Light Rifle or Carbine

Model 1907 in caliber 7.65 Browning. Fitted with a fixed stock and 6-round magazine.

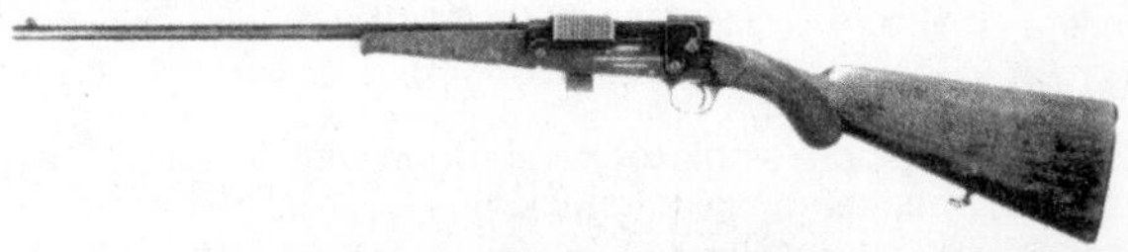

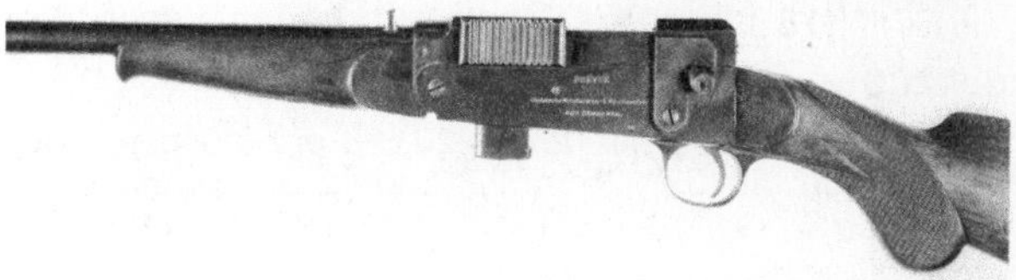

Courtesy James Rankin

NIB	Exc.	V.G.	Good	Fair	Poor
—	1850	1400	1150	700	300

RHODE ISLAND ARMS CO.

Hope Valley, Rhode Island

Morrone

A 12 or 20 gauge over-and-under boxlock shotgun with 26" or 28" barrels, single trigger and automatic ejectors. Blued with either a straight or pistol grip walnut checkered stock. 450 were made in 12 gauge and 50 in 20 gauge. Manufactured from 1949 to 1953.

NIB	Exc.	V.G.	Good	Fair	Poor
—	1700	1200	850	600	350

RICHLAND ARMS CO.

Blissfield, Michigan

This company, which ceased operation in 1986, imported a variety of Spanish-made shotguns.

Model 41 Ultra Over-and-Under

A 20, 28, or .410 bore double-barrel shotgun with 26" or 28" ventilated rib barrels, single nonselective trigger and automatic ejectors. French case hardened receiver and checkered walnut stock.

NIB	Exc.	V.G.	Good	Fair	Poor
—	300	250	200	150	100

Model 747 Over-and-Under

As above, in 20 gauge only with a single-selective trigger.

NIB	Exc.	V.G.	Good	Fair	Poor
—	425	350	300	250	175

Model 757 Over-and-Under

A Greener-style boxlock 12 gauge double-barrel shotgun with 26" or 28" ventilated rib barrels, double triggers and automatic ejectors. Finished as Model 747.

NIB	Exc.	V.G.	Good	Fair	Poor
—	300	250	200	175	125

Model 787 Over-and-Under

As above, fitted with screw-in choke tubes.

NIB	Exc.	V.G.	Good	Fair	Poor
—	450	375	325	275	200

Model 808 Over-and-Under

A 12 gauge double-barrel shotgun with 26", 28" or 30" ventilated rib barrels, single trigger and automatic ejectors. Blued with checkered walnut stock. Manufactured in Italy from 1963 to 1968.

NIB	Exc.	V.G.	Good	Fair	Poor
—	425	350	300	250	175

Model 80 LS

A 12, 20 or .410 bore single-barrel shotgun with 26" or 28" barrels. Blued with checkered walnut stock.

NIB	Exc.	V.G.	Good	Fair	Poor
—	175	125	100	80	60

Model 200

An Anson & Deeley-style 12, 16, 20, 28 or .410 bore double-barrel shotgun with 22", 26" or 28" barrels, double triggers, and automatic ejectors. Blued with a checkered walnut stock.

NIB	Exc.	V.G.	Good	Fair	Poor
—	350	300	250	200	125

Model 202

As above, with an extra set of interchangeable barrels. Imported from 1963 to 1985.

NIB	Exc.	V.G.	Good	Fair	Poor
—	325	275	225	175	100

Model 711 Magnum

As above, chambered for 3" shells and fitted with 30" or 32" barrels.

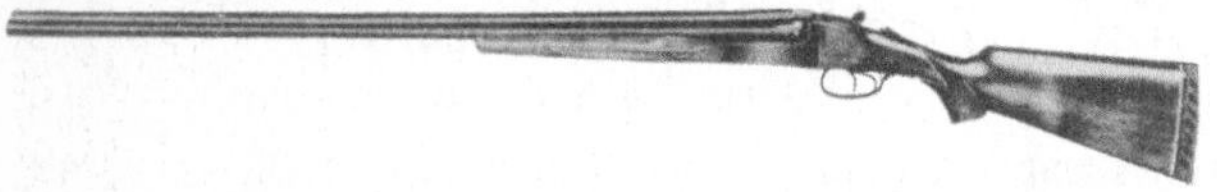

NIB	Exc.	V.G.	Good	Fair	Poor
—	350	300	250	200	150

Model 707 Deluxe

As above, more finely finished and fitted with well figured walnut stocks.

NIB	Exc.	V.G.	Good	Fair	Poor
—	350	300	250	200	150

RIEDL RIFLE CO.

Westminster, California

Single-Shot Rifle

This company produced custom order dropping block single-shot rifles in a variety of calibers and barrel lengths. Rifles were normally fitted only with telescopic or target sight bases. Blued with a checkered walnut stock. Premium for African or magnum chamberings.

NIB	Exc.	V.G.	Good	Fair	Poor
—	1750	1500	1250	750	400

RIGBY, JOHN & CO., LTD.

London, England

This company was established in the 18th century in the U.K. and has produced a wide variety of firearms over the years. It traces its roots back to 1735 in Dublin where the company was known for its percussion dueling pistols. A branch was opened in London in 1865 where some of the world's finest double rifles were made for more than 130 years, many of them made to order. In 1997 a group of investors moved the company to Paso Robles, California where production continues on a limited number of Rigby models. Current prices start at $32,000 for double rifles and $40,000 for shotguns.

RIFLES

Magazine Rifle

Utilizing a Mauser action, this rifle is available in a number of calibers, barrel lengths and with either a 3- or 5-shot magazine. Checkered walnut stock.

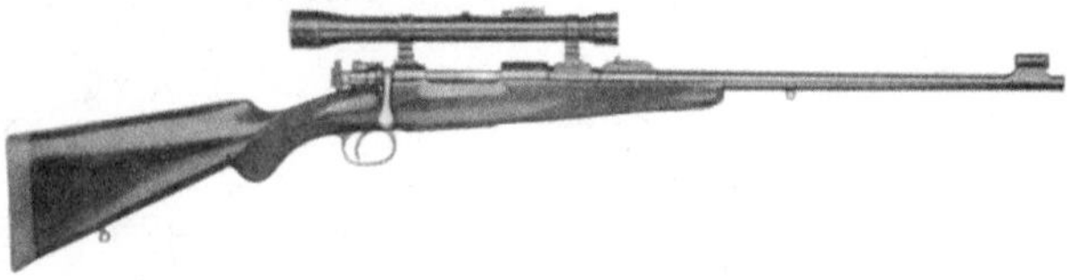

Courtesy Faintich Auction Service, Paul Goodwin photo

NIB	Exc.	V.G.	Good	Fair	Poor
—	12500	10000	7000	4000	1000

African Express Magazine Rifle

Utilizing a square bridge Mauser action, this rifle is chambered for .375 Holland & Holland, .404 Gibbs, .416 Rigby, .458 Winchester Magnum and .505 Gibbs cartridges. Barrel lengths vary from 20" to 24" and a 4-shot magazine is standard.

NIB	Exc.	V.G.	Good	Fair	Poor
—	25000	20000	15000	10000	2000

Single-Shot Rifle

Utilizing a Farquharson falling block action, this rifle is chambered for a variety of cartridges and has a 24" barrel. The receiver finely engraved and blued. Stock of well figured walnut.

NIB	Exc.	V.G.	Good	Fair	Poor
—	8000	7000	5500	2500	600

Second Quality Boxlock Double Rifle

A double-barrel rifle chambered for cartridges from .275 Magnum to .577 Nitro Express with a 24" to 28" barrel fitted with express sights. Double triggers and automatic ejectors. Blued with light engraving and a checkered walnut stock.

NIB	Exc.	V.G.	Good	Fair	Poor
—	20000	17000	11000	5500	900

Best Quality Boxlock Double Rifle

As above, but more finely engraved and with better quality walnut stocks.

NIB	Exc.	V.G.	Good	Fair	Poor
—	30000	22500	15000	7500	1000

Best Quality Sidelock Double Rifle

As above, but fitted with full sidelocks, with best bouquet engraving and finely figured walnut stocks.

NIB	Exc.	V.G.	Good	Fair	Poor
—	50000	42500	33000	15000	1500

SHOTGUNS

Sidelock Double

Offered in all gauges with choice of barrel lengths, chokes, stock dimensions, grip and fore-end styles. Double triggers and automatic ejectors. Prices shown are for Sandringham Grade. Regal Grade has higher grade wood and engraving. Made in London prior to 1998.

NIB	Exc.	V.G.	Good	Fair	Poor
9000	7500	6000	4500	3000	1000

NOTE: Add 20 percent for Regal Grade, 30 percent for 20 gauge, 40 percent for 28 or .410.

Boxlock Double

Same features and options as above except boxlock action. Prices shown are for Chatsworth Grade. Sackville Grade has higher grade wood and engraving. Made in London prior to 1998.

NIB	Exc.	V.G.	Good	Fair	Poor
4500	3700	2800	2000	1500	500

NOTE: Add 30 percent for Sackville Grade, 20 percent for 20 gauge, 30 percent for 28 or .410.

RIPOMANTI, GUY

St. Etienne, France

Side-by-Side Shotgun

A high-grade shotgun offered on a strictly made-to-order basis. There is a boxlock model that begins at $8,500 and a sidelock that is priced from $22,500. These prices rise depending on the options and embellishments desired. These guns are rarely seen on the used-gun market.

Side-by-Side Double Rifles

Extremely high-grade and basically made to order. They are rarely encountered on today's market. They have been imported since 1988. They range in price from $11,000 up.

Over-and-Under Double Rifle

A boxlock action over-and-under chambered for the 9.3x74R cartridge. The barrels are 23.5" in length and have express sights. There are double triggers and automatic ejectors. This model is highly engraved and features a high-grade, hand-checkered walnut stock.

NIB	Exc.	V.G.	Good	Fair	Poor
12500	9750	7750	5000	4000	900

RIVERSIDE ARMS CO.

Chicopee Falls, Massachusetts

SEE—Stevens, J. Arms Co.

Double-Barrel Shotguns

Brand name used by J. Stevens Arms Co. on many good quality double-barrel shotguns. Value depends on model, gauge, and condition. From $100 to $1,600. See also Stevens.

Courtesy William Hammond

RIZZINI, BATTISTA

Bresica, Italy

NOTE: There are a number of extra cost options for Rizzini guns that can greatly affect price. Extra barrels and upgraded wood are such options.

SHOTGUNS

Aurum Light

This over-and-under model features a choice of 24.5" to 27.5". Vent rib barrel. Figured oil finish walnut stock with hand checkering and pistol grip. Game scene engraved receiver. Auto ejectors and single-selective trigger. Weight is about 6 lbs.

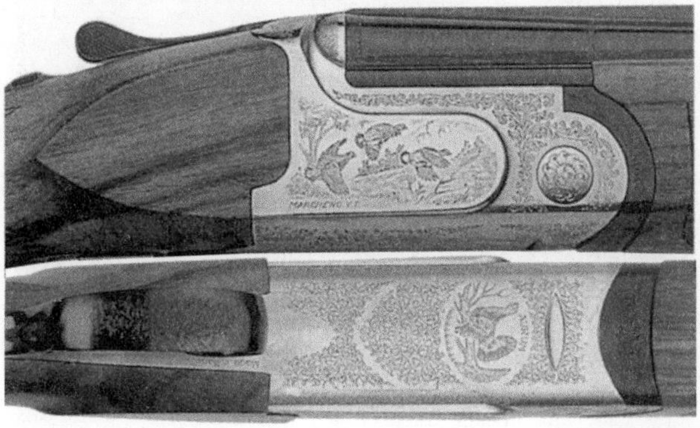

Courtesy William Larkin Moore & Co.

NIB	Exc.	V.G.	Good	Fair	Poor
2250	1650	1250	975	700	500

Artemis Classic

This model features engraved sideplates with game scenes. Offered in 12, 16, 20, 28 gauge as well as .410 bore. Barrel lengths from 24" to 27.5". Auto ejectors and single-selective trigger. Figured walnut stock with hand checkering and pistol grip. Weight is about 6 lbs.

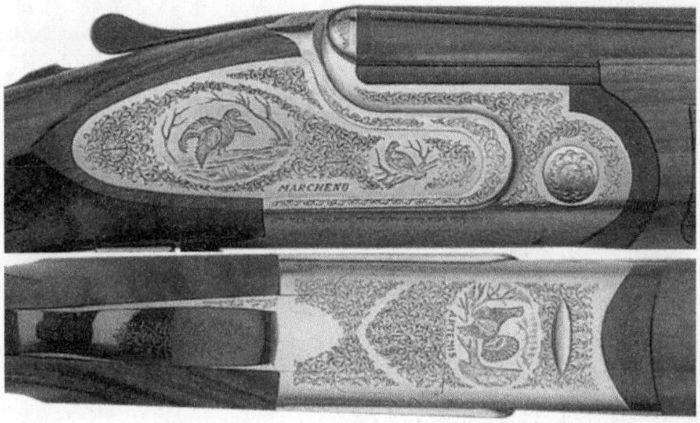

Courtesy William Larkin Moore & Co.

NIB	Exc.	V.G.	Good	Fair	Poor
3200	2700	2300	1900	1000	500

Artemis Deluxe

Similar to the standard Artemis with the addition of gold inlaid game scenes and fancy walnut stock. Cased.

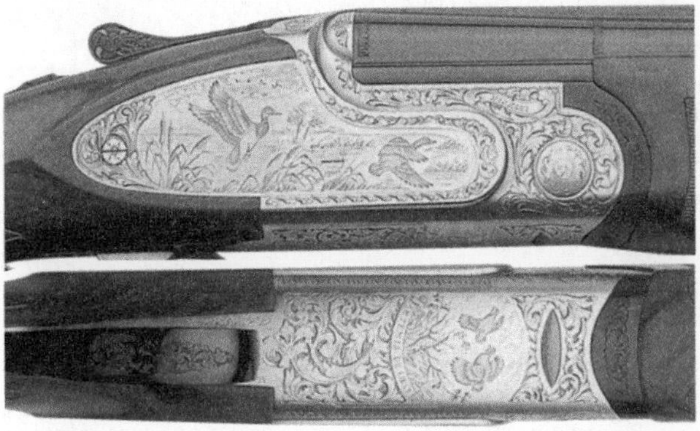

NIB	Exc.	V.G.	Good	Fair	Poor
5000	4200	3500	2500	1250	600

Artemis EL

This model features sideplates with hand engraved English scroll and game scenes. Extra fancy walnut stock. Cased.

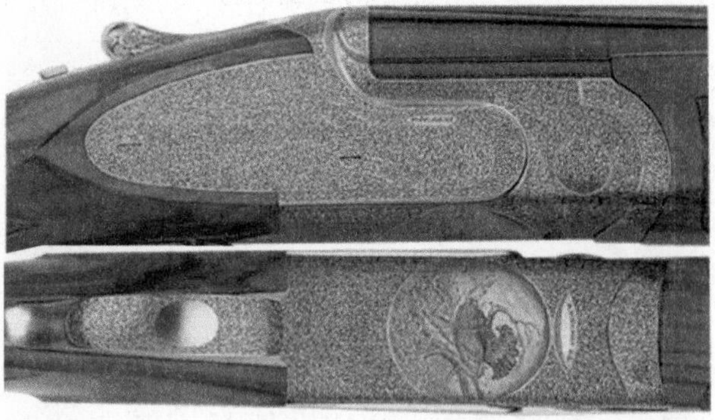

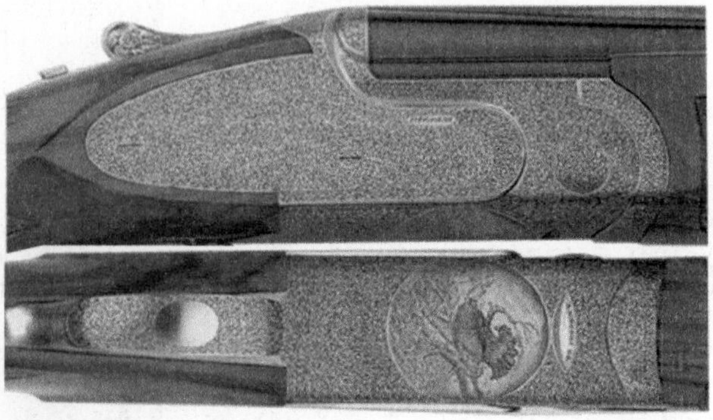

NIB	Exc.	V.G.	Good	Fair	Poor
18000	13500	10000	8000	6000	900

Upland EL

NIB	Exc.	V.G.	Good	Fair	Poor
4000	3500	3000	2500	1250	600

S780 Emel

This boxlock model is offered in 12, 16, 20, 28, or .410. Barrel lengths from 24" to 27.5". Hand engraved receiver with game scenes. Auto ejectors and single-selective trigger. Fancy walnut stock with hand checkering. Leather case. Weight for 12 gauge is about 6.8 lbs. and the smaller gauges about 6 lbs.

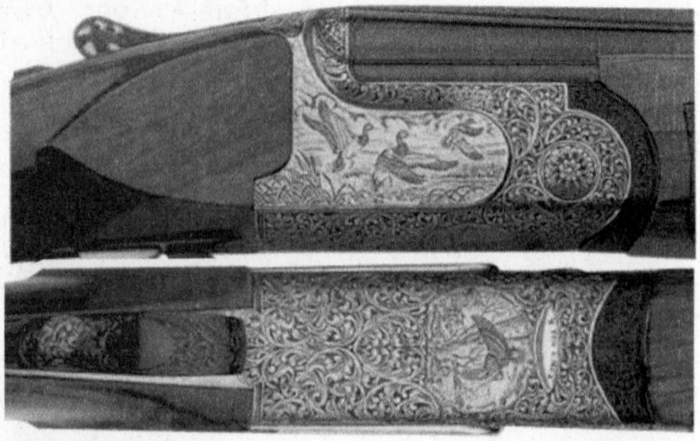

NIB	Exc.	V.G.	Good	Fair	Poor
13500	11000	8750	7000	4250	900

S782 Emel Field Classic

This model is similar to the S792 but with the addition of hand engraved gold inlaid game scenes.

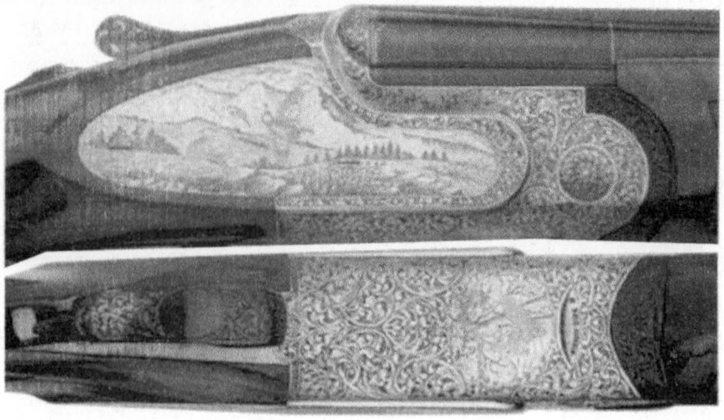

NIB	Exc.	V.G.	Good	Fair	Poor
15000	13000	10000	8750	5700	900

S790 Emel Field

This model is similar to the S780 with the exception of the engraving pattern. This model has a thistle-leaf style pattern.

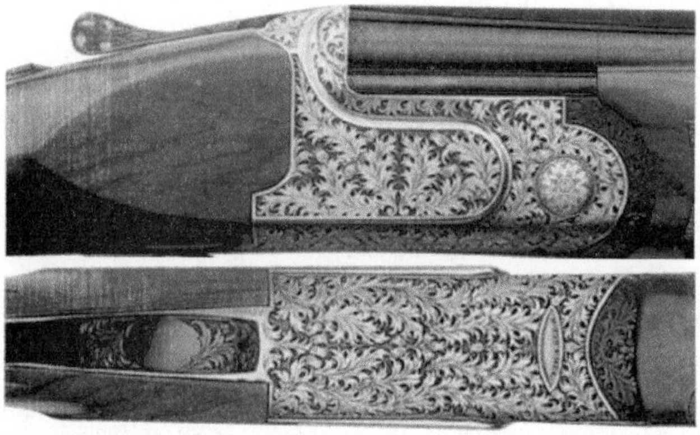

NIB	Exc.	V.G.	Good	Fair	Poor
10500	8000	6500	5000	4250	900

S792 Emel Field

This model features sideplates engraved with English scroll and game scenes. Extra select walnut stock. Available in 12, 16, 20, 28, and .410 with barrel lengths from 24" to 27.5".

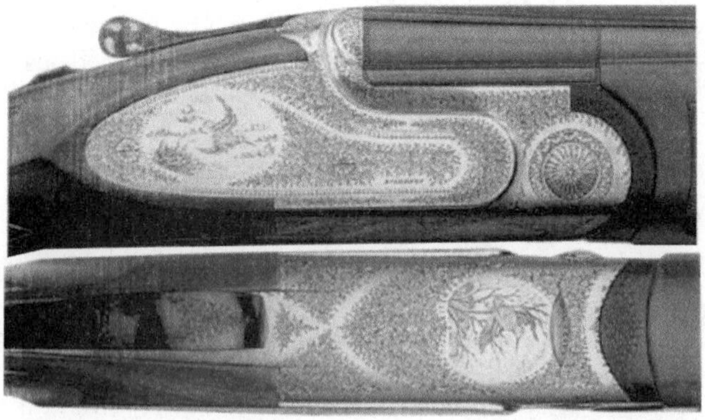

NIB	Exc.	V.G.	Good	Fair	Poor
11000	9750	8000	6750	5000	900

Premier Sporting

This model is offered in 12 or 20 gauge with choice of barrel lengths from 27.5" to 31.5". Blued boxlock action with auto ejectors and single-selective trigger. Select walnut stock with hand checkering and oil finish. Pistol grip stock and beavertail forend. Weight is about 7.5 lbs.

NIB	Exc.	V.G.	Good	Fair	Poor
3250	2750	2100	1600	900	500

Sporting EL

NIB	Exc.	V.G.	Good	Fair	Poor
3750	2800	2200	1750	975	600

S790 EL Sporting

This model is offered in 12 gauge only and choice of barrel from 27.5" to 31.5". Boxlock action with chrome plate. Auto ejectors and single-selective trigger. Pistol grip stock with fancy walnut. Weight is about 7.5 lbs.

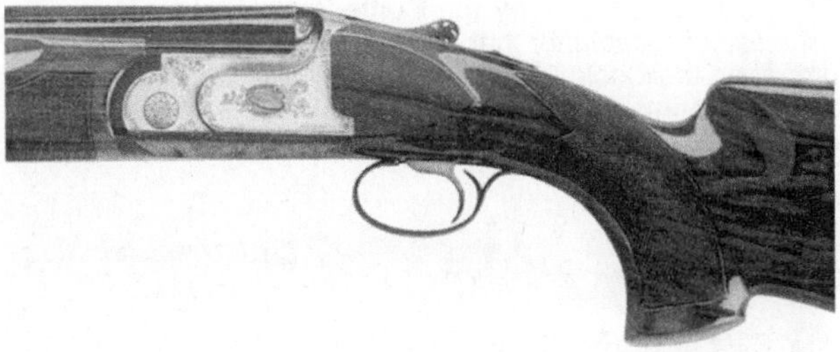

NIB	Exc.	V.G.	Good	Fair	Poor
7500	6250	5000	3750	2900	800

EXPRESS RIFLES

Express 90 L

This over-and-under rifle is chambered for the 7x65R, 8x57JRS, 9.3x74R, .30-06, .308 Win., and .444 Marlin. Barrel length is 16". Boxlock action with case colored receiver. Auto ejectors and single trigger. Pistol-grip walnut stock with Bavarian cheekpiece. Hand checkered and oil finish stock. Weight is about 8 lbs.

NIB	Exc.	V.G.	Good	Fair	Poor
4750	4250	3500	2500	1750	800

Express 92 EL

Same calibers as above model but with sideplates engraved with English scroll and game scenes. Extra select walnut stock with pistol grip and round cheekpiece.

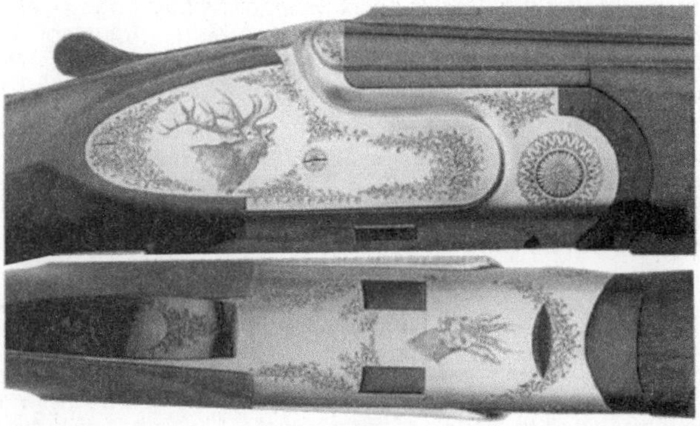

NIB	Exc.	V.G.	Good	Fair	Poor
11000	9500	8000	5500	2500	900

RIZZINI, FRATELLI

Brescia, Italy

Early guns were manufactured with Antonio Zoli. As a result, these were off-the-shelf guns of lower prices. These early guns were imported by Abercombie and Fitch of New York. Some of these guns will be stamped with the A&F address on the barrel. These side-by-side guns have a boxlock action. **NOTE:** At the present time this Italian gun company builds about 24 shotguns a year. Each gun is highly individualized for the customer. The company produces only two models. These are listed to give the reader some idea of the value of one of these models. None of these models includes the cost of engraving and multi barrel set and multi gauge sets are extra. Rizzini models with serial numbers above #1709 have their own patented action and the prices listed reflect that action. Guns listed have a H&H style action and should deduct approximately 30 percent from the prices listed.

LUSSO GRADE

12 gauge

NIB	Exc.	V.G.	Good	Fair	Poor
3200	2850	2200	1600	900	400

20 gauge

NIB	Exc.	V.G.	Good	Fair	Poor
3700	3250	2800	2200	1500	550

28 gauge and .410 bore

NIB	Exc.	V.G.	Good	Fair	Poor
4000	3600	3000	2500	1700	600

EXTRA LUSSO GRADE—SCALLOPED RECEIVER

12 gauge

NIB	Exc.	V.G.	Good	Fair	Poor
4800	4150	3250	2700	1500	700

20 gauge

NIB	Exc.	V.G.	Good	Fair	Poor
5450	4600	3500	2900	1650	700

28 gauge

NIB	Exc.	V.G.	Good	Fair	Poor
5850	4900	3750	3250	1900	700

.410 bore

NIB	Exc.	V.G.	Good	Fair	Poor
6250	5250	3900	3500	2350	750

MODEL R-1

Available in 12 to .410 bore with choice of barrels from 25" to 30". Choice of single or double trigger, pistol or straight grip, rib, barrel length and chokes are standard items on this model. This model features a Holland & Holland sidelock action.

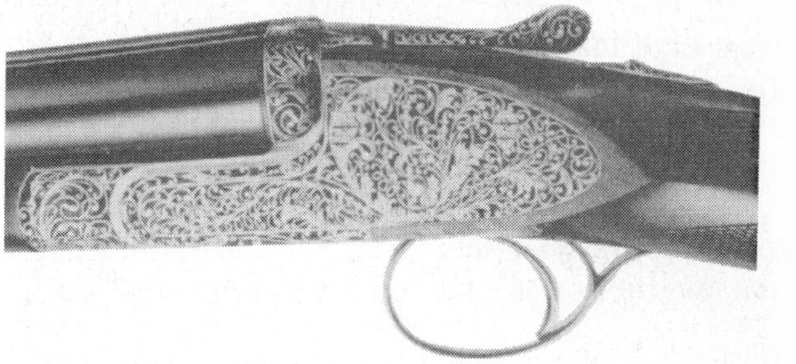

12, 16, or 20 gauge

NIB	Exc.	V.G.	Good	Fair	Poor
45000	34000	19000	—	—	—

28 gauge or .410 bore

NIB	Exc.	V.G.	Good	Fair	Poor
48500	34500	22000	—	—	—

Model R-2

This model has a boxlock action and a removable inspection plate on the bottom of the frame. The stock and forearm is fitted with Turkish Circassian walnut. Offered in 12 gauge to .410 bore.

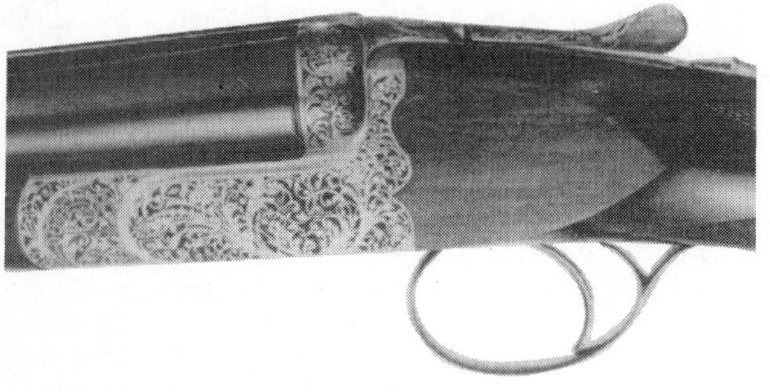

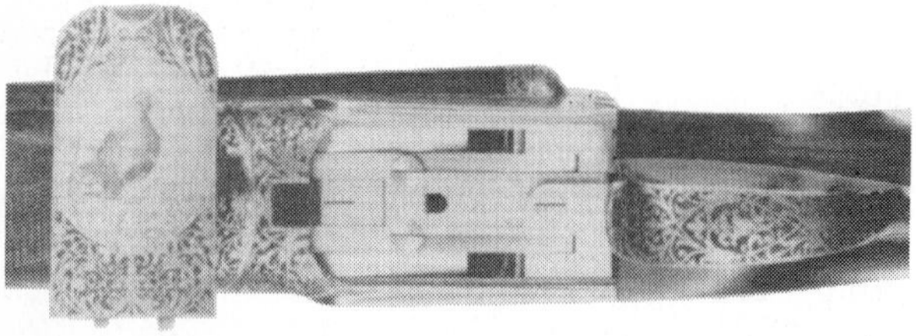

NIB	Exc.	V.G.	Good	Fair	Poor
17000	14000	1000	7500	5000	700

NOTE: Engraving extras for above models will add $8,700 for English scroll pattern and $22,000 for Fracassi style engraving. Other types of engraving are offered. Extra set of barrels in same gauge add 15 percent.

ROBAR COMPANIES

Phoenix, Arizona

This company has been building precision rifles, shotguns, and pistol since 1983.

Robar Patriot Tactical Shotgun

Built on a Remington Model 870 this model features an 18" barrel, express sights, seamless extended magazine tube, sidesaddle shell carrier, Wolff springs, etc. as well as Roguard/NP3 finish.

NIB	Exc.	V.G.	Good	Fair	Poor
765	600	500	400	300	100

Robar Spec Ops Tactical Shotgun

Similar to the model above but fitted with tactical ghost ring night sights, tactical safety, and tactical sling.

NIB	Exc.	V.G.	Good	Fair	Poor
990	800	700	600	400	100

Robar Elite Tactical Shotgun

This model features a number of special options such as Robar choke with forcing cone, modified bolt, Pachmayr pad, etc.

NIB	Exc.	V.G.	Good	Fair	Poor
1700	1350	1000	875	600	300

Robar MK I Tactical Rifle

This model is built on a Remington Model 700 action with a 24" heavy factory barrel. Chambered for the .308 or .223 cartridge. Fitted with a gray Choate Ultimate sniper stock, Robar bipod, and adjustable trigger. Roguard/MP3 finish.

NIB	Exc.	V.G.	Good	Fair	Poor
3400	2900	2250	1600	900	300

Robar MK II Tactical Rifle

As above but chambered for the .308 cartridge only. Special trigger job and special hand finish of internal parts and chamber.

NIB	Exc.	V.G.	Good	Fair	Poor
3400	2900	2250	1600	900	300

Robar SR60 Precision Rifle

This model is a fully accurized Remington Mdeol 700 action with bench rest quality barrel and chamber. Custom stock with hand bedding and pillars. Choice of .308 with 20" or 24" barrel and .223 with 24" barrel.

NIB	Exc.	V.G.	Good	Fair	Poor
3900	3500	2900	2200	1400	500

ROBINSON, S.C.

Richmond, Virginia

From December of 1862 through March 1 of 1863, S.C. Robinson produced copies of the Sharps carbine. These arms had an overall length of 38-1/2", with .52 caliber barrels 21-1/2" long. The lockplates were marked "S.C. ROBINSON/ARMS MANUFACTORY/RICHMOND VA/1862" along with the serial number. The barrels were marked forward of the rear sight "S.C. ROBINSON/ARMS MANUFACTORY," as well as "RICHMOND VA/1862" to the rear of the sight. Total number made estimated to be slightly more than 1,900.In March of 1863, the Robinson factory was taken over by the Confederate States Government. Carbines produced after that date are only stamped with the serial number on their lockplates and "RICHMOND VA" on their barrels. Total number made in excess of 3,400.

Robinson Sharps

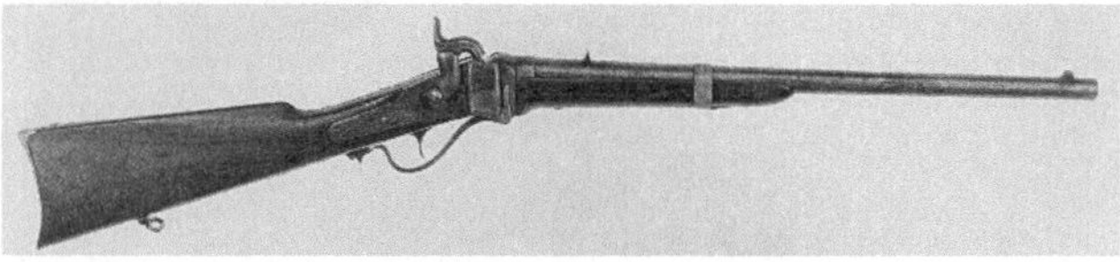

NIB	Exc.	V.G.	Good	Fair	Poor
—	—	37000	30000	9300	1500

Confederate Sharps

NIB	Exc.	V.G.	Good	Fair	Poor
—	—	32000	27500	8250	1500

ROBINSON ARMAMENT CO.

Salt Lake City, Utah

Super VEPR

This semi-automatic rifle is made in Russia and is chambered for the .308, .223, or 7.62x39mm cartridge. Uses an RPK-type receiver. Chrome lined 21.65" barrel. Walnut thumbhole stock. Black oxide finish. Weight is about 8.5 lbs.

NIB	Exc.	V.G.	Good	Fair	Poor
1200	800	675	500	400	200

M-96 Expeditonary Rifle

Chambered for the .223 or 7.62x39mm cartridge. Can use either AK or AR magazines. With quick-change barrel. Adjustable gas operating system. Can interchange calibers without tools. Built in the U.S.A.

NIB	Exc.	V.G.	Good	Fair	Poor
1750	1400	1100	800	575	300

M-96 Carbine

As above but with shorter barrel.

NIB	Exc.	V.G.	Good	Fair	Poor
1750	1400	1100	800	575	300

M-96 Top Fed

This model has the same specifications as the rifle but with the magazine fitted to the top of the receiver.

NIB	Exc.	V.G.	Good	Fair	Poor
1900	1550	1175	900	625	350

ROCK RIVER ARMS, INC.

Colona, Illinois

RIFLES

CAR A2

These are AR-15-style rifles chambered for the .223 cartridge. Fitted with a 16" barrel with CAR handguards. Two stage trigger. Choice of A2 or non-collapsible buttstock. Choice of black or green furniture. Weight is about 7 lbs.

NIB	Exc.	V.G.	Good	Fair	Poor
925	750	600	500	375	200

NOTE: Add $25 for non-collapsible buttstock.

CAR A2M

Same as above but with mid-length handguard.

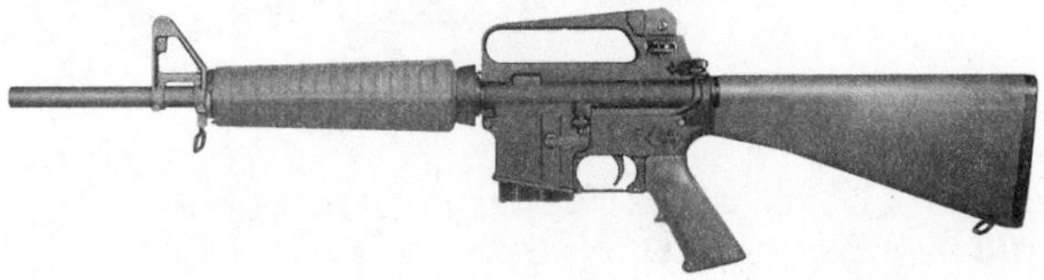

NIB	Exc.	V.G.	Good	Fair	Poor
925	750	600	500	375	200

NOTE: Add $25 for non-collapsible buttstock.

CAR A4

Similar to the models above but with flattop receiver and CAR handguard.

NIB	Exc.	V.G.	Good	Fair	Poor
925	750	600	500	375	200

NOTE: Add $25 for non-collapsible buttstock.

CAR A4M

Flattop receiver with mid-length handguard.

NIB	Exc.	V.G.	Good	Fair	Poor
925	750	600	500	375	200

NOTE: Add $25 for non-collapsible buttstock.

Standard A2

The AR-15-style rifle is fitted with a 20" barrel and chambered for the .223 cartridge. Two stage trigger. Fixed stock and full-length hand guard. Weight is about 8.2 lbs.

NIB	Exc.	V.G.	Good	Fair	Poor
925	750	600	500	375	200

National Match A2

This model features a .22 Wylde chamber with a 20" Wilson air-gauged match stainless steel barrel. A2 receiver. Two stage trigger. Free float high tempeture thermo mold handguard. Match sights. Weight is about 9.7 lbs.

NIB	Exc.	V.G.	Good	Fair	Poor
1265	950	800	650	500	300

Standard A4 Flattop

Same as Standard A2 but with flattop receiver.

NIB	Exc.	V.G.	Good	Fair	Poor
925	750	600	500	375	200

Varmint Rifle

This flattop model is fitted with a 24" stainless steel barrel without sights. Chambered for the .223 cartridge. Fixed stock. Two-stage trigger. Weight is about 9.5 lbs.

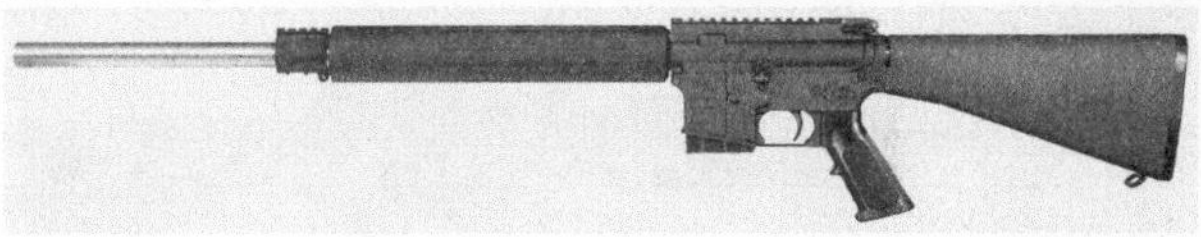

NIB	Exc.	V.G.	Good	Fair	Poor
1050	875	600	475	375	200

Varmint EOP (Elevated Optical Platform)

Chambered for the .223 with a Wylde chamber and fitted with a Wilson air-gauged bull stainless steel barrel. Choice of 16", 18", 20", and 24" barrel lengths. Free float aluminum handguard. National Match two stage trigger. Weight is about 8.2 lbs with 16" barrel and 10 lbs with 24" barrel.

NIB	Exc.	V.G.	Good	Fair	Poor
1050	875	600	475	375	200

NOTE: Add $10 for each barrel length over 16".

Advanced Hunter

Chambered for 5.56/.223 Remington. Carbine-style adjustable stock, 18-inch cryogenically treated stainless steel barrel with tactical muzzle brake. Half-quad free-floating mid-length hand guard, winter designed trigger guard, two-stage trigger. Numerous options. Introduced in 2011.

NIB	Exc.	V.G.	Good	Fair	Poor
1100	1000	850	700	400	250

NM A2-DCM Legal

Fitted with a 20" stainless steel barrel with National Match sleeve and specially selected upper and lower to ensure tight fit. Special high temp handguards. Two-stage trigger. National Match sights. Weight is about 9 lbs.

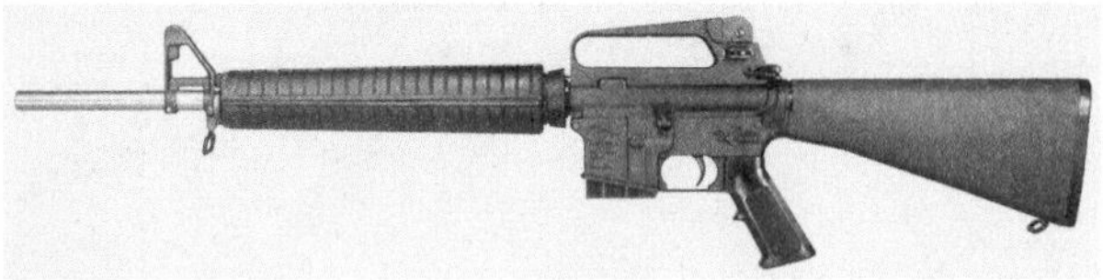

NIB	Exc.	V.G.	Good	Fair	Poor
1200	1000	825	600	450	200

Government Model

Chambered for the .223 cartridge and fitted with a 16" Wilson chrome barrel with A2 flash hider. Nation Match two stage trigger. A4 upper receiver. Flip-up rear sight. EOTech M951 light syatem. Surefire M73 Quad Rail handguard, and 6 position tactical CAR stock. Weight is about 8.2 lbs.

NIB	Exc.	V.G.	Good	Fair	Poor
2310	1750	1150	800	575	350

Tactical CAR A4

This .223 caliber rifle has a 16" Wilson chrome barrel with A2 flash hider. A4 upper receiver with detachable carry handle. Two stage National Match trigger. R-4 handguard. Six position tactical CAR stock. Weight is about 7.5 lbs.

NIB	Exc.	V.G.	Good	Fair	Poor
950	800	650	500	350	200

Elite CAR A4

As above but with mid-length handguard. Weight is about 7.7 lbs.

NIB	Exc.	V.G.	Good	Fair	Poor
950	800	650	500	350	200

Tactical CAR UTE (Universal Tactical Entry) 2

This .223 caliber rifle has a 16" Wilson chrome barrel with A2 flash hider. It has a R-2 handguard. The upper receiver is a UTE2 with standard A4 rail height. Two stage trigger and 6 position CAR tactical stock. Weight is about 7.5 lbs.

NIB	Exc.	V.G.	Good	Fair	Poor
950	800	650	500	350	200

Elite CAR UTE 2

As above but with mid-length handguard. Weight is about 7.7 lbs.

NIB	Exc.	V.G.	Good	Fair	Poor
950	800	650	500	350	200

Entry Tactical

This .223 model features a 16" Wilson chrome barrel with a R-4 profile. A4 upper receiver with detachable carry handle. National Match two stage trigger. Six position tactical CAR stock. R-4 handguard. Weight is about 7.5 lbs.

NIB	Exc.	V.G.	Good	Fair	Poor
950	800	650	500	350	200

TASC Rifle

This rifle features a 16" Wilson chrome barrel with A2 flash hider. A2 upper receiver with windage and elevation rear sight. R-4 handguard. A2 buttstock. Weight is about 7.5 lbs.

NIB	Exc.	V.G.	Good	Fair	Poor
925	750	600	500	375	200

ROGUE RIVER RIFLEWORKS

Paso Robles, California

Boxlock Double Rifle

These rifles are custom fitted and available in any barrel length or caliber from .22 Hornet to .577 NE. Anson & Deeley boxlocks. Choice of finish, forend, engraving, wood, and various other options. Each rifle should be appraised individually before a sale. Prices listed are for basic rifle with no extras.

NIB	Exc.	V.G.	Good	Fair	Poor
17500	15000	12000	9500	5000	900

Sidelock Double Rifle

These rifles are custom fitted and available in any barrel length or caliber from .22 Hornet to .577 NE. Holland & Holland pattern sidelocks. Choice of finish, forend, engraving, wood, and various other options. Each rifle should be appraised individually before a sale. Prices listed are for basic rifle with no extras.

NIB	Exc.	V.G.	Good	Fair	Poor
50000	42500	30000	17000	7500	900

ROSS RIFLE CO.

Quebec, Canada

Designed in 1896 by Sir Charles Ross, this straight pull rifle was manufactured in a variety of styles. Due to problems with the bolt design, it never proved popular and was discontinued in 1915.

Mark 1

Barrel length 28", .303 caliber with a "Harris Controlled Platform Magazine" that can be depressed by an external lever to facilitate loading.

Courtesy Buffalo Bill Historical Center, Cody, Wyoming

NIB	Exc.	V.G.	Good	Fair	Poor
—	700	550	400	175	100

Mark 1 Carbine

As above, with a 22" barrel.

NIB	Exc.	V.G.	Good	Fair	Poor
—	650	500	350	150	75

Mark 2

As above, with a modified rear sight.

NIB	Exc.	V.G.	Good	Fair	Poor
—	650	500	350	150	75

Mark 3

Introduced in 1910 with improved lockwork and stripper clip guides.

Courtesy Buffalo Bill Historical Center, Cody, Wyoming

NIB	Exc.	V.G.	Good	Fair	Poor
—	1200	875	675	375	175

Mark 3B

As above, with a magazine cut-off.

NIB	Exc.	V.G.	Good	Fair	Poor
—	650	500	350	150	75

Sporting Rifle

A .280 Ross or .303 caliber straight pole sporting rifle with a 24" barrel and open sights. Blued with a checkered walnut stock.

Courtesy Buffalo Bill Historical Center, Cody, Wyoming

NIB	Exc.	V.G.	Good	Fair	Poor
—	950	650	400	150	125

ROSSI, AMADEO

São Leopoldo, Brazil

SHOTGUNS

Overland Shotgun

An exposed hammer sidelock 12, 20 or .410 bore double-barrel shotgun with 26" or 28" barrels and double triggers. Manual extractors. Blued with a walnut stock. Discontinued in 1988.

NIB	Exc.	V.G.	Good	Fair	Poor
250	225	200	150	100	75

Squire Shotgun

A 12, 20 or .410 bore double-barrel shotgun with 20", 26", or 28" barrels, double triggers and manual ejectors. Blued with a walnut stock.

NIB	Exc.	V.G.	Good	Fair	Poor
350	300	250	200	150	100

Field Grade Shotgun

This is a single-shot tip-open gun with oil-finish hardwood stock, low profile hammer, and pistol grip. No checkering. Offered in 12 and 20 gauge, as well as .410 bore. Barrel length is 28". Weight is about 5.25 lbs. for 12 and 20 gauge and 4 lbs. for the .410 bore.

NIB	Exc.	V.G.	Good	Fair	Poor
115	75	50	25	—	10

Youth Model Shotgun

Same as above but with shorter length of pull and 22" barrel. Offered in 20 gauge and .410 bore only. Weight for 20 gauge is about 5 lbs. and 3.75 lbs. for the .410 bore.

NIB	Exc.	V.G.	Good	Fair	Poor
115	75	50	25	—	10

Matched Pair Combo Guns

This model matches a single-barrel shotgun with a .22 LR barrel. Offered in 12/.22, 20/.22, and .410/.22. Adjustable sights on the rifle barrel. Blued finish.

NIB	Exc.	V.G.	Good	Fair	Poor
165	125	100	65	50	25

Stainless Matched Pair Combo Guns

Similar to above but with stainless barrel/receiver. Introduced 2008.

NIB	Exc.	V.G.	Good	Fair	Poor
200	165	125	100	75	50

Trifecta

Similar to Matched Pair with a black synthetic stock and blued barrel; includes easily interchangeable .243 Winchester or .44 Magnum, .22 Long Rifle, and 20-gauge barrels.

NIB	Exc.	V.G.	Good	Fair	Poor
300	250	200	150	100	75

Turkey Gun

Introduced in 2008. A specialized version of Roosi's 12-ga. single-shot shotgun. Features a 3-1/2 inch chamber, fiber optic sights, drilled and tapped barrel, included scope mount base and a removable Briley™ Extended Turkey Choke.

NIB	Exc.	V.G.	Good	Fair	Poor
200	165	125	100	75	50

Rossi Circuit Judge

Revolving shotgun chambered in .410 (2-1/2- or 3-inch/.45 Colt. Based on Taurus Judge handgun. Features include 18.5-inch barrel; fiber optic front sight; 5-round cylinder; hardwood Monte Carlo stock.

NIB	Exc.	V.G.	Good	Fair	Poor
600	—	—	—	—	—

RIFLES

Model 62

A copy of the Winchester Model 62 rifle with either 16.5" or 23" round or octagonal barrels. Blued or stainless steel with a walnut stock. Imported from 1988 to 1998.

NIB	Exc.	V.G.	Good	Fair	Poor
200	165	125	100	75	50

Model 92

A copy of the Winchester Model 1892, chambered for .357 Magnum, .44 Magnum, .45 Colt or .44-40 with either a 16" or 20" barrel. Blued with a walnut stock. The engraved version of this model is worth approximately 20 percent more than the values listed.

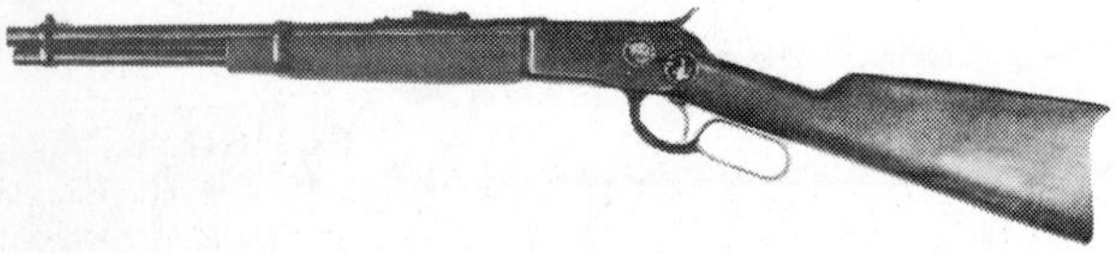

NIB	Exc.	V.G.	Good	Fair	Poor
475	350	295	225	175	100

NOTE: Add $75 for stainless steel version introduced in 1997.

Model 92 Rifle

Introduced in 1997 this model is fitted with a 24" half octagon barrel and brass blade front sight. Magazine capacity is 13 rounds of .45 Colt. Weight is about 6.8 lbs.

NIB	Exc.	V.G.	Good	Fair	Poor
500	375	325	250	200	125

Rossi Rio Grande

Variation of the Model 92 chambered for the .45-70 plus the .410-bore shotshell. Side ejection and hammer extension allow a scope to be mounted easily. Scope-mounting rail is atop the receiver. Barrel is 20-inches with adjustable rear open sight, bead front. Hardwood stock with recoil pad. Cross bolt safety.

NIB	Exc.	V.G.	Good	Fair	Poor
500	400	350	275	200	100

SHOTGUNS

RIFLES

Model 92 Large Loop

This model has a 16" barrel and is chambered for the .44 Magnum or .45 Colt cartridge. Weight is about 5.5 lbs. Finish is blue. Introduced in 1997.

NIB	Exc.	V.G.	Good	Fair	Poor
475	350	295	225	175	100

Model 65

Similar to the Model 92, but chambered for either the .44 Special or .44 Magnum cartridge. Barrel length 20". Blued with a walnut stock. Introduced in 1989.

NIB	Exc.	V.G.	Good	Fair	Poor
500	375	325	250	200	125

Single-Shot Rifle

Offered in a variety of configurations and chambered for the .22 LR, .22 Magnum, .357 Magnum, .44 Magnum, .45 Colt, .223 Rem., and .243 calibers. Fitted with 23" barrel with wood stock and choice of matte blue or stainless steel finish. Weight varies from 4.75 lbs. to 6.25 lbs. depending on caliber.

NIB	Exc.	V.G.	Good	Fair	Poor
225	175	125	100	75	50

NOTE: For stainless steel add $30, for .357 and .44 add $10. For .223 or .243 add $30.

Single Shot Rifle—Heavy Barrel

Chambered for the .223, .243, and .22-250. This rifle is fitted with a 23" heavy barrel with plain wood stock. Matte blue finish. Weight is about 7 lbs. introduced in 2005.

NIB	Exc.	V.G.	Good	Fair	Poor
230	175	125	100	75	50

Rossi Blued Synthetic Matched Pair

Single-shot combo outfit consisting of interchangeable rifle and shotgun barrels. Synthetic stock, blued barrel and receiver. Combinations include 12 or 20 ga./.22LR, .22 WMR, .17 HMR, .223, .243, .270, .308, .30-06 and .410/.22 LR or .410/.17 HMR. Youth and full-size versions available.

NIB	Exc.	V.G.	Good	Fair	Poor
250	200	150	100	75	50

Rossi Stainless Synthetic Matched Pair

Single-shot combo outfit consisting of interchangeable rifle and shotgun barrels. Synthetic stock, stainless barrel and receiver. Combinations include 12 or 20 ga./.22LR, .22 WMR, .17 HMR, .223, .243, .270, .308, .30-06 and .410/.22 LR or .410/.17 HMR. Youth and full-size versions available.

NIB	Exc.	V.G.	Good	Fair	Poor
275	225	165	115	90	50

Rossi Wizard

Single shot rifle chambered in 23 different rimfire/centerfire/shotshell/muzzleloading configurations. Featured include drop-barrel action; quick, toolless barrel interchangeability; fiber optic front sight; adjustable rear sight with barrel-mounted optics rail; hardwood or camo Monte Carlo stock.

NIB	Exc.	V.G.	Good	Fair	Poor
225	200	175	150	110	80

Rossi Ranch Hand

Based upon Rossi's R92 lever-action rifle. Calibers: .38/.357, .44 Magnum or .45 Colt. Barrel length is 12-inches, overall length 24-inches, weight 4.9 pounds (empty). Large loop lever, 6-round tubular magazine, shortened hardwood buttstock. Open buckhorn rear sight, bead front. Blue or case-hardened carbon steel receiver with saddle ring.

NIB	Exc.	V.G.	Good	Fair	Poor
450	400	325	250	200	100

ROTTWEIL
Rottweil, West Germany

Model 650

A 12 gauge over-and-under shotgun with 28" ventilated rib barrels, screw-in choke tubes, single-selective trigger, and automatic ejectors. The receiver is engraved and case hardened. Checkered stock of well figured walnut. Imported prior to 1987.

NIB	Exc.	V.G.	Good	Fair	Poor
—	900	700	550	425	150

Model 72

A 12 gauge over-and-under shotgun with 28" ventilated rib barrels, screw-in choke tubes, single-selective trigger and automatic ejectors. Blued with a well figured checkered walnut stock. Imported prior to 1988.

NIB	Exc.	V.G.	Good	Fair	Poor
—	2200	1550	975	650	350

Model 72 American Skeet

As above, with a 26.75" ventilated rib barrel, single-selective trigger, and automatic ejectors. The receiver is also engraved. Imported prior to 1988.

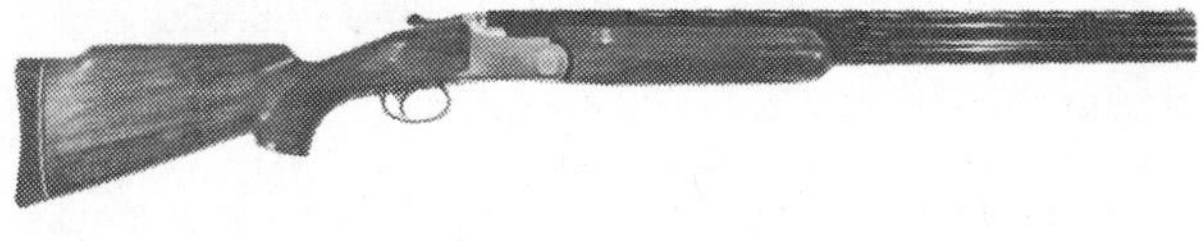

NIB	Exc.	V.G.	Good	Fair	Poor
—	2200	1550	975	650	350

Model 72 Adjustable American Trap

As above, with a 34" ventilated rib barrel, adjustable to point of impact. Imported prior to 1987.

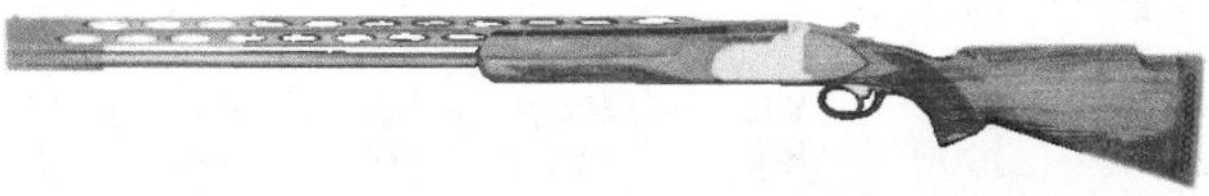

NIB	Exc.	V.G.	Good	Fair	Poor
—	2200	1550	975	650	350

Model 72 American Trap

As above, without the barrel being adjustable to the point of impact.

NIB	Exc.	V.G.	Good	Fair	Poor
—	2100	1450	875	550	300

Model 72 International Skeet

As above, with 26.75" ventilated rib barrels choked Skeet. Imported prior to 1988.

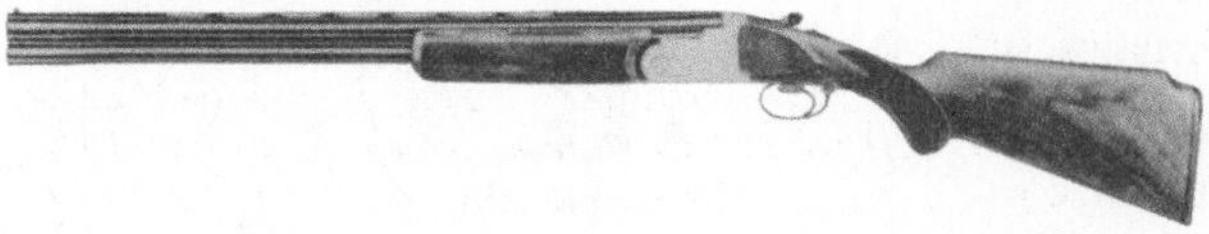

NIB	Exc.	V.G.	Good	Fair	Poor
—	2100	1450	875	550	300

Model 72 International Trap

As above, with 30" high ventilated rib barrels that are choked Improved Modified and Full. Imported prior to 1988.

NIB	Exc.	V.G.	Good	Fair	Poor
—	2100	1450	875	550	300

ROYAL AMERICAN SHOTGUNS
Woodland Hills, California

Model 100

A 12 or 20 gauge over-and-under shotgun with 26", 28", or 30" ventilated rib barrels, double triggers and extractors. Blued with a walnut stock. Imported from 1985 to 1987.

NIB	Exc.	V.G.	Good	Fair	Poor
—	550	375	250	175	150

Model 100AE

As above, with a single trigger and automatic ejectors.

NIB	Exc.	V.G.	Good	Fair	Poor
—	650	475	275	200	175

Model 600

A 12, 20, 28 or. 410 bore double-barrel shotgun with 25", 26", 28", or 30" ventilated rib barrels, double triggers and extractors. Blued with a walnut stock. Imported from 1985 to 1987.

NIB	Exc.	V.G.	Good	Fair	Poor
—	600	425	300	200	175

Model 800

A 28 or .410 bore detachable sidelock double-barrel shotgun with 24", 26", or 28" barrels, double triggers and automatic ejectors. Blued, French case hardened with an English-style walnut stock. Imported from 1985 to 1987.

NIB	Exc.	V.G.	Good	Fair	Poor
—	1550	1200	900	675	400

RWS
Nurenberg, Germany
Dynamit Nobel

Model 820 S

A .22 caliber target rifle with 24" heavy barrel and adjustable aperture sights. The trigger is fully adjustable. Three-position adjustable match stock with stippled pistol grip and forend. Discontinued in 1986.

NIB	Exc.	V.G.	Good	Fair	Poor
1650	1275	975	625	450	250

Model 820 SF

As above with a heavier barrel. Discontinued in 1986.

NIB	Exc.	V.G.	Good	Fair	Poor
1700	1350	1000	550	400	250

Model 820 K

Offhand "Running Boar" model of the above with a lighter barrel. Furnished without sights. Discontinued in 1986.

NIB	Exc.	V.G.	Good	Fair	Poor
1700	1350	1000	550	400	250

S

S.A.E.
Miami, Florida

S.A.E. was an importer of Spanish shotguns, some of very fine quality. The most notable of these is the S.A.E. line of Sarasqueta shotguns from Eibar, Spain. Not all S.A.E. shotguns are marked with the maker's name.

Model 210S

A 12, 20 or .410 bore double-barrel shotgun with 26" or 28" barrels, double triggers and manual extractors. Blued, French case hardened with a checkered walnut stock. Imported in 1988.

NIB	*Exc.*	*V.G.*	*Good*	*Fair*	*Poor*
—	475	395	300	225	150

Model 340X

A Holland & Holland-style sidelock 10 or 20 gauge double-barrel shotgun with 26" barrels, double triggers and automatic ejectors. Blued, case hardened with a checkered English style walnut stock. Imported in 1988.

NIB	*Exc.*	*V.G.*	*Good*	*Fair*	*Poor*
—	850	675	500	400	200

Model 209E

As above, with the exception that it was also chambered for .410 bore cartridges, and was more finely engraved. Imported in 1988.

NIB	*Exc.*	*V.G.*	*Good*	*Fair*	*Poor*
—	1100	850	700	550	250

Model 70

A 12 or 20 gauge over-and-under shotgun with 26" ventilated rib barrels screw-in choke tubes, single trigger and automatic ejectors. The modestly engraved receiver is either blued or French case hardened. Stock of finely figured walnut. Imported in 1988.

NIB	*Exc.*	*V.G.*	*Good*	*Fair*	*Poor*
—	500	375	250	200	100

Model 66C

A 12 gauge over-and-under shotgun with 26" or 30" ventilated rib barrels choked for skeet or trap, single trigger and automatic ejectors. The boxlock action fitted with false sideplates, which are engraved and gold inlaid. Blued with a checkered Monte Carlo-style stock and a beavertail forearm. Imported in 1988.

NIB	*Exc.*	*V.G.*	*Good*	*Fair*	*Poor*
—	1100	850	700	575	300

S.W.D., INC.
Atlanta, Georgia

M-11 Carbine

A 16.25" barrel enclosed in a shroud and fitted with a telescoping wire stock.

NIB	*Exc.*	*V.G.*	*Good*	*Fair*	*Poor*
—	800	650	550	275	100

Terminator

A 12 or 20 gauge single-shot shotgun with an 18" cylinder bored barrel. Parkerized finish. Said to be exceptionally rare but attracts little interest.

NIB	*Exc.*	*V.G.*	*Good*	*Fair*	*Poor*
—	150	80	70	60	50

SAFARI ARMS
Phoenix, Arizona

In operation from 1978 to 1987, this company was purchased by Olympic Arms of Olympia, Washington, in 1987 and the models listed are currently produced by that company under different trade names.

Counter Sniper Rifle

A .308 caliber bolt-action target rifle with a heavy 26" barrel and 20-round detachable magazine. Matte blued with a colored composite stock.

NIB	*Exc.*	*V.G.*	*Good*	*Fair*	*Poor*
1200	1050	850	650	450	200

SAKO
Riihimaki, Finland

NOTE: Arms produced by this company prior to 1972 are worth approximately 25 percent more than arms of the same type produced thereafter. Prices for fair and poor condition reflect the worth of the action.In 2000 Beretta Holding Co. purchased Sako and distributes the product line through Beretta U.S.A.

Standard Sporter

A bolt-action magazine rifle produced in a wide variety of calibers with varying barrel lengths, etc. Blued with checkered walnut stocks.

NIB	*Exc.*	*V.G.*	*Good*	*Fair*	*Poor*
—	750	650	450	400	300

Deluxe Model

As above, with an engraved floorplate and checkered Monte Carlo-style stock featuring a rosewood pistol grip cap and forend tip.

NIB	*Exc.*	*V.G.*	*Good*	*Fair*	*Poor*
—	900	750	600	450	400

Finnbear

As above, with a long action available in a variety of large bore calibers. Fitted with a 20" or 23.5" barrel. Blued with a checkered stock. For .458 Winchester Magnum (only 20 produced), values double. Add 15 percent for other magnum chamberings or Deluxe version. Add 20 percent for Mannlicher Carbine version.

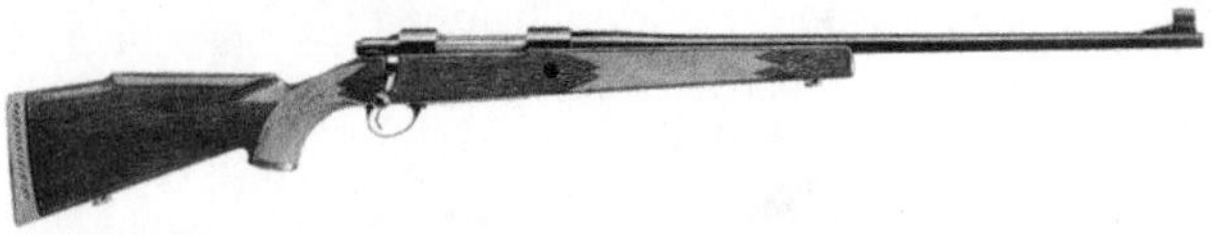

NIB	*Exc.*	*V.G.*	*Good*	*Fair*	*Poor*
—	1000	850	650	400	300

Forester

As above, with a shorter action suitable for use with intermediate cartridges. Add 20 percent for Mannlicher Carbine version.

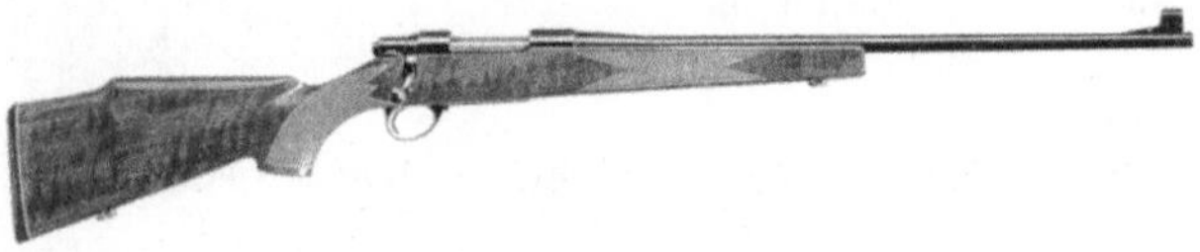

NIB	Exc.	V.G.	Good	Fair	Poor
—	1000	850	650	400	300

Vixen

As above, with a short action. Add 20 percent for Mannlicher Carbine version.

NIB	Exc.	V.G.	Good	Fair	Poor
—	1000	850	650	400	300

FN Action

Manufactured from 1950 to 1957, this model utilized a Fabrique Nationale manufactured receiver and was chambered for .270 Winchester and .30-06 cartridges. Otherwise, as above.

NIB	Exc.	V.G.	Good	Fair	Poor
—	800	600	475	400	300

FN Magnum Action

As above, with a long action for .300 and .375 Holland & Holland.

NIB	Exc.	V.G.	Good	Fair	Poor
—	900	700	550	400	300

Anniversary Model

A 7mm Remington Magnum bolt-action rifle with a 24" barrel. Blued, checkered walnut stock. A total of 1,000 were manufactured. As with any commemorative firearm, this model should be NIB to realize its full resale potential.

NIB	Exc.	V.G.	Good	Fair	Poor
2500	850	750	450	400	300

Finnwolf

A 4-shot lever-action rifle produced in .243 and .308 calibers. Blued, checkered walnut stock. Manufactured from 1962 to 1974.

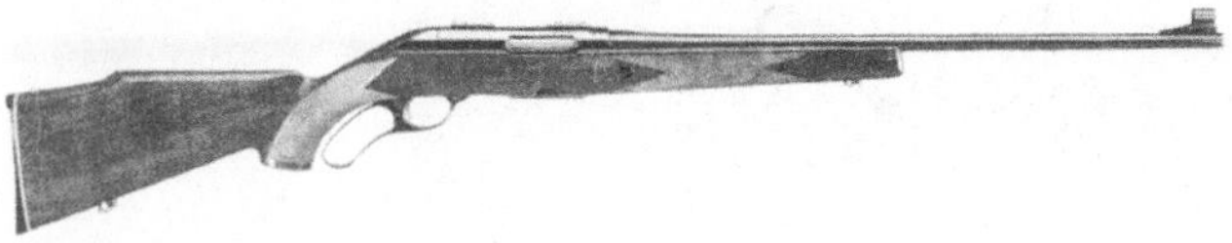

NIB	Exc.	V.G.	Good	Fair	Poor
—	1400	1200	750	450	300

Finnfire

This bolt-action rifle is chambered for the .22 long rifle cartridge. It is fitted with a 22" barrel with choice of iron sights or no sights, and a European walnut stock. A 5-shot detachable magazine is standard. Weight is about 5.25 lbs.

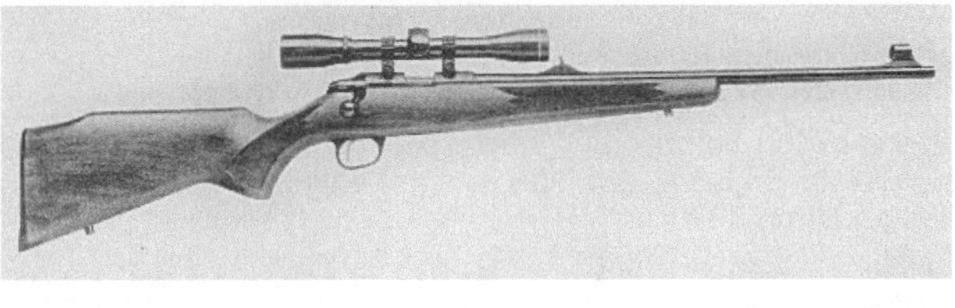

Courtesy Stoeger

NIB	Exc.	V.G.	Good	Fair	Poor
1150	950	700	575	400	300

Finnfire Heavy Barrel

Same as above but fitted with a heavy barrel.

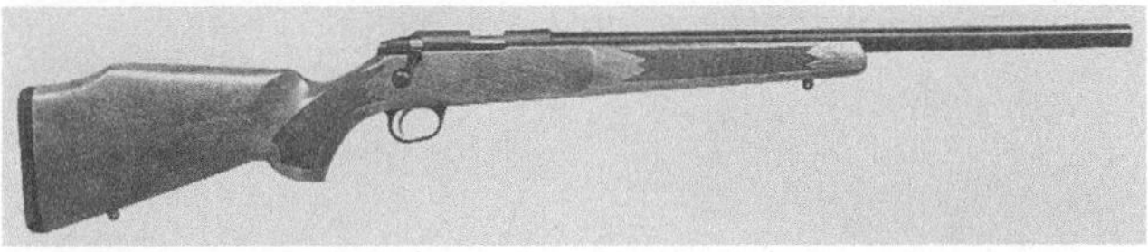

Courtesy Stoeger

NIB	Exc.	V.G.	Good	Fair	Poor
1150	950	700	575	400	300

Finnfire Hunter

Introduced in 2000 this bolt-action model is chambered for the .22 LR cartridge. It is fitted with a 22" barrel and a Sako 75 style select walnut stock. Weight is about 5.75 lbs.

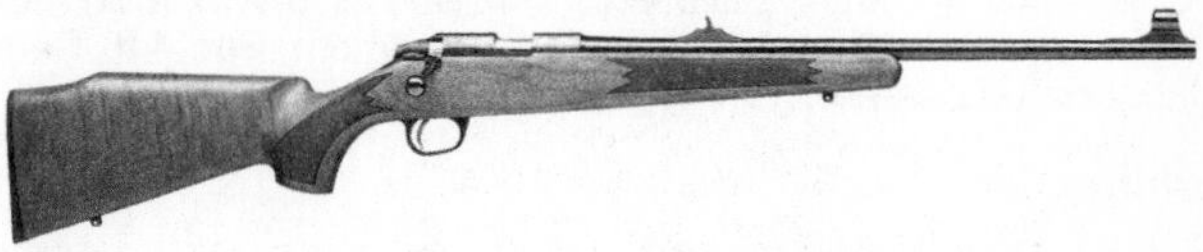

NIB	Exc.	V.G.	Good	Fair	Poor
1150	950	700	575	400	300

Finnfire Sporter

This model is chambered for the .22 LR cartridge and is built on the P94S action. It has a walnut stock with adjustable cheekpiece and buttplate spacer system that allows for length of pull and buttplate angle adjustment. Trigger is adjustable. Introduced in 1999.

NIB	Exc.	V.G.	Good	Fair	Poor
1150	950	700	575	400	300

Sako Quad Combo

Introduced in 2005 this bolt action rifle features four interchangeable barrels in four different rimfire calibers. Black synthetic stock. Detachable 5-round magazine. Included barrels are: .22 Long Rifle, .22 WMR, .17 HMR, and .17 Mach 2. All 22" in length. Blued finish. Weight is about 5.75 lbs.

NIB	Exc.	V.G.	Good	Fair	Poor
1450	1300	1075	800	500	300

NOTE: NIB price for rifles with only one barrel is $948. Extra barrels are $260 each.

HUNTER

This model is offered in three action lengths: short, medium, and long. In the short action the calibers available are .17 Rem., .222, .223 in 21.25" barrel. In medium action the calibers are: .22-250, .243, .308, and 7mm-08 in 21.75" barrel. The long action calibers are: .25-06, .270 Win., .280 Rem., .30-06 for 22" barrel length. In 24" barrel the long action calibers are: 7mm Rem. Mag., .300 Win. and .300 Wby. Mag., .338 and .375 Win. Mag., and .416 Rem. Mag. In 1996 the .270 Wthby Mag., 7mm Wthby Mag., and the .340 Wthby was added to the long action calibers. Available in left-handed version for all but short action calibers. Adjustable trigger is standard. Checkered European walnut stock. Weight for short action is 6.25 lbs., for medium action 6.5 lbs., and long action calibers 7.75 to 8.25 depending on caliber.

Medium Action

NIB	Exc.	V.G.	Good	Fair	Poor
1200	1050	875	600	500	300

Short Action

Add 10 percent to Medium Action prices for .222 Rem. and .223 Rem. For .17 Rem. add 20 percent to Medium Action prices.

Long Action

NIB	Exc.	V.G.	Good	Fair	Poor
1400	1175	1000	750	600	300

NOTE: For long action calibers in .300 and .338 Win. Mag. add 10 percent. For .375 H&H Mag. add 20 percent. For .416 Rem. Mag. add 25 percent.

Carbine

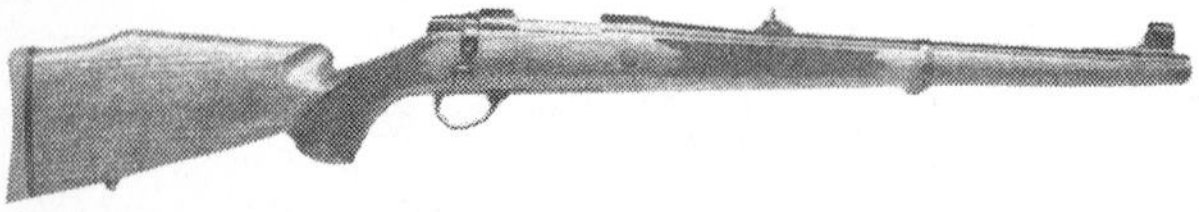

As above, with an 18.5" barrel. Produced with either a medium or long-length action.

NIB	Exc.	V.G.	Good	Fair	Poor
1200	1050	875	600	500	300

Long Range Hunting Rifle

Similar to the long action Hunter but fitted with a 26" fluted barrel. Chambered for the .25-06, .270 Win., 7mm Rem. Mag., and .300 Win. Mag. Introduced in 1996.

NIB	Exc.	V.G.	Good	Fair	Poor
1500	1300	1050	875	650	300

Laminated Model

This model features a laminated checkered hardwood stock made up of 36 layers. Solid recoil pad is standard as are quick detachable sling swivels. Available in both medium and long action calibers. Medium action calibers are: .22-250, .243, .308, and 7mm-08 with 21.75" barrel and weight of 6.5 lbs. Long action calibers are: .25-06, .270, .280, .30-06 with 22" barrel and weight of 7.75 lbs. Offered with 24" barrels are: 7mm Rem. Mag., .300 and .338 Win. Mag., and .375 H weight is 7.75 lbs.

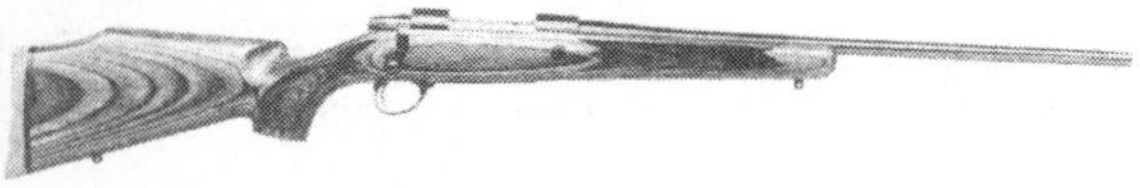

Laminated Model Medium Action

NIB	Exc.	V.G.	Good	Fair	Poor
1200	1050	875	600	500	300

Laminated Model Long Action

NIB	Exc.	V.G.	Good	Fair	Poor
1400	1175	1000	750	600	300

NOTE: For long action calibers in .300 and .338 Win. Mag. add 10 percent. For.375 H&H Mag. add 20 percent. For .416 Rem. Mag. add 25 percent.

FiberClass

This model features a black plain fiberglass stock. Offered in long action calibers only. The .25-06, .270, .280, and .30-06 are fitted with 22" barrels and weigh 7.25 lbs. The 7mm Rem. Mag., .300 Win. Mag., .338 Win. Mag., and .375 H&H are fitted with 24" barrel and weigh 7.25 lbs. The .416 Rem. Mag. has a 24" barrel and weighs 8 lbs.

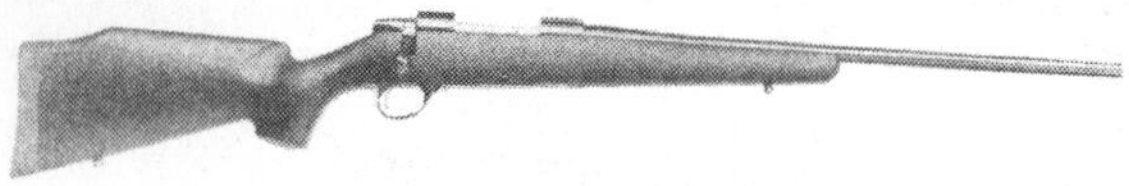

NIB	Exc.	V.G.	Good	Fair	Poor
1050	800	600	500	400	400

NOTE: For long action calibers in .300 and .338 Win. Mag. add 10 percent. For .375 H&H Mag. add 20 percent. For .416 Rem. Mag. add 25 percent.

FiberClass Carbine

NIB	Exc.	V.G.	Good	Fair	Poor
1050	800	600	500	400	400

CARBINE

This model features a Mannlicher-style stock with a two-piece forearm. It has a checkered walnut stock with oil finish. It is offered in both medium and short actions, all with 18.5" barrels. In medium action the .243 and .308 are available and weigh 6 lbs. The long action calibers are: .270, and .30-06, weighing 7.25 lbs.; and the .338 Win. Mag. and .375 H&H, weighing 7.75 lbs.

Medium Action

NIB	Exc.	V.G.	Good	Fair	Poor
1200	1050	875	600	500	300

Long Action

NIB	Exc.	V.G.	Good	Fair	Poor
1200	1050	875	600	500	300

NOTE: For long action calibers in .338 Win. Mag. add 10 percent. For .375 H&H Mag. add 20 percent.

VARMINT-HEAVY BARREL

The checkered walnut stock on this model features an extra wide beavertail forearm with oil finish. Offered in both short and medium action, all are fitted with a 23" heavy barrel weighing 8.5 lbs. Short action calibers are .17 Rem., .222, and .223. Medium action calibers are: .22-250, .243, .308, and 7mm-08.

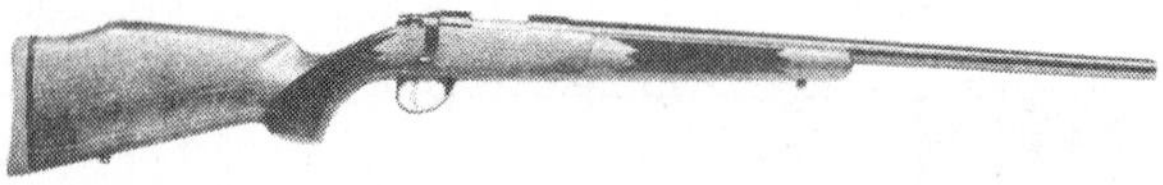

Short Action

NIB	Exc.	V.G.	Good	Fair	Poor
1200	1050	875	600	500	300

NOTE: Add 10 percent for .222 and .223 Rem. Add 20 percent for .17 Rem. to above prices.

Medium Action

NIB	Exc.	V.G.	Good	Fair	Poor
1200	1050	875	600	500	300

PPC Bench Rest/Varmint

Similar to the Varmint but single-shot. Fitted with 23.75" barrel and weighs 8.75 lbs. Available in short action special calibers .22 PPC and 6mm PPC.

NIB	Exc.	V.G.	Good	Fair	Poor
1350	1150	975	650	500	300

Classic Grade

Hand-checkered select walnut stock with matte lacquer finish is featured on this grade. Offered in medium and long action. Long action rifles are offered in left-hand model. The medium action caliber is .243 Win. with a 21.75" barrel and weight of 6 lbs. The long action calibers are: .270, .30-06, and 7mm Rem. Mag. with 24" barrels. Long action calibers weigh about 7.5 lbs.

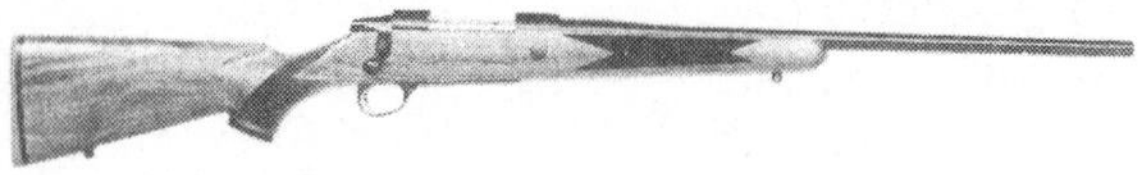

NIB	Exc.	V.G.	Good	Fair	Poor
1200	1050	875	600	500	300

DELUXE GRADE

This grade features a high grade European walnut stock with hand cut basket weave checkering. The forend tip and grip are fitted with rosewood. English-style recoil pad is standard. Long action models are offered in left-hand configuration. As with the Hunter model short, medium, and long action are available in the same calibers, barrel lengths and weights as the Hunter.

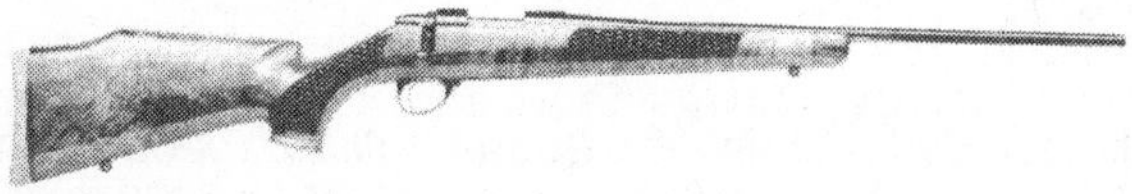

Medium Action

NIB	Exc.	V.G.	Good	Fair	Poor
1400	1175	1000	750	600	300

NOTE: Add 10 percent to above prices for .222 and .223 Rem. Add 20 percent for .17 Rem.

Long Action

NIB	Exc.	V.G.	Good	Fair	Poor
1400	1175	1000	750	600	300

NOTE: For long action calibers in .300 and .338 Win. Mag. add 10 percent. For .375 H&H Mag. add 20 percent. For .416 Rem. Mag. add 25 percent. For left-hand models add $100.

SUPER GRADE/SUPER DELUXE

Similar to Deluxe Grade but offered with fancy walnut stock with oak-leaf carving. Floor plate and trigger guard are engraved. Pistol grip cap has inlaid silver plate. Offered in same actions and calibers as Hunter and Deluxe Grades.

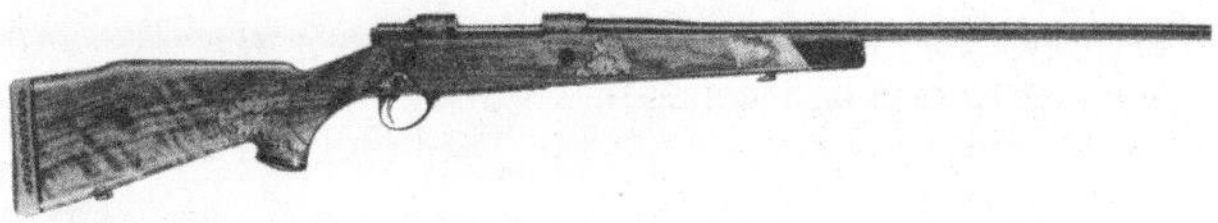

Medium Action

NIB	Exc.	V.G.	Good	Fair	Poor
2500	1750	1200	750	625	300

Add 10 percent to above prices for .222 and .223 Rem.

Long Action

NIB	Exc.	V.G.	Good	Fair	Poor
2500	1750	1200	750	625	300

NOTE: For long action calibers in .300 and .338 Win. Mag. add 10 percent. For .375 H&H Mag. add 20 percent. For .416 Rem. Mag. add 25 percent.

Safari Grade

As above, chambered for .300 Winchester Magnum, .338 Winchester Magnum, or .375 Holland & Holland cartridges.

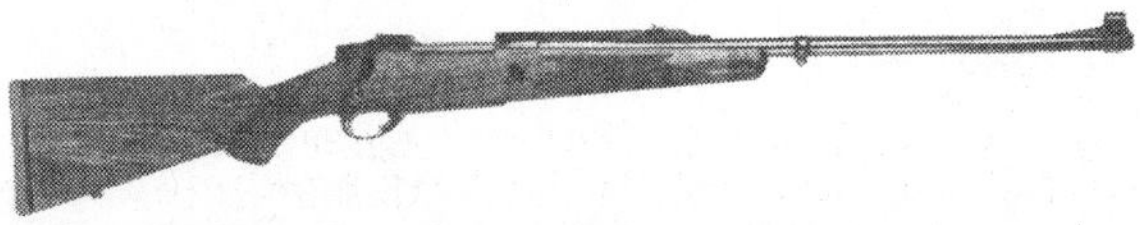

NIB	Exc.	V.G.	Good	Fair	Poor
3250	2500	1900	1100	800	400

MODEL 75 SERIES

This model was introduced in March 1997. It is based on a new design by Sako. Each of the five different action sizes is manufactured for a specific range of calibers. Its action, barrel, and stocks are all redesigned components. It is offered in a variety of configurations and calibers. Sako actions are offered separately in carbon steel, in white, and stainless steel.

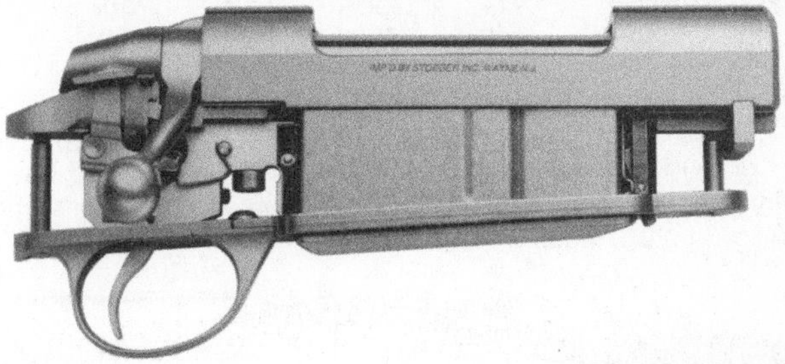

Model 75 Hunter

This model is available in five different action sizes for calibers from .17 Rem. to .416 Rem. Mag. Weight varies from 6.37 lbs. to 9 lbs. and barrel lengths from 22" to 24.37". Choice of checkered walnut stock or black synthetic stock. All Hunter models are sold without sights as standard but open sights are an option. Magazine is detachable except for .300 Rem. Ultra Mag and the .416 Rem. Mag. Single set trigger is an option. In 2003 a left-hand model was offered in .270 Win and .30-06. In 2004 the .270 WSM and .300 WSM calibers were added.

NIB	Exc.	V.G.	Good	Fair	Poor
1425	1050	700	500	400	300

NOTE: Add $30 for long action calibers from .270 to .416.

Model 75 Stainless Synthetic

Same as above but available with synthetic stock and stainless steel barrel and action. Offered in calibers from .22-250 to .375 H&H.

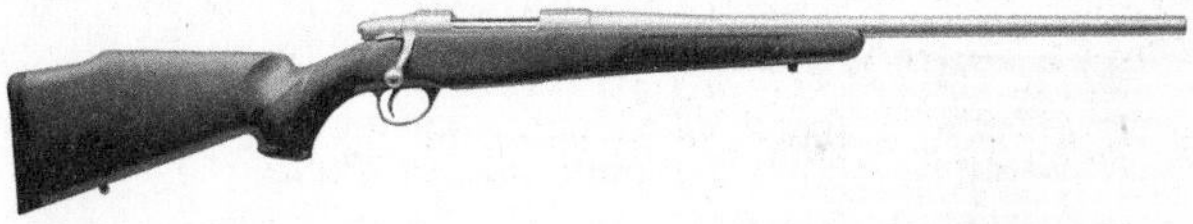

NIB	Exc.	V.G.	Good	Fair	Poor
1500	1100	750	600	400	300

NOTE: Add $30 for long action calibers.

Model 75 Deluxe

This model features all of the elements of the Hunter model with the addition of special checkering on select walnut stock with special black finish. All models have a hinged floor plate. In 2004 the .270 WSM and .300 WSM calibers were added. Weight is about 7.75 lbs.

NIB	Exc.	V.G.	Good	Fair	Poor
1600	1050	800	700	500	400

NOTE: Add $100 for long action calibers.

Model 75 Big Game Deluxe

This model is similar to the M75 Deluxe except that it is chambered for the .416 Rem. Magnum cartridge and fitted with iron sights.

NIB	Exc.	V.G.	Good	Fair	Poor
1600	1050	800	700	500	400

Model 75 Varmint

This model is chambered for the .17 Rem., .222 Rem., .223, and .22-250, all with 24" heavy barrels. In 1999 Sako added the .22 PPC and 6mm PPC calibers. Other calibers are .260 Remington, .308, and .204 Ruger. It weighs about 8.4 lbs. Walnut stock.

NIB	Exc.	V.G.	Good	Fair	Poor
1250	950	750	600	450	400

Model 75 Varmint Set Trigger

As above but with a single set trigger. Introduced in 2005.

NIB	Exc.	V.G.	Good	Fair	Poor
1550	1100	875	700	500	400

Model 75 Varmint Stainless

Introduced in 1999 this model is similar to the Varmint 75 but with stainless steel barrel. Magazine is detachable but can be loaded through the ejection port. Trigger is adjustable. Offered in all of the calibers as the standard Model 75 Varmint. Weights vary from about 8 lbs. to 8.6 lbs. The stock is laminated.

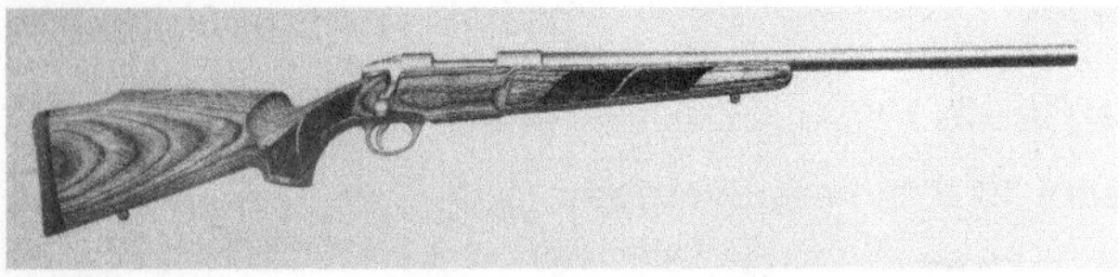

NIB	Exc.	V.G.	Good	Fair	Poor
1200	1050	875	600	500	300

Model 75 Varmint Stainless Set Trigger

As above but with stainless steel barrel and receiver and laminated stock. Weight is about 9 lbs. Introduced in 2005.

NIB	Exc.	V.G.	Good	Fair	Poor
1400	1175	1000	750	600	300

Model 75 Finnlight

Introduced in 2001 this bolt-action rifle features short, medium, and long action calibers with stainless steel barrel lengths from 20.25" to 22.5" depending on caliber. Barrels are fluted. Synthetic stock. Weight is about 6.5 lbs. depending on caliber. In 2003 this model was offered in .300 WSM caliber.

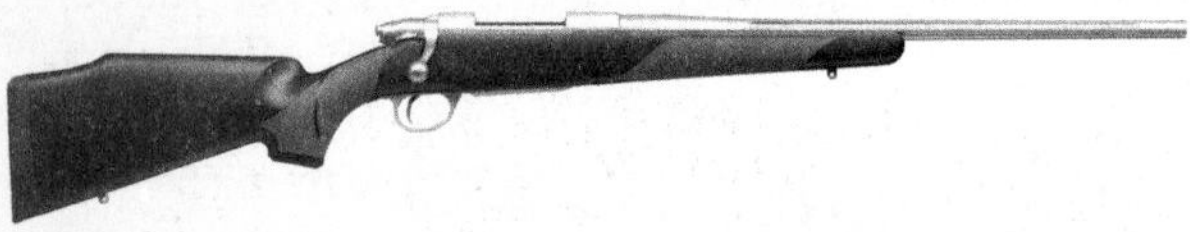

NIB	Exc.	V.G.	Good	Fair	Poor
1300	1075	900	650	500	300

Model 75 Grey Wolf

This bolt action rifle is chambered for a wide variety of calibers from .223 to 7mm WSM. Stainless steel barrel is either 22.5" or 24.3" depending on caliber without sights. The gray stock is laminated and checkered. Rubber recoil pad. Detachable magazine. Weight is about 7.75 lbs. depending on caliber. Introduced in 2005.

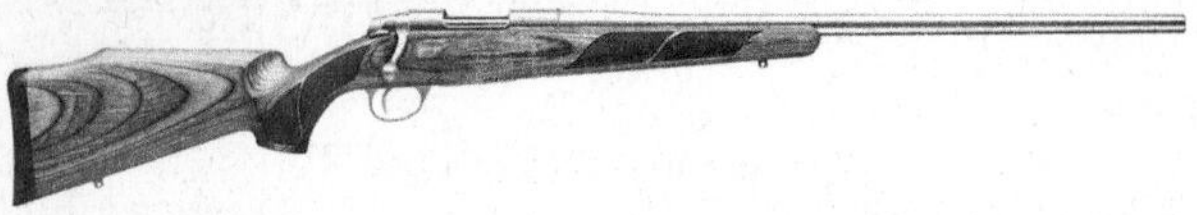

NIB	Exc.	V.G.	Good	Fair	Poor
1400	1175	1000	750	600	300

Model 75 Custom Deluxe

Introduced in 2003 this model features an oil-finished premium-grade walnut stock with special fine-line checkering pattern. Factory recoil pad. Chambered for the .270 Win or .30-06 cartridges.

NIB	Exc.	V.G.	Good	Fair	Poor
3250	2500	1900	1100	800	400

Model 75 Custom Single Shot

Introduced in 2004 this single-shot model is chambered for the .308 cartridge and fitted with a 23.625" heavy fluted stainless steel barrel with no sights. Checkered laminated stock with beavertail forearm. Weight is about 9 lbs.

NIB	Exc.	V.G.	Good	Fair	Poor
3250	2500	1900	1100	550	400

Model 75 Super Deluxe

This is a special order rifle. Advise obtaining an expert opinion before a sale. Prices listed are for the base rifle.

NIB	Exc.	V.G.	Good	Fair	Poor
3400	22750	1900	1275	600	400

Model 78

A .22 or .22 Hornet bolt-action rifle with a 22" barrel. Blued with a checkered walnut stock. Discontinued in 1986.

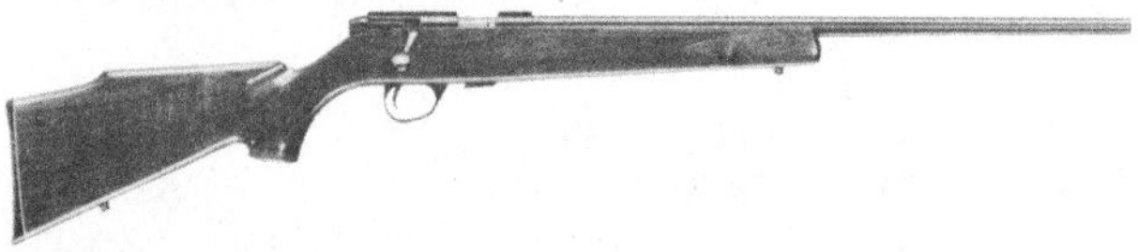

NIB	Exc.	V.G.	Good	Fair	Poor
—	850	675	500	375	250

Model 2700 Finnsport

A .270 to .300 Winchester Magnum bolt-action rifle with a 22" barrel. Blued, checkered walnut stock. Discontinued in 1985.

NIB	Exc.	V.G.	Good	Fair	Poor
—	900	750	600	475	200

Safari 80th Anniversary Model

This is a limited edition rifle. Built on the Sako 75 magnum long action and chambered for the .375 H&H cartridge. Match grade heavy barrel. Select grade walnut stock with straight comb and ebony forend tip. Quarter rib. Equipped with Swarovski PV-1 1.25x24 scope. Engraved floor plate. Supplied with hand-made leather case with cleaning accessories. Limited to 80 rifles worldwide. Serial numbers 200101 to 200180.

NIB	*Exc.*	*V.G.*	*Good*	*Fair*	*Poor*
15950	12500	8500	—	—	—

Sako 85 Hunter

Bolt-action centerfire rifle chambered in short and long calibers ranging from .223 Remington to .375 H&H Mag. Controlled round feeding, checkered walnut stock, satin blued sightless 22-7/16", 22-7/8", or 24-3/8" barrel. Introduced in 2007. Thirty percent premium for .375.

NIB	*Exc.*	*V.G.*	*Good*	*Fair*	*Poor*
1100	900	775	600	475	300

Sako 85 Stainless Synthetic

Similar to Sako 85 Hunter but with stainless steel receiver and barrel. Introduced 2007.

NIB	*Exc.*	*V.G.*	*Good*	*Fair*	*Poor*
1200	1000	875	650	525	350

Sako 85 Finnlight

Similar to Sako 85 Stainless Synthetic but with recoil pad and ultra-lightweight synthetic stock. Chambered in long and short cartridges ranging from .243 to .300 Win Mag. Introduced 2007.

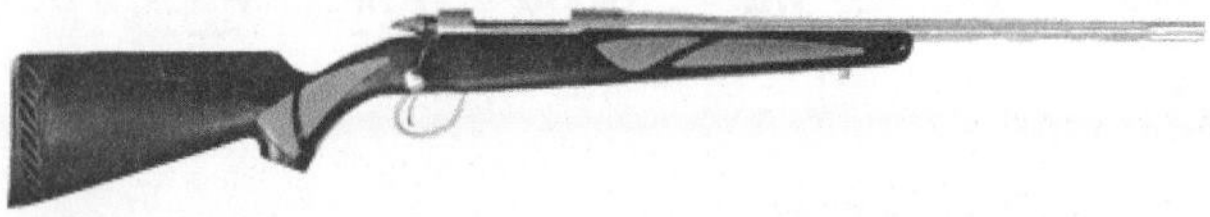

NIB	*Exc.*	*V.G.*	*Good*	*Fair*	*Poor*
1550	1100	875	700	500	400

Sako 85 Varmint

Similar to Sako 85 Hunter but with recoil pad and 7.5-oz. set trigger. Chambered in .204 Ruger, .243, .22-250 or .308. Introduced 2007.

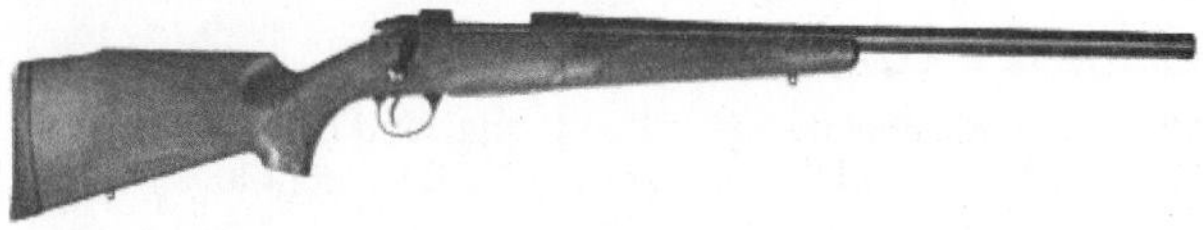

NIB	*Exc.*	*V.G.*	*Good*	*Fair*	*Poor*
1300	1075	900	650	500	300

Sako 85 Laminated SS Varmint

Similar to Sako 85 Varmint but with laminated stock and stainless steel barrel. Introduced 2007.

NIB	*Exc.*	*V.G.*	*Good*	*Fair*	*Poor*
1400	1175	1000	750	600	300

Sako A7 American Bolt-Action Rifle

Bolt-action rifle chambered in .22-250, .243 Win., .25-06, .260 Rem., .270 Win., .270 WSM, .300 WSM, .30-06, .300 WM, .308 Win., .338 Federal, .7mm Rem. Mag., 7mm-08. Features include blued or stainless barrel (22-7/16" standard, 24-3/8" magnum) and receiver, black composite stock with sling swivels and recoil pad, two-position safety, adjustable trigger, detachable 3+1 box magazine. Weight 6 lbs., 3 oz. to 6 lbs., 13 oz.

NIB	*Exc.*	*V.G.*	*Good*	*Fair*	*Poor*
850	725	575	400	300	200

Sako A-7 Tecomate

Chambered in the .270 WSM (23-inch barrel) or .300 WSM (24-1/4-inch) barrel. Magazine capacity 4 rounds. Features a new Bell & Carlson Medalist composite stock. Integral aluminum bedding system, CNC produced from aircraft quality 6061-T6 aluminum. Flat bottom receiver. Stainless action. Introduced in 2011.

NIB	*Exc.*	*V.G.*	*Good*	*Fair*	*Poor*
1200	1025	850	600	300	100

Sako Classic Deluxe

High grade version of Model 85 with oil-finished walnut stock with palm swell and cheekpiece, pronounced pistol grip, rosewood pistol and fore-end tip. Barrel band for sling swivel. Free-floating barrel. All metal parts are highly polished and blued. Medium or long action depending upon caliber. Adjustable trigger. Open sights are available. Five cartridges are available to include .270 Winchester, 7x64, .30-06, .370 Sako Magnum and .375 H&H. Introduced in 2011.

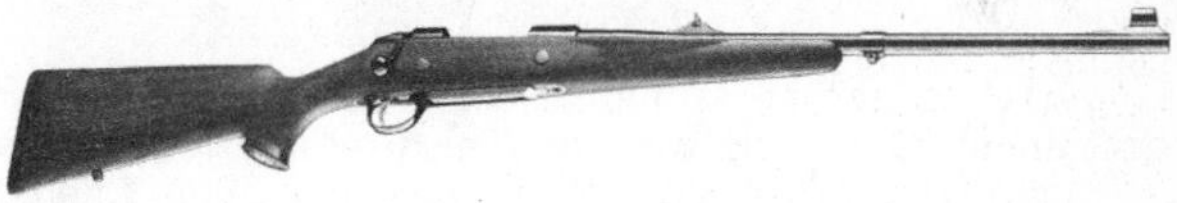

NIB	*Exc.*	*V.G.*	*Good*	*Fair*	*Poor*
3450	3100	2600	2000	1600	500

Sako Black Bear Series

Model 85 variation available in short and medium actions only. Short action is chambered in .308 Win. or .338 Federal; medium action in .30-06, 8x57 JS, 9.3x62 and 9.3x66 (.370) Sako. Controlled feeding, detachable magazine, single-stage adjustable trigger. Black injection molded stock with Soft Touch areas around pistol grip and forend. Open sights are available, scope can be mounted to integral Sako mounting system on receiver. Bull barrel, free-floating and hammer forged. Brown Bear model has similar features but with brown laminated hardwood stock and is chambered in .338 Win. Mag. or .375 H&H. Introduced in 2011.

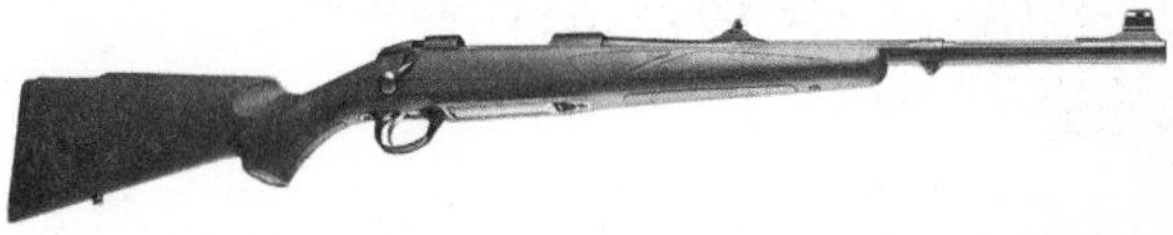

NIB	*Exc.*	*V.G.*	*Good*	*Fair*	*Poor*
1600	1350	1100	950	600	300

TRG-S

This model features a unique cold-forged receiver. The stock is a special reinforced polyurethane Monte Carlo without checkering. The recoil pad has spacer for adjustable length of pull. The trigger is adjustable and the detachable magazine holds 5 rounds. Offered in a variety of calibers from .243 to .375 H&H. Non-Magnum calibers are fitted with a 22" barrel and weigh 7.75 lbs. and magnum calibers are fitted with a 24" barrel and also weigh 7.75 lbs. In 1996 the .270 Wthby Mag., 7mm Wthby Mag., the .340 Wthby Mag., as well as the 6.5x55S, were added.

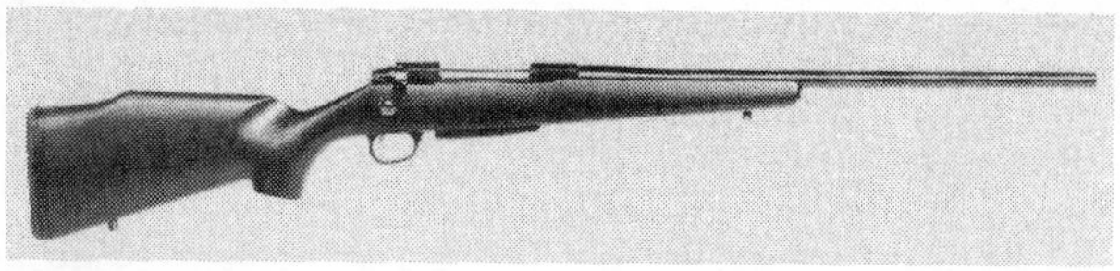

NIB	*Exc.*	*V.G.*	*Good*	*Fair*	*Poor*
1000	850	675	500	350	250

TRG-21

The receiver is similar to the TRG-S but the polyurethane stock features a unique design. Chambered for the .308 cartridge. The trigger is adjustable for length and two-stage pull and also for horizontal or vertical pitch. This model also has several options that would affect the price; muzzlebrake, one-piece scope mount, bipod, quick detachable sling swivels, and military nylon sling. The rifle is offered in .308 Win. only. It is fitted with a 25.75" barrel and weighs 10.5 lbs.

NIB	*Exc.*	*V.G.*	*Good*	*Fair*	*Poor*
3500	2750	1850	—	—	—

TRG-22

This model is similar to the TRG-21 but meets the exact specifications to comply with the Finish military requirements. Chambered for the .308 cartridge. Introduced in 2000. Offered in both green and black finish. Weight is about 10.25 lbs.

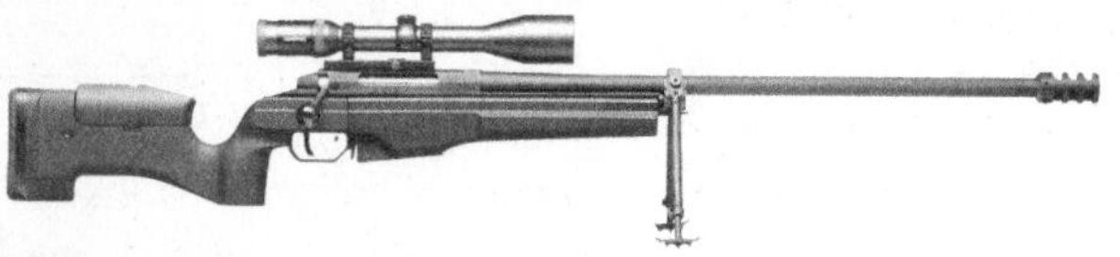

NIB	*Exc.*	*V.G.*	*Good*	*Fair*	*Poor*
3589	2650	1750	—	—	—

NOTE: Add $2,250 for folding stock version.

TRG-41

Exactly the same as the TRG-21 except chambered for the .338 Lapua Magnum cartridge.

NIB	*Exc.*	*V.G.*	*Good*	*Fair*	*Poor*
4350	3500	2500	—	—	—

TRG-42

This model is similar to the TRG-41 but meets the exact specifications to comply with the Finish military requirements. Chambered for the .338 Lapua or .300 Win. Mag cartridge. Introduced in 2000. Weight is about 11.25 lbs.

NIB	*Exc.*	*V.G.*	*Good*	*Fair*	*Poor*
4000	3000	2000	—	—	—

SAM, INC.

Special Service Arms Mfg., Inc.
Reston, Virginia

Model 88 Crossfire

A semi-automatic combination 12 gauge/.308 caliber shotgun/rifle, with a 7-shot shotgun magazine and 20-shot rifle magazine. Barrel length 20", matte black finish with a composition stock. This weapon can be fired in either mode by means of a selector switch mounted on the receiver.

NIB	*Exc.*	*V.G.*	*Good*	*Fair*	*Poor*
1900	1500	1175	800	550	300

SARASQUETA, FELIX

Eibar, Spain

Merke

A 12 gauge over-and-under double-barrel shotgun with 22" or 27" ribbed and separated barrels, nonselective trigger and manual extractors. Blued, checkered walnut stock. Imported in 1986 only.

NIB	*Exc.*	*V.G.*	*Good*	*Fair*	*Poor*
—	500	375	200	150	100

SARASQUETA, J. J.

Eibar, Spain

Model 107E

A 12, 16, or 20 gauge boxlock double-barrel shotgun with a variety of barrel lengths, double triggers and automatic ejectors. Blued with a checkered walnut stock. Discontinued in 1984.

NIB	*Exc.*	*V.G.*	*Good*	*Fair*	*Poor*
—	425	300	275	225	100

Model 119E

As above, with a more finely figured walnut stock.

NIB	*Exc.*	*V.G.*	*Good*	*Fair*	*Poor*
—	525	400	375	325	150

Model 130E

As above, but engraved.

NIB	*Exc.*	*V.G.*	*Good*	*Fair*	*Poor*
—	950	700	600	450	250

Model 131E

As above, with considerably more engraving.

NIB	*Exc.*	*V.G.*	*Good*	*Fair*	*Poor*
—	1350	900	800	650	350

Model 1882 E LUXE

As above, with a single-selective trigger and gold inlays. A silver inlaid version is sold for approximately 10 percent less.

NIB	*Exc.*	*V.G.*	*Good*	*Fair*	*Poor*
—	1750	1250	900	650	350

SARASQUETA, VICTOR

Eibar, Spain

Model 3

A 12, 16, or 20 gauge boxlock or sidelock double-barrel shotgun available in a variety of barrel lengths, with double triggers and automatic ejectors. Blued with a checkered straight stock. The sidelock version is worth approximately 20 percent more than the values listed. The basic Model 3 was offered in a variety of grades featuring different amounts of engraving and better quality wood. These shotguns are listed under the model designations of 4 to 12E.

NIB	*Exc.*	*V.G.*	*Good*	*Fair*	*Poor*
—	650	500	450	350	300

Model 4

NIB	*Exc.*	*V.G.*	*Good*	*Fair*	*Poor*
—	1200	1000	875	600	300

Model 4E (Auto-ejectors)

NIB	*Exc.*	*V.G.*	*Good*	*Fair*	*Poor*
—	1600	1400	1100	800	400

Model 203

NIB	Exc.	V.G.	Good	Fair	Poor
—	700	600	525	425	325

Model 203E

NIB	Exc.	V.G.	Good	Fair	Poor
—	900	750	625	475	375

Model 6E

NIB	Exc.	V.G.	Good	Fair	Poor
—	1400	1250	875	525	425

Model 7E

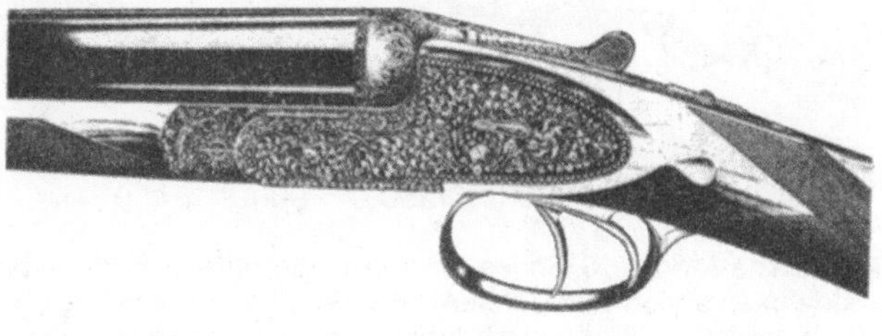

NIB	Exc.	V.G.	Good	Fair	Poor
—	1500	1350	1000	750	475

Model 10E

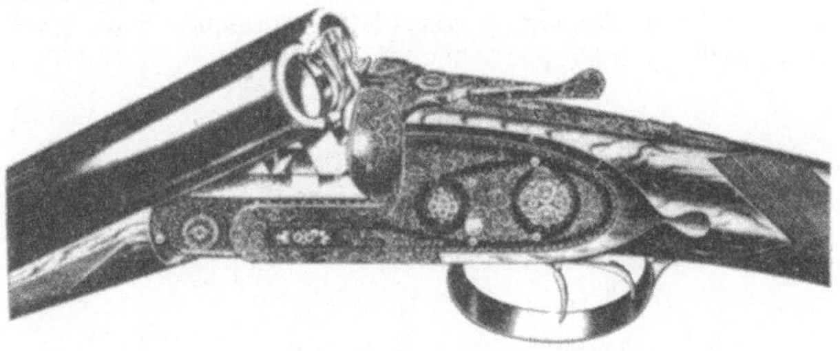

NIB	Exc.	V.G.	Good	Fair	Poor
—	2600	2100	1650	950	750

Model 11E

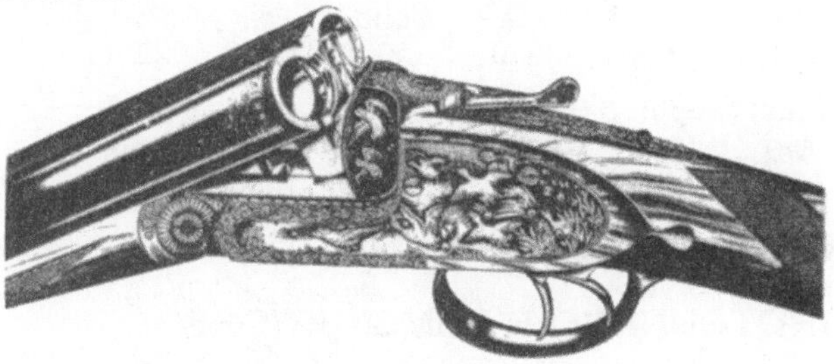

NIB	Exc.	V.G.	Good	Fair	Poor
—	3000	2600	2000	1150	850

Model 12E

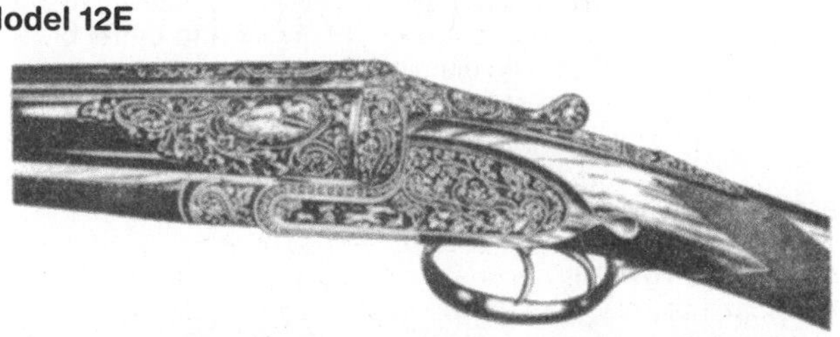

NIB	Exc.	V.G.	Good	Fair	Poor
—	3200	2850	2200	1300	1000

SAUER & SON, J. P.

Suhl and Eckernfoerde, Germany

This is the oldest firearms manufacturing firm in Germany. It was founded in 1751 in Suhl. During this period the company produced high quality handguns and long guns. In 1938 it introduced a new double-action semi-automatic pistol, the Sauer 38H. This pistol had the first decocking lever ever used on a mass produced pistol. In 1951 the company relocated to Eckernfoerde where it continued to produced high quality forearms.NOTE: The Model 90 Supreme and Model 202 are currently imported by SIGARMS Inc.

RIFLES

Bolt-Action Rifle

A Mauser action sporting rifle chambered for a variety of cartridges with either a 22" or 24" barrel featuring a raised rib. Double set triggers, express sights, blued with a checkered walnut stock. Manufactured prior to WWII.

NIB	Exc.	V.G.	Good	Fair	Poor
—	1250	900	6500	400	300

Model 200

A bolt-action rifle chambered for a variety of cartridges with short or medium length actions, 24" barrels, set trigger, 4-round magazine. Blued, checkered walnut stock. Discontinued 1987. Extra barrels add $235.

NIB	Exc.	V.G.	Good	Fair	Poor
1350	1050	700	500	425	350

Model 200 Lightweight

As above, with an alloy receiver. Discontinued in 1987.

NIB	Exc.	V.G.	Good	Fair	Poor
—	1100	900	550	325	250

Model 200 Lux

As above, with a finely figured walnut stock, rosewood pistol grip cap and forend tip, gold-plated trigger and a machine jewelled bolt. Imported prior to 1988.

NIB	Exc.	V.G.	Good	Fair	Poor
—	1200	950	700	475	400

Model 200 Carbon Fiber

The Model 200 fitted with a carbon composition stock. Imported in 1987 and 1988.

NIB	Exc.	V.G.	Good	Fair	Poor
—	1300	1100	800	500	400

Model 202 Supreme

This is a bolt-action rifle with a barrel change feature. It is fitted with an adjustable two-stage trigger, quick-change fluted barrel, black rubber recoil pad, and removable box magazine. The stock is select American claro walnut with high gloss finish and rosewood forend and grip cap. Buttstock has a Monte Carlo comb and cheekpiece. It is offered in .243, .270, .308, and .30-06. Barrel length for these calibers is 23.6". Weight for these calibers is about 7.7 lbs. In the Supreme Magnum series it is available in 7mm magnum, .300 Win. Mag., and .375 H&H Mag. Barrel for these magnum calibers is 26". Weight for these caliber is 8.4 lbs.

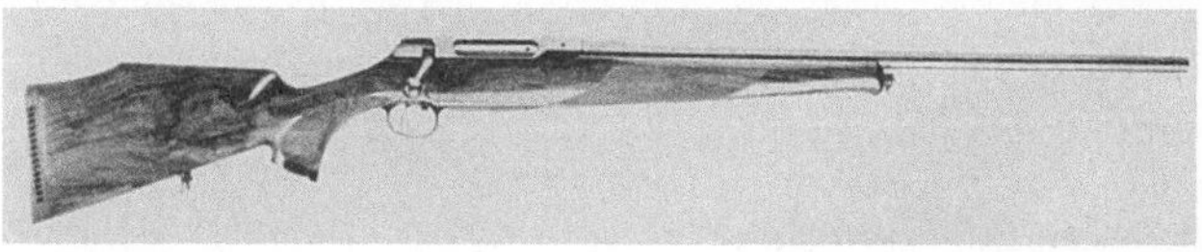

NIB	Exc.	V.G.	Good	Fair	Poor
2700	2000	1350	1000	750	400

Model 202 Takedown

This model is a true takedown. Introduced in 2003 this rifle is chambered for the .300 Win. Mag and the .375 H other calibers will be offered in the future. Fancy Turkish walnut stock with Monte Carlo and rosewood forend tip. Base price listed.

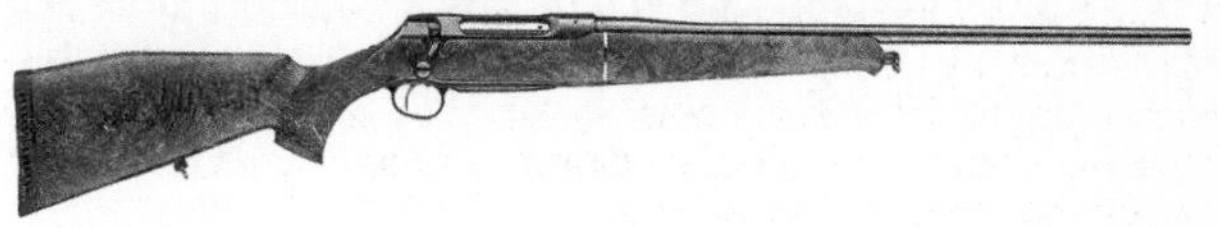

NIB	Exc.	V.G.	Good	Fair	Poor
5700	4400	2900	2000	1200	400

Model S202 Wolverine

Similar to the Model 202 Supreme above but with 25.6" barrel, beavertail forend and adjustable cheekpiece. Chambered in various varmint calibers.

NIB	Exc.	V.G.	Good	Fair	Poor
—	2300	1950	1500	1050	400

Model S202 Highland

Similar to the Model 202 Supreme above but with 20" barrel, schnabel forend and easily-detachable buttstock. Chambered in .308 Winchester and various European cartridges.

NIB	Exc.	V.G.	Good	Fair	Poor
—	2500	1950	1500	1050	400

Model S202 Forest

A carbine-style version of the Model 202 Highland above intended specifically for drive hunts. Has standard forend and 25.6" barrel and is chambered in various varmint calibers.

NIB	Exc.	V.G.	Good	Fair	Poor
—	2500	1950	1500	1050	400

Model S202 Hardwood

Similar to the Model 202 Highland above but, oddly enough, with a synthetic stock with orange inserts. Chambered in .308 Winchester and various European cartridges.

NIB	Exc.	V.G.	Good	Fair	Poor
—	2300	1950	1500	1050	400

Model S202 Match

Target version of the Model 202 with 26.8" match barrel, wide forend. Chambered in .300 Winchester Magnum and 6.5x55 Swedish.

NIB	Exc.	V.G.	Good	Fair	Poor
—	2500	1950	1500	1050	400

Model S202 Outback

Similar to the Model 202 Hardwood above but withlightweight construction and plain black synthetic stock

NIB	Exc.	V.G.	Good	Fair	Poor
—	2500	1950	1500	1050	400

Model S202 Team Sauer

Classically-styled sporter version of Model 202 with heavy medium or magnum-weight barrel and walnut Monte Carlo stock. Chambered in various European and American long-action cartridges from 6.5x55 Swedish up to .300 Winchester Magnum.

NIB	Exc.	V.G.	Good	Fair	Poor
—	1950	1600	1250	800	400

Model 90

A bolt-action rifle produced in a number of calibers in all action lengths with 23" or 26" barrels, with a detachable magazine. Blued with a checkered walnut stock.

NIB	Exc.	V.G.	Good	Fair	Poor
—	1300	1100	675	500	300

Model 90 Stutzen

As above, with a full-length Mannlicher-style stock. Imported prior to 1990.

NIB	Exc.	V.G.	Good	Fair	Poor
—	1350	1150	725	550	350

Model 90 Safari

The Model 90 made for use with the .458 Winchester Magnum cartridge and fitted with a 24" barrel. Imported from 1986 to 1988.

NIB	Exc.	V.G.	Good	Fair	Poor
—	2300	2000	1250	900	400

NOTE: The Model 90 Series of bolt-action rifles was available in a deluxe version that differed with the grade of workmanship and materials utilized. This deluxe series would be worth approximately 60 percent additional.

Model 90 Supreme

Similar to the above, with a gold-plated trigger, machine jewelled bolt and finely figured checkered walnut stock. Introduced in 1987.

NIB	Exc.	V.G.	Good	Fair	Poor
—	2500	2200	1425	1000	400

SSG-3000

NIB	Exc.	V.G.	Good	Fair	Poor
3300	2650	1950	1500	11000	500

SG 550 Sniper

NIB	Exc.	V.G.	Good	Fair	Poor
5500	4750	3875	2700	2000	500

NOTE: For other current Sauer rifles see SIGARMS.

SHOTGUN/RIFLE COMBINATIONS

Luftwaffe M30 Survival Drilling

A double-barrel 12 gauge by 9.3x74R combination shotgun/rifle with 28" barrels. Blued with a checkered walnut stock and marked with Nazi inspection. Stampings on the stock and barrel breech. Normally, furnished with an aluminum case.

NIB	Exc.	V.G.	Good	Fair	Poor
—	12000	8500	6000	3250	1500

NOTE: Add 50 percent to prices for case.

Model 3000 Drilling

This model was chambered for a variety of gauges and calibers and is built upon a boxlock action with a Greener crossbolt. The action is lightly engraved. Blued, checkered walnut stock.

NIB	Exc.	V.G.	Good	Fair	Poor
5500	3700	2750	2000	1500	1250

Model 54 Combo

A combination rifle/shotgun chambered for a variety of gauges and calibers with an action as above. Discontinued in 1986.

NIB	Exc.	V.G.	Good	Fair	Poor
—	3000	2250	1750	1400	1200

SHOTGUNS

Model 60

A 12, 16 or 20 gauge double-barrel boxlock shotgun produced in a variety of barrel lengths with double triggers and manual extractors. Blued with checkered walnut stock. Produced prior to WWII.

NIB	Exc.	V.G.	Good	Fair	Poor
—	1300	950	725	550	400

Royal Model

A 12 or 20 gauge boxlock double-barrel shotgun with 26", 28", or 30" barrels, single-selective triggers with automatic ejectors. The frame is scalloped, blued with a checkered walnut stock. Manufactured from 1955 to 1977.

NIB	Exc.	V.G.	Good	Fair	Poor
—	1500	1250	1000	750	500

Grade I Artemis

A 12 gauge sidelock double-barrel shotgun with 28" barrels, single-selective trigger and automatic ejector. Engraved, blued with checkered walnut stock. Manufactured from 1966 to 1977.

NIB	Exc.	V.G.	Good	Fair	Poor
—	5000	4250	3500	2500	2000

Grade II Artemis

As above, but more finely finished.

NIB	Exc.	V.G.	Good	Fair	Poor
—	6500	5750	4750	3500	3000

MODEL 66

A 12 gauge sidelock double-barrel shotgun with a 26", 28", or 30" barrel, single-selective trigger and automatic ejectors. Blued, checkered walnut stock. This model was produced in three different grades that have different degrees of engraving. Produced from 1966 to 1975.

Grade I

NIB	Exc.	V.G.	Good	Fair	Poor
—	2000	1800	1500	1150	800

Grade II

NIB	Exc.	V.G.	Good	Fair	Poor
—	3000	2800	2500	2150	1800

Model 66 Grade III

NIB	Exc.	V.G.	Good	Fair	Poor
—	3750	3500	2850	2500	2000

SAVAGE ARMS CORPORATION

Utica, New York
Westfield, Massachusetts

Model 1895

A .303 Savage caliber lever-action rifle with a 26" or 30" barrel and 5-shot rotary magazine. Identifiable by the hole in the breechbolt. The barrel marked "Savage Repeating Arms Co. Utica, N.Y. U.S.A. Pat. Feb. 7, 1893, July 25, 1893. CAL. .303." Blued with a walnut stock. Approximately 8,000 were manufactured between 1895 and 1899.

Courtesy Rock Island Auction Company

NIB	Exc.	V.G.	Good	Fair	Poor
—	3000	2500	1800	800	200

NOTE: For carbine version add 50 percent.

Model 1899-A 22" Barrel Short Rifle

Chambered for .303, .30-30, .25-35, .32-40, .38-55. Serial number range from 10000 to 220000. Produced from 1899 to 1922. Same cocking indicator as the 1899-A rifle.

NIB	Exc.	V.G.	Good	Fair	Poor
—	1600	100	600	300	100

NOTE: Add 50 percent for .25-35, .32-40, and .38-55 calibers.

Model 1899-A 26" Round Barrel Rifle

A .25-35, .30-30, .303 Savage, .32-40 or .38-55, .300 Savage caliber lever-action rifle with 26" barrel marked "Savage Arms Company, Utica, N.Y. Pat. Feb. 7, 1893, July 25.'93, Oct.3.'99 .CAL.30." Manufactured between 1899 and 1926/27. Blued with a walnut stock. Serial number range 10000 to 300000. Block cocking indicator on bolt to s/n 90000 then changed to pin indicator on tang.

Courtesy Rock Island Auction Company

NIB	Exc.	V.G.	Good	Fair	Poor
—	1500	1000	600	250	100

NOTE: Add 50 percent for .25-35, .32-40, and .38-55 calibers.

Model 1899-B 26" Octagon Barrel Rifle

In calibers .303, .30-30, .25-35, .32-40, .38-55. Manufactured between 1899 and 1915. Serial number range 10000 to 175000. Same cocking indicator as 1899-A rifle.

Courtesy Rock Island Auction Company

NIB	Exc.	V.G.	Good	Fair	Poor
—	1900	1300	800	350	150

NOTE: Add 50 percent for .25-35, .32-40, and .38-55 calibers.

Model 1899-C 26" Half Octagon Barrel Rifle

In calibers .303, .30-30, .25-35, .32-40, .38-55. Manufactured between 1899 and 1915. Serial number range 10000 to 175000. Same cocking indicator as 1899-A rifle.

Courtesy Rock Island Auction Company

NIB	Exc.	V.G.	Good	Fair	Poor
—	2300	1700	1100	400	150

NOTE: Add 50 percent for .25-35, .32-40, and .38-55 calibers.

Model 1899-D Military Musket

Chambered for .303 Savage only with 28" barrel. Fitted with full military stocks. Produced from 1899 to 1915. Several hundred produced for Canadian Home Guard during WWI. These will have rack number on buttplate.

NIB	Exc.	V.G.	Good	Fair	Poor
—	4300	3200	1100	700	300

Model 1899-F Saddle Ring Carbine

Fitted with 20" barrel only in calibers .303, .30-30, .25-35, .32-40, .38-55. Built from 1899 to 1919 in serial number range 19000 to 200000. Same cocking indicator as 1899-A rifle. Earliest style with barrel band is rarest variation.

Courtesy Rock Island Auction Company

NIB	Exc.	V.G.	Good	Fair	Poor
—	1800	1100	600	300	100

NOTE: Add 100 percent for .25-35, .32-40, and .38-55 calibers. Add 200 percent for barrel band carbine.

Model 1899-CD Deluxe Rifle

In calibers .303, .30-30, .25-35, .32-40, .38-55. Serial number range 50000 to 175000. Built from 1905 to 1917. Same cocking indicator as the 1899-A rifle. The standard Deluxe 1899 rifle with 26" round, octagon, or half octagon barrel with pistol grip stock and checkering. Takedown barrel or short 22" barrel.

Courtesy Rock Island Auction Company

NIB	Exc.	V.G.	Good	Fair	Poor
—	3000	2200	1600	600	250

NOTE: Add 30 percent for .25-35, .32-40, and .38-55 calibers.

Model 1899-H Featherweight Rifle

Chambered for .303, .30-30, .25-35, and .22 HP Savage in 20" barrel. Serial number range 50000 to 220000. Built from 1905 to 1919. The revolutionary .22 HP cartridge was introduced in this model in 1912. Most 1899-Hs are found with takedown barrels.

Paul Goodwin photo

NIB	Exc.	V.G.	Good	Fair	Poor
—	1900	1400	700	300	100

NOTE: Add 50 percent for .25-35, add 25 percent for .22HP.

Model 1899 .250-3000 Savage Rifle

This deluxe Model 1899 was developed to introduce the Charles Newton designed .250-3000 Savage cartridge. Fitted with a 22" featherweight takedown barrel, pistol grip, checkered perch belly stock, unique checkered trigger. Built from 1914 to 1921 in the 146500 to 237500 serial number range.

NIB	Exc.	V.G.	Good	Fair	Poor
—	1800	1500	800	350	100

Model 99-B 26"/24" Standard Weight Takedown

Chambered for .303, .30-30, and .300 Savage. Serial number range 200000 to 344000. Produced from 1920 to 1934. In 1926 a new 24" barrel with ramp front sight was introduced.

NIB	Exc.	V.G.	Good	Fair	Poor
—	1200	900	500	300	100

Model 99-C 22" Standard Weight Short Rifle

Chambered for .303, .30-30, and .300 Savage. Serial number range 238000 to 290000. Built from 1922 to 1926. This model looks like a shortened 26" rifle but with a heavily crowned muzzle.

NIB	Exc.	V.G.	Good	Fair	Poor
—	1100	800	500	200	100

Model 99-D 22" Standard Weight Takedown Rifle

Chambered for .303, .30-30, and .300 Savage. Serial number range 238000 to 290000. Built from 1922 to 1926. Same heavily crowned muzzle as 99-C.

NIB	Exc.	V.G.	Good	Fair	Poor
—	1200	900	500	200	100

Model 99-E Lightweight Rifle

Chambered for .22 HP, .30-30, .303, .250-3000, and .300 Savage. Manufactured between 1922 and 1934. Serial number range 238000 to 344000. In 1926 new ramp front sight introduced.

Courtesy Rock Island Auction Company

NIB	Exc.	V.G.	Good	Fair	Poor
—	1450	950	600	300	100

NOTE: Add 25 percent for .22 Hi Power and .250-3000 calibers.

Model 99-F Lightweight Takedown Rifle

As above, but in lightweight takedown barrels in 20", 22", and 24". Chambered for .22 HP, .30-30, .303, .250-3000, and .300 Savage. These barrels were tapered lightweight barrels. Manufactured between 1920 and 1940. Serial number range 200000 to 398000. In 1926 new ramp front sight introduced. Early versions look similar to Model 1899-H featherweight. In 1938 checkered stocks offered this option is rare.

NIB	Exc.	V.G.	Good	Fair	Poor
—	1700	1200	700	300	100

NOTE: Add 50 percent for .22 HP, and .250-3000. Add 75 percent for 1938 checkered stocks.

Model 99-G Deluxe Takedown Pistol Grip Rifle

Calibers and barrel lengths as above, with a pistol grip checkered stock. Manufactured between 1922 and 1941. Serial number range 238000 to 407000. No takedown Model 99s made after 1941.

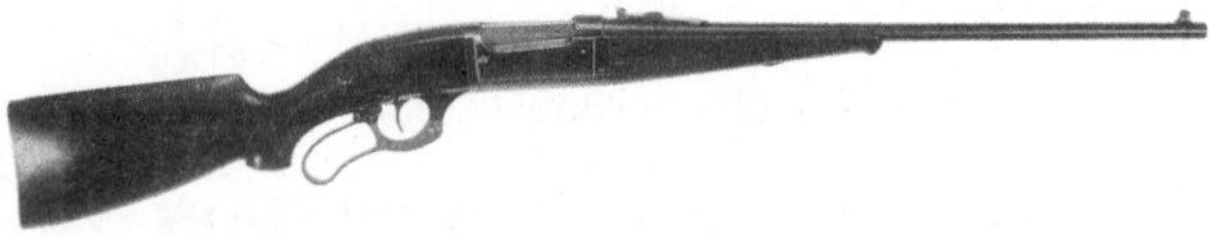

Courtesy Rock Island Auction Company

NIB	Exc.	V.G.	Good	Fair	Poor
—	1950	1400	800	300	100

NOTE: Add 50 percent for .22 Hi Power and 25 percent for .250-3000.

Model 99-H Carbine/Barrel Band Carbine

Fitted with 20" or 22" barrels and chambered for .30-30, .303,

.250-3000, and .300 Savage. serial number range 220000 to 400000. Built between 1923 and 1940. Distinctive plain stocks with no flat pads on side of buttstock. Curved carbine style buttplate. In 1931 barrel band added to forend, then commonly called the "barrel band carbine." In 1935 flat pads added to buttstock sides. Also front ramp sight added.

Courtesy Rock Island Auction Company

NIB	Exc.	V.G.	Good	Fair	Poor
—	1200	800	500	200	100

NOTE: Add 50 percent for 1935 barrel band carbine. Add 25 percent for .250-3000, and .300 Savage.

Combination Cased Set .300 Savage/.410 Barrel

Fitted with 22" or 24" barrels with .410 barrels and .300 Savage in Model 99-F, 99-G, or 99-K configuration. In black fitted case. Serial number range 240000 to 350000. built from 1922 to 1934. Be aware that the barrel address on the .410 barrel matches that on the rifle barrel and that the .410 barrel takes up correctly on the receiver, and that the case fits the .410 barrel and receiver.

Courtesy Amoskeag Auction Company

NIB	Exc.	V.G.	Good	Fair	Poor
—	4000	2500	1500	800	300

Model 99-A 24" Featherweight Rifle

Fitted with a 24" barrel with new 1926 ramp front sight. Chambered for .303, .30-30, or .300 Savage. Serial number range 290000 to 370000. Built from 1926 to 1937. Buttplate is older 1899 crescent style.

NIB	Exc.	V.G.	Good	Fair	Poor
—	900	700	5500	250	75

Model 99-K Deluxe Engraved Rifle

The premier Savage Model 99 with an engraved receiver. Fitted with a checkered pistol grip stock of select American walnut, and a takedown frame. Hand honed and hand fitted. Chambered for .22 HP, .30-30, .303, .250-3000, and .300 Savage. Fitted with 22" or 24" barrels. Serial number range 285000 to 398000. Manufactured between 1926 and 1940.

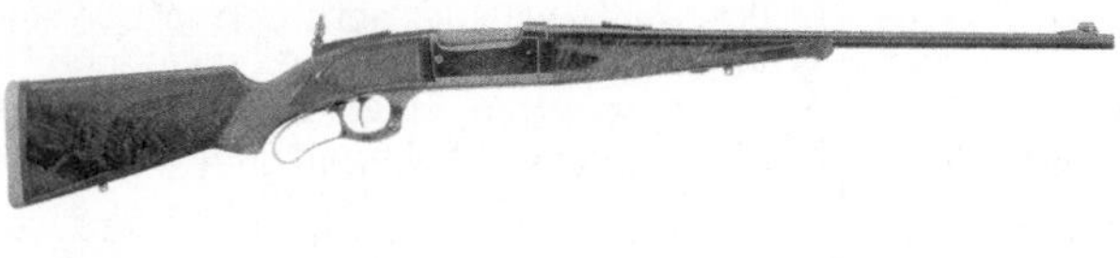

Courtesy Rock Island Auction Company

NIB	Exc.	V.G.	Good	Fair	Poor
—	3000	2500	1400	600	200

NOTE: Add 30 percent for .22 caliber Hi Power. Some of these models found with cased set with .410 barrel. Add $700 for V.G. case and barrels.

Model 99-R Heavy Stocked Rifle

This model features a heavy pistol grip checkered stock with rounded forend tip. Fitted with a 22" or 24" barrel and chambered for .250-3000, .303, .300 Savage, .308, .243, and .358 calibers. Serial number range 340000 to 1060000. Manufactured between 1932 and 1960.

Courtesy Rock Island Auction Company

NIB	Exc.	V.G.	Good	Fair	Poor
—	1300	800	550	200	100

NOTE: Add 50 percent for .358 and 100 percent for rare uncataloged .30-30. Approximately 10 made for A.F. Stoeger of N.Y.C. for N.Y. State Police in 1935 in serial number range 348600. Most of these are found with Redfield No. 102 side peep sight and 1/4" rack number stamped in stock below pistol grip.

Model 99-RS Special Sights

As above, with a Lyman aperture rear tang sight. In 1940 this was changed to a Redfield micrometer tang sight. This was the first model fitted with Savage quick release sling swivels. No .30-30 calibers made in this model. Manufactured between 1932 and 1942.

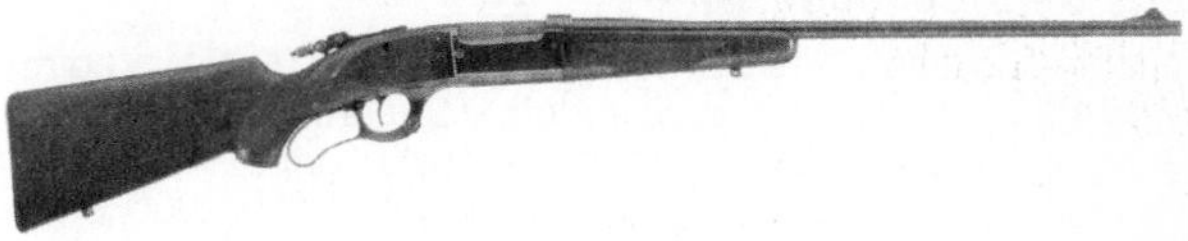

Courtesy Rock Island Auction Company

NIB	Exc.	V.G.	Good	Fair	Poor
—	1500	1000	600	350	200

NOTE: Add 50 percent for .358.

Model 99-EG Standard Weight Rifle

Produced with plain uncheckered pistol grip stock until 1940. Available in .22 Hi Power, .250 Savage, .30-30, .303 Savage. .300 Savage, .308, .243, and .358. Serial number range 350000 to 1060000. Manufactured between 1935 and 1960.

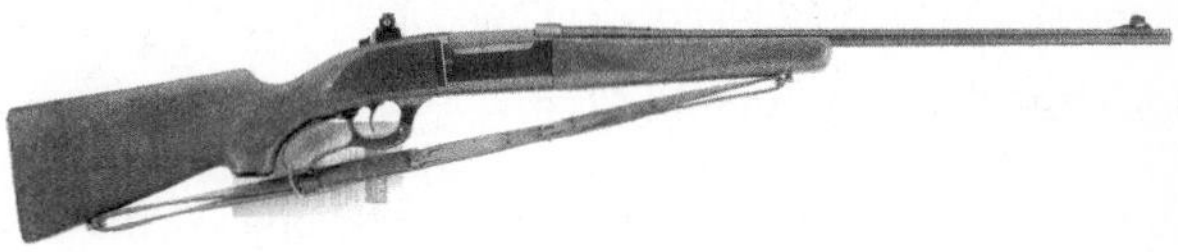

Courtesy Rock Island Auction Company

NIB	Exc.	V.G.	Good	Fair	Poor
—	900	650	400	200	75

NOTE: For pre-1940 uncheckered stocks add 20 percent. Add 100 percent for rifles chambered for .22 Hi Power and .358.

Model 99-T Deluxe Featherweight Rifle

This is the classic short barrel deluxe Model 99 with semi-beavertail forend and distinct long checkering pattern. Fitted with 20" or 22" barrels and chambered for .250-3000, .30-30, .303, .22 HP, or .300 Savage. Serial number range 350000 to 400000. Manufactured between 1935 and 1940.

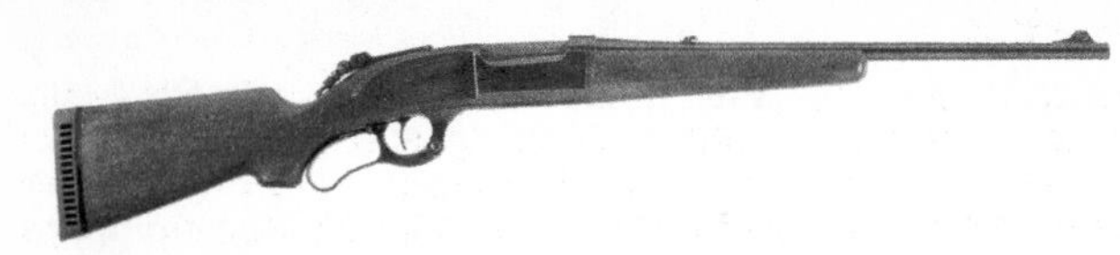

Courtesy Rock Island Auction Company

NIB	Exc.	V.G.	Good	Fair	Poor
—	1750	1200	800	450	200

NOTE: Add 100 percent for .22 Hi Power caliber, 20 percent for .250-3000.

Model 99-F Featherweight Rifle

The first Savage made with the model designation visible on the outside. Located at the rear on the right side of the barrel. A true featherweight with slender 22" barrel, lightweight stocks with butt end hollowed out. Chambered for .250-3000, .300 Savage, .308, .243, .284, and .358 calibers. Serial number range 755000 to present. Built from 1955 to 1973.

NIB	Exc.	V.G.	Good	Fair	Poor
—	1200	800	500	250	75

NOTE: Add 100 percent for .284 and .358 calibers, add 50 percent for .243 and .250-3000 Savage.

Model 99-DL Deluxe Monte Carlo Rifle

A deluxe version of the Model 99EG. Available in .243, .250 Savage, .300 Savage, .284, .358, and .308 calibers with a Monte Carlo-style stock. Serial number range 1000000 to present. Manufactured between 1960 and 1973.

NIB	Exc.	V.G.	Good	Fair	Poor
—	800	550	350	200	100

NOTE: Add 75 percent for .358 and .284 calibers.

Model 99-E Economy Rifle

The ugly duckling of the Savage line. The Model 99-E lacked many of the standard features such as left side cartridge counter, tang sight holes, walnut stocks, and capped pistol grip. Fitted with 20", 22", or 24" barrels and chambered for .250-3000, .300 Savage, .243, and .308 calibers. Serial number range 1000000 to present. Built from 1960 to 1984.

NIB	Exc.	V.G.	Good	Fair	Poor
—	750	575	375	150	50

NOTE: The Model 99-E was the last original rotary magazine Model 99 when production discontinued in 1984.

Model 99-C Clip Magazine Rifle

The recent production model in .22-250, .243, .284 Winchester, 7mm-08, or .308 caliber with a 22" barrel and open sights. Blued with a walnut stock. This model features a clip magazine and is the first modification in the Model 99 in 66 years. Introduced in 1965. Dropped from production and reintroduced in 1995 in .243 and .308 calibers. Approximate weight is 7.75 lbs.

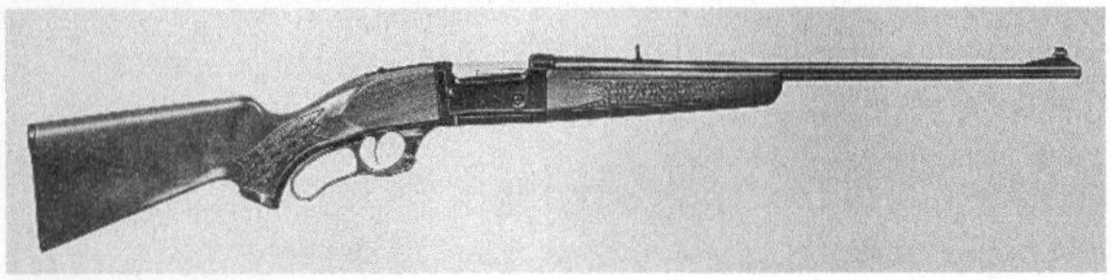

NIB	Exc.	V.G.	Good	Fair	Poor
850	550	400	250	150	50

NOTE: Add 100 percent for .22-250, .284, and 7mm-08.

Model 99-DE Citation Grade Rifle

A premier Savage with an engraved receiver with nickel-like finish and impressed checkering on select walnut stocks. Marked 99-M. Offered in .243, .284, and .308 calibers with 22" barrel only. Serial number range 1140000 to present. Manufactured between 1965 and 1970.

NIB	Exc.	V.G.	Good	Fair	Poor
—	1750	1200	700	400	200

NOTE: Add 30 percent for .284 caliber.

Model 99-PE Presentation Grade Rifle

This model is a presentation grade Model 99 with an engraved receiver as well as a hand-checkered finely figured walnut stock. Mountain lion on right side of receiver and elk on left side. Chambered for .243, .284, and .308 caliber with 22" barrel. Serial number range 1140000 to present. Manufactured between 1965 and 1970.

NIB	Exc.	V.G.	Good	Fair	Poor
—	2000	1500	800	500	300

NOTE: Add 30 percent for .284 caliber.

Model 1895 Anniversary Edition

A .308 caliber reproduction of the Model 1895 with a 24" octagonal barrel, engraved receiver and walnut stock with a schnabel forend. Brass crescent buttplate, brass medallion inlaid in stock. There were 9,999 manufactured in 1970.

NIB	Exc.	V.G.	Good	Fair	Poor
950	775	600	450	300	200

Model 99-A Saddle Gun

A variation of the original Model 99A with a 20" or 22" barrel. Chambered for the .243, .250 Savage, .300 Savage, .308, and .375. Serial number range in new "A" series on left side. Manufactured between 1971 and 1982.

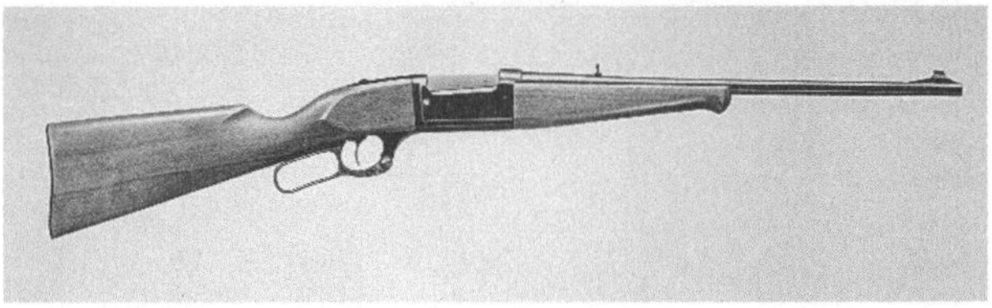

NIB	Exc.	V.G.	Good	Fair	Poor
1200	800	500	400	300	200

NOTE: Add 25 percent for .375 caliber.

Model 99-.358 and 99-.375 Brush Guns

Similar to the Model 99-A straight grip saddle gun, but in .358 and .375 Win. (1980) calibers. Has plain grooved forend, rubber recoil pad. Serial number range in the "A" series on left side. Built from 1977 to 1980.

NIB	Exc.	V.G.	Good	Fair	Poor
1200	800	500	400	300	200

NOTE: Add 25 percent for .358 Win. caliber.

Model 99-CD Deluxe Clip Model

The North American classic rifle with distinct stocks of checkered walnut with long grooved forend, deep shaped pistol grip, and Monte Carlo stock with cheekpiece. Fitted with 22" barrel and chambered for .250-3000, .308, or .243. Serial number range in new "A" series on left side. Built from 1975 to 1980.

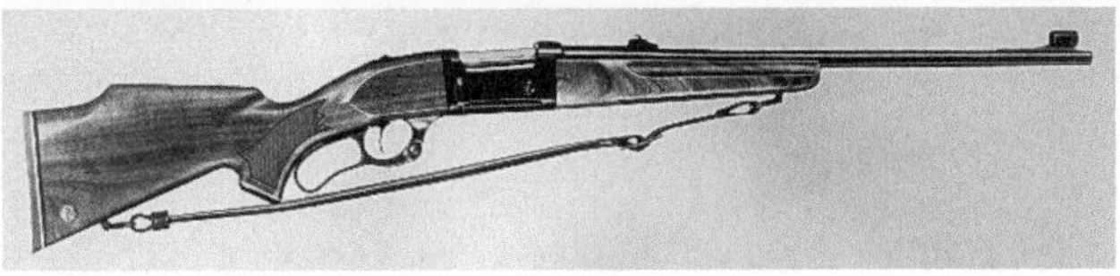

NIB	Exc.	V.G.	Good	Fair	Poor
1100	850	600	400	300	200

Model 99-CE (Centennial Edition)

Introduced in 1995 this limited edition rifle is chambered for the .300 Savage cartridge. Limited to 1,000 rifles with serial numbers from AS0001 to AS1000. Engraved receiver with gold inlays. Select American walnut stock with Monte Carlo comb.

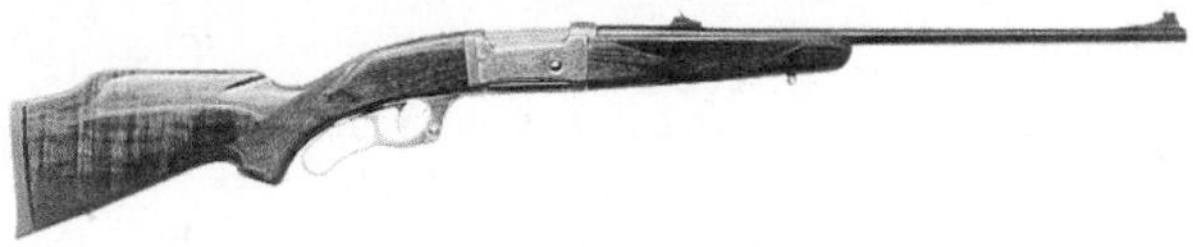

Courtesy Savage Arms

NIB	Exc.	V.G.	Good	Fair	Poor
1600	1300	900	750	500	250

Model 1903

A .22 caliber slide-action rifle with a 24" octagon barrel having open sights. Blued with a walnut stock. Manufactured between 1903 and 1922. Late model rifles have updated slide handle and pistol-grip stock in same style as Model 1914.

Courtesy Rock Island Auction Company

NIB	Exc.	V.G.	Good	Fair	Poor
—	450	350	150	100	75

Model 1903 Gallery Model

Same general specifications as Model 1903 except for a mechanical counter attached to record shots fired.

NIB	Exc.	V.G.	Good	Fair	Poor
—	550	425	200	150	100

MODEL 1903 FACTORY ENGRAVED MODELS

NOTE: These models are seldom seen. Secure a qualified appraisal prior to a sale.

Grade EF

Grade "B" checkering, fancy English walnut stock, Savage 22B front sights, and 21B rear sight.

Expert Grade

Fancy American walnut stock, Grade "A" engraving, Grade "B" checkering, and standard sights.

Grade GH

Plain American walnut stock, Grade "A" checkering, 22B front sight, and 21B rear sight.

Gold Medal Grade

Plain American walnut stock, animal ornamentation on receiver, Grade "A" checkering, and standard sights.

Model 1909

As above, with a 20" barrel. Manufactured between 1909 and 1915.

NIB	Exc.	V.G.	Good	Fair	Poor
—	450	350	175	100	75

Model 1911

Produced from 1911 to 1915 in .22 short only. Bolt-action repeater. American walnut stock. Shotgun steel buttplate, bead front sight with adjustable open rear sight. Tubular magazine is loaded through buttstock and has capacity of 20 rounds. Weight is approximately 4 lbs.

NIB	Exc.	V.G.	Good	Fair	Poor
—	475	425	225	125	100

Model 1912

A .22 caliber semi-automatic rifle with a 20" barrel, open sights and in takedown form. Magazine capacity is 7 rounds. Blued with a walnut stock. Manufactured between 1912 and 1916. Weight is about 4.5 lbs.

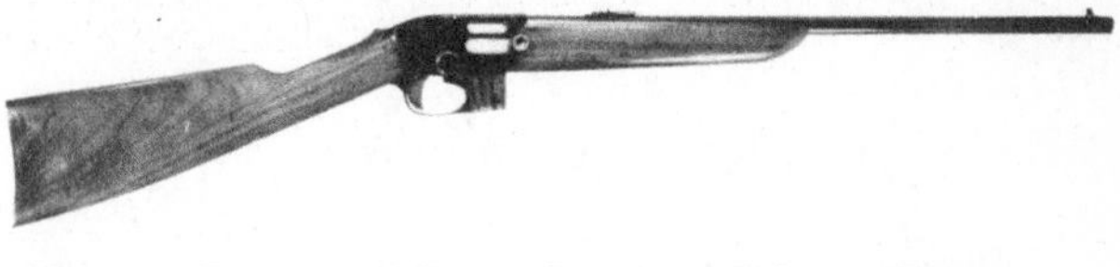

NIB	Exc.	V.G.	Good	Fair	Poor
—	550	450	300	125	90

Model 6

Similar to the above, with a 24" barrel and tubular magazine. The walnut stock checkered prior to 1938 and plain after 1965.

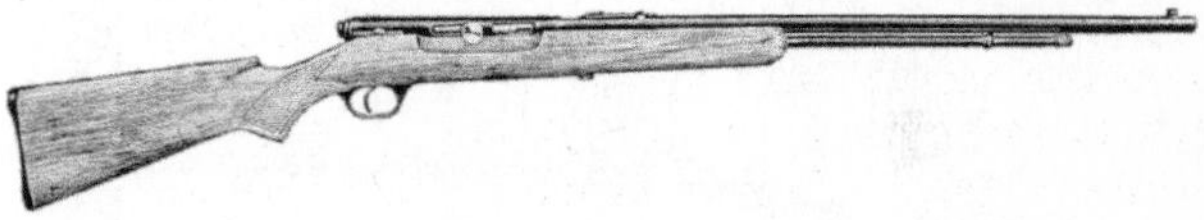

NIB	Exc.	V.G.	Good	Fair	Poor
—	350	300	200	125	50

Model 7

As above, with a detachable magazine. Manufactured between 1938 and 1954.

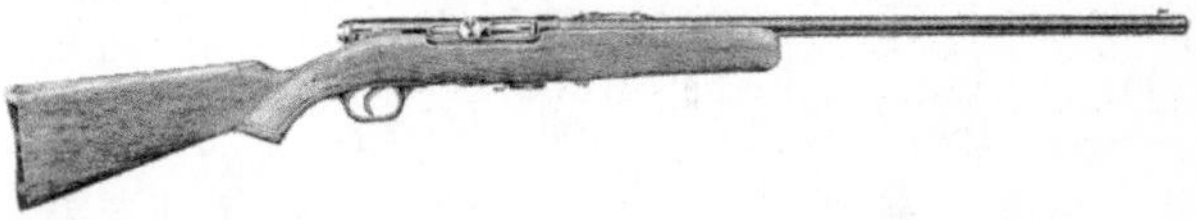

NIB	Exc.	V.G.	Good	Fair	Poor
—	350	300	200	125	50

Model 1914

As above, with a 24" octagonal barrel. Manufactured between 1914 and 1926.

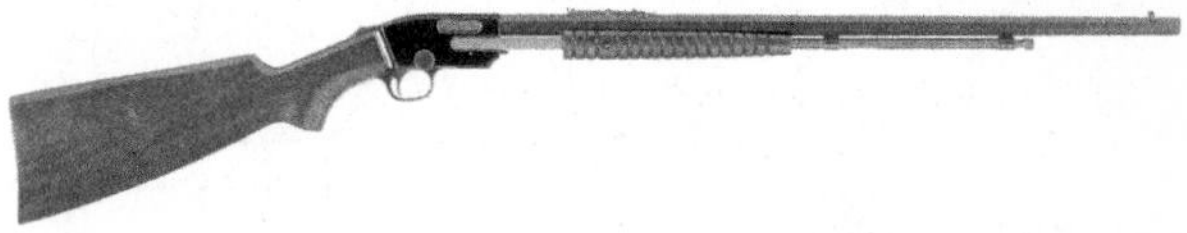

Courtesy Rock Island Auction Company

NIB	Exc.	V.G.	Good	Fair	Poor
—	350	300	200	125	50

Model 25

A .22 caliber slide-action rifle with a 24" octagonal barrel, open sights and tubular magazine. Blued with a plain walnut stock. Manufactured between 1925 and 1929.

NIB	Exc.	V.G.	Good	Fair	Poor
—	450	350	250	200	125

Model 29

Similar to above but with a 22" octagonal barrel, later changed to round on post-war rifles, and a checkered walnut stock, later changed to plain on post-war rifles. Manufactured between 1929 and 1967.

NIB	Exc.	V.G.	Good	Fair	Poor
—	450	325	200	150	100

Model 170

A .30-30 or .35 Remington caliber slide-action rifle with a 22" barrel and 3-shot tubular magazine. Blued with a walnut stock. Manufactured between 1970 and 1981.

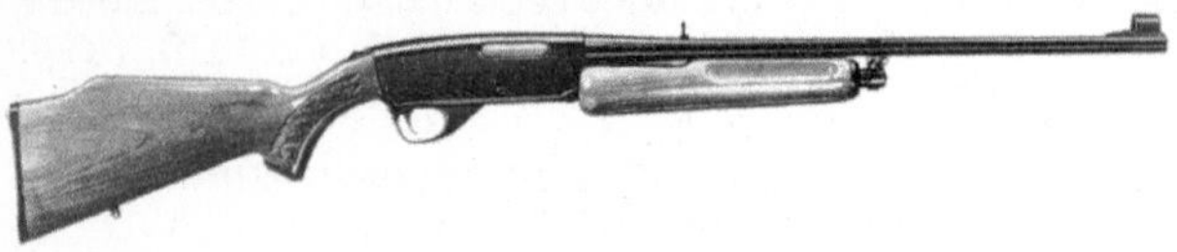

NIB	Exc.	V.G.	Good	Fair	Poor
—	550	400	250	175	100

Model 1904

A .22 caliber single-shot bolt-action rifle with an 18" barrel and walnut stock. Manufactured between 1904 and 1931. After 1915 this model became known as the Model 04.

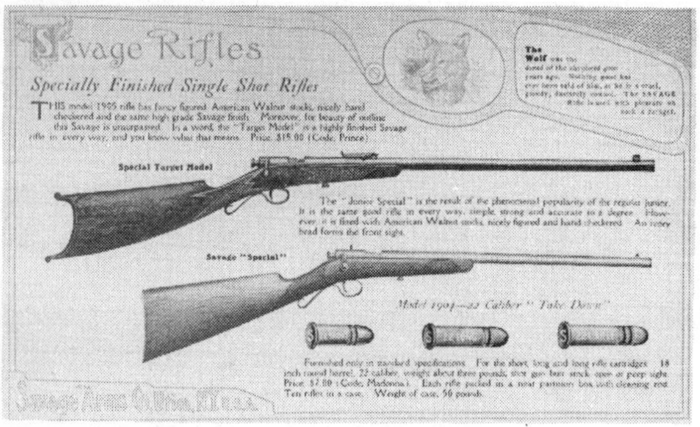

NIB	Exc.	V.G.	Good	Fair	Poor
—	200	150	100	75	50

Model 1905

As above, with a 24" barrel. Manufactured between 1905 and 1919.

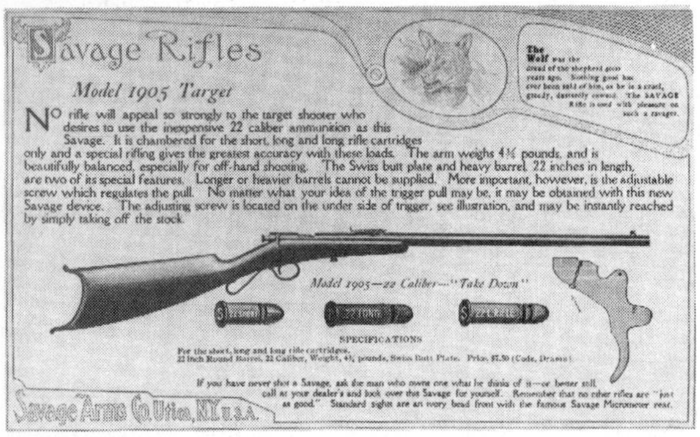

NIB	Exc.	V.G.	Good	Fair	Poor
—	200	150	100	75	50

Model 1905 Style "B"

Same as the Model 1905 target but with shotgun buttplate.

NIB	Exc.	V.G.	Good	Fair	Poor
—	375	300	200	150	50

Model 1905 Special Target Rifle

This model is the same as the Model 1905 Target Rifle except for hand checkered fancy American walnut stock.

NIB	Exc.	V.G.	Good	Fair	Poor
—	450	325	250	150	100

Model 19 NRA

A .22 caliber bolt-action rifle with a 25" barrel, detachable magazine and full-length military-style stock. Approximately 50,000 were manufactured total between 1919 and 1937.

NIB	Exc.	V.G.	Good	Fair	Poor
—	395	250	175	100	75

Model 19L

As above, with a Lyman receiver sight. Manufactured between 1933 and 1942.

NIB	Exc.	V.G.	Good	Fair	Poor
—	425	275	225	200	150

Model 19M

As above, with a 28" barrel fitted with telescope sight bases. Manufactured between 1933 and 1942.

NIB	Exc.	V.G.	Good	Fair	Poor
—	395	250	175	100	75

Model 19H

The Model 19 chambered for .22 Hornet. Manufactured between 1933 and 1942.

NIB	Exc.	V.G.	Good	Fair	Poor
—	600	475	350	300	200

Model 3

A .22 caliber single-shot bolt-action rifle with a 24" barrel, open sights and walnut stock. Manufactured between 1933 and 1952.

NIB	Exc.	V.G.	Good	Fair	Poor
—	200	150	100	75	50

Model 4

Similar to the above, with a 24" barrel and 5-shot magazine. Produced from 1932 to 1964.

NIB	Exc.	V.G.	Good	Fair	Poor
—	200	150	100	75	50

Model 4M

As above, in .22 Magnum. Produced from 1960 to 1964.

NIB	Exc.	V.G.	Good	Fair	Poor
—	225	175	110	75	50

Model 5

The Model 4 with a tubular magazine. Manufactured between 1933 and 1964.

NIB	Exc.	V.G.	Good	Fair	Poor
—	200	150	100	75	50

Model 1920

A .250-3000 or .300 Savage caliber bolt-action rifle with a 22" or 24" barrel, open sights and 5-shot magazine. Blued, with a walnut stock and schnabel forend. Manufactured between 1920 and 1929. An improved version of this rifle was introduced in 1926 that was heavier and had a Lyman #54 peep sight.

NIB	Exc.	V.G.	Good	Fair	Poor
—	1000	600	465	300	200

Model 1922

This model is a variation of the Model 19 NRA with a sporting-style stock and schnabel forend. Fitted with a 23" round barrel it was chambered for the .22 caliber cartridge. This model superceded the Model 23 and looks like a Model 23 sporter. Introduced in 1922 and discontinued in 1923. Very rare.

NIB	Exc.	V.G.	Good	Fair	Poor
—	750	600	475	300	200

Model 23A

This bolt-action .22 LR rifle was introduced in 1923 and features a 5-round detachable box magazine and 23" barrel with open sights. The large loading port on the left side of the receiver permitted easy single-shot loading. The stock was plain with pistol grip and a schnabel forend. A varnish wood finish was applied to this model. Production stopped in 1933.

NIB	Exc.	V.G.	Good	Fair	Poor
—	350	275	150	125	100

Model 23AA

This was an improved version of the Model 23A introduced in 1933. It features better speed lock, redesigned stock with oil finish. The receiver was tapped for No. 15 Savage extension peep sight. The rifle weighs approximately 6 lbs. Production ceased in 1942.

NIB	Exc.	V.G.	Good	Fair	Poor
—	395	295	200	150	125

Model 23B

Similar to the Model 23A except chambered for the .25-20 cartridge. Barrel length was 25" and forearm was a full 1.5" wide beavertail. Receiver was tapped for peep sight and magazine capacity was 4 rounds. Production on the Model 23B was from 1923 to 1940.

NIB	Exc.	V.G.	Good	Fair	Poor
—	375	325	250	200	100

Model 23C

The same configuration as the Model 23B with the exception of the caliber .32-20. Manufactured from 1923 to 1946.

NIB	Exc.	V.G.	Good	Fair	Poor
—	375	325	250	200	100

Model 23D

The same configuration as the Model 23B but chambered for the .22 Hornet cartridge. Manufactured from 1932 to 1948.

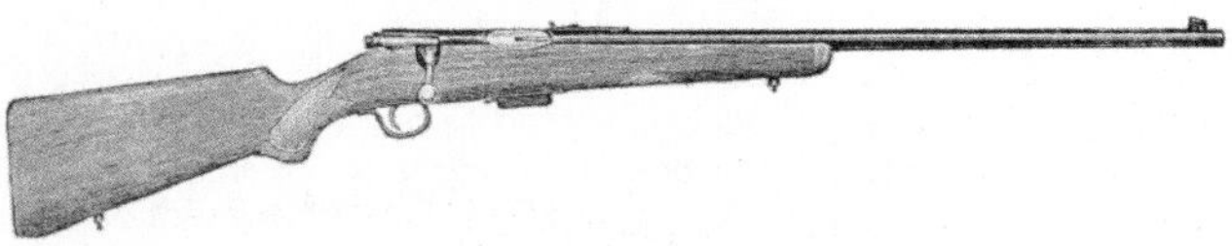

NIB	Exc.	V.G.	Good	Fair	Poor
—	375	325	250	200	100

Model 40 (Old Model)

Similar to the above but in .250-3000, .300 Savage, .30-30, and .30-06 caliber. Manufactured between 1928 and 1940.

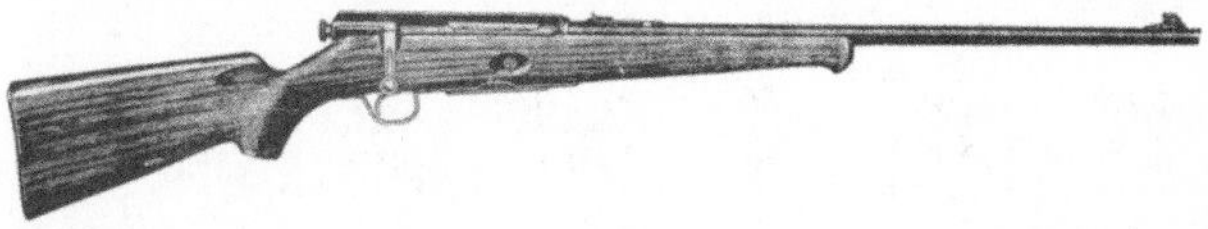

NIB	Exc.	V.G.	Good	Fair	Poor
—	425	350	295	250	175

Model 45 Super

Similar to old Model 40, with a Lyman receiver sight and checkered walnut stock. Manufactured between 1928 and 1940.

NIB	Exc.	V.G.	Good	Fair	Poor
—	400	350	300	200	150

Model 35

A .22 caliber bolt-action rifle with a 22" barrel, open sights and 5-shot magazine. Blued with a Monte Carlo-style hardwood stock.

NIB	Exc.	V.G.	Good	Fair	Poor
—	175	150	125	75	50

Model 46

As above with a tubular magazine. Manufactured between 1969 and 1973.

NIB	Exc.	V.G.	Good	Fair	Poor
—	175	150	125	75	50

Model 340

A .22 Hornet, .222 Remington, .223, or .30-30 caliber bolt-action rifle with a 22" or 24" barrel, open sights and 4- or 5-shot magazine. Blued, with a plain walnut stock. Manufactured between 1950 and 1985.

NIB	Exc.	V.G.	Good	Fair	Poor
—	375	325	250	200	100

Model 342

As above, but in .22 Hornet caliber. Manufactured between 1950 and 1955.

NIB	Exc.	V.G.	Good	Fair	Poor
—	375	325	250	200	100

MODEL 110 SERIES

Model 110 Sporter

A bolt-action rifle manufactured in a variety of calibers with a 22" barrel, open sights and 4-shot magazine. Blued with a walnut stock. Manufactured between 1958 and 1963.

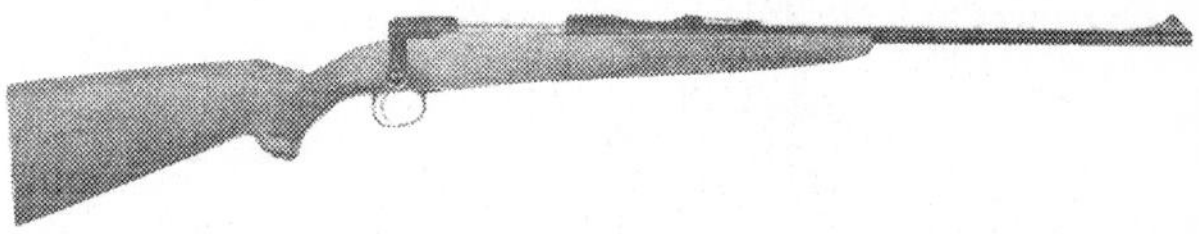

NIB	Exc.	V.G.	Good	Fair	Poor
—	375	250	175	125	100

Model 110-M

Similar to the above, in 7mm Magnum to .338 Winchester Magnum. Manufactured between 1963 and 1969.

NIB	Exc.	V.G.	Good	Fair	Poor
—	395	275	200	150	125

Model 110-D

Similar to the Model 110 in .22-250 to .338 Winchester Magnum caliber with a detachable magazine. Manufactured between 1966 and 1988.

NIB	Exc.	V.G.	Good	Fair	Poor
—	400	300	250	200	150

Model 110-P Premier Grade

As above, with a finely figured walnut stock, rosewood forend tip and pistol grip cap. Manufactured between 1964 and 1970.

NIB	Exc.	V.G.	Good	Fair	Poor
—	575	450	325	250	200

Model 110-PE

As above, with an engraved receiver, magazine floorplate and trigger guard. Manufactured between 1968 and 1970.

NIB	Exc.	V.G.	Good	Fair	Poor
—	950	700	500	400	300

NOTE: Current production Model 110-F are made in the styles listed.

Model 110-F

DuPont Rynite stock and sights. Discontinued.

NIB	Exc.	V.G.	Good	Fair	Poor
450	400	350	300	250	200

Model 110-FX

As above without sights. Discontinued.

NIB	Exc.	V.G.	Good	Fair	Poor
400	350	300	250	200	150

Model 110-FP

Composite stock and 24" heavy barrel. In 2003 the Savage AccuTrigger was added to this model. Discontinued.

NIB	Exc.	V.G.	Good	Fair	Poor
600	450	325	225	150	150

Model 110-G

Checkered hardwood stock and sights. Discontinued.

NIB	Exc.	V.G.	Good	Fair	Poor
425	325	275	225	175	125

Model 110-GX

As above without sights. Discontinued.

NIB	Exc.	V.G.	Good	Fair	Poor
400	300	250	200	150	100

Model 110-CY

A compact version of the Model 110 series. Shorter length of pull on walnut stock and 22" barrel. Overall length is 42-1/2". Weight is about 6-1/2 lbs. Chambered in .223, .243, .270, .300 Savage, and .308 calibers. Discontinued.

NIB	Exc.	V.G.	Good	Fair	Poor
400	300	250	200	150	100

Model 110-FP Tactical

Offered in calibers from .223 Rem. to .300 Win. Mag this bolt-action rifle has a 24" heavy barrel with recessed muzzle. The synthetic stock is black as are all other surfaces. Available in both right- and left-hand versions. Weight is approximately 8.5 lbs. Discontinued.

NIB	Exc.	V.G.	Good	Fair	Poor
600	450	325	225	150	150

Model 110-FP Duty

Introduced in 2002 this model is chambered for the .308 cartridge and features a 24" free-floating barrel with open sights. Black synthetic stock. Third swivel stud for bipod. Matte blue finish. Magazine capacity is 4 rounds. Weight is about 8.5 lbs. Discontinued.

NIB	Exc.	V.G.	Good	Fair	Poor
600	450	300	250	200	100

Model 110-FP-LE1

Similar to the Model 110FP-Duty (.308) but with a 20" barrel. No sights. Weight is about 8.25 lbs. Introduced in 2002. Discontinued.

NIB	Exc.	V.G.	Good	Fair	Poor
500	375	275	225	175	100

Model 110-FP-LE2

Same as the model above but fitted with a 26" barrel. Weight is about 8.75 lbs. Introduced in 2002. Discontinued.

NIB	Exc.	V.G.	Good	Fair	Poor
500	375	275	225	175	100

Model 110-Fiftieth Anniversary

Short-action rifle commemorating the 50th anniversary of the Model 10. Chambered in .300 Savage with 22-inch barrel. 1000 numbered rifles, high-luster blued barrel and action, unique checkering pattern on select walnut stock, high-grade hinged floorplate, Scroll pattern on receiver, 24-karat gold plated double barrel bands, 24-karat gold plated AccuTrigger, embossed recoil pad.

NIB	Exc.	V.G.	Good	Fair	Poor
1000	750	600	475	300	200

Axis Series

Comes in long or short action, offered in eight cartridge choices from .223 Remington to .30-06 Springfield. Stainless action, natural color. Detachable box magazine. Right-hand action only. Synthetic stock with camo or black matte finish. Drilled and tapped for scope mounts. Also available with 3-9x40 mounted scope. Previously called "The Edge".

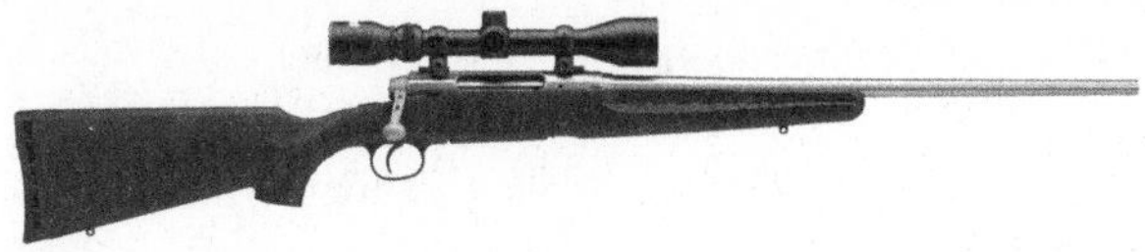

NIB	Exc.	V.G.	Good	Fair	Poor
300	265	225	200	150	100

NOTE: Add 15 percent for camo stock, 20 percent for scope.

110 BA Law Enforcement Rifle

Bolt action rifle chambered .300 Win. Mag. And .338 Lapua Mag. Features include aluminum stock that features Savage\qs innovative three-dimensional bedding system; interchangeable buttstocks and pistol grips; three-sided accessory rail; 5-round detachable magazine; high-efficiency muzzle-brake; Magpul PRS adjustable stock; 26-inch carbon steel barrel.

NIB	Exc.	V.G.	Good	Fair	Poor
1900	1650	1400	1100	700	300

MODEL 111 SERIES

Model 111 Classic Hunter Series

Allmodelsunderthisseriesarefittedwithaclassic Americandesigned straight comb stock with pistol grip. Chambered in 13 different calibers from .223 Rem. to the .338 Win. Mag. Weights vary with caliber and stock type but range from 6-3/8 to 7 lbs. Models are fitted with a detachable or internal magazine. All Hunter series rifles are drilled and tapped for scope mounts.

Model 111G

Top loading with walnut stock with recoil pad. chambered for the .25-06, .270, .30-06, 7mm Rem. Mag., or the .300 Win. Mag. Fitted with 22" or 24" barrel depending on caliber with iron sights. Weight is about 7 lbs.

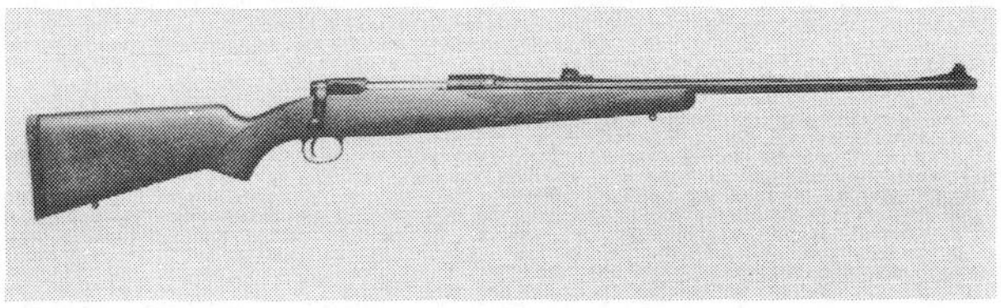

NIB	Exc.	V.G.	Good	Fair	Poor
495	375	275	200	150	100

Model 111GCNS

This is a long action model as above with 22" or 24" barrel depending on caliber with no sights. Introduced in 2005.

NIB	Exc.	V.G.	Good	Fair	Poor
515	400	325	250	175	100

Model 111GC

Detachable magazine with walnut stock and recoil pad. Discontinued.

Savage Model 111 GC

NIB	Exc.	V.G.	Good	Fair	Poor
450	350	300	250	200	150

Model 111GL

Same as the Model 111G model but with left hand action.

NIB	Exc.	V.G.	Good	Fair	Poor
485	350	250	200	150	100

Model 111F

Top loading with graphite stock. Chambered for the .25-06, .270, .30-06, 7mm Rem. Mag., .300 Win. Mag., and the .338 Win. Mag. cartridges. Fitted with either a 22" or 24" barrel depending on caliber with iron sights. Black synthetic stock. Weight is about 6.75 lbs. depending on caliber.

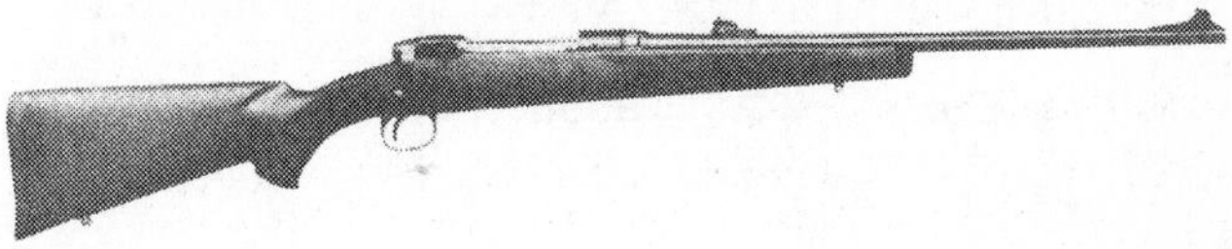

NIB	Exc.	V.G.	Good	Fair	Poor
485	350	250	200	150	100

Model 111FL

As above but with left hand action.

NIB	Exc.	V.G.	Good	Fair	Poor
485	350	250	200	150	100

Model 111FC

Detachable magazine with graphite stock. Discontinued.

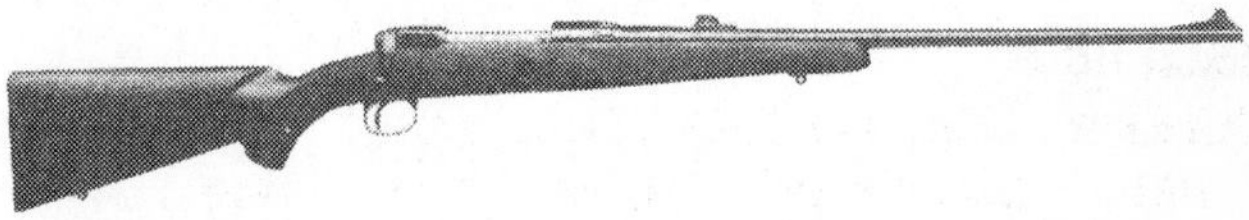

NIB	Exc.	V.G.	Good	Fair	Poor
450	350	300	250	200	150

Model 111FCNS

Introduced in 2005 this model is chambered for the .25-06, .270, .30-06, 7mm Rem. Mag., .300 Win. Mag., and the .338 Win. Mag calibers. Fitted with 22" or 24" barrel with no sights. Black synthetic stock. Weight is about 6.75 lbs. depending on caliber.

NIB	Exc.	V.G.	Good	Fair	Poor
505	375	275	—	—	—

Model 111FXP3

Top loading with graphite stock and 3x9 scope, rings, and bases, and sling.

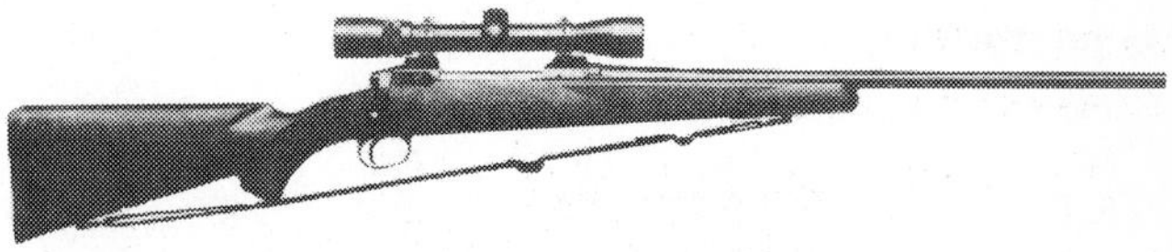

NIB	Exc.	V.G.	Good	Fair	Poor
515	400	350	300	200	150

Model 111FCXP3

Same as above but detachable magazine.

NIB	Exc.	V.G.	Good	Fair	Poor
515	400	350	300	200	150

Model 111FAK

Blued steel barrel, composite stock, muzzlebrake. Discontinued.

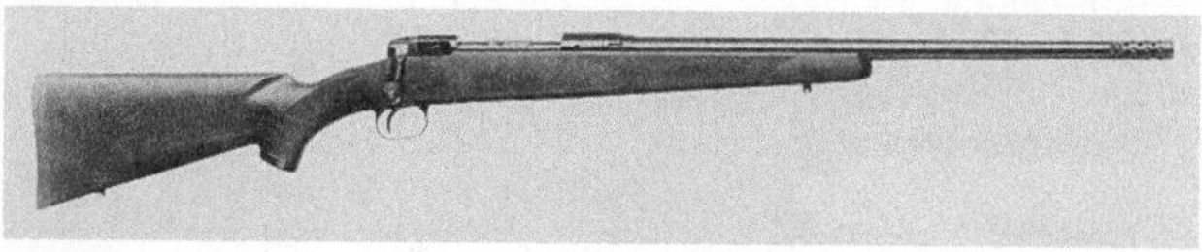

NIB	Exc.	V.G.	Good	Fair	Poor
450	350	300	250	200	150

MODEL 112 SERIES

Model 112BT / 112BT-S (Long Action)

Introduced for the first time in 1994 this model is a competition grade rifle. Chambered for the .223 Rem. and the .308 Win. it features a 26" heavy stainless steel barrel fitted to an alloy steel receiver. In 1995 the .300 Win. Magnum was added to the line referred to as the Model 112BT-S. The barrel finish is black. The stock is laminated with ambidextrous palm swell and adjustable cheek rest. Weight is about 11 lbs.

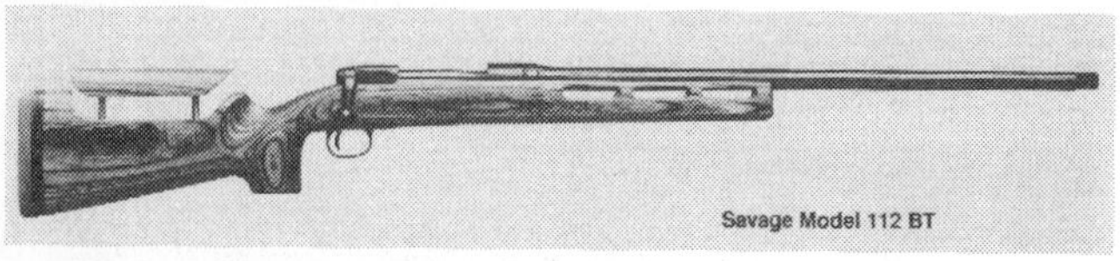

Savage Model 112 BT

NIB	Exc.	V.G.	Good	Fair	Poor
1025	850	700	500	300	250

Model 112 Series Varmint Rifles

This series of varmint rifles features 26" barrels. Offered with either composite or laminated wood stocks all Model 112s are top loading and all are drilled and tapped for scope mounting. Available in .223, .22-250, and .220 Swift the BV configuration weighs about 10-1/2 lbs. while the FV configuration weighs about 9 lbs.

Model 112BVSS (Long Action)

This model has a laminated wood stock with high comb and ambidextrous palm swell. It is fitted with a stainless steel barrel, bolt and trigger guard. In 1996 the .300 Win. Mag., 7mm Rem. Mag., .308 Win., .30-06, and .25-06 was added to this model.

NIB	Exc.	V.G.	Good	Fair	Poor
720	550	400	275	200	150

Model 112BVSS-S

Same as above but single-shot.

NIB	Exc.	V.G.	Good	Fair	Poor
600	450	325	225	150	150

Model 112FVSS

This version also is fitted with a stainless steel barrel and a composite stock This version was fitted with a stainless steel "fluted" barrel in 1995. Several new calibers were added as well: 300 Win. Mag., 7mm Rem. Mag., .25-06 Rem. In 2003 the Savage AccuTrigger was added to this model.

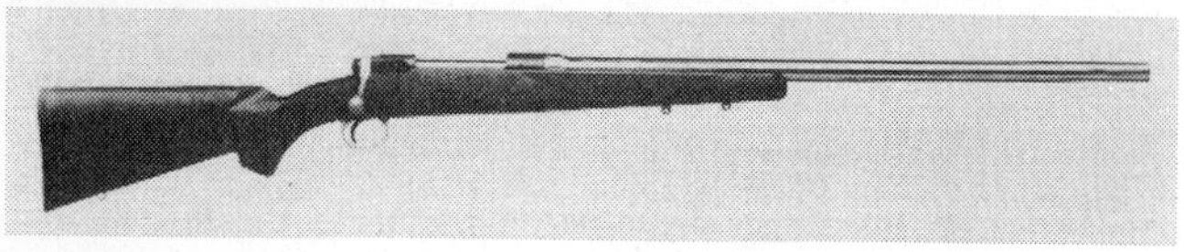

NIB	Exc.	V.G.	Good	Fair	Poor
475	400	350	300	200	150

Model 112FVSS-S

This is a single-shot version of the above model.

NIB	Exc.	V.G.	Good	Fair	Poor
475	400	350	300	200	150

Model 112FV

This is similar to the model above but with a blued barrel.

NIB	Exc.	V.G.	Good	Fair	Poor
375	300	250	200	150	100

Model 112BT—Competition Grade

This model was introduced in 1996. It is a competition rifle. It features a 26" blackened stainless steel barrel and custom target style laminated stock with adjustable cheek rest. Chambered for .223 or .308 cartridges. Weight is approximately 11 lbs. The barrel is pillar bedded.

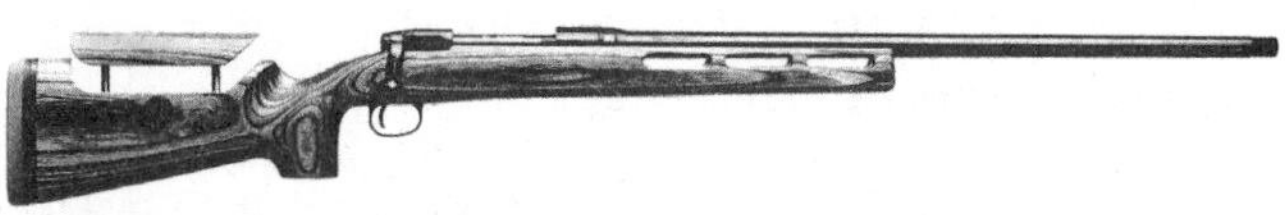

NIB	Exc.	V.G.	Good	Fair	Poor
950	850	700	500	300	250

MODEL 114 SERIES

Model 114C—Classic

This model, introduced in 2000, features a select grade oil finished walnut stock with cut checkering. No sights. Chambered for .270 and .30-06 with 22" barrel, and 7mm Mag. and .300 Win. Mag with 24" barrel.

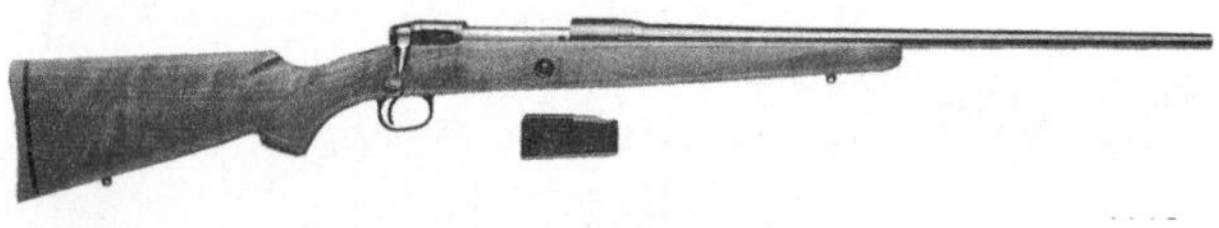

NIB	Exc.	V.G.	Good	Fair	Poor
615	450	325	225	—	—

Model 114CE—Classic European

Introduced in 1996 this rifle is chambered for the .270 Win., .30-06, 7mm Rem. Mag., and .300 Win. Mag. Barrel lengths are 22" or 24" depending on caliber. It has an oil-finished stock with skip line checkering and cheekpiece. The forend tip is a schnabel type. Rubber recoil pad and pistol grip cap are standard. High luster blue finish. Approximate weight is 7.12 lbs. Discontinued.

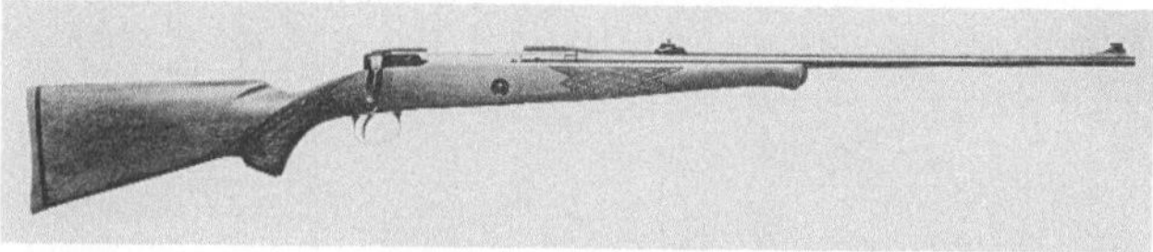

Courtesy Savage Arms

NIB	Exc.	V.G.	Good	Fair	Poor
550	475	400	350	300	150

Model 114CU

This model has a select grade walnut oil finished stock. The finish is a high polish blue and the bolt has a laser etched Savage logo. A detachable magazine is standard. The receiver is drilled and tapped for a scope mount. Offered in .270, .30-06, 7mm Rem. Mag., and .300 Win. Mag. Weights are about 7-1/8 lbs. Discontinued.

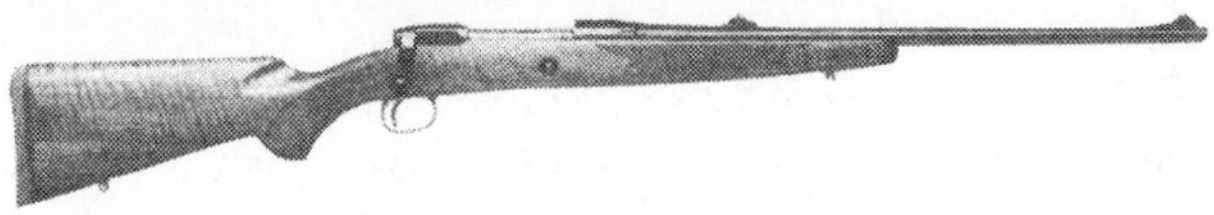

NIB	Exc.	V.G.	Good	Fair	Poor
500	425	325	250	200	150

Model 114U—Ultra

Introduced in 1999 this model features a high gloss walnut stock with custom checkering. Blued finish is high luster with a laser-etched Savage logo on the bolt body. Chambered for the .270 Win., .30-06, 7mm-08 Rem., and .300 Win. Mag cartridges. Barrel length is 22" and 24" depending on caliber. Weight is about 7 lbs.

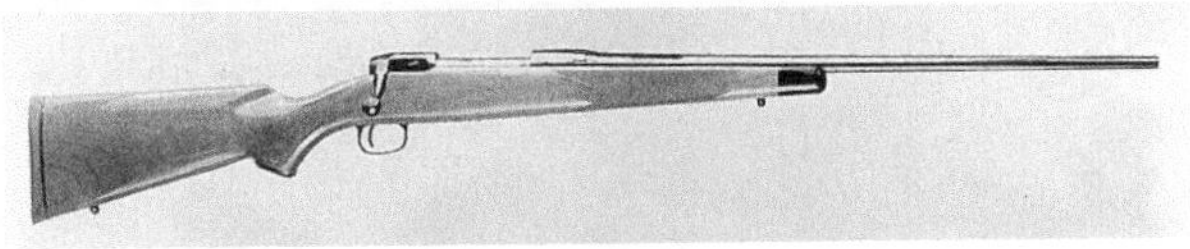

NIB	Exc.	V.G.	Good	Fair	Poor
500	425	325	250	200	150

MODEL 116 SERIES

This series of rifles feature graphite stocks and stainless steel barreled actions. An adjustable muzzlebrake is also included. All rifles in the 116 series are drilled and tapped for scope mounts.

Model 116FCSAK (Long Action)

Features a detachable box magazine. The 22" barrel is fluted. Offered in .270, .30-06, 7mm Rem. Mag., .300 Win. Mag., and .338 Win. Mag. Weighs about 6-1/2 lbs.

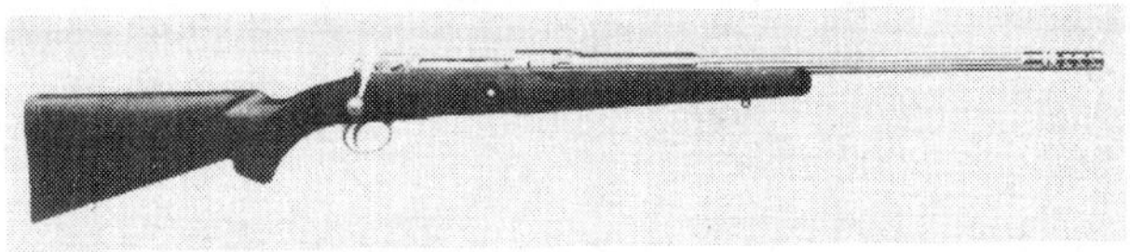

NIB	Exc.	V.G.	Good	Fair	Poor
660	500	375	250	175	175

Model 116FSAK (Long Action)

Same as model above but with on-off choice for muzzlebrake given to shooter. AccuTrigger added in 2004.

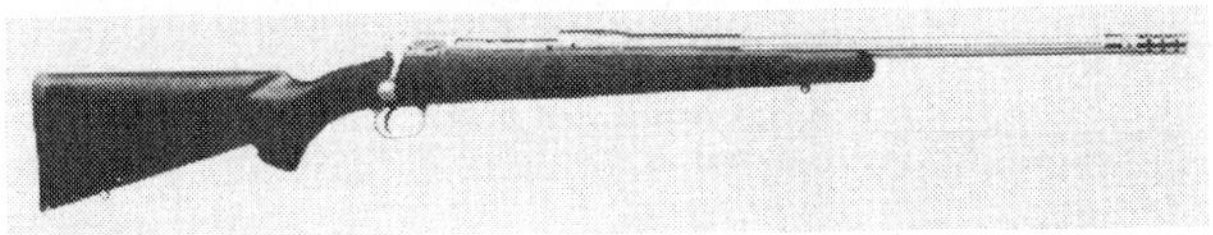

NIB	Exc.	V.G.	Good	Fair	Poor
600	450	325	225	175	175

Model 116BSS

Introduced in 2001 this model features a laminated stock. It is chambered for the .270 Win., .30-06, 7mm Rem. Mag., .300 Win. Mag., and the .300 Rem. Ultra Mag. cartridges. Fitted with either a 24" or 26" stainless steel barrel depending on caliber. No sights. Weight is about 7.5 lbs. depending on caliber. Discontinued.

NIB	Exc.	V.G.	Good	Fair	Poor
625	500	365	225	175	175

Model 116FSS (Long Action)

This is the standard configuration for the 116 series. This model features a top-loading action with 22" or 24" barrel depending on caliber. There is no muzzlebrake fitted to this model. Weight is approximately 6-3/4 lbs. Offered in 7 calibers from .223 to .338 Win. Mag. AccuTrigger added in 2004.

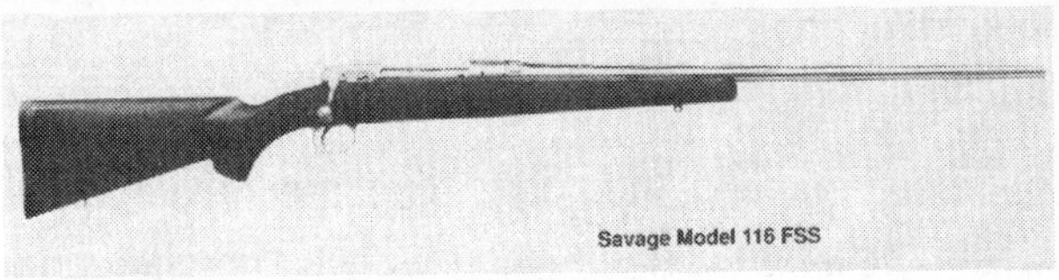

Savage Model 116 FSS

NIB	Exc.	V.G.	Good	Fair	Poor
550	475	375	300	200	150

Model 116FCS

Same as above but with stainless steel removable box magazine.

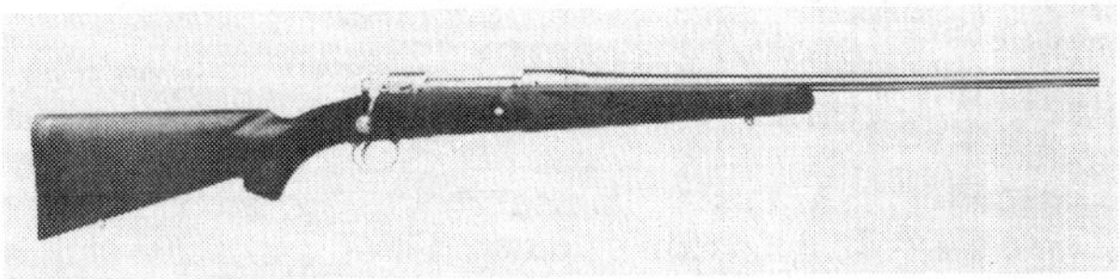

NIB	Exc.	V.G.	Good	Fair	Poor
550	475	375	300	200	150

Model 116FSK—Kodiak (Long Action)

This model features a top loading action with a 22" barrel with muzzlebrake. Weight is approximately 7.25 lbs.

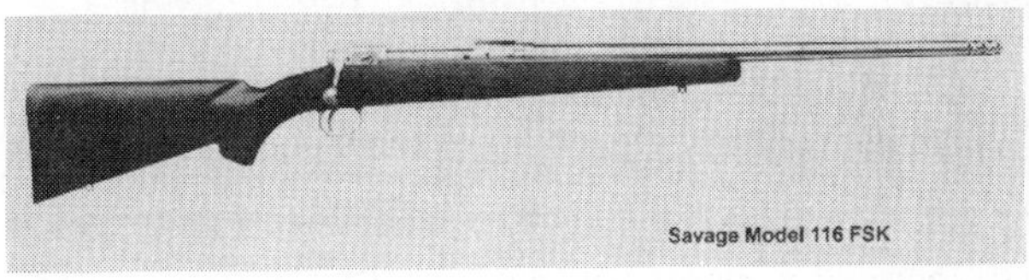

Savage Model 116 FSK

NIB	Exc.	V.G.	Good	Fair	Poor
575	495	385	300	200	150

Model 116SE—Safari Express

Introduced in 1994 this rifle features select grade walnut stock with ebony tip and deluxe checkering. Barrel and action are stainless steel with adjustable muzzlebrake. Offered in .300 Win. Mag., .338 Win. Mag., and .458 calibers. In 1995 the .425 Express cartridge was added. In 2000 this model had a stainless steel action and barrel. Weight is approximately 8-1/2 lbs. Discontinued.

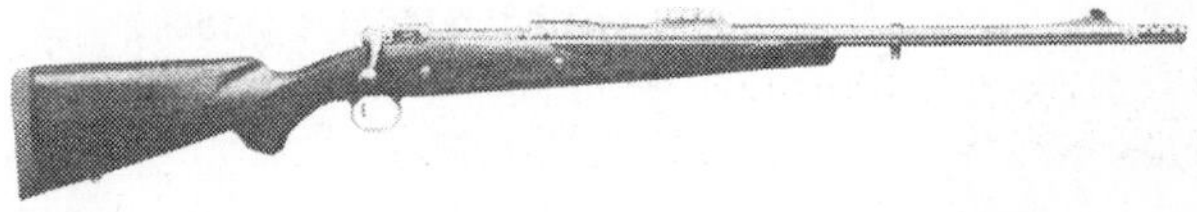

NIB	Exc.	V.G.	Good	Fair	Poor
1100	950	775	600	475	300

Model 116US

Introduced in 1995 this model features a stainless steel action and barrel with a high gloss American walnut stock with ebony tip and custom checkering. Offered in .270 Win., .30-06, 7mm Rem. Mag., and .300 Win. Mag. Barrel is 22" on the two smaller calibers and 24" on the magnum calibers. Discontinued.

NIB	Exc.	V.G.	Good	Fair	Poor
600	500	400	300	250	200

MODEL 12 SERIES VARMINT

Introduced in 1998 this series features a short action heavy barrel line of rifles designed for long-range shooting.

Model 12BVSS

This model features a 26" fluted stainless steel barrel with recessed crown and a brown laminated stock with beavertail forend. Chambered for .223, .22-250, and .308. Magazine capacity is 4 rounds. Weight is approximately 9.5 lbs. Introduced in 1998. In 2003 the Savage AccuTrigger was added to this model.

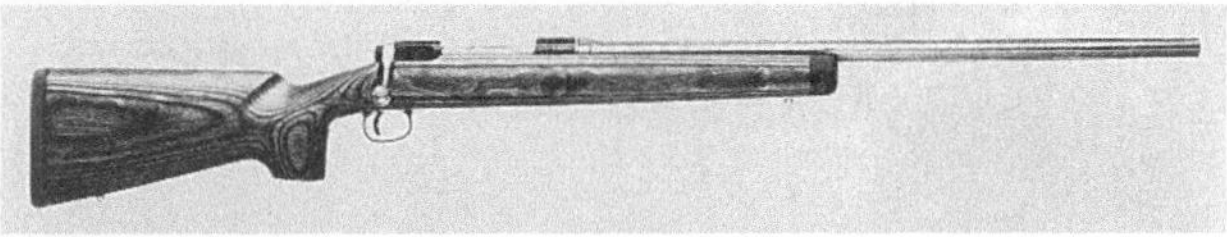

NIB	Exc.	V.G.	Good	Fair	Poor
720	550	400	275	200	100

Model 12BVSS-S

Same as above but in a single-shot version chambered for .223 and .22-250. Weight is 9 lbs. In 2003 the Savage AccuTrigger was added to this model.

NIB	Exc.	V.G.	Good	Fair	Poor
720	550	400	275	200	150

Model 12BVSS-SXP

Introduced in 2003 this single-shot model is chambered for the .223 Rem. or .22-250 Rem. cartridge. Fitted with a 26" stainless steel fluted barrel. Savage AccuTrigger. Stock is a target-style heavy prone laminate. Weight is about 12 lbs.

NIB	Exc.	V.G.	Good	Fair	Poor
675	525	400	275	200	150

Model 12BTCSS

Similar to Model 12BVSS but with laminated thumbhole Monte Carlo stock with short action and detachable box magazine.

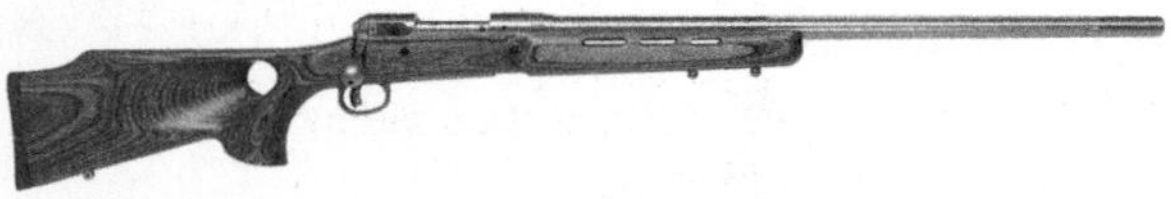

NIB	Exc.	V.G.	Good	Fair	Poor
725	550	400	275	200	100

Model 12FVSS

This model has a 26" stainless steel fluted barrel and a synthetic stock. Offered in .223, .22-250, and .308 calibers. Weight is about 9 lbs. Introduced in 1998. A left-hand version is also offered. In 2003 the Savage AccuTrigger was added to this model.

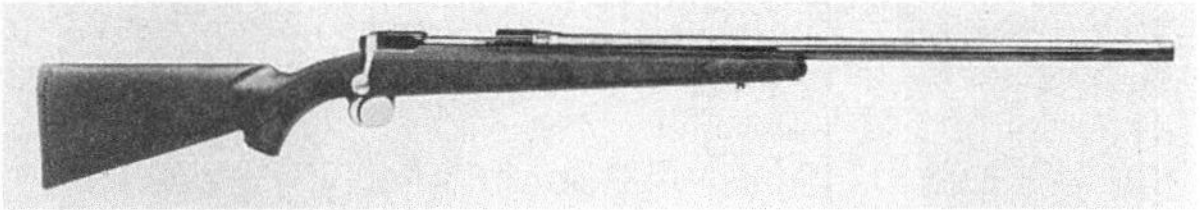

NIB	Exc.	V.G.	Good	Fair	Poor
600	500	375	250	200	100

Model 12FVSS-S

Same as above but in a single-shot configuration chambered for .223 or .22-250. Weight is about 9 lbs. In 2003 the Savage AccuTrigger was added to this model. Discontinued.

NIB	Exc.	V.G.	Good	Fair	Poor
550	450	325	225	175	100

Model 12FV (Short Action)

This model is similar to the other 12 Series rifles but with blued actions and 26" barrels that are nonfluted. Synthetic stock. Chambered for .223 or .22-250. Weight is about 9 lbs. Introduced in 1998. Offered in a left-hand model. In 2003 the Savage AccuTrigger was added to this model.

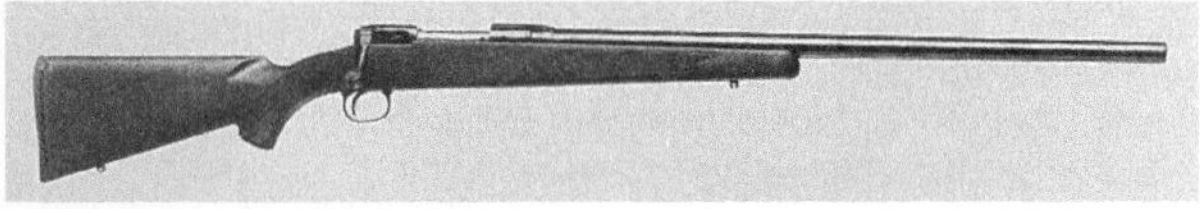

NIB	Exc.	V.G.	Good	Fair	Poor
575	495	385	300	200	150

Model 12FLV

As above but with left hand action. Introduced in 2005.

NIB	Exc.	V.G.	Good	Fair	Poor
575	495	385	300	200	150

Model 12VSS—Varminter (Short Action)

Introduced in 2000 this model features a Choate adjustable black synthetic stock. A heavy fluted stainless steel barrel. Box magazine holds 4 rounds. Chambered for .223 or .22-250 cartridges. Weight is approximately 15 lbs. In 2003 the Savage AccuTrigger was added to this model.

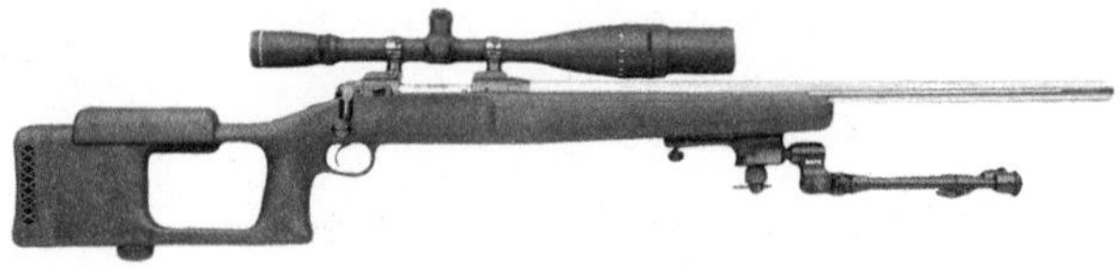

NIB	Exc.	V.G.	Good	Fair	Poor
700	525	375	275	200	100

Model 12 Varminter Low Profile

Introduced in 2004 this model is chambered for the .223 Rem. or .22-250 cartridge and fitted with a 26" heavy fluted stainless steel barrel with no sights. Low-profile laminated stock with extra wide beavertail forearm. Adjustable trigger. Available as a repeater or single shot. Weight is about 10 lbs.

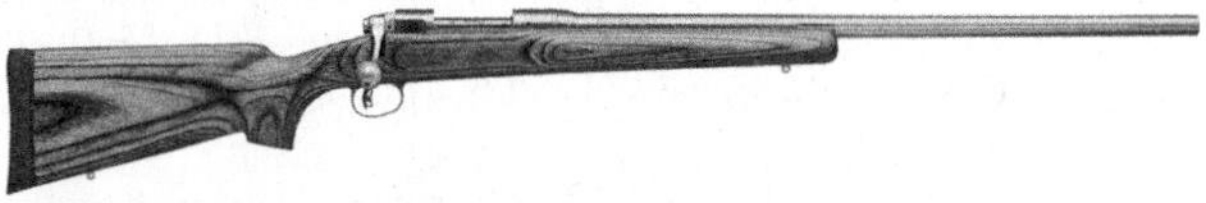

NIB	Exc.	V.G.	Good	Fair	Poor
950	800	650	500	350	175

Model 12 LRPV Long Range Precision Varminter

Similar to Model 12 FVSS but with 30" stainless bull barrel and various accurizing refinements. Chambered in .204 Ruger, .223 Remington and .22-250. Introduced in 2007. Available in single shot and 4+1 repeating versions.

NIB	Exc.	V.G.	Good	Fair	Poor
850	700	575	425	300	150

12 FCV Varmint Rifle

The new model 12 FCV varmint rifle includes the AccuStock with beavertail forend, AccuTrigger, detachable box magazine and a heavy fluted barrel.

NIB	Exc.	V.G.	Good	Fair	Poor
675	600	525	450	300	150

Model 12 F-Class Target Rifle

International-class target rifle chambered in .6.5x284 Norma. Ventilated for-end, laminated "under-hold" target stock, oversize bolt knob, AccuTrigger, 30" stainless barrel. Also available in Model 12F/TR version with conventional buttstock and elevated cheekpiece. Introduced in 2007.

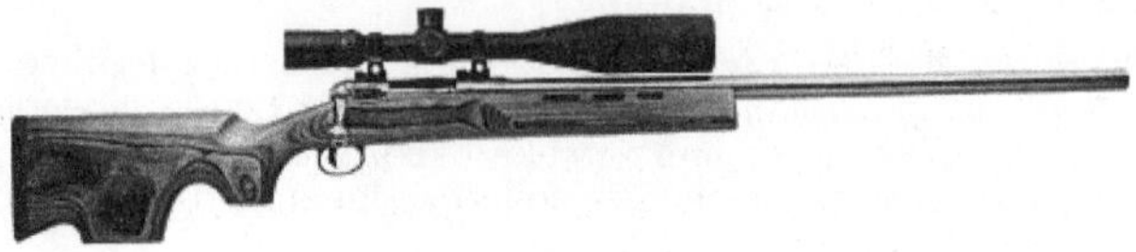

NIB	Exc.	V.G.	Good	Fair	Poor
1200	1000	750	600	475	200

Model 12 Long Range Precision

Target series rifle with target style AccuTrigger, HS Precision fiberglass matte black stock. Fluted barrel 26-inches long. Detachable magazine with 4-round capacity. Weight is 11 pounds, overall length 46-1/4-inches. Chambered for .243 winchester, .260 Remington or 6.5 Creedmoor.

NIB	Exc.	V.G.	Good	Fair	Poor
925	825	700	550	400	250

MODEL 40 VARMINT HUNTER

Model 40 Varmint Hunter

This model, introduced in 2004, is chambered for the .22 Hornet or .223 Rem. cartridge. Fitted with a 24" heavy barrel with no sights. Laminated stock with wide beavertail forearm. Blued. Single shot. Weight is about 7.75 lbs.

NIB	Exc.	V.G.	Good	Fair	Poor
400	300	250	200	150	100

NOTE: Add $30 for .223 Rem. model.

MODEL 10 SERIES

Model 10FP—Tactical (Short Action)

This is a short action model chambered for the .223 or .308 calibers. Fitted with a 24" barrel. Black synthetic stock. Drilled and tapped for scope mount. Weight is approximately 8 lbs. Introduced in 1998. In 2003 the Savage AccuTrigger was added to this model. Premium foir Choate or McMillan stock.

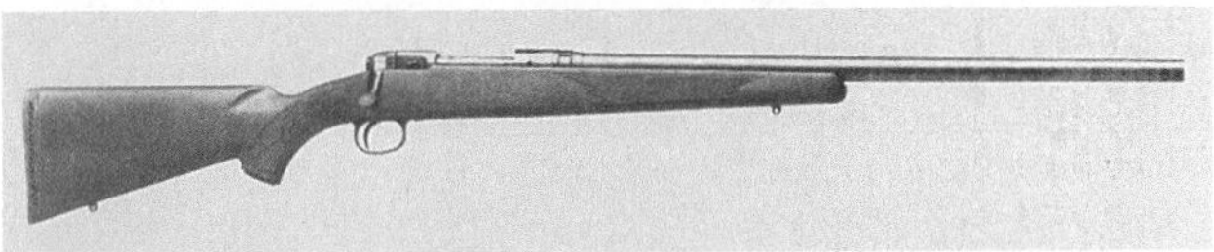

NIB	Exc.	V.G.	Good	Fair	Poor
545	450	325	225	150	100

Model 10FLP

Same as above but in left-hand. In 2003 the Savage AccuTrigger was added to this model.

NIB	Exc.	V.G.	Good	Fair	Poor
550	450	325	225	150	100

Model 10FM—Sierra

This model features a 20" barrel chambered for .223, .243, or .308 calibers. In 2002 the .300 WSM caliber was added. Black synthetic stock. Magazine capacity is 4 rounds. Weight is approximately 6 lbs. Introduced in 1998. Discontinued.

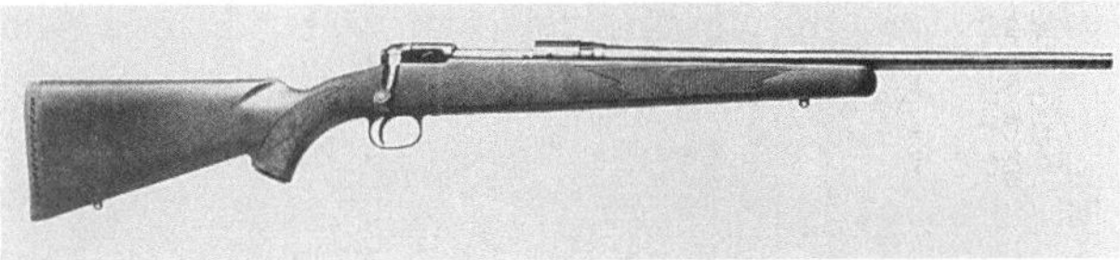

NIB	Exc.	V.G.	Good	Fair	Poor
500	400	300	150	125	100

Model 10FCM—Sierra

Introduced in 2005 this model features a 20" light barrel with detachable magazine. Chambered for the .243, 7mm-08 Rem., .308, .270, and .300 WSM calibers. Black synthetic stock. Weight is about 6.25 lbs.

NIB	Exc.	V.G.	Good	Fair	Poor
550	450	325	225	150	100

Model 10FCM—Scout Rifle

Chambered for the 7mm-08 Rem. or .308 Win. cartridge this model is fitted with a 20" barrel, removable ghost ring rear sight, one-piece scope mount, and other special features. Weight is about 6.2 lbs. Introduced in 1999. Discontinued in 2005 but reintroduced in 2007.

NIB	Exc.	V.G.	Good	Fair	Poor
545	450	325	225	150	100

Model 10GY Youth

This model is similar to the Model 10FM but features a shortened hardwood stock. It is fitted with a 22" barrel and has open sights. It is chambered for .223, .243, or .308 calibers. Weight is about 6.25 lbs. Introduced in 1998.

NIB	Exc.	V.G.	Good	Fair	Poor
450	325	225	165	125	100

NOTE: The Savage Predator line of rifles now includes a version with the new AccuStock Savage launched in 2009. This version has the AccuStock, AccuTrigger, detachable box magazine and a medium-contour fluted barrel. The stock is finished in Realtree Advantage Max 1 and the metal is matte black. MSRP is $864.

Model 10 Predator Hunter

Similar to Model 110FCM but with overall camo finish, 22" medium-contour barrel, and AccuTrigger. Chambered in .204 Ruger, .22-250 and .223. Introduced in 2007.

NIB	Exc.	V.G.	Good	Fair	Poor
600	475	350	275	200	100

Model 10XP Predator

Package rifle with factory-mounted scope, entirely covered in camo finish. 22-inch barrel, chambered in .204, .223 and .22-250. Introduced in 2008.

NIB	Exc.	V.G.	Good	Fair	Poor
650	500	395	300	225	125

Model 10XP Predator Hunter Bolt-Action Rifle Package

Bolt-action rifle similar to Model 10 but chambered in .223, .204, .22-250 or .243 Win. Includes 4-12x40 scope, 22" barrel, Accu-Trigger, choice of Realtree Snow or Mossy Oak Brush camo overall.

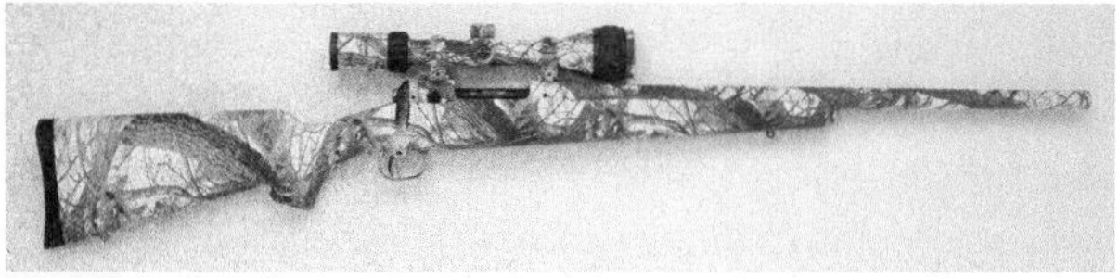

NIB	Exc.	V.G.	Good	Fair	Poor
725	575	425	325	250	150

LAW ENFORCEMENT SERIES

Model 10FP-LE1

Chambered for the .308 Win. cartridge and fitted with a 20" heavy barrel with no sights. Black synthetic stock. AccuTrigger. Weight is about 8.25 lbs. Introduced in 2003.

NIB	Exc.	V.G.	Good	Fair	Poor
550	450	325	225	150	100

Model 10FP-LE1A

As above but chambered for the .223 Rem. cartridge as well as the .308. Black synthetic Choate adjustable stock with accessory rail. Weight is about 10.75 lbs. Introduced in 2003.

NIB	Exc.	V.G.	Good	Fair	Poor
650	500	395	300	225	125

Model 10FP-LE2B

This bolt action model is chambered for the .308 Win. cartridge and fitted with a McMillan fiberglass tactical stock. Barrel is 26" with no sights. AccuTrigger. Matte blue finish. Weight is about 10 lbs. Introduced in 2003.

NIB	Exc.	V.G.	Good	Fair	Poor
800	675	525	400	300	175

Model 10FP-LE2

Introduced in 2003 this model features a 26" barrel chambered for the .308 Win. cartridge and fitted with a black synthetic stock. AccuTrigger. Weight is about 8.75 lbs.

NIB	Exc.	V.G.	Good	Fair	Poor
650	500	395	300	225	125

Model 10FP-LE2A

This model is chambered for the .223 or .308 cartridge and fitted with a 26" heavy barrel with no sights. Black synthetic Choate adjustable stock with accessory rail. Weight is about 11.25 lbs. Introduced in 2003.

NIB	Exc.	V.G.	Good	Fair	Poor
725	575	425	325	250	150

Model 10FPXP-LEA

This item is a package of both rifle and scope with accessories. Features a Model 10FP with 26" barrel and black synthetic stock, Leupold 3.5-10x40 black matte scope with Mil Dot, scope covers and one-piece base. Harris bipod and heavy duty aluminum case. Rifle weighs about 10.5 lbs. Introduced in 2003.

NIB	Exc.	V.G.	Good	Fair	Poor
1950	1450	1100	700	450	300

Model 10FPXP-LE

As above but with Choate adjustable stock with accessory rail. Rifle weighs about 11.25 lbs. Introduced in 2003.

NIB	Exc.	V.G.	Good	Fair	Poor
1805	1350	1000	600	350	200

Model 10FCP-HS Precision

Similar to Model 110FP-LE1 but with one-piece HS Precision synthetic target stock and detachable box magazine. Introduced in 2007.

NIB	Exc.	V.G.	Good	Fair	Poor
650	500	395	300	225	125

Model 10FCP Choate

Similar to Model 10FP-LE1 but with Choate synthetic stock. Introduced in 2007.

NIB	Exc.	V.G.	Good	Fair	Poor
675	535	395	300	225	125

Model 10FCP McMillan

Similar to Model 10FP-LE1 but with synthetic McMillan precision stock. Introduced in 2007.

NIB	Exc.	V.G.	Good	Fair	Poor
1100	900	725	575	400	200

Model 10FPXP-HS Precision

Similar to Model 10FPXP-LEA but with HS Precision Tactical Stock. Introduced 2006.

NIB	Exc.	V.G.	Good	Fair	Poor
1725	1500	1250	800	600	300

Model 10FP-HS

Similar to Model 10FP-LE1 but with HS Precision Tactical stock. Introduced 2006.

NIB	Exc.	V.G.	Good	Fair	Poor
950	800	625	475	300	200

Model 10 Precision Carbine

Similar to Model 10 but with 20" medium contour barrel, synthetic camo Accu-Stock. Chambered in .223/.308.

NIB	Exc.	V.G.	Good	Fair	Poor
800	675	525	400	300	175

Model 10FLCP

Similar to Model 10 FCP but in left-hand configuration, with standard stock or Accu-Stock.

NIB	Exc.	V.G.	Good	Fair	Poor
800	675	525	400	300	175

Model 10 BAT-S

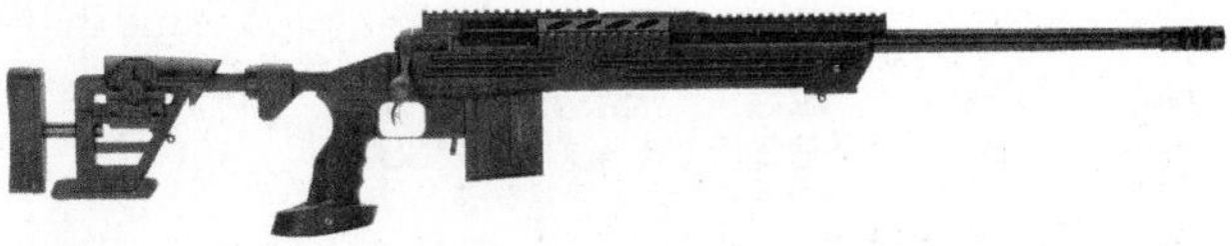

NIB	Exc.	V.G.	Good	Fair	Poor
1700	1400	1075	800	550	325

MODEL 10 SERIES MUZZLELOADER

Model 10ML-II

This model is fitted with a .50 caliber 24" barrel with adjustable sights. Synthetic stock. Blued finish. Weight is about 7.75 lbs.

NIB	Exc.	V.G.	Good	Fair	Poor
530	375	300	200	150	100

Model 10MLSS-II

As above in stainless steel.

NIB	Exc.	V.G.	Good	Fair	Poor
590	375	325	200	150	100

Model 10ML-II Camo

This model, introduced in 2002, has a camo stock finish with blued barrel and action.

NIB	Exc.	V.G.	Good	Fair	Poor
570	425	300	200	150	100

Model 10MLSS-II Camo

This model has a camo stock finish with stainless steel barrel and action. Introduced in 2002.

NIB	Exc.	V.G.	Good	Fair	Poor
625	475	350	200	150	100

Model 10MLBSS-II

This model features a brown laminate stock with stainless steel action and barrel. Weight is 8.75 lbs. Introduced in 2002.

NIB	Exc.	V.G.	Good	Fair	Poor
665	500	375	200	150	100

Model 10ML-IIXP

Introduced in 2002 this model has a blued action and barrel with a synthetic stock. Fitted with a 3-9x40mm scope. Weight is 9.25 lbs.

NIB	Exc.	V.G.	Good	Fair	Poor
570	425	300	200	150	100

Model 10MLSS-IIXP

Same as above but with stainless steel barrel and action.

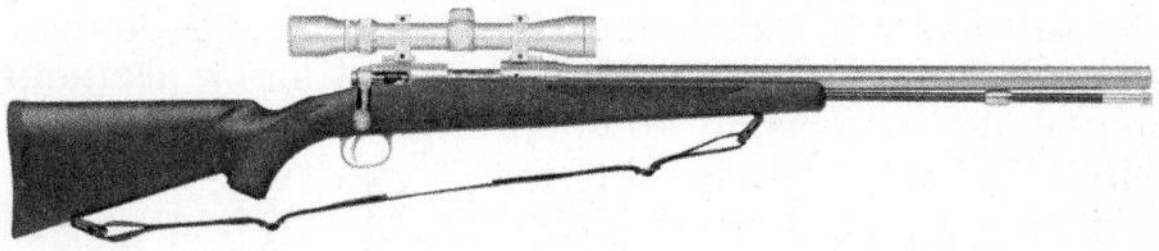

NIB	Exc.	V.G.	Good	Fair	Poor
625	475	350	200	150	100

MODEL 11 SERIES

Model 11F

This model features a short action chambered for the .223, .22-250, .243, or .308 calibers. Barrel lengths are 22" with open sights. Black synthetic stock. Weight is approximately 6.75 lbs. Introduced in 1998.

NIB	Exc.	V.G.	Good	Fair	Poor
485	350	250	175	125	100

Model 11FCNS

Introduced in 2005 this model is chambered for the .22-250, .243, 7mm-08, .308, .270 WSM, .7mm WSN, and the .300 WSM cartridges. Barrel length is 22" or 24" depending on caliber without sights. Detachable box magazine. Black synthetic stock. Weight is about 6.5 lbs. depending on caliber.

NIB	Exc.	V.G.	Good	Fair	Poor
500	375	250	175	125	100

Model 11 Lightweight Hunter

Chambered for five standard cartridges plus 6.5 Creedmoor. Lightweight at 5-1/2 pounds with a satin-finished American walnut wood stock. AccuTrigger, detachable box magazine, matte blue barrel and action with spiral fluted bolt. Barrel length is 20-inches.

NIB	Exc.	V.G.	Good	Fair	Poor
750	650	500	400	250	150

Model 11G

Chambered for .223, .243, .22-250, or .308 calibers and fitted with a 22" barrel. Wood stock has fancy checkering pattern, black recoil pad, and a gold medallion. Fitted with open sights. Weight is about 6.75 lbs. Introduced in 1998.

NIB	Exc.	V.G.	Good	Fair	Poor
500	375	250	175	125	100

Model 11BTH

Laminated, thumbhole-stock version of the Model 11 chambered in .204, .223, .22-250 and .22 Hornet. 22-inch blued barrel.

NIB	*Exc.*	*V.G.*	*Good*	*Fair*	*Poor*
625	475	350	200	150	100

Model 11GCNS

This model, introduced in 2005, is chambered for the .22-250, .243, 7mm-08, .308, .270 WSM, 7mm WSM, and the .300 WSM cartridges. Fitted with a 22" or 24" barrel depending on caliber without sights. Checkered walnut stock. Detachable box magazine. Weight is about 6.75 lbs. depending on caliber.

NIB	*Exc.*	*V.G.*	*Good*	*Fair*	*Poor*
525	400	300	200	150	100

MODEL 14 SERIES

Model 14 Classic

Short-action chambered for .22-250, .243, .270 WSM, 7mm-08, .300 WSM and .308. Barrel: 22-inch or 24-inch polished blue without sights. Stock: Select lacquered walnut with contrasting forend. Introduced 2006. Also available in American Classic version with optional left hand action.

NIB	*Exc.*	*V.G.*	*Good*	*Fair*	*Poor*
600	500	400	300	200	100

Model 14 Left Hand

Similar to above but in left hand and chambered in .250 Savage and .300 Savage only. Suggested retail price: $779.

Model 114 Classic

Similar to Model 14 Classic but long-action chambered for .270, 7mm RM and .300 WM. Introduced 2006. Also available in American Classic version with optional left hand action.

NIB	*Exc.*	*V.G.*	*Good*	*Fair*	*Poor*
625	475	350	200	150	100

Model 14 Euro Classic

Similar to Model 14 Classic but with iron sights. Introduced 2006.

NIB	*Exc.*	*V.G.*	*Good*	*Fair*	*Poor*
625	475	350	200	150	100

Model 114 Euro Classic

Similar to Model 114 Classic but with iron sights. Introduced 2006.

NIB	*Exc.*	*V.G.*	*Good*	*Fair*	*Poor*
625	475	350	200	150	100

Model 14 / 114 American Classic Stainless

Traditional design has an oil-finished American walnut stock featuring wrap-around checkering, a back fore-end tip and no Monte-Carlo. Available in short and long-action versions. Short action is chambered for .243 or .308 Win., long action in .270 Winchester, .30-06 and 7mm Rem. Magnum, all with a 22-inch barrel. Introduced in 2011.

NIB	*Exc.*	*V.G.*	*Good*	*Fair*	*Poor*
825	750	650	500	350	150

MODEL 16 SERIES

Model 16FSS

This is a short action with a top-loading design and a magazine capacity of 4 rounds. Chambered for the .223, .243, or .308 calibers. Fitted with a 22" stainless steel barrel. Black synthetic stock. Introduced in 1998.

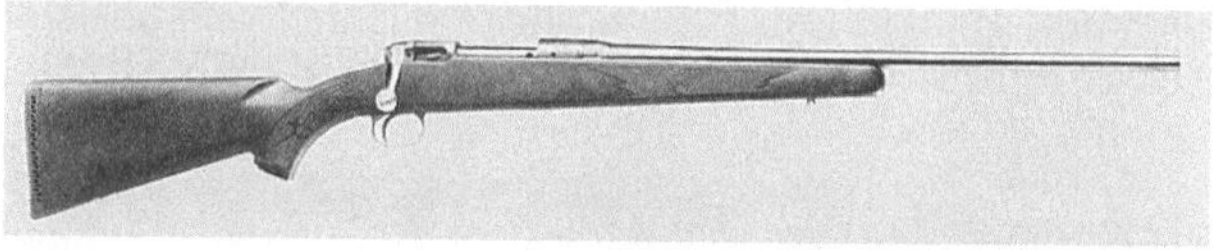

NIB	*Exc.*	*V.G.*	*Good*	*Fair*	*Poor*
550	425	325	250	200	100

Model 16FLSS

Same as above but with left-hand action.

NIB	*Exc.*	*V.G.*	*Good*	*Fair*	*Poor*
550	425	325	250	200	100

Model 16FCSAK

Introduced in 2005 this model is chambered for the .243, 7mm-08 Rem., .308, .270 WSM, 7mm WSM, and the .300 WSM cartridges. Fitted with a 22" or 24" barrel depending on caliber. Detachable box magazine. Black synthetic stock. Weights are between 7.75 and 7.25 lbs. depending on caliber.

NIB	*Exc.*	*V.G.*	*Good*	*Fair*	*Poor*
660	500	400	300	200	100

Model 16FCSS

This model is chambered for the .22-250, .243, 7mm-08 Rem., .308, .270 WSM, 7mm WSM, and the .300 WSM cartridges. Fitted with a 22" or 24" depending on caliber. Detachable box magazine. Black synthetic stock. Weight is about 6.5 lbs. depending on caliber. Introduced in 2005.

NIB	*Exc.*	*V.G.*	*Good*	*Fair*	*Poor*
570	425	375	250	175	125

Model 16BSS

Introduced in 2002 this model features a shot action chambered for the 7mm RSUM, .300 RSUM, and the .300 WSM cartridges. Fitted with a 24" stainless steel barrel drilled and tapped for scope mounts. Laminated stock with cut checkering. Weight is about 7.75 lbs. Discontinued.

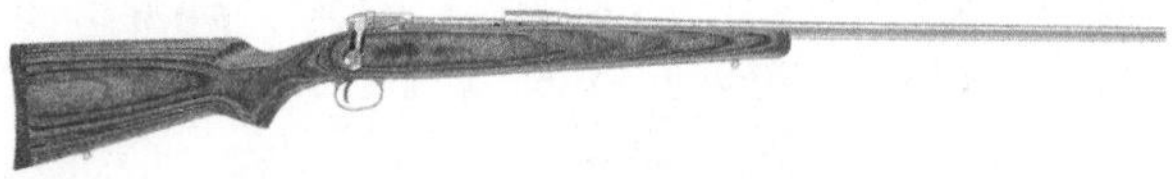

NIB	*Exc.*	*V.G.*	*Good*	*Fair*	*Poor*
640	475	400	300	200	100

Long Range Precision Varminter

Single-shot bolt action chambered in .204 Ruger, .223 or .22-250. Features include AccuTrigger and oversized bolt handle. Composite stock, sightless stainless steel fluted barrel. Weight: 11.25 lbs. Introduced 2006. about 6.5 lbs. depending on caliber. Introduced in 2005.

NIB	*Exc.*	*V.G.*	*Good*	*Fair*	*Poor*
900	750	600	450	300	200

Model 112 Varmint, Low Profile

Long-action bolt rifle chambered for .25-06 (4) and .300 WM (3). Stock: Brown laminated with recoil pad. Barrel: 26-inch sightless stainless steel bull. Weight: 11.25 lbs.

NIB	*Exc.*	*V.G.*	*Good*	*Fair*	*Poor*
600	475	350	200	150	100

Model 16FHSAK

Similar to Model 116FHSAK but short-action only. Introduced 2006.

NIB	*Exc.*	*V.G.*	*Good*	*Fair*	*Poor*
600	475	350	200	150	100

Model 16FHSS

Similar to Model 16FSS but with hinged floorplate. Introduced 2006.

NIB	*Exc.*	*V.G.*	*Good*	*Fair*	*Poor*
600	475	350	200	150	100

Model 11FYCAK

Short-action youth model chambered in .243, 7mm-08, and .308. Barrel: 22-inch blued with muzzlebrake, no sights. Stock: Black composite. Weight 6.5 lbs.; 41.5-inch overall length. Introduced 2006.

NIB	*Exc.*	*V.G.*	*Good*	*Fair*	*Poor*
515	400	300	200	125	100

Model 111FYCAK

Similar to Model 11FYCAK but long-action chambered for .25-06, .270 and .30-06. Introduced 2006.

NIB	*Exc.*	*V.G.*	*Good*	*Fair*	*Poor*
515	400	300	200	125	100

Model 11BTH

Laminated, thumbhole-stock version of the Model 11 chambered in .204, .223, .22-250 and .22 Hornet. 22-inch blued barrel.

NIB	*Exc.*	*V.G.*	*Good*	*Fair*	*Poor*
625	475	350	200	150	100

Model 111FHNS

Similar to Model 111FCNS but with hinged floorplate. Introduced 2006.

NIB	*Exc.*	*V.G.*	*Good*	*Fair*	*Poor*
515	400	300	200	125	100

Model 11FHNS

Similar to Model 11FCNS but with hinged floorplate. Introduced 2006.

NIB	*Exc.*	*V.G.*	*Good*	*Fair*	*Poor*
515	400	300	200	125	100

Model 11FCXP3

Similar to Model 111FCXP3 but in short-action. Introduced 2006.

NIB	*Exc.*	*V.G.*	*Good*	*Fair*	*Poor*
515	400	300	200	125	100

Model 11FYCXP3

Similar to Model 11FCXP3 but in youth version chambered in .243 Win.

NIB	*Exc.*	*V.G.*	*Good*	*Fair*	*Poor*
450	325	250	175	150	100

Model 25 Lightweight Varminter

Short-action rifle chambered in .204 and .223. Medium-contour fluted barrel with recessed target crown, free-floating sleved barrel, dual pillar bedding, three locking lugs, 60-degree bolt lift, AccuTrigger adjustable from 2.5 to 3.25 lbs., detachable box magazine. Weight 8.25 lbs.

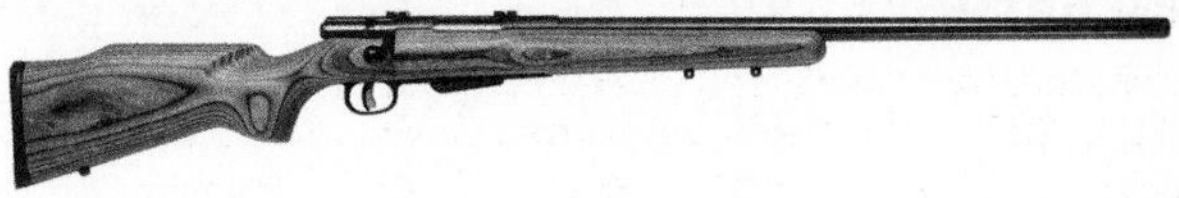

NIB	*Exc.*	*V.G.*	*Good*	*Fair*	*Poor*
575	450	325	250	150	100

Model 25 Lightweight Varminter Thumbhole

Similar to above but with thumbhole stock.

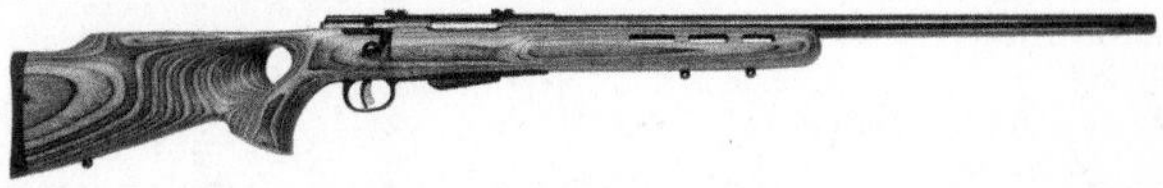

NIB	*Exc.*	*V.G.*	*Good*	*Fair*	*Poor*
650	525	400	325	275	125

Model 25 Classic Sporter

Short-action rifle chambered in .204 and .223. Free-floating sleeved barrel, Dual pillar bedding, three locking lugs, 60-degree bolt lift, AccuTrigger adjustable from 2.5 to 3.25 lbs., Detachable box magazine. Satin lacquer American walnut stock with contrasting forend tip and wraparound checkering.

NIB	*Exc.*	*V.G.*	*Good*	*Fair*	*Poor*
600	475	350	200	150	100

Model 25 Walking Varminter

Chambered for .204 Ruger, .22 Hornet, .222 Remington, .223 Remington and 5.7x28mm. Features a 22-inch barrel sleeved for rigidity. Triple pillar bedding and Weaver scope bases. Has a three-lug bolt with a 60-degree throw to allow mounting of a large diameter optic. AccuTrigger is standard, center feed detachable magazine and synthetic stock.

NIB	*Exc.*	*V.G.*	*Good*	*Fair*	*Poor*
475	425	350	250	200	150

Savage Edge Bolt Action Rifle

Entry-level bolt-action repeating rifle chambered in .223, .22-250, .243 Win., 7mm-08, .308 Win., .25-06, .270 Win., and .30-06. Features include 22-inch matte black barrel, synthetic black stock, 4-round capacity; detachable box magazine, drilled and tapped for scope mounts. Also available in camo finish (Edge Camo); XP variation (with 3x9 scope); and Camo XP (with camo finish and scope). In 2011 the name of this model was changed to the Axis.

NIB	*Exc.*	*V.G.*	*Good*	*Fair*	*Poor*
300	265	225	200	150	100

NOTE: Add 15 percent for camo stock, 20 percent for scope.

RIMFIRE RIFLES

NOTE: As of 2006, virtually all Savage rimfire rifles (with the exception of the 30G and semi-autos) were equipped with AccuTrigger as a standard feature.

Model 60

A .22 caliber semi-automatic rifle with a 20" barrel, open sights, and tubular magazine. Blued with a Monte Carlo-style walnut stock. Manufactured between 1969 and 1972.

NIB	Exc.	V.G.	Good	Fair	Poor
—	100	80	70	50	35

Model 64G

Introduced in 1996 this semi-automatic .22 long rifle has a 20.25" barrel and 10-shot detachable magazine. The finish is blue and the stock has a Monte Carlo with checkered pistol grip. Bead front sight with adjustable open rear sight is standard. Weight is about 5.5 lbs.

NIB	Exc.	V.G.	Good	Fair	Poor
160	125	90	60	50	40

Model 64GXP

As above but with 4x15mm scope.

NIB	Exc.	V.G.	Good	Fair	Poor
170	125	100	80	60	50

Model 64BTV

Similar to Model 64 but with laminated thumbhole stock.

NIB	Exc.	V.G.	Good	Fair	Poor
170	125	100	80	60	50

Model 64F

Introduced in 1997 this model features a black synthetic stock with blue finish. Chambered for .22 LR and fitted with a 20.25" barrel. Weight is approximately 5.5 lbs.

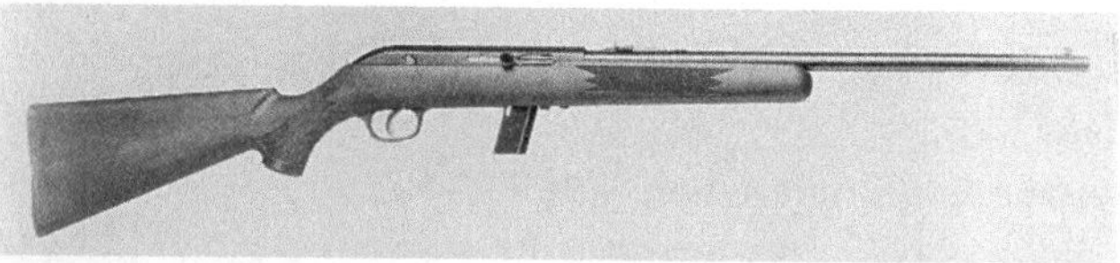

NIB	Exc.	V.G.	Good	Fair	Poor
140	120	90	65	50	25

Model 64FSS

Similar to the model above but with stainless steel action and barrel. Introduced in 2002.

NIB	Exc.	V.G.	Good	Fair	Poor
200	150	110	75	50	25

Model 64FV

Introduced in 1998 this model features a heavy 21" target barrel with no sights. A black synthetic stock is standard. Chambered for the .22 LR cartridge. Weight is about 6 lbs. Discontinued.

NIB	Exc.	V.G.	Good	Fair	Poor
150	125	90	65	50	25

Model 64FVXP

Similar to Model 64FV but with scope package. Introduced 2006.

NIB	Exc.	V.G.	Good	Fair	Poor
190	150	110	75	50	25

Model 64FVSS

Similar to the Model FV but with stainless steel action and barrel. Introduced in 2002. Discontinued.

NIB	Exc.	V.G.	Good	Fair	Poor
225	175	125	100	75	50

Model 64FXP

This is a package model that offers a .22 LR gun with 20.25" barrel with detachable 10-round magazine. It comes with a 4x15mm scope as well as open sights. Introduced in 1998. Weight is about 5.25 lbs.

NIB	Exc.	V.G.	Good	Fair	Poor
150	125	90	65	50	25

Model 88

As above, with a hardwood stock. Manufactured between 1969 and 1972.

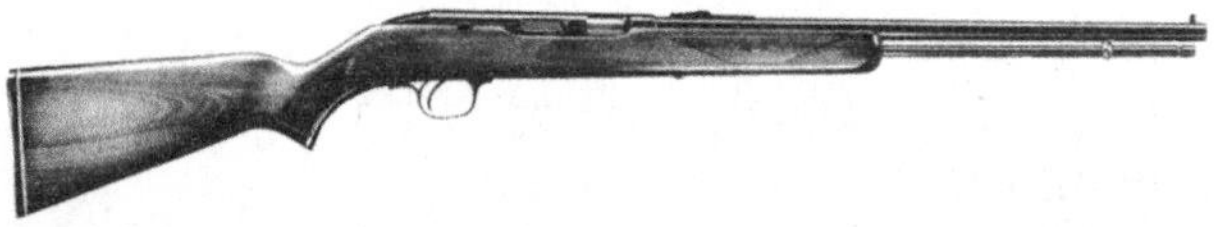

NIB	Exc.	V.G.	Good	Fair	Poor
—	100	80	70	50	35

Model 90 Carbine

As above, with a 16.5" barrel and carbine-style stock. The forend is secured to the barrel by a barrel band. Discontinued.

NIB	Exc.	V.G.	Good	Fair	Poor
—	100	80	70	50	35

Model 93G

Introduced in 1996 this model is a bolt-action repeating rifle chambered for the .22 WMR cartridge. It is fitted with a 20.75" barrel with 5-shot magazine. It has a walnut-stained hardwood stock with cut checkering. Open sights standard. Weight is about 5.75 lbs. In 2001 this model was offered in a left-hand version (Model 93GL). AccuTrigger introduced 2006.

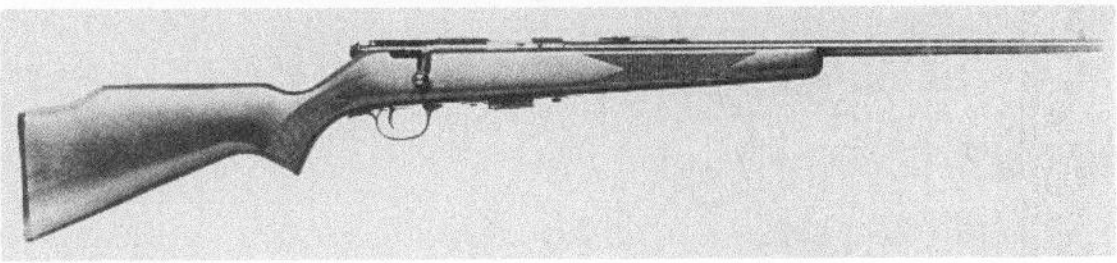

NIB	Exc.	V.G.	Good	Fair	Poor
195	150	100	75	60	50

Model 93FS

This .22 WMR model features a stainless steel finish with a 20.75" barrel and black synthetic stock. Five-round magazine. Front bead sight and sporting rear sight. Introduced in 1997. Weight is about 5.5 lbs. Discontinued.

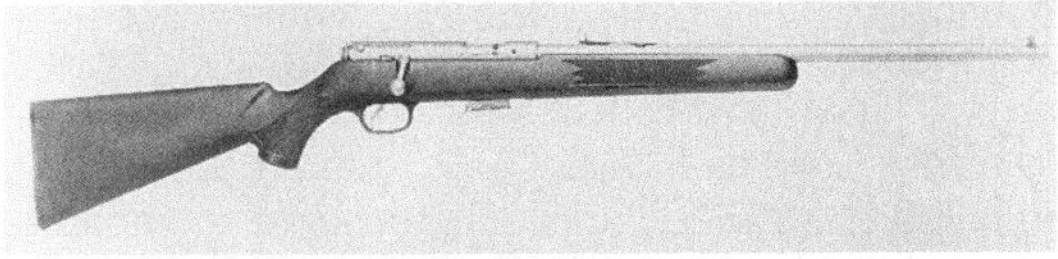

NIB	Exc.	V.G.	Good	Fair	Poor
195	150	100	75	60	50

Model 93 Classic

Similar to Model 93G but with sporter-weight barrel and oil-finished premium walnut stock. AccuTrigger. Introduced in 2007.

NIB	Exc.	V.G.	Good	Fair	Poor
475	375	325	200	150	100

Model 93 Classic Thumbhole

Similar to above but with thumbhole stock.

NIB	Exc.	V.G.	Good	Fair	Poor
515	400	300	200	125	100

Model 93XP

.22 WMR package gun with 22-inch barrel and factory-mounted 3x9 scope. Finished overall with Mossy Oak Brush stock.

NIB	Exc.	V.G.	Good	Fair	Poor
400	325	250	150	100	75

Model 93FVSS

This model features a 21" heavy barrel chambered for the .22 WMR cartridge, recessed target muzzle and stainless steel barreled action. Equipped with black synthetic stock. Magazine capacity is 5 rounds. Weight is about 6 lbs. Introduced in 1998.

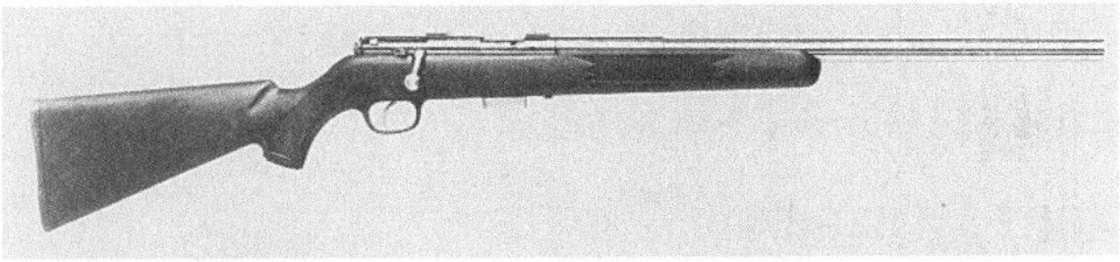

NIB	Exc.	V.G.	Good	Fair	Poor
275	200	150	100	70	50

Model 93BTVS

Similar to Model 93FVSS but with laminated thumbhole stock. Introduced in 2007.

NIB	Exc.	V.G.	Good	Fair	Poor
400	325	250	150	100	75

Model 93F

Similar to the above model but with blued finish and a synthetic stock with open sights. Weight is approximately 5 lbs. Introduced in 1998.

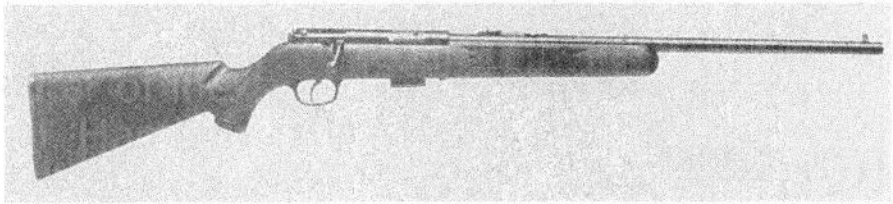

NIB	Exc.	V.G.	Good	Fair	Poor
185	125	95	65	50	25

Model 93R17-F

This bolt-action rifle is chambered for the .17 HMR cartridge and fitted with a 20.75" barrel with no sights. Black synthetic stock. Magazine capacity is 5 rounds. Blued finish. Weight is about 5 lbs. Introduced in 2003.

NIB	Exc.	V.G.	Good	Fair	Poor
225	175	125	100	75	50

Model 93R17-BVSS

Similar to the above model but with 21" stainless steel barrel with no sights and laminated hardwood stock. Weight is about 6 lbs. Introduced in 2003.

NIB	Exc.	V.G.	Good	Fair	Poor
325	250	190	125	75	50

Model 93R17-FSS

This .17 HMR caliber rifle has a 20.75" stainless steel barrel with no sights and black synthetic stock. Weight is about 5 lbs. Introduced in 2003.

NIB	Exc.	V.G.	Good	Fair	Poor
250	180	130	100	75	50

Model 93R17-Camo

As above but with Realtree Hardwoods camo stock. Weight is about 5 lbs. Introduced in 2003.

NIB	Exc.	V.G.	Good	Fair	Poor
250	180	130	100	75	50

Model 93R17-FVSS

As above but with 21" stainless steel heavy barrel. Weight is about 6 lbs. Introduced in 2003.

NIB	Exc.	V.G.	Good	Fair	Poor
275	210	150	125	75	50

Model 93R17-GV

This .17 HMR model has a walnut finished hardwood checkered stock and 21" heavy barrel with no sights. Blued finish. Weight is about 6 lbs. Introduced in 2003. A left-hand model is also available.

NIB	Exc.	V.G.	Good	Fair	Poor
230	175	125	100	75	50

Model 93R17-GVXP

Similar to Model 93R17-GV but with scope package. Introduced 2006.

NIB	Exc.	V.G.	Good	Fair	Poor
250	180	130	100	75	50

Model 93R17-FXP

Similar to Model 93R17-F but with scope package. Introduced 2006.

NIB	Exc.	V.G.	Good	Fair	Poor
250	180	130	100	75	50

Model 93FVSS-XP

Similar to Model 93FVSS but with scope package. Introduced 2006.

NIB	Exc.	V.G.	Good	Fair	Poor
300	225	150	125	75	50

Model 93FSS

Similar to discontinued Model 93FS but with no sights and AccuTrigger. Introduced 2006.

NIB	Exc.	V.G.	Good	Fair	Poor
275	210	150	125	75	50

Model 93FV

Similar to Model 93F but with AccuTrigger. Introduced 2006.

NIB	Exc.	V.G.	Good	Fair	Poor
250	180	130	100	75	50

Model 93R17-BTVS

Similar to Model 93R17-BVSS but with laminated thumbhole stock. Introduced 2006.

NIB	Exc.	V.G.	Good	Fair	Poor
350	295	245	195	150	100

Model 93R17BLTVS

Similar to above but in left hand. Suggested retail price: $441.

Model 93R17-BV

Similar to Model 93R17-GV but with brown laminated stock with wide beavertail forend. Introduced 2006.

NIB	Exc.	V.G.	Good	Fair	Poor
350	295	245	195	150	100

Model 93R17 Classic

Similar to Model 93R17 but with sporter-weight barrel and oil-finished premium walnut stock. AccuTrigger. Introduced in 2007.

NIB	Exc.	V.G.	Good	Fair	Poor
450	345	295	200	135	100

Model Mark II BRJ

Similar to Mark II, Model 93 but features spiral fluting pattern on a heavy barrel, blued finish and Royal Jacaranda wood laminate stock. In .22 LR, .22 WMR or .17 HMR.

NIB	Exc.	V.G.	Good	Fair	Poor
400	350	300	250	200	100

Model Mark II TRR-SR

Similar to Mark II, Model 93 but features heavy barrel, matte finish and a tactical-style wood stock.

NIB	Exc.	V.G.	Good	Fair	Poor
475	425	350	300	250	150

Model CUB-G (Mini-Youth)

Introduced in 2003 this single-shot bolt-action rifle is chambered for the .22 caliber cartridge. Barrel length is 16" and the walnut-stained hardwood stock is proportionally scaled down. Weight is about 3.3 lbs. In 2005 this model was offered in .17 HM2.

NIB	Exc.	V.G.	Good	Fair	Poor
155	125	100	75	50	25

Model CUB-T

Similar to Model CUB-G but with laminated thumbhole stock. Introduced in 2007.

NIB	Exc.	V.G.	Good	Fair	Poor
235	195	145	100	75	50

Model 30G "Stevens Favorite"

Based on the Stevens Favorite model, this lever-action single-shot .22 caliber rifle is fitted with a 21" half octagonal barrel. Walnut stock with schnabel forend. Blued finish. Weight is about 4.25 lbs. Introduced in 1999. Additional calibers added are .22 WMR and .22 Hornet.

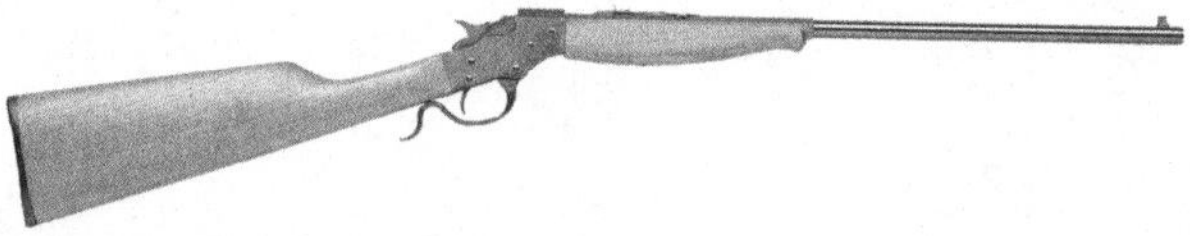

NIB	Exc.	V.G.	Good	Fair	Poor
325	275	225	150	100	50

NOTE: Add $35 for .22WMR and $60 for .22 Hornet.

Model 30G "Favorite" Takedown

Introduced in 2004 this model has a takedown feature. Offered in .17 HMR and .22 LR. The .17 HMR is fitted with a 21" full octagon barrel with sights and scope base included. The .22 LR model is fitted with a 21" half octagon barrel with sights.

NIB	Exc.	V.G.	Good	Fair	Poor
325	275	225	150	100	50

NOTE: Add $65 for .17 HMR model.

MARK I & II SERIES

Introduced in 1996 this series of .22 caliber rifles feature both single-shot and repeating models. They are available in both right- and left-hand models.

Mark I-G

This is a bolt-action single-shot rifle chambered for the .22 Short, Long, or Long Rifle cartridges. It is fitted with a 20.75" barrel and has a cut checkered walnut finished stock. Bead front sight and open adjustable rear sight. Offered in both right- and left-hand models. Weight is about 5.5 lbs.

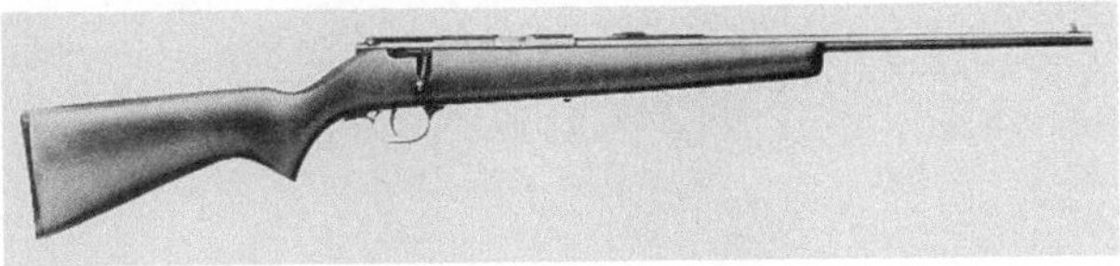

NIB	Exc.	V.G.	Good	Fair	Poor
150	100	80	70	60	50

Model Mark I-FVT

Similar to Model Mark I-G but with synthetic stock, rear peep sight and hooded front sight. Introduced 2006.

NIB	Exc.	V.G.	Good	Fair	Poor
200	150100	80	70	60	—

Mark I-GY (Youth Model)

Same as above but fitted with a 19" barrel and shorter buttstock. Weight is about 5 lbs.

MARK I GY

NIB	Exc.	V.G.	Good	Fair	Poor
150	100	80	70	60	50

Mark I-GSB Smoothbore

This version of the Mark I is a smoothbore model made for .22 caliber shot cartridges. Barrel length is 20.75" and weight is about 5.5 lbs.

NIB	Exc.	V.G.	Good	Fair	Poor
150	100	80	70	60	50

Mark II-G

This model is a bolt-action repeater with 10-shot magazine. It is chambered for the .22 LR cartridge. Checkered walnut finished stock. Open sights. Barrel length is 20.75". Offered in both right- and left-hand versions. Weight is approximately 5.5 lbs.

NIB	Exc.	V.G.	Good	Fair	Poor
170	125	90	70	60	50

Mark II-GY (Youth Model)

Same as above but with 19" barrel and shorter stock.

NIB	Exc.	V.G.	Good	Fair	Poor
170	125	90	70	60	50

Mark II-GXP

Same as the Mark II-G model but includes an unmounted 4x15mm scope. Discontinued.

NIB	Exc.	V.G.	Good	Fair	Poor
130	100	80	70	60	50

Mark II-FSS

This is a stainless steel .22 caliber rifle with 20.75" barrel and 10-round magazine. Receiver is dovetailed for scope mounting. Stock is black synthetic. Weight is about 5 lbs.

NIB	Exc.	V.G.	Good	Fair	Poor
210	150	110	75	65	45

Mark II-LV

This .22 caliber is fitted with a 21" heavy barrel. It has a laminated hardwood stock with cut checkering. Blue finish and 10-round magazine. Weight is approximately 6.5 lbs. Introduced in 1997. Discontinued.

NIB	Exc.	V.G.	Good	Fair	Poor
200	150	110	75	65	45

Mark II-F

This model has the standard Mark II barreled action with a black synthetic stock. Detachable 10-round magazine is standard. Weight is about 5 lbs. Introduced in 1998. .17 Hornady Mach 2 added in 2006.

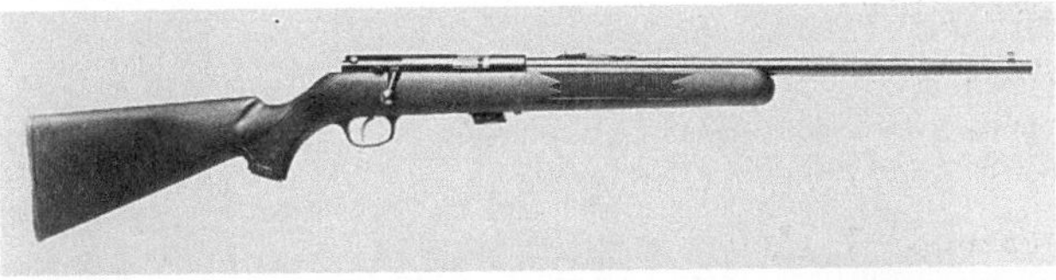

NIB	Exc.	V.G.	Good	Fair	Poor
150	110	80	70	65	45

Mark II-FXP

Similar to the Mark II-F but with a 4x15mm scope. Weight is approximately 5.25 lbs. First offered in 1998.

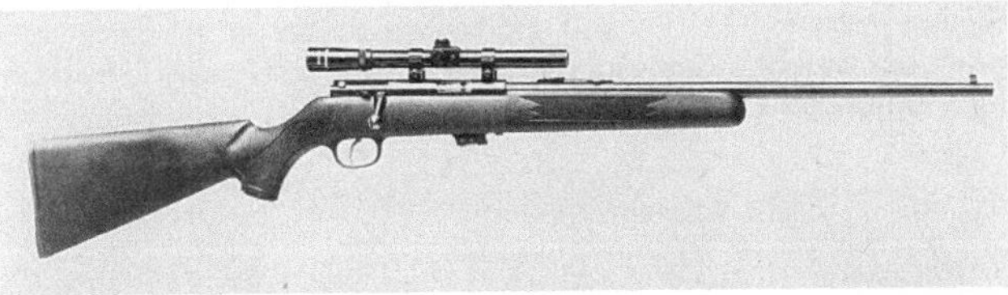

NIB	Exc.	V.G.	Good	Fair	Poor
155	110	80	70	65	45

Model Mark II Camo

Similar to Model Mark II-F but with forest camo synthetic stock. Introduced 2006.

NIB	Exc.	V.G.	Good	Fair	Poor
200	165	135	100	75	50

Mark II-FV

Introduced in 1998 this model features a 21" heavy barrel with blue alloy steel receiver. Stock is black synthetic. Magazine capacity is 5-round detachable magazine. Weight is about 6 lbs. .17 Hornady Mach 2 added in 2006.

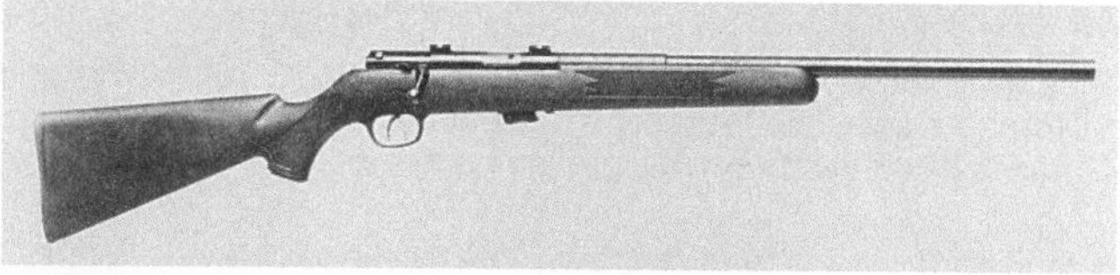

NIB	Exc.	V.G.	Good	Fair	Poor
215	150	110	80	60	45

Model Mark II-FVXP

Similar to Model Mark II-FV but with scope package. Introduced 2006.

NIB	Exc.	V.G.	Good	Fair	Poor
250	195	150	125	75	50

Model Mark II-FVT

Similar to Model Mark II-FV but with rear peep sight and hooded front sight. Introduced 2006.

NIB	Exc.	V.G.	Good	Fair	Poor
315	250	195	145	100	75

Model Mark II-BV

This model features a 21-inch stainless steel bull barrel without sights and a brown laminate stock. Chambered in .22 LR. Introduced 2006.

NIB	Exc.	V.G.	Good	Fair	Poor
300	225	175	150	100	75

Model Mark II BTV

Similar to above but with laminated thumbhole vent stock, Accu-Trigger, blued receiver and bull barrel.

NIB	Exc.	V.G.	Good	Fair	Poor
375	325	250	150	125	100

Mark II BVTS

Similar to above but with stainless barrel/receiver; available in right- or left-hand (BTVLS) configuration. Suggested retail price: $393 (standard); $441 (left hand).

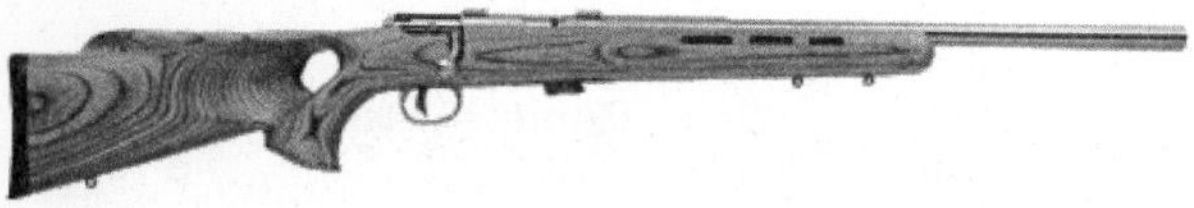

NIB	Exc.	V.G.	Good	Fair	Poor
395	350	265	165	140	125

Model Mark II Classic

Similar to Mark II-FV but with sporter-weight barrel and oil-finished premium walnut stock. AccuTrigger. Introduced in 2007. Add $50 for thumbhole stock.

NIB	Exc.	V.G.	Good	Fair	Poor
395	350	295	225	150	100

MODEL 900 SERIES

First offered in 1996 this series consists of .22 caliber rimfire target rifles in various configurations. All are available in both right- or left-hand versions.

Model 900B—Biathlon

This rifle features a hardwood stock with 5-round magazine, carrying and shooting rails, butt hook, and hand stop. The barrel length is 21" and comes with a snow cover. Receiver sight are peep variety and the front sight has 7 aperture inserts as standard. Weight is about 8.25 lbs.

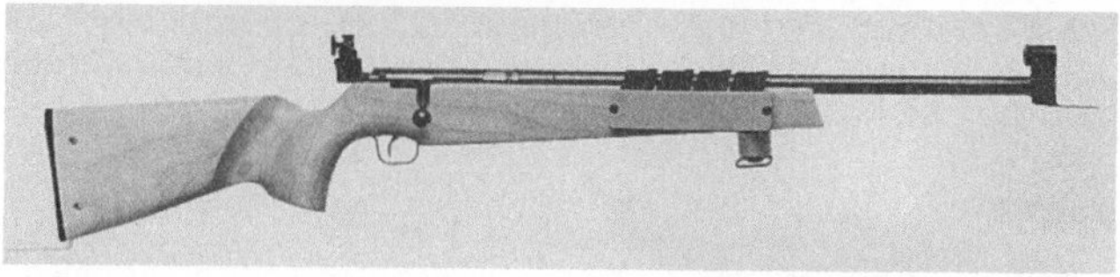

NIB	Exc.	V.G.	Good	Fair	Poor
475	400	350	300	2175	125

Model 900 TR—Target

This model has a one-piece hardwood stock with shooting rail and hand stop. Rear sight is adjustable peep and front sight has 7 aperture inserts. Barrel length is 25". Five-shot magazine is standard. Weight is about 8 lbs.

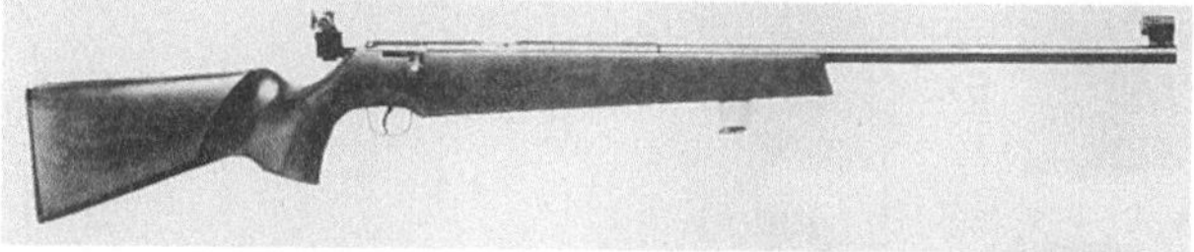

NIB	Exc.	V.G.	Good	Fair	Poor
400	325	275	225	150	100

Model 900S—Silhouette

This version features a 21" heavy barrel with recessed target style crown. Fitted with a one-piece silhouette-style stock with high comb and satin walnut finish. Receiver is drilled and tapped for scope mount. Weight is about 8 lbs.

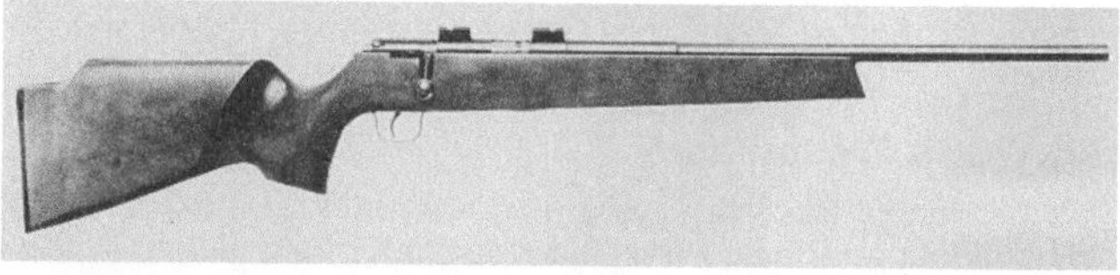

NIB	Exc.	V.G.	Good	Fair	Poor
400	325	275	225	150	100

Model 24

An external hammer combination rifle/shotgun with 24" barrels. Blued with a walnut stock. Manufactured from 1950 to 1965 in a variety of styles. The standard chambering was .22 by .410. Add 20 percent for centerfire chamberings.

NIB	Exc.	V.G.	Good	Fair	Poor
—	450	375	275	150	100

Model 24S

20 gauge.

Model 24MS

.22 Rimfire Magnum.

NIB	Exc.	V.G.	Good	Fair	Poor
—	475	395	325	175	125

Model 24DL

Satin chrome with checkered stock.

NIB	Exc.	V.G.	Good	Fair	Poor
—	450	375	325	175	125

Model 24 Field—Lightweight Version

NIB	Exc.	V.G.	Good	Fair	Poor
—	450	375	275	150	100

Model 24C

Nickel finish.

NIB	Exc.	V.G.	Good	Fair	Poor
—	450	375	275	150	100

Model 24VS

.357 Magnum or .357 Maximum/20 gauge, nickel finish.

NIB	Exc.	V.G.	Good	Fair	Poor
—	675	575	400	250	175

Model 24F

DuPont Rynite stock.

NIB	Exc.	V.G.	Good	Fair	Poor
500	400	325	250	150	100

Model 2400

A combination 12 gauge by .222 or .308 caliber over-and-under rifle/shotgun with 23.5" barrels and a Monte Carlo-style stock. Made by Valmet and imported between 1975 and 1980.

NIB	Exc.	V.G.	Good	Fair	Poor
—	700	575	450	350	275

SAVAGE SHOTGUNS

Model 411 Upland Sporter

SEE—Stevens.

Model 420

A 12, 16, or 20 gauge boxlock over-and-under shotgun with 26", 28", or 30" barrels, double triggers and extractors. Manufactured between 1937 and 1943.

Courtesy Nick Niles, Paul Goodwin photo

NIB	Exc.	V.G.	Good	Fair	Poor
—	500	400	300	200	150

Model 420 with Single Trigger

NIB	Exc.	V.G.	Good	Fair	Poor
—	500	400	300	200	150

Model 430

As above, with a checkered walnut stock and solid barrel rib. Produced from 1937 to 1943.

NIB	Exc.	V.G.	Good	Fair	Poor
—	550	450	350	200	150

Model 430 with Single Trigger

NIB	Exc.	V.G.	Good	Fair	Poor
—	600	450	300	200	150

Model 320

This is a side-by-side model.

NIB	Exc.	V.G.	Good	Fair	Poor
—	800	650	500	400	300

Model 412

.410 bore adapter.

NIB	Exc.	V.G.	Good	Fair	Poor
—	80	60	50	40	30

Model 412F

.410 bore adapter.

NIB	Exc.	V.G.	Good	Fair	Poor
—	50	45	40	35	25

Model 220

A 12, 16, 20 or .410 bore boxlock single barrel shotgun with 26" to 32" barrels. Blued with a walnut stock. Manufactured between 1938 and 1965.

NIB	Exc.	V.G.	Good	Fair	Poor
—	100	80	70	50	35

Model 210F

Introduced in 1996 this bolt-action shotgun has a 24" rifled barrel for slugs. It is chambered for the 3" 12 gauge shell. No sights. Magazine holds 2 rounds. Weight is about 7.5 lbs.

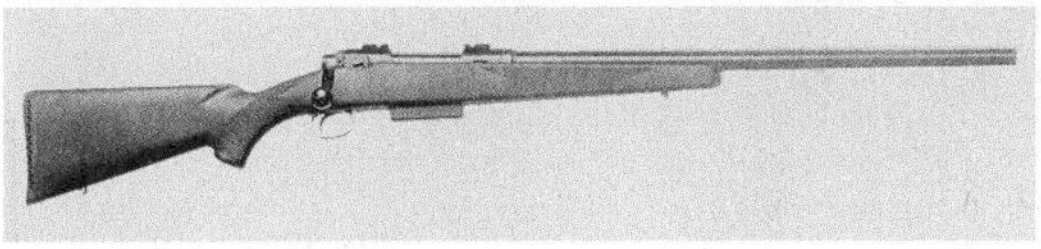

NIB	Exc.	V.G.	Good	Fair	Poor
575	500	425	350	200	125

Model 210F Slug Warrior Camo

As above but with camo stock.

NIB	Exc.	V.G.	Good	Fair	Poor
595	525	450	375	225	150

Model 210FT

Introduced in 1997 this is a 12 gauge bolt-action shotgun with a camouflage finish. Chambered for 3" shells and fitted with a 24" barrel. 2-round magazine. Approximate weight is 7.5 lbs. Drilled and tapped for scope mounting.

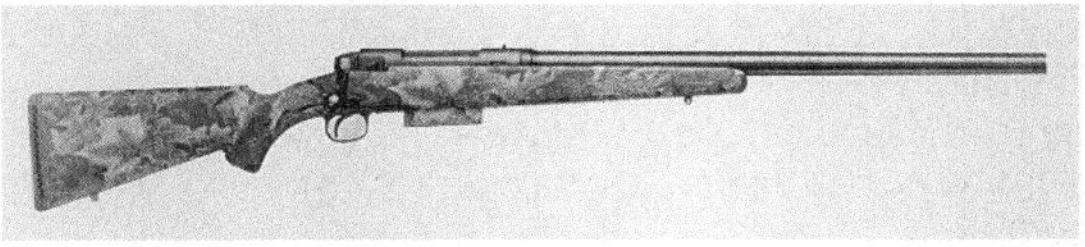

NIB	Exc.	V.G.	Good	Fair	Poor
575	500	425	350	200	125

Model 720

A 12 or 16 gauge semi-automatic shotgun with 26" to 32" barrels. Blued with a walnut stock. Manufactured between 1930 and 1949.

NIB	Exc.	V.G.	Good	Fair	Poor
—	450	375	275	225	100

Model 726 Upland Sporter

As above, with a 2-shot magazine. Manufactured between 1931 and 1949.

NIB	Exc.	V.G.	Good	Fair	Poor
—	450	375	275	225	100

Model 740C Skeet

The Model 726 with a 24.5" barrel featuring a Cutts compensator and skeet-style stock. Manufactured between 1936 and 1949.

NIB	Exc.	V.G.	Good	Fair	Poor
—	450	375	275	225	100

Model 745

The Model 720 in 12 gauge with an alloy receiver and 28" barrel. Manufactured between 1940 and 1949.

NIB	Exc.	V.G.	Good	Fair	Poor
—	450	375	275	225	100

Model 755

A 12 or 16 gauge semi-automatic shotgun with 26" to 30" barrels. Blued with a walnut stock. Also available with Savage Super Choke. Manufactured between 1949 and 1958.

NIB	Exc.	V.G.	Good	Fair	Poor
—	295	225	175	125	75

Model 775

As above, with an alloy receiver. Manufactured between 1950 and 1966.

NIB	Exc.	V.G.	Good	Fair	Poor
—	295	225	175	125	75

Model 750

A 12 gauge semi-automatic shotgun with a 26" or 28" barrel. The Model 750SC fitted with the Savage Super Choke and the Model 750AC with a Poly Choke. Blued with a walnut stock. Manufactured between 1960 and 1967.

NIB	Exc.	V.G.	Good	Fair	Poor
—	295	225	175	125	75

Model FA-1

This is Savage Fox semi-automatic shotgun imported from Japan in 1981 and 1982. Marked KTG. Offered in 12 gauge only with 28" or 30" vent rib barrels. Walnut stock with cut checkering. Magazine capacity is 4 rounds. Weight is about 7.5 lbs.

NIB	Exc.	V.G.	Good	Fair	Poor
—	350	300	250	200	150

Model FP-1

Similar to the above model but with 3" chambers and a 5-round magazine capacity.

NIB	Exc.	V.G.	Good	Fair	Poor
—	350	300	250	200	150

Model 21

This is a slide-action shotgun built between 1920 and 1928. Chambered for 12 gauge with 26", 28", 30", or 32" barrel. Walnut pistol grip stock and slide handle. Takedown. Almost identical to the famous Winchester Model 12. Offered in a number of different configurations including standard grade, Trap grade, Tournament grade, and Riot Model. About 13,000 were built.

NIB	Exc.	V.G.	Good	Fair	Poor
—	450	375	275	225	100

Model 28

This slide-action shotgun is an improved version of the Model 21. It was manufactured from 1928 to 1934. There are several variations of this gun including the Model 28-A, a standard grade; the Model 28-B, a standard grade with raised matted rib; a Model 28-C, a Riot gun; a Model 28-D, a Trap grade; and in 1931 a Model 28-3, an improved version with checkering and roll marked game scenes on the receiver.

NIB	Exc.	V.G.	Good	Fair	Poor
—	450	375	275	225	100

Model 30

A 12, 16, 20 or .410 bore slide-action shotgun with 26" to 30" ventilated rib barrels. Blued with a walnut stock. Manufactured between 1958 and 1978.

NIB	Exc.	V.G.	Good	Fair	Poor
—	300	195	150	100	75

Model 242

A .410 bore boxlock double-barrel over-and-under shotgun with 26" barrels, single trigger, extractors and exposed hammer. Manufactured between 1977 and 1981.

Courtesy Nick Niles, Paul Goodwin photo

NIB	Exc.	V.G.	Good	Fair	Poor
—	550	475	350	225	125

Model 550

A 12 or 20 gauge boxlock side-by-side double-barrel shotgun with 26", 28", or 30" barrels, single triggers and automatic ejectors. Blued with a hardwood stock. Manufactured between 1971 and 1973. Barrels were built by Valmet.

Courtesy Nick Niles, Paul Goodwin photo

NIB	Exc.	V.G.	Good	Fair	Poor
—	500	400	300	200	150

Model 440

An Italian made 12 or 20 gauge boxlock over-and-under shotgun with 26", 28", or 30" ventilated rib barrels, single-selective trigger and extractors. Blued with a walnut stock. Manufactured between 1968 and 1972.

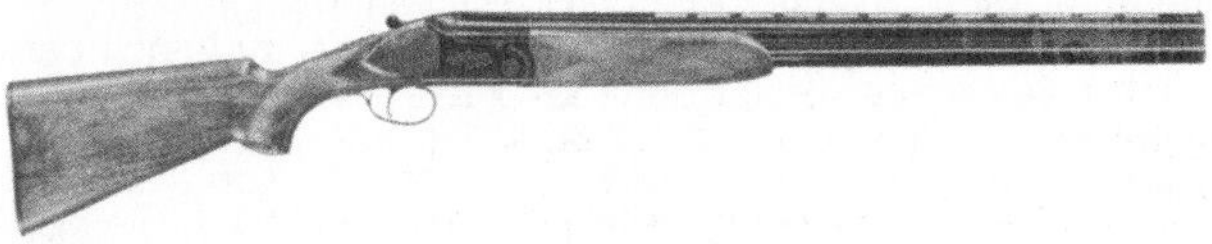

NIB	*Exc.*	*V.G.*	*Good*	*Fair*	*Poor*
—	600	500	400	300	200

Model 440A

Courtesy Nick Niles, Paul Goodwin photo

NIB	*Exc.*	*V.G.*	*Good*	*Fair*	*Poor*
—	600	500	400	300	200

Model 440B-T

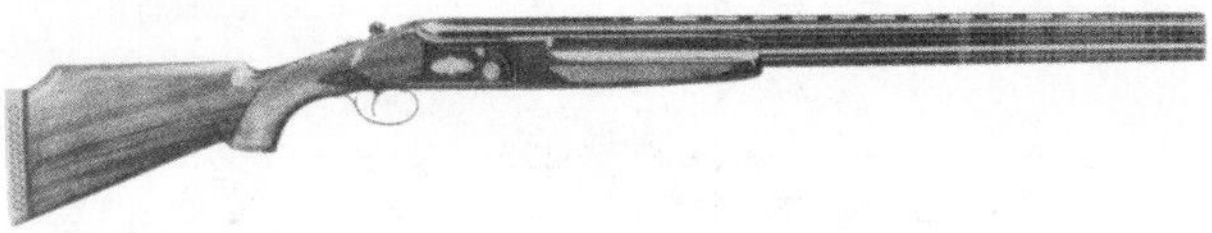

NIB	*Exc.*	*V.G.*	*Good*	*Fair*	*Poor*
—	800	650	500	350	250

Model 444 Deluxe

As above, with a more finely figured stock and automatic ejectors. Imported between 1969 and 1972.

NIB	*Exc.*	*V.G.*	*Good*	*Fair*	*Poor*
—	550	475	400	300	225

Model 444

NIB	*Exc.*	*V.G.*	*Good*	*Fair*	*Poor*
—	600	500	400	300	200

Model 444B

NIB	*Exc.*	*V.G.*	*Good*	*Fair*	*Poor*
—	700	550	400	300	250

Model 440T

A 12 gauge Model 440 with 30" barrels and a trap-style stock. Imported between 1969 and 1972.

NIB	*Exc.*	*V.G.*	*Good*	*Fair*	*Poor*
—	600	500	400	300	200

Model 330

A Valmet manufactured 12 or 20 gauge over-and-under shotgun with 26", 28", or 30" barrels, single-selective trigger and extractors. Blued with a walnut stock. Imported between 1970 and 1978.

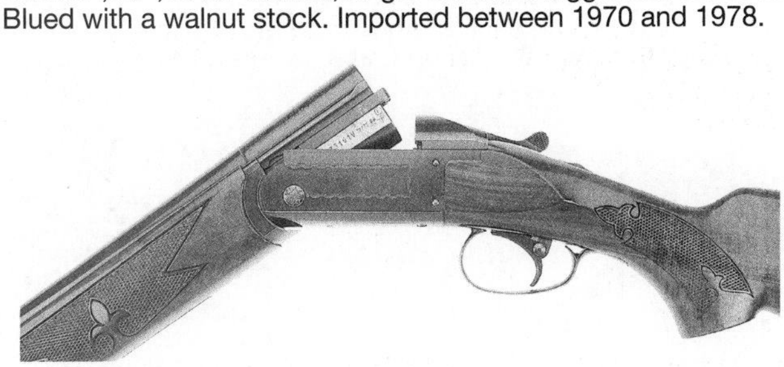

Courtesy Nick Niles, Paul Goodwin photo

NIB	*Exc.*	*V.G.*	*Good*	*Fair*	*Poor*
—	800	650	500	350	250

Model 333

As above, with a ventilated rib and automatic ejectors. Imported between 1973 and 1980.

NIB	*Exc.*	*V.G.*	*Good*	*Fair*	*Poor*
—	700	550	400	300	200

Model 333T

As above, with a 30" barrel and trap-style stock. Imported between 1972 and 1980.

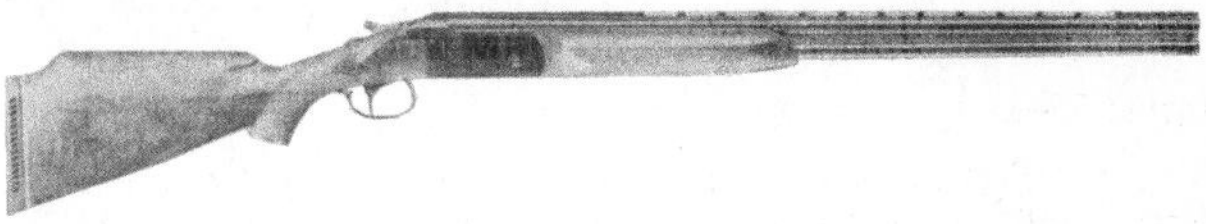

NIB	*Exc.*	*V.G.*	*Good*	*Fair*	*Poor*
—	800	650	500	350	250

Model 312 Field Over-and-Under

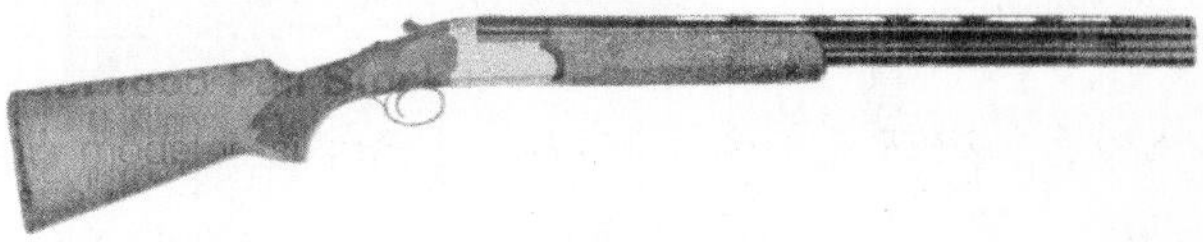

NIB	*Exc.*	*V.G.*	*Good*	*Fair*	*Poor*
—	800	600	450	300	200

Model 312 Trap

NIB	*Exc.*	*V.G.*	*Good*	*Fair*	*Poor*
—	700	600	550	350	200

Model 312 Sporting Clay

NIB	*Exc.*	*V.G.*	*Good*	*Fair*	*Poor*
—	800	600	450	300	200

Model 320 Field

NIB	*Exc.*	*V.G.*	*Good*	*Fair*	*Poor*
—	800	600	450	300	200

(SAVAGE) FOX B MODELS

The Fox Model B was introduced about 1939 by Savage for the hunter who wanted better fit and finish than offered by the Stevens brand Model 530. It was made in many variations until 1988.

Fox Model B—Utica, NY

NIB	*Exc.*	*V.G.*	*Good*	*Fair*	*Poor*
1000	800	600	450	400	350

Fox Model B—Chicopee Falls, Mass. (later Westfield, Mass.)

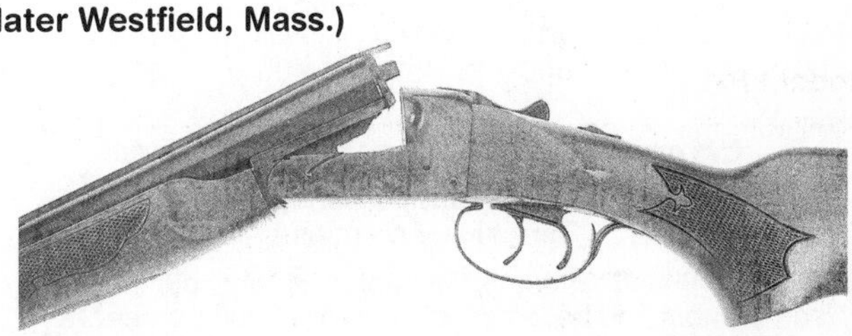

Courtesy Nick Niles, Paul Goodwin photo

NIB	*Exc.*	*V.G.*	*Good*	*Fair*	*Poor*
800	750	500	400	350	300

Fox Model B—Single Trigger

NIB	Exc.	V.G.	Good	Fair	Poor
900	800	600	500	400	300

Fox Model BDL

NIB	Exc.	V.G.	Good	Fair	Poor
1000	800	700	600	400	350

Fox Model BDE

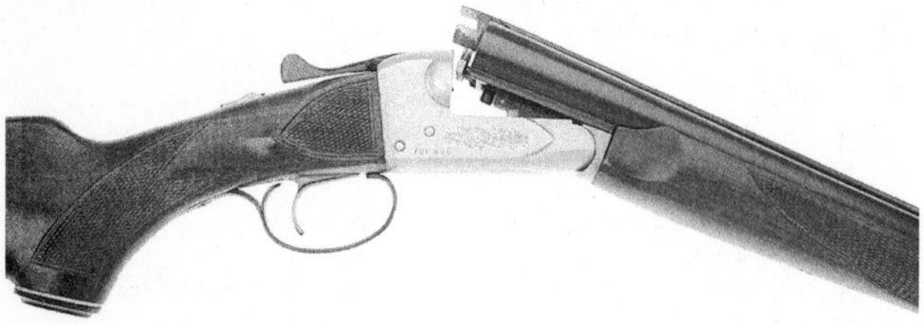

Courtesy Nick Niles, Paul Goodwin photo

NIB	Exc.	V.G.	Good	Fair	Poor
1000	800	700	600	400	350

Fox Model BST

NIB	Exc.	V.G.	Good	Fair	Poor
800	700	600	500	400	300

Fox Model BSE

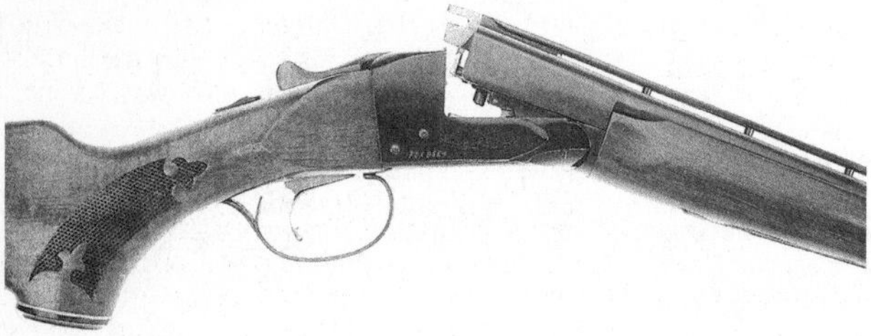

Courtesy Nick Niles, Paul Goodwin photo

NIB	Exc.	V.G.	Good	Fair	Poor
1000	750	650	550	450	350

Fox Model BE

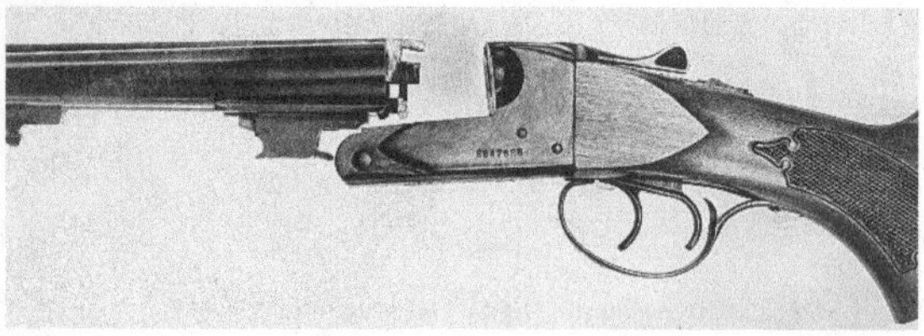

NIB	Exc.	V.G.	Good	Fair	Poor
1000	800	600	450	400	350

SCATTERGUN TECHNOLOGIES

Formerly—Nashville, Tennessee
Berryville, Arkansas

NOTE: In 1999 Scattergun Technologies was purchased by Wilson Combat and became a division of Wilson Combat.

TR-870

This model is based on the Remington Model 870 slide-action shotgun. It is offered in a wide variety of configurations with different features. The standard model is fitted with an 18" barrel and chambered for the 12 gauge shell. The stock is composite with recoil pad. Tactical forend has flashlight built in. Ghost Ring rear sight. Front sight has tritium insert. Six-round shell carrier on left side of receiver. Introduced in 1991. Weight for standard model is approximately 9 lbs. Prices listed are for the standard model.

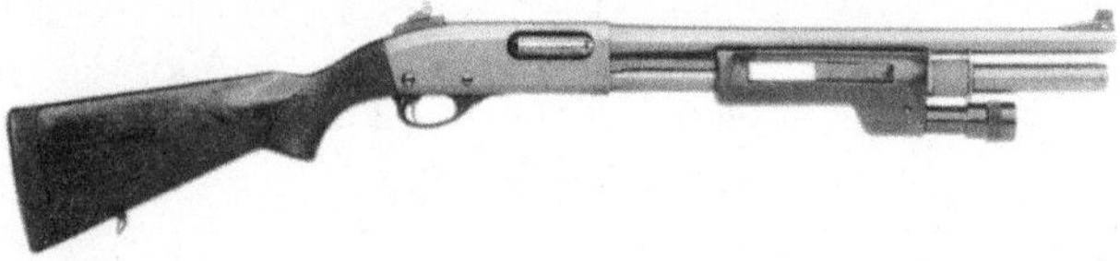

NIB	Exc.	V.G.	Good	Fair	Poor
1000	800	650	550	300	200

WILSON COMBAT CURRENT PRODUCTION MODELS

Standard Model

Based on the Remington 12 gauge 3" 870 Magnum this model is fitted with an 18" barrel with cylinder bore. Adjustable Ghost Ring rear sight with tritium front sight. Seven-round extended magazine. Side saddle shell carrier. Synthetic stock. Tactical sling is standard. Parkerized finish. Fitted with a SURE-FIRE tactical light.

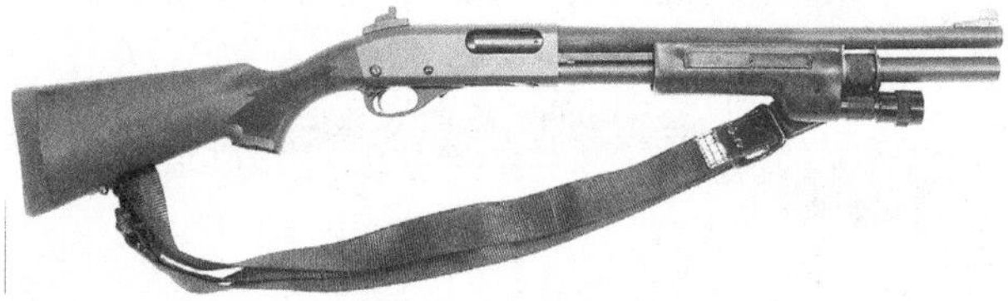

NIB	Exc.	V.G.	Good	Fair	Poor
1150	850	625	500	400	300

NOTE: Add $100 for Armor-Tuff finish.

Border Patrol Model

Similar to the standard model but without the tactical light. A 14" barrel is offered on this model but all NFA rules apply to the purchase of a short barrel shotgun.

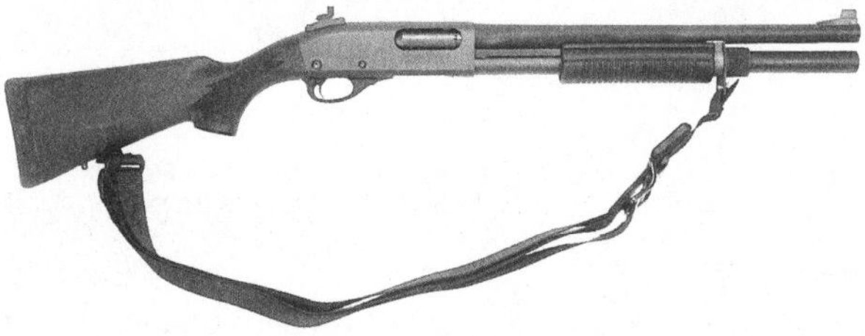

NIB	Exc.	V.G.	Good	Fair	Poor
875	650	475	300	200	150

NOTE: Add $100 for Armor-Tuff finish.

Professional Model

This model features all of the standard model components but it is fitted with a 14" barrel. Magazine capacity is 6 rounds. All NFA rules apply to purchase of short barrel shotgun.

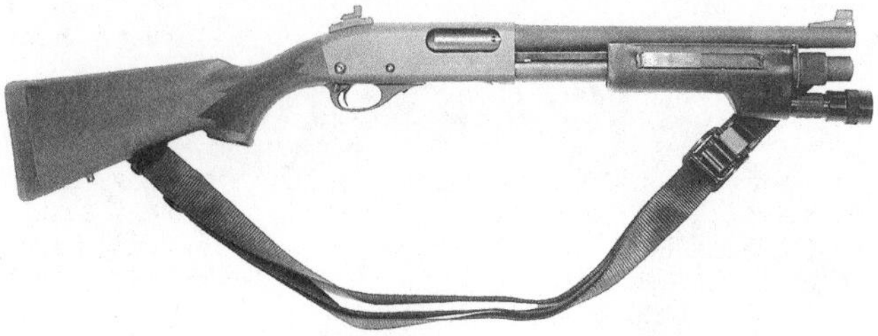

NIB	Exc.	V.G.	Good	Fair	Poor
1175	875	650	500	400	300

NOTE: Add $100 for Armor-Tuff finish.

Entry Model

This model has all the features of the standard model but is fitted with a 12.5" barrel. Magazine capacity is 5 rounds. All NFA rules apply to the purchase of a short barrel shotgun.

NIB	Exc.	V.G.	Good	Fair	Poor
950	700	600	500	400	300

NOTE: Add $100 for Armor-Tuff finish.

K-9 Model

This model is built on a Remington 12 gauge 3" 11-87 Magnum semi-automatic. Fitted with Ghost Ring rear sights and tritium front sight. Extended magazine holds 7 rounds. Barrel is 18". Synthetic stock with side saddle shell carrier. Parkerized finish.

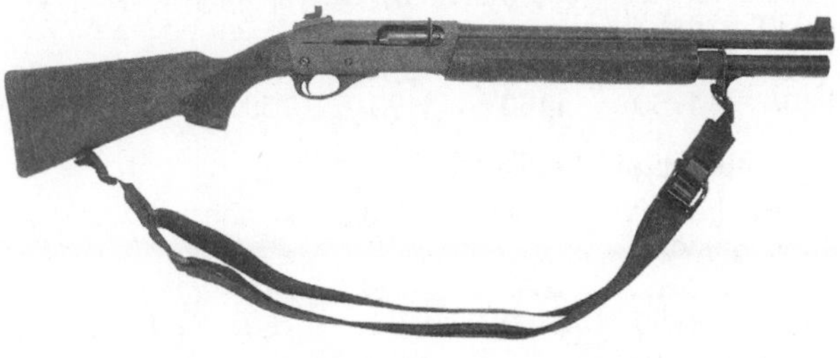

NIB	Exc.	V.G.	Good	Fair	Poor
1075	800	700	600	500	350

NOTE: Add $100 for Armor-Tuff finish.

SWAT Model

Similar to the K-9 model but fitted with a tactical light and 14" barrel. All NFA rules apply to the purchase of a short barrel shotgun.

NIB	Exc.	V.G.	Good	Fair	Poor
1350	1000	800	650	550	400

NOTE: Add $100 for Armor-Tuff finish.

SCHUERMAN ARMS, LTD.

Scottsdale, Arizona

NOTE: There are a number of extra costs options that may be ordered with this model. These options will affect price.

Model SA40

Introduced in 2004 this bolt-action rifle is chambered for a wide variety of calibers from short action to long magnum. Offered in both right-hand and left-hand models. Barrel lengths from 20" to 26" in stainless steel. No sights. Stock is laminated fiberglass sporter style.Retail prices start at $5440.

SCHULTZ & LARSEN

Ofterup, Denmark

Model 47 Match Rifle

A .22 caliber single-shot bolt-action rifle with a 28" barrel, adjustable sights and adjustable trigger. Blued with an ISU-style stock.

NIB	Exc.	V.G.	Good	Fair	Poor
—	800	650	550	400	250

Model 61 Match Rifle

As above, but fitted with a palm rest.

NIB	Exc.	V.G.	Good	Fair	Poor
—	1000	850	750	600	300

Model 62 Match Rifle

Similar to the above, but manufactured for centerfire cartridges.

NIB	Exc.	V.G.	Good	Fair	Poor
—	1250	900	750	650	350

Model 54 Free Rifle

Similar to the above, with a 27" barrel and ISU stock.

NIB	Exc.	V.G.	Good	Fair	Poor
—	950	800	700	550	300

Model 68 DL

A .22-250 to .458 Winchester Magnum bolt-action rifle with a 24" barrel, adjustable trigger and well figured walnut stock.

NIB	Exc.	V.G.	Good	Fair	Poor
—	850	700	600	450	200

SEARS, ROEBUCK & CO. BRAND

Chicago, Illinois

Double-Barrel Shotguns

Between 1892 and 1988 the world's largest mail order house carried a huge inventory of sporting doubleguns including any foreign and domestic brands whose makers did not object to Sears' famous price discounts. To increase sales volume, however, Sears also created its own brands which they supported with innovative design, extravagant advertising claims, unbeatable pricing and excellent quality control. These doubles, like many other firearms products handled by Sears, were listed in its very detailed semiannual catalog from about 1892, when the company first offered doubleguns, until about 1988 when social and political pressures made the company stop handling firearms. Sears marketing people gave birth to and successfully exploited many house and private brands which we no longer associate with Sears at all. In fact, many of these brands clearly rollmarked on guns are now unfamiliar to many collectors. Frequently seen and important in the market segment which many might describe as affordable doubles are some of the most often seen Sears trade names or brands. Listed in chronological order: T. Barker, S.R. & Co., Triumph, Thomas Barker, Sam Holt, Chicago Long Range Wonder, American Bar Lock, Meriden Fire Arms Co., Norwich, A. J. Arbrey Gun Co., New England, Gladiator, Berkshire, Ranger, Eastern Arms Co., J.C. Higgins, Sears, and Ted Williams. These guns were of good quality but sold at bargain prices which gave them tremendous appeal. They were made for Sears to Sears' specifications by a number of American firms and a few foreign ones as well, all of which produced excellent shotguns under their own names. Among the best-known American companies were J. Stevens, Savage Arms, A.H. Fox, High Standard, N.R. Davis, Crescent Firearms, Ithaca, A. Fyrberg, Colton Mfg. Co., Marlin, Hunter Gun Co., Baker Gun Co., and probably a few others. Among the foreign makers were AYA, H. Pieper, Janssen, SKB, Rossi, CBC, and A. Zoli.Sears customers were not aware of this but they did trust Sears name and bought many millions of these shotguns over the nearly 100 years that Sears was in the business. Today these guns are becoming recognized as interesting and valuable collectibles in their own special niche. Their values range from $100 to $3,500 or more depending on make, model, decoration, if any, and relative rarity.

SEDGELY, R. F., INC.

Philadelphia, Pennsylvania

R.F. Sedgely produced specialized bolt-action rifles using the Model 1903 Springfield action. As these arms were for the most part custom order pieces, it is impossible to provide standardized values. It should be noted that his prime engraver was Rudolph J. Kornbrath.Sedgely also made a .22 caliber hammerless pistol. SEE— KOLB.

SERBU FIREARMS

Tampa, Florida

BFG-50 Rifle

This is .50 caliber single-shot bolt-action rifle fitted with a 29.5" barrel. Also offered with 36" barrel. Parkerized finish. Weight is about 22 lbs.

NIB	Exc.	V.G.	Good	Fair	Poor
2195	1600	1275	1000	700	350

BFG-50 Carbine

As above but fitted with a 22" barrel. Weight is about 17 lbs.

NIB	Exc.	V.G.	Good	Fair	Poor
2195	1600	1275	1000	700	350

BFG-50A

This model is a gas operated semi-automatic takedown rifle with a 25" barrel. Parkerized finish. Magazine capacity is 10 rounds. Weight is about 25 lbs.

NIB	Exc.	V.G.	Good	Fair	Poor
6700	5200	400	2750	1700	500

SHARPS ARMS CO., C.

Big Timber, Montana

This company was founded in 1975 in Richland, Washington, and moved to Big Timber, Montana, in 1980. It also produced custom-built rifles included the Model 1877 Sharps and others to individual customer specifications. The models listed are standard production models without extras.

Model 1874 Sharps Hartford Sporting Rifle

Chambered for a number of popular blackpowder calibers and fitted with either a 26", 28", or 30" tapered octagon barrel, double set triggers. American walnut stock with Hartford semi cresent steel butt. Silver nose cap. Case colored receiver with blued barrel. Optional sights. Weight depending on barrel length is about 10 lbs.

NIB	Exc.	V.G.	Good	Fair	Poor
2300	1775	1350	1200	800	500

Model 1874 Bridgeport Sporting Rifle

As above but with Bridgeport checkered steel butt. Schnabel-style forend.

NIB	Exc.	V.G.	Good	Fair	Poor
2300	1775	1350	1200	1000	500

Model 1875 Carbine—Hunters Rifle

Offered in a variety of calibers from .38-55 to .50-70. Fitted with a choice of tapered round military-style barrels of lengths from 22", 24", or 26". Full buckhorn and silver blade sights. Semi-cresent military-style butt with slender forend. Case colored receiver and blued barrel. Double set triggers.

NIB	Exc.	V.G.	Good	Fair	Poor
2300	1775	1350	1200	1000	500

Model 1874 Boss Gun

This model features engraved receiver, XXX fancy walnut, 34" #1 heavy tapered octagon barrel, long range tang sight, buckhorn rear sight, globe with post front sight, and Hartford nose cap. Calibers offered from .38-55 to .50-100. Weight is about 13.5 lbs. with 34" #1 barrel.

NIB	Exc.	V.G.	Good	Fair	Poor
4395	3250	2250	1500	1000	500

NOTE: For Grade II add $750, for Grade III add $1,500.

Model 1875 Target & Sporting Rifle

Offered in a variety of calibers this rifle is fitted with a 30" heavy tapered round barrel. American walnut stock with pistol grip. Case colored receiver with blued barrel. Single trigger. Price listed is without sights.

NIB	Exc.	V.G.	Good	Fair	Poor
1500	1300	1075	900	775	400

Model 1875 Classic Rifle

This model features a receiver with octagon top and with tapered octagon barrel lengths from 26" to 30". American walnut stock with straight grip and crescent butt. Single trigger. German steel nose cap. Case colored receiver with blued barrel. Weight is about 9.5 lbs. with 30" barrel. Priced without sights.

NIB	Exc.	V.G.	Good	Fair	Poor
1500	1300	1075	900	775	400

Model 1885 High Wall Sporting Rifle

Offered with choice of .26", 28", or 30" tapered octagon barrel. Calibers are from .22 to .45-120. Single trigger. American walnut stock with straight grip and oil finish. Checkered steel butt plate. Schnabel forend. Priced without sights. Weight is about 9.25 lbs. with 30" barrel.

NIB	Exc.	V.G.	Good	Fair	Poor
2200	1750	1450	1195	750	400

Model 1885 High Wall Classic Rifle

As above but with crescent butt. Stock with cheek rest and silver inlay in forend.

NIB	Exc.	V.G.	Good	Fair	Poor
2200	1750	1450	1195	750	400

SHARPS RIFLE MANUFACTURING COMPANY

Hartford, Connecticut

The first Sharps rifles to be manufactured were made by A.S. Nippes of Mill Creek, Pennsylvania. Later they were made by Robbins & Lawrence of Windsor, Vermont. It was not until 1855 that Sharps established his own factory in Hartford, Connecticut. After his death in 1874, the company was reorganized as the Sharps Rifle Company and remained in Hartford until 1876 when it moved to Bridgeport, Connecticut. It effectively ceased operations in 1880.The following descriptions are just a brief guide and are by no means exhaustive.

Model 1849

A breechloading .44 caliber percussion rifle with a 30" barrel having a wooden cleaning rod mounted beneath it. The breech is activated by the trigger guard lever, and there is an automatic disk-type capping device on the right side of the receiver. The finish is blued and case colored. The stock is walnut with a brass patch box, buttplate, and forend cap. It is marked "Sharps Patent 1848." There were approximately 200 manufactured in 1849 and 1850 by the A.S. Nippes Company.

NIB	Exc.	V.G.	Good	Fair	Poor
—	—	23000	18000	7500	1500

Model 1850

As above, with a Maynard priming mechanism mounted on the breech. Marked "Sharps Patent 1848" on the breech and the barrel "Manufactured by A.S. Nippes Mill Creek, Pa." The priming device marked "Maynard Patent 1845." There were approximately 200 manufactured in 1850. This model is also known as the 2nd Model Sharps.

NIB	Exc.	V.G.	Good	Fair	Poor
—	—	21000	15000	6000	1200

Model 1851 Carbine

A single-shot breechloading percussion rifle in .36, .44, or .52 caliber with a 21.75" barrel and Maynard tape priming device. Blued and case hardened with a walnut stock and forearm held on by a single barrel band. The buttplate and barrel band are brass, and the military versions feature a brass patch box. The tang marked "C. Sharps Patent 1848," the barrel "Robbins & Lawrence," and the priming device "Edward Maynard Patentee 1845." Approximately 1,800 carbines and 180 rifles were manufactured by Robbins & Lawrence in Windsor, Vermont, in 1851.

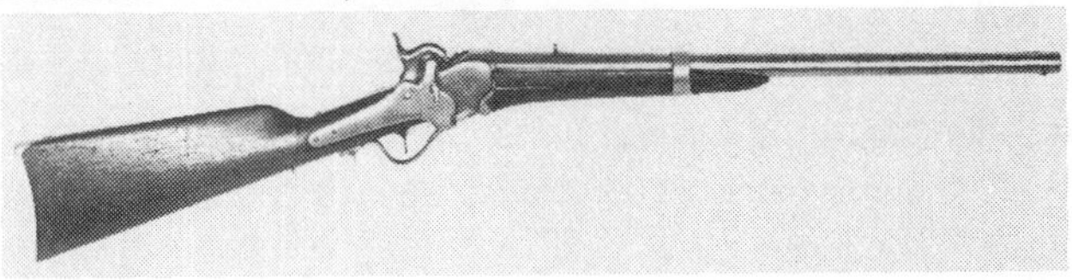

Courtesy Milwaukee Public Museum, Milwaukee, Wisconsin

NIB	Exc.	V.G.	Good	Fair	Poor
—	—	12000	9500	4250	1000

NOTE: Those bearing U.S. inspection marks are worth approximately 75 percent more than the values listed.

MODEL 1852

Similar to the above, but with Sharps' Patent Pellet Primer. The barrel marked "Sharps Rifle Manufg. Co. Hartford, Conn." Blued, case hardened, brass furniture and a walnut stock. Manufactured in carbine, rifle, sporting rifle and shotgun form. Approximately 4,600 carbines and 600 rifles were made between 1853 and 1855.

Military Carbine

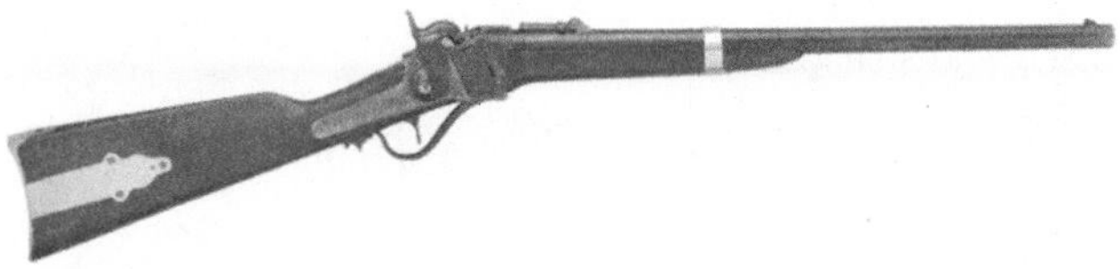

Courtesy Bonhams & Butterfields

NIB	Exc.	V.G.	Good	Fair	Poor
—	—	9000	6750	3000	750

Military Rifle

NIB	Exc.	V.G.	Good	Fair	Poor
—	—	12500	9750	4000	1000

Sporting Rifle

NIB	Exc.	V.G.	Good	Fair	Poor
—	—	6500	4250	1750	500

Shotgun

NIB	Exc.	V.G.	Good	Fair	Poor
—	—	4700	3250	1250	500

MODEL 1853

As above, but without the spring retainer for the lever hinge being mounted in the forestock. Approximately 10,500 carbines and 3,000 rifles were made between 1854 and 1858.

Military Carbine

Courtesy Milwaukee Public Museum, Milwaukee, Wisconsin

NIB	Exc.	V.G.	Good	Fair	Poor
—	—	8500	6250	2750	750

Military Rifle

NIB	Exc.	V.G.	Good	Fair	Poor
—	—	12000	9500	4000	1000

Sporting Rifle

Courtesy Bonhams & Butterfields

NIB	Exc.	V.G.	Good	Fair	Poor
—	—	4500	2750	1250	450

Shotgun

Courtesy Bonhams & Butterfields

NIB	Exc.	V.G.	Good	Fair	Poor
—	—	4300	2500	1000	450

MODEL 1855

As above, in .52 caliber and fitted with a Maynard tape primer that is marked "Edward Maynard Patentee 1845." Approximately 700 were made between 1855 and 1856.

NIB	Exc.	V.G.	Good	Fair	Poor
—	—	14500	10500	4250	1000

U.S. Navy Rifle

As above, with a 28" barrel, full-length stock and bearing U.S. Navy inspection marks. Approximately 260 were made in 1855.

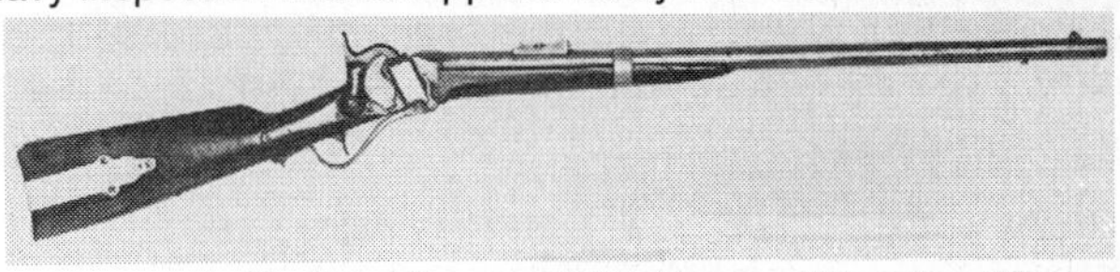

Courtesy Milwaukee Public Museum, Milwaukee, Wisconsin

NIB	Exc.	V.G.	Good	Fair	Poor
—	—	13000	10500	4000	1000

British Carbine

The Model 1855 with British inspection marks. Approximately 6,800 were made between 1855 and 1857.

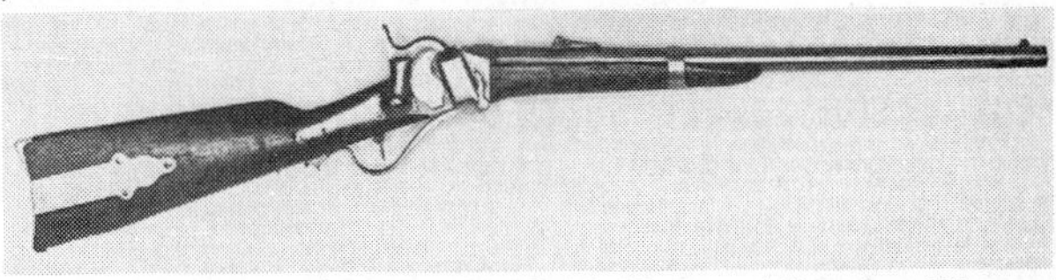

Courtesy Milwaukee Public Museum, Milwaukee, Wisconsin

NIB	Exc.	V.G.	Good	Fair	Poor
—	—	8750	6250	3000	850

SHARPS STRAIGHT BREECH MODELS

Similar to the above models, but with the breech opening cut on an almost vertical angle.

Model 1859 Carbine 22" Barrel, Brass Mountings

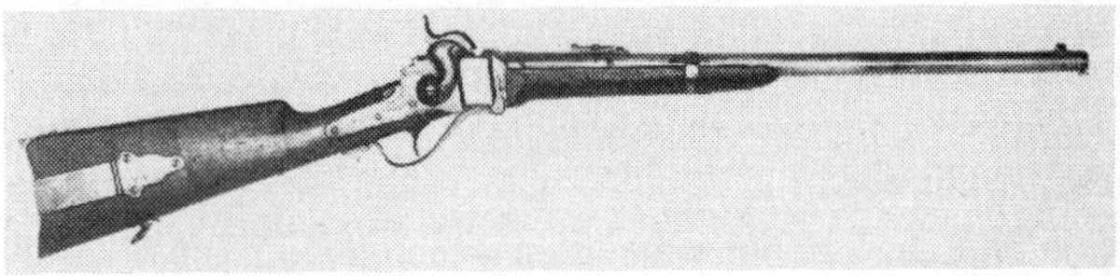

Courtesy Milwaukee Public Museum, Milwaukee, Wisconsin

NIB	Exc.	V.G.	Good	Fair	Poor
—	—	7700	6250	2500	500

Rifle 30" Barrel

NIB	Exc.	V.G.	Good	Fair	Poor
—	—	5500	4250	2000	800

Rifle 36" Barrel

NIB	Exc.	V.G.	Good	Fair	Poor
—	—	5500	4250	2000	800

Carbine Iron Mountings

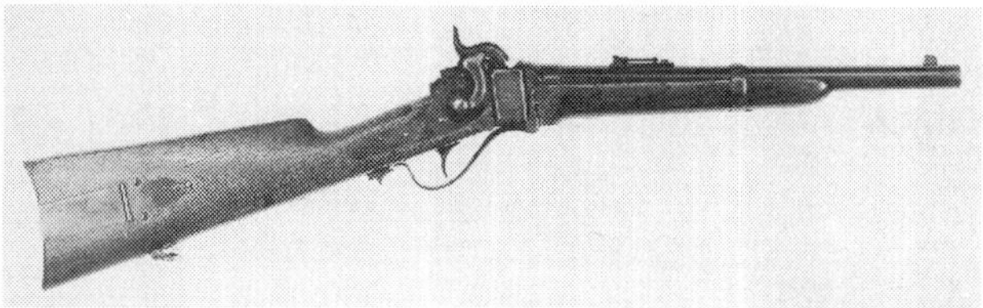

Courtesy Milwaukee Public Museum, Milwaukee, Wisconsin

NIB	Exc.	V.G.	Good	Fair	Poor
—	—	—	3250	1500	500

MODEL 1863

Rifle

Without bayonet lug.

NIB	Exc.	V.G.	Good	Fair	Poor
—	—	4500	3750	1500	500

Carbine

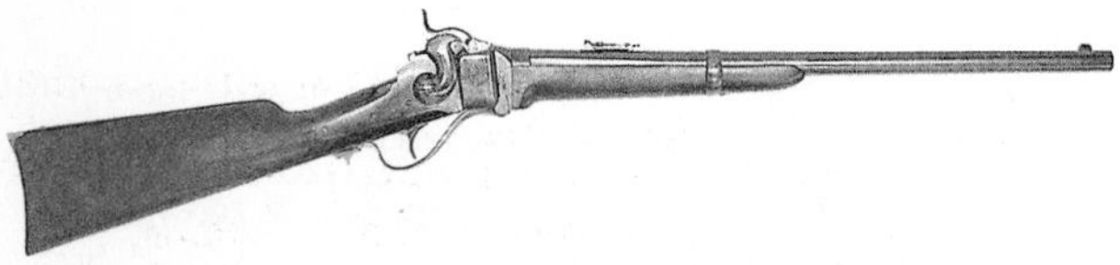

Courtesy Mike Stuckslager

NIB	Exc.	V.G.	Good	Fair	Poor
—	—	5000	3250	1500	500

MODEL 1865

Rifle

Without bayonet lug.

NIB	Exc.	V.G.	Good	Fair	Poor
—	—	4200	3250	1000	500

Carbine

NIB	Exc.	V.G.	Good	Fair	Poor
—	—	4500	3750	1750	500

Rifle 30" Barrel

NIB	Exc.	V.G.	Good	Fair	Poor
—	—	5500	4250	2000	800

Rifle 36" Barrel

NIB	Exc.	V.G.	Good	Fair	Poor
—	—	5500	4250	2000	800

Sporting Rifle

As above, with octagonal barrels, set triggers and finely figured walnut stocks. The Model 1853 Sporting rifle was built as a special order. About 32 were produced. The Model 1863 Sporting Rifle was also built on special order. About 16 were produced. No two of this model are alike. All reside in museums or collections.

Coffee-Mill Model

Some Sharps' carbines were fitted with coffee-mill style grinding devices set into their buttstocks. CAUTION: These arms are exceptionally rare and extreme caution should be exercised prior to purchase. Fakes exist.

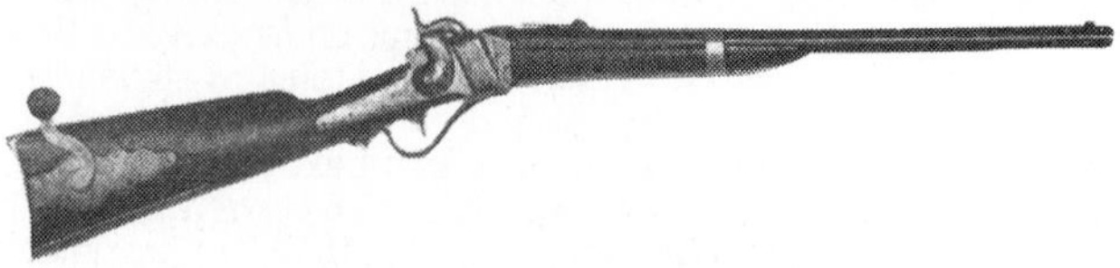

Courtesy Milwaukee Public Museum, Milwaukee, Wisconsin

NIB	Exc.	V.G.	Good	Fair	Poor
—	—	65000	42500	15000	5000

Metallic Cartridge Conversions

In 1867 approximately 32,000 Model 1859, 1863 and 1865 Sharps were altered to .52-70 rimfire and centerfire caliber.

Courtesy Mike Stuckslager

NIB	Exc.	V.G.	Good	Fair	Poor
—	—	5500	4250	2000	600

MODEL 1869

A .40-50 to .50-70 caliber model produced in a military form with 26", 28", or 30" barrels; as a carbine with 21" or 24" barrels and in a sporting version with various barrel lengths and a forend stock fitted with a pewter tip. Approximately 650 were made.

Carbine

.50-70, saddle ring on frame.

NIB	Exc.	V.G.	Good	Fair	Poor
—	—	5500	4250	1750	500

Military Rifle

.50-70, 30" barrel with three barrel bands.

NIB	Exc.	V.G.	Good	Fair	Poor
—	—	6500	5250	2000	800

Sporting Rifle

26" barrel, .44-77 and .50-70.

NIB	Exc.	V.G.	Good	Fair	Poor
—	—	8000	6500	3000	950

MODEL 1870 SPRINGFIELD ALTERED

Chambered for .50-70 caliber and fitted with a 35.5" barrel with two barrel bands, walnut stock, case hardened lock and breechlock. Buttplate stamped "US." Also built for Army trials with 22" barrel converted to centerfire.

First Type

Courtesy Bonhams & Butterfields

Most common, straight breech.

NIB	Exc.	V.G.	Good	Fair	Poor
—	—	5000	3750	1750	500

Second Type

Model 1874 action, serial #1 to 300.

NIB	Exc.	V.G.	Good	Fair	Poor
—	—	8000	6000	2750	750

Carbine

22" barrel converted to centerfire.

NIB	Exc.	V.G.	Good	Fair	Poor
—	—	10500	8250	5000	1250

MODEL 1874

This model was manufactured in a variety of calibers, barrel lengths, and stock styles. The barrel markings are of three forms: initially, "Sharps Rifle Manufg. Co. Hartford, Conn." ; then, "Sharps Rifle Co. Hartford, Conn." ; and finally "Sharps Rifle Co. Bridgeport, Conn." As of 1876 "Old Reliable" was stamped on the barrels. This marking is usually found on Bridgeport-marked rifles only. The major styles of this model are listed.

Military Carbine

.50-70, 21" barrel (460 made).

NIB	Exc.	V.G.	Good	Fair	Poor
—	—	7950	5500	2750	750

Military Rifle

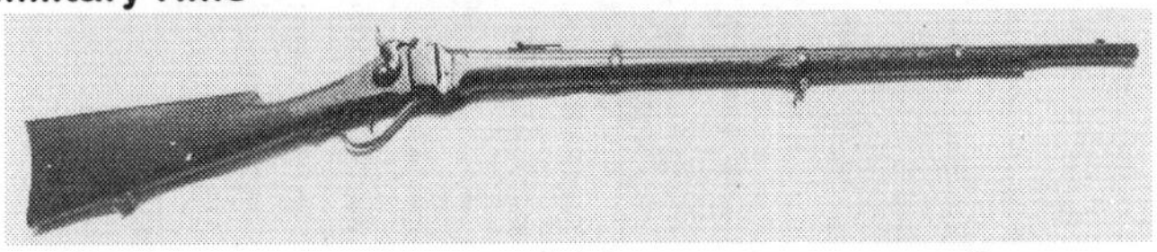

Courtesy Dennis Callender

In .45-70 and .50-70 centerfire caliber with a 30" barrel and full-length forend secured by three barrel bands. Approximately 1,800 made.

NIB	Exc.	V.G.	Good	Fair	Poor
—	—	7500	5000	2250	750

Hunter's Rifle

In .40, .44, .45-70, and .50-70 caliber with 26", 28", or 30" round barrels having open sights. Approximately 600 were manufactured.

NIB	Exc.	V.G.	Good	Fair	Poor
—	—	8000	6250	2750	800

Business Rifle

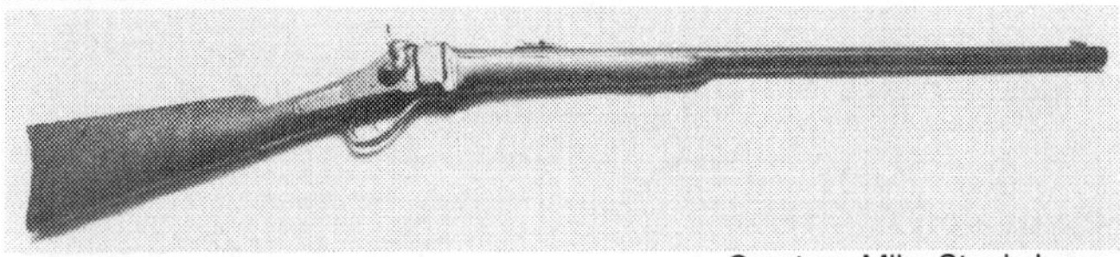

Courtesy Mike Stuckslager

In .40-70 and .45-75 Sharps caliber with a 26", 28", or 30" round barrel, adjustable sights and double-set triggers. Approximately 1,600 manufactured.

NIB	Exc.	V.G.	Good	Fair	Poor
—	—	7750	6000	3250	1000

Sporting Rifle

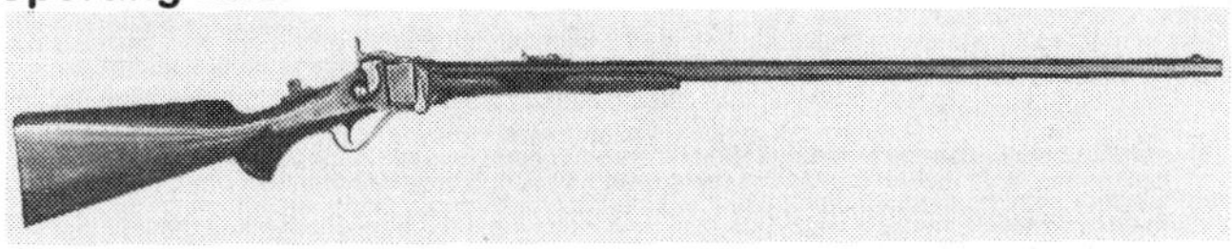

Courtesy Milwaukee Public Museum, Milwaukee, Wisconsin

Offered in a variety of calibers, barrel lengths, barrel weights, barrel styles and stock styles. Approximately 6,000 were manufactured.

NIB	Exc.	V.G.	Good	Fair	Poor
—	—	15000	8500	4000	1500

Creedmoor Rifle

With a checkered pistol grip stock, vernier sights, combination wind gauge and spirit level front sight, set trigger and shotgun style butt. Approximately 150 were made.

NIB	Exc.	V.G.	Good	Fair	Poor
—	—	24000	17500	8500	2000

Mid-Range Rifle

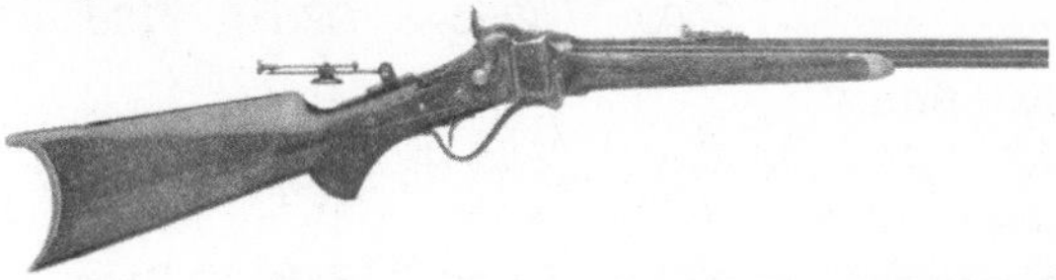

Courtesy Bonhams & Butterfields

Similar to the above, with a crescent buttplate. Approximately 180 were made.

NIB	Exc.	V.G.	Good	Fair	Poor
—	—	22500	15000	6500	1500

Long-Range Rifle

As above with a 34" octagonal barrel. Approximately 425 were manufactured.

NIB	Exc.	V.G.	Good	Fair	Poor
—	—	23000	16500	6000	1500

Schuetzen Rifle

Similar to above, with a checkered pistol grip stock and forend, a large Schuetzen style buttplate, double-set trigger and a vermier tang sight. Approximately 70 were manufactured.

Courtesy Bonhams & Butterfields

NIB	Exc.	V.G.	Good	Fair	Poor
—	—	22500	15000	6500	2000

MODEL 1877

Similar to the Model 1874, and in .45-70 caliber with a 34" or 36" barrel which is marked "Sharps Rifle Co. Bridgeport, Conn. Old Reliable." Approximately 100 were manufactured in 1877 and 1878.

NIB	Exc.	V.G.	Good	Fair	Poor
—	—	30000	10000	5000	2000

MODEL 1878 SHARPS-BORCHARDT

An internal hammer breechloading rifle manufactured from 1878 to approximately 1880. The frame marked "Borchardt Patent Sharps Rifle Co. Bridgeport Conn. U.S.A." NOTE: Be advised that the actions on Borchardt Sporting Rifles are worth a minimum of $750. Military actions are not as difficult to locate as Sporting actions. For the sake of continuity rifles in poor condition, but with usable actions, are priced at the minimum of $750.

Carbine

Approximately 385 were made in .45-70 caliber with a 24" barrel. The forend is secured by one barrel band.

Courtesy Milwaukee Public Museum, Milwaukee, Wisconsin

NIB	Exc.	V.G.	Good	Fair	Poor
—	—	4700	3750	1500	750

Military Rifle

Approximately 12,000 were made in .45-70 caliber with 32.25" barrels and full stocks secured by two barrel bands.

Courtesy Bonhams & Butterfields

NIB	Exc.	V.G.	Good	Fair	Poor
—	—	3000	1250	900	750

Sporting Rifle

Approximately 1,600 were made in .45-70 caliber with 30" round or octagonal barrels.

NIB	Exc.	V.G.	Good	Fair	Poor
—	—	6000	2500	800	750

Hunter's Rifle

Approximately 60 were made in .40 caliber with 26" barrels and plain walnut stocks.

NIB	Exc.	V.G.	Good	Fair	Poor
—	—	4500	1750	1000	750

Business Rifle

Approximately 90 were made with 28" barrels in .40 caliber.

NIB	Exc.	V.G.	Good	Fair	Poor
—	—	4500	2000	1000	750

Officer's Rifle

Approximately 50 were made in .45-70 caliber with 32" barrels and checkered walnut stocks.

NIB	Exc.	V.G.	Good	Fair	Poor
—	—	7500	3750	1500	750

Express Rifle

Approximately 30 were made in .45-70 caliber with 26" barrels, set triggers and checkered walnut stocks.

Courtesy Little John's Auction Service, Inc., Paul Goodwin photo

NIB	Exc.	V.G.	Good	Fair	Poor
—	—	12500	6000	2000	800

Short-Range Rifle

Approximately 155 were made in .40 caliber with 26" barrels, vernier rear sights, wind gauge front sight and a checkered walnut stock.

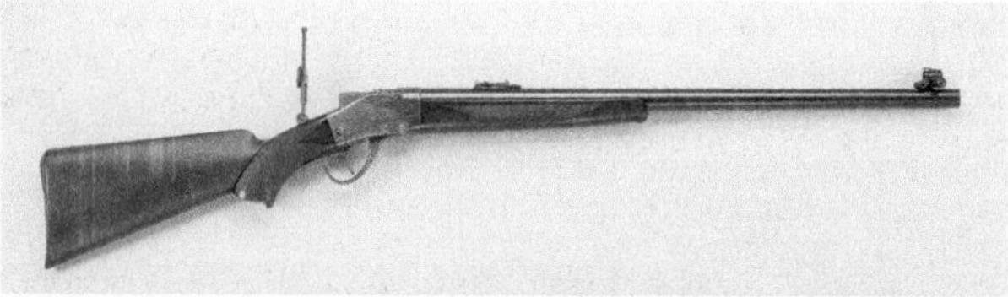

Courtesy Little John's Auction Service, Inc., Paul Goodwin photo

NIB	Exc.	V.G.	Good	Fair	Poor
—	—	7500	3750	1000	800

Mid-Range Rifle

Similar to the above, with a 30" barrel. Approximately 250 were manufactured.

Courtesy Little John's Auction Service, Inc., Paul Goodwin photo

NIB	Exc.	V.G.	Good	Fair	Poor
—	10000	7000	4000	2000	900

Long-Range Rifle

Similar to the above, with different sights. Approximately 230 were manufactured.

Courtesy Amoskeag Auction Company

NIB	Exc.	V.G.	Good	Fair	Poor
—	—	16000	6500	2500	900

C. Sharps & Company and Sharps & Hankins Company Breechloading, Single-Shot Pistol

A .31, .34, or .36 caliber breechloading percussion pistol with 5" or 6.5" round barrels. Blued, case hardened with walnut stock.

Courtesy Buffalo Bill Historical Center, Cody, Wyoming

NIB	Exc.	V.G.	Good	Fair	Poor
—	—	7000	5000	2000	600

Pistol-Grip Rifle

A .31 or .38 caliber breechloading percussion rifle resembling the above. Manufactured in a variety of barrel lengths. Blued, case hardened with a walnut stock having German silver mounts.

Courtesy Bonhams & Butterfields

NIB	Exc.	V.G.	Good	Fair	Poor
—	—	6800	4750	2500	750

Percussion Revolver

A .25 caliber percussion revolver with a 3" octagonal barrel and 6-shot cylinder. Blued with walnut grips. The barrel marked "C. Sharps & Co., Phila. Pa." Approximately 2,000 were manufactured between 1857 and 1858.

NIB	Exc.	V.G.	Good	Fair	Poor
—	—	4250	3000	1250	500

SHATTUCK, C. S.

Hatfield, Massachusetts

Double-Barrel Shotguns

In addition to single-barrel shotguns, Shattuck made about 1,000 hammerless doubles.

Courtesy Nick Niles

NIB	Exc.	V.G.	Good	Fair	Poor
—	1000	500	400	300	200

SHILEN RIFLES, INC.

Ennis, Texas

Model DGA Bench Rest Rifle

A centerfire single-shot bolt-action rifle with a 26" barrel and either fiberglass or walnut stock.

NIB	Exc.	V.G.	Good	Fair	Poor
—	1750	1400	1100	850	500

Model DGA Sporter

A .17 Remington to .308 Winchester caliber bolt-action sporting rifle with a 24" barrel furnished without sights. Blued with a walnut stock.

NIB	Exc.	V.G.	Good	Fair	Poor
—	1750	1400	1100	850	500

Model DGA Varminter

As above, in varmint calibers with a 25" barrel.

NIB	Exc.	V.G.	Good	Fair	Poor
—	1750	1400	1100	850	500

Model DGA Silhouette Rifle

As above, in .308 Winchester only.

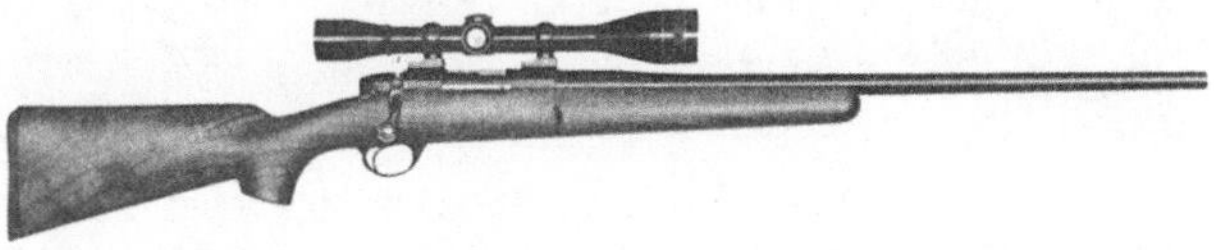

NIB	Exc.	V.G.	Good	Fair	Poor
—	1750	1400	1100	850	500

SHILOH RIFLE MFG. CO., INC.

Big Timber, Montana

Established in Farmingdale, New York, in 1976, this company moved to Big Timber, Montana, in 1983 with the name Shiloh Products. It changed its name to Shiloh Rifle Manufacturing Co. in that same year. In 1985 the company began marketing its products factory direct. In 1991 Robert, Phyllis, and Kirk Bryan purchased the company. Those interested in the Sharps reproduction rifles manufactured by this company are advised to contact them in Big Timber. **NOTE:** The company will build a rifle to customers' specifications. It is therefore possible that many of these rifles have special-order features that are not reflected in the base model price. Since Shiloh is in effect a custom (or at least semi-custom) manufacturer, the rifles listed here are representative but not inclusive.

Model 1863 Military Rifle

A .54 caliber percussion rifle with a 30" barrel, single- or double-set triggers and full-length walnut stock secured by three barrel bands.

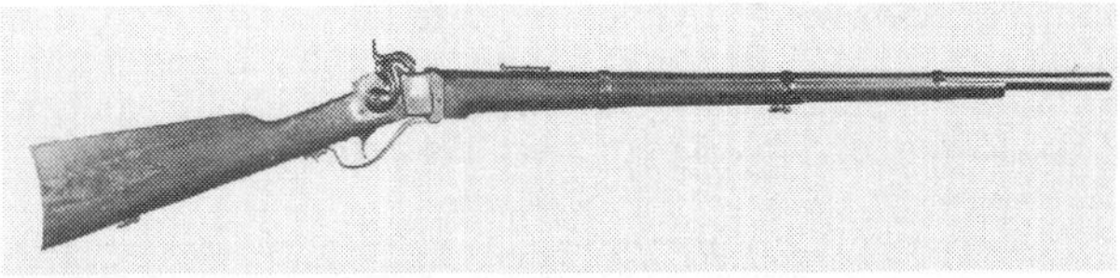

NIB	Exc.	V.G.	Good	Fair	Poor
1900	1650	1100	900	700	500

Model 1863 Sporting Rifle

As above, with a 30" octagonal barrel, sporting sights and a half-length stock.

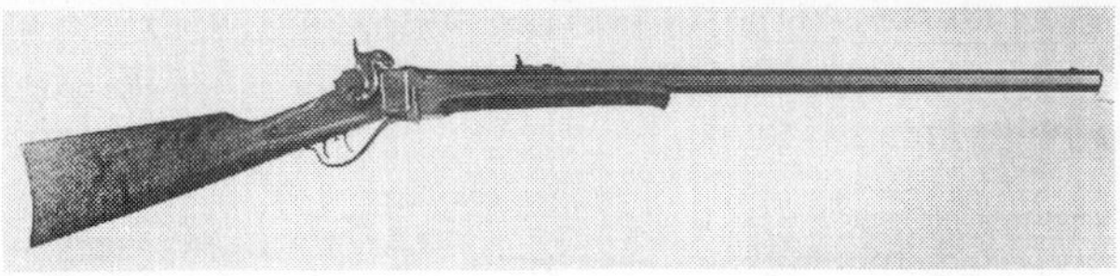

NIB	Exc.	V.G.	Good	Fair	Poor
1800	1550	1050	850	600	450

Model 1863 Military Carbine

The Model 1863 with a 22" round barrel and carbine stock secured by one barrel band.

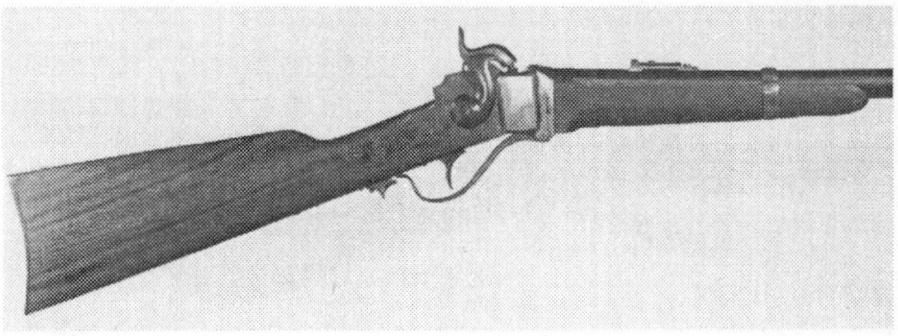

NIB	Exc.	V.G.	Good	Fair	Poor
1900	1650	1100	900	700	500

Model 1862 Confederate Robinson

As above, with a 21.5" barrel, brass buttplate and barrel band.

NIB	Exc.	V.G.	Good	Fair	Poor
1900	1650	1100	900	700	500

Model 1874 Creedmore Target Rifle

This model is furnished with a 32" 1/2 round, 1/2 octagon barrel. Extra-fancy wood stock with pistol grip, no cheek rest, and shotgun butt. Single trigger. No sights.

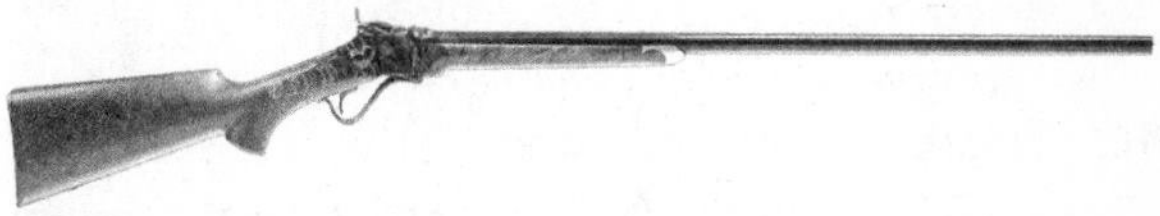

NIB	Exc.	V.G.	Good	Fair	Poor
2700	2250	1700	1300	800	500

Model 1874 Buffalo Rifle (Quigley)

Offered in .45-70 or .45-110 with 34" heavy octagon barrel. Mid-range tang sight with globe front sight. Semi buckhorn rear sight. Double-set triggers. Military buttstock with patch box. No cheek rest and straight-grip stock.

NIB	Exc.	V.G.	Good	Fair	Poor
3300	2750	2100	1700	1200	500

Model 1874 Long Range Express Rifle

Manufactured in a variety of calibers with a 34" octagonal barrel, double-set triggers, vernier rear sight and globe front sight.

NIB	Exc.	V.G.	Good	Fair	Poor
2200	1750	1450	1195	750	400

Model 1874 Montana Roughrider Rifle

As above, with either octagonal or half-octagonal barrels ranging in lengths from 24" to 34".

NIB	*Exc.*	*V.G.*	*Good*	*Fair*	*Poor*
2200	1750	1450	1195	750	400

Saddle Rifle

As above, with a 26" barrel and shotgun butt.

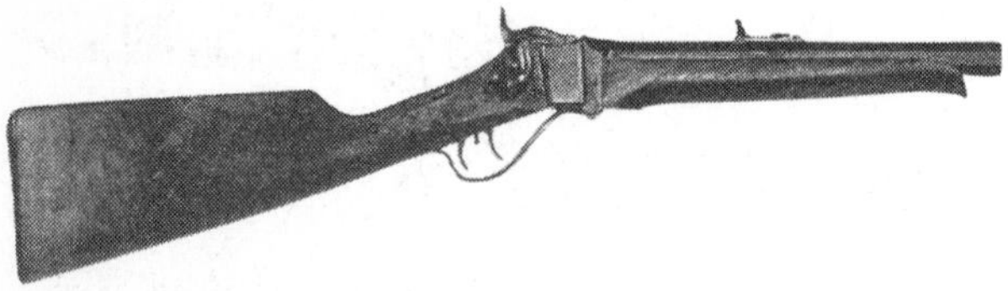

NIB	*Exc.*	*V.G.*	*Good*	*Fair*	*Poor*
2200	1750	1450	1195	750	400

No. 1 Sporter Deluxe Rifle

Similar to the above, with a 30" octagonal barrel.

NIB	*Exc.*	*V.G.*	*Good*	*Fair*	*Poor*
2200	1750	1450	1195	750	400

No. 3 Standard Sporter

As above, with a military-style stock.

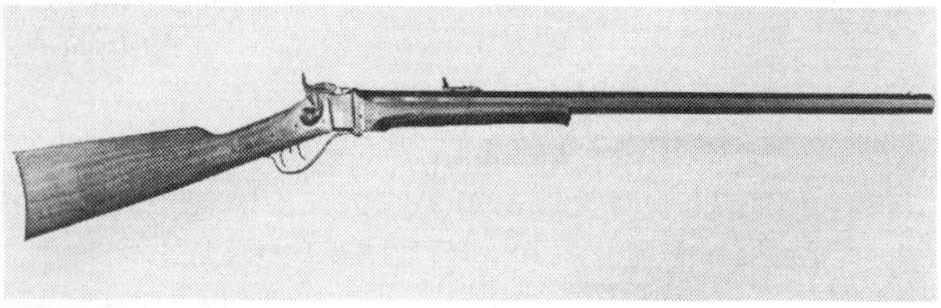

NIB	*Exc.*	*V.G.*	*Good*	*Fair*	*Poor*
2200	1750	1450	1195	750	400

The Business Rifle

As above, with a heavy 28" barrel.

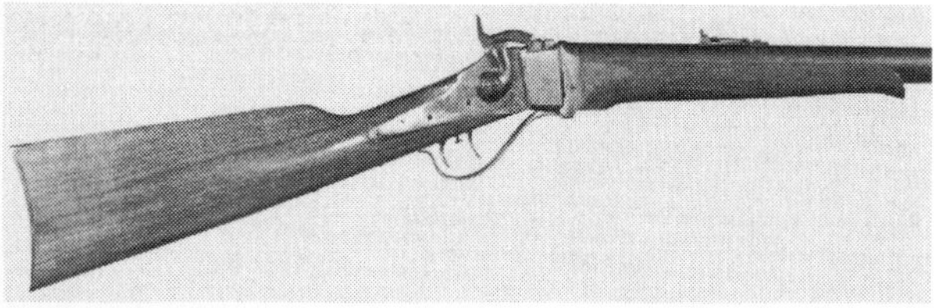

NIB	*Exc.*	*V.G.*	*Good*	*Fair*	*Poor*
2200	1750	1450	1195	750	400

Model 1874 Military Rifle

The Model 1874 with a 30" round barrel, military sights and full-length stocks secured by three barrel bands.

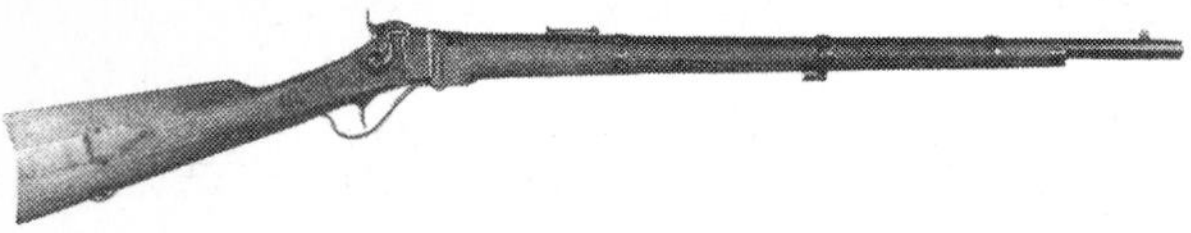

NIB	*Exc.*	*V.G.*	*Good*	*Fair*	*Poor*
2200	1750	1450	1195	750	400

Model 1874 Carbine

Similar to the above, with a 24" round barrel.

NIB	*Exc.*	*V.G.*	*Good*	*Fair*	*Poor*
2000	1550	1150	750	500	300

The Jaeger

The Model 1874 with a 26" half-octagonal barrel, open sights and pistol-grip stock with a shotgun butt.

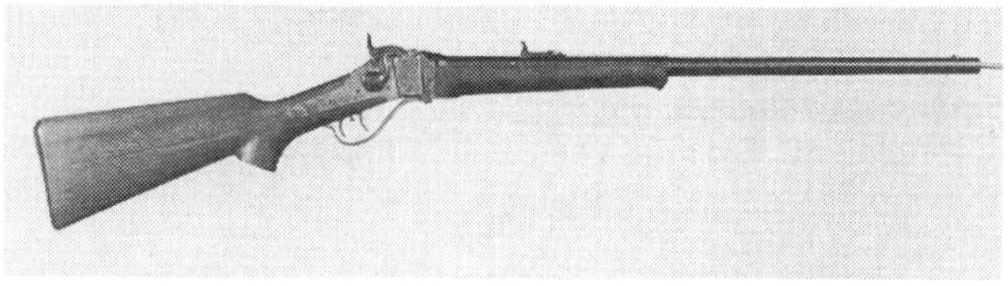

NIB	*Exc.*	*V.G.*	*Good*	*Fair*	*Poor*
2200	1750	1450	1195	750	400

Model 1874 Military Carbine

Similar to the Military Rifle, but with a 22" round barrel.

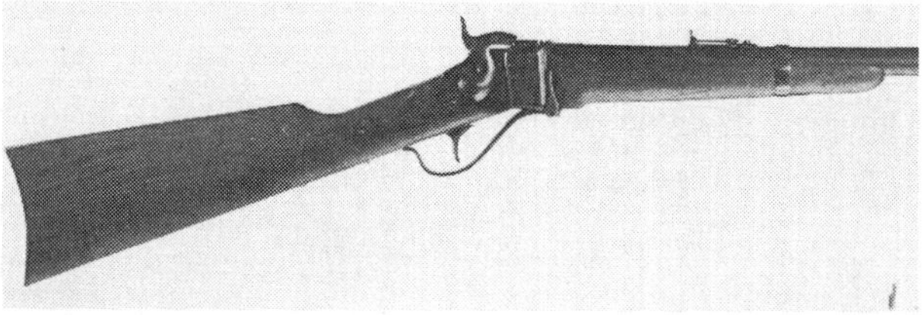

NIB	*Exc.*	*V.G.*	*Good*	*Fair*	*Poor*
2200	1750	1450	1195	750	400

SIGARMS/SIG-SAUER

Eckernforde, West Germany

SHOTGUNS

Model SA3 Hunter

Introduced in 1997 this over-and-under shotgun is chambered for the 20 gauge shell and fitted with 26" or 28" barrels. It has single-selective trigger and automatic ejectors. The stock is figured walnut with pistol grip. The receiver is polished steel with engraved game scenes. Weight is approximately 6.8 lbs.

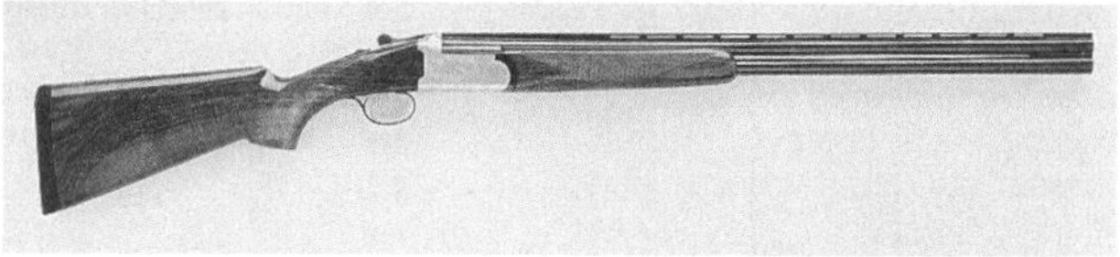

NIB	*Exc.*	*V.G.*	*Good*	*Fair*	*Poor*
1325	1050	750	600	400	300

Model SA3 Sporting

This 12 gauge over-and-under gun was introduced in 1998 and features a 28" or 29.5" barrel with wide 11mm rib and front and mid-target sights. Both barrels and action are blued. Walnut stock with pistol grip and recoil pad. Weight is about 7.3 lbs.

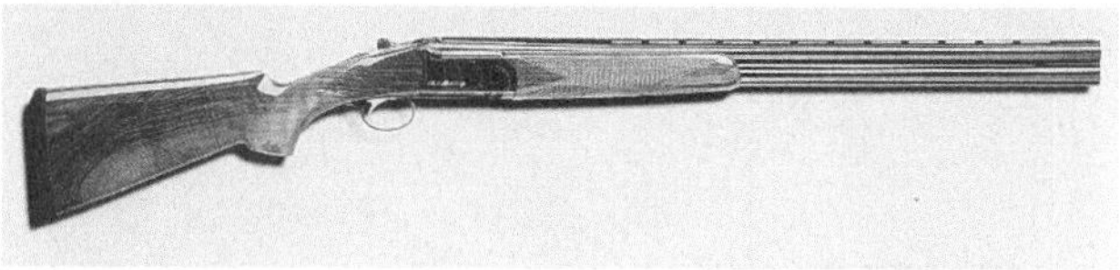

NIB	*Exc.*	*V.G.*	*Good*	*Fair*	*Poor*
1675	1250	1000	700	500	400

Model SA5 Sporting

Introduced in 1998 this 12 gauge is fitted with a choice of 28" or 29.5" barrels. Single-selective trigger and automatic ejectors are standard. Barrels are fitted with a 10mm rib. Receiver is polished steel with engraved clay target on each side. Weight is about 7.6 lbs.

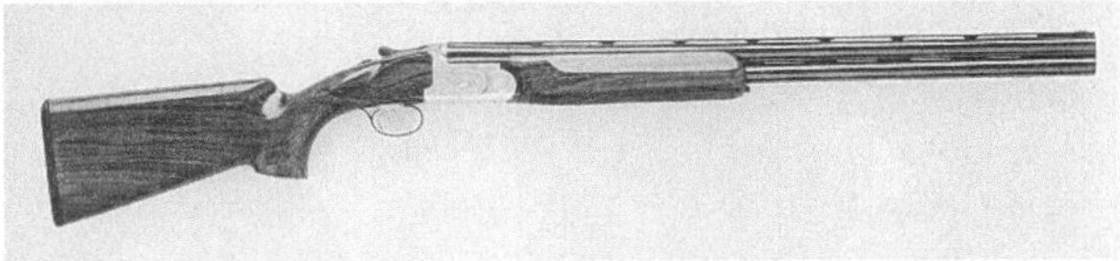

NIB	Exc.	V.G.	Good	Fair	Poor
3175	2500	1795	1100	750	500

AURORA SERIES

These shotguns were first imported and introduced into the SIG product line in 2000. They are made in Italy by B. Rizzini. All the guns in this series are over-and-under guns.

Aurora TR Field Shotguns

All of the TR field guns are offered in 12, 20, and 28 gauge as well as .410 bore. All have single triggers and ejectors. Barrel lengths are 26" or 28". Weights vary from 7 lbs. for the 12 gauge to 6 lbs. for the .410. Select walnut stock with oil finish. Cut checkering of 20 lpi. Choke tubes on the 12 and 20 gauge models and fixed chokes on the 28 and .410 models.

TR 20U

This model features a boxlock action with case hardened frame. No engraving. Straight-grip stock.

NIB	Exc.	V.G.	Good	Fair	Poor
2000	1750	1475	1200	900	400

TR 20

This model features a boxlock action with nickel finish and no engraving. Pistol grip.

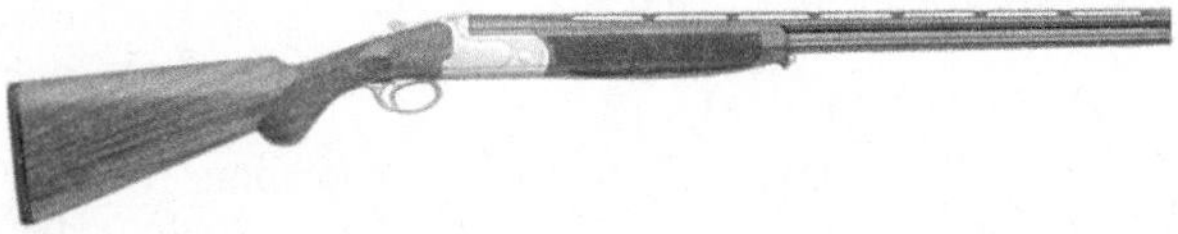

NIB	Exc.	V.G.	Good	Fair	Poor
1850	1500	1325	1000	750	300

TR 30

This model features a case hardened action with side plates. No engraving. Pistol grip.

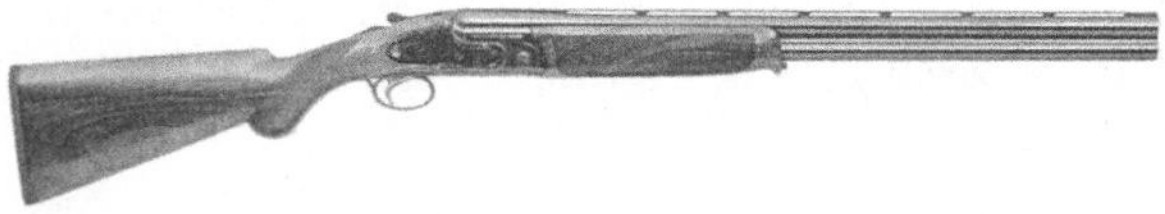

NIB	Exc.	V.G.	Good	Fair	Poor
2225	1850	1550	1375	1000	400

TR 40 Silver

This model features a silver action with side plates with gold inlaid game scenes. Pistol grip.

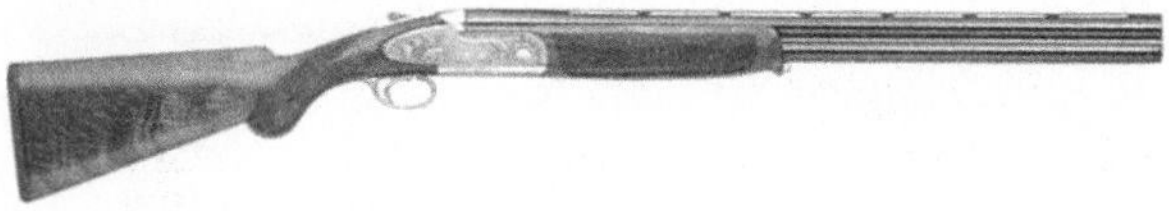

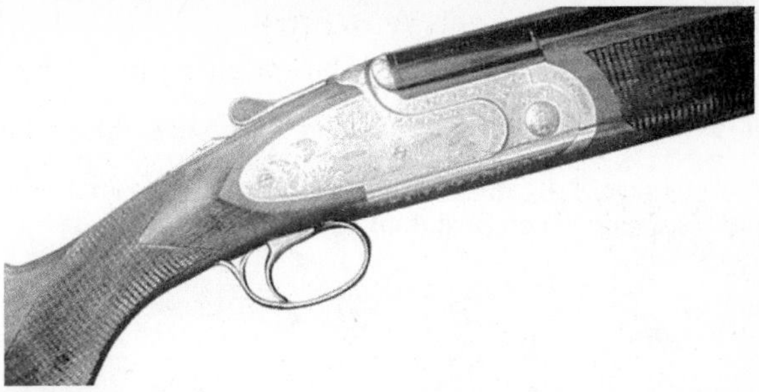

Aurora TR 40 Silver

NIB	Exc.	V.G.	Good	Fair	Poor
2575	2100	1550	1200	950	450

TR 40 Gold

This features a case hardened action with side plates and gold inlaid game scenes. Pistol grip.

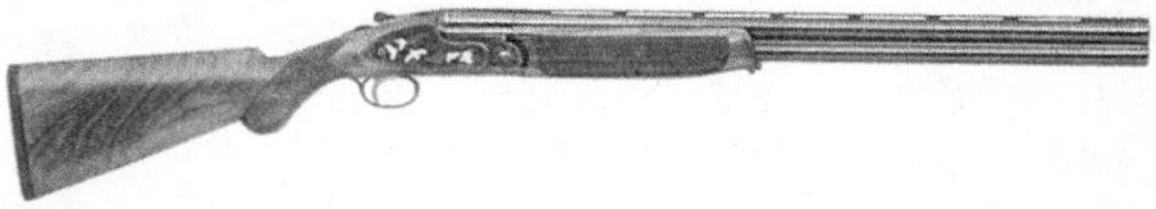

NIB	Exc.	V.G.	Good	Fair	Poor
2675	2000	1450	1100	800	500

New Englander

Introduced in 2000 jointly by SIG and L.L. Bean this over-and-under gun is chambered in 12 and 20 gauge with choice of 26" or 28" barrels. Single-selective trigger, auto ejectors, choke tubes all standard. L.L. Bean logo inlaid in gold on receiver. Select turkish walnut stock with oil finish. Prince of Wales-style pistol grip and rubber recoil pad.

NIB	Exc.	V.G.	Good	Fair	Poor
1995	1500	1200	900	700	350

AURORA TT 25 COMPETITION SHOTGUNSTT25

This model is offered in both 12 and 20 gauge with a choice of 28" to 32" barrels for the 12 gauge and 28" or 30" barrels for the 20 gauge. Choke tubes. Single-selective auto ejectors are standard. Wide competition vent rib. Pistol grip on select walnut stock with 20 lpi checkering. Weight for 12 gauge is about 7.25 lbs. while the 20 gauge weighs about 6.75 lbs.

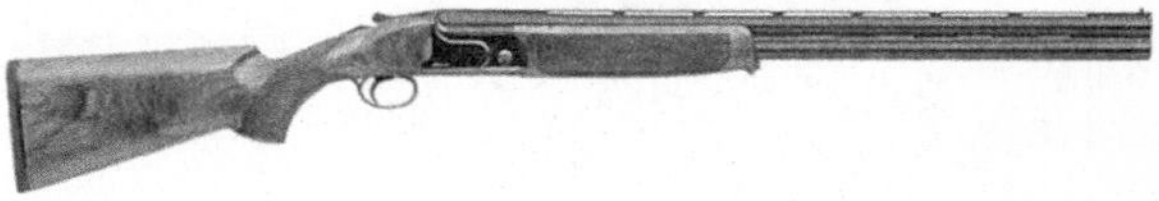

NIB	Exc.	V.G.	Good	Fair	Poor
1995	1500	1200	900	700	350

TT45

Similar to the TT25 but with the addition of a case hardened receiver and side plates with engraving and gold inlay game scenes.

NIB	Exc.	V.G.	Good	Fair	Poor
3275	2795	2200	1775	1300	450

RIFLES

SIG AMT

This is a semi-automatic rifle chambered for .308 cartridge. Fitted with a 19" barrel and wooden buttstock and forearm. Folding bipod standard. Box magazine capacity is 5, 10, or 20 rounds. Weight is about 10 lbs. Built from 1960 to 1974.

Courtesy Rock Island Auction Company

NIB	Exc.	V.G.	Good	Fair	Poor
4500	3800	3100	2500	1500	1000

SIG PE-57

Similar to the above but chambered for the 7.5x55 Swiss cartridge.

NIB	Exc.	V.G.	Good	Fair	Poor
4500	3800	3000	2500	1500	1000

SIG 550

This semi-automatic rifle is chambered for .223 cartridge and fitted with a 18" barrel.

NIB	Exc.	V.G.	Good	Fair	Poor
9000	7000	5500	3000	1800	1000

SIG 551

Same as above but fitted with a 16" barrel.

NIB	Exc.	V.G.	Good	Fair	Poor
10500	9500	7500	4000	2000	1000

SSG 2000

This is a high-grade, bolt-action, sniping-type rifle chambered for .223, 7.5mm Swiss, .300 Weatherby Magnum, and .308 Winchester. It has a 24" barrel and was furnished without sights. It has a 4-round box magazine. The finish is matte blue with a thumbhole-style stippled walnut stock with an adjustable cheekpiece. This model was discontinued in 1986.

NIB	Exc.	V.G.	Good	Fair	Poor
8000	6000	3500	2700	1500	—

SSG 3000

Chambered for the .308 Win. cartridge this model is fitted with a 23.4" barrel and ambidextrous McMillian Tactical stock. Magazine capacity is 5 rounds. Overall length is 46.5", and approximate weight is 12 lbs. This model comes in three different packages.

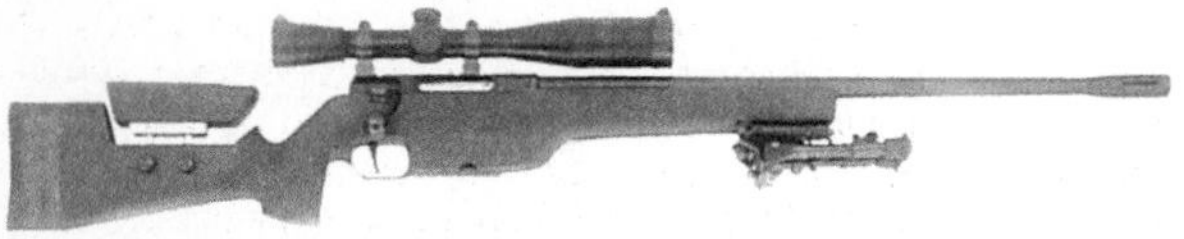

SSG 3000 Level I

Base model with no bipod or scope, but with carrying case.

NIB	Exc.	V.G.	Good	Fair	Poor
2550	2000	1600	1350	950	600

SSG 3000 Level II

At this level a Leupold Vari-X III 3.5-10x40mm Duplex scope and Harris bipod with carrying case.

NIB	Exc.	V.G.	Good	Fair	Poor
3500	2750	2300	1700	1200	600

SSG 3000 Level III

Rifle is supplied with a Leupold Mark 4 M1-10x40mm Mil-Dot Scope with Harris bipod and carrying case.

NIB	Exc.	V.G.	Good	Fair	Poor
4500	3500	2700	2400	1500	700

SSG 3000 Conversion Kit—.22 LR

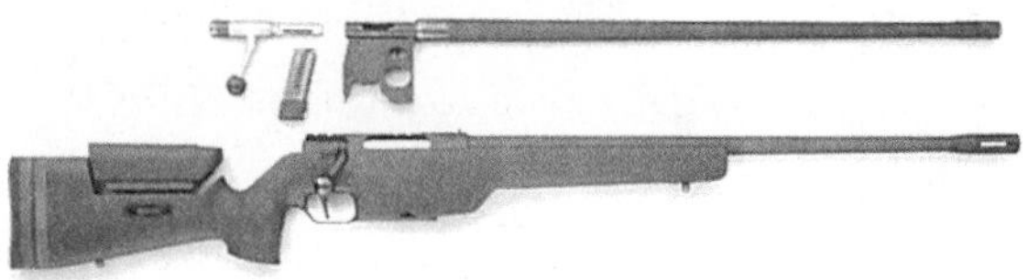

In 2001 a .22 caliber conversion was offered for the SSG 3000 rifle. The kit includes a heavy contured barrel, bolt, and 5-round magazine.

NIB	Exc.	V.G.	Good	Fair	Poor
750	—	—	—	—	—

Model SHR 970

Introduced in 1998 this bolt-action rifle is chambered for the .25-06 Rem., .270, .280 Rem., .30-06, or .308 cartridges. It has a 22" barrel and the receiver is drilled and tapped for scope mounts. Detachable box magazine. Stock is black synthetic or walnut. Barrels are interchangeable. Weight is about 7.2 lbs.

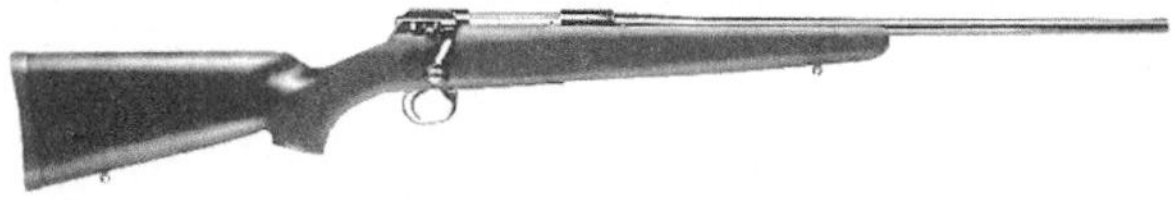

NIB	Exc.	V.G.	Good	Fair	Poor
725	650	575	400	300	200

NOTE: Add $30 for walnut stock.

Model SHR 970 Magnum

Same as above but chambered for 7mm Rem. Mag or .300 Win. Mag. Barrel length is 24". Weight is about 7.4 lbs.

NIB	Exc.	V.G.	Good	Fair	Poor
775	725	625	450	350	250

NOTE: Add $30 for walnut stock.

Model SHR 970 Tactical

This model was introduced in 2000 and features a McMillan stock, non-reflective metal coating, heavy fluted contoured barrel, integral muzzlebrake. The rifle is chambered for .308 Win. or .300 Win. Mag cartridges. Receiver is drilled and tapped for scope mount and the stock has a fitted rubber recoil pad.

NIB	Exc.	V.G.	Good	Fair	Poor
1400	1200	1000	775	600	400

Model 202 Standard

This bolt-action rifle features a choice of synthetic or Turkish walnut stock. Bolt is jeweled. Detachable 3-round box magazine. Offered in standard calibers from .22-250 to .30-06 and magnum calibers from 7mm Rem. Mag. to .375 H&H Mag. Barrel length is 24" for standard calibers and 26" for magnum calibers. Weight is about 7.5 lbs. depending on caliber.

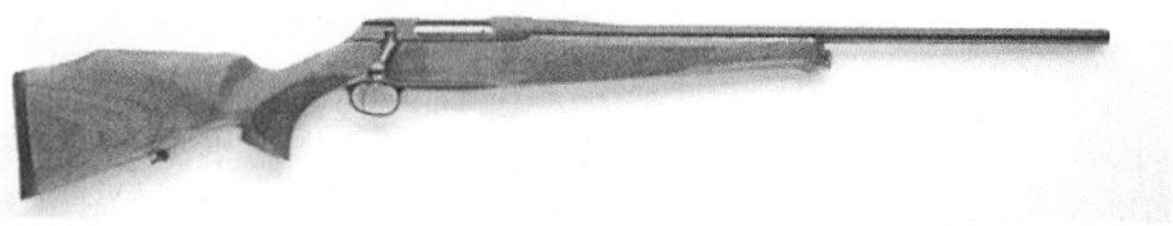

NIB	Exc.	V.G.	Good	Fair	Poor
1650	1200	975	750	600	400

Model 202 Lightweight

This model features a black synthetic stock fluted barrel chambered for the .22-250, .243, .25-06, .270, or .30-05 calibers. Barrel length is 24". Magazine capacity is 3 rounds. Alloy receiver and quick change barrel system are standard. Weight is about 6.5 lbs. Introduced in 2001.

NIB	Exc.	V.G.	Good	Fair	Poor
1600	1150	925	700	550	350

Model 202 Varmint

This model is chambered for the .22-250, .243, or .25-06 cartridge. Fitted with a 26" fluted bull barrel. Stock is Turkish walnut with adjustable cheekpiece. Three-round detachable box magazine. Quick change barrel system. Weight is approximately 9.5 lbs.

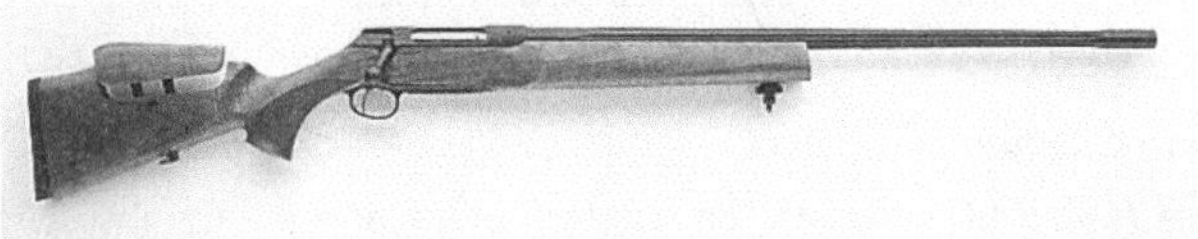

NIB	Exc.	V.G.	Good	Fair	Poor
1600	1150	925	700	550	350

Model 202 Supreme

This bolt-action model is chambered for .243, .25-06, 6.5x55 Swedish, .270 Win., .308 Win., or .30-06. It is fitted with a 24" barrel with choice of synthetic or walnut stock. Magazine capacity is 3 rounds. Weight is approximately 7.7 lbs. No sights.

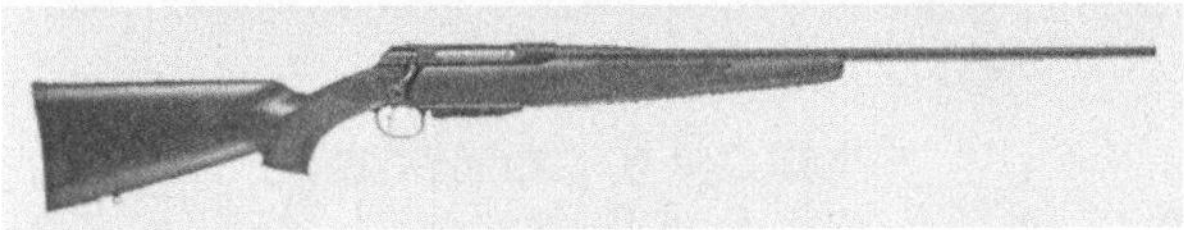

NIB	Exc.	V.G.	Good	Fair	Poor
1800	1650	1400	1100	800	400

NOTE: Add $50 for walnut stock.

Model 202 Supreme Magnum

As above but chambered for 7mm Rem. Mag, .300 Win. Mag, .300 Wby Mag., or .375 H&H Mag. Magazine capacity is 3 rounds. Choice of synthetic or walnut stock. Weight is about 8.4 lbs.

NIB	Exc.	V.G.	Good	Fair	Poor
1875	1725	1475	1150	850	450

NOTE: Add $50 for walnut stock.

SIG 556

Generally similar to the SIG 556 but made in the USA. Chambered in 5.56 NATO. Collapsible stock, 16" mil-spec barrel, picatinny rail and all the trendy tactical goodies. Introduced 2006.

NIB	Exc.	V.G.	Good	Fair	Poor
2250	1600	1300	1050	875	600

SIG 556 SWAT

The SIG556 SWAT features a 16-inch military grade cold hammer forged barrel, chambered in 5.56mm NATO, with a twist rate of 1 in 7". High performance flash suppressor, vented tactical quad rail forearm machined from aircraft grade aluminum alloy and hard coat anodized for durability, quad rail with four picatinny rails, picatinny equipped receiver. The rifle comes standard with the flip-up combat front and rear sight system. The trigger housing is machined from an aircraft grade aluminum alloy forging with a hard-coat anodized finish designed to survive extreme conditions. The rifle comes equipped with a smooth two-stage trigger, ambidextrous safety and is designed to accept standard AR magazines.

NIB	Exc.	V.G.	Good	Fair	Poor
2250	1600	1300	1050	875	600

SIG 556 HOLO

Similar to above but with holographic sight and without quad rail and other features.

NIB	Exc.	V.G.	Good	Fair	Poor
2250	1600	1300	1050	875	600

SIG 556 DMR

A sniper version of the SIG 556 SWAT with bipod and other accurizing features.

NIB	Exc.	V.G.	Good	Fair	Poor
2450	1800	1575	1300	1050	600

SIG-Sauer SIG516 Gas Piston Rifle

AR-style rifle chambered in 5.56 NATO. Features include 14.5-, 16-, 18- or 20-inch chrome-lined barrel; free-floating, aluminum quad rail fore-end with four M1913 Picatinny rails; threaded muzzle with a standard (0.5x28TPI) pattern; aluminum upper and lower receiver is machined; black anodized finish; 30-round magazine; flattop upper; various configurations available. Price: N/A.

SIG-Sauer SIG716 Tactical Patrol Rifle

AR-10 type rifle chambered in 7.62 NATO/.308 Winchester. Features include gas-piston operation with 3 round-position (4-position optional) gas valve; 16-, 18- or 20-inch chrome-lined barrel with threaded muzzle and nitride finish; free-floating aluminum quad rail fore-end with four M1913 Picatinny rails; telescroping buttstock; lower receiver is machined from a 7075-T6 Aircraft grade aluminum forging; upper receiver, machined from 7075-T6 aircraft grade aluminum with integral M1913 Picatinny rail. Price: N/A.

Sauer SSG 3000

Imported by SIGARMS. A 5-round bolt action sniper rifle chambered in .308 Winchester. The heavy-contoured, hammer forged barrel is fitted with a flash suppressor/muzzle brake to provide greater accuracy with reduced muzzle signature. Both the barrel and the receiver feature a black oxide finish to eliminate glare. The short, smooth 60 degree bolt throw allows for rapid operation and, like the safety release, the bolt action is quiet. A massive six-lug lockup system is used to give the SSG 3000 greater strength and accuracy. Pistol grip and fully adjustable stock to give the shooter a custom fit. The trigger is adjustable for trigger position, trigger take up, let-off point, and trigger pull weight. The receiver on the SSG 3000 features a dovetail that will accept a wide range of sighting systems, including a factory available M1913 rail.

NIB	Exc.	V.G.	Good	Fair	Poor
4000	3550	2700	2000	1200	600

Model 516 Series

AR-based series chambered for 5.56x45/.223 round. Short-stroke gas-piston system with adjustable, three-position regulator. Picatinny flattop upper receiver, chrome-lined and phosphate-coated barrel available in five lengths. Thirty-round capacity. Weight without magazine, 6.5 pounds. Prices shown are for Basic Patrol rifle. Other variations are available. Introduced in 2011.

NIB	Exc.	V.G.	Good	Fair	Poor
1050	900	700	500	325	150

Model 716 Series

AR-based rifle chambered for 7.62x51mm (.308) with other features similar to Model 516. Weight, without magazine, 9.3 pounds. Magazine capacity, 20 rounds. Prices shown are for Basic Patrol model. Introduced in 2011.

NIB	Exc.	V.G.	Good	Fair	Poor
1575	1400	1150	900	625	300

NOTE: Add 15 percent for Precision Marksman model.

Sig 50

Bolt-action tactical rifle chambered for the .50 BMG cartridge. Designed for ultra long-range tactical applications. Match-grade trigger that is set for 3-1/2 pounds. Stock has adjustable cheekpiece, pistol grip and length of pull. Barrel is 29-inch heavy fluted with muzzle brake. Full length machined rails allow the mounting of accessories. Fluted bolt, heavy duty steel bipod, Duracoat coating. Weight is 23.5 pounds. Introduced in 2011.

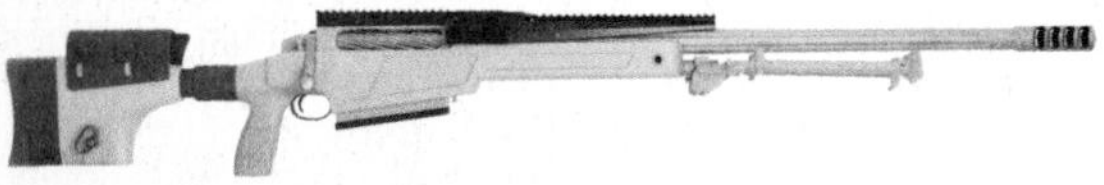

NIB	Exc.	V.G.	Good	Fair	Poor
8300	7400	6350	—	—	—

SILMA
Italy

STANDARD MODELS

MODEL 70 EJ

This over-and-under gun is chambered for the 12 or 20 gauge shell with 28" vent rib barrels with choke tubes. Single-selective trigger and auto ejectors. Checkered walnut stock. Weight for 12 gauge is about 7.6 lbs. and for the 20 gauge about 6.9 lbs. Silver engraved receiver.

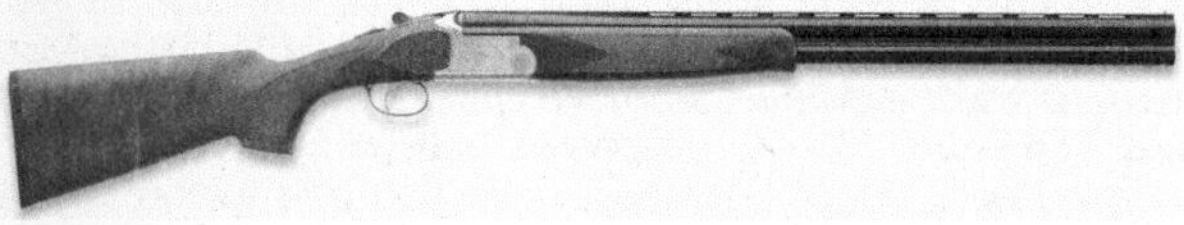

12 Gauge

NIB	Exc.	V.G.	Good	Fair	Poor
950	800	675	495	300	200

20 Gauge

NIB	Exc.	V.G.	Good	Fair	Poor
875	725	600	400	265	150

DELUXE MODELS

MODEL 70 EJ

This model is chambered for the 12, 20, 28, or .410 shell and fitted with 28" vent rib barrels. Checkered select walnut stock with deluxe engraved receiver. Weights are 7.6 lbs. for 12 gauge and 6.9 lbs. for smaller gauges.

12 Gauge

NIB	Exc.	V.G.	Good	Fair	Poor
1050	750	600	475	350	200

Model 70 EJ 20 Gauge

NIB	Exc.	V.G.	Good	Fair	Poor
950	700	550	425	300	175

Model 70 EJ 28 and .410 Gauge

NIB	Exc.	V.G.	Good	Fair	Poor
1075	800	650	525	400	250

Superlight

This model is offered in 12 or 20 gauge with 28" barrels with choke tubes. Checkered select wanut stock. Receiver is made from alloy steel. Weight for 12 gauge is about 6.7 lbs. and about 6.3 lbs. for the 20 gauge.

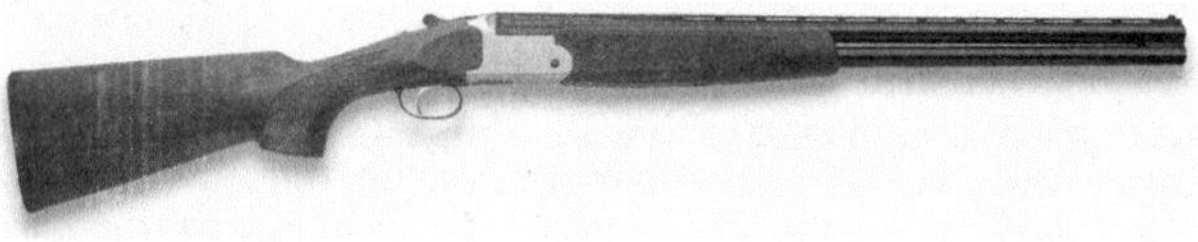

NIB	Exc.	V.G.	Good	Fair	Poor
1100	825	675	550	425	275

Clays Model

This model is designed for sporting clays and is chambered for the 12 gauge 3" shell. Fitted with a 28" barrel with choke tubes and wide ventilated rib. Checkered select walnut stock.

NIB	Exc.	V.G.	Good	Fair	Poor
1300	975	775	625	500	400

SIMSON & COMPANY
Suhl, Germany

SEE—Luger

NOTE: The models listed and pictured are taken from a mid-1930s Simson catalog. Because the company was Jewish-owned the Nazis took control in the mid-1930s changing the name to "Berlin Suhler Waffen." Prices are estimates.

SHOTGUNS

Model 235

Side-by-side shotgun chambered for 12 or 16 gauge with Anson & Deely action. Scalloped frame with scroll engraving. Walnut stock with pistol grip. Double triggers.

Courtesy Jim Cate

NIB	Exc.	V.G.	Good	Fair	Poor
—	900	700	550	400	350

Model 73

Similar to the above model but with more scroll engraving coverage.

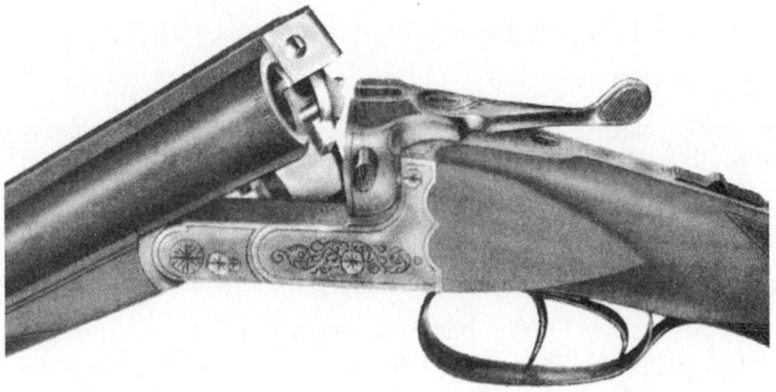

Courtesy Jim Cate

NIB	Exc.	V.G.	Good	Fair	Poor
—	950	750	600	400	350

Model 74

This model features deep cut game scene engraving. Select walnut stock with fine-line checkering.

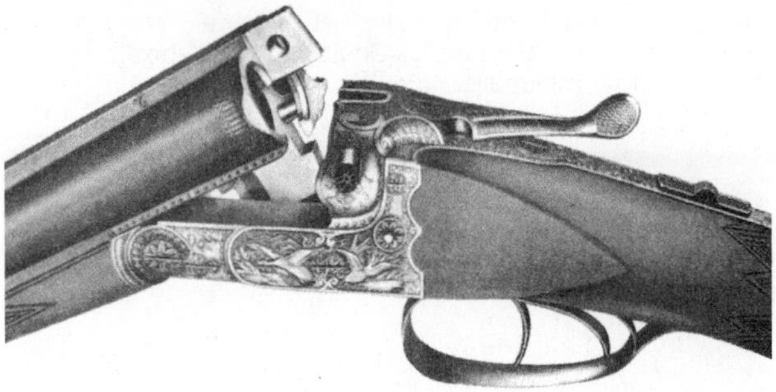

Courtesy Jim Cate

NIB	Exc.	V.G.	Good	Fair	Poor
—	1100	800	600	450	350

Model 74E

Same as above but with automatic ejectors.

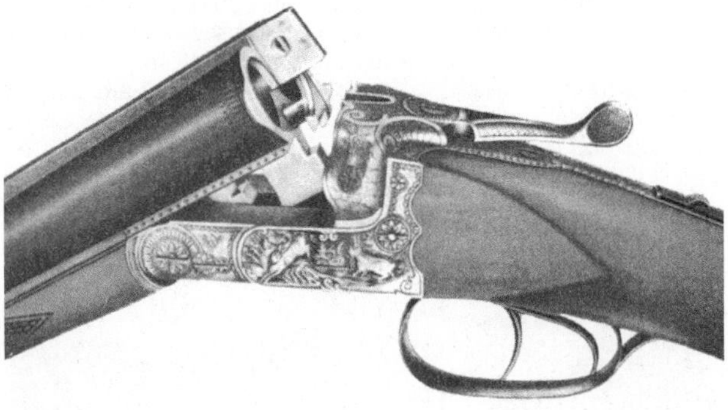

Courtesy Jim Cate

NIB	Exc.	V.G.	Good	Fair	Poor
—	1200	850	650	450	350

Model 76

This side-by-side model is fitted with game scene engraved side plates and offered in 12 or 16 gauge.

Courtesy Jim Cate

NIB	Exc.	V.G.	Good	Fair	Poor
—	1400	1100	800	550	400

Model 76E

As above but with automatic ejectors.

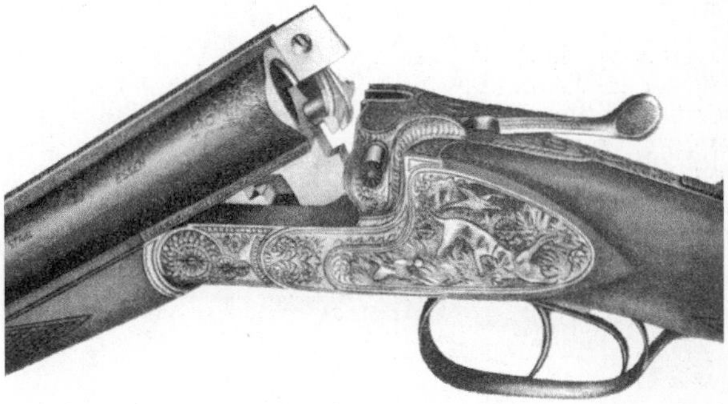

Courtesy Jim Cate

NIB	Exc.	V.G.	Good	Fair	Poor
—	1500	1200	850	550	400

SIRKIS INDUSTRIES, LTD.

Ramat-Gan, Israel

Model 35 Match Rifle

A .22 caliber single-shot bolt-action rifle with a 26" free floating barrel, adjustable rear sight and adjustable trigger. Blued with a walnut stock.

NIB	Exc.	V.G.	Good	Fair	Poor
—	600	550	500	400	200

Model 36 Sniper's Rifle

A 7.62x54mm caliber semi-automatic rifle with a 22" barrel. Matte blued with a composition stock.

NIB	Exc.	V.G.	Good	Fair	Poor
—	675	600	550	450	200

SKB ARMS COMPANY

Tokyo, Japan

SIDE-BY-SIDE GUNS

Model 100

A boxlock 12 or 20 gauge double-barrel shotgun with 25" to 30" barrels, single-selective trigger and automatic ejectors. Blued with a walnut stock. Imported prior to 1981. Discontinued.

NIB	Exc.	V.G.	Good	Fair	Poor
—	1400	1100	800	550	400

Model 150

As above, with some engraving, a beavertail forearm and a figured walnut stock. Imported from 1972 to 1974.

NIB	Exc.	V.G.	Good	Fair	Poor
—	1450	1125	800	550	400

Model 200

As above, with a French case hardened and scalloped receiver. Discontinued.

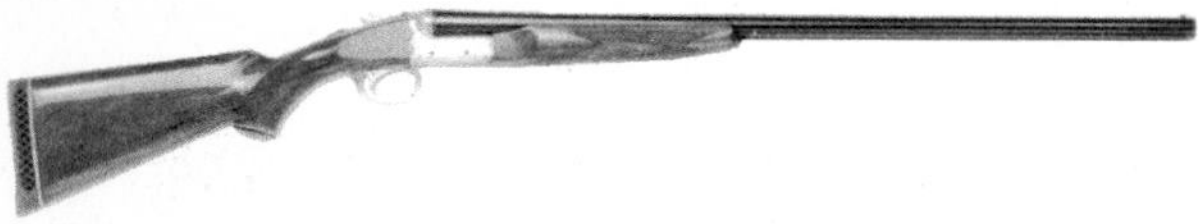

NIB	Exc.	V.G.	Good	Fair	Poor
—	1150	900	675	500	400

Model 200E

As above, with an English-style stock. Imported prior to 1989.

NIB	Exc.	V.G.	Good	Fair	Poor
—	1200	850	650	450	350

Model 280

Same as the Model 200 but fitted with a straight grip stock. Discontinued.

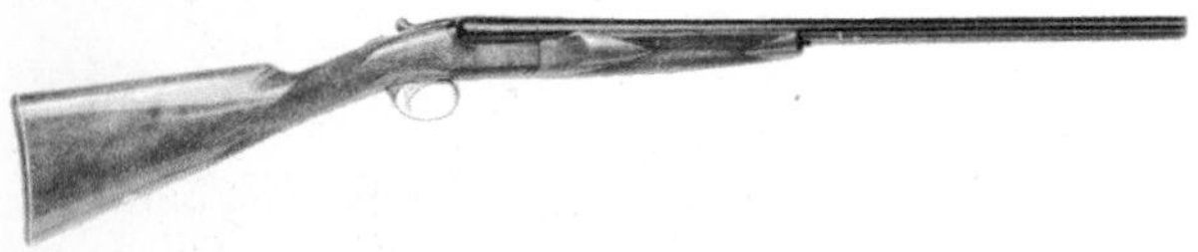

NIB	Exc.	V.G.	Good	Fair	Poor
—	1200	850	650	450	350

Model 300

As above, with more engraving and a figured walnut stock. Discontinued.

NIB	Exc.	V.G.	Good	Fair	Poor
—	1250	900	700	475	350

Model 385

Similar to the Model 300 but chambered for the 12, 20 or 28 gauge shell. Scroll engraved frame with semi-fancy walnut. Pistol-grip or straight-grip stock. Limited quantities imported. Weight is approximately 7 lbs. depending on barrel length and gauge. Discontinued.

NIB	Exc.	V.G.	Good	Fair	Poor
—	1750	1475	1100	700	400

Model 385 2 Barrel Set

Same as above but with a 20 and 28 gauge set of barrels in either 26" or 28". Discontinued.

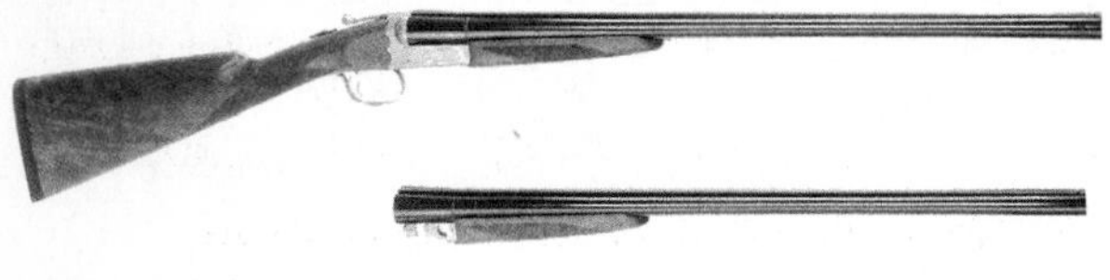

NIB	Exc.	V.G.	Good	Fair	Poor
—	2500	2250	1300	900	500

Model 385 Sporting Clays

This model is chambered for 12, 20, or 28 gauge and fitted with a 28" barrel. Pistol-grip stock. Weight is about 7 lbs. depending on gauge. Discontinued.

NIB	Exc.	V.G.	Good	Fair	Poor
—	1750	1475	1100	700	400

NOTE: For extra set of 20 or 28 gauge barrels add $900.

Model 400E

As above, with engraved false sideplates and an English-style stock. Imported prior to 1990.

NIB	Exc.	V.G.	Good	Fair	Poor
—	1750	1475	1100	700	400

Model 480E

As above, with a French case hardened receiver and more finely figured walnut stocks. Discontinued.

NIB	Exc.	V.G.	Good	Fair	Poor
—	1750	1475	1100	700	400

Model 485

This model features an engraved sideplate boxlock action chambered for 12, 20, or 28 gauge with 26" or 28" barrels. Choke tubes. Weight is approximately 7.7 lbs. Discontinued.

NIB	Exc.	V.G.	Good	Fair	Poor
2750	2100	1500	900	650	300

Model 485 2 Barrel Set

Same as above but with an extra set of barrels in 20/28 gauge combinations with 26" barrels. Choice of pistol-grip or straight-grip stock. Discontinued.

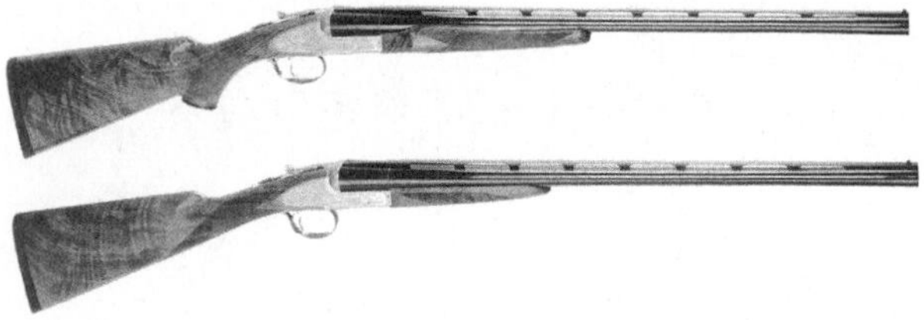

NIB	Exc.	V.G.	Good	Fair	Poor
3900	3000	1850	1500	1200	500

OVER-AND-UNDER GUNS

MODEL 85TSS SERIES

This series, introduced in 2004, features a low-profile boxlock action fitted with an inertia trigger (12 and 20 gauge), mechanical on 28 and .410 bore. Single-selective trigger with manual safety. Silver nitride finish. Barrels have automatic ejectors, ventilated rib and choke tubes. Pigeon porting is optional. Stocks are American walnut with matte finish and fitted with Pachmayr recoil pad. Adjustable comb stock is optional.

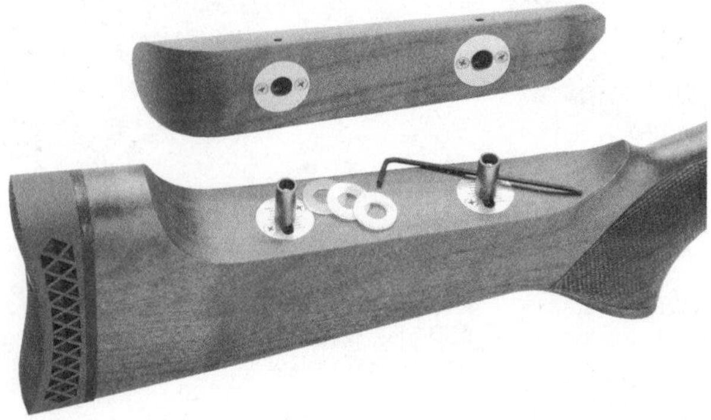

Model 85TSS Sporting Clays

Chambered for the 12, 20, 28 gauge, and .410 bore, this model features a choice of 28", 30", or 32" barrels on the 12 gauge guns and 28" or 30" barrels on the small bore guns. Choke tubes. Choice of fixed or adjustable comb. Choice of multiple barrel sets. Weight on 12 gauge guns is about 8.5 lbs. depending on barrel length and 7.5 lbs. on the smaller bore guns.

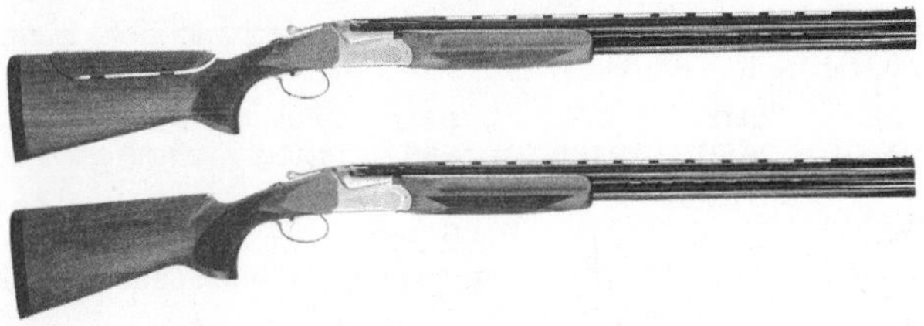

NIB	Exc.	V.G.	Good	Fair	Poor
1875	1600	1425	1075	800	450

NOTE: Add $175 for adjustable comb, $1,200 for two- barrel sets and $2,800 for three-barrel 20, 28 and .410 set.

Model 85TSS Trap

This 12 gauge 3" trap model is fitted with a choice of 30" or 32" backbored barrels with adjustable 12mm rib. Choice of fixed or adjustable comb with or without Monte Carlo. Weight is about 8.75 lbs.

NIB	Exc.	V.G.	Good	Fair	Poor
1875	1600	1425	1075	800	450

NOTE: Add $175 for adjustable comb.

Model 85TSS Trap Unsingle

This model is a single barrel trap gun with choice of 32" or 34" adjustable rib barrel with choice of standard comb or Monte Carlo with or without adjustable comb. Weight is about 9 lbs.

NIB	Exc.	V.G.	Good	Fair	Poor
2100	1900	1625	1250	1000	500

NOTE: Add $175 for adjustable comb.

Model 85TSS Trap Unsingle Combo

This model features a 32" or 34" single barrel and 30" or 32" over/under barrels. Barrel rib is adjustable. Choice of Monte Carlo or standard stock with or without adjustable comb.

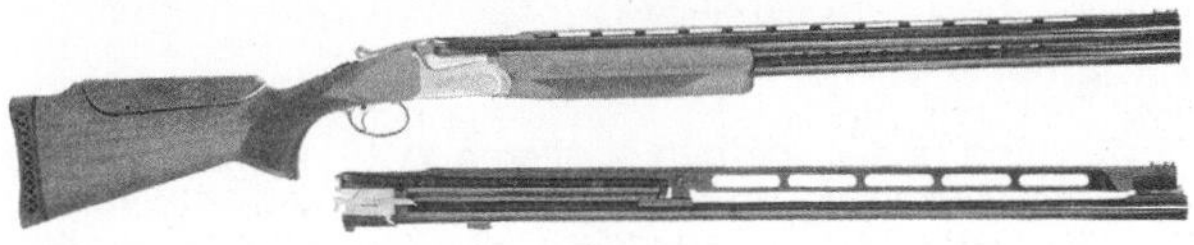

NIB	Exc.	V.G.	Good	Fair	Poor
3175	2500	2250	1875	1300	600

NOTE: Add $175 for adjustable comb.

Model 85TSS Skeet

This model is offered in 12, 20, and 28 gauge as well as .410 bore. The 12 gauge model is offered with a choice of 28", 30" or 32" backbored barrels with 9.5mm rib. Small gauges are offered with a choice of 28" or 30" backbored barrels with 8.5mm rib. Weight for 12 gauge gun is about 8.35 lbs. and 7.5 lbs. for smaller gauges. Choice of fixed or adjustable comb.

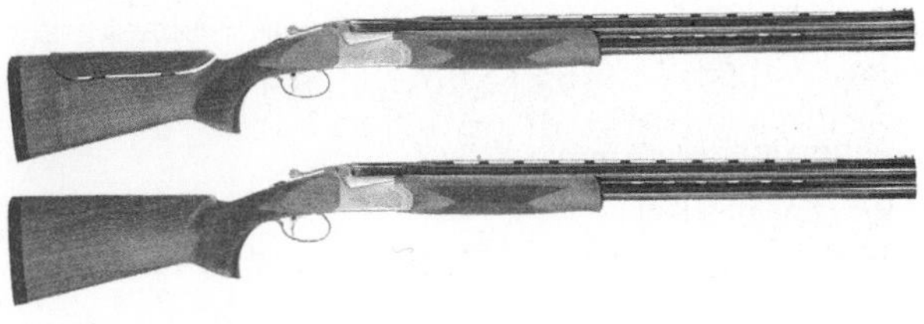

NIB	Exc.	V.G.	Good	Fair	Poor
2100	1900	1625	1250	1000	500

NOTE: Add $175 for adjustable comb. Add $2,800 for three-barrel set.

Model 500

A 12, 20, 28 gauge or .410 bore over-and-under shotgun with 26", 28" or 30" ventilated rib barrels. Blued with a walnut stock. Imported from 1966 to 1979.

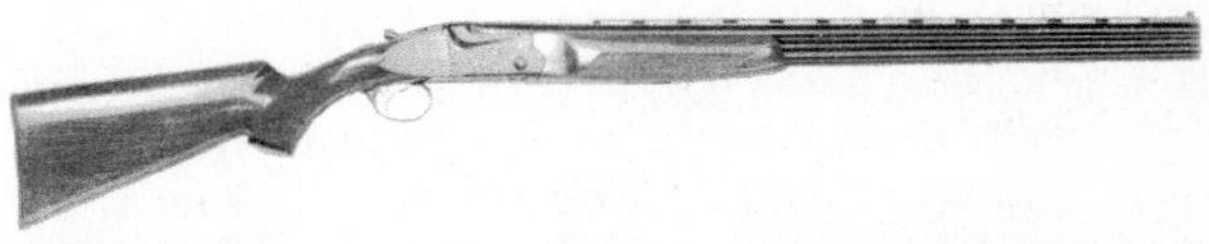

NIB	Exc.	V.G.	Good	Fair	Poor
850	700	575	400	325	200

Model 505 Field

The 505 Series is also produced in sporting clays, trap and skeet configurations, which are valued at approximately 10 percent additional.

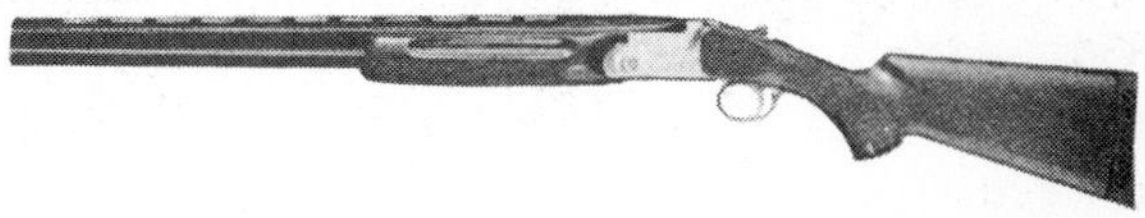

NIB	Exc.	V.G.	Good	Fair	Poor
1270	950	700	500	350	250

Model 505 3-Gauge Skeet Set

As above, with 3 sets of barrels.

NIB	Exc.	V.G.	Good	Fair	Poor
2500	1800	1400	975	650	650

Model 585

Similar to the Model 505 but offered in 12, 20, and 28 gauge and .410 bore as well. Barrel lengths are 26" or 28". Weight is about 7.25 lbs. for small bores and 8 lbs. for 12 gauge guns.

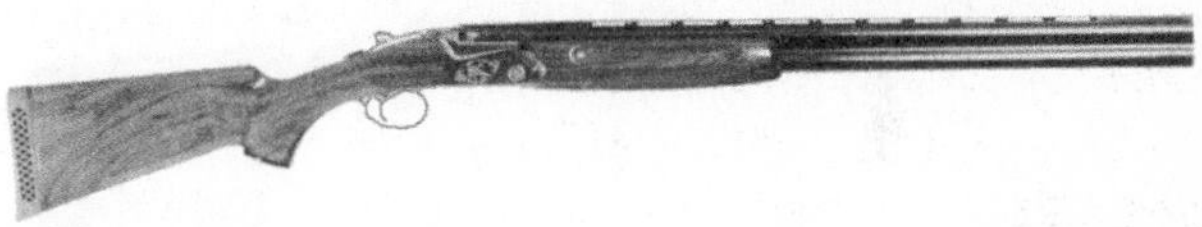

NIB	Exc.	V.G.	Good	Fair	Poor
1550	1200	950	650	400	300

Model 585 Gold Package

Has all of the features of the 585 series with the addition of a gold-plated trigger, gold-plated game scenes, and schnabel forend. Choice of blued or silver receiver.

NIB	Exc.	V.G.	Good	Fair	Poor
1600	1250	975	675	425	300

Model 585 Skeet

Offered in 12, 20, or 28 gauge as well as .410 bore with 28" barrels. Skeet stock and beavertail forearm. Black recoil pad. Weight in 12 gauge about 8 lbs.

NIB	Exc.	V.G.	Good	Fair	Poor
1600	1250	975	675	425	300

Model 585—3 Barrel Skeet Set

Fitted with 20, 28 gauge and .410 bore barrels. Skeet choked.

NIB	Exc.	V.G.	Good	Fair	Poor
2500	2250	1875	1300	600	400

Model 585—3 Barrel Skeet Set Gold Package

Same as above but with engraving and choice of silver or blued receiver.

NIB	Exc.	V.G.	Good	Fair	Poor
2600	2350	1875	675	600	400

Model 585 Youth/Ladies

This model is similar to the 585 but with a shortened length of pull to 13.5". Weight of 20 gauge model is approximately 6.6 lbs. Weight of 12 gauge is about 7.5 lbs.

NIB	Exc.	V.G.	Good	Fair	Poor
1525	1300	975	700	350	200

Model 585 Youth Gold Package

Same as above but with gold trigger, gold-plated game scenes, and schnabel forend. Choice of silver or blued receiver.

NIB	Exc.	V.G.	Good	Fair	Poor
1625	1375	1025	750	400	200

Model 585 Upland

Similar to the 585 series except for straight-grip stock. Offered in 12, 20, and 28 gauge all with 26" barrels. Weight for 12 gauge is about 7.75 lbs. and for 20 and 28 gauge about 6.75 lbs.

NIB	Exc.	V.G.	Good	Fair	Poor
1525	1300	975	700	350	200

Model 585 Upland Gold Package

This model has the additional gold package features of gold trigger, gold game scenes, and schnabel forend. Choice of silver or blued receiver.

NIB	Exc.	V.G.	Good	Fair	Poor
1600	1375	1025	750	350	225

Model 600

Similar to Model 585, with a silver-plated receiver.

NIB	Exc.	V.G.	Good	Fair	Poor
1000	875	650	500	350	200

Model 600 Magnum

As above, chambered for 3", 12 gauge cartridges. Imported from 1969 to 1972.

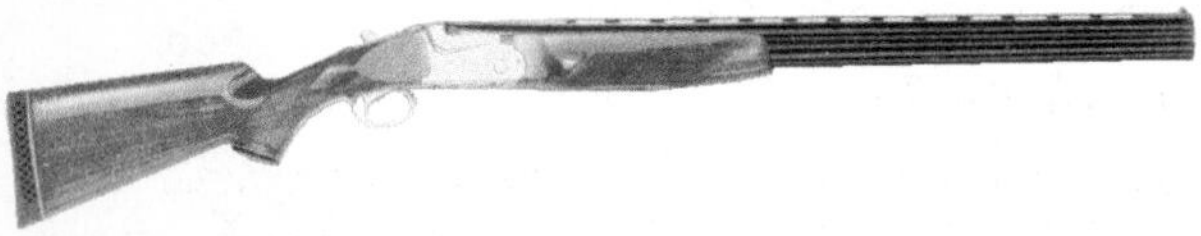

NIB	Exc.	V.G.	Good	Fair	Poor
—	900	675	525	375	200

Model 600 Trap Gun

As above, with 30" or 32" barrels trap choked, with a high comb walnut stock.

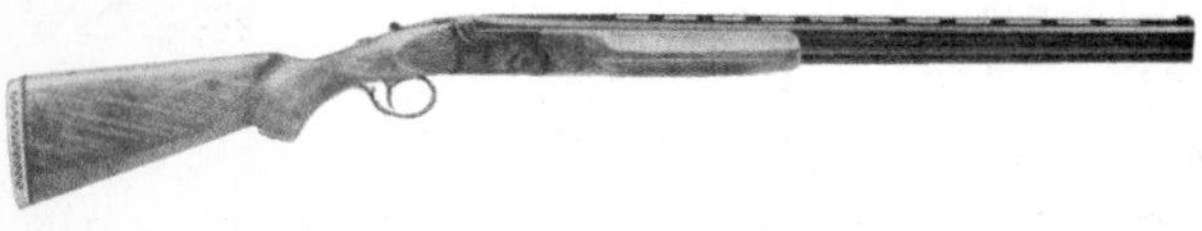

NIB	Exc.	V.G.	Good	Fair	Poor
1000	875	650	500	350	200

Model 600 Skeet Gun

As above, chambered for 12, 20, 28 or .410 bore cartridges with 26" or 28" barrels that are skeet choked.

NIB	Exc.	V.G.	Good	Fair	Poor
1000	875	650	500	350	200

Model 600 Skeet Combo Set

As above, with an extra set of three interchangeable barrels. Furnished with a carrying case.

NIB	Exc.	V.G.	Good	Fair	Poor
2900	2550	2100	1650	1200	600

Model 605

Similar to Model 600, with an engraved and French case hardened receiver.

NIB	Exc.	V.G.	Good	Fair	Poor
1250	950	700	500	400	400

NOTE: The 605 Series is also available in trap or skeet configurations. The values are similar.

Model 605 3-Gauge Skeet Set

As above, with three extra sets of barrels.

NIB	Exc.	V.G.	Good	Fair	Poor
2900	2550	2100	1650	1200	600

Model 680E

Similar to the Model 600, with an engraved receiver and English-style stock. Imported from 1973 to 1976.

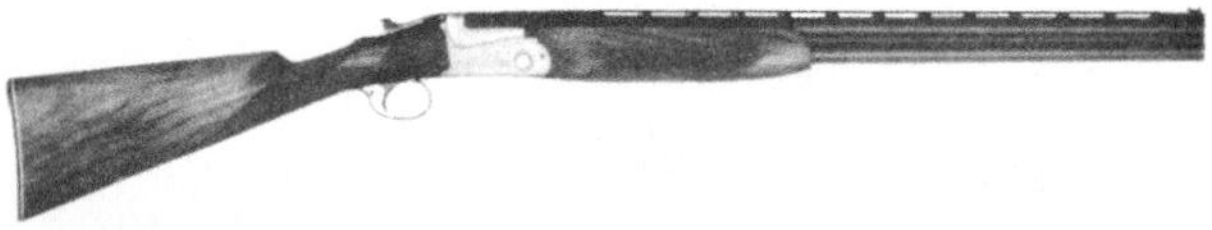

NIB	Exc.	V.G.	Good	Fair	Poor
1400	1100	850	600	500	250

Model 685

This over-and-under shotgun is offered in 12, 20, and 28 gauge as well as .410 bore. Barrel lengths are 26" or 28" with choke tubes. The engraved receiver has a silver finish with gold inlays. The walnut stock is semi-fancy.

NIB	Exc.	V.G.	Good	Fair	Poor
1400	1100	850	600	500	250

Model 700 Trap Gun

Similar to the Model 600 Trap, with a wider rib, additional engraving and a figured walnut stock. Imported from 1969 to 1975.

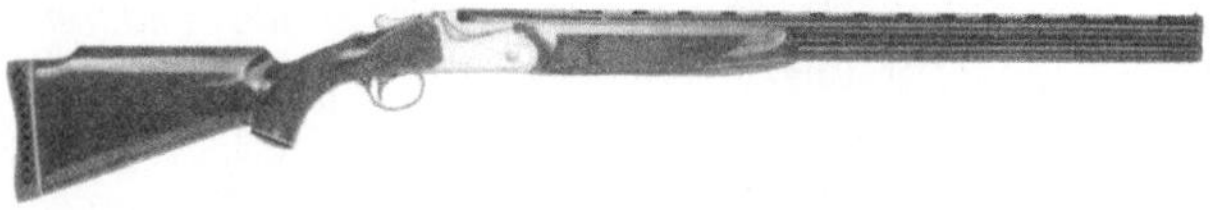

NIB	Exc.	V.G.	Good	Fair	Poor
1600	1250	975	675	425	300

Model 700 Skeet Gun

As above, with skeet chokes.

NIB	Exc.	V.G.	Good	Fair	Poor
1700	1350	1050	775	500	350

Model 785

Offered in 12, 20, and 28 gauge as well as .410 bore this over-and-under features 26" or 28" barrels with choke tubes, single trigger, ejectors, and checkered walnut stock. The silver receiver is scroll engraved. Weight is about 8 lbs. for 12 gauge and 7.25 lbs. for small bores.

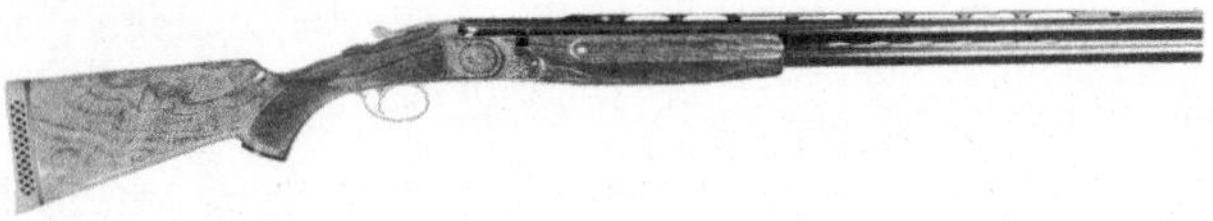

NIB	Exc.	V.G.	Good	Fair	Poor
1800	1500	900	750	500	300

Model 785—2 Barrel Set

These two barrel sets are in combination 12/20, 20/28, and 28/.410 bore with 26" and 28" barrels.

NIB	Exc.	V.G.	Good	Fair	Poor
2900	2650	2200	1775	1200	600

Model 785 Sporting Clays

Chambered for 12, 20, and 28 gauge with barrels lengths from 28" to 32" in 12 gauge and 28" in 20 and 28 gauge. Recoil pad standard.

NIB	Exc.	V.G.	Good	Fair	Poor
2250	1750	1150	1400	900	500

NOTE: For Sporting Clays set add $900.

Model 785 Skeet

Offered in 12, 20, 28, and .410 bore with 28" barrels. Recoil pad standard.

NIB	Exc.	V.G.	Good	Fair	Poor
2250	1750	1150	1400	900	500

Model 785 3-Gauge Skeet Set

This model furnished with 12, 20, and 28 gauge barrel all 28" in length. Weight is about 7.3 lbs. regardless of gauge.

NIB	Exc.	V.G.	Good	Fair	Poor
4400	3250	2500	1700	1200	600

Model 785 Trap

Offered in 12 gauge with or without Monte Carlo stock. Barrel length either 30" or 32". Ventilated recoil pad standard.

NIB	Exc.	V.G.	Good	Fair	Poor
2250	1750	1150	1400	900	500

Model 785 Trap Combo

Features a 30" or 32" over-and-under barrels with a single 32" or 34" barrel. Choice of standard stock or Monte Carlo.

NIB	Exc.	V.G.	Good	Fair	Poor
3050	2250	1250	100	700	375

Model 800 Trap Gun

As above, but with trap chokes and more engraving. Imported from 1969 to 1975.

NIB	Exc.	V.G.	Good	Fair	Poor
2000	1000	850	650	550	250

Model 800 Skeet Gun

As above, in 12 or 20 gauge with 26" or 28" skeet choked barrels. Imported from 1969 to 1975.

NIB	Exc.	V.G.	Good	Fair	Poor
2000	1000	850	650	550	250

Model 880 Crown Grade

A false sidelock 12, 20, 28 or .410 bore boxlock double-barrel shotgun with a single-selective trigger and automatic ejectors. The engraved sideplates and receiver are French case hardened, and the figured walnut stock is checkered. Imported prior to 1981.

NIB	Exc.	V.G.	Good	Fair	Poor
1900	1700	1350	1100	900	450

Model 885

A false sidelock 12, 20, 28 or .410 bore boxlock shotgun. Similar to the Model 800.

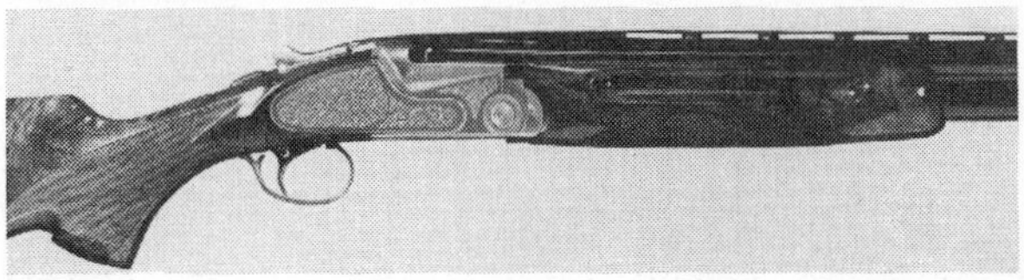

NIB	Exc.	V.G.	Good	Fair	Poor
1600	1250	1050	900	700	300

Model 5600

This over-and-under gun is offered in 12 gauge only in either trap or skeet configurations.

NIB	Exc.	V.G.	Good	Fair	Poor
875	775	650	500	400	200

Model 5700

Similar to the above but with light scroll engraving on the receiver and figured walnut stock.

NIB	Exc.	V.G.	Good	Fair	Poor
900	800	675	525	425	200

Model 5800

Similar to the Model 5600 but with more engraving coverage on the receiver and fancy walnut stock.

NIB	Exc.	V.G.	Good	Fair	Poor
950	800	700	550	450	175

Model 7300

A 12 or 20 gauge slide-action shotgun. Blued with a walnut stock. Imported prior to 1981.

NIB	Exc.	V.G.	Good	Fair	Poor
—	300	250	200	150	100

Model 7900

As above, but skeet choked.

NIB	Exc.	V.G.	Good	Fair	Poor
400	300	250	200	150	100

Model 300

A 12 or 20 gauge semi-automatic shotgun with 26", 28", or 30" barrels. Blued with a walnut stock. Imported from 1968 to 1972.

NIB	Exc.	V.G.	Good	Fair	Poor
—	450	395	350	300	200

NOTE: Ventilated rib barrel add 20 percent.

SEMI-AUTOMATICS

Model 1300

A redesigned version of the Model 300 with a ventilated rib barrel and screw-in choke tubes. Imported since 1988.

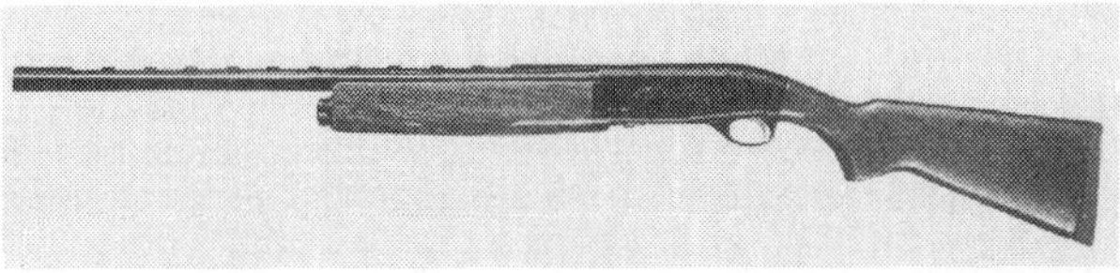

NIB	Exc.	V.G.	Good	Fair	Poor
450	400	350	300	200	150

Model XL 900 MR

A 12 gauge, semi-automatic shotgun with 26" to 30" ventilated-rib barrels, and etched alloy receiver and checkered walnut stock. Imported prior to 1981.

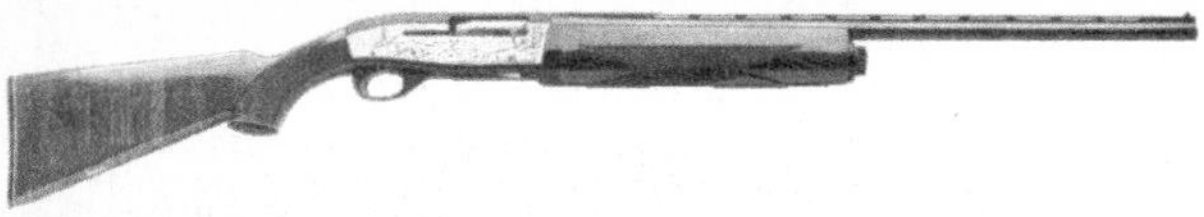

NIB	Exc.	V.G.	Good	Fair	Poor
—	475	425	375	325	200

Model 1900

As above, but also chambered for 20 gauge shells and available with 22", 26", or 28" ventilated rib barrels and screw-in choke tubes. Blued with a walnut stock.

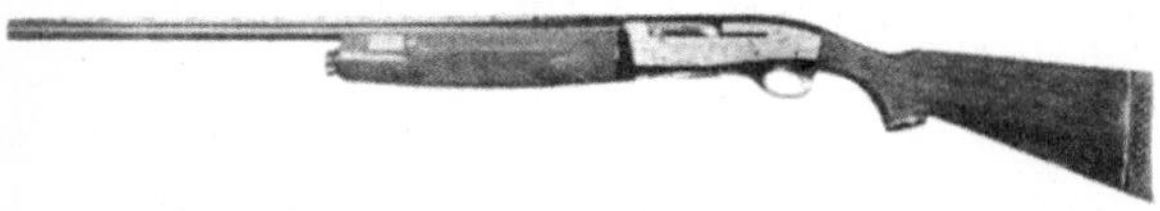

NIB	Exc.	V.G.	Good	Fair	Poor
500	425	375	300	250	175

Model 3000

Similar to the above, with a modified receiver design. Imported prior to 1990.

NIB	Exc.	V.G.	Good	Fair	Poor
—	475	400	350	250	150

SMITH AMERICAN ARMS COMPANY

Springfield, Massachusetts

Smith Carbine

A .50 caliber breechloading percussion carbine with a 21.75" round barrel having an octagonal breech. Blued, case hardened with a walnut stock. The barrel marked "Address/Poultney & Trimble/Baltimore, USA" and the frame "Smith's Patent/June 23, 1857" as well as "American Arms Co./Chicopee Falls." Approximately 30,000 were manufactured, most of which were purchased by the United States government. The sales agents were Poultney & Trimble of Baltimore, Maryland.

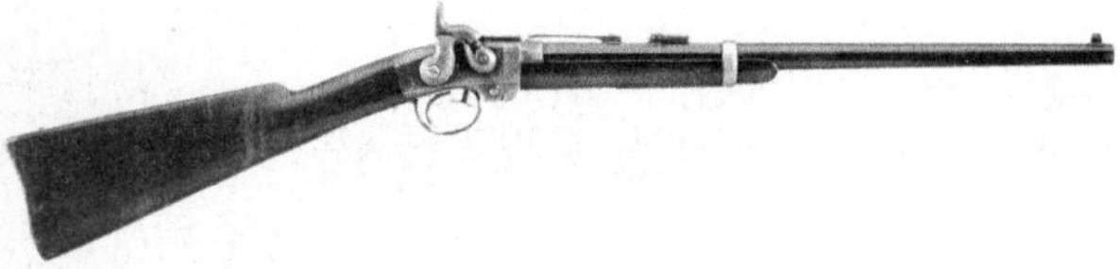

NIB	Exc.	V.G.	Good	Fair	Poor
—	—	2750	1200	500	200

SMITH, L. C.

Syracuse, New York
Hunter Arms Company
Fulton, New York

One of the finest American-made double-barrel shotguns and very collectible in today's market. It was manufactured between 1880 and 1888 in Syracuse, New York; and between 1890 and 1945 in Fulton, New York, by the Hunter Arms Company. In 1945 Marlin Firearms Company acquired Hunter Arms, and the L.C. Smith was made until 1951. In 1968 the L.C. Smith was resurrected for five years, and production ceased totally in 1973. The values given are approximate for standard production models; and we strongly feel that competent, individual appraisals should be secured, especially on the rarer and higher grade models, if a transaction is contemplated.

The values given are for fluid steel, hammerless guns only. Damascus-barreled guns have become collectible if they are in very good or better condition, and values are approximately the same as for the fluid steel models. Damascus guns in less than good condition are worth considerable less.

Early Hammerless Shotguns

The models listed were manufactured between 1890 and 1913. They are chambered for 10, 12, 16, and 20 gauge and were produced with various barrel lengths and choke combinations. They feature full sidelock actions. The difference in the models and their values is based on the degree of ornamentation and the quality of materials and workmanship utilized in their construction. The general values furnished are for 10, 12 or 16 gauge guns only.

NOTE: 20 gauge add 50 percent. A premium for 25 percent for 10 gauge and 16 gauge guns should be added. Single-selective trigger add $250. Automatic ejectors add 30 percent.

EARLY HAMMERLESS SHOTGUNS 00 GRADE

60,000 manufactured.

NIB	Exc.	V.G.	Good	Fair	Poor
—	2050	1800	1300	650	400

0 Grade

30,000 manufactured.

NIB	Exc.	V.G.	Good	Fair	Poor
—	2150	1900	1400	700	450

No. 1 Grade

10,000 manufactured.

NIB	Exc.	V.G.	Good	Fair	Poor
—	3150	2600	1950	800	550

No. 2 Grade

13,000 manufactured.

NIB	Exc.	V.G.	Good	Fair	Poor
—	7300	2900	1625	900	700

No. 3 Grade

4,000 manufactured.

NIB	Exc.	V.G.	Good	Fair	Poor
—	4250	3400	2275	1000	750

Pigeon Grade

1,200 manufactured.

NIB	Exc.	V.G.	Good	Fair	Poor
—	4250	3400	2280	1000	750

No. 4 Grade

500 manufactured.

NIB	Exc.	V.G.	Good	Fair	Poor
—	12500	8650	5800	3000	2000

A-1 GRADE

700 manufactured, all damascus, No 20 gauge.

NIB	Exc.	V.G.	Good	Fair	Poor
—	6500	4250	2750	1750	1000

No. 5 Grade

500 manufactured.

NIB	Exc.	V.G.	Good	Fair	Poor
—	9750	8100	5800	3250	2000

Monogram Grade

100 manufactured.

NIB	Exc.	V.G.	Good	Fair	Poor
—	13000	9750	6900	3750	2500

A-2 Grade

200 manufactured.

NIB	Exc.	V.G.	Good	Fair	Poor
—	17500	11500	8550	4500	3750

A-3 Grade

20 manufactured. This is too rare to generalize a value.

LATER PRODUCTION HAMMERLESS SHOTGUNS

These were manufactured at Fulton, New York, between 1914 and 1951. They are side-by-side double-barrel shotguns chambered for 12, 16, and 20 gauge, as well as the .410. They are offered with various barrel lengths and choke combinations. They feature a full sidelock action and are available with double or single triggers, extractors, and automatic ejectors. The finishes are blued and case colored, with checkered walnut stocks that are of either straight, semi-pistolgrip, or pistolgrip configurations. The various models differ as to the degree of ornamentation and the quality of materials and workmanship utilized in their construction. These are highly collectible American shotguns. Because these guns were manufactured as late as 1951, mint original specimens and even unfired new in the box guns will be offered for sale occasionally. These guns are worth considerably more than excellent condition guns and more than ever an individual, expert authentication and appraisal is recommended if a transaction is anticipated.

NOTE: The values supplied are for 12 gauge models only. For 16 gauge add 25 percent premium. For 20 gauge add 50 percent premium. For .410 bore add 200 percent premium (field grade), 300 percent to 400 percent for higher grades. Single-selective triggers add $250 premium. For automatic ejectors add 30 percent premium.

Courtesy Milwaukee Public Museum, Milwaukee, Wisconsin

20 manufactured. This is too rare to generalize a value.

Field Grade

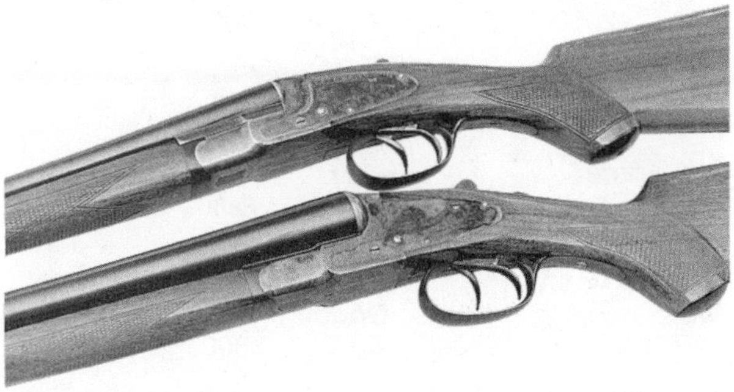

20 manufactured. This is too rare to generalize a value.

NIB	Exc.	V.G.	Good	Fair	Poor
—	1800	1500	1125	700	350

Specialty Grade

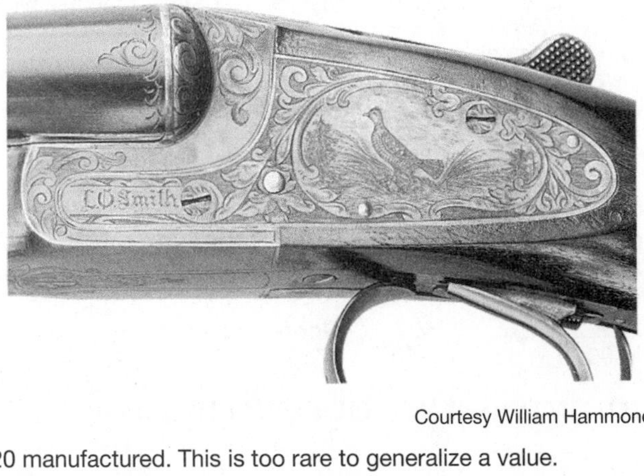

Courtesy William Hammond

20 manufactured. This is too rare to generalize a value.

NIB	Exc.	V.G.	Good	Fair	Poor
—	3400	3150	2150	1200	400

Skeet Special Grade

Courtesy William Hammond

20 manufactured. This is too rare to generalize a value.

NIB	Exc.	V.G.	Good	Fair	Poor
—	3400	3150	2225	1300	500

Premier Skeet Grade

20 manufactured. This is too rare to generalize a value.

NIB	Exc.	V.G.	Good	Fair	Poor
—	3700	3150	2250	1350	500

Eagle Grade

20 manufactured. This is too rare to generalize a value.

NIB	Exc.	V.G.	Good	Fair	Poor
—	5350	4350	3150	1700	500

Crown Grade

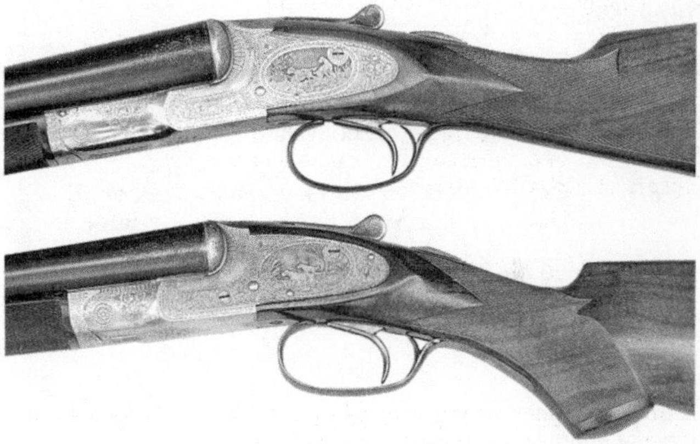

With this grade, automatic ejectors became standard equipment. The .410 is extremely rare in this model and nonexistent in higher grades; there were only six manufactured, and they cannot be generally evaluated.

NIB	Exc.	V.G.	Good	Fair	Poor
—	7000	5350	4400	2950	500

Ideal Grade

With this grade, automatic ejectors became standard equipment. The .410 is extremely rare in this model and nonexistent in higher grades; there were only six manufactured, and they cannot be generally evaluated.

NIB	Exc.	V.G.	Good	Fair	Poor
—	2350	1950	1700	900	500

Trap Grade

With this grade, automatic ejectors became standard equipment. The .410 is extremely rare in this model and nonexistent in higher grades; there were only six manufactured, and they cannot be generally evaluated.

NIB	Exc.	V.G.	Good	Fair	Poor
—	2800	2350	1900	1100	500

Monogram Grade

There were two higher grades offered: the Premier Grade and the Deluxe Grade. They are extremely rare, and there have not been enough transactions to generally evaluate them.

This version is offered standard with automatic ejectors and a single-selective trigger.

NIB	Exc.	V.G.	Good	Fair	Poor
—	15000	12000	8750	600	500

HUNTER ARMS BOXLOCKS

These shotguns are inexpensive, high quality boxlocks built with quality equal to the Field Grade L.C. Smith. The receiver, forend iron, trigger guard and triggers are all machined from forgings. Durability of these guns has proven to be excellent.

Fulton Model

A utility side-by-side boxlock shotgun chambered for 12, 16, 20 gauge and .410 bore. It was offered with various barrel length and choke combinations. It has double triggers and extractors with a non-selective single trigger option. Values given are for 12 gauge only.

NIB	Exc.	V.G.	Good	Fair	Poor
—	1150	925	600	425	150

NOTE: For 20 gauge add 50 percent premium. For .410 bore add 250 percent premium. For 16 gauge add 25 percent. For single trigger add $150.

Fulton Special

A slightly higher grade version of the Fulton Model featuring modest engraving and pointed checkering.

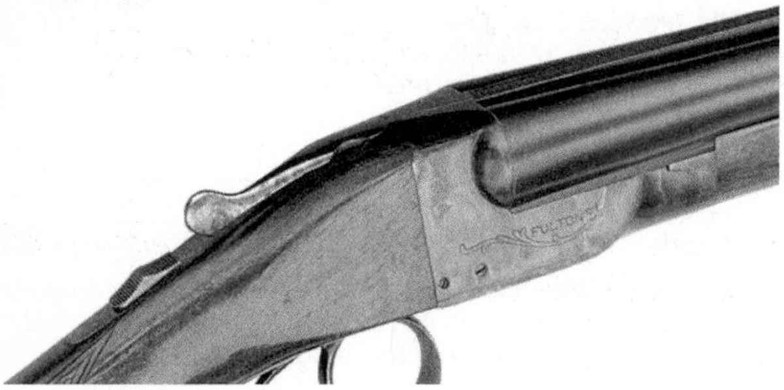

Courtesy William Hammond

NIB	Exc.	V.G.	Good	Fair	Poor
—	1400	1050	750	500	200

NOTE: For 20 gauge add 50 percent premium. For 16 gauge add 25 percent. For single trigger add $200.

Hunter Special

Similar to the Fulton Model but features the L.C. Smith rotary locking bolt.

Courtesy William Hammond

NIB	Exc.	V.G.	Good	Fair	Poor
—	1100	950	750	500	200

NOTE: For 20 gauge add 75 percent premium. For .410 bore add 300 percent premium. for 16 gauge add 25 percent.

SINGLE BARREL TRAP GUNS

High quality, break-open, single-shot trap guns chambered for 12 gauge only. They feature 32" or 34" vent rib barrels that are full-choked. They have boxlock actions and are standard with automatic ejectors. The finish is blued and case colored, and they have a checkered walnut stock with a recoil pad. The various models differ in the amount of ornamentation and the quality of the materials and workmanship utilized in their construction. There was a total of approximately 2,650 manufactured between 1917 and 1951. Although these firearms are actually rarer and just as high in quality as their side-by-side counterparts, they are simply not as collectible as the side-by-side variations.

Olympic Grade

NIB	Exc.	V.G.	Good	Fair	Poor
—	2050	1775	1300	900	500

Specialty Grade

NIB	Exc.	V.G.	Good	Fair	Poor
—	2600	1950	1400	1000	800

Crown Grade

NIB	Exc.	V.G.	Good	Fair	Poor
—	4250	3700	2800	1850	500

Monogram Grade

NIB	Exc.	V.G.	Good	Fair	Poor
—	7650	6500	4350	2800	500

1968 Model

A side-by-side double-barrel shotgun chambered for 12 gauge with a 28" vent rib barrel, choked Full and Modified. It features a sidelock action with double triggers and extractors. The finish is blued and case colored, with a checkered walnut stock. This shotgun was offered by Marlin between 1968 and 1973.These are less desirable than earlier models because of manufacturing expedients used. Investment cast receiver rather than machined forgings were used. Cyanide case-hardening replaced bone charcoal hardening and aluminum vent ribs were used. A thin brown polymer layer was used to create the fit between the lock plates and buttstock which is a departure from traditional fitting.

NIB	Exc.	V.G.	Good	Fair	Poor
1300	1075	850	650	450	300

1968 Deluxe Model

Similar to the 1968 model but features a Simmons floating rib and a beavertail-type forearm. It was manufactured by Marlin between 1971 and 1973.

NIB	Exc.	V.G.	Good	Fair	Poor
1500	1200	950	750	600	400

L.C. SMITH NEW MODEL (MARLIN)

Model LC12-DB

Introduced in 2005 this Italian-made side-by-side gun is chambered for the 12 gauge 3" shell. Single trigger, selective ejectors, and 3 choke tubes. Barrel length is 28". Checkered walnut stock with pistol grip. Beavertail forearm. Recoil pad. Weight is about 6.25 lbs.

NIB	*Exc.*	*V.G.*	*Good*	*Fair*	*Poor*
1500	1250	950	800	675	300

Model LC20-DB

As above but chambered for the 20 gauge 3" shell and fitted with a 26" barrel. Weight is about 6 lbs. Introduced in 2005.

NIB	*Exc.*	*V.G.*	*Good*	*Fair*	*Poor*
1500	1250	950	800	675	300

Model LC12-OU

This is a 12 gauge 3" over-and-under gun with 28" vent rib barrels. Checkered walnut stock with pistol grip. Choke tubes. Weight is about 7.25 lbs. Introduced in 2005.

NIB	*Exc.*	*V.G.*	*Good*	*Fair*	*Poor*
1000	875	725	600	400	300

Model LC20-OU

As above but in 20 gauge with 3" chamber. Barrel length is 26". Weight is about 6.75 lbs. Introduced in 2005.

NIB	*Exc.*	*V.G.*	*Good*	*Fair*	*Poor*
1000	875	725	600	400	300

Model LC28/LC410-DB

The 28 gauge and .410 bore models were introduced in 2007. Both have 2.75" chambers and 26" barrels. Selective automatic ejectors. Case-colored receiver with gold game bird. Three choke tubes. Weight is about 6.5 lbs.

NIB	*Exc.*	*V.G.*	*Good*	*Fair*	*Poor*
1100	975	825	675	450	350

SMITH & WESSON

Springfield, Massachusetts

RIFLES

.320 Revolving Rifle Model

This model is rare and unique—a prize to a S&W collector. The Revolving Rifle is chambered for the .320 S&W Revolving Rifle cartridge, has a 6-shot fluted cylinder and is offered with a 16", 18", and 20" barrel. Only 76 of the rifles are nickel-plated, and the remainder of the production is blued. The butt is rounded, with red hard rubber checkered grips and a forearm of the same material. There is a detachable shoulder stock with a black hard rubber buttplate featuring the S&W logo. The rifle was furnished in a leather carrying case with accessories. As fine a firearm as this was, it was a commercial failure for S and they finally came to the realization that the public did not want a revolving rifle. They manufactured only 977 of them between 1879 and 1887.

NIB	*Exc.*	*V.G.*	*Good*	*Fair*	*Poor*
—	8000	5500	3500	2000	1500

NOTE: Values are for complete unit. Deduct 40 percent without stock. Add 10 percent for 16" or 20" barrels.

Model A Rifle

A bolt-action with 23.75" barrel, chambered for .22-250, .243, .270, .308, .30-06, 7mm Magnum, and .300 Winchester Magnum. It has a folding rear sight and a checkered Monte Carlo stock with contrasting rosewood forend tip and pistol grip cap. It was manufactured for S&W by Husqvarna of Sweden. From 1969 to 1972.

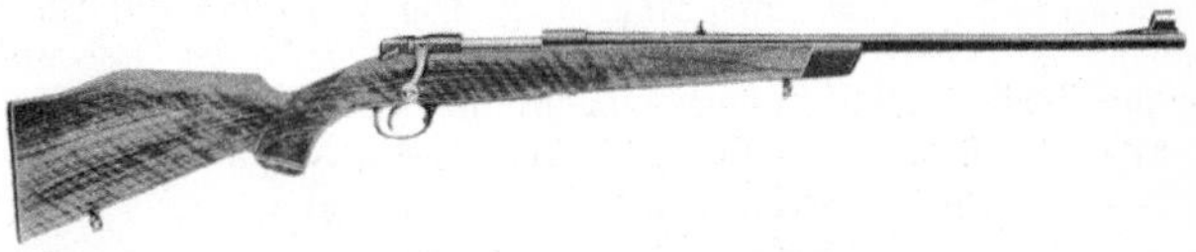

NIB	*Exc.*	*V.G.*	*Good*	*Fair*	*Poor*
400	325	275	200	150	100

Model B

As above, with a schnabel forend and 20.75" barrel.

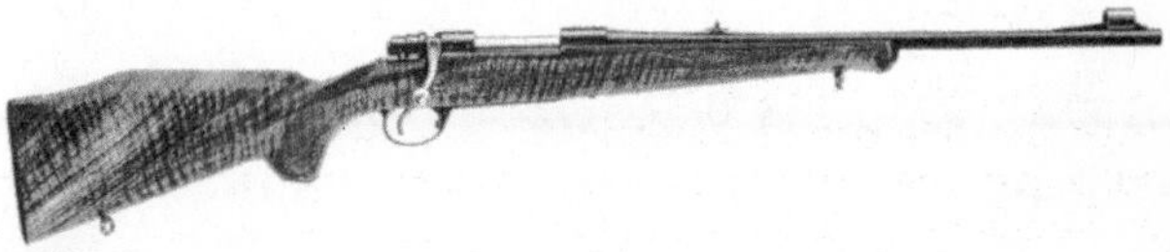

NIB	*Exc.*	*V.G.*	*Good*	*Fair*	*Poor*
425	350	295	200	150	100

Model C

As above, with a cheekpiece.

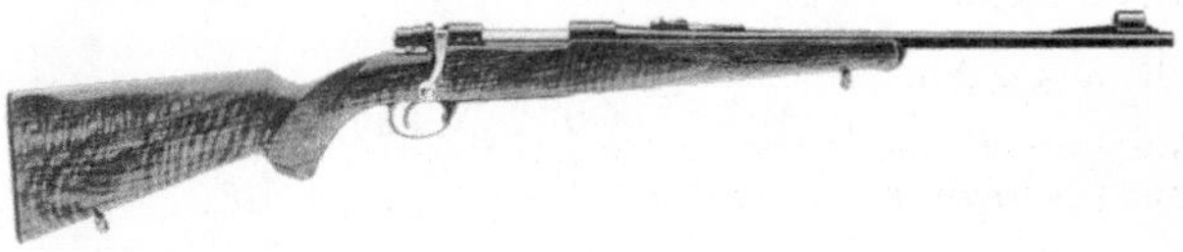

NIB	*Exc.*	*V.G.*	*Good*	*Fair*	*Poor*
425	350	295	225	175	125

Model D

As above, with a Mannlicher-style stock.

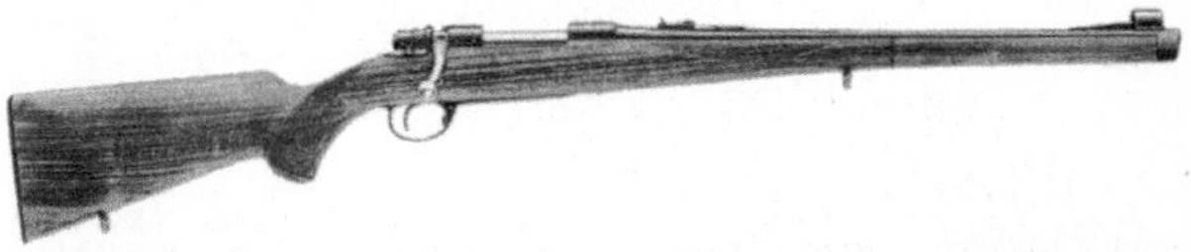

NIB	*Exc.*	*V.G.*	*Good*	*Fair*	*Poor*
700	600	400	350	250	150

Model 1500 Series

A bolt-action series of hunting rifles made for Smith & Wesson by Howa of Japan in 1983 and 1984. Calibers included .222 Rem., .223 Rem., .22-250 Rem., .243 Win., .25-06 Rem., .270 Win., 7mm Rem. Mag., .308 Win., .30-06 and .300 Win. Mag.. Offered in several variations with blue or stainless receiver, plain or checkered wood stock (Deluxe model). Barrel lengths are 22-inches except

24-inches for magnum calibers. A heavy barrel varmint version was available. The Model 1700 Classic Hunter was similar, except for a removable magazine and Schnabel fore-end.

NIB	Exc.	V.G.	Good	Fair	Poor
450	400	350	300	250	150

NOTE: Add 10 percent for Deluxe or Varmint model, 15 percent for Model 1700.

I-Bolt Rifle

This bolt-action hunting rifle was made in the U.S.A. by Smith & Wesson from 2008 to 2009 in .25-06, .270 Win., .30-06, 7mm Rem. Mag. and .300 Win. Mag.. Offered with wood, synthetic or camo stock, and blue or stainless finish. Integral Picatinny rail.

NIB	Exc.	V.G.	Good	Fair	Poor
475	425	365	300	250	150

NOTE: Add 10 percent for camo stock.

M&P15 Military and Police Tactical Rifle

Gas-operated semi-auto built along lines of AR-15. Caliber: 5.56mm NATO. Magazine capacity: 30. Barrel: 16-inch 1:9. Stock: Six-position telescoping composite. Weight: 6.74 lbs. unloaded. Sights: Adjustable front and rear. Variants: M&P15A & M&P15T (no carry handle; folding battle sight). Introduced 2006.

NIB	Exc.	V.G.	Good	Fair	Poor
1200	950	800	675	450	200

M&P 15 PC

Generally similar to the M&P rifle but with accurized tubular floated barrel, 2-stage match trigger, 20" matte stainless barrel. No sights. Introduced 2007.

NIB	Exc.	V.G.	Good	Fair	Poor
1750	1300	950	800	550	250

M&P 15 Sport

A more economical addition to the M&P rifle line. Chambered for the 5.56 NATO with a black anodized upper and lower receiver of 7075 T6 aluminum. Polymer hand guard, 16-inch 4140 steel barrel. Adjustable sights, single-stage trigger, chrome-lined gas key and bolt carrier. Flash suppressor compensator. Introduced in 2011.

NIB	Exc.	V.G.	Good	Fair	Poor
665	550	475	400	300	150

M&P 15PC Camo

AR-style semi-auto rifle chambered for .223 Remington/5.56 NATO. A2 configuration, 10-round magazine. No sights but integral front and rear optics rails. Two-stage trigger, aluminum lower, stainless 20" barrel with 1:8 twist. Finished in Realtree Advantage Max-1 camo. Overall length 38.5" , weight 8.2 lbs.

NIB	Exc.	V.G.	Good	Fair	Poor
1500	1075	875	750	500	275

M&P 15VTAC Viking Tactics

AR-style semi-auto rifle chambered in .223 Remington/5.56 NATO. Six-position CAR stock. 16" barrel. Surefire flash-hider and G2 light with VTAC light mount; VTAC/JP handguard; JP single-stage match trigger and speed hammer; three adjustable picatinny rails; VTAC padded two-point adjustable sling. Overall length 35" extended, 32" collapsed; weight 6.5 lbs. 30-round magazine.

NIB	Exc.	V.G.	Good	Fair	Poor
1750	1300	950	800	550	250

M&P 15 Piston Rifle

Similar to AR-derived M&P15 but with gas piston. Chambered in 5.56 NATO. Features include adjustable gas port, optional Troy quad mount handguard, chromed bore/gas key/bolt carrier/ chamber, 6-position telescoping or MagPul MOE stock, flattop or folding MBUS sights, aluminum receiver, alloy upper and lower, black anodized finish, 30-round magazine, 16-inch barrel with birdcage. Suggested retail price $1531 (standard handguard), $1692 (Troy quad mount handguard).

M&P 15-22

.22 LR rimfire verson of AR-derived M&P tactical autoloader. Features include blowback action, 15.5- or 16-inch barrel, 6-position telescoping or fixed stock, quad mount Picatinny rails, plain barrel or compensator, alloy upper and lower, matte black finish, 10- or 25-round magazine. Price: $589.

SHOTGUNS

Model 916

A series of slide-action shotguns made in the U.S.A. by Smith & Wesson from 1972 to 1981. Made in 12, 16 and 20 gauge in various barrel lengths with fixed chokes. Ventilated rib or plain barrel. Offered in both solid-frame and takedown versions.

NIB	Exc.	V.G.	Good	Fair	Poor
200	180	150	120	100	75

NOTE: Add 10 percent for ventilated rib, 10 percent for takedown model.

Model 3000

Slide-action shotgun made in Japan by Howa for Smith & Wesson and imported from 1982 to about 1989. In 12 or 20 gauge with a 3-inch chamber, checkered wood stock and fore-end, and fixed chokes or choke tubes. Standard barrel lengths of 26, 28 or 30-inches. Also offered in 18 or 20-inches in police model, and 22-inches in a slug gun with rifle sights.

NIB	Exc.	V.G.	Good	Fair	Poor
350	320	280	225	180	100

NOTE: Add 10 percent for choke tubes.

Model 1000

A series of gas-operated semi-auto shotguns patterned after the Remington Model 1100. Offered in 12 or 20 gauge with barrel length from 22 to 30-inches and with fixed chokes or interchangeable tubes. Checkered walnut stock and fore-end, engraved aluminum receiver. Available in several variations including waterfowl, trap and skeet models.

NIB	Exc.	V.G.	Good	Fair	Poor
400	350	285	220	150	100

NOTE: Add 25 percent for waterfowl model, 50 percent for trap gun.

Model 1012/1020

This series of gas-operated semi-autos were imported by S&W from Turkey from 2007 to 2009. Available in 12 gauge (1012) or 20 gauge (1020) with barrel lengths from 24 to 30-inches, and five choke tubes. Stock is adjustable for length and drop. Satin finished walnut or black synthetic stock, or total camo coverage.

NIB	Exc.	V.G.	Good	Fair	Poor
500	425	385	325	250	200

NOTE: Add 20 percent for camo coverage, 30 percent for 3.5-inch 12 ga. model.

Elite Gold & Silver Series

Elite Gold model is a side-by-side in 20 gauge only with quality double-gun features. Grade III checkered walnut stock with English-style straight grip or pistol grip, and a choice of single or double triggers. Automatic ejectors, color case hardened frame, fixed chokes of IC/M or M/F with barrel lengths of 26 or 28-inches. Weight is approx. 6.5 pounds. Elite Silver is over/under in 12 gauge only with features similar to Elite Gold except the O/U has five choke tubes, single trigger and recoil pad. Weight is approx. 7.5 pounds. Both of these models were imported from Turkey from 2007 to 2010.

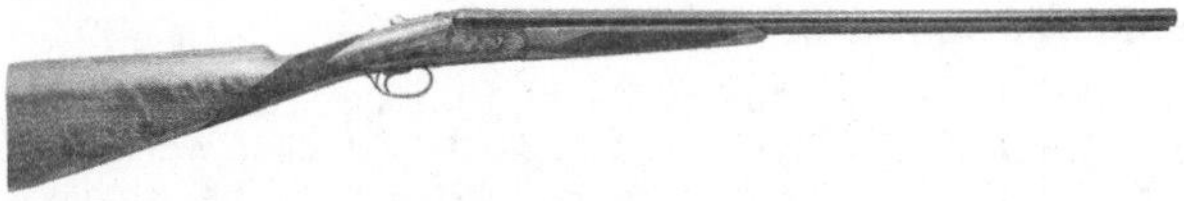

NIB	Exc.	V.G.	Good	Fair	Poor
500	425	385	325	250	200

SNAKE CHARMER

Little Field, Texas
Sporting Arms Manufacturing, Inc.

Snake Charmer

A .410 bore single-shot shotgun with an 18.5" barrel. Stainless steel with a composition stock.

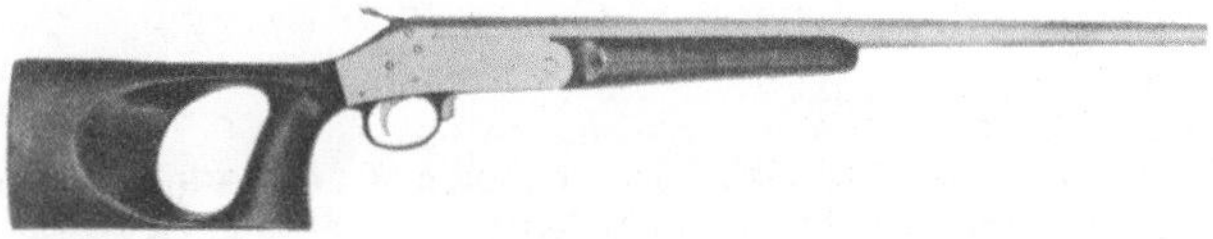

NIB	Exc.	V.G.	Good	Fair	Poor
200	125	100	75	50	25

SPENCER

Boston, Massachusetts

Spencer Carbine

This was one of the most popular firearms used by Union forces during the Civil War. It is chambered for a metallic rimfire cartridge known as the "No. 56." It is actually a .52 caliber and was made with a copper case. The barrel is 22" in length. The finish is blued, with a carbine-length walnut stock held on by one barrel band. There is a sling swivel at the butt. There were approximately 50,000 manufactured between 1863 and 1865.

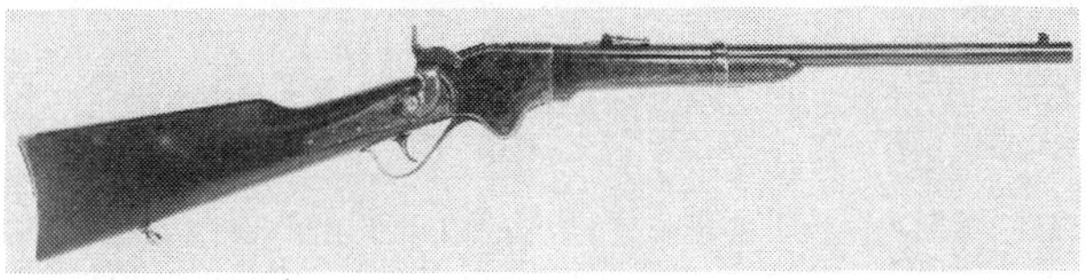

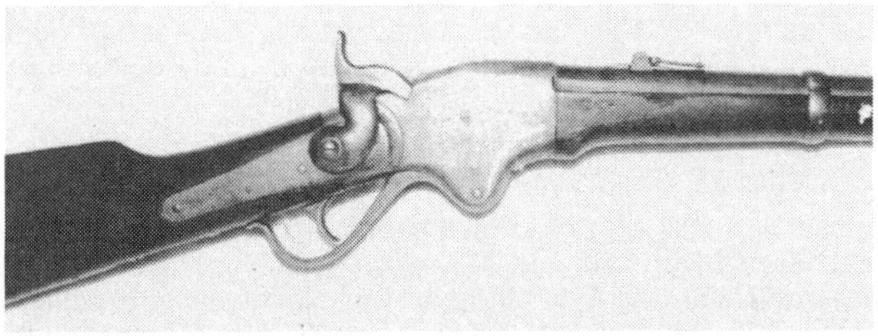

Courtesy Bonhams & Butterfields, San Francisco, California

NIB	Exc.	V.G.	Good	Fair	Poor
—	—	7500	5000	2500	500

Military Rifle—Navy Model

This model is similar to the carbine, with a 30" round barrel and a full-length walnut stock held on by three barrel bands. It features an iron for-end tip and sling swivels. The Civil War production consisted of two models. A Navy model was manufactured between 1862 and 1864 (there were approximately 1,000 of these so marked).

NIB	Exc.	V.G.	Good	Fair	Poor
—	—	10000	7500	5000	1000

Military Rifle—Army Model

There were approximately 11,450 produced for the Army during the Civil War. They are similar to the Navy model except that the front sight doubles as a bayonet lug. They were manufactured in 1863 and 1864.

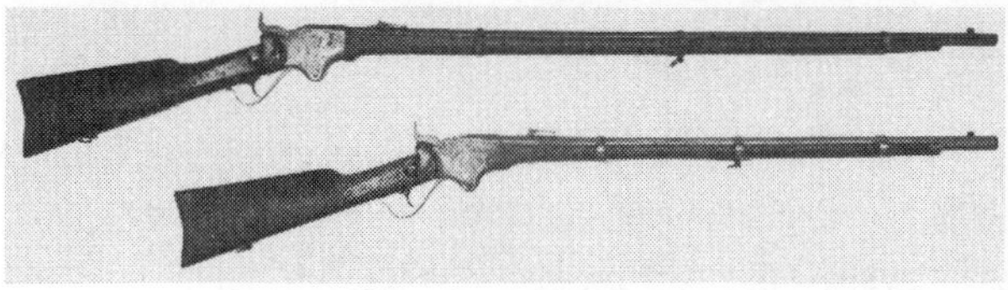

Courtesy Milwaukee Public Museum, Milwaukee, Wisconsin

NIB	Exc.	V.G.	Good	Fair	Poor
—	—	8000	6000	2500	600

Springfield Armory Post-war Alteration

After the conclusion of the Civil War, approximately 11,000 carbines were refurbished and rechambered for .50 caliber rimfire. The barrels were sleeved, and a device known as the "Stabler cut-off" was added to convert the arm to single-shot function. Often they were refinished and restocked. The inspector's marks "ESA" will be found in an oval cartouche on the left side of the stock. These alterations took place in 1867 and 1868.

NIB	Exc.	V.G.	Good	Fair	Poor
—	—	5250	3950	1700	500

Model 1865 Contract

This model was manufactured by the Burnside Rifle Company in 1865. They are similar to the Civil War-type carbine and are marked "By Burnside Rifle Co./Model 1865." There were approximately 34,000 manufactured. Old records show that 30,500 were purchased by the United States government, and 19,000 of these had the Stabler cut-off device.

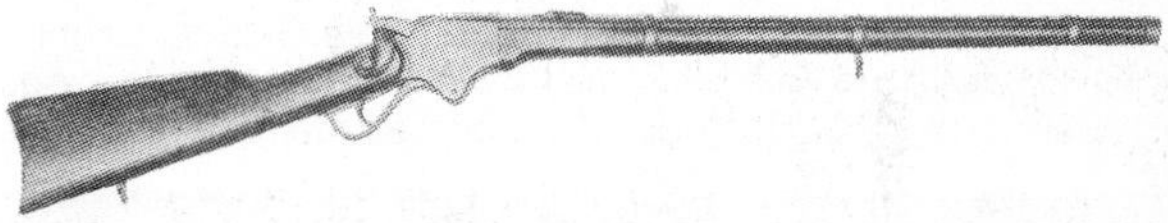

Courtesy Wallis & Wallis, Lewes, Sussex, England

NIB	Exc.	V.G.	Good	Fair	Poor
—	—	5300	3250	1250	500

SPENCER ARMS CO.

Windsor, Connecticut

Slide-Action Shotgun

From 1882 to 1889 they manufactured the first successful slide action repeating shotgun. Designed by Christopher M. Spencer who also designed the Civil War era Spencer military carbines. The shotgun came in both solid and takedown models in both 12 and 10 gauge. In 1890 Francis Bannerman & Sons of New York bought the patents and machinery and moved the operation to Brooklyn, New York. They produced what is known as the Spencer Bannerman models from 1890 to 1907. The later Bannerman models are worth 50 percent less than the Spencer models.

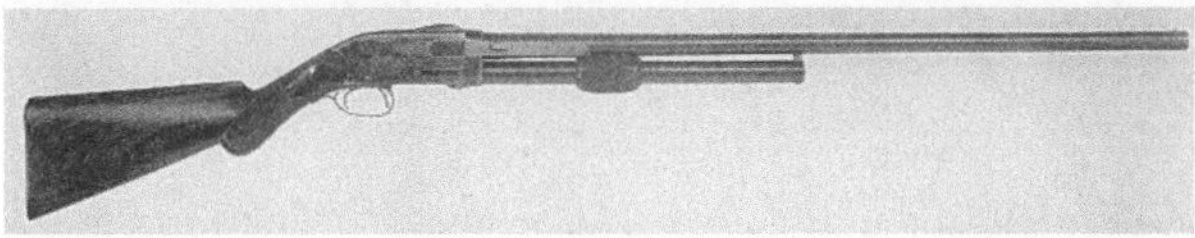

NIB	Exc.	V.G.	Good	Fair	Poor
—	—	1000	600	200	125

NOTE: The takedown model is worth 20 percent premium and 10 gauge models are worth a 10 percent premium.

SPRINGFIELD ARMORY INC.

Geneseo, Illinois

RIFLES

M1 Garand Rifle

A .270 (discontinued), .308 or .30-06 caliber semi-automatic rifle with a 24" barrel and 8-shot magazine. Patterned directly after the U.S. M1 Rifle.

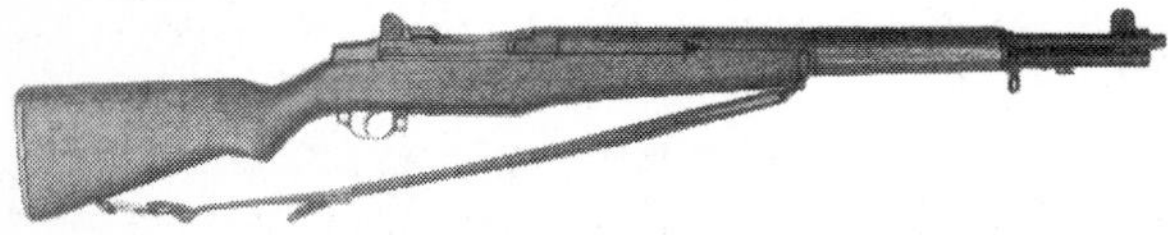

Courtesy Milwaukee Public Museum, Milwaukee, Wisconsin

NIB	Exc.	V.G.	Good	Fair	Poor
—	1000	825	550	400	300

Iwo Jima M1 Garand

Similar to standard M1 Model but shipped in reproduction WWII-era crate with signed decorative lithograph. Introduced 2006.

NIB	Exc.	V.G.	Good	Fair	Poor
1600	1300	1000	800	400	200

M1A Basic Rifle

Chambered for .308 Win. and fitted with a painted black fiberglass stock. Barrel length is 22" without flash suppressor. Front sights are military square post and rear military aperture (battle sights). Magazine capacity is 5, 10, or 20 box. Rifle weighs 9 lbs.

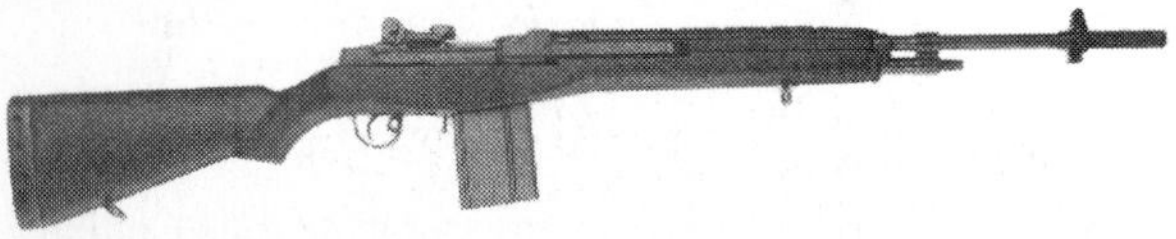

NIB	Exc.	V.G.	Good	Fair	Poor
1250	1000	850	650	400	250

D-Day M1 Garand Limited Edition

Introduced in 2005 this model is chambered for the .30-06 cartridge and fitted with a 24" barrel. Military style sights. Two-stage military trigger. Limited to 1,944 rifles, each with a military-style wooden crate. Each side of the buttstock has stamped memorials to D-Day.

NIB	Exc.	V.G.	Good	Fair	Poor
1600	1200	925	675	425	250

M1A Standard Rifle

This model is chambered for the .308 Win. or .243 cartridge. Also fitted with a 22" barrel but with adjustable rear sight. Fitted with a walnut stock with fiberglass hand guard, it comes equipped with a 20-round box magazine. Weighs 9 lbs.

NIB	Exc.	V.G.	Good	Fair	Poor
1500	1100	850	650	400	250

M1A-A1 Bush Rifle

Chambered for .308 or .243 cartridge with choice of walnut stock, black fiberglass, or folding stock (no longer produced). Fitted with 18.25" barrel. Rifle weighs 8.75 lbs.

NIB	Exc.	V.G.	Good	Fair	Poor
1400	1100	850	650	400	250

NOTE: Add $250 for folding stock.

M1A Scout Squad Rifle

This .308 model is fitted with an 18" barrel and a choice of fiberglass or walnut stock. Military sights. Supplied with 10-round magazine. Weight with fiberglass stock is about 9 lbs., with walnut stock about 9.3 pounds.

NIB	Exc.	V.G.	Good	Fair	Poor
1800	1100	750	550	300	175

M1A National Match

Chambered for .308 as standard or choice of .243 cartridge. Fitted with a medium weight National Match 22" glass bedded barrel and walnut stock. Special rear sight adjustable to half minute of angle clicks. Weighs 10.06 lbs.

NIB	Exc.	V.G.	Good	Fair	Poor
2050	1400	1000	700	500	250

M1A Super Match

This is Springfield's best match grade rifle. Chambered for .308 as standard and also .243 cartridge. Fitted with special oversize heavy walnut stock, heavy Douglas match glass bedded barrel, and special rear lugged receiver. Special rear adjustable sight. Weighs 10.125 lbs.

NIB	Exc.	V.G.	Good	Fair	Poor
2500	1850	1350	900	600	300

NOTE: For walnut stock and Douglas barrel add $165. For black McMillan stock and Douglas stainless steel barrel add $600. For Marine Corp. camo stock and Douglas stainless steel barrel add $600. For adjustable walnut stock and Douglas barrel add $535. For adjustable walnut stock and Krieger barrel add $900.

M1A Model 25 Carlos Hathcock

Introduced in 2001 this model features a match trigger, stainless steel heavy match barrel, McMillan synthetic stock with adjustable cheek pad, Harris Bi-pod, and other special featirtes. Chambered for the .308 cartridge. Weight is about 12.75 lbs. A special logo bears his signature.

NIB	Exc.	V.G.	Good	Fair	Poor
4650	3450	2500	1750	800	400

M21 Law Enforcement/Tactical Rifle

Similar to the Super Match with the addition of a special stock with rubber recoil pad and height adjustable cheekpiece. Available as a special order only. Weighs 11.875 lbs.

NIB	Exc.	V.G.	Good	Fair	Poor
2400	1750	1350	900	650	350

M1A SOCOM 16

This M1A1 rifle features a 16.25" barrel with muzzlebrake. Black fiberglass stock with steel buttplate. Forward scout-style scope mount. Front sight post has tritium insert. Weight is about 9 lbs. Introduced in 2004.

NIB	Exc.	V.G.	Good	Fair	Poor
1575	1250	875	650	400	250

M1A SOCOM II

Introduced in 2005 this model features a full length top rail and short bottom rail for accessories. Weight is about 11 lbs.

NIB	Exc.	V.G.	Good	Fair	Poor
1700	1450	950	700	450	300

M1A SOCOM Urban Rifle

Similar to the SOCOM but with black and white camo stock. Introduced in 2005.

NIB	Exc.	V.G.	Good	Fair	Poor
1725	1475	950	700	450	300

IDF Mauser Rifle Model 66SP

This is a bolt-action rifle chambered for the .308 Win. cartridge. Adjustable trigger for pull and travel. Barrel length is 27". Specially designed stock has broad forend and a thumb hole pistol grip. Cheekpiece is adjustable as is the recoil pad. Supplied with case. This rifle is military issue. Fewer than 100 imported into the U.S.

NIB	Exc.	V.G.	Good	Fair	Poor
2200	1750	950	700	450	300

SAR-48

This is the pre-ban version of the SAR-4800.

NIB	Exc.	V.G.	Good	Fair	Poor
1400	1200	850	600	500	250

SAR-4800

This is a semi-automatic gas operated rifle, similar in appearance to the FN-FAL/LAR rifle, chambered for the .308 Win. cartridge. It is fitted with a 21" barrel and has a fully adjustable rear sight. Weight is approximately 9.5 lbs. No longer imported.

NIB	Exc.	V.G.	Good	Fair	Poor
1600	1200	800	600	400	250

SAR-8

This semi-automatic rifle is similar in appearance to the HK-91. It is chambered for the .308 Win. and is of the recoil operated delayed roller-lock design. Barrel length is 18" and the rear sight is fully adjustable. Weight is about 8.7 lbs. No longer imported.

NIB	Exc.	V.G.	Good	Fair	Poor
950	750	600	400	300	200

SAR-8 Tactical

Similar to the above model but fitted with a heavy barrel. Introduced in 1996. No longer imported. Fewer than 100 imported into U.S.

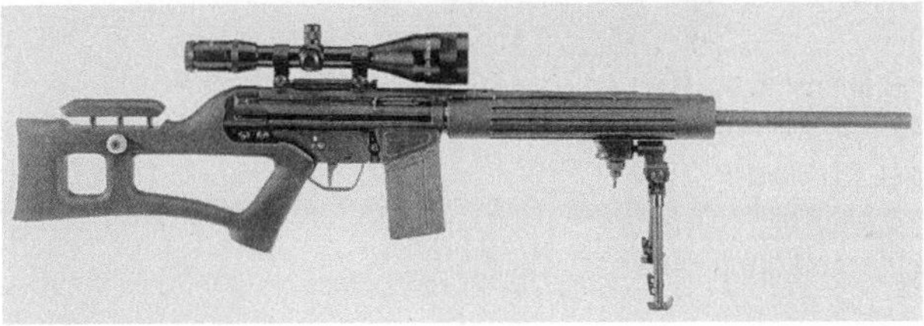

NIB	Exc.	V.G.	Good	Fair	Poor
1450	1100	750	600	400	300

M6 Scout

A .22, .22 Magnum, or .22 Hornet and .410 bore over-and-under combination shotgun rifle with an 18" barrel. Black anodized finish with a synthetic stock. Discontinued. The US-made version commands a premium over the Czech-made. Add 30 percent for Hornet. Values shown are for US-made version.

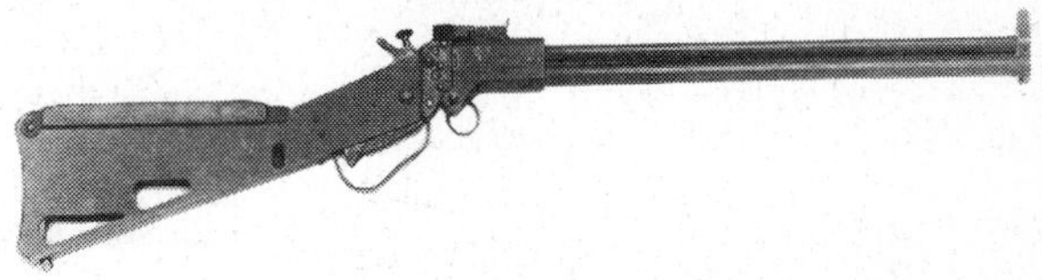

NIB	Exc.	V.G.	Good	Fair	Poor
600	450	295	200	100	50

M6 Scout—Stainless Steel

Same as above but in stainless steel. First introduced in 1996. Discontinued.

NIB	Exc.	V.G.	Good	Fair	Poor
625	475	325	225	150	75

SPRINGFIELD ARMS COMPANY

Springfield, Massachusetts

Double-Barrel Shotguns

The Springfield Arms Co. was bought by Stevens who used the Springfield brand name on many good quality single and double-barrel shotguns. Values range from $100 to $1,600 depending on model, gauge, and condition. See also Stevens.

STAG ARMS
New Britain, Connecticut

NOTE: All Stag rifles are available in left hand configuration. The prices are approximately $25-$40 higher than the right handed models listed here.

Stag-15 Model 1 Pre-Ban

Basic M-4 Carbine pattern. Cal. 5.56mm/.223. 16-inch M-4 barrel with flash hider and bayonet lug. A2 upper receiver with adjustable rear sight. Six-position collapsible buttstock.

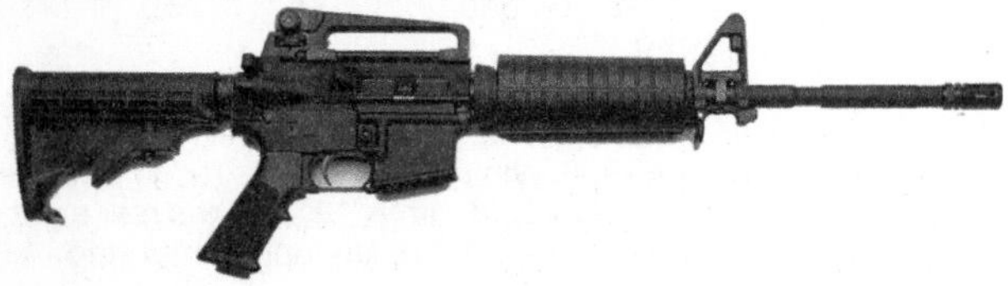

NIB	Exc.	V.G.	Good	Fair	Poor
950	800	675	500	350	200

Stag-15 Model 2 Pre-Ban

As above but with a flat top upper receiver. Includes MI ERS flip type rear sight assembly.

NIB	Exc.	V.G.	Good	Fair	Poor
950	800	675	500	350	200

Stag-15 Model 2 T

As above but with a A.R.M.S. sight system and Samson MRFS-C four sided hand guard.

NIB	Exc.	V.G.	Good	Fair	Poor
1050	900	775	600	400	250

Stag-15 Model 3 Pre-Ban

M-4 type carbine featuring a flat top receiver and gas block with picatinny rails. Six position collapsible buttstock.

NIB	Exc.	V.G.	Good	Fair	Poor
950	800	675	500	350	200

Stag-15 Model 4 Pre-Ban

An A-2 type rifle featuring a 20-inch barrel. Flash hider and bayonet lug.

NIB	Exc.	V.G.	Good	Fair	Poor
950	800	675	500	350	200

Stag 6.8 Model 5 Pre-Ban

Cal. 6.8 SPC. 16-inch barrel. Flat top receiver with picatinny rail. Six position collapsible buttstock. 25-round magazine.

NIB	Exc.	V.G.	Good	Fair	Poor
1050	900	775	600	400	250

Stag-15 Model 6 Pre-Ban Super Varminter

24-inch heavy barrel. No flash hider. Flat top receiver with picatinny rail. Two stage trigger. Free float round hand guard. A2 type fixed stock.

NIB	Exc.	V.G.	Good	Fair	Poor
1050	900	775	600	400	250

STALCAP, ALEXANDER T.F.M.
Nashville, Tennessee

First in business during the 1850s, Stalcap received a contract in 1862, to modify sporting arms for military use. Overall length 50-7/8" to 51-3/4"; octagonal barrels 35-1/4" - 36" turned round at muzzle for socket bayonets; .54 caliber. Rifles assembled with sporting locks, new stocks and brass furniture. At least 102 rifles were delivered in 1862. These arms are unmarked.

NIB	Exc.	V.G.	Good	Fair	Poor
—	—	6500	4250	2000	1000

STANDARD ARMS CO.
Wilmington, Delaware

Model G

Chambered for .25 Remington, .30 Remington, and .35 Remington, with a 22" barrel, and open sights. Integral box magazine and closable gas port that allowed the rifle to be used as a slide action. Blued with a walnut stock. Produced in limited quantities, circa 1910. A notorious jamamatic. Bronze alloy buttplate and forend.

NIB	Exc.	V.G.	Good	Fair	Poor
—	750	600	450	250	150

Model M

Manually-operated pump-only version of Model G.

NIB	Exc.	V.G.	Good	Fair	Poor
—	900	725	550	300	150

STARR ARMS COMPANY
New York, New York

Percussion Carbine

A .54 caliber breechloading percussion carbine with a 21" round barrel secured by one barrel band. Blued, case hardened with a walnut stock. The lock marked "Starr Arms Co./Yonkers, N.Y."

Courtesy Milwaukee Public Museum, Milwaukee, Wisconsin

NIB	Exc.	V.G.	Good	Fair	Poor
—	—	3500	2750	1250	400

Cartridge Carbine

Similar to the above, but in .52 rimfire caliber. Approximately 5,000 were manufactured.

Courtesy Milwaukee Public Museum, Milwaukee, Wisconsin

The frame length of this variation is of increased size.

NIB	Exc.	V.G.	Good	Fair	Poor
—	—	3750	2500	1000	350

STERLING ARMAMENT LTD.

London, England

Sterling MK 6

A semi-automatic copy of the Sterling submachine gun with a 16.1" barrel, folding metal stock and side mounted magazine. Finished as above.

The frame length of this variation is of increased size.

NIB	Exc.	V.G.	Good	Fair	Poor
1500	950	750	500	300	200

Sterling AR 180

A copy of the Armalite Model AR18, 5.56mm rifle. Finished with either black wrinkled paint or, more rarely, blued.

The frame length of this variation is of increased size.

NIB	Exc.	V.G.	Good	Fair	Poor
1100	750	600	500	350	200

STEVENS ARMS CO., J.

Chicopee Falls, Massachusetts

The J. Stevens Arms Company also produced a series of utility-grade slide-action shotguns. They are chambered for various gauges with various barrel lengths and chokes. The finishes are blued, with walnut stocks. The values are similar, and are listed for reference purposes are listed.

Stevens Tip Up Rifles

This series of rifles was produced by Stevens beginning in the 1870s through 1895. There are a number of variations, but they are all quite similar in appearance. They feature a distinctive sloped frame made of iron and nickel-plated. Most frames are similar in size, but there is a slightly lighter frame used on the "Ladies Model" rifles. These Tip Up rifles are chambered for various calibers from the .22 rimfire to the .44 centerfire cartridges. They are offered with barrel lengths of 24", 26", 28", or 30". The actions are nickel-plated, as well as the trigger guards and the buttplates. The barrels are blued, and the two-piece stocks are of walnut. They are offered with various buttplates and sights. A shotgun version is also offered. There are a number of variations that differ only slightly, and the model numbers are not marked on the rifles. We suggest securing a qualified appraisal if in doubt. The major variations and their values are as follows:

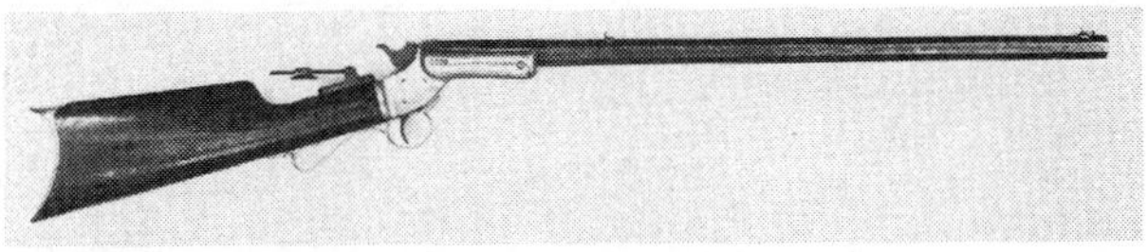

Courtesy Milwaukee Public Museum, Milwaukee, Wisconsin

Ladies Model—.22 or .25 Rimfire Only, 24" or 26" Barrel

NIB	Exc.	V.G.	Good	Fair	Poor
—	3500	3000	2100	1400	700

Tip Up Rifle—Without Forend

NIB	Exc.	V.G.	Good	Fair	Poor
—	700	600	400	250	200

Tip Up Rifle—With Forend, Swiss-Type Buttplate

NIB	Exc.	V.G.	Good	Fair	Poor
—	1150	900	550	375	250

Tip Up Shotgun—All Gauges, 30" or 32" Barrel

NIB	Exc.	V.G.	Good	Fair	Poor
—	550	400	300	150	100

Ideal Single-Shot Rifle

This excellent rifle was manufactured by Stevens between 1896 and 1933. It is a single-shot, falling-block type action that is activated by a trigger guard-action lever. It was produced in many popular calibers from .22 rimfire up to .30-40. It was also manufactured in a number of special Stevens calibers. It was offered with various length barrels in many different grades, from plain Spartan starter rifles up to some extremely high-grade Schuetzen-type target rifles with all available options. In 1901 Harry Pope of Hartford, Connecticut, went to work for Stevens and brought his highly respected barrel to the Stevens Company. He remained an employee for only two years, and the firearms produced during this period have the name "Stevens-Pope" stamped on the top of the barrel in addition to the other factory markings. Rifles marked in this manner and authenticated would be worth an approximate 50 percent premium if they are in very good to excellent condition. Due to numerous variations and options offered, we strongly recommend securing a qualified appraisal, especially on the higher-grade Ideal series rifles, before a purchase.

No. 44

This version is chambered for various calibers and is offered with a 24" or 26" barrel. It has an open rear sight with a Rocky Mountain-type front sight. The finish is blued and case colored, with a walnut stock. There were approximately 100,000 manufactured between 1896 and 1933.

NIB	Exc.	V.G.	Good	Fair	Poor
—	1200	1000	650	400	225

No. 44-1/2

This rifle is similar in appearance to the No. 44 but features an improved action. It has barrel lengths up to 34" and will be found with the Stevens-Pope barrel. It was manufactured between 1903 and 1916.

Courtesy J.B. Barnes

NIB	Exc.	V.G.	Good	Fair	Poor
—	2000	1800	1400	1000	725

No. 044-1/2

This version is also known as the English Model rifle and is similar to the No. 44-1/2 except that it has a shotgun butt and a tapered barrel. There were a number of options offered that would affect the value. It was manufactured between 1903 and 1916.

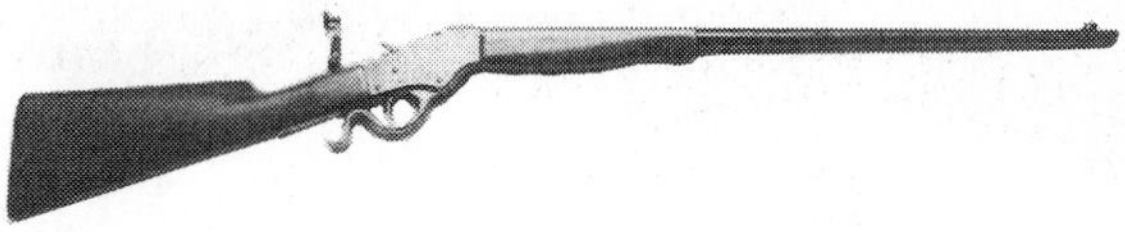

Courtesy Mike Stuckslager

NIB	Exc.	V.G.	Good	Fair	Poor
—	2000	1800	1400	1000	725

No. 45

This version is also known as the Range Rifle, It is chambered for various calibers from the .22 rimfire to .44-40. Its identifying features are the Beach sights with an additional vernier tang sight and a Swiss-type buttstock. It is offered with a 26" or 28" part-octagonal barrel. It was manufactured between 1896 and 1916. Values listed are for the standard version.

NIB	Exc.	V.G.	Good	Fair	Poor
—	2200	2000	1500	1100	825

NOTE: Deduct 25 percent for .44 action.

No. 46

Same as the No. 45 but with a fancy wood stock. Manufactured from 1896 to 1902. Built in No. 44 action-only.

NIB	Exc.	V.G.	Good	Fair	Poor
—	2500	2200	1750	1450	1100

No. 47

This version is similar to the No. 45, with a pistol grip buttstock.

NIB	Exc.	V.G.	Good	Fair	Poor
—	5000	4400	3300	2100	1200

NOTE: Deduct 25 percent for .44 action.

No. 48

Same as the No. 47 but with a fancy wood checkered stock. Manufactured from 1896 to 1902. Built in a No. 44 action-only. This is a very rare model.

NIB	Exc.	V.G.	Good	Fair	Poor
—	5500	4700	3700	2900	1800

No. 49

This model is also known as the "Walnut Hill Rifle." It is a high grade target rifle chambered for many calibers between the .22 rimfire and the .44-40. It is offered with a 28" or 30" part-octagonal barrel that is medium- or heavy-weight. It was furnished with a globe front sight and a vernier tang sight. It is blued with a case-colored frame and has a high-grade, checkered, varnished walnut stock that has a high comb and features a pistol grip, cheekpiece, Swiss-type buttplate, and a loop-type trigger guard lever that resembles that of a lever-action rifle. The receiver is engraved, and there were a number of options available that would increase the value when present. We recommend an appraisal when in doubt. This rifle was manufactured between 1896 and 1916.

Courtesy J.B. Barnes

NIB	Exc.	V.G.	Good	Fair	Poor
—	7500	7000	4200	2800	1900

Model 50

This version is identical to the Model 49 but was offered with a higher-grade walnut stock. This is a very rare model.

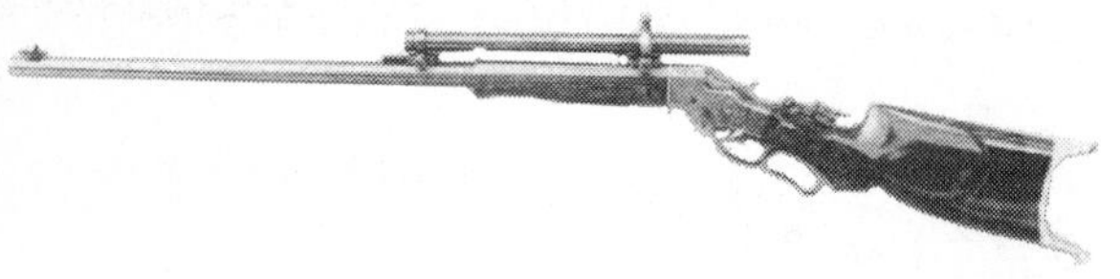

Courtesy J.B. Barnes

NIB	Exc.	V.G.	Good	Fair	Poor
—	8500	8000	4800	3300	2200

Model 51

This version is known as the "Schuetzen Rifle" and is quite similar to the No. 49 except that it features double-set triggers, a higher-grade walnut stock, a wooden insert in the trigger guard action lever, and a heavy, Schuetzen-type buttplate. There were many options available on this model, and we recommend securing an appraisal when in doubt. It was manufactured between 1896 and 1916.

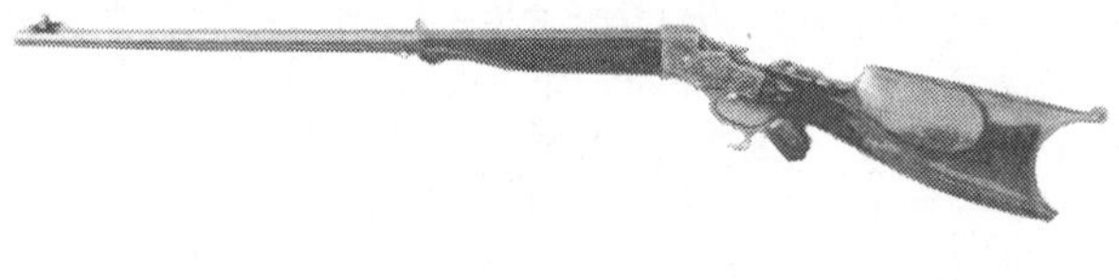

Courtesy J.B. Barnes

NIB	Exc.	V.G.	Good	Fair	Poor
—	14000	12000	7500	4000	2500

No. 52

This version is also known as the "Schuetzen Junior." It is similar to the No. 51 except that it features more engraving and a higher-grade walnut stock. It was manufactured between 1897 and 1916.

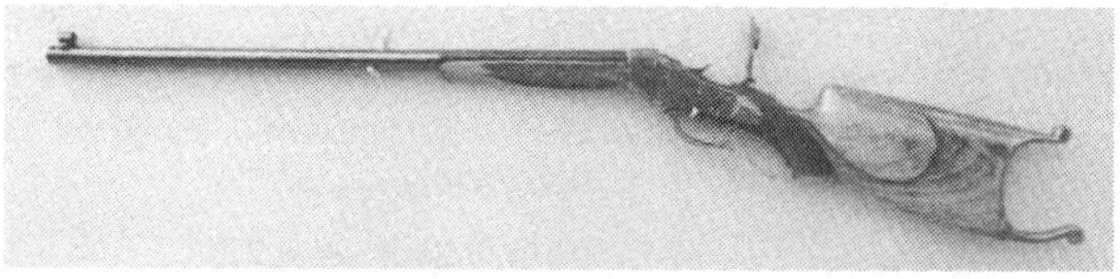

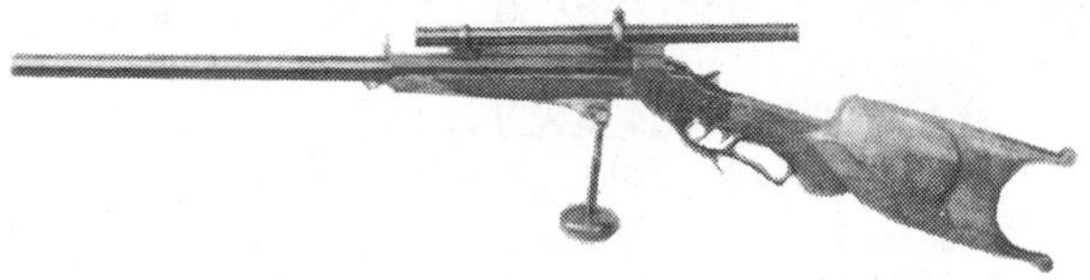

Courtesy J.B. Barnes

NIB	Exc.	V.G.	Good	Fair	Poor
—	14000	12000	7500	4000	2000

No. 53

This model is the same as the No. 51 except for the addition of a fancy wood stock and palm rest. Produced from 1896 to 1902 and offered only with a No. 44 action. This is a rare rifle.

NIB	Exc.	V.G.	Good	Fair	Poor
—	12000	9250	7800	4000	3000

No. 54

This is similar to the No. 52 except that it has double-set triggers and a palm rest, as well as a heavy, Swiss-style buttplate. It is offered with a 30" or 32" part-octagonal heavy barrel. This was Stevens' top-of-the-line rifle. It was offered with many options, and an appraisal should be secured if in doubt. It was manufactured between 1897 and 1916.

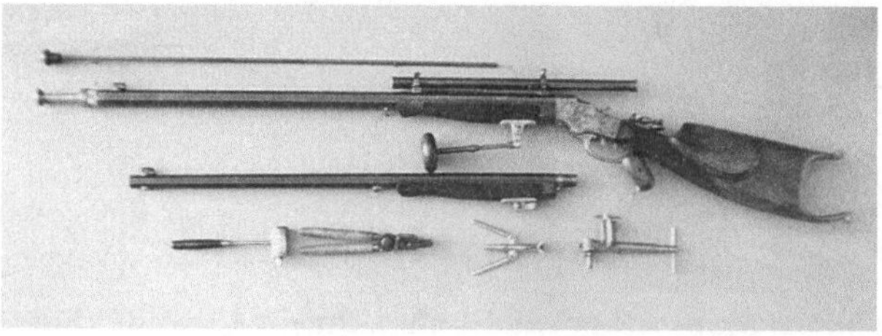

NIB	Exc.	V.G.	Good	Fair	Poor
—	18000	16000	11500	8000	5000

NOTE: The above prices are based on a No. 44-1/2 action. A No. 44 action will bring 20 percent less than the prices listed above.

No. 55

This version is one of the Stevens' Ideal Ladies Models. It is chambered for the smaller rimfire calibers between .22 Short and .32 Long rimfire. It features a 24" or 26" part-octagonal barrel with a vernier tang sight. The finish is blued and case-colored, with a checkered pistol grip walnut stock that features a Swiss-type buttplate. This is a lighter weight rifle that was manufactured between 1897 and 1916.

NIB	Exc.	V.G.	Good	Fair	Poor
—	6500	5000	3500	2000	1000

No. 56

This Ladies' Model rifle is similar to the No. 55 except that it is chambered for centerfire cartridges and has a higher-grade walnut stock. It was made on the improved No. 44-1/2 action. It was manufactured between 1906 and 1916.

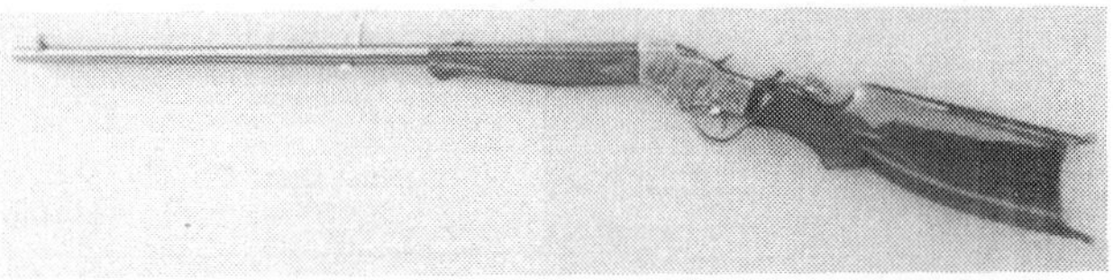

Courtesy J.B. Barnes

NIB	Exc.	V.G.	Good	Fair	Poor
—	7000	5500	4000	2200	1100

No. 404

This version is chambered for the .22 rimfire cartridge only. It features a 28" round barrel with a globe front sight and a Lyman No. 42 receiver sight. The finish is blued and case-colored. It has a walnut straight-grip stock with a semi-beavertail forend. It features a shotgun-type buttplate. It was manufactured between 1910 and 1916.

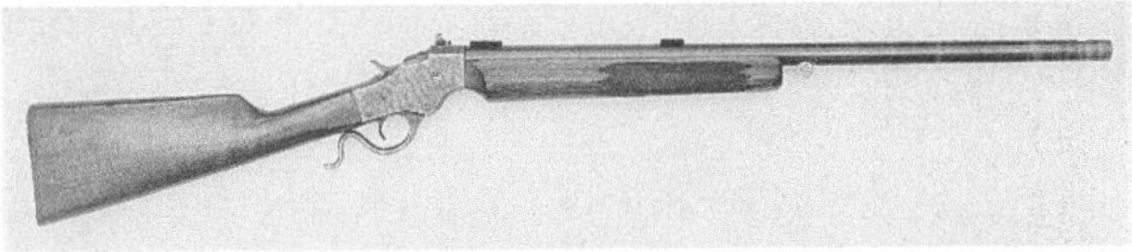

NIB	Exc.	V.G.	Good	Fair	Poor
—	1200	1000	800	700	600

No. 414

This version is also known as the Armory Model and is chambered for the .22 LR cartridge only. It was built on a No. 44 action and features a 26" round barrel. It has a Rocky Mountain front sight with a Lyman receiver sight at the rear. The finish is blued and case-colored, with a straight-grip walnut stock and forend held on by a single barrel band. It was manufactured between 1912 and 1932.

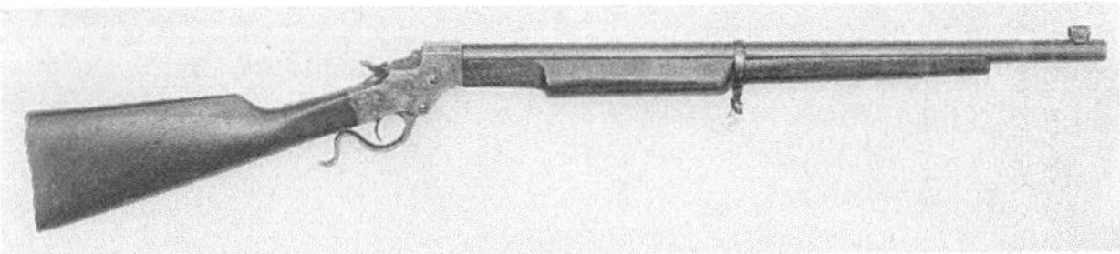

Courtesy Mike Stuckslager

NIB	Exc.	V.G.	Good	Fair	Poor
—	900	700	500	300	275

No. 417 Walnut Hill Model

This is a heavy single-shot, lever action target rifle chambered for the .22 LR, .22 Short, or .22 Hornet cartridges. Weight is approximately 10.5 lbs. Produced from 1932 to 1940.

NIB	Exc.	V.G.	Good	Fair	Poor
—	1500	1200	800	600	400

No. 417 1/2 Walnut Hill Model

This model is a sporting version of the Model 417. Weight is about 8.5 lbs. Manufactured from 1932 to 1940.

NIB	Exc.	V.G.	Good	Fair	Poor
—	1600	1300	900	700	450

No. 418 Walnut Hill Jr.

This is a light single-shot lever action target rifle chambered for .22 LR or .22 Short. Weight is about 6.5 lbs. Manufactured from 1932 to 1940.

NIB	Exc.	V.G.	Good	Fair	Poor
—	900	750	500	300	200

No. 418 1/2 Walnut Hill Jr.

Similar to the Model 418 but chambered for .25 rimfire or .22 WRF cartridges. It is also fitted with sporting sights. Manufactured from 1932 to 1940.

NIB	Exc.	V.G.	Good	Fair	Poor
—	900	750	500	300	200

BOY'S RIFLES

The Stevens Company produced an extensive line of smaller, single-shot rifles chambered for small calibers and intended primarily for use by young shooters. These firearms have become quite collectible and are considered a field of specialty by many modern collectors.NOTE: There are many variations that were available with a number of options that would affect their value. We supply information and values for the major variations but would recommend securing a qualified appraisal if in doubt.

"FAVORITE" RIFLES

This series of rifles is chambered for the .22, .25, and .32 rimfire. It has a 22" part-octagonal barrel and is blued, with a case-colored frame. It has a takedown-type action with an interchangeable barrel feature. It was available with optional sights, as well as buttplates. There were approximately 1,000,000 manufactured between 1893 and 1939. The variations are listed.

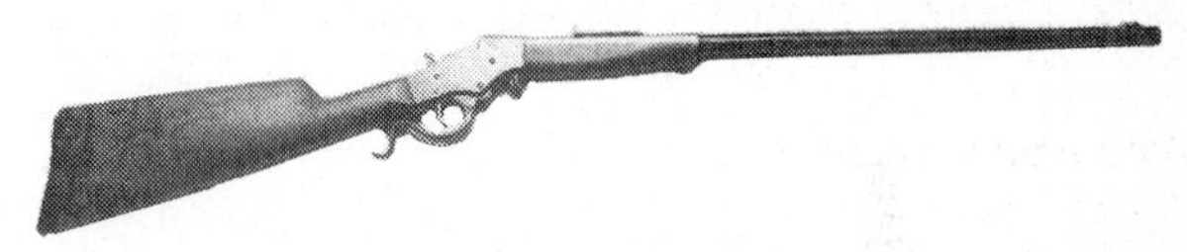

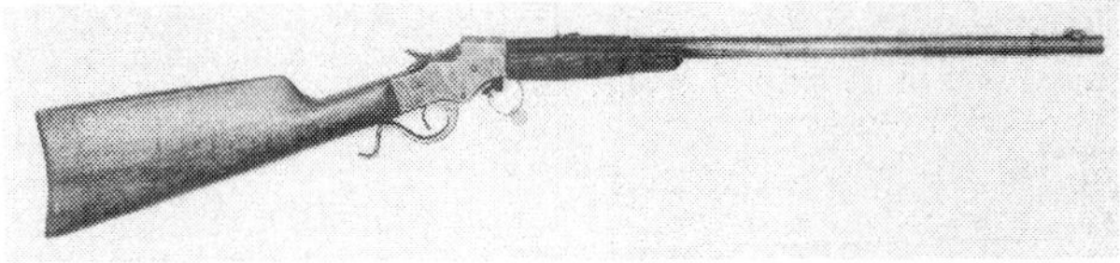

Courtesy Mike Stuckslager

1st Model Favorite

This version is chambered for the .22 or .25 rimfire cartridge. It has a removable sideplate on the right side of the receiver not found on any other variation. There were approximately 1,000 manufactured between 1893 and 1894.

NIB	Exc.	V.G.	Good	Fair	Poor
—	1200	800	650	500	350

No. 17

This is the standard, plain version with open sights.

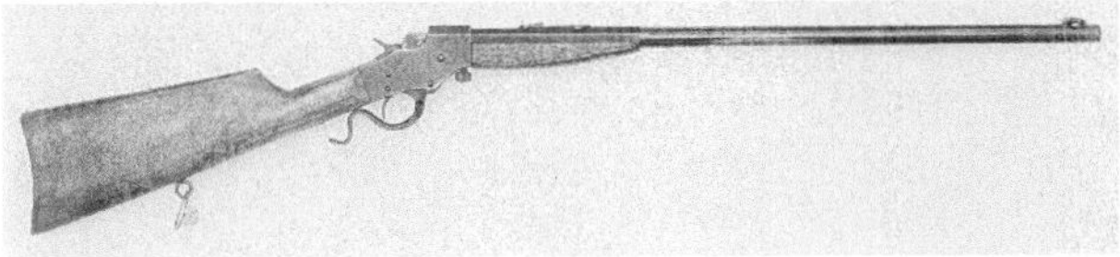

NIB	Exc.	V.G.	Good	Fair	Poor
—	550	400	300	175	125

No. 20

This version is chambered for the .22 or .32 rimfire shot cartridges and has a smoothbore barrel and no rear sight.

NIB	Exc.	V.G.	Good	Fair	Poor
—	600	450	300	175	125

No. 21

This version is known as the Bicycle rifle and features a 20" barrel with open sights standard. It was furnished with a canvas carrying case that would be worth approximately a 30 percent premium. It was manufactured between 1898 and 1903.

NIB	Exc.	V.G.	Good	Fair	Poor
—	750	575	350	150	100

No. 21 Ladies Model

This version bears the same model number as the Bicycle rifle but has a 24" barrel and a high grade, checkered walnut stock with a Swiss buttplate. It features a vernier tang sight. It was manufactured between 1910 and 1916.

NIB	Exc.	V.G.	Good	Fair	Poor
—	6500	5000	3500	2000	1000

No. 16

This version is known as the "Crack Shot." It is chambered for .22 or .32 rimfire cartridges with a 20" round barrel. It has a rolling-block-type action with a thumb lever on the side. It is a utility-type rifle with open sights, a blued and case-colored finish, and a plain two-piece walnut stock with a rubber buttplate. The barrel is marked "Crack Shot" along with the standard Stevens' barrel address markings. It was manufactured between 1900 and 1913.

NIB	Exc.	V.G.	Good	Fair	Poor
—	550	450	325	225	100

No. 16-1/2

This version is similar to the No. 16 except that it is chambered for the .32 rimfire shot cartridge with a smoothbore barrel. It was manufactured between 1900 and 1913.

NIB	Exc.	V.G.	Good	Fair	Poor
—	575	475	350	250	125

No. 23—Sure Shot

This version is chambered for the .22 rimfire cartridge. It has a 20" round barrel that pivots to the right for loading. There is a barrel release on the frame. This version is blued and case-colored, with a plain walnut buttstock and no forend. It was manufactured between 1894 and 1897.

NIB	Exc.	V.G.	Good	Fair	Poor
—	2600	2200	1400	1000	600

No. 15

This version is also known as the "Maynard Junior." It is chambered for the .22 rimfire cartridge and has an 18" part-octagonal barrel. The action is similar to the Civil War Maynard rifle with a trigger guard-activating lever. The finish is all blued, with a bored-type buttstock and no forearm. The barrel is marked "Stevens Maynard, J. R." in addition to the standard Stevens' barrel address. It was manufactured between 1902 and 1912.

Courtesy Mike Stuckslager

NIB	Exc.	V.G.	Good	Fair	Poor
—	550	450	325	225	100

No. 15-1/2

This is a smoothbore version of the No. 15.

NIB	Exc.	V.G.	Good	Fair	Poor
—	575	475	350	250	125

No. 14

This version is also known as the "Little Scout." It is a utility, takedown rifle that is blued, with a one-piece bored-type stock. It features a rolling-block-type action and was manufactured between 1906 and 1910.

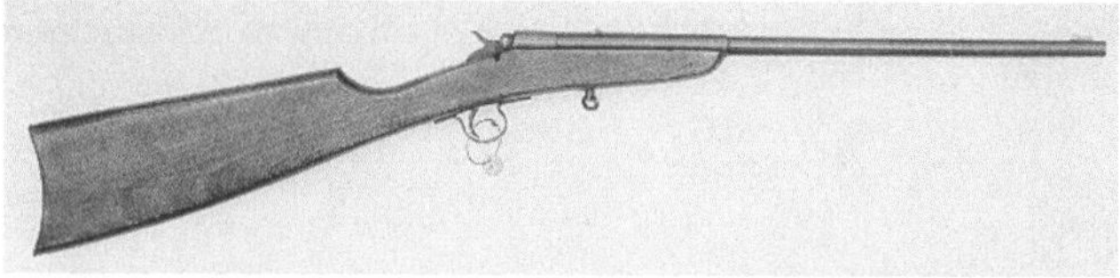

NIB	Exc.	V.G.	Good	Fair	Poor
—	500	400	300	225	100

No. 14-1/2

This version is similar to the No. 14 except that it has a two-piece stock. It is also marked "Little Scout." It was manufactured between 1911 and 1941.

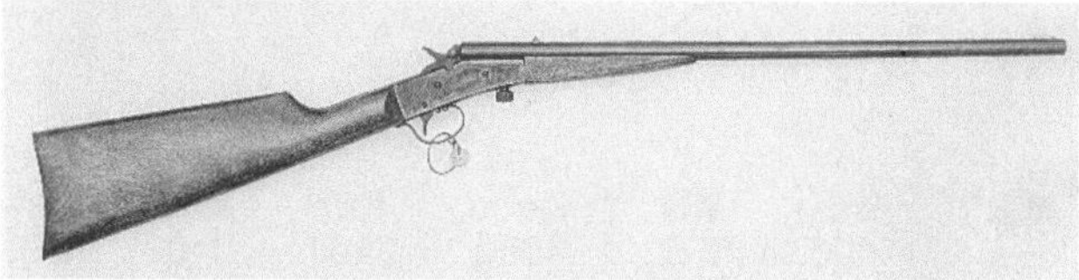

NIB	Exc.	V.G.	Good	Fair	Poor
—	450	350	200	150	100

No. 65

This version is known as the "Little Krag." It is a single-shot bolt-action rifle chambered for the .22 rimfire cartridge. It has a one-piece stock and a 20" round barrel that was marked "Little Krag." This version is quite scarce. It was manufactured between 1903 and 1910.

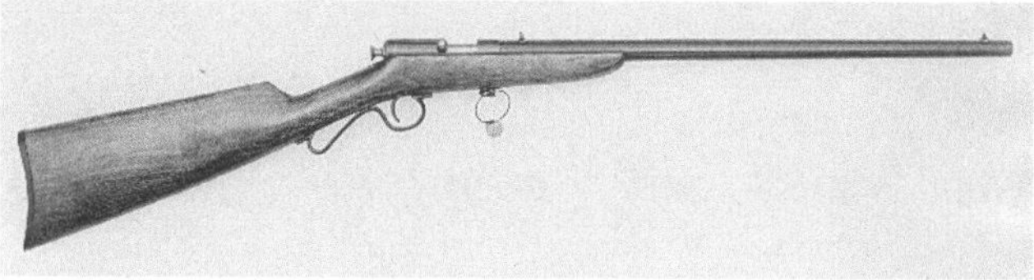

NIB	Exc.	V.G.	Good	Fair	Poor
—	550	450	300	200	100

No. 12

This version is also known as the "Marksman." It is chambered for the .22, .25, and the .32 rimfire cartridges. It has a 22" barrel that pivots upward for loading. It is activated by an S-shaped trigger guard lever. It was manufactured between 1911 and 1930.

Courtesy Mike Stuckslager

NIB	Exc.	V.G.	Good	Fair	Poor
—	500	400	300	225	100

No. 26

This version is also known as the "Crack Shot." It has a rolling block-type action and is chambered for .22 or the .32 rimfire cartridges. It is offered with an 18" or 20" round barrel. It is blued and has a two-piece stock. It was manufactured between 1912 and 1939.

Courtesy Mike Stuckslager

NIB	Exc.	V.G.	Good	Fair	Poor
—	500	400	300	225	100

No. 26-1/2

This is the smoothbore version of the No. 26.

NIB	Exc.	V.G.	Good	Fair	Poor
—	525	475	350	250	100

No. 11—Junior

This is a single-shot, rolling block rifle chambered for the .22 rimfire cartridge. It has a 20" barrel, is blued, and has a bore-type stock without a buttplate. This was the last model offered in the Boy's Rifle series. It was manufactured between 1924 and 1931.

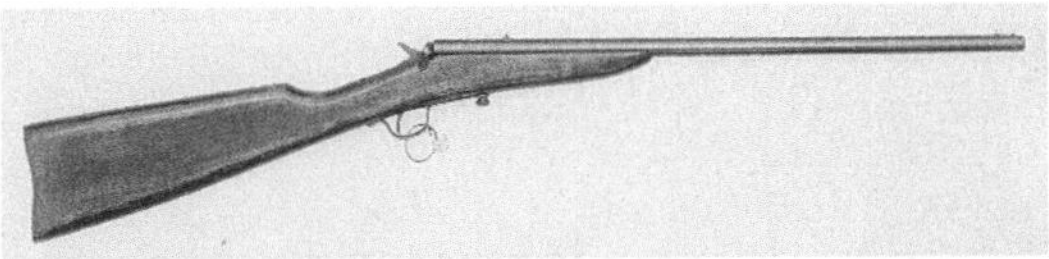

NIB	Exc.	V.G.	Good	Fair	Poor
—	500	400	300	225	100

Model 71

This was a reintroduced version of the "Stevens Favorite." It is chambered for the .22 LR cartridge and has a 22" octagonal barrel. The finish is blued and case-colored, with a plain walnut stock that has an inlaid medallion and a crescent buttplate. There were 10,000 manufactured in 1971.

NIB	Exc.	V.G.	Good	Fair	Poor
350	275	175	125	100	75

Model 72

This is a reintroduced version of the "Crack Shot" that features a single-shot, falling block action. It is chambered for the .22 rimfire cartridge and has a 22" octagon barrel with open sights. It is blued and case-colored, with a straight walnut stock. It was introduced in 1972.

NIB	Exc.	V.G.	Good	Fair	Poor
300	225	175	125	100	75

Model 70

This is a slide-action rifle chambered for the .22 rimfire cartridge. It is also known as the "Visible Loading Rifle." It features a 20" round barrel with a 3/4-length, tubular magazine. The finish is blued and case-colored, and it has a walnut stock. It features open sights but was available with other options. It was offered as the No. 70-1/2, 71, 71-1/2, 72, and 72-1/2. These different model numbers denote various sight combinations. Otherwise, they are identical. They were manufactured between 1907 and 1932.

NIB	Exc.	V.G.	Good	Fair	Poor
—	400	350	225	100	75

No. 80

This is a slide-action repeating rifle chambered for the .22 rimfire cartridge. It has a 24" round barrel with a tubular magazine. It features open sights and is blued, with a walnut stock. It was manufactured between 1906 and 1910.

NIB	Exc.	V.G.	Good	Fair	Poor
—	450	350	225	175	100

High Power Rifle

This is a series of lever-action hunting rifles chambered for the .25, .300, .32, and the .35 Remington centerfire cartridges. It features a 22" round barrel with a tubular magazine. The finish is blued, with a walnut stock. It is available in four variations: the No. 425, No. 430, No. 435, and the No. 440. These designations denote increased ornamentation and high quality materials and workmanship used in construction. There were approximately 26,000 manufactured between 1910 and 1917.

No. 425

NIB	Exc.	V.G.	Good	Fair	Poor
—	1050	800	550	300	200

No. 430

NIB	Exc.	V.G.	Good	Fair	Poor
—	1250	950	650	400	300

No. 435

NIB	Exc.	V.G.	Good	Fair	Poor
—	1600	1300	1000	600	400

No. 440

NIB	Exc.	V.G.	Good	Fair	Poor
—	3100	2800	2400	1600	850

STEVENS BOLT-ACTION UTILITY RIFLES

The Stevens Company produced a number of inexpensive, utilitarian, bolt-action rifles. These were both single-shot and repeaters. They have been popular over the years as starter rifles for young shooters. Their values are quite similar, and they are listed for reference purposes only.

NIB	Exc.	V.G.	Good	Fair	Poor
—	—	200	100	70	50

Model 416

This is a target rifle chambered for the .22 LR cartridge. It has a 24" heavy barrel with aperture sights. It features a 5-round detachable magazine and is blued, with a target-type walnut stock.

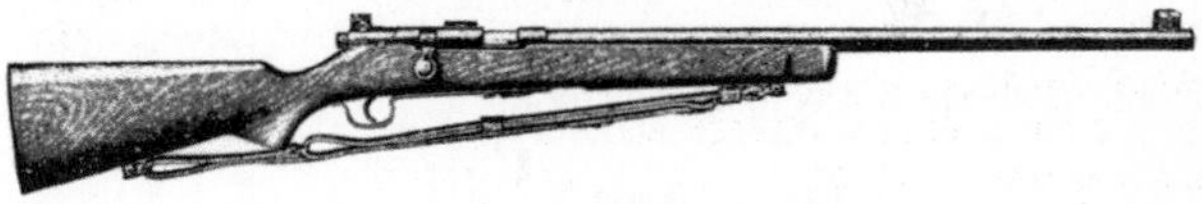

NIB	Exc.	V.G.	Good	Fair	Poor
—	450	350	200	150	100

Model 322

This is a bolt-action sporting rifle chambered for the .22 Hornet cartridge. It has a 20" barrel with open sights and a detachable box magazine. The finish is blued, with a plain walnut stock.

NIB	Exc.	V.G.	Good	Fair	Poor
—	175	125	100	75	50

Model 322-S

This version features an aperture rear sight.

NIB	Exc.	V.G.	Good	Fair	Poor
—	225	125	100	75	50

Model 89

This is a single-shot, Martini-type, falling-block rifle chambered for the .22 LR cartridge. It has an 18.5" barrel and a trigger guard loop-lever activator. The finish is blued, with a straight walnut stock. It was introduced in 1976 and is no longer manufactured.

NIB	Exc.	V.G.	Good	Fair	Poor
—	125	80	70	60	40

Model 87M

Designed to look like the M1 Garand this rifle was chambered for the .22 rimfire cartridge.

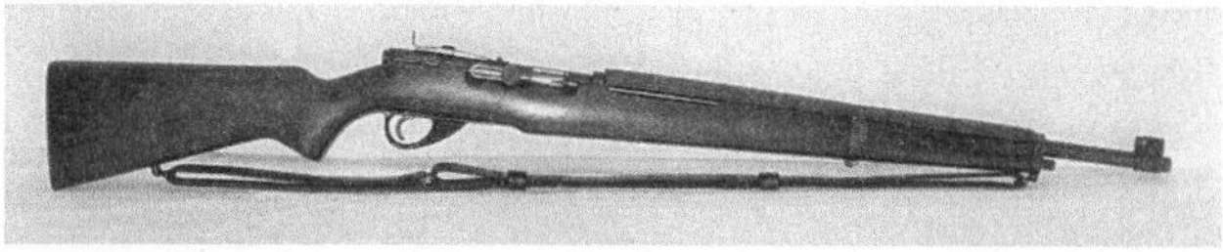

Courtesy Richard M. Kumor, Sr.

NIB	Exc.	V.G.	Good	Fair	Poor
—	600	500	375	225	150

Model 987

This is a blowback-operated semi-automatic rifle chambered for the .22 LR cartridge. It has a 20" barrel with a 15-round tubular magazine. The finish is blued, with a hardwood stock.

NIB	Exc.	V.G.	Good	Fair	Poor
—	150	100	75	50	25

STEVENS ECONOMY LINE (SAVAGE, 2006)

Stevens Model 200

Long- or short-action bolt rifle chambered in .223, .22-250, .243, 7MM-08, .308, .25-06, .270, .30-06, 7mm RM, or .300 WM. Gray checkered synthetic stock and 22-inch (short-action) or 24-inch (long-action) blued sightless barrel. Introduced 2006.

NIB	Exc.	V.G.	Good	Fair	Poor
325	275	225	175	125	100

Model 200XP Long or Short Action Package Rifle

Similar to above but with 4x12 scope.

NIB	Exc.	V.G.	Good	Fair	Poor
375	300	250	200	150	125

Model 200XP Camo

Similar to above but with camo stock.

NIB	Exc.	V.G.	Good	Fair	Poor
400	325	275	225	175	150

Stevens Cadet Mini-Youth

Similar to Savage Cub .22 rimfire. Introduced 2006.

NIB	Exc.	V.G.	Good	Fair	Poor
200	150	125	100	75	50

Stevens Model 315 Youth

Similar to Cadet Mini-Youth but with sightless barrel. Introduced 2006.

NIB	Exc.	V.G.	Good	Fair	Poor
200	150	125	100	75	50

Stevens Model 310

Five-shot bolt-action repeater chambered for .17 HMR. Detachable box magazine, synthetic stock, blued 20.75-inch sightless barrel. Introduced 2006.

NIB	Exc.	V.G.	Good	Fair	Poor
200	150	125	100	75	50

Stevens Model 310 Heavy Barrel

Similar to Stevens Model 310 but with 21-inch bull barrel. Introduced 2006.

NIB	Exc.	V.G.	Good	Fair	Poor
225	175	150	115	75	50

Stevens Model 300

Clip-fed bolt-action repeater chambered for .22 rimfire. Gray synthetic stock and 20.75-inch blued barrel. Also available with scope package (add 10 percent). Introduced 2006.

NIB	Exc.	V.G.	Good	Fair	Poor
200	150	125	100	75	50

Stevens Model 305

Similar to Model 310 but chambered in .22 WMR. Introduced 2006.

NIB	Exc.	V.G.	Good	Fair	Poor
225	175	150	115	75	50

MISCELLANEOUS STEVENS SINGLE-SHOT SHOTGUNS

This company manufactured a number of single barrel break-open, single-shot shotguns. They were produced chambered for various gauges with various-length barrels and chokes. They are quite similar in appearance and were designed as inexpensive utility-grade weapons. There is little or no collector interest in them at this time, and their values are similar. They are listed for reference purposes only.

Model 89	Model 97	Model 108	Model 170
Model 90	Model 100	Model 110	Model 180
Model 93	Model 102	Model 120	Model 944
Model 94	Model 104	Model 125	Model 958
Model 94A	Model 105	Model 140	Model 970
Model 94C	Model 106	Model 160	
Model 95	Model 107	Model 165	

Model 107

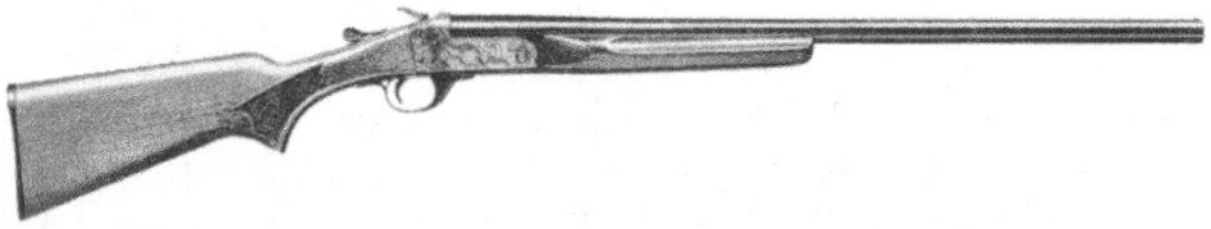

Model 94C

NIB	Exc.	V.G.	Good	Fair	Poor
—	150	100	75	50	25

Model 182

This is a single-shot, break-open shotgun chambered for 12 gauge. It is offered with a 30" or 32" trap choked barrels and features a hammerless action with an automatic ejector and a lightly engraved receiver. The finish is blued, with a checkered trap-grade stock.

NIB	Exc.	V.G.	Good	Fair	Poor
—	175	125	100	75	50

Model 185

This version features a half-octagonal barrel with an automatic ejector and a checkered walnut stock.

NIB	Exc.	V.G.	Good	Fair	Poor
—	175	125	100	75	50

NOTE: Damascus barrel deduct 25 percent.

Model 190

This is a 12-gauge hammerless gun with an automatic ejector. It is lightly engraved with a half-octagonal barrel.

NIB	Exc.	V.G.	Good	Fair	Poor
—	175	125	100	75	50

NOTE: Damascus barrel deduct 25 percent.

Model 195

This is another deluxe version that features engraving, a half-octagonal barrel, and a high-grade, checkered walnut stock.

NIB	Exc.	V.G.	Good	Fair	Poor
—	350	250	200	150	100

NOTE: Damascus barrel deduct 25 percent.

Model 240

This over-and-under model features a boxlock frame with exposed hammers.

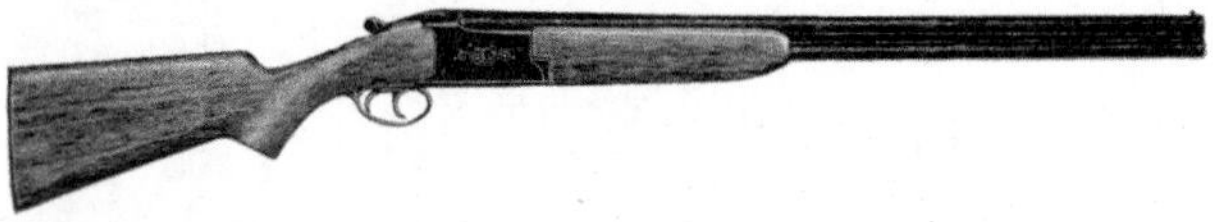

NIB	Exc.	V.G.	Good	Fair	Poor
—	400	300	250	200	150

Model .22/.410

Over/under .22/.410 combo gun with Tenite stock. Manufactured 1939-1950.

NIB	Exc.	V.G.	Good	Fair	Poor
—	350	300	250	175	100

STEVENS DOUBLE-BARREL SHOTGUNS

The firm of J. Stevens and its successors produced a number of utility-grade, side-by-side double-barrel shotguns between 1877 and 1988. They are chambered for 10, 12, 16, or 20 gauge as well as the .410 bore. Stevens shotguns in 10 gauge and .410 bore will normally bring a premium as do guns with single triggers and ejectors. They have various length barrels and choke combinations. They feature double triggers and extractors except where noted. A complete list of Stevens brand models including the three in-house brands: Riverside, Springfield, and Super Value, are listed.

STEVENS BRAND

Model 1877—Hammer Boxlock

NIB	Exc.	V.G.	Good	Fair	Poor
—	575	450	350	250	200

Model 250—Hammer Sidelock

NIB	Exc.	V.G.	Good	Fair	Poor
—	575	450	350	250	200

Model 225—Hammer Boxlock

Courtesy Nick Niles, Paul Goodwin photo

NIB	Exc.	V.G.	Good	Fair	Poor
—	575	450	350	250	200

Model 260—Hammer Sidelock

NIB	Exc.	V.G.	Good	Fair	Poor
—	575	450	350	250	200

Model 270—Hammer Sidelock

NIB	Exc.	V.G.	Good	Fair	Poor
—	575	450	350	250	200

Model 280—Hammer Sidelock

NIB	Exc.	V.G.	Good	Fair	Poor
—	575	450	350	250	200

Model 325—Hammerless Boxlock

NIB	Exc.	V.G.	Good	Fair	Poor
—	450	400	350	250	200

Model 350—Hammerless Boxlock

NIB	Exc.	V.G.	Good	Fair	Poor
—	450	400	350	250	200

Model 360—Hammerless Boxlock

NIB	Exc.	V.G.	Good	Fair	Poor
—	450	400	350	250	200

Model 370—Hammerless Boxlock

NIB	Exc.	V.G.	Good	Fair	Poor
—	450	400	350	250	200

Model 380—Hammerless Boxlock

NIB	Exc.	V.G.	Good	Fair	Poor
—	575	450	350	250	200

Model 235—Hammer Boxlock

NIB	Exc.	V.G.	Good	Fair	Poor
—	450	400	350	250	200

Model 335 (Early)—Hammerless Boxlock

Courtesy Nick Niles, Paul Goodwin photo

NIB	Exc.	V.G.	Good	Fair	Poor
—	450	400	350	250	200

Model 335 (Late)—Hammerless Boxlock

NIB	Exc.	V.G.	Good	Fair	Poor
—	450	400	350	250	200

Model 255—Hammer Sidelock

NIB	Exc.	V.G.	Good	Fair	Poor
—	450	400	350	250	200

Model 265—Hammer Sidelock

Courtesy Nick Niles, Paul Goodwin photo

NIB	Exc.	V.G.	Good	Fair	Poor
—	450	400	350	250	200

Model 355—Hammerless Boxlock

NIB	Exc.	V.G.	Good	Fair	Poor
—	800	575	450	350	250

Model 365—Hammerless Boxlock

Courtesy Nick Niles, Paul Goodwin photo

NIB	Exc.	V.G.	Good	Fair	Poor
—	925	625	500	400	300

Model 375 (London Proofs)—Hammerless Boxlock

NIB	Exc.	V.G.	Good	Fair	Poor
—	1500	950	700	450	350

Model 375 (U.S.)—Hammerless Boxlock

NIB	Exc.	V.G.	Good	Fair	Poor
—	1100	700	575	400	300

Model 385 (London Proofs)—Hammerless Boxlock

NIB	Exc.	V.G.	Good	Fair	Poor
—	1650	1050	700	450	350

Model 385 (U.S.)—Hammerless Boxlock

NIB	Exc.	V.G.	Good	Fair	Poor
—	1200	850	575	450	300

Model 345—Hammerless Boxlock

Courtesy Nick Niles, Paul Goodwin photo

NIB	Exc.	V.G.	Good	Fair	Poor
—	575	450	350	250	200

Model 330—Hammerless Boxlock

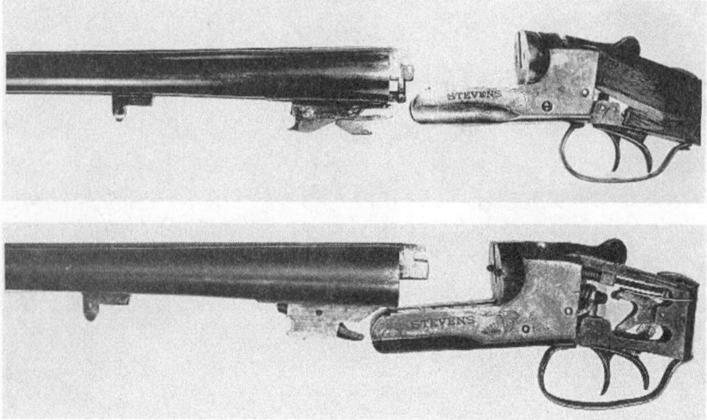

Stevens Model 330 early fork-type cocking lever

NIB	Exc.	V.G.	Good	Fair	Poor
—	450	400	350	250	200

Model 515—Hammerless Boxlock

NIB	Exc.	V.G.	Good	Fair	Poor
—	625	525	450	350	300

Model 515—Single Trigger Hammerless Boxlock

NIB	Exc.	V.G.	Good	Fair	Poor
—	750	575	450	350	300

Model 500—Skeet Hammerless Boxlock

Courtesy Nick Niles, Paul Goodwin photo

NIB	Exc.	V.G.	Good	Fair	Poor
—	1250	925	800	700	400

Model 530—Hammerless Boxlock

NIB	Exc.	V.G.	Good	Fair	Poor
—	450	400	350	250	200

Model 530M—Tenite Hammerless Boxlock

NIB	Exc.	V.G.	Good	Fair	Poor
—	450	400	350	250	200

Model 530M—Tenite Single Trigger Hammerless Boxlock

NIB	Exc.	V.G.	Good	Fair	Poor
—	750	575	450	350	300

Model 530A—Hammerless Boxlock

Courtesy Nick Niles, Paul Goodwin photo

NIB	Exc.	V.G.	Good	Fair	Poor
—	450	400	350	250	200

Model 530A—Single Trigger Hammerless Boxlock

NIB	Exc.	V.G.	Good	Fair	Poor
—	525	450	350	300	250

Model 311—Tenite Hammerless Boxlock

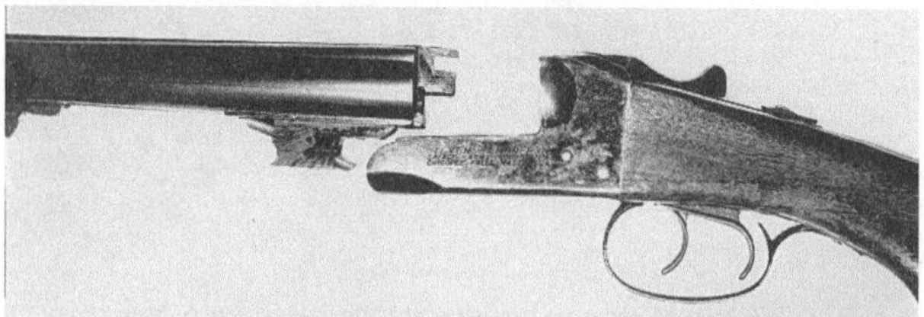

NIB	Exc.	V.G.	Good	Fair	Poor
—	450	400	350	250	200

Model 331—Single Trigger Hammerless Boxlock

NIB	Exc.	V.G.	Good	Fair	Poor
—	525	400	300	250	200

Model 311—Tenite Single Trigger Hammerless Boxlock

NIB	Exc.	V.G.	Good	Fair	Poor
—	575	500	450	350	300

Model 311A—Hammerless Boxlock

NIB	Exc.	V.G.	Good	Fair	Poor
—	525	450	350	250	200

Model 311C—Hammerless Boxlock

Courtesy Nick Niles, Paul Goodwin photo

NIB	Exc.	V.G.	Good	Fair	Poor
—	400	350	250	200	150

Model 311D—Hammerless Boxlock

Courtesy Nick Niles, Paul Goodwin photo

NIB	Exc.	V.G.	Good	Fair	Poor
—	450	400	350	250	200

Model 311E—Hammerless Boxlock

NIB	Exc.	V.G.	Good	Fair	Poor
—	600	450	400	300	250

Model 311F—Hammerless Boxlock

NIB	Exc.	V.G.	Good	Fair	Poor
—	450	400	350	250	200

Model 311H—Hammerless Boxlock

NIB	Exc.	V.G.	Good	Fair	Poor
—	450	400	350	250	200

Model 311H—Vent Rib Hammerless Boxlock

NIB	Exc.	V.G.	Good	Fair	Poor
—	500	450	350	300	250

Model 311J/R—Hammerless Boxlock

Courtesy Nick Niles, Paul Goodwin photo

NIB	Exc.	V.G.	Good	Fair	Poor
—	400	350	250	200	150

Model 311J/R—Solid Rib Hammerless Boxlock

NIB	Exc.	V.G.	Good	Fair	Poor
—	400	350	250	200	150

Model 311H—Waterfowler Hammerless Boxlock

NIB	Exc.	V.G.	Good	Fair	Poor
—	700	575	450	350	250

Model 240—.410 Over-and-Under Hammer Tenite

NIB	Exc.	V.G.	Good	Fair	Poor
700	575	450	350	250	200

RIVERSIDE BRAND

Model 215—Hammer Boxlock

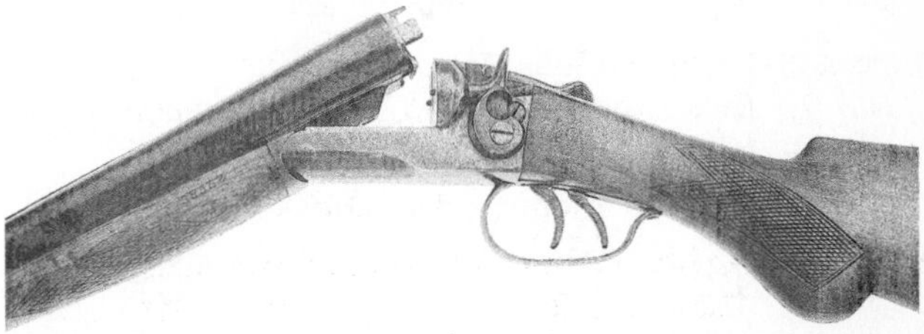

Courtesy Nick Niles, Paul Goodwin photo

NIB	Exc.	V.G.	Good	Fair	Poor
—	750	525	400	250	200

Model 315 (Early)—Hammerless Boxlock

NIB	Exc.	V.G.	Good	Fair	Poor
—	575	450	350	250	200

Model 315 (Late)—Hammerless Boxlock

NIB	Exc.	V.G.	Good	Fair	Poor
—	575	450	350	250	200

SUPER VALUE BRAND

Model 511—Hammerless Boxlock

NIB	Exc.	V.G.	Good	Fair	Poor
—	525	400	300	200	150

Model 511—Sunken Rib Hammerless Boxlock

NIB	Exc.	V.G.	Good	Fair	Poor
—	575	450	350	200	150

SPRINGFIELD BRAND

Model 215—Hammer Boxlock

NIB	Exc.	V.G.	Good	Fair	Poor
—	575	450	350	250	150

Model 311—Hammerless Boxlock

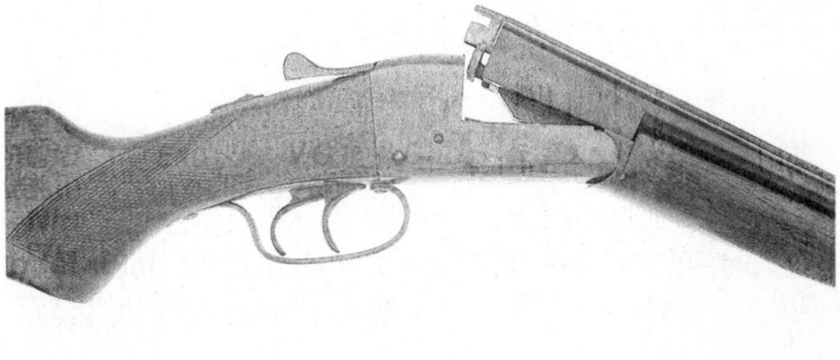

Courtesy Nick Niles, Paul Goodwin photo

NIB	Exc.	V.G.	Good	Fair	Poor
—	575	450	350	250	150

Model 315—Hammerless Boxlock

Courtesy Nick Niles, Paul Goodwin photo

NIB	Exc.	V.G.	Good	Fair	Poor
—	575	450	350	250	200

Model 3150—Hammerless Boxlock

NIB	Exc.	V.G.	Good	Fair	Poor
—	700	575	400	250	200

Model 3151—Hammerless Boxlock

NIB	Exc.	V.G.	Good	Fair	Poor
—	850	700	450	350	250

Model 3151—Single Trigger Hammerless Boxlock

NIB	Exc.	V.G.	Good	Fair	Poor
—	950	800	575	450	300

Model 311—Single Trigger Hammerless Boxlock

NIB	Exc.	V.G.	Good	Fair	Poor
—	800	700	575	450	300

Model 5151—Hammerless Boxlock

Courtesy Nick Niles, Paul Goodwin photo

NIB	Exc.	V.G.	Good	Fair	Poor
—	575	450	350	250	200

Model 5151—Single Trigger Hammerless Boxlock

NIB	Exc.	V.G.	Good	Fair	Poor
—	700	525	400	300	200

Model 311—New Style Hammerless Boxlock

Courtesy Nick Niles, Paul Goodwin photo

NIB	Exc.	V.G.	Good	Fair	Poor
—	575	450	350	250	150

Model 311—New Style Tenite Hammerless Boxlock

NIB	Exc.	V.G.	Good	Fair	Poor
—	575	450	350	250	150

Model 511—Sunken Rib Hammerless Boxlock

NIB	Exc.	V.G.	Good	Fair	Poor
—	575	450	350	250	150

Model 511—Hammerless Boxlock

NIB	Exc.	V.G.	Good	Fair	Poor
—	525	400	300	200	150

Model 511A—Hammerless Boxlock

NIB	Exc.	V.G.	Good	Fair	Poor
—	525	400	300	200	150

STEVENS/SAVAGE SHOTGUNS

Model 411 Upland Sporter

Introduced in 2003 this side-by-side shotgun is chambered for the 12 or 20 gauge, as well as the .410 bore. The 12 gauge is fitted with 28" barrels, while the 28 and .410 have 26" barrels. Single trigger with ejectors. False sideplates are laser engraved. European walnut stock with pistol grip and splinter forend. Weight is about 6.75 to 6.5 lbs. depending on gauge.

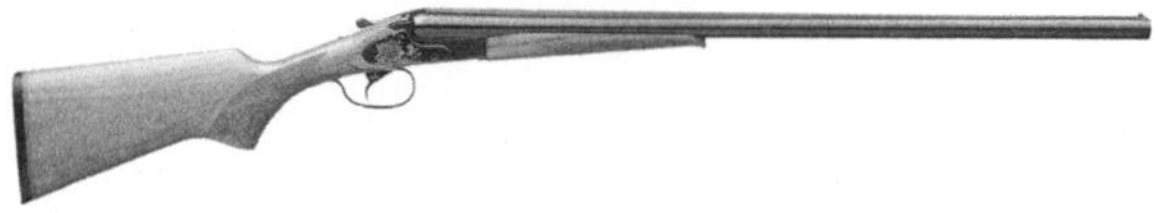

NIB	Exc.	V.G.	Good	Fair	Poor
550	425	350	300	200	125

NOTE: Add 50 percent for 20 and .410 models.

STEVENS DATE CODE

Collectors will find a date code stamped on every double-barrelshotgun in the Stevens brands produced between March 1949and December 1968. Usually, it is behind the hinge pin or aheadof the trigger guard on the bottom of the frame. It will appear asa small circle containing a number and letter. The letters correspond to the years shown in the following table. Significance ofthe numbers is not known.

DATE CODES			
A-1949	B-1950	C-1951	D-1952
E-1953	F-1954	G-1955	H-1956
I-1957	J-1958	K-1959	L-1960
M-1961	N-1962	P-1963	R-1964
S-1965	T-1966	U-1967	V-1968
W-1969	X-1970		

STEVENS BOLT-ACTION SHOTGUNS

The Stevens Company produced a number of bolt-action shotguns that are either single-shot or repeaters. They are chambered for the 20 gauge or .410 and are blued, with walnut stocks. The values for these utility-grade shotguns are similar.

Model 237—Single-Shot
Model 258—Clip Fed
Model 37—Single-Shot
Model 38—Clip Fed
Model 39—Tube Magazine
Model 58—Clip Fed
Model 59—Tube Magazine

Model 58

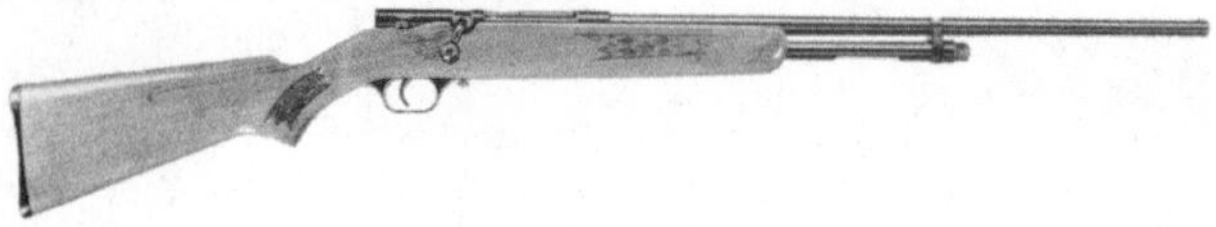

Model 59

NIB	Exc.	V.G.	Good	Fair	Poor
—	125	100	75	50	35

STEVENS SLIDE-ACTION UTILITY-GRADE SHOTGUNS

Model 67	Model 77-AC	Model 520	Model 621
Model 67-VR	Model 77-M	Model 522	Model 820
Model 77	Model 77-SC	Model 620	

NIB	Exc.	V.G.	Good	Fair	Poor
—	225	150	125	100	75

Model 620 U.S. Marked Trench Gun

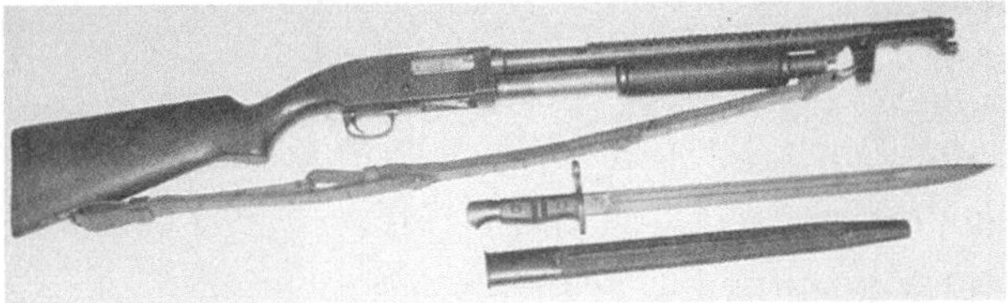

Courtesy Richard M. Kumor Sr.

NIB	Exc.	V.G.	Good	Fair	Poor
—	3000	2500	1650	1200	750

NOTE: Add $150 for bayonet.

Model 124

This is a manually-operated bolt action shotgun chambered for 12 gauge. It has a 28" barrel with various chokes, is blued, and has a brown plastic Tenite stock. Ann odd duck: it looks like a semi-auto and is often mistaken for such.

NIB	Exc.	V.G.	Good	Fair	Poor
—	225	175	75	65	50

Model 67

This is a slide-action shotgun chambered for 12 and 20 gauge, as well as .410. It has 3" chambers. It is offered with various length barrels and choke tubes with a 5-shot tube magazine. It features a steel receiver and is blued, with a walnut stock. It was discontinued in 1989.

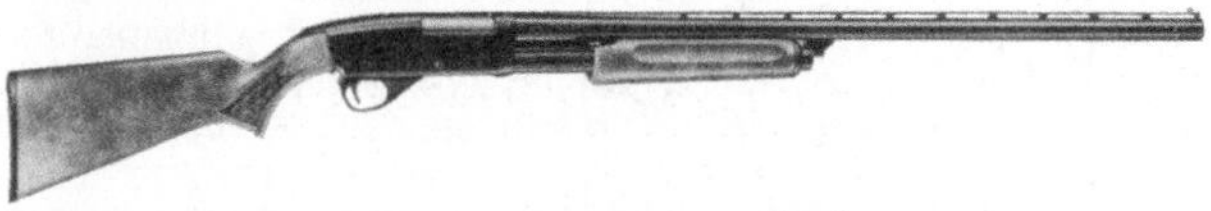

NIB	Exc.	V.G.	Good	Fair	Poor
—	250	175	150	100	75

Model 675

This is a slide-action shotgun chambered for 12 gauge with a 24" vent rib barrel with iron sights. The finish is blued, with a hardwood stock and recoil pad. It was manufactured in 1987 and 1988.

NIB	Exc.	V.G.	Good	Fair	Poor
—	275	240	200	150	100

Model 69-RXL

This is a matte-finished riot version of the Model 67 series slide-action shotgun. It has an 18.25" cylinder-bore barrel and is furnished with a recoil pad. It was discontinued in 1989.

NIB	Exc.	V.G.	Good	Fair	Poor
—	250	175	150	100	75

Stevens Model 350 Pump Shotgun

Pump-action shotgun chambered for 2.75- and 3-inch 12-ga. Features include all-steel barrel and receiver; bottom-load and -eject design; black synthetic stock; 5+1 capacity. Price: $267 (Field Model w/ 28-inch barrel, screw-in choke); $241 (Security Model w/ 18-inch barrel, fixed choke); $307 (Combo Model with Field and Security barrels); $254 (Security Model with 18.25-inch barrel w/ ghost ring rear sight).

STEYR

Steyr, Austria

RIFLES

NOTE: For earlier models see Mannlicher Schoenauer.

Steyr Mannlicher Model 1950

A .257 Roberts, .270 Winchester, or .30-06 caliber bolt-action sporting rifle with a 24" barrel and 5-shot rotary magazine. Blued with a checkered walnut stock having an ebony pistol grip cap and forend tip. Manufactured from 1950 to 1952.

NIB	Exc.	V.G.	Good	Fair	Poor
—	1800	1400	975	700	450

Model 1950 Carbine

As above, with a 20" barrel and Mannlicher-style stock. Fitted with a steel forend cap. Manufactured in 1950 to 1952.

NIB	Exc.	V.G.	Good	Fair	Poor
—	2000	1600	1100	750	400

Model 1952

Similar to the above, with a swept back bolt handle. Manufactured from 1952 to 1956.

NIB	Exc.	V.G.	Good	Fair	Poor
—	1650	1350	1000	750	600

Model 1952 Carbine

As above, with a 20" barrel and Mannlicher-style stock.

NIB	Exc.	V.G.	Good	Fair	Poor
—	2000	1600	1100	750	600

Model 1956 Rifle

Similar to the above, in various calibers from .243 and .30-06 caliber with a 22" barrel and high comb stock. Manufactured from 1956 to 1960.

NIB	Exc.	V.G.	Good	Fair	Poor
—	2000	1600	1100	800	650

Model 1956 Carbine

As above, with a 20" barrel and Mannlicher-style stock. Manufactured from 1956 to 1960.

NIB	Exc.	V.G.	Good	Fair	Poor
—	2000	1600	1100	800	650

Model 1961 MCA Rifle

As above, with a Monte Carlo-style stock.

NIB	Exc.	V.G.	Good	Fair	Poor
—	1750	1500	1100	850	700

Model 1961 MCA Carbine

As above, with a Mannlicher-style Monte Carlo stock.

NIB	Exc.	V.G.	Good	Fair	Poor
—	2000	1600	1100	700	600

NOTE: The following steyr/mannlicher guns were imported by GSI inc. Trussville, Alabama.

SPORTER SERIES

This series includes rifles that are lightweight and have a reduced overall length. All Sporter models have an interchangeable 5-round rotary magazine. The stock is oil-finished walnut in either the Mannlicher full stock design or the half stock version. In both stock configurations an oval European cheekpiece is standard. These rifles are offered in four different action lengths: SL (super light), L (light), M (medium), or S (magnum). They are also available with either single trigger or double set triggers.

Model M72 L/M

A .243, .270, 7x57mm, 7x64mm, .308 or .30-06 caliber bolt-action rifle with a 23" fluted barrel, and single or double set triggers. Blued, checkered walnut stock. Manufactured from 1972 to 1980.

NIB	Exc.	V.G.	Good	Fair	Poor
—	1325	1025	750	550	450

Model SL

This model features the super light action and is offered with 20" barrel in full stock version or 23-1/6" barrel in half stock version. A rubber buttpad is standard. This model does not have a forend tip on its half stock variation. Offered in the following calibers: .222 Rem., .222 Rem. Mag., .223, and 5.6x50 Mag. Weighs approximately 6.2 lbs. with full stock and 6.3 lbs. with half stock.

NIB	Exc.	V.G.	Good	Fair	Poor
2000	1650	1000	750	500	300

Model SL Carbine

As above, with a 20" fluted barrel and Mannlicher-style stock.

NIB	Exc.	V.G.	Good	Fair	Poor
1950	1750	1050	800	550	350

Varmint Model

This model features a heavy 26" barrel chambered for the .222 Rem., .223, 5.6x57, .243 Win., .308 Win., and .22-250. The forend of the stock is ventilated. The grip is enlarged and textured. Choice of single or double set triggers. Recoil pad is standard. Weighs about 8 lbs.

NIB	Exc.	V.G.	Good	Fair	Poor
1950	1750	1050	800	550	350

Model L

This rifle has the light action and is offered in the same stock configuration and barrel lengths as the Model SL. The calibers are: 5.6x57, .243 Win., .308, .22-250, and 6mm Rem. Weighs about 6.3 lbs. with full stock and 6.4 lbs. with half stock.

NIB	Exc.	V.G.	Good	Fair	Poor
1850	1650	1000	750	500	300

LUXUS SERIES

This luxury model offers a choice of full or half stock variations in select walnut with fine line checkering. The pistol grip is steeply angled. The Luxus rifles are fitted with a swept back European cheekpiece. A single set trigger is standard. The box magazine holds 3 rounds. Optional engraving and stock carving may be encountered on these modes that will dramatically affect price. The Luxus rifles are available with light, medium, or magnum length actions.

Luxus Model L

Same dimensions and barrel lengths as the Sporter version. The calibers are: 5.6x57, .243 Win., .308, .22-250, and 6mm Rem.

NIB	Exc.	V.G.	Good	Fair	Poor
2400	2000	1100	800	600	350

Luxus Model M

Same dimensions and barrel lengths as the Sporter Model M. Available in these calibers: 6.5x57, .270 Win., 7x64, .30-06, 9.3x 626.5x55, 7.5 Swiss, 7x57, and 8x57JS.

NIB	Exc.	V.G.	Good	Fair	Poor
2400	2000	1100	800	600	350

Luxus Model S

Same as the Sporter Model S. Offered in the following calibers: 6.5x68, 7mm Rem. Mag., .300 Win. Mag., and 8x68S.

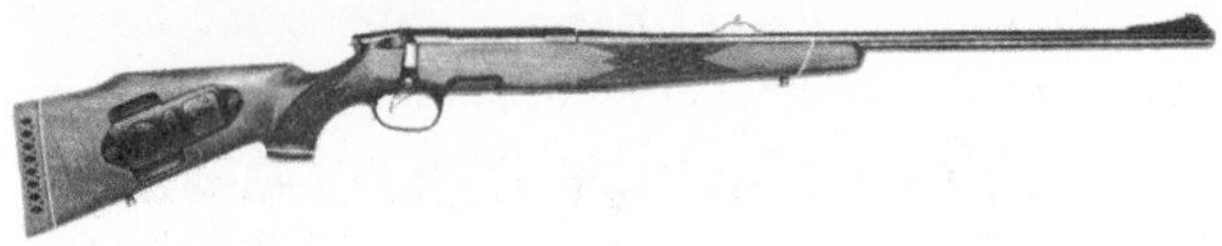

NIB	Exc.	V.G.	Good	Fair	Poor
2400	2000	1100	800	600	350

Professional Model M

This model is fitted with a medium weight action and features a black synthetic checkered stock. Comes fitted with a ventilated rubber recoil pad. Offered with 20" or 23.6" barrel it is available with single or double set trigger. Available in these calibers: 6.5x57, .270 Win., 7x64, .30-06, 9.3x62, 6.5x55, 7.5 Swiss, 7x57, and 8x57JS. Weighs approximately 7.25 lbs.

NIB	Exc.	V.G.	Good	Fair	Poor
1500	1200	950	700	600	300

Model S

This rifle is offered with half stock only and is fitted with a 26" barrel. The action is magnum length and is offered in these calibers: 6.5x68, 7mm Rem. Mag., .300 Win. Mag., and 8x68S. Rifle weighs about 8.4 lbs.

NIB	Exc.	V.G.	Good	Fair	Poor
1950	1750	1150	900	700	300

Model S/T

Similar to the model above but in a heavy barreled version. Offered in these calibers: 9.3x64, .375 H&H, and .458 Win. Mag. An optional buttstock magazine is available. Weighs about 9 lbs.

NIB	Exc.	V.G.	Good	Fair	Poor
2100	1900	1400	1100	800	500

Tropical Rifle

As above, with a 26" heavy barrel chambered for .375 Holland & Holland and .458 Winchester Magnum. Not imported after 1985.

NIB	Exc.	V.G.	Good	Fair	Poor
—	2000	1750	1100	650	450

Model MIII Professional

Introduced in 1995 this is an economy version of the Model M Professional. It is fitted with a 23.5" barrel, black synthetic stock, and choice of single or double set triggers. Offered in .25-06, .270 Win., .30-06, and 7x64 calibers. Weight is approximately 7 lb. 5 oz.

NIB	Exc.	V.G.	Good	Fair	Poor
1000	800	600	400	300	200

NOTE: With checkered walnut stock add $100.

STEYR SBS (SAFE BOLT SYSTEM)

This series was introduced in 1997 and features a newly designed bolt. It is offered in two distinct models the SBS Forester and the SBS ProHunter.

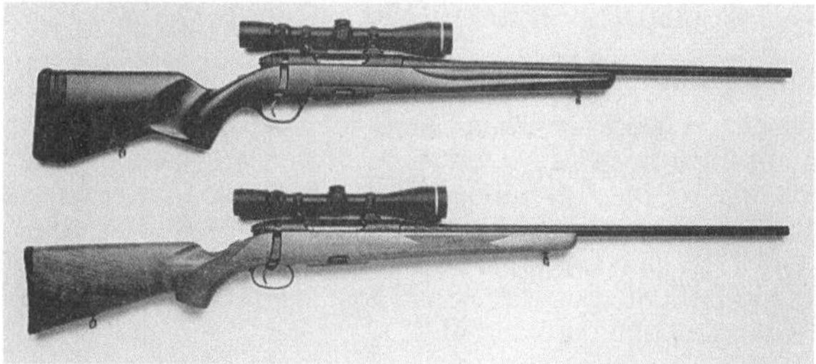

SBS ProHunter

This model has a 23.6" barrel with 4-round magazine and single adjustable trigger. Offered in .243 Win., .25-06, .270 Win., 7mm-08, .308 Win., .30-06, 7mm Rem. Mag., .300 Win. Mag., and several European calibers. Weight is approximately 7.5 lbs. This model is furnished with a black synthetic stock with recoil pad and buttspacers. Introduced in 1999.

NIB	*Exc.*	*V.G.*	*Good*	*Fair*	*Poor*
750	650	575	400	300	150

NOTE: Add $150-$300 for custom metric calibers. Add approximately $30 for 7mm Mag and .300 Win. Mag calibers.

SBS ProHunter Stainless Steel

Same as the ProHunter model but with stainless steel action and barrel. Introduced in 2000.

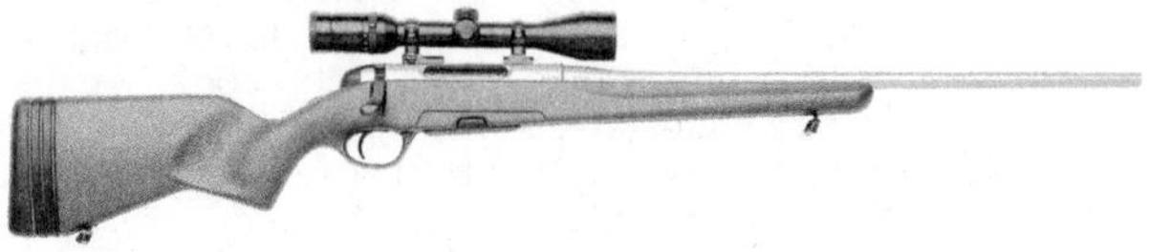

NIB	*Exc.*	*V.G.*	*Good*	*Fair*	*Poor*
900	750	675	500	400	250

NOTE: Add $150-$300 for custom metric calibers. Add approximately $30 for 7mm mag and .300 Win. Mag calibers.

SBS ProHunter Camo

Same as standard ProHunter but with camo synthetic stock.

NIB	*Exc.*	*V.G.*	*Good*	*Fair*	*Poor*
1000	850	700	575	400	200

NOTE: Add $150-$300 for custom metric calibers. Add approximately $30 for 7mm mag and .300 Win. Mag calibers.

SBS ProHunter Camo Stainless Steel

With stainless steel action and barrel.

NIB	*Exc.*	*V.G.*	*Good*	*Fair*	*Poor*
1050	900	750	600	475	250

NOTE: Add $150-$300 for custom metric calibers. Add approximately $30 for 7mm mag and .300 Win. Mag calibers.

SBS ProHunter Mountain Rifle

Chambered for .243, .25-06, .270, and 7mm-08 calibers, this model is fitted with a 20" barrel with no sights. Receiver engraved "Mountain Rifle." Synthetic stock with recoil pad standard. Weight is 7.25 lbs. Introduced in 1999.

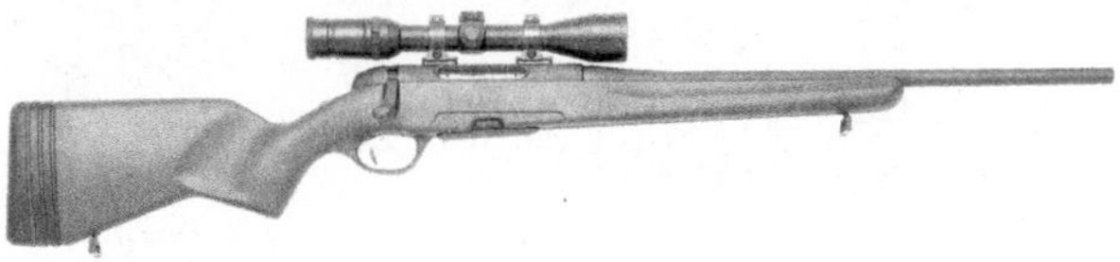

NIB	*Exc.*	*V.G.*	*Good*	*Fair*	*Poor*
1000	850	700	575	400	200

SBS ProHunter Mountain Stainless Steel

Same as the ProHunter Mountain but with stainless steel action and barrel. Introduced in 2000.

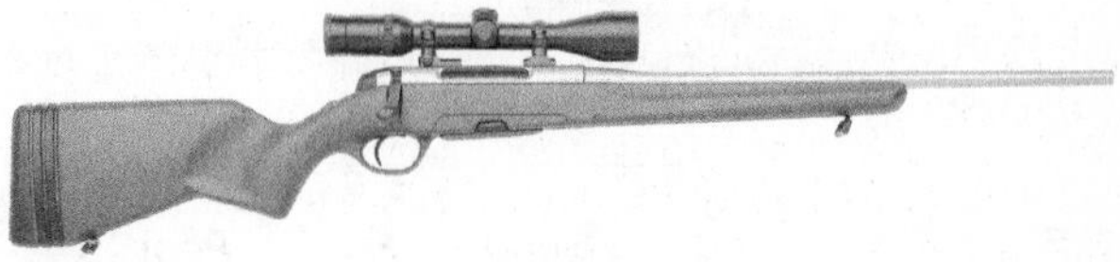

NIB	*Exc.*	*V.G.*	*Good*	*Fair*	*Poor*
1050	900	750	600	425	200

SBS ProHunter Mountain Camo

Same as the ProHunter but with camo synthetic stock. Introduced in 2000.

NIB	*Exc.*	*V.G.*	*Good*	*Fair*	*Poor*
1150	1000	850	700	475	250

SBS ProHunter Mountain Camo Stainless Steel

Same as above but with stainless steel action and barrel. Introduced in 2000.

NIB	*Exc.*	*V.G.*	*Good*	*Fair*	*Poor*
1150	1000	850	700	475	250

SBS ProHunter (Youth/Ladies)

This model is fitted with a walnut stock with buttspacers (to create a shorter length of pull) and extra thick recoil pad. Chambered for .243, 7mm-08, and .308. Weight is about 7.25 lbs. Introduced in 1999.

NIB	*Exc.*	*V.G.*	*Good*	*Fair*	*Poor*
1000	850	700	575	400	200

SBS ProHunter Compact

Same as above but with black synthetic stock. Also offered with stainless steel action and barrel.

NIB	*Exc.*	*V.G.*	*Good*	*Fair*	*Poor*
1000	850	700	575	400	200

NOTE: Add $80 for stainless steel model.

SBS ProHunter 376 Steyr

This model is chambered for the .376 Steyr cartridge. Fitted with a 20" barrel with iron sights. Synthetic stock with special thick pad. Weight is about 8 lbs. Introduced in 1999.

NIB	Exc.	V.G.	Good	Fair	Poor
1200	950	800	675	400	200

SBS Forester

Same as Pro Hunter model but furnished with a walnut stock with recoil pad.

NIB	Exc.	V.G.	Good	Fair	Poor
850	725	625	500	400	200

NOTE: Add $150-$300 for custom metric calibers. Add $30 for 7mm Rem. Mag and .300 Win. Mag.

SBS Classic American

This model features a 23.6" barrel with a single adjustable trigger and stain finish walnut stock with recoil pad. Offered in calibers from .243 to .300 Win. Mag. Weight is about 7.2 lbs. Introduced in 2000.

NIB	Exc.	V.G.	Good	Fair	Poor
1500	1100	850	650	500	300

NOTE: Add $150-$300 for custom metric calibers. Add approximately $30 for 7mm Mag and .300 Win. Mag calibers.

SBS Classic Mannlicher

Offered in the same calibers as above except for 7mm Rem. Mag and .300 Win. Mag. and fitted with a 25.6" barrel. The walnut stock is the full Mannlicher style with recoil pad. Fitted with open sights. Weight is about 7.2 lbs. Introduced in 2000.

NIB	Exc.	V.G.	Good	Fair	Poor
2300	2000	1600	1000	675	400

SBS Forester Mountain Rifle

Walnut stock with 20" barrel and no sights. Chambered for a variety of calibers including .243, .25-06, .270, 7mm-08, .308, .30-06 and 6.5x55. Receiver engraved "Mountain Rifle." Introduced in 1999.

NIB	Exc.	V.G.	Good	Fair	Poor
850	725	625	500	400	200

Mannlicher SBS European—Half Stock

Fitted with a 23.6" barrel with iron sights and chambered for a wide variety of American and European calibers from .243 to 9.3x62. European style figured walnut stock. Adjustable trigger. Recoil pad. Weight is about 7.5 lbs.

NIB	Exc.	V.G.	Good	Fair	Poor
2795	2200	1750	1200	700	400

Mannlicher SBS European—Half Stock Carbine

Same as model above but with 20" barrel.

NIB	Exc.	V.G.	Good	Fair	Poor
2795	2200	1750	1200	700	400

Mannlicher SBS European—Full Stock

Same as above but with full European stock covering a 20" barrel.

NIB	Exc.	V.G.	Good	Fair	Poor
2895	2300	1800	1250	750	450

Mannlicher SBS Magnum European—Half Stock

This model is chambered for the 7mm Rem. Mag., .300 Win. Mag., and the 6.5x68 and 8x68S calibers. Fitted with a 25.6" barrel with iron sights. Walnut stock. Weight is about 7.75 lbs.

NIB	Exc.	V.G.	Good	Fair	Poor
2895	2300	1800	1250	750	450

Steyr Scout—Jeff Cooper Package

Developed by Col. Jeff Cooper this model is chambered for the .308 Win. cartridge. It is fitted with a 19" fluted barrel. Stock is gray synthetic with removable buttspacers and folding bi-pod. Magazine capacity is 5 rounds with optional 10-round magazines available. Weight is approximately 7 lbs. with scope. Weight is 6.3 lbs. with no scope. Adjustable single trigger. Factory-installed Leupold M8 2.5x28mm scope. Introduced in 1998.

NIB	Exc.	V.G.	Good	Fair	Poor
2600	2000	1600	1100	650	400

Steyr Scout Package

Similar to the Jeff Cooper Package but without the Jeff Cooper logo. Stock is black synthetic. Also offered in .223 Rem., .243 Win., 7mm-08 as well as .308 and .375 Steyr calibers.

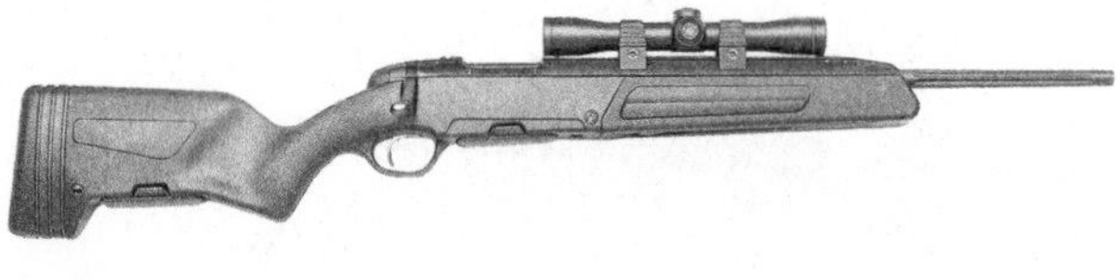

NIB	Exc.	V.G.	Good	Fair	Poor
2100	1800	1550	1000	700	400

Steyr Scout

Same as above but rifle only.

NIB	Exc.	V.G.	Good	Fair	Poor
2100	1800	1550	1000	700	400

Steyr Scout Tactical

This model has a 19.25" fluted barrel and is chambered for the .223 or .308 Win. cartridge. Integral bipod. Emergency Ghost Ring sights.

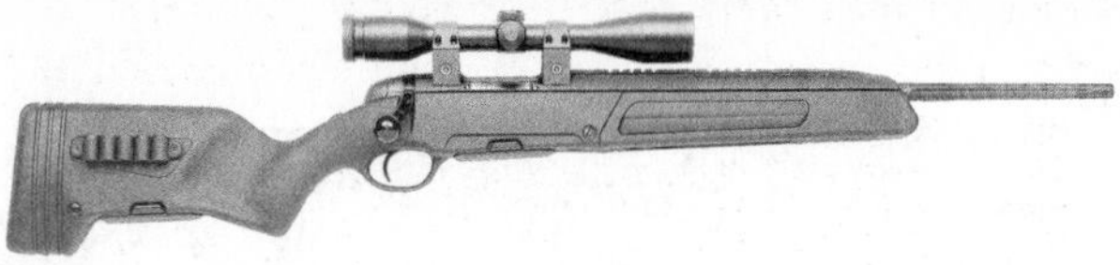

NIB	Exc.	V.G.	Good	Fair	Poor
2050	1500	1000	800	750	425

NOTE: Add $100 for stainless steel model.

PRECISION/TACTICAL RIFLES

Model SSG-PI

This model features a black synthetic stock originally designed as a military sniper rifle. Fitted with a cocking indicator, single or double set trigger, 5-round rotary magazine, or 10-round magazine. Receiver is milled to NATO specifications for Steyr ring mounts. Barrel length is 26". Rifle weighs about 9 lbs. Offered in .308 Win. **NOTE:** This model was originally called the SSG 69.

NIB	Exc.	V.G.	Good	Fair	Poor
1700	1300	1000	800	600	400

SSG-PII Police Rifle

This version of the SSG has a heavier 26" barrel and a larger knob-style bolt handle. Weighs about 10 lbs. 11 oz.

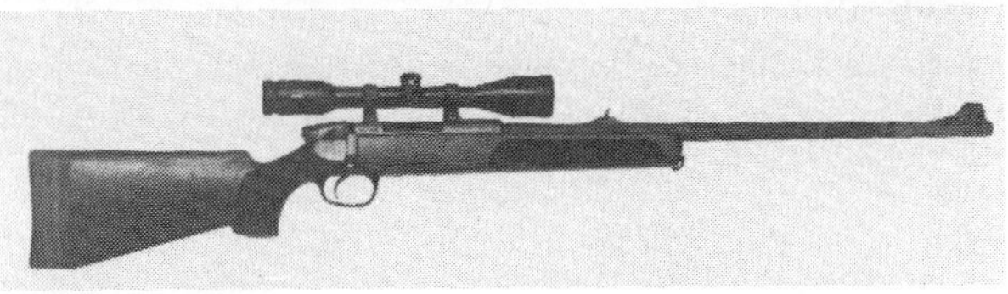

NIB	Exc.	V.G.	Good	Fair	Poor
1700	1300	1000	800	600	400

SSK-PIIK Police Kurz

Similar to the above model but with a 20" heavy barrel. Weight is about 10 lbs.

NIB	Exc.	V.G.	Good	Fair	Poor
1700	1300	1000	800	600	400

SSG-PII & PIIK McMillan

Fitted with a McMillan A-3 stock with adjustable cheekpiece and removable buttspacers. Special forearm rail.

NIB	Exc.	V.G.	Good	Fair	Poor
2300	1750	1350	950	750	500

SSG-PIV

Again similar to the above PIIK but with a 16.75" heavy barrel with a removable flash hider. Barrel is threaded. Weight is about 9 lbs. 11 oz.

NIB	Exc.	V.G.	Good	Fair	Poor
2500	2000	1500	1000	750	500

SSG-PIV Match

NIB	Exc.	V.G.	Good	Fair	Poor
3000	2500	2000	1500	800	500

Match UIT

Designed as an international target rifle this model features special shaped pistol grip, an adjustable trigger for length of pull and pressure. Enlarged bolt handle and nonglare barrel. Chambered for .308 Win. cartridge.

NIB	Exc.	V.G.	Good	Fair	Poor
3900	3500	3000	2000	1500	1000

JAGD Match

Introduced in 1995 this model features a choice of 23.5" or 20" barrel with sights. The stock is laminated. A full stock version is offered on 20" barrel models and a half stock is offered on the 23.5" barrel models. Available in a variety of configurations with calibers from .222 Rem. to .458 Win. Mag.

NIB	Exc.	V.G.	Good	Fair	Poor
1750	1250	900	500	350	200

SBS TACTICAL SERIES

SBS Tactical

Fitted with a black synthetic stock and 20" barrel with no sights. This model is chambered for the .308 cartridge. Removable buttspacers. Black bolt body. Receiver engraved "SBS Tactical." Introduced in 1999. Weight is about 7.25 lbs.

NIB	Exc.	V.G.	Good	Fair	Poor
1150	950	700	550	300	200

NOTE: Add $100 for stainless steel model (introduced 2000).

SBS Tactical Heavy Barrel

This model also has a black synthetic stock but is fitted with a 26" heavy barrel and no sights. Black bolt body. Receiver engraved "SBS Tactical HB." Weight is about 8 lbs. Introduced in 1999. Also offered with 20" barrel called "HBC." Both barrel lengths chambered for .308 cartridge.

NIB	Exc.	V.G.	Good	Fair	Poor
1250	1050	800	650	300	200

SBS Tactical Heavy Barrel Carbine

This model features a 20" heavy barrel, no sights, matte blue finish. Chambered for .308 caliber. Introduced in 2000.

NIB	Exc.	V.G.	Good	Fair	Poor
1150	950	700	550	300	200

SBS Tactical McMillan

This model is fitted with a 26" barrel chambered for the .308 cartridge and has a McMillan A-3 stock. Oversize bolt handle. Weight is about 9.8 lbs. Introduced in 1999.

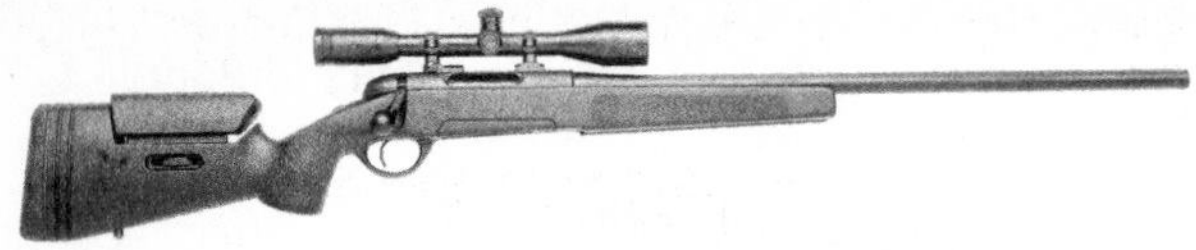

NIB	Exc.	V.G.	Good	Fair	Poor
1600	1250	950	750	60	400

SBS CISM Rifle

This model is chambered for the .308 cartridge and fitted with a 19.7" heavy barrel. The stock is laminated wood with black lacquer finish. The stock has a forearm rail with handstop, adjustable buttplate, and cheekpiece. The trigger is adjustable. Weight is approximately 10.25 lbs. Introduced in 1999.

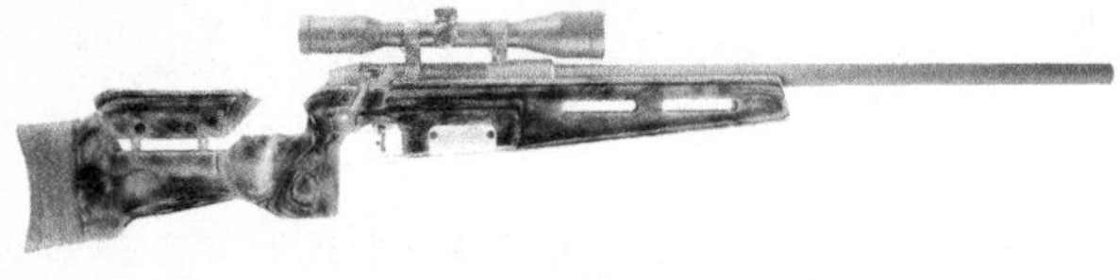

NIB	Exc.	V.G.	Good	Fair	Poor
3295	2500	1950	1600	1200	700

SBS Tactical Elite Heavy Barrel

This model, introduced in 2000, features a 26" heavy barrel, no sights, matte blue finish, Zytel stock with adjustable cheekpiece and adjustable buttplate. Full length Picatinny mounting rail. Magazine capacity is 5 or 10 rounds. Chambered for .308 cartridge.

NIB	Exc.	V.G.	Good	Fair	Poor
2400	1750	1400	1000	700	400

NOTE: Add $100 for stainless steel model. Add $1,000 for ZF optics.

SBS Tactical Elite Heavy Barrel Carbine

Same as the Tactical Elite Heavy Barrel model but fitted with a 20" heavy barrel. Introduced in 2000.

NIB	Exc.	V.G.	Good	Fair	Poor
2400	1750	—	—	—	—

Steyr AUG

A 5.56mm semi-automatic, Bullpup rifle with a 20" barrel incorporating a Swarovski 1.5x telescopic sight. Green carbon composite stock. Weight is about 8.5 lbs. Recommend independent, local appraisals.

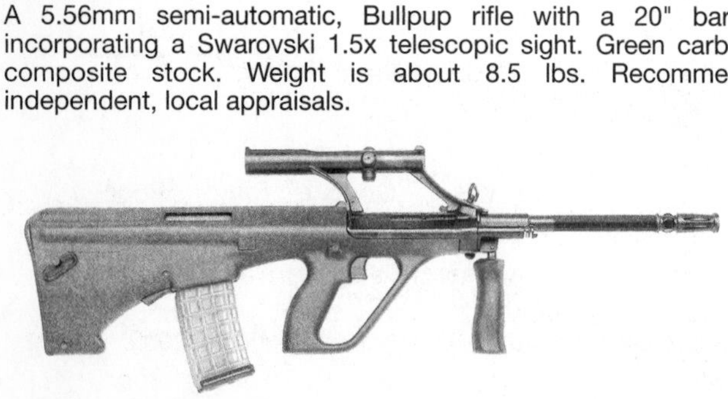

NIB	Exc.	V.G.	Good	Fair	Poor
3700	3100	2500	1600	1300	650

Steyr AUG—Police Model

Same as above but with black stock and 16" barrel.

NIB	Exc.	V.G.	Good	Fair	Poor
3700	3100	2500	1600	1300	650

Steyr AUG Special Receiver

Receiver only. Special flattop with Stanag mounting.

NIB	Exc.	V.G.	Good	Fair	Poor
3700	3100	2500	1600	1300	650

Steyr USR

This model is the post-ban version of the AUG. Fitted with a Swarovski 1.5x scope and gray synthetic stock.

NIB	Exc.	V.G.	Good	Fair	Poor
3700	3100	2500	1600	1300	650

Steyr Zephyr

This model is a .22 caliber rimfire bolt-action carbine. It has a 5-round detachable magazine, dovetailed receiver for scope rings. It is fitted with a full stock. Made from 1953 to 1968.

NIB	Exc.	V.G.	Good	Fair	Poor
—	1800	1475	1150	800	400

STI INTERNATIONAL

Georgetown, Texas

FPI 2260 Rifle

Chambered for the .22 Long Rifle cartridge. Aluminum receiver with adjustable trigger and quick magazine release. Integral scope mount.

NIB	Exc.	V.G.	Good	Fair	Poor
1000	850	675	500	300	150

Sporting Competition Rifle

AR-style semi-auto rifle chambered in 5.56 NATO. Features include 16-inch 410 stainless 1:8 barrel; mid-length gas system; Nordic Tactical Compensator and JP Trigger group; custom STI Valkyrie hand guard and gas block; flat-top design with Picatinny rail; anodized finish with black Teflon coating. Also available in Tactical configuration.

NIB	Exc.	V.G.	Good	Fair	Poor
1175	1000	825	650	350	250

STOEGER, A. F.

South Hackensack, New Jersey

SHOTGUNS

Model 2000

This is a semi-automatic shotgun chambered for the 12 gauge shell. Fitted with 26", 28", or 30" vent rib barrel. Single trigger with screw-in chokes. Weight is about 7 lbs. Introduced in 2001.

NIB	Exc.	V.G.	Good	Fair	Poor
500	400	300	200	150	75

Model 2000 Deluxe

Same as above but with high grade walnut stock and etched receiver with gold trigger.

NIB	Exc.	V.G.	Good	Fair	Poor
625	500	400	300	250	125

Model 2000 Camo

As above but with Advantage Timber HD camo stock.

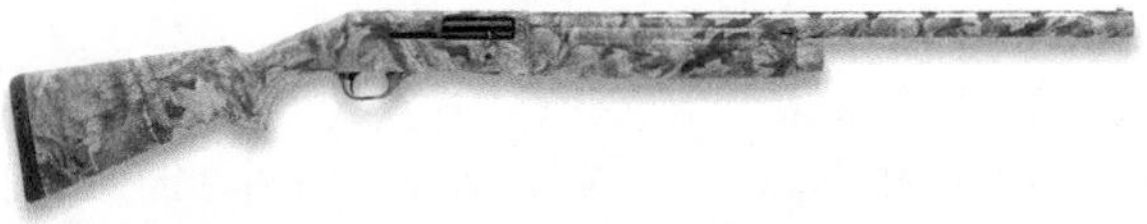

NIB	Exc.	V.G.	Good	Fair	Poor
500	400	300	200	150	75

Model 2000 Slug

This model is chambered for the 12 gauge shell with 3" chamber. Barrel length is 24". The gun is fitted with a black synthetic stock. Smooth bore barrel. Adjustable rifle-type sights. Optional field-style barrels in 24", 26", or 28". Weight is approximately 6.7 lbs. Introduced in 2003.

NIB	Exc.	V.G.	Good	Fair	Poor
450	350	250	175	125	50

Model 2000 Synthetic

As above but choice of 24", 26", or 28" vent rib barrel and black synthetic stock. Weight is about 6.8 lbs. Introduced in 2003.

NIB	Exc.	V.G.	Good	Fair	Poor
500	400	300	200	150	75

Model 3500

This 12-gauge auto-loader comes with either a 24-, 26- or 28-inch barrel fitted with a ventilated, stepped rib and fiber-optic front sight. Inertia operation. Weight is 7.5 lbs. The alloy receiver is drilled and tapped and includes a Weaver-style scope base. All M3500s come supplied with five choke tubes (Extra-full turkey, Full, Modified, Improved Cylinder and Cylinder). A shim kit provides drop and cast adjustment. A threaded steel recoil reducer (included) can be installed in the buttstock to help manage felt recoil from heavy Magnum loads. Available in three different finishes: matte black synthetic, Realtree APG or Realtree Max-4.

NIB	Exc.	V.G.	Good	Fair	Poor
535	450	385	325	250	200

NOTE: Add 20 percent for total camo coverage.

Coach Gun

This is a side-by-side gun chambered for the 12 or 20 gauge shell as well as the .410 shell. Fitted with 20" barrels with double triggers. Improved Cylinder and Modified fixed chokes. Weight is about 7 lbs.

NIB	Exc.	V.G.	Good	Fair	Poor
400	275	225	175	125	75

NOTE: Add $50 for nickel finish.

Silverado Coach Gun

Offered in 12 and 20 gauge as well as .410 bore with straight- or pistol-grip stock and matte nickel finish. Straight-stock version is offered in 12 and 20 gauge only. Weight is about 6.5 lbs.

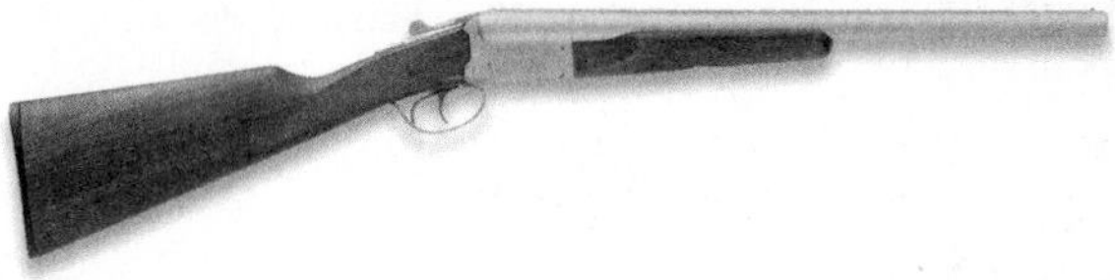

NIB	Exc.	V.G.	Good	Fair	Poor
450	320	250	175	125	75

Coach Gun Supreme

This model is similar to the above but offered with blue, stainless, or nickel receiver. Introduced in 2004.

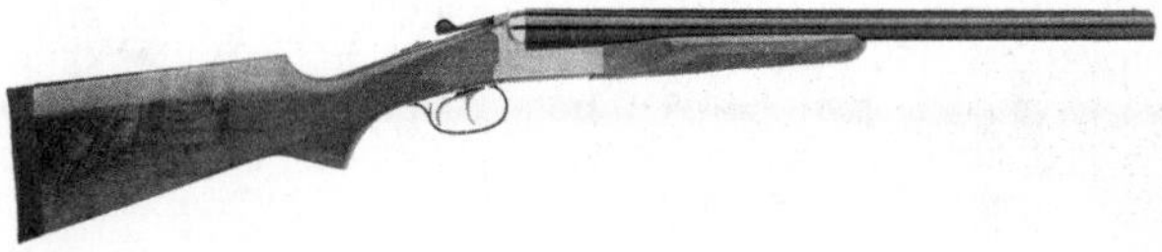

NIB	Exc.	V.G.	Good	Fair	Poor
450	320	250	175	125	75

NOTE: Add $10 for stainless and $30 for nickel.

Uplander

This side-by-side shotgun is chambered for the 12, 16, 20, 28, and .410 bores. with choice of 26" or 28" barrels. Fixed chokes. Double triggers. Weight is about 7.25 lbs.

NIB	Exc.	V.G.	Good	Fair	Poor
375	275	175	125	100	75

Uplander Special

As above but with straight grip and oil finish stock. Offered in 12, 20, or 28 gauge. Weight is about 7.3 lbs.

NIB	Exc.	V.G.	Good	Fair	Poor
395	300	200	150	100	75

Uplander Supreme

Same as above but with select wood and screw-in chokes.

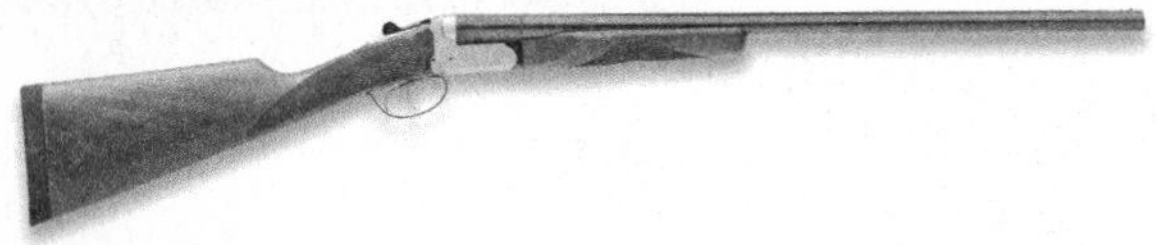

NIB	Exc.	V.G.	Good	Fair	Poor
425	350	250	175	125	100

Uplander English

This variation is fitted with a straight-grip stock and chambered for the 20 gauge or .410 bore. Fitted with 24" barrels. Weight is about 7 lbs. Also available with a short stock.

NIB	Exc.	V.G.	Good	Fair	Poor
395	300	200	150	100	75

Uplander Youth

Offered in 20 gauge or .410 bore this model features a 13" LOP with 22" barrels choked Improved Modified and Modified. Weight is about 6.75 lbs.

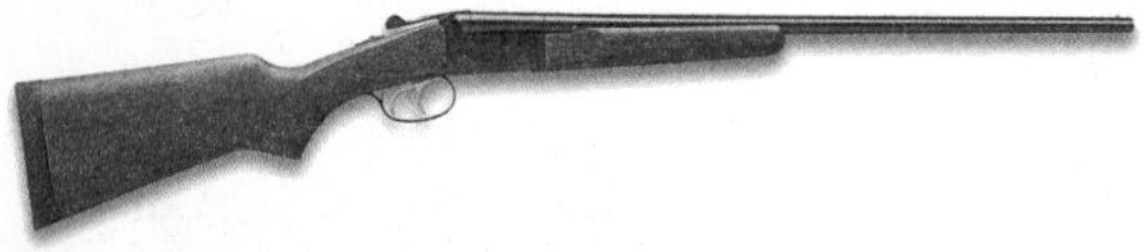

NIB	Exc.	V.G.	Good	Fair	Poor
375	275	175	125	100	75

Condor

This over-and-under shotgun is chambered 12, 16 and 20 gauges and .410 bore. Available with 26" and 28" barrels in all gauges and 26" barrel in .410 bore. Single trigger. Blued finish. The 16-gauge is chambered for 2.75" shells. All others have 3" chambers. Weights run from 6 lbs. to 7.4 lbs. depending on bore.

NIB	Exc.	V.G.	Good	Fair	Poor
375	275	175	125	100	75

Condor Special

Similar to the standard Condor model but with matte stainless receiver and rubbed oil finish stock. Introduced in 2003.

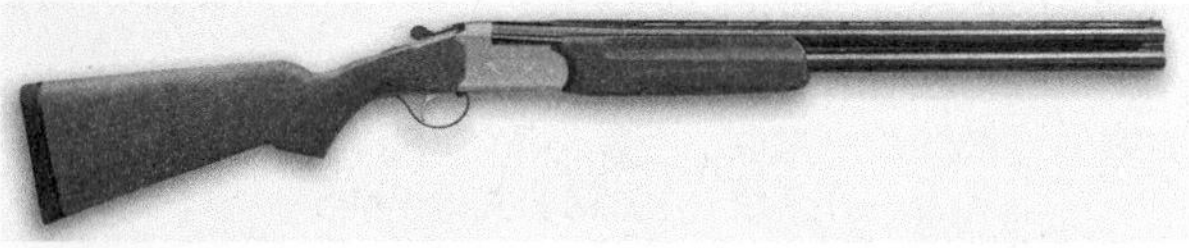

NIB	Exc.	V.G.	Good	Fair	Poor
475	375	295	200	125	100

CONDOR COMBO

This model, introduced in 2004, features a two-barrel set of 12 and 20 gauge. Barrel length on the 12 gauge is 28" and 26" on the 20 gauge. Choke tubes. Offered in 3 grades: Field, Special, and Supreme. Introduced in 2004.

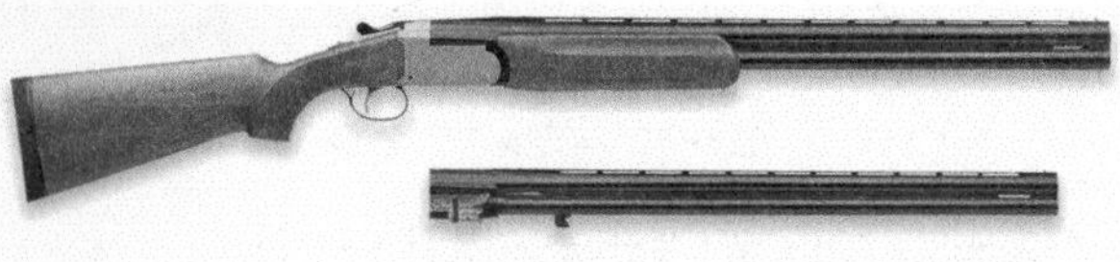

Field

NIB	Exc.	V.G.	Good	Fair	Poor
500	400	300	200	100	75

Special

NIB	Exc.	V.G.	Good	Fair	Poor
650	500	400	275	175	125

Supreme

NIB	Exc.	V.G.	Good	Fair	Poor
775	650	500	300	200	150

Condor Supreme Deluxe

Similar to the above model but with cut checkering and high polish blue. Offered in 12 and 20 gauge with 26" or 28" barrels as well as 24" barrels for the 20 gauge. Automatic ejectors.

NIB	Exc.	V.G.	Good	Fair	Poor
500	400	300	200	100	75

Condor Competition

These 3" 12 and 20 gauge over-and-unders feature 30" barrels, AA Grade wood and adjustable combs. Three choke tubes. Weight is about 7.3 lbs. in 20 gauge and 7.8 lbs. in 12 gauge.

NIB	Exc.	V.G.	Good	Fair	Poor
650	500	400	275	175	125

Condor Competition Combo

As above with 12 gauge and 20 gauge barrels.

NIB	Exc.	V.G.	Good	Fair	Poor
775	650	500	300	200	150

Condor Outback

New in 2007, the Outback comes in 12 and 20 gauge chambered for 3" shells. The finish is either A Grade satin walnut stock with blued barrels and receiver or matte black walnut stock with polished barrels and receiver. Barrels are 20" with rifle sights. Includes two choke tubes. Add $40 for black/nickel finish.

NIB	Exc.	V.G.	Good	Fair	Poor
375	275	175	125	100	75

Single Barrel Classic Youth

Available in 20 gauge or .410 bore with a 13" length of pull and 22" vent rib barrel. Straight-grip stock. Weight is about 5 lbs.

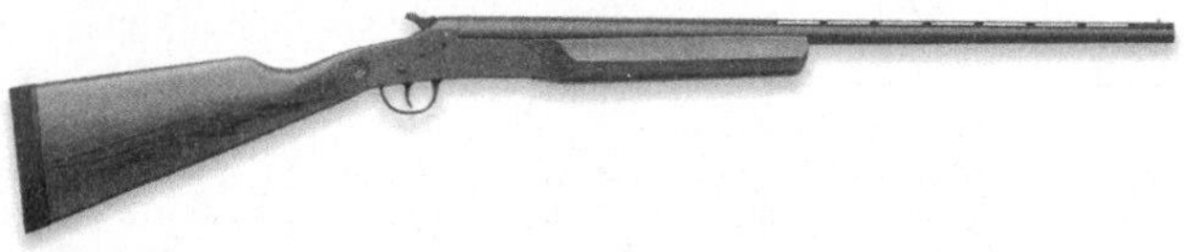

NIB	Exc.	V.G.	Good	Fair	Poor
125	100	75	50	25	10

Single Barrel Classic

As above but with standard length of pull and available in 12, 20 or .410 bore. Barrel length on 12 gauge is 26" or 28"; on 20 gauge length is 26". On .410 bore barrel length is 24". Open pistol grip. Weight is about 5.5 lbs.

NIB	Exc.	V.G.	Good	Fair	Poor
125	100	75	50	25	10

Single Barrel Special

As above but with stainless steel frame. Offered in 12, 20, or .410 bore. Weight is about 5.5 lbs.

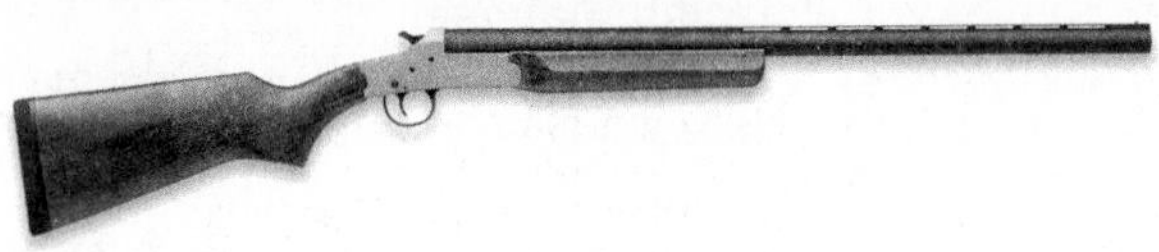

NIB	Exc.	V.G.	Good	Fair	Poor
125	100	75	50	25	10

P-350

This pump-action 12 gauge shotgun was introduced in 2005. All versions are chambered for 3.5" shells. Available with 24", 26" or 28" barrel in matte black synthetic or Advantage Timber camo finish; available with 26" or 28" barrel in Max-4 camo finish. Comes with 5 choke tubes. Weight is about 6.8 lbs. Also available is a Defense model with 18.5" barrel and fixed cylinder bore. Add 15 percent for camo models.

NIB	Exc.	V.G.	Good	Fair	Poor
275	225	175	125	100	50

P-350 Camo

This pump-action 12 gauge is chambered for 3.5" shells. It has a 24", 26" or 28" barrel and a matte black, Max-4, Timber or APG finish. There are also some pistol-grip stock offerings with 24" barrels. Includes five choke tubes. Weight is about 6.8 lbs. Add $20 for pistol-grip stock. Add $75 for camo finish.

NIB	Exc.	V.G.	Good	Fair	Poor
350	275	225	150	125	75

P-350 Defense

Same as above in a matte black finish with 18.5", fixed cylinder choke barrel. Add $20 for pistol-grip stock.

NIB	Exc.	V.G.	Good	Fair	Poor
300	225	175	125	100	50

STREET SWEEPER

Atlanta, Georgia

Street Sweeper

A 12 gauge semi-automatic double-action shotgun with an 18" barrel and 12-shot rotary, drum magazine. Matte black finish. Introduced in 1989. **NOTE:** This firearm is now on the restricted list as a Class III weapon and is subject to NFA rules. This model requires registration with the BATF to avoid federal penalties. Make sure that the shotgun is transferable prior to sale.

NIB	Exc.	V.G.	Good	Fair	Poor
2195	—	—	—	—	—

STURM, RUGER & CO.

Southport, Connecticut

SEMI-AUTOMATIC RIFLES

10/22 Standard Carbine With Walnut Stock

This model has an 18.5" barrel and is chambered for the .22 LR. It has a 10-shot, detachable rotary magazine and a folding rear sight. The stock is smooth walnut, with a barrel band and carbine-style buttplate. This rifle enjoys a fine reputation for accuracy and dependability and is considered an excellent value. It was introduced in 1964.

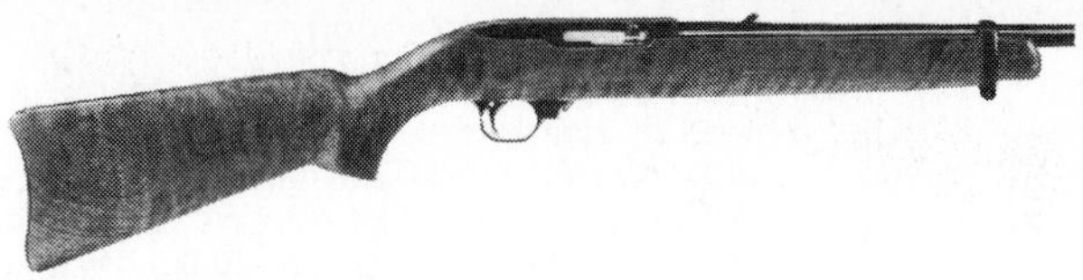

NIB	Exc.	V.G.	Good	Fair	Poor
275	225	125	100	75	50

NOTE: Birch stock deduct $20.

10/22 Standard Carbine Stainless Steel

Same as above but with stainless steel barrel and receiver.

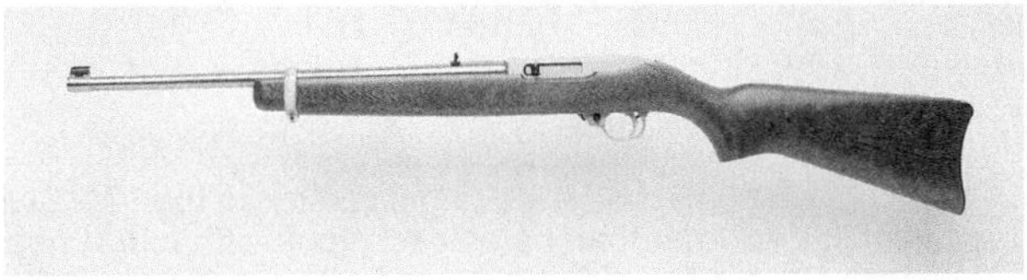

NIB	Exc.	V.G.	Good	Fair	Poor
300	250	150	125	100	75

10/22 Magnum

Introduced in 1999, this model is chambered for the .22 Magnum cartridge. Barrel length is 18.5". Folding rear sight and gold bead front sight. Hardwood stock. Weight is about 5.5 lbs. Discontinued.

NIB	Exc.	V.G.	Good	Fair	Poor
635	500	300	200	150	100

10/22 Sporter (Finger Groove Old Model)

This model is similar to the Standard Carbine except that it has a Monte Carlo stock, finger-groove forend, and no barrel band. It was manufactured between 1966 and 1971.

NIB	Exc.	V.G.	Good	Fair	Poor
—	500	400	300	175	125

NOTE: Factory hand checkering add 300 percent.

10/22 Deluxe Sporter

The same as the Sporter with a checkered stock and better buttplate. Introduced in 1971.

NIB	Exc.	V.G.	Good	Fair	Poor
325	250	150	125	100	75

10/22 International Carbine

This model is similar to the Standard Carbine, with a full-length, Mannlicher-style stock. It was manufactured between 1966 and 1971 and is fairly rare on today's market.

NIB	Exc.	V.G.	Good	Fair	Poor
—	1100	625	450	300	250

NOTE: Factory hand checkering add 50 percent.

10/22 International Carbine (New Model)

This 1994 model is a reintroduction of the older version. It is offered in either a blued or stainless steel finish. Barrel length is 18-1/2". Magazine capacity is 10 rounds. The hardwood stock had no checkering when this model was first introduced. Shortly after introduced the factory began checkering these stocks. Weight is about 5.2 lbs. Discontinued.

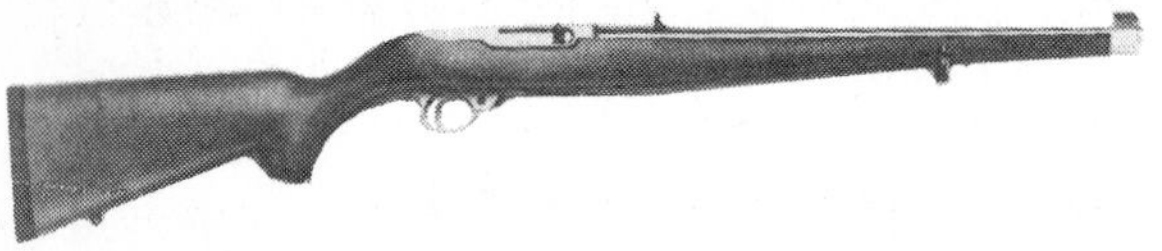

NIB	*Exc.*	*V.G.*	*Good*	*Fair*	*Poor*
465	300	225	—	—	—

Model 10/22T

Introduced in 1996 this model is a target version of the 10/22 line. It has a laminated American hardwood stock with blued heavy barrel with hammer-forged spiral finish. Rifle comes standard without sights. Barrel length is 20". Weight is approximately 7.25 lbs.

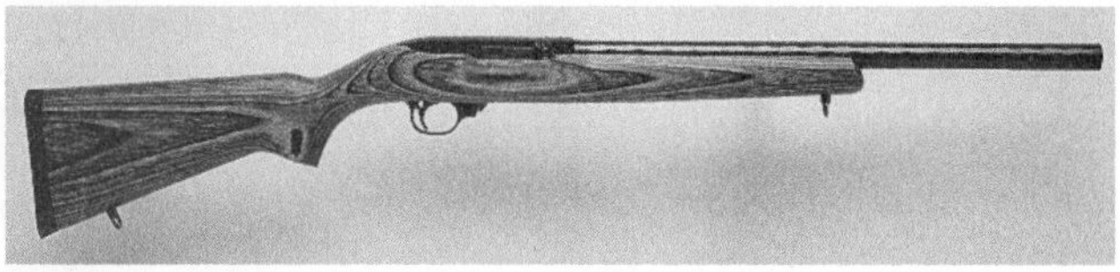

NIB	*Exc.*	*V.G.*	*Good*	*Fair*	*Poor*
450	350	275	200	150	100

Model 10/22TNZ

This target model features a 20" stainless steel barrel and receiver with laminated thumbhole stock. No sights. Weight is about 7 lbs. Introduced in 2001.

NIB	*Exc.*	*V.G.*	*Good*	*Fair*	*Poor*
500	375	275	200	150	100

MODEL 10/22 CANADIAN CENTENNIAL

In 1966 and 1967 approximately 4,500 10/22 Sporters were built for the Canadian Centennial. The first 2,000 were sold with a Remington Model 742 in .308 caliber with matching serial numbers. The Ruger Sporter may be checkered or uncheckered. The two-gun set was either boxed separately or together.

Two Gun Set

NIB	*Exc.*	*V.G.*	*Good*	*Fair*	*Poor*
700	—	—	—	—	—

10/22 Only

NIB	*Exc.*	*V.G.*	*Good*	*Fair*	*Poor*
450	—	—	—	—	—

10/22 Laminated Stock Carbine

Produced in varying quantities since 1986 these models are becoming quite collectible. The stocks range in color from dark green to gray and various shades of brown. Because there are so many different variations each should be individually appraised. Prices listed are for blued carbine models.

NIB	*Exc.*	*V.G.*	*Good*	*Fair*	*Poor*
250	200	175	150	125	100

NOTE: In stainless steel add approximately $40 to NIB price.

10/22 Laminated Stock Sporter Model

This model has a tree bark laminated stock.

NIB	*Exc.*	*V.G.*	*Good*	*Fair*	*Poor*
325	275	225	175	150	100

10/22 Laminated Stock International

This stainless steel model was an exclusive Wal-Mart product. A few of these models in blue were also produced.

10/22 Laminated Stock International Blue

NIB	*Exc.*	*V.G.*	*Good*	*Fair*	*Poor*
400	325	250	200	150	100

10/22 Laminated Stock International Stainless Steel

NIB	*Exc.*	*V.G.*	*Good*	*Fair*	*Poor*
350	275	225	175	125	100

10/22 All Weather

This model is fitted with a stainless steel barrel and action and synthetic stock. Introduced in 1997. In 2001 this model was offered with blued finish.

NIB	*Exc.*	*V.G.*	*Good*	*Fair*	*Poor*
300	225	175	125	100	70

NOTE: Deduct $40 for blued model.

Model 10/22 Carbine 40th Anniversary

This model is blued with hardwood stock. It is equipped with a 40th anniversary clear magazine with red rotor and original scope base adapter. A nickel-silver medallion is inlaid on the right side of the buttstock.

NIB	*Exc.*	*V.G.*	*Good*	*Fair*	*Poor*
280	225	175	125	100	75

Ruger 10/22 Compact Rifle 10/22 CRR

Similar to 10/22 standard rifle but with 16.25-inch blued barrel, shorter hardwood stock, fiber optic sights and 34.5-inch overall length. Introduced 2006.

NIB	*Exc.*	*V.G.*	*Good*	*Fair*	*Poor*
275	225	175	125	100	75

K10/22T Ruger 10/22 Target Stainless

Similar to 10/22 Target but with stainless steel barrel and laminated stock.

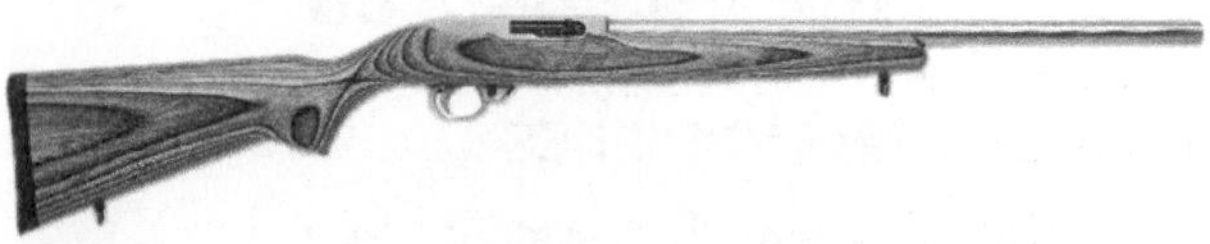

NIB	*Exc.*	*V.G.*	*Good*	*Fair*	*Poor*
495	425	350	275	200	150

10/22-T

Similar to 100/22 Target Stainless but with blued steel barrel and blued receiver. Introduced in 2007.

NIB	Exc.	V.G.	Good	Fair	Poor
450	350	275	200	150	100

10/22RPFCARH (Lipsey's Distributor's Special)

Similar to 10/22 but covered throughout with RealTree Hardwoods HD camo finish. Introduced 2008.

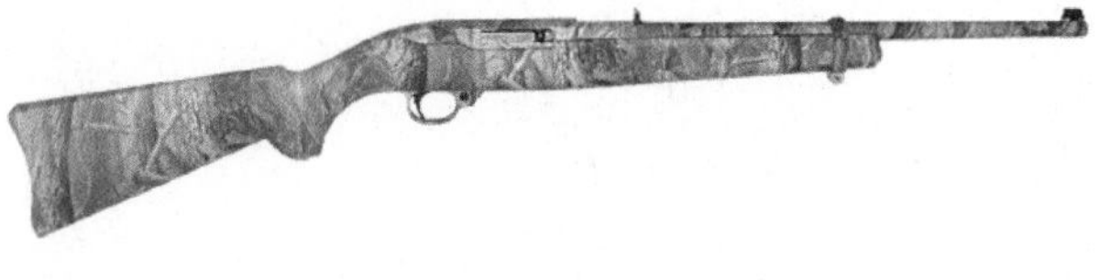

NIB	Exc.	V.G.	Good	Fair	Poor
275	225	175	125	100	75

K10/22-USST "Barracuda" (Distributor Exclusive)

Wow! A funkalicious 10/22 with red/whit/blue laminated thumbhole stock and other goodies. Introduced 2008. Pricing not available. (Note: Compare styling to that of Remington Model 592 Yellow Jacket.)

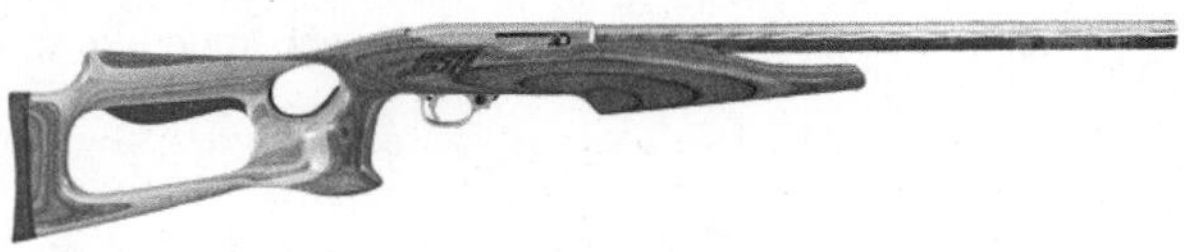

10/22VLEH Target Tactical Rifle

Semi-auto rimfire rifle chambered in .22 LR. Features include precision-rifled, cold hammer-forged, spiral-finished 16-1/8-inch crowned match barrel; Hogue® OverMolded® stock; 10/22T target trigger; precision-adjustable bipod for steady shooting from the bench; 10-round rotary magazine. Weight: 6-7/8 lbs.

NIB	Exc.	V.G.	Good	Fair	Poor
485	400	350	300	225	150

Model 10/17

Introduced in 2004 this model is chambered for the .17 HMR cartridge. Fitted with a 20" barrel. Magazine capacity is 9 rounds. Weight is about 6.5 lbs. Discontinued.

NIB	Exc.	V.G.	Good	Fair	Poor
600	475	300	200	150	100

SR-22 Rifle

AR-style semi-auto rifle chambered in .22 LR, based on 0/22 action. Features include all-aluminum chassis replicating the AR-platform dimensions between the sighting plane, buttstock height, and grip; Picatinny rail optic mount includes a six-position, telescoping M4-style buttstock (on a Mil-Spec diameter tube); Hogue Monogrip pistol grip; buttstocks and grips interchangeable with any AR-style compatible option; round, mid-length hand-guard mounted on a standard-thread AR-style barrel nut; precision-rifled, cold hammer forged 16-1/8-inch alloy steel barrel capped with an SR-556/Mini-14 flash suppressor.

NIB	Exc.	V.G.	Good	Fair	Poor
535	460	385	325	250	150

Model 44 Carbine

This model is a short, 18.5" barreled, gas-operated carbine chambered for the .44 Magnum cartridge. It has a 4-shot, nondetachable magazine, a folding rear sight, and a plain walnut stock. This is a handy deer hunting carbine manufactured between 1961 and 1985.

NIB	Exc.	V.G.	Good	Fair	Poor
550	450	350	300	200	150

Deerstalker Model

The same as the Model 44 Carbine with "Deerstalker" stamped on it. This model was manufactured in 1961 and 1962 only.

NIB	Exc.	V.G.	Good	Fair	Poor
950	800	600	400	300	200

Model 44 RS

This is the Model 44 with sling swivels and an aperture sight.

NIB	Exc.	V.G.	Good	Fair	Poor
—	600	550	350	200	150

NOTE: "Liberty" -marked 44RS carbines are extremely rare and will bring a premium.

Model 44 Sporter (Finger Groove Old Model)

This version has a Monte Carlo stock, finger groove forend, and no barrel band. It was manufactured until 1971.

NIB	Exc.	V.G.	Good	Fair	Poor
—	750	600	400	250	200

NOTE: Factory hand checkered models will bring at least a 75 percent premium.

Model 44 International Carbine

This version features a full-length, Mannlicher-style stock. It was discontinued in 1971 and is quite collectible.

NIB	Exc.	V.G.	Good	Fair	Poor
—	800	600	425	350	275

NOTE: Factory hand checkered models will bring at least a 50 percent premium.

Model 44 25th Anniversary Model

This version is lightly engraved, has a medallion in the stock and was only made in 1985, the last year of production.

NIB	Exc.	V.G.	Good	Fair	Poor
550	400	350	300	250	200

Model 99/44 Deerfield Carbine

A new and improved version, introduced in 2000, of the original Model 44 Carbine. Fitted with a 18.5" barrel this gas operated rifle has a hardwood stock and 4-round magazine capacity. Adjustable rear sight. Blued finish. Weight is about 6.2 lbs. This rifle will not cycle .44 Special ammo. Discontinued.

NIB	Exc.	V.G.	Good	Fair	Poor
700	525	400	275	200	150

Mini-14

This is a paramilitary-style carbine chambered for the .223 Remington and on a limited basis for the .222 cartridge. It has an 18.5" barrel and is gas-operated. The detachable magazines originally offered held 5, 10, or 20 rounds. The high-capacity magazines are now discontinued, and prices of them are what the market will bear. The Mini-14 has a military-style stock and aperture sight. It was introduced in 1975. 20-round magazine added 2009.

NIB	Exc.	V.G.	Good	Fair	Poor
750	550	400	275	200	150

Mini-14 Stainless Steel

The same as the Mini-14 except constructed of stainless steel.

NIB	*Exc.*	*V.G.*	*Good*	*Fair*	*Poor*
810	600	450	300	200	150

Mini-14 Target Rifle

Acccurized version of the Mini-14 but with matte stainless barrel and reciver, black laminated thumbhole stock, adjustable harmonic dampener. No sights. Also available with non-thumbhole synthetic stock. Introduced in 2007.

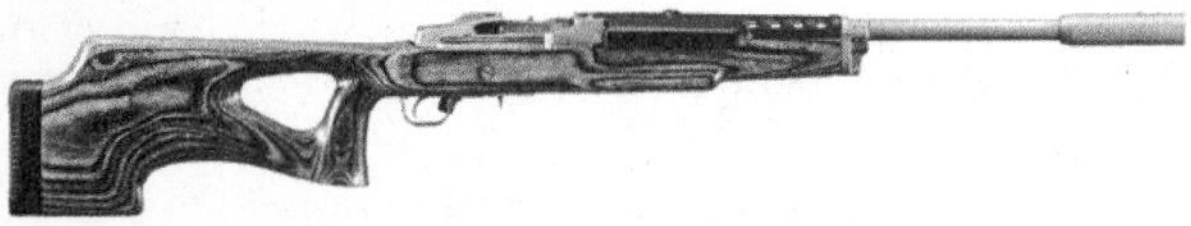

NIB	*Exc.*	*V.G.*	*Good*	*Fair*	*Poor*
1025	900	775	600	400	250

Mini-14 Ranch Rifle

This model is similar to the standard Mini-14, with a folding rear sight and the receiver milled to accept the Ruger scope-ring system. The rings are supplied with the rifle. 6.8 Remington chambering also available.

NIB	*Exc.*	*V.G.*	*Good*	*Fair*	*Poor*
625	500	450	350	250	175

NOTE: Models chambered in .222 caliber will bring a premium.

Mini-14 Stainless All-Weather Ranch Rifle

Introduced in 1999 this model has all the features of the stainless steel Ranch Rifle with the addition of a black polymer stock. Weight is about 6.5 lbs.

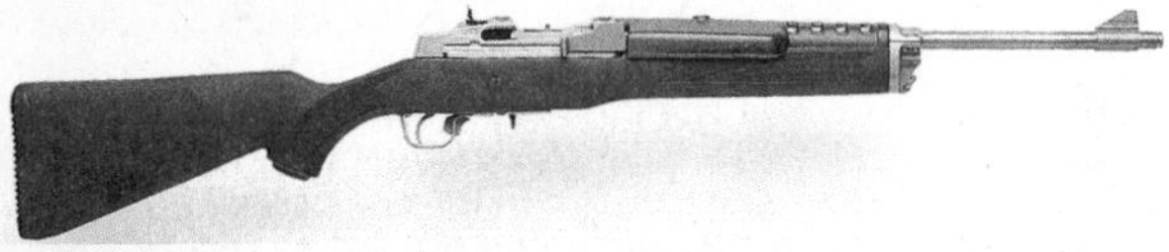

NIB	*Exc.*	*V.G.*	*Good*	*Fair*	*Poor*
810	600	450	300	200	150

NRA Mini-14

Ruger NRA Mini-14 Rifle with two 20-round magazines, gold-tone medallion in grip cap, and special serial number sequence (NRA8XXXXX). Produced in 2008 only. Also available with 5-round magazines.

NIB	*Exc.*	*V.G.*	*Good*	*Fair*	*Poor*
1000	700	575	—	—	—

Mini-14 ATI Stock

Tactical version of Mini-14 but with six-position collapsible stock or folding stock, grooved pistol grip, multiple picatinny optics/accessories rails. Suggested retail price: $872.

NIB	*Exc.*	*V.G.*	*Good*	*Fair*	*Poor*
675	550	425	300	200	150

Mini-14 Tactical Rifle

Similar to Mini-14 but with 16-12" barrel with flash hider, black synthetic stock, adjustable sights.

NIB	*Exc.*	*V.G.*	*Good*	*Fair*	*Poor*
700	525	400	275	200	150

SR-556

AR-style semi-auto rifle chambered in 5.56 NATO. Feature include two-stage piston; quad rail hand-guard; Troy Industries sights; black synthetic fixed or telescoping buttstock; 16.12-inch 1:9 steel barrel with birdcage; 10- or 30-round detachable box magazine; black matte finish overall.

NIB	*Exc.*	*V.G.*	*Good*	*Fair*	*Poor*
1750	1400	1250	900	600	250

Mini-30

This model was brought out by Ruger in 1987 and is similar in appearance to the standard Mini-14 and is supplied with Ruger scope rings. Chambered in 7.63x39. 6.8mm chambering added 2007.

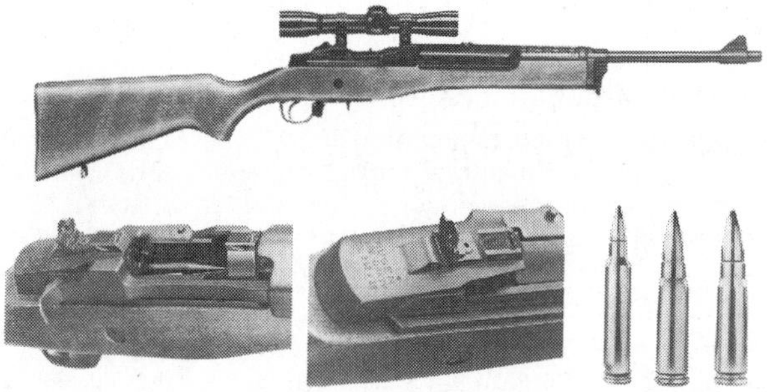

NIB	*Exc.*	*V.G.*	*Good*	*Fair*	*Poor*
550	450	300	250	200	150

Mini-30 Stainless with Synthetic Stock

NIB	*Exc.*	*V.G.*	*Good*	*Fair*	*Poor*
700	550	450	300	200	150

GB Model

This model has a factory-installed folding stock, flash suppressor, and bayonet lug. It was designed and sold by Ruger to law enforcement agencies. A number have come on the civilian market through surplus sales and police trade-ins. With the assault rifle hysteria, prices of this model have fluctuated wildly in some areas. Now that Ruger has discontinued the folding stock and the high-capacity magazines, this could become even less predictable. Note that this is a semi-automatic and totally different than the full-auto version of this weapon available only through Class 3 dealers.

NIB	*Exc.*	*V.G.*	*Good*	*Fair*	*Poor*
—	1350	1100	650	400	300

Ruger PC4/PC9 Carbine

This is a semi-automatic carbine chambered for the 9mm (PC9) or .40 S&W (PC4) cartridges. It is fitted with a 16.25" barrel and black synthetic stock. Post front sight with adjustable rear sight. A receiver is also offered. Detachable magazine has 10-round capacity. Weight is approximately 6.4 lbs. Introduced in 1998. Discontinued.

NIB	*Exc.*	*V.G.*	*Good*	*Fair*	*Poor*
625	450	325	225	150	100

NOTE: Add $30 for receiver sight.

SINGLE-SHOT RIFLES

Ruger No. 1 Light Sporter (1-A)

This model features open sights, barrel band on lightweight barrel, and Alexander Henry-style forearm. Offered with a 22" barrel in four calibers. Rifle weighs 7.25 lbs. .300 Ruger Compact Magnum added 2009.

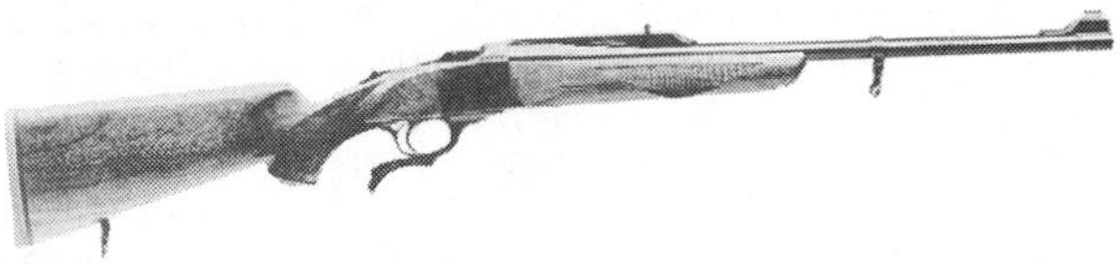

NIB	*Exc.*	*V.G.*	*Good*	*Fair*	*Poor*
965	725	550	375	250	200

Ruger Number 1 Light Standard (1-AB)

Similar to Light Sporter 1-A but with 22-inch sightless blued barrel. Chambered in .204 Ruger only; introduced 2006. MSRP: $1000.

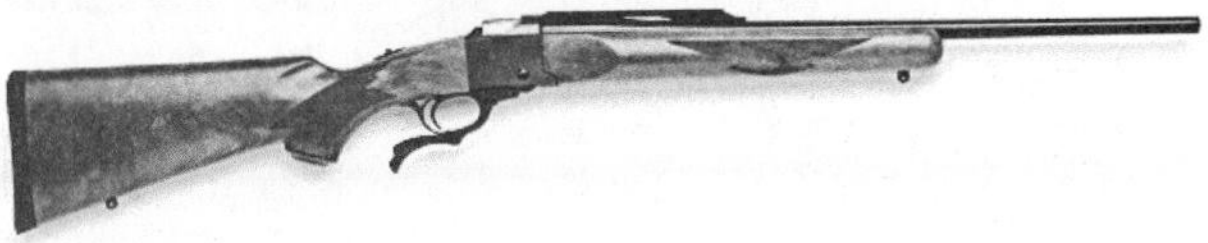

Ruger No. 1 Standard (1-B)

This model is furnished with no sights, medium barrel, semi-beavertail forearm, and quarter rib with 1" Ruger scope rings. 6.5 Creedmore added 2010. Weighs 8 lbs.

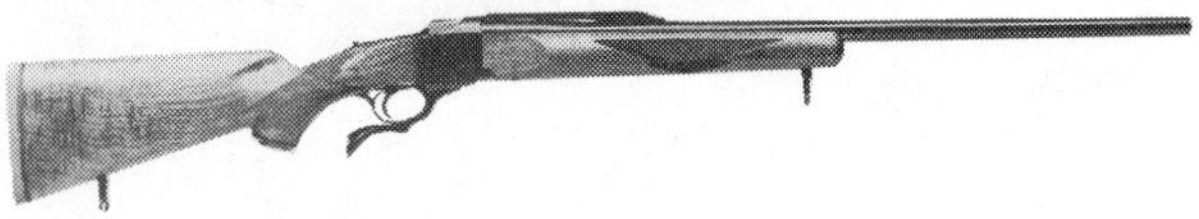

NIB	*Exc.*	*V.G.*	*Good*	*Fair*	*Poor*
965	725	550	375	250	200

Ruger No. 1 Standard Stainless (1-B-BBZ)

Introduced in 2000 this model features a laminated wood stock. It is chambered for the .243 Win., .25-06, 7mm Mag., 7mm STW, .30-06, .300 Win. Mag. Fitted with a 26" barrel. Weight is approximately 8 lbs.

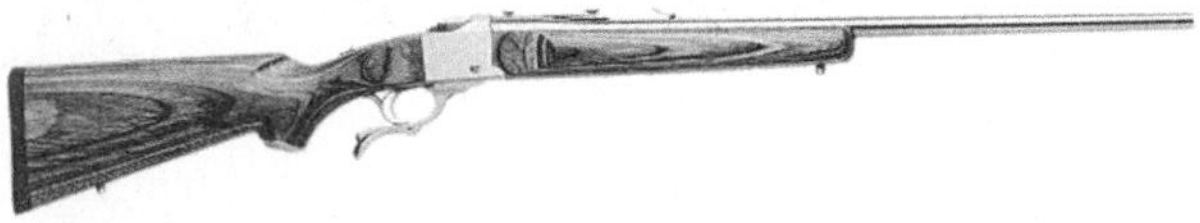

NIB	*Exc.*	*V.G.*	*Good*	*Fair*	*Poor*
995	750	550	375	250	200

Ruger No. 1 Tropical (1-H)

Fitted with open sights this model has a barrel band on a heavy barrel with Alexander Henry-style forearm. Rifle weighs 9 lbs. **NOTE:** In 2001 this model was also offered with stainless steel finish and black laminated stock in .375 H&H. In 2003 the .458 Lott and .405 Win. cartridges were added to this model. In 2008 the ..450/.400 Nitro Express was added. .416 Ruger added 2009.

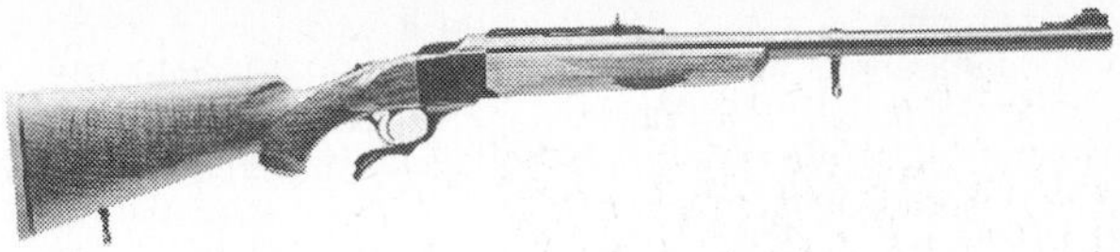

NIB	*Exc.*	*V.G.*	*Good*	*Fair*	*Poor*
965	725	550	375	250	200

NOTE: A few 24" heavy barrel 1-H rifles were chambered for the .45-70 Government cartridge up to 1976. These bring a substantial premium and should be appraised individually. The recently catalogued .404 Jeffery has been discontinued. Only a few of these rifles were produced. Add 100 percent for .404 Jeffery caliber.

Ruger No. 1 International (1-RSI)

This No. 1 rifle features a lightweight barrel with full length forearm, open sights. Rifle weighs 7.25 lbs.

NIB	*Exc.*	*V.G.*	*Good*	*Fair*	*Poor*
995	750	550	375	250	200

Ruger No. 1 Medium Sporter (1-S)

The Medium Sporter is equipped with open sights, a barrel band on a medium weight barrel, and Alexander Henry-style forearm. Rifle weighs 8 lbs. In 2001 this model was also offered in stainless steel and black laminated stock in .45-70 caliber. .300 H&H, .338 Ruger Compact Magnum, .375 Ruger, .460 S&W Magnum, .480Ruger/.475 Linebaugh added 2009.

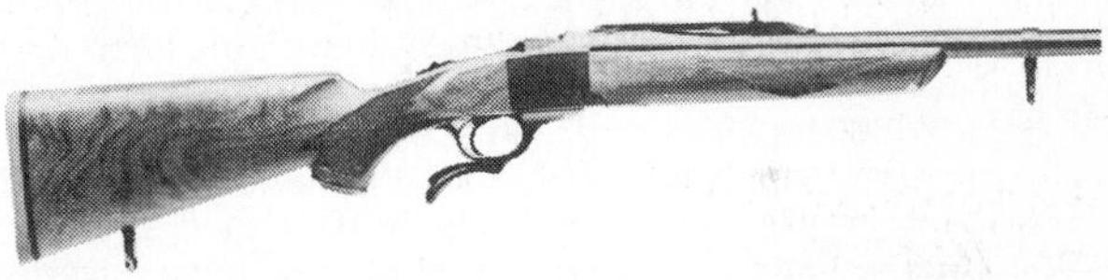

NIB	*Exc.*	*V.G.*	*Good*	*Fair*	*Poor*
965	725	550	375	250	200

Ruger No. 1 Special Varminter (1-V)

This model is furnished with no sights, a heavy barrel, target scope blocks with 1" Ruger scope rings, and semi-beavertail forearm. Rifle weighs about 9 lbs.

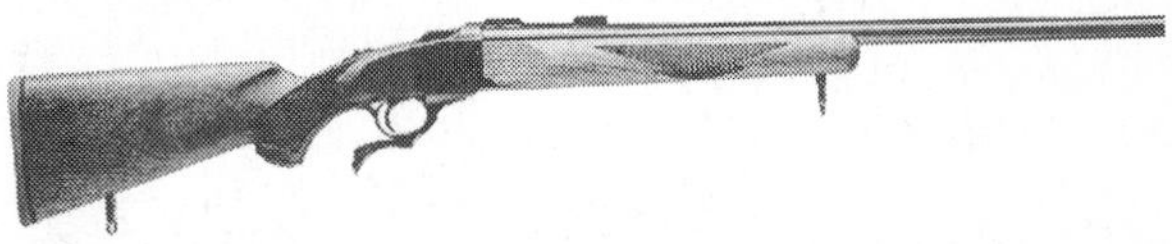

NIB	*Exc.*	*V.G.*	*Good*	*Fair*	*Poor*
965	725	550	375	250	200

Ruger No. 1 Stainless Varminter (1-V-BBZ)

Introduced in 2000 this model features a laminated wood stock and stainless steel finish. Chambered for .22-250 and fitted with a 24" barrel. Weight is approximately 9 lbs.

NIB	*Exc.*	*V.G.*	*Good*	*Fair*	*Poor*
995	750	550	375	250	200

Number 3 Carbine

This model is a less elaborate, inexpensive version of the Number 1. The action is the same except that the lever is less ornate in appearance and lacks the locking bar. The uncheckered stock is of a military carbine style with a barrel band. It is similar in appearance to the Model 44 and the 10/22. This serviceable rifle was chambered for the .45-70 when it was released in 1972. Later chamberings added the .22 Hornet, .30-40 Krag, .223, .44 Magnum, and the .375 Winchester. The barrel is 22" long, and there is a folding rear sight. This model was discontinued in 1987. Add premium for "neato" calibers.

NIB	Exc.	V.G.	Good	Fair	Poor
—	625	500	300	200	125

BOLT-ACTION RIFLES

Ruger introduced the Model 77R in 1968. It filled the need for a good quality, reasonably priced, bolt-action hunting rifle. It has been a commercial success. There are certain variations of this rifle that collectors actively seek. One should avail oneself of the specialized literature on this model and secure individual appraisals on the rare variations as the differences are slight and beyond the scope of this book.

Model 77-R/RS

This model was introduced in 1968. It is offered with a 22", 24", or 26" barrel. The Model 77 is chambered for most calibers from .22-250 through .458 Win. Mag. The action is of a modified Mauser-type, finished in blue with a checkered walnut stock and red rubber buttplate. The rifle is available milled for Ruger scope rings or in the round-top style that allows the mounting of any popular scope ring system. This model is designated 77R when supplied with rings only; and 77RS, when supplied with rings and sights. This model was replaced by the Model 77 MK II.

NIB	Exc.	V.G.	Good	Fair	Poor
500	400	350	300	250	200

Model 77-RS

NIB	Exc.	V.G.	Good	Fair	Poor
550	450	400	300	250	200

Model 77 Flat Bolt

This is an example of the slight variations that make this model collectible. This is essentially the same rifle with the knob on the bolt handle flattened. They were only produced in the configuration until 1972. Watch for fakes, and read specialized material. Calibers such as the 6.5 Rem. Mag., .284, and .350 Rem. Mag. will bring a premium especially in the RS model. **NOTE:** Nonprefixed rifles exists in calibers and configurations other than those advertised by Ruger. These should be individually appraised.

NIB	Exc.	V.G.	Good	Fair	Poor
—	650	500	400	350	275

Model 77 RL & RLS

This variation is similar to the standard model except that it features an ultralight 20" barrel and black forearm tip. This model was also available in an 18.5" carbine version with sights designated the RLS. This model was also in an 18.5" carbine version with sights designated the RLS. They were chambered for the .22-250, .243, .257, .270, .250-3000, .308, and .30-06. Weight is only 6 lbs.

NIB	Exc.	V.G.	Good	Fair	Poor
550	450	375	325	275	225

Model 77V Varmint

This variation is similar to the standard Model 77 except that it has a 24" heavy barrel that is drilled and tapped for target-scope bases and has a wider beavertail forearm. It is chambered for the .22-250, .243, 6mm, .25-06, .280, and .308. This model was also chambered for the .220 Swift in a 26" heavyweight barrel.

NIB	Exc.	V.G.	Good	Fair	Poor
500	400	350	300	250	200

Model 77 RSI

This version of the Model 77 has a full-length, Mannlicher-style stock and was chambered for the .22-250, .250-3000, .243, .270, 7mm-08, .308 and the .30-06.

NIB	Exc.	V.G.	Good	Fair	Poor
700	600	500	300	275	200

Model 77 RS African

This is a heavier-barreled version, with a steel trigger guard and floorplate. Earlier versions were stocked with fine-quality Circassian walnut. This rifle is chambered for the .458 Winchester Magnum. **NOTE:** Fewer than 50 rifles chambered for the .416 Taylor cartridge were produced up to 1976. Selling prices range from $3,000 to $5,000 and should be individually appraised.

NIB	Exc.	V.G.	Good	Fair	Poor
700	550	400	350	300	250

NOTE: Add $100 for early models with Circassian walnut stocks.

Model 77/17

Introduced in 2003, this rifle is chambered for the .17 HMR caridge and fitted with a 22" barrel with no sights. Walnut stock with blued finish. Magazine capacity is nine rounds. Weight is about 6 lbs.

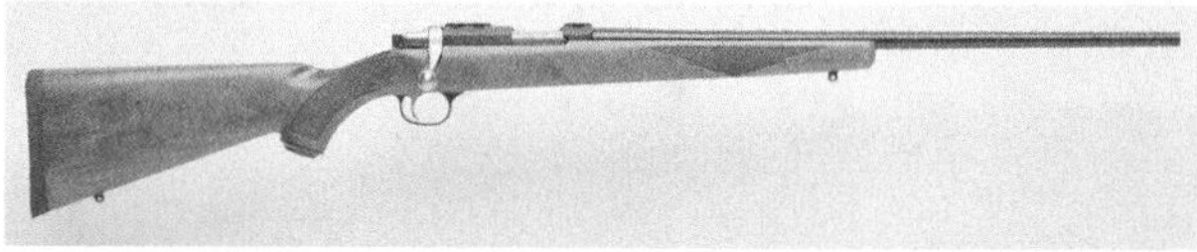

NIB	Exc.	V.G.	Good	Fair	Poor
610	475	350	250	175	125

Model 77/17 Synthetic

As above but with black synthetic stock and blued finish.

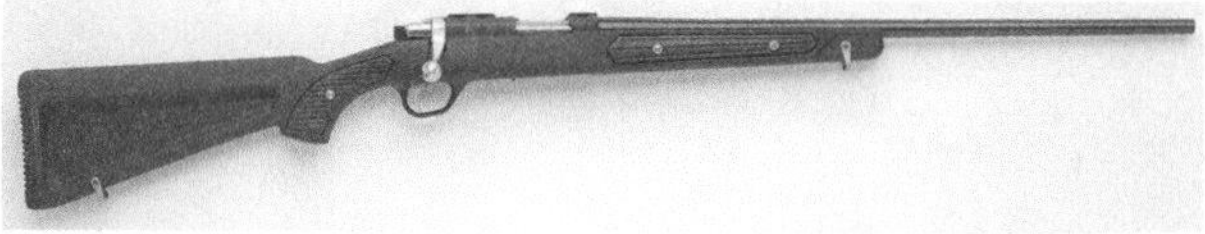

NIB	Exc.	V.G.	Good	Fair	Poor
625	475	350	250	175	125

Model 77/17 Varmint

As above but with black laminate stock and 24" stainless steel heavy barrel with no sights. Weight is about 7 lbs.

NIB	Exc.	V.G.	Good	Fair	Poor
685	500	375	265	195	145

Model 77/17RM2

Introduced in 2005 this model is chambered for the .17 Mach 2 caliber and fitted with a 20" barrel with no sights. Walnut stock with checkering. Blued finish. Weight is about 6.5 lbs.

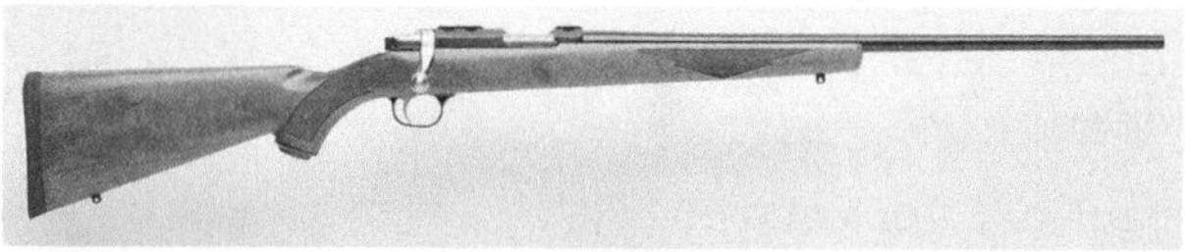

NIB	Exc.	V.G.	Good	Fair	Poor
625	475	350	250	175	125

Model 77/17RM2 Stainless Steel

As above but with stainless steel finish and black laminate stock. Weight is about 7.25 lbs. Introduced in 2005.

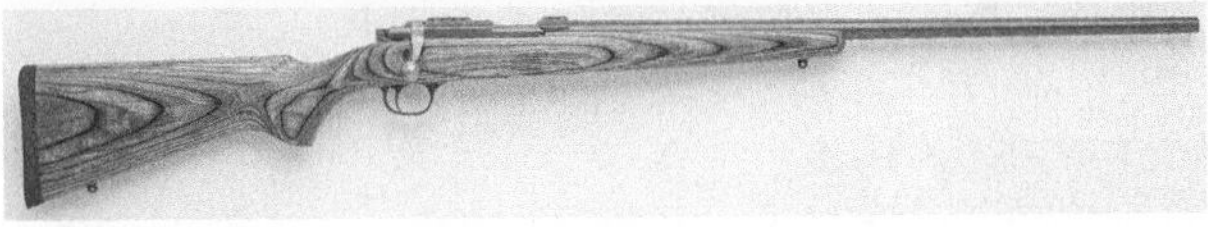

NIB	Exc.	V.G.	Good	Fair	Poor
745	625	500	400	275	150

Model 77/22

This is a high quality, .22 rimfire (LR and WMR) rifle designed for the serious shooter. This model has a 20" barrel and a 10-shot, detachable rotary magazine. It is made of steel and stocked with checkered walnut. It is available with sights, scope rings, or both as an extra-cost ($20) option. This model was introduced in 1984. Early guns without the 77/22 rollmark on the receiver will bring a premium.

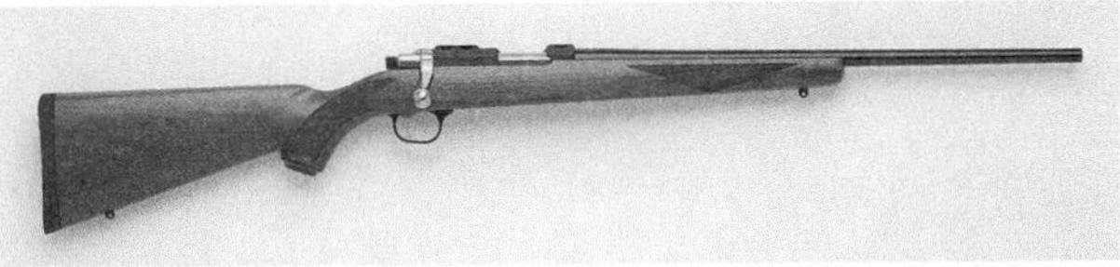

NIB	Exc.	V.G.	Good	Fair	Poor
625	450	350	250	175	125

Model 77/22 Synthetic Stock

This version is quite similar to the standard 77/22, with a black-matte-finished synthetic stock.

NIB	Exc.	V.G.	Good	Fair	Poor
625	450	350	250	200	150

Model 77/22 Stainless Steel/Synthetic Stock

This model is the same as the blued version except that it is made of stainless steel.

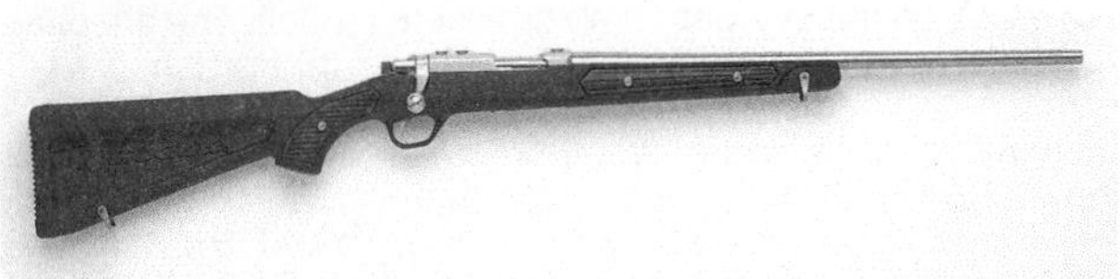

NIB	Exc.	V.G.	Good	Fair	Poor
610	475	375	275	225	150

Model 77/22 Varmint

Introduced in 1993 this model features a stainless steel finish, laminated wood stock, heavy 20" varmint barrel with no sights. Scope rings are included as standard. Chambered for the .22 LR or Win. Mag. Rimfire.

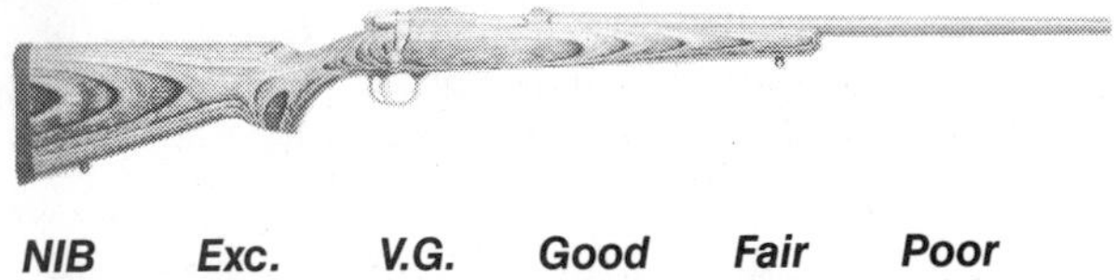

NIB	Exc.	V.G.	Good	Fair	Poor
650	525	425	300	250	150

Model 77/22M

This model is simply the 77/22 chambered for the .22 Magnum cartridge. The finish is blue, and the magazine capacity is 9 rounds.

NIB	Exc.	V.G.	Good	Fair	Poor
610	450	350	250	175	125

Model 77/22 Stainless Steel

This is the same as the blued 77/22M constructed of stainless steel.

NIB	Exc.	V.G.	Good	Fair	Poor
600	475	375	275	225	150

Model 77/22—.22 Hornet

Introduced in 1994 this version of the 77/22 series is chambered for the .22 Hornet cartridge. This model is furnished with or without sights. The barrel is 20" and it has a 6-round detachable rotary magazine. The stock is checkered walnut with sling swivels. Weight is approximately 6 lbs. **NOTE:** This model is offered with (77/22RSH) or without (77/22RH) sights.

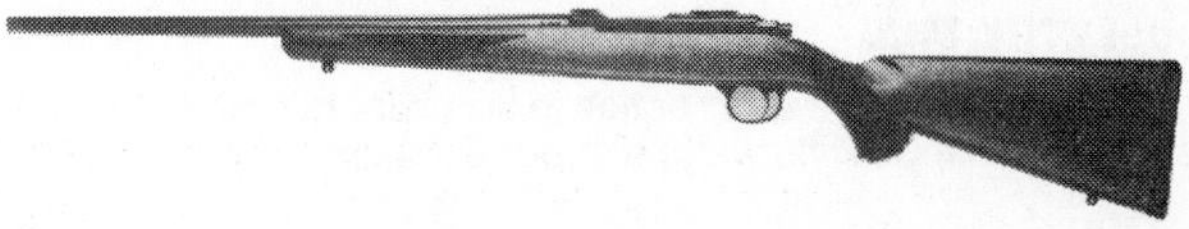

NIB	Exc.	V.G.	Good	Fair	Poor
650	500	375	275	225	150

Model K77/22VHZ

Introduced in 1995 this .22 Hornet variation features a stainless steel heavyweight barrel and laminated American hardwood stock. Offered without sights.

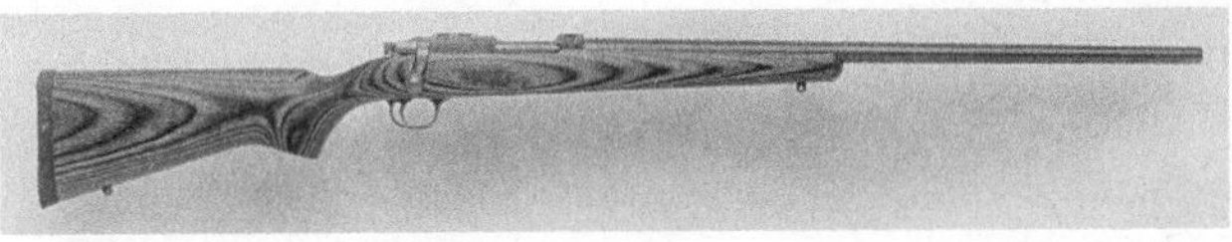

NIB	Exc.	V.G.	Good	Fair	Poor
685	525	425	300	250	150

Model 77R MKII

Introduced in 1992 this model is the basic Model 77 rifle. Features blued metal parts and no sights. Available in 15 different calibers from .223 to .338 Win. Mag. in barrel lengths from 22" to 24" depending on caliber. Comes from factory with scope bases and rings. Rifle weighs approximately 7 lbs.

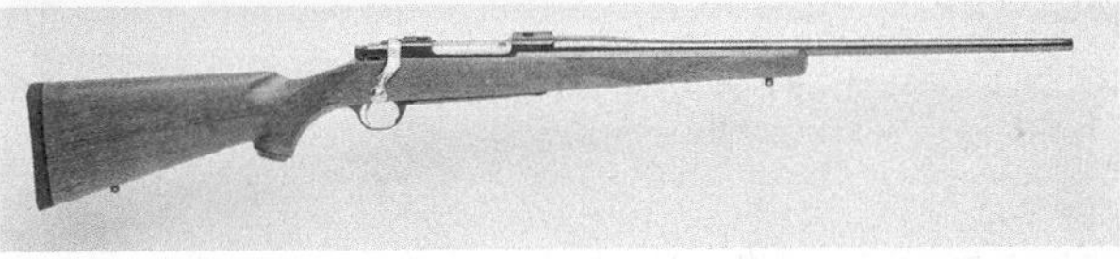

NIB	Exc.	V.G.	Good	Fair	Poor
715	525	375	250	200	150

Model 77RP MKII

This model was also introduced in 1992 and differs from the Model 77R with the addition of stainless steel barrel and receiver and synthetic stock. Available in 10 calibers. In 1998 the .25-06 caliber was added to this model.

NIB	Exc.	V.G.	Good	Fair	Poor
715	525	375	250	200	150

Model 77RS MKII

This is a blued version of the basic rifle with the addition of open sights. Available in 9 calibers from .243 Win. to .458 Win. Mag.

NIB	Exc.	V.G.	Good	Fair	Poor
760	600	450	350	250	175

Model 77RSP MKII

The stainless version of the basic rifle with the addition of a synthetic stock and open sights. Available in 6 calibers: .243, .270, 7MM Rem. Mag., .30-06, .330 Win. Mag., .338 Win. Mag. Introduced in 1993.

NIB	Exc.	V.G.	Good	Fair	Poor
500	400	350	300	250	175

Model 77RSI MKII

Also introduced in 1993 this model features a blued barrel and full-length walnut stock. Offered in four calibers, all with 18" barrel. The calibers are: .243, .270, .30-06, and .308.

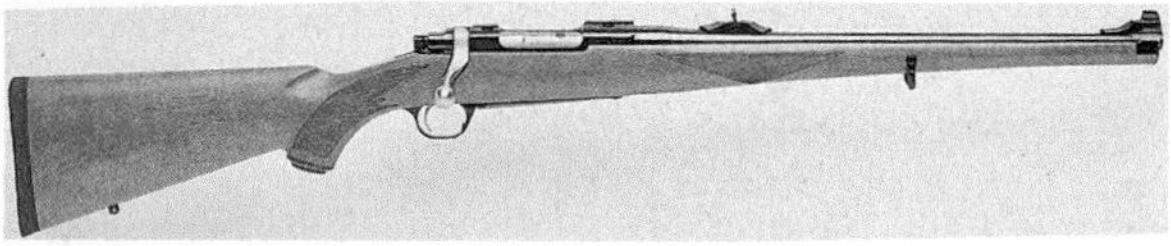

NIB	Exc.	V.G.	Good	Fair	Poor
820	600	450	350	250	175

Model 77RL MKII

This model features a short action in six calibers from .223 to .308, all with 20" barrel. Rifle weighs about 6 lbs. Introduced in 1992.

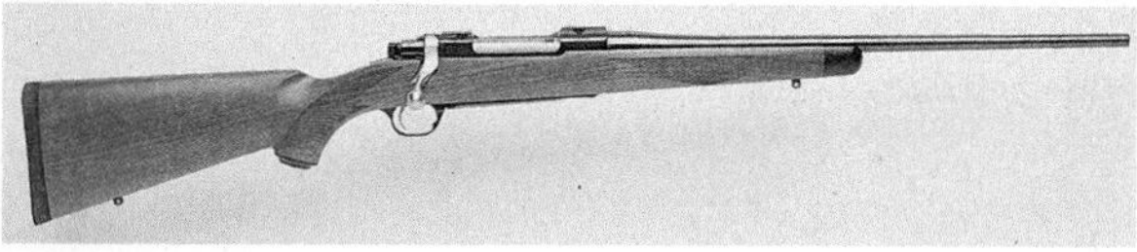

NIB	Exc.	V.G.	Good	Fair	Poor
770	575	425	300	200	150

Model 77LR MKII

This model is a left-handed rifle furnished in long action calibers: .270, 7mm Rem. Mag., .30-06, .300 Win. Mag. Introduced in 1992.

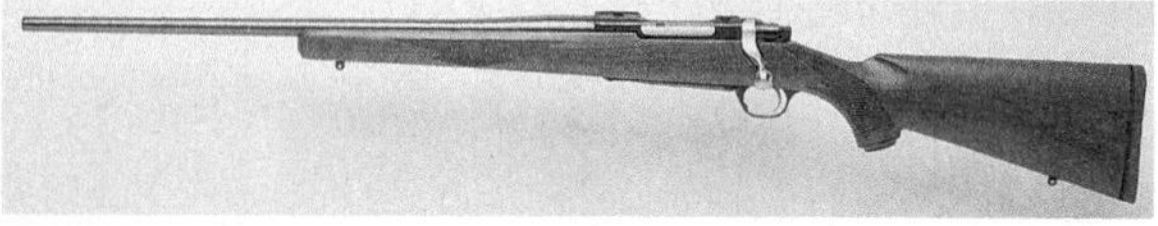

NIB	Exc.	V.G.	Good	Fair	Poor
770	575	425	300	200	150

Model 77RLP MKII

Introduced in 1999 this model is similar to the RL model above, but with an all-weather synthetic stock. Weight is about 6.5 lbs.

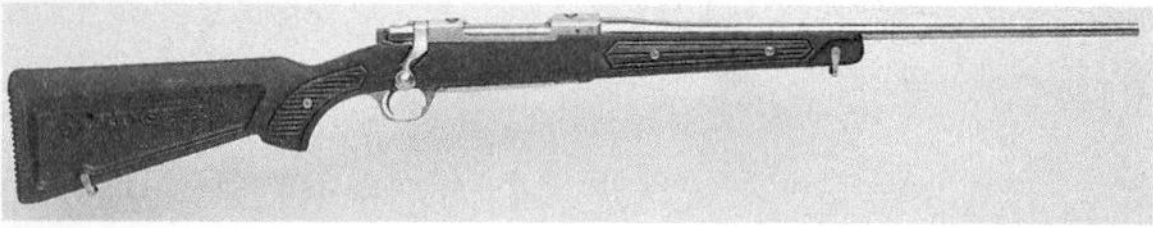

NIB	Exc.	V.G.	Good	Fair	Poor
715	525	400	275	200	150

Model 77VT MKII

This rifle was introduced in 1993 and is a target rifle. Furnished with no sights, heavy laminated wood stock with beavertail forend, and adjustable trigger. Barrel, bolt, and action are stainless steel. Weighs approximately 9.75 lbs. Furnished in eight calibers from .223 to .308.

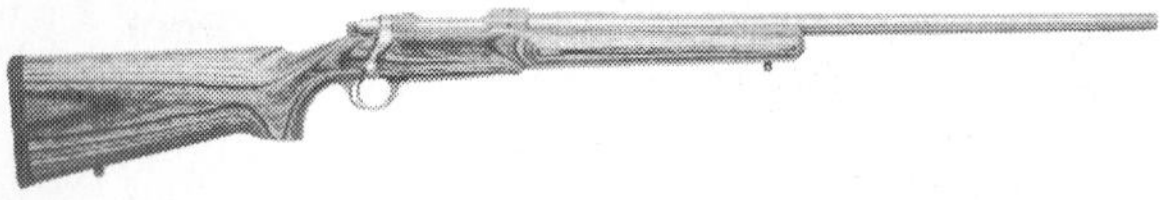

NIB	Exc.	V.G.	Good	Fair	Poor
820	650	475	350	250	175

Model 77RBZ MKII

This model features a stainless steel barrel and action fitted with laminated hardwood stock. No sights. Weight is approximately 7.25 lbs. Offered in a wide variety of calibers from .223 to .338 Win. Mag. Introduced in 1997.

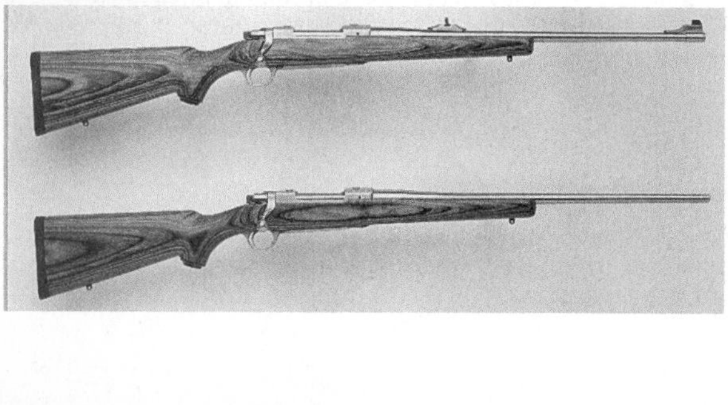

NIB	Exc.	V.G.	Good	Fair	Poor
600	500	400	300	225	175

Model 77RSBZ MKII

Same as above but fitted with open sights. Introduced in 1997.

NIB	Exc.	V.G.	Good	Fair	Poor
800	650	475	350	250	125

Model 77CR MKII Compact Rifle

Introduced in 2001 this rifle features a 16.5" barrel with four-round magazine. Chambered for the .223 Rem., .243 Win., .260 Rem., and .308 Win. cartridges. Blued model is fitted with walnut stock and stainless steel model is fitted with black laminated stock. Weight is about 5.75 lbs.

Ruger M-77 Mark II .223 Remington

NIB	Exc.	V.G.	Good	Fair	Poor
715	525	400	275	200	150

NOTE: Add $50 for stainless steel model (M77CRBBZ).

Model 77 Express MKII

Introduced in 1992 the Ruger Express Mark II rifle features a select Circassian walnut straight comb checkered stock. The checkering is 22 lpi and the buttstock is fitted with a rubber recoil pad. The pistol grip is fitted with a metal grip cap. The barrel length is 22" and features a blade front sight, V-notch rear express sights, and the receiver is machined for scope mounts, which are included. Available in these calibers: .270, .30-06, 7mm Rem. Mag., .300 Win. Mag., .338 Win. Mag. Rifle weighs about 7.5 lbs.

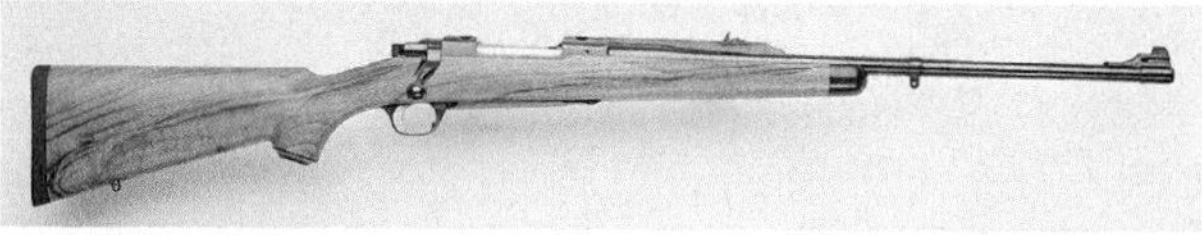

NIB	Exc.	V.G.	Good	Fair	Poor
1200	850	650	550	400	200

Model 77 Magnum MKII

Similar in all respects to the Model 77 Express MKII except offered in these calibers: .375 H&H and .416 Rigby. The .375 and weighs about 9.25 lbs. while the .416 weighs about 10.25 lbs.NOTE: In 2003 the .458 Lott cartridge was added to this model.

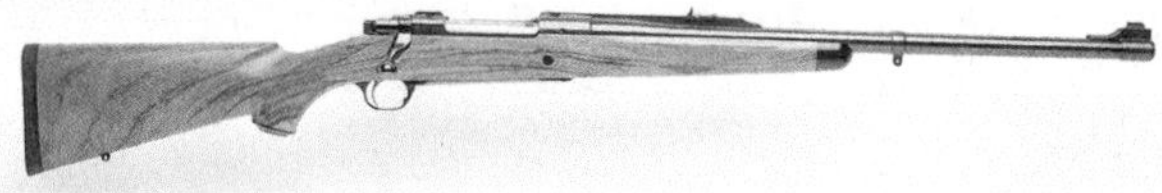

NIB	Exc.	V.G.	Good	Fair	Poor
1975	1500	1100	750	525	350

M77 MKII Frontier Rifle

Bolt-action rifle based on M77 MkII chassis but configured for "scout" -style scope mount system. Chambered in .243, .308, 7mm-08, .300 WSM, .325 WSM. 338 Federal. Gray laminated stock, 16.5-inch blued or stainless barrel (add 15 percent for stainless). Introduced 2005; stainless model introduced 2006 (add 10 percent). .338 Federal and .358 Winchester added 2008. Black laminated version discontinued 2008.

NIB	Exc.	V.G.	Good	Fair	Poor
600	500	400	300	225	175

Gunsite Scout

Based on the Ruger M77 rifle design with a 16.5-inch barrel and forward mounted Picatinny rail for intermediate eye relief scopes. Chambered in .308 Win. with a 10-round detachable magazine, integral scope mounts with rings and a flash suppressor. Adjustable ghost-ring rear sight and ramp front. Black/gray laminated stock with checkering and a soft rubber recoil pad with spacers.

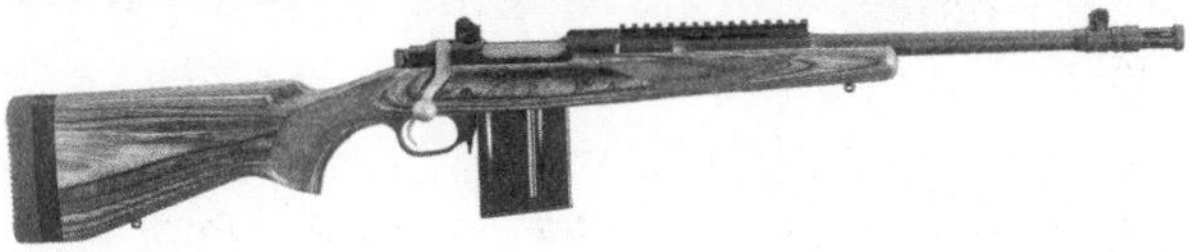

NIB	Exc.	V.G.	Good	Fair	Poor
850	750	600	450	300	200

BOLT-ACTION RIFLES

Model 77/44RS

This bolt-action is chambered for the .44 Magnum cartridge. It features an 18.5" barrel with open sights. The stock is American walnut with rubber buttpad and checkering on forearm and pistol grip. Detachable rotary magazine has 4-round capacity. Weight is approximately 6 lbs. Introduced in mid-1997.

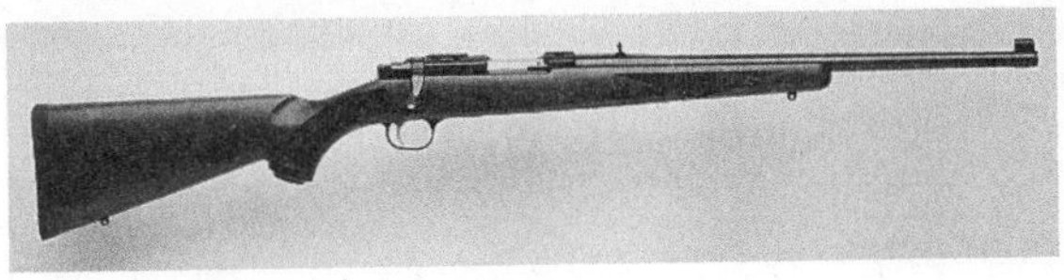

NIB	Exc.	V.G.	Good	Fair	Poor
575	465	375	250	175	125

Model 77/44RSP

Introduced in 1999 this model has a matte stainless steel barrel and action and a black synthetic stock. Chambered for .44 Magnum cartridge. Weight is about 6 lbs.

NIB	Exc.	V.G.	Good	Fair	Poor
575	465	375	250	175	125

Model 77/17RM

Similar in appearance to the .22 caliber Model 77 series this rifle is chambered for the .17 HMR and .17 Mach 2 cartridges. Fitted with a 22" barrel and walnut stock. Magazine capacity is nine rounds. Weight is about 6.25 lbs. Introduced in 2002.

NIB	Exc.	V.G.	Good	Fair	Poor
565	475	375	250	175	125

HAWKEYE SERIES

With a few exceptions, the Hawkeye Series, introduced in 2007, has replaced Ruger's M77 Mark II line. In 2010, the Hawkeye series began being offered in left-hand versions.

HM77R Hawkeye

Slimmed-down version of the M77. American walnut stock, blued barrel, Mauser-style controlled feed extractor, soft red rubber recoil pad, stainless steel bolt, new LC6 trigger, engraved solid steel floorplate. Chambered in.2506, 7mm-08, 7mm Magnum, .308, .30-06, .300 Win Mag, .338 Win Mag. Left-hand and laminate-stock versions available. Introduced in 2007. In 2008 a left-hand version (HM77LR) was introduced at no extra charge.

NIB	Exc.	V.G.	Good	Fair	Poor
550	450	350	225	175	125

M77 Hawkeye Ultra-Light

Similar to Hawkeye but with lightweight 20" blued barrel; chambered in .223, .243 Winchester, .257 Roberts, .270 Winchester, .308 Winchester and .30-06.

NIB	Exc.	V.G.	Good	Fair	Poor
600	500	400	300	225	175

M77 Hawkeye All-Weather Ultra-Light

Similar to above but with black synthetic stock and matte stainless barrel and receiver; chambered in .204, .223, .243 Winchester, .270 Winchester and .30-06.

NIB	Exc.	V.G.	Good	Fair	Poor
600	500	400	300	225	175

M77 Hawkeye Compact

Similar to M77 Hawkeye Ultra-Light but with 16.5" barrel and smaller overall dimensions; chambered in .223, .243 Winchester, .260 Remington, 7mm-08, .308 Winchester, 6.8 SPC, and 7.62x39.

NIB	Exc.	V.G.	Good	Fair	Poor
700	600	500	400	300	175

M77 Hawkeye Laminate Compact

Similar to above but with black laminate stock and matte stainless barrel and receiver.

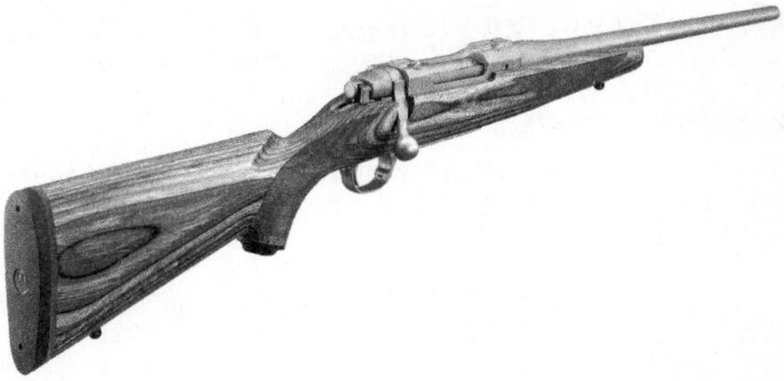

NIB	Exc.	V.G.	Good	Fair	Poor
650	525	425	300	250	150

HK77RFP Hawkeye All-Weather

All-weather version of the HM77R Hawkeye but with synthetic stock and stainless barrel. Same chamberings as HM77R but with .338 Federal and .358 Winchester as well. Introduced in 2007. Left hand version introduced in 2008.

NIB	Exc.	V.G.	Good	Fair	Poor
575	465	375	250	175	125

HKM77PRCM Hawkeye Compact Magnum

Similar to Hawkeye but with 1/2-inch shorter synthetic stock and stainless steel barrel and receiver. Chambered for .416 Ruger, .375 Ruger, .300 Ruger Compact Magnum, .338 Ruger Compact Magnum. Introduced 2008.

NIB	*Exc.*	*V.G.*	*Good*	*Fair*	*Poor*
775	675	550	450	325	195

HKM77RCM Hawkeye Compact Magnum

Similar to above but with blued barrel and walnut stock. Introduced 2008.

NIB	*Exc.*	*V.G.*	*Good*	*Fair*	*Poor*
800	700	575	475	350	200

HM77RSPHAB Hawkeye Alaskan

Similar to HK77RFP but with iron sights, Diamond black finish, stainless or matte blued barrel/receiver and Hogue stock. Chambered in .375 Ruger or .416 Ruger. Introduced in 2007. Left hand model introduced 2008.

NIB	*Exc.*	*V.G.*	*Good*	*Fair*	*Poor*
850	725	600	475	300	200

HM77RSPHAB Hawkeye African

Similar to HK77RFP but with checkered walnut stock and express-style sights. Chambered in .375 Ruger, .223 Rem., 9.3x62, .300 Win. Mag. and .338 Win. Mag. Chambered in .375 Ruger. Introduced in 2007. A left-hand version was introduced in 2008.

NIB	*Exc.*	*V.G.*	*Good*	*Fair*	*Poor*
900	775	650	525	350	225

M77 Hawkeye Tactical

Similar to M77 Hawkeye but with 20" matte blue heavy barrel, overmolded Hogue synthetic stock; chambered in .223, .243 Winchester and .308 Winchester.

NIB	*Exc.*	*V.G.*	*Good*	*Fair*	*Poor*
875	750	625	500	300	200

M77 Hawkeye Predator

Similar to M77 Hawkeye but with 24" matte stainless barrel. Green-toned Green Mountain laminate stock; chambered in .204, .223 and .22-250.

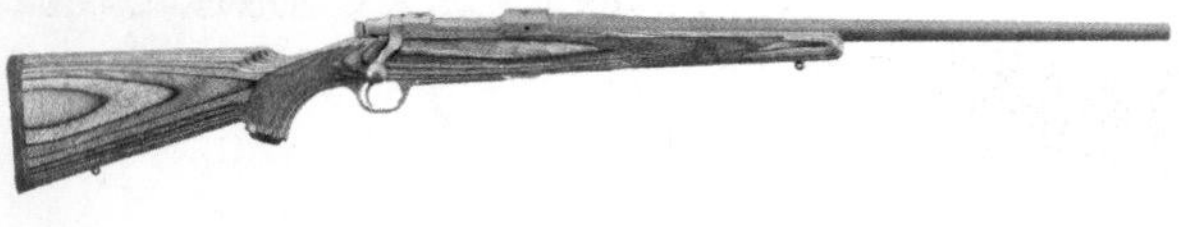

NIB	*Exc.*	*V.G.*	*Good*	*Fair*	*Poor*
775	675	550	450	325	195

M77 Hawkeye International

Similar to Hawkeye but with 18.5" barrel and full-length Mannlicher-style stock; chambered in .243, .270 and .308 Winchester and .30-06.

NIB	*Exc.*	*V.G.*	*Good*	*Fair*	*Poor*
825	725	600	475	350	225

LEVER-ACTION RIFLES

Model 96/17

Introduced in 2003 this model is chambered for the .17 HMR cartridge and fitted with an 18.5" barrel. Magazine capacity is nine rounds. Hardwood stock and open sights. Weight is about 5.25 lbs.

NIB	*Exc.*	*V.G.*	*Good*	*Fair*	*Poor*
425	300	225	175	150	100

Model 96/22

Introduced into the Ruger line in 1996 this lever action rifle is chambered for the .22 LR. The stock is American hardwood and the barrel length is 18.5". Magazine capacity is 10 rounds. Open sights are standard. Weight is approximately 5.25 lbs. Apparently discontinued.

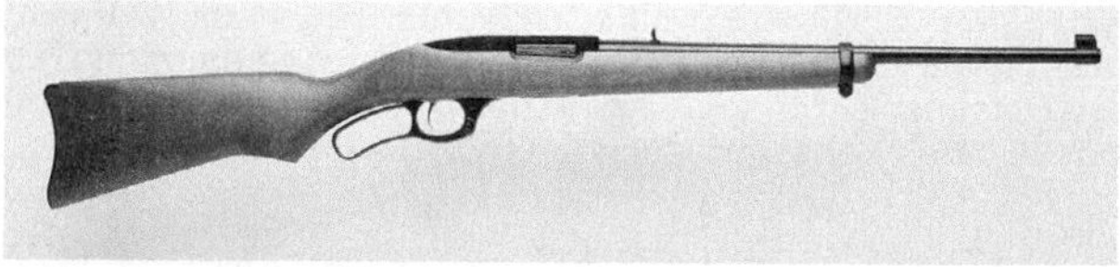

NIB	*Exc.*	*V.G.*	*Good*	*Fair*	*Poor*
325	275	200	175	150	100

Model 96/22M

Same as above but chambered for the .22 WMR cartridge. Magazine capacity is nine rounds.

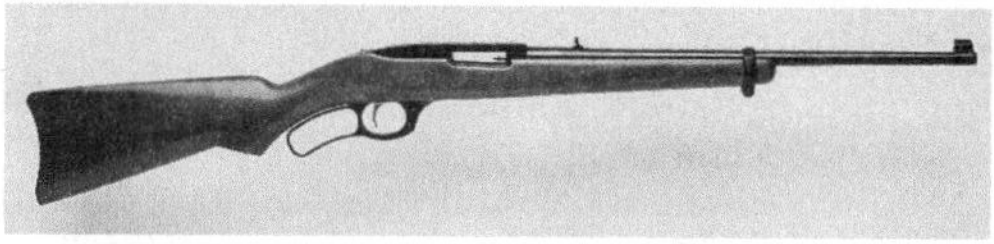

NIB	*Exc.*	*V.G.*	*Good*	*Fair*	*Poor*
350	300	225	175	150	100

Model 96/44

Same as the .22 caliber except chambered for the .44 Magnum cartridge. Magazine capacity is four rounds and the weight is about 5-7/8 lbs. Discontinued.

NIB	*Exc.*	*V.G.*	*Good*	*Fair*	*Poor*
550	450	325	250	200	125

SHOTGUNS

Red Label Over-and-Under Early Production

Ruger introduced the Red Label in 20 gauge in 1977; the 12 gauge followed five years later. This high quality shotgun is offered with 3" chambers in 26" or 28" barrel lengths. Various chokes are available. They are boxlocks with automatic ejectors. The stock is of checkered walnut. The finish is blue on the earlier guns.

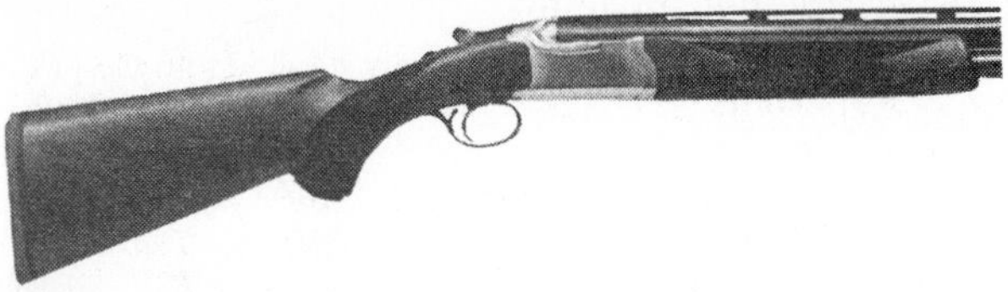

NIB	*Exc.*	*V.G.*	*Good*	*Fair*	*Poor*
1175	750	550	400	300	250

Red Label Over-and-Under Current Production

The new 12 and 20 gauge Red Label shotgun has a stainless steel receiver and blued barrels. They are offered with screw-in choke tubes. Otherwise they are similar to the earlier models. In 1994 Ruger added the 28 gauge with 26" or 28" barrels to the Red Label line.

NIB	*Exc.*	*V.G.*	*Good*	*Fair*	*Poor*
1250	850	650	400	300	250

Red Label Over-and-Under Sporting Clays

Offered in 20 gauge this model was introduced in 1994 with 3" chambers and 30" barrels. Walnut stock has checkering and pistol grip. Weight is about 7 lbs.NOTE: Factory engraved Red Label shotguns are catalogued, as of 1996, as available with three different engraving coverages. A total of 375 were produced. Prices for these engraved guns are:

Grade 1—EXC.—$2200
Grade 2 (1/3 coverage)—EXC.—$2400
Grade 3 (2/3 coverage)—EXC.—$2750

Courtesy compliments of Bill Ruger, John C. Dougan

NIB	*Exc.*	*V.G.*	*Good*	*Fair*	*Poor*
1050	950	750	500	325	225

Red Label All-Weather Over-and-Under

Offered in 12 gauge only with 26", 28", or 30" barrels this model is fitted with a black synthetic stock with pistol grip. Weight is about 7.5 lbs. Introduced in 1999.

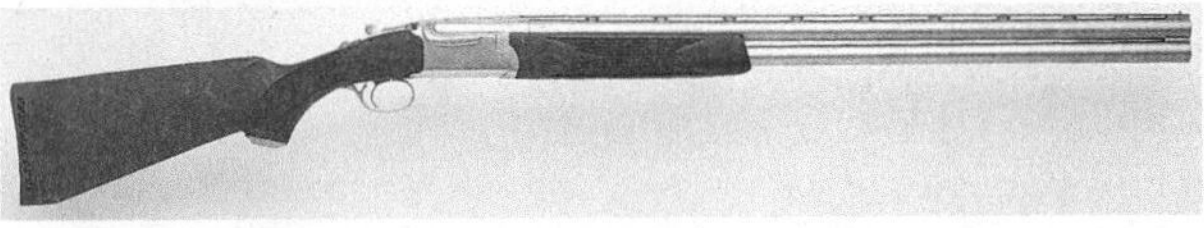

NIB	*Exc.*	*V.G.*	*Good*	*Fair*	*Poor*
1200	875	650	400	300	250

Engraved Red Label Over-and-Under

This model features a scroll engraved receiver with a gold inlaid game bird appropriate to gauge. The 12 gauge: pheasant; 20 gauge: grouse; and 28 gauge: woodcock. Walnut stock. Other specifications same as standard Red Label shotguns. Introduced in 2000. Premium for 28 ga.

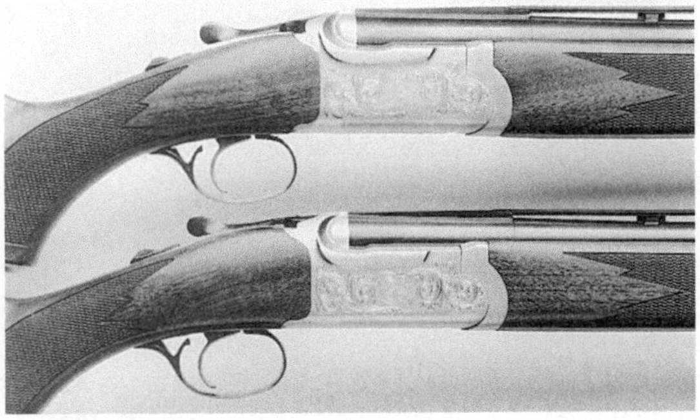

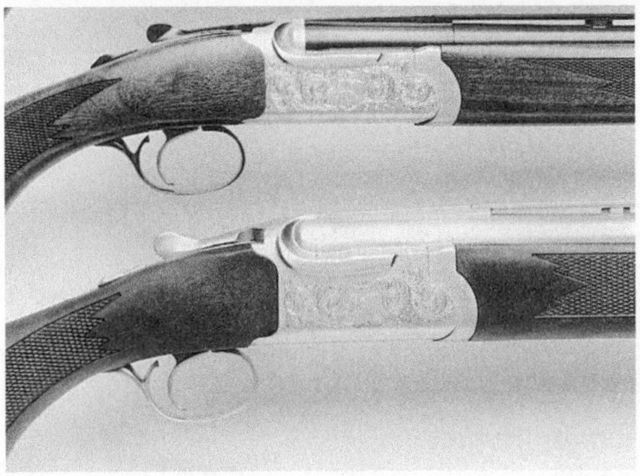

NIB	*Exc.*	*V.G.*	*Good*	*Fair*	*Poor*
1650	1300	1050	750	500	300

Engraved Red Label All-Weather Over-and-Under

Introduced in 2000 this model features a scroll engraved receiver with gold inlaid duck. Offered in 12 gauge only with 26", 28", or 30" barrel.

NIB	*Exc.*	*V.G.*	*Good*	*Fair*	*Poor*
1675	1325	1075	750	500	300

Ruger Woodside Over-and-Under

Introduced in 1995 this new model features a Circassian walnut stock with either pistol grip or straight grip. Available in 12 or 20 gauge with barrel lengths of 26", 28", or 30". Screw-in chokes are standard. **NOTE:** The Woodside shotgun is also available in three different engraving patterns.

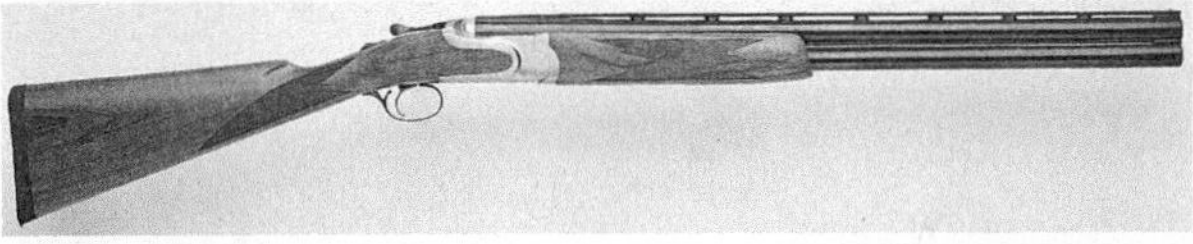

NIB	*Exc.*	*V.G.*	*Good*	*Fair*	*Poor*
1250	850	650	400	300	250

Ruger Trap Model

Introduced in 2000 this model is a 12 gauge single-barrel trap gun with a 34" barrel choked Full and Modified. It is fitted with a mechanical trigger and auto ejector. The stock is select walnut with adjustable cheekpiece and buttplate. Receiver is engraved. Weight is approximately 9 lbs.

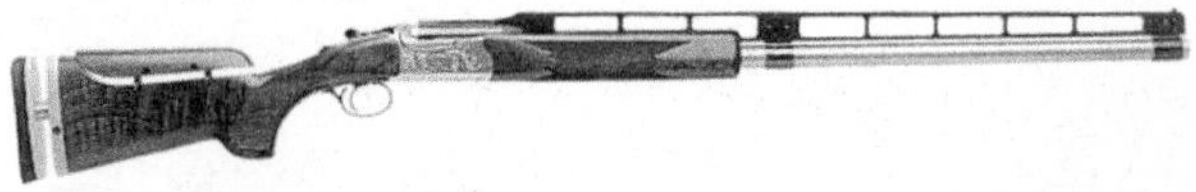

NIB	*Exc.*	*V.G.*	*Good*	*Fair*	*Poor*
3000	2500	1750	1200	900	500

Ruger Gold Label Side-by-Side

Introduced in 2002 this model is chambered for the 12 gauge 3" shell. Offered with 28" barrels with choke tubes. Choice of pistol or straight grip checkered walnut stock. Ejectors and single trigger. Weight is about 6.33 lbs. Discontinued 2008.

NIB	*Exc.*	*V.G.*	*Good*	*Fair*	*Poor*
3000	2450	1975	1300	700	450

T

TACONIC FIREARMS LTD.

Cambridge, New York

NOTE: Barrel interchangeability is acceptable for blued barrels and frames with stainless steel barrels and frames. DO NOT interchange Alloy II barrels and frames with either blued or stainless steel components.

M98 Ultimate Hunter

This bolt-action rifle is based on the M98 Mauser action. It is available in calibers from .22-250 to .358 Win. Stainless steel barrel length is 22". Titanium grip cap. Stock is XXX English walnut with cheekpiece and oil finish. Ebony forend tip. Scope bases are integral to the receiver. The prices listed is for the standard rifle. There are an extensive list of options which will greatly affect price. For example an optional quarter rib will add $1000 to the base price of the gun. Value speculative.

NIB	*Exc.*	*V.G.*	*Good*	*Fair*	*Poor*
6000 — 10000					

TALLASSEE

Tallassee, Alabama

Carbine

A .58 caliber single-shot percussion carbine with a 25" round barrel and full-length stock secured by two barrel bands. Fitted with sling swivels. Barrel and lock finished in the bright, brass furniture and walnut stock. The lock marked "C.S./Tallassee/ Ala." Approximately 500 of these carbines were manufactured in 1864. Very Rare.

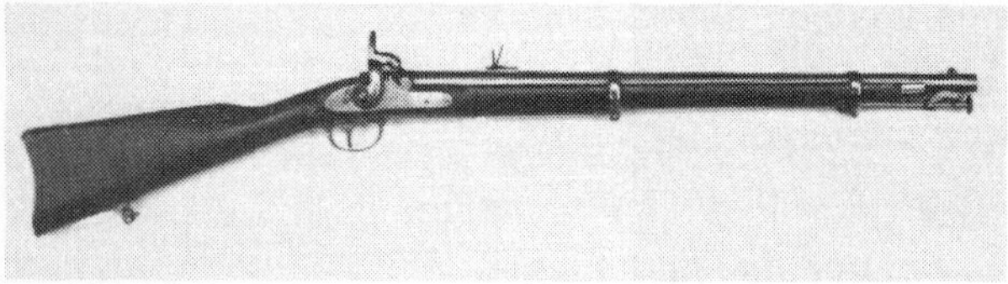

Courtesy Milwaukee Public Museum, Milwaukee, Wisconsin

NIB	*Exc.*	*V.G.*	*Good*	*Fair*	*Poor*
—	—	71250	33000	24500	10000

TANNER, ANDRE

Switzerland

Model 300 Free Rifle

A 7.5mm Swiss or .308 caliber single-shot rifle with varying length barrels having adjustable target sights, adjustable trigger, and a walnut stock fitted with a palm rest and adjustable cheekpiece. Blued.

NIB	*Exc.*	*V.G.*	*Good*	*Fair*	*Poor*
4750	3750	3000	2500	1500	750

Model 300S

As above, with a 10-shot magazine and not fitted with a palm rest. Discontinued in 1988.

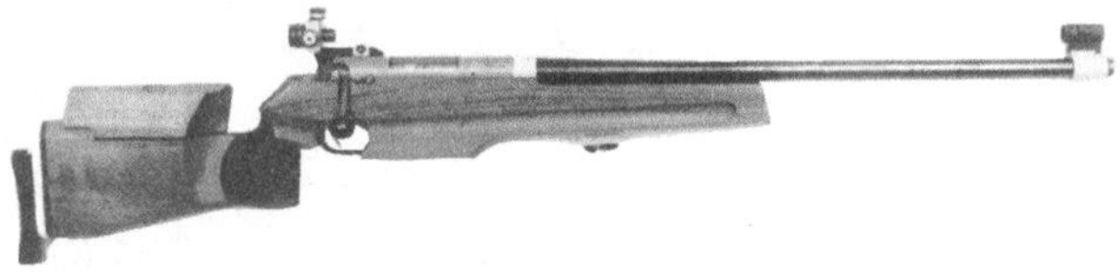

NIB	*Exc.*	*V.G.*	*Good*	*Fair*	*Poor*
4500	3500	2750	2250	1250	750

Model 50F

As above, in .22 caliber with a thumb hole stock. Discontinued in 1988.

NIB	*Exc.*	*V.G.*	*Good*	*Fair*	*Poor*
3750	3000	2500	1750	900	500

TAURUS INTERNATIONAL MFG. CO.

Porto Alegre, Brazil

TRACKER SERIES

Tracker 5mm Remington Magum Rimfire

Nine-shot double-action stainless steel revolver chambered in, of all things, 5mm Remington Magnum Rimfire. Introduced 2008. Ever produced? Doubtful.

RIFLES

Model 62 Carbine

Same as above but with a 16.5" barrel. Magazine capacity is 12 rounds. Weight is about 4.5 lbs. Introduced in 2000.

NIB	*Exc.*	*V.G.*	*Good*	*Fair*	*Poor*
350	300	225	175	125	75

NOTE: In 2003 this model was offered in .22 WMR and .17 HMR calibers. Add 10 percent for stainless.

Model 62 Upstart

This model is similar to the Model 62 above but with a shorter buttstock. Introduced in 2002.

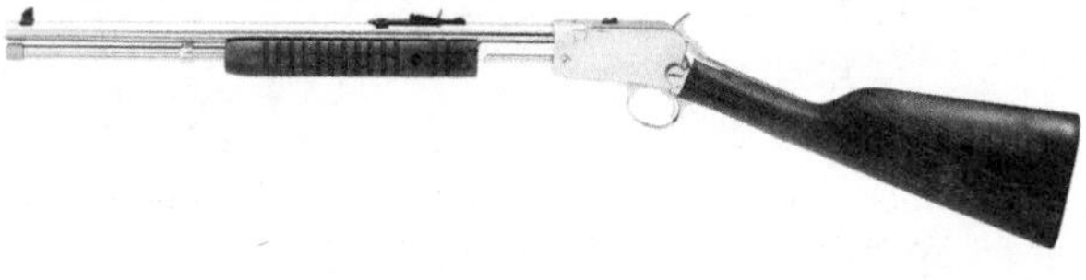

NIB	Exc.	V.G.	Good	Fair	Poor
350	300	225	175	125	75

Model 72

Same as the Model 62 but chambered for the .22 Magnum cartridge.

NIB	Exc.	V.G.	Good	Fair	Poor
350	300	225	175	125	75

NOTE: Add $15 for stainless steel.

Model 72 Carbine

Same as the Model 62 Carbine but chambered for the .22 Magnum cartridge.

NIB	Exc.	V.G.	Good	Fair	Poor
350	300	225	175	125	75

NOTE: Add $15 for stainless steel. Value speculative.

Model 174R-B

This lever action model resembles the Winchester Model 62 but without the slide action. Chambered for the .17 HMR and fitted with a 23" barrel. Checkered forearm but plain straight grip buttstock. Choice of blue of stainless steel finish. Weight is about 5 lbs. Introduced in 2005. Ever produced? Doubtful.

Model 63

Copy of the Winchester Model 63 in takedown. Chambered for the .22 LR cartridge and fitted with a 23" round barrel with adjustable rear sight. Offered in blue or stainless steel. Introduced in 2002. In 2003 this model was reportedly also offered chambered for the .17 Mach II rimfire cartridge. Was it really? Discontinued.

NIB	Exc.	V.G.	Good	Fair	Poor
300	245	200	150	100	75

Model 62LAR Lever Rifle

Lever-action rifle chambered in .22 LR. 23-inch blued barrel, walnut-finish hardwood stock. Introduced 2006. KInd of a lever-operated pump.

NIB	Exc.	V.G.	Good	Fair	Poor
450	375	300	250	195	10

NOTE: Value speculative.

Model 62LAR-SS

Similar to Model 62LAR but in stainless steel. Introduced 2006. It is unclear whether this rifle was ever actually produced.

Thunderbolt

This slide-action rifle is a knockoff of the Colt Lightning rifle and is chambered for the .45 Colt cartridge as well as the .38/.357 Magnum. Fitted with a 26" barrel with adjustable sights. Blued or stainless steel finish. Stocks are hardwood. Weight is about 8.125 lbs. Introduced in 2004.

NIB	Exc.	V.G.	Good	Fair	Poor
550	450	325	250	175	150

NOTE: Add $50 for stainless steel or bright "Sundance" stainless finish.

Taurus CT9G2

Semi-auto carbine with hybrid aluminum/polymer construction. Reinforced steel frame. Lower receiver made with high-strength polymer reinforced with steel. Upper receiver has a flat top Picatinny rail. Two-position safety lever. Adjustable rear sight, fixed front. Ambidextrous slide catch. Available in 9mm, .40 S&W, .45 ACP. Taurus Security System installed. Introduced in 2011.

NIB	Exc.	V.G.	Good	Fair	Poor
700	600	500	—	—	—

TAYLOR'S & CO., INC.

Winchester, Virginia

RIFLES

KENTUCKY RIFLE

Offered in either flintlock or percussion this rifle is .40 caliber and fitted with a 3.5" barrel. One-piece stock with brass fixtures.

Flintlock (Model 183)

NIB	Exc.	V.G.	Good	Fair	Poor
495	335	225	150	100	75

Percussion (Model 182)

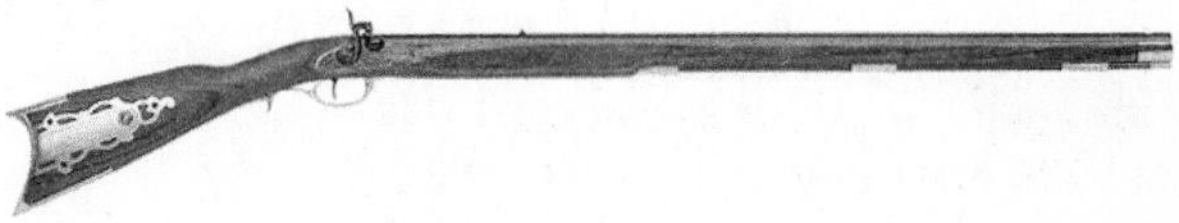

NIB	Exc.	V.G.	Good	Fair	Poor
475	325	200	150	100	75

MODEL 1842 U.S. PERCUSSION MUSKET (MODEL 125)

This model is offered as a smoothbore or rifled musket with 42" .69 caliber barrel. Finish is in the white. One-piece walnut stock.

Smoothbore

NIB	*Exc.*	*V.G.*	*Good*	*Fair*	*Poor*
450	325	250	200	150	100

Rifled Smoothbore with Rear Sight (Model 126)

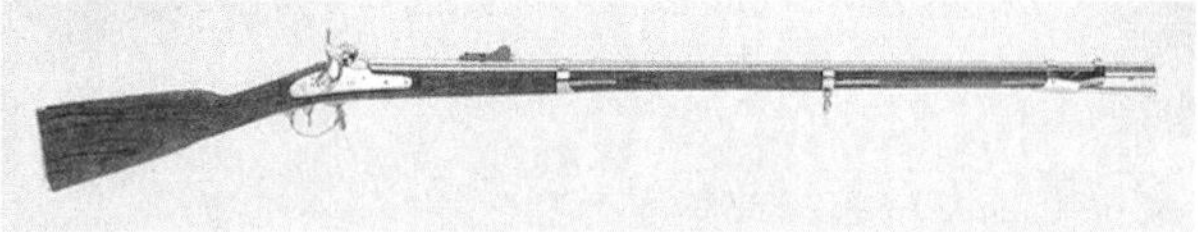

NIB	*Exc.*	*V.G.*	*Good*	*Fair*	*Poor*
450	325	250	200	150	100

Model 1855 U.S. Percussion Musket (Model 116)

This model has a .58 caliber 40" barrel with rear sight. One-piece walnut stock. White satin finish.

NIB	*Exc.*	*V.G.*	*Good*	*Fair*	*Poor*
500	375	225	175	150	125

Model 1853 3-Band Enfield Musket (Model 120)

This rifled musket has a 39" .58 caliber barrel. Blued finish. One-piece walnut stock. Brass buttplate, nosecap, and trigger guard.

NIB	*Exc.*	*V.G.*	*Good*	*Fair*	*Poor*
475	350	300	250	200	100

Model 1858 2-Band Enfield Musket (Model 121)

Similar to the above model but fitted with a .58 caliber 33" barrel.

NIB	*Exc.*	*V.G.*	*Good*	*Fair*	*Poor*
475	350	300	250	200	100

Model 1861 Springfield Musket (Model 110)

This model has a 40" .58 caliber barrel with one-piece walnut stock. White satin finish.

NIB	*Exc.*	*V.G.*	*Good*	*Fair*	*Poor*
550	425	350	300	200	100

Model 1862 C.S. Richmond Musket (Model 115)

This rifle is fitted with a 40" .58 caliber barrel with three barrel bands. Brass buttplate and nosecap. White satin finish. One-piece walnut stock.

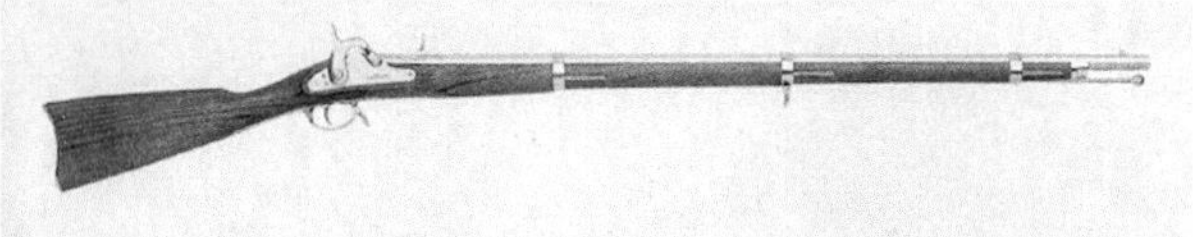

NIB	*Exc.*	*V.G.*	*Good*	*Fair*	*Poor*
550	425	350	300	200	100

Model 1863 Remington Zouave (Model 140)

Fitted with a 33" barrel chambered for the .58 caliber ball. One-piece walnut stock with blued finish, brass buttplate, nosecap, trigger guard, patchbox, and barrel bands.

NIB	*Exc.*	*V.G.*	*Good*	*Fair*	*Poor*
450	325	250	200	150	100

HENRY RIFLE

This lever-action rifle is chambered for the .44-40 or .45 Colt cartridge. Fitted with a 24.25" octagon barrel. Walnut stock. Open sights.

Brass Frame (Model 198)

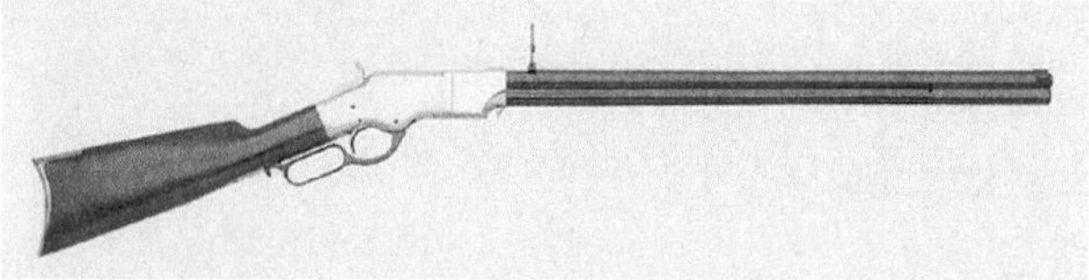

NIB	*Exc.*	*V.G.*	*Good*	*Fair*	*Poor*
875	700	600	500	400	200

Iron Frame (Model 199)

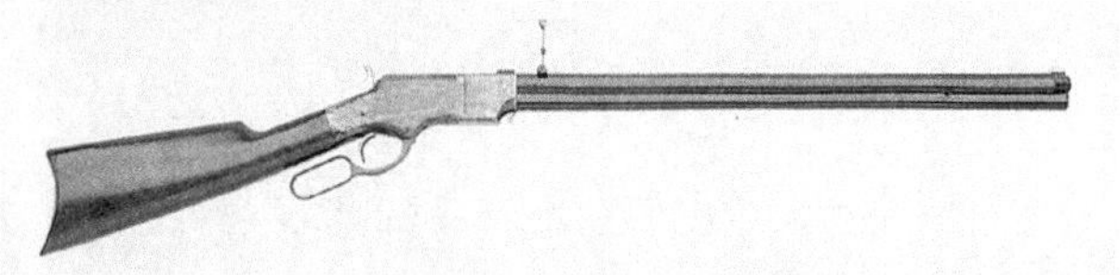

NIB	*Exc.*	*V.G.*	*Good*	*Fair*	*Poor*
925	750	650	500	400	200

Winchester Model 1866 (Model 201)

This model is chambered for the .44-40 or .45 Colt cartridge. Fitted with a 24.25" octagon barrel. Brass frame. Open sights. Made by Uberti.

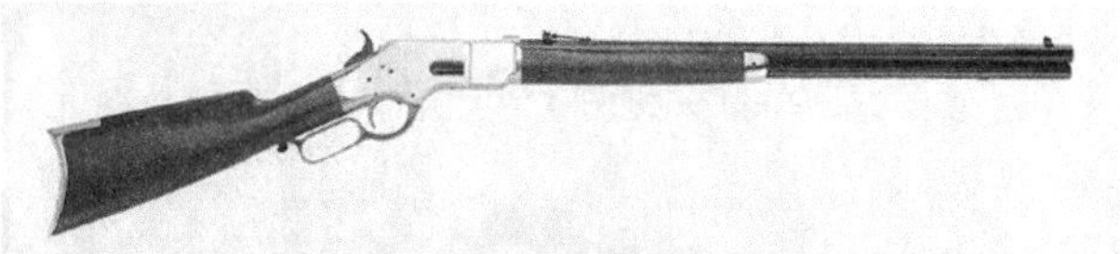

NIB	*Exc.*	*V.G.*	*Good*	*Fair*	*Poor*
830	650	575	400	300	175

Winchester Model 1866 Yellowboy Carbine (Model 202)

Same as above but with 19" round barrel and the additional .38 Special caliber. Made by Uberti.

NIB	*Exc.*	*V.G.*	*Good*	*Fair*	*Poor*
850	675	525	450	300	150

Winchester Model 1873 (Model 200)

This lever action model is chambered for the .44-40 or .45 Colt cartridge and fitted with a 24.25" octagon barrel. Made by Uberti.

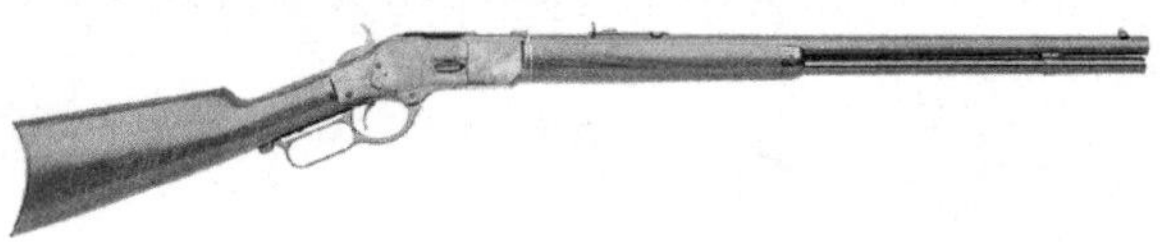

NIB	*Exc.*	*V.G.*	*Good*	*Fair*	*Poor*
900	725	600	500	400	200

Winchester Model 1873 Carbine (Model 200B)

Chambered for the .45 Long Colt cartridge and fitted with a 19" barrel. Magazine capacity is 10 rounds. Walnut stock and case colored frame.

NIB	*Exc.*	*V.G.*	*Good*	*Fair*	*Poor*
900	725	600	500	400	200

Winchester Model 1873 Sporting Rifle (Model 200C)

Chambered for the .45 Long Colt cartridge and fitted with a 30" octagon barrel. Checkered walnut stock with pistol grip. Case colored frame and blued barrel.

NIB	Exc.	V.G.	Good	Fair	Poor
900	725	600	500	400	200

Winchester Model 1885 High Wall (Model 203)

Offered with 30" or 32" barrels chambered for the .45-70 cartridge. Walnut stock.

NIB	Exc.	V.G.	Good	Fair	Poor
900	725	600	500	400	200

Winchester Model 1885 Low Wall Sporting Rifle (Model 204)

This single-shot rifle is chambered for the .22 LR, .32-20, or .38-40 cartridge. Checkered walnut stock.

NIB	Exc.	V.G.	Good	Fair	Poor
900	725	600	500	400	200

Winchester Model 92

Introduced in 2004 this lever-action rifle is chambered for the .32-20, .32 H&R Magnum, .357 Magnum, .38 Special, .38-40, .44-40, .44 S&W, or the .45 Colt. Barrel length is 20" or 24" octagon. Takedown feature. Hardwood stock with blued barrel finish and case colored frame.

NIB	Exc.	V.G.	Good	Fair	Poor
725	625	450	300	250	200

Sharps Model 1859 Infantry (Model 151)

This rifle is fitted with a 30" round barrel and is chambered for the .54 caliber cartridge. One-piece walnut with 3 barrel bands. Adjustable rear sight.

NIB	Exc.	V.G.	Good	Fair	Poor
1150	800	600	400	300	150

Sharps Model 1859 Berdan Military (Model 152)

This .54 caliber rifle is fitted with a 30" round barrel. One-piece walnut stock with 3 barrel bands. Adjustable rear sight. This model is fitted with double set triggers.

NIB	Exc.	V.G.	Good	Fair	Poor
1150	800	600	400	300	150

Sharps Model 1859 Cavalry (Model 153)

This model has a 22" round barrel with adjustable rear sight. Chambered for .54 caliber. Walnut stock is fitted with patch box.

NIB	Exc.	V.G.	Good	Fair	Poor
1150	800	600	400	300	150

Sharps Model 1863 Cavalry (Model 154)

Similar to the Model 1859 Cavalry but without the patch box.

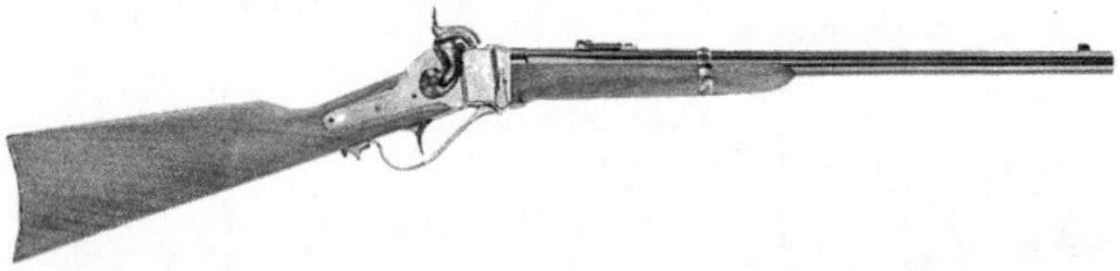

NIB	Exc.	V.G.	Good	Fair	Poor
1150	800	600	400	300	150

Sharps Model 1863 Sporting Rifle (Model 131)

This .54 caliber model is offered with either 30" or 32" octagon barrel with single or double set triggers. Walnut stock.

NIB	Exc.	V.G.	Good	Fair	Poor
1150	800	600	400	300	150

NOTE: Add $20 for double set trigger.

Sharps Model 1874 Sporting Rifle (Model 138)

This model is offered with a variety of features. Available in .45-70 with choice of 30" or 32" octagon barrel with a choice of single trigger or double set triggers. It is also available with Hartford-style pewter forend tip. In this configuration it is available in .45-70, .40-65, .45-90, or .45-120 calibers. Checkered stock with patch is optional.

NIB	Exc.	V.G.	Good	Fair	Poor
895	700	545	400	315	175

NOTE: Add $125 for Hartford-style forend tip. Add $250 for checkered stock with patch box.

Sharps Model 1874 Deluxe Sporting Rifle (Model 155)

This .45-70 caliber model features a hand checkered walnut stock with oil finish. Receiver is in the white with standard scroll engraving.

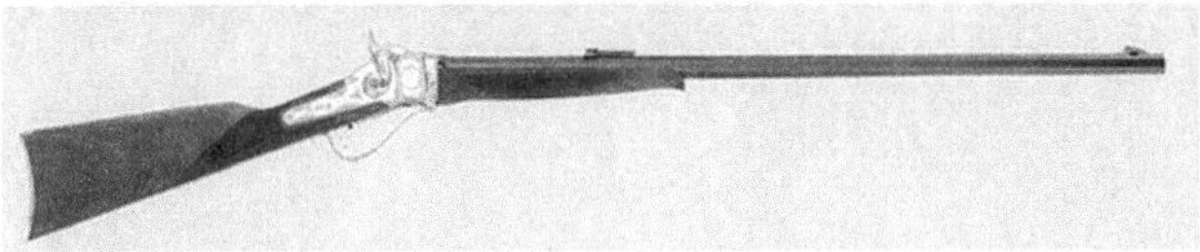

NIB	Exc.	V.G.	Good	Fair	Poor
1800	1350	1050	775	595	200

NOTE: For Deluxe Model 1874 with gold inlay add $800.

Sharps Model 1874 Infantry Rifle (Model 157)

This .45-70 caliber model features a 30" round barrel with 3 barrel bands. One-piece walnut stock. Adjustable rear sight. Single trigger. Patch box in stock.

NIB	Exc.	V.G.	Good	Fair	Poor
1325	1000	750	550	375	200

Sharps Model 1874 Berdan Rifle (Model 158)

Similar to the above model but with a double set trigger.

NIB	Exc.	V.G.	Good	Fair	Poor
1325	1000	750	550	375	200

Sharps Model 1874 Cavalry (Model 159)

This .45-70 caliber model is fitted with a 22" round barrel. Adjustable rear sight.

NIB	Exc.	V.G.	Good	Fair	Poor
1150	800	600	400	300	150

Spencer Model 1865 Carbine (Model 160)

This lever-action model is chambered in a choice of calibers: .56-50, .44 Russian, or .45 Schofield. Fitted with a 20" round barrel. Walnut stock. Case hardened receiver and blued barrel. Made by Armi Sport.

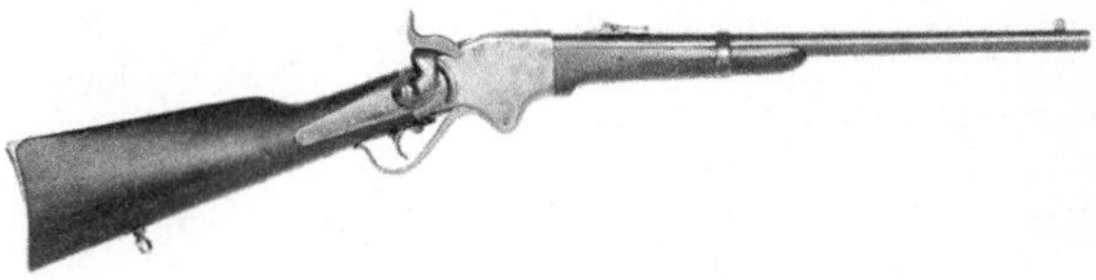

NIB	Exc.	V.G.	Good	Fair	Poor
1200	1050	875	750	500	400

Spencer Model 1865 Rifle

As above but with 30" barrel with three barrel bands. Chambered for the .56-50 cartridge.

NIB	Exc.	V.G.	Good	Fair	Poor
1200	1050	875	750	500	400

TEXAS CONTRACT RIFLES

Three contractors produced rifles for the State of Texas during 1862 and 1863. One of these patterns has a sporting back-action lock, Enfield barrel bands, an overall length of 47-3/8", heavy 32" long barrel of .58 caliber. Total deliveries by all contractors amounted to 1,464 rifles. Quality of these arms was decidedly inferior and often complained about.

THOMPSON/CENTERARMS

Rochester, New Hampshire

NOTE: In late 2006 it was announced that Thompson/Center Arms had been acquired by Smith & Wesson.

G2 Contender Rifle

This rifle is fitted with a 23" barrel with no sights and is chambered for the .17 HMR, .22 LR, .223 Rem., .30-30, and the .45-70. Walnut stock with blued finish. Weight is about 5.4 lbs. In 2004 the .375 JDJ and .204 Ruger calibers were added.

NIB	Exc.	V.G.	Good	Fair	Poor
600	500	400	325	275	200

G2 Contender Shotgun

Chambered for the .410 bore shell and fitted with a 24" ventilated rib barrel. Walnut stock. Weight is about 5.4 lbs. Introduced in 2004.

NIB	Exc.	V.G.	Good	Fair	Poor
600	500	400	325	275	200

CONTENDER CARBINE MODEL

This model is built from the same design as the Contender Model. It features completely interchangeable barrels chambered for 12 different cartridges from .22 LR to .35 Rem. A .410 bore shotgun barrel is also offered. The standard model has a 21" barrel stocked with walnut. For stainless steel models a composite stock in fitted walnut is also available. All are drilled and tapped for scope mounts. Available in blued or stainless steel.

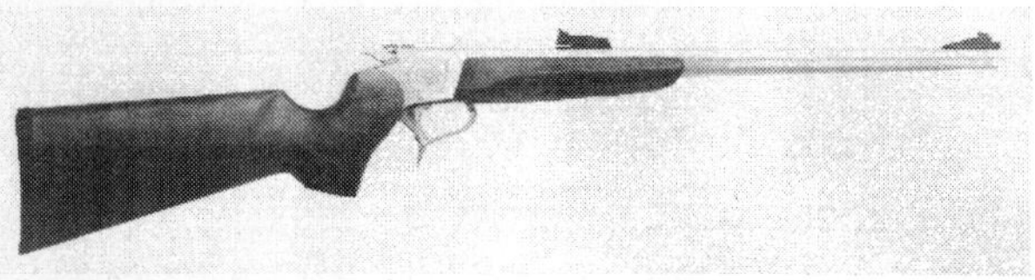

Standard 21" Carbine

This model is fitted with a 21" plain barrel and walnut stocks. Offered in these calibers as a complete gun only: .22 LR, .22 LR Match (blued only), .17 Rem. (blued only), .22 Hornet, .223 Rem., 7-30 Waters, .30-30, .35 Rem. (blued only), .375 Win. (blued only). Weighs 5 lbs. 3 oz.

NIB	Exc.	V.G.	Good	Fair	Poor
500	400	350	300	250	200

21" Carbine .410 Bore

Same as above but fitted with a vent rib barrel and screw-in choke.

NIB	Exc.	V.G.	Good	Fair	Poor
475	375	300	250	200	100

16" Youth Model Carbine

A special walnut buttstock with 12" length of pull and 16.25" barrel. Short buttstock can be replaced with standard buttstock. Blued or stainless steel finish. Complete guns are offered in the same calibers as the 21" Carbine with the exception of the .375 Win. and the addition of the .45 Long Colt/.410 bore with vent rib barrel.

NIB	Exc.	V.G.	Good	Fair	Poor
475	375	300	250	200	100

HotShot Youth Rifle

Single-shot dropping-barrel rifle chambered in .22 Long Rifle. Features include a crowned 19-inch steel barrel, exposed hammer, synthetic forend and buttstock, peep sight (receiver drilled and tapped for optics), three stock pattern options (black, Realtree AP and pink AP). Overall weight 3 lbs., 11.5-inch length of pull. Price: $229 to $249.

Encore Katahdin Carbine

This model is fitted with a heavy 18" barrel with integral muzzle-brake. Offered in .444 Marlin, .450 Marlin, and .45-70 Government calibers. Blued finish with composite stock and adjustable fiber optic sights. Weight is about 6.75 lbs. Introduced in 2002.

NIB	Exc.	V.G.	Good	Fair	Poor
650	550	425	300	225	175

Encore Katahdin Turkey Gun

This is a 12 gauge 3" chamber gun with 20" barrel and screw-in Turkey chokes. Open sights. Realtree Hardwoods HD camo composite stock. Weight is about 6 lbs. Introduced in 2005.

NIB	Exc.	V.G.	Good	Fair	Poor
750	575	450	325	225	200

Encore Shotgun 20 Gauge

Introduced in 1998 this model is fitted with a 26" 20 gauge vent rib barrel with walnut stock and forend. Choke tubes are standard.

NIB	Exc.	V.G.	Good	Fair	Poor
650	550	425	300	225	175

Encore Camo Shotgun 12 Gauge

This model features a 24" smoothbore barrel with screw-in turkey choke, camo stock and metal pattern. Blued frame with composite stock. Introduced in 2002.

NIB	Exc.	V.G.	Good	Fair	Poor
750	575	450	325	225	200

Encore Shotgun 12 Gauge

This model features a 3" 26" ventilated rib barrel with bead front sight. Blued with walnut stock. Weight is about 6.6 lbs. Introduced in 2004.

NIB	Exc.	V.G.	Good	Fair	Poor
750	575	450	325	225	200

Encore Rifled Shotgun 20 Gauge

Introduced in 2000 this model features a 26" rifled shotgun barrel chambered for the 20 gauge shell. Adjustable rear sight. Walnut stock and blued finish.

NIB	Exc.	V.G.	Good	Fair	Poor
650	550	425	300	225	175

Encore Rifled Shotgun 12 Gauge

Introduced in 2002 this model is fitted with a 24" rifled barrel with adjustable fiber optic sights. Blued with walnut stock.

NIB	Exc.	V.G.	Good	Fair	Poor
650	550	425	300	225	175

Encore Turkey Gun

Introduced in 2005 this model is chambered for the 20 gauge shell with 3" chamber, 26" barrel with open sights and screw-in Turkey chokes. Realtree Hardwoods HD camo composite stock.

NIB	*Exc.*	*V.G.*	*Good*	*Fair*	*Poor*
650	550	425	300	225	175

Thompson/Center ProHunter Predator Rifle

Contender-style break-action single shot rifle chambered in .204 Ruger, .223 Remington, .22-250 and .308 Winchester. Features include 28-inch deep-fluted interchangeable barrel, composite buttstock and for-end with non-slip inserts in cheekpiece, pistol grip and for-end. Max 1 camo finish overall. Overall length: 42.5 inches. Weight: 7-3/4 lbs.

NIB	*Exc.*	*V.G.*	*Good*	*Fair*	*Poor*
750	650	500	400	300	250

Icon

Bolt-action centerfire rifle chambered in .22-250, .243, .308 and .30 Thompson-Center. Barrel length 22" (iron sight) or 24" (sightless). Detachable box magazine, Introduced in 2007.

NIB	*Exc.*	*V.G.*	*Good*	*Fair*	*Poor*
900	800	675	525	300	200

Icon Classic Long Action Rifle

Similar to Icon but with long-action design and chambered for .270, .30-06, .300 Winchester Magnum and 7mm Remington Magnum.

NIB	*Exc.*	*V.G.*	*Good*	*Fair*	*Poor*
1000	850	700	600	400	200

Icon Weathershield Medium Action Rifle

Similar to Icon but with stainless steel barrel and receiver and black synthetic or RealTree AP Camo stock.

NIB	*Exc.*	*V.G.*	*Good*	*Fair*	*Poor*
1000	850	700	600	400	200

Thompson/Center Venture Medium Action Rifle

Bolt action rifle chambered in .204, .22-250, .223, .243, 7mm-08, .308 and 30TC. Features include a 24-inch crowned medium weight barrel, classic styled composite stock with inlaid traction grip panels, adjustable 3.5 to 5 pound trigger along with a drilled and tapped receiver (bases included). 3+1 detachable nylon box magazine. Overall length: 7 lbs. Length: 43.5 inches.

NIB	*Exc.*	*V.G.*	*Good*	*Fair*	*Poor*
500	400	325	250	175	100

Thompson/Center Venture Predator PDX Rifle

Bolt action rifle chambered in .204, .22-250, .223, .243, .308. Similar to Venture Medium action but with heavy, deep-fluted 22-inch barrel and Max-1 camo finish overall. Overall length: 8 lbs. Length: 41.5 inches.

NIB	*Exc.*	*V.G.*	*Good*	*Fair*	*Poor*
600	500	425	350	275	200

Venture Weather Shield

Advanced Weather Shield finish for durability. Classic styled composite stock with Hogue Overmolded Grip panels. Classic styled composite stock. T/C large bolt design for smooth operation. 60 degree bolt lift. Receiver drilled and tapped with bases included. Magazine capacity, 3+1. Available in short and long-action models for most standard, magnum and WSM cartridges.

NIB	*Exc.*	*V.G.*	*Good*	*Fair*	*Poor*
525	450	380	325	225	150

Model R55

This semi-automatic rifle is chambered for the .17 Mach 2 cartridge and fitted with a 20" match grade barrel with adjustable sights. Black composite or laminated hardwood stock. Receiver is blued or stainless steel. Magazine capacity is 5 rounds. Weight is about 5.5 lbs. Introduced in 2005.

NIB	*Exc.*	*V.G.*	*Good*	*Fair*	*Poor*
550	450	375	300	250	175

NOTE: Add $65 for black composite stock.

TCR 87 Hunter Model

This single-shot top lever rifle is chambered for cartridges from .22 LR to .308 Win. Fitted with a 23" barrel. The finish is blue with walnut stock. Discontinued as a regular production rifle in 1993.

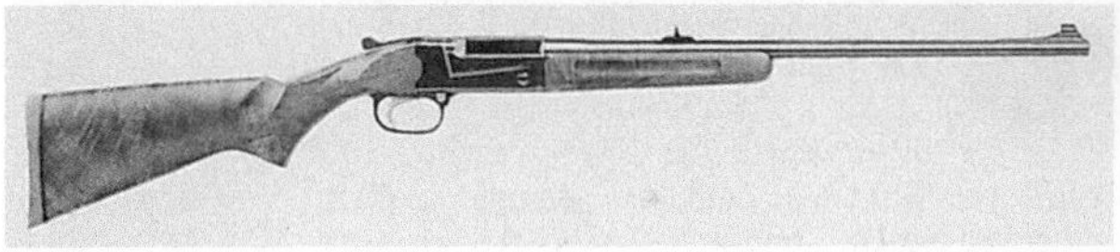

NIB	*Exc.*	*V.G.*	*Good*	*Fair*	*Poor*
650	550	425	300	225	175

T/C 22 LR Classic

Introduced in 2000 this model is a semi-automatic rifle chambered for the .22 LR cartridge. It is fitted with a 22" match grade barrel. Walnut stock with Monte Carlo comb. Adjustable rear sight. Magazine capacity is 8 rounds. Weight is about 5.5 lbs.

NIB	*Exc.*	*V.G.*	*Good*	*Fair*	*Poor*
450	350	275	225	175	100

.22 Classic Benchmark

An updated version of the Classic with an 18" heavy barrel and no sights. Wood laminated target stock. Magazine capacity is 10 rounds. Weight is about 6.8 lbs. Introduced in 2003.

NIB	*Exc.*	*V.G.*	*Good*	*Fair*	*Poor*
475	375	300	250	200	100

BLACKPOWDER FIREARMS

System 1

Introduced in 1997 this concept features a complete muzzleloading system with interchangeable barrels. Offered with .32, .50, .54, .58 caliber and 12 gauge shotgun barrels with walnut stock and blued finish. Or stainless steel with synthetic stock. Barrel lengths are 26". Approximate weight is 7.5 lbs. Sights are adjustable.

NIB	*Exc.*	*V.G.*	*Good*	*Fair*	*Poor*
350	300	225	175	125	75

NOTE: Add $30 for synthetic stock and stainless steel.

Thunder Hawk

Introduced in 1993, this rifle features a .50 caliber caplock in-line ignition with 21" round barrel. Rear sight is adjustable with ramp front sight. The stock is a plain American black walnut with rubber recoil pad. Trigger is adjustable. In 1994 this model was available in stainless steel. Weighs 6.75 lbs.

NIB	*Exc.*	*V.G.*	*Good*	*Fair*	*Poor*
225	200	175	150	100	75

Thunder Hawk Shadow

Introduced in 1996, this model features an in-line ignition in .50 or .54 caliber with a 24" round barrel. It comes standard with a black checkered composite stock. Weight is approximately 7 lbs. In 1997 this model was offered with camouflage stock and blued finish.

NIB	*Exc.*	*V.G.*	*Good*	*Fair*	*Poor*
300	250	200	150	100	75

Grey Hawk

This stainless steel composite stock rifle is a .50 caliber cap-lock with 24" round barrel. It utilizes a hooked breech system. The lock is a heavy-duty coil spring with floral engraving pattern. Adjustable rear sight and bead front sight are standard. Weighs about 7 lbs.

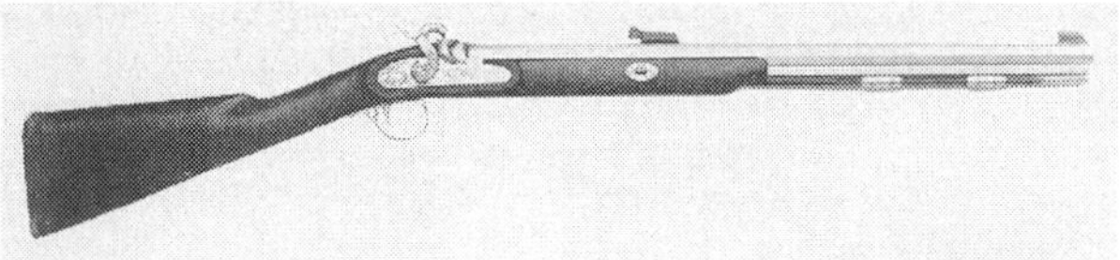

NIB	*Exc.*	*V.G.*	*Good*	*Fair*	*Poor*
225	200	175	150	100	75

Hawken Caplock Rifle

Available in .45, .50, and .54 caliber this rifle has a 28" octagonal barrel and hooked breech system. Triggers are fully adjustable and can function as double set or single stage. Adjustable sights with bead front sight are standard. Trim is solid brass and stock is select American walnut with cheekpiece. Weighs about 8.5 lbs.

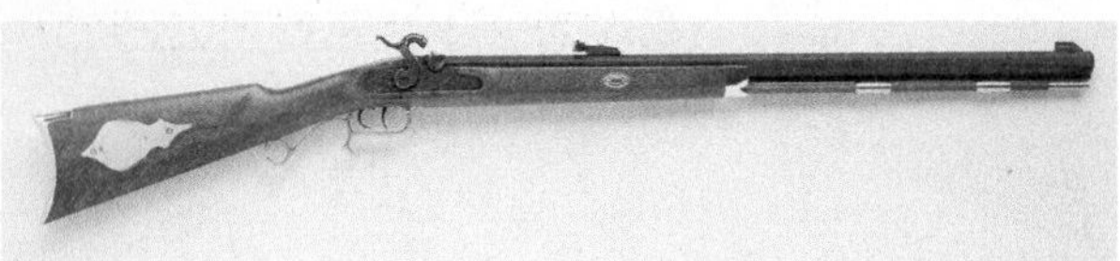

NIB	*Exc.*	*V.G.*	*Good*	*Fair*	*Poor*
300	250	200	150	100	75

Hawken Flintlock Rifle

Offered in .50 caliber with 28" octagonal barrel. All other features are the same as above.

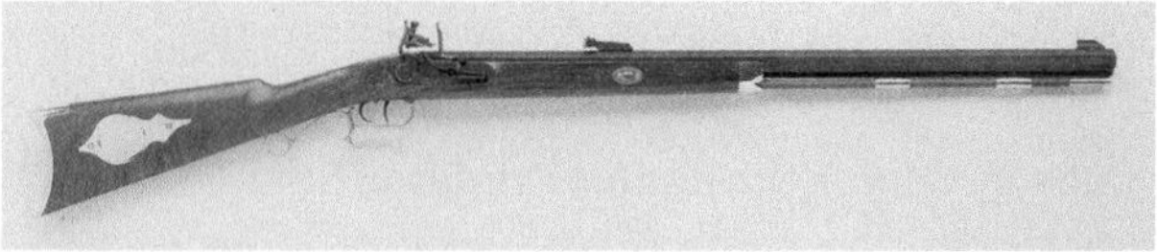

NIB	*Exc.*	*V.G.*	*Good*	*Fair*	*Poor*
310	260	200	150	100	75

Hawken Custom/Elite

Introduced in 1994 this model is a .50 caliber traditional cap-lock rifle with double set triggers, crescent butt, and select American walnut stock with no patch box. The finish is a high luster blue.

NIB	*Exc.*	*V.G.*	*Good*	*Fair*	*Poor*
400	350	275	175	100	75

Omega 45/Omega 50

This muzzleloader is chambered for .45 or .50 and fitted with a 28" round barrel. Adjustable sights. Composite or laminated stock. Weight is about 7 lbs. Introduced in 2002.

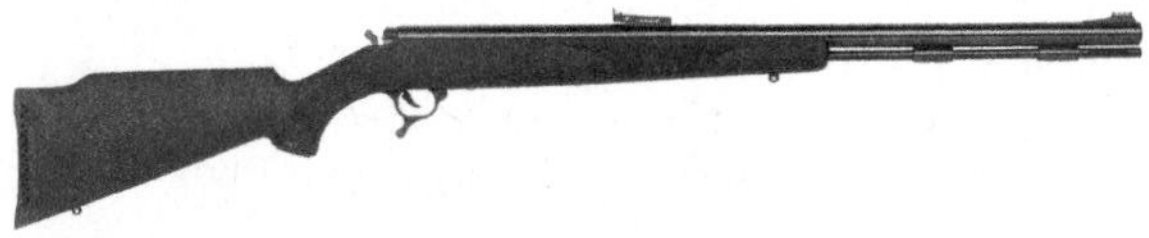

NIB	*Exc.*	*V.G.*	*Good*	*Fair*	*Poor*
535	425	325	250	150	75

NOTE: For stainless steel add $50. Add $60 for Realtree camo stock.

Omega Pivoting Breech Rifle

Introduced in 2004 this rifle has a 28" stainless steel fluted barrel bored for the .50 caliber slug. Laminated wood thumbhole stock. Fiber optic sights. Weight is about 7 lbs.

NIB	*Exc.*	*V.G.*	*Good*	*Fair*	*Poor*
400	350	275	175	100	75

Renegade Caplock Rifle

Offered in .50 or .54 caliber with 26" octagonal barrel. Adjustable triggers that can function as double set or single stage. Adjustable sights with blued trim. Walnut stock. Offered in either right hand or left hand models. Weighs about 8 lbs.

NIB	*Exc.*	*V.G.*	*Good*	*Fair*	*Poor*
460	350	250	150	100	75

Renegade Flintlock

Available in .50 caliber only and right hand only. Other features are the same as Caplock model.

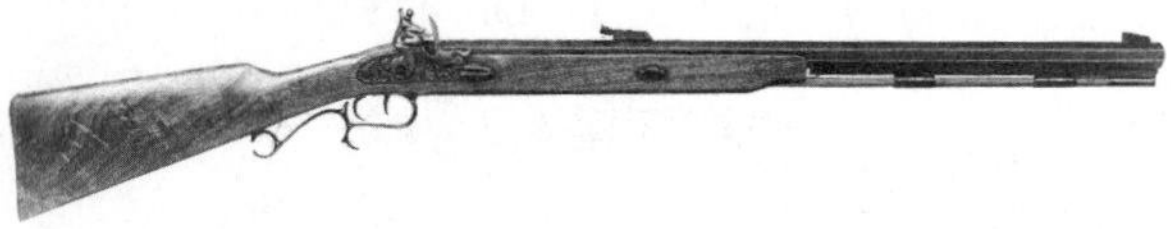

NIB	*Exc.*	*V.G.*	*Good*	*Fair*	*Poor*
460	350	250	150	100	755

Big Boar Rifle

This hooked breech model features the .58 caliber with 26" octagonal barrel. Single trigger and adjustable sights are standard. Trim is blued steel. American walnut stock with rubber pad. Weighs about 7.75 lbs.

NIB	*Exc.*	*V.G.*	*Good*	*Fair*	*Poor*
550	400	300	250	200	100

High Plains Sporter

This is a .50 caliber caplock with a 24" round barrel. The lock is case-colored. Choice of adjustable open sights or tang sight. Trim is blued. The stock is walnut with rubber recoil pad, pistol grip, and sling swivel studs. Weighs about 7 lbs.

NIB	*Exc.*	*V.G.*	*Good*	*Fair*	*Poor*
275	250	200	150	100	75

TREE HAWK

Available in either .50 caliber caplock or 12 gauge caplock. The .50 caliber carbine has a 21" barrel and is offered in camo colors. The 12 gauge shotgun is fitted with a 27" barrel and also comes in camo colors. Weight is about 6.75 lbs.

Rifle

NIB	*Exc.*	*V.G.*	*Good*	*Fair*	*Poor*
275	250	200	150	100	75

Shotgun

NIB	*Exc.*	*V.G.*	*Good*	*Fair*	*Poor*
275	250	200	150	100	75

White Mountain Carbine

Available in either .45, .50, or .54 caliber caplock or .50 flintlock. Fitted with a 20-1/2" octagon barrel. The lock is case-colored and trim is blued. Stock is walnut with rubber recoil pad. Weighs about 6.5 lbs. Discontinued.

NIB	*Exc.*	*V.G.*	*Good*	*Fair*	*Poor*
400	350	275	175	100	75

Black Mountain Magnum

Introduced in 1999 this model features a 26" round barrel with choice of walnut or composite stock. Chambered for .50 or .54 caliber or 12 gauge with 27" round barrel. All models are caplock. Blued finish. Discontinued.

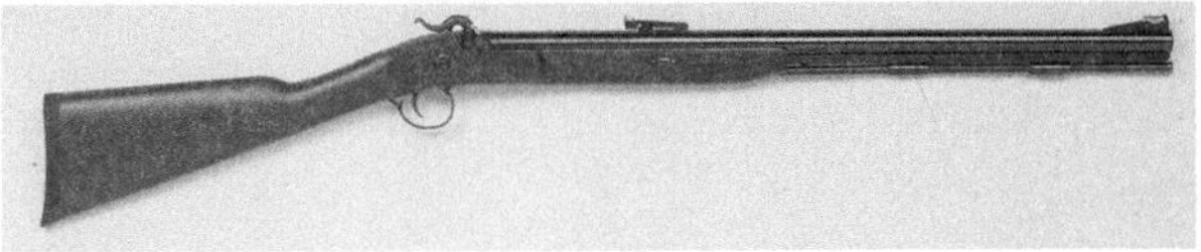

NIB	*Exc.*	*V.G.*	*Good*	*Fair*	*Poor*
400	350	275	175	100	75

Pennsylvania Hunter

Offered in .50 caliber caplock or flintlock and fitted with either a 31-1/2" octagon/round barrel or a 21-1/2" octagon/round barrel. Fully adjustable sights, walnut stock, and blued trim are standard. Rifle weighs about 7.5 lbs. while the carbine weighs about 6.5 lbs. Discontinued.

Pennsylvania Hunter Rifle

NIB	*Exc.*	*V.G.*	*Good*	*Fair*	*Poor*
400	325	250	200	150	100

Pennsylvania Hunter Carbine

NIB	*Exc.*	*V.G.*	*Good*	*Fair*	*Poor*
400	325	250	200	150	100

Pennsylvania Match Rifle

Similar to the Pennsylvania Hunter Rifle except equipped with a tang peep sight and a globe front sight. Discontinued.

NIB	*Exc.*	*V.G.*	*Good*	*Fair*	*Poor*
—	450	375	300	250	175

New Englander Rifle

Offered in either .50 or .54 caliber caplock with walnut stock and 26" round barrel. Adjustable sights. Weighs about 7 lbs. 15 oz. A 12" barrel is optional. Discontinued.

NIB	*Exc.*	*V.G.*	*Good*	*Fair*	*Poor*
350	275	200	150	100	75

NOTE: Add $150 for interchangeable shotgun barrel.

New Englander Shotgun

Same as above, but fitted with a 27" 12 gauge barrel with screw in full choke. Weighs about 6 lbs. 8 oz. Discontinued.

NIB	*Exc.*	*V.G.*	*Good*	*Fair*	*Poor*
350	275	200	150	100	75

NEW ENGLANDER COMPOSITE

Offered with composite stock. The .50 or .54 caliber rifle has a 24" barrel and the 12 gauge shotgun has a 27" barrel. Discontinued.

Rifle

NIB	*Exc.*	*V.G.*	*Good*	*Fair*	*Poor*
350	275	200	150	100	75

Shotgun

NIB	*Exc.*	*V.G.*	*Good*	*Fair*	*Poor*
350	275	200	150	100	75

ProHunter Turkey Gun

Contender-style break-action single shot shotgun chambered in 12 - or 20 gauge 3-inch shells. Features include 24-inch barrel with interchangeable choke tubes (Extra Full supplied), composite buttstock and forend with non-slip inserts in cheekpiece, pistol grip and forend. Adjustable fiber optic sights, Sims recoil pad, AP camo finish overall. Overall length: 40.5 inches. Weight: 6-1/2 lbs. Price: $799.

SCOUT CARBINE

This is a muzzleloading carbine of .50 or .54 caliber with an in-line ignition system. Offered with either walnut stock or composite stock (first offered in 1993) it is fitted with a 21" round barrel. Adjustable rear sight and fixed blade front sight. Brass barrel band and trigger guard on walnut stock and blued barrel band and trigger guard on composite stock model. Weighs about 7 lbs. 4 oz. Discontinued.

Walnut stock

NIB	*Exc.*	*V.G.*	*Good*	*Fair*	*Poor*
325	275	200	150	100	75

Composite stock

NIB	Exc.	V.G.	Good	Fair	Poor
250	225	175	150	100	75

SCOUT RIFLE

Similar to the Scout Carbine but fitted with a 24" stepped half-round, half-octagonal barrel. Weight is approximately 8 lbs. Discontinued.

Walnut Stock

NIB	Exc.	V.G.	Good	Fair	Poor
425	350	275	225	150	100

Composite Stock

NIB	Exc.	V.G.	Good	Fair	Poor
400	325	250	200	150	100

Scout Pistol

The same design as the Scout carbine this single-action pistol is available in .45, .50, or .54 caliber. Fitted with a 12" barrel, adjustable rear sight, and blued finish with brass trigger guard. Black walnut grips. Weighs 4 lbs. 6 oz. Discontinued.

NIB	Exc.	V.G.	Good	Fair	Poor
250	225	200	175	100	75

Fire Hawk Deluxe

Introduced in 1996 this is an in-line muzzleloader. Offered in either .50 or .54 caliber with blued or stainless steel. Semi-fancy checkered walnut stock has a cheekpiece. The round barrel is 24" long. Adjustable rear leaf sight with ramp style front bead. Weight is about 7 lbs.

NIB	Exc.	V.G.	Good	Fair	Poor
400	325	250	200	125	100

FIRE HAWK

Similar to the Deluxe Fire Hawk but with standard American walnut stock or composition stock.

NIB	Exc.	V.G.	Good	Fair	Poor
300	250	200	150	100	75

Fire Hawk Thumbhole Stock

NIB	Exc.	V.G.	Good	Fair	Poor
325	275	225	175	100	75

Fire Hawk Camo Stock

NIB	Exc.	V.G.	Good	Fair	Poor
325	275	225	175	100	75

Fire Hawk Bantam

NIB	Exc.	V.G.	Good	Fair	Poor
275	225	175	125	100	75

Fire Hawk .32 & .58 caliber models

NIB	Exc.	V.G.	Good	Fair	Poor
300	250	200	150	100	75

Fire Storm

Offered as a percussion or flintlock and fitted with a 26" barrel chambered for .50 caliber. Black composite stock. Adjustable fiber optics rear sight. Weight is about 7 lbs. Introduced in 2000.

NIB	Exc.	V.G.	Good	Fair	Poor
375	300	225	150	100	75

Black Diamond

This is an in-line muzzleloading rifle with removable breech plug. Fitted with a 22.5" .50 caliber barrel. Stock is Rynite. Choice of blue or stainless steel. Introduced in 1998. Discontinued.

NIB	Exc.	V.G.	Good	Fair	Poor
325	275	225	175	100	75

NOTE: Add $50 for stainless steel.

Black Diamond XR

This .45 caliber or .50 caliber muzzleloader is fitted with a 26" round barrel. Offered with blued finish, camo, or stainless steel. Weight is about 6.75 lbs. Introduced in 2002. Discontinued.

NIB	Exc.	V.G.	Good	Fair	Poor
375	300	225	150	100	75

Triumph

Fifty-caliber toggle-breech inline muzzleloader with only four moving parts. Blued/synthetic, Weathershield/synthetic, or Weathershield/stainless finish. Introduced 2007.

NIB	Exc.	V.G.	Good	Fair	Poor
425	350	275	225	150	100

Impact Muzzleloading Rifle

50-caliber single shot rifle. Features include 209 primer ignition, sliding hood to expose removable breechplug, synthetic stock adjustable from 12.5 to 13.5 inches, 26-inch blued 1:28 rifled barrel, adjustable fiber optic sights, aluminum ramrod, camo composite stock, QLA muzzle system. Weight 6.5 lbs. Price: $249 to $269.

NorthWest Explorer Muzzleloading Rifle

50-caliber single shot rifle. Features include dropping block action, #11 percussion cap ignition, 28-inch blued or Weathershield 1:48 rifled barrel, adjustable fiber optic sights, aluminum ramrod, black or camo composite stock with recoil pad, QLA muzzle system. Weight 7 lbs. Price: $329 to $399.

TIKKA

Tikkakoski, Finland

RIFLES

Whitetail Hunter

This rifle features a hand checkered walnut stock with matte lacquer finish. These rifles are furnished without sights, but receiver is grooved. Magazine is detachable box type. Three action lengths are offered: short, medium, and long. In short action calibers the choices are: .17 Rem., .223, .22-250, .243, and .308 with 22.4" barrels and weight of 7 lbs. The medium action calibers are: .270 and .30-06 with 22.4" barrels and weight of 7.3 lbs. In long are the 7mm Rem. Mag., .300 and .338 Win. Mag. with 24.4" barrel and weight of 7.5 lbs.

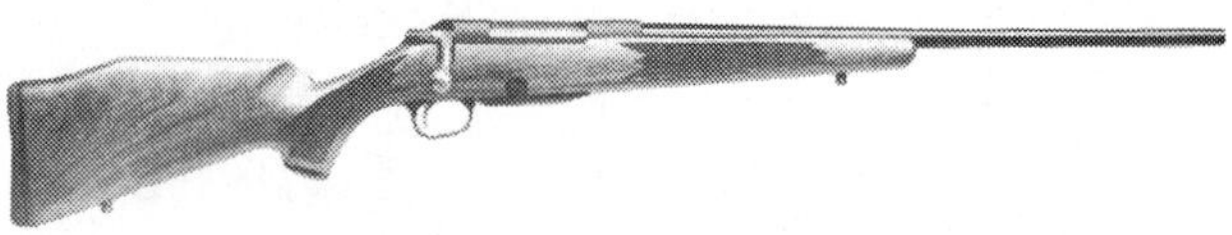

NIB	Exc.	V.G.	Good	Fair	Poor
725	600	500	400	200	150

Whitetail Hunter Deluxe

Similar to standard model above but furnished with cheekpiece, select walnut stock, rosewood pistol grip cap and forend tip. Metal surfaces are a highly polished blue. Same calibers as offered above.

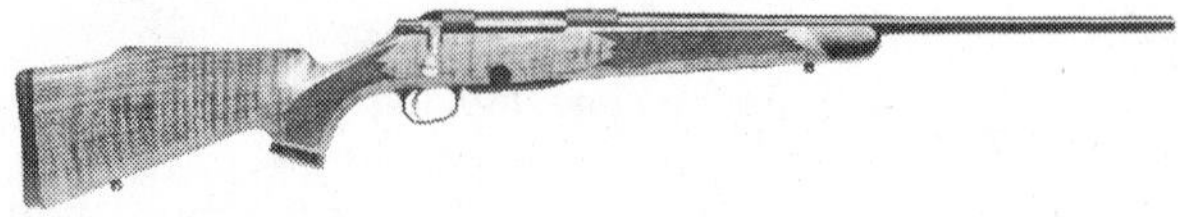

NIB	Exc.	V.G.	Good	Fair	Poor
875	700	600	400	200	150

Whitetail/Battue Rifle

This rifle was originally designed for the French market. The barrel is 20.5" long and is fitted with a raised quarter rib. The walnut is checkered with rubber recoil pad standard. A black fiberglass stock is offered as an option. In the medium action the only caliber is .308. In a long action the calibers are: .270, .30-06, 7mm Rem. Mag., .300 and .338 Win. Mag. All models weigh about 7 lbs. In 2000 this was offered in a left-hand model.

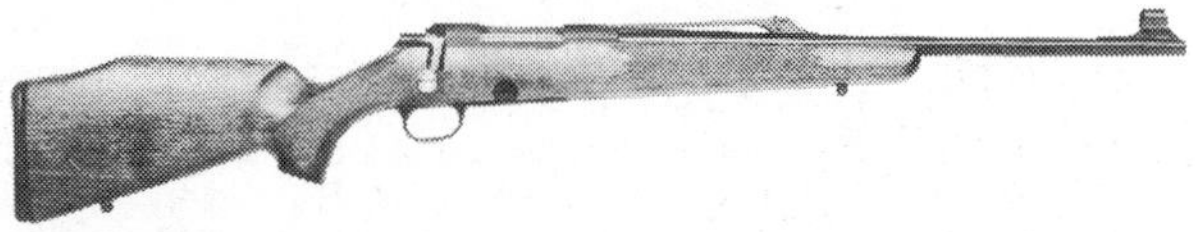

NIB	Exc.	V.G.	Good	Fair	Poor
650	500	400	275	200	100

NOTE: Add $50 for stainless steel finish. Add $20 for magnum calibers. Add $60 for left hand model.

Varmint/Continental Rifle

This model features a 23.5" heavy barrel without sights. The checkered walnut stock has a wide forend. Offered in .17 Rem., .223, .22-250, .243, and .308. Weighs approximately 8.5 lbs.

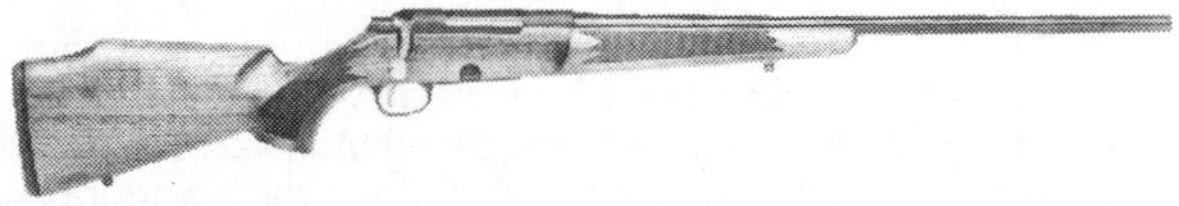

NIB	Exc.	V.G.	Good	Fair	Poor
725	600	500	400	200	150

Long Range Hunting

Same as above but in .25-06, .270, .7mm Mag., and .300 Win. Mag. Fitted with 26" heavy barrel.

NIB	Exc.	V.G.	Good	Fair	Poor
725	600	500	400	200	150

Sporter

Introduced in 1998 this model features a select walnut stock, adjustable cheekpiece, adjustable buttplate, adjustable trigger. Comes without open sights. Detachable 5-round magazine. Chambered for .223, .22-250, and .308 calibers.

NIB	Exc.	V.G.	Good	Fair	Poor
950	825	675	500	395	200

T3 Hunter

Introduced in 2003 this bolt-action rifle features a hand-forged barrel and adjustable trigger. Offered in standard and magnum calibers from .223 to .338 Win. Mag. Walnut stock with recoil pad. Detachable magazine holds three rounds for all calibers except .223 (four). No sights. Barrel lengths are 22.5" and 24.25" for standard and magnum calibers respectively. Weight is about 6.75 lbs.

NIB	Exc.	V.G.	Good	Fair	Poor
750	625	500	400	200	150

T3 Lite

As above but fitted with a black synthetic stock with blued finish. Introduced in 2003.

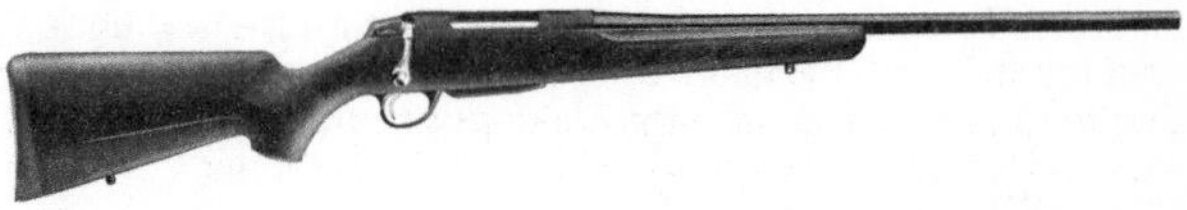

NIB	Exc.	V.G.	Good	Fair	Poor
675	550	425	325	150	100

T3 Lite Stainless

As above but with stainless steel barrel and synthetic stock.

NIB	Exc.	V.G.	Good	Fair	Poor
725	600	500	400	200	150

T3 Big Boar

This bolt action rifle is chambered for the .308, .30-06, or .300 WSM cartridges. Fitted with a 19" barrel with no sights. Black synthetic stock with recoil pad. Blued finish. Magazine capacity is 3 rounds. Weight is about 6 lbs. Introduced in 2005.

NIB	Exc.	V.G.	Good	Fair	Poor
725	600	500	400	200	150

T3 Super Varmint

This bolt action model is chambered for the .223 Rem., .22-250 Rem., or the .308 cartridge. Stainless steel receiver and barrel with Picatinny rail on receiver. Barrel length is 23.3". Black synthetic stock has adjustable comb. Adjustable trigger. Detachable magazine. Introduced in 2005.

NIB	Exc.	V.G.	Good	Fair	Poor
1575	1350	1100	750	575	300

T3 Varmint

Chambered for the .223, .22-250, and .308 cartridges. Fitted with a 23.3" barrel with no sights. Synthetic stock with blued finish. Adjustable trigger. Rubber recoil pad.

NIB	Exc.	V.G.	Good	Fair	Poor
850	725	575	400	295	150

NOTE: Add $70 for stainless steel version.

T3 Tactical

Introduced in 2004 this rifle is chambered for the .223 or .308 cartridge. Fitted with a 20" barrel with muzzlebrake. Black synthetic varmint-style stock with adjustable cheekpiece. Detachable magazine capacity is 5 rounds. Picatinny rail on receiver top.

NIB	Exc.	V.G.	Good	Fair	Poor
1500	1350	1050	850	575	350

Tikka Target

This bolt-action rifle is chambered for the .223, .22-250, 7mm-08 Rem., .308 Win., and the 6.5x55 Swedish Mauser cartridge. Fitted with a 23.25" barrel and adjustable walnut target stock, the trigger is adjustable for weight. No sights. Weight is about 9 lbs.

NIB	Exc.	V.G.	Good	Fair	Poor
950	825	675	500	395	200

SHOTGUNS/DOUBLE RIFLES (FORMERLY VALMET)

Tikka, Valmet and Sako have been merged into one company, SAKO Ltd. These firearms are now manufactured in Italy under the brand name Tikka. Parts are interchangeable between the Valmet guns, made in Finland, and the Tikka guns, made in Italy.

412S Shotgun

This over-and-under shotgun is available in 12 gauge only with 26" or 28" barrels. The stock is checkered European walnut. Weighs about 7.25 lbs.

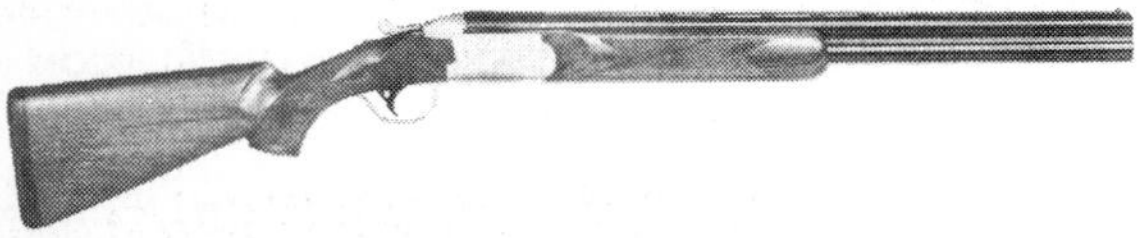

NIB	Exc.	V.G.	Good	Fair	Poor
950	800	650	500	300	200

412S Shotgun/Rifle

Same as above but with 12 gauge barrel and choice of .222 or .308 barrel. Barrel length is 24" and weighs 8 lbs.

NIB	Exc.	V.G.	Good	Fair	Poor
1000	850	700	500	300	200

412S Double Rifle

Same as above but fitted with a 24" over-and-under rifle barrel in 9.3x74R. Weighs about 8.5 lbs.

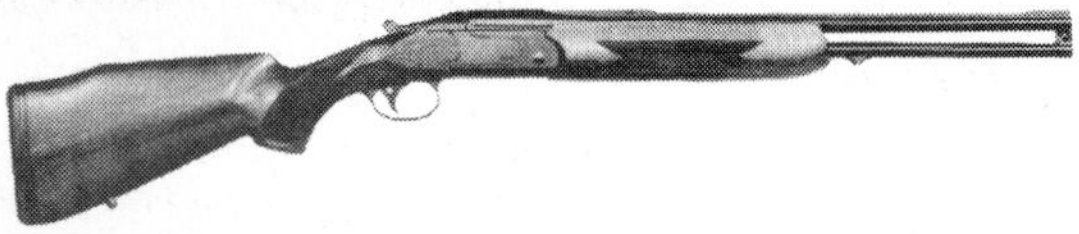

NIB	Exc.	V.G.	Good	Fair	Poor
1150	950	750	500	300	200

412S Sporting Clays

Introduced in 1993 this model is offered in 12 gauge with 28" barrels with choke tubes.

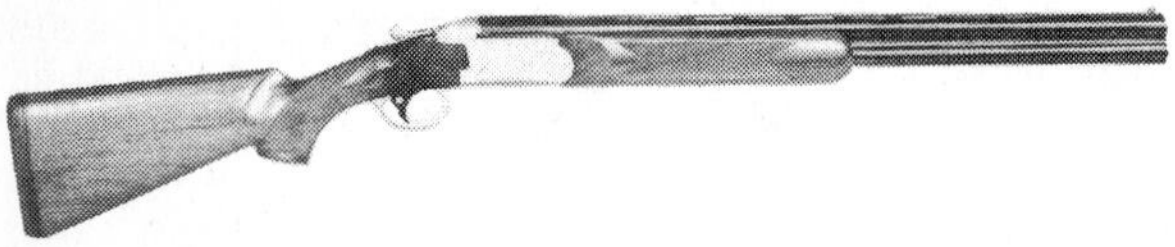

NIB	Exc.	V.G.	Good	Fair	Poor
1000	850	700	500	300	200

512S Field Grade

Introduced in 2000 this over-and-under gun is chambered for the 12 gauge 3" shell and fitted with either a 26" or 28" choke tube barrels.

NIB	Exc.	V.G.	Good	Fair	Poor
1125	850	750	500	300	200

NOTE: For shotgun/rifle barrel sets add $650 per set.

512S Sporting Clays

This 12 gauge 3" model is fitted with a 30" barrel with choke tubes.

NIB	Exc.	V.G.	Good	Fair	Poor
1175	900	750	500	300	200

TIPPMAN ARMS

Fort Wayne, Indiana

Model 1917

A .22 caliber semi-automatic one-half scale reproduction of the Browning Model 1917 water-cooled machine gun. Barrel length 10". A tripod was sold with this model. Manufactured in 1986 and 1987.

NIB	Exc.	V.G.	Good	Fair	Poor
5750	5250	—	—	—	—

Model 1919 A-4

A .22 caliber semi-automatic one-half scale reproduction of the Browning Model 1919 A-4 machine gun. Barrel length 11" and furnished with a tripod. Manufactured in 1986 and 1987.

NIB	Exc.	V.G.	Good	Fair	Poor
3000	2750	—	—	—	—

Model .50 HB

A .22 Magnum caliber semi-automatic one-half scale reproduction of the Browning .50 caliber machine gun. Barrel length 18.25", furnished with a tripod. Manufactured in 1986 and 1987.

NIB	Exc.	V.G.	Good	Fair	Poor
6000	5500	—	—	—	—

TOBIN ARMS MANUFACTURING CO.

Norwich, Connecticut and Windsor, Ontario, Canada

The Tobin Arms Manufacturing Co. operated from about 1905 to 1925 making an exposed hammer double and two hammerless models in four grades. The "Simplex" was cleverly designed (based on a patent by C.M. Wollam) side plated double-barrel internal hammer shotgun which resembled the Hopkins and Allen guns of that time. Some may have been private branded. Most of the Tobin doubles were made in Norwich, Conn., and are so marked. After 1909 operations were transferred to Windsor, Ont., Canada, and some guns will be found with that address. Tobin guns are not often seen by collectors and are highly prized because of their relative rarity and because they were considered good guns by top dealers such as C.J. Godfrey Co. of New York City and Iver Johnson Sporting Goods of Boston. Values depend on condition and range from $200 in poor condition to $1000 and up for engraved versions in good to very good condition.

NOTE: Tobin also manufactured a .22 rimfire single-shot rifle apparently during the period 1910-1925. These are rather scarce and their value is estimated to be in the $500 - $700 range, depending on condition.

A rough timeline of the Tobin Arms Manufacturing Company follows:

1903: founded by Frank M. Tobin in Norwich, CT.

1904-1909: manufactured hammer and hammerless sidelock shotguns (12ga. and 16ga.) in Norwich, Connecticut, USA

1909: purchased by a group of Canadian Investors and moved to Woodstock, ON, CAN

1910-1923/25: manufactured shotguns and rifles (entire product list unknown)

1923/25: purchased by sporting goods distributor G.B.Crandall

1923/25-1951: G.B.Crandall continued production until 1951 (possibly under the name GB Crandall)

Thanks to Jack of Florida for furnishing us with this information!

TODD, GEORGE H.

Montgomery, Alabama

Rifled Musket

A .58 caliber single-shot percussion rifle with a 40" barrel and full length stock secured by three barrel bands. Barrel and lock finished in the bright, brass furniture and walnut stock. The lock marked "George H. Todd/ Montgomery, Ala."

Too rare to price

TORKELSON ARMS CO.

Harfield, Warren, and Worcester, Massachusetts

Double-Barrel Shotguns

Reinhard T. Torkelson's company made double-barrel, boxlock, side-by-side, hammerless shotguns in four models at several locations between 1885 and 1910. He worked with Iver Johnson at Fitchburg, Mass., and also built guns carrying the Lovell (Boston) name. His "New Worcester" marked guns are quite common. they were sold by Sears and other large and well known houses.

NIB	*Exc.*	*V.G.*	*Good*	*Fair*	*Poor*
—	600	300	200	150	100

TRADEWINDS

Tacoma, Washington

Model H-170

A 12 gauge semi-automatic shotgun with a 26" or 28" ventilated rib barrel and 5-shot tubular magazine. Blued, anodized alloy receiver and walnut stock.

NIB	*Exc.*	*V.G.*	*Good*	*Fair*	*Poor*
—	300	250	225	150	100

Model 260-A

A .22 caliber semi-automatic rifle with a 22.5" barrel, open sights and 5-shot magazine. Blued with a walnut stock.

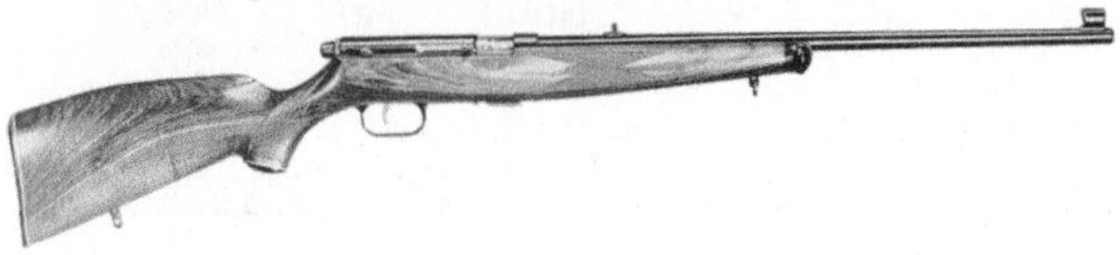

NIB	*Exc.*	*V.G.*	*Good*	*Fair*	*Poor*
—	200	175	125	100	75

Model 311-A

A .22 caliber bolt-action rifle with a 22.5" barrel, open sights and a 5-shot magazine. Blued with a walnut stock.

NIB	*Exc.*	*V.G.*	*Good*	*Fair*	*Poor*
—	175	150	100	75	50

Model 5000 "Husky"

A centerfire bolt-action rifle with a 24" barrel, adjustable sights and 4-shot magazine. Blued with a walnut stock.

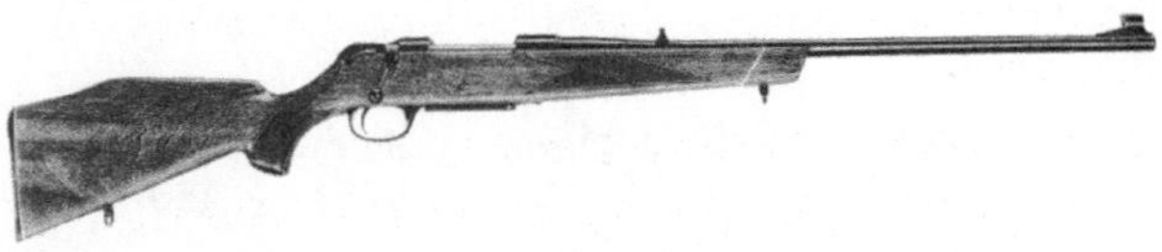

NIB	*Exc.*	*V.G.*	*Good*	*Fair*	*Poor*
—	350	300	275	200	100

TRADITIONS

Old Saybrook, Connecticut

OVER-AND-UNDER SHOTGUNS

NOTE: These shotguns are built by the Italian firm of Fausti Stefano and Emil Rizzini.

Hunter

Introduced in 2001 this model features a choice of 12 or 20 gauge chambers with 26" or 28" vent rib barrels with fixed chokes. Single-selective trigger. Extractors. Checkered walnut stock. Blued frame and barrels. Black rubber recoil pad. Weight is about 7.25 lbs. for 12 gauge and 6.75 lbs. for 20 gauge.

NIB	*Exc.*	*V.G.*	*Good*	*Fair*	*Poor*
650	525	400	300	225	150

Field I

This model is offered in 12, 20 and 28 gauge as well as .410 bore. Barrel lengths are 26". Fixed chokes. Single-selective trigger and extractors. Coin finish engraved receiver. Checkered walnut stock. Black rubber recoil pad. Weight is similar to the Hunter model with the .410 bore weighing about 6.5 lbs.

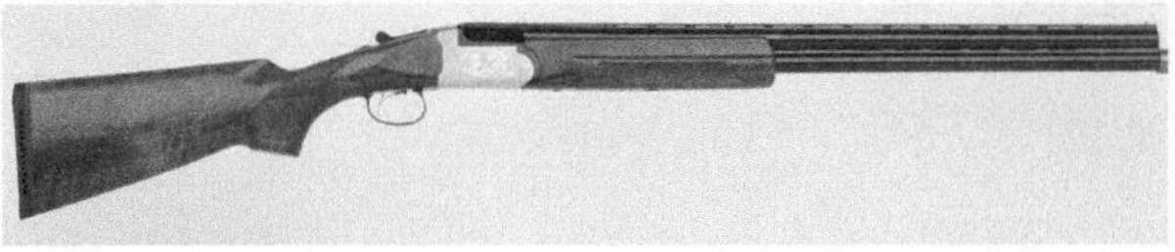

NIB	*Exc.*	*V.G.*	*Good*	*Fair*	*Poor*
575	450	375	275	200	125

Field II

Similar to the Field I but with the additional choice of a 16 gauge with 28" barrels. This model also features screw-in chokes and automatic ejectors.

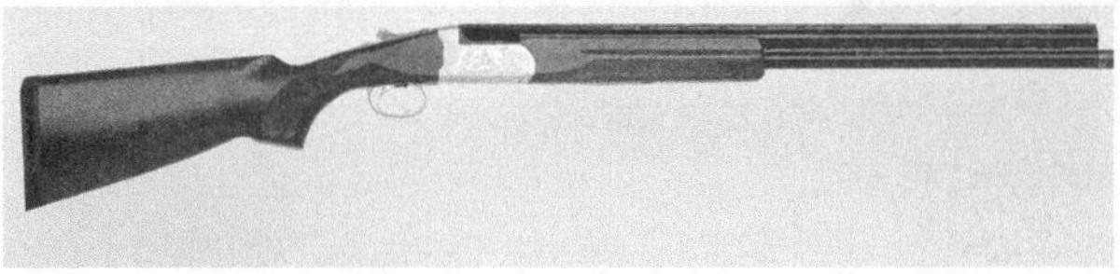

NIB	*Exc.*	*V.G.*	*Good*	*Fair*	*Poor*
750	625	500	375	250	125

Field II Combo

This model features a 20 gauge and .410 bore two barrel set. Both barrels are 26" with fixed chokes. Checkered walnut stock. Weight is about 6 lbs. Introduced in 2004.

NIB	*Exc.*	*V.G.*	*Good*	*Fair*	*Poor*
1400	1200	950	800	500	300

Field III Gold

Similar to the other Field series of guns but offered in 12 gauge only with 26" or 28" barrels. Select oil finish walnut stock. Engraved receiver with gold pheasants and woodcock.

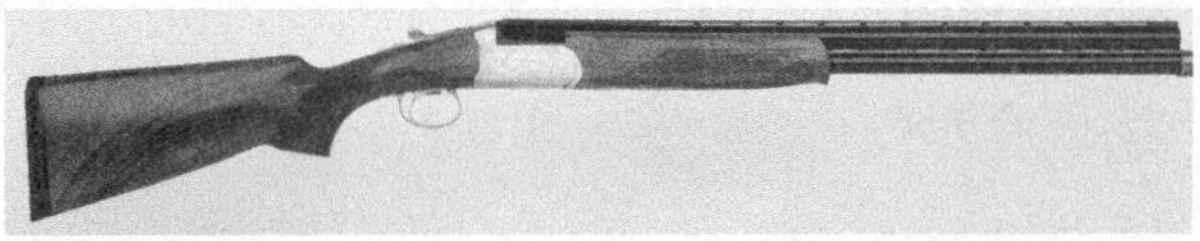

NIB	*Exc.*	*V.G.*	*Good*	*Fair*	*Poor*
1100	950	800	675	500	250

Upland II

Offered in both 12 and 20 gauge with 26" barrels in 12 gauge and 24" or 26" barrels in 20 gauge. Straight grip walnut stock. Engraved blued receiver. Schnabel forend. Choke tubes. Single-selective trigger and auto ejectors. Weight for 12 gauge gun is about 7.25 lbs. and for 20 gauge about 6.25 lbs.

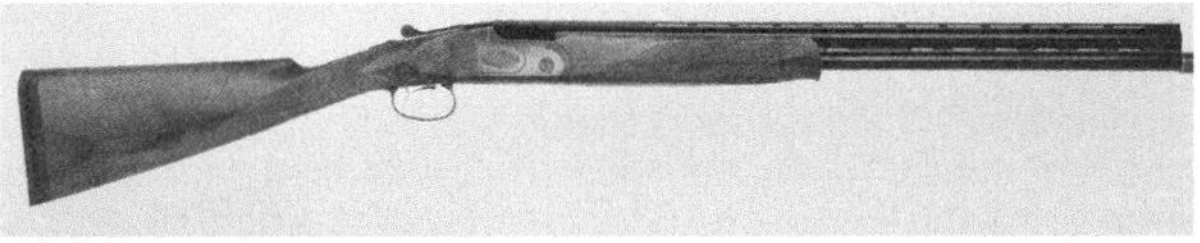

NIB	*Exc.*	*V.G.*	*Good*	*Fair*	*Poor*
800	650	500	350	275	150

Upland III

Introduced in 2001 this model features a 12 gauge gun with 26" vent rib barrels. High grade checkered walnut stock with hand engraved receiver with gold. Schnabel forend. Single-selective trigger and auto ejectors standard. Screw-in chokes. Black rubber recoil pad. Weight is about 7.25 lbs.

NIB	*Exc.*	*V.G.*	*Good*	*Fair*	*Poor*
1400	1200	950	800	500	300

Sporting Clay II

This 12 gauge gas operated model has either 28" or 30" vent rib ported barrels. Screw-in extended choke tubes. Checkered walnut stock with blued receiver and barrels. Weight is about 8 lbs.

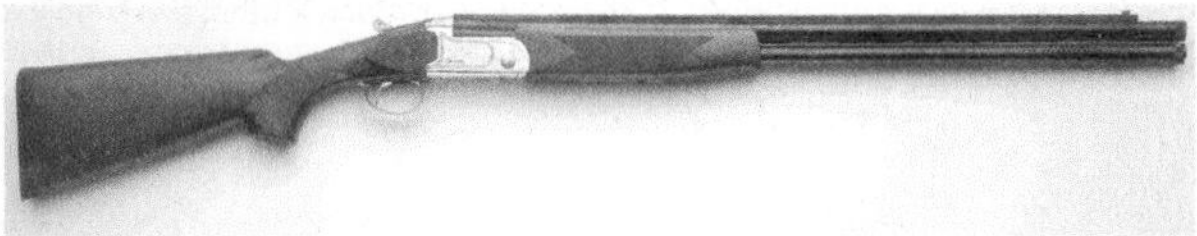

NIB	*Exc.*	*V.G.*	*Good*	*Fair*	*Poor*
900	775	650	475	300	150

Sporting Clay III

This model features a choice of 12 or 20 gauge with 28" or 30" vent rib barrels. High grade checkered walnut stock. Choke tubes. Weight is about 8.5 lbs. for 12 gauge and 8.25 lbs. for 20 gauge.

NIB	*Exc.*	*V.G.*	*Good*	*Fair*	*Poor*
1400	1200	950	800	500	300

NOTE: Add $200 for 20 gauge guns.

Waterfowl II

Introduced in 2001 this 12 gauge model is fitted with 28" vent rib barrels and 3.5" chambers. Finish on stock and barrels is Advantage Wetlands camo. Blued engraved receiver. Recoil pad. Single-selective trigger with auto ejectors. Weight is about 7.25 lbs.

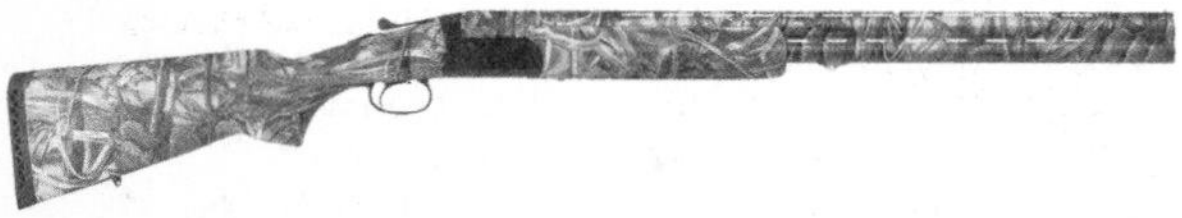

NIB	*Exc.*	*V.G.*	*Good*	*Fair*	*Poor*
800	650	500	350	275	150

Turkey II

Offered in 12 gauge with choice of 24" or 26" vent rib barrels with Mossy Oak Break-Up finish camo with blued receiver. X-Full choke. Single-selective trigger and auto ejectors. Weight is about 7 lbs.

NIB	*Exc.*	*V.G.*	*Good*	*Fair*	*Poor*
800	650	500	350	275	150

Mag Hunter II

This 12-gauge features 28" barrels with 3.5" chambers. Engraved blued receiver with walnut stock or blued receiver with Realtree Max-4 finish. Rubber recoil pad. Single selective trigger with auto ejectors. Screw-in chokes. Weight is about 7 lbs. Add 10 percent for camo model. MSRP: $1169.

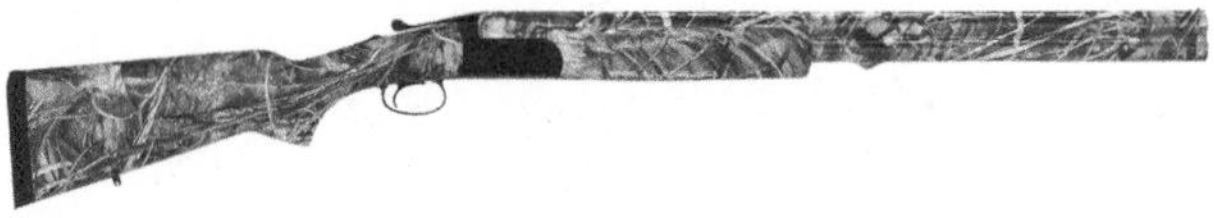

Real 16

This 16 gauge gun is fitted with 26" vent rib barrels. Checkered walnut stock. Choke tubes. Single trigger with auto ejectors. Receiver is game scene engraved. Weight is about 6.75 lbs. Introduced in 2004.

NIB	*Exc.*	*V.G.*	*Good*	*Fair*	*Poor*
1100	950	800	675	500	250

Real 16 Gold

As above but with gold-filled birds on receiver.

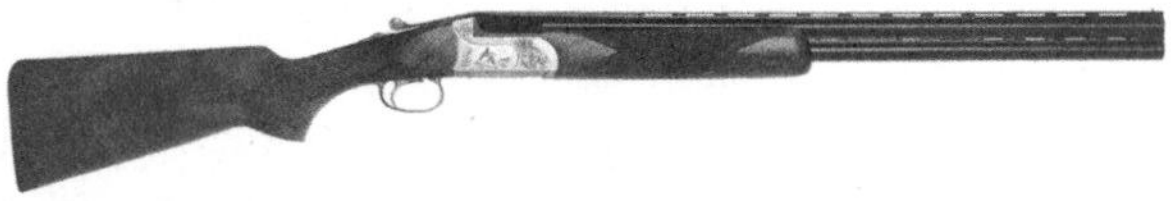

NIB	*Exc.*	*V.G.*	*Good*	*Fair*	*Poor*
1400	1200	950	800	500	300

Gold Wing II Silver

Chambered for the 12 gauge 3" shell and fitted with 28" vent rib barrels with choke tubes. Single trigger and auto ejectors. Receiver is engraved with game scenes. High grade walnut stock with oil finish. Weight is about 7.5 lbs.

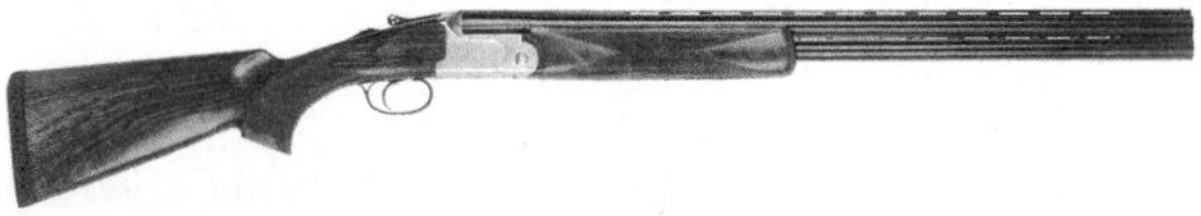

NIB	*Exc.*	*V.G.*	*Good*	*Fair*	*Poor*
1500	1300	1100	850	675	300

Gold Wing III

As above but with case colored receiver with gold inlays.

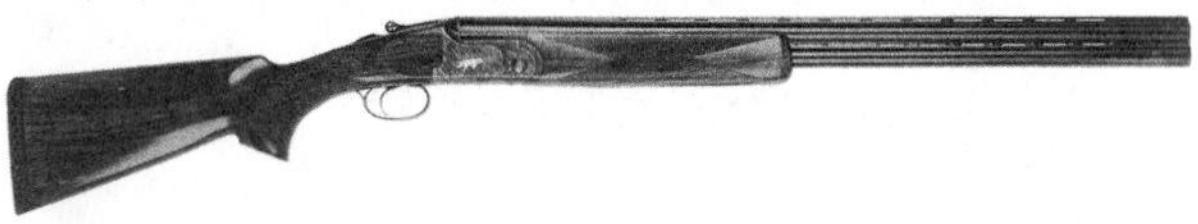

NIB	*Exc.*	*V.G.*	*Good*	*Fair*	*Poor*
2000	1750	1400	1050	800	400

Gold Wing III Silver

As above but with silver receiver with gold inlays.

NIB	*Exc.*	*V.G.*	*Good*	*Fair*	*Poor*
2100	1850	1500	1150	875	450

Gold Wing SL III

As above but with case colored side plates and gold inlays.

NIB	Exc.	V.G.	Good	Fair	Poor
2200	1950	1575	1225	950	450

Gold Wing SL III Silver

As above but with silver side plates and gold inlays.

NIB	Exc.	V.G.	Good	Fair	Poor
2300	2050	1675	1300	1000	500

SIDE-BY-SIDE SHOTGUNS

NOTE: These side-by-side guns are imported from the Italian firm of Fausti Stanfano.

Elite I DT

This model is offered in 12, 20, and 28 gauge as well as .410 bore. All gauges are fitted with 26" barrels with fixed chokes. Double triggers and extractors. Walnut stock. Weight about 6 lbs.

NIB	Exc.	V.G.	Good	Fair	Poor
750	600	400	300	200	100

NOTE: Add $60 for 28 and .410 models.

Elite I ST

Same as above but with single-selective trigger.

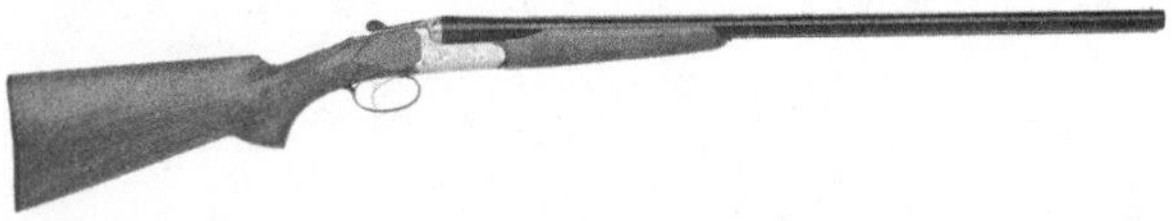

NIB	Exc.	V.G.	Good	Fair	Poor
900	750	550	425	300	150

Elite Hunter

Introduced in 2001 this model features either a 12 or 20 gauge gun with 26" barrels with screw-in chokes. Walnut stock with beavertail forend. Single non-selective trigger. Weight is about 6.5 lbs.

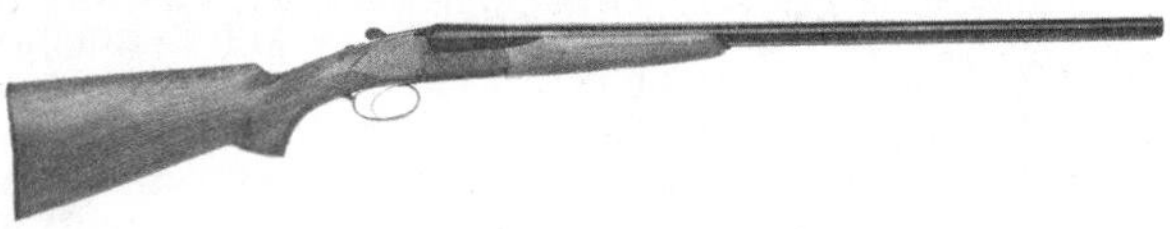

NIB	Exc.	V.G.	Good	Fair	Poor
950	800	600	475	350	200

Elite Field III ST

Introduced in 2001 this model is offered in either 28 or .410 bore with 26" barrels. High grade walnut stock with straight grip. Fixed chokes. Engraved receiver with gold. Weight is about 6.25 lbs.

NIB	Exc.	V.G.	Good	Fair	Poor
2000	1750	1400	1050	800	400

Uplander II Silver

Chambererd for the 12 gauge with 28" barrels or 20 gauge with 26" barrels. Choke tubes. Silver receiver with light scroll engraving. Checkered stock with high grade walnut. Straight grip. Single trigger and auto ejectors. Weight is about 6.75 lbs.

NIB	Exc.	V.G.	Good	Fair	Poor
2100	1850	1500	1150	875	450

Uplander III Silver

As above but with more extensive engraving with gold inlays.

NIB	Exc.	V.G.	Good	Fair	Poor
2700	2350	1950	1600	900	500

Uplander V Silver

As above but with sideplates, extensive engraving and gold inlays.

NIB	Exc.	V.G.	Good	Fair	Poor
3000	2650	2200	1800	1100	600

SEMI-AUTOMATIC SHOTGUNS

ALS Field

Introduced in 2001 this model is offered in both 12 and 20 gauge with 24", 26", or 28" vent rib barrel. Walnut stock with black pad. Blued receiver and barrels. Screw-in chokes. Weight is about 6.25 lbs.

NIB	Exc.	V.G.	Good	Fair	Poor
450	350	225	175	125	100

ALS Hunter

Same as above but with synthetic stock with 26" or 28" barrels.

NIB	Exc.	V.G.	Good	Fair	Poor
450	350	225	175	125	100

ALS Waterfowl

This 12 gauge model has Advantage Wetlands camo and is fitted with a 28" barrel with screw-in chokes. Weight is about 6.5 lbs.

NIB	Exc.	V.G.	Good	Fair	Poor
500	400	300	225	175	100

ALS Turkey

Same as above but with 21" barrel and Mossy Oak Break-up camo. Weight is about 6 lbs.

NIB	Exc.	V.G.	Good	Fair	Poor
500	400	300	225	175	100

TRIPLETT & SCOTT/MERIDEN MANUFACTURING COMPANY

Meriden, Connecticut

Repeating Carbine

A .50 caliber carbine with either a 22" or 30" round barrel and a 7-shot magazine located in the butt. This model is loaded by turning the barrel until it comes in line with the magazine. Blued, case hardened with a walnut stock. Approximately 5,000 were made in 1864 and 1865. Add 20 percent for even scarcer 22-inch barrel version.

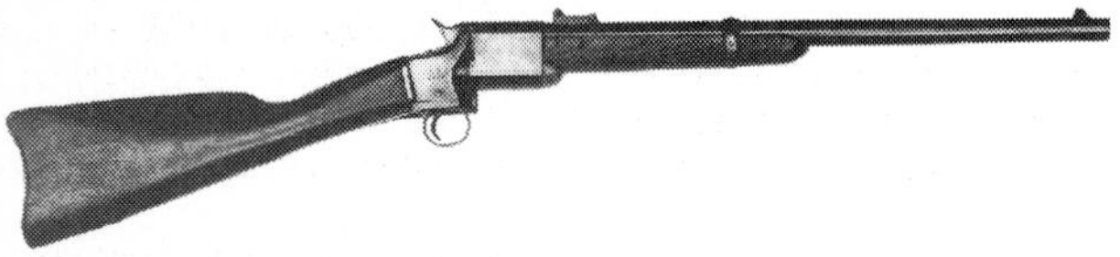

Courtesy Milwaukee Public Museum, Milwaukee, Wisconsin

NIB	Exc.	V.G.	Good	Fair	Poor
—	—	3500	1500	500	200

TRISTAR SPORTING ARMS

N. Kansas City, Missouri

Tristar 300 series over-and-under guns are imported from Turkey. Tristar Nova series are imported from Italy. **NOTE:** In 2000 Tristar bought American Arms. American Arms no longer exists but some of its models will appear under the Tristar name. For American Arms firearms built prior to the sale see that section.

SILVER SERIES

This series of over-and-under guns is produced by the Spanish company Zabala.

Silver Sporting

Offered in 12 gauge with 28" or 30" barrels with single-selective trigger, auto ejectors, choke tubes, ported barrels with target rib, checkered walnut stock with pistol grip and recoil pad.

NIB	Exc.	V.G.	Good	Fair	Poor
800	675	525	400	200	125

Specialty Magnums

This is a 12 gauge magnum chambered for the 3.5" shell and fitted with a 28" barrel. Choke tubes. Checkered black walnut stock with pistol grip.

NIB	Exc.	V.G.	Good	Fair	Poor
645	500	400	300	200	100

NOTE: In 2003 a camo finish was offered for this model. Add $85 for camo.

Silver Hunter

Offered in both 12 and 20 gauge with 26" or 28" vent rib barrels with single-selective trigger, choke tubes, engraved receiver with silver finish. Checkered walnut stock with pistol grip.

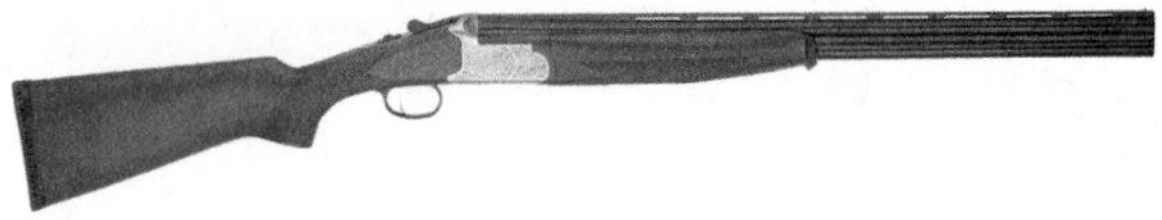

NIB	Exc.	V.G.	Good	Fair	Poor
625	500	400	300	200	100

Silver II

As above but also in 16 and 28 gauge as well as .410 bore. Fixed chokes for 16, 28, and .410 models.

NIB	Exc.	V.G.	Good	Fair	Poor
670	525	425	325	225	125

Silver Classic

This model is offered in both 12 and 20 gauge with 28" vent rib barrels and choke tubes. Frame is case colored and scroll engraved. Single-selective trigger and ejectors. Weight is about 6.75 lbs.

NIB	Exc.	V.G.	Good	Fair	Poor
800	650	500	400	300	175

BASQUE SERIES

This series of side-by-side shotguns was introduced in 2003. They are produced in Spain by Zabala.

Brittany Sporting

Offered in 12 and 20 gauge with 28" barrels with 3" chambers and choke tubes. The action is box lock with sideplates scroll engraved with case coloring. Semi-fancy checkered walnut stock with oil finish and pistol grip. Semi beavertail forend. Single-selective trigger and ejectors. Weight is around 6.75 lbs.

NIB	Exc.	V.G.	Good	Fair	Poor
750	625	500	400	300	150

Brittany

This model features a boxlock action with case-colored frame with scroll engraving. Straight grip walnut stock with semi-beavertail forend. Offered in 12, 16, 20 and 28 gauge and .410 bore with 3" chambers and choke tubes. Weight is 6.2 - 7.4 lbs. depending on gauge.

NIB	Exc.	V.G.	Good	Fair	Poor
450	325	225	175	100	75

Brittany Classic

Enhanced Brittany model features fancy walnut wood and rounded pistol grip, cut checkering, engraved case colored frame and auto selective ejectors. Available in 12, 16, 20 and 28 gauges and .410 bore, all with 3" chambers and 27" barrels. Weight is about 6.7 lbs. in 12 gauge and slightly less in sub-gauges.

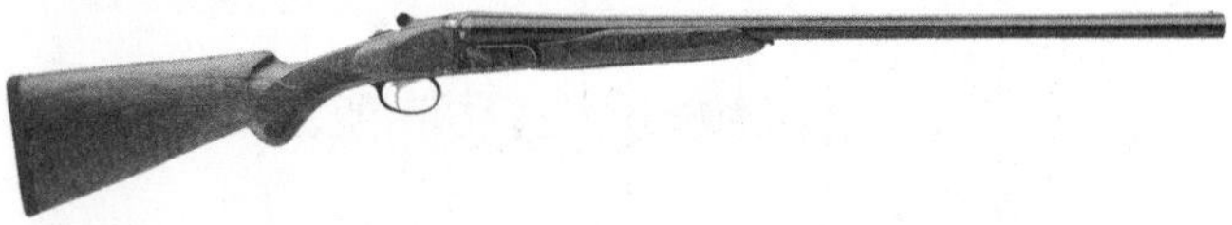

NIB	Exc.	V.G.	Good	Fair	Poor
1050	875	700	575	400	200

York

This side-by-side with blued engraved receiver and 3" chambers comes in 12 and 20 gauge with 26" or 28" barrels. Walnut, pistol grip stock and rubber recoil pad.

NIB	Exc.	V.G.	Good	Fair	Poor
625	500	400	300	200	100

Hunter Lite

Over-and-under with silver alloy engraved frame, 3" chambers, extractors, choke tubes and walnut pistol grip stock and forearm. 20-gauge with 26" barrels weighs 5.4 lbs.; 12 gauge with 28" barrels weighs 6 lbs.

NIB	Exc.	V.G.	Good	Fair	Poor
450	325	225	175	100	75

Hunter

Similar to Hunter Lite But with blued steel frame.

NIB	Exc.	V.G.	Good	Fair	Poor
450	325	225	175	100	75

Field Hunter

Based on the Hunter, this model includes selective auto ejectors and five choke tubes.

NIB	Exc.	V.G.	Good	Fair	Poor
575	450	325	250	150	100

Gentry/Gentry Coach

This model is offered in 12, 16, 20 or 28 gauge and .410 bore in the Gentry and 12 and 20 gauge in the Gentry Coach. Barrel length are 28" for the Gentry (26" for 28 and .410) and 20" for the Gentry Coach. Boxlock action with engraved antique silver finish. Walnut stock with pistol grip. Choke tubes. Single-selective trigger. Weight is about 6.5 lbs. for Gentry and Gentry Coach depending on gauge.

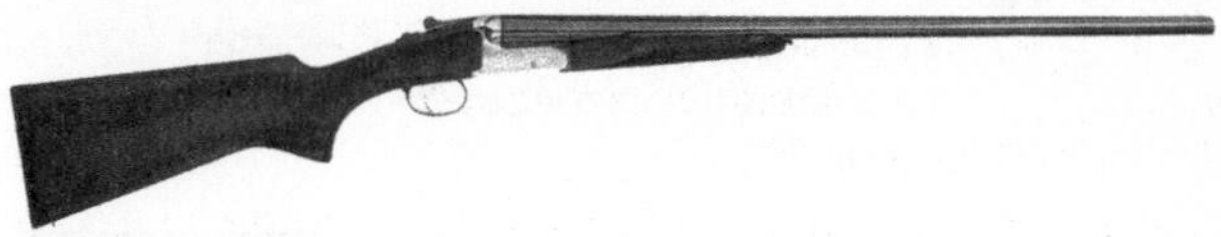

NIB	Exc.	V.G.	Good	Fair	Poor
450	325	225	175	100	75

Derby Classic

This model features a sidelock frame and action that is engraved and case colored. Offered in 12 gauge with fixed chokes in modified and full. Fitted with 28" barrel. Double trigger and automatic ejectors. Weight is approximately 7.75 lbs.

NIB	Exc.	V.G.	Good	Fair	Poor
450	325	225	175	100	75

TSA SERIES

Note: These gas-operated semi-automatics are available in 12 and 20 gauges with barrels from 24" to 26" depending on model.

TSA Field

Walnut forend and pistol grip stock, 3" chamber, 3 choke tubes and magazine-cut-off feature. Weight is around 5.7 lbs. in 20 gauge and 6.5 lbs. in 12 gauge depending on barrel length. 20 gauge available in youth model.

NIB	Exc.	V.G.	Good	Fair	Poor
375	325	275	175	125	75

TSA Synthetic and Synthetic Mag

Same features as TSA Field Model but with non-glare black synthetic stock and forend. Also available with complete Realtree Max-4 coverage. Mag model has 3.5" chamber.

NIB	Exc.	V.G.	Good	Fair	Poor
375	325	275	175	125	75

300 SERIES

NOTE: This series of over-and-under shotguns is no longer imported by Tristar.

Model 333

This over-and-under gun is available in 12 or 20 gauge with 26", 28", or 30" barrels in 12 gauge. Hand engraved frame. Fitted with 3" chambers and choke tubes. Single-selective triggers and auto ejectors. Fancy Turkish walnut stock. Weighs around 7.75 lbs. for 12 gauge and 7.5 lbs. for 20 gauge.

NIB	Exc.	V.G.	Good	Fair	Poor
650	600	425	325	225	150

Model 333SC

Similar to above model but with addition of 11mm sporting rib, recoil pad, forcing cones, and ported barrels. Extended choke tubes.

NIB	Exc.	V.G.	Good	Fair	Poor
700	650	475	375	250	175

Model 333SCL

Same features as Model 333SC but with special stock.

NIB	Exc.	V.G.	Good	Fair	Poor
700	650	475	375	250	175

Model 333L

This shotgun has the same features as the Model 333 but with a special stock designed for women. Length of pull is shorter with special Monte Carlo comb.

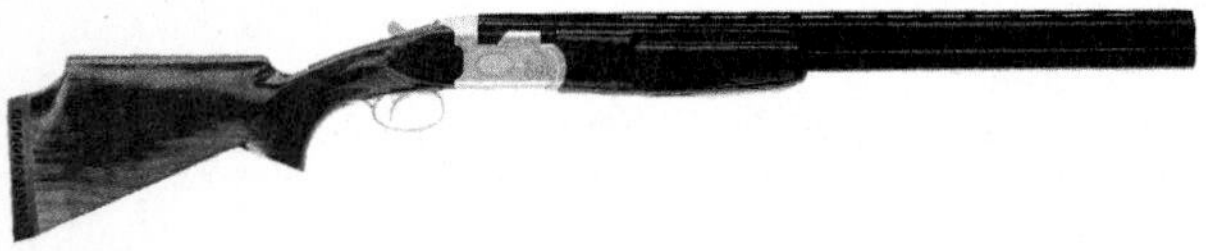

NIB	Exc.	V.G.	Good	Fair	Poor
650	600	425	325	225	150

Model 330

This over-and-under model has a standard Turkish walnut stock with etched engraved frame. Offered in 12 and 20 gauge. Single trigger with extractors and fixed chokes.

NIB	Exc.	V.G.	Good	Fair	Poor
450	325	225	175	100	75

Model 330D

This model is the same as the above but with the addition of selective auto ejectors.

NIB	Exc.	V.G.	Good	Fair	Poor
500	400	300	225	175	100

Model 300

This model features an underlug action lock with double triggers and extractors. Frame is etched. Offered in 12 gauge only with 26" or 28" barrels with fixed chokes.

NIB	Exc.	V.G.	Good	Fair	Poor
450	325	225	175	100	75

Model 311

This is a side-by-side gun in 12 or 20 gauge with 26" or 28" barrels with choke tubes. Standard Turkish walnut. Blued frame.

NIB	Exc.	V.G.	Good	Fair	Poor
500	400	300	225	175	100

Model 311R

Same as above but with 20" barrel choked Cylinder and Cylinder.

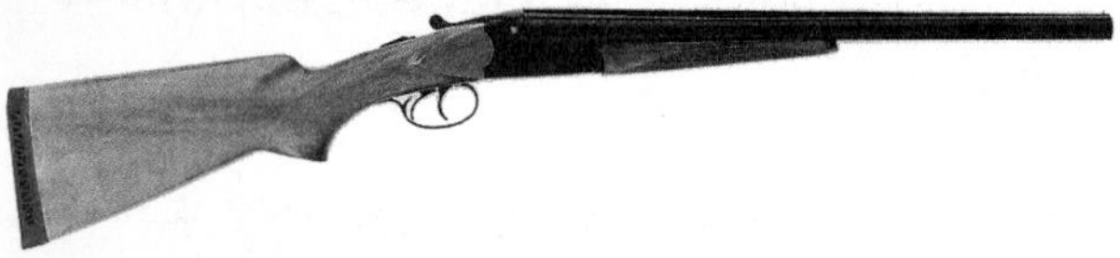

NIB	Exc.	V.G.	Good	Fair	Poor
500	400	300	225	175	100

EMILIO RIZZINI (OLD NOVA SERIES)

This gun line is no longer imported.

TR-L

Offered in 12 or 20 gauge with choice of 28" or 30" vent rib barrels. Choke tubes standard. Standard grade walnut with pistol grip. Action is silver finish boxlock with auto ejectors and single-selective trigger. Weight is approximately 7.5 lbs. Stock dimensions are made for a smaller shooter. Introduced in 1998.

NIB	Exc.	V.G.	Good	Fair	Poor
1000	850	700	575	400	200

TR-SC

Similar to the Nova L but offered in 12 gauge only with standard stock dimensions and semi-fancy walnut stock with pistol grip. Black sporting clays-style recoil pad. Weight is between 7.5 and 8 lbs. depending on barrel length. Introduced in 1998.

NIB	Exc.	V.G.	Good	Fair	Poor
1000	850	700	575	400	200

TR-I

Offered in 12 and 20 gauge with in 26" or 28" barrels with fixed chokes. Walnut stock with hand checkering and pistol grip. Beavertail forend. Boxlock action is blue with single-selective trigger and extractors. Weight is about 7.5 lbs. Introduced in 1998.

NIB	Exc.	V.G.	Good	Fair	Poor
650	600	425	325	225	150

TR-II (Nova II)

Same as above but fitted with automatic ejectors.

NIB	Exc.	V.G.	Good	Fair	Poor
700	650	475	375	250	175

TR-Mag

Similar to the Nova I but chambered for 10 and 12 gauge 3.5" shell. Choice of 24" or 28" vent rib barrels with choke tubes. Nonreflective, non-glare blue finish. Introduced in 1998.

NIB	Exc.	V.G.	Good	Fair	Poor
750	650	475	375	250	175

NOTE: Add $175 for 12 gauge with ejectors and $350 for 10 gauge guns.

TTR-Royal

This model is offered in 12, 20 or 28 gauge with 28" ported choke tube barrels, straight grip semi-fancy walnut stock, and auto ejectors. Silver receiver with gold engraving.

NIB	Exc.	V.G.	Good	Fair	Poor
1300	1250	1100	875	600	300

TR-Class SL

Top-of-the-line model with sculptured frame and engraved side plates. Offered in 12 gauge only.

NIB	Exc.	V.G.	Good	Fair	Poor
1775	1500	1250	1000	750	500

411 SERIES

These shotguns are made in Italy by R.F.M. Luciano Rota.

Model 411

This side-by-side double is imported from Italy and introduced in 1998. Chambered for 12, 20, and .410 bore with choice of 26" or 28" barrels with choke tubes or fixed chokes. Boxlock action with engraving and case coloring. Double triggers and extractors. Standard walnut stock with pistol grip and splinter forearm. Weight is between 6 and 6.5 lbs.

NIB	Exc.	V.G.	Good	Fair	Poor
850	675	500	375	250	150

Model 411R

Offered in 12 or 20 gauge with 20" barrel with fixed cylinder chokes. Extractors. Weight is about 6.5 lbs. for 12 gauge and 6 lbs. for 20 gauge.

NIB	Exc.	V.G.	Good	Fair	Poor
750	650	475	375	250	175

Model 411D

This model is similar to the Model 411 but with engraved case, colored finish on the receiver, auto ejectors, single trigger, and straight grip stock. Weight for 28 gauge is about 6.25 lbs. and for the 12 gauge about 7 lbs.

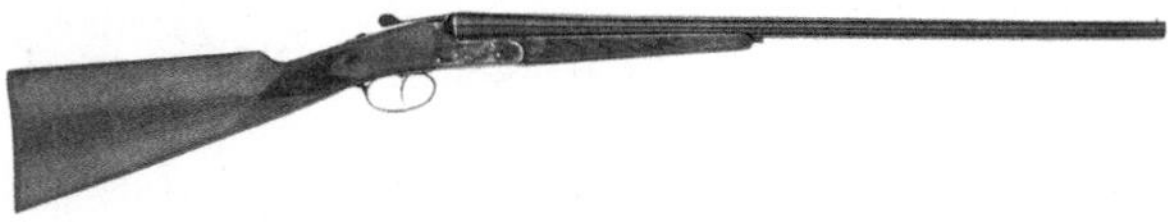

NIB	Exc.	V.G.	Good	Fair	Poor
1050	875	700	575	400	200

Model 411F

Same as the Model 411D but with silver engraved receiver.

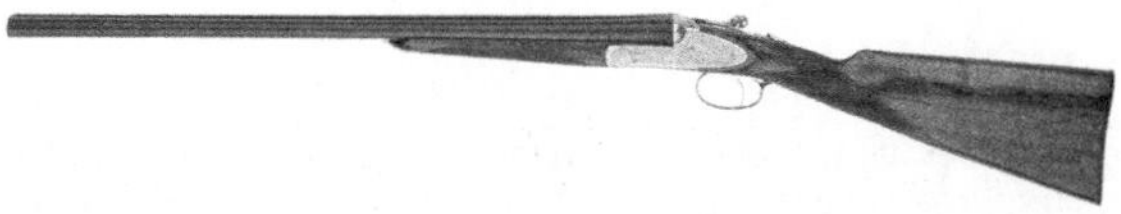

NIB	Exc.	V.G.	Good	Fair	Poor
1600	1400	1050	800	600	400

PHANTOM SERIES

These shotguns are made in Turkey by Eqsilah and have been discontinued in favor of a new redesigned gun that is found under the Diana Series.

Phantom Field

This is a gas operated semi-automatic shotgun that is chambered for the 12 gauge 2.75" or 3" shell. Fitted with 24", 26", or 28" barrel. Checkered walnut stock with pistol grip. Screw-in chokes. Five-round magazine.

NIB	Exc.	V.G.	Good	Fair	Poor
425	325	275	200	150	100

NOTE: For magnum models add $75.

Phantom Synthetic

Same as above but with synthetic stock.

NIB	Exc.	V.G.	Good	Fair	Poor
395	300	225	195	150	75

NOTE: For magnum models add $75.

Phantom HP

Same features as the phantom field except with synthetic stock, 19" barrel, and swivel studs.

NIB	Exc.	V.G.	Good	Fair	Poor
395	300	225	195	150	75

BREDA SERIES

These semi-automatic shotguns are made in Italy by Breda. This series of guns was first imported by Tristar in 2003.

ERMES

Chambered for the 12 gauge 3" shell and fitted with either a 26" or 28" vent rib barrel. Inertia operated recoil system. Checkered walnut stock with pistol grip. Choice of black, nickel, gold, or silver alloy receiver finish. Receiver is engraved with hunting scenes. Adjustable stock spacers. Weight is about 7.75 lbs.

Gold

NIB	Exc.	V.G.	Good	Fair	Poor
1935	1500	1250	1075	800	400

Silver

NIB	Exc.	V.G.	Good	Fair	Poor
1725	1350	1100	900	650	300

Nickel

NIB	Exc.	V.G.	Good	Fair	Poor
1650	1200	1050	750	500	300

Black

NIB	Exc.	V.G.	Good	Fair	Poor
1260	975	750	600	500	250

Astra 20

This is a 20 gauge model with 26" vent rib barrel. Black receiver. Walnut with pistol grip and solid rubber recoil pad. Furnished with five choke tubes. Weight is about 6 lbs.

NIB	Exc.	V.G.	Good	Fair	Poor
1140	900	750	600	465	200

Mira Sporting

This semi-automatic shotgun is gas operated and chambered for the 12 gauge shell with 3" chamber. Fitted with a 30" vent rib barrel with 10mm wide rib. Checkered walnut stock with pistol grip. Weight is approximately 7 lbs.

NIB	Exc.	V.G.	Good	Fair	Poor
875	700	550	400	300	200

Mira Camo

As above but with 28" barrel and camo finish.

NIB	Exc.	V.G.	Good	Fair	Poor
875	700	550	400	300	200

CD DIANA SERIES

These shotguns are made in Turkey by Eqsilah. This line has replaced the Phantom Series and was first imported by Tristar in 2003.

CD Diana Field

This is a gas operated semi-automatic shotgun chambered for the 12 gauge 3" shell and fitted with a 26", 28", or 30" vent rib barrel. Checkered walnut stock with pistol grip. Choke tubes. Magazine cutoff. Weight is about 7 lbs. depending on barrel length.

NIB	Exc.	V.G.	Good	Fair	Poor
425	325	275	200	150	100

CD Diana Synthetic

As above but with black synthetic stock. Also offered with 3.5" chamber. Weight is about 6.75 lbs.

NIB	Exc.	V.G.	Good	Fair	Poor
400	300	250	200	150	100

NOTE: Add $90 for 3.5" Magnum model.

CD Diana Slug

This 12 gauge gun is fitted with a 24" rifled slug barrel with open adjustable sights. Black synthetic stock. Weight is about 6.75 lbs.

NIB	Exc.	V.G.	Good	Fair	Poor
425	325	275	200	150	100

CD Diana Camo Mag

Similar to the models above but with camo stock and barrel and choice of 24" or 28" barrel with 3.5" chamber. Weight is about 6.75 lbs.

NIB	Exc.	V.G.	Good	Fair	Poor
575	450	350	225	175	100

Pee Wee

This is a single-shot bolt-action rifle chambered for .22 LR cartridges. Stock is walnut and it is about 1/2 the size of an adult rifle. Weight is about 2.75 lbs. Open sights. Finish is blue.

NIB	Exc.	V.G.	Good	Fair	Poor
200	150	100	75	50	25

TYLER ORDNANCE WORKS

Tyler, Texas

This company produced 56 Austrian rifles, 508 Enfield rifles, 423 Hill rifles and 1,009 Texas rifles during the Civil War.NOTE: These rifles are very rare.

Tyler Texas Rifle

A .57 caliber single-shot rifle with a 27" barrel and a full stock secured by two barrel bands. The lock marked "Texas Rifle/Tyler/ Cal. .57."

NIB	Exc.	V.G.	Good	Fair	Poor
—	—	62500	44000	16500	12000

Hill Rifle

A .54 caliber single-shot percussion rifle with a 27" barrel, full stock secured by two brass barrel bands and an iron trigger guard and buttplate. The lock marked "Hill Rifle/Tyler/Tex/ Cal. .54."

NIB	Exc.	V.G.	Good	Fair	Poor
—	—	58000	40000	15000	12000

U

U.S. M1 CARBINE

Various Manufacturers

NOTE: For history, techinical data, descriptions, photos, and prices see the Standard Catalog of Military Firearms under United States, Rifles. **PRICING NOTE:** The prices listed are for rifles in original, unaltered condition. For rifles that have been refinished or restored deduct about 50 percent.

Inland

NIB	Exc.	V.G.	Good	Fair	Poor
—	1500	1200	600	425	350

Underwood

NIB	Exc.	V.G.	Good	Fair	Poor
—	1600	1250	550	400	275

S.G. Saginaw

NIB	Exc.	V.G.	Good	Fair	Poor
—	2000	1400	700	450	375

IBM

NIB	Exc.	V.G.	Good	Fair	Poor
—	1800	1100	525	375	250

Quality Hardware

NIB	Exc.	V.G.	Good	Fair	Poor
—	1700	1100	525	375	250

National Postal Meter

NIB	Exc.	V.G.	Good	Fair	Poor
—	1800	1100	575	375	250

Standard Products

NIB	Exc.	V.G.	Good	Fair	Poor
—	1900	1200	600	425	250

Rockola

NIB	Exc.	V.G.	Good	Fair	Poor
—	2000	1400	750	475	350

SG Grand Rapids

NIB	Exc.	V.G.	Good	Fair	Poor
—	2000	1400	600	425	350

Winchester

NIB	Exc.	V.G.	Good	Fair	Poor
—	2000	1400	700	450	375

Irwin Pedersen

NIB	Exc.	V.G.	Good	Fair	Poor
—	4000	2200	950	650	500

M1 Carbine Cutaway

NIB	Exc.	V.G.	Good	Fair	Poor
—	2500	1500	900	600	500

M1 Carbine Sniper with infra red conversion

NIB	Exc.	V.G.	Good	Fair	Poor
—	1450	1000	800	400	300

U.S. M1 A1 Paratrooper Model

NIB	Exc.	V.G.	Good	Fair	Poor
—	4500	3500	2500	1250	750

U.S. ORDNANCE

Reno, Nevada

The models listed are machined to military specifications and are semi-automatic only.

M-60

This is a 7.62mm belt-fed semi-automatic weapon modeled after the famous machine gun used in Vietnam. Fitted with a 22" barrel, the weight of the gun is about 24 lbs.

NIB	Exc.	V.G.	Good	Fair	Poor
10000	8900	7000	5500	4000	2500

M-60E3

A shorter, more lightweight version of the standard M-60 fitted with a 17" barrel. Weight reduced to about 18 lbs.

NIB	Exc.	V.G.	Good	Fair	Poor
8900	7000	5500	4000	3000	1750

Browning Model 1919

This belt-fed model is chambered for the 7.62mm/.30-06 cartridges. Fitted with a 23" barrel. Weight is about 30 lbs. Prices listed are for gun only.

Model 1919 with A4 tripod

NIB	Exc.	V.G.	Good	Fair	Poor
2800	2400	1900	1500	1200	900

NOTE: For A6 stock, bipod, and carry handle add $125. For A4 tripod add $450.

Vickers

This model is chambered for the .303 cartridge and is belt-fed. Weight is about 40 lbs. Prices listed are for gun only.

NIB	Exc.	V.G.	Good	Fair	Poor
4800	4000	3000	2200	1700	900

NOTE: For tripod add $500.

UBERTI, ALDO/UBERTI USA

Ponte Zanano, Italy

This company manufactures high-grade reproductions of famous Western-style American firearms. Their products have been imported over the years by a number of different companies. They produce both blackpowder guns and the cartridge firearms that are included in this section. This Italian manufacturer builds high quality firearms of the American West. Featured are Colt, Winchester, and Remington. Each importer stamps its name on the firearm in addition to the Uberti address.NOTE: In 2000 Beretta Holding Company purchased Uberti.

Remington Model 1858 Target Revolving Carbine

Chambered for .44 caliber and fitted with an 18" octagon barrel. The frame is blued steel and the trigger guard is brass. Stock is select walnut. Overall length is 35" and weight is about 4.4 lbs.

NIB	Exc.	V.G.	Good	Fair	Poor
425	300	200	150	100	75

Model 1871 Rolling Block Carbine

This model is similar to the pistol, with a 22.5" half-octagonal, half-round barrel and a full-length walnut stock. trigger guard and buttplate are brass. Overall length is 35.5" and weight is approximately 4.8 lbs.

NIB	Exc.	V.G.	Good	Fair	Poor
650	525	400	275	200	125

Henry Rifle

This is a brass-framed reproduction of the famous Winchester/Henry Rifle. It is chambered for the .44-40 or .45 Colt cartridge, and this is basically the only departure from being a true and faithful copy. The octagonal barrel is 24.25" on the rifle model and 22.25" on the carbine model. There are also two Trapper models offered: an 18.5" barrel and a 16.5" version. This is a high-quality rifle and amazingly close to the original in configuration. There are three grades of engraving also available. Weights are: rifle 9.2 lbs., carbine 9 lbs., 18.5" trapper 7.9 lbs., 16.5" trapper 7.4 lbs. Finish can be steel, standard blued or charcoal blue.

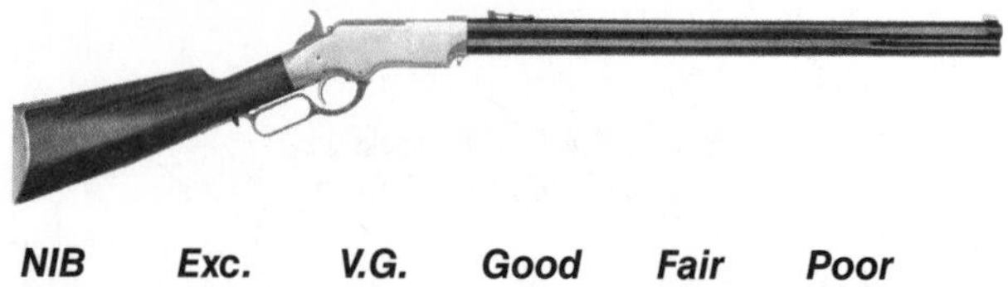

NIB	Exc.	V.G.	Good	Fair	Poor
900	700	550	450	350	200

NOTE: Grade A add $350. Grade B add $450. Grade C add $600.

Winchester Model 1866

This is a faithful replica of the Winchester 1866. It is chambered for .22 LR, .22 Magnum, .38 Special, and .44-40, and .45 Long Colt. The rifle version has a brass frame and a 24.25" tapered octagon barrel. The frame finish is brass, with a walnut stock. Weight is about 8 lbs.

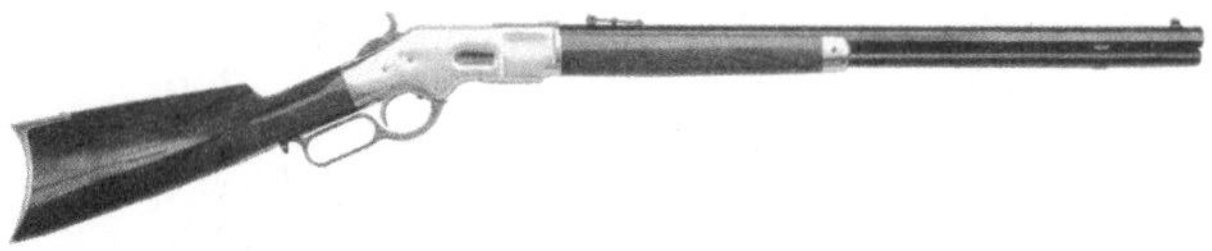

NIB	Exc.	V.G.	Good	Fair	Poor
800	650	550	450	350	200

1866 Yellowboy Carbine

This model is similar to the standard rifle, but is offered with a 19" round tapered barrel.

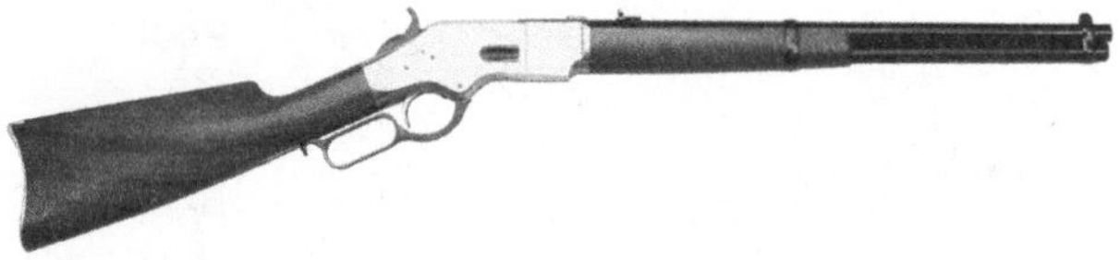

NIB	Exc.	V.G.	Good	Fair	Poor
700	600	500	450	350	200

Winchester Model 1873 Carbine

This is a reproduction of the Winchester 1873 chambered for .357 Magnum, .45 Long Colt, and .44-40. It has a case colored steel receiver and a 19" round tapered barrel. The lever is also case colored. The stock and forearm are walnut. Overall length is 38.25" and weight is about 7.4 lbs.

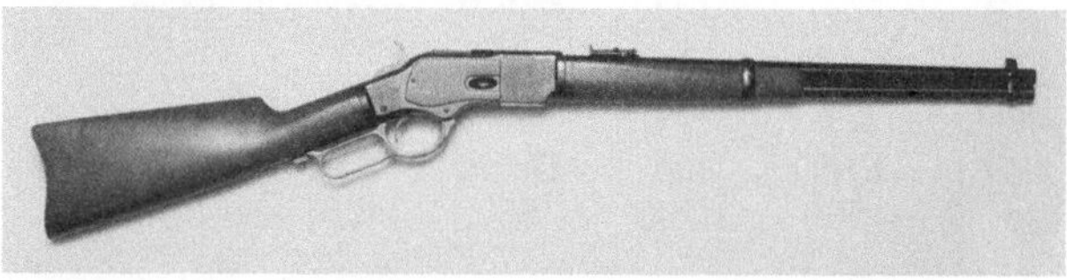

NIB	Exc.	V.G.	Good	Fair	Poor
900	700	500	450	350	200

Winchester Model 1873 Rifle

This model is similar to the Carbine, with a 24.25" octagonal barrel. Overall length is 43.25" and weight is approximately 8.2 lbs.

NIB	Exc.	V.G.	Good	Fair	Poor
950	750	600	450	350	200

NOTE: Extra barrel lengths from 30" to 20" in .45 L.C. and .44-40 are also offered at extra cost.

Winchester 1873 Short Sporting Rifle

As above but fitted with a 20" octagon barrel.

NIB	Exc.	V.G.	Good	Fair	Poor
950	800	600	450	350	200

Winchester 1873 Half-Octagon Rifle

Same as above but with 24.25" half octagon barrel. Stock has a checkered pistol grip.

NIB	Exc.	V.G.	Good	Fair	Poor
1000	800	600	450	350	200

Winchester 1873 Musket

Chambered for the .44-40 or .45 Long Colt cartridge and fitted with a 30" barrel with full stock and three barrel bands. Magazine capacity is 14 rounds. Weight is about 9 lbs.

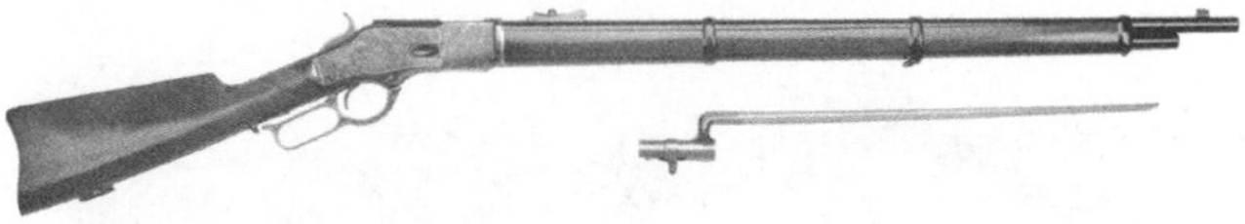

NIB	Exc.	V.G.	Good	Fair	Poor
1000	800	600	450	350	200

Model 1885 High Wall Single-Shot Carbine

Chambered for .38-55, .30-30, .44-40, .45 Colt, .40-65, or .45-70 with 28" barrel. Walnut stock.

NIB	Exc.	V.G.	Good	Fair	Poor
825	600	450	350	250	200

Model 1885 High Wall Single-Shot Rifle

Same as above but with 30" barrel.

NIB	Exc.	V.G.	Good	Fair	Poor
900	675	500	400	300	200

Model 1885 High Wall Single-Shot Rifle Pistol Grip

Fittted with a 30" or 32" barrel and checkered pistol-grip stock. Same calibers as above.

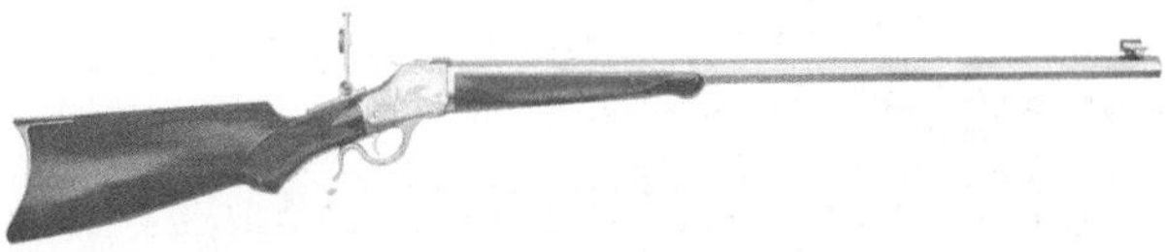

NIB	Exc.	V.G.	Good	Fair	Poor
1000	800	600	450	350	200

Winchester 1885 Low Wall Sporting Rifle

This version of the Low Wall Winchester is chambered for the .22 Hornet, .30-30, .44 Mag, or .45 Colt cartridges. Fitted with a 30" octagon barrel. Walnut stock with pistol grip. Weight is about 7.5 lbs. Introduced in 2004.

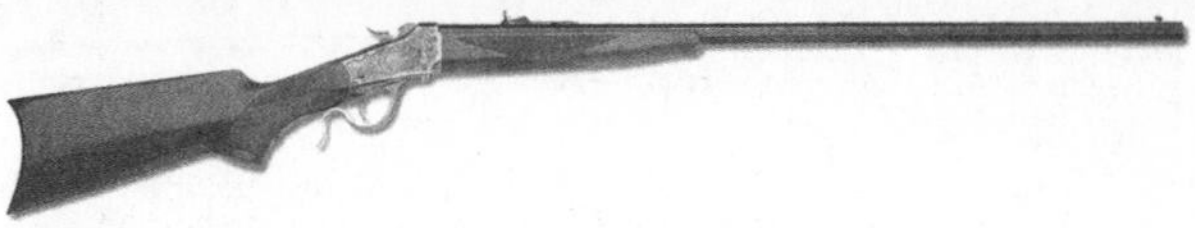

NIB	Exc.	V.G.	Good	Fair	Poor
950	800	600	450	350	200

Winchester 1885 Low Wall Schuetzen

As above but chambered for the .45 Colt cartridge and fitted with a palm rest and Swiss butt. Weight is about 7.75 lbs. Introduced in 2004.

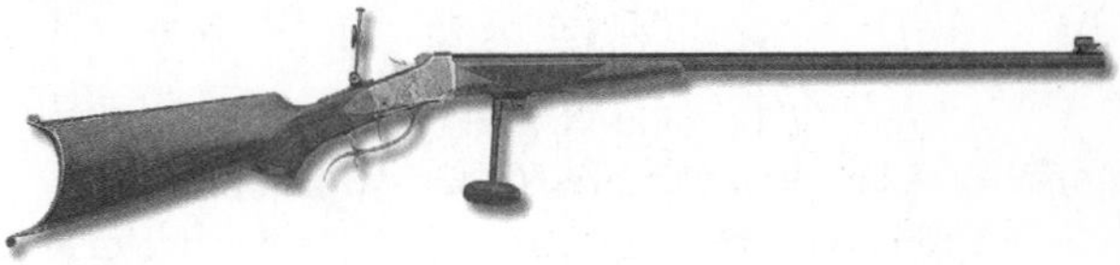

NIB	Exc.	V.G.	Good	Fair	Poor
1200	950	800	600	450	350

Buntline Carbine

This version has the 18" barrel but is fitted with a permanently mounted shoulder stock with a brass buttplate and sling swivel. Chambered for .44-40, .45 Long Colt, .357 Magnum, and .44 Magnum. Offered with fixed or adjustable sights.

NIB	Exc.	V.G.	Good	Fair	Poor
450	400	350	300	250	200

ULTRA LIGHT ARMS, INC./NEW ULTRA LIGHT ARMS

Granville, West Virginia

This maker manufactures a variety of bolt-action rifles fitted with Douglas barrels of varying lengths, custom triggers, and reinforced graphite stocks. The values for standard production models are listed.

Model 20 (Short Action)

Weight is 4.5 lbs. with 22" barrel. Composte stock with choice of colors or camo finish. Adjustable trigger. No sights. Offered in left- or right-hand.

NIB	Exc.	V.G.	Good	Fair	Poor
3100	2750	2500	1850	900	500

Model 20 RF Rimfire

Weight is about 4.5 lbs. with 22" barrel. Stock is synthetic with choice of colors or camo finish. No sights. Adjustable trigger. Available as a single-shot or repeater.

NIB	Exc.	V.G.	Good	Fair	Poor
1350	1200	800	600	400	200

Model 24 (Long Action)

Weight is approximately 5.25 lbs. with 22" barrel.

NIB	Exc.	V.G.	Good	Fair	Poor
3100	2750	2500	1850	900	500

Model 28 Magnum

Weight is about 5.75 lbs. with 24" barrel.

NIB	Exc.	V.G.	Good	Fair	Poor
3300	3050	2750	1950	900	500

Model 40 Magnum

Weight is about 7.5 lbs. with 26" barrel.

NIB	Exc.	V.G.	Good	Fair	Poor
3300	3050	2750	1950	900	500

UMAREX USA

Fort Smith, Arkansas

Umarex Colt Tactical Rimfire M4 Ops Carbine

Blowback semi-auto rifle chambered in .22 LR, styled to resemble Colt M16. Features include 16.2-inch barrel; front sight adjustable for elevation; adjustable rear sight; alloy lower; adjustable telestock; flattop receiver with removable carry handle; 10- or 30-round detachable magazine.

NIB	Exc.	V.G.	Good	Fair	Poor
500	425	365	300	225	150

Umarex Colt Tactical Rimfire M4 Carbine

Blowback semi-auto rifle chambered in .22 LR, styled to resemble Colt M4. Features include 16.2-inch barrel; front sight adjustable for elevation; adjustable rear sight; alloy lower; adjustable telestock; flattop receiver with optics rail; 10- or 30-round detachable magazine.

NIB	Exc.	V.G.	Good	Fair	Poor
550	465	400	335	250	165

Umarex Colt Tactical Rimfire M16 Rifle

Blowback sem-iauto rifle chambered in .22 LR, styled to resemble Colt M16. Features include 21.2-inch barrel; front sight adjustable for elevation; adjustable rear sight; alloy lower; fixed stock; flattop receiver; removable carry handle; 10- or 30-round detachable magazine.

NIB	Exc.	V.G.	Good	Fair	Poor
500	425	365	300	225	150

Umarex Colt Tactical Rimfire M16 SPR Rifle

Blowback semi-auto rifle chambered in .22 LR, styled to resemble Colt M16 SPR. Features include 21.2-inch barrel; front sight adjustable for elevation; adjustable rear sight; alloy lower; fixed stock; flattop receiver with optics rail; removable carry handle; 10- or 30-round detachable magazine. Price: $670.

NIB	Exc.	V.G.	Good	Fair	Poor
575	485	425	360	275	185

Umarex H&K 416-22

Blowback semi-auto rifle chambered in .22 LR, styled to resemble H&K 416. Features include metal upper and lower receivers; RIS - rail interface system; retractable stock; pistol grip with storage compartment; on-rail sights; rear sight adjustable for wind and elevation; 16.1-inch barrel; 10- or 20-round magazine. Also available in pistol version with 9-inch barrel.

NIB	Exc.	V.G.	Good	Fair	Poor
575	485	425	360	275	185

Umarex H&K MP5 A5

Blowback semi-auto rifle chambered in .22 LR, styled to resemble H&K MP5. Features include metal receiver; compensator; bolt catch; NAVY pistol grip; on-rail sights; rear sight adjustable for wind and elevation; 16.1-inch barrel; 10- or 25-round magazine. Also available in pistol version with 9-inch barrel. Also available with SD-type for-end.

NIB	Exc.	V.G.	Good	Fair	Poor
450	375	300	250	200	150

UNION FIRE ARMS COMPANY

Toledo, Ohio

This company was incorporated in 1902 and used the names of Union Fire Arms, Union Arms Company, Illinois Arms Company (made for Sears) and Bee Be Arms Company. In 1917 the company was either bought up or absorbed by Ithaca Gun Company. **NOTE:** Union Fire Arms Company (or Union Firearms Company, as it is sometimes known) slide action shotguns are not commonly seen. Though not widely collected, they seem to attract considerable interest as oddities, much as the Spencer/Bannerman slide action shotguns do. The values given below are approximate; as always, true value lies in the eyes of the buyer, not the seller.

Double Barrel Shotguns

Union's predecessor, Colton Manufacturing Co. (1894-1902) made a double for Sears. It was cleverly designed with coil mainspring striker locks set into sideplates. The Union double in 12 and 16 gauge with steel or Damascus barrels derived from it, but was a traditional hammerless sidelock side-by-side well-made gun (1902-1913) and also sold by Sears. Values depend on grade and condition.Union also offered, about 1905, an unusual boxlock hammer gun, the Model 25 in 12 gauge only. It employs external hammers but they are mounted within the frame and the spurs protrude in front of the topsnap opener. These guns are hard to find and values range from $300 to $1,200 depending on condition. They are produced with steel, twist, or Damascus barrels but only in a plain grade.

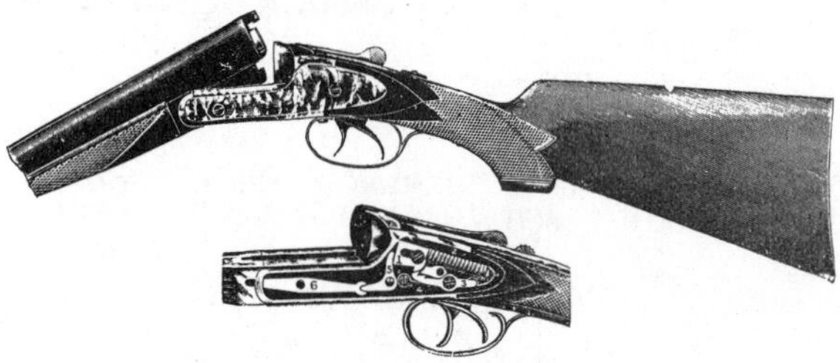

Courtesy Nick Niles

NIB	Exc.	V.G.	Good	Fair	Poor
—	1300	525	4050	300	200

Model 24

Slide action, Model 25 Peerless that was a fancy version of the Model 24 and the Model 25A, which was a trap model, were manufactured from 1902 to 1913 in 12 or 16 gauge with 24", 26", 28", or 32" steel or Damascus barrels. This gun had a unique double trigger. The front trigger cocked and decocked an internal firing pin and the back trigger fired the gun. The gun is marked on the left side of the frame and the pump release is on the right side. This model had one serious drawback, in that the slide that extracted a spent shell extended back over the comb of the stock. This often hit the shooter's thumb knuckle and caused injury. In 1907 Union redesigned their slide by reducing its length and shielding it behind a steel plate that covered the rear half of the opening. These are the Model 24, 25, and 25A improved versions. Approximately 17,000 of all models combined were made.

NIB	Exc.	V.G.	Good	Fair	Poor
—	—	750	300	200	100

Model 50

Manufactured 1911 to 1913. This was basically a redesign of the Model 24. The main distinguishing feature of the Model 50 was that the frame sloped down to meet the comb of the stock and the double trigger system was replaced by a single trigger. It came in 12 or 16 gauge with a 26", 28", 30", or 32" Krupp steel barrel. Fewer than 3,000 were made.

NIB	Exc.	V.G.	Good	Fair	Poor
—	—	850	400	300	200

Model 22

This was essentially a no frills Model 23. It had the same barrel length and steel options, but it had a plain walnut stock and no engraving. There were fewer than 10,000 Model 22 and 23s made.

NIB	Exc.	V.G.	Good	Fair	Poor
—	—	300	100	75	50

Model 23

Hammerless double, manufactured between 1902 and 1913 with or without automatic ejectors. With some engraving, it came in both single and double trigger models; this was their top grade gun. Came in 12 and 16 gauge with 28", 30", or 32" steel, twist, or Damascus barrels.

NIB	Exc.	V.G.	Good	Fair	Poor
—	—	450	150	125	100

Diamond Grade

Single-shot, manufactured between 1905 and 1910. It had a unique octagonal breech in 12 gauge only with 30" steel, laminated, or Damascus barrel. This was their premium grade single-shot. Few of these were made.

NIB	Exc.	V.G.	Good	Fair	Poor
—	—	450	200	100	50

Model 18

Single-shot, manufactured 1906 to 1913 came in 12 or 16 gauge. 30", 32", 34", or 36" steel barrel. A plain single-shot. Very few made.

NIB	Exc.	V.G.	Good	Fair	Poor
—	—	200	75	50	25

UNITED STATES FIRE ARMS MFG.

(Formerly United States Patent Firearms Mfg. Co.)
Hartford, Connecticut

This company began business in 1992. The company uses parts manufactured in the U.S. and fits, finishes, and assembles the gun in Hartford. Produces a wide variety of extremely high-quality replica arms. **NOTE:** This company offers a wide variety of special order options on its revolvers, from special bluing to grips to engraving. These special order options will affect price to a significant degree.

RIFLES

Cowboy Action Lightning

This is a copy of the Colt Lightning rifle chambered for the .44-40, .45 Colt, or the .38 WCF cartridge. Fitted with a 26" round barrel and walnut stock with crescent butt. Magazine capacity is 15 rounds. Introduced in the fall of 2003. Discontinued.

NIB	Exc.	V.G.	Good	Fair	Poor
1625	1450	1200	900	675	400

Cowboy Action Carbine

As above but with 20" round barrel. Magazine capacity is 12 rounds. Discontinued.

NIB	Exc.	V.G.	Good	Fair	Poor
1625	1450	1200	900	675	400

Lightning Magazine Rifle

This model is a premium version of the Cowboy Action Lightning and features a choice of 26" round, half round, or octagon barrel. Checkered American walnut forearm with non-checkered stock with oil finish. Many extra cost options are offered for this model. Discontinued.

NIB	Exc.	V.G.	Good	Fair	Poor
1625	1450	1200	900	675	400

NOTE: Add $200 for half round barrel. Fancy wood, pistol grip, finish and engraving offered for this rifle.

Lightning Magazine Carbine

As above but with 20" round barrel. Discontinued.

NIB	Exc.	V.G.	Good	Fair	Poor
1625	1450	1200	900	675	400

Lightning Baby Carbine

This model is fitted with a 20" special round tapered barrel. Lightweight carbine forearm with border line. Discontinued.

NIB	Exc.	V.G.	Good	Fair	Poor
1995	1825	1600	1250	950	650

UNIVERSAL FIREARMS

Hialeah, Florida/Jacksonville, Arkansas

NOTE: Universal merged with Iver-Johnson in 1985 and relocated to Arkansas in 1986. Universal operated out of Florida from the late 1950s to 1985.

Model 7312

A 12 gauge Over/Under shotgun with separated 30" ventilated rib barrels, single-selective trigger and automatic ejectors. The case hardened receiver engraved. Blued with a walnut stock. Imported from Italy.

NIB	Exc.	V.G.	Good	Fair	Poor
—	1250	900	450	300	175

Model 7412

As above, with extractors. Imported from Italy.

NIB	Exc.	V.G.	Good	Fair	Poor
—	1000	750	400	250	150

Model 7712

As above, with 26" or 28" barrels, nonselective single trigger and extractors. Imported from Italy.

NIB	Exc.	V.G.	Good	Fair	Poor
—	550	400	350	250	100

Model 7812

As above, with more detailed engraving and automatic ejectors. Imported from Italy.

NIB	Exc.	V.G.	Good	Fair	Poor
—	700	550	450	350	150

Model 7912

As above, with a gold wash frame and single-selective trigger. Imported from Italy.

NIB	Exc.	V.G.	Good	Fair	Poor
—	1350	1000	750	600	300

Model 7112

A 12 gauge double-barrel boxlock shotgun with 26" or 28" barrels, double triggers and extractors. Blued, case hardened with a walnut stock. Imported from Italy.

NIB	Exc.	V.G.	Good	Fair	Poor
—	450	300	250	200	100

Double Wing

A 10, 12, 20 or .410 bore boxlock double-barrel shotgun with 26", 28", or 30" barrels, double triggers and extractors. Blued with a walnut stock. Imported from Italy. Premium for .410 and 10 ga.

NIB	Exc.	V.G.	Good	Fair	Poor
—	450	300	250	200	100

Model 7212

A 12 gauge single-barrel trap shotgun with a 30" ventilated-rib ported barrel, and automatic ejector. Engraved, case hardened receiver and walnut stock. Imported from Italy.

NIB	Exc.	V.G.	Good	Fair	Poor
—	1200	850	650	450	300

Model 1000 Military Carbine

A copy of the U.S. M1 Carbine with an 18" barrel. Blued with a birch wood stock.

NIB	Exc.	V.G.	Good	Fair	Poor
—	400	250	200	100	75

Model 1003

As above, with a 16", 18", or 20" barrel.

NIB	Exc.	V.G.	Good	Fair	Poor
—	350	200	150	100	75

Model 1010

As above, but nickel-plated.

NIB	Exc.	V.G.	Good	Fair	Poor
—	375	225	175	125	100

Model 1015

As above, but gold-plated.

NIB	Exc.	V.G.	Good	Fair	Poor
—	400	250	200	150	125

Model 1005 Deluxe

As above, with a polished blue finish and Monte Carlo-style stock.

NIB	Exc.	V.G.	Good	Fair	Poor
—	375	225	150	100	75

Model 1006 Stainless

As the Model 1000, but in stainless steel.

NIB	Exc.	V.G.	Good	Fair	Poor
—	450	300	225	125	100

Model 1020 Teflon

As above, with a black or gray Dupont Teflon-S finish.

NIB	Exc.	V.G.	Good	Fair	Poor
—	375	225	175	125	100

Model 1256 Ferret

The Model 1000 in .256 Winchester Magnum caliber.

NIB	Exc.	V.G.	Good	Fair	Poor
—	350	200	175	125	100

Model 5000 Paratrooper

The Model 1000, with a 16" or 18" barrel and folding stock. This model, in stainless steel, is known as the Model 5006.

NIB	Exc.	V.G.	Good	Fair	Poor
—	400	250	200	125	100

1981 Commemorative Carbine

A limited production version of the Model 1000 cased with accessories. Produced in 1981.

NIB	Exc.	V.G.	Good	Fair	Poor
500	350	250	200	100	75

Model 2200 Leatherneck

A .22 caliber version of the U.S. M1 Carbine with an 18" barrel and blowback action. Blued with a birch wood stock.

NIB	Exc.	V.G.	Good	Fair	Poor
—	300	175	150	100	75

USAS 12 DAEWOO PRECISION IND., LTD.

South Korea

USAS 12

A 12 gauge semi-automatic shotgun with a 18.25" cylinder-bored barrel, and either a 10-shot box magazine or 20-shot drum magazine. Parkerized, with a composition stock. This model is no longer imported.WARNING: As of May 1, 2001 this firearm must be registered with the ATF and a transfer tax of $200 paid. This firearm is classified as a destructive device. Unregistered guns will be considered contraband after this date, and persons in possession will be in violation of federal law.

UZI ISRAELI MILITARY INDUSTRIES

SEE—Vector Arms, Inc.

Uzi Carbine Model A

Chambered for 9mm cartridge and fitted with a 16" barrel with 25-round magazine. Gray Parkerized finish. Built from 1980 to 1983.

NIB	Exc.	V.G.	Good	Fair	Poor
1600	1450	1200	800	600	450

Uzi Carbine Model B

A 9mm, .41 Action Express or .45 caliber semi-automatic carbine with a 16.1" barrel and 20-, 25-, or 32-shot box magazines. A 50-shot drum magazine is available in 9mm caliber. Black Parkerized finish, plastic grips and a folding stock. It is strongly suggested that a buyer or seller seek a qualified local appraisal. First produced in 1983. This model was no longer imported as of 1989.

NIB	Exc.	V.G.	Good	Fair	Poor
1500	1350	1100	750	550	400

Uzi Mini-Carbine

As above, in 9mm or .45 caliber with a 19.75" barrel. This model is no longer imported.

NIB	Exc.	V.G.	Good	Fair	Poor
2250	1600	1150	800	600	400

V

VALKYRIE ARMS, LTD.
Olympia, Washington

NOTE: Valkyrie Arms filed for bankruptcy in early 2008.

Browning 1919 A4 .30 Caliber

This is a semi-automatic version of the famous Browning machine gun. It is chambered for the .30-06 or the .308 cartridge. It come equipped with a tripod, pintle, T&E, belly linker and 200 links. An A6 configuration is available. Introduced in1996.

NIB	Exc.	V.G.	Good	Fair	Poor
2850	2000	1500	1100	750	600

U.S. M3-A1

A re-creation of the famous "grease gun" but in semi-auto. Barrel length is 16.5". Supplied with three 30-round magazines.

NIB	Exc.	V.G.	Good	Fair	Poor
1500	1250	1000	750	500	300

NOTE: For dummy suppressor add $50. For real suppressor add $300 plus transfer tax of $200. All NFA rules and state laws must be followed for suppressors.

DeLisle Carbine

A copy of the famous World War II commando carbine used by British forces. Chambered for .45 ACP. Integral suppressor. All NFA rules must be followed. Only 167 original WWII carbines were produced.

NIB	Exc.	V.G.	Good	Fair	Poor
1575	1250	1000	750	500	300

NOTE: For dummy suppressor deduct $300.

VALMET, INC.
Jyvaskyla, Finland

M-62S

A semi-automatic copy of the Finnish M-62 service rifle in 7.62x39 caliber that is patterned after the Russian AK47. Fitted with a walnut or tubular steel stock. Manufactured after 1962.

NIB	Exc.	V.G.	Good	Fair	Poor
—	3000	2800	2300	900	750

M-71S

As above, in 5.56mm caliber and available with a composition stock.

NIB	Exc.	V.G.	Good	Fair	Poor
—	1350	1000	850	650	450

MODEL 76S

As above, in 5.56mm, 7.62x39mm, or 7.62x51mm with either a 16.75" or 20.5" barrel.

5.56mm

NIB	Exc.	V.G.	Good	Fair	Poor
—	1750	1500	1250	750	600

7.62x39mm or 7.62x51mm

NIB	Exc.	V.G.	Good	Fair	Poor
—	3000	2750	2500	2000	1250

Model 78

As above, in 7.62x51mm, 7.62x39, or .223 with a 24.5" barrel, wood stock, and integral bipod.

NIB	Exc.	V.G.	Good	Fair	Poor
—	2150	1700	1300	850	600

Model 212 Lion

A 12 gauge Over/Under shotgun with 26", 28", or 30" barrels, single-selective trigger and extractors. Blued with a walnut stock. Manufactured from 1947 to 1968. Amazingly similar to the Savage Model 330 over/under. Values shown are for standard field grade.

NIB	Exc.	V.G.	Good	Fair	Poor
—	750	625	500	400	300

Model 412 Combination Gun

A 12 ga./.30-06 over/under combination gun built on the frame of the 12-ga. Lion shotgun. Discontinued.

NIB	Exc.	V.G.	Good	Fair	Poor
—	1900	1475	1200	1050	700

VALTRO
Italy

Tactical 98 Shotgun

Chambered for 12 gauge and fitted with a 18.5" or 20" ported barrel. Choice of pistol grip or standard stock. Extended magazine with 5 or 7 rounds. Ghost ring sights.

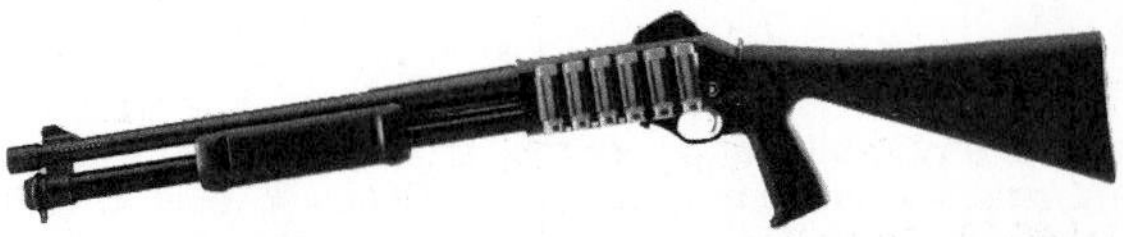

NIB	Exc.	V.G.	Good	Fair	Poor
—	900	750	675	500	325

PM5

This is a slide-action shotgun chambered for the 12 gauge 3" shell. Barrel length is 20" choked Cylinder. Box-fed magazine. Value shown is for pre-ban model.

NIB	Exc.	V.G.	Good	Fair	Poor
—	1200	1050	800	675	500

VARNER SPORTING ARMS, INC.

Marietta, Georgia

NOTE: This company made several over-and-under shotguns and rifle/shotgun combination guns for the Savage Company. These are no longer being imported into this country.The rifles listed are all patterned after the Stevens Favorite model.

Hunter

.22 caliber single-shot rifle with a 21.5" half-octagonal, takedown barrel fitted with an aperture rear sight. Blued with well-figured walnut stocks. Introduced in 1988.

NIB	*Exc.*	*V.G.*	*Good*	*Fair*	*Poor*
375	300	250	200	150	100

Hunter Deluxe

As above, with a case hardened receiver and a more finely figured stock.

NIB	*Exc.*	*V.G.*	*Good*	*Fair*	*Poor*
500	400	350	250	175	125

PRESENTATION GRADE

As above, with a target hammer and trigger, and a hand checkered stock.

NIB	*Exc.*	*V.G.*	*Good*	*Fair*	*Poor*
575	475	425	350	250	200

No. 1 Grade

NIB	*Exc.*	*V.G.*	*Good*	*Fair*	*Poor*
650	550	500	450	350	200

No. 2 Grade

NIB	*Exc.*	*V.G.*	*Good*	*Fair*	*Poor*
775	650	600	500	400	200

No. 3 Grade

NIB	*Exc.*	*V.G.*	*Good*	*Fair*	*Poor*
1100	850	700	550	350	200

VECTOR ARMS, INC.

North Salt Lake, Utah

MINI UZI

A smaller version of the full size Uzi chambered for the 9mm cartridge only. Fitted with 18" barrel.

Pre-Ban

NIB	*Exc.*	*V.G.*	*Good*	*Fair*	*Poor*
—	2000	1700	1400	1050	700

Post-Ban

NIB	*Exc.*	*V.G.*	*Good*	*Fair*	*Poor*
—	1500	1250	1050	700	500

UZI

This is a semi-automatic, pre-ban Uzi carbine with 18" barrel chambered for the 9mm cartridge. Receiver built by Group Industries of Louisville, Ky., prior to May 1986. Receiver fixed parts manufacturing and receiver assembly by Vector Arms. Only 97 of these semi-automatic receivers were manufactured.

Pre-Ban

NIB	*Exc.*	*V.G.*	*Good*	*Fair*	*Poor*
—	1500	1250	1050	700	500

Post-Ban

NIB	*Exc.*	*V.G.*	*Good*	*Fair*	*Poor*
—	1200	1050	800	675	500

NOTE: For .45 ACP or .22 caliber conversion kit, add $200.

VEKTOR

South Africa

No longer in business.

Vektor H5 Pump-Action Rifle

This pump-action rifle is chambered for the .233 cartridge. It is fitted with a thumbhole stock and a 22" barrel. Magazine capacity is 5 rounds.

NIB	*Exc.*	*V.G.*	*Good*	*Fair*	*Poor*
850	725	600	475	300	200

Vektor 98

Built on a Mauser action, this rifle is chambered for a variety of calibers from .243 to .375 H&H. Fitted with a one-piece walnut stock with hand checkering. Magazine capacity is five rounds. Open sights on magnum calibers only.

NIB	*Exc.*	*V.G.*	*Good*	*Fair*	*Poor*
1200	950	800	575	400	300

Vektor Lyttelton

This rifle features numerous special features and is fitted with a classic walnut stock with wraparound checkering. Fixed sights. Calibers offered are from .243 to .375 H&H.

NIB	*Exc.*	*V.G.*	*Good*	*Fair*	*Poor*
1595	1400	1100	800	575	300

VERNEY-CARRON

St. Etienne, France

Concours

A 12 gauge Over/Under boxlock shotgun with 26" or 28" ventilated rib barrels, single-selective triggers, automatic ejectors and profuse engraving. Blued, French case hardened with checkered walnut stock. First imported in 1978.

NIB	*Exc.*	*V.G.*	*Good*	*Fair*	*Poor*
—	1450	900	700	600	300

Skeet Model

As above, with a 28" Skeet-choked barrel and a pistol-grip stock.

NIB	*Exc.*	*V.G.*	*Good*	*Fair*	*Poor*
—	1600	1050	700	600	300

Snake Charmer II

A .410 single-barrel break-action shotgun with stainless steel barrel and receiver and black ABS stock. Overall length 29 inches.

NIB	*Exc.*	*V.G.*	*Good*	*Fair*	*Poor*
—	175	150	100	75	50

VERONA
Italy

HUNTING SHOTGUNS

Model SX401/S

This 12 gauge 3" semi-automatic model is offered with either a 26" or 28" vent rib barrel with choke tubes. Checkered Turkish walnut stock. Weight is about 6.75 lbs.

NIB	Exc.	V.G.	Good	Fair	Poor
425	325	275	225	150	100

Model SX405/S/L

As above but with black composite stock. Weight is about 6.5 lbs.

NIB	Exc.	V.G.	Good	Fair	Poor
350	275	225	150	100	75

Model SX405W/H/SW/SH

This 12 gauge 3" Magnum semi-automatic gun is offered with a choice of 26" or 28" vent-rib barrel with wetland or hardwood camo pattern. Weight is about 6.5 lbs.

NIB	Exc.	V.G.	Good	Fair	Poor
440	340	295	225	150	100

Model SX405T

This 12 gauge 3" semi-auto model features a 24" vent-rib barrel with hardwood camo pattern. Weight is about 6.5 lbs.

NIB	Exc.	V.G.	Good	Fair	Poor
440	340	295	225	150	100

Model SX405 Combo

This model features a 12 gauge 22" slug barrel and a 12 gauge 3" 26" vent-rib smoothbore barrel. Weight is about 6.5 lbs.

NIB	Exc.	V.G.	Good	Fair	Poor
500	400	300	225	150	125

Model SX405 Slug

This model features a hardwood camo stock with 22" slug barrel. Weight is about 6.5 lbs.

NIB	Exc.	V.G.	Good	Fair	Poor
425	325	275	225	150	100

LX501

This over-and-under shotgun is chambered for the 12, 20, 28, and .410 bore. Single-selective trigger. Ejectors. Blued steel receiver. Walnut stock with machine checkering. It is offered with 28" vent-rib barrels. Screw-in chokes for 12 and 20 gauges models. Fixed chokes for 28 and .410 bore. Chambers are 3" for all gauges except 28 gauge. Weight is between 6.25 lbs. and 6.75 lbs. depending on gauge.

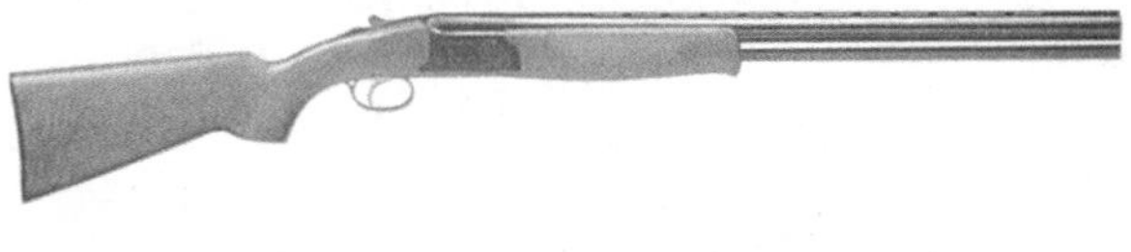

NIB	Exc.	V.G.	Good	Fair	Poor
800	675	525	400	300	225

NOTE: For 28 gauge and .410 bore add $30.

LX692G

This model is also offered in 12, 20, 28, and .410 bore with 28" vent-rib barrels. Receiver is fitted with sideplates with gold inlaid hunting scenes on three sides. Matte finish walnut stock with schnabel forearm, hand-cut checkering. Weight is between 7.25 lbs. and 7.75 lbs. depending on gauge.

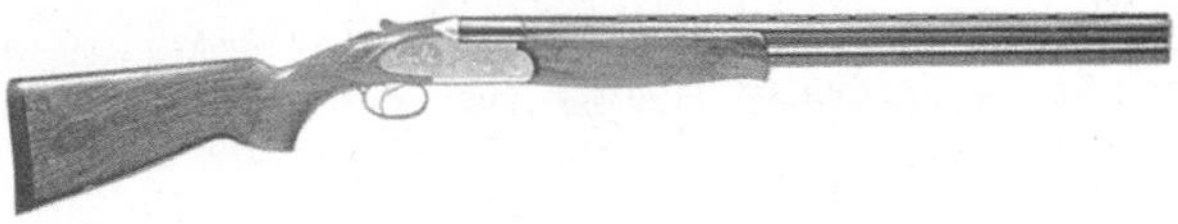

NIB	Exc.	V.G.	Good	Fair	Poor
1250	1100	875	725	500	300

NOTE: For 28 gauge add $40; for .410 bore add $25.

LX692G-20/28

This model has the features as above but features a 20 gauge gun with extra set of 28 gauge barrels. Choke tubes standard. Weight is about 7.5 lbs. with 20 gauge barrels.

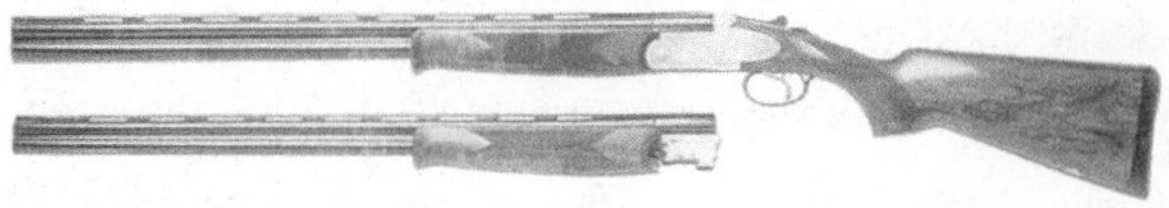

NIB	Exc.	V.G.	Good	Fair	Poor
2000	1800	1500	1200	900	500

Model LX1001 Express Combo

This over-and-under gun features two sets of barrels; one for 20 gauge 2.75" and the other for either .223, .243, .270, .308, or .30-06. The 20 gauge barrels are 28" vent rib and the rifle barrels are 22". Checkered walnut stock with oil finish. Engraved receiver.

NIB	Exc.	V.G.	Good	Fair	Poor
2580	2300	1975	1600	900	600

LX702G

This model is offered in both 12 and 20 gauge with 28" barrel chambered for 3" shells. This model features a case colored receiver with side plates. The reciever is engraved on three sides with gold inlaid upland bird hunting scenes. Full-figured Turkish walnut with hand checkering and oil finish. Single-selective trigger, black recoil pad, ejectors and schnabel forearm. Weight for 12 gauge is about 7 lbs. For the 20 gauge about 6 lbs.

NIB	Exc.	V.G.	Good	Fair	Poor
1375	1200	950	700	500	350

SIDE-BY-SIDE SHOTGUNS

Model SS662GL

This side-by-side gun is offered in 20 or 28 gauge with 28" barrels choked Modified and Full. Double triggers. Engraved receiver. Checkered walnut stock with straight grip. Weight is about 6 lbs. Made by Bernardelli. Add 20 percent for 28-gauge.

NIB	Exc.	V.G.	Good	Fair	Poor
2200	2000	1750	1400	1000	500

Model SS772GL

As above but with slightly more engraving. Add 20 percent for 28-gauge.

NIB	Exc.	V.G.	Good	Fair	Poor
2450	2200	1850	1550	1175	550

SPORTING/COMPETITION SHOTGUNS

LX680

Chambered for 12 or 20 gauge shells with 2.75" chambers. Single-selective trigger, ejectors, lightly engraved steel receiver. Walnut stock with beavertail firearm and hand-cut checkering. Ventilated recoil pad standard. Fitted with 28" barrels with ventilated rib between barrels. Choke tubes. Weight is about 6.5 lbs. depending on gauge.

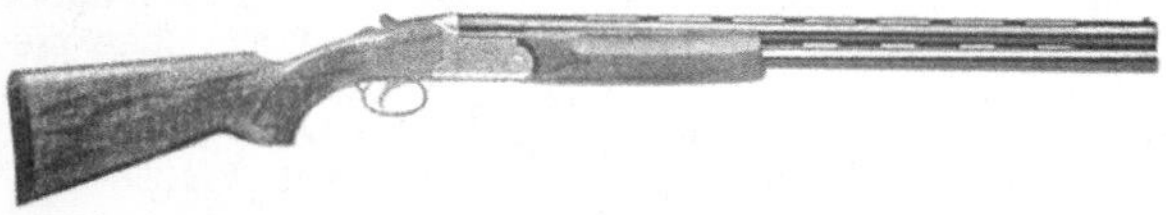

NIB	Exc.	V.G.	Good	Fair	Poor
1075	900	700	525	375	250

LX692GS

Similar to the above model but fitted with sideplates with gold inlaid hunting scenes.

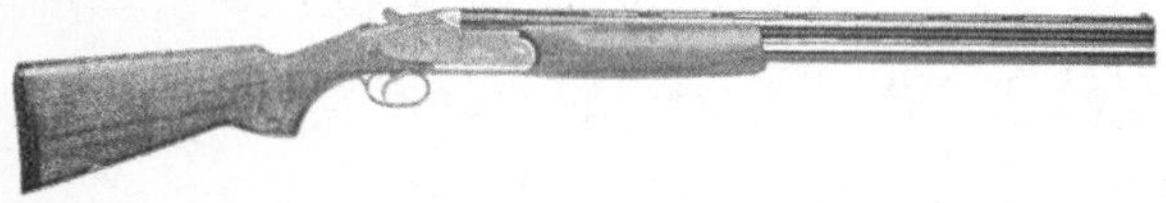

NIB	Exc.	V.G.	Good	Fair	Poor
1425	1300	1050	750	500	350

LX680C S&T

This over-and-under model features a choice of 28" or 30" 11mm vent-rib barrels on a 12 gauge frame. Single-selective trigger, ejectors. Matte finish Turkish walnut stock with hand-cut checkering, beavertail forearm, wider comb. Lightly engraved steel receiver. Ventilated rib between barrels. Choke tubes. Weight is approximately 7.75 lbs. depending on barrel length. The 28" barrel model is designated as Skeet/Sporting and the 30" model is designated Trap.

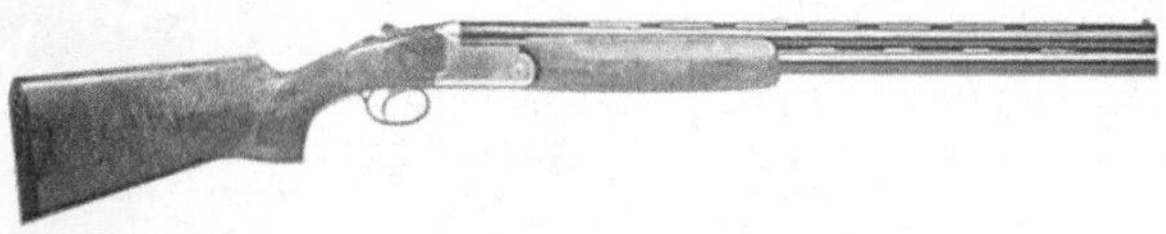

NIB	Exc.	V.G.	Good	Fair	Poor
1175	1000	800	600	425	275

LX692GC S&T

Same as above but with sideplates with gold inlaid game scenes.

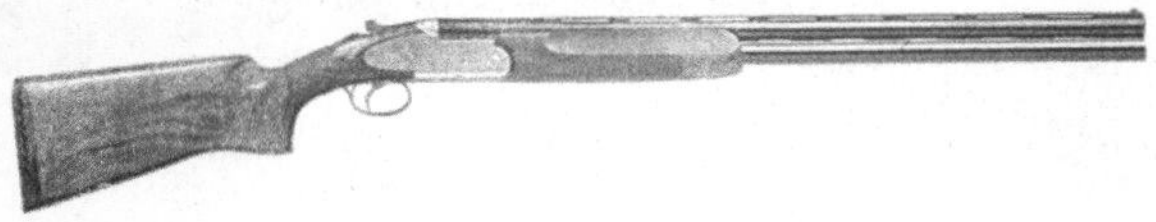

NIB	Exc.	V.G.	Good	Fair	Poor
1550	1400	1150	850	600	350

LX702GC S&T

This model features a case colored receiver and sideplates with gold inlaid birds. Offered in 12 gauge only with choice of 28" or 30" barrels. Weight is about 7.5 lbs.

NIB	Exc.	V.G.	Good	Fair	Poor
1625	1475	1175	800	600	350

Model SX801/L

This semi-automatic 12 gauge 2.75" shotgun is fitted with a choice of 28" or 30" vent-rib ported barrels with choke tubes and Hi-Viz sights. Walnut stock with choice of Monte Carlo comb or adjustable comb. Weight is about 6.75 lbs.

NIB	Exc.	V.G.	Good	Fair	Poor
865	700	575	400	275	200

Model SX801G/GL

As above but with higher grade walnut stock.

NIB	Exc.	V.G.	Good	Fair	Poor
1060	900	725	600	450	200

Model LX980CS

This 12 gauge 2.75" over-and-under gun is fitted with 30" ported barrels with extended choke tubes. Removable trigger assembly. Black receiver. Checkered select walnut stock. Weight is about 7.5 lbs.

NIB	Exc.	V.G.	Good	Fair	Poor
3525	3200	2500	2000	1550	600

Model LX980GCS/GCT

As above but with choice of 30" ported barrels or 32" ported barrels. Select walnut stock has adjustable comb. Weight is about 7.5 lbs.

NIB	Exc.	V.G.	Good	Fair	Poor
3775	3400	2800	2250	1700	650

VICKERS, LTD.

Crayford/Kent, England

Jubilee

A .22 caliber single-shot Martini-action rifle with a 28" barrel, adjustable sights and pistol grip walnut stock. Blued. Manufactured prior to WWII.

NIB	Exc.	V.G.	Good	Fair	Poor
—	1000	700	550	375	200

Empire

As above, with a 27" or 30" barrel and a straight stock.

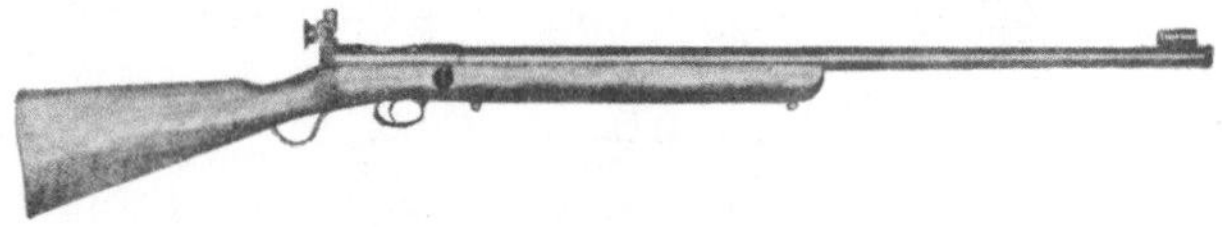

NIB	Exc.	V.G.	Good	Fair	Poor
—	1000	700	550	375	200

VOERE

Kufstein, Austria

In 1987 this company was purchased by Mauser-Werke. Voere actions are used in rifles made and sold by KDF, Inc. (Kleinguenther), of Seguin, Texas. Values for older-production rifles are listed.

Model 1007

Bolt-action rifle chambered for .22 LR cartridge and fitted with an 18" barrel. Open sights. Beech stock. Introduced in 1984. Discontinued in 1991.

NIB	Exc.	V.G.	Good	Fair	Poor
450	375	300	200	150	75

Model 1013

This bolt-action rifle is chambered for the .22 WMR cartridge and fitted with an 18" barrel. Magazine capacity is 8 rounds. Open sight with adjustable rear. Military-style stock is oil finished. Double set triggers.

NIB	Exc.	V.G.	Good	Fair	Poor
650	575	500	375	250	125

Model 2107

This .22 LR bolt-action rifle has a 19.5" barrel with Monte Carlo stock. Eight-round magazine. Weight is about 6 lbs.

NIB	Exc.	V.G.	Good	Fair	Poor
650	575	500	375	250	125

Model 2107 Deluxe

Bolt-action rifle chambered for .22 LR cartridge has checkered stock with raised cheekpiece. Discontinued in 1988.

NIB	Exc.	V.G.	Good	Fair	Poor
650	575	500	375	250	125

Model 2114S

This is a semi-automatic rifle chambered for .22 LR cartridge and fitted with a 18" barrel. Magazine capacity is 15 rounds. Open sight. Stock is beechwood. Single-stage trigger. No longer in production.

NIB	Exc.	V.G.	Good	Fair	Poor
450	375	300	200	150	75

Model 2115

Similar to the model above but with checkered stock. Weight is about 5.75 lbs. Discontinued in 1995.

NIB	Exc.	V.G.	Good	Fair	Poor
500	425	350	250	200	100

Model 2150

This is a bolt-action centerfire rifle chambered for calibers from .22-250 to .338 Win. Mag. Fitted with 22" barrels (24" on magnums). Open sights with adjustable rear sight. Checkered walnut stock with oil finish. Built on M98 Mauser action. Weight is about 8 lbs. depending on caliber. Discontinued in 1995.

NIB	Exc.	V.G.	Good	Fair	Poor
—	1500	1200	850	550	300

Model 2155

Similar to the Model 2150 but with no sights and double set triggers. Discontinued in 1995.

NIB	Exc.	V.G.	Good	Fair	Poor
—	1650	1350	1000	700	225

Model 2165

Similar to the above model but with open sights, walnut stock with Bavarian cheekpiece and schnabel forearm. Rosewood grip cap. Discontinued.

NIB	Exc.	V.G.	Good	Fair	Poor
—	1650	1350	1000	700	225

Model 2185

This is a semi-automatic centerfire rifle chambered for 7x64, .308, and .30-06 cartridges. Fitted with a 20" barrel and open sights with adjustable rear sight. Checkered walnut stock. Available with full stock as well.

NIB	Exc.	V.G.	Good	Fair	Poor
—	1500	1200	950	850	400

NOTE: Add $100 for Mannlicher stock.

Model 2185 Match

Same as the Model 2185 except for a 5-round magazine, hooded front sight, laminated stock with adjustable cheekpiece. Discontinued in 1994.

NIB	Exc.	V.G.	Good	Fair	Poor
4000	3400	2750	1150	650	400

Model Titan

This is a centerfire bolt-action rifle chambered in calibers from .243 to .375 H&H. Fitted with 24" or 26" barrels depending on caliber. No sights. Checkered Monte Carlo walnut stock with oil finish. Discontinued in 1988.

NIB	Exc.	V.G.	Good	Fair	Poor
—	1200	1000	775	500	350

Model Titan Menor

Bolt-action rifle chambered for .222 Rem, .223 Rem. Fitted with a 23.5" barrel and 3-round magazine. No sights. Checkered Monte Carlo walnut stock with rosewood grip cap. Introduced in 1986 and dropped in 1988.

NIB	Exc.	V.G.	Good	Fair	Poor
—	1000	800	600	400	250

Model VEC-91 Lightning

Bolt-action rifle that fires caseless 6mm ammo. Adjustable rear sight on a 20" barrel. Checkered walnut stock with cheekpiece. Electronic trigger. Introduced in 1991. Value Speculative.

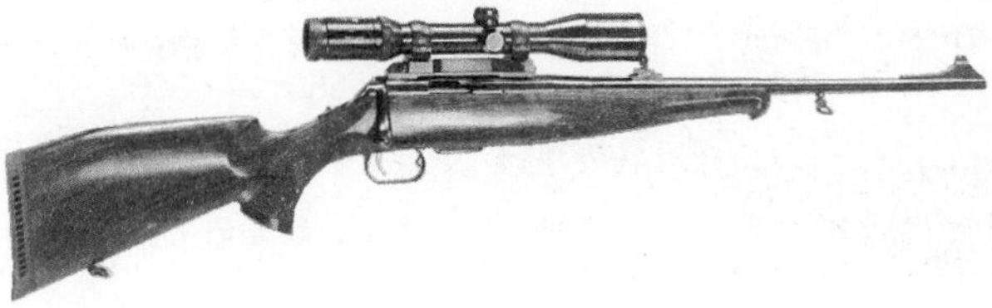

Model VEC-91BR

Same as model above but in single-shot with heavy 20" barrel. Synthetic target stock. Introduced in 1995.

Model VEC-91HB

Same as the VEC-91 except single-shot with heavy 22" barrel. Choice of synthetic stock or laminated wood stock. Introduced in 1995. Value Speculative.

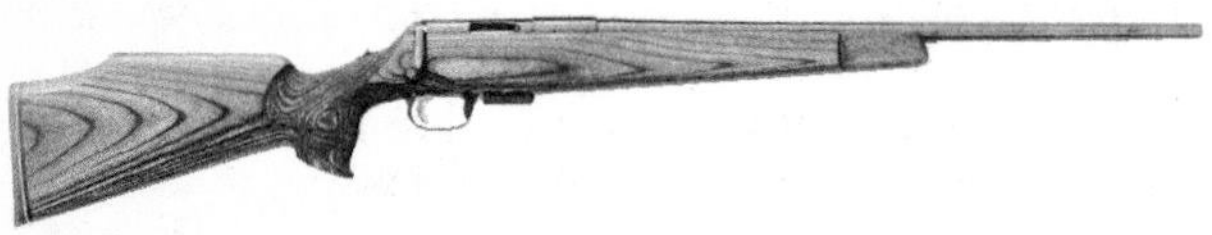

Model VEC-91SS

This version has no sights and a synthetic stock. Introduced in 1995. Value Speculative.

VOLQUARTSEN CUSTOM

Carroll, Iowa

This company was started in 1973, and began specializing in Ruger 10/22 aftermarket conversions. In 1997 the company began producing its own receivers. **NOTE:** Volquartsen offers beaucoup options on a wide variety of rifles. The values shown below are for the more-or-less base models.

SEMI-AUTO RIFLES

These rifles are based on the Ruger 10/22 design. They are chambered for the .22 LR or .22 WMR cartridge.

Standard

Fitted with an 18.5" stainless steel barrel and either a Hogue rubber stock or brown laminated stock. No sights. Integral Weaver rail.

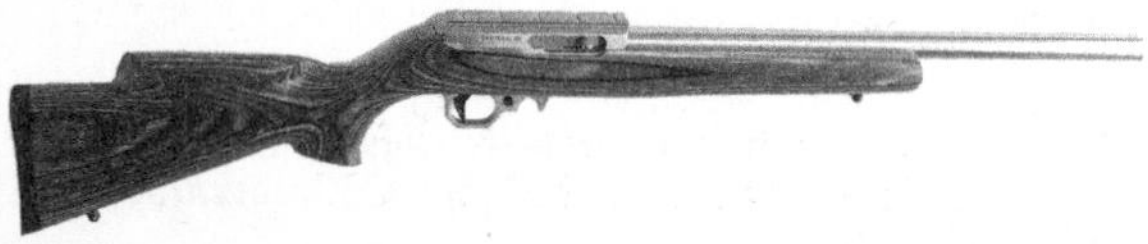

NIB	*Exc.*	*V.G.*	*Good*	*Fair*	*Poor*
1350	1200	950	700	550	300

Lightweight

This model has a 16.5" carbon-fiber barrel. Choice of rubber or laminated stock. Integral Weaver rail.

NIB	*Exc.*	*V.G.*	*Good*	*Fair*	*Poor*
1370	1220	975	725	550	300

Deluxe

This model has a 20" stainless steel fluted and compensated barrel. Choice of laminated or rubber stock.

NIB	*Exc.*	*V.G.*	*Good*	*Fair*	*Poor*
1360	1200	950	700	550	300

Signature Series

Fitted with a 20" stainless steel fluted and compensated barrel. Engraved receiver, trigger guard and rings. Comes with a Nikon 3.3x10 Titanium scope. Fancy walnut stock.

NIB	*Exc.*	*V.G.*	*Good*	*Fair*	*Poor*
3000	2650	2200	1600	1200	500

VG-1

This model has a 20" stainless steel fluted and compensated barrel. Fitted with a green McMillan fiberglass stock. Finish is black epoxy powder coating. Offered in .22 WMR only.

NIB	*Exc.*	*V.G.*	*Good*	*Fair*	*Poor*
1900	1700	1400	1150	900	500

VOUZELAUD

Paris, France

Model 315 E

A 12, 16, or 20 gauge boxlock shotgun with 20" barrels, double triggers, and straight-gripped stock. Blued, case hardened. Imported prior to 1988.

NIB	*Exc.*	*V.G.*	*Good*	*Fair*	*Poor*
—	7500	6000	4000	2000	900

Model 315 EL

As above, with more engraving and also available in .28 or .410 bore, which are worth approximately $1,000 more than the values listed.

NIB	*Exc.*	*V.G.*	*Good*	*Fair*	*Poor*
—	10000	8000	5000	2500	1100

Model 315 EGL

As above, with a French case hardened receiver. Discontinued in 1987.

NIB	*Exc.*	*V.G.*	*Good*	*Fair*	*Poor*
—	15000	12000	8500	4000	1500

Model 315 EGL-S

As above, with engraved hunting scenes. Discontinued in 1987.

NIB	*Exc.*	*V.G.*	*Good*	*Fair*	*Poor*
—	5500	4500	3500	2000	1000

W

WALTHER, CARL
Zella Mehilis and Ulm/Donau, Germany

RIFLES

Model B

A .30-06 caliber bolt-action rifle with a 22" barrel, 4-shot magazine and single or double set triggers. Double set triggers are worth approximately 20 percent more than the values listed. Blued with a walnut stock.

NIB	Exc.	V.G.	Good	Fair	Poor
—	775	700	450	250	175

Olympic Single-Shot

A .22 caliber bolt-action rifle with a 26" barrel, adjustable target sights and a walnut stock fitted with a palm rest and adjustable buttplate. Blued.

NIB	Exc.	V.G.	Good	Fair	Poor
—	1150	950	800	500	400

Model V

A .22 caliber single-shot bolt-action rifle with a 26" barrel and adjustable sights. Blued with a plain walnut stock. Manufactured before WWII.

NIB	Exc.	V.G.	Good	Fair	Poor
—	550	450	300	200	150

Model V Champion

As above, with a checkered walnut stock.

NIB	Exc.	V.G.	Good	Fair	Poor
—	600	500	350	250	200

Model KKM International Match

A .22 caliber single-shot bolt-action rifle with a 28" barrel and adjustable sights. Blued with a walnut stock fitted for a palm rest and with an adjustable buttplate. Manufactured after WWII.

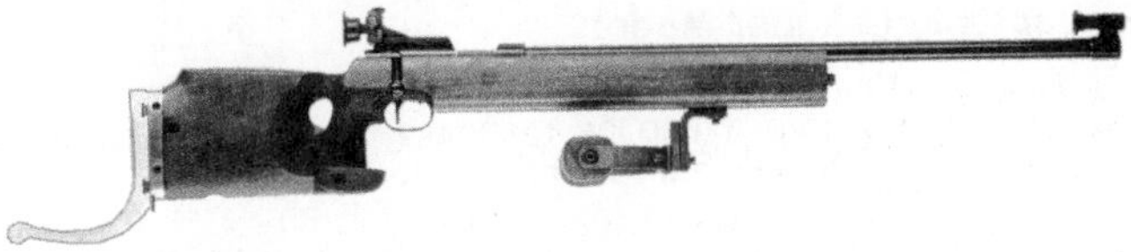

NIB	Exc.	V.G.	Good	Fair	Poor
—	1550	1275	850	450	350

Model KKM-S

As above, with an adjustable cheekpiece.

NIB	Exc.	V.G.	Good	Fair	Poor
—	1625	1350	850	500	400

Model KKW

As above, with a military-style stock.

NIB	Exc.	V.G.	Good	Fair	Poor
—	1250	975	600	250	175

Model KKJ Sporter

A .22 caliber bolt action rifle with a 22.5" barrel and 5-shot magazine. Blued with a checkered walnut stock. This model was available with double set triggers and their presence would add approximately 20 percent to the values listed. Manufactured after WWII.

NIB	Exc.	V.G.	Good	Fair	Poor
—	900	800	550	350	300

Model KKJ-MA

As above, in .22 Magnum rimfire.

NIB	Exc.	V.G.	Good	Fair	Poor
—	850	750	550	350	300

Model KKJ-HO

As above, in .22 Hornet.

NIB	Exc.	V.G.	Good	Fair	Poor
—	950	850	650	450	350

Model SSV Varmint

A .22 caliber bolt action single-shot rifle with a 25.5" barrel not fitted with sights and Monte Carlo-style stock. Blued. Manufactured after WWII.

NIB	Exc.	V.G.	Good	Fair	Poor
—	700	600	475	375	300

Model UIT BV Universal

As above, with adjustable target sights and a walnut stock fitted with a palm rest and adjustable buttplate.

NIB	Exc.	V.G.	Good	Fair	Poor
1750	1500	1250	900	650	500

Model UIT Match

As above, with a stippled pistol grip and forend. Also available with an electronic trigger that would add approximately $50 to the values listed.

NIB	Exc.	V.G.	Good	Fair	Poor
1350	1100	800	600	450	400

GX 1

As above, with an adjustable Free Rifle stock.

NIB	Exc.	V.G.	Good	Fair	Poor
2250	2000	1750	1250	850	700

Prone Model 400

Target rifle in .22 caliber with a prone position stock.

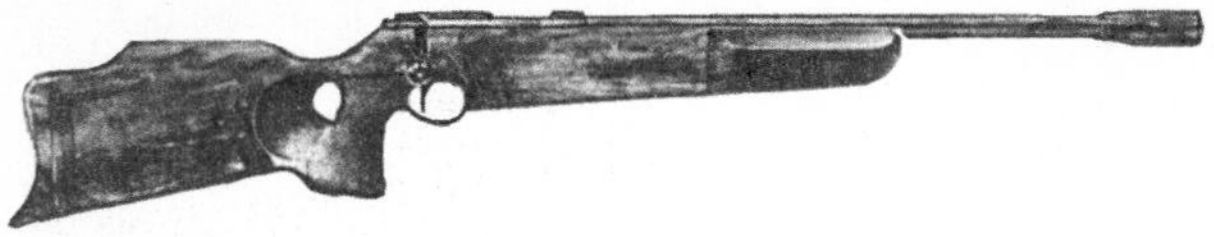

NIB	Exc.	V.G.	Good	Fair	Poor
800	700	600	450	350	300

Model KK/MS Silhouette

A .22 caliber bolt-action rifle with a 25.5" front-weighted barrel furnished without sights and a thumbhole stock with an adjustable buttplate. Introduced in 1984.

NIB	Exc.	V.G.	Good	Fair	Poor
1300	1100	850	700	550	400

Running Boar Model 500

As above, with a 23.5" barrel.

NIB	Exc.	V.G.	Good	Fair	Poor
1550	1350	950	750	600	450

Model WA-2000

A .300 Winchester Magnum or .308 caliber bolt-action sporting rifle produced on custom order. Imported prior to 1989.

NIB	Exc.	V.G.	Good	Fair	Poor
—	6500	4750	3500	3000	2000

Model G22

This is a .22 caliber rifle with a 20" barrel with adjustable sights. This model features a cocking indicator, integrated lock, slide safety, and multi function rail. Black or green finish. Weight is about 6 lbs. This model is also sold as a package.

NIB	Exc.	V.G.	Good	Fair	Poor
450	350	225	175	125	100

Model G22 Package A1 with Walther rifle scope

NIB	Exc.	V.G.	Good	Fair	Poor
500	400	275	225	175	150

Model G22 Package A2 with laser

NIB	Exc.	V.G.	Good	Fair	Poor
500	400	275	225	175	150

Model G22 Package A3 with Walther rifle scope & laser

NIB	Exc.	V.G.	Good	Fair	Poor
500	400	275	225	175	150

Model G22 Package A4 with Walther PS22 red-dot sight

NIB	Exc.	V.G.	Good	Fair	Poor
500	400	275	225	175	150

SHOTGUNS

Model SF

A 12 or 16 gauge boxlock double-barrel shotgun fitted with double triggers and extractors. Blued with a checkered walnut stock fitted with sling swivels.

NIB	Exc.	V.G.	Good	Fair	Poor
—	1150	900	750	600	450

Model SFD

As above, with the stock having a cheekpiece.

NIB	Exc.	V.G.	Good	Fair	Poor
—	1150	900	750	600	450

WARNER, JAMES

Springfield, Massachusetts

REVOLVING CARBINES

A variety of revolving carbines were made by this maker, nearly all of which are of .40 caliber, with octagonal barrels measuring 20" to 24" in length. The most commonly encountered variations are listed.

Manually Revolved Grooved Cylinder

This model is fitted with two triggers, one of which is a release so that the cylinder can be manually turned. Not fitted with a loading lever. The top strap marked "James Warner/Springfield, Mass." Approximately 75 were made in 1849.

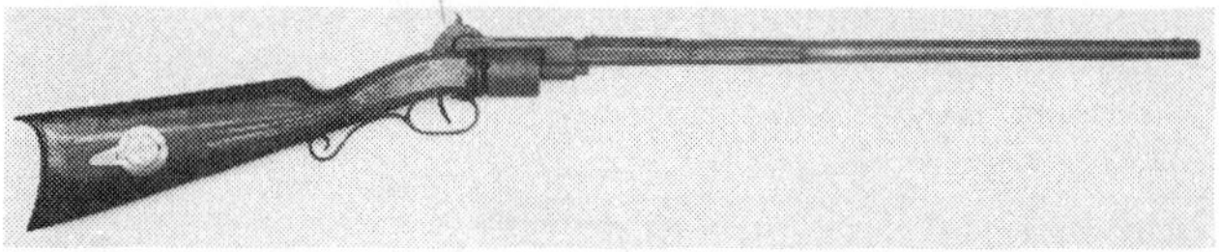

Courtesy Milwaukee Public Museum, Milwaukee, Wisconsin

NIB	Exc.	V.G.	Good	Fair	Poor
—	—	7500	4700	2200	500

Retractable Cylinder Model

This version has a cylinder that fits over the breech, and it must be retracted before it can be manually rotated. The cylinder release is a button located in front of the trigger. It is marked "James Warner/Springfield Mass" and with an eagle over the letters "U.S." The cylinder is etched, and there is no loading lever. It also has a walnut stock with patch box and no forearm. There were approximately 25 manufactured in 1849.

NIB	Exc.	V.G.	Good	Fair	Poor
—	—	9500	6900	3000	800

Automatic Revolving Cylinder

The cylinder is automatically turned when the hammer is cocked. This model is fitted with a loading lever and is marked "Warner's Patent/Jan. 1851" and "Springfield Arms Co." Approximately 200 were made during the 1850s.

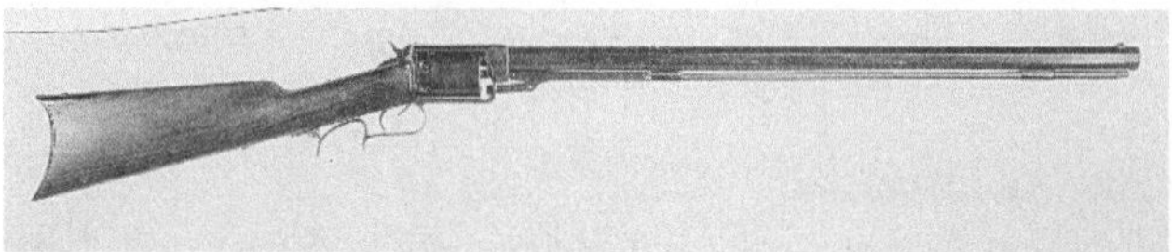

Courtesy Milwaukee Public Museum, Milwaukee, Wisconsin

NIB	Exc.	V.G.	Good	Fair	Poor
—	—	7500	4700	1900	500

WARNER ARMS CORPORATION

Brooklyn, New York and Norwich, Connecticut

Established in 1912, this firm marketed revolvers, rifles, semi-automatic pistols and shotguns made for them by other companies (including N.R. Davis & Sons, Ithaca Gun Company and so forth). In 1917, the company was purchased by N.R. Davis & Company. See also Davis-Warner.The arms marketed by Warner Prior to 1917 are listed.

SHOTGUNS

Single Trigger Hammerless Utica Special Double-Barrel

In 12 gauge with 28", 30", or 32" barrels.

Double Trigger Hammerless Double-Barrel

In 12 or 16 gauge with 28", 30", or 32" barrels.

Grade X, SF, XT, SFT, XD and XDF Hammer Guns

In 12, 16 or 20 gauge with 28", 30", or 32" barrels.

Field Grade Hammer Gun

In 12 or 16 gauge with 28" or 30" barrels.

Boxlock Hammerless

In 12 or 16 gauge with 28", 30", or 32" barrels.

RIFLES

Number 522

A .22 caliber single-shot rifle with an 18" barrel.

WEATHERBY

Atascadero, California

This corporation was founded in 1945 by Roy Weatherby. He pioneered the high-velocity hunting rifle. His rifles were designed to fire cartridges that he also produced. They are examples of fine craftsmanship and have been used to take some of the top trophy animals from all around the world. Formerly these rifles were manufactured in West Germany. They are currently produced in Japan. Although the Japanese rifles are, in the opinion of the editors, every bit as fine a firearm as the German versions, collectors have given an approximate 25 percent premium to the German-manufactured versions. The values given are for the current-production Japanese weapons. Simply add the premium for a German-manufactured rifle. There are other premiums that collectors are paying in 1994 and these are listed.
NOTE: For German manufacture in calibers .224 through .300 add 25 percent for 24" barrels and 35 percent for 26" barrels.

Mark V

This is a deluxe, bolt-action repeating rifle chambered for various popular standard calibers, as well as the full line of Weatherby cartridges from .240 Weatherby Magnum to .300 Weatherby Magnum. It is furnished with either a 24" or 26" barrel without sights. It has either a 3- or 5-round magazine, depending on the caliber. It has a deluxe, high-polish blued finish with a select, skip-line checkered walnut stock with a rosewood forearm tip and pistol grip cap. This rifle is available with a left-hand action.

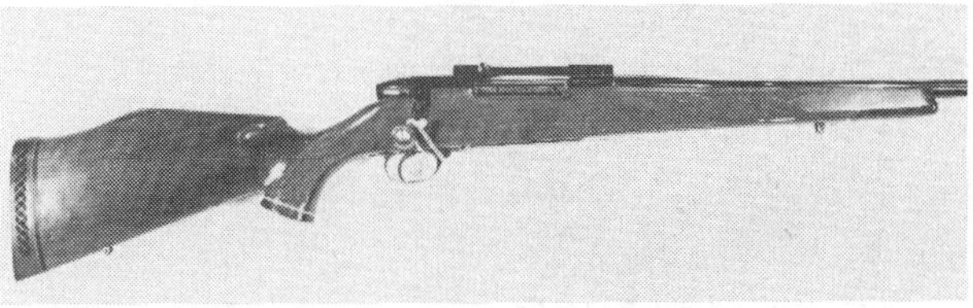

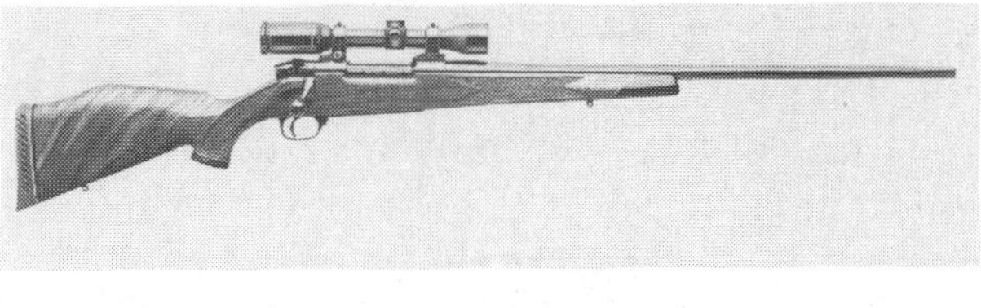

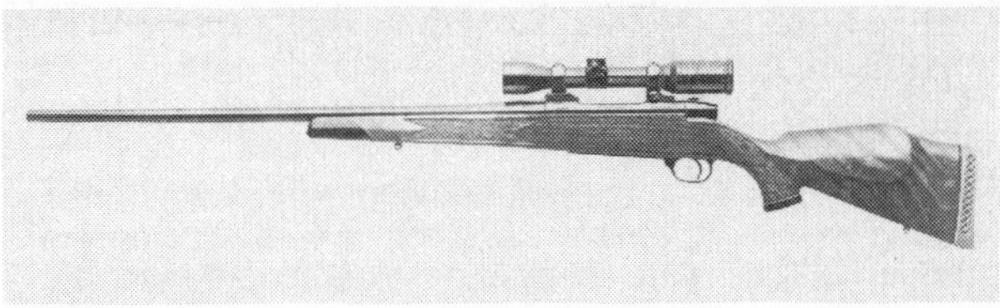

NIB	*Exc.*	*V.G.*	*Good*	*Fair*	*Poor*
1200	1050	800	600	500	250

Weatherby Mark V Deluxe

Step-up version of classic Mark V. Features include deluxe Claro walnut Monte Carlo stock with rosewood for-end, 26-inch or 28-inch high-polish blued sightless barrel. Chambered in .257, .270, 7mm, .300, .30-378, .340, .378, .416, and .460 Weatherby Magnum. Also available in short-action model in .22-250, .243 Win., .240 Weatherby, .25-06, .270 Win., 7mm-08, .280 Rem., .308 Win., .30-06.

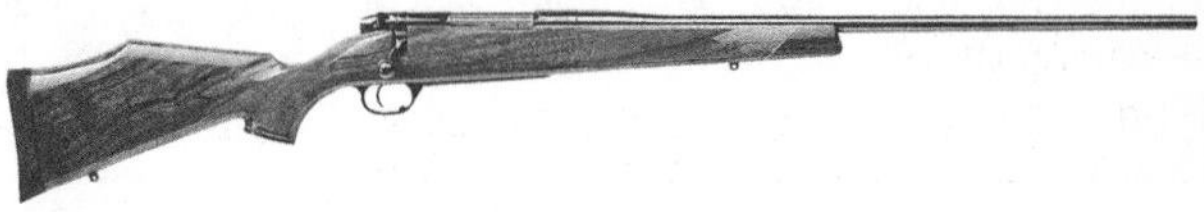

NIB	*Exc.*	*V.G.*	*Good*	*Fair*	*Poor*
1750	1475	1300	1075	800	350

NOTE: Add 25 percent for .30-378 Weatherby Magnum.

Mark V Sporter

Introduced in 1993 this model is identical to the Mark V Deluxe without the custom features. The metal is a low luster finish, the stock is Claro walnut with high gloss finish. A Monte Carlo comb with raised cheekpiece and black 1" recoil pad are standard features on this model. Available in Weatherby calibers from .257 through .340 plus .270 Win., .30-06, 7mm Rem. Mag., .300 Win Mag., .338 Win. Mag. Weighs 8 to 8.5 lbs. depending on caliber.

NIB	*Exc.*	*V.G.*	*Good*	*Fair*	*Poor*
1100	950	800	650	500	300

Mark V .375 Weatherby Magnum

This version was manufactured in Germany only and is chambered for the currently obsolete .375 Weatherby Magnum cartridge. This version has become very collectible.

NIB	*Exc.*	*V.G.*	*Good*	*Fair*	*Poor*
5000	3500	3000	2500	2000	1500

Mark V .378 Weatherby Magnum

This version is chambered for the .378 Weatherby Magnum cartridge. It is furnished with a 26" barrel only.

NIB	*Exc.*	*V.G.*	*Good*	*Fair*	*Poor*
2000	1825	1550	1200	850	500

NOTE: For German guns in this caliber add 50 percent.

Mark V .416 Weatherby Magnum

This is an extremely powerful rifle suitable for hunting the biggest game. It was introduced in 1989.

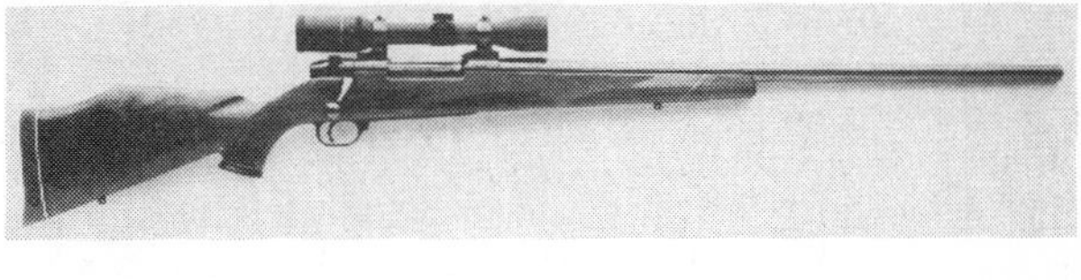

NIB	Exc.	V.G.	Good	Fair	Poor
2000	1825	1550	1200	850	500

Mark V .460 Weatherby Magnum

This is said to be the most powerful commercial rifle available in the world, with the possible exception of some of the recently-reintroduced British nitro chamberings. It is available with a 24" or 26" heavy barrel with an integral, recoil-reducing muzzlebrake. It has a custom reinforced stock.

NIB	Exc.	V.G.	Good	Fair	Poor
2500	2200	1850	1500	1000	600

NOTE: For German guns in this caliber add 100 percent.

Mark V Dangerous Game Rifle

This model was introduced in 2001 and features a synthetic stock with Monte Carlo and 24" or 26" barrel with barrel band and hooded front sight depending on caliber. Chambered for the .378 Weatherby Mag., .416 Weatherby Mag., and the .460 Weatherby Mag. Adjustable trigger. Weight is between 8.74 and 9.5 lbs. depending on caliber. In 2003 the .458 Lott was offered for this model.

NIB	Exc.	V.G.	Good	Fair	Poor
2500	2200	1850	1500	1000	600

Mark V Euromark

This model features a hand-checkered, oil-finished, Claro walnut stock with an ebony forend tip and pistol grip cap. It has a satin blued finish. It was introduced in 1986.

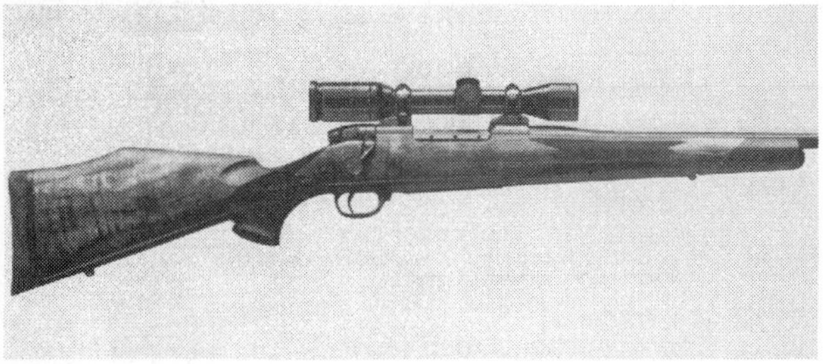

NIB	Exc.	V.G.	Good	Fair	Poor
1500	1300	1050	800	575	350

Mark V Fluted Stainless

Introduced late in 1996 this model features a fluted stainless steel barrel chambered for the .257 Weatherby Magnum to the .300 Weatherby Magnum calibers as well as the 7mm Rem. Mag. and the .300 Win. Mag. The stock is synthetic with raised comb and checkered stock. Weight varies depending on caliber.

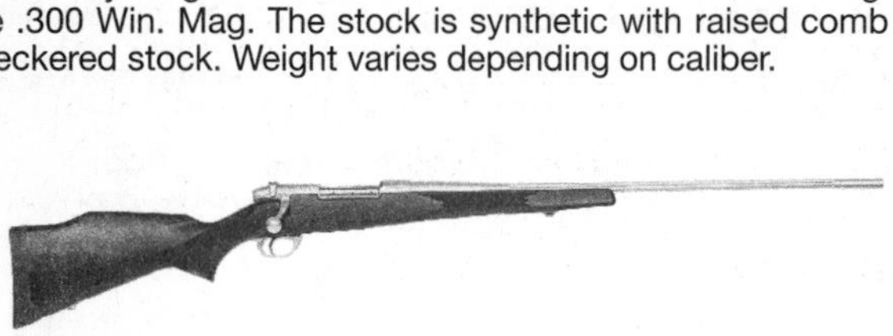

NIB	Exc.	V.G.	Good	Fair	Poor
1200	1050	800	600	500	250

Mark V Fluted Synthetic

This model is similar to the above model with a blued carbon steel action and barrel with synthetic stock. Introduced late in 1996.

NIB	Exc.	V.G.	Good	Fair	Poor
1000	850	650	450	400	200

Mark V SLS

This model features a stainless steel barreled action with laminated wood stock fitted with a 1" black recoil pad. Rifle is chambered for .257 through .340 Weatherby Magnum calibers as well as 7mm Rem. Mag., .300 and .338 Win. Mag., and the .375 H&H Mag. Weight is about 8.25 lbs. depending on caliber. Introduced in late 1996.

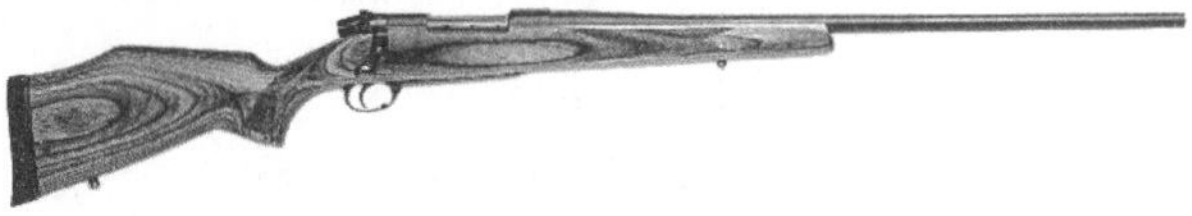

NIB	Exc.	V.G.	Good	Fair	Poor
1200	1050	800	600	500	250

Mark V Varmint

This version is chambered for the .22-250 and the .224 Weatherby cartridge. It is offered with a 24" or 26" heavy barrel.

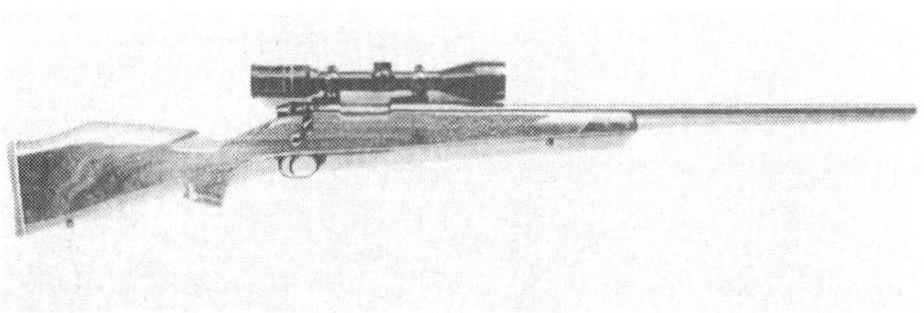

NIB	Exc.	V.G.	Good	Fair	Poor
975	800	750	550	450	400

NOTE: For German built add 50 percent.

Mark V Lazermark

This version had a laser-carved pattern on the stock and forearm in place of the usual checkering. It was introduced in 1985.

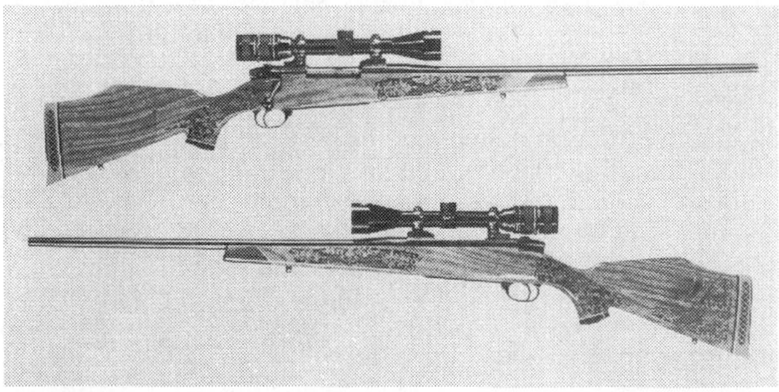

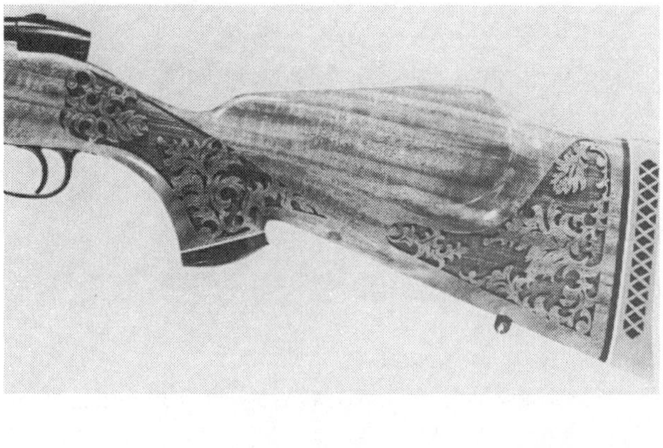

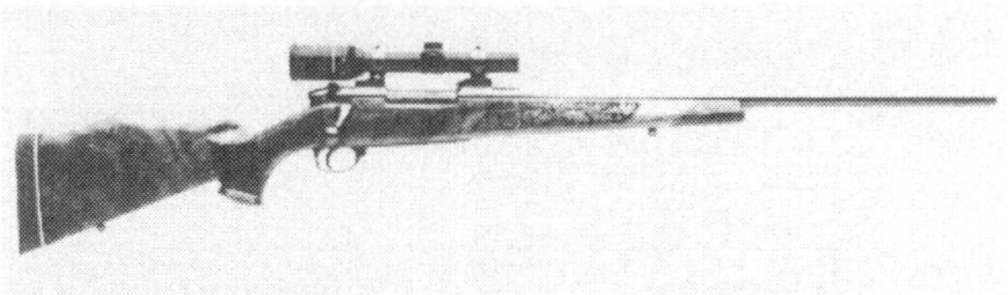

NIB	Exc.	V.G.	Good	Fair	Poor
2000	1750	1500	1100	600	300

Mark V Fibermark Composite

This version has a matte blue finish and is furnished with a synthetic black, wrinkle-finished stock. Chambered for calibers from .22-250 to .375 H&H with barrel lengths from 24" to 26" depending on caliber.

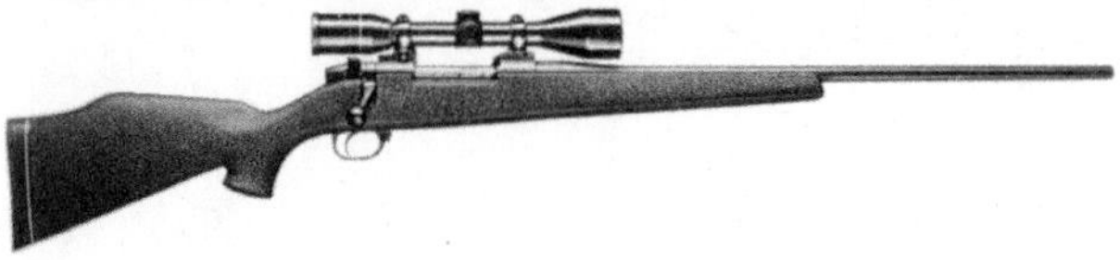

NIB	Exc.	V.G.	Good	Fair	Poor
1250	1000	800	550	400	250

Mark V Ultramark

This is a custom-finished version with a glass-bedded action and a special, high-polish blue. The action is hand-honed, and the walnut stock features basket weave checkering. It was introduced in 1989.

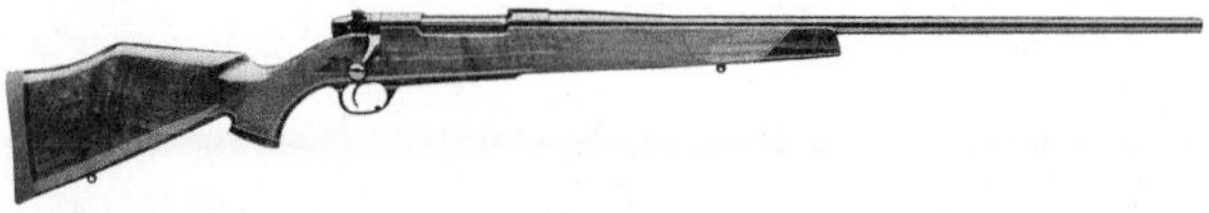

NIB	Exc.	V.G.	Good	Fair	Poor
2400	2000	1650	1200	800	500

Mark V Accumark

Introduced in 1995 this rifle features a Mark V Magnum action. The trigger is preset at the factory for 3.5 lbs. of pull. It is fully adjustable for sear engagement at let-off weight. The action metal is black oxide coated with a bead blast matte finish. The stainless steel barrel is 26" in length with a low luster brushed finish. Weight is approximately 8 lbs. and is offered in caliber from .257 to .340 Weatherby Magnum, 7mm Rem. Magnum, and .300 Win. Magnum. In August the company announced that this model would also be offered in the .30-.378 Weatherby caliber. In 1997 this model was offered chambered for the 7mm STW cartridge. Available in right-hand only.

Mark V Accumark

NIB	Exc.	V.G.	Good	Fair	Poor
1400	1100	950	800	500	300

Mark V Accumark Left-Hand

This is a left-hand version of the Accumark. Introduced in 1999.

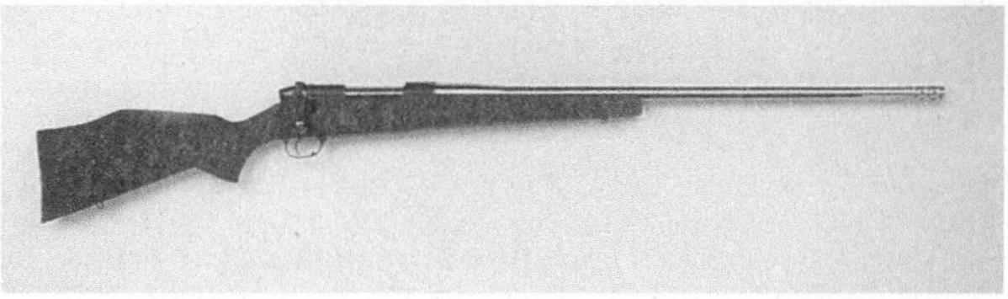

NIB	Exc.	V.G.	Good	Fair	Poor
1400	1100	950	800	500	300

35th Anniversary Commemorative Mark V

This specially embellished rifle commemorated the 35th anniversary of the company. There were 1,000 produced in 1980. As with all commemoratives, it must be NIB with all furnished materials to be worth top dollar.

NIB	Exc.	V.G.	Good	Fair	Poor
1600	1300	1050	750	500	350

1984 Olympic Commemorative Mark V

This is a specially embellished Mark V rifle that has gold-plated accents and an exhibition-grade walnut stock with a star inlay. There were 1,000 manufactured in 1984. This is a commemorative rifle and must be NIB to bring premium value.

NIB	Exc.	V.G.	Good	Fair	Poor
1600	1300	1050	750	500	350

Safari Grade Mark V

This is a custom-order version that is available chambered from the .300 Weatherby Magnum through the .460 Weatherby Magnum. It is available with a number of custom options and can be ordered with an 8- to 10-month delivery delay.

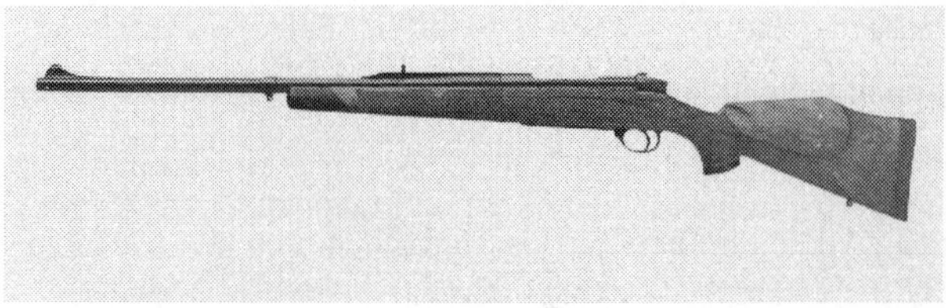

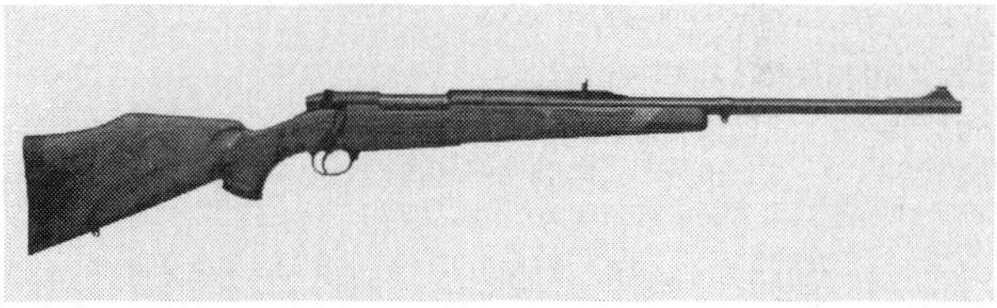

NIB	Exc.	V.G.	Good	Fair	Poor
3500	3000	2750	2000	1200	600

Crown Grade Mark V

This is Weatherby's best-grade rifle and is available on a custom-order basis only. It features an engraved receiver and barrel with an exhibition-grade, hand-checkered walnut stock. It is also furnished with an engraved scope mount.

NIB	Exc.	V.G.	Good	Fair	Poor
6500	5000	3500	2750	1500	500

Mark V Super Varmint Master (SVM)

Introduced in 2000 this model features a 26" stainless steel barrel. The stock is laminated with Monte Carlo comb. Fully adjustable trigger. Chambered for .220 Swift, .223 Rem., .22-250, .243 Win., 7mm-08, and .308 Win. Also offered in a single-shot configuration. Weight is about 8.5 lbs.

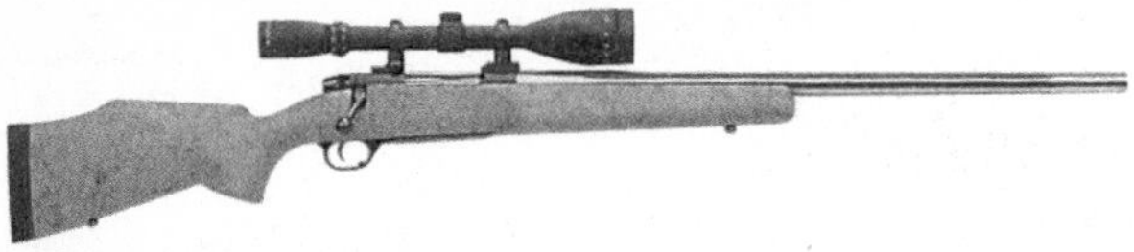

NIB	*Exc.*	*V.G.*	*Good*	*Fair*	*Poor*
1675	1400	1200	900	600	350

Mark V Special Varmint Rifle (SVR)

Introduced in 2003 this model features a 22" Krieger heavy barrel, a Monte Carlo composite stock, a black recoil pad and matte black finish. Adjustable trigger is standard. Available in .223 Rem. and .22-250. Weight is approximately 7.25 lbs.

NIB	*Exc.*	*V.G.*	*Good*	*Fair*	*Poor*
1100	1000	800	700	500	300

MARK V LIGHTWEIGHT RIFLES

Mark V Synthetic Lightweight

Chambered in calibers from .22-250 to .308 Win. fitted with a 24" barrel. Synthetic stock with Monte Carlo comb. Magazine capacity is 5 rounds. Weight is approximately 6.5 lbs. A carbine version is offered with 20" barrel in .243, 7mm-08, and .308. Weight is about 6 lbs.

NIB	*Exc.*	*V.G.*	*Good*	*Fair*	*Poor*
900	750	600	475	350	250

Mark V Stainless Lightweight

Similar to the model above but with stainless steel barrel and action. Weight is about 6.5 lbs. Carbine version also available.

NIB	*Exc.*	*V.G.*	*Good*	*Fair*	*Poor*
1100	950	800	650	525	300

Mark V Sporter Lightweight

Chambered for calibers ranging from .22-250 to .308 Win. and fitted with a 24" barrel. Stock is Claro walnut with Monte Carlo comb. Weight is approximately 6.75 lbs.

NIB	*Exc.*	*V.G.*	*Good*	*Fair*	*Poor*
1050	900	750	600	475	250

Mark V Accumark Lightweight

Chambered for calibers from .22-250 to .300 Wby. and fitted with a 24" barrel. Magazine capacity is 5 rounds. Special laminated synthetic stock. Weight is approximately 7 lbs. Introduced in 1998.

NIB	*Exc.*	*V.G.*	*Good*	*Fair*	*Poor*
1250	1000	900	800	650	400

Mark V Ultra Lightweight

Similar to the above model but with lightened components. Calibers begin with .243 and go to .300 Wby. Fitted with a 24" or 26" barrel depending on caliber. Weight is about 5.75 lbs. Introduced in 1998. In 2000 this model was offered in a left-hand version. In 2001 this model was available chambered for the .338-06 A-Square cartridge.

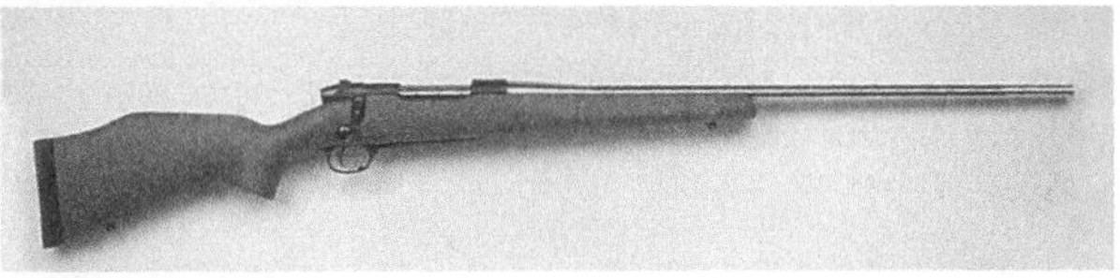

NIB	*Exc.*	*V.G.*	*Good*	*Fair*	*Poor*
1450	1200	950	700	450	300

Mark V Deluxe Lightweight

This model, in its lightweight configuration, is offered in calibers from .22-25- to .30-06. These calibers are fitted to a 24" barrel. Fitted with hand select walnut Monte Carlo stock with rosewood forend tip and pistol grip cap. Fine line checkering. Weight is about 6.75 lbs. Introduced in 1999.

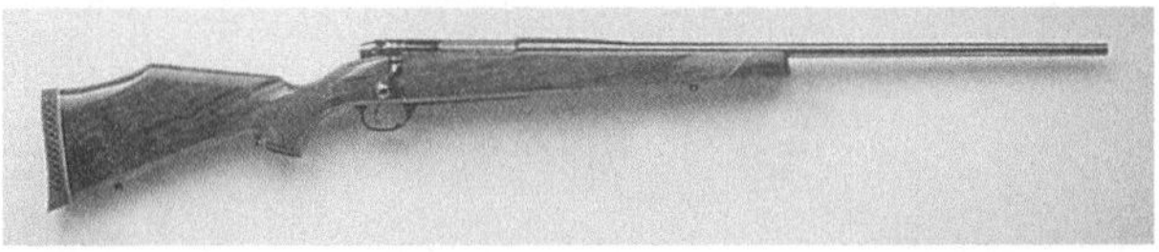

NIB	*Exc.*	*V.G.*	*Good*	*Fair*	*Poor*
1650	1250	1000	800	600	400

Mark V SPM (Super Predator Master)

Introduced in 2001 this rifle features a 24" blackened stainless steel fluted barrel. Chambered for the .223 Rem., .22-250 Rem., .243 Win., 7mm-08 Rem., and the .308 Win. cartridges. Fully adjustable trigger. Synthetic stock. Weight is about 6.5 lbs. Right-hand only.

NIB	*Exc.*	*V.G.*	*Good*	*Fair*	*Poor*
1600	1300	1050	750	500	350

Mark V SBGM (Super Big Game Master)

This model features a 24" blackened stainless steel barrel Krieger fluted barrel (26" for magnum calibers). Fully adjustable trigger. Tan composite stock with raised comb Monte Carlo. Pachmayr Decelerator recoil pad. Offered in a wide variety of caliber from .240 Weatherby Mag. to .300 Weatherby Mag. Weight is about 5.75 lbs. and 6.75 lbs. for magnum rifles. Introduced in 2002.

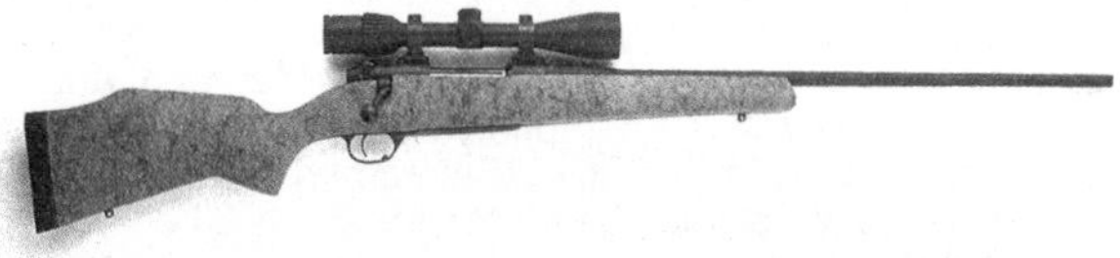

NIB	*Exc.*	*V.G.*	*Good*	*Fair*	*Poor*
1650	1250	1000	800	600	400

NOTE: Add $60 for magnum calibers.

THREAT RESPONSE RIFLE SERIES

These rifles are based on the Mark V action.

TRR

Chambered for the .223 or .308 Win. cartridge and fitted with a 22" heavy-contour black Krieger barrel. Black composite stock with raised comb Monte Carlo. Flat-bottom forearm. Fully adjustable trigger. Recoil pad. Introduced in 2002.

NIB	Exc.	V.G.	Good	Fair	Poor
1250	1000	900	800	650	400

TRR Magnum

As above but chambered for the .300 Win. Mag., .300 Wby. Mag., .30-378 Wby. Mag., or the .338-378 Wby. Mag. Barrel length is 26".

NIB	Exc.	V.G.	Good	Fair	Poor
1450	1200	950	700	450	300

NOTE: Add $150 for .30-378 and .338-378 calibers.

TRR Magnum Custom

This model has all the features of the TRR Magnum with the addition of a fully adjustable stock.

NIB	Exc.	V.G.	Good	Fair	Poor
2500	2200	1900	1600	1250	500

NOTE: Add $150 for .30-378 or .338-378 calibers.

WARNING: WEATHERBY VANGUARD

DO NOT use this model until the company performs a safety upgrade to the bolt. The rifle can accidentally discharge without the bolt being fully engaged. The affected rifles bear serial numbers from one of these series on the receiver: 00001 through 03810; V00001 through V80966; VX00001 through VX44065; VS00001 through VS23699; VL00001 through VL46984; W00001 through W0099; NV0001 through NV0099. For more information contact Weatherby at 800-227-2018

Vanguard (early production)

This was Weatherby's Japanese-manufactured economy rifle. It is chambered for various popular standard American cartridges from .22-50 to the .300 Winchester Magnum cartridge. It is a bolt-action repeater with a 24" barrel furnished without sights. It has either a 3-shot or 5-shot magazine; and the finish is polished blue, with a select, checkered walnut stock with a rosewood forend tip and pistol-grip cap. This model was discontinued in 1988.

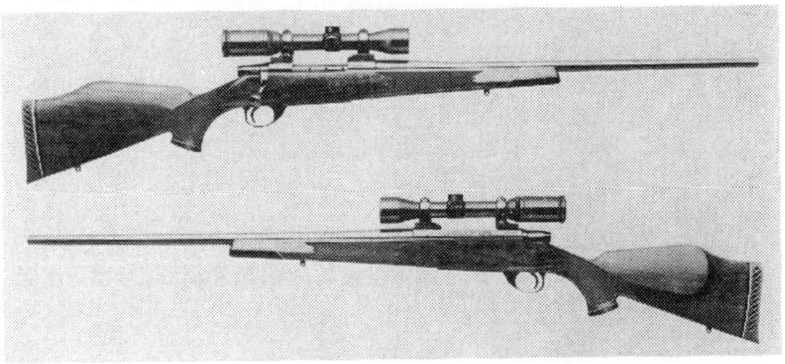

NIB	Exc.	V.G.	Good	Fair	Poor
—	1100	925	750	600	350

Vanguard VGS

This satin-finish version was also discontinued in 1988.

NIB	Exc.	V.G.	Good	Fair	Poor
—	1000	825	650	500	300

Vanguard VGL

This is a lightweight carbine version that has a 20" barrel. It was discontinued in 1988.

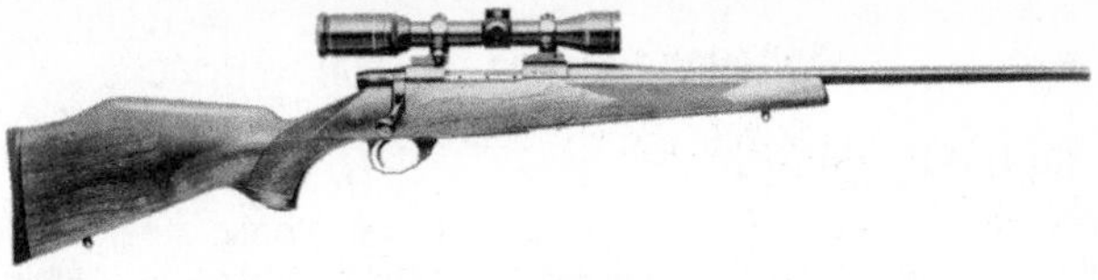

NIB	Exc.	V.G.	Good	Fair	Poor
—	900	725	550	400	250

Fiberguard

This version has a matte-blued finish with a green fiberglass stock. It was discontinued in 1988.

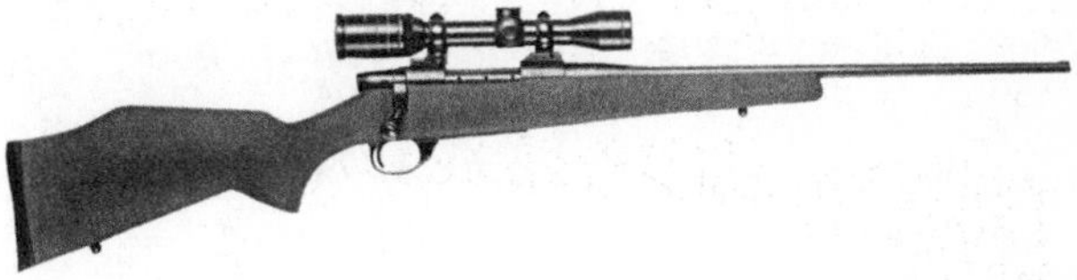

NIB	Exc.	V.G.	Good	Fair	Poor
—	750	575	400	300	200

Vanguard Classic I

This version is chambered for various popular standard calibers and has a 24" barrel and either a 3- or 5-shot magazine. It has a satin blue finish and a select checkered, oil-finished walnut stock. It was introduced in 1989.

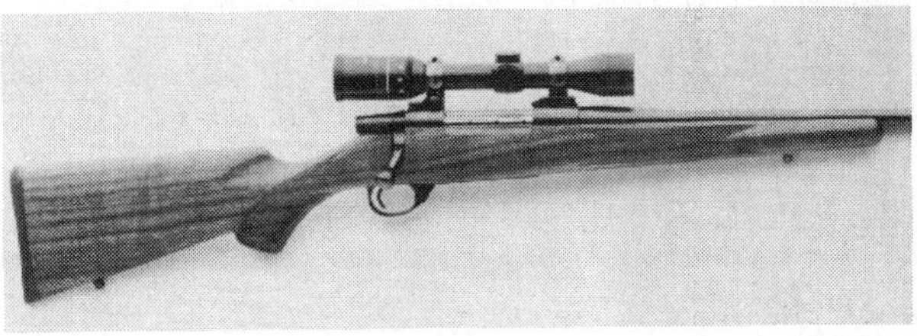

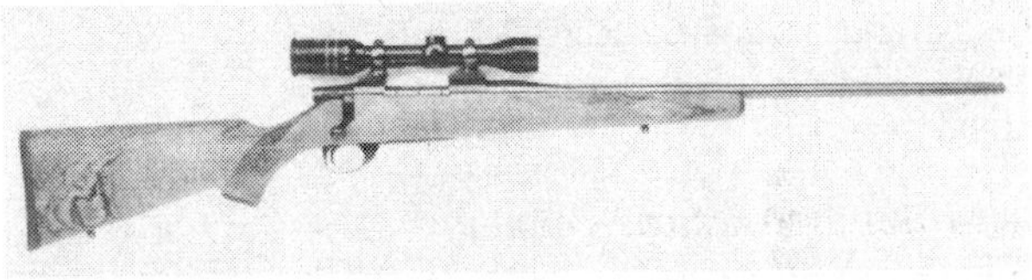

NIB	Exc.	V.G.	Good	Fair	Poor
700	600	500	400	300	200

Vanguard Classic II

This is a more deluxe version with a higher-grade walnut stock.

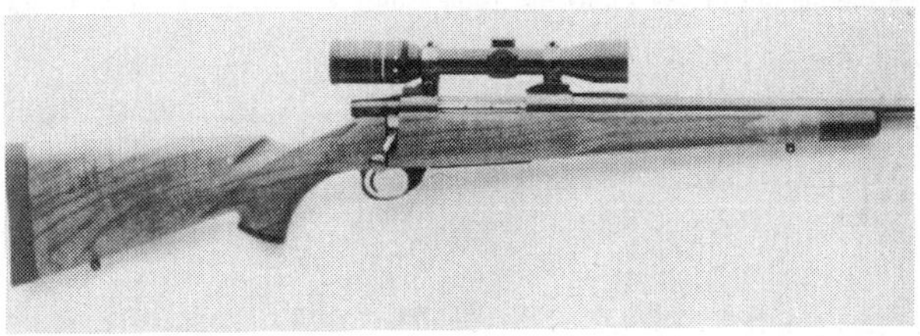

NIB	Exc.	V.G.	Good	Fair	Poor
725	625	525	425	325	225

Vanguard VGX Deluxe

This version has a high-gloss, Monte Carlo-type stock and a high-polished blued finish. It was introduced in 1989.

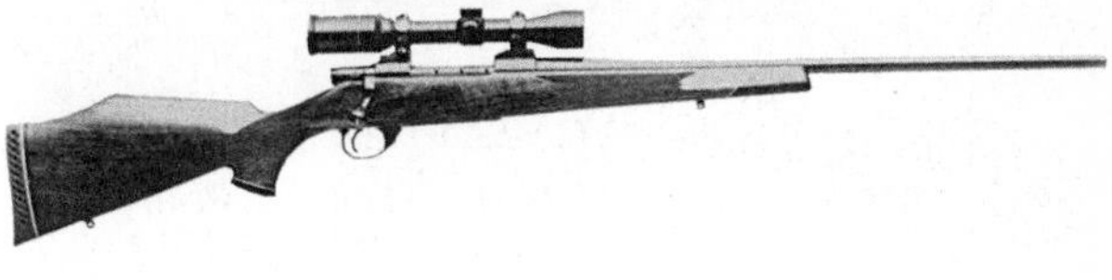

NIB	Exc.	V.G.	Good	Fair	Poor
800	700	600	500	400	300

Vanguard Weatherguard

This version has a wrinkle-finished, black synthetic stock. It was introduced in 1989. In 2003 this model was offered in stainless steel.

NIB	Exc.	V.G.	Good	Fair	Poor
650	500	400	300	225	175

NOTE: Add $120 for stainless steel.

Vanguard Synthetic

This model features an upgraded composite stock with Monte Carlo comb, a ring/base scope mounting system, a 24" barrel, and calibers from .223 Rem. to .338 Win. Mag., including the .257 Weatherby. Weight is about 7.75 lbs. Introduced in 2004.

NIB	Exc.	V.G.	Good	Fair	Poor
400	350	300	250	175	100

Vanguard Stainless

Similar to Vanguard Synthetic but with stainless steel barrel and receiver.

NIB	Exc.	V.G.	Good	Fair	Poor
575	500	450	350	275	125

Vanguard Sporter

Similar to the model above but with a figured walnut stock, rosewood forend tip and fine line checkering. Chambered for calibers from .270 to .338 Win. Mag. Barrel length is 24". Weight is about 8 lbs. Introduced in 2004. Also available with detachable magazine.

NIB	Exc.	V.G.	Good	Fair	Poor
550	450	350	250	175	100

Vanguard Sporter SS

Similar to Vanguard Sporter but with stainless steel barrel and receiver.

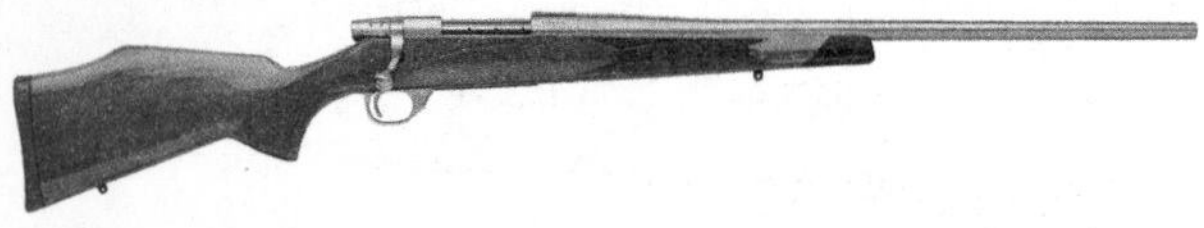

NIB	Exc.	V.G.	Good	Fair	Poor
675	575	475	375	275	125

Vanguard Varmint Special

Chambered in .223, .22-250, or .308. 22-inch blued #3 contour heavy crowned barrel, adjustable trigger, synthetic tan composite stock with black spiderweb pattern. Introduced 2006.

NIB	Exc.	V.G.	Good	Fair	Poor
575	475	375	275	195	125

Vanguard Synthetic Package

Introduced in 2004 this model features a 24" barrel with adjustable trigger. Chambered for a variety of calibers from the .223 Rem. to the .338 Win. Mag. Supplied with a Bushnell Banner 3-9x40 scope, sling, and hard case. Weight is about 7.75 lbs.

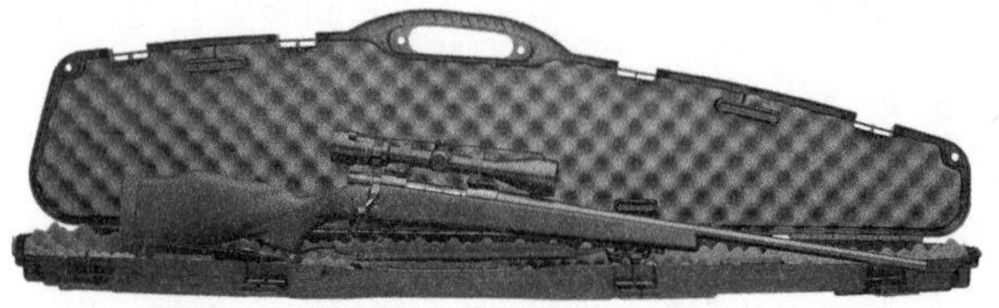

NIB	Exc.	V.G.	Good	Fair	Poor
650	550	350	275	225	150

Vanguard Sub-MOA Matte or Stainless

Introduced in 2005 this model features a guarantee to shoot .99" at 100 yards. Calibers from .223 Rem. to .338 Win. Mag. Barrel length is 24" with Monte Carlo Fiberguard stock. Adjustable trigger. Weight is about 7.75 lbs. Also available in stainless steel.

NIB	Exc.	V.G.	Good	Fair	Poor
800	700	600	500	300	200

NOTE: Add $120 for stainless steel.

Vanguard Sub-MOA Varmint

Similar to Vanguard Varmint Special but with ventilated beavertail for-end. Chambered in .204, .223, .22-250, and .308. Introduced 2006.

NIB	Exc.	V.G.	Good	Fair	Poor
925	800	650	500	300	200

Vanguard Compact

This model, chambered for the ..223, 22-250, .243, or .308, is fitted with a 20" barrel and scaled-down hardwood stock with shorter length of pull. Also included is a full size composite stock. Weight is about 6.75 lbs. Introduced in 2005.

NIB	Exc.	V.G.	Good	Fair	Poor
550	450	350	250	175	100

Vanguard Youth Compact

Similar to above but with synthetic stock. Introduced 2008.

NIB	Exc.	V.G.	Good	Fair	Poor
550	450	350	250	175	100

Vanguard Deluxe

Similar to Vanguard but features 24-inch polished blued barrel, glossy select Monte Carlo walnut stock with rosewood forend, adjustable trigger. Chambered in .270, .30-06, .257 Weatherby Mag., and .300 Weatherby Mag. Introduced 2006.

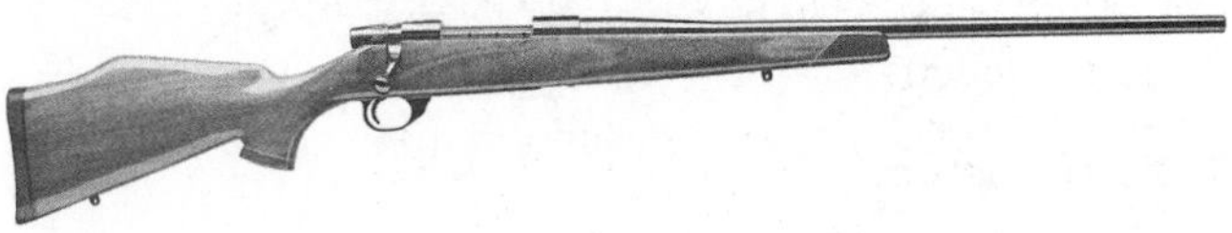

NIB	Exc.	V.G.	Good	Fair	Poor
750	650	550	450	325	225

Vanguard Series II

Proven Mauser-style bolt, twin-locking lugs, 3-position safety. Available in 15 popular calibers from .223 Rem. to .338 Win. Mag., including .257 and .300 Weatherby Magnums. Adjustable match-quality two-stage trigger, 24-inch barrel on all models. Sub-MOA guaranteed. New stock design with Griptonite inserts, raised comb, right-hand side palm swell. Matte bead blast blue finish or stainless.

NIB	Exc.	V.G.	Good	Fair	Poor
425	375	325	275	200	150

NOTE: Add 35 percent for stainless finish.

Weathermark

Introduced in 1993 this model features a checkered composite stock with matte blue metal finish. Available in Weatherby calibers from .257 through .340 and .270 Win., 7mm Rem. Mag., .30-06, .300 and .338 Win. Mag. Weighs 7.5 lbs.

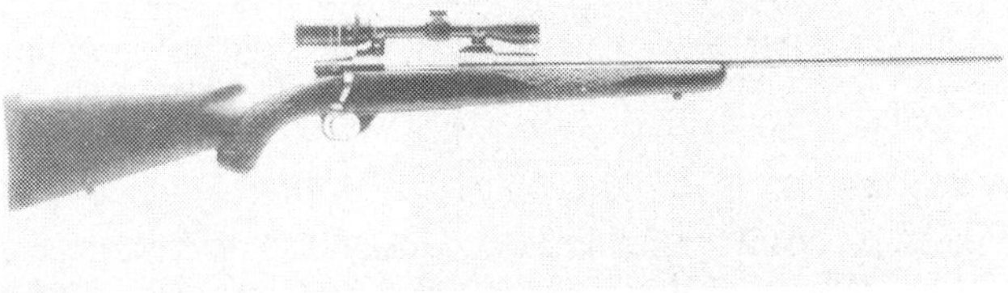

NIB	Exc.	V.G.	Good	Fair	Poor
550	450	350	250	175	100

Weathermark Alaskan

Similar to the Weathermark with checkered composite stock the barreled action is electroless nickel with nonglare finish. Muzzlebrake is optional. Available in same calibers as Weathermark. Weighs 7.7 lbs.

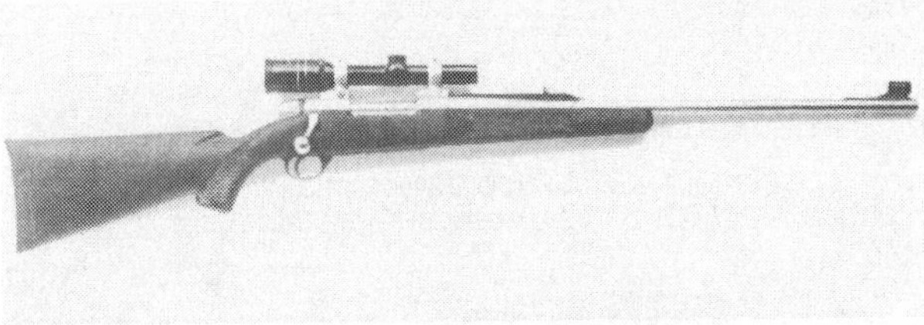

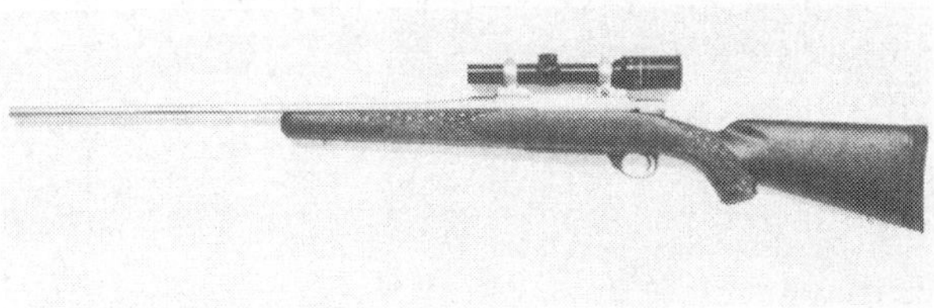

NIB	Exc.	V.G.	Good	Fair	Poor
750	650	550	450	325	225

Mark XXII

This is a semi-automatic rifle chambered for the .22 LR cartridge. There are two versions—one with a detachable magazine and the other with a tubular magazine. It has a 24" barrel with adjustable sights and a select checkered walnut stock with a rosewood forearm tip and pistol-grip cap. This model was originally produced in Italy and was later manufactured in Japan. Introduced in 1965 and discontinued in 1989.

Mark XXII Clip Model

Mark XXII Tube Model

NIB	Exc.	V.G.	Good	Fair	Poor
550	450	350	275	225	200

NOTE: Premium for Italian guns.

Mark XXII Bolt Action

Based on Anschutz design. Available in .22 Long Rifle or .17 HMR. Classic Mark V-style high-gloss walnut Monte Carlo stock with precision cut checkering, rosewood fore-end tip and grip cap. Target-grade barrel is 23-inches, weight 6.5 pounds. Fully adjustable single-stage trigger. Introduced in 2007.

NIB	Exc.	V.G.	Good	Fair	Poor
800	685	560	450	400	300

NOTE: Add 10 percent for .17 HMR.

CUSTOM RIFLES

NOTE: Weatherby custom rifles are offered with many different options that will affect price. Consult an expert prior to a sale.

Vanguard Sage Country Custom

Introduced in 2008, this is similar to the Vanguard Synthetic but with injection-molded Desert Camo stock. Available in a variety of chamberings from .223 to .338 Winchester Magnum.

NIB	Exc.	V.G.	Good	Fair	Poor
600	500	400	300	225	175

Vanguard Back Country Custom

Introduced in 2008, this is a lightweight version of the Vanguard Synthetic with a fluted barrel, textured stock and overall weight of 6-3/4 lbs. Available in a variety of chamberings from .257 Weatherby Magnum to .300 Weatherby Magnum.

NIB	Exc.	V.G.	Good	Fair	Poor
950	850	725	625	425	200

Classic Custom

This model features an oil-finished French walnut stock with 20 lpi checkering, ebony forend tip, metal grip cap, and skeltonized steel buttplate. All metal work is matte blue. Calibers are all Weatherby from .257 Wby. Mag to .340 Wby. Mag.

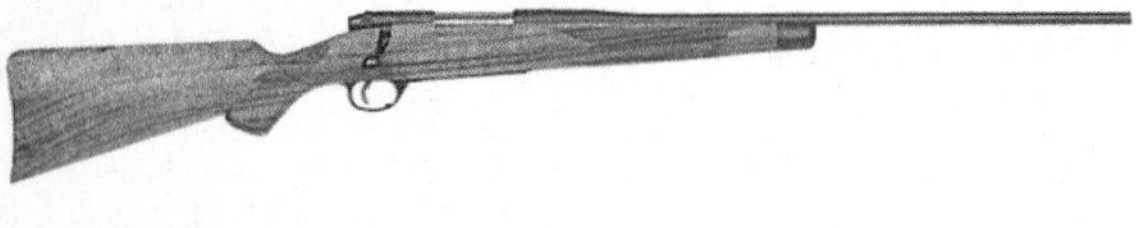

NIB	Exc.	V.G.	Good	Fair	Poor
5100	4600	3500	2250	900	500

Safari Grade Custom

This model features an oil-finish French walnut stock with Monte Carlo comb with fleur-de-lis checkering. Ebony forend tip and pistol-grip cap. Damascened bolt and follower with checkered bolt handle. Quarter rib. Engraved floorplate "Safari Custom." Calibers from .257 Wby. Mag. to .460 Wby. Mag.

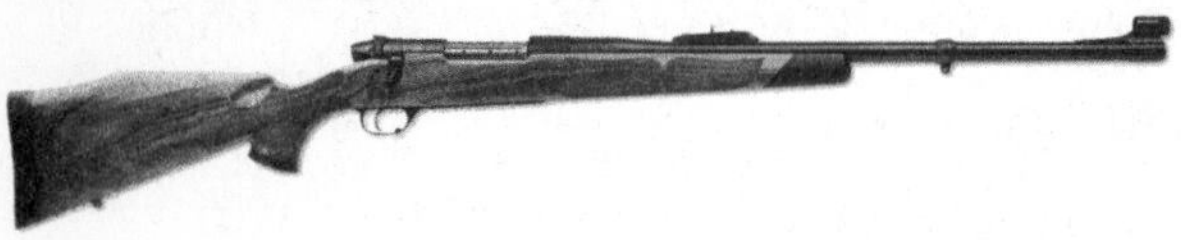

NIB	Exc.	V.G.	Good	Fair	Poor
5300	4800	3700	2450	1050	550

Crown Custom

This model features a hand-carved walnut stock with buttstock inlay, damascened bolt and follower with checkered bolt handle. Engraved barrel, receiver and trigger guard. Floorplate engraved with gold inlays.

NIB	Exc.	V.G.	Good	Fair	Poor
7000	6250	4500	3000	1500	750

Royal Custom

Introduced in 2002 this model features a Monte Carlo hand-checkered stock of fancy Claro walnut with high-gloss finish. Engraved receiver, bolt sleeve, and floorplate. Barrel length is 26". Available in a wide variety of calibers.

NIB	Exc.	V.G.	Good	Fair	Poor
5300	4800	3700	2450	1050	550

Outfitter Custom

This model features a Bell & Carlson synthetic stock with custom camo and Pachmayr pad. Lightweight stainless steel fluted barrel. Titanium nitride finish on all metalwork.

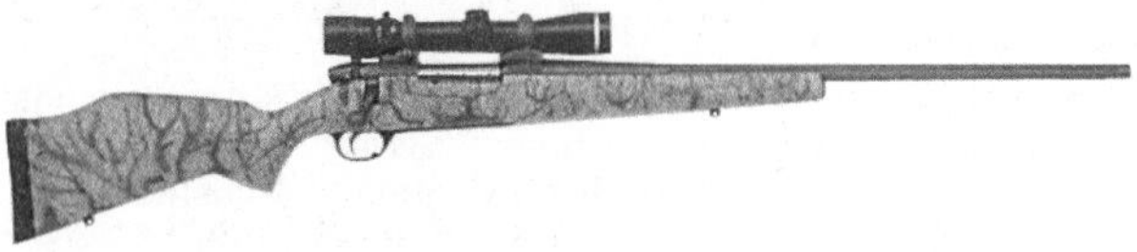

NIB	Exc.	V.G.	Good	Fair	Poor
2250	1700	1400	1100	700	400

Outfitter Krieger Custom

This model features a Bell & Carlson synthetic stock with custom camo and Pachmayr pad. Custom Krieger stainless steel fluted barrel. Titanium nitride finish on all metalwork.

NIB	Exc.	V.G.	Good	Fair	Poor
3500	3000	2500	2000	1300	600

SHOTGUNS

PA-08 SERIES

Weatherby introduced this line of pump-action shotguns in 2008. All models come in 12 gauge with 3" chambers and have chrome-lined barrels. Knoxx stock models reduced recoil and are adjustable in length.

PA-08 Upland

This model has a walnut stock and forend with low-lustre finish and matte black metal work. Available with 28" or 26" barrel. Includes three choke tubes.

NIB	Exc.	V.G.	Good	Fair	Poor
325	275	225	175	125	75

PA-08 Knoxx Strutter X

Strutter models feature a synthetic stock and 24" vent rib barrel. Three choke tubes included. Add 15 percent for Apparition Excel camo pattern.

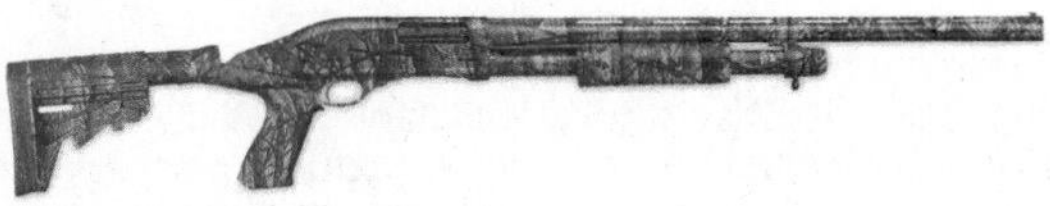

NIB	Exc.	V.G.	Good	Fair	Poor
425	375	325	250	175	100

PA-08 Knoxx HD

Home defense model features an 18" non-vent-rib barrel and cylinder choke.

NIB	Exc.	V.G.	Good	Fair	Poor
425	375	325	250	175	100

PA-08 Field/Slug Combo

Field and Slug-gun Combo pump features both a 28-inch field barrel for hunting birds and a 24-inch rifled slug barrel for deer. The field barrel is chrome lined and has a ventilated rib. Integral choke system features Briley thread pattern, and comes with improved cylinder, Modified and full-choked tubes. The 8-groove Slug barrel has a Weaver-compatible cantilevered scope mount base. Matte black finish. Weight: approx. 6-3/4 lbs. Introduced in 2011.

NIB	Exc.	V.G.	Good	Fair	Poor
430	380	340	300	270	220

PA-459 Turkey Camo

This pump gun features Mothwing Camo's Spring Mimicry pattern on stock and fore-end. The 12-gauge gun has a 19-inch barrel, a 13-1/2-inch length of pull and overall length of 40-inches. Weight: approx. 6-1/2 lbs. Integral Picatinny rail allows mounting optical sights or other accessories. The rail has a clamp-style LPA ghost-ring rear sight adjustable for windage and elevation.

NIB	Exc.	V.G.	Good	Fair	Poor
450	390	360	320	290	250

Centurion

This is a gas-operated semi-automatic shotgun chambered for 12 gauge. It is offered with various barrel lengths and chokes. It has a checkered walnut stock. It was manufactured between 1972 and 1981.

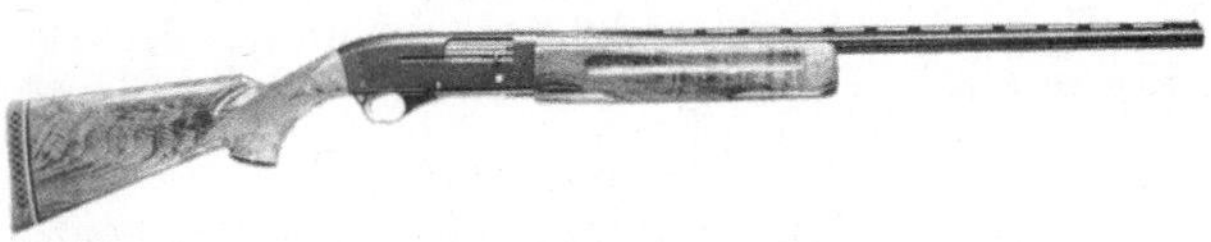

NIB	Exc.	V.G.	Good	Fair	Poor
—	575	300	250	200	150

Centurion Deluxe

This version is slightly engraved and features a vent-ribbed barrel and higher-grade wood.

NIB	Exc.	V.G.	Good	Fair	Poor
—	600	325	275	225	175

Model 82

This is a gas-operated semi-automatic shotgun chambered for 12 gauge with 2.75" or 3" chambers. It has various barrel lengths with vent-ribs and screw-in choke tubes. It features an alloy receiver and a deluxe, checkered walnut stock. It is also available as the Buckmaster with a 22" open-choked barrel. This model was introduced in 1983.

NIB	Exc.	V.G.	Good	Fair	Poor
500	450	400	350	300	250

Model SAS Field

Introduced in 1999 this gas-operated semi-automatic model features a high-grade Claro walnut stock with black pistol-grip cap. Fine-line checkering. Chambered for 12 or 20 gauge and fitted with 26", 28", or 30" vent-rib barrels in 12 gauge and 26" or 28" vent-rib barrels in 20 gauge. The 12 gauge models weigh around 7.5 lbs. depending on barrel length, and the 20 gauge weighs around 7 lbs. depending on barrel length. Fitted with Briley choke tubes.

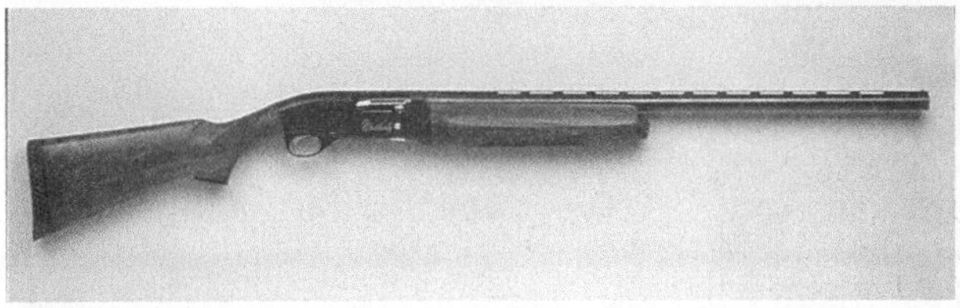

NIB	Exc.	V.G.	Good	Fair	Poor
700	550	450	325	250	200

Model SAS Camo

This model is offered with either Shadowgrass or Superflaugecamo stocks. Available in 12 gauge only with 3" chambers. Shadowgrass model offered with 26" or 28" barrels; the Superflauge model with 24" or 26" barrels. Weight is about 7.5 lbs.

Model SAS Camo Shadow Grass

NIB	Exc.	V.G.	Good	Fair	Poor
750	600	500	375	300	225

Model SAS Camo Superflauge

NIB	Exc.	V.G.	Good	Fair	Poor
750	600	500	375	300	225

Model SAS Slug Gun

This model features a 22" rifled barrel chambered for the 3" 12 gauge shell. The barrel has a cantilever base for scope mounts. Walnut stock has a raised Monte Carlo comb. Sling swivel studs. Weight is about 7.25 lbs. Introduced in 2003.

NIB	Exc.	V.G.	Good	Fair	Poor
750	600	500	375	300	225

Model SAS Sporting Clays

This 12 gauge gun is fitted with a 28" or 30" vent-rib ported barrel. Walnut stock with pistol grip. Choke tubes standard. Weight is about 7.5 lbs. Introduced in 2002.

NIB	Exc.	V.G.	Good	Fair	Poor
800	650	550	425	350	250

Model SAS Synthetic

This model features a black synthetic stock chambered for 12 or 20 gauge barrels as above. Introduced in 2000.

NIB	Exc.	V.G.	Good	Fair	Poor
650	525	425	325	250	175

SA-08 Upland

This semi-automatic was new in 2008. It features a walnut stock with oil finish. Available in 12 and 20 gauge with 3" chambers and 28" or 26" barrels. Three choke tubes included.

NIB	Exc.	V.G.	Good	Fair	Poor
575	450	325	250	175	150

SA-08 Youth

As above but in 20 gauge with 26" barrel only and shorter 12.5" length of pull.

NIB	Exc.	V.G.	Good	Fair	Poor
550	425	300	250	175	150

SA-08 Entré Rios

The Entré Rios autoloader has a scaled-down frame for the 28 gauge. Features include a select, cut-checkered walnut stock, and a high-gloss finish on barrel and receiver. Comes equipped with skeet, improved cylinder and modified choke tubes. Weight: 5-1/4 lbs. Available with 26 or 28-inch barrel.

NIB	Exc.	V.G.	Good	Fair	Poor
600	500	425	365	310	200

SA-459 TR

This gas-operated autoloader features a bolt with an oversized hourglass design that's easily located in the dark. It comes equipped with a new TR accessory rail for mounting tactical lights or laser sights. Also has a fully adjustable, LPA-style ghost ring sight. Pistol-grip buttstock has rubber-textured grip. Available in 12 or 20 gauge. Barrel length: 18-1/2-inches. Weight: 7 lbs.

NIB	Exc.	V.G.	Good	Fair	Poor
515	450	385	325	250	150

Patrician

This is a slide-action shotgun chambered for 12 gauge. It is offered with various barrel lengths and choke combinations. It has a vent-rib barrel, a blued finish, and a checkered walnut stock. It was manufactured between 1972 and 1981.

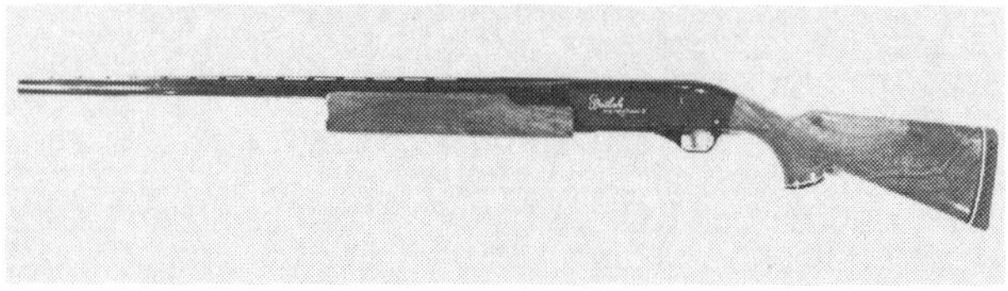

NIB	Exc.	V.G.	Good	Fair	Poor
—	550	425	300	250	175

Patrician Deluxe

This is a slightly engraved version with fancier-grade walnut.

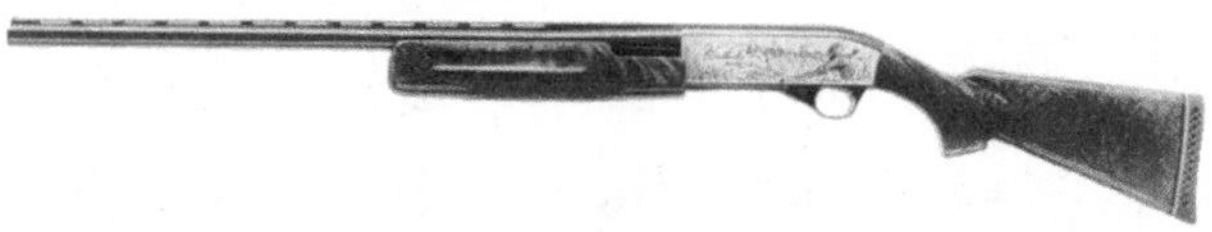

NIB	Exc.	V.G.	Good	Fair	Poor
—	600	475	350	275	200

Model 92

This is a slide-action shotgun chambered for 12 gauge with 2.75" or 3" chambers. It is offered with 26", 28", or 30" ventilated rib barrels with screw-in choke tubes. It features a short, twin-rail slide action and an engraved alloy receiver. The finish is blued, with a deluxe checkered walnut stock. A Buckmaster model with a 22" open-choke barrel and rifle sights is also available.

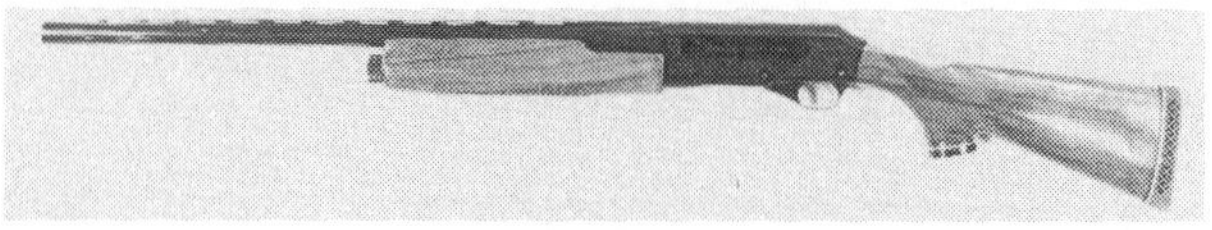

NIB	Exc.	V.G.	Good	Fair	Poor
350	300	250	200	175	125

SIDE-BY-SIDE SHOTGUNS

These shotgun are built in Spain.

Athena SBS

Introduced in 2002 this model features a case colored boxlock receiver with false sideplates with scroll engraving. Offered in 12 or 20 gauge with 26" or 28" barrels. Choke tubes. Turkish walnut stock with straight grip and recoil pad. Checkering is 22 lpi. Single trigger and ejectors. Weight is about 7 lbs.

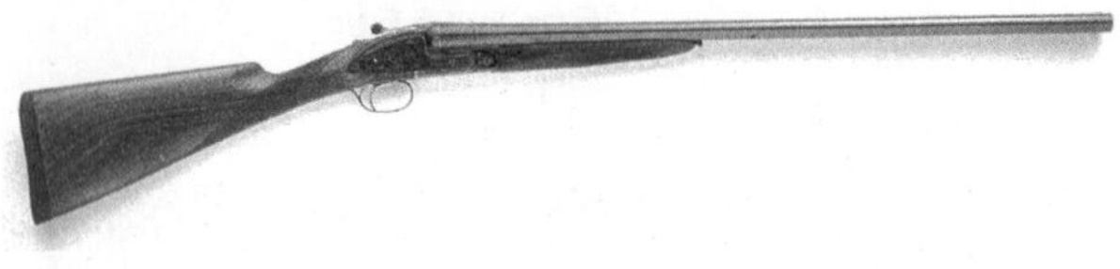

NIB	Exc.	V.G.	Good	Fair	Poor
1550	1200	1000	750	500	400

Athena D'Italia

Introduced in 2005 this gun is chambered for the 12, 20, or 28 gauge and fitted with 28" barrels for the 12 gauge and 26" barrels for the 20 and 28 gauge guns. Receiver has silver sideplates with scroll engraving. Checkered walnut stock with straight grip. Weight is about 7 lbs.

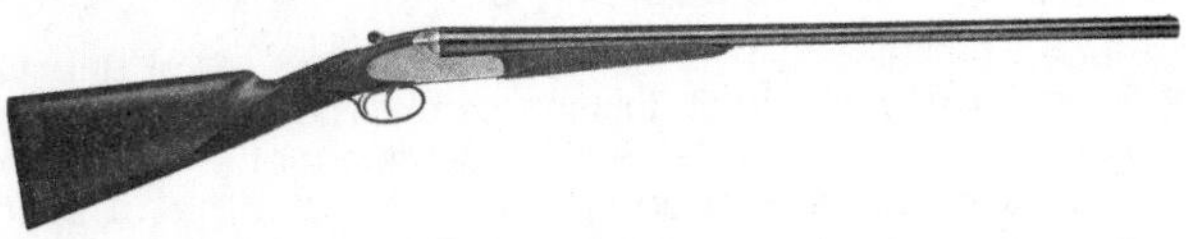

NIB	Exc.	V.G.	Good	Fair	Poor
2840	2100	1600	1100	750	500

NOTE: Add $135 for 28 gauge.

Athena D'Italia PG

Introduced in 2006, this model is offered in the same configurations as the D'Italia. It is identical in action and frame to the D'Italia but with a rounded pistol grip stock and single gold trigger. Laser-cut checkering at 20 lpi. Introduced 2006. Pricing is for 12 and 20 gauges. Add $200 for 28 ga.

NIB	Exc.	V.G.	Good	Fair	Poor
3200	2500	2000	1500	1050	500

Athena D'Italia Deluxe

Renaissance floral engraving with Bolino style game scene and AAA Fancy Turkish walnut with 24 lpi hand checkering adorn this straight grip stocked model. Available in 12, 20 and 28 gauges with 26" or 28" barrels with fixed IC and Mod. chokes. Single trigger. Introduced 2006.

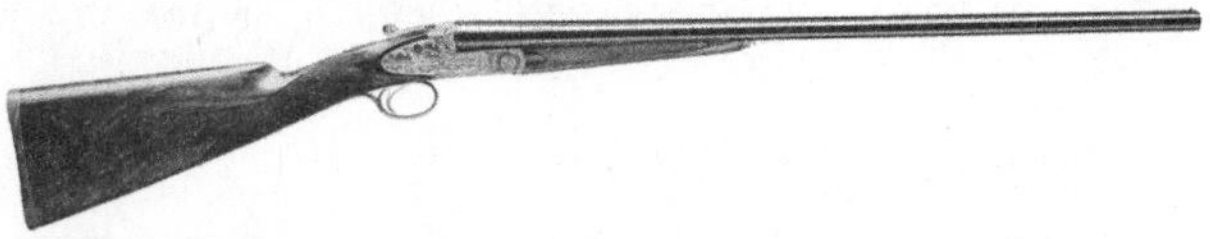

NIB	Exc.	V.G.	Good	Fair	Poor
7600	6000	4750	3000	2200	600

Orion SBS

This model is a lower cost alternative to the Athena. Turkish walnut stock with pistol grip and 18 lpi checkering. Case colored boxlock receiver. Offered in 12, 20, and 28 gauge as well as .410 bore. Choke tubes except for .410. Choice of 26" or 28" barrels. Weight is about 7 lbs. Introduced in 2002.

NIB	Exc.	V.G.	Good	Fair	Poor
1400	1100	900	650	475	300

OVER-AND-UNDER SHOTGUNS

Regency Field Grade

This is an over-and-under double-barrel shotgun chambered for 12 or 20 gauge. It has various length vent-ribbed barrels and a boxlock action with engraved false sideplates. It features a single-selective trigger and automatic ejectors. The finish is blued, with a checkered walnut stock. This model was imported from Italy between 1972 and 1980. It is also offered as a trap grade with the same value.

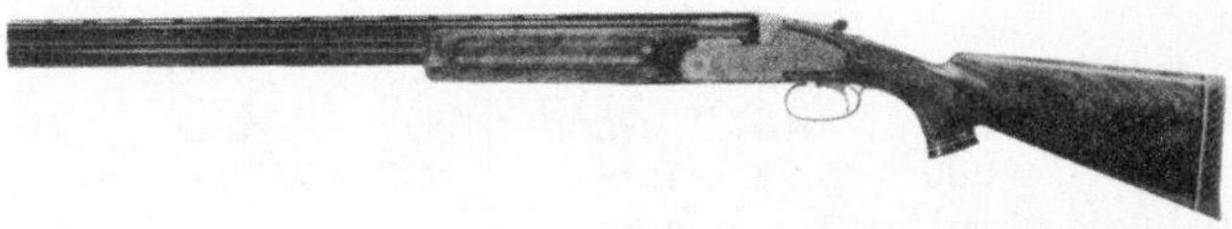

NIB	Exc.	V.G.	Good	Fair	Poor
—	1500	1300	900	600	300

Olympian

This model is similar to the Regency, with less engraving. It was not imported after 1980. A skeet and a trap model, as well as a field-grade model, were available. The values were similar.

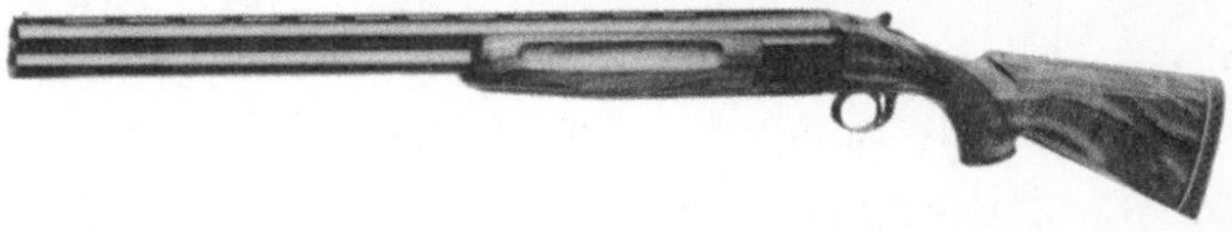

NIB	Exc.	V.G.	Good	Fair	Poor
—	1250	1050	650	500	275

Orion Upland

This 12 or 20 gauge model features a Claro walnut stock with rounded pistol grip and slim forearm. Plain blued receiver. Choice of 26" or 28" vent-rib barrel with 3" chambers. Multi-choke system. Introduced in 1999.

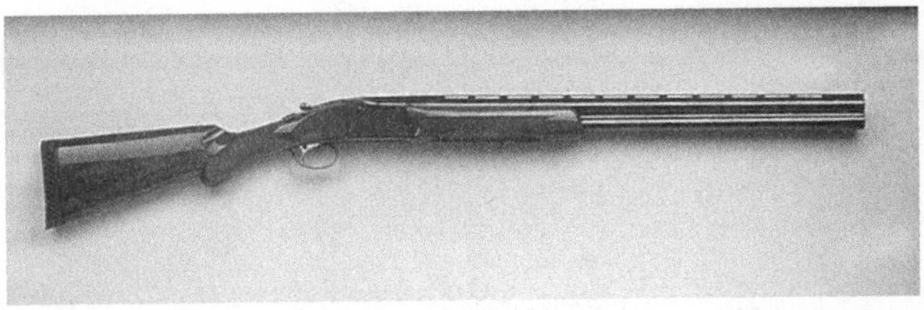

NIB	Exc.	V.G.	Good	Fair	Poor
1200	1000	800	600	450	300

Orion Grade I

This is an over-and-under double-barrel shotgun chambered for 12 or 20 gauge with 3" chambers. It is offered with 26" or 28" vent-rib barrels with screw-in chokes. It has a single-selective trigger and automatic ejectors. The boxlock action features no engraving. The finish is blued, with a checkered walnut stock. It was introduced in 1989.

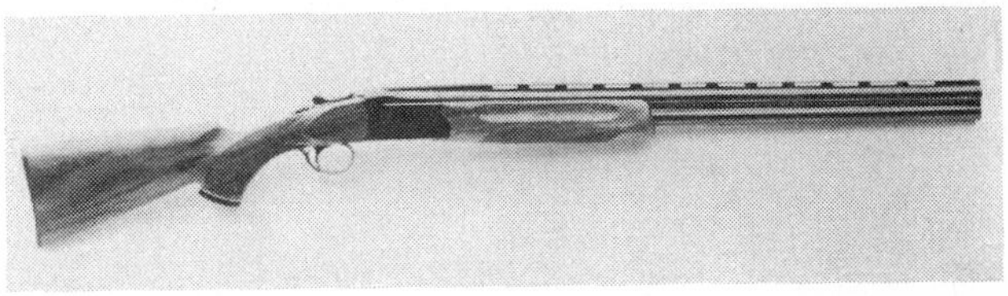

NIB	Exc.	V.G.	Good	Fair	Poor
1000	850	750	700	600	300

Orion Grade II Skeet

This model is supplied with a Claro walnut checkered stock with full pistol grip with rosewood grip cap. The receiver is matte blue with scroll engraving. The barrel has a matte vent-rib with side vents and mid-point head with white bead front sight. Special ventilated recoil pad. Offered in 12 gauge and 20 gauge with 26" barrels. Fixed Skeet chokes are standard. The 12 gauge weighs 7.5 lbs. while the 20 gauge weighs 7.25 lbs.

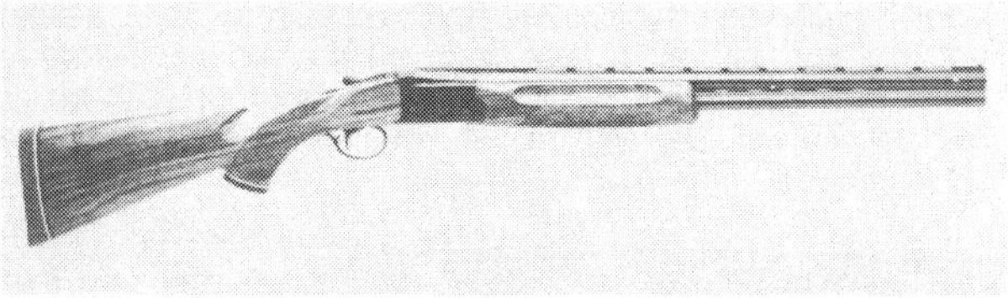

NIB	Exc.	V.G.	Good	Fair	Poor
950	800	700	600	400	200

Orion Grade II Sporting Clays

Similar to the Classic model but with a full pistol grip with rosewood grip cap. The receiver is silver gray with scroll engraving. The Claro walnut stock is checkered with a high-gloss finish. Offered in 12 gauge with 28" to 30" vent-rib barrels. Supplied with five screw-in choke tubes.

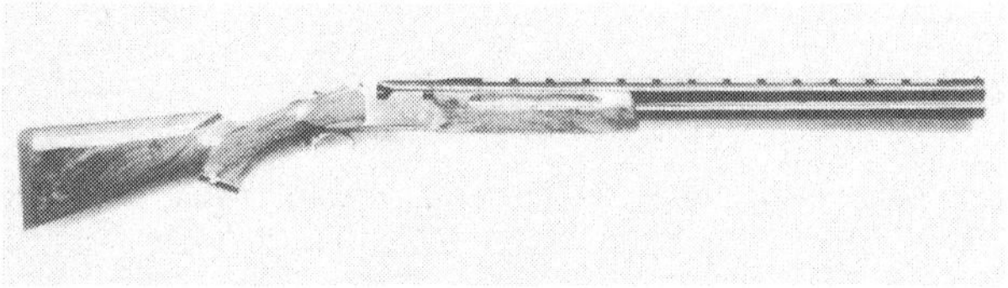

NIB	Exc.	V.G.	Good	Fair	Poor
1000	850	750	600	400	200

Orion Grade II Double Trap

This model features an integral multi-choke tube. The Monte Carlo stock has a rosewood pistol grip cap with diamond shaped inlay. The receiver is blue with scroll engraving. Available with 30" or 32" vent-rib barrels. Weighs 8 lbs.

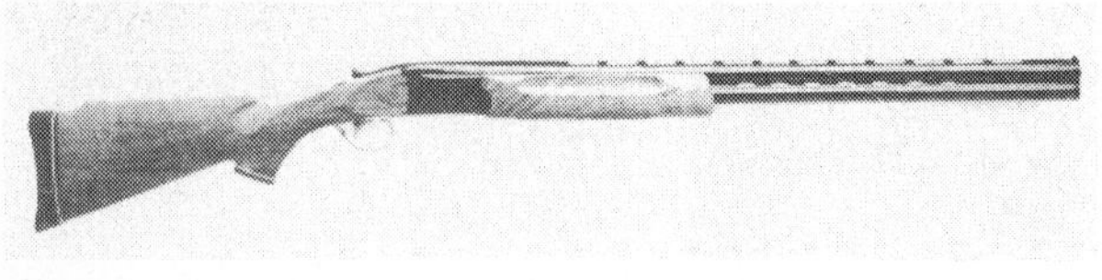

NIB	Exc.	V.G.	Good	Fair	Poor
950	800	700	550	400	200

Orion Grade II Single Trap

Similar to the Double Trap but furnished with a single 32" barrel. Weighs 8 lbs.

NIB	Exc.	V.G.	Good	Fair	Poor
950	800	700	550	400	200

Orion Grade II

This version is lightly engraved and has a high-gloss finish. Otherwise, it is similar to the Grade I.

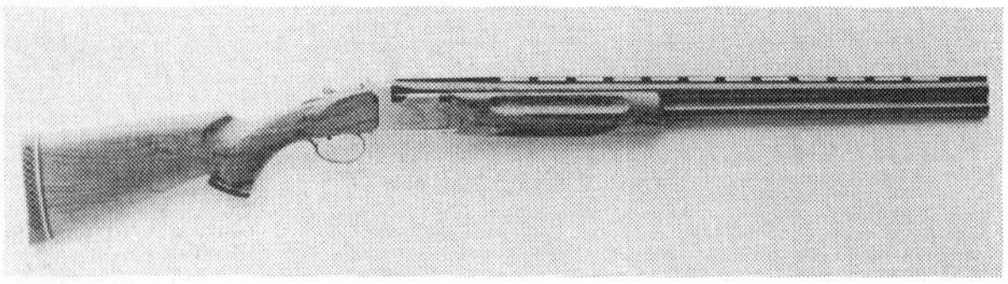

NIB	Exc.	V.G.	Good	Fair	Poor
1200	1050	925	800	600	250

Orion Grade II Classic Field

Introduced in 1993 this model features a rounded pistol grip and slim forearm design. The walnut stock is oil finished. The receiver is blued with game scene engraving. A solid recoil pad is standard. Available in 12 gauge, 20 gauge, and 28 gauge with vent-rib barrel lengths from 26" to 30" depending on gauge. Screw-in choke tubes standard. Weighs 6.5 lbs. to 8 lbs. depending on gauge.

NIB	Exc.	V.G.	Good	Fair	Poor
950	800	700	550	400	200

Orion Grade II Classic Sporting Clays

Introduced in 1993 this model has a rounded pistol grip with slender forearm with an oil-finished stock. The receiver is blued with scroll engraving. A stepped competition matte vent-rib with additional side vents is supplied. The recoil pad has a special radius heel. Offered in 12 gauge with 28" barrel. Furnished with five screw-in choke tubes. Weighs 7.5 lbs.

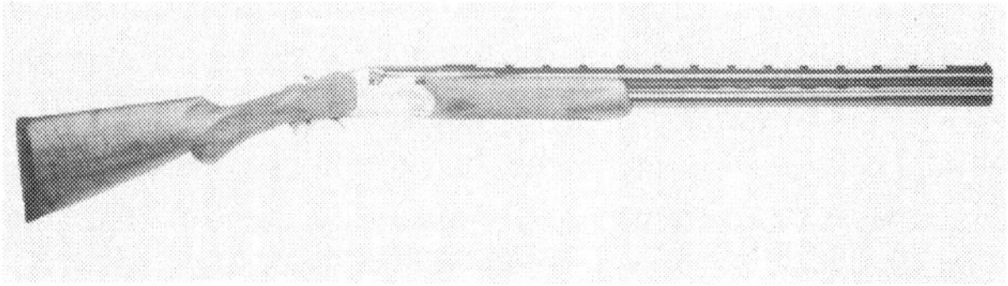

NIB	Exc.	V.G.	Good	Fair	Poor
1000	850	750	600	400	200

Orion Super Sporting Clays (SSC)

Introduced in 1999 this 12 gauge model features a walnut stock with sporter-style pistol grip and cast off. Barrel lengths are 28", 30" or 32" with 3" chambers and 12mm grooved rib. Barrels are also ported and backbored. Comes with five choke tubes. Weight is approximately 8 lbs.

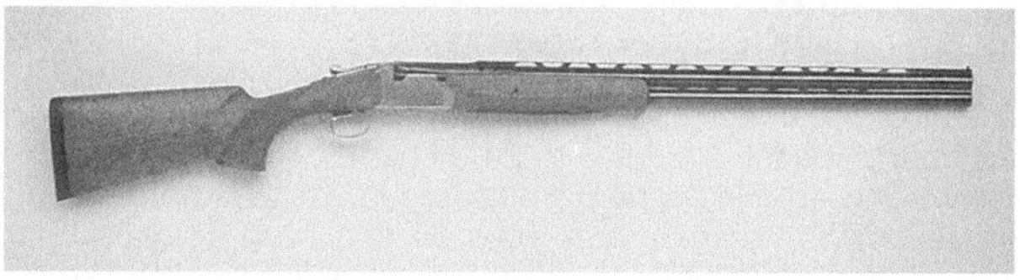

NIB	Exc.	V.G.	Good	Fair	Poor
1750	1400	1150	925	750	350

Orion Grade III

This version has a game scene-engraved, coin-finished receiver and higher-grade walnut. It was introduced in 1989.

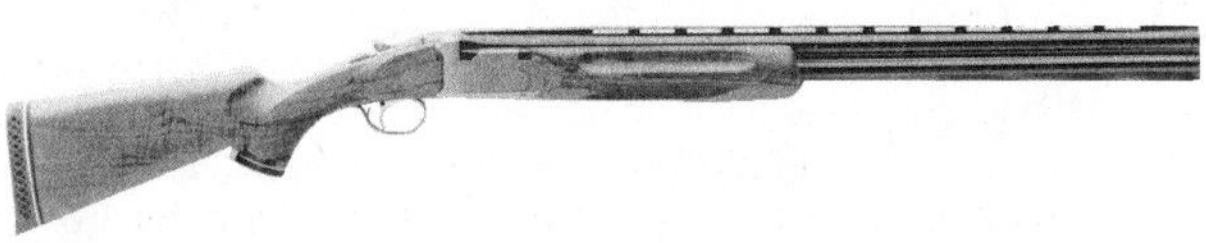

NIB	Exc.	V.G.	Good	Fair	Poor
1100	950	850	650	500	300

Orion Grade III Classic Field

New for 1993 this model features a rounded pistol grip and slim forearm with oil finish Claro walnut with fine line checkering. The receiver is silver gray with scroll engraving and gold game bird overlays. Available in 12 gauge with 28" vent-rib barrels and 20 gauge with 26" vent-rib barrels. Screw-in choke tubes standard.

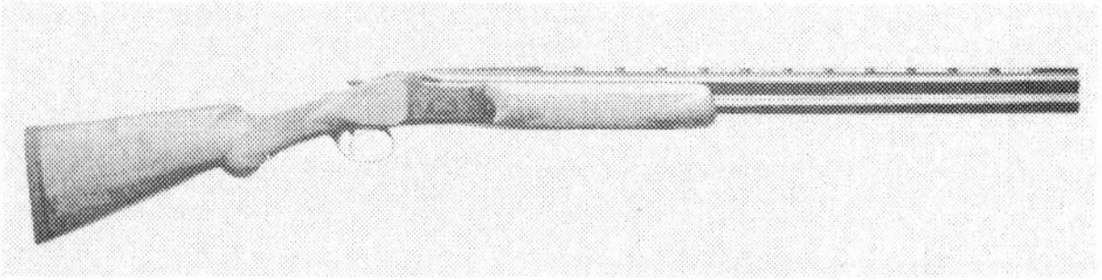

NIB	Exc.	V.G.	Good	Fair	Poor
1100	950	850	650	500	300

Orion Grade III Classic English Field

This model features an English-style straight-grip stock with a choice of 12 gauge with 28" barrel or 20 gauge with 26" or 28" barrels. The receiver is engraved and the stock is oil-finished hand-checkered. Weight of 12 gauge gun is about 7 lbs. and 20 gauge gun is about 6.5 lbs. Introduced in 1996.

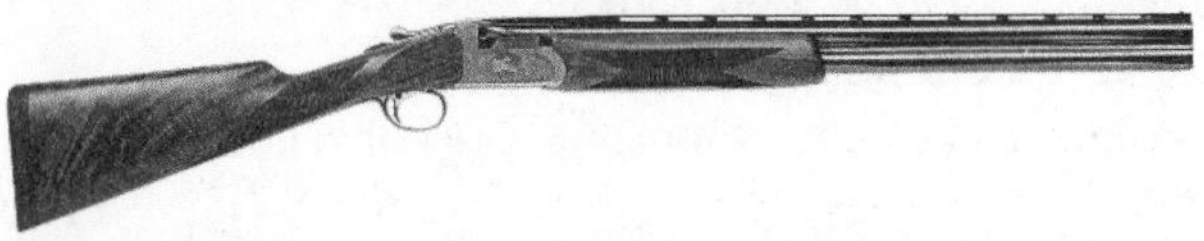

NIB	*Exc.*	*V.G.*	*Good*	*Fair*	*Poor*
1250	1050	925	800	600	250

Orion D\qltalia

Engraved silver-finish metalwork and fineline, 20 lpi checkering. Turkish walnut stock with high-gloss finish. Available in 12 gauge with 28" barrel and 20 gauge with 26" barrel.

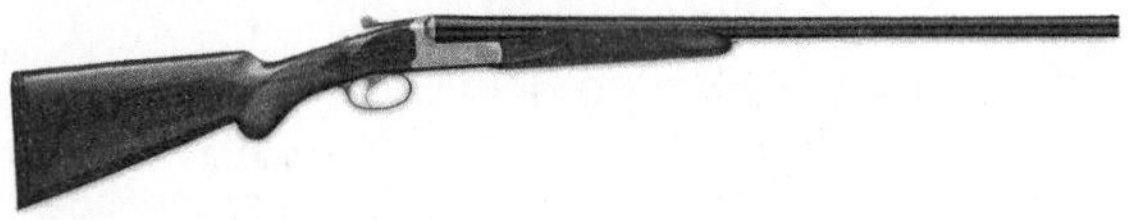

NIB	*Exc.*	*V.G.*	*Good*	*Fair*	*Poor*
1650	1400	1100	900	750	400

Athena Grade III Classic Field

Offered in 12 or 20 gauge this model features a hand select Claro walnut stock with oil finish. The pistol grip is rounded. The silver-gray sideplates feature a rose and scroll engraving pattern with gold overlaid hunting scenes. Available with 26" or 28" vent-rib barrels with multi-choke system. Weight is around 7.5 lbs. for 12 gauge and 7 lbs. for 20 gauge. Introduced in 1999. In 2001 a 28 gauge version was offered with 26" or 28" barrels.

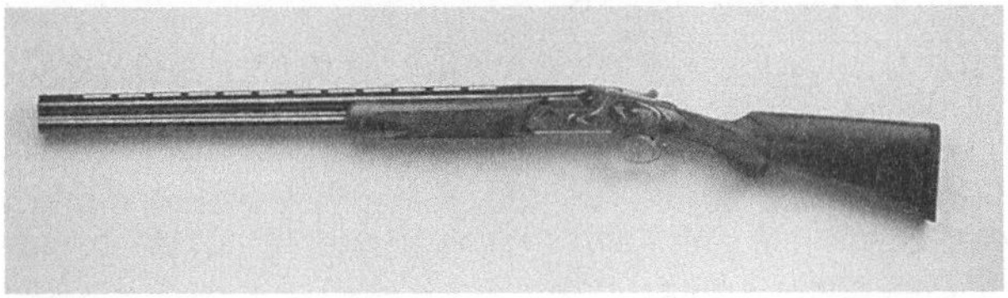

NIB	*Exc.*	*V.G.*	*Good*	*Fair*	*Poor*
1700	1500	1250	900	600	350

Athena Grade IV

This is an over/under double-barrel shotgun chambered for 12, 20, and 28 gauge, as well as .410. It has 3" chambers. It is offered with various barrel lengths with vent-ribs and screw-in choke tubes. It has a boxlock action with Greener crossbolt, single-selective trigger, and automatic ejectors. It has engraved false sideplates and a satin nickel-plated action. The barrels are blued, with a select checkered walnut stock. This model was introduced in 1989.

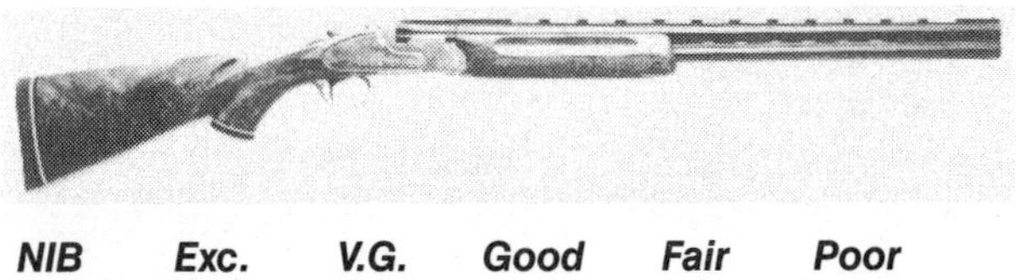

NIB	*Exc.*	*V.G.*	*Good*	*Fair*	*Poor*
2100	1700	1500	1100	750	450

Athena Grade V Classic Field

Introduced in 1993 this model features a rounded pistol grip with slender forearm. The high-grade Claro walnut stock is oil finished with fine line checkering. The receiver has a side plate that is silver gray with rose and scroll engraving. The vent-rib barrels also have side vents. An Old English recoil pad is supplied. Offered in 12 gauge with 26", 28", or 30" barrels and 20 gauge with 26" and 28" barrels. Choke tubes are standard. Weatherby Athena Master skeet tube set, 12 gauge 28" skeet shotgun, plus two each 20, 28 and .410 gauge fitted, full-length Briley tubes with integral extractors. Packed in custom fitted aluminum case (not shown).

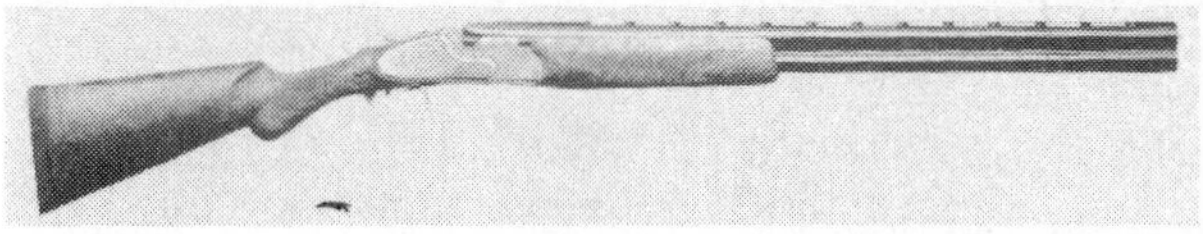

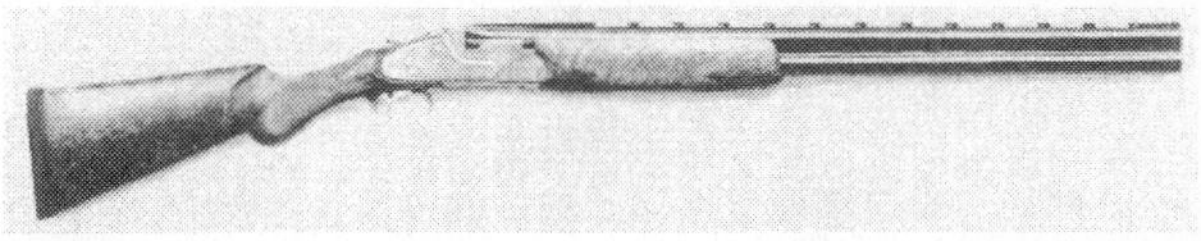

NIB	*Exc.*	*V.G.*	*Good*	*Fair*	*Poor*
2800	2400	1800	1400	900	500

NOTE: Add 50 percent for Master Skeet Set.

Competition Model Athena

This is either a trap or skeet version with stock dimensions designed for either skeet or trap and competition-type ribs.

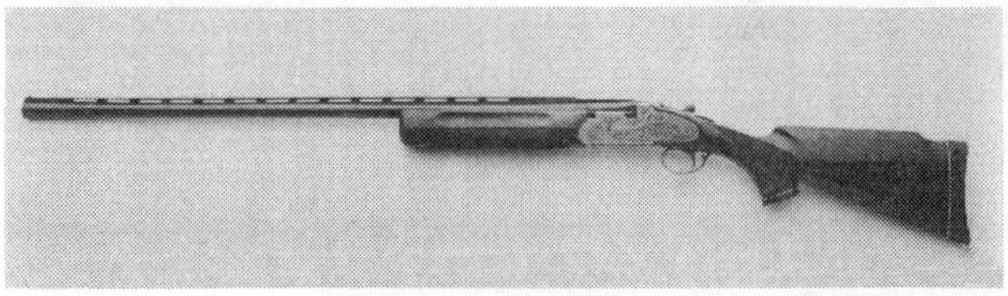

NIB	*Exc.*	*V.G.*	*Good*	*Fair*	*Poor*
1650	1400	1150	1000	750	600

WEAVER ARMS

Escondido, California

Nighthawk Carbine

With a 16.1" barrel, retractable shoulder stock, 25-, 32-, 40-, or 50-shot magazine. Introduced in 1984.

NIB	*Exc.*	*V.G.*	*Good*	*Fair*	*Poor*
600	500	450	350	300	150

WEIHRAUCH, HANS HERMANN

Melrichstadt, West Germany

Model HW 60M

A .22 caliber single-shot bolt action rifle with a 26.75" barrel and adjustable sights. Blued with a walnut stock.

NIB	*Exc.*	*V.G.*	*Good*	*Fair*	*Poor*
800	650	550	400	350	250

Model HW 66

A .22 Hornet or .222 Remington bolt action rifle with a stainless steel 26" barrel and single- or double-set triggers. Blued with a walnut stock.

NIB	*Exc.*	*V.G.*	*Good*	*Fair*	*Poor*
700	550	500	350	300	200

WESSON & LEAVITT

Chicopee Falls, Massachusetts

Revolving Rifle

A .40 caliber percussion revolving rifle with a 16" to 24" round barrel and 6-shot cylinder. Blued with a walnut stock. Approximately 25 were made in 1849.

NIB	Exc.	V.G.	Good	Fair	Poor
—	—	13000	7500	3500	950

WESSON FIREARMS, DAN

Norwich, New York

In 1996 the assets of the Wesson Firearms Co. were purchased by the New York International Corp. All interchangeable barrel models were produced. There are no plans at this time to build fixed barrel models. At the present time, parts and service for original Dan Wesson revolvers are available from the new company. Full production of new models occurred in 1997. These firearms are laser marked on the barrel or frame with: "NYI" in an oval and below "DAN WESSON FIREARMS" on the next line "NORWICH, NEW YORK USA." NOTE: In April, 2005 Dan Wesson Firearms was acquired by CZ-USA. Production continues (somewhat irregularly) at the Norwich, New York, facility.

Coyote Target

Chambered for the.22 LR or .22 Magnum cartridge and fitted with an 18.375" heavy bull barrel. Receiver is drilled and tapped for scope mount. Hardwood stock with high comb and flat-bottom forend. Magazine capacity is 6 or 10 rounds.**NOTE:** It is unknown whether the Dan Wesson Coyote rifles were ever actually produced; we suspect not. The values shown are based on 2002 suggested retail prices.

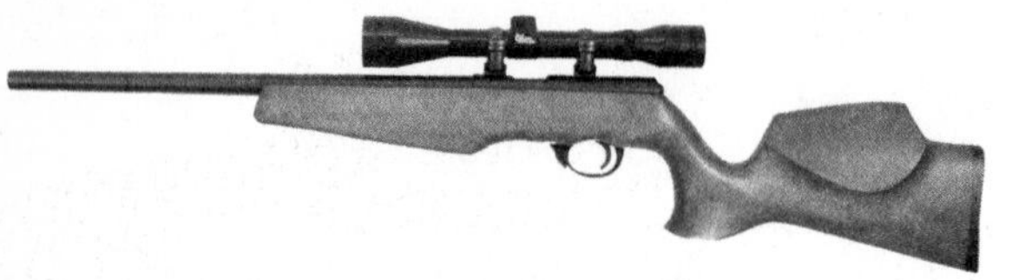

NIB	Exc.	V.G.	Good	Fair	Poor
275	—	—	—	—	—

Coyote Classic

This model is also chambered for the .22 LR or .22 Magnum cartridge. Fitted with a 22.75" barrel with open sights. Drilled and tapped for scope mount. Checkered hardwood stock. Magazine capacity is 6 or 10 rounds. Introduced in 2002.

NIB	Exc.	V.G.	Good	Fair	Poor
235	—	—	—	—	—

WESSON, FRANK

Worcester & Springfield, Massachusetts

Small Frame Pocket Rifle

A .22 caliber spur trigger single-shot pistol with a 6" half octagonal barrel and narrow brass frame. This model is adopted for use with a detachable skeleton shoulder stock. The barrel marked "Frank Wesson Worcester, Mass." Manufactured from 1865 to 1875 with approximately 5,000 made. Prices are for pistol only.

NIB	Exc.	V.G.	Good	Fair	Poor
—	—	1500	925	350	100

NOTE: Matching shoulder stock add 100 percent.

1870 Medium Frame Pocket Rifle First Type

As above, but with a slightly larger frame chambered for .32 rimfire. Approximately 5,000 were made from 1870 to 1893.

1870 Large Frame Pocket Rifle First Type

As above, in .32, .38, .42, or .44 rimfire with an octagonal barrel from 15" to 24" in length. The barrel marked "Frank Wesson Worcester, Mass Patented May 31, 1870." Fewer than 250 of these rifles were made between 1870 and 1880.

No. 1 Long Range Rifle

A .44-100 or .45-100 caliber single-shot dropping block rifle with a 34" octagonal barrel. Blued with a checkered walnut stock. The barrel marked "F. Wesson Mfr. Worcester, Mass. Long Range Rifle Creedmoor." Manufactured in 1876.

NIB	Exc.	V.G.	Good	Fair	Poor
—	—	12500	4500	2000	500

No. 2 Mid-Range or Hunting Rifle

Similar to the above, with the firing pin located in a bolster on the right side of the receiver. The trigger guard has a rear finger loop. Standard barrel length 28", 32", and 34" and marked "F. Wesson Maker Worcester, Mass." The 32" and 34" barrels are occasionally marked "Long Range Rifle Creedmoor." Approximately 100 were made.

Courtesy Buffalo Bill Historical Center, Cody, Wyoming

NIB	Exc.	V.G.	Good	Fair	Poor
—	—	7250	3750	1750	500

No. 2 Sporting Rifle

A .38-100, .40-100, or .45-100 caliber single-shot dropping-barrel-action rifle with barrels ranging from 28" to 34" in length. Approximately 25 were made.

Courtesy Buffalo Bill Historical Center, Cody, Wyoming

NIB	Exc.	V.G.	Good	Fair	Poor
—	—	8250	3750	1750	500

Military Carbine

Fitted with a 24" barrel with sling swivels and chambered for the .44 caliber rimfire cartridge. Approximately 4,500 were manufactured.

NIB	Exc.	V.G.	Good	Fair	Poor
—	—	6000	2500	1100	500

NOTE: Add 100 percent for martially marked examples.

WHITNEY ARMS COMPANY

INCLUDING ELI WHITNEY, SR. / P. & E.W. BLAKE / ELI WHITNEY, JR.

As the United States' first major commercial arms maker, Eli Whitney's New Haven plant, which began production in 1798 and continued under family control for the next 90 years, was one of the more important American arms manufactories of the 19th century. Its products, accordingly, are eminently collectible. Moreover, during its 90 years of operation, the Whitney clan produced a number of unusual arms, some exact copies of regulation U.S. martial longarms, others variations and derivatives of U.S. and foreign longarms, a variety of percussion revolvers, and finally a variety of single-shot and repeating breechloading rifles in an attempt to capture a portion of the burgeoning market in these cartridge arms during the post-Civil War period. Contrary to the prevailing myth, Eli Whitney, Sr., who also invented the cotton gin, did NOT perfect a system of interchangeability of parts in the arms industry. His contributions in this line were more as a propagandist for the concept that was brought to fruition by others, notably Simeon North and John Hall.

Eli Whitney, Sr. Armory Muskets, 1798-1824. 1798 U.S. Contract Muskets, Types I-IV

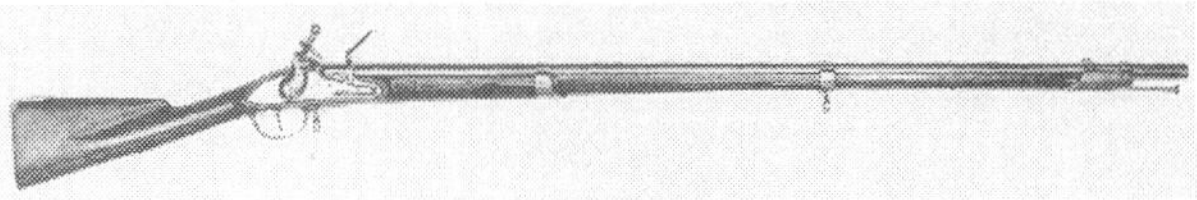

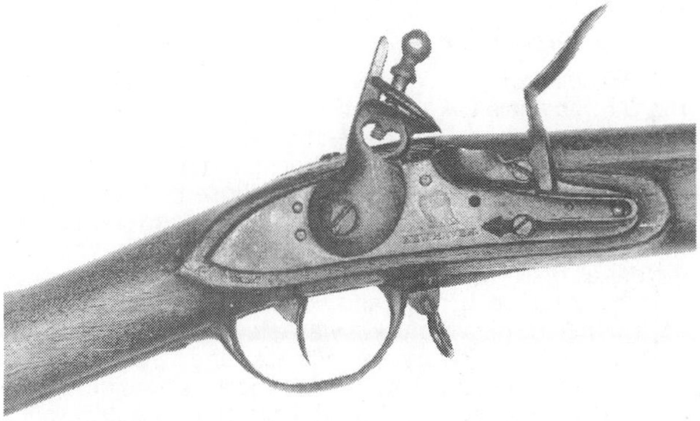

On 14 January 1798, Eli Whitney, Sr., having convinced the U.S. War Department that he could mass-produce interchangeable parts muskets, was awarded a contract for 10,000 muskets following the "Charlesville" (French M1766) pattern, then also being copied at the newly opened Springfield Armory and most of the U.S. musket contractors. Whitney's 1798 contract muskets measure between 58-7/8" and 57-3/4" in overall length, with the longer arms delivered earlier. The .69-caliber smoothbore barrels measure approximately 44", though most are shy of that length by anywhere from 1/16" to a maximum of 1-1/4". Lockplates are flat with a beveled edge and are marked "U.STATES" in a curve on the pointed tail and with a perched eagle with down folded wings over "NEW HAVEN" forward of the cock. Four differences in the material and manner of attachment of the pan distinguish the subtypes. The first deliver of 500 muskets in September of 1801 had an integral, faceted iron pan (Type I); the second delivery of 500 muskets in June of 1802 also had faceted iron pans, but were detachable (Type II). The 1,000 muskets delivered in September of 1802 and March of 1803 had faceted, detachable pans, but these were made of brass instead of iron (Type III). The final 8,000 muskets, delivered between 1803 and 1809, had detachable brass pans with a rounded bottom that Whitney copied from the French M1777 musket (Type IV) and a rounded cock, also copied from the French M1777 musket. Generally speaking, due to the limited production of Types I - III, they should command a higher price; prices are given for the more common Type IV 1798 contract musket. It should be noted however, that about 1804 Whitney delivered 112 Type IV muskets to Connecticut's "1st Company of Governor's Foot Guards." Although similar to the Type IV musket, these 112 arms are distinguished by the absence of the "U.STATES" on the tail of the lock and the addition of the name "CONNECTICUT" to the left side plate. Such an arm should demand a considerable premium over the usual Type IV musket.

NIB	*Exc.*	*V.G.*	*Good*	*Fair*	*Poor*
—	—	7500	4500	2000	500

Whitney Connecticut, New York, and U.S. 1812 Contract Muskets

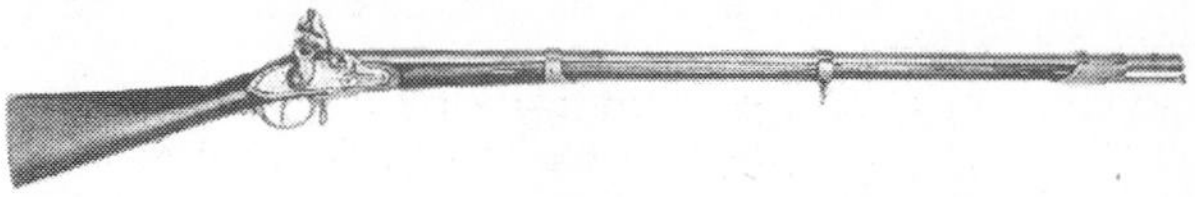

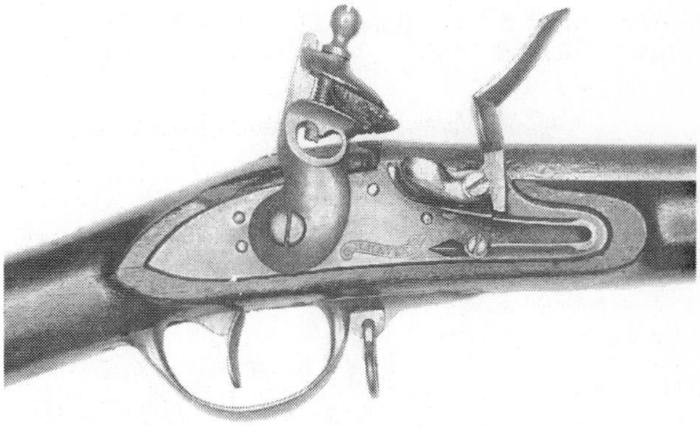

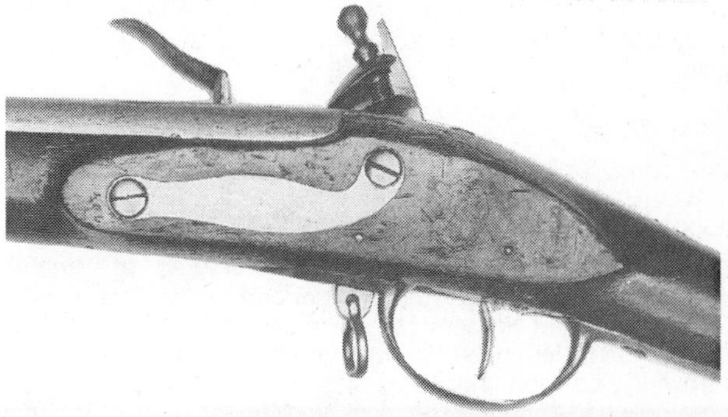

In 1808, Whitney received a contract from the state of New York for 2,000 muskets. In 1810, he received a second contract from the same source for an additional 2,000 muskets, all of which were eventually delivered by mid-1813. In the interim, in 1809, the state of Connecticut contracted with Whitney to deliver 700 muskets per year over the next three years. With the outbreak of the War of 1812, in July of 1812, a contract was let to Eli Whitney for 15,000 muskets (later extended by another 3,000 muskets), conforming to the pattern he had made for the state of New York, but with 42"-long barrels. All of these contract muskets shared most of the same features. Overall length was 58". The .69-caliber smoothbore barrel was nominally 42", though the two state contracts did not rigidly enforce that dimension. The lockplate of these muskets bore the inscription "NEW HAVEN" within a curving scroll forward of the cock. Like the Type III 1798 U.S. contract muskets, the lockplates incorporated a detachable round-bottomed brass pan and a round faced cock. The stock was distinguished by having a low, virtually nonexistent comb similar to that of the 1816 musket pattern. The New York state contract muskets are distinguished by having the state ownership mark "SNY" on the axis of the barrel near the breech. (It should be noted that the first 1,000 muskets delivered under the U.S. 1812 contract were also delivered to New York, but these have the mark across the breech at right angles to the axis of the barrel.) The Connecticut contract muskets are distinguishable by having the state-ownership mark "S.C." (for "state of Connecticut" on the barrel and the top of the comb of the stock. On Connecticut muskets in better condition, the Connecticut coat of arms (a shield with three clusters of grape vines) should also be visible struck into the wood on the left side of the musket opposite the lock. Verifiable Connecticut and New York contract muskets should bring a premium over the U.S. contract muskets.

NIB	*Exc.*	*V.G.*	*Good*	*Fair*	*Poor*
—	—	6000	3250	1500	500

Whitney (and P. & E.W. Blake) U.S. M1816/1822 Contract Muskets

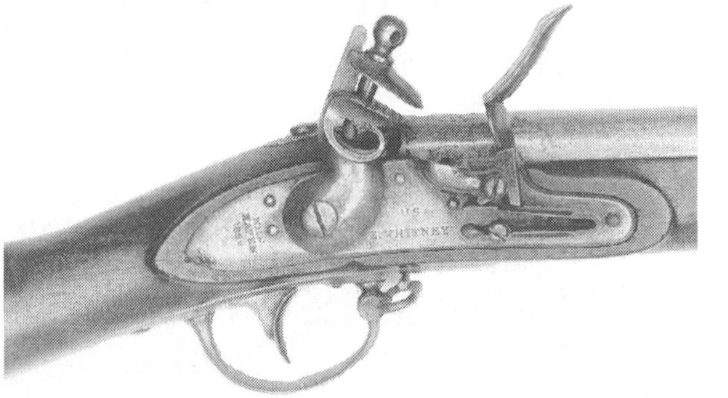

The U.S. M1816/1822 muskets manufactured at Whitney's Armory were identical to those produced at the U.S. Armories at Springfield and Harpers Ferry. The overall length was 57-3/4". The 42"-long, .69-caliber smoothbore barrels were finished with a browning solution until 1831; after that date the metal was left in the polished "bright." The stock and the lock reflect Whitney's earlier attempts impart his design elements into the U.S. patterns. The stock had the low comb of his M1812 musket and the lock incorporated the rounded cock and round bottomed brass pan that he had championed from the French M1777 musket. The lock markings varied during the period that the arm was produced, though all were marked on the pointed tail with the vertical stamp: "NEW HAVEN" arced around the date (1825-1830), or in three vertical lines: "NEW / HAVEN / (date: 1831-1842)." Those made between 1825 and 1830 under the direct supervision of Whitney's nephews bore the two line mark "U.S. / P. & E.W. BLAKE" forward of the cock; those made from 1830 to 1837 bear the "U.S" over "E. WHITNEY" with a crossed arrow and olive branch between; after 1837 the crossed arrow and olive branch motif was eliminated in favor of the simple two lines. In addition to the Whitney Armory's federal contracts, Whitney executed at least one contract with the state of South Carolina in the mid-1830s for an estimated 800 to 2,000 muskets. Basically identical in configuration to the federal contract muskets, the South Carolina muskets were distinguished by the substitution of "S.C." for "U.S." over the "E. WHITNEY" stamp of the lockplate. They also bear the state ownership mark "So. CAROLINA" on the top of the barrel. Due to their relative rarity and Confederate usage (especially if altered to percussion by means of a brazed bolster), the South Carolina contract arms should bring a considerable premium.

NIB	*Exc.*	*V.G.*	*Good*	*Fair*	*Poor*
—	—	6500	3500	1500	500

Whitney Armory U.S. M1816/M1822 Muskets, Flintlock or Altered to Percussion and Adapted with "Sea Fencible" Heavy Buttplates

A number of the Whitney U.S. M1816/M1822 muskets were delivered to the Commonwealth of Massachusetts under the terms of the 1808 Militia Act. Many of these were subsequently altered to percussion at the Watertown Arsenal near Boston for the state after 1850. At some time in their career both some of the flintlock arms and those that had been altered to percussion were adapted to a heavy brass buttplate with a peculiar knob at its heel. In the process the buttstock was usually narrowed to conform to the width of the new buttplate. Because many of the muskets encountered with this buttplate bore the inspection mark of Samuel Fuller ("SF/V" within a lozenge), these arms were initially considered to have been made for the Massachusetts "Sea Fencible" organizations formed during and after the War of 1812. That appellation, however, has been dismissed, although the exact purpose of the new buttplate and the date of its application are not known. These butt-plates are usually (but not necessarily) found on Whitney contract muskets and invariably are marked with the Massachusetts state ownership mark "MS" on the barrel as well as rack numbers on the tang of the buttplate itself. Despite the unknown purpose of these arms, they command a considerable premium over standard flintlock or altered to percussion Whitney muskets.

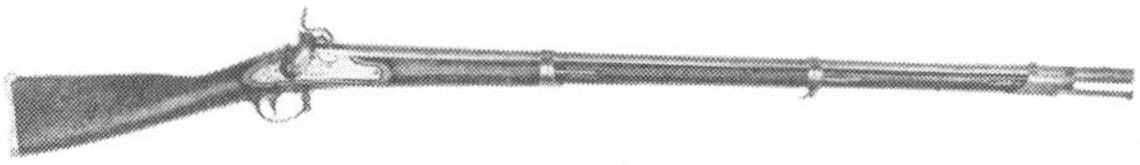

NIB	*Exc.*	*V.G.*	*Good*	*Fair*	*Poor*
—	—	6500	3500	1250	400

Whitney Armory U.S. M1816/M1822 Muskets, Altered to Percussion

From 1850 through 1856, many of the contract muskets in store at the U.S. arsenals were altered from flintlock to percussion by means of the "Belgian" or "cone-in barrel" method. The system of alteration involved the removal of the flintlock battery from the lock, filing in the screw holes from those parts, substituting a percussion hammer for the cock, plugging the vent, removing the breech plug so as to "upset" the upper, right-hand side top of the barrel, drilling and threading the "upset" section for a cone, reinserting the breech plug, and screwing in a new percussion cone. The percussioned musket was effective but the barrel was considerably weakened by the process, and while some were rifled during the American Civil War, most saw service in that conflict as smoothbores. As a general rule, the muskets so altered generally command about one-third the price of the arm in original flintlock. Exceptions are those with state ownership marks (eg. "OHIO" in the stock), with regimental marks, or with the so-called "Sea Fencible" buttplate.

Whitney Armory Muskets, 1825-1842

Eli Whitney died in 1825. Although he had a son destined to take over the family business, Eli Whitney, Jr. was only 5 years old when his father passed away and could not assume legal possession until he turned 21 in 1842. In the interim, the company was administered by the senior Whitney's trustees, Henry Edwards and James Goodrich, while the plant itself was run by Whitney's nephews, Philo and Eli Whitney Blake. During their control of the factory, three contracts were fulfilled for the U.S. government, one awarded in August of 1822 for 15,000 muskets (delivered between 1826 and 1830), a second awarded in March of 1830 for 8,750 muskets (delivered between 1831 and 1836) and a final contract in January of 1840 for 3,000 muskets (delivered between 1840 and 1842). An additional 6,750 were delivered under annual allotments granted by the War Department between 1835 and 1839 over and above the contracts for distribution to the states under the 1808 Militia Act. Although the 1840 contract had originally called for U.S. M1840 muskets, in April of that year, the contract was altered so that Whitney's plant could continue to deliver what it had delivered consistently from 1824, the U.S. M1816/1822 flintlock musket.

Eli Whitney, Jr. Armory Rifles and Rifle-Muskets, 1842-1865

Upon reaching the age of 21 in 1842, Eli Whitney, Jr. assumed command of his late father's gun making empire. Although he realized that the armory required updating to meet the improved tolerances adopted by the U.S. War Department, he also realized that a profit might be made in turning out arms of lesser standards for independent sale to the militia or the states. As a result, the younger Whitney's product line included not only several of the regulation U.S. longarms, but also a number of "good and serviceable" militia arms, including:

Whitney U.S. M1841 Contract Rifle (unaltered)

Between 1842 and 1855 Eli Whitney, Jr. received five contracts from the U.S. War Department to manufacture the newly adopted U.S. M1841 percussion rifle: 7,500 on October of 1842 (delivered between 1844 and 1847), 7,500 in March of 1848, subsequently extended to 10,000 in January of 1849 (delivered between 1849 and 1853) 5,000 (previously contracted for by Edward K. Tryon) in October of 1848 (delivered contiguous with the 1848 contract for 10,000), 5,000 in 1853 (delivered between 1853 and 1855), and 100 in 1855 (delivered that year). All except the final 1,100 delivered in 1855 conformed to the model made at Harpers Ferry, and of those 1,100, the only difference of 500 of them was the ramrod. This rifle was 49" in length, overall, having a 33" long browned barrel with .54 caliber rifled (7 groove) bore. The barrel bears the stamp of inspection at the breech, usually "U S /(inspectors' initials) / P," while the left flat (after mid-1848 for Whitney rifles) should also bear the stamping "STEEL" to indicate that the barrel had been rolled from "cast steel." Furniture is brass, the buttplate bearing the stamped letters, "U S." The lockplate is flat with a beveled edge and bears the horizontal two line inscription "E. WHITNEY" / "U S" forward of the hammer and the vertical, two line inscription "N. HAVEN" / (date) on the tail. (The date also appears on the breech plug tang). As originally made, the M1841 rifle was not adapted for a bayonet, though several modifications were made to the rifle between 1855 and 1862 to affect that adaptation.

NIB	Exc.	V.G.	Good	Fair	Poor
—	—	7500	4750	1750	500

Whitney U.S. M1841/1855 Contract Rifle, Adapted to Saber Bayonet and Long Range Sights

Before the final 600 rifles (of the 2,600 made in 1855) left the factory, the U.S. War Department contracted with Whitney to bring them up to the standards of the modified U.S. M1841 rifle then being produced or adapted at the Harpers Ferry Armory. The adaptation was two fold. First, a long range rear "ladder" style rear sight, having a 2-1/4" base was soldered to the top of the barrel; then a 1/2" long bayonet lug with 1" guide was brazed to the right side of the barrel, 2-1/2" from the muzzle. To permit disassembly, the old front band was removed and replaced with a shortened version. A new ramrod (also applied to 500 rifles without this adaptation), having an integral iron head cupped for the newly adopted "Minie ball" replaced the flat brass headed ramrod to complete the process; the rifle remained in .54 caliber with 7 grooves. Neither was the front sight modified. Bayonets were furnished by the Ames Manufacturing Company on a separate contract. Rifles so adapted at the Whitney Armory are among the rarer variants of the U.S. M1841 line and prices reflect that rarity.

NIB	Exc.	V.G.	Good	Fair	Poor
—	—	7500	4750	1750	650

Whitney U.S. M1841 Contract Rifles, Adapted to Saber Bayonets and Long Range Rear Sights (Colt 1862 Adaptation)

A large number of unaltered U.S. M1841 rifles remained on hand in U.S. Arsenals when the Civil War broke out, primarily those of Whitney's and Robbins & Lawrence's manufacture. To upgrade these rifles, revolver maker, Samuel Colt arranged to purchase 10,500 and adapt them to bayonets and long-range sights. The sight that he affixed consisted of the two leaf rear sight he had been using on his revolving rifles, with one leaf flopping forward and one flopping backward from the 100 yard block. The saber bayonet lug he attached consisted of a blued clamping ring with integral 1/2"-long lug attached that could fastened to the barrel so that the lug projected from the right side. These lugs were numbered both to the bayonet and the rifle's barrel, the number appearing on the lower surface of the barrel just behind the location of the clamping ring. Colt also bored the rifles up to .58 caliber, leaving some with 7 grooves but rerifling others with 3 wide grooves. An estimated half of the 10,200 rifles so modified by Colt were of Whitney's earlier production. Due to the Colt association, rifles so modified usually command slightly higher prices than other Civil War adaptations for saber or socket bayonets.

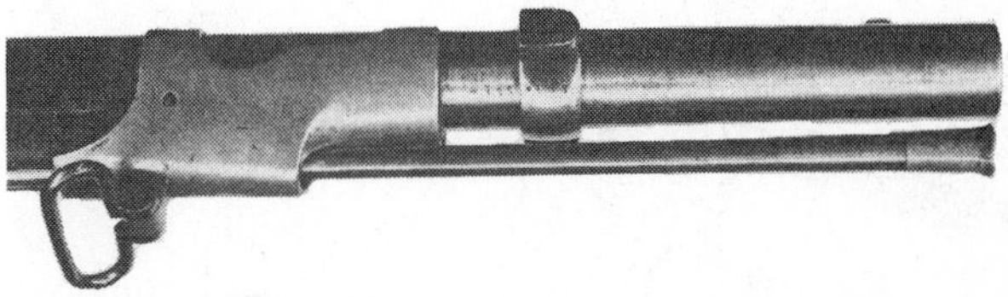

NIB	Exc.	V.G.	Good	Fair	Poor
—	—	7500	4750	1750	650

Whitney South Carolina Contract M1841 Rifle

To meet the perceived needs of South Carolina during the anti-slavery debates following the Mexican War Annexation, Whitney produced a variant of the U.S. M1841 rifle for that state, delivering only 274 in 1849. The marking of this rifle differed only in having the letters "S C" on the plate beneath the "E. WHITNEY" stamp. Because South Carolina had previously contracted for 1,000 variant M1841 rifles from William Glaze & Co. in 1853 which accepted a socket bayonet, Whitney provided the 274 1849 dated rifles with that provision also, although the lug was located under the barrel instead of atop it. Because the socket bayonet dominated the forward 3" of the barrel, the front sight was relocated to the top of the upper strap of the front band. Rifles from this contract are exceedingly rare.

NIB	Exc.	V.G.	Good	Fair	Poor
—	—	10000	6500	3250	950

Whitney "Good & Serviceable" M1841 Derivatives

Type IV. M1841 rifle unadapted using modified parts.Rifles of this configuration use the same markings as the type III rifles but delete entirely the patch box and its lid (like the type II rifles). The trigger guard strap is iron and the lock screws seem to be the same as Whitney used for his Whitney short Enfield derivative rifles. It is suspected that these rifles were purchased from New York dealers and sold to Georgia during the secession crisis of 1860-1861, thereby enhancing their collector's value, though in general Whitney M1841 derivative rifles are equal in pricing:

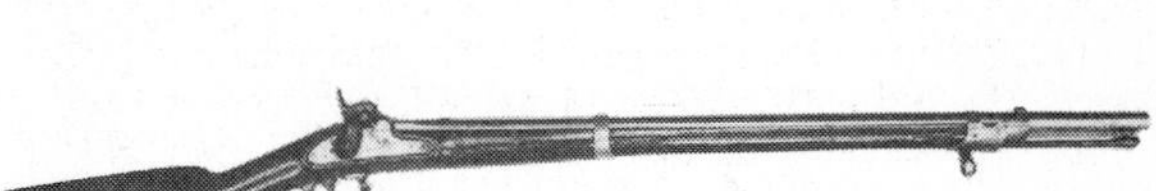

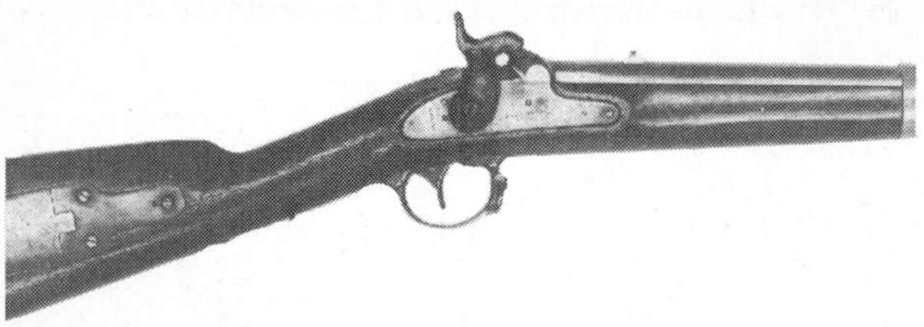

These late-production (1859-1860) derivatives of the M1841 rifle are adapted to the Sharps long-range sight used on the Type II. rifles but have a patch box. Unlike standard production, however, it is covered with an iron lid and hingle. The trigger guard strap is also iron. Lock plates delete both the date from the tail and the "US" under "E. WHITNEY." An iron stud is added below the barrel near the muzzle for a socket bayonet, necessitating the relocation of the brass blade front sight to the upper strap of the forward band. Probably fewer than 100 of this configuration were made, making it the most desirable of the derivative M1841 rifles.

NIB	*Exc.*	*V.G.*	*Good*	*Fair*	*Poor*
—	—	6500	3250	1250	500

Whitney M1842 Rifled Musket Derivative

Using rejected U.S. M1842 barrels sold at auction by the Springfield Armory, Whitney assembled approximately 2,000 .69 caliber rifled muskets that he exchanged with the state of New Hampshire in 1858 for a number of old flintlock muskets owned by that state. These rifled muskets exhibit a number of anomalies from the U.S. M1842 musket, although overall length (57-3/4") and the barrel length (42") remain the same as that musket, the bores are rifles with 7 narrow grooves, and in addition to the dates and inspection marks placed at Springfield usually bear the state ownership mark "NEW HAMPSHIRE" on the top of the barrel. In finishing these rifled muskets, Whitney utilized a number of parts from other gun makers, including Sharps M1853 "ladder" style carbine rear sights, bands from the Robbins & Lawrence P1853 Enfield rifle-musket contract, and internal lock parts remaining from his M1841 rifles. Parts that are unique to these arms include the iron nosecap and the flat lockplate. The lockplates are unmarked, but the barrels usually show a letter/number code common to Whitney's production during this period. Despite a production of approximately 2,000 muskets, the survival rate for this type of arm is quite low.

NIB	*Exc.*	*V.G.*	*Good*	*Fair*	*Poor*
—	—	6500	3250	1250	400

Whitney P1853 "Long Enfield" Rifle-Musket Derivative

Having secured a number of bands and other furniture from the Robbins & Lawrence contract for P1853 Enfield rifle-muskets, about 1859 Whitney developed a derivative of that arm that combined those bands with a 40"-barrel .58 caliber, rifled with 7 grooves that basically resembled the configuration of the U.S. M1855 rifle-musket, a copy of which Whitney was also making. The 56"-long rifle-musket that resulted was sold to state militia companies and two states, Maryland purchasing 2,000 and Georgia contracting for 1,700 (of which 1,225 were delivered). Although several of the components of the furniture were from the Robbins & Lawrence contract, the nosecap was pewter (Enfield style), and the iron buttplate and brass trigger guard bow/iron strap were of a style peculiar to Whitney' Enfield series. The rear sight resembled the ladder pattern of the U.S. M1855 rifle musket. The unique flat, unbeveled lockplate simply bears the one line stamp, "E. WHITNEY" forward of the hammer.

NIB	*Exc.*	*V.G.*	*Good*	*Fair*	*Poor*
—	—	6500	3250	1250	600

Whitney P1853 "Short Enfield" Rifle Derivative

Total production of these rifles is estimated to have been between 800 and 1,000, with approximately half of the number going to southern states. Prices should not vary between the four types; however, confirmed Confederate usage will increase the value significantly.

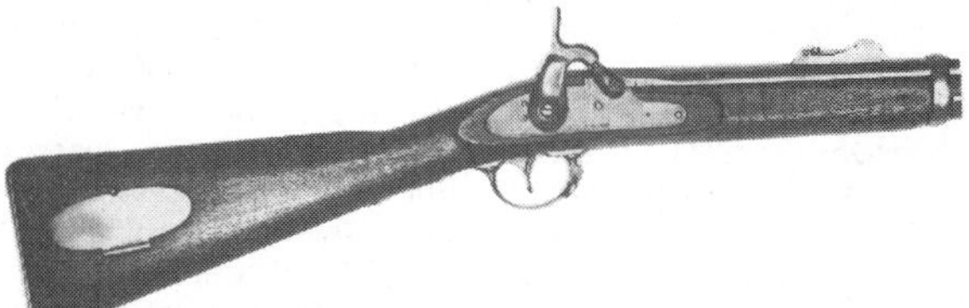

Type IV. Identical to Type III but with a new single leaf rear sight on a 1-1/4" long base.

NIB	*Exc.*	*V.G.*	*Good*	*Fair*	*Poor*
—	—	8500	4250	2000	600

Whitney M1855 Rifle Derivative

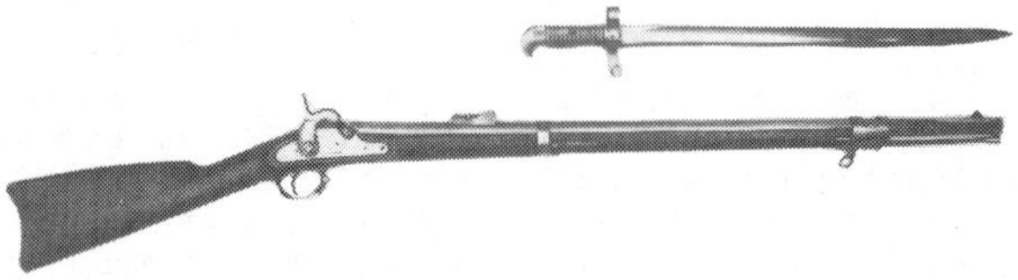

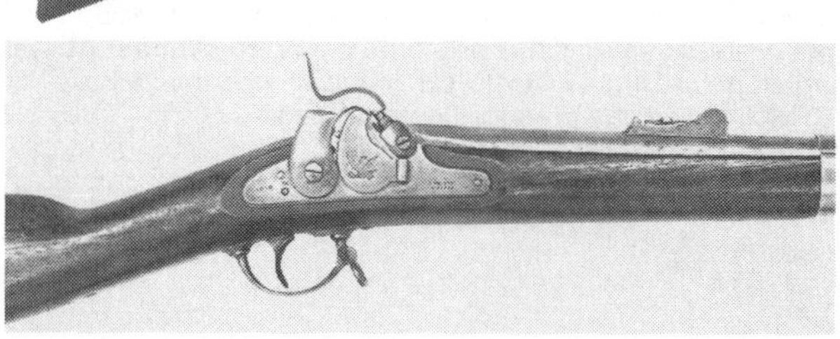

At the same time that Whitney advertised his Enfield derivative series of rifle-muskets and rifles, he also indicated the availability of a short rifle with saber bayonet. This rifle combined rejected barrels made at Harpers Ferry in 1858 for the U.S. M1855 rifles with rejected, unmilled Maynard tape primer lockplates that had been shaved of their top "hump," marked forward of the hammer with the single line stamp, "E. WHITNEY." The buttplate and the trigger guard also conform to that of the U.S. M1855 rifle, but the bands are brass, remaining from Whitney's M1841/1855 rifle contract. Early in production these rifles used round brass lock screw washers following the M1855 pattern; later production used the winged brass lock screw washers that Whitney inherited from the Robbins & Lawrence P1853 rifle-musket contract and which he used on his Enfield series derivatives. At least two patterns of saber bayonet were used on this rifle.

NIB	Exc.	V.G.	Good	Fair	Poor
—	—	7000	3500	1250	500

Whitney M1855 Rifle-Musket Derivative

In 1861, Whitney accepted a U.S. contract to produce 40,000 U.S. "M1855" rifle-muskets. What Whitney had in mind under this contract and what the War Department demanded were two different arms. Whitney's product was similar to the U.S. M1855 rifle-musket but differed in a number of respects. The 40" barrel was .58 caliber but was rifled with 7 rather than 3 grooves and was adapted to the English P1853 socket bayonet he had been using on his Enfield derivative rifle-muskets. The initial rear sight, while similar to the U.S. M1855 type, was slightly shorter, having a 2-5/16" base. (On later production, Whitney substituted a shorter, 1-1/4"-long base with a single, pierced leaf sight.) The nosecap, moreover, was made of pewter and followed the Enfield pattern rather than being malleable iron of the U.S. M1855 pattern. On later production, Whitney also substituted brass winged lock screw washers from his Enfield derivative series. The lockplates for these arms were drawn from complete Maynard locks made at the federal armories in 1858 and 1859 but later rejected for flaws. Upon these plates Whitney stamped "E. WHITNEY / N. HAVEN," as on his early Connecticut contract M1861 derivative rifle-muskets. Except for the letter/number code, the barrels are unmarked. Examples are known whose stocks bear indications of issue to the 8th Connecticut Infantry during the Civil War, suggesting Whitney may have sold the few made to Connecticut under his first state contract. Arms with these regimental marks should command a premium over unmarked arms.

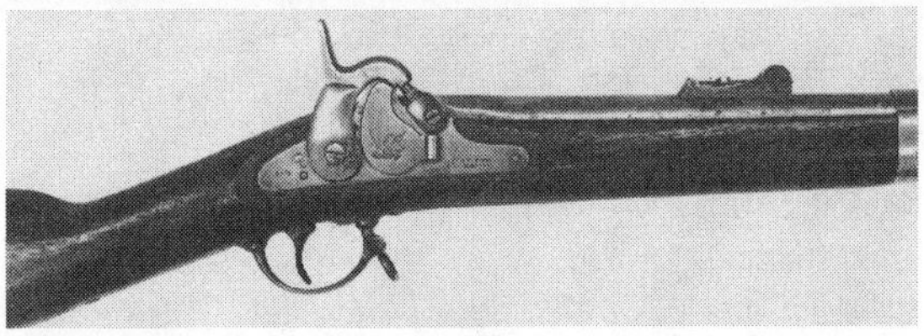

NIB	Exc.	V.G.	Good	Fair	Poor
—	—	7000	3500	1250	500

Whitney M1861 Connecticut Contract Rifle-Musket Derivative

In 1861 and 1862, Eli Whitney, Jr. entered into two contracts with his home state of Connecticut for respectively 6,000 and 8,000 rifle-muskets generally conforming to the U.S. M1861 rifle musket. A number of exceptions to the U.S. model, however, were permitted. On the first contract, the 40" barrels were in .58 caliber but were made with 7 groove rifling instead of 3 groove; on the second contract, the arms were made with 3-groove rifling. Nosecaps for both contracts were of the U.S. M1855/1861 pattern but were cast in pewter instead of malleable iron. An exception was also permitted in the rear sights, which initially were the same 1-1/4" long base with pierced single leaf that Whitney had used on his Type IV short Enfield derivative rifles, though later the base was changed to conform to the pattern adopted for the U.S. M1861 rifle-musket but still retaining the single leaf. Lockplates were M1861-style, marked forward of the hammer "E. WHITNEY / N. HAVEN" on early production and with an eagle surmounting a panoply of flags and trophies over "WHITNEYVILLE" on later production. The barrels bore the typical Whitney letter/number code and were adapted to the Enfield pattern socket bayonets rather than the U.S. M1855 socket bayonets. Later production occasionally bears the inspection letters "G.W.Q."

NIB	Exc.	V.G.	Good	Fair	Poor
—	—	6000	2750	1150	400

Whitney "High Humpback" Lockplate M1861 Rifle-Musket Derivative

With the completion of his Connecticut contracts, Whitney combined the excess parts from its production with some of the unmilled and unshaved lockplates that he still had on hand from his M1855 Rifle Derivatives. The 56"-long rifle-muskets that resulted have 40" barrels in .58 caliber with 3-groove rifling and a rear sight that conforms to the U.S. M1861 pattern that Whitney began making in 1863. The flat, beveled unmilled lockplates bear the two line stamp "E. WHITNEY / N. HAVEN" that Whitney had used on his M1855 rifle-musket derivative and on the early M1861 Connecticut contract rifle-muskets, but showing considerable wear, to the extent that the second line is often incomplete or missing entirely. Photograph evidence indicates that the 21st Connecticut Infantry received some of these rifle-muskets. They are often mistaken as a southern purchase, which artificially raises the asking prices.

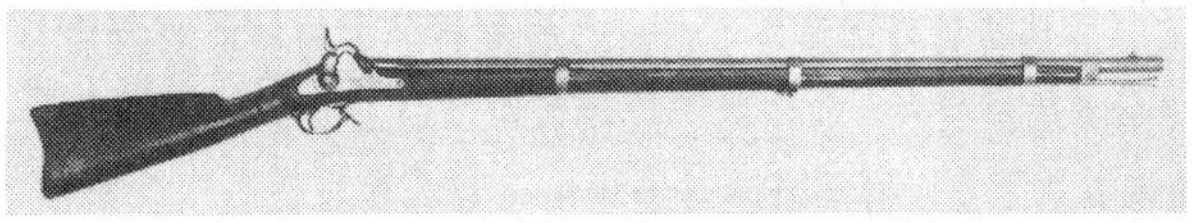

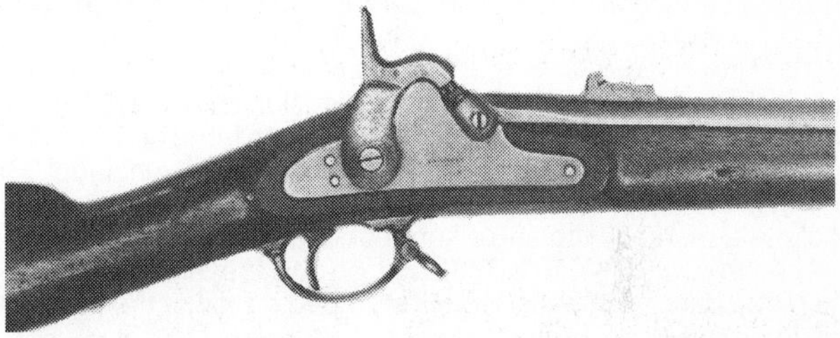

NIB	Exc.	V.G.	Good	Fair	Poor
—	—	7000	3250	1250	500

Whitney "Manton" M1861 Rifle-Musket Derivative

In order to dispose of some of his inferior arms from the second Connecticut state contract, Whitney assembled at least 1,300 bearing a fictitious Old English lock stamp "Manton" forward of the hammer and the date "1862" on its tail. In most respects this arm resembled the U.S. M1861 rifle musket, complete with 3-groove rifling in its .58-caliber, 40" barrel with typical Whitney letter/number code near the muzzle (and often also marked "G.W.Q. on its left flat). Nosecaps, in typical Whitney style, were case from pewter instead of being formed from malleable iron. The rear sight closely follows the M1861 pattern but lacks the step on its side walls since it utilized a simple pierced leaf instead of the compound double leaf of the M1861 rifle-musket. These arms were disposed of in the New York City market after the 1863 Draft Riot and issued to the New York National Guard.

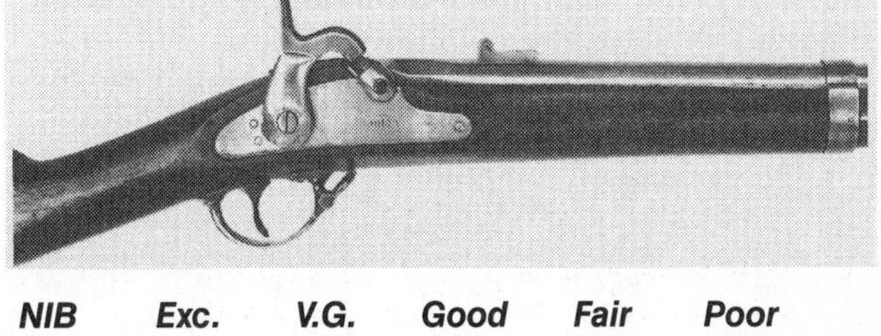

NIB	Exc.	V.G.	Good	Fair	Poor
—	—	8250	4250	2000	600

Whitney "Direct Vent" M1861 Rifle-Musket Derivatives

In his continued efforts to dispose of surplus and rejected parts from his Connecticut and federal contracts, Whitney devised in 1863 a rifle-musket generally conforming to the M1861 rifle-musket except in two notable features. The bolster, instead of projecting considerably away from the barrel and having a clean-out screw was relatively short and flat faced. The process of making this bolster eliminated one production sequence, since it was not possible to drill the hole for the cone directly to the barrel. To accommodate the new cone position, the lockplates were made flat, without the bevel, and inletted flush with the stock. Lockplates bear the eagle surmounting the panoply of flags and trophies over "WHITNEYVILLE" stamp forward of the hammer, and are known with "1863" on the tail or without any date. The rear sight is the same as used on the "Manton" rifle-musket derivative. Arms with barrels than 40", 39", and 30" exist, all in .58 caliber with 3-groove rifling; however, the shortest of these may be post-war modifications for cadet use. Quantities made are not known, but surviving examples suggest limited production, probably to use faulty parts from the 1863 federal contract.

NIB	*Exc.*	*V.G.*	*Good*	*Fair*	*Poor*
—	—	7000	3250	1250	400

Whitney U.S. M1861 Contract Rifle-Musket

In October of 1863, Whitney secured a contract with the U.S. War Department to produce 15,000 U.S. M1861 rifle-muskets. The arms manufactured under this contract conform in all respects to the Springfield Model adopted in 1861. The 40" barrel is in .58 caliber and rifled with 3 grooves; its rear sight conforms to the two-leaf model with stepped side walls. Nosecap is M1861 style and made of malleable iron. Socket bayonets furnished with them conform to the U.S. M1855/M1861 pattern. Marks include "US" on buttplate and standard inspection marks on barrel and stock. Lockplate marked with eagle surmounting letters "US" forward of the hammer and "WHITNEYVILLE" on the forward projection of the plate; date, "1863" or "1864" stamped on tail of the plate.

NIB	*Exc.*	*V.G.*	*Good*	*Fair*	*Poor*
—	—	7000	3250	1250	400

Whitney U.S. Navy Contract Rifle

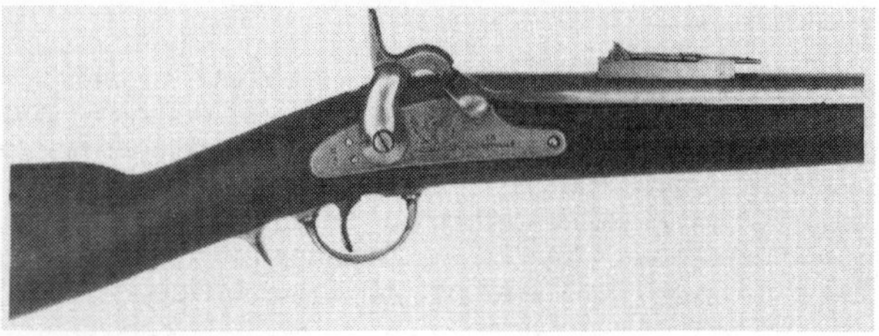

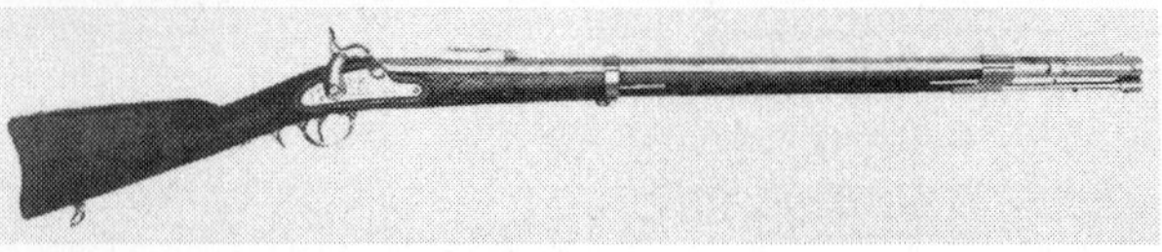

In July of 1861, Whitney entered a contact with the U.S. Navy to produce 10,000 rifles of the "Plymouth Pattern." So called after the U.S. Navy warship whereupon the first Harpers Ferry trial rifles had been developed, the new Navy rifle borrowed many of its characteristics from the French M1846 "carbine a tige." Overall length was 50" with a 34"-long barrel bearing a saber bayonet lug with guide extending nearly to the muzzle on its right side. The bore was .69 caliber, rifled with three broad lands and grooves. The rear sight copied the French M1846 and M1859 styles, i.e. it has an elevating ladder but no sidewalls. On early production the sights are serially numbered to the rifle's serial number (appearing on the breech plug tang). Barrels bear the standard U.S. inspection marks on the left quarter flat and the production date ("1863" or "1864") on the top of the barrel near the breech. Two lock markings have been encountered. The earlier production uses flat beveled plate marked with the date "1863" on its tail and an eagle surmounting a panoply of flags and trophies over the name "WHITNEYVILLE." In later (after serial no. 3,000) the lock's tail is marked "1864" and the stamping forward of the hammer matches that on the U.S. M1861 Whitney contract rifle-muskets, i.e. a small eagle over "U S" and "WHITNEYVILLE" in the forward projection of the plate. Inspector's initials (F.C.W.) appear on the barrel and in a cartouche on the stock.

NIB	*Exc.*	*V.G.*	*Good*	*Fair*	*Poor*
—	—	8250	4250	1750	600

The Whitney Arms Company, 1865-1888

With the close of the American Civil War, Eli Whitney, Jr. again turned his eyes to the manufacture of inexpensive arms from parts remaining on hand from his Civil War contracts. Extra barrels were turned into inexpensive muzzleloading shotguns, and a few breechloading designs were toyed with. Following Remington's example, Whitney soon realized that a substantial profit could be made in the production of single-shot martial arms for foreign governments. The result was a series of breechloading arms that copied many salient features of the Remington line, including a direct copy after the expiration of the Remington patent for the "rolling block" mechanism. Not until the late 1870s did Whitney acquire the rights to several patents that led to the production of a lever-action repeating rifle. During the post-war period, revolver production, which had begun with evasions of Colt's patents in the decade prior to the Civil War, mushroomed with the production of small spur-trigger rimfire cartridge revolvers. Despite the variety of arms produced, by 1883 Whitney was considering the sale of his company. Business reverses over the next five years necessitated the sale of the firm to Winchester in 1888. Primarily interested securing in the patent rights for Whitney's lever-action series of rifles, Winchester closed the plant and moved its machinery to New Haven. After 90 years of production, the Whitneyville Armory ceased to exist.

Single Barreled Percussion Shotgun

This firearm was manufactured by Whitney out of surplus .58 caliber rifle barrels that were opened up and converted to smoothbore .60-caliber shotgun barrels. They are offered in lengths of 28" to 36" and are marked "Whitney Arms Co., Whitneyville, Conn. Homogeneous Wrought Steel." The finish is blued, with varnished walnut stocks that are crudely checkered. There were approximately 2,000 manufactured between 1866 and 1869. These guns are rarely encountered on today's market.

NIB	*Exc.*	*V.G.*	*Good*	*Fair*	*Poor*
—	—	1300	950	400	150

Double-Barreled Percussion Shotgun

The specifications for this version are similar to that of the single barrel except that there are two side-by-side barrels with double locks and hammers and double triggers. They are slightly more common than the single barreled version.

NIB	*Exc.*	*V.G.*	*Good*	*Fair*	*Poor*
—	—	1300	950	400	150

Swing-Breech Carbine

This is a single-shot breechloading carbine chambered for the .46-caliber rimfire cartridge. It has a 22" round barrel with a button-released breechblock that swings to the side for loading. The finish is blued, with a walnut stock. There were fewer than 50 manufactured in 1866.

NIB	*Exc.*	*V.G.*	*Good*	*Fair*	*Poor*
—	—	6000	3250	1750	600

Whitney-Cochran Carbine

This is a single-shot breechloading carbine chambered for the .44 rimfire cartridge. It has a 28" round barrel with a lever-activated breechblock that raises upward for loading. It was manufactured under license from J.W. Cochran. The finish is blued, with a walnut stock. There is a saddle ring on the left side of the frame. It is marked "Whitney Arms Co. - Whitneyville, Conn." This gun was produced for the 1867 Government Carbine Trials. There were fewer than 50 manufactured in 1866 and 1867.

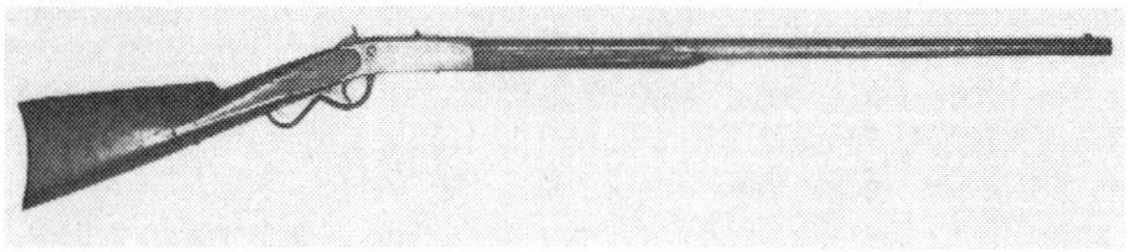

Courtesy Milwaukee Public Museum, Milwaukee, Wisconsin

NIB	Exc.	V.G.	Good	Fair	Poor
—	—	7000	3500	1500	600

Excelsior

This is a single-shot rifle chambered for the .38, .44, or .50 rimfire cartridges. It is found with various-length octagonal or round barrels. The finish is blued, with a walnut stock and forearm held on by one barrel band. The breechblock pivots downward for loading. There is a center-mounted hammer. It is marked "Whitney Arms Co. Whitneyville Conn." The shorter barreled carbine versions have a saddle ring on the frame. There were approximately 200 manufactured between 1866 and 1870.

NIB	Exc.	V.G.	Good	Fair	Poor
—	—	6700	2750	1150	400

Whitney-Howard Lever Action ("Thunderbolt)

This is a single-shot breechloader that is chambered for the .44 rimfire cartridge. It has also been noted as a shotgun chambered for 20 gauge smoothbore with barrels from 30" to 40" in length. The rifle version has barrel lengths from 22" to 28". The breechblock is opened by means of a combination lever and trigger guard. There is also a carbine version with barrel lengths of 18.5" or 19". There were approximately 2,000 manufactured totally between 1866 and 1870.

Whitney-Howard Lever Action ("Thunderbolt) Shotgun

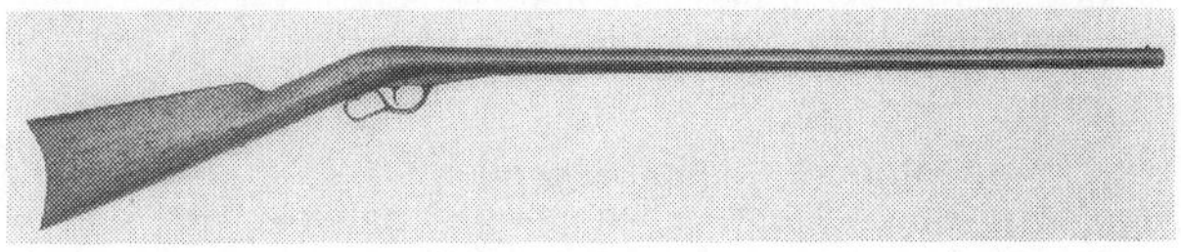

Courtesy Buffalo Bill Historical Center, Cody, Wyoming

NIB	Exc.	V.G.	Good	Fair	Poor
—	—	1400	650	300	100

Whitney-Howard Lever Action ("Thunderbolt) Rifle

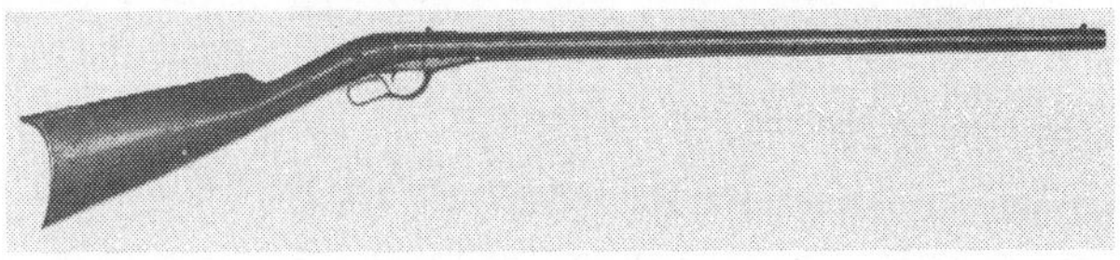

Courtesy Milwaukee Public Museum, Milwaukee, Wisconsin

NIB	Exc.	V.G.	Good	Fair	Poor
—	—	1600	900	450	150

Whitney-Howard Lever Action ("Thunderbolt) Carbine

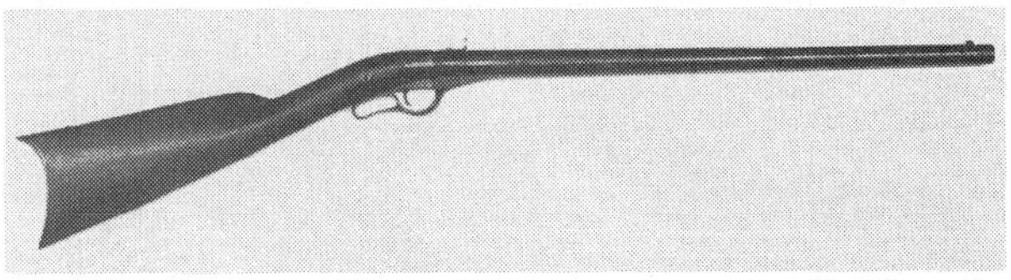

Courtesy Milwaukee Public Museum, Milwaukee, Wisconsin

NIB	Exc.	V.G.	Good	Fair	Poor
—	—	2000	1250	500	200

Whitney Phoenix

There is little known about the origin of this model. It is built on a patent issued to Whitney in 1874. There are a number of variations that are all marked "Phoenix, Patent May 24, 74." The Whitney name is not marked on any of the versions. They are all single-shot breechloaders with a breechblock that lifts to the right side and upward for loading. The barrels are all blued, with either case colored or blued receivers and walnut stocks. There were approximately 25,000 total manufactured between 1867 and 1881. The models and values are listed.

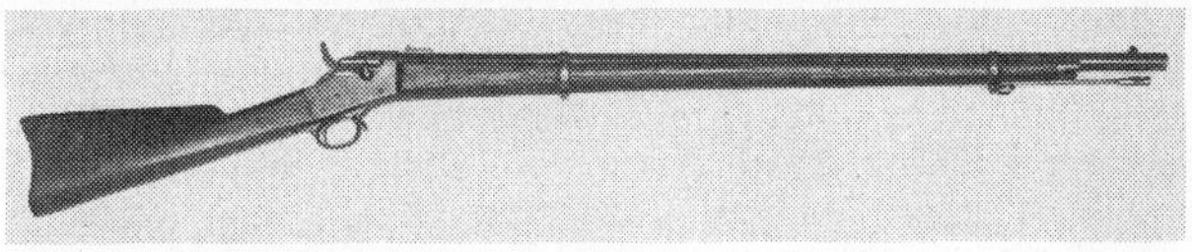

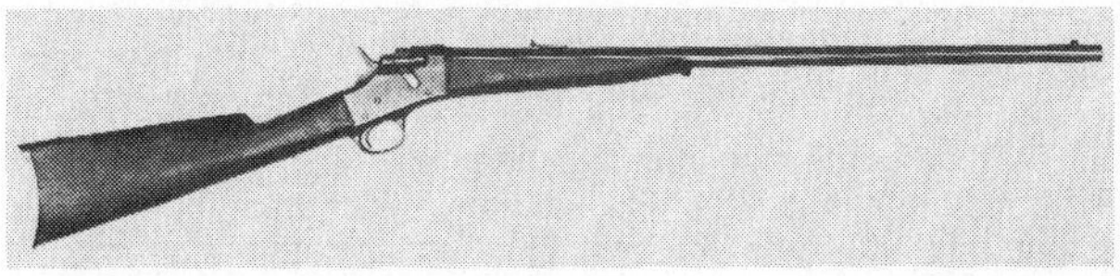

Courtesy Milwaukee Public Museum, Milwaukee, Wisconsin

Whitney Phoenix Gallery Rifle

This version is chambered for the .22 rimfire caliber and has a 24" half-octagonal barrel. Its production was quite limited.

NIB	Exc.	V.G.	Good	Fair	Poor
—	—	3250	1500	600	200

Whitney Phoenix Shotgun

This is a smoothbore version chambered for 10, 12, 14, 16, or 22 gauge. It has smoothbore barrels between 26" and 32" in length. There were approximately 5,000 manufactured.

NIB	Exc.	V.G.	Good	Fair	Poor
—	—	1100	600	250	100

Whitney Phoenix Military Rifle

This version is chambered for the .433, .45, or .50 caliber centerfire cartridges. It has a 35" round barrel with a full-length, two-piece walnut stock held on by three barrel bands. There were approximately 15,000 manufactured. Many were sent to Central or South America.

NIB	Exc.	V.G.	Good	Fair	Poor
—	—	5750	3000	1250	400

Whitney Phoenix Schuetzen Rifle

This is a target-shooting version chambered for the .38, .40, or .44 centerfire cartridges. It has either a 30" or 32" octagonal barrel with a Schuetzen-type walnut stock and forearm that features hand checkering. It has a nickel-plated, Swiss-style buttplate and adjustable sights with a spirit level. This model has been noted with double-set triggers. There were few manufactured.

NIB	Exc.	V.G.	Good	Fair	Poor
—	—	6000	3250	1250	400

Whitney Phoenix Civilian Carbine

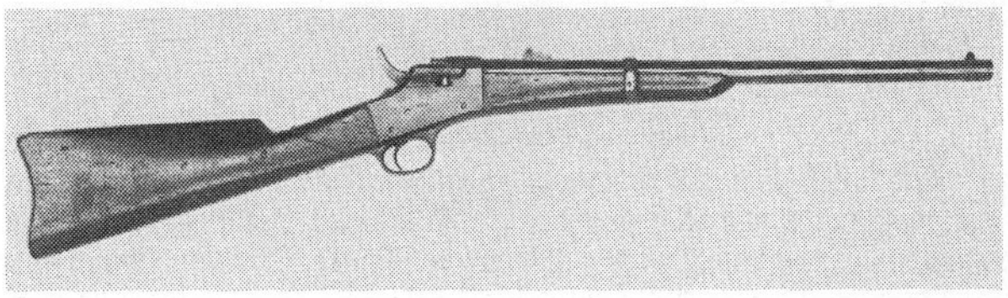

Courtesy Milwaukee Public Museum, Milwaukee, Wisconsin

This version is chambered for the .44 caliber centerfire and has a 24" round barrel. The finish is blued, with a case colored frame and a walnut stock and forearm held on by one barrel band. It has military-type sights, buttplate, and a saddle ring mounted on the frame. There were approximately 500 manufactured.

NIB	Exc.	V.G.	Good	Fair	Poor
—	—	4800	2500	850	400

Whitney Phoenix Military Carbine

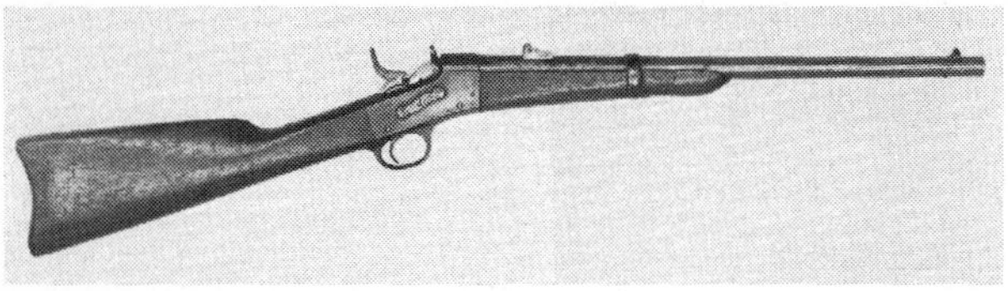

Courtesy Milwaukee Public Museum, Milwaukee, Wisconsin

This version is chambered for the .433, .45, or .50 centerfire cartridges. It has a 20.5" round barrel and was manufactured for Central and South America. It is very rarely encountered on today's market.

NIB	Exc.	V.G.	Good	Fair	Poor
—	—	5000	2750	1000	400

WHITNEY-LAIDLEY MODEL I ROLLING BLOCK

Whitney acquired manufacturing rights for this model from the inventors T. Laidley and C.A. Emery, who had received the patent in 1866. Whitney immediately started to modify the action to become competitive with the Remington Rolling Block. There were approximately 50,000 manufactured total between 1871 and 1881. There are a number of variations of this model.

Military Carbine

There were approximately 5,000 manufactured chambered for the .433, .45, or .50 centerfire cartridges. It has a 20.5" round barrel with military-type sights and a saddle ring on the receiver. The finish is blued, with a case colored frame and a walnut stock. Most of them were shipped to Central or South America.

NIB	Exc.	V.G.	Good	Fair	Poor
—	—	3500	1750	700	250

Civilian Carbine

This version is chambered for .44 rimfire or centerfire and .46 rimfire. It has either an 18.5" or 19.5" barrel. It is blued, with a case colored frame. The stock is walnut. A nickel-plated version is also available. There were approximately 1,000 of this version manufactured.

NIB	Exc.	V.G.	Good	Fair	Poor
—	—	2800	1750	700	250

Military Rifle

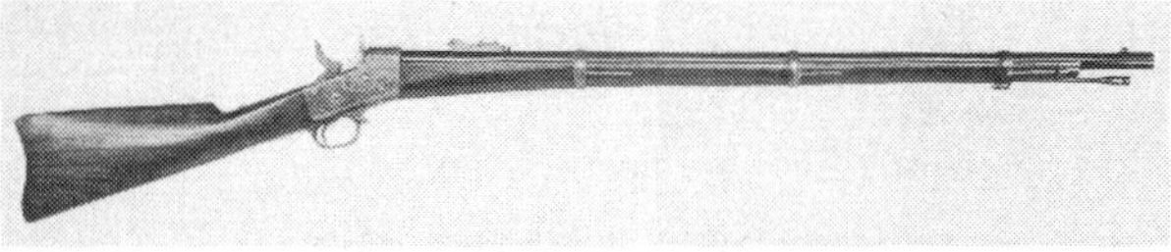

Courtesy Milwaukee Public Museum, Milwaukee, Wisconsin

This version is chambered the same as the Military Carbine but has either a 32.5" or 35" round barrel with a full-length two-piece stock held on by three barrel bands. The finish is blued, with a case colored receiver and a walnut stock. There were approximately 30,000 manufactured. Most were shipped to Central or South America.

NIB	Exc.	V.G.	Good	Fair	Poor
—	—	3950	2000	800	300

Gallery Rifle

This is a .22 caliber sporting-rifle version with a 24" octagonal barrel. The finish is similar to the Military Rifle. There were approximately 500 manufactured.

NIB	Exc.	V.G.	Good	Fair	Poor
—	—	3400	1750	700	250

Sporting Rifle

This version is chambered for .38, .40, .44, .45, or .50 centerfire, as well as .32, .38, or .44 rimfire. It features barrel lengths from 24" to 30" in either round or octagonal configurations. The finish is similar to the Military Rifle, and there were approximately 5,000 manufactured.

NIB	Exc.	V.G.	Good	Fair	Poor
—	—	3950	2000	750	300

Creedmoor No. 1 Rifle

This version is chambered for the .44 caliber cartridge and has a 32" or 34" barrel that is either round or octagonal in configuration. It has a blued finish with case colored frame and a hand checkered, select walnut stock and forearm. It features vernier adjustable sights with a spirit level. It is marked "Whitney Creedmoor." There were fewer than 100 manufactured.

NIB	Exc.	V.G.	Good	Fair	Poor
—	—	11500	6250	2750	850

Creedmoor No. 2 Rifle

This version is similar to the No. 1 Rifle except that it is chambered for the .40 caliber cartridge with either a 30" or 32" barrel.

NIB	Exc.	V.G.	Good	Fair	Poor
—	—	9500	4250	1750	500

WHITNEY-REMINGTON MODEL 2 ROLLING BLOCK

When Remington's patent for the Rolling Block action expired, Whitney was quick to reproduce the action, labeling it his "New Improved System." It is essentially quite similar to Remington's Rolling Block and is easily recognized when compared with the Model 1 because it has only two parts — the hammer and the breechblock. The frame is also rounded. The tang on this model is marked "Whitney Arms Company, New Haven Ct USA." There were approximately 50,000 total manufactured between 1881 and 1888. There are a number of variations are listed.

Shotgun

This is a smoothbore version chambered for 12, 14, 16, or 20 gauge. It is offered with barrel lengths between 26" and 30". Twenty inch barrels have also been noted.

NIB	Exc.	V.G.	Good	Fair	Poor
—	—	1300	650	250	100

Military Carbine

This version is chambered for the .433 and .45 centerfire cartridges. It has a 20.5" barrel and is blued, with a case colored receiver and walnut stock. There were approximately 5,000 manufactured. Most were sent to South or Central America.

NIB	Exc.	V.G.	Good	Fair	Poor
—	—	3400	1750	700	300

Civilian Carbine

This version is chambered for the .44 rimfire or centerfire cartridge with an 18.5" round barrel. The finish is similar to the Military Carbine. There were approximately 2,000 manufactured.

NIB	Exc.	V.G.	Good	Fair	Poor
—	—	3100	1600	600	250

Military Rifle

Courtesy Buffalo Bill Historical Center, Cody, Wyoming

This version is chambered for the .433, .45, or .50 centerfire cartridge. It has a 32.5" or 35" barrel. It is finished similarly to the Military Carbine. There were approximately 39,000 manufactured.

NIB	Exc.	V.G.	Good	Fair	Poor
—	—	3950	2000	750	300

No. 1 Sporting Rifle

This version is chambered for various popular sporting cartridges and is offered with barrel lengths from 26" to 30", either round or octagonal in configuration. The finish is blued, with a case colored receiver and a varnished walnut stock. There were many options available that could radically affect the value, and a qualified appraisal would be advisable. There were approximately 3,000 manufactured.

NIB	Exc.	V.G.	Good	Fair	Poor
—	—	4850	2500	1000	400

No. 2 Sporting Rifle

This is a smaller version of the No. 1 Rifle, chambered for the .22 rimfire, .32, .38, and .44-40 centerfire cartridges. Again, a qualified appraisal would be helpful, as many options can affect the value.

NIB	Exc.	V.G.	Good	Fair	Poor
—	—	3400	1750	700	250

WHITNEY-BURGESS-MORSE RIFLE

This is a lever action repeating rifle chambered for the .45-70 Government cartridge. There are three variations. All have a magazine tube mounted beneath the barrel with blued finishes and walnut stocks. The barrels are marked "G. W. Morse Patented Oct. 28th 1856." The tang is marked "A. Burgess Patented Jan. 7th, 1873, Patented Oct 19th 1873." There were approximately 3,000 total manufactured between 1878 and 1882. The variations are listed.

Sporting Rifle

This version has a 28" octagonal or round barrel. The magazine tube holds 9 rounds. There are a number of options available that can increase the value drastically; and we recommend competent, individual appraisal. Value given is for a standard model.

NIB	Exc.	V.G.	Good	Fair	Poor
—	—	6500	3250	1250	400

Military Rifle

This version has a 33" round barrel with a full-length forearm held on by two barrel bands. It features military sights and has an 11-round tubular magazine. It has a bayonet lug and sling swivels. This variation is also found chambered for the .43 Spanish and .42 Russian cartridges. There were approximately 1,000 manufactured.

NIB	Exc.	V.G.	Good	Fair	Poor
—	—	8000	4250	2000	700

Carbine

This version has a 22" round barrel with a full-length forearm held on by one barrel band. It has a 7-round tubular magazine and a saddle ring attached to the frame. There were approximately 500 manufactured.

NIB	Exc.	V.G.	Good	Fair	Poor
—	—	9000	4750	2250	750

WHITNEY-KENNEDY RIFLE

This is a lever action repeating rifle that was manufactured in two sizes. It has a magazine tube mounted under the barrel and a blued finish with a case colored lever. The stock is walnut. The barrel is marked "Whitney Arms Co New Haven, Conn. U.S.A." Occasionally, the word "Kennedy" is marked after the Whitney name. There are two major variations. One features a standard-type action lever; and the other, the same "S" -shaped lever that is found on the Burgess model. This version would be worth approximately 10 percent additional. As with many of the rifles of this era, there were many options available that will affect the values. We strongly recommend securing a qualified appraisal for all but the standard models if a transaction is contemplated. There were approximately 15,000 manufactured between 1879 and 1886. The variations of the Whitney-Kennedy and their values are listed.

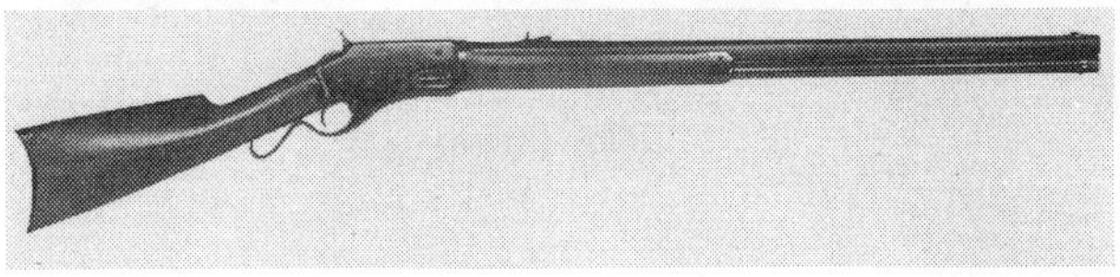

Courtesy Buffalo Bill Historical Center, Cody, Wyoming

Small Frame Sporting Rifle

This version is chambered for the .32-20, .38-40, and the .40-40 cartridges. It has a 24" barrel that is either round or octagonal in configuration. Examples will be noted with either a full-length or half-length tubular magazine.

NIB	Exc.	V.G.	Good	Fair	Poor
—	—	5000	2750	1200	500

Large Frame Sporting Rifle

This version is chambered for the .40-60, .45-60, .45-75, and the .50-90 cartridges. The .50-caliber version is uncommon and will bring a 20 percent premium. The barrel lengths offered are 26" or 28".

NIB	Exc.	V.G.	Good	Fair	Poor
—	—	6000	3000	1350	500

Military Rifle

This is a large-frame model, chambered for the .40-.60, .44-.40, and the .45-60 cartridges. It has a 32.25" round barrel and either an 11- or 16-round tubular magazine. It has a full-length walnut forend held on by two barrel bands and features a bayonet lug and sling swivels. There were approximately 1,000 manufactured. Most were shipped to Central or South America.

NIB	Exc.	V.G.	Good	Fair	Poor
—	—	6400	3750	1750	550

Military Carbine

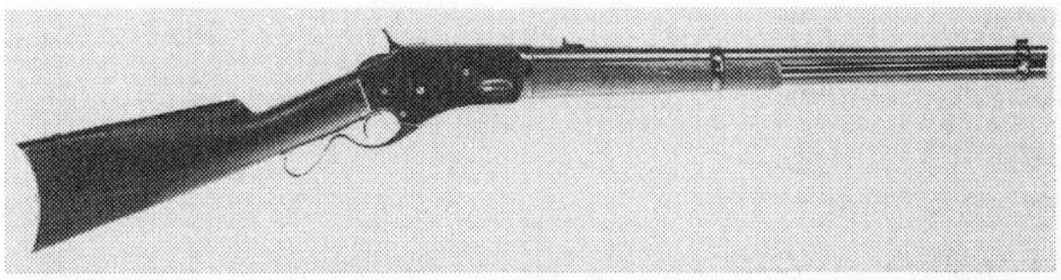

Courtesy Buffalo Bill Historical Center, Cody, Wyoming

This is built on either the small-frame or large-frame action and is chambered for the .38-40, .44-40, .40-60, or .45-60 cartridges. It has either a 20" or 22" round barrel and a 9- or 12-round tubular magazine, depending on the caliber. It has a short forend held on by a single barrel band. There were approximately 1,000 manufactured. Most were sent to Central or South America.

NIB	Exc.	V.G.	Good	Fair	Poor
—	—	6400	3750	1750	550

WICHITA ARMS, INC.

Wichita, Kansas

Classic Rifle

A single-shot bolt-action rifle produced in a variety of calibers with a 21" octagonal barrel. Offered with Canjar adjustable triggers. Blued with a checkered walnut stock.

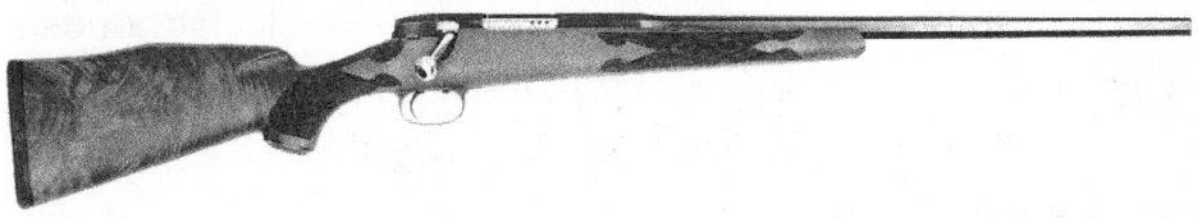

NIB	Exc.	V.G.	Good	Fair	Poor
3000	2500	2250	1850	1250	1000

Varmint Rifle

As above, with a round barrel.

NIB	Exc.	V.G.	Good	Fair	Poor
2000	1750	1500	1250	1000	800

Silhouette Rifle

As above, with a 24" heavy barrel, gray composition stock and 2-oz. Canjar trigger.

NIB	Exc.	V.G.	Good	Fair	Poor
2200	1900	1700	1000	850	650

Wichita Classic Engraved

As above, but embellished.

NIB	Exc.	V.G.	Good	Fair	Poor
5000	4250	3500	2500	2000	1500

WICKLIFFE RIFLES

Triple S Development
Wickliffe, Ohio/Austinburg, Ohio

NOTE: The Wickliffe Rifle Company has been reorganized as a maker of custom single-shot rifles. Values below are for the original Wickliffe guns.

Model 76

A single-shot falling-block rifle produced in a variety of calibers from .22 Hornet to .45-70 with a 22" lightweight or 26" heavyweight barrel. Blued with a walnut stock. Introduced in 1976. Discontinued.

NIB	Exc.	V.G.	Good	Fair	Poor
—	1200	1000	750	550	300

Model 76 Deluxe

As above, with a nickel-silver pistol grip cap, machine jeweled breechblock and more finely figured walnut stock. Introduced in 1976.

NIB	Exc.	V.G.	Good	Fair	Poor
—	1450	1250	900	700	450

Traditionalist

The Model 76 in .30-06 or .45-70 caliber with a 24" barrel having open sights and a checkered walnut buttstock. Introduced in 1979.

NIB	Exc.	V.G.	Good	Fair	Poor
—	1200	1000	750	550	300

Stinger

Similar to the Model 76, but chambered for .22 Hornet or .223 Remington with a 22" barrel fitted with a Burris 6X power telescope. Blued with a checkered Monte Carlo-style stock. Introduced in 1979.

NIB	Exc.	V.G.	Good	Fair	Poor
—	1200	1000	750	550	300

Stinger Deluxe

As above, with a superior grade of finish and more finely figured walnut stock.

NIB	Exc.	V.G.	Good	Fair	Poor
—	1250	1050	800	575	300

WILKINSON ARMS CO.

Covina, California

Terry Carbine

A 9mm caliber semi-automatic carbine with a 16.25" barrel, adjustable sights, and 30-shot magazine. Matte blued with either a black composition or maple stock.

NIB	Exc.	V.G.	Good	Fair	Poor
—	675	450	325	200	125

WILSON COMBAT

Berryville, Arkansas

UT-15 Urban Tactical

This semi-auto rifle is fitted with a 16.25" fluted barrel with tactical muzzlebrake. Flattop receiver. Aluminum handguard. Chambered for the .223 cartridge. Parkerized finish. Accepts all M-16/AR-15 magazines. Weight is about 6.5 lbs.

NIB	Exc.	V.G.	Good	Fair	Poor
1900	1700	1450	1100	900	500

NOTE: Add $100 for Armor-Tuff finish.

Tactical Hunter LW 6.8

Chambered for the Remington 6.8 SPC with 15-round magazine. Stainless lightweight match-grade 16- or 18-inch barrel. Forged upper and lower receivers. Enhanced bolt and carrier with NP3 coating. Wilson Combat Quadrail, Accu-Tac flash hider. Armor Tuff polymer finish in black, gray or tan. Collapsible stock.

NIB	Exc.	V.G.	Good	Fair	Poor
2000	1700	1450	1150	750	300

TACTICAL RIFLES

TPR-15 Tactical Precision Rifle

This model is fitted with a match-grade 18" fluted barrel. Free-floating aluminum handguard. Chambered for .223 cartridge. Weight is about 6.5 lbs. Parkerized finish.

NIB	Exc.	V.G.	Good	Fair	Poor
2500	2300	1950	1300	1100	600

NOTE: Add $100 for Armor-Tuff finish.

M-4T Tactical Carbine

This model features a 16.25" M-4 style heavy barrel with muzzlebrake. Flattop receiver. Chambered for .223 cartridge. Parkerized finish. Weight is about 6.5 lbs.

NIB	Exc.	V.G.	Good	Fair	Poor
1900	1700	1450	1100	900	500

NOTE: Add $100 for Armor-Tuff finish.

TL-15 Tactical Lightweight

Introduced in 2002, this flattop model features a match-grade 16.25" lightweight barrel with muzzlebrake. Aluminum handguard and fixed buttstock. Chambered for the .223 cartridge. Black Mil-Spec finish.

NIB	Exc.	V.G.	Good	Fair	Poor
1900	1700	1450	1100	900	500

NOTE: Add $100 for Armor-Tuff finish.

Super Sniper

Fitted with a 20" stainless steel match grade barrel with a 1 in 8 twist. Flat top receiver. Offered in Parkerized or Armor-Tuff finish.

NIB	Exc.	V.G.	Good	Fair	Poor
2350	2100	1800	1500	1150	600

NOTE: Add $100 for Armor-Tuff finish.

WINCHESTER REPEATING ARMS COMPANY

New Haven, Connecticut

The prices given here are for the most part standard guns without optional features that were so often furnished by the factory. These optional or extra-cost features are too numerous to list and can affect the price of a shotgun or rifle to an enormous degree. In some cases these options are one of a kind. Collectors and those interested in Winchester firearms have the benefit of some of the original factory records. These records are now stored in the Cody Firearms Museum, Buffalo Bill Historical Center, P.O. Box 1000, Cody, Wyoming (307) 587-4771. For a $25 fee the museum will provide factory letters containing the original specifications of certain Winchester models using the original factory records.

CAUTION: Buyers should confirm by Cody letter any special-order feature on any Winchester within the Cody record range before paying a premium for a scarce feature.

Hunt Repeating Rifle

Walter Hunt described his repeating rifle as the Volition Repeater. Hunt was granted U.S. patent number 6663 in August 1849 for his repeating rifle that was to pave the way for future generations of Winchester repeating rifles. Hunt's rifle design was unique and innovative as was his patent number 5701 for a conical lead bullet that was to be fired in his rifle. This ingenious bullet had a hole in its base filled with powder and closed by a disc with an opening in the middle to expel the ignition from an independent priming source that used priming pellets made of fulminate of mercury. The rifle actually worked but only the patent model was built; it is now in the Cody Firearms Museum.

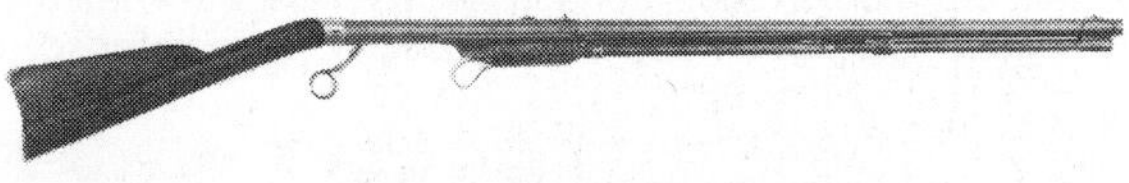

JENNINGS

Second in the evolutionary line of Winchester rifles is the Jennings. Made by Robbins & Lawrence of Windsor, Vermont, this rifle incorporated the original concept of the Hunt design with the additional improvements utilized by Lewis Jennings. The Jennings rifle is important not only as a link in the chain of repeating-rifle development but also because it introduced Benjamin Henry Tyler to the concept of the tubular magazine lever-action repeating rifle. The Jennings rifle was built in three separate and distinct models. While total production of the three types was contracted for 5,000 guns, it is probable that only about 1,000 were actually produced.

First Model

The First Model Jennings was built in a .54 caliber, breech-loading, single-shot configuration with a ring trigger, oval trigger guard, and 26" barrel. A ramrod was fixed to the underside of the barrel as well. This variation was made from 1850 to 1851.

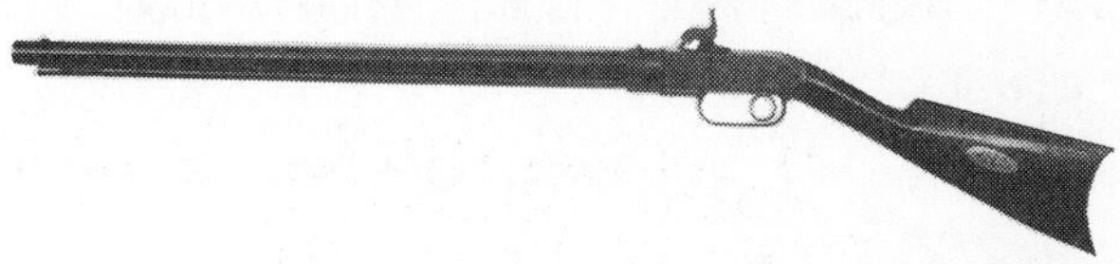

Courtesy Milwaukee Public Museum, Milwaukee, Wisconsin

NIB	Exc.	V.G.	Good	Fair	Poor
—	—	35000	25000	7000	1500

Second Model

The Second Model Jennings was produced adopting the improvements made by Horace Smith. This Second Model is a breech-loading repeating rifle with an under barrel magazine tube and a 26" barrel. The frame is sculpted, unlike the First Model. The ring trigger is still present, but the trigger guard was removed as part of the design change. The caliber remained a .54, and the rifle was fitted with a 25" barrel. The Second Model was produced in 1851 and 1852.

Courtesy Milwaukee Public Museum, Milwaukee, Wisconsin

NIB	Exc.	V.G.	Good	Fair	Poor
—	—	30000	20000	5000	1200

Third Model

The Third Model represents an attempt by investors to use the remaining parts and close out production. The .54 caliber Third Model was a muzzleloading rifle with a ramrod mounted under the barrel and a 26-1/2" barrel. The frame was the same as that used on the First Model, but the trigger was more of the conventional type. The trigger guard had a bow in the middle giving this model a distinctive appearance. This variation was produced in 1852 and marks the end of the early conceptual period in repeating rifle development.

NIB	Exc.	V.G.	Good	Fair	Poor
—	—	23500	9500	4500	1500

SMITH & WESSON VOLCANIC FIREARMS

An interesting connection in the evolution of the lever-action repeating firearm is found in the production of a small group of pistols and rifles built in Norwich, Connecticut, by Horace Smith and Daniel Wesson under the firm name of Smith & Wesson. The company produced a lever-action repeating rifle. These rifles are exceedingly rare with fewer than 10 having been built. They were chambered for the .528 caliber and were fitted with 23" barrels. Because of the small number of rifles built, no value is offered.

LEVER ACTION CARBINE

New Haven Arms introduced, for the first time, a Volcanic rifle that featured a full-length slotted magazine tube with a spring-activated thumbpiece follower that moved along the entire length of the magazine tube. These rifles were chambered for .38 caliber cartridge and were offered in three barrel lengths: 16", 20", and 24".

Courtesy Buffalo Bill Historical Center, Cody, Wyoming

16" Barrel

NIB	Exc.	V.G.	Good	Fair	Poor
—	40000	26000	16000	6000	2000

20" Barrel

NIB	Exc.	V.G.	Good	Fair	Poor
—	45000	23000	19000	8000	3000

24" Barrel

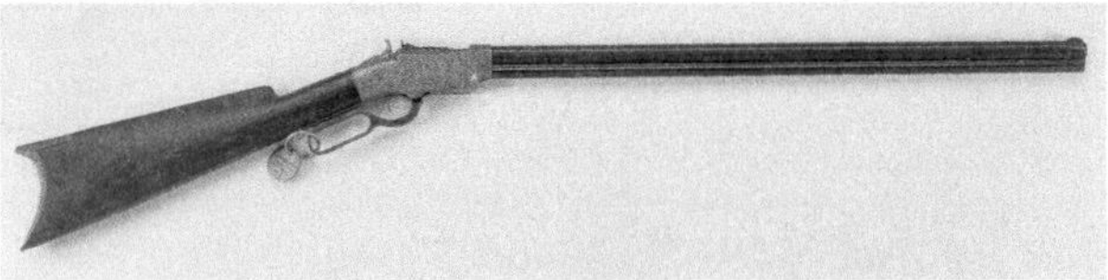

Courtesy Little John's Auction Service, Inc., Paul Goodwin photo

NIB	Exc.	V.G.	Good	Fair	Poor
—	55000	37000	22500	10000	3000

HENRY RIFLE

With the development of B. Tyler Henry's improvements in the metallic rimfire cartridge and his additional improvements in the Volcanic frame, the direct predecessor to the Winchester lever-action repeater was born. The new cartridge was the .44 caliber rimfire, and the Henry rifle featured a 24" octagon barrel with a tubular magazine holding 15 shells. The rifle had no forearm, but was furnished with a walnut buttstock with two styles of buttplates: an early rounded heel crescent shape seen on guns produced from 1860 to 1862 and the later sharper heel crescent butt found on guns built from 1863 to 1866. The early models, produced from 1860 to 1861, were fitted with an iron frame, and the later models, built from 1861 to 1866, were fitted with brass frames. About 14,000 Henry rifles were made during the entire production period; only about 300 were iron frame rifles.

Iron Frame Rifle

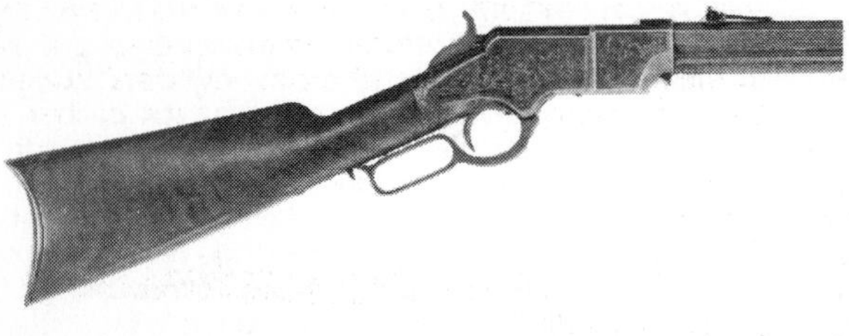

Courtesy Bonhams & Butterfields, San Francisco, California

NIB	Exc.	V.G.	Good	Fair	Poor
—	—	85000	65000	30000	13000

Brass Frame Rifle

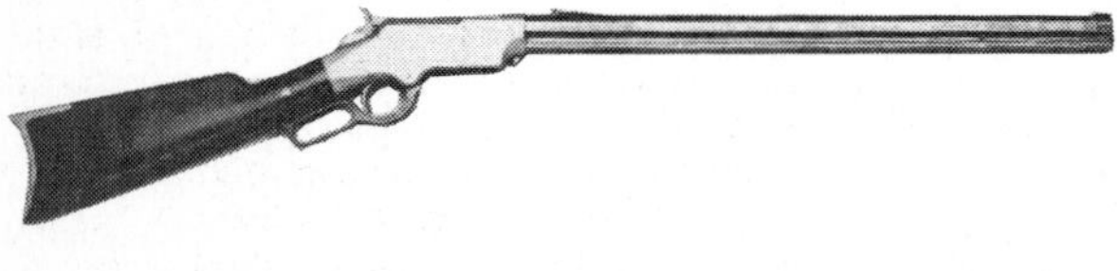

Courtesy Bonhams & Butterfields, San Francisco, California

NIB	Exc.	V.G.	Good	Fair	Poor
—	—	53000	37500	17500	9000

Martially Inspected Henry Rifles

Beginning in 1863 the Federal Government ordered 1,730 Henry Rifles for use in the Civil War. Most of these government-inspected rifles fall into serial number range 3000 to 4000 while the balance are close to this serial-number range. They are marked "C.G.C." for Charles G. Chapman, the government inspector. These Henry rifles were used under actual combat conditions and for that reason it is doubtful that there are any rifles that would fall into the excellent condition category. Therefore no price is given.

NOTE: There are many counterfeit examples of these rifles. It is strongly advised that an expert in this field be consulted prior to a sale.

NIB	Exc.	V.G.	Good	Fair	Poor
—	—	45000	34000	17500	12000

Winchester's Improvement Carbine

Overall length 43-1/2"; barrel length 24"; caliber .44 rimfire. Walnut stock with a brass buttplate; the receiver and magazine cover/forend of brass; the barrel and magazine tube blued. The magazine loading port is exposed by sliding the forend forward. This design was protected by O.F. Winchester's British Patent Number 3285 issued December 19, 1865. Unmarked except for internally located serial numbers. Approximately 700 manufactured in December of 1865 and early 1866, the majority of which were sold to Maximilian of Mexico. Prospective purchasers are strongly advised to secure an expert appraisal prior to acquisition.

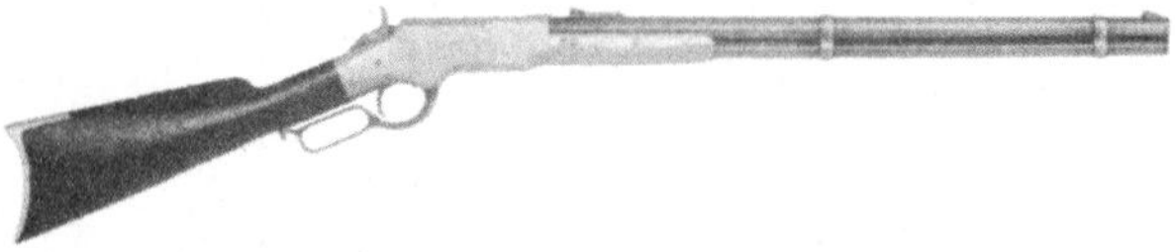

NIB	Exc.	V.G.	Good	Fair	Poor
—	35000	27500	19500	13000	9000

MODEL 1866

In 1866 the New Haven Arms Company changed its name to the Winchester Repeating Arms Company. The first firearm to be built under the Winchester name was the Model 1866. This first Winchester was a much-improved version of the Henry. A new magazine tube developed by Nelson King, Winchester's plant superintendent, was a vast improvement over the slotted magazine tube used on the Henry and its predecessor. The old tube allowed dirt to enter through the slots and was weakened because of it. King's patent, assigned to Winchester, featured a solid tube that was much stronger and reliable. His patent also dealt with an improved loading system for the rifle. The rifle now featured a loading port on the right side of the receiver with a spring-loaded cover. The frame continued to be made from brass. The Model 1866 was chambered for the .44 caliber Flat Rimfire or the .44 caliber Pointed Rimfire. Both cartridges could be used interchangeably.

The barrel on the Model 1866 was marked with two different markings. The first, which is seen on early guns up to serial number 23000, reads "HENRY'S PATENT-OCT. 16, 1860 KING'S PATENT-MARCH 29, 1866." The second marking reads, "WINCHESTER'S-REPEATING-ARMS.NEW HAVEN, CT. KING'S-IMPROVEMENT-PATENTED MARCH 29, 1866 OCTOBER 16, 1860." There are three basic variations of the Model 1866:

1. Sporting Rifle round or octagon barrel. Approximately 28,000 were produced.
2. Carbine round barrel. Approximately 127,000 were produced.
3. Musket round barrel. Approximately 14,000 were produced

The rifle and musket held 17 cartridges, and the carbine had a capacity of 13 cartridges. Unlike the Henry, Model 1866s were fitted with a walnut forearm. The Model 1866 was discontinued in 1898 with approximately 170,000 guns produced. The Model 1866 was sold in various special order configurations, such as barrels longer or shorter than standard, including engraved guns. The prices listed represent only standard-model 1866s. For guns with special-order features, an independent appraisal from an expert is highly recommended.

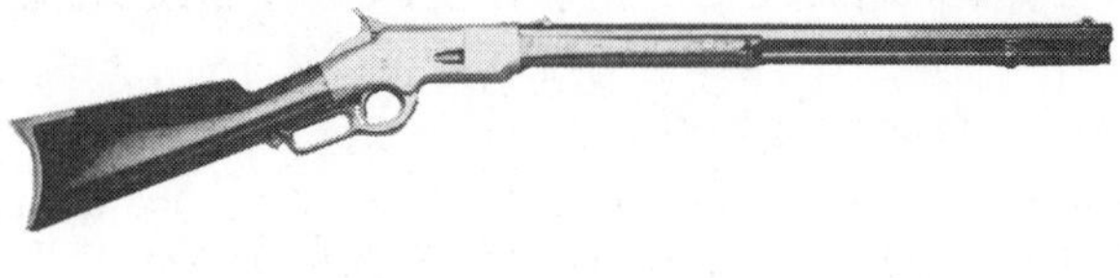

Courtesy Milwaukee Public Museum, Milwaukee, Wisconsin

First Model Rifle

This first style has both the Henry and King patent dates stamped on the barrel, a flat-loading port cover, and a two-screw upper tang. Perhaps the most distinctive feature of the First Model is the rapid drop at the top rear of the receiver near the hammer. This is often referred to as the "Henry Drop," a reference to the same receiver drop found on the Henry rifle. First Models will be seen up through the 15000 serial number range.

NIB	Exc.	V.G.	Good	Fair	Poor
—	45000	30000	19000	13000	4000

Carbine

NIB	Exc.	V.G.	Good	Fair	Poor
—	40000	26000	17000	11000	3000

Second Model Rifle

The second style differs from the first most noticeably in its single screw upper tang and a flare at the front of the receiver to meet the forearm. The Second Model also has a more gradual drop at the rear of the receiver than the First Model. The Second Style Model 1866 appears through serial number 25000.

NIB	Exc.	V.G.	Good	Fair	Poor
—	25000	19000	10500	7500	4000

Carbine

NIB	Exc.	V.G.	Good	Fair	Poor
—	25000	16000	9500	6750	3500

Third Model Rifle

The third style's most noticeable characteristic is the more moderately curved receiver shape at the rear of the frame. The serial number is now stamped in block numerals behind the trigger, thus allowing the numbers to be seen for the first time without removing the stock. The barrel marking is stamped with the Winchester address. The Third Model is found between serial numbers 25000 and 149000. For the first time, a musket version was produced in this serial-number range.

WINCHESTER CORPORATE AND DIVISIONAL NAME CHANGES 1931-1991

WINCHESTER REPEATING ARMS COMPANY
Dec. 22, 1931—Dec. 31, 1938

WINCHESTER REPEATING ARMS COMPANY
A Division of Western Cartridge Company
Dec. 31, 1938—Dec. 30, 1944

WINCHESTER REPEATING ARMS COMPANY
A Division of Olin Industries, Inc.
Dec. 30, 1944—January 1952

WINCHESTER-WESTERN DIVISION
Olin Industries, Inc.
January 1952—Aug. 31, 1954

WINCHESTER-WESTERN DIVISION
Olin Mathieson Chemical Corporation
Aug. 31, 1954—Sept. 1, 1969

WINCHESTER-WESTERN DIVISION
OLIN CORPORATION
Sept. 1, 1969—July 21, 1981

U.S REPEATING ARMS COMPANY
July 21, 1981—Present

NIB	Exc.	V.G.	Good	Fair	Poor
—	22000	15000	8000	5000	3000

Carbine

NIB	Exc.	V.G.	Good	Fair	Poor
—	25000	17000	9500	5500	3500

Musket

NIB	Exc.	V.G.	Good	Fair	Poor
—	12000	10000	8000	4500	2500

Fourth Model Rifle

The fourth style has an even less pronounced drop at the top rear of the frame, and the serial number is stamped in script on the lower tang under the lever. The Fourth Model is seen between serial number 149000 and 170100 with the late guns having an iron buttplate instead of brass.

NIB	Exc.	V.G.	Good	Fair	Poor
—	12000	10000	8500	4000	3000

Carbine

NIB	Exc.	V.G.	Good	Fair	Poor
—	18000	13000	11000	3500	2500

Musket

NIB	Exc.	V.G.	Good	Fair	Poor
—	14500	11000	8000	3500	2500

Model 1866 Iron Frame Rifle Musket

Overall length 54-1/2"; barrel length 33-1/4"; caliber .45 centerfire. Walnut stock with case hardened furniture, barrel burnished bright, the receiver case hardened. The finger lever catch mounted within a large bolster at the rear of the lever. Unmarked except for serial numbers that appear externally on the receiver and often the buttplate tang. Approximately 25 made during the early autumn of 1866.

Value speculative.

Model 1866 Iron Frame Swiss Sharpshooters Rifle

As above, but in .41 Swiss caliber and fitted with a Scheutzen style stock supplied by the firm of Weber Ruesch in Zurich. Marked Weber Ruesch, Zurich on the barrel and serial numbered externally. Approximately 400 to 450 manufactured in 1866 and 1867.

Value speculative.

Model 1867 Iron Frame Carbine

Overall length 39-1/4"; barrel length 20"; caliber .44 rimfire. Walnut stock with case hardened furniture; the barrel and magazine tube blued; the receiver case hardened. The finger lever catch mounted within the rear curl of the lever. Unmarked except for serial numbers that appear externally on the receiver and often the buttplate tang. Approximately 20 manufactured. Prospective purchasers are strongly advised to secure an expert appraisal prior to acquisition.

Value speculative.

Model 1868 Iron Frame Rifle Musket

Overall length 49-1/2" (.455 cal.), 50-1/2" or 53" (.45 and .47 cal.); barrel length 29-1/2" (.455 cal.) and 30-1/4" or 33" (.45 and .47 cal.); calibers .45, .455, and .47 centerfire. Walnut stock with case hardened or burnished bright (.45 and .47 cal.) furniture; the barrel burnished bright; the receiver case hardened or burnished bright (.45 and .47 cal.). The finger lever catch mounted on the lower receiver tang. The rear of the finger lever machined with a long flat extension on its upper surface. Unmarked except for serial number. Approximately 30 examples made in .45 and .455 caliber and 250 in .47 caliber.

Value speculative.

Model 1868 Iron Frame Carbine

Overall length 40"; barrel length 20"; caliber .44 centerfire. Walnut stock with case hardened furniture; barrel and magazine tube blued; the receiver case hardened. The finger lever catch as above. Unmarked except for serial numbers (receiver and buttplate tang). Approximately 25 manufactured.

Value speculative.

MODEL 1873

This Winchester rifle was one of the most popular lever-actions the company ever produced. This is the "gun that won the West" and with good reason. It was chambered for the more powerful centerfire cartridge, the .44-40. Compared to the .44 Henry, this cartridge was twice as good. With the introduction of the single-action Colt pistol in 1878, chambered for the same cartridge, the individual had the convenience of a pistol for protection and the accuracy of the Winchester for food and protection. The .44-40 was the standard cartridge for the Model 1873. Three additional cartridges were offered but were not as popular as the .44. The .38-40 was first offered in 1879 and the.32-20 was introduced in 1882. In 1884 the Model 1873 was offered in .22 caliber rimfire, with a few special order guns built in .22 extra long rimfire. Approximately 19,552 .22 caliber Model 1873s were produced.

Early Model 1873s were fitted with an iron receiver until 1884, when a steel receiver was introduced. The Model 1873 was offered in three styles:

1. Sporting Rifle, 24" round, octagon, or half-octagon barrel. Equipped standard with a crescent iron buttplate, straight-grip stock and capped forearm.
2. Carbine, 20" round barrel. Furnished standard with a rounded iron buttplate, straight-grip stock, and carbine style forend fastened to the barrel with a single barrel band.
3. Musket, 30" round barrel. Standard musket is furnished with a nearly full-length forearm fastened to the barrel with three barrel bands. The buttstock has a rounded buttplate.

The upper tang was marked with the model designation and the serial number was stamped on the lower tang. Caliber stampings on the Model 1873 are found on the bottom of the frame and on the breech end of the barrel. Winchester discontinued the Model 1873 in 1919, after producing about 720,000 guns.

The Winchester Model 1873 was offered with a large number of extra-cost options that greatly affect the value of the gun. For example, Winchester built two sets of special Model 1873s: the 1-of-100 and the 1-of-1000. Winchester sold only eight 1-of-100 Model 1873s, and 136 of the 1-of-1000 guns that were built. In 1991 a few of these special guns were sold at auction and brought prices exceeding $75,000. The prices listed here are for standard guns only. For Model 1873 with special features, it is best to secure an expert appraisal. Model 1873s with case colored receivers will bring a premium.

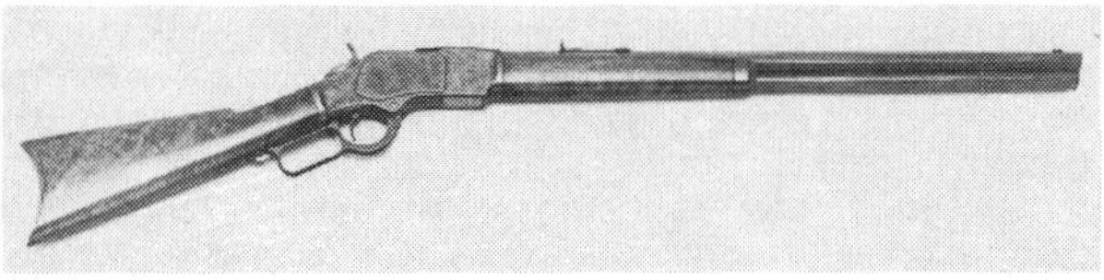

Courtesy Bonhams & Butterfields, San Francisco, California

First Model Rifle

The primary difference between the various styles of the Model 1873 is found in the appearance and construction of the dust cover. The First Model has a dust cover held in place with grooved guides on either side. A checkered oval finger grip is found on top of the dust cover. The latch that holds the lever firmly in place is anchored into the lower tang with visible threads. On later First Models, these threads are not visible. First Models appear from serial number 1 to about 31000.

NIB	Exc.	V.G.	Good	Fair	Poor
—	18000	15000	6000	3000	1400

Carbine

NIB	Exc.	V.G.	Good	Fair	Poor
—	22000	18000	7500	4000	2500

Musket

NIB	Exc.	V.G.	Good	Fair	Poor
—	14000	12000	5000	2500	1000

Second Model Rifle

The dust cover on the Second Model operates on one central guide secured to the receiver with two screws. The checkered oval finger grip is still used, but on later Second Models this is changed to a serrated finger grip on the rear of the dust cover. Second Models are found in the 31000 to 90000 serial number range.

NIB	Exc.	V.G.	Good	Fair	Poor
—	10000	8000	4000	2000	1250

Carbine

NIB	Exc.	V.G.	Good	Fair	Poor
—	15000	13000	7000	3000	1000

Musket

NIB	Exc.	V.G.	Good	Fair	Poor
—	5000	4000	2000	1250	900

Third Model Rifle

The central guide rail is still present on the Third Model, but it is now integrally machined as part of the receiver. The serrated rear edges of the dust cover are still present on the Third Model.

NIB	Exc.	V.G.	Good	Fair	Poor
—	6000	4000	2000	1000	750

Carbine

NIB	Exc.	V.G.	Good	Fair	Poor
—	12500	8000	5000	2000	800

Musket

NIB	Exc.	V.G.	Good	Fair	Poor
—	7000	2700	1500	850	500

Model 1873 .22 Rimfire Rifle

Winchester's first .22 caliber rifle and the first .22 caliber repeating rifle made in America was introduced in 1884 and discontinued in 1904. Its drawback was the small caliber. The general preference during this period of time was for the larger-caliber rifles. Winchester sold a little more than 19,000 .22 caliber Model 1873s.

NIB	Exc.	V.G.	Good	Fair	Poor
—	8000	6500	3000	1700	750

MODEL 1876

Winchester's Model 1876, sometimes referred to as the Centennial Model, was the company's response to the public's demand for a repeater rifle capable of handling larger and more potent calibers. Many single-shot rifles were available at this time to shoot more powerful cartridges, and Winchester redesigned the earlier Model 1873 to answer this need. The principal changes made to the Model 1873 were a larger and stronger receiver to handle more powerful cartridges. Both the carbine and the musket had their forearms extended to cover the full length of the magazine tube. The carbine barrel was increased in length from 20" to 22", and the musket barrel length was increased from 30 to 32". The Model 1876 was the first Winchester to be offered with a pistol-grip stock on its special Sporting Rifle. The Model 1876 was available in these calibers: .45-77 W.C.F., .50-95 Express, .45-60 W.C.F., .40-60 W.C.F. The Model 1876 was offered in four different styles:

1. Sporting Rifle, 28" round, octagon, or half-octagon barrel. This rifle was fitted with a straight-grip stock with crescent iron buttplate. A special sporting rifle was offered with a pistol-grip stock.

2. Express Rifle, 26" round, octagon, or half-octagon barrel. The same sporting rifle stock was used.
3. Carbine, 22" round barrel with full length forearm secured by one barrel band and straight-grip stock.
4. Musket, 32" round barrel with full-length forearm secured by one barrel band and straight-grip stock. Stamped on the barrel is the Winchester address with King's patent date. The caliber marking is stamped on the bottom of the receiver near the magazine tube and the breech end of the barrel. Winchester also furnished the Model 1876 in 1-of-100 and 1-of-1000 special guns. Only 8 1-of-100 Model 1876s were built and 54 1-of-1000 76s were built. As with their Model 1873 counterparts, these rare guns often sell in the $75,000 range or more. Approximately 64,000 Model 1876s were built by Winchester between 1876 and 1897. As with other Winchesters, the prices given are for standard guns.

First Model Rifle

As with the Model 1873, the primary difference in model types lies in the dust cover. The First Model has no dust cover and is seen between serial number 1 and 3000.

NIB	Exc.	V.G.	Good	Fair	Poor
—	17500	12000	6000	2750	1000

Carbine

NIB	Exc.	V.G.	Good	Fair	Poor
—	12000	9500	6500	2500	1000

Musket

NIB	Exc.	V.G.	Good	Fair	Poor
—	20000	19000	10000	5000	1500

Second Model Rifle

The Second Model has a dust cover with guide rail attached to the receiver with two screws. On the early Second Model an oval finger guide is stamped on top of the dust cover while later models have a serrated finger guide along the rear edge of the dust cover. Second Models range from serial numbers 3000 to 30000.

NIB	Exc.	V.G.	Good	Fair	Poor
—	11000	7500	4000	2000	1000

Carbine

NIB	Exc.	V.G.	Good	Fair	Poor
—	11000	7500	4000	2000	1000

Musket

NIB	Exc.	V.G.	Good	Fair	Poor
—	20000	15000	8000	1750	1000

Northwest Mounted Police Carbine

The folding rear sight is graduated in meters instead of yards.

Courtesy Little John's Auction Service, Inc., Paul Goodwin photo

NIB	Exc.	V.G.	Good	Fair	Poor
—	15000	9000	4500	2000	1250

NOTE: Deduct 50 percent from prices if factory records do not confirm NPW use. A Model 1876 NWP in excellent condition is very rare. Proceed with caution.

Third Model Rifle

The dust cover guide rail on Third Model 76s is integrally machined as part of the receiver with a serrated rear edge on the dust cover. Third Model will be seen from serial numbers 30000 to 64000.

NIB	Exc.	V.G.	Good	Fair	Poor
—	9000	5500	3250	1500	750

Carbine

NIB	Exc.	V.G.	Good	Fair	Poor
—	12500	8000	3000	2000	1250

Musket

NIB	Exc.	V.G.	Good	Fair	Poor
—	14000	10000	7500	4000	1000

Winchester Hotchkiss Bolt-Action Rifle

This model is also known as the Hotchkiss Magazine Gun or the Model 1883. This rifle was designed by Benjamin Hotchkiss in 1876, and Winchester acquired the manufacturing rights to the rifle in 1877. In 1879 the first guns were delivered for sale. The Hotchkiss rifle was a bolt-action firearm designed for military and sporting use. It was the first bolt-action rifle made by Winchester. The rifle was furnished in .45-70 Government, and although the 1884 Winchester catalog lists a .40-65 Hotchkiss as being available, no evidence exists that such a chamber was ever actually furnished. The Model 1883 was available in three different styles:

1. Sporting Rifle, 26" round, octagon, or half-octagon barrel fitted with a rifle-type stock that included a modified pistol grip or straight-grip stock.
2. Carbine, 24" round or 22-1/2" round barrel with military-style straight-grip stock.
3. Musket, 32" or 28" round barrel with almost full-length military-style straight-grip stock. Winchester produced the Model 1883 until 1899, having built about 85,000 guns.

First Model Sporting Rifle

This model has the safety and a turn button magazine cut-off located above the trigger guard on the right side. The Sporting Rifle is furnished with a 26" round or octagon barrel while the carbine has a 24" round barrel with a saddle ring on the left side of the stock. The musket has a 32" round barrel with two barrel bands, a steel forearm tip, and bayonet attachment under the barrel. The serial number range for the First Model is between 1 and about 6419.

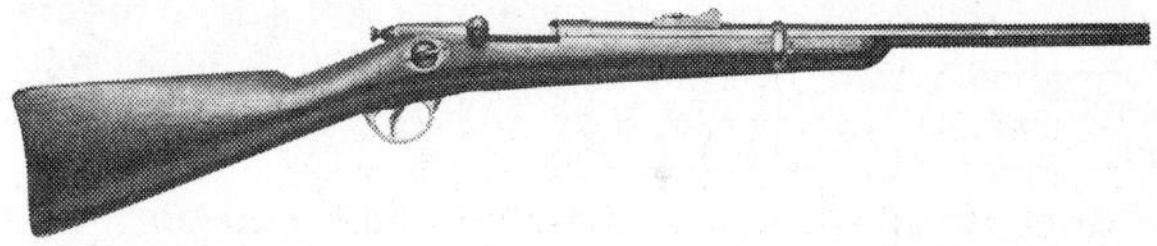

Courtesy Bonhams & Butterfields, San Francisco, California

Courtesy George Hoyem

NIB	Exc.	V.G.	Good	Fair	Poor
—	2000	1650	1250	800	400

Carbine

NIB	Exc.	V.G.	Good	Fair	Poor
—	5500	2500	1500	900	500

Musket

NIB	Exc.	V.G.	Good	Fair	Poor
—	2000	1650	1250	800	400

Second Model Sporting Rifle

On this model the safety is located on the top left side of the receiver, and the magazine cutoff is located on the top right side of the receiver to the rear of the bolt handle. The sporting rifle remains unchanged from the First Model with the above exceptions. The carbine has a 22-1/2" round barrel with a nickeled forearm cap. The musket now has a 28" barrel. Serial number range for the Second Model runs from 6420 to 22521.

Courtesy Milwaukee Public Museum, Milwaukee, Wisconsin

Courtesy George Hoyem

NIB	Exc.	V.G.	Good	Fair	Poor
—	1750	1400	900	600	300

Carbine

NIB	Exc.	V.G.	Good	Fair	Poor
—	1750	1400	900	600	300

Musket

NIB	Exc.	V.G.	Good	Fair	Poor
—	4500	2250	1000	750	500

Third Model Sporting Rifle

The Third Model is easily identified by the two-piece stock separated by the receiver. The specifications for the sporting rifle remain the same as before, while the carbine is now fitted with a 20" barrel with saddle ring and bar on the left side of the frame. The musket remains unchanged from the Second Model with the exception of the two-piece stock. Serial numbers of the Third Model range from 22552 to 84555.

NIB	Exc.	V.G.	Good	Fair	Poor
—	1650	1250	800	500	300

Carbine

NIB	Exc.	V.G.	Good	Fair	Poor
—	1650	1250	800	500	300

Musket

NIB	Exc.	V.G.	Good	Fair	Poor
—	1650	1250	800	500	300

MODEL 1885 (SINGLE-SHOT)

The Model 1885 marks an important development between Winchester and John M. Browning. The Single-Shot rifle was the first of many Browning patents that Winchester would purchase and provided the company with the opportunity to diversify its firearms line. The Model 1885 was the first single-shot rifle built by Winchester. The company offered more calibers in this model than any other. A total of 45 centerfire calibers were offered from the .22 extra long to the 50-110 Express, as well as 14 rimfire caliber from .22 B.B. cap to the .44 Flat Henry. Numerous barrel lengths, shapes, and weights were available as were stock configurations, sights, and finishes. These rifles were also available in solid frame and takedown styles. One could almost argue that each of the 139,725 Model 1885s built are unique. Many collectors of the Winchester Single-Shot specialize in nothing else. For this reason it is difficult to provide pricing that will cover most of the Model 1885s that the collector will encounter. However the prices given here are for standard guns in standard configurations.

The Model 1885 was offered in two basic frame types:

A. The High Wall was the first frame type produced and is so called because the frame covers the breech and hammer except for the hammer spur.
B. The breech and hammer are visible on the Low Wall frame with its low sides. This frame type was first introduced around the 5000 serial number range.

Both the High Wall and the Low Wall were available in two type frame profiles; the Thickside and the Thinside. The Thickside frame has flat sides that do not widen out to meet the stock. The Thickside is more common on the low wall rifle and rare on the High Walls.

The Thinside frame has shallow milled sides that widen out to meet the stock. Thinside frames are common on High Wall guns and rare on Low Wall rifles.

1. The standard High Wall rifle was available with octagon or round barrel with length determined by caliber. The butt stock and forearm were plain walnut with crescent buttplate and blued frame.
2. The standard Low Wall featured a round or octagon barrel with length determined by caliber and a plain walnut stock and forearm with crescent buttplate.
3. The High Wall musket most often had a 26" round barrel chambered for the .22 caliber cartridge. Larger calibers were available as were different barrel lengths. The High Wall Musket featured an almost full length forearm fastened to the barrel with a single barrel band and rounded buttplate.
4. The Low Wall musket is most often referred to as the Winder Musket named after the distinguished marksman, Colonel C.B. Winder. This model features a Lyman receiver sight and was made in .22 caliber.
5. The High Wall Schuetzen rifle was designed for serious target shooting and was available with numerous extras including a 30" octagon barrel medium weight without rear sight seat; fancy walnut checkered pistol grip Schuetzen-style cheekpiece; Schuetzen-style buttplate; checkered forearm; double set triggers; spur finger lever, and adjustable palm rest.
6. The Low Wall carbine was available in 15", 16", 18", and 20" round barrels. The carbine featured a saddle ring on the left side of the frame and a rounded buttplate.
7. The Model 1885 was also available in a High Wall shotgun in 20 gauge with 26" round barrel and straight-grip stock with shotgun style rubber buttplate. The Model 1885 was manufactured between 1885 and 1920 with a total production of about 140,000 guns.

CALIBER NOTE: As stated above it is difficult to provide pricing on specific rifles, especially calibers, because of the wide range of variables. However, the collector may find it useful to know that the most common rimfire calibers were the .22 Short, .22 WCF, and .22 Long, in that order, with the .22 Long Rifle a distant fourth. The most common centerfire chambers were the .32 WCF and the .32-40. Other popular centerfire calibers were the .38-55, .25-20, .44 WCF, .32 Long WCF, and the .45-70. There were a number of chamberings that are extremely rare (one of each built). It is strongly recommended that research is done prior to a sale.

Courtesy Bonhams & Butterfields, San Francisco, California

Standard High Wall Rifle

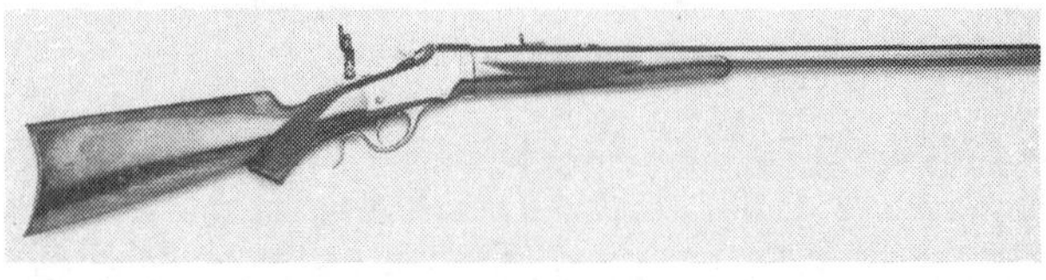

Deluxe High Wall

Courtesy Bonhams & Butterfields, San Francisco, California

NIB	Exc.	V.G.	Good	Fair	Poor
—	5000	3500	2200	1500	950

Standard Low Wall Rifle

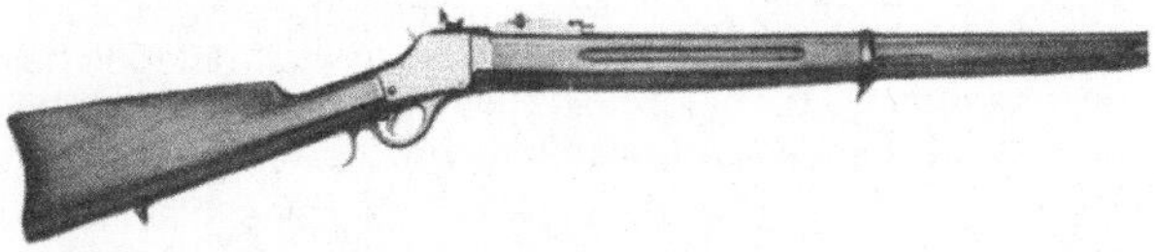

Courtesy Bonhams & Butterfields, San Francisco, California

NIB	Exc.	V.G.	Good	Fair	Poor
—	2500	1800	1200	1400	900

High Wall Musket

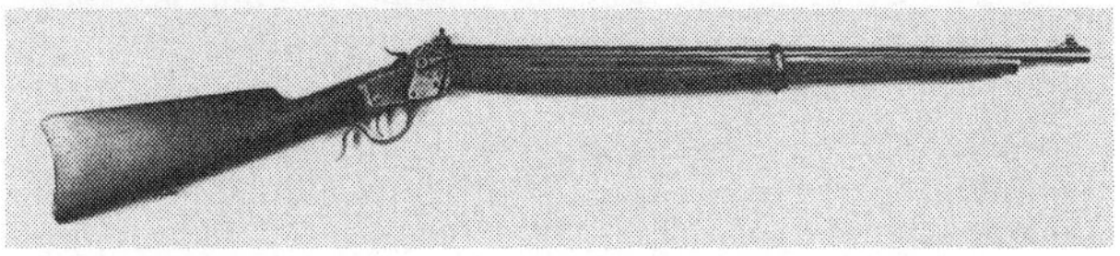

NIB	Exc.	V.G.	Good	Fair	Poor
—	2200	1500	1000	700	425

Low Wall Musket (Winder Musket)

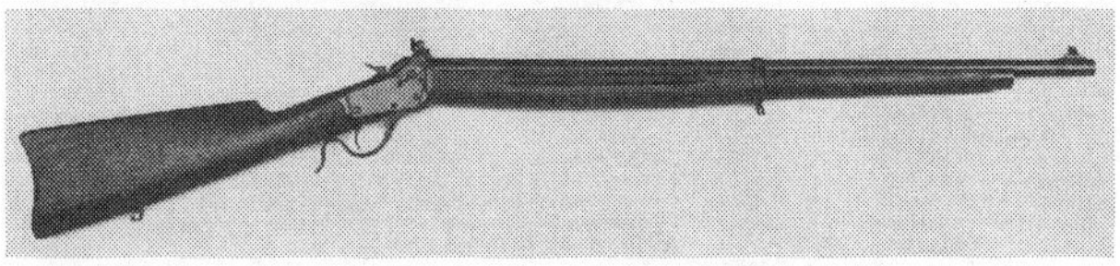

Courtesy Buffalo Bill Historical Center, Cody, Wyoming

NIB	Exc.	V.G.	Good	Fair	Poor
—	1700	1200	800	500	300

High Wall Schuetzen Rifle

NIB	Exc.	V.G.	Good	Fair	Poor
—	14000	7000	3000	1850	1000

Low Wall Carbine

NIB	Exc.	V.G.	Good	Fair	Poor
—	7500	5000	3500	2750	1500

High Wall Shotgun

Courtesy Buffalo Bill Historical Center, Cody, Wyoming

NIB	Exc.	V.G.	Good	Fair	Poor
—	4500	3000	2250	1250	850

NOTE: Model 1885s with case colored frames bring a premium of 25 percent over guns with blued frames. Model 1885s in calibers .50-110 and .50-100 will bring a premium depending on style and configuration.

MODEL 1886

Based on a John Browning patent, the Model 1886 was one of the finest and strongest lever-actions ever utilized in a Winchester rifle. Winchester introduced the Model 1886 in order to take advantage of the more powerful centerfire cartridges of the time.

Model 1886 rifles and carbines were furnished with walnut stocks, case hardened frames, and blued barrels and magazine tubes. In 1901 Winchester discontinued the use of case hardened frames on all its rifles and used blued frames instead. For this reason, case hardened Model 1886 rifles will bring a premium. Winchester provided a large selection of extra cost options on the Model 1886, and for rifles with these options, a separate valuation should be made by a reliable source. The Model 1886 was produced from 1886 to 1935 with about 160,000 in production.

The rifle was available in 10 different chambers:

.45-70 U.S. Government	.50-110 Express
.45-90 W.C.F.	.40-70 W.C. F.
.40-82 W.C.F.	.38-70 W.C. F.
.40-65 W.C.F.	.50-100-450
.38-56 W.C.F.	.33 W.C. F.

The most popular caliber was the .45-70 Government. Prices of the Model 1886 are influenced by caliber, with the larger calibers bringing a premium. The 1886 was available in several different configurations.

1. Sporting Rifle, 26", round, octagon, or half-octagon barrel, full or half magazine and straight-grip stock with plain forearm.
2. Fancy Sporting Rifle, 26", round or octago n barrel, full or half magazine and fancy checkered walnut pistol-grip stock with checkered forearm.
3. Takedown Rifle, 24" round barrel, full or half magazine with straight-grip stock fitted with shotgun rubber buttplate and plain forearm.
4. Extra Lightweight Takedown Rifle, 22" round barrel, full or half magazine with straight-grip stock fitted with shotgun rubber buttplate and plain forearm.
5. Extra Lightweight Rifle, 22" round barrel, full or half magazine with straight-grip stock fitted with a shotgun rubber butt-plate and plain forearm.
6. Carbine, 22" round barrel, full or half magazine, with straight-grip stock and plain forearm.
7. Musket, 30" round barrel, musket-style forearm with one barrel band. Military-style sights. About 350 Model 1886 Muskets were produced.

Sporting Rifle

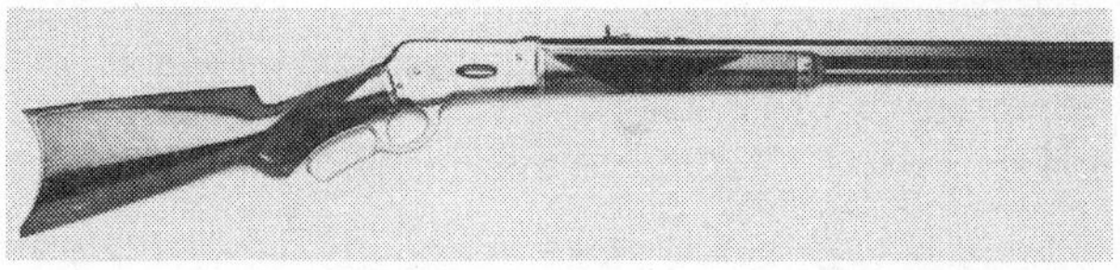

Courtesy Bonhams & Butterfields, San Francisco, California

NIB	Exc.	V.G.	Good	Fair	Poor
—	15000	15000	7500	5000	2500

Fancy Sporting Rifle

NIB	Exc.	V.G.	Good	Fair	Poor
—	25000	14500	8000	6000	3000

Takedown Rifle—Standard

NIB	Exc.	V.G.	Good	Fair	Poor
—	12500	900	4200	2000	700

Extra Lightweight Takedown Rifle—.33 caliber

NIB	Exc.	V.G.	Good	Fair	Poor
—	9000	5000	2000	750	400

Extra Lightweight Takedown Rifle—Other Calibers

NIB	Exc.	V.G.	Good	Fair	Poor
—	8750	6000	1800	1250	500

Extra Lightweight Rifle—.33 caliber

NIB	Exc.	V.G.	Good	Fair	Poor
—	6000	4000	1800	1000	500

Extra Lightweight Rifle—Other Calibers

NIB	Exc.	V.G.	Good	Fair	Poor
—	7000	5500	3000	950	500

Carbine

Courtesy Bonhams & Butterfields, San Francisco, California

Model 1886 carbine barrels are 22". A few were Trappers with 20" barrels. Add 50 percent if Trapper.

NIB	Exc.	V.G.	Good	Fair	Poor
—	19000	11000	7500	4500	2000

Musket

NIB	Exc.	V.G.	Good	Fair	Poor
—	19000	15000	9000	3500	1500

NOTE: For .50 Express add a premium of 20 percent. Case colored Model 1886s will bring a premium of 20 percent.

MODEL 71

When Winchester dropped the Model 1886 from its line in 1935, the company replaced its large-bore lever-action rifle with the Model 71 chambered for the .348 caliber. The Model 71 is similar in appearance to the Model 1886 with some internal parts strengthened to handle the powerful .348 cartridge. The rifle was available in three basic configurations:

1. Standard Rifle, 24" round barrel, 3/4 magazine, plain walnut pistol-grip stock and semi-beavertail forearm.
2. Standard Rifle (Carbine), 20" round barrel, 3/4 magazine, plain walnut pistol-grip stock and semi-beavertail forearm.
3. Deluxe Rifle, 24" round barrel, 3/4 magazine, checkered walnut pistol-grip stock and checkered semi-beavertail forearm. The frames and barrels were blued on all models of this rifle.
4. Deluxe Rifle (Carbine), 20" round barrel, 3/4 magazine, checkered walnut pistol-grip stock and checkered semi-beavertail forearm. The frames and barrels were blued on all models of this rifle.

The Model 71 was produced from 1935 to 1957 with about 47,000 built.

Standard Rifle

NIB	Exc.	V.G.	Good	Fair	Poor
—	1500	1200	800	400	300

Standard Rifle (Carbine)

NIB	Exc.	V.G.	Good	Fair	Poor
—	3250	2000	1600	1200	650

Deluxe Rifle

NIB	Exc.	V.G.	Good	Fair	Poor
—	3500	3050	800	525	425

Deluxe Rifle (Carbine)

NIB	Exc.	V.G.	Good	Fair	Poor
—	4100	3500	2000	1250	700

NOTE: For pre-war Model 71s add a premium of 20 percent. The pre-war Model 71 has a longer tang than its post-war equivalent. For a bolt peep sight add 10 percent.

MODEL 1892

The Model 1892 was an updated successor to the Model 1873 using a scaled down version of the Model 1886 action. The rifle was chambered for the popular smaller cartridges of the day, namely the .25-20, .32-20, .38-40, .44-40, and the rare .218 Bee.The rifle was available in several different configurations:

1. Sporting Rifle, solid frame or takedown (worth an extra premium of about 20 percent), 24" round, octagon, or half-octagon barrel with 1/2, 2/3, or full magazines. Plain straight-grip walnut stock with capped forearm.
2. Fancy Sporting Rifle, solid frame or takedown (worth 20 percent premium), 24" round, octagon, or half-octagon barrel with 1/2, 2/3, or full magazine. Checkered walnut pistol-grip stock with checkered capped forearm.
3. Carbine, 20" round barrel, full or half magazine, plain walnut straight-grip stock with one barrel band forearm. Carbines were offered only with solid frames.
4. Trapper's Carbine, 18", 16", 15", or 14" round barrel with the same dimensions of standard carbine. Federal law prohibits the possession of rifles with barrel lengths shorter than 16". The Model 1892 Trapper's Carbine can be exempted from this law as a curio and relic with a federal permit providing the trapper is an original trapper and left the factory with the short trapper barrel.
5. Musket, 30" round barrel with full magazine. Almost full-length forearm held by two barrel bands. Buttstock is plain walnut with straight grip.

The Model 1892 was built between 1892 and 1932 with slightly more than 1 million sold. The Model 1892 carbine continued to be offered for sale until 1941.

NOTE: Antique Winchester Model 1892s (pre-1898 manufacture) will bring a premium of 10 percent.

Sporting Rifle

Courtesy Bonhams & Butterfields, San Francisco, California

NIB	Exc.	V.G.	Good	Fair	Poor
—	5000	3500	1250	700	350

Fancy Sporting Rifle

Courtesy Bonhams & Butterfields, San Francisco, California

NIB	Exc.	V.G.	Good	Fair	Poor
—	12000	7500	4000	2500	1000

Carbine

Courtesy Bonhams & Butterfields, San Francisco, California

NIB	Exc.	V.G.	Good	Fair	Poor
—	3500	2500	1700	1200	600

Trapper's Carbine

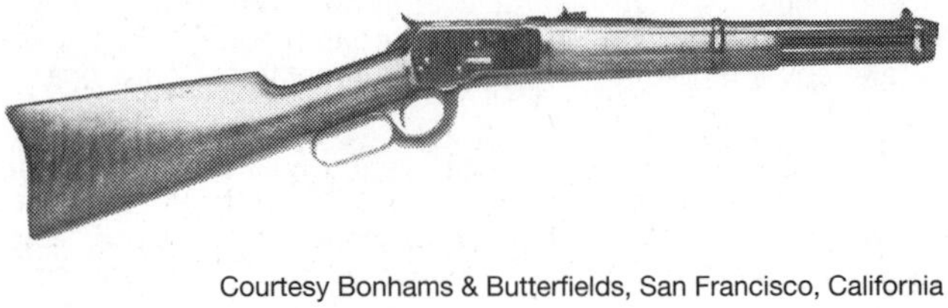

Courtesy Bonhams & Butterfields, San Francisco, California

NIB	Exc.	V.G.	Good	Fair	Poor
—	12000	8500	4000	2500	1250

NOTE: Add 20 percent for 15" barrel. Add 50 percent for carbines chambered for .25-20 cartridge.

Musket

NIB	Exc.	V.G.	Good	Fair	Poor
—	—	9500	4500	2500	1500

MODEL 1894

Based on a John M. Browning patent, the Model 1894 was the most successful centerfire rifle Winchester ever produced. This model is still in production, and the values given here reflect those rifles produced before 1964, or around serial number 2550000. The Model 1894 was the first Winchester developed especially for smokeless powder and was chambered for these cartridges: .32-40, .38-55, .25-35 Winchester, .30-30 Winchester, and the .32 Winchester Special. The rifle was available in several different configurations:

1. Sporting Rifle, 26" round, octagon, or half-octagon barrel, in solid frame or takedown. Full, 2/3 or 1/2 magazines were available. Plain walnut straight or pistol-grip stock with crescent buttplate and plain capped forearm.
2. Fancy Sporting Rifle, 26" round, octagon, or half-octagon barrel, in solid frame or takedown. Full, 2/3, or 1/2 magazines were available. Fancy walnut checkered straight or pistol-grip stock with crescent buttplate and checkered fancy capped forearm.
3. Extra lightweight Rifle, 22" or 26" round barrel with half magazine. Plain walnut straight-grip stock with shotgun buttplate and plain capped forearm.
4. Carbine, 20" round barrel, plain walnut straight-grip stock with carbine style buttplate. Forearm was plain walnut uncapped with one barrel band. Carbines were available with solid frame only. Carbines made prior to 1925 were fitted with a saddle ring on the left side of receiver and worth a premium over carbines without saddle ring.
5. Trapper's Carbine, 18", 16", 15", or 14". Buttstock, forearm, and saddle ring specifications same as standard carbine. All Model 1894s were furnished with blued frames and barrels, although case hardened frames were available as an extra-cost option. Case colored Model 1894s are rare and worth a considerable premium, perhaps as much as 1,000 percent. Guns with extra-cost options should be evaluated by an expert to determine proper value. Between 1894 and 1963, approximately 2,550,000 Model 1894s were sold.

NOTE: Antique Winchester Model 1894s (pre-1898 manufacture) will bring a premium of 10 percent. First year production guns, October 1894 to December 1894, documented by the Cody Museum will command a 100 percent premium.

First Model Sporting Rifle

Very early model that incorporates a screw entering the receiver over the loading port from the outside. Rare.

NIB	Exc.	V.G.	Good	Fair	Poor
—	7000	4000	2000	1250	500

Sporting Rifle

Courtesy Bonhams & Butterfields, San Francisco, California

NIB	Exc.	V.G.	Good	Fair	Poor
—	4000	3000	1500	850	450

NOTE: Takedown versions are worth approximately 20 percent more.

Fancy Sporting Rifle

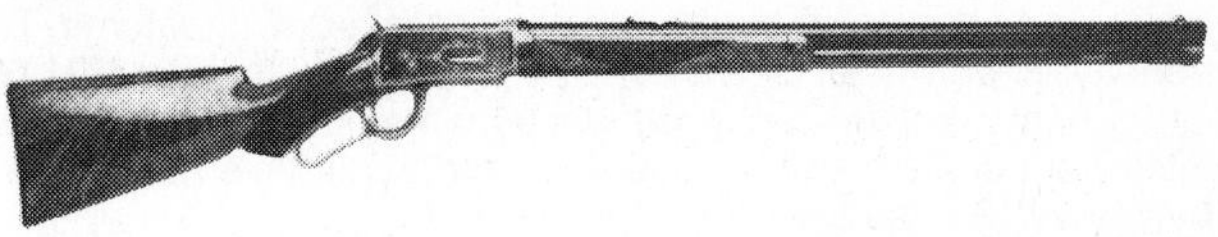

Courtesy Bonhams & Butterfields, San Francisco, California

NIB	Exc.	V.G.	Good	Fair	Poor
—	12000	7500	3500	2000	900

NOTE: Takedown versions are worth approximately 20 percent more. Fancy Sporting Rifles were also engraved at the customer's request. Check factory where possible and proceed with caution. Factory engraved Model 1894s are extremely valuable.

Extra Lightweight Rifle

Courtesy Bonhams & Butterfields, San Francisco, California

NIB	Exc.	V.G.	Good	Fair	Poor
—	5000	3500	1500	1000	450

Carbine

NIB	Exc.	V.G.	Good	Fair	Poor
—	3000	2000	600	400	200

NOTE: Above values are for guns with saddle rings. For carbines without saddle rings deduct 35 percent. Add 25 percent for carbines chambered for .25-35 or .38-55 cartridge.

Trapper's Carbine

Courtesy Bonhams & Butterfields, San Francisco, California

NIB	Exc.	V.G.	Good	Fair	Poor
—	6500	4250	2500	1500	700

NOTE: Add 30 percent for carbines chambered for .25-35 or .38-55 calibers.

Model 53

This model was in fact a slightly more modern version of the Model 1892 offered in these calibers: .25-20, .32-20, and the .44-40. It was available in only one style: the Sporting Rifle, 22" round barrel, half magazine, straight- or pistol-grip plain walnut stock with shotgun butt. It was available in solid frame or takedown with blued frame and barrel. The Model 53 was produced from 1924 to 1932 with about 25,000 built.

NIB	Exc.	V.G.	Good	Fair	Poor
—	3000	2000	1000	500	300

NOTE: Add 10 percent for takedown model. Add 40 percent for rifles chambered for .44-40 cartridge. A few of these rifles were fitted with stainless steel barrel in the early 1930s. If the black paint on these barrels is in good condition, they will bring a substantial premium.

Model 55

This model was a continuation of the Model 1894 except in a simplified version. Available in the same calibers as the Model

1894, this rifle could be ordered only with a 24" round barrel, plain walnut straight-grip stock with plain forend and shotgun butt. Frame and barrel were blued with solid or takedown features. This model was produced between 1924 and 1932 with about 21,000 sold. Serial numbers for the Model 55 were numbered separately until about serial number 4500; then the guns were numbered in the Model 1894 sequence.

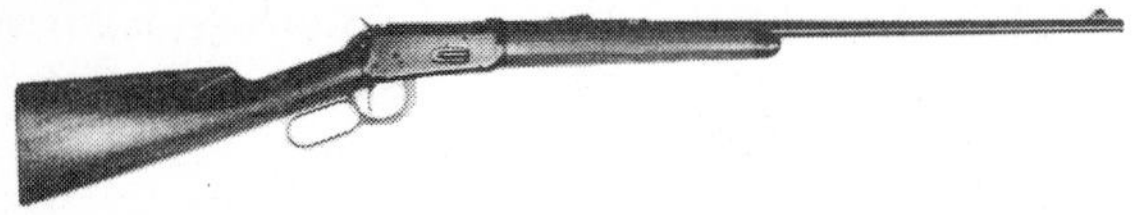

NIB	*Exc.*	*V.G.*	*Good*	*Fair*	*Poor*
—	1500	1000	650	450	200

NOTE: .25-35 caliber will bring about a 60 percent premium. Add 10 percent for models with solid frame.

Model 64

An improved version of the Model 55, this gun featured a larger magazine, pistol-grip stock, and forged front sight ramp. The trigger pull was also improved. Frame and barrel were blued. Chambered for the .25-35 Win., .30-30 Win., .32 Win. Special, and the .219 zipper added in 1938 (and discontinued in the Model 64 in 1941). Serial number of the Model 64 was concurrent with the Model 1894. Built between 1933 and 1957, approximately 67,000 were sold. This model was reintroduced in 1972 and discontinued in 1973. The values listed are for the early version only.

Courtesy Bonhams & Butterfields, San Francisco, California

NIB	*Exc.*	*V.G.*	*Good*	*Fair*	*Poor*
—	1200	900	500	300	200

Carbine

20" barrel.

NIB	*Exc.*	*V.G.*	*Good*	*Fair*	*Poor*
—	1550	1000	650	500	250

NOTE: For Deluxe model add 50 percent to above prices. For Carbine model add 50 percent to above prices. For rifles chambered for the .219 Zipper and .25-35 cartridges add 100 percent. Add 10 percent for bolt peep sight. Model 64s in .219 Zipper left the factory with bolt peep sights as original equipment.

Model 65

This model was a continuation of the Model 53 and was offered in three calibers: .25-20, .32-20, and .218 Bee. It had several improvements over the Model 53, namely the magazine capacity was increased to seven cartridges, forged ramp for front sight, and a lighter trigger pull. The Model 65 was available only in solid blued frame with blued barrel and pistol grip with plain walnut stock. Only about 5,700 of these rifles were built between 1933 and 1947.

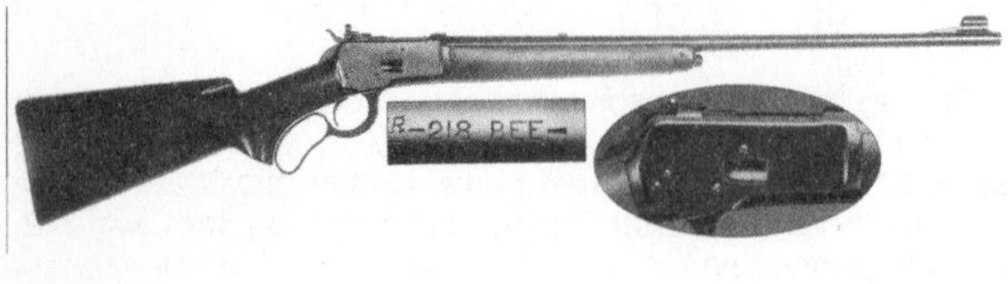

Model 65 in .218 Bee

NIB	*Exc.*	*V.G.*	*Good*	*Fair*	*Poor*
—	4000	3500	2000	1000	500

NOTE: Add 10 percent for bolt peep sight. Model 65s in .218 Bee left the factory with bolt peep sights as original equipment.

MODEL 1895

The Model 1895 was the first nondetachable box magazine rifle offered by Winchester. Built on a John M. Browning patent, this rifle was introduced by Winchester to meet the demand for a rifle that could handle the new high-power, smokeless hunting cartridges of the period. The Model 1895 was available in these calibers: .30-40 Krag, .38-72 Winchester, .40-72 Winchester, .303 British, .35 Winchester, .405 Government, 7.62 Russian, .30-03, and .30-06. The rifle gained fame as a favorite hunting rifle of Theodore Roosevelt. Because of its box magazine, the Model 1895 has a distinctive look like no other Winchester lever-action rifle. The rifle was available in several different configurations:

1. Sporting Rifle, 28" or 24" (depending on caliber) round barrel, plain walnut straight-grip stock with plain forend. The first 5,000 rifles were manufactured with flat-sided receivers, and the balance of production were built with the receiver sides contoured. After serial-number 60000, a takedown version was available.
2. Fancy Sporting Rifle, 28" round barrel, fancy walnut checkered straight-grip stock and fancy walnut checkered forearm. Rifles with serial numbers below 5000 had flat sided frames.
3. Carbine, 22" round barrel, plain walnut straight-grip stock with military-style hand guard forend. Some carbines are furnished with saddle rings on left side of receiver.
4. Musket:
   - A. Standard Musket, 28" round, plain walnut straight-grip stock with musket style forend with two barrel bands.
   - B. U.S. Army N.R.A. Musket, 30" round barrel, Model 1901 Krag-Jorgensen rear sight. Stock similar to the standard musket. This musket could be used for "Any Military Arm" matches under the rules of the National Rifle Association.
   - C. N.R.A. Musket, Models 1903 and 1906, 24" round barrel with special buttplate. Also eligible for all matches under "Any Military Arm" sponsored by the NRA. This musket was fitted with the same stock as listed above.
   - D. U.S. Army Musket, 28" round barrel chambered for the .30-40 Krag. Came equipped with or without knife bayonet. These muskets were furnished to the U.S. Army for use during the Spanish-American War and are "US" marked on the receiver.
   - E. Russian Musket, similar to standard musket but fitted with clip guides in the top of the receiver and with bayonet. Approximately 294,000 Model 1895 Muskets were sold to the Imperial Russian Government between 1915 and 1916. The first 15,000 Russian Muskets had 8" knife bayonets, and the rest were fitted with 16" bayonets.

The Model 1895 was produced from 1895 to 1931 with about 426,000 sold.

NOTE: Add a 10 percent premium for rifles built before 1898.

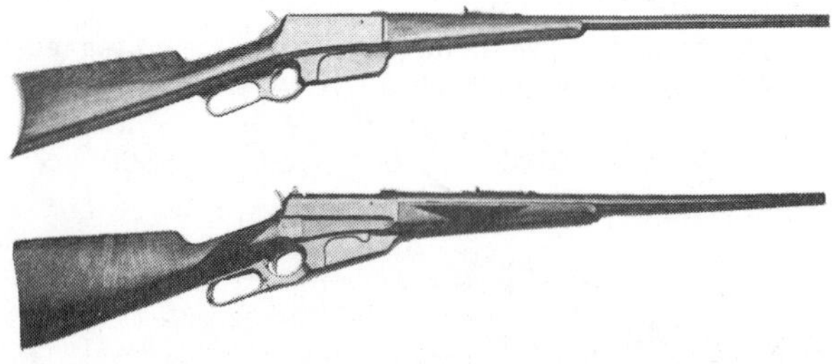

Courtesy Bonhams & Butterfields, San Francisco, California

Flat-side rifle

NIB	*Exc.*	*V.G.*	*Good*	*Fair*	*Poor*
—	5000	3000	1200	700	300

NOTE: Flat-side rifles will bring a premium of 100 percent. Takedown rifles will add an additional 15 percent.

Fancy Sporting Rifles

NIB	Exc.	V.G.	Good	Fair	Poor
—	7000	5000	1500	1100	500

NOTE: Flat-side rifles will bring a premium of 100 percent. Takedown rifles will add an additional 15 percent.

Carbine

Courtesy Bonhams & Butterfields, San Francisco, California

NIB	Exc.	V.G.	Good	Fair	Poor
—	5500	3250	1550	900	300

Standard Musket

NIB	Exc.	V.G.	Good	Fair	Poor
—	3200	1800	1000	600	300

U.S. Army N.R.A. Musket

NIB	Exc.	V.G.	Good	Fair	Poor
—	4500	2000	1200	800	400

N.R.A. Musket, Model 1903 and 1906

NIB	Exc.	V.G.	Good	Fair	Poor
—	5500	2500	1200	800	400

U.S. Army Musket

NIB	Exc.	V.G.	Good	Fair	Poor
—	5000	3000	1500	850	450

Russian Musket

NIB	Exc.	V.G.	Good	Fair	Poor
—	4000	2500	1000	500	250

Breechloading Double-Barrel Shotgun

Winchester imported an English-made shotgun sold under the Winchester name between 1879 and 1884. The gun was available in 10 and 12 gauge with 30" or 32" Damascus barrels. It was sold in five separate grades referred to as "classes." The lowest grade was the "D" and the best grade was called the "Match Grade." These were marked on the sidelocks. The center rib was stamped "Winchester Repeating Arms Co., New Haven, Connecticut, U.S.A." Prices shown for "D" grade. Add 10 percent for "C" grade; 20 percent for "B" grade; and 30 percent for "A" grade. About 10,000 of these guns were imported by Winchester.

Class A, B, C, and D

NIB	Exc.	V.G.	Good	Fair	Poor
—	2500	2250	1250	850	500

Match Gun

NIB	Exc.	V.G.	Good	Fair	Poor
—	5000	4000	1800	850	500

MODEL 1887 SHOTGUN

Winchester enjoyed a great deal of success with its imported English shotgun, and the company decided to manufacture a shotgun of its own. In 1885 it purchased the patent for a lever-action shotgun designed by John M. Browning. By 1887 Winchester had delivered the first model 1887 in 12 gauge and shortly after offered the gun in 10 gauge. Both gauges were offered with 30" or 32" Full choked barrels, with the 30" standard on the 12 gauge and 32" standard on the 10 gauge. A Riot Gun was offered in 1898 both in 10, and 12 gauge with 20" barrels choked cylinder. Both variations of the Model 1887 were offered with plain walnut pistol-grip stocks with plain forend. The frame was case hardened and the barrel blued. Between 1887 and 1901 Winchester sold approximately 65,000 Model 1887 shotguns.

Standard Shotgun

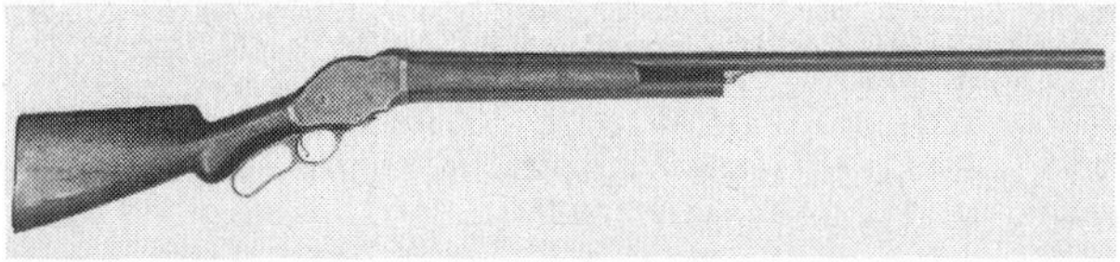

Courtesy Milwaukee Public Museum, Milwaukee, Wisconsin

NIB	Exc.	V.G.	Good	Fair	Poor
—	2500	1500	850	500	300

Riot Shotgun

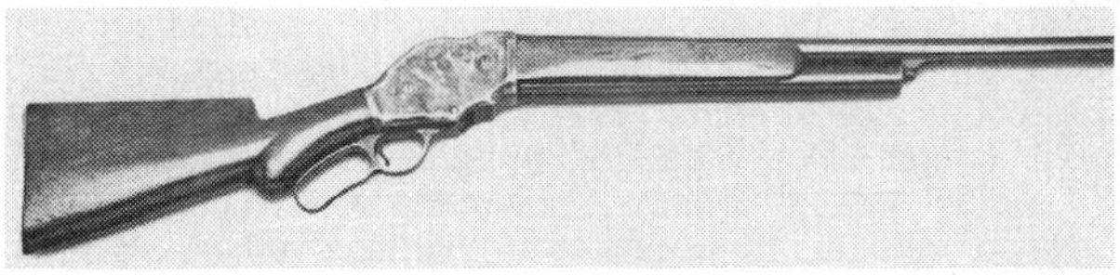

Courtesy Bonhams & Butterfields, San Francisco, California

NIB	Exc.	V.G.	Good	Fair	Poor
—	3000	2000	950	600	400

Model 1901 Shotgun

This model is a redesign of the Model 1887 shotgun and was offered in 10 gauge only with a 32" barrel choked Full, Modified, or Cylinder. The barrel was reinforced to withstand the new smokeless powder loads and the frame was blued instead of case hardened. The stock was of plain walnut with a modified pistol and plain forearm. The Model 1901 was built between 1901 and 1920 with about 65,000 guns sold.

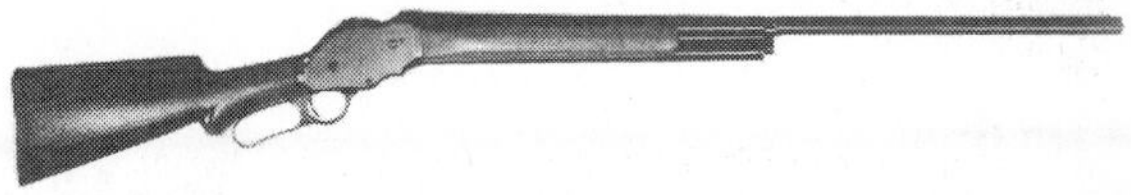

NIB	Exc.	V.G.	Good	Fair	Poor
—	1500	1000	600	400	250

Model 1893

This was the first slide-action repeating shotgun built by Winchester. It featured an exposed hammer and side ejection. Based on a John M. Browning patent, this model was not altogether satisfactory. The action proved to be too weak to handle smokeless loads, even though the gun was designed for black powder. The gun was offered in 12 gauge with 30" or 32" barrels choked Full. Other chokes were available on special order and will command a premium. The stock was plain walnut with a modified pistol grip, grooved slide handle, and hard rubber buttplate. The receiver and barrel were blued. Winchester produced the Model 1893 between 1893 and 1897, selling about 31000 guns.

Courtesy Bonhams & Butterfields, San Francisco, California

NIB	Exc.	V.G.	Good	Fair	Poor
—	1000	700	600	325	250

MODEL 1897

The Model 1897 replaced the Model 1893, and while similar to the Model 1893, the new model had several improvements such as a stronger frame, chamber made longer to handle 23/4" shells, frame top was covered to force complete side ejection, the stock was made longer and with less drop. The Model 1897 was available in 12 or 16 gauge with the 12 gauge offered either in solid or takedown styles and the 16 gauge available in takedown only. The Model 1897 was available with barrel lengths of 20",

26", 28", 30", and 32" and in practically all choke options from full to cylinder. The shotgun could be ordered in several different configurations:

1. Standard Gun, 12 or 16 gauge, 30" barrel in 12 gauge and 28" barrel in 16 gauge, with plain walnut modified pistol-grip stock and grooved slide handle. Steel buttplate standard.
2. Trap Gun 12 or 16 gauge, 30" barrel in 12 gauge and 28" barrel in 16 gauge, fancy walnut stock with oil finish checkered pistol-grip or straight-grip stock with checkered slide handle. Marked "TRAP" on bottom of frame.
3. Pigeon Gun, 12 or 16 gauge, 28" barrel on both 12 and 16 gauge, straight- or pistol-grip stock same as Trap gun, receiver hand engraved.
4. Tournament Gun, 12 gauge only with 30" barrel, select walnut checkered straight-grip stock and checkered slide handle, top of receiver is matted to reduce glare.
5. Brush Gun, 12 or 16 gauge, 26" barrel, Cylinder choke, has a slightly shorter magazine tube than standard gun, plain walnut modified pistol-grip stock with grooved slide handle.
6. Brush Gun, Takedown, same as above with takedown feature and standard length magazine tube.
7. Riot Gun, 12 gauge, 20" barrel bored to shoot buckshot, plain walnut modified pistol-grip stock with grooved slide handle. Solid frame or takedown.
8. Trench Gun, same as Riot Gun but fitted with barrel hand guard and bayonet.

The Winchester Model 1897 was a great seller for Winchester. During its 60-year production span, 1,025,000 guns were sold.

Standard Gun

NIB	Exc.	V.G.	Good	Fair	Poor
—	1300	850	650	300	200

Trap Gun

NIB	Exc.	V.G.	Good	Fair	Poor
—	1500	1200	800	500	400

Pigeon Gun

NIB	Exc.	V.G.	Good	Fair	Poor
—	1600	1300	800	750	400

Tournament Gun

NIB	Exc.	V.G.	Good	Fair	Poor
—	2000	1700	900	750	400

Brush Gun

NIB	Exc.	V.G.	Good	Fair	Poor
—	950	750	600	500	400

Riot Gun

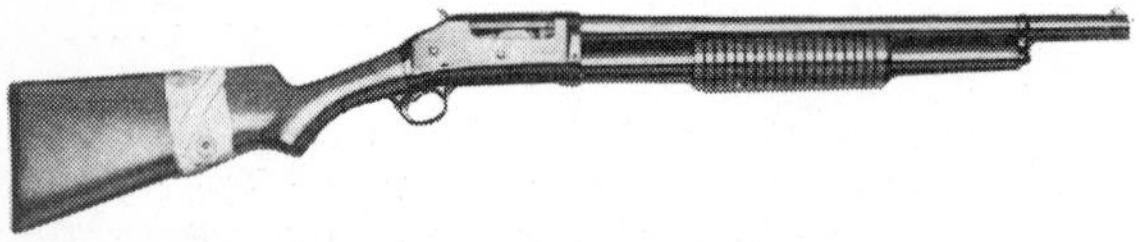

Courtesy Bonhams & Butterfields, San Francisco, California

NIB	Exc.	V.G.	Good	Fair	Poor
—	1600	1050	750	450	300

Trench Gun

Courtesy Bonhams & Butterfields, San Francisco, California

NIB	Exc.	V.G.	Good	Fair	Poor
—	3500	2900	2250	1500	600

NOTE: Add 100 percent for 16 gauge guns in excellent, very good, and good condition.

WINCHESTER-LEE STRAIGHT PULL RIFLE

U.S. Navy Musket

NIB	Exc.	V.G.	Good	Fair	Poor
—	2500	2000	1500	700	500

Commercial Musket

NIB	Exc.	V.G.	Good	Fair	Poor
—	2500	2000	1500	700	500

Sporting Rifle

Courtesy Amoskeag Auction Company

NIB	Exc.	V.G.	Good	Fair	Poor
—	2500	2000	1500	700	500

MODEL 1890

The Model 1890 was the first slide-action rifle ever produced by Winchester. Designed by John and Matthew Browning, this rifle was chambered for the .22 Short, Long, and Winchester Rimfire cartridges (the WRF cartridge was developed by Winchester specifically for the Model 1890) not on an interchangeable basis. In 1919 the .22 LR cartridge was offered as well. The rifle was a slide-action top ejecting rifle with an 18" under barrel magazine tube. All Model 1890s were furnished standard with plain walnut straight stocks with crescent buttplate and 12 groove slide handle. This rifle was one of the company's best selling small caliber firearms and was in worldwide use. The Model 1890 came in three separate and distinct variations that greatly affect its value:

1. First Model, solid frame, 24" octagon barrel, case hardened frame, and fixed rear sight. Approximately 15,552 of these First Model guns were produced, and their distinctive feature is concealed locking lugs and solid frame. Serial numbered on the lower tang only. Built from 1890 to 1892.
2. Second Model, takedown, 24" octagon barrel, case hardened frame, and adjustable rear sight. Serial numbered from 15553 to 112970 (on lower tang only) these Second Model guns feature the same concealed locking lugs but with the added takedown feature. A Deluxe version was offered with fancy walnut checkered straight- or pistol-grip stock and grooved slide handle.

2A. Second Model (blued frame variation), same as above but with blued frame. Serial numbered from 112971 to 325250 (on lower tang until 232328, then also on bottom front end of receiver) these blued frame Second Models are much more numerous than the case hardened variety. A Deluxe version was offered with fancy walnut checkered straight- or pistol-grip stock and grooved slide handle.

3. Third Model, takedown, 24" octagon barrel, blued frame, adjustable rear sight. Serial numbered from 325251 to as high as 853000 (numbered on both the lower tang and bottom front of receiver) the distinctive feature of the Third Model is the locking cut made on the front top of the receiver to allow the breech bolt to lock externally. A Deluxe version was offered with fancy walnut checkered stock, straight or

pistol grip with grooved slide handle. Winchester offered many extra-cost options for this rifle that will greatly affect the value. Secure an expert appraisal before proceeding. The Model 1890 was produced from 1890 to 1932 with approximately 775,000 guns sold.

First Model—Standard Grade

NIB	Exc.	V.G.	Good	Fair	Poor
—	9000	5000	2500	1250	750

Second Model—Case Hardened FrameStandard

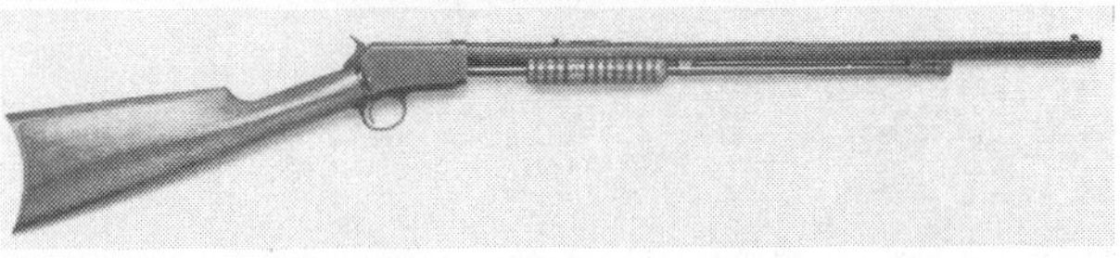

Courtesy Bonhams & Butterfields, San Francisco, California

NIB	Exc.	V.G.	Good	Fair	Poor
—	6000	3500	2000	1000	500

Deluxe

NIB	Exc.	V.G.	Good	Fair	Poor
—	10000	7000	3500	2000	1000

Second Model—Blued FrameStandard

NIB	Exc.	V.G.	Good	Fair	Poor
—	2500	1700	1500	750	250

Deluxe

NIB	Exc.	V.G.	Good	Fair	Poor
—	7500	5500	3000	1500	750

Third Model

Standard

NIB	Exc.	V.G.	Good	Fair	Poor
—	2000	1400	900	450	250

Deluxe

NIB	Exc.	V.G.	Good	Fair	Poor
—	6500	4000	2000	1000	750

NOTE: For Third Models chambered for .22 LR add 25 percent premium.

MODEL 1906

In 1906 Winchester decided to offer a lower-cost version of the Model 1890. The Model 1906 used the same receiver but was fitted with a 20" round barrel and plain gumwood straight-grip stock. When the Model 1906 was first introduced, it sold for two-thirds of the price of the Model 1890. For the first two years the gun was chambered for the .22 Short cartridge only. In 1908 the rifle was modified to shoot .22 Short, Long, and LR cartridges interchangeably. This modification ensured the Model 1906's success, and between 1906 and 1932 about 800,000 were sold. All Model 1906s were of the takedown variety. The Model 1906 is available in three important variations:

1. 22 Short Only, 20" round barrel, straight-grip gumwood stock and smooth slide handle. These were built from serial number 1 to around 113000.
2. Standard Model 1906, 20" round barrel, straight-grip gumwood stock with 12 groove slide handle. Serial numbered from 113000 to 852000.
3. Model 1906 Expert, 20" round barrel, pistol-grip gumwood stock with fluted smooth slide handle. Expert was available from 1918 to 1924 and was offered in three different finishes regular blued finish, half nickel (receiver, guard, and bolt), and full nickel (receiver, guard, bolt, and barrel nickeled).

.22 Short Only

Courtesy Bonhams & Butterfields, San Francisco, California

NIB	Exc.	V.G.	Good	Fair	Poor
—	2500	1750	750	500	200

Standard

Courtesy Bonhams & Butterfields, San Francisco, California

NIB	Exc.	V.G.	Good	Fair	Poor
2000	1500	750	400	400	200

Expert

Courtesy Bonhams & Butterfields, San Francisco, California

NIB	Exc.	V.G.	Good	Fair	Poor
—	2500	1850	950	500	300

NOTE: Prices are for half-nickel Experts. Add 10 percent for blued guns and 100 percent for full nickel.

MODEL 61

Winchester developed the Model 61 in an attempt to keep pace with its competitors' hammerless .22 rifles. The Model 61 featured a 24" round or octagonal barrel and could be ordered by the customer in a variety of configurations. Collector interest in this rifle is high because of the fairly large number of variations. The Model 61 is often considered a companion to the Winchester Model 12 and Model 42 shotguns.The following is a list of chamber and barrel variations found in this model:

1. 24" round barrel, .22 Short, Long, LR
2. 24" octagonal barrel, .22 Short only add 200 percent.
3. 24" octagonal barrel, .22 LR only add 200 percent.
4. 24" octagonal barrel, .22 W.R.F. only add 200 percent.
5. 24" round barrel, .22 LR Shot only add 300 percent.

5A. 24" round barrel, shot only Routledge bore add 300 percent.

6. 24" round barrel, .22 W.R.F. only add 200 percent.
7. 24" round barrel, .22 LR only add 200 percent.
8. 24" round barrel, .22 Winchester Magnum add 200 percent.
9. 24" round barrel, .22 Short only add 200 percent.

The Model 61 was fitted with a plain walnut pistol-grip stock with grooved slide handle. All Model 61s were of the take down variety. Pre-war models will have a short slide handle. Manufactured between 1932 and 1963, approximately 342,000 guns were sold.

Pre-war Model 61

NIB	Exc.	V.G.	Good	Fair	Poor
3000	1500	800	600	325	200

NOTE: Single caliber models will command a premium of 50 percent depending on caliber. Octagon barrel models will command a premium of 75 percent. .22 LR shot only models will bring a premium of 250 percent.

Post-war

Courtesy Bonhams & Butterfields, San Francisco, California

NIB	Exc.	V.G.	Good	Fair	Poor
—	2000	1200	800	450	250

Magnum

NIB	Exc.	V.G.	Good	Fair	Poor
—	1950	950	775	600	400

NOTE: This variation (Model 61 Magnum) was produced from 1960 to 1963.

MODEL 62 AND 62A

When the Model 1890 and Model 1906 were dropped from the Winchester product line in 1932, the company introduced the Model 62 to take their place. An updated version of the earlier slide-action .22 rifles, the Model 62 was fitted with a 23" round barrel and was capable of shooting .22 Short, Long, and LR cartridges interchangeably. Winchester offered a Gallery version of the Model 62 that was chambered for .22 Short only. Some of these Gallery guns have "Winchester" stamped on the left side of the receiver. Winchester Model 62 Gallery rifles have a triangular loading port on the loading tube that the standard models did not have. A change in the breech bolt mechanism brought about a change in the name designation from Model 62 to Model 62A. This occurred around serial number 98000. The letter "A" now appears behind the serial number. This model stayed in production until 1958, and collectors will concede a premium for guns built prior to WWII with small slide handles. The stock was of plain walnut with straight grip and grooved slide handle. Both the receiver and barrel were blued. All Model 62 and 62As were takedown. Approximately 409,000 guns were sold.

Pre-war

NIB	Exc.	V.G.	Good	Fair	Poor
2400	1750	850	400	250	150

NOTE: Barrels marked with Model 62 are worth more than barrels marked with Model 62A by approximately 15 percent. Gallery models will bring a premium of 300 percent.

Post-war

Courtesy Bonhams & Butterfields, San Francisco, California

NIB	Exc.	V.G.	Good	Fair	Poor
1300	600	450	325	225	125

Gallery

.22 Short only with triangular loading port & "winchester" stamped on side of receiver.

NIB	Exc.	V.G.	Good	Fair	Poor
3200	2000	1000	650	400	200

NOTE: A Model 62 with "winchester" stamped on the side of the receiver is more desirable than one without the stamping. Deduct 10 percent for Gallery rifles without this stamping.

MODEL 1903

The first semi-automatic rifle produced by Winchester was designed by T.C. Johnson. This rifle was offered in a takedown version only and was available in a 20" round barrel chambered for the .22 Winchester Automatic Rimfire. This ammunition is no longer produced and when found is very expensive. The tubular magazine is located in the buttstock and holds 10 cartridges. The rifle was available in two different configurations:

1. Standard Rifle, 20" round barrel, plain walnut straight-grip stock with plain forend. Steel crescent butt was standard.
2. Deluxe Rifle, 20" round barrel, fancy checkered walnut pistol-grip stock with checkered forearm. Manufactured from 1903 to 1932, about 126,000 were sold.

Standard Rifle

NIB	Exc.	V.G.	Good	Fair	Poor
—	850	550	325	200	100

Deluxe Rifle

Courtesy Bonhams & Butterfields, San Francisco, California

NIB	Exc.	V.G.	Good	Fair	Poor
—	1800	1100	700	500	250

NOTE: The first 5,000 guns were built without safeties, and the first 15,000 guns were furnished with bronze firing pins instead of steel. These early Model 1903s will bring a premium of 30 percent.

Model 63

The Model 63 took the place of the Model 1903 in 1933 in an attempt by Winchester to solve the problem of having to use a special .22 caliber cartridge in the gun to operate the blowback system. It is a very high quality semi-automatic rifle. Many collectors and shooters considered it the best rimfire semi-automatic rifle ever produced.The Model 63 was chambered for the .22 LR cartridge and was available in a 20" barrel for the first four years or until about serial number 9800. Thereafter, the model was offered with a 23" round barrel for the remainder of the production period. The gun was fitted with a plain walnut pistol-grip stock and forearm. The tubular magazine was located in the buttstock that came with a steel buttplate. The last 10,000 Model 63s were sold with a grooved receiver top to make the addition of a scope easier. Manufactured between 1933 and 1958, about 175,000 guns were sold.

20" Barrel

Courtesy Bonhams & Butterfields, San Francisco, California

NIB	Exc.	V.G.	Good	Fair	Poor
2750	1400	800	500	400	250

23" Barrel

Courtesy Bonhams & Butterfields, San Francisco, California

NIB	Exc.	V.G.	Good	Fair	Poor
1600	1000	700	600	400	200

NOTE: Grooved top receivers command a premium of 20 percent.

MODEL 1905

The Model 1905 was a larger version of the Model 1903, developed by T.C. Johnson to handle the more powerful centerfire cartridges. It was chambered for the .32 Winchester Self-Loading and .35 Self-Loading cartridges, loading by means of a detachable box magazine. Available in takedown only, this model was offered in two different styles:

1. Sporting Rifle, 22" round barrel, plain walnut straight grip (changed to pistol grip in 1908) stock with plain forend.
2. Fancy Sporting Rifle, 22" round barrel, fancy walnut checkered pistol-grip stock with checkered forend. This

model was the first Winchester semi-automatic rifle to fire centerfire cartridges. Produced from 1905 to 1920 with about 30,000 rifles sold.

Sporting

NIB	*Exc.*	*V.G.*	*Good*	*Fair*	*Poor*
—	700	550	350	175	125

Fancy Sporting

NIB	*Exc.*	*V.G.*	*Good*	*Fair*	*Poor*
—	900	750	500	200	150

MODEL 1907

The Model 1907 was an improved version of the Model 1905 and chambered for the new .351 Winchester Self-Loading cartridge. Outward appearance was the same as Model 1905 except for 20" round barrel. This rifle was available in three different styles:

1. Sporting Rifle, 20" round barrel, plain walnut pistol-grip stock with plain forend. Discontinued in 1937.
2. Fancy Sporting Rifle, 20" round barrel, fancy walnut checkered pistol-grip stock and checkered forend.
3. Police Rifle, 20" round barrel, plain walnut pistol-grip stock and beavertail forend. This version was fitted with a leather sling and with or without knife bayonet. First introduced in 1937. Winchester discontinued this model in 1957 after having sold about 59,000 guns.

NOTE: Post-WWII Model 1907s command a premium over the values shown below.

Sporting

NIB	*Exc.*	*V.G.*	*Good*	*Fair*	*Poor*
—	750	500	350	175	125

Fancy Sporting

NIB	*Exc.*	*V.G.*	*Good*	*Fair*	*Poor*
—	850	650	450	200	150

Police

NIB	*Exc.*	*V.G.*	*Good*	*Fair*	*Poor*
—	950	750	575	300	250

MODEL 1910

This model was similar to the Model 1907 but the action was made stronger to handle the new Winchester .401 Self-Loading cartridge. The specifications for this model are the same as the Model 1907. Built between 1907 and 1936, only about 21,000 of these guns were sold.

Sporting

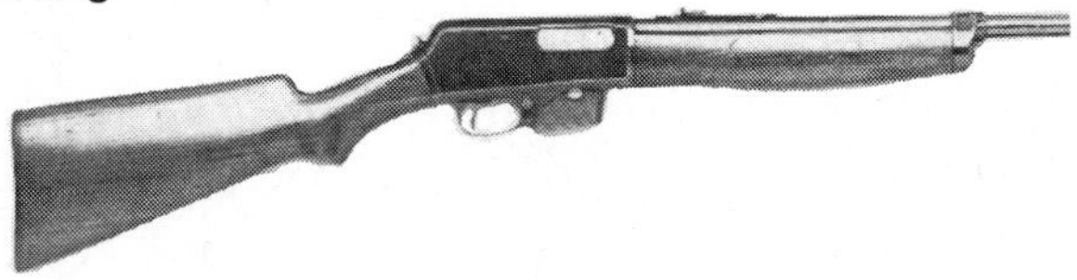

Courtesy Bonhams & Butterfields, San Francisco, California

NIB	*Exc.*	*V.G.*	*Good*	*Fair*	*Poor*
—	900	750	550	400	200

Fancy Sporting

NIB	*Exc.*	*V.G.*	*Good*	*Fair*	*Poor*
—	1000	800	600	450	250

Model 55 (Rimfire Rifle)

Not to be confused with the lever-action model, this .22 caliber rifle was a semi-automatic (auto-ejecting, actually) single-shot with a 22" round barrel. Fitted with a plain walnut pistol-grip one-piece stock and forend. The safety goes on when each cartridge is inserted into the chamber. This model was not serial numbered and was produced from 1957 to 1961 with about 45,000 guns sold.

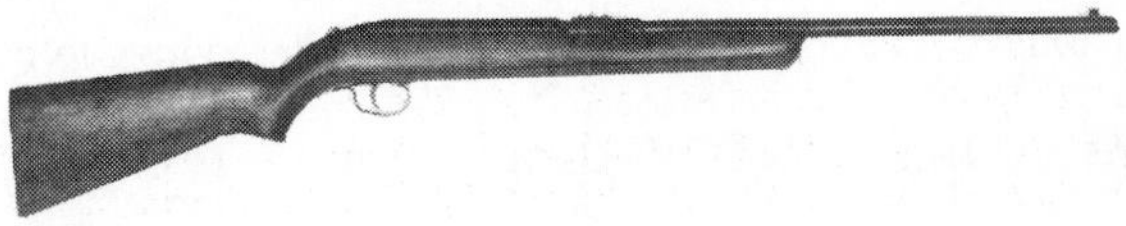

NIB	*Exc.*	*V.G.*	*Good*	*Fair*	*Poor*
—	400	350	225	150	75

MODEL 74

This was a semi-automatic chambered for either the .22 Short or the .22 LR. The rifle has a tubular magazine in the buttstock and a 24" round barrel. The bolt on this rifle was designed to be easily removed for cleaning or repair. The stock was plain walnut pistol-grip with semi-beavertail forend. A Gallery Special was offered that was chambered for the .22 Short and fitted with a steel shell deflector. This gallery model was also available with chrome trimmings at extra cost.

Sporting

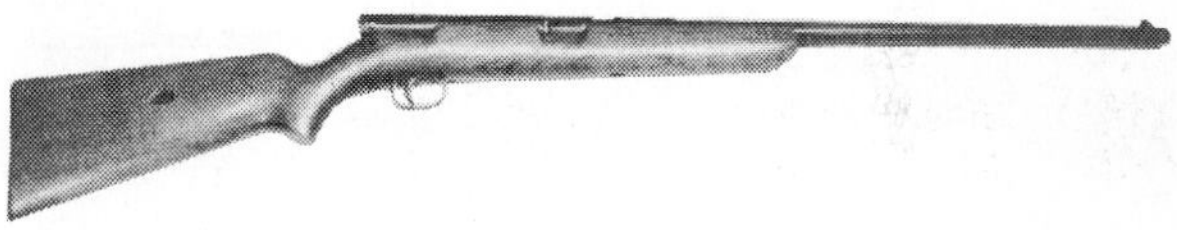

Courtesy C.H. Wolfersberger

NIB	*Exc.*	*V.G.*	*Good*	*Fair*	*Poor*
—	400	300	225	150	100

Gallery Special—.22 Short Only

NIB	*Exc.*	*V.G.*	*Good*	*Fair*	*Poor*
—	800	600	325	225	150

NOTE: For Gallery models with chrome trimmings, add a premium of 50 percent.

Model 77

This rifle was built on the blow-back design for semi-automatic rifles and is chambered for the .22 LR. It features a 22" round barrel and either a detachable box magazine or under barrel tubular magazine. The rifle has a trigger guard made of nylon. It has a plain walnut pistol-grip stock with semi-beavertail forend and composition buttplate. Built between 1955 and 1963, Winchester sold about 217,000 of these rifles.

NIB	*Exc.*	*V.G.*	*Good*	*Fair*	*Poor*
—	500	375	250	175	75

NOTE: Models with tubular magazines will bring a premium of 10 percent to 20 percent.

MODEL 100

This rifle is a gas operated semi-automatic and chambered for the .243, .308, and .284 caliber cartridges. The Model 100 was the first commercial Winchester self-loading, centerfire rifle made since the Winchester Model 1905, the Model 1907, and the Model 1910. These models were produced until 1936/37. Winchester did produce the M1 Carbine during WWII. It was available in a rifle version with a 22" round barrel and a carbine version with a 19" barrel. Both were furnished with a detachable box magazine. The stock was a one-piece design with pistol grip and was offered in either hand-cut checkering or pressed basket weave checkering. Rifles were introduced in 1960 and the carbine in 1967. The Model 100 was last produced in 1973 with about 263,000 guns sold.

Rifle

NIB	Exc.	V.G.	Good	Fair	Poor
—	600	475	350	250	200

NOTE: Pre-1964 models 15 percent premium. Prices given are for .308 caliber; for .243 add 15 percent, for .284 add 20 percent.

Carbine

Only about 53,000 carbines were made, about one for every five rifles.

NIB	Exc.	V.G.	Good	Fair	Poor
—	675	525	400	325	225

NOTE: Add 25 percent premium for .243, and 100 percent for .284.

Model 88 "Centennial Model" (1855/1955)

The Model 88 was a modern short-stroke lever-action chambered for the .243, .308, 284, and .358 calibers. It was available in a rifle version with 22" round barrel and a carbine version with 19" round barrel. The carbine model was not chambered for the .358 cartridge. Both were furnished with a detachable box magazine. The stock was a one-piece design with pistol grip and was offered with hand-cut checkering or pressed basket weave checkering after 1964. The rifle was introduced in 1955 and the carbine was first offered in 1968. Both versions were discontinued in 1973 with about 283,000 sold.

Rifle

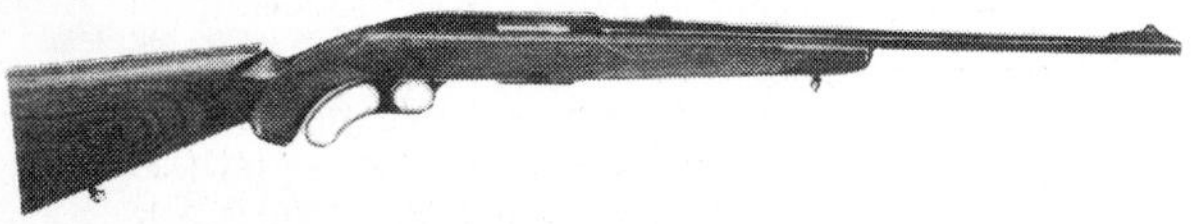

NIB	Exc.	V.G.	Good	Fair	Poor
—	900	750	500	300	250

NOTE: Pre-1964 models add 25 percent premium. Prices above are for .308 caliber; for .243 add 15 percent, .284 add 75 percent, and for 358 add 100 percent. This model was offered with no front or rear sights (Gopher Special) for a few years prior to 1962. Add 100 percent for this variant. Beware of fakes.

Carbine

Only 28,000 carbines were built, about 1 for every 10 rifles. Rarely encountered.

NIB	Exc.	V.G.	Good	Fair	Poor
—	1300	1150	900	650	300

NOTE: Add 25 percent for .243, add 100 percent for .284 calibers. The carbine was not offered in .358 caliber.

Model 99 or Thumb Trigger

This rifle was a modification of the Model 1902 without a traditional trigger. The rifle was fired by depressing the trigger with the thumb, which was part of the sear and extractor located behind the bolt. The rifle was chambered for the .22 Short and Long until 1914 when it was also chambered for the .22 Extra Long. All cartridges could be shot interchangeably. The stock was the same as the Model 1902, Gumwood stained walnut, without the trigger or trigger guard. This model was not serial numbered. Built between 1904 and 1923. Winchester sold about 76,000 rifles.

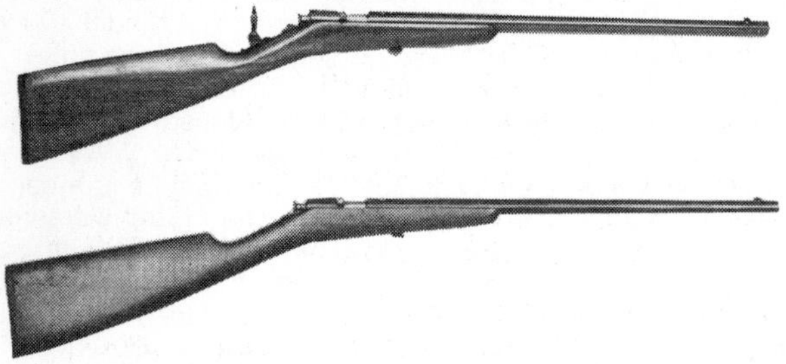

Courtesy Bonhams & Butterfields, San Francisco, California

NIB	Exc.	V.G.	Good	Fair	Poor
—	3500	2000	1000	700	500

Model 1900

This single-shot bolt-action .22 caliber rifle was based on a John M. Browning design. The rifle was furnished with an 18" round barrel and chambered for the .22 Short and Long interchangeably. The stock was a one-piece plain gumwood straight grip without a buttplate. The rifle was not serial numbered. It was produced from 1899 to 1902 with about 105,000 sold.

Courtesy Buffalo Bill Historical Center, Cody, Wyoming

NIB	Exc.	V.G.	Good	Fair	Poor
—	2000	1000	450	300	200

Model 1902

Also a single-shot, this model was of the same general design as the Model 1900 with several improvements: a special shaped metal trigger guard was added, a shorter trigger pull, a steel buttplate, a rear peep sight, and the barrel was made heavier at the muzzle. The rifle was chambered for the .22 Short and Long cartridges until 1914 when the .22 Extra Long was added. In 1927 the .22 Extra Long was dropped in favor of the more popular .22 LR. All of these cartridges were interchangeable. The stock was a one-piece plain gumwood with straight grip (the metal trigger guard added a pistol grip feel) and steel buttplate, which was changed to composition in 1907. This model was not serial numbered. About 640,000 Model 1902s were sold between 1902 and 1931 when it was discontinued.

NIB	Exc.	V.G.	Good	Fair	Poor
—	1000	750	400	225	125

Model 1904

This model was a slightly more expensive version of the Model 1902. It featured a 21" round barrel, a one-piece plain gumwood straight-grip stock (the metal trigger guard gave the rifle a pistol grip feel) with a small lip on the forend. Rifle was chambered for the .22 Short and Long until 1914 when the .22 Extra Long was added. The .22 LR cartridge was added in place of the Extra Long in 1927. This model was not serial numbered. Produced between 1904 and 1931, about 303,000 rifles were sold.

NIB	Exc.	V.G.	Good	Fair	Poor
—	850	600	350	200	100

Model D Military Rifle

Overall length 46-3/8"; barrel length 26"; caliber 7.62mm. Walnut stock with blued barrel, receiver, magazine housing and furniture. Receiver ring over barrel breech stamped with serial number and Winchester proofmark. A total of 500 Model D Rifles were shipped to Russia for trial in March of 1917.

Value speculative.

Imperial Bolt-Action Magazine Rifle (Model 51)

Designed by T.C. Johnson, approximately 25 of these rifles were made during 1919 and 1920 in two different styles and three calibers. The takedown variation has an overall length of 42-1/4", barrel length 22" and was made in .27, .30-06 and .35 Newton calibers. The solid frame version is identical in form, dimensions and calibers. Sight configurations and markings vary.

Value speculative.

MODEL 43

Introduced in 1949, this rifle was chambered for the .218 Bee, .22 Hornet, .25-20 Winchester, and the .32-20 Winchester. The rifle was a bolt-action with detachable box magazine, fitted with a 24" round barrel and front sight ramp forged integrally with barrel. **This model was not drilled and tapped for scope blocks except for a few late rifles.** This model was available in two styles:

1. Standard Rifle, 24" round barrel, plain walnut pistol-grip stock and forend. One inch sling swivels are standard.
2. Special Rifle, 24" round barrel, select walnut checkered pistol-grip stock and checkered forend. Furnished with either open sporting rear sight or Lyman 57A micrometer receiver sight.

The Model 43 was produced from 1949 to 1957 with about 63,000 sold.

Standard

NIB	*Exc.*	*V.G.*	*Good*	*Fair*	*Poor*
—	800	700	550	300	200

Special or Deluxe

NIB	*Exc.*	*V.G.*	*Good*	*Fair*	*Poor*
—	1000	850	675	450	175

NOTE: For rifles chambered for .25-20 and .32-20 add a 50 percent premium. For rifles with non-factory drilled and tapped scope holes deduct 40 percent.

Model 47

This model was a single-shot bolt-action rifle chambered for the .22 Short, Long, and LR interchangeably. The rifle was furnished with a 25" round barrel, plain walnut pistol-grip stock and forend. The bolt, bolt handle, and trigger are chrome plated. This model has a special bolt with a post on the underside. This moves into the safety position when the bolt is closed.This model was not serial numbered. Produced between 1948 and 1954, Winchester sold about 43,000 guns.

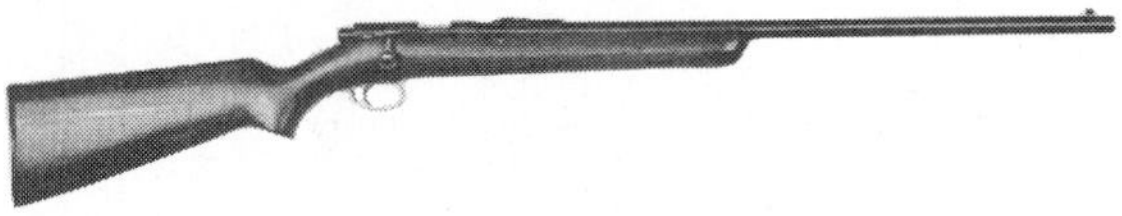

Courtesy Buffalo Bill Historical Center, Cody, Wyoming

NIB	*Exc.*	*V.G.*	*Good*	*Fair*	*Poor*
—	450	350	250	200	150

Model 47 Target Rifle

Fitted with a 28" round standard weight or heavyweight barrel, plain walnut modified pistol-grip stock with correct bolt.

NIB	*Exc.*	*V.G.*	*Good*	*Fair*	*Poor*
—	750	600	450	250	150

NOTE: Add 10 percent premium for Model 47 with factory peep sight.

MODEL 52

EDITOR'S COMMENT: According to Winchester factory records, Model 52 barrels were, "originally drilled and tapped for Winchester telescope bases designed for use with the Winchester 3A, 5A, and Lyman telescopes." These bases had a 6.2" center-to-center spacing ... a change in the bases and the spacing to be used was authorized on January 11, 1933. These new bases had a specially shaped Fecker-type notch added on the right-hand side of both bases. They are known as Winchester Combination Telescope Sight Bases and are satisfactory for use with Winchester, Lyman, Fecker, and Unertl telescopes. Bases are spaced 7.2" center to center ... All Model 52 targets were factory drilled for scope mounting but only the "C" series Sporters were factory drilled for scopes. One of the finest small-caliber bolt-action rifles ever built, the Model 52 was Winchester's answer to the increased demand for a military-style target rifle following WWI. The Model 52 was a well-made quality-built bolt-action rifle. The rifle was chambered for the .22 LR cartridge. Designed by T.C. Johnson, this rifle was built in several different configurations over its production life:

1. Model 52 with finger groove in forend and one barrel band. Produced from 1920 to 1929.
2. Model 52 Target Rifle, same as above but without finger groove in forend and has first speed lock. Made from 1929 to 1932.
3. Model 52A Target Rifle, same as above with addition of reinforced receiver and locking lug. Made from 1932 to 1935.
4. Model 52B Target Rifle, same as above with addition of adjustable sling swivel and single-shot adaptor. Made from 1935 to 1947.
5. Model 52C Target Rifle, same as above with addition of an easily adjustable vibration-free trigger mechanism. Made from 1947 to 1961.
6. Model 52D Target Rifle, this is a single-shot rifle with free-floating barrel and new design stock with adjustable hand-stop channel.
7. Model 52 Bull Gun, same as target rifle but fitted with extra heavyweight barrel. Made from 1939 to 1960. The Bull Barrel measures 1.125" at the receiver juncture while the heavyweight measures 1". Both barrels measure .875" at the muzzle.
8. Model 52 International Match, a free-style stock with thumb hole and adjustable buttstock and forend introduced in 1969. International Prone model with no thumb hole or adjustable buttplate and forend was introduced in 1975. Both discontinued in 1980.
9. Model 52 Sporter, 24" round barrel, select walnut checkered pistol-grip stock with cheekpiece and forend with black plastic tip. Pistol grip was furnished with hard-rubber grip cap. The Model 52 Sporter was introduced in 1934 and discontinued in 1958. It went through the same improvements as the Target Rifle, thus the designation Model 52A Sporter, etc.

Standard

NIB	*Exc.*	*V.G.*	*Good*	*Fair*	*Poor*
—	1250	1000	750	250	300

Target

Courtesy Rock Island Auction Company

NIB	*Exc.*	*V.G.*	*Good*	*Fair*	*Poor*
—	1750	1500	1150	900	350

Target—Speed Lock

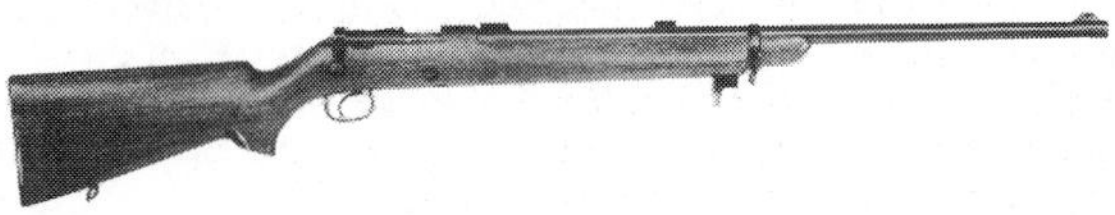

NIB	*Exc.*	*V.G.*	*Good*	*Fair*	*Poor*
—	1700	1400	1050	900	350

Model 52A Target Heavy Barrel—Rare

NIB	*Exc.*	*V.G.*	*Good*	*Fair*	*Poor*
—	1700	1400	1050	900	350

Model 52B Target Heavy & Standard Barrel

NIB	*Exc.*	*V.G.*	*Good*	*Fair*	*Poor*
—	1500	1300	950	700	300

Model 52B Target Bull Barrel

NIB	*Exc.*	*V.G.*	*Good*	*Fair*	*Poor*
—	1700	1400	1050	900	350

Model 52C Target

Courtesy Amoskeag Auction Company

NIB	Exc.	V.G.	Good	Fair	Poor
—	1700	1400	1050	800	500

Model 52D Target

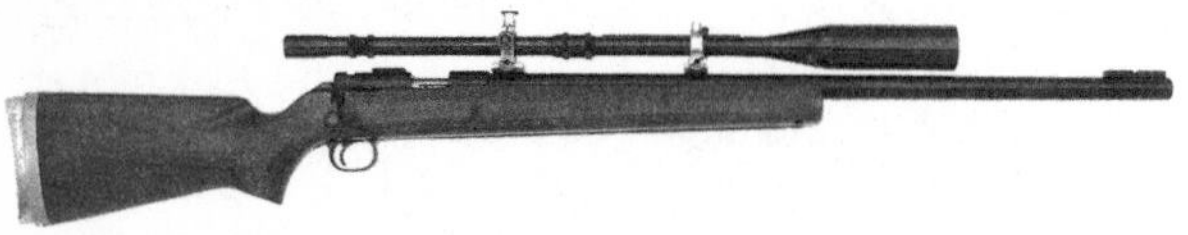

Courtesy Amoskeag Auction Company

NIB	Exc.	V.G.	Good	Fair	Poor
—	1800	1500	1300	1050	500

Model 52B Bull Gun

NIB	Exc.	V.G.	Good	Fair	Poor
—	1800	1500	1300	1050	500

Model 52C Bull Gun

NIB	Exc.	V.G.	Good	Fair	Poor
—	1800	1500	1300	1050	500

International Match

Approximately 300 manufactured.

Free Style

NIB	Exc.	V.G.	Good	Fair	Poor
—	3550	2900	2050	1200	600

Prone

NIB	Exc.	V.G.	Good	Fair	Poor
—	1600	1350	1150	800	600

Sporter—B & C Models

NIB	Exc.	V.G.	Good	Fair	Poor
—	4100	3400	2300	1800	900

NOTE: Add 50 percent to above prices for "A" or pre-" A" series sporters. These are very rare early models in the Sporter Series.

MODEL 54

The Model 54 was to centerfire cartridges what the Model 52 was to rimfire cartridges. The Model 54 was also a quality-made bolt-action rifle with a nondetachable box magazine and was chambered for a variety of calibers: .270, .30-06, .30-30, 7mm, 7.65, 9.mm, .250-3000, .22 Hornet, .220 Swift, and .257 Roberts. This was Winchester's first bolt-action rifle built for heavy, high velocity ammunition. The rifle was available in several different styles:

1. Standard Rifle, 24" or 20" round barrel (except .220 Swift which was 26"), plain walnut checkered pistol-grip stock and forend.
2. Carbine, 20" round barrel, plain walnut pistol-grip stock with finger groove on each side of forend.
3. Sniper's Rifle, 26" round heavyweight barrel, plain walnut pistol-grip stock and forend.
4. N.R.A. Rifle, 24" round barrel, select walnut checkered pistol-grip stock and forend.
5. Super Grade Rifle, 24" round barrel, select walnut checkered pistol-grip stock with cheekpiece and checkered forend with black plastic tip. Pistol grip was capped with hard rubber cap. Super Grade was equipped with 1" detachable sling swivels.
6. Target Rifle, 24" round heavyweight barrel, plain walnut checkered pistol-grip stock and forend.
7. National Match Rifle, 24" round barrel, plain walnut special target stock and forend.

The Model 54 was introduced in 1925 and was discontinued in 1936 with about 50,000 guns sold.

Standard

NIB	Exc.	V.G.	Good	Fair	Poor
—	1300	1100	800	600	425

Carbine

NIB	Exc.	V.G.	Good	Fair	Poor
—	1400	1200	900	700	475

Sniper's

NIB	Exc.	V.G.	Good	Fair	Poor
—	1800	1500	1200	1000	550

N.R.A.

NIB	Exc.	V.G.	Good	Fair	Poor
—	1800	1500	1200	1000	550

Super Grade

NIB	Exc.	V.G.	Good	Fair	Poor
—	2400	1950	1600	1350	600

Target

NIB	Exc.	V.G.	Good	Fair	Poor
—	1800	1500	1200	1000	550

National Match

NIB	Exc.	V.G.	Good	Fair	Poor
—	1800	1500	1200	1000	550

NOTE: The rare calibers are the 7mm, 7.65mm and the 9mm, which bring considerable premiums (in some cases as much as 250 percent) over standard calibers. Popular calibers such as .22 Hornet, .220 Swift, .30-30, and .257 Roberts will also bring a premium. Proceed with caution on Model 54s with rare caliber markings.

MODEL 56

This model was designed to be a medium-priced bolt-action rimfire rifle. It featured a detachable box magazine and was chambered for the .22 Short or .22 LR cartridges. The rifle was offered in two styles:

1. Sporting Rifle, 22" round barrel, plain walnut pistol-grip stock and forend.
2. Fancy Sporting Rifle, 22" round barrel, fancy walnut checkered pistol-grip stock and forend.

Both styles had a forend with a distinctive lip on the forend tip. The rifle was introduced in 1926 and was discontinued in 1929 with about 8,500 rifles sold.

Sporting

NIB	Exc.	V.G.	Good	Fair	Poor
—	1500	1000	750	525	400

Fancy Sporting

Very rare, use caution.

NIB	Exc.	V.G.	Good	Fair	Poor
—	3000	2000	1500	900	750

NOTE: Add a 50 percent premium for rifles chambered for .22 Short only.

MODEL 57

The Model 57 was close in appearance to the Model 56 with the addition of a heavier stock, target sights, and swivel bows attached to the stock. The rifle was chambered for the .22 Short or .22 LR and featured a 22" round barrel with detachable box magazine. The stock was plain walnut with pistol grip and plain forend. The rifle was introduced in 1927 and dropped from the Winchester line in 1936 having sold only about 19,000 guns.

NIB	Exc.	V.G.	Good	Fair	Poor
—	950	700	450	325	250

NOTE: Add 20 percent premium for web sling.

Model 58

This model was an attempt by the company to market a low-priced .22 caliber rimfire rifle in place of its Models 1902 and 1904. This was a single-shot bolt-action, cocked by pulling the firing pin head to the rear. It had an 18" round barrel and was chambered for the .22 Short, Long, and LR interchangeably. The stock was a one-piece plain wood with straight grip. This model was not serial-numbered. The Model 58 was introduced in 1928 and discontinued in 1931. About 39,000 were sold.

NIB	Exc.	V.G.	Good	Fair	Poor
—	800	700	450	300	200

Model 59

The Model 59 was essentially a Model 58 with the addition of a pistol-grip stock and a 23" round barrel. Introduced in 1930, it was dropped from the product line in the same year with a total sales of about 9,000 guns.

NIB	Exc.	V.G.	Good	Fair	Poor
—	1000	800	550	400	200

MODEL 60 AND 60A

This rifle used the same action as that of the Model 59. When the rifle was first introduced in 1931, it was furnished with a 23" round barrel which was changed to 27" in 1933. Several other mechanical improvements were included with this model; perhaps the most noticeable were the chrome-plated bolt, bolt handle, and trigger. The stock was plain wood with pistol grip. In 1933 the Model 60A was added, which was the same rifle but in a target configuration. The front sight was a square top military blade with a Lyman 55W receiver sight. The Model 60 was discontinued in 1934 with about 166,000 rifles sold. The Model 60A was dropped in 1939 with only about 6,100 rifles sold.

Courtesy Buffalo Bill Historical Center, Cody, Wyoming

Model 60

NIB	Exc.	V.G.	Good	Fair	Poor
—	375	250	200	150	100

Model 60A

NIB	Exc.	V.G.	Good	Fair	Poor
—	500	425	300	200	100

MODEL 67

Winchester again upgraded and improved the Model 60 with an expansion of the styles offered to the shooting public. The standard chamber for the rifle was .22 Short, Long, and LR interchangeably with the W.R.F. only added in 1935:

1. Sporting Rifle, 27" round barrel, stock similar to the Model 60.
2. Smoothbore Rifle, 27" barrel, chambered for the .22 long shot or .22 LR shot.
3. Junior Rifle, 20" round barrel and shorter stock.
4. Rifle with miniature target boring, 24" round barrel, chambered for .22 LR shot.

Model 67s were not serial numbered for domestic sales but were numbered for foreign sales. Introduced in 1934 the gun was dropped from the line in 1963 having sold about 384,000. Many of these models were fitted at the factory with telescopes, and the bases were mounted on the rifle and the scope was packed separately.

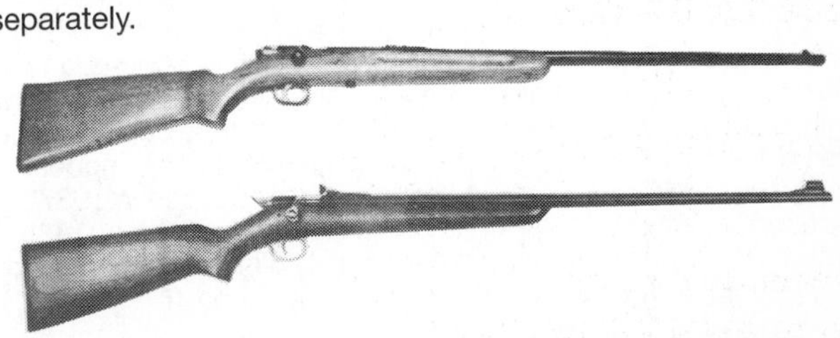

Courtesy C.H. Wolfersberger

Sporting Rifle

NIB	Exc.	V.G.	Good	Fair	Poor
—	300	250	175	125	75

Smoothbore Rifle

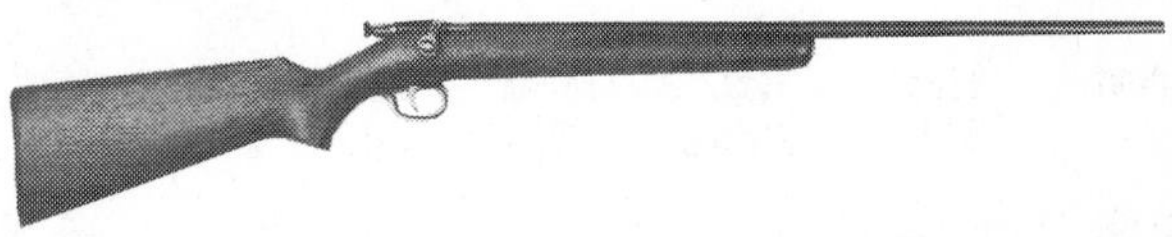

Courtesy Buffalo Bill Historical Center, Cody, Wyoming

NIB	Exc.	V.G.	Good	Fair	Poor
—	800	600	400	250	200

Junior Rifle

NIB	Exc.	V.G.	Good	Fair	Poor
—	350	300	225	175	125

Miniature Target Rifle

This model is marked "for shot only" and has beads instead of standard iron rifle sights.

NIB	Exc.	V.G.	Good	Fair	Poor
—	1200	900	700	400	300

Model 677

This model looked the same as the Model 67 but was manufactured without iron sights and therefore will have no sight cuts in the barrel. The rifle was furnished with either 2-3/4 power scopes or 5 power scopes. This model was not serial numbered. Introduced in 1937 and discontinued in 1939.

NIB	Exc.	V.G.	Good	Fair	Poor
—	2250	1350	900	600	300

NOTE: Add 100 percent premium for rifles chambered for .22 WRF.

MODEL 68

Another takeoff on the Model 67, this model differed only in the sight equipment offered. Winchester fitted this rifle with its own

5-power telescopes. First sold in 1934 the Model 68 was dropped in 1946 with sales of about 101,000.

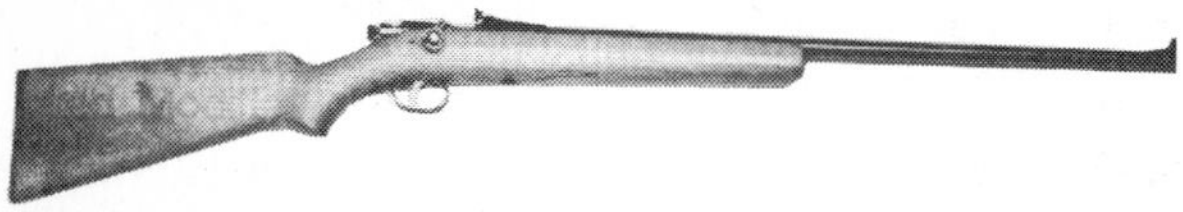

Courtesy C.H. Wolfersberger

With Scope

NIB	Exc.	V.G.	Good	Fair	Poor
—	750	500	300	200	150

Without Scope

NIB	Exc.	V.G.	Good	Fair	Poor
—	300	225	150	100	75

NOTE: Rifles with factory scopes and no sights add 50 percent. For rifles with factory scopes and no sights chambered for .22 WRF add 200 percent.

Model 69 and 69A

This model was designed by Winchester to answer the demand for a medium-priced hunting and target .22 rimfire bolt-action rifle. The rifle had a detachable box magazine, and many were offered with factory-installed telescopes in 2-3/4 and 5 power. The stock was plain walnut with pistol grip and plain forend. This model was not serial numbered. The 69A version was introduced in 1937 and featured an improved cocking mechanism. Introduced in 1935 as the Model 69, this gun was dropped in 1963 with sales of about 355,000 guns.

NIB	Exc.	V.G.	Good	Fair	Poor
—	450	375	300	200	100

NOTE: Add 25 percent for Target Model. Add 20 percent for grooved receiver.

Model 697

The Model 697 was similar in appearance to the Model 69 except it was equipped exclusively for a telescope. Winchester offered either a 2-3/4 or 5-power scope with the bases attached at the factory and the scope packed separately. Built between 1937 and 1941 with small sales, this model was not serial numbered.

NIB	Exc.	V.G.	Good	Fair	Poor
—	2000	1200	800	600	400

NOTE: For factory scopes with no sights add 50 percent.

MODEL 70

Considered by many as the finest bolt-action rifle ever built in the United States, the pre-1964 Model 70 is highly sought after by shooters and collectors alike. Its smooth, strong action has no peer. It is often referred to as "The Riflemen's Rifle." The Model 70 is an updated and improved version of the Model 54 and features a hinged floorplate, new speed locks, new safety design that does not interfere with telescope, manually releasable bolt stop, more attractive buttstock and forend, and forged steel trigger guard. Like many Winchesters, the Model 70 was available with several extra-cost options that should be evaluated by an expert. The values listed are given for pre-1964 Model 70s with serial numbers from 1 to 581471. This rifle was available in several different styles:

1. Standard Grade, 24" round barrel (except 26" round barrel for .220 Swift and .300 H&H Magnum—25" round barrel for .375 H&H Magnum after 1937), plain walnut checkered pistol stock and forend. Built from 1936 to 1963.
2. Standard Grade Carbine, 20" round barrel, chambered for .22 Hornet, .250-3000, .257 Roberts, .270, 7mm, and .30-06, same stock as Standard Grade. Built from 1936 to 1946.
3. Super Grade Rifle, same barrel and calibers as Standard Grade, select walnut checkered and capped pistol-grip stock with cheekpiece and checkered forend with plastic tip. Built from 1936 to 1960.
4. Featherweight, 22" round barrel chambered for .243, .264, .270, .308, .30-06, and .358. Fitted with aluminum trigger guard, aluminum buttplate, and aluminum floor plate. Later versions with plastic buttplate. Built from 1952 to 1963.
5. Featherweight Super Grade, same as above except not chambered for the .358 cartridge, but fitted with Super Grade stock. Built from 1952 to 1963.
6 National Match, same as Standard Grade but fitted with target type stock and telescope bases. Chambered for .30-06 only. Discontinued in 1960.
7. Target, 24" round medium-weight barrel with same stock as National Match in .243 and .30-06 calibers. Discontinued in 1963.
8. Varmint, 26" round heavy barrel, with heavier varmint stock, chambered for .243 and the rare .220 Swift. Built from 1956 to 1963.
9. Westerner, 26" round barrel with Standard Grade stock, chambered for .264 Winchester Magnum. Built from 1960 to 1963. Fitted with a solid rubber pad for early production guns and a vented pad for later guns.
10. Alaskan, 25" round barrel, with Standard Grade stock, chambered for .338 Winchester Magnum and .375 H&H Magnum. Built from 1960 to 1963. Fitted with a solid rubber pad marked Winchester for early production guns and a vented pad both marked Winchester for later guns.
11. Bull Gun, 28" round barrel, same stock as National Match, chambered for .30-06 and .300 H&H Magnum. Built from 1936 to 1963.

The standard calibers offered for the Model 70 are these, in order of rarity: .300 Savage, .35 Rem., .458 Win Magnum, 7mm, .358 Win., .250-3000 Savage, .300 Win Magnum, .338 Win. Magnum, .375 H&H Magnum, .257 Roberts, .220 Swift, .22 Hornet, .264 Win. Magnum, .300 H&H Magnum, .308 Win., .243 Win., .270 W.C.F., .30-06.

NOTE: Prices for the Model 70 are, in many cases, based on the caliber of the rifle; the more rare the caliber, the more premium the gun will command. Many pre-1964 Model 70s are still available in new condition in the original box with all papers. Add 100 percent if the box is serial numbered to the gun. Use caution prior to purchase of NIB guns due to fake boxes and papers.

PRICING NOTE: The asterisk (*) signifies the value of the rifle with respect to a usable action. Model 70 unaltered receivers bring $500 regardless of the condition of the barrel and stock. If the receiver is unusable then the rifle is worth the value of its usable parts, i.e. less than $500.

For Model 70s with "X" or "D" prefex add a collector premium of 10 percent. These letters indicate that there were two rifles mistakenly stamped with the same serial number.

STANDARD RIFLE.30-06 SPRINGFIELD (1937-1963)

Pre-War

NIB	Exc.	V.G.	Good	Fair	Poor
—	1900	1200	900	500*	500*

Post-War

NIB	Exc.	V.G.	Good	Fair	Poor
—	1450	1125	700	500*	500*

.270 WIN. (1937-1963)

Pre-War

NIB	Exc.	V.G.	Good	Fair	Poor
—	2100	1850	900	500*	500*

.243. Win. (1955-1963)

NIB	Exc.	V.G.	Good	Fair	Poor
—	3050	2200	1100	500*	500*

.300 H&H MAGNUM (1937-1963)

Pre-War

NIB	Exc.	V.G.	Good	Fair	Poor
—	3000	2000	1700	1000	500*

Post-War

NIB	Exc.	V.G.	Good	Fair	Poor
—	2500	1750	1400	850	500*

.264 Win. Magnum (1959-1963)

NIB	Exc.	V.G.	Good	Fair	Poor
—	2400	1850	1200	850	500*

.22 HORNET (1937-1958)

Pre-War

NIB	Exc.	V.G.	Good	Fair	Poor
—	2400	2100	1400	1000	500*

Post-War

NIB	Exc.	V.G.	Good	Fair	Poor
—	2000	1600	1150	750	500*

.220 SWIFT (1937-1963)

Pre-War

NIB	Exc.	V.G.	Good	Fair	Poor
—	3000	2400	1750	900	500*

Post-War

NIB	Exc.	V.G.	Good	Fair	Poor
—	2500	1750	1200	650	500*

.257 ROBERTS (1937-1959)

Pre-War

NIB	Exc.	V.G.	Good	Fair	Poor
—	2900	2400	1250	950	500*

Post-War

NIB	Exc.	V.G.	Good	Fair	Poor
—	2100	1700	1200	750	500*

.375 H&H MAGNUM (1937-1963)

Pre-War

NIB	Exc.	V.G.	Good	Fair	Poor
—	4300	3700	2200	1350	500*

Post-War

NIB	Exc.	V.G.	Good	Fair	Poor
—	2900	2300	1550	900	500*

.338 Win. Magnum (1959-1963)

NIB	Exc.	V.G.	Good	Fair	Poor
—	3150	2550	1550	900	500*

.300 Win. Magnum (1962-1963)

NIB	Exc.	V.G.	Good	Fair	Poor
—	2650	2250	1200	750	500*

.250-3000 Savage (1937-1949)

NIB	Exc.	V.G.	Good	Fair	Poor
—	4400	3300	1850	950	500*

7mm (1937-1949)

NIB	Exc.	V.G.	Good	Fair	Poor
—	5900	4800	2700	1700	700

.35 Rem. (1944-1947)

NIB	Exc.	V.G.	Good	Fair	Poor
—	8900	6050	3700	2000	950

.300 Savage (1944-1950s?)

NIB	Exc.	V.G.	Good	Fair	Poor
—	9400	8300	3800	2000	950

.458 African

Built in Supergrade only, 1956-1963.

NIB	Exc.	V.G.	Good	Fair	Poor
—	7400	5350	4200	2750	1350

Featherweight

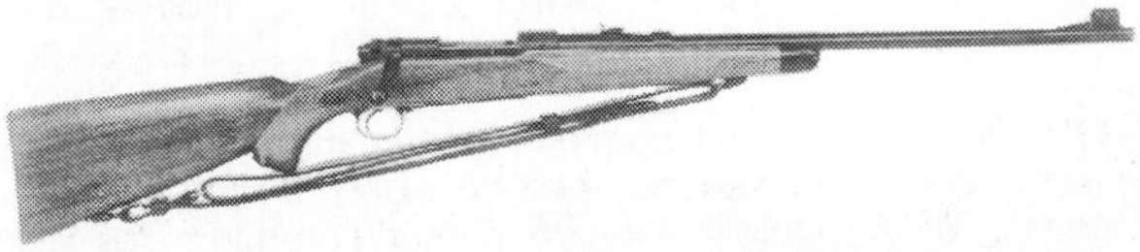

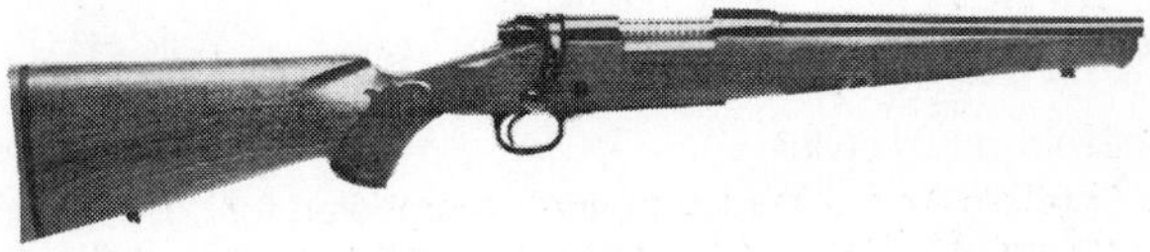

NIB	Exc.	V.G.	Good	Fair	Poor
—	2200	1450	1075	700	450

NOTE: Add 100 percent for .358 Win. For .264 and .270 calibers add 25 percent.

Featherweight Super Grade

NIB	Exc.	V.G.	Good	Fair	Poor
—	5400	4300	3200	1650	1000

Standard Grade Carbine

NIB	Exc.	V.G.	Good	Fair	Poor
—	2900	2000	1400	950	650

NOTE: For Supergrade rifles add 100 percent.

National Match

NIB	Exc.	V.G.	Good	Fair	Poor
—	3400	2550	1850	950	600

Target

NIB	Exc.	V.G.	Good	Fair	Poor
—	2450	2100	1150	750	550

Varmint

NIB	Exc.	V.G.	Good	Fair	Poor
—	2350	1950	950	600	375*

NOTE: Add 40 percent premium for .220 Swift.

Bull Gun

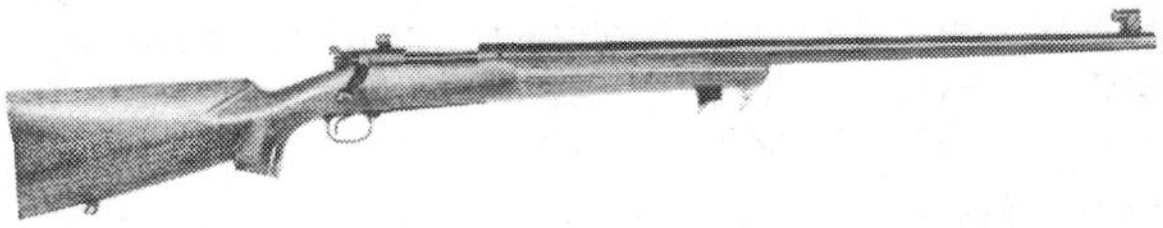

NIB	Exc.	V.G.	Good	Fair	Poor
—	3900	3200	2450	850	600

Model 72

This model is a bolt-action rifle with tubular magazine. It is chambered for the .22 Short, Long, and LR cartridges interchangeably. Early rifles were available with 2-3/4 or 5 power telescopes, but the majority were furnished with either open sights or peep sights. This rifle was available in two different configurations:

1. Sporting Rifle, 25" round barrel, chambered for the .22 Short, Long, and LR cartridges, one-piece plain walnut pistol-grip stock and forend.
2. Gallery Special, 25" round barrel, chambered for .22 Short only, stock same as Sporting Rifle.

This model was not serial numbered. It was built between 1938 and 1959 with about 161,000 rifles sold.

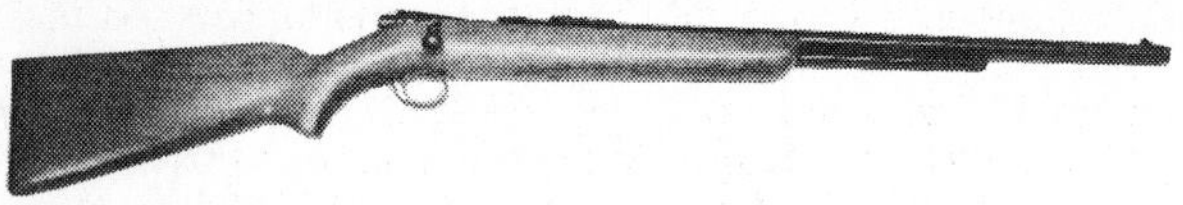

Courtesy C.H. Wolfersberger

NIB	Exc.	V.G.	Good	Fair	Poor
—	425	350	275	200	125

NOTE: Gallery Special will command a premium of 100 percent. For rifles with factory scopes and no sights add 200 percent depending on condition. Add 25 percent premium for peep sights. Add 20 percent for Model 72A with grooved receiver.

MODEL 75

Available in two styles:

1. Sporting Rifle, 24" round barrel, chambered for .22 LR, select walnut checkered pistol-grip stock and forend. This rifle was furnished with either open rear sights or a Lyman 57E receiver sight.
2. Target Rifle, 28" round barrel, chambered for .22 LR, plain walnut pistol-grip stock and forend. The Target Rifle was furnished with either a Winchester 8-power telescope or a variety of target sights.

This model was discontinued in 1958 with about 89,000 sold.

Sporter

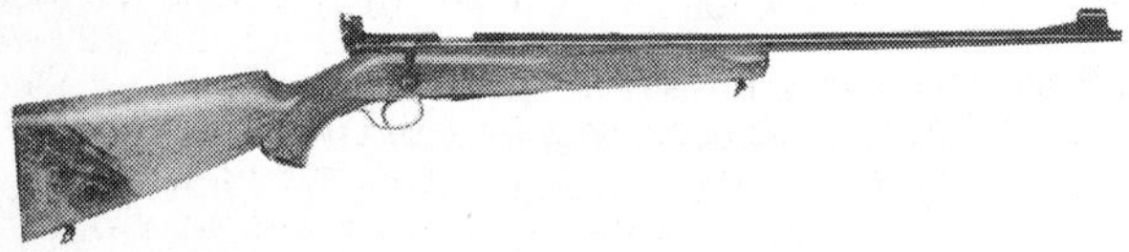

NIB	Exc.	V.G.	Good	Fair	Poor
—	1400	900	700	500	350

Target

NIB	Exc.	V.G.	Good	Fair	Poor
—	900	700	600	500	200

Model SXR Super X Rifle

Gas-operated semi-automatic patterned after Browning BAR ShortTrac and LongTrac. Calibers: .30-06 (4), .300WM (3), .270 WSM (3), .300 WSM (3). Barrel: 22-inch (.30-06), 24-inch. Weight: 7-1/4 lbs. Stock: Two-piece checkered walnut. Introduced 2006.

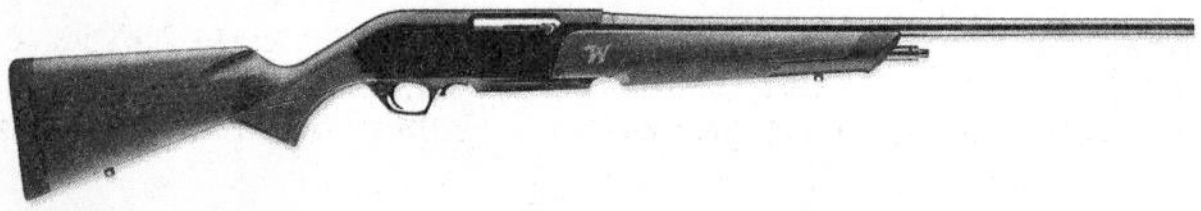

NIB	Exc.	V.G.	Good	Fair	Poor
600	500	400	325	250	125

SHOTGUNS

MODEL 12

This model was designed by T.C. Johnson and was the first slide-action hammerless shotgun built by Winchester. The Model 12 has enjoyed great success in its 51-year history, and over 1,900,000 were sold. This was a high quality, well-made shotgun that is still in use in the hunting and shooting fields across the country. All Model 12s were of the takedown variety. The Model 12 was dropped from regular product line in 1963, but a special model was produced in the Custom Shop until 1979. In 1972 Winchester resurrected the Model 12 in its regular production line in 12 gauge only and ventilated rib. This reintroduced Model 12 was dropped in 1980. The prices listed are for guns made prior to 1964 or for guns with serial numbers below 1968307. This shotgun was offered in several different styles:

1. Standard Grade, 12, 16, 20, and 28 gauge, with plain, solid rib, or vent rib round barrels of standard lengths (26", 28", 30", 32"), plain walnut pistol-grip stock with grooved slide handle. Built from 1912 to 1963.
2. Featherweight, same as above with lightweight alloy trigger guard. Built between 1959 and 1962.
3. Riot Gun, in 12 gauge only with 20" round choked cylinder, stock same as Standard Grade. Built between 1918 and 1963.
4. Trench Gun, chambered for 12 gauge only with 20" round barrel with ventilated hand guard over barrel, fitted with bayonet lug. All metal surfaces are "Parkerized," and these shotguns should be U.S. marked as a military firearm. Introduced in 1918 and built for U.S. Armed Forces on special order.
5. Skeet Grade, chambered for 12, 16, 20, and 28 gauge with 26" round barrel with solid or ventilated rib, select walnut checkered pistol stock and special checkered extension slide handle (longer than standard). Built from 1933 to 1963.
6. Trap Grade, chambered for 12 gauge only with 30" round barrel with solid rib or ventilated rib, select walnut pistol or straight-grip stock, checkered extension slide handle. Built from 1914 to 1963.
7. Heavy Duck Gun, chambered in 12 gauge only with 30" or 32" round barrel with plain, solid, or ventilated rib, plain walnut pistol-grip stock fitted with Winchester solid red rubber recoil pad, plain grooved slide handle. Built from 1935 to 1963.
8. Pigeon Grade, chambered for 12, 16, 20, and 28 gauges with standard barrel lengths and choice of ribs. This was a special order shotgun and will be seen in many different variations, most of these guns were factory engraved. Built 1914 to 1963.

The Model 12 shotgun will be seen in many different combinations of gauges, barrel lengths, ribs, and stocks, all of which determine value. The more rare a particular combination, the higher the price. The buyer is urged to be extremely cautious before purchasing the more rare combinations, such as a 28 gauge. The best advice is to seek assistance from an expert and get as many opinions as possible. The prices listed are for guns in standard configurations.

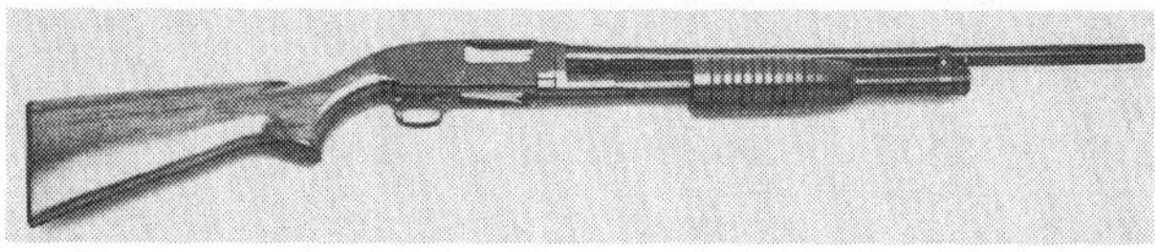

Courtesy Bonhams & Butterfields, San Francisco, California

Standard Grade—12 gauge

NIB	Exc.	V.G.	Good	Fair	Poor
—	1000	800	600	500	200

Featherweight

NIB	Exc.	V.G.	Good	Fair	Poor
—	1300	900	700	575	200

Riot Gun

NIB	Exc.	V.G.	Good	Fair	Poor
—	1800	1300	900	700	250

Trench Gun

NIB	Exc.	V.G.	Good	Fair	Poor
—	3050	2550	1400	900	400

Skeet Grade

NIB	Exc.	V.G.	Good	Fair	Poor
—	1500	1200	900	600	350

Trap Grade

NIB	Exc.	V.G.	Good	Fair	Poor
—	1400	1000	800	550	400

Heavy Duck Gun

NIB	Exc.	V.G.	Good	Fair	Poor
—	1150	900	350	425	300

NOTE: For Heavy Duck Guns with solid ribs add 25 percent premium.

Pigeon Grade

NIB	Exc.	V.G.	Good	Fair	Poor
—	3500	2300	1600	750	500

NOTE: For 16 gauge add 10 percent. For 20 gauge add 50 percent. For 28 gauge add 600 percent. For guns with solid rib add 20 percent. For guns with Winchester Special ventilated rib add 30 percent. For guns with milled rib add 40 percent. Add 20 percent for 32" barrels on any Model 12 model. Add 30 percent premium for original box and papers.

Model 25

This model is similar in appearance to the Model 12 but does not have the takedown feature. All guns were solid frame. The Model 25 was furnished in 12 gauge with 26" or 28" plain round barrel, plain walnut pistol-grip stock with grooved slide handle. This was an attempt by Winchester to introduce a less expensive version of the Model 12. Introduced in 1949 it was dropped from the product line in 1954 having sold about 88,000 guns.

NIB	Exc.	V.G.	Good	Fair	Poor
—	700	550	400	250	100

Model 20

In order to utilize the expanded production facilities left over from WWI, Winchester introduced a series of three different models of single-shot shotguns; the Model 20 was the first of the three. This model has a visible hammer and a top lever frame. It was the first Winchester to have this type of breakdown action. It was chambered for the .410, 2-1/2" shell. The barrel is 26" round choked full, plain walnut pistol-grip stock with hard rubber buttplate. The forend has a small lip on the front end. The Model 20 was dropped from the product line in 1924 having sold about 24,000 guns.

Courtesy C.H. Wolfersberger

NIB	Exc.	V.G.	Good	Fair	Poor
—	700	500	350	200	150

Model 36

The Model 36 was the second of the single-shot shotguns to be introduced in 1920. This model features a bolt-action that is cocked by pulling the firing pin head to the rear. It is fitted with an 18" round barrel, chambered for the 9mm Long Shot, 9mm Short Shot, and 9mm Ball interchangeably, plain gumwood straight-grip stock with special metal pistol grip trigger guard. Winchester referred to this model as the "Garden Gun" for use against birds and pests around the house and barn. This model was not serial numbered. It was dropped from the product line in 1927 having sold about 20,000 guns.

NIB	Exc.	V.G.	Good	Fair	Poor
—	900	775	475	300	225

Model 41

This was the third of the low-priced single-shot shotguns to be announced in 1920. Like the Model 36, the Model 41 was a bolt-action arrangement but of much stronger construction and design. It features a 24" round barrel, chambered for the .410 2-1/2" shell, plain walnut pistol-grip stock and forend. Straight-grip stock was furnished at no extra charge. This model was not serial numbered. It was discontinued in 1934 having sold about 22,000 guns.

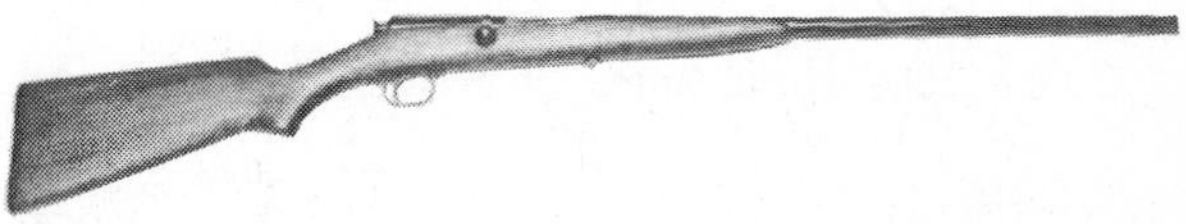

Courtesy C.H. Wolfersberger

NIB	Exc.	V.G.	Good	Fair	Poor
—	600	500	350	300	200

MODEL 21

The Model 21 was Winchester's finest effort with regard to quality, reliability, and strength. Developed in the late 1920s the introduction of this fine side-by-side shotgun was delayed by the company's financial troubles. When Winchester was purchased by the Olin family, the Model 21 was assured the attention it richly deserved due to John M. Olin's love for the gun. Despite the Model 21 being offered as a production gun it was, in fact, a hand-built custom-made shotgun. Almost each Model 21 built has a personality of its own because each shotgun is slightly different with regard to chokes, barrel lengths, stock dimensions, and embellishments. The gun was introduced in 1931. From 1931 to 1959 the Model 21 was considered a production line gun and about 30,000 were sold. In 1960, when the Custom Shop was opened, the Model 21 was built there using the same procedures. Sales during the Custom Shop era were about 1,000 guns. Winchester changed the name of some of the Model 21 styles but the production methods stayed the same. In 1981 Winchester sold its firearms division to U.S. Repeating Arms Company including the right to build the Model 21. Again the production procedures stayed the same as did many of the former employees. U.S. Repeating Arms expanded and changed some of the style designations for the Model 21. Production was discontinued in about 1991. No sales figures are available for this time period. Collectors and shooters will be given the price breakdown for all three eras of production separately.

NOTE: Fewer than 50 .410 Model 21s were built between 1931 and 1959 in all grades. The number of 28 gauge Model 21s built is unknown but the number is probably no greater than the .410 bore.

EDITOR'S COMMENT: There were eight 28 gauge Model 21s built during this period and five .410 bores built. These guns obviously command a large premium. Factory letters are available on these guns.

Model 21—1931 to 1959

The Model 21 was available in several different styles and configurations:

1. Standard Grade, chambered in 12, 16, and 20 gauge with barrel length from 26", 28", 30", and 32" with matted rib or ventilated rib, select walnut checkered pistol- or straight-grip stock with checkered beavertail forend. Built from 1931 to 1959.
2. Tournament Grade, same as above with special dimension stock. Marked "TOURNAMENT" on bottom of trigger plate. Built from 1933 to 1934.
3. Trap Grade, same as above with slightly better-grade wood and stock made to customers' dimensions. Marked "TRAP" on trigger plate. Built from 1932 to 1959.
4. Skeet Grade, same as above with the addition of the 28 gauge, stock furnished with checkered butt. Marked "SKEET" on trigger plate. Built from 1936 to 1959.

5. Duck Gun, chambered for 12 gauge 3" magnum shells, 30" or 32" barrels, Standard Grade stock except for shorter length of pull. Marked "DUCK" on trigger plate. Built from 1940 to 1952.
6. Magnum Gun, chambered for 3" 12 or 20 gauge, same stock as Duck Gun. Not marked on trigger plate. Built from 1953 to 1959.
7. Custom Built/Deluxe Grade, chambered for 12, 16, 20, 28, and .410, barrel lengths from 26" to 32", stock built to customer's specifications using fancy walnut. Marked "CUSTOM BUILT" on top of rib or "DELUXE" on trigger plate. These grades are frequently but not always engraved. Built from 1933 to 1959.

NOTE: Some early Model 21s were furnished with double triggers, extractors, and splinter forends. This combination reduces the price of the gun regardless of grade. Deduct about 25 percent.

Standard Grade - 12 gauge

NIB	*Exc.*	*V.G.*	*Good*	*Fair*	*Poor*
—	5000	4000	3000	2400	2000

Standard Grade - 16 gauge

NIB	*Exc.*	*V.G.*	*Good*	*Fair*	*Poor*
—	7900	6700	5650	4700	4200

Standard Grade - 20 gauge

NIB	*Exc.*	*V.G.*	*Good*	*Fair*	*Poor*
—	8500	7500	6500	5100	4700

Tournament Grade - 12 gauge

NIB	*Exc.*	*V.G.*	*Good*	*Fair*	*Poor*
—	6500	5200	4150	3500	3300

Tournament Grade - 16 gauge

NIB	*Exc.*	*V.G.*	*Good*	*Fair*	*Poor*
—	8500	7200	6000	5000	4500

Tournament Grade - 20 gauge

NIB	*Exc.*	*V.G.*	*Good*	*Fair*	*Poor*
—	9000	8200	7200	6000	4800

Trap Grade - 12 gauge

NIB	*Exc.*	*V.G.*	*Good*	*Fair*	*Poor*
—	6800	5300	4250	3800	3600

Trap Grade - 16 gauge

NIB	*Exc.*	*V.G.*	*Good*	*Fair*	*Poor*
—	8500	7300	6100	5300	4900

Trap Grade - 20 gauge

NIB	*Exc.*	*V.G.*	*Good*	*Fair*	*Poor*
—	8700	7500	6550	5800	5300

Skeet Grade - 12 gauge

NIB	*Exc.*	*V.G.*	*Good*	*Fair*	*Poor*
—	6500	5000	3950	3400	3200

Skeet Grade - 16 gauge

NIB	*Exc.*	*V.G.*	*Good*	*Fair*	*Poor*
—	7900	6300	5450	4900	4400

Skeet Grade - 20 gauge

NIB	*Exc.*	*V.G.*	*Good*	*Fair*	*Poor*
—	8200	7200	6000	5000	4500

Duck/Magnum Gun

NIB	*Exc.*	*V.G.*	*Good*	*Fair*	*Poor*
—	6500	5100	4450	4000	3800

NOTE: Add 30 percent for 20 gauge Magnum. Factory ventilated ribs command a premium of about $1,800 on 12 gauge guns and $2,500 on 20 and 16 gauge guns. Models 21s with factory furnished extra barrels will bring an additional premium of about $2,500. Refinished and restored Model 21s are in a somewhat unique category of American-made collectible shotguns. A gun that has been professionally refinished by a master craftsman will approximate 90 percent of the value of factory original guns.

CUSTOM BUILT/DELUXE GRADE

The prices paid for guns of this grade are determined by gauge, barrel and choke combinations, rib type, stock specifications, and engraving. Expert appraisal is recommended. It is best to secure a factory letter from the Cody Firearms Museum. With respect to such letter, it is important to note that these records are incomplete and may be inaccurate in a few cases. Records for Model 21s built during the 1930s may be missing. Special-order guns may have incomplete records. In such cases, a written appraisal from an authoritative collector or dealer may be helpful.

12 gauge

NIB	*Exc.*	*V.G.*	*Good*	*Fair*	*Poor*
—	8000	7000	5750	4500	4000

16 gauge

NIB	*Exc.*	*V.G.*	*Good*	*Fair*	*Poor*
—	9000	8000	6750	5500	4500

20 gauge

NIB	*Exc.*	*V.G.*	*Good*	*Fair*	*Poor*
—	9500	8500	7250	6000	5000

.410 Bore

NIB	*Exc.*	*V.G.*	*Good*	*Fair*	*Poor*
—	47500	36500	31000	26000	22000

CUSTOM SHOP MODEL 21S—1960 TO 1981

When Winchester moved the production of the Model 21 into the Custom Shop, the number of styles was greatly reduced. There were now three distinct styles:

1. Custom Grade, chambered in 12, 16, 20, 28 gauge, and .410 bore in barrel lengths from 26" to 32". Matted rib, fancy walnut checkered pistol- or straight-grip stock with checkered forend. Guns with pistol grips furnished with steel grip cap. A small amount of scroll engraving was provided on the frame of this grade.
2. Pigeon Grade, same chambers and barrel lengths as above with the addition of choice of matted or ventilated rib, leather-covered recoil pad, style "A" carving on stock and forend, and gold engraved pistol grip cap. The frame was engraved with the 21-6 engraving pattern.
3. Grand American Grade, same chambers and barrel lengths as Pigeon Grade with the addition of "B" carving on the stock and forend, 21-6 engraving with gold inlays, extra set of interchangeable barrels with extra forend. All of this was enclosed in a leather trunk case.

Custom Grade—12 Gauge

NIB	*Exc.*	*V.G.*	*Good*	*Fair*	*Poor*
—	10000	8500	7300	6000	5200

NOTE: Add $4,000 for 16 gauge. Add $5,000 for 20 gauge.

Pigeon Grade—12 Gauge

NIB	*Exc.*	*V.G.*	*Good*	*Fair*	*Poor*
—	19000	16500	12500	10000	8000

NOTE: Add $6,000 for 16 gauge. Add $5,000 for 20 gauge.

Grand American—12 Gauge

NIB	*Exc.*	*V.G.*	*Good*	*Fair*	*Poor*
—	27500	22500	16500	14000	13000

NOTE: Add $15,000 for 16 gauge (extremely rare). Add $5,000 for 20 gauge.

EDITOR'S COMMENT: According to Ned Schwing's excellent book, "Winchester's Finest, The Model 21", there were only eight 28 gauge and five .410-bore models made during the Custom

Shop production era from 1960 to 1981. Any price estimates would be highly speculative.

ENGRAVED MODEL 21S

Winchester catalogued a number of special-order engraving patterns which ranged from a small amount of scroll (#1) to full-coverage game scene and scroll (#6). In addition, there were a few guns engraved on special order to the customer's request. Engraved guns are extremely rare, and the value added will vary with the rarity of the gauge and the date of manufacture. The following table represents the value added for various standard engraving patterns on 12 gauge guns for the "Custom Shop" (1960-1982) and "Pre-Custom Shop" (1932-1959) periods. However, it is advisable to seek the opinion of an authorative collector or dealer prior to a sale.

Engraving Pattern	*Pre-Custom Shop*	*Custom Shop*
#1	30 percent	20 percent
#2	40 percent	30 percent
#3	60 percent	45 percent
#4	70 percent	50 percent
#5	90 percent	70 percent
#6	100 percent	80 percent

Custom Shop Model 21s—1982 to 1993

When U.S. Repeating Arms Company took over the production of the Model 21, the Pigeon Grade was dropped from the line. The Grand American Grade was retained with all the features of its predecessor but with the addition of a small-bore set featuring a 28 gauge and .410 bore set of barrels. Two new grades were introduced in 1983: the Standard Custom Grade and the Special Custom Built. In addition to these grades, the factory would undertake to build for its customers whatever was desired. Due to the unique nature of these guns, it is advised that an expert appraisal be sought to establish a value. While the changeover from Winchester to U.S. Repeating Arms was a transfer of business assets and the craftsmen and personnel remained the same, collectors are reluctant to assign the same values to U.S. Repeating Arms Model 21s as those produced by Winchester. No official production figures are available for U.S.R.A. Model 21s, but the number is most likely small; perhaps around 200 guns.

Standard Custom Built

NIB	*Exc.*	*V.G.*	*Good*	*Fair*	*Poor*
9000	7000	6000	5000	4500	4000

Grand American

NIB	*Exc.*	*V.G.*	*Good*	*Fair*	*Poor*
19000	14000	10500	8500	6000	5000

Grand American Small Gauge Set—28 or .410 bore

NIB	*Exc.*	*V.G.*	*Good*	*Fair*	*Poor*
62500	46500	37500	27000	22000	20000

CURRENT MODEL 21 PRODUCTION

In 1995, Connecticut Shotgun Mfg. Co. purchased the assets of the Winchester Model 21 Custom Shop. Beginning in 2002, Winchester licensed CSMC to build Model 21s on a custom-order basis in a wide variety of grades and models, made to the buyer's specifications. For more information, see the listing for Connecticut Shotgun Mfg. Co. in this edition.

Model 24

The Model 24 was Winchester's attempt to develop a medium-priced double-barrel shotgun. Like the Model 21, it was a top lever breakdown model that was available in 12, 16, and 20 gauge in various barrel lengths from 26" to 30". Offered in a Standard model only with double triggers, raised matted rib, plain walnut pistol- or straight-grip stock with semi-beavertail forend, the Model 24 was introduced in 1939 and was discontinued in 1957 with about 116,000 guns sold.

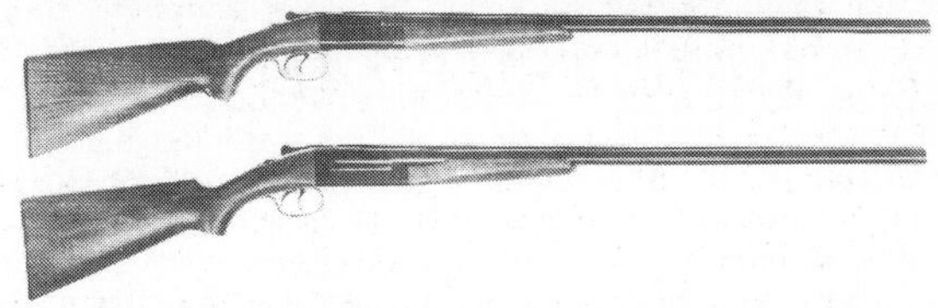

NIB	*Exc.*	*V.G.*	*Good*	*Fair*	*Poor*
—	650	500	400	250	200

NOTE: Add 10 percent for 16 gauge. Add 25 percent for 20 gauge.

MODEL 37

This model was developed to keep pace with Winchester's competitors in the low-price single-barrel exposed-hammer shotgun market. The shotgun was available in 12, 16, 20, 28 gauge, and .410 bore with barrel lengths from 26" to 30". The stock was plain walnut with pistol grip and semi-beavertail forend. This model was not serial numbered. Introduced in 1936 it stayed in the company line until 1963, having sold slightly over 1,000,000 guns.NOTE: Add 15 percent premium for so-called "red letter" (red-filled "W" on bottom of receiver). Do not confuse this model with the Model 37A.

Courtesy C.H. Wolfersberger

NIB	*Exc.*	*V.G.*	*Good*	*Fair*	*Poor*
—	12 gauge	350	300	250	100

Youth Model

26" Modified choke barrel, Win. red factory pad.

NIB	*Exc.*	*V.G.*	*Good*	*Fair*	*Poor*
—	20 gauge	550	450	350	125

NOTE: For 12 and 16 gauge guns add a 50 percent premium for 32" barrels. Use caution for 28 gauge guns. Many fakes are seen for sale.

MODEL 42

Commentary and values by Bud Bugni.

This was the first slide-action shotgun ever developed exclusively for the .410 bore. Invented by William Roemer, the Model 42 was in effect, at least in outward appearance, a miniature Model 12. This shotgun was a quality-built, fast-handling, racy looking shotgun that many refer to as "Everybody's Sweetheart." The Model 42 was the first American .410 bore chambered for the new 3" shell as well as the 2.5" shell. The Model 42 was offered in several different configurations throughout its production. These configurations will greatly influence value:

1. Standard Grade, 26" or 28" plain or solid rib barrel, plain walnut pistol-grip stock with grooved slide handle, fitted with composition buttplate. A straight grip was offered on the Standard Grade on a special order basis, but it is extremely rare. Built from 1933 to 1963.
2. Skeet Grade, 26" or 28" plain, solid rib, or ventilated rib barrel, select walnut checkered pistol or straight-grip stock with checkered extension slide handle. The Skeet Grade was offered in Full, Modified, Improved Cylinder, Cylinder as well as Skeet chokes. Built from 1933 to 1963.
3. Trap Grade, 26" or 28" plain or solid rib barrel, fancy walnut special checkered pistol or straight-grip stock with special checkered extension slide handle. The Trap Grade checkering pattern has one closed diamond on each side of the pistol grip or, in the case of the straight grip, the diamond is located on the underside of the grip. The extension slide handle has two uncut diamonds on each side. Most were stamped "TRAP" on the bottom of the receiver under the

serial number. Built from 1934 to 1939.

4. Deluxe Grade, a continuation of the Trap Grade, available with ventilated rib in 1954. Some early models stamped "DELUXE" on bottom of receiver. This stamping is seldom seen and was probably discontinued around 1949. Built from 1940 to 1963.
5. Pigeon Grade, same as above Deluxe Grade but engraved with a pigeon on the lower magazine tube. Very few of this grade were built by Winchester, and the majority were done in the late 1940s. Authentic Pigeon Grade 42s appear to have been built between 1945 and 1949. Some estimate that less than 50 were produced. this is a rare Model 42. Seek an expert opinion before a sale.

NOTE: Engraved Model 42s will occasionally be seen. Collectors are urged to seek expert advice on these rare and expensive guns. The Model 42 was produced from 1933 to 1963. About 164,000 were sold. Factory service and repair for this model were discontinued in February of 1972.Extra Barrels: Winchester offered extra interchangeable barrels for its Model 42s at the customer's request beginning in 1934. These extra sets of barrels are a rare option. Both barrels should have the same barrel markings and matching serial numbers before originality can be considered. Values are difficult to determine, but as a general rule add 60 percent to the price of a Model 42 if it has a factory-original extra barrel.Editor's Comment: Contrary to traditional views, Winchester did install factory ventilated ribs on its Model 42. Former employees and factory drawings substantiate this fact. However, the subject of what is a factory rib and what is not has been covered in great detail in an excellent book on the Model 42. Seek expert advice before selling or purchasing any Model 42 with a ventilated rib.

Standard Grade

NIB	Exc.	V.G.	Good	Fair	Poor
2500	1850	100	850	650	350

NOTE: For Standard Grade guns with solid ribs add 50 percent. For pre-war guns add 30 percent.

Skeet Grade—Solid Rib

NIB	Exc.	V.G.	Good	Fair	Poor
6500	4000	3500	2400	1650	950

NOTE: Add 25 percent guns chambered for 2-1/2" shells. For pre-war guns add 30 percent. For Skeet Grade guns with no rib deduct 25 percent.

Skeet Grade—Ventilated Rib

NIB	Exc.	V.G.	Good	Fair	Poor
7000	5250	3850	3000	2200	1250

NOTE: Add 25 percent of guns chambered for 2-1/2" shells.

Trap Grade - Plain or Solid Rib

NIB	Exc.	V.G.	Good	Fair	Poor
—	10000	8750	8250	5500	3000

Deluxe Grade—Solid Rib

NIB	Exc.	V.G.	Good	Fair	Poor
—	8500	7000	5750	3500	1250

Deluxe Grade—Ventilated Rib

NIB	Exc.	V.G.	Good	Fair	Poor
—	10000	8250	7000	4750	2200

NOTE: For Pigeon Grade Model 42s with documentation on expert authentication add 100 percent.

Cutts Compensator Guns: Approximately 66 original Cutts Compensator guns were produced in the factory, making this one of the rarest options on the Model 42. These original guns will have ***no choke markings***, and were only offered with a vent rib. Add 25 percent for original Cutts guns, deduct 50 percent for non-original Cutts guns.

MODEL 1911

This was Winchester's first self-loading shotgun and was developed by T.C. Johnson in order to keep pace with the Remington Auto-Loading Shotgun Model 11, which was developed by John M. Browning with help from T.C. Johnson. Because of the delays involved in developing a brand new design, the Model 1911 was introduced on October 7, 1911. The shotgun was a recoil operated mechanism, had a tubular magazine and had the takedown feature. The shotgun was available in two styles:

1. Plain Model 1911, 26" or 28" barrel, 12 gauge, choked full, modified, or cylinder, plain birch laminated pistol-grip stock and forend with hard rubber buttplate.
2. Fancy Model 1911, same as above with fancy birch laminated stock.

Because of the hurry in getting the model ready for production, the shotgun demonstrated design weakness and never proved satisfactory. It was discontinued in 1925 with about 83,000 guns sold.

Plain

NIB	Exc.	V.G.	Good	Fair	Poor
—	550	375	300	250	200

Fancy

NIB	Exc.	V.G.	Good	Fair	Poor
—	800	500	400	300	250

MODEL 40

This model represents Winchester's second attempt to build a self-loading long recoil-operated repeating shotgun. This shotgun was a hammerless tubular magazine gun without the hump at the rear of the receiver. Available in 12 gauge only with barrel lengths from 28" to 30". The Standard Grade had plain walnut pistol-grip stock and forend. The Skeet Grade was fitted with select walnut checkered pistol-grip stock and checkered forend. The Model 40 suffered from the same design problems as the Model 11, and sales were small. Introduced in 1940 and discontinued in 1941, Winchester sold about 12,000 guns.

Standard Grade

NIB	Exc.	V.G.	Good	Fair	Poor
—	600	500	400	275	200

Skeet Grade

NIB	Exc.	V.G.	Good	Fair	Poor
—	800	600	500	300	250

MODEL 50

The Model 50 was the company's third attempt to produce a satisfactory self-loading repeating shotgun. Winchester went to the short recoil system, utilizing a floating chamber design. This model was available in several different styles:

1. Standard Grade, 12 or 20 gauge with plain or ventilated rib in lengths from 26" to 30", plain walnut checkered pistol-grip stock and forend.
2. Skeet Grade, 12 or 20 gauge with 26" ventilated rib barrel. Walnut checkered pistol-grip stock and forend.
3. Trap Grade, 12 gauge with 30" ventilated rib barrel, walnut checkered Monte Carlo stock and forend.
4. Pigeon Grade, 12 or 20 gauge with barrel lengths to customers' specifications. Fancy walnut checkered stock and forend. Made on special orders only.
5. Featherweight, a lighter version of all the above except Trap Grade.

This model begins with serial number 1000. This model was successful and was built between 1954 and 1961. Winchester sold about 200,000 guns.

Standard Grade

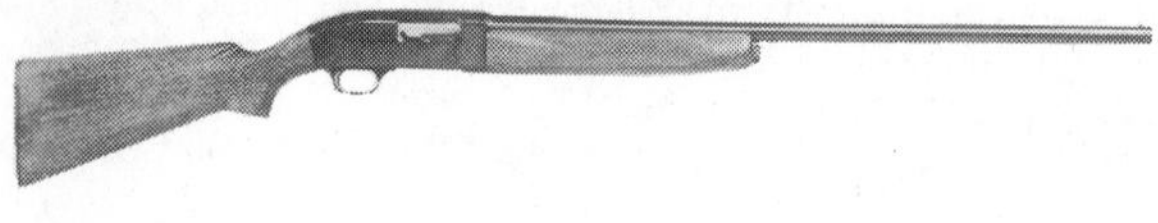

NIB	Exc.	V.G.	Good	Fair	Poor
—	500	400	300	200	150

Skeet Grade

NIB	Exc.	V.G.	Good	Fair	Poor
—	600	500	350	250	200

Trap Grade

NIB	Exc.	V.G.	Good	Fair	Poor
—	600	500	350	250	200

Pigeon Grade

NIB	Exc.	V.G.	Good	Fair	Poor
—	1250	900	750	450	250

Featherweight

NIB	Exc.	V.G.	Good	Fair	Poor
—	600	500	350	250	200

NOTE: Add 10 percent for 20 gauge. Add 20 percent for vent rib on standard grade guns.

MODEL 59

The fourth and final pre-1964 Winchester self-loading shotgun featured a steel and fiberglass barrel with aluminum alloy receiver. The gun was available in 12 gauge only with barrel lengths from 26" to 30" with a variety of chokes. In 1961 Winchester introduced the "Versalite" choke tube, which gave the shooter a choice of Full, Modified, or Improved Cylinder chokes in the same barrel. This model was available in two different styles:

1. Standard Grade, plain walnut checkered pistol-grip stock and forend.
2. Pigeon Grade, select walnut checkered pistol-grip and forend.

Winchester sold about 82,000 of these guns between 1960 and 1965.

NOTE: This shotgun was also made in 10 gauge (very rare), 20 gauge, and 14 gauge. If any of these very low production or prototype guns are encountered, use extreme caution and seek an expert appraisal.

Standard Grade

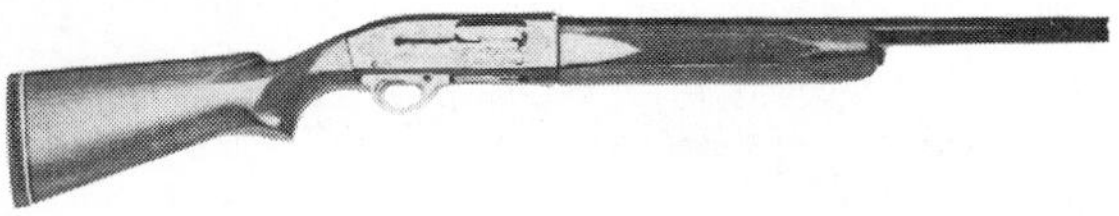

Courtesy Bonhams & Butterfields, San Francisco, California

NIB	Exc.	V.G.	Good	Fair	Poor
—	650	550	450	350	250

Pigeon Grade

NIB	Exc.	V.G.	Good	Fair	Poor
—	1500	1100	850	600	300

NOTE: Add 40 percent premium for barrels with three Versalite chokes and wrench. Add 20 percent premium for original box and papers.

POST-1963 RIFLES

Model 121

This is a single-shot, bolt-action rifle chambered for the .22 rimfire cartridge. It has a 20.75" barrel with open sights. The finish is blued, with a plain walnut stock. It was manufactured between 1967 and 1973. A youth model with a shorter stock was designated the 121Y and is valued the same.

Courtesy Buffalo Bill Historical Center, Cody, Wyoming

NIB	Exc.	V.G.	Good	Fair	Poor
—	225	150	100	60	40

Model 131

This is a bolt-action repeater chambered for the .22 rimfire cartridge. It has a 20.75" barrel with open sights and a 7-round, detachable magazine. The finish is blued, with a plain walnut stock. It was manufactured between 1967 and 1973. A tubular magazine version was designated the Model 141 and is valued the same.

NIB	Exc.	V.G.	Good	Fair	Poor
—	250	175	100	60	40

Model 310

This is a single-shot, bolt-action rifle chambered for the .22 rimfire cartridge. It features a 22" barrel with open sights. The finish is blued, with a checkered walnut stock. It was manufactured between 1972 and 1975.

Courtesy Buffalo Bill Historical Center, Cody, Wyoming

NIB	Exc.	V.G.	Good	Fair	Poor
—	250	150	125	100	75

Model 320

This is a bolt-action repeating rifle that is similar in configuration to the Model 310 single-shot. It has a 5-round, detachable box magazine. It was manufactured between 1972 and 1974.

NIB	Exc.	V.G.	Good	Fair	Poor
—	400	300	250	175	125

Model 250

This is a lever-action repeating rifle with a hammerless action. It is chambered for the .22 rimfire cartridge and has a 20.5" barrel with open sights and a tubular magazine. The finish is blued, with a checkered pistol-grip stock. It was manufactured between 1963 and 1973.

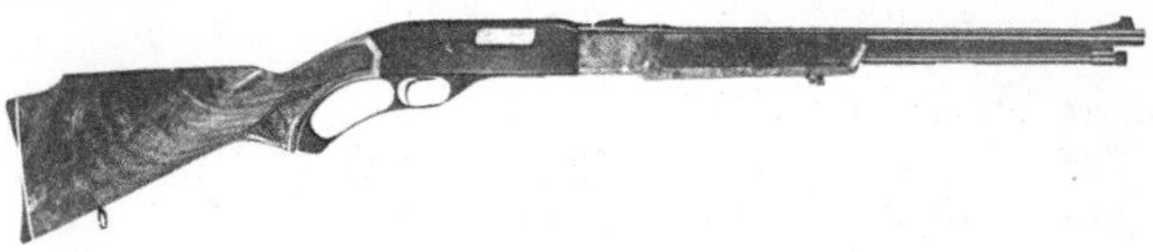

NIB	Exc.	V.G.	Good	Fair	Poor
—	200	125	80	60	40

Model 250 Deluxe

This version is similar to the Model 250 and is furnished with select walnut and sling swivels. It was manufactured between 1965 and 1971.

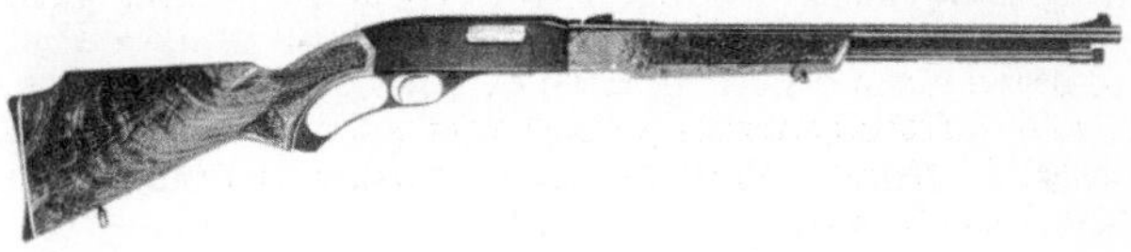

NIB	Exc.	V.G.	Good	Fair	Poor
—	275	195	125	100	75

Model 255

This version is simply the Model 250 chambered for the .22 WMR cartridge. It was manufactured between 1964 and 1970.

NIB	Exc.	V.G.	Good	Fair	Poor
—	225	150	100	70	50

Model 255 Deluxe

This version was offered with select walnut and sling swivels. It was manufactured between 1965 and 1973.

NIB	Exc.	V.G.	Good	Fair	Poor
—	375	250	175	125	75

Model 490

This is a blowback-operated, semi-automatic rifle chambered for the .22 LR cartridge. It has a 22" barrel with open sights and a 5-round, detachable magazine. The finish is blued, with a checkered stock. It was manufactured between 1975 and 1980.

NIB	Exc.	V.G.	Good	Fair	Poor
—	350	225	165	100	75

Model 270

This is a slide-action rifle chambered for the .22 rimfire cartridge. It has a 20.5" barrel and a tubular magazine. The finish is blued, with a checkered walnut stock. It was manufactured between 1963 and 1973.

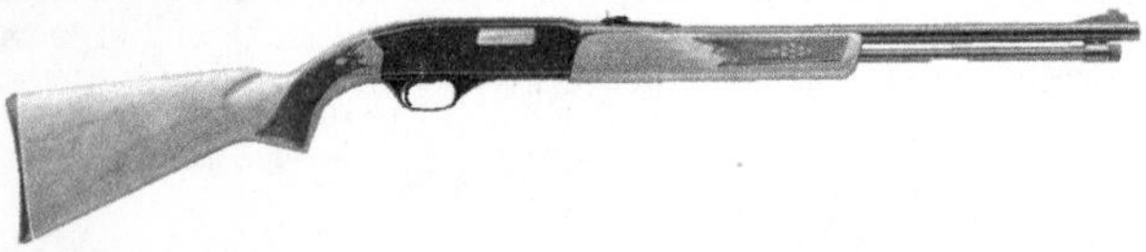

NIB	Exc.	V.G.	Good	Fair	Poor
—	350	225	165	100	75

MODEL 63 (1997)

Introduced in 1997 this is a re-creation of the famous Model 63 .22 caliber auto. Fitted with a 23" barrel and 10-round tubular magazine. The receiver top is grooved for scope mounting.

Grade I

NIB	Exc.	V.G.	Good	Fair	Poor
800	525	—	—	—	—

High Grade

Engraved receiver with gold accents and select walnut stock.

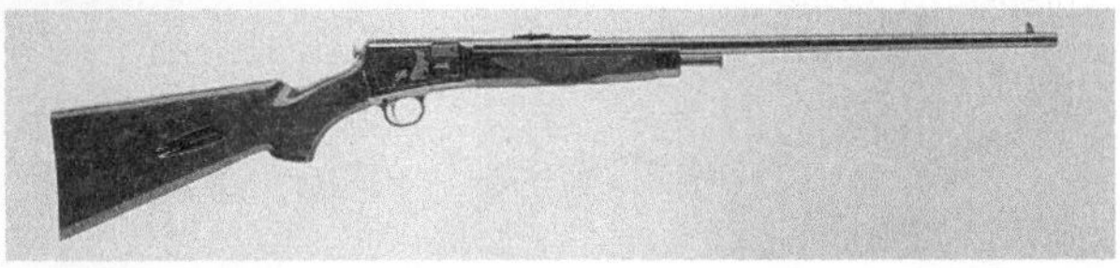

NIB	Exc.	V.G.	Good	Fair	Poor
1050	850	700	575	400	300

Wildcat

Bolt-action repeater styled after Mosin-Nagant military sporter. Caliber: .22 LR. Magazine: 5- and 10-round detachable. Stock: checkered walnut with schnabel. Barrel: 21-inch blued. Weight: 4.5 lbs. Imported. Introduced 2006. Sporter and Target/Varmint versions available. Add 5 percent for Target/Varmint.

NIB	Exc.	V.G.	Good	Fair	Poor
240	175	150	125	95	50

Model 94

This is the post-1964 lever-action carbine chambered for the .30-30, 7-30 Waters, and the .44 Magnum cartridges. It is offered with a 20" or 24" barrel and has a 6- or 7-round, tubular magazine depending on barrel length. The round barrel is offered with open sights. The forearm is held on by a single barrel band. The finish is blued, with a straight-grip walnut stock. In 1982 it was modified to angle ejection to simplify scope mounting. It was introduced as a continuation of the Model 94 line in 1964. In 2003 a top-tang safety was installed and the .480 Ruger caliber was added. The Model 94 series was discontinued in 2006. Premium for unusual chamberings such as 7-30 Waters, etc.

NIB	Exc.	V.G.	Good	Fair	Poor
800	600	425	300	200	100

Model 94 Traditional—CW

As above but with checkered walnut stock. Chambered for the .30-30, .44 Mag., and the .480 Ruger cartridge.

NIB	Exc.	V.G.	Good	Fair	Poor
850	575	450	325	225	125

NOTE: For .44 Mag. add $20. For the .480 Ruger add $70.

Model 94 Ranger

Chambered for .30-30 cartridge and fitted with a 20" barrel. Weight is about 6.25 lbs. In 2003 a top-tang safety was installed.

NIB	Exc.	V.G.	Good	Fair	Poor
—	450	300	225	150	100

Model 94 Ranger Compact

Introduced in 1998 this model features a 16" barrel with 12.5" lop. Chambered for .30-30 or .357 Magnum. Furnished with black recoil pad. Post-style front sight with adjustable rear sight. Hardwood stock. Weight is approximately 5.87 lbs

NIB	Exc.	V.G.	Good	Fair	Poor
—	475	352	250	150	100

Model 94 Black Shadow

This model features a black synthetic stock with nonglare finish and black recoil pad. Offered in .30-30, .44 Magnum, or .444 Marlin. Fitted with a 20" barrel. Weight is about 6.5 lbs. Introduced in 1998.

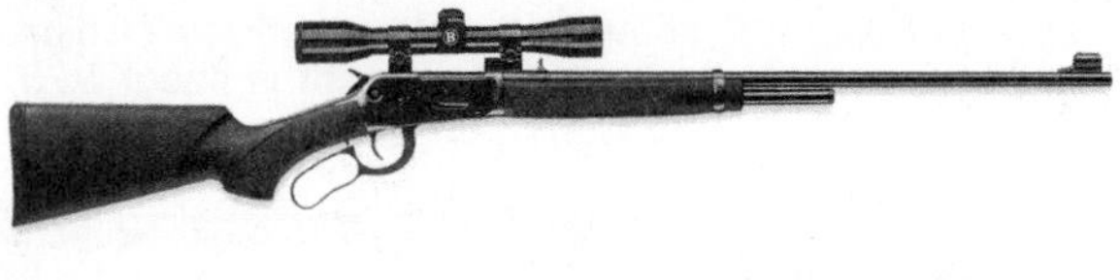

NIB	Exc.	V.G.	Good	Fair	Poor
600	475	375	250	225	175

Model 94 Deluxe

Checkered stock.

NIB	Exc.	V.G.	Good	Fair	Poor
850	675	550	400	300	200

Model 94 Win-Tuff

Laminated stock.

NIB	Exc.	V.G.	Good	Fair	Poor
500	400	275	225	165	125

Model 94 XTR

Select, checkered walnut stock, discontinued 1988.

NIB	Exc.	V.G.	Good	Fair	Poor
—	700	450	350	250	175

Model 94 XTR Deluxe

Fancy checkering.

NIB	Exc.	V.G.	Good	Fair	Poor
—	725	475	375	275	200

Model 94 Trapper

16" barrel. Chambered for the .30-30, .357 Mag., .44 Mag, or .45 Colt cartridge. In 2003 a top-tang safety was installed.

NIB	Exc.	V.G.	Good	Fair	Poor
750	575	450	350	250	150

Model 94 Antique Carbine

Gold-plated saddle ring.

NIB	Exc.	V.G.	Good	Fair	Poor
—	80	0	600	475	200

Model 94 Wrangler

.32 Win. Special.

NIB	Exc.	V.G.	Good	Fair	Poor
—	900	725	525	400	250

Model 94 Wrangler II

Loop lever.

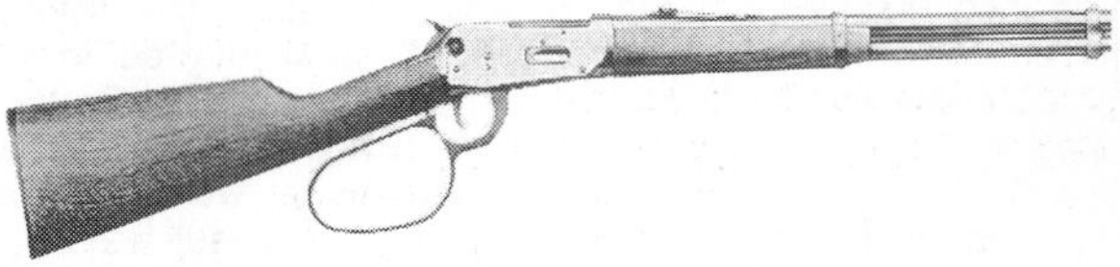

NIB	Exc.	V.G.	Good	Fair	Poor
700	525	425	300	150	—

Model 94 Legacy 20-inch

This Model 94 is fitted with a 20" barrel and chambered for the .30-30 Win. but it is fitted with a half pistol-grip stock. Both walnut buttstock and forearm are cut checkered. Weight is 6.5 lbs. In 2003 a top-tang safety was installed.

NIB	Exc.	V.G.	Good	Fair	Poor
900	750	600	475	300	200

Model 94 Legacy 24-inch

Introduced in 2005 this model features a 24" round barrel with full length magazine. Checkered walnut stock with semi-pistol grip. Chambered for the .30-30, .357 Mag., .44 Rem. Mag. or the .45 Colt cartridge. Drilled and tapped for scope mount. Blued finish. Weight is about 6.75 lbs.

NIB	Exc.	V.G.	Good	Fair	Poor
900	750	600	475	300	200

Model 94 Legacy 26-inch

Similar to the model above but offered in both round and octagon barrel and blue or case colored receiver. Marbles' tang sight. Chambered for the .30-30 or .38-55 calibers. Weight is about 7 lbs. Introduced in 2005. Premium for .38-55.

NIB	Exc.	V.G.	Good	Fair	Poor
1100	875	750	575	400	300

NOTE: Add $55 for case colored receiver. Add $100 for octagon barrel.

Model 94 XTR Big Bore

This version is chambered for the .307, .356, or the .375 Win. cartridges. It features the angle-ejection and is blued with a walnut, Monte Carlo-type stock and recoil pad. The round barrel is 20" in length. It has a 6-round, tubular magazine. It was introduced in 1978. Deduct 12.5 percent for .375.

NIB	Exc.	V.G.	Good	Fair	Poor
1050	900	775	575	400	300

MODEL 94 CENTENNIAL LIMITED EDITIONS

Introduced in 1994 these models celebrate the 100-year anniversary of the Winchester Model 1894. Offered in three grades, these models are of limited production. The Grade I is limited to 12,000 rifles while the High Grade is limited to 3,000 rifles. Only 94 of the Custom Limited model were produced. Each Limited model has different grades of select walnut and engraving coverage. All are chambered for the .30-30 Winchester cartridge.

Grade I

NIB	Exc.	V.G.	Good	Fair	Poor
1600	1250	900	700	575	400

High Grade

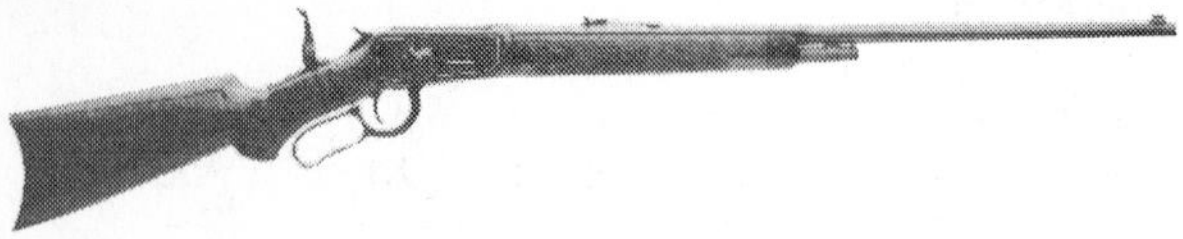

NIB	Exc.	V.G.	Good	Fair	Poor
1900	1300	1075	900	750	600

Custom High Grade

NIB	Exc.	V.G.	Good	Fair	Poor
4750	3900	2500	1000	750	450

Model 94 Heritage—Limited 1 of 1000

Introduced in 2002 and limited to 1,000 rifles. Fitted with half round/half octagon 26" barrel. Engraved with #3 pattern with gold plate. Fancy walnut stock. Chambered for the .38-55 cartridge.

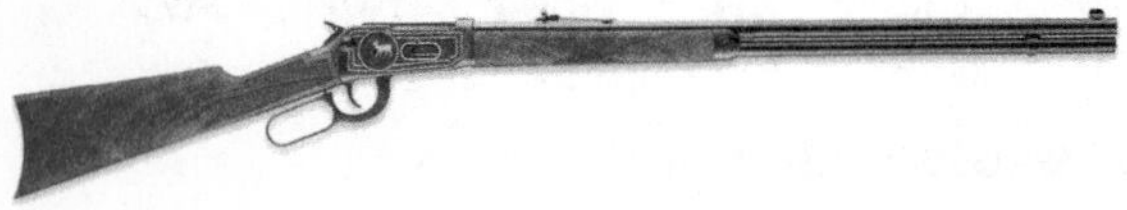

NIB	Exc.	V.G.	Good	Fair	Poor
5000	4000	3000	1750	1200	600

Model 94 Heritage—Custom 1 of 100

Similar to the above model but with finer wood and engraved with #2 pattern with gold. Limited to 100 rifles. Introduced in 2002.

NIB	Exc.	V.G.	Good	Fair	Poor
7500	—	—	—	—	—

Model 94 Trails End

This model is chambered for the .357 Mag., .44 Mag., and .45 Colt. Offered with standard-size loop lever or Wrangler-style loop. Introduced in 1997. Add $500 to NIB for .25-35 Win.

NIB	Exc.	V.G.	Good	Fair	Poor
1375	1050	825	600	450	300

Model 94 Trails End Octagon

As above but with 20" octagon barrel and choice of blued or case colored receiver. Crescent butt. Weight is about 6.75 lbs. Introduced in 2004.

NIB	Exc.	V.G.	Good	Fair	Poor
1395	1100	850	600	450	300

NOTE: Add $60 for case colored receiver.

Model 94 Trails End Hunter

Offered in .25-35 Win, .30-30 Win, or .38-55 Win and fitted with a 20" round or octagon barrel. Plain walnut stock. Blued finish on round barrel model and case colored finish on octagon model. Weight is about 6.5 lbs. Introduced in 2005.

NIB	Exc.	V.G.	Good	Fair	Poor
1375	1050	825	600	450	300

NOTE: Add $290 for octagon barrel model.

Model 94 Timber Carbine

Introduced in 1999 this model is chambered for the .444 Marlin cartridge. Barrel is 17.75" long and ported. Hooded front sight. Magazine capacity is 5 rounds. Weight is about 6 lbs. Finish is blue. Walnut stock. In 2004 this rifle was chambered for the .450 Marlin cartridge.

NIB	Exc.	V.G.	Good	Fair	Poor
1000	850	700	600	400	300

Model 94 Timber Scout

This model, introduced in 2005, features an 18" barrel chambered for the .30-30 Win. or .44 Rem. Mag. cartridges with a quick detachable scope mount attached to the barrel for long eye relief. Plain walnut stock with pistol grip. Blued finish. Weight is about 6 lbs. Scope not included.

NIB	Exc.	V.G.	Good	Fair	Poor
900	750	600	475	300	200

Model 94 Pack Rifle

This lever-action model features an 18" barrel chambered for the .30-30 or .44 Magnum. It has a walnut stock with pistol grip and no checkering. Magazine is 3/4-style and has a 4-round capacity for the .30-30, and five rounds for the .44 Mag. Open sights. Weight is about 6.25 lbs. Introduced in 2000.

NIB	Exc.	V.G.	Good	Fair	Poor
900	750	600	475	300	200

Winchester Model 1894 Custom Grade

Lever-action rifle chambered in .30-30. Features include 24-inch half-round, half octagon deeply blued barrel; buckhorn rear sight with Marble\qs gold bead front sight; Grade IV/V walnut stock and forend with a rich, high gloss finish; deep scroll engraving on both sides of the blued receiver. Commemorates the 200th anniversary of Oliver F. Winchester\qs birth. An early Winchester Repeating Arms crest graces the left side of the receiver, with the right side bearing the words, "Two Hundred Years, Oliver F. Winchester," and the dates, "1810 - 2010," in gold. The barrel is deeply polished, with the signature of Oliver F. Winchester in gold on the top of the bolt. Sold individually in limited quantities and in 500 sets with the High Grade. Price (single rifle): $1959.

Winchester Model 1894 High Grade

Lever-action rifle chambered in .30-30. Features include 24-inch half-round, half octagon deeply blued barrel; buckhorn rear sight with Marble\qs gold bead front sight; silver nitride receiver; Grade II/III high gloss walnut stock and forend with a rich, high gloss finish; delicate scroll work, with Oliver F. Winchester\qs signature in gold on top of the bolt. The left side of receiver bears an early Winchester Repeating Arms crest; on right side are the words, "Two Hundred Years, Oliver F. Winchester," and the dates, "1810 - 2010." Sold individually in limited quantities and in 500 sets with the Custom Grade. Price (single rifle): $1469.

Model 71

A true reproduction of the original. Drilled and tapped for a receiver sight. Barrel is 24-inches, polished blue and round. Oil finished American walnut stock for fore-end cap, no checkering. Marble gold bead front sight, buckhorn rear sight. Chambered for original caliber only, .348 WCF. Introduced in 2011.

NIB	Exc.	V.G.	Good	Fair	Poor
1300	1100	—	—	—	—

Model 94 Short Rifle

New for 2011, the latest incarnation of the famous Model 94 Carbine with 20-inch round barrel and straight grip walnut stock. Rifle-styled fore-end has black grip cap and full-length magazine. Receiver drilled and tapped for scope mounts with hammer extension included. Marble gold bead front sight, semi-buckhorn rear. Overall length 38-inches and weight is 6-3/4 pounds. Chambered in .30-30 Winchester only.

NIB	Exc.	V.G.	Good	Fair	Poor
1000	875	750	—	—	—

Model 94 Sporter

Reminiscent of the original Model 1894 Rifle, this new for 2011 model has a 24-inch half-round, half-octagon blued barrel, and a satin oil-finished American walnut stock with steel crescent buttplate and double-line bordering checkering pattern. Blue receiver drilled and tapped for optical sights. Gold bead front sight, buckhorn sight at rear. Hammer extension included. Available in .30-30 or .38-55 Winchester.

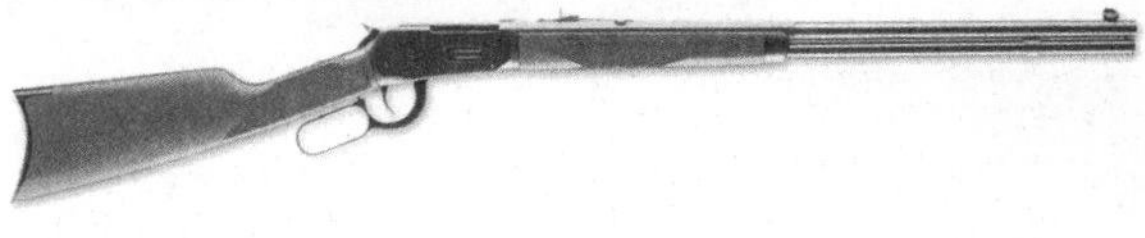

NIB	Exc.	V.G.	Good	Fair	Poor
1175	1000	850	—	—	—

Model 1886 Short Rifle

Reintroduction of a version of the famed Model 1886 with Grade I American walnut stock. Blue steel fore-end cap and crescent buttplate. Barrel is 24-inches with full-length tubular magazine that holds six cartridges. Chambered in .45-70 Government. Elegant satin finish on all wood, no checkering. Deep blue receiver, barrel and lever. Top tang safety, adjustable rear buckhorn sight with fine gold Marble front sight.

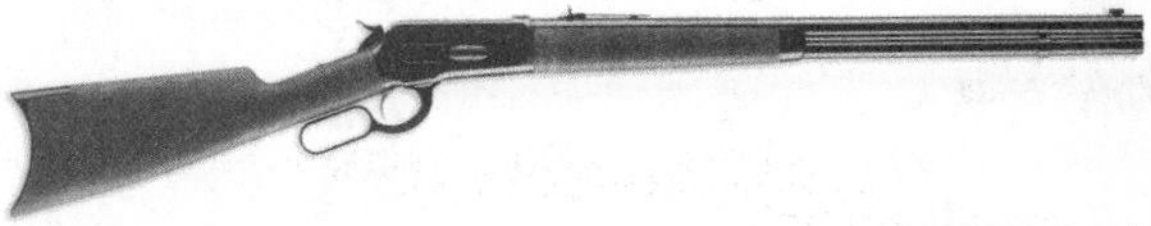

NIB	Exc.	V.G.	Good	Fair	Poor
1125	975	825	—	—	—

Model 1892 Carbine

New version of the rifle made famous by actor John Wayne. Chambered for .357 Magnum, .44 Remington Magnum or .45 Colt. American walnut stock with straight grip. Twenty-inch round barrel, receiver and lever are deeply polished and blued. Full-length magazine. Front and rear iron sights.

NIB	Exc.	V.G.	Good	Fair	Poor
950	800	700	—	—	—

MODEL 9400 SERIES

Model 9410

Introduced in 2001 this model features a .410 shotgun in a lever-action configuration. Barrel length is 24" and is smoothbore with Cylinder choke. Chambered is 2.5". Magazine capacity is nine rounds. Tru-glo front sight. Weight is about 6.75 lbs. In 2003 a top-tang safety was installed.

NIB	Exc.	V.G.	Good	Fair	Poor
1450	1100	900	750	600	400

Model 9410 Semi-Fancy

As above but with semi-fancy walnut stock with checkering. Introduced in 2004.

NIB	Exc.	V.G.	Good	Fair	Poor
1600	1200	975	825	650	400

Model 9410 Packer

Introduced in 2002 this model features a 20" barrel with 3/4 magazine and pistol-grip stock. Weight is about 6.5 lbs.

NIB	Exc.	V.G.	Good	Fair	Poor
1000	850	700	600	400	300

Model 9410 Packer Compact

Introduced in 2003 this model features a reduced length of pull to 12-1/2". Fitted with Invector chokes. Weight is about 6.25 lbs.

NIB	Exc.	V.G.	Good	Fair	Poor
1000	850	700	600	400	300

Model 9410 Ranger

This version is the same as the standard or traditional Model 9410 but hardwood stock without checkering. Weight is about 6.75 lbs. Fitted with top-tang safety. Introduced in 2003.

NIB	Exc.	V.G.	Good	Fair	Poor
900	750	575	450	300	250

Model 9422

Introduced in 1972 this model is chambered for the .22 rimfire and .22 Magnum rimfire cartridges. It was fitted with a 20.5" barrel, front ramp sight with hood, and adjustable semi-buckhorn rear sight. Tubular magazine holds 21 Shorts, 17 Longs, and 15 LR cartridges. The Magnum version holds 11 cartridges. Weight is about 6.25 lbs. Two-piece American walnut stock with no checkering. Between 1972 and 1992 approximately 750,000 Model 9422s were produced.

NIB	Exc.	V.G.	Good	Fair	Poor
850	675	525	375	225	125

Model 9422 XTR

This is a deluxe lever-action rifle chambered for the .22 rimfire cartridge. It is a takedown rifle with a 20.5", round barrel and a tubular magazine. The finish is blued with a checkered, high-gloss, straight-grip walnut stock. It was introduced in 1978. A .22 Magnum version is also available and would be worth approximately $100 additional.

NIB	Exc.	V.G.	Good	Fair	Poor
1000	850	700	600	400	300

Model 9422 XTR Classic

This version is similar to the standard Model 9422 XTR except that it features a 22.5" barrel and a satin-finished, plain, pistol-grip walnut stock. It was manufactured between 1985 and 1987.

NIB	Exc.	V.G.	Good	Fair	Poor
1100	925	750	650	450	325

Model 9422 WinTuff

This model features an uncheckered laminated wood stock that is brown in color. Chambered for both the .22 Rimfire and the .22 Winchester Magnum Rimfire. Weighs 6.25 lbs. Other features are the same as the standard Model 9422.

NIB	Exc.	V.G.	Good	Fair	Poor
850	675	525	375	225	125

Model 9422 WinCam

This model is chambered only for the .22 Winchester Magnum Rimfire. The laminated stock is a green color. Weighs 6.25 lbs.

NIB	Exc.	V.G.	Good	Fair	Poor
850	675	525	375	225	125

Model 9422 Trapper

Introduced in 1996 this model features a 16.5" barrel. It has an overall length of 33". Weight is 5.5 lbs.

NIB	Exc.	V.G.	Good	Fair	Poor
850	675	525	375	225	125

Model 9422 High Grade

This variation of the Model 9422 series features a specially engraved receiver and fancy wood stock. Barrel length is 20.5". Weight is about 6 lbs.

NIB	Exc.	V.G.	Good	Fair	Poor
1000	850	700	600	400	300

MODEL 9422 25TH ANNIVERSARY RIFLE

Introduced in 1997 this model features 20.5" barrel. Limited quantities.

Grade I

Engraved receiver.

NIB	Exc.	V.G.	Good	Fair	Poor
1000	850	700	600	400	300

High Grade

Engraved receiver with silver border.

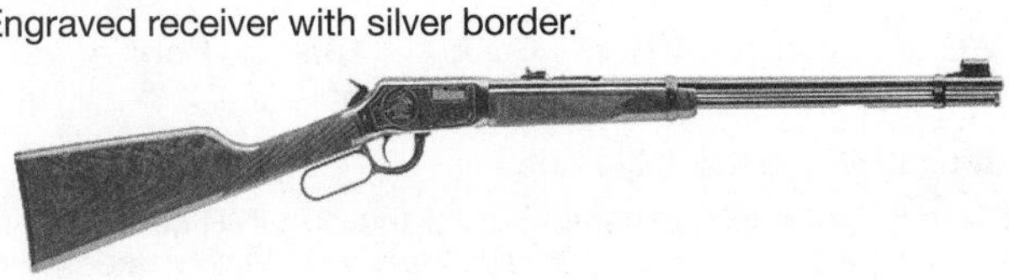

NIB	Exc.	V.G.	Good	Fair	Poor
1450	1100	900	750	600	400

Model 9422 Legacy

This model has a semi-pistol-grip stock of checkered walnut. Will shoot .22 caliber LR, L, or S cartridges. Fitted with a 16" barrel. Weight is about 6 lbs. Introduced in 1998.

NIB	Exc.	V.G.	Good	Fair	Poor
850	675	525	375	225	125

Model 9422 Large Loop & Walnut

Introduced in 1998 this model features a walnut stock with large loop lever. Large loop offered on .22 LR, L, or S model. Standard lever on .22 WMR version. Fitted with 16" barrel. Weight is about 6 lbs.

NIB	Exc.	V.G.	Good	Fair	Poor
900	750	575	450	300	250

Model 9422 High Grade Series II

This model features a high-grade walnut stock with cut checkering. Receiver engraved with dogs and squirrels. Fitted with 16" barrel. Weight is about 6 lbs. Introduced in 1998.

NIB	Exc.	V.G.	Good	Fair	Poor
1450	1100	900	750	600	400

Model 9417 Traditional

Introduced in 2003 this model is chambered for the .17 HMR cartridge and fitted with a 20.5" barrel. Adjustable sights. Checkered walnut stock with straight grip. Weight is about 6 lbs.

NIB	Exc.	V.G.	Good	Fair	Poor
1200	975	850	675	400	300

Model 9417 Legacy

Similar to the model above but fitted with a 22.5" barrel and checkered walnut with pistol grip. Weight is about 6 lbs. Introduced in 2003.

NIB	Exc.	V.G.	Good	Fair	Poor
1200	975	850	675	400	300

MODEL 9422 TRIBUTE SERIES

As of 2005 the Model 9422 production will end. These final production Model 9422s will be limited to a total production of 9,422 rifles. Each rifle will have the Winchester Horse and Rider on one side and the Model 9422 tribute logo on the other side.

High Grade Traditional Tribute

This model features a 20.5" barrel with high grade checkered walnuty stock. Blued receiver with high-relief silver inlay on both sides of the receiver.

NIB	Exc.	V.G.	Good	Fair	Poor
1400	1200	975	825	650	300

High Grade Legacy Tribute

Similar to the model above but with semi-pistol grip and 22.5" barrel.

NIB	Exc.	V.G.	Good	Fair	Poor
1500	1300	1075	925	650	300

Custom Traditional Tribute

walnut stock. High-relief scroll engraved receiver with gold logos on both sides. Limited to 222 rifles.

NIB	Exc.	V.G.	Good	Fair	Poor
2600	2200	1650	1200	800	500

Special Edition Traditional Tribute

This model has a 20.5" barrel with checkered walnut straight grip stock and engraved blued receiver. Engraved logos on both sides of receiver.

NIB	Exc.	V.G.	Good	Fair	Poor
1200	975	850	675	400	300

Special Edition Legacy Tribute

This 22.5" barrel model has a checkered semi-pistol grip stock Blued receiver with engraved logos on both sides.

NIB	Exc.	V.G.	Good	Fair	Poor
1200	975	850	675	400	300

Model 64 (Post-'64)

This is a post-1964 version of the lever-action Model 64. It is chambered for the .30-30 cartridge and has a 24" round barrel with open sights and a 5-round, 2/3-length tubular magazine. The finish is blued with a plain walnut pistol-grip stock. It was manufactured between 1972 and 1974.

NIB	Exc.	V.G.	Good	Fair	Poor
—	800	650	550	375	250

MODEL 1885 LOW WALL

Introduced in fall of 1999 this single-shot model is chambered for the .22 LR or .17 Mach II cartridge. It is fitted with a 24.5" half octagon barrel with leaf rear sight. Drilled and tapped for a tang sight. Crescent steel buttplate. Walnut stock. Weight is about 8 lbs. Limited to 2,400 rifles.

Grade I

NIB	Exc.	V.G.	Good	Fair	Poor
1050	900	750	600	500	300

High Grade

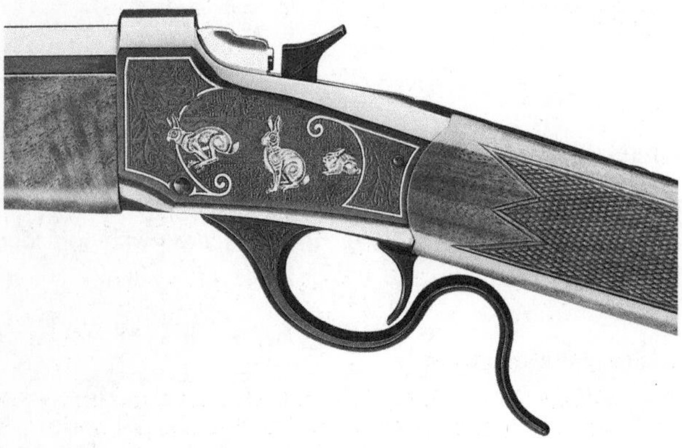

Left side detail of High Grade 1885 Low Wall

NIB	Exc.	V.G.	Good	Fair	Poor
1300	1050	875	750	600	400

Model 1885 High Wall Hunter

Single-shot; patterned after original Model 1885 designed by John Browning. Calibers: .223, .22-250, .270 WSM, 7mm WSM, .300 WSM, .325 WSM. Stock: Checkered walnut. Barrel: 28-inch blued, sightless octagon with Pachmayr pad. Weight: 8-1/2 lbs.

NIB	Exc.	V.G.	Good	Fair	Poor
1100	925	750	650	450	325

Model 1885 .30-06 Centennial High Wall Hunter

Similar to Model 1885 High Wall Hunter but with premium wood and gold inlay on receiver. Commemorates centennial of .30-06 cartridge. Introduced 2006.

NIB	Exc.	V.G.	Good	Fair	Poor
1300	1125	875	750	550	325

Model 1885 Low Wall Classic

This single-shot rifle is chambered for the .17 HMR cartridge and fitted with a 24" octagon barrel. Checkered walnut stock with straight grip and schnabel forend. Adjustable sights. Weight is about 8 lbs. Introduced in 2003. In 2005 the .17 Mach 2 caliber was offered in this model.

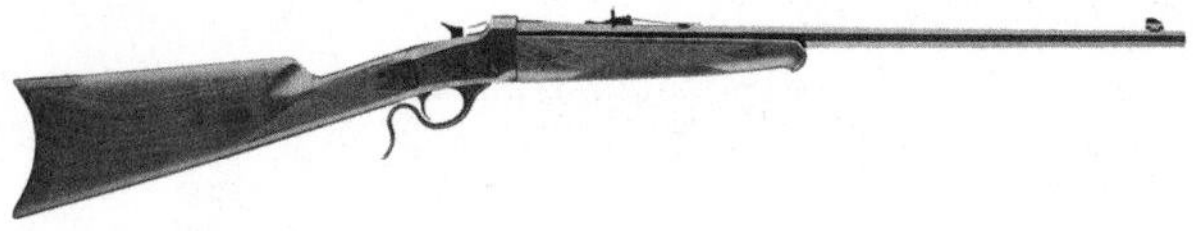

NIB	Exc.	V.G.	Good	Fair	Poor
1100	925	750	650	450	325

Model 1885 Low Wall 17 Mach 2

Similar to Model 1885 High Wall but with low-profile receiver, crescent buttplate, and 24-inch barrel. Chambered for 17 Mach 2 rimfire cartridge. Introduced 2006.

NIB	Exc.	V.G.	Good	Fair	Poor
1050	900	750	600	500	300

MODEL 1892

Introduced in mid-1997 this model is chambered for the .45 Colt cartridge. It features a straight grip, full magazine, and crescent buttplate.

Grade I

2,500 rifles with engraved receiver.

NIB	Exc.	V.G.	Good	Fair	Poor
1100	925	750	650	450	325

High Grade

1,000 rifle with gold accents.

NIB	Exc.	V.G.	Good	Fair	Poor
1500	1300	1075	925	650	300

Model 1892 Short Rifle

This model is fitted with a 20" barrel and chambered for the .45 Colt, .357 Magnum, .44 Magnum, and .44-40 cartridges. Walnut stock and blued barrel and receiver. Weight is about 6.25 lbs. Introduced in 1999.

NIB	Exc.	V.G.	Good	Fair	Poor
1200	975	850	675	400	300

MODEL 1886

Introduced to the Winchester line in 1997 this was a noncatalogued item. This model features a 26" octagon barrel, semi-pistol grip, and crescent buttplate.

Grade I

2,500 rifles with blued receiver.

NIB	Exc.	V.G.	Good	Fair	Poor
1050	900	750	600	500	300

High Grade

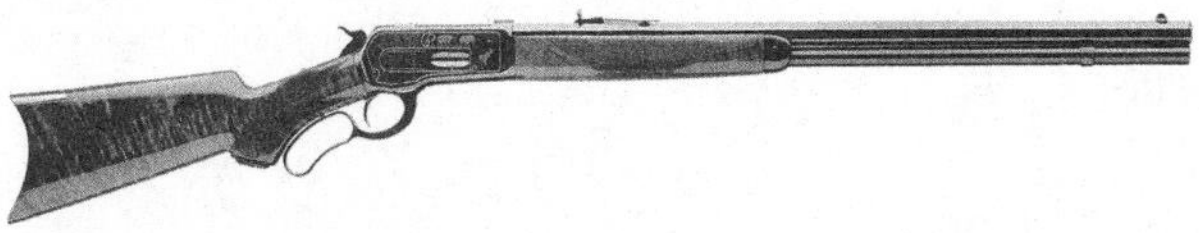

1,000 rifles with gold accents on receiver.

NIB	Exc.	V.G.	Good	Fair	Poor
1500	1300	1075	925	650	300

Model 1886 Take Down Classic

Introduced in 1999 this model is chambered for the .45-70 cartridge and features a 26" barrel with takedown feature. Walnut stock with pistol grip and crescent butt. Magazine capacity is 8 rounds. Weight is about 9.25 lbs.

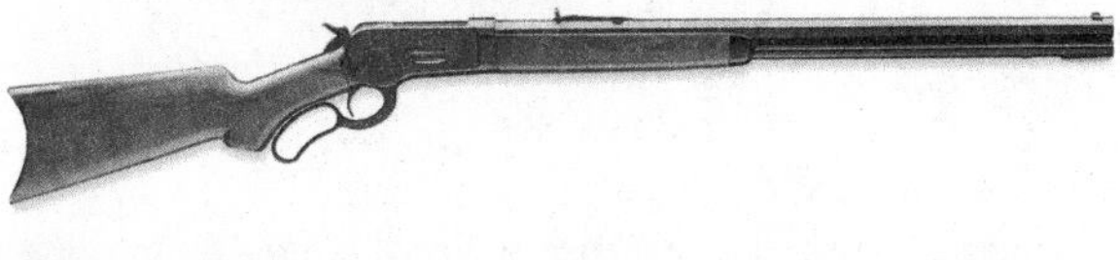

NIB	Exc.	V.G.	Good	Fair	Poor
1300	1125	875	750	550	325

MODEL 1886 EXTRA LIGHT

This model is similar to the Model 1886 Classic but fitted with a 22" round tapered barrel and half magazine. Chambered for the .45-70 cartridge. Shotgun butt. Weight is about 7.25 lbs. Limited edition. Introduced in 2000.

Grade I (3,500)

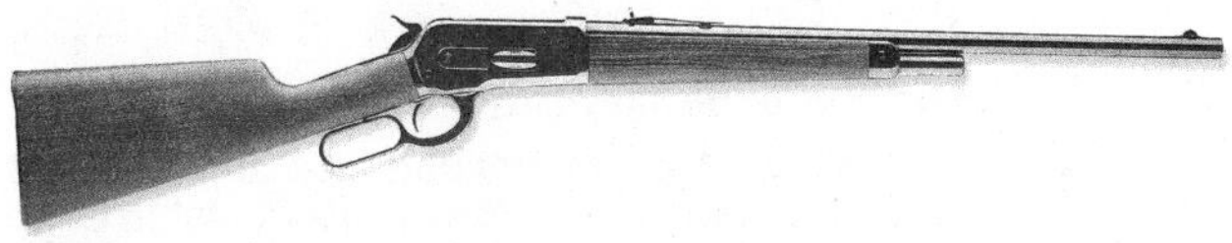

NIB	Exc.	V.G.	Good	Fair	Poor
1100	925	750	650	450	325

High Grade (1,000)

NIB	Exc.	V.G.	Good	Fair	Poor
1500	1300	1075	925	650	300

MODEL 1895 LIMITED EDITION

Introduced in 1995 this reproduction of the famous Model 1895 is offered in .30-06 caliber with 24" barrel. Magazine capacity is 4 rounds. Weight is approximately 8 lbs. Available in two grades, each limited to 4,000 rifles. Reintroduced in 2010 in .30-40 Krag caliber.

Grade I

NIB	Exc.	V.G.	Good	Fair	Poor
1050	900	750	600	500	300

High Grade

NIB	Exc.	V.G.	Good	Fair	Poor
1500	1300	1075	925	650	300

MODEL 1895—LIMITED EDITION FOR THE YEAR 2000

Same as above but chambered for the .405 Win. cartridge. Introduced in 2000.

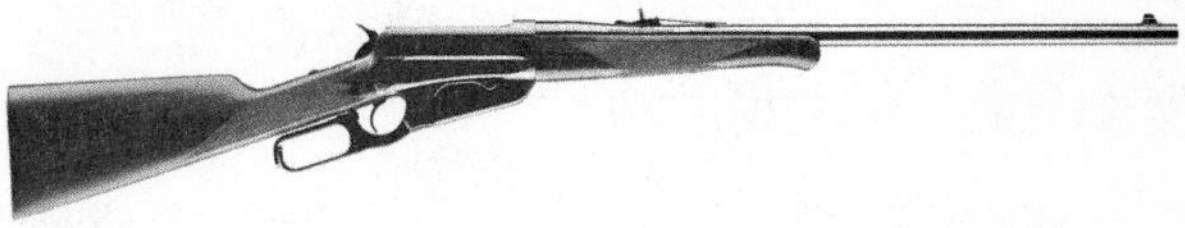

Grade I

NIB	Exc.	V.G.	Good	Fair	Poor
1100	925	750	650	450	325

High Grade

NIB	Exc.	V.G.	Good	Fair	Poor
1500	1300	1075	925	650	300

Model 1895 Saddle Ring Carbine

Patterned after original Model 1895 carbine. Features include blued 22-inch barrel, ladder style rear sight; D&T for Lyman side mount; saddle ring on left side of receiver; rollmarked -inch.30 Gov't \xd4 06.-inch Chambered in .30-06 only; commemorates centennial of .30-06 cartridge. Introduced 2006.

NIB	Exc.	V.G.	Good	Fair	Poor
1200	975	850	675	400	300

Winchester Model 1895 Safari Centennial High Grade

Lever-action rifle patterned after original Winchester Model 1895. Chambered in .405 Winchester; commemorates Theodore Roosevelt's 1909 African Safari. 24" blued round barrel, four-round box magazine, checkered walnut forend and buttstock with inlaid "TR" medallion, engraved and silvered receiver. Weight: 8 lbs.

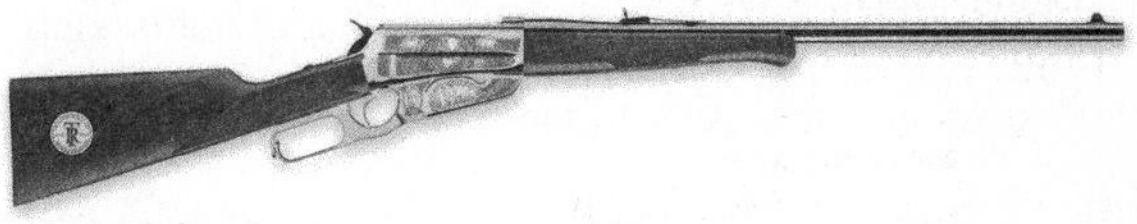

NIB	Exc.	V.G.	Good	Fair	Poor
1600	1375	1075	925	650	300

Custom Grade

Similar to above but with jeweled hammer, fancier wood and engraving, gold-filled highlights and numerous accessories. Production limited to 1000 sets.

NIB	Exc.	V.G.	Good	Fair	Poor
3000	2500	1950	1575	1200	700

Model 52B Sporting Rifle

A 1993 limited-edition rifle (6,000 guns) that is a faithful reproduction of the famous Winchester Model 52 Sporter. Equipped with a 24" barrel, adjustable trigger, and "B" style cheekpiece. This model was reissued in 1997 and limited to 3,000 rifles.

NIB	Exc.	V.G.	Good	Fair	Poor
750	600	475	350	225	150

Express Rifle

This is an Over/Under, double-barreled rifle chambered for the .257 Roberts, .270, 7.7x65R, .30-06, and the 9.3x74R cartridges. It features 23.5" barrels with a solid rib and express sights. It is engraved with game scenes and has a satin-finished receiver. The stock is checkered select walnut. It was manufactured in 1984 and 1985.

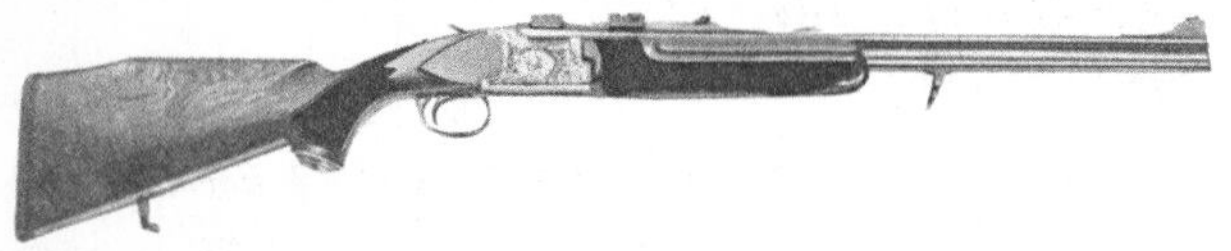

NIB	Exc.	V.G.	Good	Fair	Poor
—	3500	3000	2100	1700	900

POST-1964 MODEL 70

These post-Model 70 rifles were fitted with redesigned actions and bolt with free-floating barrels, and new style stock with impressed checkering.

NOTE: *In 1994, U.S. Repeating Arms reintroduced the pre-1964 Model 70 action on many of its Model 70 rifles. At the present time this new action does not affect values but may do so in the future depending on shooter reaction.*

In 2006, the Model 70 was discontinued by US Repeating Arms. It is uncertain whether the bulk of post-'64 Model 70s will become truly collectible, although the potential is there.

In the editor's opinion, there was never anything really wrong with the post-'64 Model 70. It might even be argued that in "dumbing down" the M70, Winchester was simply ahead of its time, as many of the manufacturing "shortcuts" that characterized the post-'64 M70 have come to be accepted as commonplace.

Nevertheless, as the M70 reached the end of its seven-decade run, it had lost much of its premium status. The Ruger M77, the Remington M700 and Model Seven, the Browning A-Bolt and other high-end bolt rifles gave it a serious run for its money.

In October of 2007, Winchester Repeating Arms announced that the pre-'64-style Model 70 would once again be produced – this time at the FN plant in Columbia, SC. We wish it well!

Model 70—Standard Grade

This is a bolt-action sporting rifle chambered for various popular calibers such as the .22-250, .222 Rem., .243 Win., .270 Win., .30-06, and .308 Win. It features a 22" barrel with open sights and a 5-round, integral box magazine. The finish is blued with a Monte Carlo-type stock furnished with sling swivels. It was manufactured between 1964 and 1971.

NIB	Exc.	V.G.	Good	Fair	Poor
—	600	475	325	175	110

Model 70 Varmint

Chambered for the .22-25, .222 Rem., and .243 Win. cartridges this rifle is fitted with a 24" heavyweight barrel with no sights. Magazine capacity is 5 rounds. Weight is about 9.75 lbs. Built from 1964 to 1971.

NIB	Exc.	V.G.	Good	Fair	Poor
—	600	450	300	150	100

Model 70 Westerner

This model is chambered for the .264 Win. Magnum and .300 Win. Magnum cartridges. Open sights, 24" barrel. Ventilated recoil pad. Weight is about 7.25 lbs. Built from 1964 to 1971.

NIB	Exc.	V.G.	Good	Fair	Poor
—	650	475	325	175	110

Model 70 African

Chambered for the .458 Win. Magnum cartridge this rifle is fitted with a 22" barrel with open sights. Magazine capacity is 3 rounds. Weight is about 8.5 lbs. Built from 1964 to 1971.

NIB	Exc.	V.G.	Good	Fair	Poor
—	925	750	485	275	175

Model 70 Magnum

Chambered for the 7mm Rem. Mag., .300 Win. Mag., and .375 H&H cartridges. Barrel length is 24". Weight is about 7.75 lbs. Built from 1964 to 1971.

NIB	Exc.	V.G.	Good	Fair	Poor
—	750	585	375	225	175

Model 70 Deluxe

Built from 1964 to 1971, this rifle features a Monte Carlo stock with hand checkering and ebony forend tip. Offered in .243, .270, .30-06, .300 Win. Mag. Fitted with 22" barrel except magnums, which have 24" barrel. Weight is about 7.5 lbs.

NIB	Exc.	V.G.	Good	Fair	Poor
—	750	575	350	175	125

Model 70 Mannlicher

This is a full-length, Mannlicher-type stocked version of the Model 70 bolt-action rifle that is chambered for the .243, .270, .308, and the .30-06 cartridges. It was introduced in 1969. It features a 19" barrel with open sights. The finish is blued. It was discontinued in 1972. Only 2,401 were produced. Excellent quality.

NIB	Exc.	V.G.	Good	Fair	Poor
—	975	825	625	425	310

Model 70 Target Rifle

This version is chambered for the .308 or the .30-06 cartridges. It was offered with a 24" heavy barrel without sights. It is furnished with bases for a target scope. The finish is blued with a heavy walnut target stock with a palm rest. Weight is approximately 10.25 lbs.

NIB	Exc.	V.G.	Good	Fair	Poor
—	875	775	575	375	260

Model 70 International Match Army

This version is chambered for the .308 cartridge and has a 24" heavy barrel furnished without sights. It has an adjustable trigger and is blued, with a target-type heavy stock that had an accessory rail and an adjustable butt.

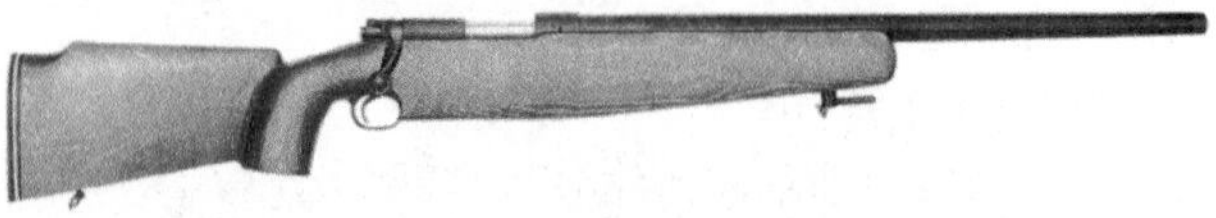

NIB	Exc.	V.G.	Good	Fair	Poor
—	950	850	600	400	300

Model 70A

This is a utility version of the bolt-action post-1964 Model 70. It was furnished without a hinged floorplate. The finish is blued, with a walnut stock. It was manufactured between 1972 and 1978.

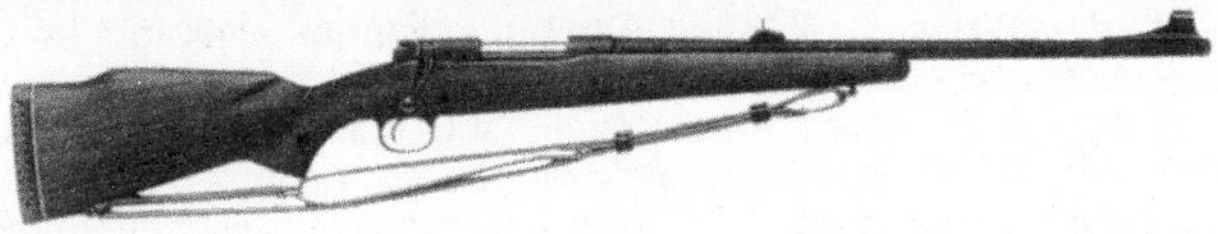

NIB	Exc.	V.G.	Good	Fair	Poor
—	500	400	350	300	125

Model 670

Economy-grade version of the Model 70. Hardwood stock, iron sights, non-hinged floorplate, 22" blued barrel. Manufactured from 1967 to 1973.

NIB	Exc.	V.G.	Good	Fair	Poor
—	450	400	300	250	100

Model 70 XTR Featherweight

This gun was built after the takeover by the U.S.R.A. Company. It is a bolt-action sporting rifle chambered for various calibers from .22-250 up to the .30-06 cartridges. It has a 22" barrel that is furnished without sights and features either a short- or medium-length action. It has a 5-round, integral magazine. The finish is blued, with a checkered walnut stock. It was introduced in 1981.

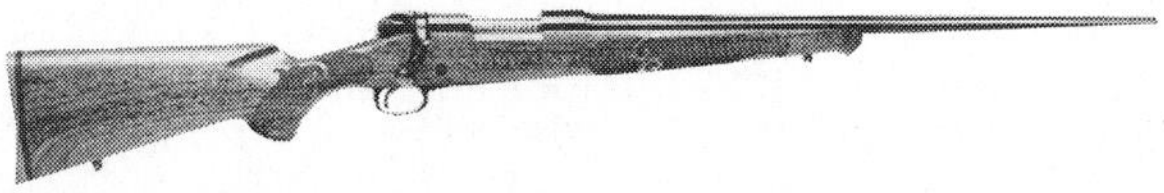

NIB	Exc.	V.G.	Good	Fair	Poor
—	725	625	450	325	265

Model 70 Fiftieth Anniversary Model

This is a commemorative version of the post-1964 Model 70 bolt-action rifle. It is chambered for the .300 Win. Mag. and is offered with a 24" barrel. It is engraved and high-gloss blued with a deluxe, checkered walnut stock. There were 500 manufactured in 1987. In order to realize collector potential, it must be NIB with all supplied materials.

NIB	Exc.	V.G.	Good	Fair	Poor
1500	1400	1200	900	500	300

Model 70 XTR Super Express

This is a heavy-duty version of the post-1964 Model 70 chambered for the .375 H&H and the .458 Win. Mag. cartridges. It is offered with a 22" or 24" heavy barrel and a 3-round, integral box magazine. This version has extra recoil lugs mounted in the stock and is blued with a select, straight-grain walnut stock and a recoil pad standard.

NIB	Exc.	V.G.	Good	Fair	Poor
1100	925	750	650	450	325

Model 70 XTR Varmint

This version is chambered for the .22-250, .223, and the .243 cartridges. It has a 24" heavy barrel and is furnished without sights. It has a 5-round magazine and is blued with a heavy walnut stock. It was introduced in 1972.

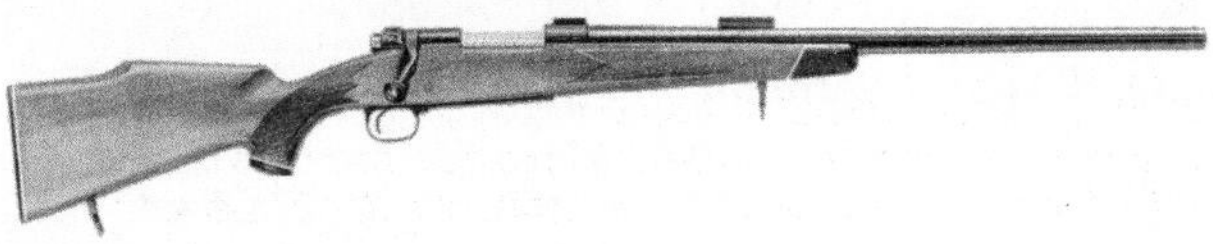

NIB	Exc.	V.G.	Good	Fair	Poor
650	550	400	250	200	100

Model 70 Winlight

This version is offered in various calibers between .270 and the .338 Win. Mag. It features a matte-blue finish and a fiberglass stock. It is offered with a 22" or a 24" barrel and a 3- or 4-round magazine. It was introduced in 1986.

NIB	Exc.	V.G.	Good	Fair	Poor
700	550	400	250	200	100

Ranger (Model 70)

This is a utility-grade, bolt-action rifle chambered for the .270 Win., .30-06, and the 7mm Rem. Mag. cartridges. It is offered with a 22" or a 24" barrel with open sights and has a 3- or 4-round box magazine. The finish is blued with a plain hardwood stock.

NIB	Exc.	V.G.	Good	Fair	Poor
450	300	275	225	150	100

Model 70 Featherweight

Bolt-action rifle chambered in .22-250, .243, 7mm-08, .308, .270 WSM, 7mm WSM, .300 WSM, .325 WSM, .25-06, .270, .30-06, 7mm Remington Magnum, .300 Winchester Magnum, .338 Winchester Magnum. 22" blued barrel (24" in magnum chamberings), satin-finished checkered Grade I walnut stock, controlled round feeding. Capacity 5 rounds (short action) or 3 rounds (long action). Weight: 6-1/2 to 7-1/4 lbs. Pachmayr Decelerator pad. No sights but drilled and tapped for scope mounts. Values shown are for long action. Deduct 15 percent for short action.

NIB	Exc.	V.G.	Good	Fair	Poor
850	650	450	375	225	125

NOTE: In 2003 a left-hand model was offered. Add $35. For stainless steel model add $60.

Model 70 Featherweight Classic All-Terrain

Introduced in 1996, this model features a weather-resistant stainless steel barrel and action with fiberglass/graphite black synthetic stock. Offered in .270 Win., .30-06, 7mm Rem. Mag., .330 Win. Mag. Weight is about 7.25 lbs. Also offered with the BOSS system.

NIB	Exc.	V.G.	Good	Fair	Poor
950	650	450	325	225	125

NOTE: Add $100 for BOSS.

Model 70 Featherweight Super Short

Introduced in 2003 this rifle features a shorter receiver to handle the .223 WSSM and .243 WSSM cartridges. Fitted with a 22" barrel and a checkered walnut stock with solid recoil pad. Weight is about 6 lbs.

NIB	Exc.	V.G.	Good	Fair	Poor
770	600	500	400	300	200

Model 70 Classic Laredo

First offered in 1996, this model features a heavy 26" barrel with pre-1964 action on a gray synthetic stock. Chambered for the 7mm Rem. Mag and the .300 Win. Mag. The forearm is a beavertail. Finish is matte blue. In 1997 this model was offered chambered for the 7mm STW cartridge. In 1998 this model was offered with fluted barrel.

NIB	Exc.	V.G.	Good	Fair	Poor
750	650	550	500	400	300

NOTE: Add $100 for BOSS. Add $125 for fluted barrel.

Model 70 Classic Compact

Introduced in 1998, this model is a scaled-down version of the Featherweight. It has a length of pull of 12.5" and a 20" barrel. Chambered for .243, .308, and 7mm-08 calibers. Checkered walnut stock. Weight is about 6.5 lbs.

NIB	Exc.	V.G.	Good	Fair	Poor
750	650	550	500	400	300

Model 70 Classic Sporter LT

Introduced in 1999, this model is chambered for a wide variety of calibers from .25-06 to .338 Win. Mag. Fitted with a 24" or 26" barrel depending on caliber and no sights. Walnut stock with butt pad. Blued finish. Also offered in left-hand models from .270 to .338 Win. Mag. Weight is about 8 lbs.

NIB	Exc.	V.G.	Good	Fair	Poor
750	650	550	500	400	300

NOTE: Add $30 for left-hand models.

Model 70 Classic Safari Express

This model is chambered for the .375 H&H Mag, .416 Rem. Mag, and .458 Win. Mag. fitted with a 24" barrel magazine capacity is 4 rounds. Walnut stock with open sights. Left-hand model offered in .375 H&H. Weight is about 8.5 lbs. Introduced in 1999.

NIB	Exc.	V.G.	Good	Fair	Poor
1200	950	875	650	500	300

NOTE: Add $30 for .375 H&H left-hand model.

Model 70 Super Grade

Another U.S.R.A. rifle that features a select walnut stock, claw-controlled round feed, a single reinforced cross bolt, 24" barrel shipped with bases and rings. The buttstock has a straight comb with classic cheekpiece and deep-cut checkering. Available in .270, .30-06, 7mm Rem. Mag., .300 Win. Mag., .338 Win. Mag.,.270 WSM, .300 WSM. Rifle weighs approximately 7.75 lbs. Currently in production.

NIB	Exc.	V.G.	Good	Fair	Poor
1500	1300	1075	925	650	300

Model 70 RMEF Super Grade

As above but with stainless steel action and barrel. Chambered for the .300 Win. Mag. cartridge. Fitted with a 26" barrel. Checkered walnut stock with solid recoil pad. Weight is about 8 lbs. Introduced in 2003. Special RMEF (Rock Mountain Elk Foundation) emblem on grip cap. Limited production.

NIB	Exc.	V.G.	Good	Fair	Poor
1600	1400	1175	975	650	300

Model 70 RMEF Super Grade III

This model is chambered for the .325 WSM or .300 WSM calibers and fitted with a 24" stainless steel barrel without sights. Super Grade walnut checkered stock with shadow line cheek piece. Weight is about 7.75 lbs. RMEF grip cap medallion. Introduced in 2005.

NIB	Exc.	V.G.	Good	Fair	Poor
1200	950	875	650	500	300

Model 70 Classic Super Grade III

Similar to the model above but chambered for a variety of short action calibers including WSM calibers. Fitted with a 24" barrel with no sights except for .300 Win. Mag. and .338 Win. Mag. which have 26" barrels. Weight is about 7.75 to 8 lbs. depending on caliber. Introduced in 2005.

NIB	Exc.	V.G.	Good	Fair	Poor
1200	950	875	650	500	300

Model 70 Super Express

A U.S.R.A. version of the post-1964 XTR Super Express. Specifications are the same as the earlier model. Rifle weighs 8.5 lbs. Introduced in 1993.

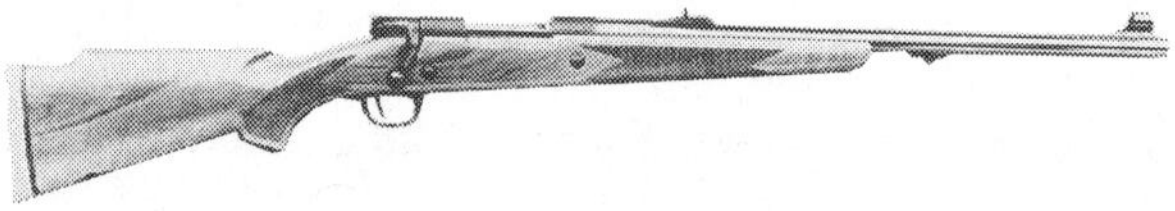

NIB	Exc.	V.G.	Good	Fair	Poor
1500	1200	1075	975	650	300

Model 70 Heavy Varmint

Introduced by U.S.R.A. in 1993, this rifle features a fiberglass/graphite stock with heavy 26" stainless steel barrel. Offered in .223,

.22-250, .243, and .308. In 1997, this model was offered chambered for the .222 Rem. cartridge. Rifle weighs about 10.75 lbs.

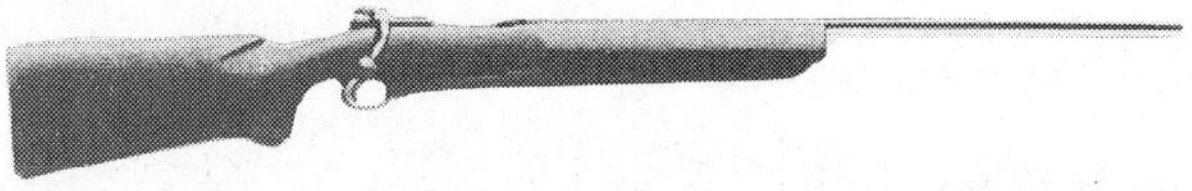

NIB	Exc.	V.G.	Good	Fair	Poor
750	575	500	425	375	200

Model 70 Heavy Varmint—Fluted Barrel

Introduced in 1997, this model is similar to the above Varmint with the addition of a fluted barrel. Calibers are also the same as the above model.

NIB	Exc.	V.G.	Good	Fair	Poor
825	625	500	475	350	250

Model 70 Stainless

All-metal parts are stainless steel, including the barrel, with synthetic stock. Available with 24" barrel and chambered for .270, .30-06, 7mm Rem. Mag., .300 Win. Mag., and .338 Win. Mag. Weighs about 7.5 lbs. Currently in production. In 2001 this model was offered chambered for the .300 Winchester Short Magnum (WSM) cartridge.

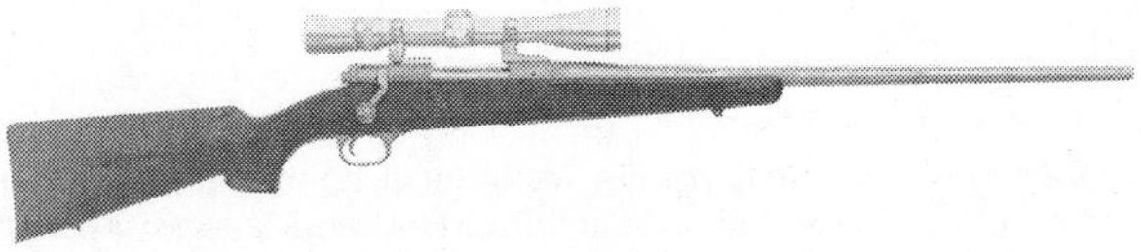

NIB	Exc.	V.G.	Good	Fair	Poor
850	650	450	375	225	125

Model 70 Classic Laminated Stainless

Introduced in 1998 this model features a laminated stock and stainless steel barrel and action. Offered in .270, .30-06, 7mm Rem. Mag., .300 Win. Mag., and .338 Win. Mag. Pre-1964 action. Bolt is jeweled and bolt handle is knurled. Barrel lengths are 24" and 26", depending on caliber. Weight is about 8 lbs. In 2001, this model was offered chambered for the .300 Winchester Short Magnum (WSM) cartridge.

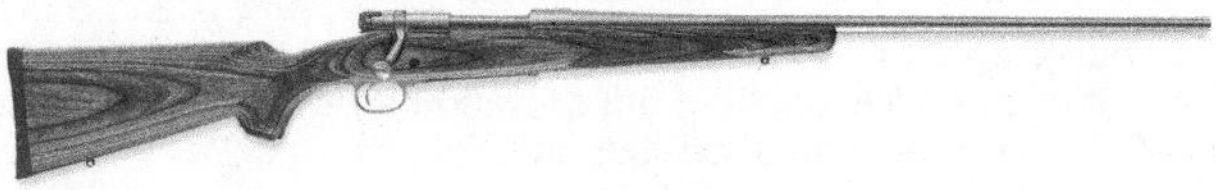

NIB	Exc.	V.G.	Good	Fair	Poor
850	650	450	375	225	125

Model 70 Classic Camo Stainless

This model features a Sporter-style stock with 24" or 26" barrel and Mossy Oak Treestand camo on the stock. Chambered for .270 Win., .30-06, 7mm Rem. Mag., and .300 Win Mag. Magazine capacity is 5 rounds. Weight is about 7.5 lbs. Introduced in 1998.

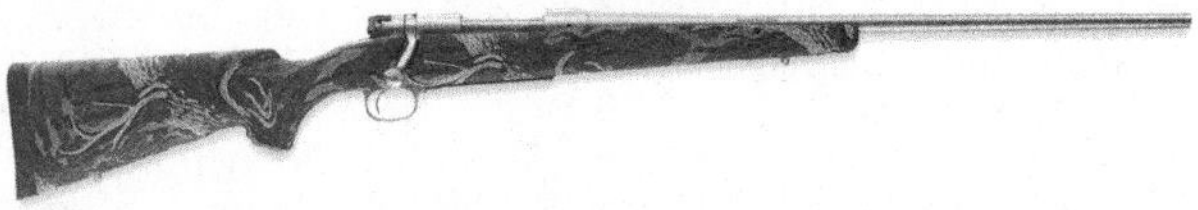

NIB	Exc.	V.G.	Good	Fair	Poor
850	650	450	375	225	125

Model 70 SM

This rifle features a synthetic stock with black matte finish. Barrel length is 24". Available in 10 calibers from .223 Rem. to .375 H&H Mag. Depending on caliber, rifle weighs between 7 and 8 lbs.

NIB	Exc.	V.G.	Good	Fair	Poor
850	650	450	375	225	125

Model 70 DBM-S

Similar to Model 70 SM but fitted with detachable box magazine. The metal parts are blued and the stock is synthetic. Offered in eight calibers from .223 Rem. to .338 Win. Mag. Furnished with scope bases and rings are open sights. Rifle weighs about 7.25 lbs., depending on caliber. Introduced in 1993.

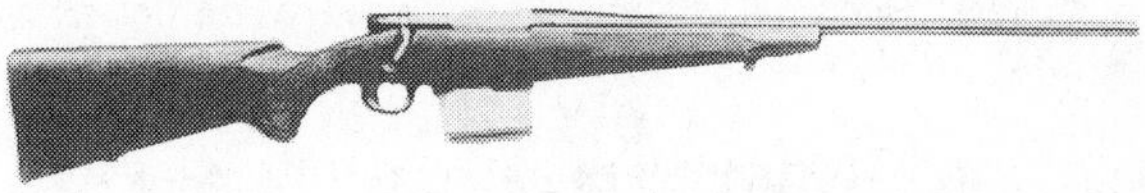

NIB	Exc.	V.G.	Good	Fair	Poor
650	550	450	375	225	125

Model 70 Varmint

Similar to the Model 70 Heavy Varmint but furnished with a traditional walnut stock and 26" medium-heavy barrel. Offered in .223 Rem., .22-250, .243, and .308. Weighs 9 lbs.

NIB	Exc.	V.G.	Good	Fair	Poor
700	600	450	325	225	150

Model 70 DBM

DBM stands for detachable box magazine. Fitted with a straight-comb walnut stock. Jeweled bolt with blued receiver. Shipped with scope bases and rings or open sights. Rifle offered in eight calibers from .223 Rem. to .300 Win. Mag. Rifle weighs about 7.35 lbs., depending on caliber. Introduced in 1993.

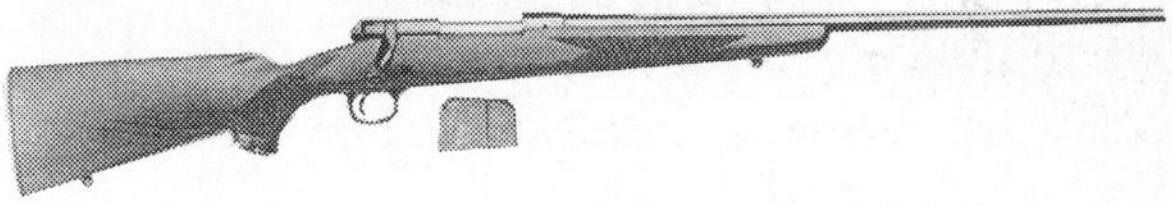

NIB	Exc.	V.G.	Good	Fair	Poor
700	600	450	325	225	150

Model 70 Sporter

U.S.R.A.'s basic Model 70 offering. Straight-comb walnut stock with checkering, jeweled bolt and blued receiver and barrel are standard. Available in 12 calibers from .223 Rem. to .338 Win. Mag. including .270 Weatherby Mag. and .300 Weatherby Mag. Barrel length is 24" and is available with either scope bases and rings or open sights. Rifle weighs about 7.5 lbs.

NIB	Exc.	V.G.	Good	Fair	Poor
700	600	450	325	225	150

Model 70 WinTuff

Similar to the Sporter except fitted with a laminated hardwood straight-comb stock with cheekpiece. Offered in 24" barrel lengths with a choice of 6 calibers from .270 Win. to .338 Win. Mag. Furnished with scope bases and rings. Rifle weighs about 7.65 lbs., depending on caliber.

NIB	Exc.	V.G.	Good	Fair	Poor
700	600	450	325	225	150

Model 70 Lightweight

Similar to the Model 70 Winlight. Offered with straight-comb checkered walnut stock with knurled bolt and blued receiver and barrel. The barrel is 22" without sights. Offered in 5 calibers: .223, .243, .270, .308, and .30-06. Rifle weighs about 7 lbs., depending on caliber.

NIB	Exc.	V.G.	Good	Fair	Poor
700	600	450	325	225	150

Model 70 Black Shadow

Chambered for the .270, .30-06, 7mm Rem. Mag., and .300 Win. Mag. and fitted with a 22" or 24" barrel, depending on caliber. Finish is matte black with composite stock. Push-feed action. Weight is 7.25 lbs. Introduced in 1998.

NIB	Exc.	V.G.	Good	Fair	Poor
550	450	375	325	225	150

Model 70 Ultimate Shadow

Introduced in 2003 this bolt-action model features a new black synthetic stock design with improved gripping surfaces and soft recoil pad. This model has a blued action and barrel. Chambered for the .300 WSM, .270 WSM, or the 7mm WSM cartridges. Fitted with a 24" barrel. Weight is about 6.75 lbs. Also offered with stainless action and barrel.

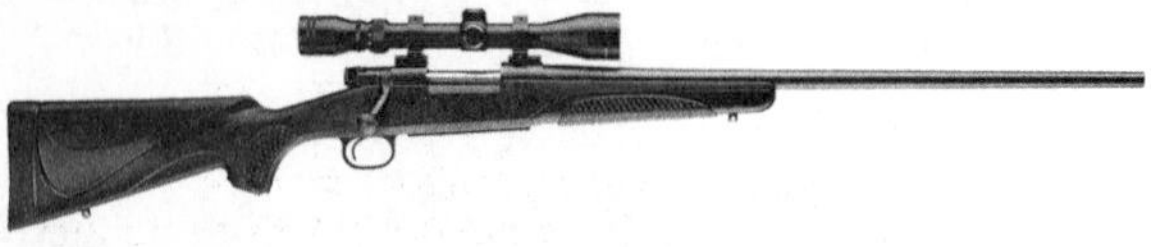

NIB	Exc.	V.G.	Good	Fair	Poor
800	700	425	350	275	125

NOTE: For stainless steel model add $45.

Model 70 Ultimate Shadow Camo

As above but with Mossy Oak New Break-Up camo. Introduced in 2004.

NIB	Exc.	V.G.	Good	Fair	Poor
900	800	525	450	375	150

Model 70 Super Shadow Super Short

Similar to the above model but chambered for the .223 WSM or .243 WSM cartridge. Fitted with a 22" barrel and blind magazine. Weight is about 6 lbs. Introduced in 2003.

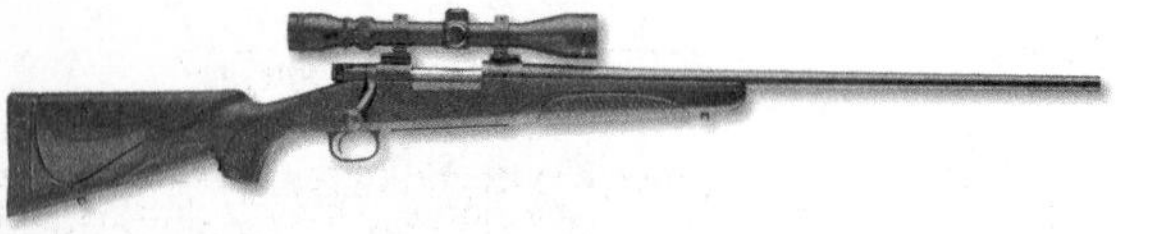

NIB	Exc.	V.G.	Good	Fair	Poor
700	600	450	325	225	150

Model 70 Super Shadow

Similar to the Ultimate Shadow but fitted with a controlled round push feed bolt. Chambered for the .300 WSM, .270 WSM, or the 7mm WSM cartridge. Fitted with a 22" barrel, composite stock and blind magaziine. Weight is about 6.75 lbs. Introduced in 2003. New calibers: .243, .308, .270, .30-06, .300WM.

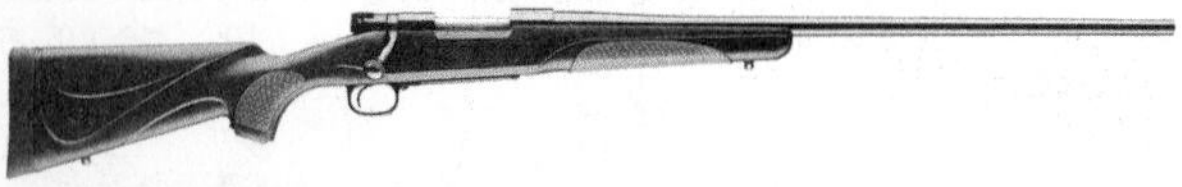

NIB	Exc.	V.G.	Good	Fair	Poor
700	600	450	325	225	150

Model 70 Stealth

This is a varmint model with 26" heavy barrel chambered for .223 Rem., .22-250, or .308 Win. It has a push-feed bolt-action. Black synthetic stock. Matte black finish. Weight is approximately 10.85 lbs. In 2004 the .223 WSSM, .243 WSSM and the .25 WSSM calibers were added.

NIB	Exc.	V.G.	Good	Fair	Poor
850	650	450	375	225	125

Model 70 Coyote

This model, introduced in 2000, has a push-feed bolt-action and is chambered for the .223 Rem, .22-250, and .243 Win. calibers. Fitted with a medium-heavy 24" stainless steel barrel with laminated stock and large forend. Weight is about 9 lbs. In 2002 the rifle was offered in .270 WSM, 7mm WSM, and .300 WSM. In 2005 the .325 WSM was added to this model. Discontinued 2006.

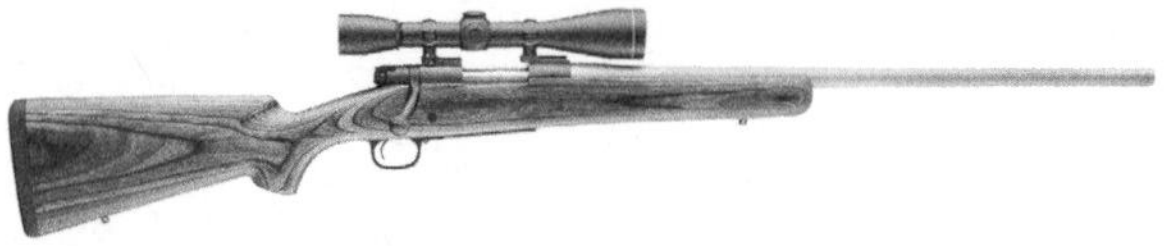

NIB	Exc.	V.G.	Good	Fair	Poor
750	650	450	375	225	125

Model 70 Coyote Lite

Introduced in 2005 this model features a lightweight composite stock with skeletonized aluminum block bedding. Recoil pad. Fluted 24" medium-heavy barrel with no sights. Offered in .223 Rem and all WSSM and WSM calibers. New calibers: .22-250, .243, .308.

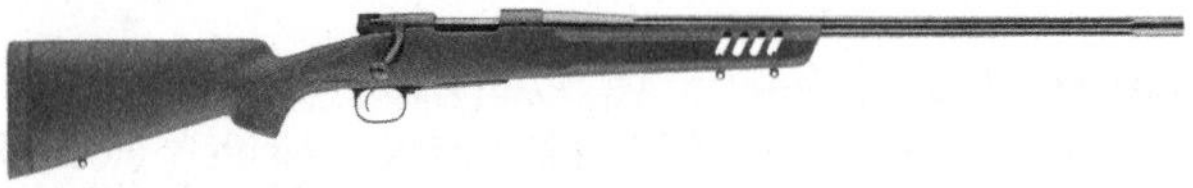

NIB	Exc.	V.G.	Good	Fair	Poor
850	650	450	375	225	125

NOTE: Add $40 for stainless steel.

Model 70 Ladies/Youth Ranger

A scaled-down version of the Ranger. Length of pull is 1" shorter than standard. Rifle weighs 6.5 lbs. Chambered in .243 and .308. In 1997 this model was offered chambered for the .223 Rem. and the 7mm-08 Rem. cartridges.

NIB	Exc.	V.G.	Good	Fair	Poor
450	300	275	225	150	100

Model 70 Shadow Elite Stainless

Bolt-action rifle. Calibers: .22-250, .243, .308, .270, .30-06, .300 WM, .338 WM, .375 H&H, .270 WSM, 7mm WSM, .300 WSM, .325 WSM. Barrel: Stainless steel, 24-inch or 26-inch (.300, .338 WM). Stock: Overmolded composite. Weight: 6-1/2 – 7-3/4 lbs. Magazine capacity: 3 or 5 (.22-250, .243, .308, .270, .30-06). Introduced 2006.

NIB	Exc.	V.G.	Good	Fair	Poor
800	700	425	350	275	125

Model 70 Shadow Elite Camo Stainless

Similar to Shadow Elite Stainless but with Mossy Oak New Break Up camo synthetic stock.

NIB	Exc.	V.G.	Good	Fair	Poor
850	750	475	350	275	125

Model 70 Pro Shadow Blued

Bolt-action rifle. Calibers: .22-250, .243, .308, .270, .30-06, 7mm RM, .300 WM, .270 WSM, 7mm WSM, .300 WSM, .325 WSM. Barrel: Blued steel, 22-inch (standard) or 24-inch (magnum). Stock: Overmolded composite. Weight: 6-1/2 – 7 lbs. Magazine capacity: 3 (magnum) or 5 (standard). Introduced 2006.

NIB	Exc.	V.G.	Good	Fair	Poor
650	550	375	250	175	125

Model 70 Pro Shadow Stainless

Similar to Pro Shadow blued but with stainless steel barrel and .338 WM and .375 H&H chamberings.

NIB	Exc.	V.G.	Good	Fair	Poor
700	600	450	325	225	150

Model 70 Laminated Coyote Outback Stainless

Similar to Model 70 Coyote Lite but with skeletonized laminated stock and stainless steel only. Calibers: .22-250, .243, .308, .270, .30-06, 7mm RM, .300 WM, .270 WSM, 7mm WSM, .300 WSM, .325 WSM. Weight: 7-3/4 lbs. Introduced 2006.

NIB	Exc.	V.G.	Good	Fair	Poor
750	650	450	375	225	125

Model 70 Laminated Coyote Gray or Brown Stainless

Similar to Model 70 Laminated Coyote Outback but with non-fluted barrel and choice of brown or gray laminated stock.

NIB	Exc.	V.G.	Good	Fair	Poor
700	600	450	325	225	150

POST-2007 MODEL 70

In 2006, Winchester closed its factory in New Haven, CT and discontinued production of the Model 70 and Model 94 rifles. Late in 2007, it was announced that production of the Model 70 would resume at the FN plant in Columbia, SC. FN (Fabrique Nationale of Belgium) is the parent company of Winchester. The following models are produced at the South Carolina plant.

Model 70 Featherweight Deluxe

Pre-64 action, three-position safety, jewelled bolt, knurled bolt handle, walnut stock with slight schnabel, cut checkering, Pachmayr Decelerator recoil pad., 22- or 24-inch barrel depending on caliber. Chambered for a variety of cartridges from .243 to .325 Winchester Short Magnum. Weight 6.5 to 7 lbs. Introduced in 2008.

NIB	Exc.	V.G.	Good	Fair	Poor
950	650	450	325	225	125

Model 70 Sporter Deluxe

Similar to above but with non-schnabel forend and cheekpiece.

NIB	Exc.	V.G.	Good	Fair	Poor
950	650	450	325	225	125

New Model 70 Super Grade Special Limited Edition

Very fancy version of the Model 70 featuring post-'64 action, ultra-premium walnut, gold-filled engraving, black forend cap, steel grip cap, and shadowline cheekpiece. Only 250 produced in 2008. Chambered in .300 Winchester Magnum only.

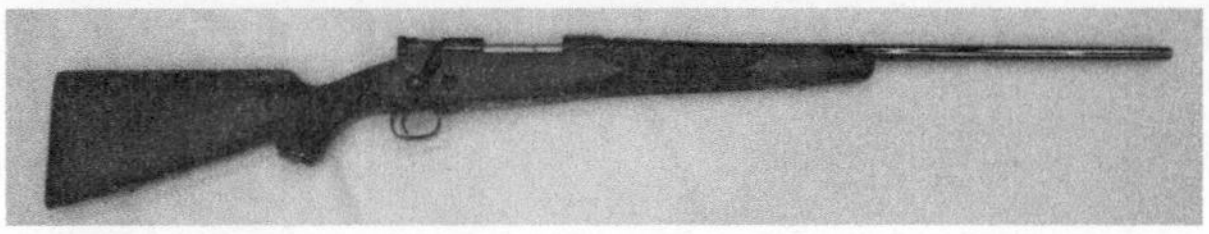

NIB	Exc.	V.G.	Good	Fair	Poor
2400	2000	1650	1300	900	500

Model 70 Extreme Weather SS

Post-'64 style action with 22-, 24- or 26-inch barrel depending on chambering. Three-position safety, fluted stainless barrel and Bell and Carlson composite stock. Chambered for a variety of cartridges from .243 to .325 Winchester Short Magnum.

NIB	Exc.	V.G.	Good	Fair	Poor
1000	750	550	425	275	175

Model 70 FW Compact

Featherweight Compact made for smaller-framed shooters. Light mountain type rifle weighing 6.5 pounds with 20-inch barrel. Pre-'64 Controlled Round Feed and three-position safety. M.O.A. adjustable trigger system. Jeweled bolt body with knurled bolt handle. Walnut stock with fancy checkering pattern. Chambered for .22-250 Remington, .243 Winchester, 7mm-08 Remington or .308 Winchester. Introduced in 2011.

NIB	Exc.	V.G.	Good	Fair	Poor
765	650	550	450	350	200

Model 70 Safari Express

Designed for dangerous game, calibers include .375 H&H, .416 Rem. Mag. or .458 Win. Mag. Express sights, 24-inch barrel, satin finished and checkered walnut stock. Other features include reinforced crossbolts, dual recoil lugs and Pachmayr Decelerator recoil pad. Weight: 9- pounds.

NIB	Exc.	V.G.	Good	Fair	Poor
1200	1000	800	650	500	350

WINCHESTER CUSTOM GUN SHOP

NOTE: There were a number of special order options offered by the Custom shop that greatly affect price, such as special-order engraving, stock carving, wood, sights, etc. It is strongly suggested that an independent appraisal be secured prior to a sale.

Model 94 Custom Limited Edition New Generation

This lever-action rifle is stocked with fancy checkered walnut with pistol grip and long nose forend. Custom engraved with gold inlaid moose on right side and gold inlaid buck and doe on the left side. Fitted with tang safety. Barrel is 20" and chambered for the .30-30 cartridge. Introduced in 2003. Weight is about 6.25 lbs.

NIB	Exc.	V.G.	Good	Fair	Poor
4000	—	—	—	—	—

Model 70 Featherweight Ultra Grade

Limited to 1,000 rifles, this model is profusely engraved with game scene and gold line inlaid. Serial number inlaid in gold. Offered in .270 caliber with very fine-figured walnut stock with fine line checkering. Mahogany fitted case. Strongly suggest a qualified appraisal before sale.

NIB	*Exc.*	*V.G.*	*Good*	*Fair*	*Poor*
5000	—	—	—	—	—

Model 70 Custom Featherweight

Introduced in 2003 this rifle is chambered for the .270, 7mm Win. Mag., or the .30-06. Fitted with a 22" barrel. Semi-fancy walnut stock with schnabel forend. Offered in blued or stainless steel finish in either right- or left-hand models. Weight is about 7.25 lbs.

NIB	*Exc.*	*V.G.*	*Good*	*Fair*	*Poor*
3500	—	—	—	—	—

Model 70 Custom Carbon

This rifle features a stainless steel action with Shilen barrel wrapped in graphite epoxy. Fitted with a black composite stock. Chambered for the .270 WSM, 7mm WSM, .300 WSM, .25-06 Rem., or the .338 Win. Mag. cartridge. Fitted with a 24" barrel on all calibers but the .338 (26"). Weight is about 6.5 lbs. on the WSM calibers and 7 lbs. of the others. Magazine capacity is three rounds. Introduced in 2003.

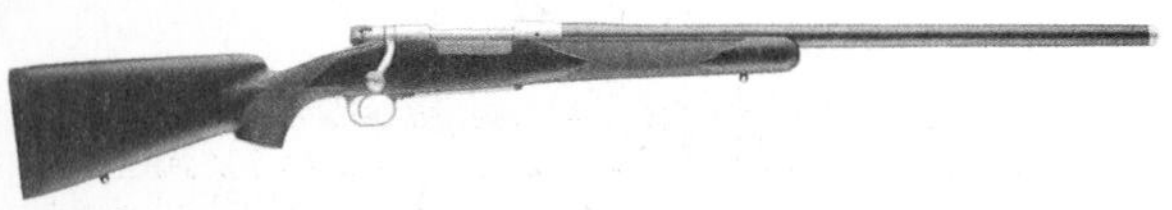

NIB	*Exc.*	*V.G.*	*Good*	*Fair*	*Poor*
3200	—	—	—	—	—

Model 70 Custom Sharpshooter

A U.S.R.A. Custom Shop gun. This model is fitted with a stainless steel Schneider barrel with hand-honed action and hand fitted. The stock is a custom McMillan A-2 glass bedded stock. Offered in .223 Rem., .22-250 Rem., .308 Win. and .300 Win. Mag. Comes from the factory with a hard case. Currently in production.

NIB	*Exc.*	*V.G.*	*Good*	*Fair*	*Poor*
2500	—	—	—	—	—

Model 70 Custom Classic Sharpshooter II

Same as above but introduced in 1996 with an H-S heavy target stock, a pre-1964 action stainless steel H-S barrel. Weight is about 11 lbs. Offered in .22-250, .308, .30-06, and .300 Win. Mag.

NIB	*Exc.*	*V.G.*	*Good*	*Fair*	*Poor*
2250	—	—	—	—	—

Model 70 Custom Sporting Sharpshooter

Essentially a take-off on the Custom Sharpshooter but configured for hunting. Fitted with a McMillan sporter-style gray stock and Schneider stainless steel barrel. Offered in .270 Win., .300 Win., and 7mm STW. Introduced in 1993.

NIB	*Exc.*	*V.G.*	*Good*	*Fair*	*Poor*
2000	—	—	—	—	—

Model 70 Custom Classic Sporting Sharpshooter II

Introduced in 1996 this is an updated version of the model above. It features a pre-1964 action with H-S special fiberglass stock and stainless steel barrel. Available in 7mm STW, .300 Win. Mag. Weight is about 8.5 lbs.

NIB	*Exc.*	*V.G.*	*Good*	*Fair*	*Poor*
2500	—	—	—	—	—

Model 70 Custom Grade

This custom built Model 70 is hand finished, polished, and fitted in the Custom Shop. Internal parts are hand honed while the barrel is lead lapped. The customer can order individual items to his or her own taste, including engraving, special stock dimensions and carvings, etc. Each Custom Grade Model 70 should be priced on an individual basis.

Model 70 Custom Express

Also built in the Custom Shop this model features figured walnut, hand-honed internal parts, bolt and follower are engine turned. A special 3-leaf rear sight is furnished also. Offered in .375 H&H Mag., .375 JRS, .416 Rem. Mag., .458 Win. Mag., and .470 Capstick.

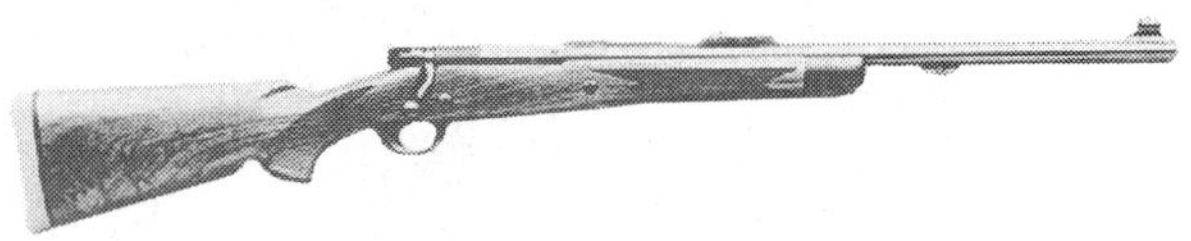

NIB	*Exc.*	*V.G.*	*Good*	*Fair*	*Poor*
3000	—	—	—	—	—

Model 70 Custom African Express

Introduced in 1999 this model is chambered for the .340 Wby., .358 STA, .375 H&H, .416 Rem. Mag., and the .458 Win. Mag. Fitted with a 24" barrel and a magazine capacity of 4 rounds. Express sights. Weight is about 9.75 lbs. Ebony pistol grip cap, and select walnut stock.

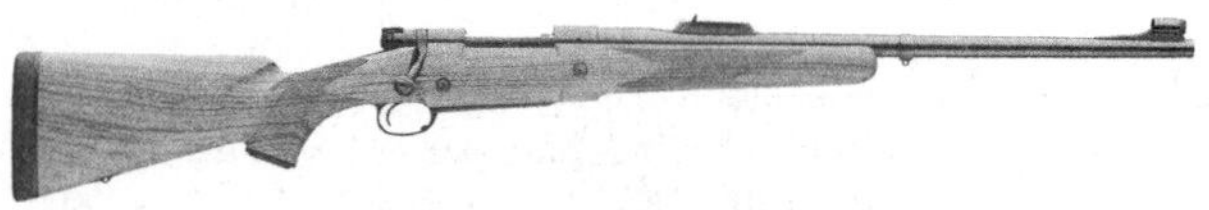

NIB	*Exc.*	*V.G.*	*Good*	*Fair*	*Poor*
3850	—	—	—	—	—

Model 70 Custom Safari Express

This model has a figured walnut stock with the bolt and follower engine turned. Express sights. Chambered in .340 Wby., .358 STA, .375 H&H, .416 Rem. Mag., and .458 Win. Mag. Barrel length is 24". Weight is about 9.5 lbs. Introduced in 1999.

NIB	*Exc.*	*V.G.*	*Good*	*Fair*	*Poor*
2500	—	—	—	—	—

Model 70 Custom "Ultra Light" Mannlicher

This model features a full-length stock of figured walnut with smooth tapered barrel and blued action. Chambered for .260 Rem., .308 Win., and 7mm-08. Fitted with a 19" barrel with optional open sights. Weight is about 6.75 lbs. Introduced in 1999.

NIB	Exc.	V.G.	Good	Fair	Poor
2500	—	—	—	—	—

Model 70 Ultimate Classic

This model features a number of special options as standard. Included is a pre-1964 action, choice of round, round fluted, 1/2 octagon 1/2 round barrel, full tapered octagon barrel, blued or stainless steel barrel actions, fancy American walnut stock, special Custom Shop serial numbers and proof stamp, inletted swivel bases, red recoil pad, fine cut checkering, and a hard case. Offered in a wide variety of calibers from .25-06 to .338 Win. Mag. Weight is about 7.5 to 7.75 lbs. depending on caliber. Also available in stainless steel.

NIB	Exc.	V.G.	Good	Fair	Poor
2450	—	—	—	—	—

NOTE: In 1997 this model was introduced in a left-hand version.

Model 70 Custom Short Action

This custom shop model is fitted with a 22" match-grade barrel Controlled feed. Chambered for short-action calibers from .243 to .358. Semi-fancy walnut stock. Hand-cut checkering. Supplied with hard case. Weight is about 7.5 lbs. Introduced in 2000. In 2003 this model was offered in a left-hand version.

NIB	Exc.	V.G.	Good	Fair	Poor
2700	—	—	—	—	—

Model 70 Custom Extreme Weather

This custom shop model is fitted with a round or fluted 24" match-grade barrel. Both barrel and action are stainless steel. McMillan fiberglass stock with cheekpiece. Chambered in calibers from .25-06 to .338 Win. Mag. Weight is about 7.5 lbs. Introduced in 2000. Lightweight Extreme Weather II model introduced 2006 (6-1/4 – 7 lbs.). MSRP: $2800.

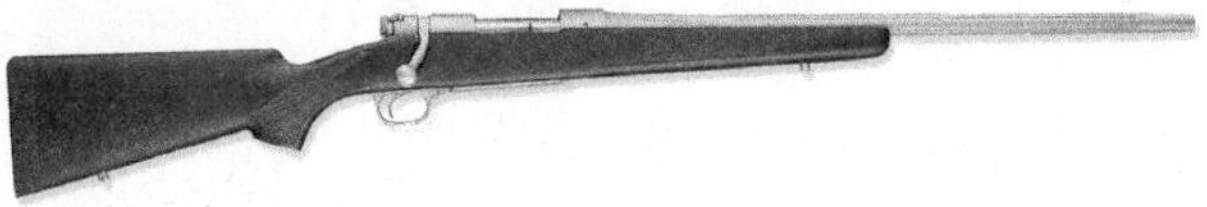

NIB	Exc.	V.G.	Good	Fair	Poor
1950	—	—	—	—	—

Model 70 Custom Take Down

Introduced in 1998 this composite stock rifle has a special take down feature. Chambered for .375 H&H, .416 Rem. Mag., .300 Win Mag., 7mm STW. Magazine capacity is 3 rounds. Barrel length is 26". Weight is between 8.5 and 9 lbs. Offered in fluted barrel in .300 Win. Mag. and 7mm STW.

NIB	Exc.	V.G.	Good	Fair	Poor
3300	—	—	—	—	—

Model 70 Custom 100th Anniversary .30-06

Semi-fancy walnut Featherweight stock with single steel crossbolt, one-piece engraved floorplate, high-lustre blued and engraved 22-inch barrel. Commemorates centennial of .30-06 cartridge. Introduced 2006; only 100 manufactured.

NIB	Exc.	V.G.	Good	Fair	Poor
2700	—	—	—	—	—

Model 70 Custom Special "70 Years of the Model 70"

Calibers: .270, .30-06 Springfield, .300 WM. Barrel: 24-inch or 26-inch (.300 WM) blued sightless. Engraved floorplate and barrel. Stock: semi-fancy checkered walnut. Introduced 2006, only 70 manufactured per caliber.

NIB	Exc.	V.G.	Good	Fair	Poor
2800	—	—	—	—	—

Model 70 Custom Maple

Calibers: .284, .270, .308, .30-06. Barrel: 24-inch blued. Weight: 7-3/4 lbs. Stocked in fiddleback maple with pre-'64 pattern checkering. Quantities "very limited." Introduced 2006.

NIB	Exc.	V.G.	Good	Fair	Poor
4400	—	—	—	—	—

Model 70 Custom Continental Hunter

Calibers: .284, .270, .308, .30-06. Barrel: 22-inch blued or stainless Krieger. Stock: glossy claro walnut, round knob pistol grip, schnabel forend.

NIB	Exc.	V.G.	Good	Fair	Poor
5300	—	—	—	—	—

Model 70 Custom Stainless Laminate

Calibers: .270 WSM, 7mm WSM, .300 WSM, .325 WSM. Barrel: 24-inch stainless sporter. Stock: black/gray or brown Featherweight laminated with Schnabel and Pachmayr pad.

NIB	Exc.	V.G.	Good	Fair	Poor
2300	—	—	—	—	—

Model 94 Custom Limited Edition

This is essentially a special order Model 94 with choice of engraving and stock carving. Chambered for the .44-40 and fitted with a 24" octagonal barrel. Fancy walnut stock. Limited to 75 rifles. Weight is about 7.75 lbs. Suggest an appraisal prior to a sale.

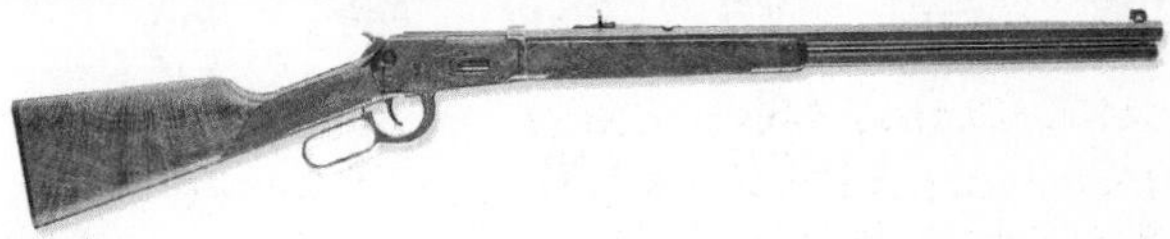

NIB	Exc.	V.G.	Good	Fair	Poor
2300	—	—	—	—	—

Model 9410 Custom

Introduced in 2005 this .410 shotgun is fitted with a 24" round barrel and full length magazine. Case colored receiver with semi-fancy checkered walnut stock. Weight is about 7 lbs.

NIB	Exc.	V.G.	Good	Fair	Poor
2300	—	—	—	—	—

POST-1964 SHOTGUNS

MODEL 12 "Y" SERIES

Model 12 Field Grade

This is a later version of the slide-action Model 12, chambered for 12 gauge only. It was offered with a 26", 28", or 30" vent rib barrel with various chokes. The finish is blued with a jeweled bolt and a hand-checkered, select walnut stock. This version is easily recognizable as it has the letter Y serial number prefix. It was manufactured between 1972 and 1976.

NIB	Exc.	V.G.	Good	Fair	Poor
—	950	800	650	485	300

Model 12 Super Pigeon Grade

This is a deluxe version that features extensive engraving and fancy checkering. It was offered with a turned action and select, fancy-grade walnut. It was a limited-production item produced between 1964 and 1972. It was briefly reintroduced in 1984 and discontinued again in 1985.

NIB	Exc.	V.G.	Good	Fair	Poor
—	3000	2400	1850	1400	950

Model 12 Skeet

This version is similar to the Field Grade but is offered with a 26", vent rib, skeet-bored barrel. The finish is blued, with a skeet-type stock and recoil pad. It was manufactured between 1972 and 1975.

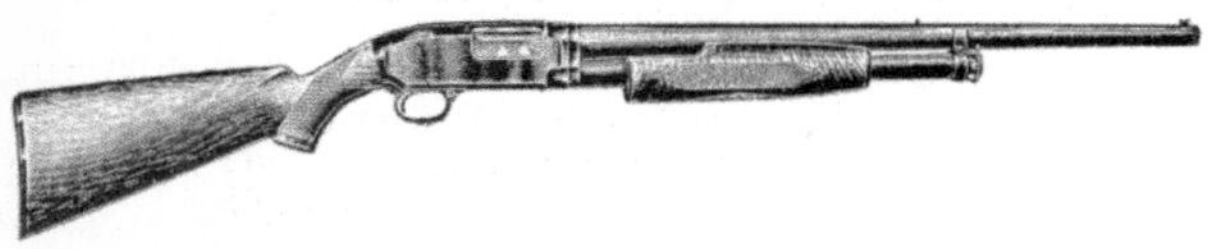

NIB	Exc.	V.G.	Good	Fair	Poor
—	950	850	750	450	300

Model 12 Trap Grade

This version features a 30" vent rib barrel with a Full choke. It is blued with a trap-type, standard, or Monte Carlo stock with a recoil pad. It was manufactured between 1972 and 1980.

NIB	Exc.	V.G.	Good	Fair	Poor
—	935	830	725	425	215

MODEL 12 (LIMITED EDITION)

Available in 20 gauge only. Furnished with a 26" vent rib barrel choked Improved Cylinder. The walnut stock is checkered with pistol grip. Introduced in 1993 and available in three different grades.

Grade I

4,000 guns.

NIB	Exc.	V.G.	Good	Fair	Poor
1000	800	650	450	200	100

Grade IV

1,000 guns, gold highlights.

NIB	Exc.	V.G.	Good	Fair	Poor
1400	1100	850	500	200	100

Model 42 (Limited Edition)

A reproduction of the famous Winchester Model 42 .410 bore slide-action shotgun. Furnished with a 26" ventilated rib barrel choked Full. The receiver is engraved with gold border. Introduced in 1993 and limited to 850 guns.

NIB	Exc.	V.G.	Good	Fair	Poor
1800	1400	1000	500	300	150

Model 1200

This is a slide-action shotgun chambered for 12, 16, or 20 gauge. It was offered with a 26", 28", or 30", vent rib barrel with various chokes. It has an alloy receiver and is blued, with a checkered walnut stock and recoil pad. It was manufactured between 1964 and 1981. This model was offered with the plastic Hydrocoil stock, and this would add approximately 35 percent to the values given.

NIB	Exc.	V.G.	Good	Fair	Poor
—	300	250	200	150	100

Ducks Unlimited Model

Available through Ducks Unlimited chapters. An independent appraisal is suggested.

MODEL 1300 SERIES Discontinued in 2006.

Model 1300 XTR

Chambered for 12 and 20 gauge with 3" chambers. It is a takedown gun that is offered with various-length vent rib barrels with screw-in choke tubes. It has an alloy frame and is blued with a walnut stock. It was introduced in 1978.

NIB	Exc.	V.G.	Good	Fair	Poor
475	350	275	200	150	100

Model 1300 Waterfowl

This version is chambered for 12 gauge, 3" only. It has a 30" vent rib barrel with screw-in choke tubes. It is matte-blued, with a satin-finished walnut stock and a recoil pad. It was introduced in 1984. A laminated WinTuff stock was made available in 1988 and would add $10 to the value.

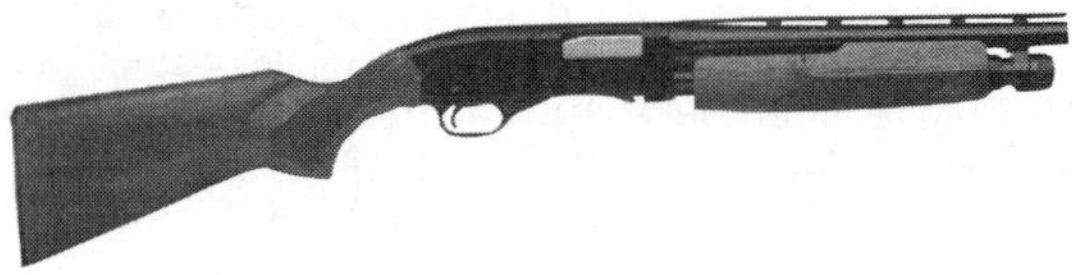

NIB	Exc.	V.G.	Good	Fair	Poor
400	300	250	200	150	100

Model 1300 New Shadow Grass

Introduced in 2004 this 12 gauge 3" gun is fitted with either a 26" or 28" vent rib barrel with choke tubes. Composite stock has New Shadow Grass camo pattern. Weight is about 7 lbs.

NIB	Exc.	V.G.	Good	Fair	Poor
470	370	250	200	150	100

Model 1300 WinCam Turkey Gun

This version is similar to the Model 1300 Turkey Gun, with a green, laminated hardwood stock. It was introduced in 1987. A WinTuff version is also available and would add $20 to the values given.

NIB	Exc.	V.G.	Good	Fair	Poor
475	350	275	200	150	100

Model 1300 Stainless Security

This version is chambered for 12 or 20 gauge and is constructed of stainless steel. It has an 18" cylinder-bore barrel and a 7- or

8-shot tubular magazine. It is available with a pistol-grip stock, which would add approximately 50 percent to the values given.

NIB	*Exc.*	*V.G.*	*Good*	*Fair*	*Poor*
475	350	275	200	150	100

Model 1300 Turkey

This slide-action model features a 22" vent rib barrel chambered for 3" 12 gauge shells. Supplied with choke tubes. Gun weighs 7.25 lbs.

NIB	*Exc.*	*V.G.*	*Good*	*Fair*	*Poor*
475	350	275	200	150	100

Model 1300 Realtree Turkey

Introduced in 1994, this model features a synthetic stock camouflaged with Realtree. The receiver and 22" barrel are matte finish.

NIB	*Exc.*	*V.G.*	*Good*	*Fair*	*Poor*
475	350	275	200	150	100

Model 1300 Mossy Oak Break-Up Turkey

Same as above but with Mossy Oak Break-Up camo stock and gun. Introduced in 2000.

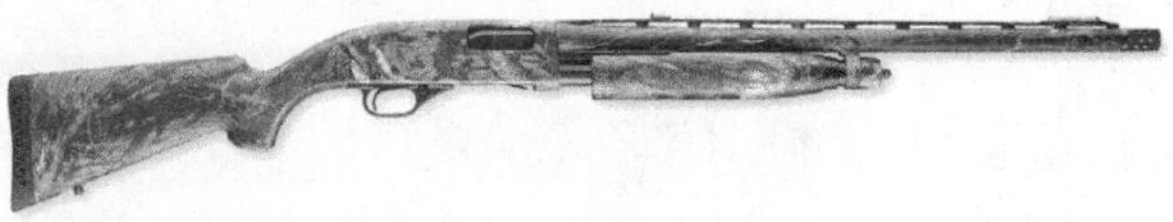

NIB	*Exc.*	*V.G.*	*Good*	*Fair*	*Poor*
475	350	275	200	150	100

Model 1300 Black Shadow Turkey

This model was also introduced in 1994 and features a black composite stock with a nonglare finish on the barrel, receiver, bolt, and magazine. Barrel has vent rib and is 22" in length.

NIB	*Exc.*	*V.G.*	*Good*	*Fair*	*Poor*
475	350	275	200	150	100

Model 1300 National Wild Turkey Federation Series III

Engraved receiver, camo stock, open sights on a 22" plain barrel, and all metal and wood parts are nonglare. Comes with a quick detachable sling. Offered in 12 gauge only. Gun weighs 7.25 lbs.

NIB	*Exc.*	*V.G.*	*Good*	*Fair*	*Poor*
575	420	350	250	150	100

Model 1300 National Wild Turkey Federation Series IV

Introduced in 1993, this model is similar to the Series II with the addition of a 22" vent rib barrel. Stock is black laminated. Comes with quick detachable sling. Gun weight 7 lbs.

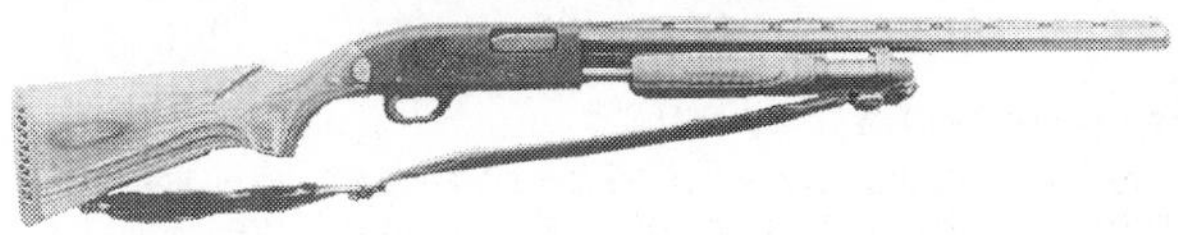

NIB	*Exc.*	*V.G.*	*Good*	*Fair*	*Poor*
600	520	350	250	150	100

Model 1300 NWTF Short Turkey

This 12 gauge gun is fitted with an 18" barrel with extended choke tubes. Fiber Optic sights. Mossy Oak camo stock. NWTF medallion on pistol grip cap. Weight is about 6.5 lbs. Introduced in 2005.

NIB	*Exc.*	*V.G.*	*Good*	*Fair*	*Poor*
475	350	275	200	150	100

Model 1300 Whitetails Unlimited Slug Hunter

This slide-action model features a full-length rifle barrel chambered for 3" 12 gauge shells. Barrel is choked Cylinder. Fitted with a checkered walnut stock with engraved receiver. Receiver is drilled and tapped for bases and rings, which are included. Comes equipped with camo sling. Weighs 7.25 lbs.

NIB	*Exc.*	*V.G.*	*Good*	*Fair*	*Poor*
475	350	275	200	150	100

Model 1300 Slug Hunter

Similar to the Whitetails Unlimited model, but without the engraved receiver.

NIB	*Exc.*	*V.G.*	*Good*	*Fair*	*Poor*
475	350	275	200	150	100

Model 1300 Buck and Tom

Introduced in 2002 for both deer and turkey. Camo stock. Fitted with a 22" barrel with choke tubes for both deer and turkey. Receiver drilled and tapped for scope mount. Weight is about 6.75 lbs.

NIB	*Exc.*	*V.G.*	*Good*	*Fair*	*Poor*
525	400	325	250	175	125

Model 1300 Universal Hunter

Introduced in 2002, this model features a camo stock with 26" vent rib barrel. Choke tubes. Weight is about 7 lbs.

NIB	*Exc.*	*V.G.*	*Good*	*Fair*	*Poor*
550	425	375	275	225	125

Model 1300 Black Shadow Deer

Introduced in 1994, this 12 gauge Model 1300 features a black composite stock with nonglare finish on the bolt, barrel, receiver, and magazine. Barrel is 22" with ramp front sight and adjustable rear sight. In 2000 this model was offered with a rifled barrel for shooting sabot slugs.

NIB	*Exc.*	*V.G.*	*Good*	*Fair*	*Poor*
475	350	275	200	150	100

NOTE: Add $25 for rifled barrel.

Model 1300 Black Shadow Field

Same as above but fitted with a 26" or 28" vent rib barrel chambered for 3" Mag. shells. Weight is about 7 lbs.

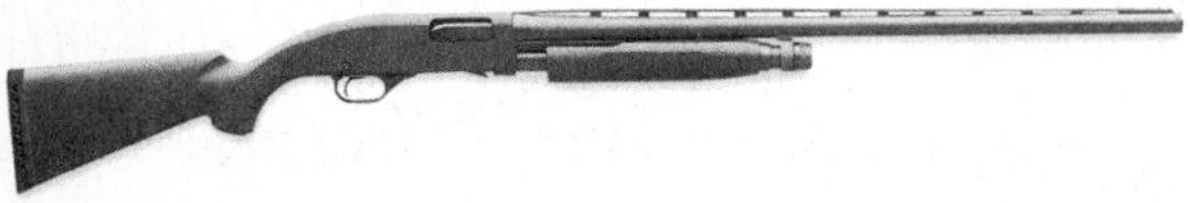

NIB	Exc.	V.G.	Good	Fair	Poor
475	350	275	200	150	100

Model 1300 Sporting/Field

This 12 gauge gun has a 28" vent rib barrel with five choke tubes. Checkered walnut stock. Black recoil pad. Weight is about 7.5 lbs. Introduced in 2002.

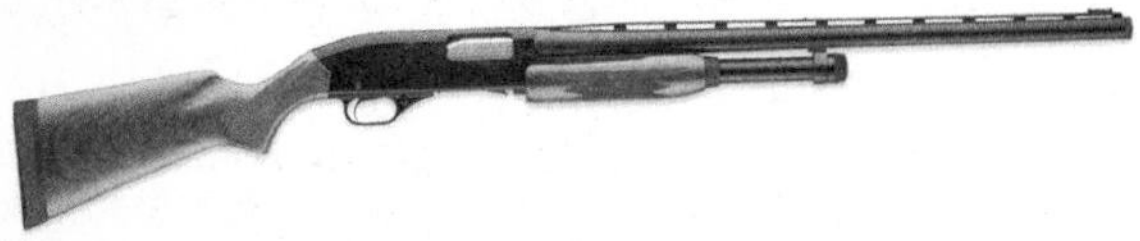

NIB	Exc.	V.G.	Good	Fair	Poor
475	350	275	200	150	100

Model 1300 Sporting/Field Compact

As above but with 24" barrel and 1" shorter length of pull. Introduced in 2002.

NIB	Exc.	V.G.	Good	Fair	Poor
475	350	275	200	150	100

Model 1300 Walnut Field

This 12 gauge 3" gun is fitted with either 26" or 28" vent rib barrels with choke tubes. Checkered walnut stock with recoil pad. Weight is about 7.25 lbs. Introduced in 2004.

NIB	Exc.	V.G.	Good	Fair	Poor
475	350	275	200	150	100

Model 1300 Slug Hunter Sabot (Smoothbore)

Similar to the Slug Hunter but furnished with a smoothbore barrel with a special extended screw-in choke tube that is rifled.

NIB	Exc.	V.G.	Good	Fair	Poor
425	300	225	150	125	100

Model 1300 Upland Special

This 12 gauge slide-action shotgun is fitted with a 24" vent rib barrel and straight-grip walnut stock. Weight is about 7 lbs. Introduced in 1999. In 2000 this model was offered in 20 gauge with 24" vent rib barrel.

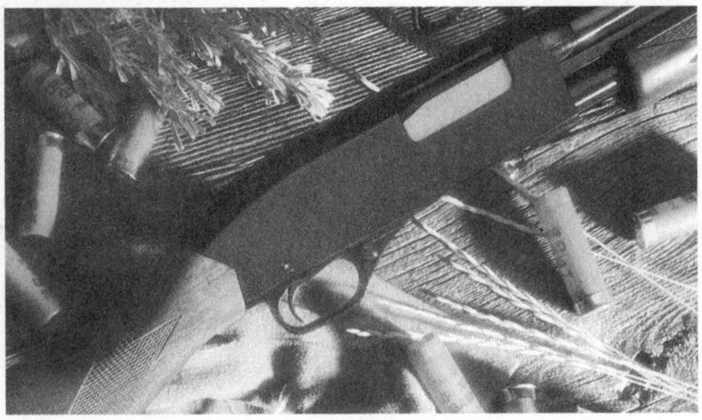

NIB	Exc.	V.G.	Good	Fair	Poor
600	500	400	300	200	100

Model 1300 Upland Special Field

This model, introduced in 2004, features a choice of 12 or 20 gauge 3" guns with 24" vent rib barrel with choke tube. Checkered walnut stock with straight grip. Weight is about 6.75 lbs.

NIB	Exc.	V.G.	Good	Fair	Poor
600	500	400	300	200	100

Model 1300 Ranger

This slide-action shotgun is a lower-cost version of the Model 1300. Furnished with a hardwood stock and available in 12 or 20 gauge with 26" or 28" vent rib barrel. WinChokes are included.

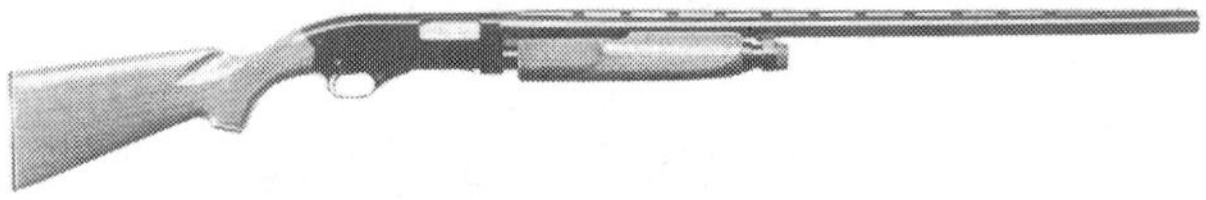

NIB	Exc.	V.G.	Good	Fair	Poor
300	225	190	165	125	100

Model 1300 Ranger Ladies/Youth-Compact

Available in 20 gauge only this model has a 1" shorter than standard length of pull and a 22" vent rib barrel. Choke tubes are included. Gun weighs 6.75 lbs.

NIB	Exc.	V.G.	Good	Fair	Poor
300	225	190	165	125	100

Model 1300 Ranger Deer Slug

Comes in two principal configurations: a 12 gauge 22" smooth barrel with Cylinder choke; and a 12 gauge 22" rifled barrel. Both are chambered for 3" shells and weigh 6.75 lbs.

NIB	Exc.	V.G.	Good	Fair	Poor
300	200	175	150	125	100

MODEL 1300 RANGER DEER COMBO

The Model 1300 Ranger Deer Combos are available in three different configurations. One: 12 gauge 22" smooth barrel and 28" vent rib barrel with WinChokes. Two: 12 gauge 22" rifled barrel with 28" vent rib barrel with WinChokes. Three: 20 gauge 22" smooth barrel with 28" vent rib barrel with WinChokes.

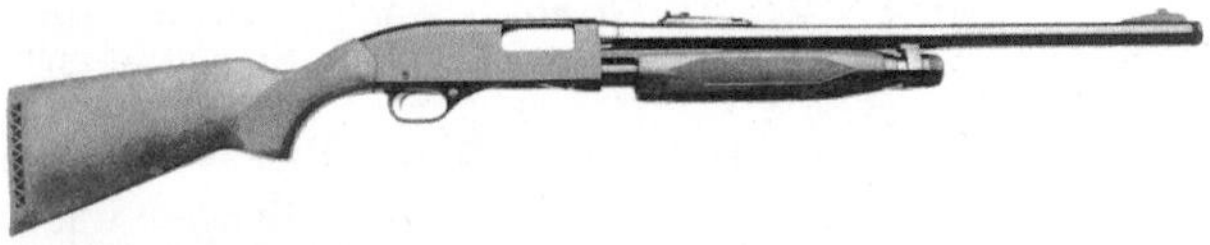

12 Gauge Combo

NIB	Exc.	V.G.	Good	Fair	Poor
375	275	225	190	165	100

20 Gauge Combo

NIB	Exc.	V.G.	Good	Fair	Poor
375	275	225	190	165	100

Model 1300 Defender Combo

This personal defense slide-action shotgun features an 18" Cylinder choked barrel and a 28" vent rib barrel with modified WinChoke and an accessory pistol grip. A hardwood stock comes fitted to the gun.

NIB	Exc.	V.G.	Good	Fair	Poor
425	300	225	150	125	100

Model 1300 Defender 5-Shot

Same as above but furnished with a hardwood stock only and 18" barrel.

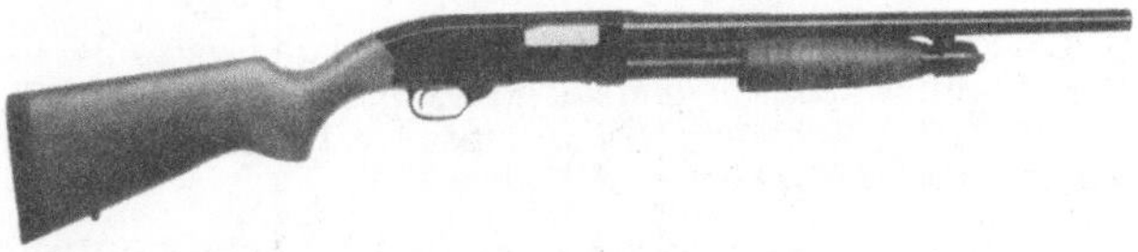

NIB	Exc.	V.G.	Good	Fair	Poor
425	300	225	150	125	100

Model 1300 Camp Defender

Introduced in 1999 this 12 gauge model features a 22" barrel and walnut stock. Magazine capacity is five rounds. Barrel fitted with rifle sights. Weight is about 7 lbs. Comes with Cylinder choke tube.

NIB	Exc.	V.G.	Good	Fair	Poor
425	300	225	150	125	100

Model 1300 Defender 8-Shot

Same as above but furnished with an 18" barrel with extended magazine tube.

NIB	Exc.	V.G.	Good	Fair	Poor
425	300	225	150	125	100

Model 1300 Defender Synthetic Stock

Same as above but fitted with a black synthetic full stock. Available in either 12 or 20 gauge.

NIB	Exc.	V.G.	Good	Fair	Poor
425	300	225	150	125	100

Model 1300 Defender Pistol Grip

Same as above but fitted with a black synthetic pistol grip and extended magazine tube.

NIB	Exc.	V.G.	Good	Fair	Poor
425	300	225	150	125	100

Model 1300 Lady Defender

Chambered for the 20 gauge shell, this model features an 18" barrel with 8-round capacity. Pistol-grip stock. Introduced in 1997.

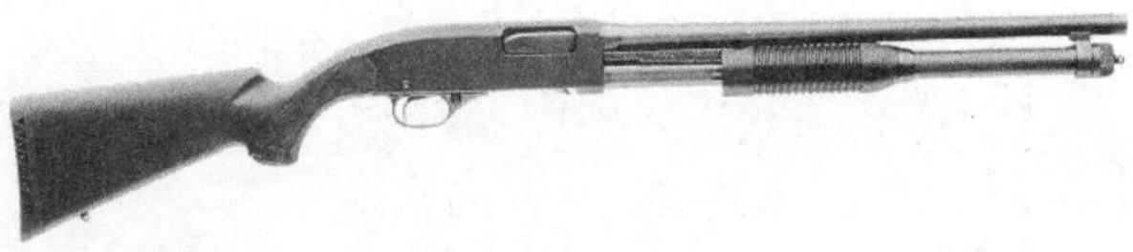

NIB	Exc.	V.G.	Good	Fair	Poor
425	300	225	150	125	100

Model 1300 Stainless Marine

This 12 gauge slide-action shotgun comes with a black synthetic full stock with all metal parts chrome plated. Barrel is 18" and magazine tube holds 7 rounds. Gun weighs 6.75 lbs.

NIB	Exc.	V.G.	Good	Fair	Poor
600	500	400	300	200	100

Model 1300 Stainless Marine with Pistol Grip

Same as above with black synthetic pistol grip in place of full buttstock. Gun weighs 5.75 lbs.

NIB	Exc.	V.G.	Good	Fair	Poor
600	500	400	300	200	100

SPEED PUMP SERIES

This family of inertia-assisted slide-action shotguns was introduced in 2008 to take the place of the discontinued Model 1300. The 3" 12 gauge is available with a 26" or 28" barrel. Three choke tubes included. Weight is 7 to 7.25 lbs.

Speed Pump Walnut Field

High-gloss walnut with traditional checkering.

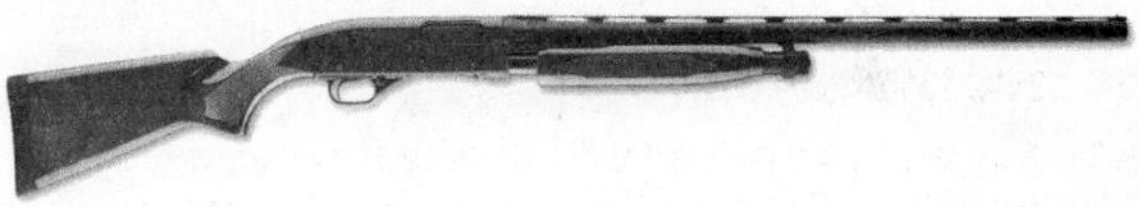

NIB	Exc.	V.G.	Good	Fair	Poor
375	325	275	200	150	100

Speed Pump Black Shadow Field

Synthetic stock and forend with matte black metal.

NIB	Exc.	V.G.	Good	Fair	Poor
375	325	275	200	150	100

Speed Pump Defender

This home-security 12 gauge has an 18" , cylinder choke barrel and 5-round magazine tube. Weight is about 6.5 lbs.

NIB	Exc.	V.G.	Good	Fair	Poor
375	325	275	200	150	100

Model SXP Series

The Super X Pump is successor to Speed Pump series and features the same inertia-assisted action. Comes in 12 gauge only, with 3-inch chamber, 26 or 28-inch back-bored barrel with Invector choke tubes. Weight is approx. 6.8 pounds. Field grade model has Black Shadow composite stock. Waterfowl variation (shown) has full coverage Mossy Oak Duck Blind camo. Also available with 18-inch, straight cylinder barrel as Defender model. Prices are for Black Shadow field model.

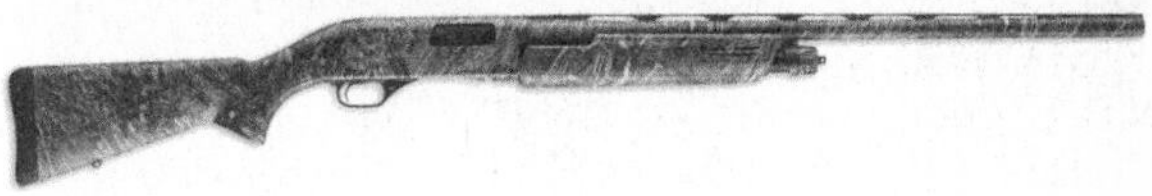

NIB	Exc.	V.G.	Good	Fair	Poor
400	360	325	275	225	150

NOTE: Add 20 percent for Waterfowl model, deduct 20 percent for Defender.

Model 9410

A variation of the Model 94 lever-action rifle chambered for the .410-bore shotgun. Available in several versions. **SEE:** Model 9400 Series in the lever-action rifle section.

Model 1500 XTR

This is a gas-operated, semi-automatic shotgun chambered for 12 or 20 gauge, with a 28" vent rib barrel with screw-in chokes. The finish is blued, with a walnut stock. It was manufactured between 1978 and 1982.

NIB	Exc.	V.G.	Good	Fair	Poor
550	425	325	225	175	150

Super X Model 1

This is a self-compensating, gas-operated, semi-automatic shotgun chambered for 12 gauge. It was offered with a 26", 28", or 30" vent rib barrel with various chokes. It features all-steel construction and is blued, with a checkered walnut stock. It was manufactured between 1974 and 1981.

NIB	Exc.	V.G.	Good	Fair	Poor
—	800	675	525	400	250

Super X Model 1 Custom Competition

This is a custom-order trap or skeet gun that features the self compensating, gas-operated action. It is available in 12 gauge only from the Custom Shop. It is offered with a heavy degree of engraving on the receiver and a fancy, checkered walnut stock. Gold inlays are available and would add approximately 50 percent to the values given. This model was introduced in 1987.

NIB	Exc.	V.G.	Good	Fair	Poor
1450	1100	925	775	650	500

Super X2 3.5" Magnum

Introduced in 1999, this model is a gas-operated design chambered for 3.5" 12 gauge shells. Fitted with a black synthetic stock and choice of 24", 26", or 28" vent rib barrels. Invector chokes. Magazine capacity is five rounds. Weight is about 7.5 lbs. depending on barrel length. Matte black finish.

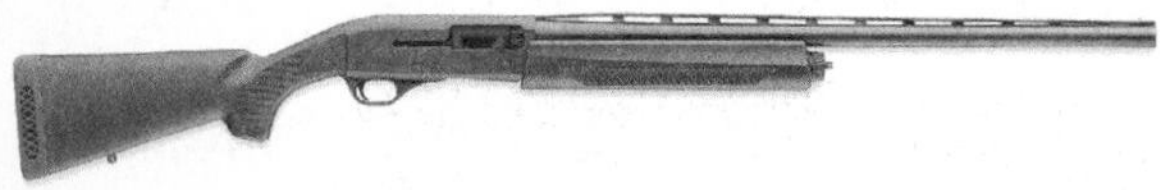

NIB	Exc.	V.G.	Good	Fair	Poor
950	875	700	525	450	300

Super X2 Turkey

Similar to the X2 Magnum but with 24" vent rib barrel with truglo sights. Extra-Full choke. Weight is about 7.25 lbs. Black synthetic stock. Introduced in 1999.

NIB	Exc.	V.G.	Good	Fair	Poor
950	875	700	525	450	300

Super X2 Turkey Mossy Oak Break-Up

Same as above but with Mossy Oak Break-Up camo on stock and gun. Introduced in 2000.

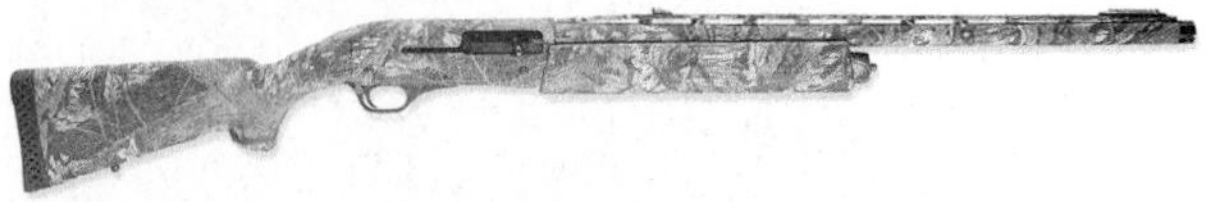

NIB	Exc.	V.G.	Good	Fair	Poor
1025	900	700	525	450	350

Super X2 NWTF Turkey

Introduced in 2005 this 3.5" 12 gauge gun is fitted with a 24" vent rib barrel with extra full extended choke tubes. Three dot TRUGLO sights. Mossy Oak camo stock. A brass NWTF medallion on the pistol grip cap. Weight is about 7.5 lbs.

NIB	Exc.	V.G.	Good	Fair	Poor
1235	950	1025	900	700	450

Super X2 Universal Hunter

Similar to the Super X2 Turkey but with a 26" barrel with Extra-Full choke tube. Weight is about 7.75 lbs. Introduced in 2002.

NIB	Exc.	V.G.	Good	Fair	Poor
1025	900	700	525	450	350

Super X2 Camo Waterfowl

Chambered for 12 gauge 3.5" shells and fitted with a 28" vent rib barrel, this model features a Mossy Oak camo finish. Weight is about 8 lbs. Introduced in 1999. In 2004 a New Shadow Grass camo pattern was added.

NIB	Exc.	V.G.	Good	Fair	Poor
1025	900	700	525	450	350

Super X2 Magnum Greenhead

Introduced in 2002, this model is chambered for the 12 gauge 3.5" shell and has a composite stock that is green in color. Fitted with 28" barrel. Weight is about 8 lbs.

NIB	Exc.	V.G.	Good	Fair	Poor
1025	900	700	525	450	350

Super X2 Magnum Field

This model is chambered for the 12 gauge 3" shell and is offered with either a walnut stock or black synthetic stock. Choice of 26" or 28" vent rib barrel with invector chokes. Weight is about 7.25 lbs. Introduced in 1999.

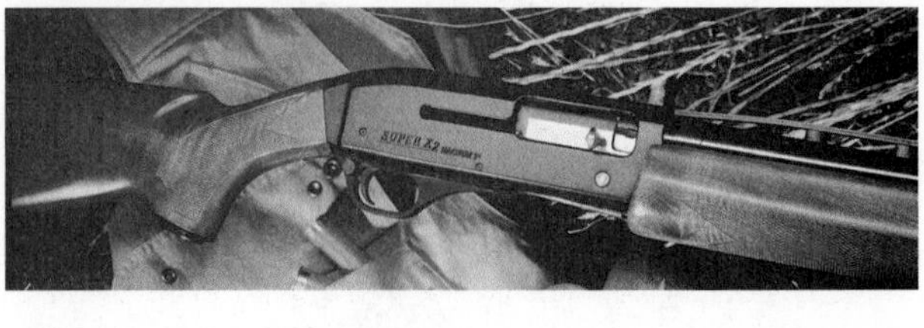

NIB	Exc.	V.G.	Good	Fair	Poor
950	875	700	525	450	300

Super X2 Light Field

Checkered walnut stock with choice of 26" or 28" vent rib barrel with choke tubes are featured on this 12 gauge gun. Weight is about 6.5 lbs. Introduced in 2005.

Super X2 Cantilever Deer

This 12 gauge model has a 22" fully rifled barrel with fold-down rear sight and scope mount. Black composite stock. Weight is about 7.25 lbs. Introduced in 2002.

NIB	Exc.	V.G.	Good	Fair	Poor
950	875	700	525	450	300

Super X2 Practical

Introduced in 2002, this model is designed for competition shooting. Fitted with a 22" barrel with ghost ring sight and 8-round magazine. Black composite stock. Weight is about 8 lbs.

NIB	Exc.	V.G.	Good	Fair	Poor
1025	900	700	525	450	350

Super X2 Sporting Clays

Introduced in 2001, this model features a 12 gauge gun with choice of 28" or 30" barrels with high post rib. Barrels are back bore with Invector chokes. Adjustable comb. Weight is about 8 lbs.

NIB	Exc.	V.G.	Good	Fair	Poor
1200	950	750	575	500	350

Super X2 Sporting Clays Signature II

This 3" 12 gauge gun is fitted with a 30" barrel with choke tubes. The hardwood stock is painted black metallic. The receiver is a red anodized alloy. Weight is about 8.25 lbs. Introduced in 2005.

NIB	Exc.	V.G.	Good	Fair	Poor
1025	900	700	525	450	350

Super X2 Signature Red Sporting

This 12 gauge 3" shell model features a hardwood stock with red Dura-Touch coating. Fitted with a 30" vent rib barrel with five choke tubes. Weight is about 8 lbs. Introduced in 2003.

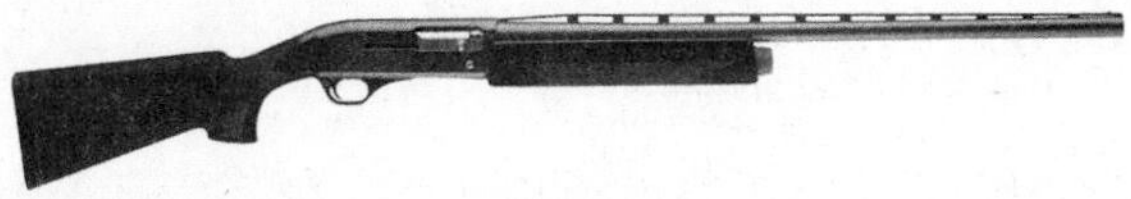

NIB	Exc.	V.G.	Good	Fair	Poor
950	875	700	525	450	300

SUPER X3 SERIES

Introduced in 2006, The Super X3 12 gauge features weight and recoil reducing features and a .742" back-bored barrel. It is available in a variety of configurations weighing under 7 lbs. in the 3" Field model and about 7.5 lbs. in composite, camo and 3.5" models. All models except Cantilever Deer included three choke tubes.

Super X3 Field

Walnut stock and 26" or 28" barrel.

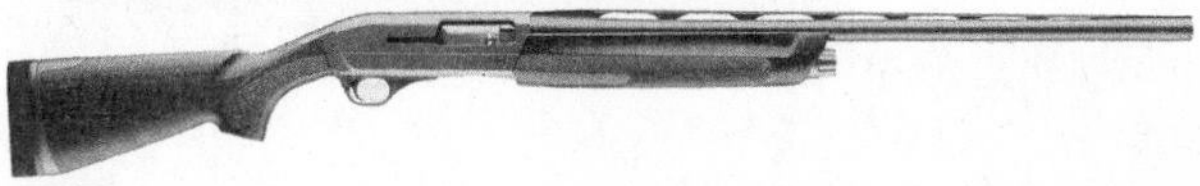

NIB	Exc.	V.G.	Good	Fair	Poor
1200	950	750	575	500	350

Super X3 Composite

Matte black stock and forend. Available in 26" or 28" barrel and 3" or 3.5" chamber. Add 100 for 3.5" model.

NIB	Exc.	V.G.	Good	Fair	Poor
1200	950	750	575	500	350

Super X3 Camo

Composite camo stock with 3.5" chamber. Available in various camo patterns with 26" and 28" barrel.

NIB	Exc.	V.G.	Good	Fair	Poor
1200	950	750	575	500	350

Super X3 Cantilever Deer

Slug gun with 22" barrel with cantilever scope mount and 3" chamber.

NIB	Exc.	V.G.	Good	Fair	Poor
950	875	700	525	450	300

Super X3 "Flanigun" Exhibition/Sporting

With a red receiver and forend cap, this is a duplicate of the gun used by exhibition shooter Patrick Flanigan but with a shorter magazine tube. It has a 3" chamber and 28" barrel.

NIB	Exc.	V.G.	Good	Fair	Poor
1200	950	750	575	500	350

Super X3 Classic Field

Introduced in 2008, the Classic Field is similar to the Super X3 Field but with traditional sharp checkering on pistol grip and forend. Barrel length is 26" or 28" .

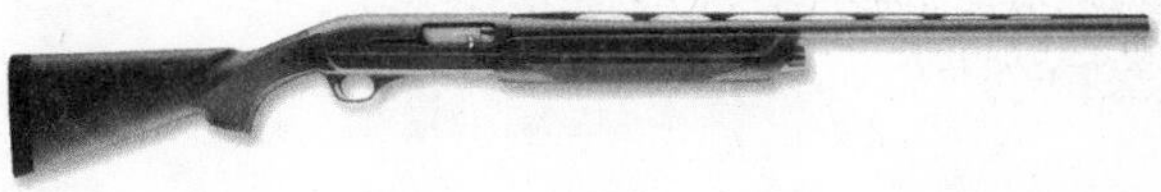

NIB	Exc.	V.G.	Good	Fair	Poor
950	875	700	525	450	300

Super X3 Turkey

New in 2008, this dedicated turkey model has a 3.5" chamber, 24" barrel, extra-full choke tube and complete coverage in Mossy Oak New Breakup camo. Price includes a TruGlo red-dot scope. Weight is 7.5 lbs.

NIB	Exc.	V.G.	Good	Fair	Poor
1200	950	750	575	500	350

Model 1400

This is a gas-operated, semi-automatic shotgun chambered for 12, 16, or 20 gauge. It was offered with a 26", 28", or 30" vent rib barrel with various chokes. The finish is blued, with a checkered walnut stock. It was manufactured between 1964 and 1981. The Hydrocoil plastic stock was available on this model and would add approximately 35 percent to the values given.

NIB	Exc.	V.G.	Good	Fair	Poor
450	350	300	250	200	125

New Model 1400

This is a gas-operated, semi-automatic shotgun chambered for 12 or 20 gauge. It is offered with a 22" or 28" vent rib barrel with screw-in chokes. The finish is blued, with a checkered walnut stock. It was introduced in 1989.

NIB	Exc.	V.G.	Good	Fair	Poor
450	350	300	250	200	125

Model 1400 Ranger

This is a utility-grade, gas-operated, semi-automatic shotgun chambered for 12 or 20 gauge. It is offered with a 28" vent rib barrel with screw-in chokes, as well as a 24" slug barrel with rifle sights. The finish is blued, with a checkered stock. A combination two-barrel set that includes the deer barrel would be worth approximately 20 percent additional. This model was introduced in 1983.

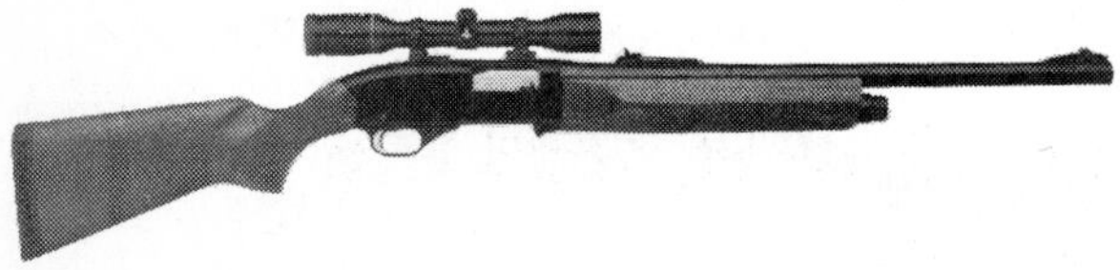

NIB	Exc.	V.G.	Good	Fair	Poor
400	300	250	200	150	100

Model 1400 Quail Unlimited

This 12 gauge semi-automatic shotgun model was introduced in 1993. It features compact engraved receiver with 26" vent rib barrel supplied with WinChoke tubes. Stock is checkered walnut. Gun weighs 7.25 lbs.

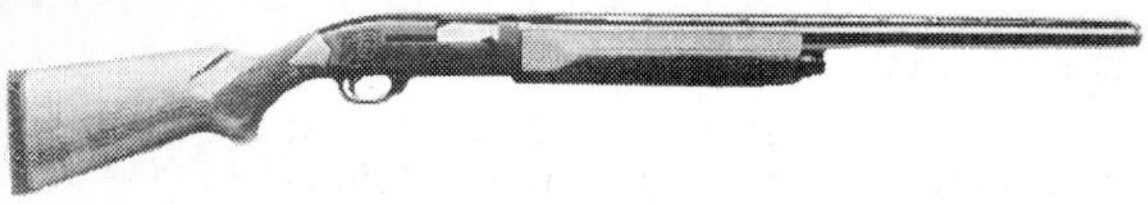

NIB	Exc.	V.G.	Good	Fair	Poor
400	300	250	200	150	100

Model 1400 Ranger Deer Combo

This model features a 12 gauge 22" smooth barrel and a 28" vent rib barrel with three WinChokes.

NIB	Exc.	V.G.	Good	Fair	Poor
400	300	250	200	150	100

Model 37A

Introduced in 1973. It is single-shot shotgun with exposed hammer. Offered in 12, 16, 20, and 28 gauge as well as .410 bore. All guns choked Full except youth model choked Modified. Walnut finish on wardwood stock. Pistol-grip cap with white spacer. Weight is about 6 lbs. About 395,000 were produced until 1980.

NIB	Exc.	V.G.	Good	Fair	Poor
—	350	250	225	175	115

Model 22

Introduced in 1975 this side-by-side shotgun was manufactured by Laurona in Spain to Winchester's specifications for the European market. It had an oil-finished stock with checkered pistol grip semi-beavertail forearm and hand engraved receiver. The finish was black chrome. The gun was fitted with double triggers, matted rib and offered in 12 gauge only with 28" barrels. It weighs 6-3/4 lbs. Rare.

NIB	Exc.	V.G.	Good	Fair	Poor
1250	950	700	550	400	200

Model 91

This over-and-under shotgun was built for Winchester by Laurona for its European markets. Offered in 12 gauge only with 28" barrels the barrels were fitted with a ventilated rib. The gun was offered with single or double triggers with hand-checkered walnut stock with oil finish and hand-engraved receiver. The finish was black chrome. Gun weighs 7-1/2 lbs. Rare.

NIB	Exc.	V.G.	Good	Fair	Poor
1100	800	600	500	400	200

Supreme Field

Introduced in 2000, this over-and-under gun is chambered for the 12 gauge 3" shell and fitted with 28" vent rib barrels with Invector chokes. Walnut stock with pistol grip and blued engraved receiver. Weight is about 7.5 lbs.

NIB	Exc.	V.G.	Good	Fair	Poor
1025	900	700	525	450	350

Supreme Sporting

Similar to the above model but fitted with a choice of 28" or 30" barrels chambered for 12 gauge 2.75" shells. Barrels are ported. Adjustable trigger. Polished silver receiver with blued barrels. Weight is about 7.5 lbs. Introduced in 2000.

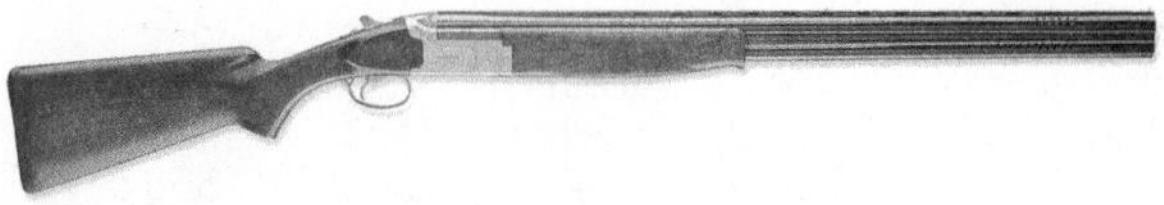

NIB	Exc.	V.G.	Good	Fair	Poor
1200	950	750	575	500	350

Supreme Elegance

Introduced in 2003 this over-and-under model is chambered for the 12 gauge 3" shell. Choice of 26" or 28" vent rib barrels with three choke tubes. Grayed receiver with scroll and bird scenes. Weight is about 7 lbs. depending on barrel length.

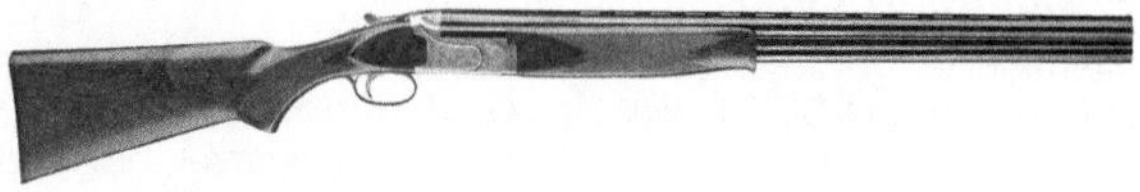

NIB	Exc.	V.G.	Good	Fair	Poor
1400	1100	850	500	200	100

MODEL 23 SERIES

Model 23 XTR Grade I

This is a side-by-side, double-barrel shotgun chambered for 12 or 20 gauge. It is offered with 25.5", 26", 28", or 30" vent rib barrels with 3" chambers and various choke combinations. It is a boxlock gun that features a single trigger and automatic ejectors. It is scroll-engraved with a coin-finished receiver, blued barrels, and a checkered, select walnut stock. It was introduced in 1978. This model is available in a number of configurations that differ in the amount of ornamentation and the quality of materials and workmanship utilized in their construction. These models and their values are listed. Discontinued.

NIB	Exc.	V.G.	Good	Fair	Poor
—	1500	1250	1050	850	500

Model 23 XTR Pigeon Grade

With WinChokes.

NIB	Exc.	V.G.	Good	Fair	Poor
—	2300	1950	1600	1300	5000

Model 23 XTR Pigeon Grade Lightweight

Straight stock.

NIB	Exc.	V.G.	Good	Fair	Poor
—	2450	2100	1750	1400	500

Model 23 Golden Quail

This series was available in 28 gauge and .410, as well as 12 or 20 gauge. It features 25.5" barrels that are choked improved cylinder/modified. It features a straight-grip, English-style stock with a recoil pad. The .410 version would be worth approximately 10 percent more than the values given. This series was discontinued in 1987.

NIB	Exc.	V.G.	Good	Fair	Poor
—	4500	3700	2400	1200	500

Model 23 Light Duck

This version is chambered for 20 gauge and was offered with a 28" Full and Full-choked barrel. There were 500 manufactured in 1985.

NIB	Exc.	V.G.	Good	Fair	Poor
—	3400	2600	1800	800	500

Model 23 Heavy Duck

This version is chambered for 12 gauge with 30" Full and Full-choked barrels. There were 500 manufactured in 1984.

NIB	Exc.	V.G.	Good	Fair	Poor
—	3400	2600	1800	800	500

Model 21

This is a high-quality, side-by-side, double-barrel shotgun that features a boxlock action and is chambered for 12, 16, 20, and 28 gauges, as well as .410. See previous Model 21 entry.

MODEL 101 SERIES

Model 101 Field Grade

This is an Over/Under, double-barrel shotgun chambered for 12, 20, and 28 gauge, as well as .410. It was offered with 26", 28", or 30" vent rib barrels with various choke combinations. Since 1983 screw-in chokes have been standard, and models so furnished would be worth approximately $50 additional. This is a boxlock gun with a single-selective trigger and automatic ejectors. The receiver is engraved; the finish, blued with a checkered walnut stock. It was manufactured between 1963 and 1987.

NIB	Exc.	V.G.	Good	Fair	Poor
—	1525	1260	1050	850	500

NOTE: 28 gauge add 40 percent; .410 add 50 percent.

Waterfowl Model

This version of the Model 101 is chambered for 12 gauge with 3" chambers. It has 30" or 32" vent rib barrels and a matte finish.

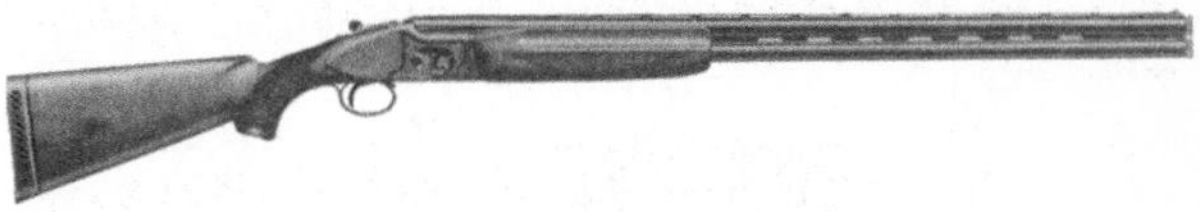

NIB	Exc.	V.G.	Good	Fair	Poor
—	1900	1675	1400	800	400

Model 101 Magnum

This version is similar to the Field Grade, chambered for 12 or 20 gauge with 3" Magnum chambers. It was offered with 30" barrels with various chokes. The stock is furnished with a recoil pad. It was manufactured between 1966 and 1981.

Model 101 Skeet Grade

This version was offered with 26" skeet-bored barrels with a competition rib and a skeet-type walnut stock. It was manufactured between 1966 and 1984.

NIB	Exc.	V.G.	Good	Fair	Poor
—	1500	1250	1050	850	500

Model 101 Three-Gauge Skeet Set

This combination set was offered with three barrels, chambered for 20 and 28 gauge, as well as .410. It was furnished with a fitted case and manufactured between 1974 and 1984.

NIB	Exc.	V.G.	Good	Fair	Poor
—	3500	2600	1800	800	500

Model 101 Trap Grade

This version is chambered for 12 gauge only and was offered with 30" or 32" competition ribbed barrels, choked for trap shooting. It is furnished with a competition-type stock. It was manufactured between 1966 and 1984.

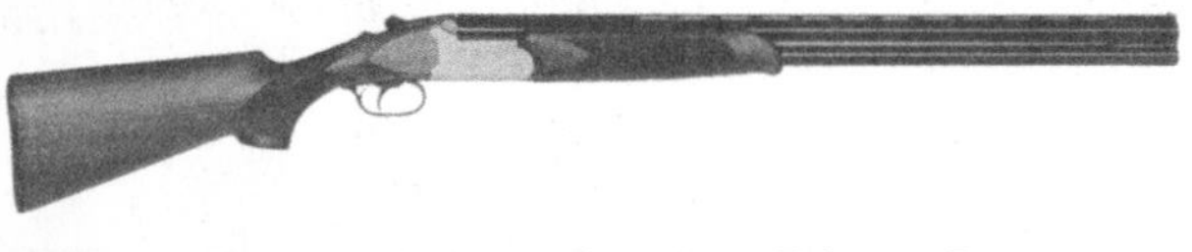

NIB	Exc.	V.G.	Good	Fair	Poor
—	1400	1100	925	700	500

Model 101 Pigeon Grade

This is a more deluxe-engraved version of the Model 101, chambered for 12, 20, or 28 gauge, as well as .410. It features a coin-finished receiver with a fancy checkered walnut stock. It was introduced in 1974.

NIB	Exc.	V.G.	Good	Fair	Poor
—	3000	2600	1800	1275	750

Model 101 Super Pigeon Grade

This is a deluxe version of the Model 101, chambered for 12 gauge. It is heavily engraved with several gold inlays. The receiver is blued, and it features a high-grade walnut stock with fleur-de-lis checkering. It was imported between 1985 and 1987.

NIB	Exc.	V.G.	Good	Fair	Poor
—	5500	4200	3500	2800	1000

Model 101 Diamond Grade

This is a competition model, chambered for all four gauges. It was offered in either a trap or skeet configuration with screw-in chokes, an engraved matte-finished receiver, and a select checkered walnut stock. The skeet model features recoil-reducing muzzle vents.

NIB	Exc.	V.G.	Good	Fair	Poor
—	2000	1625	1250	900	680

Model 101 Pigeon Grade Trap

This deluxe dedicated trap gun was introduced in 2008. It features a Grade III/IV walnut stock with a high-gloss finish and a raised comb. Barrels are 30" or 32" . Three choke tubes included. Weight is 7.5 to 7.75 lbs. Add 5 percent for adjustable comb stock.

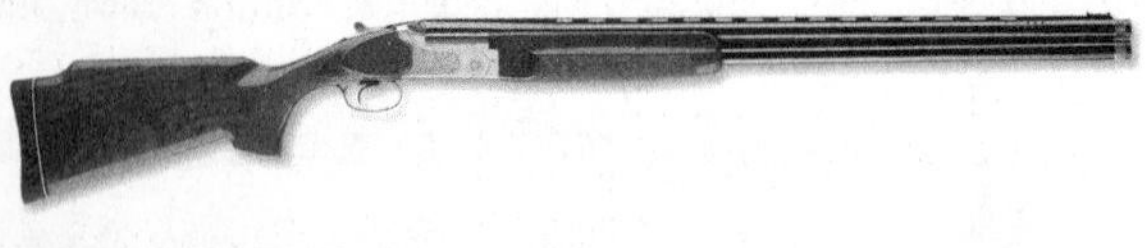

NIB	Exc.	V.G.	Good	Fair	Poor
1750	1500	1300	975	600	400

Model 501 Grand European

This is an Over/Under, double-barrel shotgun chambered for 12 or 20 gauge. It was available in trap or skeet configurations and was offered with a 27", 30", or 32" vent rib barrel. It is heavily engraved and matte-finished, with a select checkered walnut stock. It was manufactured between 1981 and 1986.

NIB	Exc.	V.G.	Good	Fair	Poor
—	2700	2100	1700	1300	500

Model 501 Presentation Grade

This is a deluxe version chambered in 12 gauge only. It is ornately engraved and gold-inlaid. The stock is made out of presentation-grade walnut. It was furnished with a fitted case. It was manufactured between 1984 and 1987.

NIB	Exc.	V.G.	Good	Fair	Poor
—	3400	2750	2200	1600	500

Select Model 101 Field

This Belgian-made version of Winchester\qs popular Model 101 was introduced in 2007. It features Grade II/III walnut, 26" or 28" barrels and deep-relief engraving on the blued receiver that mimics the original 101. Classic white line spacer and vented recoil pad. Three choke tubes. Weight is about 7.2 lbs. Introduced in 2007.

NIB	Exc.	V.G.	Good	Fair	Poor
1600	1400	1150	900	650	400

Select Model 101 Sporting

Similar to Field model plus competition features such as a wider rib, adjustable trigger, white mid-bead and five extended Signature choke tubes. Ported barrels are 28", 30" or 32".

NIB	Exc.	V.G.	Good	Fair	Poor
1675	1475	1225	1050	775	450

Combination Gun

This is an Over/Under rifle/shotgun combination chambered for 12 gauge over .222, .223, .30-06, and the 9.3x74R cartridges. It features 25" barrels. The shotgun tube has a screw-in choke. It is engraved in the fashion of the Model 501 Grand European and features a select checkered walnut stock. It was manufactured between 1983 and 1985.

NIB	Exc.	V.G.	Good	Fair	Poor
—	3000	2500	1600	1200	700

Model 96 Xpert

This is a utility-grade, Over/Under, double-barrel shotgun that is mechanically similar to the Model 101. Chambered for 12 or 20 gauge and offered with various barrel lengths and choke combinations. It has a boxlock action with single-selective trigger and automatic ejectors. The plain receiver is blued, with a checkered walnut stock. Manufactured between 1976 and 1982. A competition-grade model for trap or skeet was also available and would be worth approximately the same amount.

NIB	Exc.	V.G.	Good	Fair	Poor
—	1025	900	700	525	350

Model 1001 Field

A new addition to the U.S.R.A. product line for 1993. This Over/Under shotgun was available in 12 gauge only, with a 28" ventilated rib barrel furnished with WinPlus choke tubes. A walnut checkered pistol stock is standard. The finish is blued with scroll engraving on the receiver. The receiver top has a matte finish. The gun weighs 7 lbs. subject to a 1995 recall.

NIB	Exc.	V.G.	Good	Fair	Poor
1000	850	700	500	350	200

Model 1001 Sporting Clays I & II

This model features different stock dimensions, a fuller pistol grip, a radiused recoil pad, and a wider vent rib fitted on a 28" barrel (Sporting Clays I model, the Sporting Clays II features a 30" barrel). Comes complete with choke tubes. The frame has a silver nitrate finish and special engraving featuring a flying clay target. Introduced in 1993. Gun weighs 7.75 lbs. Subject to a 1995 recall.

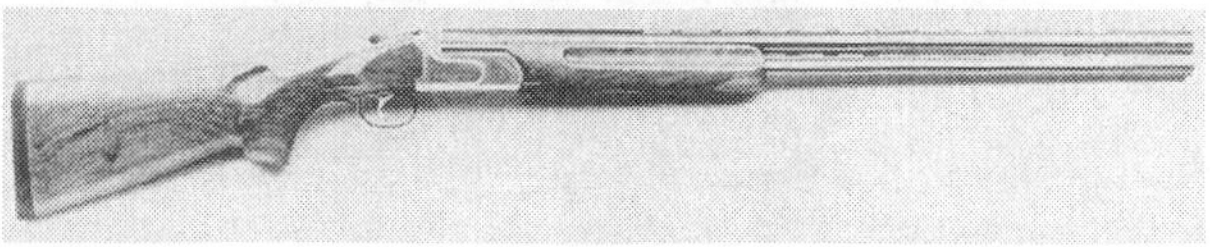

NIB	Exc.	V.G.	Good	Fair	Poor
1100	950	800	600	350	200

SELECT OVER/UNDER SERIES

This series of over-and-under shotguns was introduced into the Winchester line in 2004. The series features a low-profile receiver with unique engraving, lightweight barrels, and contoured walnut stocks with distinctive checkering patterns.

Select Midnight

High-gloss bluing on receiver and barrels with gold accent game bird pattern on both sides and bottom of the receiver. Satin finished Grade II/III walnut. Oval checkering pattern. Choke tubes. Introduced 2006. Available in 26" and 28" barrels.

NIB	Exc.	V.G.	Good	Fair	Poor
1600	1400	1150	900	650	400

Select White Field

An engraved silver nitride receiver is featured on both versions of the White Field. The Traditional model has traditional checkering and the Extreme model features the Select Series' unique oval checkering pattern. Both versions have choke tubes and are available in 26" and 28" barrels. Introduced 2006.

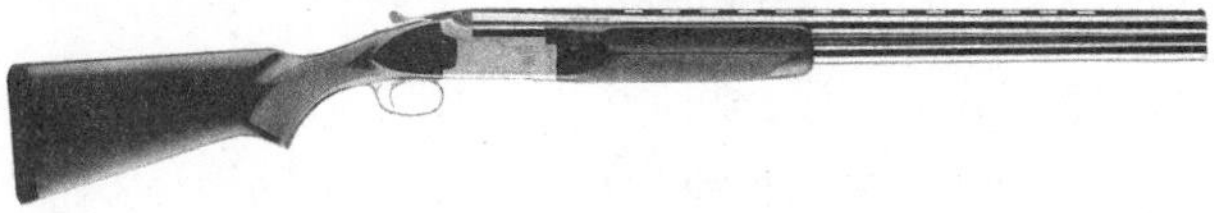

NIB	Exc.	V.G.	Good	Fair	Poor
1600	1400	1150	900	650	400

Select Energy Sporting

Chambered for the 12 gauge 2.75" shell and offered with a choice of 28", 30", or 32" vent rib barrels with choke tubes and porting. Truglo front sight. Adjustable trigger shoe. Walnut stock with recoil pad. Weight is about 7.62 lbs. Adjustable comb available.

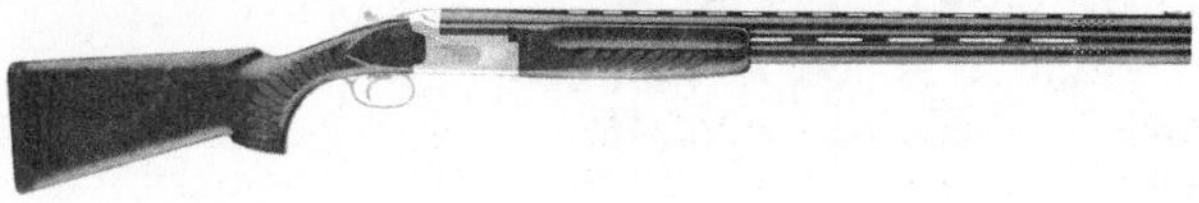

NIB	Exc.	V.G.	Good	Fair	Poor
1600	1400	1150	900	650	400

NOTE: Add $150 for adjustable comb.

Select Energy Trap

This 12 gauge model is fitted with a choice of 30" or 32" back-bored ported barrels. Wide vent rib. Choke tubes. Walnut stock with Monte Carlo comb. Weight is about 7.8 lbs. Adjustable comb available.

NIB	Exc.	V.G.	Good	Fair	Poor
1600	1400	1150	900	650	400

NOTE: Add $150 for adjustable comb.

Select Extreme Elegance

This 12 gauge gun features full coverage engraving with game scenes. Choice of 26" or 28" vent rib barrels with choke tubes. Walnut stock with unique checkering pattern. Weight is about 7 lbs.

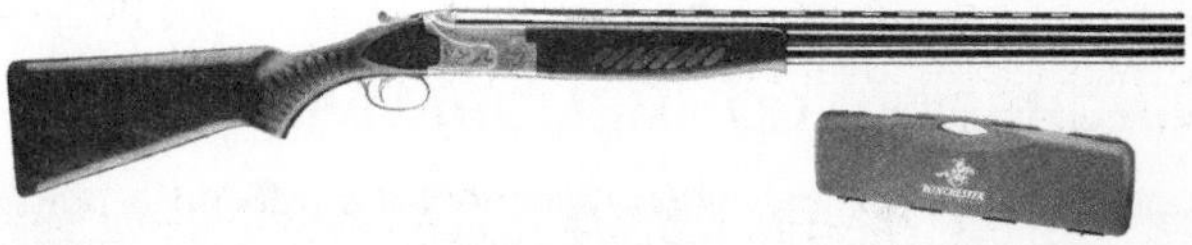

NIB	Exc.	V.G.	Good	Fair	Poor
1600	1400	1150	900	650	400

Select Field

This 12 gauge 3" gun is fitted with a choice of 26" or 28" vent ribs barrels with choke tubes. Engraved receiver with oval checkering pattern. Weight is about 7 lbs.

NIB	Exc.	V.G.	Good	Fair	Poor
1400	1200	950	700	450	300

Select Traditional Elegance

Similar to the Extreme Elegance but with traditional checkering pattern.

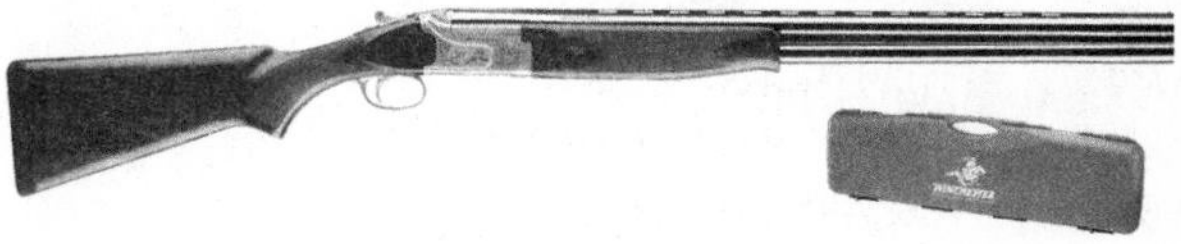

NIB	Exc.	V.G.	Good	Fair	Poor
1400	1200	950	700	450	300

Select Deluxe Field

New in 2007, this Belgian-made 3" 12 gauge features an engraved steel receiver with silver nitride finish and Grade II walnut. Barrels are 26", 28" or 30". Three chokes included. Weight is about 7.25 lbs.

NIB	Exc.	V.G.	Good	Fair	Poor
1600	1400	1150	900	650	400

Select Platinum Field

This 3" 12 gauge was introduced in 2007. It is Belgian-made and comes with 28" or 30" barrels, Grade II/III walnut and deep relief engraving. Includes three Signature extended choke tubes and hard case.

NIB	Exc.	V.G.	Good	Fair	Poor
2050	1800	1575	1200	900	500

Select Platinum Sporting

Similar to the Platinum Field with 28", 30" or 32" ported barrels, wide rib, adjustable trigger shoe and five Signature extended choke tubes and hard case.

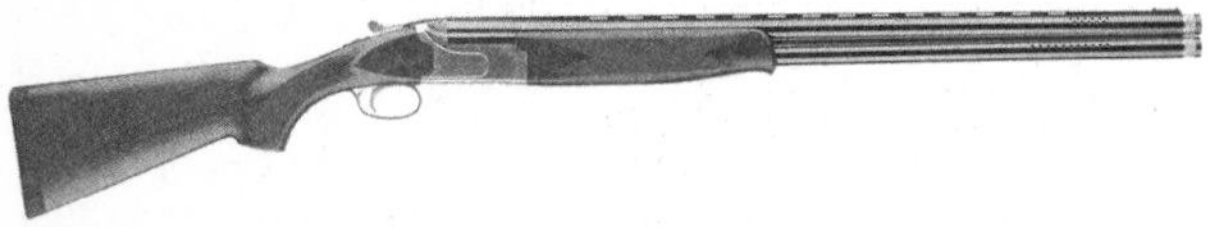

NIB	Exc.	V.G.	Good	Fair	Poor
2200	1950	1725	1375	1075	500

WINCHESTER COMMEMORATIVE RIFLES

Beginning in the early 1960s, Winchester produced a number of special Model 1894 rifles and carbines that commemorated certain historic events, places, or individuals. In some cases they are slightly embellished and in others are quite ornate. If a Winchester commemorative rifle has been cocked leaving a line on the hammer or the lever, many collectors will show little or no interest in its acquisition. If they have been fired, they will realize little premium over a standard, Post-1964 Model 94. A number of commemoratives have been ordered by outside concerns and are technically not factory issues. Most have less collectibility than the factory-issued models. There are a number of concerns that specialize in marketing the total range of Winchester commmemorative rifles. Listed are the factory-issue commemoratives with their current value, their issue price, and the number manufactured.

NOTE: Since the Model 94 was discontinued in 2006, values of Model 94 commemoratives have risen right along with values for Model 94s in general. We expect this situation to moderate over time but for the present, it's a seller's market.

1964 Wyoming Diamond Jubilee—Carbine

NIB	Issue	Amt. Mfg.
1400	100	1,500

1966 Centennial—Rifle

NIB	Issue	Amt. Mfg.
900	125	102,309

1966 Centennial—Carbine

NIB	Issue	Amt. Mfg.
900	125	102,309

1966 Nebraska Centennial—Rifle

NIB	Issue	Amt. Mfg.
1400	100	2,500

1967 Canadian Centennial—Rifle

NIB	Issue	Amt. Mfg.
900	125	—

1967 Canadian Centennial—Carbine

NIB	Issue	Amt. Mfg.
900	125	90,301

1967 Alaskan Purchase Centennial—Carbine

NIB	Issue	Amt. Mfg.
1400	125	1,500

1968 Illinois Sesquicentennial—Carbine

NIB	Issue	Amt. Mfg.
800	110	37,648

1968 Buffalo Bill—Carbine

NIB	Issue	Amt. Mfg.
900	130	112,923

1968 Buffalo Bill—Rifle

NIB	Issue	Amt. Mfg.
900	130	—

1968 Buffalo Bill "1 or 300"—Rifle

NIB	Issue	Amt. Mfg.
3800	1000	300

1969 Theodore Roosevelt—Rifle

NIB	Issue	Amt. Mfg.
900	135	—

1969 Theodore Roosevelt—Carbine

NIB	Issue	Amt. Mfg.
900	135	52,386

1969 Golden Spike Carbine

NIB	Issue	Amt. Mfg.
900	120	69,996

1970 Cowboy Commemorative Carbine

NIB	Issue	Amt. Mfg.
900	125	27,549

1970 Cowboy Carbine "1 of 300"

NIB	Issue	Amt. Mfg.
3800	1000	300

1970 Northwest Territories (Canadian)

NIB	Issue	Amt. Mfg.
1600	150	2,500

1970 Northwest Territories Deluxe (Canadian)

NIB	Issue	Amt. Mfg.
2000	250	500

1970 Lone Star—Rifle

NIB	Issue	Amt. Mfg.
900	140	—

1970 Lone Star—Carbine

NIB	Issue	Amt. Mfg.
900	140	38,385

1971 NRA Centennial—Rifle

NIB	Issue	Amt. Mfg.
900	150	21,000

1971 NRA Centennial—Musket

NIB	Issue	Amt. Mfg.
900	150	23,400

1971 Yellow Boy (European)

NIB	Issue	Amt. Mfg.
2200	250	500

1971 Royal Canadian Mounted Police (Canadian)

NIB	Issue	Amt. Mfg.
1500	190	9,500

1971 Mounted Police (Canadian)

NIB	Issue	Amt. Mfg.
1500	190	5,100

1971 Mounted Police, Presentation

NIB	Issue	Amt. Mfg.
14000	—	10

1974 Texas Ranger—Carbine

NIB	Issue	Amt. Mfg.
1300	135	4,850

1974 Texas Ranger Presentation Model

NIB	Issue	Amt. Mfg.
5000	1000	150

1974 Apache (Canadian)

NIB	Issue	Amt. Mfg.
1400	150	8,600

1974 Commanche (Canadian)

NIB	Issue	Amt. Mfg.
1400	230	11,500

1974 Klondike Gold Rush (Canadian)

NIB	Issue	Amt. Mfg.
1400	240	10,500

1975 Klondike Gold Rush—Dawson City Issue (Canadian)

NIB	Issue	Amt. Mfg.
13000	—	25

1976 Sioux (Canadian)

NIB	Issue	Amt. Mfg.
1400	280	10,000

1976 Little Bighorn (Canadian)

NIB	Issue	Amt. Mfg.
1400	300	11,000

1976 U.S. Bicentennial Carbine

NIB	Issue	Amt. Mfg.
1100	325	19,999

1977 Wells Fargo

NIB	Issue	Amt. Mfg.
1100	350	19,999

1977 Legendary Lawman

NIB	Issue	Amt. Mfg.
495	375	19,999

1977 Limited Edition I

NIB	Issue	Amt. Mfg.
2500	1500	1,500

1977 Cheyenne—.22 Cal. (Canadian)

NIB	Issue	Amt. Mfg.
1400	320	5,000

1977 Cheyenne—.44-40 Cal. (Canadian)

NIB	Issue	Amt. Mfg.
1400	300	11,225

1977 Cherokee—.22 Cal. (Canadian)

NIB	Issue	Amt. Mfg.
1400	385	3,950

1977 Cherokee—.30-30 Cal. (Canadian)

NIB	Issue	Amt. Mfg.
1400	385	9,000

1978 "One of One Thousand" (European)

NIB	Issue	Amt. Mfg.
12500	5000	250

1978 Antler Game Carbine

NIB	Issue	Amt. Mfg.
1100	375	19,999

1979 Limited Edition II

NIB	Issue	Amt. Mfg.
2500	1500	1,500

1979 Legendary Frontiersman Rifle

NIB	Issue	Amt. Mfg.
1100	425	19,999

1979 Matched Set of 1,000

NIB	Issue	Amt. Mfg.
4000	3000	1,000

1979 Bat Masterson (Canadian)

NIB	Issue	Amt. Mfg.
1400	650	8,000

1980 Alberta Diamond Jubilee (Canadian)

NIB	Issue	Amt. Mfg.
1400	650	2,700

1980 Alberta Diamond Jubilee Deluxe (Canadian)

NIB	Issue	Amt. Mfg.
2800	1900	300

1980 Saskatchewan Diamond Jubilee (Canadian)

NIB	Issue	Amt. Mfg.
1400	695	2,700

1980 Saskatchewan Diamond Jubilee Deluxe (Canadian)

NIB	Issue	Amt. Mfg.
2800	1995	300

1980 Oliver Winchester

NIB	Issue	Amt. Mfg.
1300	375	19,999

1981 U.S. Border Patrol

NIB	Issue	Amt. Mfg.
1100	1195	1,000

1981 U.S. Border Patrol—Member's Model

NIB	Issue	Amt. Mfg.
1100	695	800

1981 Calgary Stampede (Canadian)

NIB	Issue	Amt. Mfg.
2500	2200	1,000

1981 Canadian Pacific Centennial (Canadian)

NIB	Issue	Amt. Mfg.
1100	800	2,000

1981 Canadian Pacific Centennial Presentation (Canadian)

NIB	Issue	Amt. Mfg.
2200	2200	300

1981 Canadian Pacific Employee's Model (Canadian)

NIB	Issue	Amt. Mfg.
1100	800	2,000

1981 John Wayne (Canadian)

NIB	Issue	Amt. Mfg.
2800	995	1,000

1981 John Wayne

NIB	Issue	Amt. Mfg.
2600	600	49,000

1981 Duke

NIB	Issue	Amt. Mfg.
7000	2250	1,000

1981 John Wayne "1 of 300" Set

NIB	Issue	Amt. Mfg.
12500	10000	300

1982 Great Western Artist I

NIB	Issue	Amt. Mfg.
2400	2200	999

1982 Great Western Artist II

NIB	Issue	Amt. Mfg.
2400	2200	999

1982 Annie Oakley

NIB	Issue	Amt. Mfg.
1400	699	6,000

1983 Chief Crazy Horse

NIB	Issue	Amt. Mfg.
1200	600	19,999

1983 American Bald Eagle

NIB	Issue	Amt. Mfg.
1100	895	2,800

1983 American Bald Eagle—Deluxe

NIB	Issue	Amt. Mfg.
7500	2995	200

1983 Oklahoma Diamond Jubilee

NIB	Issue	Amt. Mfg.
2600	2250	1,001

1984 Winchester—Colt Commemorative Set

NIB	Issue	Amt. Mfg.
4400	3995	2,300

1985 Boy Scout 75th Anniversary .22 Cal.

NIB	Issue	Amt. Mfg.
1500	615	15,000

1985 Boy Scout 75th Anniversary—Eagle Scout

NIB	Issue	Amt. Mfg.
8000	2140	1,000

Texas Sesquicentennial Model—Rifle .38-55 Cal.

NIB	Issue	Amt. Mfg.
4000	2995	1,500

Texas Sesquicentennial Model—Carbine .38-55 Cal.

NIB	Issue	Amt. Mfg.
1300	695	15,000

Texas Sesquicentennial Model Set with Bowie Knife

NIB	Issue	Amt. Mfg.
9000	7995	150

1986 Model 94 Ducks Unlimited

NIB	Issue	Amt. Mfg.
1200	—	2,800

1986 Statue of Liberty

NIB	Issue	Amt. Mfg.
10000	6500	100

1986 120th Anniversary Model—Carbine .44-40 Cal.

NIB	Issue	Amt. Mfg.
1600	995	1,000

1986 European 1 of 1,000 Second Series (European)

NIB	Issue	Amt. Mfg.
1300	6000	150

1987 U.S. Constitution 200th Anniversary 44-40

NIB	Issue	Amt. Mfg.
20000	12000	17

1990 Wyoming Centennial-30-30

NIB	Issue	Amt. Mfg.
2800	895	500

1991 Winchester 125th Anniversary

NIB	Issue	Amt. Mfg.
10000	4995	61

1992 Arapaho—30-30

NIB	Issue	Amt. Mfg.
2800	895	500

1992 Ontario Conservation-30-30

NIB	Issue	Amt. Mfg.
2800	1195	400

1992 Kentucky Bicentennial-30-30

NIB	Issue	Amt. Mfg.
2800	995	500

1993 Nez Perce—30-30

NIB	Issue	Amt. Mfg.
2800	995	600

1995 Florida Sesquicentennial Carbine

NIB	Issue	Amt. Mfg.
2800	1195	360

1996 Wild Bill Hickok Carbine

NIB	Issue	Amt. Mfg.
2800	1195	350

WINDSOR

Windsor, Vermont
Robbins & Lawrence
Hartford, Connecticut

Windsor Rifle-Musket

A .577 caliber single-shot percussion rifle with a 39" round barrel secured by three barrel bands. The lock marked "Windsor." Rifles of this pattern were contracted for by the British Government. The lock and barrel finished in the white, brass furniture, and a walnut stock. Approximately 16,000 were made from 1855 to 1858.

NIB	Exc.	V.G.	Good	Fair	Poor
—	—	3750	3000	950	300

WINSLOW ARMS CO.

Camden, South Carolina

BOLT ACTION RIFLE

A high-grade, semi-custom sporting rifle built upon a number of actions and offered in all popular calibers from .17 Remington to the .458 Winchester Magnum with a 24" barrel and a 3-shot magazine. The larger Magnum models have a 26" barrel and a 2-shot magazine. Two basic stocks are offered—the Conventional Bushmaster, which features a standard pistol grip and a beavertail forearm; and also the Plainsmaster, which has a full curled, hooked pistol grip and a wide, flat beavertail forearm. Both have Monte Carlo-style stocks with recoil pads and sling swivels. Offered in a choice of popular woods with rosewood forend tips and pistol gripcaps. Eight different grades of this rifle are available and the following lists the values applicable for each.

Commander Grade

Figured walnut stock. Rosewood forearm tip and grip cap. White line recoil pad. FN Supreme action.

NIB	Exc.	V.G.	Good	Fair	Poor
—	1450	1050	925	700	550

Regal Grade

All features of Commander Grade plus ivory and ebony inlay on stock, French-style checkering, jeweled bolt.

NIB	Exc.	V.G.	Good	Fair	Poor
—	2200	1800	1225	900	600

Regent Grade

As above with addition of hand-carved checkering.

NIB	Exc.	V.G.	Good	Fair	Poor
—	2375	1850	1250	900	600

Regimental Grade

As above but with addition of basket weave carving, two ivory stock inlays and large ivory and ebony inlay on both side of butt stock with animal silhouette.

NIB	Exc.	V.G.	Good	Fair	Poor
—	3000	2200	1500	1200	650

Crown Grade

As above but with more elaborate ivory inlays on stock.

NIB	Exc.	V.G.	Good	Fair	Poor
—	3700	2550	1800	1500	650

Royal Grade

As above but with addition even more elaborate stock carving and ivory and ebony inlay.

NIB	Exc.	V.G.	Good	Fair	Poor
—	4500	3250	2000	1600	650

Imperial Grade

As above but with addition of engraved barrel from receiver to 11" forward. Engraved receiver ring, bolt handle and trigger guard. Engraved scope mounts and rings.

NIB	Exc.	V.G.	Good	Fair	Poor
—	5000	3750	2500	2000	700

Emperor Grade

As above but with addition of gold raised relief animals engraved receiver and forward part of barrel with muzzle tip engraved engraved as well. Highest Winslow grade.

NIB	Exc.	V.G.	Good	Fair	Poor
—	6250	5000	4000	3000	700

WOODWARD, JAMES & SONS

London, England

Prior to WWII, this company produced a variety of boxlock and sidelock shotguns that are regarded as some of the best made. Prospective purchasers should secure a qualified appraisal prior to acquisition.

WURFFLEIN, ANDREW & WILLIAM

Philadelphia, Pennsylvania

Single-Shot Rifle

A single-shot rifle produced in a variety of calibers with octagonal barrels of 24" to 28" length. This rifle was available with a wide variety of optional features.

NIB	Exc.	V.G.	Good	Fair	Poor
—	—	2400	1250	350	150

Mid-range Model

As above, with a 28" or 30" half-octagonal barrel.

NIB	Exc.	V.G.	Good	Fair	Poor
—	—	4250	3000	950	400

Model No. 25

The highest grade rifle manufactured by Wurfflein.

NIB	Exc.	V.G.	Good	Fair	Poor
—	—	4500	3500	1250	600

X

XPERT

Norwich, Connecticut

Xpert Pocket Rifle

Similar to the derringer with the same size frame but fitted with a 7.5" barrel and chambered for the .22 cartridge, as well as the .30 caliber rimfire. Supplied with wire stock. Values are for gun with stock. Produced from about 1870 to 1890s.

NIB	*Exc.*	*V.G.*	*Good*	*Fair*	*Poor*
—	—	1475	1150	500	150

Z

Z-B RIFLE CO.

Brno, Czechoslovakia

Model ZKW-465 Varmint Rifle

A Mauser bolt-action rifle chambered for the .22 Hornet cartridge. It has a 23" barrel with a three-leaf, folding rear sight. It is offered standard with double-set triggers. The finish is blued, with a select walnut checkered stock.

NIB	*Exc.*	*V.G.*	*Good*	*Fair*	*Poor*
—	1600	1150	975	800	500

ZANOTTI, FABIO

Brescia, Italy

Model 625

A 12 to .410 bore boxlock double-barrel shotgun with automatic ejectors and single-selective trigger. Blued with checkered walnut stock.

NIB	*Exc.*	*V.G.*	*Good*	*Fair*	*Poor*
6500	5200	4700	3500	2500	500

Model 626

As above, engraved with either scroll work or hunting scenes.

NIB	*Exc.*	*V.G.*	*Good*	*Fair*	*Poor*
7000	5700	5200	4000	2800	500

Giacinto

An external hammer boxlock shotgun produced in a variety of gauges with double triggers.

NIB	*Exc.*	*V.G.*	*Good*	*Fair*	*Poor*
6500	5200	4700	3500	2500	500

Maxim

Similar to the Model 625, but fitted with detachable sidelocks.

NIB	*Exc.*	*V.G.*	*Good*	*Fair*	*Poor*
7000	5700	5200	4000	2800	500

Edward

As above, but more intricately engraved.

NIB	*Exc.*	*V.G.*	*Good*	*Fair*	*Poor*
12000	9000	6500	4500	3000	1500

Cassiano I

As above, with exhibition grade engraving.

NIB	*Exc.*	*V.G.*	*Good*	*Fair*	*Poor*
13000	9000	7000	6000	4000	2000

Cassiano II

As above, with gold inlays.

NIB	*Exc.*	*V.G.*	*Good*	*Fair*	*Poor*
14500	12000	9500	7000	5000	2500

Cassiano Executive

A strictly custom-made shotgun produced to the client's specifications.

NIB	*Exc.*	*V.G.*	*Good*	*Fair*	*Poor*
45000	—	—	—	—	—

ZEPHYR

Eibar, Spain

Importer—Stoegers

Woodlander II

A 12 or 20 gauge boxlock shotgun with varying length barrels, double triggers and extractors. Blued with a walnut stock.

NIB	*Exc.*	*V.G.*	*Good*	*Fair*	*Poor*
600	450	400	300	200	100

Uplander

A 12, 16, 20, 28 or .410 bore sidelock double-barrel shotgun with varying length barrels, double triggers, and automatic ejectors. Blued with a walnut stock.

NIB	*Exc.*	*V.G.*	*Good*	*Fair*	*Poor*
850	700	500	400	300	150

Upland King

As above, in 12 or 16 gauge with ventilated-rib barrels.

NIB	*Exc.*	*V.G.*	*Good*	*Fair*	*Poor*
1150	800	700	600	400	250

Vandalia

A 12 gauge single-barrel trap gun with a 32" Full choked barrel. Blued with a walnut stock.

NIB	*Exc.*	*V.G.*	*Good*	*Fair*	*Poor*
750	600	550	450	300	150

Sterlingworth II

Identical to the Woodlander, but with sidelocks.

NIB	*Exc.*	*V.G.*	*Good*	*Fair*	*Poor*
850	700	550	450	300	150

Victor Special

A 12 gauge boxlock double-barrel shotgun with 25", 28", or 30" barrels, double triggers and extractors. Blued with a walnut stock.

NIB	*Exc.*	*V.G.*	*Good*	*Fair*	*Poor*
525	400	300	250	175	100

Thunderbird

A 10 gauge Magnum boxlock double-barrel shotgun with 32" full choked barrels, double triggers, and automatic ejectors. Blued with a walnut stock.

NIB	*Exc.*	*V.G.*	*Good*	*Fair*	*Poor*
950	700	600	500	400	200

Honker

A 10 gauge Magnum single-barrel shotgun with a 36" full choked and ventilated-rib barrel. Blued with a walnut stock.

NIB	*Exc.*	*V.G.*	*Good*	*Fair*	*Poor*
600	450	400	300	200	100

ZM WEAPONS

Bernardton, Massachusetts

LR-300 Sport Rifle

This is a highly modified AR-15 chambered for the .223 cartridge. It is fitted with a 16.25" barrel and a true folding stock. A Ghost Ring rear sight and an adjustable post front sight with tritium insert is standard. Weight is approximately 7.2 pounds. Introduced in 1997.

NIB	*Exc.*	*V.G.*	*Good*	*Fair*	*Poor*
—	1600	1200	950	775	500

ZOLI, ANTONIO

Brescia, Italy

Silver Hawk

A 12 or 20 gauge boxlock double-barrel shotgun produced in a variety of barrel lengths and chokes with a double trigger. Engraved, blued with walnut stock.

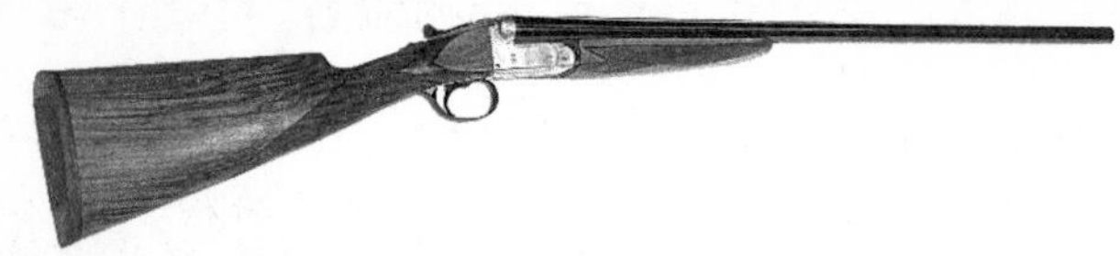

NIB	Exc.	V.G.	Good	Fair	Poor
—	1025	900	850	600	450

Ariete M2

A 12 gauge boxlock double-barrel shotgun with 26" or 28" barrels, non-selective single trigger and automatic ejectors. Engraved, blued with a walnut stock.

NIB	Exc.	V.G.	Good	Fair	Poor
—	1150	1000	850	700	350

Empire

As above, in 12 or 20 gauge with 27" or 28" barrels. Engraved, French case hardened, blued with a walnut stock.

NIB	Exc.	V.G.	Good	Fair	Poor
—	2300	1950	1400	1250	400

Volcano Record

A 12 gauge sidelock double-barrel shotgun with 28" barrels available in a variety of chokes, single-selective trigger and automatic ejectors. Engraved, French case hardened, blued with a walnut stock.

NIB	Exc.	V.G.	Good	Fair	Poor
—	7000	6000	5000	4000	500

Volcano Record ELM

This model is strictly a custom-ordered shotgun produced to the purchaser's specifications. Value speculative.

NIB	Exc.	V.G.	Good	Fair	Poor
—	16000	13500	10500	8500	500

Silver Snipe

A 12 or 20 gauge over-and-under shotgun produced with varying lengths, ventilated rib barrels, single trigger and extractors. Engraved, blued with a walnut stock.

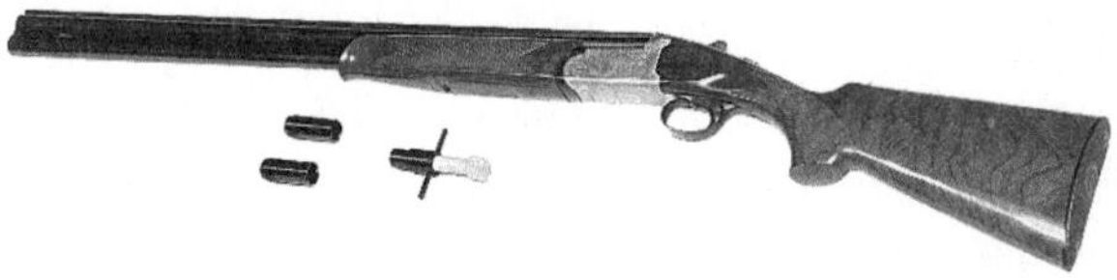

NIB	Exc.	V.G.	Good	Fair	Poor
—	600	450	400	325	275

Golden Snipe

As above, but more finely finished and fitted with automatic ejectors.

NIB	Exc.	V.G.	Good	Fair	Poor
—	650	500	450	350	300

Delfino

As above, in 12 or 20 gauge Magnum with 26" or 28" ventilated rib barrels, non-selective single trigger and automatic ejectors. Engraved, blued with walnut stock.

NIB	Exc.	V.G.	Good	Fair	Poor
—	575	425	325	275	250

Ritmo Hunting Gun

As above, in 12 gauge Magnum with 26" or 28" separated ventilated rib barrels, single-selective trigger and automatic ejectors. Engraved, blued with a walnut stock.

NIB	Exc.	V.G.	Good	Fair	Poor
—	650	500	450	400	350

Condor Model

As above, in 12 gauge with 28" skeet bored barrels having a wide competition rib, single-selective trigger and automatic ejectors. Engraved, French case hardened, blued with a walnut stock.

NIB	Exc.	V.G.	Good	Fair	Poor
—	1100	800	650	500	400

Angel Model

As above, in a field grade version.

NIB	Exc.	V.G.	Good	Fair	Poor
—	1100	800	600	500	400

Ritmo Pigeon Grade IV

As above, with 28" separated ventilated rib barrels, single-selective trigger, automatic ejectors and extensively engraved. French case hardened, blued with a finely figured walnut stock.

NIB	Exc.	V.G.	Good	Fair	Poor
—	2250	1600	1200	800	600

Model 208 Target

As above, with 28" or 30" trap or skeet bored barrels fitted with a wide ventilated rib.

NIB	Exc.	V.G.	Good	Fair	Poor
—	1200	850	700	600	500

Model 308 Target

As above, but more finely finished.

NIB	Exc.	V.G.	Good	Fair	Poor
—	1500	1100	850	700	500

Combination

A .222 or .243 and 12 or 20 gauge over-and-under combination rifle/shotgun with an engraved boxlock-action, double triggers, and a folding rear sight. French case hardened, blued with a walnut stock.

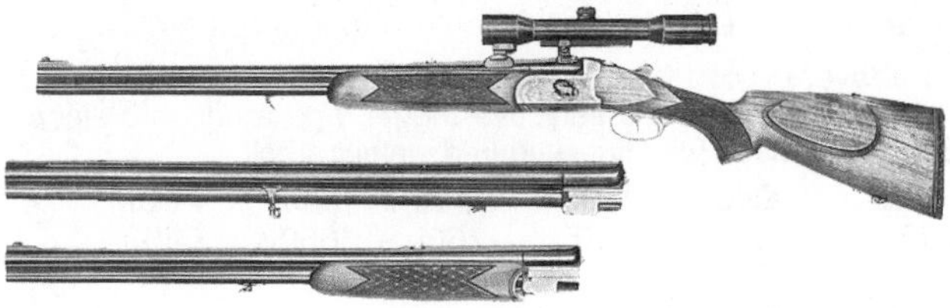

NIB	Exc.	V.G.	Good	Fair	Poor
—	2500	1700	1250	950	500

Safari Deluxe

As above, but with false sidelocks that are engraved with scrolls or hunting scenes.

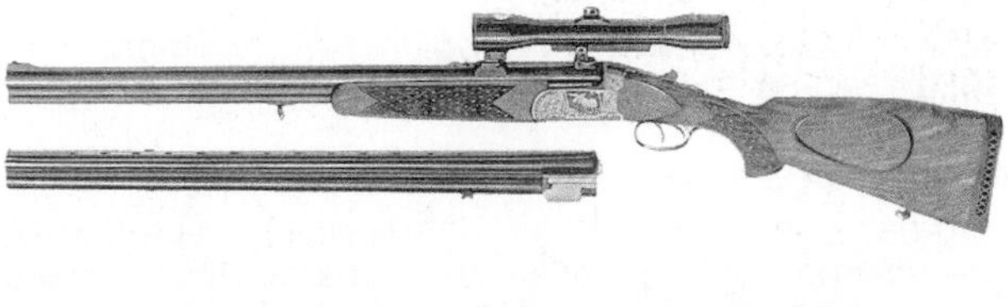

NIB	Exc.	V.G.	Good	Fair	Poor
—	5000	4000	2850	1500	650

ZOLI USA, ANGELO

Brescia, Italy

Slide-Action Shotgun

A 12 gauge Magnum slide-action shotgun produced with a variety of barrel lengths with detachable choke tubes. Blued with a walnut stock.

NIB	Exc.	V.G.	Good	Fair	Poor
400	300	250	200	150	100

Diano I

A 12, 20 or .410 bore single-shot folding barrel shotgun. Produced in a variety of barrel lengths. Blued with a walnut stock.

NIB	Exc.	V.G.	Good	Fair	Poor
175	100	90	80	60	40

Diano II

As above, but with a bottom lever instead of a top release lever.

NIB	Exc.	V.G.	Good	Fair	Poor
175	100	90	80	60	40

Apache

A 12 gauge Magnum lever-action shotgun with a 20" barrel fitted with detachable choke tubes. Blued with a walnut stock.

NIB	Exc.	V.G.	Good	Fair	Poor
500	400	350	300	250	150

Quail Special

A .410 Magnum bore double-barrel shotgun with 28" barrels and a single trigger. Blued with a walnut stock.

NIB	Exc.	V.G.	Good	Fair	Poor
325	200	150	125	100	75

Falcon II

As above with 26" or 28" barrels and double triggers.

NIB	Exc.	V.G.	Good	Fair	Poor
325	200	150	125	100	75

Pheasant

A 12 gauge Magnum double-barrel shotgun with 28" barrels, single trigger, and automatic ejectors. Blued with a walnut stock.

NIB	Exc.	V.G.	Good	Fair	Poor
450	350	300	250	200	150

Classic

As above, with 26" to 30" barrels fitted with detachable choke tubes, single-selective trigger, and automatic ejectors. Blued with a walnut stock.

NIB	Exc.	V.G.	Good	Fair	Poor
850	700	600	500	300	200

Snipe

A .410 bore over-and-under shotgun with 26" or 28" barrels and a single trigger.

NIB	Exc.	V.G.	Good	Fair	Poor
400	300	200	175	150	100

Dove

Similar to the above.

NIB	Exc.	V.G.	Good	Fair	Poor
400	300	200	175	150	100

Texas

A 12, 20 or .410 bore over-and-under shotgun with 26" or 28" barrels, double triggers, and a bottom barrel release lever.

NIB	Exc.	V.G.	Good	Fair	Poor
350	250	200	150	100	75

Field Special

A 12 or 20 gauge Magnum double-barrel shotgun produced in a variety of barrel lengths with a single trigger and extractors. Blued with a walnut stock.

NIB	Exc.	V.G.	Good	Fair	Poor
550	400	300	250	200	100

Pigeon Model

As above, but more finely finished.

NIB	Exc.	V.G.	Good	Fair	Poor
550	400	300	250	200	100

Standard Model

Similar to the above but in 12 and 20 gauge only.

NIB	Exc.	V.G.	Good	Fair	Poor
500	400	300	250	200	100

Special Model

As above, with detachable choke tubes and a single-selective trigger.

NIB	Exc.	V.G.	Good	Fair	Poor
600	450	300	250	200	100

Deluxe Model

As above, but engraved and with better quality walnut.

NIB	Exc.	V.G.	Good	Fair	Poor
800	600	500	400	300	150

Presentation Model

As above, with false sidelocks and finely figured walnut stock.

NIB	Exc.	V.G.	Good	Fair	Poor
950	700	600	450	350	200

St. George's Target

A 12 gauge over-and-under shotgun trap or skeet bore with various length barrels, single-selective trigger, and automatic ejectors. Blued with a walnut stock.

NIB	Exc.	V.G.	Good	Fair	Poor
1200	900	700	600	550	250

St. George Competition

A 12 gauge single-barrel gun with an extra set of over and under barrels.

NIB	Exc.	V.G.	Good	Fair	Poor
1950	1600	1200	950	500	300

Express Rifle

A .30-06, 7x65Rmm or 9.3x74Rmm over-and-under double-barrel rifle with single triggers and automatic ejectors. Blued with a walnut stock.

NIB	Exc.	V.G.	Good	Fair	Poor
4250	3500	2500	1750	1200	600

Express EM

As above, but more finely finished.

NIB	Exc.	V.G.	Good	Fair	Poor
5500	4000	3000	1500	1000	750

Savana E

As above, with double triggers.

NIB	Exc.	V.G.	Good	Fair	Poor
6500	5250	4500	3500	2750	1500

Savana Deluxe

As above, but engraved with hunting scenes.

NIB	Exc.	V.G.	Good	Fair	Poor
8000	7000	6000	4750	3500	2000

AZ 1900C

A .243, .270, 6.5x55mm, .308, or .30-06 bolt-action rifle with a 24" barrel having open sights. Blued with a walnut stock.

NIB	Exc.	V.G.	Good	Fair	Poor
850	700	500	400	300	150

AZ 1900M

Same as above but fitted with a Bell & Carlson composite stock.

NIB	Exc.	V.G.	Good	Fair	Poor
750	600	450	350	275	200

AZ 1900 Deluxe

As above, but more finely finished.

NIB	Exc.	V.G.	Good	Fair	Poor
1100	800	650	500	400	200

AZ 1900 Super Deluxe

As above, but engraved with a finely figured walnut stock.

NIB	Exc.	V.G.	Good	Fair	Poor
1500	1000	800	600	450	250

Patricia Model

As above, in .410 Magnum bore with 28" ventilated rib barrels, various chokes, single-selective trigger, and automatic ejectors. Engraved, blued with finely figured walnut stock.

NIB	Exc.	V.G.	Good	Fair	Poor
1500	1100	950	750	650	400

Condor

A .30-06 or .308 and 12 gauge over-and-under combination shotgun rifle with double triggers, extractors and sling swivels. Blued with a walnut stock.

NIB	Exc.	V.G.	Good	Fair	Poor
1500	1050	850	700	500	300

Airone

As above, with false sidelocks.

NIB	Exc.	V.G.	Good	Fair	Poor
1650	1250	1000	800	600	300

Leopard Express

A .30-06, .308, 7x65Rmm, or .375 Holland & Holland over-and-under double-barrel rifle with 24" barrels having express sights, double triggers and extractors. Blued with a walnut stock.

NIB	Exc.	V.G.	Good	Fair	Poor
1750	1400	1000	800	600	300

MANUFACTURER & MODEL INDEX

A

B

BERNARDELLI, VINCENZO 76

BERTUZZI... 79

BIG HORN ARMORY 79

BIGHORN ARMS CO............................. 79

BIGHORN RIFLE CO. 79

BILHARZ, HALL & CO........................... 79

BINGHAM LTD. 80

C

D

E

F

G

H

I

J

K

L

M

MAROCCHI ARMI 342

MASQUELIER S. A. 342

MASSACHUSETTS ARMS CO. 343

MATEBA ARMS 343

MAUNZ MFG., INC. 343

MAUSER WERKE 344

N

O

P

Q

R

STI INTERNATIONAL.......................... 554

STOEGER, A. F................................ 554

STREET SWEEPER............................ 557

STURM, RUGER & CO. 557

T

V

W

X

Z